2018 County and City Extra
Annual Metro, City, and County Data Book
26th Edition

2018 County and City Extra

Annual Metro, City, and County Data Book

26th Edition

Edited by Deirdre A. Gaquin
and Mary Meghan Ryan

Lanham, MD

Published by Bernan Press
An imprint of The Rowman & Littlefield Publishing Group, Inc.
4501 Forbes Boulevard, Suite 200, Lanham, Maryland 20706
www.rowman.com
800-462-6420

6 Tinworth Street, London SE11 5AL, United Kingdom

ISBN: 978-1-64143-273-3
E-ISBN: 978-1-64143-274-0

♾™ The paper used in this publication meets the minimum requirements of American National Standard for Information Sciences—Permanence of Paper for Printed Library Materials, ANSI/NISO Z39.48-1992.

Printed in the United States of America.

Contents

INTRODUCTION

County and City Extra is an annual publication that provides the most up-to-date statistical information available for every state, county, metropolitan area, and congressional district, as well as all cities in the United States with a 2010 census population of 25,000 or more. Data for places, including towns and cities with populations of fewer than 25,000 people are published by Bernan Press in a separate companion volume, *Places, Towns and Townships,* now in its sixth edition. These two volumes are designed to meet the needs of libraries, businesses, and other organizations or individuals who desire convenient and timely sources of the most frequently sought information about geographic entities within the United States. The annual updating of *County and City Extra* for 26 years ensures its stature as a reliable and authoritative source for statistical information.

Bernan Press also publishes a companion volume, the *State and Metropolitan Area Data Book,* previously published by the Census Bureau. The recently published second edition provides an expanded collection of data about states and metropolitan areas, including micropolitan areas and their component counties. Another recent addition is the *County and City Extra: Special Historical Edition, 1790-2010* with data from the earliest days of the nation, and states, counties, and cities from their beginnings.

County and City Extra, Places, Towns and Townships, and *State and Metropolitan Area Data Book* are large volumes, but are not big enough to accommodate the wealth of information from the decennial census and the American Community Survey. Two additional volumes in the *County and City Extra* series include this information. *County and City Extra—Special Decennial Census Edition* provides detailed population and housing data from the 2010 census and was published by Bernan Press in December 2011. *The Who, What, and Where of America—Understanding the American Community Survey,* recently released in its sixth edition, includes social and economic details from the ongoing American Community Survey, and the *County and City Extra* Series includes additional books on special topics, such as the recently published *Education and the American Workforce.*

The American Community Survey (ACS) is a national survey that has replaced the census long form as the key source of detailed social and economic data. *County and City Extra* includes data from both the 2010 census and the ACS.

New and Updated Information for the 2018 Edition

This edition includes IRS income tax data for counties from the Statistics of Income program of the Internal Revenue Service. Expanded ACS data on income and earnings as well as data on commuting and availability of computers are now included for cities. Internet access is included for cities and metropolitan areas. Updated data include 2017 population estimates for states, counties, metropolitan areas, and cities. Also included are the latest available data for education, vital statistics, income and poverty, employment and unemployment, residential construction, production by industry, health resources, crime, land use, city government finances, and many other topics.

Table E (Congressional Districts) includes a wide selection of 2016 American Community Survey data, Business Patterns, and Social Security data for the 115th Congress, as well as data from the 2012 Census of Agriculture for the congressional districts of the 114th Congress, along with the 115th Congressional representatives. Only four states had revised boundaries between the 114th and 115th Congresses.

In August 2017, the Office of Management and Budget released an updated list of Core Based Statistical Areas (metropolitan and micropolitan areas) based on the 2010 census and some changes in the way these areas are defined. Only one new metropolitan area was delineated, as the Twin Falls Idaho micropolitan area gained enough population to be designated metropolitan. Because most data sources in this book still followed the 2015 metropolitan area delineations, those are used in Table C. Appendixes B and C provide details about the component counties of these metropolitan and micropolitan areas and their 2010 census and 2017 estimated populations. Appendix D has a map for each state showing the metropolitan and micropolitan areas.

This edition includes data from the 2010 census, 2016 and 2017 population estimates, and the ACS. Annual ACS data are available for all states and almost all metropolitan areas (all geographic areas with populations of 65,000 or more), but five years are needed to build a sample large enough for reliable estimates for all counties The Census Bureau no longer releases 3-year data which were previously available for areas with populations of 20,000 or more. These have now been replaced with 1-year Supplemental Estimates which are used in this book for Table D, cities with populations of 25,000 or more.

With the now annual release of 1-year and 5-year estimates, *County and City Extra* uses ACS data for all geographic areas. ACS 1-year data for 2016 are included in Table A (States), Table C (metropolitan areas) and Table E (Congressional Districts)—all areas with populations of 65,000 or more. Table D (cities) uses the 1-year supplemental estimates which are less detailed than the regular 1-year estimates. Table B (Counties) includes 5-year data (2012-2016). The release of 5-year data for even the smallest geographic areas means that annual social and economic characteristics are available for all counties and cities. .

Although some of the state data are also included in Table B (States and Counties), the separate state data table offers several important features:

- Additional data not available at the county level are provided. Examples include population projections, health insurance coverage, number of immigrants, personal tax payments, information about health service firms not subject to federal tax, and exports by state of origin.

- Additional data that exceeds the space limitations for counties can be found for states. Examples are age of householder, more detailed information about employment in retail trade and services, and detailed government employment and finance data.

- State totals can be found more quickly and compared more readily.

Appendix F, **Source Notes and Explanations**, includes internet references for all data sources. This is especially helpful in today's environment where the data sources are updated at a faster pace. The sources referenced here can be used to track down additional information too cumbersome for this book. Some of the data can be directly found in data tables on the websites; some can be assembled through on-line access tools; others can be obtained by downloading files and processing them with statistical software; and some need to be ordered from the agencies.

Rankings

The rankings present the geography types by various subjects, including population, land area, population density, population change, age, immigration, birth rate, housing characteristics, race, Hispanic origin, educational attainment, income, unemployment rate, per capita local taxes, poverty rate, defense contracts, value of agricultural products, and violent crime rate.

Subjects Covered and Volume Organization

A summary of the **subjects covered** in each of the five tables appears on **page xi**. The **colored map** portfolio begins on **page xv**.

The main body of this volume contains five basic parts. Each part includes a table that is preceded by highlights and rankings, as well as the complete column headings for the table. **Part A**, which begins on **page 1**, contains data for states. **Part B**, beginning on **page 51**, contains information for states and counties. The county geography codes include county typology codes from the Economic Research Service of the

Department of Agriculture. These codes characterize counties by size of the largest place as well as by other criteria for nonmetropolitan counties. (See Appendix A for the definition of each code.) **Part C**, beginning on **page 773**, contains information for metropolitan areas. Statistics for cities with a 2010 census population of 25,000 or more can be found in **Part D**, which begins on **page 895**. **Part E**, beginning on **page 1175**, contains data for the congressional districts of the 115th Congress.

A contents page preceding tables B through E lists the page number on which the data for a given geographic area begin. Counties and cities are listed alphabetically by state. Metropolitan areas are listed alphabetically, except that metropolitan divisions are listed alphabetically within the metropolitan statistical area of which they are components. Congressional districts are listed in numeric order within states.

The appendixes include definitions of geographic concepts (**Appendix A**), sources and definitions of each data item included in this volume (**Appendix F**), an alphabetical listing of metropolitan areas with their component counties delineated as of July 2015, with 2010 census populations (**Appendix B**), a listing of metropolitan and micropolitan areas and their component counties as of August 2017, with 2010 census populations and 2017 estimated populations (**Appendix C**), a list of cities by county (**Appendix E**), and maps showing congressional districts in the United States; and metropolitan areas, counties and selected places within each state (**Appendix D**).

Symbols

D   Indicates that the number has been withheld to avoid disclosure of information pertaining to a specific organization or individual, or because the number does not meet statistical standards for publication.

NA   Indicates that data are not available.

X   Indicates that data are not applicable or are not meaningful for this geographic unit.

In this volume, a figure that is less than half the unit of measure shown will appear as zero.

Sources

All of the data in this volume have been obtained from federal government sources. For a complete list of these sources, see **Appendix F**.

Data included in this volume meet the publication standards established by the U.S. Census Bureau and the other federal statistical agencies from which they were obtained. Every effort has been made to select data that are accurate, meaningful, and useful. All data from censuses, surveys, and administrative records are subject to errors arising from factors such as sampling variability, reporting errors, incomplete coverage, nonresponse, imputations, and processing error. Responsibility of the editors and publishers of this volume is limited to reasonable care in the reproduction and presentation of data obtained from sources believed to be reliable.

County and City Extra: Annual Metro, City, and County Data Book is part of Bernan Press's *County and City Extra* series. The editors of *County and City Extra* acknowledge the contributions of the late Courtenay Slater and George Hall, the originators of this publication. Their initial contributions continue to enrich the *County and City Extra* series. As always, we are especially grateful to the many federal agency personnel who assisted us in obtaining the data, provided excellent resources on their websites, and patiently answered questions.

Deirdre A. Gaquin has been a data use consultant to private organizations, government agencies, and universities for over 30 years. Prior to that, she was Director of Data Access Services at Data Use & Access Laboratories, a pioneer in private sector distribution of federal statistical data. A former President of the Association of Public Data Users, Ms. Gaquin has served on numerous boards, panels, and task forces concerned with federal statistical data and has worked on five decennial censuses. She holds a Master of Urban Planning (MUP) degree from Hunter College. Ms. Gaquin is also an editor of Bernan Press's *The Who, What, and Where of America: Understanding the American Community Survey*; *Places, Towns and Townships*; *The Congressional District Atlas*, *The Almanac of American Education, Race and Employment in America,* and *the State and Metropolitan Area Data Book*.

Mary Meghan Ryan is the senior research editor for Bernan Press. She is also the editor for the *Handbook of U.S. Labor Statistics*, and the associate editor for *Business Statistics of the United States*.

SUBJECTS COVERED, BY GEOGRAPHY TYPE

State data begin on page 1
County data begin on page 51
Metropolitan area data begin on page 773
City data begin on page 895
Congressional district data begin on page 1175

Subject	Column number				
	Table A. States	Table B. States and Counties	Table C. Metropolitan Areas	Table D. Cities	Table E. Congressional Districts
Land area	1	1	1	1	1
Population					
Total persons, 1990	31				
Total persons, 2000	32	20	20	23	
Total persons, 2010	33	21	21	24	
Total persons, 2016					2
Total persons, 2017	2	2	2	2	
Rank, 2017	3	3	3	3	
Persons per square mile	4	4	4	4	
Race and Hispanic or Latino origin, 2010	45-50				
Race and Hispanic or Latino origin, 2016				5-10	4-11
Race and Hispanic or Latino origin, 2017	5–9	5-9	5-9		
Percent female	21	19	19	22	12
Foreign-born population	22			11	13
Percent born in state of residence	23				14
Immigrants	24				
Age distribution, 2010	52-61				
Age distribution, 2016				12-20	15-23
Age distribution, 2017	10-19	10-18	10-18		
Median age	20, 62			21	24
Percent population change, 1990–2000	34				
Percent population change, 2000–2010	35	22	22	25	
Percent population change, 2010–2017	36	23	23	26	
Components of population change	37-41	24-26	24-26		
Daytime population		33-34	33-34		
Population projections	42-44				
Households					
Total households, 2010	64				
Total households, 2016	25	27	27	27	28
Total households, 2012–2016		27-31			
Percent change in number of households	26, 65				
Household type	28-30, 67-68	29-31	29-31	29-33	30-33
Persons per household	27, 66	28	28	28	29
Persons in group quarters		32	32	34	34-39
Housing					
Housing units in 2010	69-78			47-49	
Housing units in 2016	79-92		89-96	50-58	40-45
Housing units in 2017		87-88	87-88		
Housing units in 2012–2016		89-96			
Percent change in number of housing units	70, 80	88	88	48	
Housing costs	73-77, 83-90	91-95	91-95	52	43-45
Substandard housing units	78, 91	96			
Percent with computer and internet access			96	57-58	
Commuting patterns				55-56	
Percent who lived in same house one year ago	92			59	
Percent who lived in different place one year ago				60	
New residential construction	93-95	169-170	169-170	69-71	
Manufactured housing	96				

SUBJECTS COVERED, BY GEOGRAPHY TYPE — Continued

State data begin on page 1
County data begin on page 51
Metropolitan area data begin on page 773
City data begin on page 895
Congressional district data begin on page 1175

Subject	Column number				
	Table A. States	Table B. States and Counties	Table C. Metropolitan Areas	Table D. Cities	Table E. Congressional Districts
Vital statistics					
Births	97-98	35-36	35-36		
Deaths	99-103	37-38	37-38		
Health					
Persons in nursing facilities				33	37
Medicare enrollees	106	41-43	41-43		
Persons lacking health insurance	104-105	39-40	39-40		59
Crime	107-110	44-47	44-47	35-38	
Education					
School enrollment	111-112	48-49	48-49		25
Educational attainment	113-116	50-51	50-51	39-41	26-27
Expenditures for education	117-118	52-53	52-53		
Income					
Personal income	134-149	62-71	62-71		
Per capita income	122, 136, 149	54, 64	54, 64		46
Household income	123-126	55-58	55-58	42-44	47-48
Family and non-family income				45-46	
Earnings by gender				47-49	
Poverty	127-133	59-61	59-61		49-50
Food stamps					51
Personal income by type	138-140	66-70	66-70		
Earnings by industry	150-158	72-83	72-83		
Transfer payments	141-146	71	71		
Gross state product	159				
Personal tax payments	147				
Disposable personal income	148-149				
Social Security	160-162	84-86	84-86		60-62
Individual income taxes		197-199	197-199		
Labor Force and Employment					
Labor force and unemployment	167-171	97-100	97-100	61-68	52-54
Employment in selected occupations	163-166	101-103	101-103		55-58
Employment by industry	172-183, 207-216	104-112	104-112		73-84
Exports of goods produced	119-121				
Establishments, employment, sales, and payroll					
Manufacturing	207-216	151-154	151-154	88-91	
Construction	217-221				
Wholesale trade	222-226	135-138	135-138	72-75	
Retail trade	227-235	139-142	139-142	76-79	
Information	236-246				
Utilities	247-251				
Transportation and warehousing	252-256				
Finance and insurance	257-261				
Real estate and rental and leasing	262-266	143-146	143-146	80-83	
Professional, scientific, and technical services	267-275	147-150	147-150	84-87	
Health care and social assistance	276-289	159-162	159-162	100-103	

SUBJECTS COVERED, BY GEOGRAPHY TYPE — Continued

State data begin on page 1
County data begin on page 51
Metropolitan area data begin on page 773
City data begin on page 895
Congressional district data begin on page 1175

Subject	Column number				
	Table A. States	Table B. States and Counties	Table C. Metropolitan Areas	Table D. Cities	Table E. Congressional Districts
Arts, entertainment and recreation	290-294			96-99	
Accommodation and food services	295-300	155-158	155-158	92-95	
Other services, except public administration	301-308	163-166	163-166	104-108	
Nonemployer businesses		167-168	167-168		
Government employment	309-314	171, 194-196	171, 194-196	108	
Government payroll	315-330	172-179	172-179	109-116	
Government finances	331-350	180-193	180-193	117-139	
Agriculture	184-202	113-132	113-132		63-72
Land and water	203-206	133-134	133-134		
Voting and elections	351-355				
Climate				140-146	

Population Change
2010–2017

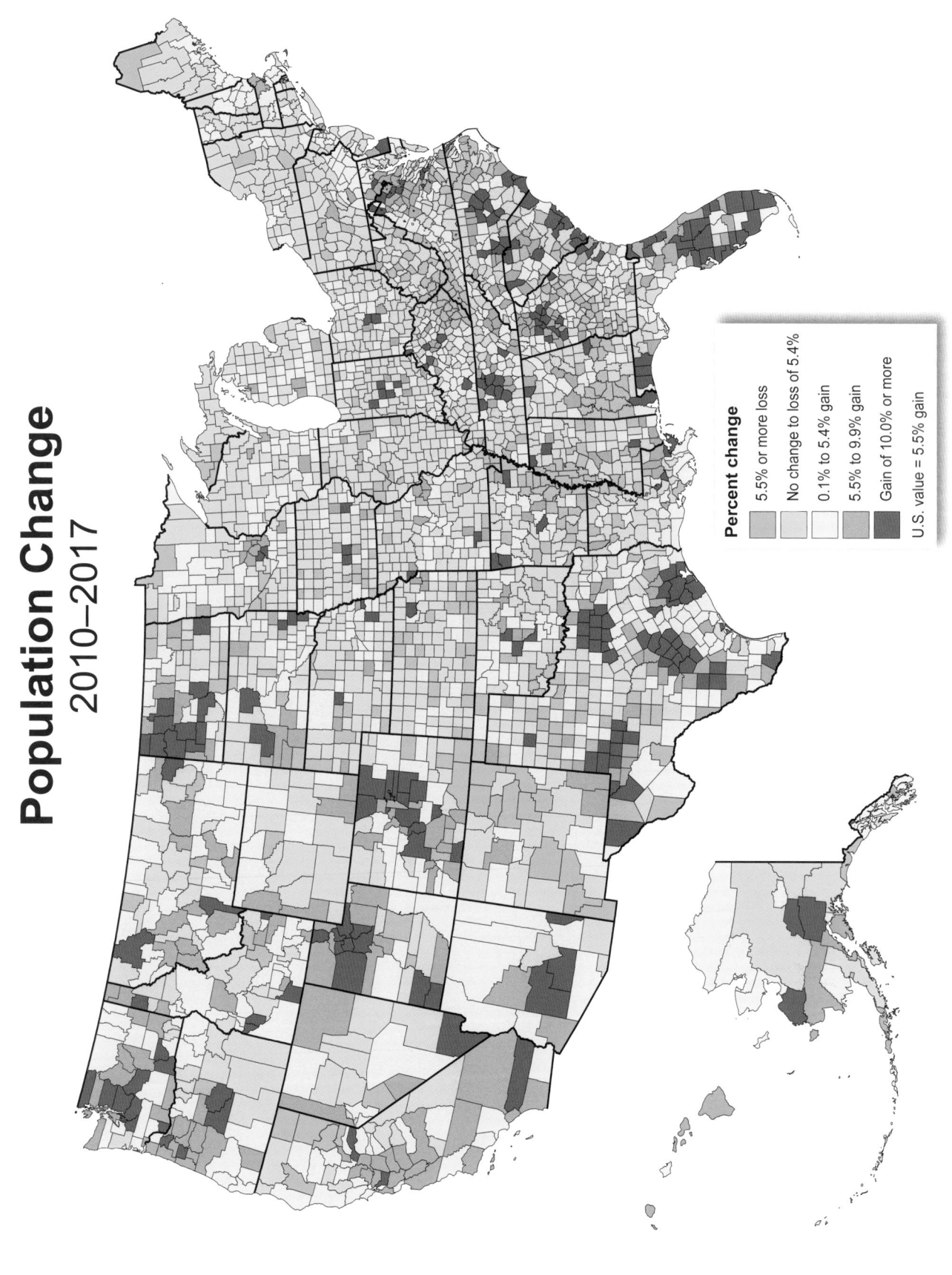

Percent change

- 5.5% or more loss
- No change to loss of 5.4%
- 0.1% to 5.4% gain
- 5.5% to 9.9% gain
- Gain of 10.0% or more

U.S. value = 5.5% gain

Black, Not Hispanic or Latino, Population
2017

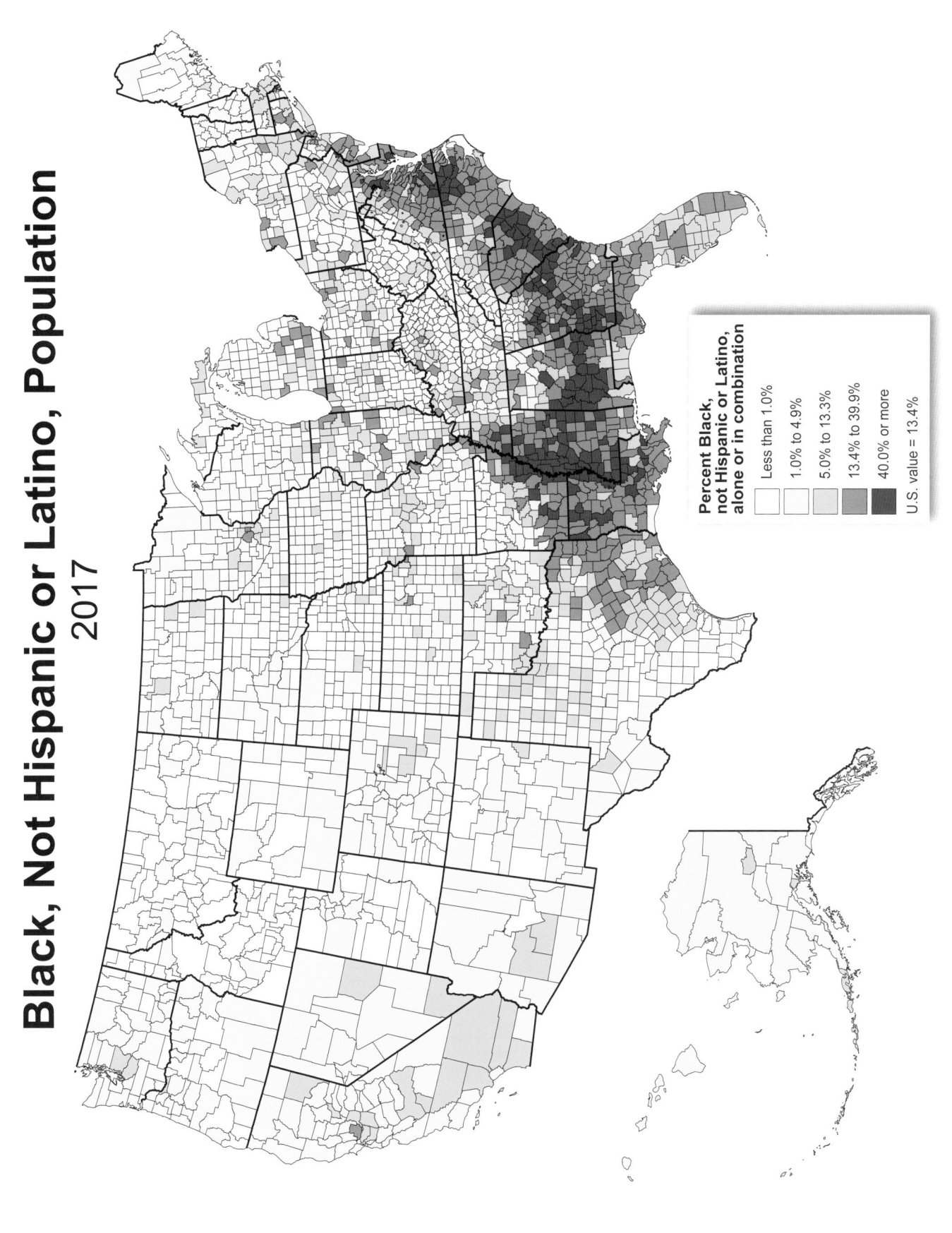

Percent Black, not Hispanic or Latino, alone or in combination

Less than 1.0%
1.0% to 4.9%
5.0% to 13.3%
13.4% to 39.9%
40.0% or more

U.S. value = 13.4%

Hispanic or Latino Population
2017

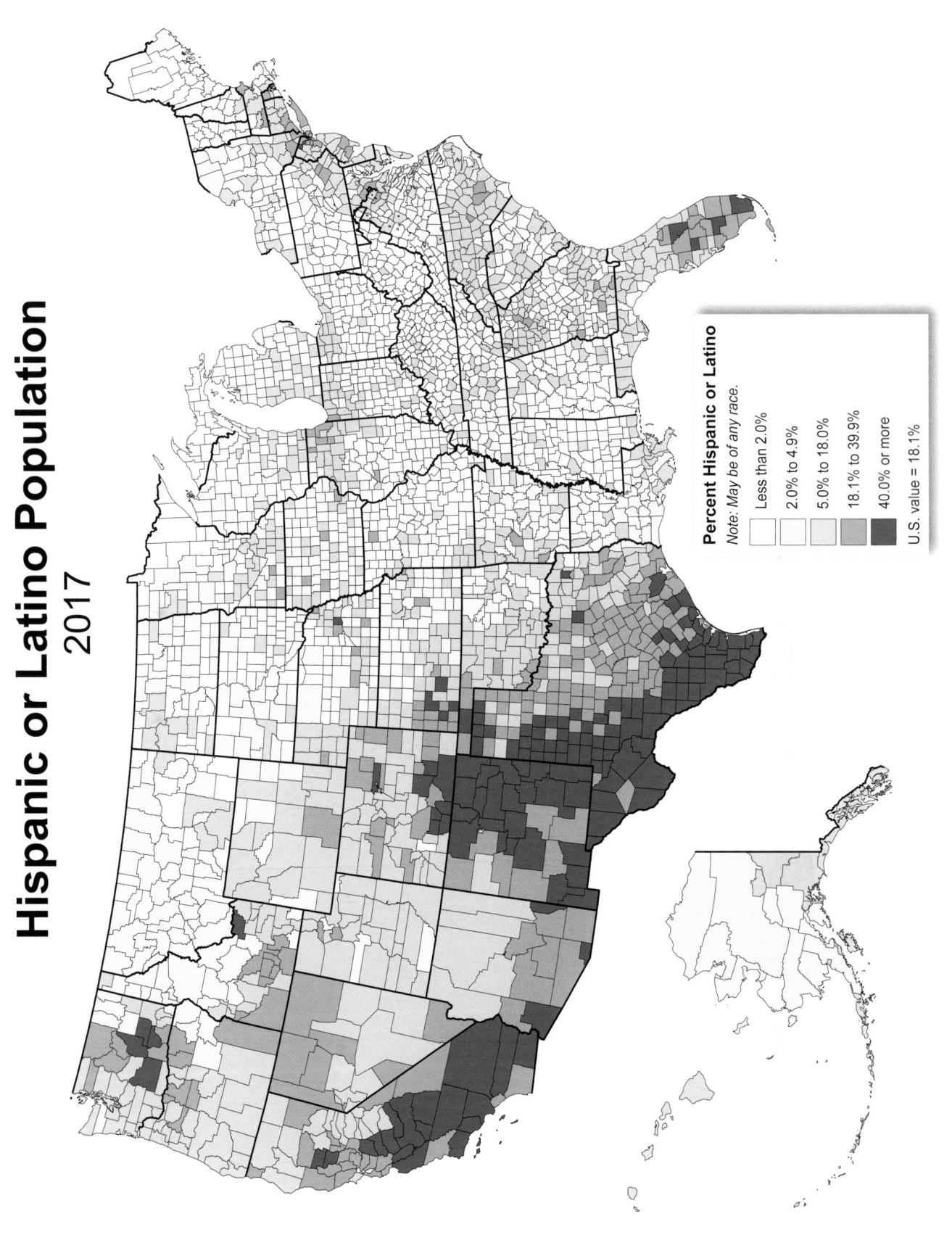

Percent Hispanic or Latino

Note: May be of any race.

- Less than 2.0%
- 2.0% to 4.9%
- 5.0% to 18.0%
- 18.1% to 39.9%
- 40.0% or more

U.S. value = 18.1%

Population Under 18 Years Old
2017

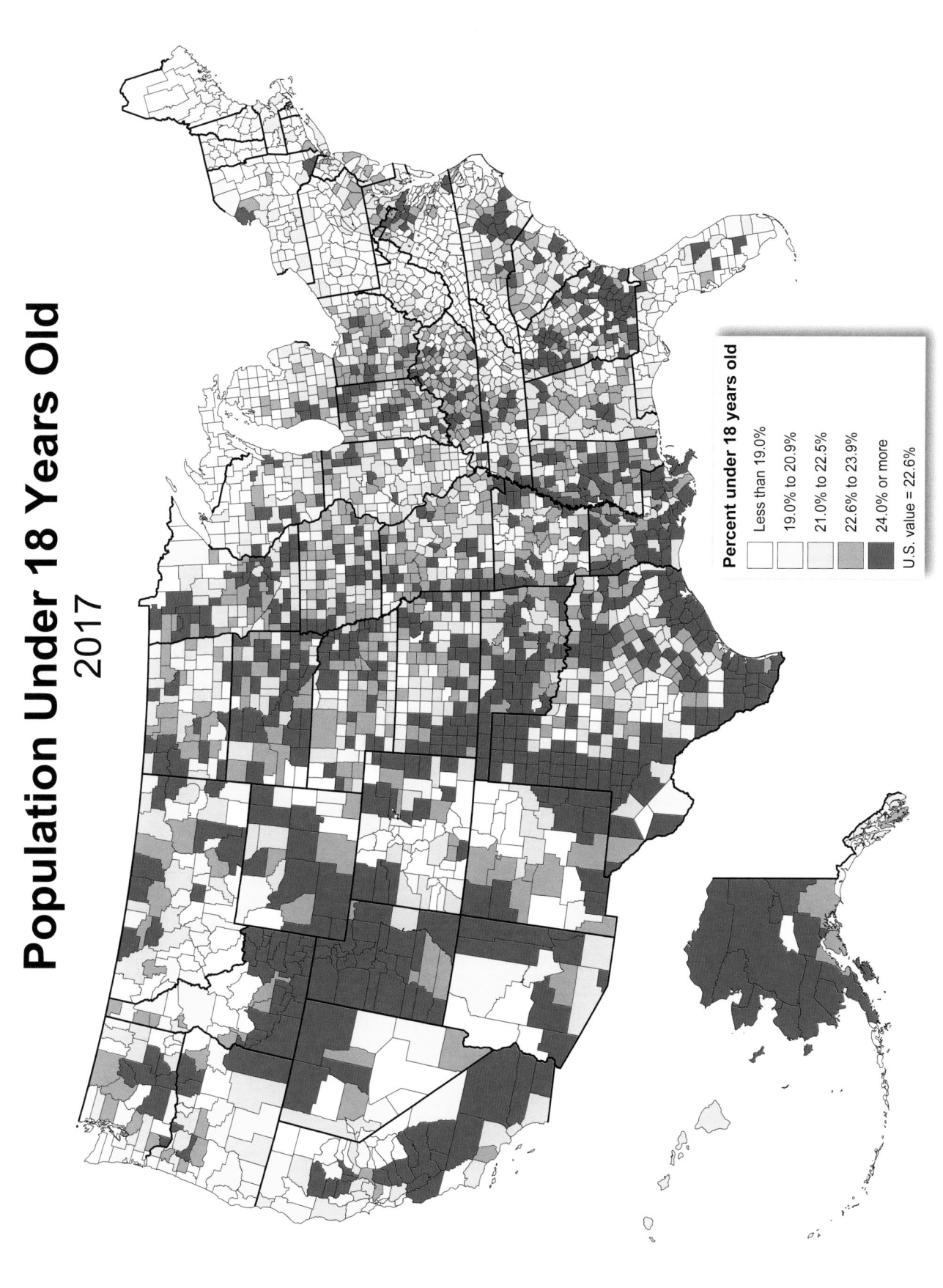

Percent under 18 years old

- Less than 19.0%
- 19.0% to 20.9%
- 21.0% to 22.5%
- 22.6% to 23.9%
- 24.0% or more

U.S. value = 22.6%

Population 65 Years Old and Over

2017

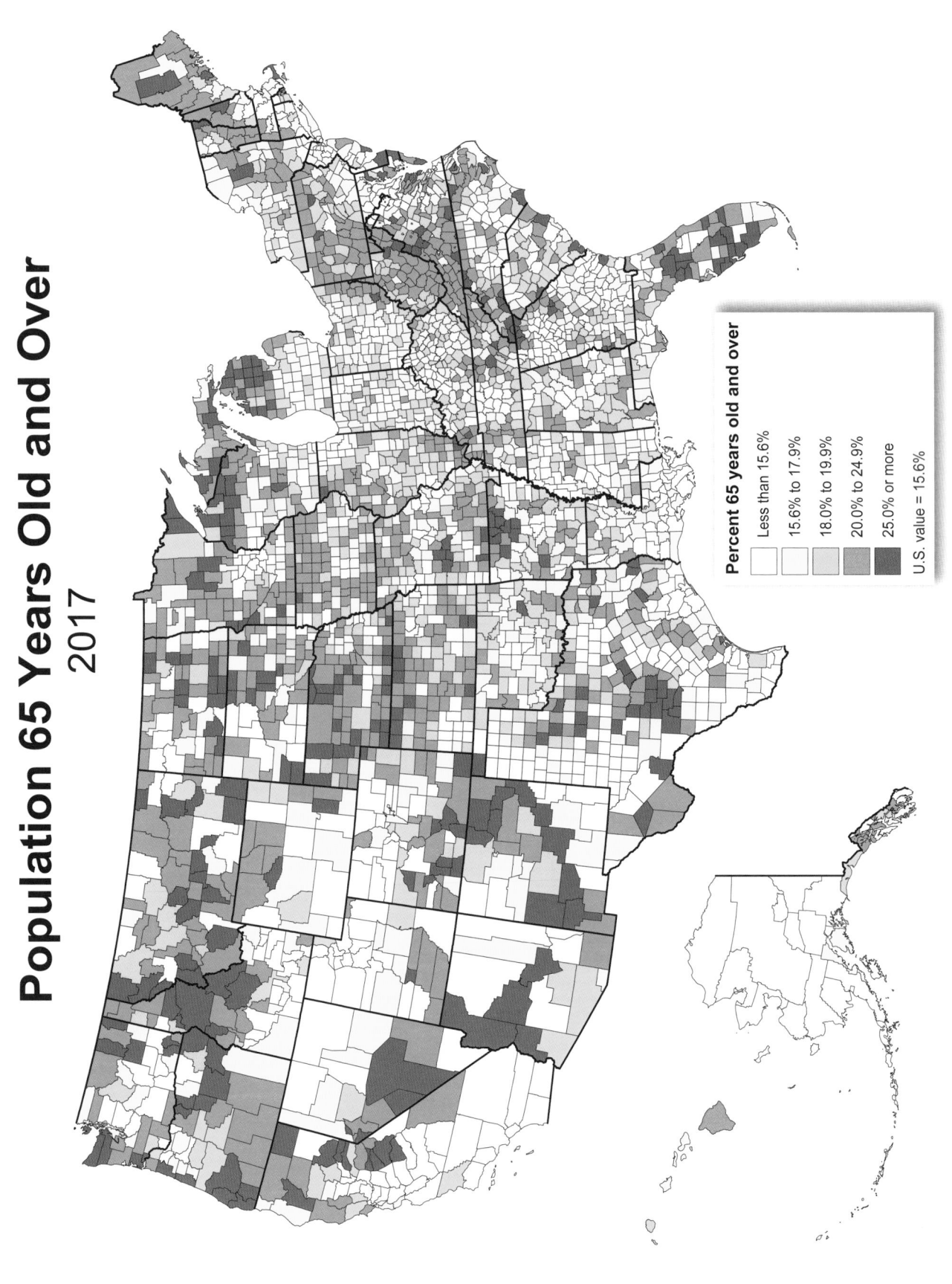

Percent 65 years old and over

Less than 15.6%
15.6% to 17.9%
18.0% to 19.9%
20.0% to 24.9%
25.0% or more

U.S. value = 15.6%

Population Density
2017

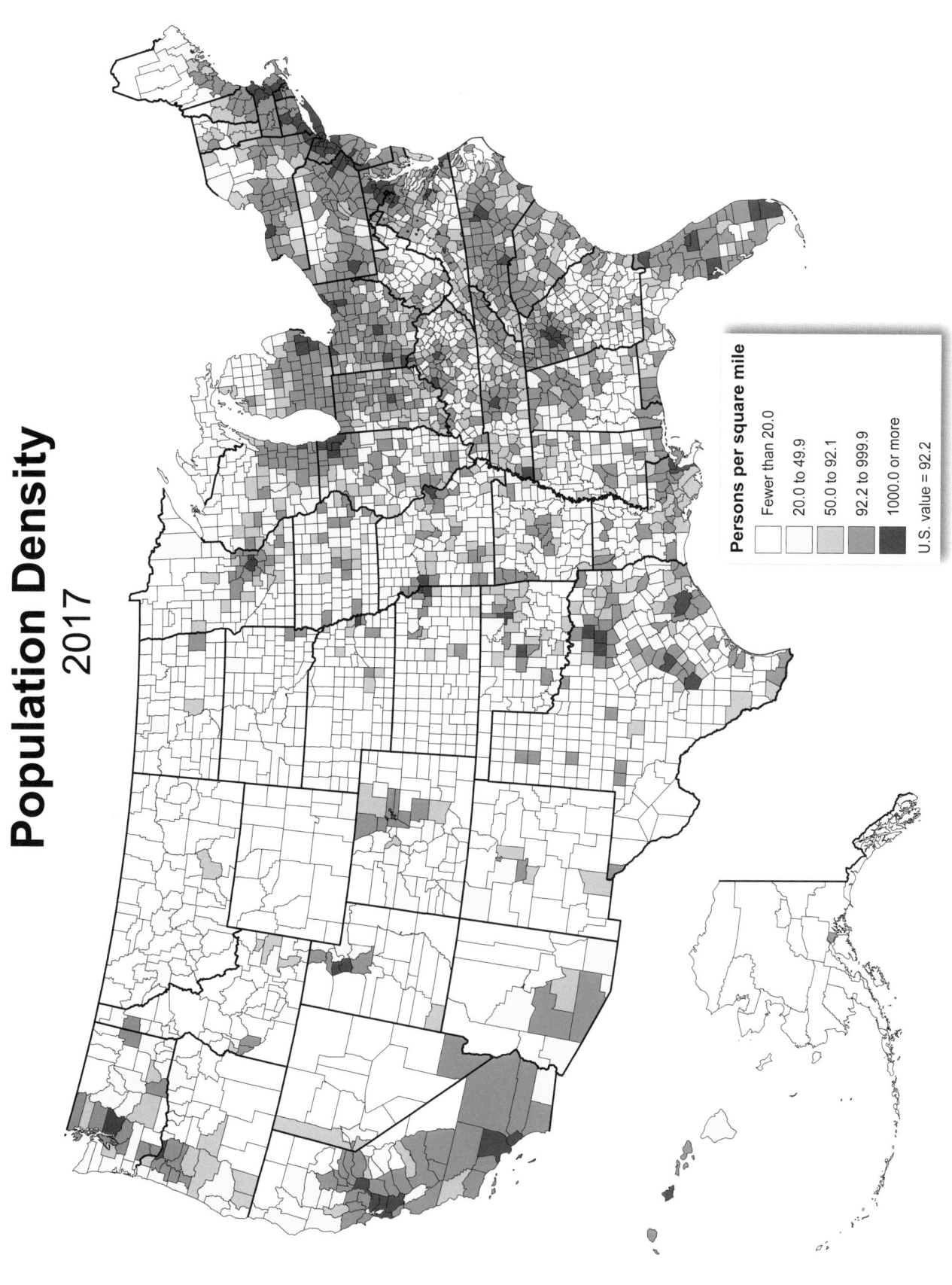

Persons per square mile

Fewer than 20.0
20.0 to 49.9
50.0 to 92.1
92.2 to 999.9
1000.0 or more

U.S. value = 92.2

xix

Unemployment Rate
2017

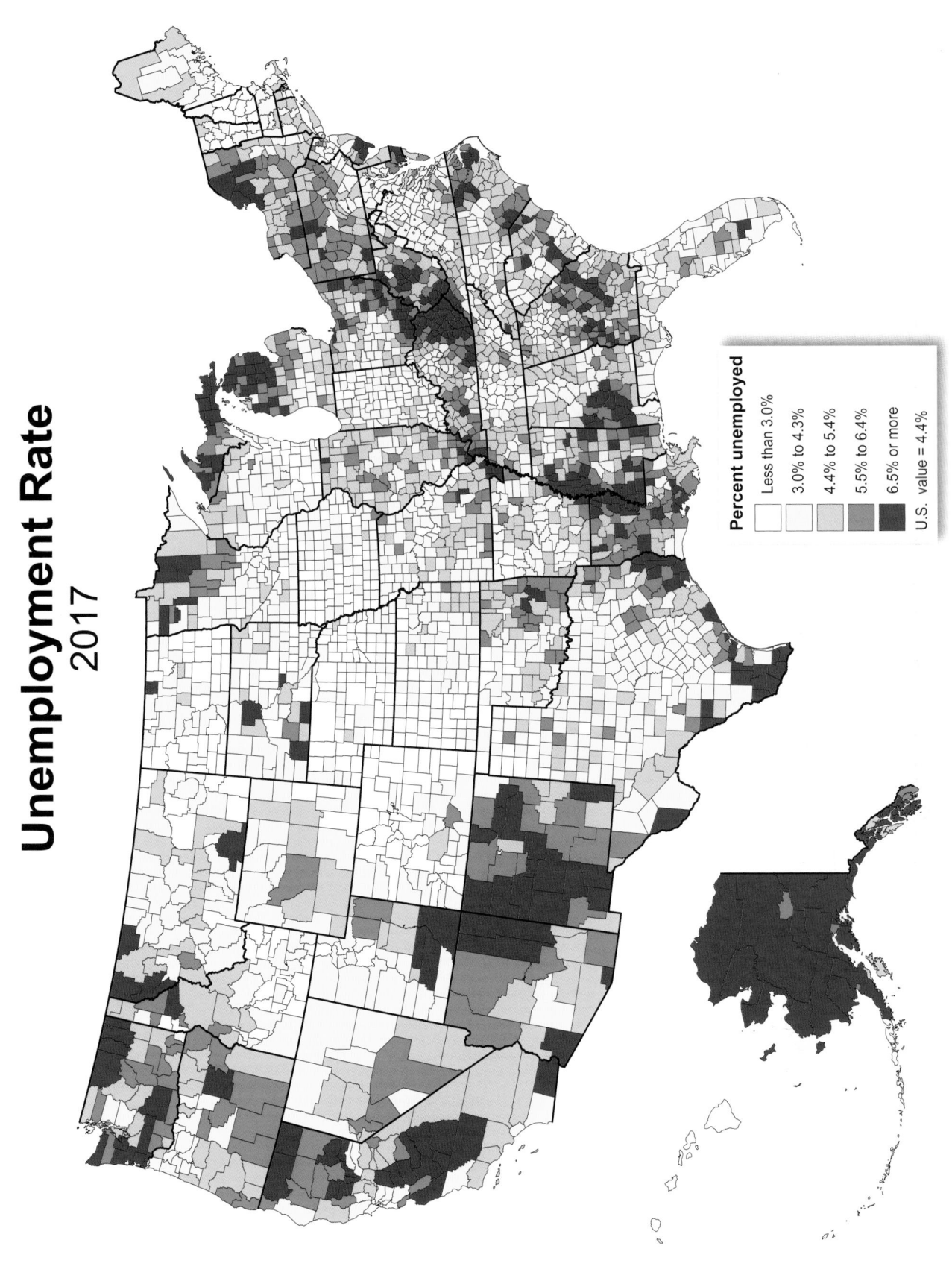

Percent unemployed

Less than 3.0%
3.0% to 4.3%
4.4% to 5.4%
5.5% to 6.4%
6.5% or more

U.S. value = 4.4%

Earnings from Manufacturing
2016

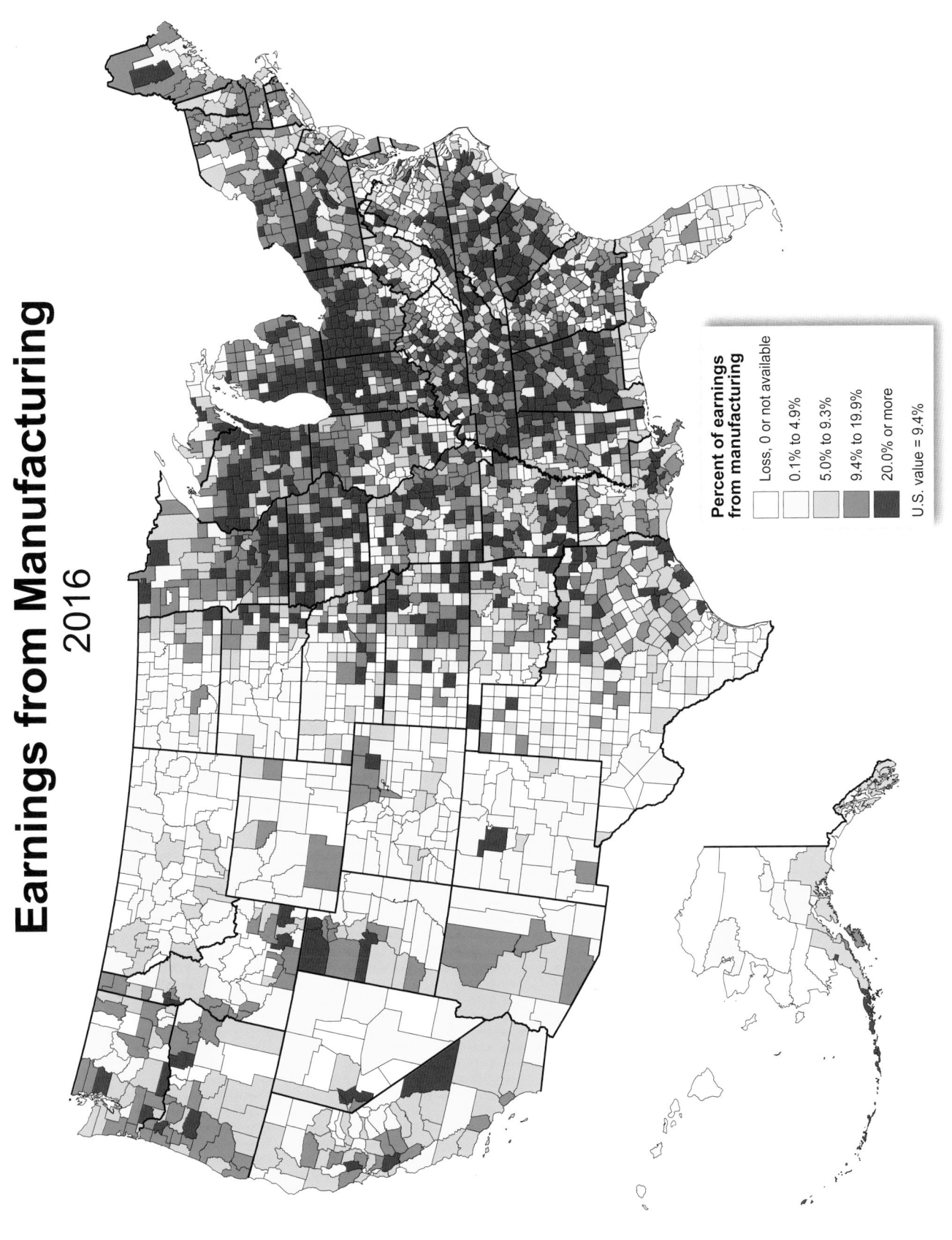

Percent of earnings from manufacturing

- Loss, 0 or not available
- 0.1% to 4.9%
- 5.0% to 9.3%
- 9.4% to 19.9%
- 20.0% or more

U.S. value = 9.4%

States

(For explanation of symbols, see page viii)

Part A — States

State Highlights and Rankings

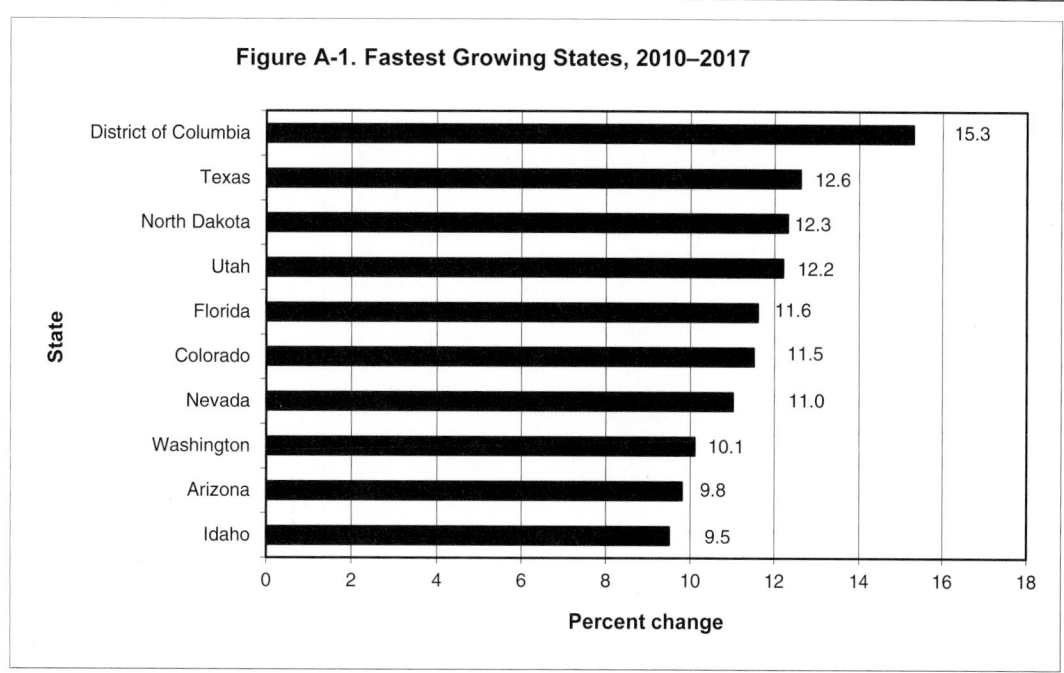

Figure A-1. Fastest Growing States, 2010–2017

State	Percent change
District of Columbia	15.3
Texas	12.6
North Dakota	12.3
Utah	12.2
Florida	11.6
Colorado	11.5
Nevada	11.0
Washington	10.1
Arizona	9.8
Idaho	9.5

There is no simple relationship between population size and land area for most of the geographic entities included in this publication. According to the Census Bureau's 2017 estimates, state populations ranged from a high of over 39 million in California to a low of 579,315 in Wyoming. (The median population for states—with half having a larger population and half having a smaller population—was over 4.4 million people.) California was also one of the largest states in land area (ranking third). Alaska was by far the largest state in area; it was more than twice the size of Texas, the second-largest state, even though its population rank was close to the bottom (ranked 48th). Texas was also the second-largest state in terms of total population with over 28.0 million residents. At the other end of the geographic size spectrum were many of the New England states (with Rhode Island ranking as the smallest), plus Delaware, Hawaii, and New Jersey. As a consequence of differing area size and population rank, New Jersey was the most densely settled state, with 1,224.4 persons per square mile while Alaska was the least densely settled, with about 1.3 persons per square mile. California, which had the largest population and third-largest land area, ranked 12th in terms of population density (253.8 persons per square mile). The 15 most populous states remained almost unchanged between 2010 and 2017—Arizona moved into the top 15 while Indiana dropped out—but there were changes within their ranks. Florida became the 3rd most populous state, pushing ahead of New York while Georgia became the 8th most populous state. North Carolina moved up to 9th place while Michigan dropped to 10th.

Not surprisingly, states with higher population density also had higher proportions of developed land. According to the Department of Agriculture's most recent National Resources Inventory, 35.4 percent of New Jersey's land was developed. Connecticut had the second highest proportion with 33.9 percent, followed by Massachusetts at 33.1 percent. Among the reporting states,

Nevada had the lowest proportion of developed land, at just 0.8 percent, followed by Montana and Wyoming, with 1.1 percent and 1.2 percent of their land developed. Nearly 85 percent of Nevada's land was owned by the federal government. This was by far the highest percentage in the nation. Federal land accounted for almost 21 percent of the United States' total land area. (Estimates are not available for Alaska, and the District of Columbia. See Appendix F for definitions and additional information.)

The total population of the United States increased 5.5 percent between 2010 and 2017, with 20 states matching or exceeding this rate of growth and the remainder growing more slowly. The District of Columbia experienced a higher growth rate than any of the states (15.3 percent). Texas, North Dakota and Utah all had growth rates above 12 percent. The District of Columbia ranked 49th by population size and gained more than 92,000 residents in the 7-year period. Texas has the second largest population among all the states and gained more than 3 million residents. Despite its growth, North Dakota ranked 47th for total population and 48th for density, with only 10.9 persons per square mile. Texas and Florida ranked among the top 10 states for total population and for population growth from 2010 to 2017. Florida, with the third-largest population, grew by 11.6 percent, increasing its population by nearly 2.2 million people. Rhode Island and Vermont both ranked among the 10 least populous states, as well as among the 10 states with the lowest population growth between 2010 and 2017. While most states have increased their populations in the seven years, the populations of West Virginia, Illinois, and Vermont declined by a small amount. Six other states experienced increases below one percent. Louisiana's population has rebounded from a loss of about 250,000 residents after Hurricane Katrina hit the state in August 2005. Its 2017 population of over 4.6 million is slightly higher than its 2005 estimated population on July 1 of that year.

3

States and the District of Columbia, Selected Rankings

Population, 2017			Land Area, 2017				Population density, 2017			
Population rank	State	Population [col 2]	Population rank	Land area	State	Land area (square miles) [col 1]	Population rank	Density rank	State	Density (per square mile) [col 4]
	United States	325,719,178			United States	3,532,316			United States	92.2
1	California	39,536,653	48	1	Alaska	570,886	49	1	District of Columbia	11,358.0
2	Texas	28,304,596	2	2	Texas	261,253	11	2	New Jersey	1,224.4
3	Florida	20,984,400	1	3	California	155,786	43	3	Rhode Island	1,024.8
4	New York	19,849,399	44	4	Montana	145,545	15	4	Massachusetts	879.4
5	Pennsylvania	12,805,537	36	5	New Mexico	121,310	29	5	Connecticut	740.9
6	Illinois	12,802,023	14	6	Arizona	113,591	19	6	Maryland	623.2
7	Ohio	11,658,609	33	7	Nevada	109,780	45	7	Delaware	493.6
8	Georgia	10,429,379	21	8	Colorado	103,640	4	8	New York	421.2
9	North Carolina	10,273,419	51	9	Wyoming	97,091	3	9	Florida	391.3
10	Michigan	9,962,311	27	10	Oregon	95,987	5	10	Pennsylvania	286.2
11	New Jersey	9,005,644	39	11	Idaho	82,645	7	11	Ohio	285.3
12	Virginia	8,470,020	31	12	Utah	82,195	1	12	California	253.8
13	Washington	7,405,743	35	13	Kansas	81,758	6	13	Illinois	230.6
14	Arizona	7,016,270	22	14	Minnesota	79,626	40	14	Hawaii	222.3
15	Massachusetts	6,859,819	37	15	Nebraska	76,818	12	15	Virginia	214.5
16	Tennessee	6,715,984	46	16	South Dakota	75,809	9	16	North Carolina	211.3
17	Indiana	6,666,818	47	17	North Dakota	69,001	17	17	Indiana	186.1
18	Missouri	6,113,532	18	18	Missouri	68,746	8	18	Georgia	181.1
19	Maryland	6,052,177	28	19	Oklahoma	68,597	10	19	Michigan	176.1
20	Wisconsin	5,795,483	13	20	Washington	66,453	23	20	South Carolina	167.1
21	Colorado	5,607,154	8	21	Georgia	57,598	16	21	Tennessee	162.9
22	Minnesota	5,576,606	10	22	Michigan	56,559	41	22	New Hampshire	150.0
23	South Carolina	5,024,369	30	23	Iowa	55,855	26	23	Kentucky	112.8
24	Alabama	4,874,747	6	24	Illinois	55,515	13	24	Washington	111.4
25	Louisiana	4,684,333	20	25	Wisconsin	54,161	25	25	Louisiana	108.4
26	Kentucky	4,454,189	3	26	Florida	53,634	2	26	Texas	108.3
27	Oregon	4,142,776	32	27	Arkansas	52,034	20	27	Wisconsin	107.0
28	Oklahoma	3,930,864	24	28	Alabama	50,647	24	28	Alabama	96.3
29	Connecticut	3,588,184	9	29	North Carolina	48,618	18	29	Missouri	88.9
30	Iowa	3,145,711	4	30	New York	47,123	38	30	West Virginia	75.5
31	Utah	3,101,833	34	31	Mississippi	46,923	22	31	Minnesota	70.0
32	Arkansas	3,004,279	5	32	Pennsylvania	44,742	50	32	Vermont	67.7
33	Nevada	2,998,039	25	33	Louisiana	43,207	34	33	Mississippi	63.6
34	Mississippi	2,984,100	16	34	Tennessee	41,235	14	34	Arizona	61.8
35	Kansas	2,913,123	7	35	Ohio	40,863	32	35	Arkansas	57.7
36	New Mexico	2,088,070	26	36	Kentucky	39,485	28	36	Oklahoma	57.3
37	Nebraska	1,920,076	12	37	Virginia	39,481	30	37	Iowa	56.3
38	West Virginia	1,815,857	17	38	Indiana	35,826	21	38	Colorado	54.1
39	Idaho	1,716,943	42	39	Maine	30,844	42	39	Maine	43.3
40	Hawaii	1,427,538	23	40	South Carolina	30,063	27	40	Oregon	43.2
41	New Hampshire	1,342,795	38	41	West Virginia	24,041	31	41	Utah	37.7
42	Maine	1,335,907	19	42	Maryland	9,711	35	42	Kansas	35.6
43	Rhode Island	1,059,639	50	43	Vermont	9,218	33	43	Nevada	27.3
44	Montana	1,050,493	41	44	New Hampshire	8,953	37	44	Nebraska	25.0
45	Delaware	961,939	15	45	Massachusetts	7,801	39	45	Idaho	20.8
46	South Dakota	869,666	11	46	New Jersey	7,355	36	46	New Mexico	17.2
47	North Dakota	755,393	40	47	Hawaii	6,423	46	47	South Dakota	11.5
48	Alaska	739,795	29	48	Connecticut	4,843	47	48	North Dakota	10.9
49	District of Columbia	693,972	45	49	Delaware	1,949	44	49	Montana	7.2
50	Vermont	623,657	43	50	Rhode Island	1,034	51	50	Wyoming	6.0
51	Wyoming	579,315	49	51	District of Columbia	61.1	48	51	Alaska	1.3

States and the District of Columbia, Selected Rankings

	Percent population change, 2010–2017				Percent Under 18 years old, 2017				Percent 65 years old and over, 2017		
Population rank	Percent change rank	State	Percent change [col 36]	Population rank	Under 18 years old rank	State	Percent under 18 years old [cols 10 + 11]	Population rank	65 years old and over rank	State	Percent 65 years old and over [cols 17 + 18 + 19]
		United States	5.5			United States	22.6			United States	15.6
49	1	District of Columbia	15.3	31	1	Utah	29.8	3	1	Florida	20.1
2	2	Texas	12.6	2	2	Texas	26.0	42	2	Maine	19.9
47	3	North Dakota	12.3	39	3	Idaho	25.8	38	3	West Virginia	19.4
31	4	Utah	12.2	48	4	Alaska	25.0	50	4	Vermont	18.7
3	5	Florida	11.6	37	5	Nebraska	24.7	45	5	Delaware	18.1
21	6	Colorado	11.5	46	5	South Dakota	24.7	44	5	Montana	18.1
33	7	Nevada	11.0	35	7	Kansas	24.4	40	7	Hawaii	17.8
13	8	Washington	10.1	28	7	Oklahoma	24.4	5	7	Pennsylvania	17.8
14	9	Arizona	9.8	8	9	Georgia	24.1	41	9	New Hampshire	17.6
39	10	Idaho	9.5	34	10	Mississippi	23.9	23	10	South Carolina	17.2
23	11	South Carolina	8.6	25	11	Louisiana	23.7	14	11	Arizona	17.1
27	12	Oregon	8.1	17	12	Indiana	23.6	27	11	Oregon	17.1
8	13	Georgia	7.7	51	12	Wyoming	23.6	36	13	New Mexico	16.9
9	13	North Carolina	7.7	32	14	Arkansas	23.5	29	14	Connecticut	16.8
45	15	Delaware	7.1	22	15	Minnesota	23.3	43	14	Rhode Island	16.8
46	16	South Dakota	6.8	36	15	New Mexico	23.3	30	16	Iowa	16.7
44	17	Montana	6.2	47	15	North Dakota	23.3	10	16	Michigan	16.7
1	18	California	6.1	14	18	Arizona	23.2	7	16	Ohio	16.7
12	19	Virginia	5.9	30	18	Iowa	23.2	32	19	Arkansas	16.6
16	20	Tennessee	5.8	1	20	California	23.0	24	20	Alabama	16.5
22	21	Minnesota	5.1	33	21	Nevada	22.9	18	20	Missouri	16.5
37	21	Nebraska	5.1	26	22	Kentucky	22.7	20	22	Wisconsin	16.4
40	23	Hawaii	4.9	6	23	Illinois	22.6	46	23	South Dakota	16.3
19	24	Maryland	4.8	18	23	Missouri	22.6	15	24	Massachusetts	16.1
15	24	Massachusetts	4.8	24	25	Alabama	22.5	16	24	Tennessee	16.1
28	24	Oklahoma	4.8	21	25	Colorado	22.5	26	26	Kentucky	16.0
48	27	Alaska	4.2	16	25	Tennessee	22.5	4	27	New York	15.9
30	28	Iowa	3.3	9	28	North Carolina	22.4	9	27	North Carolina	15.9
25	28	Louisiana	3.3	7	28	Ohio	22.4	11	29	New Jersey	15.8
32	30	Arkansas	3.0	19	30	Maryland	22.3	51	29	Wyoming	15.8
17	31	Indiana	2.8	13	31	Washington	22.2	39	31	Idaho	15.5
51	31	Wyoming	2.8	20	32	Wisconsin	22.1	34	31	Mississippi	15.5
26	33	Kentucky	2.6	11	33	New Jersey	22.0	17	33	Indiana	15.4
11	34	New Jersey	2.4	12	33	Virginia	22.0	35	33	Kansas	15.4
4	34	New York	2.4	10	35	Michigan	21.9	22	33	Minnesota	15.4
35	36	Kansas	2.1	23	35	South Carolina	21.9	33	33	Nevada	15.4
18	36	Missouri	2.1	44	37	Montana	21.8	37	37	Nebraska	15.3
24	38	Alabama	2.0	40	38	Hawaii	21.4	28	37	Oklahoma	15.3
41	38	New Hampshire	2.0	45	39	Delaware	21.2	6	39	Illinois	15.2
20	40	Wisconsin	1.9	27	40	Oregon	21.1	12	40	Virginia	15.1
36	41	New Mexico	1.4	4	41	New York	21.0	13	40	Washington	15.1
7	42	Ohio	1.1	5	42	Pennsylvania	20.8	47	42	North Dakota	15.0
10	43	Michigan	0.8	29	43	Connecticut	20.7	25	43	Louisiana	14.9
5	43	Pennsylvania	0.8	38	44	West Virginia	20.3	19	43	Maryland	14.9
43	45	Rhode Island	0.7	3	45	Florida	20.0	1	45	California	14.0
42	46	Maine	0.6	15	45	Massachusetts	20.0	21	46	Colorado	13.7
34	46	Mississippi	0.6	43	47	Rhode Island	19.6	8	47	Georgia	13.6
29	48	Connecticut	0.4	41	48	New Hampshire	19.3	2	48	Texas	12.3
6	49	Illinois	-0.2	42	49	Maine	18.9	49	49	District of Columbia	12.0
50	50	Vermont	-0.3	50	50	Vermont	18.7	48	50	Alaska	11.2
38	51	West Virginia	-2.0	49	51	District of Columbia	17.9	31	51	Utah	10.8

States and the District of Columbia, Selected Rankings

Percent born in state of residence, 2016

Population rank	Born in state of residence rank	State	Percent born in state of residence [col 23]
		United States	58.3
25	1	Louisiana	78.2
10	2	Michigan	76.3
7	3	Ohio	75.0
5	4	Pennsylvania	72.4
34	5	Mississippi	71.5
20	6	Wisconsin	71.5
30	7	Iowa	70.5
24	8	Alabama	69.5
26	9	Kentucky	68.9
38	10	West Virginia	68.9
17	11	Indiana	68.2
22	12	Minnesota	68.0
6	13	Illinois	67.1
18	14	Missouri	66.3
37	15	Nebraska	64.7
46	16	South Dakota	64.5
4	17	New York	62.7
42	18	Maine	62.6
47	19	North Dakota	62.5
31	20	Utah	62.0
28	21	Oklahoma	61.4
32	22	Arkansas	61.2
16	23	Tennessee	61.2
15	24	Massachusetts	60.9
2	25	Texas	59.7
35	26	Kansas	59.1
23	27	South Carolina	57.0
9	28	North Carolina	56.8
43	29	Rhode Island	56.4
29	30	Connecticut	55.2
1	31	California	55.0
44	32	Montana	54.7
8	33	Georgia	54.6
40	34	Hawaii	53.3
36	35	New Mexico	52.9
11	36	New Jersey	52.2
50	37	Vermont	50.2
12	38	Virginia	49.4
39	39	Idaho	48.3
19	40	Maryland	47.6
13	41	Washington	46.8
27	42	Oregon	46.3
45	43	Delaware	45.0
21	44	Colorado	42.8
51	45	Wyoming	42.7
41	46	New Hampshire	41.7
48	47	Alaska	40.7
14	48	Arizona	39.5
49	49	District of Columbia	37.2
3	50	Florida	35.8
33	51	Nevada	26.4

Number of immigrants, 2016

Population rank	Immigrant rank	State	Number of immigrants [col 24]
		United States	1,183,505
1	1	California	223,141
4	2	New York	159,878
3	3	Florida	136,337
2	4	Texas	110,651
11	5	New Jersey	56,187
6	6	Illinois	43,207
15	7	Massachusetts	35,706
8	8	Georgia	29,572
12	9	Virginia	29,242
13	10	Washington	27,304
5	11	Pennsylvania	27,217
19	12	Maryland	26,077
10	13	Michigan	22,569
9	14	North Carolina	20,811
14	15	Arizona	20,694
7	16	Ohio	17,251
22	17	Minnesota	15,603
21	18	Colorado	14,225
29	19	Connecticut	12,669
33	20	Nevada	11,555
27	21	Oregon	10,033
16	22	Tennessee	10,032
17	23	Indiana	9,946
31	24	Utah	7,271
20	25	Wisconsin	7,111
26	26	Kentucky	7,098
18	27	Missouri	6,868
40	28	Hawaii	6,285
28	29	Oklahoma	5,960
25	30	Louisiana	5,784
35	31	Kansas	5,709
37	32	Nebraska	5,654
30	33	Iowa	5,299
23	34	South Carolina	5,104
24	35	Alabama	4,736
43	36	Rhode Island	4,194
36	37	New Mexico	4,104
32	38	Arkansas	3,158
49	39	District of Columbia	3,114
39	40	Idaho	2,562
41	41	New Hampshire	2,332
45	42	Delaware	2,204
34	43	Mississippi	2,149
42	44	Maine	1,748
48	45	Alaska	1,726
47	46	North Dakota	1,595
46	47	South Dakota	1,229
38	48	West Virginia	928
50	49	Vermont	886
44	50	Montana	566
51	51	Wyoming	462

Birth rate, 2016

Population rank	Birth rate rank	State	Birth rate (per 1,000 population) [col 98]
		United States	12.2
31	1	Utah	16.5
48	2	Alaska	15.1
47	3	North Dakota	15.0
49	4	District of Columbia	14.5
2	5	Texas	14.3
46	6	South Dakota	14.2
37	7	Nebraska	13.9
25	8	Louisiana	13.5
39	9	Idaho	13.4
28	9	Oklahoma	13.4
35	11	Kansas	13.1
32	12	Arkansas	12.8
34	13	Mississippi	12.7
8	14	Georgia	12.6
40	14	Hawaii	12.6
30	14	Iowa	12.6
22	14	Minnesota	12.6
51	14	Wyoming	12.6
1	19	California	12.5
17	19	Indiana	12.5
26	19	Kentucky	12.5
13	22	Washington	12.4
18	23	Missouri	12.3
33	23	Nevada	12.3
24	25	Alabama	12.2
14	25	Arizona	12.2
19	25	Maryland	12.2
12	25	Virginia	12.2
6	29	Illinois	12.1
16	29	Tennessee	12.1
21	31	Colorado	12.0
36	32	New Mexico	11.9
4	32	New York	11.9
9	32	North Carolina	11.9
7	32	Ohio	11.9
44	36	Montana	11.8
23	37	South Carolina	11.6
45	38	Delaware	11.5
11	38	New Jersey	11.5
20	38	Wisconsin	11.5
10	41	Michigan	11.4
27	42	Oregon	11.1
3	43	Florida	10.9
5	43	Pennsylvania	10.9
15	45	Massachusetts	10.5
38	46	West Virginia	10.4
43	47	Rhode Island	10.2
29	48	Connecticut	10.1
42	49	Maine	9.5
41	50	New Hampshire	9.2
50	50	Vermont	9.2

States and the District of Columbia, Selected Rankings

Population rank	Percent high school graduates rank	State	Percent high school graduates [col 115]	Population rank	Percent college graduates rank	State	Percent college graduates [col 116]	Population rank	Median income rank	State	Median income (dollars) [col 123]
		United States	87.0			United States	30.3			United States	57,617
44	1	Montana	92.9	49	1	District of Columbia	55.4	19	1	Maryland	78,945
22	2	Minnesota	92.6	15	2	Massachusetts	41.2	48	2	Alaska	76,440
41	2	New Hampshire	92.6	21	3	Colorado	38.7	11	3	New Jersey	76,126
51	4	Wyoming	92.4	19	4	Maryland	38.4	49	4	District of Columbia	75,506
48	5	Alaska	92.3	29	5	Connecticut	38.0	15	5	Massachusetts	75,297
47	6	North Dakota	92.0	11	6	New Jersey	37.5	40	6	Hawaii	74,511
42	7	Maine	91.9	12	7	Virginia	36.9	29	7	Connecticut	73,433
50	7	Vermont	91.9	50	8	Vermont	36.2	41	8	New Hampshire	70,936
30	9	Iowa	91.7	41	9	New Hampshire	35.5	12	9	Virginia	68,114
31	10	Utah	91.5	4	10	New York	34.7	1	10	California	67,739
20	11	Wisconsin	91.4	22	11	Minnesota	34.2	13	11	Washington	67,106
40	12	Hawaii	91.3	13	12	Washington	33.6	31	12	Utah	65,977
46	13	South Dakota	91.2	6	13	Illinois	32.9	21	13	Colorado	65,685
21	14	Colorado	91.0	43	14	Rhode Island	32.5	22	14	Minnesota	65,599
37	15	Nebraska	90.7	1	15	California	32.0	4	15	New York	62,909
13	16	Washington	90.6	31	16	Utah	31.7	45	16	Delaware	61,757
35	17	Kansas	90.3	35	17	Kansas	31.6	6	17	Illinois	60,960
29	18	Connecticut	90.1	40	18	Hawaii	31.4	47	18	North Dakota	60,656
15	18	Massachusetts	90.1	27	18	Oregon	31.4	43	19	Rhode Island	60,596
49	20	District of Columbia	90.0	45	20	Delaware	30.5	51	20	Wyoming	59,882
39	20	Idaho	90.0	37	21	Nebraska	30.0	50	21	Vermont	57,677
27	20	Oregon	90.0	44	22	Montana	29.9	27	22	Oregon	57,532
10	23	Michigan	89.9	8	23	Georgia	29.4	37	23	Nebraska	56,927
19	24	Maryland	89.6	42	24	Maine	29.3	5	24	Pennsylvania	56,907
7	25	Ohio	89.5	5	24	Pennsylvania	29.3	20	25	Wisconsin	56,811
5	25	Pennsylvania	89.5	9	26	North Carolina	29.0	2	26	Texas	56,565
11	27	New Jersey	88.9	48	27	Alaska	28.8	30	27	Iowa	56,247
45	28	Delaware	88.8	20	28	Wisconsin	28.4	33	28	Nevada	55,180
18	28	Missouri	88.8	47	29	North Dakota	28.2	35	29	Kansas	54,935
12	30	Virginia	88.6	2	30	Texas	28.1	46	30	South Dakota	54,467
6	31	Illinois	88.3	14	31	Arizona	28.0	8	31	Georgia	53,559
17	32	Indiana	88.1	3	32	Florida	27.9	14	32	Arizona	53,558
28	33	Oklahoma	87.3	18	33	Missouri	27.6	42	33	Maine	53,079
3	34	Florida	87.2	46	34	South Dakota	27.5	10	34	Michigan	52,492
43	35	Rhode Island	87.0	10	35	Michigan	27.4	7	35	Ohio	52,334
9	36	North Carolina	86.3	30	36	Iowa	27.2	17	36	Indiana	52,314
14	37	Arizona	86.2	36	37	New Mexico	26.7	39	37	Idaho	51,807
23	38	South Carolina	86.0	7	37	Ohio	26.7	18	38	Missouri	51,746
16	38	Tennessee	86.0	23	39	South Carolina	26.5	3	39	Florida	50,860
4	40	New York	85.9	39	40	Idaho	26.2	9	40	North Carolina	50,584
8	41	Georgia	85.8	51	41	Wyoming	26.0	44	41	Montana	50,027
33	42	Nevada	85.4	16	42	Tennessee	25.4	23	42	South Carolina	49,501
38	43	West Virginia	85.3	17	43	Indiana	24.6	28	43	Oklahoma	49,176
32	44	Arkansas	85.2	28	44	Oklahoma	24.5	16	44	Tennessee	48,547
24	45	Alabama	84.8	24	45	Alabama	24.0	36	45	New Mexico	46,748
26	46	Kentucky	84.6	33	46	Nevada	23.2	26	46	Kentucky	46,659
36	46	New Mexico	84.6	25	47	Louisiana	23.0	24	47	Alabama	46,257
25	48	Louisiana	83.8	26	48	Kentucky	22.7	25	48	Louisiana	45,146
34	49	Mississippi	83.0	32	49	Arkansas	21.5	32	49	Arkansas	44,334
2	50	Texas	82.3	34	50	Mississippi	21.0	38	50	West Virginia	43,385
1	51	California	82.1	38	51	West Virginia	19.6	34	51	Mississippi	41,754

1. Population 25 years and older.

States and the District of Columbia, Selected Rankings

Unemployment rate, 2017

Population rank	Unemployment rate rank	State	Unemployment rate [col 171]
		United States	4.4
48	1	Alaska	7.2
36	2	New Mexico	6.2
49	3	District of Columbia	6.1
38	4	West Virginia	5.2
25	5	Louisiana	5.1
34	5	Mississippi	5.1
6	7	Illinois	5.0
33	7	Nevada	5.0
7	7	Ohio	5.0
14	10	Arizona	4.9
26	10	Kentucky	4.9
5	10	Pennsylvania	4.9
1	13	California	4.8
13	13	Washington	4.8
29	15	Connecticut	4.7
8	15	Georgia	4.7
4	15	New York	4.7
45	18	Delaware	4.6
10	18	Michigan	4.6
11	18	New Jersey	4.6
9	18	North Carolina	4.6
43	22	Rhode Island	4.5
24	23	Alabama	4.4
28	24	Oklahoma	4.3
23	24	South Carolina	4.3
2	24	Texas	4.3
3	27	Florida	4.2
51	27	Wyoming	4.2
19	29	Maryland	4.1
27	29	Oregon	4.1
44	31	Montana	4.0
18	32	Missouri	3.8
12	32	Virginia	3.8
32	34	Arkansas	3.7
15	34	Massachusetts	3.7
16	34	Tennessee	3.7
35	37	Kansas	3.6
17	38	Indiana	3.5
22	38	Minnesota	3.5
42	40	Maine	3.3
46	40	South Dakota	3.3
20	40	Wisconsin	3.3
39	43	Idaho	3.2
31	43	Utah	3.2
30	45	Iowa	3.1
50	46	Vermont	3.0
37	47	Nebraska	2.9
21	48	Colorado	2.8
41	49	New Hampshire	2.7
47	50	North Dakota	2.6
40	51	Hawaii	2.4

Per capita state taxes, 2016

Population rank	State taxes rank	State	State taxes per capita (dollars) [col 337]
		United States	X
50	1	Vermont	$4,941
47	2	North Dakota	$4,894
40	3	Hawaii	$4,843
22	4	Minnesota	$4,563
29	5	Connecticut	$4,263
4	6	New York	$4,120
15	7	Massachusetts	$4,004
1	8	California	$3,955
45	9	Delaware	$3,700
11	10	New Jersey	$3,527
19	11	Maryland	$3,473
51	12	Wyoming	$3,268
32	13	Arkansas	$3,163
42	14	Maine	$3,102
43	15	Rhode Island	$3,091
13	16	Washington	$3,057
30	17	Iowa	$3,049
20	18	Wisconsin	$3,047
6	19	Illinois	$3,039
5	20	Pennsylvania	$2,925
38	21	West Virginia	$2,800
35	22	Kansas	$2,772
10	23	Michigan	$2,763
33	24	Nevada	$2,730
27	25	Oregon	$2,698
37	26	Nebraska	$2,683
26	27	Kentucky	$2,655
17	28	Indiana	$2,652
36	29	New Mexico	$2,625
9	30	North Carolina	$2,582
34	31	Mississippi	$2,563
12	32	Virginia	$2,523
44	33	Montana	$2,521
39	34	Idaho	$2,499
7	35	Ohio	$2,471
31	36	Utah	$2,321
21	37	Colorado	$2,309
28	38	Oklahoma	$2,164
14	39	Arizona	$2,117
8	40	Georgia	$2,081
24	41	Alabama	$2,040
46	42	South Dakota	$2,019
16	43	Tennessee	$2,013
18	44	Missouri	$2,010
25	45	Louisiana	$1,989
41	46	New Hampshire	$1,979
23	47	South Carolina	$1,926
2	48	Texas	$1,871
3	49	Florida	$1,826
48	50	Alaska	$1,405
49	X	District of Columbia	X

Exports of goods by state of origin, 2017

Population rank	Exports rank	State	Exports (millions of dollars) [col 119]
		United States	1,546,762
2	1	Texas	264,086
1	2	California	171,929
13	3	Washington	77,001
4	4	New York	75,278
6	5	Illinois	64,901
10	6	Michigan	59,796
25	7	Louisiana	56,494
3	8	Florida	55,030
7	9	Ohio	50,067
5	10	Pennsylvania	38,650
17	11	Indiana	37,805
8	12	Georgia	37,224
11	13	New Jersey	34,523
16	14	Tennessee	33,200
9	15	North Carolina	32,551
23	16	South Carolina	32,232
26	17	Kentucky	30,881
15	18	Massachusetts	27,536
20	19	Wisconsin	22,300
27	20	Oregon	21,922
24	21	Alabama	21,702
14	22	Arizona	20,867
22	23	Minnesota	20,648
12	24	Virginia	16,524
29	25	Connecticut	14,758
18	26	Missouri	14,172
30	27	Iowa	13,209
33	28	Nevada	12,162
31	29	Utah	11,614
35	30	Kansas	11,251
34	31	Mississippi	11,192
19	32	Maryland	9,196
21	33	Colorado	8,062
37	34	Nebraska	7,208
38	35	West Virginia	7,129
32	36	Arkansas	6,325
28	37	Oklahoma	5,407
47	38	North Dakota	5,324
41	39	New Hampshire	5,148
48	40	Alaska	4,934
45	41	Delaware	4,561
39	42	Idaho	3,858
36	43	New Mexico	3,623
50	44	Vermont	2,775
42	45	Maine	2,647
43	46	Rhode Island	2,393
44	47	Montana	1,602
49	48	District of Columbia	1,483
46	49	South Dakota	1,361
51	50	Wyoming	1,196
40	51	Hawaii	938

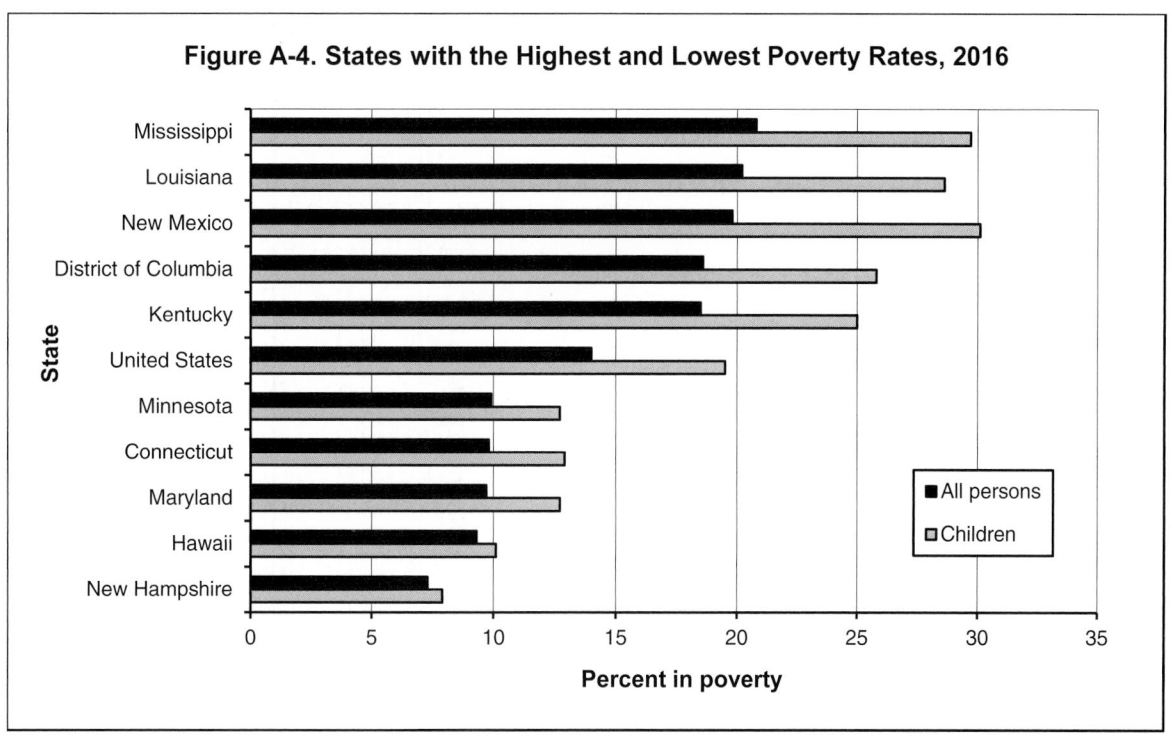

Figure A-4. States with the Highest and Lowest Poverty Rates, 2016

Nationally, 87 percent of the population 25 years old and over had graduated from high school. Twenty-one states and the District of Columbia had high school attainment levels of 90 percent or more, led by Montana with 92.9 percent. States in the Midwest and the West tended to have above average high school attainment rates although California had the lowest rate at 82.1 percent, followed by Texas at 82.3 percent. States with above average high school attainment levels do not necessarily have high proportions of college graduates. Nationally, 30.3 percent of the population held bachelor's degrees. In the District of Columbia, 55.4 percent of the population had graduated from college. Even when compared with other large cities, the District of Columbia had among the 10 highest proportions of college graduates in the nation. Of the 50 states, Massachusetts, Colorado, Maryland, Connecticut, New Jersey, Virginia, New Hampshire, and Vermont each had 35 percent or more of their populations holding bachelor's degrees or more. States in the Northeast tended to have above average college attainment levels, while states in the South had below average rates.

Median household income ranged from $41,754 in Mississippi to $78,945 in Maryland. Nationally, the median household income was $57,617. In Mississippi 31.3 percent of households had incomes below $25,000. The District of Columbia and Maryland had the highest proportions of households earning $100,000 or more, at 40.2 percent and 38.7 percent respectively, followed by New Jersey at 38.4 percent.

The poverty threshold for an individual was $12,228 in 2016. Mississippi had the highest poverty rate in the nation, with 20.8 percent of its population living in poverty. Mississippi, Louisiana, and New Mexico all had poverty rates of 19 percent or higher. The poverty threshold for a four-person family was $24,563. Among children under 18 years old, 19.5 percent were living in poverty. Over 30 percent of children in New Mexico lived in poverty. New Hampshire had the lowest proportion of children in poverty, at 7.9 percent. The District of Columbia had the highest proportion of residents 65 years and over living in poverty at 13.4 percent, followed by Louisiana at 13.0 percent.

The United States labor force increased by 1.0 percent between 2016 and 2017. From 2000 to 2008, it grew about an average of 1 percent a year but then declined from 2009 to 2011 followed by small increases in recent years. Thirteen states experienced a decline in their labor force between 2016 and 2017. Wyoming experienced the largest decline, dropping 2.5 percent. Meanwhile, the labor force in Utah and Colorado grew by more than 3 percent in the same period. In 2017, the unemployment rate was 4.4 percent, down from 4.9 percent in 2016. Two states and the District of Columbia had an unemployment rate at 6.0 percent or higher. Alaska had the highest unemployment rate in the nation at 7.2 percent followed by New Mexico at 6.2 percent. Hawaii and North Dakota had the lowest unemployment rates in 2017, at 2.4 percent and 2.6 percent respectively. Nebraska, Colorado, and New Hampshire each also had an unemployment rate below three percent.

States and the District of Columbia, Selected Rankings

Percent of persons below the poverty level, 2016				Percent of children under 18 years old below the poverty level, 2016				Percent of persons lacking health insurance, 2016			
Population rank	Poverty rate rank	State	Poverty rate [col 127]	Population rank	Poverty rate rank	State	Poverty rate [col 128]	Population rank	Percent lacking health insurance rank	State	Percent lacking health insurance [col 104]
		United States	14.0			United States	19.5			United States	8.6
34	1	Mississippi	20.8	36	1	New Mexico	30.1	2	1	Texas	16.6
25	2	Louisiana	20.2	34	2	Mississippi	29.7	48	2	Alaska	14.0
36	3	New Mexico	19.8	25	3	Louisiana	28.6	28	3	Oklahoma	13.8
49	4	District of Columbia	18.6	49	4	District of Columbia	25.8	8	4	Georgia	12.9
26	5	Kentucky	18.5	26	5	Kentucky	25.0	3	5	Florida	12.5
38	6	West Virginia	17.9	24	6	Alabama	24.5	34	6	Mississippi	11.8
32	7	Arkansas	17.2	38	7	West Virginia	24.0	51	7	Wyoming	11.5
24	8	Alabama	17.1	32	8	Arkansas	23.8	33	8	Nevada	11.4
14	9	Arizona	16.4	14	9	Arizona	23.6	9	9	North Carolina	10.4
28	10	Oklahoma	16.3	23	10	South Carolina	23.0	25	10	Louisiana	10.3
8	11	Georgia	16.0	8	11	Georgia	22.9	39	11	Idaho	10.1
16	12	Tennessee	15.8	28	11	Oklahoma	22.9	14	12	Arizona	10.0
2	13	Texas	15.6	16	13	Tennessee	22.6	23	12	South Carolina	10.0
9	14	North Carolina	15.4	2	14	Texas	22.4	36	14	New Mexico	9.2
23	15	South Carolina	15.3	9	15	North Carolina	21.7	24	15	Alabama	9.1
10	16	Michigan	15.0	3	16	Florida	21.0	16	16	Tennessee	9.0
3	17	Florida	14.7	10	17	Michigan	20.7	18	17	Missouri	8.9
4	17	New York	14.7	4	17	New York	20.7	31	18	Utah	8.8
7	19	Ohio	14.6	7	19	Ohio	20.5	35	19	Kansas	8.7
39	20	Idaho	14.4	1	20	California	19.9	46	19	South Dakota	8.7
1	21	California	14.3	17	21	Indiana	19.5	12	19	Virginia	8.7
17	22	Indiana	14.1	18	22	Missouri	19.2	37	22	Nebraska	8.6
18	23	Missouri	14.0	33	23	Nevada	19.1	17	23	Indiana	8.1
33	24	Nevada	13.8	5	24	Pennsylvania	18.5	44	23	Montana	8.1
44	25	Montana	13.3	39	25	Idaho	17.7	42	25	Maine	8.0
27	25	Oregon	13.3	6	25	Illinois	17.7	11	25	New Jersey	8.0
46	25	South Dakota	13.3	45	27	Delaware	17.4	32	27	Arkansas	7.9
6	28	Illinois	13.0	42	28	Maine	17.2	21	28	Colorado	7.5
5	29	Pennsylvania	12.9	27	29	Oregon	17.0	1	29	California	7.3
43	30	Rhode Island	12.8	43	29	Rhode Island	17.0	47	30	North Dakota	7.0
42	31	Maine	12.5	46	31	South Dakota	16.9	6	31	Illinois	6.5
35	32	Kansas	12.1	20	32	Wisconsin	15.7	27	32	Oregon	6.2
50	33	Vermont	11.9	44	33	Montana	15.1	19	33	Maryland	6.1
30	34	Iowa	11.8	30	34	Iowa	14.8	4	33	New York	6.1
20	34	Wisconsin	11.8	50	34	Vermont	14.8	13	35	Washington	6.0
45	36	Delaware	11.7	11	36	New Jersey	14.6	41	36	New Hampshire	5.9
37	37	Nebraska	11.4	12	37	Virginia	14.3	45	37	Delaware	5.7
13	38	Washington	11.3	37	38	Nebraska	14.2	7	38	Ohio	5.6
51	38	Wyoming	11.3	48	39	Alaska	14.1	5	38	Pennsylvania	5.6
21	40	Colorado	11.0	35	39	Kansas	14.1	10	40	Michigan	5.4
12	40	Virginia	11.0	13	41	Washington	13.7	38	41	West Virginia	5.3
47	42	North Dakota	10.7	15	42	Massachusetts	13.6	20	41	Wisconsin	5.3
15	43	Massachusetts	10.4	21	43	Colorado	13.4	26	43	Kentucky	5.1
11	43	New Jersey	10.4	29	44	Connecticut	12.9	29	44	Connecticut	4.9
31	45	Utah	10.2	19	45	Maryland	12.7	30	45	Iowa	4.3
48	46	Alaska	9.9	22	45	Minnesota	12.7	43	45	Rhode Island	4.3
22	46	Minnesota	9.9	47	47	North Dakota	12.4	22	47	Minnesota	4.1
29	48	Connecticut	9.8	31	48	Utah	11.1	49	48	District of Columbia	3.9
19	49	Maryland	9.7	51	48	Wyoming	11.1	50	49	Vermont	3.7
40	50	Hawaii	9.3	40	50	Hawaii	10.1	40	50	Hawaii	3.5
41	51	New Hampshire	7.3	41	51	New Hampshire	7.9	15	51	Massachusetts	2.5

States and the District of Columbia, Selected Rankings

	State government employment, 2016				Value of agricultural products sold, 2012				Violent crime rate, 2016		
Popu-rank	State government employment rank	State	State government employment [col 312]	Popu-lation rank	Agricultural sales rank	State	Value of sales (millions of dollars) [col 197]	Popu-lation rank	Violent crime rate rank	State	Violent crime rate (per 100,000 population) [col 108]
		United States	4,360,635			United States	394,644			United States	397.1
1	1	California	414,679	1	1	California	42,627	49	1	District of Columbia	1,205.9
2	2	Texas	309,862	30	2	Iowa	30,822	48	2	Alaska	804.2
4	3	New York	242,184	2	3	Texas	25,376	36	3	New Mexico	702.5
3	4	Florida	178,571	37	4	Nebraska	23,069	33	4	Nevada	678.1
5	5	Pennsylvania	162,573	22	5	Minnesota	21,280	16	5	Tennessee	632.9
10	6	Michigan	144,350	35	6	Kansas	18,461	25	6	Louisiana	566.1
9	7	North Carolina	140,047	6	7	Illinois	17,187	32	7	Arkansas	550.9
11	8	New Jersey	139,043	9	8	North Carolina	12,588	24	8	Alabama	532.3
7	9	Ohio	137,846	20	9	Wisconsin	11,744	18	9	Missouri	519.4
8	10	Georgia	128,151	17	10	Indiana	11,211	45	10	Delaware	508.8
13	11	Washington	126,970	47	11	North Dakota	10,951	23	11	South Carolina	501.8
12	12	Virginia	126,741	46	12	South Dakota	10,170	19	12	Maryland	472.0
6	13	Illinois	123,611	7	13	Ohio	10,064	14	13	Arizona	470.1
15	14	Massachusetts	99,315	32	14	Arkansas	9,776	10	14	Michigan	459.0
24	15	Alabama	90,141	8	15	Georgia	9,255	28	15	Oklahoma	449.8
17	16	Indiana	89,278	18	16	Missouri	9,165	1	16	California	445.3
21	17	Colorado	87,844	13	17	Washington	9,121	6	17	Illinois	436.3
18	18	Missouri	87,140	10	18	Michigan	8,678	2	18	Texas	434.4
19	19	Maryland	85,928	39	19	Idaho	7,801	3	19	Florida	430.3
26	20	Kentucky	85,606	21	20	Colorado	7,781	46	20	South Dakota	418.4
22	21	Minnesota	82,697	3	21	Florida	7,702	17	21	Indiana	404.7
23	22	South Carolina	79,917	5	22	Pennsylvania	7,401	8	22	Georgia	397.6
16	23	Tennessee	78,599	28	23	Oklahoma	7,130	35	23	Kansas	380.4
25	24	Louisiana	73,796	34	24	Mississippi	6,441	15	24	Massachusetts	376.9
20	25	Wisconsin	72,676	24	25	Alabama	5,571	4	25	New York	376.2
14	26	Arizona	72,316	4	26	New York	5,415	9	26	North Carolina	372.2
28	27	Oklahoma	68,649	26	27	Kentucky	5,067	44	27	Montana	368.3
27	28	Oregon	68,128	27	28	Oregon	4,884	38	28	West Virginia	358.1
29	29	Connecticut	62,863	44	29	Montana	4,230	21	29	Colorado	342.6
32	30	Arkansas	62,476	25	30	Louisiana	3,809	5	30	Pennsylvania	316.4
40	31	Hawaii	58,777	12	31	Virginia	3,753	40	31	Hawaii	309.2
31	32	Utah	57,733	14	32	Arizona	3,732	20	32	Wisconsin	305.9
34	33	Mississippi	56,841	16	33	Tennessee	3,611	13	33	Washington	302.2
35	34	Kansas	52,118	23	34	South Carolina	3,040	7	34	Ohio	300.3
30	35	Iowa	51,005	36	35	New Mexico	2,550	37	35	Nebraska	291.0
36	36	New Mexico	45,775	19	36	Maryland	2,271	30	36	Iowa	290.6
38	37	West Virginia	41,422	31	37	Utah	1,816	34	37	Mississippi	280.5
37	38	Nebraska	31,924	51	38	Wyoming	1,689	27	38	Oregon	264.6
33	39	Nevada	28,314	45	39	Delaware	1,274	47	39	North Dakota	251.1
45	40	Delaware	25,881	11	40	New Jersey	1,007	11	40	New Jersey	245.0
48	41	Alaska	25,073	38	41	West Virginia	807	51	41	Wyoming	244.2
39	42	Idaho	24,025	50	42	Vermont	776	31	42	Utah	242.8
42	43	Maine	20,647	33	43	Nevada	764	22	43	Minnesota	242.6
44	44	Montana	20,392	42	44	Maine	763	43	44	Rhode Island	238.9
47	45	North Dakota	19,321	40	45	Hawaii	661	26	45	Kentucky	232.3
41	46	New Hampshire	19,092	29	46	Connecticut	551	39	46	Idaho	230.3
43	47	Rhode Island	18,302	15	47	Massachusetts	492	29	47	Connecticut	227.1
50	48	Vermont	14,388	41	48	New Hampshire	191	12	48	Virginia	217.6
46	49	South Dakota	14,106	43	49	Rhode Island	60	41	49	New Hampshire	197.6
51	50	Wyoming	13,502	48	50	Alaska	59	50	50	Vermont	158.3
49	X	District of Columbia	X	49	X	District of Columbia	X	42	51	Maine	123.8

15

Table A. States — **Land Area and Population Characteristics**

State code	STATE	Population, 2017				Population characteristics, 2017										
						Race alone or in combination, not Hispanic or Latino (percent)					Age (percent)					
		Land area,[1] 2017 (sq mi)	Total persons, 2017	Rank	Per square mile	White	Black	American Indian, Alaska Native	Asian and Pacific Islander	Hispanic or Latino[2] (percent)	Under 5 years	5 to 17 years	18 to 24 years	25 to 34 years	35 to 44 years	45 to 54 years
		1	2	3	4	5	6	7	8	9	10	11	12	13	14	15

1. Dry land or land partially or temporarily covered by water. 2. May be of any race.

Table A. States — **Population Characteristics, Immigration, and Households**

STATE	Population characteristics, 2017 (cont.)						Percent foreign born 2016	Percent born in state of residence 2016	Immigrants admitted to legal status, 2016	Households, 2016					
	Age (percent) (cont.)												Household type		
	55 to 64 years	65 to 74 years	75 to 84 years	85 years and over	Median age	Percent female				Number	Percent change, 2015–2016	Persons per house-hold	Married Couple family	Female house-holder family[1]	House-holder living alone
	16	17	18	19	20	21	22	23	24	25	26	27	28	29	30

1. No spouse present.

Table A. States — **Population Change**

STATE	Population, 1990–2010			Population change, 1990–2017								Population, 2020–2030		
	Census counts			Percent change			Components of change, 2010–2017					Projections		
									Migration					
	1990	2000	2010	1990–2000	2000–2010	2010–2017	Births	Deaths	Net migration	Inter-national	Net internal	2020	2025	2030
	31	32	33	34	35	36	37	38	39	40	41	42	43	44

Table A. States — **Population Characteristics**

STATE	Population characteristics, 2010																		
	Race (percent)							Age (percent)										
	White alone	Black alone	American Indian, Alaska Native alone	Asian and Pacific Islander alone	Some other race or two or more races	Percent Hispanic or Latino[1]	Percent foreign born	Under 5 years	5 to 17 years	18 to 24 years	25 to 34 years	35 to 44 years	45 to 54 years	55 to 64 years	65 to 74 years	75 to 84 years	85 years and over	Median age	Percent female
	45	46	47	48	49	50	51	52	53	54	55	56	57	58	59	60	61	62	63

1. May be of any race.

Table A. States — **Households and Housing Units**

STATE	Households, 2010					Housing units, 2010									
				Percent				Occupied units							
								Owner-occupied				Renter-occupied			
										Median owner cost as a percent of income					
	Number	Percent change, 2000-2010	Persons per household	Female family householder[1]	One-person households	Total	Percent change, 2000–2010	Total	Percent	Median value[2] (dollars)	With a mortgage	Without a mortgage[3]	Median gross rent[4] (dollars)	Median rent as a percent of income	Substandard units[5] (percent)
	64	65	66	67	68	69	70	71	72	73	74	75	76	77	78

1. No spouse present.　2. Specified owner-occupied units.　3. Median monthly costs is often in the minimum category—10.0 percent or less, which is indicated as 10.0 percent.
4. Specified renter-occupied units.　5. Overcrowded or lacking complete plumbing facilities.

Table A. States — **Housing Units**

STATE	Housing units, 2016													
			Occupied units											
					Percent who pay 30 percent or more of income for housing expenses[1]		Median owner cost as a percent of income							
	Total	Percent change, 2015–2016	Total	Percent owner-occupied	Owners with a mortgage	Renter	With a mortgage	Without a mortgage[2]	Median monthly housing costs (dollars)	Median value of units[3] (dollars)	Percent valued over $500,000	Median gross rent[4] (dollars)	Substandard units[5] (percent)	Percent living in a different house than 1 year ago
	79	80	81	82	83	84	85	86	87	88	89	90	91	92

1. Excludes units where owner costs or gross rent as a percentage of houshold income cannot be calculated.　2. Median monthly costs is often in the minimum category—10.0 percent or less, which is indicated as 10.0 percent.　3. Specified owner-occupied units.　4. Specified renter-occupied units. 5. Overcrowded or lacking complete plumbing facilities.

Table A. States — **Residential Contruction, Vital Statistics, and Health**

STATE	Value of residential construction authorized by building permits, 2017				Births, 2016		Deaths, 2015					Percent lacking health insurance, 2016		
							Number		Rate					
									Total					
	New construction ($1,000)	Number of housing units	Percent single family	Manufactured homes placed by state, 2017	Total	Rate[1]	Total	Infant[2]	Crude[1]	Age-adjusted[1]	Infant[3]	All persons	Children under 18 years	Medicare beneficiaries, 2017
	93	94	95	96	97	98	99	100	101	102	103	104	105	106

1. Per 1,000 resident population.　2. Deaths of infants under 1 year old.　3. Deaths of infants under 1 year old per 1,000 live births.

Table A. States — **Crime and Education**

STATE	Serious crime known to police,[1] 2016				Public elementary and secondary school enrollment, 2015–2016		Educational attainment[1] (percent)				Local government expenditures for education, 2014-2015	
	Violent crime		Property crime				2010		2016			
	Number	Rate[2]	Number	Rate[2]	Total	Student/ teacher ratio	High school graduate or more	Bachelor's degree or more	High school graduate or more	Bachelor's degree or more	Total current expenditures (mil dol)	Current expenditures per student (dollars)
	107	108	109	110	111	112	113	114	115	116	117	118

1. Data for serious crimes have not been adjusted for underreporting; this may affect comparability between geographic areas and over time.　2. Per 100,000 population estimated by the FBI.

Table A. States — Exports, Income, and Poverty

STATE	Exports of goods by state of origin, 2017 (mil dol)		Income, 2016						Percent below poverty level, 2016						
			Per capita income (dollars)	Households			Median income of family of four					Families with related children under 18 years		
	Total	Manu-factured	Non-manu-factured		Median income (dollars)	Percent with income of $24,999 or less	Percent with income of $100,000 or more		All persons	Children under 18 years	Persons 65 years and over	All families	Married-couple families	Male house-holder[1] families	Female house-holder[1] families
	119	120	121	122	123	124	125	126	127	128	129	130	131	132	133

1. No spouse present.

Table A. States — Personal Income

STATE	Personal income													
		Per capita[1], 2017		Sources of personal income (mil dol)										
									Transfer payments, 2016					
										Government payments to individuals				
	Total, 2017 (mil dol)	Percent change, 2016–2017	Dollars	Rank	Wages and salaries[2], 2017	Proprietors' income, 2017	Dividends, interest, and rent, 2017	Total	Total	Social Security	Medical payments	Income main-tenance	Unemploy-ment insurance
	134	135	136	137	138	139	140	141	142	143	144	145	146	

1. Based on the resident population estimated as of July 1 of the year shown.   2. Includes supplements to wages and salaries.

Table A. States — Personal Income and Earnings

STATE		Disposable personal income, 2016		Earnings, 2017									Gross state product, 2017 (mil dol)
					Percent by selected industries								
						Goods-related[2]		Service-related and other[3]					
	Personal tax payments, 2016 (mil dol)	Total (mil dol)	Per capita[1] (dollars)	Total (mil dol)	Farm	Total	Manu-facturing	Total	Retail trade	Finance, insurance, real estate, rental and leasing	Health care and social assistance	Government	
	147	148	149	150	151	152	153	154	155	156	157	158	159

1. Based on the resident population estimated as of July 1 of the year shown.   2. Includes mining, construction, and manufacturing.   3. Includes private sector earnings in forestry, fishing, related activities, and other; utilities; wholesale trade; transportation and warehousing; and information.

Table A. States — Social Security, Employment, and Labor Force

STATE	Social Security beneficiaries, December 2016		Supple-mental Security Income recipients, December 2016	Civilian employment and selected occupations,[2] 2016				Civilian labor force (annual average), 2017				
					Percent						Unemployed	
	Number	Rate[1]		Total	Management, business, science, and arts occupations	Services, sales, and office	Construction and production	Total	Percent change, 2016–2017	Employed	Total	Rate[3]
	160	161	162	163	164	165	166	167	168	169	170	171

1. Per 1,000 resident population estimated as of July 1 of the year shown.   2. Persons 16 years old and over.   3. Percent of civilian labor force.

Table A. States — **Nonfarm Employment and Earnings**

STATE	Nonfarm employment and earnings, 2017											
	Employed		Manufacturing			Employment (1,000)						
				Average earnings of production workers								
	Total (1,000)	Percent change, 2016–2017	Employment (1,000)	Hourly	Weekly	Construction	Transportation, warehousing, and utilities	Wholesale trade	Retail trade	Information	Financial activities	Services[1]
	172	173	174	175	176	177	178	179	180	181	182	183

1. Includes professional and business services, educational and health services, leisure and hospitality, and other services.

Table A. States — **Agriculture**

STATE	Agriculture, 2012											
	Farms					Land in farms					Value of land and buildings (dollars)	
		Percent with:						Acres				
	Number	Fewer than 50 acres	500 acres or more	Farm operators whose principal occupation is farming (percent)	Government payments, average per farm (dollars)	Acreage (1,000)	Percent change, 2007–2012	Average size of farm	Total irrigated (1,000)	Total cropland (1,000)	Average per farm	Average per acre
	184	185	186	187	188	189	190	191	192	193	194	195

Table A. States — **Agriculture, Land, and Water**

STATE	Agriculture, 2012 (cont.)							Land, 2012			
		Value of products sold				Percent of farms with sales of:					
				Percent from:							
	Value of machinery and equipment, average per farm (dollars)	Total (mil dol)	Average per farm (dollars)	Crops	Livestock and poultry products	$10,000 or more	$100,000 or more	Cropland (percent)	Owned by the federal government (percent)	Developed (percent)	Public water supply withdrawn, 2015 (mil gal per day)
	196	197	198	199	200	201	202	203	204	205	206

Table A. States — **Manufactures and Construction**

STATE	Manufactures, 2016										Construction, 2012			
	All employees			Production workers								Employees		
							Annual Wages							
	Number (1,000)	Percent change, 2015–2016	Annual payroll (mil dol)	Number (1,000)	Work hours (millions)	Total (mil dol)	Average per worker (dollars)	Value added by manufacture (mil dol)	Value of shipments (mil dol)	Total cost of materials (mil dol)	Number of establishments	Number	Percent change, 2007–2012	Value (mil dol)	Annual payroll (mil dol)
	207	208	209	210	211	212	213	214	215	216	217	218	219	220	221

Table A. States — Wholesale Trade and Retail Trade

STATE	Wholesale trade, 2012					Retail trade,[1] 2012								
		Employees						Employees						
	Number of estab-lishments	Number	Percent change, 2007–2012	Sales (mil dol)	Annual payroll (mil dol)	Number of estab-lishments	Total	Percent change, 2007–2012	Motor vehicle and parts dealers	Food and beverage stores	Clothing and clothing accessory stores	General merchan-dise stores	Sales (mil dol)	Annual payroll (mil dol)
	222	223	224	225	226	227	228	229	230	231	232	233	234	235

1. Establishments with payroll.

Table A. States — Information

STATE	Information, 2012										
		Employees									
	Number of establishments	Number	Percent change, 2007–2012	Publishing, except Internet	Motion picture and sound recording	Broad-casting, except Internet	Internet publishing and broad-casting and web search portals	Telecom-munications	Data processing, hosting, and related services	Receipts (mil dol)	Annual payroll (mil dol)
	236	237	238	239	240	241	242	243	244	245	246

Table A. States — Utilities, Transportation and Warehousing, and Finance and Insurance

STATE	Utilities, 2012					Transportation and warehousing, 2012					Finance and insurance, 2012				
		Employees					Employees					Employees			
	Number of estab-lishments	Number	Percent change, 2007–2012	Receipts (mil dol)	Annual payroll (mil dol)	Number of estab-lishments	Number	Percent change, 2007–2012	Receipts (mil dol)	Annual payroll (mil dol)	Number of estab-lishments	Number	Percent change, 2007–2012	Receipts (mil dol)	Annual payroll (mil dol)
	247	248	249	250	251	252	253	254	255	256	257	258	259	260	261

Table A. States — Real Estate and Rental and Leasing and Professional, Scientific, and Technical Services

STATE	Real estate and rental and leasing, 2012					Professional, scientific, and technical services, 2012								
		Employees						Employees						
	Number of estab-lishments	Number	Percent change, 2007–2012	Receipts (mil dol)	Annual payroll (mil dol)	Number of estab-lishments	Total	Percent change, 2007–2012	Legal services	Accounting, tax preparation, bookkeeping, and payroll services	Architectural, engineering, and related services	Computer systems design and related services	Receipts (mil dol)	Annual payroll (mil dol)
	262	263	264	265	266	267	268	269	270	271	272	273	274	275

Table A. States — Health Care and Social Assistance

STATE	Health care and social assistance, 2012													
	Subject to federal tax						Tax-exempt							
		Employees							Employees						
	Number of establishments	Total	Percent change, 2007–2012	Ambulatory health care services	Hospitals	Receipts (mil dol)	Annual payroll (mil dol)	Number of establishments	Total	Percent change, 2007–2012	Ambulatory health care services	Hospitals	Receipts (mil dol)	Annual payroll (mil dol)
	276	277	278	279	280	281	282	283	284	285	286	287	288	289

Table A. States — Arts, Entertainment, and Recreation and Accommodation and Food Services

STATE	Arts, entertainment, and recreation, 2012					Accommodation and food services, 2012				
		Employees					Employees			
	Number of establishments	Number	Percent change, 2007–2012	Receipts (mil dol)	Annual payroll (mil dol)	Number of establishments	Total	Percent change, 2007–2012	Food services and drinking places	Receipts (mil dol)	Annual payroll (mil dol)
	290	291	292	293	294	295	296	297	298	299	300

Table A. States — Other services, Except Public Administration and Government Employment

STATE	Other services, except public administration, 2012								Government employment, 2016		
		Employees									
	Number of establishments	Total	Percent change, 2007–2012	Repair and maintenance	Personal and laundry services	Religious, civic, and similar services	Receipts (mil dol)	Annual payroll (mil dol)	Federal civilian	Federal military	State and local
	301	302	303	304	305	306	307	308	309	310	311

Table A. States — State Government Employment and Payroll

STATE	State government employment and payroll, 2016										
	State government employment, 2016			State government payroll, 2016			Full-time equivalent payroll (1000 dollars)					
								Percent of total for:				
	Full-time equivalent employees	Full-time employees	Part-time employees	Full-time March payroll (1000 dollars)	Part-time March payroll (1000 dollars)	Total March payroll (1000 dollars)[1]	Administration	Judicial and legal	Police	Corrections	Highways	Welfare
	312	313	314	315	316	317	318	319	320	321	322	323

1. Includes program categories not shown separately.

Table A. States — **State Government Employment and Payroll and State Government Finances**

STATE	State government employment and payroll, 2016 (cont.)							State government finances, 2016							
	Full-time equivalent payroll (1000 dollars) (cont.)							General revenue (mil dol)							
	Percent of total for:								From federal government		From own sources				
												Taxes		Taxes per capita[1] (dollars)	
	Health	Hospitals	Social Insurance administration	Natural resources and parks	Utilities, sewerge, and waste management	Elementary and secondary education and libraries	Higher education	Total	Total	Per capita[1] (dollars)	Total	Total	Sales and gross receipts	Total	Sales and gross receipts
	324	325	326	327	328	329	330	331	332	333	334	335	336	337	338

1. Based on resident population estimated as of July 1 of the year shown.

Table A. States — **State Government Finances and Voting**

STATE	State government finances, 2016 (cont.)										Debt outstanding		Voting and registration, November 2016		Presidential election, 2016 (percent of vote cast)		
	General expenditures (mil dol) (cont.)																
			Direct expenditures		By selected function												
	Total	To local govern-ments	Total	Per capita[1] (dollars)	Educa-tion	Health and hospitals	Highways	Public safety	Public welfare	Natural resources, parks, and recreation	Total (mil dol)	Per capita[1]	Percent registered	Percent voted	Demo-cratic	Repub-lican	All other
	339	340	341	342	343	344	345	346	347	348	349	350	351	352	353	354	355

1. Based on resident population estimated as of July 1 of the year shown.

Table A. States — Land Area and Population Characteristics

State code	STATE	Land area,[1] 2017 (sq mi)	Total persons, 2017	Rank	Per square mile	White	Black	American Indian, Alaska Native	Asian and Pacific Islander	Hispanic or Latino[2] (percent)	Under 5 years	5 to 17 years	18 to 24 years	25 to 34 years	35 to 44 years	"45 to 54 years"
		1	2	3	4	5	6	7	8	9	10	11	12	13	14	15
00	United States............	3,532,315.6	325,719,178	X	92.2	62.6	13.4	1.3	6.8	18.1	6.1	16.5	9.4	13.9	12.5	13.0
01	Alabama.....................	50,646.7	4,874,747	24	96.3	67.0	27.3	1.2	1.9	4.3	6.0	16.5	9.4	13.1	12.1	13.1
02	Alaska.......................	570,886.1	739,795	48	1.3	66.7	4.7	18.8	10.0	7.1	7.3	17.7	9.8	16.2	12.6	12.3
04	Arizona.....................	113,590.7	7,016,270	14	61.8	56.7	5.1	4.6	4.4	31.4	6.2	17.0	9.6	13.6	12.2	12.1
05	Arkansas	52,034.3	3,004,279	32	57.7	74.2	16.2	1.6	2.3	7.6	6.4	17.1	9.4	13.2	12.2	12.5
06	California..................	155,785.7	39,536,653	1	253.8	39.6	6.5	1.0	16.8	39.1	6.3	16.7	9.6	15.2	13.2	13.1
08	Colorado...................	103,639.8	5,607,154	21	54.1	70.3	4.9	1.3	4.4	21.5	6.0	16.5	9.3	15.5	13.6	12.8
09	Connecticut...............	4,842.7	3,588,184	29	740.9	68.5	11.1	0.6	5.4	16.1	5.1	15.6	9.8	12.4	11.8	14.3
10	Delaware...................	1,948.8	961,939	45	493.6	64.2	23.2	0.9	4.8	9.3	5.7	15.5	8.8	13.4	11.5	13.0
11	District of Columbia	61.1	693,972	49	11,358.0	38.5	46.9	0.8	5.3	11.0	6.5	11.4	10.8	23.4	14.7	11.0
12	Florida	53,634.0	20,984,400	3	391.3	55.4	16.5	0.6	3.6	25.6	5.4	14.6	8.3	13.1	12.0	13.2
13	Georgia.....................	57,597.8	10,429,379	8	181.1	54.3	32.4	0.7	4.8	9.6	6.3	17.8	9.6	13.9	13.1	13.6
15	Hawaii.......................	6,422.5	1,427,538	40	222.3	36.2	3.0	1.7	75.2	10.5	6.3	15.1	8.7	14.5	12.6	12.3
16	Idaho........................	82,644.5	1,716,943	39	20.8	83.9	1.1	1.9	2.5	12.5	6.8	19.0	9.2	13.1	12.4	11.6
17	Illinois......................	55,515.4	12,802,023	6	230.6	62.8	14.9	0.5	6.3	17.3	6.0	16.6	9.3	13.9	12.8	13.1
18	Indiana......................	35,825.6	6,666,818	17	186.1	80.9	10.5	0.7	2.8	7.0	6.3	17.3	9.9	13.0	12.3	12.8
19	Iowa.........................	55,855.1	3,145,711	30	56.3	87.3	4.6	0.7	3.2	6.0	6.3	16.9	10.2	12.6	11.9	12.1
20	Kansas	81,758.4	2,913,123	35	35.6	78.2	7.0	1.7	3.8	11.9	6.6	17.8	10.2	13.2	12.1	11.9
21	Kentucky...................	39,485.2	4,454,189	26	112.8	86.3	9.2	0.7	2.0	3.7	6.2	16.5	9.4	13.0	12.4	13.2
22	Louisiana	43,206.7	4,684,333	25	108.4	59.9	33.0	1.2	2.3	5.2	6.7	17.0	9.3	14.5	12.3	12.4
23	Maine........................	30,844.1	1,335,907	42	43.3	94.9	2.0	1.4	1.7	1.6	4.8	14.1	8.2	11.9	11.3	13.9
24	Maryland...................	9,710.7	6,052,177	19	623.2	52.9	31.1	0.8	7.7	10.1	6.1	16.2	8.9	13.8	12.7	13.9
25	Massachusetts	7,800.9	6,859,819	15	879.4	73.8	8.0	0.6	7.6	11.9	5.3	14.7	10.2	14.2	12.1	13.8
26	Michigan...................	56,559.4	9,962,311	10	176.1	77.2	15.0	1.3	3.8	5.1	5.8	16.1	9.7	12.7	11.6	13.3
27	Minnesota.................	79,625.5	5,576,606	22	70.0	82.0	7.4	1.8	5.8	5.4	6.4	16.9	9.1	13.6	12.5	12.8
28	Mississippi................	46,923.1	2,984,100	34	63.6	57.7	38.1	0.9	1.4	3.2	6.3	17.6	9.8	13.2	12.2	12.6
29	Missouri....................	68,746.3	6,113,532	18	88.9	81.4	12.7	1.2	2.7	4.2	6.1	16.5	9.3	13.4	12.0	12.6
30	Montana....................	145,545.4	1,050,493	44	7.2	88.6	1.0	7.7	1.5	3.8	6.0	15.8	9.4	12.9	11.7	11.7
31	Nebraska...................	76,818.1	1,920,076	37	25.0	80.7	5.7	1.4	3.2	11.0	6.9	17.8	9.9	13.3	12.2	11.7
32	Nevada.....................	109,780.2	2,998,039	33	27.3	51.9	10.2	1.5	11.3	28.8	6.2	16.7	8.3	14.7	13.2	13.2
33	New Hampshire.................	8,952.7	1,342,795	41	150.0	92.0	1.8	0.8	3.3	3.7	4.8	14.5	9.5	12.2	11.3	14.6
34	New Jersey................	7,355.1	9,005,644	11	1,224.4	56.4	13.7	0.5	10.7	20.4	5.8	16.2	8.7	13.0	12.8	14.2
35	New Mexico...............	121,310.0	2,088,070	36	17.2	38.8	2.3	9.5	2.1	48.8	6.1	17.2	9.5	13.5	11.8	11.8
36	New York...................	47,123.4	19,849,399	4	421.2	56.7	15.5	0.7	9.8	19.2	5.9	15.1	9.4	14.8	12.4	13.4
37	North Carolina...........	48,617.9	10,273,419	9	211.3	64.8	22.5	1.7	3.6	9.5	5.9	16.5	9.5	13.3	12.6	13.5
38	North Dakota.............	69,000.5	755,393	47	10.9	86.4	3.6	6.1	2.2	3.7	7.2	16.1	11.4	15.1	11.7	10.9
39	Ohio.........................	40,862.6	11,658,609	7	285.3	81.0	13.9	0.7	2.8	3.8	6.0	16.4	9.2	13.1	11.8	13.0
40	Oklahoma..................	68,596.6	3,930,864	28	57.3	70.8	8.9	12.4	3.1	10.6	6.7	17.7	9.7	13.9	12.3	11.9
41	Oregon	95,986.7	4,142,776	27	43.2	78.8	2.7	2.4	6.5	13.1	5.7	15.4	8.8	14.2	13.2	12.4
42	Pennsylvania.............	44,742.1	12,805,537	5	286.2	78.0	11.8	0.5	4.1	7.3	5.5	15.3	9.2	13.2	11.6	13.3
44	Rhode Island	1,034.0	1,059,639	43	1,024.8	74.3	7.1	1.1	4.3	15.5	5.2	14.4	10.7	13.7	11.7	13.5
45	South Carolina...........	30,063.0	5,024,369	23	167.1	65.2	27.8	0.9	2.2	5.7	5.8	16.1	9.3	13.1	12.0	12.9
46	South Dakota.............	75,809.3	869,666	46	11.5	84.2	2.7	9.6	2.0	3.8	7.1	17.6	9.5	13.1	11.6	11.4
47	Tennessee.................	41,234.9	6,715,984	16	162.9	75.5	17.7	0.8	2.3	5.5	6.1	16.4	9.1	13.6	12.4	13.3
48	Texas.......................	261,252.9	28,304,596	2	108.3	43.3	12.6	0.7	5.5	39.4	7.2	18.8	9.8	14.7	13.4	12.5
49	Utah.........................	82,195.3	3,101,833	31	37.7	80.4	1.6	1.4	4.8	14.0	8.2	21.6	11.1	14.7	13.6	10.2
50	Vermont....................	9,217.6	623,657	50	67.7	94.6	1.8	1.2	2.4	1.9	4.8	13.9	10.7	11.7	11.2	13.4
51	Virginia.....................	39,480.6	8,470,020	12	214.5	64.2	20.4	0.8	8.0	9.4	6.0	16.0	9.5	14.0	12.9	13.6
53	Washington	66,452.7	7,405,743	13	111.4	72.4	5.1	2.5	11.7	12.7	6.2	16.0	8.8	15.1	13.1	12.8
54	West Virginia	24,040.9	1,815,857	38	75.5	93.8	4.4	0.7	1.2	1.6	5.4	14.9	8.7	11.9	12.1	13.2
55	Wisconsin..................	54,160.7	5,795,483	20	107.0	82.9	7.2	1.4	3.4	6.9	5.8	16.3	9.6	12.6	12.0	13.1
56	Wyoming	97,091.4	579,315	51	6.0	85.7	1.6	2.9	1.6	10.0	6.4	17.2	9.1	13.7	12.4	11.5

1. Dry land or land partially or temporarily covered by water.   2. May be of any race.

24

Table A. States — **Population Characteristics, Immigration, and Households**

STATE	Population characteristics, 2017 (cont.) Age (percent) (cont.)						Percent foreign born 2016	Percent born in state of residence 2016	Immigrants admitted to legal status, 2016	Households, 2016			Household type		
	55 to 64 years	65 to 74 years	75 to 84 years	85 years and over	Median age	Percent female				Number	Percent change, 2015–2016	Persons per house-hold	Married Couple family	Female house-holder family[1]	House-holder living alone
	16	17	18	19	20	21	22	23	24	25	26	27	28	29	30
United States	12.9	9.1	4.5	2.0	38.0	50.8	13.5	58.3	1,183,505	118,860,065	0.6	2.65	47.9	12.6	28.0
Alabama	13.3	9.8	4.9	1.8	39.0	51.6	3.4	69.5	4,736	1,852,518	0.3	2.56	46.7	14.2	30.7
Alaska	12.9	7.6	2.7	0.9	34.3	47.7	7.7	40.7	1,726	248,468	-0.7	2.87	49.2	11.1	25.1
Arizona	12.1	10.0	5.2	1.9	37.7	50.3	13.5	39.5	20,694	2,519,052	2.3	2.69	47.4	12.6	27.3
Arkansas	12.7	9.7	5.0	1.9	38.1	50.9	4.6	61.2	3,158	1,142,718	-0.2	2.54	48.1	13.2	29.3
California	12.0	8.1	4.0	1.9	36.6	50.3	27.2	55.0	223,141	12,944,178	0.4	2.97	49.5	13.2	23.9
Colorado	12.6	8.5	3.7	1.5	36.8	49.7	9.8	42.8	14,225	2,108,992	1.7	2.57	49.9	9.4	27.3
Connecticut	14.2	9.4	4.8	2.6	40.9	51.2	14.4	55.2	12,669	1,357,269	1.0	2.55	47.8	12.7	28.7
Delaware	13.8	10.9	5.2	2.0	40.4	51.6	9.4	45.0	2,204	351,085	-0.4	2.64	47.7	14.6	27.6
District of Columbia	10.1	6.9	3.4	1.7	34.0	52.6	13.3	37.2	3,114	281,241	-0.2	2.28	25.3	15.0	43.8
Florida	13.3	11.2	6.3	2.6	42.1	51.1	20.6	35.8	136,337	7,573,456	1.5	2.66	46.4	13.0	28.8
Georgia	12.1	8.4	3.8	1.4	36.7	51.3	10.1	54.6	29,572	3,686,135	0.8	2.73	47.4	15.1	27.2
Hawaii	12.8	10.2	4.8	2.8	39.0	49.8	18.4	53.3	6,285	455,868	2.2	3.04	51.8	11.7	24.5
Idaho	12.3	9.4	4.4	1.7	36.3	49.9	5.8	48.3	2,562	610,872	2.3	2.71	53.8	9.1	26.6
Illinois	13.0	8.7	4.4	2.1	38.1	50.8	13.9	67.1	43,207	4,822,046	0.6	2.59	47.0	12.6	29.6
Indiana	13.1	9.0	4.4	2.0	37.7	50.7	5.3	68.2	9,946	2,533,270	0.7	2.54	48.4	11.8	28.6
Iowa	13.3	9.3	4.9	2.5	38.1	50.3	5.1	70.5	5,299	1,247,932	0.1	2.43	50.6	9.1	29.4
Kansas	12.8	8.8	4.4	2.2	36.6	50.2	7.1	59.1	5,709	1,110,407	-0.1	2.55	50.1	10.0	29.6
Kentucky	13.3	9.6	4.6	1.8	38.8	50.7	3.5	68.9	7,098	1,717,706	0.1	2.51	47.3	13.2	28.8
Louisiana	12.9	8.9	4.3	1.7	36.8	51.1	4.1	78.2	5,784	1,720,801		2.65	42.7	16.0	30.2
Maine	15.8	11.9	5.6	2.4	44.7	51.0	3.8	62.6	1,748	531,660	-2.5	2.44	48.2	9.1	30.0
Maryland	13.4	8.8	4.2	1.9	38.7	51.5	15.3	47.6	26,077	2,194,657	0.8	2.68	47.4	14.0	27.3
Massachusetts	13.6	9.3	4.5	2.3	39.5	51.5	16.5	60.9	35,706	2,579,398	0.8	2.54	46.3	12.5	28.9
Michigan	14.1	9.8	4.8	2.1	39.8	50.8	6.7	76.3	22,569	3,884,153	0.7	2.5	46.8	12.3	29.7
Minnesota	13.4	8.8	4.4	2.2	37.9	50.2	8.2	68.0	15,603	2,148,725	0.1	2.51	50.3	8.9	29.2
Mississippi	12.9	9.2	4.6	1.7	37.4	51.5	2.0	71.5	2,149	1,091,245	-1.2	2.65	44.9	17.7	28.8
Missouri	13.5	9.5	4.9	2.1	38.6	50.9	4.1	66.3	6,868	2,372,190	-0.1	2.49	48.0	11.8	29.2
Montana	14.5	10.9	5.1	2.1	39.8	49.6	2.1	54.7	566	416,125	0.3	2.44	49.9	7.9	30.7
Nebraska	12.6	8.7	4.4	2.2	36.4	50.1	7.0	64.7	5,654	747,562	0.5	2.48	49.4	10.4	29.9
Nevada	12.4	9.6	4.4	1.4	37.9	49.8	20.0	26.4	11,555	1,055,158	1.3	2.75	44.4	13.0	28.6
New Hampshire	15.6	10.6	4.8	2.2	43.1	50.5	5.7	41.7	2,332	520,643	0.6	2.48	52.1	9.3	26.4
New Jersey	13.5	8.9	4.6	2.3	39.8	51.2	22.5	52.2	56,187	3,194,519	0.2	2.74	50.8	13.1	26.3
New Mexico	13.2	10.1	4.9	1.9	37.8	50.5	9.5	52.9	4,104	758,364	-0.5	2.69	44.1	14.0	30.4
New York	13.1	9.0	4.6	2.3	38.7	51.4	23.0	62.7	159,878	7,209,054	-0.3	2.66	43.8	14.1	29.9
North Carolina	12.9	9.6	4.5	1.8	38.7	51.3	7.8	56.8	20,811	3,882,423	1.0	2.55	48.0	13.1	28.5
North Dakota	12.6	8.2	4.3	2.5	35.1	48.7	3.2	62.5	1,595	315,134	0.5	2.32	47.7	7.2	32.3
Ohio	13.8	9.6	4.9	2.2	39.4	51.0	4.4	75.0	17,251	4,624,669	0.4	2.44	45.9	12.7	30.3
Oklahoma	12.5	8.9	4.6	1.8	36.5	50.5	5.8	61.4	5,960	1,469,342	0.2	2.6	48.3	11.9	28.7
Oregon	13.2	10.4	4.7	2.0	39.3	50.4	9.6	46.3	10,033	1,571,678	1.2	2.55	48.7	10.1	27.4
Pennsylvania	14.1	10.0	5.2	2.6	40.7	51.0	6.8	72.4	27,217	4,937,771	-0.4	2.5	47.4	11.7	30.0
Rhode Island	14.0	9.5	4.7	2.6	39.9	51.4	14.1	56.4	4,194	408,239	0.2	2.48	42.3	13.9	32.3
South Carolina	13.3	10.6	4.9	1.7	39.4	51.5	4.8	57.0	5,104	1,877,887	1.1	2.57	46.4	14.2	29.3
South Dakota	13.4	9.3	4.6	2.4	37.1	49.5	3.6	64.5	1,229	334,003	-1.6	2.49	49.3	9.3	31.0
Tennessee	13.1	9.6	4.7	1.8	38.7	51.2	4.8	61.2	10,032	2,556,332	1.0	2.54	47.8	13.0	28.7
Texas	11.3	7.4	3.5	1.4	34.6	50.3	17.0	59.7	110,651	9,535,612	1.2	2.86	49.9	14.1	25.2
Utah	9.6	6.5	3.1	1.2	30.9	49.7	8.3	62.0	7,271	943,147	1.3	3.19	61.3	9.6	18.7
Vermont	15.5	11.3	5.1	2.3	42.9	50.6	4.5	50.2	886	254,851	0.0	2.35	47.2	9.0	30.2
Virginia	12.9	9.0	4.3	1.8	38.2	50.8	12.3	49.4	29,242	3,120,692	0.4	2.62	49.9	11.8	27.4
Washington	12.9	9.2	4.1	1.8	37.7	50.0	14.0	46.8	27,304	2,768,076	1.4	2.58	50.2	9.8	27.0
West Virginia	14.4	11.5	5.7	2.2	42.5	50.5	1.7	68.9	928	722,125	-1.7	2.47	48.1	12.1	29.7
Wisconsin	14.1	9.5	4.7	2.2	39.4	50.3	5.0	71.5	7,111	2,326,998	0.3	2.42	48.5	9.7	29.8
Wyoming	14.0	9.7	4.3	1.8	37.7	49.0	3.2	42.7	462	223,619	-2.3	2.55	52.3	7.8	27.7

STATE	Population, 1990–2010			Population change, 1990–2017								Population, 2020–2030		
	Census counts			Percent change			Components of change, 2010–2017					Projections		
										Migration				
	1990	2000	2010	1990–2000	2000–2010	2010–2017	Births	Deaths	Net migration	Inter-national	Net internal	2020	2025	2030
	31	32	33	34	35	36	37	38	39	40	41	42	43	44
United States	248,709,873	281,421,906	308,745,538	13.2	9.7	5.5	28,703,158	18,975,711	7,233,626	7,233,626	(X)	335,804,546	349,439,199	363,584,435
Alabama	4,040,587	4,447,100	4,779,736	10.1	7.5	2.0	426,951	365,095	33,238	32,085	1,153	4,728,915	4,800,092	4,874,243
Alaska	550,043	626,932	710,231	14.0	13.3	4.2	82,228	30,233	-23,089	14,403	-37,492	774,421	820,881	867,674
Arizona	3,665,228	5,130,632	6,392,017	40.0	24.6	9.8	622,449	376,768	376,659	98,369	278,290	8,456,448	9,531,537	10,712,397
Arkansas	2,350,725	2,673,400	2,915,918	13.7	9.1	3.0	278,204	219,415	28,860	21,638	7,222	3,060,219	3,151,005	3,240,208
California	29,760,021	33,871,648	37,253,956	13.8	10.0	6.1	3,606,215	1,825,645	515,366	1,072,076	-556,710	42,206,743	44,305,177	46,444,861
Colorado	3,294,394	4,301,261	5,029,196	30.6	16.9	11.5	478,843	250,768	345,091	68,606	276,485	5,278,867	5,522,803	5,792,357
Connecticut	3,287,116	3,405,565	3,574,097	3.6	4.9	0.4	263,119	215,683	-33,328	119,948	-153,276	3,675,650	3,691,016	3,688,630
Delaware	666,168	783,600	897,934	17.6	14.6	7.1	80,315	59,863	43,628	17,804	25,824	963,209	990,694	1,012,658
District of Columbia	606,900	572,059	601,723	-5.7	5.2	15.3	68,412	35,349	57,912	27,125	30,787	480,540	455,108	433,414
Florida	12,937,926	15,982,378	18,801,310	23.5	17.6	11.6	1,582,037	1,346,983	1,936,102	910,841	1,025,261	23,406,525	25,912,458	28,685,769
Georgia	6,478,216	8,186,453	9,687,653	26.4	18.3	7.7	948,960	549,905	338,202	174,666	163,536	10,843,753	11,438,622	12,017,838
Hawaii	1,108,229	1,211,537	1,360,301	9.3	12.3	4.9	135,275	79,396	12,149	54,605	-42,456	1,412,373	1,438,720	1,466,046
Idaho	1,006,749	1,293,953	1,567,582	28.5	21.1	9.5	165,299	89,455	72,816	11,484	61,332	1,741,333	1,852,627	1,969,624
Illinois	11,430,602	12,419,293	12,830,632	8.6	3.3	-0.2	1,148,820	755,145	-423,770	219,051	-642,821	13,236,720	13,340,507	13,432,892
Indiana	5,544,159	6,080,485	6,483,802	9.7	6.6	2.8	605,118	435,449	14,929	72,793	-57,864	6,627,008	6,721,322	6,810,108
Iowa	2,776,755	2,926,324	3,046,355	5.4	4.1	3.3	282,560	207,721	24,342	42,037	-17,695	3,020,496	2,993,222	2,955,172
Kansas	2,477,574	2,688,418	2,853,118	8.5	6.1	2.1	284,693	183,971	-40,572	42,586	-83,158	2,890,566	2,919,002	2,940,084
Kentucky	3,685,296	4,041,769	4,339,367	9.7	7.4	2.6	402,569	320,325	33,351	45,944	-12,593	4,424,431	4,489,662	4,554,998
Louisiana	4,219,973	4,468,976	4,533,372	5.9	1.4	3.3	457,569	311,323	3,585	51,286	-47,701	4,719,160	4,762,398	4,802,633
Maine	1,227,928	1,274,923	1,328,361	3.8	4.2	0.6	92,150	97,623	13,783	9,815	3,968	1,408,665	1,414,402	1,411,097
Maryland	4,781,468	5,296,486	5,773,552	10.8	9.0	4.8	529,515	334,205	85,909	198,001	-112,092	6,497,626	6,762,732	7,022,251
Massachusetts	6,016,425	6,349,097	6,547,629	5.5	3.1	4.8	522,461	399,744	193,318	292,266	-98,948	6,855,546	6,938,636	7,012,070
Michigan	9,295,297	9,938,444	9,883,640	6.9	-0.6	0.8	822,434	669,034	-74,546	150,756	-225,302	10,695,993	10,713,730	10,694,172
Minnesota	4,375,099	4,919,479	5,303,925	12.4	7.8	5.1	501,335	297,508	71,202	103,720	-32,518	5,900,769	6,108,787	6,306,130
Mississippi	2,573,216	2,844,658	2,967,297	10.5	4.3	0.6	279,716	219,202	-45,155	14,512	-59,667	3,044,812	3,069,420	3,092,410
Missouri	5,117,073	5,595,211	5,988,927	9.3	7.0	2.1	545,020	416,536	-2,166	55,209	-57,375	6,199,882	6,315,366	6,430,173
Montana	799,065	902,195	989,415	12.9	9.7	6.2	89,362	68,289	39,807	2,503	37,304	1,022,735	1,037,387	1,044,898
Nebraska	1,578,385	1,711,263	1,826,341	8.4	6.7	5.1	190,243	113,743	17,758	30,047	-12,289	1,802,678	1,812,787	1,820,247
Nevada	1,201,833	1,998,257	2,700,551	66.3	35.1	11.0	259,181	158,713	196,123	50,992	145,131	3,452,283	3,863,298	4,282,102
New Hampshire	1,109,252	1,235,786	1,316,470	11.4	6.5	2.0	90,742	80,817	17,085	14,210	2,875	1,524,751	1,586,348	1,646,471
New Jersey	7,730,188	8,414,350	8,791,894	8.9	4.5	2.4	751,661	519,932	-18,209	376,951	-395,160	9,461,635	9,636,644	9,802,440
New Mexico	1,515,069	1,819,046	2,059,179	20.1	13.2	1.4	191,186	124,116	-38,193	17,710	-55,903	2,084,341	2,106,584	2,099,708
New York	17,990,455	18,976,457	19,378,102	5.5	2.1	2.4	1,728,230	1,102,746	-152,501	869,570	-1,022,071	19,576,920	19,540,179	19,477,429
North Carolina	6,628,637	8,049,313	9,535,483	21.4	18.5	7.7	872,453	614,104	474,259	146,628	327,631	10,709,289	11,449,153	12,227,739
North Dakota	638,800	642,200	672,591	0.5	4.7	12.3	76,402	44,256	49,131	9,953	39,178	630,112	620,777	606,566
Ohio	10,847,115	11,353,140	11,536,504	4.7	1.6	1.1	1,004,081	824,167	-54,642	137,973	-192,615	11,644,058	11,605,738	11,550,528
Oklahoma	3,145,585	3,450,654	3,751,351	9.7	8.7	4.8	383,013	278,633	74,597	46,472	28,125	3,735,690	3,820,994	3,913,251
Oregon	2,842,321	3,421,399	3,831,074	20.4	12.0	8.1	330,894	246,980	227,565	46,313	181,252	4,260,393	4,536,418	4,833,918
Pennsylvania	11,881,643	12,281,054	12,702,379	3.4	3.4	0.8	1,025,691	935,944	20,444	234,870	-214,426	12,787,354	12,801,945	12,768,184
Rhode Island	1,003,464	1,048,319	1,052,567	4.5	0.4	0.7	79,313	70,559	-1,819	31,796	-33,615	1,154,230	1,157,855	1,152,941
South Carolina	3,486,703	4,012,012	4,625,364	15.1	15.3	8.6	417,195	325,675	304,789	40,008	264,781	4,822,577	4,989,550	5,148,569
South Dakota	696,004	754,844	814,180	8.5	7.9	6.8	87,872	53,467	20,859	8,969	11,890	801,939	801,845	800,462
Tennessee	4,877,185	5,689,283	6,346,105	16.7	11.5	5.8	584,236	459,851	244,537	66,412	178,125	6,780,670	7,073,125	7,380,634
Texas	16,986,510	20,851,820	25,145,561	22.8	20.6	12.6	2,842,169	1,312,326	1,616,768	672,750	944,018	28,634,896	30,865,134	33,317,744
Utah	1,722,850	2,233,169	2,763,885	29.6	23.8	12.2	372,364	117,476	83,776	33,614	50,162	2,990,094	3,225,680	3,485,367
Vermont	562,758	608,827	625,741	8.2	2.8	-0.3	43,526	40,432	-4,827	5,352	-10,179	690,686	703,288	711,867
Virginia	6,187,358	7,078,515	8,001,024	14.4	13.0	5.9	743,716	459,403	183,742	237,242	-53,500	8,917,395	9,364,304	9,825,019
Washington	4,866,692	5,894,121	6,724,540	21.1	14.1	10.1	639,401	379,922	421,907	172,855	249,052	7,432,136	7,996,400	8,624,801
West Virginia	1,793,477	1,808,344	1,852,994	0.8	2.5	-2.0	146,363	159,967	-23,089	5,291	-28,380	1,801,112	1,766,435	1,719,959
Wisconsin	4,891,769	5,363,675	5,686,986	9.6	6.0	1.9	486,526	358,238	-17,782	50,956	-68,738	6,004,954	6,088,374	6,150,764
Wyoming	453,588	493,782	563,626	8.9	14.1	2.8	55,071	33,611	-6,275	2,563	-8,838	530,948	529,031	522,979

Table A. States — **Personal Income**

STATE	Personal income												
		Per capita[1], 2017			Sources of personal income (mil dol)								
									Transfer payments, 2016				
										Government payments to individuals			
	Total, 2017 (mil dol)	Percent change, 2016–2017	Dollars	Rank	Wages and salaries[2], 2017	Proprietors' income, 2017	Dividends, interest, and rent, 2017	Total	Total	Social Security	Medical payments	Income main-tenance	Unemploy-ment insurance
	134	135	136	137	138	139	140	141	142	143	144	145	146
United States	16,413,551	3.1	50,392	(X)	8,344,886	1,384,901	3,180,511	2,768,331	2,688,162	896,470	1,244,651	267,621	31,770
Alabama	194,871	3.0	39,976	47	92,797	13,441	33,507	43,949	42,740	16,334	16,907	4,634	219
Alaska	41,460	0.4	56,042	11	20,196	3,594	7,427	6,615	6,434	1,352	2,859	900	109
Arizona	292,108	4.3	41,633	43	145,909	19,876	55,364	58,072	56,348	19,459	25,078	4,991	334
Arkansas	122,546	3.2	40,791	44	55,360	8,448	26,640	28,348	27,610	9,668	12,693	2,488	196
California	2,303,870	4.1	58,272	7	1,169,628	213,223	477,981	334,664	324,884	85,046	166,247	35,247	5,247
Colorado	300,006	4.1	53,504	14	159,120	28,956	63,801	38,191	36,811	12,510	16,862	2,852	513
Connecticut	251,608	1.5	70,121	2	113,232	26,008	55,589	32,738	31,857	11,006	15,653	2,591	652
Delaware	47,256	3.7	49,125	22	25,576	3,705	8,375	9,312	9,076	3,255	4,264	664	75
District of Columbia	53,426	3.1	76,986	1	72,450	6,954	9,939	6,594	6,431	1,140	3,950	931	57
Florida	983,294	3.8	46,858	27	439,679	52,749	265,154	187,912	182,772	66,283	78,933	17,278	517
Georgia	451,281	3.8	43,270	41	243,032	35,614	76,171	75,561	73,003	25,779	28,580	9,418	378
Hawaii	74,144	3.1	51,939	18	36,885	5,328	15,767	11,311	10,959	3,910	4,653	1,278	135
Idaho	69,548	4.7	40,507	45	30,972	7,941	14,401	12,251	11,831	4,727	4,567	1,004	120
Illinois	676,053	1.9	52,808	16	363,303	48,418	135,263	100,687	97,507	34,023	43,538	11,264	1,792
Indiana	294,440	3.0	44,165	35	147,632	26,471	44,483	55,885	54,245	20,592	23,960	4,976	332
Iowa	144,691	0.3	45,996	29	72,636	11,991	27,380	25,206	24,434	9,542	10,623	1,937	411
Kansas	138,673	1.0	47,603	25	67,941	14,471	27,019	21,920	21,201	8,265	8,929	1,850	222
Kentucky	175,464	1.6	39,393	48	89,373	10,153	27,516	42,316	41,220	13,864	19,366	3,977	368
Louisiana	203,725	2.9	43,491	38	96,358	17,386	34,312	43,058	41,896	12,343	20,527	4,781	290
Maine	60,212	2.7	45,072	32	28,476	4,491	10,532	13,130	12,800	4,675	5,787	973	112
Maryland	360,251	3.1	59,524	6	171,381	29,988	67,803	49,208	47,714	15,284	23,493	4,477	601
Massachusetts	451,994	3.3	65,890	3	251,844	35,056	88,090	65,391	63,722	19,074	33,729	6,111	1,369
Michigan	450,847	2.6	45,255	31	229,335	28,550	78,036	93,520	91,053	34,436	41,532	8,177	890
Minnesota	295,798	3.0	53,043	15	163,164	21,520	54,811	45,579	44,209	15,416	20,830	4,000	789
Mississippi	108,460	2.3	36,346	51	47,856	8,726	16,506	28,348	27,610	9,138	12,859	3,208	129
Missouri	266,921	2.1	43,661	37	141,676	18,314	48,604	53,104	51,598	18,793	23,476	4,274	314
Montana	46,124	3.0	43,907	36	20,481	4,536	10,784	8,662	8,404	3,188	3,436	608	126
Nebraska	96,762	1.4	50,395	21	47,967	13,441	18,182	13,932	13,461	5,034	5,503	1,158	84
Nevada	133,789	4.4	44,626	33	67,147	7,190	30,856	21,652	20,914	7,560	8,893	2,098	344
New Hampshire	77,309	3.5	57,574	8	36,945	6,878	13,411	11,322	10,993	4,610	4,820	602	77
New Jersey	563,339	2.5	62,554	4	261,939	52,237	103,704	79,080	76,852	26,628	35,487	6,820	1,914
New Mexico	81,484	1.8	39,023	49	38,338	4,868	15,449	19,367	18,848	5,823	9,009	2,110	192
New York	1,210,641	2.9	60,991	5	657,368	99,687	249,505	205,912	201,035	55,174	109,358	21,729	2,178
North Carolina	444,872	3.8	43,303	40	229,753	34,210	79,593	84,955	82,439	30,221	33,728	8,468	258
North Dakota	41,277	-0.3	54,643	12	21,953	4,093	9,231	5,521	5,335	1,852	2,173	436	147
Ohio	531,811	2.7	45,615	30	279,373	40,006	83,965	104,012	101,136	34,537	48,742	9,321	964
Oklahoma	170,791	2.0	43,449	39	77,031	21,995	31,089	32,324	31,354	11,205	12,794	3,118	378
Oregon	192,064	3.3	46,361	28	99,699	15,625	38,020	36,636	35,617	12,630	16,124	3,186	510
Pennsylvania	667,118	2.8	52,096	17	320,824	61,980	114,513	128,605	125,461	43,173	60,949	11,172	2,209
Rhode Island	54,575	2.4	51,503	19	26,918	3,699	9,864	10,649	10,391	3,338	4,907	1,097	157
South Carolina	203,088	3.6	40,421	46	97,756	13,357	34,893	44,246	43,019	16,369	17,081	4,307	195
South Dakota	41,988	1.4	48,281	23	18,910	5,714	9,397	6,298	6,087	2,453	2,447	529	34
Tennessee	297,293	3.2	44,266	34	147,401	39,770	42,192	58,416	56,763	20,821	24,379	6,073	257
Texas	1,328,683	3.1	46,942	26	693,065	159,067	228,837	199,477	192,542	58,389	89,503	21,820	3,067
Utah	130,410	4.4	42,043	42	71,494	10,519	24,628	16,746	15,981	5,825	6,007	1,763	181
Vermont	31,878	2.1	51,114	20	14,702	2,333	6,563	6,449	6,296	2,157	3,038	580	68
Virginia	459,449	3.1	54,244	13	237,806	25,385	92,950	61,446	59,368	22,494	23,588	5,251	394
Washington	416,816	4.8	56,283	10	215,491	30,441	91,879	59,662	57,844	20,126	24,087	5,495	1,020
West Virginia	68,864	2.7	37,924	50	30,672	3,890	10,133	19,477	19,024	6,966	8,315	1,692	257
Wisconsin	277,317	2.6	47,850	24	142,485	19,257	50,156	46,307	44,874	18,356	18,873	3,678	473
Wyoming	32,861	1.8	56,724	9	13,559	3,435	10,252	4,307	4,161	1,625	1,522	232	115

1. Based on the resident population estimated as of July 1 of the year shown.   2. Includes supplements to wages and salaries.

Table A. States — Personal Income and Earnings

STATE	Personal tax payments, 2016 (mil dol)	Disposable personal income, 2016		Earnings, 2017 — Percent by selected industries									Gross state product, 2017 (mil dol)
		Total (mil dol)	Per capita[1] (dollars)	Total (mil dol)	Farm	Goods-related[2]		Service-related and other[3]					
						Total	Manu-facturing	Total	Retail trade	Finance, insurance, real estate, rental and leasing	Health care and social assistance	Government	
	147	148	149	150	151	152	153	154	155	156	157	158	159
United States	1,958,362	13,954,415	43,148	11,678,482	0.6	16.5	9.3	66.4	5.9	9.1	11.3	16.5	19,263,350
Alabama	18,196	170,965	35,174	129,088	1.3	20.5	14.2	57.4	6.5	6.6	11.5	20.8	210,954
Alaska	3,634	37,649	50,772	30,435	0.1	17.1	3.1	51.1	5.6	4.0	12.1	31.7	52,789
Arizona	28,465	251,655	36,426	198,374	0.9	14.6	7.8	68.2	7.3	10.3	12.7	16.4	319,850
Arkansas	11,580	107,118	35,847	76,363	2.5	19.0	12.8	61.2	6.8	5.7	12.9	17.2	124,918
California	318,242	1,894,449	48,209	1,654,959	0.8	14.7	9.1	67.6	5.5	8.2	9.6	16.9	2,746,873
Colorado	36,465	251,638	45,503	220,569	0.4	17.9	5.9	65.9	5.4	8.6	9.3	15.9	342,748
Connecticut	38,789	209,097	58,282	164,605	0.1	17.7	12.2	68.8	5.7	15.4	11.5	13.3	260,827
Delaware	5,114	40,461	42,470	35,617	1.1	12.0	5.9	70.5	5.7	17.2	13.8	16.0	73,541
District of Columbia	7,858	43,985	64,273	98,887	0.0	1.7	0.2	59.3	1.0	5.0	5.7	39.0	131,010
Florida	105,110	842,097	40,767	584,847	0.3	11.5	4.8	73.2	7.7	9.5	12.8	15.0	967,337
Georgia	49,207	385,470	37,375	334,405	0.9	14.8	9.0	68.0	6.0	7.9	9.8	16.4	554,269
Hawaii	7,766	64,180	44,923	52,683	0.5	10.0	1.8	59.7	6.1	6.2	10.1	29.8	88,136
Idaho	6,700	59,734	35,555	47,028	4.8	19.6	11.2	58.9	8.6	6.1	11.9	16.7	71,886
Illinois	85,080	578,258	45,051	495,732	0.0	16.0	10.7	70.3	5.2	11.0	10.6	13.7	820,362
Indiana	29,699	256,165	38,614	211,068	0.5	27.0	20.6	60.2	6.2	8.6	13.1	12.3	359,122
Iowa	15,512	128,684	41,102	103,584	2.1	23.8	16.9	57.3	6.1	10.0	10.7	16.8	190,191
Kansas	14,098	123,207	42,372	98,837	1.7	19.8	12.5	61.1	5.6	9.1	11.2	17.4	157,797
Kentucky	18,745	153,969	34,708	122,068	0.0	21.5	14.9	59.5	6.2	7.0	12.5	19.0	202,507
Louisiana	17,791	180,234	38,461	137,475	0.3	23.6	9.4	58.8	6.6	6.0	12.3	17.4	246,264
Maine	6,135	52,520	39,482	40,108	0.3	16.3	9.2	65.4	7.8	6.9	16.3	18.0	61,404
Maryland	47,238	302,029	50,131	244,057	0.1	11.2	4.3	64.5	5.2	9.7	11.0	24.2	393,632
Massachusetts	68,422	369,130	54,095	340,843	0.0	14.0	7.8	73.6	4.7	10.8	13.5	12.4	527,455
Michigan	50,264	389,098	39,170	312,930	0.3	22.0	16.1	63.5	5.9	7.2	12.4	14.2	504,967
Minnesota	40,257	246,993	44,704	221,754	0.9	18.7	12.3	67.4	5.4	9.8	13.3	13.1	351,113
Mississippi	8,827	97,226	32,567	68,294	2.4	20.1	13.2	55.1	7.9	5.0	11.6	22.4	111,707
Missouri	29,519	232,029	38,093	191,880	0.1	17.0	10.8	67.1	6.2	8.4	12.5	15.8	304,898
Montana	4,969	39,804	38,323	30,006	1.0	16.6	4.2	62.5	8.3	7.2	14.6	20.0	48,098
Nebraska	9,929	85,482	44,811	73,085	5.0	15.6	9.2	63.4	5.7	8.4	10.7	16.0	121,774
Nevada	13,422	114,668	39,013	90,244	0.1	13.3	3.8	69.3	6.9	4.7	9.5	17.3	156,313
New Hampshire	7,845	66,842	50,069	51,877	0.1	19.2	11.5	68.0	8.0	8.4	12.7	12.7	80,516
New Jersey	75,785	474,051	52,799	372,711	0.1	13.4	7.4	71.7	6.1	10.3	11.5	14.8	591,743
New Mexico	7,172	72,893	34,954	53,499	1.6	13.9	2.6	57.8	6.8	5.1	12.5	26.7	97,090
New York	199,117	976,963	49,251	915,298	0.1	9.0	4.2	74.8	5.0	17.1	11.3	16.1	1,547,116
North Carolina	48,995	379,644	37,379	316,492	1.3	17.7	11.5	62.2	6.0	8.2	10.3	18.9	538,291
North Dakota	3,957	37,448	49,565	31,643	1.5	22.3	5.6	58.4	6.4	7.8	12.1	17.8	55,493
Ohio	57,234	460,684	39,637	387,196	0.1	20.9	14.3	63.6	5.8	7.4	13.1	15.4	649,127
Oklahoma	16,065	151,438	38,620	118,433	0.8	21.3	8.2	58.4	6.0	5.3	10.7	19.5	189,160
Oregon	24,419	161,421	39,506	138,373	1.2	18.4	11.6	64.3	6.7	6.4	12.7	16.0	236,219
Pennsylvania	77,287	571,407	44,686	463,950	0.2	16.5	9.6	70.1	5.3	7.6	14.1	13.2	752,071
Rhode Island	6,091	47,182	44,614	37,161	0.0	14.0	8.4	69.1	6.3	11.1	13.9	16.6	59,458
South Carolina	19,848	176,201	35,526	134,686	0.1	20.5	13.7	58.9	6.8	7.4	9.5	20.5	219,093
South Dakota	3,824	37,574	43,613	29,409	2.2	18.1	11.2	62.1	7.6	9.9	15.7	17.6	49,928
Tennessee	24,598	263,572	39,638	221,641	-0.1	18.6	12.0	68.0	7.0	7.4	16.2	13.5	345,218
Texas	130,059	1,159,251	41,543	999,191	0.4	22.5	8.5	62.3	6.1	8.6	9.5	14.7	1,696,206
Utah	14,005	110,866	36,417	100,059	0.2	18.5	9.8	64.8	8.0	8.9	8.9	16.6	165,526
Vermont	3,233	27,987	44,898	21,127	0.5	18.1	10.4	61.8	7.5	5.5	15.1	19.6	32,197
Virginia	56,914	388,548	46,177	318,603	0.0	11.4	5.6	64.4	5.1	6.9	9.2	24.2	508,662
Washington	43,354	354,418	48,678	295,114	1.3	16.1	9.2	64.3	8.6	5.9	10.3	18.3	506,353
West Virginia	6,475	60,587	33,132	42,546	-0.2	20.2	8.1	58.3	6.9	4.5	16.6	21.7	76,794
Wisconsin	31,793	238,433	41,302	198,637	1.2	23.9	17.6	60.3	6.0	7.6	12.7	14.7	324,061
Wyoming	3,262	29,009	49,595	21,009	0.1	23.9	4.1	50.3	5.9	5.5	7.4	25.7	40,286

1. Based on the resident population estimated as of July 1 of the year shown.   2. Includes mining, construction, and manufacturing.   3. Includes private sector earnings in forestry, fishing, related activities, and other; utilities; wholesale trade; transportation and warehousing; and information.

Table A. States — Social Security, Employment, and Labor Force

STATE	Social Security beneficiaries, December 2016		Supplemental Security Income recipients, December 2016	Civilian employment and selected occupations,[2] 2016				Civilian labor force (annual average), 2017				
					Percent						Unemployed	
	Number	Rate[1]		Total	Management, business, science, and arts occupations	Services, sales, and office	Construction and production	Total	Percent change, 2016–2017	Employed	Total	Rate[3]
	160	161	162	163	164	165	166	167	168	169	170	171
United States	59,373,422	183.7	8,250,117	152,571,041	37.6	41.4	21.0	160,588,786	1.0	153,594,231	6,994,555	4.4
Alabama	1,120,486	230.4	167,349	2,078,325	34.2	40.6	25.2	2,168,448	-0.2	2,073,106	95,342	4.4
Alaska	95,500	128.7	12,449	357,098	37.2	39.9	22.9	362,786	-0.1	336,808	25,978	7.2
Arizona	1,274,815	183.9	119,079	3,031,781	36.1	45.2	18.6	3,312,721	2.7	3,151,407	161,314	4.9
Arkansas	685,361	229.4	108,580	1,282,676	33.5	40.9	25.6	1,354,272	0.9	1,304,437	49,835	3.7
California	5,754,771	146.6	1,275,744	18,343,258	38.3	41.7	20.0	19,311,960	1.1	18,393,077	918,883	4.8
Colorado	830,604	149.9	72,623	2,827,340	41.7	40.0	18.3	2,992,307	3.4	2,907,470	84,837	2.8
Connecticut	664,688	185.9	64,637	1,811,769	42.8	40.9	16.3	1,918,576	0.7	1,828,857	89,719	4.7
Delaware	201,748	211.9	16,905	444,321	39.9	39.9	20.2	477,350	0.7	455,428	21,922	4.6
District of Columbia	81,274	119.3	26,769	364,797	61.4	31.5	7.2	400,894	1.6	376,633	24,261	6.1
Florida	4,431,473	215.0	575,473	9,219,488	34.3	46.9	18.8	10,100,268	2.6	9,680,822	419,446	4.2
Georgia	1,751,227	169.9	258,698	4,735,947	36.4	40.8	22.7	5,061,413	2.7	4,821,627	239,786	4.7
Hawaii	261,513	183.1	24,224	686,487	33.6	47.8	18.7	685,419	0.2	669,242	16,177	2.4
Idaho	325,247	193.2	30,770	762,788	35.0	41.7	23.2	833,467	2.5	807,163	26,304	3.2
Illinois	2,196,032	171.5	272,102	6,231,419	37.6	41.1	21.3	6,492,591	-0.9	6,170,683	321,908	5.0
Indiana	1,318,046	198.7	128,383	3,165,016	33.1	39.6	27.3	3,320,417	-0.2	3,203,355	117,062	3.5
Iowa	630,014	201.0	50,942	1,613,618	36.1	38.6	25.4	1,678,567	-1.0	1,626,043	52,524	3.1
Kansas	535,673	184.3	48,072	1,426,134	38.1	39.1	22.8	1,478,791	-0.4	1,425,217	53,574	3.6
Kentucky	972,352	219.1	180,613	1,954,642	33.4	40.0	26.6	2,052,374	2.0	1,952,068	100,306	4.9
Louisiana	882,185	188.4	177,524	2,020,951	33.4	43.3	23.3	2,112,322	-0.6	2,004,005	108,317	5.1
Maine	334,291	251.1	37,294	658,476	37.2	41.3	21.5	700,102	1.1	677,145	22,957	3.3
Maryland	966,632	160.7	120,710	3,073,923	45.1	39.0	15.8	3,219,461	1.3	3,086,249	133,212	4.1
Massachusetts	1,246,936	183.1	186,896	3,571,010	45.6	39.1	15.4	3,657,172	1.3	3,521,480	135,692	3.7
Michigan	2,162,113	217.8	273,999	4,586,513	35.8	40.5	23.7	4,883,821	0.9	4,657,277	226,544	4.6
Minnesota	994,806	180.2	93,856	2,921,646	40.0	39.1	20.9	3,063,608	0.9	2,957,840	105,768	3.5
Mississippi	653,352	218.6	120,647	1,227,812	31.2	41.4	27.4	1,280,081	0.1	1,215,122	64,959	5.1
Missouri	1,269,508	208.4	138,530	2,892,864	35.6	41.9	22.5	3,050,725	-0.9	2,936,132	114,593	3.8
Montana	223,401	214.3	18,276	503,850	36.3	41.8	21.9	525,457	0.7	504,280	21,177	4.0
Nebraska	335,361	175.8	27,893	987,794	36.7	40.0	23.3	1,007,021	-0.2	977,449	29,572	2.9
Nevada	506,324	172.2	55,549	1,375,164	28.9	51.9	19.2	1,462,952	2.3	1,389,370	73,582	5.0
New Hampshire	294,322	220.5	19,246	719,923	39.9	40.6	19.4	746,551	0.0	726,608	19,943	2.7
New Jersey	1,597,052	178.6	182,022	4,410,393	42.1	40.1	17.9	4,518,837	-0.3	4,309,710	209,127	4.6
New Mexico	416,674	200.2	63,596	880,676	35.9	44.9	19.1	929,572	0.1	872,383	57,189	6.2
New York	3,546,954	179.6	644,377	9,503,468	40.3	43.2	16.5	9,704,700	0.4	9,249,226	455,474	4.7
North Carolina	2,020,386	199.1	233,432	4,646,249	37.1	40.4	22.5	4,941,702	1.8	4,716,834	224,868	4.6
North Dakota	127,962	168.8	8,214	407,369	36.1	39.1	24.8	414,405	-0.0	403,614	10,791	2.6
Ohio	2,311,984	199.1	310,474	5,543,802	36.0	40.6	23.4	5,780,032	0.7	5,491,179	288,853	5.0
Oklahoma	768,889	196.0	96,315	1,742,747	34.1	41.8	24.0	1,834,320	0.3	1,755,606	78,714	4.3
Oregon	836,215	204.3	87,402	1,940,682	38.8	40.7	20.5	2,104,086	2.7	2,017,297	86,789	4.1
Pennsylvania	2,768,956	216.6	363,735	6,097,349	38.0	40.8	21.2	6,427,376	-0.4	6,111,636	315,740	4.9
Rhode Island	220,420	208.6	33,215	521,879	39.3	42.3	18.4	554,658	0.2	529,867	24,791	4.5
South Carolina	1,089,728	219.7	117,325	2,229,274	33.9	41.9	24.1	2,312,655	0.8	2,213,898	98,757	4.3
South Dakota	171,594	198.3	14,725	437,627	36.7	39.4	23.9	455,182	0.7	440,029	15,153	3.3
Tennessee	1,412,299	212.3	180,145	3,024,597	34.4	40.9	24.7	3,198,773	2.0	3,080,213	118,560	3.7
Texas	4,024,516	144.4	657,899	12,927,456	36.0	41.4	22.6	13,538,411	1.7	12,960,611	577,800	4.3
Utah	385,942	126.5	31,368	1,453,401	37.8	41.6	20.6	1,560,850	3.3	1,510,210	50,640	3.2
Vermont	144,889	232.0	15,574	324,824	40.6	38.7	20.7	344,762	0.1	334,376	10,386	3.0
Virginia	1,471,294	174.9	156,608	4,115,486	43.5	38.6	17.9	4,307,758	1.5	4,146,135	161,623	3.8
Washington	1,291,198	177.2	150,658	3,496,141	40.6	38.4	21.0	3,724,721	2.5	3,547,429	177,292	4.8
West Virginia	470,240	256.8	74,665	740,513	33.8	43.1	23.1	778,832	-0.4	738,317	40,515	5.2
Wisconsin	1,189,455	205.8	117,813	2,962,695	35.9	39.2	24.9	3,151,915	0.7	3,048,245	103,670	3.3
Wyoming	106,720	182.3	6,723	287,583	33.0	39.2	27.7	293,345	-2.5	281,016	12,329	4.2

1. Per 1,000 resident population estimated as of July 1 of the year shown.   2. Persons 16 years old and over.   3. Percent of civilian labor force.

Table A. States — Nonfarm Employment and Earnings

	Nonfarm employment and earnings, 2017											
	Employed		Manufacturing			Employment (1,000)						
				Average earnings of production workers								
STATE	Total (1,000)	Percent change, 2016–2017	Employment (1,000)	Hourly	Weekly	Construction	Transportation, warehousing, and utilities	Wholesale trade	Retail trade	Information	Financial activities	Services[1]
	172	173	174	175	176	177	178	179	180	181	182	183
United States	148,530	1.5	12,444	19.86	875.71	6,955	5,721	5,904.0	15,869	2,795	8,455	65,481
Alabama	2,016	1.0	263.3	19.89	861.24	85.0	73.7	73.6	231.5	20.9	96.6	776.0
Alaska	329	-1.4	13.2	21.60	857.52	15.3	21.9	6.4	36.1	6.0	11.9	124.1
Arizona	2,773	2.4	164.3	17.50	707.00	145.4	97.9	95.2	331.1	45.2	213.9	1,254.6
Arkansas	1,239	0.9	157.1	16.11	649.23	51.3	63.4	46.8	140.5	13.2	53.0	496.8
California	16,813	2.0	1,311.9	22.74	925.52	809.1	626.0	723.0	1,693.6	528.7	830.5	7,714.3
Colorado	2,659	2.2	144.0	27.52	1,128.32	163.6	83.7	106.6	270.1	71.7	167.5	1,188.8
Connecticut	1,681	0.1	159.4	25.01	1,040.42	58.2	51.9	62.7	183.1	31.4	128.0	772.9
Delaware	456	0.6	25.9	19.17	795.56	21.9	17.0	10.7	53.1	4.6	47.9	208.4
District of Columbia	790	1.0	1.3	–	–	15.4	5.2	5.0	23.3	17.9	30.1	451.8
Florida	8,567	2.1	363.6	21.47	884.56	504.5	287.1	343.8	1,111.8	138.1	561.9	4,143.8
Georgia	4,452	1.8	397.5	18.42	792.06	184.0	222.0	221.8	495.9	116.2	242.0	1,875.9
Hawaii	653	1.0	14.2	20.50	813.85	36.4	32.7	17.9	70.7	9.2	28.5	317.4
Idaho	717	3.3	66.9	18.57	770.66	45.1	24.3	29.2	86.6	9.0	35.3	293.5
Illinois	6,062	0.7	576.7	20.22	853.28	220.2	294.5	307.5	611.1	97.1	391.1	2,725.5
Indiana	3,105	1.0	530.9	19.90	833.81	137.6	144.7	119.1	333.1	31.4	135.8	1,239.9
Iowa	1,572	0.1	216.3	19.37	813.54	75.8	66.6	66.5	181.6	22.0	109.2	571.7
Kansas	1,404	-0.0	161.6	19.14	805.79	60.3	61.0	59.7	147.0	19.4	78.1	553.6
Kentucky	1,920	0.6	250.1	20.29	856.24	77.1	110.2	76.2	215.2	22.7	93.3	749.4
Louisiana	1,971	-0.1	134.4	21.88	921.15	146.3	80.3	69.9	231.0	22.9	91.8	832.5
Maine	623	0.7	51.1	22.18	913.82	28.0	19.0	19.7	81.4	7.4	31.4	282.5
Maryland	2,721	0.9	106.7	20.61	859.44	161.9	92.0	85.9	288.6	37.3	146.1	1,297.0
Massachusetts	3,608	1.2	244.2	23.71	991.08	151.8	99.4	125.8	353.8	91.3	221.7	1,866.5
Michigan	4,371	1.2	614.7	20.74	893.89	162.8	141.8	173.1	473.1	56.5	218.1	1,920.1
Minnesota	2,930	1.3	318.3	20.76	849.08	119.6	106.2	132.5	298.9	50.4	180.1	1,293.8
Mississippi	1,152	0.5	144.0	20.58	856.13	43.3	56.3	34.9	140.4	11.6	44.3	427.7
Missouri	2,869	1.1	266.2	22.38	931.01	123.3	110.8	121.2	313.6	51.5	173.1	1,270.0
Montana	472	0.9	19.9	19.23	736.13	27.7	18.2	17.2	59.1	6.4	24.4	201.3
Nebraska	1,018	0.2	98.1	19.16	802.80	50.8	52.7	40.9	109.2	18.2	74.0	400.1
Nevada	1,341	3.2	47.8	19.51	782.35	83.4	67.3	36.1	145.7	14.7	65.1	705.3
New Hampshire	675	1.0	69.2	21.57	914.57	26.6	16.6	28.0	95.7	12.6	34.9	300.6
New Jersey	4,127	1.3	244.6	21.68	861.09	155.0	204.1	217.8	462.3	70.7	248.8	1,908.0
New Mexico	831	0.3	26.4	17.31	661.24	45.7	24.5	21.1	91.0	12.3	34.0	368.3
New York	9,517	1.2	445.9	20.55	824.06	383.8	294.8	338.7	940.0	268.8	716.6	4,673.9
North Carolina	4,415	1.7	467.4	17.74	746.85	208.6	143.6	185.6	497.9	79.1	232.4	1,861.7
North Dakota	431	-0.9	24.7	20.28	779.14	27.0	23.1	24.0	47.7	6.5	24.4	153.0
Ohio	5,526	0.8	686.8	21.11	897.18	216.3	213.5	236.2	574.5	71.6	306.5	2,426.9
Oklahoma	1,662	0.5	128.2	18.94	782.22	77.2	66.0	58.1	179.2	20.5	79.1	656.0
Oregon	1,873	2.1	189.4	20.66	836.73	97.1	62.9	76.5	210.9	34.2	99.7	786.1
Pennsylvania	5,946	1.1	561.5	20.34	838.01	248.6	282.9	219.0	624.5	83.0	321.2	2,875.4
Rhode Island	494	0.9	40.5	19.00	758.10	18.4	11.7	16.5	48.4	6.2	36.1	255.6
South Carolina	2,091	1.8	240.6	19.08	820.44	100.8	78.2	72.5	246.4	27.6	101.9	852.7
South Dakota	434	0.5	43.1	18.75	772.50	22.4	13.2	20.9	52.8	5.7	29.3	166.9
Tennessee	3,010	1.5	348.8	19.40	820.62	119.9	165.1	121.1	334.8	45.6	158.1	1,282.2
Texas	12,226	1.8	851.0	23.13	992.28	714.5	538.5	588.5	1,326.3	201.8	756.3	5,087.1
Utah	1,468	2.9	129.3	20.62	824.80	97.5	59.6	50.7	167.7	38.6	84.0	588.8
Vermont	314	0.3	29.4	21.09	837.27	15.2	8.0	9.3	37.8	4.5	12.1	141.4
Virginia	3,951	0.9	234.1	19.42	796.22	193.3	133.4	111.3	417.7	67.8	205.3	1,863.1
Washington	3,325	2.6	283.9	27.38	1,141.75	199.8	107.4	134.5	384.9	126.6	153.5	1,342.4
West Virginia	745	-0.3	46.7	21.15	867.15	31.8	26.2	20.8	84.7	8.6	26.8	324.0
Wisconsin	2,945	0.6	468.2	20.25	838.35	116.6	108.3	125.5	307.9	47.8	152.7	1,206.0
Wyoming	281	-1.0	9.4	22.78	936.26	19.5	14.3	8.2	29.7	3.7	10.9	96.0

1. Includes professional and business services, educational and health services, leisure and hospitality, and other services.

Table A. States — **Agriculture**

STATE	Farms — Number	Farms — Percent with: Fewer than 50 acres	Farms — Percent with: 500 acres or more	Farm operators whose principal occupation is farming (percent)	Government payments, average per farm (dollars)	Land in farms — Acreage (1,000)	Land in farms — Percent change, 2007–2012	Land in farms — Acres — Average size of farm	Land in farms — Acres — Total irrigated (1,000)	Land in farms — Acres — Total cropland (1,000)	Value of land and buildings (dollars) — Average per farm	Value of land and buildings (dollars) — Average per acre
	184	185	186	187	188	189	190	191	192	193	194	195
United States...................	2,109,303	38.6	15.0	47.8	9,925	914,528	-0.8	434	55,822	389,690	1,075,491	2,481
Alabama.........................	43,223	37.4	8.6	44.2	6,802	8,903	-1.4	206	113	2,759	547,524	2,658
Alaska............................	762	56.2	11.3	54.1	12,473	834	-5.4	1,094	2	84	681,479	623
Arizona..........................	20,005	79.9	8.1	66.1	10,245	26,249	0.5	1,312	881	1,151	844,065	643
Arkansas........................	45,071	30.8	13.0	47.3	20,013	13,811	-0.4	306	4,804	7,931	807,965	2,637
California........................	77,857	64.8	9.9	54.5	19,349	25,569	0.8	328	7,862	9,592	2,061,792	6,278
Colorado........................	36,180	39.4	24.3	49.6	14,897	31,887	0.9	881	2,517	10,650	1,128,277	1,280
Connecticut....................	5,977	69.8	1.8	46.3	9,328	437	7.6	73	9	151	809,375	11,082
Delaware........................	2,451	56.5	9.8	63.9	10,553	509	-0.3	208	127	439	1,694,584	8,166
District of Columbia	X	X	X	X	X	X	X	X	X	X	X	X
Florida............................	47,740	68.6	5.6	48.0	10,158	9,548	3.4	200	1,493	2,744	1,040,259	5,201
Georgia..........................	42,257	39.9	10.4	47.0	9,793	9,621	-5.2	228	1,125	4,191	702,282	3,085
Hawaii............................	7,000	88.1	2.6	52.0	8,325	1,129	0.7	161	82	174	1,461,342	9,058
Idaho.............................	24,816	47.9	17.1	49.8	10,673	11,497	2.3	474	3,365	5,793	1,052,941	2,222
Illinois...........................	75,087	34.1	20.4	50.4	9,829	26,775	0.6	359	522	23,753	2,261,778	6,305
Indiana..........................	58,695	46.6	12.8	43.7	8,331	14,773	-0.4	251	437	12,591	1,342,826	5,354
Iowa..............................	88,637	30.9	22.4	54.1	11,262	30,748	-0.4	345	172	26,256	2,207,220	6,389
Kansas...........................	61,773	19.0	31.6	48.3	10,426	46,346	-0.4	747	2,881	28,503	1,218,662	1,632
Kentucky........................	77,064	36.5	6.2	41.7	5,087	13,993	-6.7	169	74	6,336	512,033	3,024
Louisiana	28,093	43.7	11.6	43.2	14,625	8,110	-2.6	281	1,093	4,276	718,179	2,554
Maine.............................	8,173	43.0	6.7	48.5	7,629	1,348	7.9	178	31	477	410,633	2,308
Maryland........................	12,256	49.2	7.6	48.9	7,784	2,052		166	105	1,396	1,148,268	6,930
Massachusetts................	7,755	67.5	1.5	50.0	10,416	518	1.1	68	23	161	704,071	10,430
Michigan	52,194	43.9	8.8	48.4	7,567	10,032	-0.8	191	592	7,669	766,148	4,020
Minnesota	74,542	25.2	18.2	52.9	8,962	26,918	-3.3	349	524	21,597	1,474,057	4,220
Mississippi	38,076	28.1	11.8	43.0	10,983	11,456	-4.6	287	1,652	5,076	652,593	2,273
Missouri.........................	99,171	25.5	13.7	44.2	7,834	29,027	-2.6	285	1,181	15,259	795,444	2,791
Montana.........................	28,008	28.1	42.2	55.1	16,865	61,388	-2.7	2,134	1,903	17,022	1,674,568	785
Nebraska........................	49,969	23.3	37.7	59.7	11,436	45,480	-0.3	907	8,297	21,597	2,159,268	2,380
Nevada..........................	4,137	53.2	18.9	53.0	9,566	5,865	0.8	1,429	688	757	1,324,673	927
New Hampshire...............	4,391	55.5	3.5	48.0	7,434	472	0.5	108	3	98	449,848	4,167
New Jersey.....................	9,071	71.2	3.1	49.5	7,332	733	-2.5	79	88	457	1,008,402	12,792
New Mexico.....................	24,721	51.3	25.3	50.1	12,829	43,238	-0.1	1,748	680	1,977	755,185	432
New York........................	35,537	32.6	8.4	57.4	7,955	7,175	0.1	202	60	4,217	525,587	2,600
North Carolina	50,218	48.1	6.8	48.9	8,332	8,475	-0.7	168	175	4,745	726,944	4,338
North Dakota	30,961	11.0	48.8	56.6	15,398	39,675		1,268	218	27,147	1,808,801	1,426
Ohio..............................	75,462	41.1	8.3	43.9	6,603	13,957	0.0	185	47	10,749	894,933	4,837
Oklahoma.......................	80,245	25.0	19.0	42.1	8,634	35,087	-2.1	428	480	11,279	573,858	1,340
Oregon...........................	35,439	61.5	10.6	49.9	16,054	16,400	-0.6	460	1,630	4,690	865,613	1,882
Pennsylvania..................	59,309	39.3	4.1	51.7	5,395	7,809	-1.3	130	39	4,546	704,712	5,425
Rhode Island	1,243	71.1	0.9	49.8	12,344	68	2.6	56	4	23	786,093	14,041
South Carolina................	25,266	44.1	8.1	41.0	6,867	4,889	1.7	197	159	1,967	586,518	2,981
South Dakota..................	31,989	19.6	43.6	58.9	12,451	43,666	-0.9	1,352	379	19,147	2,281,026	1,687
Tennessee......................	68,050	39.4	5.5	41.8	4,184	10,970	-0.9	160	146	5,330	569,416	3,565
Texas............................	248,809	37.7	15.8	42.1	12,293	130,399	-0.2	523	4,489	29,148	876,614	1,676
Utah..............................	18,027	57.9	12.3	38.5	8,584	11,095	-1.1	609	1,104	1,646	888,886	1,460
Vermont.........................	7,338	39.2	7.3	51.5	8,929	1,233	1.5	171	4	488	546,627	3,205
Virginia..........................	46,030	38.6	7.7	45.1	7,719	8,104	2.4	180	69	2,991	776,719	4,306
Washington.....................	37,249	63.2	11.0	47.4	22,014	14,973	-1.5	396	1,634	7,527	910,249	2,299
West Virginia	21,489	28.3	5.8	42.6	3,203	3,698	-2.5	168	2	804	413,407	2,463
Wisconsin.......................	69,754	32.2	8.8	49.8	6,093	15,191	-4.1	209	422	9,911	819,551	3,924
Wyoming........................	11,736	28.8	36.3	49.8	10,027	30,170	0.6	2,587	1,436	2,419	1,759,200	680

37

Table A. States — Agriculture, Land, and Water

STATE	Value of machinery and equipment, average per farm (dollars)	Value of products sold — Total (mil dol)	Value of products sold — Average per farm (dollars)	Percent from: Crops	Percent from: Livestock and poultry products	Percent of farms with sales of: $10,000 or more	Percent of farms with sales of: $100,000 or more	Land, 2012 — Cropland (percent)	Land, 2012 — Owned by the federal government (percent)	Land, 2012 — Developed (percent)	Public water supply withdrawn, 2015 (mil gal per day)
	196	197	198	199	200	201	202	203	204	205	206
United States	115,706	394,644	187,097	53.8	46.2	43.4	18.4	18.7	20.9	5.8	38,595.83
Alabama	71,211	5,571	128,894	23.6	76.4	33.8	11.2	6.9	2.8	8.6	761.53
Alaska..............................	87,445	59	77,329	42.2	57.8	42.3	11.4				99.18
Arizona	63,624	3,732	186,559	55.6	44.4	20.3	7.3	1.2	41.5	2.9	1,195.15
Arkansas...........................	115,438	9,776	216,897	49.5	50.5	44.0	16.7	21.0	9.6	5.4	363.06
California	124,720	42,627	547,510	71.2	28.8	57.0	26.4	9.0	46.7	6.2	5,147.74
Colorado	110,134	7,781	215,060	31.3	68.7	37.7	15.6	11.9	36.1	2.9	843.95
Connecticut.......................	58,958	551	92,123	70.7	29.3	30.0	7.7	5.4	0.5	33.9	239.93
Delaware	161,559	1,274	519,794	33.7	66.3	64.6	41.7	26.8	1.6	19.0	86.35
District of Columbia	X	X	X	X	X	X	X	NA	NA	NA	0.00
Florida..............................	60,845	7,702	161,322	77.5	22.5	34.3	11	7.6	10.3	14.6	2,384.85
Georgia.............................	93,146	9,255	219,020	39.7	60.3	37.4	17.3	11.1	5.5	12.3	1,069.91
Hawaii..............................	43,999	661	94,478	81.5	18.5	41.6	7.2	2.1	14.8	5.9	266.92
Idaho................................	143,835	7,801	314,372	44.1	55.9	44.3	20.5	10.1	62.5	1.7	275.79
Illinois..............................	203,192	17,187	228,895	82.3	17.7	54.5	33.0	66.3	1.4	9.5	1,475.66
Indiana.............................	143,252	11,211	191,001	67.2	32.8	48.3	24.4	57.5	2.1	10.9	627.84
Iowa.................................	213,856	30,822	347,728	56.3	43.7	62.8	41.0	72.1	0.6	5.4	390.38
Kansas..............................	156,740	18,461	298,845	37.8	62.2	56.0	25.5	49.1	0.9	4.0	351.15
Kentucky...........................	70,190	5,067	65,755	45.0	55.0	36.5	8.2	21.1	4.9	8.2	552.83
Louisiana..........................	104,418	3,809	135,600	73.1	26.9	33.0	11.7	15.8	4.0	6.1	708.92
Maine...............................	69,780	763	93,364	62.1	37.9	34.6	9.5	1.7	1.0	4.1	84.97
Maryland...........................	115,879	2,271	185,329	46.3	53.7	43.1	20.6	17.6	2.1	19.2	749.52
Massachusetts...................	53,948	492	63,470	77.8	22.2	32.7	9.8	4.1	1.4	33.1	648.06
Michigan	122,533	8,678	166,265	63.5	36.5	44.0	18.0	21.4	8.6	11.3	1,030.44
Minnesota	197,715	21,280	285,479	65.2	34.8	60.0	33.5	39.0	6.4	4.5	515.24
Mississippi	91,917	6,441	169,162	46.2	53.8	33.0	12.4	15.6	5.5	6.1	400.36
Missouri	88,960	9,165	92,415	49.8	50.2	46.8	12.5	31.3	4.5	6.7	797.09
Montana............................	137,625	4,230	151,031	53.3	46.7	50.4	26.2	15.4	28.7	1.1	153.19
Nebraska...........................	230,222	23,069	461,661	49.3	50.7	68.5	43.0	40.4	1.2	2.4	275.18
Nevada	134,658	764	184,710	47.9	52.1	42.0	21.2	0.9	84.1	0.8	558.26
New Hampshire.................	56,439	191	43,477	52.8	47.2	26.6	6.0	2.0	13.5	12.3	95.52
New Jersey........................	81,470	1,007	111,006	88.5	11.5	36.1	12.3	9.3	3.4	35.4	1,175.42
New Mexico	60,610	2,550	103,157	24.2	75.8	24.4	7.0	2.0	33.9	1.7	254.10
New York	117,163	5,415	152,380	41.5	58.5	49.2	20.0	16.3	0.7	12.2	2,424.65
North Carolina	92,887	12,588	250,670	34.2	65.8	37.3	16.6	15.3	7.1	14.2	938.01
North Dakota	300,334	10,951	353,693	88.3	11.7	59.0	40.6	54.7	3.9	2.2	84.18
Ohio.................................	116,899	10,064	133,366	65.6	34.4	47.4	20.3	42.0	1.4	15.8	1,306.28
Oklahoma	74,212	7,130	88,848	26.3	73.7	40.8	10.0	19.6	2.7	4.9	611.24
Oregon	90,222	4,884	137,805	66.5	33.5	35.6	13.1	5.6	51.7	2.3	567.04
Pennsylvania	89,735	7,401	124,783	37.6	62.4	48.1	19.9	17.4	2.3	15.2	1,391.70
Rhode Island	56,065	60	47,990	82.1	17.9	35.7	8.7	2.1	0.5	28.4	97.46
South Carolina...................	72,400	3,040	120,323	42.6	57.4	27.0	8.6	11.0	5.3	13.5	633.39
South Dakota....................	241,388	10,170	317,929	59.7	40.3	65.0	40.7	35.7	5.6	1.9	71.95
Tennessee.........................	69,248	3,611	53,064	57.8	42.2	30.2	6.1	16.8	5.2	11.6	849.69
Texas...............................	72,185	25,376	101,988	29.0	71.0	29.7	7.0	14.0	1.8	5.2	2,885.33
Utah.................................	84,537	1,816	100,746	31.6	68.4	37.2	11.0	2.7	64.1	1.6	785.91
Vermont............................	86,947	776	105,765	22.9	77.1	40.6	15.1	8.6	7.4	6.5	42.66
Virginia.............................	72,561	3,753	81,540	36.2	63.8	37.9	9.6	10.3	8.7	11.7	695.63
Washington.......................	98,588	9,121	244,859	71.2	28.8	34.2	16.4	13.2	28.5	5.8	866.53
West Virginia	50,027	807	37,544	17.2	82.8	25.3	4.0	4.6	8.2	7.4	184.96
Wisconsin	129,561	11,744	168,370	39.2	60.8	52.3	24.6	28.9	5.1	7.7	479.38
Wyoming...........................	114,212	1,689	143,952	26.0	74.0	48.8	23.5	3.4	47.2	1.2	101.35

Table A. States — Real Estate and Rental and Leasing and Professional, Scientific, and Technical Services

STATE	Real estate and rental and leasing, 2012					Professional, scientific, and technical services, 2012								
	Number of estab-lishments	Employees Number	Employees Percent change, 2007–2012	Receipts (mil dol)	Annual payroll (mil dol)	Number of estab-lishments	Employees Total	Employees Percent change, 2007–2012	Legal services	Accounting, tax preparation, bookkeeping, and payroll services	Architectural, engineering, and related services	Computer systems design and related services	Receipts (mil dol)	Annual payroll (mil dol)
	262	263	264	265	266	267	268	269	270	271	272	273	274	275
United States	354,106	1,923,770	-12.1	487,655	85,326	856,463	8,203,735	4.2	1,148,683	1,443,462	1,354,603	1,473,241	1,480,277	581,406
Alabama	3,858	22,852	-15.7	3,919	820	9,109	89,988	-4.3	13,755	12,456	24,527	18,294	16,320	5,725
Alaska	872	4,212	-3.6	1,023	188	1,898	17,648	37.4	D	1,917	8,171	1,253	3,175	1,178
Arizona	8,089	40,479	-23.1	9,330	1,693	16,198	121,381	-6.2	17,690	20,352	21,731	22,873	19,268	7,379
Arkansas.........................	2,802	12,867	-8.8	1,923	410	5,678	32,210	-0.5	D	6,889	5,762	2,813	4,528	1,567
California	49,276	273,511	-12.5	78,740	13,467	114,321	1,303,232	3.4	141,018	384,308	162,594	200,809	234,371	90,437
Colorado.........................	9,295	38,706	-18.6	8,482	1,570	23,872	180,064	12.1	19,729	20,420	39,432	41,352	33,741	12,932
Connecticut.....................	3,219	19,778	-11.9	5,349	958	9,220	97,578	-4.4	12,910	14,369	12,982	16,920	17,994	8,364
Delaware	1,111	5,402	-7.0	5,471	265	2,543	D	D	D	3,109	2,585	5,393	D	D
District of Columbia	1,112	10,103	4.6	3,214	674	5,061	97,555	9.6	31,675	4,829	8,003	14,685	31,866	11,196
Florida............................	29,845	139,955	-18.1	30,560	5,337	70,785	440,858	2.5	93,530	73,188	60,374	76,034	70,176	27,100
Georgia...........................	10,484	55,551	-15.7	14,232	2,704	28,112	D	D	31,571	42,729	33,823	56,588	D	D
Hawaii............................	1,919	11,369	-32.2	3,411	484	3,226	21,629	-3.7	D	3,385	5,251	2,847	3,334	1,266
Idaho.............................	2,033	6,268	-25.1	1,040	184	4,198	32,076	1.3	D	3,702	7,951	2,623	4,274	1,728
Illinois............................	12,035	76,794	-12.2	23,649	3,816	38,673	364,336	-1.3	57,212	62,779	44,413	62,613	70,263	28,315
Indiana...........................	5,729	31,715	-7.5	6,548	1,172	12,829	99,962	3.9	14,668	19,194	18,906	12,437	14,702	5,491
Iowa..............................	2,742	12,031	-18.0	2,268	426	6,204	48,521	14.5	7,489	9,878	5,908	7,957	6,421	2,467
Kansas...........................	2,999	14,256	-6.0	2,743	508	7,110	60,989	8.3	7,462	12,290	12,765	8,129	8,716	3,596
Kentucky.........................	3,534	18,250	-9.4	4,846	637	8,101	62,851	1.5	10,848	15,446	9,866	8,447	7,782	2,817
Louisiana	4,500	31,298	1.2	7,486	1,461	11,728	88,093	3.1	19,363	16,839	26,874	6,092	13,546	5,023
Maine.............................	1,580	6,242	-10.1	1,100	221	3,492	22,943	3.2	4,025	3,317	4,866	2,813	3,353	1,238
Maryland.........................	6,001	42,838	-13.9	13,410	2,253	19,714	244,710	-2.8	D	20,872	44,204	67,825	50,025	20,161
Massachusetts..................	6,485	42,788	-11.9	13,628	2,358	21,422	255,022	0.8	29,271	25,343	38,428	51,240	60,370	23,827
Michigan	7,826	48,706	-11.2	11,974	1,807	21,650	D	D	26,862	38,730	59,343	32,723	D	D
Minnesota........................	6,300	34,499	-12.5	7,828	1,396	16,348	140,927	-0.6	D	18,988	17,814	24,040	23,449	9,739
Mississippi	2,374	10,235	0.6	1,709	334	4,747	30,205	-2.6	D	6,904	5,529	3,438	4,023	1,450
Missouri..........................	6,165	33,447	-15.6	6,730	1,298	13,279	137,981	4.3	21,063	22,228	18,976	30,349	24,293	8,615
Montana..........................	1,726	5,207	-18.8	835	162	3,545	16,660	-1.4	2,972	3,236	4,129	1,185	2,192	799
Nebraska	2,001	10,068	0.9	1,732	389	4,448	74,514	82.5	D	42,825	5,660	8,215	5,727	3,639
Nevada	3,866	22,412	-29.1	4,981	815	8,102	47,934	-17.5	9,894	7,385	8,885	4,681	7,759	2,832
New Hampshire.................	1,338	7,044	-3.1	1,593	310	3,825	30,159	2.4	D	6,571	4,357	5,756	3,948	1,697
New Jersey......................	8,749	53,751	-16.0	17,328	2,813	29,390	307,549	-7.3	38,055	44,203	39,728	88,570	58,738	24,013
New Mexico......................	2,369	9,754	-16.5	1,960	369	4,687	44,175	-0.3	5,449	4,647	8,101	4,058	7,619	2,772
New York.........................	32,033	166,315	-3.1	56,410	8,654	59,302	588,820	4.2	121,085	97,246	59,318	77,105	133,639	49,200
North Carolina	10,140	47,155	-12.0	9,302	1,943	22,855	196,287	6.1	23,399	29,415	28,778	36,677	31,948	12,940
North Dakota	912	5,157	37.6	1,445	248	1,722	13,715	40.0	1,902	1,821	3,213	2,586	1,847	736
Ohio..............................	9,932	60,966	-9.1	16,133	2,442	23,961	233,876	2.3	34,707	36,624	40,381	39,420	35,971	14,220
Oklahoma	4,000	21,261	-14.6	4,270	898	9,470	71,997	9.3	12,250	11,842	21,414	7,113	10,991	4,115
Oregon...........................	5,644	26,016	-16.0	4,650	903	11,663	84,493	-0.9	11,773	11,963	12,941	11,952	11,386	5,841
Pennsylvania	9,438	58,585	-15.0	13,364	2,618	29,297	316,658	6.0	51,348	50,126	58,713	42,585	54,834	22,622
Rhode Island	1,058	5,615	-13.5	1,120	219	2,997	21,165	-7.5	4,086	3,091	3,470	4,696	3,338	1,310
South Carolina..................	4,692	23,189	-23.8	4,334	826	9,721	79,824	6.5	13,690	11,165	20,796	10,923	12,722	4,817
South Dakota....................	962	3,526	-8.3	583	106	1,822	11,144	9.3	1,820	2,570	2,277	1,305	1,315	482
Tennessee.......................	5,470	30,593	-18.9	6,178	1,220	10,863	104,552	3.7	D	22,269	18,445	11,327	14,200	6,129
Texas............................	26,639	169,941	-2.2	38,757	7,752	62,322	639,561	18.3	81,308	90,410	171,740	110,640	122,086	47,256
Utah..............................	4,446	16,197	-20.7	3,226	605	9,009	76,345	11.5	9,137	16,734	11,239	10,085	10,555	3,909
Vermont..........................	741	3,092	-8.9	510	104	2,113	15,948	-3.5	D	5,838	2,056	1,874	1,782	740
Virginia...........................	8,862	54,246	-10.3	11,759	2,378	29,368	429,690	11.0	27,122	35,371	73,172	162,320	92,776	36,365
Washington......................	9,913	45,209	-11.7	9,695	1,895	20,047	167,512	4.9	D	20,084	30,768	32,431	28,284	11,977
West Virginia	1,405	6,011	-14.8	1,256	204	2,974	24,816	11.6	6,084	4,068	4,320	2,733	3,105	1,143
Wisconsin	4,509	23,762	-12.7	4,359	801	11,301	99,162	1.1	14,704	18,173	17,021	13,998	15,135	5,738
Wyoming..........................	1,076	4,546	-2.3	1,259	216	2,141	9,134	3.5	D	1,324	2,603	419	1,297	467

Table A. States — Health Care and Social Assistance

	Health care and social assistance, 2012												
	Subject to federal tax						Tax-exempt						
		Employees							Employees					
STATE	Number of establishments	Total	Percent change, 2007–2012	Ambulatory health care services	Hospitals	Receipts (mil dol)	Annual payroll (mil dol)	Number of establishments	Total	Percent change, 2007–2012	Ambulatory health care services	Hospitals	Receipts (mil dol)	Annual payroll (mil dol)
	276	277	278	279	280	281	282	283	284	285	286	287	288	289
United States	690,525	9,542,138	14.7	5,687,621	677,114	1,008,745	409,812	140,778	8,872,619	4.8	787,378	5,074,227	1,031,697	391,428
Alabama	8,489	142,386	5.5	76,205	20,349	14,628	5,995	1,816	100,808	-2.3	8,624	67,461	11,412	4,244
Alaska..............................	1,851	21,389	38.7	12,315	1,849	2,810	1,098	581	27,312	8.4	4,359	12,617	3,565	1,336
Arizona	15,041	184,186	19.6	106,247	15,871	20,221	7,975	1,831	130,921	4.9	13,850	79,719	16,835	6,261
Arkansas..........................	5,936	86,999	12.7	42,556	12,408	8,541	3,496	1,549	79,456	5.0	6,689	42,744	7,252	2,823
California	89,999	1,005,201	13.8	630,526	66,982	127,356	48,373	13,208	771,239	8.8	72,024	466,701	121,598	42,767
Colorado	12,701	140,738	10.8	82,675	7,852	14,693	6,167	2,168	117,160	4.7	18,826	64,999	14,795	5,710
Connecticut......................	7,876	131,732	7.6	73,550	D	13,333	6,059	2,420	139,540	6.6	13,781	D	16,240	6,475
Delaware	1,964	30,400	20.1	18,888	D	3,174	1,435	560	31,497	7.1	2,618	D	3,830	1,561
District of Columbia	1,353	24,356	23.6	13,997	3,244	2,871	1,203	712	43,386	4.9	2,717	23,473	6,093	2,393
Florida.............................	51,567	614,004	14.1	360,507	77,106	76,786	27,914	5,092	377,250	3.1	34,574	224,905	47,276	16,521
Georgia............................	20,166	256,945	12.2	158,607	D	28,196	11,171	2,568	191,515	0.7	11,486	134,809	23,604	8,344
Hawaii.............................	2,794	26,788	-7.7	20,436	D	3,180	1,347	765	39,984	15.5	4,777	21,720	4,957	1,943
Idaho..............................	4,271	49,613	11.5	26,127	2,924	4,281	1,636	594	33,892	15.1	1,393	25,236	3,614	1,535
Illinois.............................	27,624	383,980	18.1	240,920	15,441	39,270	16,151	5,431	386,504	1.3	22,524	230,249	44,161	16,423
Indiana............................	12,360	206,531	13.8	113,641	15,020	21,191	8,626	2,796	190,392	1.0	12,842	119,354	17,028	5,804
Iowa................................	5,582	78,961	12.4	43,888	D	7,151	3,357	2,549	127,945	-0.1	7,799	D	D	D
Kansas............................	5,977	93,121	11.5	52,953	6,761	9,678	3,955	1,957	99,151	4.4	6,359	51,968	6,152	2,429
Kentucky..........................	9,449	127,446	10.2	69,066	8,611	11,985	5,178	1,976	124,432	4.0	11,499	80,486	11,418	3,868
Louisiana	10,240	167,792	15.6	88,911	19,565	15,870	6,157	1,759	117,187	5.7	4,258	77,104	9,939	3,613
Maine..............................	3,071	41,700	4.9	23,055	D	3,487	1,613	1,659	67,531	4.9	7,036	D	D	D
Maryland..........................	13,217	168,241	17.1	105,879	D	18,823	7,785	2,783	191,493	11.3	9,804	D	D	D
Massachusetts..................	13,136	237,631	17.2	138,145	18,506	26,639	12,209	5,250	349,854	13.5	32,003	169,964	25,847	10,415
Michigan..........................	21,447	270,655	18.4	173,860	14,278	27,435	11,944	4,784	314,875	-1.8	31,655	191,187	27,028	10,346
Minnesota	11,233	189,308	20.6	108,030	D	15,774	7,259	3,874	250,887	9.5	23,077	D	D	D
Mississippi	5,149	84,441	16.3	43,908	11,822	8,731	3,451	1,062	73,179	-1.5	3,226	54,427	6,833	2,684
Missouri	14,644	184,918	15.9	95,013	14,471	17,917	7,525	3,122	215,022	6.0	18,417	129,225	17,263	6,202
Montana	2,545	24,420	12.2	15,400	D	2,508	1,041	967	41,237	14.2	2,978	D	D	D
Nebraska	4,282	57,239	16.0	31,302	2,328	5,707	2,398	1,128	68,230	4.0	3,575	40,591	5,495	1,806
Nevada	5,766	77,665	6.8	42,411	14,806	9,937	3,598	542	30,920	29.3	2,120	20,737	3,216	1,223
New Hampshire..................	2,775	35,400	8.2	21,181	2,347	444	1,770	803	51,699	1.4	9,014	25,218	5,615	2,317
New Jersey.......................	23,088	297,847	17.7	198,143	10,677	1,468	13,028	3,847	243,028	-2.9	20,746	136,380	27,740	11,297
New Mexico......................	3,970	67,477	17.5	34,002	8,324	1,176	2,450	997	49,080	2.1	5,093	26,723	5,166	2,138
New York.........................	43,548	540,067	17.4	397,708	3,366	237	22,401	13,186	928,920	7.3	102,840	443,108	100,067	42,779
North Carolina	19,152	292,709	2.0	168,931	7,693	1,090	11,432	3,825	236,861	0.2	16,895	151,084	27,922	10,325
North Dakota	1,235	15,038	6.4	9,934	D	D	776	621	41,601	9.3	1,630	D	3,609	1,638
Ohio................................	22,945	393,909	13.7	231,564	12,043	1,530	15,471	5,292	404,861	2.5	32,022	254,046	46,278	17,670
Oklahoma	8,868	128,437	6.0	63,736	19,773	3,626	4,996	1,786	84,789	6.5	5,726	49,730	9,413	3,293
Oregon............................	9,829	105,341	14.7	65,396	D	D	4,534	2,646	112,243	11.8	11,445	D	13,940	5,156
Pennsylvania	27,983	433,818	17.7	266,329	28,531	3,968	19,364	8,569	521,661	3.1	48,929	245,857	52,550	19,962
Rhode Island	2,470	35,597	2.4	20,571	D	D	1,536	766	48,470	2.7	4,687	D	4,756	2,020
South Carolina..................	8,346	132,360	14.4	70,689	16,924	2,886	5,385	1,502	80,084	-5.3	3,855	51,861	9,119	3,302
South Dakota....................	1,544	20,514	17.9	11,889	D	D	830	754	42,980	10.0	3,975	D	4,189	1,729
Tennessee.......................	12,286	220,313	18.7	123,165	30,315	4,700	9,564	2,611	160,140	5.2	13,454	100,602	17,842	6,664
Texas..............................	55,176	945,659	21.2	552,817	118,155	20,879	36,493	6,166	400,005	3.6	30,342	268,014	51,047	18,077
Utah...............................	6,601	77,036	14.9	44,035	7,957	8,254	3,017	684	49,139	7.8	5,381	32,987	5,109	1,573
Vermont...........................	1,370	14,976	-2.6	8,847	D	1,297	578	726	29,222	10.1	6,615	D	D	D
Virginia............................	16,070	236,459	15.9	139,138	17,223	25,556	10,868	2,704	174,649	4.5	13,334	102,848	15,825	5,535
Washington.......................	16,888	194,136	12.9	115,714	D	20,414	8,703	2,945	180,091	4.0	23,965	D	D	D
West Virginia	3,734	57,400	10.8	27,271	5,215	5,125	2,108	1,205	71,675	14.0	8,152	43,463	5,810	2,094
Wisconsin	11,460	175,153	6.1	99,434	1,679	16,357	7,785	3,199	210,988	3.3	23,362	112,126	17,578	5,514
Wyoming..........................	1,457	13,706	17.3	8,109	1,159	1,486	608	441	17,634	0.4	1,026	9,743	1,408	561

Table A. States — Arts, Entertainment, and Recreation and Accommodation and Food Services

STATE	Arts, entertainment, and recreation, 2012					Accommodation and food services, 2012					
	Number of establishments	Employees		Receipts (mil dol)	Annual payroll (mil dol)	Number of establishments	Employees		Food services and drinking places	Receipts (mil dol)	Annual payroll (mil dol)
		Number	Percent change, 2007–2012				Total	Percent change, 2007–2012			
	290	291	292	293	294	295	296	297	298	299	300
United States	124,591	2,081,668	1.0	201,193	64,052	662,489	12,007,689	3.5	10,057,608	708,139	196,103
Alabama	1,086	17,170	-4.5	1,194	297	8,339	157,337	4.3	142,339	7,576	2,071
Alaska	545	5,055	13.4	407	91	2,126	26,836	4.7	20,057	2,221	626
Arizona	1,764	42,407	-8.8	3,810	1,263	11,669	251,455	0.3	203,083	13,997	4,030
Arkansas	781	8,881	-3.6	704	160	5,473	95,854	6.6	85,388	4,307	1,183
California	21,191	303,838	0.6	39,179	13,419	78,560	1,394,984	2.1	1,160,464	90,830	25,148
Colorado	2,433	51,235	3.1	3,783	1,323	12,744	240,484	3.8	194,749	13,618	3,995
Connecticut	1,610	26,476	5.2	2,298	715	8,263	134,546	1.9	107,171	9,542	2,591
Delaware	409	8,102	18.2	651	208	1,987	35,609	10.6	31,519	2,148	567
District of Columbia	301	7,510	2.6	1,021	412	2,371	60,370	13.9	45,949	5,102	1,505
Florida	7,562	169,796	1.8	16,453	4,904	37,118	786,082	5.3	621,439	49,818	13,598
Georgia	2,733	42,851	-4.9	3,780	1,262	18,815	353,638	-0.5	313,419	18,977	5,173
Hawaii	495	10,623	-11.4	844	249	3,518	98,364	0.0	59,938	9,537	2,536
Idaho	712	8,944	-0.8	455	138	3,564	54,257	-4.2	43,787	2,680	726
Illinois	4,520	77,153	-3.1	7,401	2,348	27,117	469,870	0.2	415,659	27,937	7,707
Indiana	2,069	33,726	-6.0	3,652	941	13,057	255,223	0.4	224,519	13,077	3,433
Iowa	1,466	21,233	-2.0	1,626	364	7,047	115,134	-1.5	96,648	5,469	1,467
Kansas	1,000	14,341	-8.3	884	252	5,943	106,850	2.0	95,624	4,873	1,343
Kentucky	1,242	17,360	-6.4	1,207	349	7,678	156,965	3.6	143,432	7,500	2,084
Louisiana	1,376	23,386	-5.6	2,661	720	9,019	193,928	7.6	157,059	11,698	3,111
Maine	849	7,305	-6.3	527	155	3,958	49,672	0.6	40,538	2,901	851
Maryland	1,960	35,932	-4.2	3,391	1,062	11,344	204,222	6.0	181,041	12,517	3,411
Massachusetts	3,130	55,585	5.4	5,012	1,788	16,898	273,185	6.2	243,840	17,509	5,020
Michigan	3,369	46,255	-16.1	3,709	1,416	19,491	347,337	2.4	302,053	17,962	4,872
Minnesota	2,714	42,320	0.6	3,127	1,191	11,345	221,859	0.4	184,868	11,723	3,238
Mississippi	656	8,840	8.1	587	161	5,177	116,238	-2.8	82,085	6,999	1,765
Missouri	2,095	38,190	1.8	3,716	1,341	12,459	239,264	-0.9	206,309	12,430	3,409
Montana	1,126	10,903	5.9	785	170	3,458	46,251	0.2	35,921	2,420	650
Nebraska	842	13,090	15.2	780	206	4,326	70,128	1.4	62,732	3,094	855
Nevada	1,290	26,705	-11.8	3,645	772	5,815	296,762	-8.8	102,621	27,482	8,556
New Hampshire	724	12,946	11.7	793	235	3,606	54,047	-2.2	44,957	2,942	891
New Jersey	3,421	56,427	10.5	4,632	1,606	20,127	291,933	0.2	233,932	19,674	5,387
New Mexico	652	12,259	-14.5	1,353	268	4,177	82,601	2.7	64,280	4,350	1,250
New York	11,615	162,729	2.8	21,929	6,900	49,731	679,146	14.8	584,408	49,286	13,734
North Carolina	3,471	58,185	5.2	4,774	1,535	19,496	358,602	4.5	318,217	18,622	5,041
North Dakota	421	4,901	7.0	242	64	1,935	35,698	17.8	26,990	2,045	521
Ohio	3,810	60,704	-7.1	5,432	1,977	23,432	437,293	0.2	403,421	20,653	5,743
Oklahoma	1,052	26,375	0.5	2,791	672	7,403	143,561	11.2	125,756	7,121	1,908
Oregon	1,636	24,031	-1.2	1,607	570	10,610	150,482	0.0	126,327	8,467	2,438
Pennsylvania	4,402	99,568	19.1	8,748	2,742	27,646	439,159	4.5	386,349	23,504	6,377
Rhode Island	537	8,798	-0.4	780	216	2,973	44,063	-0.8	40,040	2,481	706
South Carolina	1,525	24,918	-1.5	1,813	432	9,828	185,282	1.3	158,300	9,764	2,650
South Dakota	668	6,204	-3.6	437	103	2,363	37,974	3.4	29,328	1,874	514
Tennessee	2,326	32,490	0.2	3,355	1,150	12,004	241,348	0.8	211,928	12,499	3,546
Texas	6,304	119,132	8.6	10,287	3,309	48,721	976,390	12.7	868,360	54,481	14,744
Utah	923	20,749	12.2	1,181	401	5,108	95,933	4.5	78,587	4,789	1,363
Vermont	451	7,147	-10.8	352	116	1,920	31,365	0.6	18,803	1,564	494
Virginia	2,744	54,248	6.0	4,244	1,268	16,832	320,514	6.0	273,558	17,796	4,909
Washington	2,744	58,770	2.0	5,093	1,553	16,333	234,145	0.4	198,551	14,297	4,160
West Virginia	756	8,349	-22.7	632	128	3,629	66,302	7.4	52,982	4,036	976
Wisconsin	2,655	43,555	1.8	3,182	1,053	14,137	221,567	-2.6	189,520	10,303	2,764
Wyoming	428	3,971	-1.8	248	79	1,799	27,580	2.2	18,763	1,645	469

Other Services, Except Public Administration and Government Employment

STATE	Other services, except public administration, 2012								Government employment, 2016		
		Employees									
	Number of establishments	Total	Percent change, 2007–2012	Repair and mainte-nance	Personal and laundry services	Religious, civic, and similar services	Receipts (mil dol)	Annual payroll (mil dol)	Federal civilian	Federal military	State and local
	301	302	303	304	305	306	307	308	309	310	311
United States	529,691	3,430,711	-1.4	1,194,122	1,349,371	887,218	426,694	108,186	2,852,000	1,927,000	19,521,000
Alabama	6,087	37,291	-7.9	17,145	14,117	6,029	4,378	1,117	53,482	29,134	317,597
Alaska	1,355	7,238	-4.3	2,579	2,228	2,431	905	236	15,245	25,257	63,008
Arizona	8,503	62,073	-9.2	23,444	23,403	15,226	6,232	1,736	55,453	32,799	357,744
Arkansas...........................	3,961	21,830	-5.9	8,514	8,577	4,739	2,339	586	20,353	15,839	192,764
California	57,009	395,836	-0.9	143,971	155,062	96,803	50,439	12,251	248,686	206,029	2,296,556
Colorado	10,246	64,398	2.6	22,061	23,944	18,393	8,519	2,100	54,254	52,336	379,677
Connecticut.......................	7,282	43,384	-9.6	13,274	20,799	9,311	4,904	1,382	17,932	13,715	223,879
Delaware	1,513	9,841	-1.7	2,963	4,705	2,173	975	290	5,678	8,603	59,403
District of Columbia	3,357	58,982	18.3	638	7,081	51,263	19,773	4,239	196,574	14,087	40,368
Florida.............................	34,843	195,176	-3.2	60,133	84,877	50,166	20,799	5,415	137,843	92,399	946,374
Georgia............................	13,828	89,302	-8.9	35,769	36,220	17,313	10,617	2,703	100,803	89,733	577,918
Hawaii..............................	2,808	19,348	-3.8	3,202	7,812	8,334	2,005	539	33,283	56,456	93,739
Idaho...............................	2,553	12,188	-10.9	5,569	4,257	2,362	1,118	311	12,895	8,687	109,708
Illinois..............................	23,334	165,366	-1.4	58,058	59,330	47,978	21,356	5,827	80,468	41,771	747,214
Indiana............................	10,777	72,937	-3.1	28,900	25,835	18,202	8,910	2,107	37,734	20,696	385,713
Iowa................................	5,866	30,672	-3.8	11,925	11,612	7,135	3,343	848	17,789	11,639	240,343
Kansas.............................	5,147	29,521	-6.8	10,781	10,367	8,373	3,433	849	25,127	33,131	233,851
Kentucky..........................	5,849	38,364	-6.3	16,863	14,589	6,912	4,071	1,090	36,803	44,555	270,518
Louisiana..........................	6,293	43,500	3.0	21,958	14,140	7,402	5,409	1,479	30,863	35,744	294,194
Maine...............................	2,786	13,755	3.4	4,907	4,517	4,331	1,463	376	15,056	6,805	84,822
Maryland...........................	9,978	79,391	2.6	25,219	31,858	22,314	10,880	2,929	175,205	50,125	343,113
Massachusetts...................	14,008	93,489	3.6	25,127	42,404	25,958	10,455	2,931	46,394	19,311	397,187
Michigan...........................	15,919	96,150	-5.3	37,715	37,999	20,436	10,408	2,720	52,304	17,692	539,920
Minnesota.........................	10,832	72,715	-11.1	22,221	29,525	20,969	7,877	2,017	32,015	20,023	373,591
Mississippi	3,540	19,232	-5.8	8,304	6,723	4,205	1,952	549	25,432	26,991	221,591
Missouri	10,357	62,825	-6.9	25,284	24,124	13,417	6,980	1,835	58,526	35,042	377,849
Montana	2,278	10,917	5.8	4,644	2,731	3,542	1,222	303	13,326	7,836	75,220
Nebraska	3,989	21,832	-3.2	9,171	7,747	4,914	2,841	612	16,803	12,643	146,708
Nevada	3,538	25,386	-6.8	8,561	12,023	4,802	2,609	706	18,935	17,920	135,048
New Hampshire	2,879	16,603	2.8	5,699	6,736	4,168	1,555	473	7,672	4,710	82,737
New Jersey........................	18,327	108,216	2.4	32,991	56,552	18,673	11,608	3,150	49,520	25,197	533,081
New Mexico	2,962	17,464	-3.3	7,474	5,336	4,654	1,799	501	29,438	17,159	162,324
New York..........................	45,646	271,689	8.9	56,633	111,369	103,687	39,709	9,395	116,717	55,158	1,275,405
North Carolina	13,716	80,710	-5.4	32,784	31,859	16,067	9,141	2,321	71,813	127,883	659,692
North Dakota	1,716	9,232	-0.3	3,515	3,137	2,580	1,064	254	9,450	11,567	68,278
Ohio.................................	18,851	127,366	-5.8	44,260	55,364	27,742	13,221	3,491	77,791	35,432	688,476
Oklahoma	5,411	32,388	2.3	13,280	12,874	6,234	4,037	940	48,263	33,005	289,623
Oregon.............................	6,894	37,941	-3.0	14,717	13,486	9,738	4,435	1,149	28,391	11,582	248,090
Pennsylvania	25,231	154,319	0.0	51,110	63,740	39,469	17,737	4,367	97,071	35,446	640,913
Rhode Island	2,276	13,046	-9.3	4,172	5,690	3,184	1,445	391	10,755	6,772	54,309
South Carolina...................	6,666	44,374	-2.5	19,017	15,909	9,448	4,465	1,302	33,515	52,060	321,878
South Dakota.....................	1,805	8,371	-1.7	3,569	2,586	2,216	939	214	11,362	7,888	65,999
Tennessee.........................	8,117	55,990	-10.3	20,581	23,773	11,636	6,526	1,711	49,819	20,953	374,358
Texas...............................	34,116	259,128	2.2	120,606	95,613	42,909	30,172	8,454	198,786	171,371	1,676,937
Utah.................................	4,259	26,026	-0.8	11,864	9,841	4,321	2,544	723	36,195	16,147	197,779
Vermont............................	1,588	7,211	-0.8	2,223	2,032	2,956	755	199	6,968	4,179	46,997
Virginia.............................	14,726	112,430	1.2	34,521	41,520	36,389	17,079	4,471	198,064	138,123	537,803
Washington........................	12,425	69,976	-1.7	24,072	29,997	15,907	13,185	2,203	74,800	75,029	491,330
West Virginia	2,661	16,583	0.3	6,969	5,759	3,855	1,773	444	23,649	8,517	124,519
Wisconsin	10,210	62,054	-6.5	21,698	25,964	14,392	6,407	1,732	29,157	15,820	392,371
Wyoming...........................	1,373	6,655	2.0	3,467	1,628	1,560	885	215	7,543	6,004	62,484

Table A. States — State Government Employment and Payroll

	State government employment and payroll, 2016											
	State government employment, 2016			State government payroll, 2016		Full-time equivalent payroll (1000 dollars)						
							Percent of total for:					
STATE	Full-time equivalent employees	Full-time employees	Part-time employees	Full-time March payroll (1000 dollars)	Part-time March payroll (1000 dollars)	Total March payroll (1000 dollars)[1]	Administration	Judicial and legal	Police	Corrections	Highways	Welfare
	312	313	314	315	316	317	318	319	320	321	322	323
United States	4,360,635	3,763,727	1,604,731	19,850,430	2,298,248	22,148,678	5.3	4.9	3.1	10.1	5.1	4.8
Alabama	90,141	78,048	32,820	358,987	37,759	396,746	3.6	3.8	1.4	4.8	4.3	3.9
Alaska	25,073	23,274	4,885	136,941	6,287	143,228	7.7	6.7	3.1	9.8	13.5	6.4
Arizona	72,316	60,479	31,237	296,763	34,354	331,117	4.1	3.8	3.3	11.8	3.9	7.1
Arkansas	62,476	56,651	16,428	235,294	15,280	250,573	5.3	2.6	2.0	7.7	5.9	5.5
California	414,679	345,411	175,986	2,432,641	393,539	2,826,181	6.5	1.8	3.9	16.7	6.0	0.8
Colorado	87,844	60,312	48,392	344,773	92,118	436,891	3.6	7.9	2.2	9.1	4.2	3.0
Connecticut	62,863	52,844	24,295	335,832	45,520	381,353	6.0	8.5	4.2	10.1	5.5	9.8
Delaware	25,881	22,628	8,031	105,117	12,031	117,148	4.2	8.0	6.9	11.6	4.7	4.5
District of Columbia	X	X	X	X	X	X	X	X	X	X	X	X
Florida	178,571	159,594	49,279	698,927	61,643	760,570	4.5	11.5	2.3	10.2	4.1	4.0
Georgia	128,151	112,660	50,877	479,920	49,625	529,545	3.4	3.3	2.1	9.2	2.9	4.2
Hawaii	58,777	52,248	19,613	247,472	21,951	269,423	2.6	5.2	0.0	4.9	1.7	0.7
Idaho	24,025	20,642	10,563	106,667	11,848	118,516	7.5	4.7	2.3	12.0	5.2	6.6
Illinois	123,611	102,044	50,836	594,783	88,576	683,359	6.1	3.9	3.8	12.5	6.4	8.6
Indiana	89,278	75,588	43,179	333,168	35,660	368,828	3.3	2.9	2.4	5.3	3.5	5.0
Iowa	51,005	41,359	28,324	261,559	23,913	285,472	3.5	4.8	2.2	5.4	4.4	5.0
Kansas	52,118	46,519	18,059	217,346	20,125	237,471	3.8	4.1	2.2	4.9	4.4	4.7
Kentucky	85,606	74,313	25,571	332,405	27,919	360,324	4.1	5.9	2.4	3.9	4.8	6.7
Louisiana	73,796	66,308	20,529	314,490	20,649	335,139	6.6	2.4	4.0	7.1	6.6	6.2
Maine	20,647	18,201	7,952	79,469	8,494	87,963	8.0	4.3	3.2	5.6	10.0	13.2
Maryland	85,928	77,139	13,230	405,368	40,211	445,579	5.5	7.3	3.5	13.8	5.7	6.8
Massachusetts	99,315	88,728	34,785	524,724	49,506	574,231	5.9	10.8	5.0	13.0	3.5	7.6
Michigan	144,350	115,407	72,358	671,807	122,743	794,550	4.5	1.5	2.2	9.4	2.0	7.8
Minnesota	82,697	68,694	34,091	401,628	51,638	453,266	8.8	5.0	1.2	5.1	5.8	2.2
Mississippi	56,841	51,813	13,515	202,453	14,209	216,662	4.0	1.3	2.4	3.4	4.8	6.0
Missouri	87,140	77,082	29,500	300,426	26,790	327,216	4.4	5.4	3.6	10.8	5.9	6.1
Montana	20,392	17,258	9,409	80,017	10,118	90,135	7.6	4.6	2.9	5.8	11.9	8.3
Nebraska	31,924	26,492	10,345	115,843	12,398	128,241	3.7	3.6	3.1	9.3	6.5	6.9
Nevada	28,314	25,177	9,860	124,985	11,497	136,482	8.5	4.0	4.4	13.3	6.1	7.1
New Hampshire	19,092	15,014	11,259	79,045	13,765	92,809	6.8	4.4	3.5	6.8	8.0	10.1
New Jersey	139,043	126,626	29,984	791,589	48,512	840,100	4.3	10.1	6.3	6.3	4.0	6.5
New Mexico	45,775	40,851	13,857	190,956	18,334	209,290	3.1	7.7	1.7	7.2	4.5	3.3
New York	242,184	224,566	46,386	1,397,285	79,349	1,476,634	8.2	9.9	3.8	12.9	3.9	1.6
North Carolina	140,047	123,990	43,332	578,840	54,626	633,466	3.5	5.4	2.6	12.1	6.3	0.7
North Dakota	19,321	16,322	9,712	79,411	10,839	90,250	5.3	4.8	1.4	4.7	7.0	2.0
Ohio	137,846	108,195	76,670	583,493	87,835	671,329	6.8	3.1	2.4	10.3	4.7	2.5
Oklahoma	68,649	60,316	26,097	256,943	22,729	279,672	5.3	5.1	3.9	5.8	4.2	9.6
Oregon	68,128	60,704	24,666	311,498	41,286	352,783	7.9	5.2	2.5	8.7	6.3	10.5
Pennsylvania	162,573	141,062	64,338	720,039	112,934	832,973	5.6	3.9	5.8	11.8	7.0	5.9
Rhode Island	18,302	16,855	7,366	100,494	6,628	107,122	9.0	7.2	2.7	10.2	3.7	7.9
South Carolina	79,917	71,611	21,472	303,986	24,272	328,257	4.7	1.5	2.7	7.4	5.2	5.4
South Dakota	14,106	12,380	6,326	56,836	5,707	62,544	7.0	5.6	2.7	5.3	7.6	11.7
Tennessee	78,599	69,961	26,479	305,276	24,904	330,179	6.1	4.7	2.8	7.1	4.2	8.8
Texas	309,862	274,945	90,324	1,414,733	132,677	1,547,410	3.4	2.2	3.4	9.5	4.2	5.9
Utah	57,733	48,902	28,318	245,571	32,466	278,038	5.5	3.2	1.5	4.8	2.8	3.4
Vermont	14,388	13,162	4,002	68,493	7,029	75,523	7.6	5.2	5.1	7.5	7.2	11.8
Virginia	126,741	107,381	60,157	545,010	73,946	618,955	4.3	3.5	2.8	8.6	6.7	2.5
Washington	126,970	106,882	53,506	576,345	88,858	665,203	3.5	2.2	1.9	6.2	6.0	8.1
West Virginia	41,422	37,331	12,652	141,691	12,252	153,943	4.7	5.4	3.0	6.4	12.1	6.5
Wisconsin	72,676	57,564	50,233	306,705	49,309	356,014	4.8	4.3	1.5	13.1	2.8	2.8
Wyoming	13,502	12,194	3,646	56,387	3,590	59,977	8.2	5.2	2.5	8.3	13.5	3.9

1. Includes program categories not shown separately.

Table A. States — Federal Funds and State Government Finances

	State government employment and payroll, 2016 (cont.)							State government finances, 2016							
	Full-time equivalent payroll (1000 dollars) (cont.)							General revenue (mil dol)							
	Percent of total for:											From own sources			
									From federal government			Taxes		Taxes per capita[1] (dollars)	
STATE	Health	Hospitals	Social Insurance administration	Natural resources and parks	Utilities, sewerge, and waste management	Elementary and secondary education and libraries	Higher education	Total	Total	Per capita[1] (dollars)	Total	Total	Sales and gross receipts	Total	Sales and gross receipts
	324	325	326	327	328	329	330	331	332	333	334	335	336	337	338
United States	4.3	8.8	1.6	3.5	0.1	1.1	39.5	X	X	X	X	X	X	X	X
Alabama	4.9	14.4	0.9	2.2	-	-	48.9	25,250	9,522	1,958	15,728	9,920	5,106	2,040	1,050
Alaska	2.9	1.1	1.0	9.8	-	8.6	16.7	7,629	2,853	3,846	4,775	1,042	261	1,405	352
Arizona	3.2	0.9	2.0	2.3	-	-	49.2	34,583	14,540	2,098	20,042	14,676	8,680	2,117	1,252
Arkansas	5.5	10.3	1.8	3.7	-	-	44.5	20,346	7,432	2,487	12,915	9,453	4,590	3,163	1,536
California	3.9	11.3	2.8	4.2	0.2	-	36.1	282,908	94,336	2,403	188,572	155,231	53,366	3,955	1,360
Colorado	2.2	6.6	1.3	2.9	-	-	51.0	27,530	8,704	1,571	18,826	12,795	4,897	2,309	884
Connecticut	6.6	10.0	1.2	1.4	0.1	-	27.2	26,172	7,321	2,047	18,851	15,245	6,150	4,263	1,720
Delaware	7.5	4.4	1.0	2.4	0.5	-	30.5	7,963	2,231	2,344	5,732	3,522	539	3,700	566
District of Columbia	X	X	X	X	X	X	X	X	X	X	X	X	X	X	X
Florida	7.5	1.9	1.3	4.2	-	-	43.6	80,261	27,390	1,329	52,871	37,640	30,429	1,826	1,476
Georgia	3.1	6.0	0.9	4.9	-	20.6	53.9	42,279	14,572	1,413	27,707	21,454	8,408	2,081	816
Hawaii	3.9	9.0	0.4	1.7	-	-	20.2	12,919	2,943	2,060	9,976	6,919	4,316	4,843	3,021
Idaho	8.0	1.8	2.9	9.1	-	-	30.4	8,151	2,722	1,617	5,429	4,206	2,117	2,499	1,258
Illinois	2.5	8.7	1.5	2.4	-	-	36.3	68,847	20,265	1,583	48,582	38,907	18,524	3,039	1,447
Indiana	1.9	1.7	1.0	2.5	-	-	66.8	36,260	13,042	1,966	23,218	17,588	10,608	2,652	1,599
Iowa	1.0	17.0	0.9	3.3	-	-	45.2	21,074	6,646	2,120	14,429	9,559	4,593	3,049	1,465
Kansas	1.9	21.0	0.2	2.3	-	-	45.4	16,460	3,828	1,317	12,631	8,059	4,325	2,772	1,488
Kentucky	4.5	9.3	1.1	3.7	-	0.1	48.0	28,198	11,564	2,606	16,635	11,779	5,603	2,655	1,263
Louisiana	5.6	12.0	1.2	6.3	-	-	34.4	24,110	10,362	2,213	13,748	9,310	5,353	1,989	1,143
Maine	5.2	2.6	1.7	6.8	-	-	29.9	8,310	2,894	2,173	5,417	4,130	2,078	3,102	1,561
Maryland	6.7	3.9	1.0	2.9	-	3.1	31.1	39,160	12,290	2,043	26,869	20,894	8,939	3,473	1,486
Massachusetts	6.8	4.8	1.4	2.4	1.1	-	26.6	54,701	16,401	2,408	38,300	27,277	8,684	4,004	1,275
Michigan	3.8	10.3	0.5	2.3	-	-	51.4	61,246	20,908	2,106	40,338	27,437	13,239	2,763	1,333
Minnesota	4.3	4.4	1.2	4.4	1.0	-	44.0	41,213	11,321	2,051	29,892	25,189	10,121	4,563	1,833
Mississippi	5.3	18.1	1.0	5.3	-	-	40.9	18,954	8,299	2,777	10,655	7,660	4,778	2,563	1,599
Missouri	3.3	10.6	0.5	2.8	-	-	40.5	28,850	10,988	1,803	17,863	12,245	5,302	2,010	870
Montana	4.4	2.6	4.0	8.4	-	-	30.7	6,011	2,446	2,346	3,566	2,628	562	2,521	540
Nebraska	2.1	11.0	0.8	5.8	-	-	38.5	10,130	3,162	1,658	6,968	5,117	2,363	2,683	1,239
Nevada	5.2	5.0	1.4	3.7	-	-	31.9	13,904	4,558	1,550	9,346	8,025	6,348	2,730	2,159
New Hampshire	5.0	3.0	1.4	3.0	-	117.0	36.6	6,997	2,609	1,955	4,388	2,642	983	1,979	736
New Jersey	2.8	8.1	0.9	1.9	0.4	-	25.0	60,953	17,976	2,010	42,977	31,547	13,173	3,527	1,473
New Mexico	5.1	16.6	0.6	3.6	-	-	40.1	16,537	7,030	3,378	9,507	5,462	2,930	2,625	1,408
New York	3.5	15.2	2.9	2.0	-	-	19.8	164,399	56,823	2,878	107,576	81,354	24,790	4,120	1,255
North Carolina	1.6	13.2	0.9	3.5	0.3	-	43.7	51,110	15,909	1,568	35,202	26,202	11,149	2,582	1,099
North Dakota	8.3	3.3	1.4	6.3	-	-	44.2	6,699	1,641	2,166	5,058	3,709	1,497	4,894	1,975
Ohio	2.8	10.3	1.3	2.1	-	-	47.9	67,466	24,258	2,089	43,209	28,695	18,231	2,471	1,570
Oklahoma	8.3	1.2	1.3	2.9	0.2	-	44.6	20,921	7,246	1,847	13,674	8,491	3,778	2,164	963
Oregon	3.4	9.7	4.1	4.4	-	-	33.3	28,109	10,027	2,450	18,081	11,043	1,532	2,698	374
Pennsylvania	1.2	5.3	2.3	4.4	-	0.3	38.6	79,738	26,240	2,053	53,498	37,395	19,284	2,925	1,508
Rhode Island	5.5	4.3	2.1	2.5	2.0	-	22.1	7,430	2,518	2,384	4,912	3,266	1,665	3,091	1,576
South Carolina	6.1	7.1	1.2	3.0	-	-	44.5	24,905	8,272	1,667	16,633	9,556	4,621	1,926	931
South Dakota	4.6	2.1	1.4	6.6	-	-	36.2	4,251	1,475	1,705	2,775	1,748	1,440	2,019	1,664
Tennessee	6.1	4.4	1.3	5.7	-	-	42.8	28,984	11,239	1,690	17,746	13,386	9,704	2,013	1,459
Texas	6.4	6.6	1.0	3.6	-	-	49.3	122,795	43,751	1,570	79,044	52,133	46,371	1,871	1,664
Utah	3.4	17.6	1.6	2.4	-	-	47.9	16,441	4,234	1,388	12,207	7,083	3,032	2,321	994
Vermont	3.8	1.7	1.7	5.4	-	-	30.3	6,121	2,139	3,425	3,982	3,086	1,031	4,941	1,651
Virginia	5.5	9.5	0.8	2.6	-	-	47.1	45,426	10,228	1,216	35,198	21,220	6,886	2,523	819
Washington	5.2	9.0	2.9	4.4	0.5	-	44.8	43,629	13,705	1,880	29,924	22,280	17,636	3,057	2,420
West Virginia	1.9	3.1	1.2	4.9	-	-	41.3	12,845	4,846	2,646	7,999	5,128	2,567	2,800	1,402
Wisconsin	2.6	4.6	1.1	3.3	-	-	49.7	34,643	9,318	1,612	25,325	17,608	7,722	3,047	1,336
Wyoming	7.2	4.2	0.9	9.4	-	-	27.2	5,090	2,143	3,661	2,947	1,914	820	3,268	1,401

1. Based on resident population estimated as of July 1 of the year shown.

Table A. States — State Government Finances and Voting

	State government finances, 2016 (cont.)												Voting and registration, November 2016		Presidential election, 2016 (percent of vote cast)		
	General expenditures (mil dol) (cont.)										Debt outstanding						
			Direct expenditures		By selected function												
STATE	Total	To local govern-ments	Total	Per capita[1] (dollars)	Educa-tion	Health and hospitals	Highways	Public safety	Public welfare	Natural resources, parks, and recreation	Total (mil dol)	Per capita[1]	Percent registered	Percent voted	Demo-cratic	Repub-lican	All other
	339	340	341	342	343	344	345	346	347	348	349	350	351	352	353	354	355
United States	X	X	X	X	X	X	X	X	X	X	X	X	64.2	56.0	48.0	45.8	6.2
Alabama	26,349	6,672	19,677	4,046	11,376	3,154	1,653	712	7,203	293	8,969	1,844	68.0	56.4	34.4	62.1	3.6
Alaska	10,873	2,038	8,835	11,909	2,864	280	1,291	473	2,373	495	5,728	7,721	69.1	59.4	36.6	51.3	12.2
Arizona	37,788	10,904	26,884	3,879	12,806	2,693	2,194	1,321	14,280	369	14,244	2,055	60.5	53.3	45.1	48.7	6.2
Arkansas	20,975	5,883	15,092	5,050	8,449	1,318	1,443	549	6,980	395	4,985	1,668	65.7	56.0	33.7	60.6	5.8
California	276,187	103,512	172,675	4,399	93,606	20,022	10,923	11,449	107,044	7,531	151,715	3,865	53.8	48.2	61.7	31.6	6.7
Colorado	29,100	7,311	21,789	3,933	11,793	1,535	1,863	1,320	8,640	444	17,200	3,104	68.2	63.8	48.2	43.3	8.6
Connecticut	26,929	5,438	21,491	6,009	8,529	2,501	1,414	935	7,727	304	35,352	9,885	63.9	57.5	54.6	40.9	4.5
Delaware	8,563	1,512	7,052	7,407	3,082	502	603	441	2,455	144	4,965	5,215	66.8	57.2	53.4	41.9	4.7
District of Columbia	X	X	X	X	X	X	X	X	X	X	X	0	75.9	68.7	90.5	4.1	5.4
Florida	79,066	20,408	58,658	2,846	26,633	4,570	8,007	2,875	25,597	1,268	33,315	1,616	59.3	52.9	47.8	49.0	3.2
Georgia	41,408	11,836	29,572	2,868	18,583	2,742	2,772	1,667	12,005	702	13,248	1,285	64.1	55.7	45.6	50.8	3.6
Hawaii	10,805	135	10,670	7,469	3,386	1,143	457	306	2,758	248	8,758	6,130	49.8	43.3	61.0	29.4	9.6
Idaho	8,097	2,277	5,820	3,458	3,042	200	682	331	2,429	269	3,685	2,190	64.5	58.3	27.5	59.3	13.2
Illinois	63,958	18,109	45,849	3,581	17,795	3,329	6,746	1,453	21,878	434	64,221	5,017	68.5	58.8	55.8	38.8	5.4
Indiana	36,675	9,712	26,964	4,065	15,895	723	2,543	965	12,709	458	22,464	3,387	66.1	56.0	37.8	56.9	5.3
Iowa	21,011	5,471	15,540	4,958	7,225	2,050	2,179	398	6,501	329	6,120	1,952	69.2	60.7	41.8	51.2	7.1
Kansas	16,856	4,800	12,057	4,147	7,247	2,220	1,336	456	4,150	279	7,581	2,608	67.1	58.0	36.1	56.7	7.3
Kentucky	30,914	4,780	26,133	5,890	10,372	2,347	2,414	880	11,266	565	13,785	3,107	67.3	55.3	32.7	62.5	4.8
Louisiana	26,954	5,766	21,188	4,526	9,564	953	1,613	993	8,805	1,136	17,594	3,758	70.6	59.7	38.4	58.1	3.5
Maine	8,336	1,289	7,047	5,293	2,211	301	716	263	3,343	207	5,012	3,764	78.5	71.3	46.3	43.5	10.2
Maryland	38,756	9,398	29,358	4,880	12,924	2,836	2,557	2,091	11,933	647	26,593	4,420	67.3	59.2	60.3	33.9	5.8
Massachusetts	53,641	9,081	44,561	6,542	13,605	2,433	3,006	2,027	20,186	650	75,308	11,056	68.1	61.7	59.1	32.3	8.7
Michigan	62,217	20,788	41,429	4,173	25,726	5,380	2,743	2,389	18,707	492	33,245	3,349	71.3	61.8	47.3	47.5	5.2
Minnesota	40,870	13,144	27,727	5,023	15,132	833	3,196	1,067	14,874	971	16,756	3,035	72.9	65.3	46.4	44.9	8.6
Mississippi	19,322	5,252	14,070	4,708	6,516	1,892	1,337	475	6,633	305	7,470	2,500	78.3	66.7	40.1	57.9	1.9
Missouri	28,241	6,173	22,068	3,622	10,024	3,830	1,375	1,045	8,666	389	19,350	3,176	72.1	62.8	38.1	56.8	5.1
Montana	6,071	1,094	4,977	4,774	1,901	292	646	251	1,697	237	3,207	3,076	72.8	65.2	35.9	56.5	7.6
Nebraska	10,286	2,418	7,869	4,126	3,993	731	906	458	2,638	274	1,809	949	71.7	63.4	33.7	58.7	7.6
Nevada	12,686	4,429	8,257	2,808	4,886	493	718	367	4,035	133	3,352	1,140	61.4	53.5	47.9	45.5	6.6
New Hampshire	6,390	461	5,930	4,442	1,536	207	477	184	2,389	91	8,210	6,151	73.1	66.9	46.8	46.5	6.7
New Jersey	56,487	11,672	44,814	5,010	18,628	3,645	3,310	2,099	18,457	684	66,923	7,482	60.7	53.4	55.5	41.4	3.2
New Mexico	17,849	4,986	12,863	6,181	6,048	1,638	716	635	5,631	273	6,738	3,238	59.2	49.4	48.3	40.0	11.7
New York	160,856	61,640	99,216	5,025	47,037	13,789	5,271	4,371	63,587	1,159	137,369	6,957	59.0	50.7	56.1	32.4	11.5
North Carolina	47,759	12,859	34,900	3,440	20,827	3,337	3,884	1,982	12,939	728	17,464	1,721	68.1	61.6	46.2	49.8	4.0
North Dakota	7,369	2,112	5,257	6,936	2,472	299	1,316	128	1,571	164	2,064	2,723	72.8	62.1	27.2	63.0	9.8
Ohio	69,003	18,552	50,451	4,344	22,907	6,262	4,077	2,122	25,748	648	33,109	2,851	69.5	61.4	43.6	51.7	4.8
Oklahoma	21,228	4,459	16,769	4,274	8,489	1,200	2,144	804	6,572	252	8,899	2,268	63.7	53.2	28.9	65.3	5.7
Oregon	28,512	5,552	22,960	5,609	9,255	3,043	1,171	1,056	10,391	671	13,061	3,191	67.4	61.0	50.1	39.1	10.8
Pennsylvania	82,457	20,051	62,407	4,882	25,179	8,221	8,685	3,147	27,934	1,002	47,052	3,680	69.2	60.2	47.9	48.6	3.6
Rhode Island	7,190	1,237	5,953	5,635	2,164	249	316	283	2,702	99	9,005	8,524	64.4	55.5	54.4	38.9	6.7
South Carolina	26,640	6,394	20,246	4,081	9,558	2,952	1,664	686	7,429	359	15,122	3,048	69.0	59.8	40.7	54.9	4.4
South Dakota	4,521	775	3,746	4,329	1,464	214	726	173	1,046	214	3,286	3,797	69.3	57.3	31.7	61.5	6.7
Tennessee	29,839	7,618	22,221	3,341	10,268	1,075	1,552	1,216	12,327	457	6,025	906	64.3	52.0	34.7	60.7	4.6
Texas	130,549	31,763	98,785	3,545	56,424	10,433	9,522	5,132	37,548	1,234	48,238	1,731	58.1	47.7	43.2	52.2	4.5
Utah	17,585	3,512	14,073	4,612	8,601	2,088	836	494	3,406	236	7,480	2,451	66.7	58.9	27.5	45.5	27.0
Vermont	6,325	1,772	4,553	7,290	2,736	408	454	228	1,770	123	3,341	5,348	70.2	61.0	55.7	29.8	14.5
Virginia	48,164	12,467	35,697	4,244	16,743	6,242	4,900	2,384	11,248	391	28,232	3,356	69.4	62.6	49.8	44.4	5.8
Washington	46,238	11,871	34,366	4,715	18,877	4,686	2,797	1,435	12,654	1,141	32,232	4,423	69.9	60.5	52.5	36.8	10.6
West Virginia	12,939	2,385	10,553	5,763	4,437	456	1,163	385	4,452	314	7,124	3,890	63.6	50.4	26.5	68.6	4.9
Wisconsin	33,172	9,032	24,140	4,177	12,137	2,610	1,707	1,259	10,757	590	22,087	3,822	74.4	68.7	46.5	47.2	6.3
Wyoming	5,374	1,868	3,506	5,988	1,983	270	504	193	825	388	835	1,426	69.7	63.5	21.6	67.4	11.0

1. Based on resident population estimated as of July 1 of the year shown.

PART B.

States and Counties

(For explanation of symbols, see page viii)

Page

County Highlights and Rankings

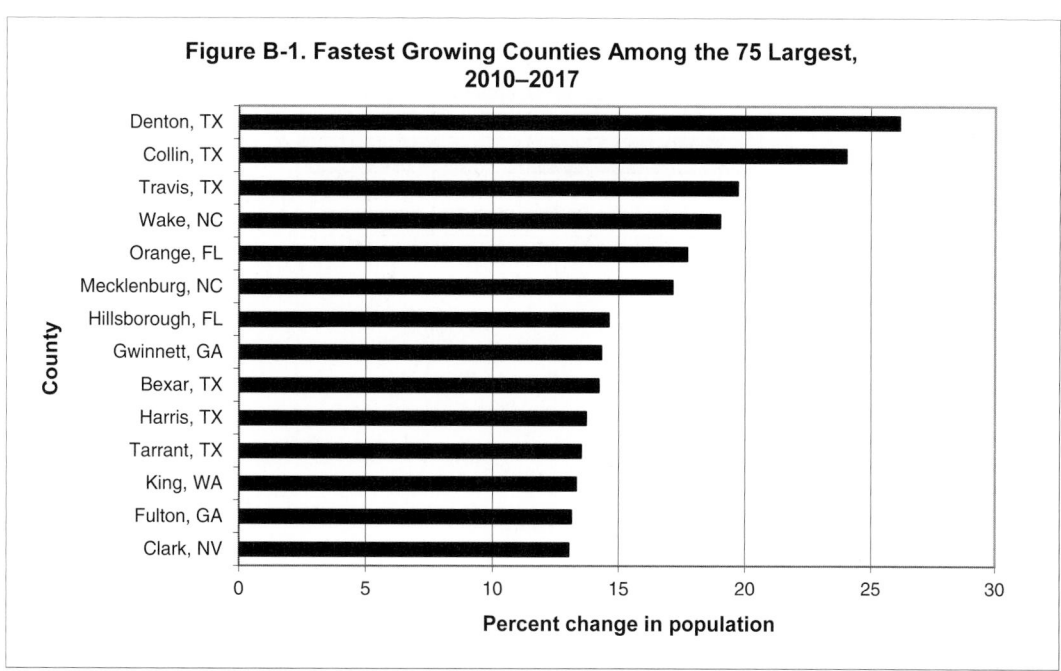

Figure B-1. Fastest Growing Counties Among the 75 Largest, 2010–2017

Seven years after the 2010 census, the 2017 population estimates show that Los Angeles County, CA, remains, by far, the most populous county, with more than 10 million residents. Next is Cook County, IL, which includes Chicago, with over 5.2 million people. Its population declined 3.4 percent from 2000 to 2010 but increased 0.3 percent from 2010 to 2017. New York City consists of five counties (the five boroughs), with Kings (Brooklyn) and Queens each with over 2 million residents, New York (Manhattan) and the Bronx each with about 1.5 million. Queens County moved out of the top 10 in 2014 but Brooklyn's nearly 6.0 percent growth keeps Kings the 8th most populous county in the nation.

Among the 75 most populous counties, the highest growth rates from 2010 to 2017 were found in the South, with five of the ten top growth rates in Texas. From 2010 to 2017, the fastest-growing of these large counties was Denton, TX, in the Dallas-Fort Worth metropolitan area. During the past six years, Denton County's population increased by 26.2 percent followed by Collin County, TX (also Dallas) at 24.0 percent. In 2017, Denton County ranked 71st among the most populous counties. Six other counties in Texas also had growth rates over 10 percent: Travis (Austin), Bexar (San Antonio), Harris (Houston), Tarrant (Fort Worth.), Hidalgo (McAllen) and Dallas. Other large counties that experienced more than 10 percent growth in the six-year period were found mainly in the South and the West. Nearly 1,700 counties lost population during this period. The largest proportional losses were in counties with very small populations. Among the largest counties, only St. Louis, MO, New Haven, CT, Cuyahoga, OH (Cleveland), and Wayne, MI

(Detroit), declined in population between 2010 and 2017. Two hundred fifty-eight counties had population growth rates at or above 10 percent from 2010 to 2017. One hundred eighty-nine of these fast-growing counties had more than 50,000 residents and 151 counties had more than 100,000 residents.

Within states, the number and physical size of counties varied considerably: Delaware had three counties while Texas had 254 counties. For the 3,142 counties (and county equivalents—see Appendix A) in the United States, population in 2017 ranged from nearly 10.2 million in Los Angeles, CA, to 88 in Kalawao County, HI. Other particularly large counties in terms of population are Cook County, IL (over 5.2 million people), encompassing Chicago and its suburbs, Harris County, TX (containing Houston) with more than 4.6 million people, and Maricopa County, AZ (containing Phoenix), with over 4.3 million people. There were 44 counties with a population of 1,000,000 or more; these counties combined contain more than one-fourth of the U.S. population. Over half of the U.S. population lived in the 155 largest counties, those with a population of 450,000 or more. At the other extreme, there were 35 counties with fewer than 1,000 people in 2017. The median county population size was 25,839.

In terms of land area, counties range from the nearly 145,573 square miles of Yukon-Koyukuk Census Area, AK; to Kalawao County, HI, with 12 square miles; New York County, NY (Manhattan), with 22.7 square miles; Bristol County, RI, with 24.1 square miles; and Arlington County, VA, with 26 square miles.[1] Counties tend to be larger in the western United States

---

[1] Several independent cities in Virginia, which are treated as counties for tabulation purposes, were excluded here.

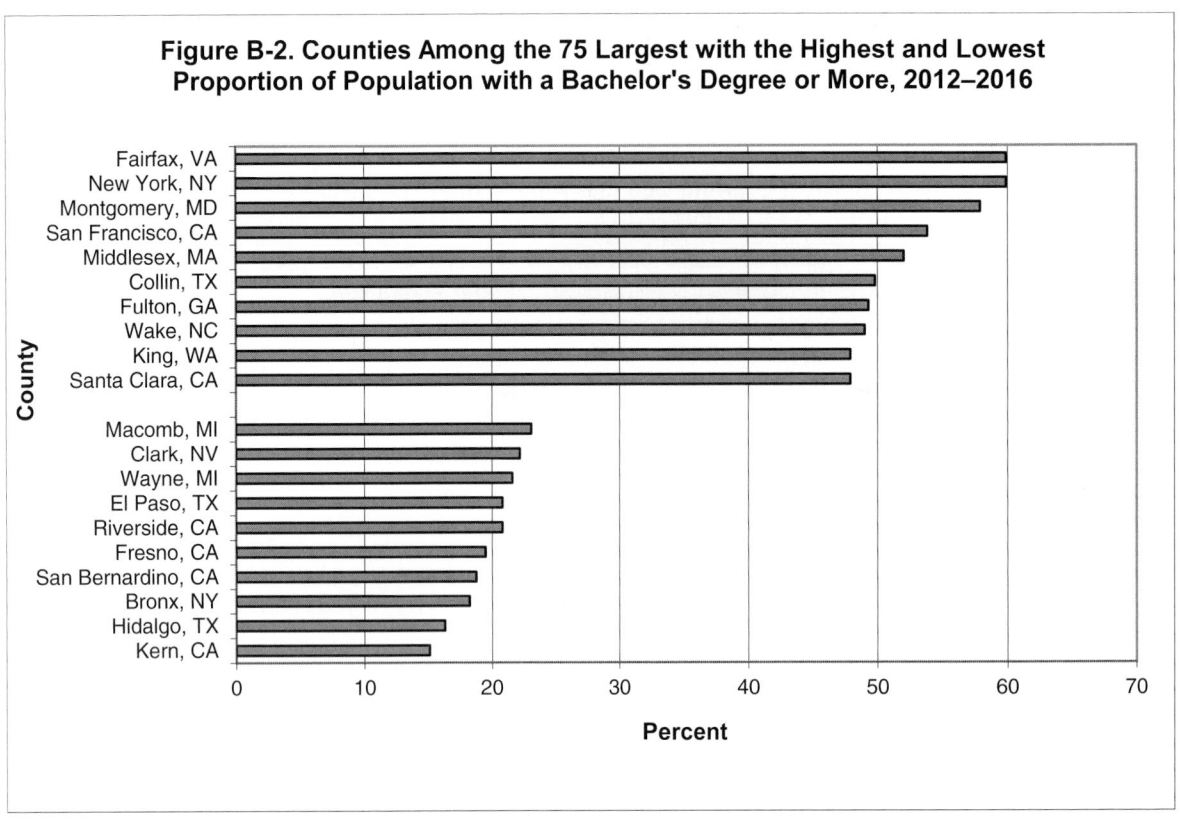

Figure B-2. Counties Among the 75 Largest with the Highest and Lowest Proportion of Population with a Bachelor's Degree or More, 2012–2016

(most of the largest 50 in size are in that region). The median land area for all U.S. counties was about 616 square miles in 2017.

While New York County, NY, had one of the smallest land areas, it had by far the highest population density among U.S. counties in 2017, with over 73,000 persons per square mile. No other county approached that density (although three other New York City boroughs were among the top five counties in population density). San Francisco had the highest population density outside of New York City, with Suffolk County, MA (Boston); Philadelphia County, PA; and Washington, DC, also among the top 10 counties. The median county had nearly 45 persons per square mile, with 266 counties having more than 500 persons per square mile. The nation's largest county in terms of population (Los Angeles) had a population density of 2,504 persons per square mile. This density ranked 20th among the 75 most populous U.S. counties.

Proportionally large year-to-year labor force changes are not unusual for counties with small populations. The 2017 annual averages reflect a national labor force that increased by 1.0 percent. Among the 75 most populous counties, 13 counties' labor forces grew by 3.0 percent or more between 2016 and 2017. Miami-Dade Country, FL and Orange County, FL experienced the largest increases among the 75 most populous counties, at 3.8 percent and 3.5 percent respectively. Duval County, FL followed with an increase of 3.4 percent. Over 1,400 counties experienced declines in their labor forces from 2016 to 2017, with 70 counties losing 5 percent or more. Among the most populous 75 counties, 7

counties had decreases in their labor forces, led by Kern County, CA (Bakersfield) and St. Louis County, MO at -0.9 percent each.

The national annual average unemployment rate was 4.4 percent in 2017—the lowest it has been since 2007. The unemployment rate was down from 4.9 percent in 2016, 5.3 percent in 2015, and 6.2 percent in 2014. Nearly 1,500 counties had unemployment rates above the national average of 4.4 percent in 2017 and 35 counties had unemployment rates greater than 10 percent, down from 1,100 counties in 2010, 82 counties in 2015, and 62 counties in 2016. Of the 10 counties with the highest unemployment rates, only Imperial County, CA, and Yuma County, AZ had populations over 100,000. Among the 75 most populous counties, 28 exceeded the national unemployment rate of 4.4 percent and one county equaled it, with the highest in two California counties—9.2 percent in Kern County and 8.5 percent in Fresno County. Honolulu, HI had the lowest unemployment rate at 2.2 percent, followed by San Francisco, CA at 2.9 percent. Among all smaller counties in 2017, nine counties in Colorado, eight counties in North Dakota, and one county each in Iowa, Kansas, Idaho, Nebraska, and Texas had unemployment rates of less than 2 percent.

Among the 75 largest counties, the two counties with the highest unemployment rates, Fresno and Kern counties in CA, ranked among the top counties for agricultural sales. Meanwhile, Wayne County, MI which ranked second highest in manufacturing employment had the seventh highest unemployment rate among the 75 most populous counties. Three of the ten lowest unemployment

75 Largest Counties by 2017 Population
Selected Rankings

Percent Hispanic or Latino,[1] 2017				Percent under 18 years old, 2017				Percent 65 years old and over, 2017			
Population rank	Hispanic or Latino rank	County	Percent Hispanic or Latino [col 9]	Population rank	Under 18 years old rank	County	Percent under 18 years old [cols 10 and 11]	Population rank	65 years old and over rank	County	Percent 65 years old and over [cols 17 and 18]
66	1	Hidalgo, TX	92.2	66	1	Hidalgo, TX	33.0	49	1	Pinellas, FL	24.2
70	2	El Paso, TX	82.8	62	2	Kern, CA	29.0	27	2	Palm Beach, FL	23.6
7	3	Miami-Dade, FL	68.6	46	3	Fresno, CA	28.5	44	3	Pima, AZ	19.2
16	4	Bexar, TX	60.3	39	4	Salt Lake, UT	27.5	36	4	Allegheny, PA	18.4
26	5	Bronx, NY	56.2	70	4	El Paso, TX	27.5	34	5	Cuyahoga, OH	17.8
14	6	San Bernardino, CA	53.4	59	6	Gwinnett, GA	27.3	45	6	St. Louis, MO	17.7
62	6	Kern, CA	53.4	3	7	Harris, TX	26.9	58	7	Erie, NY	17.5
46	8	Fresno, CA	53.2	14	8	San Bernardino, CA	26.5	29	8	Nassau, NY	17.4
10	9	Riverside, CA	49.1	15	8	Tarrant, TX	26.5	74	9	Montgomery, PA	17.3
1	10	Los Angeles, CA	48.6	9	10	Dallas, TX	26.4	47	10	Honolulu, HI	17.2
3	11	Harris, TX	43.0	50	11	Collin, TX	26.3	54	11	Bergen, NJ	16.9
68	12	Ventura, CA	42.9	16	12	Bexar, TX	25.8	67	11	New Haven, CT	16.9
9	13	Dallas, TX	40.2	10	13	Riverside, CA	25.5	61	13	Hartford, CT	16.8
44	14	Pima, AZ	37.3	71	14	Denton, TX	25.2	72	14	Baltimore, MD	16.7
6	15	Orange, CA	34.2	56	15	Shelby, TN	25.0	48	15	Westchester, NY	16.6
5	16	San Diego, CA	33.9	26	16	Bronx, NY	24.9	65	15	Macomb, MI	16.6
35	16	Travis, TX	33.9	52	17	Marion, IN	24.7	25	17	Suffolk, NY	16.4
30	18	Orange, FL	31.4	4	18	Maricopa, AZ	24.3	33	17	Oakland, MI	16.4
12	19	Clark, NV	31.3	41	19	Wake, NC	24.2	18	19	Broward, FL	16.2
4	20	Maricopa, AZ	31.1	51	20	Milwaukee, WI	24.0	7	20	Miami-Dade, FL	16.0
18	21	Broward, FL	29.7	40	21	Mecklenburg, NC	23.9	20	20	New York, NY	16.0
15	22	Tarrant, TX	28.9	19	22	Wayne, MI	23.8	53	22	Fairfield, CT	15.5
28	23	Hillsborough, FL	28.6	24	22	Sacramento, CA	23.8	63	23	San Francisco, CA	15.4
11	24	Queens, NY	28.0	64	24	Pierce, WA	23.6	38	24	Contra Costa, CA	15.3
20	25	New York, NY	26.1	31	25	Franklin, OH	23.4	73	24	Worcester, MA	15.3
38	26	Contra Costa, CA	25.7	37	25	Fairfax, VA	23.4	19	26	Wayne, MI	15.1
17	27	Santa Clara, CA	25.6	12	27	Clark, NV	23.3	75	26	Hamilton, OH	15.1
2	28	Cook, IL	25.5	42	28	Montgomery, MD	23.2	11	28	Queens, NY	15.0
48	29	Westchester, NY	24.9	68	28	Ventura, CA	23.2	22	28	Middlesex, MA	15.0
24	30	Sacramento, CA	23.3	75	30	Hamilton, OH	23.1	57	28	Du Page, IL	15.0
21	31	Alameda, CA	22.5	8	31	Kings, NY	22.9	68	28	Ventura, CA	15.0
27	32	Palm Beach, FL	22.3	28	32	Hillsborough, FL	22.8	42	32	Montgomery, MD	14.9
59	33	Gwinnett, GA	21.2	38	32	Contra Costa, CA	22.8	4	33	Maricopa, AZ	14.8
69	33	Middlesex, NJ	21.2	57	32	Du Page, IL	22.8	69	34	Middlesex, NJ	14.5
53	35	Fairfield, CT	19.9	53	35	Fairfield, CT	22.7	12	35	Clark, NV	14.4
54	35	Bergen, NJ	19.9	55	36	Duval, FL	22.6	6	36	Orange, CA	14.3
42	37	Montgomery, MD	19.6	30	37	Orange, FL	22.4	2	37	Cook, IL	14.2
25	38	Suffolk, NY	19.5	43	38	Fulton, GA	22.3	10	38	Riverside, CA	14.0
71	39	Denton, TX	19.4	60	38	Prince George's, MD	22.3	28	38	Hillsborough, FL	14.0
8	40	Kings, NY	19.1	6	40	Orange, CA	22.2	24	40	Sacramento, CA	13.7
60	41	Prince George's, MD	18.5	17	40	Santa Clara, CA	22.2	32	40	Hennepin, MN	13.7
39	42	Salt Lake, UT	18.3	35	40	Travis, TX	22.2	55	40	Duval, FL	13.7
67	43	New Haven, CT	18.1	48	43	Westchester, NY	22.1	5	43	San Diego, CA	13.6
61	44	Hartford, CT	18.0	2	44	Cook, IL	22.0	8	44	Kings, NY	13.5
29	45	Nassau, NY	17.2	32	44	Hennepin, MN	22.0	21	44	Alameda, CA	13.5
37	46	Fairfax, VA	16.2	45	44	St. Louis, MO	22.0	23	46	Philadelphia, PA	13.4
50	47	Collin, TX	15.3	1	47	Los Angeles, CA	21.9	64	46	Pierce, WA	13.4
63	48	San Francisco, CA	15.2	5	47	San Diego, CA	21.9	51	48	Milwaukee, WI	13.3
51	49	Milwaukee, WI	15.1	23	49	Philadelphia, PA	21.8	1	49	Los Angeles, CA	13.2
23	50	Philadelphia, PA	14.8	69	50	Middlesex, NJ	21.6	17	49	Santa Clara, CA	13.2
57	51	Du Page, IL	14.4	72	50	Baltimore, MD	21.6	56	49	Shelby, TN	13.2
40	52	Mecklenburg, NC	13.3	74	50	Montgomery, PA	21.6	37	52	Fairfax, VA	13.1
73	53	Worcester, MA	11.5	29	53	Nassau, NY	21.5	13	53	King, WA	12.9
64	54	Pierce, WA	10.9	25	54	Suffolk, NY	21.4	60	54	Prince George's, MD	12.8
52	55	Marion, IN	10.5	33	55	Oakland, MI	21.3	26	55	Bronx, NY	12.3
41	56	Wake, NC	10.2	54	55	Bergen, NJ	21.3	52	55	Marion, IN	12.3
47	57	Honolulu, HI	9.9	65	55	Macomb, MI	21.3	46	57	Fresno, CA	12.0
13	58	King, WA	9.7	73	55	Worcester, MA	21.3	16	58	Bexar, TX	11.9
49	58	Pinellas, FL	9.7	18	59	Broward, FL	21.2	70	58	El Paso, TX	11.9
55	58	Duval, FL	9.7	44	59	Pima, AZ	21.2	30	60	Orange, FL	11.7
22	61	Middlesex, MA	8.0	47	59	Honolulu, HI	21.2	31	60	Franklin, OH	11.7
43	62	Fulton, GA	7.3	61	62	Hartford, CT	21.1	43	62	Fulton, GA	11.4
32	63	Hennepin, MN	7.0	34	63	Cuyahoga, OH	20.9	14	63	San Bernardino, CA	11.3
56	64	Shelby, TN	6.4	21	64	Alameda, CA	20.8	41	64	Wake, NC	11.2
19	65	Wayne, MI	5.9	13	65	King, WA	20.4	15	65	Tarrant, TX	11.1
34	65	Cuyahoga, OH	5.9	58	65	Erie, NY	20.4	40	66	Mecklenburg, NC	10.9
31	67	Franklin, OH	5.5	67	65	New Haven, CT	20.4	66	67	Hidalgo, TX	10.8
58	67	Erie, NY	5.5	7	68	Miami-Dade, FL	20.3	50	68	Collin, TX	10.7
72	67	Baltimore, MD	5.5	11	69	Queens, NY	20.1	62	68	Kern, CA	10.7
74	70	Montgomery, PA	5.2	22	70	Middlesex, MA	19.9	39	70	Salt Lake, UT	10.6
33	71	Oakland, MI	4.0	27	71	Palm Beach, FL	19.2	9	71	Dallas, TX	10.5
75	72	Hamilton, OH	3.3	36	72	Allegheny, PA	18.8	3	72	Harris, TX	10.2
45	73	St. Louis, MO	2.9	49	73	Pinellas, FL	16.4	71	73	Denton, TX	9.8
65	74	Macomb, MI	2.6	20	74	New York, NY	14.4	59	74	Gwinnett, GA	9.6
36	75	Allegheny, PA	2.1	63	75	San Francisco, CA	13.4	35	75	Travis, TX	9.5

75 Largest Counties by 2017 Population
Selected Rankings

Percent female-headed family households, 2012–2016				Birth rate, 2017				Percent under 65 who have no health insurance, 2016			
Popu-lation rank	Female households rank	County	Percent female households [col 30]	Popu-lation rank	Live birth rate rank	County	Birth rate [col 36]	Popu-lation rank	No health insurance rank	County	Percent with no health insurance [col 40]
26	1	Bronx, NY	30.5	66	1	Hidalgo, TX	18.1	66	1	Hidalgo, TX	29.7
66	2	Hidalgo, TX	21.3	3	2	Harris, TX	15.7	9	2	Dallas, TX	21.6
23	3	Philadelphia, PA	20.4	70	2	El Paso, TX	15.7	70	3	El Paso, TX	21.2
56	3	Shelby, TN	20.4	9	4	Dallas, TX	15.5	3	4	Harris, TX	20.7
60	5	Prince George's, MD	20.0	8	5	Kings, NY	15.4	7	5	Miami-Dade, FL	19.4
19	6	Wayne, MI	19.5	39	5	Salt Lake, UT	15.4	15	6	Tarrant, TX	17.0
70	7	El Paso, TX	19.2	46	5	Fresno, CA	15.4	59	7	Gwinnett, GA	16.7
8	8	Kings, NY	19.1	62	8	Kern, CA	15.3	16	8	Bexar, TX	16.6
7	9	Miami-Dade, FL	18.2	52	9	Marion, IN	15.1	27	9	Palm Beach, FL	16.3
46	10	Fresno, CA	17.9	31	10	Franklin, OH	14.7	18	10	Broward, FL	15.3
14	11	San Bernardino, CA	17.0	16	11	Bexar, TX	14.5	35	11	Travis, TX	15.2
51	12	Milwaukee, WI	16.7	26	12	Bronx, NY	14.3	30	12	Orange, FL	14.9
16	13	Bexar, TX	16.5	14	13	San Bernardino, CA	14.1	28	13	Hillsborough, FL	14.0
62	14	Kern, CA	16.4	15	13	Tarrant, TX	14.1	49	14	Pinellas, FL	13.9
52	15	Marion, IN	16.2	51	13	Milwaukee, WI	14.1	12	15	Clark, NV	13.5
11	16	Queens, NY	16.1	56	13	Shelby, TN	14.1	43	16	Fulton, GA	13.0
9	17	Dallas, TX	16.0	55	17	Duval, FL	14.0	55	17	Duval, FL	12.8
34	18	Cuyahoga, OH	15.9	40	18	Mecklenburg, NC	13.9	40	18	Mecklenburg, NC	12.1
55	19	Duval, FL	15.8	23	19	Philadelphia, PA	13.8	4	19	Maricopa, AZ	11.7
3	20	Harris, TX	15.6	64	20	Pierce, WA	13.4	56	20	Shelby, TN	11.6
18	20	Broward, FL	15.6	35	21	Travis, TX	13.3	71	20	Denton, TX	11.6
1	22	Los Angeles, CA	15.4	75	21	Hamilton, OH	13.3	11	22	Queens, NY	11.3
30	23	Orange, FL	15.3	32	23	Hennepin, MN	13.2	44	23	Pima, AZ	11.0
75	24	Hamilton, OH	15.1	5	24	San Diego, CA	13.1	39	24	Salt Lake, UT	10.9
2	25	Cook, IL	14.8	19	24	Wayne, MI	13.1	50	25	Collin, TX	10.8
24	25	Sacramento, CA	14.8	47	24	Honolulu, HI	13.1	60	25	Prince George's, MD	10.8
61	27	Hartford, CT	14.5	60	24	Prince George's, MD	13.1	1	27	Los Angeles, CA	10.7
59	28	Gwinnett, GA	14.4	2	28	Cook, IL	12.8	52	28	Marion, IN	10.6
72	28	Baltimore, MD	14.4	4	28	Maricopa, AZ	12.8	10	29	Riverside, CA	9.8
43	30	Fulton, GA	14.3	24	30	Sacramento, CA	12.7	23	30	Philadelphia, PA	9.7
15	31	Tarrant, TX	14.2	59	30	Gwinnett, GA	12.7	68	30	Ventura, CA	9.7
28	31	Hillsborough, FL	14.2	10	32	Riverside, CA	12.6	2	32	Cook, IL	9.4
31	31	Franklin, OH	14.2	11	32	Queens, NY	12.6	26	32	Bronx, NY	9.4
40	34	Mecklenburg, NC	14.1	12	34	Clark, NV	12.5	46	32	Fresno, CA	9.4
45	34	St. Louis, MO	14.1	28	34	Hillsborough, FL	12.5	37	35	Fairfax, VA	9.3
12	36	Clark, NV	13.9	30	34	Orange, FL	12.5	41	36	Wake, NC	9.2
67	36	New Haven, CT	13.9	43	34	Fulton, GA	12.5	14	37	San Bernardino, CA	9.1
58	38	Erie, NY	13.5	71	38	Denton, TX	12.4	8	38	Kings, NY	8.8
10	39	Riverside, CA	13.4	41	39	Wake, NC	12.2	69	39	Middlesex, NJ	8.7
65	40	Macomb, MI	13.1	42	39	Montgomery, MD	12.2	54	40	Bergen, NJ	8.5
44	41	Pima, AZ	12.9	1	41	Los Angeles, CA	12.1	6	41	Orange, CA	8.2
48	41	Westchester, NY	12.9	37	41	Fairfax, VA	12.1	5	42	San Diego, CA	8.1
4	43	Maricopa, AZ	12.7	13	43	King, WA	11.9	45	42	St. Louis, MO	8.1
53	44	Fairfield, CT	12.4	17	43	Santa Clara, CA	11.9	62	42	Kern, CA	8.1
47	45	Honolulu, HI	12.3	72	43	Baltimore, MD	11.8	31	45	Franklin, OH	7.9
68	45	Ventura, CA	12.3	6	46	Orange, CA	11.7	53	45	Fairfield, CT	7.9
38	47	Contra Costa, CA	12.2	21	46	Alameda, CA	11.7	51	47	Milwaukee, WI	7.8
73	47	Worcester, MA	12.2	34	46	Cuyahoga, OH	11.7	48	48	Westchester, NY	7.7
5	49	San Diego, CA	12.1	7	49	Miami-Dade, FL	11.6	42	49	Montgomery, MD	7.4
6	50	Orange, CA	12.0	18	49	Broward, FL	11.6	19	50	Wayne, MI	7.1
21	50	Alameda, CA	12.0	68	49	Ventura, CA	11.6	64	51	Pierce, WA	6.5
27	50	Palm Beach, FL	12.0	45	52	St. Louis, MO	11.5	72	51	Baltimore, MD	6.5
25	53	Suffolk, NY	11.8	50	52	Collin, TX	11.5	20	53	New York, NY	6.3
69	53	Middlesex, NJ	11.8	57	52	Du Page, IL	11.5	34	53	Cuyahoga, OH	6.3
29	55	Nassau, NY	11.7	44	55	Pima, AZ	11.2	65	55	Macomb, MI	6.2
64	56	Pierce, WA	11.6	58	56	Contra Costa, CA	11.0	75	55	Hamilton, OH	6.2
36	57	Allegheny, PA	11.4	33	57	Oakland, MI	10.8	25	57	Suffolk, NY	6.0
41	57	Wake, NC	11.4	36	58	Allegheny, PA	10.8	38	58	Contra Costa, CA	5.9
42	59	Montgomery, MD	11.3	65	58	Macomb, MI	10.8	24	59	Sacramento, CA	5.8
20	60	New York, NY	11.1	22	61	Middlesex, MA	10.7	57	59	Du Page, IL	5.8
54	60	Bergen, NJ	11.1	48	61	Westchester, NY	10.7	13	61	King, WA	5.6
71	60	Denton, TX	11.1	69	61	Middlesex, NJ	10.7	67	61	New Haven, CT	5.6
49	63	Pinellas, FL	11.0	74	61	Montgomery, PA	10.7	21	63	Alameda, CA	5.3
39	64	Salt Lake, UT	10.8	20	65	New York, NY	10.6	33	64	Oakland, MI	5.2
35	65	Travis, TX	10.7	25	66	Suffolk, NY	10.4	17	65	Santa Clara, CA	5.1
17	66	Santa Clara, CA	10.4	29	66	Nassau, NY	10.4	29	66	Nassau, NY	5.0
33	67	Oakland, MI	10.3	53	66	Fairfield, CT	10.4	32	66	Hennepin, MN	5.0
22	68	Middlesex, MA	9.9	73	66	Worcester, MA	10.4	61	66	Hartford, CT	5.0
32	69	Hennepin, MN	9.8	27	70	Palm Beach, FL	10.2	36	69	Allegheny, PA	4.9
50	69	Collin, TX	9.8	61	70	Hartford, CT	10.2	63	70	San Francisco, CA	4.7
74	71	Montgomery, PA	9.4	63	70	San Francisco, CA	10.2	74	71	Montgomery, PA	4.6
37	72	Fairfax, VA	9.3	67	73	New Haven, CT	10.1	58	72	Erie, NY	4.5
57	73	Du Page, IL	9.2	54	74	Bergen, NJ	9.9	47	73	Honolulu, HI	3.8
13	74	King, WA	8.8	49	75	Pinellas, FL	8.9	73	74	Worcester, MA	2.8
63	75	San Francisco, CA	8.1					22	75	Middlesex, MA	2.7

Table B. States and Counties — Land Area and Population

State / county code	CBSA code[1]	County code[2]	STATE County	Land area[3] (sq. mi)	Total persons 2017	Rank	Per square mile	White	Black	American Indian, Alaska Native	Asian and Pacific Islander	Percent Hispanic or Latino[4]	Under 5 years	5 to 17 years	18 to 24 years	25 to 34 years	35 to 44 years	45 to 54 years
					Population, 2017			Race alone or in combination, not Hispanic or Latino (percent)					Age (percent)					
				1	2	3	4	5	6	7	8	9	10	11	12	13	14	15

1. CBSA = Core Based Statistical Area. See Appendix A for explanation. See Appendix B for list of metropolitan areas with component counties. 2. County type code from the Economic Research Service of USDA Rural-Urban Continuum Codes. See Appendix A for definition. 3. Dry land or land partially or temporarily covered by water. 4. May be of any race.

Table B. States and Counties — Population and Households

STATE County	55 to 64 years	65 to 74 years	75 years and over	Percent female	2000	2010	2000-2010	2010-2017	Births	Deaths	Net Migration	Number	Persons per household	Family households	Female family householder[1]	One person
	Age (percent) (cont.)				Total persons		Percent change		Components of change, 2010-2017					Percent		
	16	17	18	19	20	21	22	23	24	25	26	27	28	29	30	31

1. No spouse present.

Table B. States and Counties — Population, Vital Statistics, Health, and Crime

STATE County	Persons in group quarters, 2017	Number	Employment/ residence ratio	Total	Rate[1]	Number	Rate[1]	Number	Percent	Total beneficiaries	Enrolled in Original Medicare	Enrolled in Medicare Advantage	Number	Rate[3]
		Daytime Population, 2012-2016		Births, 2017		Deaths, 2017		Persons under 65 with no health insurance, 2016		Medicare, 2017			Serious crimes known to police[2], 2016 — Total	
	32	33	34	35	36	37	38	39	40	41	42	43	44	45

1. Per 1,000 estimated resident population. 2. Data for serious crimes have not been adjusted for underreporting; this may affect comparability between geographic areas and over time.
3. Per 100,000 population estimated by the FBI.

Table B. States and Counties — Crime, Education, Money Income, and Poverty

STATE County	Violent	Property	Total	Percent private	High school graduate or less	Bachelor's degree or more	Total current spending (mil dol)	Current spending per student (dollars)	Per capita income[6]	Median income (dollars)	with income of less than $50,000	with income of $200,000 or more	Median household income (dollars)	All persons	Children under 18 years	Children 5 to 17 years in families
	Rate		Enrollment[3]		Attainment[4] (percent)		Local government expenditures,[5] 2013-2014			Households	Percent			Percent below poverty level		
	Serious crimes known to police, 2016 (cont.)[1]		Education						Money income, 2012-2016				Income and poverty, 2016			
	46	47	48	49	50	51	52	53	54	55	56	57	58	59	60	61

1. Data for serious crimes have not been adjusted for underreporting; this may affect comparability between geographic areas and over time. 2. Per 100,000 population estimated by the FBI.
3. All persons 3 years old and over enrolled in nursery school through college. 4. Persons 25 years old and over. 5. Elementary and secondary education expenditures.
6. Based on population estimated by the American Community Survey, 2011–2015.

Table B. States and Counties — **Personal Income and Earnings**

STATE County	Personal income, 2016										Earnings, 2016		
	Total (mil dol)	Percent change 2015-2016	Per capita[1]		Wages and salaries (mil dol)	Pension and insurance	Supplements to wages and salaries, employer contributions (mil dol) Government social insurance	Proprietors' income (mil dol)	Dividends, interest, and rent (mil dol)	Personal transfer reecipts (mil dol)	Total (mil dol)	Contributions for government social insurance (mil dol)	
			Dollars	Rank								From employee and self-employed	From employer
	62	63	64	65	66	67	68	69	70	71	72	73	74

1. Based on the resident population estimated as of July 1 of the year shown.

Table B. States and Counties — **Earnings, Social Security , and Housing**

STATE County	Earnings, 2016 (cont.)									Social Security beneficiaries, December 2016		Supplemental Security Income recipients, 2016	Housing units, 2017	
	Percent by selected industries													
	Farm	Mining, quarrying, and extracting	Construction	Manufacturing	Information; professional, scientific, technical services	Retail trade	Finance, insurance, real estate, and leasing	Health care and social assistance	Government	Number	Rate[1]		Total	Percent change, 2010-2017
	75	76	77	78	79	80	81	82	83	84	85	86	87	88

1. Per 1,000 resident population estimated as of July 1 of the year shown.

Table B. States and Counties — **Housing, Labor Force, and Employment**

STATE County	Housing units, 2017 (cont.)									Civilian labor force, 2017				Civilian employment[6], 2012-2016		
	Occupied units											Unemployment		Percent		
			Owner-occupied				Renter-occupied									
	Total	Percent	Median value[1]	Median owner cost as a percent of income		Median rent[3]	Median rent as a percent of income[2]	Substandard units[4] (percent)		Total	Percent change, 2016-2017	Total	Rate[5]	Total	Management, business, science, and arts	Construction, production, and maintenance occupations
				With a mortgage	Without a mortgage[2]											
	89	90	91	92	93	94	95	96		97	98	99	100	101	102	103

1. Specified owner-occupied units.   2. A value of 10.0 represents 10 percent or less; a value of 50.0 represents 50 percent or more.   3. Specified renter-occupied units.
4. Overcrowded or lacking complete plumbing facilities.   5. Percent of civilian labor force.   6. Civilian employed persons 16 years old and over.

Table B. States and Counties — **Nonfarm Employment and Agriculture**

STATE County	Private nonfarm establishments, employment and payroll, 2016									Agriculture, 2012			
		Employment						Annual payroll		Farms			Farm operators whose principal occupation is farming (percent)
	Number of establishments	Total	Health care and social assistance	Manufacturing	Retail trade	Finance and insurance	Professional, scientific, and technical services	Total (mil dol)	Average per employee (dollars)	Number	Percent with:		
											Fewer than 50 acres	500 acres or more	
	104	105	106	107	108	109	110	111	112	113	114	115	116

Table B. States and Counties — Agriculture

STATE County	Land in farms					Value of land and buildings (dollars)		Value of machinery and equiopmnet, average per farm (dollars)	Value of products sold:				Percent of farms with sales of:		Government payments	
			Acres									Percent from:					
	Acreage (1,000)	Percent change, 2007-2012	Average size of farm	Total irrigated (1,000)	Total cropland (1,000)	Average per farm	Average per acre		Total (mil dol)	Average per farm (acres)	Crops	Live-stock and poultry products	$10,000 or more	$100,000 or more	Total ($1,000)	Percent of farms
	117	118	119	120	121	122	123	124	125	126	127	128	129	130	131	132

Table B. States and Counties — Water Use, Wholesale Trade, Retail Trade, and Real Estate

STATE County	Water use, 2015		Wholesale Trade[1], 2012				Retail Trade[2], 2012				Real estate and rental and leasing,[2] 2012			
	Public supply water withdrawn (mil gal/ day)	Public supply gallons withdrawn per person per day	Number of establish-ments	Number of employees	Sales (mil dol)	Annual payroll (mil dol)	Number of establishments	Number of employees	Sales (mil dol)	Annual payroll (mil dol)	Number of establish-ments	Number of employees	Sales (mil dol)	Annual payroll (mil dol)
	133	134	135	136	137	138	139	140	141	142	143	144	145	146

1 Merchant wholesalers, except manufacturers' sales branches and offices. 2. Employer establishments.

Table B. States and Counties — Professional Services, Manufacturing, and Accommodation and Food Services

STATE County	Professional, scientific, and technical services, 2012				Manufacturing, 2012				Accommodation and food services, 2012			
	Number of establishments	Number of employees	Sales (mil dol)	Annual payroll (mil dol)	Number of establishments	Number of employees	Sales (mil dol)	Annual payroll (mil dol)	Number of establishments	Number of employees	Sales (mil dol)	Annual payroll (mil dol)
	147	148	149	150	151	152	153	154	155	156	157	158

Table B. States and Counties — Health Care and Social Assistance, Other Services, Nonemployer Businesses, and Residential Construction

STATE County	Health care and social assistance, 2012				Other services, 2012				Nonemployer businesses, 2015		Value of residential construction authorized by building permits, 2017	
	Number of establishments	Number of employees	Receipts (mil dol)	Annual payroll (mil dol)	Number of establishments	Number of employees	Receipts (mil dol)	Annual payroll (mil dol)	Number	Receipts (mil dol)	New construction ($1,000)	Number of housing units
	159	160	161	162	163	164	165	166	167	168	169	170

Table B. States and Counties — **Government Employment and Payroll, and Local Government Finances**

STATE County	Government employment and payroll, 2012									Local government finances				
			March payroll (percent of total)							General revenue				
												Taxes		
													Per capita[1] (dollars)	
	Full-time equivalent employees	March payroll (dollars)	Administration, judicial, and legal	Police and corrections	Fire protection	Highways and transportation	Health and welfare	Natural resources and utilities	Education and libraries	Total (mil dol)	Inter-govern-mental (mil dol)	Total (mil dol)	Total	Property
	171	172	173	174	175	176	177	178	179	180	181	182	183	184

1. Based on the resident population estimated as of July 1 of the year shown.

Table B. States and Counties — **Local Government Finances, Government Employment, and Income Taxes**

STATE County	Local governmnet finances, 2012 (cont.)							Debt outstanding		Government employment, 2016			Individual income tax returns, 2015		
			Direct general expenditure												
				Percent of total for:											
	Total (mil dol)	Per capita[1] (dollars)	Education	Health and hospitals	Police protection	Public welfare	Highways	Total (mil dol)	Per capita[1] (dollars)	Federal civilian	Federal military	State and local	Number of returns	Mean adjusted gross income	Mean income tax
	185	186	187	188	189	190	191	192	193	194	195	196	197	198	199

1. Based on the resident population estimated as of July 1 of the year shown.

Table B. States and Counties — **Land Area and Population**

State / county code	CBSA code[1]	County code[2]	STATE County	Land area[3] (sq. mi)	Total persons 2017	Rank	Per square mile	White	Black	American Indian, Alaska Native	Asian and Pacific Islancer	Percent Hispanic or Latino[4]	Under 5 years	5 to 17 years	18 to 24 years	25 to 34 years	35 to 44 years	45 to 54 years
				1	2	3	4	5	6	7	8	9	10	11	12	13	14	15
00000		0	UNITED STATES........	3,532,315.6	325,719,178	X	92.2	62.6	13.4	1.3	6.8	18.1	6.1	16.5	9.4	13.9	12.5	13.0
01000		0	ALABAMA	50,646.7	4,874,747	X	96.3	67.0	27.3	1.2	1.9	4.3	6.0	16.5	w9.4	13.1	12.1	13.1
01001	33,860	2	Autauga..................	594.4	55,504	914	93.4	76.0	20.1	0.9	1.9	2.9	5.9	18.0	8.2	12.9	13.1	14.2
01003	19,300	3	Baldwin	1,589.8	212,628	313	133.7	84.5	9.6	1.4	1.6	4.6	5.6	16.2	7.3	11.4	12.0	13.4
01005	21,640	6	Barbour	885.0	25,270	1,595	28.6	46.8	48.6	0.7	0.8	4.2	5.2	15.6	8.0	14.1	12.1	13.2
01007	13,820	1	Bibb	622.5	22,668	1,692	36.4	75.2	22.0	0.8	0.5	2.6	5.9	14.7	8.1	14.9	13.2	14.6
01009	13,820	1	Blount....................	644.8	58,013	889	90.0	88.1	1.9	1.2	0.5	9.6	6.0	17.4	7.8	12.0	12.2	13.7
01011		6	Bullock...................	622.8	10,309	2,402	16.6	22.1	69.6	0.6	0.4	8.2	6.0	14.7	8.2	15.0	13.1	13.3
01013		6	Butler.....................	776.8	19,825	1,836	25.5	52.5	45.2	0.7	1.2	1.4	5.9	16.9	7.8	11.9	11.8	11.9
01015	11,500	3	Calhoun..................	605.9	114,728	538	189.4	73.9	21.7	1.0	1.6	3.7	5.7	16.1	9.1	13.2	12.0	12.8
01017	46,740	6	Chambers	596.5	33,713	1,335	56.5	56.5	40.2	0.6	1.4	2.4	6.0	15.1	8.2	12.5	11.2	13.4
01019		6	Cherokee	553.8	25,857	1,570	46.7	93.2	4.8	1.5	0.6	1.6	4.7	15.0	7.1	10.4	10.8	13.9
01021	13,820	1	Chilton	692.9	44,067	1,090	63.6	81.2	10.7	0.8	0.7	7.8	6.2	17.6	8.1	12.4	12.5	13.2
01023		9	Choctaw..................	913.5	12,945	2,231	14.2	57.0	41.9	0.4	0.4	1.0	5.4	14.7	7.7	9.8	10.9	13.5
01025		7	Clarke....................	1,238.4	24,083	1,641	19.4	53.5	44.6	0.7	0.7	1.3	5.7	16.2	8.5	10.9	11.8	13.4
01027		9	Clay......................	604.0	13,367	2,202	22.1	82.2	14.8	1.2	0.5	3.1	5.2	15.4	8.3	10.9	11.4	14.3
01029		8	Cleburne	560.1	14,900	2,104	26.6	93.8	3.6	0.9	0.4	2.4	5.6	17.3	7.3	11.5	11.7	13.8
01031	21,460	4	Coffee	679.0	51,874	962	76.4	72.5	18.4	2.1	2.5	7.1	6.3	17.4	8.1	12.8	13.5	13.5
01033	22,520	3	Colbert	592.6	54,500	929	92.0	80.1	17.0	1.3	0.8	2.6	5.7	15.3	7.9	12.4	11.5	13.6
01035		7	Conecuh..................	850.2	12,469	2,260	14.7	51.0	46.8	1.0	0.5	2.0	5.8	15.2	8.1	10.8	10.2	12.4
01037	45,180	8	Coosa.....................	650.9	10,754	2,368	16.5	66.8	30.6	0.9	0.4	2.4	4.3	12.1	7.3	10.1	11.0	14.8
01039		6	Covington................	1,030.5	37,092	1,247	36.0	84.8	13.2	1.2	0.6	1.7	6.0	15.8	7.1	11.8	11.0	12.9
01041		8	Crenshaw................	608.9	13,871	2,174	22.8	72.8	24.4	1.1	1.3	2.1	5.8	17.3	7.7	11.6	11.7	13.0
01043	18,980	4	Cullman..................	734.8	82,755	685	112.6	93.3	1.6	1.3	0.8	4.3	6.1	16.4	7.7	12.8	12.1	13.2
01045	37,120	4	Dale	561.4	49,226	998	87.7	70.7	21.5	1.5	2.2	6.5	6.6	16.4	8.7	14.7	11.7	12.3
01047	42,820	4	Dallas	978.7	39,215	1,197	40.1	28.0	70.6	0.5	0.7	1.1	6.1	18.2	8.8	11.9	11.0	12.1
01049	22,840	6	DeKalb	777.1	71,617	755	92.2	82.0	1.9	2.6	0.6	14.8	6.0	18.5	8.1	11.8	12.5	13.3
01051	33,860	2	Elmore	618.4	81,677	691	132.1	74.6	21.8	1.0	1.2	3.0	5.8	16.5	8.5	14.1	13.4	13.9
01053	12,120	6	Escambia	945.1	37,447	1,240	39.6	61.8	32.8	4.4	0.6	2.3	5.9	16.3	7.8	13.7	12.7	13.1
01055	23,460	3	Etowah...................	535.3	102,755	588	192.0	79.5	16.2	1.0	1.0	3.8	5.7	15.9	8.3	12.0	12.2	13.6
01057		6	Fayette...................	627.7	16,468	2,013	26.2	85.9	12.4	0.8	0.4	1.7	5.6	15.5	8.0	11.2	11.0	13.2
01059		6	Franklin..................	633.9	31,495	1,393	49.7	78.1	4.5	1.1	0.6	17.0	6.6	18.0	7.9	12.6	12.7	13.4
01061	20,020	3	Geneva	574.5	26,421	1,551	46.0	85.4	10.2	1.6	0.6	4.0	5.5	16.6	7.1	11.3	11.5	13.7
01063		8	Greene	647.0	8,330	2,562	12.9	18.4	79.9	0.5	0.4	1.5	5.6	16.3	8.0	11.5	10.2	11.3
01065	46,220	3	Hale.......................	644.0	14,812	2,108	23.0	40.1	58.1	0.4	0.4	1.5	6.8	16.5	8.8	11.5	11.0	12.1
01067	20,020	3	Henry	561.8	17,147	1,969	30.5	70.2	27.0	0.8	0.6	2.7	5.2	15.5	7.2	10.4	12.2	13.2
01069	20,020	3	Houston..................	579.9	104,346	578	179.9	68.3	27.7	1.0	1.5	3.4	6.0	17.2	7.7	13.1	12.3	13.1
01071	42,460	6	Jackson...................	1,078.0	51,909	961	48.2	91.7	4.0	3.1	0.7	3.0	5.3	15.9	7.4	11.3	12.1	13.6
01073	13,820	1	Jefferson.................	1,111.2	659,197	101	593.2	50.9	43.8	0.6	2.1	3.9	6.4	16.5	8.9	14.5	12.6	12.4
01075		8	Lamar.....................	604.8	13,946	2,167	23.1	87.4	11.4	0.8	0.3	1.6	5.4	16.4	7.0	10.7	11.5	13.1
01077	22,520	3	Lauderdale..............	668.2	92,538	633	138.5	86.1	10.9	0.9	1.0	2.7	5.1	14.7	11.5	11.8	10.8	12.8
01079	19,460	3	Lawrence	690.7	33,049	1,357	47.8	81.1	11.6	9.3	0.5	2.2	5.5	16.1	7.7	12.1	11.3	14.7
01081	12,220	3	Lee	607.6	161,604	405	266.0	68.8	23.8	0.7	4.6	3.8	5.9	15.4	18.4	14.5	12.0	11.8
01083	26,620	2	Limestone	560.0	94,402	624	168.6	78.3	14.1	1.4	2.1	6.1	5.7	17.2	7.5	13.0	13.5	14.9
01085	33,860	2	Lowndes..................	715.9	10,076	2,425	14.1	25.3	72.7	0.6	0.4	1.7	6.0	16.5	7.8	12.4	10.9	13.2
01087		6	Macon	608.8	18,755	1,883	30.8	16.7	81.2	0.7	0.9	1.8	4.8	12.5	17.9	11.3	9.0	11.4
01089	26,620	2	Madison	801.6	361,046	195	450.4	66.9	25.6	1.6	3.6	4.9	5.8	16.2	9.5	13.9	12.1	14.0
01091		7	Marengo..................	976.9	19,375	1,860	19.8	45.7	51.7	0.6	0.5	2.5	6.3	16.5	8.3	11.7	11.0	12.8
01093		7	Marion	742.3	29,833	1,436	40.2	92.9	4.3	0.9	0.5	2.5	5.2	15.7	7.5	11.0	11.5	14.2
01095	10,700	4	Marshall	565.8	95,548	618	168.9	82.3	3.1	1.3	0.9	13.9	6.9	18.1	8.0	12.5	11.7	13.1
01097	33,660	2	Mobile	1,229.4	413,955	169	336.7	58.3	36.5	1.5	2.5	2.9	6.5	17.0	9.1	14.0	11.9	12.4
01099		7	Monroe	1,025.7	21,327	1,761	20.8	55.8	41.8	1.9	0.7	1.4	5.1	16.8	8.5	10.5	11.3	13.3
01101	33,860	2	Montgomery.............	785.2	226,646	296	288.6	34.9	58.9	0.6	3.6	3.5	6.8	16.8	9.9	14.5	12.6	12.3
01103	19,460	3	Morgan...................	579.4	118,818	523	205.1	77.6	13.4	1.7	1.0	8.3	5.9	16.9	7.9	12.3	12.3	14.0
01105		8	Perry	719.7	9,339	2,478	13.0	30.3	67.4	0.4	0.7	1.7	5.8	15.9	14.8	10.4	10.3	10.7
01107	46,220	3	Pickens...................	881.4	20,176	1,816	22.9	54.7	40.7	0.5	0.4	4.6	5.3	14.7	8.6	13.4	11.5	13.8
01109	45,980	6	Pike.......................	672.1	33,267	1,347	49.5	57.5	38.3	1.3	2.6	2.2	5.6	13.7	22.6	12.1	9.7	10.3
01111		6	Randolph.................	580.5	22,670	1,690	39.1	76.6	20.4	0.9	0.6	2.9	5.7	15.9	8.6	10.5	11.0	13.5
01113	17,980	2	Russell....................	641.1	57,045	898	89.0	48.3	45.7	1.0	1.7	5.4	7.0	17.5	8.5	14.7	12.5	12.9
01115	13,820	1	St. Clair	631.9	88,199	656	139.6	87.1	9.9	0.8	1.1	2.4	6.1	16.8	7.1	13.3	12.9	13.9
01117	13,820	1	Shelby	785.4	213,605	311	272.0	79.2	13.1	0.7	2.6	5.8	5.9	17.9	8.1	12.3	13.8	14.3
01119		8	Sumter	903.8	12,687	2,248	14.0	25.2	72.3	0.3	1.8	1.1	5.7	13.7	19.5	9.9	8.6	10.6
01121	45,180	4	Talladega	736.8	80,065	701	108.7	64.1	33.4	0.9	0.9	2.3	5.3	16.2	8.3	12.7	12.0	13.8
01123	10,760	6	Tallapoosa	716.5	40,681	1,162	56.8	69.8	27.4	0.8	0.8	2.4	5.6	15.4	7.7	11.1	10.5	13.4
01125	46,220	3	Tuscaloosa..............	1,320.9	207,811	318	157.3	62.6	32.3	0.6	2.0	3.7	6.1	15.1	16.9	14.7	11.8	11.2
01127	13,820	1	Walker	791.0	64,058	828	81.0	90.3	6.9	1.0	0.7	2.6	6.1	16.1	7.8	11.7	11.5	13.6

1. CBSA = Core Based Statistical Area. See Appendix A for explanation. See Appendix B for list of metropolitan areas with component counties.   2. County type code from the Economic Research Service of USDA Rural-Urban Continuum Codes. See Appendix A for definition.   3. Dry land or land partially or temporarily covered by water.   4. May be of any race.

Table B. States and Counties — Population and Households

STATE County	Population, 2017 (cont.) Age (percent) (cont.)				Population change, 2000-2017							Households, 2012-2016				
	55 to 64 years	65 to 74 years	75 years and over	Percent female	Total persons		Percent change		Components of change, 2010-2017				Persons per house-hold	Family house-holds	Female family house-holder[1]	One person
					2000	2010	2000-2010	2010-2017	Births	Deaths	Net Migration	Number			Percent	
	16	17	18	19	20	21	22	23	24	25	26	27	28	29	30	31
UNITED STATES..........	12.9	9.1	6.5	50.8	281,421,906	308,758,105	9.7	5.5	28,703,158	18,975,711	7,233,626	117,716,237	2.64	65.9	12.9	27.7
ALABAMA	13.3	9.8	6.7	51.6	4,447,100	4,780,135	7.5	2.0	426,951	365,095	33,238	1,851,061	2.55	66.6	14.9	29.2
Autauga...........................	12.6	8.7	6.4	51.3	43,671	54,571	25.0	1.7	4,593	3,977	317	20,800	2.62	70.4	11.3	26.2
Baldwin...........................	14.2	12.1	7.9	51.5	140,415	182,265	29.8	16.7	16,068	14,356	28,263	75,149	2.62	66.8	9.9	29.0
Barbour...........................	13.0	11.4	7.4	47.2	29,038	27,457	-5.4	-8.0	2,065	2,229	-2,031	9,122	2.60	65.4	18.8	32.4
Bibb.................................	12.5	9.6	6.5	46.5	20,826	22,919	10.0	-1.1	1,879	1,782	-342	7,048	2.92	74.8	14.7	23.1
Blount..............................	13.2	10.7	7.2	50.7	51,024	57,324	12.3	1.2	4,980	4,416	171	20,619	2.77	74.9	9.9	22.9
Bullock............................	13.9	9.2	6.7	45.5	11,714	10,911	-6.9	-5.5	994	906	-707	3,556	2.84	65.2	24.0	31.3
Butler..............................	14.3	10.7	8.8	53.4	21,399	20,946	-2.1	-5.4	1,776	1,939	-953	7,675	2.60	67.0	17.9	29.0
Calhoun...........................	13.9	10.3	7.0	51.9	112,249	118,586	5.6	-3.3	9,755	10,129	-3,450	45,071	2.51	68.1	16.4	27.2
Chambers	14.5	11.3	7.8	52.1	36,583	34,170	-6.6	-1.3	2,900	3,262	-78	13,851	2.42	62.5	15.6	33.6
Cherokee.........................	15.5	13.9	8.7	50.3	23,988	25,988	8.3	-0.5	1,714	2,474	649	10,999	2.32	72.0	11.3	26.1
Chilton.............................	13.5	9.9	6.4	50.8	39,593	43,631	10.2	1.0	3,962	3,540	40	16,619	2.61	70.0	12.1	26.4
Choctaw..........................	15.3	13.0	9.7	52.7	15,922	13,858	-13.0	-6.6	969	1,222	-659	5,562	2.36	64.8	16.2	32.3
Clarke..............................	14.3	10.6	8.7	52.8	27,867	25,833	-7.3	-6.8	1,979	2,111	-1,634	9,554	2.56	63.8	12.2	33.7
Clay.................................	14.4	11.6	8.6	51.1	14,254	13,932	-2.3	-4.1	1,012	1,320	-257	5,363	2.47	70.5	12.5	27.0
Cleburne..........................	13.7	11.2	7.9	50.4	14,123	14,972	6.0	-0.5	1,249	1,327	9	5,834	2.54	66.6	9.1	29.7
Coffee..............................	12.6	9.8	6.7	50.7	43,615	49,948	14.5	3.9	4,619	3,593	890	19,375	2.60	68.0	13.7	28.4
Colbert............................	13.9	11.1	8.5	52.0	54,984	54,428	-1.0	0.1	4,442	5,069	747	22,105	2.44	68.1	13.8	28.4
Conecuh..........................	15.4	12.6	9.4	52.0	14,089	13,228	-6.1	-5.7	1,055	1,221	-594	5,090	2.48	67.7	17.6	31.5
Coosa..............................	17.6	13.5	9.3	49.8	12,202	11,758	-3.6	-8.5	677	957	-727	4,206	2.50	61.8	13.2	34.5
Covington........................	14.8	11.5	9.1	51.8	37,631	37,765	0.4	-1.8	3,235	3,664	-213	15,179	2.45	66.6	13.7	29.8
Crenshaw........................	14.3	11.5	7.2	51.6	13,665	13,900	1.7	-0.2	1,124	1,261	113	5,426	2.53	67.2	16.4	29.9
Cullman...........................	13.5	10.8	7.4	50.6	77,483	80,410	3.8	2.9	7,125	7,003	2,279	31,081	2.58	69.5	11.1	27.4
Dale.................................	13.1	9.5	6.9	50.7	49,129	50,247	2.3	-2.0	4,813	3,546	-2,296	18,794	2.58	66.5	14.6	28.6
Dallas..............................	14.6	10.4	7.0	53.9	46,365	43,820	-5.5	-10.5	3,851	3,850	-4,648	16,099	2.54	62.4	25.4	33.7
DeKalb............................	12.9	10.2	6.6	50.3	64,452	71,115	10.3	0.7	6,142	5,523	-67	24,811	2.82	70.5	11.4	27.0
Elmore.............................	13.1	9.1	5.6	51.5	65,874	79,296	20.4	3.0	6,820	5,407	1,007	28,890	2.64	71.8	13.1	25.5
Escambia.........................	13.1	10.0	7.3	48.8	38,440	38,319	-0.3	-2.3	3,237	3,399	-690	13,536	2.61	65.0	14.9	33.2
Etowah............................	13.8	11.2	7.4	51.6	103,459	104,427	0.9	-1.6	8,579	10,030	-133	39,522	2.58	68.6	13.9	27.9
Fayette............................	14.5	12.3	8.8	50.9	18,495	17,236	-6.8	-4.5	1,278	1,689	-347	6,850	2.40	69.4	10.7	28.4
Franklin...........................	12.4	9.5	7.0	49.7	31,223	31,709	1.6	-0.7	3,019	2,787	-437	11,697	2.67	69.3	13.3	27.8
Geneva............................	14.3	11.8	8.3	51.1	25,764	26,788	4.0	-1.4	2,166	2,558	38	10,657	2.49	70.3	15.1	25.6
Greene............................	15.8	12.3	9.0	52.8	9,974	9,045	-9.3	-7.9	741	781	-684	3,107	2.75	62.8	22.3	35.8
Hale.................................	14.5	11.0	7.8	52.5	17,185	15,762	-8.3	-6.0	1,431	1,301	-1,097	5,948	2.51	64.1	20.1	33.1
Henry...............................	14.1	13.7	8.5	51.7	16,310	17,300	6.1	-0.9	1,278	1,558	136	6,831	2.48	66.3	11.0	30.7
Houston...........................	13.2	10.2	7.2	52.0	88,787	101,555	14.4	2.7	9,387	7,618	1,092	39,363	2.61	66.0	16.2	28.1
Jackson............................	14.9	11.7	7.9	50.9	53,926	53,226	-1.3	-2.5	4,069	4,942	-402	19,945	2.60	69.5	9.7	28.1
Jefferson.........................	13.3	9.0	6.4	52.7	662,047	658,352	-0.6	0.1	63,608	50,672	-11,702	261,773	2.46	63.3	18.0	31.9
Lamar..............................	14.4	12.1	9.4	51.1	15,904	14,564	-8.4	-4.2	1,067	1,423	-256	6,010	2.31	68.5	11.2	29.7
Lauderdale.......................	13.7	11.3	8.3	52.1	87,966	92,709	5.4	-0.2	6,769	7,929	1,056	38,361	2.36	64.7	12.0	29.8
Lawrence.........................	14.5	11.0	7.2	51.3	34,803	34,339	-1.3	-3.8	2,626	2,872	-1,041	13,321	2.49	71.0	11.7	26.0
Lee..................................	10.5	7.2	4.3	50.7	115,092	140,296	21.9	15.2	13,181	7,240	15,188	57,901	2.56	62.7	14.2	27.7
Limestone.......................	13.3	9.1	5.8	49.8	65,676	82,782	26.0	14.0	7,289	5,253	9,449	32,073	2.72	71.3	10.7	25.9
Lowndes..........................	15.1	10.3	7.9	52.6	13,473	11,289	-16.2	-10.7	963	958	-1,232	4,238	2.47	65.5	26.6	32.4
Macon.............................	13.8	11.7	7.7	54.4	24,105	21,448	-11.0	-12.6	1,432	1,713	-2,454	7,915	2.20	58.3	23.8	36.7
Madison...........................	13.8	8.5	6.2	51.1	276,700	334,811	21.0	7.8	29,995	20,921	17,235	139,949	2.44	64.4	12.1	30.9
Marengo..........................	14.0	10.8	8.6	52.9	22,539	21,036	-6.7	-7.9	1,750	1,885	-1,541	8,149	2.43	58.9	17.8	37.8
Marion.............................	13.9	11.8	9.2	50.5	31,214	30,776	-1.4	-3.1	2,211	2,917	-214	12,486	2.37	71.5	13.0	25.8
Marshall...........................	12.9	9.9	6.9	50.7	82,231	93,019	13.1	2.7	9,444	7,910	1,077	34,461	2.71	69.7	11.9	26.6
Mobile.............................	13.3	9.5	6.3	52.3	399,843	413,143	3.3	0.2	40,422	30,886	-8,517	154,261	2.62	66.7	18.2	29.0
Monroe............................	14.9	11.1	8.5	52.4	24,324	23,070	-5.2	-7.6	1,659	1,854	-1,566	8,316	2.61	62.0	13.0	35.6
Montgomery.....................	12.5	8.6	6.0	52.8	223,510	229,385	2.6	-1.2	22,656	15,038	-10,409	90,281	2.44	63.2	20.4	32.0
Morgan............................	13.6	10.0	7.1	50.8	111,064	119,486	7.6	-0.6	10,270	9,111	-1,761	46,164	2.55	68.7	13.3	28.4
Perry...............................	13.1	10.3	8.8	53.2	11,861	10,579	-10.8	-11.7	881	952	-1,182	3,198	2.84	65.0	30.7	33.8
Pickens	14.2	10.4	8.0	50.3	20,949	19,746	-5.7	2.2	1,613	1,797	557	7,618	2.50	63.0	14.1	36.1
Pike.................................	11.1	8.7	6.2	51.8	29,605	32,899	11.1	1.1	2,787	2,307	-137	12,802	2.45	58.4	16.2	32.7
Randolph..........................	14.6	11.7	8.6	51.5	22,380	22,914	2.4	-1.1	1,768	2,060	50	8,691	2.55	68.5	12.5	28.1
Russell............................	12.9	8.5	5.5	52.0	49,756	52,951	6.4	7.7	6,273	4,129	1,774	22,333	2.60	64.4	19.1	30.9
St. Clair...........................	13.6	10.0	6.3	50.3	64,742	83,593	29.1	5.5	7,574	6,438	3,503	31,832	2.65	73.4	10.6	22.9
Shelby.............................	12.9	9.2	5.6	51.5	143,293	195,214	36.2	9.4	17,407	9,840	10,857	75,942	2.67	71.4	9.6	24.6
Sumter............................	14.5	9.4	8.0	54.4	14,798	13,763	-7.0	-7.8	1,043	1,144	-982	4,878	2.55	55.0	22.9	41.4
Talladega.........................	14.2	10.7	6.9	51.6	80,321	82,291	2.5	-2.8	6,239	7,094	-1,336	31,461	2.47	67.7	17.2	29.1
Tallapoosa.......................	15.2	12.7	8.3	51.4	41,475	41,618	0.3	-2.3	3,387	3,830	-483	16,338	2.47	69.5	16.3	28.3
Tuscaloosa.......................	11.5	7.8	5.0	51.8	164,875	194,662	18.1	6.8	17,906	12,237	7,508	70,440	2.73	66.0	15.6	27.6
Walker.............................	14.1	11.4	7.6	51.2	70,713	67,023	-5.2	-4.4	5,804	7,191	-1,541	25,194	2.57	71.9	15.5	24.3

1. No spouse present.

Table B. States and Counties — Population, Vital Statistics, Health, and Crime

STATE County	Daytime Population, 2012-2016			Births, 2017		Deaths, 2017		Persons under 65 with no health insurance, 2016		Medicare, 2017			Serious crimes known to police[2], 2016 Total	
	Persons in group quarters, 2017	Number	Employment/ residence ratio	Total	Rate[1]	Number	Rate[1]	Number	Percent	Total beneficiaries	Enrolled in Original Medicare	Enrolled in Medicare Advantage	Number	Rate[3]
	32	33	34	35	36	37	38	39	40	41	42	43	44	45
UNITED STATES..........	8,087,237	318,558,162	1.00	3,946,000	12.1	2,744,040	8.4	26,749,668	10.0	57,281,023	37,680,865	19,600,168	9,202,093	2,848
ALABAMA	118,973	4,793,491	0.98	58,389	12.0	52,390	10.7	427,972	10.8	1,009,065	637,901	371,164	169,248	3,480
Autauga............................	455	43,875	0.54	664	12.0	510	9.2	4,002	8.5	9,946	5,447	4,499	1,875	3,440
Baldwin............................	2,278	183,903	0.82	2,325	10.9	2,090	9.8	17,733	10.7	48,928	28,205	20,723	4,456	2,147
Barbour............................	2,979	26,432	0.98	270	10.7	286	11.3	2,252	12.5	5,643	3,848	1,795	714	2,770
Bibb................................	2,209	18,929	0.56	270	11.9	233	10.3	1,646	9.7	4,751	2,385	2,366	216	961
Blount..............................	489	45,414	0.42	685	11.8	653	11.3	5,704	12.1	9,768	4,783	4,985	1,649	2,865
Bullock	1,729	9,752	0.81	138	13.4	118	11.4	937	13.2	1,486	969	517	193	1,815
Butler..............................	333	19,593	0.91	228	11.5	253	12.8	1,703	10.7	4,639	3,636	1,003	672	3,368
Calhoun............................	2,759	116,189	1.01	1,342	11.7	1,427	12.4	10,386	11.2	28,874	21,358	7,516	4,766	4,180
Chambers	458	28,436	0.60	384	11.4	468	13.9	2,876	10.7	8,958	6,588	2,370	1,362	4,000
Cherokee	290	22,250	0.63	244	9.4	338	13.1	2,366	11.9	5,895	3,948	1,947	719	2,790
Chilton	393	37,004	0.61	523	11.9	476	10.8	5,181	14.2	8,251	3,764	4,487	1,473	3,356
Choctaw	129	12,475	0.80	143	11.0	174	13.4	1,136	11.3	3,535	2,876	658	68	523
Clarke..............................	280	24,846	1.00	270	11.2	321	13.3	2,219	11.4	6,812	4,267	2,546	589	2,413
Clay................................	255	12,415	0.80	134	10.0	184	13.8	1,416	13.4	3,422	2,589	834	155	1,152
Cleburne	178	12,170	0.49	154	10.3	190	12.8	1,427	11.9	3,295	2,581	713	191	1,274
Coffee	543	47,056	0.82	643	12.4	517	10.0	4,583	10.8	10,087	8,120	1,967	1,209	2,357
Colbert	474	56,174	1.08	618	11.3	684	12.6	4,221	9.7	13,007	9,963	3,044	1,489	2,748
Conecuh...........................	45	12,074	0.83	148	11.9	166	13.3	1,225	12.8	3,335	2,557	778	217	1,731
Coosa	256	8,513	0.35	86	8.0	114	10.6	1,097	13.3	2,895	2,180	714	223	2,123
Covington.........................	575	36,545	0.92	443	11.9	511	13.8	3,635	12.3	9,858	7,922	1,936	934	2,474
Crenshaw	132	12,346	0.72	163	11.8	183	13.2	1,293	11.5	3,429	2,275	1,154	183	1,344
Cullman............................	1,044	76,936	0.86	991	12.0	1,014	12.3	8,562	12.8	19,157	12,580	6,577	1,691	2,059
Dale................................	931	51,253	1.08	638	13.0	543	11.0	4,460	11.0	11,200	8,902	2,299	1,501	3,129
Dallas..............................	855	41,219	0.99	492	12.5	552	14.1	3,369	10.4	10,782	7,326	3,456	2,344	5,785
DeKalb	782	67,370	0.87	839	11.7	770	10.8	9,705	16.6	14,605	10,234	4,371	1,713	2,496
Elmore.............................	5,313	66,733	0.57	889	10.9	803	9.8	5,531	8.5	16,582	10,012	6,570	1,992	2,439
Escambia	3,173	38,926	1.09	429	11.5	499	13.3	3,680	13.2	8,415	5,628	2,788	944	2,511
Etowah............................	2,085	99,313	0.90	1,192	11.6	1,444	14.1	9,476	11.5	25,537	15,836	9,701	4,367	4,325
Fayette............................	291	14,758	0.67	165	10.0	230	14.0	1,401	10.8	4,008	2,980	1,028	151	908
Franklin............................	272	30,141	0.88	421	13.4	365	11.6	3,419	13.1	6,995	5,609	1,386	760	2,426
Geneva	229	22,614	0.59	279	10.6	359	13.6	2,978	14.1	6,669	5,365	1,304	669	2,505
Greene	45	8,005	0.75	95	11.4	95	11.4	738	11.1	2,169	1,731	438	184	2,201
Hale................................	221	12,829	0.53	187	12.6	195	13.2	1,341	11.2	4,464	3,539	925	243	1,631
Henry	199	14,558	0.62	175	10.2	202	11.8	1,559	11.7	4,534	3,100	1,434	268	1,561
Houston...........................	1,417	110,760	1.16	1,286	12.3	1,116	10.7	9,498	11.1	22,229	15,884	6,345	4,108	3,947
Jackson............................	597	49,633	0.86	554	10.7	686	13.2	5,240	12.6	13,439	9,858	3,581	NA	NA
Jefferson	16,603	724,149	1.22	8,532	12.9	7,192	10.9	53,889	9.9	144,445	70,864	73,581	30,102	4,566
Lamar..............................	217	12,919	0.77	155	11.1	189	13.6	1,204	11.1	3,946	3,303	642	105	765
Lauderdale........................	2,117	87,611	0.87	925	10.0	1,128	12.2	7,267	9.9	22,032	16,450	5,582	2,044	2,220
Lawrence..........................	229	27,659	0.54	366	11.1	403	12.2	3,804	14.0	6,073	4,502	1,571	485	1,502
Lee.................................	4,894	142,132	0.83	1,947	12.0	1,048	6.5	14,359	10.5	20,419	14,042	6,377	5,053	3,157
Limestone	2,840	78,954	0.70	1,020	10.8	772	8.2	8,497	11.1	14,341	10,137	4,204	1,860	1,995
Lowndes...........................	96	9,473	0.68	120	11.9	147	14.6	937	11.4	2,420	1,153	1,267	282	3,268
Macon	1,683	18,521	0.84	189	10.1	262	14.0	1,435	10.4	5,016	3,131	1,885	695	3,822
Madison	8,122	382,694	1.20	4,174	11.6	3,193	8.8	26,207	8.8	64,581	47,935	16,646	14,967	4,207
Marengo	254	19,789	0.96	237	12.2	271	14.0	1,571	10.1	4,625	3,662	963	535	2,735
Marion..............................	808	29,207	0.91	300	10.1	388	13.0	2,644	11.4	6,949	5,501	1,447	746	2,489
Marshall	1,063	95,128	1.02	1,335	14.0	1,146	12.0	10,702	13.7	21,576	16,291	5,285	2,940	3,101
Mobile	7,403	423,487	1.05	5,475	13.2	4,481	10.8	42,679	12.4	81,181	37,817	43,365	19,105	4,606
Monroe............................	230	21,746	0.96	212	9.9	247	11.6	2,128	12.3	4,857	3,606	1,251	528	2,471
Montgomery......................	8,989	262,665	1.35	3,038	13.4	2,158	9.5	20,575	11.1	43,095	23,998	19,097	10,690	4,744
Morgan............................	2,108	119,965	1.01	1,398	11.8	1,280	10.8	10,877	11.2	26,946	20,040	6,906	3,672	3,079
Perry	780	9,355	0.80	126	13.5	129	13.8	786	11.3	2,230	1,834	396	NA	NA
Pickens	1,788	17,375	0.60	226	11.2	251	12.4	1,734	11.7	4,817	3,980	837	109	518
Pike................................	2,155	35,593	1.17	378	11.4	330	9.9	3,347	12.8	6,430	4,013	2,417	1,457	4,417
Randolph..........................	387	20,026	0.69	232	10.2	280	12.4	2,121	12.0	5,325	4,017	1,308	470	2,079
Russell............................	574	48,539	0.58	821	14.4	642	11.3	5,370	10.8	12,443	8,733	3,711	2,303	3,821
St. Clair...........................	1,633	69,964	0.56	1,038	11.8	970	11.0	6,805	9.4	15,772	7,820	7,952	2,018	2,305
Shelby.............................	2,558	187,457	0.82	2,363	11.1	1,534	7.2	13,311	7.4	23,173	11,651	11,521	3,678	1,744
Sumter.............................	897	12,799	0.88	139	11.0	157	12.4	1,276	12.9	2,988	2,425	563	127	981
Talladega	3,048	81,711	1.02	838	10.5	1,044	13.0	6,266	9.8	18,815	11,402	7,413	3,394	4,220
Tallapoosa	576	39,362	0.89	452	11.1	561	13.8	3,417	10.7	10,793	7,869	2,924	1,380	3,466
Tuscaloosa	10,821	210,922	1.10	2,537	12.2	1,799	8.7	15,705	9.2	33,645	22,733	10,912	7,236	3,524
Walker.............................	851	62,581	0.87	777	12.1	974	15.2	5,959	11.5	19,165	9,981	9,184	2,422	3,738

1. Per 1,000 estimated resident population.   2.   Data for serious crimes have not been adjusted for underreporting; this may affect comparability between geographic areas and over time.
3. Per 100,000 population estimated by the FBI.

Table B. States and Counties — Crime, Education, Money Income, and Poverty

STATE County	Serious crimes known to police, 2016 (cont.)[1] Rate Violent	Property	Education — School enrollment and attainment, 2012-2016 Enrollment[3] Total	Percent private	Attainment[4] (percent) High school graduate or less	Bachelor's degree or more	Local government expenditures,[5] 2013-2014 Total current spending (mil dol)	Current spending per student (dollars)	Money income, 2012-2016 Per capita income[6]	Median income (dollars)	Households Percent with income of less than $50,000	with income of $200,000 or more	Income and poverty, 2016 Median household income (dollars)	Percent below poverty level All persons	Children under 18 years	Children 5 to 17 years in families
	46	47	48	49	50	51	52	53	54	55	56	57	58	59	60	61
UNITED STATES	397	2,451	82,148,370	16.2	40.6	30.3	544,544.8	10,932	29,829	55,322	45.5	5.7	57,617	14.0	19.5	18.3
ALABAMA	532	2,948	1,193,757	13.9	46.2	24.0	6,728.2	9,017	24,736	44,758	54.3	2.9	46,309	17.2	24.7	23.5
Autauga	281	3,160	13,933	18.2	46.7	24.6	71.0	7,434	26,168	53,099	46.4	2.3	54,487	13.5	19.3	18.4
Baldwin	211	1,936	44,157	15.7	38.7	29.5	267.2	8,824	28,069	51,365	48.5	4.3	56,460	11.7	17.6	16.6
Barbour	407	2,362	5,536	10.3	61.2	12.9	34.1	8,918	17,249	33,956	66.0	0.5	32,884	29.9	39.6	36.8
Bibb	67	894	4,942	8.7	61.1	12.0	28.0	8,107	18,988	39,776	60.3	0.8	43,079	20.1	27.5	26.8
Blount	752	2,112	12,535	6.7	52.9	13.0	75.7	7,780	21,033	46,212	53.8	1.2	47,213	14.1	19.4	17.6
Bullock	320	1,495	2,196	10.5	67.6	10.3	16.7	11,094	17,909	29,335	68.6	1.2	34,278	32.6	45.7	43.6
Butler	586	2,782	4,387	11.1	58.8	16.1	28.4	8,622	19,011	34,315	64.8	0.6	35,409	24.8	36.6	34.2
Calhoun	897	3,283	28,439	10.0	49.7	17.7	166.0	9,003	22,231	41,954	57.4	1.6	41,778	17.1	25.7	24.2
Chambers	552	3,448	7,262	9.7	59.1	12.5	42.8	9,133	21,532	36,027	64.5	1.1	39,530	19.9	32.5	32.2
Cherokee	369	2,421	5,026	4.9	54.7	14.0	36.0	8,895	22,544	38,925	60.8	1.2	41,456	16.8	27.5	25.4
Chilton	688	2,668	9,670	8.1	61.2	14.9	61.5	8,016	22,045	42,594	57.2	1.3	44,188	18.3	26.3	24.8
Choctaw	115	407	2,785	27.4	58.4	12.0	15.2	9,102	20,773	32,622	64.5	1.3	32,691	22.7	32.6	30.4
Clarke	471	1,942	5,228	18.6	64.1	12.1	41.2	9,037	20,543	32,735	63.4	1.9	34,061	29.0	38.9	34.4
Clay	305	847	2,780	10.3	60.0	11.1	17.2	8,565	21,115	38,815	63.7	1.8	38,512	18.9	28.2	26.2
Cleburne	100	1,174	3,208	9.1	63.8	11.5	23.5	8,826	19,791	36,316	62.3	0.9	43,483	17.2	24.5	23.2
Coffee	263	2,094	11,851	9.8	44.2	23.7	82.9	8,797	25,325	47,872	51.4	1.9	48,632	14.4	21.3	19.1
Colbert	328	2,419	11,530	7.0	51.4	18.5	80.3	9,711	23,318	43,786	55.0	1.0	46,572	16.7	25.1	22.9
Conecuh	287	1,444	2,529	11.7	66.8	8.7	18.5	11,862	16,004	27,609	73.4	0.6	29,758	28.1	43.9	42.1
Coosa	276	1,847	1,891	4.0	63.4	9.9	10.7	9,681	18,080	31,910	68.7	0.6	36,441	17.5	29.3	28.3
Covington	400	2,074	8,086	6.1	53.5	14.9	52.5	8,484	21,738	37,313	60.5	1.5	35,010	19.6	28.1	27.9
Crenshaw	154	1,190	3,073	11.9	60.2	14.6	19.0	8,477	20,455	37,557	62.7	1.7	37,374	20.5	28.8	26.7
Cullman	113	1,946	17,066	9.1	53.0	15.0	112.6	8,844	21,041	39,297	61.7	1.8	41,543	14.9	20.7	18.8
Dale	559	2,570	12,229	10.6	47.2	16.1	57.1	8,863	22,834	44,093	55.7	1.9	40,523	20.6	29.7	27.4
Dallas	1,046	4,738	10,585	14.2	57.4	13.8	70.8	9,297	17,611	28,136	71.7	1.8	30,488	35.4	58.3	55.8
DeKalb	329	2,167	16,163	9.2	61.6	11.4	101.5	8,559	18,685	38,248	61.6	1.3	37,128	20.5	30.9	28.8
Elmore	249	2,190	19,308	20.4	48.6	22.2	102.7	7,803	24,771	53,398	47.0	2.4	54,553	13.5	20.2	19.6
Escambia	471	2,040	7,989	12.0	63.0	11.6	53.3	9,452	17,420	32,334	67.0	1.5	35,096	23.3	30.7	30.0
Etowah	709	3,616	23,298	8.1	50.1	16.5	135.2	8,415	21,287	40,478	58.1	1.8	40,972	17.5	26.8	25.7
Fayette	72	836	3,651	9.7	59.8	14.1	21.8	8,964	20,201	36,205	64.9	1.5	38,403	20.3	29.0	27.6
Franklin	281	2,145	7,219	8.3	61.0	12.4	52.5	9,068	18,193	36,138	65.7	1.2	37,049	20.1	29.4	28.6
Geneva	431	2,074	5,400	5.5	58.3	11.7	33.3	8,277	20,189	36,519	63.3	1.3	36,976	20.9	31.4	29.1
Greene	610	1,591	1,870	8.5	64.0	10.0	13.2	10,950	13,679	21,339	80.3	0.0	26,559	34.0	49.3	47.2
Hale	255	1,376	3,716	12.0	61.4	14.0	24.9	8,822	19,296	33,351	64.5	1.8	35,381	23.7	34.8	32.4
Henry	204	1,357	3,552	18.5	55.4	16.1	21.4	8,156	22,825	41,456	58.6	1.1	41,426	18.7	28.9	26.1
Houston	649	3,297	24,930	15.1	47.2	21.0	138.3	8,839	24,086	41,945	57.3	3.2	42,910	19.4	28.7	26.4
Jackson	NA	NA	10,727	10.2	61.7	12.6	77.4	9,252	20,487	38,422	61.7	1.8	41,407	17.5	23.6	21.7
Jefferson	874	3,692	165,397	16.4	37.5	31.4	1,023.1	9,802	28,162	47,220	52.0	4.4	50,109	15.3	22.0	21.8
Lamar	80	684	2,910	7.8	58.0	13.1	19.6	8,218	20,206	34,298	67.6	1.2	38,358	18.6	27.1	24.6
Lauderdale	261	1,959	22,484	10.8	49.7	21.7	117.6	9,033	24,893	43,657	56.1	2.4	44,124	15.2	20.9	19.7
Lawrence	257	1,245	7,181	5.2	62.3	10.3	46.4	9,186	21,911	42,339	56.4	0.5	43,107	16.8	24.0	23.1
Lee	572	2,584	54,316	8.9	35.8	34.4	196.8	8,933	24,951	45,056	53.9	3.2	47,749	18.3	18.2	17.8
Limestone	190	1,805	21,487	12.1	48.8	23.3	113.7	9,280	26,086	51,115	48.9	3.7	52,181	12.8	17.8	15.8
Lowndes	591	2,677	2,347	14.6	62.9	12.3	22.3	13,130	18,434	27,914	71.0	1.3	32,011	31.7	57.5	60.7
Macon	759	3,063	6,109	47.8	50.7	20.0	24.3	10,994	18,385	32,390	69.4	0.3	30,681	30.0	45.2	43.5
Madison	653	3,554	93,203	16.1	30.1	40.7	489.7	9,248	33,264	60,150	42.6	5.7	61,193	13.5	18.4	16.4
Marengo	440	2,296	4,970	11.9	56.4	14.8	36.0	8,971	20,359	30,713	68.2	1.1	34,794	25.8	36.8	33.8
Marion	280	2,209	6,202	9.2	55.1	12.5	41.2	8,653	20,998	34,074	65.3	1.9	36,386	18.5	27.2	26.4
Marshall	354	2,746	22,233	5.0	53.3	16.6	150.0	8,762	21,767	39,831	60.3	2.6	42,117	21.0	32.1	30.0
Mobile	585	4,021	103,330	19.6	46.8	22.5	563.2	8,839	23,318	44,263	54.5	2.5	45,233	19.5	30.4	29.5
Monroe	416	2,054	4,837	9.2	63.0	12.4	32.9	8,900	16,556	28,182	69.9	0.8	36,639	25.7	34.6	32.2
Montgomery	592	4,152	59,845	23.4	39.9	31.5	266.7	8,385	26,255	45,358	54.0	3.4	45,111	18.8	28.6	26.5
Morgan	221	2,858	27,470	10.2	47.6	21.4	186.4	9,575	24,415	46,883	52.8	2.1	46,843	15.8	23.2	21.6
Perry	NA	NA	2,712	19.5	63.1	14.5	16.3	9,759	14,033	24,912	76.2	1.1	25,221	35.0	51.6	48.9
Pickens	147	370	4,284	19.8	58.8	11.1	24.9	9,195	19,188	31,679	66.3	1.8	35,968	25.8	36.6	33.5
Pike	676	3,741	11,295	6.0	52.7	24.0	40.9	9,592	20,180	33,193	67.3	1.3	35,172	25.1	36.7	34.9
Randolph	288	1,792	4,977	10.4	59.1	15.4	32.2	8,744	19,584	37,496	62.0	1.2	40,283	21.8	34.5	31.3
Russell	582	3,238	15,534	12.4	48.6	17.0	88.5	8,396	20,760	38,400	60.4	0.9	38,617	19.3	28.1	28.1
St. Clair	448	1,858	19,085	11.7	52.6	16.1	106.2	8,186	24,474	54,042	45.5	1.8	57,856	12.0	17.1	16.5
Shelby	297	1,447	55,778	20.0	29.5	41.4	262.1	9,059	34,117	72,310	34.2	6.3	74,212	7.9	9.9	9.6
Sumter	263	718	4,193	6.3	61.6	18.1	18.2	10,338	13,929	20,428	76.1	0.4	26,814	32.4	44.1	44.6
Talladega	533	3,686	18,037	9.6	55.9	13.1	111.0	8,987	20,430	37,923	62.7	1.1	40,555	18.0	24.6	22.8
Tallapoosa	881	2,584	8,632	8.6	55.6	17.3	52.9	8,781	21,410	39,395	59.0	1.3	40,169	20.2	30.3	27.7
Tuscaloosa	395	3,129	60,949	8.8	42.2	29.4	256.9	9,145	23,896	48,022	51.8	3.0	47,483	17.6	21.9	22.1
Walker	491	3,247	13,638	7.0	58.1	10.5	97.9	9,040	20,410	37,025	62.3	1.7	39,511	20.5	29.9	28.8

1. Data for serious crimes have not been adjusted for underreporting; this may affect comparability between geographic areas and over time.   2. Per 100,000 population estimated by the FBI.
3. All persons 3 years old and over enrolled in nursery school through college.   4. Persons 25 years old and over.   5. Elementary and secondary education expenditures.
6. Based on population estimated by the American Community Survey, 2011–2015.

Table B. States and Counties — Personal Income and Earnings

STATE County	Personal income, 2016										Earnings, 2016		
			Per capita[1]			Supplements to wages and salaries, employer contributions (mil dol)						Contributions for government social insurance (mil dol)	
	Total (mil dol)	Percent change 2015-2016	Dollars	Rank	Wages and salaries (mil dol)	Pension and insurance	Government social insurance	Proprietors' income (mil dol)	Dividends, interest, and rent (mil dol)	Personal transfer receipts (mil dol)	Total (mil dol)	From employee and self-employed	From employer
	62	63	64	65	66	67	68	69	70	71	72	73	74
UNITED STATES..........	15,912,777	2.3	49,204	X	8,079,770	1,303,804	582,633	1,338,565	3,079,782	2,768,331	11,304,772	660,739	582,633
ALABAMA	189,162	2.0	38,918	X	90,592	15,666	6,651	12,241	32,583	43,949	125,150	8,207	6,651
Autauga........................	2,201	3.7	39,721	1,396	443	79	32	94	323	458	649	81	32
Baldwin	8,611	4.0	41,286	1,202	2,671	421	197	538	1,685	1,858	3,827	473	197
Barbour	825	-0.7	31,788	2,643	302	61	22	65	128	274	450	54	22
Bibb..............................	663	1.6	29,264	2,913	183	35	13	23	71	205	254	34	13
Blount............................	1,816	-0.2	31,470	2,680	316	61	23	98	220	478	498	67	23
Bullock	276	0.3	26,661	3,039	97	22	7	17	41	91	143	17	7
Butler............................	674	0.0	33,694	2,363	252	48	19	34	99	215	352	44	19
Calhoun.........................	3,943	2.0	34,401	2,263	1,774	381	133	197	711	1,164	2,485	300	133
Chambers	1,080	2.0	31,925	2,628	314	61	23	29	145	355	428	58	23
Cherokee	850	0.7	33,057	2,465	185	39	14	50	123	273	287	38	14
Chilton	1,408	1.8	32,041	2,610	360	68	27	62	173	393	517	68	27
Choctaw.........................	415	2.1	31,926	2,627	173	28	12	36	58	167	249	31	12
Clarke............................	807	1.9	33,096	2,457	333	61	24	55	119	263	473	59	24
Clay..............................	451	0.4	33,452	2,402	138	28	10	31	65	139	208	26	10
Cleburne	476	0.5	31,917	2,630	109	20	8	34	55	142	171	21	8
Coffee	2,045	1.9	39,923	1,375	557	104	42	151	378	481	855	98	42
Colbert	1,975	1.7	36,422	1,927	1,097	206	84	115	294	570	1,501	185	84
Conecuh.........................	376	0.7	30,349	2,811	129	27	10	24	56	153	190	24	10
Coosa...........................	310	1.6	29,276	2,910	55	11	4	9	46	104	80	12	4
Covington.......................	1,211	1.6	32,340	2,561	453	93	35	76	179	403	656	82	35
Crenshaw.......................	469	-2.6	33,684	2,366	148	29	11	53	61	148	241	27	11
Cullman.........................	2,995	0.3	36,315	1,949	1,150	198	84	238	424	791	1,670	201	84
Dale..............................	1,707	1.2	34,673	2,212	1,246	302	106	72	313	472	1,726	201	106
Dallas...........................	1,343	2.9	33,578	2,387	506	94	39	96	195	514	735	92	39
DeKalb..........................	2,099	-0.5	29,610	2,879	783	148	59	129	298	633	1,119	139	59
Elmore...........................	3,209	3.6	39,226	1,462	729	143	54	132	498	706	1,058	133	54
Escambia	1,176	2.5	31,174	2,722	526	103	38	51	192	381	719	89	38
Etowah..........................	3,583	1.7	34,932	2,177	1,382	240	103	208	530	1,097	1,934	245	103
Fayette	518	1.4	31,296	2,704	141	33	10	18	75	199	203	28	10
Franklin	1,019	0.7	32,203	2,580	373	78	28	50	141	295	530	66	28
Geneva	863	0.5	32,418	2,556	174	38	13	75	121	278	300	36	13
Greene	272	1.5	32,245	2,573	65	15	5	23	44	103	109	13	5
Hale..............................	529	-0.1	35,388	2,099	106	22	8	52	72	170	188	21	8
Henry............................	634	3.1	36,952	1,828	142	26	10	47	97	181	225	28	10
Houston.........................	4,092	2.5	39,321	1,452	2,039	359	148	256	711	1,001	2,802	331	148
Jackson.........................	1,781	1.4	34,151	2,297	607	116	46	93	305	507	862	110	46
Jefferson........................	32,571	1.7	49,386	450	19,609	3,013	1,396	3,520	6,524	5,901	27,539	3,126	1,396
Lamar............................	431	1.3	30,954	2,740	136	26	10	18	62	155	190	26	10
Lauderdale	3,276	1.5	35,485	2,082	1,085	197	81	181	620	848	1,544	195	81
Lawrence........................	1,039	0.2	31,245	2,713	177	37	13	37	121	317	264	39	13
Lee	5,465	4.1	34,372	2,268	2,288	456	166	237	960	994	3,147	363	166
Limestone	3,517	2.7	37,913	1,677	1,146	223	87	165	492	732	1,623	197	87
Lowndes........................	384	-3.4	37,049	1,816	117	25	9	36	48	121	187	21	9
Macon...........................	599	1.4	31,579	2,664	214	61	16	9	97	197	300	37	16
Madison	16,811	3.1	47,095	600	11,670	1,908	882	724	3,273	2,672	15,183	1,793	882
Marengo.........................	719	1.0	36,551	1,909	300	55	21	41	112	232	418	51	21
Marion	878	0.7	29,273	2,912	350	66	27	54	141	291	496	63	27
Marshall	3,201	1.6	33,640	2,375	1,319	250	98	198	525	860	1,865	226	98
Mobile...........................	14,914	1.9	35,951	2,008	8,412	1,369	617	1,023	2,354	3,754	11,423	1,361	617
Monroe..........................	694	2.2	32,219	2,576	276	49	20	28	129	226	372	47	20
Montgomery....................	9,372	2.2	41,404	1,184	6,582	1,245	492	554	1,951	2,036	8,873	1,020	492
Morgan..........................	4,373	1.7	36,746	1,869	2,162	378	160	221	717	1,068	2,922	355	160
Perry	288	1.5	30,099	2,836	74	17	6	30	38	118	126	15	6
Pickens	609	-2.1	29,966	2,849	148	34	11	26	83	210	220	29	11
Pike	1,175	0.7	35,287	2,123	598	117	44	81	191	308	840	96	44
Randolph........................	728	-0.7	32,160	2,586	167	35	13	38	110	237	252	33	13
Russell	1,758	2.5	30,214	2,824	542	98	39	54	255	557	734	94	39
St. Clair	3,052	1.7	34,676	2,211	777	133	57	121	357	707	1,088	141	57
Shelby...........................	10,620	2.6	50,421	398	4,801	664	334	685	1,718	1,400	6,483	746	334
Sumter...........................	402	-0.5	30,845	2,752	130	28	9	40	53	141	208	23	9
Talladega	2,577	1.1	32,172	2,583	1,399	241	103	82	336	808	1,823	230	103
Tallapoosa	1,520	1.5	37,320	1,762	489	89	37	85	283	465	700	90	37
Tuscaloosa......................	7,401	2.1	35,909	2,013	4,241	796	307	376	1,319	1,610	5,720	664	307
Walker...........................	2,416	0.6	37,191	1,794	699	133	52	118	435	763	1,002	131	52

1. Based on the resident population estimated as of July 1 of the year shown.

Table B. States and Counties — Earnings, Social Security, and Housing

STATE County	Earnings, 2016 (cont.) Percent by selected industries									Social Security beneficiaries, December 2016		Supplemental Security Income recipients, 2016	Housing units, 2017	
	Farm	Mining, quarrying, and extracting	Construction	Manu-facturing	Information; professional, scientific, technical services	Retail trade	Finance, insurance, real estate, and leasing	Health care and social assistance	Govern-ment	Number	Rate[1]		Total	Percent change, 2010-2017
	75	76	77	78	79	80	81	82	83	84	85	86	87	88
UNITED STATES	0.6	1.1	6.0	9.4	13.7	6.0	9.0	11.2	16.7	59,373,422	184	8,250,117	137,403,460	4.3
ALABAMA	0.8	0.4	6.0	14.4	9.4	6.6	6.6	11.5	21.0	1,120,486	231	167,349	2,258,596	4.0
Autauga	0.6	0.7	7.6	18.3	3.4	8.1	4.3	10.1	19.0	11,670	211	1,467	23,495	6.1
Baldwin	0.2	0.2	9.4	6.6	5.7	12.8	7.2	13.0	14.4	52,270	252	3,521	114,162	9.7
Barbour	6.9	2.8	3.0	24.9	D	8.0	3.2	D	19.5	7,145	277	1,469	11,970	1.2
Bibb	0.7	D	27.5	7.7	D	6.1	1.9	D	27.2	5,565	246	966	9,187	2.3
Blount	3.2	D	11.4	11.8	4.6	8.2	3.5	D	21.5	13,670	237	1,282	24,314	1.8
Bullock	10.5	0.0	D	22.1	D	3.5	1.7	12.9	25.8	2,100	201	598	4,535	1.0
Butler	3.3	0.0	5.6	21.0	D	8.0	2.7	13.1	14.3	5,425	272	1,099	10,055	0.9
Calhoun	0.6	D	3.1	15.1	4.5	8.1	3.4	10.8	33.0	30,285	263	4,684	53,771	0.9
Chambers	3.3	D	3.5	27.9	3.2	7.7	2.2	D	22.9	9,860	292	1,483	17,000	0.0
Cherokee	5.8	0.0	4.3	18.0	D	11.6	3.4	D	23.3	7,845	304	876	16,576	1.9
Chilton	0.0	D	10.6	21.9	D	9.9	3.4	D	18.6	10,305	235	1,398	19,672	2.1
Choctaw	0.9	0.2	D	D	2.0	7.4	2.2	D	9.9	4,295	329	820	7,363	1.3
Clarke	0.7	0.5	4.0	26.0	D	9.3	5.7	D	20.8	7,195	295	1,419	12,764	1.0
Clay	4.6	-0.1	3.8	40.5	1.3	4.8	3.1	D	21.9	4,000	298	523	6,817	0.6
Cleburne	8.4	0.0	27.5	11.9	D	7.8	2.1	2.0	24.3	3,920	264	512	6,820	1.5
Coffee	6.5	D	3.3	17.0	D	10.3	3.8	11.4	17.2	11,490	224	1,408	23,150	3.7
Colbert	0.0	0.6	8.0	29.3	2.1	8.1	3.8	8.2	21.1	15,200	280	2,024	26,585	3.2
Conecuh	7.1	D	1.9	13.4	1.3	4.0	D	D	20.7	4,000	320	733	7,154	0.9
Coosa	0.8	0.0	2.8	38.9	D	3.1	D	D	20.9	2,930	271	453	6,567	1.2
Covington	3.7	D	5.1	15.2	D	9.6	4.7	D	17.0	10,780	288	1,440	18,935	0.6
Crenshaw	12.9	0.0	4.1	24.2	1.3	3.2	2.7	D	13.4	3,940	283	644	6,804	1.1
Cullman	3.4	D	7.0	21.2	3.3	8.5	4.5	12.6	13.7	21,760	264	2,602	37,808	2.0
Dale	1.3	D	3.1	22.9	2.9	2.1	1.5	2.7	48.6	11,470	233	1,859	23,083	1.8
Dallas	5.3	D	4.2	25.5	2.5	7.6	3.2	13.7	18.4	11,080	276	4,139	20,340	0.7
DeKalb	2.9	D	5.6	29.4	3.2	7.7	2.4	10.6	15.8	17,375	244	2,131	31,525	1.3
Elmore	0.0	D	7.9	16.4	4.9	10.9	4.4	9.6	23.8	18,325	226	2,268	34,245	4.9
Escambia	0.8	2.7	5.6	19.3	1.9	7.7	3.9	8.8	30.8	9,970	266	1,445	16,623	0.8
Etowah	0.2	0.1	5.2	15.9	3.6	8.5	5.1	22.8	15.2	28,835	281	4,711	47,746	0.6
Fayette	2.9	0.9	3.9	23.6	2.0	9.0	3.5	D	29.6	5,470	331	764	8,485	0.6
Franklin	1.2	0.9	3.7	39.5	D	5.0	4.0	D	19.7	7,660	243	1,178	14,195	1.2
Geneva	13.8	0.0	5.4	10.7	D	6.8	4.1	5.0	22.8	7,545	285	1,194	12,807	1.0
Greene	18.9	0.0	2.3	21.0	D	4.5	D	D	29.3	2,575	303	764	5,087	1.6
Hale	25.2	D	5.8	17.1	1.3	4.4	3.0	D	23.7	4,570	308	1,087	7,802	1.9
Henry	6.6	0.0	6.3	12.2	D	4.4	2.4	D	16.5	5,090	298	615	9,133	2.7
Houston	0.8	D	4.8	7.0	4.8	10.4	4.3	18.3	19.3	25,195	242	4,043	47,438	4.7
Jackson	1.7	D	5.4	32.9	2.6	8.4	3.2	D	21.3	14,425	277	1,684	25,171	1.6
Jefferson	0.0	0.4	6.7	6.7	11.1	5.1	10.9	16.9	16.0	141,280	214	23,903	308,822	2.8
Lamar	0.9	D	3.8	37.5	D	5.7	3.6	7.1	16.2	4,335	311	644	7,410	0.8
Lauderdale	-0.2	D	8.0	10.5	5.2	11.3	5.1	17.7	19.2	23,880	259	2,642	44,839	2.4
Lawrence	-0.5	D	10.6	3.2	D	10.0	5.4	D	27.2	9,010	271	1,300	15,414	1.2
Lee	0.0	0.2	6.0	12.7	5.5	6.9	4.0	6.6	34.2	24,690	155	3,326	68,915	10.4
Limestone	0.2	D	14.9	13.8	4.4	8.8	2.6	4.3	34.0	18,785	202	2,130	36,240	3.6
Lowndes	14.0	D	7.3	39.5	D	2.5	D	D	15.1	3,140	307	776	5,196	1.1
Macon	0.8	D	D	D	D	3.8	0.8	D	66.6	4,830	253	1,105	10,270	0.1
Madison	0.0	D	2.9	12.0	25.6	5.1	3.4	7.5	28.6	64,460	181	6,815	161,760	10.5
Marengo	3.6	0.0	7.3	23.0	D	6.3	4.4	D	19.1	6,055	310	1,503	10,346	1.0
Marion	3.8	D	2.6	31.3	1.3	6.8	5.0	D	16.4	8,040	269	1,068	14,890	1.0
Marshall	1.4	D	6.3	27.8	4.0	9.5	3.7	7.0	18.2	22,620	238	3,084	40,691	0.9
Mobile	0.2	0.4	7.1	15.6	9.0	6.7	7.5	12.5	15.1	90,530	218	15,207	183,897	3.2
Monroe	2.1	D	3.5	25.4	D	6.8	3.4	D	19.9	6,065	281	950	11,419	0.7
Montgomery	0.5	0.0	4.4	10.6	9.5	5.5	6.0	11.8	30.6	45,910	203	9,707	104,858	3.2
Morgan	0.3	0.1	7.8	33.4	4.8	6.5	3.9	7.6	13.9	28,470	240	3,419	52,093	1.8
Perry	11.5	0.2	3.2	18.4	D	3.6	3.5	7.8	21.4	2,785	291	1,009	4,762	0.6
Pickens	5.3	D	2.8	19.2	D	5.8	D	D	36.4	5,630	277	1,211	9,587	1.1
Pike	3.1	0.1	2.7	23.8	3.0	5.7	4.0	7.8	22.8	6,825	205	1,559	16,123	5.6
Randolph	4.9	D	5.4	21.4	2.9	8.7	4.2	D	24.0	6,210	276	828	12,074	0.8
Russell	1.4	0.2	6.4	25.0	D	9.3	5.1	11.1	21.1	12,700	218	1,914	27,636	12.4
St. Clair	0.8	D	9.5	20.2	4.9	8.5	3.8	8.6	15.6	19,450	222	1,954	36,978	4.0
Shelby	0.0	0.5	7.6	5.7	11.0	7.2	18.3	7.8	8.0	37,125	176	2,499	87,243	7.7
Sumter	15.7	0.0	2.9	10.7	D	3.3	1.8	D	34.1	3,395	263	1,105	6,875	1.3
Talladega	0.1	D	3.6	42.2	2.7	4.6	2.1	D	15.3	21,545	268	4,060	37,780	1.9
Tallapoosa	0.3	D	6.2	17.5	5.9	7.7	3.7	D	15.9	12,500	308	1,588	22,396	1.3
Tuscaloosa	0.1	1.8	5.3	20.5	5.7	6.0	4.8	7.8	28.7	39,345	191	6,264	91,804	8.2
Walker	0.4	1.8	5.3	9.5	3.5	12.4	4.5	19.9	17.2	20,270	314	3,329	31,131	1.0

1. Per 1,000 resident population estimated as of July 1 of the year shown.

Table B. States and Counties — Housing, Labor Force, and Employment

STATE County	Housing units, 2017 (cont.) Occupied units — Owner-occupied					Renter-occupied			Civilian labor force, 2017		Unemployment		Civilian employment[6], 2012-2016 Percent		
	Total	Percent	Median value[1]	With a mortgage	Without a mortgage[2]	Median rent[3]	Median rent as a percent of income[2]	Sub-standard units[4] (percent)	Total	Percent change, 2016-2017	Total	Rate[5]	Total	Management, business, science, and arts	Construction, production, and maintenance occupations
	89	90	91	92	93	94	95	96	97	98	99	100	101	102	103
UNITED STATES..........	117,716,237	63.6	184,700	22.5	11.8	949	30.6	3.7	160,588,786	1.0	6,994,555	4.4	148,001,326	37.0	21.1
ALABAMA	1,851,061	68.5	128,500	20.4	10.6	728	29.9	2.0	2,168,448	-0.2	95,342	4.4	2,042,025	33.6	25.8
Autauga.........................	20,800	73.2	141,000	20.8	10.0	896	33.0	1.8	25,909	0.0	1,001	3.9	24,262	33.8	24.5
Baldwin.........................	75,149	71.7	173,400	21.6	10.0	889	29.9	1.5	91,567	1.2	3,652	4.0	87,753	34.2	22.0
Barbour.........................	9,122	63.9	90,300	19.6	12.1	588	31.0	1.9	8,236	-2.0	486	5.9	8,993	26.7	35.6
Bibb.............................	7,048	72.6	97,200	21.7	10.9	654	27.2	0.6	8,506	-1.2	373	4.4	8,354	21.3	41.8
Blount...........................	20,619	78.8	124,200	20.4	10.6	631	27.5	2.3	24,494	-0.3	985	4.0	21,593	29.3	34.3
Bullock.........................	3,556	73.1	68,000	24.4	12.6	564	31.5	1.1	4,812	-0.2	237	4.9	4,174	17.5	45.6
Butler...........................	7,675	70.3	83,000	23.8	12.1	563	28.7	1.8	8,946	-2.7	491	5.5	7,810	28.1	34.6
Calhoun.........................	45,071	69.0	107,900	19.8	10.4	635	29.0	1.8	45,582	-0.5	2,249	4.9	47,010	28.3	30.5
Chambers	13,851	67.6	83,000	21.5	12.3	658	29.6	4.4	15,176	1.3	619	4.1	14,031	23.1	38.1
Cherokee	10,999	79.2	112,500	22.6	12.9	601	28.9	2.0	11,174	-1.4	453	4.1	10,193	31.0	35.5
Chilton	16,619	76.0	99,100	21.6	10.6	646	29.4	3.3	19,118	-0.3	774	4.0	17,627	26.3	34.1
Choctaw	5,562	80.5	64,600	19.1	12.7	497	33.5	2.1	4,336	0.2	277	6.4	4,260	25.4	39.8
Clarke	9,554	67.2	85,900	19.4	12.5	540	30.6	1.9	7,720	-2.9	655	8.5	8,159	21.4	40.3
Clay	5,363	75.1	90,000	23.6	10.0	441	22.9	2.8	5,721	1.7	250	4.4	5,470	20.1	45.4
Cleburne	5,834	75.6	108,100	21.5	12.6	582	25.8	2.9	5,742	-0.7	256	4.5	5,823	25.8	38.9
Coffee	19,375	66.7	142,800	19.3	10.0	701	27.1	1.7	20,671	0.4	907	4.4	21,353	31.5	27.7
Colbert	22,105	72.1	102,500	19.3	10.9	638	30.1	0.7	23,092	-1.5	1,203	5.2	22,056	27.4	30.7
Conecuh........................	5,090	78.5	72,300	21.9	12.1	528	34.0	3.3	4,446	-2.2	273	6.1	3,794	17.7	40.1
Coosa...........................	4,206	79.5	76,500	23.5	12.9	567	25.1	2.9	4,348	-0.7	201	4.6	3,747	17.7	38.9
Covington......................	15,179	74.7	93,700	20.3	11.0	585	26.2	2.0	15,646	1.0	820	5.2	14,441	27.9	34.7
Crenshaw......................	5,426	70.1	77,600	18.6	11.7	515	28.9	0.8	6,417	-0.5	287	4.5	5,693	26.0	37.8
Cullman........................	31,081	75.9	118,700	23.0	12.0	626	28.9	2.1	37,637	-0.7	1,398	3.7	32,232	28.4	32.4
Dale.............................	18,794	60.7	103,800	19.8	10.0	636	28.6	1.6	19,868	-0.4	881	4.4	18,495	27.7	30.8
Dallas...........................	16,099	58.3	81,000	22.3	13.2	581	34.1	5.7	14,935	-3.1	1,124	7.5	14,379	26.6	33.8
DeKalb..........................	24,811	72.3	99,600	21.3	11.2	552	24.3	3.1	29,038	-0.7	1,304	4.5	27,980	21.9	39.9
Elmore..........................	28,890	73.4	152,500	19.8	10.0	817	28.3	1.6	37,236	0.0	1,356	3.6	33,355	33.7	26.7
Escambia.......................	13,536	71.2	93,900	19.3	12.6	564	32.3	2.8	14,352	-1.4	722	5.0	11,977	23.7	30.8
Etowah..........................	39,522	71.0	101,900	20.9	11.4	623	29.1	1.8	42,894	-0.8	1,962	4.6	41,540	28.6	31.5
Fayette.........................	6,850	77.9	76,400	20.3	10.9	483	32.3	1.6	6,529	-1.0	309	4.7	6,217	26.8	37.5
Franklin.........................	11,697	68.8	87,000	20.0	12.2	553	25.9	4.7	13,960	0.7	591	4.2	12,298	22.9	43.0
Geneva..........................	10,657	75.2	81,500	19.8	11.5	567	27.2	1.8	10,817	0.1	462	4.3	10,216	24.5	37.3
Greene..........................	3,107	70.5	68,100	34.1	17.8	414	32.1	4.7	2,833	-1.3	217	7.7	2,349	20.3	34.5
Hale.............................	5,948	75.1	89,400	25.0	12.6	449	35.6	3.5	6,007	0.4	354	5.9	5,039	26.3	31.6
Henry...........................	6,831	80.1	101,800	21.4	10.6	582	28.0	1.3	6,697	-0.4	326	4.9	7,049	32.1	30.0
Houston........................	39,363	64.4	124,800	20.0	10.0	707	29.3	1.3	44,411	-0.3	1,927	4.3	43,805	31.2	24.0
Jackson........................	19,945	72.8	103,800	19.7	10.2	591	26.0	2.6	23,066	-2.2	1,100	4.8	20,965	24.7	40.0
Jefferson	261,773	63.0	145,700	21.1	11.0	820	31.3	1.7	309,076	-0.7	13,106	4.2	297,470	38.6	18.9
Lamar...........................	6,010	73.1	71,100	19.4	10.3	432	27.7	1.7	5,703	0.3	241	4.2	5,148	26.8	39.2
Lauderdale.....................	38,361	68.6	124,100	19.6	10.1	601	27.9	1.4	41,868	-1.5	1,931	4.6	39,275	29.8	27.0
Lawrence.......................	13,321	79.8	97,600	19.9	11.4	557	23.7	1.6	13,640	-0.6	666	4.9	12,625	24.8	43.1
Lee..............................	57,901	58.8	156,400	20.0	10.0	806	36.0	2.2	73,520	1.6	2,877	3.9	70,851	40.4	20.0
Limestone......................	32,073	76.0	142,500	19.0	10.0	628	28.3	2.6	41,092	1.0	1,635	4.0	38,289	34.0	28.5
Lowndes........................	4,238	73.6	68,900	27.4	17.8	589	33.0	2.7	3,750	-1.3	300	8.0	3,562	22.2	41.3
Macon...........................	7,915	66.0	77,000	24.9	12.9	592	31.7	2.3	7,892	0.3	456	5.8	7,594	29.0	26.9
Madison.........................	139,949	68.0	171,200	18.2	10.0	783	28.4	1.5	175,153	0.9	6,741	3.8	167,515	46.1	16.5
Marengo.........................	8,149	69.7	87,900	23.5	13.3	511	30.0	2.8	7,623	-0.6	431	5.7	6,636	26.7	34.2
Marion...........................	12,486	76.5	85,500	18.9	11.7	482	29.2	2.1	12,517	0.2	599	4.8	11,749	25.7	34.1
Marshall........................	34,461	70.6	115,700	21.2	10.2	604	27.7	3.6	42,108	1.3	1,602	3.8	38,366	27.7	34.0
Mobile...........................	154,261	66.0	123,500	21.3	11.2	801	32.5	2.3	186,239	-0.8	9,652	5.2	171,733	32.2	24.4
Monroe..........................	8,316	61.3	87,700	21.6	10.8	506	30.8	1.1	7,165	-2.0	483	6.7	6,473	25.4	36.8
Montgomery....................	90,281	58.7	122,000	20.4	10.0	825	31.6	2.2	105,505	-0.2	4,541	4.3	101,005	36.7	20.1
Morgan..........................	46,164	70.9	124,900	20.1	10.0	613	26.6	2.1	54,840	0.0	2,252	4.1	50,615	30.0	30.7
Perry	3,198	73.3	73,700	29.7	16.8	516	34.5	4.8	3,402	-1.8	270	7.9	2,551	22.2	26.6
Pickens	7,618	72.7	89,100	21.3	12.1	420	32.0	1.8	7,783	0.2	412	5.3	6,886	21.9	39.0
Pike..............................	12,802	59.3	102,300	19.8	10.0	613	33.8	2.2	15,238	2.0	743	4.9	14,336	29.8	28.0
Randolph........................	8,691	71.0	85,600	22.3	10.4	606	29.1	4.5	9,373	-0.6	412	4.4	8,477	24.8	41.4
Russell..........................	22,333	58.7	114,000	22.3	12.8	742	28.9	3.5	23,457	-0.3	1,008	4.3	23,398	28.4	26.0
St. Clair........................	31,832	81.1	142,800	19.4	10.8	702	25.8	1.2	38,946	-0.3	1,546	4.0	38,399	29.4	28.5
Shelby...........................	75,942	79.3	195,400	19.9	10.0	954	26.6	1.1	109,331	-0.2	3,527	3.2	102,705	43.5	15.5
Sumter..........................	4,878	66.1	73,400	24.8	17.3	589	39.2	1.9	5,016	-1.8	328	6.5	4,331	27.2	24.0
Talladega	31,461	72.2	94,200	21.6	11.7	598	29.4	1.8	34,501	-0.9	1,712	5.0	30,853	28.1	34.5
Tallapoosa	16,338	70.8	105,200	19.4	10.9	565	32.3	4.3	18,279	-1.6	760	4.2	15,098	27.5	36.9
Tuscaloosa.....................	70,440	63.0	160,000	20.9	10.0	784	32.2	2.3	99,237	0.0	4,110	4.1	90,243	35.1	25.6
Walker...........................	25,194	74.5	84,800	20.3	11.3	607	31.2	1.9	25,145	-1.6	1,262	5.0	23,795	26.6	32.3

1. Specified owner-occupied units. lacking complete plumbing facilities.   2. A value of 10.0 represents 10 percent or less; a value of 50.0 represents 50 percent or more.   3. Specified renter-occupied units.   4. Overcrowded or
5. Percent of civilian labor force.   6. Civilian employed persons 16 years old and over.

Table B. States and Counties — Nonfarm Employment and Agriculture

STATE County	Number of establish-ments	Total	Health care and social assistance	Manufac-turing	Retail trade	Finance and insurance	Professional, scientific, and technical services	Total (mil dol)	Average per employee (dollars)	Number	Fewer than 50 acres	500 acres or more	Farm operators whose principal occupation is farming (percent)
	104	105	106	107	108	109	110	111	112	113	114	115	116
UNITED STATES	7,757,807	126,752,238	19,735,708	11,590,420	15,967,893	6,336,795	8,799,893	6,435,142	50,769	2,109,303	38.6	15.0	47.8
ALABAMA	99,584	1,673,249	245,766	250,252	237,123	70,109	100,476	68,971	41,220	43,223	37.4	8.6	44.2
Autauga.........................	851	10,790	1,639	984	2,715	392	266	332	30,815	389	31.6	14.4	51.2
Baldwin	5,235	61,341	7,858	4,120	13,738	1,607	2,120	1,960	31,955	989	52.6	8.1	45.8
Barbour..........................	452	6,857	679	2,355	877	145	116	233	34,044	571	13.8	17.3	46.1
Bibb................................	290	3,387	628	313	484	74	99	135	39,891	189	29.6	13.8	38.6
Blount.............................	675	6,286	838	1,093	1,308	201	231	199	31,609	1,241	40.6	3.1	48.8
Bullock...........................	107	2,097	399	D	207	54	17	65	31,207	273	17.2	30.4	40.7
Butler.............................	409	6,157	921	1,413	977	145	56	195	31,619	407	25.1	8.6	45.2
Calhoun..........................	2,326	35,843	6,020	5,985	6,561	977	926	1,188	33,139	592	45.4	3.5	46.1
Chambers	547	6,276	620	1,939	1,158	146	178	208	33,188	301	22.6	15.6	38.9
Cherokee	361	3,905	434	1,088	933	113	58	124	31,636	561	32.1	11.6	45.6
Chilton	738	7,609	767	1,812	1,445	206	112	252	33,172	543	37.9	7.0	41.1
Choctaw.........................	252	2,835	404	D	360	64	55	140	49,376	248	37.1	14.5	40.3
Clarke............................	595	6,821	922	1,638	1,634	361	70	222	32,591	263	38.8	9.9	35.4
Clay...............................	190	3,277	508	1,786	294	84	59	102	31,227	401	24.7	7.7	39.7
Cleburne	160	1,703	65	303	289	55	11	71	41,695	341	36.7	5.3	47.8
Coffee	986	13,388	1,933	3,417	2,399	488	785	436	32,541	899	27.9	9.1	50.5
Colbert	1,229	22,474	2,658	7,039	2,942	654	292	855	38,066	687	39.6	9.0	36.7
Conecuh.........................	188	2,441	441	437	275	40	29	81	33,143	346	19.1	8.4	44.8
Coosa.............................	93	944	110	385	110	12	20	35	36,630	152	23.7	11.8	52.6
Covington.......................	808	10,187	1,687	2,123	1,861	343	297	336	33,006	1,051	31.4	6.8	40.3
Crenshaw.......................	214	3,355	458	1,331	276	101	33	113	33,830	575	21.6	12.3	40.2
Cullman..........................	1,729	25,274	3,709	5,451	4,124	768	437	882	34,881	2,007	47.6	2.1	48.6
Dale................................	739	11,146	1,248	560	1,277	351	896	536	48,119	487	27.9	12.7	30.8
Dallas.............................	738	10,487	1,772	2,858	1,627	305	223	356	33,930	506	22.9	25.7	45.7
DeKalb...........................	1,091	17,745	2,433	7,025	2,449	423	375	611	34,460	2,035	44.9	3.4	50.7
Elmore............................	1,167	14,359	2,058	2,764	2,836	396	394	485	33,809	552	46.4	7.8	40.9
Escambia	732	10,055	1,193	1,975	1,838	404	157	349	34,698	454	44.1	13.9	39.6
Etowah...........................	1,974	30,834	7,349	5,344	4,951	1,039	580	1,018	33,028	853	51.1	2.9	40.3
Fayette...........................	314	3,175	664	862	628	76	40	101	31,952	414	24.6	8.0	38.9
Franklin	523	9,646	1,029	5,420	910	381	130	322	33,385	825	25.7	7.8	47.5
Geneva...........................	407	3,934	584	714	825	131	106	119	30,130	1,017	31.6	9.8	43.1
Greene	111	1,379	285	456	175	31	D	48	34,539	304	26.0	24.0	50.3
Hale................................	180	1,854	388	496	260	64	21	70	37,538	456	27.0	16.0	49.8
Henry	298	2,513	176	308	358	96	151	92	36,508	498	19.5	17.1	43.0
Houston..........................	2,704	43,799	9,656	4,360	8,031	1,185	1,142	1,696	38,722	816	38.8	12.3	44.5
Jackson..........................	846	13,259	1,782	5,546	1,960	314	198	428	32,298	1,376	40.1	6.0	37.4
Jefferson........................	16,484	314,992	54,315	22,626	40,644	22,620	15,623	15,783	50,105	394	59.9	3.0	46.7
Lamar.............................	240	3,141	328	1,503	366	107	47	115	36,709	353	31.7	8.5	33.4
Lauderdale.....................	2,031	25,563	4,830	2,460	5,641	984	834	762	29,807	1,466	45.9	5.2	44.8
Lawrence	387	3,138	798	150	762	113	73	86	27,492	1,551	41.5	4.3	43.2
Lee.................................	2,726	43,945	6,191	6,940	7,084	1,100	1,608	1,395	31,746	315	32.7	7.6	37.1
Limestone	1,372	16,958	2,551	3,448	2,840	383	738	609	35,887	1,230	40.6	6.9	46.6
Lowndes.........................	103	1,969	D	975	194	27	10	80	40,666	441	24.5	21.8	48.5
Macon............................	200	5,244	1,655	653	470	36	27	213	40,611	352	26.4	15.9	48.3
Madison..........................	8,325	158,629	24,786	16,258	20,392	3,721	36,754	7,895	49,772	1,033	48.4	8.0	49.5
Marengo.........................	467	6,045	1,009	1,408	952	228	75	226	37,382	499	27.3	16.8	33.9
Marion............................	531	7,656	1,123	2,828	1,106	403	73	243	31,729	715	32.3	3.8	37.5
Marshall.........................	1,805	30,833	3,723	10,569	5,037	789	636	1,003	32,533	1,505	53.2	3.1	41.9
Mobile............................	8,736	151,652	21,180	16,379	21,503	5,636	9,969	6,435	42,432	698	60.9	4.4	48.6
Monroe...........................	392	5,400	671	1,298	914	164	45	217	40,094	480	37.1	12.1	44.6
Montgomery....................	5,592	103,893	17,353	13,125	13,066	4,161	5,661	4,341	41,783	603	28.0	19.2	50.4
Morgan...........................	2,573	42,737	5,844	11,942	5,610	1,377	1,529	1,800	42,110	1,237	44.2	3.7	42.1
Perry..............................	117	1,561	137	434	197	63	17	45	28,775	389	26.2	19.0	39.8
Pickens	266	2,639	526	600	449	126	90	86	32,599	433	28.4	9.9	46.9
Pike................................	647	11,135	1,095	2,250	1,546	352	481	426	38,229	600	21.5	14.7	39.5
Randolph.........................	329	3,809	435	1,215	727	156	45	104	27,176	611	27.8	8.3	52.2
Russell...........................	781	11,156	1,389	3,005	2,245	347	199	374	33,490	280	28.9	21.8	35.4
St. Clair..........................	1,281	16,848	1,859	3,621	2,920	489	786	586	34,764	540	44.3	3.3	51.1
Shelby............................	5,132	83,416	7,145	5,705	9,198	9,926	5,438	4,111	49,284	401	45.4	6.7	44.6
Sumter	196	2,991	392	191	252	56	D	117	39,043	428	22.7	22.9	46.0
Talladega	1,229	24,080	2,709	9,007	2,835	498	431	1,058	43,926	519	38.2	8.5	50.3
Tallapoosa......................	740	10,844	2,271	2,626	1,590	251	236	329	30,372	345	35.1	5.5	42.0
Tuscaloosa.....................	4,085	78,617	12,223	14,983	10,572	1,667	2,316	3,093	39,347	497	43.7	9.5	37.0
Walker............................	1,221	14,913	3,422	2,088	3,427	475	442	509	34,161	482	46.9	3.7	33.8

Table B. States and Counties — **Agriculture**

STATE County	Land in farms Acreage (1,000)	Percent change, 2007-2012	Acres Average size of farm	Total irrigated (1,000)	Total cropland (1,000)	Value of land and buildings (dollars) Average per farm	Average per acre	Value of machinery and equiopmnet, average per farm (dollars)	Value of products sold: Total (mil dol)	Average per farm (acres)	Percent from: Crops	Livestock and poultry products	Percent of farms with sales of: $10,000 or more	$100,000 or more	Government payments Total ($1,000)	Percent of farms
	117	118	119	120	121	122	123	124	125	126	127	128	129	130	131	132
UNITED STATES..........	914,528	-0.8	434	55,822.2	389,690.4	1,075,491	2,481	115,662	394,644.5	187,097	53.8	46.2	43.4	18.4	8,053,346	38.5
ALABAMA	8,903	-1.4	206	113.0	2,758.5	547,524	2,658	71,210	5,571.2	128,894	23.6	76.4	33.8	11.2	88,145	30.0
Autauga....................	112	0.9	287	1.6	41.3	655,057	2,285	73,658	19.8	50,928	D	D	33.7	6.9	1,245	31.9
Baldwin	192	1.3	194	7.7	100.9	773,980	3,980	107,905	135.6	137,070	85.3	14.7	35.2	11.7	2,649	26.7
Barbour	204	2.6	358	2.3	41.3	808,758	2,261	80,371	104.4	182,760	14.1	85.9	32.7	9.6	1,806	62.5
Bibb...........................	56	47.7	298	0.1	12.6	624,810	2,098	66,159	D	D	D	D	23.8	1.6	138	14.3
Blount.......................	146	-3.4	118	0.5	37.1	427,880	3,632	58,512	178.2	143,587	7.0	93.0	37.4	12.7	897	19.1
Bullock	165	22.9	603	1.4	26.1	1,312,890	2,178	107,813	54.5	199,813	62.0	38.0	38.8	13.6	721	31.5
Butler........................	88	-4.5	217	0.0	21.3	527,472	2,429	65,489	110.1	270,634	D	D	28.7	10.8	355	26.3
Calhoun.....................	81	6.6	137	0.9	21.4	418,128	3,046	61,630	92.4	156,052	11.8	88.2	30.1	7.3	406	17.4
Chambers	96	-8.2	320	0.1	15.3	832,784	2,602	61,761	8.3	27,708	24.3	75.7	35.2	5.3	397	15.6
Cherokee	124	-6.5	221	1.3	58.8	757,134	3,419	84,629	120.0	213,913	30.0	70.0	36.4	17.3	1,985	38.1
Chilton	91	-8.8	168	0.5	23.7	493,578	2,933	55,048	16.0	29,538	63.8	36.2	36.8	5.3	296	10.3
Choctaw....................	68	24.5	276	0.0	8.0	517,085	1,872	53,851	D	D	D	D	18.5	2.0	194	11.3
Clarke........................	47	-35.6	181	0.0	7.7	369,251	2,045	38,399	2.6	9,863	49.1	50.9	24.3	0.8	153	17.5
Clay..........................	78	4.6	194	0.0	13.0	480,421	2,474	54,217	58.1	144,850	1.8	98.2	38.4	8.7	585	19.5
Cleburne	50	1.4	147	0.3	7.7	404,111	2,745	60,522	84.3	247,170	3.9	96.1	45.2	18.5	106	12.6
Coffee	202	-4.2	225	3.3	85.5	593,148	2,636	90,236	258.2	287,171	14.3	85.7	37.9	19.7	3,459	57.7
Colbert	153	18.5	222	3.7	65.7	626,991	2,820	80,017	67.0	97,531	54.3	45.7	32.3	8.7	1,996	31.4
Conecuh....................	94	8.6	271	0.1	20.1	539,208	1,991	72,494	16.4	47,436	44.6	55.4	35.0	6.4	770	41.0
Coosa........................	36	-20.8	236	D	4.3	489,967	2,072	52,934	2.1	13,763	D	D	30.3	2.0	39	5.9
Covington	209	4.2	198	1.4	65.5	447,436	2,255	67,858	119.8	114,025	26.0	74.0	30.9	12.9	2,582	43.8
Crenshaw	130	-1.9	226	0.9	29.0	458,381	2,029	80,572	143.8	250,132	3.5	96.5	36.2	17.0	919	51.0
Cullman	194	-15.5	97	0.5	58.4	403,876	4,176	64,375	417.1	207,820	3.8	96.2	43.3	21.1	567	12.0
Dale..........................	130	-6.1	267	2.6	49.6	668,934	2,510	86,197	118.0	242,400	21.6	78.4	32.6	15.8	1,495	55.6
Dallas	255	-0.7	504	2.0	76.8	925,310	1,835	106,532	70.2	138,800	39.5	60.5	32.6	12.3	2,616	45.8
DeKalb	229	-2.5	113	0.3	72.3	427,088	3,790	70,291	461.7	226,882	5.3	94.7	37.4	17.5	2,652	24.1
Elmore.......................	90	-12.1	164	3.1	30.2	519,685	3,175	64,795	26.5	47,986	65.6	34.4	29.3	4.3	959	15.9
Escambia	107	-4.8	236	0.8	47.7	537,068	2,271	93,018	40.9	89,991	88.5	11.5	28.4	11.5	2,602	48.9
Etowah......................	86	-8.6	101	0.1	19.5	359,368	3,559	51,635	83.7	98,161	6.5	93.5	27.8	8.2	450	11.8
Fayette	81	2.9	196	D	27.6	415,915	2,124	83,215	36.3	87,751	D	D	30.2	7.0	903	37.4
Franklin	150	6.8	182	0.8	35.0	383,861	2,104	57,796	132.7	160,807	5.6	94.4	39.3	13.8	782	21.8
Geneva	219	-0.8	215	2.7	93.1	465,026	2,161	89,514	178.5	175,499	26.4	73.6	36.0	15.6	4,741	59.2
Greene	120	-11.3	396	0.3	21.8	803,934	2,030	58,648	22.4	73,658	7.7	92.3	28.0	9.2	790	35.5
Hale..........................	161	-5.2	352	D	29.9	735,855	2,091	81,908	65.2	142,934	D	D	39.9	11.4	797	32.0
Henry	170	2.5	341	8.1	72.9	762,197	2,235	108,992	75.0	150,647	53.5	46.5	38.4	15.5	3,315	64.3
Houston....................	198	-3.3	243	9.1	97.4	631,875	2,604	89,566	89.2	109,336	71.7	28.3	31.1	14.8	5,065	59.3
Jackson.....................	232	-4.5	168	0.4	89.4	440,304	2,613	65,429	117.2	85,181	30.5	69.5	35.0	8.6	1,849	34.4
Jefferson	39	-3.6	99	0.2	9.1	446,142	4,507	49,924	10.4	26,277	10.5	89.5	20.6	1.3	98	8.1
Lamar	82	-2.8	233	D	13.9	344,326	1,477	42,527	7.5	21,337	20.7	79.3	21.5	2.0	203	27.5
Lauderdale.................	212	-7.1	144	0.4	100.0	428,690	2,970	56,675	72.4	49,385	55.6	44.4	30.7	6.8	2,973	34.7
Lawrence	244	9.6	157	4.7	114.7	480,849	3,059	81,876	192.1	123,829	29.4	70.6	32.0	13.9	4,764	40.4
Lee............................	59	-6.6	187	0.9	12.2	707,330	3,775	71,403	D	D	D	D	32.4	4.8	692	19.0
Limestone	247	4.0	201	13.1	146.1	815,963	4,068	103,711	132.7	107,913	64.2	35.8	36.3	10.7	3,605	34.6
Lowndes....................	218	16.6	494	3.8	40.0	852,254	1,726	73,297	76.3	173,052	D	D	41.0	10.0	880	34.7
Macon	103	-11.5	294	1.9	20.1	721,324	2,458	81,386	15.2	43,230	80.5	19.5	31.5	4.0	622	33.2
Madison	209	5.0	203	5.1	125.4	752,873	3,715	88,137	74.2	71,833	86.2	13.8	31.0	8.3	3,156	34.1
Marengo....................	165	-7.1	332	0.4	32.8	591,148	1,783	59,990	19.4	38,964	27.5	72.5	34.7	5.6	912	28.9
Marion	114	-2.9	159	0.0	21.8	353,441	2,221	47,490	100.1	139,948	3.2	96.8	27.6	11.2	599	29.0
Marshall	163	5.5	108	0.2	46.7	410,550	3,791	61,688	256.5	170,433	2.9	97.1	34.2	12.3	2,102	23.7
Mobile	89	-21.9	127	2.8	36.6	516,701	4,062	78,354	84.7	121,289	90.7	9.3	33.2	8.5	796	12.2
Monroe	141	18.3	293	0.2	53.9	576,181	1,967	103,242	44.5	92,663	72.1	27.9	34.6	10.0	2,925	59.2
Montgomery..............	220	-1.4	365	1.7	61.2	957,657	2,624	76,778	77.4	128,421	21.5	78.5	40.6	11.8	927	23.7
Morgan......................	153	-5.5	123	0.3	52.6	460,337	3,732	52,647	109.3	88,335	12.7	87.3	32.7	9.1	1,462	19.6
Perry.........................	157	-5.1	404	0.3	39.5	709,424	1,755	68,270	29.6	76,177	32.6	67.4	31.1	11.8	1,428	53.5
Pickens	103	-21.5	237	D	24.6	490,279	2,068	68,935	110.6	255,370	6.0	94.0	39.5	20.6	511	20.1
Pike..........................	167	-6.6	279	3.2	35.2	635,038	2,278	66,467	130.4	217,322	8.9	91.1	42.5	16.0	1,573	54.2
Randolph...................	114	-0.7	186	0.1	14.4	523,882	2,810	66,257	111.5	182,509	1.9	98.1	40.4	13.9	831	21.1
Russell	117	24.6	419	3.4	29.4	947,768	2,261	83,646	28.9	103,057	56.0	44.0	29.6	8.6	738	34.6
St. Clair	67	-5.8	125	0.3	13.6	479,537	3,839	55,039	64.8	120,028	15.2	84.8	30.4	9.1	119	6.1
Shelby.......................	58	6.6	146	1.1	18.7	612,140	4,199	68,581	12.2	30,347	80.4	19.6	25.9	6.2	659	10.5
Sumter	240	32.5	560	1.5	33.3	797,215	1,423	58,586	30.5	71,199	D	D	33.2	10.0	1,057	36.4
Talladega	100	-16.1	192	4.8	39.7	559,618	2,909	63,229	40.7	78,428	41.8	58.2	28.3	5.8	717	17.1
Tallapoosa	61	-4.9	177	1.1	8.4	426,409	2,414	53,971	10.6	30,635	32.2	67.8	24.6	3.2	266	10.4
Tuscaloosa................	86	-22.2	173	1.1	25.3	512,952	2,965	60,022	27.7	55,682	33.8	66.2	27.0	6.0	493	17.1
Walker.......................	55	-22.5	113	0.0	13.1	291,614	2,578	51,429	33.1	68,683	11.4	88.6	24.3	5.6	105	4.8

STATE County	Water use, 2015		Wholesale Trade[1], 2012				Retail Trade[2], 2012				Real estate and rental and leasing,[2] 2012			
	Public supply water withdrawn (mil gal/day)	Public supply gallons withdrawn per person per day	Number of establishments	Number of employees	Sales (mil dol)	Annual payroll (mil dol)	Number of establishments	Number of employees	Sales (mil dol)	Annual payroll (mil dol)	Number of establishments	Number of employees	Sales (mil dol)	Annual payroll (mil dol)
	133	134	135	136	137	138	139	140	141	142	143	144	145	146
UNITED STATES	38,595.83	120.1	355,983	4,880,666	5,208,023.5	287,549.6	1,062,083	14,703,529	4,219,821.9	369,001.4	354,106	1,923,770	487,655.2	85,326.0
ALABAMA	761.53	156.7	4,600	60,332	57,746.6	2,894.7	18,211	218,531	58,565.0	5,123.1	3,858	22,852	3,919.4	819.6
Autauga........................	3.64	65.8	22	D	D	D	166	2,385	607.9	54.6	31	D	D	D
Baldwin	23.67	116.2	175	1,868	1,118.2	84.1	950	12,072	3,145.8	280.0	292	1,760	250.3	53.8
Barbour	3.23	121.9	16	181	114.0	4.0	94	868	206.5	18.2	15	20	3.3	0.6
Bibb..............................	5.18	229.4	14	52	41.0	2.3	58	474	118.9	11.3	6	8	1.9	0.3
Blount...........................	56.86	985.9	36	290	153.7	10.5	135	1,255	298.7	28.6	11	19	3.3	0.5
Bullock.........................	2.11	197.3	5	D	D	D	23	244	92.6	5.3	4	12	0.9	0.1
Butler...........................	2.28	113.1	13	44	63.5	2.0	97	914	209.0	19.5	13	18	2.8	0.5
Calhoun........................	25.25	218.4	97	1,792	1,808.8	73.6	477	5,954	1,463.5	134.1	73	299	48.9	8.0
Chambers.....................	4.20	123.1	13	104	32.6	4.2	120	1,172	282.0	23.6	14	50	5.1	0.9
Cherokee	3.20	123.7	12	48	55.2	2.0	88	859	200.2	17.9	12	49	5.7	1.8
Chilton.........................	4.40	100.1	20	320	260.5	12.6	152	1,397	442.8	32.0	19	52	6.4	1.2
Choctaw........................	1.21	91.9	9	D	D	D	54	337	100.0	7.1	6	D	D	D
Clarke...........................	2.58	104.6	13	126	75.2	3.8	138	1,311	341.0	28.4	13	48	6.6	1.2
Clay.............................	1.78	131.3	6	D	D	D	34	291	67.7	5.4	6	9	0.6	0.1
Cleburne	0.48	32.0	5	49	6.6	0.8	36	275	64.0	6.9	3	4	0.5	0.2
Coffee	6.34	123.8	29	250	213.2	10.5	195	2,129	610.1	55.5	47	212	21.5	4.4
Colbert	8.26	152.0	78	853	657.4	32.1	228	2,829	1,011.3	76.5	31	144	17.8	3.5
Conecuh........................	1.32	104.2	5	236	103.9	8.8	41	280	136.4	5.6	3	3	0.2	0.1
Coosa...........................	0.27	25.2	5	D	D	D	22	161	37.9	3.5	3	1	0.6	0.1
Covington......................	4.09	108.1	34	445	470.5	17.9	202	1,834	452.0	40.3	27	97	12.3	3.1
Crenshaw......................	1.93	138.2	12	405	309.0	15.2	38	301	72.7	5.9	6	20	1.6	0.4
Cullman........................	23.24	283.4	93	896	1,068.8	37.9	332	3,264	896.4	76.1	47	195	21.6	5.6
Dale.............................	5.90	119.0	18	169	41.0	4.3	138	1,170	323.5	26.4	30	199	33.7	7.4
Dallas...........................	5.91	143.7	28	215	107.1	8.5	179	1,630	413.1	37.0	30	88	13.5	2.2
DeKalb..........................	5.91	83.1	37	415	161.0	13.7	246	2,173	579.7	53.2	24	140	9.3	3.3
Elmore..........................	12.19	149.6	37	282	136.1	9.7	224	2,649	711.6	61.0	48	D	D	D
Escambia	5.00	132.3	22	129	134.1	6.1	176	1,542	374.9	30.3	15	63	6.2	1.2
Etowah.........................	16.85	163.5	82	837	549.9	31.2	392	4,675	1,236.5	96.1	62	367	57.2	10.5
Fayette.........................	1.70	101.4	7	24	34.8	0.6	62	562	131.2	12.2	4	D	D	D
Franklin........................	5.94	187.4	19	92	44.3	3.5	100	1,116	277.7	28.0	13	33	4.7	0.6
Geneva.........................	1.78	66.5	20	D	D	D	91	713	160.8	14.6	7	14	1.4	0.4
Greene..........................	1.39	163.9	2	D	D	D	23	164	40.3	2.8	1	D	D	D
Hale..............................	3.10	205.7	7	24	29.4	0.9	43	317	76.5	6.4	8	D	D	D
Henry...........................	1.66	96.4	8	101	40.6	3.9	55	364	100.3	7.9	3	3	0.3	0.0
Houston........................	18.94	181.8	168	D	D	D	570	7,598	2,164.9	182.5	100	423	73.0	16.0
Jackson.........................	11.79	224.9	27	D	D	D	185	1,873	454.9	40.1	25	D	D	D
Jefferson.......................	48.98	74.2	977	15,345	15,668.5	816.2	2,806	38,691	10,154.0	961.4	681	6,526	1,138.7	283.7
Lamar...........................	1.42	102.3	7	D	D	D	51	344	80.9	7.1	3	D	D	D
Lauderdale	12.39	133.8	76	1,244	577.6	39.2	419	4,920	1,190.8	104.5	96	378	52.2	10.5
Lawrence	7.73	233.4	12	64	38.9	2.2	85	793	218.0	17.0	5	11	2.6	0.3
Lee...............................	15.83	100.8	75	613	504.3	28.3	477	6,450	1,632.1	141.6	113	544	81.0	16.0
Limestone	11.52	125.7	45	447	332.7	17.3	261	2,804	777.1	64.3	52	166	30.7	5.5
Lowndes........................	0.95	90.8	2	D	D	D	21	177	100.8	3.2	2	D	D	D
Macon	3.31	173.3	6	D	D	D	45	392	93.2	7.1	5	18	1.1	0.3
Madison	67.15	190.2	331	4,111	3,768.8	222.9	1,316	18,653	4,958.0	450.2	409	1,706	339.9	60.9
Marengo........................	2.77	138.3	19	151	105.9	5.3	102	883	199.7	17.8	10	72	20.9	2.9
Marion..........................	6.06	200.9	23	176	222.1	8.0	102	976	229.0	19.9	14	28	4.7	0.7
Marshall........................	23.76	250.8	81	1,253	1,177.7	47.8	419	4,559	1,280.0	102.0	58	591	34.1	9.6
Mobile..........................	66.10	159.1	499	6,116	3,680.0	283.8	1,454	19,204	5,102.6	454.7	410	2,125	419.1	83.2
Monroe.........................	2.31	106.6	16	151	101.0	7.0	89	863	211.0	17.6	13	39	4.8	1.2
Montgomery...................	28.00	123.6	299	5,401	4,140.8	257.0	911	12,148	3,258.7	302.9	228	1,907	342.5	65.5
Morgan..........................	25.60	214.1	152	2,080	1,417.0	89.2	498	5,507	1,673.5	127.6	82	340	76.2	12.4
Perry	2.02	209.3	5	59	14.7	1.5	32	174	34.7	3.6	4	D	D	D
Pickens.........................	3.00	143.8	10	69	29.8	2.2	59	427	100.6	9.0	2	D	D	D
Pike..............................	4.58	138.6	29	D	D	D	143	1,465	373.6	31.3	26	91	17.8	2.0
Randolph.......................	1.22	53.8	5	D	D	D	70	704	158.3	15.0	10	27	3.2	0.6
Russell..........................	8.45	141.6	13	D	D	D	155	1,810	499.7	40.7	39	D	D	D
St. Clair........................	8.93	102.6	69	1,160	476.4	49.2	223	2,613	704.4	56.9	36	101	22.6	3.3
Shelby	14.21	68.1	353	4,260	4,651.3	272.0	610	8,195	2,567.4	210.9	205	1,318	396.0	59.9
Sumter	2.06	157.2	11	105	60.2	3.5	46	283	62.1	4.4	7	16	1.9	0.3
Talladega	16.00	197.9	52	D	D	D	275	2,748	743.4	60.8	37	210	22.2	4.6
Tallapoosa	11.87	290.6	20	D	D	D	169	1,503	361.8	32.3	27	92	20.9	3.6
Tuscaloosa.....................	31.43	154.1	143	1,681	1,180.8	83.5	733	9,622	2,619.3	218.3	182	1,485	164.6	44.3
Walker..........................	43.88	672.0	44	406	279.4	18.2	297	3,216	963.5	78.7	38	158	28.5	5.5

1. Merchant wholesalers, except manufacturers' sales branches and offices.   2. Employer establishments.

Table B. States and Counties — Land Area and Population

State / county code	CBSA code[1]	County code[2]	STATE County	Population, 2017				Population and population characteristics, 2017										
								Race alone or in combination, not Hispanic or Latino (percent)					Age (percent)					
				Land area[3] (sq. mi)	Total persons 2017	Rank	Per square mile	White	Black	American Indian, Alaska Native	Asian and Pacific Islander[4]	Percent Hispanic or Latino[4]	Under 5 years	5 to 17 years	18 to 24 years	25 to 34 years	35 to 44 years	45 to 54 years
				1	2	3	4	5	6	7	8	9	10	11	12	13	14	15
			ALABAMA—Cont'd															
01129		8	Washington	1,080.2	16,531	2,006	15.3	66.2	24.2	8.3	1.1	1.6	5.4	16.9	8.4	11.1	11.2	14.0
01131		9	Wilcox	888.5	10,719	2,373	12.1	27.4	71.0	0.5	0.4	1.4	6.4	17.6	9.5	10.5	11.2	12.1
01133		6	Winston	613.0	23,722	1,654	38.7	95.0	1.2	1.4	0.6	3.1	5.1	15.4	7.3	10.5	11.2	14.4
02000		0	ALASKA	570,886.1	739,795	X	1.3	66.7	4.7	18.8	10.0	7.1	7.3	17.7	9.8	16.2	12.6	12.3
02013		9	Aleutians East	6,985.1	3,370	2,944	0.5	12.5	10.8	22.1	44.3	13.7	2.6	6.1	10.1	14.8	20.8	21.7
02016		9	Aleutians West	4,392.5	5,763	2,775	1.3	26.1	7.3	12.6	44.4	13.6	3.1	8.6	9.1	17.4	18.2	20.8
02020	11,260	2	Anchorage	1,706.4	294,356	233	172.5	64.4	7.4	11.9	15.2	9.2	7.3	17.2	10.1	17.5	12.9	12.4
02050		7	Bethel	40,629.1	18,076	1,915	0.4	13.1	1.2	85.3	1.9	2.4	11.1	24.6	10.6	15.5	10.3	10.4
02060		9	Bristol Bay	482.0	867	3,113	1.8	59.4	2.8	44.2	5.3	5.4	6.1	13.0	8.9	15.1	10.0	14.6
02068		8	Denali	12,637.0	2,074	3,042	0.2	84.5	2.5	8.1	5.6	3.8	5.3	13.6	6.7	16.0	14.6	17.3
02070		9	Dillingham	18,331.2	4,932	2,837	0.3	23.7	1.6	78.4	2.3	3.3	10.2	21.1	10.6	15.9	9.5	11.2
02090	21,820	3	Fairbanks North Star	7,329.1	99,703	600	13.6	75.5	6.3	10.8	5.8	8.1	7.7	16.3	13.4	19.0	12.2	10.6
02100		9	Haines	2,406.6	2,526	3,001	1.0	84.5	1.6	15.6	2.3	3.5	3.4	14.0	5.8	10.6	11.3	14.0
02105		9	Hoonah-Angoon	6,556.6	2,145	3,033	0.3	55.2	1.9	43.7	3.1	5.5	4.2	14.6	5.6	9.8	10.0	13.9
02110	27,940	5	Juneau	2,636.8	32,094	1,379	12.2	72.1	2.1	17.8	11.3	6.6	5.9	15.7	8.8	15.2	13.4	13.7
02122		7	Kenai Peninsula	16,023.2	58,617	881	3.7	85.5	1.2	11.7	3.3	4.2	6.2	16.5	7.6	12.8	11.6	12.6
02130	28,540	7	Ketchikan Gateway	4,857.0	13,856	2,175	2.9	71.7	1.6	20.0	10.7	5.2	5.7	16.4	7.6	14.0	12.3	13.3
02150		7	Kodiak Island	6,615.5	13,448	2,197	2.0	55.6	1.7	16.4	23.8	9.3	7.9	18.0	9.2	15.9	13.5	12.3
02158		0	Kusilvak	17,072.8	8,202	2,577	0.5	5.9	0.8	93.3	0.8	1.8	13.2	27.9	11.2	15.5	8.5	9.3
02164		9	Lake and Peninsula	23,897.6	1,620	3,075	0.1	31.7	2.7	68.1	4.8	3.1	9.0	19.1	8.7	15.2	12.8	11.7
02170	11,260	2	Matanuska-Susitna	24,618.1	106,532	566	4.3	85.2	2.1	10.9	3.9	4.9	7.3	19.8	8.2	14.4	13.2	12.6
02180		7	Nome	22,971.7	9,921	2,436	0.4	20.4	1.1	79.8	2.4	2.4	9.9	24.9	9.9	16.0	11.0	10.6
02185		7	North Slope	88,825.1	9,782	2,446	0.1	35.1	2.3	54.7	9.0	4.3	7.8	18.4	7.7	16.6	12.7	15.9
02188		7	Northwest Arctic	35,647.5	7,684	2,617	0.2	16.1	1.9	83.0	2.3	2.9	10.9	24.9	10.2	16.0	10.4	10.9
02195		9	Petersburg	2,900.8	3,281	2,953	1.1	77.1	2.9	15.1	6.0	6.0	6.0	15.4	7.7	11.5	11.5	13.7
02198		9	Prince of Wales-Hyder	5,262.7	6,443	2,718	1.2	52.1	1.5	47.2	3.2	3.9	6.0	17.2	6.8	12.6	11.2	14.1
02220		7	Sitka	2,870.0	8,689	2,532	3.0	69.3	1.8	21.2	10.0	6.7	4.9	16.8	8.3	14.3	13.8	12.0
02230		9	Skagway	434.0	1,157	3,102	2.7	86.7	1.8	7.3	4.4	4.9	5.1	9.3	6.0	18.0	17.9	14.3
02240		9	Southeast Fairbanks	24,822.6	6,888	2,683	0.3	78.0	2.4	14.9	3.3	6.0	7.5	17.8	7.3	13.7	12.0	13.4
02261		9	Valdez-Cordova	34,222.5	9,278	2,482	0.3	75.2	1.5	18.3	6.4	5.1	6.8	16.7	7.4	13.4	11.8	13.5
02275		9	Wrangell	2,555.8	2,521	3,002	1.0	77.2	1.7	23.7	5.2	2.5	4.9	14.7	7.7	9.6	8.4	12.3
02282		9	Yakutat	7,624.3	605	3,134	0.1	45.3	4.0	48.6	12.1	5.0	6.6	12.6	7.8	12.9	11.1	15.0
02290		9	Yukon-Koyukuk	145,572.5	5,365	2,805	0.0	27.2	1.2	73.4	1.5	2.6	7.6	20.1	8.3	13.7	11.3	10.6
04000		0	ARIZONA	113,590.7	7,016,270	X	61.8	56.7	5.1	4.6	4.4	31.4	6.2	17.0	9.6	13.6	12.2	12.1
04001		6	Apache	11,197.5	71,606	757	6.4	19.2	1.1	74.1	0.8	6.3	6.9	20.7	9.8	12.8	10.6	11.7
04003	43,420	3	Cochise	6,164.6	124,756	507	20.2	57.1	4.7	1.6	3.5	35.6	6.1	15.8	8.4	12.4	10.9	11.0
04005	22,380	3	Coconino	18,618.7	140,776	459	7.6	56.2	1.9	27.2	3.1	14.1	5.7	15.2	19.9	14.1	10.9	10.4
04007	37,740	4	Gila	4,758.0	53,501	944	11.2	63.5	0.9	17.0	1.1	18.7	5.8	14.5	6.6	9.8	8.4	10.8
04009	40,940	7	Graham	4,622.7	37,466	1,238	8.1	52.2	2.0	13.3	1.2	32.8	7.4	19.9	10.3	14.6	12.8	10.8
04011		7	Greenlee	1,842.0	9,455	2,468	5.1	48.1	2.2	3.3	1.2	46.8	7.7	20.0	9.0	14.4	13.1	11.5
04012		6	La Paz	4,499.6	20,601	1,792	4.6	59.6	1.4	13.1	1.1	26.9	4.9	12.1	5.9	8.8	7.7	8.5
04013	38,060	1	Maricopa	9,199.2	4,307,033	4	468.2	57.4	6.3	2.2	5.4	31.1	6.5	17.8	9.2	14.5	13.0	12.7
04015	29,420	3	Mohave	13,311.1	207,200	321	15.6	79.0	1.5	2.9	2.0	16.4	4.4	13.1	6.3	10.1	9.0	11.3
04017	43,320	4	Navajo	9,949.9	108,956	555	11.0	43.1	1.3	44.9	1.1	11.3	7.1	19.9	8.5	12.1	10.5	11.3
04019	46,060	2	Pima	9,187.2	1,022,769	44	111.3	53.6	4.1	3.0	4.1	37.3	5.8	15.4	11.9	12.6	11.3	11.2
04021	38,060	1	Pinal	5,365.8	430,237	164	80.2	58.7	5.3	5.3	2.8	30.1	5.8	17.2	7.8	13.2	13.1	11.2
04023	35,700	4	Santa Cruz	1,236.9	46,212	1,047	37.4	15.2	0.6	0.5	0.7	83.4	6.9	20.4	9.7	10.8	10.7	11.7
04025	39,140	3	Yavapai	8,123.5	228,168	291	28.1	82.1	1.1	2.3	1.8	14.5	4.2	12.3	6.6	9.1	8.7	10.9
04027	49,740	3	Yuma	5,514.0	207,534	319	37.6	31.7	2.3	1.4	1.9	63.9	7.3	18.1	11.4	13.8	10.8	10.4
05000		0	ARKANSAS	52,034.3	3,004,279	X	57.7	74.2	16.2	1.6	2.3	7.6	6.4	17.1	9.4	13.2	12.2	12.5
05001		6	Arkansas	988.8	17,967	1,921	18.2	71.1	25.6	0.8	1.2	3.1	6.5	16.3	7.6	11.5	11.8	12.6
05003		7	Ashley	925.4	20,283	1,811	21.9	69.4	25.1	0.8	0.4	5.4	6.0	16.9	7.9	10.8	11.5	13.2
05005	34,260	7	Baxter	554.2	41,355	1,143	74.6	96.1	0.6	1.6	0.8	2.4	4.5	13.2	5.7	9.4	8.9	11.7
05007	22,220	2	Benton	847.5	266,300	258	314.2	75.5	2.3	2.7	5.2	16.7	7.1	19.5	8.1	14.7	14.2	12.6
05009	25,460	7	Boone	590.0	37,381	1,241	63.4	95.6	0.7	2.1	1.0	2.5	6.2	16.4	7.7	11.6	11.5	12.7
05011		7	Bradley	649.2	10,864	2,359	16.7	56.3	27.9	0.9	0.5	15.6	6.2	17.9	7.1	11.9	11.9	12.7
05013	15,780	9	Calhoun	628.6	5,247	2,819	8.3	73.8	22.1	1.1	0.8	4.2	4.9	13.8	7.9	12.0	10.6	13.9
05015		6	Carroll	630.0	27,944	1,495	44.4	81.3	0.9	2.2	2.1	15.3	5.7	16.3	7.2	10.5	10.5	12.1
05017		7	Chicot	644.3	10,636	2,382	16.5	40.4	53.7	0.6	0.8	5.4	5.5	16.7	8.4	10.9	11.0	12.4
05019	11,660	7	Clark	866.1	22,293	1,715	25.7	70.0	24.8	1.0	0.9	4.8	5.1	13.8	22.0	10.8	9.7	10.9
05021		7	Clay	639.5	14,920	2,103	23.3	96.5	1.2	1.1	0.4	2.1	5.7	15.8	7.6	11.0	11.2	13.6
05023		6	Cleburne	553.7	25,048	1,606	45.2	96.0	0.7	1.6	0.7	2.4	4.6	14.5	6.3	9.8	10.5	12.8

1. CBSA = Core Based Statistical Area. See Appendix A for explanation. See Appendix B for list of metropolitan areas with component counties. 2. County type code from the Economic Research Service of USDA Rural-Urban Continuum Codes. See Appendix A for definition. 3. Dry land or land partially or temporarily covered by water. 4. May be of any race.

Table B. States and Counties — **Population and Households**

STATE County	55 to 64 years	65 to 74 years	75 years and over	Percent female	2000	2010	2000-2010	2010-2017	Births	Deaths	Net Migration	Number	Persons per household	Family households	Female family householder[1]	One person
	16	17	18	19	20	21	22	23	24	25	26	27	28	29	30	31
ALABAMA—Cont'd																
Washington	14.5	11.1	7.3	51.0	18,097	17,583	-2.8	-6.0	1,229	1,461	-827	6,113	2.74	74.1	14.9	23.6
Wilcox	13.6	11.1	7.9	52.3	13,183	11,665	-11.5	-8.1	970	1,062	-871	3,792	2.86	62.0	22.3	35.2
Winston	14.5	12.6	8.8	50.6	24,843	24,484	-1.4	-3.1	1,745	2,224	-269	9,436	2.51	67.7	10.8	29.6
ALASKA	12.9	7.6	3.6	47.7	626,932	710,249	13.3	4.2	82,228	30,233	-23,089	250,235	2.83	66.6	10.9	25.7
Aleutians East	14.9	6.3	2.7	32.0	2,697	3,141	16.5	7.3	109	46	162	788	2.36	63.3	12.7	27.5
Aleutians West	16.2	5.5	1.0	33.4	5,465	5,561	1.8	3.6	235	88	43	1,186	3.47	58.8	8.1	30.3
Anchorage	12.1	6.9	3.6	49.0	260,283	291,829	12.1	0.9	33,680	11,767	-19,562	104,969	2.77	66.6	12.1	25.0
Bethel	10.1	4.9	2.4	48.2	16,006	17,013	6.3	6.2	3,150	855	-1,238	4,555	3.79	74.1	18.7	18.2
Bristol Bay	18.8	8.5	4.8	46.1	1,258	997	-20.7	-13.0	78	56	-154	360	2.48	64.2	8.3	26.9
Denali	16.6	7.5	2.6	44.2	1,893	1,822	-3.8	13.8	156	56	151	707	2.29	55.2	4.1	36.5
Dillingham	12.5	6.0	3.0	49.5	4,922	4,847	-1.5	1.8	744	267	-395	1,375	3.43	70.3	19.4	25.8
Fairbanks North Star	11.0	6.8	2.9	46.0	82,840	97,585	17.8	2.2	12,364	3,417	-7,011	35,303	2.72	63.1	8.2	27.9
Haines	19.5	14.9	6.5	51.0	2,392	2,508	4.8	0.7	136	124	5	1,170	2.11	57.3	5.0	30.0
Hoonah-Angoon	19.5	15.2	7.0	46.8	NA	2,135	NA	0.5	147	88	-51	836	2.35	64.6	11.4	30.6
Juneau	14.6	8.7	3.9	49.1	30,711	31,275	1.8	2.6	2,792	1,325	-657	12,138	2.62	65.7	10.4	25.0
Kenai Peninsula	16.3	11.2	5.2	47.8	49,691	55,400	11.5	5.8	5,228	3,007	1,000	21,481	2.60	63.8	8.0	29.5
Ketchikan Gateway	15.6	9.9	5.1	48.7	14,070	13,491	-4.1	2.7	1,242	644	-237	5,209	2.58	63.2	10.7	29.2
Kodiak Island	12.9	6.9	3.3	46.8	13,913	13,606	-2.2	-1.2	1,609	404	-1,388	4,585	2.96	72.1	10.5	23.3
Kusilvak	8.5	4.0	1.9	47.8	7,028	7,459	6.1	10.0	1,699	474	-486	1,734	4.52	84.1	27.6	13.3
Lake and Peninsula	13.1	7.0	3.5	48.1	1,823	1,635	-10.3	-0.9	233	92	-160	468	2.84	68.8	19.9	24.6
Matanuska-Susitna	13.3	7.7	3.4	47.9	59,322	88,992	50.0	19.7	10,293	3,989	11,098	30,839	3.14	71.0	8.2	22.7
Nome	10.1	5.3	2.2	47.3	9,196	9,492	3.2	4.5	1,604	577	-609	2,879	3.30	76.0	19.8	19.9
North Slope	14.3	4.8	1.9	37.8	7,385	9,430	27.7	3.7	1,226	350	-528	2,018	3.25	75.1	22.2	20.3
Northwest Arctic	9.5	4.2	3.0	45.9	7,208	7,523	4.4	2.1	1,326	379	-793	1,904	3.93	78.4	21.6	16.0
Petersburg	15.8	12.4	6.0	46.9	NA	3,207	NA	2.3	274	121	-78	1,237	2.47	62.7	10.6	31.3
Prince of Wales-Hyder	16.3	11.3	4.6	45.2	NA	6,172	NA	4.4	572	336	34	2,267	2.77	64.1	12.0	29.2
Sitka	14.9	9.1	5.8	48.7	8,835	8,881	0.5	-2.2	691	443	-449	3,504	2.46	58.3	9.8	35.0
Skagway	14.7	9.6	5.2	48.3	NA	968	NA	19.5	79	23	129	428	2.07	46.3	5.6	35.0
Southeast Fairbanks	14.3	9.5	4.5	44.4	6,174	7,029	13.8	-2.0	809	316	-645	2,085	3.15	68.7	8.8	28.5
Valdez-Cordova	17.4	9.4	3.5	47.8	10,195	9,636	-5.5	-3.7	914	401	-891	2,937	3.14	67.2	8.5	27.9
Wrangell	19.9	13.9	8.4	47.3	NA	2,365	NA	6.6	172	131	118	1,045	2.25	62.4	10.0	29.9
Yakutat	15.7	11.6	6.8	44.6	808	662	-18.1	-8.6	58	20	-99	247	2.34	60.3	13.8	34.0
Yukon-Koyukuk	14.3	9.6	4.4	46.6	6,551	5,588	-14.7	-4.0	608	437	-398	1,981	2.75	64.0	17.2	30.6
ARIZONA	12.1	10.0	7.1	50.3	5,130,632	6,392,309	24.6	9.8	622,449	376,768	376,659	2,448,919	2.69	65.4	12.6	27.3
Apache	12.6	8.8	6.0	50.6	69,423	71,524	3.0	0.1	7,356	4,318	-2,979	19,351	3.67	68.9	21.6	27.4
Cochise	13.5	12.7	9.3	49.3	117,755	131,356	11.6	-5.0	11,814	9,110	-9,495	49,230	2.38	65.8	12.5	29.4
Coconino	11.7	7.8	4.3	50.6	116,320	134,435	15.6	4.7	12,182	5,634	-227	47,366	2.67	62.5	12.8	24.4
Gila	15.9	16.4	11.8	50.5	51,335	53,597	4.4	-0.2	4,450	5,464	959	21,408	2.44	65.8	12.5	29.0
Graham	10.3	8.0	5.8	46.7	33,489	37,220	11.1	0.7	4,150	1,985	-1,944	10,915	3.04	70.6	12.3	25.3
Greenlee	11.4	7.3	5.6	48.4	8,547	8,437	-1.3	12.1	951	406	447	3,295	2.77	71.5	13.1	24.0
La Paz	12.8	19.1	20.3	48.7	19,715	20,489	3.9	0.5	1,468	1,723	380	9,181	2.18	63.3	9.4	30.5
Maricopa	11.5	8.7	6.1	50.5	3,072,149	3,817,361	24.3	12.8	395,365	203,437	296,877	1,465,840	2.75	65.4	12.7	27.0
Mohave	16.1	17.1	12.6	49.6	155,032	200,185	29.1	3.5	13,400	19,892	13,393	82,145	2.40	63.2	11.2	28.6
Navajo	13.1	10.7	6.9	50.0	97,470	107,489	10.3	1.4	11,615	6,889	-3,243	34,090	3.10	72.4	19.5	23.4
Pima	12.6	11.0	8.2	50.8	843,746	980,260	16.2	4.3	85,585	65,749	23,510	395,390	2.47	61.5	12.9	30.7
Pinal	11.8	12.2	7.6	47.9	179,727	375,768	109.1	14.5	33,386	19,612	40,019	130,801	2.86	71.4	11.5	23.8
Santa Cruz	12.4	10.2	7.2	51.9	38,381	47,423	23.6	-2.6	4,731	2,091	-3,918	15,538	2.97	75.0	17.3	21.3
Yavapai	17.4	18.4	12.3	51.1	167,517	211,015	26.0	8.1	13,498	20,140	23,582	93,445	2.29	63.8	8.5	29.8
Yuma	9.9	9.2	9.1	48.4	160,026	195,750	22.3	6.0	22,498	10,318	-702	70,924	2.78	75.1	13.0	20.2
ARKANSAS	12.7	9.7	6.9	50.9	2,673,400	2,916,031	9.1	3.0	278,204	219,415	28,860	1,141,480	2.53	66.4	13.1	28.5
Arkansas	14.8	10.8	8.2	51.4	20,749	19,015	-8.4	-5.5	1,777	1,681	-1,151	7,685	2.38	63.5	14.6	31.2
Ashley	13.8	11.6	8.2	51.4	24,209	21,851	-9.7	-7.2	1,839	1,834	-1,584	8,338	2.49	71.1	14.1	26.6
Baxter	15.6	16.5	14.3	51.7	38,386	41,513	8.1	-0.4	2,576	4,855	2,135	18,061	2.24	65.7	8.2	30.0
Benton	10.6	7.7	5.4	50.3	153,406	221,364	44.3	20.3	25,055	12,139	31,685	88,014	2.76	74.1	10.3	21.0
Boone	13.5	11.7	8.7	50.7	33,948	36,910	8.7	1.3	3,268	3,193	421	14,883	2.47	69.0	9.8	27.6
Bradley	13.4	10.4	8.5	51.2	12,600	11,505	-8.7	-5.6	989	1,083	-548	4,550	2.39	64.4	14.2	33.0
Calhoun	15.8	12.3	8.8	49.9	5,744	5,368	-6.5	-2.3	342	409	-54	2,079	2.44	67.3	9.8	31.3
Carroll	14.9	14.0	8.7	50.5	25,357	27,445	8.2	1.8	2,290	2,169	388	10,874	2.52	65.4	9.0	30.4
Chicot	15.5	10.3	9.3	49.9	14,117	11,800	-16.4	-9.9	1,005	1,142	-1,034	4,384	2.39	65.9	20.1	33.0
Clark	11.5	8.8	7.3	52.6	23,546	22,993	-2.3	-3.0	1,727	1,852	-570	8,783	2.25	62.6	14.3	31.6
Clay	13.5	11.8	9.7	51.3	17,609	16,083	-8.7	-7.2	1,219	1,713	-667	6,453	2.34	64.6	11.7	31.1
Cleburne	15.1	14.2	12.3	50.9	24,046	25,981	8.0	-3.6	1,737	2,675	23	10,360	2.44	68.4	10.6	28.4

1. No spouse present.

Table B. States and Counties — **Population, Vital Statistics, Health, and Crime**

STATE County	Daytime Population, 2012-2016			Births, 2017		Deaths, 2017		Persons under 65 with no health insurance, 2016		Medicare, 2017			Serious crimes known to police[2], 2016 Total	
	Persons in group quarters, 2017	Number	Employment/ residence ratio	Total	Rate[1]	Number	Rate[1]	Number	Percent	Total beneficiaries	Enrolled in Original Medicare	Enrolled in Medicare Advantage	Number	Rate[3]
	32	33	34	35	36	37	38	39	40	41	42	43	44	45
ALABAMA—Cont'd														
Washington	147	15,781	0.80	170	10.3	201	12.2	1,783	13.1	3,923	2,848	1,075	244	1,469
Wilcox	108	11,102	0.99	131	12.2	123	11.5	919	10.5	3,179	2,549	630	257	2,350
Winston	301	23,386	0.93	231	9.7	321	13.5	2,403	12.9	6,219	4,730	1,489	296	1,248
ALASKA	27545	745,006	1.02	11,163	15.1	4,543	6.1	100,787	15.5	92,209	90,748	1,461	30,842	4,157
Aleutians East	1728	3,431	1.05	12	3.6	6	1.8	1,019	33.5	NA	NA	NA	NA	NA
Aleutians West	2526	6,682	1.24	34	5.9	8	1.4	1,134	22.3	0	0	0	NA	NA
Anchorage	7927	308,230	1.06	4,479	15.2	1,773	6.0	33,891	12.9	37,547	36,879	668	18,071	6,042
Bethel	342	18,032	1.03	424	23.5	146	8.1	3,931	23.9	949	D	D	NA	NA
Bristol Bay	16	1,163	1.41	10	11.5	8	9.2	178	22.9	719	D	D	NA	NA
Denali	105	2,621	1.38	29	14.0	7	3.4	255	14.5	D	D	D	NA	NA
Dillingham	50	5,059	1.04	104	21.1	38	7.7	943	20.9	566	D	D	NA	NA
Fairbanks North Star	4909	99,491	0.99	1,700	17.1	494	5.0	11,887	13.6	10,029	9,930	99	NA	NA
Haines	0	2,466	0.95	17	6.7	6	2.4	413	20.5	557	D	D	NA	NA
Hoonah-Angoon	0	2,139	1.03	16	7.5	12	5.6	430	25.3	96	D	D	NA	NA
Juneau	1036	32,861	1.02	357	11.1	175	5.5	3,658	13.1	5,124	5,074	51	1,877	5,694
Kenai Peninsula	1688	56,689	0.96	732	12.5	486	8.3	8,646	17.9	10,860	10,597	264	NA	NA
Ketchikan Gateway	264	13,881	1.02	148	10.7	82	5.9	1,937	16.6	2,473	2,450	23	NA	NA
Kodiak Island	385	14,285	1.05	208	15.5	43	3.2	2,639	21.7	1,027	D	D	NA	NA
Kusilvak	18	8,170	1.08	233	28.4	90	11.0	1,683	22.2	519	D	D	NA	NA
Lake and Peninsula	37	1,555	1.24	36	22.2	12	7.4	397	28.0	NA	NA	NA	NA	NA
Matanuska-Susitna	2289	85,749	0.68	1,568	14.7	589	5.5	14,355	15.7	11,674	11,463	211	NA	NA
Nome	184	9,952	1.02	209	21.1	117	11.8	1,938	21.5	815	D	D	NA	NA
North Slope	2651	18,244	2.62	154	15.7	60	6.1	1,774	19.6	496	D	D	NA	NA
Northwest Arctic	380	8,098	1.15	166	21.6	84	10.9	1,694	24.0	557	D	D	NA	NA
Petersburg	43	3,191	1.00	29	8.8	21	6.4	575	21.4	1,226	1,213	13	NA	NA
Prince of Wales-Hyder	49	6,386	1.00	77	12.0	56	8.7	1,346	24.3	776	D	D	NA	NA
Sitka	254	9,013	1.02	83	9.6	41	4.7	1,471	19.7	1,390	1,379	12	NA	NA
Skagway	32	1,015	1.00	13	11.2	14	12.1	142	14.7	659	D	D	NA	NA
Southeast Fairbanks	372	7,305	1.11	101	14.7	33	4.8	1,271	21.4	666	D	D	NA	NA
Valdez-Cordova	192	10,500	1.22	131	14.1	40	4.3	1,408	17.0	1,741	1,718	23	NA	NA
Wrangell	19	2,406	1.00	20	7.9	24	9.5	372	19.0	NA	NA	NA	NA	NA
Yakutat	18	686	1.11	8	13.2	2	3.3	119	23.2	D	D	D	NA	NA
Yukon-Koyukuk	31	5,706	1.05	65	12.1	76	14.2	1,281	27.6	1,267	1,253	14	NA	NA
ARIZONA	155143	6,702,334	0.99	85,634	12.2	57,553	8.2	669,819	11.9	1,223,619	748,849	474,770	239,015	3,448
Apache	913	70,837	0.92	1,073	15.0	684	9.6	12,002	19.5	11,370	10,515	855	334	467
Cochise	4820	128,815	1.01	1,498	12.0	1,292	10.4	9,801	10.5	30,376	20,882	9,494	2,939	2,609
Coconino	11486	137,479	0.99	1,615	11.5	888	6.3	15,639	13.8	23,282	19,929	3,353	4,716	3,361
Gila	939	53,868	1.04	589	11.0	831	15.5	5,448	14.4	16,025	13,802	2,223	2,087	3,923
Graham	2806	36,131	0.88	565	15.1	276	7.4	3,025	10.2	5,559	3,615	1,944	682	1,802
Greenlee	35	11,187	1.55	150	15.9	35	3.7	703	8.4	1,249	1,052	197	105	1,071
La Paz	300	20,993	1.11	212	10.3	268	13.0	2,420	19.6	5,276	4,194	1,082	557	2,766
Maricopa	62769	4,130,907	1.02	55,050	12.8	31,286	7.3	418,740	11.7	651,276	378,843	272,433	144,667	3,405
Mohave	4540	193,564	0.85	1,798	8.7	3,169	15.3	17,171	12.1	61,030	42,546	18,484	6,743	3,351
Navajo	2065	108,780	1.02	1,523	14.0	1,029	9.4	12,345	13.9	22,481	17,969	4,512	2,339	2,153
Pima	25202	1,002,090	1.00	11,490	11.2	9,881	9.7	88,068	11.0	214,923	115,262	99,661	48,215	4,737
Pinal	25460	345,547	0.62	4,542	10.6	3,090	7.2	35,200	11.3	66,945	39,508	27,437	7,086	1,727
Santa Cruz	399	46,579	1.00	628	13.6	324	7.0	5,598	14.9	9,552	4,573	4,979	768	1,656
Yavapai	4202	214,452	0.95	1,887	8.3	2,895	12.7	19,797	12.8	71,186	50,556	20,630	4,926	2,189
Yuma	9207	201,105	0.97	3,014	14.5	1,605	7.7	23,862	15.1	32,992	25,536	7,456	4,418	2,143
ARKANSAS	84942	2,967,141	1.00	38,236	12.7	30,395	10.1	228,342	9.4	616,804	477,290	139,515	114,134	3,819
Arkansas	247	20,212	1.21	233	13.0	223	12.4	1,300	8.9	4,253	3,671	581	783	4,278
Ashley	191	20,922	0.99	214	10.6	250	12.3	1,321	8.1	5,085	4,477	608	573	2,778
Baxter	595	41,938	1.06	372	9.0	678	16.4	2,408	8.5	14,859	10,624	4,234	1,378	3,367
Benton	2151	253,027	1.07	3,692	13.9	1,701	6.4	22,490	10.0	38,029	25,442	12,587	5,738	2,313
Boone	465	38,179	1.06	450	12.0	457	12.2	2,501	8.5	10,647	8,132	2,514	1,089	2,923
Bradley	224	10,703	0.90	135	12.4	134	12.3	1,010	11.6	2,508	2,189	319	207	1,880
Calhoun	175	4,838	0.83	45	8.6	48	9.1	335	8.6	1,034	841	192	80	1,537
Carroll	230	27,393	0.97	324	11.6	296	10.6	2,967	14.0	6,759	4,674	2,085	546	1,970
Chicot	770	11,346	1.04	124	11.7	165	15.5	757	9.5	2,693	2,211	483	324	2,980
Clark	2892	21,855	0.92	225	10.1	255	11.4	1,371	8.5	4,792	3,748	1,045	725	3,215
Clay	125	13,725	0.76	166	11.1	200	13.4	1,030	9.0	4,022	3,410	612	204	1,368
Cleburne	339	24,614	0.90	227	9.1	382	15.3	1,774	9.6	7,554	6,332	1,222	730	2,881

1. Per 1,000 estimated resident population.   2. Data for serious crimes have not been adjusted for underreporting; this may affect comparability between geographic areas and over time.
3. Per 100,000 population estimated by the FBI.

Table B. States and Counties — Crime, Education, Money Income, and Poverty

STATE County	Serious crimes known to police, 2016 (cont.)[1] Rate		Education School enrollment and attainment, 2012-2016 Enrollment[3]		Attainment[4] (percent)		Local government expenditures,[5] 2013-2014		Money income, 2012-2016		Households Percent		Income and poverty, 2016	Percent below poverty level	
	Violent	Property	Total	Percent private	High school graduate or less	Bachelor's degree or more	Total current spending (mil dol)	Current spending per student (dollars)	Per capita income[6]	Median income (dollars)	with income of less than $50,000	with income of $200,000 or more	Median household income (dollars)	All persons	Children under 18 years	Children 5 to 17 years in families
	46	47	48	49	50	51	52	53	54	55	56	57	58	59	60	61

ALABAMA—Cont'd

Washington	289	1,180	3,882	5.8	66.1	9.6	27.2	8,832	19,598	40,293	61.4	0.9	37,575	18.2	26.5	24.8
Wilcox	640	1,710	2,702	15.9	65.1	11.3	19.0	10,143	14,800	24,442	73.8	0.8	24,216	31.9	48.8	46.7
Winston	101	1,147	4,991	4.4	58.3	13.1	39.8	9,288	19,299	33,896	65.6	0.9	38,644	17.3	25.1	24.2
ALASKA	804	3,353	192,109	12.2	35.4	28.8	2,404.0	18,359	34,191	74,444	32.5	6.8	76,144	9.9	13.6	12.3
Aleutians East	NA	NA	395	2.3	57.7	11.9	9.4	37,811	31,025	65,926	35.7	4.2	63,991	14.8	13.5	11.4
Aleutians West	NA	NA	951	5.4	52.8	15.7	12.8	25,643	35,083	86,964	26.4	8.2	78,151	8.0	8.2	6.9
Anchorage	1144	4,898	79,402	13.4	30.7	34.3	758.6	15,641	37,864	80,862	28.7	8.8	83,959	7.2	10.2	9.1
Bethel	NA	NA	5,424	0.8	64.5	11.4	150.3	29,466	18,231	53,296	47.3	2.7	46,634	25.5	33.8	32.0
Bristol Bay	NA	NA	228	9.2	42.2	19.1	20.3	39,420	41,420	88,000	28.1	5.0	68,026	11.4	14.2	14.4
Denali	NA	NA	355	22.0	27.1	38.5	10.0	11,793	38,337	81,302	28.6	5.8	72,378	6.3	8.5	7.7
Dillingham	NA	NA	1,372	3.4	50.1	17.6	33.7	29,813	23,520	56,055	44.9	3.2	52,250	19.6	31.9	31.9
Fairbanks North Star	NA	NA	28,690	12.8	27.8	33.4	276.0	17,678	34,182	73,831	32.4	5.9	73,427	8.5	9.9	9.3
Haines	NA	NA	405	4.9	30.2	40.4	6.3	23,352	32,673	53,125	46.3	6.7	53,471	10.3	16.8	14.2
Hoonah-Angoon	NA	NA	343	16.3	43.3	24.3	9.1	33,793	31,451	54,091	44.5	1.1	53,884	19.1	35.4	31.2
Juneau	855	4,838	7,924	8.3	25.6	39.4	85.5	17,617	40,592	87,436	22.6	7.8	82,011	7.4	9.9	8.2
Kenai Peninsula	NA	NA	12,778	13.2	39.5	23.7	165.2	18,437	32,556	64,891	37.3	4.9	68,501	12.0	16.2	14.8
Ketchikan Gateway	NA	NA	3,033	10.1	39.7	23.8	42.1	18,364	32,694	64,162	38.4	5.9	67,125	9.2	12.9	11.3
Kodiak Island	NA	NA	3,584	16.2	36.6	24.8	51.3	20,336	32,066	73,068	32.3	4.7	74,683	7.3	9.3	8.3
Kusilvak	NA	NA	2,614	1.2	73.8	4.8	73.9	29,600	11,701	38,160	64.5	0.5	34,341	37.8	45.4	43.5
Lake and Peninsula	NA	NA	398	1.0	56.2	12.5	NA	NA	22,684	43,864	55.1	1.7	44,310	20.9	32.7	32.7
Matanuska-Susitna	NA	NA	26,717	16.2	39.4	20.6	273.0	15,349	30,078	73,908	33.7	5.6	71,793	9.5	10.2	9.3
Nome	NA	NA	2,875	1.3	58.2	13.9	81.2	31,209	20,033	51,563	48.5	3.4	55,974	24.0	30.6	28.2
North Slope	NA	NA	2,226	4.2	49.5	14.2	74.2	36,981	49,982	72,027	35.7	7.9	74,998	11.9	14.8	13.4
Northwest Arctic	NA	NA	2,205	2.4	65.8	10.8	67.6	32,679	21,028	61,341	40.8	4.1	53,692	27.8	36.6	33.3
Petersburg	NA	NA	686	11.5	41.3	25.0	13.5	25,030	34,788	63,940	36.9	4.5	60,540	8.4	13.0	12.3
Prince of Wales-Hyder	NA	NA	1,370	8.3	48.6	15.8	31.1	23,992	25,564	51,887	48.3	1.7	48,888	17.5	25.2	22.5
Sitka	NA	NA	1,970	7.8	33.0	32.4	26.4	14,989	35,655	70,160	33.1	4.9	72,795	7.9	9.4	8.0
Skagway	NA	NA	157	7.6	28.4	33.7	2.7	24,935	39,412	64,853	29.7	2.1	65,112	4.4	9.2	8.5
Southeast Fairbanks	NA	NA	1,658	22.0	42.7	19.2	27.1	21,574	30,757	63,713	37.9	2.7	59,412	11.8	16.9	15.3
Valdez-Cordova	NA	NA	2,294	12.7	34.5	30.1	31.5	22,678	35,457	82,511	32.3	7.5	69,755	9.2	11.3	10.5
Wrangell	NA	NA	480	5.0	46.2	20.3	8.0	23,308	29,782	52,986	47.2	2.4	56,747	11.5	18.4	16.1
Yakutat	NA	NA	128	11.7	46.3	19.7	3.0	31,082	31,084	66,875	39.7	1.2	57,687	16.8	31.7	32.9
Yukon-Koyukuk	NA	NA	1,447	4.0	57.0	12.3	60.3	10,819	20,812	38,451	60.0	1.3	37,906	23.0	28.1	26.5
ARIZONA	470	2,978	1,750,958	11.0	38.0	28.0	8,167.8	7,412	26,686	51,340	48.7	4.2	53,481	16.4	23.6	22.6
Apache	87	380	21,074	4.2	55.3	11.1	138.9	12,177	13,428	32,460	67.5	0.5	34,040	33.2	41.1	40.9
Cochise	348	2,261	30,847	10.0	36.6	23.2	158.8	8,084	23,757	45,383	54.4	2.7	45,151	21.1	33.2	33.5
Coconino	367	2,994	47,769	7.1	32.7	34.2	170.0	8,991	24,711	51,106	49.1	4.0	53,643	17.8	20.7	20.4
Gila	773	3,151	10,197	10.0	44.4	17.7	69.5	8,870	21,470	40,563	61.1	1.4	40,747	20.3	33.5	32.9
Graham	103	1,699	10,453	6.0	47.5	13.3	51.2	7,413	17,710	47,422	52.2	1.2	46,714	22.9	26.5	25.7
Greenlee	20	1,050	2,510	8.1	48.9	12.2	15.0	8,920	23,778	51,813	48.4	1.7	61,110	12.0	13.6	11.1
La Paz	273	2,493	3,338	4.2	61.3	10.4	24.1	9,638	21,447	36,321	64.6	0.8	34,285	24.8	37.9	36.6
Maricopa	432	2,973	1,091,668	11.6	36.0	31.0	5,144.8	7,156	28,791	55,676	44.8	5.2	58,742	15.0	21.5	20.7
Mohave	239	3,112	37,908	15.0	52.1	11.9	172.2	7,050	22,026	39,856	61.3	1.6	42,003	18.3	28.7	27.3
Navajo	248	1,906	28,692	6.0	48.8	14.5	177.1	9,619	16,564	36,868	61.8	1.4	37,440	28.2	37.7	36.1
Pima	495	4,242	263,261	10.3	34.8	30.8	1,149.6	7,936	26,204	46,764	52.8	3.3	47,644	18.2	26.8	25.1
Pinal	214	1,513	93,373	10.8	44.3	18.5	384.7	7,025	21,982	51,190	48.8	2.0	52,642	15.4	21.5	20.2
Santa Cruz	147	1,509	13,110	7.2	51.4	22.5	75.2	7,502	18,860	38,941	60.7	1.9	39,090	20.9	34.5	32.8
Yavapai	288	1,901	43,373	15.8	35.6	25.5	185.5	7,628	26,584	46,638	53.5	2.3	49,824	13.3	19.7	19.1
Yuma	290	1,853	53,385	6.1	53.8	14.4	251.2	6,748	19,483	41,467	58.8	1.8	42,998	19.3	29.0	28.0
ARKANSAS	551	3,269	745,905	11.1	49.5	21.5	4,688.2	9,568	23,401	42,336	57.1	2.6	44,406	17.2	24.0	22.3
Arkansas	486	3,791	4,013	8.5	58.1	14.4	27.9	9,190	23,287	37,330	64.3	2.7	39,726	18.1	27.9	26.0
Ashley	315	2,463	5,065	6.0	55.8	13.6	34.8	8,829	20,290	36,352	63.3	1.4	41,277	17.9	29.8	27.5
Baxter	225	3,142	7,381	10.4	47.1	17.7	46.0	8,909	23,068	38,115	64.0	1.5	40,147	12.7	22.2	20.1
Benton	312	2,001	61,893	12.9	43.3	30.7	378.3	9,173	28,996	59,016	42.3	5.8	64,072	9.1	11.9	10.9
Boone	690	2,233	7,973	8.7	49.6	15.0	54.5	8,688	21,719	38,664	62.8	2.8	39,881	15.4	24.1	21.7
Bradley	309	1,572	2,619	6.2	61.6	14.2	22.0	10,633	20,465	34,665	64.0	1.3	34,114	23.5	34.2	32.2
Calhoun	250	1,287	1,091	7.6	66.4	12.0	6.1	11,424	21,093	35,446	63.8	0.6	33,507	17.1	24.3	23.0
Carroll	361	1,609	5,490	13.3	51.1	17.7	36.9	9,262	20,888	38,145	62.2	1.6	37,145	17.2	28.1	25.7
Chicot	340	2,640	2,800	12.4	62.0	13.1	18.9	11,515	18,853	29,628	68.3	1.7	29,527	30.1	44.0	39.6
Clark	399	2,816	7,607	16.7	44.3	24.7	39.3	13,778	19,500	35,595	61.6	1.5	37,247	22.3	27.8	25.3
Clay	221	1,146	3,161	5.4	63.3	11.3	21.4	8,304	19,192	32,404	68.9	0.9	36,037	19.1	26.8	24.4
Cleburne	462	2,419	4,714	9.9	54.9	15.4	31.5	9,188	25,078	41,717	57.4	2.7	42,397	16.3	24.9	22.9

1. Data for serious crimes have not been adjusted for underreporting; this may affect comparability between geographic areas and over time.   2. Per 100,000 population estimated by the FBI.
3. All persons 3 years old and over enrolled in nursery school through college.   4. Persons 25 years old and over.   5. Elementary and secondary education expenditures.
6. Based on population estimated by the American Community Survey, 2011–2015.

STATE County	Personal income, 2016										Earnings, 2016		
			Per capita[1]			Supplements to wages and salaries, employer contributions (mil dol)						Contributions for government social insurance (mil dol)	
	Total (mil dol)	Percent change 2015-2016	Dollars	Rank	Wages and salaries (mil dol)	Pension and insurance	Government social insurance	Proprietors' income (mil dol)	Dividends, interest, and rent (mil dol)	Personal transfer reecipts (mil dol)	Total (mil dol)	From employee and self-employed	From employer
	62	63	64	65	66	67	68	69	70	71	72	73	74
ALABAMA—Cont'd													
Washington	568	0.6	33,889	2,341	226	48	16	27	63	164	317	38	16
Wilcox	314	0.9	28,553	2,947	126	25	9	18	49	142	178	23	9
Winston	791	1.8	33,215	2,442	270	50	20	82	120	251	422	52	20
ALASKA	41283	-1.0	55,674	X	20,529	5,170	1,520	3,532	7,236	6,615	30,751	1,588	1,520
Aleutians East	199	17.6	60,284	146	138	30	11	16	14	11	196	21	11
Aleutians West	317	5.1	56,105	209	232	49	18	21	27	21	319	34	18
Anchorage	18582	-1.9	62,317	121	9,955	2,228	763	1,782	3,394	2,668	14,728	1,545	763
Bethel	734	3.0	40,826	1,255	317	125	21	21	67	238	485	42	21
Bristol Bay	58	-1.5	64,069	101	67	17	5	10	13	9	99	10	5
Denali	136	3.2	69,535	69	108	23	9	7	20	38	147	17	9
Dillingham	267	1.4	53,923	271	122	37	10	25	46	49	193	19	10
Fairbanks North Star	5397	0.6	53,647	275	2,620	736	207	298	988	826	3,861	392	207
Haines	126	-0.4	50,667	386	39	11	3	17	36	28	69	7	3
Hoonah-Angoon	115	-0.5	55,511	223	31	12	2	10	25	28	56	5	2
Juneau	2048	0.2	63,070	111	1,033	338	66	156	388	237	1,593	137	66
Kenai Peninsula	2966	-3.1	50,691	385	1,051	302	74	222	577	568	1,648	164	74
Ketchikan Gateway	869	0.4	63,222	109	386	113	28	125	145	147	652	61	28
Kodiak Island	808	-1.8	58,843	166	350	101	28	134	152	111	613	58	28
Kusilvak	252	3.2	31,301	2,703	72	48	3	3	21	113	126	8	3
Lake and Peninsula	85	-2.2	54,491	253	36	15	2	4	19	18	57	5	2
Matanuska-Susitna	4684	-0.8	44,880	787	1,100	307	81	371	661	701	1,859	185	81
Nome	498	3.2	50,254	404	200	73	13	43	50	145	329	27	13
North Slope	359	-3.7	37,332	1,757	1,457	230	94	7	85	60	1,789	191	94
Northwest Arctic	369	1.9	48,039	532	201	54	13	10	31	119	278	27	13
Petersburg	198	-4.1	62,773	116	61	21	4	42	47	40	129	11	4
Prince of Wales-Hyder	259	1.1	40,750	1,267	94	38	6	22	48	59	159	13	6
Sitka	552	-5.2	62,537	117	215	64	16	75	132	75	369	34	16
Skagway	85	4.4	77,977	33	38	10	3	10	17	9	61	6	3
Southeast Fairbanks	299	0.0	43,473	941	178	44	12	23	53	75	256	27	12
Valdez-Cordova	574	-2.3	61,337	132	288	81	20	57	99	77	446	42	20
Wrangell	114	0.4	47,105	598	37	13	3	14	24	28	66	6	3
Yakutat	33	-11.2	54,161	266	12	5	1	4	6	7	21	2	1
Yukon-Koyukuk	303	5.4	54,850	243	93	46	5	5	50	108	149	11	5
ARIZONA	280120	3.6	40,546	X	139,321	20,901	10,047	18,776	53,502	58,072	189,044	11,982	10,047
Apache	2174	3.3	29,737	2,867	784	202	60	44	304	961	1,090	130	60
Cochise	4900	1.7	38,962	1,501	1,840	429	150	255	978	1,563	2,673	316	150
Coconino	5926	2.8	42,057	1,095	2,746	577	205	362	1,290	1,139	3,891	437	205
Gila	1944	1.4	36,294	1,954	613	123	46	69	395	802	851	113	46
Graham	1116	1.0	29,689	2,874	370	81	27	50	140	399	527	61	27
Greenlee	355	0.5	36,936	1,833	289	47	19	8	33	88	364	40	19
La Paz	646	7.0	31,781	2,647	219	46	16	43	118	238	324	40	16
Maricopa	185112	3.9	43,628	914	103,249	14,031	7,327	12,835	34,715	31,420	137,442	15,864	7,327
Mohave	6167	2.9	30,045	2,840	1,878	321	142	333	1,080	2,218	2,675	370	142
Navajo	3236	3.7	29,408	2,901	1,185	240	97	132	516	1,333	1,654	215	97
Pima	40182	2.4	39,541	1,419	17,526	3,140	1,295	2,294	8,946	9,879	24,256	2,879	1,295
Pinal	11690	5.0	27,930	2,983	2,661	523	194	501	1,569	3,463	3,878	487	194
Santa Cruz	1612	2.6	35,052	2,155	624	131	49	216	306	405	1,019	116	49
Yavapai	8200	3.9	36,353	1,941	2,495	433	185	546	2,139	2,566	3,659	481	185
Yuma	6861	6.1	33,365	2,416	2,842	576	234	1,088	974	1,598	4,740	479	234
ARKANSAS	118698	2.1	39,722	X	53,993	8,094	4,099	7,637	25,810	28,348	73,822	4,922	4,099
Arkansas	787	4.3	43,192	979	433	66	35	127	101	190	660	74	35
Ashley	684	1.9	33,361	2,417	309	45	25	47	82	244	425	55	25
Baxter	1418	0.8	34,537	2,236	548	92	43	67	286	538	750	107	43
Benton	19773	0.6	76,554	39	7,072	783	493	462	10,261	1,697	8,809	1,056	493
Boone	1232	2.4	33,026	2,467	561	91	43	70	199	393	765	100	43
Bradley	358	-1.9	32,521	2,545	136	23	11	35	45	142	205	25	11
Calhoun	163	3.1	31,737	2,654	141	20	10	4	19	50	175	22	10
Carroll	866	1.5	31,339	2,701	347	59	28	53	167	262	487	63	28
Chicot	368	4.5	33,652	2,370	117	19	9	43	49	146	188	21	9
Clark	729	3.1	32,165	2,584	346	62	28	34	109	234	469	59	28
Clay	510	3.2	34,214	2,288	115	20	9	59	66	176	203	24	9
Cleburne	867	0.3	34,327	2,279	236	42	19	50	198	288	346	49	19

1. Based on the resident population estimated as of July 1 of the year shown.

Table B. States and Counties — Earnings, Social Security, and Housing

STATE County	Earnings, 2016 (cont.) Percent by selected industries									Social Security beneficiaries, December 2016			Housing units, 2017	
	Farm	Mining, quarrying, and extracting	Construction	Manu-facturing	Information; professional, scientific, technical services	Retail trade	Finance, insurance, real estate, and leasing	Health care and social assistance	Govern-ment	Number	Rate[1]	Supple-mental Security Income recipients, 2016	Total	Percent change, 2010-2017
	75	76	77	78	79	80	81	82	83	84	85	86	87	88
ALABAMA—Cont'd														
Washington	2.7	D	4.5	40.0	D	2.1	D	D	14.1	4,720	284	695	8,537	1.5
Wilcox	5.0	0.0	3.6	36.1	D	4.4	2.7	D	21.4	3,765	346	1,425	5,747	1.8
Winston	2.8	D	4.3	39.5	D	6.3	3.3	8.2	13.9	6,885	288	1,027	13,679	1.6
ALASKA	0.1	8.0	7.2	3.1	7.2	5.5	4.0	11.5	31.4	95,500	129	12,449	316,952	3.3
Aleutians East	0.0	0.1	D	74.0	D	1.0	D	D	10.9	160	48	11	753	0.8
Aleutians West	1.9	D	1.9	44.7	D	4.3	D	2.4	14.2	240	42	15	1,958	1.5
Anchorage	0.0	5.5	6.4	1.0	10.9	5.6	5.4	13.6	27.5	35,940	121	5,879	117,289	3.8
Bethel	0.0	D	2.8	D	D	4.9	4.9	D	46.6	1,780	99	412	6,025	1.8
Bristol Bay	0.0	0.0	D	42.9	D	D	D	D	21.8	120	133	8	976	0.8
Denali	0.0	D	D	0.6	8.7	0.9	D	0.6	23.0	250	122	12	1,764	-0.3
Dillingham	0.0	D	2.4	D	D	3.8	D	24.7	28.3	560	113	109	2,452	1.0
Fairbanks North Star	0.1	3.2	10.2	1.1	4.0	5.4	2.9	9.9	47.3	10,830	108	1,075	44,302	6.0
Haines	0.0	D	13.0	8.2	D	8.8	D	9.6	22.7	595	235	48	1,670	2.4
Hoonah-Angoon	0.0	0.0	D	3.6	D	4.9	D	D	48.5	465	217	44	1,780	1.4
Juneau	0.0	D	6.4	1.3	5.5	5.3	3.5	7.3	47.9	4,445	137	521	13,734	5.2
Kenai Peninsula	0.1	7.2	7.6	5.7	4.3	6.7	3.8	12.7	30.1	11,340	194	1,009	31,250	2.2
Ketchikan Gateway	0.0	D	7.9	5.4	2.5	9.0	4.7	9.8	32.6	2,330	170	243	6,377	3.3
Kodiak Island	0.0	0.7	4.1	13.6	1.7	3.3	2.4	D	33.2	1,660	121	153	5,410	2.0
Kusilvak	0.0	0.0	D	D	0.0	6.5	D	D	71.0	815	100	201	2,239	2.6
Lake and Peninsula	0.0	0.2	D	6.7	D	0.8	D	D	47.4	185	115	25	1,512	0.4
Matanuska-Susitna	0.3	0.6	18.8	0.9	5.9	9.9	3.7	14.1	26.7	13,845	133	1,608	41,877	1.3
Nome	0.0	D	6.7	D	1.4	4.3	2.8	D	43.2	1,115	112	211	4,103	2.4
North Slope	0.0	61.1	D	D	D	0.7	D	D	11.9	670	69	28	2,625	5.0
Northwest Arctic	0.0	D	D	0.1	D	D	D	D	30.8	750	98	100	2,741	1.3
Petersburg	0.0	D	4.8	9.0	2.3	6.1	1.7	2.0	37.3	720	220	46	1,689	2.7
Prince of Wales-Hyder	0.0	D	2.9	5.9	D	7.3	3.4	3.8	51.3	1,020	157	110	3,434	2.3
Sitka	0.0	0.8	8.3	8.0	2.1	6.3	2.4	11.7	35.0	1,330	152	90	4,220	2.9
Skagway	0.0	0.0	3.7	5.2	D	16.4	D	D	27.2	125	111	0	689	8.3
Southeast Fairbanks	0.0	D	4.8	D	4.7	5.0	0.6	D	32.4	1,250	183	152	3,906	-0.2
Valdez-Cordova	0.0	D	6.9	7.2	3.7	4.3	D	4.9	29.2	1,425	153	108	6,175	1.2
Wrangell	0.0	0.3	3.7	8.2	D	7.2	1.5	D	40.6	510	204	32	1,452	2.3
Yakutat	0.0	1.1	D	D	D	D	0.0	1.0	54.2	115	188	0	457	1.6
Yukon-Koyukuk	0.0	2.0	D	D	D	4.1	D	10.5	64.8	910	168	190	4,093	1.4
ARIZONA	0.8	0.8	5.6	8.0	10.3	7.4	10.2	12.5	16.6	1,274,815	185	119,079	2,999,157	5.4
Apache	0.5	0.9	1.5	0.6	1.8	D	2.1	13.0	61.2	12,735	178	4,216	32,867	1.1
Cochise	3.7	0.2	3.6	1.3	8.1	5.9	3.0	8.6	49.2	31,755	253	3,040	61,062	3.4
Coconino	0.2	0.2	4.3	10.3	3.5	6.9	4.3	14.9	32.4	19,780	141	2,518	66,071	4.3
Gila	0.1	10.3	5.6	12.0	D	7.1	2.0	9.3	33.8	17,110	321	1,416	33,545	2.6
Graham	3.0	D	2.5	2.1	4.9	9.0	D	11.1	35.7	6,250	165	772	13,489	3.9
Greenlee	0.9	D	1.5	0.0	D	D	D	D	8.7	1,520	158	117	4,460	2.0
La Paz	5.1	0.2	2.1	2.3	4.4	10.4	D	D	41.4	5,730	279	483	16,294	1.5
Maricopa	0.2	0.5	6.0	8.1	11.5	7.4	12.3	12.2	12.0	672,860	159	60,980	1,738,157	6.0
Mohave	0.2	0.2	6.2	6.6	5.1	12.2	4.7	21.0	17.7	65,910	321	4,718	114,500	3.2
Navajo	0.5	2.8	6.6	0.8	6.8	8.4	2.4	13.8	35.2	23,460	217	4,629	57,823	1.6
Pima	0.2	0.8	4.6	10.6	9.4	6.6	5.9	14.8	24.9	214,365	212	20,366	459,915	4.3
Pinal	4.3	2.2	4.9	6.0	3.7	7.7	3.5	7.4	35.5	80,960	195	6,159	173,681	9.1
Santa Cruz	0.5	0.2	2.5	2.8	2.9	8.6	3.0	3.5	34.9	9,490	206	1,416	18,311	1.7
Yavapai	0.2	2.6	8.2	6.0	5.6	9.5	5.3	16.0	19.6	77,005	343	3,740	116,541	5.5
Yuma	17.1	0.1	3.4	3.1	4.5	7.3	2.9	9.6	28.9	35,885	175	4,509	92,441	5.2
ARKANSAS	1.8	0.6	5.7	12.8	6.3	7.0	5.8	12.7	17.5	685,361	229	108,580	1,370,111	4.1
Arkansas	10.5	0.1	3.0	34.8	3.0	7.0	3.4	7.1	8.9	4,645	255	734	9,458	0.3
Ashley	4.7	0.0	9.8	33.0	D	5.2	2.5	D	12.2	5,775	282	913	10,167	0.3
Baxter	-0.2	D	5.2	16.9	4.8	9.5	8.3	27.0	11.5	16,020	389	1,034	22,880	1.3
Benton	0.5	0.1	5.0	6.9	8.9	4.9	2.9	5.9	6.7	43,625	169	3,515	105,269	13.1
Boone	-0.4	0.0	D	12.9	4.1	9.4	4.2	9.1	22.2	11,075	298	1,148	16,986	0.9
Bradley	5.4	D	4.2	19.8	1.7	5.3	3.8	16.3	19.1	2,860	260	539	5,797	-1.1
Calhoun	0.3	D	3.9	72.4	D	D	D	1.8	7.3	1,360	263	169	2,913	0.6
Carroll	3.5	D	7.4	28.9	2.6	7.1	5.1	9.8	12.3	5,720	287	605	13,708	1.1
Chicot	20.7	0.1	6.2	1.9	D	5.6	6.3	D	24.1	3,000	275	914	5,431	0.2
Clark	0.9	0.0	2.0	20.6	D	9.3	3.6	D	24.1	5,020	223	776	10,523	1.3
Clay	21.2	0.0	5.7	2.8	2.1	6.7	3.6	9.8	19.5	4,675	310	650	8,017	-0.2
Cleburne	0.8	3.6	8.3	17.2	4.2	8.8	6.1	D	14.5	8,465	336	729	16,061	1.5

1. Per 1,000 resident population estimated as of July 1 of the year shown.

Table B. States and Counties — Housing, Labor Force, and Employment

STATE County	Housing units, 2017 (cont.)								Civilian labor force, 2017				Civilian employment[6], 2012-2016		
	Occupied units										Unemployment			Percent	
			Owner-occupied			Renter-occupied									
				Median owner cost as a percent of income			Median rent as a percent of income[2]	Sub-standard units[4] (percent)		Percent change, 2016-2017				Management, business, science, and arts	Construction, production, and maintenance occupations
	Total	Percent	Median value[1]	With a mortgage	Without a mortgage[2]	Median rent[3]			Total		Total	Rate[5]	Total		
	89	90	91	92	93	94	95	96	97	98	99	100	101	102	103
ALABAMA—Cont'd															
Washington	6113	83.7	81,100	19.9	11.9	615	24.9	3.3	6,656	-1.2	455	6.8	5,644	19.7	45.7
Wilcox	3792	62.7	81,600	21.4	15.0	457	32.3	0.9	2,808	-0.4	320	11.4	2,977	27.6	32.4
Winston	9436	75.9	77,700	22.6	13.1	540	27.3	2.0	9,646	1.2	482	5.0	8,934	24.6	38.5
ALASKA	250235	63.7	257,100	22.3	10.2	1,173	28.2	9.6	362,786	-0.1	25,978	7.2	353,954	36.7	23.4
Aleutians East	788	56.2	124,500	18.8	10.0	939	21.6	3.6	2,584	-0.3	65	2.5	2,466	14.9	65.3
Aleutians West	1186	28.3	211,400	19.7	14.1	1,257	18.3	13.0	3,861	-3.1	140	3.6	4,083	16.5	51.8
Anchorage	104969	60.3	298,000	22.2	10.6	1,231	29.0	4.5	155,462	-0.2	9,287	6.0	153,197	40.2	18.5
Bethel	4555	64.1	151,400	19.5	11.4	1,175	24.7	54.2	7,445	2.4	1,027	13.8	6,040	35.4	20.9
Bristol Bay	360	54.7	199,000	19.9	10.0	1,040	18.1	6.9	426	2.9	27	6.3	533	28.0	30.4
Denali	707	75.4	228,600	20.9	10.0	933	12.8	19.9	1,130	3.1	106	9.4	1,312	31.9	26.8
Dillingham	1375	60.5	196,400	21.9	12.8	1,018	23.6	31.7	2,055	-1.3	191	9.3	1,933	41.9	22.1
Fairbanks North Star	35303	59.5	224,000	23.6	11.3	1,240	30.2	11.0	46,708	0.3	2,940	6.3	47,009	37.6	23.0
Haines	1170	68.6	198,400	24.1	10.0	882	22.1	19.0	1,089	1.1	99	9.1	1,360	33.5	22.7
Hoonah-Angoon	836	71.4	235,100	24.0	10.0	785	24.3	12.4	1,140	-5.6	144	12.6	1,046	33.2	30.8
Juneau	12138	64.4	329,500	22.4	10.0	1,184	25.4	5.3	17,435	0.4	828	4.7	17,899	45.4	17.8
Kenai Peninsula	21481	71.6	229,200	21.7	10.0	970	25.8	7.9	27,095	-0.5	2,300	8.5	25,696	31.2	28.3
Ketchikan Gateway	5209	59.5	257,100	22.0	12.1	1,078	28.8	5.3	7,104	0.9	448	6.3	6,822	30.1	25.9
Kodiak Island	4585	60.7	266,700	25.7	10.0	1,254	27.6	9.3	6,447	0.3	329	5.1	7,273	27.3	32.9
Kusilvak	1734	74.0	101,300	16.8	13.2	607	17.6	67.1	2,805	2.6	563	20.1	2,156	29.4	25.5
Lake and Peninsula	468	67.9	143,800	21.7	12.8	743	17.7	26.3	723	10.0	86	11.9	618	32.8	33.2
Matanuska-Susitna	30839	75.8	230,100	22.1	10.0	1,079	29.2	8.7	47,397	-0.3	4,105	8.7	42,025	32.9	28.2
Nome	2879	60.2	138,300	20.1	13.5	1,260	26.5	42.5	4,089	-0.1	514	12.6	3,589	34.0	20.0
North Slope	2018	50.0	154,100	14.3	10.0	1,057	16.5	37.2	3,670	-7.4	273	7.4	5,393	27.8	38.6
Northwest Arctic	1904	54.8	146,400	19.2	14.1	1,226	19.0	46.5	2,961	-0.4	498	16.8	2,562	34.5	23.9
Petersburg	1237	67.9	213,400	18.6	10.0	912	30.2	3.6	1,413	-2.8	132	9.3	1,632	28.9	42.5
Prince of Wales-Hyder	2267	71.7	171,100	19.3	10.0	834	23.3	10.5	2,836	2.2	324	11.4	2,782	26.7	36.3
Sitka	3504	55.9	341,600	24.3	10.0	1,019	26.4	5.0	4,449	1.6	208	4.7	4,766	41.6	22.0
Skagway	428	54.4	305,700	23.2	10.7	1,028	20.7	4.9	824	2.0	87	10.6	699	27.5	27.5
Southeast Fairbanks	2085	71.7	201,600	20.3	10.0	1,132	24.0	14.1	2,969	-1.2	310	10.4	2,990	30.2	32.4
Valdez-Cordova	2937	71.7	227,900	19.6	10.0	879	19.6	8.1	4,898	1.6	390	8.0	4,518	29.8	32.3
Wrangell	1045	68.5	183,300	23.8	10.8	759	26.9	3.8	1,050	-0.6	81	7.7	1,096	31.4	28.1
Yakutat	247	60.3	165,800	22.0	11.9	975	25.5	9.3	235	-4.1	22	9.4	369	25.2	32.5
Yukon-Koyukuk	1981	70.9	90,800	19.8	11.3	631	22.2	45.9	2,486	2.3	454	18.3	2,090	35.0	26.3
ARIZONA	2448919	62.6	176,900	22.2	10.3	937	29.8	5.0	3,312,721	2.7	161,314	4.9	2,879,372	35.4	18.8
Apache	19351	76.9	77,900	21.4	10.0	503	18.0	25.8	20,419	1.0	2,127	10.4	18,258	29.7	24.9
Cochise	49230	67.8	140,700	20.8	10.0	790	29.2	3.7	49,373	0.0	2,771	5.6	42,925	33.8	17.3
Coconino	47366	59.1	231,300	22.6	10.0	1,025	32.1	10.0	75,381	2.1	4,186	5.6	65,260	36.5	18.3
Gila	21408	71.9	139,800	23.6	11.5	762	28.0	5.1	21,362	2.2	1,295	6.1	18,016	31.1	24.9
Graham	10915	69.4	121,400	20.0	10.7	794	26.9	8.7	14,423	0.8	785	5.4	12,014	28.6	26.5
Greenlee	3295	45.5	81,600	19.6	10.0	421	10.0	6.4	3,992	2.8	204	5.1	3,561	26.4	45.0
La Paz	9181	75.0	71,200	22.6	10.0	562	26.5	7.2	8,681	3.0	467	5.4	6,343	26.1	29.7
Maricopa	1465840	60.4	204,900	21.9	10.2	989	29.6	4.7	2,134,987	3.1	89,102	4.2	1,871,139	37.0	17.9
Mohave	82145	66.8	130,000	24.1	10.5	791	29.3	4.4	82,407	2.8	4,828	5.9	67,179	24.7	22.5
Navajo	34090	69.8	106,100	21.3	10.0	681	28.9	14.5	41,337	0.5	3,131	7.6	32,364	29.1	23.4
Pima	395390	61.3	160,800	22.5	10.8	831	31.7	4.3	475,622	1.7	21,330	4.5	428,188	35.8	17.2
Pinal	130801	72.5	142,200	22.0	10.7	990	28.9	4.1	168,806	3.4	8,473	5.0	140,965	30.2	22.8
Santa Cruz	15538	66.2	135,200	23.9	11.8	627	29.6	6.9	19,001	-0.5	1,807	9.5	17,393	27.6	23.0
Yavapai	93445	70.1	199,300	25.9	11.1	892	30.7	3.0	101,763	2.7	4,583	4.5	82,934	31.5	21.4
Yuma	70924	67.4	113,400	23.7	10.1	831	29.6	6.6	95,167	1.7	16,225	17.0	72,833	24.8	28.8
ARKANSAS	1141480	65.7	114,700	19.6	10.2	689	28.8	3.1	1,354,272	0.9	49,835	3.7	1,266,552	32.4	26.9
Arkansas	7685	64.6	77,600	21.9	10.0	632	27.8	1.1	9,013	-2.9	294	3.3	8,033	28.0	34.2
Ashley	8338	75.1	70,900	18.6	11.0	616	28.6	2.3	7,695	-0.7	441	5.7	8,062	27.9	35.4
Baxter	18061	75.3	123,100	22.4	11.0	638	27.4	1.8	16,401	1.7	694	4.2	15,427	30.1	28.6
Benton	88014	66.9	155,900	18.6	10.0	814	23.6	3.1	132,496	3.4	3,849	2.9	114,951	36.6	23.2
Boone	14883	72.0	114,400	20.4	10.6	606	27.3	3.0	15,821	-0.9	543	3.4	15,255	27.5	26.8
Bradley	4550	64.5	72,500	18.8	10.5	575	30.8	4.9	4,379	1.8	205	4.7	4,041	28.5	37.4
Calhoun	2079	81.8	71,800	18.6	10.0	645	34.7	1.4	2,361	-0.8	93	3.9	2,216	22.3	45.6
Carroll	10874	76.0	118,500	23.1	11.1	585	24.7	5.7	13,097	1.6	431	3.3	11,555	28.2	33.7
Chicot	4384	66.2	59,600	19.8	14.4	571	29.8	2.8	3,505	-2.3	229	6.5	3,688	28.6	24.5
Clark	8783	63.1	92,700	17.6	10.6	584	30.7	2.4	9,470	0.7	377	4.0	10,042	33.8	22.3
Clay	6453	72.6	66,700	19.6	11.8	513	31.3	3.3	5,908	-2.3	269	4.6	6,270	22.9	36.1
Cleburne	10360	75.3	126,100	20.3	10.3	679	30.3	2.2	9,351	-1.5	458	4.9	9,767	26.4	34.2

1. Specified owner-occupied units.   2. A value of 10.0 represents 10 percent or less; a value of 50.0 represents 50 percent or more.   3. Specified renter-occupied units.   4. Overcrowded or lacking complete plumbing facilities.   5. Percent of civilian labor force.   6. Civilian employed persons 16 years old and over.

Table B. States and Counties — Nonfarm Employment and Agriculture

STATE County	Private nonfarm establishments, employment and payroll, 2016									Agriculture, 2012			
	Number of establish-ments	Employment						Annual payroll		Farms			Farm operators whose principal occupation is farming (percent)
		Total	Health care and social assistance	Manufac-turing	Retail trade	Finance and insurance	Professional, scientific, and technical services	Total (mil dol)	Average per employee (dollars)	Number	Percent with:		
											Fewer than 50 acres	500 acres or more	
	104	105	106	107	108	109	110	111	112	113	114	115	116
ALABAMA—Cont'd													
Washington	210	4,979	283	3,417	264	55	32	377	75,753	371	31.3	6.2	43.4
Wilcox	180	1,918	268	D	233	86	19	88	45,973	316	30.7	24.1	44.9
Winston	448	6,393	731	2,765	884	174	90	195	30,454	520	32.3	3.3	51.0
ALASKA	21077	266,072	49,799	12,701	35,101	7,602	19,498	15,239	57,275	762	56.2	11.3	54.1
Aleutians East	55	2,265	D	D	57	D	NA	92	40,677	NA	NA	NA	NA
Aleutians West	115	3,720	103	2,600	154	D	11	154	41,447	NA	NA	NA	NA
Anchorage	8798	147,302	25,839	1,845	16,111	5,015	15,488	8,950	60,759	291	56.7	5.8	56.4
Bethel	261	3,189	1,129	48	768	32	18	142	44,457	NA	NA	NA	NA
Bristol Bay	77	392	D	98	44	D	D	48	123,000	NA	NA	NA	NA
Denali	104	459	13	NA	32	D	4	48	105,303	NA	NA	NA	NA
Dillingham	89	1,182	670	42	187	10	D	69	58,485	NA	NA	NA	NA
Fairbanks North Star	2466	27,962	6,101	616	5,205	760	1,201	1,430	51,124	217	39.2	20.7	47.9
Haines	141	589	127	33	113	D	12	28	47,195	NA	NA	NA	NA
Hoonah-Angoon	74	212	30	D	59	NA	D	11	50,396	NA	NA	NA	NA
Juneau	1151	11,456	2,335	297	1,904	329	562	571	49,830	52	92.3	0.0	63.5
Kenai Peninsula	2104	15,364	3,880	748	2,736	280	571	790	51,408	162	67.9	4.9	57.4
Ketchikan Gateway	602	5,102	821	294	803	210	117	287	56,230	NA	NA	NA	NA
Kodiak Island	482	5,634	717	2,622	453	72	58	201	35,737	NA	NA	NA	NA
Kusilvak	76	674	D	D	308	D	NA	18	26,932	NA	NA	NA	NA
Lake and Peninsula	58	240	NA	63	24	D	NA	15	63,154	NA	NA	NA	NA
Matanuska-Susitna	2204	18,400	4,078	286	3,632	500	790	927	50,383	NA	NA	NA	NA
Nome	174	2,080	949	D	357	50	7	105	50,509	NA	NA	NA	NA
North Slope	157	4,698	326	D	236	D	41	415	88,233	NA	NA	NA	NA
Northwest Arctic	81	1,917	D	NA	146	D	D	157	81,696	NA	NA	NA	NA
Petersburg	172	994	177	195	227	22	13	46	45,997	NA	NA	NA	NA
Prince of Wales-Hyder	148	982	184	153	233	28	D	39	39,732	NA	NA	NA	NA
Sitka	375	2,920	796	413	415	60	52	141	48,337	NA	NA	NA	NA
Skagway	117	375	9	1	94	D	NA	30	79,288	NA	NA	NA	NA
Southeast Fairbanks	167	1,215	110	16	202	15	45	85	69,640	NA	NA	NA	NA
Valdez-Cordova	496	2,806	447	162	311	D	94	196	69,708	NA	NA	NA	NA
Wrangell	91	594	D	D	129	D	14	22	37,439	NA	NA	NA	NA
Yakutat	28	143	17	D	39	NA	NA	6	40,084	NA	NA	NA	NA
Yukon-Koyukuk	96	338	32	NA	121	NA	D	14	42,849	NA	NA	NA	NA
ARIZONA	139134	2,379,409	359,183	144,208	320,561	147,682	148,267	106,431	44,730	20,005	79.9	8.1	66.1
Apache	442	6,722	2,692	84	1,268	74	102	252	37,461	5,591	85.6	4.2	73.3
Cochise	2150	25,795	4,892	391	5,343	469	3,563	928	35,983	1,093	43.8	22.4	56.1
Coconino	3650	51,713	8,356	5,590	8,259	905	1,713	2,002	38,720	2,239	92.0	3.8	72.5
Gila	994	11,611	2,421	159	2,112	163	268	481	41,443	195	65.6	13.3	58.5
Graham	476	6,814	1,712	212	1,629	112	502	246	36,120	412	61.4	15.8	45.4
Greenlee	86	3,848	122	NA	176	17	19	237	61,471	159	52.8	15.1	57.9
La Paz	341	4,077	611	198	944	65	44	116	28,504	125	35.2	28.8	73.6
Maricopa	91270	1,623,299	233,035	100,313	207,576	122,111	114,799	78,086	48,103	2,479	84.6	5.7	50.9
Mohave	3697	41,954	8,666	2,965	9,654	1,002	947	1,362	32,464	335	59.1	23.9	51.3
Navajo	1734	19,173	4,355	372	4,191	355	387	687	35,823	3,846	91.3	3.4	75.5
Pima	20180	316,661	61,442	22,850	48,632	12,820	17,161	12,446	39,305	855	79.4	9.4	49.0
Pinal	3488	48,859	8,582	4,079	8,931	963	969	1,695	34,692	938	56.5	22.8	62.8
Santa Cruz	1163	11,420	1,240	363	2,420	205	265	383	33,519	236	53.0	19.5	58.9
Yavapai	5825	60,153	13,238	3,508	10,771	1,234	1,768	2,052	34,110	940	69.9	13.1	64.1
Yuma	2963	42,536	7,324	3,124	8,262	1,014	1,250	1,379	32,412	562	64.4	14.4	54.8
ARKANSAS	65611	1,023,854	170,777	153,952	147,616	36,831	37,811	40,969	40,015	45,071	30.8	13.0	47.3
Arkansas	510	8,786	964	3,790	1,115	248	72	339	38,541	492	17.9	41.7	53.7
Ashley	383	5,844	952	1,854	748	153	75	250	42,735	376	47.9	12.2	40.4
Baxter	1033	13,145	3,812	2,275	2,275	555	533	452	34,402	561	38.5	6.4	44.9
Benton	6063	115,639	9,403	11,315	13,112	2,875	7,645	6,779	58,619	2,157	43.2	5.1	47.8
Boone	878	12,035	2,277	1,711	2,115	345	224	428	35,575	1,282	32.2	9.2	52.7
Bradley	254	2,848	521	739	293	113	29	80	27,925	185	39.5	2.7	36.8
Calhoun	59	421	D	D	59	14	D	16	38,941	92	20.7	5.4	28.3
Carroll	695	9,000	816	3,016	1,206	195	D	309	34,329	1,126	27.5	10.7	49.4
Chicot	207	2,029	653	9	355	92	33	65	32,019	313	17.6	41.5	57.5
Clark	499	6,919	1,129	1,310	1,251	217	176	216	31,260	381	26.0	10.0	44.1
Clay	288	2,473	715	113	505	91	43	72	29,061	610	24.6	26.6	52.5
Cleburne	563	5,649	865	1,326	1,084	184	155	164	29,045	797	32.4	7.0	40.0

STATE County	Acreage (1,000)	Percent change, 2007-2012	Average size of farm	Total irrigated (1,000)	Total cropland (1,000)	Average per farm	Average per acre	Value of machinery and equipment, average per farm (dollars)	Total (mil dol)	Average per farm (acres)	Crops	Livestock and poultry products	$10,000 or more	$100,000 or more	Total ($1,000)	Percent of farms
	117	118	119	120	121	122	123	124	125	126	127	128	129	130	131	132
ALABAMA—Cont'd																
Washington	96	14.3	258	0.0	12.6	435,148	1,689	62,544	31.7	85,329	15.3	84.7	26.7	7.0	373	17.5
Wilcox	120	-29.2	379	D	22.3	636,839	1,682	51,880	D	D	D	D	25.9	3.2	1,142	44.9
Winston	58	-10.2	111	D	13.5	289,904	2,601	51,921	57.6	110,785	1.4	98.6	36.7	13.8	135	7.3
ALASKA	834	-5.4	1,094	2.5	84.1	681,479	623	87,445	58.9	77,329	42.2	57.8	42.3	11.4	2,432	25.6
Aleutians East	NA	NA	NA	NA	NA	NA	NA	NA	NA	NA	NA	NA	NA	NA	NA	NA
Aleutians West	NA	NA	NA	NA	NA	NA	NA	NA	NA	NA	NA	NA	NA	NA	NA	NA
Anchorage	36	-5.2	125	1.3	17.1	879,979	7,039	92,491	30.0	103,158	47.3	52.7	46.0	14.8	354	17.5
Bethel	NA	NA	NA	NA	NA	NA	NA	NA	NA	NA	NA	NA	NA	NA	NA	NA
Bristol Bay	NA	NA	NA	NA	NA	NA	NA	NA	NA	NA	NA	NA	NA	NA	NA	NA
Denali	NA	NA	NA	NA	NA	NA	NA	NA	NA	NA	NA	NA	NA	NA	NA	NA
Dillingham	NA	NA	NA	NA	NA	NA	NA	NA	NA	NA	NA	NA	NA	NA	NA	NA
Fairbanks North Star	100	-10.1	459	1.0	61.4	580,382	1,264	94,359	9.1	42,120	84.8	15.2	42.4	10.6	1,354	30.9
Haines	NA	NA	NA	NA	NA	NA	NA	NA	NA	NA	NA	NA	NA	NA	NA	NA
Hoonah-Angoon	NA	NA	NA	NA	NA	NA	NA	NA	NA	NA	NA	NA	NA	NA	NA	NA
Juneau	1	37.5	14	0.0	0.1	740,712	54,479	152,173	12.4	238,692	7.4	92.6	51.9	23.1	25	13.5
Kenai Peninsula	29	-23.9	180	0.1	4.5	435,877	2,423	46,315	D	D	D	D	30.9	3.7	353	33.3
Ketchikan Gateway	NA	NA	NA	NA	NA	NA	NA	NA	NA	NA	NA	NA	NA	NA	NA	NA
Kodiak Island	NA	NA	NA	NA	NA	NA	NA	NA	NA	NA	NA	NA	NA	NA	NA	NA
Kusilvak	NA	NA	NA	NA	NA	NA	NA	NA	NA	NA	NA	NA	NA	NA	NA	NA
Lake and Peninsula	NA	NA	NA	NA	NA	NA	NA	NA	NA	NA	NA	NA	NA	NA	NA	NA
Matanuska-Susitna	NA	NA	NA	NA	NA	NA	NA	NA	NA	NA	NA	NA	NA	NA	NA	NA
Nome	NA	NA	NA	NA	NA	NA	NA	NA	NA	NA	NA	NA	NA	NA	NA	NA
North Slope	NA	NA	NA	NA	NA	NA	NA	NA	NA	NA	NA	NA	NA	NA	NA	NA
Northwest Arctic	NA	NA	NA	NA	NA	NA	NA	NA	NA	NA	NA	NA	NA	NA	NA	NA
Petersburg	NA	NA	NA	NA	NA	NA	NA	NA	NA	NA	NA	NA	NA	NA	NA	NA
Prince of Wales-Hyder	NA	NA	NA	NA	NA	NA	NA	NA	NA	NA	NA	NA	NA	NA	NA	NA
Sitka	NA	NA	NA	NA	NA	NA	NA	NA	NA	NA	NA	NA	NA	NA	NA	NA
Skagway	NA	NA	NA	NA	NA	NA	NA	NA	NA	NA	NA	NA	NA	NA	NA	NA
Southeast Fairbanks	NA	NA	NA	NA	NA	NA	NA	NA	NA	NA	NA	NA	NA	NA	NA	NA
Valdez-Cordova	NA	NA	NA	NA	NA	NA	NA	NA	NA	NA	NA	NA	NA	NA	NA	NA
Wrangell	NA	NA	NA	NA	NA	NA	NA	NA	NA	NA	NA	NA	NA	NA	NA	NA
Yakutat	NA	NA	NA	NA	NA	NA	NA	NA	NA	NA	NA	NA	NA	NA	NA	NA
Yukon-Koyukuk	NA	NA	NA	NA	NA	NA	NA	NA	NA	NA	NA	NA	NA	NA	NA	NA
ARIZONA	26249	0.5	1,312	880.6	1,150.8	844,064	643	62,708	3,732.1	186,559	55.6	44.4	20.3	7.3	31,329	15.3
Apache	5598	D	1,001	9.8	26.5	192,667	192	18,893	24.2	4,327	54.5	45.5	7.5	0.6	973	14.9
Cochise	917	11.2	839	65.5	123.3	1,175,308	1,401	81,234	150.0	137,235	D	D	37.6	13.3	2,594	16.9
Coconino	5816	-4.7	2,597	1.9	8.3	543,406	209	23,731	25.8	11,528	9.1	90.9	9.6	1.4	987	23.0
Gila	1189	1.9	6,098	0.8	2.8	1,993,174	327	55,646	3.8	19,241	9.1	90.9	33.8	4.6	323	10.8
Graham	1251	-7.0	3,037	36.9	41.7	1,752,109	577	143,189	170.9	414,769	97.1	2.9	33.5	15.8	3,056	38.3
Greenlee	52	48.5	329	5.4	5.2	514,126	1,561	70,818	9.7	61,239	24.8	75.2	38.2	15.1	337	32.7
La Paz	D	D	D	93.2	120.0	2,513,648	D	345,968	183.2	1,465,944	D	D	64.8	45.6	2,011	34.4
Maricopa	476	-2.0	192	192.9	222.5	1,087,145	5,663	113,576	1,003.5	404,790	44.5	55.5	32.2	14.1	5,379	9.7
Mohave	1244	45.0	3,714	20.8	29.1	1,792,487	483	75,743	30.2	90,102	68.9	31.1	33.7	11.9	1,242	11.3
Navajo	4323	-4.0	1,124	6.5	20.1	291,214	259	20,164	64.5	16,775	9.0	91.0	7.6	0.6	832	13.1
Pima	D	D	D	32.4	36.7	1,651,870	D	64,622	97.3	113,786	76.8	23.2	31.2	10.3	1,085	5.3
Pinal	1175	12.2	1,252	223.6	302.6	2,979,541	2,379	188,860	927.7	989,059	34.0	66.0	49.7	30.0	9,558	27.8
Santa Cruz	215	65.9	911	1.8	1.2	1,390,784	1,527	35,631	14.7	62,110	4.7	95.3	43.6	12.7	996	15.7
Yavapai	825	29.0	877	7.6	10.7	1,382,518	1,576	51,250	41.6	44,285	25.5	74.5	32.2	12.0	141	3.2
Yuma	215	2.0	382	181.4	200.1	2,758,098	7,220	372,064	985.0	1,752,685	D	D	61.7	28.5	1,815	17.1
ARKANSAS	13811	-0.4	306	4,803.9	7,931.1	807,965	2,637	115,436	9,775.8	216,897	49.5	50.5	44.0	16.7	262,967	29.2
Arkansas	402	-0.7	817	314.6	360.2	2,168,250	2,653	320,372	298.2	606,043	99.7	0.3	55.5	46.5	17,373	83.9
Ashley	112	-27.7	297	70.8	83.7	861,694	2,905	127,370	72.8	193,734	91.6	8.4	31.4	15.2	3,123	31.1
Baxter	92	-5.4	164	0.1	12.8	436,902	2,668	46,217	20.4	36,305	3.0	97.0	29.8	4.1	948	16.8
Benton	305	19.7	141	0.6	88.0	626,853	4,435	68,418	529.1	245,307	1.0	99.0	46.5	17.8	1,832	13.7
Boone	257	6.2	201	0.4	38.7	515,837	2,572	54,509	124.1	96,775	1.1	98.9	45.1	10.8	3,730	34.8
Bradley	20	-21.7	107	D	5.5	372,924	3,492	57,232	43.6	235,854	D	D	41.1	16.2	133	13.0
Calhoun	14	-15.4	151	0.1	3.4	370,859	2,459	57,957	6.0	64,761	6.5	93.5	28.3	7.6	32	21.7
Carroll	256	5.7	228	0.1	48.2	579,130	2,543	70,987	307.0	272,652	0.6	99.4	56.6	20.4	2,464	25.3
Chicot	290	1.4	925	197.1	254.9	2,465,096	2,665	340,051	204.7	654,054	96.4	3.6	60.4	44.7	7,640	83.7
Clark	90	10.3	237	D	26.5	437,554	1,848	53,113	15.1	39,588	13.9	86.1	34.6	5.0	342	22.8
Clay	331	0.3	543	235.6	298.0	1,737,748	3,198	263,780	246.2	403,561	98.6	1.4	48.9	32.0	9,792	77.2
Cleburne	157	21.3	198	0.8	37.0	540,846	2,738	62,587	47.9	60,064	2.5	97.5	33.9	6.9	1,013	23.5

Table B. States and Counties — Water Use, Wholesale Trade, Retail Trade, and Real Estate

STATE County	Water use, 2015		Wholesale Trade[1], 2012				Retail Trade[2], 2012				Real estate and rental and leasing,[2] 2012			
	Public supply water withdrawn (mil gal/day)	Public supply gallons withdrawn per person per day	Number of establishments	Number of employees	Sales (mil dol)	Annual payroll (mil dol)	Number of establishments	Number of employees	Sales (mil dol)	Annual payroll (mil dol)	Number of establishments	Number of employees	Sales (mil dol)	Annual payroll (mil dol)
	133	134	135	136	137	138	139	140	141	142	143	144	145	146
ALABAMA—Cont'd														
Washington	2.81	167.2	3	D	D	D	34	232	75.7	5.5	1	D	D	D
Wilcox	2.80	253.2	7	D	D	D	47	269	72.8	5.5	3	D	D	D
Winston	0.81	33.9	22	171	207.7	6.8	98	754	165.0	16.3	8	22	3.5	0.6
ALASKA	99.18	134.3	638	7,734	5,216.3	440.9	2,508	33,721	10,474.3	977.4	872	4,212	1,022.7	187.6
Aleutians East	1.22	365.2	1	D	D	D	8	D	D	D	3	7	1.3	0.2
Aleutians West	2.27	398.1	13	111	145.9	7.8	11	148	53.4	4.7	4	34	11.9	1.9
Anchorage	44.49	148.9	336	5,228	3,147.7	296.6	860	15,253	4,966.8	462.2	383	2,403	631.3	112.1
Bethel	0.30	16.7	5	28	6.9	0.6	54	855	162.8	15.4	7	D	D	D
Bristol Bay	0.07	78.5	4	D	D	D	9	52	15.8	1.6	1	D	D	D
Denali	0.04	20.8	NA	NA	NA	NA	13	99	13.4	1.1	NA	NA	NA	NA
Dillingham	0.25	50.0	2	D	D	D	18	214	58.4	4.6	6	D	D	D
Fairbanks North Star	14.12	141.7	69	666	413.5	36.5	301	4,758	1,732.5	153.1	144	661	159.6	33.2
Haines	0.29	114.4	1	D	D	D	19	115	21.6	3.5	5	3	0.8	0.1
Hoonah-Angoon	0.53	248.7	NA	NA	NA	NA	14	48	11.4	1.0	2	D	D	D
Juneau	4.80	146.5	36	265	196.9	12.8	142	1,821	491.4	53.0	61	249	42.2	7.0
Kenai Peninsula	3.63	62.5	44	383	262.4	18.2	266	2,482	804.2	69.7	66	238	68.9	12.7
Ketchikan Gateway	5.70	415.8	10	D	D	D	121	856	235.9	28.1	28	103	17.5	3.3
Kodiak Island	7.64	550.1	22	93	78.1	4.1	41	463	115.9	12.2	13	71	6.2	1.6
Kusilvak	0.48	59.1	2	D	D	D	25	339	46.6	4.6	2	D	D	D
Lake and Peninsula	0.12	76.8	1	D	D	D	4	D	D	D	4	8	1.0	0.1
Matanuska-Susitna	2.69	26.6	40	298	134.9	14.8	244	3,415	1,039.1	89.3	75	181	38.3	6.2
Nome	0.68	69.1	4	D	D	D	34	360	78.7	7.9	5	18	4.0	0.5
North Slope	0.38	39.2	9	234	354.0	19.2	20	240	94.9	6.8	8	49	10.9	2.5
Northwest Arctic	0.57	73.5	1	D	D	D	12	D	D	D	4	6	0.7	0.0
Petersburg	0.65	204.6	8	33	22.2	1.8	28	231	44.2	6.0	5	D	D	D
Prince of Wales-Hyder	0.34	53.6	2	D	D	D	25	204	48.2	5.1	3	D	D	D
Sitka	1.22	137.7	9	48	38.3	1.9	57	424	98.5	12.4	16	47	4.3	1.2
Skagway	0.24	227.1	2	D	D	D	38	118	32.2	4.3	2	D	D	D
Southeast Fairbanks	0.24	35.1	4	D	D	D	34	248	78.6	6.3	8	11	0.7	0.1
Valdez-Cordova	4.83	515.9	8	44	62.7	4.9	52	372	114.0	9.5	10	21	3.0	0.9
Wrangell	0.64	268.7	2	D	D	D	20	180	27.7	4.7	3	2	0.5	0.0
Yakutat	0.51	832.0	1	D	D	D	5	41	5.2	0.9	1	D	D	D
Yukon-Koyukuk	0.24	43.4	2	D	D	D	33	130	32.9	2.4	3	3	1.1	0.1
ARIZONA	1195.15	175.0	5,570	73,496	69,437.3	4,144.3	17,479	286,184	84,716.5	7,367.8	8,089	40,479	9,329.7	1,693.2
Apache	5.77	80.7	15	D	D	D	105	1,133	324.3	22.2	12	D	D	D
Cochise	16.15	127.7	47	269	133.9	10.1	408	5,266	1,267.3	115.2	113	424	57.1	11.4
Coconino	19.87	142.8	95	738	439.3	33.8	590	7,337	1,896.5	164.8	188	667	137.3	28.1
Gila	4.83	90.9	23	169	68.5	8.6	169	2,005	486.0	46.0	61	149	27.0	4.1
Graham	3.80	100.9	15	D	D	D	93	1,524	381.8	33.6	25	80	17.4	2.6
Greenlee	1.70	178.4	3	D	D	D	16	143	44.2	3.1	3	D	D	D
La Paz	2.89	143.4	11	94	64.2	4.2	81	924	436.0	19.8	21	72	10.7	1.5
Maricopa	776.54	186.3	3,957	57,945	60,841.1	3,426.0	10,415	183,609	57,296.7	4,930.7	5,398	29,825	7,607.5	1,352.0
Mohave	47.86	233.8	114	816	391.1	30.5	593	8,918	2,712.7	211.4	199	628	83.2	15.6
Navajo	14.50	133.9	36	291	170.0	12.1	300	3,935	1,120.3	89.1	94	211	36.0	7.0
Pima	175.40	173.7	703	6,172	3,099.3	269.6	2,770	43,642	11,377.2	1,094.8	1,250	6,042	973.5	205.5
Pinal	63.24	155.5	101	1,633	785.6	123.5	484	8,142	2,375.2	184.3	180	574	105.4	15.6
Santa Cruz	5.17	111.3	150	D	D	D	219	2,344	498.3	47.8	45	192	23.9	3.2
Yavapai	21.14	95.1	163	1,385	880.4	59.1	787	9,854	2,504.3	233.3	341	941	153.0	27.7
Yuma	36.29	177.7	137	2,433	1,439.8	102.5	449	7,408	1,996.0	171.9	159	639	91.9	18.0
ARKANSAS	363.06	121.9	2,884	34,492	31,256.1	1,630.8	10,923	135,448	36,815.3	3,061.5	2,802	12,867	1,922.7	409.8
Arkansas	1.18	64.0	36	428	300.4	19.8	99	1,066	336.0	26.0	22	67	10.0	1.7
Ashley	1.20	57.6	12	136	198.7	6.8	85	863	185.2	17.2	12	26	3.1	0.8
Baxter	3.46	84.3	21	D	D	D	210	2,105	476.6	43.4	36	150	43.7	13.8
Benton	64.74	259.3	237	2,550	2,366.0	150.5	660	10,143	2,906.0	241.3	245	897	173.2	35.7
Boone	0.99	26.6	36	D	D	D	143	1,739	493.3	42.2	37	D	D	D
Bradley	0.21	18.9	10	96	54.9	3.0	39	338	98.9	7.6	7	14	0.8	0.2
Calhoun	0.24	45.9	2	D	D	D	17	78	17.8	1.5	1	D	D	D
Carroll	8.60	310.4	9	94	33.5	3.9	147	1,142	230.2	24.0	26	72	4.3	1.0
Chicot	0.62	56.2	12	109	169.1	6.4	49	379	75.9	7.6	11	D	D	D
Clark	1.84	81.3	10	D	D	D	96	1,158	273.7	27.0	29	94	10.9	1.5
Clay	0.91	60.2	15	258	192.9	8.3	55	485	179.4	11.4	6	D	D	D
Cleburne	11.15	437.8	21	D	D	D	108	1,052	313.1	23.4	21	D	D	D

1. Merchant wholesalers, except manufacturers' sales branches and offices. 2. Employer establishments.

Table B. States and Counties — Professional Services, Manufacturing, and Accommodation and Food Services

STATE County	Professional, scientific, and technical services, 2012				Manufacturing, 2012				Accommodation and food services, 2012			
	Number of establishments	Number of employees	Sales (mil dol)	Annual payroll (mil dol)	Number of establishments	Number of employees	Receipts (mil dol)	Annual payroll (mil dol)	Number of establishments	Number of employees	Receipts (mil dol)	Annual payroll (mil dol)
	147	148	149	150	151	152	153	154	155	156	157	158
ALABAMA—Cont'd												
Washington	13	50	6.4	3.5	14	3,022	D	236.0	11	D	D	D
Wilcox	10	D	D	D	8	471	D	32.9	12	D	D	D
Winston	28	78	8.5	2.4	53	2,624	608.2	79.4	36	D	D	D
ALASKA	1898	17,648	3,175.2	1,178.3	527	12,450	D	514.5	2,126	26,836	2,221.3	626.0
Aleutians East	NA	NA	NA	NA	5	D	D	D	11	D	D	D
Aleutians West	1	D	D	D	15	2,120	598.5	81.6	7	118	14.2	4.1
Anchorage	1141	13,516	2,523.8	958.8	182	2,049	479.8	95.7	788	14,957	1,106.2	338.1
Bethel	6	D	D	D	4	10	D	0.4	18	D	D	D
Bristol Bay	1	D	D	D	6	509	D	17.1	19	57	15.7	4.0
Denali	6	5	1.2	0.3	NA	NA	NA	NA	34	106	63.9	17.3
Dillingham	3	D	D	D	4	267	D	8.5	12	49	4.7	0.9
Fairbanks North Star	237	1,683	293.4	86.5	67	641	1,941.2	36.2	213	3,092	255.3	66.4
Haines	5	8	0.9	0.2	8	44	26.3	3.3	20	94	5.7	1.6
Hoonah-Angoon	NA	NA	NA	NA	NA	NA	NA	NA	16	48	8.4	1.8
Juneau	89	514	79.7	31.4	26	236	75.4	11.7	119	1,329	81.5	24.1
Kenai Peninsula	122	541	65.0	27.6	63	758	D	49.6	265	1,646	149.4	37.4
Ketchikan Gateway	28	93	12.7	4.6	11	648	152.4	27.0	66	560	45.7	11.8
Kodiak Island	24	72	26.5	5.7	22	1,744	D	59.6	47	453	31.5	8.7
Kusilvak	NA	NA	NA	NA	NA	NA	NA	NA	NA	NA	NA	NA
Lake and Peninsula	NA	NA	NA	NA	4	237	57.1	6.7	11	11	9.8	2.6
Matanuska-Susitna	165	915	122.7	45.4	45	222	53.8	9.1	200	1,782	135.5	35.3
Nome	6	7	1.4	0.5	3	D	D	D	18	176	14.8	3.4
North Slope	6	46	12.7	5.9	NA	NA	NA	NA	33	783	132.9	31.7
Northwest Arctic	3	D	D	D	NA	NA	NA	NA	7	99	6.1	2.1
Petersburg	5	10	0.5	0.2	8	D	104.9	9.8	16	63	5.2	1.1
Prince of Wales-Hyder	1	D	D	D	8	161	D	5.6	26	108	10.6	2.6
Sitka	18	74	5.5	2.0	14	325	D	11.8	39	358	30.3	7.9
Skagway	2	D	D	D	3	6	D	D	22	69	13.0	3.7
Southeast Fairbanks	8	25	4.0	2.0	6	23	D	0.8	24	212	16.5	4.8
Valdez-Cordova	17	90	17.6	5.0	14	385	D	14.7	72	462	41.4	10.1
Wrangell	3	D	D	D	4	59	D	D	6	31	2.9	0.7
Yakutat	NA	NA	NA	NA	NA	NA	NA	NA	6	14	3.7	0.9
Yukon-Koyukuk	1	D	D	D	NA	NA	NA	NA	11	54	5.1	1.1
ARIZONA	16198	121,381	19,268.1	7,378.7	4,269	131,941	51,243.5	8,193.2	11,669	251,455	13,996.6	4,030.3
Apache	27	D	D	D	10	86	D	D	70	816	47.1	12.6
Cochise	217	4,592	586.7	254.7	43	279	141.0	14.2	277	3,875	173.4	48.4
Coconino	331	1,584	178.5	65.3	90	4,025	2,181.3	312.0	545	11,436	765.7	191.8
Gila	81	354	44.5	15.4	18	723	D	32.2	130	1,673	94.6	26.5
Graham	24	227	7.3	16.4	13	167	D	5.4	57	866	36.2	9.0
Greenlee	3	D	D	D	NA	NA	NA	NA	16	D	D	D
La Paz	13	D	D	D	12	199	D	D	79	D	D	D
Maricopa	11557	90,488	15,557.1	5,822.6	2,889	91,348	34,583.4	5,426.8	6,776	159,029	9,105.9	2,655.2
Mohave	239	931	72.4	30.8	133	2,566	D	109.5	382	5,787	256.7	74.3
Navajo	113	364	30.7	9.8	31	402	179.8	22.1	225	3,197	186.6	48.1
Pima	2531	16,514	2,241.1	940.0	640	24,297	8,686.6	1,906.7	1,787	42,311	2,154.7	637.4
Pinal	255	1,430	101.7	42.7	111	2,713	2,244.1	133.8	345	6,125	350.5	90.1
Santa Cruz	64	167	20.6	6.8	27	289	211.0	10.2	103	1,413	58.6	17.4
Yavapai	522	1,748	190.9	74.3	184	2,765	706.9	130.8	548	8,223	407.5	130.8
Yuma	221	1,364	132.3	68.0	68	2,084	884.3	79.8	329	5,736	307.5	76.2
ARKANSAS	5678	32,210	4,528.0	1,567.0	2,688	153,706	62,712.9	6,290.8	5,473	95,854	4,307.3	1,182.5
Arkansas	23	78	9.6	2.4	27	3,628	1,927.2	126.1	39	D	D	D
Ashley	27	71	10.0	2.4	29	2,172	1,339.9	135.4	27	425	17.3	4.4
Baxter	75	401	30.1	12.1	50	2,201	574.4	86.7	99	1,372	61.6	16.1
Benton	619	6,232	1,062.7	402.1	160	9,219	D	363.0	401	8,290	366.8	105.1
Boone	61	D	D	D	54	1,700	493.7	69.0	68	D	D	D
Bradley	11	31	2.7	0.8	8	459	127.9	18.9	11	D	D	D
Calhoun	2	D	D	D	NA	NA	NA	NA	6	17	1.0	0.2
Carroll	36	130	9.7	3.4	32	3,546	741.9	102.5	133	1,185	56.7	17.0
Chicot	13	35	3.6	1.4	6	81	D	1.7	17	187	7.5	1.9
Clark	28	463	74.8	23.9	23	1,186	392.7	53.9	55	1,025	41.5	12.1
Clay	17	39	3.0	0.9	16	341	D	12.0	19	D	D	D
Cleburne	43	167	13.8	4.9	31	1,183	190.3	42.6	59	766	33.9	8.6

Health Care and Social Assistance, Other Services, Nonemployer Businesses, and Residential Construction

STATE County	Health care and social assistance, 2012				Other services, 2012				Nonemployer businesses, 2015		Value of residential construction authorized by building permits, 2017	
	Number of establish-ments	Number of employees	Receipts (mil dol)	Annual payroll (mil dol)	Number of establish-ments	Number of employees	Receipts (mil dol)	Annual payroll (mil dol)	Number	Receipts (mil dol)	New construction ($1,000)	Number of housing units
	159	160	161	162	163	164	165	166	167	168	169	170
ALABAMA—Cont'd												
Washington	19	D	D	D	9	D	D	D	1,060	30.6	0	0
Wilcox	18	262	16.0	6.7	8	31	3.1	0.8	622	18.5	188	1
Winston	36	684	57.9	21.4	20	D	D	D	1,642	72.9	470	4
ALASKA	2432	48,701	6,375.5	2,434.2	1,355	7,238	904.6	235.8	55,521	2,601.8	395,668	1,539
Aleutians East	10	D	D	D	4	D	D	D	243	24.5	0	0
Aleutians West	14	D	D	D	6	D	D	D	236	13.9	589	6
Anchorage	1165	25,616	3,656.2	1,347.8	580	3,863	514.2	136.0	20,364	1,067.2	285,957	1,019
Bethel	47	D	D	D	14	56	8.4	1.1	887	20.8	3,522	15
Bristol Bay	2	D	D	D	2	D	D	D	206	9.2	0	0
Denali	3	12	1.0	0.6	3	D	D	D	182	6.7	NA	NA
Dillingham	8	D	D	D	6	17	1.5	0.6	780	18.4	592	3
Fairbanks North Star	290	5,748	746.9	305.5	185	842	88.8	25.6	5,587	230.5	2,950	15
Haines	10	134	9.2	4.0	7	D	D	D	428	14.6	2,506	9
Hoonah-Angoon	7	44	3.6	1.5	3	D	D	D	278	11.1	0	0
Juneau	144	2,458	275.5	112.4	82	406	46.5	12.9	2,773	136.7	14,033	64
Kenai Peninsula	226	3,651	352.9	144.4	138	648	78.5	19.9	6,622	284.7	20,296	104
Ketchikan Gateway	36	799	90.1	39.3	42	142	14.1	3.8	1,311	74.0	7,592	30
Kodiak Island	39	733	79.7	35.4	30	150	19.1	4.4	1,498	77.7	10,074	48
Kusilvak	19	D	D	D	4	D	D	D	510	4.0	0	0
Lake and Peninsula	NA	NA	NA	NA	1	D	D	D	272	11.1	NA	NA
Matanuska-Susitna	267	3,621	411.5	161.6	123	572	64.4	16.7	6,940	311.1	23,504	129
Nome	27	D	D	D	13	D	D	D	504	15.6	73	1
North Slope	9	D	D	D	7	D	D	D	273	7.9	1,644	6
Northwest Arctic	4	D	D	D	9	D	D	D	252	8.1	2,920	7
Petersburg	11	176	17.5	6.4	13	D	D	D	775	53.5	1,872	13
Prince of Wales-Hyder	10	197	13.4	6.4	7	D	D	D	534	23.4	2,950	15
Sitka	25	937	111.5	47.7	25	100	8.3	2.3	1,327	71.3	3,438	19
Skagway	4	4	0.3	0.1	5	22	1.3	0.4	147	7.5	1,074	8
Southeast Fairbanks	11	D	D	D	7	D	D	D	529	16.6	NA	NA
Valdez-Cordova	24	455	46.1	18.7	28	109	10.7	3.4	1,191	52.2	9,438	23
Wrangell	7	D	D	D	7	D	D	D	360	14.0	612	3
Yakutat	3	D	D	D	NA	NA	NA	NA	124	5.1	30	2
Yukon-Koyukuk	10	32	2.3	1.2	4	D	D	D	388	10.3	0	0
ARIZONA	16872	315,107	37,055.9	14,236.1	8,503	62,073	6,231.7	1,736.0	451,951	20,709.1	8,701,276	39,472
Apache	64	3,300	412.8	148.1	19	75	7.7	1.6	2,859	61.6	10,612	46
Cochise	273	4,896	408.9	167.4	150	684	53.1	16.1	6,628	206.3	34,350	202
Coconino	381	6,995	1,040.7	354.3	230	1,307	105.8	32.7	9,015	375.9	155,762	697
Gila	133	2,479	259.1	97.6	57	225	18.2	5.3	3,339	118.0	36,883	156
Graham	78	822	61.3	25.1	33	219	31.2	8.0	1,452	53.9	17,336	97
Greenlee	7	D	D	D	2	D	D	D	255	5.0	180	1
La Paz	21	D	D	D	15	D	D	D	802	32.0	2,145	22
Maricopa	10811	199,139	23,736.9	9,260.4	5,265	42,665	4,489.1	1,246.0	298,614	14,750.9	5,797,176	25,731
Mohave	478	8,222	995.0	364.2	290	1,394	110.3	29.4	10,592	461.3	189,366	913
Navajo	241	3,832	439.1	177.5	117	525	46.0	11.4	5,359	173.5	81,563	361
Pima	2777	56,539	6,617.5	2,441.8	1,483	10,691	1,008.6	281.2	64,179	2,556.9	1,025,886	4,495
Pinal	420	8,118	786.3	313.8	240	1,249	120.5	33.1	17,428	645.2	705,819	3,581
Santa Cruz	70	1,135	146.0	41.0	44	154	13.4	3.7	4,237	176.1	20,702	93
Yavapai	759	11,555	1,245.1	517.8	364	1,717	142.9	41.0	18,282	750.9	447,425	1,976
Yuma	359	7,092	794.1	282.4	194	1,099	77.8	25.0	8,910	341.6	176,071	1,101
ARKANSAS	7485	166,455	15,792.6	6,318.7	3,961	21,830	2,339.4	586.3	198,380	8,380.3	1,766,488	10,795
Arkansas	46	988	63.6	27.6	30	112	7.6	3.0	1,358	62.3	2,034	19
Ashley	46	931	64.3	26.8	25	100	9.3	2.6	1,084	33.8	65	1
Baxter	170	3,490	337.5	133.3	80	326	25.4	6.5	3,023	126.3	5,413	80
Benton	472	8,091	751.6	281.5	256	1,613	145.1	44.1	17,040	750.8	657,044	3,331
Boone	126	2,336	195.6	74.3	48	227	24.5	6.5	2,799	113.8	7,522	34
Bradley	25	530	38.6	14.9	21	69	6.7	1.8	510	23.1	341	3
Calhoun	4	D	D	D	2	D	D	D	184	6.3	0	0
Carroll	50	752	57.9	24.0	39	114	10.7	2.8	2,492	85.1	3,641	57
Chicot	36	900	51.2	26.7	10	58	6.5	1.6	577	21.6	170	2
Clark	59	934	65.9	26.4	27	92	10.7	2.4	1,291	50.7	1,688	18
Clay	33	695	42.1	19.8	29	D	D	D	787	33.5	312	3
Cleburne	45	828	54.1	21.5	33	121	10.7	2.4	2,151	88.8	4,027	11

Table B. States and Counties — Government Employment and Payroll, and Local Government Finances

STATE County	Government employment and payroll, 2012									Local government finances				
			March payroll (percent of total)							General revenue				
												Taxes		
													Per capita[1] (dollars)	
	Full-time equivalent employees	March payroll (dollars)	Adminis-tration, judicial, and legal	Police and corrections	Fire protection	Highways and transpor-tation	Health and welfare	Natural resources and utilities	Education and libraries	Total (mil dol)	Inter-govern-mental (mil dol)	Total (mil dol)	Total	Property
	171	172	173	174	175	176	177	178	179	180	181	182	183	184
ALABAMA—Cont'd														
Washington	673	2,075,254	4.0	4.1	0.0	2.0	21.7	3.3	64.7	40.9	25.0	11.8	691	514
Wilcox	583	1,459,476	6.1	7.4	0.0	6.3	11.1	6.3	60.3	29.0	18.4	7.7	674	358
Winston	1387	3,355,200	3.1	5.2	0.8	2.7	29.1	3.2	54.4	62.5	36.3	16.1	667	283
ALASKA	X	X	X	X	X	X	X	X	X	X	X	X	X	X
Aleutians East	184	728,454	19.1	7.1	0.2	11.9	2.3	7.0	41.2	34.8	17.1	10.2	3,215	0
Aleutians West	278	1,422,298	17.8	11.2	3.2	9.9	3.0	15.4	24.7	56.1	18.9	21.5	3,872	853
Anchorage	10003	52,917,485	4.5	7.7	6.5	5.4	2.3	9.8	62.6	1,313.0	582.8	546.6	1,831	1,623
Bethel	302	1,160,315	19.0	13.8	3.3	7.0	2.2	43.9	0.1	65.9	43.9	9.6	543	0
Bristol Bay	78	333,504	12.5	13.6	0.7	18.6	2.8	5.7	46.1	16.8	7.9	5.5	5,590	3,083
Denali	82	322,133	9.4	0.0	0.0	0.0	4.0	0.0	85.9	11.0	7.8	2.8	1,472	0
Dillingham	293	1,115,865	13.8	10.5	0.7	3.7	2.6	29.8	35.5	40.8	28.5	5.7	1,140	460
Fairbanks North Star	2949	14,833,210	7.9	3.4	2.6	2.4	1.8	5.3	75.9	380.0	201.2	148.5	1,481	1,335
Haines	105	554,027	8.6	6.3	0.8	5.6	0.6	5.8	68.5	20.5	12.5	5.3	2,089	1,020
Hoonah-Angoon	90	310,388	14.5	8.3	2.0	8.6	2.0	9.8	54.0	12.4	8.3	1.7	814	39
Juneau	2061	10,714,562	5.3	5.1	2.9	7.0	24.9	13.7	41.0	338.0	110.1	83.0	2,549	1,125
Kenai Peninsula	2080	9,477,210	10.6	5.1	7.7	3.9	1.5	4.4	61.5	445.9	125.4	111.8	1,965	1,014
Ketchikan Gateway	699	3,359,138	10.3	7.2	4.6	11.2	1.5	15.2	47.8	123.4	42.9	28.8	2,087	994
Kodiak Island	637	2,986,849	7.4	6.7	2.5	6.1	0.9	9.3	64.9	102.4	55.1	27.0	1,893	1,004
Kusilvak	286	832,391	24.5	17.3	0.7	6.1	0.8	19.3	17.7	58.3	48.1	1.6	208	0
Lake and Peninsula	163	640,681	11.6	0.0	0.1	1.6	1.2	2.7	78.9	24.1	18.4	2.8	1,706	0
Matanuska-Susitna	2847	12,057,275	8.3	3.7	1.6	2.4	3.8	2.2	76.5	386.7	229.3	136.9	1,458	1,165
Nome	378	1,484,923	12.5	9.6	0.1	4.9	2.6	23.5	37.5	50.2	28.5	9.5	963	231
North Slope	1749	8,359,644	27.7	5.0	3.3	11.1	11.6	11.4	26.8	503.2	75.9	366.0	37,957	37,888
Northwest Arctic	630	2,686,215	7.5	8.0	1.7	3.7	1.1	9.5	61.6	100.8	72.5	4.2	541	0
Petersburg	512	2,386,453	4.4	6.0	0.8	10.0	32.9	10.6	32.3	82.3	42.5	9.6	2,490	1,229
Prince of Wales-Hyder	289	1,128,652	6.7	2.6	1.0	2.1	2.2	19.6	61.2	30.3	21.8	3.3	576	89
Sitka	525	2,686,315	6.2	5.6	2.0	2.6	30.9	12.2	35.9	89.4	30.2	15.4	1,705	671
Skagway	66	277,303	9.2	10.8	6.1	7.0	16.4	6.9	36.1	19.8	9.1	8.4	8,710	2,132
Southeast Fairbanks	12	40,359	51.1	0.0	0.0	7.5	18.3	0.0	17.1	1.8	1.3	0.0	0	0
Valdez-Cordova	506	2,285,718	8.9	9.3	3.5	9.2	14.4	12.9	38.6	103.7	27.4	50.7	5,213	4,747
Wrangell	NA	NA	NA	NA	NA	NA	NA	NA	NA	NA	NA	NA	NA	NA
Yakutat	56	174,101	20.5	10.7	0.0	9.9	2.5	2.0	50.3	6.3	4.3	1.3	1,936	647
Yukon-Koyukuk	365	1,481,198	10.8	1.7	0.6	2.6	1.1	7.6	73.3	41.9	35.8	0.9	148	52
ARIZONA	X	X	X	X	X	X	X	X	X	X	X	X	X	X
Apache	2657	8,600,597	5.6	5.3	1.9	2.9	2.7	1.1	79.6	168.2	116.4	31.5	431	379
Cochise	4879	16,984,358	11.7	10.2	5.2	2.9	3.0	3.3	61.1	397.9	175.5	144.2	1,092	821
Coconino	4575	17,536,070	11.8	13.5	9.2	3.5	4.5	6.4	48.1	469.7	159.1	223.4	1,643	979
Gila	2222	7,331,024	14.5	15.3	7.8	3.9	2.3	5.8	48.1	194.4	80.9	87.8	1,652	1,207
Graham	2165	7,913,958	6.9	8.1	0.2	2.5	26.5	4.9	50.0	137.7	81.5	29.0	774	382
Greenlee	376	1,216,974	14.2	15.2	0.0	7.6	5.4	1.1	53.9	32.1	12.7	13.6	1,545	1,283
La Paz	799	2,443,896	12.2	19.6	6.3	4.6	4.4	6.2	44.6	60.9	26.7	21.8	1,075	779
Maricopa	129919	553,767,788	8.2	13.2	5.3	2.8	6.3	12.4	50.5	14,121.0	4,763.7	5,936.1	1,506	958
Mohave	5613	20,393,845	13.0	13.4	11.7	4.5	2.0	5.6	47.4	538.5	183.2	229.9	1,131	849
Navajo	4056	13,281,721	8.7	9.6	5.1	2.8	1.5	3.5	67.5	523.9	174.9	109.2	1,020	745
Pima	31634	115,785,276	10.5	14.5	6.6	3.5	2.2	7.1	52.9	3,257.1	1,214.5	1,427.3	1,438	1,057
Pinal	9793	33,904,548	13.3	15.5	5.5	3.5	3.8	5.1	52.2	961.4	426.5	329.1	850	624
Santa Cruz	2004	6,229,659	10.5	13.1	10.4	3.9	2.5	1.8	56.6	161.7	83.6	52.4	1,108	737
Yavapai	6155	23,081,009	10.4	13.4	9.4	4.0	2.1	5.5	45.2	648.3	201.2	335.8	1,579	1,029
Yuma	7924	25,609,990	12.0	12.1	3.1	2.2	2.4	7.3	59.9	638.9	314.0	221.6	1,108	716
ARKANSAS	X	X	X	X	X	X	X	X	X	X	X	X	X	X
Arkansas	988	2,636,492	5.7	8.3	2.3	3.4	19.7	5.4	51.8	59.0	32.8	17.1	906	316
Ashley	866	2,414,339	4.8	9.8	2.9	4.1	2.0	4.2	71.6	63.9	38.0	15.5	719	291
Baxter	1228	3,503,816	4.6	8.5	3.2	6.2	1.3	7.6	68.0	81.3	46.3	22.7	553	251
Benton	7214	24,863,912	5.8	8.5	5.2	2.0	0.5	6.6	70.3	624.9	346.9	196.3	845	405
Boone	1391	3,599,052	4.9	7.8	2.9	3.4	0.3	7.1	72.7	96.8	61.2	19.7	527	210
Bradley	467	1,184,067	4.0	5.4	0.9	4.3	3.1	2.7	79.4	35.7	24.9	6.9	603	215
Calhoun	169	422,712	9.1	11.0	0.0	8.6	4.4	3.4	61.8	17.3	7.1	2.7	511	302
Carroll	1012	2,598,555	4.9	8.8	2.4	5.9	2.4	9.3	64.4	71.0	38.3	16.2	585	295
Chicot	716	2,139,884	6.2	8.0	0.0	2.0	31.0	4.0	48.8	35.1	21.3	8.7	762	307
Clark	763	2,247,437	7.0	17.2	2.0	3.9	2.5	9.0	58.1	67.1	41.9	13.1	572	219
Clay	859	3,044,204	5.9	15.6	0.0	4.6	23.1	14.3	35.5	49.8	25.0	7.5	478	259
Cleburne	801	2,107,158	6.7	9.2	0.5	4.7	1.5	7.6	69.0	57.0	31.3	15.0	583	313

1. Based on the resident population estimated as of July 1 of the year shown.

STATE County	Total (mil dol)	Per capita[1] (dollars)	Education	Health and hospitals	Police protection	Public welfare	Highways	Total (mil dol)	Per capita[1] (dollars)	Federal civilian	Federal military	State and local	Number of returns	Mean adjusted gross income	Mean income tax
	185	186	187	188	189	190	191	192	193	194	195	196	197	198	199
ALABAMA—Cont'd															
Washington	42.8	2,504	67.0	3.3	3.6	0.1	11.2	186.5	10,900	30	72	941	6,550	50,447	4,582
Wilcox	31.8	2,786	61.3	2.7	5.4	0.0	7.4	45.1	3,945	68	47	712	4,450	35,769	2,876
Winston	67.7	2,809	62.8	0.9	3.3	0.0	6.0	53.1	2,204	70	102	1,083	9,010	44,493	4,375
ALASKA	X	X	X	X	X	X	X	X	X	15,245	25,257	63,008	362,220	69,166	9,800
Aleutians East	35.1	11,095	24.9	0.3	3.1	0.0	6.3	40.2	12,717	23	11	248	900	49,644	5,036
Aleutians West	55.3	9,975	16.7	0.1	7.8	0.0	12.5	41.9	7,550	15	29	449	2,240	61,003	7,765
Anchorage	1268.0	4,246	52.5	2.1	9.8	0.0	5.8	1,857.9	6,222	8,617	11,753	19,847	154,130	77,266	11,936
Bethel	70.7	3,986	0.0	0.1	6.7	0.0	3.2	8.4	476	77	118	2,921	7,020	37,839	3,762
Bristol Bay	15.8	15,960	28.3	4.7	6.6	0.0	2.4	1.0	993	51	0	177	530	56,019	6,370
Denali	10.7	5,696	75.8	0.1	0.0	0.0	0.0	0	0	203	28	159	1,200	65,554	8,671
Dillingham	39.6	7,872	29.2	2.5	8.2	2.1	5.2	15.1	2,990	44	33	666	2,320	44,267	4,453
Fairbanks North Star	342.4	3,415	63.0	1.6	2.3	0.0	6.2	170.2	1,698	3,031	9,510	7,715	48,780	66,787	8,999
Haines	15.3	5,980	38.0	1.6	3.3	0.0	6.3	16.4	6,424	11	17	169	1,340	53,659	6,368
Hoonah-Angoon	11.8	5,536	49.2	1.1	4.3	0.0	4.8	3.0	1,396	101	14	255	1,010	44,592	4,800
Juneau	318.0	9,768	26.7	30.7	5.4	0.0	4.2	225.5	6,927	699	458	5,784	17,350	72,558	9,927
Kenai Peninsula	437.7	7,692	32.5	38.4	2.0	0.0	2.4	171.8	3,019	355	474	4,505	29,000	67,675	9,493
Ketchikan Gateway	133.0	9,654	26.9	0.8	3.6	0.0	4.1	145.8	10,581	235	269	1,686	7,270	62,376	8,262
Kodiak Island	95.8	6,729	46.7	0.6	5.3	0.0	3.3	62.8	4,413	291	985	1,129	6,950	60,899	7,217
Kusilvak	70.2	8,985	80.8	0.2	1.6	0.0	1.3	3.8	489	18	54	1,542	3,170	22,673	1,211
Lake and Peninsula	20.2	12,184	72.3	0.1	0.5	0.0	0.8	3.8	2,267	44	10	382	740	34,755	2,827
Matanuska-Susitna	393.6	4,190	61.3	2.3	2.6	0.0	6.9	404.7	4,309	235	684	5,007	45,510	68,762	8,923
Nome	44.7	4,511	29.0	1.0	4.3	0.0	6.8	12.3	1,244	45	65	1,633	3,800	50,733	5,950
North Slope	459.1	47,609	17.7	2.7	3.1	1.5	3.7	510.2	52,913	21	47	2,003	3,760	56,345	6,957
Northwest Arctic	89.1	11,410	62.5	0.1	1.7	0.0	2.2	72.5	9,289	43	49	1,009	2,570	51,804	6,034
Petersburg	85.2	22,155	24.0	26.0	3.2	1.2	7.1	28.2	7,342	102	47	378	1,920	52,032	6,099
Prince of Wales-Hyder	28.0	4,867	53.2	1.1	4.5	0.0	2.7	4.0	704	87	42	969	2,400	48,560	5,363
Sitka	79.2	8,752	28.6	27.3	5.4	0.0	1.8	117.1	12,949	127	235	1,002	4,700	63,768	8,836
Skagway	17.6	18,327	12.7	9.9	7.3	0.1	9.4	6.5	6,776	55	0	120	810	57,912	6,841
Southeast Fairbanks	1.9	262	0.2	0.1	0.0	0.0	8.6	0.9	119	418	44	431	3,320	57,206	6,605
Valdez-Cordova	84.7	8,716	25.8	23.7	2.1	0.0	3.8	37.8	3,895	142	211	1,128	5,180	61,764	7,776
Wrangell	NA	NA	NA	NA	NA	NA	NA	NA	NA	45	16	273	1,170	50,476	5,477
Yakutat	6.6	9,847	45.8	2.9	9.1	0.0	7.6	1.0	1,548	22	0	108	270	49,304	4,974
Yukon-Koyukuk	46.4	8,035	79.2	0.3	1.0	0.0	1.2	6.9	1,200	88	37	1,313	2,900	35,668	3,270
ARIZONA	X	X	X	X	X	X	X	X	X	55,453	32,799	357,744	2,904,290	59,031	7,572
Apache	161.6	2,208	65.6	3.6	3.3	0.0	6.5	280.9	3,837	2,610	160	8,050	24,580	37,067	2,895
Cochise	407.1	3,082	44.0	3.5	12.3	4.9	7.3	161.6	1,223	5,016	4,063	6,370	51,930	47,457	4,645
Coconino	457.2	3,361	35.9	3.4	6.5	1.6	7.6	377.9	2,779	2,792	305	16,138	59,740	54,238	6,385
Gila	163.2	3,071	37.4	1.4	11.8	2.5	6.1	46.8	881	354	117	4,914	21,510	45,213	4,403
Graham	132.6	3,543	64.5	0.4	8.6	1.6	4.9	28.1	752	406	76	2,525	11,310	47,134	4,216
Greenlee	31.0	3,517	44.5	5.9	11.6	0.0	6.8	16.8	1,911	37	21	511	3,470	59,816	5,929
La Paz	82.5	4,069	27.8	3.1	9.7	0.6	7.2	44.7	2,204	336	44	2,018	6,510	35,942	3,074
Maricopa	13916.1	3,530	41.6	5.1	8.2	1.5	4.1	27,988.0	7,100	20,647	13,078	194,844	1,821,940	64,480	8,917
Mohave	555.1	2,730	33.9	2.7	6.9	0.1	8.7	627.7	3,087	449	445	7,090	80,250	41,725	4,049
Navajo	397.5	3,712	44.4	24.0	5.0	0.8	4.3	156.9	1,465	1,728	239	7,756	38,670	40,613	3,298
Pima	3531.8	3,559	37.0	3.1	9.1	2.7	5.3	5,788.9	5,833	12,829	7,908	66,739	439,010	55,216	6,392
Pinal	1130.4	2,918	46.7	4.4	9.1	1.6	3.8	1,030.3	2,660	1,639	874	18,455	138,990	48,569	4,475
Santa Cruz	148.9	3,149	48.5	3.1	10.0	0.0	3.8	161.3	3,410	1,619	101	2,094	20,080	41,813	3,989
Yavapai	653.7	3,074	36.5	2.1	7.2	1.8	9.0	725.7	3,413	1,558	500	9,292	102,360	51,178	5,813
Yuma	616.3	3,081	47.8	2.1	6.0	2.5	4.6	668.5	3,342	3,433	4,868	10,948	84,000	40,613	3,708
ARKANSAS	X	X	X	X	X	X	X	X	X	20,353	15,839	192,764	1,229,010	54,196	6,388
Arkansas	54.5	2,887	54.8	0.8	6.7	0.0	6.5	53.2	2,814	190	73	942	7,850	49,421	5,869
Ashley	63.4	2,945	60.9	0.2	5.8	0.0	6.5	95.2	4,425	70	83	1,012	8,190	44,438	4,022
Baxter	82.1	2,001	58.9	0.0	7.5	0.1	8.6	143.9	3,507	133	166	1,483	17,620	47,106	5,099
Benton	620.5	2,672	61.2	0.2	5.6	0.0	5.6	1,204.1	5,184	459	1,048	9,501	109,690	94,901	14,217
Boone	94.8	2,540	65.0	0.1	4.7	0.0	4.2	59.7	1,600	150	151	3,039	15,460	44,924	4,282
Bradley	34.0	2,985	65.5	0.0	5.4	0.1	7.3	14.7	1,294	33	44	826	4,360	40,512	3,823
Calhoun	20.8	3,913	57.2	1.1	3.3	0.5	6.0	106.6	20,089	10	20	264	1,880	45,876	4,170
Carroll	75.8	2,746	55.7	0.1	5.3	0.0	7.5	76.9	2,784	87	112	1,089	11,990	37,627	3,309
Chicot	34.4	3,008	57.3	2.8	6.4	0.1	7.0	15.4	1,344	45	42	900	4,040	36,944	3,553
Clark	65.6	2,861	64.3	0.1	4.3	0.0	5.6	101.8	4,437	87	81	2,458	8,430	45,116	4,391
Clay	49.7	3,171	48.6	25.1	4.0	0.0	5.7	31.5	2,010	55	61	827	5,890	37,937	3,674
Cleburne	54.0	2,093	60.3	0.2	4.9	0.1	9.9	57.4	2,225	89	102	931	10,360	46,997	4,835

1. Based on the resident population estimated as of July 1 of the year shown.

— **Land Area and Population**

State / county code	CBSA code[1]	County code[2]	STATE County	Land area[3] (sq. mi)	Total persons 2017	Rank	Per square mile	White	Black	American Indian, Alaska Native	Asian and Pacific Islander	Percent Hispanic or Latino[4]	Under 5 years	5 to 17 years	18 to 24 years	25 to 34 years	35 to 44 years	45 to 54 years
				1	2	3	4	5	6	7	8	9	10	11	12	13	14	15
			ARKANSAS—Cont'd															
05025	38,220	3	Cleveland	597.8	8,202	2,577	13.7	85.8	11.9	0.9	0.4	2.3	5.0	17.0	7.4	11.1	11.6	13.2
05027	31,620	7	Columbia	766.0	23,627	1,658	30.8	60.3	36.0	0.8	1.4	2.6	6.0	14.7	17.4	11.0	10.1	11.3
05029		6	Conway	552.3	20,916	1,780	37.9	83.5	12.2	1.8	0.8	3.9	6.0	16.7	7.4	11.7	11.4	13.3
05031	27,860	3	Craighead	707.3	107,115	562	151.4	77.8	16.3	0.8	1.6	5.2	7.2	17.8	10.5	15.5	12.7	11.7
05033	22,900	2	Crawford	591.2	62,996	840	106.6	86.8	2.1	3.9	2.1	7.9	6.4	18.2	7.8	12.6	12.2	13.2
05035	32,820	1	Crittenden	610.3	48,750	1,009	79.9	43.0	54.1	0.7	1.0	2.6	7.9	19.6	8.9	13.1	11.8	12.5
05037		6	Cross	616.4	16,863	1,985	27.4	73.7	23.8	0.9	0.9	2.0	6.6	17.1	8.3	11.2	12.2	12.8
05039		6	Dallas	667.4	7,393	2,635	11.1	54.3	42.4	1.1	0.6	3.2	5.1	16.1	7.4	10.7	10.7	12.0
05041		6	Desha	768.1	11,764	2,306	15.3	46.3	46.6	0.8	0.7	6.7	6.9	19.0	7.8	11.2	10.9	11.2
05043		6	Drew	828.4	18,547	1,892	22.4	67.4	28.8	0.8	0.8	3.5	6.0	15.7	14.3	11.8	10.8	11.7
05045	30,780	2	Faulkner	647.9	123,654	510	190.9	82.0	12.8	1.3	1.9	4.1	6.1	17.1	15.2	14.5	12.3	11.8
05047		6	Franklin	608.9	17,890	1,923	29.4	93.4	1.4	2.3	1.4	3.1	5.7	17.5	8.2	11.4	12.0	12.5
05049		9	Fulton	618.2	12,055	2,287	19.5	97.0	1.2	1.7	0.6	1.3	5.3	15.5	6.3	9.0	9.4	12.8
05051	26,300	3	Garland	677.7	98,658	602	145.6	84.2	9.6	1.5	1.3	5.7	5.4	14.8	7.2	11.3	11.0	12.2
05053	30,780	2	Grant	631.8	18,165	1,910	28.8	93.7	3.0	1.2	0.6	2.6	5.4	17.2	7.5	11.9	12.7	13.8
05055	37,500	4	Greene	577.7	45,053	1,072	78.0	94.3	2.1	1.1	1.0	2.8	6.5	18.0	8.1	13.3	13.0	13.4
05057	26,260	6	Hempstead	727.5	21,861	1,732	30.0	56.7	30.6	1.0	0.9	12.8	7.0	18.7	7.8	11.2	11.6	12.2
05059	31,680	6	Hot Spring	615.2	33,574	1,339	54.6	84.4	11.8	1.4	0.8	3.5	4.9	15.6	8.1	12.7	12.3	13.7
05061		6	Howard	588.6	13,478	2,195	22.9	65.4	20.9	1.6	0.8	12.9	7.5	18.8	7.6	12.0	11.2	12.7
05063	12,900	7	Independence	764.0	37,504	1,237	49.1	90.0	2.8	1.1	1.2	6.5	6.5	17.6	8.5	12.0	12.4	12.6
05065		9	Izard	580.6	13,686	2,185	23.6	94.2	2.3	1.7	0.7	2.5	4.4	13.9	6.8	10.5	10.8	13.6
05067		6	Jackson	633.9	17,135	1,971	27.0	78.6	18.2	1.3	0.8	2.9	5.6	14.7	7.9	14.5	12.9	13.4
05069	38,220	3	Jefferson	870.0	69,115	771	79.4	39.9	57.3	0.8	1.2	2.1	6.1	16.2	10.3	12.8	11.4	12.5
05071		7	Johnson	659.9	26,552	1,544	40.2	80.9	2.2	2.0	2.5	14.3	6.8	18.1	9.2	12.7	11.7	12.6
05073		8	Lafayette	528.3	6,862	2,686	13.0	60.2	36.9	0.9	0.6	2.5	4.9	13.9	7.8	10.5	10.2	13.2
05075		6	Lawrence	587.6	16,525	2,007	28.1	96.6	1.4	1.4	0.5	1.5	5.5	16.4	9.3	11.8	11.3	12.9
05077		7	Lee	602.6	9,176	2,491	15.2	42.0	54.8	1.1	0.8	2.6	5.1	13.5	8.3	15.2	12.6	13.1
05079	38,220	3	Lincoln	561.6	13,646	2,188	24.3	65.4	31.0	0.9	0.4	3.6	4.7	12.9	10.1	16.9	14.5	14.4
05081	45,500	3	Little River	532.3	12,359	2,267	23.2	75.0	20.4	2.4	0.6	3.7	5.6	16.3	7.4	10.9	12.0	13.2
05083		6	Logan	708.1	21,722	1,741	30.7	91.8	2.1	2.1	2.6	3.2	5.9	16.1	8.1	11.1	11.3	14.1
05085	30,780	2	Lonoke	770.9	72,898	746	94.6	87.5	6.9	1.2	1.5	4.7	6.8	19.2	8.2	14.3	13.6	13.1
05087	22,220	2	Madison	834.3	16,339	2,022	19.6	91.2	0.9	2.5	1.4	5.7	6.3	17.2	7.5	11.7	11.3	12.9
05089		9	Marion	597.0	16,428	2,017	27.5	95.8	0.8	2.0	0.9	2.2	4.9	13.2	5.6	8.9	8.9	12.0
05091	45,500	3	Miller	625.6	43,984	1,093	70.3	70.4	25.9	1.4	0.8	3.4	6.8	17.1	7.9	13.5	12.3	12.8
05093	14,180	4	Mississippi	900.6	42,159	1,128	46.8	59.3	36.4	0.7	0.7	4.3	7.2	19.1	9.0	13.0	11.9	12.4
05095		7	Monroe	607.1	7,085	2,661	11.7	55.9	41.1	1.2	0.9	2.8	6.3	14.9	7.5	10.1	9.8	12.6
05097		8	Montgomery	779.9	8,919	2,511	11.4	92.6	1.0	2.5	1.6	4.4	4.7	14.1	6.7	8.4	8.9	14.0
05099	26,260	7	Nevada	617.8	8,327	2,563	13.5	64.3	31.9	0.8	0.6	4.2	5.9	16.6	7.2	11.0	10.9	13.3
05101	25,460	9	Newton	820.9	7,828	2,610	9.5	96.0	1.0	2.8	0.5	2.0	5.0	14.6	6.0	10.1	10.1	12.2
05103	15,780	7	Ouachita	732.8	23,868	1,650	32.6	57.1	40.8	0.9	0.7	2.3	5.8	16.9	7.2	11.2	10.8	12.7
05105	30,780	2	Perry	551.6	10,348	2,399	18.8	94.1	2.6	1.8	0.6	2.9	5.9	16.3	7.5	10.6	11.5	13.8
05107	25,760	6	Phillips	695.5	18,572	1,890	26.7	35.5	62.4	0.7	0.6	2.0	7.5	18.4	8.7	11.1	10.2	11.4
05109		9	Pike	600.6	10,726	2,372	17.9	89.0	4.0	1.5	0.7	6.5	5.3	16.4	8.1	10.8	12.0	13.7
05111	27,860	3	Poinsett	758.4	24,154	1,635	31.8	88.1	9.0	0.9	0.5	3.0	6.7	17.4	8.1	12.6	11.5	13.1
05113		7	Polk	857.7	20,118	1,819	23.5	90.1	0.9	3.5	1.1	6.7	6.0	17.0	7.2	10.3	10.4	12.4
05115	40,780	5	Pope	812.5	63,835	833	78.6	85.9	3.8	1.6	1.6	9.1	6.2	16.4	13.1	13.5	11.1	12.2
05117		8	Prairie	647.9	8,248	2,573	12.7	85.8	12.4	0.9	0.2	1.8	5.5	15.1	7.1	10.9	9.8	13.9
05119	30,780	2	Pulaski	758.9	393,956	178	519.1	54.0	38.0	1.0	2.9	6.2	6.8	16.6	8.8	14.9	12.8	12.3
05121		7	Randolph	652.2	17,557	1,947	26.9	95.9	1.5	1.3	0.7	2.1	6.0	17.0	7.3	12.3	11.3	12.7
05123	22,620	6	St. Francis	634.8	25,930	1,564	40.8	41.3	52.9	0.9	0.9	5.3	6.3	15.3	8.0	14.8	14.3	12.6
05125	30,780	2	Saline	723.5	119,323	522	164.9	85.9	8.1	1.0	1.6	4.8	6.0	17.5	7.2	12.8	13.6	13.2
05127		6	Scott	892.3	10,445	2,392	11.7	86.3	1.2	3.2	3.4	7.7	5.6	17.7	7.3	11.3	10.5	13.4
05129		9	Searcy	666.1	7,938	2,602	11.9	95.2	0.9	3.0	0.6	2.5	5.0	15.3	6.4	9.8	10.2	12.7
05131	22,900	2	Sebastian	531.9	128,107	495	240.8	72.4	7.8	3.4	5.4	14.4	6.6	17.6	8.9	13.5	12.2	13.0
05133		6	Sevier	565.1	17,115	1,973	30.3	59.0	4.6	3.2	1.5	33.8	7.4	20.9	9.2	12.4	11.9	12.5
05135		7	Sharp	604.4	17,393	1,954	28.8	95.4	1.3	2.2	0.8	2.2	5.9	15.3	6.6	9.2	10.1	12.4
05137		9	Stone	606.4	12,537	2,254	20.7	96.1	0.8	2.0	0.7	2.1	4.8	14.6	6.4	9.4	10.1	11.3
05139	20,980	7	Union	1,039.2	39,449	1,190	38.0	62.1	33.3	1.0	0.9	4.1	6.8	17.4	7.8	11.8	11.8	12.7
05141		8	Van Buren	709.7	16,506	2,008	23.3	95.2	1.0	1.9	0.6	3.0	4.7	15.2	5.9	9.4	10.1	12.7
05143	22,220	2	Washington	942.0	231,996	283	246.3	73.7	4.2	2.3	5.6	16.8	6.9	17.7	14.6	15.2	13.0	11.1
05145	42,620	4	White	1,035.1	79,016	707	76.3	89.8	5.4	1.2	1.1	4.4	6.2	17.3	11.6	12.6	11.6	12.7
05147		9	Woodruff	586.8	6,571	2,706	11.2	71.4	27.0	1.0	0.5	1.7	5.5	15.5	7.5	10.3	10.7	12.9
05149	40,780	6	Yell	930.1	21,523	1,754	23.1	76.1	2.1	1.2	1.4	20.4	6.2	18.5	7.9	11.3	12.1	13.4

1. CBSA = Core Based Statistical Area. See Appendix A for explanation. See Appendix B for list of metropolitan areas with component counties. Service of USDA Rural-Urban Continuum Codes. See Appendix A for definition.   3. Dry land or land partially or temporarily covered by water.   2. County type code from the Economic Research Service of USDA Rural-Urban Continuum Codes. See Appendix A for definition.   4. May be of any race.

Table B. States and Counties — **Population and Households**

STATE County	Age (percent) (cont.)				Population change, 2000-2017							Households, 2012-2016				
					Total persons		Percent change		Components of change, 2010-2017					Percent		
	55 to 64 years	65 to 74 years	75 years and over	Percent female	2000	2010	2000-2010	2010-2017	Births	Deaths	Net Migration	Number	Persons per house-hold	Family house-holds	Female family house-holder[1]	One person
	16	17	18	19	20	21	22	23	24	25	26	27	28	29	30	31
ARKANSAS—Cont'd																
Cleveland	14.2	12.0	8.5	50.7	8,571	8,692	1.4	-5.6	587	690	-388	3,342	2.50	72.4	13.6	26.0
Columbia	12.4	9.4	7.9	51.6	25,603	24,552	-4.1	-3.8	2,124	2,230	-846	9,518	2.36	67.4	16.5	27.1
Conway	14.0	10.9	8.6	50.9	20,336	21,267	4.6	-1.7	1,841	1,797	-382	8,360	2.49	66.9	13.0	29.7
Craighead	11.0	7.9	5.7	51.4	82,148	96,443	17.4	11.1	10,670	6,482	6,454	39,042	2.54	66.4	14.7	26.6
Crawford	13.2	9.5	6.7	50.6	53,247	61,949	16.3	1.7	5,593	4,455	-64	23,548	2.60	75.5	12.7	21.5
Crittenden	12.5	8.1	5.5	52.5	50,866	50,906	0.1	-4.2	5,842	3,506	-4,544	18,496	2.64	66.4	23.6	27.8
Cross	13.5	10.8	7.6	51.8	19,526	17,866	-8.5	-5.6	1,613	1,562	-1,065	6,703	2.55	70.6	14.9	25.5
Dallas	16.0	12.2	9.9	50.8	9,210	8,122	-11.8	-9.0	570	752	-550	3,222	2.22	63.9	14.4	35.3
Desha	14.6	10.8	7.6	53.0	15,341	13,000	-15.3	-9.5	1,218	1,150	-1,325	5,224	2.32	63.1	20.7	33.6
Drew	12.7	9.2	7.8	51.2	18,723	18,518	-1.1	0.2	1,722	1,403	-306	7,094	2.50	66.0	14.0	25.5
Faulkner	10.8	7.4	4.7	51.1	86,014	113,242	31.7	9.2	11,203	6,332	5,473	43,451	2.66	65.9	10.9	25.7
Franklin	13.7	10.4	8.6	50.1	17,771	18,122	2.0	-1.3	1,418	1,595	-52	6,779	2.58	68.1	8.9	27.3
Fulton	15.5	14.8	11.3	50.8	11,642	12,236	5.1	-1.5	834	1,293	282	5,240	2.29	72.7	12.0	23.2
Garland	14.4	13.4	10.3	51.9	88,068	96,011	9.0	2.8	8,021	9,763	4,404	40,353	2.35	63.5	13.0	30.0
Grant	13.9	10.3	7.3	50.5	16,464	17,842	8.4	1.8	1,392	1,317	255	6,869	2.60	73.3	11.1	24.9
Greene	11.9	9.3	6.5	50.7	37,331	42,090	12.7	7.0	4,129	3,406	2,235	16,766	2.57	69.9	11.9	24.9
Hempstead	13.8	9.7	7.9	52.1	23,587	22,596	-4.2	-3.3	2,333	1,732	-1,343	7,729	2.83	68.0	15.4	29.6
Hot Spring	14.1	11.1	7.5	47.8	30,353	33,009	8.8	1.7	2,505	2,735	775	12,226	2.57	72.2	12.8	23.6
Howard	12.9	9.7	7.7	51.7	14,300	13,784	-3.6	-2.2	1,394	1,176	-527	5,068	2.62	69.7	18.0	28.6
Independence	13.1	9.7	7.6	51.2	34,233	36,642	7.0	2.4	3,417	3,027	485	14,316	2.51	68.3	10.9	27.7
Izard	14.6	13.8	11.5	48.0	13,249	13,701	3.4	-0.1	821	1,350	517	5,349	2.36	66.2	6.2	31.5
Jackson	13.5	10.4	7.2	50.6	18,418	17,998	-2.3	-4.8	1,429	1,614	-689	6,219	2.29	60.6	14.7	36.0
Jefferson	13.9	10.0	6.8	50.6	84,278	77,444	-8.1	-10.8	6,685	6,092	-9,049	27,660	2.41	61.5	19.1	35.1
Johnson	12.6	9.6	6.7	50.3	22,781	25,540	12.1	4.0	2,581	1,879	330	10,014	2.53	68.0	9.7	27.9
Lafayette	16.4	12.4	10.7	51.1	8,559	7,643	-10.7	-10.2	521	699	-604	2,947	2.37	61.8	18.2	33.7
Lawrence	13.4	10.8	8.8	50.7	17,774	17,411	-2.0	-5.1	1,340	1,725	-510	6,603	2.47	67.2	11.8	29.4
Lee	13.1	10.9	8.3	43.5	12,580	10,428	-17.1	-12.0	744	861	-1,142	3,541	2.30	61.3	16.9	35.5
Lincoln	11.5	8.3	6.7	38.1	14,492	14,142	-2.4	-3.5	972	919	-564	3,940	2.35	72.1	14.7	24.0
Little River	13.9	12.1	8.6	51.9	13,628	13,168	-3.4	-6.1	970	1,176	-609	5,191	2.40	63.8	14.7	30.9
Logan	14.2	11.1	8.3	50.3	22,486	22,350	-0.6	-2.8	1,900	2,079	-445	8,401	2.54	70.0	11.7	25.2
Lonoke	11.8	7.9	5.2	50.6	52,828	68,352	29.4	6.7	6,978	4,528	2,127	25,993	2.72	74.3	12.7	21.5
Madison	14.4	11.2	7.6	50.0	14,243	15,722	10.4	3.9	1,411	1,207	417	6,279	2.50	73.5	10.0	24.0
Marion	18.3	17.2	11.0	50.6	16,140	16,648	3.1	-1.3	1,130	1,788	449	6,667	2.44	68.8	8.3	26.9
Miller	13.0	9.6	6.9	50.7	40,443	43,462	7.5	1.2	4,428	3,125	-756	17,003	2.49	65.3	16.4	29.2
Mississippi	12.9	8.6	5.8	51.4	51,979	46,480	-10.6	-9.3	4,732	3,649	-5,462	16,835	2.58	66.2	20.0	28.7
Monroe	15.7	12.8	10.2	53.1	10,254	8,155	-20.5	-13.1	696	782	-997	3,306	2.26	60.2	17.3	35.9
Montgomery	16.2	15.2	11.9	50.2	9,245	9,493	2.7	-6.0	624	930	-263	3,735	2.40	67.8	6.2	27.8
Nevada	14.7	11.4	9.0	50.3	9,955	9,017	-9.4	-7.7	751	832	-611	3,509	2.42	61.1	13.4	36.8
Newton	16.1	15.7	10.1	49.3	8,608	8,327	-3.3	-6.0	555	709	-351	3,243	2.44	67.0	6.5	30.3
Ouachita	15.7	11.4	8.4	52.5	28,790	26,121	-9.3	-8.6	2,114	2,576	-1,804	10,313	2.36	63.4	15.8	34.3
Perry	14.6	11.5	8.2	50.5	10,209	10,441	2.3	-0.9	809	904	6	3,730	2.69	72.9	8.3	22.1
Phillips	14.3	10.7	7.6	52.9	26,445	21,755	-17.7	-14.6	2,201	1,957	-3,476	7,953	2.48	61.2	23.0	35.2
Pike	13.9	11.3	8.4	49.9	11,303	11,287	-0.1	-5.0	841	1,024	-373	4,298	2.52	68.7	9.3	28.6
Poinsett	13.0	10.3	7.3	51.4	25,614	24,583	-4.0	-1.7	2,276	2,458	-237	9,471	2.51	69.4	16.9	29.0
Polk	14.2	13.1	9.4	51.3	20,229	20,658	2.1	-2.6	1,691	1,955	-264	7,925	2.54	65.7	12.1	30.3
Pope	12.1	8.9	6.5	50.5	54,469	61,754	13.4	3.4	5,744	4,158	500	22,919	2.60	65.2	10.0	29.0
Prairie	14.8	12.3	10.6	49.9	9,539	8,719	-8.6	-5.4	634	767	-339	3,846	2.13	65.4	14.5	30.2
Pulaski	13.0	9.0	5.9	52.1	361,474	382,786	5.9	2.9	40,471	25,899	-3,151	155,440	2.48	60.3	15.7	34.2
Randolph	13.3	11.1	9.0	50.8	18,195	17,970	-1.2	-2.3	1,478	1,756	-126	7,318	2.35	69.4	12.1	27.5
St. Francis	13.1	9.4	6.1	44.9	29,329	28,254	-3.7	-8.2	2,536	2,025	-2,869	9,308	2.52	61.6	18.2	34.6
Saline	12.6	10.3	6.9	50.9	83,529	107,123	28.2	11.4	9,730	7,469	9,837	42,633	2.68	71.1	10.8	24.8
Scott	13.8	11.8	8.7	49.1	10,996	11,218	2.0	-6.9	928	864	-848	3,965	2.67	70.7	13.0	24.5
Searcy	15.8	14.0	10.7	49.6	8,261	8,190	-0.9	-3.1	554	824	21	3,194	2.46	67.2	6.9	28.9
Sebastian	12.7	9.1	6.5	51.2	115,071	125,766	9.3	1.9	12,408	8,988	-1,026	50,437	2.49	64.4	12.8	30.8
Sevier	11.4	8.2	6.0	49.7	15,757	17,058	8.3	0.3	1,903	1,133	-709	6,005	2.84	70.4	15.6	26.3
Sharp	14.8	14.5	11.2	50.4	17,119	17,264	0.8	0.7	1,440	1,835	526	7,320	2.30	60.1	10.0	33.9
Stone	16.4	15.2	11.7	50.7	11,499	12,396	7.8	1.1	880	1,225	488	4,966	2.49	65.4	7.4	31.2
Union	14.3	10.0	7.4	51.2	45,629	41,639	-8.7	-5.3	3,880	3,836	-2,249	16,383	2.43	67.1	15.5	28.8
Van Buren	15.9	14.3	11.8	50.5	16,192	17,285	6.8	-4.5	1,202	1,641	-325	6,825	2.45	67.7	9.8	28.6
Washington	10.1	6.9	4.6	50.8	157,715	203,041	28.7	14.3	23,375	10,584	16,030	83,467	2.54	61.6	9.3	28.3
White	12.2	9.3	6.7	51.3	67,165	77,076	14.8	2.5	7,044	5,894	801	29,108	2.58	70.8	12.9	24.9
Woodruff	14.9	13.4	9.5	51.9	8,741	7,264	-16.9	-9.5	519	719	-498	2,919	2.31	62.0	16.0	34.5
Yell	13.2	9.8	7.6	49.9	21,139	22,185	4.9	-3.0	2,028	1,832	-858	7,492	2.85	72.5	12.9	23.6

1. No spouse present.

Table B. States and Counties — Government Employment and Payroll, and Local Government Finances

	Government employment and payroll, 2012									Local government finances				
			March payroll (percent of total)								General revenue			
													Taxes	
													Per capita[1] (dollars)	
STATE County	Full-time equivalent employees	March payroll (dollars)	Adminis-tration, judicial, and legal	Police and corrections	Fire protection	Highways and transpor-tation	Health and welfare	Natural resources and utilities	Education and libraries	Total (mil dol)	Inter-govern-mental (mil dol)	Total (mil dol)	Total	Property
	171	172	173	174	175	176	177	178	179	180	181	182	183	184

ARKANSAS—Cont'd

Cleveland	330	806,962	9.0	5.0	0.0	5.3	0.7	2.9	76.0	20.0	15.3	2.4	280	186
Columbia	810	2,122,431	5.9	8.7	1.9	4.1	0.6	7.5	70.9	84.2	34.7	16.8	686	216
Conway	751	2,035,580	5.2	11.1	0.6	3.9	0.8	8.1	70.0	72.1	44.8	15.9	748	377
Craighead	3565	10,924,637	4.8	9.2	2.9	3.7	1.2	10.0	67.7	285.0	164.7	77.8	780	344
Crawford	2079	8,936,720	9.1	2.8	0.0	1.4	5.5	24.0	57.1	156.8	108.4	28.6	461	213
Crittenden	2243	7,239,687	5.6	10.1	4.1	1.8	1.6	6.1	67.6	182.3	109.3	39.6	792	258
Cross	603	1,548,890	10.4	9.4	1.4	3.4	1.1	2.8	71.5	51.1	33.6	9.9	562	280
Dallas	261	612,066	9.1	13.5	0.3	5.1	2.7	7.1	61.9	19.8	11.6	4.3	544	186
Desha	795	2,143,489	5.0	5.6	0.5	2.7	22.4	3.6	59.5	57.2	28.7	12.9	1,031	405
Drew	969	2,684,507	3.1	4.7	1.1	2.3	30.7	2.1	55.8	79.4	41.6	12.6	671	211
Faulkner	3393	11,696,206	5.6	8.1	3.7	2.3	1.7	2.7	75.5	324.2	171.2	77.9	656	297
Franklin	616	1,780,777	6.6	4.8	0.5	3.5	2.3	1.9	77.8	48.5	35.0	9.5	525	268
Fulton	446	1,158,320	4.4	3.4	0.7	4.9	23.0	2.8	60.2	31.9	18.9	3.9	319	163
Garland	2929	9,379,603	4.7	8.8	4.0	3.5	3.4	5.5	68.3	270.5	155.0	62.1	640	262
Grant	736	2,167,090	4.0	5.7	0.2	2.7	0.5	2.6	83.3	54.6	40.7	8.6	480	234
Greene	1593	4,613,388	4.1	5.9	2.2	3.0	2.1	8.3	68.5	112.0	67.4	19.6	455	189
Hempstead	991	2,866,901	6.3	9.8	1.5	3.8	2.3	7.5	64.3	63.0	40.8	14.1	629	190
Hot Spring	1020	3,135,235	4.3	4.3	1.6	3.0	1.9	5.9	78.5	75.0	50.6	15.7	471	242
Howard	721	2,467,138	7.2	17.5	1.7	5.0	3.5	21.0	42.7	46.1	28.6	9.7	704	226
Independence	1442	3,864,054	4.6	7.4	0.9	3.5	2.2	8.2	72.6	113.1	69.9	22.7	614	314
Izard	479	1,132,741	7.6	7.8	0.2	5.9	1.2	5.3	71.6	32.9	23.1	5.4	399	259
Jackson	623	1,641,667	7.2	8.7	4.1	4.3	2.8	5.1	65.5	43.2	27.4	9.3	528	229
Jefferson	2803	8,103,678	6.2	13.3	4.7	3.4	1.8	1.9	66.2	217.6	136.9	51.2	686	285
Johnson	832	2,711,188	3.4	5.5	0.7	2.3	0.4	12.2	75.6	63.8	42.9	12.1	466	209
Lafayette	324	1,024,900	6.7	6.5	0.5	5.3	1.6	2.4	77.1	19.1	12.6	3.8	516	258
Lawrence	1057	2,598,077	3.2	3.6	0.8	2.1	33.0	2.4	54.7	79.8	45.0	7.8	459	210
Lee	422	1,112,758	5.2	7.2	1.9	5.4	2.5	8.4	68.7	24.4	17.7	4.1	401	201
Lincoln	362	919,481	6.2	5.9	0.1	3.6	0.2	2.7	80.4	24.4	16.8	4.2	297	152
Little River	689	1,796,446	3.9	4.0	0.1	2.7	34.8	3.7	50.8	44.7	19.0	7.9	615	273
Logan	771	2,027,835	5.6	7.0	0.2	4.0	2.6	4.4	76.0	49.8	33.4	9.6	437	237
Lonoke	2693	7,148,935	4.2	6.7	2.0	2.1	0.5	4.6	79.3	189.2	129.4	38.9	558	260
Madison	571	1,449,917	5.1	4.6	0.0	6.7	5.3	2.7	75.2	31.5	20.9	6.6	420	180
Marion	420	1,177,227	8.0	10.7	0.3	8.0	1.6	5.5	65.4	26.6	17.6	6.1	370	207
Miller	1370	3,792,335	7.1	17.4	7.1	4.8	0.8	2.2	58.3	120.6	70.4	29.4	674	250
Mississippi	2048	5,872,177	5.4	9.7	2.9	3.6	2.1	9.0	65.1	191.6	104.8	32.2	707	241
Monroe	360	1,055,919	8.0	11.9	0.8	5.2	0.9	10.4	61.7	25.7	17.8	4.5	571	283
Montgomery	294	752,749	7.1	6.2	0.0	6.4	2.9	4.0	72.7	19.1	14.5	3.0	317	201
Nevada	405	978,364	8.6	11.3	0.0	8.2	3.9	6.8	59.4	20.3	14.7	3.3	374	180
Newton	434	1,232,173	2.8	2.8	0.0	2.9	1.0	1.0	89.0	59.7	55.7	2.4	298	215
Ouachita	1097	3,081,016	5.9	8.9	2.9	5.3	2.7	5.6	68.4	75.4	51.1	15.8	623	202
Perry	344	973,732	8.1	7.6	0.0	4.4	0.3	3.1	72.6	20.7	15.2	3.5	334	164
Phillips	872	2,319,840	6.4	8.7	2.9	4.6	0.0	7.6	68.3	70.5	48.6	14.3	689	239
Pike	507	1,198,447	2.9	2.6	0.0	2.3	0.6	3.0	88.0	32.5	23.2	6.0	533	207
Poinsett	959	2,599,342	5.4	11.1	1.0	3.7	0.5	5.4	72.6	69.5	51.1	10.0	411	173
Polk	1139	3,233,326	3.5	4.4	0.5	3.3	0.1	3.1	84.0	84.7	45.1	10.6	516	173
Pope	2245	7,108,185	4.8	9.2	3.2	2.4	3.2	4.5	71.3	165.6	100.1	42.3	674	270
Prairie	351	1,159,649	15.7	11.7	0.5	12.8	1.1	5.2	52.5	20.8	12.8	4.0	470	235
Pulaski	15078	52,069,152	6.0	12.7	6.6	4.5	3.5	11.7	52.8	1,476.7	724.3	418.1	1,075	551
Randolph	552	1,387,909	7.5	7.1	2.0	4.5	1.7	6.7	68.7	37.2	24.0	9.9	551	358
St. Francis	1036	3,954,323	5.7	6.9	1.6	2.0	2.7	7.1	73.4	75.8	52.5	14.7	527	164
Saline	2671	8,478,497	6.2	7.9	4.2	2.4	0.6	6.1	71.0	238.1	147.9	54.6	489	267
Scott	364	909,428	4.1	3.6	0.0	5.1	1.8	4.7	79.2	25.0	18.3	4.3	391	127
Searcy	296	714,402	4.4	5.2	0.0	5.9	1.5	2.7	80.0	16.3	12.2	2.5	308	178
Sebastian	4285	15,121,933	5.9	9.8	4.3	4.0	2.6	7.8	65.5	399.0	208.5	123.0	966	364
Sevier	764	2,036,880	4.0	5.6	0.4	2.6	1.5	12.6	72.8	59.3	43.9	8.4	490	157
Sharp	745	1,804,388	5.9	6.5	3.5	5.1	0.2	6.1	71.2	44.2	31.2	7.0	408	175
Stone	424	1,109,650	6.3	5.7	0.0	5.5	1.2	9.6	70.0	26.1	18.0	5.4	423	148
Union	1719	4,970,357	4.4	7.3	3.6	3.5	2.6	4.4	72.2	125.7	71.2	35.1	859	292
Van Buren	757	1,902,959	7.4	21.6	1.0	6.7	1.1	2.5	58.5	49.1	26.5	14.0	822	502
Washington	7560	23,284,035	5.1	10.7	3.9	4.1	1.3	4.1	69.5	691.8	396.1	183.9	870	333
White	2609	7,296,125	4.8	6.2	2.5	2.4	2.0	5.5	75.7	192.0	122.5	42.8	545	227
Woodruff	367	874,741	9.7	5.0	0.3	4.3	1.5	8.7	68.2	25.9	19.0	3.7	521	309
Yell	877	2,241,720	3.8	7.4	0.3	4.0	0.5	4.0	79.4	58.7	42.0	10.7	489	268

1. Based on the resident population estimated as of July 1 of the year shown.

Table B. States and Counties — Local Government Finances, Government Employment, and Income Taxes

STATE County	Direct general expenditure Total (mil dol)	Per capita[1] (dollars)	Education	Health and hospitals	Police protection	Public welfare	Highways	Debt outstanding Total (mil dol)	Per capita[1] (dollars)	Government employment, 2016 Federal civilian	Federal military	State and local	Individual income tax returns, 2015 Number of returns	Mean adjusted gross income	Mean income tax
	185	186	187	188	189	190	191	192	193	194	195	196	197	198	199
ARKANSAS—Cont'd															
Cleveland	19.8	2,299	72.2	0.7	3.3	0.2	9.2	7.9	916	12	33	343	3,150	48,092	4,183
Columbia	85.3	3,484	43.3	28.4	3.6	0.1	3.9	107.4	4,388	37	90	2,033	9,050	50,419	5,741
Conway	70.4	3,308	65.7	1.5	5.0	0.2	8.3	39.8	1,868	60	84	1,484	8,340	49,868	5,135
Craighead	279.3	2,800	56.9	0.3	5.7	0.1	5.4	482.8	4,841	320	422	8,127	42,270	52,679	6,314
Crawford	160.3	2,588	67.2	0.0	5.0	0.0	7.4	203.0	3,277	101	252	2,166	23,860	45,365	3,994
Crittenden	177.1	3,540	57.7	0.2	7.9	0.0	4.9	305.8	6,114	98	197	2,666	21,030	41,324	3,816
Cross	50.3	2,847	65.6	4.4	4.9	0.2	5.5	15.3	867	59	88	1,068	7,260	41,436	3,909
Dallas	18.2	2,276	53.5	0.2	7.1	0.0	9.3	15.1	1,887	21	29	380	2,900	38,463	3,212
Desha	54.8	4,365	49.1	21.1	6.0	0.1	3.4	43.6	3,478	62	48	952	4,980	38,969	3,553
Drew	81.1	4,329	53.9	22.7	3.7	0.2	6.4	39.5	2,108	53	72	2,032	7,260	47,111	4,809
Faulkner	340.2	2,866	58.3	0.1	4.3	0.0	5.9	686.1	5,780	200	493	7,664	49,210	54,748	5,890
Franklin	46.2	2,558	73.0	3.3	3.8	0.3	6.5	43.4	2,406	156	70	872	6,670	44,277	3,973
Fulton	30.6	2,485	53.3	24.1	3.1	0.1	8.4	14.3	1,159	28	49	609	4,240	36,468	2,888
Garland	268.9	2,775	57.5	0.3	5.6	0.0	3.6	344.1	3,551	493	391	4,040	43,240	49,824	5,745
Grant	54.3	3,022	74.8	0.6	4.5	0.1	4.4	31.4	1,747	30	73	777	7,330	52,415	5,209
Greene	119.5	2,769	59.8	0.2	3.6	0.1	4.4	136.1	3,152	93	180	2,036	17,410	46,401	4,413
Hempstead	64.4	2,877	60.7	0.2	4.3	0.1	5.2	53.7	2,402	84	89	1,708	8,610	36,871	2,728
Hot Spring	76.2	2,283	72.0	1.7	3.4	0.1	4.0	94.3	2,823	70	127	1,964	12,480	42,597	3,509
Howard	46.0	3,350	63.9	0.8	4.9	0.1	4.2	74.9	5,451	65	54	808	5,550	38,872	3,467
Independence	118.5	3,202	52.8	0.2	3.5	0.1	6.2	274.1	7,403	104	148	2,139	14,590	46,441	4,574
Izard	33.6	2,497	65.3	1.3	4.8	0.2	6.9	26.2	1,942	25	51	1,001	4,660	38,700	3,094
Jackson	41.6	2,363	54.0	1.4	7.4	0.1	6.9	23.9	1,357	44	61	1,502	5,870	38,946	3,648
Jefferson	217.7	2,914	59.7	0.1	7.5	0.1	4.0	226.1	3,025	1,487	289	6,928	29,590	41,117	3,743
Johnson	65.1	2,514	63.3	0.2	4.4	0.0	7.2	48.8	1,883	85	105	1,089	9,840	39,860	3,208
Lafayette	20.9	2,805	68.4	0.2	6.4	0.1	6.3	10.0	1,344	26	28	335	2,500	37,383	3,466
Lawrence	75.1	4,412	56.5	22.2	3.3	4.3	3.1	40.2	2,361	49	66	1,158	6,210	37,863	3,002
Lee	21.6	2,110	53.3	0.4	9.2	0.2	10.8	5.6	551	34	31	710	2,920	38,523	4,379
Lincoln	25.2	1,788	68.0	0.1	4.2	0.0	7.9	12.9	913	23	40	1,238	3,960	42,491	3,830
Little River	45.4	3,511	41.4	20.9	4.1	6.7	4.1	77.9	6,027	44	50	803	4,950	44,156	3,853
Logan	50.5	2,295	64.1	5.2	5.3	0.1	5.4	41.6	1,893	98	87	1,335	8,510	39,381	3,240
Lonoke	184.1	2,636	69.9	0.2	4.3	0.0	2.8	172.0	2,463	127	293	2,692	29,700	53,619	5,306
Madison	31.6	2,021	66.4	3.3	5.6	0.0	11.6	24.7	1,576	40	65	554	6,300	40,888	3,592
Marion	28.0	1,688	60.5	0.2	8.4	0.2	11.9	19.4	1,172	32	66	526	6,320	40,745	3,356
Miller	112.1	2,568	56.8	0.3	9.6	0.0	4.3	109.3	2,504	58	173	2,000	17,630	46,074	4,813
Mississippi	189.3	4,154	49.4	0.5	5.1	0.1	2.9	796.0	17,471	102	172	2,690	16,800	41,150	3,828
Monroe	25.5	3,252	52.9	1.3	5.1	0.2	10.3	10.9	1,390	33	29	418	3,050	33,470	2,989
Montgomery	18.0	1,926	60.2	0.1	3.4	0.0	10.6	13.6	1,457	44	36	479	3,120	37,058	2,908
Nevada	20.5	2,300	61.8	0.3	6.5	0.2	8.5	12.4	1,394	25	34	439	3,320	39,772	3,334
Newton	30.3	3,746	81.8	0.1	1.5	0.1	7.3	72.1	8,919	46	32	431	2,890	34,704	2,346
Ouachita	71.1	2,801	66.5	0.1	4.9	0.0	5.4	60.6	2,386	95	97	1,874	9,710	43,451	3,999
Perry	19.2	1,861	72.5	0.1	5.9	0.3	7.5	14.0	1,359	22	41	393	3,990	45,306	3,993
Phillips	71.5	3,442	65.5	0.1	5.3	0.1	3.5	34.7	1,670	59	77	1,296	7,220	34,216	2,915
Pike	30.8	2,738	73.7	0.4	3.3	0.2	7.6	17.3	1,541	48	44	572	4,110	38,673	3,307
Poinsett	65.0	2,676	70.6	0.2	6.9	0.1	4.4	35.9	1,479	63	97	1,158	8,940	38,709	3,274
Polk	82.4	4,025	54.6	28.8	2.5	0.0	3.6	60.1	2,937	89	82	1,120	7,590	38,819	3,168
Pope	163.1	2,599	67.0	1.6	6.5	0.1	6.0	190.1	3,029	262	245	4,425	25,530	49,821	5,209
Prairie	19.8	2,343	62.2	2.0	6.4	0.0	9.5	17.3	2,050	39	33	324	3,280	42,489	3,596
Pulaski	1448.1	3,723	46.0	4.2	6.9	0.0	3.8	1,780.8	4,578	9,174	5,430	44,886	182,050	63,625	9,055
Randolph	35.5	1,979	57.5	0.0	7.8	0.0	9.3	8.9	498	37	70	1,237	6,720	38,136	3,349
St. Francis	73.2	2,628	65.4	0.5	5.9	0.1	4.9	21.2	759	682	90	1,373	8,980	34,617	2,840
Saline	246.7	2,206	68.6	0.3	4.4	0.0	5.3	376.7	3,368	83	480	4,171	50,340	57,620	5,951
Scott	25.5	2,315	68.6	0.5	4.5	0.0	7.8	31.9	2,901	81	42	559	3,890	34,382	2,449
Searcy	16.1	2,010	62.9	0.2	4.8	0.2	10.4	2.8	353	40	32	399	2,950	31,390	2,198
Sebastian	398.6	3,131	51.6	0.2	5.7	0.1	6.2	717.8	5,639	939	545	6,694	53,490	52,368	6,214
Sevier	59.7	3,477	77.9	0.0	3.5	0.1	3.6	19.8	1,151	69	68	1,140	6,130	38,582	2,960
Sharp	43.7	2,563	62.6	0.1	5.0	0.0	10.0	23.8	1,398	52	69	777	6,410	36,169	2,823
Stone	24.5	1,931	63.3	0.1	5.7	0.2	9.7	8.6	681	68	51	528	4,560	37,188	3,018
Union	124.9	3,056	60.5	0.1	5.9	0.0	7.4	143.9	3,521	143	162	2,443	17,450	56,853	7,017
Van Buren	45.8	2,692	53.0	4.9	8.6	0.2	14.4	61.6	3,616	33	67	736	6,390	42,531	3,653
Washington	690.9	3,268	59.8	0.3	5.5	0.0	3.8	886.2	4,192	1,977	913	18,099	95,260	56,609	7,342
White	187.6	2,389	67.8	0.2	5.9	0.1	5.3	228.1	2,907	164	310	3,434	30,120	49,530	5,062
Woodruff	27.6	3,888	46.7	0.3	3.9	20.3	8.1	12.6	1,776	36	27	459	2,600	34,892	3,596
Yell	56.6	2,581	70.7	0.1	6.1	0.0	5.0	53.5	2,439	122	87	1,199	8,240	39,581	3,300

1. Based on the resident population estimated as of July 1 of the year shown.

Table B. States and Counties — **Land Area and Population**

State / county code	CBSA code[1]	County code[2]	STATE County	Land area[3] (sq. mi)	Total persons 2017	Rank	Per square mile	White	Black	American Indian, Alaska Native	Asian and Pacific Islander	Percent Hispanic or Latino[4]	Under 5 years	5 to 17 years	18 to 24 years	25 to 34 years	35 to 44 years	45 to 54 years
								\<-- Race alone or in combination, not Hispanic or Latino (percent) --\>					\<-- Age (percent) --\>					
				1	2	3	4	5	6	7	8	9	10	11	12	13	14	15
			COLORADO—Cont'd															
08013	14,500	2	Boulder................	726.4	322,514	214	444.0	80.0	1.5	0.9	6.1	13.9	4.6	14.8	14.8	13.9	12.5	13.0
08014	19,740	1	Broomfield.............	33.0	68,341	781	2,070.9	79.1	1.8	1.0	8.1	12.4	5.5	18.1	7.5	15.1	14.9	14.2
08015		7	Chaffee................	1,013.4	19,638	1,842	19.4	86.4	1.8	1.6	1.3	10.1	3.5	11.5	6.4	12.5	12.0	12.3
08017		9	Cheyenne...............	1,778.3	1,845	3,064	1.0	86.0	1.4	1.2	0.6	11.8	7.6	17.7	6.4	10.7	10.9	11.5
08019	19,740	1	Clear Creek............	395.2	9,574	2,461	24.2	90.2	1.3	1.6	1.5	7.1	3.9	11.8	5.6	11.2	12.9	15.7
08021		9	Conejos................	1,287.4	8,184	2,581	6.4	46.0	0.7	1.5	0.9	52.1	6.8	19.7	8.5	10.6	10.3	11.2
08023		9	Costilla...............	1,227.6	3,776	2,916	3.1	34.4	1.1	2.1	1.5	62.2	4.3	14.5	7.1	9.3	8.6	11.3
08025		8	Crowley................	787.4	5,810	2,772	7.4	55.5	10.7	2.3	1.5	31.2	2.8	9.4	9.7	20.7	17.5	15.6
08027		8	Custer.................	738.6	4,874	2,841	6.6	91.7	1.6	1.6	0.9	5.6	3.0	11.1	4.8	7.7	8.2	10.8
08029		6	Delta..................	1,142.1	30,568	1,419	26.8	82.6	1.0	1.5	1.2	15.2	4.9	15.2	6.6	9.8	10.1	11.4
08031	19,740	1	Denver.................	153.3	704,621	90	4,596.4	56.4	10.1	1.3	4.9	29.9	6.1	13.7	8.1	23.0	15.8	11.6
08033		9	Dolores................	1,067.2	2,067	3,043	1.9	90.0	1.1	4.1	0.8	6.5	4.2	15.3	6.4	8.5	11.3	11.9
08035	19,740	1	Douglas................	840.2	335,299	207	399.1	84.7	1.9	0.7	6.3	8.7	5.9	20.7	7.4	10.9	15.0	16.4
08037	20,780	5	Eagle..................	1,684.5	54,772	926	32.5	67.8	1.2	0.6	1.5	29.7	5.6	16.6	7.4	16.3	15.5	15.1
08039	19,740	1	Elbert.................	1,850.8	25,642	1,576	13.9	90.3	1.3	1.2	1.7	7.1	4.5	16.9	7.2	8.9	11.1	16.6
08041	17,820	2	El Paso................	2,126.8	699,232	93	328.8	72.7	7.8	1.5	5.1	17.1	6.8	17.6	10.9	15.9	12.6	12.1
08043	15,860	4	Fremont................	1,533.1	47,559	1,025	31.0	80.5	4.2	2.3	1.2	13.3	4.1	12.2	6.7	14.4	13.0	13.5
08045	24,060	5	Garfield...............	2,947.5	59,118	876	20.1	69.4	1.0	1.1	1.3	28.6	6.9	18.5	8.1	13.8	13.8	13.0
08047	19,740	1	Gilpin.................	149.9	6,013	2,748	40.1	89.3	1.3	1.8	2.3	7.1	3.5	12.5	4.9	10.5	14.4	17.1
08049		7	Grand..................	1,846.4	15,321	2,076	8.3	89.2	1.1	1.2	1.6	8.5	4.0	13.1	7.0	13.7	12.6	13.9
08051		7	Gunnison...............	3,239.1	16,939	1,982	5.2	88.5	0.9	1.4	1.4	9.2	4.4	12.7	18.4	14.6	12.8	12.0
08053		9	Hinsdale...............	1,117.2	794	3,118	0.7	92.8	1.9	2.4	1.3	4.4	4.4	14.1	6.5	8.6	9.6	10.7
08055		6	Huerfano...............	1,591.0	6,662	2,700	4.2	63.0	1.1	2.2	1.1	34.5	3.5	12.5	5.3	8.2	8.3	11.3
08057		9	Jackson................	1,613.7	1,385	3,086	0.9	85.1	0.4	1.3	1.2	13.1	5.0	12.0	5.7	11.5	12.2	12.9
08059	19,740	1	Jefferson..............	764.2	574,613	114	751.9	80.1	1.6	1.1	3.8	15.4	5.2	14.8	7.7	14.6	13.3	13.6
08061		9	Kiowa..................	1,767.8	1,376	3,088	0.8	90.0	0.9	0.8	0.4	8.9	7.0	15.0	7.6	10.4	9.4	10.1
08063		7	Kit Carson.............	2,160.8	7,158	2,654	3.3	79.7	1.0	1.1	1.0	18.4	6.9	18.5	8.0	11.4	10.9	11.0
08065		6	Lake...................	376.9	7,778	2,612	20.6	61.6	1.0	1.7	1.0	36.2	5.6	15.6	9.4	16.5	13.7	12.9
08067	20,420	4	La Plata...............	1,689.8	55,589	913	32.9	80.3	0.8	6.7	1.2	12.8	5.2	13.9	9.6	13.7	13.2	12.4
08069	22,660	2	Larimer................	2,595.8	343,976	203	132.5	84.7	1.5	1.1	3.4	11.4	5.2	14.7	14.3	14.5	12.2	11.2
08071		7	Las Animas.............	4,772.9	14,238	2,145	3.0	54.3	2.0	2.0	1.2	41.8	4.7	14.2	8.3	11.2	10.7	11.4
08073		8	Lincoln................	2,577.7	5,546	2,791	2.2	79.2	5.5	1.6	1.4	13.8	5.4	14.8	8.3	15.7	12.1	13.7
08075	44,540	7	Logan..................	1,838.6	21,896	1,730	11.9	78.3	4.1	1.4	1.4	16.1	5.5	13.0	11.4	15.5	12.3	12.1
08077	24,300	3	Mesa...................	3,328.9	151,616	435	45.5	83.0	1.3	1.4	1.6	14.6	5.8	16.0	9.4	13.2	11.8	11.3
08079		9	Mineral................	875.8	766	3,123	0.9	91.9	1.0	0.8	0.8	6.4	4.3	9.5	4.3	11.2	7.4	11.9
08081	18,780	7	Moffat.................	4,743.2	13,131	2,224	2.8	81.9	1.3	1.6	1.3	15.7	7.3	18.5	7.4	13.1	12.0	12.3
08083		6	Montezuma..............	2,029.3	26,140	1,559	12.9	74.3	0.8	13.2	1.1	12.6	6.0	16.4	6.8	11.1	10.6	11.8
08085	33,940	4	Montrose...............	2,240.9	41,784	1,136	18.6	77.4	0.8	1.4	1.2	20.6	5.8	16.2	7.1	10.4	10.8	11.9
08087	22,820	6	Morgan.................	1,280.5	28,192	1,486	22.0	59.6	3.3	0.8	0.9	36.3	7.5	18.5	8.9	13.4	11.7	11.8
08089		6	Otero..................	1,262.1	18,326	1,904	14.5	55.5	1.4	1.5	1.2	41.9	6.0	18.0	8.9	11.2	11.3	11.2
08091		9	Ouray..................	541.6	4,794	2,848	8.9	92.2	0.7	1.3	1.2	6.2	3.7	12.7	4.9	7.9	10.7	13.5
08093	19,740	1	Park...................	2,193.9	17,905	1,922	8.2	91.0	1.3	1.9	1.8	6.1	3.5	12.0	5.1	8.9	11.7	15.8
08095		9	Phillips...............	687.9	4,292	2,877	6.2	77.0	0.9	0.7	0.9	21.3	6.6	17.7	7.4	10.2	10.5	11.2
08097	24,060	7	Pitkin.................	970.7	17,890	1,923	18.4	86.7	1.3	0.6	2.4	10.1	3.6	11.6	6.7	14.8	13.4	15.4
08099		7	Prowers................	1,638.4	12,070	2,285	7.4	60.1	1.2	1.3	0.7	38.1	7.0	18.7	10.0	11.0	11.2	10.7
08101	39,380	3	Pueblo.................	2,386.1	166,475	388	69.8	53.5	2.3	1.4	1.3	43.0	5.8	16.9	8.9	13.0	11.6	12.2
08103		9	Rio Blanco.............	3,221.0	6,420	2,720	2.0	87.2	2.1	2.2	1.4	9.6	5.6	18.4	9.9	12.8	11.9	11.6
08105		7	Rio Grande.............	912.0	11,301	2,333	12.4	53.6	0.9	1.8	0.8	44.1	6.0	17.1	8.1	12.2	11.4	10.9
08107	44,460	5	Routt..................	2,362.0	25,220	1,599	10.7	90.9	1.1	0.8	1.5	7.0	4.6	13.7	8.1	15.1	14.1	14.0
08109		9	Saguache...............	3,168.6	6,626	2,701	2.1	60.7	1.4	2.5	1.4	36.1	5.4	15.9	6.3	8.3	11.0	11.9
08111		9	San Juan...............	387.5	715	3,127	1.8	86.0	0.6	1.8	1.7	12.2	2.9	8.7	4.5	11.3	14.1	13.7
08113		9	San Miguel.............	1,286.7	7,967	2,596	6.2	87.6	0.9	1.1	1.3	10.3	4.1	13.5	5.8	15.7	14.9	16.4
08115		9	Sedgwick...............	548.0	2,344	3,018	4.3	82.9	1.3	1.2	1.2	15.1	6.3	14.2	6.3	10.6	10.8	9.7
08117	14,720	5	Summit.................	608.3	30,585	1,418	50.3	83.5	1.3	0.6	1.7	14.0	4.3	11.8	7.5	19.8	15.2	14.3
08119	17,820	2	Teller.................	557.0	24,646	1,620	44.2	90.9	1.3	1.8	1.8	6.3	4.1	13.3	6.2	9.2	10.1	14.8
08121		9	Washington.............	2,518.1	4,938	2,836	2.0	87.4	1.6	0.7	0.9	10.7	5.8	17.6	7.4	11.6	11.1	11.9
08123	24,540	2	Weld...................	3,986.0	304,633	230	76.4	67.4	1.6	1.1	2.3	29.3	7.4	19.1	9.2	15.2	13.5	12.3
08125		7	Yuma...................	2,364.4	10,075	2,426	4.3	75.3	0.7	0.8	0.5	23.5	7.3	19.0	7.7	12.1	11.3	12.1
09000		0	CONNECTICUT	4,842.7	3,588,184	X	740.9	68.5	11.1	0.6	5.4	16.1	5.1	15.6	9.8	12.4	11.8	14.3
09001	14,860	2	Fairfield..............	625.0	949,921	53	1,519.9	63.2	11.7	0.4	6.4	19.9	5.5	17.2	9.2	11.4	12.4	15.0
09003	25,540	1	Hartford...............	735.1	895,388	61	1,218.0	62.8	14.2	0.6	6.2	18.0	5.3	15.8	9.1	13.2	12.2	13.8
09005	45,860	4	Litchfield.............	920.5	182,177	359	197.9	89.9	2.1	0.6	2.5	6.3	4.1	14.4	7.6	10.2	10.4	15.5
09007	25,540	1	Middlesex..............	369.3	163,410	398	442.5	85.5	5.7	0.6	3.8	6.3	4.2	13.9	8.8	11.4	10.7	15.2
09009	35,300	2	New Haven	604.5	860,435	67	1,423.4	64.5	13.8	0.6	4.8	18.1	5.2	15.2	10.1	13.3	11.7	13.8
09011	35,980	2	New London.............	665.1	269,033	254	404.5	78.1	7.3	1.7	5.5	10.6	4.9	14.6	10.3	13.0	11.0	13.8

1. CBSA = Core Based Statistical Area. See Appendix A for explanation. See Appendix B for list of metropolitan areas with component counties.   2. County type code from the Economic Research Service of USDA Rural-Urban Continuum Codes. See Appendix A for definition.   3. Dry land or land partially or temporarily covered by water.   4. May be of any race.

Items 1—15

Table B. States and Counties — Population and Households

STATE County	55 to 64 years	65 to 74 years	75 years and over	Percent female	2000	2010	2000-2010	2010-2017	Births	Deaths	Net Migration	Number	Persons per house-hold	Family house-holds	Female family house-holder[1]	One person
	16	17	18	19	20	21	22	23	24	25	26	27	28	29	30	31
COLORADO—Cont'd																
Boulder	12.7	8.6	5.2	49.7	269,814	294,572	9.2	9.5	21,163	12,227	18,871	123,669	2.45	58.8	7.7	28.0
Broomfield	11.5	8.1	5.2	50.3	38,272	55,858	46.0	22.3	5,055	2,492	9,777	24,581	2.53	67.7	7.0	25.4
Chaffee	17.2	15.4	9.3	47.1	16,242	17,809	9.6	10.3	985	1,224	2,048	7,736	2.24	68.7	7.5	24.3
Cheyenne	14.6	10.8	9.6	49.7	2,231	1,833	-17.8	0.7	194	132	-50	776	2.61	65.9	3.0	29.9
Clear Creek	19.6	13.7	5.7	47.5	9,322	9,075	-2.6	5.5	494	411	408	4,411	2.07	60.0	7.3	33.6
Conejos	14.0	11.2	7.7	49.7	8,400	8,256	-1.7	-0.9	821	572	-324	2,900	2.81	68.2	9.0	30.3
Costilla	17.7	16.3	10.9	47.7	3,663	3,524	-3.8	7.2	210	259	295	1,506	2.38	57.8	10.2	39.0
Crowley	11.0	8.1	5.3	26.6	5,518	5,823	5.5	-0.2	264	280	-38	1,174	3.69	68.4	18.6	21.9
Custer	23.4	22.3	8.7	48.5	3,503	4,255	21.5	14.5	167	257	703	1,950	2.24	70.7	4.2	27.1
Delta	16.8	14.7	10.6	49.9	27,834	30,952	11.2	-1.2	2,232	2,578	-42	12,027	2.42	67.2	9.3	28.1
Denver	10.0	7.0	4.6	49.9	554,636	599,813	8.1	17.5	68,525	31,338	65,613	281,072	2.31	48.8	10.4	39.0
Dolores	17.6	14.9	9.7	47.0	1,844	2,064	11.9	0.1	128	114	-13	720	2.48	65.7	14.2	29.3
Douglas	12.4	7.5	3.8	50.1	175,766	285,468	62.4	17.5	25,323	8,292	32,558	114,017	2.75	77.9	7.1	17.4
Eagle	12.6	7.9	2.9	47.0	41,659	52,197	25.3	4.9	4,743	755	-1,445	17,613	3.00	65.5	7.4	22.6
Elbert	19.1	11.3	4.6	49.5	19,872	23,086	16.2	11.1	1,343	887	2,094	8,568	2.82	77.3	4.6	18.5
El Paso	11.8	7.7	4.7	49.5	516,929	622,259	20.4	12.4	67,606	29,587	38,910	249,279	2.60	68.5	11.0	25.4
Fremont	14.9	12.5	8.6	42.2	46,145	46,824	1.5	1.6	2,721	3,891	1,881	16,327	2.22	65.9	9.6	28.9
Garfield	13.5	8.2	4.3	49.1	43,791	56,389	28.8	4.8	5,926	2,212	-1,019	20,771	2.72	72.4	10.1	21.0
Gilpin	21.6	11.8	3.8	47.3	4,757	5,441	14.4	10.5	302	183	439	2,508	2.23	56.2	2.1	36.5
Grand	18.8	12.2	4.7	46.6	12,442	14,843	19.3	3.2	844	422	21	5,788	2.45	62.6	6.9	26.6
Gunnison	12.5	8.9	3.8	45.9	13,956	15,324	9.8	10.5	1,094	492	986	6,577	2.28	56.8	8.1	26.6
Hinsdale	17.6	18.4	10.1	48.7	790	843	6.7	-5.8	38	28	-60	401	2.12	68.3	1.2	27.7
Huerfano	19.4	18.3	13.2	48.9	7,862	6,711	-14.6	-0.7	345	702	306	3,132	2.02	55.0	9.5	38.9
Jackson	18.7	13.1	9.0	47.2	1,577	1,394	-11.6	-0.6	87	75	-25	616	2.10	57.0	1.9	37.8
Jefferson	14.7	9.8	6.2	50.1	525,507	534,774	1.8	7.4	42,034	29,867	27,586	225,320	2.44	64.5	9.3	27.6
Kiowa	16.8	12.1	11.7	51.7	1,622	1,398	-13.8	-1.6	113	137	0	581	2.47	68.8	6.2	31.2
Kit Carson	14.2	10.1	9.1	49.9	8,011	8,270	3.2	-13.4	704	541	-1,311	2,975	2.45	69.0	6.2	28.4
Lake	13.0	9.1	4.3	46.0	7,812	7,310	-6.4	6.4	596	276	139	3,121	2.32	59.0	4.0	31.9
La Plata	15.6	11.0	5.4	49.5	43,941	51,335	16.8	8.3	3,985	2,332	2,570	21,605	2.41	59.9	7.9	30.5
Larimer	12.7	9.3	5.8	50.1	251,494	299,628	19.1	14.8	24,843	14,873	33,905	127,067	2.49	62.6	7.9	24.3
Las Animas	15.8	14.2	9.5	47.8	15,207	15,507	2.0	-8.2	992	1,247	-1,040	6,090	2.22	62.8	8.5	31.2
Lincoln	12.4	9.1	8.7	42.3	6,087	5,469	-10.2	1.4	419	366	19	1,502	2.34	66.6	12.3	29.6
Logan	13.1	9.2	8.0	44.2	20,504	22,709	10.8	-3.6	1,669	1,468	-1,098	8,029	2.58	60.1	9.3	33.6
Mesa	14.0	10.7	7.7	50.5	116,255	146,717	26.2	3.3	13,110	10,149	2,003	59,501	2.43	65.0	11.7	27.4
Mineral	20.4	20.0	11.0	49.9	831	712	-14.3	7.6	42	34	45	409	1.88	63.8	3.4	31.5
Moffat	14.5	9.2	5.6	48.6	13,184	13,795	4.6	-4.8	1,334	684	-1,345	4,927	2.62	63.9	7.1	29.4
Montezuma	16.1	13.0	8.3	50.5	23,830	25,541	7.2	2.3	2,220	1,920	315	10,305	2.50	62.2	8.3	31.1
Montrose	15.2	13.0	9.7	50.7	33,432	41,278	23.5	1.2	3,295	3,010	226	16,587	2.43	67.6	10.3	27.8
Morgan	12.8	8.2	7.2	49.5	27,171	28,159	3.6	0.1	3,185	1,848	-1,313	10,493	2.66	73.4	13.9	23.2
Otero	13.5	10.9	9.1	50.8	20,311	18,831	-7.3	-2.7	1,605	1,699	-409	7,449	2.41	67.5	13.3	30.2
Ouray	20.5	18.2	7.8	49.3	3,742	4,434	18.5	8.1	230	210	331	2,166	2.15	64.3	4.9	26.0
Park	23.7	14.7	4.7	47.3	14,523	16,201	11.6	10.5	800	622	1,499	7,398	2.21	63.6	4.7	29.5
Phillips	14.1	10.2	12.0	50.6	4,480	4,442	-0.8	-3.4	414	365	-205	1,731	2.47	65.2	6.5	31.0
Pitkin	16.1	12.6	5.9	48.0	14,872	17,148	15.3	4.3	1,011	353	76	7,601	2.29	50.0	7.6	36.2
Prowers	14.0	9.9	7.3	50.0	14,483	12,551	-13.3	-3.8	1,196	885	-805	4,897	2.40	67.8	11.5	27.7
Pueblo	13.5	10.4	7.6	50.7	141,472	159,063	12.4	4.7	13,621	12,057	5,924	62,899	2.51	64.2	14.0	30.2
Rio Blanco	14.8	8.6	6.5	48.8	5,986	6,669	11.4	-3.7	575	358	-473	2,450	2.59	66.1	5.9	29.3
Rio Grande	14.7	11.6	8.0	50.1	12,413	11,982	-3.5	-5.7	1,013	880	-817	4,582	2.49	67.5	10.8	29.0
Routt	16.0	10.1	4.3	47.8	19,690	23,506	19.4	7.3	1,603	729	811	9,437	2.50	59.7	4.6	30.0
Saguache	19.4	15.1	6.8	49.8	5,917	6,108	3.2	8.5	515	298	295	2,530	2.46	61.5	9.7	34.3
San Juan	21.4	15.8	7.6	42.9	558	699	25.3	2.3	34	29	9	284	1.94	44.7	7.7	46.1
San Miguel	16.0	10.6	2.9	46.4	6,594	7,359	11.6	8.3	500	166	273	3,258	2.37	52.8	7.1	36.6
Sedgwick	16.5	12.9	12.5	50.6	2,747	2,379	-13.4	-1.5	193	260	32	1,012	2.30	61.2	8.5	32.8
Summit	14.2	9.6	3.3	46.2	23,548	27,994	18.9	9.3	2,057	411	901	9,714	2.97	58.4	6.6	28.4
Teller	21.4	15.3	5.6	49.1	20,555	23,356	13.6	5.5	1,362	1,117	1,041	9,762	2.39	71.1	7.8	24.0
Washington	14.6	10.5	9.5	47.9	4,926	4,814	-2.3	2.6	333	357	146	2,005	2.27	68.1	8.9	29.1
Weld	11.6	7.5	4.4	49.6	180,926	252,839	39.7	20.5	29,146	11,697	33,972	96,616	2.81	73.3	10.3	20.6
Yuma	12.5	9.9	8.1	50.3	9,841	10,043	2.1	0.3	1,067	712	-330	4,009	2.50	58.7	6.1	35.7
CONNECTICUT	14.2	9.4	7.4	51.2	3,405,565	3,574,114	4.9	0.4	263,119	215,683	-33,328	1,354,713	2.56	66.0	12.8	28.0
Fairfield	13.8	8.5	7.0	51.3	882,567	916,846	3.9	3.6	73,454	47,770	7,582	335,209	2.75	70.1	12.4	24.5
Hartford	13.8	9.3	7.5	51.4	857,183	894,031	4.3	0.2	68,198	57,275	-9,634	347,207	2.50	65.2	14.5	28.9
Litchfield	17.3	12.1	8.5	50.6	182,193	189,926	4.2	-4.1	10,589	12,769	-5,572	74,339	2.45	66.8	8.9	26.8
Middlesex	16.1	11.3	8.4	51.2	155,071	165,676	6.8	-1.4	10,152	10,640	-1,703	66,467	2.39	64.3	8.7	28.8
New Haven	13.9	9.5	7.4	51.7	824,008	862,462	4.7	-0.2	64,732	55,491	-11,253	326,487	2.55	62.9	13.9	31.1
New London	14.8	10.2	7.4	49.9	259,088	274,059	5.8	-1.8	19,518	17,252	-7,365	106,170	2.44	65.4	12.3	28.6

1. No spouse present.

Table B. States and Counties — Professional Services, Manufacturing, and Accommodation and Food Services

STATE County	Professional, scientific, and technical services, 2012				Manufacturing, 2012				Accommodation and food services, 2012			
	Number of establishments	Number of employees	Sales (mil dol)	Annual payroll (mil dol)	Number of establishments	Number of employees	Receipts (mil dol)	Annual payroll (mil dol)	Number of establishments	Number of employees	Receipts (mil dol)	Annual payroll (mil dol)
	147	148	149	150	151	152	153	154	155	156	157	158
COLORADO—Cont'd												
Boulder	2679	27,395	4,767.9	2,011.5	536	14,305	5,061.5	998.4	866	15,855	842.2	252.2
Broomfield	325	6,060	1,252.4	496.8	82	3,087	3,918.4	188.5	143	2,944	169.6	54.7
Chaffee	96	223	24.1	7.6	29	199	25.3	6.0	108	1,172	58.9	19.7
Cheyenne	4	5	0.3	0.1	NA	NA	NA	NA	4	28	1.1	0.2
Clear Creek	48	78	11.7	3.9	8	D	D	D	42	540	30.3	8.8
Conejos	5	9	0.8	0.2	5	53	D	2.6	11	38	3.9	1.0
Costilla	NA	NA	NA	NA	NA	NA	NA	NA	6	D	D	D
Crowley	3	D	D	D	NA	NA	NA	NA	3	12	0.8	0.0
Custer	16	21	3.8	0.8	7	32	D	1.3	12	56	3.2	0.7
Delta	76	D	D	D	50	619	168.1	27.4	76	623	27.2	8.0
Denver	4291	42,123	9,140.6	3,409.8	759	17,032	5,343.9	761.4	1,982	42,906	2,884.9	823.2
Dolores	4	2	0.3	0.1	NA	NA	NA	NA	8	39	2.5	1.0
Douglas	1623	10,273	2,561.7	798.6	133	2,169	460.4	119.3	522	10,295	541.8	167.0
Eagle	401	1,289	183.9	65.7	50	238	73.8	11.2	259	7,998	477.8	175.3
Elbert	87	176	22.0	8.5	21	143	D	6.5	26	190	9.3	2.5
El Paso	2417	19,740	2,983.8	1,258.0	465	10,425	3,375.9	560.5	1,300	26,734	1,443.2	389.2
Fremont	64	178	14.1	4.3	34	409	116.8	20.5	85	878	39.2	11.2
Garfield	300	1,004	137.6	55.1	46	246	41.1	9.4	201	2,727	161.3	49.1
Gilpin	23	34	5.7	1.8	4	D	D	D	10	2,408	404.7	81.0
Grand	81	247	75.4	42.1	14	136	18.6	3.7	136	1,826	84.3	29.4
Gunnison	125	312	28.7	10.0	25	80	9.5	2.2	121	1,339	87.0	16.1
Hinsdale	1	D	D	D	NA	NA	NA	NA	17	75	4.1	1.3
Huerfano	14	35	2.7	1.2	3	26	D	1.4	26	172	9.0	2.4
Jackson	5	10	0.6	0.1	NA	NA	NA	NA	11	51	2.9	0.7
Jefferson	2985	23,587	4,908.0	1,823.0	448	12,913	6,119.0	907.3	1,160	20,616	1,069.2	318.1
Kiowa	2	D	D	D	NA	NA	NA	NA	2	D	D	D
Kit Carson	18	41	3.8	1.2	8	165	D	4.6	23	261	12.8	3.4
Lake	11	40	3.6	1.6	4	36	D	D	37	268	13.1	3.7
La Plata	326	1,100	139.8	55.3	57	518	84.9	21.1	206	4,226	209.2	68.4
Larimer	1493	8,727	1,031.1	450.9	403	10,163	4,275.7	642.6	847	14,821	756.5	218.0
Las Animas	24	93	7.2	2.8	6	56	9.0	2.6	50	656	30.9	8.4
Lincoln	10	25	2.2	0.6	NA	NA	NA	NA	19	222	9.6	2.3
Logan	30	101	10.9	3.4	20	308	213.0	11.9	46	595	26.2	7.5
Mesa	561	2,529	289.0	119.8	159	2,388	520.6	95.1	300	6,052	282.6	88.8
Mineral	3	4	0.3	0.1	NA	NA	NA	NA	19	66	7.9	2.5
Moffat	31	129	10.1	4.0	11	50	D	1.6	33	454	20.7	5.9
Montezuma	80	281	30.1	11.8	32	264	49.9	9.2	85	1,263	83.2	22.8
Montrose	110	438	46.3	20.6	66	1,167	210.7	39.2	78	1,007	49.6	15.4
Morgan	36	120	10.4	3.1	42	3,147	2,444.1	105.4	57	693	29.5	8.4
Otero	32	105	7.3	2.4	15	465	75.9	18.2	52	603	22.9	6.4
Ouray	47	78	10.4	3.7	11	36	4.9	1.2	47	280	21.5	6.3
Park	57	86	10.2	3.3	15	55	D	1.7	40	230	18.4	3.8
Phillips	10	18	2.2	0.5	3	16	4.1	0.7	15	76	2.6	0.8
Pitkin	224	636	154.3	43.7	17	104	16.7	4.5	160	5,089	305.3	118.2
Prowers	28	95	11.2	3.5	14	150	31.5	5.4	35	414	17.6	4.2
Pueblo	238	1,744	435.3	157.3	90	4,221	2,333.3	216.8	356	5,698	236.0	67.8
Rio Blanco	15	51	4.8	1.6	3	10	D	D	30	200	11.5	3.1
Rio Grande	28	72	6.1	2.1	10	59	10.5	2.4	32	278	12.8	3.9
Routt	193	531	81.9	25.5	24	118	17.4	4.8	146	5,159	241.4	80.0
Saguache	9	13	1.1	0.5	5	45	D	2.0	5	30	1.1	0.3
San Juan	6	D	D	D	3	8	D	0.4	24	86	6.2	1.5
San Miguel	75	129	19.7	5.6	14	84	10.9	4.9	72	1,439	77.2	29.2
Sedgwick	5	17	1.0	0.3	3	29	D	0.7	4	53	1.4	0.5
Summit	258	575	89.3	30.4	26	166	40.6	7.9	250	6,201	311.3	101.3
Teller	88	411	57.8	22.6	14	46	6.5	1.7	71	1,649	110.8	38.1
Washington	7	18	1.7	0.4	6	100	D	D	6	27	1.0	0.3
Weld	533	2,362	311.5	113.7	284	11,102	5,991.4	485.8	400	5,794	273.9	76.2
Yuma	27	62	6.6	2.0	11	78	164.8	2.8	26	231	8.5	2.5
CONNECTICUT	9220	97,578	17,993.7	8,364.1	4,350	163,847	55,160.1	10,546.2	8,263	134,546	9,542.1	2,590.8
Fairfield	3481	40,694	8,738.6	3,975.9	837	35,507	13,412.5	2,338.2	2,266	30,574	2,153.3	604.6
Hartford	2238	26,427	5,239.4	1,968.7	1,261	57,332	16,965.5	3,899.3	2,043	32,877	1,905.3	549.8
Litchfield	372	D	D	D	382	9,062	2,615.3	463.3	411	4,426	265.2	75.3
Middlesex	374	2,735	425.1	166.9	243	8,920	3,605.4	543.1	421	5,434	329.5	99.3
New Haven	1907	16,222	2,461.1	1,216.8	1,151	31,792	10,818.1	1,879.2	1,969	26,342	1,487.2	411.3
New London	529	8,100	666.1	862.0	172	12,435	4,693.7	950.2	698	28,347	3,023.8	748.7

Items 147—158

STATE County	Health care and social assistance, 2012				Other services, 2012				Nonemployer businesses, 2015		Value of residential construction authorized by building permits, 2017	
	Number of establishments	Number of employees	Receipts (mil dol)	Annual payroll (mil dol)	Number of establishments	Number of employees	Receipts (mil dol)	Annual payroll (mil dol)	Number	Receipts (mil dol)	New construction ($1,000)	Number of housing units
	159	160	161	162	163	164	165	166	167	168	169	170
COLORADO—Cont'd												
Boulder	1332	18,386	2,129.6	841.9	717	4,415	670.1	176.7	38,414	1,972.3	417,268	1,667
Broomfield	145	1,611	172.9	64.4	109	704	141.8	23.7	5,513	241.1	124,041	416
Chaffee	66	791	76.3	31.3	40	175	11.7	3.7	2,362	89.4	38,791	154
Cheyenne	1	D	D	D	4	6	1.0	0.2	196	7.0	378	3
Clear Creek	19	67	5.8	2.2	10	27	1.8	0.5	605	26.6	7,692	30
Conejos	11	254	17.1	6.9	4	D	D	D	605	26.6	3,049	24
Costilla	7	37	1.7	0.9	3	D	D	D	277	11.4	0	0
Crowley	3	D	D	D	1	D	D	D	178	4.8	720	3
Custer	2	D	D	D	10	120	5.3	2.6	649	28.0	18,304	74
Delta	89	1,716	115.7	48.9	50	185	15.2	4.1	2,774	119.0	8,919	46
Denver	2093	54,161	7,316.9	3,008.8	1,607	13,247	1,868.2	472.2	66,449	3,542.0	1,561,486	10,525
Dolores	5	D	D	D	NA	NA	NA	NA	151	5.5	0	0
Douglas	743	8,339	1,137.4	412.4	508	3,075	270.0	80.6	30,353	1,582.1	919,323	3,742
Eagle	168	2,052	384.1	115.8	189	1,278	119.3	37.3	7,226	449.1	140,045	426
Elbert	25	132	8.2	3.9	42	118	11.9	3.2	2,770	138.5	49,655	163
El Paso	1897	D	D	D	1,086	8,419	1,805.3	323.0	48,394	1,927.3	1,620,008	4,855
Fremont	93	1,982	128.3	60.6	46	214	13.1	4.4	2,797	103.3	23,366	119
Garfield	161	D	D	D	152	692	91.3	20.8	6,108	304.6	46,516	194
Gilpin	6	43	4.0	1.5	3	7	0.4	0.1	561	20.3	9,490	34
Grand	36	324	35.9	13.3	46	103	12.0	2.6	1,889	97.0	64,153	198
Gunnison	64	494	50.3	18.0	64	221	27.3	5.7	2,307	95.1	41,389	142
Hinsdale	1	D	D	D	6	D	D	D	145	6.6	3,371	8
Huerfano	18	424	31.2	15.3	7	D	D	D	601	23.0	7,810	42
Jackson	3	7	0.5	0.2	1	D	D	D	176	7.0	1,106	9
Jefferson	1565	24,678	2,717.4	1,084.2	1,121	6,073	628.1	172.8	54,185	2,433.9	490,604	2,373
Kiowa	2	D	D	D	4	4	0.5	0.1	148	5.8	0	0
Kit Carson	26	284	22.2	9.0	13	D	D	D	685	29.4	560	3
Lake	14	195	18.3	6.8	12	32	2.1	0.5	649	25.0	8,271	24
La Plata	237	2,737	335.0	125.2	143	612	53.9	16.6	6,396	298.4	183,340	564
Larimer	1021	18,142	1,988.2	783.2	658	3,536	374.1	96.2	30,473	1,392.6	660,383	2,935
Las Animas	36	D	D	D	36	129	11.0	3.0	955	34.7	2,091	17
Lincoln	7	245	21.3	8.4	11	41	3.4	0.9	386	13.8	1,640	11
Logan	65	1,027	88.3	33.5	53	203	21.5	5.2	1,232	61.4	1,763	11
Mesa	426	10,176	1,029.0	427.2	293	1,883	182.6	47.8	11,373	489.7	142,442	755
Mineral	2	D	D	D	3	D	D	D	159	12.7	3,490	19
Moffat	40	440	50.3	19.1	37	219	18.5	6.7	984	39.3	2,153	11
Montezuma	90	1,422	109.3	45.2	47	173	15.7	3.6	2,305	88.6	5,032	23
Montrose	172	2,338	221.5	83.5	86	368	36.5	9.4	3,602	150.6	33,688	210
Morgan	57	1,186	118.5	46.1	40	139	14.1	3.2	1,871	92.5	16,420	90
Otero	57	921	50.8	24.8	27	81	7.1	1.8	1,037	32.0	485	4
Ouray	18	52	3.9	1.6	8	35	2.6	0.8	945	49.8	16,689	49
Park	23	96	4.6	2.1	24	76	9.1	2.4	1,804	76.2	33,032	154
Phillips	9	298	21.2	8.8	12	24	3.2	0.7	390	20.6	2,361	18
Pitkin	74	D	D	D	115	913	122.3	36.8	3,677	282.4	197,995	53
Prowers	30	625	48.8	20.7	23	87	10.5	2.1	809	37.0	610	3
Pueblo	419	11,404	1,063.1	458.0	238	1,222	93.1	28.2	8,177	323.3	62,271	368
Rio Blanco	10	176	19.0	8.8	12	25	3.0	0.8	552	22.4	8,169	13
Rio Grande	34	420	28.7	11.9	24	94	12.6	2.9	1,048	37.4	4,860	23
Routt	118	1,170	141.6	51.0	86	438	37.7	10.9	3,709	185.0	85,303	115
Saguache	6	D	D	D	8	D	D	D	610	21.3	6,282	93
San Juan	3	D	D	D	3	17	0.7	0.4	117	4.4	1,307	7
San Miguel	28	132	10.0	4.2	44	270	29.1	7.8	1,745	99.1	83,127	68
Sedgwick	5	D	D	D	5	10	1.6	0.2	184	8.2	600	2
Summit	104	852	134.8	39.9	121	420	60.5	12.3	4,424	258.6	204,658	475
Teller	58	D	D	D	42	129	11.5	3.1	2,542	101.3	31,498	110
Washington	8	32	1.7	0.5	8	D	D	D	368	17.2	1,442	8
Weld	435	7,951	893.1	325.4	329	1,537	175.9	44.5	20,948	980.3	794,426	3,646
Yuma	26	584	53.7	22.6	22	D	D	D	961	43.4	260	1
CONNECTICUT	10296	271,272	29,573.1	12,533.5	7,282	43,384	4,904.0	1,382.4	272,809	16,122.8	1,185,527	4,547
Fairfield	2827	63,963	8,087.6	3,291.8	2,103	13,041	1,654.3	420.8	91,902	6,611.0	667,495	1,719
Hartford	2771	79,917	8,536.4	3,723.3	1,935	12,855	1,454.4	450.4	58,242	3,174.9	157,760	957
Litchfield	515	9,500	929.2	374.9	359	1,621	163.1	46.6	17,074	956.7	47,549	142
Middlesex	470	13,869	1,411.2	645.8	339	1,650	163.1	49.9	13,359	728.6	124,211	750
New Haven	2408	73,162	7,788.2	3,238.4	1,717	9,881	977.8	297.8	59,574	3,112.0	124,211	750
New London	734	17,357	1,728.0	751.2	459	2,498	274.7	61.9	16,548	788.9	65,433	295

Government Employment and Payroll, and Local Government Finances

STATE County	Full-time equivalent employees	March payroll (dollars)	Adminis-tration, judicial, and legal	Police and corrections	Fire protection	Highways and transpor-tation	Health and welfare	Natural resources and utilities	Education and libraries	Total (mil dol)	Inter-govern-mental (mil dol)	Total (mil dol)	Total	Property
	171	172	173	174	175	176	177	178	179	180	181	182	183	184
COLORADO—Cont'd														
Boulder	11666	48,102,144	8.2	10.8	5.0	2.7	5.3	10.3	53.3	1,374.3	334.5	816.3	2,674	1,840
Broomfield	687	3,465,698	16.4	35.0	0.0	2.4	10.3	27.3	3.9	167.6	16.5	123.6	2,120	775
Chaffee	981	3,205,729	12.3	6.1	0.6	3.3	43.6	2.3	30.5	122.6	43.2	31.0	1,707	1,041
Cheyenne	186	506,783	7.0	5.9	0.0	7.9	25.6	3.5	46.1	11.6	3.9	4.8	2,562	2,163
Clear Creek	426	1,607,157	17.1	24.4	1.0	10.4	10.2	4.5	29.9	55.5	7.7	41.0	4,539	4,152
Conejos	417	1,165,848	8.0	8.9	0.0	4.9	9.9	3.0	62.1	35.4	24.9	8.0	965	500
Costilla	216	594,990	12.8	7.1	0.6	14.3	13.6	6.0	39.9	21.5	11.8	7.4	2,049	1,959
Crowley	149	372,979	13.1	7.4	0.2	7.6	12.0	7.9	49.2	13.0	9.3	3.0	554	412
Custer	188	561,207	16.3	10.1	0.7	9.8	17.6	3.0	41.1	14.0	3.5	7.4	1,741	1,402
Delta	1667	6,363,576	6.3	7.6	0.1	3.4	39.9	9.2	32.0	159.9	41.2	32.5	1,067	738
Denver	31444	153,513,001	5.5	11.6	4.4	12.7	23.1	10.5	30.8	5,569.5	1,334.4	2,071.4	3,266	1,406
Dolores	125	332,266	21.5	7.7	0.0	17.4	6.7	1.6	42.7	5.7	2.5	2.8	1,418	1,324
Douglas	8978	36,551,403	6.0	11.8	1.8	3.0	0.7	5.6	68.6	1,187.6	326.8	623.8	2,092	1,621
Eagle	1753	9,241,964	10.1	13.6	8.4	9.4	9.0	14.1	30.0	388.1	36.2	240.3	4,632	3,109
Elbert	793	2,420,569	5.3	13.3	4.8	6.6	3.6	3.3	61.8	68.8	28.9	26.5	1,132	853
El Paso	24223	94,407,600	4.8	9.4	3.9	2.0	15.6	15.5	46.2	2,544.0	807.4	804.8	1,248	728
Fremont	1361	4,257,494	6.5	12.3	3.9	5.6	7.8	6.9	53.3	113.3	43.1	39.2	837	567
Garfield	2715	10,773,217	7.9	10.4	4.9	3.5	18.8	8.7	43.3	377.7	79.3	217.3	3,815	3,060
Gilpin	323	1,493,439	17.4	31.0	11.0	10.9	2.8	6.6	15.7	64.3	18.7	33.2	6,047	1,928
Grand	899	3,399,937	11.0	8.9	1.9	8.6	29.9	12.4	25.0	112.4	11.3	66.9	4,715	3,643
Gunnison	938	4,262,174	12.1	9.1	1.5	9.8	23.1	10.8	16.9	118.1	21.2	51.6	3,335	2,295
Hinsdale	78	213,518	22.4	6.9	0.0	16.9	17.4	4.9	28.8	6.8	1.9	3.5	4,346	3,385
Huerfano	683	2,657,574	9.1	15.2	0.3	8.0	42.0	6.2	18.4	59.2	16.3	13.5	2,049	1,649
Jackson	109	283,034	16.2	7.4	0.3	12.1	6.1	7.8	43.4	7.5	4.3	2.3	1,700	1,447
Jefferson	16292	67,925,819	8.0	14.5	6.3	2.7	4.7	8.0	53.4	1,796.8	529.1	959.0	1,758	1,296
Kiowa	195	518,331	6.2	3.4	0.1	6.2	53.7	0.0	26.7	13.7	4.6	3.5	2,400	2,321
Kit Carson	599	1,765,320	8.1	7.1	2.1	6.4	30.3	7.6	36.2	45.5	15.1	12.7	1,565	1,397
Lake	1036	3,786,124	2.2	2.4	4.0	1.7	9.4	2.1	76.3	123.9	28.5	61.1	8,331	7,915
La Plata	2067	7,718,347	12.2	16.8	4.4	5.9	9.2	7.1	41.1	215.9	60.0	121.8	2,324	1,552
Larimer	10782	47,317,101	8.8	11.5	1.1	2.8	7.5	18.4	46.2	1,178.8	292.6	577.8	1,861	1,211
Las Animas	790	3,154,143	13.1	10.3	5.0	7.2	4.0	23.0	36.5	67.9	34.0	24.1	1,610	1,155
Lincoln	433	1,393,504	11.8	4.7	0.0	8.0	44.9	2.8	25.9	42.3	17.3	9.6	1,763	1,199
Logan	1057	3,288,524	7.3	7.7	3.0	24.9	6.5	4.7	43.0	98.6	25.5	33.4	1,475	969
Mesa	5197	18,735,519	8.2	13.3	5.0	4.1	7.0	9.6	48.8	498.4	180.8	228.0	1,542	966
Mineral	54	178,882	27.1	10.8	0.0	16.4	3.6	2.1	40.0	2.9	0.6	1.5	2,123	1,523
Moffat	596	2,538,838	9.9	13.4	0.2	10.3	6.2	10.3	44.2	92.8	17.6	36.4	2,760	2,173
Montezuma	1215	5,805,045	11.6	22.2	1.0	7.2	7.7	14.6	27.4	95.8	39.0	40.1	1,577	1,113
Montrose	2104	7,665,788	7.4	9.0	2.9	5.0	34.2	6.0	34.1	212.1	63.1	64.1	1,574	943
Morgan	1340	3,811,946	7.6	9.5	0.4	4.0	9.8	9.7	57.0	108.9	39.6	44.8	1,573	1,252
Otero	1005	2,762,692	7.5	7.2	2.0	3.8	7.9	18.7	51.8	77.3	47.6	18.6	995	589
Ouray	217	778,899	20.7	8.6	4.2	8.7	4.3	7.5	43.5	24.2	6.0	13.1	2,889	2,250
Park	565	1,709,266	7.9	11.7	9.4	8.8	7.9	2.6	45.3	79.9	43.2	27.9	1,739	1,620
Phillips	387	1,231,524	5.8	2.8	0.0	4.9	50.9	5.0	28.5	41.2	11.7	7.9	1,819	1,329
Pitkin	1617	8,457,732	10.5	7.7	1.5	20.9	24.6	13.9	14.7	334.3	32.9	154.4	8,946	4,437
Prowers	976	3,070,921	6.7	5.7	0.9	3.5	37.0	8.6	32.8	89.1	35.2	16.6	1,340	781
Pueblo	5698	21,434,409	5.8	12.3	11.0	3.0	6.6	9.0	49.7	552.8	247.0	223.3	1,388	895
Rio Blanco	743	2,764,159	6.3	7.4	0.2	5.5	52.7	8.3	15.4	118.7	16.4	59.8	8,716	7,064
Rio Grande	594	2,555,313	11.1	23.0	0.0	5.2	6.7	1.8	52.0	64.6	42.5	16.8	1,408	981
Routt	1184	5,565,786	14.7	11.9	5.9	17.1	2.2	12.5	30.0	144.8	31.4	79.2	3,394	2,136
Saguache	347	1,034,643	14.8	8.6	0.3	8.8	6.1	10.3	48.3	55.6	45.0	6.6	1,042	909
San Juan	40	161,715	24.7	12.1	0.0	15.7	7.6	8.1	30.7	9.6	6.5	2.6	3,820	2,945
San Miguel	502	2,269,390	18.4	15.3	2.9	13.4	5.4	10.0	33.5	93.6	14.2	55.2	7,283	5,078
Sedgwick	255	812,165	5.4	2.7	1.9	4.4	48.8	7.8	27.6	22.9	7.9	4.8	2,001	1,581
Summit	1631	6,095,822	12.4	10.1	11.6	10.3	3.7	14.3	28.7	206.4	13.5	141.5	5,044	2,991
Teller	955	3,818,256	16.1	19.9	2.6	7.0	8.6	7.5	33.5	87.9	28.6	45.4	1,942	1,236
Washington	385	1,126,606	13.3	11.8	0.0	8.2	7.0	2.5	56.0	43.4	28.9	10.2	2,145	1,945
Weld	8663	35,763,495	8.2	17.4	4.0	5.2	6.6	11.0	45.5	919.9	308.8	411.9	1,562	1,194
Yuma	749	2,253,233	4.4	5.3	0.0	6.1	43.0	5.1	34.4	88.3	21.8	23.8	2,349	2,036
CONNECTICUT	X	X	X	X	X	X	X	X	X	X	X	X	X	X
Fairfield	32029	179,963,079	3.5	9.1	5.1	3.1	3.2	3.7	70.6	4,597.7	963.2	3,193.1	3,419	3,370
Hartford	31675	164,755,032	3.0	8.6	3.8	2.4	3.4	4.9	72.4	4,279.2	1,571.4	2,306.6	2,571	2,541
Litchfield	5578	26,405,841	4.3	6.4	1.8	5.2	1.9	2.5	76.6	698.9	167.1	476.8	2,542	2,521
Middlesex	5503	26,698,181	4.2	7.4	4.5	3.5	3.5	3.2	71.4	656.2	154.4	441.0	2,663	2,643
New Haven	28448	140,929,161	3.5	10.1	6.3	2.6	2.7	5.4	68.7	3,790.8	1,443.5	2,034.2	2,358	2,333
New London	8967	42,369,410	4.4	7.7	3.8	3.8	2.3	8.0	68.3	1,101.6	386.5	598.5	2,183	2,159

1. Based on the resident population estimated as of July 1 of the year shown.

STATE County	Total (mil dol) 185	Per capita[1] (dollars) 186	Education 187	Health and hospitals 188	Police protection 189	Public welfare 190	Highways 191	Total (mil dol) 192	Per capita[1] (dollars) 193	Federal civilian 194	Federal military 195	State and local 196	Number of returns 197	Mean adjusted gross income 198	Mean income tax 199
COLORADO—Cont'd															
Boulder	1414.6	4,633	43.6	2.5	8.2	2.3	4.6	1,940.0	6,354	2,070	954	31,869	157,860	95,378	16,085
Broomfield	144.5	2,479	0.0	1.3	11.0	7.9	6.3	650.9	11,165	162	172	1,416	32,300	87,882	12,995
Chaffee	126.2	6,953	33.9	30.5	2.8	4.5	3.0	96.2	5,298	73	46	1,898	8,950	56,300	6,520
Cheyenne	10.0	5,359	50.3	1.1	4.3	21.9	4.7	4.3	2,284	13	0	285	800	45,911	5,488
Clear Creek	50.3	5,569	22.6	4.4	10.8	5.5	14.8	19.7	2,186	32	24	647	4,620	76,558	11,143
Conejos	32.7	3,950	48.7	4.8	3.1	18.2	5.7	7.1	857	43	21	541	2,990	38,066	2,935
Costilla	19.3	5,383	36.1	8.6	3.1	5.2	18.0	10.6	2,962	10	10	371	1,330	34,100	2,872
Crowley	12.3	2,296	34.8	0.9	4.5	16.8	7.5	5.3	989	0	0	511	1,110	35,114	2,795
Custer	14.0	3,302	29.4	21.6	5.5	3.1	12.9	5.3	1,249	14	13	248	2,010	57,127	6,759
Delta	164.5	5,405	28.7	38.1	3.5	2.1	6.4	79.3	2,607	180	87	2,227	12,870	44,707	4,357
Denver	4720.3	7,442	20.3	15.1	4.8	3.6	3.3	12,146.9	19,151	14,760	2,457	57,069	347,940	77,720	12,555
Dolores	8.4	4,230	38.7	1.5	9.3	1.7	28.9	3.1	1,535	0	0	228	830	45,037	4,225
Douglas	1073.0	3,598	46.7	0.7	5.5	1.9	8.1	1,832.6	6,145	423	853	12,500	150,070	116,290	19,049
Eagle	360.2	6,944	19.9	3.1	5.6	0.9	7.0	691.4	13,329	125	140	3,162	28,730	81,610	13,063
Elbert	66.6	2,849	52.4	1.1	2.8	6.7	8.4	163.8	7,006	33	65	908	11,540	84,508	11,682
El Paso	2502.2	3,880	37.1	21.9	6.0	2.0	8.1	4,398.1	6,819	12,649	36,974	37,617	314,020	60,205	7,096
Fremont	111.0	2,373	42.2	0.5	8.6	5.0	5.7	106.8	2,282	1,093	102	4,205	17,570	46,342	4,718
Garfield	343.8	6,036	29.4	12.6	5.3	5.4	6.2	453.7	7,965	265	151	5,237	27,410	68,503	10,221
Gilpin	50.9	9,270	11.0	2.3	12.0	3.9	11.8	57.5	10,467	11	15	453	2,680	64,712	7,966
Grand	101.5	7,151	19.1	14.0	6.2	1.0	9.3	159.5	11,235	127	38	1,234	7,520	61,200	8,308
Gunnison	122.5	7,917	13.3	24.8	4.1	3.0	11.9	140.6	9,086	169	40	1,959	7,940	56,641	7,035
Hinsdale	7.9	9,716	19.4	25.6	3.8	0.3	8.5	0.7	895	0	0	91	380	58,405	6,413
Huerfano	56.4	8,549	15.8	41.7	1.6	2.4	10.2	12.0	1,821	14	17	489	2,680	39,432	3,655
Jackson	7.0	5,173	38.5	4.4	6.1	2.3	23.7	0.7	487	34	0	132	610	47,033	4,897
Jefferson	1793.4	3,289	42.8	1.2	9.3	2.3	4.8	1,397.5	2,563	8,658	1,531	27,887	293,390	77,653	11,094
Kiowa	14.6	10,098	23.1	43.2	3.7	4.8	11.6	4.6	3,195	20	0	227	580	43,426	4,307
Kit Carson	45.0	5,561	31.8	27.5	3.7	5.2	8.8	19.9	2,455	38	19	741	3,320	41,810	4,628
Lake	135.4	18,454	79.4	5.5	1.1	1.4	2.2	36.4	4,957	55	19	697	3,390	45,183	4,162
La Plata	202.8	3,869	35.0	1.1	7.0	2.7	5.9	291.6	5,566	330	140	5,408	26,800	69,736	9,560
Larimer	1080.2	3,479	37.9	4.5	6.4	3.0	9.0	1,388.6	4,472	2,532	887	33,875	163,360	70,915	9,900
Las Animas	67.0	4,482	36.8	3.7	4.8	14.4	8.4	26.1	1,744	70	34	1,537	5,880	43,999	4,591
Lincoln	47.4	8,698	36.7	27.0	2.8	5.8	9.1	9.7	1,786	22	12	1,016	2,050	44,755	4,249
Logan	73.2	3,236	40.5	1.4	5.0	4.8	10.0	99.6	4,400	62	48	2,399	8,540	58,959	7,967
Mesa	517.8	3,502	35.4	1.7	13.1	5.6	9.4	476.5	3,223	1,522	398	8,447	68,170	55,231	6,406
Mineral	2.9	4,056	57.4	0.8	5.3	0.0	15.9	1.2	1,746	0	0	91	430	58,867	6,533
Moffat	93.2	7,060	24.3	30.6	5.6	6.2	10.7	40.3	3,050	146	34	968	5,910	54,982	5,752
Montezuma	95.7	3,762	36.0	3.0	10.1	11.6	6.2	60.5	2,379	348	70	2,409	11,490	49,879	5,662
Montrose	215.1	5,283	25.1	29.4	6.1	3.0	9.2	127.2	3,123	313	106	2,774	18,370	48,212	4,899
Morgan	102.1	3,585	44.8	1.5	4.7	4.6	7.3	72.8	2,556	112	72	2,084	12,740	48,452	4,964
Otero	73.8	3,949	48.8	9.4	2.9	2.4	5.4	37.0	1,981	111	46	1,761	7,520	38,291	3,334
Ouray	18.2	4,027	38.4	1.5	6.2	7.7	14.2	11.3	2,485	13	13	373	2,440	70,458	9,413
Park	79.6	4,968	50.7	2.8	3.8	4.7	6.8	28.9	1,800	50	44	791	7,290	61,149	6,995
Phillips	43.4	9,946	35.1	40.0	2.6	1.2	5.0	19.5	4,468	24	11	578	2,010	53,687	6,139
Pitkin	271.6	15,734	9.3	32.7	4.0	1.8	4.6	380.2	22,024	90	46	2,184	10,440	134,329	27,045
Prowers	85.2	6,880	36.9	27.3	5.4	4.4	4.5	184.4	14,887	39	30	1,345	4,870	41,970	3,962
Pueblo	566.4	3,521	40.3	1.5	6.6	5.3	3.7	456.3	2,837	1,107	436	11,579	69,500	48,503	5,118
Rio Blanco	94.0	13,703	15.7	31.1	5.7	2.8	9.7	113.7	16,584	70	16	1,176	2,720	60,453	6,347
Rio Grande	62.5	5,236	64.5	2.5	4.3	3.9	5.0	22.1	1,851	117	29	819	5,780	44,165	4,588
Routt	151.7	6,501	26.1	0.5	3.9	3.9	7.2	168.4	7,217	109	63	1,843	12,940	85,017	14,682
Saguache	54.4	8,636	66.9	1.8	1.8	8.1	6.5	14.0	2,225	44	17	487	1,860	32,396	3,315
San Juan	9.9	14,307	73.7	1.8	5.2	0.9	5.5	1.8	2,645	0	0	71	360	45,217	5,044
San Miguel	78.7	10,376	17.1	8.1	5.4	1.7	11.2	104.6	13,797	34	21	774	4,310	102,689	18,763
Sedgwick	21.9	9,187	35.7	36.4	2.6	2.8	4.4	1.7	700	19	0	336	1,070	42,843	4,141
Summit	193.3	6,894	18.6	1.3	5.5	1.0	7.9	128.1	4,569	49	78	2,629	17,240	75,448	11,451
Teller	84.7	3,621	35.6	6.2	7.8	2.8	8.5	55.5	2,371	60	62	1,335	11,620	60,399	6,772
Washington	40.7	8,539	68.2	2.8	2.6	6.4	6.5	14.9	3,135	50	12	448	2,010	45,165	4,053
Weld	839.9	3,185	42.6	1.2	7.3	4.0	6.6	868.6	3,294	632	754	16,389	127,150	62,806	7,515
Yuma	77.9	7,698	25.5	39.3	3.2	4.7	6.7	65.7	6,497	45	26	978	4,420	53,779	6,233
CONNECTICUT	X	X	X	X	X	X	X	X	X	17,932	13,715	223,879	1,760,990	95,153	16,422
Fairfield	4616.9	4,944	50.9	1.2	6.6	1.0	3.1	4,013.1	4,297	2,798	1,917	44,253	461,240	157,516	33,952
Hartford	4219.6	4,703	56.1	0.9	6.3	0.8	4.1	2,673.7	2,980	5,561	1,825	66,306	446,770	74,926	10,827
Litchfield	765.4	4,081	66.1	1.3	3.5	0.2	6.7	390.3	2,081	439	369	7,820	94,770	75,671	10,616
Middlesex	673.0	4,064	63.2	0.8	4.2	0.4	4.0	355.1	2,144	379	326	9,898	84,260	82,985	12,305
New Haven	4427.8	5,132	58.4	0.6	4.3	0.3	2.5	3,649.0	4,229	5,462	1,921	44,592	414,980	71,056	9,891
New London	1142.0	4,165	60.1	0.7	5.5	0.6	6.1	911.5	3,324	2,758	6,808	28,172	135,500	68,060	8,828

1. Based on the resident population estimated as of July 1 of the year shown.

Table B. States and Counties — Land Area and Population

State / county code	CBSA code[1]	County code[2]	STATE County	Land area[3] (sq. mi)	Total persons 2017	Rank	Per square mile	White	Black	American Indian, Alaska Native	Asian and Pacific Islancer	Percent Hispanic or Latino[4]	Under 5 years	5 to 17 years	18 to 24 years	25 to 34 years	35 to 44 years	45 to 54 years
				1	2	3	4	5	6	7	8	9	10	11	12	13	14	15
			CONNECTICUT—Cont'd															
09013	25,540	1	Tolland	410.4	151,461	437	369.1	86.1	3.9	0.6	5.6	5.6	4.0	13.4	19.1	10.7	10.1	13.5
09015	49,340	2	Windham	512.8	116,359	531	226.9	84.5	2.7	1.0	2.0	11.7	4.8	15.0	9.8	12.8	11.8	14.4
10000		0	**DELAWARE**	1,948.8	961,939	X	493.6	64.2	23.2	0.9	4.8	9.3	5.7	15.5	8.8	13.4	11.5	13.0
10001	20,100	3	Kent	586.3	176,824	372	301.6	64.4	27.2	1.3	3.4	7.2	6.3	16.6	10.1	13.6	11.5	12.6
10003	37,980	1	New Castle	426.3	559,793	121	1,313.1	59.2	26.0	0.7	6.4	10.0	5.8	15.9	9.4	14.6	12.2	13.6
10005	41,540	2	Sussex	936.1	225,322	299	240.7	76.7	13.3	1.0	1.7	9.4	5.0	13.8	6.4	10.3	9.6	12.0
11000		0	**DISTRICT OF COLUMBIA**	61.1	693,972	X	11,358.0	38.5	46.9	0.8	5.3	11.0	6.5	11.4	10.8	23.4	14.7	11.0
11001	47,900	1	District of Columbia	61.1	693,972	95	11,358.0	38.5	46.9	0.8	5.3	11.0	6.5	11.4	10.8	23.4	14.7	11.0
12000		0	**FLORIDA**	53,634.0	20,984,400	X	391.3	55.4	16.5	0.6	3.6	25.6	5.4	14.6	8.3	13.1	12.0	13.2
12001	23,540	2	Alachua	875.1	266,944	255	305.0	63.6	21.3	0.6	7.3	9.8	5.3	12.6	21.1	15.7	10.7	10.0
12003	27,260	1	Baker	585.2	28,283	1,481	48.3	82.6	14.4	1.0	1.0	2.6	6.4	17.7	8.1	15.0	13.0	13.7
12005	37,460	3	Bay	758.5	183,563	354	242.0	79.2	12.2	1.5	3.6	6.6	6.2	15.3	8.0	14.5	11.9	13.2
12007		6	Bradford	294.0	27,038	1,525	92.0	75.9	19.9	0.9	1.1	4.1	5.8	14.7	7.6	14.9	12.7	12.9
12009	37,340	2	Brevard	1,015.2	589,162	112	580.3	76.6	11.1	0.8	3.6	10.4	4.7	13.7	7.2	11.3	10.3	13.2
12011	33,100	1	Broward	1,204.6	1,935,878	18	1,607.1	37.7	29.3	0.4	4.7	29.7	5.8	14.5	7.9	13.6	13.3	14.4
12013		6	Calhoun	567.3	14,483	2,131	25.5	79.1	13.9	2.1	1.1	5.9	5.0	15.2	7.3	14.4	13.0	14.2
12015	39,460	3	Charlotte	681.1	182,033	360	267.3	85.4	6.3	0.7	1.9	7.2	3.1	9.3	5.1	7.7	7.4	10.9
12017	26,140	3	Citrus	581.9	145,647	447	250.3	89.4	3.5	0.9	2.0	5.7	3.8	11.1	5.4	8.4	7.7	11.3
12019	27,260	1	Clay	604.8	212,230	314	350.9	75.3	12.2	1.0	4.5	9.9	5.7	18.0	8.0	12.5	12.9	14.1
12021	34,940	2	Collier	1,998.8	372,880	187	186.6	63.7	7.2	0.4	1.9	27.8	4.5	12.9	6.6	9.6	9.7	11.8
12023	29,380	4	Columbia	797.5	69,612	769	87.3	74.4	18.7	1.1	1.5	6.2	6.1	15.9	8.6	13.0	11.7	12.4
12027	11,580	6	DeSoto	637.1	36,862	1,253	57.9	56.2	12.7	0.6	0.8	30.7	5.0	14.3	8.9	13.7	12.1	12.1
12029		6	Dixie	705.1	16,673	1,998	23.6	85.1	10.1	1.3	0.7	4.4	4.8	13.6	6.5	11.8	11.8	12.8
12031	27,260	1	Duval	762.8	937,934	55	1,229.6	55.3	30.7	0.8	6.2	9.7	6.8	15.8	9.0	16.6	12.6	12.8
12033	37,860	2	Escambia	656.9	313,512	220	477.3	67.0	24.1	1.6	4.9	5.6	6.1	14.9	11.6	14.7	10.8	11.9
12035	19,660	2	Flagler	485.5	110,510	546	227.6	76.4	11.0	0.8	3.2	10.4	4.0	13.3	6.3	9.0	9.7	12.2
12037		6	Franklin	545.1	11,727	2,311	21.5	80.5	14.4	1.1	0.7	5.3	4.4	11.6	6.9	15.3	11.7	12.9
12039	45,220	2	Gadsden	516.3	46,071	1,051	89.2	33.3	55.8	0.5	0.9	10.4	5.9	16.1	8.2	12.1	12.6	13.5
12041	23,540	2	Gilchrist	349.7	17,743	1,932	50.7	87.8	5.8	1.1	1.0	5.9	5.8	14.7	11.0	10.6	10.2	12.8
12043		6	Glades	806.7	13,754	2,181	17.0	61.6	13.3	4.4	0.9	20.7	3.1	12.4	6.6	13.2	12.1	12.6
12045	37,460	3	Gulf	553.6	16,160	2,031	29.2	77.3	17.9	1.2	0.9	4.5	4.0	11.6	7.2	14.6	12.8	14.7
12047		6	Hamilton	513.8	14,184	2,151	27.6	56.4	33.3	1.2	1.0	9.6	5.4	14.2	11.0	14.0	11.2	13.2
12049	48,100	6	Hardee	637.8	27,411	1,512	43.0	48.1	7.3	0.7	1.4	43.7	7.0	19.4	9.9	13.4	11.5	12.1
12051	17,500	4	Hendry	1,156.2	40,347	1,169	34.9	33.3	11.5	1.6	1.1	53.2	7.7	19.4	9.1	14.2	12.6	12.8
12053	45,300	1	Hernando	472.9	186,553	352	394.5	79.8	5.9	0.8	1.9	13.3	4.6	13.9	6.7	10.3	10.0	12.6
12055	42,700	3	Highlands	1,016.6	102,883	587	101.2	68.5	10.3	0.9	1.8	19.8	4.6	12.7	6.1	9.5	8.6	10.1
12057	45,300	1	Hillsborough	1,020.3	1,408,566	28	1,380.5	50.8	17.0	0.6	5.1	28.6	6.3	16.5	9.0	15.2	13.5	13.5
12059		6	Holmes	478.8	19,558	1,848	40.8	88.7	7.6	2.2	1.0	2.9	5.2	14.6	6.5	12.6	11.8	13.5
12061	42,680	3	Indian River	502.8	154,383	426	307.0	76.6	9.7	0.6	2.0	12.5	4.2	12.2	6.5	9.2	8.8	11.6
12063		6	Jackson	918.2	48,330	1,014	52.6	67.0	27.6	1.3	1.2	4.8	5.0	13.8	8.4	13.4	13.9	13.1
12065	45,220	2	Jefferson	598.1	14,144	2,154	23.6	60.7	34.8	0.9	0.9	4.0	4.6	12.9	6.2	11.7	11.4	14.4
12067		9	Lafayette	543.4	8,451	2,552	15.6	72.9	14.3	0.7	0.6	12.9	4.2	16.0	10.4	13.9	14.3	13.8
12069	36,740	1	Lake	940.9	346,017	202	367.8	71.6	11.1	0.8	2.8	15.4	5.0	14.4	6.7	10.8	10.7	12.4
12071	15,980	2	Lee	784.1	739,224	89	942.8	68.7	8.8	0.5	2.2	21.2	4.7	13.2	6.8	11.0	10.2	12.0
12073	45,220	2	Leon	666.9	290,292	238	435.3	58.4	32.1	0.7	4.4	6.4	5.1	13.6	21.6	14.6	10.8	10.4
12075		6	Levy	1,118.2	40,355	1,168	36.1	81.3	9.8	1.2	1.0	8.3	5.0	14.6	6.5	11.1	9.8	12.6
12077		8	Liberty	835.6	8,242	2,574	9.9	73.6	19.4	1.3	0.5	6.6	4.6	13.5	8.2	16.6	15.5	14.5
12079		6	Madison	696.1	18,449	1,899	26.5	55.7	38.3	1.0	0.7	5.6	5.3	13.8	7.4	14.0	12.0	13.4
12081	35,840	2	Manatee	743.1	385,571	181	518.9	72.8	9.3	0.6	2.6	16.3	4.8	13.8	6.6	10.6	10.3	12.4
12083	36,100	2	Marion	1,588.5	354,353	196	223.1	72.0	13.4	0.8	2.2	13.2	5.0	13.7	6.6	10.8	9.8	11.7
12085	38,940	2	Martin	543.7	159,923	407	294.1	79.4	5.7	0.5	1.8	13.8	4.1	12.4	6.2	9.3	9.2	12.7
12086	33,100	1	Miami-Dade	1,898.7	2,751,796	7	1,449.3	13.7	16.3	0.2	1.9	68.6	5.8	14.5	8.5	14.3	13.8	14.9
12087	28,580	4	Monroe	983.0	77,013	721	78.3	67.5	6.7	0.9	1.9	24.5	4.6	10.6	6.3	12.8	12.3	14.8
12089	27,260	1	Nassau	648.6	82,721	686	127.5	88.6	6.4	0.9	1.5	4.2	5.2	14.7	6.6	11.5	11.3	13.5
12091	18,880	3	Okaloosa	930.3	202,970	327	218.2	77.1	11.1	1.3	5.3	9.2	6.7	15.5	8.9	16.2	11.8	11.9
12093	36,380	4	Okeechobee	768.9	41,605	1,140	54.1	64.3	8.9	1.2	1.3	25.3	5.9	15.3	7.8	13.0	12.1	12.7
12095	36,740	1	Orange	903.1	1,348,975	30	1,493.7	42.0	21.5	0.6	6.6	31.4	6.2	16.2	10.6	16.8	14.1	13.3
12097	36,740	1	Osceola	1,327.7	352,180	198	265.3	33.4	10.4	0.5	3.4	53.7	6.3	18.3	9.3	14.4	14.4	13.4
12099	33,100	1	Palm Beach	1,966.3	1,471,150	27	748.2	55.9	19.3	0.4	3.5	22.3	5.1	14.1	7.5	12.0	11.4	13.1
12101	45,300	1	Pasco	747.6	525,643	132	703.1	76.6	6.3	0.7	3.3	15.1	5.3	15.2	7.0	11.1	12.0	13.5
12103	45,300	1	Pinellas	273.8	970,637	49	3,545.1	75.9	11.4	0.7	4.3	9.7	4.4	12.0	6.7	12.1	10.9	13.7
12105	29,460	2	Polk	1,796.8	686,483	99	382.1	60.7	15.7	0.7	2.4	22.3	5.8	16.5	8.4	12.9	11.8	12.2

1. CBSA = Core Based Statistical Area. See Appendix A for explanation. See Appendix B for list of metropolitan areas with component counties. Service of USDA Rural-Urban Continuum Codes. See Appendix A for definition.   3. Dry land or land partially or temporarily covered by water.   2. County type code from the Economic Research   4. May be of any race.

Table B. States and Counties — **Population and Households**

STATE County	55 to 64 years	65 to 74 years	75 years and over	Percent female	Total persons 2000	Total persons 2010	Percent change 2000-2010	Percent change 2010-2017	Components of change, 2010-2017 Births	Components of change, 2010-2017 Deaths	Components of change, 2010-2017 Net Migration	Number	Persons per household	Family households	Female family householder[1]	One person
	16	17	18	19	20	21	22	23	24	25	26	27	28	29	30	31
CONNECTICUT—Cont'd																
Tolland	13.8	9.1	6.3	49.8	136,364	152,691	12.0	-0.8	8,286	7,240	-2,345	54,573	2.48	65.3	9.3	25.4
Windham	15.1	9.7	6.6	50.3	109,091	118,423	8.6	-1.7	8,190	7,246	-3,038	44,261	2.52	67.5	12.6	25.7
DELAWARE	13.8	10.9	7.2	51.6	783,600	897,936	14.6	7.1	80,315	59,863	43,628	348,051	2.61	66.8	13.9	26.8
Kent	12.6	9.9	6.8	51.8	126,697	162,349	28.1	8.9	16,074	10,887	9,267	62,140	2.68	69.2	15.8	24.5
New Castle	13.3	8.8	6.3	51.5	500,265	538,477	7.6	4.0	47,845	32,246	6,152	202,524	2.64	65.6	14.1	27.7
Sussex	16.1	16.7	10.0	51.6	156,638	197,110	25.8	14.3	16,396	16,730	28,209	83,387	2.50	67.9	12.1	26.4
DISTRICT OF COLUMBIA	10.1	6.9	5.1	52.6	572,059	601,766	5.2	15.3	68,412	35,349	57,912	276,546	2.24	43.8	15.3	43.4
District of Columbia	10.1	6.9	5.1	52.6	572,059	601,766	5.2	15.3	68,412	35,349	57,912	276,546	2.24	43.8	15.3	43.4
FLORIDA	13.3	11.2	8.9	51.1	15,982,378	18,804,594	17.7	11.6	1,582,037	1,346,983	1,936,102	7,393,262	2.64	64.4	13.2	29.0
Alachua	10.9	8.2	5.4	51.6	217,955	247,337	13.5	7.9	20,901	13,260	12,022	96,336	2.49	53.4	11.3	33.8
Baker	12.2	8.5	5.4	47.3	22,259	27,115	21.8	4.3	2,508	1,691	351	8,270	2.99	74.2	12.6	20.3
Bay	14.0	9.8	7.0	50.3	148,217	168,852	13.9	8.7	16,544	12,958	11,045	67,939	2.59	64.4	12.1	29.2
Bradford	13.4	10.1	7.9	45.9	26,088	28,520	9.3	-5.2	2,220	2,129	-1,631	8,704	2.71	65.0	15.0	29.9
Brevard	16.3	12.7	10.6	51.2	476,230	543,378	14.1	8.4	37,369	48,286	56,706	224,373	2.47	63.8	11.9	30.3
Broward	13.3	9.1	7.1	51.2	1,623,018	1,748,146	7.7	10.7	157,674	107,121	138,204	672,988	2.74	63.9	15.6	29.1
Calhoun	13.1	10.2	7.6	45.4	13,017	14,625	12.4	-1.0	1,039	1,129	-47	4,555	2.75	67.7	12.9	28.0
Charlotte	17.1	21.2	18.2	51.3	141,627	159,968	13.0	13.8	7,408	17,598	31,901	73,299	2.27	64.4	7.7	29.8
Citrus	16.4	19.6	16.3	51.6	118,085	141,236	19.6	3.1	7,532	17,698	14,568	61,350	2.25	63.2	9.6	31.8
Clay	13.6	9.6	5.6	50.8	140,814	190,865	35.5	11.2	15,504	11,626	17,527	70,527	2.82	75.2	13.2	20.4
Collier	13.4	15.9	15.6	50.8	251,377	321,520	27.9	16.0	23,497	22,522	50,154	133,331	2.58	67.0	9.0	27.6
Columbia	14.0	10.9	7.6	48.5	56,513	67,530	19.5	3.1	5,822	5,607	1,886	23,911	2.65	63.7	13.0	31.6
DeSoto	12.1	11.3	10.5	43.5	32,209	34,862	8.2	5.7	2,752	2,178	1,431	11,419	2.75	60.9	12.7	26.0
Dixie	15.2	13.7	9.7	44.7	13,827	16,422	18.8	1.5	1,124	1,518	643	6,221	2.34	62.4	12.5	30.0
Duval	12.8	8.4	5.3	51.5	778,879	864,277	11.0	8.5	92,121	55,743	37,688	341,906	2.58	61.7	15.8	31.2
Escambia	13.5	9.8	6.7	50.5	294,410	297,620	1.1	5.3	28,223	23,333	11,109	115,984	2.50	59.4	13.0	32.8
Flagler	15.5	17.7	12.4	51.8	49,832	95,697	92.0	15.5	5,879	8,538	17,290	38,150	2.68	69.8	9.2	24.2
Franklin	14.4	14.4	8.5	43.3	11,057	11,549	4.4	1.5	746	941	368	4,250	2.33	66.2	9.8	28.7
Gadsden	14.5	10.4	6.8	52.4	45,087	47,744	5.9	-3.5	4,066	3,339	-2,428	16,885	2.50	68.1	22.3	27.9
Gilchrist	14.5	11.6	8.8	48.8	14,437	16,939	17.3	4.7	1,373	1,289	721	6,254	2.52	67.8	11.0	28.0
Glades	12.9	14.5	12.5	44.3	10,576	12,884	21.8	6.8	510	787	1,133	4,019	2.99	64.6	10.3	30.3
Gulf	14.5	12.6	8.2	41.4	13,332	15,863	19.0	1.9	887	1,230	631	5,349	2.53	69.1	13.0	27.4
Hamilton	13.4	10.8	6.9	42.5	13,327	14,799	11.0	-4.2	1,140	945	-853	4,717	2.32	70.7	20.2	25.3
Hardee	10.6	8.8	7.3	47.2	26,938	27,731	2.9	-1.2	2,850	1,486	-1,709	7,558	3.32	74.3	13.4	21.5
Hendry	10.9	7.5	5.8	47.4	36,210	39,140	8.1	3.1	4,310	2,046	-1,154	11,817	3.07	70.3	19.6	23.3
Hernando	14.4	15.0	12.5	52.0	130,802	172,775	32.1	8.0	11,035	18,569	21,225	70,918	2.46	67.2	12.2	27.0
Highlands	13.5	16.7	18.0	51.3	87,366	98,786	13.1	4.1	6,607	10,669	8,214	40,500	2.40	64.1	9.4	31.3
Hillsborough	11.9	8.4	5.6	51.2	998,948	1,229,179	23.0	14.6	122,243	72,604	128,728	495,841	2.63	63.3	14.2	28.8
Holmes	14.0	10.9	8.8	46.8	18,564	19,924	7.3	-1.8	1,425	1,847	64	6,809	2.60	67.0	11.4	29.8
Indian River	15.4	17.0	15.2	52.1	112,947	138,028	22.2	11.8	9,141	13,815	20,896	57,829	2.49	62.6	8.4	32.3
Jackson	13.3	10.8	8.2	44.9	46,755	49,761	6.4	-2.9	3,597	4,171	-853	16,744	2.44	64.8	14.8	31.0
Jefferson	16.0	14.0	8.8	47.7	12,902	14,753	14.3	-4.1	923	1,127	-417	5,564	2.08	63.5	15.3	33.0
Lafayette	11.4	9.2	6.9	41.8	7,022	8,870	26.3	-4.7	534	513	-454	2,320	3.04	70.4	13.3	26.4
Lake	13.5	14.4	12.1	51.6	210,528	297,047	41.1	16.5	22,680	26,948	52,733	122,036	2.57	68.3	10.5	26.5
Lee	14.1	15.5	12.5	51.0	440,888	618,754	40.3	19.5	47,191	47,340	119,306	258,084	2.60	66.1	10.6	27.7
Leon	11.0	8.1	4.8	52.5	239,452	275,490	15.1	5.4	21,961	12,746	5,531	111,111	2.44	52.5	13.0	30.4
Levy	15.8	14.7	9.8	51.2	34,450	40,801	18.4	-1.1	2,857	3,846	546	15,372	2.55	64.1	13.7	31.1
Liberty	12.6	8.7	5.8	38.8	7,021	8,365	19.1	-1.5	568	439	-262	2,363	2.87	67.7	9.7	29.8
Madison	14.2	11.9	8.1	47.0	18,733	19,226	2.6	-4.0	1,491	1,617	-652	6,665	2.47	64.4	13.7	33.1
Manatee	14.7	14.7	12.1	51.7	264,002	322,878	22.3	19.4	24,922	26,754	63,788	135,990	2.57	65.7	10.8	28.2
Marion	13.7	15.7	12.9	52.0	258,916	331,301	28.0	7.0	24,716	33,906	32,200	132,277	2.50	65.2	11.7	29.4
Martin	15.7	15.2	15.2	50.6	126,731	146,852	15.9	8.9	8,856	13,345	17,460	62,980	2.38	61.3	8.2	33.4
Miami-Dade	12.3	8.6	7.4	51.4	2,253,362	2,498,018	10.9	10.2	228,834	139,779	163,914	853,624	3.07	68.1	18.2	26.4
Monroe	16.8	13.6	8.1	48.0	79,589	73,090	-8.2	5.4	5,284	5,050	3,670	29,549	2.53	56.8	7.0	32.5
Nassau	15.6	13.7	7.9	50.8	57,663	73,317	27.1	12.8	5,609	5,460	9,202	29,214	2.62	72.5	10.7	23.1
Okaloosa	13.3	9.2	6.5	49.3	170,498	180,821	6.1	12.2	19,738	12,003	14,262	76,140	2.50	66.4	11.2	27.5
Okeechobee	12.7	11.1	9.5	46.2	35,910	39,996	11.4	4.0	3,810	2,993	797	12,850	2.82	67.4	13.9	27.0
Orange	11.2	7.1	4.6	50.9	896,344	1,145,951	27.8	17.7	116,252	53,625	139,982	444,852	2.75	64.5	15.3	26.6
Osceola	10.9	7.9	5.0	50.8	172,493	268,683	55.8	31.1	29,201	14,136	68,123	93,324	3.32	74.3	16.7	19.8
Palm Beach	13.1	11.6	12.0	51.5	1,131,184	1,320,135	16.7	11.4	103,987	101,133	148,026	538,549	2.56	62.5	12.0	30.9
Pasco	13.4	12.5	10.0	51.4	344,765	464,703	34.8	13.1	35,470	41,659	66,725	189,292	2.54	66.0	11.3	28.0
Pinellas	15.9	13.1	11.1	52.0	921,482	916,812	-0.5	5.9	61,679	84,355	76,379	405,788	2.27	55.6	11.0	37.1
Polk	12.3	11.4	8.7	51.0	483,924	602,095	24.4	14.0	53,892	45,696	76,000	223,060	2.80	68.6	13.7	25.7

1. No spouse present.

STATE County	Housing units, 2017 (cont.)								Civilian labor force, 2017				Civilian employment[6], 2012-2016		
	Occupied units										Unemployment			Percent	
			Owner-occupied			Renter-occupied									
				Median owner cost as a percent of income											
	Total	Percent	Median value[1]	With a mort-gage	Without a mort-gage[2]	Median rent[3]	Median rent as a percent of income[2]	Sub-standard units[4] (percent)	Total	Percent change, 2016-2017	Total	Rate[5]	Total	Management, business, science, and arts	Construction, production, and maintenance occupations
	89	90	91	92	93	94	95	96	97	98	99	100	101	102	103
CONNECTICUT—Cont'd															
Tolland	54573	72.7	247,800	22.4	13.1	1,061	30.8	1.1	86,570	1.1	3,463	4.0	80,477	41.7	18.0
Windham	44261	69.9	196,900	23.9	14.1	852	30.7	1.8	64,159	1.4	3,220	5.0	58,997	31.8	23.7
DELAWARE	348051	70.9	233,100	22.3	10.8	1,039	29.8	2.0	477,350	0.7	21,922	4.6	438,292	38.9	18.9
Kent	62140	69.3	199,800	23.2	10.8	1,006	31.3	2.3	78,132	0.7	3,886	5.0	76,158	33.1	24.0
New Castle	202524	68.7	244,300	21.8	10.5	1,064	29.5	1.8	296,289	0.4	13,330	4.5	270,270	43.0	15.5
Sussex	83387	77.7	231,600	23.2	11.2	968	29.4	2.3	102,929	1.6	4,706	4.6	91,864	31.5	24.6
DISTRICT OF COLUMBIA	276546	40.7	506,100	21.6	10.2	1,362	29.4	3.8	400,894	1.6	24,261	6.1	348,225	60.9	6.5
District of Columbia	276546	40.7	506,100	21.6	10.2	1,362	29.4	3.8	400,894	1.6	24,261	6.1	348,225	60.9	6.5
FLORIDA	7393262	64.8	166,800	24.6	12.6	1,032	33.9	3.2	10,100,268	2.6	419,446	4.2	8,755,427	34.3	18.2
Alachua	96336	53.7	165,700	21.7	10.6	885	35.6	2.1	136,013	2.5	5,033	3.7	117,507	46.2	11.3
Baker	8270	79.3	108,600	19.4	10.0	695	26.2	3.4	11,794	3.2	478	4.1	10,336	30.4	24.8
Bay	67939	61.7	162,500	23.2	11.3	943	31.5	2.1	88,900	1.1	3,639	4.1	79,570	32.1	20.5
Bradford	8704	72.8	92,000	19.4	10.0	734	32.7	2.2	11,293	3.9	408	3.6	9,161	31.5	20.9
Brevard	224373	71.7	150,500	23.3	11.7	936	31.7	1.6	268,757	2.3	11,392	4.2	233,874	37.1	17.8
Broward	672988	62.8	202,300	27.6	15.7	1,226	35.9	4.1	1,026,330	2.2	39,744	3.9	910,527	35.4	16.8
Calhoun	4555	82.7	80,300	24.2	10.0	652	23.8	3.4	4,933	-1.1	241	4.9	4,618	25.5	25.6
Charlotte	73299	78.1	154,400	26.8	12.7	905	33.7	1.6	70,269	1.4	3,241	4.6	57,294	28.6	19.4
Citrus	61350	81.8	114,300	23.7	11.8	775	33.7	2.1	47,901	0.1	2,767	5.8	44,047	28.9	22.3
Clay	70527	74.8	157,600	22.1	10.2	1,028	28.8	2.3	104,588	3.5	3,971	3.8	89,254	33.3	21.7
Collier	133331	72.0	291,900	26.1	12.8	1,125	32.5	4.1	171,979	1.6	7,005	4.1	145,216	30.0	20.4
Columbia	23911	72.2	105,100	22.8	10.3	781	27.5	4.1	29,419	-1.2	1,259	4.3	25,292	30.7	24.4
DeSoto	11419	68.6	82,300	23.3	10.9	666	31.1	7.5	13,833	2.6	608	4.4	12,520	14.5	44.5
Dixie	6221	77.4	69,600	25.6	10.9	644	31.1	3.7	5,800	2.6	264	4.6	4,979	22.3	32.4
Duval	341906	58.2	146,400	23.1	11.4	962	31.8	2.2	483,717	3.4	19,993	4.1	418,435	36.0	18.3
Escambia	115984	60.3	121,800	22.0	11.2	901	30.4	1.3	144,784	2.7	5,987	4.1	131,454	32.0	18.3
Flagler	38150	76.9	174,700	26.7	11.9	1,079	30.0	1.8	46,377	2.2	2,157	4.7	37,758	30.4	17.6
Franklin	4250	72.7	124,500	26.9	11.4	723	25.3	4.1	4,770	0.7	171	3.6	4,296	30.5	29.1
Gadsden	16885	71.1	105,100	23.8	10.8	693	31.7	5.0	18,477	1.4	982	5.3	16,343	31.6	21.4
Gilchrist	6254	82.4	94,400	22.3	11.2	624	30.8	1.9	6,839	2.4	288	4.2	6,270	26.4	27.9
Glades	4019	74.7	79,200	24.5	11.3	710	33.2	3.0	5,043	6.9	261	5.2	3,627	24.5	30.8
Gulf	5349	74.6	131,400	24.1	12.6	836	32.0	2.4	6,024	0.9	232	3.9	5,610	27.6	24.9
Hamilton	4717	72.6	71,000	23.0	10.3	571	28.6	3.2	4,438	-4.7	211	4.8	3,883	27.4	27.6
Hardee	7558	68.5	78,800	22.8	11.1	645	28.8	8.1	9,378	1.3	520	5.5	9,481	20.7	37.1
Hendry	11817	67.7	70,600	23.4	10.0	692	26.2	7.3	15,652	1.6	1,134	7.2	15,312	22.1	46.2
Hernando	70918	78.0	112,300	23.7	11.5	904	33.5	1.9	69,356	2.1	3,557	5.1	60,732	30.2	21.1
Highlands	40500	75.6	86,600	23.4	11.3	731	33.3	3.0	35,921	0.5	2,019	5.6	31,556	27.6	22.8
Hillsborough	495841	57.9	167,400	22.7	10.9	992	31.8	3.7	723,973	2.3	27,695	3.8	627,149	38.1	17.2
Holmes	6809	79.8	90,700	23.5	10.7	656	39.2	2.3	6,801	1.3	324	4.8	6,434	26.1	28.2
Indian River	57829	74.6	160,900	24.4	12.3	881	34.1	1.8	63,322	1.8	3,153	5.0	53,936	32.3	19.1
Jackson	16744	70.9	92,200	23.1	12.5	624	29.0	3.1	17,307	-0.2	770	4.4	15,966	26.4	20.1
Jefferson	5564	78.5	123,300	25.9	12.2	823	37.4	1.7	5,444	1.0	235	4.3	4,823	41.9	15.3
Lafayette	2320	82.2	112,400	23.0	11.3	675	28.5	4.6	2,955	-0.4	110	3.7	2,548	30.4	29.7
Lake	122036	74.0	145,100	23.4	11.8	956	32.6	2.6	151,015	3.3	6,151	4.1	125,218	31.2	20.0
Lee	258084	69.0	171,100	24.6	12.9	984	31.6	2.7	335,542	1.8	13,362	4.0	274,224	30.6	19.4
Leon	111111	52.2	183,800	21.8	10.0	941	35.6	2.4	152,544	1.5	5,893	3.9	141,908	45.0	10.0
Levy	15372	75.1	86,700	24.2	11.5	651	30.6	3.0	16,967	1.9	737	4.3	14,324	23.5	28.1
Liberty	2363	75.7	69,500	19.5	10.0	574	20.1	3.4	2,632	-0.3	118	4.5	2,759	29.0	25.3
Madison	6665	78.5	81,100	23.9	14.9	650	37.8	4.3	7,407	1.1	324	4.4	6,048	28.1	28.3
Manatee	135990	69.9	178,700	23.7	12.1	993	33.1	2.7	174,945	2.5	6,784	3.9	145,477	32.9	19.1
Marion	132277	74.8	114,400	24.0	11.8	819	31.7	2.1	133,553	1.1	6,619	5.0	118,503	27.4	20.3
Martin	62980	75.6	209,700	24.8	13.5	996	32.5	1.9	72,370	2.0	2,979	4.1	62,343	36.1	16.9
Miami-Dade	853624	52.6	221,100	29.1	14.8	1,143	39.2	6.4	1,384,224	3.8	66,731	4.8	1,235,165	31.5	19.7
Monroe	29549	60.2	400,800	31.9	13.7	1,466	35.3	3.5	45,317	-2.5	1,501	3.3	39,635	30.8	18.6
Nassau	29214	76.1	192,600	22.6	10.0	1,050	31.5	1.4	39,078	3.4	1,484	3.8	33,095	33.7	23.9
Okaloosa	76140	63.3	191,800	22.8	10.6	1,035	30.1	2.0	95,850	2.7	3,237	3.4	85,253	34.3	18.2
Okeechobee	12850	70.8	90,800	22.6	11.2	700	30.9	5.4	18,691	3.0	782	4.2	13,475	20.8	34.2
Orange	444852	54.3	173,700	24.2	12.1	1,064	33.9	3.1	731,398	3.5	26,683	3.6	620,484	35.7	16.0
Osceola	93324	60.2	146,500	26.5	13.2	1,074	36.0	3.6	169,949	3.4	7,181	4.2	137,599	24.9	20.4
Palm Beach	538549	68.6	222,700	26.0	14.6	1,206	35.5	3.3	724,465	2.1	29,486	4.1	636,646	35.9	16.2
Pasco	189292	72.8	122,100	23.7	11.7	946	32.0	2.1	227,732	2.3	9,933	4.4	193,633	36.2	17.4
Pinellas	405788	64.6	157,500	24.4	13.9	967	32.3	1.9	490,061	2.4	18,206	3.8	429,839	37.6	15.5
Polk	223060	68.0	110,400	23.4	12.0	883	30.9	3.7	293,587	2.3	13,643	4.6	252,785	29.6	23.6

1. Specified owner-occupied units. lacking complete plumbing facilities.   2. A value of 10.0 represents 10 percent or less; a value of 50.0 represents 50 percent or more.   3. Specified renter-occupied units.   4. Overcrowded or
5. Percent of civilian labor force.   6. Civilian employed persons 16 years old and over.

Table B. States and Counties — Nonfarm Employment and Agriculture

	Private nonfarm establishments, employment and payroll, 2016									Agriculture, 2012			
		Employment						Annual payroll		Farms			
												Percent with:	
STATE County	Number of establishments	Total	Health care and social assistance	Manufacturing	Retail trade	Finance and insurance	Professional, scientific, and technical services	Total (mil dol)	Average per employee (dollars)	Number	Fewer than 50 acres	500 acres or more	Farm operators whose principal occupation is farming (percent)
	104	105	106	107	108	109	110	111	112	113	114	115	116
CONNECTICUT—Cont'd													
Tolland	2458	28,239	6,338	3,313	4,967	670	1,238	1,118	39,588	578	64.5	2.4	34.3
Windham	2057	30,696	7,083	5,572	5,223	681	562	1,211	39,436	692	62.0	3.0	51.3
DELAWARE	25366	400,069	67,806	27,189	56,173	42,232	29,556	21,196	52,982	2,451	56.5	9.8	63.9
Kent	3422	53,196	10,879	4,810	9,317	1,581	2,452	2,040	38,349	863	54.5	9.0	56.8
New Castle	16056	272,403	45,065	12,441	33,234	37,768	23,916	16,312	59,882	374	64.7	9.4	57.8
Sussex	5601	66,704	11,674	9,938	13,615	1,897	1,853	2,470	37,035	1,214	55.4	10.5	70.8
DISTRICT OF COLUMBIA	23177	526,879	68,675	1,258	22,143	17,729	102,780	39,834	75,603	NA	NA	NA	NA
District of Columbia	23177	526,879	68,675	1,258	22,143	17,729	102,780	39,834	75,603	NA	NA	NA	NA
FLORIDA	546218	8,169,642	1,086,559	306,700	1,088,564	355,395	499,518	363,336	44,474	47,740	68.6	5.6	48.0
Alachua	6114	93,371	25,190	3,708	14,191	4,130	5,637	3,662	39,225	1,662	69.7	4.9	42.3
Baker	383	5,728	1,865	153	888	137	72	187	32,635	381	74.8	3.4	35.7
Bay	4627	61,535	9,768	4,101	11,712	1,464	6,833	2,125	34,529	115	71.3	2.6	42.6
Bradford	430	4,240	891	171	988	144	100	124	29,345	470	68.3	1.9	46.0
Brevard	13927	176,190	29,695	18,301	29,198	4,653	14,471	7,665	43,506	513	80.3	5.1	38.8
Broward	60204	693,194	93,960	24,305	110,165	34,234	53,439	32,246	46,518	615	93.7	1.3	50.1
Calhoun	184	1,782	653	43	307	56	12	47	26,520	218	51.8	8.3	31.2
Charlotte	3883	37,640	8,823	499	9,256	1,091	1,401	1,263	33,560	284	61.3	12.0	51.1
Citrus	2732	29,803	10,283	303	5,686	673	853	1,004	33,683	559	73.9	3.4	49.7
Clay	3806	40,089	8,730	1,027	8,626	1,006	3,136	1,359	33,906	403	75.9	2.0	44.7
Collier	11698	124,868	18,374	3,290	21,838	4,000	5,248	5,238	41,949	319	74.0	10.3	43.9
Columbia	1320	19,130	4,538	716	3,279	486	586	709	37,055	945	65.4	4.6	46.5
DeSoto	466	5,491	1,104	485	1,048	159	150	188	34,198	836	63.0	9.4	48.4
Dixie	179	1,533	272	447	275	47	24	46	30,234	204	60.3	6.4	30.9
Duval	25219	434,531	60,408	21,876	53,961	44,776	27,861	21,041	48,422	352	76.4	3.1	59.9
Escambia	6813	104,620	21,384	3,986	16,067	7,901	7,478	4,217	40,303	729	68.2	4.5	43.2
Flagler	2071	17,869	3,282	1,108	3,625	637	629	563	31,512	118	46.6	14.4	54.2
Franklin	313	2,265	296	D	447	63	73	63	27,955	20	65.0	0.0	40.0
Gadsden	664	8,956	2,494	1,010	1,260	148	128	328	36,583	402	56.5	5.2	39.6
Gilchrist	229	1,682	618	117	200	42	48	56	33,373	581	66.3	5.3	44.8
Glades	112	788	86	122	56	13	11	28	35,317	331	53.5	15.7	39.3
Gulf	286	2,749	551	41	418	86	181	87	31,476	34	41.2	5.9	52.9
Hamilton	169	1,846	255	D	444	20	20	79	42,746	292	36.0	9.6	64.4
Hardee	384	4,129	1,260	302	661	238	78	140	33,850	982	57.3	9.4	50.2
Hendry	579	6,115	1,060	792	1,305	211	352	215	35,175	406	49.8	22.7	51.2
Hernando	3177	33,835	8,704	1,952	7,837	741	1,296	1,080	31,924	799	76.0	3.3	51.2
Highlands	1913	20,419	5,793	764	4,643	596	690	635	31,108	969	64.3	11.0	49.3
Hillsborough	36533	587,224	83,095	21,301	70,169	47,963	61,718	29,071	49,506	2,466	80.3	2.1	51.7
Holmes	251	1,865	570	94	392	51	57	50	26,559	801	41.7	4.2	52.6
Indian River	4249	43,224	9,241	1,655	9,199	1,417	1,932	1,623	37,545	461	73.1	7.2	49.0
Jackson	768	9,305	1,840	556	1,998	331	258	288	30,898	1,160	39.0	8.7	42.1
Jefferson	236	1,596	239	42	363	111	61	47	29,430	617	56.1	6.6	37.0
Lafayette	97	686	137	50	78	52	21	18	26,246	221	29.9	13.6	59.7
Lake	7132	81,265	18,500	3,086	16,098	2,034	2,881	2,718	33,451	1,784	76.7	3.3	43.9
Lee	18143	209,788	35,633	5,278	40,208	6,018	12,271	8,205	39,111	844	79.5	4.5	48.1
Leon	7603	98,267	18,175	1,563	16,690	4,414	10,354	3,882	39,506	284	63.4	4.6	38.4
Levy	722	5,867	792	512	1,482	232	184	177	30,174	1,053	64.7	4.4	49.9
Liberty	85	1,156	431	308	145	10	D	39	33,533	80	30.0	5.0	30.0
Madison	308	2,863	627	472	584	67	85	86	29,993	669	36.2	10.3	38.6
Manatee	8729	99,027	16,031	8,002	19,583	2,498	4,309	3,614	36,498	689	62.6	9.6	43.4
Marion	7004	79,752	15,888	6,725	16,289	2,094	2,894	2,751	34,496	3,870	76.7	2.2	49.5
Martin	5462	57,067	11,133	2,542	10,111	1,904	3,696	2,201	38,566	587	74.3	9.7	54.7
Miami-Dade	83903	972,716	138,060	35,960	142,824	49,973	69,970	46,078	47,370	2,954	92.8	1.2	56.5
Monroe	3816	31,794	2,352	346	6,217	693	925	1,068	33,601	28	92.9	0.0	25.0
Nassau	1845	17,090	2,589	1,250	3,158	387	591	604	35,337	444	74.1	2.9	45.0
Okaloosa	5280	59,443	8,502	1,817	12,372	2,425	6,423	2,255	37,937	477	52.0	4.8	37.9
Okeechobee	791	7,042	1,352	430	1,827	190	214	241	34,198	678	47.9	25.1	56.6
Orange	36801	704,627	71,638	25,170	86,283	22,237	50,550	31,203	44,283	662	80.5	4.1	51.8
Osceola	6000	76,881	11,810	1,637	16,364	1,246	1,804	2,456	31,941	365	58.1	15.9	58.9
Palm Beach	47613	512,940	83,736	12,886	79,890	21,465	42,150	24,473	47,711	1,409	90.0	3.5	56.7
Pasco	9377	96,501	20,997	3,206	23,363	2,547	4,221	3,332	34,531	1,065	75.1	5.3	52.1
Pinellas	28117	374,390	72,554	29,033	52,728	24,657	29,654	16,585	44,298	118	91.5	0.0	45.8
Polk	11530	181,761	28,214	16,638	27,610	11,624	6,072	7,236	39,810	2,415	64.4	7.2	45.3

Table B. States and Counties — Land Area and Population

State / county code	CBSA code[1]	County code[2]	STATE County	Land area[3] (sq. mi)	Total persons 2017	Rank	Per square mile	White	Black	American Indian, Alaska Native	Asian and Pacific Islancer	Percent Hispanic or Latino[4]	Under 5 years	5 to 17 years	18 to 24 years	25 to 34 years	35 to 44 years	45 to 54 years
				1	2	3	4	5	6	7	8	9	10	11	12	13	14	15
			GEORGIA—Cont'd															
13103	42,340	2	Effingham	477.7	59,982	871	125.6	80.4	14.5	0.9	1.6	4.4	7.0	19.6	8.0	14.0	13.8	13.9
13105		6	Elbert	351.1	19,109	1,868	54.4	64.5	29.2	0.6	1.1	5.8	5.9	15.9	7.4	12.2	10.8	13.0
13107		7	Emanuel	680.6	22,530	1,704	33.1	60.0	35.1	0.5	0.9	4.5	6.8	18.2	9.0	13.5	12.1	11.8
13109		6	Evans	182.9	10,775	2,364	58.9	57.2	30.1	0.6	1.2	12.0	7.0	19.7	7.6	13.3	11.9	12.2
13111		8	Fannin	387.1	25,322	1,592	65.4	95.8	1.0	1.0	0.8	2.5	4.1	12.7	6.0	8.8	9.5	12.4
13113	12,060	1	Fayette	194.4	112,549	543	579.0	64.0	24.0	0.7	5.9	7.4	4.5	18.9	8.8	8.7	11.3	15.3
13115	40,660	3	Floyd	509.8	97,613	610	191.5	72.6	15.3	0.6	1.9	11.2	6.2	17.1	10.0	12.9	12.0	12.7
13117	12,060	1	Forsyth	224.2	227,967	292	1,016.8	73.2	4.1	0.6	14.1	9.6	6.1	21.8	7.2	9.8	16.1	16.8
13119		8	Franklin	261.5	22,820	1,684	87.3	84.7	9.9	0.7	1.3	4.7	5.9	16.1	9.3	12.1	11.0	12.9
13121	12,060	1	Fulton	526.7	1,041,423	43	1,977.3	41.2	44.8	0.6	8.0	7.3	6.0	16.3	10.2	16.8	14.3	13.9
13123		6	Gilmer	426.2	30,674	1,414	72.0	86.0	1.0	1.0	0.8	12.4	5.6	13.9	7.1	9.7	11.2	12.7
13125		9	Glascock	143.7	3,062	2,963	21.3	88.2	9.8	1.2	0.5	1.8	5.2	17.6	8.4	10.9	12.4	14.1
13127	15,260	3	Glynn	419.4	85,282	670	203.3	64.9	27.1	0.7	2.1	7.0	5.8	16.4	8.2	12.0	11.4	12.7
13129	15,660	4	Gordon	355.8	57,089	897	160.5	78.5	4.6	0.6	1.4	16.2	6.1	18.6	8.5	12.7	13.1	14.5
13131		6	Grady	454.5	24,819	1,617	54.6	58.8	28.8	1.0	0.7	11.7	6.8	18.4	7.6	12.1	11.5	12.8
13133		6	Greene	387.4	17,281	1,959	44.6	58.3	34.6	0.8	1.3	6.1	5.3	13.7	5.9	9.3	10.6	11.2
13135	12,060	1	Gwinnett	430.4	920,260	59	2,138.2	39.2	28.3	0.7	13.0	21.2	6.7	20.6	9.0	13.3	14.6	14.9
13137	18,460	6	Habersham	276.8	44,567	1,082	161.0	78.7	4.3	0.8	2.8	14.9	5.8	16.8	9.2	12.6	12.0	13.0
13139	23,580	3	Hall	393.0	199,335	335	507.2	61.9	7.9	0.6	2.3	28.6	6.5	19.1	8.9	13.1	12.6	13.7
13141	33,300	7	Hancock	471.1	8,561	2,538	18.2	25.2	71.3	0.6	1.4	2.3	3.8	12.1	8.0	14.2	11.2	13.2
13143	12,060	1	Haralson	282.2	29,256	1,450	103.7	92.5	5.4	0.9	1.1	1.7	6.2	17.9	7.8	12.9	11.9	14.7
13145	17,980	2	Harris	463.9	33,915	1,329	73.1	78.2	17.2	0.8	1.6	3.7	4.7	16.9	7.8	10.1	11.7	15.3
13147		6	Hart	232.4	25,794	1,573	111.0	76.0	19.9	0.5	1.2	3.9	5.4	15.9	7.4	11.3	10.9	13.5
13149	12,060	1	Heard	296.0	11,730	2,309	39.6	86.4	11.0	0.9	0.8	2.7	5.5	17.1	8.4	11.7	12.1	13.9
13151	12,060	1	Henry	318.6	225,813	298	708.8	45.4	45.2	0.8	4.2	6.9	5.8	20.2	9.3	12.0	13.9	15.6
13153	47,580	3	Houston	375.6	153,479	430	408.6	58.5	32.4	0.9	4.2	6.7	6.7	19.1	8.7	14.9	13.1	13.1
13155		7	Irwin	354.4	9,410	2,473	26.6	67.6	28.2	0.3	1.0	3.8	4.9	15.8	8.8	13.9	13.0	13.7
13157	27,600	4	Jackson	339.7	67,519	788	198.8	83.3	7.8	0.7	2.4	7.5	6.5	19.0	7.4	12.8	13.7	14.1
13159	12,060	1	Jasper	368.2	13,964	2,164	37.9	75.4	20.6	0.7	0.6	4.1	6.0	17.7	7.3	11.4	11.5	14.0
13161		7	Jeff Davis	330.8	15,025	2,097	45.4	72.5	15.4	0.5	0.8	11.9	7.0	19.8	8.3	12.2	12.3	13.0
13163		6	Jefferson	526.5	15,648	2,060	29.7	42.9	53.0	0.4	0.7	3.9	6.3	17.5	8.3	12.3	11.3	12.9
13165		6	Jenkins	347.3	8,767	2,527	25.2	51.5	42.7	0.5	0.6	5.6	5.4	15.3	9.6	14.6	12.6	12.9
13167	20,140	7	Johnson	303.0	9,788	2,445	32.3	63.3	34.1	0.5	0.6	2.4	4.7	13.9	7.8	13.4	13.4	14.5
13169	31,420	3	Jones	393.9	28,470	1,472	72.3	72.4	25.7	0.7	0.9	1.7	5.2	18.1	7.9	11.1	12.5	14.4
13171	12,060	1	Lamar	183.5	18,599	1,889	101.4	66.8	30.7	0.8	1.0	2.5	5.8	15.2	13.0	12.4	11.0	12.7
13173	46,660	3	Lanier	185.3	10,425	2,393	56.3	70.9	22.7	1.3	2.0	5.9	7.1	17.5	7.9	16.0	13.1	12.5
13175	20,140	5	Laurens	807.3	47,330	1,029	58.6	59.2	37.6	0.5	1.2	2.6	6.6	18.1	8.0	12.2	11.9	12.9
13177	10,500	3	Lee	355.9	29,470	1,442	82.8	73.1	21.6	0.7	3.1	2.9	6.1	20.2	7.8	12.9	14.7	13.7
13179	25,980	3	Liberty	515.9	61,386	851	119.0	42.0	44.4	1.2	3.9	12.8	10.3	17.9	14.0	19.7	10.9	9.3
13181	12,260	2	Lincoln	210.4	7,880	2,604	37.5	67.3	30.7	0.9	0.9	1.9	5.3	14.0	7.2	11.0	9.7	12.8
13183	25,980	3	Long	400.4	19,014	1,872	47.5	60.5	27.9	1.3	3.0	11.0	7.7	20.1	8.7	17.1	14.1	12.4
13185	46,660	3	Lowndes	496.2	115,489	534	232.7	55.4	37.3	0.7	2.8	5.8	6.9	17.1	17.1	15.1	11.1	10.6
13187		6	Lumpkin	282.9	32,873	1,362	116.2	92.1	2.1	1.4	1.2	4.9	4.5	13.3	19.2	11.1	10.2	11.4
13189	12,260	2	McDuffie	257.5	21,498	1,757	83.5	54.9	42.3	0.7	0.8	3.0	6.6	18.8	8.0	12.0	10.9	12.8
13191	15,260	3	McIntosh	424.4	14,106	2,158	33.2	63.5	34.4	0.8	0.7	2.1	4.1	12.3	6.8	10.3	9.7	13.5
13193		6	Macon	400.6	13,314	2,211	33.2	33.6	60.4	0.4	1.8	4.5	5.1	14.2	9.3	14.8	12.1	13.2
13195	12,020	3	Madison	282.3	29,302	1,449	103.8	83.5	9.7	0.7	2.2	5.4	6.2	16.9	8.0	12.0	12.2	14.0
13197	17,980	2	Marion	366.0	8,450	2,553	23.1	60.1	31.4	1.2	1.3	7.4	5.0	16.6	7.4	10.9	10.4	14.3
13199	12,060	1	Meriwether	501.2	21,049	1,772	42.0	57.7	40.0	0.7	0.8	2.1	5.9	15.7	8.2	11.7	10.7	12.8
13201		8	Miller	282.4	5,838	2,767	20.7	68.4	28.4	0.8	0.8	2.9	5.4	17.8	7.5	11.3	10.5	13.7
13205		6	Mitchell	512.1	22,292	1,716	43.5	46.9	48.0	0.6	1.0	4.5	5.8	17.0	8.6	13.2	12.7	13.1
13207	31,420	3	Monroe	396.1	27,113	1,520	68.4	73.5	23.6	0.6	1.2	2.4	5.0	15.7	8.5	11.4	11.7	14.2
13209	47,080	9	Montgomery	239.5	9,031	2,500	37.7	67.2	26.2	0.4	0.9	6.6	5.6	15.2	11.3	12.9	11.8	13.0
13211	12,060	1	Morgan	347.4	18,412	1,901	53.0	73.2	23.4	0.7	1.0	3.1	5.7	17.0	7.5	10.5	11.1	13.9
13213	19,140	3	Murray	344.5	39,782	1,182	115.5	83.2	1.3	0.6	0.7	15.2	6.3	18.6	8.4	12.7	12.7	14.5
13215	17,980	2	Muscogee	216.4	194,058	341	896.8	42.5	47.9	0.9	3.8	7.6	7.3	17.5	10.2	16.1	12.4	11.7
13217	12,060	1	Newton	273.7	108,078	556	394.9	48.2	45.9	0.7	1.6	5.6	6.5	19.8	9.5	12.5	13.0	14.4
13219	12,020	3	Oconee	184.3	38,028	1,224	206.3	85.6	5.6	0.4	4.8	5.0	5.6	21.0	7.9	9.2	13.5	14.8
13221	12,020	3	Oglethorpe	439.0	14,877	2,105	33.9	77.3	17.9	0.7	1.2	4.8	5.4	15.6	7.6	12.1	11.7	14.7
13223	12,060	1	Paulding	312.3	159,445	411	510.6	72.9	20.4	0.8	1.8	6.3	6.4	20.2	8.5	13.3	14.4	15.8
13225	47,580	3	Peach	150.3	27,099	1,521	180.3	46.8	44.7	0.7	1.5	8.0	5.7	15.7	13.8	12.5	10.6	12.6
13227	12,060	1	Pickens	232.1	31,588	1,392	136.1	94.5	1.6	0.9	1.1	3.2	5.1	15.6	7.0	11.0	11.2	13.6
13229	48,180	6	Pierce	340.2	19,307	1,862	56.8	85.1	9.1	0.9	0.9	5.3	6.4	18.7	7.7	11.5	12.7	13.6
13231	12,060	1	Pike	216.1	18,217	1,909	84.3	88.1	10.2	0.8	0.8	1.6	4.9	18.3	8.5	11.1	12.8	15.4
13233	16,340	4	Polk	310.3	42,085	1,129	135.6	73.2	13.4	0.6	0.9	13.5	6.8	18.8	8.3	13.6	11.9	12.7
13235	47,580	3	Pulaski	249.2	11,201	2,340	44.9	63.2	32.7	0.6	1.2	3.5	3.9	14.6	7.6	12.5	11.8	14.3

1. CBSA = Core Based Statistical Area. See Appendix A for explanation. See Appendix B for list of metropolitan areas with component counties. 2. County type code from the Economic Research Service of USDA Rural-Urban Continuum Codes. See Appendix A for definition. 3. Dry land or land partially or temporarily covered by water. 4. May be of any race.

STATE County	55 to 64 years (16)	65 to 74 years (17)	75 years and over (18)	Percent female (19)	Total persons 2000 (20)	Total persons 2010 (21)	2000-2010 (22)	2010-2017 (23)	Births (24)	Deaths (25)	Net Migration (26)	Number (27)	Persons per house-hold (28)	Family house-holds (29)	Female family house-holder[1] (30)	One person (31)
GEORGIA—Cont'd																
Effingham	12.1	7.4	4.1	50.2	37,535	52,257	39.2	14.8	5,319	2,833	5,214	18,695	2.97	76.2	11.0	18.5
Elbert	14.3	11.7	8.8	52.0	20,511	20,166	-1.7	-5.2	1,649	1,837	-871	7,611	2.52	68.4	16.1	28.3
Emanuel	12.8	9.5	6.4	50.9	21,837	22,594	3.5	-0.3	2,290	2,016	-343	8,227	2.67	65.5	19.6	30.1
Evans	12.6	9.0	6.8	51.1	10,495	11,002	4.8	-2.1	1,143	794	-591	3,950	2.59	71.4	17.3	22.6
Fannin	17.8	17.8	10.9	51.5	19,798	23,696	19.7	6.9	1,460	2,249	2,406	9,927	2.40	67.2	9.0	28.0
Fayette	14.9	11.0	6.6	51.4	91,263	106,566	16.8	5.6	6,101	5,867	5,744	38,933	2.80	77.4	9.2	21.0
Floyd	12.5	9.5	7.1	51.7	90,565	96,316	6.4	1.3	8,725	7,504	123	35,114	2.62	67.7	14.4	26.8
Forsyth	10.6	7.4	4.3	50.3	98,407	175,511	78.4	29.9	16,531	7,407	42,781	66,500	3.06	81.8	8.4	14.6
Franklin	13.9	11.1	7.7	50.9	20,285	22,084	8.9	3.3	1,935	2,018	822	8,260	2.61	68.8	10.8	26.5
Fulton	11.2	7.0	4.4	51.6	816,006	920,451	12.8	13.1	92,191	44,459	72,410	385,103	2.50	54.0	14.3	38.5
Gilmer	15.6	15.3	8.8	49.7	23,456	28,281	20.6	8.5	2,320	1,986	2,045	11,131	2.58	70.5	8.5	24.3
Glascock	14.0	10.1	7.3	50.5	2,556	3,082	20.6	-0.6	201	274	49	1,105	2.68	67.6	10.1	28.1
Glynn	14.0	11.8	7.6	52.7	67,568	79,626	17.8	7.1	7,153	5,962	4,485	32,623	2.49	67.3	16.0	28.4
Gordon	12.4	8.5	5.6	50.5	44,104	55,186	25.1	3.4	5,113	3,556	369	19,779	2.80	74.9	13.3	21.4
Grady	13.5	10.4	7.0	51.7	23,659	25,012	5.7	-0.8	2,539	1,814	-914	9,165	2.72	71.5	15.4	23.9
Greene	15.5	18.3	10.3	51.5	14,406	15,996	11.0	8.0	1,202	1,391	1,470	6,673	2.45	68.6	15.2	27.2
Gwinnett	11.4	6.3	3.3	51.1	588,448	805,297	36.9	14.3	84,282	28,313	59,320	278,996	3.12	76.2	14.4	19.5
Habersham	12.7	10.5	7.5	52.6	35,902	43,041	19.9	3.5	3,637	3,071	960	14,856	2.75	70.0	7.9	26.0
Hall	11.5	8.8	5.9	50.1	139,277	179,697	29.0	10.9	18,736	9,918	10,845	62,327	3.02	74.0	12.5	21.3
Hancock	15.6	13.1	8.8	44.6	10,076	9,402	-6.7	-8.9	553	675	-744	2,813	2.40	58.5	22.3	37.6
Haralson	12.4	9.7	6.5	51.3	25,690	28,776	12.0	1.7	2,503	2,533	510	10,886	2.60	73.8	13.2	22.6
Harris	15.2	12.0	6.4	50.1	23,695	32,000	35.0	6.0	2,110	1,812	1,631	11,699	2.78	77.8	10.5	19.8
Hart	14.2	12.4	9.0	50.6	22,997	25,213	9.6	2.3	1,989	2,072	675	10,016	2.46	69.3	14.7	26.3
Heard	14.4	10.5	6.4	50.3	11,012	11,825	7.4	-0.8	916	911	-99	4,364	2.62	69.1	13.0	25.7
Henry	11.8	7.4	4.0	52.4	119,341	203,867	70.8	10.8	17,545	9,742	14,171	71,000	3.00	77.6	17.3	19.5
Houston	12.1	7.5	4.9	51.5	110,765	139,909	26.3	9.7	14,786	7,879	6,655	54,188	2.72	70.0	15.2	25.4
Irwin	12.2	9.6	8.1	47.9	9,931	9,532	-4.0	-1.3	723	717	-153	3,279	2.72	63.5	13.1	32.5
Jackson	11.9	8.9	5.5	50.7	41,589	60,460	45.4	11.7	5,752	3,934	5,226	21,115	2.91	75.8	11.8	19.5
Jasper	15.0	10.7	6.4	51.1	11,426	13,900	21.7	0.5	1,234	944	-233	5,154	2.61	75.0	12.3	25.2
Jeff Davis	12.1	9.5	6.0	50.8	12,684	15,068	18.8	-0.3	1,520	1,136	-425	5,216	2.84	75.0	16.2	20.7
Jefferson	13.7	10.4	7.2	51.7	17,266	16,930	-1.9	-7.6	1,533	1,595	-1,230	5,855	2.67	63.6	18.1	33.9
Jenkins	13.0	9.8	6.8	46.4	8,575	8,336	-2.8	5.2	728	737	384	3,554	2.53	60.9	16.9	33.8
Johnson	13.9	10.5	7.9	43.7	8,560	9,984	16.6	-2.0	656	651	-198	3,168	2.98	70.4	16.7	27.4
Jones	13.6	10.6	6.6	51.6	23,639	28,669	21.3	-0.7	2,165	1,860	-506	10,367	2.74	76.3	14.4	20.6
Lamar	12.9	10.3	6.6	51.9	15,912	18,311	15.1	1.6	1,446	1,475	297	6,287	2.69	64.4	14.9	33.5
Lanier	12.5	8.1	5.2	49.9	7,241	10,070	39.1	3.5	979	620	-19	3,733	2.70	70.9	16.2	27.7
Laurens	12.9	9.9	7.3	52.6	44,874	48,434	7.9	-2.3	4,681	3,964	-1,822	17,622	2.65	66.5	17.6	30.0
Lee	12.3	8.2	4.0	49.8	24,757	28,298	14.3	4.1	2,564	1,402	-8	10,126	2.76	78.0	12.6	19.8
Liberty	9.3	5.8	3.0	49.3	61,610	63,482	3.0	-3.3	10,427	2,383	-10,535	22,780	2.72	71.8	16.9	22.8
Lincoln	16.8	14.2	9.0	51.1	8,348	7,996	-4.2	-1.1	545	618	-46	3,457	2.20	61.4	15.3	34.9
Long	11.0	5.8	3.2	49.6	10,304	14,437	40.1	31.7	1,791	647	3,364	5,173	3.31	72.0	16.5	23.2
Lowndes	10.1	7.2	4.8	51.3	92,115	109,243	18.6	5.7	11,905	6,084	271	39,809	2.76	63.9	15.9	27.6
Lumpkin	13.5	10.7	6.2	50.3	21,016	29,965	42.6	9.7	2,207	1,799	2,447	11,255	2.63	64.9	9.6	24.9
McDuffie	13.7	10.5	6.7	53.3	21,231	21,869	3.0	-1.7	2,139	1,709	-801	8,067	2.63	71.9	20.4	25.1
McIntosh	17.4	15.7	10.2	50.9	10,847	14,332	32.1	-1.6	860	862	-234	5,207	2.66	69.2	15.1	25.4
Macon	14.5	10.7	6.2	45.6	14,074	14,740	4.7	-9.7	1,007	1,080	-1,377	4,546	2.63	64.2	21.6	33.3
Madison	14.1	10.3	6.3	50.7	25,730	28,118	9.3	4.2	2,453	2,034	778	10,348	2.72	74.8	11.1	24.0
Marion	15.8	12.0	7.6	50.4	7,144	8,742	22.4	-3.3	656	555	-399	3,021	2.83	66.4	13.6	31.2
Meriwether	15.0	12.0	8.0	52.1	22,534	21,991	-2.4	-4.3	1,826	1,887	-883	7,982	2.62	71.4	17.9	25.6
Miller	12.8	10.6	10.4	51.8	6,383	6,129	-4.0	-4.7	493	571	-213	2,251	2.55	68.9	16.1	26.5
Mitchell	13.3	9.4	6.9	48.1	23,932	23,498	-1.8	-5.1	2,003	1,715	-1,511	8,041	2.55	67.3	21.7	30.1
Monroe	15.5	10.6	7.3	50.3	21,757	26,159	20.2	3.6	1,984	1,917	903	9,589	2.70	71.2	12.1	25.2
Montgomery	13.4	10.3	6.4	48.4	8,270	9,176	11.0	-1.6	716	590	-278	3,149	2.62	65.3	10.4	29.5
Morgan	14.7	11.7	7.9	51.8	15,457	17,866	15.6	3.1	1,380	1,261	428	6,648	2.67	76.9	13.9	20.5
Murray	12.6	9.1	5.1	50.8	36,506	39,628	8.6	0.4	3,575	2,644	-774	14,266	2.74	72.9	12.0	22.7
Muscogee	11.7	7.7	5.5	51.3	186,291	190,571	2.3	1.8	22,381	13,339	-5,898	73,449	2.60	63.3	19.2	31.9
Newton	11.5	8.1	4.6	52.7	62,001	99,985	61.3	8.1	9,754	5,838	4,214	35,090	2.92	71.3	18.5	24.0
Oconee	12.8	9.4	5.7	50.9	26,225	32,817	25.1	15.9	2,428	1,584	4,358	12,288	2.84	80.2	9.7	18.0
Oglethorpe	14.5	10.8	7.5	50.6	12,635	14,875	17.7	0.0	1,134	988	-151	5,723	2.55	69.6	13.2	25.7
Paulding	11.2	6.7	3.6	51.2	81,678	142,383	74.3	12.0	13,528	6,017	9,542	50,017	2.98	78.3	13.6	18.3
Peach	13.6	9.4	6.2	51.8	23,668	27,695	17.0	-2.2	2,229	1,767	-1,077	9,966	2.48	65.2	18.5	29.6
Pickens	15.2	13.6	7.6	50.8	22,983	29,421	28.0	7.4	2,190	2,261	2,228	11,377	2.61	75.5	8.3	19.5
Pierce	12.4	10.2	6.7	50.6	15,636	18,762	20.0	2.9	1,742	1,414	223	6,947	2.71	75.9	17.2	20.4
Pike	13.3	9.5	6.2	50.8	13,688	17,869	30.5	1.9	1,161	1,177	367	6,026	2.92	77.7	10.2	20.7
Polk	12.3	9.3	6.1	50.6	38,127	41,475	8.8	1.5	4,098	3,417	-66	14,868	2.75	70.0	14.3	25.7
Pulaski	13.8	12.5	9.0	57.0	9,588	12,001	25.2	-6.7	649	786	-671	3,829	2.58	67.9	18.1	28.2

1. No spouse present.

Table B. States and Counties — Population, Vital Statistics, Health, and Crime

STATE County	Persons in group quarters, 2017	Daytime Population, 2012-2016 Number	Employment/ residence ratio	Births, 2017 Total	Rate[1]	Deaths, 2017 Number	Rate[1]	Persons under 65 with no health insurance, 2016 Number	Percent	Medicare, 2017 Total beneficiaries	Enrolled in Original Medicare	Enrolled in Medicare Advantage	Serious crimes known to police[2], 2016 Total Number	Rate[3]
	32	33	34	35	36	37	38	39	40	41	42	43	44	45
GEORGIA—Cont'd														
Effingham............	577	41,373	0.43	788	13.1	442	7.4	6,031	11.7	7,545	5,124	2,422	932	1,606
Elbert.................	263	19,054	0.95	215	11.3	259	13.6	2,538	16.9	5,018	3,136	1,881	648	3,375
Emanuel.............	1185	22,184	0.93	291	12.9	280	12.4	3,066	17.2	4,791	3,057	1,735	772	3,481
Evans.................	398	11,116	1.09	141	13.1	107	9.9	1,531	18.1	2,079	1,290	789	130	1,211
Fannin...............	159	23,268	0.91	210	8.3	328	13.0	3,283	18.2	7,635	5,630	2,005	327	1,340
Fayette..............	521	106,994	0.95	895	8.0	864	7.7	9,056	9.8	21,353	14,580	6,773	1,624	1,458
Floyd.................	4027	101,217	1.13	1,217	12.5	1,079	11.1	12,532	16.2	20,189	14,110	6,079	3,133	3,249
Forsyth..............	672	185,306	0.81	2,367	10.4	1,228	5.4	19,170	9.8	21,212	13,589	7,624	1,836	834
Franklin.............	791	22,728	1.07	265	11.6	272	11.9	3,260	18.8	5,665	3,725	1,940	385	1,886
Fulton...............	34299	1,378,582	1.80	13,053	12.5	7,127	6.8	114,269	13.0	121,481	72,664	48,817	54,405	5,296
Gilmer..............	181	26,103	0.75	337	11.0	337	11.0	5,204	23.1	7,470	5,444	2,026	580	1,960
Glascock...........	84	2,385	0.48	28	9.1	34	11.1	315	12.9	672	457	215	22	719
Glynn...............	1452	87,673	1.14	953	11.2	893	10.5	11,809	17.4	18,210	12,992	5,218	3,071	3,644
Gordon..............	743	55,672	0.98	716	12.5	519	9.1	9,670	20.1	10,169	7,473	2,696	1,520	2,676
Grady...............	172	21,669	0.63	335	13.5	263	10.6	3,951	19.6	4,586	3,079	1,507	500	1,983
Greene..............	164	17,189	1.11	158	9.1	207	12.0	2,253	18.7	5,208	3,608	1,600	347	2,061
Gwinnett............	5093	824,284	0.88	11,700	12.7	4,475	4.9	136,064	16.7	90,571	54,643	35,928	21,647	2,370
Habersham.........	2525	42,920	0.95	512	11.5	459	10.3	6,342	18.7	9,465	5,954	3,510	741	1,679
Hall.................	3119	193,307	1.03	2,700	13.5	1,539	7.7	33,060	20.0	32,527	21,477	11,051	10,248	5,224
Hancock............	1323	7,647	0.49	66	7.7	115	13.4	761	13.7	2,072	1,105	968	175	2,088
Haralson...........	347	26,985	0.85	342	11.7	355	12.1	3,575	14.8	5,944	3,887	2,057	1,097	3,804
Harris..............	441	23,796	0.38	295	8.7	307	9.1	2,925	10.7	5,152	3,438	1,714	388	1,155
Hart................	665	22,933	0.73	267	10.4	300	11.6	3,153	16.2	4,693	3,283	1,410	791	3,174
Heard...............	132	9,165	0.47	115	9.8	130	11.1	1,500	15.7	1,783	1,129	654	191	1,666
Henry...............	946	184,887	0.68	2,512	11.1	1,526	6.8	24,528	12.5	30,712	18,175	12,536	5,903	2,682
Houston.............	1487	150,262	1.02	2,018	13.1	1,234	8.0	17,758	13.5	22,797	17,788	5,009	6,309	4,156
Irwin...............	1065	8,795	0.82	91	9.7	106	11.3	946	13.9	1,507	1,002	506	238	2,596
Jackson.............	706	58,666	0.87	850	12.6	579	8.6	7,955	14.3	15,479	10,191	5,288	1,382	2,231
Jasper..............	95	10,626	0.46	150	10.7	118	8.5	1,988	17.6	2,283	1,447	836	222	2,024
Jeff Davis..........	111	14,170	0.86	212	14.1	164	10.9	2,371	19.0	2,643	1,875	767	428	2,878
Jefferson...........	529	15,728	0.91	210	13.4	222	14.2	2,283	18.3	3,772	2,439	1,333	440	2,761
Jenkins.............	1194	7,921	0.64	93	10.6	100	11.4	1,113	18.1	1,630	988	641	NA	NA
Johnson.............	1723	8,281	0.63	93	9.5	96	9.8	912	14.4	1,673	1,093	580	76	793
Jones...............	279	21,419	0.41	248	8.7	285	10.0	3,097	13.1	3,317	1,969	1,348	498	1,751
Lamar...............	1088	16,263	0.71	212	11.4	220	11.8	2,061	14.5	3,544	2,109	1,435	433	2,383
Lanier..............	180	8,394	0.46	127	12.2	100	9.6	1,463	16.5	1,221	897	324	248	2,397
Laurens............	996	49,247	1.09	634	13.4	560	11.8	5,443	14.2	10,515	7,027	3,488	1,641	3,633
Lee.................	878	21,344	0.41	320	10.9	218	7.4	2,984	11.9	3,783	2,671	1,111	616	2,340
Liberty.............	1666	70,821	1.25	1,436	23.4	352	5.7	6,684	12.3	6,613	4,691	1,922	2,102	3,370
Lincoln.............	67	6,048	0.45	88	11.2	95	12.1	1,005	16.7	1,859	1,170	690	232	3,050
Long................	328	12,460	0.25	257	13.5	97	5.1	2,978	17.9	1,138	828	309	203	1,104
Lowndes............	6261	121,581	1.16	1,630	14.1	917	7.9	14,561	15.4	18,294	13,735	4,559	4,380	3,862
Lumpkin............	2882	26,550	0.68	280	8.5	269	8.2	4,274	17.9	5,044	3,605	1,439	473	1,497
McDuffie...........	286	20,897	0.92	283	13.2	248	11.5	2,562	14.6	4,456	2,373	2,084	266	1,240
McIntosh...........	71	11,751	0.58	107	7.6	119	8.4	1,672	15.8	2,842	1,714	1,128	359	2,584
Macon..............	1901	13,287	0.87	135	10.1	154	11.6	1,779	18.9	2,265	1,332	933	222	1,712
Madison............	252	21,348	0.38	344	11.7	265	9.0	4,156	17.4	5,994	3,857	2,137	511	1,795
Marion.............	66	7,532	0.62	85	10.1	81	9.6	1,173	17.2	1,058	631	427	81	925
Meriwether.........	245	19,367	0.76	248	11.8	271	12.9	2,747	16.4	4,411	2,513	1,898	483	2,436
Miller..............	141	5,275	0.72	61	10.4	77	13.2	729	15.7	1,276	896	381	78	1,347
Mitchell............	2249	23,397	1.08	249	11.2	224	10.0	2,862	17.2	4,233	2,673	1,560	632	2,830
Monroe.............	1133	24,390	0.75	261	9.6	312	11.5	3,001	13.9	4,324	2,894	1,430	528	1,941
Montgomery.........	694	6,987	0.42	88	9.7	78	8.6	1,200	17.6	1,681	1,088	593	NA	NA
Morgan.............	145	20,127	1.29	199	10.8	152	8.3	2,074	14.2	4,077	2,497	1,580	NA	NA
Murray.............	259	34,030	0.67	463	11.6	410	10.3	6,470	19.3	6,828	5,517	1,312	1,255	3,175
Muscogee	6412	226,100	1.30	2,860	14.7	1,961	10.1	20,378	12.3	36,066	23,915	12,151	10,884	5,379
Newton.............	1633	87,835	0.63	1,407	13.0	850	7.9	13,465	14.7	18,606	10,850	7,757	2,771	2,603
Oconee.............	151	31,470	0.78	357	9.4	226	5.9	3,046	9.6	5,878	4,056	1,821	605	1,654
Oglethorpe.........	176	10,628	0.34	149	10.0	145	9.7	2,034	16.8	1,826	1,188	638	339	2,283
Paulding...........	475	108,789	0.41	1,777	11.1	975	6.1	16,778	12.0	14,099	8,857	5,242	3,000	1,947
Peach..............	1259	24,811	0.81	329	12.1	273	10.1	3,509	16.1	6,708	4,578	2,130	891	3,363
Pickens............	370	28,073	0.85	295	9.3	351	11.1	3,601	14.9	8,240	5,718	2,522	610	2,052
Pierce.............	149	16,340	0.63	249	12.9	204	10.6	2,725	17.1	4,138	2,937	1,200	473	2,471
Pike................	230	13,541	0.41	163	8.9	180	9.9	2,136	14.2	3,407	2,179	1,228	247	1,378
Polk................	623	38,430	0.83	577	13.7	501	11.9	5,972	17.2	9,108	6,167	2,941	1,564	3,771
Pulaski.............	1197	11,478	1.00	84	7.5	126	11.2	1,311	16.8	2,159	1,567	592	287	2,544

1. Per 1,000 estimated resident population.   2. Data for serious crimes have not been adjusted for underreporting; this may affect comparability between geographic areas and over time.
3. Per 100,000 population estimated by the FBI.

Items 32—45

Table B. States and Counties — Crime, Education, Money Income, and Poverty

STATE County	Serious crimes known to police, 2016 (cont.)[1] Rate		Education — School enrollment and attainment, 2012-2016				Local government expenditures,[5] 2013-2014		Money income, 2012-2016 — Households				Income and poverty, 2016			
			Enrollment[3]		Attainment[4] (percent)						Percent			Percent below poverty level		
	Violent	Property	Total	Percent private	High school graduate or less	Bachelor's degree or more	Total current spending (mil dol)	Current spending per student (dollars)	Per capita income[6]	Median income (dollars)	with income of less than $50,000	with income of $200,000 or more	Median household income (dollars)	All persons	Children under 18 years	Children 5 to 17 years in families
	46	47	48	49	50	51	52	53	54	55	56	57	58	59	60	61
GEORGIA—Cont'd																
Effingham	138	1,468	15,588	13.3	50.7	18.3	96.6	8,372	25,553	62,820	37.6	2.7	63,776	10.3	14.9	13.8
Elbert	406	2,969	4,395	8.6	66.8	11.7	31.2	10,078	21,039	35,739	65.5	2.1	37,131	22.3	32.3	31.8
Emanuel	469	3,012	5,534	4.2	62.4	11.7	39.6	9,048	16,681	31,522	69.6	1.0	32,495	27.4	40.3	38.7
Evans	196	1,016	2,684	18.1	62.6	15.1	17.0	9,143	20,710	40,594	59.6	2.6	34,689	24.4	36.4	35.4
Fannin	107	1,233	4,519	13.5	55.8	17.7	32.5	10,994	22,425	39,011	58.7	1.2	41,487	14.1	27.3	25.3
Fayette	71	1,387	30,775	16.9	26.1	45.8	174.7	8,668	38,493	81,689	29.1	10.3	83,145	6.0	8.6	7.5
Floyd	328	2,922	24,925	21.1	51.3	19.8	159.0	9,665	22,284	42,955	55.9	2.2	46,634	15.8	23.5	22.7
Forsyth	55	779	60,928	16.3	25.4	48.3	323.3	7,946	37,686	91,842	25.4	12.6	101,804	5.7	6.6	5.5
Franklin	162	1,724	4,821	12.8	63.4	12.6	30.4	8,306	18,642	37,298	64.4	1.1	41,543	21.4	29.3	26.8
Fulton	736	4,560	278,014	21.6	26.8	49.8	1,587.6	10,700	39,101	58,851	43.4	10.9	62,824	16.0	24.3	22.3
Gilmer	250	1,710	5,456	7.2	55.5	17.8	44.0	10,223	22,893	43,775	56.9	2.2	46,332	15.2	28.2	25.8
Glascock	131	588	731	3.1	64.7	8.2	6.2	9,868	19,037	43,884	59.5	0.5	41,412	18.5	25.2	21.8
Glynn	438	3,206	19,468	11.4	40.0	28.2	122.1	9,525	27,819	46,475	53.4	4.2	48,691	19.1	29.8	27.1
Gordon	264	2,412	13,388	6.2	59.9	12.9	92.4	8,679	20,009	41,390	59.7	1.8	45,705	16.1	24.6	23.2
Grady	179	1,805	6,246	3.5	60.1	12.8	38.7	8,326	17,764	35,518	64.7	1.2	40,234	21.0	31.8	31.1
Greene	303	1,758	2,813	7.0	51.2	24.7	31.7	13,884		44,299	55.0	6.3	47,194	18.2	30.5	29.6
Gwinnett	247	2,123	260,445	13.2	35.8	34.9	1,630.7	9,240	26,749	61,865	39.6	5.1	67,197	11.3	16.5	15.5
Habersham	174	1,504	10,375	13.6	56.0	17.5	65.4	9,403	19,171	41,600	57.8	1.7	46,828	15.6	21.0	18.9
Hall	452	4,772	50,659	9.3	50.4	22.5	295.5	8,539	24,099	51,902	47.9	3.8	55,308	13.7	19.5	18.2
Hancock	334	1,754	1,503	4.6	67.4	10.9	14.5	14,579	13,898	26,386	75.2	0.7	30,616	33.5	47.8	45.2
Haralson	583	3,221	6,960	6.0	58.4	13.8	52.3	9,130	21,838	42,281	55.9	1.1	43,196	18.5	26.1	22.9
Harris	173	982	7,870	8.8	37.2	26.6	45.9	8,831	30,703	65,336	39.8	5.2	70,724	8.7	13.1	11.9
Hart	365	2,809	5,383	12.5	56.8	13.7	31.8	9,075	20,866	37,983	61.6	1.7	41,247	17.3	25.3	24.2
Heard	201	1,465	2,786	9.1	64.7	10.5	19.4	9,526	20,404	44,185	56.7	0.3	41,994	19.7	29.1	25.9
Henry	177	2,505	64,784	15.7	40.5	27.5	334.8	8,222	25,727	62,561	39.4	3.4	67,150	9.6	14.7	12.9
Houston	433	3,723	44,253	11.1	39.5	24.0	258.3	9,242	25,289	55,480	45.3	2.8	61,795	14.9	20.8	18.5
Irwin	240	2,356	2,012	2.8	58.8	11.1	16.6	9,184	18,514	29,846	68.1	4.4	35,866	23.6	35.2	32.6
Jackson	289	1,942	15,779	8.9	51.6	19.1	103.7	8,741	23,982	54,246	45.2	2.7	55,426	12.7	17.0	15.1
Jasper	511	1,514	3,070	13.6	64.0	10.4	19.7	8,500	20,685	41,434	62.5	1.0	48,473	16.9	27.2	25.9
Jeff Davis	282	2,596	4,288	4.6	60.2	10.7	24.8	7,947	17,981	36,566	63.4	0.7	35,538	23.9	33.7	31.7
Jefferson	358	2,404	3,865	7.9	66.9	10.4	27.0	9,634	16,986	28,417	69.0	1.2	33,680	25.2	37.7	34.8
Jenkins	NA	NA	2,434	13.6	61.9	13.0	14.4	10,578	18,288	27,398	69.8	1.0	30,611	34.2	44.8	41.9
Johnson	167	626	2,364	7.1	63.3	8.7	11.3	9,871	16,693	32,685	68.0	0.0	32,201	29.4	37.2	31.2
Jones	98	1,653	7,054	9.8	50.6	20.2	49.9	9,101	26,602	54,020	47.8	2.5	54,155	12.3	18.9	17.1
Lamar	303	2,080	5,226	11.4	54.7	17.2	25.2	9,596	19,143	40,364	60.5	1.2	44,575	18.2	27.3	25.5
Lanier	435	1,962	2,815	9.9	50.5	15.4	16.7	9,186	17,403	31,682	64.8	0.3	35,690	22.8	34.0	31.6
Laurens	456	3,177	11,174	7.3	61.1	15.2	81.5	9,033	19,826	33,632	64.7	2.2	39,037	25.6	37.5	35.7
Lee	152	2,188	8,917	11.2	40.3	24.2	50.6	7,933	28,175	62,797	38.7	3.3	62,972	11.2	16.9	15.4
Liberty	561	2,809	18,343	10.9	41.8	18.9	95.5	9,356	20,065	42,484	58.1	1.2	44,154	15.3	24.3	25.9
Lincoln	421	2,629	1,508	4.6	59.1	13.2	12.1	10,063	23,582	34,720	64.6	1.9	41,494	19.1	30.1	28.5
Long	38	1,066	5,100	8.2	47.3	15.2	25.3	8,033	19,176	50,848	48.7	1.1	44,542	18.6	26.4	25.1
Lowndes	282	3,580	36,671	9.3	44.8	23.9	160.2	8,646	20,428	38,915	60.2	2.2	41,331	22.1	29.4	29.3
Lumpkin	38	1,459	9,499	6.1	44.8	27.0	35.1	9,263	21,814	40,634	59.6	2.9	47,287	16.2	21.5	20.2
McDuffie	144	1,095	5,252	6.1	59.8	14.2	41.6	9,579	19,497	37,021	61.1	1.6	39,642	22.8	36.6	33.5
McIntosh	180	2,404	2,822	11.0	52.7	13.8	16.5	9,958	23,826	45,248	55.2	1.3	40,788	20.6	34.5	32.0
Macon	247	1,465	3,017	9.4	62.6	8.5	17.4	10,606	14,039	28,285	74.9	0.6	31,358	32.1	46.0	41.4
Madison	207	1,588	6,379	12.6	57.0	15.5	47.3	9,895	21,883	45,063	55.0	2.5	47,151	14.9	23.8	22.4
Marion	57	868	1,935	6.6	60.1	11.1	13.5	9,837	17,522	35,484	64.5	0.4	38,734	23.4	37.5	33.6
Meriwether	368	2,068	4,638	12.0	61.8	10.1	31.5	10,096	19,626	34,989	61.4	2.4	34,508	21.2	33.0	31.9
Miller	104	1,243	1,256	11.2	59.7	11.4	10.5	9,523	21,093	36,463	63.0	3.3	42,771	23.1	34.6	31.2
Mitchell	246	2,584	5,614	9.5	64.3	12.0	36.4	9,234	15,027	31,111	70.0	0.6	33,490	29.9	41.1	38.9
Monroe	140	1,801	6,235	21.9	51.2	22.2	41.0	10,182	29,053	50,625	49.0	4.9	55,626	12.2	19.2	17.5
Montgomery	NA	NA	2,132	23.7	56.5	15.6	10.5	6,681	19,131	38,111	64.0	2.4	39,074	22.7	32.5	30.8
Morgan	NA	NA	4,213	7.1	51.6	20.8	29.5	8,978	26,298	54,506	46.1	3.2	55,347	13.1	21.2	19.2
Murray	673	2,502	9,326	7.4	67.0	10.9	61.7	8,097	17,856	38,136	61.6	0.7	43,203	18.1	26.6	23.2
Muscogee	601	4,778	57,434	11.1	40.2	25.0	321.3	10,001	23,747	42,661	56.1	3.2	40,895	21.5	29.4	29.3
Newton	422	2,181	30,239	13.8	47.0	19.8	166.2	8,515	22,478	51,068	48.8	1.8	51,167	17.5	27.9	24.4
Oconee	118	1,537	10,570	16.2	27.6	46.6	59.3	8,750	37,054	75,946	32.5	9.7	88,570	6.8	8.4	7.1
Oglethorpe	310	1,973	3,309	8.4	57.4	16.6	21.9	9,677	20,987	44,403	57.3	0.6	45,319	15.4	23.5	21.7
Paulding	134	1,813	44,027	13.0	43.9	24.6	229.8	8,084	25,655	60,971	39.0	2.4	65,480	8.6	12.5	11.7
Peach	506	2,858	8,780	9.6	45.8	20.2	34.9	9,264	20,746	41,128	56.8	0.8	44,330	21.4	30.7	29.0
Pickens	235	1,817	6,405	9.0	46.5	24.8	44.7	10,288	28,637	56,769	44.5	3.9	57,637	11.3	20.0	18.1
Pierce	475	1,996	4,391	7.4	58.4	12.9	31.7	8,503	23,470	42,730	55.7	1.6	42,908	17.3	26.7	23.6
Pike	67	1,311	4,692	13.5	53.7	15.3	26.7	7,826	23,783	50,819	49.1	2.5	56,901	11.7	15.8	13.9
Polk	304	3,467	10,389	11.5	61.5	13.0	64.1	8,315	21,582	39,356	59.8	1.6	42,670	18.6	27.1	26.5
Pulaski	479	2,065	2,348	11.4	62.5	11.8	13.6	9,702	17,587	38,880	61.7	0.4	36,611	25.0	33.1	29.0

1. Data for serious crimes have not been adjusted for underreporting; this may affect comparability between geographic areas and over time.   2. Per 100,000 population estimated by the FBI.
3. All persons 3 years old and over enrolled in nursery school through college.   4. Persons 25 years old and over.   5. Elementary and secondary education expenditures.
6. Based on population estimated by the American Community Survey, 2011–2015.

Table B. States and Counties — Personal Income and Earnings

STATE County	Personal income, 2016										Earnings, 2016		
			Per capita[1]			Supplements to wages and salaries, employer contributions (mil dol)						Contributions for government social insurance (mil dol)	
	Total (mil dol)	Percent change 2015-2016	Dollars	Rank	Wages and salaries (mil dol)	Pension and insurance	Government social insurance	Proprietors' income (mil dol)	Dividends, interest, and rent (mil dol)	Personal transfer reecipts (mil dol)	Total (mil dol)	From employee and self-employed	From employer
	62	63	64	65	66	67	68	69	70	71	72	73	74

GEORGIA—Cont'd

STATE County	62	63	64	65	66	67	68	69	70	71	72	73	74
Effingham	2227	3.6	37,934	1,672	436	95	29	63	211	379	623	70	29
Elbert	629	1.8	32,857	2,507	212	48	15	50	109	204	325	38	15
Emanuel	649	1.8	28,687	2,941	235	60	16	25	90	241	337	39	16
Evans	344	1.6	32,219	2,576	155	33	10	29	51	94	227	24	10
Fannin	800	4.5	32,139	2,591	217	43	15	71	157	277	345	43	15
Fayette	6336	4.2	56,759	191	2,013	314	140	248	1,123	826	2,715	311	140
Floyd	3522	2.5	36,470	1,919	1,746	314	124	286	558	938	2,470	279	124
Forsyth	12900	7.7	58,369	174	3,950	537	268	1,279	1,546	1,003	6,034	629	268
Franklin	781	0.6	35,011	2,161	305	57	22	117	110	220	502	52	22
Fulton	75824	4.9	74,095	50	66,545	8,090	4,356	12,535	16,451	6,334	91,525	9,547	4,356
Gilmer	926	0.3	31,148	2,725	245	52	17	105	167	299	419	46	17
Glascock	90	1.6	29,809	2,862	12	4	1	5	12	27	22	3	1
Glynn	3473	2.6	41,105	1,219	1,710	307	122	185	900	749	2,324	266	122
Gordon	1834	2.5	32,234	2,574	852	145	62	143	213	439	1,201	136	62
Grady	750	-3.9	30,230	2,823	228	49	16	48	124	209	341	39	16
Greene	820	2.7	48,216	517	231	40	16	59	289	203	346	41	16
Gwinnett	35050	4.7	38,638	1,554	20,084	2,694	1,364	2,674	4,431	4,526	26,817	2,926	1,364
Habersham	1342	1.9	30,330	2,815	561	130	39	78	227	369	808	90	39
Hall	7682	4.5	39,065	1,487	4,039	663	266	584	1,267	1,416	5,552	601	266
Hancock	229	1.7	26,448	3,046	60	18	4	3	37	93	85	11	4
Haralson	938	1.4	32,295	2,568	289	59	20	51	119	261	419	50	20
Harris	1472	3.6	43,730	903	156	38	10	47	282	262	252	31	10
Hart	860	1.1	33,650	2,372	255	54	19	79	155	247	407	47	19
Heard	326	0.8	28,406	2,956	109	28	8	15	36	97	160	18	8
Henry	7980	5.1	35,985	2,005	2,320	439	165	259	964	1,426	3,183	368	165
Houston	6185	3.3	40,656	1,282	3,054	798	235	189	1,131	1,201	4,276	468	235
Irwin	264	2.6	28,025	2,978	71	18	5	12	47	91	106	13	5
Jackson	2397	5.3	37,092	1,807	1,047	183	74	128	296	485	1,431	162	74
Jasper	472	3.1	34,535	2,237	73	19	5	36	68	121	134	16	5
Jeff Davis	426	1.4	28,602	2,944	163	35	12	20	61	131	230	28	12
Jefferson	522	4.4	32,820	2,515	188	42	13	35	74	175	277	31	13
Jenkins	242	1.3	27,342	3,014	50	14	3	11	40	84	78	9	3
Johnson	232	3.0	24,364	3,084	56	16	4	7	30	87	84	10	4
Jones	1007	2.3	35,176	2,137	181	40	13	29	131	235	263	33	13
Lamar	566	3.3	30,651	2,774	139	35	10	33	71	175	217	25	10
Lanier	260	4.0	24,964	3,073	52	15	3	6	34	83	77	9	3
Laurens	1645	4.7	34,611	2,227	757	161	55	75	266	470	1,048	123	55
Lee	1272	3.1	43,364	960	238	49	17	48	163	201	352	38	17
Liberty	2153	1.5	34,404	2,262	1,732	500	159	30	512	465	2,422	262	159
Lincoln	267	3.0	34,167	2,294	48	12	3	11	46	77	75	10	3
Long	417	4.5	22,599	3,104	37	13	2	11	52	108	64	7	2
Lowndes	3907	2.5	34,088	2,307	2,126	481	157	170	734	891	2,934	317	157
Lumpkin	1037	3.9	32,972	2,474	282	73	19	56	168	269	429	47	19
McDuffie	722	2.0	33,592	2,385	252	52	18	30	103	215	352	41	18
McIntosh	382	2.6	27,398	3,010	63	17	4	14	73	120	98	13	4
Macon	392	-1.1	29,136	2,921	115	25	7	57	61	115	206	19	7
Madison	947	1.6	32,867	2,504	114	31	8	76	125	252	229	26	8
Marion	219	0.3	25,673	3,064	40	10	3	11	37	72	64	8	3
Meriwether	676	2.2	32,091	2,600	200	47	14	18	96	223	279	35	14
Miller	217	3.6	36,610	1,896	64	18	4	13	40	61	99	10	4
Mitchell	771	1.6	34,351	2,274	248	58	17	147	115	208	469	43	17
Monroe	1134	2.5	41,516	1,164	324	81	21	58	186	232	484	51	21
Montgomery	255	2.2	28,150	2,972	65	14	4	9	34	74	91	11	4
Morgan	795	2.3	43,769	900	261	47	18	48	162	165	374	42	18
Murray	1097	2.2	27,904	2,985	400	72	30	58	116	317	560	69	30
Muscogee	8022	1.7	40,620	1,288	4,658	905	330	267	1,992	1,867	6,160	683	330
Newton	3354	4.5	31,347	2,699	1,064	213	74	96	389	792	1,448	170	74
Oconee	2166	4.4	58,811	167	459	81	31	149	464	227	721	77	31
Oglethorpe	498	-0.5	33,400	2,409	63	16	4	67	69	121	150	13	4
Paulding	5324	5.1	34,167	2,294	922	177	64	152	508	855	1,315	154	64
Peach	962	2.1	36,079	1,992	387	81	30	55	165	259	553	62	30
Pickens	1295	3.5	41,987	1,104	363	61	24	71	247	320	519	63	24
Pierce	632	4.1	32,943	2,483	163	33	11	24	83	186	232	28	11
Pike	637	2.8	35,496	2,081	109	25	8	26	85	139	168	21	8
Polk	1253	2.8	30,002	2,845	447	86	32	46	155	396	610	75	32
Pulaski	307	0.7	27,326	3,015	113	24	8	7	66	92	152	17	8

1. Based on the resident population estimated as of July 1 of the year shown.

STATE County	Earnings, 2016 (cont.)									Social Security beneficiaries, December 2016		Supplemental Security Income recipients, 2016	Housing units, 2017	
	Percent by selected industries													
	Farm	Mining, quarrying, and extracting	Construction	Manufacturing	Information; professional, scientific, technical services	Retail trade	Finance, insurance, real estate, and leasing	Health care and social assistance	Government	Number	Rate[1]		Total	Percent change, 2010-2017
	75	76	77	78	79	80	81	82	83	84	85	86	87	88
GEORGIA—Cont'd														
Effingham	0.1	D	6.0	18.2	6.0	6.1	4.2	D	28.9	9,255	158	878	22,844	14.9
Elbert	2.9	3.6	3.7	28.0	2.5	6.3	4.9	5.7	22.5	5,500	287	852	9,595	0.1
Emanuel	0.5	0.0	3.1	23.0	3.1	7.0	3.4	D	32.2	5,315	237	1,087	9,924	-0.4
Evans	4.7	0.3	6.7	36.5	D	6.1	D	D	16.2	2,315	217	454	4,737	1.5
Fannin	0.8	0.0	D	4.5	4.5	14.4	6.7	16.5	16.3	8,300	332	694	17,223	6.2
Fayette	0.1	D	10.3	11.3	8.5	7.6	5.1	15.1	14.1	21,870	197	1,039	42,503	4.2
Floyd	0.6	D	2.7	17.4	D	7.0	4.7	24.6	14.1	22,035	228	3,315	40,587	0.1
Forsyth	0.1	0.1	10.6	8.9	23.8	5.4	5.0	8.8	8.7	26,320	120	898	81,271	26.9
Franklin	13.0	0.0	3.2	18.3	3.6	6.3	5.0	D	12.0	5,975	268	873	10,630	0.7
Fulton	0.0	0.2	2.9	3.9	30.8	3.9	12.1	7.5	10.2	130,250	127	27,227	473,166	8.3
Gilmer	11.9	D	7.9	14.2	D	9.5	3.7	6.3	16.6	8,485	283	626	17,074	3.1
Glascock	3.9	D	D	3.1	D	5.5	D	D	36.7	675	226	98	1,524	0.3
Glynn	0.0	D	4.1	6.4	5.7	7.6	4.3	15.3	23.9	19,315	229	1,907	43,051	5.7
Gordon	3.0	0.0	6.3	31.3	2.2	5.9	3.7	9.3	14.0	11,360	199	1,512	22,496	1.0
Grady	4.4	0.3	6.0	18.1	D	6.9	3.1	8.1	21.1	5,485	220	1,051	10,843	0.8
Greene	4.2	0.5	12.3	8.5	5.5	8.1	8.8	10.1	13.8	5,600	331	594	9,641	11.0
Gwinnett	0.0	D	8.7	8.6	15.9	7.9	8.3	7.1	9.5	101,690	112	12,558	309,255	6.1
Habersham	3.3	D	4.1	28.4	D	7.6	3.6	5.4	21.1	10,150	230	917	18,383	1.3
Hall	0.2	D	6.4	20.2	4.2	6.2	6.0	17.0	11.7	35,530	181	3,129	73,080	6.2
Hancock	0.9	D	D	D	D	3.3	D	D	47.5	2,430	281	454	5,379	0.8
Haralson	2.1	0.0	9.3	27.3	3.6	6.3	3.7	8.3	21.5	6,885	239	998	12,449	1.3
Harris	-0.1	0.0	10.8	15.0	D	2.6	7.0	D	27.0	6,950	207	466	14,163	5.8
Hart	8.1	0.7	5.6	26.5	4.5	7.2	3.0	5.3	16.2	6,730	263	564	13,126	0.9
Heard	2.8	D	8.1	22.5	D	1.9	1.3	D	22.6	2,470	213	345	5,205	1.2
Henry	0.0	0.4	6.0	7.9	4.5	10.2	4.2	13.4	21.3	34,370	155	4,142	81,354	6.3
Houston	0.0	D	2.7	9.1	7.0	5.4	2.3	6.3	56.6	25,045	165	3,614	62,917	7.9
Irwin	7.1	0.1	6.0	8.8	D	6.1	D	4.7	32.1	2,225	238	386	4,076	1.1
Jackson	2.2	D	7.6	23.8	D	6.5	5.6	3.9	11.9	13,070	201	1,807	25,351	6.8
Jasper	3.1	0.0	7.8	17.5	D	4.1	3.3	D	25.2	3,210	232	454	6,443	4.7
Jeff Davis	0.6	0.0	2.2	26.6	D	7.7	4.9	D	19.8	3,195	213	508	6,505	0.3
Jefferson	5.6	9.8	5.2	17.0	D	6.3	3.3	D	20.2	4,215	267	954	7,267	-0.4
Jenkins	7.0	0.0	2.5	3.0	0.0	5.0	D	6.0	36.3	1,900	217	482	4,229	0.2
Johnson	0.0	0.0	7.6	6.6	0.0	5.0	D	17.8	37.5	2,105	216	571	4,114	-0.2
Jones	0.6	D	14.6	0.8	D	5.2	5.5	D	25.3	6,105	214	376	11,840	1.3
Lamar	4.9	D	3.7	18.3	1.9	6.8	5.7	5.7	30.9	4,260	231	541	7,602	1.7
Lanier	2.5	0.3	1.5	10.4	D	5.4	D	2.3	45.6	1,715	164	344	4,424	4.2
Laurens	-0.9	D	6.1	13.1	D	7.8	3.9	D	29.9	11,465	243	2,136	21,504	0.6
Lee	9.4	D	12.4	4.5	D	7.1	3.2	D	23.4	4,930	169	465	11,121	8.2
Liberty	0.1	0.0	D	6.5	D	2.7	1.4	1.9	75.9	7,730	126	1,222	28,171	5.3
Lincoln	0.5	0.0	22.3	4.8	0.0	4.9	6.7	3.2	27.9	2,205	280	233	4,889	2.2
Long	3.3	D	7.1	D	D	2.2	1.7	2.5	58.0	1,860	100	252	6,915	14.8
Lowndes	0.3	D	6.5	8.3	6.5	7.4	3.7	9.1	36.2	19,230	168	3,936	47,568	8.3
Lumpkin	0.7	D	8.5	10.0	3.4	7.4	3.2	7.7	37.5	6,555	208	504	13,634	5.5
McDuffie	4.7	D	6.0	23.9	3.7	9.4	3.9	D	21.3	5,135	239	954	9,343	0.3
McIntosh	2.9	D	5.3	D	D	7.5	1.1	1.8	36.0	3,215	228	410	9,554	3.6
Macon	22.0	D	4.9	23.0	D	4.0	2.4	D	21.4	2,485	184	437	6,091	-0.7
Madison	15.6	D	12.2	5.1	D	5.5	4.4	D	29.1	6,855	238	1,001	12,004	1.9
Marion	7.8	D	4.4	17.4	D	4.8	D	D	29.0	1,740	204	264	4,204	1.2
Meriwether	0.9	0.0	9.9	21.4	D	4.5	2.5	D	26.0	5,370	255	878	10,005	0.5
Miller	6.5	0.1	4.0	1.9	D	7.6	D	D	46.1	1,465	249	320	2,759	-1.2
Mitchell	14.7	D	1.3	31.6	D	4.8	2.9	D	17.5	4,885	218	1,086	9,069	0.8
Monroe	2.9	D	7.2	1.8	D	5.1	3.5	5.6	31.6	6,145	229	539	11,119	5.3
Montgomery	0.8	0.0	3.7	4.0	0.0	4.7	6.0	D	22.0	1,920	214	322	3,961	0.6
Morgan	5.2	0.1	5.5	19.8	D	7.3	7.4	3.4	16.6	4,665	257	436	7,737	3.6
Murray	2.1	D	2.5	44.8	D	6.4	2.7	D	14.7	8,325	211	1,147	16,074	0.6
Muscogee	0.0	D	3.1	7.4	7.3	5.9	18.0	12.7	25.6	37,405	191	7,480	84,743	2.5
Newton	0.0	D	8.6	25.3	4.4	6.8	3.0	8.6	20.2	19,280	181	3,044	39,153	2.1
Oconee	2.3	D	4.3	4.8	10.5	6.5	11.2	14.9	13.2	6,440	175	334	14,256	15.1
Oglethorpe	35.3	3.1	10.9	6.2	D	2.5	3.7	D	19.3	3,360	228	303	6,637	2.5
Paulding	0.2	D	13.3	4.7	4.9	11.1	4.7	10.6	25.4	21,505	138	1,531	56,445	8.2
Peach	4.8	0.0	6.2	35.6	D	6.0	3.5	5.0	21.6	5,580	207	1,182	11,571	4.7
Pickens	1.6	D	7.9	9.9	5.3	7.5	5.6	24.6	15.0	9,085	296	586	13,993	2.3
Pierce	3.1	0.0	9.1	9.4	D	6.7	3.4	D	20.7	4,215	219	715	8,149	2.0
Pike	0.3	D	17.4	11.1	D	6.0	4.2	D	24.3	3,830	214	394	6,974	2.3
Polk	0.8	D	6.2	31.3	D	10.2	1.8	7.8	17.2	9,525	228	1,625	17,033	0.7
Pulaski	4.3	0.0	D	D	D	6.8	D	D	22.7	2,225	197	390	5,166	0.3

1. Per 1,000 resident population estimated as of July 1 of the year shown.

Table B. States and Counties — Population, Vital Statistics, Health, and Crime

STATE County	Persons in group quarters, 2017	Daytime Population, 2012-2016 Number	Employment/ residence ratio	Births, 2017 Total	Rate[1]	Deaths, 2017 Number	Rate[1]	Persons under 65 with no health insurance, 2016 Number	Percent	Medicare, 2017 Total beneficiaries	Enrolled in Original Medicare	Enrolled in Medicare Advantage	Serious crimes known to police[2], 2016 Total Number	Rate[3]
	32	33	34	35	36	37	38	39	40	41	42	43	44	45
GEORGIA—Cont'd														
Putnam	171	19,298	0.78	231	10.6	256	11.8	2,895	17.7	5,025	3,376	1,649	591	2,767
Quitman	0	1,813	0.56	28	11.9	16	6.8	274	16.8	177	110	67	41	1,813
Rabun	414	16,863	1.09	157	9.5	217	13.1	2,628	22.0	4,777	3,558	1,219	364	2,238
Randolph	443	7,205	0.99	76	10.7	74	10.5	758	14.6	1,550	964	586	120	1,691
Richmond	11542	242,627	1.51	2,939	14.6	2,005	9.9	23,417	14.3	39,989	25,004	14,984	9,891	4,902
Rockdale	831	88,832	1.03	1,012	11.2	684	7.6	11,717	15.4	14,258	8,019	6,239	2,614	2,922
Schley	0	4,285	0.59	52	10.0	31	5.9	689	16.1	761	484	277	53	1,020
Screven	441	12,889	0.77	161	11.5	162	11.6	1,871	16.8	3,107	1,994	1,113	280	2,111
Seminole	81	8,378	0.89	86	10.4	114	13.7	942	14.5	2,189	1,532	656	162	1,879
Spalding	1230	61,586	0.90	802	12.3	767	11.7	8,322	15.9	14,282	8,678	5,604	2,992	4,677
Stephens	572	25,556	1.00	333	12.9	329	12.7	3,106	15.4	7,728	5,251	2,478	837	3,289
Stewart	1556	5,690	0.92	41	6.9	59	9.9	604	18.2	1,027	541	486	NA	NA
Sumter	1650	32,211	1.10	372	12.5	341	11.4	3,799	16.0	5,976	3,593	2,383	1,601	5,271
Talbot	0	4,607	0.30	44	7.0	68	10.9	744	15.3	1,555	919	636	84	1,347
Taliaferro	7	1,502	0.37	13	8.0	19	11.7	231	19.2	474	263	211	NA	NA
Tattnall	4543	24,149	0.85	280	11.1	239	9.4	3,225	18.6	4,063	2,561	1,501	417	1,658
Taylor	147	7,778	0.79	78	9.6	81	9.9	1,080	16.6	1,989	1,251	738	106	1,287
Telfair	3339	16,816	1.09	127	7.9	164	10.3	1,568	15.5	2,576	1,706	870	NA	NA
Terrell	269	8,438	0.78	102	11.7	97	11.1	1,136	16.4	2,153	1,271	882	260	2,881
Thomas	771	46,910	1.11	567	12.7	512	11.4	5,829	16.0	11,413	7,648	3,765	1,568	3,687
Tift	1541	45,858	1.32	580	14.3	410	10.1	5,796	17.4	8,147	5,514	2,633	1,966	4,815
Toombs	403	29,254	1.21	389	14.4	318	11.8	3,814	16.9	6,118	4,297	1,821	NA	NA
Towns	1035	10,675	0.92	95	8.3	182	15.8	1,031	15.8	4,667	3,261	1,406	215	1,902
Treutlen	391	5,516	0.56	69	10.2	63	9.3	771	14.6	1,266	769	497	NA	NA
Troup	2245	79,159	1.34	913	13.1	738	10.6	8,481	14.7	13,188	9,141	4,047	2,851	4,059
Turner	374	7,716	0.85	117	14.7	91	11.4	1,105	18.1	2,074	1,229	845	274	3,396
Twiggs	89	7,638	0.70	80	9.8	125	15.3	1,021	16.0	1,809	1,099	710	161	1,946
Union	303	22,777	1.10	170	7.2	270	11.5	2,633	17.3	7,683	5,508	2,175	290	1,292
Upson	371	25,339	0.89	315	12.1	375	14.3	3,131	14.8	5,814	3,423	2,391	928	3,542
Walker	1266	56,112	0.57	751	10.9	794	11.5	7,921	14.3	15,822	10,854	4,968	1,841	2,714
Walton	698	73,071	0.62	1,181	12.9	843	9.2	10,825	14.2	19,380	11,901	7,478	2,203	2,469
Ware	2407	39,731	1.31	501	14.0	423	11.8	4,075	14.7	9,067	6,424	2,643	1,748	4,975
Warren	85	4,560	0.53	51	9.6	64	12.1	649	15.4	1,289	737	552	NA	NA
Washington	1677	21,011	1.04	216	10.6	237	11.7	2,155	14.0	4,139	2,390	1,749	464	2,266
Wayne	1854	29,828	0.98	382	12.8	341	11.4	3,549	15.1	5,577	3,812	1,765	1,621	5,515
Webster	0	2,263	0.63	24	9.2	17	6.5	335	16.5	385	214	171	8	305
Wheeler	2556	7,992	1.04	63	7.9	64	8.0	631	14.6	1,082	719	363	81	1,022
White	626	25,547	0.76	272	9.2	280	9.5	3,479	15.7	6,553	4,203	2,351	641	2,248
Whitfield	1084	114,124	1.23	1,423	13.6	812	7.8	19,233	21.5	17,435	14,142	3,294	2,892	2,787
Wilcox	1961	8,358	0.79	92	10.5	100	11.4	921	16.8	1,740	1,156	584	159	1,923
Wilkes	141	9,519	0.89	98	9.9	138	14.0	1,249	16.7	2,710	1,776	934	52	534
Wilkinson	114	9,154	0.95	100	11.2	139	15.5	1,016	13.9	2,313	1,467	847	78	1,012
Worth	147	16,511	0.48	211	10.3	217	10.6	2,915	17.4	3,494	2,374	1,120	640	3,125
HAWAII	44435	1,414,739	1.00	18,019	12.6	12,303	8.6	48,641	4.2	259,275	141,632	117,643	47,170	3,302
Hawaii	3864	193,144	0.99	2,347	11.7	1,930	9.6	8,067	5.0	41,362	27,029	14,333	5,395	2,747
Honolulu	36580	988,649	1.00	12,927	13.1	8,401	8.5	30,330	3.8	175,363	91,340	84,023	32,558	3,270
Kalawao	3	90	0.99	0	0.0	0	0.0	NA	NA	0	0	0	NA	NA
Kauai	1172	70,437	1.00	867	12.0	662	9.2	2,770	4.7	14,334	8,687	5,647	1,661	2,313
Maui	2816	162,419	1.00	1,878	11.3	1,310	7.9	7,474	5.4	28,158	14,532	13,627	6,191	3,757
IDAHO	29946	1,613,262	0.97	22,981	13.4	12,653	7.4	165,164	11.8	306,630	209,431	97,200	33,233	1,974
Ada	11087	447,483	1.11	5,170	11.3	2,899	6.3	33,709	8.9	73,277	39,125	34,152	8,759	1,966
Adams	21	3,479	0.74	30	7.2	24	5.8	412	14.7	1,190	987	203	37	962
Bannock	2028	82,046	0.95	1,210	14.2	662	7.8	6,949	9.8	14,846	10,466	4,380	2,459	2,913
Bear Lake	31	5,420	0.79	80	13.3	59	9.8	463	9.8	1,357	1,299	58	85	1,429
Benewah	70	9,357	1.08	106	11.5	113	12.3	910	13.1	2,619	2,549	71	NA	NA
Bingham	323	42,276	0.84	702	15.3	363	7.9	5,574	14.5	7,189	5,696	1,493	748	1,658
Blaine	258	22,442	1.09	222	10.1	104	4.7	2,922	16.2	4,279	3,504	775	187	858
Boise	34	5,891	0.62	42	5.8	54	7.4	621	11.5	1,435	833	602	86	1,209
Bonner	353	40,170	0.92	415	9.5	422	9.7	3,889	12.0	10,875	7,737	3,138	866	2,047
Bonneville	1242	114,179	1.11	1,975	17.2	828	7.2	9,066	9.3	17,775	14,332	3,443	2,453	2,192
Boundary	73	10,890	0.93	161	13.5	126	10.6	1,460	16.1	2,990	2,171	819	141	1,231
Butte	18	4,470	2.96	29	11.1	15	5.8	273	14.0	660	647	12	3	123
Camas	0	876	0.80	10	9.1	5	4.5	134	15.9	232	186	46	8	752
Canyon	3322	182,283	0.76	3,206	14.8	1,443	6.7	27,270	15.3	35,031	17,601	17,430	4,809	2,262

1. Per 1,000 estimated resident population. 2. Data for serious crimes have not been adjusted for underreporting; this may affect comparability between geographic areas and over time.
3. Per 100,000 population estimated by the FBI.

Table B. States and Counties — Crime, Education, Money Income, and Poverty

STATE County	Serious crimes known to police, 2016 (cont.)[1] Rate Violent	Property	Education School enrollment and attainment, 2012-2016 Enrollment[3] Total	Percent private	Attainment[4] (percent) High school graduate or less	Bachelor's degree or more	Local government expenditures,[5] 2013-2014 Total current spending (mil dol)	Current spending per student (dollars)	Money income, 2012-2016 Per capita income[6]	Households Median income (dollars)	Percent with income of less than $50,000	with income of $200,000 or more	Income and poverty, 2016 Median household income (dollars)	Percent below poverty level All persons	Children under 18 years	Children 5 to 17 years in families
	46	47	48	49	50	51	52	53	54	55	56	57	58	59	60	61
GEORGIA—Cont'd																
Putnam	262	2,504	4,276	22.6	54.2	18.3	31.2	11,164	25,164	45,762	53.0	2.7	44,785	18.4	32.4	28.8
Quitman	221	1,592	461	10.8	65.7	8.6	4.6	13,717	18,499	29,773	72.5	0.7	30,483	27.1	44.8	41.3
Rabun	123	2,115	2,975	20.6	47.5	26.3	28.0	12,344	24,374	38,277	60.6	2.7	41,913	17.1	29.4	28.0
Randolph	268	1,424	1,588	13.5	60.8	13.4	12.0	10,718	26,198	30,358	76.8	2.0	31,662	30.5	45.9	43.9
Richmond	429	4,474	53,254	14.0	47.2	21.0	293.1	9,159	20,956	38,595	61.9	1.8	41,128	25.6	38.9	39.9
Rockdale	319	2,603	24,225	10.8	45.1	26.0	150.6	9,384	23,003	51,072	49.0	2.1	56,689	14.7	23.8	21.3
Schley	115	905	1,567	2.6	53.0	14.9	13.7	9,919	21,202	41,227	58.5	1.9	43,396	18.5	27.6	22.8
Screven	256	1,855	3,390	10.5	59.4	14.4	22.3	9,420	19,801	35,047	61.4	2.1	36,414	27.6	44.4	42.5
Seminole	383	1,496	1,872	8.2	57.2	14.9	15.6	9,344	21,484	35,410	66.1	1.3	34,986	23.4	39.4	38.3
Spalding	586	4,090	14,420	10.0	58.6	15.4	101.2	9,520	19,899	40,548	58.4	1.7	43,065	22.4	32.4	30.0
Stephens	271	3,018	6,461	14.0	56.2	17.6	40.7	10,112	20,125	37,088	60.7	1.6	37,920	20.8	29.9	28.3
Stewart	NA	NA	812	5.4	73.2	10.4	6.6	12,153	13,883	20,882	74.0	0.5	24,945	39.2	45.0	43.8
Sumter	691	4,580	9,292	6.5	53.6	19.9	48.3	9,849	18,487	33,534	65.1	1.5	35,764	28.9	43.8	41.4
Talbot	112	1,235	1,238	16.6	66.4	12.6	6.2	11,916	20,366	36,957	67.1	1.1	36,482	23.5	38.3	34.8
Taliaferro	NA	NA	262	8.8	78.2	8.8	3.2	16,020	15,469	28,152	72.9	0.0	35,567	29.8	41.8	38.0
Tattnall	155	1,503	5,062	9.9	64.5	11.4	32.4	8,797	15,632	35,578	64.3	1.7	31,637	24.7	37.5	34.8
Taylor	121	1,166	1,998	17.6	59.7	11.3	13.9	9,135	17,321	27,114	73.0	2.0	31,637	24.7	37.5	34.8
Telfair	NA	NA	2,835	3.8	75.3	9.1	15.8	9,136	17,657	27,657	78.0	0.3	32,327	30.8	38.5	34.7
Terrell	377	2,504	2,284	12.1	56.2	12.1	15.1	10,176	17,246	30,438	67.3	1.3	34,018	31.1	48.4	45.2
Thomas	238	3,450	11,476	15.3	50.8	19.5	79.9	9,299	22,178	38,241	61.2	2.5	40,199	21.1	30.1	28.9
Tift	578	4,237	11,414	5.2	53.2	17.5	72.9	9,272	20,642	37,613	61.8	2.8	39,982	22.1	35.8	33.5
Toombs	NA	NA	7,199	6.8	59.8	17.0	48.0	8,362	20,309	33,081	64.8	2.3	36,765	23.4	35.8	34.1
Towns	354	1,548	2,451	23.8	42.5	25.1	12.7	11,730	21,671	39,321	62.9	1.1	42,439	15.1	26.9	25.9
Treutlen	NA	NA	1,404	5.6	62.3	16.5	9.7	8,116	21,307	40,204	58.7	1.9	32,100	27.1	39.8	36.4
Troup	356	3,703	17,802	14.6	51.9	18.8	113.5	8,953	21,942	42,545	56.2	2.8	42,955	20.3	29.9	29.3
Turner	582	2,813	1,938	13.7	61.0	12.3	16.1	10,786	17,149	34,667	64.6	0.7	31,969	30.4	46.7	45.3
Twiggs	205	1,741	1,562	14.3	66.7	11.6	10.9	12,003	18,255	31,625	67.7	0.5	38,507	23.5	35.7	33.0
Union	103	1,190	3,627	19.4	46.4	22.4	28.3	10,577	23,603	41,686	56.2	1.3	47,948	15.4	27.4	24.2
Upson	359	3,183	6,079	6.5	57.2	13.4	39.7	9,106	19,511	35,699	64.5	1.3	34,039	19.8	31.3	30.5
Walker	293	2,421	15,384	14.5	57.0	15.0	94.4	8,943	21,588	41,539	59.2	2.5	40,814	18.6	25.2	23.3
Walton	241	2,228	22,922	14.0	49.9	18.6	127.7	8,290	24,141	54,459	44.7	3.1	55,267	12.8	18.9	17.7
Ware	524	4,451	8,245	6.5	59.2	12.8	61.5	10,226	18,396	34,705	65.6	1.2	34,643	25.5	37.2	34.7
Warren	NA	NA	998	17.0	70.8	12.1	7.4	10,919	18,381	31,875	68.3	0.9	36,789	28.2	45.8	43.8
Washington	220	2,046	4,721	11.1	62.1	12.3	32.9	10,620	18,662	37,417	63.4	1.4	35,542	26.9	36.6	34.2
Wayne	694	4,821	7,205	8.7	58.4	13.3	47.5	8,696	18,663	39,908	59.0	1.4	42,017	22.2	31.5	29.3
Webster	38	267	725	9.2	66.9	9.4	4.4	10,555	20,834	37,072	59.7	1.7	36,329	20.8	34.1	31.0
Wheeler	50	971	1,212	5.9	76.8	4.9	10.5	10,035	9,688	27,779	71.6	0.0	29,532	39.1	38.8	36.5
White	193	2,055	6,242	10.3	46.8	20.8	58.4	11,613	22,055	42,264	57.9	1.5	44,980	14.3	21.8	20.0
Whitfield	309	2,478	27,690	4.9	59.6	13.6	190.2	9,073	21,158	41,764	57.8	2.9	46,796	16.1	21.9	19.7
Wilcox	230	1,693	1,648	13.5	71.6	9.5	12.8	10,518	14,536	34,071	66.2	0.3	33,858	31.0	41.4	41.0
Wilkes	308	226	2,075	8.0	64.0	13.8	18.5	11,107	19,129	33,462	66.0	1.3	33,735	22.9	35.7	34.6
Wilkinson	195	817	2,176	13.7	67.4	8.6	18.1	11,543	19,173	38,827	59.3	0.4	47,309	20.9	34.5	32.4
Worth	498	2,627	5,035	9.2	63.2	10.2	30.6	8,997	20,068	38,684	62.8	1.8	40,122	21.1	33.4	31.4
HAWAII	309	2,993	333,842	23.0	36.5	31.4	2,327.5	12,458	30,970	71,977	34.0	7.3	74,659	9.5	11.2	10.4
Hawaii	238	2,509	43,059	16.4	40.1	27.6	(7)	(7)	25,827	53,936	46.9	3.9	54,684	15.4	19.3	17.8
Honolulu	238	3,033	241,375	25.0	35.1	33.4	(7) 2,327.5	(7) 12,458	32,194	77,161	30.7	8.4	80,012	8.5	9.5	8.9
Kalawao	NA	NA	4	50.0	46.4	29.8	(7)	(7)	45,812	65,625	30.9	0.0	0.0	0.0	0.0	0.0
Kauai	235	2,077	14,075	16.3	39.2	27.8	(7)	(7)	28,791	68,224	37.3	5.6	63,164	8.1	10.8	10.6
Maui	273	3,484	35,329	19.4	39.6	25.7	(7)	(7)	30,599	68,777	35.9	6.5	69,699	9.5	11.7	10.0
IDAHO	230	1,744	445,695	13.5	37.6	26.2	1,934.0	6,527	24,280	49,174	50.8	2.9	51,647	13.8	16.6	15.0
Ada	233	1,732	117,463	12.6	27.3	37.0	492.2	6,339	30,086	58,099	42.8	5.0	61,571	10.8	11.3	10.3
Adams	104	858	719	9.6	48.0	22.7	3.7	8,773	22,741	41,335	59.6	0.1	42,310	15.0	23.9	22.6
Bannock	285	2,628	25,857	7.8	34.6	27.5	88.6	6,247	22,885	45,216	54.2	1.9	48,453	16.8	19.1	17.2
Bear Lake	84	1,345	1,340	5.4	45.4	19.5	7.7	6,848	22,985	46,863	53.6	1.4	45,875	13.9	18.9	17.3
Benewah	NA	NA	1,859	15.4	52.1	13.6	12.6	9,378	22,055	42,600	58.2	1.4	45,285	18.0	27.1	22.6
Bingham	226	1,432	13,231	6.3	44.6	18.1	64.9	6,199	20,199	49,943	50.1	1.7	51,586	13.8	17.5	15.6
Blaine	202	656	4,406	8.0	29.4	41.8	54.4	15,791	34,330	58,086	44.8	6.8	66,210	9.8	12.6	10.5
Boise	211	998	1,303	16.0	33.9	27.0	8.0	9,034	28,273	44,591	53.7	2.3	50,123	13.6	21.2	18.2
Bonner	208	1,839	8,222	17.4	40.2	22.1	42.6	7,746	24,507	43,697	57.3	2.3	48,097	15.4	22.9	19.6
Bonneville	361	1,831	31,387	10.2	35.8	27.8	133.1	5,706	24,889	52,831	47.0	3.6	59,293	11.7	15.2	14.0
Boundary	114	1,118	2,169	21.9	48.3	17.5	10.5	7,027	22,822	39,279	59.1	3.5	42,725	17.0	23.7	22.9
Butte	0	123	600	10.5	44.7	14.9	3.3	7,345	25,209	39,653	59.7	3.6	41,706	18.2	23.5	20.2
Camas	0	752	233	0.0	41.5	20.5	1.8	11,865	26,544	42,708	57.8	8.7	49,153	9.9	14.1	11.1
Canyon	267	1,995	57,575	13.5	48.2	18.4	227.6	5,648	18,639	44,860	55.9	1.2	48,461	15.1	18.2	16.2

1. Data for serious crimes have not been adjusted for underreporting; this may affect comparability between geographic areas and over time.   2. Per 100,000 population estimated by the FBI.
3. All persons 3 years old and over enrolled in nursery school through college.   4. Persons 25 years old and over.   5. Elementary and secondary education expenditures.
6. Based on population estimated by the American Community Survey, 2011–2015.   7. Hawaii, Kalawao, Kauai, and Maui counties are included with Honolulu county.

Table B. States and Counties — Personal Income and Earnings

STATE County	Personal income, 2016										Earnings, 2016		
			Per capita[1]			Supplements to wages and salaries, employer contributions (mil dol)						Contributions for government social insurance (mil dol)	
	Total (mil dol)	Percent change 2015-2016	Dollars	Rank	Wages and salaries (mil dol)	Pension and insurance	Government social insurance	Proprietors' income (mil dol)	Dividends, interest, and rent (mil dol)	Personal transfer receipts (mil dol)	Total (mil dol)	From employee and self-employed	From employer
	62	63	64	65	66	67	68	69	70	71	72	73	74
GEORGIA—Cont'd													
Putnam	727	2.6	33,840	2,345	193	46	13	25	167	214	277	34	13
Quitman	64	2.0	27,531	2,998	12	4	1	4	8	27	22	3	1
Rabun	616	3.4	37,215	1,791	164	34	12	45	187	179	255	31	12
Randolph	215	1.9	30,007	2,843	65	17	5	22	32	76	109	12	5
Richmond	7164	2.4	35,526	2,079	5,839	1,320	439	420	1,445	1,924	8,018	864	439
Rockdale	2978	3.9	33,329	2,423	1,573	253	109	118	406	691	2,054	235	109
Schley	140	-1.7	27,381	3,012	38	11	3	6	22	36	58	6	3
Screven	399	2.6	28,408	2,955	125	30	9	19	64	141	182	22	9
Seminole	321	5.3	37,878	1,682	88	19	6	75	45	99	187	19	6
Spalding	2107	3.8	32,512	2,547	848	180	60	105	321	645	1,193	139	60
Stephens	885	0.5	34,356	2,273	378	75	27	55	144	271	535	62	27
Stewart	133	1.1	23,277	3,095	51	11	4	6	23	49	73	9	4
Sumter	939	-0.3	30,905	2,746	376	93	27	35	180	298	530	60	27
Talbot	203	1.8	32,962	2,479	30	8	2	4	37	71	43	7	2
Taliaferro	42	-1.1	26,161	3,052	6	3	0	4	8	18	13	1	0
Tattnall	733	-1.2	29,215	2,915	224	58	15	82	96	189	379	34	15
Taylor	256	16.9	31,068	2,731	93	19	7	10	38	82	129	16	7
Telfair	328	3.2	20,541	3,109	114	29	9	27	46	122	178	21	9
Terrell	332	2.7	37,020	1,822	87	20	6	24	71	99	137	15	6
Thomas	1832	2.0	40,486	1,300	926	161	64	104	367	467	1,255	143	64
Tift	1442	-6.0	35,309	2,114	762	174	50	139	226	361	1,126	114	50
Toombs	907	1.0	33,343	2,420	444	85	32	47	128	270	609	71	32
Towns	367	3.3	32,214	2,578	115	29	8	21	100	152	173	23	8
Treutlen	182	2.8	27,416	3,008	37	9	3	9	23	68	58	7	3
Troup	2432	3.1	34,734	2,201	1,795	294	133	81	400	601	2,303	270	133
Turner	264	0.0	32,869	2,503	75	17	5	20	35	94	118	13	5
Twiggs	291	1.6	35,665	2,052	67	13	5	34	32	97	118	14	5
Union	817	4.7	35,642	2,056	256	60	17	48	168	270	382	46	17
Upson	863	2.5	32,766	2,523	253	50	18	39	135	276	360	45	18
Walker	2085	1.9	30,715	2,766	483	121	36	116	287	620	756	93	36
Walton	3251	4.4	36,044	2,000	995	174	70	133	452	689	1,372	161	70
Ware	1123	3.9	31,418	2,688	649	128	52	41	162	396	871	109	52
Warren	177	2.5	32,477	2,552	67	13	5	6	29	61	91	12	5
Washington	622	0.0	30,424	2,801	266	66	18	21	126	200	372	42	18
Wayne	941	0.1	31,272	2,707	341	76	24	53	124	283	495	57	24
Webster	72	4.9	27,686	2,995	21	4	1	8	13	20	34	4	1
Wheeler	130	1.8	16,267	3,113	43	10	3	12	18	52	69	8	3
White	906	2.5	31,355	2,696	270	52	20	64	151	258	405	49	20
Whitfield	3772	4.1	36,068	1,994	2,671	409	197	460	715	760	3,737	417	197
Wilcox	235	3.0	26,827	3,032	40	13	3	30	35	79	86	8	3
Wilkes	292	-0.3	29,758	2,865	111	26	8	25	59	111	169	19	8
Wilkinson	294	1.0	32,319	2,562	163	29	11	15	37	100	218	25	11
Worth	659	4.5	31,758	2,650	127	28	8	21	103	177	184	22	8
HAWAII	71946	3.3	50,358	X	35,884	7,391	2,818	5,146	15,250	11,311	51,239	3,036	2,818
Hawaii	7619	5.0	38,392	1,586	3,084	627	231	547	1,791	1,847	4,489	522	231
Honolulu	53828	2.9	54,229	262	27,812	5,904	2,221	3,633	11,156	7,637	39,569	4,511	2,221
Kalawao	(2) 7360	(2) 4.6	(2) 44,478	(2) 833	(2) 3,555	(2) 604	(2) 260	(2) 722	(2) 1,594	(2) 1,201	(2) 5,140	(2) 584	(2) 260
Kauai	3139	3.5	43,585	920	1,433	256	107	244	709	626	2,041	238	107
Maui	(2)	(2)	(2)	(2)	(2)	(2)	(2)	(2)	(2)	(2)	(2)	(2)	(2)
IDAHO	66433	3.5	39,543	X	29,444	5,121	2,572	7,457	13,929	12,251	44,593	2,773	2,572
Ada	20890	3.9	47,046	604	11,359	1,776	960	2,375	4,390	2,891	16,470	1,985	960
Adams	145	3.0	37,301	1,769	48	10	4	16	43	38	78	10	4
Bannock	2929	4.1	34,709	2,205	1,313	276	120	155	478	674	1,865	243	120
Bear Lake	218	2.6	36,620	1,895	57	14	6	14	40	54	91	12	6
Benewah	300	1.4	33,035	2,466	146	30	13	22	58	89	211	28	13
Bingham	1540	2.0	34,065	2,314	551	108	48	204	262	317	912	101	48
Blaine	2016	1.2	92,495	16	546	75	49	191	1,127	144	862	103	49
Boise	271	5.1	38,027	1,657	47	11	4	17	61	65	80	11	4
Bonner	1555	4.4	36,553	1,908	507	101	48	109	471	374	764	104	48
Bonneville	4795	4.7	42,728	1,020	1,898	319	171	770	971	778	3,158	366	171
Boundary	358	1.3	30,653	2,773	135	28	13	32	82	101	208	27	13
Butte	89	1.8	35,479	2,085	700	56	52	9	18	23	818	104	52
Camas	40	-3.6	37,328	1,758	22	3	2	4	11	8	31	4	2
Canyon	6204	4.7	29,305	2,908	2,321	417	211	482	913	1,499	3,431	443	211

1. Based on the resident population estimated as of July 1 of the year shown.   2. Kalawao county is included with Maui county

STATE County	Farm	Mining, quarrying, and extracting	Construction	Manu-facturing	Information; professional, scientific, technical services	Retail trade	Finance, insurance, real estate, and leasing	Health care and social assistance	Govern-ment	Number	Rate[1]	Supple-mental Security Income recipients, 2016	Total	Percent change, 2010-2017
	75	76	77	78	79	80	81	82	83	84	85	86	87	88
GEORGIA—Cont'd														
Putnam	1.6	0.0	8.6	9.6	D	9.2	6.7	D	30.2	5,875	273	529	13,114	2.4
Quitman	11.7	0.0	1.5	D	D	D	D	D	35.4	760	326	125	2,052	0.2
Rabun	1.0	D	12.5	8.6	3.3	13.4	6.4	D	19.4	5,165	313	412	12,634	2.6
Randolph	8.0	0.0	D	D	D	6.3	D	D	27.5	1,775	246	403	4,105	-1.1
Richmond	0.0	D	3.5	7.8	6.7	4.6	4.3	14.6	41.2	39,380	195	8,135	88,638	2.7
Rockdale	0.0	D	12.4	16.7	8.5	7.8	6.4	12.4	14.0	16,215	181	2,055	33,619	1.1
Schley	6.1	0.1	D	28.5	D	3.1	D	D	33.8	905	175	137	2,206	-0.1
Screven	5.0	0.1	4.1	26.2	D	6.5	3.5	D	28.4	3,535	252	714	6,766	0.4
Seminole	7.8	0.0	2.1	25.1	D	3.9	4.9	11.2	12.9	2,485	294	427	4,833	0.8
Spalding	-0.2	D	4.1	16.5	D	7.4	4.4	15.7	22.8	15,545	241	2,772	27,415	2.4
Stephens	2.1	D	D	22.5	2.7	7.7	2.7	D	18.7	7,165	279	1,231	12,631	-0.2
Stewart	6.5	0.0	D	D	D	1.6	D	26.6	32.8	1,075	183	258	2,341	-1.8
Sumter	1.9	D	2.8	9.4	D	7.8	3.5	D	28.0	6,690	220	1,356	13,885	-0.2
Talbot	-1.1	14.3	26.9	0.6	D	1.8	D	D	28.2	1,695	267	307	3,413	0.4
Taliaferro	26.6	0.0	D	D	0.0	D	D	D	48.9	465	286	95	1,015	0.0
Tattnall	20.9	0.1	3.9	2.3	2.8	4.3	3.5	D	29.2	4,420	175	937	10,004	0.4
Taylor	2.6	D	31.3	2.8	D	6.6	2.1	11.2	17.5	1,980	241	404	4,599	0.8
Telfair	2.4	1.0	3.9	D	1.8	4.6	3.9	4.9	23.7	2,735	171	589	7,290	-0.1
Terrell	10.2	0.2	2.7	13.5	D	8.7	5.3	D	23.3	2,435	274	548	4,168	0.2
Thomas	0.4	D	3.1	17.2	3.5	6.0	6.6	19.9	15.7	11,115	247	2,227	20,755	2.9
Tift	1.6	0.1	3.3	6.6	3.8	9.1	4.2	8.4	14.5	6,190	228	1,329	12,207	0.7
Toombs	2.1	0.0	5.2	9.8	4.4	5.5	6.6	D	16.1	4,795	423	254	8,264	6.9
Towns	-0.2	D	6.8	4.1	4.4	5.5	6.6	D	32.0	1,555	231	315	3,009	0.6
Treutlen	5.7	0.0	D	D	0.0	10.3	D	D	10.2	14,200	204	2,370	28,536	1.8
Troup	0.0	D	5.1	37.1	3.5	4.8	4.4	8.5	26.0	2,200	276	476	3,957	3.0
Turner	11.0	0.0	1.0	13.8	D	7.0	5.1	4.4						
Twiggs	2.6	D	D	D	D	D	D	D	14.4	2,535	308	415	4,237	0.1
Union	1.1	D	6.4	4.5	D	8.8	5.4	D	25.9	8,490	375	474	14,641	4.2
Upson	4.0	0.1	5.0	19.5	4.5	7.9	4.2	19.7	20.6	7,195	274	1,156	12,130	-0.3
Walker	2.2	D	5.9	31.6	D	5.5	5.3	4.8	23.4	16,330	239	2,212	30,370	0.9
Walton	0.3	0.2	15.2	14.0	4.1	10.2	3.6	7.3	17.4	17,085	190	1,624	33,740	4.0
Ware	0.3	0.0	3.0	10.4	2.6	10.0	3.8	18.7	21.1	8,115	227	1,792	16,687	2.2
Warren	1.9	D	1.6	29.0	D	4.1	0.7	D	14.3	1,525	283	275	2,974	-0.4
Washington	0.3	3.6	5.0	9.5	3.0	6.1	4.9	D	30.4	4,895	241	903	9,302	2.8
Wayne	1.4	0.0	8.8	19.9	D	8.2	2.8	9.1	30.7	6,560	219	1,093	12,257	0.5
Webster	19.0	D	D	D	0.0	6.6	1.2	D	20.1	575	220	91	1,531	0.5
Wheeler	10.2	0.0	4.3	0.0	D	2.3	D	D	22.3	1,230	153	235	2,620	-0.2
White	4.4	D	13.8	12.7	3.7	9.3	4.1	D	16.5	7,455	259	595	16,248	1.2
Whitfield	0.2	D	1.8	37.1	7.7	7.3	4.3	9.2	9.1	18,590	178	2,514	39,955	0.1
Wilcox	28.4	0.0	D	D	D	3.3	D	2.9	34.9	1,790	202	345	3,520	0.3
Wilkes	9.3	D	7.6	18.2	D	6.4	4.0	7.5	23.8	2,985	304	467	5,163	0.1
Wilkinson	0.3	46.2	9.4	7.2	D	1.7	D	3.1	11.7	2,550	282	353	4,477	-0.2
Worth	8.4	0.0	6.1	10.1	D	7.2	4.0	D	27.3	4,540	219	694	9,325	0.8
HAWAII	0.5	0.1	8.7	1.8	6.9	6.0	6.1	9.9	30.1	261,513	183	24,224	542,904	4.5
Hawaii	2.1	D	9.6	D	D	8.4	4.3	D	24.8	43,595	219	5,255	88,096	7.0
Honolulu	0.2	0.1	8.5	1.9	7.6	5.4	6.4	10.3	32.8	173,410	175	16,014	350,786	4.1
Kalawao	(2) 1.5	(2) D	(2) 9.3	(2) 1.4	(2) 4.3	(2) 8.2	(2) 5.6	(2) 7.1	(2) 17.1	10	114	0	113	0.0
Kauai	0.9	D	9.2	D	D	8.5	5.1	D	20.2	15,020	209	921	30,947	3.9
Maui	(2)	(2)	(2)	(2)	(2)	(2)	(2)	(2)	(2)	29,480	178	2,034	72,962	3.7
IDAHO	4.6	1.0	7.3	10.9	8.4	8.7	6.2	12.3	17.0	325,247	194	30,770	721,820	8.1
Ada	0.3	1.2	7.6	11.5	9.8	8.1	8.4	14.8	14.2	74,995	169	6,595	180,722	13.3
Adams	6.4	0.2	6.8	12.1	D	4.7	2.6	D	25.3	1,320	334	62	2,684	1.7
Bannock	0.7	D	6.3	7.9	5.2	8.1	7.1	15.6	25.7	14,650	174	1,971	34,233	3.1
Bear Lake	6.4	D	2.6	3.7	3.9	7.8	D	4.8	38.2	1,465	247	99	4,108	5.0
Benewah	1.5	D	4.0	18.0	D	4.3	2.3	9.9	21.4	2,760	306	242	4,728	2.2
Bingham	14.1	D	6.2	14.0	2.0	4.7	5.8	7.8	11.2	8,315	184	872	16,744	3.7
Blaine	1.0	D	14.6	3.3	D	7.6	8.6	D	35.1	4,170	192	108	15,428	2.5
Boise	0.9	0.6	10.3	2.9	D	4.7	D	4.5		2,125	300	108	5,534	4.6
Bonner	0.3	1.3	8.5	18.6	D	10.5	4.8	7.8	19.3	12,135	287	829	25,123	1.8
Bonneville	1.5	D	5.8	7.4	6.8	19.1	4.7	17.2	12.1	18,895	169	2,301	42,815	7.8
Boundary	3.4	0.3	8.8	11.5	4.1	7.5	5.9	8.3	29.5	3,200	275	256	5,467	5.6
Butte	1.1	0.0	0.3	D	D	0.2	D	D	2.0	670	260	80	1,380	1.8
Camas	10.2	D	D	D	D	2.1	D	D	19.3	240	221	0	854	2.8
Canyon	3.4	0.1	11.3	15.6	4.8	9.6	4.0	9.7	15.5	37,240	176	4,753	76,102	9.6

1. Per 1,000 resident population estimated as of July 1 of the year shown.   2. Kalawao county is included with Maui county

STATE County	Housing units, 2017 (cont.)								Civilian labor force, 2017				Civilian employment[6], 2012-2016		
	Occupied units										Unemployment			Percent	
			Owner-occupied			Renter-occupied									
				Median owner cost as a percent of income											
	Total	Percent	Median value[1]	With a mortgage	Without a mortgage[2]	Median rent[3]	Median rent as a percent of income[2]	Sub-standard units[4] (percent)	Total	Percent change, 2016-2017	Total	Rate[5]	Total	Management, business, science, and arts	Construction, production, and maintenance occupations
	89	90	91	92	93	94	95	96	97	98	99	100	101	102	103
GEORGIA—Cont'd															
Putnam	8322	74.1	156,000	20.9	12.0	678	32.8	1.3	8,145	2.3	475	5.8	9,260	27.0	28.3
Quitman	916	74.0	69,700	28.5	13.8	676	50.0	0.5	827	1.3	49	5.9	655	14.2	38.0
Rabun	6629	72.7	158,800	28.7	11.6	678	34.9	1.9	6,915	3.1	345	5.0	6,213	33.5	26.2
Randolph	2819	57.6	71,600	31.8	13.1	588	28.1	5.2	2,510	1.4	167	6.7	2,556	26.7	32.5
Richmond	72470	52.6	100,600	22.8	11.2	794	33.0	2.5	86,601	2.0	5,151	5.9	77,373	30.0	21.0
Rockdale	29940	67.8	143,100	23.1	10.0	922	33.0	2.9	44,641	3.1	2,357	5.3	37,607	32.8	25.1
Schley	1895	66.5	99,300	20.4	13.7	659	26.2	2.3	2,130	0.6	119	5.6	2,021	27.0	31.8
Screven	5214	69.3	77,800	24.0	12.5	591	28.3	3.1	5,275	0.6	336	6.4	5,532	27.9	31.0
Seminole	3312	74.4	76,800	27.3	11.7	681	31.6	3.2	3,124	0.9	205	6.6	2,943	33.0	23.3
Spalding	22914	61.0	110,300	23.4	12.1	804	34.8	2.5	28,529	2.5	1,659	5.8	24,094	27.0	30.7
Stephens	9189	71.4	95,900	21.7	11.2	585	30.8	3.1	11,020	-0.2	582	5.3	10,086	25.8	31.0
Stewart	1775	62.5	52,200	22.3	19.1	482	38.3	2.0	2,266	5.9	133	5.9	1,314	29.1	27.3
Sumter	11698	55.8	86,900	23.3	11.8	643	34.7	3.1	12,941	0.6	898	6.9	11,615	33.5	29.9
Talbot	2729	81.7	75,000	26.1	15.1	563	29.6	2.4	2,797	1.8	172	6.1	2,600	19.2	37.8
Taliaferro	748	69.0	57,000	26.5	19.7	535	30.0	2.1	572	4.2	39	6.8	637	17.7	40.7
Tattnall	7899	66.9	85,600	23.2	12.4	528	23.3	3.5	9,626	3.0	479	5.0	7,617	29.1	28.9
Taylor	3368	68.8	60,200	23.1	16.4	593	24.2	4.8	2,844	-14.5	249	8.8	2,856	26.9	36.7
Telfair	5110	61.5	57,700	29.5	12.8	580	24.8	3.4	4,800	-0.4	376	7.8	4,431	24.9	39.3
Terrell	3312	59.1	86,500	24.5	14.7	632	36.8	2.6	3,759	2.7	225	6.0	3,259	23.3	32.4
Thomas	17269	60.6	126,500	24.2	12.8	738	33.6	3.0	17,273	-1.6	1,018	5.9	17,684	33.5	23.0
Tift	14451	57.6	118,300	22.1	10.0	592	28.6	1.8	19,253	3.7	914	4.7	16,596	31.6	27.9
Toombs	10376	61.1	93,600	21.9	11.8	555	31.7	5.8	12,005	1.8	782	6.5	10,370	27.5	34.4
Towns	4611	79.5	189,400	29.0	13.3	653	32.8	1.0	3,839	-6.6	251	6.5	3,934	29.3	20.0
Treutlen	2586	69.7	71,300	25.4	10.7	531	17.9	2.1	2,752	0.3	183	6.6	2,772	22.5	34.9
Troup	24619	57.7	120,300	21.8	12.1	800	30.8	2.2	37,665	2.1	1,669	4.4	29,508	29.6	32.8
Turner	3071	69.7	73,000	22.4	15.5	566	36.7	7.0	3,305	2.0	189	5.7	2,985	30.2	28.8
Twiggs	2887	79.9	58,600	23.1	14.9	479	32.6	2.2	2,973	0.7	226	7.6	2,502	23.1	38.6
Union	8873	78.2	185,400	21.2	12.0	685	29.8	0.9	10,188	-2.6	456	4.5	7,509	31.3	25.3
Upson	10078	66.9	83,600	21.8	12.3	643	31.0	2.9	11,295	1.3	626	5.5	9,823	27.7	31.2
Walker	25581	71.5	107,500	20.6	11.7	665	28.9	4.3	30,728	2.5	1,402	4.6	28,058	27.0	34.0
Walton	30048	72.5	157,400	22.2	10.5	898	31.9	2.1	44,747	3.0	1,934	4.3	38,412	29.8	26.7
Ware	13847	61.4	77,100	19.8	11.7	652	30.4	2.6	15,972	3.0	729	4.6	13,134	27.1	30.6
Warren	2204	66.7	62,100	22.1	16.2	591	33.6	1.6	2,725	0.9	162	5.9	2,092	18.8	39.8
Washington	7381	69.8	79,400	21.0	12.8	615	32.7	4.0	7,373	2.5	443	6.0	7,633	28.5	26.6
Wayne	10016	65.4	98,600	21.1	10.3	599	28.3	2.1	11,371	0.6	657	5.8	9,958	32.1	33.1
Webster	1025	81.1	50,700	21.4	10.0	563	22.3	1.2	988	2.2	75	7.6	1,112	29.9	28.8
Wheeler	2065	66.0	48,300	21.2	10.8	482	28.7	1.9	1,758	1.3	157	8.9	1,559	22.9	39.8
White	11016	72.4	155,200	24.1	11.0	759	32.2	2.3	15,745	8.6	612	3.9	11,169	31.8	24.6
Whitfield	34814	63.3	120,200	21.0	10.1	669	28.5	5.9	45,297	1.1	2,476	5.5	45,576	21.4	43.0
Wilcox	2698	72.5	67,300	19.1	11.7	479	33.8	3.2	2,742	0.7	163	5.9	2,510	29.4	29.6
Wilkes	3975	67.8	87,200	24.2	15.1	603	33.4	1.3	3,836	3.4	218	5.7	3,670	25.0	35.8
Wilkinson	3297	76.2	69,600	19.3	10.8	602	32.2	3.0	3,845	5.2	220	5.7	3,376	22.8	34.4
Worth	7873	70.3	77,800	21.8	11.8	636	33.4	1.1	9,353	2.4	460	4.9	8,672	25.0	36.7
HAWAII	452030	57.5	538,400	27.0	10.0	1,456	33.1	9.5	685,419	0.2	16,177	2.4	664,616	34.0	18.4
Hawaii	66094	66.6	306,000	26.2	10.0	1,095	32.9	8.1	91,412	-0.1	2,565	2.8	83,482	31.6	19.9
Honolulu	309548	55.0	602,700	26.7	10.0	1,587	34.0	9.5	471,330	0.1	10,554	2.2	463,513	35.9	17.8
Kalawao	55	3.6	0	0.0	0.0	960	16.3	0.0	NA	NA	NA	NA	72	25.0	23.6
Kauai	22430	63.3	493,800	30.0	10.5	1,279	29.2	8.4	36,132	0.7	859	2.4	34,868	28.2	19.7
Maui	53903	58.3	528,500	28.5	10.0	1,308	29.8	12.0	86,545	0.8	2,199	2.5	82,681	28.3	20.0
IDAHO	596107	68.9	167,900	22.0	10.0	764	28.9	3.3	833,467	2.5	26,304	3.2	731,170	33.8	24.2
Ada	160398	67.5	200,200	20.7	10.0	871	29.0	1.7	232,954	3.6	6,469	2.8	207,753	42.3	15.5
Adams	1655	79.5	160,700	20.7	12.0	548	28.0	2.5	1,748	0.4	99	5.7	1,514	31.7	27.3
Bannock	30424	68.1	146,600	20.3	10.0	645	29.1	3.0	41,733	1.8	1,258	3.0	36,903	34.7	21.5
Bear Lake	2395	78.0	136,700	18.7	10.0	553	25.8	2.4	2,803	-0.1	91	3.2	2,527	25.2	31.6
Benewah	3592	73.7	147,800	23.6	11.4	676	24.2	5.7	3,993	-0.3	221	5.5	3,614	23.4	37.7
Bingham	14712	74.1	143,500	20.2	10.0	652	24.6	4.7	22,946	0.9	678	3.0	19,053	32.3	32.1
Blaine	8708	67.3	384,800	27.2	10.7	964	29.2	2.1	12,277	3.8	311	2.5	11,795	32.3	18.9
Boise	2994	81.3	188,300	22.9	11.0	688	28.6	2.7	3,200	3.5	153	4.8	2,729	37.7	22.4
Bonner	17109	73.0	212,100	27.8	10.0	734	28.8	4.6	19,131	1.5	859	4.5	16,574	27.0	30.6
Bonneville	37138	71.5	157,100	20.1	10.0	733	27.9	3.2	53,517	2.3	1,430	2.7	47,674	34.5	23.0
Boundary	4393	71.0	174,500	23.0	10.8	654	28.3	4.4	5,135	0.7	244	4.8	3,877	27.7	34.0
Butte	1061	82.8	101,300	19.1	11.7	622	26.8	0.9	1,314	1.8	40	3.0	966	34.2	29.6
Camas	379	71.8	170,600	27.3	10.0	659	25.7	3.2	676	2.9	18	2.7	462	25.1	34.6
Canyon	67155	67.8	131,300	23.2	10.1	773	29.4	4.4	96,377	3.1	3,422	3.6	85,579	26.0	30.2

1. Specified owner-occupied units.   2. A value of 10.0 represents 10 percent or less; a value of 50.0 represents 50 percent or more.   3. Specified renter-occupied units.   4. Overcrowded or lacking complete plumbing facilities.   5. Percent of civilian labor force.   6. Civilian employed persons 16 years old and over.

Table B. States and Counties — Nonfarm Employment and Agriculture

	Private nonfarm establishments, employment and payroll, 2016									Agriculture, 2012			
	Employment						Annual payroll		Farms			
											Percent with:		
STATE County	Number of establishments	Total	Health care and social assistance	Manufacturing	Retail trade	Finance and insurance	Professional, scientific, and technical services	Total (mil dol)	Average per employee (dollars)	Number	Fewer than 50 acres	500 acres or more	Farm operators whose principal occupation is farming (percent)
	104	105	106	107	108	109	110	111	112	113	114	115	116
GEORGIA—Cont'd													
Putnam	425	4,365	416	475	973	144	72	130	29,750	165	37.0	6.7	41.2
Quitman	36	224	D	D	50	12	NA	5	23,674	21	19.0	23.8	23.8
Rabun	476	4,113	507	277	1,071	120	123	126	30,661	114	57.0	0.9	62.3
Randolph	130	1,393	297	D	159	38	26	45	32,385	197	11.2	27.4	45.7
Richmond	4321	87,599	24,760	7,475	11,791	2,189	4,390	3,670	41,898	123	77.7	1.0	58.3
Rockdale	1973	31,053	4,082	5,034	4,615	933	887	1,322	42,581	103	77.7	1.0	58.3
Schley	67	627	26	286	73	D	D	26	42,252	92	17.4	19.6	41.3
Screven	204	2,344	306	883	355	96	40	72	30,561	344	14.8	26.2	48.5
Seminole	195	1,478	340	26	295	75	77	48	32,702	149	28.2	27.5	67.1
Spalding	1137	17,206	4,313	3,119	3,057	420	414	585	34,004	258	63.6	1.9	49.2
Stephens	544	7,942	1,384	2,242	1,158	177	116	263	33,116	218	45.0	0.9	53.7
Stewart	63	682	101	D	62	20	3	22	32,028	108	7.4	36.1	36.1
Sumter	625	8,586	2,610	957	1,482	212	257	265	30,818	369	19.2	19.0	38.2
Talbot	60	543	D	D	48	31	D	21	38,392	90	22.2	23.3	43.3
Taliaferro	18	48	D	D	10	D	NA	1	28,063	55	16.4	10.9	43.6
Tattnall	296	3,304	848	116	402	139	152	108	32,666	565	35.6	8.3	59.1
Taylor	121	1,176	197	65	117	52	D	51	43,113	224	21.0	15.2	46.9
Telfair	180	2,730	207	D	340	94	27	67	24,552	300	29.3	9.0	36.7
Terrell	171	1,701	160	351	318	82	39	57	33,396	248	21.4	24.2	42.3
Thomas	1113	16,241	3,576	2,557	2,344	614	295	676	41,596	407	35.4	21.1	54.3
Tift	1022	15,846	2,357	1,421	2,694	427	542	543	34,271	285	39.6	15.4	43.2
Toombs	669	9,226	2,220	1,092	1,762	299	187	315	34,162	268	36.9	12.7	29.9
Towns	263	3,167	605	41	413	68	48	80	25,284	109	58.7	0.0	49.5
Treutlen	86	680	172	66	216	27	D	19	28,454	149	31.5	11.4	27.5
Troup	1416	33,465	3,021	11,593	3,095	1,121	633	1,456	43,511	212	48.1	7.1	50.5
Turner	151	1,441	158	394	192	72	51	45	31,048	262	34.7	20.2	40.8
Twiggs	69	1,502	166	NA	62	D	D	52	34,849	108	36.1	12.0	37.0
Union	547	5,755	1,290	330	1,275	613	160	193	33,537	249	51.8	2.8	42.6
Upson	453	5,659	1,385	1,118	1,109	201	159	194	34,229	296	43.6	5.1	39.9
Walker	666	10,329	792	4,215	1,337	304	161	359	34,718	528	40.3	6.3	53.4
Walton	1602	16,593	2,086	2,297	2,725	407	550	608	36,617	477	50.3	3.4	54.3
Ware	852	11,299	2,759	1,054	2,546	324	265	389	34,448	280	44.3	8.9	43.9
Warren	68	894	132	448	82	9	7	34	38,056	134	26.1	13.4	38.1
Washington	343	5,174	885	530	750	150	173	199	38,381	408	22.5	13.0	36.8
Wayne	551	5,769	1,146	913	1,217	181	104	199	34,459	287	37.3	13.9	41.5
Webster	26	280	D	D	48	5	D	13	45,043	102	19.6	22.5	39.2
Wheeler	64	821	55	NA	52	D	D	27	32,464	136	15.4	17.6	25.7
White	603	6,522	1,006	776	1,187	145	128	204	31,322	299	64.2	2.7	53.8
Whitfield	2187	49,178	4,763	17,621	5,015	750	1,349	1,997	40,602	378	45.2	2.6	49.2
Wilcox	84	504	163	8	74	55	D	13	26,720	365	21.6	23.6	47.9
Wilkes	190	2,047	506	427	318	73	29	66	32,305	317	24.0	13.2	47.0
Wilkinson	130	2,175	187	681	165	40	33	102	47,041	114	29.8	4.4	39.5
Worth	255	2,607	380	555	528	63	70	85	32,642	487	27.3	28.5	51.1
HAWAII	32350	528,415	71,052	13,040	70,647	19,060	22,782	22,892	43,323	7,000	88.1	2.6	52.0
Hawaii	4032	54,561	8,508	1,489	9,654	1,151	1,485	2,028	37,167	4,282	87.6	2.3	48.2
Honolulu	21404	359,766	53,010	10,060	47,049	16,355	18,257	16,369	45,499	999	90.6	2.1	66.3
Kalawao	2	D	NA	NA	NA	NA	NA	D	D	NA	NA	NA	NA
Kauai	2087	27,328	3,239	345	4,216	365	928	1,063	38,915	591	85.3	4.2	52.3
Maui	4618	64,146	6,280	1,146	9,699	806	1,597	2,510	39,124	1,128	89.0	3.5	54.0
IDAHO	45826	562,282	91,190	60,078	84,071	22,432	32,852	22,243	39,559	24,816	47.9	17.1	49.8
Ada	13187	194,215	32,282	14,137	25,025	9,494	13,724	9,097	46,840	1,233	80.0	3.1	43.6
Adams	100	476	47	124	109	35	13	16	33,065	234	35.5	20.1	53.4
Bannock	2017	24,676	5,215	1,738	4,517	2,435	1,289	806	32,660	819	46.6	16.1	42.6
Bear Lake	122	942	306	49	238	37	9	27	28,604	493	25.2	24.7	46.9
Benewah	235	2,170	392	D	286	64	39	82	37,629	274	35.0	16.8	45.6
Bingham	843	9,916	1,661	2,327	1,275	271	204	359	36,184	1,265	56.4	17.1	58.5
Blaine	1412	11,001	889	430	1,429	268	700	437	39,734	186	39.2	30.1	58.6
Boise	157	609	26	14	110	D	11	15	25,348	105	43.8	12.4	57.1
Bonner	1509	11,969	1,648	2,081	2,188	269	482	421	35,146	686	51.0	3.4	42.9
Bonneville	3451	47,476	8,752	3,305	8,041	1,299	7,362	2,020	42,552	893	53.1	18.6	39.0
Boundary	367	2,458	528	438	434	54	100	82	33,340	370	44.3	12.2	41.4
Butte	56	942	D	D	78	11	D	34	35,872	214	21.5	31.3	71.0
Camas	31	174	10	D	21	D	NA	6	33,638	114	24.6	36.8	56.1
Canyon	3979	50,955	7,072	9,198	8,488	1,057	1,400	1,707	33,507	2,331	71.3	6.0	45.6

Table B. States and Counties — **Agriculture**

STATE County	Acreage (1,000) [117]	Percent change, 2007-2012 [118]	Average size of farm [119]	Total irrigated (1,000) [120]	Total cropland (1,000) [121]	Average per farm [122]	Average per acre [123]	Value of machinery and equipment, average per farm (dollars) [124]	Total (mil dol) [125]	Average per farm (acres) [126]	Crops [127]	Livestock and poultry products [128]	$10,000 or more [129]	$100,000 or more [130]	Total ($1,000) [131]	Percent of farms [132]
GEORGIA—Cont'd																
Putnam	28	-24.5	173	0.8	9.6	656,891	3,803	91,436	38.0	230,521	3.8	96.2	35.8	13.3	567	20.0
Quitman	9	-20.0	433	0.0	2.4	924,667	2,133	66,762	D	D	D	D	14.3	9.5	D	57.1
Rabun	8	1.7	71	D	3.6	500,658	7,078	73,737	21.3	186,719	20.8	79.2	50.9	21.9	138	11.4
Randolph	119	32.4	605	22.0	64.7	1,171,264	1,935	185,523	50.3	255,442	95.8	4.2	40.1	22.3	2,025	79.7
Richmond	14	11.1	113	0.1	3.9	299,699	2,650	58,967	2.0	16,276	45.6	54.4	28.5	6.5	42	12.2
Rockdale	5	-13.6	53	0.0	0.9	370,515	6,982	38,777	0.5	4,660	56.5	43.5	11.7	1.0	4	6.8
Schley	35	-2.3	385	0.8	7.1	875,543	2,273	56,413	18.1	196,239	11.2	88.8	34.8	15.2	284	58.7
Screven	180	1.0	525	17.9	103.0	1,119,872	2,134	170,779	66.6	193,669	92.3	7.7	37.5	18.3	2,076	75.0
Seminole	88	-14.8	592	38.9	62.0	1,600,074	2,703	268,034	74.7	501,631	90.7	9.3	63.1	35.6	1,883	65.1
Spalding	19	-28.8	73	0.0	5.1	381,438	5,229	37,888	5.2	20,298	19.2	80.8	17.4	3.9	60	12.8
Stephens	18	19.7	84	0.0	4.8	445,170	5,272	96,917	79.7	365,583	0.6	99.4	50.5	25.7	189	12.4
Stewart	59	28.6	549	4.4	19.7	1,076,824	1,963	127,593	14.6	135,417	80.6	19.4	30.6	17.6	917	68.5
Sumter	160	4.8	435	44.3	90.4	983,650	2,264	167,710	123.3	334,236	68.4	31.6	36.3	18.4	3,044	68.6
Talbot	34	-18.7	377	D	4.9	784,578	2,084	42,133	0.7	8,200	37.0	63.1	18.9	2.2	266	21.1
Taliaferro	14	-2.1	251	0.1	3.6	552,345	2,202	66,745	8.5	153,709	5.0	95.0	40.0	18.2	75	23.6
Tattnall	108	-20.7	190	13.8	49.2	528,524	2,778	97,715	236.2	418,099	36.7	63.3	49.4	27.1	1,594	36.5
Taylor	62	-29.0	275	6.0	21.7	556,027	2,025	65,634	22.7	101,505	55.5	44.5	29.0	6.7	510	51.3
Telfair	67	7.9	222	4.0	13.8	422,643	1,903	46,887	6.1	20,390	78.8	21.2	25.7	4.7	581	57.3
Terrell	121	-11.6	487	25.8	73.2	1,150,536	2,364	163,758	68.2	274,843	96.7	3.3	33.9	26.2	3,795	81.5
Thomas	173	-15.2	426	11.5	81.6	1,423,002	3,344	159,329	83.5	205,061	77.8	22.2	43.7	22.6	2,676	56.3
Tift	84	-36.4	296	20.6	50.0	941,074	3,176	135,681	70.6	247,653	94.0	6.0	43.5	23.5	1,695	50.5
Toombs	73	-18.5	273	9.9	30.6	647,821	2,371	84,123	58.9	219,746	78.3	21.7	31.3	11.2	745	48.5
Towns	8	12.3	77	0.0	2.1	456,587	5,913	50,862	3.2	29,367	36.6	63.4	30.3	8.3	35	4.6
Treutlen	35	16.7	236	D	9.7	423,060	1,794	64,107	8.3	55,376	95.0	5.0	20.1	3.4	259	60.4
Troup	32	-14.4	153	0.2	5.2	608,769	3,981	52,245	4.2	19,660	23.6	76.3	25.9	2.4	94	8.0
Turner	87	-25.0	332	19.1	47.5	791,313	2,384	141,511	58.4	223,050	86.8	13.2	39.7	19.8	2,000	72.1
Twiggs	39	-13.9	358	5.1	14.3	895,907	2,501	93,389	9.3	85,685	93.5	6.5	23.1	7.4	738	30.6
Union	21	-1.2	83	0.0	6.1	500,076	6,015	65,426	19.4	77,751	23.5	76.5	39.8	5.6	221	15.7
Upson	45	-6.1	151	D	8.2	478,044	3,160	51,111	23.0	77,770	8.5	91.5	20.9	5.7	193	14.5
Walker	80	12.0	151	0.3	28.5	589,797	3,907	71,972	108.2	204,932	8.1	91.9	42.8	13.6	1,049	16.3
Walton	52	-2.3	110	0.9	14.3	590,239	5,367	39,698	29.4	61,660	21.2	78.8	32.1	7.5	371	21.0
Ware	57	12.8	203	4.9	18.5	499,896	2,468	72,825	30.6	109,114	65.6	34.4	40.4	10.4	339	32.9
Warren	34	-7.5	257	0.1	9.2	518,627	2,019	54,731	5.6	41,694	58.0	42.0	27.6	8.2	225	23.1
Washington	100	-9.3	245	7.8	42.8	506,213	2,067	88,184	27.5	67,507	73.8	26.2	32.8	9.8	1,104	52.0
Wayne	62	9.6	217	6.6	35.6	595,854	2,746	115,289	44.3	154,456	59.8	40.2	42.5	19.5	748	42.5
Webster	48	-12.1	471	4.8	22.2	834,667	1,772	59,471	17.2	168,471	88.7	11.3	32.4	16.7	619	74.5
Wheeler	51	-11.4	372	2.5	11.6	556,206	1,493	60,529	8.1	59,706	95.5	4.5	28.7	6.6	473	66.9
White	23	11.8	79	0.1	5.9	539,097	6,866	50,181	77.4	258,957	2.9	97.1	45.2	27.1	129	9.7
Whitfield	39	-8.5	103	0.0	10.6	501,405	4,846	66,577	144.2	381,362	1.2	98.8	36.0	17.2	85	7.4
Wilcox	115	14.5	316	28.4	75.2	771,348	2,439	146,175	104.9	287,512	64.5	35.5	41.9	26.3	2,491	80.3
Wilkes	94	4.4	296	0.1	19.7	820,962	2,777	62,407	58.7	185,306	5.6	94.4	45.1	16.7	662	33.1
Wilkinson	16	-46.8	140	0.5	4.8	297,851	2,134	40,939	4.5	39,614	29.3	70.7	24.6	8.8	42	23.7
Worth	229	19.1	471	47.2	137.4	1,216,889	2,584	177,600	153.5	315,187	90.6	9.4	42.5	28.7	5,342	67.8
HAWAII	1129	0.7	161	81.8	174.0	1,461,342	9,058	43,999	661.3	94,478	81.5	18.5	41.6	7.2	5,228	9.0
Hawaii	687	0.4	160	7.0	72.0	1,280,898	7,985	36,698	247.2	57,741	63.3	36.7	40.6	6.1	4,153	8.2
Honolulu	69	14.5	69	10.8	22.2	1,396,597	20,171	56,908	161.5	161,650	90.0	10.0	54.6	12.7	283	6.1
Kalawao	NA	NA	NA	NA	NA	NA	NA	NA	NA	NA	NA	NA	NA	NA	NA	NA
Kauai	144	-4.9	244	22.5	30.2	1,853,486	7,600	57,464	64.5	109,161	86.3	13.7	35.2	6.6	234	16.2
Maui	229	1.6	203	41.5	49.6	1,998,207	9,836	53,229	188.1	166,755	96.5	3.5	37.1	7.1	558	10.5
IDAHO	11760	2.3	474	3,365.3	5,793.3	1,052,941	2,222	143,835	7,801.4	314,372	44.1	55.9	44.3	20.5	99,789	37.7
Ada	144	-24.8	117	55.3	53.4	616,596	5,278	70,942	221.0	179,229	20.2	79.8	26.8	7.9	704	10.2
Adams	136	-8.6	582	19.0	19.8	885,517	1,521	67,226	13.5	57,902	25.1	74.9	41.9	11.5	104	16.7
Bannock	295	-8.3	360	52.6	164.1	651,077	1,807	83,179	54.3	66,267	66.6	33.4	29.4	9.2	3,067	37.0
Bear Lake	258	10.6	523	54.5	112.5	743,225	1,421	101,310	29.5	59,850	35.4	64.6	52.7	15.8	1,316	47.1
Benewah	147	-4.5	535	0.9	81.7	849,000	1,587	106,938	23.9	87,058	96.9	3.1	29.6	10.9	1,516	45.6
Bingham	870	-4.7	687	333.4	369.5	1,536,482	2,235	194,538	453.3	358,314	82.7	17.3	46.5	23.7	5,568	33.9
Blaine	179	-6.7	963	41.9	47.6	2,752,371	2,858	165,301	38.6	207,376	72.2	27.8	62.9	32.8	415	40.3
Boise	D	D	D	2.4	3.0	667,895	D	34,914	3.1	29,133	39.8	60.3	29.5	6.7	D	6.7
Bonner	81	-14.6	118	1.2	26.1	513,108	4,366	43,496	10.2	14,940	60.1	39.9	24.2	1.9	96	4.7
Bonneville	409	-9.7	458	133.6	278.8	1,061,908	2,317	134,569	204.2	228,641	71.8	28.2	39.9	17.9	5,044	43.2
Boundary	75	2.3	203	2.1	46.7	694,997	3,420	72,922	27.8	75,203	84.1	15.8	41.1	15.7	785	23.5
Butte	125	3.3	585	58.7	68.6	901,136	1,540	148,860	39.3	183,640	82.4	17.6	71.0	38.8	1,539	67.3
Camas	168	21.1	1,471	20.4	82.7	2,182,649	1,484	176,982	21.6	189,500	83.5	16.5	51.8	26.3	406	55.3
Canyon																

Table B. States and Counties — Water Use, Wholesale Trade, Retail Trade, and Real Estate

STATE County	Water use, 2015		Wholesale Trade[1], 2012				Retail Trade[2], 2012				Real estate and rental and leasing,[2] 2012			
	Public supply water withdrawn (mil gal/day)	Public supply gallons withdrawn per person per day	Number of establishments	Number of employees	Sales (mil dol)	Annual payroll (mil dol)	Number of establishments	Number of employees	Sales (mil dol)	Annual payroll (mil dol)	Number of establishments	Number of employees	Sales (mil dol)	Annual payroll (mil dol)
	133	134	135	136	137	138	139	140	141	142	143	144	145	146
GEORGIA—Cont'd														
Putnam	3.76	176.1	16	68	57.9	2.7	75	668	157.4	14.1	12	225	9.7	3.9
Quitman	0.17	73.8	1	D	D	D	10	55	12.1	0.9	1	D	D	D
Rabun	1.60	98.3	4	6	0.5	0.1	76	902	247.7	22.3	19	D	D	D
Randolph	0.88	122.3	5	40	70.8	1.7	27	191	47.6	4.2	5	5	1.8	0.1
Richmond	39.17	194.1	182	1,856	864.7	81.5	812	10,830	2,627.3	229.5	201	1,069	248.9	37.9
Rockdale	11.76	132.3	80	636	525.7	34.1	293	4,625	1,239.6	116.2	77	327	83.0	14.9
Schley	0.45	87.1	4	56	44.4	2.1	14	76	19.3	1.6	NA	NA	NA	NA
Screven	0.74	52.3	8	D	D	D	49	360	74.5	6.9	4	7	0.7	0.2
Seminole	0.50	57.8	13	76	109.1	4.2	52	331	73.0	6.4	4	7	1.4	0.1
Spalding	6.83	106.6	39	428	467.1	17.9	224	2,669	638.8	59.4	48	185	29.9	5.7
Stephens	3.38	132.1	19	D	D	D	99	1,113	262.5	24.5	14	46	6.2	1.2
Stewart	0.78	133.3	2	D	D	D	15	42	17.1	1.0	1	D	D	D
Sumter	2.48	80.6	35	425	305.9	13.2	137	1,382	311.0	29.1	22	57	8.1	1.3
Talbot	1.33	209.9	3	11	8.8	0.2	12	65	11.7	0.8	1	D	D	D
Taliaferro	0.05	30.5	NA	NA	NA	NA	5	10	2.3	0.1	1	D	D	D
Tattnall	1.22	48.4	21	459	212.9	18.1	64	444	103.0	8.0	6	17	2.0	0.3
Taylor	0.62	74.4	4	D	D	D	29	152	36.9	2.6	3	8	0.7	0.1
Telfair	1.22	74.4	11	48	35.7	1.4	43	290	59.8	4.8	1	D	D	D
Terrell	1.44	158.0	7	162	250.1	4.0	45	316	68.0	6.0	4	D	D	D
Thomas	5.64	125.2	60	441	406.8	18.4	218	2,154	564.6	48.0	42	123	82.2	4.6
Tift	4.78	117.3	67	1,041	634.1	42.8	221	2,405	805.6	54.4	36	136	21.8	4.5
Toombs	2.84	104.3	28	566	996.3	20.8	149	1,640	406.4	35.5	24	59	7.6	1.3
Towns	1.54	137.7	8	19	2.9	0.4	57	344	87.1	6.9	15	22	7.0	0.8
Treutlen	0.30	44.2	2	D	D	D	22	140	29.9	2.6	1	D	D	D
Troup	8.54	122.4	58	D	D	D	258	3,072	911.1	73.7	61	272	41.3	7.5
Turner	0.79	96.2	13	148	81.6	5.3	32	179	66.7	4.0	2	D	D	D
Twiggs	0.45	53.6	3	D	D	D	16	68	27.9	1.1	1	D	D	D
Union	1.82	81.7	9	57	26.8	1.9	93	1,007	242.9	22.0	32	71	9.9	2.1
Upson	3.02	114.5	7	D	D	D	93	970	207.9	20.6	11	26	3.4	0.6
Walker	6.62	97.3	34	D	D	D	151	1,441	355.1	28.1	16	29	4.4	1.0
Walton	3.16	35.7	74	620	295.0	28.5	196	2,403	744.5	57.9	65	149	23.0	5.0
Ware	2.74	77.5	33	D	D	D	204	2,356	627.4	52.4	26	85	10.2	2.2
Warren	0.32	58.6	1	D	D	D	14	86	14.5	1.7	3	10	0.5	0.2
Washington	2.00	96.1	12	105	133.5	4.1	72	766	187.0	17.3	14	117	9.2	3.2
Wayne	1.50	50.8	12	99	71.0	2.9	120	1,201	293.1	25.4	16	57	5.3	1.3
Webster	0.10	37.8	3	D	D	D	5	38	9.0	1.1	NA	NA	NA	NA
Wheeler	0.18	22.8	3	5	6.5	0.3	14	70	21.2	1.2	2	D	D	D
White	1.47	51.9	15	79	30.7	2.1	119	1,097	279.7	23.0	18	59	6.1	1.0
Whitfield	23.96	229.9	191	2,604	1,196.6	103.0	435	4,690	1,302.4	107.7	63	D	D	D
Wilcox	0.44	49.7	7	38	34.3	1.5	19	90	23.4	1.6	NA	NA	NA	NA
Wilkes	1.01	102.4	9	81	24.1	3.2	48	406	70.4	7.4	4	11	0.9	0.3
Wilkinson	0.70	76.5	8	35	8.4	1.1	24	150	32.5	2.4	1	D	D	D
Worth	1.01	48.8	22	D	D	D	56	430	117.1	10.9	9	D	D	D
HAWAII	266.92	186.4	1,561	16,686	9,608.0	724.5	4,643	68,360	18,901.7	1,835.0	1,919	11,369	3,411.2	483.9
Hawaii	39.70	202.1	178	D	D	D	648	9,084	2,390.8	241.3	245	1,172	226.5	39.1
Honolulu	168.78	169.0	1,167	13,446	8,052.8	596.9	2,889	46,165	13,036.4	1,233.1	1,219	7,213	2,553.5	340.7
Kalawao	0.01	112.4	NA	NA	NA	NA	1	D	D	D	NA	NA	NA	NA
Kauai	16.34	227.8	76	D	D	D	347	3,937	1,013.5	102.4	149	962	176.9	33.3
Maui	42.09	255.7	140	1,141	714.6	50.4	758	D	D	D	306	2,022	454.4	70.8
IDAHO	275.79	166.6	1,739	21,470	17,906.0	960.8	5,815	72,980	20,444.3	1,794.0	2,033	6,268	1,039.9	184.2
Ada	72.71	167.5	550	8,141	7,352.5	419.6	1,410	20,428	5,766.7	538.7	712	2,578	456.9	85.2
Adams	0.53	137.9	1	D	D	D	12	D	D	D	7	4	0.4	0.1
Bannock	16.91	201.9	80	D	D	D	299	4,330	1,155.3	95.7	80	221	31.5	5.2
Bear Lake	0.37	62.5	5	54	13.8	1.4	26	232	58.8	4.0	5	14	1.1	0.2
Benewah	0.52	57.4	4	D	D	D	34	286	76.5	7.3	6	9	1.2	0.2
Bingham	1.99	44.2	50	1,047	635.9	33.6	111	1,132	256.2	23.6	19	37	5.7	1.1
Blaine	5.44	251.9	31	D	D	D	183	1,348	298.6	38.7	92	D	D	D
Boise	0.48	68.0	1	D	D	D	15	107	20.0	1.5	5	11	1.4	0.2
Bonner	1.71	40.9	28	157	45.5	5.5	199	1,960	438.0	45.4	68	220	30.9	6.9
Bonneville	36.62	332.6	169	2,021	3,049.6	90.5	477	6,757	1,956.5	157.1	134	460	80.6	13.8
Boundary	0.39	34.5	7	D	D	D	47	386	100.1	9.0	7	5	0.8	0.1
Butte	1.43	571.8	3	D	D	D	13	86	21.8	1.6	2	D	D	D
Camas	0.14	131.3	NA	NA	NA	NA	3	D	D	D	NA	NA	NA	NA
Canyon	15.92	76.7	148	1,600	1,089.0	71.7	485	7,102	2,149.4	182.5	149	434	49.0	10.6

1. Merchant wholesalers, except manufacturers' sales branches and offices. 2. Employer establishments.

Table B. States and Counties — **Professional Services, Manufacturing, and Accommodation and Food Services**

STATE County	Professional, scientific, and technical services, 2012				Manufacturing, 2012				Accommodation and food services, 2012			
	Number of establishments	Number of employees	Sales (mil dol)	Annual payroll (mil dol)	Number of establishments	Number of employees	Receipts (mil dol)	Annual payroll (mil dol)	Number of establishments	Number of employees	Receipts (mil dol)	Annual payroll (mil dol)
	147	148	149	150	151	152	153	154	155	156	157	158
GEORGIA—Cont'd												
Putnam	32	66	8.6	1.7	21	612	127.2	18.6	23	399	16.4	4.7
Quitman	1	D	D	D	NA	NA	NA	NA	1	D	D	D
Rabun	36	122	10.2	3.7	21	336	D	11.8	62	736	47.2	12.7
Randolph	8	28	2.5	0.6	4	D	D	D	11	66	2.7	0.7
Richmond	478	4,251	569.6	213.8	111	7,884	5,452.2	451.0	424	9,448	447.0	125.6
Rockdale	181	952	100.6	43.4	84	4,746	2,292.2	252.3	175	3,708	179.0	51.3
Schley	2	D	D	D	7	416	123.7	18.7	4	15	0.9	0.2
Screven	13	37	2.3	0.8	13	829	173.4	36.5	17	D	D	D
Seminole	8	D	D	D	3	6	D	D	15	D	D	D
Spalding	85	374	47.2	14.5	56	3,005	2,404.7	152.9	111	1,718	86.9	23.9
Stephens	39	205	28.1	15.2	54	1,807	511.6	73.5	42	595	24.9	6.4
Stewart	2	D	D	D	NA	NA	NA	NA	6	25	1.3	0.2
Sumter	39	D	D	D	25	1,103	492.5	37.8	59	882	37.2	10.2
Talbot	3	7	0.3	0.1	3	9	D	D	2	D	D	D
Taliaferro	NA	NA	NA	NA	NA	NA	NA	NA	1	D	D	D
Tattnall	20	76	5.4	1.7	9	59	7.3	1.5	15	D	D	D
Taylor	3	D	D	D	6	74	D	2.1	6	20	1.2	0.3
Telfair	10	37	2.7	1.0	8	D	D	D	15	D	D	D
Terrell	9	D	D	D	6	493	D	13.4	13	D	D	D
Thomas	74	331	41.1	12.2	41	2,677	674.9	109.0	82	1,240	59.3	15.0
Tift	81	533	47.6	23.0	39	1,289	528.1	51.5	98	2,175	100.8	26.9
Toombs	48	402	26.4	10.4	34	1,558	D	44.8	63	1,032	49.5	12.1
Towns	19	61	6.4	2.3	9	41	D	1.3	30	621	32.4	9.2
Treutlen	2	D	D	D	4	79	D	1.4	3	37	1.4	0.6
Troup	96	965	66.2	29.0	88	10,356	12,011.1	522.6	122	2,187	96.7	26.8
Turner	8	29	2.9	0.9	10	300	92.8	11.5	19	208	8.8	1.9
Twiggs	5	D	D	D	NA	NA	NA	NA	3	D	D	D
Union	43	165	15.3	5.5	27	260	54.0	10.2	46	547	28.4	7.1
Upson	30	126	15.3	3.8	19	1,252	D	51.1	39	512	25.3	6.6
Walker	51	497	16.1	7.1	55	3,652	1,753.7	129.3	49	D	D	D
Walton	158	516	65.3	18.8	56	1,800	777.9	84.4	103	1,603	72.9	19.9
Ware	61	252	23.2	6.9	31	1,118	D	35.1	66	1,317	59.3	14.8
Warren	4	6	0.7	0.2	NA	NA	NA	NA	3	7	0.4	0.1
Washington	24	170	14.2	7.8	17	565	157.5	21.4	27	409	18.3	5.0
Wayne	32	141	9.7	8.2	20	1,161	D	69.7	51	690	34.5	8.2
Webster	NA	NA	NA	NA	NA	NA	NA	NA	NA	NA	NA	NA
Wheeler	1	D	D	D	NA	NA	NA	NA	5	17	1.0	0.1
White	41	95	11.9	3.4	29	715	122.9	31.9	88	956	63.9	14.4
Whitfield	169	D	D	D	265	14,310	5,805.3	546.3	172	D	D	D
Wilcox	1	D	D	D	NA	NA	NA	NA	4	11	0.6	0.2
Wilkes	11	30	2.3	0.7	16	549	175.7	21.1	16	184	6.7	1.8
Wilkinson	5	38	2.9	0.9	12	763	D	52.9	6	25	1.0	0.2
Worth	16	55	5.4	1.7	11	256	D	10.2	14	D	D	D
HAWAII	3226	21,629	3,334.1	1,265.6	796	11,440	D	465.0	3,518	98,364	9,536.7	2,536.0
Hawaii	294	1,502	193.3	72.1	112	1,182	283.3	46.4	430	12,297	1,124.5	324.7
Honolulu	2399	18,234	2,895.1	1,105.4	544	9,076	D	370.8	2,355	57,486	5,273.2	1,333.0
Kalawao	NA	NA	NA	NA	NA	NA	NA	NA	NA	NA	NA	NA
Kauai	143	512	59.3	21.1	41	185	D	6.8	234	8,638	831.5	252.5
Maui	390	1,381	186.4	67.0	99	997	D	41.1	499	19,943	2,307.5	625.7
IDAHO	4198	32,076	4,273.6	1,728.0	1,759	52,084	20,201.4	2,445.5	3,564	54,257	2,680.2	726.1
Ada	1634	12,378	1,827.8	721.2	373	14,538	D	931.7	947	16,660	763.1	220.7
Adams	8	D	D	D	7	98	D	3.4	14	D	D	D
Bannock	165	1,277	84.2	40.3	44	1,633	916.3	67.7	197	3,199	135.5	37.2
Bear Lake	5	5	0.7	0.2	3	25	6.7	1.2	14	117	4.9	1.4
Benewah	9	D	D	D	11	548	D	D	23	D	D	D
Bingham	51	197	16.3	5.7	41	2,384	768.9	91.5	46	D	D	D
Blaine	154	652	91.7	45.5	45	298	57.8	12.8	111	2,628	138.2	49.2
Boise	9	8	0.6	0.1	4	13	4.2	0.7	23	D	D	D
Bonner	139	D	D	D	79	1,647	369.4	77.9	113	1,816	65.0	20.2
Bonneville	377	8,397	1,371.6	583.9	134	2,447	631.0	90.6	235	4,462	198.3	57.1
Boundary	23	90	6.0	2.2	24	293	D	11.6	23	D	D	D
Butte	2	D	D	D	NA	NA	NA	NA	11	D	D	D
Camas	NA	NA	NA	NA	NA	NA	NA	NA	7	32	1.4	0.2
Canyon	255	1,212	113.0	48.5	189	7,267	D	273.4	254	4,257	180.1	49.5

Items 147—158

GA(Putnam)—ID(Canyon) 195

Health Care and Social Assistance, Other Services, Nonemployer Businesses, and Residential Construction

STATE County	Health care and social assistance, 2012				Other services, 2012				Nonemployer businesses, 2015		Value of residential construction authorized by building permits, 2017	
	Number of establish-ments	Number of employees	Receipts (mil dol)	Annual payroll (mil dol)	Number of establis-hments	Number of employees	Receipts (mil dol)	Annual payroll (mil dol)	Number	Receipts (mil dol)	New construction ($1,000)	Number of housing units
	159	160	161	162	163	164	165	166	167	168	169	170
GEORGIA—Cont'd												
Putnam	30	476	36.2	14.9	21	165	5.9	5.1	1,858	77.9	37,910	158
Quitman	3	D	D	D	2	D	D	D	142	3.6	472	6
Rabun	34	532	41.8	18.5	36	113	13.3	3.2	1,803	73.7	22,960	62
Randolph	8	D	D	D	8	18	2.8	0.4	450	12.3	1,000	4
Richmond	645	24,184	3,260.4	1,241.3	275	1,816	196.3	53.1	12,412	388.8	78,733	641
Rockdale	242	3,648	392.9	138.9	135	804	89.1	22.6	8,507	277.4	63,235	280
Schley	4	D	D	D	5	D	D	D	318	9.8	1,915	9
Screven	14	222	11.5	5.2	23	91	7.3	1.5	953	29.0	3,218	21
Seminole	22	D	D	D	11	D	D	D	629	27.9	645	4
Spalding	132	4,459	351.5	122.9	76	415	32.4	9.5	5,089	158.8	28,732	242
Stephens	52	1,390	110.8	47.2	29	222	12.1	3.9	1,646	63.9	0	0
Stewart	9	171	13.0	4.4	7	54	3.3	0.9	247	5.7	491	2
Sumter	80	D	D	D	45	D	D	D	1,908	58.7	2,591	17
Talbot	3	D	D	D	6	13	1.1	0.3	450	12.9	1,785	10
Taliaferro	1	D	D	D	4	D	D	D	88	3.4	NA	NA
Tattnall	27	720	99.8	26.5	15	D	D	D	1,239	52.5	3,415	26
Taylor	16	198	10.2	4.2	7	D	D	D	599	18.6	1,829	13
Telfair	18	476	25.2	12.3	14	51	6.4	1.4	708	27.4	150	1
Terrell	15	D	D	D	14	D	D	D	749	23.7	633	5
Thomas	146	3,668	404.9	149.3	63	483	52.9	11.5	3,211	143.5	18,374	96
Tift	110	3,122	399.3	149.5	56	290	26.7	7.8	1,915	82.4	3,188	43
Toombs	106	1,982	197.9	78.5	40	215	22.9	6.1	1,168	50.5	11,276	27
Towns	25	548	34.2	14.7	10	17	1.5	0.4	1,168	50.5	11,276	57
Treutlen	9	131	7.3	3.1	7	25	1.5	0.5	443	12.5	0	0
Troup	131	3,139	300.6	128.6	81	636	66.4	18.2	5,536	167.6	31,247	152
Turner	8	170	7.2	3.3	7	D	D	D	666	21.0	1,690	8
Twiggs	7	D	D	D	6	D	D	D	600	15.0	1,692	17
Union	66	1,110	97.3	39.7	28	168	20.5	4.3	2,224	84.3	44,985	170
Upson	65	1,433	130.3	53.2	40	D	D	D	1,705	51.1	3,853	19
Walker	53	957	64.0	26.6	39	258	22.2	7.7	4,121	157.5	23,260	160
Walton	133	1,554	176.9	57.5	113	346	33.7	8.0	7,927	295.7	82,552	599
Ware	119	2,883	284.9	112.7	53	261	25.1	7.1	1,886	70.9	15,347	124
Warren	5	134	6.5	3.2	4	D	D	D	344	10.6	0	0
Washington	33	1,001	56.1	27.1	29	71	6.4	1.7	1,248	40.2	8,491	73
Wayne	65	1,036	102.4	35.3	31	160	16.3	3.7	1,745	58.1	7,008	42
Webster	1	D	D	D	1	D	D	D	157	6.1	835	4
Wheeler	5	D	D	D	3	3	0.4	0.1	373	14.6	0	0
White	34	418	26.6	11.1	41	168	13.5	3.4	2,503	98.1	16,997	88
Whitfield	192	4,275	482.4	180.7	117	855	76.7	25.8	5,998	296.0	28,290	246
Wilcox	12	D	D	D	7	D	D	D	559	17.4	NA	NA
Wilkes	24	547	32.2	13.1	10	37	3.5	0.7	646	22.1	252	3
Wilkinson	15	D	D	D	10	29	2.2	0.6	627	17.9	1,158	10
Worth	26	D	D	D	27	64	7.4	1.8	1,266	45.1	3,738	26
HAWAII	3559	66,772	8,136.9	3,290.6	2,808	19,348	2,004.8	538.7	104,707	5,039.0	1,132,364	4,035
Hawaii	469	7,503	781.2	356.4	288	1,387	166.1	41.0	17,400	759.9	272,882	894
Honolulu	2520	50,049	6,302.6	2,481.0	2,012	14,967	1,522.4	411.8	64,258	3,187.6	504,266	1,968
Kalawao	NA	NA	NA	NA	NA	NA	NA	NA	NA	NA	NA	NA
Kauai	177	3,082	311.6	145.0	125	809	78.2	23.9	6,875	303.0	145,266	312
Maui	393	6,138	741.5	308.2	383	2,185	238.1	62.0	16,174	788.5	209,950	861
IDAHO	4865	83,505	7,895.6	3,171.2	2,553	12,188	1,118.2	311.4	122,221	5,332.7	2,791,489	14,183
Ada	1387	29,953	3,174.3	1,355.9	768	4,121	377.4	112.2	35,880	1,675.9	1,309,089	5,942
Adams	5	D	D	D	3	D	D	D	375	13.2	6,018	10
Bannock	335	3,819	314.1	115.4	120	591	61.6	15.7	5,007	198.7	29,436	223
Bear Lake	13	314	24.7	10.4	5	D	D	D	445	15.2	13,760	49
Benewah	16	391	28.2	12.2	14	D	D	D	541	23.0	5,497	24
Bingham	96	1,817	155.9	67.8	51	279	33.8	8.4	2,792	124.6	14,218	113
Blaine	72	687	73.4	31.9	89	299	46.6	11.2	3,504	207.7	68,383	69
Boise	5	18	1.3	0.5	8	D	D	D	612	19.6	15,814	70
Bonner	141	1,640	130.6	53.4	79	322	22.6	6.5	3,983	152.5	23,941	134
Bonneville	537	7,680	846.0	289.1	174	852	87.1	22.0	8,231	374.0	130,254	989
Boundary	28	536	30.2	14.8	18	40	3.4	0.9	931	36.9	15,102	63
Butte	7	D	D	D	6	D	D	D	208	6.2	98	1
Camas	4	13	0.4	0.2	NA	NA	NA	NA	105	2.9	1,137	8
Canyon	374	6,754	530.8	216.1	206	1,039	93.0	26.7	12,342	509.1	281,535	1,801

Table B. States and Counties — **Personal Income and Earnings**

STATE County	Personal income, 2016										Earnings, 2016		
			Per capita[1]			Supplements to wages and salaries, employer contributions (mil dol)						Contributions for government social insurance (mil dol)	
	Total (mil dol)	Percent change 2015-2016	Dollars	Rank	Wages and salaries (mil dol)	Pension and insurance	Government social insurance	Proprietors' income (mil dol)	Dividends, interest, and rent (mil dol)	Personal transfer reecipts (mil dol)	Total (mil dol)	From employee and self-employed	From employer
	62	63	64	65	66	67	68	69	70	71	72	73	74
IDAHO—Cont'd													
Caribou	264	3.0	38,319	1,602	187	37	16	18	46	52	259	32	16
Cassia	1,004	-0.7	42,718	1,023	415	71	36	296	144	158	818	73	36
Clark	22	1.4	26,099	3,053	17	3	1	3	6	4	25	3	1
Clearwater	292	1.7	34,370	2,269	110	26	10	17	61	94	163	22	10
Custer	167	0.1	40,683	1,278	52	12	5	17	50	38	85	10	5
Elmore	930	2.3	35,734	2,039	440	114	42	76	237	191	672	74	42
Franklin	439	2.8	32,713	2,529	114	26	10	57	64	83	207	22	10
Fremont	445	3.1	34,370	2,269	115	25	10	79	94	93	230	22	10
Gem	579	3.3	33,690	2,364	129	27	12	31	132	162	199	29	12
Gooding	806	-1.0	53,068	301	230	39	19	314	99	117	602	36	19
Idaho	521	-0.1	32,263	2,571	164	38	15	54	138	134	270	33	15
Jefferson	871	4.6	31,276	2,706	222	43	20	105	127	156	391	44	20
Jerome	834	-1.3	36,275	1,959	340	57	30	212	113	147	638	58	30
Kootenai	6,145	4.5	39,820	1,390	2,336	425	211	452	1,344	1,269	3,424	445	211
Latah	1,489	4.0	37,996	1,660	533	144	45	117	334	241	840	96	45
Lemhi	293	2.2	37,885	1,679	86	20	8	21	91	82	136	17	8
Lewis	181	1.4	46,986	609	56	12	5	25	31	67	98	12	5
Lincoln	182	-2.0	34,543	2,234	55	12	5	52	25	33	123	9	5
Madison	939	3.1	24,054	3,088	497	100	45	105	146	213	748	88	45
Minidoka	774	2.4	37,542	1,730	304	54	26	118	138	139	502	54	26
Nez Perce	1,644	4.2	40,723	1,274	930	165	80	137	317	367	1,312	167	80
Oneida	139	2.0	32,085	2,603	35	9	3	8	23	36	56	7	3
Owyhee	366	-0.5	32,118	2,595	97	18	8	64	69	84	186	17	8
Payette	848	3.8	36,818	1,851	245	46	22	128	155	189	441	50	22
Power	278	1.7	36,360	1,938	147	27	13	48	48	53	235	24	13
Shoshone	437	0.1	35,065	2,154	201	34	17	11	84	136	264	37	17
Teton	352	6.2	32,088	2,601	115	19	10	31	96	51	175	21	10
Twin Falls	3,001	2.5	35,934	2,012	1,360	235	122	383	550	625	2,100	252	122
Valley	484	4.8	46,130	679	164	31	15	43	169	85	253	32	15
Washington	360	1.1	35,386	2,100	96	21	9	35	69	96	161	20	9
ILLINOIS	663,338	1.6	51,679	X	355,280	57,130	24,264	48,178	131,012	100,687	484,853	26,958	24,264
Adams	2,811	0.2	42,220	1,073	1,416	269	101	186	560	597	1,973	218	101
Alexander	207	-0.5	31,951	2,625	72	21	4	9	31	92	106	11	4
Bond	560	0.1	33,276	2,430	210	52	15	18	106	145	295	34	15
Boone	2,254	1.6	42,128	1,087	844	160	64	64	320	370	1,133	132	64
Brown	191	1.5	28,195	2,966	189	36	12	11	37	40	248	26	12
Bureau	1,306	2.5	39,139	1,478	507	104	36	42	257	289	689	79	36
Calhoun	180	1.8	36,878	1,840	26	7	2	8	31	45	44	5	2
Carroll	605	2.4	41,616	1,150	159	36	11	38	127	153	244	28	11
Cass	485	1.6	38,229	1,613	225	48	17	42	74	108	332	36	17
Champaign	8,926	1.4	42,829	1,009	4,788	1,183	294	1,021	1,736	1,172	7,286	639	294
Christian	1,261	2.6	37,872	1,685	410	89	30	108	215	319	637	68	30
Clark	606	3.1	38,053	1,648	190	46	13	30	111	145	280	31	13
Clay	472	1.8	35,471	2,087	208	50	15	3	82	147	277	33	15
Clinton	1,586	0.5	42,028	1,099	419	92	30	102	272	296	642	67	30
Coles	1,904	0.7	36,374	1,936	1,025	235	70	118	367	424	1,449	147	70
Cook	294,876	1.7	56,669	194	177,803	25,915	11,988	26,213	64,532	43,891	241,918	25,355	11,988
Crawford	825	1.0	42,754	1,017	369	111	25	124	139	168	629	58	25
Cumberland	422	2.1	38,856	1,525	99	22	7	32	66	89	161	17	7
DeKalb	3,843	2.1	36,762	1,865	1,739	422	114	137	708	643	2,413	238	114
De Witt	708	3.0	43,632	913	277	62	18	63	113	146	420	41	18
Douglas	878	0.6	44,749	797	358	73	27	115	146	153	573	59	27
DuPage	61,405	1.6	66,072	81	41,084	5,558	2,869	4,452	11,945	5,930	53,964	5,842	2,869
Edgar	716	7.0	40,746	1,269	303	64	22	41	116	179	431	47	22
Edwards	228	-0.3	34,932	2,177	93	22	7	20	45	55	142	15	7
Effingham	1,524	3.0	44,312	847	838	152	61	129	318	272	1,180	129	61
Fayette	665	1.8	30,531	2,785	185	44	13	46	124	189	288	31	13
Ford	670	2.0	49,344	452	201	43	14	150	100	121	408	35	14
Franklin	1,323	-0.1	33,791	2,353	320	75	24	71	204	425	491	59	24
Fulton	1,218	0.9	34,286	2,285	313	81	21	39	208	338	453	52	21
Gallatin	224	4.7	42,903	1,004	76	13	5	41	39	60	134	11	5
Greene	464	2.3	35,426	2,096	86	22	6	38	70	128	152	16	6
Grundy	2,421	-0.8	48,004	537	1,127	221	78	253	313	330	1,679	168	78
Hamilton	343	2.2	42,543	1,037	86	20	6	51	59	85	163	14	6
Hancock	759	1.1	41,033	1,228	147	37	10	69	129	172	263	27	10

1. Based on the resident population estimated as of July 1 of the year shown.

STATE County	Farm	Mining, quarrying, and extracting	Construction	Manufacturing	Information; professional, scientific, technical services	Retail trade	Finance, insurance, real estate, and leasing	Health care and social assistance	Government	Number	Rate[1]	Supplemental Security Income recipients, 2016	Total	Percent change, 2010-2017
	75	76	77	78	79	80	81	82	83	84	85	86	87	88
IDAHO—Cont'd														
Caribou	6.9	D	8.3	34.0	D	2.9	1.8	D	14.6	1,435	208	75	3,287	1.9
Cassia	30.8	1.1	4.8	9.8	D	6.9	4.3	8.3	9.5	4,265	182	419	8,754	4.6
Clark	17.2	0.0	D	D	D	D	D	D	27.3	125	146	0	554	4.3
Clearwater	-0.6	D	6.2	5.9	2.2	5.8	1.6	D	35.5	2,820	330	244	4,617	3.7
Custer	10.0	D	8.3	D	5.5	5.3	D	D	29.2	1,300	316	60	3,133	1.0
Elmore	9.9	0.0	2.8	3.9	D	4.9	1.8	5.3	57.5	4,625	177	582	12,505	2.8
Franklin	14.7	D	8.7	7.2	5.2	9.5	4.4	D	21.5	2,345	176	161	4,829	6.6
Fremont	26.1	D	11.2	2.2	D	4.7	2.5	D	24.6	2,625	204	156	8,978	5.3
Gem	2.5	D	12.2	3.1	3.3	7.5	4.1	16.3	26.4	4,805	283	443	7,347	3.5
Gooding	58.2	0.1	2.1	8.7	D	2.2	D	D	9.5	3,060	203	285	6,194	1.7
Idaho	5.9	1.5	10.9	7.5	2.9	6.8	3.5	9.5	29.7	4,295	265	325	8,765	0.2
Jefferson	11.8	0.0	11.3	13.1	2.3	7.7	6.0	D	14.2	4,165	150	301	9,368	7.4
Jerome	32.5	0.0	4.1	13.3	2.1	6.0	1.8	4.3	8.4	3,650	157	382	8,523	5.2
Kootenai	0.1	0.9	9.4	8.4	7.0	10.7	7.0	12.7	20.9	36,890	241	2,691	70,758	12.0
Latah	1.1	D	4.9	2.5	7.4	7.9	3.7	10.2	44.3	6,205	160	501	16,863	5.5
Lemhi	5.3	D	11.7	3.1	5.8	8.4	2.8	7.5	37.3	2,670	345	191	4,877	3.1
Lewis	15.5	D	5.0	12.9	4.0	5.8	4.9	3.9	22.3	2,070	539	221	1,929	2.6
Lincoln	46.4	0.0	D	D	D	1.9	D	4.8	20.1	915	174	82	2,000	1.3
Madison	3.6	D	5.4	6.0	6.0	8.4	4.4	6.9	15.1	3,030	78	289	14,112	25.0
Minidoka	18.0	0.4	4.7	17.0	D	4.9	2.1	D	14.1	3,975	193	366	8,197	7.0
Nez Perce	0.3	D	5.7	22.1	4.4	8.2	8.0	16.5	17.9	10,240	255	998	17,822	2.2
Oneida	9.6	D	D	2.1	2.6	6.5	8.0	5.6	32.5	1,045	242	51	1,994	4.6
Owyhee	38.9	D	5.5	4.6	D	3.9	D	D	17.0	2,450	216	264	4,905	2.6
Payette	14.1	D	5.2	14.0	9.0	4.0	6.5	D	12.0	5,545	242	568	9,426	5.4
Power	23.7	0.2	1.4	29.3	D	D	D	D	13.0	1,425	186	98	3,008	2.2
Shoshone	-0.1	26.2	5.2	2.3	5.0	20.1	2.6	8.1	18.3	3,940	317	472	7,132	0.8
Teton	3.4	D	14.7	3.1	10.8	6.9	5.3	8.8	15.5	1,315	119	57	5,783	5.6
Twin Falls	6.3	D	4.8	14.4	5.9	8.8	5.0	17.9	12.0	16,120	193	1,804	33,252	7.0
Valley	0.8	D	12.3	1.1	D	9.2	6.8	D	25.2	2,680	257	122	12,330	4.6
Washington	16.0	0.1	4.1	15.1	8.6	6.1	2.9	D	22.9	3,035	302	274	4,656	2.8
ILLINOIS	0.3	0.2	5.1	10.8	13.8	5.2	10.9	10.4	13.8	2,196,032	171	272,102	5,359,557	1.2
Adams	0.0	0.9	5.7	16.5	4.7	8.3	7.6	18.7	11.9	15,370	231	1,340	30,233	1.3
Alexander	3.6	D	1.7	8.5	D	2.1	D	D	46.1	1,735	267	420	3,978	-0.7
Bond	-0.7	0.0	5.2	25.1	3.1	3.1	2.8	D	25.7	3,695	219	331	7,279	2.7
Boone	0.4	D	7.7	49.2	2.7	4.4	2.2	3.9	12.7	10,065	188	563	20,071	0.5
Brown	1.4	D	6.8	0.7	D	1.5	D	4.5	13.0	1,080	160	79	2,452	-0.4
Bureau	-0.3	D	5.2	17.0	3.1	5.2	3.4	D	19.9	8,065	241	428	15,689	-0.2
Calhoun	3.1	D	10.3	2.6	D	9.0	D	D	32.4	1,320	272	78	2,879	1.6
Carroll	2.0	D	7.4	18.6	D	6.5	6.6	4.9	19.6	4,245	291	236	8,465	0.3
Cass	7.9	0.1	3.5	D	D	3.9	4.7	D	14.8	2,605	205	230	5,827	-0.1
Champaign	0.3	0.1	4.1	6.2	7.5	12.3	5.2	13.2	36.0	27,370	131	3,140	92,744	5.9
Christian	7.5	D	5.6	14.5	D	7.4	4.0	14.7	17.2	8,195	246	644	15,605	0.3
Clark	3.2	2.7	8.0	32.6	D	5.3	3.9	4.6	16.8	3,870	244	278	7,810	0.5
Clay	-6.4	2.8	3.0	39.9	D	5.9	3.8	D	22.3	3,395	255	312	6,429	0.4
Clinton	5.5	D	11.9	8.9	3.4	9.5	5.4	11.3	22.5	7,265	193	303	15,858	3.6
Coles	1.4	0.2	4.8	13.0	D	6.2	4.9	17.9	25.6	9,835	188	1,146	23,499	0.3
Cook	0.0	0.0	4.1	6.7	18.6	4.6	14.6	9.9	11.9	793,930	152	152,761	2,193,073	0.6
Crawford	2.7	1.4	7.2	43.4	6.1	3.9	3.1	D	16.6	4,515	236	320	8,694	0.4
Cumberland	11.0	D	4.1	20.2	D	8.5	D	D	18.2	2,475	227	162	4,876	0.0
DeKalb	-0.8	D	8.8	11.0	3.3	7.2	4.2	12.4	32.9	14,830	142	988	41,195	0.3
De Witt	8.3	D	8.4	8.0	D	5.7	2.6	D	14.2	3,695	229	243	7,576	0.7
Douglas	3.6	D	8.9	43.3	D	5.8	3.1	3.5	10.2	3,980	201	236	8,456	0.8
DuPage	0.0	0.1	5.7	9.3	16.2	4.6	9.9	9.8	7.8	143,965	155	8,025	360,146	1.1
Edgar	5.1	0.0	3.8	37.5	2.5	4.4	8.8	D	14.0	4,465	256	442	8,841	0.4
Edwards	6.0	D	D	D	D	3.6	D	1.8	10.3	1,615	247	71	3,190	0.1
Effingham	1.0	D	7.2	13.8	D	8.4	4.3	20.0	10.0	7,540	221	472	14,872	2.1
Fayette	6.9	2.0	5.0	6.7	3.2	7.8	5.2	D	23.7	4,855	223	456	9,313	0.1
Ford	11.9	D	4.7	8.7	1.7	3.9	2.3	D	10.9	3,030	227	200	6,344	1.0
Franklin	2.5	1.3	8.9	5.9	D	9.1	3.8	11.1	27.1	10,390	266	1,328	18,630	-0.4
Fulton	-0.6	D	6.6	3.1	3.4	8.4	5.7	19.3	30.8	8,655	244	705	16,340	0.9
Gallatin	26.9	D	3.8	1.9	D	2.2	D	D	10.7	1,555	301	205	2,751	0.2
Greene	14.8	D	6.4	3.1	D	8.3	D	D	24.9	3,220	245	372	6,426	0.6
Grundy	1.9	D	12.4	13.1	D	8.4	3.4	8.7	11.0	9,075	181	401	20,936	4.7
Hamilton	18.2	D	7.6	2.9	D	3.7	5.2	4.1	20.5	1,970	240	198	4,096	-0.2
Hancock	13.7	D	7.3	6.3	7.2	4.4	7.2	D	21.1	4,870	267	310	9,245	-0.3

1. Per 1,000 resident population estimated as of July 1 of the year shown.

Table B. States and Counties — Housing, Labor Force, and Employment

STATE County	Housing units, 2017 (cont.)								Civilian labor force, 2017				Civilian employment[6], 2012-2016		
	Occupied units										Unemployment			Percent	
	Owner-occupied					Renter-occupied									
				Median owner cost as a percent of income			Median rent as a percent of income[2]	Sub-standard units[4] (percent)		Percent change, 2016-2017				Management, business, science, and arts	Construction, production, and maintenance occupations
	Total	Percent	Median value[1]	With a mort-gage	Without a mort-gage[2]	Median rent[3]			Total		Total	Rate[5]	Total		
	89	90	91	92	93	94	95	96	97	98	99	100	101	102	103
IDAHO—Cont'd															
Caribou	2,553	82.9	125,900	18.3	10.0	581	18.3	2.3	3,814	0.7	121	3.2	3,091	32.1	33.7
Cassia	7,717	71.2	130,100	21.0	10.0	606	25.3	5.1	11,718	1.3	289	2.5	9,866	27.3	36.5
Clark	287	58.9	103,600	27.5	13.1	375	12.3	16.7	403	2.5	11	2.7	425	23.3	45.6
Clearwater	3,668	76.9	129,500	23.7	11.4	652	24.3	1.7	3,039	-0.2	209	6.9	2,851	29.7	34.9
Custer	1,801	78.8	166,800	25.0	10.0	629	29.1	2.1	2,151	0.6	91	4.2	1,735	34.1	27.0
Elmore	9,832	57.5	137,800	20.7	10.0	766	27.4	3.4	11,144	1.9	403	3.6	9,952	28.0	32.0
Franklin	4,226	79.5	164,100	23.5	10.9	707	24.0	2.4	6,723	1.4	153	2.3	5,526	28.7	36.8
Fremont	4,466	80.7	147,500	22.7	10.1	680	28.5	5.4	7,583	3.1	202	2.7	5,228	28.0	34.2
Gem	6,287	72.0	143,000	23.2	11.7	808	29.6	2.9	7,934	2.8	311	3.9	5,964	28.6	25.2
Gooding	5,476	66.8	132,200	22.9	10.0	742	28.3	7.2	8,054	0.5	197	2.4	6,857	27.0	40.3
Idaho	6,443	79.2	161,300	25.8	11.3	660	22.3	4.4	6,246	-1.3	309	4.9	6,155	24.9	34.7
Jefferson	8,150	81.4	160,300	22.0	10.0	669	22.5	4.0	13,057	2.0	327	2.5	11,451	34.4	31.5
Jerome	7,647	66.5	139,700	24.0	10.9	719	28.1	7.0	11,763	2.2	321	2.7	9,725	25.0	40.2
Kootenai	57,213	69.8	193,300	23.2	10.0	878	29.4	2.9	75,457	2.4	2,900	3.8	66,141	31.2	22.3
Latah	15,218	54.0	195,800	20.3	10.0	661	36.1	2.0	20,140	1.4	534	2.7	18,873	42.3	17.7
Lemhi	3,698	70.7	178,300	24.3	10.7	541	31.5	2.8	3,472	2.0	181	5.2	3,076	27.7	30.8
Lewis	1,624	71.7	116,400	21.8	11.7	598	26.8	3.7	1,604	-1.1	94	5.9	1,576	30.0	28.2
Lincoln	1,596	69.4	128,900	23.3	10.0	738	26.0	6.0	2,710	2.8	87	3.2	2,365	21.7	41.9
Madison	10,508	48.2	185,200	22.6	10.0	653	43.7	9.4	21,269	3.6	403	1.9	16,626	40.2	17.2
Minidoka	7,261	71.3	117,400	18.7	10.0	559	21.4	4.4	11,000	1.3	293	2.7	9,214	21.8	41.7
Nez Perce	16,127	69.2	169,500	21.6	10.3	673	27.2	2.8	21,264	2.1	602	2.8	18,584	30.1	26.2
Oneida	1,551	78.3	142,700	29.3	12.7	606	24.4	4.1	2,254	2.6	64	2.8	1,637	28.8	35.5
Owyhee	4,068	66.6	120,500	24.1	10.0	557	24.9	6.9	5,178	-1.7	207	4.0	4,484	24.3	43.3
Payette	8,195	76.1	136,400	23.7	11.6	669	26.4	5.5	11,512	2.5	451	3.9	9,348	27.1	28.9
Power	2,465	74.2	125,100	20.7	10.0	631	21.7	3.2	3,952	0.7	134	3.4	3,081	26.2	38.7
Shoshone	5,660	68.7	117,600	20.3	12.2	647	26.5	3.4	5,041	-1.3	316	6.3	5,071	27.3	28.7
Teton	3,725	71.5	254,600	22.7	12.0	860	30.1	2.9	6,088	2.0	166	2.7	5,526	35.6	24.6
Twin Falls	29,200	67.0	149,100	23.4	10.0	735	29.0	3.4	41,351	2.6	1,195	2.9	37,584	28.4	29.0
Valley	3,446	76.8	246,300	26.3	10.0	762	32.0	2.6	5,131	3.5	225	4.4	4,420	33.9	27.0
Washington	3,886	73.1	140,600	24.4	10.0	649	33.7	2.8	4,611	0.4	215	4.7	3,718	25.3	34.3
ILLINOIS	4,802,124	66.0	174,800	22.7	13.1	925	29.8	2.9	6,492,591	-0.9	321,908	5.0	6,134,121	37.2	21.2
Adams	27,240	70.0	116,400	18.7	10.3	590	27.4	1.2	32,237	-0.6	1,229	3.8	32,362	31.3	24.8
Alexander	2,534	68.5	50,100	25.0	14.1	464	27.0	4.1	2,161	-1.8	172	8.0	2,283	22.8	24.0
Bond	6,051	76.3	107,200	19.7	12.8	665	25.0	3.0	7,817	-0.6	339	4.3	7,457	25.3	29.1
Boone	18,405	79.0	146,600	22.7	12.5	750	27.9	2.6	25,978	-1.3	1,709	6.6	24,755	30.7	31.2
Brown	2,130	77.5	87,400	17.7	10.8	573	23.5	2.7	2,842	-0.3	81	2.9	2,643	27.4	29.5
Bureau	14,017	75.6	105,300	19.6	11.9	641	26.5	1.6	17,319	-0.1	829	4.8	16,168	28.2	30.4
Calhoun	1,936	81.7	118,100	23.1	11.6	608	27.6	2.6	2,352	-0.7	125	5.3	2,152	28.3	35.1
Carroll	6,649	75.6	98,300	19.5	11.7	603	24.9	1.5	7,607	-3.1	344	4.5	6,852	30.5	34.8
Cass	5,124	72.3	77,200	18.2	10.3	595	25.4	2.8	6,157	-1.1	275	4.5	6,113	24.2	37.0
Champaign	80,442	55.0	151,400	19.9	11.0	828	33.1	3.5	104,527	-0.7	4,427	4.2	103,721	45.5	15.4
Christian	13,901	74.7	85,200	18.2	11.3	624	27.2	1.2	14,687	-4.2	768	5.2	15,142	28.8	28.9
Clark	6,673	74.6	84,600	18.7	12.6	640	24.8	2.0	7,845	-3.7	375	4.8	7,429	27.4	34.8
Clay	5,588	77.6	76,500	18.8	10.4	515	19.9	3.4	6,623	-1.0	346	5.2	6,265	25.6	40.4
Clinton	14,012	82.4	141,200	19.0	11.6	751	24.4	1.4	20,251	-0.8	704	3.5	18,820	33.8	27.3
Coles	21,094	61.3	92,800	19.5	12.0	637	34.0	1.2	24,429	-0.2	1,121	4.6	24,960	29.8	24.7
Cook	1,951,606	56.6	219,800	25.0	15.0	999	30.7	3.9	2,653,153	-0.6	139,040	5.2	2,492,088	38.7	19.2
Crawford	7,597	79.3	82,000	17.4	10.4	576	26.8	1.6	8,778	-2.6	455	5.2	8,267	27.9	35.1
Cumberland	4,208	79.7	91,600	18.7	12.2	522	23.2	2.2	6,096	2.1	238	3.9	4,883	26.6	37.3
DeKalb	37,367	57.5	166,000	22.7	13.4	877	32.0	2.9	54,651	-0.6	2,471	4.5	52,327	34.3	22.3
De Witt	6,721	78.5	99,500	18.4	10.1	573	22.9	1.3	7,740	-2.0	354	4.6	8,154	28.6	29.3
Douglas	7,562	73.6	101,700	19.0	10.0	658	24.1	2.1	10,120	-0.9	406	4.0	9,353	27.1	33.1
DuPage	338,987	72.9	283,500	23.4	13.8	1,178	28.6	2.6	515,683	-0.4	21,039	4.1	482,850	45.1	15.9
Edgar	7,644	74.1	79,300	19.0	10.7	593	28.8	1.1	9,426	-2.7	452	4.8	7,795	28.7	33.8
Edwards	2,768	82.8	71,500	18.2	10.0	479	24.5	1.3	2,838	-4.3	128	4.5	3,066	24.4	38.3
Effingham	13,316	78.3	132,900	19.2	11.1	598	23.8	1.2	18,787	0.7	704	3.7	17,182	29.2	28.6
Fayette	7,650	82.1	81,400	18.7	11.0	597	27.0	2.5	9,585	-1.5	520	5.4	8,973	24.6	32.3
Ford	5,666	73.0	97,300	19.2	10.9	591	24.0	1.9	6,483	-0.8	305	4.7	6,221	30.7	33.4
Franklin	16,180	72.5	68,300	19.4	11.0	605	27.9	1.8	16,425	-1.4	1,045	6.4	15,474	25.9	31.2
Fulton	14,131	76.7	82,100	17.9	12.5	631	27.7	1.4	15,430	-2.2	966	6.3	15,299	29.9	29.8
Gallatin	2,295	77.8	67,200	16.8	10.7	397	26.1	1.9	2,455	-2.9	139	5.7	2,124	34.3	30.1
Greene	5,278	77.0	77,100	19.7	12.2	589	25.6	1.5	5,965	-1.5	299	5.0	5,884	28.8	30.2
Grundy	18,509	73.8	183,200	22.1	12.5	928	25.3	2.0	25,658	-0.6	1,522	5.9	24,264	28.8	30.4
Hamilton	3,394	79.2	94,100	18.8	10.9	564	28.0	1.1	4,416	3.9	195	4.4	3,571	27.0	33.6
Hancock	7,726	79.1	84,700	18.3	10.3	580	22.2	1.5	8,483	-3.7	432	5.1	8,470	29.5	30.5

1. Specified owner-occupied units. 2. A value of 10.0 represents 10 percent or less; a value of 50.0 represents 50 percent or more. 3. Specified renter-occupied units. 4. Overcrowded or lacking complete plumbing facilities.
5. Percent of civilian labor force. 6. Civilian employed persons 16 years old and over.

Table B. States and Counties — Nonfarm Employment and Agriculture

STATE County	Private nonfarm establishments, employment and payroll, 2016									Agriculture, 2012			
	Number of establishments	Employment						Annual payroll		Farms			Farm operators whose principal occupation is farming (percent)
		Total	Health care and social assistance	Manufacturing	Retail trade	Finance and insurance	Professional, scientific, and technical services	Total (mil dol)	Average per employee (dollars)	Number	Percent with:		
											Fewer than 50 acres	500 acres or more	
	104	105	106	107	108	109	110	111	112	113	114	115	116

IDAHO—Cont'd													
Caribou	186	2,744	278	751	244	48	26	178	64,868	436	19.3	40.4	55.3
Cassia	655	7,845	1,218	1,231	1,544	217	173	263	33,468	668	42.7	27.1	56.1
Clark	16	85	NA	D	40	D	D	3	29,965	72	12.5	41.7	61.1
Clearwater	231	1,812	486	297	240	39	37	69	38,312	256	35.5	11.7	34.8
Custer	165	704	63	27	169	20	30	26	36,700	272	36.4	23.9	52.9
Elmore	434	4,303	799	461	1,069	344	96	136	31,620	349	53.9	21.2	47.6
Franklin	299	2,120	308	303	545	60	83	67	31,766	834	40.0	19.2	43.5
Fremont	293	1,626	232	57	236	39	36	55	33,954	601	33.8	22.1	52.2
Gem	359	2,519	776	109	461	65	71	71	28,382	830	68.1	7.3	48.3
Gooding	356	2,683	559	539	397	71	73	99	36,820	596	53.4	14.1	52.0
Idaho	467	3,529	719	564	514	151	224	143	40,640	731	24.5	33.0	51.8
Jefferson	488	3,820	235	865	594	81	115	127	33,220	776	53.5	16.8	43.9
Jerome	538	6,351	463	1,544	899	104	90	234	36,767	560	46.3	15.4	63.2
Kootenai	4,659	50,135	9,532	5,278	8,929	2,194	2,233	1,915	38,196	824	58.4	6.7	48.1
Latah	888	8,870	1,347	383	1,935	225	485	258	29,131	1,053	30.6	15.9	43.3
Lemhi	277	1,728	492	61	400	31	79	50	28,752	350	46.6	20.0	48.6
Lewis	119	814	64	151	182	25	D	23	28,526	216	13.9	44.9	54.6
Lincoln	89	553	96	D	84	10	11	20	35,656	310	27.1	23.5	57.7
Madison	875	18,151	1,598	1,067	1,987	282	815	397	21,892	472	48.3	19.7	46.2
Minidoka	408	4,686	518	949	503	84	122	177	37,839	622	51.1	14.0	56.6
Nez Perce	1,108	17,627	3,120	4,260	2,579	1,043	498	679	38,534	430	41.4	30.0	52.1
Oneida	86	757	205	68	171	D	5	21	27,485	503	28.2	27.8	45.5
Owyhee	188	1,787	214	142	191	25	42	52	29,342	578	41.0	26.6	67.6
Payette	500	5,099	581	1,313	431	230	145	179	35,082	655	65.8	6.6	52.1
Power	170	2,150	160	D	156	51	46	81	37,694	308	24.4	50.3	63.3
Shoshone	354	4,176	519	128	1,114	61	161	184	44,134	36	61.1	0.0	33.3
Teton	462	2,348	326	114	336	42	134	93	39,773	291	30.2	21.3	42.3
Twin Falls	2,584	30,292	6,409	3,479	5,105	937	1,112	999	32,979	1,294	42.9	13.4	55.3
Valley	593	3,296	487	91	488	80	95	105	31,962	117	35.9	22.2	47.0
Washington	208	1,892	356	478	268	43	53	58	30,777	559	42.4	20.9	54.4
ILLINOIS	319,605	5,513,071	805,338	535,830	631,937	346,002	389,970	295,308	53,565	75,087	34.1	20.4	50.4
Adams	1,802	30,925	5,757	5,177	4,997	1,495	693	1,203	38,916	1,298	28.2	18.3	44.5
Alexander	91	1,047	150	164	107	18	35	44	41,564	144	25.0	19.4	56.9
Bond	318	3,743	489	739	391	117	68	126	33,594	661	39.2	16.5	46.1
Boone	848	15,589	951	8,485	1,431	231	532	667	42,795	479	49.9	15.7	53.0
Brown	106	3,487	201	D	129	45	32	165	47,178	413	23.2	16.7	41.2
Bureau	744	9,992	2,097	1,697	1,100	346	293	403	40,342	1,056	26.1	26.1	55.8
Calhoun	87	541	93	13	83	57	7	13	24,140	478	30.5	10.0	39.3
Carroll	396	3,648	452	949	549	188	47	132	36,175	643	26.7	22.4	56.9
Cass	235	4,788	352	2,334	461	182	73	172	35,887	446	29.6	24.2	48.2
Champaign	4,176	69,416	12,845	6,788	10,071	3,112	2,751	2,840	40,919	1,312	29.3	30.6	57.7
Christian	701	8,282	1,679	861	1,385	332	445	297	35,803	816	34.1	27.2	51.6
Clark	333	3,979	361	1,274	477	148	138	141	35,550	677	34.0	21.4	47.6
Clay	374	4,763	582	2,235	521	153	94	179	37,512	774	35.4	18.7	49.6
Clinton	867	9,055	1,892	826	1,754	302	175	283	31,208	915	29.0	16.3	47.9
Coles	1,188	18,865	4,793	2,680	2,539	548	413	675	35,756	704	37.2	23.2	56.7
Cook	133,150	2,401,662	370,018	179,530	242,401	196,257	226,870	145,680	60,658	127	81.1	3.9	44.1
Crawford	417	6,949	760	1,772	768	227	310	284	40,800	599	32.4	18.9	51.3
Cumberland	187	2,086	583	544	202	118	12	56	26,905	733	40.5	13.5	38.5
DeKalb	1,957	27,297	5,332	3,875	4,448	901	1,053	1,044	38,241	880	32.7	26.9	61.1
De Witt	374	4,683	578	585	672	111	233	238	50,883	511	42.3	24.7	55.4
Douglas	589	6,620	319	2,624	1,207	194	90	252	38,015	735	40.7	21.1	54.8
DuPage	33,932	598,889	68,872	54,919	62,140	35,224	44,827	35,357	59,038	74	82.4	2.7	35.1
Edgar	357	6,651	884	2,669	653	202	94	271	40,766	673	27.3	31.1	54.4
Edwards	143	2,042	90	D	180	79	23	75	36,785	365	41.4	16.4	39.7
Effingham	1,219	24,806	2,823	2,993	2,723	490	421	940	37,912	1,302	37.6	12.5	47.2
Fayette	464	4,394	802	344	817	225	119	129	29,363	1,240	39.2	12.6	42.7
Ford	356	4,184	1,172	657	480	142	113	158	37,859	546	26.4	35.7	53.5
Franklin	720	6,377	888	345	1,485	270	207	218	34,147	711	42.9	10.4	38.8
Fulton	626	6,325	1,909	176	1,402	329	168	182	28,852	970	29.7	20.2	53.1
Gallatin	98	715	95	15	67	26	25	25	34,425	203	24.1	36.0	56.2
Greene	218	1,760	343	105	394	142	93	66	37,385	689	30.2	22.9	52.8
Grundy	1,125	17,171	2,418	1,298	1,967	356	851	963	56,098	431	23.2	29.5	63.8
Hamilton	205	1,539	456	71	158	40	46	58	37,532	695	37.6	12.5	25.6
Hancock	382	2,767	501	306	425	184	157	102	36,995	1,090	28.4	21.5	50.0

Table B. States and Counties — **Agriculture**

STATE County	Land in farms					Value of land and buildings (dollars)		Value of machinery and equipment, average per farm (dollars)	Value of products sold:				Percent of farms with sales of:		Government payments	
	Acreage (1,000)	Percent change, 2007-2012	Acres			Average per farm	Average per acre		Total (mil dol)	Average per farm (acres)	Percent from:		$10,000 or more	$100,000 or more	Total ($1,000)	Percent of farms
			Average size of farm	Total irrigated (1,000)	Total cropland (1,000)						Crops	Livestock and poultry products				
	117	118	119	120	121	122	123	124	125	126	127	128	129	130	131	132
IDAHO—Cont'd																
Caribou	395	-6.4	905	66.0	215.4	1,267,638	1,401	196,009	88.0	201,934	76.8	23.2	51.6	27.3	4,068	62.8
Cassia	611	-5.2	915	237.8	333.8	2,143,115	2,343	350,045	953.7	1,427,737	27.0	73.0	58.5	37.3	5,934	43.9
Clark	151	-4.2	2,101	29.2	52.5	3,059,583	1,456	304,333	35.2	488,792	75.1	24.9	66.7	38.9	572	56.9
Clearwater	73	4.4	284	0.2	28.9	534,063	1,883	59,699	9.7	38,078	74.6	25.4	25.8	6.3	797	43.0
Custer	143	15.0	525	51.6	44.4	1,208,224	2,302	107,033	26.2	96,471	33.6	66.4	50.4	22.8	588	23.2
Elmore	345	-0.5	988	89.9	117.9	2,021,562	2,046	204,605	350.6	1,004,536	26.9	73.1	41.0	21.5	838	20.9
Franklin	263	16.8	315	61.2	140.8	632,061	2,007	117,307	106.1	127,228	23.1	76.9	45.1	18.5	3,420	48.7
Fremont	316	9.8	526	124.8	207.8	1,175,121	2,233	216,087	158.6	263,942	89.5	10.5	47.4	24.0	3,473	52.1
Gem	179	-6.2	216	34.2	31.7	595,434	2,761	57,441	42.4	51,031	39.1	60.9	34.5	9.3	517	19.9
Gooding	240	7.4	402	142.0	150.7	1,539,908	3,830	272,973	942.8	1,581,904	10.7	89.3	59.9	33.7	1,873	29.0
Idaho	639	8.2	874	5.0	209.8	1,219,897	1,395	99,766	80.8	110,564	77.4	22.6	47.2	23.1	5,658	50.5
Jefferson	323	-0.8	416	175.3	191.1	1,089,749	2,620	162,642	257.2	331,387	57.8	42.2	51.3	25.4	2,332	41.0
Jerome	188	-0.4	336	149.0	148.9	1,289,525	3,840	304,766	617.1	1,101,943	23.5	76.5	65.9	36.4	1,880	47.3
Kootenai	124	-5.1	151	13.8	64.3	624,138	4,139	57,726	23.7	28,750	83.8	16.2	19.5	4.1	1,075	20.1
Latah	416	20.9	396	0.5	254.2	713,039	1,803	102,611	87.9	83,435	94.5	5.5	26.7	12.6	8,001	69.0
Lemhi	187	-1.2	535	56.7	49.7	1,189,800	2,222	89,217	32.2	91,863	15.1	84.9	44.6	20.0	533	12.6
Lewis	221	-10.0	1,024	D	158.7	1,437,389	1,403	201,764	62.5	289,292	95.4	4.6	57.4	40.7	3,763	80.6
Lincoln	130	10.5	418	71.4	72.6	1,098,352	2,625	208,332	175.6	566,510	21.8	78.2	64.2	33.2	1,703	44.2
Madison	201	-4.4	427	122.3	167.4	1,413,886	3,314	232,362	131.1	277,674	94.2	5.8	54.0	26.9	2,678	49.4
Minidoka	244	7.9	392	204.5	217.4	1,360,826	3,468	253,349	368.9	593,125	72.6	27.4	57.2	33.9	2,782	52.6
Nez Perce	322	-8.8	749	0.8	181.4	1,261,165	1,683	150,307	81.2	188,777	89.0	11.0	46.0	26.3	5,030	56.0
Oneida	329	4.7	653	34.1	175.7	775,891	1,187	106,209	32.5	64,545	58.1	41.9	42.5	12.1	3,972	66.4
Owyhee	749	31.5	1,295	133.5	140.7	1,590,689	1,228	183,332	291.6	504,424	32.2	67.8	66.8	36.7	2,041	40.1
Payette	157	-5.5	240	56.9	51.6	724,612	3,021	117,252	236.2	360,676	21.3	78.7	43.4	16.9	652	22.1
Power	467	3.5	1,517	120.9	361.7	2,293,497	1,512	378,549	238.3	773,747	85.4	14.6	48.7	31.5	6,836	67.9
Shoshon	D	D	D	D	0.8	387,167	D	43,778	0.1	3,944	32.4	66.9	11.1	0.0	D	2.8
Teton	133	8.8	458	56.4	87.6	1,506,742	3,292	137,058	35.8	123,086	83.9	16.1	44.0	18.6	1,206	44.0
Twin Falls	484	10.1	374	257.0	275.1	1,155,801	3,090	159,620	599.6	463,355	36.0	64.0	63.3	36.9	3,657	48.1
Valley	61	-1.3	524	26.2	8.8	1,294,667	2,473	72,564	6.6	56,675	18.2	81.8	36.8	11.1	62	12.8
Washington	426	2.3	763	42.7	79.5	762,163	999	96,005	75.3	134,664	49.1	50.9	48.3	20.4	1,036	39.9
ILLINOIS	26,938	0.6	359	522.5	23,752.8	2,261,778	6,305	203,184	17,187.1	228,895	82.3	17.7	54.5	33.0	553,300	75.0
Adams	389	3.9	299	2.3	294.2	1,479,562	4,940	147,340	174.0	134,044	74.9	25.1	55.5	27.4	7,898	73.2
Alexander	62	31.1	434	5.0	51.8	1,433,333	3,306	145,569	25.7	178,771	97.9	2.1	39.6	20.8	778	66.0
Bond	198	-11.8	300	0.0	176.7	1,941,345	6,470	174,467	66.0	99,800	82.0	18.0	46.3	24.5	3,940	74.7
Boone	135	-1.8	281	0.9	126.9	1,926,883	6,849	204,127	99.0	206,676	89.1	10.9	56.8	35.5	3,391	51.4
Brown	138	-9.0	333	0.4	85.5	1,327,644	3,987	105,603	42.0	101,717	79.4	20.6	40.2	20.1	3,102	87.9
Bureau	450	-5.9	426	10.6	410.8	3,125,461	7,332	246,925	420.2	397,908	89.9	10.1	68.7	49.0	8,943	80.8
Calhoun	88	-0.2	184	0.0	48.5	697,808	3,801	80,816	23.7	49,513	83.1	16.9	35.8	11.1	2,053	76.4
Carroll	256	-3.4	398	11.3	218.8	2,723,677	6,838	250,918	270.7	421,009	69.6	30.4	57.5	43.7	6,884	81.3
Cass	183	5.3	410	21.3	151.1	2,290,363	5,592	209,209	123.7	277,296	77.8	22.2	53.1	29.8	3,866	80.5
Champaign	616	12.0	470	17.9	591.1	3,740,816	7,961	294,914	424.2	323,295	94.5	5.5	73.5	50.7	11,068	84.7
Christian	374	-16.9	458	D	352.7	3,469,135	7,576	240,299	288.7	353,750	90.6	9.4	60.2	44.2	5,962	79.0
Clark	267	11.8	394	6.6	230.3	1,935,795	4,912	234,895	130.8	193,163	69.9	30.1	47.1	25.1	6,033	79.8
Clay	270	28.8	349	0.1	235.2	1,663,978	4,764	148,499	66.7	86,142	81.2	18.8	38.6	19.3	6,246	85.5
Clinton	285	6.4	312	1.9	259.6	1,824,631	5,848	228,694	206.0	225,184	42.9	57.1	62.4	33.1	5,669	81.5
Coles	267	4.7	379	0.0	245.9	2,671,436	7,050	235,723	136.0	193,229	96.3	3.7	54.5	34.8	4,927	77.6
Cook	8	3.7	67	0.4	7.5	700,701	10,471	76,598	10.7	84,150	79.4	20.6	51.2	18.1	104	15.0
Crawford	215	4.7	359	8.3	186.7	1,793,496	4,997	228,519	65.9	110,018	86.3	13.7	43.4	22.7	6,248	85.1
Cumberland	170	17.4	232	0.1	143.5	1,262,847	5,440	150,681	89.1	121,583	68.5	31.5	41.9	21.4	4,423	84.2
DeKalb	398	7.3	452	3.3	383.5	3,549,751	7,853	289,255	474.9	539,677	70.8	29.2	70.2	55.3	11,835	76.1
De Witt	196	-1.6	383	0.1	182.6	2,749,990	7,188	228,883	154.9	303,139	89.0	11.0	53.8	36.6	3,265	73.6
Douglas	263	0.5	358	0.3	247.8	2,721,101	7,609	214,850	166.7	226,789	85.4	14.6	61.6	40.5	4,948	63.8
DuPage	7	-8.8	98	0.1	5.9	680,851	6,947	82,162	10.0	135,514	95.3	4.7	37.8	14.9	80	14.9
Edgar	352	-0.2	523	D	326.3	3,432,028	6,568	287,382	205.1	304,807	D	D	62.3	42.9	6,450	83.2
Edwards	107	-8.5	292	D	88.1	1,176,600	4,024	173,096	33.7	92,282	85.7	14.3	39.7	18.4	2,276	80.8
Effingham	287	18.6	220	1.7	241.9	1,277,618	5,796	157,144	165.8	127,337	50.5	49.5	49.9	27.3	6,722	80.2
Fayette	303	0.0	244	0.3	248.2	1,089,291	4,456	131,927	97.4	78,521	86.1	13.9	40.0	18.8	5,615	73.7
Ford	308	13.8	564	0.8	298.0	4,278,846	7,581	312,397	191.7	351,125	82.5	17.5	74.4	50.0	5,740	85.3
Franklin	181	-12.8	255	0.1	152.7	946,098	3,709	113,533	55.8	78,457	73.0	27.0	27.3	12.8	3,330	66.5
Fulton	355	-7.9	366	2.1	266.4	1,921,065	5,249	166,037	212.1	218,637	71.7	28.3	53.8	28.9	6,943	67.1
Gallatin	186	0.3	917	25.9	170.3	4,030,990	4,394	455,074	90.1	443,606	98.8	1.2	69.5	40.9	2,545	83.3
Greene	290	6.2	421	8.8	233.4	2,373,734	5,637	220,164	186.2	270,305	77.0	23.0	55.7	32.4	6,005	74.0
Grundy	217	0.7	504	0.0	206.0	3,835,093	7,617	315,223	128.9	298,993	96.7	3.3	74.9	54.1	3,667	80.0
Hamilton	223	1.6	321	0.0	195.3	1,163,304	3,620	146,839	55.7	80,098	98.0	2.0	26.9	14.5	4,621	84.7
Hancock	386	-1.7	354	2.6	315.7	2,029,171	5,726	194,508	317.2	290,977	66.7	33.3	57.7	35.0	8,365	78.3

Table B. States and Counties — Water Use, Wholesale Trade, Retail Trade, and Real Estate

STATE County	Public supply water withdrawn (mil gal/day)	Public supply gallons withdrawn per person per day	Number of establishments	Number of employees	Sales (mil dol)	Annual payroll (mil dol)	Number of establishments	Number of employees	Sales (mil dol)	Annual payroll (mil dol)	Number of establishments	Number of employees	Sales (mil dol)	Annual payroll (mil dol)
	Water use, 2015		**Wholesale Trade[1], 2012**				**Retail Trade[2], 2012**				**Real estate and rental and leasing,[2] 2012**			
	133	134	135	136	137	138	139	140	141	142	143	144	145	146
IDAHO—Cont'd														
Caribou	1.56	230.4	12	88	134.6	3.5	33	279	79.2	7.4	4	5	0.7	0.1
Cassia	3.66	155.7	30	360	702.9	15.6	116	1,301	323.9	29.8	23	38	6.0	0.8
Clark	0.17	193.2	1	D	D	D	4	D	D	D	1	D	D	D
Clearwater	1.04	122.4	4	94	54.1	5.5	36	279	55.5	6.4	6	10	0.5	0.1
Custer	0.95	232.4	NA	NA	NA	NA	29	212	39.4	3.5	6	D	D	D
Elmore	5.62	217.2	13	83	36.5	3.0	76	974	256.3	22.2	13	28	3.7	0.5
Franklin	11.62	888.8	10	D	D	D	45	511	116.4	9.7	9	D	D	D
Fremont	1.34	104.5	8	195	114.5	5.8	33	241	73.4	6.8	6	7	1.2	0.2
Gem	0.86	51.0	12	D	D	D	43	412	93.6	8.8	9	23	2.6	0.4
Gooding	3.59	234.9	21	178	217.6	6.4	44	355	91.5	7.1	7	D	D	D
Idaho	0.93	57.2	11	101	54.1	4.0	57	455	94.8	11.1	10	17	2.1	0.4
Jefferson	1.07	39.4	25	D	D	D	44	464	116.4	10.0	11	D	D	D
Jerome	3.67	160.9	36	308	217.3	14.1	71	845	277.0	20.3	22	73	8.0	1.9
Kootenai	34.69	230.7	132	D	D	D	574	7,996	2,501.7	207.0	201	623	122.6	19.1
Latah	4.20	108.3	21	D	D	D	139	1,874	356.1	37.2	44	159	19.3	3.5
Lemhi	1.63	210.7	5	D	D	D	42	335	98.4	8.0	16	33	2.5	0.7
Lewis	0.53	139.9	5	D	D	D	23	133	26.5	2.5	5	13	1.2	0.2
Lincoln	0.40	75.5	NA	NA	NA	NA	12	D	D	D	3	D	D	D
Madison	3.39	88.6	37	533	221.2	15.5	118	1,607	370.7	34.2	56	174	25.1	3.2
Minidoka	2.81	137.3	46	661	430.9	27.8	62	418	157.9	9.3	12	37	6.1	1.2
Nez Perce	10.07	251.4	42	D	D	D	200	2,249	682.9	56.9	39	137	25.5	4.5
Oneida	0.72	168.2	1	D	D	D	18	142	30.4	2.3	4	15	1.0	0.1
Owyhee	0.73	64.5	6	D	D	D	24	169	42.6	3.9	4	9	0.2	0.0
Payette	1.94	84.7	21	203	113.5	6.0	61	483	136.4	10.7	21	26	3.8	0.6
Power	2.15	281.1	13	212	221.7	7.3	16	164	29.6	3.1	7	D	D	D
Shoshone	2.48	199.5	11	D	D	D	61	846	518.2	31.2	13	35	4.4	0.4
Teton	0.78	73.8	9	D	D	D	38	299	66.1	6.3	34	51	7.6	1.5
Twin Falls	15.74	191.1	111	1,096	492.8	42.6	380	4,789	1,233.5	112.8	112	313	49.7	8.5
Valley	1.55	153.4	10	65	20.0	2.2	69	462	105.9	10.3	38	58	10.0	1.4
Washington	0.74	74.1	9	194	26.4	3.6	33	276	83.7	6.5	11	27	2.3	0.4
ILLINOIS	1,475.66	114.7	16,036	255,531	295,457.0	15,973.3	39,947	592,942	166,634.5	14,576.1	12,035	76,794	23,649.1	3,816.1
Adams	10.35	154.4	120	D	D	D	299	4,790	1,066.5	101.4	61	D	D	D
Alexander	1.61	237.5	5	16	8.0	0.5	23	135	24.2	2.3	3	8	0.8	0.2
Bond	1.30	76.7	21	247	182.4	11.2	46	363	124.2	6.5	8	D	D	D
Boone	3.56	66.4	31	239	202.6	12.4	108	1,369	395.4	31.6	24	61	9.9	1.6
Brown	0.04	5.9	10	D	D	D	20	149	32.8	3.0	NA	NA	NA	NA
Bureau	2.96	88.1	53	896	1,472.5	39.3	97	1,166	299.8	23.2	16	D	D	D
Calhoun	0.41	83.7	5	D	D	D	15	116	27.3	2.5	1	D	D	D
Carroll	1.03	70.5	28	243	285.8	9.1	50	427	95.5	8.8	7	21	1.5	0.2
Cass	1.10	85.6	18	179	501.0	8.7	48	491	119.8	10.3	5	16	2.0	0.4
Champaign	24.42	116.9	176	2,872	2,589.6	126.5	626	10,256	2,472.7	220.2	201	2,986	557.4	117.9
Christian	2.55	75.8	45	605	845.6	30.5	111	1,377	410.3	31.4	20	94	12.9	2.7
Clark	1.60	100.1	19	191	257.9	6.0	51	445	141.7	10.9	5	22	4.4	0.7
Clay	0.01	0.7	26	196	172.8	6.8	46	464	113.3	8.9	7	49	3.9	0.9
Clinton	6.98	184.7	48	541	451.0	20.9	141	1,561	425.9	40.3	21	181	14.7	8.9
Coles	4.10	78.1	50	553	627.4	25.3	198	2,645	701.3	59.5	50	166	29.4	4.8
Cook	834.08	159.2	6,130	94,754	100,829.6	6,169.4	15,225	222,918	62,767.4	5,733.8	5,629	40,439	12,377.8	2,244.4
Crawford	2.18	112.3	19	181	179.3	6.2	61	796	187.1	16.2	14	D	D	D
Cumberland	0.27	24.8	16	153	188.2	5.0	24	188	38.6	2.9	1	D	D	D
DeKalb	7.64	73.2	60	586	353.2	27.1	280	4,404	1,052.7	91.7	69	447	100.2	14.2
De Witt	1.31	80.6	30	352	603.6	23.8	52	677	220.6	17.3	9	30	2.5	0.4
Douglas	0.67	33.8	30	329	478.1	16.6	120	1,173	218.7	19.1	12	38	8.3	1.0
DuPage	6.80	7.3	2,322	45,595	65,510.4	3,110.6	3,336	59,068	17,758.8	1,543.7	1,310	11,880	6,433.2	673.0
Edgar	1.58	89.4	13	148	227.4	9.4	51	623	157.0	13.6	9	30	4.6	0.9
Edwards	0.04	6.1	15	D	D	D	28	202	55.0	3.9	2	D	D	D
Effingham	2.06	59.9	62	D	D	D	203	2,977	934.7	66.1	43	214	32.0	7.0
Fayette	1.27	57.6	25	321	398.4	13.1	85	929	256.4	19.5	12	25	3.1	0.7
Ford	1.44	104.8	34	354	566.7	19.9	51	537	119.1	10.1	8	D	D	D
Franklin	15.39	389.8	34	265	126.3	13.3	143	1,549	408.1	35.0	15	69	6.4	1.6
Fulton	2.55	71.4	22	247	184.1	11.7	115	1,378	316.6	27.8	15	49	6.7	1.1
Gallatin	3.25	617.3	4	43	25.0	1.5	13	76	16.1	1.7	1	D	D	D
Greene	0.70	52.9	18	152	321.5	5.9	49	408	125.6	9.1	3	2	0.1	0.0
Grundy	3.41	67.5	47	490	738.0	27.1	144	1,744	524.7	38.1	28	71	15.7	2.4
Hamilton	0.00	0.0	8	81	64.5	3.2	34	161	45.4	3.4	7	15	1.3	0.3
Hancock	1.32	71.2	31	233	361.4	9.8	67	474	97.0	9.0	4	10	1.2	0.2

1. Merchant wholesalers, except manufacturers' sales branches and offices.   2. Employer establishments.

STATE County	Persons in group quarters, 2017	Daytime Population, 2012-2016		Births, 2017		Deaths, 2017		Persons under 65 with no health insurance, 2016		Medicare, 2017			Serious crimes known to police[2], 2016 — Total	
		Number	Employment/ residence ratio	Total	Rate[1]	Number	Rate[1]	Number	Percent	Total beneficiaries	Enrolled in Original Medicare	Enrolled in Medicare Advantage	Number	Rate[3]
	32	33	34	35	36	37	38	39	40	41	42	43	44	45
ILLINOIS— Cont'd														
Hardin	111	3,822	0.75	34	8.4	60	14.8	201	6.8	1,036	874	162	42	1029
Henderson	51	5,174	0.45	51	7.5	83	12.2	350	6.7	1,584	1,323	261	NA	NA
Henry	722	41,932	0.66	570	11.6	540	10.9	2,137	5.4	10,406	7,580	2,825	710	1584
Iroquois	468	25,806	0.77	283	10.2	327	11.7	1,551	7.0	6,896	5,807	1,089	462	1874
Jackson	3,843	62,189	1.12	705	12.1	455	7.8	3,570	7.5	10,600	8,151	2,449	1,929	3309
Jasper	54	8,033	0.66	115	12.0	92	9.6	472	6.1	1,933	1,690	243	NA	NA
Jefferson	2,213	43,750	1.33	485	12.7	432	11.3	1,691	5.8	8,449	7,307	1,142	1,233	3237
Jersey	818	18,434	0.59	178	8.1	193	8.8	844	4.8	3,977	3,324	653	414	1870
Jo Daviess	167	20,192	0.81	178	8.2	245	11.3	1,015	6.3	5,985	3,129	2,856	220	1023
Johnson	1,798	11,636	0.71	99	7.7	134	10.4	498	5.8	3,098	2,382	716	109	934
Kane	6,799	492,060	0.86	6,577	12.3	3,369	6.3	43,137	9.4	82,295	61,986	20,309	7,537	1445
Kankakee	5,160	107,973	0.93	1,295	11.8	1,126	10.3	5,918	6.6	21,344	16,933	4,411	2,624	2718
Kendall	208	94,536	0.56	1,585	12.6	543	4.3	5,466	4.9	10,408	8,163	2,245	1,452	1167
Knox	3,972	51,652	1.00	539	10.6	579	11.4	2,171	5.8	12,265	8,381	3,884	1,314	3016
Lake	18,498	719,537	1.05	7,588	10.8	4,579	6.5	43,171	7.2	104,642	88,803	15,839	10,255	1527
LaSalle	3,562	107,974	0.92	1,255	11.4	1,216	11.0	5,115	5.8	22,980	19,742	3,238	1,868	1754
Lawrence	2,590	16,893	1.07	160	9.9	225	13.9	695	6.2	3,157	2,863	295	NA	NA
Lee	2,971	34,142	0.96	324	9.4	389	11.3	1,337	5.3	7,520	6,079	1,441	500	1464
Livingston	2,713	37,336	1.00	400	11.0	361	9.9	1,495	5.4	6,868	5,265	1,602	567	1572
Logan	4,325	28,358	0.87	302	10.3	312	10.7	951	4.7	5,702	4,210	1,492	434	1575
McDonough	3,837	33,009	1.09	250	8.1	274	8.9	1,458	6.5	5,670	4,177	1,494	498	1610
McHenry	1,648	258,100	0.69	3,256	10.5	2,015	6.5	14,516	5.5	54,873	46,946	7,927	3,218	1070
McLean	10,605	178,566	1.06	2,078	12.1	1,181	6.9	6,133	4.3	25,446	17,976	7,469	3,141	1826
Macon	4,210	114,924	1.14	1,313	12.4	1,156	10.9	4,653	5.6	23,955	20,208	3,747	3,388	3227
Macoupin	835	37,890	0.58	435	9.6	577	12.7	2,060	5.7	11,217	9,645	1,572	623	1515
Madison	3,825	248,050	0.85	2,990	11.3	2,773	10.4	11,491	5.2	53,134	35,587	17,547	5,661	2377
Marion	758	37,507	0.94	483	12.7	409	10.8	1,706	5.6	10,035	8,845	1,190	1,135	3125
Marshall	255	10,415	0.70	138	11.8	141	12.0	478	5.2	2,677	2,120	556	127	1083
Mason	206	12,469	0.75	137	10.0	164	12.0	649	6.1	3,713	3,048	666	NA	NA
Massac	292	13,297	0.72	154	10.7	182	12.7	639	5.6	3,355	3,007	348	352	2416
Menard	154	8,692	0.36	113	9.2	143	11.7	488	4.8	2,558	1,713	845	124	1006
Mercer	185	12,057	0.47	123	7.9	180	11.5	639	5.2	3,469	2,399	1,070	121	772
Monroe	343	26,118	0.56	357	10.5	314	9.2	1,065	3.8	6,334	3,986	2,347	171	505
Montgomery	2,468	28,943	0.96	315	10.9	378	13.1	1,251	5.9	6,879	5,918	961	439	1633
Morgan	2,906	35,322	1.03	351	10.4	367	10.9	1,252	4.9	7,396	5,782	1,614	793	2407
Moultrie	395	13,608	0.81	170	11.6	155	10.6	824	6.9	3,470	2,928	543	NA	NA
Ogle	525	45,457	0.73	520	10.2	480	9.4	2,376	5.7	9,964	7,431	2,534	447	1069
Peoria	4,881	208,545	1.26	2,578	14.1	1,758	9.6	8,871	5.8	35,203	23,896	11,307	6,780	3668
Perry	2,421	19,661	0.76	209	9.8	218	10.2	851	5.6	4,367	3,346	1,021	171	827
Piatt	72	12,514	0.53	178	10.8	170	10.3	603	4.5	3,709	2,314	1,395	178	1244
Pike	627	14,472	0.77	176	11.1	181	11.4	938	7.7	3,700	3,234	466	193	1219
Pope	370	3,922	0.74	23	5.3	22	5.1	222	7.3	1,000	822	178	NA	NA
Pulaski	21	6,163	1.20	51	9.3	60	10.9	312	7.1	1,438	1,272	167	NA	NA
Putnam	2	4,812	0.68	53	9.3	57	10.0	253	5.7	1,324	1,043	281	NA	NA
Randolph	4,531	33,441	1.04	311	9.6	383	11.8	1,127	5.0	6,964	5,315	1,649	128	424
Richland	364	15,960	0.98	189	11.9	183	11.5	726	5.8	3,812	3,377	435	412	2589
Rock Island	4,647	158,296	1.18	1,893	13.1	1,443	10.0	7,706	6.7	30,622	19,731	10,892	4,409	3038
St. Clair	4,699	251,662	0.88	3,305	12.6	2,637	10.0	13,536	6.1	46,769	30,819	15,950	7,830	3021
Saline	882	24,679	1.00	332	13.8	329	13.7	1,156	6.1	6,402	5,326	1,076	561	2468
Sangamon	3,909	213,128	1.15	2,235	11.4	2,097	10.7	7,407	4.6	39,813	25,312	14,502	7,726	3989
Schuyler	463	6,343	0.71	63	9.0	70	10.0	386	7.0	1,540	1,264	277	42	609
Scott	43	4,246	0.60	55	11.0	45	9.0	229	5.7	1,014	829	185	NA	NA
Shelby	205	18,336	0.64	242	11.1	255	11.7	864	5.1	4,986	4,448	539	32	189
Stark	92	5,095	0.70	68	12.5	87	16.0	238	5.5	1,388	1,038	350	NA	NA
Stephenson	836	44,677	0.92	497	11.0	553	12.3	2,064	5.8	11,821	7,265	4,555	872	2116
Tazewell	2,733	127,507	0.88	1,490	11.2	1,419	10.6	4,415	4.1	27,977	20,207	7,770	2,458	1930
Union	580	15,540	0.74	192	11.3	226	13.3	933	6.9	4,146	3,176	969	243	1568
Vermilion	2,924	78,831	0.98	1,031	13.2	909	11.7	3,564	5.8	17,589	11,149	6,440	3,347	4337
Wabash	88	10,138	0.72	133	11.6	125	10.9	554	6.0	2,493	2,182	311	214	1875
Warren	1,013	16,938	0.92	235	13.7	180	10.5	980	7.5	3,562	2,801	761	312	1792
Washington	246	14,229	0.98	182	13.0	137	9.8	587	5.2	2,857	2,447	410	163	1219
Wayne	76	14,821	0.77	229	13.9	200	12.1	869	6.7	3,699	3,367	331	NA	NA
White	391	14,128	0.95	154	11.0	210	15.1	682	6.2	3,756	3,292	464	NA	NA
Whiteside	1,010	53,184	0.85	641	11.4	616	11.0	2,587	5.8	14,027	11,488	2,540	975	1768
Will	9,198	608,464	0.77	7,753	11.2	4,527	6.5	34,207	5.7	87,807	66,864	20,943	9,409	1386
Williamson	2,136	68,385	1.04	819	12.2	777	11.5	3,006	5.6	13,629	10,981	2,648	1,055	1652

1. Per 1,000 estimated resident population.　　2. Data for serious crimes have not been adjusted for underreporting; this may affect comparability between geographic areas and over time.
3. Per 100,000 population estimated by the FBI.

Table B. States and Counties — Crime, Education, Money Income, and Poverty

STATE County	Serious crimes known to police, 2016 (cont.)[1] Rate		Education School enrollment and attainment, 2012-2016 Enrollment[3]		Attainment[4] (percent)		Local government expenditures,[5] 2013-2014		Money income, 2012-2016		Households		Income and poverty, 2016	Percent below poverty level		
	Violent	Property	Total	Percent private	High school graduate or less	Bachelor's degree or more	Total current spending (mil dol)	Current spending per student (dollars)	Per capita income[6]	Median income (dollars)	Percent with income of less than $50,000	Percent with income of $200,000 or more	Median household income (dollars)	All persons	Children under 18 years	Children 5 to 17 years in families
	46	47	48	49	50	51	52	53	54	55	56	57	58	59	60	61
ILLINOIS— Cont'd																
Hardin	147	882	849	5.8	51.8	11.3	5.3	8,188	21,573	39,926	58.8	2.5	39,143	21.9	35.5	30.1
Henderson	NA	NA	1,334	11.0	56.4	13.3	9.3	9,956	26,504	46,216	53.2	0.8	47,792	11.7	18.7	18.3
Henry	132	1,452	11,469	10.9	44.8	21.3	90.7	9,718	27,777	54,757	45.6	2.5	55,287	11.5	16.2	15.1
Iroquois	154	1,720	6,416	9.8	52.3	14.6	57.8	12,486	25,562	47,823	51.7	2.6	47,589	13.3	17.8	16.2
Jackson	410	2,899	22,357	5.4	32.5	35.9	96.4	13,089	21,948	33,845	64.2	2.4	34,982	23.4	27.5	27.7
Jasper	NA	NA	2,071	13.2	47.3	18.3	19.5	13,547	25,811	56,305	43.2	1.1	51,120	10.7	15.0	14.0
Jefferson	635	2,602	8,665	14.5	46.2	16.4	63.9	10,410	23,054	43,467	56.1	1.6	45,746	15.8	25.4	24.0
Jersey	163	1,707	5,897	26.9	45.5	18.4	26.9	9,734	26,346	52,738	46.9	2.1	57,243	11.2	15.8	14.0
Jo Daviess	153	869	4,596	13.1	45.1	24.1	42.1	12,581	29,892	54,702	44.9	2.8	54,169	9.9	13.8	12.3
Johnson	291	643	2,518	6.4	47.5	16.7	18.9	9,534	20,928	44,179	54.1	1.2	48,359	14.4	18.1	15.6
Kane	170	1,274	149,936	15.6	40.1	32.1	1,431.3	11,609	31,774	71,602	34.5	7.6	73,684	10.5	14.7	13.8
Kankakee	305	2,414	29,918	20.0	46.7	19.0	211.6	11,118	25,111	54,697	45.0	2.3	54,624	14.2	21.2	18.9
Kendall	109	1,058	36,170	13.1	31.0	34.3	292.6	11,093	31,920	85,736	24.2	6.4	91,952	4.6	6.0	5.4
Knox	372	2,644	11,841	18.5	48.7	18.1	79.5	10,213	22,939	40,605	59.5	1.4	43,277	17.1	24.1	22.3
Lake	153	1,374	195,484	16.1	31.1	43.7	2,046.8	14,912	40,655	79,886	31.2	13.4	83,344	8.7	10.9	10.4
LaSalle	130	1,625	26,041	11.0	48.1	17.0	212.6	12,589	26,228	51,684	48.4	2.1	56,543	13.3	19.6	18.1
Lawrence	NA	NA	3,392	11.7	56.3	10.1	21.2	9,174	16,417	42,650	55.9	1.0	44,774	18.6	24.8	24.2
Lee	190	1,274	7,652	16.6	48.1	17.7	50.7	11,649	27,021	55,067	45.5	2.8	55,563	13.3	17.0	16.6
Livingston	175	1,397	8,481	8.6	53.2	15.2	79.0	12,330	26,777	54,074	46.1	2.2	54,339	14.3	17.6	15.1
Logan	163	1,412	7,162	16.6	47.2	18.4	38.3	11,318	23,410	52,676	46.7	2.2	53,052	13.7	18.7	17.8
McDonough	285	1,326	11,906	7.3	36.1	33.5	47.8	13,691	22,387	41,484	56.5	1.9	44,460	20.2	22.4	21.1
McHenry	98	972	83,317	14.0	34.3	33.2	626.6	12,214	34,589	79,836	29.7	7.3	81,570	7.3	9.2	8.4
McLean	285	1,541	57,085	13.5	29.9	44.5	285.1	10,909	31,752	63,420	39.9	5.3	64,271	12.6	11.8	10.8
Macon	413	2,813	25,428	19.4	45.1	22.8	215.8	13,117	27,010	47,477	52.4	2.7	47,786	17.3	27.9	24.4
Macoupin	178	1,337	11,177	13.1	48.3	18.2	79.7	9,084	26,779	52,337	47.8	2.6	52,483	13.3	20.4	18.2
Madison	298	2,079	68,198	15.5	39.2	25.7	424.0	10,164	29,100	54,573	45.4	3.4	56,297	13.3	18.0	15.8
Marion	388	2,737	8,410	10.1	47.3	15.0	82.1	11,783	23,366	43,427	55.9	1.3	45,698	15.8	25.1	24.2
Marshall	128	955	2,356	9.8	48.6	16.1	15.3	11,281	28,279	54,189	44.6	2.5	54,807	9.8	15.5	14.4
Mason	NA	NA	2,909	5.4	55.4	14.3	29.9	10,511	25,166	43,125	55.2	1.7	46,962	15.1	23.4	21.8
Massac	329	2,086	3,314	3.7	49.0	13.3	24.4	9,880	23,673	42,706	58.0	2.1	42,833	20.6	28.1	24.5
Menard	89	916	2,817	8.4	43.0	23.9	22.4	9,260	31,323	60,420	41.8	4.2	62,966	9.7	15.4	14.3
Mercer	96	676	3,493	6.5	49.6	17.5	27.2	9,166	27,566	55,750	44.5	2.8	56,661	10.2	13.7	12.2
Monroe	24	481	8,192	20.1	36.9	29.8	49.5	9,373	35,699	72,956	32.9	6.4	83,139	4.8	5.3	4.3
Montgomery	104	1,529	6,320	8.1	54.4	13.9	40.7	8,808	21,072	45,173	54.9	2.2	46,997	16.0	22.7	20.3
Morgan	246	2,161	9,111	29.9	51.1	20.6	55.9	11,325	25,201	47,760	51.9	2.0	48,600	15.7	23.0	21.9
Moultrie	NA	NA	3,475	12.7	50.8	17.1	15.7	9,296	25,351	51,432	49.0	1.7	57,447	10.0	13.6	12.0
Ogle	60	1,010	12,784	9.5	45.5	19.8	119.7	12,819	28,026	55,832	44.3	2.6	58,812	10.2	14.6	13.2
Peoria	575	3,093	48,353	25.8	37.4	29.8	337.0	11,528	29,055	51,632	48.5	4.1	52,380	15.2	21.0	19.7
Perry	155	672	4,451	6.6	53.4	13.4	28.8	10,311	22,650	43,308	55.1	1.3	48,423	15.6	21.9	19.7
Piatt	189	1,055	3,926	11.1	39.3	29.9	31.9	10,058	33,197	69,160	37.7	4.5	65,797	6.8	8.4	7.6
Pike	95	1,124	3,519	8.3	53.6	15.3	26.7	10,144	22,048	40,157	59.8	1.1	41,671	16.4	22.3	20.7
Pope	NA	NA	715	7.0	45.1	13.7	5.1	9,083	21,427	39,243	58.2	1.3	42,917	18.2	29.3	28.2
Pulaski	NA	NA	1,253	10.8	52.0	11.0	13.2	13,434	18,924	32,538	67.4	1.0	35,875	21.1	33.5	31.4
Putnam	NA	NA	1,279	11.2	48.0	14.4	10.7	11,540	32,584	64,085	42.7	5.2	65,902	8.0	14.4	13.2
Randolph	70	354	6,428	15.0	56.5	13.0	47.4	11,429	23,424	48,343	51.6	2.2	50,681	13.7	19.4	18.2
Richland	390	2,199	3,707	12.5	46.1	20.6	23.3	9,370	23,972	45,597	54.8	2.3	46,497	14.4	19.7	19.2
Rock Island	365	2,673	35,531	18.4	42.5	22.0	251.4	11,347	26,893	50,208	49.8	2.6	50,952	15.6	25.1	24.9
St. Clair	590	2,430	71,556	14.9	37.9	26.1	472.0	11,255	27,683	50,006	50.0	3.5	50,598	15.4	23.0	22.0
Saline	405	2,063	5,164	4.9	45.4	16.0	40.4	9,437	21,917	40,290	58.7	1.6	40,690	20.4	30.5	30.9
Sangamon	793	3,197	50,441	16.0	35.6	34.3	352.1	11,768	31,904	56,742	44.4	4.4	55,090	13.8	20.6	19.8
Schuyler	145	464	1,379	4.8	48.0	18.9	11.4	9,442	24,323	48,396	52.3	1.5	49,566	12.1	16.7	15.1
Scott	NA	NA	1,191	13.3	57.9	12.1	9.4	10,185	25,568	46,210	52.3	2.4	52,386	11.5	17.0	15.3
Shelby	12	177	4,602	14.1	54.7	15.2	23.6	9,794	23,974	48,572	51.6	0.8	51,069	11.7	15.9	15.0
Stark	NA	NA	1,222	13.7	49.6	16.7	10.7	11,294	28,545	52,058	47.8	5.0	56,414	11.5	18.5	17.2
Stephenson	138	1,977	10,580	12.0	44.5	17.9	82.8	12,221	24,529	45,624	54.7	1.3	45,863	15.4	24.0	21.6
Tazewell	285	1,645	31,980	17.3	40.1	25.0	214.3	10,584	30,700	60,187	41.1	3.6	60,590	8.8	11.5	10.3
Union	219	1,349	3,733	7.0	46.9	21.3	28.1	9,815	24,296	45,464	55.1	2.3	45,476	17.4	24.7	22.6
Vermilion	813	3,525	17,858	7.0	53.4	14.0	148.2	11,198	22,733	43,552	55.8	1.6	45,247	20.2	29.9	27.4
Wabash	131	1,743	2,692	14.5	43.0	17.2	15.4	8,693	24,697	46,871	52.7	1.7	50,195	13.5	18.6	17.6
Warren	253	1,540	5,007	28.5	47.3	21.9	24.3	8,921	23,350	44,067	56.0	2.3	48,346	13.6	18.2	17.4
Washington	247	972	3,206	19.8	41.9	20.9	19.6	10,076	29,548	54,936	44.9	2.7	58,587	9.3	13.3	12.3
Wayne	NA	NA	3,479	9.1	47.9	14.0	25.8	10,000	24,342	46,903	53.8	1.9	45,583	13.9	21.6	19.7
White	NA	NA	2,854	6.2	48.6	13.7	33.5	13,286	25,065	43,678	56.3	2.1	44,874	16.2	23.3	21.4
Whiteside	205	1,563	10,212	11.7	47.4	17.3	104.7	10,963	26,155	49,151	50.6	2.2	51,567	11.9	17.8	16.0
Will	161	1,225	197,136	15.6	36.0	33.5	1,388.0	11,845	32,311	77,507	30.4	7.5	81,640	7.2	10.2	9.0
Williamson	135	1,517	14,793	9.3	40.3	22.1	104.7	10,104	25,238	45,902	54.1	1.9	48,112	15.9	22.3	19.8

1. Data for serious crimes have not been adjusted for underreporting; this may affect comparability between geographic areas and over time.   2. Per 100,000 population estimated by the FBI.
3. All persons 3 years old and over enrolled in nursery school through college.   4. Persons 25 years old and over.   5. Elementary and secondary education expenditures.
6. Based on population estimated by the American Community Survey, 2011–2015.

Table B. States and Counties — **Personal Income and Earnings**

STATE County	Personal income, 2016										Earnings, 2016		
			Per capita[1]			Supplements to wages and salaries, employer contributions (mil dol)						Contributions for government social insurance (mil dol)	
	Total (mil dol)	Percent change 2015-2016	Dollars	Rank	Wages and salaries (mil dol)	Pension and insurance	Government social insurance	Proprietors' income (mil dol)	Dividends, interest, and rent (mil dol)	Personal transfer receipts (mil dol)	Total (mil dol)	From employee and self-employed	From employer
	62	63	64	65	66	67	68	69	70	71	72	73	74
ILLINOIS— Cont'd													
Hardin	138	-2.4	34,290	2,282	28	8	2	14	20	53	51	6	2
Henderson	272	3.8	39,603	1,412	39	11	3	23	52	63	75	8	3
Henry	2,110	0.7	42,819	1,011	576	132	41	112	406	402	860	95	41
Iroquois	1,185	2.7	41,809	1,123	291	65	21	133	223	281	510	50	21
Jackson	2,009	1.1	34,125	2,301	1,179	330	71	120	411	459	1,699	151	71
Jasper	374	3.0	39,193	1,469	88	25	6	51	75	82	169	15	6
Jefferson	1,414	1.1	36,765	1,864	895	165	66	64	233	365	1,190	135	66
Jersey	833	1.6	37,822	1,692	192	45	13	35	134	194	285	32	13
Jo Daviess	998	0.0	45,829	711	301	66	22	58	251	202	447	52	22
Johnson	336	0.7	26,033	3,057	85	25	5	12	58	109	128	14	5
Kane	24,566	2.5	46,202	672	10,918	1,932	771	1,302	3,668	3,140	14,923	1,584	771
Kankakee	4,199	1.6	38,171	1,625	1,919	385	138	193	578	992	2,635	289	138
Kendall	5,555	3.6	44,552	822	1,209	247	83	214	564	566	1,752	180	83
Knox	1,958	1.1	38,438	1,578	829	168	72	82	349	550	1,150	146	72
Lake	51,291	1.6	72,956	55	26,357	3,997	1,681	3,235	12,349	4,382	35,270	3,593	1681
LaSalle	4,494	1.9	40,616	1,289	2,001	393	143	202	756	950	2,739	305	143
Lawrence	559	-5.9	34,116	2,304	179	43	13	50	98	154	285	30	13
Lee	1,321	1.1	38,575	1,562	557	110	39	47	236	302	753	86	39
Livingston	1,478	1.6	40,451	1,308	645	132	44	171	242	299	992	97	44
Logan	1,044	3.9	35,353	2,105	374	81	26	106	170	244	588	58	26
McDonough	1,072	0.5	34,587	2,231	496	148	29	60	219	235	734	64	29
McHenry	15,428	2.2	50,252	405	4,777	870	340	559	2,390	1,867	6,546	718	340
McLean	7,883	1.6	45,718	722	5,031	847	316	497	1,259	999	6,691	675	316
Macon	4,742	0.1	44,507	829	2,672	471	197	333	803	1,051	3,673	411	197
Macoupin	1,706	1.7	37,155	1,800	410	92	28	61	300	429	590	70	28
Madison	11,305	1.3	42,540	1,038	4,527	913	331	544	1,848	2,312	6,315	704	331
Marion	1,487	0.3	38,981	1,499	554	120	43	99	244	445	815	93	43
Marshall	498	3.2	41,748	1,134	127	27	9	31	92	116	194	22	9
Mason	512	2.4	37,870	1,686	119	33	7	51	89	141	211	20	7
Massac	515	1.1	35,133	2,145	193	41	12	20	84	162	266	29	12
Menard	521	3.5	41,609	1,155	67	19	4	29	90	99	120	13	4
Mercer	647	1.4	41,119	1,218	111	27	8	15	127	141	161	21	8
Monroe	1,782	1.8	52,318	327	320	65	22	97	313	243	504	55	22
Montgomery	997	2.8	34,447	2,251	352	80	25	85	196	274	542	57	25
Morgan	1,290	1.9	37,639	1,718	614	126	43	83	259	322	866	94	43
Moultrie	758	0.2	51,145	368	170	34	12	210	100	125	425	37	12
Ogle	2,134	1.6	41,616	1,150	793	172	54	56	357	414	1,075	120	54
Peoria	8,820	0.0	47,673	553	5,592	908	398	347	1,661	1,544	7,245	810	398
Perry	765	1.6	35,837	2,026	191	51	13	126	122	186	381	35	13
Piatt	762	3.7	45,991	691	133	32	9	22	124	133	197	23	9
Pike	602	3.5	37,720	1,702	160	36	11	91	103	149	298	27	11
Pope	126	-2.4	30,338	2,814	23	7	1	5	22	38	37	4	1
Pulaski	200	1.4	35,537	2,076	81	24	5	11	28	74	120	11	5
Putnam	266	-5.2	47,409	573	95	17	6	32	51	47	151	15	6
Randolph	1,114	1.7	34,144	2,299	491	116	33	44	209	284	684	73	33
Richland	598	-0.3	37,526	1,733	243	53	17	48	115	159	361	39	17
Rock Island	6,034	0.7	41,677	1,144	4,271	779	296	254	1,290	1,230	5,600	616	296
St. Clair	10,910	0.7	41,521	1,161	4,713	1,030	361	439	1,999	2,404	6,543	728	361
Saline	906	-0.4	37,279	1,775	329	76	24	69	146	284	498	54	24
Sangamon	8,793	0.9	44,523	827	5,009	991	340	483	1,720	1,621	6,823	707	340
Schuyler	284	-0.7	41,062	1,224	77	20	4	38	43	59	139	12	4
Scott	185	2.6	36,529	1,912	40	11	3	18	30	39	72	7	3
Shelby	799	4.1	36,781	1,858	177	40	13	78	137	191	308	32	13
Stark	214	3.7	37,038	1,818	56	13	4	14	44	51	88	10	4
Stephenson	1,800	1.4	39,443	1,428	774	147	56	101	349	436	1,079	125	56
Tazewell	5,912	1.2	43,991	879	3,505	556	236	245	1,066	1,086	4,542	501	236
Union	625	1.4	36,339	1,943	167	43	12	39	101	199	261	29	12
Vermilion	2,871	1.5	36,760	1,866	1,246	275	91	188	442	780	1,800	199	91
Wabash	484	0.9	42,076	1,094	128	35	8	33	90	107	205	20	8
Warren	641	2.5	36,876	1,841	239	49	17	54	115	142	358	38	17
Washington	688	1.2	48,641	489	306	69	22	87	121	120	484	47	22
Wayne	620	-0.5	37,824	1,691	153	38	11	106	113	155	308	27	11
White	633	0.5	44,298	848	176	38	13	97	117	153	324	32	13
Whiteside	2,263	0.9	40,025	1,362	851	206	59	82	424	558	1,198	132	59
Will	33,098	2.5	48,000	538	11,982	2,134	860	1,387	4,311	4,182	16,364	1,776	860
Williamson	2,760	1.2	40,850	1,251	1,221	279	89	143	443	613	1,732	190	89

1. Based on the resident population estimated as of July 1 of the year shown.

Table B. States and Counties — **Earnings, Social Security, and Housing**

STATE County	Farm	Mining, quarrying, and extracting	Construction	Manu-facturing	Information; professional, scientific, technical services	Retail trade	Finance, insurance, real estate, and leasing	Health care and social assistance	Govern-ment	Number	Rate[1]	Supple-mental Security Income recipients, 2016	Total	Percent change, 2010-2017
	75	76	77	78	79	80	81	82	83	84	85	86	87	88
ILLINOIS— Cont'd	-1.5	D	D	D	D	4.1	D	20.9	24.8	1,320	322	177	2,479	-0.4
Hardin	21.6	D	6.6	D	D	3.8	6.6	7.2	23.1	1,795	261	105	3,872	1.2
Henderson	0.4	D	11.6	14.0	4.4	7.6	5.7	10.5	23.4	11,480	232	616	22,173	0.1
Henry	17.2	0.3	8.1	6.2	2.3	7.2	6.0	D	16.2	7,205	255	564	13,503	0.4
Iroquois	0.5	D	4.7	3.1	4.1	6.2	3.1	17.2	43.9	9,795	166	1,600	29,020	1.5
Jackson	18.0	2.5	5.6	5.2	1.5	4.6	5.0	D	18.3	2,310	241	154	4,343	0.0
Jasper	0.0	0.6	2.5	24.6	3.9	6.2	5.8	19.7	13.2	8,755	229	952	16,964	0.1
Jefferson	1.7	0.0	8.8	2.6	D	9.6	4.6	D	28.3	5,330	243	337	10,145	3.0
Jersey	2.1	D	8.9	15.0	D	7.1	5.2	D	19.2	6,290	288	195	13,721	1.1
Jo Daviess	-0.5	D	6.8	1.2	3.2	4.4	D	D	51.5	3,185	246	260	5,636	0.7
Johnson	0.0	0.1	7.7	17.0	9.0	5.0	5.9	10.6	17.1	73,975	139	5,077	187,813	3.1
Kane	2.5	D	4.4	19.2	D	6.6	5.3	17.8	15.6	22,465	204	2,655	45,507	0.6
Kankakee	1.0	D	9.3	15.5	6.1	8.3	3.8	6.0	23.0	15,595	125	750	41,921	3.9
Kendall	0.6	D	3.6	6.1	D	9.4	3.8	D	18.4	12,185	239	1,321	23,908	-0.7
Knox	0.0	D	5.0	22.5	9.7	7.3	6.9	6.5	12.6	103,610	147	8,229	263,771	1.3
Lake	0.8	3.1	6.9	19.8	3.9	7.5	4.6	9.3	15.2	25,255	229	1,661	50,123	0.3
LaSalle	0.1	18.7	5.0	20.3	1.8	3.8	9.5	9.8	18.8	3,480	213	304	7,125	2.7
Lawrence	-1.6	0.9	3.5	29.5	2.9	6.4	4.2	16.8	17.3	8,045	234	491	15,105	0.4
Lee	8.6	D	6.0	16.4	10.1	8.3	3.8	9.4	17.5	8,095	222	526	15,902	0.0
Livingston	11.6	D	3.2	17.9	3.2	6.0	4.5	10.8	16.6	6,235	213	412	12,057	-0.4
Logan	3.1	D	4.4	11.5	2.8	6.1	3.6	D	50.2	5,680	181	565	14,424	0.0
McDonough	-0.4	0.1	11.0	17.4	6.3	8.3	3.7	10.8	16.1	50,065	163	1,979	118,485	2.1
McHenry	0.8	0.0	3.4	3.5	4.9	5.0	38.7	9.3	15.0	25,920	150	1,766	72,388	3.9
McLean	0.7	D	7.0	30.4	4.7	5.1	4.3	13.1	10.4	25,110	235	3,273	50,432	-0.1
Macon	-0.7	D	7.7	7.6	D	9.2	4.9	D	22.5	11,550	253	1,011	21,745	0.7
Macoupin	0.3	0.2	8.7	14.8	7.9	7.1	4.9	11.7	17.0	56,040	211	5,831	119,364	1.9
Madison	3.1	2.1	6.6	17.7	D	5.1	4.1	16.5	17.0	9,295	244	1,216	18,222	-0.4
Marion	5.9	0.8	7.6	33.0	2.7	4.0	D	7.0	14.6	3,155	265	132	5,906	-0.1
Marshall	16.3	D	4.1	1.9	D	5.5	4.6	5.8	32.9	3,665	267	299	7,050	-0.4
Mason	3.6	0.1	2.4	21.8	1.2	3.8	2.6	5.8	23.8	4,075	282	480	7,132	0.3
Massac	8.0	D	12.1	1.4	D	6.9	D	3.0	30.1	2,790	225	159	5,734	1.4
Menard	-5.6	0.0	8.6	14.2	2.9	8.8	5.9	13.9	26.2	4,155	266	163	7,427	0.9
Mercer	0.3	D	9.7	4.6	D	9.1	12.4	6.8	17.6	6,595	195	164	14,166	5.8
Monroe	6.8	1.5	6.0	7.0	3.2	9.1	5.6	16.5	19.0	7,105	244	626	13,143	0.5
Montgomery	2.3	0.1	4.8	18.9	4.3	7.0	6.6	13.2	18.8	8,135	238	867	15,469	-0.3
Morgan	2.6	D	8.7	42.8	4.7	2.6	D	D	7.0	3,165	217	166	6,485	3.6
Moultrie	-1.4	D	6.6	20.7	D	5.0	6.7	D	17.2	11,065	216	586	22,652	0.4
Ogle	-0.1	0.1	4.5	10.4	15.8	4.9	6.5	20.9	11.3	37,210	201	4,982	83,732	0.8
Peoria	3.7	D	4.7	22.8	2.6	4.9	D	D	25.5	4,910	230	432	9,627	2.1
Perry	-5.6	0.3	8.1	7.4	D	7.6	8.0	12.4	28.2	3,555	215	120	7,408	1.9
Piatt	20.1	D	5.8	1.9	D	8.9	8.2	10.4	17.9	3,765	237	357	7,993	0.5
Pike	4.3	D	2.7	D	D	2.6	D	D	46.6	1,060	247	99	2,493	0.1
Pope	5.1	0.0	2.0	3.7	D	3.4	D	D	54.9	1,610	287	285	3,165	0.3
Pulaski	6.1	D	D	24.1	D	3.6	4.4	D	10.5	1,430	250	49	3,153	2.6
Putnam	0.3	D	6.2	21.0	D	7.5	3.4	D	25.8	7,105	218	506	13,938	1.7
Randolph	3.5	4.0	4.1	7.9	2.5	6.2	5.4	16.4	16.7	3,885	245	427	7,516	0.0
Richland	0.1	0.4	4.6	11.8	7.4	5.2	4.4	10.6	20.4	31,490	216	2,720	66,171	0.6
Rock Island	0.3	0.1	5.1	6.3	8.9	6.6	4.1	13.8	31.6	49,110	187	8,010	120,201	3.4
St. Clair	2.1	D	9.1	3.6	D	8.0	6.0	15.0	22.0	6,535	269	1,059	11,691	-0.1
Saline	0.4	D	4.9	3.2	9.8	6.2	8.5	20.2	24.5	41,845	212	4,544	91,745	2.1
Sangamon	17.0	D	6.6	4.0	1.3	5.0	D	4.7	31.2	1,635	232	87	3,452	-0.2
Schuyler	16.3	0.0	D	D	D	4.3	D	D	21.6	1,025	203	73	2,457	-0.1
Scott	11.9	D	5.8	15.2	D	5.9	8.8	8.2	14.5	5,420	249	348	10,612	2.1
Shelby	3.2	0.1	13.5	20.0	D	8.4	D	4.2	21.0	1,405	255	87	2,658	-0.6
Stark	-0.7	0.3	12.2	25.7	4.1	5.4	6.9	14.6	15.0	11,915	262	1,127	21,946	-0.6
Stephenson	0.4	0.0	6.5	42.5	3.2	5.5	4.2	5.2	10.6	29,560	221	1,872	59,009	2.6
Tazewell	5.9	D	5.2	6.0	3.0	8.5	4.1	D	29.5	4,625	270	617	7,999	0.9
Union	2.8	D	3.7	21.0	2.5	6.7	4.6	9.8	22.1	18,785	239	2,790	36,071	-0.7
Vermilion	5.0	5.5	10.2	7.2	4.4	7.5	4.6	D	31.4	2,770	241	189	5,564	-0.4
Wabash	6.7	D	3.8	33.4	D	5.5	4.4	D	12.3	3,600	208	299	7,694	0.1
Warren	8.6	0.1	4.5	21.4	2.7	9.6	3.9	D	9.9	3,115	219	150	6,651	1.8
Washington	20.4	6.2	5.0	5.1	2.9	7.3	3.6	D	17.9	4,085	246	299	7,972	0.0
Wayne	11.6	20.1	5.1	4.5	D	9.2	4.7	D	14.2	3,995	284	400	7,171	-0.1
White	-0.9	D	4.2	21.8	4.3	6.7	4.6	6.7	27.7	14,380	254	1,075	25,800	0.1
Whiteside	0.0	0.2	8.8	12.4	6.9	6.6	3.9	10.7	15.2	101,385	147	6,766	243,959	2.7
Will	0.2	D	4.6	11.6	D	7.4	5.9	18.0	25.7	15,335	227	1,609	31,275	3.0
Williamson	0.4	1.8	5.3	9.5	3.5	12.4	4.5	19.9	17.2	20,270	314	3,329	31,131	1.0

1. Per 1,000 resident population estimated as of July 1 of the year shown.

Table B. States and Counties — Professional Services, Manufacturing, and Accommodation and Food Services

STATE County	Professional, scientific, and technical services, 2012				Manufacturing, 2012				Accommodation and food services, 2012			
	Number of establish-ments	Number of employees	Sales (mil dol)	Annual payroll (mil dol)	Number of establishments	Number of employees	Receipts (mil dol)	Annual payroll (mil dol)	Number of establishments	Number of employees	Receipts (mil dol)	Annual payroll (mil dol)
	147	148	149	150	151	152	153	154	155	156	157	158
ILLINOIS— Cont'd												
Hardin	4	D	D	D	NA	NA	NA	NA	9	D	D	D
Henderson	6	29	2.3	0.7	NA	NA	NA	NA	11	D	D	D
Henry	69	289	21.2	7.2	55	4,230	D	155.3	85	D	D	D
Iroquois	33	206	12.6	4.4	30	642	515.2	21.9	60	537	22.5	6.6
Jackson	108	689	68.5	27.1	39	673	178.3	25.8	140	2,927	111.5	31.4
Jasper	10	22	1.9	0.5	12	288	101.6	10.7	15	122	4.4	1.2
Jefferson	76	523	48.4	20.2	32	2,998	D	144.3	81	1,647	71.1	20.9
Jersey	20	146	13.5	6.7	14	62	D	2.2	44	644	26.3	7.4
Jo Daviess	56	250	36.1	12.2	37	1,018	480.2	45.1	108	1,656	73.6	22.5
Johnson	13	259	5.4	2.5	9	36	D	1.7	17	D	D	D
Kane	1,539	9,323	1,603.3	573.6	799	30,327	10,338.7	1,548.3	850	15,058	720.3	207.4
Kankakee	152	735	64.1	24.5	100	4,889	4,842.8	269.7	219	3,675	160.3	47.4
Kendall	199	D	D	D	79	2,298	719.2	108.9	163	2,865	139.4	38.1
Knox	64	307	27.7	11.0	38	D	321.4	36.3	124	1,715	76.3	21.3
Lake	3,052	26,120	3,483.8	2,220.4	846	35,174	12,046.0	1,950.0	1,498	24,702	1,399.2	405.5
LaSalle	166	1,098	120.8	43.7	143	4,665	2,345.6	246.9	318	4,213	188.6	52.3
Lawrence	13	45	4.8	1.2	11	541	D	20.7	22	D	D	D
Lee	38	256	32.0	13.0	36	2,775	1,193.6	117.0	82	722	38.9	8.8
Livingston	55	229	27.4	9.1	60	3,376	1,210.5	166.3	76	855	36.2	9.2
Logan	34	180	16.6	6.4	18	1,034	555.3	46.3	63	853	31.0	9.5
McDonough	44	258	20.2	8.5	20	1,538	420.9	68.9	96	1,599	71.6	17.9
McHenry	898	D	D	D	491	15,508	5,163.2	820.7	558	9,074	435.7	125.5
McLean	363	2,852	280.7	125.2	92	3,881	1,590.2	199.5	379	8,136	393.0	108.7
Macon	157	1,216	142.7	54.0	109	8,240	13,379.3	435.3	225	4,331	189.8	55.6
Macoupin	40	149	15.3	4.3	33	567	D	24.6	89	D	D	D
Madison	549	3,711	748.1	216.0	193	12,308	19,140.5	841.4	582	9,920	431.2	124.6
Marion	60	250	18.1	8.2	42	2,567	710.6	101.5	77	848	38.2	11.1
Marshall	12	24	2.2	0.7	12	888	D	37.1	30	281	7.4	2.4
Mason	9	23	2.5	0.7	12	80	24.6	3.5	41	D	D	D
Massac	9	D	D	D	10	522	D	29.5	28	D	D	D
Menard	15	79	7.2	2.5	5	24	D	1.1	21	231	5.5	1.5
Mercer	11	28	2.5	0.7	12	669	D	25.8	22	D	D	D
Monroe	81	596	89.9	40.9	23	264	D	11.3	63	1,134	43.0	12.7
Montgomery	35	198	17.2	6.6	23	679	313.6	29.4	63	875	37.3	10.8
Morgan	39	642	60.3	29.9	30	1,867	D	82.1	90	1,353	63.7	15.9
Moultrie	16	67	5.9	3.1	36	1,621	533.4	65.0	26	D	D	D
Ogle	68	210	16.0	7.5	62	3,356	1,530.9	146.0	110	1,063	52.9	12.0
Peoria	429	5,236	719.2	311.0	157	7,747	6,197.5	466.3	470	8,372	383.5	109.8
Perry	19	52	4.9	1.4	19	412	D	19.0	37	492	15.5	4.8
Piatt	28	96	8.5	3.7	13	183	D	7.0	31	D	D	D
Pike	17	73	8.0	2.2	19	143	62.4	6.2	37	350	14.0	3.6
Pope	5	D	D	D	NA	NA	NA	NA	5	9	0.6	0.1
Pulaski	1	D	D	D	NA	NA	NA	NA	6	D	D	D
Putnam	5	20	1.7	0.6	8	440	D	16.8	14	69	2.5	0.5
Randolph	36	227	24.2	8.3	28	2,902	609.3	77.6	64	806	29.6	8.5
Richland	25	135	50.1	9.9	28	438	143.5	17.2	36	D	D	D
Rock Island	291	2,847	667.4	163.6	153	8,245	6,845.4	451.8	342	5,592	344.4	75.6
St. Clair	511	5,662	870.2	364.7	158	4,922	2,779.9	241.6	561	10,416	589.3	155.9
Saline	39	160	16.3	5.5	24	348	D	11.5	47	776	37.2	8.3
Sangamon	527	4,381	549.2	224.9	109	2,834	D	139.1	523	9,447	439.2	129.0
Schuyler	7	23	2.4	0.7	6	95	D	2.4	12	D	D	D
Scott	3	9	1.1	0.3	4	163	D	6.8	11	56	2.7	0.6
Shelby	21	184	21.6	8.5	21	1,042	D	45.2	41	375	14.2	4.0
Stark	8	66	5.0	1.9	7	248	D	11.5	3	6	0.3	0.1
Stephenson	81	454	55.4	19.6	62	3,037	1,145.2	155.4	89	1,033	47.6	12.0
Tazewell	180	1,187	118.5	52.8	110	8,215	5,850.3	443.8	306	6,143	358.5	92.3
Union	19	80	6.7	2.9	12	164	D	5.4	30	D	D	D
Vermilion	84	428	46.7	16.6	96	5,168	2,353.2	256.1	143	2,161	86.0	25.4
Wabash	22	140	14.2	5.7	9	188	43.3	8.9	21	296	11.8	3.5
Warren	20	85	8.1	2.2	17	1,803	632.7	71.2	36	481	20.6	5.4
Washington	22	105	12.2	3.9	14	D	445.6	D	30	D	D	D
Wayne	21	58	4.2	1.4	16	607	D	24.6	22	D	D	D
White	19	71	6.0	1.8	12	304	D	10.6	26	D	D	D
Whiteside	81	341	36.1	12.6	88	3,955	1,453.2	198.3	124	1,589	66.5	18.6
Will	1,586	D	D	D	588	20,377	20,627.2	1,191.0	1,108	20,582	1,313.5	320.8
Williamson	121	636	65.4	21.4	42	1,748	793.0	78.5	148	2,724	123.7	35.4

Table B. States and Counties — Health Care and Social Assistance, Other Services, Nonemployer Businesses, and Residential Construction

STATE County	Health care and social assistance, 2012				Other services, 2012				Nonemployer businesses, 2015		Value of residential construction authorized by building permits, 2017	
	Number of establish-ments	Number of employees	Receipts (mil dol)	Annual payroll (mil dol)	Number of establis-hments	Number of employees	Receipts (mil dol)	Annual payroll (mil dol)	Number	Receipts (mil dol)	New construction ($1,000)	Number of housing units
	159	160	161	162	163	164	165	166	167	168	169	170
ILLINOIS— Cont'd												
Hardin	12	252	18.3	7.9	3	3	0.3	0.1	220	5.2	0	0
Henderson	8	153	7.3	3.4	7	D	D	D	393	16.2	152	2
Henry	88	1,640	123.4	49.0	97	380	31.0	8.7	2,781	93.0	6,778	33
Iroquois	66	1,588	105.2	44.6	48	148	19.7	3.2	1,980	70.8	4,686	28
Jackson	167	3,463	517.9	159.6	93	396	41.7	8.4	3,224	110.3	1,656	12
Jasper	14	143	6.6	2.2	19	61	5.6	1.0	813	27.4	150	1
Jefferson	146	3,518	391.1	145.4	82	416	43.0	11.2	2,275	87.7	4,782	48
Jersey	48	D	D	D	35	109	8.5	2.3	1,256	38.8	4,776	30
Jo Daviess	41	656	43.1	17.8	57	247	22.8	6.0	1,958	76.6	8,955	37
Johnson	19	209	12.6	4.7	10	D	D	D	765	23.7	0	0
Kane	1,153	21,559	2,406.9	968.7	821	5,885	596.9	169.7	33,140	1,449.5	296,771	1986
Kankakee	311	7,349	753.9	294.5	180	956	100.3	25.1	6,193	214.8	32,539	198
Kendall	177	D	D	D	164	795	73.6	21.5	8,000	306.9	61,112	299
Knox	122	3,696	338.7	125.8	77	562	125.9	15.1	2,330	71.1	4,458	24
Lake	1,949	33,669	4,026.3	1,549.4	1,276	7,626	728.2	224.2	53,924	3,000.8	362,138	1713
LaSalle	284	5,993	448.1	188.7	237	1,205	109.6	31.7	5,888	199.6	21,171	103
Lawrence	23	617	30.3	13.5	22	111	11.0	3.5	806	27.9	8,798	51
Lee	80	2,137	166.8	72.1	60	345	33.1	9.5	1,893	66.0	6,075	26
Livingston	74	2,090	144.5	62.4	66	334	29.3	8.3	1,900	60.1	8,418	40
Logan	58	1,330	111.3	41.5	54	206	15.9	4.2	1,405	46.5	1,460	7
McDonough	71	1,768	138.8	58.5	65	D	D	D	1,494	49.6	99	1
McHenry	718	D	D	D	634	3,300	260.3	77.6	22,100	957.8	89,141	486
McLean	371	8,547	969.7	368.4	259	2,311	212.2	74.8	9,529	395.8	49,453	370
Macon	291	8,193	886.2	332.1	176	1,170	239.1	37.3	5,713	183.7	8,271	39
Macoupin	91	1,920	115.8	48.0	85	318	25.5	6.3	2,574	93.1	14,103	69
Madison	677	13,914	1,194.9	486.2	456	2,888	272.1	79.6	14,373	550.9	107,047	449
Marion	113	3,009	249.3	94.0	73	268	21.7	5.6	2,150	71.5	1,300	13
Marshall	19	468	22.1	9.5	15	D	D	D	616	22.7	2,611	9
Mason	26	506	36.7	16.5	27	90	6.8	1.6	710	27.7	844	4
Massac	26	755	53.8	24.4	21	65	7.9	1.8	843	25.7	530	21
Menard	12	75	6.3	2.1	16	64	5.6	1.3	785	23.7	3,610	21
Mercer	24	344	23.5	9.3	16	64	5.9	1.6	903	29.5	2,290	8
Monroe	79	846	57.1	24.2	71	407	25.0	9.6	2,135	86.2	47,503	213
Montgomery	73	D	D	D	57	233	20.8	5.6	1,580	51.0	4,657	18
Morgan	121	D	D	D	64	260	18.4	4.8	1,949	69.5	528	5
Moultrie	32	735	36.2	16.8	17	D	D	D	1,032	35.9	4,642	55
Ogle	82	1,505	103.9	41.0	75	343	36.6	10.3	3,352	117.0	13,634	71
Peoria	516	22,518	2,665.0	1,057.0	304	4,714	449.2	206.3	9,715	367.7	10,740	46
Perry	45	890	63.7	25.9	46	161	11.9	3.1	1,059	28.8	6,561	31
Piatt	21	D	D	D	18	D	D	D	1,145	41.9	8,757	38
Pike	25	586	49.0	18.0	26	109	12.8	3.2	1,073	40.7	3,121	21
Pope	11	D	D	D	3	D	D	D	226	6.3	0	0
Pulaski	14	151	6.8	2.6	14	43	3.6	0.9	302	9.0	900	9
Putnam	4	18	1.5	0.6	4	D	D	D	368	15.6	2,006	15
Randolph	73	2,170	260.4	123.7	61	266	28.4	8.6	1,436	44.9	6,607	31
Richland	50	1,014	71.7	31.3	40	162	17.2	4.0	1,159	40.1	526	3
Rock Island	416	8,883	802.3	345.0	265	1,600	138.9	43.0	6,816	264.8	19,777	116
St. Clair	595	15,933	1,363.8	594.9	387	2,528	213.0	73.6	14,301	467.3	121,592	538
Saline	78	1,808	143.9	60.3	47	172	22.0	4.0	1,542	58.7	0	0
Sangamon	445	20,510	2,559.6	892.3	474	3,319	416.7	124.8	12,205	472.0	63,637	301
Schuyler	14	323	28.2	10.7	12	D	D	D	478	14.4	0	0
Scott	4	D	D	D	4	10	1.4	0.3	304	8.1	NA	NA
Shelby	33	674	42.3	18.7	32	93	11.9	2.5	1,311	42.4	7,498	26
Stark	8	167	8.9	3.7	4	D	D	D	335	14.0	1,403	8
Stephenson	104	2,545	329.3	92.9	95	642	46.2	16.0	2,866	96.7	2,701	14
Tazewell	246	5,435	388.8	155.2	242	1,270	113.7	37.2	6,471	239.7	30,246	123
Union	52	1,215	72.6	30.4	22	80	7.1	2.1	1,066	38.2	2,547	17
Vermilion	143	4,736	514.4	235.4	121	540	47.4	13.3	4,239	136.9	13,889	104
Wabash	26	832	62.0	22.6	22	94	6.5	1.5	799	27.7	364	4
Warren	37	694	48.6	19.5	31	115	11.8	2.2	892	31.3	1,237	8
Washington	26	616	39.9	15.4	27	61	7.0	1.3	938	34.1	4,868	23
Wayne	32	799	53.9	22.2	27	113	14.4	3.2	1,232	45.8	510	8
White	43	638	36.5	14.9	33	160	16.2	4.7	1,109	45.9	847	4
Whiteside	99	3,068	261.2	99.1	109	608	54.1	13.5	2,810	102.1	11,749	67
Will	1,406	24,364	2,467.6	967.5	1,053	6,884	681.5	195.1	46,617	2,042.4	336,007	1387
Williamson	204	5,977	677.0	251.1	93	519	52.4	14.1	4,230	155.0	15,142	118

Table B. States and Counties — Government Employment and Payroll, and Local Government Finances

STATE County	Full-time equivalent employees	March payroll (dollars)	Administration, judicial, and legal	Police and corrections	Fire protection	Highways and transportation	Health and welfare	Natural resources and utilities	Education and libraries	Total (mil dol)	Intergovernmental (mil dol)	Total (mil dol)	Per capita[1] (dollars) Total	Per capita[1] (dollars) Property
			March payroll (percent of total)									Taxes		
	171	172	173	174	175	176	177	178	179	180	181	182	183	184
ILLINOIS— Cont'd														
Hardin	285	791,768	2.8	3.0	0.0	56.6	0.9	4.7	31.7	16.6	13.4	1.6	384	331
Henderson	266	806,748	8.3	7.3	0.3	7.4	10.9	2.4	62.8	21.4	9.7	7.4	1,047	1030
Henry	1,997	6,801,070	4.9	8.8	1.9	3.9	16.2	5.8	57.8	199.6	66.8	68.8	1,372	1289
Iroquois	1,017	3,877,441	5.9	6.3	0.5	4.2	0.4	1.9	79.8	90.3	38.3	39.1	1,337	1242
Jackson	2,101	6,263,626	8.2	10.9	3.5	4.0	8.7	8.4	55.9	187.5	83.7	70.9	1,181	879
Jasper	379	1,198,050	10.1	7.5	0.4	7.8	10.7	3.7	59.8	34.3	16.7	13.8	1,437	1424
Jefferson	1,638	5,345,187	5.0	7.6	2.9	4.0	1.2	3.6	74.9	147.2	83.4	43.3	1,119	882
Jersey	837	3,076,248	4.5	7.9	0.3	2.8	30.8	3.6	48.9	78.3	24.9	21.1	926	828
Jo Daviess	997	3,300,597	8.1	8.4	0.4	5.4	17.9	2.0	56.6	94.9	21.9	52.5	2,329	2191
Johnson	372	1,081,737	6.4	5.0	0.0	5.0	0.2	4.9	77.4	26.5	15.8	7.0	547	545
Kane	21,805	101,252,430	5.2	10.1	5.2	2.0	0.9	6.8	68.3	2,745.0	798.1	1,591.7	3,046	2837
Kankakee	4,413	16,356,166	7.8	13.5	3.6	3.7	1.5	3.4	65.4	441.9	208.0	169.2	1,496	1433
Kendall	3,451	14,665,867	5.1	10.4	5.3	1.3	0.8	4.9	71.6	446.4	125.8	268.8	2,276	2192
Knox	2,362	8,240,583	5.2	9.0	3.0	3.3	7.4	6.1	64.9	191.6	87.1	68.2	1,306	1155
Lake	27,930	134,406,176	5.8	8.4	4.0	2.3	3.7	6.6	68.5	3,687.1	912.8	2,300.4	3,276	3089
LaSalle	4,146	16,025,437	6.1	10.7	2.6	3.3	2.5	3.9	69.6	433.1	147.6	217.8	1,928	1756
Lawrence	525	1,443,702	5.9	7.2	0.3	7.5	2.8	3.7	71.9	44.1	29.2	8.7	523	515
Lee	1,249	4,093,940	7.1	9.2	4.8	4.5	2.0	3.9	68.0	116.7	37.8	58.8	1,677	1531
Livingston	1,564	5,591,107	6.4	8.8	1.4	4.2	3.1	3.6	72.0	146.1	52.6	67.2	1,738	1641
Logan	897	2,996,965	7.7	10.0	3.8	5.0	4.3	2.9	65.3	74.1	29.9	31.4	1,045	1003
McDonough	1,625	5,796,187	4.2	7.7	1.7	2.8	51.0	3.4	28.6	163.5	47.6	32.0	983	944
McHenry	11,260	47,454,823	5.9	10.6	5.0	2.9	2.6	5.6	65.8	1,313.1	295.8	821.5	2,666	2473
McLean	6,296	24,583,518	6.5	10.3	4.7	4.3	5.2	5.3	61.6	657.7	182.2	354.7	2,059	1702
Macon	4,204	17,133,160	5.9	11.8	4.5	3.0	2.0	8.2	63.3	407.1	180.7	163.9	1,488	1260
Macoupin	1,579	5,464,855	7.7	8.5	0.5	3.9	2.1	5.6	71.2	159.2	103.8	40.1	850	818
Madison	8,550	34,777,691	7.6	11.4	3.9	3.8	1.5	6.9	63.4	966.9	418.8	400.7	1,496	1338
Marion	1,941	6,738,024	6.0	6.5	2.0	6.9	1.1	4.0	73.0	188.6	94.3	42.9	1,104	1038
Marshall	389	1,147,988	11.1	7.9	0.1	5.9	0.0	3.3	70.7	32.3	9.0	19.1	1,547	1484
Mason	923	2,905,218	5.6	6.6	1.1	4.1	31.2	2.1	49.0	70.8	24.6	21.1	1,473	1402
Massac	642	2,312,058	4.9	5.8	3.7	5.1	27.2	5.6	47.5	66.0	26.3	12.5	822	786
Menard	629	1,816,714	5.1	6.6	0.0	3.4	18.6	6.4	58.9	48.9	20.5	18.4	1,447	1400
Mercer	808	2,500,408	4.4	7.5	0.1	4.2	27.9	2.7	52.0	60.4	20.7	22.0	1,356	1324
Monroe	1,183	4,219,452	6.0	6.8	0.1	3.0	9.8	5.0	68.2	102.0	27.3	50.1	1,503	1423
Montgomery	1,039	3,506,922	6.9	10.8	2.5	5.7	5.0	6.3	61.4	82.3	39.4	28.5	963	919
Morgan	1,212	4,876,454	5.8	9.2	2.8	3.7	1.9	5.1	70.1	101.9	48.0	40.0	1,135	1038
Moultrie	521	1,796,777	7.8	7.6	2.7	4.3	1.3	9.1	66.3	36.7	14.6	17.0	1,135	1079
Ogle	2,397	8,623,161	5.6	8.6	3.0	3.7	0.9	6.5	71.3	242.2	66.1	126.2	2,388	2325
Peoria	6,795	26,829,973	7.0	12.3	5.0	5.9	4.2	8.9	54.4	819.7	356.0	319.4	1,706	1383
Perry	777	2,700,659	4.7	8.5	1.5	3.8	27.6	5.4	47.3	84.4	42.3	13.8	627	594
Piatt	763	2,418,221	6.8	10.0	0.5	5.3	14.9	3.4	57.7	66.5	26.6	26.9	1,631	1599
Pike	558	1,854,503	4.9	7.2	0.0	8.0	4.7	8.8	66.1	46.6	23.4	15.2	932	910
Pope	138	448,003	20.0	12.1	0.0	2.4	0.2	11.1	54.2	9.3	5.8	2.3	545	536
Pulaski	327	899,884	7.1	8.9	0.0	20.1	0.0	3.3	59.6	25.7	17.3	2.4	395	366
Putnam	225	602,290	16.8	7.7	4.2	6.1	0.0	5.9	58.5	21.9	11.9	8.0	1,357	1315
Randolph	1,307	4,546,917	4.9	6.9	0.2	2.7	38.8	4.6	41.3	133.8	44.5	27.5	833	774
Richland	975	3,144,076	4.3	4.3	0.6	2.4	0.2	3.1	84.3	57.1	27.3	13.0	807	742
Rock Island	5,596	23,551,782	5.9	9.4	3.6	6.1	4.6	7.6	61.4	620.9	245.3	250.9	1,701	1489
St. Clair	9,810	39,541,919	4.8	9.2	1.9	2.6	2.2	3.8	73.7	1,194.0	627.0	382.0	1,421	1216
Saline	1,108	4,428,993	4.7	6.7	0.9	2.6	0.3	6.0	77.8	90.8	50.3	23.2	930	837
Sangamon	8,380	36,468,884	5.0	9.4	3.8	4.6	1.2	19.7	56.0	774.9	316.2	329.5	1,654	1429
Schuyler	476	1,475,450	5.3	4.7	0.2	4.4	42.6	3.1	38.9	44.3	11.9	8.0	1,069	1046
Scott	279	678,856	8.7	3.5	0.5	4.1	18.9	5.6	57.3	16.8	8.0	4.6	873	829
Shelby	598	1,947,657	9.5	8.9	1.8	7.6	2.8	6.4	62.1	47.8	23.5	17.9	808	790
Stark	247	745,997	7.9	3.6	5.2	4.9	5.8	1.4	71.0	24.8	11.5	10.9	1,837	1825
Stephenson	2,084	7,077,197	4.5	9.2	3.6	2.9	5.4	4.5	68.9	190.9	85.0	73.4	1,563	1449
Tazewell	4,864	18,067,473	5.1	9.0	3.1	2.4	2.6	4.8	70.8	521.3	190.4	225.1	1,655	1450
Union	758	2,771,148	9.5	6.1	0.8	5.1	0.0	5.2	72.8	60.0	30.9	17.9	1,015	992
Vermilion	3,642	12,242,579	7.0	7.8	2.7	3.5	3.6	4.2	67.9	289.5	151.8	91.4	1,132	940
Wabash	629	2,227,140	2.9	4.6	1.3	1.8	48.4	3.1	37.5	63.3	16.1	9.7	830	795
Warren	522	1,914,920	7.4	10.5	4.1	3.6	0.2	4.0	69.9	49.1	22.4	18.5	1,044	1001
Washington	568	1,952,729	6.8	5.6	0.6	5.3	31.1	4.1	46.3	61.8	13.6	15.4	1,056	1044
Wayne	680	1,956,742	7.1	7.6	1.1	3.6	2.2	8.9	66.5	46.0	28.5	12.0	724	652
White	705	2,274,585	7.3	7.6	0.6	4.7	1.6	8.1	69.3	49.9	30.9	10.9	747	707
Whiteside	3,387	13,850,341	3.2	4.6	1.2	1.9	52.6	3.0	32.7	404.5	98.0	74.4	1,287	1222
Will	22,376	101,738,743	4.7	11.4	5.8	2.2	2.7	5.6	66.5	2,654.5	767.6	1,489.2	2,182	2004
Williamson	2,123	8,108,041	5.1	8.0	3.0	3.7	0.5	5.2	72.9	224.1	117.2	75.8	1,137	974

1. Based on the resident population estimated as of July 1 of the year shown.

Table B. States and Counties — Local Government Finances, Government Employment, and Income Taxes

STATE County	Total (mil dol)	Per capita[1] (dollars)	Education	Health and hospitals	Police protection	Public welfare	Highways	Total (mil dol)	Per capita[1] (dollars)	Federal civilian	Federal military	State and local	Number of returns	Mean adjusted gross income	Mean income tax
			Percent of total for:					Debt outstanding		Government employment, 2016			Individual income tax returns, 2015		
	185	186	187	188	189	190	191	192	193	194	195	196	197	198	199
ILLINOIS— Cont'd															
Hardin	9.4	2,219	53.6	4.3	2.9	0.3	6.9	3.9	917	0	0	212	1,520	46,138	4838
Henderson	23.7	3,370	36.9	8.9	3.5	0.0	12.3	3.3	465	34	14	332	3,290	47,733	4919
Henry	218.5	4,357	39.3	20.6	5.2	2.4	5.6	98.2	1,957	119	99	3,542	24,060	58,364	6821
Iroquois	91.6	3,132	53.4	3.1	3.5	0.1	7.9	32.1	1,098	96	57	1,592	13,690	50,497	5490
Jackson	186.2	3,100	49.6	4.1	7.0	4.9	4.5	96.1	1,600	152	126	11,416	23,150	48,674	5515
Jasper	35.9	3,739	55.0	4.2	2.9	0.1	13.9	9.9	1,031	37	19	533	4,610	49,880	4804
Jefferson	141.2	3,647	60.3	0.7	5.4	0.0	6.2	65.0	1,679	142	74	2,188	16,750	48,401	5088
Jersey	88.3	3,885	32.7	37.7	3.8	0.1	7.5	73.1	3,212	42	43	1,133	10,100	52,864	5446
Jo Daviess	84.9	3,767	44.0	15.8	6.1	0.0	11.0	34.5	1,528	65	44	1,349	13,100	48,794	5452
Johnson	27.3	2,141	60.1	1.3	4.1	0.1	8.6	19.6	1,535	68	23	775	5,000	49,063	4515
Kane	2,646.1	5,064	55.1	0.4	6.5	0.1	5.6	4,427.4	8,474	1,660	1,075	29,696	245,900	71,973	9817
Kankakee	442.3	3,912	52.1	0.7	6.1	0.1	5.9	327.2	2,894	238	214	5,758	50,580	53,622	5762
Kendall	434.1	3,676	60.8	0.5	5.2	0.9	3.7	902.1	7,638	113	255	5,863	57,050	70,392	8087
Knox	198.6	3,801	51.6	1.5	5.0	4.2	8.6	156.9	3,002	164	96	3,135	23,240	49,719	5413
Lake	3,519.2	5,012	56.6	2.1	5.9	0.6	4.2	3,079.5	4,386	5,375	12,066	36,867	345,220	111,065	21,082
LaSalle	473.9	4,195	57.8	1.3	5.1	1.1	6.6	284.6	2,520	357	220	5,989	54,290	53,881	6175
Lawrence	51.2	3,083	63.6	1.4	3.9	0.1	9.0	34.7	2,091	45	28	822	6,350	46,089	4445
Lee	113.4	3,238	58.0	1.7	5.2	0.1	7.1	71.5	2,040	85	65	1,826	16,260	53,685	6056
Livingston	169.3	4,381	47.9	3.0	3.8	0.2	5.0	65.3	1,689	105	69	2,291	17,060	54,934	6050
Logan	71.3	2,376	51.1	5.0	5.4	0.1	7.6	26.9	895	98	52	1,384	12,570	52,197	5414
McDonough	169.8	5,218	27.4	39.5	3.7	3.4	9.6	21.4	657	97	62	5,362	12,260	49,104	5137
McHenry	1,256.5	4,078	49.3	2.2	6.5	1.2	7.2	1,209.9	3,926	480	625	14,748	154,590	73,381	9762
McLean	663.9	3,853	46.3	1.2	4.8	1.3	5.4	781.5	4,536	453	337	14,764	77,850	70,047	9291
Macon	452.8	4,112	52.8	2.0	7.8	0.1	8.1	462.5	4,200	323	218	5,330	49,070	55,299	6619
Macoupin	129.5	2,741	63.8	2.0	7.1	0.2	7.8	66.0	1,397	118	92	2,198	21,030	51,985	5437
Madison	939.6	3,507	50.9	0.8	6.8	1.6	6.8	839.9	3,135	568	541	15,669	125,400	59,623	7154
Marion	186.5	4,794	59.6	11.4	3.2	0.2	3.5	110.6	2,844	114	76	2,068	17,900	45,584	4402
Marshall	33.3	2,698	45.3	2.0	5.5	0.1	16.2	9.4	759	36	24	450	6,020	53,005	5788
Mason	72.0	5,027	41.2	33.1	3.0	0.0	4.5	27.4	1,914	62	27	1,078	6,340	49,727	5274
Massac	63.9	4,197	33.1	34.0	4.6	0.0	6.8	35.3	2,315	45	29	904	6,360	45,916	4224
Menard	46.5	3,652	52.7	4.5	4.3	13.7	7.4	27.0	2,121	30	25	659	6,140	62,081	6983
Mercer	59.7	3,679	42.8	21.8	3.5	0.1	6.2	15.9	978	56	32	719	7,810	55,991	6002
Monroe	99.7	2,990	44.6	3.1	5.8	10.1	10.9	136.3	4,085	72	69	1,433	16,830	75,000	9728
Montgomery	84.4	2,851	51.5	3.4	7.1	0.1	10.4	52.7	1,779	105	54	1,469	12,570	51,838	5438
Morgan	103.7	2,940	52.8	1.6	5.8	3.3	9.0	36.7	1,040	83	64	2,254	15,710	52,468	5859
Moultrie	39.7	2,658	46.1	1.8	4.8	0.0	9.9	11.4	763	28	30	492	6,710	56,789	6841
Ogle	280.5	5,307	64.6	0.8	3.1	0.0	5.5	269.6	5,101	114	104	2,906	25,220	56,255	6165
Peoria	776.9	4,149	41.7	1.1	6.6	3.2	6.5	850.1	4,540	1,639	440	9,315	88,910	66,485	9149
Perry	91.6	4,151	51.3	22.3	3.7	0.2	4.4	32.0	1,453	47	39	1,271	8,860	46,401	4234
Piatt	65.0	3,940	47.2	2.6	3.6	12.4	9.9	36.4	2,205	40	34	967	8,080	64,471	7796
Pike	48.7	2,986	53.6	6.0	6.0	0.3	9.7	27.7	1,701	55	31	866	6,960	44,881	4518
Pope	9.6	2,241	48.1	0.0	2.7	0.0	16.4	0.3	64	71	0	190	1,570	44,766	4066
Pulaski	23.9	3,981	59.8	1.8	6.4	0.3	6.2	12.7	2,118	64	11	834	2,350	41,256	3311
Putnam	21.7	3,688	43.8	2.5	4.8	0.3	13.3	3.0	508	13	11	309	2,940	58,201	6548
Randolph	140.7	4,269	35.0	36.0	4.5	2.8	6.9	54.6	1,657	88	57	2,435	13,680	51,097	5221
Richland	75.7	4,677	78.3	0.4	3.6	0.1	5.2	28.2	1,746	52	32	926	7,500	46,630	4376
Rock Island	636.7	4,318	45.3	1.1	6.6	3.0	5.2	418.1	2,835	4,989	702	7,621	70,640	53,403	6071
St. Clair	1,159.8	4,314	54.3	1.3	5.1	0.1	4.2	908.3	3,378	6,024	4,890	12,903	121,150	57,661	6898
Saline	95.1	3,814	54.7	1.0	5.6	0.6	5.5	54.8	2,197	98	48	1,811	10,340	48,638	5069
Sangamon	823.4	4,132	52.9	1.4	7.6	0.2	4.4	2,513.3	12,612	1,800	445	18,178	99,740	64,062	8430
Schuyler	47.2	6,325	29.5	48.7	2.2	0.1	10.2	10.5	1,403	23	13	662	3,130	50,330	5174
Scott	17.4	3,281	46.2	2.2	3.3	13.9	8.8	6.2	1,174	16	10	318	2,420	50,879	4962
Shelby	50.5	2,273	53.6	3.0	5.5	0.1	12.8	14.9	670	96	44	783	10,170	49,799	4774
Stark	18.9	3,183	55.8	0.5	5.0	0.5	11.8	11.4	1,922	24	12	314	2,660	53,488	5969
Stephenson	184.9	3,937	57.2	2.4	4.7	3.3	6.3	98.3	2,092	127	92	2,651	22,200	48,445	5009
Tazewell	547.5	4,028	52.3	1.6	5.5	0.1	6.4	349.0	2,567	517	269	7,273	64,240	62,714	7560
Union	60.8	3,445	72.9	2.7	4.1	0.0	5.3	53.7	3,042	60	34	1,112	7,720	48,697	4917
Vermilion	308.3	3,819	56.4	0.7	6.4	3.5	6.3	102.1	1,265	1,517	154	4,274	34,040	45,644	4494
Wabash	60.5	5,156	29.5	47.7	4.0	0.5	5.0	14.7	1,254	22	23	1,046	5,230	55,604	6447
Warren	53.0	2,987	53.6	0.4	5.3	0.0	6.7	45.8	2,584	67	33	851	7,970	48,314	4899
Washington	72.8	4,985	42.5	34.2	2.5	0.1	6.1	55.0	3,766	49	28	813	7,100	55,981	6385
Wayne	47.3	2,854	59.1	1.9	4.8	0.1	9.4	21.3	1,285	55	33	943	7,360	47,037	4355
White	56.9	3,908	63.4	1.7	4.0	0.1	9.2	23.5	1,610	49	28	821	6,360	51,479	5466
Whiteside	392.0	6,777	27.5	52.5	2.6	0.2	2.3	129.8	2,244	162	114	4,779	28,020	50,381	5376
Will	2,568.4	3,763	52.2	1.6	6.9	0.8	5.1	3,781.8	5,541	1,010	1,406	33,297	331,460	71,829	9339
Williamson	279.8	4,196	65.4	0.0	3.9	0.1	4.9	229.8	3,447	1,681	134	4,127	30,090	51,933	5734

1. Based on the resident population estimated as of July 1 of the year shown.

Table B. States and Counties — Land Area and Population

State / county code	CBSA code[1]	County code[2]	STATE County	Land area[3] (sq. mi)	Total persons 2017	Rank	Per square mile	White	Black	American Indian, Alaska Native	Asian and Pacific Islander	Percent Hispanic or Latino[4]	Under 5 years	5 to 17 years	18 to 24 years	25 to 34 years	35 to 44 years	45 to 54 years
				1	2	3	4	5	6	7	8	9	10	11	12	13	14	15
			ILLINOIS— Cont'd															
1,7201	40,420	2	Winnebago	513.4	284,778	243	554.7	71.4	14.1	0.6	3.4	12.8	6.3	17.2	8.2	12.6	11.7	13.2
1,7203	37,900	2	Woodford	527.8	38,726	1,210	73.4	96.4	1.3	0.5	1.1	1.9	5.9	18.5	8.4	10.8	12.1	12.8
1,8000		0	INDIANA	35,825.6	6,666,818	X	186.1	80.9	10.5	0.7	2.8	7.0	6.3	17.3	9.9	13.0	12.3	12.8
1,8001	19,540	6	Adams	339.0	35,491	1,289	104.7	94.5	0.9	0.4	0.5	4.5	9.4	21.8	8.6	11.5	10.6	11.1
1,8003	23,060	2	Allen	657.3	372,877	188	567.3	76.4	13.4	0.8	4.7	7.5	7.1	18.8	9.0	13.8	12.3	12.4
1,8005	18,020	3	Bartholomew	406.9	82,040	689	201.6	83.8	2.9	0.6	7.6	6.7	6.6	17.2	8.0	14.5	12.4	12.9
1,8007	29,200	3	Benton	406.4	8,613	2,534	21.2	93.5	1.3	0.6	0.6	5.3	6.4	18.5	7.5	11.0	11.7	13.2
1,8009		6	Blackford	165.1	11,976	2,296	72.5	97.2	1.3	0.8	0.6	1.6	5.5	16.3	7.6	11.0	10.6	13.2
1,8011	26,900	1	Boone	422.9	65,875	812	155.8	92.1	2.4	0.6	3.4	3.0	6.8	19.8	7.8	11.9	13.7	14.3
1,8013	26,900	1	Brown	312.0	15,035	2,094	48.2	96.9	0.9	1.0	0.7	1.7	3.9	14.4	6.5	9.1	10.3	14.5
1,8015	29,200	3	Carroll	372.2	20,039	1,825	53.8	94.9	1.0	0.6	0.3	4.2	5.4	16.9	7.6	10.9	11.8	13.3
1,8017	30,900	4	Cass	412.2	37,994	1,225	92.2	80.7	2.1	0.7	2.1	15.6	6.4	16.8	8.3	11.5	12.3	13.3
1,8019	31,140	1	Clark	372.8	116,973	529	313.8	85.5	9.2	0.7	1.6	5.4	6.4	16.3	7.8	13.8	13.4	13.6
1,8021	45,460	3	Clay	357.6	26,198	1,558	73.3	97.3	1.2	0.7	0.6	1.4	6.2	16.8	7.7	12.1	12.2	13.1
1,8023	23,140	6	Clinton	405.1	32,317	1,373	79.8	82.8	0.9	0.4	0.5	16.1	7.1	19.3	8.0	11.9	11.7	12.4
1,8025		8	Crawford	305.6	10,566	2,388	34.6	97.2	0.9	1.0	0.6	1.6	5.3	16.6	7.0	10.7	11.8	13.5
1,8027	47,780	7	Daviess	429.5	33,113	1,353	77.1	92.5	2.4	0.5	0.6	5.0	8.1	21.1	8.3	12.6	11.2	11.3
1,8029	17,140	1	Dearborn	305.1	49,741	991	163.0	97.4	1.1	0.5	0.7	1.2	5.3	17.4	7.9	11.0	12.0	14.4
1,8031	24,700	6	Decatur	372.6	26,737	1,536	71.8	95.6	0.9	0.5	1.9	2.0	6.5	17.9	8.2	12.0	11.9	13.3
1,8033	12,140	4	DeKalb	362.8	42,836	1,118	118.1	96.0	0.9	0.6	0.8	2.8	6.3	17.9	8.4	12.3	11.9	13.5
1,8035	34,620	3	Delaware	392.1	115,184	536	293.8	88.7	8.3	0.7	1.9	2.5	5.1	13.5	19.3	11.5	10.0	11.7
1,8037	27,540	5	Dubois	427.3	42,558	1,123	99.6	91.0	0.8	0.4	0.7	7.6	6.6	17.6	8.2	11.1	11.5	13.4
1,8039	21,140	3	Elkhart	463.2	205,032	323	442.6	76.8	7.0	0.7	1.5	16.0	7.6	20.1	8.9	12.7	12.1	12.4
1,8041	18,220	6	Fayette	215.0	23,209	1,671	107.9	96.8	2.0	0.7	0.6	1.1	5.3	16.7	7.6	10.6	12.3	13.6
1,8043	31,140	1	Floyd	148.0	77,071	719	520.8	89.9	6.7	0.7	1.6	3.3	5.8	17.0	8.3	12.5	12.5	13.8
1,8045		6	Fountain	395.7	16,505	2,009	41.7	96.4	0.8	0.8	0.7	2.5	6.0	16.4	7.8	11.1	10.7	13.9
1,8047		6	Franklin	384.4	22,619	1,698	58.8	97.5	0.6	0.5	1.1	1.1	5.5	17.5	8.0	10.2	11.9	14.1
1,8049		7	Fulton	368.4	20,059	1,824	54.4	92.9	1.4	0.9	0.8	5.3	6.2	17.6	7.6	11.0	11.6	12.5
1,8051		6	Gibson	487.5	33,576	1,338	68.9	95.5	3.2	0.7	0.8	1.6	6.2	17.2	8.1	12.0	11.9	13.4
1,8053	31,980	4	Grant	414.1	66,491	803	160.6	87.2	8.7	0.8	1.3	4.4	5.6	15.3	12.9	10.8	10.4	12.4
1,8055		6	Greene	542.5	32,177	1,375	59.3	97.5	0.6	0.8	0.6	1.5	5.4	16.7	7.4	10.9	11.7	14.2
1,8057	26,900	1	Hamilton	394.3	323,747	213	821.1	85.5	4.9	0.4	7.0	4.1	6.7	20.7	7.6	11.9	14.9	14.9
1,8059	26,900	1	Hancock	306.0	74,985	739	245.0	93.8	3.2	0.6	1.3	2.4	5.9	17.7	7.8	11.8	13.0	14.5
1,8061	31,140	1	Harrison	484.5	39,898	1,177	82.3	96.8	1.1	0.7	0.8	1.8	5.9	16.6	7.1	11.8	12.3	14.2
1,8063	26,900	1	Hendricks	406.9	163,685	397	402.3	86.3	7.7	0.5	3.5	3.9	6.0	19.5	7.9	12.4	14.4	14.1
1,8065	35,220	4	Henry	391.9	48,476	1,013	123.7	94.8	3.3	0.6	0.7	1.9	5.1	15.5	7.9	12.2	12.3	14.2
1,8067	29,020	3	Howard	293.0	82,363	688	281.1	87.8	8.9	0.9	1.6	3.4	6.2	16.5	8.2	11.8	11.4	12.9
1,8069	26,540	6	Huntington	382.6	36,337	1,266	95.0	95.8	1.2	0.9	0.9	2.4	5.7	16.0	10.0	12.0	11.7	12.9
1,8071	42,980	4	Jackson	509.3	43,884	1,095	86.2	89.6	1.5	0.8	2.4	6.9	6.7	17.8	7.6	12.3	13.1	13.2
1,8073	16,980	1	Jasper	559.6	33,447	1,342	59.8	92.5	1.2	0.6	0.7	6.0	5.7	17.8	9.6	10.9	12.3	12.7
1,8075		6	Jay	383.9	20,945	1,778	54.6	95.8	0.7	0.6	0.7	3.2	7.2	18.6	8.1	11.0	11.0	13.4
1,8077	31,500	6	Jefferson	360.6	32,089	1,380	89.0	94.2	2.6	0.7	1.2	2.8	5.5	15.0	10.2	11.5	12.1	13.5
1,8079	35,860	6	Jennings	376.6	27,626	1,507	73.4	96.2	1.2	0.7	0.5	2.5	6.1	17.0	8.5	11.9	11.7	14.9
1,8081	26,900	1	Johnson	320.4	153,897	429	480.3	90.8	2.9	0.6	3.7	3.7	6.6	18.3	8.6	13.4	13.5	13.3
1,8083	47,180	5	Knox	516.0	37,508	1,236	72.7	93.8	3.7	0.7	1.2	2.0	6.0	15.4	13.7	11.6	10.6	11.8
1,8085	47,700	4	Kosciusko	531.4	79,206	704	149.1	89.5	1.5	0.6	1.6	8.0	6.5	17.6	9.4	12.7	11.5	12.6
1,8087		6	LaGrange	379.6	39,303	1,196	103.5	94.7	0.7	0.5	0.8	4.1	9.2	23.7	8.9	12.1	11.0	10.9
1,8089	16,980	1	Lake	498.9	485,640	143	973.4	55.5	24.4	0.6	2.0	19.1	6.1	17.6	8.8	12.2	12.6	12.8
1,8091	33,140	3	LaPorte	598.3	110,029	549	183.9	81.3	12.5	0.7	1.0	6.6	6.0	15.6	8.2	13.1	12.2	13.4
1,8093	13,260	6	Lawrence	449.2	45,666	1,060	101.7	96.7	0.8	1.0	1.0	1.7	5.6	16.4	7.5	11.1	11.7	13.7
1,8095	26,900	1	Madison	451.9	129,498	491	286.6	86.7	9.4	0.6	0.9	4.1	5.7	16.2	8.4	12.6	12.3	13.6
1,8097	26,900	1	Marion	396.3	950,082	52	2,397.4	57.8	29.7	0.7	4.0	10.5	7.3	17.4	9.3	16.8	12.8	12.0
1,8099	38,500	6	Marshall	443.6	46,498	1,040	104.8	88.2	1.1	0.6	0.8	10.4	6.4	18.7	8.5	11.0	11.6	12.9
1,8101		7	Martin	335.8	10,215	2,411	30.4	98.0	0.7	0.6	0.6	1.1	6.7	15.8	7.6	10.9	11.4	13.0
1,8103	37,940	6	Miami	373.8	35,845	1,281	95.9	90.6	5.7	1.6	0.8	3.2	5.3	16.3	8.2	12.8	13.1	13.7
1,8105	14,020	3	Monroe	394.5	146,986	444	372.6	85.7	4.5	0.7	8.1	3.5	4.5	11.4	26.6	14.5	10.4	9.6
1,8107	18,820	6	Montgomery	504.6	38,525	1,215	76.3	93.0	1.6	0.7	1.1	4.9	6.1	17.0	9.3	11.8	11.1	13.3
1,8109	26,900	1	Morgan	404.0	69,713	768	172.6	97.1	0.9	0.7	0.8	1.6	5.5	17.2	7.9	11.3	11.8	14.8
1,8111	16,980	1	Newton	401.8	14,130	2,156	35.2	91.9	1.1	0.7	0.8	6.4	5.6	16.2	7.6	11.1	11.7	13.5
1,8113	28,340	6	Noble	410.8	47,452	1,027	115.5	88.2	1.0	0.6	0.8	10.4	6.7	18.3	8.6	11.9	12.1	13.3
1,8115	17,140	1	Ohio	86.2	5,828	2,769	67.6	97.4	1.1	0.6	0.6	1.4	4.7	14.3	6.4	10.7	10.8	14.3
1,8117		6	Orange	398.4	19,426	1,855	48.8	96.2	1.8	0.6	0.6	1.7	6.0	16.9	7.7	10.9	11.2	13.3
1,8119	14,020	3	Owen	385.3	20,839	1,783	54.1	97.4	0.9	0.9	0.8	1.2	5.4	16.0	7.4	10.7	11.1	14.3
1,8121		6	Parke	444.7	16,886	1,984	38.0	95.4	2.9	0.6	0.4	1.5	6.2	15.6	7.6	12.7	11.3	13.2
1,8123		6	Perry	381.7	19,081	1,869	50.0	95.2	3.0	0.6	0.7	1.5	5.6	15.6	7.9	12.8	12.2	12.9

1. CBSA = Core Based Statistical Area. See Appendix A for explanation. See Appendix B for list of metropolitan areas with component counties. 2. County type code from the Economic Research Service of USDA Rural-Urban Continuum Codes. See Appendix A for definition. 3. Dry land or land partially or temporarily covered by water. 4. May be of any race.

STATE County	55 to 64 years	65 to 74 years	75 years and over	Percent female	2000	2010	2000-2010	2010-2017	Births	Deaths	Net Migration	Number	Persons per house-hold	Family house-holds	Female family house-holder[1]	One person
	16	17	18	19	20	21	22	23	24	25	26	27	28	29	30	31
ILLINOIS— Cont'd																
Winnebago	13.8	9.9	7.2	51.2	278,418	295,264	6.1	-3.6	26,157	20,155	-16,667	114,299	2.49	65.4	14.7	29.5
Woodford	14.3	9.5	7.9	50.2	35,469	38,664	9.0	0.2	3,194	2,735	-383	14,489	2.63	73.8	8.2	23.9
INDIANA	13.1	9.0	6.4	50.7	6,080,485	6,484,125	6.6	2.8	605,118	435,449	14,929	2,513,828	2.55	65.8	12.2	28.2
Adams	11.7	8.2	7.1	50.2	33,625	34,387	2.3	3.2	4,858	2,155	-1,608	12,260	2.79	69.6	10.1	26.5
Allen	12.5	8.4	5.8	51.2	331,849	355,327	7.1	4.9	37,908	21,798	1,709	141,483	2.54	64.9	13.2	29.5
Bartholomew	12.3	9.3	6.7	49.8	71,435	76,786	7.5	6.8	7,712	5,243	2,817	31,073	2.55	66.7	9.8	27.6
Benton	14.1	9.9	7.7	50.3	9,421	8,836	-6.2	-2.5	755	614	-368	3,388	2.53	68.4	9.5	26.5
Blackford	14.8	11.8	9.2	50.5	14,048	12,766	-9.1	-6.2	964	1,117	-641	5,207	2.34	67.1	11.5	28.4
Boone	12.6	7.8	5.2	50.2	46,107	56,638	22.8	16.3	5,416	3,532	7,291	23,427	2.61	73.5	9.6	22.6
Brown	17.7	15.4	8.2	50.6	14,957	15,245	1.9	-1.4	837	1,093	52	5,953	2.49	70.6	9.6	23.3
Carroll	14.9	11.3	7.9	49.9	20,165	20,159	0.0	-0.6	1,516	1,287	-349	7,770	2.56	69.8	8.2	25.1
Cass	13.9	9.7	7.7	49.9	40,930	38,966	-4.8	-2.5	3,571	2,834	-1,728	14,536	2.56	65.9	9.9	30.4
Clark	13.4	9.4	5.9	51.2	96,472	110,230	14.3	6.1	10,600	8,159	4,311	43,074	2.60	65.9	12.6	28.9
Clay	14.6	10.0	7.4	50.5	26,556	26,887	1.2	-2.6	2,317	2,167	-836	10,541	2.48	71.8	11.1	23.1
Clinton	13.3	8.8	7.6	50.2	33,866	33,223	-1.9	-2.7	3,253	2,563	-1,612	11,769	2.72	69.7	10.6	24.8
Crawford	15.9	12.0	7.2	49.3	10,743	10,713	-0.3	-1.4	835	831	-149	4,076	2.57	67.9	11.1	27.2
Daviess	12.1	8.7	6.5	49.7	29,820	31,654	6.2	4.6	3,837	2,399	41	11,483	2.79	72.4	8.1	24.8
Dearborn	14.9	10.4	6.7	50.1	46,109	50,035	8.5	-0.6	3,790	3,230	-839	18,639	2.63	73.4	9.1	22.8
Decatur	13.8	9.2	7.1	50.2	24,555	25,731	4.8	3.9	2,439	1,866	455	10,120	2.57	71.3	10.4	23.8
DeKalb	13.7	9.4	6.5	50.3	40,285	42,219	4.8	1.5	3,823	2,877	-304	16,221	2.59	68.7	10.6	27.6
Delaware	12.1	9.4	7.4	51.7	118,769	117,669	-0.9	-2.1	8,897	8,676	-2,674	46,104	2.36	59.6	12.5	29.6
Dubois	14.6	9.3	7.6	50.1	39,674	41,889	5.6	1.6	3,938	2,886	-366	16,311	2.54	70.4	7.3	25.6
Elkhart	11.8	8.2	6.2	50.6	182,791	197,561	8.1	3.8	22,299	11,706	-3,049	70,822	2.80	71.6	12.3	23.2
Fayette	14.0	11.4	8.4	50.4	25,588	24,302	-5.0	-4.5	1,763	2,232	-614	9,420	2.46	69.4	13.5	24.8
Floyd	14.3	9.5	6.2	51.5	70,823	74,578	5.3	3.3	6,485	5,313	1,359	29,034	2.58	67.2	12.6	27.9
Fountain	14.1	10.9	9.0	50.0	17,954	17,243	-4.0	-4.3	1,411	1,429	-719	6,963	2.38	64.5	9.9	28.6
Franklin	15.0	10.5	7.4	49.9	22,151	23,095	4.3	-2.1	1,729	1,523	-682	8,710	2.60	75.6	8.9	20.6
Fulton	14.4	11.0	8.2	50.2	20,511	20,851	1.7	-3.8	1,843	1,709	-922	7,962	2.53	66.3	7.9	29.3
Gibson	14.1	9.7	7.6	50.1	32,500	33,501	3.1	0.2	2,961	2,588	-278	13,297	2.47	69.0	10.5	25.6
Grant	13.9	10.4	8.3	52.2	73,403	70,063	-4.6	-5.1	5,525	5,893	-3,203	26,227	2.40	64.3	13.6	30.2
Greene	14.6	11.0	8.2	49.9	33,157	33,164	0.0	-3.0	2,467	2,757	-682	12,688	2.55	66.1	8.1	30.6
Hamilton	11.5	7.3	4.5	51.2	182,740	274,569	50.3	17.9	28,024	10,851	31,759	111,443	2.71	73.6	8.4	21.6
Hancock	13.5	9.6	6.2	50.8	55,391	70,043	26.5	7.1	5,713	4,420	3,687	26,680	2.67	73.0	9.8	22.4
Harrison	14.9	10.6	6.7	49.8	34,325	39,364	14.7	1.4	3,092	2,725	183	14,524	2.69	69.2	9.6	25.8
Hendricks	12.3	8.2	5.2	50.0	104,093	145,412	39.7	12.6	12,724	7,534	13,072	55,744	2.75	73.6	9.0	21.9
Henry	14.0	10.8	8.0	48.1	48,508	49,466	2.0	-2.0	3,440	4,111	-296	17,926	2.54	66.6	11.1	27.9
Howard	14.0	10.8	8.3	51.5	84,964	82,752	-2.6	-0.5	7,153	6,834	-655	34,411	2.37	64.6	12.3	30.7
Huntington	15.0	9.3	7.5	50.7	38,075	37,124	-2.5	-2.1	3,072	2,915	-936	14,532	2.43	68.0	8.7	26.7
Jackson	13.1	9.2	6.8	50.0	41,335	42,376	2.5	3.6	4,180	3,296	643	16,517	2.60	70.9	10.4	25.0
Jasper	14.0	10.1	6.9	50.3	30,043	33,478	11.4	-0.1	2,795	2,329	-484	12,091	2.69	66.2	9.2	23.5
Jay	13.3	9.9	7.3	50.2	21,806	21,253	-2.5	-1.4	2,202	1,661	-850	8,062	2.59	67.9	10.5	27.1
Jefferson	14.6	10.6	7.0	51.7	31,705	32,404	2.2	-1.0	2,618	2,672	-243	12,642	2.37	68.3	12.6	27.2
Jennings	13.9	9.9	6.1	49.7	27,554	28,529	3.5	-3.2	2,416	2,077	-1,247	10,519	2.63	68.4	11.8	26.0
Johnson	12.1	8.4	5.8	50.6	115,209	139,865	21.4	10.0	13,446	8,998	9,624	53,713	2.70	72.9	11.3	22.3
Knox	13.7	9.6	7.6	49.4	39,256	38,440	-2.1	-2.4	3,316	3,212	-1,023	14,655	2.42	63.5	11.2	31.5
Kosciusko	13.6	9.5	6.7	50.2	74,057	77,356	4.5	2.4	7,435	5,029	-502	30,078	2.56	71.8	9.3	23.0
LaGrange	10.8	8.0	5.3	49.3	34,909	37,130	6.4	5.9	5,420	1,893	-1,355	11,850	3.21	79.3	7.4	16.8
Lake	13.9	9.2	6.9	51.6	484,564	496,050	2.4	-2.1	43,610	34,254	-19,778	184,140	2.63	66.9	16.9	28.3
LaPorte	14.1	10.5	7.0	48.5	110,106	111,467	1.2	-1.3	9,584	8,432	-2,529	43,052	2.37	66.0	13.1	27.5
Lawrence	14.4	11.4	8.2	50.5	45,922	46,129	0.5	-1.0	3,503	3,961	38	18,426	2.44	70.6	11.9	25.2
Madison	13.4	10.4	7.5	50.1	133,358	131,636	-1.3	-1.6	10,918	10,702	-2,288	51,441	2.40	65.3	13.2	29.8
Marion	12.1	7.3	5.0	51.8	860,454	903,389	5.0	5.2	104,776	56,214	-1,348	365,472	2.50	57.0	16.2	35.4
Marshall	13.8	9.6	7.6	50.2	45,128	47,047	4.3	-1.2	4,242	3,299	-1,492	17,093	2.69	69.4	9.5	26.5
Martin	15.4	11.2	8.0	49.4	10,369	10,378	0.1	-1.6	940	754	-347	4,219	2.39	62.0	9.6	33.3
Miami	13.3	10.1	7.1	46.3	36,082	36,908	2.3	-2.9	2,698	2,593	-1,179	13,268	2.56	68.7	11.3	27.9
Monroe	10.4	7.3	5.2	50.2	120,563	137,959	14.4	6.5	9,556	6,409	5,912	54,278	2.37	51.0	9.3	33.5
Montgomery	13.9	9.6	7.9	49.4	37,629	38,121	1.3	1.1	3,346	2,787	-135	14,852	2.48	68.5	8.8	26.1
Morgan	15.1	10.1	6.4	50.4	66,689	68,935	3.4	1.1	5,518	4,720	33	25,655	2.68	73.0	11.0	21.2
Newton	15.4	10.8	8.0	49.5	14,566	14,244	-2.2	-0.8	1,071	1,106	-73	5,482	2.52	70.9	9.6	24.8
Noble	13.9	9.4	6.0	49.9	46,275	47,540	2.7	-0.2	4,434	3,216	-1,293	18,013	2.60	71.1	10.4	25.9
Ohio	17.5	12.7	8.7	50.0	5,623	6,107	8.6	-4.6	384	449	-216	2,427	2.45	69.8	7.6	26.9
Orange	14.8	11.4	7.9	50.2	19,306	19,840	2.8	-2.1	1,664	1,573	-501	7,720	2.50	68.7	11.0	26.7
Owen	16.1	11.9	7.1	49.6	21,786	21,582	-0.9	-3.4	1,647	1,658	-735	8,581	2.43	70.0	9.9	25.1
Parke	14.5	11.5	7.5	52.5	17,241	17,354	0.7	-2.7	1,455	1,174	-761	6,150	2.52	70.4	8.6	23.7
Perry	14.7	10.6	7.7	46.8	18,899	19,338	2.3	-1.3	1,511	1,442	-317	7,318	2.40	68.6	10.7	26.6

1. No spouse present.

Table B. States and Counties — Population, Vital Statistics, Health, and Crime

STATE County	Persons in group quarters, 2017	Daytime Population, 2012-2016 Number	Employment/ residence ratio	Births, 2017 Total	Rate[1]	Deaths, 2017 Number	Rate[1]	Persons under 65 with no health insurance, 2016 Number	Percent	Medicare, 2017 Total beneficiaries	Enrolled in Original Medicare	Enrolled in Medicare Advantage	Serious crimes known to police[2], 2016 Total Number	Rate[3]
	32	33	34	35	36	37	38	39	40	41	42	43	44	45
ILLINOIS— Cont'd														
Winnebago	4,715	293,777	1.04	3,531	12.4	2,724	9.6	15,892	6.7	57,130	38,832	18,298	11,052	3939
Woodford	1,022	31,904	0.61	437	11.3	411	10.6	1,373	4.3	6,449	5,111	1,339	261	808
INDIANA	18,7,264	6,535,512	0.98	83,021	12.5	60,476	9.1	518,435	9.5	1,206,841	880,016	326,826	198,604	2994
Adams	421	34,232	0.96	666	18.8	248	7.0	3,671	12.4	5,683	3,831	1,852	NA	NA
Allen	6,108	378,542	1.08	5,234	14.0	3,067	8.2	29,398	9.3	62,687	34,735	27,952	11,396	3078
Bartholomew	1,147	89,980	1.25	1,109	13.5	700	8.5	6,720	9.8	15,998	13,010	2,988	2,578	3148
Benton	92	7,405	0.68	106	12.3	80	9.3	834	11.7	1,896	1,560	335	NA	NA
Blackford	163	10,980	0.73	117	9.8	164	13.7	947	10.0	3,047	2,314	733	118	980
Boone	574	55,223	0.78	804	12.2	473	7.2	3,587	6.4	9,551	7,002	2,549	NA	NA
Brown	163	11,231	0.46	121	8.0	138	9.2	1,220	10.6	2,188	1,563	624	284	1906
Carroll	106	16,476	0.62	190	9.5	188	9.4	1,618	10.0	3,285	2,552	733	NA	NA
Cass	1,041	36,631	0.90	473	12.4	409	10.8	3,678	11.9	7,548	5,869	1,679	682	1809
Clark	1,327	109,071	0.91	1,463	12.5	1,143	9.8	8,332	8.5	22,692	17,243	5,449	3,805	3277
Clay	341	22,336	0.64	326	12.4	288	11.0	2,019	9.4	6,251	5,138	1,113	NA	NA
Clinton	831	29,512	0.79	456	14.1	319	9.9	2,862	10.7	6,329	4,953	1,376	769	2372
Crawford	62	8,439	0.50	113	10.7	115	10.9	908	10.6	2,654	2,170	484	144	1383
Daviess	581	30,909	0.88	523	15.8	318	9.6	4,865	17.5	5,132	4,612	520	598	1808
Dearborn	530	40,920	0.65	524	10.5	440	8.8	3,214	7.8	10,018	7,693	2,325	NA	NA
Decatur	377	28,878	1.20	351	13.1	272	10.2	1,913	8.6	5,371	4,094	1,277	NA	NA
DeKalb	615	43,664	1.06	518	12.1	402	9.4	3,185	8.9	8,789	4,982	3,806	530	1245
Delaware	8,413	118,303	1.04	1,168	10.1	1,181	10.3	8,520	9.6	23,716	18,792	4,924	3,732	3205
Dubois	894	47,508	1.24	570	13.4	401	9.4	3,038	8.6	8,133	7,321	812	NA	NA
Elkhart	3,796	227,089	1.28	3,145	15.3	1,621	7.9	25,222	14.7	33,583	23,812	9,770	NA	NA
Fayette	392	21,347	0.76	239	10.3	284	12.2	1,857	10.0	6,055	5,081	974	NA	NA
Floyd	1,330	69,454	0.82	910	11.8	748	9.7	4,683	7.3	15,447	12,141	3,306	1,642	2226
Fountain	172	15,238	0.79	205	12.4	187	11.3	1,231	9.4	4,447	3,626	821	NA	NA
Franklin	187	17,317	0.48	216	9.5	202	8.9	1,707	9.0	3,677	2,685	992	190	834
Fulton	224	18,115	0.75	250	12.5	202	10.1	1,963	12.1	4,200	2,704	1,496	NA	NA
Gibson	738	38,810	1.32	380	11.3	381	11.3	1,945	7.1	6,679	4,815	1,864	NA	NA
Grant	4,930	70,293	1.07	735	11.1	795	12.0	4,879	9.8	15,717	12,273	3,444	1,756	2603
Greene	281	26,843	0.59	330	10.3	407	12.6	2,540	9.8	6,935	5,790	1,145	451	1625
Hamilton	1,876	280,332	0.86	3,901	12.0	1,744	5.4	14,924	5.3	38,610	27,850	10,761	NA	NA
Hancock	649	58,938	0.63	847	11.3	606	8.1	4,261	6.9	13,827	9,372	4,456	958	1315
Harrison	461	32,889	0.64	446	11.2	348	8.7	2,976	9.1	8,171	6,566	1,606	NA	NA
Hendricks	3,889	138,868	0.78	1,784	10.9	1,061	6.5	9,146	6.7	23,068	15,979	7,090	2,360	1471
Henry	3,611	43,087	0.70	466	9.6	548	11.3	3,111	8.6	10,792	7,893	2,900	NA	NA
Howard	1,282	87,472	1.13	964	11.7	936	11.4	5,775	8.7	19,610	16,025	3,585	2,565	3157
Huntington	1,336	34,330	0.87	420	11.6	386	10.6	2,612	8.9	8,606	4,691	3,915	NA	NA
Jackson	595	45,664	1.10	574	13.1	447	10.2	3,687	10.1	8,920	6,334	2,587	1,288	2909
Jasper	931	31,647	0.88	382	11.4	320	9.6	2,435	9.0	7,013	5,646	1,367	NA	NA
Jay	243	20,614	0.94	292	13.9	217	10.4	1,691	9.8	4,411	3,265	1,147	161	853
Jefferson	1,946	32,015	0.97	361	11.2	341	10.6	2,371	9.5	7,603	6,336	1,267	NA	NA
Jennings	298	24,322	0.71	300	10.9	299	10.8	2,186	9.4	5,371	4,074	1,298	593	2139
Johnson	2,556	127,651	0.72	1,915	12.4	1,292	8.4	10,013	7.8	26,597	18,961	7,636	4,678	3120
Knox	2,560	38,856	1.05	417	11.1	393	10.5	2,635	9.1	8,362	7,455	907	1,062	3046
Kosciusko	1,803	78,986	1.01	1,019	12.9	694	8.8	7,497	11.5	13,771	8,022	5,749	1,171	1588
LaGrange	325	36,894	0.91	753	19.2	254	6.5	7,422	22.0	5,680	3,739	1,941	196	502
Lake	6,480	475,483	0.93	5,761	11.9	4,859	10.0	34,921	8.6	90,665	66,209	24,457	15,238	3352
LaPorte	6,281	106,497	0.90	1,314	11.9	1,184	10.8	8,090	9.5	21,975	18,183	3,793	3,106	2893
Lawrence	653	40,687	0.75	489	10.7	535	11.7	3,227	8.9	10,428	8,352	2,076	724	1764
Madison	5,927	118,574	0.79	1,477	11.4	1,422	11.0	9,612	9.5	29,867	21,087	8,780	3,378	2668
Marion	17,299	1,056,753	1.28	14,323	15.1	7,915	8.3	86,091	10.6	146,421	101,230	45,191	55,553	5884
Marshall	670	45,668	0.94	591	12.7	476	10.2	5,224	13.6	8,796	5,503	3,293	NA	NA
Martin	133	13,736	1.74	124	12.1	95	9.3	768	9.3	2,386	2,139	247	NA	NA
Miami	3,287	32,022	0.72	370	10.3	353	9.8	2,502	9.4	7,183	5,667	1,516	715	2008
Monroe	15,072	151,272	1.12	1,352	9.2	894	6.1	10,522	9.2	20,672	16,512	4,160	4,366	2997
Montgomery	1,174	37,087	0.94	467	12.1	378	9.8	3,257	10.7	8,260	5,895	2,365	NA	NA
Morgan	591	54,770	0.55	753	10.8	657	9.4	5,097	8.8	13,838	9,931	3,907	NA	NA
Newton	169	11,409	0.58	167	11.8	135	9.6	1,320	11.7	2,394	1,961	433	94	675
Noble	816	45,959	0.93	646	13.6	453	9.5	4,264	10.7	8,189	4,667	3,521	646	1355
Ohio	52	4,761	0.56	51	8.8	75	12.9	371	7.9	1,175	912	263	NA	NA
Orange	258	18,911	0.92	230	11.8	212	10.9	1,596	10.3	4,288	3,453	835	NA	NA
Owen	197	17,526	0.62	236	11.3	237	11.4	1,851	11.0	4,160	3,164	995	NA	NA
Parke	1,461	14,481	0.61	213	12.6	170	10.1	1,532	12.5	3,263	2,622	641	NA	NA
Perry	1,355	18,617	0.92	229	12.0	172	9.0	1,210	8.4	3,942	3,451	491	NA	NA

1. Per 1,000 estimated resident population.   2.   Data for serious crimes have not been adjusted for underreporting; this may affect comparability between geographic areas and over time.
3.   Per 100,000 population estimated by the FBI.

Table B. States and Counties — Crime, Education, Money Income, and Poverty

STATE County	Serious crimes known to police, 2016 (cont.)[1] Rate		Education School enrollment and attainment, 2012-2016				Local government expenditures,[5] 2013-2014		Money income, 2012-2016		Households		Income and poverty, 2016			
			Enrollment[3]		Attainment[4] (percent)							Percent			Percent below poverty level		
	Violent	Property	Total	Percent private	High school graduate or less	Bachelor's degree or more	Total current spending (mil dol)	Current spending per student (dollars)	Per capita income[6]	Median income (dollars)	with income of less than $50,000	with income of $200,000 or more	Median household income (dollars)	All persons	Children under 18 years	Children 5 to 17 years in families
	46	47	48	49	50	51	52	53	54	55	56	57	58	59	60	61
ILLINOIS— Cont'd																
Winnebago	1,012	2,926	72,337	19.7	44.9	22.4	571.6	12,294	26,187	49,468	50.5	2.7	50,296	15.6	23.4	20.9
Woodford	68	740	10,440	15.8	38.8	30.4	87.0	10,897	32,360	68,040	34.9	4.9	73,055	6.6	8.2	7.6
INDIANA	405	2,589	1,717,877	16.3	46.2	24.6	9,907.7	9,475	26,117	50,433	49.6	3.0	52,289	14.0	19.1	17.9
Adams	NA	NA	8,719	30.1	57.4	15.6	45.2	10,264	21,173	47,572	52.5	2.1	51,517	15.2	26.7	25.9
Allen	334	2,744	99,536	22.3	39.9	27.4	513.6	9,498	26,058	49,574	50.4	3.0	51,329	15.0	21.1	19.7
Bartholomew	82	3,067	19,522	15.1	44.6	29.7	115.0	9,146	28,631	55,874	44.6	3.6	59,765	11.7	15.1	14.0
Benton	NA	NA	2,052	13.9	55.4	17.1	19.1	10,083	23,181	48,069	52.3	1.2	47,218	11.5	17.4	15.9
Blackford	58	922	2,612	4.4	61.2	11.0	16.7	9,241	21,980	38,791	61.2	1.2	42,588	12.8	22.4	22.2
Boone	NA	NA	16,226	11.8	32.2	44.5	107.1	9,262	40,487	72,774	34.0	10.8	80,634	7.0	7.7	6.9
Brown	309	1,597	3,229	6.5	46.5	23.5	23.6	11,082	30,279	56,323	42.9	2.5	56,323	10.9	19.0	17.2
Carroll	NA	NA	4,699	13.6	52.8	17.4	23.1	8,787	25,647	54,140	45.9	2.2	55,708	10.3	14.2	13.1
Cass	45	1,764	9,193	9.9	56.7	13.9	68.0	10,289	22,625	43,918	55.9	1.6	46,287	12.5	18.9	18.0
Clark	320	2,957	26,881	15.0	46.2	20.2	151.8	8,880	25,693	51,844	48.1	2.1	51,837	10.5	15.7	14.8
Clay	NA	NA	5,916	8.3	55.0	16.9	39.9	9,145	22,913	49,735	50.2	1.3	50,185	14.2	21.2	18.9
Clinton	102	2,270	7,764	8.1	59.2	14.9	56.2	8,959	23,260	50,096	49.9	2.0	53,862	13.7	19.5	17.4
Crawford	240	1,143	2,241	4.6	65.0	9.8	15.8	10,023	19,756	41,173	59.2	0.0	46,210	17.2	26.2	24.6
Daviess	136	1,672	7,183	24.2	61.6	14.0	42.2	9,330	21,472	47,939	51.4	2.0	49,237	14.2	19.6	18.6
Dearborn	NA	NA	12,140	13.8	49.5	20.0	76.8	8,764	28,471	60,834	40.0	3.2	63,876	8.2	12.9	11.3
Decatur	NA	NA	6,248	14.3	54.5	18.2	40.8	9,204	24,175	51,185	48.0	1.7	51,999	11.5	16.9	15.9
DeKalb	66	1,180	10,919	16.1	52.2	17.4	91.3	12,539	25,132	50,398	49.4	2.1	52,599	9.0	13.2	11.9
Delaware	261	2,944	36,443	6.2	46.1	23.3	158.9	9,851	21,566	39,537	60.2	1.6	41,404	21.6	25.7	23.7
Dubois	NA	NA	9,968	9.7	52.4	19.7	69.0	9,371	27,331	55,154	44.5	2.5	62,852	6.6	8.3	7.7
Elkhart	NA	NA	50,659	14.0	56.2	18.3	340.2	9,409	22,387	49,692	50.3	2.1	54,582	13.2	16.7	16.4
Fayette	NA	NA	5,200	6.9	61.8	10.7	40.1	10,673	21,716	40,851	60.2	1.5	44,673	17.8	22.0	20.2
Floyd	107	2,119	18,965	15.4	42.5	26.9	110.1	9,303	29,350	57,494	44.4	4.1	58,703	10.3	14.7	13.7
Fountain	NA	NA	3,696	5.6	56.2	14.5	26.7	8,945	25,086	45,924	53.3	1.5	43,571	13.2	18.5	16.7
Franklin	39	794	5,621	16.7	54.7	19.1	43.1	8,694	24,748	52,128	48.2	1.9	57,674	10.7	13.9	12.5
Fulton	NA	NA	4,657	10.7	56.1	13.7	22.6	8,560	23,507	46,310	54.5	0.9	46,662	12.5	19.6	18.8
Gibson	NA	NA	7,925	16.2	49.5	15.6	47.4	9,445	25,990	49,669	50.4	2.1	54,690	10.8	13.8	12.6
Grant	251	2,353	18,105	34.3	54.5	16.7	110.4	9,956	20,348	40,272	60.2	1.1	40,177	20.3	29.1	26.0
Greene	43	1,582	6,989	10.8	54.7	14.3	50.9	9,775	23,189	45,153	54.1	1.4	46,019	16.1	20.9	19.4
Hamilton	NA	NA	87,002	17.4	19.8	56.3	503.0	8,832	42,361	87,782	26.1	12.1	92,406	4.8	4.9	4.4
Hancock	150	1,166	18,599	14.6	39.0	29.0	104.7	8,310	30,011	68,449	36.4	3.9	70,655	7.3	8.8	7.3
Harrison	NA	NA	8,514	14.0	53.3	16.9	55.5	9,223	25,319	52,926	46.9	2.2	57,573	10.2	13.6	12.9
Hendricks	144	1,327	41,626	14.4	35.0	34.7	229.2	8,145	31,335	73,042	32.2	4.4	78,464	5.8	6.7	5.9
Henry	NA	NA	10,626	7.6	55.6	15.7	73.0	9,585	22,182	44,509	56.4	1.4	45,356	16.2	21.8	20.3
Howard	639	2,518	19,671	10.3	48.0	19.5	129.9	9,199	25,507	45,928	53.5	2.4	49,204	14.8	21.3	20.5
Huntington	NA	NA	9,088	21.9	53.3	18.9	49.7	8,885	23,396	47,042	52.3	1.2	50,138	11.1	16.0	15.0
Jackson	237	2,672	10,618	18.7	58.9	16.2	61.1	9,051	23,098	48,546	51.2	1.2	51,871	13.1	15.7	14.8
Jasper	NA	NA	8,455	17.9	54.3	16.5	42.4	8,130	24,839	55,485	44.3	1.7	56,034	9.4	12.6	11.7
Jay	101	752	4,917	10.8	63.6	10.9	36.5	10,531	20,234	42,322	58.2	1.0	46,949	13.9	22.4	21.4
Jefferson	NA	NA	7,425	25.3	52.7	17.0	43.4	9,732	23,006	47,065	53.0	0.9	51,534	13.4	20.3	19.4
Jennings	202	1,937	6,615	14.1	62.7	9.6	47.2	10,039	22,374	47,236	51.9	1.1	50,425	12.7	19.7	18.9
Johnson	308	2,812	38,616	15.0	41.2	29.5	229.0	8,947	29,877	63,023	38.9	4.4	67,215	7.6	9.8	8.8
Knox	109	2,937	10,127	6.1	48.1	15.2	48.7	9,365	22,976	44,624	55.0	1.8	43,897	17.0	23.4	21.0
Kosciusko	187	1,401	18,645	16.7	52.2	21.2	134.1	9,713	26,854	54,482	44.6	3.2	56,010	10.4	14.5	13.5
LaGrange	110	392	8,677	34.6	67.7	11.2	57.6	9,803	21,774	53,947	44.8	3.1	60,402	10.0	13.6	13.1
Lake	339	3,013	126,888	15.2	47.7	20.9	834.8	9,864	25,483	50,905	49.1	2.6	53,600	16.6	25.7	23.7
LaPorte	293	2,600	25,178	15.4	51.4	17.6	179.0	9,931	24,340	48,165	51.6	2.6	52,763	15.7	26.7	23.1
Lawrence	356	1,408	10,161	13.1	54.1	14.3	66.8	9,702	23,743	46,044	53.3	1.6	47,997	13.7	20.8	18.8
Madison	243	2,426	29,782	18.6	51.7	17.4	170.8	8,954	22,997	44,795	55.4	1.3	45,853	17.5	24.7	23.6
Marion	1,274	4,610	246,707	18.8	42.5	29.0	1,534.7	10,067	25,208	43,369	55.9	2.8	45,300	18.9	28.0	28.1
Marshall	NA	NA	11,202	17.0	56.1	18.5	71.8	9,341	23,372	49,725	50.2	1.9	53,767	12.0	15.8	14.4
Martin	NA	NA	2,355	9.5	58.4	11.4	14.5	9,450	23,913	47,457	52.3	1.1	51,008	12.4	17.4	16.9
Miami	129	1,879	8,386	5.3	57.5	11.9	46.0	8,470	21,940	45,646	53.7	1.1	47,650	15.7	24.4	22.9
Monroe	329	2,668	59,348	7.6	30.4	45.1	130.3	9,326	25,488	43,389	55.4	4.1	44,442	23.8	17.6	16.1
Montgomery	NA	NA	8,905	15.2	55.0	16.8	59.9	10,012	24,095	50,253	49.7	1.7	51,527	11.3	16.2	14.7
Morgan	NA	NA	16,635	13.7	53.7	15.5	100.1	8,619	26,556	57,521	42.9	2.0	60,482	10.5	15.5	13.6
Newton	22	653	3,124	8.2	60.7	10.5	22.9	9,830	24,061	50,058	49.9	2.7	51,183	12.2	18.6	16.9
Noble	210	1,145	11,752	14.5	56.4	14.1	67.6	8,974	23,792	49,657	50.4	1.7	52,318	11.4	15.8	14.6
Ohio	NA	NA	1,204	9.1	58.2	13.8	8.1	9,656	25,278	54,653	46.6	0.0	54,422	10.1	15.6	14.0
Orange	NA	NA	4,193	8.2	61.7	11.9	37.4	11,190	21,295	41,438	59.1	0.9	41,077	16.3	24.3	23.9
Owen	NA	NA	4,353	15.7	58.9	12.0	25.9	9,490	22,675	45,388	53.7	1.5	46,069	13.8	21.6	20.0
Parke	NA	NA	3,514	6.8	56.9	11.8	22.7	10,288	22,247	42,664	55.9	1.1	47,599	16.3	25.1	24.1
Perry	NA	NA	3,948	7.2	64.2	13.4	28.4	9,687	21,634	47,396	52.2	1.6	48,905	14.9	20.0	15.3

1. Data for serious crimes have not been adjusted for underreporting; this may affect comparability between geographic areas and over time. 2. Per 100,000 population estimated by the FBI.
3. All persons 3 years old and over enrolled in nursery school through college. 4. Persons 25 years old and over. 5. Elementary and secondary education expenditures.
6. Based on population estimated by the American Community Survey, 2011–2015.

Table B. States and Counties — Agriculture

STATE County	Land in farms Acreage (1,000) 117	Percent change, 2007-2012 118	Acres Average size of farm 119	Total irrigated (1,000) 120	Total cropland (1,000) 121	Value of land and buildings (dollars) Average per farm 122	Average per acre 123	Value of machinery and equiopmnet, average per farm (dollars) 124	Value of products sold: Total (mil dol) 125	Average per farm (acres) 126	Percent from: Crops 127	Livestock and poultry products 128	Percent of farms with sales of: $10,000 or more 129	$100,000 or more 130	Government payments Total ($1,000) 131	Percent of farms 132
ILLINOIS— Cont'd																
Winnebago	183	-0.4	227	0.5	159.6	1,434,529	6,329	127,939	106.4	131,822	79.1	20.9	43.2	23.4	5,109	61.6
Woodford	323	12.0	337	0.5	291.6	2,612,922	7,750	210,760	240.6	251,196	78.5	21.5	62.3	40.6	6,107	79.2
INDIANA	14,720	-0.4	251	437.4	12,590.6	1,342,826	5,354	143,235	11,210.8	191,001	67.2	32.8	48.3	24.4	267,287	54.7
Adams	210	15.2	142	0.1	186.0	825,272	5,794	92,331	250.3	169,571	48.1	51.9	55.8	25.1	3,765	37.6
Allen	271	6.6	157	0.4	241.5	969,217	6,174	87,928	187.6	108,776	79.6	20.4	48.8	20.6	6,302	52.5
Bartholomew	172	3.2	275	13.5	153.4	1,619,191	5,878	151,406	95.6	153,387	89.5	10.5	54.9	27.1	4,647	63.7
Benton	254	-6.1	667	D	247.4	4,308,843	6,457	328,864	210.9	553,499	80.8	19.2	73.5	59.8	4,782	85.0
Blackford	88	4.0	335	D	81.2	1,414,730	4,228	176,620	71.5	271,764	D	D	56.3	28.9	1,380	66.2
Boone	222	-0.5	365	0.9	210.3	2,253,794	6,171	194,476	146.0	240,486	88.5	11.5	52.9	32.6	3,428	54.7
Brown	15	-14.0	84	0.1	6.6	337,468	4,002	37,514	4.2	24,486	D	D	16.8	2.9	156	28.3
Carroll	204	6.1	416	0.4	189.5	2,837,483	6,826	234,244	221.4	450,982	61.5	38.5	65.4	46.4	3,497	63.7
Cass	200	-12.2	291	1.9	181.6	1,575,185	5,412	185,317	158.4	230,281	78.2	21.8	55.8	30.5	4,080	73.3
Clark	79	-9.4	153	0.4	54.2	644,767	4,228	83,882	32.1	62,418	82.4	17.6	37.9	11.5	1,034	48.2
Clay	163	3.4	281	0.2	137.4	1,226,095	4,358	143,682	60.3	104,079	92.2	7.8	42.8	22.3	2,433	76.0
Clinton	223	-12.5	374	D	211.6	2,497,002	6,672	245,072	251.5	421,293	71.0	29.0	61.1	40.7	4,216	69.5
Crawford	46	2.2	137	0.0	16.2	351,639	2,561	40,038	7.2	21,323	D		17.2	2.4	288	29.6
Daviess	225	12.9	170	5.8	189.4	1,100,902	6,479	108,929	190.1	143,498	41.9	58.1	44.5	17.1	3,949	24.0
Dearborn	57	-14.1	101	0.1	26.8	410,578	4,071	46,287	12.4	22,191	74.9	25.1	27.3	6.1	650	33.9
Decatur	187	-8.9	306	0.0	162.6	1,627,090	5,321	166,746	159.4	261,293	58.0	42.0	62.8	37.0	3,721	74.1
DeKalb	161	0.1	174	0.8	136.8	771,247	4,429	92,135	106.9	115,738	65.5	34.5	35.8	16.6	4,689	73.6
Delaware	175	13.5	287	0.0	160.4	1,522,762	5,300	152,951	125.6	205,836	93.2	6.8	52.1	26.9	3,980	67.4
Dubois	175	-4.0	243	0.2	130.0	1,086,538	4,473	142,382	241.0	334,742	21.8	78.2	55.7	25.1	3,256	63.5
Elkhart	173	5.8	100	25.5	140.2	808,782	8,067	83,012	296.8	172,178	28.0	72.0	51.8	27.4	2,785	20.1
Fayette	78	-15.4	225	D	63.8	1,047,712	4,647	117,945	40.1	115,651	82.7	17.3	49.3	25.1	1,421	61.1
Floyd	21	-10.6	77	0.0	12.2	413,040	5,331	53,170	4.6	16,621	78.7	21.4	17.3	3.2	299	23.8
Fountain	214	13.6	466	D	190.5	2,236,072	4,797	218,709	116.7	253,644	D	D	52.4	30.9	3,690	68.9
Franklin	125	-1.1	172	0.1	85.1	786,644	4,577	92,254	54.0	142,304	78.8	21.2	47.3	17.6	2,101	61.9
Fulton	188	1.9	289	22.9	169.4	1,449,573	5,024	178,933	140.7	215,464	84.9	15.1	57.7	31.1	3,180	61.1
Gibson	268	16.0	455	4.8	250.3	2,426,261	5,329	255,418	146.4	248,542	87.7	12.3	63.2	35.5	4,803	70.6
Grant	183	-9.3	367	D	171.5	2,046,020	5,579	209,740	138.0	275,964	90.4	9.6	60.0	36.8	3,298	68.4
Greene	181	6.7	224	2.2	132.9	881,351	3,942	108,274	97.4	120,212	55.7	44.3	37.9	12.3	2,470	40.7
Hamilton	131	5.9	219	3.7	120.9	1,406,630	6,428	132,154	116.2	194,256	97.1	2.9	45.8	21.7	1,833	44.1
Hancock	166	-3.4	275	0.2	156.6	1,570,192	5,718	148,467	110.4	182,821	83.7	16.3	47.2	24.8	3,001	50.8
Harrison	135	-12.9	140	0.0	85.0	513,898	3,681	71,044	58.0	59,968	47.1	52.9	29.2	8.0	1,556	38.8
Hendricks	218	27.2	315	0.1	200.9	1,835,824	5,834	163,981	89.4	128,772	92.0	8.0	42.9	20.7	3,783	48.4
Henry	176	1.2	251	0.0	158.4	1,244,617	4,952	157,963	115.5	164,479	74.6	25.4	49.1	23.8	3,282	58.4
Howard	144	-11.1	303	D	134.5	1,924,391	6,353	182,880	140.4	294,874	81.1	18.9	68.1	37.2	2,993	67.0
Huntington	189	-5.1	272	0.7	172.6	1,481,458	5,452	216,573	174.8	251,550	65.7	34.3	50.5	28.2	4,185	71.7
Jackson	184	-12.1	247	2.9	139.9	1,132,552	4,582	174,212	184.4	247,907	42.2	57.8	50.8	24.5	3,876	66.7
Jasper	283	-16.9	460	21.1	256.7	2,819,873	6,132	250,876	357.4	581,142	58.3	41.7	61.3	40.0	4,736	72.8
Jay	176	-10.9	210	D	156.3	1,380,341	6,565	137,579	282.0	337,292	35.2	64.8	53.7	29.3	3,621	64.6
Jefferson	95	-6.9	155	0.0	61.7	549,182	3,540	72,820	40.4	65,737	76.7	23.3	32.4	8.8	1,907	53.3
Jennings	123	-10.8	234	0.1	87.7	910,475	3,896	126,716	79.7	150,917	57.8	42.2	37.5	16.9	3,214	57.4
Johnson	145	1.7	257	3.1	131.6	1,567,699	6,091	140,655	70.6	125,575	87.1	12.9	42.7	23.5	2,779	50.5
Knox	329	0.6	664	34.9	304.0	3,748,448	5,646	405,099	218.1	439,627	83.4	16.6	70.8	45.8	5,837	72.6
Kosciusko	255	1.4	204	18.0	219.6	1,198,890	5,866	110,144	282.1	226,226	47.0	53.0	42.4	20.8	4,140	51.7
LaGrange	204	26.2	84	25.6	147.4	628,366	7,448	56,611	262.6	108,542	26.1	73.9	55.2	23.1	2,276	12.5
Lake	133	3.6	309	8.1	124.2	1,755,500	5,673	178,735	100.8	234,374	98.1	1.9	44.4	30.0	2,419	49.1
LaPorte	228	-11.0	312	54.4	209.3	1,896,432	6,084	188,253	223.1	305,215	80.5	19.5	55.7	33.8	4,036	58.4
Lawrence	135	0.0	168	D	70.8	534,073	3,172	64,313	33.2	44,313	68.1	31.9	31.5	5.3	2,091	48.1
Madison	205	-5.6	278	0.9	191.5	1,677,897	6,028	169,689	164.4	223,026	91.7	8.3	53.5	29.0	3,565	58.8
Marion	20	16.5	87	0.2	16.0	558,134	6,422	60,861	27.3	117,991	D	D	29.4	10.8	220	16.5
Marshall	206	15.2	235	13.4	181.8	1,222,325	5,202	140,648	147.6	168,141	73.5	26.5	49.7	26.9	3,430	49.2
Martin	63	2.0	221	0.4	39.0	892,177	4,037	105,095	54.3	191,735	24.9	75.1	36.7	13.4	701	33.2
Miami	175	-1.5	263	3.1	158.1	1,333,943	5,069	145,643	156.9	235,605	67.1	32.9	55.0	32.6	3,696	68.8
Monroe	53	-1.4	114	0.1	27.6	551,762	4,831	55,294	13.0	28,134	66.7	33.3	28.4	5.6	754	29.0
Montgomery	287	-4.8	392	1.0	264.6	2,189,187	5,585	199,959	175.4	239,638	83.9	16.1	53.4	30.6	6,178	68.6
Morgan	137	20.2	235	0.0	114.2	1,158,144	4,922	130,446	51.8	88,768	87.9	12.1	36.4	14.8	2,146	46.0
Newton	192	0.8	552	6.3	174.3	3,131,055	5,674	315,417	242.6	697,187	53.1	46.9	66.1	46.3	3,086	79.6
Noble	181	13.5	156	13.7	150.1	754,298	4,834	95,800	143.7	123,588	57.4	42.6	44.3	18.4	4,236	52.5
Ohio	21	-0.2	126	0.2	10.5	446,731	3,560	57,649	4.2	24,462	74.7	25.3	28.7	4.1	368	34.5
Orange	98	0.9	206	0.0	56.9	717,036	3,488	102,278	64.0	133,902	22.4	77.6	30.3	8.6	1,599	47.9
Owen	96	8.8	174	0.1	62.5	590,885	3,396	76,073	23.5	42,805	82.7	17.3	29.0	8.0	1,537	49.7
Parke	177	-0.4	308	2.7	120.9	1,282,422	4,169	131,817	64.2	111,779	81.9	18.1	43.7	22.1	2,785	50.7
Perry	66	-5.9	160	0.0	30.7	481,276	2,999	62,182	20.3	49,208	47.4	52.6	35.1	7.5	605	42.4

Table B. States and Counties — Water Use, Wholesale Trade, Retail Trade, and Real Estate

STATE County	Water use, 2015		Wholesale Trade[1], 2012				Retail Trade[2], 2012				Real estate and rental and leasing,[2] 2012			
	Public supply water withdrawn (mil gal/day)	Public supply gallons withdrawn per person per day	Number of establish-ments	Number of employees	Sales (mil dol)	Annual payroll (mil dol)	Number of establish-ments	Number of employees	Sales (mil dol)	Annual payroll (mil dol)	Number of establish-ments	Number of employees	Sales (mil dol)	Annual payroll (mil dol)
	133	134	135	136	137	138	139	140	141	142	143	144	145	146
ILLINOIS— Cont'd														
Winnebago	29.23	101.8	333	4,123	2,700.4	207.0	986	14,298	3,752.1	326.5	212	1,512	169.0	43.7
Woodford	7.26	185.1	44	578	608.0	31.7	95	956	337.8	25.6	17	30	2.6	0.5
INDIANA	627.84	94.8	6,460	91,474	81,173.4	4,650.5	21,601	309,552	85,858.0	7,078.7	5,729	31,715	6,547.9	1171.7
Adams	2.31	66.0	35	267	240.0	9.9	133	1,500	377.2	33.3	19	D	D	D
Allen	35.70	96.9	506	7,683	9,187.6	368.3	1,273	19,912	5,197.7	467.2	382	1,863	361.6	66.5
Bartholomew	9.49	116.9	77	998	774.4	52.7	306	4,701	1,113.1	99.4	72	303	57.0	9.4
Benton	0.40	46.1	15	201	203.4	8.0	31	199	53.3	3.8	3	2	0.3	0.1
Blackford	1.04	84.6	10	D	D	D	38	406	96.7	9.0	12	33	3.5	0.5
Boone	2.01	31.7	58	901	1,684.0	45.1	160	2,238	1,137.9	72.0	52	170	35.1	5.4
Brown	0.00	0.0	5	46	2.6	0.6	77	343	58.4	6.4	11	76	5.4	1.5
Carroll	1.31	66.0	18	161	302.4	7.1	51	395	99.8	8.0	11	38	5.1	1.3
Cass	5.94	156.4	39	434	570.0	19.0	118	1,502	341.6	33.5	17	59	8.2	1.3
Clark	22.11	191.6	95	1,011	1,024.5	52.3	426	6,966	1,814.3	158.5	79	502	87.5	17.1
Clay	0.33	12.5	13	D	D	D	84	878	312.7	19.0	15	24	5.2	0.6
Clinton	3.68	112.9	24	D	D	D	102	992	239.1	21.3	11	38	4.8	0.8
Crawford	1.64	156.4	5	80	42.5	2.5	24	201	89.9	3.8	3	D	D	D
Daviess	3.55	107.9	31	336	227.3	14.3	122	1,502	485.9	37.9	18	58	6.9	1.1
Dearborn	4.41	89.2	31	207	311.2	9.3	140	1,962	576.5	48.7	36	103	14.2	2.7
Decatur	2.59	97.7	32	391	455.7	17.2	110	1,259	357.2	27.8	17	45	8.1	1.2
DeKalb	3.17	74.4	41	D	D	D	125	1,469	383.3	32.2	25	118	14.5	4.9
Delaware	9.58	82.0	92	894	805.8	32.1	428	6,189	1,519.9	131.9	95	447	90.7	16.5
Dubois	5.84	137.5	74	1,053	637.0	50.3	217	3,332	919.2	79.8	31	D	D	D
Elkhart	12.95	63.6	340	5,803	3,329.9	249.5	678	8,754	2,440.4	206.9	157	768	134.5	25.4
Fayette	2.42	103.3	14	114	110.9	5.5	75	1,070	234.4	23.6	20	68	7.1	1.3
Floyd	1.21	15.8	69	579	323.3	23.3	206	3,146	772.3	69.6	69	205	34.4	5.9
Fountain	0.88	53.0	12	77	127.3	3.6	64	572	148.3	10.8	5	12	1.1	0.3
Franklin	2.62	114.6	7	33	14.8	1.3	68	662	170.2	13.4	8	14	1.6	0.3
Fulton	1.07	52.7	18	141	98.2	5.6	79	913	214.0	19.3	15	39	4.3	0.9
Gibson	1.71	50.6	20	267	188.5	11.3	120	1,643	557.6	37.8	17	47	11.8	1.4
Grant	3.95	58.1	37	367	251.0	15.6	244	3,113	793.3	65.7	43	154	17.7	3.8
Greene	2.87	88.5	17	130	107.2	4.5	103	1,054	252.4	20.2	19	59	5.2	1.3
Hamilton	35.69	115.2	357	4,138	3,403.7	291.1	865	15,746	4,338.4	397.7	395	2,349	1,394.5	144.2
Hancock	3.18	43.8	42	624	737.6	27.2	162	2,102	600.8	48.3	45	167	32.4	4.6
Harrison	2.64	66.7	20	D	D	D	114	1,423	470.2	30.7	18	36	5.8	0.8
Hendricks	5.10	32.2	101	2,980	2,723.4	141.5	441	8,760	2,561.4	201.3	108	506	82.6	16.7
Henry	4.68	95.5	31	D	D	D	152	1,551	466.2	33.1	25	73	7.5	1.7
Howard	8.47	102.6	62	559	512.7	31.6	328	4,927	1,193.3	104.0	71	311	50.4	8.9
Huntington	3.73	101.8	36	D	D	D	135	1,347	318.1	26.9	30	73	12.2	1.6
Jackson	5.39	122.3	35	D	D	D	183	2,225	592.7	49.9	45	115	17.7	2.5
Jasper	0.91	27.2	33	251	529.3	14.7	123	1,449	572.1	31.3	20	89	23.1	2.2
Jay	1.52	72.0	15	185	230.3	7.3	66	650	136.9	14.1	6	9	2.2	0.3
Jefferson	5.63	173.7	19	D	D	D	128	1,550	390.9	35.3	30	70	11.6	2.1
Jennings	1.03	36.9	15	D	D	D	66	751	196.9	16.9	10	32	3.2	0.8
Johnson	10.04	67.1	103	1,981	1,174.7	114.6	494	8,639	2,324.6	192.1	117	356	84.5	10.3
Knox	4.20	110.7	54	588	463.0	23.6	161	2,062	459.1	40.1	38	197	21.5	4.2
Kosciusko	3.33	42.4	89	D	D	D	298	3,566	921.5	82.7	72	162	24.7	3.8
LaGrange	0.97	25.0	33	313	182.4	10.4	151	1,127	284.4	24.7	26	47	7.4	1.2
Lake	76.05	155.9	413	4,472	4,599.1	219.2	1,513	23,986	7,495.3	551.0	373	2,090	371.9	74.3
LaPorte	9.35	84.3	100	1,161	694.9	46.8	457	5,845	1,367.8	116.2	84	367	95.2	10.6
Lawrence	5.05	111.0	22	D	D	D	160	1,897	519.2	42.6	21	68	8.1	1.8
Madison	14.98	115.5	73	974	1,301.2	50.0	346	4,944	1,378.7	107.9	81	348	58.2	10.3
Marion	111.30	118.5	1,295	23,766	18,700.3	1,359.0	2,952	46,739	14,421.7	1,155.9	1,244	11,355	2,105.2	465.9
Marshall	2.85	60.8	53	523	430.5	21.5	172	1,993	568.6	45.0	30	86	10.9	2.1
Martin	0.63	61.6	4	D	D	D	34	350	150.1	7.8	3	10	0.2	0.1
Miami	2.66	74.2	29	D	D	D	94	900	226.2	18.1	17	44	4.9	0.8
Monroe	15.78	109.0	82	D	D	D	458	7,390	1,661.3	145.2	163	865	152.5	27.7
Montgomery	3.61	94.4	41	343	365.7	16.0	129	1,651	446.6	34.4	29	63	12.0	1.9
Morgan	10.52	151.0	33	275	139.3	13.8	196	2,374	638.0	49.7	44	97	15.6	2.8
Newton	0.56	40.0	19	178	214.9	7.2	40	336	88.0	6.4	5	13	0.6	0.2
Noble	2.30	48.2	39	507	450.7	22.7	139	1,543	392.9	33.4	34	87	12.2	2.2
Ohio	0.74	124.6	4	D	D	D	13	88	15.3	1.3	3	D	D	D
Orange	0.00	0.0	12	74	63.7	2.9	61	668	156.0	13.6	11	35	2.3	0.6
Owen	1.40	67.1	10	D	D	D	38	424	111.9	9.3	7	7	1.5	0.2
Parke	0.93	55.0	7	97	47.6	2.8	43	304	70.1	5.7	11	66	6.2	2.2
Perry	0.33	17.1	9	66	13.3	1.9	65	718	157.2	13.2	11	33	4.3	0.7

1. Merchant wholesalers, except manufacturers' sales branches and offices.   2. Employer establishments.

Table B. States and Counties — Professional Services, Manufacturing, and Accommodation and Food Services

STATE County	Professional, scientific, and technical services, 2012				Manufacturing, 2012				Accommodation and food services, 2012			
	Number of establish-ments	Number of employees	Sales (mil dol)	Annual payroll (mil dol)	Number of establishments	Number of employees	Receipts (mil dol)	Annual payroll (mil dol)	Number of establishments	Number of employees	Receipts (mil dol)	Annual payroll (mil dol)
	147	148	149	150	151	152	153	154	155	156	157	158
ILLINOIS— Cont'd												
Winnebago......................	608	3,779	660.0	191.5	600	25,024	8,145.6	1,491.8	566	10,168	490.0	137.0
Woodford	47	205	20.5	8.5	45	2,464	1,363.6	122.9	61	830	28.5	8.2
INDIANA.....................	12,829	99,962	14,702.0	5,490.6	8,141	452,513	242,763.8	23,041.3	13,057	255,223	13,076.6	3432.7
Adams.........................	45	215	19.0	8.0	63	4,246	2,200.6	172.8	55	800	27.7	7.3
Allen...........................	874	5,326	720.8	254.0	501	24,975	16,200.1	1,336.5	712	15,250	643.1	190.1
Bartholomew..................	159	3,550	299.0	234.7	142	11,663	5,636.4	553.6	201	4,243	198.6	54.2
Benton.........................	8	31	3.5	0.8	15	341	D	13.3	9	51	1.8	0.4
Blackford......................	11	97	13.3	3.5	24	1,056	255.6	43.8	20	221	7.7	2.2
Boone..........................	166	645	120.2	33.5	69	1,759	D	70.7	117	1,686	71.4	20.3
Brown..........................	32	80	9.5	4.0	15	111	D	2.7	33	D	D	D
Carroll	23	90	7.0	2.2	25	1,963	D	76.1	32	407	19.4	5.6
Cass............................	44	224	17.7	5.9	50	4,197	1,768.1	144.2	79	1,062	40.8	11.0
Clark...........................	177	1,021	126.2	37.9	143	7,708	2,376.6	340.7	219	D	D	D
Clay............................	23	D	D	D	33	2,198	520.4	82.3	45	531	21.4	5.7
Clinton.........................	44	144	12.6	4.1	37	3,035	3,192.7	143.0	52	680	27.5	7.9
Crawford	4	12	0.4	0.1	5	D	D	D	21	D	D	D
Daviess........................	42	554	125.3	42.0	73	1,726	848.1	56.0	56	981	35.3	9.4
Dearborn......................	69	320	24.6	9.3	46	1,460	385.1	64.9	69	D	D	D
Decatur........................	31	131	12.6	4.2	56	4,722	4,663.4	208.9	51	953	38.1	10.8
DeKalb.........................	71	449	40.5	14.5	111	8,128	4,742.1	414.3	81	1,387	53.1	14.7
Delaware......................	163	1,522	240.5	63.4	130	4,205	1,591.3	191.2	211	4,417	172.7	49.6
Dubois.........................	83	355	34.8	12.1	103	9,834	D	363.1	100	1,727	65.8	18.1
Elkhart.........................	313	2,004	220.2	81.0	795	53,705	14,833.3	2,288.0	348	6,500	280.7	75.8
Fayette........................	28	214	10.5	4.1	30	1,195	489.7	60.2	43	D	D	D
Floyd...........................	195	1,068	151.9	45.7	108	5,421	1,726.9	264.2	130	D	D	D
Fountain.......................	17	75	4.8	1.5	21	2,368	615.1	96.6	38	370	13.0	3.7
Franklin	17	52	9.1	1.3	18	551	258.0	26.2	40	589	27.1	7.3
Fulton..........................	32	142	43.4	4.5	43	1,751	513.9	75.7	45	488	18.9	4.8
Gibson.........................	48	281	29.9	16.3	41	6,144	6,041.4	368.0	68	1,192	45.9	13.2
Grant...........................	75	359	31.6	10.8	68	4,770	2,013.0	278.8	129	2,061	89.8	24.7
Greene.........................	47	253	25.7	9.6	23	449	118.7	23.9	54	702	22.1	6.5
Hamilton.......................	1,260	6,790	1,168.3	472.1	196	5,171	1,641.7	242.7	579	11,974	588.2	166.1
Hancock.......................	124	4,210	274.6	186.2	56	2,998	1,183.9	124.7	98	1,872	80.7	23.3
Harrison.......................	40	159	11.1	4.6	41	1,613	473.0	64.4	61	2,442	349.8	49.6
Hendricks.....................	285	1,105	127.4	44.7	96	3,336	2,660.1	148.1	298	6,387	292.8	82.5
Henry..........................	50	209	17.5	5.4	42	1,845	579.9	78.3	64	921	42.8	11.5
Howard........................	114	631	61.2	22.6	70	7,671	D	593.4	186	3,866	159.9	46.1
Huntington....................	43	180	15.6	5.4	64	3,417	1,740.6	170.7	87	1,207	47.3	13.3
Jackson........................	54	294	25.9	8.4	64	5,395	2,307.5	268.1	86	1,536	65.4	18.3
Jasper.........................	49	203	16.0	4.9	35	1,426	650.4	65.8	64	868	34.5	9.5
Jay..............................	22	83	4.7	1.7	34	3,042	1,059.2	119.1	33	545	19.9	5.4
Jefferson......................	42	242	15.3	7.4	43	2,754	1,548.4	132.8	83	1,408	50.6	14.6
Jennings.......................	19	88	11.1	3.3	37	1,712	425.6	68.3	31	453	17.8	4.9
Johnson........................	270	1,332	166.6	51.7	123	4,932	2,024.1	237.4	282	6,135	263.6	75.4
Knox............................	46	216	18.9	6.1	40	1,789	464.0	66.8	84	1,508	63.5	16.8
Kosciusko.....................	138	475	44.8	14.4	173	13,247	7,235.4	750.6	167	2,452	113.3	31.3
LaGrange......................	39	178	10.8	4.3	134	5,141	1,416.3	234.2	68	907	39.6	11.2
Lake............................	886	6,003	709.3	261.6	349	23,122	30,831.9	1,746.0	983	18,097	1,167.0	265.5
LaPorte........................	158	1,069	85.0	40.4	172	7,589	2,644.0	350.5	235	4,992	357.0	78.7
Lawrence......................	66	784	87.5	34.2	60	2,008	437.3	100.3	69	1,177	52.2	13.6
Madison........................	182	769	70.8	23.0	94	2,701	1,391.1	129.3	229	3,885	165.5	47.6
Marion..........................	2,747	32,947	5,954.4	2,344.4	881	42,808	28,049.4	2,579.2	2,130	47,455	2,645.5	734.8
Marshall........................	62	334	24.4	8.9	130	5,712	1,816.5	240.3	90	1,343	56.6	16.7
Martin..........................	20	1,107	163.2	64.4	10	324	64.2	15.9	25	243	8.8	2.7
Miami	31	111	8.6	3.1	38	1,542	D	68.7	55	796	31.2	8.7
Monroe.........................	289	2,014	240.8	98.8	94	6,578	1,548.5	283.0	368	7,805	335.9	92.3
Montgomery...................	53	187	15.3	5.1	64	4,658	2,719.5	230.0	91	1,150	49.5	12.6
Morgan.........................	94	323	31.4	10.1	64	1,847	649.4	86.0	71	D	D	D
Newton.........................	17	61	5.8	1.9	24	663	156.2	24.9	28	209	8.7	2.2
Noble...........................	46	165	16.6	5.0	123	8,351	2,937.7	337.5	74	1,046	38.5	10.5
Ohio............................	4	D	D	D	4	16	D	D	12	D	D	D
Orange.........................	18	75	4.5	1.8	24	1,216	208.9	43.5	39	1,921	148.8	37.4
Owen...........................	22	68	5.3	1.9	27	1,117	169.4	48.8	18	363	12.3	3.4
Parke...........................	10	62	4.0	1.4	13	402	D	20.2	24	211	9.1	2.3
Perry...........................	24	78	10.4	2.9	29	1,883	945.5	102.1	40	500	23.7	6.1

STATE County	Health care and social assistance, 2012				Other services, 2012				Nonemployer businesses, 2015		Value of residential construction authorized by building permits, 2017	
	Number of establishments	Number of employees	Receipts (mil dol)	Annual payroll (mil dol)	Number of establishments	Number of employees	Receipts (mil dol)	Annual payroll (mil dol)	Number	Receipts (mil dol)	New construction ($1,000)	Number of housing units
	159	160	161	162	163	164	165	166	167	168	169	170
ILLINOIS— Cont'd												
Winnebago	665	19,871	2,398.9	923.1	534	3,186	306.6	82.3	18,120	642.5	26,084	195
Woodford	51	2,063	112.3	60.6	48	213	24.0	6.6	2,495	90.4	16,553	71
INDIANA	15,156	396,923	42,493.1	16,208.7	10,777	72,937	8,909.7	2,106.7	403,546	16,458.7	4,583,499	21,664
Adams	53	1,475	100.3	47.7	76	392	31.2	7.6	3,132	169.9	10,141	85
Allen	947	28,368	2,803.4	1,195.5	661	4,571	441.6	133.1	23,179	947.1	292,414	1522
Bartholomew	221	4,824	512.8	203.1	111	692	82.5	19.7	4,184	169.7	49,578	204
Benton	13	67	4.0	2.2	10	29	3.5	0.8	609	22.1	2,652	17
Blackford	22	385	27.6	10.6	21	65	7.0	1.5	625	21.7	470	3
Boone	120	2,318	207.4	87.6	98	606	44.7	11.8	5,192	264.8	163,114	539
Brown	22	311	18.8	8.2	18	97	7.2	2.5	1,448	53.6	20,097	79
Carroll	26	255	18.4	7.9	26	85	6.8	1.8	1,307	56.1	9,341	60
Cass	65	2,332	180.8	88.4	59	328	22.5	5.1	1,786	62.9	4,282	27
Clark	239	5,916	591.2	239.0	173	1,192	138.5	33.2	6,718	302.4	113,703	554
Clay	44	574	59.5	17.3	40	360	23.0	6.4	1,420	50.3	0	0
Clinton	50	1,162	79.5	34.0	48	303	26.9	7.6	1,680	61.3	10,660	121
Crawford	14	D	D	D	8	D	D	D	625	24.3	0	0
Daviess	75	1,452	99.5	42.3	69	325	81.7	12.4	2,144	90.0	2,997	23
Dearborn	117	D	D	D	71	328	29.3	8.1	3,000	126.0	29,305	130
Decatur	59	1,064	99.7	42.2	40	242	22.8	4.7	1,557	61.1	12,473	54
DeKalb	87	1,613	126.8	53.2	70	353	26.5	6.2	2,527	103.9	29,383	154
Delaware	313	9,158	873.1	318.7	174	1,043	105.9	26.2	5,649	206.4	15,205	72
Dubois	124	3,358	314.6	124.1	82	462	58.1	13.4	2,751	107.5	20,969	83
Elkhart	362	10,105	1,160.8	413.6	336	2,069	261.0	61.1	12,754	562.7	97,970	560
Fayette	61	1,773	127.7	57.0	39	171	13.6	3.8	1,042	36.7	502	3
Floyd	238	5,715	577.4	218.7	127	864	81.9	18.4	5,174	226.7	69,374	231
Fountain	24	511	36.2	11.8	33	82	7.4	1.7	977	35.0	4,787	58
Franklin	52	833	55.8	19.3	38	107	10.4	2.6	1,598	66.8	10,987	47
Fulton	45	847	78.6	26.9	38	126	14.1	3.0	1,303	53.0	3,376	14
Gibson	77	1,923	150.9	61.2	53	246	21.9	6.2	1,652	58.6	21,224	148
Grant	192	5,281	508.2	211.7	106	475	50.7	13.4	3,308	112.1	10,615	54
Greene	66	1,049	75.4	27.6	50	176	14.2	3.2	1,821	54.5	NA	NA
Hamilton	897	16,978	2,311.3	740.4	498	3,201	249.8	74.1	27,498	1,409.9	929,813	3089
Hancock	136	2,511	256.0	93.5	94	391	36.8	9.4	5,045	199.2	106,783	528
Harrison	68	1,346	103.6	39.4	39	127	13.8	3.4	2,553	90.9	24,877	120
Hendricks	296	7,036	763.3	293.4	206	1,574	114.9	37.1	10,736	442.3	279,775	1504
Henry	90	2,718	194.9	82.2	66	323	31.9	6.7	2,407	85.8	7,339	34
Howard	221	5,417	456.4	182.6	129	922	68.2	18.9	4,225	150.6	15,545	92
Huntington	66	1,812	141.2	53.9	75	369	23.1	6.4	1,827	64.6	14,286	71
Jackson	106	2,528	237.0	87.4	75	435	38.5	9.3	2,139	83.7	20,329	182
Jasper	47	1,400	85.1	40.8	55	D	D	D	1,791	75.7	18,960	84
Jay	28	819	62.4	25.5	35	99	10.6	1.8	1,347	59.3	3,208	15
Jefferson	74	1,963	187.1	80.7	53	257	19.9	4.8	1,818	73.7	6,425	37
Jennings	74	933	70.5	30.0	24	84	6.5	1.7	1,444	53.2	5,723	45
Johnson	331	7,291	632.2	272.9	222	1,587	160.0	49.9	9,886	453.4	220,393	1097
Knox	110	3,345	327.7	129.2	69	347	36.4	9.9	1,866	68.8	8,085	43
Kosciusko	149	3,711	321.4	118.8	145	934	108.8	24.1	5,019	192.4	44,439	277
LaGrange	46	807	69.7	25.4	44	197	20.3	5.8	3,653	162.0	30,046	152
Lake	1,254	31,946	3,812.7	1,353.0	876	6,336	638.4	185.0	28,274	1,056.4	320,402	1399
LaPorte	228	5,626	611.2	208.3	194	1,090	79.0	22.5	5,858	206.4	37,400	157
Lawrence	94	2,646	202.8	80.1	73	361	30.7	8.6	2,577	92.2	1,722	16
Madison	251	6,498	697.3	262.5	199	1,088	77.1	21.6	6,670	235.0	30,140	169
Marion	2,414	83,226	10,235.0	4,151.7	1,625	17,182	3,477.5	665.9	61,844	2,452.5	361,223	1632
Marshall	72	1,809	156.9	50.9	84	501	50.6	14.3	2,818	114.1	37,776	133
Martin	9	D	D	D	12	63	6.2	2.2	618	21.6	610	6
Miami	40	1,148	98.7	36.7	44	349	34.5	9.2	1,668	62.7	3,616	20
Monroe	329	8,906	927.6	356.4	204	1,905	265.5	55.8	9,182	348.7	102,546	557
Montgomery	84	1,332	106.2	43.3	83	304	24.1	5.8	2,084	81.8	11,947	57
Morgan	109	2,069	235.0	74.2	97	452	42.8	11.5	4,482	181.4	36,544	142
Newton	13	253	13.1	6.2	18	D	D	D	736	30.1	3,854	19
Noble	73	1,347	132.7	43.6	81	280	42.4	7.7	2,553	94.0	20,694	109
Ohio	8	D	D	D	6	D	D	D	343	12.1	2,668	21
Orange	42	862	69.7	25.6	31	138	11.1	2.3	1,153	44.9	270	2
Owen	23	422	22.9	10.0	27	68	4.8	1.1	1,374	51.8	10,523	47
Parke	19	D	D	D	29	71	8.0	1.6	1,082	60.7	6,056	39
Perry	36	846	80.3	26.4	26	83	6.8	1.8	882	35.3	5,333	31

Table B. States and Counties — Government Employment and Payroll, and Local Government Finances

	Government employment and payroll, 2012									Local government finances				
			March payroll (percent of total)							General revenue				
												Taxes		
													Per capita[1] (dollars)	
STATE County	Full-time equivalent employees	March payroll (dollars)	Adminis-tration, judicial, and legal	Police and corrections	Fire protection	Highways and transpor-tation	Health and welfare	Natural resources and utilities	Education and libraries	Total (mil dol)	Inter-govern-mental (mil dol)	Total (mil dol)	Total	Property
	171	172	173	174	175	176	177	178	179	180	181	182	183	184
ILLINOIS— Cont'd														
Winnebago	10,237	41,731,581	5.0	11.9	6.0	3.7	3.9	7.5	61.2	1,183.6	493.6	527.0	1,804	1627
Woodford	1,508	5,339,422	4.9	6.4	1.3	4.5	0.9	2.8	78.6	119.7	45.6	61.2	1,570	1555
INDIANA	X	X	X	X	X	X	X	X	X	X	X	X	X	X
Adams	1,561	4,888,145	4.7	5.9	0.8	2.1	44.7	3.1	37.8	145.4	46.1	31.4	914	779
Allen	10,511	40,339,187	6.4	12.9	4.3	4.7	1.4	5.9	62.8	1,115.0	515.1	426.4	1,183	960
Bartholomew	4,371	15,688,309	3.2	6.6	2.9	1.3	44.5	3.1	37.7	469.7	111.3	106.7	1,348	1076
Benton	555	1,313,464	8.3	7.4	0.0	6.3	5.5	2.3	69.0	40.6	19.2	16.2	1,838	1489
Blackford	419	1,328,279	7.1	13.0	1.8	3.7	2.2	4.2	65.8	39.7	21.9	11.2	898	707
Boone	2,618	9,699,681	4.3	6.4	4.6	1.8	30.1	1.6	50.8	311.1	88.4	80.6	1,367	1089
Brown	487	1,429,248	8.6	9.6	0.0	3.1	3.6	3.8	70.3	49.6	24.3	20.7	1,373	893
Carroll	613	1,723,537	7.5	7.8	0.0	5.1	6.1	5.3	66.8	54.7	26.6	20.7	1,030	776
Cass	2,403	7,224,020	3.1	5.7	1.4	1.6	31.7	7.4	48.9	182.8	62.7	46.0	1,192	797
Clark	4,732	18,084,071	3.7	7.9	2.7	2.4	38.3	3.7	41.0	466.1	142.4	134.5	1,201	884
Clay	1,049	2,619,145	6.8	6.9	1.9	3.0	1.0	5.5	72.4	75.7	42.8	22.3	831	529
Clinton	1,323	4,321,114	6.4	5.1	2.9	2.8	0.7	8.5	67.5	112.5	54.4	40.9	1,238	878
Crawford	416	1,229,568	6.6	5.4	0.0	4.7	3.2	1.7	77.0	32.3	18.4	8.3	783	640
Daviess	1,354	4,234,993	5.9	7.5	1.3	3.1	36.1	7.1	38.5	148.6	57.8	30.0	937	730
Dearborn	2,410	9,132,488	4.4	7.5	0.7	1.6	40.1	3.6	41.5	318.7	143.7	50.2	1,007	864
Decatur	1,237	4,252,343	4.4	5.2	2.3	2.0	40.2	2.9	42.7	119.2	37.5	26.3	1,009	794
DeKalb	1,614	5,058,353	9.1	8.5	2.6	3.0	1.3	8.0	66.9	153.8	68.7	51.5	1,216	955
Delaware	3,335	10,832,587	6.2	9.0	3.6	4.7	3.7	4.2	64.9	345.4	171.1	109.1	930	778
Dubois	1,643	4,804,962	7.3	8.1	0.8	5.6	2.5	16.6	59.1	155.2	64.9	49.7	1,180	905
Elkhart	6,985	24,411,992	5.4	8.4	4.1	2.5	1.6	3.6	73.6	630.5	315.1	218.4	1,094	907
Fayette	815	2,807,530	4.2	10.7	4.2	2.9	3.8	5.1	67.2	77.2	42.2	24.8	1,032	701
Floyd	4,128	15,144,305	3.0	3.9	2.2	0.8	54.1	2.1	33.3	467.4	119.9	81.4	1,081	846
Fountain	702	1,835,852	6.6	8.5	1.6	5.5	6.2	3.5	67.3	53.7	31.0	15.9	930	767
Franklin	568	1,607,664	8.0	8.8	0.0	4.5	1.5	2.6	73.5	47.8	26.1	16.2	704	477
Fulton	976	3,541,251	3.8	5.5	1.3	2.2	47.4	1.8	37.3	96.4	27.9	20.7	1,000	751
Gibson	1,093	3,390,759	8.4	7.1	3.0	3.7	4.8	4.6	68.3	107.6	54.3	38.1	1,140	1012
Grant	2,226	7,247,230	7.6	13.8	3.6	3.3	0.8	2.9	67.7	198.6	103.6	70.9	1,023	759
Greene	1,299	4,191,866	4.9	6.2	1.0	2.4	23.5	4.2	56.9	123.7	53.8	24.9	756	573
Hamilton	9,749	38,707,131	4.7	8.4	7.3	2.0	14.0	2.7	59.9	1,219.3	387.4	488.6	1,688	1330
Hancock	2,896	9,851,360	4.6	8.2	3.9	1.7	31.8	2.5	45.9	327.9	103.5	93.6	1,319	977
Harrison	1,349	4,713,395	5.2	4.9	0.0	2.6	36.7	2.0	47.0	155.4	72.7	26.9	689	469
Hendricks	6,025	22,075,204	3.7	5.6	5.8	1.4	30.4	2.6	50.1	681.2	209.2	213.8	1,421	1074
Henry	2,369	7,555,604	4.3	5.2	1.2	2.3	32.1	3.4	50.6	241.5	75.8	42.1	853	643
Howard	4,091	15,459,399	5.0	6.2	3.5	2.0	35.8	3.0	42.2	435.8	136.7	118.7	1,433	1170
Huntington	1,237	3,734,687	5.5	8.0	4.3	3.5	1.1	5.4	69.0	101.2	49.3	39.0	1,055	770
Jackson	2,118	8,012,413	3.8	6.5	2.3	1.6	47.5	1.4	36.3	212.1	54.8	30.5	707	506
Jasper	1,433	4,507,418	5.5	8.1	0.3	2.6	29.7	5.3	47.8	131.9	42.0	40.9	1,224	719
Jay	1,099	3,415,778	5.2	6.1	1.4	1.7	36.1	3.1	45.2	123.7	55.6	25.5	1,196	860
Jefferson	902	3,038,763	7.5	7.5	0.7	2.5	2.6	4.5	74.2	89.4	47.0	26.9	826	757
Jennings	908	2,922,410	4.4	7.4	0.6	3.0	2.6	5.4	75.0	78.7	47.6	22.3	793	611
Johnson	4,964	16,948,881	4.8	8.7	2.9	1.9	18.6	2.7	59.4	506.1	198.1	162.0	1,131	885
Knox	2,489	8,335,443	2.7	4.6	1.9	1.6	60.2	2.8	25.4	286.7	52.9	33.9	890	737
Kosciusko	2,569	8,158,465	6.1	8.0	0.4	2.3	0.9	3.7	77.8	243.0	119.1	85.5	1,101	909
LaGrange	1,149	3,367,799	4.8	6.5	0.3	3.1	0.6	2.5	80.6	95.5	51.4	32.4	865	663
Lake	18,892	64,877,066	9.2	9.9	4.1	4.4	2.1	8.2	60.1	2,367.0	1,042.1	989.0	2,003	1956
LaPorte	4,264	12,639,630	5.9	11.9	4.3	3.5	3.5	6.6	63.1	369.8	180.5	137.0	1,231	1055
Lawrence	1,833	6,258,969	4.2	7.1	2.2	2.7	24.3	3.4	55.6	143.8	73.1	50.7	1,100	799
Madison	3,695	12,894,572	8.1	13.7	4.5	3.9	1.5	11.3	55.4	411.1	191.4	142.7	1,095	811
Marion	34,223	145,267,021	3.8	7.6	6.1	1.6	14.0	18.4	48.0	4,321.3	1,815.1	1,329.5	1,447	1014
Marshall	1,390	4,686,571	6.2	10.5	1.5	4.0	1.4	5.1	69.8	140.9	76.1	48.0	1,020	856
Martin	313	962,585	8.0	8.2	0.0	3.8	2.8	1.5	67.8	29.8	16.1	7.1	689	541
Miami	1,311	4,091,188	4.5	6.1	2.6	3.8	0.7	6.7	70.0	119.6	65.2	34.0	931	637
Monroe	3,589	12,483,781	10.4	10.4	5.5	5.0	2.7	8.7	56.9	339.2	139.6	147.6	1,046	827
Montgomery	1,366	4,441,185	3.7	7.5	4.2	3.9	1.0	10.2	68.9	131.4	58.1	56.2	1,468	1078
Morgan	2,356	7,692,514	4.7	7.9	3.4	3.0	18.5	1.3	60.5	238.5	98.7	72.4	1,044	538
Newton	607	1,789,217	10.0	9.0	0.0	3.9	4.7	2.6	67.9	61.2	25.8	18.1	1,291	1109
Noble	1,526	4,688,687	7.9	9.1	1.0	3.1	0.3	4.9	73.3	132.6	63.7	46.2	972	770
Ohio	248	804,741	9.9	6.7	0.0	5.5	3.4	20.4	52.3	29.4	20.3	4.8	786	579
Orange	656	2,087,602	7.2	6.3	0.2	4.7	1.4	5.5	73.3	74.2	49.7	16.5	838	620
Owen	478	1,467,231	7.6	11.8	0.0	5.3	4.5	1.2	68.4	51.9	27.2	15.9	742	538
Parke	550	1,469,526	6.3	9.1	0.8	4.5	3.5	4.2	69.9	47.3	28.5	14.7	862	531
Perry	892	2,938,269	4.0	4.8	0.4	4.2	35.8	7.7	42.5	92.9	30.5	18.1	929	744

1. Based on the resident population estimated as of July 1 of the year shown.

Table B. States and Counties — Local Government Finances, Government Employment, and Income Taxes

	Local government finances (cont.)							Debt outstanding		Government employment, 2016			Individual income tax returns, 2015		
	Direct general expenditure														
			Percent of total for:												
STATE County	Total (mil dol)	Per capita[1] (dollars)	Education	Health and hospitals	Police protection	Public welfare	Highways	Total (mil dol)	Per capita[1] (dollars)	Federal civilian	Federal military	State and local	Number of returns	Mean adjusted gross income	Mean income tax
	185	186	187	188	189	190	191	192	193	194	195	196	197	198	199
ILLINOIS— Cont'd															
Winnebago	1,135.0	3,886	50.2	1.7	8.1	3.0	5.4	750.7	2,570	828	598	13,933	136,190	52,202	5850
Woodford	116.2	2,982	68.7	1.1	3.9	0.0	7.1	40.0	1,026	73	78	1,806	18,270	73,685	9659
INDIANA	X	X	X	X	X	X	X	X	X	37,734	20,696	385,713	3,104,390	55,910	6780
Adams	133.8	3,893	35.3	41.5	1.9	0.6	3.0	120.4	3,505	62	106	2,042	15,150	48,349	5092
Allen	969.6	2,690	50.6	0.7	6.5	0.4	3.3	1,061.3	2,945	2,008	1,144	16,929	176,860	55,800	7070
Bartholomew	465.6	5,883	32.7	40.9	1.8	0.5	0.9	364.3	4,603	169	245	6,263	39,920	62,456	7509
Benton	35.9	4,079	50.7	2.9	2.6	0.5	7.6	27.8	3,163	25	26	584	4,110	45,012	4425
Blackford	31.6	2,526	55.3	0.6	5.0	0.9	4.4	22.9	1,830	24	37	530	5,850	40,774	3598
Boone	254.2	4,312	38.4	34.0	3.4	0.2	3.0	422.2	7,162	97	196	3,471	30,460	103,128	18,283
Brown	46.1	3,056	59.2	0.2	2.0	0.2	4.2	23.3	1,545	14	45	830	7,660	51,657	5591
Carroll	44.9	2,233	56.6	1.7	3.2	1.1	6.3	15.9	791	68	61	795	9,570	50,343	4975
Cass	169.3	4,387	43.5	32.2	4.5	0.2	2.9	80.8	2,094	94	113	3,063	17,920	43,808	4163
Clark	456.8	4,081	34.1	34.1	3.8	0.2	1.1	411.3	3,674	1,575	353	4,620	56,840	49,657	4990
Clay	70.5	2,627	57.4	1.1	2.7	0.5	3.4	38.3	1,426	70	79	1,223	11,980	45,792	4250
Clinton	106.0	3,210	57.5	0.5	2.8	0.7	3.5	96.4	2,919	61	97	1,682	15,350	45,517	4171
Crawford	28.5	2,676	60.9	2.8	2.1	0.1	4.3	20.9	1,955	21	32	515	4,610	39,746	3148
Daviess	136.7	4,263	34.6	34.7	1.9	0.2	4.2	136.4	4,253	75	99	1,746	14,520	48,474	5064
Dearborn	292.4	5,869	28.3	29.1	2.1	0.0	1.6	199.3	3,999	108	149	2,938	24,880	57,155	6413
Decatur	123.9	4,759	32.1	32.1	1.8	0.1	1.8	144.4	5,545	60	80	1,546	12,860	47,185	4491
DeKalb	141.5	3,344	61.2	0.3	3.3	0.3	3.6	92.5	2,185	83	129	1,978	20,480	50,321	5350
Delaware	323.3	2,755	48.4	0.8	3.9	0.5	2.7	191.9	1,635	290	334	10,595	48,930	46,410	4997
Dubois	122.5	2,913	62.4	0.6	3.1	0.1	4.8	195.3	4,641	100	127	2,135	22,470	66,281	9669
Elkhart	609.8	3,055	58.2	1.0	3.9	0.2	3.5	758.8	3,801	267	611	8,457	94,480	55,585	6900
Fayette	72.1	3,001	59.5	1.8	4.9	0.2	5.4	37.9	1,577	44	70	1,082	10,180	40,609	3510
Floyd	441.6	5,865	25.8	49.3	1.8	0.0	1.1	309.6	4,113	215	231	6,396	38,010	65,878	9035
Fountain	45.0	2,632	61.9	2.3	2.9	0.3	7.1	40.9	2,387	60	50	754	7,930	43,504	3971
Franklin	38.8	1,688	69.0	0.1	2.0	0.3	4.9	26.8	1,166	44	69	932	10,840	55,012	6102
Fulton	83.1	4,008	31.5	45.7	2.8	0.1	2.5	22.8	1,097	46	61	1,326	9,440	47,896	4899
Gibson	99.3	2,969	54.6	1.5	3.1	0.1	6.2	186.7	5,581	89	101	1,348	16,120	51,201	5197
Grant	175.3	2,529	54.4	0.3	7.8	0.2	3.4	108.6	1,566	1,041	190	2,819	29,420	41,992	3809
Greene	110.5	3,356	48.9	22.9	1.7	0.1	3.4	52.3	1,587	74	98	1,752	14,310	45,727	4237
Hamilton	1,098.2	3,794	43.5	16.9	3.8	0.1	2.9	2,131.8	7,364	396	962	13,225	147,240	104,443	17,831
Hancock	259.1	3,652	38.3	36.3	2.5	0.1	3.7	430.2	6,065	112	223	3,807	36,040	62,480	7230
Harrison	142.1	3,631	38.8	32.2	0.5	0.1	1.6	105.0	2,682	99	120	2,084	18,220	50,385	4973
Hendricks	586.7	3,900	37.8	29.3	2.6	0.1	1.7	985.7	6,552	267	480	8,036	75,730	66,707	7886
Henry	226.4	4,588	34.1	40.7	1.5	0.1	1.6	118.3	2,397	96	137	2,945	21,790	44,547	4268
Howard	406.5	4,907	32.7	36.7	3.9	0.3	1.8	200.3	2,417	186	248	4,950	40,320	49,427	5167
Huntington	90.3	2,442	58.2	0.3	3.7	0.1	4.3	59.5	1,608	88	107	1,390	17,620	47,197	4562
Jackson	185.0	4,294	31.0	55.4	1.0	0.1	1.1	103.4	2,400	93	133	2,999	21,670	49,065	4980
Jasper	124.9	3,732	37.4	35.2	2.1	0.1	2.1	207.7	6,207	92	99	1,424	15,480	54,157	5591
Jay	94.3	4,414	38.3	35.4	2.3	0.6	3.7	67.3	3,148	48	64	1,314	9,560	40,304	3636
Jefferson	77.9	2,394	64.1	1.2	3.5	0.2	4.5	52.1	1,600	79	93	2,337	14,880	49,130	5333
Jennings	82.7	2,935	66.8	0.7	2.7	0.2	2.8	49.5	1,758	73	84	1,184	12,910	41,632	3651
Johnson	466.1	3,255	49.3	17.5	3.5	0.1	2.7	489.4	3,417	407	771	6,792	72,230	62,834	7669
Knox	274.0	7,186	18.6	63.3	1.2	0.1	2.8	128.9	3,381	166	108	4,843	16,690	47,725	4962
Kosciusko	216.4	2,788	61.0	1.0	3.8	0.1	4.8	226.2	2,915	163	236	3,004	38,470	61,945	8483
LaGrange	85.5	2,278	67.1	0.1	1.4	0.1	3.8	71.2	1,896	59	119	1,243	17,050	49,273	4647
Lake	1,850.2	3,748	45.8	0.6	5.4	1.1	1.8	1,929.7	3,909	1,388	1,467	24,020	229,360	52,843	5951
LaPorte	330.9	2,974	53.0	1.0	4.1	0.3	2.3	311.4	2,799	171	336	6,700	51,640	49,502	5409
Lawrence	114.9	2,494	59.2	0.4	4.2	0.2	6.0	97.1	2,107	115	137	2,069	20,940	45,123	4260
Madison	322.0	2,470	48.2	0.7	5.0	0.2	3.7	497.2	3,814	253	378	6,018	59,480	44,355	4291
Marion	4,896.8	5,329	31.1	23.0	4.5	0.2	0.9	11,765.5	12,803	15,161	3,109	65,339	458,140	50,994	6222
Marshall	129.3	2,749	63.4	1.7	4.8	0.2	5.4	98.6	2,098	105	146	2,059	22,130	49,263	5214
Martin	26.7	2,598	58.5	0.8	2.4	0.3	8.0	14.6	1,421	4,359	71	456	4,710	46,873	4354
Miami	111.4	3,054	57.5	0.2	2.1	0.2	4.7	101.3	2,777	637	115	1,940	15,580	42,729	3739
Monroe	289.9	2,055	45.2	1.2	4.9	0.4	4.3	383.5	2,719	310	430	21,865	57,780	57,913	7358
Montgomery	110.0	2,875	52.3	0.3	3.9	0.5	5.8	103.4	2,703	77	113	1,855	18,290	47,110	4518
Morgan	210.4	3,033	48.5	21.5	2.5	0.1	2.6	96.0	1,385	96	211	2,638	33,520	53,937	5568
Newton	55.2	3,932	46.4	2.3	2.3	0.2	6.4	34.2	2,435	26	42	708	6,680	49,138	4715
Noble	113.5	2,385	60.5	0.3	5.9	0.1	4.5	94.3	1,982	77	143	1,852	22,130	46,958	4360
Ohio	23.6	3,888	36.5	0.1	3.4	0.1	3.1	15.6	2,573	14	18	351	2,810	47,833	4648
Orange	63.7	3,235	54.0	0.2	0.9	0.1	3.8	72.0	3,654	42	69	935	8,730	40,808	3588
Owen	40.1	1,878	63.7	0.0	2.5	0.2	4.4	41.4	1,939	35	63	759	9,580	42,783	3739
Parke	44.2	2,588	55.1	0.9	2.6	0.1	6.9	39.4	2,308	50	47	1,049	6,940	44,673	4219
Perry	80.3	4,126	33.1	41.5	1.7	0.0	3.6	65.0	3,340	73	54	1,430	8,640	46,006	4376

1. Based on the resident population estimated as of July 1 of the year shown.

Table B. States and Counties — **Land Area and Population**

State / county code	CBSA code[1]	County code[2]	STATE County	Land area[3] (sq. mi)	Total persons 2017	Rank	Per square mile	White	Black	American Indian, Alaska Native	Asian and Pacific Islander[4]	Percent Hispanic or Latino[4]	Under 5 years	5 to 17 years	18 to 24 years	25 to 34 years	35 to 44 years	45 to 54 years
				1	2	3	4	5	6	7	8	9	10	11	12	13	14	15
			INDIANA— Cont'd															
1,8125	27,540	8	Pike	334.2	12,365	2,266	37.0	97.1	0.9	0.6	0.6	1.6	5.6	16.0	6.9	11.0	11.3	13.6
1,8127	16,980	1	Porter	418.1	168,404	382	402.8	84.4	4.4	0.6	1.9	10.0	5.4	16.9	9.1	12.2	13.0	13.3
1,8129	21,780	2	Posey	409.6	25,595	1,581	62.5	97.0	1.7	0.5	0.8	1.2	5.8	16.4	7.7	11.2	11.5	13.4
1,8131		6	Pulaski	433.6	12,534	2,255	28.9	95.5	1.3	0.9	0.5	2.9	5.4	16.8	7.6	11.0	11.6	13.5
1,8133	26,900	1	Putnam	480.5	37,702	1,231	78.5	93.0	4.2	0.6	1.5	1.9	5.0	14.7	14.2	12.5	11.1	13.4
1,8135		6	Randolph	452.4	24,922	1,613	55.1	95.3	1.2	0.7	0.6	3.3	5.9	17.1	7.7	10.3	11.7	13.1
1,8137		6	Ripley	446.4	28,442	1,476	63.7	96.5	0.8	0.7	1.2	1.9	5.8	18.1	8.3	10.6	12.0	13.7
1,8139		6	Rush	408.1	16,645	2,000	40.8	96.8	1.6	0.5	0.5	1.6	5.6	17.1	8.2	11.0	11.3	13.9
1,8141	43,780	2	St. Joseph	457.9	270,434	252	590.6	75.3	14.7	0.9	3.2	8.8	6.4	17.2	11.0	13.2	11.7	12.1
1,8143	31,140	1	Scott	190.4	23,870	1,649	125.4	96.0	0.9	0.5	1.0	2.4	6.0	16.8	8.0	12.0	12.4	14.4
1,8145	26,900	1	Shelby	411.2	44,395	1,084	108.0	93.4	1.6	0.6	1.2	4.3	5.7	17.1	7.7	11.9	12.0	13.9
1,8147		8	Spencer	396.8	20,394	1,805	51.4	95.8	1.2	0.5	0.5	3.0	5.3	16.8	7.6	10.4	11.4	13.9
1,8149		6	Starke	309.1	22,893	1,681	74.1	95.1	0.9	0.8	0.4	3.8	5.9	16.9	7.5	11.4	11.7	13.3
1,8151	11,420	7	Steuben	308.8	34,484	1,311	111.7	94.6	1.2	0.6	1.0	3.7	5.6	15.0	10.2	10.5	10.3	13.4
1,8153	45,460	3	Sullivan	447.1	20,746	1,786	46.4	93.1	5.1	0.7	0.5	1.8	5.2	14.5	8.2	14.1	13.5	13.8
1,8155		8	Switzerland	220.7	10,696	2,376	48.5	96.0	1.8	0.6	0.5	2.1	6.3	19.0	6.8	11.1	11.7	14.4
1,8157	29,200	3	Tippecanoe	498.9	190,587	345	382.0	77.5	6.2	0.6	9.2	8.5	6.1	14.8	23.6	14.2	10.5	9.9
1,8159		6	Tipton	260.5	15,128	2,087	58.1	95.9	1.1	0.5	0.8	2.7	4.9	15.9	8.0	10.5	10.7	14.2
1,8161	17,140	1	Union	161.2	7,200	2,651	44.7	96.6	1.5	0.7	0.8	1.8	5.2	16.0	8.1	11.0	11.4	14.7
1,8163	21,780	2	Vanderburgh	233.7	181,616	361	777.1	86.0	11.2	0.6	2.0	2.7	5.9	15.7	10.0	14.3	11.7	12.0
1,8165	45,460	3	Vermillion	256.9	15,505	2,066	60.4	97.7	1.0	0.6	0.6	1.3	5.3	16.9	7.6	10.9	11.9	13.3
1,8167	45,460	3	Vigo	403.5	107,516	561	266.5	87.7	8.6	0.8	2.5	2.7	5.8	14.7	15.0	13.0	11.4	11.9
1,8169	47,340	6	Wabash	412.4	31,443	1,395	76.2	95.4	1.2	1.1	0.7	2.7	5.3	15.6	10.1	10.7	10.9	12.5
1,8171		8	Warren	364.7	8,201	2,579	22.5	96.9	0.9	0.5	0.9	1.8	5.0	16.8	7.0	10.5	11.1	14.4
1,8173	21,780	2	Warrick	384.8	62,530	843	162.5	93.7	2.3	0.5	3.1	1.9	5.8	18.6	7.5	10.8	12.8	13.6
1,8175	31,140	1	Washington	513.7	27,827	1,502	54.2	97.6	0.8	0.6	0.5	1.4	6.0	16.9	7.8	11.4	12.2	14.3
1,8177	39,980	5	Wayne	401.7	66,185	807	164.8	90.7	6.7	0.8	1.7	2.9	5.8	16.9	9.0	11.4	11.6	13.2
1,8179	23,060	2	Wells	368.1	27,984	1,494	76.0	95.2	1.1	0.6	0.9	3.2	6.3	18.3	7.7	11.4	11.4	12.6
1,8181		6	White	505.1	24,182	1,633	47.9	90.0	0.9	0.8	0.8	8.6	6.3	17.2	7.7	10.5	10.9	12.7
1,8183	23,060	2	Whitley	335.6	33,756	1,333	100.6	96.8	0.8	0.7	0.8	2.0	5.9	17.1	7.6	11.7	11.9	12.9
1,9000		0	IOWA	55,855.1	3,145,711	X	56.3	87.3	4.6	0.7	3.2	6.0	6.3	16.9	10.2	12.6	11.9	12.1
1,9001		8	Adair	569.3	7,054	2,666	12.4	96.8	0.9	0.5	0.6	1.9	5.1	16.3	6.7	10.8	10.5	12.2
1,9003		9	Adams	423.4	3,686	2,925	8.7	97.3	0.6	0.7	0.9	1.3	6.1	15.1	6.0	11.0	10.0	12.1
1,9005		6	Allamakee	639.1	13,884	2,173	21.7	90.9	1.9	0.4	0.8	6.6	6.8	16.4	7.0	9.9	11.4	11.8
1,9007		7	Appanoose	497.3	12,352	2,268	24.8	96.4	1.2	0.8	1.0	1.9	5.8	16.2	6.5	10.5	10.5	12.4
1,9009		8	Audubon	443.0	5,578	2,790	12.6	97.5	0.7	0.4	0.9	1.4	5.8	14.7	7.2	9.3	9.2	12.4
1,9011	16,300	2	Benton	716.3	25,642	1,576	35.8	97.3	1.1	0.5	0.6	1.5	6.1	17.3	7.4	10.3	14.1	14.1
1,9013	47,940	3	Black Hawk	565.8	132,648	480	234.4	83.8	10.6	0.6	3.1	4.3	6.4	15.4	15.2	12.9	11.1	10.7
1,9015	14,340	6	Boone	571.6	26,484	1,546	46.3	95.2	1.6	0.7	0.9	2.7	5.5	16.2	7.4	12.2	12.4	12.8
1,9017	47,940	3	Bremer	435.5	24,911	1,614	57.2	96.0	1.7	0.4	1.3	1.6	5.8	16.6	11.8	10.4	11.8	11.7
1,9019		6	Buchanan	571.0	21,202	1,767	37.1	97.1	1.0	0.5	0.9	1.6	6.8	19.7	6.9	11.3	11.9	12.1
1,9021	44,740	7	Buena Vista	574.9	20,110	1,822	35.0	60.6	3.5	0.5	11.0	25.8	7.6	18.0	11.4	12.5	10.9	12.1
1,9023		8	Butler	580.1	14,606	2,122	25.2	97.2	0.8	0.4	1.1	1.5	5.2	17.6	6.8	9.9	11.6	12.1
1,9025		9	Calhoun	569.8	9,746	2,449	17.1	95.4	2.3	0.7	0.5	2.0	6.0	15.3	7.7	11.2	10.7	11.1
1,9027	16,140	7	Carroll	569.4	20,320	1,808	35.7	95.7	1.7	0.5	0.7	2.4	6.5	17.9	7.7	10.6	10.8	11.9
1,9029		6	Cass	564.3	13,145	2,222	23.3	96.1	0.7	0.4	0.9	2.6	5.5	17.0	7.0	10.1	10.9	11.5
1,9031		6	Cedar	579.4	18,543	1,893	32.0	96.5	1.1	0.6	1.0	2.0	5.4	17.2	6.9	10.5	12.4	13.3
1,9033	32,380	5	Cerro Gordo	568.3	43,006	1,113	75.7	92.0	2.6	0.6	1.6	4.9	5.5	15.4	8.0	11.4	10.9	12.1
1,9035		6	Cherokee	576.9	11,316	2,330	19.6	94.4	1.4	0.7	0.9	3.7	6.0	15.4	6.4	10.3	10.0	11.7
1,9037		6	Chickasaw	504.4	12,005	2,293	23.8	96.6	0.9	0.4	0.5	2.3	5.9	17.8	7.4	9.6	10.7	12.4
1,9039		6	Clarke	431.2	9,374	2,475	21.7	83.7	1.2	0.9	1.0	14.3	7.2	18.2	7.2	11.9	11.1	12.0
1,9041	43,980	7	Clay	567.2	16,170	2,029	28.5	94.6	1.4	0.6	1.1	3.6	6.2	16.3	7.0	11.7	11.7	11.5
1,9043		8	Clayton	778.5	17,637	1,941	22.7	96.9	1.0	0.5	0.6	1.9	5.6	15.8	7.0	9.8	10.0	12.0
1,9045	17,540	4	Clinton	694.9	47,010	1,033	67.7	92.7	4.2	0.6	1.0	3.2	6.1	17.0	7.7	11.0	11.1	12.9
1,9047		7	Crawford	714.2	17,056	1,976	23.9	66.7	3.3	0.6	2.3	27.9	6.9	18.2	9.3	11.5	11.6	11.8
1,9049	19,780	2	Dallas	588.3	87,235	662	148.3	86.8	2.6	0.5	5.4	6.1	8.0	20.1	7.1	14.5	15.6	12.8
1,9051	36,900	9	Davis	502.2	8,966	2,506	17.9	97.8	0.4	0.8	0.6	1.5	8.4	20.6	7.9	10.8	10.8	11.2
1,9053		9	Decatur	531.9	7,950	2,601	14.9	94.0	2.1	1.0	1.2	2.9	6.4	15.5	17.0	9.5	9.0	10.2
1,9055		6	Delaware	577.7	17,153	1,968	29.7	97.2	1.1	0.4	0.4	1.6	6.4	17.4	7.7	9.8	10.8	13.1
1,9057	15,460	5	Des Moines	416.1	39,417	1,191	94.7	89.8	7.4	0.8	1.4	3.1	6.0	16.6	7.5	11.4	11.4	12.5
1,9059	44,020	7	Dickinson	380.5	17,199	1,963	45.2	96.8	0.8	0.5	1.0	2.0	5.0	14.4	6.2	10.0	10.5	11.8
1,9061	20,220	3	Dubuque	608.3	97,041	614	159.5	92.1	4.3	0.5	2.2	2.5	6.3	16.7	10.2	12.7	10.9	12.2
1,9063		7	Emmet	395.9	9,432	2,470	23.8	88.1	1.4	0.9	0.9	9.6	5.5	15.6	6.4	11.6	11.3	11.2
1,9065		6	Fayette	730.8	19,796	1,837	27.1	95.0	2.1	0.5	1.4	2.3	5.3	15.3	10.1	10.6	10.0	12.2
1,9067		7	Floyd	500.6	15,744	2,055	31.5	93.2	3.0	0.4	1.7	2.8	6.0	16.9	7.8	10.4	10.5	12.5

1. CBSA = Core Based Statistical Area. See Appendix A for explanation. See Appendix B for list of metropolitan areas with component counties. Service of USDA Rural-Urban Continuum Codes. See Appendix A for definition.   3. Dry land or land partially or temporarily covered by water.   2. County type code from the Economic Research   4. May be of any race.

Table B. States and Counties — Population and Households

STATE County	55 to 64 years (16)	65 to 74 years (17)	75 years and over (18)	Percent female (19)	2000 (20)	2010 (21)	2000-2010 (22)	2010-2017 (23)	Births (24)	Deaths (25)	Net Migration (26)	Number (27)	Persons per household (28)	Family households (29)	Female family householder[1] (30)	One person (31)
INDIANA— Cont'd																
Pike	15.8	11.3	8.5	49.8	12,837	12,764	-0.6	-3.1	1,004	1,024	-376	4,957	2.48	70.4	8.5	26.7
Porter	14.2	9.8	6.1	50.5	146,798	164,347	12.0	2.5	12,660	10,323	1,849	62,429	2.62	70.7	11.4	23.9
Posey	16.1	10.7	7.3	50.3	27,061	25,912	-4.2	-1.2	2,020	1,745	-597	10,017	2.52	73.2	9.0	22.9
Pulaski	15.0	10.7	8.4	48.9	13,755	13,388	-2.7	-6.4	985	1,085	-760	5,174	2.46	68.7	9.9	27.6
Putnam	13.1	9.1	7.1	47.6	36,019	37,952	5.4	-0.7	2,572	2,499	-318	12,962	2.47	69.4	11.8	24.5
Randolph	14.3	10.9	9.0	50.9	27,401	26,169	-4.5	-4.8	2,184	2,074	-1,370	10,483	2.39	65.6	9.9	29.1
Ripley	13.9	10.2	7.3	50.5	26,523	28,811	8.6	-1.3	2,379	2,227	-517	10,981	2.56	72.7	9.9	23.6
Rush	14.8	10.0	8.1	50.7	18,261	17,392	-4.8	-4.3	1,317	1,377	-690	6,747	2.47	70.8	11.8	24.3
St. Joseph	12.9	8.8	6.6	51.3	265,559	266,929	0.5	1.3	25,403	18,440	-3,397	100,861	2.53	63.6	13.1	30.4
Scott	14.1	10.0	6.3	50.8	22,960	24,185	5.3	-1.3	2,069	2,174	-207	8,844	2.64	70.3	10.2	24.8
Shelby	14.9	9.7	7.1	50.3	43,445	44,406	2.2	0.0	3,655	3,179	-463	17,309	2.52	66.6	11.1	26.9
Spencer	15.7	11.1	7.9	49.6	20,391	20,952	2.8	-2.7	1,559	1,426	-693	8,065	2.54	73.1	6.4	23.1
Starke	15.2	10.9	7.2	50.0	23,556	23,362	-0.8	-2.0	1,891	2,003	-343	8,727	2.64	70.5	12.4	25.0
Steuben	15.2	12.0	7.7	49.3	33,214	34,183	2.9	0.9	2,776	2,229	-223	13,451	2.45	68.4	8.6	25.5
Sullivan	13.3	10.3	7.1	45.8	21,751	21,475	-1.3	-3.4	1,631	1,714	-647	7,713	2.45	71.1	10.4	24.6
Switzerland	13.8	10.0	6.9	48.5	9,065	10,666	17.7	0.3	905	757	-121	4,102	2.53	72.5	11.5	21.5
Tippecanoe	9.6	6.6	4.7	48.9	148,955	172,803	16.0	10.3	16,674	8,178	9,356	68,172	2.46	56.4	10.4	29.9
Tipton	15.2	11.9	8.7	50.1	16,577	15,932	-3.9	-5.0	1,069	1,237	-641	6,401	2.38	68.4	9.1	27.4
Union	14.8	11.2	7.5	50.4	7,349	7,516	2.3	-4.2	516	495	-341	2,917	2.46	63.0	9.1	32.1
Vanderburgh	14.1	9.2	7.2	51.6	171,922	179,703	4.5	1.1	16,357	13,845	-453	74,313	2.35	60.2	12.9	33.2
Vermillion	14.4	11.6	8.1	50.2	16,788	16,210	-3.4	-4.3	1,185	1,543	-348	6,600	2.35	63.3	11.0	31.2
Vigo	12.2	9.0	6.9	49.4	105,848	107,848	1.9	-0.3	9,351	8,314	-1,315	40,753	2.42	61.5	12.4	30.7
Wabash	14.6	10.7	9.7	51.5	34,960	32,885	-5.9	-4.4	2,476	3,000	-915	12,767	2.37	67.4	9.9	28.0
Warren	15.2	11.1	8.8	50.3	8,419	8,508	1.1	-3.6	628	548	-390	3,327	2.47	73.6	7.8	23.0
Warrick	13.9	10.2	6.7	50.7	52,383	59,689	13.9	4.8	4,784	3,909	2,001	23,290	2.60	73.5	8.3	23.2
Washington	14.5	10.2	6.6	50.1	27,223	28,262	3.8	-1.5	2,290	2,159	-557	10,540	2.61	71.4	12.6	24.7
Wayne	14.0	10.3	8.4	51.6	71,097	69,003	-2.9	-4.1	5,722	6,066	-2,462	26,664	2.43	64.8	13.8	29.7
Wells	14.5	9.9	8.0	50.5	27,600	27,636	0.1	1.3	2,476	1,955	-161	10,828	2.52	70.7	10.5	26.4
White	14.7	11.6	8.3	50.3	25,267	24,643	-2.5	-1.9	2,110	1,969	-593	9,670	2.48	69.5	7.6	25.7
Whitley	15.3	10.3	7.2	50.1	30,707	33,291	8.4	1.4	2,818	2,178	-159	13,232	2.49	71.1	9.3	24.9
IOWA	13.3	9.3	7.5	50.3	2,926,324	3,046,869	4.1	3.2	282,560	207,721	24,342	1,242,641	2.42	64.3	9.2	28.9
Adair	16.1	11.0	11.3	50.5	8,243	7,682	-6.8	-8.2	503	776	-356	3,228	2.22	65.6	8.9	29.1
Adams	16.9	11.7	11.2	50.1	4,482	4,029	-10.1	-8.5	321	351	-318	1,681	2.19	65.6	4.1	27.8
Allamakee	15.7	12.3	10.0	49.1	14,675	14,328	-2.4	-3.1	1,308	1,162	-592	6,035	2.26	64.2	5.5	30.1
Appanoose	15.6	12.2	10.2	50.6	13,721	12,887	-6.1	-4.2	1,085	1,225	-387	5,430	2.29	60.1	6.8	34.8
Audubon	16.9	11.9	12.5	51.0	6,830	6,119	-10.4	-8.8	453	576	-420	2,667	2.12	60.9	7.0	34.4
Benton	14.9	9.8	8.3	50.1	25,308	26,076	3.0	-1.7	2,105	1,657	-887	10,155	2.50	69.7	7.1	25.3
Black Hawk	12.3	9.0	7.0	51.0	128,012	131,090	2.4	1.2	12,406	8,617	-2,136	52,506	2.42	59.2	10.2	31.6
Boone	15.7	10.2	7.6	49.5	26,224	26,306	0.3	0.7	2,157	2,135	170	10,943	2.33	63.7	6.8	30.6
Bremer	12.6	10.1	9.2	50.6	23,325	24,276	4.1	2.6	1,858	1,522	315	9,343	2.47	69.2	5.4	26.5
Buchanan	13.6	9.8	7.7	50.2	21,093	20,958	-0.6	1.2	2,080	1,457	-368	8,246	2.51	66.6	7.9	28.1
Buena Vista	12.9	8.3	7.5	49.2	20,411	20,260	-0.7	-0.7	2,294	1,355	-1,101	7,504	2.59	68.3	10.0	27.3
Butler	14.7	11.8	10.2	50.2	15,305	14,867	-2.9	-1.8	1,110	1,312	-49	6,282	2.34	68.2	4.9	27.4
Calhoun	15.4	11.3	11.3	48.4	11,115	10,177	-8.4	-4.2	802	1,029	-200	4,249	2.15	62.9	8.8	31.6
Carroll	14.8	9.7	10.1	50.8	21,421	20,816	-2.8	-2.4	1,897	1,756	-637	8,580	2.35	64.0	7.2	33.0
Cass	15.4	11.5	11.1	50.8	14,684	13,956	-5.0	-5.8	1,037	1,389	-455	6,076	2.16	62.4	8.6	33.3
Cedar	15.2	10.3	8.8	50.1	18,187	18,455	1.7	0.3	1,338	1,311	28	7,599	2.38	67.3	6.1	28.0
Cerro Gordo	15.6	11.4	9.9	51.1	46,447	44,151	-4.9	-2.6	3,413	3,619	-929	19,250	2.19	59.4	9.4	35.0
Cherokee	16.7	11.6	12.0	49.9	13,035	12,072	-7.4	-6.3	934	1,166	-529	5,317	2.13	60.7	9.6	32.6
Chickasaw	15.7	11.0	9.5	49.6	13,095	12,439	-5.0	-3.5	1,001	969	-464	5,244	2.28	64.7	5.5	29.7
Clarke	14.2	9.9	8.2	49.5	9,133	9,286	1.7	0.9	895	774	-28	3,837	2.37	63.2	6.5	31.2
Clay	15.2	10.2	10.1	50.7	17,372	16,667	-4.1	-3.0	1,411	1,378	-520	7,281	2.22	62.9	9.0	30.3
Clayton	17.1	12.0	10.9	49.7	18,678	18,129	-2.9	-2.7	1,371	1,406	-451	7,622	2.28	64.1	7.6	30.2
Clinton	14.9	10.5	8.7	51.0	50,149	49,116	-2.1	-4.3	4,191	3,969	-2,334	19,871	2.37	64.4	10.5	29.9
Crawford	13.2	9.3	8.2	48.3	16,942	17,096	0.9	-0.2	1,728	1,147	-621	6,430	2.58	71.3	10.6	23.8
Dallas	10.0	6.8	5.0	50.7	40,750	66,137	62.3	31.9	8,682	2,942	15,129	30,026	2.58	69.4	6.9	25.3
Davis	12.7	9.3	8.4	50.5	8,541	8,753	2.5	2.4	1,017	616	-186	3,230	2.68	72.6	7.7	23.4
Decatur	13.0	10.1	9.3	49.9	8,689	8,457	-2.7	-6.0	674	676	-507	3,166	2.35	63.0	9.2	31.4
Delaware	16.1	9.8	9.0	49.7	18,404	17,764	-3.5	-3.4	1,479	1,244	-851	6,882	2.50	72.4	7.7	23.3
Des Moines	14.3	11.2	9.1	51.2	42,351	40,325	-4.8	-2.3	3,374	3,349	-924	16,659	2.37	63.9	12.0	32.2
Dickinson	16.7	14.1	11.3	50.0	16,424	16,667	1.5	3.2	1,199	1,416	754	8,008	2.10	62.6	5.8	33.2
Dubuque	13.6	9.3	8.1	50.6	89,143	93,653	5.1	3.6	8,753	6,419	1,120	38,006	2.42	64.4	9.6	27.7
Emmet	15.5	10.9	10.0	49.8	11,027	10,302	-6.6	-8.4	796	889	-787	4,127	2.19	63.7	9.3	30.8
Fayette	15.4	10.9	10.2	49.5	22,008	20,880	-5.1	-5.2	1,545	1,798	-833	8,333	2.35	64.5	8.8	30.6
Floyd	14.2	11.5	10.3	50.9	16,900	16,303	-3.5	-3.4	1,386	1,385	-557	6,891	2.28	65.1	10.5	31.8

1. No spouse present.

Table B. States and Counties — **Population, Vital Statistics, Health, and Crime**

STATE County	Persons in group quarters, 2017	Daytime Population, 2012-2016		Births, 2017		Deaths, 2017		Persons under 65 with no health insurance, 2016		Medicare, 2017			Serious crimes known to police[2], 2016 Total	
		Number	Employment/ residence ratio	Total	Rate[1]	Number	Rate[1]	Number	Percent	Total beneficiaries	Enrolled in Original Medicare	Enrolled in Medicare Advantage	Number	Rate[3]
	32	33	34	35	36	37	38	39	40	41	42	43	44	45
INDIANA— Cont'd														
Pike	213	10,416	0.63	133	10.8	143	11.6	886	9.0	2,706	2,084	622	46	452
Porter	3,415	154,021	0.83	1,667	9.9	1,579	9.4	10,151	7.3	29,964	22,581	7,382	1,240	772
Posey	242	23,245	0.81	284	11.1	244	9.5	1,479	7.0	4,593	3,443	1,151	NA	NA
Pulaski	193	12,296	0.89	127	10.1	134	10.7	1,018	10.1	2,911	2,364	548	NA	NA
Putnam	4,968	35,807	0.88	364	9.7	340	9.0	2,197	8.2	6,517	4,732	1,786	NA	NA
Randolph	329	22,380	0.73	289	11.6	266	10.7	1,914	9.6	5,928	4,975	953	NA	NA
Ripley	449	26,264	0.82	307	10.8	314	11.0	2,086	8.9	6,768	5,350	1,418	NA	NA
Rush	178	14,351	0.67	181	10.9	185	11.1	1,568	11.6	3,385	2,707	678	NA	NA
St. Joseph	11,386	269,352	1.01	3,467	12.8	2,438	9.0	22,735	10.4	50,059	34,028	16,031	10,248	3830
Scott	312	20,835	0.72	297	12.4	303	12.7	1,794	9.2	5,658	4,571	1,087	437	2244
Shelby	683	41,901	0.88	480	10.8	433	9.8	3,427	9.4	8,060	5,838	2,222	1,176	2648
Spencer	368	18,776	0.79	185	9.1	238	11.7	1,378	8.3	4,278	3,503	775	NA	NA
Starke	16	18,867	0.55	256	11.2	281	12.3	1,951	10.4	5,020	3,953	1,067	NA	NA
Steuben	1,305	32,942	0.92	404	11.7	312	9.0	2,403	9.0	7,569	4,440	3,129	NA	NA
Sullivan	2,174	19,221	0.78	197	9.5	202	9.7	1,398	9.2	4,227	3,480	747	200	1201
Switzerland	107	8,548	0.56	117	10.9	109	10.2	961	11.2	1,742	1,441	301	NA	NA
Tippecanoe	14,470	194,686	1.13	2,394	12.6	1,138	6.0	16,330	10.6	24,271	19,213	5,058	4,800	2583
Tipton	205	13,884	0.78	143	9.5	160	10.6	972	8.1	3,168	2,507	661	179	1184
Union	67	5,457	0.46	61	8.5	65	9.0	548	9.4	1,639	1,359	280	NA	NA
Vanderburgh	7,552	202,114	1.24	2,163	11.9	1,856	10.2	12,807	8.7	37,253	27,099	10,154	7,337	4033
Vermillion	209	14,207	0.76	166	10.7	200	12.9	1,104	8.8	3,554	3,023	530	NA	NA
Vigo	9,518	116,706	1.19	1,271	11.8	1,158	10.8	7,731	9.4	21,062	17,729	3,333	4,369	4143
Wabash	1,841	31,637	0.96	326	10.4	410	13.0	2,367	9.9	7,635	4,600	3,035	NA	NA
Warren	84	6,678	0.58	70	8.5	84	10.2	523	8.0	1,221	1,058	163	NA	NA
Warrick	727	49,116	0.58	685	11.0	618	9.9	3,572	6.9	11,816	8,691	3,125	831	1336
Washington	261	22,628	0.56	324	11.6	291	10.5	2,336	10.2	5,420	4,029	1,391	NA	NA
Wayne	2,705	69,435	1.07	772	11.7	861	13.0	5,813	11.1	16,061	14,228	1,834	NA	NA
Wells	472	25,882	0.85	335	12.0	245	8.8	1,780	7.8	5,193	3,105	2,088	536	1917
White	307	22,782	0.87	293	12.1	292	12.1	2,204	11.6	5,974	4,809	1,165	103	426
Whitley	436	29,554	0.77	387	11.5	296	8.8	2,249	8.1	7,106	3,518	3,588	NA	NA
IOWA	10,0,003	3,109,383	1.00	39,076	12.4	28,310	9.0	126,746	5.0	599,730	489,227	110,503	74,501	2377
Adair	151	6,714	0.83	70	9.9	91	12.9	246	4.5	1,487	1,380	107	56	785
Adams	82	3,499	0.83	33	9.0	39	10.6	172	6.0	879	856	23	33	881
Allamakee	294	12,655	0.80	192	13.8	167	12.0	758	7.2	3,308	2,868	439	119	864
Appanoose	121	12,226	0.93	150	12.1	157	12.7	552	5.8	3,199	2,637	562	387	3110
Audubon	115	5,094	0.76	68	12.2	71	12.7	245	5.8	1,438	1,387	51	59	1035
Benton	314	19,395	0.51	301	11.7	228	8.9	855	4.0	4,821	3,789	1,032	85	333
Black Hawk	5,540	141,828	1.14	1,692	12.8	1,205	9.1	5,661	5.3	25,424	17,391	8,033	3,786	2832
Boone	750	23,226	0.76	291	11.0	290	11.0	881	4.1	5,122	4,284	838	280	1050
Bremer	1,607	24,011	0.95	267	10.7	214	8.6	642	3.4	5,295	4,154	1,141	285	1151
Buchanan	305	18,747	0.77	283	13.3	184	8.7	823	4.8	4,253	3,066	1,186	232	1102
Buena Vista	879	21,435	1.09	295	14.7	165	8.2	1,514	9.3	3,592	3,385	207	409	1996
Butler	211	11,956	0.60	135	9.2	173	11.8	517	4.5	3,680	3,014	665	6	40
Calhoun	730	8,685	0.73	111	11.4	135	13.9	371	5.2	2,393	2,264	128	83	853
Carroll	441	21,771	1.12	262	12.9	240	11.8	627	3.8	4,982	4,585	398	253	1240
Cass	303	13,332	0.98	131	10.0	173	13.2	587	5.8	3,526	3,198	329	158	1187
Cedar	313	14,344	0.58	190	10.2	191	10.3	569	3.8	3,521	2,849	672	108	591
Cerro Gordo	1,086	45,895	1.12	461	10.7	505	11.7	1,402	4.2	11,033	10,604	429	1,476	3454
Cherokee	350	11,319	0.93	131	11.6	169	14.9	487	5.7	2,842	2,575	267	115	1004
Chickasaw	99	11,311	0.86	133	11.1	114	9.5	523	5.5	2,473	2,274	198	75	624
Clarke	155	9,382	1.02	123	13.1	98	10.5	418	5.6	1,850	1,691	160	172	1862
Clay	235	17,040	1.07	176	10.9	159	9.8	581	4.5	3,900	3,835	65	292	1774
Clayton	276	16,450	0.85	177	10.0	190	10.8	853	6.3	4,352	3,433	919	47	268
Clinton	635	48,313	1.02	580	12.3	520	11.1	1,559	4.1	10,253	8,416	1,837	1,707	3599
Crawford	567	16,968	0.98	236	13.8	146	8.6	1,287	9.3	3,209	2,904	305	58	340
Dallas	701	68,241	0.77	1,312	15.0	474	5.4	2,817	3.7	7,987	6,478	1,510	1,325	1596
Davis	99	8,095	0.82	151	16.8	80	8.9	618	8.6	1,667	1,374	294	14	160
Decatur	708	7,693	0.86	92	11.6	80	10.1	386	6.6	1,734	1,538	196	24	294
Delaware	224	15,747	0.81	203	11.8	171	10.0	694	5.0	3,277	2,538	739	209	1208
Des Moines	652	43,343	1.17	452	11.5	432	11.0	1,512	4.8	9,535	8,697	838	1,805	4518
Dickinson	186	17,439	1.04	168	9.8	172	10.0	535	4.1	4,746	4,511	235	207	1205
Dubuque	4,301	104,246	1.16	1,219	12.6	865	8.9	3,175	4.1	20,086	9,429	10,656	2,325	2382
Emmet	416	9,080	0.85	106	11.2	112	11.9	511	7.0	2,238	2,166	72	172	1781
Fayette	900	19,177	0.88	213	10.8	227	11.5	811	5.3	4,577	3,849	728	178	885
Floyd	289	15,089	0.88	195	12.4	183	11.6	689	5.6	3,633	3,384	249	198	1248

1. Per 1,000 estimated resident population.   2. Data for serious crimes have not been adjusted for underreporting; this may affect comparability between geographic areas and over time.
3. Per 100,000 population estimated by the FBI.

Table B. States and Counties — Crime, Education, Money Income, and Poverty

STATE County	Serious crimes known to police, 2016 (cont.)[1] Rate Violent	Property	Education School enrollment and attainment, 2012-2016 Enrollment[3] Total	Percent private	Attainment[4] (percent) High school graduate or less	Bachelor's degree or more	Local government expenditures,[5] 2013-2014 Total current spending (mil dol)	Current spending per student (dollars)	Money income, 2012-2016 Per capita income[6]	Households Median income (dollars)	Percent with income of less than $50,000	with income of $200,000 or more	Income and poverty, 2016 Percent below poverty level Median household income (dollars)	All persons	Children under 18 years	Children 5 to 17 years in families
	46	47	48	49	50	51	52	53	54	55	56	57	58	59	60	61
INDIANA— Cont'd																
Pike	138	314	2,873	7.1	59.6	12.6	20.8	10,636	24,367	48,076	51.4	0.7	49,578	11.4	15.6	14.0
Porter	54	718	43,190	19.4	43.2	26.1	234.8	8,509	30,615	64,874	38.4	4.0	67,302	7.8	9.9	9.3
Posey	NA	NA	5,976	18.7	44.5	20.6	39.2	10,892	30,396	59,918	40.2	2.8	61,619	8.7	12.1	11.3
Pulaski	NA	NA	2,896	7.3	59.0	10.7	22.4	10,545	23,958	44,884	55.9	1.5	47,243	11.5	19.4	18.3
Putnam	NA	NA	9,310	30.3	53.2	15.0	59.0	9,838	23,040	52,465	47.8	2.3	50,896	12.6	16.1	14.7
Randolph	NA	NA	5,713	6.2	57.3	13.1	42.1	9,771	22,817	42,418	58.8	0.9	46,750	15.4	24.6	25.0
Ripley	NA	NA	6,683	13.2	56.4	17.4	36.9	11,487	23,980	52,372	47.5	1.3	55,129	12.2	17.9	16.0
Rush	NA	NA	3,754	8.8	63.3	14.0	23.9	9,588	24,267	46,380	53.7	2.2	50,412	13.9	18.8	17.3
St. Joseph	506	3,323	75,166	31.6	43.2	28.2	379.1	9,713	24,748	46,174	53.3	3.2	48,960	16.2	22.4	20.4
Scott	144	2,100	5,438	18.7	58.0	13.0	36.0	9,087	23,103	46,368	53.6	0.6	47,738	15.8	23.7	22.4
Shelby	572	2,076	10,791	8.6	55.3	16.6	64.4	8,672	25,478	52,651	46.7	1.7	53,019	12.3	16.4	14.5
Spencer	NA	NA	4,586	6.9	54.6	15.3	29.1	8,708	25,914	54,870	45.2	1.7	58,217	9.1	11.2	10.1
Starke	NA	NA	5,221	12.3	58.6	11.6	39.4	10,478	21,343	43,401	56.5	0.9	46,602	16.1	23.7	21.7
Steuben	NA	NA	8,476	23.5	49.5	19.9	36.4	9,134	25,497	50,418	49.5	2.5	54,071	10.7	16.7	15.8
Sullivan	108	1,093	3,953	12.0	56.3	12.7	30.0	9,410	20,219	43,786	56.0	0.7	46,706	14.2	19.8	18.6
Switzerland	NA	NA	2,338	6.5	65.6	8.3	14.5	9,650	20,698	43,456	57.5	1.1	45,337	17.2	27.8	26.2
Tippecanoe	258	2,326	70,868	9.4	35.9	35.3	210.1	9,396	24,221	47,406	52.0	2.9	51,385	17.6	16.3	15.1
Tipton	106	1,078	3,421	13.0	51.1	21.1	21.1	8,160	27,556	54,023	45.0	1.9	60,756	8.5	12.2	10.7
Union	NA	NA	1,685	5.5	56.5	18.6	16.0	10,876	22,918	45,104	54.4	0.7	46,862	12.8	19.7	18.3
Vanderburgh	450	3,584	44,149	20.0	44.0	24.9	236.0	10,139	25,666	43,311	55.7	2.2	46,750	17.4	22.8	21.5
Vermillion	NA	NA	3,592	8.1	56.3	13.0	25.1	9,841	22,932	44,409	55.9	1.1	51,425	13.3	18.2	16.5
Vigo	202	3,941	30,572	13.2	45.3	23.2	143.9	9,237	22,079	41,221	58.7	2.0	43,560	17.8	22.4	21.6
Wabash	NA	NA	7,817	20.1	54.1	18.3	54.8	10,347	23,745	47,473	52.8	1.5	51,561	11.5	17.3	15.8
Warren	NA	NA	1,688	11.2	52.2	19.6	10.9	9,626	28,690	58,623	39.0	3.4	55,466	9.1	14.6	13.0
Warrick	215	1,121	15,628	14.1	40.1	28.0	87.1	8,712	31,021	61,542	39.7	5.1	65,809	7.5	9.4	8.6
Washington	NA	NA	6,267	8.9	60.1	12.7	40.1	9,228	22,096	44,883	55.3	1.3	48,939	14.3	21.8	20.2
Wayne	NA	NA	15,876	17.0	54.5	17.1	96.0	8,867	22,227	39,691	60.0	2.1	42,983	17.0	25.2	23.3
Wells	21	1,895	6,689	13.6	49.2	17.4	41.1	8,655	24,544	51,568	47.3	1.4	56,054	9.7	13.9	12.8
White	91	335	5,246	7.8	53.6	15.7	44.8	9,380	25,859	51,547	48.4	1.7	47,439	10.9	16.9	16.1
Whitley	NA	NA	7,851	18.2	51.2	18.3	40.8	8,492	27,062	54,837	43.1	2.2	54,873	9.0	11.5	10.7
IOWA	291	2,086	810,892	15.8	40.2	27.2	5,352.7	10,645	28,872	54,570	45.7	3.5	56,354	11.7	14.6	13.0
Adair	140	645	1,551	6.1	49.8	16.6	9.4	10,412	27,358	48,765	51.3	2.4	53,416	10.7	15.4	13.1
Adams	0	881	788	6.2	47.6	16.7	6.8	12,660	26,991	48,598	51.1	1.7	46,939	12.3	22.0	21.5
Allamakee	80	784	2,937	17.6	52.2	17.0	22.5	9,813	27,027	48,089	51.3	2.5	49,439	13.2	19.2	18.0
Appanoose	217	2,893	2,590	11.6	45.8	18.1	19.7	9,490	23,617	40,817	60.1	2.2	39,124	18.7	26.5	24.6
Audubon	70	965	1,204	14.7	52.8	13.1	8.2	10,154	30,085	47,048	52.6	3.0	49,560	11.1	17.5	15.5
Benton	74	258	6,193	14.7	43.0	21.8	36.4	9,454	30,888	61,222	40.7	3.1	63,069	7.8	9.0	7.8
Black Hawk	465	2,366	37,647	11.0	41.9	27.0	235.9	12,528	26,571	50,348	49.6	2.4	50,887	16.1	18.4	16.7
Boone	244	806	6,526	10.5	40.0	22.4	38.2	9,761	28,412	54,513	44.7	2.1	60,421	9.2	12.0	10.6
Bremer	505	646	7,087	29.3	39.2	27.9	48.8	9,626	31,001	64,264	37.3	3.9	65,733	6.7	6.7	6.0
Buchanan	86	1,017	5,143	18.6	48.3	18.0	30.2	9,823	30,216	55,881	44.8	3.9	57,228	10.1	14.3	13.1
Buena Vista	327	1,669	5,584	14.9	52.3	18.7	42.6	10,233	25,035	49,942	50.1	2.7	52,344	12.1	17.3	16.4
Butler	13	27	3,368	6.9	48.4	15.7	11.8	6,064	27,085	52,204	47.2	2.2	54,970	9.8	13.0	11.6
Calhoun	51	801	1,963	6.8	44.1	18.4	17.5	10,056	26,210	44,635	54.7	3.1	50,767	12.4	16.4	16.1
Carroll	39	1,201	4,751	26.5	46.5	21.4	25.8	10,044	28,307	53,785	47.6	2.3	56,292	8.8	11.0	10.3
Cass	233	954	2,785	6.6	52.5	19.8	30.4	11,621	26,411	45,469	55.7	2.3	47,897	12.8	18.8	16.2
Cedar	126	465	4,338	6.7	42.8	22.0	33.7	9,677	29,271	60,435	37.9	3.2	63,672	6.6	9.1	8.0
Cerro Gordo	152	3,302	9,234	14.1	38.1	21.9	64.0	10,250	28,763	47,788	51.8	3.1	53,109	11.7	15.3	14.0
Cherokee	210	795	2,328	9.0	44.2	19.2	17.0	9,706	28,783	51,590	48.5	3.6	53,534	10.9	14.6	13.3
Chickasaw	150	474	2,816	16.5	53.9	14.5	20.5	10,107	26,915	48,013	52.3	1.9	49,197	10.9	14.6	13.0
Clarke	152	1,711	1,783	4.4	53.6	15.4	16.4	8,899	23,742	46,510	55.1	0.5	47,753	11.6	18.0	17.1
Clay	134	1,641	3,706	14.8	41.3	20.9	24.5	9,896	27,883	48,888	50.8	1.7	53,549	9.1	12.6	10.9
Clayton	40	228	3,793	11.4	53.7	15.3	47.7	19,706	26,960	48,482	52.0	2.0	53,809	9.9	14.8	13.5
Clinton	555	3,044	11,462	13.0	44.9	19.4	82.0	10,340	27,116	50,067	49.9	2.4	49,850	13.5	18.3	16.3
Crawford	47	293	4,221	19.0	59.2	11.7	37.9	10,000	26,693	49,699	50.2	3.0	51,473	14.1	16.9	15.6
Dallas	194	1,402	20,825	19.1	23.9	47.4	147.6	9,361	40,468	78,918	29.9	9.8	82,123	4.9	5.5	4.9
Davis	46	114	1,876	25.4	51.5	16.6	12.1	9,777	24,405	49,696	50.4	3.1	49,636	12.9	21.8	21.3
Decatur	98	196	2,361	37.5	50.2	20.1	11.9	10,879	20,808	38,467	61.5	1.5	36,808	20.0	28.1	26.7
Delaware	139	1,069	4,060	16.7	52.8	15.1	22.0	9,667	29,978	59,452	39.6	2.5	56,747	9.5	13.3	12.1
Des Moines	576	3,942	8,834	10.9	42.8	19.6	65.8	9,973	25,151	44,516	56.1	1.9	48,991	16.1	23.2	19.9
Dickinson	186	1,019	3,449	4.8	33.7	29.0	25.5	9,993	36,042	57,914	42.8	5.4	58,019	7.8	9.6	8.0
Dubuque	243	2,139	25,470	33.4	42.3	29.2	154.8	10,616	28,526	56,154	44.8	3.2	59,403	10.5	13.1	11.6
Emmet	394	1,388	2,521	4.8	44.5	17.5	17.4	9,930	27,807	45,536	53.3	2.8	48,035	10.9	16.8	15.8
Fayette	174	711	4,862	22.5	48.7	19.6	38.2	10,360	26,002	47,711	52.4	2.0	52,192	12.8	18.1	16.6
Floyd	170	1,078	3,482	10.7	46.3	19.7	21.6	10,310	26,929	46,406	52.3	2.3	49,771	12.9	17.8	16.3

1. Data for serious crimes have not been adjusted for underreporting; this may affect comparability between geographic areas and over time.   2. Per 100,000 population estimated by the FBI.
3. All persons 3 years old and over enrolled in nursery school through college.   4. Persons 25 years old and over.   5. Elementary and secondary education expenditures.
6. Based on population estimated by the American Community Survey, 2011–2015.

Table B. States and Counties — **Personal Income and Earnings**

STATE County	Personal income, 2016										Earnings, 2016		
	Total (mil dol)	Percent change 2015-2016	Per capita[1]		Wages and salaries (mil dol)	Supplements to wages and salaries, employer contributions (mil dol)		Proprietors' income (mil dol)	Dividends, interest, and rent (mil dol)	Personal transfer receipts (mil dol)	Total (mil dol)	Contributions for government social insurance (mil dol)	
			Dollars	Rank		Pension and insurance	Government social insurance					From employee and self-employed	From employer
	62	63	64	65	66	67	68	69	70	71	72	73	74

INDIANA— Cont'd													
Pike	455	3.7	36,589	1,899	154	34	11	29	58	125	228	26	11
Porter	7,880	2.7	46,965	614	2,804	468	211	429	1,162	1,344	3,911	460	211
Posey	1,145	2.9	44,931	784	483	108	34	80	180	220	704	75	34
Pulaski	523	3.9	41,309	1,200	190	38	13	51	96	122	292	31	13
Putnam	1,301	5.4	34,742	2,200	521	99	40	87	177	295	748	88	40
Randolph	963	6.0	38,378	1,589	294	56	22	109	134	253	482	54	22
Ripley	1,179	4.7	40,863	1,250	579	108	42	57	174	227	786	91	42
Rush	697	6.4	41,879	1,113	203	42	15	92	100	156	352	35	15
St. Joseph	11,995	2.7	44,568	821	5,827	983	442	1,273	1,940	2,249	8,525	954	442
Scott	828	3.3	34,889	2,184	304	60	23	36	93	249	422	53	23
Shelby	1,788	4.6	40,348	1,318	825	141	62	119	251	397	1,148	133	62
Spencer	867	2.2	42,013	1,103	283	58	21	64	110	171	426	48	21
Starke	736	4.7	31,967	2,621	156	34	12	59	87	247	262	32	12
Steuben	1,298	2.7	38,033	1,654	579	113	45	65	231	296	802	98	45
Sullivan	684	5.1	32,892	2,499	237	55	17	30	94	199	340	40	17
Switzerland	306	2.5	29,081	2,926	82	13	6	15	38	78	117	15	6
Tippecanoe	6,733	4.3	35,804	2,033	4,170	823	305	425	1,164	1,097	5,723	633	305
Tipton	634	3.9	41,777	1,130	186	34	14	36	114	145	270	33	14
Union	254	6.1	35,175	2,138	47	10	3	26	36	65	86	10	3
Vanderburgh	7,637	2.1	42,024	1,101	5,051	827	379	546	1,407	1,710	6,804	794	379
Vermillion	575	4.9	36,743	1,871	214	42	16	37	82	166	308	36	16
Vigo	3,827	2.3	35,457	2,088	2,087	400	160	190	658	1,067	2,838	338	160
Wabash	1,294	1.2	40,737	1,270	462	89	35	129	213	353	714	81	35
Warren	342	4.1	41,856	1,116	76	15	6	44	47	73	141	14	6
Warrick	3,115	3.5	49,836	422	775	132	56	228	478	497	1,191	134	56
Washington	970	0.6	35,051	2,156	226	45	17	69	121	258	358	43	17
Wayne	2,505	3.6	37,624	1,720	1,214	227	92	153	364	748	1,686	201	92
Wells	1,097	2.3	39,264	1,457	427	84	33	84	181	232	626	72	33
White	975	3.7	40,640	1,284	370	70	28	82	161	229	549	61	28
Whitley	1,362	3.8	40,731	1,271	527	104	39	79	197	266	748	87	39
IOWA	14,4,196	1.0	46,056	X	71,817	12,896	5,571	13,130	26,636	25,206	103,414	6,386	5571
Adair	317	-1.6	44,765	794	106	21	9	28	63	62	164	19	9
Adams	223	-2.4	60,450	144	49	11	4	82	36	38	145	12	4
Allamakee	573	0.4	41,262	1,203	181	41	14	85	110	121	320	34	14
Appanoose	452	1.9	36,236	1,968	170	36	14	32	73	131	252	32	14
Audubon	280	-2.4	49,397	448	61	13	4	48	60	57	127	12	4
Benton	1,240	1.9	48,239	515	225	48	17	154	206	202	444	48	17
Black Hawk	5,427	0.9	40,837	1,252	3,376	605	265	286	971	1,135	4,532	550	265
Boone	1,192	-0.3	44,926	785	408	85	33	78	216	254	604	73	33
Bremer	1,104	-0.6	44,514	828	418	83	32	58	223	194	590	71	32
Buchanan	915	0.5	43,607	918	242	51	19	81	198	175	393	45	19
Buena Vista	889	-7.1	43,740	902	415	82	31	156	152	154	684	69	31
Butler	659	-0.9	44,540	825	133	29	10	95	120	141	268	26	10
Calhoun	451	-0.2	45,833	710	115	24	9	69	87	93	216	21	9
Carroll	991	-2.0	48,514	498	453	83	34	163	199	180	733	78	34
Cass	581	-2.4	44,134	864	228	49	18	56	129	140	350	40	18
Cedar	865	0.7	46,851	622	212	41	17	79	178	133	349	40	17
Cerro Gordo	2,284	-0.4	53,035	303	1,026	176	81	467	408	427	1,751	196	81
Cherokee	653	-1.2	56,784	190	189	39	14	223	109	106	465	42	14
Chickasaw	608	-1.3	50,537	391	193	36	15	120	126	105	364	39	15
Clarke	343	1.4	36,869	1,843	169	34	13	25	52	93	241	28	13
Clay	747	-7.9	45,719	721	359	67	27	101	156	140	555	61	27
Clayton	833	-0.1	47,348	582	262	53	21	117	188	166	453	49	21
Clinton	1,960	1.0	41,427	1,179	875	163	72	127	327	470	1,237	154	72
Crawford	666	-1.2	39,296	1,454	292	57	21	70	137	132	440	48	21
Dallas	5,169	5.5	61,159	136	2,229	313	166	308	917	414	3,017	352	166
Davis	300	-0.9	33,812	2,347	75	17	6	47	45	67	145	16	6
Decatur	270	0.5	33,196	2,445	78	19	6	25	41	71	128	15	6
Delaware	757	-1.5	43,681	905	277	58	22	91	160	133	448	49	22
Des Moines	1,911	1.9	48,092	526	964	172	82	299	330	398	1,516	180	82
Dickinson	925	-1.5	53,622	276	355	73	28	97	259	164	554	65	28
Dubuque	4,372	1.1	45,068	772	2,555	429	199	263	907	788	3,445	422	199
Emmet	388	-9.1	40,194	1,339	149	31	11	32	67	92	222	26	11
Fayette	796	-1.2	39,709	1,399	260	53	21	84	157	213	417	48	21
Floyd	663	-1.1	41,741	1,135	249	54	19	48	133	158	370	44	19

1. Based on the resident population estimated as of July 1 of the year shown.

STATE County	Earnings, 2016 (cont.) — Percent by selected industries									Social Security beneficiaries, December 2016		Supplemental Security Income recipients, 2016	Housing units, 2017	
	Farm	Mining, quarrying, and extracting	Construction	Manufacturing	Information; professional, scientific, technical services	Retail trade	Finance, insurance, real estate, and leasing	Health care and social assistance	Government	Number	Rate[1]		Total	Percent change, 2010-2017
	75	76	77	78	79	80	81	82	83	84	85	86	87	88
INDIANA— Cont'd														
Pike	7.1	4.5	11.7	5.2	D	2.9	D	6.5	12.9	3,295	265	236	5,821	2.1
Porter	0.1	D	9.3	21.7	5.9	6.7	4.5	13.8	9.7	33,880	202	1,931	68,773	3.9
Posey	5.5	0.4	5.9	45.4	3.9	4.7	2.2	D	8.4	5,775	225	345	11,501	2.6
Pulaski	14.3	D	3.8	30.7	D	4.8	4.1	D	19.7	3,295	261	260	6,111	0.9
Putnam	3.4	0.6	6.2	22.4	3.1	4.8	3.2	D	16.7	6,485	259	514	11,697	-0.4
Randolph	5.0	D	8.4	30.5	5.2	3.6	2.4	D	11.9	5,840	206	350	12,385	3.6
Ripley	1.8	0.2	5.3	19.0	4.1	4.1	2.9	D	8.6	3,990	240	309	7,499	-0.1
Rush	14.2	D	7.6	22.0	2.7	6.5	3.5	D	15.9					
St. Joseph	0.0	D	5.3	15.3	10.1	6.0	5.4	15.3	9.1	51,620	191	5,870	116,460	1.4
Scott	0.7	D	3.9	37.0	2.1	7.6	3.0	D	14.4	6,240	263	852	10,600	1.5
Shelby	3.5	0.3	7.5	32.7	2.7	5.1	2.5	6.6	13.2	9,525	215	679	19,292	1.1
Spencer	5.5	0.0	5.6	21.4	D	3.4	2.9	4.8	11.3	4,775	233	259	9,099	2.6
Starke	9.8	0.0	6.2	19.0	2.5	7.8	2.5	D	18.3	6,295	274	563	11,149	1.7
Steuben	0.7	0.1	5.0	37.6	2.8	7.7	2.5	D	9.1	8,150	237	442	20,002	3.2
Sullivan	1.3	D	3.7	11.4	3.8	5.7	2.6	D	27.9	4,785	231	386	8,933	-0.1
Switzerland	-0.7	D	8.2	D	D	2.9	D	D	20.4	1,970	185	190	5,319	6.7
Tippecanoe	0.4	D	4.6	23.0	5.1	5.3	4.9	13.5	26.9	25,450	135	2,263	75,912	6.8
Tipton	4.1	0.0	10.2	29.0	5.1	6.8	4.7	D	13.9	3,780	249	144	6,995	0.0
Union	7.1	0.0	7.9	16.2	1.9	7.6	D	D	23.3	1,675	234	129	3,254	0.5
Vanderburgh	0.2	0.2	7.7	16.1	7.0	6.7	4.7	18.9	9.2	39,205	216	4,573	84,322	1.6
Vermillion	5.5	D	16.1	23.2	1.9	6.8	D	10.5	10.6	4,155	266	343	7,497	0.1
Vigo	0.6	0.6	6.1	15.6	4.0	7.5	4.7	18.7	18.7	23,280	216	3,178	47,349	2.9
Wabash	6.9	D	5.9	30.3	3.4	7.1	4.0	D	10.6	8,720	276	596	14,178	0.1
Warren	22.9	D	5.1	20.2	D	4.0	1.8	11.6	13.3	1,995	244	86	3,743	1.7
Warrick	0.6	2.1	8.1	18.0	6.1	4.9	6.1	26.1	10.1	13,135	212	699	25,942	7.2
Washington	6.9	D	9.7	24.2	3.2	9.1	3.5	D	16.9	6,590	237	633	12,401	1.5
Wayne	1.0	D	3.9	21.2	3.2	7.5	4.5	21.3	13.7	17,435	262	2,196	31,389	0.5
Wells	6.4	D	5.4	28.7	D	5.1	4.3	10.7	10.4	6,265	225	324	11,871	1.8
White	9.6	D	8.4	28.0	D	7.2	3.7	D	11.6	5,975	248	340	13,108	1.1
Whitley	2.4	0.0	7.2	45.1	1.8	5.5	3.8	6.0	10.0	7,390	221	365	14,769	3.4
IOWA	3.3	0.2	7.7	16.3	6.3	6.0	9.8	10.5	16.4	630,014	201	50,942	1,398,016	4.6
Adair	8.1	D	D	D	2.6	5.6	4.9	D	15.4	1,720	245	90	3,713	0.4
Adams	19.8	D	3.1	26.9	D	3.9	D	10.7	8.1	970	261	68	2,012	0.1
Allamakee	11.4	0.3	8.0	16.3	2.0	8.4	3.5	7.9	18.8	3,585	258	163	7,795	2.4
Appanoose	-0.3	D	5.2	24.0	2.9	7.9	3.5	D	15.7	3,490	279	435	6,647	0.2
Audubon	30.2	0.0	5.3	8.9	D	4.5	4.4	D	17.1	1,570	279	74	3,014	1.4
Benton	6.4	D	11.3	20.1	D	7.9	5.5	D	20.0	5,565	217	315	11,155	0.5
Black Hawk	0.3	D	5.0	24.3	5.8	6.9	5.9	13.7	16.1	26,730	201	3,214	57,856	3.5
Boone	5.0	D	10.4	6.0	5.7	6.7	4.0	8.5	25.6	5,825	220	324	11,943	1.6
Bremer	1.1	D	6.1	19.6	3.5	7.1	16.1	D	19.4	5,400	218	187	10,411	5.0
Buchanan	5.3	D	11.3	19.1	3.0	7.6	5.7	6.1	21.5	4,430	211	292	9,087	1.3
Buena Vista	12.7	0.0	4.4	26.9	D	5.7	4.3	D	15.0	3,645	180	265	8,292	0.7
Butler	24.6	D	3.8	15.3	3.7	5.0	3.8	D	17.4	2,645	270	150	5,124	0.3
Calhoun	22.2	0.0	10.2	2.8	2.0	5.4	4.2	D	9.6	4,780	235	247	9,509	1.4
Carroll	9.2	D	7.2	11.0	3.4	7.5	9.8	D	25.4	3,695	280	301	6,583	-0.1
Cass	6.7	D	8.5	13.2	D	7.5	5.3	9.4		3,975	216	163	8,221	2.0
Cedar	8.2	0.0	8.5	13.6	7.5	5.2	3.7	D						
Cerro Gordo	0.7	0.1	5.0	24.9	5.4	6.4	5.1	21.2	10.3	11,265	262	804	22,362	0.9
Cherokee	12.8	D	5.3	30.9	3.0	4.2	2.5	D	12.8	3,000	263	127	5,776	0.0
Chickasaw	4.9	D	7.7	34.3	2.7	5.4	3.7	D	10.5	2,905	241	130	5,705	0.5
Clarke	2.9	D	D	33.1	1.4	7.0	2.4	6.7	19.2	2,135	230	140	4,220	3.3
Clay	7.6	D	6.5	9.5	D	12.5	3.5	11.5	18.3	3,985	244	217	8,278	2.7
Clayton	14.7	D	16.2	13.4	2.8	5.4	3.9	D	16.5	4,745	269	221	9,124	1.4
Clinton	2.4	D	6.5	27.1	3.6	6.6	4.6	14.7	11.8	11,135	236	1,114	21,989	1.2
Crawford	9.3	0.0	5.2	29.3	2.6	5.5	4.5	5.4	18.5	3,560	209	203	7,058	1.7
Dallas	0.4	D	5.8	4.7	5.9	7.3	42.1	8.0	8.0	11,080	132	434	36,844	35.2
Davis	-0.5	D	15.1	13.5	D	7.0	3.8	D	24.1	1,780	200	120	3,602	0.1
Decatur	8.0	D	9.1	4.1	D	5.5	D	D	23.3	1,790	222	188	3,856	0.6
Delaware	9.6	0.0	8.9	26.7	2.7	4.7	4.0	D	17.6	3,650	211	208	8,114	1.1
Des Moines	1.0	D	6.3	34.5	4.3	6.4	3.2	14.5	10.5	9,700	245	999	18,590	0.3
Dickinson	3.4	D	10.1	23.6	3.9	9.9	5.4	6.8	12.9	5,025	294	173	13,890	8.1
Dubuque	1.2	D	6.2	19.3	7.7	6.6	10.5	14.6	8.6	20,820	215	1,634	41,334	6.1
Emmet	6.1	0.0	8.1	17.5	D	6.7	D	D	19.0	2,350	246	130	4,820	1.3
Fayette	11.9	D	8.6	6.9	2.7	6.2	3.7	D	15.5	5,105	255	488	9,578	0.2
Floyd	3.9	D	5.2	31.2	3.3	6.6	5.7	D	15.9	4,060	256	329	7,592	0.9

1. Per 1,000 resident population estimated as of July 1 of the year shown.

Table B. States and Counties — Population, Vital Statistics, Health, and Crime

STATE County	Daytime Population, 2012-2016			Births, 2017		Deaths, 2017		Persons under 65 with no health insurance, 2016		Medicare, 2017			Serious crimes known to police[2], 2016 Total	
	Persons in group quarters, 2017	Number	Employment/ residence ratio	Total	Rate[1]	Number	Rate[1]	Number	Percent	Total beneficiaries	Enrolled in Original Medicare	Enrolled in Medicare Advantage	Number	Rate[3]
	32	33	34	35	36	37	38	39	40	41	42	43	44	45
IOWA— Cont'd														
Franklin	178	10,175	0.95	120	11.8	113	11.1	549	6.9	1,967	1,904	63	20	196
Fremont	123	6,149	0.74	84	12.1	78	11.2	242	4.5	1,715	1,534	181	91	1339
Greene	85	8,637	0.90	115	12.8	122	13.6	361	5.2	2,202	1,889	313	148	1654
Grundy	156	10,416	0.68	119	9.6	130	10.5	345	3.5	2,546	2,066	479	82	661
Guthrie	168	9,194	0.71	106	9.9	109	10.2	458	5.5	2,691	2,221	470	35	330
Hamilton	203	14,222	0.87	189	12.5	167	11.0	626	5.2	3,301	2,966	335	172	1141
Hancock	185	10,871	0.98	115	10.7	123	11.4	416	4.9	2,337	2,278	60	82	753
Hardin	771	17,096	0.97	192	11.3	216	12.7	677	5.2	4,320	3,968	352	220	1271
Harrison	283	11,854	0.65	161	11.4	171	12.1	562	5.0	3,282	2,900	383	116	822
Henry	1,496	19,724	0.98	225	11.3	193	9.7	695	4.7	4,375	4,032	343	323	1624
Howard	199	9,135	0.94	115	12.5	109	11.8	420	5.7	2,249	2,193	57	100	1068
Humboldt	114	9,081	0.88	105	11.0	109	11.4	350	4.7	2,101	1,993	108	82	864
Ida	120	7,575	1.15	80	11.7	105	15.3	253	4.7	1,617	1,458	159	46	656
Iowa	284	16,605	1.03	185	11.5	185	11.5	532	4.0	3,341	2,769	572	108	659
Jackson	200	16,952	0.72	224	11.6	206	10.6	806	5.2	4,462	3,140	1,322	200	1034
Jasper	1,712	31,225	0.68	407	11.0	361	9.8	1,120	3.9	7,473	6,296	1,178	786	2138
Jefferson	1,721	18,737	1.14	159	8.6	174	9.4	938	7.3	3,952	3,469	483	394	2229
Johnson	8,617	150,560	1.11	1,821	12.2	761	5.1	6,676	5.4	18,240	15,468	2,772	3,192	2175
Jones	1,097	18,000	0.73	213	10.4	195	9.5	725	4.7	4,154	3,305	849	194	951
Keokuk	127	8,518	0.64	121	11.9	105	10.3	487	6.1	2,544	2,141	403	69	684
Kossuth	238	15,467	1.03	171	11.4	154	10.3	511	4.4	3,545	3,455	91	94	624
Lee	1,391	37,606	1.15	403	11.8	406	11.8	1,142	4.3	7,844	7,239	605	1,215	3483
Linn	5,169	229,195	1.10	2,818	12.6	1,744	7.8	6,611	3.6	39,743	28,607	11,136	7,036	3180
Louisa	122	9,568	0.69	141	12.6	111	9.9	722	7.9	2,199	1,896	303	100	898
Lucas	70	8,538	0.96	94	11.0	91	10.7	355	5.3	2,017	1,720	296	205	2376
Lyon	169	10,701	0.82	166	14.1	101	8.6	530	5.5	2,116	1,948	167	80	680
Madison	171	12,095	0.54	178	11.1	154	9.6	600	4.6	2,923	2,394	529	160	1017
Mahaska	685	20,135	0.80	272	12.2	231	10.4	788	4.4	4,276	3,668	608	456	2047
Marion	1,378	34,667	1.09	371	11.2	318	9.6	990	3.8	6,743	5,898	845	273	1049
Marshall	1,297	41,041	1.02	506	12.6	452	11.2	2,422	7.6	8,863	7,503	1,360	1,154	2836
Mills	565	12,195	0.63	150	10.0	122	8.1	495	4.1	3,100	2,678	423	245	1658
Mitchell	246	10,428	0.94	109	10.3	119	11.2	532	6.4	2,573	2,545	27	75	693
Monona	203	8,085	0.78	92	10.5	140	16.0	364	5.5	2,247	1,829	418	83	931
Monroe	115	7,788	0.95	84	10.7	89	11.3	341	5.4	1,657	1,345	313	108	1357
Montgomery	186	10,562	1.04	120	11.8	118	11.6	477	6.0	2,627	2,386	241	NA	NA
Muscatine	556	45,305	1.11	530	12.4	366	8.5	2,014	5.7	8,058	6,167	1,891	857	1993
O'Brien	376	13,339	0.90	184	13.3	183	13.3	554	5.0	3,269	3,107	162	131	944
Osceola	95	5,523	0.80	74	12.2	80	13.2	312	6.5	1,337	1,266	71	65	1068
Page	1,456	16,442	1.13	158	10.4	198	13.0	592	5.5	3,704	3,376	327	307	1991
Palo Alto	274	8,862	0.94	110	12.1	108	11.9	345	5.0	2,249	2,201	47	92	1015
Plymouth	349	23,684	0.90	296	11.7	229	9.1	981	4.8	4,590	3,896	695	270	1092
Pocahontas	104	6,867	0.94	78	11.4	84	12.3	315	6.0	1,845	1,762	83	65	936
Polk	9,554	500,137	1.17	7,006	14.5	3,464	7.2	20,758	5.1	74,741	58,775	15,966	15,540	3276
Pottawattamie	2,043	86,389	0.85	1,145	12.3	944	10.1	3,869	5.1	18,948	14,371	4,578	4,492	4800
Poweshiek	1,602	20,094	1.16	167	9.1	205	11.2	699	5.2	4,079	3,566	513	352	1908
Ringgold	175	4,692	0.83	62	12.3	66	13.1	270	7.2	1,215	1,143	72	33	654
Sac	174	9,048	0.80	111	11.3	115	11.7	399	5.3	2,480	2,387	93	35	448
Scott	3,373	174,479	1.04	2,171	12.6	1,449	8.4	6,038	4.2	31,795	23,698	8,097	6,722	3889
Shelby	212	12,034	1.01	112	9.6	133	11.4	424	4.7	2,820	2,591	228	10	84
Sioux	2,358	37,081	1.13	479	13.7	261	7.5	1,583	5.7	5,616	5,262	354	168	478
Story	11,534	98,088	1.07	890	9.1	514	5.3	3,529	4.7	13,151	11,440	1,711	1,659	1836
Tama	299	15,218	0.73	218	12.8	180	10.6	887	6.4	3,781	3,072	709	240	1393
Taylor	73	5,479	0.76	74	12.0	60	9.7	312	6.5	1,589	1,560	29	28	454
Union	443	13,098	1.09	123	9.9	137	11.0	472	4.9	3,418	3,121	298	239	1921
Van Buren	57	6,612	0.77	84	11.7	96	13.4	361	6.4	1,908	1,658	251	37	507
Wapello	890	36,487	1.08	440	12.6	365	10.4	2,000	7.1	8,111	6,420	1,691	1,347	3846
Warren	1,588	35,704	0.50	570	11.4	430	8.6	1,338	3.3	8,415	6,722	1,693	874	1783
Washington	314	19,895	0.80	299	13.4	225	10.1	944	5.3	4,850	4,236	614	240	1075
Wayne	95	6,084	0.88	90	13.9	84	13.0	368	7.4	1,489	1,270	219	64	1004
Webster	2,688	38,681	1.10	443	12.1	419	11.4	1,383	5.0	8,197	7,324	873	1,268	3441
Winnebago	454	10,992	1.08	109	10.3	117	11.1	334	4.1	2,657	2,536	122	31	294
Winneshiek	2,084	21,325	1.04	170	8.4	188	9.3	620	4.3	4,339	3,701	638	126	611
Woodbury	2,620	101,858	0.99	1,501	14.7	879	8.6	6,143	7.2	18,739	14,298	4,441	3,918	3815
Worth	78	6,120	0.61	82	11.0	75	10.0	271	4.5	1,577	1,457	120	25	331
Wright	206	13,223	1.06	170	13.3	154	12.0	635	6.4	3,084	2,920	164	108	852

1. Per 1,000 estimated resident population. 2. Data for serious crimes have not been adjusted for underreporting; this may affect comparability between geographic areas and over time.
3. Per 100,000 population estimated by the FBI.

Table B. States and Counties — Local Government Finances, Government Employment, and Income Taxes

STATE County	Local government finances (cont.) — Direct general expenditure							Debt outstanding		Government employment, 2016			Individual income tax returns, 2015		
	Total (mil dol)	Per capita[1] (dollars)	Percent of total for:					Total (mil dol)	Per capita[1] (dollars)	Federal civilian	Federal military	State and local	Number of returns	Mean adjusted gross income	Mean income tax
			Education	Health and hospitals	Police protection	Public welfare	Highways								
	185	186	187	188	189	190	191	192	193	194	195	196	197	198	199
IOWA— Cont'd															
Franklin	74.7	7,078	38.7	27.4	2.8	0.1	7.5	53.7	5,092	43	37	756	4,660	55,868	6383
Fremont	36.0	5,034	46.9	4.3	4.1	0.1	19.2	10.1	1,415	27	26	443	3,190	54,915	5552
Greene	58.6	6,398	31.8	39.4	3.0	0.2	8.2	19.5	2,133	37	34	792	4,290	50,472	4985
Grundy	60.9	4,889	35.4	29.1	3.1	0.1	12.1	34.5	2,773	33	46	704	5,710	65,472	7222
Guthrie	64.7	6,005	45.4	24.0	2.4	0.1	9.0	71.3	6,614	59	39	847	5,030	58,461	6559
Hamilton	89.3	5,820	41.9	27.7	3.4	0.2	7.1	95.4	6,215	40	56	1,177	7,170	57,121	6014
Hancock	59.9	5,378	31.9	38.4	3.3	0.1	11.3	36.3	3,260	40	40	608	5,280	53,458	5528
Hardin	98.1	5,668	39.4	22.8	3.6	0.1	10.4	60.0	3,470	77	62	1,764	7,930	55,931	6201
Harrison	56.0	3,853	56.3	5.5	3.7	0.3	12.4	33.4	2,299	71	52	810	6,710	54,522	5580
Henry	99.5	4,919	39.9	36.4	3.0	0.3	4.6	76.0	3,758	67	69	1,596	8,880	49,126	4419
Howard	49.9	5,214	37.9	32.9	2.9	0.4	8.5	14.5	1,518	28	34	707	4,540	48,517	4898
Humboldt	60.5	6,223	36.7	23.4	2.9	0.2	10.8	37.9	3,894	47	35	664	4,540	59,055	6883
Ida	25.1	3,531	55.4	4.9	4.2	0.2	13.6	14.0	1,973	28	26	370	3,370	60,961	7906
Iowa	74.5	4,600	48.3	23.2	3.7	0.4	9.2	69.2	4,275	51	60	996	8,050	53,470	5727
Jackson	75.2	3,817	46.3	20.7	4.1	0.1	9.2	36.7	1,860	78	72	1,008	9,540	50,269	5379
Jasper	146.8	4,011	39.1	28.3	4.3	0.3	6.0	102.6	2,802	95	131	2,142	16,720	55,077	5600
Jefferson	72.9	4,323	28.0	30.9	3.6	0.2	10.0	71.8	4,254	62	61	1,070	7,410	48,083	5487
Johnson	524.4	3,847	35.0	4.1	4.1	0.9	6.0	708.3	5,196	2,049	559	35,267	64,670	70,926	9628
Jones	81.7	3,958	56.2	5.0	3.3	0.1	12.9	52.6	2,548	51	72	1,329	9,090	54,231	5728
Keokuk	46.7	4,504	42.3	19.6	2.4	0.1	11.3	24.3	2,344	44	37	538	4,560	47,163	4147
Kossuth	92.1	6,004	26.6	34.3	2.6	0.2	10.8	73.1	4,765	62	56	1,078	7,590	59,418	6747
Lee	137.2	3,851	55.0	7.3	5.0	0.5	5.8	121.6	3,414	99	141	1,945	15,810	50,308	5293
Linn	1,336.0	6,206	46.5	3.0	3.7	1.2	4.7	1,559.7	7,244	1,048	817	12,687	106,870	66,739	8400
Louisa	54.0	4,790	58.9	3.9	3.7	0.1	10.4	92.9	8,237	57	41	655	5,130	49,165	4390
Lucas	45.7	5,216	36.3	40.7	2.3	0.2	8.8	77.6	8,862	36	32	631	3,950	45,625	4191
Lyon	43.5	3,701	45.1	4.4	4.6	0.1	20.2	26.6	2,260	40	43	661	5,240	60,068	6568
Madison	80.3	5,130	45.0	29.6	2.4	0.1	8.2	120.8	7,718	39	59	938	7,200	66,238	7717
Mahaska	103.0	4,588	32.3	43.1	3.7	0.2	7.0	35.6	1,584	58	81	1,430	9,710	53,255	5438
Marion	110.4	3,302	53.4	5.1	4.5	0.3	11.9	105.0	3,142	132	119	1,685	14,840	61,234	6703
Marshall	192.9	4,722	64.1	3.0	4.2	0.3	6.4	177.1	4,335	116	146	3,278	18,120	52,767	5227
Mills	49.6	3,346	58.3	5.0	5.7	1.1	10.6	46.3	3,118	36	54	1,574	6,750	63,976	7448
Mitchell	58.6	5,460	27.5	34.6	2.8	0.1	12.4	39.9	3,723	36	39	727	4,810	54,355	5826
Monona	39.6	4,341	49.5	4.3	4.7	0.4	17.8	19.2	2,100	38	33	532	4,160	51,317	5731
Monroe	25.6	3,175	52.7	6.3	5.3	0.3	19.1	18.5	2,294	40	29	537	3,470	46,124	4517
Montgomery	75.5	7,150	27.3	38.4	8.7	0.2	5.5	34.3	3,246	40	38	935	4,820	47,958	4682
Muscatine	169.3	3,949	47.2	3.6	5.1	0.4	6.8	78.4	1,828	86	159	2,620	20,690	55,117	5797
O'Brien	67.2	4,738	61.1	4.1	3.9	0.2	8.1	45.7	3,226	44	51	1,062	6,730	57,041	6827
Osceola	20.4	3,288	41.6	8.9	9.7	0.1	18.2	8.6	1,389	27	22	290	2,960	49,370	4840
Page	86.1	5,483	33.4	39.4	2.8	0.1	7.4	65.9	4,192	69	52	1,264	6,570	49,211	4784
Palo Alto	64.4	6,948	31.7	32.8	2.9	0.1	15.3	37.1	4,003	38	33	983	4,280	51,757	5566
Plymouth	123.5	4,958	40.4	28.0	3.4	2.2	7.8	86.7	3,483	82	93	1,453	12,270	61,208	7448
Pocahontas	41.8	5,851	31.5	27.7	4.1	0.5	11.0	23.7	3,313	34	25	548	3,400	50,262	5197
Polk	2,428.8	5,474	46.0	7.6	4.5	1.5	5.2	2,789.0	6,286	5,986	1,861	29,972	225,010	68,533	9029
Pottawattamie	475.8	5,121	56.9	3.4	5.2	0.3	4.5	433.2	4,662	212	345	5,317	43,020	54,429	5792
Poweshiek	66.2	3,533	47.3	5.0	4.5	0.2	10.8	65.3	3,483	60	63	861	8,250	54,515	5810
Ringgold	38.2	7,503	25.9	44.8	2.8	0.2	9.0	42.2	8,280	30	18	430	2,040	46,873	5129
Sac	42.6	4,196	49.4	6.2	4.3	0.1	13.4	17.5	1,720	44	36	596	4,790	53,389	5608
Scott	760.2	4,504	54.4	2.6	4.9	0.1	3.6	683.1	4,047	587	637	8,415	81,930	65,538	8441
Shelby	87.3	7,233	22.6	50.5	1.7	0.1	7.8	52.5	4,348	43	43	1,043	5,810	57,269	6641
Sioux	160.8	4,691	31.1	29.5	3.1	0.1	6.7	182.6	5,329	97	122	2,198	14,580	65,299	8396
Story	440.2	4,830	30.3	42.8	3.2	0.5	3.7	391.5	4,295	954	344	19,451	37,020	65,374	7984
Tama	71.1	4,056	60.3	5.1	3.5	0.1	12.6	36.6	2,088	67	64	1,968	8,350	49,963	4782
Taylor	30.7	4,937	39.9	4.5	3.6	0.1	25.2	25.0	4,034	42	23	372	2,790	41,266	3775
Union	122.3	9,707	35.7	41.6	1.4	0.1	4.0	91.1	7,230	53	45	1,338	5,610	47,144	4470
Van Buren	35.9	4,821	31.7	41.5	2.3	0.1	11.2	9.2	1,230	33	27	520	3,150	43,757	4100
Wapello	204.9	5,795	64.7	3.0	2.8	0.3	9.3	88.9	2,514	115	128	2,532	15,660	46,864	4515
Warren	173.5	3,701	60.2	4.1	4.2	0.3	5.2	262.4	5,595	88	180	1,482	22,690	66,833	7711
Washington	127.8	5,831	38.9	20.4	2.8	0.3	9.4	155.3	7,085	68	82	583	10,480	55,104	5399
Wayne	43.2	6,809	20.6	52.3	2.4	0.2	7.7	24.6	3,877	35	24	713	2,730	39,381	3386
Webster	231.6	6,213	65.0	3.5	2.6	0.2	5.7	235.4	6,314	188	128	2,803	16,590	52,153	5628
Winnebago	54.8	5,168	50.8	4.8	4.2	0.1	18.2	51.9	4,900	50	42	713	5,160	52,117	5284
Winneshiek	175.5	8,333	54.9	26.3	1.7	0.1	5.5	125.4	5,954	70	69	2,109	9,530	55,663	6197
Woodbury	498.8	4,875	56.0	4.2	4.6	0.6	3.9	465.5	4,550	685	376	6,334	47,290	51,070	5475
Worth	37.0	4,920	43.7	3.8	4.3	0.1	12.6	25.7	3,424	28	28	374	3,630	50,223	4752
Wright	134.7	10,370	22.1	58.1	1.8	0.2	4.2	130.1	10,011	63	47	1,300	5,980	50,994	4959

1. Based on the resident population estimated as of July 1 of the year shown.

Table B. States and Counties — **Land Area and Population**

State / county code	CBSA code[1]	County code[2]	STATE County	Land area[3] (sq. mi)	Total persons 2017	Rank	Per square mile	White	Black	American Indian, Alaska Native	Asian and Pacific Islander	Percent Hispanic or Latino[4]	Under 5 years	5 to 17 years	18 to 24 years	25 to 34 years	35 to 44 years	45 to 54 years
				1	2	3	4	5	6	7	8	9	10	11	12	13	14	15
			KANSAS— Cont'd															
2,0133		7	Neosho	571.5	16,015	2,038	28.0	91.9	2.0	1.9	1.0	5.2	6.5	17.9	8.8	10.9	10.5	11.9
2,0135		9	Ness	1,074.7	2,869	2,980	2.7	88.8	1.2	0.7	0.5	10.0	5.6	16.2	7.6	8.2	9.6	10.3
2,0137		7	Norton	878.0	5,441	2,801	6.2	90.3	4.0	0.8	1.2	5.3	5.0	13.8	8.2	13.0	11.8	14.3
2,0139	45,820	3	Osage	705.5	15,772	2,050	22.4	94.8	1.5	1.5	0.8	3.3	5.6	17.6	7.3	10.0	11.0	12.8
2,0141		9	Osborne	892.5	3,610	2,931	4.0	95.4	0.7	1.0	1.7	2.2	6.3	15.0	6.8	11.1	9.4	10.7
2,0143	41,460	9	Ottawa	720.7	5,863	2,763	8.1	95.2	1.9	1.0	0.5	2.8	5.2	17.5	7.8	9.5	11.5	12.8
2,0145		7	Pawnee	754.3	6,680	2,698	8.9	85.6	6.4	1.2	0.7	7.9	4.2	13.0	8.3	12.5	12.6	13.5
2,0147		7	Phillips	885.9	5,370	2,804	6.1	94.9	1.0	0.7	1.0	3.4	5.5	17.2	7.3	10.1	9.9	11.5
2,0149	31,740	3	Pottawatomie	840.8	23,908	1,646	28.4	91.8	2.0	1.5	1.6	5.3	7.7	21.2	8.4	12.7	13.0	11.0
2,0151		7	Pratt	735.0	9,547	2,463	13.0	90.2	2.2	1.3	0.9	7.2	7.0	17.4	9.6	11.2	10.5	10.4
2,0153		9	Rawlins	1,069.4	2,497	3,004	2.3	91.7	1.3	0.6	0.6	7.0	5.6	14.6	6.6	10.0	8.7	10.6
2,0155	26,740	4	Reno	1,255.3	62,510	844	49.8	86.3	4.2	1.4	0.9	9.4	5.5	17.1	8.5	12.5	11.3	11.8
2,0157		9	Republic	717.4	4,691	2,852	6.5	96.8	1.3	0.7	0.5	1.9	5.4	15.0	6.5	8.9	9.1	10.7
2,0159		7	Rice	726.2	9,660	2,455	13.3	85.4	2.1	1.6	1.2	11.6	6.4	17.1	11.6	11.2	10.0	10.7
2,0161	31,740	3	Riley	609.7	74,172	743	121.7	79.5	7.9	1.2	6.3	8.3	5.6	11.0	32.6	17.8	9.5	6.7
2,0163		9	Rooks	890.5	5,043	2,829	5.7	95.3	1.5	0.9	1.1	2.7	6.0	16.4	7.1	11.1	10.4	11.7
2,0165		9	Rush	717.8	3,103	2,959	4.3	94.6	0.9	1.3	0.5	4.0	5.3	15.7	6.3	9.5	9.6	11.7
2,0167		7	Russell	886.3	6,915	2,680	7.8	93.9	2.2	1.3	0.9	3.3	5.9	15.6	6.6	10.5	10.0	11.9
2,0169	41,460	5	Saline	720.2	54,734	928	76.0	82.6	4.7	1.1	3.0	11.3	6.4	17.0	9.0	12.3	11.4	12.5
2,0171		7	Scott	717.6	4,961	2,834	6.9	79.2	1.1	1.0	1.5	18.2	6.3	20.3	7.6	11.1	10.8	12.0
2,0173	48,620	5	Sedgwick	997.5	513,687	135	515.0	71.0	10.5	1.9	5.4	14.6	7.1	18.8	9.3	14.3	12.1	11.7
2,0175	30,580	5	Seward	639.3	22,159	1,720	34.7	31.2	4.5	0.9	3.0	61.6	8.8	22.5	11.0	14.8	12.1	11.6
2,0177	45,820	3	Shawnee	544.0	178,187	370	327.5	77.0	10.0	2.1	2.1	12.4	6.4	17.5	8.4	12.6	11.6	12.2
2,0179		9	Sheridan	896.0	2,527	3,000	2.8	93.9	0.8	0.6	0.6	5.0	5.9	18.7	6.5	9.2	10.3	10.6
2,0181		7	Sherman	1,056.1	5,930	2,758	5.6	86.0	1.7	0.9	0.8	12.3	6.9	17.1	8.5	12.2	10.9	10.5
2,0183		9	Smith	895.5	3,668	2,927	4.1	96.6	1.1	1.4	0.8	2.2	5.2	14.9	6.6	7.8	10.0	11.1
2,0185		9	Stafford	792.0	4,207	2,887	5.3	84.8	1.1	1.6	0.7	13.5	6.5	17.9	7.5	9.9	9.6	11.9
2,0187		9	Stanton	680.4	2,060	3,044	3.0	59.9	1.6	1.7	0.6	38.1	8.1	20.0	8.2	10.5	11.5	12.3
2,0189		7	Stevens	727.3	5,612	2,786	7.7	61.8	1.0	1.4	0.7	36.3	7.0	22.3	8.2	11.3	11.0	12.9
2,0191	48,620	2	Sumner	1,181.6	23,159	1,672	19.6	91.8	1.8	2.4	0.8	5.4	6.2	18.5	7.7	11.4	11.3	11.7
2,0193		7	Thomas	1,074.7	7,788	2,611	7.2	91.2	1.4	1.1	1.2	6.4	6.8	16.3	13.2	12.9	10.5	9.8
2,0195		9	Trego	889.5	2,884	2,979	3.2	96.0	1.4	0.9	1.0	2.2	6.2	13.4	6.4	10.6	9.6	11.8
2,0197	45,820	3	Wabaunsee	794.4	6,874	2,684	8.7	94.5	1.4	1.7	0.8	3.7	6.7	17.3	6.8	9.7	10.9	12.6
2,0199		9	Wallace	913.7	1,524	3,079	1.7	90.5	1.2	0.7	0.3	8.5	6.8	18.5	7.4	10.0	9.2	10.2
2,0201		9	Washington	894.8	5,485	2,797	6.1	95.1	1.3	0.7	0.9	3.4	7.1	15.4	7.5	9.7	10.0	12.0
2,0203		9	Wichita	718.6	2,125	3,037	3.0	69.0	1.3	0.5	0.5	29.7	6.2	20.1	7.5	10.0	10.8	11.7
2,0205		7	Wilson	570.4	8,675	2,533	15.2	94.2	1.2	2.6	1.3	3.2	6.0	18.0	7.0	10.4	10.8	11.4
2,0207		9	Woodson	497.8	3,147	2,958	6.3	94.9	1.5	2.2	0.5	3.2	4.8	15.9	6.5	10.3	10.4	11.4
2,0209	28,140	1	Wyandotte	151.6	165,288	394	1,090.3	43.0	23.7	1.4	5.5	29.0	8.2	19.8	8.6	15.0	13.0	11.6
2,1000		0	**KENTUCKY**	39,485.2	4,454,189	X	112.8	86.3	9.2	0.7	2.0	3.7	6.2	16.5	9.4	13.0	12.4	13.2
2,1001		7	Adair	405.3	19,485	1,852	48.1	94.4	3.8	0.7	0.5	1.9	5.5	14.8	12.8	11.2	10.8	13.2
2,1003	14,540	3	Allen	344.3	20,933	1,779	60.8	96.4	1.7	0.8	0.5	2.0	6.2	17.3	7.5	12.2	11.8	14.0
2,1005	23,180	6	Anderson	201.8	22,544	1,702	111.7	95.4	2.8	0.7	0.9	1.8	6.2	17.8	7.5	11.8	12.9	15.0
2,1007	37,140	9	Ballard	246.7	8,039	2,591	32.6	94.5	4.8	0.9	0.8	1.4	5.3	16.2	7.7	10.5	11.8	13.4
2,1009	23,980	6	Barren	487.5	43,801	1,098	89.8	91.7	4.9	0.6	1.0	3.2	6.5	17.1	7.7	12.1	12.0	13.3
2,1011	34,460	8	Bath	278.8	12,378	2,264	44.4	96.6	2.1	0.6	0.4	1.6	7.1	18.4	7.9	10.7	12.1	13.8
2,1013	33,180	7	Bell	359.0	26,894	1,529	74.9	95.9	3.2	1.1	0.6	1.1	5.9	15.2	8.1	12.5	11.6	13.7
2,1015	17,140	1	Boone	246.3	130,728	488	530.8	89.5	4.2	0.6	3.4	4.3	6.7	19.6	8.0	12.4	13.6	14.3
2,1017	30,460	2	Bourbon	289.7	20,029	1,826	69.1	87.0	7.0	0.6	0.6	6.6	5.6	17.0	8.1	11.1	11.8	14.0
2,1019	26,580	2	Boyd	159.9	47,979	1,021	300.1	94.2	3.7	0.7	0.9	1.9	6.0	15.5	6.9	12.0	12.5	13.5
2,1021	19,220	7	Boyle	180.3	29,924	1,434	166.0	87.8	9.0	0.7	1.3	3.4	5.3	14.8	11.9	11.8	11.4	13.1
2,1023	17,140	1	Bracken	205.6	8,267	2,570	40.2	97.4	1.2	0.7	0.4	1.7	6.5	17.6	7.1	12.1	11.7	14.1
2,1025		7	Breathitt	492.4	12,946	2,230	26.3	97.6	0.9	0.6	0.9	1.0	6.1	14.4	7.9	12.1	12.8	14.9
2,1027		8	Breckinridge	567.2	20,111	1,821	35.5	95.9	2.8	0.9	0.5	1.4	5.9	17.3	7.2	10.3	11.3	13.8
2,1029	31,140	1	Bullitt	297.0	80,246	699	270.2	95.9	1.6	0.9	1.0	2.0	5.2	17.0	8.0	12.8	13.2	14.9
2,1031	14,540	3	Butler	426.1	12,831	2,235	30.1	95.9	0.9	0.7	0.4	3.2	6.0	16.6	6.6	12.0	12.6	13.6
2,1033		7	Caldwell	344.8	12,639	2,250	36.7	92.2	6.4	0.8	0.5	1.6	5.7	16.4	7.3	11.3	11.6	12.9
2,1035	34,660	7	Calloway	385.0	38,919	1,208	101.1	91.0	4.5	0.6	2.7	2.6	5.1	12.9	20.3	12.0	9.9	11.1
2,1037	17,140	1	Campbell	151.3	92,488	634	611.3	93.8	3.9	0.6	1.4	2.0	5.9	15.2	9.9	14.8	12.0	12.9
2,1039		9	Carlisle	189.4	4,846	2,843	25.6	95.3	2.3	1.2	0.6	2.5	7.0	16.2	6.7	11.6	11.4	12.8
2,1041		6	Carroll	128.6	10,713	2,374	83.3	91.1	2.7	0.9	0.9	6.3	7.4	18.5	7.9	12.1	12.2	12.9
2,1043		6	Carter	409.5	27,144	1,518	66.3	97.6	0.9	0.7	0.4	1.3	6.5	16.1	8.8	11.4	11.7	13.5
2,1045		9	Casey	444.2	15,750	2,054	35.5	95.6	1.3	0.7	0.5	3.0	6.3	16.2	7.7	11.5	11.7	13.3
2,1047	17,300	2	Christian	717.5	70,416	764	98.1	68.1	23.4	1.1	2.7	7.8	9.5	18.5	15.9	16.5	10.1	9.0
2,1049	30,460	2	Clark	252.5	36,046	1,272	142.8	91.7	5.5	0.6	0.8	2.8	6.3	16.3	7.8	11.8	12.3	14.2

1. CBSA = Core Based Statistical Area. See Appendix A for explanation. See Appendix B for list of metropolitan areas with component counties.   2. County type code from the Economic Research Service of USDA Rural-Urban Continuum Codes. See Appendix A for definition.   3. Dry land or land partially or temporarily covered by water.   4. May be of any race.

Table B. States and Counties — Population and Households

STATE County	Age (percent) (cont.) 55 to 64 years	65 to 74 years	75 years and over	Percent female	Population change, 2000-2017 Total persons 2000	2010	Percent change 2000-2010	2010-2017	Components of change, 2010-2017 Births	Deaths	Net Migration	Households, 2012-2016 Number	Persons per house-hold	Family house-holds	Percent Female family house-holder[1]	One person
	16	17	18	19	20	21	22	23	24	25	26	27	28	29	30	31
KANSAS— Cont'd																
Neosho	14.1	10.2	9.2	50.1	16,997	16,517	-2.8	-3.0	1,503	1,423	-581	6,407	2.48	67.0	11.5	30.1
Ness	17.7	11.1	13.6	51.0	3,454	3,107	-10.0	-7.7	244	321	-160	1,325	2.26	67.3	5.3	31.1
Norton	13.6	10.0	10.4	44.1	5,953	5,669	-4.8	-4.0	386	440	-172	2,019	2.35	68.4	11.5	29.7
Osage	16.1	10.9	8.5	49.8	16,712	16,295	-2.5	-3.2	1,187	1,400	-307	6,444	2.45	68.0	7.4	28.6
Osborne	16.1	11.2	13.3	49.4	4,452	3,858	-13.3	-6.4	335	405	-179	1,713	2.13	59.5	6.9	35.8
Ottawa	16.0	10.7	9.0	48.4	6,163	6,091	-1.2	-3.7	434	475	-185	2,446	2.42	70.0	6.1	26.0
Pawnee	15.5	10.7	9.7	44.1	7,233	6,971	-3.6	-4.2	477	548	-219	2,598	2.22	59.9	13.9	33.4
Phillips	15.4	12.6	10.5	49.8	6,001	5,642	-6.0	-4.8	421	511	-182	2,345	2.29	64.1	6.4	33.4
Pottawatomie	12.1	8.1	5.8	50.3	18,209	21,610	18.7	10.6	2,619	1,251	940	8,364	2.70	72.2	6.0	24.1
Pratt	14.4	9.6	10.0	50.3	9,647	9,651	0.0	-1.1	1,000	820	-281	3,778	2.47	63.3	10.7	32.6
Rawlins	16.2	14.1	13.7	49.1	2,966	2,519	-15.1	-0.9	181	255	52	1,178	2.14	64.1	4.8	32.4
Reno	14.0	10.4	9.0	49.7	64,790	64,511	-0.4	-3.1	5,220	5,360	-1,826	25,028	2.44	65.0	11.1	30.1
Republic	16.8	13.1	14.5	51.1	5,835	4,980	-14.7	-5.8	337	625	1	2,238	2.09	55.2	4.3	41.5
Rice	14.5	9.5	9.0	49.6	10,761	10,082	-6.3	-4.2	909	866	-463	3,968	2.35	65.7	5.2	30.5
Riley	7.5	5.3	3.9	46.7	62,843	71,132	13.2	4.3	7,634	2,422	-2,384	26,544	2.48	54.2	7.2	29.0
Rooks	15.4	11.6	10.5	51.9	5,685	5,181	-8.9	-2.7	439	463	-110	2,192	2.27	63.6	9.2	32.7
Rush	16.9	12.3	12.6	49.4	3,551	3,307	-6.9	-6.2	218	337	-87	1,424	2.16	59.3	7.2	34.4
Russell	15.5	12.6	11.5	50.8	7,370	6,970	-5.4	-0.8	599	651	0	3,195	2.15	64.7	9.6	29.5
Saline	13.9	9.6	7.8	50.4	53,597	55,638	3.8	-1.6	5,444	3,790	-2,544	22,400	2.41	64.3	12.0	29.2
Scott	13.2	9.7	9.0	49.3	5,120	4,936	-3.6	0.5	440	400	-14	2,139	2.28	63.8	4.1	28.5
Sedgwick	12.7	8.3	5.8	50.5	452,869	498,358	10.0	3.1	54,693	30,749	-8,434	193,927	2.59	64.4	12.2	30.5
Seward	9.5	5.4	4.3	48.7	22,510	22,950	2.0	-3.4	3,188	944	-3,068	7,381	3.08	71.6	15.7	23.0
Shawnee	13.8	10.1	7.5	51.5	169,871	177,934	4.7	0.1	17,113	12,804	-3,976	71,015	2.45	62.4	10.8	31.7
Sheridan	16.0	11.2	11.6	49.4	2,813	2,544	-9.6	-0.7	195	220	10	1,151	2.17	66.6	6.9	31.2
Sherman	15.0	10.1	9.0	49.8	6,760	6,010	-11.1	-1.3	582	534	-131	2,804	2.11	62.7	11.7	33.9
Smith	17.0	12.9	14.5	50.4	4,536	3,853	-15.1	-4.8	261	415	-31	1,698	2.14	62.0	4.4	35.1
Stafford	15.5	10.4	10.7	48.8	4,789	4,439	-7.3	-5.2	353	407	-179	1,770	2.35	68.5	6.5	28.0
Stanton	12.5	8.6	8.3	49.7	2,406	2,236	-7.1	-7.9	236	134	-283	810	2.57	69.5	3.5	28.0
Stevens	12.3	7.8	7.1	50.9	5,463	5,726	4.8	-2.0	588	311	-401	1,910	2.96	75.0	6.9	22.6
Sumner	15.2	10.0	8.1	49.9	25,946	24,137	-7.0	-4.1	2,006	1,887	-1,106	9,103	2.53	66.2	8.5	30.6
Thomas	13.6	8.8	8.1	51.2	8,180	7,902	-3.4	-1.4	802	537	-382	3,233	2.34	66.7	6.6	30.3
Trego	17.4	13.0	11.5	49.2	3,319	3,006	-9.4	-4.1	260	324	-56	1,334	2.13	64.9	9.1	32.0
Wabaunsee	16.8	11.1	8.2	49.2	6,885	7,051	2.4	-2.5	631	455	-353	2,707	2.54	70.8	6.6	26.0
Wallace	15.5	11.1	11.4	50.4	1,749	1,485	-15.1	2.6	134	132	36	587	2.67	61.7	3.6	36.3
Washington	14.5	11.3	12.4	49.0	6,483	5,795	-10.6	-5.3	525	522	-319	2,412	2.26	66.8	7.0	30.4
Wichita	14.0	10.3	9.4	48.7	2,531	2,234	-11.7	-4.9	185	176	-117	839	2.55	70.3	11.3	26.8
Wilson	15.3	12.0	9.1	50.8	10,332	9,409	-8.9	-7.8	790	908	-617	3,878	2.27	65.1	11.7	30.3
Woodson	16.7	13.6	10.5	49.3	3,788	3,309	-12.6	-4.9	237	353	-46	1,521	2.08	57.8	8.3	35.2
Wyandotte	11.9	7.1	4.8	50.5	157,882	157,505	-0.2	4.9	19,848	9,944	-2,047	59,067	2.72	63.6	17.5	30.4
KENTUCKY	13.3	9.6	6.4	50.7	4,041,769	4,339,340	7.4	2.6	402,569	320,325	33,351	1,718,217	2.49	66.2	12.8	28.3
Adair	13.7	10.6	7.3	50.2	17,244	18,655	8.2	4.4	1,522	1,407	703	7,126	2.51	69.2	10.3	28.0
Allen	13.5	10.5	6.8	50.6	17,800	19,967	12.2	4.8	1,846	1,576	705	7,705	2.62	72.2	10.6	24.9
Anderson	13.4	9.3	6.0	51.0	19,111	21,421	12.1	5.2	1,832	1,443	748	8,554	2.54	70.3	10.6	24.4
Ballard	14.7	11.6	8.8	49.9	8,286	8,247	-0.5	-2.5	604	746	-62	3,252	2.49	65.6	9.3	30.5
Barren	13.8	9.9	7.4	51.6	38,033	42,173	10.9	3.9	3,982	3,502	1,170	16,766	2.54	68.9	12.6	27.6
Bath	13.5	9.8	6.8	50.2	11,085	11,585	4.5	6.8	1,189	1,005	613	4,450	2.70	70.2	13.3	23.9
Bell	14.3	11.2	7.6	51.1	30,060	28,691	-4.6	-6.3	2,507	2,740	-1,571	10,978	2.43	64.7	16.6	30.7
Boone	12.3	8.2	4.8	50.6	85,991	118,815	38.2	10.0	11,909	5,754	5,807	45,649	2.73	75.7	11.8	19.9
Bourbon	13.8	10.6	8.2	51.3	19,360	19,980	3.2	0.2	1,608	1,532	-16	8,043	2.46	65.2	13.3	29.1
Boyd	14.4	10.9	8.2	50.2	49,752	49,538	-0.4	-3.1	4,298	4,272	-1,568	19,386	2.40	68.1	11.7	27.5
Boyle	12.9	10.5	8.3	50.2	27,697	28,416	2.6	5.3	2,259	2,234	1,457	10,882	2.47	65.6	10.9	30.1
Bracken	14.9	9.9	6.2	49.9	8,279	8,488	2.5	-2.6	741	683	-278	3,412	2.45	65.1	10.3	28.9
Breathitt	14.9	10.6	6.1	50.0	16,100	13,876	-13.8	-6.7	1,228	1,405	-755	5,304	2.48	64.9	15.9	32.4
Breckinridge	15.2	11.8	7.4	49.8	18,648	20,042	7.5	0.3	1,625	1,643	90	7,343	2.68	69.1	8.5	25.3
Bullitt	13.8	9.7	5.5	50.4	61,236	74,319	21.4	8.0	5,593	3,996	4,323	28,533	2.71	74.1	12.2	21.3
Butler	14.2	10.8	7.6	49.8	13,010	12,690	-2.5	1.1	1,093	1,000	52	5,153	2.45	69.8	11.7	26.1
Caldwell	14.3	11.7	8.9	51.6	13,060	12,984	-0.6	-2.7	1,050	1,204	-183	5,322	2.37	72.2	16.9	24.4
Calloway	11.9	9.6	7.1	51.2	34,177	37,191	8.8	4.6	2,835	2,864	1,752	15,002	2.32	57.9	8.9	34.4
Campbell	14.2	8.9	6.2	50.8	88,616	90,336	1.9	2.4	7,725	5,995	462	35,954	2.46	66.1	13.0	28.7
Carlisle	13.7	11.0	9.6	51.0	5,351	5,104	-4.6	-5.1	487	484	-263	2,088	2.34	66.1	8.0	30.3
Carroll	13.7	9.1	6.0	49.8	10,155	10,809	6.4	-0.9	1,180	924	-360	4,030	2.59	64.7	9.9	28.5
Carter	13.7	10.9	7.4	50.5	26,889	27,718	3.1	-2.1	2,580	2,264	-875	10,647	2.50	70.6	13.4	25.5
Casey	13.3	12.1	7.8	51.4	15,447	15,956	3.3	-1.3	1,396	1,393	-201	6,412	2.42	67.9	8.1	29.5
Christian	9.2	6.8	5.4	47.0	72,265	73,939	2.3	-4.8	11,046	4,290	-10,372	25,382	2.66	69.0	14.1	26.3
Clark	13.9	10.4	7.0	50.9	33,144	35,609	7.4	1.2	3,149	2,883	188	14,183	2.49	69.2	13.0	24.0

1. No spouse present.

Table B. States and Counties — Population, Vital Statistics, Health, and Crime

STATE County	Persons in group quarters, 2017	Daytime Population, 2012-2016 Number	Daytime Population Employment/ residence ratio	Births, 2017 Total	Births, 2017 Rate[1]	Deaths, 2017 Number	Deaths, 2017 Rate[1]	Persons under 65 with no health insurance, 2016 Number	Persons under 65 Percent	Medicare, 2017 Total beneficiaries	Medicare Enrolled in Original Medicare	Medicare Enrolled in Medicare Advantage	Serious crimes known to police[2], 2016 Total Number	Serious crimes Rate[3]
	32	33	34	35	36	37	38	39	40	41	42	43	44	45
KANSAS— Cont'd														
Neosho	450	16,063	0.96	178	11.1	169	10.6	1,075	8.5	3,462	3,246	216	346	2132
Ness	70	3,193	1.10	31	10.8	43	15.0	289	13.0	793	772	21	35	1179
Norton	821	5,611	1.02	57	10.5	66	12.1	343	9.4	1,147	1,089	58	44	800
Osage	194	12,012	0.43	155	9.8	204	12.9	1,213	9.5	3,575	3,210	365	188	1332
Osborne	100	3,569	0.90	54	15.0	37	10.2	348	12.8	928	903	25	69	1899
Ottawa	98	4,668	0.55	64	10.9	60	10.2	394	8.3	1,219	1,177	41	103	1740
Pawnee	1,025	7,440	1.21	64	9.6	79	11.8	408	9.2	750	738	12	144	2125
Phillips	68	5,492	1.00	46	8.6	64	11.9	427	10.2	1,393	1,349	44	31	578
Pottawatomie	299	22,339	0.95	371	15.5	191	8.0	1,474	7.2	3,332	2,994	337	343	1459
Pratt	380	10,070	1.08	129	13.5	91	9.5	788	10.5	1,856	1,817	39	417	4322
Rawlins	40	2,575	1.02	24	9.6	19	7.6	253	13.6	679	647	32	45	1804
Reno	3,115	63,133	0.98	657	10.5	683	10.9	5,013	10.3	14,003	13,070	933	2,522	3990
Republic	103	4,582	0.92	45	9.6	62	13.2	344	10.2	1,334	1,292	43	48	1031
Rice	650	9,555	0.92	131	13.6	96	9.9	802	10.7	2,063	1,988	75	95	1035
Riley	10,247	72,835	0.95	934	12.6	354	4.8	5,104	8.7	8,110	7,634	476	1,519	2009
Rooks	72	5,082	0.97	55	10.9	70	13.9	403	10.2	1,243	1,200	44	14	272
Rush	66	2,911	0.84	37	11.9	26	8.4	228	9.9	842	825	17	78	2534
Russell	89	6,687	0.91	71	10.3	91	13.2	616	11.5	1,791	1,756	35	140	1997
Saline	1,465	57,258	1.06	696	12.7	482	8.8	4,811	10.7	11,416	10,354	1,061	2,204	3980
Scott	105	4,829	0.95	55	11.1	66	13.3	459	11.3	606	D	D	60	1214
Sedgwick	7,263	524,821	1.07	7,186	14.0	4,374	8.5	48,714	11.2	83,796	65,992	17,804	27,261	5331
Seward	476	24,296	1.10	407	18.4	116	5.2	4,111	20.6	2,264	2,207	56	391	1695
Shawnee	4,394	192,136	1.16	2,206	12.4	1,784	10.0	13,191	9.1	37,824	32,424	5,400	9,064	5096
Sheridan	33	2,514	0.99	28	11.1	22	8.7	302	15.9	533	521	12	6	241
Sherman	102	5,961	0.97	80	13.5	84	14.2	484	10.3	1,265	1,241	24	94	1581
Smith	56	3,669	0.98	45	12.3	44	12.0	299	11.4	1,077	1,038	39	15	410
Stafford	69	3,939	0.83	51	12.1	46	10.9	492	14.9	1,549	1,508	41	35	838
Stanton	47	2,140	1.02	39	18.9	17	8.3	270	16.1	353	D	D	0	0
Stevens	72	5,807	1.03	76	13.5	29	5.2	709	14.9	814	787	27	NA	NA
Sumner	409	20,897	0.75	280	12.1	247	10.7	1,753	9.3	5,464	4,729	735	618	2652
Thomas	353	8,098	1.04	108	13.9	60	7.7	588	9.2	1,406	1,343	63	145	1846
Trego	64	2,744	0.89	46	16.0	44	15.3	174	8.1	692	D	D	43	1483
Wabaunsee	90	5,313	0.51	92	13.4	50	7.3	427	7.7	1,411	1,291	120	98	1534
Wallace	19	1,555	0.96	18	11.8	14	9.2	116	10.0	368	D	D	0	0
Washington	114	5,074	0.81	85	15.5	84	15.3	511	12.2	1,442	1,387	55	28	506
Wichita	26	2,251	1.08	18	8.5	21	9.9	330	19.3	409	D	D	31	1455
Wilson	121	8,769	0.95	92	10.6	113	13.0	735	10.8	2,125	2,012	112	161	1850
Woodson	39	2,678	0.66	33	10.5	43	13.7	277	11.4	803	748	55	61	1992
Wyandotte	1,335	176,619	1.21	2,716	16.4	1,392	8.4	24,087	17.0	24,797	15,610	9,187	NA	NA
KENTUCKY	13,1,983	4,435,449	1.01	54,895	12.3	44,749	10.0	218,900	6.0	897,353	634,052	263,301	107,466	2422
Adair	1,408	17,053	0.73	221	11.3	223	11.4	1,037	7.2	3,920	3,053	866	41	215
Allen	197	17,964	0.70	255	12.2	240	11.5	1,127	6.7	4,121	3,175	946	262	1263
Anderson	108	16,454	0.48	267	11.8	197	8.7	907	4.8	4,191	2,543	1,649	165	748
Ballard	127	7,291	0.73	80	10.0	106	13.2	360	5.7	2,459	1,940	520	62	757
Barren	702	43,229	1.00	570	13.0	514	11.7	2,470	6.9	9,104	6,880	2,225	687	1568
Bath	103	10,139	0.55	170	13.7	154	12.4	762	7.5	2,505	1,670	834	45	365
Bell	931	28,831	1.16	321	11.9	355	13.2	1,560	7.4	6,958	5,493	1,465	755	2792
Boone	835	146,245	1.33	1,649	12.6	929	7.1	4,303	3.8	21,043	12,824	8,219	2,557	1977
Bourbon	236	18,765	0.86	204	10.2	229	11.4	1,239	7.7	4,087	2,618	1,469	353	1754
Boyd	2,320	56,666	1.44	565	11.8	574	12.0	1,886	5.0	11,056	8,156	2,901	1,126	2345
Boyle	3,252	32,721	1.25	315	10.5	312	10.4	1,145	5.3	7,255	5,262	1,992	383	1276
Bracken	41	6,536	0.45	98	11.9	103	12.5	419	6.0	1,980	1,362	618	52	628
Breathitt	320	12,891	0.85	155	12.0	193	14.9	752	7.0	3,482	2,635	848	28	209
Breckinridge	300	17,028	0.60	236	11.7	200	9.9	1,232	7.7	4,255	3,458	797	84	420
Bullitt	340	63,385	0.62	757	9.4	627	7.8	3,182	4.7	11,895	7,902	3,994	1,477	1858
Butler	203	11,285	0.70	144	11.2	125	9.7	766	7.4	2,491	1,711	781	105	810
Caldwell	148	12,335	0.92	128	10.1	152	12.0	573	5.8	3,142	2,429	713	318	2522
Calloway	3,231	39,821	1.09	381	9.8	404	10.4	2,070	7.1	7,432	5,338	2,094	962	2498
Campbell	3,237	76,374	0.67	1,068	11.5	890	9.6	3,751	4.9	15,820	9,379	6,441	1,789	1939
Carlisle	60	3,991	0.53	67	13.8	59	12.2	280	7.4	1,220	918	301	24	497
Carroll	325	13,796	1.69	166	15.5	122	11.4	566	6.4	2,265	1,577	688	84	787
Carter	632	24,193	0.68	333	12.3	342	12.6	1,436	6.6	4,861	3,544	1,317	162	600
Casey	476	14,336	0.72	180	11.4	209	13.3	1,004	8.2	3,319	2,650	669	54	343
Christian	5,368	97,806	1.77	1,459	20.7	615	8.7	3,777	6.5	11,299	8,880	2,419	1,789	2448
Clark	458	33,775	0.88	467	13.0	360	10.0	1,550	5.3	7,620	4,947	2,673	1,287	3600

1. Per 1,000 estimated resident population.   2. Data for serious crimes have not been adjusted for underreporting; this may affect comparability between geographic areas and over time.
3. Per 100,000 population estimated by the FBI.

Table B. States and Counties — Crime, Education, Money Income, and Poverty

	Serious crimes known to police, 2016 (cont.)[1]		Education						Money income, 2012-2016				Income and poverty, 2016		
	Rate		School enrollment and attainment, 2012-2016				Local government expenditures,[5] 2013-2014			Households			Percent below poverty level		
			Enrollment[3]		Attainment[4] (percent)						Percent				
STATE County	Violent	Property	Total	Percent private	High school graduate or less	Bachelor's degree or more	Total current spending (mil dol)	Current spending per student (dollars)	Per capita income[6]	Median income (dollars)	with income of less than $50,000	with income of $200,000 or more	Median household income (dollars)	All persons	Children under 18 years	Children 5 to 17 years in families
	46	47	48	49	50	51	52	53	54	55	56	57	58	59	60	61

KANSAS— Cont'd																
Neosho..........	277	1,855	4,044	6.2	40.0	18.9	25.3	10,141	22,759	43,867	55.6	2.0	42,441	16.4	21.9	20.4
Ness..........	67	1,111	679	18.0	42.8	20.1	5.8	12,467	28,184	47,298	52.8	2.0	46,439	11.3	13.9	13.2
Norton..........	73	727	1,154	4.3	46.3	13.8	10.3	11,185	23,039	47,651	52.7	0.9	45,845	13.7	16.8	16.0
Osage..........	170	1,162	3,697	7.7	48.4	19.9	30.3	10,934	25,880	52,171	48.3	1.5	54,760	10.9	15.1	13.5
Osborne..........	138	1,761	741	18.1	44.0	21.0	6.4	14,432	27,824	41,432	56.9	2.0	41,967	14.2	20.8	19.0
Ottawa..........	34	1,706	1,473	7.1	41.4	21.5	14.0	10,932	26,749	52,241	47.9	1.8	52,808	10.7	14.4	12.1
Pawnee..........	295	1,830	1,425	9.8	38.1	22.4	12.4	9,671	25,193	46,227	52.3	2.4	46,961	14.7	18.6	15.9
Phillips..........	205	373	1,228	4.3	42.1	22.3	9.6	12,044	25,364	45,940	55.2	1.2	49,386	12.6	16.6	15.1
Pottawatomie	238	1,221	6,380	19.7	34.7	32.0	40.7	10,051	27,199	62,500	38.4	3.0	64,704	8.2	9.1	8.2
Pratt..........	197	4,125	2,264	11.6	36.4	25.5	16.4	9,464	25,745	48,995	51.1	2.1	51,419	11.4	15.1	14.3
Rawlins..........	200	1,604	479	5.6	37.1	23.9	4.2	12,772	27,250	49,327	50.6	1.3	47,377	12.4	16.1	15.6
Reno..........	343	3,646	15,292	14.1	42.3	19.2	101.2	9,960	24,313	46,000	53.7	2.1	46,208	14.7	18.0	16.3
Republic..........	107	923	911	11.0	39.0	21.0	8.3	11,608	26,029	41,489	60.1	1.1	43,921	11.4	16.7	16.2
Rice..........	120	915	2,671	17.5	40.4	22.4	22.0	11,521	22,596	46,335	52.2	1.3	47,737	12.8	16.6	14.7
Riley..........	274	1,735	30,458	6.1	21.5	46.0	75.6	10,067	25,087	46,609	53.5	3.5	49,901	18.2	12.3	12.6
Rooks..........	19	253	1,088	9.3	42.0	24.3	10.4	12,235	24,919	46,750	54.2	2.1	45,268	11.9	13.5	12.8
Rush..........	130	2,404	662	4.8	38.5	23.7	6.6	12,551	25,002	40,395	56.6	1.2	45,281	12.0	17.6	16.0
Russell..........	371	1,626	1,349	3.3	41.0	24.2	9.0	10,970	24,181	42,656	54.7	1.2	43,857	14.5	19.6	18.8
Saline..........	417	3,563	14,382	15.4	43.5	23.8	89.2	10,424	26,477	48,497	52.1	3.1	48,748	12.0	15.3	14.0
Scott..........	263	951	1,116	21.2	46.0	26.3	9.8	10,067	31,280	61,886	39.5	1.8	60,540	7.5	10.8	10.4
Sedgwick..........	842	4,489	141,978	15.7	37.6	30.0	838.1	9,944	26,672	51,157	48.9	3.6	52,612	14.9	17.8	16.8
Seward..........	225	1,470	7,030	4.3	60.0	11.6	55.6	9,719	20,844	47,507	52.3	2.8	48,648	13.6	17.7	16.7
Shawnee..........	459	4,638	45,477	13.1	39.8	29.3	293.4	10,261	27,534	52,088	47.7	2.6	55,387	10.9	14.1	13.4
Sheridan..........	0	241	481	1.9	40.3	22.9	6.6	10,973	29,604	50,822	48.9	2.9	49,860	11.5	18.0	16.0
Sherman..........	185	1,396	1,445	1.5	39.1	19.0	10.3	9,489	24,494	47,036	51.9	1.4	48,456	14.4	18.9	17.2
Smith..........	27	383	738	3.5	42.8	22.0	8.5	13,244	27,870	43,913	57.4	3.9	40,006	14.2	17.2	15.2
Stafford..........	168	670	992	4.8	41.0	21.7	11.7	12,071	25,046	46,830	53.4	2.6	46,104	13.3	19.8	18.8
Stanton..........	0	0	614	6.2	44.9	24.8	5.5	11,965	22,383	44,567	51.7	0.2	58,135	10.9	15.6	14.0
Stevens..........	NA	NA	1,663	8.4	49.3	16.5	15.5	11,236	23,579	54,333	44.8	2.3	57,432	10.0	13.4	12.0
Sumner..........	163	2,489	6,086	8.7	43.5	19.4	41.6	10,802	24,764	50,950	49.0	1.5	52,186	13.5	17.2	15.3
Thomas..........	76	1,770	1,994	9.5	34.1	28.4	11.6	10,971	26,241	52,074	48.9	4.0	46,756	11.0	14.5	14.9
Trego..........	345	1,138	588	7.8	38.2	25.8	4.3	10,523	29,651	54,630	44.2	0.7	61,502	8.1	11.1	10.0
Wabaunsee..........	156	1,377	1,564	13.2	42.0	23.7	11.9	12,179	25,194	57,791	44.1	0.8	47,844	12.1	11.9	10.7
Wallace..........	0	0	403	2.7	41.8	24.9	4.3	14,890	28,875	45,804	52.3	3.7	45,077	10.8	13.9	13.0
Washington..........	72	434	1,213	12.0	44.8	18.4	9.4	11,260	24,241	47,045	54.7	1.0				
Wichita..........	47	1,408	544	2.4	46.5	18.3	5.3	12,176	26,194	57,596	44.8	2.5	55,336	11.7	17.6	15.7
Wilson..........	207	1,643	1,811	7.0	49.3	15.3	18.5	11,475	23,869	43,594	57.0	1.9	43,134	16.4	23.1	21.4
Woodson..........	261	1,731	616	2.8	48.5	13.7	5.9	12,154	20,499	35,321	64.0	0.9	35,417	18.4	23.5	20.9
Wyandotte..........	NA	NA	42,201	9.5	54.7	16.3	319.5	10,508	19,282	40,757	60.2	0.7	43,396	19.4	24.4	22.5
KENTUCKY.......	232	2,190	1,085,773	15.0	48.7	22.7	6,396.7	9,443	24,802	44,811	54.5	2.9	46,610	18.2	24.4	23.0
Adair..........	16	199	4,981	29.1	60.4	16.5	23.1	8,542	18,463	33,873	64.1	0.9	33,925	26.1	36.7	35.1
Allen..........	121	1,143	4,444	13.1	59.4	13.6	25.5	8,528	20,607	41,166	58.6	1.3	41,368	18.6	28.0	25.6
Anderson..........	73	675	4,965	9.7	51.0	18.9	32.0	8,185	24,891	53,513	46.9	1.8	57,448	10.6	15.3	14.0
Ballard..........	61	696	1,890	10.9	50.6	15.3	12.7	9,013	24,459	43,923	55.4	1.8	45,074	16.2	24.3	21.9
Barren..........	119	1,449	10,030	8.2	58.8	15.5	52.3	8,793	20,130	39,034	62.5	1.0	40,274	21.8	30.4	29.5
Bath..........	16	348	2,861	7.6	64.4	12.1	17.7	8,359	19,590	34,986	65.8	1.9	36,468	24.9	34.4	33.2
Bell..........	163	2,629	6,020	7.7	68.4	9.5	44.8	9,209	13,654	22,603	78.5	0.4	26,014	38.7	47.4	46.7
Boone..........	111	1,866	34,245	17.7	34.6	31.1	182.2	8,430	31,593	69,165	34.0	5.5	72,942	7.6	10.3	8.8
Bourbon..........	99	1,654	4,345	12.5	53.4	17.8	33.3	9,043	24,433	44,232	54.7	1.8	46,231	17.6	27.3	24.9
Boyd..........	135	2,209	10,665	10.8	46.0	19.1	68.1	8,961	25,939	44,140	54.8	2.6	44,569	18.2	26.1	25.0
Boyle..........	97	1,179	7,515	28.6	49.3	23.0	42.3	8,982	23,276	40,758	58.8	3.1	44,834	17.1	23.2	22.0
Bracken..........	12	616	1,825	13.3	60.6	14.6	12.8	8,145	21,569	35,887	58.1	1.2	47,182	16.7	23.8	23.1
Breathitt..........	7	202	2,634	13.3	63.0	12.2	25.2	10,015	15,798	25,484	74.5	1.2	26,659	34.3	44.2	45.5
Breckinridge..........	55	365	4,425	14.1	64.2	10.5	30.2	9,139	19,984	43,390	56.6	0.6	43,053	17.3	26.2	24.2
Bullitt..........	112	1,746	18,220	14.6	54.3	14.2	104.2	7,803	25,805	58,702	42.2	1.8	63,570	10.4	14.4	12.8
Butler..........	39	771	2,628	17.9	65.7	10.4	18.4	8,053	20,591	38,427	60.9	0.5	41,701	17.8	27.4	25.8
Caldwell..........	182	2,340	2,655	3.3	58.4	15.2	16.8	7,852	23,308	43,491	55.8	2.1	40,327	20.4	33.6	35.0
Calloway	161	2,337	12,857	4.9	43.1	28.6	63.4	9,129	21,109	36,692	62.0	1.7	39,438	21.2	24.9	26.0
Campbell..........	112	1,827	23,436	21.0	40.7	30.6	112.1	9,537	29,834	56,772	44.6	4.1	61,490	12.5	16.7	16.0
Carlisle..........	21	477	1,040	13.4	52.1	15.7	7.5	9,094	23,456	40,913	57.7	1.4	45,362	14.5	25.3	24.5
Carroll..........	66	722	2,344	6.7	63.3	12.5	22.1	10,656	21,639	42,882	57.8	1.9	47,726	20.8	32.3	30.7
Carter..........	37	563	6,534	15.7	61.1	13.1	41.6	8,632	19,170	37,367	64.1	0.3	37,406	22.6	31.6	30.0
Casey..........	6	336	3,274	16.4	63.0	12.4	21.5	9,418	18,146	32,315	68.7	0.9	29,417	27.8	36.6	36.5
Christian..........	205	2,243	18,764	11.5	47.5	16.7	84.3	9,038	19,962	40,253	61.5	1.9	41,081	20.8	27.0	29.4
Clark..........	173	3,427	7,934	15.0	51.6	20.5	48.8	8,431	25,674	49,069	50.7	2.1	48,474	15.9	24.8	23.5

1. Data for serious crimes have not been adjusted for underreporting; this may affect comparability between geographic areas and over time. 2. Per 100,000 population estimated by the FBI.
3. All persons 3 years old and over enrolled in nursery school through college. 4. Persons 25 years old and over. 5. Elementary and secondary education expenditures.
6. Based on population estimated by the American Community Survey, 2011–2015.

Table B. States and Counties — **Personal Income and Earnings**

	Personal income, 2016										Earnings, 2016		
			Per capita[1]			Supplements to wages and salaries, employer contributions (mil dol)						Contributions for government social insurance (mil dol)	
STATE County	Total (mil dol)	Percent change 2015-2016	Dollars	Rank	Wages and salaries (mil dol)	Pension and insurance	Government social insurance	Proprietors' income (mil dol)	Dividends, interest, and rent (mil dol)	Personal transfer receipts (mil dol)	Total (mil dol)	From employee and self-employed	From employer
	62	63	64	65	66	67	68	69	70	71	72	73	74
KANSAS— Cont'd													
Neosho	528	1.9	32,715	2,528	227	45	17	46	85	163	336	40	17
Ness	151	-2.1	50,894	377	45	9	3	38	35	29	96	9	3
Norton	222	7.7	40,460	1,305	97	21	7	41	47	43	166	17	7
Osage	624	2.4	39,372	1,441	91	21	7	37	89	143	156	19	7
Osborne	151	-3.6	41,519	1,163	49	10	3	22	33	37	83	9	3
Ottawa	236	2.2	39,886	1,381	48	10	3	29	35	50	90	9	3
Pawnee	270	2.8	40,001	1,364	116	27	8	52	49	63	203	18	8
Phillips	247	-6.4	45,511	740	93	24	7	23	58	55	147	16	7
Pottawatomie	1,156	3.4	48,860	478	405	71	31	85	157	149	592	66	31
Pratt	437	1.7	45,604	733	176	32	13	91	84	80	312	30	13
Rawlins	116	1.9	45,614	732	37	7	3	18	31	28	65	7	3
Reno	2,424	1.1	38,345	1,599	1,041	185	77	192	462	566	1,496	175	77
Republic	230	3.5	49,012	466	66	14	5	67	37	48	152	12	5
Rice	400	-6.9	40,675	1,279	141	29	10	74	67	81	255	24	10
Riley	2,904	-0.4	39,592	1,414	1,245	271	91	197	700	359	1,804	193	91
Rooks	201	-6.6	39,524	1,421	72	15	5	25	41	46	118	13	5
Rush	129	-4.1	42,088	1,092	40	9	3	16	27	32	68	7	3
Russell	288	-9.5	41,142	1,216	98	23	7	41	60	72	169	18	7
Saline	2,467	2.0	44,732	800	1,244	213	94	349	446	457	1,899	209	94
Scott	316	0.7	62,849	113	90	14	6	130	51	42	240	14	6
Sedgwick	25,197	0.2	49,213	457	12,517	2,039	965	3,501	5,874	3,736	19,022	2,092	965
Seward	756	-3.8	33,310	2,425	431	82	30	118	88	126	662	67	30
Shawnee	7,928	2.8	44,504	830	4,749	787	356	549	1,306	1,672	6,440	759	356
Sheridan	133	2.8	52,887	309	43	8	3	33	27	22	87	7	3
Sherman	220	-4.3	36,876	1,841	95	18	7	16	44	59	135	15	7
Smith	160	1.4	44,166	859	44	9	3	34	37	39	90	8	3
Stafford	208	-3.9	49,489	442	45	10	3	66	38	38	124	10	3
Stanton	114	-4.7	55,331	229	37	7	2	22	28	15	68	6	2
Stevens	217	-7.3	38,816	1,530	78	15	6	40	41	33	139	12	6
Sumner	863	0.7	37,084	1,808	278	51	23	85	133	192	437	51	23
Thomas	317	5.6	40,139	1,349	160	28	11	37	58	58	236	26	11
Trego	119	-5.9	41,476	1,171	45	11	3	15	22	32	75	8	3
Wabaunsee	337	2.2	48,849	479	47	10	4	20	93	55	81	9	4
Wallace	70	4.1	46,635	644	21	4	1	16	14	13	43	3	1
Washington	249	0.9	44,950	783	64	14	4	52	45	55	135	11	4
Wichita	158	-3.1	75,038	48	33	6	2	72	30	18	114	5	2
Wilson	358	2.7	41,063	1,223	144	33	11	47	58	97	236	26	11
Woodson	108	-0.7	34,049	2,318	22	6	2	10	21	32	40	5	2
Wyandotte	4,998	-15.4	30,508	2,788	5,130	816	406	291	576	1,316	6,643	809	406
KENTUCKY	17,2,714	1.4	38,934	X	87,794	15,253	6,868	9,791	26,869	42,316	119,705	7,579	6868
Adair	501	-0.6	25,994	3,058	155	34	12	14	65	208	215	29	12
Allen	617	0.3	29,902	2,857	171	33	13	40	70	194	257	33	13
Anderson	815	2.4	36,774	1,861	177	36	14	19	103	177	246	33	14
Ballard	285	-2.0	35,378	2,101	91	15	7	15	44	83	127	16	7
Barren	1,539	0.7	34,987	2,164	634	113	51	160	211	429	958	116	51
Bath	347	-0.3	28,154	2,971	72	16	6	8	35	127	102	15	6
Bell	784	-0.4	28,923	2,930	291	63	23	22	91	385	399	54	23
Boone	5,592	2.9	43,507	935	4,114	592	319	202	645	816	5,227	633	319
Bourbon	762	-0.7	38,049	1,650	289	47	22	41	146	185	400	50	22
Boyd	1,737	0.0	36,096	1,990	1,140	210	88	66	228	566	1,505	185	88
Boyle	1,050	2.1	34,967	2,168	587	104	49	49	196	283	789	101	49
Bracken	280	2.0	33,301	2,426	56	12	4	10	30	78	81	11	4
Breathitt	392	-1.5	29,488	2,894	114	27	9	8	36	211	158	22	9
Breckinridge	644	-0.8	32,269	2,570	125	28	10	39	108	200	201	26	10
Bullitt	2,996	3.9	37,848	1,688	903	151	73	115	282	607	1,243	160	73
Butler	411	0.6	31,967	2,621	111	25	9	25	45	138	171	22	9
Caldwell	435	1.3	34,629	2,223	145	27	12	33	63	138	217	27	12
Calloway	1,297	0.5	33,745	2,358	588	141	44	90	208	320	863	96	44
Campbell	4,058	1.8	44,008	877	1,353	235	102	152	635	737	1,842	221	102
Carlisle	193	-2.5	39,708	1,400	55	9	4	31	30	53	99	11	4
Carroll	413	-2.9	38,716	1,546	402	57	32	44	45	111	535	65	32
Carter	811	-0.3	29,984	2,847	188	39	14	28	83	309	270	38	14
Casey	439	0.2	27,783	2,989	133	29	11	13	52	187	186	26	11
Christian	2,615	-3.1	36,146	1,985	3,033	794	292	161	557	597	4,280	484	292
Clark	1,334	1.3	37,240	1,783	636	103	51	52	192	346	843	108	51

1. Based on the resident population estimated as of July 1 of the year shown.

Table B. States and Counties — Earnings, Social Security, and Housing

STATE County	Farm	Mining, quarrying, and extracting	Construction	Manu- facturing	Information; professional, scientific, technical services	Retail trade	Finance, insurance, real estate, and leasing	Health care and social assistance	Govern- ment	Number	Rate[1]	Supple- mental Security Income recipients, 2016	Total	Percent change, 2010-2017
	Earnings, 2016 (cont.) — Percent by selected industries									Social Security beneficiaries, December 2016			Housing units, 2017	
	75	76	77	78	79	80	81	82	83	84	85	86	87	88
KANSAS— Cont'd														
Neosho	2.1	5.3	5.0	18.3	D	7.9	5.2	10.3	28.3	3,815	238	356	7,742	3.0
Ness	12.0	27.4	3.7	2.1	D	2.6	D	D	21.3	780	264	19	1,727	-0.7
Norton	5.1	D	3.5	9.7	3.7	4.9	D	9.7	25.7	1,240	225	53	2,550	0.4
Osage	7.1	D	10.5	4.5	D	6.5	5.9	D	31.4	3,870	245	336	7,582	1.1
Osborne	8.2	5.0	4.2	D	D	8.8	D	8.9	18.4	1,015	280	45	2,182	-1.1
Ottawa	19.4	D	4.4	8.9	D	3.1	8.7	11.6	21.1	1,400	237	96	2,780	0.0
Pawnee	19.2	D	6.7	1.4	0.0	3.0	5.3	7.3	43.3	1,505	223	71	3,155	0.1
Phillips	-2.6	2.7	2.9	22.9	3.7	4.7	D	2.3	26.3	1,475	274	45	3,092	1.4
Pottawatomie	4.1	0.2	10.5	22.9	4.9	8.8	6.5	7.8	10.0	3,985	169	207	9,644	11.8
Pratt	15.2	5.5	5.2	2.5	D	11.5	6.0	D	17.2	2,070	216	132	4,481	-0.7
Rawlins	-7.1	0.3	7.0	4.1	8.1	16.5	D	6.0	21.7	730	292	26	1,458	0.0
Reno	2.6	0.7	6.3	12.4	6.2	7.3	6.8	14.9	17.8	14,730	234	1,278	28,526	0.9
Republic	34.1	D	5.5	8.3	3.6	5.1	3.2	D	13.2	1,435	309	64	2,885	0.3
Rice	19.2	6.2	3.4	14.3	4.0	3.7	D	D	18.6	2,200	224	124	4,600	1.2
Riley	0.9	D	5.7	2.2	6.8	5.9	8.6	11.3	40.7	7,500	101	547	31,208	10.6
Rooks	2.7	13.5	D	D	4.1	4.2	2.4	4.8	25.5	1,310	256	66	2,753	-0.5
Rush	7.1	D	4.1	22.0	D	4.0	3.0	3.6	21.8	870	283	55	1,850	-1.0
Russell	1.2	16.8	5.6	16.7	4.6	4.4	4.2	D	15.8	1,870	268	146	3,873	-0.9
Saline	1.4	D	5.5	16.1	7.0	6.9	5.5	18.3	11.7	11,680	212	1,046	24,394	1.1
Scott	50.5	D	2.2	1.7	D	3.3	D	D	7.2	1,045	209	55	2,222	1.3
Sedgwick	0.2	4.9	5.7	21.1	7.1	5.6	7.2	11.2	12.0	90,375	176	10,969	218,975	3.5
Seward	4.5	3.7	D	D	D	7.1	6.7	D	19.3	2,510	110	337	8,224	2.0
Shawnee	0.2	0.2	5.4	6.9	9.2	5.0	11.1	15.6	22.3	38,620	217	4,782	80,074	1.2
Sheridan	17.8	4.1	D	D	D	3.2	D	D	18.1	590	238	14	1,256	-0.4
Sherman	6.4	D	3.1	3.3	3.5	10.0	D	D	29.9	1,380	232	132	3,122	-0.8
Smith	30.7	D	4.1	1.3	1.7	4.6	2.9	11.7	16.3	1,150	313	57	2,242	0.4
Stafford	15.4	36.3	1.5	2.5	D	1.0	2.9	D	19.9	990	236	61	2,337	0.7
Stanton	15.9	2.0	D	D	D	3.7	D	D	23.3	345	164	14	991	0.0
Stevens	22.2	D	D	D	D	4.4	6.5	D	25.3	860	152	36	2,322	0.7
Sumner	10.2	0.6	3.5	17.2	5.2	6.2	4.9	D	19.5	5,175	223	366	10,967	0.9
Thomas	1.7	D	6.4	3.2	5.3	9.8	10.4	D	15.7	1,460	187	78	3,603	1.9
Trego	5.5	D	3.0	3.0	D	4.5	D	D	29.9	800	279	35	1,667	-1.0
Wabaunsee	7.9	2.9	14.2	10.9	D	2.0	D	D	24.5	1,560	226	85	3,295	2.1
Wallace	33.7	0.5	D	D	D	4.1	D	D	18.1	350	233	16	776	-0.6
Washington	31.5	D	5.1	7.5	D	4.0	D	4.7	20.9	1,505	270	59	2,939	-0.5
Wichita	60.5	D	1.7	3.0	0.2	1.9	D	0.7	12.1	430	202	23	1,050	-0.4
Wilson	3.0	1.2	7.1	36.7	2.8	3.6	D	9.3	19.5	2,430	280	234	4,657	-0.5
Woodson	2.5	15.7	3.9	4.5	D	8.5	D	6.2	27.0	825	258	71	2,020	-0.1
Wyandotte	0.0	D	6.3	14.7	7.1	4.6	2.5	15.3	21.1	26,080	159	5,321	68,107	2.0
KENTUCKY	0.1	0.6	5.9	15.1	7.1	6.3	7.0	12.4	19.1	972,352	219	180,613	1,984,150	3.0
Adair	-2.6	0.3	7.3	7.3	D	10.4	7.8	D	23.3	4,645	240	972	8,604	0.4
Allen	2.3	0.0	6.6	27.2	D	6.0	3.8	D	16.9	4,865	235	845	9,477	1.8
Anderson	-2.5	D	7.8	31.6	3.5	9.3	4.4	4.5	19.5	4,820	218	439	9,399	3.0
Ballard	7.2	0.0	22.2	21.6	10.6	5.3	1.2	4.6	16.1	2,145	266	284	3,920	0.9
Barren	-0.1	0.0	4.4	19.5	4.1	8.8	3.3	15.1	13.3	10,835	247	1,757	19,660	2.5
Bath	-3.1	0.0	16.0	D	D	3.5	1.9	6.3	28.0	3,170	258	893	5,484	1.5
Bell	-0.1	6.4	3.0	11.8	D	11.6	5.3	D	22.8	7,675	282	2,948	13,224	0.5
Boone	-0.1	D	3.9	17.9	5.2	6.4	5.3	6.1	8.5	20,800	161	1,683	49,444	7.1
Bourbon	0.9	D	6.0	19.9	D	9.3	4.9	8.4	13.6	4,790	239	617	9,045	1.3
Boyd	-0.2	0.5	7.7	13.9	6.9	7.5	3.2	23.6	13.4	12,585	261	2,510	21,643	-0.7
Boyle	-1.1	D	3.6	16.4	D	7.8	4.7	D	13.3	7,140	239	1,165	12,484	1.4
Bracken	-4.5	0.0	7.7	D	D	3.0	2.5	7.4	25.6	2,065	247	318	3,873	0.8
Breathitt	0.1	D	D	D	2.2	9.9	4.2	29.4	34.4	3,835	291	1,986	6,337	1.7
Breckinridge	1.5	0.6	14.4	8.1	2.2	9.0	5.5	12.0	23.2	5,265	264	852	10,788	1.6
Bullitt	-0.3	D	11.0	15.6	3.0	5.1	2.9	4.8	13.3	16,310	206	1,313	31,505	7.5
Butler	4.2	D	8.0	34.0	1.4	3.0	3.5	D	18.8	3,275	258	495	5,950	1.2
Caldwell	4.8	D	3.7	22.5	3.8	10.3	5.1	D	15.7	3,510	278	508	6,281	-0.2
Calloway	3.4	D	5.7	16.7	4.5	7.5	3.5	5.0	31.0	8,220	212	794	18,885	4.5
Campbell	-0.1	0.2	D	10.6	7.6	7.7	4.8	12.4	22.6	16,860	183	1,886	40,383	2.2
Carlisle	14.6	0.0	32.3	2.3	0.0	3.9	D	6.2	12.3	1,385	288	166	2,465	1.0
Carroll	0.0	0.1	D	46.6	17.4	3.8	1.3	D	7.6	2,675	252	522	4,713	0.4
Carter	-2.1	1.8	9.7	11.8	D	17.4	4.6	D	25.2	7,230	265	1,638	12,502	1.6
Casey	-3.2	D	7.9	26.4	D	6.8	D	12.3	18.4	4,160	264	905	7,510	0.3
Christian	-0.1	0.1	1.4	9.0	2.3	2.3	1.6	5.4	67.7	12,350	172	2,313	29,958	1.7
Clark	-0.9	D	6.1	22.4	6.3	7.6	3.7	11.5	10.9	8,465	236	1,362	15,892	1.2

1. Per 1,000 resident population estimated as of July 1 of the year shown.

Table B. States and Counties — Housing, Labor Force, and Employment

	Housing units, 2017 (cont.)								Civilian labor force, 2017				Civilian employment[6], 2012-2016		
	Occupied units										Unemployment		Percent		
		Owner-occupied				Renter-occupied									
				Median owner cost as a percent of income											
STATE County	Total	Percent	Median value[1]	With a mort-gage[2]	Without a mort-gage[2]	Median rent[3]	Median rent as a percent of income[2]	Sub-standard units[4] (percent)	Total	Percent change, 2016-2017	Total	Rate[5]	Total	Management, business, science, and arts	Construction, production, and maintenance occupations
	89	90	91	92	93	94	95	96	97	98	99	100	101	102	103
KANSAS— Cont'd															
Neosho	6,407	71.3	74,500	18.4	11.3	592	26.8	3.0	6,053	0.0	317	5.2	7,800	29.2	32.0
Ness	1,325	79.8	68,800	18.6	10.0	605	19.3	1.5	1,368	-3.9	40	2.9	1,491	32.5	32.2
Norton	2,019	73.9	69,700	17.4	11.6	675	21.0	2.7	2,820	-1.8	63	2.2	2,645	32.6	23.8
Osage	6,444	76.0	101,800	20.2	13.0	632	26.9	2.5	7,961	-1.2	315	4.0	7,152	31.6	29.1
Osborne	1,713	75.2	60,100	19.4	10.0	489	21.4	1.6	2,008	-2.5	56	2.8	1,792	41.3	25.8
Ottawa	2,446	82.4	92,800	20.1	13.3	667	24.5	0.9	3,060	-3.3	94	3.1	3,005	34.7	27.2
Pawnee	2,598	70.9	77,200	21.6	10.8	534	19.2	0.3	3,035	-5.4	101	3.3	2,949	37.2	20.6
Phillips	2,345	76.4	76,500	18.9	10.4	521	25.1	1.4	2,811	-1.6	83	3.0	2,781	35.5	27.3
Pottawatomie	8,364	77.6	165,900	19.8	11.4	745	23.8	3.1	12,168	0.1	373	3.1	10,727	39.8	25.8
Pratt	3,778	68.1	86,300	17.9	10.4	697	23.7	2.0	4,931	-3.4	162	3.3	4,423	31.7	29.0
Rawlins	1,178	75.0	81,500	18.5	11.7	590	20.6	0.3	1,463	-5.3	33	2.3	1,219	42.5	23.9
Reno	25,028	66.6	96,100	19.7	11.7	676	26.9	3.0	30,028	-0.4	1,161	3.9	29,367	29.7	27.3
Republic	2,238	78.2	55,400	19.6	10.5	487	21.0	1.9	2,460	-3.3	69	2.8	2,420	35.5	28.2
Rice	3,968	73.7	74,200	18.6	10.8	528	19.3	2.0	5,406	1.9	174	3.2	4,811	31.8	31.2
Riley	26,544	41.8	184,500	21.5	11.2	905	31.9	5.3	35,023	0.4	1,049	3.0	35,128	43.3	15.3
Rooks	2,192	76.7	74,600	20.9	10.6	548	24.0	2.0	2,505	-6.1	96	3.8	2,546	35.3	29.1
Rush	1,424	77.8	66,700	17.8	10.5	555	32.5	1.3	1,634	-5.7	52	3.2	1,502	37.5	26.7
Russell	3,195	74.7	85,100	18.0	12.4	584	28.2	0.9	3,501	-2.0	117	3.3	3,464	32.4	32.7
Saline	22,400	66.7	123,200	21.6	11.8	719	30.2	1.1	30,674	1.9	981	3.2	28,159	31.6	29.1
Scott	2,139	73.1	133,500	22.3	10.0	770	24.5	2.7	2,851	-1.2	62	2.2	2,600	41.0	32.5
Sedgwick	19,3,927	63.7	128,000	20.1	10.9	750	28.1	2.3	244,662	-1.1	10,335	4.2	241,895	35.2	24.2
Seward	7,381	68.8	89,400	20.6	11.0	699	23.5	6.7	9,873	-3.5	347	3.5	10,800	22.0	46.3
Shawnee	71,015	64.2	125,900	19.4	11.8	738	28.9	2.5	90,915	-0.8	3,330	3.7	84,380	37.3	20.8
Sheridan	1,151	77.9	91,400	17.1	11.2	503	19.3	0.6	1,363	-5.9	31	2.3	1,269	39.9	30.3
Sherman	2,804	62.9	80,400	21.5	11.5	637	24.0	0.2	2,882	-2.0	85	2.9	2,936	38.1	24.5
Smith	1,698	77.5	65,200	19.6	11.0	449	25.0	1.5	1,971	-3.1	55	2.8	1,790	38.5	22.9
Stafford	1,770	84.7	64,900	17.2	10.9	629	24.3	2.2	2,003	-4.4	66	3.3	2,058	35.3	24.6
Stanton	810	77.8	76,900	23.5	10.1	575	22.1	1.0	992	-7.4	27	2.7	1,115	37.8	26.3
Stevens	1,910	74.3	98,600	19.3	10.5	676	25.4	0.8	2,657	-8.6	85	3.2	2,575	30.1	38.8
Sumner	9,103	75.3	84,200	19.5	12.4	647	25.6	2.4	10,761	-1.6	409	3.8	10,685	31.0	31.7
Thomas	3,233	73.3	110,100	18.5	12.4	457	24.4	1.2	4,266	-2.0	110	2.6	4,395	34.6	21.9
Trego	1,334	78.8	82,000	19.1	10.0	540	26.5	0.0	1,435	-2.8	48	3.3	1,691	33.4	26.6
Wabaunsee	2,707	85.3	112,700	20.0	12.3	685	24.1	2.1	3,637	-1.9	116	3.2	3,355	36.0	25.9
Wallace	587	75.5	82,500	19.0	10.0	438	17.6	0.3	847	-1.5	21	2.5	747	41.2	16.2
Washington	2,412	79.3	73,900	18.1	10.7	440	17.3	0.6	2,962	-4.0	89	3.0	2,831	29.3	36.7
Wichita	839	75.0	81,800	16.8	13.9	674	17.7	5.8	1,168	-3.2	28	2.4	1,056	33.0	40.0
Wilson	3,878	75.2	61,700	19.9	11.1	578	31.1	2.6	3,998	-2.9	188	4.7	4,200	30.5	30.7
Woodson	1,521	80.2	52,100	18.6	14.5	542	26.1	2.8	1,589	-1.7	71	4.5	1,519	31.0	38.2
Wyandotte	59,067	57.2	90,100	23.2	15.2	799	30.3	4.2	77,204	1.0	4,010	5.2	72,378	22.3	32.0
KENTUCKY	17,1,8217	66.8	126,100	20.0	10.5	690	28.7	2.3	2,052,374	2.0	100,306	4.9	1,914,189	33.0	26.5
Adair	7,126	75.5	86,100	20.1	10.6	499	30.2	3.4	6,854	0.3	434	6.3	8,076	28.9	34.1
Allen	7,705	70.1	98,200	20.7	10.0	607	24.1	4.7	8,954	2.3	365	4.1	8,452	24.7	37.6
Anderson	8,554	75.4	136,300	19.7	10.0	728	27.6	1.4	11,573	1.8	481	4.2	10,443	31.0	26.6
Ballard	3,252	81.4	108,400	20.3	10.0	615	31.0	2.5	3,650	-0.2	279	7.6	3,427	29.5	31.5
Barren	16,766	66.8	108,300	20.2	11.6	595	29.1	2.4	19,257	0.9	880	4.6	18,680	28.1	36.1
Bath	4,450	73.1	73,500	22.0	11.8	591	30.2	3.4	4,755	-0.6	371	7.8	4,491	25.9	39.0
Bell	10,978	65.5	59,800	24.5	11.3	490	37.1	3.4	8,790	0.3	690	7.8	7,598	24.2	33.3
Boone	45,649	72.0	178,300	19.1	10.0	922	26.7	1.1	68,431	2.9	2,670	3.9	63,757	39.0	21.0
Bourbon	8,043	61.6	140,500	21.6	10.0	674	27.3	1.5	9,921	1.4	458	4.6	9,061	30.0	29.1
Boyd	19,386	69.6	100,700	19.1	10.0	624	30.5	1.3	18,497	0.8	1,320	7.1	18,472	35.8	23.8
Boyle	10,882	64.3	136,900	19.7	11.3	652	27.9	0.8	12,701	3.2	637	5.0	12,392	33.5	26.6
Bracken	3,412	75.3	96,200	21.8	11.7	576	31.6	2.8	3,878	2.3	226	5.8	3,469	30.4	33.4
Breathitt	5,304	75.0	49,600	23.0	12.3	475	29.0	5.0	3,942	0.4	336	8.5	4,119	29.7	22.5
Breckinridge	7,343	79.3	91,600	19.1	10.0	535	24.4	4.1	8,206	3.3	481	5.9	7,682	26.8	38.7
Bullitt	28,533	82.5	149,000	20.7	10.2	784	27.6	1.2	41,337	2.9	1,756	4.2	38,026	27.0	32.5
Butler	5,153	73.7	92,300	18.7	10.3	580	28.2	3.4	5,257	3.0	287	5.5	5,193	26.4	40.9
Caldwell	5,322	70.0	95,600	20.0	10.0	541	26.4	1.5	5,467	-0.1	285	5.2	5,306	28.7	34.0
Calloway	15,002	62.6	123,400	19.8	11.6	585	36.8	1.1	18,597	0.2	826	4.4	16,899	32.1	24.1
Campbell	35,954	68.2	156,600	19.8	10.8	777	27.4	1.5	49,517	2.8	1,882	3.8	46,233	37.8	19.9
Carlisle	2,088	78.8	78,800	19.8	10.0	609	26.3	2.3	2,432	-9.2	166	6.8	2,088	27.6	29.9
Carroll	4,030	60.9	104,200	17.4	10.0	659	29.2	6.2	4,919	-4.2	232	4.7	4,445	21.6	38.6
Carter	10,647	77.1	81,000	19.9	11.9	563	27.5	3.1	10,232	0.5	979	9.6	9,968	24.9	32.5
Casey	6,412	79.1	76,000	21.9	11.9	481	24.0	2.6	6,943	0.8	325	4.7	5,848	30.1	35.0
Christian	25,382	47.3	109,200	20.3	10.0	763	29.5	2.7	25,091	1.9	1,528	6.1	23,827	27.0	31.0
Clark	14,183	63.9	138,000	20.4	10.6	695	27.8	2.3	17,258	2.4	803	4.7	16,045	34.6	27.3

1. Specified owner-occupied units, lacking complete plumbing facilities.   2. A value of 10.0 represents 10 percent or less; a value of 50.0 represents 50 percent or more.   3. Specified renter-occupied units.   4. Overcrowded or
5. Percent of civilian labor force.   6. Civilian employed persons 16 years old and over.

Table B. States and Counties — Nonfarm Employment and Agriculture

	Private nonfarm establishments, employment and payroll, 2016									Agriculture, 2012			
		Employment						Annual payroll		Farms			
												Percent with:	
STATE County	Number of establish-ments	Total	Health care and social assistance	Manufac-turing	Retail trade	Finance and insurance	Professional, scientific, and technical services	Total (mil dol)	Average per employee (dollars)	Number	Fewer than 50 acres	500 acres or more	Farm operators whose principal occupation is farming (percent)
	104	105	106	107	108	109	110	111	112	113	114	115	116

KANSAS— Cont'd													
Neosho	446	5,064	1,174	891	815	202	144	171	33,736	702	23.4	19.8	43.2
Ness	137	915	257	38	68	54	24	33	35,730	557	8.3	45.6	44.0
Norton	184	1,784	458	242	198	93	37	65	36,708	367	12.3	48.2	59.7
Osage	247	1,678	484	D	357	116	53	42	25,078	1,014	22.9	21.0	43.0
Osborne	146	1,087	290	106	176	50	26	33	29,959	343	10.2	50.1	65.0
Ottawa	129	842	271	45	107	50	38	25	29,512	525	12.0	35.4	49.9
Pawnee	151	1,973	1,081	D	205	71	79	73	36,787	401	13.7	45.4	53.1
Phillips	235	1,648	266	204	225	116	117	60	36,108	441	17.7	46.3	58.3
Pottawatomie	607	8,699	1,338	1,420	1,690	202	181	341	39,216	890	22.5	23.7	42.9
Pratt	387	3,452	671	119	678	151	115	123	35,772	543	7.6	37.9	45.1
Rawlins	106	632	180	42	88	30	14	23	35,853	307	6.2	67.1	63.2
Reno	1,616	22,381	4,179	3,699	3,234	893	600	805	35,970	1,633	20.6	23.6	49.0
Republic	188	1,418	361	167	204	55	36	40	28,054	575	13.0	34.6	60.7
Rice	273	2,623	357	477	251	134	143	87	33,316	532	15.0	38.9	54.5
Riley	1,608	21,283	3,461	814	4,327	995	1,232	658	30,908	493	24.3	22.7	44.6
Rooks	189	1,477	286	107	210	73	48	47	31,819	440	10.9	50.0	48.2
Rush	99	1,052	152	338	68	40	17	35	33,538	528	12.3	40.7	47.0
Russell	257	1,803	323	98	262	72	46	55	30,546	504	11.1	36.5	48.2
Saline	1,512	27,684	5,107	4,975	4,154	892	1,140	998	36,055	674	19.7	30.1	46.7
Scott	205	1,497	415	50	282	92	55	47	31,594	269	14.5	51.7	64.3
Sedgwick	12,161	227,567	33,526	42,283	30,242	7,250	10,958	10,025	44,053	1,344	36.5	19.0	46.1
Seward	556	8,792	1,070	D	1,351	197	142	315	35,791	363	8.8	39.7	44.6
Shawnee	4,216	80,123	18,478	7,473	10,192	5,466	4,672	3,441	42,944	826	39.8	11.3	39.3
Sheridan	107	674	D	D	84	53	26	26	38,297	384	6.0	60.4	67.7
Sherman	256	1,977	382	68	379	99	64	66	33,275	416	6.3	51.2	58.7
Smith	139	873	263	12	166	59	27	23	26,216	497	12.3	47.3	62.2
Stafford	138	659	204	D	88	61	17	21	31,244	536	9.0	45.0	51.3
Stanton	66	496	D	D	61	50	20	19	38,133	278	0.7	54.0	52.5
Stevens	155	2,176	D	173	252	65	19	76	34,782	315	6.0	41.0	38.4
Sumner	481	4,328	932	849	634	211	68	145	33,580	1,096	17.5	33.2	51.8
Thomas	342	2,943	475	84	702	137	62	100	33,989	460	10.0	51.5	58.5
Trego	130	888	D	38	128	36	24	29	32,927	384	9.9	47.9	50.3
Wabaunsee	132	799	112	143	95	48	1	24	29,852	617	18.2	27.9	43.9
Wallace	56	356	53	D	40	15	D	13	36,806	294	6.1	57.5	54.1
Washington	211	1,591	397	189	189	70	57	42	26,593	732	15.6	37.6	52.3
Wichita	80	461	D	55	61	24	5	19	41,358	265	7.9	60.0	62.6
Wilson	215	3,699	743	1,005	246	87	49	153	41,327	423	13.0	33.1	52.2
Woodson	84	467	145	D	67	D	10	11	23,606	315	14.0	41.9	53.0
Wyandotte	3,171	70,230	14,555	10,468	7,981	1,109	2,509	3,420	48,692	164	70.7	1.8	39.6
KENTUCKY	92,000	1,603,173	255,345	235,487	214,356	74,742	74,749	65,243	40,696	77,064	36.5	6.2	41.7
Adair	301	4,138	521	564	718	185	50	104	25,175	1,243	33.8	3.8	38.5
Allen	249	3,194	443	514	378	126	111	102	32,033	1,080	35.7	4.6	48.0
Anderson	328	3,585	358	1,098	755	104	97	125	34,930	676	38.2	3.4	40.4
Ballard	124	1,419	107	601	152	17	101	58	40,955	408	36.5	11.3	46.1
Barren	878	14,811	2,426	3,966	2,483	332	269	481	32,496	1,869	39.5	4.4	51.1
Bath	140	1,612	204	D	152	62	22	48	29,694	690	23.9	8.4	47.4
Bell	474	6,854	1,457	1,159	1,485	259	124	207	30,152	81	56.8	3.7	48.1
Boone	3,086	79,697	4,725	13,819	10,100	3,779	1,630	3,410	42,781	608	53.5	3.5	40.3
Bourbon	399	5,236	704	1,434	927	229	237	224	42,692	907	38.4	11.4	53.3
Boyd	1,352	22,665	5,867	1,730	4,152	578	729	1,003	44,262	214	37.9	1.4	35.5
Boyle	718	14,916	2,978	2,209	1,802	344	325	473	31,685	620	38.7	8.5	39.0
Bracken	94	911	76	D	134	31	12	29	31,786	587	28.4	3.7	42.2
Breathitt	243	3,055	925	33	458	116	92	90	29,573	120	34.2	10.0	26.7
Breckinridge	308	2,489	478	273	546	165	71	76	30,561	1,304	27.2	7.6	37.3
Bullitt	1,105	19,147	1,350	2,712	2,139	273	360	645	33,664	488	54.5	1.8	43.9
Butler	184	1,892	334	652	232	68	29	59	31,332	697	23.4	8.3	36.4
Caldwell	287	3,838	513	871	725	127	56	113	29,314	538	32.5	8.0	34.6
Calloway	823	14,516	2,308	2,531	1,960	405	291	433	29,851	821	40.4	9.4	38.4
Campbell	1,663	24,559	3,297	2,081	4,155	478	1,122	873	35,553	504	48.0	1.6	42.1
Carlisle	93	656	90	85	113	66	14	19	28,203	325	41.2	14.2	39.7
Carroll	233	5,893	385	2,767	625	64	93	337	57,154	278	20.1	5.4	37.4
Carter	441	4,891	539	700	923	194	117	132	27,031	786	30.8	3.7	31.3
Casey	217	3,259	538	1,523	382	85	156	88	27,133	1,118	27.4	4.1	52.6
Christian	1,356	24,095	3,127	6,616	3,279	655	715	862	35,764	1,179	27.1	10.7	45.9
Clark	745	12,839	1,582	2,825	1,626	293	1,145	483	37,584	883	42.7	7.1	39.2

Table B. States and Counties — **Agriculture**

	Agriculture, 2012 (cont.)														
	Land in farms					Value of land and buildings (dollars)			Value of products sold:				Percent of farms with sales of:		Government payments
			Acres								Percent from:				
STATE County	Acreage (1,000)	Percent change, 2007-2012	Average size of farm	Total irrigated (1,000)	Total cropland (1,000)	Average per farm	Average per acre	Value of machinery and equiopmnet, average per farm (dollars)	Total (mil dol)	Average per farm (acres)	Crops	Livestock and poultry products	$10,000 or more	$100,000 or more	Total ($1,000)	Percent of farms
	117	118	119	120	121	122	123	124	125	126	127	128	129	130	131	132
KANSAS— Cont'd																
Neosho	308	-4.2	439	0.1	175.4	657,053	1,497	105,855	68.0	96,806	60.8	39.2	50.1	15.1	2,284	57.0
Ness	678	9.4	1,218	4.8	412.3	1,267,795	1,041	143,088	63.5	114,077	71.7	28.3	55.1	28.4	7,435	90.7
Norton	502	-5.5	1,368	14.5	270.6	1,812,496	1,325	210,428	146.1	397,976	34.9	65.1	66.5	32.7	3,716	85.3
Osage	442	16.3	436	0.0	251.4	709,350	1,626	105,941	71.0	70,021	52.4	47.6	43.3	14.9	4,728	64.1
Osborne	440	4.7	1,283	6.7	232.5	1,758,099	1,370	162,679	69.6	202,854	67.6	32.4	70.0	42.3	3,088	85.1
Ottawa	420	-4.0	800	4.2	239.0	1,505,440	1,883	167,135	99.0	188,631	60.6	39.4	64.4	28.0	3,509	82.3
Pawnee	480	-1.4	1,198	78.5	398.5	2,184,032	1,823	247,526	362.3	903,614	25.4	74.6	61.3	35.4	5,993	90.3
Phillips	495	0.0	1,123	7.5	232.2	1,404,333	1,251	170,676	100.4	227,633	48.7	51.3	63.7	34.9	3,275	76.9
Pottawatomie	410	-4.4	460	21.9	164.9	878,335	1,908	101,524	117.0	131,421	44.8	55.2	53.9	17.9	2,860	57.2
Pratt	465	-3.3	855	86.2	356.8	1,368,877	1,600	188,613	273.4	503,547	46.0	54.0	53.6	33.0	7,049	86.6
Rawlins	609	3.1	1,984	17.7	354.9	3,461,316	1,744	266,081	91.4	297,700	75.7	24.3	85.7	54.1	4,191	87.9
Reno	790	1.1	483	58.4	591.7	868,492	1,796	138,632	267.3	163,698	56.7	43.3	50.6	22.3	9,785	73.1
Republic	361	-11.2	628	46.5	258.5	1,664,624	2,651	228,520	197.3	343,073	58.8	41.2	71.7	37.7	4,144	78.6
Rice	458	6.8	860	28.6	360.9	1,373,859	1,597	238,983	258.2	485,303	38.3	61.7	62.8	37.8	5,201	79.3
Riley	218	-5.9	443	4.1	99.4	809,619	1,829	107,047	54.4	110,404	66.7	33.3	54.6	22.7	1,265	64.9
Rooks	551	-1.8	1,253	6.9	316.9	1,644,650	1,312	187,098	85.3	193,841	66.6	33.4	58.2	35.7	3,975	85.2
Rush	453	11.6	858	13.2	321.9	1,112,680	1,297	166,716	66.8	126,566	71.4	28.6	55.7	25.9	5,200	86.7
Russell	436	-1.8	864	0.5	234.9	986,889	1,142	129,329	56.8	112,649	64.6	35.4	56.0	22.8	4,283	83.9
Saline	364	-15.5	541	4.8	236.2	1,068,445	1,976	155,677	84.4	125,258	70.5	29.5	58.6	25.4	3,461	77.0
Scott	453	0.0	1,686	36.5	363.4	2,556,929	1,517	344,584	979.8	3,642,543	6.6	93.4	71.7	46.5	4,947	76.6
Sedgwick	487	-4.6	362	45.4	396.0	860,281	2,376	133,063	148.5	110,479	87.7	12.3	52.8	20.4	4,973	58.3
Seward	402	1.5	1,107	101.0	307.7	1,274,033	1,151	214,950	465.3	1,281,838	20.6	79.4	46.3	26.4	4,481	77.4
Shawnee	194	-5.8	235	19.0	117.7	585,475	2,489	78,510	50.3	60,844	83.0	17.0	39.5	10.4	2,350	40.8
Sheridan	562	7.6	1,463	79.3	363.5	2,808,255	1,919	288,505	328.7	855,951	33.3	66.7	79.7	51.0	5,406	83.6
Sherman	595	-9.6	1,430	87.0	498.7	2,441,558	1,707	280,512	170.2	409,043	77.2	22.8	63.5	41.8	7,341	86.8
Smith	500	9.4	1,007	7.3	334.4	1,633,296	1,622	212,620	111.0	223,270	67.2	32.8	71.6	38.6	5,354	84.3
Stafford	499	-0.7	931	103.4	396.5	1,644,125	1,767	234,315	197.6	368,696	60.8	39.2	55.6	36.4	6,769	85.6
Stanton	429	3.6	1,544	76.7	390.6	1,708,899	1,107	304,309	163.7	588,986	48.6	51.4	54.7	36.3	6,864	91.4
Stevens	456	-9.5	1,446	145.2	354.3	1,982,368	1,371	373,492	328.5	1,042,711	44.0	56.0	47.3	31.4	5,414	84.4
Sumner	720	1.4	657	16.1	592.9	1,177,329	1,793	178,303	168.7	153,935	88.8	11.2	62.9	28.2	7,384	77.0
Thomas	675	2.7	1,468	90.0	576.5	3,128,313	2,132	332,954	253.4	550,976	57.6	42.4	73.3	47.0	8,819	80.7
Trego	447	4.0	1,163	6.7	258.7	1,525,997	1,312	157,602	58.9	153,425	60.8	39.2	62.8	28.4	3,651	89.6
Wabaunsee	396	-15.8	642	7.0	107.6	944,000	1,470	92,042	58.3	94,561	36.9	63.1	53.3	21.1	1,959	56.7
Wallace	488	13.6	1,660	58.0	353.3	2,093,398	1,261	233,490	97.2	330,708	66.2	33.8	64.3	40.5	6,452	85.0
Washington	490	-10.6	669	9.7	298.2	1,562,583	2,334	197,657	187.1	255,668	53.2	46.8	69.5	36.9	5,492	79.5
Wichita	464	-10.8	1,750	67.5	351.2	2,375,000	1,357	320,019	624.8	2,357,736	D	D	72.1	49.1	5,701	87.2
Wilson	255	-23.6	602	2.2	142.4	865,076	1,437	129,043	55.4	131,021	84.4	15.6	62.4	23.6	1,636	65.0
Woodson	295	12.6	935	0.0	153.9	1,286,667	1,376	140,746	54.6	173,343	49.5	50.5	60.0	28.9	1,856	69.5
Wyandotte	12	-33.7	73	D	7.3	352,140	4,809	42,561	3.3	20,067	82.2	17.8	22.6	3.0	106	9.8
KENTUCKY	13,049	-6.7	169	73.6	6,336.2	512,033	3,024	70,188	5,067.3	65,755	45.0	55.0	36.5	8.2	169,821	43.3
Adair	170	-9.5	137	0.1	66.6	350,537	2,560	49,813	53.4	42,936	25.9	74.1	37.4	7.1	2,392	54.9
Allen	146	-12.6	135	0.3	52.3	398,629	2,955	51,991	53.2	49,291	26.5	73.5	39.4	6.9	2,086	44.4
Anderson	81	-7.5	120	0.2	29.4	373,490	3,116	48,127	12.7	18,857	33.7	66.3	29.6	3.3	625	22.9
Ballard	107	-2.7	263	0.4	85.2	893,627	3,402	150,120	57.6	141,206	54.7	45.3	42.6	14.7	1,937	65.9
Barren	249	-6.1	133	0.2	130.0	391,780	2,945	68,049	113.0	60,474	33.4	66.6	45.2	8.2	4,232	40.6
Bath	142	10.2	206	0.0	47.9	402,174	1,951	58,223	19.3	27,915	46.7	53.3	42.6	5.8	1,041	41.6
Bell	8	-20.9	100	0.0	1.8	193,704	1,945	25,827	0.5	6,037	D	D	21.0	0.0	7	7.4
Boone	67	-10.1	111	0.2	28.3	682,016	6,170	64,265	12.4	20,467	66.2	33.8	26.3	4.6	450	26.2
Bourbon	184	-0.3	203	0.4	74.8	862,352	4,256	90,714	108.4	119,568	34.5	65.5	50.3	13.2	1,916	39.6
Boyd	22	-24.1	102	0.0	4.8	237,617	2,333	53,234	1.9	8,813	27.0	73.0	13.6	0.9	22	6.5
Boyle	102	7.8	164	0.2	41.9	557,629	3,405	64,198	31.0	49,953	22.9	77.1	41.5	9.8	687	33.5
Bracken	87	-13.8	148	0.2	29.0	309,826	2,095	53,532	10.9	18,547	62.5	37.5	31.9	3.4	837	39.0
Breathitt	22	-49.0	185	0.0	4.8	264,842	1,430	58,558	1.7	14,261	43.0	57.0	14.2	3.3	192	39.2
Breckinridge	260	-5.4	199	0.0	116.6	477,849	2,399	64,376	79.5	60,995	42.8	57.2	40.3	8.2	3,246	58.2
Bullitt	46	-9.8	95	D	20.2	344,717	3,645	48,629	7.7	15,873	59.6	40.4	21.5	2.7	369	23.0
Butler	153	-12.3	219	0.2	62.8	442,750	2,023	59,912	42.4	60,822	54.7	45.3	29.6	7.9	2,052	48.6
Caldwell	133	-6.5	248	D	85.5	678,645	2,735	83,006	38.5	71,561	86.7	13.3	33.1	7.4	2,270	60.4
Calloway	176	11.6	214	3.8	131.9	636,456	2,968	109,851	109.7	133,619	57.3	42.7	35.8	16.2	5,573	68.7
Campbell	42	-10.9	84	0.1	15.0	367,526	4,393	49,331	6.9	13,718	45.7	54.3	24.4	3.2	179	16.3
Carlisle	99	3.0	303	0.6	79.6	858,588	2,829	151,486	73.1	224,939	46.6	53.4	38.2	20.0	2,245	74.2
Carroll	54	-15.9	193	0.1	21.7	508,050	2,637	55,694	6.4	23,169	69.9	30.1	36.0	2.5	354	41.7
Carter	106	-15.7	135	0.1	22.6	236,774	1,758	40,621	9.5	12,080	32.7	67.3	21.5	1.7	400	23.9
Casey	179	-6.5	160	0.1	60.6	325,356	2,031	49,997	29.6	26,471	47.1	52.9	38.2	5.1	1,559	47.5
Christian	360	4.0	306	3.3	252.3	1,055,497	3,454	121,645	185.8	157,625	80.2	19.8	48.3	20.6	7,302	56.4
Clark	137	-7.9	156	0.2	50.5	510,663	3,282	63,019	34.8	39,361	31.7	68.3	40.1	8.3	790	25.3

Table B. States and Counties — Water Use, Wholesale Trade, Retail Trade, and Real Estate

STATE County	Water use, 2015 Public supply water withdrawn (mil gal/day)	Public supply gallons withdrawn per person per day	Wholesale Trade[1], 2012 Number of establishments	Number of employees	Sales (mil dol)	Annual payroll (mil dol)	Retail Trade[2], 2012 Number of establishments	Number of employees	Sales (mil dol)	Annual payroll (mil dol)	Real estate and rental and leasing,[2] 2012 Number of establishments	Number of employees	Sales (mil dol)	Annual payroll (mil dol)
	133	134	135	136	137	138	139	140	141	142	143	144	145	146
KANSAS— Cont'd														
Neosho	1.08	66.1	28	223	96.2	8.2	86	800	197.7	18.8	11	18	2.0	0.4
Ness	0.32	106.5	16	D	D	D	19	98	15.4	1.6	1	D	D	D
Norton	0.75	135.1	8	68	38.3	2.5	27	183	51.2	3.9	1	D	D	D
Osage	1.52	95.9	15	73	48.6	2.9	42	360	74.0	5.8	5	D	D	D
Osborne	0.45	122.2	14	136	157.7	5.9	31	212	46.6	3.2	NA	NA	NA	NA
Ottawa	0.53	88.7	10	D	D	D	14	79	16.2	1.3	3	2	1.3	0.1
Pawnee	0.94	137.5	9	100	130.3	5.0	28	224	50.1	4.7	4	16	1.9	0.3
Phillips	0.98	180.5	13	63	69.7	2.8	35	227	51.5	4.1	1	D	D	D
Pottawatomie	6.22	267.0	30	549	224.8	23.5	81	1,819	338.9	48.4	18	D	D	D
Pratt	1.67	172.3	25	190	230.6	9.2	54	734	173.3	16.4	13	36	2.7	0.6
Rawlins	0.30	119.7	9	109	108.6	6.4	15	103	25.1	1.8	1	D	D	D
Reno	7.61	119.4	84	D	D	D	265	3,345	818.1	74.6	67	167	26.8	4.6
Republic	0.65	137.6	15	120	181.0	3.9	39	237	48.2	4.2	2	D	D	D
Rice	1.16	116.3	18	113	113.7	4.9	39	280	50.0	4.7	3	5	0.5	0.1
Riley	3.03	40.3	26	176	82.3	7.3	272	4,389	903.9	81.6	111	D	D	D
Rooks	0.68	131.4	17	159	178.2	6.9	28	200	69.2	3.8	2	D	D	D
Rush	0.51	162.9	14	74	58.6	2.9	10	65	29.1	1.8	NA	NA	NA	NA
Russell	0.44	62.5	14	114	101.2	4.3	39	267	76.5	4.7	8	25	3.1	0.6
Saline	5.90	105.9	95	1,195	996.5	54.7	250	3,989	1,120.4	87.4	64	208	52.5	6.4
Scott	0.84	169.2	19	126	192.1	6.1	33	223	56.8	3.9	4	3	0.5	0.1
Sedgwick	51.98	101.6	589	8,367	8,308.4	478.6	1,720	27,362	7,201.5	646.4	554	3,997	582.4	133.0
Seward	4.87	210.3	36	407	264.4	19.7	91	1,262	317.1	28.5	20	54	10.3	2.1
Shawnee	14.34	80.2	154	1,992	1,376.1	100.0	653	9,678	2,364.3	212.6	202	903	134.7	26.3
Sheridan	0.48	191.1	14	124	160.6	7.1	19	89	21.0	1.6	NA	NA	NA	NA
Sherman	1.34	224.0	23	225	341.0	9.3	34	409	132.3	8.9	4	D	D	D
Smith	0.49	132.3	10	134	128.2	4.8	24	169	67.4	3.4	2	D	D	D
Stafford	0.35	82.6	8	D	D	D	17	125	34.8	2.3	1	D	D	D
Stanton	0.40	193.1	9	D	D	D	5	D	D	D	1	D	D	D
Stevens	1.37	236.0	11	95	128.0	4.2	14	144	37.0	3.3	2	D	D	D
Sumner	2.10	89.2	28	167	157.4	7.0	65	592	159.8	11.1	12	D	D	D
Thomas	1.27	160.7	28	296	388.2	16.2	63	666	233.5	14.3	8	34	8.5	0.8
Trego	0.68	232.3	11	78	104.2	2.7	24	154	47.7	3.1	3	D	D	D
Wabaunsee	0.54	77.7	4	34	20.5	1.5	18	88	36.7	1.7	4	D	D	D
Wallace	0.22	144.9	5	D	D	D	7	42	7.6	1.0	2	D	D	D
Washington	0.78	139.3	21	183	264.8	6.3	36	215	45.6	4.1	6	9	0.4	0.0
Wichita	0.29	134.4	11	93	111.4	3.8	14	70	19.8	1.5	NA	NA	NA	NA
Wilson	1.36	153.6	5	20	31.7	0.7	43	234	57.7	4.5	3	3	0.2	0.0
Woodson	0.30	96.3	5	44	25.9	1.7	17	69	22.0	1.7	3	D	D	D
Wyandotte	62.15	380.4	225	5,758	5,611.1	302.2	452	6,929	1,769.4	172.6	136	593	112.2	20.2
KENTUCKY	552.83	124.9	3,690	57,630	71,745.9	3,090.3	15,224	202,615	54,870.0	4,619.2	3,534	18,250	4,845.5	637.3
Adair	0.00	0.0	15	72	42.1	1.6	64	691	204.3	16.2	5	D	D	D
Allen	0.95	46.0	9	D	D	D	59	410	111.3	8.4	9	23	2.4	0.6
Anderson	2.21	100.6	6	33	10.1	1.4	51	738	188.9	15.4	14	49	4.3	1.0
Ballard	0.58	70.6	4	D	D	D	26	162	57.6	3.6	3	D	D	D
Barren	7.76	178.1	39	D	D	D	188	2,193	562.8	49.5	23	71	9.9	1.6
Bath	0.00	0.0	3	D	D	D	31	182	47.8	3.8	8	D	D	D
Bell	3.83	140.1	18	189	212.9	5.9	128	1,515	365.1	31.2	19	71	9.2	1.6
Boone	0.04	0.3	170	6,614	21,688.2	542.7	470	9,132	2,564.6	208.6	102	719	175.3	25.2
Bourbon	2.10	104.4	4	D	D	D	65	876	248.2	21.8	10	16	4.0	0.5
Boyd	11.09	229.5	65	904	1,288.6	39.3	239	3,719	1,010.4	78.8	45	408	52.6	14.6
Boyle	5.58	187.2	20	140	114.1	5.7	134	1,717	431.4	39.6	23	66	8.7	1.5
Bracken	0.65	78.1	2	D	D	D	18	131	25.6	2.2	2	D	D	D
Breathitt	1.41	104.6	1	D	D	D	45	499	118.3	10.4	8	21	2.6	0.5
Breckinridge	1.80	89.9	8	72	36.0	2.3	55	543	148.2	12.2	9	23	2.2	0.8
Bullitt	0.00	0.0	28	564	519.7	22.0	144	1,550	586.4	36.0	31	118	19.6	4.0
Butler	1.21	93.5	6	D	D	D	33	232	49.9	4.3	4	5	0.3	0.1
Caldwell	0.00	0.0	9	D	D	D	57	687	159.9	15.0	6	9	1.7	0.3
Calloway	3.47	90.5	39	D	D	D	153	1,987	523.8	41.4	37	188	20.8	4.5
Campbell	26.34	286.1	60	1,036	835.3	60.6	265	4,285	1,105.2	94.3	62	544	93.9	26.4
Carlisle	0.14	28.7	4	20	4.2	0.5	12	81	19.9	1.6	7	8	2.3	0.2
Carroll	1.87	174.8	8	53	17.0	1.8	49	629	187.8	13.7	3	D	D	D
Carter	4.09	150.6	11	289	209.6	7.6	96	881	272.8	17.6	13	D	D	D
Casey	1.01	63.9	12	136	33.7	3.1	56	375	83.1	6.7	4	11	0.5	0.1
Christian	12.19	166.3	67	886	1,060.4	33.1	249	3,239	1,019.9	77.6	58	D	D	D
Clark	6.90	193.0	34	623	873.0	27.9	127	1,623	471.5	37.0	28	71	12.0	1.7

1. Merchant wholesalers, except manufacturers' sales branches and offices.   2. Employer establishments.

Table B. States and Counties — Professional Services, Manufacturing, and Accommodation and Food Services

STATE County	Professional, scientific, and technical services, 2012				Manufacturing, 2012				Accommodation and food services, 2012			
	Number of establishments	Number of employees	Sales (mil dol)	Annual payroll (mil dol)	Number of establishments	Number of employees	Receipts (mil dol)	Annual payroll (mil dol)	Number of establishments	Number of employees	Receipts (mil dol)	Annual payroll (mil dol)
	147	148	149	150	151	152	153	154	155	156	157	158
KANSAS— Cont'd												
Neosho	33	123	42.9	5.5	31	922	223.1	39.6	27	D	D	D
Ness	5	20	1.7	0.5	4	23	7.5	1.0	7	D	D	D
Norton	14	46	3.8	0.8	5	D	D	D	13	140	6.1	1.8
Osage	17	54	6.0	1.6	3	D	D	D	20	D	D	D
Osborne	7	42	12.6	1.6	6	113	D	4.5	12	D	D	D
Ottawa	14	D	D	D	8	84	D	2.2	10	41	1.2	0.3
Pawnee	16	74	8.1	2.2	NA	NA	NA	NA	16	153	5.5	1.5
Phillips	16	97	11.6	4.0	10	178	D	11.1	14	140	4.3	1.0
Pottawatomie	52	198	15.5	5.8	30	1,368	377.5	74.6	35	422	17.7	4.5
Pratt	28	115	11.7	4.7	9	78	42.6	3.4	32	438	25.0	5.1
Rawlins	11	16	1.3	0.3	7	31	9.4	1.2	5	25	0.5	0.1
Reno	102	642	61.8	24.5	87	3,752	1,232.8	168.4	117	2,141	91.6	26.3
Republic	13	25	3.4	0.6	10	168	D	6.3	11	D	D	D
Rice	16	143	9.4	2.6	14	328	291.2	14.9	22	D	D	D
Riley	146	D	D	D	30	480	94.5	18.9	166	3,903	146.8	42.1
Rooks	13	43	4.9	1.9	6	130	D	4.1	17	88	3.1	0.8
Rush	6	14	1.4	0.7	6	320	D	11.3	7	36	1.5	0.3
Russell	12	44	4.7	1.2	7	114	D	5.1	18	283	11.6	3.3
Saline	112	D	D	D	75	5,497	D	237.2	137	3,047	119.6	31.8
Scott	19	52	7.7	1.6	6	20	D	1.0	14	D	D	D
Sedgwick	1,155	10,100	1,586.7	570.9	533	40,629	15,547.1	2,316.4	1,102	22,151	1,029.8	287.6
Seward	22	139	12.0	5.0	7	D	D	D	45	789	40.4	10.4
Shawnee	449	D	D	D	105	5,291	2,588.3	244.4	362	D	D	D
Sheridan	3	16	1.0	0.3	3	6	D	D	6	D	D	D
Sherman	22	79	6.6	1.9	5	46	D	2.1	25	D	D	D
Smith	8	21	2.6	0.4	6	107	D	3.3	8	D	D	D
Stafford	6	11	2.0	0.7	NA	NA	NA	NA	10	D	D	D
Stanton	5	16	1.2	0.4	NA	NA	NA	NA	4	D	D	D
Stevens	11	40	3.3	0.9	4	22	D	1.9	12	144	5.0	1.3
Sumner	32	114	13.9	5.6	37	827	D	35.6	42	458	19.3	5.0
Thomas	28	65	7.2	2.1	9	45	D	1.8	31	464	21.8	6.2
Trego	8	24	1.4	0.4	6	41	D	1.4	11	119	4.8	1.2
Wabaunsee	7	8	1.2	0.3	7	D	D	D	8	30	1.3	0.2
Wallace	3	D	D	D	NA	NA	NA	NA	3	D	D	D
Washington	10	24	3.4	0.8	8	174	35.1	5.4	12	110	3.2	0.8
Wichita	4	6	0.3	0.1	4	62	D	2.3	4	D	D	D
Wilson	13	34	4.1	1.1	19	888	181.5	35.0	20	D	D	D
Woodson	5	D	D	D	3	13	D	0.5	8	D	D	D
Wyandotte	191	2,703	305.9	93.5	174	10,537	11,105.9	666.4	265	5,206	284.6	75.1
KENTUCKY	8,101	62,851	7,782.5	2,816.7	3,782	213,545	129,284.4	10,140.1	7,678	156,965	7,500.1	2083.5
Adair	17	D	D	D	25	323	153.1	10.9	19	D	D	D
Allen	7	84	3.4	1.7	10	D	D	D	16	D	D	D
Anderson	29	96	11.1	3.1	26	1,130	746.5	70.8	30	403	20.4	5.5
Ballard	10	D	D	D	11	678	D	49.0	10	D	D	D
Barren	47	265	22.5	7.9	45	3,480	929.5	139.8	86	1,554	71.9	18.6
Bath	10	D	D	D	8	D	D	4.8	12	D	D	D
Bell	29	104	9.2	3.3	19	1,075	304.4	34.6	44	855	36.7	9.5
Boone	224	2,184	228.4	72.6	188	12,910	5,069.7	653.0	286	D	D	D
Bourbon	32	321	35.0	14.7	24	1,731	1,066.6	78.2	27	D	D	D
Boyd	96	720	73.9	33.4	34	2,798	D	218.5	120	2,704	129.4	35.0
Boyle	55	275	34.6	10.2	22	1,881	673.6	77.7	61	1,325	59.6	17.2
Bracken	4	12	0.6	0.3	NA	NA	NA	NA	8	D	D	D
Breathitt	10	D	D	D	5	25	D	1.0	10	D	D	D
Breckinridge	19	77	6.0	2.0	13	248	29.7	9.4	15	195	8.7	2.4
Bullitt	77	336	31.4	11.4	42	2,117	811.5	85.7	90	1,930	82.9	22.4
Butler	10	31	1.6	0.7	13	573	185.8	24.0	13	D	D	D
Caldwell	18	45	3.5	0.8	12	864	391.2	31.8	25	393	13.2	3.5
Calloway	65	357	29.6	12.5	30	2,548	828.7	93.4	87	1,679	60.4	16.1
Campbell	146	950	125.1	41.8	78	2,651	994.7	123.9	208	D	D	D
Carlisle	2	D	D	D	4	80	10.4	1.8	6	31	1.3	0.3
Carroll	16	93	10.0	4.6	13	2,452	D	177.2	28	D	D	D
Carter	28	111	6.9	2.6	15	791	253.5	23.6	32	636	28.1	7.3
Casey	10	D	D	D	31	1,266	237.7	28.4	12	192	7.6	2.6
Christian	111	958	100.0	41.0	72	4,647	1,894.8	207.8	113	D	D	D
Clark	55	293	31.4	13.5	40	2,378	1,016.0	108.4	58	1,148	56.5	15.6

Table B. States and Counties — Health Care and Social Assistance, Other Services, Nonemployer Businesses, and Residential Construction

STATE County	Health care and social assistance, 2012				Other services, 2012				Nonemployer businesses, 2015		Value of residential construction authorized by building permits, 2017	
	Number of establishments	Number of employees	Receipts (mil dol)	Annual payroll (mil dol)	Number of establishments	Number of employees	Receipts (mil dol)	Annual payroll (mil dol)	Number	Receipts (mil dol)	New construction ($1,000)	Number of housing units
	159	160	161	162	163	164	165	166	167	168	169	170
KANSAS— Cont'd												
Neosho	52	1,148	94.8	36.3	31	102	8.7	1.7	1,098	41.8	390	3
Ness	9	257	15.5	7.4	14	D	D	D	316	11.4	350	1
Norton	22	497	26.3	13.1	11	D	D	D	432	12.8	150	1
Osage	27	1,648	40.6	25.0	18	D	D	D	1,035	41.1	4,350	28
Osborne	13	334	16.2	8.1	10	33	4.5	0.9	353	10.4	475	2
Ottawa	12	D	D	D	11	D	D	D	500	18.3	2,415	12
Pawnee	16	1,210	87.4	43.8	14	30	2.7	0.5	431	22.2	500	3
Phillips	19	346	21.3	10.5	25	84	11.0	1.6	489	16.1	235	2
Pottawatomie	50	1,048	78.1	29.6	53	152	14.6	3.8	1,756	79.5	49,940	209
Pratt	36	713	64.2	27.4	34	107	9.5	2.3	806	35.3	294	1
Rawlins	9	210	12.3	5.8	7	11	1.2	0.2	265	9.2	847	4
Reno	176	4,895	441.4	176.7	115	514	46.5	12.0	3,896	136.5	10,228	40
Republic	15	296	16.8	8.1	15	42	4.0	0.8	420	15.0	0	0
Rice	20	400	22.1	11.7	19	62	8.2	1.7	649	19.2	1,317	6
Riley	180	3,201	313.2	112.9	119	1,100	208.7	44.9	3,366	144.5	36,144	172
Rooks	12	245	17.8	7.2	10	39	3.5	0.7	568	21.5	175	1
Rush	7	163	9.1	3.7	5	D	D	D	280	9.8	0	0
Russell	13	132	8.1	3.6	18	71	7.4	1.7	828	38.9	2,697	25
Saline	181	D	D	D	113	D	D	D	3,459	143.2	14,469	87
Scott	11	341	19.6	10.4	17	42	6.5	1.0	475	17.9	1,706	6
Sedgwick	1,358	34,266	3,501.4	1,450.6	796	5,733	677.1	172.7	31,576	1,463.2	310,214	2333
Seward	74	1,079	91.4	35.5	44	166	23.0	4.5	1,290	76.1	2,686	28
Shawnee	523	16,404	1,706.2	740.6	371	3,580	322.3	102.6	9,505	414.2	46,146	218
Sheridan	7	D	D	D	10	58	1.8	0.3	285	12.0	NA	NA
Sherman	38	353	23.9	11.7	20	71	7.4	1.7	453	17.5	0	0
Smith	7	D	D	D	13	D	D	D	327	9.5	0	0
Stafford	15	168	10.1	4.7	13	21	1.7	0.3	391	15.7	2,029	11
Stanton	3	D	D	D	5	D	D	D	197	8.8	0	0
Stevens	6	D	D	D	8	D	D	D	360	19.5	176	1
Sumner	58	947	58.2	25.4	39	116	9.9	2.6	1,474	53.7	4,660	31
Thomas	34	407	33.1	13.4	29	121	10.8	2.9	838	29.3	480	4
Trego	6	D	D	D	9	22	1.7	0.5	332	12.8	0	0
Wabaunsee	8	D	D	D	6	D	D	D	501	19.2	5,735	24
Wallace	4	D	D	D	6	D	D	D	169	4.8	0	0
Washington	25	317	16.3	7.6	19	D	D	D	462	17.8	0	0
Wichita	6	D	D	D	8	D	D	D	197	9.9	0	0
Wilson	33	695	46.6	18.8	17	35	3.8	0.8	630	23.1	847	4
Woodson	10	126	5.7	2.1	5	D	D	D	290	12.1	489	7
Wyandotte	320	13,552	1,568.6	707.1	222	1,320	270.7	42.0	7,442	291.3	50,646	311
KENTUCKY	11,425	251,878	26,264.7	10,184.1	5,849	38,364	4,071.4	1,090.0	280,835	11,996.9	1,974,160	12,630
Adair	36	739	48.8	20.2	14	D	D	D	1,568	61.8	280	2
Allen	23	D	D	D	17	D	D	D	1,448	61.6	1,050	11
Anderson	34	329	19.1	8.4	30	84	8.6	2.3	1,447	49.3	13,804	66
Ballard	6	D	D	D	5	D	D	D	474	16.0	NA	NA
Barren	105	D	D	D	59	223	14.9	4.7	3,223	121.5	15,410	144
Bath	9	296	10.1	4.3	8	D	D	D	791	22.6	0	0
Bell	78	D	D	D	35	154	11.2	2.9	1,393	40.0	2,767	28
Boone	243	4,772	446.2	181.8	180	D	D	D	7,374	322.3	94,837	655
Bourbon	47	714	59.3	22.2	21	D	D	D	1,364	60.9	11,333	57
Boyd	245	7,292	993.0	372.3	96	D	D	D	2,545	107.0	421	4
Boyle	132	2,917	297.4	130.9	53	208	16.8	4.2	2,031	76.8	7,463	38
Bracken	8	D	D	D	5	D	D	D	587	19.2	NA	NA
Breathitt	48	1,277	97.7	42.7	10	34	5.2	1.3	584	18.4	0	0
Breckinridge	31	589	39.9	13.5	19	38	3.7	0.8	1,247	55.3	122	1
Bullitt	108	1,386	95.1	39.7	90	1,584	46.3	42.7	4,335	176.4	101,803	465
Butler	20	352	19.9	9.7	18	D	D	D	841	34.1	0	0
Caldwell	34	570	44.7	16.4	17	D	D	D	723	28.3	0	0
Calloway	110	2,119	190.7	73.4	47	182	13.1	3.8	2,446	107.9	8,167	92
Campbell	158	3,490	334.3	130.9	126	D	D	D	5,476	213.3	51,067	276
Carlisle	6	D	D	D	5	10	1.1	0.2	436	16.4	NA	NA
Carroll	20	373	32.0	13.9	14	D	D	D	574	25.8	0	0
Carter	44	519	38.8	14.9	30	D	D	D	1,765	63.9	330	3
Casey	21	527	35.4	16.0	8	34	3.0	0.7	1,140	53.4	0	0
Christian	157	3,130	300.4	106.2	87	D	D	D	3,258	136.2	8,889	94
Clark	126	1,518	139.2	51.2	45	181	15.1	4.4	2,179	85.7	12,117	86

Table B. States and Counties — **Agriculture**

STATE County	Land in farms		Acres			Value of land and buildings (dollars)		Value of machinery and equipment, average per farm (dollars)	Value of products sold:		Percent from:		Percent of farms with sales of:		Government payments	
	Acreage (1,000)	Percent change, 2007-2012	Average size of farm	Total irrigated (1,000)	Total cropland (1,000)	Average per farm	Average per acre		Total (mil dol)	Average per farm (acres)	Crops	Livestock and poultry products	$10,000 or more	$100,000 or more	Total ($1,000)	Percent of farms
	117	118	119	120	121	122	123	124	125	126	127	128	129	130	131	132
LOUISIANA— Cont'd																
Orleans	111	D	8	0.0	0.0	122,786	15,486	114,143	0.5	37,143	41.2	59.0	42.9	7.1	D	7.1
Ouachita	93	9.1	207	12.1	47.4	603,420	2,916	72,287	49.1	109,047	54.9	45.1	29.3	9.8	1,933	25.8
Plaquemines	89	-26.8	635	0.1	8.5	801,564	1,262	64,250	15.0	107,457	39.1	61.0	61.4	15.0	60	7.9
Pointe Coupee	182	-4.4	464	6.1	143.8	1,272,481	2,744	240,089	130.1	331,163	95.8	4.2	58.8	18.3	2,786	41.0
Rapides	211	19.0	247	21.1	132.1	628,930	2,543	99,732	132.2	154,972	88.3	11.7	42.3	16.4	3,644	22.2
Red River	135	31.0	537	3.0	34.3	1,049,234	1,954	129,516	38.6	153,024	33.5	66.5	41.3	15.5	1,506	34.9
Richland	279	-4.2	366	85.1	189.5	840,475	2,296	126,639	127.3	167,038	93.5	6.5	37.1	18.2	10,171	76.1
Sabine	52	2.5	132	0.1	12.0	420,495	3,180	71,528	142.1	362,612	0.9	99.1	37.8	14.0	441	11.5
St. Bernard	32	-0.5	569	0.0	4.3	946,804	1,663	68,750	5.8	103,482	2.7	97.3	32.1	12.5	19	14.3
St. Charles	16	D	232	D	1.9	501,871	2,166	57,929	1.2	16,571	12.8	87.3	44.3	0.0	D	8.6
St. Helena	53	1.4	142	1.4	17.0	476,399	3,346	62,539	25.6	68,542	8.3	91.7	28.4	7.5	298	18.2
St. James	40	-7.7	634	0.0	37.1	2,231,444	3,520	369,730	33.2	526,270	98.8	1.2	58.7	28.6	84	17.5
St. John the Baptist	11	-21.5	468	0.0	8.0	1,361,261	2,910	240,391	9.3	402,696	98.6	1.4	43.5	13.0	D	4.3
St. Landry	301	0.8	225	29.8	223.9	540,722	2,405	90,250	125.0	93,408	91.7	8.3	28.3	9.7	5,809	39.3
St. Martin	76	-3.8	223	6.7	58.2	552,229	2,473	154,956	52.8	155,250	91.0	9.0	37.1	14.1	506	17.6
St. Mary	76	4.6	594	0.0	63.0	1,490,961	2,508	392,164	65.8	513,867	98.4	1.6	43.8	27.3	173	21.1
St. Tammany	34	-25.0	56	0.4	7.9	413,126	7,315	44,215	11.3	18,685	61.1	38.9	22.2	4.0	38	2.5
Tangipahoa	107	-13.8	100	0.7	36.3	410,570	4,117	54,967	45.7	42,694	40.2	59.8	29.1	7.2	790	17.3
Tensas	197	-12.8	783	40.3	168.2	1,721,227	2,197	275,825	129.2	514,558	99.8	0.2	37.5	29.5	7,350	86.5
Terrebonne	93	-47.9	492	0.6	21.5	1,102,540	2,243	147,534	37.1	224,986	43.6	56.4	37.0	13.2	95	9.0
Union	63	-7.0	152	0.0	16.8	441,254	2,909	75,138	92.9	224,986	1.5	98.5	40.7	15.3	166	9.2
Vermilion	284	-2.3	240	59.2	171.9	622,631	2,599	100,574	141.1	119,207	69.7	30.3	36.7	10.3	6,832	57.3
Vernon	49	-3.2	104	0.0	8.9	328,764	3,160	43,987	3.2	6,794	29.0	70.9	14.0	0.6	89	4.0
Washington	81	-16.7	99	0.4	28.6	349,438	3,545	54,988	28.3	34,259	40.2	59.8	23.0	4.4	434	14.6
Webster	52	5.6	117	D	10.1	407,367	3,483	51,532	10.1	22,501	17.3	82.7	27.1	2.2	81	7.2
West Baton Rouge	30	17.4	286	0.1	25.6	1,071,953	3,750	222,868	31.4	295,934	88.7	11.3	39.6	17.9	181	33.0
West Carroll	166	-15.8	226	45.2	115.9	482,630	2,135	86,151	72.5	98,966	97.1	2.9	19.9	11.3	5,879	83.8
West Feliciana	101	51.9	621	0.0	28.9	1,639,712	2,639	99,767	18.7	114,497	76.8	23.2	41.1	8.0	273	30.7
Winn	25	16.7	139	0.0	4.1	337,184	2,418	59,615	18.0	100,575	4.0	96.0	24.6	4.5	118	14.0
MAINE	1,454	7.9	178	30.9	477.3	410,633	2,308	69,762	763.1	93,364	62.1	37.9	34.6	9.5	10,162	16.3
Androscoggin	59	16.9	128	0.8	22.0	329,181	2,564	72,955	53.8	116,266	22.1	77.9	32.8	8.0	445	15.6
Aroostook	351	-6.6	392	11.4	187.5	559,514	1,427	157,318	210.5	235,215	91.6	8.4	42.9	21.5	2,492	43.0
Cumberland	63	21.2	87	0.7	18.0	428,535	4,907	61,922	26.3	36,635	65.6	34.4	33.7	7.5	497	8.1
Franklin	49	21.3	127	0.1	9.6	276,724	2,172	47,778	D	D	D	D	22.4	5.4	595	17.8
Hancock	53	1.2	132	0.2	12.0	444,960	3,369	51,351	D	D	D	D	38.6	6.9	187	14.9
Kennebec	78	-5.3	129	0.4	32.8	370,354	2,866	69,992	49.8	82,505	28.9	71.1	36.8	8.8	711	12.3
Knox	29	-2.3	94	0.3	7.5	355,739	3,798	35,876	D	D	D	D	31.2	4.1	116	14.6
Lincoln	32	5.2	92	0.1	7.4	320,218	3,489	43,009	10.2	29,541	51.2	48.8	32.8	5.5	269	7.8
Oxford	75	9.5	137	0.4	15.7	347,443	2,543	48,483	19.2	34,880	75.4	24.6	27.0	5.3	488	12.5
Penobscot	113	-1.4	167	2.3	35.6	336,186	2,015	63,316	50.2	74,084	32.3	67.7	33.4	9.0	1,044	13.3
Piscataquis	47	37.1	230	0.2	12.4	394,502	1,715	49,310	D	D	D	D	29.1	9.4	405	22.2
Sagadahoc	20	7.9	88	0.2	5.2	331,555	3,779	39,664	D	D	D	D	30.1	5.7	139	7.4
Somerset	140	25.7	242	0.2	30.2	512,425	2,119	92,294	86.4	149,278	64.1	35.9	44.7	19.2	1,053	16.6
Waldo	131	91.5	206	0.2	24.8	384,874	1,865	39,363	D	D	D	D	29.1	6.5	837	16.6
Washington	149	-5.9	380	12.1	35.7	594,518	1,564	79,079	154.6	394,508	D	D	45.7	9.4	526	18.6
York	65	8.7	83	1.3	21.0	403,257	4,869	58,392	27.5	35,239	D	D	31.8	6.4	358	5.9
MARYLAND	2,031	-1.0	166	104.9	1,396.1	1,148,268	6,930	115,879	2,271.4	185,329	46.3	53.7	43.1	20.6	36,024	37.8
Allegany	36	-1.0	125	0.0	11.8	435,282	3,493	52,261	3.1	10,735	59.5	40.5	30.6	1.0	253	31.6
Anne Arundel	28	-3.9	74	0.3	14.7	854,334	11,579	71,680	19.7	51,627	84.0	16.0	25.7	5.8	160	10.0
Baltimore	70	-10.0	110	0.5	44.6	1,038,656	9,440	91,152	76.3	119,228	88.6	11.4	34.5	12.5	840	18.3
Calvert	33	24.4	122	0.2	21.2	921,743	7,536	72,149	11.1	41,416	95.3	4.7	37.2	9.7	523	23.8
Caroline	150	14.5	229	27.0	121.4	1,395,853	6,109	155,213	257.9	391,968	33.1	66.9	68.2	46.0	3,335	61.7
Carroll	133	-6.6	121	1.4	97.2	989,130	8,144	101,499	111.6	102,232	67.3	32.7	34.5	12.6	3,440	40.2
Cecil	77	-9.8	155	0.6	54.8	1,121,347	7,255	132,554	113.8	229,466	60.3	39.7	43.8	19.4	1,505	30.4
Charles	47	-10.5	122	0.5	25.3	788,220	6,453	70,134	11.9	31,272	89.8	10.2	26.4	6.5	508	22.8
Dorchester	126	-5.1	299	22.4	92.0	1,557,508	5,211	204,546	187.1	442,215	37.3	62.7	51.1	40.0	2,501	75.9
Frederick	182	-10.2	139	1.4	127.1	1,053,941	7,595	108,462	150.5	115,030	49.5	50.5	41.1	17.9	3,060	33.6
Garrett	95	-0.3	143	0.0	41.5	600,378	4,207	80,346	31.5	47,168	34.7	65.3	46.0	14.4	540	18.9
Harford	65	-12.9	112	0.5	40.4	929,613	8,264	89,722	46.0	79,041	68.1	31.9	33.8	12.9	894	28.5
Howard	37	27.6	128	0.2	20.9	1,401,898	10,961	84,051	31.9	108,816	86.9	13.1	32.4	11.9	309	20.8
Kent	133	3.9	363	8.3	104.6	2,472,676	6,813	197,866	112.3	305,858	69.8	30.2	61.3	33.2	2,931	77.9
Montgomery	63	-6.1	118	1.0	45.6	1,195,894	10,171	101,435	48.3	89,520	86.6	13.4	29.1	10.6	836	17.2
Prince George's	33	-11.9	94	0.8	14.4	741,326	7,889	56,916	18.0	51,873	91.3	8.7	30.0	5.2	157	11.5
Queen Anne's	157	6.8	296	15.8	129.9	2,204,232	7,444	181,240	166.9	314,821	61.9	38.1	53.2	35.1	4,242	73.6

Table B. States and Counties — **Water Use, Wholesale Trade, Retail Trade, and Real Estate**

STATE County	Water use, 2015 — Public supply water withdrawn (mil gal/ day)	Water use, 2015 — Public supply gallons withdrawn per person per day	Wholesale Trade[1], 2012 — Number of establish-ments	Wholesale Trade[1], 2012 — Number of employees	Wholesale Trade[1], 2012 — Sales (mil dol)	Wholesale Trade[1], 2012 — Annual payroll (mil dol)	Retail Trade[2], 2012 — Number of establish-ments	Retail Trade[2], 2012 — Number of employees	Retail Trade[2], 2012 — Sales (mil dol)	Retail Trade[2], 2012 — Annual payroll (mil dol)	Real estate and rental and leasing,[2] 2012 — Number of establish-ments	Real estate and rental and leasing,[2] 2012 — Number of employees	Real estate and rental and leasing,[2] 2012 — Sales (mil dol)	Real estate and rental and leasing,[2] 2012 — Annual payroll (mil dol)
	133	134	135	136	137	138	139	140	141	142	143	144	145	146
LOUISIANA— Cont'd														
Orleans	140.90	361.6	256	3,794	2,687.0	191.5	1,275	12,371	3,245.1	337.8	379	2,156	411.6	79.1
Ouachita	24.18	154.2	182	D	D	D	710	9,203	2,387.1	205.9	185	1,145	228.0	37.9
Plaquemines	7.14	303.9	54	982	2,228.3	57.5	66	499	134.1	13.3	41	364	116.3	23.0
Pointe Coupee	3.54	159.1	10	140	436.2	6.3	77	775	201.2	17.0	12	37	10.7	1.7
Rapides	18.91	143.1	123	D	D	D	584	7,769	2,211.5	188.3	137	D	D	D
Red River	1.00	116.4	7	70	22.9	2.3	18	154	37.3	2.6	3	D	D	D
Richland	3.64	177.4	21	234	529.8	13.8	65	715	250.4	16.9	16	113	8.1	2.0
Sabine	2.34	96.8	14	123	55.8	4.6	79	860	217.2	19.3	13	23	3.1	0.4
St. Bernard	7.16	157.7	26	D	D	D	137	1,432	392.2	35.7	19	60	8.9	2.2
St. Charles	9.09	172.1	73	1,944	4,939.9	105.6	112	1,184	402.9	31.0	35	172	49.9	9.3
St. Helena	0.90	85.2	2	D	D	D	29	345	80.0	4.4	2	D	D	D
St. James	4.00	185.5	10	D	D	D	50	490	128.6	10.7	6	14	1.8	0.3
St. John the Baptist	7.45	170.8	29	D	D	D	118	1,586	479.2	36.4	29	199	58.2	8.7
St. Landry	10.31	123.0	59	578	782.4	24.5	305	3,806	976.8	86.8	53	674	124.3	31.0
St. Martin	4.67	86.7	52	795	458.3	43.5	142	1,615	559.0	33.9	38	814	352.9	59.5
St. Mary	9.32	176.5	75	D	D	D	198	2,295	605.2	54.2	80	1,141	259.8	65.0
St. Tammany	23.64	94.5	244	2,224	5,060.2	125.1	915	12,433	3,550.7	301.2	215	1,112	250.7	55.5
Tangipahoa	15.06	117.0	86	1,701	1,300.4	68.5	438	6,290	1,769.7	144.7	94	498	86.5	18.5
Tensas	1.16	244.7	9	72	195.4	3.7	15	78	27.7	1.8	NA	NA	NA	NA
Terrebonne	1.88	16.5	196	2,102	996.0	113.8	503	7,070	1,929.4	170.2	167	1,690	471.5	101.9
Union	4.40	195.8	5	D	D	D	66	609	141.3	14.4	5	9	1.3	0.2
Vermilion	7.07	118.1	33	307	235.8	15.1	180	2,057	577.3	47.8	39	224	41.9	9.0
Vernon	4.35	85.6	18	90	57.3	3.3	134	1,537	426.7	34.7	31	268	70.5	11.3
Washington	4.63	99.8	20	118	128.3	3.5	138	1,152	297.0	26.5	15	41	4.0	0.8
Webster	5.36	133.9	34	394	204.7	15.4	163	2,193	549.4	47.2	33	155	34.4	6.7
West Baton Rouge	7.21	282.9	43	755	967.9	41.2	85	1,173	455.5	25.3	11	121	29.2	5.9
West Carroll	1.39	123.1	5	D	D	D	34	397	87.4	7.8	5	12	1.8	0.3
West Feliciana	1.67	108.5	3	D	D	D	28	283	86.6	5.7	6	D	D	D
Winn	2.01	138.0	10	108	65.2	3.8	48	543	113.9	11.3	8	29	3.3	0.8
MAINE	84.97	63.9	1,344	14,753	12,961.3	691.5	6,351	80,155	21,521.7	1,884.6	1,580	6,242	1,100.4	220.6
Androscoggin	7.92	73.9	102	1,236	473.9	54.6	439	6,018	1,818.1	138.5	111	376	62.9	11.6
Aroostook	4.11	59.9	72	503	308.9	21.8	346	4,186	1,119.4	90.0	76	252	50.4	6.5
Cumberland	25.35	87.4	456	5,956	5,925.3	308.3	1,448	21,738	5,751.4	522.3	516	2,787	519.6	109.3
Franklin	1.36	45.3	14	D	D	D	161	1,623	395.5	34.4	27	68	8.2	1.6
Hancock	6.69	122.4	59	464	244.5	14.7	379	3,471	852.6	86.4	80	185	27.2	5.5
Kennebec	6.15	51.3	96	1,990	1,613.7	96.4	526	8,111	2,179.3	201.2	99	429	65.5	14.1
Knox	3.02	75.8	49	256	165.9	9.6	257	2,656	632.9	60.7	69	151	22.2	5.5
Lincoln	0.73	21.5	30	D	D	D	210	1,648	421.7	39.6	49	114	15.2	3.2
Oxford	2.85	49.8	34	D	D	D	224	2,212	611.4	53.6	37	129	14.6	3.5
Penobscot	4.79	31.4	162	1,794	955.4	82.3	735	10,931	3,203.1	249.6	172	692	123.3	22.9
Piscataquis	0.88	52.0	8	D	D	D	91	823	212.2	19.0	12	27	3.3	0.6
Sagadahoc	1.41	40.1	22	108	43.5	3.8	141	1,864	465.5	42.8	32	60	8.7	1.9
Somerset	1.82	35.6	28	176	61.1	6.6	213	2,353	611.0	51.9	31	219	48.7	10.0
Waldo	0.99	25.3	23	D	D	D	163	1,479	365.7	34.4	29	59	7.1	2.1
Washington	1.57	49.6	45	230	125.4	5.2	150	1,670	433.1	37.1	20	46	4.1	1.2
York	15.33	76.2	144	1,163	818.2	55.2	868	9,372	2,448.7	223.0	220	648	119.4	21.0
MARYLAND	749.52	124.8	4,768	73,369	60,734.2	4,378.5	18,179	281,678	76,379.7	7,168.5	6,001	42,838	13,410.1	2253.2
Allegany	0.67	9.2	45	D	D	D	288	3,854	922.8	81.5	52	199	29.3	5.6
Anne Arundel	39.49	70.0	492	8,187	7,606.5	484.5	2,005	33,052	8,758.8	831.2	566	4,232	1,254.5	203.5
Baltimore	209.46	252.0	749	10,796	5,548.5	609.6	2,745	47,973	12,645.7	1,235.1	855	6,432	3,201.7	344.6
Calvert	2.49	27.5	42	268	91.8	13.6	205	2,955	848.4	72.4	80	285	79.2	15.3
Caroline	0.98	30.1	21	186	118.9	8.3	86	980	476.2	28.7	15	D	D	D
Carroll	7.05	42.1	150	1,286	723.9	61.7	495	7,901	2,245.2	184.3	137	474	83.1	15.7
Cecil	3.60	35.2	60	D	D	D	264	3,895	1,146.3	87.9	72	191	27.7	5.5
Charles	7.32	46.9	56	435	950.4	21.1	495	8,729	2,245.0	207.7	107	394	97.3	13.3
Dorchester	2.65	81.8	32	276	234.2	12.2	100	1,133	288.7	25.4	37	92	8.3	2.6
Frederick	13.79	56.2	199	2,212	1,185.8	119.4	736	11,814	3,267.7	299.3	246	864	207.0	39.8
Garrett	2.74	93.0	23	D	D	D	136	1,714	517.9	39.1	34	D	D	D
Harford	9.84	39.3	170	1,865	2,420.7	99.4	723	13,420	3,792.9	342.6	215	751	192.9	27.9
Howard	0.01	0.0	478	11,707	9,266.7	784.1	854	15,811	4,867.7	427.7	379	3,356	1,025.9	181.9
Kent	1.09	55.1	24	172	127.1	6.9	99	848	185.9	18.6	25	57	12.0	2.0
Montgomery	354.94	341.3	676	9,113	10,456.8	672.7	2,702	46,240	13,706.2	1,333.7	1,324	12,342	4,534.5	829.3
Prince George's	52.34	57.5	536	11,108	7,639.8	651.0	2,217	36,414	9,358.1	907.2	640	6,216	1,186.5	281.3
Queen Anne's	1.77	36.2	70	778	353.0	37.8	210	2,305	547.5	49.1	47	155	36.1	4.8

1. Merchant wholesalers, except manufacturers' sales branches and offices.   2. Employer establishments.

Table B. States and Counties — Professional Services, Manufacturing, and Accommodation and Food Services

STATE County	Professional, scientific, and technical services, 2012				Manufacturing, 2012				Accommodation and food services, 2012			
	Number of establishments	Number of employees	Sales (mil dol)	Annual payroll (mil dol)	Number of establishments	Number of employees	Receipts (mil dol)	Annual payroll (mil dol)	Number of establishments	Number of employees	Receipts (mil dol)	Annual payroll (mil dol)
	147	148	149	150	151	152	153	154	155	156	157	158
LOUISIANA— Cont'd												
Orleans	1,450	13,212	2,613.2	971.7	144	6,049	4,352.7	335.6	1,300	35,510	2,765.4	764.7
Ouachita	435	2,696	373.8	123.8	126	D	D	D	294	D	D	D
Plaquemines	51	382	114.7	28.9	37	2,174	D	192.2	61	737	59.8	18.8
Pointe Coupee	30	99	15.8	5.4	8	385	D	16.0	37	344	18.5	3.8
Rapides	285	D	D	D	72	3,851	D	217.3	237	4,330	216.8	58.3
Red River	9	29	4.0	1.0	4	194	D	8.2	10	D	D	D
Richland	27	92	10.4	2.8	11	904	396.5	37.5	24	D	D	D
Sabine	50	185	19.8	7.6	16	753	D	36.1	25	D	D	D
St. Bernard	34	148	14.2	4.3	33	1,195	11,904.0	109.8	81	D	D	D
St. Charles	95	1,402	162.3	75.5	40	4,695	29,174.8	471.2	82	995	49.3	12.7
St. Helena	6	16	2.2	0.4	5	257	D	D	8	D	D	D
St. James	17	75	8.0	3.3	24	2,156	D	201.7	25	D	D	D
St. John the Baptist	57	335	46.3	15.3	24	2,788	D	234.5	75	1,235	58.5	14.4
St. Landry	142	553	78.8	25.3	57	1,353	3,421.2	60.8	99	1,594	76.6	21.0
St. Martin	100	325	50.6	13.5	69	1,911	D	86.0	75	1,321	63.2	15.5
St. Mary	104	614	97.7	34.5	81	4,170	1,901.2	249.1	107	2,823	201.1	55.7
St. Tammany	844	5,154	700.8	292.6	123	3,676	D	205.3	556	9,615	443.8	128.0
Tangipahoa	208	889	93.5	33.6	79	2,389	681.2	84.4	213	4,285	185.8	50.9
Tensas	2	D	D	D	3	13	D	D	6	D	D	D
Terrebonne	287	2,797	353.6	138.9	143	6,301	1,538.3	343.2	235	5,138	295.2	84.7
Union	14	41	5.3	1.4	10	D	D	D	16	D	D	D
Vermilion	118	291	33.0	11.6	40	636	D	24.9	61	928	49.4	11.3
Vernon	86	725	70.3	32.6	14	200	D	6.4	66	1,412	58.8	16.2
Washington	43	133	19.4	5.2	27	1,027	616.1	65.5	61	713	33.5	8.5
Webster	53	247	21.0	6.4	29	1,436	D	D	61	807	34.8	8.7
West Baton Rouge	26	238	22.2	8.1	36	2,300	7,272.3	151.5	56	878	49.1	10.9
West Carroll	11	D	D	D	3	D	D	D	11	186	6.3	1.8
West Feliciana	26	77	7.9	4.3	8	324	D	D	27	341	14.7	3.9
Winn	21	47	4.4	1.4	14	606	D	28.1	18	D	D	D
MAINE	3,492	22,943	3,352.6	1,238.0	1,650	49,238	16,044.5	2,424.3	3,958	49,672	2,901.3	850.8
Androscoggin	183	1,652	359.2	80.1	150	5,205	1,886.9	251.6	209	3,021	153.3	44.5
Aroostook	97	343	31.4	11.9	92	2,689	1,037.9	121.1	156	1,897	83.2	23.9
Cumberland	1,410	10,188	1,627.5	641.9	380	8,691	D	433.9	973	15,001	839.9	254.8
Franklin	43	D	D	D	25	1,454	D	72.7	92	1,114	41.4	12.8
Hancock	138	1,773	268.7	99.5	90	1,463	520.2	73.7	301	2,040	211.1	54.9
Kennebec	302	D	D	D	95	2,386	634.2	114.8	302	4,055	222.9	66.8
Knox	132	440	53.5	20.8	94	1,443	377.8	63.4	166	1,663	96.8	30.9
Lincoln	108	D	D	D	72	742	D	31.9	149	1,127	84.6	24.3
Oxford	75	307	32.8	10.9	61	2,434	860.6	138.6	133	2,562	103.8	32.5
Penobscot	328	1,831	179.4	84.5	134	3,749	977.7	164.0	315	5,639	313.9	86.7
Piscataquis	13	D	D	D	22	1,045	177.5	37.8	47	259	14.9	3.6
Sagadahoc	99	917	103.0	52.7	39	D	D	D	81	1,053	54.9	17.1
Somerset	59	332	37.1	13.4	72	3,330	1,607.3	177.8	92	846	43.8	12.8
Waldo	60	187	15.7	7.1	45	1,163	168.4	36.4	93	789	46.2	13.3
Washington	31	D	D	D	36	994	359.2	40.7	80	558	28.2	7.8
York	414	2,078	356.0	106.6	243	D	2,763.3	D	769	8,048	562.4	164.0
MARYLAND	19,714	244,710	50,024.9	20,161.2	3,096	100,079	39,533.0	5,908.9	11,344	204,222	12,516.8	3410.5
Allegany	96	486	42.7	18.3	52	2,547	D	119.2	181	D	D	D
Anne Arundel	2,027	24,815	5,787.2	2,467.9	275	11,547	4,456.9	993.6	1,158	25,939	1,564.0	419.4
Baltimore	2,692	24,678	3,990.9	1,657.7	451	16,807	8,066.7	1,003.7	1,578	27,158	1,555.8	415.4
Calvert	215	1,286	162.5	54.7	38	455	84.1	18.8	146	D	D	D
Caroline	38	D	D	D	28	1,167	302.3	42.8	36	D	D	D
Carroll	494	2,471	324.9	125.6	124	3,402	1,019.4	178.4	262	5,810	246.8	73.1
Cecil	155	570	52.7	19.1	49	4,496	1,989.3	312.3	176	2,792	154.1	41.7
Charles	273	1,979	311.6	127.5	43	399	84.0	18.4	244	D	D	D
Dorchester	53	169	17.8	5.2	44	2,546	843.1	93.7	58	D	D	D
Frederick	845	6,686	1,098.7	427.9	163	6,026	3,236.1	354.3	441	8,452	449.6	130.0
Garrett	53	397	37.4	17.3	50	1,128	D	39.6	74	D	D	D
Harford	697	D	D	D	137	4,058	1,866.8	207.2	394	7,960	390.9	104.7
Howard	1,883	35,086	10,616.5	3,126.2	186	5,013	1,538.2	276.8	543	11,000	610.9	177.1
Kent	51	D	D	D	29	945	360.0	50.7	74	D	D	D
Montgomery	5,701	74,255	14,389.9	6,751.1	381	8,233	2,172.6	619.7	1,818	31,526	2,080.0	571.8
Prince George's	1,662	26,331	4,349.1	1,903.9	264	7,291	2,216.8	424.1	1,269	23,872	1,685.5	436.2
Queen Anne's	158	D	D	D	49	921	208.3	41.8	94	2,111	113.0	33.7

Table B. States and Counties — Health Care and Social Assistance, Other Services, Nonemployer Businesses, and Residential Construction

STATE County	Health care and social assistance, 2012				Other services, 2012				Nonemployer businesses, 2015		Value of residential construction authorized by building permits, 2017	
	Number of establishments	Number of employees	Receipts (mil dol)	Annual payroll (mil dol)	Number of establishments	Number of employees	Receipts (mil dol)	Annual payroll (mil dol)	Number	Receipts (mil dol)	New construction ($1,000)	Number of housing units
	159	160	161	162	163	164	165	166	167	168	169	170
LOUISIANA— Cont'd												
Orleans	861	21,761	2,667.4	964.2	578	4,297	791.8	139.5	37,229	1,549.0	137,093	660
Ouachita	629	14,085	1,354.2	483.6	229	1,533	141.0	41.4	12,655	515.3	119,797	612
Plaquemines	21	468	40.0	17.7	44	D	D	D	2,408	135.4	11,412	45
Pointe Coupee	35	709	49.3	19.3	28	D	D	D	1,526	59.9	14,177	52
Rapides	506	14,112	1,514.4	554.9	198	1,018	104.1	27.5	7,967	363.6	52,426	246
Red River	15	444	37.8	11.4	6	D	D	D	486	14.5	0	0
Richland	80	1,783	100.9	40.6	18	D	D	D	1,453	53.5	2,918	34
Sabine	44	846	53.5	20.5	22	79	19.5	2.2	1,324	56.0	7,628	43
St. Bernard	51	D	D	D	37	D	D	D	3,502	138.9	19,931	112
St. Charles	65	D	D	D	50	D	D	D	4,022	168.8	27,704	130
St. Helena	14	D	D	D	7	D	D	D	839	19.7	7,304	41
St. James	28	764	69.8	29.3	16	D	D	D	1,316	41.3	14,995	55
St. John the Baptist	70	D	D	D	39	367	57.3	16.1	3,124	90.6	7,591	46
St. Landry	289	6,071	433.5	172.0	77	361	31.7	8.9	5,723	215.5	25,717	121
St. Martin	79	1,675	79.2	37.7	44	126	20.5	4.3	4,364	154.9	31,903	174
St. Mary	115	2,094	164.1	64.7	89	523	65.0	19.2	3,865	142.9	5,419	21
St. Tammany	791	14,504	1,581.8	607.7	356	1,993	219.0	60.3	23,003	1,185.3	333,801	1438
Tangipahoa	301	8,143	655.2	261.4	149	966	98.1	25.5	9,340	324.9	135,452	983
Tensas	9	66	5.1	2.1	2	D	D	D	372	11.5	1,129	14
Terrebonne	284	6,992	704.8	288.9	175	1,449	232.6	73.0	8,102	373.6	34,730	139
Union	32	851	53.6	20.7	14	35	3.3	0.7	1,450	58.1	32,449	140
Vermilion	101	1,764	122.8	46.2	56	252	24.6	6.2	4,386	158.2	28,659	154
Vernon	77	2,010	222.5	85.8	41	170	15.3	3.6	2,034	77.2	10,646	54
Washington	84	2,309	171.6	73.6	28	106	10.0	2.3	2,905	101.6	13,886	89
Webster	86	2,332	173.5	65.1	39	250	29.9	7.2	2,563	103.3	9,274	40
West Baton Rouge	32	443	26.4	11.3	38	263	40.4	10.7	1,570	64.8	40,156	262
West Carroll	16	549	35.9	14.9	15	60	4.2	1.1	645	22.1	1,748	9
West Feliciana	24	462	36.9	13.6	10	D	D	D	753	24.8	17,990	50
Winn	38	957	67.2	29.2	18	D	D	D	668	38.1	0	0
MAINE	4,730	109,231	10,297.0	4,393.0	2,786	13,755	1,462.8	376.3	113,012	5,075.9	827,749	4358
Androscoggin	385	9,531	947.5	402.8	211	1,024	84.6	23.5	6,137	288.8	38,329	252
Aroostook	229	6,120	471.8	207.2	122	397	45.8	9.1	4,035	166.0	10,221	71
Cumberland	1,339	33,687	3,348.8	1,475.2	734	4,502	518.8	130.4	28,144	1,428.0	277,463	1404
Franklin	106	1,882	156.4	74.4	44	214	19.8	4.8	2,391	82.3	19,100	96
Hancock	159	3,144	306.6	127.7	140	686	101.2	21.7	7,621	356.1	37,028	172
Kennebec	464	13,374	1,293.6	552.0	289	1,265	139.0	37.9	8,395	321.4	46,363	283
Knox	163	3,022	256.5	104.8	126	593	66.9	19.1	5,919	306.2	18,187	95
Lincoln	113	1,800	144.6	51.5	81	547	51.7	16.2	4,652	183.0	24,071	97
Oxford	125	2,777	198.2	85.1	90	335	31.1	8.4	4,401	183.4	30,286	168
Penobscot	547	14,740	1,570.2	624.9	273	1,395	142.7	36.9	9,201	361.0	56,273	304
Piscataquis	36	1,508	106.4	51.6	25	92	6.6	1.9	1,149	41.1	6,283	11
Sagadahoc	116	1,375	80.7	36.0	59	266	27.3	6.9	3,213	126.0	21,817	124
Somerset	144	2,809	208.6	96.4	88	286	26.2	6.3	3,188	115.6	7,648	65
Waldo	113	1,622	148.9	65.4	82	264	26.3	6.4	3,853	134.2	17,901	93
Washington	108	2,058	137.6	66.4	51	209	19.7	4.3	3,776	185.8	5,893	41
York	583	9,782	920.8	371.5	371	1,680	155.0	42.5	16,937	797.2	198,536	989
MARYLAND	16,000	359,734	40,821.9	16,319.9	9,978	79,391	10,879.7	2,928.5	475,518	20,715.5	3,257,334	16,224
Allegany	250	6,283	616.1	235.0	139	780	58.0	16.9	3,031	109.0	4,533	21
Anne Arundel	1,272	26,683	2,975.3	1,196.9	1,077	8,665	902.9	291.8	41,227	1,986.8	358,970	2406
Baltimore	2,619	58,216	6,062.4	2,458.5	1,376	9,983	1,044.2	295.7	65,395	2,916.2	289,120	1376
Calvert	181	3,475	342.2	149.7	122	773	59.6	20.1	6,447	274.2	60,380	263
Caroline	46	826	44.6	23.3	48	226	23.7	7.6	2,575	109.0	13,030	55
Carroll	459	9,821	950.3	358.3	355	2,195	180.2	57.5	12,230	536.0	86,351	312
Cecil	196	4,679	534.5	259.0	164	867	68.1	20.9	5,613	246.1	22,865	99
Charles	325	4,598	456.6	190.4	213	1,353	113.6	35.7	10,522	363.0	155,274	682
Dorchester	84	1,826	158.1	65.8	68	360	19.7	5.3	2,410	93.5	8,835	43
Frederick	613	11,380	1,206.1	516.3	426	2,837	348.7	93.7	18,267	839.1	424,948	1893
Garrett	76	1,797	118.6	52.0	73	1,219	106.6	47.9	2,373	106.7	23,687	67
Harford	594	10,550	1,029.1	406.1	422	2,691	227.0	90.5	16,506	712.2	161,547	886
Howard	928	14,235	1,406.4	600.2	509	4,399	552.9	179.8	26,462	1,379.7	239,659	1219
Kent	74	1,374	115.6	47.4	44	172	19.5	4.8	1,768	83.5	8,782	33
Montgomery	3,584	61,807	7,227.2	3,069.1	1,891	19,109	4,325.3	1,001.8	108,980	5,622.5	385,024	1637
Prince George's	1,812	31,493	3,126.4	1,249.8	1,126	8,923	996.2	297.7	73,775	2,181.5	507,945	2618
Queen Anne's	85	1,064	74.1	34.4	103	526	45.1	12.7	4,704	272.1	50,339	203

Table B. States and Counties — Government Employment and Payroll, and Local Government Finances

STATE County	Government employment and payroll, 2012									Local government finances				
			March payroll (percent of total)							General revenue				
												Taxes		
													Per capita[1] (dollars)	
	Full-time equivalent employees	March payroll (dollars)	Administration, judicial, and legal	Police and corrections	Fire protection	Highways and transportation	Health and welfare	Natural resources and utilities	Education and libraries	Total (mil dol)	Inter-governmental (mil dol)	Total (mil dol)	Total	Property
	171	172	173	174	175	176	177	178	179	180	181	182	183	184
LOUISIANA— Cont'd														
Orleans	7,189	28,500,562	12.7	30.3	9.1	2.5	3.8	25.1	9.9	1,968.9	669.4	766.2	2,075	1020
Ouachita	7,210	21,316,630	7.2	10.3	3.6	2.2	3.7	5.2	67.2	636.4	302.9	268.8	1,730	618
Plaquemines	1,620	5,259,702	13.4	13.1	0.6	7.9	7.0	6.2	48.6	320.9	176.8	96.4	4,031	2274
Pointe Coupee	1,063	2,905,856	7.3	13.8	0.0	1.6	21.6	5.3	50.2	93.0	34.1	31.6	1,391	766
Rapides	5,615	17,417,361	10.4	15.6	7.9	3.6	1.4	5.7	52.6	487.4	230.0	195.3	1,475	567
Red River	533	1,454,876	5.8	37.4	0.0	1.9	0.9	1.0	50.4	43.6	18.0	22.1	2,455	992
Richland	1,229	3,799,353	5.9	17.8	0.1	3.2	35.8	2.3	34.3	105.4	49.7	25.9	1,238	508
Sabine	818	2,028,527	9.4	18.3	0.0	4.8	3.6	7.0	55.7	96.4	47.5	40.6	1,668	405
St. Bernard	1,804	5,761,067	8.7	16.2	6.9	6.4	1.4	5.2	54.8	484.3	396.4	68.9	1,655	655
St. Charles	3,451	12,023,950	5.4	15.1	0.0	1.8	10.8	8.5	57.6	387.0	80.9	211.6	4,016	2217
St. Helena	456	1,219,647	8.6	9.7	0.0	3.8	45.3	1.3	30.5	32.8	13.8	7.5	676	349
St. James	1,306	4,803,097	7.4	11.1	0.0	2.6	16.4	8.2	49.6	231.2	42.5	70.5	3,247	1994
St. John the Baptist	1,701	5,496,602	10.6	10.0	0.0	8.8	0.1	9.7	60.5	229.3	53.3	82.6	1,845	913
St. Landry	4,416	14,852,877	5.9	10.1	3.0	2.4	26.6	3.1	48.4	409.3	165.3	100.0	1,196	372
St. Martin	1,824	5,579,531	5.5	14.8	0.1	2.7	7.9	2.9	65.6	147.8	80.2	54.1	1,026	489
St. Mary	3,043	9,174,661	6.1	12.3	1.5	2.5	10.9	8.1	57.1	251.5	102.3	102.4	1,907	1061
St. Tammany	10,707	35,822,862	5.7	10.3	0.3	2.6	33.9	2.1	44.3	1,250.6	404.2	450.6	1,882	995
Tangipahoa	6,393	23,444,209	4.2	6.0	1.2	1.7	46.4	1.8	37.5	621.2	213.8	128.9	1,044	366
Tensas	264	627,291	16.3	4.0	0.0	4.9	1.7	3.9	68.6	27.3	17.2	7.3	1,474	872
Terrebonne	5,509	18,140,503	3.6	8.6	1.2	1.4	31.1	4.6	49.2	603.6	234.4	173.9	1,554	551
Union	834	2,308,579	6.3	18.6	0.2	2.1	11.0	6.9	53.9	62.9	32.1	20.7	923	359
Vermilion	2,406	8,239,940	6.2	8.3	1.8	3.2	23.4	6.7	50.2	227.6	95.5	73.9	1,258	572
Vernon	2,133	5,249,110	6.4	9.9	1.2	3.6	0.1	1.9	76.0	155.1	98.2	46.0	855	294
Washington	1,946	5,729,429	5.2	6.2	1.5	2.7	14.9	1.9	66.9	160.0	81.0	45.0	964	454
Webster	1,523	4,175,873	6.3	15.2	1.4	3.3	0.1	7.0	65.3	133.5	64.2	57.4	1,402	613
West Baton Rouge	1,000	3,133,887	7.9	4.1	2.2	2.9	2.9	12.2	62.7	112.9	36.3	55.4	2,296	1199
West Carroll	438	1,121,168	6.5	2.8	0.0	4.1	3.9	2.4	79.0	46.7	23.8	13.0	1,133	428
West Feliciana	748	2,572,616	10.2	10.9	0.2	3.9	16.8	3.4	53.6	68.8	21.1	29.6	1,922	1366
Winn	679	1,633,669	7.5	13.5	1.8	3.1	0.7	8.9	63.3	42.7	25.9	13.6	909	416
MAINE	X	X	X	X	X	X	X	X	X	X	X	X	X	X
Androscoggin	3,959	13,779,680	4.1	8.3	4.8	4.2	2.0	5.1	70.2	355.6	153.6	163.3	1,517	1507
Aroostook	3,302	10,418,372	5.5	4.9	2.0	3.8	16.3	5.3	61.4	264.2	111.0	83.6	1,180	1174
Cumberland	10,861	40,790,587	5.2	9.0	5.8	4.8	5.4	6.8	61.0	1,129.5	280.4	610.0	2,149	2117
Franklin	1,043	3,602,511	5.4	8.2	1.3	4.4	1.5	4.1	73.6	80.5	29.1	43.4	1,418	1414
Hancock	1,982	6,326,482	6.8	6.5	2.5	3.7	1.0	4.2	73.3	197.6	39.3	137.4	2,518	2502
Kennebec	4,312	13,281,549	5.2	7.6	3.0	3.6	1.2	5.8	72.6	343.2	144.3	155.9	1,280	1266
Knox	1,307	4,815,634	8.9	8.8	3.1	4.4	3.3	2.5	67.5	129.9	19.5	90.5	2,283	2267
Lincoln	1,389	4,505,799	5.7	4.0	0.5	2.0	2.2	3.4	80.2	135.6	34.2	88.2	2,582	2572
Oxford	2,319	7,212,500	4.7	5.3	2.5	4.9	0.8	2.5	78.4	186.7	69.4	103.9	1,807	1800
Penobscot	5,352	18,128,721	5.6	7.8	5.2	7.6	1.3	6.1	64.9	466.9	185.2	205.7	1,338	1324
Piscataquis	1,109	4,071,817	4.7	4.0	0.2	1.9	47.9	1.9	38.2	99.6	35.5	26.2	1,514	1504
Sagadahoc	1,209	4,568,672	5.0	6.6	2.7	2.7	1.0	3.8	74.9	131.3	38.0	73.7	2,093	2078
Somerset	2,667	8,560,527	3.4	6.5	1.2	2.5	0.5	1.6	82.6	185.9	90.8	84.4	1,626	1622
Waldo	1,256	3,892,726	8.1	6.4	0.8	2.8	1.9	2.4	74.8	102.4	36.3	56.7	1,460	1455
Washington	1,219	3,492,782	6.9	7.3	1.2	2.6	3.5	5.0	70.9	100.0	42.2	47.1	1,450	1445
York	7,047	25,948,699	5.4	9.0	4.1	3.0	1.2	5.9	70.5	637.1	181.5	390.3	1,961	1938
MARYLAND	X	X	X	X	X	X	X	X	X	X	X	X	X	X
Allegany	2,826	11,858,505	3.5	6.0	2.0	3.5	0.4	6.3	75.4	272.3	133.1	86.3	1,167	773
Anne Arundel	17,468	83,267,035	4.0	8.6	6.2	4.4	2.8	3.8	67.7	2,076.5	568.1	1,135.3	2,062	1152
Baltimore	26,532	122,265,325	4.1	12.0	5.2	1.3	3.0	2.6	69.5	2,786.6	910.6	1,567.3	1,917	1039
Calvert	3,256	15,584,064	4.8	7.8	0.1	1.9	2.8	4.8	74.3	388.6	117.7	224.0	2,500	1684
Caroline	1,269	4,767,293	5.8	8.2	0.0	2.2	3.3	4.6	71.4	117.5	59.9	45.1	1,379	973
Carroll	5,844	23,979,765	5.5	5.5	0.7	1.6	1.0	2.9	80.6	641.8	205.1	366.2	2,190	1331
Cecil	3,436	14,149,378	4.6	8.1	1.2	1.6	2.8	2.0	76.9	375.0	153.4	172.0	1,691	1137
Charles	5,864	27,330,417	4.8	12.4	0.0	0.6	3.1	3.7	73.5	663.0	226.7	318.3	2,114	1346
Dorchester	1,251	4,831,214	5.1	13.0	0.0	3.8	4.8	2.5	66.5	134.8	62.3	54.8	1,683	1219
Frederick	10,553	47,827,090	4.3	6.4	4.0	1.9	4.9	3.7	73.1	1,033.9	315.3	529.5	2,210	1385
Garrett	1,283	4,466,807	6.7	4.8	0.8	10.6	1.8	3.9	70.1	214.5	59.8	111.5	3,734	2998
Harford	8,483	39,111,192	6.1	9.6	0.3	2.6	1.8	4.3	73.8	952.9	307.2	524.4	2,109	1291
Howard	12,202	62,646,998	4.3	7.7	1.9	1.0	4.2	4.1	75.2	1,532.5	372.1	962.2	3,214	1692
Kent	708	2,731,612	8.4	10.5	0.0	4.3	1.1	5.9	64.0	74.9	18.1	46.4	2,298	1677
Montgomery	38,590	236,750,984	3.3	7.6	4.0	3.0	6.2	10.6	64.3	5,240.0	1,125.4	3,182.9	3,168	1422
Prince George's	27,062	140,810,958	4.4	15.2	3.4	1.2	4.0	1.6	67.6	3,399.7	1,344.2	1,551.8	1,761	1007
Queen Anne's	1,906	8,133,110	4.6	6.4	0.2	2.6	7.3	5.6	72.6	207.2	65.4	111.4	2,293	1412

1. Based on the resident population estimated as of July 1 of the year shown.

Table B. States and Counties — Local Government Finances, Government Employment, and Income Taxes

	Local government finances (cont.)							Debt outstanding		Government employment, 2016			Individual income tax returns, 2015		
	Direct general expenditure														
				Percent of total for:											
STATE County	Total (mil dol)	Per capita[1] (dollars)	Education	Health and hospitals	Police protection	Public welfare	Highways	Total (mil dol)	Per capita[1] (dollars)	Federal civilian	Federal military	State and local	Number of returns	Mean adjusted gross income	Mean income tax
	185	186	187	188	189	190	191	192	193	194	195	196	197	198	199
LOUISIANA— Cont'd															
Orleans	1,848.6	5,006	12.2	0.7	7.8	0.1	6.6	2,707.7	7,333	9,377	3,742	25,363	164,320	60,569	9283
Ouachita	687.9	4,428	53.4	2.3	5.8	0.1	2.6	489.7	3,152	441	652	10,277	66,160	52,335	6301
Plaquemines	321.2	13,429	37.8	2.1	4.1	0.5	1.0	163.7	6,844	658	440	1,673	10,110	68,275	9472
Pointe Coupee	90.9	4,001	37.3	22.2	6.6	0.4	2.1	45.9	2,021	61	95	1,082	9,710	51,999	6026
Rapides	504.4	3,810	49.3	0.1	8.4	0.1	5.3	504.4	3,811	2,196	554	9,829	57,260	52,477	6057
Red River	47.2	5,251	59.8	0.0	3.7	0.0	1.4	5.0	560	25	36	509	3,360	50,189	4885
Richland	109.4	5,231	36.1	29.1	3.4	0.1	5.6	51.6	2,464	82	83	958	8,240	46,592	5086
Sabine	85.0	3,493	69.8	0.2	4.8	0.0	5.6	27.9	1,145	39	101	1,261	8,740	53,276	5392
St. Bernard	516.0	12,393	31.7	3.5	2.5	0.2	1.3	186.9	4,490	47	195	2,280	16,950	40,305	3669
St. Charles	382.3	7,256	43.1	9.6	4.8	0.3	5.3	894.4	16,978	150	225	3,270	24,090	64,644	8101
St. Helena	32.3	2,917	31.4	38.0	4.6	0.0	8.8	5.1	457	10	45	612	5,310	39,558	3297
St. James	156.3	7,194	43.5	11.8	3.9	0.6	2.5	1,439.8	66,281	38	92	1,440	9,860	55,950	6178
St. John the Baptist	252.0	5,630	34.8	0.5	4.6	0.5	5.1	1,281.3	28,626	101	186	2,052	19,720	47,665	4756
St. Landry	414.8	4,958	43.1	29.0	4.8	0.0	3.0	98.9	1,182	168	357	5,070	35,620	53,025	6355
St. Martin	141.4	2,682	59.3	0.9	8.4	0.2	5.1	123.9	2,349	65	229	1,839	23,240	48,695	5193
St. Mary	245.0	4,562	42.6	10.2	6.7	0.2	3.8	139.7	2,602	134	341	4,411	22,840	48,650	5309
St. Tammany	1,244.6	5,198	37.0	28.1	5.6	0.3	4.8	977.9	4,084	501	1,086	13,678	111,730	70,694	10,391
Tangipahoa	692.4	5,610	29.5	47.0	3.7	0.0	2.7	361.5	2,929	366	547	10,182	50,700	48,472	5160
Tensas	26.2	5,284	36.9	2.0	4.8	0.0	4.9	26.6	5,361	20	20	306	1,830	38,578	4268
Terrebonne	620.6	5,546	29.9	28.6	4.4	0.3	2.9	301.9	2,698	277	524	5,175	47,880	57,991	7499
Union	60.2	2,685	49.1	8.9	5.4	0.2	6.0	5.9	265	94	95	725	8,920	48,098	4751
Vermilion	223.8	3,812	42.2	20.8	4.9	2.1	5.1	37.7	643	152	268	2,978	24,620	53,049	5933
Vernon	159.1	2,953	69.0	0.3	5.5	0.1	5.4	78.1	1,451	2,132	7,795	2,328	20,700	46,502	3963
Washington	160.8	3,445	54.9	14.8	4.7	0.0	5.1	63.6	1,363	102	192	2,525	16,330	40,442	3351
Webster	135.1	3,299	55.0	0.5	6.2	0.1	4.2	123.2	3,010	105	165	1,992	16,410	45,938	4798
West Baton Rouge	118.0	4,896	36.6	0.9	8.9	0.6	4.0	182.2	7,559	94	109	1,574	11,680	58,466	6774
West Carroll	47.4	4,114	52.9	20.0	3.8	2.1	3.9	8.1	701	33	46	723	4,230	45,100	4134
West Feliciana	67.9	4,410	41.6	23.6	6.1	0.1	2.4	71.0	4,612	16	43	2,386	4,570	66,946	8929
Winn	46.7	3,110	63.7	0.5	5.9	0.0	4.7	11.5	766	56	54	739	5,050	50,890	4724
MAINE	X	X	X	X	X	X	X	X	X	15,056	6,805	84,822	645,700	55,104	6279
Androscoggin	348.5	3,239	53.0	0.2	4.0	0.4	5.6	353.5	3,285	274	329	5,065	49,210	47,646	4629
Aroostook	269.7	3,805	46.4	17.9	2.8	0.3	7.2	101.0	1,426	1,205	206	4,918	30,290	43,159	3953
Cumberland	1,113.8	3,923	43.9	0.9	4.4	2.5	5.5	1,208.5	4,257	1,954	2,259	18,120	151,910	69,930	9539
Franklin	104.7	3,419	60.2	0.7	3.7	0.2	8.5	100.7	3,287	108	90	2,010	13,080	45,184	4343
Hancock	188.4	3,453	54.5	0.6	3.0	0.2	9.3	154.0	2,823	338	263	2,945	27,280	53,877	5872
Kennebec	348.6	2,861	58.7	0.5	3.4	0.3	6.1	214.9	1,764	2,184	407	14,300	58,130	50,905	5333
Knox	129.2	3,257	48.4	1.5	4.4	0.2	9.5	77.3	1,950	112	199	2,459	20,240	53,728	6124
Lincoln	134.0	3,920	66.7	0.7	2.9	0.4	7.8	90.9	2,659	80	128	1,544	17,700	53,466	5802
Oxford	185.2	3,222	64.2	0.5	2.9	0.4	8.6	87.1	1,516	132	176	3,025	25,590	42,906	3825
Penobscot	527.2	3,429	48.1	1.1	3.8	0.2	4.2	409.3	2,662	1,187	465	12,617	67,800	50,967	5551
Piscataquis	98.3	5,686	30.4	44.3	1.9	0.2	4.5	37.9	2,194	51	52	1,331	7,230	41,169	3687
Sagadahoc	124.2	3,528	56.8	0.2	3.5	0.3	5.7	98.8	2,807	359	126	1,494	18,280	57,846	6329
Somerset	179.7	3,461	69.3	0.2	2.5	0.2	6.3	81.7	1,574	186	157	2,375	22,040	43,672	4066
Waldo	97.2	2,504	58.5	1.5	3.5	0.6	10.7	48.3	1,244	88	129	1,500	18,220	46,382	4457
Washington	103.7	3,194	54.3	2.0	2.7	0.1	8.6	31.8	979	345	155	2,363	13,980	40,588	3609
York	629.4	3,163	57.4	0.5	5.3	0.3	6.4	355.5	1,787	6,453	1,664	8,756	104,780	56,962	6356
MARYLAND	X	X	X	X	X	X	X	X	X	175,205	50,125	343,113	2,963,510	75,003	10,302
Allegany	267.9	3,619	60.6	0.8	3.3	0.6	4.9	173.8	2,348	500	260	5,587	29,180	46,609	4521
Anne Arundel	2,207.3	4,010	54.8	2.4	5.2	1.0	4.4	1,723.1	3,130	42,402	17,916	33,824	283,920	83,396	11,821
Baltimore	3,004.9	3,676	56.3	1.7	6.9	0.4	2.5	3,573.5	4,372	15,125	2,668	40,657	414,570	74,043	10,379
Calvert	401.4	4,479	58.4	0.8	3.8	1.0	3.2	210.1	2,344	132	330	4,076	44,430	80,010	9999
Caroline	111.8	3,416	59.2	0.3	4.3	0.1	4.2	60.3	1,842	71	105	1,688	15,400	46,780	4413
Carroll	634.2	3,793	62.1	0.8	3.5	1.2	4.4	467.0	2,793	300	537	7,910	83,670	76,828	9572
Cecil	362.9	3,569	58.9	0.9	5.1	1.4	5.0	330.6	3,251	1,873	327	4,658	46,800	60,414	6601
Charles	647.7	4,301	63.4	0.9	8.5	0.6	1.8	442.9	2,941	2,286	1,077	7,428	78,770	69,879	7733
Dorchester	119.9	3,683	50.4	0.7	6.1	0.1	5.4	66.4	2,040	178	103	2,140	15,230	45,109	4442
Frederick	1,022.3	4,267	56.6	0.7	5.2	3.4	3.4	1,148.1	4,792	3,679	1,922	11,662	122,180	75,181	9488
Garrett	204.6	6,852	39.8	0.8	9.6	0.1	12.7	131.5	4,404	64	93	1,609	13,560	47,948	4857
Harford	983.7	3,957	58.8	0.5	6.5	0.7	5.0	907.9	3,652	11,062	2,231	9,475	124,900	72,563	8845
Howard	1,583.8	5,289	57.3	0.6	5.3	0.9	2.7	1,520.4	5,078	640	1,175	16,329	152,850	105,370	16,546
Kent	68.7	3,405	43.8	1.6	9.3	1.4	5.8	56.0	2,776	64	59	1,011	9,330	66,485	6601
Montgomery	5,475.9	5,450	50.5	1.8	5.2	3.2	3.5	5,936.8	5,909	48,314	7,703	42,116	527,500	104,549	17,630
Prince George's	3,659.3	4,153	49.8	1.7	6.7	0.8	3.4	2,724.6	3,092	26,706	7,641	64,970	487,090	54,933	5421
Queen Anne's	220.6	4,540	56.7	1.1	3.1	1.6	2.2	152.9	3,146	91	157	2,541	24,200	78,842	10,592

1. Based on the resident population estimated as of July 1 of the year shown.

Table B. States and Counties — Land Area and Population

State / county code	CBSA code[1]	County code[2]	STATE County	Land area[3] (sq. mi)	Total persons 2017	Rank	Per square mile	White	Black	American Indian, Alaska Native	Asian and Pacific Islancer	Percent Hispanic or Latino[4]	Under 5 years	5 to 17 years	18 to 24 years	25 to 34 years	35 to 44 years	45 to 54 years
				1	2	3	4	5	6	7	8	9	10	11	12	13	14	15
			MARYLAND— Cont'd															
2,4037	15,680	3	St. Mary's	358.6	112,667	542	314.2	77.0	16.1	0.9	4.1	5.2	6.5	18.0	9.3	14.0	12.4	14.5
2,4039	41,540	2	Somerset	319.7	25,918	1,565	81.1	53.2	43.2	0.9	1.4	3.6	4.8	12.3	17.0	13.5	11.0	12.0
2,4041	20,660	6	Talbot	268.5	37,103	1,246	138.2	79.0	13.2	0.5	1.8	7.1	4.6	13.7	6.2	10.0	9.2	12.4
2,4043	25,180	2	Washington	457.8	150,578	438	328.9	81.4	13.1	0.6	2.5	5.0	5.8	16.3	8.0	13.0	12.3	14.5
2,4045	41,540	2	Wicomico	374.4	102,923	586	274.9	64.9	27.7	0.6	3.8	5.4	6.0	16.0	14.9	12.1	10.9	11.9
2,4047	41,540	2	Worcester	468.3	51,690	966	110.4	81.5	14.1	0.6	2.0	3.5	4.4	13.1	6.6	10.3	9.3	13.1
2,4510	12,580	1	Baltimore city	80.9	611,648	108	7,560.5	29.1	63.3	0.9	3.4	5.3	6.4	14.3	9.7	19.2	12.3	12.0
2,5000		0	MASSACHUSETTS	7,800.9	6,859,819	X	879.4	73.8	8.0	0.6	7.6	11.9	5.3	14.7	10.2	14.2	12.1	13.8
2,5001	12,700	3	Barnstable	394.2	213,444	312	541.5	91.8	3.8	1.2	2.1	3.0	3.6	11.5	7.1	8.9	8.7	12.8
2,5003	38,340	3	Berkshire	926.9	126,313	500	136.3	90.4	4.2	0.6	2.3	4.6	4.2	12.9	9.6	10.5	10.3	13.5
2,5005	39,300	1	Bristol	553.1	561,483	120	1,015.2	84.9	5.4	0.7	3.0	8.0	5.2	15.5	9.2	12.7	12.2	14.6
2,5007	47,240	7	Dukes	103.2	17,325	1,958	167.9	89.7	5.4	2.3	1.9	3.5	4.6	13.0	6.6	10.7	11.1	14.0
2,5009	14,460	1	Essex	492.4	785,205	81	1,594.6	71.7	4.1	0.4	4.1	21.0	5.6	15.8	9.3	12.3	11.8	14.2
2,5011	24,640	4	Franklin	699.2	70,702	762	101.1	92.5	2.0	1.0	2.4	4.0	4.4	13.2	7.1	11.8	11.5	13.5
2,5013	44,140	2	Hampden	617.0	469,818	147	761.5	64.1	8.8	0.6	3.0	25.3	5.5	16.2	10.5	13.2	11.4	13.1
2,5015	44,140	2	Hampshire	527.2	161,834	404	307.0	85.4	3.6	0.6	6.8	5.6	3.5	11.4	23.4	10.6	9.6	11.8
2,5017	14,460	1	Middlesex	817.7	1,602,947	22	1,960.3	74.3	5.9	0.4	13.5	8.0	5.4	14.5	9.9	15.4	13.0	13.8
2,5019		7	Nantucket	46.1	11,229	2,339	243.6	74.3	10.6	0.5	1.8	14.4	6.5	14.4	6.5	14.4	15.4	15.1
2,5021	14,460	1	Norfolk	396.1	700,322	92	1,768.0	77.0	7.5	0.4	12.4	4.6	5.4	15.8	8.7	12.7	12.5	14.5
2,5023	14,460	1	Plymouth	658.8	515,142	134	781.9	83.8	11.3	0.7	2.2	3.9	5.3	16.3	8.6	10.8	11.4	15.1
2,5025	14,460	1	Suffolk	58.2	797,939	79	13,710.3	47.0	21.7	0.7	9.9	22.9	5.3	11.5	13.7	23.3	12.9	11.3
2,5027	49,340	2	Worcester	1,510.6	826,116	73	546.9	78.5	5.5	0.6	5.8	11.5	5.4	15.9	9.8	12.8	12.0	14.7
2,6000		0	MICHIGAN	56,559.4	9,962,311	X	176.1	77.2	15.0	1.3	3.8	5.1	5.8	16.1	9.7	12.7	11.6	13.3
2,6001		9	Alcona	674.7	10,351	2,398	15.3	96.9	0.9	1.3	0.6	1.5	3.0	9.7	5.1	6.8	7.6	12.0
2,6003		7	Alger	915.0	9,121	2,492	10.0	86.7	8.0	6.3	0.7	1.4	3.6	11.5	7.0	11.3	11.1	12.8
2,6005	26,090	4	Allegan	825.2	116,447	530	141.1	89.9	2.0	1.2	1.1	7.4	6.2	18.2	7.9	11.8	11.8	13.7
2,6007	10,980	7	Alpena	571.9	28,462	1,473	49.8	97.0	1.0	1.1	0.8	1.3	4.8	14.0	7.2	10.2	10.6	13.0
2,6009		9	Antrim	475.7	23,292	1,666	49.0	96.1	0.7	1.8	0.6	2.3	4.6	13.8	6.7	8.9	9.1	12.7
2,6011		8	Arenac	363.2	15,045	2,093	41.4	96.0	0.9	1.8	0.7	2.1	4.7	13.4	6.7	9.7	9.8	12.6
2,6013		9	Baraga	898.4	8,441	2,554	9.4	76.8	8.5	16.7	0.8	1.6	4.1	14.0	8.2	11.9	11.6	13.6
2,6015	24,340	2	Barry	553.1	60,586	862	109.5	95.5	1.0	1.0	0.7	3.0	5.5	16.7	7.9	11.1	11.4	13.9
2,6017	13,020	3	Bay	442.3	104,239	579	235.7	91.9	2.7	1.1	0.9	5.4	5.0	15.4	7.7	12.2	11.3	13.1
2,6019	45,900	9	Benzie	319.7	17,573	1,944	55.0	94.8	1.0	2.2	0.7	2.6	4.6	13.8	6.3	10.0	9.7	12.7
2,6021	35,660	2	Berrien	567.8	154,259	427	271.7	77.0	16.0	1.2	2.7	5.5	5.9	16.1	8.2	11.6	11.3	13.0
2,6023	17,740	6	Branch	506.4	43,410	1,105	85.7	92.1	2.6	1.0	1.3	4.7	6.0	17.4	7.5	11.8	11.8	13.1
2,6025	12,980	3	Calhoun	706.3	134,128	474	189.9	80.5	12.8	1.4	3.3	5.3	6.3	16.8	8.9	12.1	11.7	12.9
2,6027	43,780	2	Cass	490.1	51,381	968	104.8	88.9	6.8	2.1	1.3	3.9	5.0	15.9	7.8	10.2	10.9	14.2
2,6029		7	Charlevoix	416.3	26,139	1,560	62.8	95.5	0.9	2.5	0.9	1.9	4.3	15.0	7.0	9.7	9.8	13.1
2,6031		7	Cheboygan	715.3	25,369	1,589	35.5	94.6	1.1	4.7	0.8	1.5	4.0	12.8	6.6	9.3	9.6	13.1
2,6033	42,300	7	Chippewa	1,558.5	37,711	1,230	24.2	74.5	7.4	19.7	1.7	1.9	4.8	13.6	11.9	13.1	12.5	12.9
2,6035		6	Clare	564.4	30,653	1,417	54.3	96.2	1.1	1.6	0.6	2.0	5.5	14.3	6.8	10.4	10.2	12.6
2,6037	29,620	2	Clinton	566.4	78,443	709	138.5	91.6	2.6	1.0	2.1	4.5	5.5	17.0	8.5	12.2	12.1	14.1
2,6039		7	Crawford	556.4	13,907	2,171	25.0	95.9	1.1	1.3	1.0	2.0	4.6	13.7	6.4	9.2	9.2	13.7
2,6041	21,540	5	Delta	1,171.1	35,965	1,275	30.7	95.2	0.9	4.1	0.9	1.3	5.1	14.9	6.8	9.7	10.5	12.7
2,6043	27,020	7	Dickinson	760.9	25,415	1,587	33.4	96.5	0.9	1.5	1.0	1.5	5.3	14.7	7.1	10.5	10.5	13.3
2,6045	29,620	2	Eaton	575.2	109,027	554	189.5	85.2	7.9	1.2	2.8	5.3	5.4	15.6	8.6	12.9	11.6	13.1
2,6047		7	Emmet	467.5	33,193	1,349	71.0	93.3	1.2	5.0	1.0	1.7	4.8	14.8	7.8	11.1	10.7	12.6
2,6049	22,420	2	Genesee	637.0	407,385	173	639.5	74.8	21.6	1.3	1.5	3.4	5.9	16.8	8.7	12.0	11.7	13.5
2,6051		6	Gladwin	501.8	25,234	1,597	50.3	96.8	0.8	1.1	0.6	1.7	5.2	13.6	6.4	9.2	9.3	13.0
2,6053		7	Gogebic	1,102.1	15,342	2,074	13.9	91.0	4.9	3.8	0.6	1.4	4.0	11.7	7.7	11.1	10.7	13.1
2,6055	45,900	5	Grand Traverse	464.3	91,807	640	197.7	94.5	1.3	1.9	1.2	2.9	5.3	15.1	7.5	12.7	11.7	13.0
2,6057	10,940	2	Gratiot	568.4	41,018	1,152	72.2	86.8	6.3	1.0	0.8	6.2	4.9	15.1	11.1	13.1	12.5	13.4
2,6059	25,880	6	Hillsdale	598.2	45,879	1,055	76.7	96.1	1.1	1.2	0.7	2.3	5.6	16.1	9.5	10.6	10.8	12.8
2,6061	26,340	5	Houghton	1,009.1	36,305	1,267	36.0	93.8	1.3	1.4	3.6	1.6	5.2	15.0	21.8	10.1	9.2	10.0
2,6063		7	Huron	836.1	31,280	1,401	37.4	96.1	0.8	0.8	0.8	2.4	4.8	14.4	7.0	9.5	9.7	13.0
2,6065	29,620	2	Ingham	556.1	290,186	239	521.8	73.3	13.7	1.3	7.8	7.7	5.7	14.2	19.6	14.1	11.0	10.9
2,6067	26,960	4	Ionia	571.3	64,291	825	112.5	89.5	5.2	1.0	0.8	4.9	5.8	16.7	9.3	13.6	13.0	13.9
2,6069		7	Iosco	549.1	25,162	1,602	45.8	95.5	1.2	1.7	1.1	2.2	4.6	12.1	6.0	9.1	8.6	12.3
2,6071		7	Iron	1,166.0	11,124	2,345	9.5	95.8	0.8	2.0	0.8	2.1	4.2	12.2	5.7	7.8	9.1	11.6
2,6073	34,380	4	Isabella	572.7	71,063	759	124.1	88.0	3.9	4.5	2.5	3.9	4.6	12.6	27.9	12.5	9.6	9.9
2,6075	27,100	3	Jackson	701.7	158,640	414	226.1	87.3	9.7	1.0	1.2	3.5	5.7	16.1	8.8	12.5	11.6	13.7
2,6077	28,020	2	Kalamazoo	562.2	262,985	260	467.8	80.5	13.3	1.2	3.5	4.9	6.0	15.7	15.6	13.5	11.5	11.3
2,6079	45,900	7	Kalkaska	559.7	17,634	1,942	31.5	95.9	1.1	1.9	0.9	2.1	5.2	15.7	6.9	11.3	11.2	13.4
2,6081	24,340	2	Kent	847.7	648,594	102	765.1	76.2	11.2	1.0	3.7	10.6	6.8	17.6	9.5	15.7	12.4	12.4

1. CBSA = Core Based Statistical Area. See Appendix A for explanation. See Appendix B for list of metropolitan areas with component counties. 2. County type code from the Economic Research Service of USDA Rural-Urban Continuum Codes. See Appendix A for definition. 3. Dry land or land partially or temporarily covered by water. 4. May be of any race.

STATE County	Age (percent) (cont.) 55 to 64 years	65 to 74 years	75 years and over	Percent female	Total persons 2000	2010	Percent change 2000-2010	2010-2017	Components of change, 2010-2017 Births	Deaths	Net Migration	Households, 2012-2016 Number	Persons per house-hold	Family house-holds	Percent Female family house-holder[1]	One person
	16	17	18	19	20	21	22	23	24	25	26	27	28	29	30	31
MARYLAND— Cont'd																
St. Mary's	12.7	7.5	5.0	50.1	86,211	105,148	22.0	7.2	10,397	5,532	2,666	38,978	2.77	71.5	11.3	22.7
Somerset	13.0	9.5	6.8	46.2	24,747	26,470	7.0	-2.1	1,848	1,908	-510	8,328	2.32	61.8	18.1	31.8
Talbot	15.5	15.2	13.1	52.5	33,812	37,782	11.7	-1.8	2,403	3,213	163	16,481	2.26	66.7	12.2	27.8
Washington	13.3	9.4	7.4	49.1	131,923	147,430	11.8	2.1	12,523	10,759	1,436	56,094	2.51	67.0	12.9	27.1
Wicomico	12.8	9.1	6.3	52.5	84,644	98,733	16.6	4.2	8,944	6,742	2,043	37,170	2.62	66.0	13.9	25.7
Worcester	16.1	15.5	11.8	51.4	46,543	51,451	10.5	0.5	3,192	4,456	1,544	21,010	2.41	63.9	10.6	30.4
Baltimore city	12.7	8.0	5.5	53.0	651,154	620,951	-4.6	-1.5	63,580	46,011	-26,559	242,416	2.46	51.4	21.8	39.0
MASSACHUSETTS	13.6	9.3	6.9	51.5	6,349,097	6,547,808	3.1	4.8	522,461	399,744	193,318	2,558,889	2.54	63.6	12.5	28.6
Barnstable	17.6	17.0	12.9	52.2	222,230	215,868	-2.9	-1.1	11,326	20,671	7,104	94,351	2.25	61.9	8.9	32.4
Berkshire	16.2	12.9	9.9	51.6	134,953	131,272	-2.7	-3.8	7,882	10,462	-2,325	54,854	2.22	59.9	12.2	33.7
Bristol	13.9	9.5	7.1	51.5	534,678	548,265	2.5	2.4	41,213	37,361	9,809	212,933	2.53	65.6	14.0	28.2
Dukes	16.6	15.2	8.1	50.9	14,987	16,535	10.3	4.8	1,161	1,016	643	6,134	2.75	61.8	9.5	32.6
Essex	14.3	9.6	7.1	51.8	723,419	743,172	2.7	5.7	61,278	47,032	28,395	288,291	2.61	66.8	13.7	27.5
Franklin	17.3	13.4	7.7	51.3	71,535	71,372	-0.2	-0.9	4,452	4,953	-134	30,389	2.28	59.2	9.8	31.1
Hampden	13.7	9.3	7.1	51.7	456,228	463,625	1.6	1.3	38,148	31,544	-329	177,153	2.56	64.9	17.7	29.0
Hampshire	13.3	10.1	6.5	53.4	152,251	158,078	3.8	2.4	7,817	8,838	4,707	58,448	2.36	58.1	10.2	30.5
Middlesex	13.0	8.5	6.5	51.1	1,465,396	1,503,017	2.6	6.6	126,845	80,858	55,092	587,735	2.57	64.7	9.9	26.7
Nantucket	13.2	8.9	5.8	49.1	9,520	10,172	6.8	10.4	1,065	445	425	3,836	2.72	60.0	7.4	31.2
Norfolk	13.9	9.2	7.4	51.9	650,308	670,968	3.2	4.4	52,516	41,189	18,514	260,061	2.59	65.9	9.9	27.4
Plymouth	14.8	10.5	7.1	51.4	472,822	494,949	4.7	4.1	37,309	31,775	15,075	182,252	2.72	71.2	12.8	24.1
Suffolk	10.4	6.7	5.0	51.6	689,807	722,136	4.7	10.5	68,574	34,278	41,738	299,658	2.40	49.6	16.7	36.1
Worcester	14.1	8.9	6.4	50.7	750,963	798,379	6.3	3.5	62,875	49,322	14,604	302,794	2.59	66.1	12.2	27.1
MICHIGAN	14.1	9.8	6.9	50.8	9,938,444	9,884,129	-0.5	0.8	822,434	669,034	-74,546	3,860,394	2.51	64.7	12.6	29.1
Alcona	20.1	19.9	16.0	49.6	11,719	10,942	-6.6	-5.4	440	1,331	302	4,973	2.08	62.7	5.8	33.3
Alger	17.9	14.8	10.0	45.0	9,862	9,601	-2.6	-5.0	418	829	-64	3,433	2.43	64.6	5.9	31.3
Allegan	14.4	9.8	6.2	50.1	105,665	111,410	5.4	4.5	9,839	6,765	1,998	42,097	2.67	73.2	9.1	21.8
Alpena	17.2	12.7	10.3	50.8	31,314	29,598	-5.5	-3.8	1,916	2,620	-413	12,670	2.24	63.0	10.7	31.7
Antrim	17.7	15.5	11.0	50.2	23,110	23,580	2.0	-1.2	1,440	1,957	245	9,841	2.33	69.9	7.4	25.4
Arenac	18.4	14.5	10.1	49.6	17,269	15,899	-7.9	-5.4	910	1,497	-255	6,514	2.32	65.9	8.5	29.3
Baraga	15.4	12.4	8.9	44.7	8,746	8,860	1.3	-4.7	552	737	-232	2,962	2.15	61.2	9.9	34.2
Barry	15.4	10.9	7.2	49.6	56,755	59,175	4.3	2.4	4,565	3,797	667	22,858	2.56	71.4	6.0	23.2
Bay	15.4	11.4	8.5	50.8	110,157	107,771	-2.2	-3.3	7,706	8,546	-2,644	43,714	2.39	63.6	11.9	30.1
Benzie	17.3	14.9	10.7	50.4	15,998	17,525	9.5	0.3	1,100	1,527	483	7,169	2.39	65.2	8.1	29.8
Berrien	14.7	11.0	8.3	51.0	162,453	156,817	-3.5	-1.6	13,168	12,229	-3,467	62,282	2.41	65.5	13.5	29.4
Branch	14.6	10.4	7.4	48.4	45,787	45,248	-1.2	-4.1	3,819	3,130	-2,570	16,118	2.57	67.7	9.5	26.2
Calhoun	13.9	9.9	7.5	51.1	137,985	136,148	-1.3	-1.5	11,991	10,605	-3,406	53,089	2.46	63.7	14.0	31.0
Cass	15.7	12.7	7.7	49.9	51,104	52,286	2.3	-1.7	3,484	3,737	-623	20,246	2.54	69.1	9.6	25.8
Charlevoix	17.4	14.1	9.5	50.6	26,090	25,949	-0.5	0.7	1,692	1,988	505	11,043	2.34	65.1	8.2	29.5
Cheboygan	17.9	15.6	11.0	50.2	26,448	26,150	-1.1	-3.0	1,456	2,321	102	11,185	2.26	66.6	10.1	29.0
Chippewa	13.7	10.0	7.4	44.6	38,543	38,673	0.3	-2.5	2,559	2,615	-924	13,905	2.44	61.7	9.3	30.9
Clare	16.7	14.2	9.3	50.1	31,252	30,926	-1.0	-0.9	2,348	2,857	249	12,918	2.33	64.5	10.8	30.6
Clinton	14.3	9.8	6.6	50.5	64,753	75,382	16.4	4.1	5,747	4,262	1,612	28,919	2.64	70.4	8.4	23.3
Crawford	18.3	14.7	10.3	49.4	14,273	14,080	-1.4	-1.2	865	1,227	199	6,064	2.25	65.0	8.3	28.8
Delta	16.7	13.2	10.4	50.3	38,520	37,069	-3.8	-3.0	2,647	3,073	-655	15,816	2.28	63.4	8.9	31.3
Dickinson	17.0	11.7	9.9	50.1	27,472	26,168	-4.7	-2.9	1,812	2,222	-332	11,175	2.28	65.9	10.3	29.9
Eaton	14.6	11.0	7.1	51.0	103,655	107,759	4.0	1.2	8,460	7,040	-90	43,908	2.43	64.7	10.8	29.7
Emmet	16.4	13.0	8.8	50.5	31,437	32,694	4.0	1.5	2,203	2,443	767	14,144	2.30	65.2	8.0	27.9
Genesee	14.3	9.9	7.1	51.8	436,141	425,788	-2.4	-4.3	35,720	31,707	-22,658	166,244	2.45	64.3	16.2	29.9
Gladwin	16.9	15.5	10.8	49.6	26,023	25,692	-1.3	-1.8	1,841	2,445	156	10,838	2.32	65.2	9.1	30.3
Gogebic	16.8	13.9	10.9	45.8	17,370	16,427	-5.4	-6.6	897	1,540	-440	6,636	2.12	58.5	9.9	35.9
Grand Traverse	15.5	11.5	7.7	51.0	77,654	86,986	12.0	5.5	6,706	5,900	4,002	35,708	2.46	64.2	8.9	29.4
Gratiot	12.9	9.2	7.7	46.3	42,285	42,476	0.5	-3.4	2,957	3,175	-1,246	14,721	2.44	66.8	11.3	27.6
Hillsdale	15.4	11.2	7.9	50.3	46,527	46,688	0.3	-1.7	3,912	3,342	-1,366	17,775	2.50	66.8	8.7	28.3
Houghton	11.8	9.7	7.3	45.9	36,016	36,628	1.7	-0.9	2,732	2,540	-533	13,378	2.57	57.7	7.2	31.7
Huron	16.9	13.5	11.1	50.5	36,079	33,118	-8.2	-5.5	2,183	3,215	-789	13,885	2.27	65.3	8.7	31.1
Ingham	11.5	8.0	5.1	51.3	279,320	280,891	0.6	3.3	23,896	14,980	285	111,118	2.39	54.8	12.1	32.9
Ionia	13.4	8.9	5.5	46.2	61,518	63,905	3.9	0.6	5,347	3,679	-1,264	22,293	2.70	70.6	10.0	23.9
Iosco	18.2	16.5	12.5	50.2	27,339	25,885	-5.3	-2.8	1,641	2,868	508	11,483	2.18	61.6	8.6	32.9
Iron	19.2	16.4	13.7	50.3	13,138	11,817	-10.1	-5.9	648	1,335	6	5,401	2.04	54.9	7.9	39.9
Isabella	10.8	7.1	4.9	51.4	63,351	70,311	11.0	1.1	4,785	3,364	-693	24,712	2.59	55.7	10.8	27.3
Jackson	14.4	10.2	7.1	49.0	158,422	160,248	1.2	-1.0	12,936	11,671	-2,805	60,803	2.47	66.1	13.1	28.8
Kalamazoo	11.8	8.5	6.1	51.0	238,603	250,327	4.9	5.1	22,767	14,976	5,054	101,589	2.46	59.6	11.1	30.1
Kalkaska	16.0	12.6	7.6	48.8	16,571	17,147	3.5	2.8	1,248	1,314	557	7,031	2.43	65.1	7.1	28.7
Kent	12.4	7.7	5.5	50.7	574,335	602,622	4.9	7.6	64,044	32,694	14,933	234,570	2.64	66.2	12.6	26.1

1. No spouse present.

Table B. States and Counties — Population, Vital Statistics, Health, and Crime

STATE County	Persons in group quarters, 2017	Daytime Population, 2012-2016		Births, 2017		Deaths, 2017		Persons under 65 with no health insurance, 2016		Medicare, 2017			Serious crimes known to police[2], 2016 — Total	
		Number	Employment/ residence ratio	Total	Rate[1]	Number	Rate[1]	Number	Percent	Total beneficiaries	Enrolled in Original Medicare	Enrolled in Medicare Advantage	Number	Rate[3]
	32	33	34	35	36	37	38	39	40	41	42	43	44	45
MARYLAND— Cont'd														
St. Mary's	2,779	105,922	0.91	1,441	12.8	843	7.5	5,412	5.6	15,946	15,199	747	2,302	2057
Somerset	5,333	24,803	0.86	246	9.5	271	10.5	1,537	9.2	5,138	4,825	313	607	2382
Talbot	373	41,808	1.24	319	8.6	474	12.8	2,147	8.0	10,848	10,190	658	790	2122
Washington	8,246	151,636	1.03	1,675	11.1	1,498	9.9	8,448	7.1	29,752	26,440	3,312	3,632	2436
Wicomico	4,862	102,730	1.03	1,243	12.1	1,046	10.2	6,734	8.1	18,848	17,936	912	3,505	3420
Worcester	721	53,903	1.11	422	8.2	660	12.8	2,733	7.3	14,221	13,282	939	1,985	3873
Baltimore city	26,111	727,239	1.39	8,340	13.6	6,711	11.0	39,346	7.6	106,698	88,691	18,007	40,689	6580
MASSACHUSETTS	25,0,594	6,813,001	1.02	71,168	10.4	57,119	8.3	165,417	3.0	1,278,484	977,850	300,634	132,016	1938
Barnstable	4,134	211,547	0.97	1,519	7.1	2,832	13.3	4,663	3.1	73,410	63,392	10,018	4,118	1933
Berkshire	5,920	130,284	1.03	1,012	8.0	1,387	11.0	3,117	3.3	33,789	31,425	2,364	2,756	2387
Bristol	15,836	506,525	0.82	5,627	10.0	5,271	9.4	14,881	3.3	117,542	95,943	21,599	12,520	2252
Dukes	141	17,234	1.01	162	9.4	138	8.0	566	4.2	4,548	4,414	134	278	1600
Essex	19,498	711,118	0.85	8,430	10.7	6,760	8.6	21,253	3.3	152,210	119,055	33,156	13,297	1715
Franklin	1,556	63,163	0.79	588	8.3	681	9.6	1,587	2.8	17,040	13,382	3,658	1,080	1770
Hampden	15,384	463,920	0.98	5,004	10.7	4,345	9.2	13,665	3.6	99,624	67,863	31,760	14,913	3236
Hampshire	22,691	155,971	0.94	1,016	6.3	1,231	7.6	2,992	2.6	30,979	24,625	6,354	2,700	1717
Middlesex	56,724	1,633,523	1.08	17,193	10.7	11,702	7.3	35,016	2.7	264,291	198,669	65,622	21,430	1347
Nantucket	60	10,812	1.02	165	14.7	54	4.8	387	4.1	1,772	1,727	45	335	3036
Norfolk	17,436	671,384	0.94	7,240	10.3	5,900	8.4	11,891	2.1	123,658	97,776	25,882	8,779	1354
Plymouth	11,692	449,287	0.77	5,211	10.1	4,688	9.1	10,660	2.5	104,535	86,584	17,951	7,368	1552
Suffolk	50,981	1,023,426	1.63	9,391	11.8	5,159	6.5	25,518	3.9	104,416	75,667	28,749	23,645	3009
Worcester	28,541	764,807	0.88	8,610	10.4	6,971	8.4	19,221	2.8	150,615	97,287	53,328	16,130	2085
MICHIGAN	22,9,856	9,873,322	0.99	112,143	11.3	93,495	9.4	519,190	6.4	1,984,465	1,234,708	749,758	235,192	2369
Alcona	127	9,356	0.66	55	5.3	165	15.9	563	8.5	4,053	2,877	1,176	112	1094
Alger	1,050	9,073	0.90	57	6.2	117	12.8	474	7.9	2,531	1,755	776	76	813
Allegan	954	105,357	0.84	1,356	11.6	919	7.9	6,171	6.4	19,182	9,643	9,539	1,710	1484
Alpena	513	29,500	1.05	258	9.1	341	12.0	1,341	6.1	9,092	7,096	1,996	494	1725
Antrim	226	20,351	0.69	201	8.6	263	11.3	1,333	7.9	6,360	4,159	2,201	406	1759
Arenac	207	14,464	0.85	127	8.4	202	13.4	872	7.7	5,070	3,570	1,501	160	1057
Baraga	1,010	8,865	1.11	66	7.8	103	12.2	523	8.9	2,152	1,551	601	NA	NA
Barry	607	46,437	0.52	627	10.3	554	9.1	2,736	5.6	10,462	5,444	5,018	648	1101
Bay	1,439	96,411	0.79	1,019	9.8	1,162	11.1	5,048	6.0	25,201	17,342	7,859	2,378	2260
Benzie	252	15,065	0.68	156	8.9	211	12.0	970	7.5	4,752	3,065	1,687	179	1026
Berrien	3,492	155,386	1.00	1,718	11.1	1,639	10.6	9,340	7.6	37,973	24,716	13,257	4,304	2792
Branch	1,963	41,298	0.87	507	11.7	407	9.4	2,766	8.1	8,680	6,094	2,586	835	1926
Calhoun	4,137	140,958	1.11	1,620	12.1	1,397	10.4	7,020	6.5	29,911	20,490	9,421	5,109	3815
Cass	625	42,307	0.57	481	9.4	535	10.4	3,129	7.7	7,708	5,116	2,592	848	1856
Charlevoix	279	25,243	0.92	221	8.5	274	10.5	1,495	7.4	7,163	4,863	2,299	375	1426
Cheboygan	391	23,007	0.74	209	8.2	355	14.0	1,674	9.1	6,969	4,891	2,078	367	1451
Chippewa	4,826	38,365	1.00	333	8.8	353	9.4	2,387	8.9	8,092	5,619	2,474	563	1485
Clare	391	28,376	0.79	307	10.0	376	12.3	2,038	8.8	8,489	5,957	2,532	597	1961
Clinton	630	62,041	0.58	802	10.2	575	7.3	2,939	4.5	10,999	7,121	3,878	707	909
Crawford	197	13,216	0.88	118	8.5	167	12.0	731	7.2	3,273	2,377	896	247	1797
Delta	623	35,940	0.96	345	9.6	421	11.7	1,956	7.1	10,611	6,996	3,615	781	2156
Dickinson	435	27,944	1.19	253	10.0	302	11.9	1,127	5.7	6,742	4,555	2,187	NA	NA
Eaton	1,631	103,897	0.91	1,149	10.5	979	9.0	4,661	5.2	16,953	11,256	5,698	1,872	1718
Emmet	505	36,249	1.20	298	9.0	309	9.3	1,907	7.4	9,260	6,497	2,762	364	1095
Genesee	5,893	398,227	0.91	4,675	11.5	4,444	10.9	21,574	6.4	90,271	54,461	35,810	11,919	2922
Gladwin	289	22,246	0.64	269	10.7	366	14.5	1,549	8.4	8,084	5,436	2,649	278	1110
Gogebic	1,481	15,653	1.00	122	8.0	206	13.4	751	7.3	4,530	2,968	1,562	175	1149
Grand Traverse	1,362	99,104	1.19	922	10.0	830	9.0	5,027	6.8	23,776	14,855	8,920	1,199	1295
Gratiot	5,540	41,250	0.97	388	9.5	434	10.6	1,768	6.0	8,698	6,209	2,489	613	1483
Hillsdale	1,654	43,133	0.85	525	11.4	453	9.9	2,449	6.8	9,675	6,853	2,822	516	1127
Houghton	3,103	36,308	0.98	368	10.1	348	9.6	1,945	7.0	6,781	4,187	2,594	470	1295
Huron	524	32,606	1.04	313	10.0	449	14.4	1,656	7.0	8,791	6,572	2,219	321	1053
Ingham	18,395	318,958	1.26	3,315	11.4	2,174	7.5	16,185	6.9	56,554	40,629	15,925	8,377	2919
Ionia	5,376	55,741	0.68	725	11.3	528	8.2	3,192	6.4	10,820	6,808	4,011	780	1214
Iosco	400	26,323	1.11	222	8.8	386	15.3	1,383	7.8	8,770	6,177	2,594	464	1838
Iron	355	10,939	0.89	86	7.7	184	16.5	538	6.9	3,554	2,462	1,093	167	1484
Isabella	6,236	73,789	1.10	650	9.1	453	6.4	5,075	8.9	10,942	7,822	3,119	1,167	1650
Jackson	8,664	155,036	0.93	1,711	10.8	1,599	10.1	7,513	6.1	33,693	24,228	9,465	4,338	2761
Kalamazoo	8,146	265,437	1.05	3,173	12.1	2,184	8.3	14,403	6.6	46,556	25,469	21,087	9,213	3515
Kalkaska	138	15,237	0.70	168	9.5	168	9.5	1,042	7.6	3,430	2,398	1,032	337	1950
Kent	11,526	678,814	1.16	8,839	13.6	4,668	7.2	38,088	6.9	104,739	49,599	55,140	14,339	2230

1. Per 1,000 estimated resident population.   2. Data for serious crimes have not been adjusted for underreporting; this may affect comparability between geographic areas and over time.
3. Per 100,000 population estimated by the FBI.

Table B. States and Counties — Crime, Education, Money Income, and Poverty

STATE County	Serious crimes known to police, 2016 (cont.)[1] Rate Violent	Property	Education School enrollment and attainment, 2012-2016 Enrollment[3] Total	Percent private	Attainment[4] (percent) High school graduate or less	Bachelor's degree or more	Local government expenditures,[5] 2013-2014 Total current spending (mil dol)	Current spending per student (dollars)	Money income, 2012-2016 Per capita income[6]	Households Median income (dollars)	Percent with income of less than $50,000	with income of $200,000 or more	Income and poverty, 2016 Median household income (dollars)	Percent below poverty level All persons	Children under 18 years	Children 5 to 17 years in families
	46	47	48	49	50	51	52	53	54	55	56	57	58	59	60	61
MARYLAND— Cont'd																
St. Mary's	203	1,854	30,436	15.8	40.4	29.9	222.3	12,463	36,814	86,810	27.0	8.4	80,049	9.1	11.5	10.7
Somerset	451	1,931	7,625	7.9	62.6	14.0	42.3	14,359	17,143	35,886	61.1	1.2	38,546	24.3	31.9	30.6
Talbot	220	1,902	7,651	21.0	37.1	35.8	54.8	12,085	40,533	61,395	41.8	8.1	62,264	10.4	16.0	14.9
Washington	302	2,134	34,599	13.3	51.1	20.1	287.3	12,771	27,586	56,316	44.5	3.5	54,643	13.2	17.6	16.0
Wicomico	489	2,931	30,641	10.2	44.9	27.4	191.3	13,255	26,498	53,508	47.2	2.9	50,015	18.0	24.1	22.6
Worcester	297	3,576	10,029	15.4	42.7	29.9	109.4	16,449	32,988	57,227	43.5	4.7	53,509	11.4	19.9	18.3
Baltimore city	1,802	4,778	158,883	23.7	46.1	29.7	1,318.7	15,490	27,129	44,262	54.7	4.1	46,604	21.8	31.3	31.6
MASSACHUSETTS	377	1,561	1,748,398	26.6	35.0	41.2	14,467.9	15,138	38,069	70,954	36.8	9.6	75,207	10.5	13.6	12.4
Barnstable	367	1,565	40,016	15.2	29.8	41.1	441.9	17,258	39,104	65,382	38.7	6.2	67,374	7.6	12.0	10.6
Berkshire	534	1,853	29,097	24.9	40.1	32.6	278.8	16,553	31,417	52,253	47.9	4.5	56,011	10.9	14.9	14.1
Bristol	464	1,788	136,658	17.5	46.3	26.5	1,080.6	13,624	30,525	59,343	43.3	4.9	65,154	10.7	14.7	12.4
Dukes	294	1,306	3,093	22.5	31.8	39.8	60.0	26,385	40,051	63,534	39.7	8.9	66,528	7.6	12.1	10.9
Essex	350	1,365	192,564	20.9	36.4	38.0	1,667.1	14,483	37,210	70,886	36.7	9.6	73,503	10.7	14.2	13.4
Franklin	380	1,390	15,054	13.9	34.8	35.9	156.9	16,230	31,689	56,347	44.8	3.7	56,544	10.0	15.2	13.5
Hampden	633	2,603	122,028	17.1	45.0	26.2	1,088.5	14,886	27,057	51,005	49.1	3.6	51,589	16.5	26.7	24.1
Hampshire	278	1,439	57,132	20.6	30.0	44.7	283.1	15,041	31,051	62,608	41.0	5.7	64,425	11.9	10.8	9.3
Middlesex	180	1,167	413,835	32.0	27.9	53.0	3,383.3	15,613	45,579	89,019	29.0	14.6	94,977	7.7	8.6	7.6
Nantucket	236	2,800	2,303	27.9	30.4	42.0	30.7	20,743	46,009	89,428	23.8	11.2	82,324	6.4	7.1	6.6
Norfolk	194	1,160	180,418	31.5	27.1	51.2	1,519.0	14,821	47,306	90,226	28.2	15.2	92,606	6.1	6.0	5.5
Plymouth	379	1,173	127,644	16.7	36.5	35.0	1,149.2	13,380	37,188	77,627	32.3	9.3	81,483	8.0	10.6	9.6
Suffolk	734	2,276	216,973	45.5	38.5	42.7	1,560.5	19,688	35,844	57,439	44.8	8.2	61,367	19.5	28.2	28.3
Worcester	438	1,646	211,583	20.3	38.9	34.8	1,768.3	13,690	33,272	67,005	38.3	7.1	69,064	9.6	11.7	10.6
MICHIGAN	459	1,910	2,562,133	13.0	39.7	27.4	16,471.5	10,912	27,549	50,803	49.2	3.8	52,436	14.9	20.7	18.9
Alcona	146	947	1,407	5.5	51.6	14.5	7.1	9,531	23,380	38,160	64.3	1.1	37,900	16.2	29.6	26.6
Alger	161	653	1,555	14.5	54.9	18.1	11.3	10,379	20,993	41,270	58.5	0.7	43,693	13.9	19.5	17.5
Allegan	277	1,207	27,149	13.3	47.8	21.4	176.2	9,990	25,840	55,630	44.4	2.5	58,311	9.0	11.8	10.9
Alpena	342	1,382	6,061	10.1	43.2	16.8	44.8	11,016	22,776	39,832	61.7	0.9	42,332	15.5	24.1	21.4
Antrim	91	1,668	4,387	8.0	42.5	26.7	33.4	9,599	28,180	48,825	51.3	3.9	50,356	11.7	20.3	18.4
Arenac	271	786	2,721	6.2	56.6	11.4	21.0	9,195	21,602	39,240	61.9	1.3	44,187	16.5	24.0	22.3
Baraga	NA	NA	1,336	11.5	59.0	15.6	11.9	10,369	17,664	42,810	59.0	2.5	60,818	8.4	12.4	11.3
Barry	204	897	13,803	10.8	45.7	18.9	82.4	8,959	25,909	56,883	43.8	1.8	45,731	15.2	22.7	19.3
Bay	373	1,888	24,561	11.9	46.4	18.1	162.7	11,191	24,753	45,851	54.0	1.7	50,323	10.8	18.4	16.8
Benzie	138	889	3,203	10.3	42.0	25.6	19.9	9,290	25,506	48,694	51.1	1.8	47,237	16.7	26.1	24.9
Berrien	453	2,339	38,296	21.2	40.5	26.8	276.6	10,920	26,309	45,980	53.3	3.3	48,321	16.8	25.0	22.0
Branch	272	1,654	9,830	12.1	52.4	13.6	74.6	11,344	21,838	46,428	53.6	1.5	46,423	16.8	25.2	22.8
Calhoun	742	3,074	32,910	12.8	45.2	20.8	246.4	12,173	23,812	44,681	54.8	1.9	51,530	12.9	19.7	18.1
Cass	232	1,624	11,551	8.8	46.9	17.4	68.3	10,167	25,955	47,991	52.0	2.7	52,944	11.5	18.2	15.9
Charlevoix	179	1,247	5,458	9.3	39.2	28.5	58.4	15,310	29,581	48,603	51.3	3.8	41,667	18.0	31.1	27.8
Cheboygan	146	1,305	4,716	9.2	49.5	18.3	43.6	11,926	24,220	41,023	60.2	1.8	43,683	16.0	20.9	20.0
Chippewa	303	1,182	8,687	9.2	48.3	19.7	62.2	12,504	20,839	42,287	57.1	1.3	37,646	21.7	34.1	32.1
Clare	378	1,583	6,024	10.9	55.1	11.4	54.1	12,254	20,418	34,911	65.6	0.7	66,396	8.4	9.9	8.2
Clinton	108	801	21,268	11.5	34.3	30.7	103.8	10,431	31,170	62,646	39.3	5.0	39,208	21.4	34.6	30.5
Crawford	269	1,528	2,495	7.4	47.9	16.7	15.3	9,329	22,348	41,034	58.5	0.3	43,835	14.3	19.0	17.7
Delta	215	1,941	7,520	9.6	41.2	20.6	51.7	10,835	24,182	42,353	56.7	1.3	46,094	12.8	17.3	15.8
Dickinson	NA	NA	5,119	10.4	45.4	23.4	43.3	11,624	25,136	44,373	56.0	1.9	57,807	11.2	16.4	15.1
Eaton	279	1,439	26,254	15.5	35.8	25.2	177.3	10,136	28,624	56,472	43.8	2.5	51,122	11.8	14.7	12.7
Emmet	144	950	7,423	10.6	31.9	32.9	50.1	9,963	30,250	51,096	48.4	3.6	44,174	20.3	29.1	25.6
Genesee	653	2,270	105,610	10.0	42.7	19.9	748.7	10,893	23,755	43,246	56.6	2.2	41,251	18.0	29.1	26.5
Gladwin	228	882	4,647	11.9	55.5	13.4	26.7	8,813	22,255	39,629	62.1	1.6	36,429	20.4	30.0	26.0
Gogebic	112	1,037	2,744	7.4	46.1	17.5	10.8	10,435	21,464	35,833	64.4	1.2	57,367	10.0	12.9	11.4
Grand Traverse	231	1,064	20,435	14.2	31.7	31.7	165.7	13,049	30,024	55,597	43.6	4.3	42,642	18.8	22.1	20.6
Gratiot	189	1,294	9,918	21.4	51.8	14.3	76.7	11,371	20,358	42,145	57.4	1.8	49,049	14.5	20.1	19.2
Hillsdale	186	941	11,338	26.7	51.8	16.7	66.9	10,700	22,435	44,458	56.1	1.7	38,603	20.2	18.1	16.1
Houghton	193	1,102	12,433	6.7	42.4	31.0	55.1	10,331	20,248	39,080	59.9	1.7	44,845	14.2	23.1	20.1
Huron	125	929	6,279	12.2	54.5	14.9	58.7	11,639	24,455	43,082	57.0	1.9	49,387	20.1	19.2	21.8
Ingham	632	2,287	100,764	7.7	29.3	37.7	480.9	11,587	26,083	46,842	52.7	3.5	50,383	14.5	19.7	17.1
Ionia	252	962	15,248	13.5	49.7	15.6	94.8	11,376	21,526	50,037	50.0	1.3	39,721	18.2	31.2	29.0
Iosco	321	1,517	4,342	8.7	51.2	16.3	40.3	10,278	23,723	38,900	64.5	1.5	38,913	15.4	25.6	23.7
Iron	231	1,253	1,853	6.1	53.0	18.1	12.7	9,666	22,454	33,137	66.6	1.0	42,924	23.4	18.9	18.2
Isabella	312	1,337	30,266	5.5	39.7	28.2	60.4	9,503	21,387	40,706	58.6	2.2	50,809	13.6	20.4	18.2
Jackson	537	2,224	38,515	15.6	43.8	20.6	267.1	11,433	24,444	47,709	51.8	2.4	53,370	16.6	19.6	17.8
Kalamazoo	569	2,947	80,730	10.1	29.3	36.1	376.3	10,943	27,370	49,693	50.2	3.8	48,426	15.3	24.7	24.1
Kalkaska	411	1,539	3,511	10.8	53.7	13.6	21.4	9,624	22,508	42,612	58.9	1.4	59,649	12.1	14.9	13.1
Kent	380	1,850	170,943	20.3	35.4	33.7	1,171.1	10,741	28,070	54,673	45.7	4.1				

1. Data for serious crimes have not been adjusted for underreporting; this may affect comparability between geographic areas and over time.   2. Per 100,000 population estimated by the FBI.
3. All persons 3 years old and over enrolled in nursery school through college.   4. Persons 25 years old and over.   5. Elementary and secondary education expenditures.
6. Based on population estimated by the American Community Survey, 2011–2015.

Table B. States and Counties — **Agriculture**

STATE County	Land in farms Acreage (1,000)	Percent change, 2007-2012	Acres Average size of farm	Total irrigated (1,000)	Total cropland (1,000)	Value of land and buildings (dollars) Average per farm	Average per acre	Value of machinery and equipment, average per farm (dollars)	Value of products sold: Total (mil dol)	Average per farm (acres)	Percent from: Crops	Livestock and poultry products	Percent of farms with sales of: $10,000 or more	$100,000 or more	Government payments Total ($1,000)	Percent of farms
	117	118	119	120	121	122	123	124	125	126	127	128	129	130	131	132
MARYLAND— Cont'd																
St. Mary's	67	-2.3	106	0.7	41.2	700,921	6,603	80,758	21.8	34,494	87.4	12.6	42.6	6.6	783	30.1
Somerset	65	8.2	228	0.4	36.4	1,247,458	5,471	182,073	219.0	765,559	12.2	87.8	58.0	50.0	1,653	61.9
Talbot	119	9.6	364	7.6	98.2	2,408,598	6,612	177,098	89.5	272,893	71.2	28.8	58.5	34.8	2,380	69.2
Washington	130	13.6	151	0.8	85.3	901,269	5,981	117,867	107.7	125,219	42.2	57.8	47.6	24.2	1,078	26.2
Wicomico	84	-9.8	164	9.4	56.1	1,031,771	6,284	134,363	236.3	463,375	22.7	77.3	54.9	35.5	2,360	53.7
Worcester	99	-10.4	266	5.0	71.3	1,585,529	5,971	163,979	199.3	532,794	25.8	74.2	52.7	39.6	1,733	58.6
Baltimore city	NA	NA	NA	NA	NA	NA	NA	NA	NA	NA	NA	NA	NA	NA	NA	NA
MASSACHUSETTS	524	1.1	68	23.4	160.8	704,071	10,430	53,920	492.2	63,470	77.8	22.2	32.7	9.8	8,124	10.1
Barnstable	5	-10.6	14	1.2	1.5	500,691	35,657	50,009	19.1	57,438	50.8	49.2	40.5	11.4	358	7.5
Berkshire	62	-7.1	117	0.2	18.4	824,924	7,024	51,476	22.5	42,796	45.1	54.9	29.5	6.7	268	9.3
Bristol	35	-11.2	49	1.6	11.9	709,223	14,584	51,411	37.7	52,522	79.4	20.6	36.3	8.6	1,527	12.7
Dukes	13	60.6	145	0.2	D	1,416,193	9,800	84,943	3.5	39,671	71.9	28.1	34.1	6.8	D	3.4
Essex	22	-19.5	43	0.6	9.2	893,351	20,821	56,138	25.2	48,205	71.7	28.3	31.0	8.0	207	4.0
Franklin	90	13.0	115	2.1	22.5	700,144	6,083	68,964	55.1	70,585	71.0	29.0	31.9	10.3	1,987	16.4
Hampden	39	5.1	67	0.9	11.1	488,323	7,343	45,735	23.6	40,564	73.6	26.4	26.5	6.5	480	9.1
Hampshire	54	2.3	68	0.9	21.5	544,950	8,071	53,222	49.2	61,613	75.6	24.4	30.5	10.1	682	11.9
Middlesex	28	-16.7	38	1.7	10.7	730,977	19,135	50,583	76.6	103,593	89.7	10.3	35.7	10.1	482	9.3
Nantucket	1	100.3	62	D	0.6	1,642,150	26,658	20,950	1.7	82,800	84.0	15.9	55.0	15.0	0	0.0
Norfolk	9	-18.9	39	0.6	3.4	936,188	24,277	47,890	12.5	51,012	75.8	24.2	33.5	12.7	D	6.9
Plymouth	64	29.1	78	12.0	17.3	893,370	11,510	65,783	108.1	130,986	92.2	7.8	46.9	19.2	1,306	12.4
Suffolk	0	-75.8	1	D	D	246,000	205,000	7,700	0.2	8,100	96.3	4.3	40.0	0.0	0	0.0
Worcester	102	-4.3	65	1.3	32.2	609,428	9,338	47,396	57.5	36,845	68.9	31.1	25.4	7.0	690	8.1
MICHIGAN	9,949	-0.8	191	592.2	7,669.1	766,148	4,020	122,528	8,678.1	166,265	63.5	36.5	44.0	18.0	155,919	39.5
Alcona	38	-15.6	163	0.0	23.8	394,591	2,421	78,426	11.4	48,511	40.3	59.7	31.9	9.8	263	24.3
Alger	18	-3.1	191	0.0	8.7	395,710	2,070	54,075	3.0	32,527	29.4	70.6	38.7	6.5	119	29.0
Allegan	270	-1.8	194	28.1	223.3	927,485	4,790	152,066	580.8	416,071	33.4	66.6	45.1	19.7	3,286	27.1
Alpena	69	-19.4	151	0.0	44.1	367,974	2,433	82,430	23.7	51,644	40.2	59.8	37.3	11.4	694	32.8
Antrim	64	-4.7	155	3.4	33.9	554,149	3,584	77,942	21.0	50,593	73.0	27.0	29.9	8.7	1,324	31.1
Arenac	82	-13.7	194	D	63.0	539,781	2,782	114,143	51.2	121,620	70.0	30.0	33.0	17.8	1,570	72.2
Baraga	18	-4.9	311	0.0	7.9	574,842	1,848	71,667	1.5	25,825	53.2	46.9	38.6	7.0	79	26.3
Barry	165	-1.8	160	4.3	119.4	637,736	3,980	89,944	140.1	135,859	33.9	66.1	35.3	11.2	2,853	37.1
Bay	194	4.0	253	6.3	174.5	1,015,918	4,017	198,977	165.3	215,789	95.1	4.9	58.6	31.9	2,628	68.0
Benzie	21	-2.0	114	0.3	9.8	475,486	4,169	65,177	6.4	35,337	51.9	48.1	30.9	8.8	808	20.4
Berrien	156	-7.5	147	18.1	126.1	822,736	5,591	123,913	161.5	151,968	90.3	9.7	51.6	20.6	3,303	29.4
Branch	244	-2.4	232	44.5	197.7	823,531	3,554	132,288	175.3	166,362	71.5	28.5	44.0	20.3	4,329	54.2
Calhoun	225	-1.4	220	10.7	175.6	807,980	3,676	117,543	133.0	130,044	64.6	35.4	43.4	17.5	3,618	47.7
Cass	189	-0.9	236	57.6	148.0	936,370	3,960	147,259	187.2	234,535	67.1	32.9	43.1	19.9	2,666	47.9
Charlevoix	38	-9.4	126	0.2	20.8	465,684	3,684	52,899	9.9	33,391	60.3	39.7	30.6	6.4	182	14.5
Cheboygan	46	-4.2	146	0.5	21.8	361,479	2,483	51,425	9.3	29,633	60.5	39.5	25.2	3.2	221	20.1
Chippewa	93	-6.0	227	0.1	57.4	368,870	1,622	60,252	12.6	30,724	41.7	58.3	39.6	6.8	934	31.5
Clare	63	-8.6	136	D	30.7	385,265	2,835	54,583	20.4	44,263	30.3	69.7	31.1	8.3	438	24.8
Clinton	244	-10.2	216	4.2	205.7	939,125	4,345	133,106	262.6	232,828	46.7	53.3	49.6	21.5	3,797	54.2
Crawford	3	9.2	56	0.0	0.8	185,959	3,307	54,816	0.3	5,306	26.9	73.1	14.3	0.0	0	0.0
Delta	71	-8.9	250	0.6	35.0	488,406	1,951	83,208	15.0	52,883	51.0	49.0	38.5	13.1	588	35.7
Dickinson	29	15.0	177	0.3	15.5	390,512	2,211	77,451	5.6	34,759	51.6	48.4	34.0	7.4	186	30.2
Eaton	223	0.5	192	1.5	176.1	714,449	3,722	119,525	119.0	102,364	83.8	16.2	46.9	19.8	3,008	46.6
Emmet	40	0.6	139	0.3	17.9	438,456	3,161	55,383	6.7	23,429	66.1	33.9	34.1	4.9	117	12.5
Genesee	123	-4.6	148	1.5	102.6	570,910	3,867	107,984	91.3	109,389	88.7	11.3	38.4	12.9	2,131	32.2
Gladwin	67	-0.7	126	0.5	40.1	355,311	2,820	61,334	19.3	36,300	70.6	29.4	34.5	4.7	599	38.3
Gogebic	6	55.6	98	0.0	2.4	257,194	2,624	34,226	0.5	8,016	72.8	27.2	25.8	0.0	D	3.2
Grand Traverse	55	-12.8	108	3.0	36.4	577,258	5,333	79,274	18.2	36,202	76.3	23.7	40.1	9.7	1,273	28.8
Gratiot	289	0.9	330	9.5	259.5	1,486,503	4,510	209,694	345.0	392,976	57.7	42.3	56.3	31.7	4,522	68.6
Hillsdale	262	-2.8	171	9.1	207.9	590,512	3,444	101,482	161.5	105,577	71.8	28.2	35.6	14.5	6,159	57.7
Houghton	27	15.0	154	0.1	10.8	272,254	1,772	42,633	4.0	22,678	53.0	47.0	27.7	2.3	101	18.1
Huron	452	2.6	375	2.0	406.0	1,952,800	5,202	304,740	654.6	543,207	51.1	48.9	62.5	43.8	9,479	79.6
Ingham	201	7.7	212	1.7	167.4	866,715	4,079	128,773	131.3	139,131	77.4	22.6	42.2	17.2	2,925	27.2
Ionia	248	4.2	224	6.0	203.1	934,093	4,170	154,311	406.1	366,228	31.6	68.4	50.9	25.4	4,662	51.9
Iosco	38	-20.4	134	0.0	23.7	358,890	2,673	85,230	17.1	60,364	36.4	63.6	29.3	7.8	467	30.4
Iron	23	-17.3	196	0.5	9.5	390,043	1,989	50,376	3.7	31,222	87.3	12.7	25.6	6.8	25	17.9
Isabella	188	-3.9	203	3.4	148.9	772,920	3,806	104,693	119.4	128,664	65.7	34.3	46.7	19.2	2,703	52.3
Jackson	183	0.4	171	3.9	136.0	652,247	3,822	85,794	78.2	72,866	69.2	30.8	36.4	12.0	4,210	32.1
Kalamazoo	144	-0.9	196	39.1	112.9	909,857	4,653	148,903	244.0	332,383	79.7	20.3	48.5	21.5	2,473	26.7
Kalkaska	26	10.0	115	1.6	12.9	350,875	3,044	45,339	8.8	39,299	92.1	7.9	23.2	3.1	104	17.0
Kent	157	-7.4	136	10.0	120.5	795,991	5,858	111,424	231.9	200,053	77.8	22.2	42.6	16.6	2,417	22.7

Table B. States and Counties — Water Use, Wholesale Trade, Retail Trade, and Real Estate

STATE County	Water use, 2015		Wholesale Trade[1], 2012				Retail Trade[2], 2012				Real estate and rental and leasing,[2] 2012			
	Public supply water withdrawn (mil gal/day)	Public supply gallons withdrawn per person per day	Number of establishments	Number of employees	Sales (mil dol)	Annual payroll (mil dol)	Number of establishments	Number of employees	Sales (mil dol)	Annual payroll (mil dol)	Number of establishments	Number of employees	Sales (mil dol)	Annual payroll (mil dol)
	133	134	135	136	137	138	139	140	141	142	143	144	145	146
MARYLAND— Cont'd														
St. Mary's	4.15	37.2	39	397	189.5	17.6	294	4,835	1,227.0	109.5	83	312	94.7	11.4
Somerset	1.09	42.3	14	D	D	D	61	434	112.2	9.5	17	42	4.8	0.7
Talbot	2.24	59.7	56	443	277.4	19.9	222	2,635	670.2	64.6	55	179	34.7	6.3
Washington	17.27	115.5	137	1,917	1,804.2	89.0	612	9,244	2,457.6	207.6	141	755	216.5	29.4
Wicomico	6.86	67.0	108	1,122	1,231.4	49.9	390	6,375	1,608.3	145.0	126	624	86.3	20.7
Worcester	7.68	149.0	47	D	D	D	401	3,370	835.6	81.9	152	467	75.3	15.1
Baltimore city	0.00	0.0	544	8,592	7,954.3	495.2	1,839	15,747	3,647.7	379.0	596	4,055	883.7	187.6
MASSACHUSETTS	648.06	95.4	6,619	114,195	123,904.4	8,035.1	24,311	351,598	92,915.4	9,161.7	6,485	42,788	13,628.4	2357.9
Barnstable	31.84	148.6	178	1,152	563.1	57.0	1,503	14,395	3,856.9	401.4	331	1,361	260.5	53.1
Berkshire	14.33	112.1	105	1,242	455.0	58.0	711	8,482	1,916.5	201.7	108	715	99.5	23.1
Bristol	26.60	47.8	517	10,556	9,375.8	626.2	2,192	33,806	8,403.5	813.8	418	1,382	293.7	53.1
Dukes	3.07	177.5	16	D	D	D	205	1,276	373.6	43.7	63	142	41.6	6.6
Essex	77.15	99.4	726	11,128	15,101.2	768.2	2,585	37,792	10,037.9	995.4	602	2,734	629.9	113.9
Franklin	3.73	52.8	64	D	D	D	262	2,903	703.7	73.3	37	110	16.9	2.9
Hampden	45.38	96.4	385	6,581	6,028.9	355.0	1,573	22,637	5,753.0	540.3	364	1,839	289.2	66.0
Hampshire	18.09	112.2	85	1,676	1,807.0	81.2	546	7,914	1,750.0	187.6	114	435	279.8	15.5
Middlesex	70.26	44.3	1,760	36,339	46,631.4	3,169.0	5,156	80,738	21,344.6	2,155.0	1,567	11,979	5,087.1	616.2
Nantucket	2.00	183.1	7	D	D	D	155	998	317.5	35.8	53	157	59.7	7.9
Norfolk	35.88	51.6	890	15,930	13,702.9	1,083.4	2,548	43,010	11,801.1	1,163.3	774	6,263	1,778.1	382.1
Plymouth	68.09	133.4	488	5,947	9,622.7	353.9	1,892	26,703	6,889.6	698.5	364	1,550	341.1	69.6
Suffolk	0.00	0.0	630	11,314	12,840.7	809.3	2,411	31,965	8,851.0	892.5	1,093	11,366	3,821.2	826.9
Worcester	251.64	307.3	768	11,502	7,126.8	636.8	2,572	38,979	10,916.5	959.5	597	2,755	630.2	120.8
MICHIGAN	1,030.44	103.8	9,392	132,490	115,704.9	7,474.6	34,858	441,190	119,302.0	10,527.3	7,826	48,706	11,974.5	1806.9
Alcona	0.06	5.8	4	14	3.2	0.4	35	236	52.5	4.9	3	5	0.8	0.1
Alger	0.41	43.7	3	D	D	D	45	272	64.6	5.6	3	4	0.7	0.1
Allegan	4.03	35.2	106	1,354	609.4	130.1	335	3,354	949.9	76.3	69	210	38.9	8.0
Alpena	2.02	70.1	32	409	223.9	17.6	146	1,731	448.8	41.5	18	111	7.3	2.1
Antrim	1.19	51.4	9	40	15.7	1.2	88	530	169.6	13.4	22	D	D	D
Arenac	42.16	2,762.6	10	D	D	D	71	459	150.8	9.6	5	D	D	D
Baraga	0.51	59.5	3	9	3.3	0.2	29	275	53.1	5.3	5	D	D	D
Barry	1.57	26.5	26	179	122.5	7.3	124	1,198	286.0	24.0	24	68	8.1	2.8
Bay	8.97	84.9	87	D	D	D	419	5,526	1,303.0	124.5	65	212	29.3	4.7
Benzie	0.68	39.0	5	D	D	D	73	535	128.0	11.2	15	33	3.3	0.7
Berrien	12.42	80.3	133	D	D	D	587	6,783	1,681.1	147.2	152	614	78.3	19.5
Branch	2.77	63.4	28	265	124.3	11.3	132	1,612	435.2	39.0	31	77	15.0	2.8
Calhoun	12.53	93.3	94	D	D	D	488	5,858	1,702.3	133.4	87	373	53.9	10.5
Cass	1.15	22.3	45	321	316.2	15.8	116	876	256.9	18.9	28	48	7.9	1.0
Charlevoix	2.66	101.4	15	51	9.6	1.4	116	823	196.8	18.0	29	115	18.0	3.9
Cheboygan	0.98	38.5	13	89	37.4	3.1	147	1,161	310.2	27.3	17	D	D	D
Chippewa	2.69	70.7	25	295	145.4	11.0	148	1,725	454.1	36.8	26	96	8.9	1.8
Clare	1.12	36.7	11	D	D	D	118	1,027	261.3	22.5	9	24	2.5	0.4
Clinton	1.16	15.0	52	869	659.2	39.7	170	2,090	749.2	53.0	53	204	34.7	6.8
Crawford	0.66	47.8	4	34	21.5	1.3	60	531	214.6	12.0	13	22	3.7	0.7
Delta	2.81	77.2	45	331	157.1	12.3	183	2,160	507.1	45.0	29	64	6.8	1.2
Dickinson	2.35	91.1	42	D	D	D	154	1,824	431.2	40.4	28	D	D	D
Eaton	2.63	24.2	71	1,474	1,076.7	65.4	330	5,619	1,453.0	129.9	79	380	78.8	12.4
Emmet	3.84	115.8	34	217	95.8	9.4	293	2,606	627.8	63.5	41	204	24.8	3.9
Genesee	4.22	10.3	272	3,969	3,673.6	218.5	1,459	19,368	5,307.9	444.9	318	1,843	255.8	57.1
Gladwin	0.45	17.9	7	38	11.2	1.4	82	598	141.0	11.6	13	102	6.1	2.6
Gogebic	1.48	95.9	9	66	74.3	2.1	79	764	159.6	15.1	14	104	7.2	1.6
Grand Traverse	7.33	80.0	134	1,146	454.0	52.5	560	7,184	1,767.8	174.8	151	488	96.5	17.0
Gratiot	1.60	38.5	27	D	D	D	135	1,339	344.2	28.2	19	60	7.5	1.3
Hillsdale	2.01	43.8	33	301	407.9	12.7	139	1,330	370.2	32.1	25	54	12.0	1.4
Houghton	3.87	106.4	21	D	D	D	149	1,638	329.4	32.7	25	D	D	D
Huron	2.58	80.9	38	518	523.6	26.4	161	1,481	361.9	29.1	9	11	2.6	0.4
Ingham	26.09	91.2	204	2,701	5,407.9	130.9	916	13,217	3,260.5	293.0	253	1,946	236.4	68.8
Ionia	4.99	77.7	26	D	D	D	143	1,589	430.4	34.8	17	45	6.9	1.1
Iosco	1.20	47.3	5	D	D	D	115	1,302	327.2	28.8	19	37	4.3	0.6
Iron	1.26	111.0	10	44	11.7	1.3	61	433	101.6	9.1	17	37	3.5	0.7
Isabella	3.01	42.6	51	504	362.3	19.7	215	3,322	769.9	71.5	55	1,077	70.7	27.6
Jackson	10.84	68.0	137	D	D	D	526	7,003	1,841.7	163.5	99	567	82.0	15.5
Kalamazoo	24.35	93.6	234	3,668	1,553.7	197.3	863	12,708	3,129.4	284.2	210	2,328	223.7	71.6
Kalkaska	0.41	23.8	18	167	75.7	7.1	54	525	155.9	12.7	9	D	D	D
Kent	9.01	14.2	976	22,090	17,703.0	1,235.3	2,116	31,615	8,698.6	803.1	640	3,990	698.0	143.7

1. Merchant wholesalers, except manufacturers' sales branches and offices.   2. Employer establishments.

Table B. States and Counties — **Land Area and Population**

					Population, 2017			Population and population characteristics, 2017									
								Race alone or in combination, not Hispanic or Latino (percent)					Age (percent)					
State / county code	CBSA code[1]	County code[2]	STATE County	Land area[3] (sq. mi)	Total persons 2017	Rank	Per square mile	White	Black	American Indian, Alaska Native	Asian and Pacific Islander	Percent Hispanic or Latino[4]	Under 5 years	5 to 17 years	18 to 24 years	25 to 34 years	35 to 44 years	45 to 54 years
				1	2	3	4	5	6	7	8	9	10	11	12	13	14	15
			MICHIGAN— Cont'd															
2,6083	26,340	9	Keweenaw	540.1	2,105	3,040	3.9	98.1	0.6	1.0	0.2	1.2	3.6	11.9	4.5	7.1	8.4	10.5
2,6085		9	Lake	567.6	12,013	2,291	21.2	86.9	10.5	1.9	0.6	2.7	4.4	11.7	6.0	8.8	9.4	12.6
2,6087	19,820	1	Lapeer	644.2	88,174	657	136.9	93.1	1.6	1.0	0.9	4.7	4.9	16.1	8.3	10.6	11.1	15.2
2,6089	45,900	9	Leelanau	347.2	21,657	1,746	62.4	91.4	1.0	3.9	0.9	4.4	4.2	12.3	6.5	8.4	8.7	11.2
2,6091	10,300	4	Lenawee	749.6	98,623	603	131.6	88.4	3.5	1.1	0.8	8.0	5.5	15.8	9.2	11.6	11.6	13.5
2,6093	19,820	1	Livingston	565.1	189,651	346	335.6	95.6	0.9	0.9	1.5	2.4	5.1	16.6	8.2	10.7	11.4	15.7
2,6095		7	Luce	899.1	6,358	2,725	7.1	81.2	12.6	7.5	0.6	1.6	3.9	12.6	7.9	13.1	13.1	13.4
2,6097		7	Mackinac	1,021.9	10,712	2,375	10.5	78.2	3.4	20.6	1.0	1.7	3.8	12.2	6.4	9.0	9.6	13.4
2,6099	19,820	1	Macomb	479.2	871,375	65	1,818.4	81.3	12.8	0.9	4.8	2.6	5.5	15.8	8.2	13.2	12.0	14.4
2,6101		7	Manistee	542.3	24,427	1,629	45.0	91.0	3.8	3.2	0.7	3.1	4.2	13.3	7.3	10.1	9.7	12.8
2,6103	32,100	5	Marquette	1,809.0	66,502	802	36.8	94.2	2.1	3.0	1.3	1.5	4.8	13.3	15.4	11.5	10.8	11.3
2,6105	31,220	7	Mason	494.9	29,073	1,456	58.7	92.9	1.6	1.7	1.0	4.6	5.1	15.2	7.2	10.6	10.3	12.3
2,6107	13,660	6	Mecosta	555.1	43,391	1,107	78.2	93.3	3.8	1.5	1.3	2.2	4.8	13.9	18.9	10.8	9.3	10.9
2,6109	31,940	7	Menominee	1,044.0	23,046	1,679	22.1	94.3	1.2	3.4	0.8	1.8	4.4	13.9	6.8	9.7	10.4	13.4
2,6111	33,220	3	Midland	516.3	83,411	683	161.6	92.9	2.0	0.9	2.9	2.8	5.4	16.2	8.4	12.3	11.7	13.8
2,6113	15,620	9	Missaukee	564.8	14,998	2,100	26.6	95.3	1.1	1.4	0.8	2.9	6.3	16.8	7.4	10.8	10.1	13.1
2,6115	33,780	3	Monroe	549.5	149,649	440	272.3	93.0	3.2	0.9	1.0	3.6	5.3	16.2	8.0	11.7	11.6	14.3
2,6117	24,340	2	Montcalm	705.3	63,550	838	90.1	93.2	2.9	1.2	0.7	3.5	5.8	16.8	8.0	12.4	12.0	13.7
2,6119		9	Montmorency	546.7	9,250	2,484	16.9	97.4	1.0	1.4	0.5	1.3	3.6	11.5	5.5	7.6	8.2	12.0
2,6121	34,740	3	Muskegon	501.4	173,693	375	346.4	78.7	15.6	1.6	1.1	5.7	6.1	17.2	8.5	12.9	11.9	12.7
2,6123		6	Newaygo	815.7	48,242	1,016	59.1	92.0	1.6	1.4	0.7	5.8	5.8	16.7	7.6	11.4	10.6	13.3
2,6125	19,820	1	Oakland	867.5	1,250,836	33	1,441.9	74.1	14.9	0.8	8.4	4.0	5.5	15.8	8.2	13.0	12.4	14.4
2,6127		6	Oceana	523.4	26,442	1,549	50.5	83.0	1.4	1.6	0.4	14.9	5.7	17.4	7.7	10.5	10.3	12.6
2,6129		9	Ogemaw	563.5	20,981	1,776	37.2	95.8	0.7	1.7	0.8	2.2	4.5	14.1	6.5	9.5	9.7	12.1
2,6131		9	Ontonagon	1,311.0	5,881	2,762	4.5	96.1	0.9	1.9	0.9	1.6	2.8	9.8	4.6	5.6	7.6	13.5
2,6133		9	Osceola	566.3	23,260	1,668	41.1	96.3	1.6	1.5	0.7	1.8	5.7	16.9	7.1	10.8	10.8	12.6
2,6135		9	Oscoda	565.7	8,287	2,568	14.6	97.0	0.9	1.7	0.5	1.6	5.7	13.7	6.3	8.5	8.2	11.1
2,6137		7	Otsego	515.0	24,538	1,622	47.6	96.0	1.2	1.6	1.2	1.7	5.5	16.0	7.7	11.2	10.4	13.5
2,6139	24,340	2	Ottawa	563.6	286,383	241	508.1	85.5	2.3	0.7	3.5	9.7	6.3	17.9	13.5	12.0	11.6	12.0
2,6141		7	Presque Isle	658.7	12,791	2,239	19.4	96.6	1.0	1.4	0.7	1.4	3.9	12.1	6.0	7.4	8.9	11.7
2,6143		7	Roscommon	519.6	23,895	1,648	46.0	96.1	1.0	1.5	0.9	1.8	3.6	11.3	5.2	8.0	7.8	11.9
2,6145	40,980	3	Saginaw	800.5	191,934	344	239.8	71.2	19.8	0.9	1.7	8.4	5.7	15.8	9.7	12.2	10.9	12.8
2,6147	19,820	1	St. Clair	721.2	159,350	412	221.0	93.0	3.5	1.1	1.0	3.4	5.0	16.1	7.9	10.9	11.2	14.9
2,6149	44,780	4	St. Joseph	500.6	60,947	858	121.7	88.5	3.8	1.0	1.1	7.9	6.5	18.1	8.0	11.7	11.3	12.5
2,6151		6	Sanilac	962.6	41,269	1,146	42.9	95.0	1.0	0.9	0.5	3.6	5.5	16.2	7.5	10.1	10.4	13.3
2,6153		7	Schoolcraft	1,171.3	8,049	2,590	6.9	88.9	1.3	11.7	0.6	1.1	3.9	12.9	6.8	7.8	9.7	12.8
2,6155	37,020	4	Shiawassee	530.8	68,446	779	128.9	95.4	1.1	1.1	0.8	2.9	5.3	16.0	8.6	11.3	11.4	14.4
2,6157		6	Tuscola	803.4	52,764	951	65.7	94.5	1.6	1.1	0.5	3.4	5.2	15.4	7.7	10.9	11.0	14.0
2,6159	28,020	2	Van Buren	607.8	75,353	736	124.0	83.2	4.8	1.6	1.1	11.6	6.1	17.5	7.9	10.9	11.6	13.2
2,6161	11,460	2	Washtenaw	706.0	367,627	190	520.7	73.3	13.8	1.0	10.7	4.7	4.9	13.8	18.9	14.4	11.3	11.9
2,6163	19,820	1	Wayne	612.0	1,753,616	19	2,865.4	51.5	39.8	1.1	4.2	5.9	6.6	17.2	8.9	13.8	11.8	13.3
2,6165	15,620	7	Wexford	565.0	33,276	1,346	58.9	96.1	1.2	1.3	1.0	1.9	6.2	17.3	7.4	11.5	11.0	12.9
2,7000		0	MINNESOTA	79,625.5	5,576,606	X	70.0	82.0	7.4	1.8	5.8	5.4	6.4	16.9	9.1	13.6	12.5	12.8
2,7001		8	Aitkin	1,821.7	15,829	2,047	8.7	95.1	1.0	3.1	0.7	1.5	3.6	13.2	5.4	7.6	8.3	11.3
2,7003	33,460	1	Anoka	423.0	351,373	199	830.7	83.7	7.5	1.4	5.6	4.6	6.3	17.7	7.9	13.1	13.2	14.4
2,7005		6	Becker	1,315.1	34,098	1,323	25.9	89.4	1.1	9.7	0.9	2.1	6.3	18.2	7.3	10.4	11.2	11.4
2,7007	13,420	7	Beltrami	2,504.7	46,513	1,039	18.6	75.0	1.6	23.0	1.3	2.3	7.3	18.0	13.6	12.6	10.6	10.2
2,7009	41,060	3	Benton	408.3	39,937	1,176	97.8	91.9	4.8	1.0	1.8	2.4	7.4	18.1	8.1	15.0	13.5	12.5
2,7011		9	Big Stone	499.0	5,026	2,831	10.1	96.9	0.7	1.0	0.5	1.7	5.6	15.4	6.6	9.5	8.9	11.3
2,7013	31,860	3	Blue Earth	747.8	66,973	793	89.6	89.7	4.9	0.7	3.1	3.6	5.6	14.2	21.9	13.7	10.6	9.7
2,7015	35,580	6	Brown	611.1	25,194	1,601	41.2	94.1	0.9	0.4	1.1	4.5	5.6	16.5	9.5	10.8	10.4	11.5
2,7017	20,260	2	Carlton	861.3	35,498	1,288	41.2	90.4	2.1	7.2	1.0	1.7	5.3	17.3	7.5	12.0	12.6	13.8
2,7019	33,460	1	Carver	354.2	102,119	594	288.3	90.6	2.4	0.5	3.9	4.2	6.6	20.5	8.1	10.8	14.1	15.4
2,7021	14,660	9	Cass	2,021.5	29,355	1,448	14.5	85.1	0.9	13.4	0.9	2.1	5.8	15.7	6.1	9.4	9.4	11.5
2,7023		7	Chippewa	581.1	11,980	2,295	20.6	88.8	1.3	1.8	2.6	7.2	7.2	16.5	7.7	11.1	10.7	11.5
2,7025	33,460	1	Chisago	414.9	55,308	916	133.3	94.7	1.9	1.2	1.6	2.1	5.7	17.3	7.7	12.1	12.1	15.5
2,7027	22,020	3	Clay	1,045.2	63,569	837	60.8	89.4	4.1	2.2	2.1	4.5	7.3	17.1	15.1	13.8	12.4	10.5
2,7029		8	Clearwater	999.0	8,878	2,514	8.9	87.7	1.1	11.3	0.9	2.4	6.2	18.5	6.6	10.7	11.0	11.7
2,7031		9	Cook	1,452.4	5,398	2,803	3.7	88.8	1.4	9.5	1.4	2.5	4.9	11.0	5.8	10.1	10.1	11.6
2,7033		7	Cottonwood	639.9	11,295	2,334	17.7	87.2	1.3	0.9	4.2	7.7	7.1	17.0	7.6	9.6	10.2	11.6
2,7035	14,660	4	Crow Wing	998.4	64,424	824	64.5	96.2	1.3	1.6	0.9	1.5	5.7	16.1	7.0	11.0	10.8	12.1
2,7037	33,460	1	Dakota	562.4	421,751	166	749.9	81.0	7.8	0.9	6.0	7.1	6.5	18.0	8.0	13.0	13.2	14.0
2,7039	40,340	3	Dodge	439.3	20,762	1,785	47.3	93.2	1.0	0.9	1.3	5.1	6.4	19.9	7.9	11.5	13.3	13.5
2,7041	10,820	6	Douglas	636.8	37,575	1,234	59.0	96.8	0.9	0.7	0.9	1.8	5.8	15.6	7.1	11.6	10.9	11.8
2,7043		6	Faribault	712.5	13,784	2,180	19.3	91.9	0.8	0.8	0.7	6.9	5.5	16.5	6.9	9.9	11.1	11.6

1. CBSA = Core Based Statistical Area. See Appendix A for explanation. See Appendix B for list of metropolitan areas with component counties. 2. County type code from the Economic Research Service of USDA Rural-Urban Continuum Codes. See Appendix A for definition. 3. Dry land or land partially or temporarily covered by water. 4. May be of any race.

Table B. States and Counties — **Population and Households**

STATE County	Age (percent) (cont.)				Population change, 2000-2017							Households, 2012-2016				
					Total persons		Percent change		Components of change, 2010-2017						Percent	
	55 to 64 years	65 to 74 years	75 years and over	Percent female	2000	2010	2000-2010	2010-2017	Births	Deaths	Net Migration	Number	Persons per house-hold	Family house-holds	Female family house-holder[1]	One person
	16	17	18	19	20	21	22	23	24	25	26	27	28	29	30	31

STATE County	16	17	18	19	20	21	22	23	24	25	26	27	28	29	30	31
MICHIGAN— Cont'd																
Keweenaw	18.9	21.1	14.0	48.7	2,301	2,156	-6.3	-2.4	130	144	-38	1,023	2.13	61.9	9.0	34.5
Lake	19.7	16.8	10.6	48.5	11,333	11,539	1.8	4.1	712	1,113	864	4,394	2.51	60.3	9.1	34.7
Lapeer	16.3	10.9	6.6	49.3	87,904	88,307	0.5	-0.2	5,884	5,832	-171	32,757	2.64	73.7	9.2	22.3
Leelanau	18.9	17.4	12.5	50.7	21,119	21,708	2.8	-0.2	1,230	1,685	408	8,984	2.38	69.3	6.1	26.4
Lenawee	14.4	11.0	7.4	49.4	98,890	99,892	1.0	-1.3	7,601	7,102	-1,765	37,856	2.47	66.1	11.1	29.0
Livingston	15.8	10.4	6.1	49.9	156,951	180,964	15.3	4.8	12,831	10,062	6,042	69,763	2.65	73.8	8.0	21.5
Luce	15.7	11.0	9.4	40.9	7,024	6,631	-5.6	-4.1	373	517	-134	2,316	2.33	62.7	8.2	32.9
Mackinac	18.4	15.9	11.4	49.0	11,943	11,113	-6.9	-3.6	603	984	-17	5,230	2.05	60.3	8.5	33.3
Macomb	14.3	9.5	7.1	51.3	788,149	841,047	6.7	3.6	67,193	60,337	24,081	338,893	2.51	66.1	13.1	28.8
Manistee	17.3	14.7	10.5	48.4	24,527	24,751	0.9	-1.3	1,416	2,230	488	9,977	2.31	62.4	8.2	33.2
Marquette	14.3	10.9	7.6	49.7	64,634	67,077	3.8	-0.9	4,642	4,725	-460	26,293	2.38	60.1	8.3	31.2
Mason	16.5	13.2	9.7	50.3	28,274	28,687	1.5	1.3	2,133	2,366	641	12,171	2.32	66.1	10.8	28.3
Mecosta	13.5	10.7	7.3	49.8	40,553	42,798	5.5	1.4	3,062	2,695	231	15,528	2.59	60.7	8.6	29.3
Menominee	17.6	13.4	10.4	49.1	25,326	24,029	-5.1	-4.1	1,464	1,925	-507	10,586	2.19	60.2	8.2	35.6
Midland	14.3	9.8	8.1	50.7	82,874	83,629	0.9	-0.3	6,180	5,126	-1,258	33,757	2.44	67.9	8.7	26.3
Missaukee	15.1	12.0	8.2	49.3	14,478	14,849	2.6	1.0	1,280	1,191	65	5,843	2.54	69.0	7.7	27.0
Monroe	15.5	10.4	7.2	50.6	145,945	152,021	4.2	-1.6	11,068	10,098	-3,353	58,516	2.54	68.6	10.4	26.5
Montcalm	14.3	10.0	7.1	48.4	61,266	63,342	3.4	0.3	5,243	4,277	-752	23,057	2.61	69.4	10.8	26.4
Montmorency	20.2	18.4	13.1	49.3	10,315	9,765	-5.3	-5.3	483	1,118	123	4,122	2.22	62.2	9.7	32.1
Muskegon	14.3	9.7	6.7	50.2	170,200	172,188	1.2	0.9	15,282	12,202	-1,614	64,914	2.55	67.4	14.7	27.1
Newaygo	15.7	11.1	7.7	49.7	47,874	48,460	1.2	-0.4	3,952	3,552	-604	18,394	2.57	68.8	9.4	25.0
Oakland	14.3	9.7	6.7	51.1	1,194,156	1,202,386	0.7	4.0	97,310	74,250	26,128	496,727	2.46	64.8	10.3	29.6
Oceana	15.2	12.1	8.3	49.5	26,873	26,570	-1.1	-0.5	2,239	1,884	-479	10,043	2.53	72.2	9.7	23.4
Ogemaw	18.3	14.7	10.7	50.3	21,645	21,699	0.2	-3.3	1,356	2,158	102	9,318	2.23	65.1	11.3	30.1
Ontonagon	20.8	20.5	14.9	49.0	7,818	6,780	-13.3	-13.3	223	706	-419	2,969	2.05	57.2	4.5	37.6
Osceola	15.3	12.0	8.7	49.6	23,197	23,528	1.4	-1.1	1,903	1,740	-421	8,847	2.57	67.8	11.8	26.8
Oscoda	19.6	15.6	11.1	49.1	9,418	8,640	-8.3	-4.1	633	895	-90	3,662	2.27	62.5	5.1	33.4
Otsego	15.3	12.1	8.4	50.2	23,301	24,164	3.7	1.5	1,821	1,903	472	9,809	2.42	69.5	10.2	24.8
Ottawa	12.0	8.4	6.2	50.7	238,314	263,801	10.7	8.6	24,362	12,957	11,307	97,687	2.74	73.4	8.6	20.6
Presque Isle	19.3	17.1	13.6	50.0	14,411	13,376	-7.2	-4.4	685	1,392	131	5,911	2.15	66.0	6.1	30.0
Roscommon	20.1	19.2	12.9	50.2	25,469	24,449	-4.0	-2.3	1,242	2,808	1,004	11,344	2.08	61.7	11.0	33.5
Saginaw	14.2	10.7	8.1	51.4	210,039	200,169	-4.7	-4.1	16,380	14,912	-9,783	77,928	2.42	63.1	14.9	31.3
St. Clair	15.7	10.8	7.4	50.3	164,235	163,040	-0.7	-2.3	11,407	12,346	-2,741	64,529	2.45	66.8	10.9	27.7
St. Joseph	14.2	10.3	7.3	50.3	62,422	61,295	-1.8	-0.6	5,877	4,472	-1,746	23,198	2.59	69.2	11.0	26.0
Sanilac	16.1	12.0	8.9	50.3	44,547	43,114	-3.2	-4.3	3,214	3,372	-1,698	16,881	2.44	65.5	8.6	29.2
Schoolcraft	19.7	15.2	11.2	50.7	8,903	8,485	-4.7	-5.1	478	776	-134	3,318	2.42	62.6	7.7	32.9
Shiawassee	15.2	10.6	7.3	50.6	71,687	70,648	-1.4	-3.1	5,144	5,099	-2,265	27,480	2.48	69.6	10.6	24.8
Tuscola	16.0	11.5	8.3	49.7	58,266	55,729	-4.4	-5.3	3,989	4,154	-2,825	21,459	2.46	69.4	8.8	25.6
Van Buren	15.3	10.8	6.8	50.3	76,263	76,263	0.0	-1.2	6,559	5,288	-2,201	28,623	2.58	67.6	11.3	27.5
Washtenaw	11.5	8.2	5.2	50.4	322,895	345,066	6.9	6.5	27,004	15,734	11,512	138,672	2.44	57.8	9.3	30.0
Wayne	13.4	8.8	6.3	51.9	2,061,162	1,820,573	-11.7	-3.7	169,496	130,264	-107,979	669,412	2.61	62.2	19.5	32.8
Wexford	15.0	11.0	7.7	50.1	30,484	32,735	7.4	1.7	2,953	2,543	148	12,975	2.50	68.1	10.8	26.4
MINNESOTA	13.4	8.8	6.6	50.2	4,919,479	5,303,924	7.8	5.1	501,335	297,508	71,202	2,135,310	2.49	64.7	9.5	28.3
Aitkin	18.2	18.6	13.8	49.3	15,301	16,202	5.9	-2.3	823	1,522	333	7,640	2.02	65.3	6.9	29.5
Anoka	13.9	8.4	5.2	50.0	298,084	330,858	11.0	6.2	30,294	13,784	4,221	125,260	2.70	72.1	10.6	22.1
Becker	15.1	11.8	8.3	50.2	30,000	32,504	8.3	4.9	3,049	2,477	1,050	13,495	2.44	67.8	9.8	26.4
Beltrami	12.2	8.9	6.7	50.2	39,650	44,442	12.1	4.7	5,034	2,946	7	16,906	2.57	63.5	14.1	29.7
Benton	11.8	7.5	6.2	50.0	34,226	38,451	12.3	3.9	4,153	2,404	-249	15,726	2.45	65.6	10.6	26.1
Big Stone	17.2	11.8	13.7	50.3	5,820	5,269	-9.5	-4.6	401	534	-109	2,226	2.22	64.7	5.8	31.9
Blue Earth	10.9	7.4	6.0	49.5	55,941	64,013	14.4	4.6	5,388	3,416	1,008	25,081	2.46	57.3	7.5	27.1
Brown	15.1	10.2	10.4	50.2	26,911	25,893	-3.8	-2.7	1,991	2,118	-569	10,641	2.27	63.9	7.3	30.8
Carlton	14.5	9.5	7.5	47.8	31,671	35,386	11.7	0.3	2,660	2,680	158	13,289	2.54	66.3	8.6	28.0
Carver	13.0	6.9	4.6	50.4	70,205	91,086	29.7	12.1	8,408	3,376	6,034	34,990	2.75	74.7	6.8	20.6
Cass	17.0	15.1	10.1	49.0	27,150	28,567	5.2	2.8	2,447	2,250	597	12,806	2.21	69.6	9.9	25.3
Chippewa	14.3	10.9	10.2	50.3	13,088	12,441	-4.9	-3.7	1,192	1,073	-584	4,997	2.37	65.2	9.0	31.3
Chisago	14.4	9.1	5.9	48.3	41,101	53,887	31.1	2.6	4,075	2,768	117	19,790	2.64	71.7	7.6	22.5
Clay	10.9	6.9	6.1	50.6	51,229	58,999	15.2	7.7	6,047	3,325	1,871	23,034	2.49	64.7	8.8	27.7
Clearwater	14.8	11.1	9.3	49.1	8,423	8,695	3.2	2.1	777	692	101	3,435	2.52	65.8	7.5	28.9
Cook	19.2	17.6	9.7	50.3	5,168	5,176	0.2	4.3	342	318	198	2,661	1.93	62.1	6.1	30.7
Cottonwood	14.1	11.3	11.5	50.3	12,167	11,687	-3.9	-3.4	1,098	967	-526	4,822	2.34	64.2	7.7	32.4
Crow Wing	15.3	12.6	9.4	50.2	55,099	62,500	13.4	3.1	5,245	4,680	1,418	26,398	2.37	66.9	9.0	27.3
Dakota	13.6	8.2	5.4	50.7	355,904	398,581	12.0	5.8	37,883	17,031	2,459	157,696	2.59	69.3	10.1	24.4
Dodge	13.2	8.1	6.3	50.0	17,731	20,087	13.3	3.4	1,835	977	-180	7,583	2.66	74.7	9.5	21.8
Douglas	14.9	12.1	10.2	50.0	32,821	36,009	9.7	4.3	2,979	2,913	1,522	15,688	2.31	65.6	5.3	29.2
Faribault	15.8	11.5	11.2	50.0	16,181	14,553	-10.1	-5.3	1,073	1,368	-477	6,347	2.17	63.7	8.9	31.4

1. No spouse present.

Table B. States and Counties — Housing, Labor Force, and Employment

STATE County	Housing units, 2017 (cont.) — Occupied units								Civilian labor force, 2017		Unemployment		Civilian employment[6], 2012-2016		
	Owner-occupied			Median owner cost as a percent of income		Renter-occupied								Percent	
	Total	Percent	Median value[1]	With a mortgage	Without a mortgage[2]	Median rent[3]	Median rent as a percent of income[2]	Sub-standard units[4] (percent)	Total	Percent change, 2016-2017	Total	Rate[5]	Total	Management, business, science, and arts	Construction, production, and maintenance occupations
	89	90	91	92	93	94	95	96	97	98	99	100	101	102	103
MICHIGAN— Cont'd															
Keweenaw	1,023	88.5	98,800	21.9	14.5	552	33.6	4.1	940	-0.1	82	8.7	857	33.8	19.1
Lake	4,394	83.0	79,100	27.8	14.1	574	37.5	2.4	3,772	0.6	307	8.1	3,338	21.0	31.4
Lapeer	32,757	82.2	141,200	22.8	12.2	793	31.7	2.3	41,114	1.1	2,208	5.4	38,038	28.5	31.7
Leelanau	8,984	86.0	243,500	24.8	11.7	865	30.1	1.1	10,655	0.8	522	4.9	9,665	36.8	21.5
Lenawee	37,856	77.7	119,400	22.3	13.0	754	29.9	1.3	47,363	0.1	2,274	4.8	43,293	29.0	28.7
Livingston	69,763	84.9	204,000	20.3	11.2	939	27.5	1.1	101,400	1.5	3,362	3.3	93,195	38.9	20.8
Luce	2,316	75.3	80,300	20.0	12.2	620	29.8	1.9	2,431	1.2	168	6.9	1,992	27.8	24.8
Mackinac	5,230	73.3	124,100	21.8	13.2	579	25.7	2.8	5,282	1.9	541	10.2	4,547	24.8	25.6
Macomb	33,8,893	73.0	134,800	20.5	13.1	884	30.6	1.7	441,491	1.5	18,931	4.3	408,439	34.1	23.3
Manistee	9,977	81.6	109,800	23.0	12.6	619	30.0	1.5	10,448	-0.7	694	6.6	9,060	28.8	24.0
Marquette	26,293	70.1	137,700	19.0	11.7	644	31.8	1.5	32,799	-1.5	1,868	5.7	29,589	32.3	21.7
Mason	12,171	75.9	123,200	24.1	13.0	681	29.7	1.8	14,163	-0.7	823	5.8	12,384	30.5	26.7
Mecosta	15,528	73.1	111,300	21.9	12.0	631	33.3	2.7	18,905	-1.0	1,097	5.8	17,694	27.5	28.9
Menominee	10,586	78.6	93,700	21.1	12.1	538	27.9	1.8	11,018	-2.0	554	5.0	10,405	25.3	35.5
Midland	33,757	74.7	131,100	19.3	11.4	748	28.6	1.8	40,489	-1.2	1,924	4.8	37,904	38.7	21.3
Missaukee	5,843	82.7	103,900	22.9	12.9	718	28.6	3.7	7,033	0.2	420	6.0	6,196	24.4	38.0
Monroe	58,516	79.6	141,500	20.5	11.9	786	29.0	1.4	76,449	0.1	3,713	4.9	68,233	29.8	31.4
Montcalm	23,057	78.3	96,500	22.3	12.9	668	29.5	1.9	28,183	1.0	1,430	5.1	25,269	24.2	35.6
Montmorency	4,122	84.8	95,100	24.4	12.3	592	33.8	1.5	3,037	-0.7	328	10.8	2,819	22.0	33.0
Muskegon	64,914	74.1	101,400	20.3	12.2	692	34.6	2.3	78,193	1.0	4,232	5.4	71,549	27.4	29.0
Newaygo	18,394	83.2	101,200	22.1	13.3	670	32.5	2.7	23,456	0.6	1,174	5.0	18,878	25.3	35.9
Oakland	49,6,727	70.3	191,500	20.0	12.2	968	27.7	1.4	662,752	1.7	22,784	3.4	619,073	48.2	14.1
Oceana	10,043	79.9	104,800	23.4	13.0	660	29.1	5.2	12,397	0.7	887	7.2	10,319	26.3	38.6
Ogemaw	9,318	82.5	88,600	23.9	14.0	646	34.2	2.6	8,238	0.1	646	7.8	7,689	24.7	27.6
Ontonagon	2,969	87.6	69,500	24.6	13.1	431	29.8	1.6	2,166	-1.6	197	9.1	1,959	26.3	30.1
Osceola	8,847	79.0	89,400	22.6	13.0	592	29.5	2.7	10,624	1.9	646	6.1	8,772	24.6	38.7
Oscoda	3,662	85.1	80,700	23.3	13.8	586	31.3	3.2	2,941	1.2	220	7.5	2,826	21.3	33.3
Otsego	9,809	80.9	121,600	19.7	12.5	743	31.3	1.7	11,668	-0.1	714	6.1	11,045	27.9	25.1
Ottawa	97,687	77.2	160,500	19.4	10.8	807	28.4	2.4	157,285	1.3	5,263	3.3	139,418	33.5	27.7
Presque Isle	5,911	88.1	94,000	20.8	12.4	577	28.4	1.4	5,190	-1.8	493	9.5	4,495	27.1	32.2
Roscommon	11,344	80.8	92,400	24.8	12.4	629	33.7	1.7	7,957	1.2	709	8.9	7,645	24.1	27.3
Saginaw	77,928	72.1	92,800	20.7	12.8	709	32.1	1.5	87,662	-1.0	4,842	5.5	81,750	30.6	23.1
St. Clair	64,529	75.6	126,900	21.7	12.8	751	31.1	1.5	75,420	1.1	3,748	5.0	71,019	27.4	30.9
St. Joseph	23,198	73.4	109,700	21.3	11.5	669	28.9	3.2	28,855	-0.9	1,240	4.3	26,968	24.0	41.6
Sanilac	16,881	79.1	98,500	21.4	12.8	622	29.2	1.6	19,457	0.3	1,170	6.0	17,430	26.0	36.4
Schoolcraft	3,318	80.7	98,700	21.8	13.6	586	34.1	1.4	3,370	-0.5	288	8.5	2,739	27.6	26.1
Shiawassee	27,480	75.9	105,500	21.2	12.3	683	29.0	1.5	33,525	0.2	1,763	5.3	29,921	27.9	31.6
Tuscola	21,459	82.0	95,200	22.1	13.0	650	30.5	1.9	24,039	-0.7	1,535	6.4	23,102	26.1	32.5
Van Buren	28,623	77.5	121,400	22.0	13.0	666	29.2	2.7	35,459	0.0	2,064	5.8	32,533	28.7	29.9
Washtenaw	13,8,672	59.6	218,100	20.3	11.9	980	31.7	1.8	193,566	1.1	6,968	3.6	180,182	52.6	12.8
Wayne	66,9,412	62.1	86,000	21.4	14.2	808	34.6	2.8	789,088	1.4	42,673	5.4	710,658	31.4	23.9
Wexford	12,975	75.4	92,400	22.9	13.2	718	29.8	2.4	14,776	0.6	840	5.7	13,503	26.4	34.9
MINNESOTA	21,3,5310	71.4	191,500	20.9	11.0	873	28.9	2.4	3,063,608	0.9	105,768	3.5	2,864,441	39.8	20.9
Aitkin	7,640	82.6	165,300	26.6	12.7	632	29.9	3.5	7,195	2.0	448	6.2	6,284	29.6	25.5
Anoka	12,5,260	79.9	193,200	21.0	10.1	1,000	29.8	2.1	195,328	1.4	6,520	3.3	184,997	36.8	23.1
Becker	13,495	79.0	177,600	21.6	11.7	681	27.2	2.3	18,589	-0.2	772	4.2	16,139	31.9	30.5
Beltrami	16,906	68.9	148,600	22.2	12.2	686	30.1	2.8	23,722	-0.2	1,155	4.9	20,609	32.1	21.3
Benton	15,726	69.1	158,400	22.8	11.8	668	30.6	2.7	22,088	1.1	886	4.0	20,381	30.2	29.4
Big Stone	2,226	78.8	96,900	18.9	11.0	499	24.3	1.6	2,599	-4.2	114	4.4	2,432	31.5	30.3
Blue Earth	25,081	63.0	166,200	20.5	10.2	784	31.0	1.5	40,188	1.1	1,169	2.9	36,614	33.6	22.4
Brown	10,641	78.8	132,300	19.3	10.7	596	27.5	1.5	14,473	-0.7	538	3.7	13,534	31.4	30.4
Carlton	13,289	78.9	160,900	21.9	12.2	714	27.0	2.7	17,854	0.3	857	4.8	16,855	30.7	26.8
Carver	34,990	79.8	277,600	20.8	10.4	976	26.1	1.2	57,261	1.3	1,672	2.9	54,114	45.6	15.5
Cass	12,806	80.7	174,000	23.4	11.6	684	29.6	3.0	14,554	2.4	852	5.9	12,237	29.6	25.9
Chippewa	4,997	71.3	102,400	18.7	10.2	576	23.8	1.1	6,969	-0.3	281	4.0	6,389	30.9	29.2
Chisago	19,790	85.1	195,600	22.5	11.8	796	29.3	1.4	29,638	1.3	1,171	4.0	27,555	34.1	25.9
Clay	23,034	69.8	166,600	20.5	10.9	747	33.6	1.7	35,875	0.4	1,152	3.2	33,480	35.4	21.7
Clearwater	3,435	78.7	116,500	22.2	12.7	543	27.9	4.6	4,631	-2.1	402	8.7	3,625	27.3	37.6
Cook	2,661	74.0	242,200	24.4	10.0	655	25.7	5.3	3,194	2.9	119	3.7	2,709	35.6	20.5
Cottonwood	4,822	78.3	88,800	18.5	11.1	592	25.3	2.7	5,636	1.4	301	5.3	5,396	29.2	34.9
Crow Wing	26,398	75.2	181,800	22.3	11.5	758	29.5	1.1	32,486	1.7	1,450	4.5	29,695	31.9	22.5
Dakota	15,7,696	74.3	226,900	20.3	10.0	1,003	28.1	1.6	239,345	1.4	7,228	3.0	227,582	42.4	17.3
Dodge	7,583	83.1	162,000	20.4	11.3	624	25.3	1.6	11,657	0.5	396	3.4	11,082	34.5	28.7
Douglas	15,688	77.0	189,900	22.0	12.3	723	28.8	0.9	20,653	1.7	658	3.2	19,015	33.6	25.8
Faribault	6,347	76.2	85,400	18.9	11.0	564	23.2	1.2	7,235	-1.5	305	4.2	7,060	32.1	32.2

1. Specified owner-occupied units. lacking complete plumbing facilities. 2. A value of 10.0 represents 10 percent or less; a value of 50.0 represents 50 percent or more. 3. Specified renter-occupied units. 4. Overcrowded or 5. Percent of civilian labor force. 6. Civilian employed persons 16 years old and over.

Table B. States and Counties — Nonfarm Employment and Agriculture

	Private nonfarm establishments, employment and payroll, 2016									Agriculture, 2012			
	Employment							Annual payroll		Farms			
											Percent with:		
STATE County	Number of establishments	Total	Health care and social assistance	Manufacturing	Retail trade	Finance and insurance	Professional, scientific, and technical services	Total (mil dol)	Average per employee (dollars)	Number	Fewer than 50 acres	500 acres or more	Farm operators whose principal occupation is farming (percent)
	104	105	106	107	108	109	110	111	112	113	114	115	116
MICHIGAN— Cont'd													
Keweenaw	60	204	NA	D	16	D	D	6	29,093	6	66.7	0.0	33.3
Lake	160	1,115	249	91	257	63	D	32	28,576	200	38.0	5.0	49.5
Lapeer	1,639	18,318	2,788	5,282	3,300	428	546	642	35,059	1,133	52.8	7.2	51.3
Leelanau	751	4,572	629	393	669	210	217	188	41,113	494	38.3	2.6	55.5
Lenawee	1,805	23,382	2,997	5,219	3,825	824	454	854	36,507	1,618	45.7	11.7	39.3
Livingston	4,319	51,969	5,915	9,509	9,311	3,525	2,725	2,029	39,035	734	58.3	4.6	54.8
Luce	171	1,526	383	253	284	57	19	54	35,193	43	44.2	16.3	44.2
Mackinac	440	2,112	385	106	350	88	38	113	53,545	103	30.1	11.7	57.3
Macomb	18,905	298,365	40,754	69,651	42,581	6,029	29,648	14,497	48,589	502	59.4	6.4	53.8
Manistee	563	5,891	1,015	871	1,255	167	104	218	37,088	324	35.2	2.5	43.8
Marquette	1,625	21,405	5,712	928	3,800	979	635	818	38,218	168	41.1	6.0	48.8
Mason	732	9,263	1,326	2,233	1,510	222	165	343	37,056	440	34.5	8.2	45.2
Mecosta	716	9,471	1,446	2,359	2,041	209	274	325	34,273	779	31.8	5.9	48.1
Menominee	459	5,125	230	1,709	676	143	137	181	35,322	398	25.6	9.8	47.5
Midland	2,081	35,682	6,644	6,859	4,066	1,125	978	2,271	63,646	555	47.9	7.0	46.7
Missaukee	297	2,383	405	399	406	55	36	75	31,648	433	38.6	10.6	48.3
Monroe	2,285	37,503	4,751	7,359	4,933	810	1,285	1,623	43,270	1,144	53.0	10.9	46.3
Montcalm	995	12,232	3,044	2,382	2,467	355	235	425	34,746	1,127	41.3	9.4	54.3
Montmorency	203	1,647	247	438	229	73	19	57	34,508	151	31.1	8.6	36.4
Muskegon	3,114	52,661	10,271	13,060	7,940	1,075	1,474	2,129	40,422	514	56.6	4.9	48.4
Newaygo	803	9,374	1,664	1,525	1,615	583	348	337	35,961	923	45.8	5.1	45.1
Oakland	38,944	692,833	107,764	52,089	76,020	37,676	100,586	41,487	59,880	537	70.9	2.0	51.6
Oceana	492	4,878	705	1,522	644	126	93	161	32,914	609	37.9	9.4	52.7
Ogemaw	547	5,268	1,086	300	1,434	129	111	169	32,166	280	24.6	11.4	49.3
Ontonagon	161	894	208	D	225	58	10	25	27,885	109	12.8	14.7	45.0
Osceola	425	6,073	1,010	2,170	591	119	94	245	40,378	750	34.0	4.9	35.9
Oscoda	176	1,459	136	328	230	36	20	47	31,920	145	43.4	2.1	52.4
Otsego	754	8,863	1,794	1,054	2,128	176	167	308	34,739	180	37.2	9.4	47.2
Ottawa	6,013	109,415	10,969	37,004	10,396	2,557	4,027	4,586	41,916	1,363	55.2	5.6	51.5
Presque Isle	321	2,300	326	222	374	102	40	79	34,183	323	22.9	9.9	55.1
Roscommon	539	4,716	561	591	1,335	158	57	130	27,607	58	44.8	3.4	34.5
Saginaw	4,261	78,672	17,499	11,722	12,759	2,770	2,470	3,159	40,154	1,318	41.0	12.1	48.9
St. Clair	3,096	42,187	7,816	8,957	7,219	1,281	1,012	1,608	38,123	1,049	46.1	7.9	56.0
St. Joseph	1,161	19,614	1,678	9,511	2,525	371	474	761	38,813	967	44.9	10.9	41.8
Sanilac	816	8,346	1,290	2,791	1,582	362	185	286	34,294	1,467	29.9	17.3	55.6
Schoolcraft	236	1,877	447	69	358	188	35	69	36,643	65	27.7	6.2	50.8
Shiawassee	1,126	13,299	2,533	2,202	2,525	332	270	458	34,447	1,033	42.1	10.6	51.2
Tuscola	824	8,628	2,401	1,271	1,614	293	199	305	35,372	1,322	40.0	12.3	48.6
Van Buren	1,303	16,763	2,651	2,954	2,861	327	1,914	672	40,079	1,113	49.5	4.4	53.2
Washtenaw	8,119	150,135	37,479	15,005	17,704	3,911	15,217	8,233	54,838	1,236	55.3	6.9	48.8
Wayne	32,224	637,407	107,608	84,269	69,675	34,809	41,534	34,371	53,924	287	77.7	1.4	59.9
Wexford	840	12,142	1,795	3,120	2,036	316	245	435	35,813	357	42.6	3.4	37.5
MINNESOTA	15,0,115	2,661,627	460,279	305,782	307,266	163,505	183,069	137,136	51,523	74,542	25.2	18.2	52.9
Aitkin	400	3,180	832	397	610	95	34	103	32,529	471	19.7	12.5	40.8
Anoka	7,750	114,048	17,467	20,998	16,803	2,257	3,987	5,292	46,400	396	58.3	4.5	44.7
Becker	932	10,740	2,441	2,285	1,984	267	178	383	35,689	1,107	17.3	15.4	54.9
Beltrami	1,170	14,490	3,793	950	3,090	406	417	501	34,565	573	15.5	17.6	44.9
Benton	900	15,199	2,473	3,260	2,098	202	225	610	40,107	958	29.7	7.8	51.8
Big Stone	190	1,646	762	14	196	89	32	60	36,615	400	14.8	34.0	63.0
Blue Earth	1,956	36,969	8,851	4,233	6,371	974	1,096	1,346	36,410	1,070	26.9	22.4	53.7
Brown	772	13,095	2,370	3,015	1,717	439	447	502	38,330	1,055	21.0	19.9	55.9
Carlton	710	8,015	2,033	1,283	1,397	429	168	318	39,719	501	21.6	5.8	43.7
Carver	2,517	39,358	5,610	10,723	3,734	753	2,053	1,968	50,009	789	38.3	9.6	51.3
Cass	820	7,007	1,254	305	1,016	190	557	212	30,212	546	20.1	12.6	54.0
Chippewa	387	5,030	1,188	1,025	653	194	80	174	34,673	674	23.7	30.4	67.1
Chisago	1,246	13,579	3,976	2,149	1,899	271	872	573	42,216	832	44.2	4.7	37.6
Clay	1,317	17,915	4,377	800	2,901	422	543	604	33,737	804	20.5	33.6	52.6
Clearwater	211	2,478	592	D	234	70	60	127	51,204	519	12.5	15.4	36.0
Cook	278	2,022	221	58	306	42	29	67	32,917	18	50.0	5.6	16.7
Cottonwood	346	3,921	742	1,278	501	95	73	124	31,603	813	23.1	31.1	66.8
Crow Wing	2,178	26,295	6,154	2,353	4,694	1,307	983	980	37,251	533	28.5	8.1	50.5
Dakota	10,530	177,935	24,923	17,404	24,775	12,181	9,356	8,817	49,552	892	42.2	13.6	56.8
Dodge	414	4,759	355	1,682	453	106	94	207	43,400	621	39.6	19.5	58.5
Douglas	1,348	18,089	3,863	3,899	3,146	404	423	730	40,332	1,091	24.6	11.2	39.4
Faribault	415	4,094	739	1,226	608	235	78	150	36,659	824	21.4	32.0	67.4

Table B. States and Counties — **Agriculture**

STATE County	Acreage (1,000) 117	Percent change, 2007-2012 118	Average size of farm 119	Total irrigated (1,000) 120	Total cropland (1,000) 121	Average per farm 122	Average per acre 123	Value of machinery and equipment, average per farm (dollars) 124	Total (mil dol) 125	Average per farm (acres) 126	Crops 127	Livestock and poultry products 128	$10,000 or more 129	$100,000 or more 130	Total ($1,000) 131	Percent of farms 132
MICHIGAN— Cont'd																
Keweenaw	0	-80.1	53	0.0	0.0	133,333	2,516	34,167	D	D	D	D	0.0	0.0	0	0.0
Lake	26	21.7	130	0.0	11.5	338,075	2,598	55,965	4.1	20,305	56.4	43.6	22.0	4.0	88	12.0
Lapeer	176	-0.4	155	2.1	137.1	708,546	4,572	126,049	113.4	100,049	80.6	19.4	41.8	15.3	2,214	23.1
Leelanau	59	6.7	120	2.2	33.3	810,441	6,731	96,296	20.5	41,486	86.7	13.3	43.1	9.1	2,363	31.0
Lenawee	344	-1.2	213	4.4	299.3	863,720	4,058	134,226	204.6	126,435	70.4	29.6	42.0	17.4	10,028	62.1
Livingston	86	-10.7	117	1.4	61.0	569,114	4,849	88,651	52.3	71,187	74.1	25.9	36.0	10.4	1,090	16.5
Luce	12	31.5	270	D	4.3	619,116	2,295	97,233	3.6	84,070	81.7	18.3	39.5	11.6	79	20.9
Mackinac	22	3.3	218	0.0	11.5	452,359	2,078	57,767	5.4	52,039	22.1	77.9	45.6	7.8	142	21.4
Macomb	68	9.6	135	2.5	58.4	747,673	5,523	120,797	73.2	145,900	79.7	20.3	53.4	24.7	956	23.5
Manistee	44	-3.8	137	1.3	20.1	393,093	2,875	41,111	7.6	23,543	85.1	14.9	28.4	5.9	241	13.0
Marquette	31	2.0	183	0.1	9.2	372,268	2,038	68,690	2.3	13,679	35.5	64.5	26.8	1.2	209	8.9
Mason	79	3.4	180	3.0	56.7	512,948	2,855	109,655	52.9	120,184	59.9	40.1	43.0	15.0	828	27.0
Mecosta	123	7.2	158	14.4	79.7	471,610	2,987	90,709	113.3	145,388	40.6	59.4	46.5	13.0	904	36.5
Menominee	92	-11.3	231	0.0	50.3	463,201	2,006	84,543	41.4	104,025	19.1	80.9	37.7	14.6	1,131	37.4
Midland	90	-1.2	161	1.0	69.5	580,838	3,600	98,339	70.1	126,285	67.9	32.1	39.1	14.1	2,310	44.3
Missaukee	100	12.6	230	7.5	71.7	695,275	3,025	154,582	126.0	290,998	24.8	75.2	41.6	18.7	1,568	28.6
Monroe	215	3.2	188	9.8	196.2	853,688	4,553	135,682	173.9	152,008	95.5	4.5	54.6	20.3	3,653	50.8
Montcalm	237	-2.3	211	55.9	181.1	702,214	3,336	131,319	213.9	189,831	72.1	27.9	41.1	17.9	2,577	40.6
Montmorency	24	11.6	161	D	14.6	366,252	2,272	84,497	8.1	53,854	52.8	47.2	37.7	9.9	175	25.2
Muskegon	74	-6.8	144	9.5	49.0	741,080	5,130	95,333	76.0	147,860	61.6	38.4	38.9	15.6	658	21.8
Newaygo	126	-5.8	136	7.5	83.4	484,268	3,557	91,385	113.8	123,346	39.9	60.1	39.5	13.8	1,193	20.8
Oakland	32	-2.4	59	0.7	18.8	506,358	8,572	54,261	25.9	48,244	87.5	12.5	25.1	6.9	226	6.9
Oceana	128	3.6	210	10.4	89.4	675,791	3,221	124,509	101.2	166,141	63.3	36.7	48.6	18.7	2,529	31.2
Ogemaw	68	11.8	243	0.1	40.2	645,025	2,650	129,246	46.3	165,218	29.1	70.9	42.1	18.9	927	47.1
Ontonagon	29	-5.7	267	0.0	13.9	451,716	1,694	61,257	2.2	20,220	75.1	24.9	40.4	4.6	91	12.8
Osceola	111	-9.5	147	1.4	64.7	373,809	2,536	65,007	45.7	60,912	28.5	71.5	30.0	8.5	1,124	22.8
Oscoda	17	-4.7	116	0.0	7.9	303,648	2,629	48,641	6.9	47,635	17.1	82.9	45.5	13.8	44	6.2
Otsego	32	-3.9	179	1.2	14.3	453,122	2,526	72,189	7.1	39,250	85.5	14.5	39.4	6.1	88	32.2
Ottawa	186	9.2	137	18.1	138.1	881,996	6,458	142,875	534.4	392,080	56.2	43.8	56.9	26.9	2,689	25.5
Presque Isle	82	14.7	252	1.4	45.4	541,449	2,145	82,938	22.8	70,653	76.5	23.5	39.6	10.8	684	31.0
Roscommon	7	56.2	128	0.3	2.7	336,517	2,626	56,966	D	D	D	D	24.1	0.0	6	6.9
Saginaw	310	-4.5	235	2.3	274.5	896,656	3,816	144,832	243.6	184,855	91.7	8.3	55.8	27.6	6,093	71.6
St. Clair	180	12.1	172	0.4	151.6	640,936	3,736	122,904	107.9	102,895	90.7	9.3	47.5	17.8	1,714	32.6
St. Joseph	222	2.9	229	112.4	188.2	1,090,049	4,754	158,897	238.1	246,177	80.2	19.8	48.4	25.0	4,196	46.8
Sanilac	457	9.5	311	1.8	405.5	1,365,955	4,386	217,288	421.0	286,957	66.5	33.5	61.0	36.3	7,213	60.3
Schoolcraft	19	-27.2	299	D	5.3	485,169	1,624	59,031	2.2	33,354	63.0	37.1	32.3	9.2	93	10.8
Shiawassee	223	-1.4	216	0.8	195.2	773,484	3,577	136,423	145.2	140,532	78.1	21.9	52.6	22.0	3,634	55.3
Tuscola	325	-5.1	246	5.4	284.5	1,117,802	4,542	168,867	274.4	207,599	82.4	17.6	48.9	26.2	4,778	56.9
Van Buren	175	-5.5	157	34.0	125.1	699,335	4,445	132,358	194.7	174,900	82.9	17.1	46.6	16.4	2,425	21.5
Washtenaw	170	2.0	138	3.6	133.5	701,358	5,095	92,338	87.8	71,004	77.0	23.0	42.5	14.6	3,466	31.7
Wayne	16	-9.6	55	0.3	10.9	408,840	7,442	80,902	26.5	92,456	98.2	1.8	36.9	8.4	102	9.4
Wexford	40	4.8	113	0.9	23.7	321,616	2,847	47,675	9.7	27,104	49.9	50.1	26.1	5.0	122	15.1
MINNESOTA	26,036	-3.3	349	524.0	21,597.1	1,474,057	4,220	197,702	21,280.2	285,479	65.2	34.8	60.0	33.5	467,867	70.0
Aitkin	123	-7.6	260	3.1	61.8	458,718	1,762	64,280	15.7	33,395	52.4	47.6	36.9	6.8	275	22.1
Anoka	45	-2.5	113	2.6	33.0	683,038	6,032	84,725	47.5	119,922	81.5	18.5	35.6	11.6	329	23.7
Becker	435	9.9	393	10.4	309.9	1,067,005	2,716	145,055	261.5	236,218	67.8	32.2	45.9	21.0	6,592	62.9
Beltrami	181	-14.4	315	2.6	88.2	535,471	1,699	70,642	32.4	56,518	66.0	34.0	41.2	10.3	1,146	32.6
Benton	189	1.5	197	11.5	139.9	676,684	3,435	130,284	167.5	174,846	44.1	55.9	59.5	24.5	3,168	63.9
Big Stone	249	-1.4	622	2.1	215.7	2,426,078	3,901	304,623	164.6	411,560	84.0	16.0	72.0	47.5	3,512	85.8
Blue Earth	376	-9.4	352	1.7	338.8	2,256,415	6,413	234,723	505.4	472,358	51.8	48.2	65.8	46.4	7,732	80.4
Brown	326	-8.1	309	2.4	296.4	1,705,125	5,518	216,063	382.9	362,955	57.5	42.5	76.5	51.5	7,384	88.3
Carlton	93	-5.5	185	D	42.4	345,838	1,872	55,281	11.0	21,878	49.3	50.7	39.1	2.4	D	12.2
Carver	155	-8.3	197	0.2	131.6	1,139,812	5,793	194,842	134.4	170,340	65.4	34.6	59.6	28.9	3,149	62.4
Cass	157	-7.1	288	8.8	61.3	549,962	1,910	68,947	38.2	69,877	27.5	72.5	44.3	8.1	542	23.4
Chippewa	335	-8.9	497	4.3	310.6	2,569,132	5,167	332,969	333.2	494,408	79.3	20.7	66.5	48.5	6,261	87.5
Chisago	114	-1.3	137	1.6	76.2	595,308	4,354	79,403	56.5	67,945	77.7	22.3	47.8	12.6	1,081	38.6
Clay	611	-0.5	760	9.9	555.2	2,673,295	3,519	311,899	398.1	495,118	90.3	9.7	62.3	41.3	8,241	75.7
Clearwater	167	-14.0	322	4.0	76.2	539,944	1,679	79,719	31.1	59,836	48.3	51.7	48.4	9.8	886	41.0
Cook	2	-5.4	126	0.0	0.2	598,778	4,744	28,444	0.3	14,278	90.3	9.7	27.8	5.6	D	5.6
Cottonwood	373	-2.2	459	1.4	336.4	2,519,027	5,494	312,232	374.1	460,135	62.6	37.4	70.6	53.4	7,918	83.9
Crow Wing	100	-17.9	188	2.2	44.8	485,445	2,588	75,574	24.8	46,593	58.6	41.5	36.8	8.8	546	30.6
Dakota	220	-10.6	246	50.4	192.7	1,398,640	5,675	195,370	241.0	270,188	77.8	22.2	63.9	32.5	3,892	54.4
Dodge	225	-9.2	363	D	202.5	2,231,597	6,148	237,108	288.1	463,976	61.6	38.4	63.6	40.3	4,124	68.9
Douglas	268	1.8	245	3.4	197.8	754,903	3,078	113,163	120.9	110,813	73.7	26.3	52.6	23.1	4,467	77.7
Faribault	390	-14.0	473	0.3	370.2	2,662,949	5,624	317,608	414.2	502,671	77.9	22.1	78.9	61.0	7,763	82.8

STATE County	Water use, 2015 Public supply water withdrawn (mil gal/day)	Public supply gallons withdrawn per person per day	Wholesale Trade[1], 2012 Number of establishments	Number of employees	Sales (mil dol)	Annual payroll (mil dol)	Retail Trade[2], 2012 Number of establishments	Number of employees	Sales (mil dol)	Annual payroll (mil dol)	Real estate and rental and leasing,[2] 2012 Number of establishments	Number of employees	Sales (mil dol)	Annual payroll (mil dol)
	133	134	135	136	137	138	139	140	141	142	143	144	145	146
MICHIGAN— Cont'd														
Keweenaw	0.05	23.1	2	D	D	D	11	39	3.9	0.5	1	D	D	D
Lake	0.26	22.8	4	D	D	D	30	243	60.2	4.8	4	D	D	D
Lapeer	0.40	4.5	50	438	282.1	20.7	239	2,859	867.1	66.0	56	219	24.5	5.2
Leelanau	0.50	22.7	11	D	D	D	124	568	139.3	12.4	30	D	D	D
Lenawee	6.10	61.9	56	D	D	D	304	3,804	961.6	86.9	57	169	30.5	8.2
Livingston	6.92	36.9	198	2,435	3,092.5	144.1	599	8,695	2,410.2	205.7	124	544	95.4	18.5
Luce	0.50	77.9	4	D	D	D	26	256	84.2	5.9	7	36	2.4	0.6
Mackinac	1.29	118.5	8	48	65.3	1.9	93	366	121.9	10.3	12	D	D	D
Macomb	3.97	4.6	787	10,277	5,776.1	580.9	2,786	40,305	11,304.2	1,006.0	617	3,018	572.1	99.2
Manistee	1.54	63.0	13	117	225.6	6.6	107	905	231.9	19.0	18	42	5.8	0.9
Marquette	5.16	76.8	47	370	203.2	15.9	275	3,741	789.3	77.2	64	266	37.8	6.3
Mason	2.45	85.1	19	135	190.9	5.8	113	1,428	370.3	32.4	30	560	117.8	31.7
Mecosta	1.27	29.5	19	D	D	D	142	1,881	488.2	40.3	38	94	15.8	2.4
Menominee	1.07	45.4	18	297	144.1	11.9	68	584	155.5	11.9	16	D	D	D
Midland	0.14	1.7	44	297	703.7	16.7	314	4,050	1,015.7	88.4	63	257	36.8	8.4
Missaukee	0.38	25.5	16	111	69.6	4.5	39	332	120.0	8.9	4	5	0.5	0.1
Monroe	9.27	62.0	89	D	D	D	377	4,977	1,471.2	110.5	78	306	43.8	7.9
Montcalm	3.06	48.6	39	314	144.6	12.0	214	2,231	601.8	50.2	22	64	9.5	1.4
Montmorency	0.12	13.0	2	D	D	D	33	224	66.7	4.9	3	D	D	D
Muskegon	16.08	93.1	121	D	D	D	552	7,597	1,919.4	171.2	91	457	71.7	14.8
Newaygo	1.87	39.0	29	201	105.1	8.7	149	1,423	377.1	31.9	26	65	9.0	1.7
Oakland	19.11	15.4	2,048	28,521	25,910.5	1,806.5	4,880	70,570	20,886.2	1,879.2	1,644	15,464	3,085.1	678.8
Oceana	1.16	44.4	10	65	31.2	2.7	88	606	160.5	12.8	17	43	6.2	1.2
Ogemaw	0.38	18.1	21	441	155.5	17.4	119	1,574	387.6	35.3	21	58	9.0	1.6
Ontonagon	0.44	73.2	4	9	1.9	0.3	30	242	48.4	5.2	3	5	0.3	0.2
Osceola	1.37	59.4	13	116	134.7	5.2	73	601	176.1	15.4	9	9	2.3	0.4
Oscoda	0.07	8.5	2	D	D	D	37	241	59.5	4.6	7	14	1.8	0.2
Otsego	1.11	45.8	42	379	167.4	15.1	148	2,025	528.6	46.1	21	66	9.7	1.8
Ottawa	88.23	315.2	295	3,659	2,645.2	190.1	764	9,714	2,666.6	230.5	196	825	143.8	27.3
Presque Isle	0.46	35.8	5	8	2.0	0.2	64	388	110.9	8.6	7	D	D	D
Roscommon	0.28	11.7	10	48	12.6	1.4	111	1,220	331.4	28.7	15	63	9.7	1.6
Saginaw	0.42	2.2	181	1,975	1,264.9	96.7	870	12,210	2,913.3	262.8	132	602	101.1	16.3
St. Clair	137.89	862.5	89	924	548.7	40.4	532	6,745	1,760.0	148.7	94	272	56.4	8.2
St. Joseph	3.25	53.3	42	D	D	D	196	2,254	631.8	51.7	40	133	18.7	2.7
Sanilac	1.56	37.6	33	315	248.9	16.9	156	1,502	374.2	30.7	18	41	5.3	1.0
Schoolcraft	0.35	42.8	6	5	2.8	0.1	46	376	124.6	7.9	1	D	D	D
Shiawassee	2.89	42.1	40	457	201.1	18.2	200	2,413	713.9	58.1	35	77	11.2	2.0
Tuscola	1.89	35.1	39	465	404.6	23.0	157	1,581	481.9	34.8	19	75	8.7	1.4
Van Buren	3.55	47.3	53	D	D	D	252	2,285	634.6	54.1	32	102	15.3	1.9
Washtenaw	18.36	51.2	276	3,580	4,695.9	221.8	1,106	16,577	4,461.1	411.4	306	2,409	727.2	115.9
Wayne	466.55	265.2	1,483	23,525	25,358.3	1,417.5	6,091	65,409	17,409.4	1,539.9	1,070	6,044	4,464.6	225.3
Wexford	2.65	80.3	25	409	162.6	19.5	163	1,922	497.4	42.8	34	105	15.6	2.9
MINNESOTA	515.24	93.9	6,569	108,467	104,485.1	7,170.1	19,109	288,888	78,898.2	6,857.5	6,300	34,499	7,827.9	1396.0
Aitkin	0.27	17.2	12	114	125.1	4.8	69	647	173.3	13.3	9	9	1.4	0.2
Anoka	108.23	314.5	326	12,633	7,485.0	1,617.5	884	15,209	3,982.1	355.7	345	1,149	249.9	34.9
Becker	1.66	49.7	37	263	150.8	10.1	132	1,731	459.7	38.9	34	77	17.8	2.5
Beltrami	1.45	31.7	44	D	D	D	220	3,106	702.7	66.5	30	83	14.5	2.4
Benton	2.08	52.4	42	1,130	911.7	58.9	119	1,800	510.3	42.9	35	80	13.5	2.4
Big Stone	0.49	97.2	8	74	208.2	3.9	27	209	38.2	3.7	3	3	0.3	0.1
Blue Earth	6.23	94.7	89	1,383	953.2	65.6	321	6,061	1,413.1	128.0	83	557	66.5	13.3
Brown	1.07	42.3	28	376	701.3	19.2	109	1,606	347.1	32.6	18	59	7.5	1.5
Carlton	1.51	42.5	17	287	226.0	11.4	107	1,344	351.8	28.3	16	51	10.5	1.1
Carver	8.32	84.3	127	2,247	1,699.4	200.5	210	3,484	907.8	80.6	96	603	123.4	29.1
Cass	0.54	18.8	14	187	87.9	10.0	131	913	255.7	19.8	37	236	13.3	5.9
Chippewa	1.17	96.6	19	313	532.2	15.7	54	650	198.9	13.9	14	122	6.5	2.4
Chisago	2.00	36.8	45	435	176.2	18.3	154	1,722	469.2	37.1	44	D	D	D
Clay	4.92	78.9	68	900	1,175.4	47.0	160	2,682	665.1	57.7	41	160	19.2	3.7
Clearwater	0.22	25.0	2	D	D	D	34	245	48.8	4.1	NA	NA	NA	NA
Cook	0.29	55.8	3	D	D	D	52	337	66.7	7.8	15	43	4.3	0.9
Cottonwood	1.76	152.4	25	168	287.4	9.6	51	506	102.8	9.8	6	19	3.3	0.8
Crow Wing	3.40	53.6	67	450	265.1	18.4	365	4,518	1,125.0	101.2	89	203	46.4	6.3
Dakota	40.71	98.2	524	7,768	11,786.0	484.9	1,122	21,719	6,485.6	576.6	479	2,310	439.8	83.3
Dodge	0.92	45.2	21	521	406.7	28.5	48	452	87.9	7.1	7	D	D	D
Douglas	2.20	59.3	48	997	502.2	44.5	234	3,078	743.4	65.8	43	146	36.6	4.5
Faribault	0.92	65.5	25	227	227.0	6.6	66	618	122.3	11.8	5	10	1.0	0.2

1. Merchant wholesalers, except manufacturers' sales branches and offices. 2. Employer establishments.

Table B. States and Counties — Land Area and Population

					Population, 2017			Population and population characteristics, 2017										
								Race alone or in combination, not Hispanic or Latino (percent)					Age (percent)					
State / county code	CBSA code[1]	County code[2]	STATE County	Land area[3] (sq. mi)	Total persons 2017	Rank	Per square mile	White	Black	American Indian, Alaska Native	Asian and Pacific Islander	Percent Hispanic or Latino[4]	Under 5 years	5 to 17 years	18 to 24 years	25 to 34 years	35 to 44 years	45 to 54 years
				1	2	3	4	5	6	7	8	9	10	11	12	13	14	15
			MINNESOTA— Cont'd															
2,7045	40,340	3	Fillmore	861.3	20,980	1,777	24.4	97.1	0.7	0.5	0.8	1.7	6.5	18.0	6.9	10.1	11.1	12.0
2,7047	10,660	7	Freeborn	707.1	30,535	1,420	43.2	86.5	1.6	0.7	2.8	9.7	5.7	16.2	6.9	11.1	10.9	12.0
2,7049	39,860	4	Goodhue	756.9	46,304	1,043	61.2	93.4	1.9	1.7	1.2	3.4	5.7	16.8	7.3	11.2	11.5	13.1
2,7051		9	Grant	547.8	5,941	2,755	10.8	96.2	1.0	0.9	0.7	2.5	6.5	16.3	6.1	10.8	11.2	10.9
2,7053	33,460	1	Hennepin	553.6	1,252,024	32	2,261.6	71.5	14.7	1.4	8.5	7.0	6.5	15.5	8.6	17.1	13.4	12.6
2,7055	29,100	3	Houston	552.0	18,660	1,887	33.8	97.3	1.4	0.6	1.0	1.2	5.5	16.2	6.8	10.0	11.0	12.8
2,7057		7	Hubbard	925.9	21,018	1,774	22.7	94.5	1.0	3.2	0.9	2.2	5.4	15.6	6.0	8.8	10.4	12.2
2,7059	33,460	1	Isanti	435.7	39,582	1,186	90.8	95.5	1.3	1.2	1.7	2.1	6.1	17.7	7.7	12.5	12.4	13.9
2,7061	24,330	6	Itasca	2,667.1	45,137	1,070	16.9	94.0	1.0	5.1	0.8	1.4	5.3	15.7	6.8	9.8	11.0	12.9
2,7063		7	Jackson	703.0	9,946	2,435	14.1	93.7	1.2	0.8	2.0	3.7	5.6	16.3	6.9	10.4	11.4	11.9
2,7065		6	Kanabec	521.6	16,024	2,037	30.7	96.5	1.1	1.7	1.0	1.6	5.3	16.1	7.1	10.1	11.3	13.2
2,7067	48,820	4	Kandiyohi	797.3	42,743	1,119	53.6	81.2	5.5	0.6	1.2	12.3	6.8	17.6	8.0	12.3	11.0	11.5
2,7069		9	Kittson	1,098.8	4,250	2,883	3.9	96.8	0.8	0.5	0.9	2.1	5.0	15.9	7.3	8.5	9.1	12.6
2,7071		6	Koochiching	3,104.2	12,528	2,256	4.0	95.0	1.1	3.7	0.7	1.4	4.2	14.3	6.9	9.3	10.2	12.9
2,7073		9	Lac qui Parle	765.0	6,685	2,697	8.7	96.1	1.1	0.7	1.2	2.2	4.6	15.4	6.9	8.2	10.0	11.1
2,7075		6	Lake	2,109.3	10,524	2,390	5.0	96.6	0.8	1.5	0.9	1.6	4.8	13.6	6.1	9.4	10.4	11.7
2,7077		9	Lake of the Woods	1,297.9	3,744	2,920	2.9	95.1	1.3	2.8	2.4	1.4	5.0	13.4	6.4	8.4	9.9	12.8
2,7079	33,460	1	Le Sueur	448.7	28,111	1,488	62.6	92.4	1.0	0.8	0.9	6.0	5.8	18.2	7.4	10.8	12.2	13.9
2,7081		9	Lincoln	536.8	5,678	2,782	10.6	96.8	0.7	0.5	0.7	2.0	6.3	17.2	6.3	9.7	10.2	11.0
2,7083	32,140	7	Lyon	714.4	25,831	1,572	36.2	85.4	4.1	0.8	4.6	6.5	7.3	17.8	10.4	13.1	11.9	11.4
2,7085	26,780	6	McLeod	491.5	35,884	1,276	73.0	92.1	1.0	0.7	1.1	6.1	6.1	17.2	7.7	11.9	11.6	13.5
2,7087		8	Mahnomen	557.9	5,596	2,787	10.0	53.8	1.4	48.4	0.7	4.4	8.9	22.7	7.3	10.1	10.2	10.6
2,7089		8	Marshall	1,775.1	9,356	2,477	5.3	94.4	0.8	1.0	0.5	4.4	6.3	16.5	7.4	10.5	10.5	12.5
2,7091	21,860	7	Martin	712.3	19,850	1,835	27.9	94.0	1.0	0.6	0.9	4.4	5.7	16.0	7.1	10.4	10.0	11.6
2,7093		6	Meeker	608.2	23,131	1,675	38.0	94.6	1.1	0.5	0.7	4.1	6.2	18.2	7.4	10.1	11.1	12.2
2,7095	33,460	1	Mille Lacs	572.3	25,872	1,568	45.2	90.7	1.2	6.6	0.9	2.4	6.4	17.9	6.9	11.6	11.8	13.3
2,7097		6	Morrison	1,125.1	33,064	1,356	29.4	96.8	1.0	0.8	0.7	1.7	6.1	17.5	7.1	10.9	11.4	12.9
2,7099	12,380	4	Mower	711.3	39,566	1,187	55.6	80.8	4.2	0.6	4.6	11.4	6.4	18.4	7.6	12.3	11.7	12.0
2,7101		9	Murray	704.7	8,346	2,559	11.8	94.0	0.7	0.5	1.6	4.0	5.6	16.3	6.7	9.3	9.1	11.8
2,7103	31,860	3	Nicollet	448.6	33,966	1,327	75.7	90.2	3.9	0.7	2.2	4.5	5.8	16.2	12.7	12.9	12.6	11.3
2,7105	49,380	7	Nobles	715.1	21,944	1,727	30.7	59.9	5.3	0.7	7.0	28.3	8.0	18.6	9.4	12.4	11.3	11.7
2,7107		8	Norman	872.8	6,597	2,704	7.6	91.9	1.2	3.4	0.9	5.0	6.0	17.7	7.4	9.6	11.4	12.0
2,7109	40,340	3	Olmsted	653.5	154,930	424	237.1	82.3	6.9	0.6	7.4	5.0	7.0	17.5	7.8	14.6	13.0	12.1
2,7111	22,260	1	Otter Tail	1,972.0	58,345	883	29.6	93.6	2.0	1.3	1.0	3.5	6.0	15.9	7.1	9.7	10.0	11.6
2,7113		6	Pennington	616.6	14,238	2,145	23.1	92.4	2.1	2.3	1.4	3.7	6.2	16.7	8.3	13.2	11.9	12.0
2,7115		6	Pine	1,411.3	29,203	1,454	20.7	91.1	2.7	4.2	1.1	2.9	4.7	15.2	6.9	11.0	12.1	13.7
2,7117		6	Pipestone	465.1	9,087	2,496	19.5	89.7	1.9	2.1	1.2	6.8	6.7	18.6	7.3	10.0	10.4	11.8
2,7119	24,220	3	Polk	1,971.1	31,619	1,388	16.0	88.3	3.2	2.4	1.4	6.6	7.0	17.2	9.1	12.1	11.0	11.8
2,7121		8	Pope	669.6	10,970	2,355	16.4	97.2	1.0	0.7	0.8	1.4	5.6	15.5	6.2	11.1	10.4	11.2
2,7123	33,460	1	Ramsey	152.2	547,974	122	3,600.4	64.6	13.6	1.4	16.2	7.6	7.0	16.3	10.0	16.7	12.2	11.5
2,7125		8	Red Lake	432.4	4,030	2,899	9.3	93.6	1.4	2.3	0.5	3.7	6.3	18.3	6.1	9.2	12.1	11.8
2,7127		7	Redwood	878.6	15,272	2,081	17.4	89.2	1.1	5.1	3.1	3.4	6.3	18.2	7.5	10.3	10.5	11.8
2,7129		8	Renville	982.9	14,645	2,121	14.9	88.7	1.1	1.5	1.1	8.8	6.3	16.8	7.4	10.0	10.6	12.3
2,7131	22,060	4	Rice	495.8	65,968	810	133.1	84.1	5.6	0.7	3.1	8.1	5.7	16.1	14.7	11.3	11.5	12.7
2,7133		6	Rock	482.5	9,490	2,466	19.7	94.6	1.4	0.9	1.2	3.2	6.1	19.7	7.4	10.1	11.6	11.5
2,7135		7	Roseau	1,671.6	15,327	2,075	9.2	93.4	1.2	2.5	3.2	1.4	6.2	18.2	7.8	10.2	10.1	14.3
2,7137	20,260	2	St. Louis	6,247.6	200,000	334	32.0	93.3	2.5	3.3	1.7	1.7	5.1	14.0	12.6	11.6	11.1	11.6
2,7139	33,460	1	Scott	356.3	145,827	446	409.3	83.2	5.1	1.4	7.3	5.2	7.0	20.9	7.7	12.2	14.7	15.3
2,7141	33,460	1	Sherburne	432.9	94,570	623	218.5	93.2	3.3	1.0	1.8	2.5	6.9	19.7	8.2	13.3	13.9	14.8
2,7143	33,460	1	Sibley	588.8	14,869	2,106	25.3	89.3	1.3	0.5	0.9	9.2	5.7	18.3	7.4	10.8	11.7	13.3
2,7145	41,060	3	Stearns	1,342.8	157,822	416	117.5	87.9	6.8	0.6	2.9	3.4	6.3	16.7	15.2	12.3	11.0	11.7
2,7147	36,940	5	Steele	429.6	36,887	1,252	85.9	87.4	3.9	0.5	1.4	8.0	6.6	18.6	7.8	11.9	11.5	12.9
2,7149		7	Stevens	563.6	9,634	2,457	17.1	89.9	1.6	2.3	2.4	5.9	5.6	15.0	20.7	10.9	9.8	9.2
2,7151		7	Swift	742.0	9,407	2,474	12.7	92.1	1.9	0.8	1.3	5.2	5.8	16.9	6.9	10.9	10.8	12.3
2,7153		6	Todd	945.0	24,515	1,625	25.9	92.4	1.0	1.0	1.1	5.9	6.7	17.1	7.4	9.7	10.2	12.4
2,7155		9	Traverse	573.9	3,319	2,948	5.8	91.0	1.5	5.9	0.5	2.9	5.2	15.3	7.7	8.8	9.9	12.1
2,7157	40,340	3	Wabasha	522.9	21,608	1,749	41.3	95.7	1.1	0.7	0.9	2.8	5.7	16.2	7.0	10.4	10.8	13.5
2,7159		7	Wadena	536.3	13,669	2,186	25.5	95.9	1.8	1.4	0.7	1.8	6.8	18.5	7.2	10.2	11.0	11.2
2,7161		6	Waseca	423.4	18,787	1,879	44.4	90.2	3.0	1.0	1.2	6.0	5.8	17.7	7.7	12.4	12.6	12.6
2,7163	33,460	1	Washington	384.4	256,348	265	666.9	84.7	5.6	0.9	6.9	4.2	6.1	18.6	8.0	11.5	13.0	14.5
2,7165		6	Watonwan	435.0	10,840	2,361	24.9	73.1	1.1	0.5	1.3	24.8	6.8	17.5	8.5	10.2	11.2	11.1
2,7167	47,420	6	Wilkin	751.0	6,324	2,729	8.4	94.3	1.3	2.1	0.8	2.9	5.8	16.9	7.5	10.4	11.6	13.0
2,7169	49,100	4	Winona	626.1	50,873	979	81.3	92.1	2.3	0.7	3.0	2.9	4.9	13.2	20.4	11.3	10.0	10.6
2,7171	33,460	1	Wright	661.2	134,286	473	203.1	94.0	2.0	0.7	1.9	3.0	7.1	21.1	7.5	11.7	14.2	14.2
2,7173		9	Yellow Medicine	759.1	9,867	2,440	13.0	90.4	1.0	4.1	0.9	4.9	6.2	17.3	7.8	11.1	10.3	11.8

1. CBSA = Core Based Statistical Area. See Appendix A for explanation. See Appendix B for list of metropolitan areas with component counties. Service of USDA Rural-Urban Continuum Codes. See Appendix A for definition. 2. County type code from the Economic Research 3. Dry land or land partially or temporarily covered by water. 4. May be of any race.

Table B. States and Counties — **Population and Households**

STATE County	55 to 64 years	65 to 74 years	75 years and over	Percent female	2000	2010	2000-2010	2010-2017	Births	Deaths	Net Migration	Number	Persons per house-hold	Family house-holds	Female family house-holder[1]	One person
	16	17	18	19	20	21	22	23	24	25	26	27	28	29	30	31
MINNESOTA— Cont'd																
Fillmore	14.8	10.8	9.8	49.8	21,122	20,866	-1.2	0.5	1,847	1,672	-53	8,540	2.40	67.9	6.1	27.8
Freeborn	15.2	11.3	10.6	50.1	32,584	31,255	-4.1	-2.3	2,479	2,611	-578	13,046	2.31	63.9	10.4	29.3
Goodhue	15.4	10.6	8.5	50.2	44,127	46,182	4.7	0.3	3,742	3,433	-164	19,051	2.39	67.1	9.1	27.2
Grant	15.0	12.1	11.2	49.6	6,289	6,018	-4.3	-1.3	506	516	-66	2,547	2.30	68.7	7.1	26.7
Hennepin	12.7	8.0	5.7	50.5	1,116,200	1,152,381	3.2	8.6	119,191	59,239	40,345	493,832	2.40	57.6	9.8	33.0
Houston	17.0	11.5	9.2	49.9	19,718	19,027	-3.5	-1.9	1,370	1,244	-493	7,989	2.32	67.6	8.2	28.3
Hubbard	16.8	14.9	10.0	49.3	18,376	20,428	11.2	2.9	1,584	1,431	446	8,741	2.34	70.2	7.0	24.8
Isanti	14.3	9.0	6.5	49.6	31,287	37,810	20.8	4.7	3,286	2,176	670	14,403	2.63	69.4	10.0	24.5
Itasca	16.6	13.2	9.5	49.5	43,992	45,058	2.4	0.2	3,393	3,743	474	19,126	2.31	67.7	8.0	27.0
Jackson	16.0	10.6	10.9	48.8	11,268	10,266	-8.9	-3.1	802	773	-349	4,335	2.31	67.2	7.8	28.1
Kanabec	16.6	12.0	8.3	49.3	14,996	16,239	8.3	-1.3	1,101	1,090	-221	6,290	2.49	68.3	8.6	25.9
Kandiyohi	14.5	10.0	8.4	49.7	41,203	42,239	2.5	1.2	4,213	2,763	-944	16,737	2.48	68.9	9.2	26.1
Kittson	17.3	12.3	12.0	49.5	5,285	4,552	-13.9	-6.6	329	467	-161	1,913	2.23	61.8	8.1	34.9
Koochiching	18.1	13.7	10.5	49.8	14,355	13,311	-7.3	-5.9	769	1,099	-452	5,732	2.20	63.7	8.0	32.0
Lac qui Parle	17.0	12.5	14.3	49.8	8,067	7,259	-10.0	-7.9	468	637	-408	3,111	2.18	64.7	6.9	30.1
Lake	18.5	13.8	11.7	48.6	11,058	10,866	-1.7	-3.1	776	1,012	-99	5,207	2.01	63.1	5.9	31.1
Lake of the Woods	20.0	13.7	10.2	48.6	4,522	4,045	-10.5	-7.4	248	330	-220	1,551	2.48	62.7	4.2	33.2
Le Sueur	14.4	9.9	7.4	49.6	25,426	27,703	9.0	1.5	2,273	1,556	-305	10,805	2.52	69.7	6.8	24.9
Lincoln	14.8	10.9	13.5	49.5	6,429	5,896	-8.3	-3.7	499	574	-140	2,477	2.26	63.8	4.6	31.8
Lyon	12.9	7.9	7.4	50.0	25,425	25,857	1.7	-0.1	2,655	1,603	-1,104	10,072	2.42	63.7	8.5	29.8
McLeod	13.6	9.8	8.5	50.1	34,898	36,651	5.0	-2.1	3,063	2,408	-1,436	14,780	2.40	66.9	8.2	28.1
Mahnomen	13.0	9.3	7.9	49.7	5,190	5,413	4.3	3.4	749	418	-147	1,977	2.74	67.8	15.8	27.8
Marshall	15.4	10.4	10.5	49.5	10,155	9,439	-7.1	-0.9	797	565	-315	3,991	2.33	66.8	6.5	28.4
Martin	16.0	11.5	11.5	50.5	21,802	20,840	-4.4	-4.8	1,610	1,820	-776	8,777	2.26	63.9	9.2	32.1
Meeker	15.1	10.7	8.8	49.2	22,644	23,300	2.9	-0.7	1,998	1,560	-609	9,119	2.49	68.9	6.4	27.1
Mille Lacs	14.3	9.8	8.1	49.7	22,330	26,097	16.9	-0.9	2,348	2,115	-455	10,012	2.52	67.3	11.6	27.3
Morrison	15.2	10.3	8.6	49.5	31,712	33,198	4.7	-0.4	2,798	2,287	-635	13,275	2.43	67.8	8.4	27.8
Mower	13.1	9.3	9.2	49.9	38,603	39,163	1.5	1.0	3,647	2,723	-504	15,414	2.51	65.1	8.3	29.5
Murray	15.2	12.9	12.1	49.8	9,165	8,725	-4.8	-4.3	631	724	-286	3,715	2.23	63.9	4.7	30.8
Nicollet	12.6	9.0	6.8	49.5	29,771	32,727	9.9	3.8	2,784	1,571	34	12,559	2.41	67.1	8.7	26.3
Nobles	12.4	8.2	8.1	48.4	20,832	21,378	2.6	2.6	2,642	1,275	-828	7,890	2.70	69.6	9.3	26.4
Norman	15.0	10.5	10.3	49.3	7,442	6,852	-7.9	-3.7	510	680	-84	2,696	2.41	67.1	8.6	28.6
Olmsted	13.1	8.2	6.8	51.2	124,277	144,260	16.1	7.4	15,676	7,100	2,156	58,692	2.51	66.6	9.8	27.1
Otter Tail	16.5	12.9	10.4	49.7	57,159	57,303	0.3	1.8	4,707	4,901	1,293	23,962	2.36	67.4	6.8	29.0
Pennington	14.0	9.2	8.5	50.1	13,584	13,930	2.5	2.2	1,321	958	-46	5,923	2.35	60.1	9.5	34.3
Pine	16.4	11.5	8.6	46.5	26,530	29,750	12.1	-1.8	2,051	1,986	-608	10,993	2.49	63.7	7.7	30.0
Pipestone	14.3	9.5	11.4	51.3	9,895	9,596	-3.0	-5.3	865	787	-592	3,998	2.28	65.9	8.9	30.4
Polk	14.1	9.4	8.3	49.9	31,369	31,600	0.7	0.1	2,974	2,478	-466	12,608	2.39	63.2	7.5	32.1
Pope	16.4	13.0	10.6	48.9	11,236	10,995	-2.1	-0.2	895	920	7	4,815	2.23	65.5	4.9	29.8
Ramsey	12.3	8.2	5.9	51.3	511,035	508,639	-0.5	7.7	55,985	29,036	12,717	207,327	2.49	58.5	12.1	32.9
Red Lake	16.0	10.6	9.6	49.2	4,299	4,089	-4.9	-1.4	373	255	-178	1,676	2.39	63.1	7.6	32.6
Redwood	14.2	10.5	10.6	50.1	16,815	16,059	-4.5	-4.9	1,373	1,345	-814	6,262	2.43	63.8	7.4	32.5
Renville	16.1	10.2	10.3	49.0	17,154	15,730	-8.3	-6.9	1,285	1,382	-1,001	6,188	2.37	64.9	5.7	30.9
Rice	12.9	8.5	6.6	49.0	56,665	64,142	13.2	2.8	5,272	3,371	-63	22,654	2.51	68.6	9.0	26.5
Rock	14.0	9.9	9.7	50.6	9,721	9,687	-0.3	-2.0	801	860	-137	3,932	2.36	67.7	6.6	29.8
Roseau	15.6	9.2	7.5	48.5	16,338	15,629	-4.3	-1.9	1,386	988	-715	6,106	2.52	68.4	6.7	27.7
St. Louis	15.2	10.8	7.9	49.9	200,528	200,226	-0.2	-0.1	14,688	15,004	267	85,059	2.24	58.0	9.4	33.8
Scott	11.8	6.4	4.0	50.2	89,498	129,916	45.2	12.3	13,732	4,395	6,636	47,154	2.93	77.1	8.7	18.3
Sherburne	12.0	6.9	4.1	48.7	64,417	88,492	37.4	6.9	8,608	3,509	1,002	30,781	2.89	76.7	8.6	17.1
Sibley	14.9	9.5	8.5	49.8	15,356	15,226	-0.8	-2.3	1,214	1,062	-511	6,009	2.45	68.5	7.0	27.0
Stearns	12.1	8.2	6.5	49.5	133,166	150,642	13.1	4.8	14,160	7,026	82	57,695	2.52	64.3	8.9	26.0
Steele	13.5	9.1	8.1	50.3	33,680	36,576	8.6	0.9	3,387	2,154	-930	14,354	2.51	67.5	8.4	28.1
Stevens	11.4	8.3	9.0	50.1	10,053	9,726	-3.3	-0.9	819	601	-307	3,567	2.62	60.8	4.3	30.7
Swift	14.7	10.9	10.8	49.7	11,956	9,783	-18.2	-3.8	789	777	-390	4,177	2.23	63.7	8.4	33.0
Todd	15.5	11.7	9.3	48.7	24,426	24,895	1.9	-1.5	2,307	1,522	-1,176	9,866	2.43	66.6	6.2	29.5
Traverse	15.6	10.9	14.4	49.9	4,134	3,558	-13.9	-6.7	230	371	-99	1,544	2.14	63.5	5.8	33.7
Wabasha	15.2	11.9	9.3	50.0	21,610	21,664	0.2	-0.3	1,705	1,313	-444	9,004	2.34	68.9	7.8	26.0
Wadena	14.0	10.7	10.4	50.5	13,713	13,843	0.9	-1.3	1,286	1,399	-54	5,657	2.36	61.6	10.6	34.4
Waseca	13.6	9.8	7.8	52.0	19,526	19,136	-2.0	-1.8	1,567	1,175	-743	7,329	2.43	68.1	8.6	26.6
Washington	13.9	8.7	5.7	50.5	201,130	238,128	18.4	7.7	20,597	10,568	8,358	91,282	2.68	72.6	9.8	22.2
Watonwan	14.5	9.6	10.5	50.5	11,876	11,211	-5.6	-3.3	1,090	856	-607	4,465	2.43	63.9	9.9	32.3
Wilkin	16.2	9.4	9.2	48.5	7,138	6,576	-7.9	-3.8	508	558	-205	2,871	2.20	63.6	7.2	34.3
Winona	13.1	9.3	7.1	50.4	49,985	51,461	3.0	-1.1	3,440	2,954	-1,081	19,078	2.45	60.2	7.3	30.4
Wright	11.9	7.4	4.9	49.6	89,986	124,697	38.6	7.7	13,100	5,305	1,875	45,887	2.81	76.1	8.7	19.6
Yellow Medicine	15.5	9.4	10.5	49.7	11,080	10,438	-5.8	-5.5	842	858	-561	4,174	2.33	68.5	8.2	27.0

1. No spouse present.

Table B. States and Counties — Population, Vital Statistics, Health, and Crime

STATE County	Persons in group quarters, 2017	Daytime Population, 2012-2016 Number	Employment/ residence ratio	Births, 2017 Total	Rate[1]	Deaths, 2017 Number	Rate[1]	Persons under 65 with no health insurance, 2016 Number	Percent	Medicare, 2017 Total beneficiaries	Enrolled in Original Medicare	Enrolled in Medicare Advantage	Serious crimes known to police[2], 2016 Total Number	Rate[3]
	32	33	34	35	36	37	38	39	40	41	42	43	44	45
MINNESOTA— Cont'd														
Fillmore	359	17,810	0.70	260	12.4	226	10.8	1,254	7.6	4,959	2,269	2,689	83	399
Freeborn	637	28,869	0.87	320	10.5	351	11.5	1,314	5.6	7,218	2,859	4,359	432	1418
Goodhue	894	45,817	0.97	500	10.8	454	9.8	1,796	4.8	9,843	4,014	5,829	909	1958
Grant	110	5,401	0.81	68	11.4	59	9.9	258	5.7	1,585	689	896	16	272
Hennepin	25,653	1,433,213	1.34	16,588	13.2	8,526	6.8	52,533	5.0	195,599	82,239	113,360	40,613	3286
Houston	257	15,179	0.63	188	10.1	169	9.1	704	4.7	4,384	2,188	2,197	116	620
Hubbard	154	18,559	0.77	204	9.7	185	8.8	907	5.9	5,196	2,245	2,950	545	2636
Isanti	465	31,278	0.63	446	11.3	315	8.0	1,464	4.5	6,380	2,535	3,845	778	2021
Itasca	1,020	44,019	0.93	463	10.3	475	10.5	2,239	6.5	11,447	5,233	6,214	460	1012
Jackson	110	10,580	1.08	107	10.8	106	10.7	341	4.4	2,648	1,510	1,137	43	429
Kanabec	246	13,239	0.63	153	9.5	159	9.9	704	5.6	3,300	1,532	1,768	259	1645
Kandiyohi	1,046	43,384	1.04	589	13.8	348	8.1	1,920	5.6	8,422	3,216	5,206	658	1546
Kittson	111	4,259	0.92	37	8.7	57	13.4	171	5.2	1,112	487	625	23	523
Koochiching	241	12,693	0.96	98	7.8	146	11.7	635	6.7	3,667	1,697	1,970	58	455
Lac qui Parle	154	6,232	0.80	59	8.8	92	13.8	273	5.5	1,671	631	1,039	47	694
Lake	224	10,461	0.94	101	9.6	131	12.4	337	4.3	2,827	1,360	1,467	39	369
Lake of the Woods	53	3,501	0.80	37	9.9	37	9.9	187	6.4	1,048	494	554	7	180
Le Sueur	270	22,436	0.64	310	11.0	218	7.8	1,164	5.1	6,265	2,428	3,836	303	1097
Lincoln	135	5,105	0.76	67	11.8	77	13.6	239	5.6	1,421	816	605	12	209
Lyon	1,050	27,460	1.13	374	14.5	228	8.8	1,113	5.3	5,372	3,146	2,226	321	1254
McLeod	476	34,579	0.93	418	11.6	341	9.5	1,282	4.4	9,193	3,353	5,840	530	1482
Mahnomen	79	5,784	1.14	98	17.5	47	8.4	371	8.4	1,165	691	474	1	18
Marshall	76	7,757	0.65	111	11.9	82	8.8	425	5.8	2,068	919	1,148	49	521
Martin	348	19,910	0.97	228	11.5	221	11.1	839	5.5	5,341	2,538	2,803	242	1220
Meeker	354	20,048	0.73	270	11.7	202	8.7	957	5.2	4,872	1,638	3,234	247	1072
Mille Lacs	523	24,631	0.90	318	12.3	295	11.4	1,338	6.5	6,992	2,806	4,187	711	2767
Morrison	527	29,744	0.81	397	12.0	336	10.2	1,473	5.6	7,450	2,778	4,672	212	649
Mower	632	38,358	0.95	508	12.8	369	9.3	2,028	6.4	8,713	4,605	4,109	758	1941
Murray	163	7,770	0.83	90	10.8	87	10.4	355	5.7	2,047	1,172	875	100	1198
Nicollet	2,878	31,410	0.90	362	10.7	238	7.0	986	3.8	5,289	2,251	3,038	388	1161
Nobles	385	22,452	1.07	377	17.2	165	7.5	1,802	10.0	3,574	2,323	1,251	245	1123
Norman	149	5,971	0.78	71	10.8	91	13.8	315	6.2	1,520	765	755	2	30
Olmsted	2,445	166,238	1.20	2,145	13.8	1,032	6.7	6,011	4.6	25,324	14,755	10,568	3,024	1981
Otter Tail	1,184	54,572	0.89	681	11.7	671	11.5	2,367	5.4	14,779	5,742	9,036	915	1585
Pennington	327	16,797	1.35	170	11.9	129	9.1	524	4.5	2,802	1,150	1,652	126	884
Pine	1,625	26,847	0.82	252	8.6	273	9.3	1,405	6.5	6,621	2,812	3,808	942	3259
Pipestone	205	9,386	1.02	119	13.1	113	12.4	518	7.2	2,138	1,314	824	63	685
Polk	1,262	29,156	0.85	432	13.7	331	10.5	1,294	5.1	6,339	2,912	3,427	531	1687
Pope	184	10,335	0.88	118	10.8	117	10.7	386	4.6	2,764	1,083	1,681	64	580
Ramsey	17,532	593,914	1.23	7,744	14.1	4,077	7.4	24,725	5.5	121,073	50,339	70,734	18,798	3459
Red Lake	34	3,395	0.67	43	10.7	21	5.2	193	6.0	882	244	638	8	198
Redwood	373	15,554	1.00	194	12.7	176	11.5	840	7.1	3,501	1,580	1,922	251	1636
Renville	342	14,225	0.90	176	12.0	180	12.3	710	6.2	3,322	1,661	1,660	262	1780
Rice	7,255	61,786	0.90	761	11.5	479	7.3	2,801	5.7	11,112	4,424	6,689	1,012	1544
Rock	260	8,797	0.84	110	11.6	105	11.1	385	5.2	2,299	1,224	1,075	106	1107
Roseau	191	16,324	1.09	181	11.8	130	8.5	640	5.0	2,952	1,008	1,944	169	1070
St. Louis	8,918	208,798	1.09	1,956	9.8	2,048	10.2	6,849	4.3	44,703	20,573	24,130	6,622	3307
Scott	1,314	115,960	0.69	1,843	12.6	666	4.6	4,744	3.7	13,987	5,354	8,633	2,161	1503
Sherburne	2,159	68,866	0.53	1,235	13.1	524	5.5	3,113	3.8	9,871	3,746	6,125	1,378	1495
Sibley	230	12,293	0.66	147	9.9	141	9.5	706	5.9	2,733	1,127	1,607	101	683
Stearns	7,620	165,722	1.15	1,972	12.5	968	6.1	5,828	4.6	31,794	13,633	18,162	4,154	2674
Steele	594	38,739	1.12	442	12.0	304	8.2	1,285	4.2	7,054	2,760	4,294	761	2070
Stevens	1,003	10,666	1.18	102	10.6	71	7.4	340	4.8	1,804	1,047	757	141	1439
Swift	150	9,203	0.94	112	11.9	96	10.2	402	5.5	2,282	1,094	1,189	47	508
Todd	346	21,061	0.71	318	13.0	201	8.2	1,400	7.3	5,079	1,672	3,407	304	1261
Traverse	100	3,243	0.90	32	9.6	27	8.1	156	6.3	984	531	452	64	1899
Wabasha	246	17,800	0.68	237	11.0	166	7.7	778	4.6	5,403	2,305	3,098	164	776
Wadena	482	14,431	1.12	178	13.0	179	13.1	642	6.1	3,747	1,439	2,308	46	332
Waseca	1,021	16,943	0.78	214	11.4	149	7.9	718	4.9	3,765	1,500	2,265	267	1410
Washington	3,562	211,170	0.71	2,819	11.0	1,613	6.3	6,455	3.0	24,876	9,020	15,857	5,311	2092
Watonwan	150	10,159	0.85	152	14.0	102	9.4	732	8.5	2,433	1,250	1,183	130	1194
Wilkin	152	5,857	0.81	74	11.7	83	13.1	224	4.4	1,377	639	738	87	1370
Winona	4,202	50,752	0.99	479	9.4	433	8.5	1,871	4.8	9,382	4,945	4,437	1,046	2062
Wright	1,105	105,379	0.64	1,735	12.9	815	6.1	3,989	3.4	18,344	6,626	11,717	2,233	1686
Yellow Medicine	290	9,682	0.93	124	12.6	111	11.2	465	5.9	2,499	1,346	1,153	84	861

1. Per 1,000 estimated resident population.   2. Data for serious crimes have not been adjusted for underreporting; this may affect comparability between geographic areas and over time.
3. Per 100,000 population estimated by the FBI.

Table B. States and Counties — Crime, Education, Money Income, and Poverty

STATE County	Serious crimes known to police, 2016 (cont.)[1] Rate		Education						Money income, 2012-2016				Income and poverty, 2016			
			School enrollment and attainment, 2012-2016				Local government expenditures,[5] 2013-2014			Households			Percent below poverty level			
			Enrollment[3]		Attainment[4] (percent)							Percent					
	Violent	Property	Total	Percent private	High school graduate or less	Bachelor's degree or more	Total current spending (mil dol)	Current spending per student (dollars)	Per capita income[6]	Median income (dollars)	with income of less than $50,000	with income of $200,000 or more	Median household income (dollars)	All persons	Children under 18 years	Children 5 to 17 years in families
	46	47	48	49	50	51	52	53	54	55	56	57	58	59	60	61
MINNESOTA— Cont'd																
Fillmore	38	360	4,715	13.1	43.5	20.4	25.4	10,186	27,777	54,358	45.9	2.3	60,575	12.3	19.1	17.2
Freeborn	72	1,346	6,673	7.6	47.2	16.8	48.0	11,834	27,332	48,827	51.2	2.2	48,943	11.0	15.9	14.6
Goodhue	151	1,807	10,626	13.9	39.9	24.3	74.6	11,095	31,830	60,452	42.2	3.5	66,038	7.7	9.7	8.9
Grant	17	255	1,210	10.2	40.7	19.6	11.7	10,764	29,446	53,828	46.9	3.7	51,274	12.0	18.7	17.5
Hennepin	470	2,816	307,188	17.9	24.7	47.6	2,024.7	12,471	39,939	67,989	37.6	9.0	71,184	10.9	14.0	13.1
Houston	37	583	4,126	17.6	40.2	22.6	46.4	10,105	29,007	55,550	44.7	2.3	58,201	8.5	10.5	8.6
Hubbard	140	2,496	4,209	9.6	39.9	25.4	24.2	10,120	26,417	49,742	50.3	2.4	49,129	13.1	20.4	19.2
Isanti	104	1,917	9,412	12.1	45.6	17.7	60.7	10,054	28,676	62,733	39.0	2.4	68,303	7.7	10.6	9.7
Itasca	119	893	9,888	10.1	37.7	22.3	76.4	11,558	25,862	49,507	50.4	1.5	51,644	13.3	18.8	16.8
Jackson	20	409	2,315	7.7	40.8	21.2	15.8	10,132	28,958	55,114	46.2	3.6	58,849	8.7	12.1	11.3
Kanabec	140	1,506	3,524	6.8	52.2	13.8	21.0	9,151	24,582	48,042	51.8	1.9	51,347	13.2	20.0	17.5
Kandiyohi	169	1,377	9,762	10.0	38.3	22.5	60.3	10,926	28,165	53,514	46.2	3.3	53,034	11.5	16.7	15.0
Kittson	23	500	878	9.7	44.4	20.7	9.5	13,712	29,939	51,484	48.5	1.9	50,012	11.0	14.8	13.6
Koochiching	71	385	2,523	13.8	46.0	18.4	22.5	12,317	26,814	44,929	54.3	2.3	49,393	14.3	22.6	20.5
Lac qui Parle	15	679	1,379	6.8	46.0	18.3	14.7	11,384	30,816	49,800	50.9	4.5	49,669	9.7	13.8	12.6
Lake	19	350	1,964	5.9	38.1	27.2	14.6	10,378	31,215	52,320	47.9	2.3	62,746	9.1	13.1	11.3
Lake of the Woods	26	154	661	6.5	52.3	17.0	6.2	13,400	23,234	45,732	54.5	0.0	47,584	10.9	15.9	14.8
Le Sueur	36	1,061	6,605	14.0	45.2	21.4	41.4	9,632	29,714	62,462	39.5	3.6	63,451	8.4	10.7	9.7
Lincoln	209	0	1,219	10.6	48.8	18.9	11.4	11,671	27,946	49,438	50.6	2.0	46,445	12.7	18.4	16.5
Lyon	82	1,172	7,152	12.1	41.1	26.8	73.5	17,004	28,860	51,920	47.3	3.6	52,989	12.8	14.9	13.8
McLeod	92	1,390	8,312	14.1	45.4	17.3	54.1	10,148	28,241	57,738	42.3	2.1	58,393	7.4	9.5	8.6
Mahnomen	0	18	1,419	5.8	48.9	12.6	18.2	13,588	20,233	41,597	56.7	1.0	41,640	17.5	29.8	29.0
Marshall	53	468	1,925	8.3	47.6	20.0	18.7	14,307	28,194	56,340	43.7	1.8	54,651	9.8	12.8	11.8
Martin	106	1,114	4,258	15.2	48.7	18.5	35.2	11,979	29,034	51,984	48.7	3.8	48,326	12.1	17.5	15.4
Meeker	104	968	5,338	10.0	45.3	18.9	25.5	10,155	27,974	58,574	41.6	2.6	61,374	7.1	10.0	9.3
Mille Lacs	117	2,650	5,938	12.4	48.0	15.6	62.1	9,736	24,489	51,232	48.6	1.7	53,407	12.1	17.3	16.6
Morrison	21	628	7,404	12.1	48.5	16.2	53.1	10,088	26,442	51,456	48.5	2.6	51,422	11.9	16.1	13.7
Mower	197	1,744	10,105	9.5	44.7	20.0	70.5	11,474	27,459	51,778	48.2	3.1	53,302	13.2	14.9	13.6
Murray	60	1,138	1,712	11.0	47.5	17.8	12.4	11,530	29,084	51,801	48.0	2.7	52,373	9.3	12.7	11.4
Nicollet	60	1,101	9,860	37.6	33.5	32.3	35.9	14,884	28,089	61,501	40.3	3.1	66,868	8.0	10.7	9.6
Nobles	115	1,008	5,197	6.9	56.0	13.5	41.7	10,962	24,188	53,269	46.5	2.5	56,069	11.6	15.3	14.4
Norman	0	30	1,390	8.1	50.7	15.7	13.0	11,984	26,270	52,083	48.1	2.2	49,572	12.1	18.9	17.1
Olmsted	174	1,807	38,704	17.7	26.2	42.0	237.4	10,246	36,143	69,308	35.5	6.9	72,511	8.6	9.9	9.4
Otter Tail	80	1,505	11,904	13.3	38.9	24.1	134.1	17,728	28,781	53,351	46.7	3.1	51,252	10.5	14.0	13.2
Pennington	56	828	3,294	7.0	44.5	17.4	76.4	34,598	26,992	51,156	48.7	1.8	52,724	9.8	11.8	11.3
Pine	270	2,989	6,142	13.2	52.2	13.8	39.9	10,299	22,817	45,379	54.6	1.6	50,962	12.2	17.1	15.4
Pipestone	33	652	1,995	14.4	48.6	19.9	17.0	11,064	27,489	48,944	51.0	2.9	51,050	10.9	15.1	14.0
Polk	178	1,509	7,857	9.6	39.9	23.9	53.8	10,598	27,231	53,059	46.8	2.6	50,893	14.5	19.9	16.9
Pope	45	534	2,181	8.1	40.2	22.5	15.2	12,294	30,485	55,180	44.8	2.9	58,892	9.1	12.1	11.8
Ramsey	425	3,034	145,036	24.9	31.6	41.0	1,177.4	13,642	31,256	57,717	43.7	5.3	60,287	13.9	20.2	20.9
Red Lake	0	198	840	5.6	48.9	15.0	9.9	13,209	25,732	49,800	50.1	1.5	50,625	9.8	11.9	11.0
Redwood	143	1,493	3,645	12.5	49.1	17.8	27.0	10,852	26,716	48,891	51.1	2.5	54,918	9.1	13.7	12.5
Renville	136	1,644	3,181	13.5	47.5	14.8	19.3	10,171	30,089	54,824	46.1	3.5	56,724	9.9	14.6	13.9
Rice	154	1,390	20,007	38.0	41.1	27.2	89.3	10,646	27,856	61,683	40.2	4.2	67,726	9.7	12.4	11.0
Rock	376	731	2,338	17.0	47.9	20.6	14.8	9,337	27,634	52,835	46.5	2.6	57,518	9.4	11.4	9.8
Roseau	6	1,064	3,524	6.4	44.7	18.7	30.6	10,423	27,307	54,827	45.2	2.9	55,879	7.8	11.0	10.0
St. Louis	236	3,071	49,958	12.9	35.7	27.8	276.3	11,046	28,013	49,395	50.5	2.9	50,156	14.7	16.6	14.7
Scott	105	1,398	39,430	18.3	28.1	38.8	230.1	9,810	37,113	90,198	24.6	10.1	91,046	5.5	6.6	5.8
Sherburne	115	1,380	25,398	11.7	32.7	26.7	184.4	9,316	31,182	78,081	28.3	4.5	83,304	6.3	7.3	6.3
Sibley	108	575	3,487	16.4	50.4	16.7	24.4	10,238	28,811	59,596	42.0	2.7	60,978	9.1	12.2	10.4
Stearns	211	2,463	46,262	20.6	37.7	25.9	261.7	10,551	27,792	56,977	43.5	3.6	57,881	11.7	12.6	11.4
Steele	144	1,926	9,214	11.8	43.3	24.8	61.3	9,418	28,736	58,141	42.7	3.0	60,619	9.1	12.2	11.0
Stevens	163	1,276	3,360	7.2	35.2	28.2	16.3	10,632	26,625	55,941	45.6	4.7	58,179	11.1	9.7	8.7
Swift	86	422	1,971	2.7	46.8	17.3	14.9	9,962	28,969	49,956	50.0	3.3	50,954	10.2	14.7	13.5
Todd	120	1,141	5,324	15.9	48.9	15.4	48.3	14,963	24,410	47,549	52.5	1.6	46,255	12.5	18.4	17.1
Traverse	178	1,721	666	2.9	45.3	18.1	6.0	11,976	30,992	50,333	49.6	4.7	50,416	12.7	20.5	18.9
Wabasha	66	710	4,651	14.1	43.9	21.2	41.9	9,262	31,464	58,865	40.6	3.5	63,115	7.6	9.9	9.2
Wadena	36	296	3,208	3.7	48.9	13.0	28.5	9,581	22,283	42,689	57.9	1.1	40,963	14.6	19.2	17.1
Waseca	100	1,310	4,375	11.5	44.3	19.9	35.2	9,734	27,179	53,191	45.5	2.5	53,383	9.3	12.5	11.1
Washington	103	1,989	66,984	16.4	25.6	42.3	401.7	10,144	39,873	86,689	25.7	10.1	90,755	4.5	5.3	4.7
Watonwan	202	992	2,417	6.5	55.8	16.3	21.0	11,504	26,273	50,068	49.9	2.1	49,482	11.3	16.5	15.6
Wilkin	79	1,291	1,458	8.5	37.1	21.3	11.6	10,662	27,814	52,963	47.1	1.6	54,373	8.9	11.9	10.8
Winona	120	1,942	16,124	17.3	36.7	29.3	67.5	12,602	25,967	52,840	47.8	3.0	56,499	11.5	11.7	10.8
Wright	91	1,596	35,057	11.4	34.5	26.8	256.8	9,688	31,154	75,705	30.5	3.9	76,256	5.3	5.7	5.1
Yellow Medicine	133	728	2,276	8.0	46.2	16.2	18.9	12,663	27,686	54,717	44.7	2.7	55,690	9.9	14.1	13.1

1. Data for serious crimes have not been adjusted for underreporting; this may affect comparability between geographic areas and over time.   2. Per 100,000 population estimated by the FBI.
3. All persons 3 years old and over enrolled in nursery school through college.   4. Persons 25 years old and over.   5. Elementary and secondary education expenditures.
6. Based on population estimated by the American Community Survey, 2011–2015.

Table B. States and Counties — Personal Income and Earnings

	Personal income, 2016										Earnings, 2016		
			Per capita[1]			Supplements to wages and salaries, employer contributions (mil dol)						Contributions for government social insurance (mil dol)	
STATE County	Total (mil dol)	Percent change 2015-2016	Dollars	Rank	Wages and salaries (mil dol)	Pension and insurance	Government social insurance	Proprietors' income (mil dol)	Dividends, interest, and rent (mil dol)	Personal transfer receipts (mil dol)	Total (mil dol)	From employee and self-employed	From employer
	62	63	64	65	66	67	68	69	70	71	72	73	74
MINNESOTA— Cont'd													
Fillmore	887	-0.4	42,246	1,068	221	44	18	115	161	188	398	47	18
Freeborn	1,219	1.2	40,045	1,361	510	88	39	46	238	312	684	89	39
Goodhue	2,282	2.1	48,888	475	1,013	181	77	255	392	405	1,526	175	77
Grant	280	-0.1	47,079	602	77	14	6	46	58	72	143	15	6
Hennepin	83,103	2.7	67,427	74	65,022	8,396	4,628	6,523	18,579	9,821	84,569	9,636	4628
Houston	890	2.5	47,315	585	185	40	15	69	158	171	308	36	15
Hubbard	807	4.2	38,935	1,504	221	42	17	62	165	226	342	44	17
Isanti	1,557	3.7	39,909	1,378	446	86	35	70	201	324	637	79	35
Itasca	1,725	0.5	38,125	1,635	666	130	53	81	332	520	929	119	53
Jackson	496	-4.9	49,859	419	209	44	17	71	108	95	341	36	17
Kanabec	619	4.4	39,122	1,479	153	31	12	62	87	165	258	31	12
Kandiyohi	2,168	2.2	51,006	374	932	167	74	354	379	411	1,527	169	74
Kittson	250	1.4	57,735	180	62	13	5	59	51	47	138	11	5
Koochiching	470	0.5	37,209	1,792	190	37	16	16	79	161	259	35	16
Lac qui Parle	365	1.0	54,426	255	81	18	6	88	75	83	193	16	6
Lake	459	1.6	43,168	982	170	33	14	24	85	127	241	31	14
Lake of the Woods	171	-1.3	44,756	796	56	12	4	19	33	47	92	11	4
Le Sueur	1,225	1.5	44,382	841	393	72	32	68	220	220	566	69	32
Lincoln	266	-1.8	46,011	690	66	14	5	34	56	61	119	12	5
Lyon	1,146	-1.8	44,580	819	631	117	47	106	224	218	900	101	47
McLeod	1,561	1.2	43,559	926	762	131	59	106	265	310	1,058	128	59
Mahnomen	192	3.6	35,129	2,146	72	17	5	15	34	65	109	12	5
Marshall	454	2.1	48,686	487	103	20	8	59	82	95	190	19	8
Martin	937	-2.9	47,255	591	362	65	27	98	243	223	551	61	27
Meeker	958	1.2	41,449	1,174	284	54	22	70	159	213	430	52	22
Mille Lacs	985	3.1	38,091	1,642	341	68	26	59	139	276	494	61	26
Morrison	1,252	0.5	38,149	1,630	408	84	32	106	214	321	629	74	32
Mower	1,734	1.6	44,274	851	855	131	57	118	316	386	1,162	133	57
Murray	442	-5.5	53,013	304	115	24	9	101	84	87	248	22	9
Nicollet	1,537	1.1	45,777	714	634	122	48	107	318	255	911	103	48
Nobles	925	-3.9	42,329	1,057	446	77	33	147	174	175	703	73	33
Norman	283	-2.0	43,065	992	71	14	5	34	64	74	124	13	5
Olmsted	8,049	4.3	52,571	320	5,729	800	416	411	1,294	1,113	7,356	857	416
Otter Tail	2,529	2.3	43,545	929	912	180	71	232	516	613	1,395	166	71
Pennington	697	1.3	48,997	468	473	81	37	29	153	133	621	75	37
Pine	993	3.4	34,379	2,267	276	63	22	50	155	299	411	52	22
Pipestone	468	-4.2	50,828	380	165	32	13	117	87	89	327	30	13
Polk	1,436	3.2	45,345	751	504	95	41	158	231	322	798	88	41
Pope	519	0.4	46,981	611	194	34	15	35	117	119	279	34	15
Ramsey	26,916	3.0	49,785	423	21,105	3,088	1,516	1,627	5,267	4,855	27,334	3,148	1516
Red Lake	179	-0.6	44,633	815	39	9	3	26	25	37	77	8	3
Redwood	782	-5.6	51,227	358	253	52	19	164	158	157	488	48	19
Renville	741	-4.2	50,529	392	235	43	18	119	172	154	416	40	18
Rice	2,636	2.4	40,167	1,345	1,130	190	88	141	464	490	1,549	188	88
Rock	449	-6.7	46,901	618	143	28	10	89	88	90	270	24	10
Roseau	695	0.9	44,447	835	350	71	27	54	146	128	503	57	27
St. Louis	8,624	0.6	43,126	985	4,466	792	350	427	1,543	2,132	6,036	739	350
Scott	7,662	3.9	53,325	293	2,449	375	193	520	992	747	3,538	411	193
Sherburne	4,028	4.3	43,067	991	1,162	213	93	194	464	587	1,663	199	93
Sibley	640	-2.4	43,192	979	158	33	13	53	122	133	257	30	13
Stearns	6,626	1.1	42,572	1,034	4,034	689	313	486	1,160	1,252	5,522	645	313
Steele	1,600	3.4	43,470	943	959	159	72	59	276	311	1,249	151	72
Stevens	470	-3.0	48,530	497	226	44	17	84	111	79	372	36	17
Swift	452	-4.2	48,008	535	145	31	11	109	81	103	296	29	11
Todd	879	0.0	36,270	1,960	239	47	18	83	136	251	386	47	18
Traverse	179	-5.2	53,319	294	46	9	3	29	49	42	88	8	3
Wabasha	947	1.8	44,534	826	258	51	20	85	169	187	413	47	20
Wadena	501	2.4	36,429	1,926	232	47	18	48	85	171	344	41	18
Waseca	819	-4.1	43,306	968	267	52	22	135	136	168	476	53	22
Washington	15,124	3.1	59,749	151	3,962	640	299	819	2,699	1,673	5,720	667	299
Watonwan	440	2.9	40,331	1,323	157	31	12	50	85	103	250	27	12
Wilkin	337	1.9	53,057	302	92	15	7	76	60	66	190	19	7
Winona	2,260	1.1	44,354	843	1,043	216	81	125	576	399	1,465	167	81
Wright	5,997	3.1	45,245	757	1,830	327	146	387	748	818	2,691	318	146
Yellow Medicine	532	-7.8	53,519	281	153	33	12	110	116	112	307	29	12

1. Based on the resident population estimated as of July 1 of the year shown.

Table B. States and Counties — **Earnings, Social Security, and Housing**

| STATE County | Earnings, 2016 (cont.) Percent by selected industries | | | | | | | | | Social Security beneficiaries, December 2016 | | | Housing units, 2017 | |
	Farm	Mining, quarrying, and extracting	Construction	Manu-facturing	Information; professional, scientific, technical services	Retail trade	Finance, insurance, real estate, and leasing	Health care and social assistance	Govern-ment	Number	Rate[1]	Supple-mental Security Income recipients, 2016	Total	Percent change, 2010-2017
	75	76	77	78	79	80	81	82	83	84	85	86	87	88
MINNESOTA— Cont'd														
Fillmore	1.1	D	10.4	23.5	3.1	6.7	5.6	D	16.0	4,990	239	170	9,970	2.4
Freeborn	-1.6	D	6.2	21.8	D	10.1	8.3	D	13.7	8,005	263	546	14,368	1.0
Goodhue	1.6	D	6.5	25.6	2.7	5.4	3.3	11.8	16.0	10,385	225	488	20,622	1.4
Grant	18.6	0.0	10.9	6.0	D	4.3	6.2	D	15.4	1,705	287	66	3,306	-0.5
Hennepin	0.0	0.1	4.0	8.5	19.1	4.5	14.3	10.1	9.4	184,640	149	26,864	533,411	4.7
Houston	6.0	0.0	11.8	10.3	D	5.6	3.5	10.2	20.0	4,560	244	214	8,747	1.7
Hubbard	1.8	D	10.1	18.5	2.6	8.8	4.4	D	17.7	6,035	291	363	14,808	1.3
Isanti	-0.6	0.0	8.0	15.6	D	8.6	3.8	D	19.5	7,685	198	424	15,963	4.2
Itasca	0.0	4.8	7.9	7.5	2.9	7.8	4.8	16.9	22.2	12,935	286	910	27,743	2.5
Jackson	13.9	0.0	3.5	29.7	D	2.4	2.9	D	11.7	2,390	240	105	5,080	1.8
Kanabec	0.0	0.5	23.8	9.3	2.2	6.9	4.8	8.8	29.2	4,210	265	221	7,924	1.0
Kandiyohi	4.3	D	7.9	21.3	4.2	6.9	4.7	D	16.2	9,530	224	741	19,882	2.1
Kittson	35.7	D	D	5.7	D	3.3	D	D	14.7	1,155	267	51	2,614	0.3
Koochiching	0.9	0.0	6.1	24.0	2.4	7.1	4.1	D	24.0	3,870	307	295	7,921	0.3
Lac qui Parle	32.3	0.0	6.3	5.0	D	5.4	5.5	7.8	20.0	1,905	283	82	3,697	0.1
Lake	0.0	D	4.7	17.3	2.7	4.9	4.2	D	21.4	3,115	296	123	7,959	3.6
Lake of the Woods	0.5	0.0	D	14.7	D	6.1	D	10.6	19.4	1,130	298	28	3,781	3.0
Le Sueur	1.4	D	10.0	37.8	3.0	4.5	4.7	5.5	12.6	5,330	192	297	12,682	2.2
Lincoln	20.9	0.1	13.7	2.7	3.0	4.2	2.8	D	13.5	1,500	263	56	3,148	1.3
Lyon	2.0	0.1	5.4	16.4	3.9	7.1	11.9	8.5	20.9	4,930	191	417	11,259	1.5
McLeod	0.1	D	5.7	36.9	2.7	6.0	4.2	14.9	10.7	7,790	218	350	15,849	0.6
Mahnomen	8.2	0.0	3.9	D	D	3.3	D	D	55.1	975	177	142	2,781	-0.2
Marshall	20.1	D	9.5	11.1	2.2	4.1	D	6.9	19.3	2,235	239	86	4,811	0.0
Martin	10.8	0.0	6.0	13.0	3.7	6.8	6.8	D	12.8	5,540	279	378	9,969	-0.4
Meeker	5.4	0.2	11.7	19.8	D	5.9	5.2	8.6	17.2	5,255	227	218	10,864	1.8
Mille Lacs	-1.0	D	10.0	9.2	4.7	6.6	4.2	D	35.2	6,470	253	447	12,918	1.3
Morrison	6.9	0.2	9.5	9.9	5.9	7.9	3.9	D	23.6	7,795	237	625	16,176	2.8
Mower	-0.3	0.0	4.1	18.4	D	4.2	2.8	D	13.8	8,980	228	756	17,056	0.2
Murray	29.5	0.6	9.0	10.0	2.6	5.1	D	D	14.2	2,185	263	81	4,647	2.0
Nicollet	4.2	0.0	3.7	23.9	D	4.3	3.9	D	22.1	5,870	174	343	13,547	5.2
Nobles	9.4	0.2	4.6	28.5	4.4	6.7	5.4	D	12.3	4,050	184	312	8,669	1.6
Norman	22.2	0.0	5.7	0.2	7.1	4.4	D	14.2	18.3	1,725	264	120	3,435	0.4
Olmsted	0.1	0.0	4.6	8.9	4.1	5.1	3.1	53.7	8.6	26,250	171	2,167	65,539	8.3
Otter Tail	3.7	0.1	10.4	18.0	4.3	6.9	3.8	14.2	16.1	15,975	276	778	36,165	1.6
Pennington	0.9	0.0	2.9	9.5	D	4.8	2.3	D	13.3	2,895	203	197	6,546	4.0
Pine	1.1	D	10.5	2.7	D	6.9	3.6	9.4	41.2	7,090	246	543	17,534	1.5
Pipestone	17.5	D	9.7	7.7	6.7	5.4	D	6.0	15.4	2,045	222	150	4,502	0.4
Polk	12.2	0.2	8.6	14.0	3.2	6.4	3.8	D	19.5	6,795	215	591	14,966	2.4
Pope	5.5	0.0	6.3	18.4	2.6	7.0	5.0	D	18.7	2,725	249	126	6,645	3.3
Ramsey	0.0	0.0	4.3	10.9	9.7	4.1	9.1	13.1	16.9	86,135	159	16,668	220,443	1.5
Red Lake	22.1	D	7.8	D	D	4.6	D	2.7	19.9	925	231	42	1,940	-0.4
Redwood	14.2	D	4.2	23.3	2.0	4.4	6.1	5.7	19.8	3,600	236	193	7,340	0.9
Renville	24.3	D	5.1	17.0	3.6	2.8	D	D	15.4	3,575	245	214	7,355	0.0
Rice	0.4	0.2	7.5	21.6	3.0	5.7	3.7	10.5	15.2	11,760	179	756	24,987	2.2
Rock	25.1	D	5.2	7.4	1.9	5.0	13.4	10.5	14.3	2,320	246	98	4,308	1.1
Roseau	5.9	0.0	1.6	50.9	D	4.1	4.5	D	12.9	3,280	211	139	7,604	1.8
St. Louis	0.1	5.3	5.8	5.0	6.5	7.3	5.4	25.5	17.9	46,905	235	5,089	104,691	1.6
Scott	0.2	0.2	15.6	16.7	6.1	5.6	3.6	7.9	17.5	17,175	120	1,217	51,013	8.3
Sherburne	0.4	D	12.8	15.0	3.5	7.5	3.3	10.5	17.7	13,440	144	499	33,888	4.7
Sibley	10.5	0.0	13.4	13.2	2.2	2.7	3.4	D	15.8	3,170	214	142	6,596	0.2
Stearns	1.7	D	8.5	12.8	6.1	7.5	6.8	19.1	15.1	26,915	172	2,405	64,690	4.4
Steele	-0.7	D	3.7	30.2	D	7.4	16.9	10.1	11.3	7,635	208	514	15,578	1.5
Stevens	16.6	D	6.4	19.3	3.9	5.3	3.5	10.4	19.6	1,715	176	118	4,254	2.3
Swift	9.5	D	5.9	27.6	2.9	4.6	3.4	D	16.8	2,240	237	153	4,835	0.0
Todd	4.8	D	5.5	29.4	2.0	4.8	4.1	D	19.2	5,955	244	384	13,232	2.4
Traverse	28.3	0.0	3.1	3.2	D	5.4	2.8	9.5	18.8	980	295	81	2,102	1.4
Wabasha	8.0	D	6.7	22.1	2.4	5.1	5.0	D	15.3	4,950	231	210	10,217	2.2
Wadena	3.9	0.0	7.5	8.4	2.9	5.3	3.3	D	21.7	3,845	283	405	7,114	3.1
Waseca	5.0	D	6.1	38.1	D	4.4	4.4	8.3	17.9	4,195	223	232	7,949	0.6
Washington	0.3	0.1	7.4	13.9	7.7	7.8	7.7	13.9	13.5	41,115	163	2,054	98,256	6.4
Watonwan	12.7	D	8.3	24.9	1.8	3.7	4.4	9.2	16.3	2,335	214	133	5,053	0.1
Wilkin	9.2	D	4.0	1.7	D	2.7	D	11.1	12.2	1,435	226	104	3,116	1.2
Winona	3.5	D	4.1	28.2	D	5.6	3.9	9.5	15.6	9,545	188	626	21,197	2.1
Wright	0.1	D	16.0	15.9	3.1	7.8	4.3	11.5	14.0	19,910	150	898	51,778	5.7
Yellow Medicine	16.5	D	8.0	10.7	3.1	4.1	D	D	23.0	2,470	250	148	4,768	0.2

1. Per 1,000 resident population estimated as of July 1 of the year shown.

Table B. States and Counties — **Housing, Labor Force, and Employment**

STATE County	Housing units, 2017 (cont.) Occupied units Owner-occupied Total	Percent	Median value[1]	Median owner cost as a percent of income With a mortgage	Without a mortgage[2]	Renter-occupied Median rent[3]	Median rent as a percent of income[2]	Sub-standard units[4] (percent)	Civilian labor force, 2017 Total	Percent change, 2016-2017	Unemployment Total	Rate[5]	Civilian employment[6], 2012-2016 Total	Percent Management, business, science, and arts	Construction, production, and maintenance occupations
	89	90	91	92	93	94	95	96	97	98	99	100	101	102	103
MINNESOTA— Cont'd															
Fillmore	8,540	78.9	143,700	21.5	11.2	607	26.5	3.3	11,521	-0.2	402	3.5	10,597	35.2	28.7
Freeborn	13,046	75.6	106,600	19.5	10.7	616	25.3	1.6	16,182	-1.0	593	3.7	15,280	27.3	32.7
Goodhue	19,051	75.6	185,800	21.1	12.2	757	28.4	1.9	26,916	-0.1	874	3.2	23,841	35.3	27.2
Grant	2,547	80.1	100,800	19.8	11.6	533	28.0	1.4	3,281	-0.5	135	4.1	2,879	33.9	29.1
Hennepin	49,3,832	62.2	235,800	21.0	11.6	982	29.0	2.8	698,457	1.5	21,118	3.0	661,175	48.2	13.6
Houston	7,989	80.8	162,300	21.4	11.7	644	27.9	1.2	10,613	-0.3	359	3.4	9,988	34.2	29.4
Hubbard	8,741	81.6	177,800	23.4	12.7	624	27.6	3.1	9,924	0.9	552	5.6	9,339	31.0	27.2
Isanti	14,403	81.3	166,900	22.9	12.2	874	29.2	2.4	21,034	1.4	910	4.3	19,715	29.3	31.0
Itasca	19,126	80.2	155,400	22.4	11.9	651	29.7	2.8	21,781	-1.5	1,527	7.0	20,115	31.6	26.5
Jackson	4,335	77.6	115,100	17.5	10.1	575	22.9	1.5	5,779	-5.6	211	3.7	5,408	36.1	29.9
Kanabec	6,290	80.6	136,600	23.9	14.7	776	30.3	2.6	9,022	0.0	548	6.1	7,411	27.7	31.0
Kandiyohi	16,737	72.6	164,300	21.5	11.7	672	28.6	2.3	24,834	2.3	811	3.3	21,732	32.0	29.4
Kittson	1,913	81.6	72,400	17.8	10.0	497	24.8	1.6	2,381	-1.3	90	3.8	2,204	32.8	33.0
Koochiching	5,732	79.3	105,500	19.3	11.1	585	32.9	1.4	6,026	-2.6	424	7.0	5,851	27.6	30.0
Lac qui Parle	3,111	80.2	81,000	18.4	10.0	569	24.6	0.8	3,528	-2.9	124	3.5	3,478	35.7	28.6
Lake	5,207	80.6	164,700	21.9	10.8	690	28.8	4.0	5,591	2.8	218	3.9	4,844	37.8	25.8
Lake of the Woods	1,551	84.4	122,400	22.5	14.2	635	32.0	2.3	2,387	-0.2	112	4.7	2,027	24.7	41.8
Le Sueur	10,805	81.2	182,000	21.9	11.5	696	27.3	2.0	15,803	1.2	737	4.7	14,710	32.2	32.3
Lincoln	2,477	79.3	89,600	20.7	11.1	584	26.1	1.0	3,321	-2.2	111	3.3	2,885	33.3	30.9
Lyon	10,072	67.7	134,500	18.9	10.0	614	26.1	2.8	14,987	-1.7	481	3.2	13,862	34.7	28.6
McLeod	14,780	77.0	148,400	21.3	11.7	752	25.2	1.4	19,578	-1.4	747	3.8	19,253	30.0	32.1
Mahnomen	1,977	71.7	96,800	21.1	12.6	532	26.8	4.4	2,367	-1.3	117	4.9	2,246	27.8	23.5
Marshall	3,991	81.1	99,100	18.3	10.4	551	22.7	1.6	5,498	-2.5	387	7.0	4,783	33.4	31.3
Martin	8,777	74.5	108,500	19.0	10.0	591	28.8	2.3	10,424	-0.7	367	3.5	10,189	30.2	31.2
Meeker	9,119	79.6	157,600	22.1	11.8	720	27.2	2.2	13,301	-0.1	540	4.1	11,516	32.7	34.1
Mille Lacs	10,012	74.1	143,500	23.3	13.7	751	28.2	2.8	12,918	1.2	713	5.5	11,994	27.7	33.0
Morrison	13,275	78.9	155,600	22.4	12.4	661	28.8	2.0	17,713	-1.2	948	5.4	16,684	28.9	32.1
Mower	15,414	72.8	114,100	19.1	10.0	693	28.9	1.9	20,575	-0.1	584	2.8	19,061	28.5	32.9
Murray	3,715	80.7	105,000	19.6	11.5	565	20.2	0.6	4,898	-1.5	212	4.3	4,234	35.9	29.0
Nicollet	12,559	72.8	174,200	21.3	10.1	812	27.0	1.3	20,625	0.9	524	2.5	18,503	38.5	21.6
Nobles	7,890	70.9	113,100	19.7	10.0	640	23.7	4.8	11,344	-1.3	363	3.2	10,509	25.1	42.2
Norman	2,696	81.3	86,000	18.1	11.3	549	29.2	3.0	3,408	-1.4	162	4.8	3,127	34.4	28.7
Olmsted	58,692	73.8	178,000	19.4	10.0	845	29.1	2.2	86,420	1.0	2,335	2.7	80,136	48.9	15.6
Otter Tail	23,962	78.7	168,900	20.5	11.4	645	27.6	1.9	31,757	1.1	1,259	4.0	27,950	33.1	29.4
Pennington	5,923	73.2	123,300	19.3	10.5	602	25.8	1.0	8,831	-2.7	505	5.7	7,580	29.0	30.4
Pine	10,993	77.8	144,800	24.7	13.3	703	29.4	3.4	15,044	1.0	846	5.6	12,607	24.6	30.4
Pipestone	3,998	75.9	92,400	20.1	10.0	559	25.6	3.0	4,909	-0.2	168	3.4	4,458	28.2	34.6
Polk	12,608	72.9	145,100	19.7	11.6	663	30.0	1.5	17,043	-1.0	722	4.2	15,882	34.3	25.3
Pope	4,815	80.2	153,000	21.7	11.8	610	25.3	1.7	6,371	0.7	195	3.1	5,406	35.6	26.9
Ramsey	20,7,327	59.0	199,200	21.4	11.3	892	29.9	4.4	287,472	1.4	9,262	3.2	270,977	43.4	16.8
Red Lake	1,676	80.5	103,700	18.9	11.3	477	27.6	1.8	2,255	-1.9	148	6.6	2,034	29.8	31.2
Redwood	6,262	79.3	96,900	19.6	10.3	602	25.8	1.2	7,702	-7.8	317	4.1	7,580	33.3	28.2
Renville	6,188	79.2	99,300	19.2	10.0	594	25.2	1.3	8,900	5.4	400	4.5	7,499	33.0	33.4
Rice	22,654	74.1	184,400	22.9	10.8	760	28.4	1.9	36,629	1.1	1,163	3.2	34,123	35.9	25.9
Rock	3,932	74.1	131,700	20.2	11.1	668	25.3	1.6	5,912	-0.3	122	2.1	4,748	34.1	26.9
Roseau	6,106	79.5	115,700	20.5	10.3	659	24.5	2.8	8,157	-1.5	399	4.9	8,420	28.1	42.6
St. Louis	85,059	70.7	143,200	20.6	11.3	698	31.0	2.1	102,698	-0.3	4,761	4.6	97,461	34.6	21.0
Scott	47,154	82.9	258,400	20.7	10.0	1,084	29.0	1.6	82,194	1.5	2,370	2.9	76,197	41.0	20.4
Sherburne	30,781	82.7	193,300	21.2	10.6	946	30.7	2.1	51,601	1.4	1,926	3.7	48,754	34.8	25.9
Sibley	6,009	78.2	134,300	20.1	11.0	628	24.9	1.4	8,513	-0.1	305	3.6	7,991	30.3	36.2
Stearns	57,695	68.8	168,200	20.8	10.7	754	27.6	2.5	90,157	1.0	3,041	3.4	84,285	32.3	25.0
Steele	14,354	76.0	149,700	20.3	10.9	726	29.5	2.5	20,561	-3.3	694	3.4	18,676	32.4	27.4
Stevens	3,567	67.6	146,400	17.7	10.0	645	38.6	0.9	5,526	-2.6	147	2.7	5,177	34.8	23.3
Swift	4,177	70.9	97,100	18.1	10.8	615	24.8	1.6	5,045	-0.4	207	4.1	4,832	31.5	32.6
Todd	9,866	81.5	132,100	23.1	12.9	587	26.0	4.4	13,476	4.0	538	4.0	11,476	28.1	37.3
Traverse	1,544	82.1	72,800	18.7	10.0	547	23.9	1.0	1,789	4.4	63	3.5	1,615	39.0	23.5
Wabasha	9,004	80.3	160,900	21.5	11.7	698	26.8	1.5	12,078	0.2	404	3.3	11,312	34.2	28.9
Wadena	5,657	75.2	113,400	22.6	13.3	601	27.1	2.0	5,831	-7.0	329	5.6	5,971	24.1	35.3
Waseca	7,329	76.3	142,800	19.2	10.4	598	27.2	1.6	9,392	-1.2	367	3.9	9,525	32.7	30.0
Washington	91,282	80.4	253,300	20.6	10.0	1,192	28.7	1.5	141,336	1.4	4,230	3.0	132,292	45.5	16.1
Watonwan	4,465	73.8	94,900	19.2	10.0	593	23.6	1.3	6,491	-1.7	286	4.4	5,757	29.3	38.3
Wilkin	2,871	76.7	110,800	20.1	10.0	498	26.5	1.3	3,574	-4.3	112	3.1	3,325	35.9	28.0
Winona	19,078	70.4	156,500	21.0	10.5	629	29.3	2.0	29,057	-1.1	905	3.1	28,474	34.1	25.2
Wright	45,887	81.8	201,500	20.8	10.2	915	28.6	2.2	74,355	1.3	2,606	3.5	69,613	34.5	26.7
Yellow Medicine	4,174	78.3	98,100	18.8	10.1	568	27.6	1.1	5,345	-2.8	189	3.5	5,084	33.5	29.5

1. Specified owner-occupied units.   2. A value of 10.0 represents 10 percent or less; a value of 50.0 represents 50 percent or more.   3. Specified renter-occupied units.   4. Overcrowded or lacking complete plumbing facilities.   5. Percent of civilian labor force.   6. Civilian employed persons 16 years old and over.

Table B. States and Counties — Nonfarm Employment and Agriculture

STATE County	Number of establishments	Employment Total	Health care and social assistance	Manufacturing	Retail trade	Finance and insurance	Professional, scientific, and technical services	Total (mil dol)	Average per employee (dollars)	Number	Fewer than 50 acres	500 acres or more	Farm operators whose principal occupation is farming (percent)
	104	105	106	107	108	109	110	111	112	113	114	115	116
MINNESOTA— Cont'd													
Fillmore	600	4,686	850	857	757	239	133	158	33,653	1,553	24.8	14.8	50.4
Freeborn	781	11,569	2,498	2,739	1,999	522	192	428	36,999	1,122	33.9	23.4	54.0
Goodhue	1,312	20,628	3,478	4,808	2,562	442	453	875	42,428	1,536	34.2	11.4	47.7
Grant	199	1,431	360	104	247	72	37	51	35,324	542	23.4	25.1	42.3
Hennepin	40,301	888,172	135,045	74,644	77,584	84,038	85,258	55,619	62,622	627	60.3	6.2	65.1
Houston	426	4,023	1,010	476	575	103	98	126	31,374	920	14.9	11.3	48.5
Hubbard	575	4,545	822	853	1,036	146	106	161	35,533	406	18.7	11.1	51.5
Isanti	835	8,978	2,009	1,395	1,890	309	205	340	37,863	844	43.4	7.8	44.1
Itasca	1,164	14,132	3,641	1,009	2,424	421	558	520	36,815	401	23.2	8.0	45.6
Jackson	312	4,767	1,287	1,169	355	91	53	174	36,460	826	21.3	30.0	59.9
Kanabec	292	2,966	912	525	543	91	77	114	38,316	648	23.1	8.6	50.8
Kandiyohi	1,408	19,658	5,419	2,674	3,104	547	565	709	36,083	1,310	27.0	14.8	44.7
Kittson	143	1,261	325	203	298	57	22	44	35,256	544	10.8	36.2	43.0
Koochiching	392	3,788	680	D	779	129	63	136	35,916	187	9.1	17.6	43.9
Lac qui Parle	204	1,717	553	144	300	92	18	53	30,824	852	18.7	35.2	57.4
Lake	298	2,868	490	507	343	115	50	110	38,259	44	50.0	2.3	29.5
Lake of the Woods	159	1,373	D	165	236	30	14	42	30,744	196	15.3	19.9	36.2
Le Sueur	702	7,406	779	2,945	717	219	186	327	44,112	1,051	35.8	11.4	40.6
Lincoln	211	1,515	520	19	244	53	35	42	27,496	699	17.6	24.5	54.6
Lyon	807	12,785	2,381	1,928	1,945	1,106	373	523	40,946	904	17.7	30.6	64.8
McLeod	978	16,258	3,118	5,590	2,264	412	412	687	42,280	966	32.6	16.6	62.6
Mahnomen	101	1,785	340	D	143	56	17	54	30,055	310	15.8	37.1	52.6
Marshall	260	1,573	305	223	249	119	28	67	42,429	1,148	8.1	33.0	44.9
Martin	635	8,078	1,706	1,478	1,317	331	189	316	39,135	897	20.3	33.2	67.8
Meeker	565	6,467	1,353	1,777	922	199	96	235	36,350	1,147	31.8	13.1	49.4
Mille Lacs	696	8,547	1,823	1,057	1,309	206	112	263	30,777	731	31.5	7.4	43.2
Morrison	871	7,919	1,530	1,124	1,592	260	182	274	34,566	1,957	18.3	8.7	50.3
Mower	846	14,602	2,624	3,817	1,733	312	226	700	47,936	1,053	30.7	22.5	64.1
Murray	307	2,650	433	D	326	153	75	87	32,797	895	20.7	31.1	59.1
Nicollet	658	12,832	2,359	3,641	1,040	215	434	511	39,808	764	23.6	20.9	62.6
Nobles	601	9,148	1,450	3,011	1,558	242	255	323	35,309	995	22.7	26.1	65.7
Norman	183	1,284	439	D	185	82	30	51	39,665	610	7.9	43.9	64.6
Olmsted	3,575	95,956	19,904	4,307	11,594	1,703	D	5,349	55,741	1,150	35.6	11.6	50.3
Otter Tail	1,673	18,780	3,997	4,099	2,862	546	398	666	35,456	3,033	17.0	13.9	46.6
Pennington	397	9,350	1,290	941	1,143	130	335	371	39,652	515	12.6	25.2	37.5
Pine	616	7,223	1,464	332	1,106	177	114	191	26,409	870	16.6	10.6	47.2
Pipestone	339	3,114	480	491	591	112	81	103	33,199	637	25.1	25.0	57.1
Polk	768	9,406	2,199	1,726	1,478	243	210	329	34,978	1,322	11.6	37.3	56.1
Pope	370	3,858	642	915	376	120	248	156	40,501	931	21.6	16.6	37.1
Ramsey	13,536	307,529	62,278	23,081	27,738	18,528	15,057	16,980	55,214	97	96.9	0.0	83.5
Red Lake	103	607	91	D	118	61	20	21	34,578	322	8.4	29.8	57.1
Redwood	525	5,721	877	904	813	339	80	195	34,037	1,163	19.9	31.2	68.5
Renville	467	4,632	892	1,245	554	174	162	177	38,154	1,061	20.2	32.9	63.4
Rice	1,543	24,908	3,308	4,014	2,864	450	470	889	35,702	1,304	40.9	7.7	45.6
Rock	264	2,826	863	292	408	276	91	91	32,176	689	26.6	23.9	62.1
Roseau	415	6,854	772	3,812	850	174	79	248	36,249	977	9.6	27.2	41.2
St. Louis	5,339	88,503	24,822	4,126	12,618	4,411	3,721	3,668	41,449	685	26.1	6.6	38.4
Scott	3,338	44,084	4,949	6,688	5,215	709	2,411	2,141	48,568	847	41.0	6.8	51.6
Sherburne	2,039	22,123	4,271	3,559	3,199	417	610	942	42,590	455	41.1	12.5	42.2
Sibley	350	3,520	610	898	366	136	56	125	35,453	949	25.7	20.9	63.8
Stearns	4,428	83,525	16,872	11,748	11,363	4,135	2,864	3,615	43,282	3,501	23.0	8.4	55.4
Steele	1,005	19,226	2,665	4,997	2,729	2,168	247	864	44,962	796	38.4	14.2	55.5
Stevens	314	4,675	1,461	1,031	557	102	108	167	35,754	560	25.2	31.1	56.3
Swift	304	3,041	641	611	398	105	82	104	34,312	801	22.2	26.0	55.2
Todd	544	5,796	1,559	1,758	783	208	83	210	36,188	1,931	18.4	6.8	52.9
Traverse	123	839	282	47	191	39	2	25	29,757	458	22.7	36.7	62.7
Wabasha	552	5,448	1,013	1,237	789	157	111	197	36,170	909	24.1	14.2	58.7
Wadena	402	4,040	944	306	746	154	120	144	35,639	643	15.7	6.4	42.8
Waseca	460	5,133	889	1,657	710	170	167	200	38,956	805	31.3	18.8	55.8
Washington	5,870	81,510	12,925	8,466	14,185	6,193	3,818	3,409	41,822	602	54.0	6.5	57.3
Watonwan	294	3,721	498	1,343	458	130	40	117	31,561	503	25.0	27.4	60.2
Wilkin	156	1,763	463	D	183	55	D	61	34,832	391	14.8	49.9	68.3
Winona	1,156	23,755	3,467	5,109	2,844	549	489	899	37,855	1,115	22.6	11.9	52.6
Wright	3,285	36,834	5,711	5,744	7,255	731	1,013	1,515	41,141	1,463	39.2	8.3	48.8
Yellow Medicine	328	3,329	876	224	384	121	D	133	39,837	885	22.7	32.3	60.8

Table B. States and Counties — Government Employment and Payroll, and Local Government Finances

STATE County	Government employment and payroll, 2012									Local government finances				
			March payroll (percent of total)							General revenue				
													Taxes	
													Per capita[1] (dollars)	
	Full-time equivalent employees	March payroll (dollars)	Adminis-tration, judicial, and legal	Police and corrections	Fire protection	Highways and transpor-tation	Health and welfare	Natural resources and utilities	Education and libraries	Total (mil dol)	Inter-govern-mental (mil dol)	Total (mil dol)	Total	Property
	171	172	173	174	175	176	177	178	179	180	181	182	183	184
MINNESOTA— Cont'd														
Fillmore	743	2,541,608	12.4	9.9	0.0	8.7	11.1	6.0	50.3	79.4	42.2	20.8	999	988
Freeborn	1,073	4,355,329	8.3	11.4	1.9	7.2	10.0	5.7	54.1	127.7	69.2	36.7	1,183	1110
Goodhue	1,720	6,840,668	9.9	13.6	2.1	4.3	9.2	6.0	53.4	204.8	92.0	69.5	1,500	1468
Grant	273	953,527	13.2	7.0	0.0	7.4	8.2	5.8	57.5	34.1	18.5	9.7	1,624	1620
Hennepin	35,312	195,123,070	8.9	12.4	2.0	3.7	9.4	8.3	54.2	6,392.6	2,496.9	2,262.3	1,910	1724
Houston	731	2,758,225	7.6	7.3	0.3	4.4	7.9	2.9	66.7	81.1	51.4	19.2	1,022	1012
Hubbard	660	2,206,385	9.8	10.0	0.0	6.0	8.6	2.6	59.7	84.9	48.1	26.6	1,305	1278
Isanti	1,257	4,796,343	6.7	9.3	0.1	4.0	7.5	2.3	68.0	131.8	76.3	35.3	924	904
Itasca	1,538	7,554,704	6.6	8.1	0.4	8.7	15.2	3.8	55.3	301.4	126.6	54.1	1,196	1185
Jackson	515	1,776,829	11.8	7.0	0.2	8.4	20.7	6.0	44.4	50.6	24.7	15.9	1,544	1531
Kanabec	867	2,925,087	5.0	6.1	0.0	4.3	35.1	1.6	43.5	90.0	33.3	14.7	920	889
Kandiyohi	2,286	9,769,471	6.3	8.2	0.4	2.9	40.7	4.1	36.3	282.7	84.2	49.6	1,170	1089
Kittson	282	1,417,262	8.1	3.9	0.0	6.1	5.8	4.7	69.0	29.6	16.1	6.4	1,432	1411
Koochiching	528	2,114,323	5.7	6.7	1.6	5.8	7.4	7.8	61.4	61.1	35.8	8.3	632	626
Lac qui Parle	625	1,888,050	6.9	3.8	0.0	5.1	33.9	3.0	45.7	46.7	21.4	8.4	1,176	1141
Lake	361	1,980,601	12.9	10.1	0.3	9.4	6.4	8.7	48.8	64.0	33.4	15.7	1,454	1414
Lake of the Woods	143	726,420	14.0	7.3	0.0	9.2	10.2	5.3	51.7	20.3	13.0	5.1	1,272	1255
Le Sueur	871	2,940,497	8.0	8.1	0.0	4.7	11.3	5.1	60.6	96.7	50.3	31.2	1,128	1088
Lincoln	199	603,609	18.2	11.9	0.1	15.9	1.7	6.8	38.3	21.7	9.6	8.1	1,392	1384
Lyon	1,012	3,496,744	7.5	9.5	0.1	6.3	1.3	11.7	60.6	145.6	71.4	30.6	1,199	1151
McLeod	1,516	6,615,440	5.8	6.3	0.2	3.2	37.7	10.6	34.8	212.6	66.7	39.1	1,084	1063
Mahnomen	413	1,411,273	11.1	5.4	0.0	2.8	22.1	3.6	50.5	40.8	24.5	6.0	1,085	1083
Marshall	459	1,668,424	9.8	5.5	0.5	7.6	16.1	9.7	49.9	55.9	36.6	9.4	991	982
Martin	655	3,114,449	10.3	9.8	0.1	7.4	3.2	9.6	56.8	92.7	49.5	24.0	1,170	1158
Meeker	1,226	4,903,007	5.1	5.4	0.1	2.7	21.6	3.2	60.7	139.5	63.7	28.6	1,239	1222
Mille Lacs	1,239	4,213,762	8.0	10.1	0.2	3.3	6.5	3.4	67.4	113.5	71.6	30.4	1,182	1162
Morrison	1,124	4,203,099	7.6	8.2	0.9	5.8	10.1	2.5	63.7	118.8	71.3	29.8	903	875
Mower	1,542	6,255,175	7.7	8.0	0.8	4.4	8.9	12.3	56.6	166.8	93.6	36.0	915	853
Murray	420	2,070,204	5.7	4.9	0.0	4.6	33.5	2.7	42.5	54.5	22.6	10.9	1,273	1259
Nicollet	835	3,375,650	8.8	10.9	0.1	6.1	20.8	7.8	43.0	108.0	39.0	29.6	899	839
Nobles	747	5,019,216	4.9	6.5	0.1	3.1	5.4	4.5	73.5	104.9	59.6	21.9	1,019	964
Norman	410	1,309,952	11.1	4.4	0.2	8.7	6.0	6.0	61.5	40.3	26.4	8.4	1,266	1263
Olmsted	4,101	28,521,111	5.6	8.4	2.3	3.1	9.3	7.4	60.7	672.3	289.4	201.9	1,373	1242
Otter Tail	2,164	8,240,552	8.0	7.4	0.2	4.7	21.9	3.4	52.3	298.8	109.1	62.1	1,083	1068
Pennington	640	2,304,729	5.4	8.5	1.6	4.2	7.5	11.0	56.5	114.3	37.7	13.8	984	963
Pine	879	3,660,809	9.4	7.3	0.3	7.0	4.0	1.4	67.8	103.3	61.8	27.4	938	920
Pipestone	661	2,186,364	6.7	4.4	0.1	5.7	33.1	2.8	46.0	72.9	31.8	11.0	1,175	1146
Polk	1,733	5,824,889	5.7	5.8	1.5	3.5	29.5	8.1	43.7	191.1	112.8	36.5	1,161	1082
Pope	553	2,333,307	3.9	5.8	0.0	8.4	42.6	1.9	32.2	48.8	23.1	14.2	1,302	1287
Ramsey	16,492	141,646,187	5.1	8.3	2.7	4.8	6.3	4.1	67.7	2,881.4	1,248.1	805.8	1,549	1417
Red Lake	258	709,610	7.9	6.0	0.0	6.6	6.3	5.2	67.6	24.0	15.3	4.3	1,044	1038
Redwood	739	3,232,367	9.3	5.7	0.2	4.8	7.0	5.7	65.2	101.1	39.6	20.4	1,287	1261
Renville	704	2,316,532	18.7	8.2	0.0	9.5	12.1	4.4	43.1	88.9	34.9	21.9	1,424	1401
Rice	2,519	10,254,560	4.8	6.6	0.7	2.9	41.2	2.9	39.9	352.9	102.9	62.2	959	916
Rock	396	1,387,361	10.8	6.2	0.1	8.3	1.0	11.6	59.9	45.4	21.6	11.5	1,203	1152
Roseau	687	2,591,371	8.0	6.4	0.0	5.4	6.6	3.1	69.0	74.6	50.8	14.1	909	899
St. Louis	7,560	37,760,893	7.0	10.6	2.8	7.2	13.4	8.3	44.2	1,073.0	545.0	233.2	1,164	1026
Scott	3,486	17,619,282	8.6	9.3	0.5	3.5	6.2	5.2	64.4	500.4	232.5	180.8	1,338	1287
Sherburne	3,233	14,013,536	5.6	10.8	0.4	2.4	4.7	3.2	71.3	366.7	185.3	126.0	1,408	1391
Sibley	636	2,194,050	9.3	7.3	0.3	6.5	27.2	1.9	46.6	76.3	33.5	18.9	1,250	1235
Stearns	4,907	24,879,439	7.5	10.1	1.5	2.8	14.9	4.1	56.2	676.6	322.4	196.7	1,297	1129
Steele	1,297	5,726,547	5.5	10.8	0.9	4.1	6.2	10.3	60.3	147.4	81.6	42.4	1,167	1112
Stevens	479	1,791,149	11.2	17.4	0.6	6.2	9.0	11.6	40.3	43.2	23.3	12.2	1,258	1229
Swift	748	2,235,013	8.5	5.5	0.0	5.7	37.9	3.6	34.8	82.8	25.2	13.2	1,379	1363
Todd	994	3,435,036	8.2	8.5	0.0	4.5	12.5	2.3	58.8	94.8	59.3	21.3	869	840
Traverse	251	735,078	9.6	10.4	0.1	13.3	21.2	2.5	41.3	26.6	9.8	7.7	2,242	2236
Wabasha	717	2,663,637	12.2	9.5	0.1	4.8	7.6	8.0	55.6	95.1	50.4	27.4	1,278	1244
Wadena	723	2,230,614	6.7	2.7	0.1	5.3	11.7	4.2	66.3	67.0	41.7	12.2	887	870
Waseca	839	2,685,918	9.1	9.2	1.4	6.3	7.1	5.6	60.1	83.8	42.3	21.8	1,133	1094
Washington	6,573	28,742,198	7.5	9.9	1.5	2.6	4.9	4.1	68.0	850.9	369.3	318.3	1,304	1251
Watonwan	544	1,961,440	9.4	7.3	0.3	6.3	9.4	7.3	57.7	52.1	29.2	12.3	1,097	1083
Wilkin	308	1,120,394	10.9	8.0	0.0	10.2	10.2	7.3	51.6	36.4	21.4	9.3	1,417	1407
Winona	1,299	5,244,944	8.6	10.3	2.2	4.6	9.2	8.7	54.4	161.3	88.3	44.7	866	816
Wright	4,086	18,042,110	5.5	7.7	0.2	3.1	16.3	2.4	60.5	548.1	243.1	150.9	1,185	1154
Yellow Medicine	412	1,492,491	12.8	9.7	0.0	10.5	8.7	6.7	48.7	72.8	27.5	13.9	1,364	1345

1. Based on the resident population estimated as of July 1 of the year shown.

STATE County	Local government finances (cont.)							Debt outstanding		Government employment, 2016			Individual income tax returns, 2015		
	Direct general expenditure														
			Percent of total for:												
	Total (mil dol)	Per capita[1] (dollars)	Education	Health and hospitals	Police protection	Public welfare	Highways	Total (mil dol)	Per capita[1] (dollars)	Federal civilian	Federal military	State and local	Number of returns	Mean adjusted gross income	Mean income tax
	185	186	187	188	189	190	191	192	193	194	195	196	197	198	199
MINNESOTA— Cont'd															
Fillmore	76.1	3,651	36.6	4.1	4.6	4.1	17.1	66.9	3,213	80	74	1,187	9,890	50,922	5077
Freeborn	125.1	4,028	42.5	2.8	6.6	6.1	15.4	132.0	4,249	75	107	1,419	15,120	51,255	5521
Goodhue	204.0	4,403	43.7	3.7	6.0	4.9	10.8	184.3	3,977	123	164	4,056	23,580	62,708	7364
Grant	31.2	5,248	38.6	0.9	4.1	11.4	16.0	31.1	5,236	27	21	361	2,960	53,604	5781
Hennepin	7,135.3	6,024	29.8	13.2	5.5	5.6	5.3	9,944.8	8,395	13,301	4,735	85,710	634,140	89,296	14,594
Houston	81.7	4,339	53.8	2.6	5.0	5.5	10.5	57.5	3,052	70	67	1,132	9,540	55,029	6093
Hubbard	78.2	3,842	35.6	0.3	3.6	14.6	18.2	83.3	4,093	40	74	1,083	9,330	52,223	5220
Isanti	136.1	3,558	50.4	3.4	6.9	7.7	11.0	169.3	4,426	77	139	2,037	18,860	55,210	5604
Itasca	350.2	7,744	24.1	20.6	2.5	8.1	14.2	319.0	7,054	167	159	3,394	20,890	52,685	5366
Jackson	50.2	4,887	33.0	4.1	3.8	7.8	19.0	50.8	4,943	27	35	772	5,150	57,350	6169
Kanabec	84.8	5,300	27.0	37.5	2.3	6.2	8.2	63.2	3,950	39	56	1,233	7,240	48,591	4607
Kandiyohi	300.9	7,100	20.9	38.3	5.5	4.8	6.1	333.7	7,875	140	149	3,887	21,320	55,981	6308
Kittson	33.3	7,415	39.2	0.7	3.3	4.6	22.4	21.5	4,785	47	15	294	2,140	53,211	5713
Koochiching	70.6	5,344	34.8	3.6	4.7	13.7	11.0	39.7	3,002	179	45	809	6,110	48,942	5032
Lac qui Parle	48.9	6,880	33.1	26.2	3.0	4.0	16.2	28.8	4,046	38	24	728	3,440	54,494	6031
Lake	63.2	5,838	24.4	5.5	5.8	10.5	17.5	119.8	11,076	22	37	852	5,260	52,540	5199
Lake of the Woods	20.1	5,071	32.1	0.5	4.1	7.7	23.1	304.4	76,625	31	14	288	2,000	48,344	4966
Le Sueur	119.9	4,333	53.4	2.4	3.8	5.4	10.2	161.8	5,845	81	98	1,323	13,920	59,328	6505
Lincoln	25.1	4,309	25.1	0.5	6.1	11.4	20.4	39.0	6,710	32	20	292	2,680	49,486	4808
Lyon	146.3	5,727	52.4	0.4	7.1	3.1	11.6	165.7	6,486	118	89	2,814	12,290	57,577	6408
McLeod	206.8	5,737	26.6	34.0	4.4	4.9	10.2	191.4	5,309	80	127	1,811	18,380	54,460	5620
Mahnomen	39.5	7,142	44.6	20.1	5.7	5.9	9.3	26.1	4,718	28	19	1,323	2,300	41,741	3360
Marshall	64.2	6,790	36.8	0.4	2.9	5.0	21.2	37.9	4,006	51	33	587	4,550	54,353	5917
Martin	94.4	4,613	46.0	0.5	6.6	4.8	14.2	96.9	4,732	58	70	1,312	10,370	54,173	6203
Meeker	131.9	5,719	44.6	17.9	4.5	5.3	7.4	173.9	7,539	75	82	1,205	11,060	55,531	5799
Mille Lacs	118.0	4,583	57.3	0.6	3.7	6.4	6.8	133.7	5,195	63	91	3,372	12,200	47,103	4423
Morrison	121.6	3,680	48.7	1.8	3.7	7.1	14.7	122.4	3,704	416	116	1,979	15,730	47,125	4410
Mower	168.0	4,268	46.1	1.1	4.6	8.4	11.8	1,198.8	30,447	140	138	2,524	18,890	56,740	7000
Murray	54.4	6,337	23.7	28.8	4.7	2.0	15.6	37.9	4,418	44	29	539	4,160	54,993	5682
Nicollet	111.3	3,380	30.7	17.7	4.8	6.8	10.6	144.3	4,383	31	110	2,915	15,830	62,939	7482
Nobles	104.2	4,852	42.9	3.4	7.6	7.3	10.8	69.0	3,210	87	77	1,430	10,620	49,183	4719
Norman	40.7	6,134	33.4	1.1	3.5	8.1	19.4	17.3	2,601	33	23	445	3,170	49,867	4810
Olmsted	687.5	4,675	34.2	1.9	4.8	7.4	9.9	2,857.8	19,432	817	546	7,929	77,160	72,663	9717
Otter Tail	312.8	5,461	45.3	8.8	3.2	5.1	10.5	310.4	5,419	222	204	3,579	28,270	56,293	6153
Pennington	122.4	8,695	70.1	0.0	2.8	3.6	4.7	105.6	7,504	62	50	1,605	7,110	52,305	5433
Pine	95.3	3,262	45.6	1.9	5.8	7.4	12.1	136.2	4,662	303	98	3,046	12,710	45,389	4017
Pipestone	70.7	7,570	36.9	25.0	2.8	5.3	9.6	31.4	3,359	47	32	891	4,580	50,430	5278
Polk	182.0	5,792	29.6	1.4	3.7	10.5	14.8	169.8	5,406	98	109	2,688	14,880	53,893	5597
Pope	48.7	4,470	30.5	12.3	9.7	6.5	14.2	36.7	3,368	39	39	796	5,550	57,456	6995
Ramsey	2,823.6	5,428	39.6	2.3	6.4	6.6	5.2	4,373.6	8,408	2,351	1,950	55,151	266,050	66,469	8827
Red Lake	25.7	6,285	56.4	0.3	4.3	4.4	15.8	18.7	4,565	21	14	281	1,930	48,531	4283
Redwood	94.9	5,987	30.0	25.7	4.1	7.3	11.4	93.1	5,876	56	53	1,968	7,760	52,181	5445
Renville	96.1	6,251	25.3	21.0	3.3	5.9	14.5	80.0	5,207	60	51	1,072	7,580	54,775	6267
Rice	342.7	5,285	25.9	37.7	3.6	2.9	5.8	303.1	4,673	138	210	3,419	29,410	61,859	7287
Rock	42.6	4,461	42.5	0.6	4.4	8.4	12.8	74.6	7,811	30	33	710	4,460	53,103	5243
Roseau	80.9	5,225	41.7	0.5	3.6	5.4	18.9	44.4	2,870	97	55	1,000	7,920	60,199	7993
St. Louis	1,223.1	6,106	33.5	5.6	5.4	6.8	9.4	959.9	4,792	1,374	818	15,359	94,880	57,602	6670
Scott	487.6	3,608	45.0	0.4	4.6	4.1	15.6	1,025.8	7,590	126	511	9,563	68,360	86,284	12,565
Sherburne	342.7	3,831	57.6	0.7	4.6	4.0	8.4	655.5	7,328	126	328	4,367	43,900	65,522	7384
Sibley	82.9	5,484	34.0	16.4	4.2	4.8	14.5	70.1	4,636	40	52	753	7,440	53,076	5175
Stearns	692.0	4,565	39.7	8.6	5.0	4.9	11.1	994.2	6,558	2,264	537	9,546	72,700	60,271	7545
Steele	144.4	3,975	47.3	1.6	5.1	5.6	14.0	145.9	4,016	76	130	2,170	18,550	55,600	5727
Stevens	43.9	4,548	36.6	0.3	5.8	5.7	19.8	77.2	7,986	77	31	1,388	4,440	61,390	7008
Swift	86.6	9,024	19.1	41.7	2.8	4.8	8.8	45.2	4,715	49	33	901	4,660	51,244	5538
Todd	111.4	4,544	53.4	2.6	3.5	6.4	11.8	81.6	3,330	82	86	1,311	10,860	43,170	3768
Traverse	29.5	8,562	21.2	13.2	3.7	4.8	17.5	15.5	4,502	25	12	317	1,640	54,751	6745
Wabasha	100.8	4,696	37.3	2.8	5.5	4.0	15.3	103.1	4,800	56	76	1,041	11,040	55,024	5775
Wadena	92.1	6,693	61.5	1.4	3.3	12.6	6.8	28.2	2,051	52	48	1,405	6,300	43,705	3944
Waseca	84.8	4,408	42.7	2.1	5.7	11.6	9.7	75.0	3,897	258	64	1,089	9,120	51,126	5217
Washington	872.4	3,574	51.1	1.8	5.9	3.6	8.8	1,195.5	4,898	398	898	10,784	127,010	88,988	13,063
Watonwan	57.4	5,127	43.4	1.2	4.2	7.5	11.1	64.3	5,747	55	39	734	5,410	48,883	4725
Wilkin	36.2	5,494	38.6	2.9	5.1	6.0	20.9	19.1	2,900	18	22	396	3,300	55,415	6300
Winona	157.7	3,054	44.7	2.6	5.6	6.4	13.8	84.9	1,645	144	168	3,607	22,670	56,179	6436
Wright	554.0	4,351	45.4	11.5	4.5	3.5	7.8	1,170.5	9,192	198	474	5,801	62,580	67,855	8172
Yellow Medicine	83.2	8,190	26.8	22.5	2.0	9.0	12.3	76.0	7,477	38	35	1,456	4,960	52,160	5424

1. Based on the resident population estimated as of July 1 of the year shown.

Table B. States and Counties — Land Area and Population

State / county code	CBSA code[1]	County code[2]	STATE County	Land area[3] (sq. mi)	Total persons 2017	Rank	Per square mile	White	Black	American Indian, Alaska Native	Asian and Pacific Islander	Percent Hispanic or Latino[4]	Under 5 years	5 to 17 years	18 to 24 years	25 to 34 years	35 to 44 years	45 to 54 years
				1	2	3	4	5	6	7	8	9	10	11	12	13	14	15
2,8000		0	MISSISSIPPI............	46,923.1	2,984,100	X	63.6	57.7	38.1	0.9	1.4	3.2	6.3	17.6	9.8	13.2	12.2	12.6
2,8001	35,020	5	Adams.....................	462.3	31,003	1,408	67.1	36.7	53.9	0.6	0.8	9.0	5.9	14.7	8.0	13.1	12.5	12.1
2,8003	18,420	7	Alcorn...................	400.0	37,210	1,244	93.0	83.8	12.9	0.6	0.6	3.2	6.0	17.3	7.9	12.4	12.5	13.2
2,8005	32,620	8	Amite....................	730.1	12,447	2,263	17.0	57.9	40.5	0.6	0.3	1.4	5.1	15.5	6.9	10.3	10.1	12.4
2,8007		6	Attala...................	735.0	18,477	1,897	25.1	54.2	43.3	0.5	0.6	2.1	6.6	19.0	7.9	11.3	11.1	12.5
2,8009	32,820	1	Benton...................	406.6	8,312	2,565	20.4	61.8	35.6	0.9	0.3	2.7	5.9	15.7	8.1	11.5	11.8	14.2
2,8011	17,380	7	Bolivar..................	876.7	31,945	1,381	36.4	33.2	63.9	0.3	1.1	2.1	6.7	17.6	11.0	14.1	11.2	11.7
2,8013		9	Calhoun..................	586.6	14,492	2,130	24.7	65.6	28.7	0.6	0.3	5.9	5.9	17.8	7.8	11.2	11.3	13.6
2,8015	24,900	9	Carroll..................	628.2	10,139	2,416	16.1	65.0	33.2	0.6	0.4	1.7	4.4	14.8	7.3	10.8	11.5	12.9
2,8017		7	Chickasaw................	501.8	17,146	1,970	34.2	50.8	44.4	0.5	0.6	4.8	6.9	18.0	9.1	12.7	11.4	12.4
2,8019		9	Choctaw..................	418.2	8,278	2,569	19.8	68.0	30.0	0.6	0.7	1.7	5.6	16.3	7.3	11.2	11.2	12.8
2,8021	46,980	8	Claiborne................	487.4	8,950	2,508	18.4	12.0	85.8	0.5	1.0	1.5	6.1	15.2	19.6	10.8	10.2	9.8
2,8023	32,940	3	Clarke...................	691.6	15,828	2,048	22.9	63.7	34.8	0.6	0.3	1.1	5.6	17.0	7.9	11.5	11.1	12.8
2,8025	48,500	7	Clay.....................	410.1	19,640	1,841	47.9	39.5	58.9	0.4	0.4	1.4	5.7	17.3	8.6	12.9	11.5	11.9
2,8027	17,260	7	Coahoma..................	552.5	23,154	1,673	41.9	21.4	76.6	0.3	0.7	1.5	8.1	19.0	10.3	12.5	10.8	11.4
2,8029	27,140	2	Copiah...................	777.2	28,516	1,470	36.7	44.7	51.9	0.5	0.6	3.2	6.1	17.2	10.2	12.0	11.3	12.0
2,8031		8	Covington................	413.8	19,079	1,870	46.1	61.3	36.3	0.5	0.6	2.4	6.8	18.1	8.3	13.2	11.5	12.9
2,8033	32,820	1	DeSoto...................	476.3	178,751	367	375.3	65.7	28.4	0.6	1.9	4.8	6.1	19.8	8.7	12.9	14.1	14.2
2,8035	25,620	3	Forrest..................	466.0	75,471	735	162.0	57.9	38.5	0.6	1.5	2.9	6.6	16.5	14.9	15.0	11.6	11.1
2,8037		9	Franklin	564.0	7,765	2,613	13.8	64.1	34.8	0.6	0.4	1.1	5.3	18.1	7.7	10.5	11.2	12.5
2,8039		6	George...................	478.7	24,094	1,640	50.3	87.8	8.1	0.9	1.1	3.1	7.6	19.1	8.4	13.5	11.8	13.1
2,8041		8	Greene...................	712.8	13,345	2,207	18.7	73.5	25.0	0.6	0.3	1.3	4.5	15.2	9.0	16.0	14.2	14.1
2,8043	24,980	7	Grenada..................	422.1	21,087	1,769	50.0	55.3	43.0	0.6	0.6	1.4	6.3	17.4	8.3	12.1	11.7	13.0
2,8045	25,060	2	Hancock..................	474.0	47,053	1,032	99.3	86.6	8.8	1.4	1.4	3.9	5.3	15.9	7.3	11.8	11.3	13.9
2,8047	25,060	2	Harrison.................	574.0	205,027	324	357.2	66.0	26.3	1.0	4.0	5.4	6.6	17.5	9.6	14.3	12.3	12.5
2,8049	27,140	2	Hinds....................	869.8	239,497	281	275.3	25.1	72.9	0.4	1.0	1.6	6.5	18.1	11.1	14.5	12.0	11.7
2,8051		6	Holmes...................	756.7	17,739	1,933	23.4	16.2	82.6	0.4	0.4	1.1	6.7	19.1	11.8	12.9	10.6	11.5
2,8053		6	Humphreys................	418.5	8,342	2,560	19.9	21.5	75.2	0.5	0.5	3.2	6.0	20.4	8.5	12.0	10.5	11.7
2,8055		8	Issaquena	413.0	1,339	3,092	3.2	35.7	62.0	0.5	0.6	1.5	3.1	9.0	13.3	15.9	12.1	14.6
2,8057	46,180	7	Itawamba.................	532.8	23,508	1,661	44.1	90.7	7.3	0.7	0.6	1.6	6.5	16.5	10.6	12.4	11.7	13.4
2,8059	25,060	2	Jackson..................	722.8	142,152	455	196.7	69.3	22.1	0.9	3.0	6.5	5.8	17.8	8.1	13.3	12.7	13.4
2,8061	29,860	9	Jasper...................	676.2	16,582	2,004	24.5	45.4	53.4	0.5	0.3	1.3	6.2	16.4	8.3	11.6	11.0	12.3
2,8063		8	Jefferson................	519.9	7,262	2,645	14.0	13.7	85.4	0.5	0.3	0.8	6.7	16.0	9.0	13.3	11.9	11.9
2,8065		8	Jefferson Davis	408.4	11,314	2,332	27.7	38.5	59.9	0.6	0.4	1.4	5.4	14.7	8.3	11.0	11.2	12.6
2,8067	29,860	4	Jones....................	694.8	67,930	783	97.8	65.4	29.6	0.8	0.7	4.4	7.0	18.4	8.7	12.5	11.6	12.0
2,8069	32,940	9	Kemper...................	766.2	9,883	2,438	12.9	34.8	60.8	3.9	0.3	1.0	4.4	14.7	12.4	12.0	10.9	12.3
2,8071	37,060	4	Lafayette................	631.7	54,374	932	86.1	71.3	24.1	0.5	2.7	2.6	5.1	13.1	23.8	14.4	11.5	10.0
2,8073	25,620	3	Lamar....................	497.1	61,374	852	123.5	75.4	20.9	0.6	1.8	2.6	6.5	18.4	8.6	14.8	14.0	12.7
2,8075	32,940	5	Lauderdale...............	703.7	76,155	726	108.2	53.4	43.9	0.5	1.1	2.2	6.4	17.2	8.9	13.3	11.8	12.5
2,8077		8	Lawrence	430.7	12,643	2,249	29.4	65.4	32.4	0.5	0.5	2.0	6.2	18.2	7.8	11.3	12.0	12.6
2,8079		6	Leake....................	582.9	22,715	1,687	39.0	47.6	42.2	5.8	0.5	4.8	6.6	19.6	8.3	12.8	12.1	12.3
2,8081	46,180	5	Lee......................	450.0	84,933	676	188.7	66.5	30.4	0.5	1.2	2.6	6.8	18.7	8.2	13.4	12.8	13.3
2,8083	24,900	5	Leflore..................	593.4	29,223	1,453	49.2	22.6	74.2	0.4	0.7	2.7	7.7	19.8	11.4	12.8	11.5	10.9
2,8085	15,020	6	Lincoln..................	586.1	34,347	1,316	58.6	68.0	30.8	0.5	0.6	1.0	6.2	17.7	8.2	12.0	12.7	13.0
2,8087	18,060	5	Lowndes..................	505.4	59,186	875	117.1	52.3	44.7	0.5	1.3	2.2	6.5	17.3	9.7	14.0	11.7	12.2
2,8089	27,140	2	Madison	714.4	104,618	577	146.4	56.1	38.4	0.4	3.0	3.0	6.3	18.8	8.8	13.1	13.6	13.6
2,8091		6	Marion...................	542.4	25,069	1,604	46.2	66.0	32.2	0.5	0.7	1.6	5.9	17.6	7.9	12.5	12.4	12.5
2,8093	32,820	1	Marshall.................	706.2	35,619	1,283	50.4	48.5	47.8	0.6	0.4	3.7	5.9	15.6	9.5	12.2	11.7	13.3
2,8095		7	Monroe...................	765.1	35,872	1,277	46.9	67.5	31.1	0.5	0.4	1.3	5.7	17.1	7.9	12.2	11.5	13.1
2,8097		7	Montgomery...............	407.0	10,173	2,413	25.0	52.8	45.2	0.6	0.7	1.4	6.3	16.7	7.6	11.4	10.4	12.2
2,8099		7	Neshoba..................	570.1	29,369	1,446	51.5	59.7	22.1	17.2	0.8	2.0	7.2	21.1	8.5	12.0	11.7	11.7
2,8101		7	Newton...................	577.9	21,185	1,768	36.7	61.8	31.3	5.5	0.7	1.9	6.5	18.9	9.6	11.9	11.9	12.7
2,8103		7	Noxubee..................	695.2	10,742	2,369	15.5	26.2	72.2	0.5	0.4	1.4	7.0	17.5	9.6	13.1	11.0	12.1
2,8105	44,260	5	Oktibbeha................	458.2	49,799	989	108.7	57.5	37.9	0.5	3.7	1.7	5.2	12.5	30.9	14.2	9.0	8.2
2,8107		6	Panola...................	685.1	33,994	1,326	49.6	47.6	50.5	0.6	0.4	1.9	6.9	18.2	8.9	12.9	11.5	12.8
2,8109	38,100	6	Pearl River..............	810.9	55,270	917	68.2	83.4	13.1	1.3	0.9	3.1	5.8	17.0	8.9	11.7	11.4	13.1
2,8111	25,620	3	Perry....................	647.2	12,032	2,290	18.6	78.4	20.3	0.7	0.4	1.5	5.8	17.0	8.5	11.5	12.3	12.9
2,8113	32,620	6	Pike.....................	409.0	39,468	1,189	96.5	44.0	53.7	0.6	0.8	1.7	6.6	19.6	9.1	11.8	11.6	11.7
2,8115	46,180	7	Pontotoc.................	497.7	31,640	1,386	63.6	78.0	15.6	0.7	0.6	6.5	7.1	19.5	8.0	13.0	12.3	13.0
2,8117		7	Prentiss.................	415.0	25,261	1,596	60.9	83.7	15.1	0.4	0.4	1.5	5.8	16.7	10.1	12.4	11.4	13.0
2,8119		6	Quitman..................	405.0	7,269	2,643	17.9	27.3	71.2	0.6	0.5	1.6	6.0	17.4	9.2	11.4	11.8	13.1
2,8121	27,140	2	Rankin...................	775.4	152,080	433	196.1	75.1	21.1	0.5	1.7	2.7	6.1	17.4	7.6	14.2	14.2	13.3
2,8123		6	Scott....................	609.2	28,420	1,479	46.7	50.6	38.3	0.6	0.6	11.0	7.6	18.9	8.4	12.9	12.1	12.4
2,8125		8	Sharkey..................	431.7	4,435	2,863	10.3	26.9	70.8	0.3	0.6	2.0	5.6	18.8	7.9	10.3	10.8	12.0
2,8127	27,140	2	Simpson..................	589.2	26,947	1,528	45.7	62.4	35.5	0.5	0.7	1.8	5.5	18.5	8.2	12.2	12.0	12.6
2,8129		8	Smith....................	636.3	16,078	2,033	25.3	74.3	24.1	0.3	0.2	1.7	5.8	17.6	7.9	11.5	11.4	12.9
2,8131		6	Stone....................	445.5	18,112	1,913	40.7	77.2	20.2	0.9	0.7	2.1	5.7	16.3	11.7	12.4	12.0	12.9

1. CBSA = Core Based Statistical Area. See Appendix A for explanation. See Appendix B for list of metropolitan areas with component counties. 2. County type code from the Economic Research Service of USDA Rural-Urban Continuum Codes. See Appendix A for definition. 3. Dry land or land partially or temporarily covered by water. 4. May be of any race.

Table B. States and Counties — **Population and Households**

STATE County	55 to 64 years	65 to 74 years	75 years and over	Percent female	2000	2010	2000-2010	2010-2017	Births	Deaths	Net Migration	Number	Persons per house-hold	Family house-holds	Female family house-holder[1]	One person
	16	17	18	19	20	21	22	23	24	25	26	27	28	29	30	31
MISSISSIPPI..................	12.9	9.2	6.3	51.5	2,844,658	2,968,103	4.3	0.5	279,716	219,202	-45,155	1,098,803	2.63	68.0	18.3	27.8
Adams............................	15.4	10.6	7.8	49.0	34,340	32,297	-5.9	-4.0	2,748	2,973	-1,110	11,586	2.53	65.2	24.0	33.0
Alcorn...........................	12.9	10.5	7.4	51.1	34,558	37,057	7.2	0.4	3,197	3,285	271	14,776	2.49	68.1	14.1	27.6
Amite.............................	17.1	12.9	9.8	51.5	13,599	13,128	-3.5	-5.2	938	1,060	-561	4,957	2.54	58.8	13.4	39.7
Attala............................	13.2	10.2	8.2	52.6	19,661	19,564	-0.5	-5.6	1,808	2,028	-866	7,268	2.58	69.5	22.3	29.1
Benton..........................	14.0	10.6	8.2	50.7	8,026	8,730	8.8	-4.8	682	730	-380	3,126	2.66	71.4	14.5	27.0
Bolivar..........................	12.4	9.7	5.6	53.5	40,633	34,148	-16.0	-6.5	3,680	2,961	-2,935	12,598	2.54	63.2	27.9	31.4
Calhoun.........................	13.9	10.2	8.2	51.9	15,069	14,962	-0.7	-3.1	1,273	1,304	-430	5,820	2.49	66.6	16.3	30.9
Carroll..........................	15.7	13.4	9.3	49.4	10,769	10,597	-1.6	-4.3	642	757	-340	3,674	2.76	76.9	10.3	22.5
Chickasaw....................	12.8	9.6	7.2	51.1	19,440	17,392	-10.5	-1.4	1,804	1,315	-734	6,398	2.66	67.6	18.9	30.0
Choctaw........................	14.2	12.0	9.4	51.2	9,758	8,548	-12.4	-3.2	653	637	-284	3,184	2.57	64.3	15.4	34.3
Claiborne......................	12.3	9.4	6.5	52.7	11,831	9,598	-18.9	-6.8	849	700	-826	3,134	2.75	66.0	30.2	32.2
Clarke...........................	14.3	11.7	8.2	53.0	17,955	16,732	-6.8	-5.4	1,356	1,501	-759	6,598	2.45	69.2	17.6	28.4
Clay...............................	14.1	10.5	7.5	53.2	21,979	20,634	-6.1	-4.8	1,652	1,687	-959	7,781	2.56	69.9	24.3	27.6
Coahoma	12.9	8.7	6.2	53.8	30,622	26,145	-14.6	-11.4	3,070	2,190	-3,910	9,084	2.65	66.1	30.5	30.3
Copiah..........................	14.2	10.1	7.0	51.9	28,757	29,449	2.4	-3.2	2,677	2,338	-1,276	9,851	2.81	70.3	20.0	27.5
Covington......................	12.9	9.5	6.9	51.5	19,407	19,571	0.8	-2.5	1,922	1,894	-516	6,950	2.77	68.8	17.8	27.3
DeSoto..........................	11.6	7.8	4.8	51.7	107,199	161,264	50.4	10.8	15,174	9,017	11,343	60,575	2.81	73.8	15.3	21.7
Forrest..........................	10.9	7.7	5.7	52.5	72,604	74,932	3.2	0.7	7,775	5,262	-1,988	28,022	2.58	63.0	19.5	28.7
Franklin	15.4	10.5	8.7	51.0	8,448	8,118	-3.9	-4.3	619	721	-255	3,096	2.49	72.7	15.4	26.4
George..........................	11.8	9.1	5.4	49.7	19,144	22,579	17.9	6.7	2,655	1,820	688	7,410	3.08	74.0	10.1	24.3
Greene..........................	12.3	8.8	6.1	42.7	13,299	14,395	8.2	-7.3	917	919	-1,063	4,164	2.55	68.4	9.1	28.6
Grenada........................	13.5	10.5	7.1	52.4	23,263	21,906	-5.8	-3.7	1,972	2,076	-710	7,508	2.82	66.4	20.8	30.1
Hancock........................	15.4	11.7	7.4	51.1	42,967	44,014	2.4	6.9	3,497	3,374	2,903	18,782	2.43	67.6	12.8	26.9
Harrison........................	12.7	8.8	5.6	50.9	189,601	187,105	-1.3	9.6	20,089	13,528	11,374	76,660	2.53	65.6	17.9	28.3
Hinds............................	12.5	8.1	5.5	53.3	250,800	245,365	-2.2	-2.4	24,049	15,154	-14,905	89,335	2.65	64.8	25.0	30.3
Holmes..........................	12.8	8.3	6.4	52.2	21,609	19,478	-9.9	-8.9	1,928	1,563	-2,129	6,314	2.83	66.6	36.3	31.6
Humphreys	14.2	9.6	7.2	52.7	11,206	9,375	-16.3	-11.0	871	674	-1,251	3,058	2.86	62.6	28.8	34.0
Issaquena	15.4	8.2	8.4	42.7	2,274	1,406	-38.2	-4.8	87	77	-79	478	2.22	70.3	20.5	22.6
Itawamba	12.3	9.9	7.6	50.7	22,770	23,401	2.8	0.5	1,914	1,971	176	8,858	2.53	70.0	12.6	26.5
Jackson........................	13.6	9.3	6.1	50.8	131,420	139,668	6.3	1.8	11,765	9,491	263	50,365	2.77	67.0	14.9	27.7
Jasper...........................	14.5	11.2	8.4	51.6	18,149	17,062	-6.0	-2.8	1,613	1,417	-682	6,771	2.43	75.8	20.2	23.3
Jefferson	14.9	8.7	7.5	50.8	9,740	7,732	-20.6	-6.1	778	591	-670	2,457	2.88	62.0	28.0	36.5
Jefferson Davis	14.8	13.0	9.0	52.7	13,962	12,480	-10.6	-9.3	1,002	1,105	-1,069	4,903	2.37	62.1	22.4	34.5
Jones	13.2	9.7	6.9	51.4	64,958	67,761	4.3	0.2	7,061	5,349	-1,508	24,870	2.67	70.0	15.8	26.7
Kemper	13.3	10.7	9.4	50.3	10,453	10,461	0.1	-5.5	628	705	-510	3,552	2.58	60.9	21.2	35.3
Lafayette	10.3	7.4	4.5	51.4	38,744	47,359	22.2	14.8	4,031	2,695	5,560	18,788	2.50	56.6	13.0	30.8
Lamar............................	11.7	8.0	5.4	51.9	39,070	55,675	42.5	10.2	5,659	2,977	2,963	21,800	2.72	72.3	15.9	22.1
Lauderdale....................	13.1	9.6	7.3	51.5	78,161	80,261	2.7	-5.1	7,419	6,245	-5,298	29,689	2.56	65.4	19.3	30.6
Lawrence	14.3	10.2	7.3	51.4	13,258	12,929	-2.5	-2.2	1,175	1,038	-428	4,859	2.59	72.2	15.7	26.4
Leake	12.4	9.3	6.7	48.3	20,940	23,803	13.7	-4.6	2,194	1,804	-1,483	8,259	2.69	69.8	21.1	27.9
Lee...............................	12.4	8.5	5.9	52.1	75,755	82,910	9.4	2.4	8,421	6,608	243	32,591	2.59	68.5	15.6	27.7
Leflore..........................	11.9	8.0	5.9	53.3	37,947	32,382	-14.7	-9.8	3,538	2,651	-4,114	10,671	2.72	60.8	28.1	36.6
Lincoln..........................	13.5	9.8	7.0	52.4	33,166	34,869	5.1	-1.5	3,211	2,928	-789	12,936	2.63	72.5	17.7	24.7
Lowndes........................	13.1	9.0	6.5	52.4	61,586	59,779	-2.9	-1.0	5,753	4,277	-2,057	22,821	2.55	67.8	17.9	28.5
Madison	13.2	8.1	4.6	52.1	74,674	95,203	27.5	9.9	9,375	7,167	7,170	37,415	2.67	72.4	15.5	24.5
Marion	13.4	10.3	7.6	51.6	25,595	27,081	5.8	-7.4	2,316	2,510	-1,828	9,659	2.60	71.7	16.6	25.4
Marshall	14.8	10.5	6.4	50.4	34,993	37,139	6.1	-4.1	3,173	2,974	-1,721	13,213	2.59	70.5	17.4	24.4
Monroe..........................	13.7	10.8	8.1	52.3	38,014	36,989	-2.7	-3.0	3,030	3,039	-1,104	13,949	2.55	69.3	16.3	28.0
Montgomery...................	14.4	12.2	8.8	52.4	12,189	10,925	-10.4	-6.9	933	1,041	-648	4,351	2.35	65.7	20.3	31.1
Neshoba........................	12.2	9.1	6.4	52.4	28,684	29,673	3.4	-1.0	3,105	2,667	-731	10,777	2.70	69.0	20.1	29.0
Newton..........................	12.0	9.5	7.0	52.1	21,838	21,720	-0.5	-2.5	2,074	1,987	-617	7,984	2.62	72.6	19.7	26.1
Noxubee........................	13.9	9.0	6.7	52.6	12,548	11,545	-8.0	-7.0	1,121	884	-1,056	4,012	2.72	71.3	26.3	25.8
Oktibbeha......................	9.1	6.1	4.8	50.0	42,902	47,671	11.1	4.5	4,051	2,162	214	17,109	2.57	52.4	12.4	33.6
Panola..........................	13.3	9.3	6.1	51.8	34,274	34,699	1.2	-2.0	3,643	2,907	-1,433	12,184	2.80	67.8	19.9	30.1
Pearl River	13.6	11.3	7.1	50.7	48,621	55,747	14.7	-0.9	4,626	4,464	-625	20,494	2.61	69.9	13.8	26.7
Perry	14.4	10.6	7.1	51.2	12,138	12,250	0.9	-1.8	1,036	967	-286	4,431	2.72	68.2	14.7	29.7
Pike..............................	12.8	9.9	7.0	52.8	38,940	40,407	3.8	-2.3	4,001	3,591	-1,336	14,717	2.65	64.5	19.2	31.9
Pontotoc........................	12.3	8.5	6.3	51.0	26,726	29,957	12.1	5.6	3,172	2,052	557	10,801	2.83	71.0	12.8	26.2
Prentiss........................	12.5	10.1	8.1	50.9	25,556	25,276	-1.1	-0.1	2,318	2,039	-289	9,572	2.54	70.2	16.3	26.5
Quitman........................	14.3	9.6	7.1	53.2	10,117	8,223	-18.7	-11.6	717	708	-979	3,047	2.45	61.7	23.6	35.3
Rankin...........................	12.3	9.0	5.9	51.8	115,327	142,061	23.2	7.1	13,620	7,816	4,283	54,377	2.61	72.8	13.8	22.9
Scott.............................	12.8	8.6	6.3	51.3	28,423	28,260	-0.6	0.6	3,327	2,033	-1,133	9,848	2.84	69.4	21.9	28.1
Sharkey.........................	16.1	10.5	8.0	52.7	6,580	4,916	-25.3	-9.8	460	424	-527	1,804	2.51	65.9	26.9	29.6
Simpson........................	14.0	10.0	7.2	51.5	27,639	27,502	-0.5	-2.0	2,346	2,155	-735	9,418	2.82	71.0	17.5	25.7
Smith............................	14.0	10.7	8.0	51.8	16,182	16,493	1.9	-2.5	1,377	1,194	-597	5,895	2.72	72.2	15.2	26.0
Stone............................	13.4	9.9	5.6	49.6	13,622	17,786	30.6	1.8	1,532	1,271	63	5,805	2.98	77.0	16.5	19.9

1. No spouse present.

Table B. States and Counties — Population, Vital Statistics, Health, and Crime

STATE County	Persons in group quarters, 2017	Daytime Population, 2012-2016 Number	Employment/ residence ratio	Births, 2017 Total	Rate[1]	Deaths, 2017 Number	Rate[1]	Persons under 65 with no health insurance, 2016 Number	Percent	Medicare, 2017 Total beneficiaries	Enrolled in Original Medicare	Enrolled in Medicare Advantage	Serious crimes known to police[2], 2016 Total Number	Rate[3]
	32	33	34	35	36	37	38	39	40	41	42	43	44	45
MISSISSIPPI	92,944	2,938,295	0.96	37,373	12.5	30,875	10.3	342,668	14.0	582,423	479,662	102,761	91,115	3049
Adams	2,409	32,716	1.09	374	12.1	421	13.6	3,274	14.1	7,370	6,192	1,178	NA	NA
Alcorn	740	37,464	1.01	443	11.9	445	12.0	4,278	14.2	8,869	8,497	372	NA	NA
Amite	116	10,715	0.55	111	8.9	149	12.0	1,648	17.2	2,750	2,371	379	NA	NA
Attala	341	17,564	0.77	240	13.0	264	14.3	2,069	13.8	4,551	3,636	915	NA	NA
Benton	79	6,522	0.37	100	12.0	96	11.5	981	14.8	2,027	1,741	286	NA	NA
Bolivar	1,754	33,594	1.00	434	13.6	400	12.5	3,652	14.1	7,378	6,498	881	NA	NA
Calhoun	212	13,157	0.70	165	11.4	168	11.6	2,232	18.9	3,252	2,958	294	NA	NA
Carroll	377	7,668	0.29	80	7.9	100	9.9	1,206	15.8	2,223	2,056	167	NA	NA
Chickasaw	495	16,720	0.90	236	13.8	208	12.1	2,406	17.3	4,422	3,853	569	NA	NA
Choctaw	122	7,437	0.69	82	9.9	105	12.7	888	13.7	1,610	1,437	174	99	1204
Claiborne	1,101	9,667	1.20	112	12.5	101	11.3	923	14.0	1,800	1,394	406	95	1245
Clarke	52	13,795	0.59	193	12.2	203	12.8	1,887	14.8	4,010	3,392	618	NA	NA
Clay	303	18,321	0.76	227	11.6	232	11.8	2,498	15.7	4,131	3,582	550	373	1875
Coahoma	706	24,852	1.01	377	16.3	283	12.2	2,585	13.1	4,981	4,453	528	NA	NA
Copiah	996	26,660	0.78	350	12.3	329	11.5	3,324	14.4	6,585	4,816	1,768	NA	NA
Covington	221	17,676	0.74	257	13.5	237	12.4	2,643	16.6	4,232	3,418	814	NA	NA
DeSoto	609	144,058	0.68	2,169	12.1	1,360	7.6	15,900	10.3	26,066	21,164	4,902	4,120	2351
Forrest	3,248	86,093	1.31	1,047	13.9	765	10.1	9,723	15.5	18,173	14,591	3,582	2,817	3711
Franklin	67	6,871	0.67	78	10.0	75	9.7	869	13.8	1,696	1,528	168	NA	NA
George	559	20,058	0.59	377	15.6	238	9.9	2,713	13.8	5,158	3,988	1,170	NA	NA
Greene	2,402	12,445	0.60	121	9.1	140	10.5	1,392	15.1	1,814	1,578	237	26	202
Grenada	246	23,060	1.19	276	13.1	259	12.3	2,590	15.0	5,446	4,705	741	NA	NA
Hancock	548	44,505	0.92	473	10.1	484	10.3	5,749	15.1	8,645	5,881	2,764	NA	NA
Harrison	5,064	210,822	1.14	2,724	13.3	1,894	9.2	26,077	15.4	39,335	31,028	8,307	9,390	4611
Hinds	8,977	260,140	1.15	3,137	13.1	2,150	9.0	27,658	13.8	42,242	29,823	12,419	10,255	4835
Holmes	900	17,064	0.71	230	13.0	227	12.8	2,239	15.7	4,159	3,324	836	NA	NA
Humphreys	83	8,460	0.86	100	12.0	100	12.0	1,045	14.9	1,898	1,660	238	NA	NA
Issaquena	284	1,316	0.90	10	7.5	2	1.5	144	17.8	160	139	21	NA	NA
Itawamba	993	20,848	0.70	258	11.0	266	11.3	2,874	15.5	3,961	3,704	257	NA	NA
Jackson	1,365	137,747	0.95	1,611	11.3	1,336	9.4	16,058	13.4	24,566	18,433	6,133	4,365	3417
Jasper	87	14,422	0.65	210	12.7	193	11.6	2,098	15.9	3,901	3,156	745	NA	NA
Jefferson	384	7,117	0.79	92	12.7	82	11.3	981	17.1	1,490	1,244	246	NA	NA
Jefferson Davis	111	9,862	0.52	122	10.8	154	13.6	1,581	17.9	2,403	2,087	316	NA	NA
Jones	1,872	71,088	1.10	952	14.0	777	11.4	8,816	15.9	14,120	11,744	2,376	1,835	2923
Kemper	951	10,478	1.10	80	8.1	100	10.1	1,350	19.0	1,900	1,581	319	68	772
Lafayette	6,120	53,312	1.05	577	10.6	385	7.1	5,719	13.8	6,761	6,215	546	NA	NA
Lamar	308	52,725	0.76	793	12.9	422	6.9	6,692	12.5	5,923	4,665	1,259	1,119	1896
Lauderdale	3,533	84,280	1.16	964	12.7	837	11.0	7,910	12.8	15,484	13,207	2,277	2,704	3470
Lawrence	0	11,067	0.67	166	13.1	149	11.8	1,626	15.4	3,775	3,235	540	NA	NA
Leake	1,601	20,347	0.67	293	12.9	263	11.6	3,383	19.3	4,617	3,669	949	NA	NA
Lee	1,059	98,619	1.36	1,147	13.5	993	11.7	9,147	12.7	18,307	16,637	1,670	NA	NA
Leflore	1,406	33,862	1.36	465	15.9	374	12.8	3,379	13.9	6,321	5,945	376	NA	NA
Lincoln	700	33,398	0.90	401	11.7	396	11.5	4,077	14.3	6,935	5,815	1,120	NA	NA
Lowndes	1,391	62,971	1.13	798	13.5	602	10.2	6,984	14.2	12,224	10,854	1,370	NA	NA
Madison	1,746	107,873	1.12	1,328	12.7	1,097	10.5	8,648	9.5	16,429	13,051	3,377	1,361	1527
Marion	719	25,929	1.01	293	11.7	332	13.2	3,197	15.9	5,615	4,554	1,061	337	1770
Marshall	1,853	30,446	0.59	405	11.4	411	11.5	3,897	13.9	8,391	6,638	1,753	600	1686
Monroe	406	32,321	0.74	394	11.0	416	11.6	3,912	13.5	7,648	6,899	748	NA	NA
Montgomery	99	9,410	0.75	129	12.7	129	12.7	1,278	15.8	2,947	2,778	169	NA	NA
Neshoba	394	29,712	1.02	419	14.3	388	13.2	4,278	17.3	4,627	4,085	542	NA	NA
Newton	552	19,592	0.74	277	13.1	299	14.1	2,832	16.3	5,934	5,057	877	NA	NA
Noxubee	158	10,415	0.83	149	13.9	134	12.5	1,748	19.5	2,414	2,297	117	NA	NA
Oktibbeha	4,702	50,499	1.05	557	11.2	356	7.1	5,663	14.2	7,194	6,512	683	1,117	2230
Panola	315	33,205	0.91	485	14.3	420	12.4	4,200	14.7	7,265	5,955	1,310	1,207	3765
Pearl River	1,327	46,926	0.59	613	11.1	636	11.5	6,289	14.3	12,288	9,068	3,220	NA	NA
Perry	101	10,856	0.67	129	10.7	119	9.9	1,700	17.1	2,396	2,088	308	NA	NA
Pike	845	40,776	1.06	522	13.2	506	12.8	4,679	14.5	9,270	7,289	1,981	NA	NA
Pontotoc	236	28,922	0.85	452	14.3	262	8.3	4,311	16.1	5,374	4,848	525	NA	NA
Prentiss	875	23,164	0.77	311	12.3	252	10.0	3,140	15.6	6,520	6,139	382	NA	NA
Quitman	137	6,903	0.67	89	12.2	89	12.2	984	16.5	1,657	1,483	175	NA	NA
Rankin	5,097	141,473	0.91	1,801	11.8	1,155	7.6	12,832	10.2	24,158	19,062	5,096	1,227	1068
Scott	227	29,230	1.09	462	16.3	302	10.6	4,572	19.2	6,298	5,001	1,297	NA	NA
Sharkey	107	4,370	0.80	48	10.8	46	10.4	573	15.5	1,070	939	130	NA	NA
Simpson	628	24,007	0.68	292	10.8	295	10.9	3,211	14.6	5,522	4,388	1,134	14	57
Smith	105	13,848	0.63	178	11.1	168	10.4	1,935	14.9	2,619	2,143	476	NA	NA
Stone	1,409	16,201	0.75	206	11.4	183	10.1	1,886	13.5	4,106	3,128	978	424	2349

1. Per 1,000 estimated resident population. 2. Data for serious crimes have not been adjusted for underreporting; this may affect comparability between geographic areas and over time.
3. Per 100,000 population estimated by the FBI.

Table B. States and Counties — Crime, Education, Money Income, and Poverty

STATE County	Serious crimes known to police, 2016 (cont.)[1] Rate		Education School enrollment and attainment, 2012-2016				Local government expenditures,[5] 2013-2014		Money income, 2012-2016	Households			Income and poverty, 2016	Percent below poverty level		
			Enrollment[3]		Attainment[4] (percent)						Percent					
	Violent	Property	Total	Percent private	High school graduate or less	Bachelor's degree or more	Total current spending (mil dol)	Current spending per student (dollars)	Per capita income[6]	Median income (dollars)	with income of less than $50,000	with income of $200,000 or more	Median household income (dollars)	All persons	Children under 18 years	Children 5 to 17 years in families
	46	47	48	49	50	51	52	53	54	55	56	57	58	59	60	61
MISSISSIPPI	280	2,768	802,804	13.0	47.5	21.0	4,075.5	8,268	21,651	40,528	58.6	2.3	41,793	21.0	30.2	29.1
Adams	NA	NA	7,654	11.7	53.7	18.1	33.2	9,074	18,091	31,283	68.5	1.9	32,956	31.4	46.1	46.4
Alcorn	NA	NA	9,334	12.0	53.5	16.6	46.0	7,633	20,006	38,892	64.1	1.4	38,675	16.9	26.8	25.9
Amite	NA	NA	2,954	31.0	61.5	12.2	11.3	10,664	17,954	27,334	71.9	1.0	34,986	24.0	33.9	34.1
Attala	NA	NA	4,491	8.1	52.8	14.8	28.6	8,240	20,283	33,018	66.0	2.2	31,722	23.8	34.5	34.1
Benton	NA	NA	1,838	6.0	60.5	11.4	11.0	8,897	20,261	36,302	65.2	1.6	36,400	25.3	36.2	35.2
Bolivar	NA	NA	10,216	6.9	50.4	21.5	59.2	9,006	16,595	27,457	71.6	1.2	29,633	35.3	42.2	42.0
Calhoun	NA	NA	3,505	8.7	59.6	10.9	19.8	7,676	17,203	31,141	68.4	0.5	34,417	21.9	32.7	31.6
Carroll	NA	NA	2,443	32.4	55.1	16.1	8.3	8,222	22,519	40,278	55.6	3.7	39,622	17.4	26.3	24.8
Chickasaw	NA	NA	4,019	6.7	64.0	11.0	25.0	8,226	18,514	31,048	70.0	1.7	34,611	22.2	34.2	32.8
Choctaw	73	1,131	2,170	9.2	54.6	15.4	14.2	9,992	18,434	32,953	65.2	0.2	36,194	23.1	35.5	33.9
Claiborne	288	956	2,901	6.4	51.2	19.2	15.9	9,803	12,944	25,000	76.5	0.5	29,266	38.2	52.4	56.5
Clarke	NA	NA	3,850	5.0	55.7	14.1	24.7	8,139	20,431	36,441	63.3	1.1	37,814	20.9	33.5	32.7
Clay	206	1,669	5,447	14.9	53.3	18.9	28.8	8,467	19,097	33,142	64.6	1.5	34,408	23.9	37.7	35.3
Coahoma	NA	NA	7,429	11.6	48.8	17.2	45.7	9,351	16,066	28,217	71.9	1.1	26,815	41.2	66.3	71.6
Copiah	NA	NA	7,603	11.2	53.7	12.9	34.2	7,568	18,188	34,738	67.1	1.5	34,450	27.1	38.6	38.1
Covington	NA	NA	4,513	11.7	58.7	14.4	24.3	8,215	16,941	31,684	68.3	0.3	33,348	23.5	36.4	36.7
DeSoto	118	2,234	48,822	12.8	40.0	23.2	220.5	6,671	27,135	60,111	40.3	2.9	64,138	10.2	14.6	13.5
Forrest	196	3,514	24,355	13.6	42.4	25.7	107.4	9,263	20,194	37,017	60.9	1.7	36,709	25.4	36.8	37.4
Franklin	NA	NA	1,795	9.6	53.8	16.7	13.1	9,061	22,769	40,081	57.8	1.8	37,533	20.2	30.1	27.0
George	NA	NA	5,759	12.3	59.7	13.1	29.5	7,144	20,640	47,313	52.7	1.7	50,705	16.1	23.2	22.6
Greene	16	186	2,630	5.3	61.5	7.8	17.2	8,170	15,659	40,069	60.9	1.6	39,559	24.1	27.9	24.9
Grenada	NA	NA	5,293	13.8	51.9	16.8	32.7	7,595	20,562	33,026	63.8	1.9	37,419	22.5	34.6	35.5
Hancock	NA	NA	10,465	15.1	44.1	20.9	54.2	8,344	23,221	46,542	52.9	1.7	45,369	17.2	26.7	24.9
Harrison	248	4,363	49,527	12.9	43.1	21.5	260.5	8,369	22,517	43,095	56.8	1.7	42,988	20.5	32.8	30.3
Hinds	739	4,096	74,751	17.0	38.8	28.0	339.7	8,355	21,672	38,773	60.3	2.5	42,903	20.8	31.4	30.3
Holmes	NA	NA	5,616	8.0	66.1	11.6	30.1	8,518	12,408	20,800	80.8	0.5	22,045	42.5	51.3	51.2
Humphreys	NA	NA	2,451	7.9	62.3	13.9	14.2	8,069	13,977	23,442	79.9	2.0	25,506	38.9	56.8	52.8
Issaquena	NA	NA	170	31.8	67.9	9.0	NA	NA	17,282	24,306	80.1	2.1	26,957	40.5	54.0	52.8
Itawamba	NA	NA	6,096	3.8	54.1	13.1	26.7	7,557	19,707	35,380	64.1	1.0	40,644	18.1	22.9	21.7
Jackson	197	3,219	37,014	13.3	43.6	20.5	217.6	8,845	24,350	49,158	50.9	2.9	53,288	17.6	25.3	25.4
Jasper	NA	NA	3,646	14.3	54.5	13.7	22.0	9,051	19,363	34,993	67.2	2.3	34,806	22.7	33.8	32.7
Jefferson	NA	NA	1,809	0.2	57.4	17.8	12.2	9,235	13,703	23,773	73.5	0.9	26,731	33.7	44.8	46.4
Jefferson Davis	NA	NA	2,486	17.1	58.2	14.6	16.0	10,166	16,859	26,429	75.5	1.3	30,815	26.9	43.0	41.9
Jones	352	2,571	16,745	13.4	48.8	18.7	92.8	7,968	20,957	37,846	61.3	2.3	40,283	20.5	29.4	27.1
Kemper	114	659	2,738	4.9	53.0	11.4	12.1	10,405	14,715	29,925	76.4	0.4	31,018	28.3	39.3	36.4
Lafayette	NA	NA	20,382	4.5	31.5	39.7	58.5	8,749	23,833	43,162	55.1	4.4	42,287	20.7	19.0	18.6
Lamar	191	1,704	17,735	15.0	32.1	36.8	80.8	7,921	28,101	53,888	45.9	4.7	57,419	12.6	18.5	17.6
Lauderdale	368	3,102	20,486	9.6	45.1	19.2	108.0	8,336	21,575	38,399	62.0	2.1	40,949	23.7	34.8	33.0
Lawrence	NA	NA	2,976	8.8	56.7	13.6	17.4	7,910	20,700	38,155	60.8	1.4	42,291	19.7	29.6	28.0
Leake	NA	NA	6,106	13.9	60.2	12.3	22.8	7,745	18,178	32,657	65.0	3.8	35,644	24.9	38.5	37.6
Lee	NA	NA	21,915	10.5	43.4	23.1	131.7	8,552	22,741	43,224	56.6	2.3	43,834	17.0	21.9	22.5
Leflore	NA	NA	9,215	9.1	56.3	18.8	50.8	9,009	15,370	25,356	70.5	0.7	27,573	35.6	46.7	47.0
Lincoln	NA	NA	8,286	10.9	51.6	14.8	46.3	7,388	19,418	36,250	61.6	1.4	39,701	20.0	27.2	27.4
Lowndes	NA	NA	15,935	11.5	46.1	22.4	81.3	8,257	22,143	41,219	57.3	1.6	44,142	21.2	30.9	29.0
Madison	141	1,385	29,074	24.0	26.0	45.7	130.5	8,192	35,435	65,924	38.1	8.8	65,870	12.0	16.6	15.3
Marion	215	1,554	5,940	20.6	59.4	12.7	36.7	9,280	19,707	30,914	65.4	1.7	33,416	27.0	35.5	31.7
Marshall	374	1,312	8,597	14.8	60.3	13.0	38.9	7,953	19,104	40,598	60.3	0.6	37,561	23.0	32.5	32.1
Monroe	NA	NA	8,172	7.6	56.3	15.6	54.4	7,991	19,905	37,345	61.0	1.4	38,208	19.4	27.4	27.2
Montgomery	NA	NA	2,211	20.7	58.6	18.3	13.8	9,379	19,706	31,207	65.3	0.7	34,946	24.2	36.4	36.1
Neshoba	NA	NA	8,076	7.1	54.6	14.4	33.4	7,319	19,030	35,991	62.8	2.1	37,195	22.5	32.2	29.7
Newton	NA	NA	6,042	7.8	46.3	15.8	32.0	8,235	20,896	35,527	63.9	1.6	37,468	21.7	31.2	29.5
Noxubee	NA	NA	2,800	14.9	63.0	14.5	16.8	9,323	16,108	31,472	68.9	0.8	29,330	31.6	47.7	49.0
Oktibbeha	168	2,063	23,276	8.4	33.8	42.0	48.1	9,362	20,128	33,431	62.1	2.5	36,105	28.3	31.2	31.1
Panola	377	3,388	8,592	13.5	57.0	15.6	52.4	8,567	20,098	37,556	62.0	1.6	35,570	22.7	37.0	35.4
Pearl River	NA	NA	13,630	13.4	46.7	14.2	71.5	8,296	20,653	41,598	57.3	1.1	43,654	18.6	27.5	25.0
Perry	NA	NA	2,988	7.5	58.0	9.0	16.1	8,400	18,188	34,774	65.2	1.3	38,064	21.4	33.1	31.6
Pike	NA	NA	10,422	12.8	53.7	15.7	60.5	8,637	17,316	31,511	67.0	1.2	32,485	30.1	42.9	40.7
Pontotoc	NA	NA	8,021	6.6	56.8	14.7	43.9	7,482	19,743	39,869	59.2	1.6	41,455	18.4	24.8	24.9
Prentiss	NA	NA	6,345	2.8	55.4	12.0	29.8	8,126	18,313	33,500	67.3	1.1	36,558	24.2	30.0	27.4
Quitman	NA	NA	1,948	13.3	63.6	12.9	11.8	9,678	14,928	24,835	76.5	0.6	26,210	34.3	50.5	48.9
Rankin	64	1,004	37,634	20.8	37.4	29.6	184.2	7,855	27,822	59,370	41.7	3.7	62,284	9.5	14.2	13.6
Scott	NA	NA	7,113	8.3	61.9	11.8	40.8	7,253	17,203	32,615	67.6	1.5	34,452	22.6	30.7	31.7
Sharkey	NA	NA	1,190	13.9	53.6	19.0	9.2	9,984	15,430	28,878	76.2	1.2	27,880	35.0	52.9	51.3
Simpson	4	53	7,241	18.7	57.5	12.8	33.5	8,101	18,495	37,285	65.8	1.6	39,568	23.1	34.3	32.7
Smith	NA	NA	3,597	7.6	61.7	11.9	24.0	8,530	22,129	33,696	62.3	2.4	38,521	18.9	28.1	26.3
Stone	227	2,122	4,560	11.2	53.1	14.0	21.6	7,987	19,588	44,995	54.7	1.1	41,884	20.3	29.9	30.0

1. Data for serious crimes have not been adjusted for underreporting; this may affect comparability between geographic areas and over time.   2. Per 100,000 population estimated by the FBI.
3. All persons 3 years old and over enrolled in nursery school through college.   4. Persons 25 years old and over.   5. Elementary and secondary education expenditures.
6. Based on population estimated by the American Community Survey, 2011–2015.

Table B. States and Counties — Agriculture

| | | Land in farms | | | Value of land and buildings (dollars) | | | Value of products sold: | | | | Percent of farms with sales of: | | Government payments | |
| | | | Acres | | | | | | | Percent from: | | | | | |
STATE County	Acreage (1,000)	Percent change, 2007-2012	Average size of farm	Total irrigated (1,000)	Total cropland (1,000)	Average per farm	Average per acre	Value of machinery and equipment, average per farm (dollars)	Total (mil dol)	Average per farm (acres)	Crops	Livestock and poultry products	$10,000 or more	$100,000 or more	Total ($1,000)	Percent of farms
	117	118	119	120	121	122	123	124	125	126	127	128	129	130	131	132
MISSISSIPPI	10,931	-4.6	287	1,652.0	5,075.6	652,593	2,273	91,910	6,441.0	169,162	46.2	53.8	33.0	12.4	181,205	43.3
Adams	66	-5.6	349	D	20.3	757,720	2,170	73,026	9.9	52,228	85.4	14.6	18.5	4.2	1,107	38.1
Alcorn	94	-0.3	185	D	43.3	345,842	1,866	59,352	20.9	41,461	84.6	15.4	25.1	3.6	795	50.7
Amite	121	10.2	205	0.1	23.0	690,939	3,365	66,768	68.4	115,958	5.6	94.4	32.4	8.8	1,025	43.4
Attala	125	-8.6	275	0.4	29.1	495,542	1,801	48,726	23.1	50,686	54.8	45.2	22.4	4.2	1,359	52.0
Benton	82	-4.3	264	D	29.2	421,772	1,596	49,298	14.5	46,596	72.8	27.2	19.6	6.7	740	56.4
Bolivar	390	-8.8	932	247.8	362.0	2,254,100	2,419	463,976	277.0	661,122	99.9	0.1	70.9	50.1	12,645	85.0
Calhoun	175	-13.3	282	1.2	80.1	520,758	1,844	98,725	78.5	126,446	92.9	7.1	34.5	12.1	3,146	73.4
Carroll	169	-11.1	336	12.3	57.8	631,318	1,879	75,996	36.5	72,620	86.9	13.1	30.0	8.3	2,451	46.1
Chickasaw	166	-7.0	289	3.0	67.2	533,009	1,847	69,757	60.9	105,897	49.6	50.4	34.6	10.3	2,924	65.0
Choctaw	63	-12.0	250	1.0	9.0	492,768	1,973	41,854	11.4	44,945	11.1	88.9	18.9	4.3	444	49.2
Claiborne	83	-11.5	334	D	22.0	671,028	2,011	54,072	11.4	45,864	77.2	22.8	25.3	3.6	1,125	55.0
Clarke	56	-12.9	171	0.4	13.9	404,097	2,358	59,161	33.5	101,763	4.5	95.5	24.9	5.2	160	17.6
Clay	130	-8.6	310	0.8	30.8	507,521	1,639	66,540	92.3	219,655	7.8	92.2	33.3	8.3	1,554	48.6
Coahoma	261	-13.8	956	138.0	226.8	2,411,634	2,523	406,249	179.6	657,799	96.1	3.9	62.3	50.2	10,498	86.4
Copiah	116	-11.8	229	0.2	18.4	523,654	2,286	58,763	61.4	121,336	10.4	89.6	29.1	6.7	527	32.8
Covington	106	-9.0	215	0.6	24.6	631,521	2,941	97,406	203.5	412,838	3.1	96.9	46.5	22.1	617	26.4
DeSoto	119	-16.2	274	17.2	81.2	723,771	2,641	84,483	50.0	115,386	90.2	9.8	24.5	9.0	1,866	25.4
Forrest	43	-6.1	119	0.8	9.8	406,844	3,416	65,822	20.8	58,075	22.8	77.2	27.9	5.8	598	24.2
Franklin	50	6.8	266	0.0	8.8	680,487	2,562	74,143	10.5	55,667	21.7	78.3	27.5	6.3	254	39.7
George	61	-10.6	106	0.5	19.3	357,428	3,361	75,084	22.7	39,620	84.8	15.2	27.2	4.4	421	16.6
Greene	69	34.8	174	0.2	16.2	379,203	2,175	91,420	32.8	83,139	30.5	69.5	26.6	6.8	300	13.2
Grenada	88	-20.8	280	1.1	25.8	511,345	1,828	51,522	11.6	36,775	59.4	40.6	26.9	4.7	1,414	63.6
Hancock	25	-40.2	102	0.1	4.8	403,952	3,964	38,907	2.7	10,988	D	D	27.4	1.6	175	14.1
Harrison	24	12.6	73	0.1	5.6	452,586	6,199	37,532	3.4	10,417	45.8	54.2	19.6	2.1	63	6.9
Hinds	251	-3.5	240	0.5	61.8	549,542	2,292	58,127	73.4	70,106	34.0	66.0	22.0	3.2	3,055	41.2
Holmes	238	4.2	447	51.1	119.8	938,991	2,098	99,501	93.4	175,972	97.7	2.3	25.4	9.8	5,781	66.9
Humphreys	194	-0.5	740	82.7	161.4	1,633,874	2,209	292,195	132.7	506,458	87.2	12.8	55.7	42.4	5,952	84.0
Issaquena	124	2.7	1,282	19.7	75.2	2,458,216	1,917	298,340	53.3	549,691	D	D	52.6	36.1	2,396	88.7
Itawamba	95	1.7	214	0.0	30.2	429,835	2,007	59,011	17.6	39,623	67.5	32.5	29.3	5.9	786	48.8
Jackson	38	-9.3	92	0.2	14.3	347,257	3,778	60,181	14.4	35,164	87.3	12.7	22.0	3.2	277	8.8
Jasper	97	7.1	218	0.0	14.1	436,222	1,998	73,629	97.2	218,366	1.6	98.4	36.2	16.0	545	27.0
Jefferson	86	-14.7	310	0.6	29.9	655,975	2,119	67,863	31.7	114,484	46.7	53.3	32.1	10.8	815	37.5
Jefferson Davis	59	-13.2	175	0.3	10.6	347,445	1,985	54,522	36.0	106,831	4.9	95.1	30.3	7.7	460	36.5
Jones	126	14.7	136	0.4	25.5	433,357	3,189	62,438	217.0	234,063	2.2	97.8	37.6	19.2	1,212	21.6
Kemper	124	-9.1	328	0.1	18.0	569,079	1,738	52,138	20.5	54,119	9.1	90.9	31.2	4.5	619	28.6
Lafayette	109	-4.8	242	0.6	26.9	543,419	2,242	56,581	8.9	19,904	73.3	26.7	22.7	3.1	1,120	50.3
Lamar	64	-12.3	151	0.2	13.2	544,656	3,602	64,014	25.0	59,033	13.8	86.2	36.3	6.4	565	25.0
Lauderdale	69	-17.4	185	0.1	14.6	441,753	2,387	46,413	5.4	14,453	50.1	49.9	21.4	0.8	252	17.2
Lawrence	73	-9.1	183	D	18.2	492,441	2,689	75,239	79.4	199,970	7.3	92.7	40.8	10.3	804	35.5
Leake	106	-16.7	167	0.1	22.6	446,077	2,678	58,912	283.3	444,706	0.9	99.1	38.9	21.4	711	34.5
Lee	133	-9.2	253	0.4	84.7	484,651	1,913	65,162	45.0	85,766	89.3	10.7	31.0	6.9	880	39.2
Leflore	293	-6.9	977	164.1	235.8	1,970,613	2,017	381,793	241.9	806,193	78.3	21.7	55.0	41.0	7,438	81.3
Lincoln	109	-12.8	183	0.2	20.1	547,086	2,997	65,555	69.9	117,405	4.6	95.4	37.3	9.2	615	25.7
Lowndes	119	-8.3	289	4.8	57.3	613,637	2,122	89,651	43.1	104,276	62.2	37.8	33.9	12.1	1,478	47.7
Madison	203	-8.8	296	0.1	68.6	776,399	2,619	67,238	33.3	48,600	82.6	17.4	19.9	6.7	3,611	45.5
Marion	82	-11.3	148	D	18.2	438,998	2,966	75,457	97.3	176,281	2.1	97.9	28.4	13.0	1,259	37.9
Marshall	203	5.3	355	3.5	70.0	699,567	1,972	81,276	32.7	57,079	84.1	15.9	30.7	7.7	1,667	47.3
Monroe	228	14.8	314	0.5	99.6	549,209	1,749	77,127	55.2	76,070	82.2	17.8	28.0	9.6	2,655	54.8
Montgomery	97	-0.1	282	0.7	26.8	501,565	1,779	64,942	20.1	58,339	54.5	45.5	26.4	7.2	1,257	52.2
Neshoba	101	-16.0	150	0.0	20.6	461,393	3,081	79,096	246.5	364,069	0.9	99.1	43.7	21.9	249	16.2
Newton	109	-9.4	194	0.6	22.6	404,137	2,083	65,811	102.4	182,242	4.2	95.8	37.0	15.5	659	22.1
Noxubee	213	-3.8	377	17.3	105.9	815,425	2,161	147,076	140.3	248,235	48.3	51.7	49.7	31.5	2,547	59.6
Oktibbeha	105	3.3	260	0.3	21.7	573,619	2,203	56,042	15.1	37,674	15.0	85.0	24.9	4.7	912	37.8
Panola	273	1.1	366	30.4	134.8	704,463	1,924	87,615	71.9	96,451	91.6	8.4	31.3	9.8	5,745	61.9
Pearl River	118	-12.8	146	1.0	23.0	465,647	3,200	48,637	17.6	21,654	45.7	54.3	28.2	3.4	735	14.8
Perry	44	5.8	140	0.5	12.1	401,719	2,862	68,168	21.8	70,442	23.7	76.3	31.6	7.4	513	23.9
Pike	72	-1.9	136	0.1	14.6	481,913	3,552	55,004	74.4	140,021	2.3	97.7	32.8	7.7	984	38.4
Pontotoc	153	4.7	172	D	64.2	312,294	1,819	55,052	24.7	27,747	76.8	23.2	24.9	5.2	2,249	64.2
Prentiss	93	-8.1	185	0.0	38.4	290,214	1,569	45,899	15.5	30,835	83.6	16.4	23.6	5.6	966	69.4
Quitman	209	-5.3	601	68.7	155.8	1,210,934	2,014	188,674	85.1	245,130	D	D	38.6	24.5	8,654	91.4
Rankin	126	-10.3	188	0.0	28.5	561,387	2,990	65,404	111.2	165,990	8.2	91.8	32.4	12.2	829	20.4
Scott	115	-9.2	161	0.1	27.8	406,497	2,528	85,180	270.8	378,270	1.7	98.3	41.3	16.9	476	20.3
Sharkey	155	-13.5	1,214	61.0	135.2	2,782,797	2,292	455,836	108.2	844,969	96.1	3.9	61.7	45.3	3,767	88.3
Simpson	110	-6.9	181	1.2	28.2	495,135	2,739	80,403	202.4	334,068	3.4	96.6	44.2	21.5	396	16.7
Smith	108	-1.3	170	0.1	26.2	502,821	2,956	74,466	251.1	394,133	3.0	97.0	49.1	25.9	427	11.8
Stone	46	-11.9	169	0.1	7.5	615,882	3,655	58,841	10.7	39,410	D	D	32.5	2.6	298	18.1

Table B. States and Counties — Water Use, Wholesale Trade, Retail Trade, and Real Estate

STATE County	Water use, 2015		Wholesale Trade[1], 2012				Retail Trade[2], 2012				Real estate and rental and leasing,[2] 2012			
	Public supply water withdrawn (mil gal/day)	Public supply gallons withdrawn per person per day	Number of establish-ments	Number of employees	Sales (mil dol)	Annual payroll (mil dol)	Number of establish-ments	Number of employees	Sales (mil dol)	Annual payroll (mil dol)	Number of establish-ments	Number of employees	Sales (mil dol)	Annual payroll (mil dol)
	133	134	135	136	137	138	139	140	141	142	143	144	145	146
MISSISSIPPI................	400.36	133.8	2,484	30,351	28,303.0	1,373.6	11,594	136,032	37,053.2	2,968.4	2,374	10,235	1,709.3	334.1
Adams....................	4.92	157.4	35	265	169.6	10.0	176	2,119	488.7	47.6	36	135	17.6	3.9
Alcorn....................	4.75	127.0	35	D	D	D	172	2,119	538.0	49.0	23	225	12.2	3.8
Amite.....................	1.34	106.6	7	62	14.0	1.5	30	162	39.2	3.5	3	4	0.5	0.1
Attala....................	2.24	117.6	13	D	D	D	78	807	192.5	15.5	10	29	3.8	0.8
Benton...................	0.49	59.9	NA	NA	NA	NA	16	112	24.4	2.5	NA	NA	NA	NA
Bolivar...................	4.16	124.8	29	329	763.8	15.0	161	1,535	371.2	31.5	45	126	18.6	3.2
Calhoun..................	2.28	154.9	14	175	81.1	5.2	58	401	95.2	8.1	4	10	0.7	0.3
Carroll	0.86	84.0	4	D	D	D	15	87	22.1	1.5	1	D	D	D
Chickasaw...............	1.81	104.5	15	90	69.8	3.1	83	687	153.4	11.7	8	17	2.6	0.5
Choctaw..................	0.96	115.7	2	D	D	D	27	152	25.1	2.7	1	D	D	D
Claiborne................	0.66	72.1	1	D	D	D	24	152	35.3	3.4	NA	NA	NA	NA
Clarke...................	2.00	125.0	4	D	D	D	51	322	63.6	5.5	2	D	D	D
Clay.....................	2.53	126.2	12	119	158.4	5.8	78	792	165.4	15.2	8	20	3.5	0.6
Coahoma..................	3.83	155.6	28	D	D	D	117	1,043	295.4	24.6	42	255	23.4	5.0
Copiah...................	3.79	131.7	15	87	46.3	2.8	83	834	181.5	15.7	8	75	5.0	1.6
Covington................	1.86	95.2	12	68	116.9	2.4	68	522	188.3	12.1	8	27	3.2	0.5
DeSoto...................	19.51	112.6	120	2,840	3,232.4	127.2	495	7,957	2,320.9	193.3	97	331	83.8	11.6
Forrest..................	12.10	159.3	86	857	574.3	32.9	367	4,470	3,680.2	107.7	92	377	66.1	12.8
Franklin.................	0.98	126.6	4	D	D	D	17	113	29.0	2.4	4	30	1.1	0.8
George...................	1.23	52.6	11	75	54.2	2.5	77	900	229.5	17.2	6	D	D	D
Greene...................	1.86	137.6	3	D	D	D	26	211	48.3	3.9	3	11	0.6	0.1
Grenada..................	3.96	183.5	28	D	D	D	120	1,305	415.1	32.2	17	61	13.0	2.4
Hancock..................	4.39	94.6	15	64	10.3	3.3	126	1,328	346.2	30.2	28	90	10.0	2.3
Harrison.................	20.84	103.5	161	1,537	664.4	65.1	805	10,872	2,859.1	243.0	249	1,100	210.9	35.5
Hinds....................	50.54	208.1	270	3,476	2,274.4	166.5	869	11,093	3,072.3	276.4	278	1,544	319.8	66.3
Holmes...................	2.20	120.0	8	26	32.7	1.0	66	467	98.1	8.9	13	29	2.8	0.4
Humphreys................	0.92	106.1	4	D	D	D	34	288	100.4	6.9	2	D	D	D
Issaquena................	0.12	89.8	2	D	D	D	NA	NA	NA	NA	NA	NA	NA	NA
Itawamba.................	10.39	440.1	8	138	41.9	4.6	70	614	157.1	13.2	4	10	0.7	0.2
Jackson..................	14.50	102.5	60	564	236.3	22.5	426	4,828	1,220.5	109.0	98	424	49.4	12.7
Jasper...................	3.29	198.6	5	D	D	D	39	360	73.0	7.8	5	47	5.2	1.2
Jefferson................	0.72	95.9	NA	NA	NA	NA	14	108	22.0	1.5	1	D	D	D
Jefferson Davis..........	1.45	124.3	2	D	D	D	39	207	61.6	4.4	2	D	D	D
Jones....................	11.75	172.2	75	D	D	D	241	3,000	796.4	61.7	54	228	64.8	13.0
Kemper...................	1.78	178.6	3	D	D	D	25	156	37.8	2.8	4	D	D	D
Lafayette................	5.28	99.3	31	249	161.2	9.1	211	2,576	548.8	53.2	43	97	24.5	3.3
Lamar....................	5.92	97.7	36	D	D	D	282	4,802	1,041.4	86.7	61	D	D	D
Lauderdale...............	10.95	139.4	78	1,649	1,701.4	74.1	406	5,061	1,488.2	113.4	75	266	58.2	7.9
Lawrence.................	1.72	136.3	1	D	D	D	36	342	62.5	6.1	1	D	D	D
Leake....................	2.21	97.1	6	60	16.9	1.8	78	776	173.0	15.9	4	6	0.2	0.1
Lee......................	4.29	50.3	153	1,526	1,049.1	63.6	510	7,242	1,628.1	154.7	96	413	76.0	12.7
Leflore..................	4.15	133.9	31	D	D	D	154	1,637	465.6	36.2	42	D	D	D
Lincoln..................	4.04	116.6	31	D	D	D	159	1,783	540.6	40.8	26	86	13.8	2.9
Lowndes..................	8.37	140.2	80	D	D	D	311	3,578	736.5	73.2	63	186	26.3	4.8
Madison	16.52	159.7	135	2,220	4,549.4	118.2	497	6,698	1,616.9	148.1	139	909	133.7	32.4
Marion...................	3.62	141.6	16	163	121.6	5.1	134	1,182	280.1	25.6	25	110	18.3	3.6
Marshall.................	2.53	70.4	17	180	96.9	9.5	95	881	185.4	16.8	9	16	1.8	0.3
Monroe...................	3.63	101.3	18	182	150.2	8.0	136	1,213	259.2	22.9	14	51	6.0	1.6
Montgomery...............	1.30	128.1	3	D	D	D	51	478	144.4	9.0	4	18	1.7	0.4
Neshoba..................	4.47	151.7	20	277	448.0	13.2	110	1,180	288.5	25.0	11	256	9.3	6.8
Newton...................	2.47	113.6	8	39	8.0	1.1	70	707	137.4	14.2	5	12	1.9	0.2
Noxubee..................	1.37	124.1	10	80	58.4	1.8	43	320	93.5	7.0	NA	NA	NA	NA
Oktibbeha................	7.58	152.2	15	436	187.3	17.5	163	1,924	472.0	38.3	59	178	30.5	4.8
Panola...................	3.35	98.0	31	536	576.6	24.2	170	1,555	471.8	33.0	15	66	10.0	2.1
Pearl River..............	4.58	83.0	25	D	D	D	172	1,793	477.3	43.4	19	52	7.7	1.1
Perry....................	1.23	100.2	4	D	D	D	34	250	62.4	4.4	3	D	D	D
Pike.....................	5.89	147.4	52	383	206.4	13.9	223	2,458	603.8	51.1	39	140	27.1	3.6
Pontotoc.................	3.45	111.6	16	148	65.2	3.9	88	950	259.3	19.6	8	18	1.9	0.3
Prentiss.................	3.28	128.8	15	72	11.5	1.2	103	948	189.1	17.1	32	61	7.6	1.2
Quitman..................	0.74	98.9	4	D	D	D	23	128	28.6	2.3	6	D	D	D
Rankin...................	17.66	118.5	224	3,551	2,354.5	186.9	509	8,324	2,361.2	190.2	167	818	143.3	28.9
Scott....................	8.02	283.7	17	72	56.4	2.3	126	1,188	243.8	23.6	9	35	4.0	1.0
Sharkey..................	0.52	113.4	9	82	86.7	3.4	24	174	31.5	3.1	13	24	2.7	0.4
Simpson..................	3.60	132.2	13	79	27.0	2.6	90	1,020	234.7	20.5	12	41	5.8	1.0
Smith....................	1.18	73.5	5	42	15.5	1.2	35	210	47.2	4.0	NA	NA	NA	NA
Stone....................	1.46	80.8	10	29	10.9	1.0	54	582	166.6	13.4	8	22	1.5	0.3

1. Merchant wholesalers, except manufacturers' sales branches and offices. 2. Employer establishments.

Table B. States and Counties — **Land Area and Population**

State / county code	CBSA code[1]	County code[2]	STATE County	Land area[3] (sq. mi)	Total persons 2017	Rank	Per square mile	White	Black	American Indian, Alaska Native	Asian and Pacific Islancer	Percent Hispanic or Latino[4]	Under 5 years	5 to 17 years	18 to 24 years	25 to 34 years	35 to 44 years	45 to 54 years
				1	2	3	4	5	6	7	8	9	10	11	12	13	14	15
			MISSISSIPPI— Cont'd															
28,133	26,940	7	Sunflower......................	697.8	25,981	1,563	37.2	24.2	73.7	0.5	0.5	1.8	5.7	17.1	10.2	16.2	12.7	13.0
28,135		7	Tallahatchie....................	645.2	14,125	2,157	21.9	35.9	56.5	0.7	1.2	6.8	5.2	14.3	10.5	17.0	13.5	12.6
28,137	32,820	1	Tate.............................	404.8	28,441	1,477	70.3	65.8	31.7	0.6	0.6	2.5	5.6	17.5	11.4	11.8	11.4	13.0
28,139		6	Tippah..........................	457.8	21,969	1,726	48.0	78.2	17.7	0.5	0.5	4.7	6.3	18.2	9.0	11.7	12.2	13.3
28,141		8	Tishomingo	424.3	19,542	1,849	46.1	94.0	3.0	0.5	0.3	3.1	5.5	16.3	8.0	11.4	11.1	14.0
28,143	32,820	1	Tunica..........................	454.7	10,024	2,431	22.0	19.9	76.9	0.6	1.0	2.5	8.9	20.2	9.0	13.7	12.9	11.8
28,145		6	Union...........................	415.6	28,556	1,469	68.7	79.3	15.9	0.6	1.5	4.2	6.8	18.4	8.2	12.4	13.0	12.9
28,147		9	Walthall	403.9	14,499	2,129	35.9	53.6	44.1	0.8	0.8	2.0	5.8	17.2	8.7	11.2	12.2	12.1
28,149	46,980	4	Warren..........................	588.5	46,768	1,037	79.5	47.6	49.5	0.5	1.1	2.2	6.6	17.5	8.4	12.5	12.2	12.5
28,151	24,740	5	Washington	724.7	46,221	1,046	63.8	25.4	72.3	0.3	1.0	1.6	7.5	18.6	9.2	12.4	11.2	12.0
28,153		7	Wayne..........................	810.7	20,446	1,801	25.2	57.9	40.4	0.6	0.5	1.7	6.9	17.9	8.4	12.6	11.6	12.2
28,155		9	Webster.........................	420.9	9,765	2,448	23.2	78.9	19.9	0.5	0.4	1.5	6.1	17.7	7.6	12.2	11.3	13.3
28,157		8	Wilkinson.......................	678.1	8,804	2,520	13.0	28.6	70.3	0.5	0.3	1.0	5.7	15.7	8.4	15.1	11.7	12.1
28,159		7	Winston.........................	607.2	18,246	1,908	30.0	50.6	47.4	1.4	0.4	1.2	5.3	17.8	7.4	11.8	11.7	12.3
28,161		7	Yalobusha	467.1	12,497	2,259	26.8	59.1	39.4	0.6	0.4	1.6	6.4	16.3	7.6	11.5	11.5	12.5
28,163	27,140	2	Yazoo	922.0	27,057	1,523	29.3	36.1	57.6	0.6	0.8	5.8	6.0	17.4	8.7	16.3	14.6	11.8
29,000		0	**MISSOURI**.................	68,746.3	6,113,532	X	88.9	81.4	12.7	1.2	2.7	4.2	6.1	16.5	9.3	13.4	12.0	12.6
29,001	28,860	7	Adair............................	567.3	25,377	1,588	44.7	91.6	3.7	0.8	3.3	2.5	5.0	13.5	28.1	10.1	8.5	9.8
29,003	41,140	3	Andrew..........................	432.7	17,555	1,948	40.6	95.9	1.4	0.8	0.8	2.4	5.8	17.1	7.4	11.1	11.9	13.3
29,005		9	Atchison	547.3	5,275	2,818	9.6	97.2	0.8	0.9	0.9	1.3	5.2	14.8	6.3	10.3	10.9	13.0
29,007	33,020	6	Audrain..........................	692.2	25,641	1,578	37.0	88.8	8.1	0.7	0.9	3.1	6.4	16.5	8.2	13.2	12.6	12.5
29,009		6	Barry............................	778.3	35,668	1,282	45.8	86.8	0.9	2.1	2.2	9.7	6.0	16.9	7.6	11.1	10.7	12.8
29,011		6	Barton	591.9	11,850	2,302	20.0	94.5	1.3	2.8	1.2	2.8	6.0	18.0	7.8	10.4	11.2	12.0
29,013	28,140	1	Bates............................	836.7	16,334	2,023	19.5	95.6	1.7	1.5	0.6	2.3	5.9	17.8	7.5	11.1	11.4	12.4
29,015		7	Benton	704.0	19,074	1,871	27.1	96.3	0.8	1.6	0.7	2.1	4.4	12.7	5.6	7.8	8.4	12.6
29,017	16,020	3	Bollinger	617.9	12,306	2,270	19.9	97.2	0.7	1.3	0.6	1.3	5.3	16.7	6.8	10.7	11.3	13.9
29,019	17,860	3	Boone...........................	685.5	178,271	369	260.1	81.7	11.0	1.0	5.9	3.4	5.9	14.4	19.6	15.3	11.5	10.7
29,021	41,140	3	Buchanan........................	408.0	89,065	653	218.3	85.1	7.3	1.0	2.2	6.8	6.3	16.4	9.3	14.5	12.3	12.5
29,023	38,740	5	Butler............................	694.7	42,666	1,120	61.4	90.8	6.8	1.6	1.2	2.1	6.3	17.2	7.6	12.5	11.6	12.5
29,025	28,140	1	Caldwell	426.4	9,100	2,494	21.3	96.3	1.3	1.4	0.8	2.1	5.8	18.1	7.8	10.0	11.1	13.4
29,027	27,620	3	Callaway	834.6	45,032	1,073	54.0	92.2	5.4	1.3	1.1	2.1	5.5	15.5	10.8	13.4	12.2	13.3
29,029		7	Camden	656.0	45,632	1,062	69.6	95.1	1.0	1.1	1.0	2.9	4.7	13.3	5.8	9.3	9.2	12.3
29,031	16,020	3	Cape Girardeau	578.5	78,161	711	135.1	88.0	8.9	0.8	2.0	2.4	5.8	15.7	14.0	12.7	11.2	11.5
29,033		6	Carroll	694.6	8,796	2,523	12.7	96.0	2.6	0.7	0.6	1.6	5.9	16.8	7.7	10.3	11.3	12.6
29,035		9	Carter	507.4	6,169	2,739	12.2	95.8	0.9	1.9	0.6	2.6	6.3	17.4	7.3	10.5	11.5	12.7
29,037	28,140	1	Cass.............................	696.6	103,724	580	148.9	90.1	4.8	1.4	1.6	4.5	6.0	18.4	7.7	11.7	12.7	13.3
29,039		6	Cedar	474.5	14,073	2,160	29.7	96.3	0.7	1.7	0.8	2.2	6.8	17.1	6.9	9.8	9.9	12.2
29,041		9	Chariton	751.2	7,480	2,629	10.0	96.1	3.0	0.7	0.4	1.0	6.3	16.6	6.3	9.7	10.3	11.5
29,043	44,180	2	Christian.........................	562.6	85,432	669	151.9	95.0	1.3	1.3	1.2	2.9	6.3	19.1	7.3	13.0	13.4	12.8
29,045	22,800	7	Clark.............................	504.7	6,723	2,692	13.3	98.0	0.7	0.8	0.7	1.0	6.0	16.6	6.7	10.3	11.0	13.3
29,047	28,140	1	Clay.............................	397.7	242,874	278	610.7	83.5	7.5	1.2	3.5	6.9	6.5	17.8	8.1	14.6	13.7	13.2
29,049	28,140	1	Clinton	419.0	20,554	1,794	49.1	95.4	2.1	1.3	0.8	2.1	5.8	17.7	7.3	11.4	11.6	13.7
29,051	27,620	3	Cole.............................	391.5	76,708	723	195.9	83.2	13.2	0.8	1.8	3.0	6.1	16.4	8.6	13.6	12.8	13.2
29,053		6	Cooper	564.8	17,644	1,940	31.2	89.8	7.9	1.2	1.1	2.0	5.4	16.3	9.8	13.5	11.7	12.2
29,055		6	Crawford	742.5	24,102	1,637	32.5	96.5	0.9	1.4	0.6	2.0	6.0	17.0	7.3	11.1	11.3	13.0
29,057		8	Dade............................	490.0	7,588	2,620	15.5	96.1	0.8	2.5	1.0	2.1	4.9	16.3	6.7	9.5	10.9	12.7
29,059	44,180	2	Dallas	540.8	16,673	1,998	30.8	96.5	0.7	2.0	0.6	2.0	6.4	17.5	7.1	10.7	10.6	12.4
29,061		8	Daviess	563.3	8,361	2,558	14.8	97.0	1.1	1.2	0.6	1.6	6.5	19.3	7.8	9.9	10.6	11.6
29,063	41,140	3	DeKalb..........................	421.4	12,588	2,251	29.9	84.8	12.1	0.7	0.7	2.5	4.7	12.3	7.9	16.4	14.9	14.9
29,065		7	Dent	752.8	15,480	2,068	20.6	95.9	1.0	1.9	1.1	1.8	6.1	16.4	6.6	10.9	10.6	12.7
29,067		6	Douglas	813.6	13,300	2,213	16.3	96.9	0.8	2.1	0.6	1.6	5.5	16.0	6.1	9.8	9.9	12.2
29,069	28,380	7	Dunklin..........................	541.1	30,119	1,429	55.7	82.2	11.1	0.9	0.8	6.8	7.1	18.7	7.7	11.3	11.3	12.3
29,071	41,180	1	Franklin.........................	922.7	103,330	582	112.0	96.4	1.5	0.9	0.9	1.7	6.1	17.1	7.6	12.3	11.4	13.7
29,073		6	Gasconade......................	519.0	14,726	2,114	28.4	97.3	0.9	0.9	0.8	1.4	5.1	15.6	7.1	10.5	10.3	13.0
29,075		8	Gentry	491.4	6,665	2,699	13.6	96.9	1.2	0.8	0.7	1.8	7.4	17.6	7.3	12.0	10.2	12.2
29,077	44,180	2	Greene	675.3	289,805	240	429.2	90.2	4.5	1.6	2.9	3.8	6.1	14.8	13.7	14.1	11.6	11.5
29,079		7	Grundy	435.3	9,949	2,434	22.9	95.7	1.3	1.2	1.1	2.2	7.4	16.7	8.0	12.3	9.5	11.5
29,081		7	Harrison	722.5	8,524	2,546	11.8	96.3	1.0	1.0	0.7	2.2	6.4	17.9	6.9	10.5	10.3	11.4
29,083		6	Henry	696.9	21,718	1,743	31.2	95.2	1.8	1.5	0.7	2.4	6.1	16.2	6.5	11.2	10.9	12.4
29,085		8	Hickory	398.8	9,475	2,467	23.8	96.5	0.9	2.1	0.5	1.7	4.2	12.7	5.1	7.4	8.2	12.4
29,087		8	Holt..............................	462.7	4,413	2,867	9.5	96.9	0.7	1.6	0.6	1.3	5.1	15.0	5.4	10.0	10.4	13.8
29,089		6	Howard..........................	463.8	10,139	2,416	21.9	92.5	5.8	1.4	0.7	1.6	6.0	15.7	12.3	11.3	10.2	11.5
29,091	48,460	7	Howell	927.1	40,103	1,174	43.3	96.0	0.9	1.7	1.1	2.1	6.4	17.5	7.7	12.0	11.2	12.3
29,093		7	Iron..............................	550.3	10,226	2,409	18.6	95.9	2.0	1.6	0.4	1.8	4.8	16.1	6.9	10.3	11.8	13.2
29,095	28,140	1	Jackson.........................	604.5	698,895	94	1,156.2	64.8	25.0	1.3	2.8	9.2	6.7	17.0	8.3	15.5	12.4	12.5

1.   CBSA = Core Based Statistical Area. See Appendix A for explanation. See Appendix B for list of metropolitan areas with component counties.   2.   County type code from the Economic Research Service of USDA Rural-Urban Continuum Codes. See Appendix A for definition.   3.   Dry land or land partially or temporarily covered by water.   4.   May be of any race.

Table B. States and Counties — **Population and Households**

STATE County	Age (percent) (cont.) 55 to 64 years	65 to 74 years	75 years and over	Percent female	Total persons 2000	2010	Percent change 2000-2010	2010-2017	Components of change, 2010-2017 Births	Deaths	Net Migration	Households, 2012-2016 Number	Persons per household	Family households	Female family householder[1]	One person
	16	17	18	19	20	21	22	23	24	25	26	27	28	29	30	31
MISSISSIPPI— Cont'd																
Sunflower	12.1	7.8	5.3	47.2	34,369	29,385	-14.5	-11.6	2,374	2,141	-3,733	8,507	2.76	67.5	29.6	29.1
Tallahatchie	12.0	8.4	6.4	44.5	14,903	15,383	3.2	-8.2	1,143	1,110	-1,304	4,313	2.48	61.2	24.1	36.0
Tate	13.0	10.0	6.3	52.0	25,370	28,882	13.8	-1.5	2,414	2,015	-853	9,919	2.68	72.9	18.5	23.4
Tippah	12.8	9.8	6.4	51.2	20,826	22,232	6.8	-1.2	1,979	1,920	-314	8,400	2.59	73.3	11.5	22.8
Tishomingo	13.7	11.8	8.3	51.5	19,163	19,596	2.3	-0.3	1,454	2,049	551	7,768	2.48	71.7	13.0	25.0
Tunica	11.8	7.5	4.3	53.0	9,227	10,778	16.8	-7.0	1,398	730	-1,441	3,999	2.57	66.4	26.3	30.9
Union	11.9	9.6	6.8	51.0	25,362	27,134	7.0	5.2	2,652	2,037	818	10,298	2.69	69.8	12.2	27.3
Walthall	13.7	10.5	8.6	51.8	15,156	15,443	1.9	-6.1	1,297	1,330	-917	5,879	2.50	60.9	14.9	37.1
Warren	14.2	9.7	6.3	52.4	49,644	48,773	-1.8	-4.1	4,514	3,794	-2,732	18,476	2.56	66.8	20.1	29.3
Washington	14.1	9.3	5.7	53.5	62,977	51,135	-18.8	-9.6	5,509	4,280	-6,216	18,148	2.66	65.0	28.1	31.7
Wayne	13.7	9.5	7.2	51.8	21,216	20,747	-2.2	-1.5	2,106	1,593	-813	7,496	2.72	72.9	18.4	24.0
Webster	14.2	10.2	7.4	51.3	10,294	10,252	-0.4	-4.8	882	1,006	-364	3,950	2.49	73.3	15.5	25.5
Wilkinson	14.1	9.8	7.3	46.8	10,312	9,878	-4.2	-10.9	793	836	-1,047	2,877	2.85	63.8	24.3	33.7
Winston	14.2	10.9	8.6	51.1	20,160	19,198	-4.8	-5.0	1,441	1,605	-782	7,634	2.36	70.8	22.1	27.1
Yalobusha	14.8	11.6	7.8	51.9	13,051	12,678	-2.9	-1.4	1,135	1,226	-91	5,146	2.37	65.9	16.7	30.8
Yazoo	11.7	7.5	6.0	44.9	28,149	28,065	-0.3	-3.6	2,526	2,081	-1,469	8,754	2.72	66.0	26.6	30.7
MISSOURI	13.5	9.5	7.0	50.9	5,595,211	5,988,925	7.0	2.1	545,020	416,536	-2,166	2,372,362	2.48	64.5	12.0	29.3
Adair	10.5	8.1	6.4	51.7	24,977	25,607	2.5	-0.9	1,880	1,540	-571	9,462	2.41	54.2	7.3	35.3
Andrew	14.8	10.6	8.1	50.3	16,492	17,291	4.8	1.5	1,329	1,201	138	6,837	2.51	72.9	6.2	21.7
Atchison	14.6	13.7	11.2	50.3	6,430	5,685	-11.6	-7.2	388	548	-257	2,494	2.11	58.0	6.2	34.0
Audrain	13.3	9.8	7.6	54.5	25,853	25,529	-1.3	0.4	2,495	2,117	-253	9,255	2.58	64.0	10.8	30.5
Barry	14.8	11.7	8.4	49.5	34,010	35,597	4.7	0.2	3,034	2,959	18	13,248	2.67	70.6	9.1	24.7
Barton	15.0	10.8	8.9	50.7	12,541	12,402	-1.1	-4.5	1,034	1,011	-582	4,910	2.43	69.6	9.7	26.0
Bates	14.8	10.2	8.9	50.5	16,653	17,049	2.4	-4.2	1,361	1,509	-572	6,617	2.45	66.5	9.4	29.3
Benton	17.9	17.9	12.6	49.9	17,180	19,056	10.9	0.1	1,140	2,068	951	8,128	2.29	66.6	8.1	29.3
Bollinger	15.5	11.6	8.2	50.0	12,029	12,363	2.8	-0.5	967	951	-71	4,805	2.51	68.4	10.4	26.9
Boone	10.8	7.2	4.7	51.5	135,454	162,643	20.1	9.6	15,274	7,406	7,756	67,833	2.41	56.9	9.3	30.1
Buchanan	13.1	8.8	6.8	49.5	85,998	89,201	3.7	-0.2	8,499	6,851	-1,772	33,330	2.56	62.1	14.1	31.2
Butler	13.7	10.4	8.2	51.5	40,867	42,794	4.7	-0.3	4,022	4,044	-70	16,616	2.52	66.4	14.7	26.8
Caldwell	14.5	11.0	8.4	49.4	8,969	9,424	5.1	-3.4	693	717	-307	3,738	2.37	66.9	8.0	28.4
Callaway	13.5	9.6	6.2	48.7	40,766	44,330	8.7	1.6	3,657	2,725	-210	16,018	2.54	65.4	10.9	29.8
Camden	17.9	17.4	10.1	50.4	37,051	44,001	18.8	3.7	2,964	3,375	2,029	16,389	2.66	71.4	7.8	24.6
Cape Girardeau	12.6	9.2	7.3	51.5	68,693	75,674	10.2	3.3	6,612	5,458	1,379	29,831	2.50	63.2	9.1	28.2
Carroll	14.0	12.0	9.3	51.4	10,285	9,295	-9.6	-5.4	765	868	-398	3,703	2.40	66.9	9.5	29.2
Carter	14.9	11.7	7.8	51.6	5,941	6,265	5.5	-1.5	558	553	-102	2,480	2.50	61.5	12.1	32.7
Cass	13.7	9.3	7.2	51.2	82,092	99,505	21.2	4.2	8,651	6,506	2,136	38,045	2.64	73.5	9.7	21.9
Cedar	14.1	12.7	10.4	50.1	13,733	13,982	1.8	0.7	1,259	1,473	311	5,886	2.34	62.4	9.2	33.4
Chariton	15.9	11.8	11.6	50.1	8,438	7,827	-7.2	-4.4	623	675	-296	2,905	2.54	64.9	6.0	31.9
Christian	12.7	9.3	6.0	51.1	54,285	77,417	42.6	10.4	7,351	4,230	4,878	30,093	2.70	75.7	11.1	20.2
Clark	15.1	11.5	9.4	49.3	7,416	7,129	-3.9	-5.7	573	612	-370	2,837	2.39	66.8	7.2	28.0
Clay	12.4	8.4	5.5	50.9	184,006	221,950	20.6	9.4	22,153	12,015	10,843	88,389	2.61	67.2	11.0	26.2
Clinton	14.6	10.1	7.8	49.7	18,979	20,743	9.3	-0.9	1,656	1,794	-56	8,118	2.47	73.0	9.7	22.5
Cole	13.3	9.5	6.5	49.4	71,397	75,983	6.4	1.0	6,699	4,587	-1,356	29,658	2.42	64.3	12.1	29.6
Cooper	13.5	9.8	7.8	47.9	16,670	17,601	5.6	0.2	1,390	1,378	38	6,550	2.45	64.4	10.6	30.6
Crawford	15.1	11.3	7.8	50.5	22,804	24,696	8.3	-2.4	2,061	2,118	-528	9,290	2.60	66.5	10.4	28.5
Dade	15.8	13.1	10.1	49.1	7,923	7,882	-0.5	-3.7	492	750	-41	3,099	2.40	68.4	9.9	26.4
Dallas	15.7	11.2	8.5	50.1	15,661	16,777	7.1	-0.6	1,475	1,366	-213	6,150	2.65	74.2	10.4	20.4
Daviess	14.1	12.0	8.1	49.4	8,016	8,433	5.2	-0.9	825	643	-252	3,040	2.65	67.2	6.8	27.5
DeKalb	12.5	8.2	8.1	37.2	11,597	12,892	11.2	-2.4	795	837	-263	3,774	2.43	66.0	6.6	29.7
Dent	15.4	11.6	9.9	50.4	14,927	15,654	4.9	-1.1	1,296	1,399	-66	5,889	2.61	66.2	8.6	28.5
Douglas	16.5	13.7	10.3	50.0	13,084	13,686	4.6	-2.8	1,078	1,168	-293	5,110	2.61	70.4	5.7	27.9
Dunklin	13.5	10.1	8.1	52.0	33,155	31,953	-3.6	-5.7	3,222	3,134	-1,931	12,680	2.41	63.6	16.2	32.1
Franklin	15.1	9.8	7.0	50.3	93,807	101,492	8.2	1.8	8,987	7,165	84	40,197	2.52	70.1	10.7	25.2
Gasconade	16.1	12.0	10.3	50.1	15,342	15,215	-0.8	-3.2	1,132	1,452	-158	6,168	2.37	68.1	7.7	27.3
Gentry	13.7	9.4	10.2	51.9	6,861	6,738	-1.8	-1.1	683	621	-134	2,677	2.43	64.0	8.0	29.3
Greene	11.9	9.0	7.1	51.2	240,391	275,178	14.5	5.3	25,764	19,391	8,340	119,141	2.30	58.4	10.2	31.5
Grundy	13.2	10.8	10.7	51.4	10,432	10,261	-1.6	-3.0	1,066	994	-381	4,056	2.44	64.7	11.3	30.2
Harrison	14.4	11.3	10.8	50.9	8,850	8,957	1.2	-4.8	800	821	-410	3,586	2.33	66.1	9.5	28.8
Henry	15.0	12.4	9.3	50.9	21,997	22,272	1.3	-2.5	1,869	2,246	-161	9,420	2.30	64.4	9.9	28.9
Hickory	16.8	19.6	13.7	50.7	8,940	9,627	7.7	-1.6	550	1,059	358	3,962	2.32	67.5	6.9	27.7
Holt	15.4	12.9	12.0	50.8	5,351	4,912	-8.2	-10.2	368	448	-423	2,109	2.10	65.8	8.0	29.8
Howard	14.7	10.1	8.3	50.0	10,212	10,148	-0.6	-0.1	866	692	-185	3,760	2.50	65.7	9.9	29.9
Howell	13.3	11.1	8.4	51.2	37,238	40,400	8.5	-0.7	3,703	3,625	-349	16,214	2.45	66.0	11.9	27.4
Iron	15.9	11.9	9.1	50.1	10,697	10,628	-0.6	-3.8	765	1,018	-151	4,050	2.43	66.2	11.5	28.1
Jackson	13.0	8.5	6.1	51.6	654,880	674,124	2.9	3.7	68,895	44,728	1,098	276,857	2.43	58.9	15.0	33.9

1. No spouse present.

STATE County	Housing units, 2017 (cont.)								Civilian labor force, 2017				Civilian employment[6], 2012-2016		
	Occupied units										Unemployment		Percent		
	Owner-occupied					Renter-occupied									
				Median owner cost as a percent of income			Median rent as a percent of income[2]	Sub-standard units[4] (percent)		Percent change, 2016-2017				Management, business, science, and arts	Construction, production, and maintenance occupations
	Total	Percent	Median value[1]	With a mort-gage	Without a mort-gage[2]	Median rent[3]			Total		Total	Rate[5]	Total		
	89	90	91	92	93	94	95	96	97	98	99	100	101	102	103
MISSISSIPPI— Cont'd															
Sunflower	8,507	56.6	71,100	25.7	12.9	586	33.2	4.7	8,091	-3.1	666	8.2	8,471	27.8	29.9
Tallahatchie	4,313	75.8	61,500	23.1	13.1	415	27.4	3.1	5,631	-1.9	298	5.3	3,599	34.6	29.6
Tate	9,919	74.3	110,000	22.7	11.0	691	26.2	5.3	12,138	0.4	608	5.0	11,235	30.0	30.9
Tippah	8,400	75.5	82,700	22.5	10.5	537	25.9	2.4	9,486	0.8	425	4.5	8,752	25.1	40.8
Tishomingo	7,768	75.0	79,300	20.8	10.5	522	25.9	2.9	8,308	0.5	415	5.0	7,951	22.6	38.1
Tunica	3,999	39.5	87,500	24.3	10.2	708	30.7	8.1	4,597	-0.4	267	5.8	4,176	23.4	18.2
Union	10,298	71.7	86,700	20.9	10.3	665	25.7	4.0	13,976	2.2	502	3.6	11,211	25.0	35.9
Walthall	5,879	85.5	93,300	27.1	14.0	550	29.0	5.4	5,008	-0.7	341	6.8	5,359	29.3	35.0
Warren	18,476	63.1	109,500	20.9	10.4	655	33.0	2.8	20,649	-0.9	1,182	5.7	19,481	35.4	23.8
Washington	18,148	55.6	73,000	22.2	12.7	637	36.8	2.6	17,237	-3.0	1,281	7.4	17,128	31.2	24.2
Wayne	7,496	81.7	74,000	19.8	12.6	506	30.6	2.6	7,505	-0.5	471	6.3	7,558	21.0	40.6
Webster	3,950	72.6	79,900	21.5	10.7	484	35.0	3.8	3,908	-0.1	204	5.2	3,754	36.2	30.8
Wilkinson	2,877	80.5	61,900	24.8	17.1	435	29.7	1.5	2,836	-0.1	247	8.7	2,591	29.6	30.6
Winston	7,634	68.0	80,400	21.6	12.5	630	32.5	3.9	7,245	1.9	432	6.0	7,211	30.1	33.2
Yalobusha	5,146	74.4	72,300	21.1	12.5	503	25.8	2.8	5,005	2.3	275	5.5	5,038	19.6	41.2
Yazoo	8,754	60.3	72,100	24.6	12.9	583	35.3	5.2	9,212	-0.5	555	6.0	8,188	25.8	29.3
MISSOURI	237,2,362	66.8	141,200	20.4	11.4	759	28.9	2.0	3,050,725	-0.9	114,593	3.8	2,835,183	35.4	22.2
Adair	9,462	59.0	112,100	19.2	10.8	598	36.8	1.4	10,204	-1.7	445	4.4	11,138	37.1	20.6
Andrew	6,837	77.1	131,800	21.6	10.0	736	25.7	2.6	9,919	-1.2	311	3.1	8,515	32.5	27.1
Atchison	2,494	69.3	81,700	21.1	12.5	540	21.6	0.6	2,817	-1.0	99	3.5	2,645	33.6	27.2
Audrain	9,255	68.6	93,400	19.8	11.2	636	26.2	1.8	10,937	-1.9	387	3.5	10,640	26.5	31.8
Barry	13,248	74.9	112,900	21.3	12.4	583	27.7	3.1	15,109	-0.7	519	3.4	14,201	24.2	40.1
Barton	4,910	68.4	94,900	22.4	12.0	498	29.4	2.4	5,116	-3.9	215	4.2	5,059	30.3	33.6
Bates	6,617	70.7	107,500	20.4	12.3	619	26.8	2.1	8,116	-0.6	354	4.4	7,271	27.9	31.1
Benton	8,128	81.6	110,000	23.5	12.7	593	32.4	3.2	7,120	-2.0	369	5.2	6,176	28.7	31.4
Bollinger	4,805	81.0	94,400	21.2	10.1	586	27.8	2.9	5,382	-1.5	238	4.4	4,854	23.7	39.5
Boone	67,833	54.6	171,400	19.4	10.0	803	32.3	1.5	97,496	-0.8	2,543	2.6	91,504	46.1	13.5
Buchanan	33,330	63.0	112,400	19.7	11.3	715	28.8	2.0	46,169	-1.2	1,601	3.5	41,752	27.6	27.8
Butler	16,616	64.0	97,200	20.5	12.2	659	30.5	1.8	18,085	-3.9	835	4.6	17,121	29.0	27.1
Caldwell	3,738	74.9	99,100	20.5	13.2	622	27.5	4.0	4,465	-0.3	179	4.0	3,842	30.9	31.4
Callaway	16,018	72.1	124,900	19.9	10.0	666	25.9	2.7	21,514	-1.5	746	3.5	19,749	30.8	26.4
Camden	16,389	77.6	171,700	23.0	10.6	697	29.9	2.0	18,475	-1.4	889	4.8	17,044	29.0	21.9
Cape Girardeau	29,831	64.4	147,400	19.4	10.9	716	28.4	1.9	40,154	-1.6	1,382	3.4	37,365	34.0	21.5
Carroll	3,703	74.4	79,900	18.3	12.3	530	30.3	2.7	4,716	-1.2	196	4.2	3,814	28.8	31.8
Carter	2,480	70.1	95,600	23.0	10.6	555	29.5	4.8	2,471	-2.9	148	6.0	2,430	33.3	28.0
Cass	38,045	75.2	161,000	21.0	11.6	924	27.6	2.2	54,502	-0.1	1,897	3.5	49,212	34.1	25.8
Cedar	5,886	68.2	87,800	22.4	13.3	602	32.0	0.9	5,667	-2.3	233	4.1	5,071	29.1	29.1
Chariton	2,905	76.6	80,200	18.5	12.4	517	26.8	1.7	3,780	-2.0	132	3.5	3,303	27.8	32.5
Christian	30,093	73.3	148,000	20.5	10.9	786	29.4	2.3	43,119	-0.6	1,329	3.1	38,307	35.7	20.4
Clark	2,837	75.3	85,900	20.5	11.1	532	20.4	2.8	3,160	-6.3	179	5.7	3,178	26.1	41.2
Clay	88,389	69.9	156,600	19.9	11.4	851	26.2	1.3	134,548	0.3	4,827	3.6	120,744	36.8	20.3
Clinton	8,118	73.8	138,400	19.5	11.6	772	24.0	1.7	11,051	0.3	432	3.9	9,863	27.9	30.9
Cole	29,658	67.9	150,700	19.7	10.0	608	23.5	1.4	38,860	-1.5	1,140	2.9	36,537	38.4	19.2
Cooper	6,550	70.6	122,900	19.2	11.4	655	27.1	1.7	7,348	-1.9	271	3.7	7,845	28.8	25.7
Crawford	9,290	72.3	116,500	20.9	13.2	610	30.5	2.7	10,644	-1.8	498	4.7	9,425	25.8	33.3
Dade	3,099	77.5	80,300	22.8	11.6	600	29.1	3.0	3,544	-1.3	121	3.4	3,274	33.0	31.1
Dallas	6,150	73.0	101,300	23.0	10.0	594	25.4	3.5	6,917	-0.7	324	4.7	5,813	24.2	32.7
Daviess	3,040	78.1	97,700	21.2	12.1	546	26.1	4.3	4,031	-2.1	134	3.3	3,419	29.7	31.3
DeKalb	3,774	63.0	104,600	18.9	12.4	507	22.3	1.6	5,031	-1.1	192	3.8	4,178	31.5	31.2
Dent	5,889	71.4	100,300	22.3	10.9	479	25.9	2.7	6,040	-2.7	258	4.3	5,962	25.6	31.7
Douglas	5,110	77.7	99,900	23.0	12.5	546	31.3	3.7	4,971	-2.3	235	4.7	4,998	18.8	38.1
Dunklin	12,680	62.7	68,500	19.3	12.3	530	31.5	2.7	12,219	-4.9	813	6.7	11,537	26.3	31.2
Franklin	40,197	72.9	152,500	21.3	11.0	706	26.5	2.0	52,277	-0.9	1,891	3.6	49,147	29.1	32.8
Gasconade	6,168	74.6	126,600	19.9	10.8	599	29.6	2.9	7,678	-0.4	300	3.9	6,573	26.9	35.5
Gentry	2,677	74.0	84,800	18.8	13.0	576	24.8	2.9	3,572	-0.6	102	2.9	3,065	33.6	28.0
Greene	119,141	58.3	133,700	20.1	10.0	707	30.8	1.5	147,999	-0.5	4,502	3.0	136,536	35.3	19.1
Grundy	4,056	68.7	83,300	18.4	11.7	570	24.9	5.2	4,744	-3.3	172	3.6	4,390	29.9	33.7
Harrison	3,586	71.2	73,900	21.2	12.1	565	27.4	4.9	3,863	-2.8	137	3.5	3,804	32.6	26.8
Henry	9,420	74.9	88,600	21.7	12.7	691	28.6	3.6	9,663	-2.4	405	4.2	9,160	28.1	31.2
Hickory	3,962	80.8	89,800	25.3	12.8	564	35.1	1.8	3,691	-0.2	166	4.5	2,976	27.3	30.6
Holt	2,109	69.7	90,200	20.1	10.8	454	23.8	2.1	2,669	-0.7	78	2.9	2,140	33.0	31.1
Howard	3,760	75.7	107,600	20.6	10.0	648	29.1	2.0	4,987	-1.0	192	3.9	4,805	35.2	27.0
Howell	16,214	69.5	103,500	22.1	11.4	577	28.5	2.8	15,467	-4.1	758	4.9	16,415	28.4	28.2
Iron	4,050	69.5	81,800	19.5	11.4	542	26.8	3.0	3,486	-6.3	228	6.5	3,851	20.3	31.9
Jackson	276,857	58.5	127,400	21.0	12.6	820	29.6	1.9	363,854	-0.2	15,851	4.4	331,990	36.2	20.1

1. Specified owner-occupied units.　2. A value of 10.0 represents 10 percent or less; a value of 50.0 represents 50 percent or more.　3. Specified renter-occupied units.　4. Overcrowded or lacking complete plumbing facilities.　5. Percent of civilian labor force.　6. Civilian employed persons 16 years old and over.

Table B. States and Counties — Nonfarm Employment and Agriculture

	Private nonfarm establishments, employment and payroll, 2016									Agriculture, 2012			
		Employment						Annual payroll		Farms			
												Percent with:	
STATE County	Number of establishments	Total	Health care and social assistance	Manufacturing	Retail trade	Finance and insurance	Professional, scientific, and technical services	Total (mil dol)	Average per employee (dollars)	Number	Fewer than 50 acres	500 acres or more	Farm operators whose principal occupation is farming (percent)
	104	105	106	107	108	109	110	111	112	113	114	115	116
MISSISSIPPI— Cont'd													
Sunflower	439	5,439	1,022	354	1,005	242	57	179	32,841	350	22.6	44.0	59.7
Tallahatchie	173	1,814	446	D	270	34	44	59	32,626	509	13.6	28.7	38.9
Tate	378	3,923	600	491	830	175	89	118	30,156	569	25.3	14.1	38.8
Tippah	356	5,280	564	2,151	650	137	78	165	31,187	691	25.2	5.4	32.0
Tishomingo	358	5,003	588	2,287	631	119	101	156	31,112	287	22.0	3.8	36.2
Tunica	204	7,319	227	513	342	70	18	215	29,427	108	7.4	62.0	64.8
Union	507	9,608	1,090	3,901	1,179	218	95	351	36,579	688	29.1	6.4	25.3
Walthall	214	1,911	256	369	352	66	14	58	30,221	684	30.7	4.8	49.9
Warren	1,013	16,058	2,452	3,066	2,557	375	394	621	38,679	238	18.5	19.7	39.9
Washington	1,136	14,338	2,922	1,173	2,853	343	340	456	31,812	284	18.7	47.5	71.1
Wayne	373	4,226	654	808	975	217	98	143	33,810	508	34.4	5.5	48.0
Webster	155	1,363	289	209	210	50	73	52	38,081	362	20.7	11.0	32.9
Wilkinson	134	1,359	318	132	271	37	11	39	28,472	198	17.7	23.7	41.4
Winston	378	4,990	663	1,465	941	92	74	166	33,335	506	27.1	9.5	40.9
Yalobusha	182	2,429	354	984	328	96	12	75	30,891	364	21.2	13.7	50.5
Yazoo	386	4,116	977	546	769	140	148	136	33,017	672	14.3	25.9	49.9
MISSOURI	160,912	2,494,720	420,073	260,451	324,717	131,863	156,958	112,072	44,924	99,171	25.5	13.7	44.2
Adair	630	7,929	2,105	586	1,485	216	275	252	31,784	822	19.6	16.7	44.0
Andrew	314	1,758	334	32	352	59	52	51	29,176	826	29.5	12.8	42.1
Atchison	202	1,296	282	18	292	87	29	38	29,171	395	12.9	36.5	66.6
Audrain	545	6,998	1,063	1,819	1,135	248	129	256	36,579	1,015	18.6	25.1	55.8
Barry	738	14,648	2,180	4,963	1,605	291	D	573	39,146	1,427	31.1	8.4	43.5
Barton	264	2,667	473	358	506	145	107	80	30,126	940	24.0	22.8	45.7
Bates	365	2,773	785	70	581	219	77	86	30,887	1,169	23.4	18.1	46.6
Benton	383	2,254	365	172	738	115	63	54	23,963	800	18.5	13.1	52.8
Bollinger	215	1,443	364	167	307	49	31	40	27,541	788	16.9	12.8	42.4
Boone	4,671	77,527	17,549	4,133	12,833	7,279	3,869	2,946	38,005	1,171	39.5	8.6	38.3
Buchanan	2,284	44,180	8,638	10,317	5,713	1,680	1,315	1,837	41,574	727	29.4	13.1	44.4
Butler	1,242	15,479	4,266	2,345	3,006	575	332	508	32,834	509	23.8	24.6	47.9
Caldwell	143	1,118	109	38	410	57	18	35	30,979	1,035	24.3	10.6	41.0
Callaway	738	12,098	2,515	1,734	1,319	277	308	490	40,492	1,417	28.4	9.7	35.5
Camden	1,442	13,229	2,420	430	3,246	401	914	434	32,783	533	16.3	12.0	42.2
Cape Girardeau	2,446	38,503	10,591	3,735	6,207	1,253	1,231	1,430	37,149	1,139	29.5	10.2	47.8
Carroll	223	1,636	400	191	285	103	36	48	29,373	1,112	18.4	18.2	39.8
Carter	182	1,006	265	210	164	53	12	24	23,762	196	23.5	17.9	45.4
Cass	1,972	21,209	3,084	2,799	4,439	605	493	675	31,848	1,495	41.1	9.2	46.3
Cedar	281	2,420	586	364	414	94	59	65	26,788	819	19.9	10.4	45.2
Chariton	218	1,354	295	90	274	77	28	41	30,604	1,120	17.1	21.3	47.8
Christian	1,760	14,957	1,777	1,468	2,891	598	965	446	29,820	1,177	36.4	5.6	43.8
Clark	145	943	130	43	266	68	11	22	23,558	673	13.5	20.8	40.9
Clay	5,079	100,582	13,915	14,301	12,441	2,342	15,693	5,114	50,842	578	48.8	10.2	42.6
Clinton	378	2,968	992	157	467	125	77	96	32,389	758	35.1	8.8	38.5
Cole	2,262	35,026	6,746	2,289	5,586	1,963	1,533	1,373	39,190	1,055	24.1	5.4	38.2
Cooper	403	3,934	841	220	800	137	76	112	28,538	928	16.4	17.3	42.8
Crawford	505	5,741	896	2,014	650	155	129	197	34,371	679	20.2	12.8	40.4
Dade	141	1,251	41	304	165	35	18	37	29,644	734	21.5	16.5	47.0
Dallas	316	2,440	1,000	161	533	116	40	45	18,373	1,188	31.7	7.6	46.8
Daviess	150	924	83	214	230	57	29	26	27,708	1,199	23.4	12.9	36.8
DeKalb	215	1,956	400	38	515	218	20	64	32,755	863	22.7	12.6	40.3
Dent	397	3,632	839	665	509	175	48	125	34,544	673	21.0	13.5	35.7
Douglas	204	2,090	283	615	463	69	33	51	24,454	984	18.6	10.9	43.2
Dunklin	797	7,157	2,203	458	1,394	302	137	185	25,790	345	22.6	42.6	63.5
Franklin	2,663	35,408	4,735	8,946	4,983	1,054	926	1,315	37,125	1,841	33.6	5.1	32.6
Gasconade	415	4,246	878	964	673	174	84	110	25,928	859	14.6	10.0	39.1
Gentry	192	1,818	808	D	275	60	13	47	26,004	708	20.2	16.2	40.8
Greene	8,671	154,610	29,063	12,645	20,178	7,371	7,111	6,132	39,663	1,752	48.8	4.5	43.9
Grundy	246	2,631	632	725	469	75	51	84	32,089	689	23.1	12.0	42.7
Harrison	204	2,004	513	48	660	115	22	50	25,128	1,051	18.5	17.4	42.7
Henry	581	6,900	1,830	1,083	1,202	229	126	246	35,658	894	21.8	21.5	54.7
Hickory	152	842	213	D	311	41	21	20	23,633	487	14.4	18.1	56.5
Holt	135	928	179	182	161	40	D	32	35,001	408	20.3	26.7	49.3
Howard	204	2,226	615	270	266	72	66	63	28,464	765	17.0	19.0	36.6
Howell	1,123	12,416	3,268	2,265	2,207	406	319	386	31,075	1,535	24.8	10.1	41.3
Iron	239	1,839	618	73	299	63	16	61	33,331	273	15.4	13.6	46.2
Jackson	19,144	338,535	56,859	24,887	37,550	24,955	28,012	17,037	50,325	701	57.5	5.6	38.7

STATE County	Government employment and payroll, 2012									Local government finances				
			March payroll (percent of total)							General revenue				
												Taxes		
													Per capita[1] (dollars)	
	Full-time equivalent employees	March payroll (dollars)	Adminis-tration, judicial, and legal	Police and corrections	Fire protection	Highways and transpor-tation	Health and welfare	Natural resources and utilities	Education and libraries	Total (mil dol)	Inter-govern-mental (mil dol)	Total (mil dol)	Total	Property
	171	172	173	174	175	176	177	178	179	180	181	182	183	184
MISSISSIPPI— Cont'd														
Sunflower	2,017	5,682,629	3.7	5.0	1.7	2.5	30.7	1.5	53.7	155.8	63.4	20.6	724	694
Tallahatchie	772	1,986,175	8.5	7.5	0.2	4.7	29.5	0.9	48.6	34.1	21.3	8.2	542	517
Tate	1,430	4,623,219	2.1	2.6	1.1	1.1	0.9	1.2	90.6	106.6	62.4	20.6	724	690
Tippah	915	2,435,046	6.8	3.3	0.2	2.1	22.7	2.8	61.0	68.1	38.2	11.3	512	467
Tishomingo	694	1,807,779	8.5	7.3	1.2	2.3	1.2	4.4	73.2	46.2	29.7	10.1	515	495
Tunica	738	1,778,465	10.4	23.6	0.0	4.7	6.1	9.7	45.3	86.8	57.0	21.4	2,043	1,507
Union	1,025	2,626,662	4.5	7.6	2.0	3.0	1.3	10.2	71.3	61.0	37.8	16.4	596	576
Walthall	518	1,141,649	3.1	5.7	0.2	3.0	2.1	0.6	83.4	45.4	21.5	8.4	559	539
Warren	1,819	5,138,472	4.6	6.1	7.5	3.0	0.3	7.0	69.2	170.1	68.3	68.7	1,429	1,171
Washington	3,566	9,118,481	5.7	7.2	2.5	3.0	32.4	4.6	43.1	298.0	98.6	52.7	1,060	977
Wayne	1,112	3,158,182	4.3	5.0	0.4	2.8	39.5	1.7	44.9	88.7	32.9	10.5	508	496
Webster	496	1,240,223	6.4	4.4	0.1	3.7	24.5	1.5	58.9	36.7	19.1	6.3	623	599
Wilkinson	427	1,032,081	12.7	10.5	0.3	7.1	2.1	3.0	61.9	56.6	14.2	5.9	630	607
Winston	620	1,506,689	8.7	16.0	2.1	4.3	1.9	2.4	64.2	46.2	24.1	11.5	602	576
Yalobusha	708	1,878,214	6.3	4.5	1.3	4.5	39.0	4.3	40.1	42.2	18.6	8.6	691	675
Yazoo	1,019	2,766,051	5.8	9.4	4.3	6.7	2.3	10.2	60.9	70.1	40.4	21.3	755	728
MISSOURI	X	X	X	X	X	X	X	X	X	X	X	X	X	X
Adair	916	2,496,611	7.3	5.8	2.8	3.2	13.2	5.6	59.0	68.7	23.1	26.9	1,051	570
Andrew	515	1,433,245	5.1	4.2	0.9	3.0	4.0	5.7	76.7	48.4	17.6	23.4	1,345	1,199
Atchison	319	829,091	7.7	5.0	0.1	22.0	10.0	5.1	49.6	22.0	10.2	9.7	1,755	1,294
Audrain	1,347	4,107,516	4.1	5.9	0.2	2.5	49.7	3.5	33.4	133.2	34.7	34.4	1,343	940
Barry	1,307	3,855,776	4.7	5.7	1.8	2.3	1.6	5.6	77.7	94.7	45.3	37.8	1,063	636
Barton	723	2,240,324	3.5	2.9	0.7	1.9	43.2	5.8	41.8	83.5	14.1	10.7	866	674
Bates	840	2,585,067	4.7	5.8	0.3	2.0	37.0	4.7	45.0	42.1	19.9	13.4	805	577
Benton	748	1,949,137	5.2	5.4	0.1	2.8	27.9	2.2	53.8	41.5	16.6	13.2	696	514
Bollinger	361	902,476	5.5	5.4	0.3	4.6	0.0	1.6	82.4	21.6	12.4	7.2	585	414
Boone	6,008	20,052,275	7.9	5.3	3.3	2.8	2.7	11.3	63.5	497.3	161.0	228.2	1,354	805
Buchanan	3,079	9,642,143	5.9	9.4	5.3	3.7	2.5	5.0	66.6	296.5	114.1	129.1	1,439	812
Butler	1,617	4,243,462	2.3	5.6	2.5	3.4	0.0	4.2	79.9	124.9	58.1	43.7	1,015	498
Caldwell	485	1,279,896	6.3	9.6	0.0	2.5	7.8	5.3	68.5	29.5	14.3	7.8	847	648
Callaway	1,265	3,154,685	6.9	9.5	2.6	4.3	5.4	8.0	63.0	88.2	36.4	34.7	782	576
Camden	1,451	4,272,326	7.8	13.4	5.1	5.6	4.2	2.2	60.3	116.5	32.4	68.3	1,557	990
Cape Girardeau	2,602	6,797,882	6.6	9.1	5.9	6.5	1.2	10.3	58.6	207.7	74.1	101.6	1,320	702
Carroll	390	1,096,814	9.3	3.7	1.4	4.2	4.3	6.6	70.1	26.7	11.7	10.0	1,101	852
Carter	278	723,988	1.6	5.8	0.0	2.9	3.2	2.5	72.4	15.4	9.6	3.9	625	446
Cass	4,195	14,748,324	5.3	6.9	4.3	2.7	12.2	4.5	63.7	380.9	126.2	139.6	1,391	927
Cedar	643	1,585,692	4.7	5.5	0.2	3.0	25.1	6.6	54.3	50.4	15.5	11.7	850	590
Chariton	295	762,719	8.8	6.7	0.2	3.7	5.8	6.0	68.4	20.7	8.4	9.5	1,240	969
Christian	2,200	6,653,224	5.3	7.1	2.0	1.8	0.2	4.7	77.8	188.4	89.3	71.0	890	611
Clark	372	840,780	6.1	5.8	0.0	4.4	21.9	7.3	53.6	21.0	7.2	6.3	911	738
Clay	12,186	43,650,964	3.1	4.3	2.0	0.8	42.4	2.3	44.6	1,333.0	239.3	340.1	1,495	1,078
Clinton	670	2,036,971	7.0	9.3	0.4	4.7	2.3	8.2	67.6	52.6	24.6	20.4	993	788
Cole	2,439	7,947,888	7.8	8.8	4.1	4.5	3.5	5.9	65.1	213.9	62.0	116.3	1,523	890
Cooper	744	2,121,619	5.8	7.9	1.4	3.1	23.2	4.8	52.9	62.0	16.7	23.7	1,353	687
Crawford	756	1,998,530	5.7	8.1	0.0	3.7	7.3	5.6	68.1	45.1	21.5	17.0	683	512
Dade	452	949,754	5.1	2.9	0.0	1.2	37.3	2.9	50.6	20.8	9.6	6.2	824	608
Dallas	463	1,037,873	7.3	5.8	0.3	5.2	0.8	2.2	78.1	31.3	18.2	10.5	627	394
Daviess	341	863,936	7.8	3.3	0.0	3.1	2.5	7.8	74.9	20.0	9.8	7.4	895	719
DeKalb	227	666,095	6.8	3.3	0.0	4.5	3.8	6.9	74.5	18.0	7.8	6.8	522	356
Dent	677	1,899,125	6.9	2.7	0.2	3.0	33.8	4.1	48.4	46.0	16.0	9.7	622	406
Douglas	383	1,073,499	10.7	2.4	0.0	4.9	5.0	5.3	70.1	32.6	12.6	16.6	1,225	824
Dunklin	1,473	3,567,888	5.4	6.8	1.4	3.0	1.6	10.3	68.2	82.8	44.0	27.3	859	614
Franklin	3,292	11,002,286	4.9	8.8	2.3	3.4	4.3	2.7	72.9	276.7	102.6	133.5	1,317	868
Gasconade	880	2,347,282	3.9	4.6	0.0	3.4	28.6	4.8	53.1	70.3	15.8	18.8	1,257	905
Gentry	345	893,935	12.0	4.7	0.4	7.4	4.6	5.3	65.1	20.8	9.7	7.8	1,144	911
Greene	10,039	36,380,689	4.7	8.2	3.7	4.6	1.4	13.2	55.1	880.5	308.6	410.2	1,462	763
Grundy	761	1,960,447	2.6	5.1	1.0	3.5	14.2	6.8	64.8	55.4	22.3	10.8	1,048	654
Harrison	594	1,570,497	5.2	2.6	0.2	3.0	37.3	7.0	42.9	43.2	13.0	10.7	1,229	806
Henry	1,267	4,585,264	3.2	3.7	1.3	1.0	61.3	2.7	26.7	117.2	50.1	23.1	1,045	588
Hickory	326	851,720	6.0	4.2	0.0	2.3	0.0	2.3	84.9	21.9	12.6	6.7	714	572
Holt	184	461,150	11.3	6.1	0.0	5.3	1.7	7.2	68.0	16.0	6.1	7.4	1,595	1,143
Howard	396	983,070	7.8	7.5	0.4	5.0	4.3	9.4	64.8	23.9	8.7	11.5	1,135	911
Howell	1,537	3,973,191	5.5	5.3	1.4	3.4	4.8	7.9	71.2	100.7	49.7	31.7	781	439
Iron	459	1,303,360	4.7	4.4	0.6	6.5	6.1	1.8	75.7	26.1	13.0	10.3	991	765
Jackson	27,447	101,433,064	7.4	14.7	9.5	6.2	0.7	5.5	54.6	3,343.9	905.1	1,696.2	2,504	1,116

1. Based on the resident population estimated as of July 1 of the year shown.

Table B. States and Counties — Local Government Finances, Government Employment, and Income Taxes

STATE County	Local government finances (cont.)									Government employment, 2016			Individual income tax returns, 2015		
	Direct general expenditure							Debt outstanding							
	Total (mil dol)	Per capita[1] (dollars)	Percent of total for:					Total (mil dol)	Per capita[1] (dollars)	Federal civilian	Federal military	State and local	Number of returns	Mean adjusted gross income	Mean income tax
			Education	Health and hospitals	Police protection	Public welfare	Highways								
	185	186	187	188	189	190	191	192	193	194	195	196	197	198	199
MISSISSIPPI— Cont'd															
Sunflower	160.1	5,631	46.7	34.5	2.9	0.1	5.4	30.8	1,085	52	131	3,438	9,750	33,994	2,983
Tallahatchie	39.2	2,596	54.2	1.1	5.0	0.0	7.9	12.7	843	43	69	1,000	5,020	32,801	2,456
Tate	144.1	5,057	68.2	0.5	2.9	0.0	3.0	96.6	3,389	86	156	1,556	11,670	44,071	4,084
Tippah	68.2	3,095	49.3	23.7	3.2	0.2	8.8	13.9	629	61	127	1,228	8,780	40,260	3,291
Tishomingo	53.8	2,746	50.8	1.1	4.8	0.0	7.0	25.8	1,315	62	112	854	7,460	42,013	3,403
Tunica	103.7	9,896	24.0	1.9	8.0	0.7	5.8	114.9	10,965	21	59	811	4,740	30,680	2,375
Union	59.7	2,178	65.6	1.4	6.1	0.0	5.6	32.4	1,180	44	163	1,215	11,420	42,938	3,692
Walthall	45.0	2,981	52.1	26.1	4.3	0.2	4.8	1.9	128	29	84	619	5,590	39,747	3,110
Warren	169.5	3,526	45.5	1.1	6.6	0.2	7.1	264.3	5,496	2,283	315	2,266	21,100	47,188	4,774
Washington	305.6	6,143	28.7	43.2	3.9	0.1	4.1	140.1	2,816	420	289	3,628	20,010	38,163	3,647
Wayne	70.5	3,414	47.5	34.9	3.4	0.1	5.6	14.5	700	36	118	1,231	8,260	46,511	4,736
Webster	31.4	3,130	63.8	1.3	4.6	0.0	7.8	7.1	706	32	56	439	3,970	41,742	3,445
Wilkinson	55.4	5,871	26.6	28.9	2.5	0.1	3.6	35.9	3,804	0	46	528	3,500	37,807	2,955
Winston	45.6	2,397	54.2	1.3	6.9	0.1	7.3	5.2	272	36	103	770	7,460	40,184	3,724
Yalobusha	40.4	3,257	39.3	27.4	4.0	0.0	10.5	17.9	1,447	67	72	824	5,300	37,028	2,823
Yazoo	75.1	2,663	51.5	1.3	5.5	0.3	5.8	42.6	1,510	849	134	1,434	9,570	39,204	3,517
MISSOURI	X	X	X	X	X	X	X	X	X	58,526	35,042	377,849	2,787,570	58,387	7,412
Adair	66.2	2,589	44.3	3.2	5.6	7.5	7.7	43.5	1,700	80	80	2,385	9,530	44,308	4,386
Andrew	36.8	2,114	65.6	3.0	5.9	1.0	6.2	25.6	1,468	32	58	723	8,330	55,303	5,884
Atchison	22.0	3,990	52.6	2.6	2.8	0.0	17.0	6.5	1,173	32	18	342	2,540	50,656	5,456
Audrain	139.4	5,440	36.1	40.4	2.1	3.8	3.0	68.4	2,669	77	80	2,282	10,650	43,146	3,937
Barry	100.1	2,815	59.9	3.2	4.9	0.0	15.0	67.2	1,892	106	122	1,455	14,070	43,158	4,317
Barton	83.6	6,780	22.2	65.7	1.4	0.0	2.7	35.3	2,861	40	40	844	5,060	42,796	3,933
Bates	44.5	2,660	58.6	0.1	9.7	6.8	7.3	46.0	2,754	59	61	1,102	7,060	44,045	4,002
Benton	41.9	2,209	51.5	5.5	3.4	22.2	5.5	22.9	1,210	101	63	946	7,870	38,224	3,254
Bollinger	21.1	1,700	73.8	1.0	4.3	0.0	7.9	3.1	248	24	40	443	4,640	38,597	2,763
Boone	580.4	3,444	44.8	3.1	4.3	0.2	6.2	2,592.5	15,382	2,513	597	28,974	78,330	61,780	8,208
Buchanan	261.5	2,915	51.6	2.2	9.4	0.7	5.3	599.9	6,688	539	309	6,419	39,150	48,760	5,220
Butler	122.1	2,837	60.0	0.0	6.4	0.0	5.4	48.6	1,129	742	142	2,783	17,570	41,492	4,139
Caldwell	28.6	3,124	59.8	1.8	3.5	5.7	7.6	9.9	1,087	41	30	603	3,850	46,465	3,988
Callaway	85.8	1,936	53.8	4.3	8.4	0.0	6.7	57.3	1,293	125	140	3,760	19,590	46,865	4,457
Camden	113.7	2,593	47.6	3.7	9.0	0.0	11.7	112.7	2,570	78	148	1,822	19,930	49,294	5,621
Cape Girardeau	211.7	2,751	54.0	0.3	5.4	0.0	9.9	197.3	2,564	405	282	5,930	35,320	56,141	6,738
Carroll	27.9	3,076	59.3	3.2	3.9	0.0	11.1	12.4	1,360	43	30	566	4,110	44,886	4,259
Carter	15.8	2,520	74.5	2.8	1.9	0.0	3.9	29.2	4,657	88	21	374	2,400	34,934	2,599
Cass	400.2	3,987	50.4	13.7	3.1	0.3	5.8	468.7	4,669	268	346	4,721	48,240	60,661	6,921
Cedar	37.7	2,733	50.1	29.0	5.1	0.0	2.8	32.6	2,361	68	47	707	5,460	36,700	3,045
Chariton	22.7	2,968	52.9	4.1	2.8	0.0	14.2	3.5	456	40	25	447	3,470	43,939	4,031
Christian	179.8	2,252	67.4	0.5	4.7	1.0	5.5	246.9	3,093	110	285	3,051	36,680	55,449	6,000
Clark	23.6	3,386	46.2	6.2	1.8	17.9	8.0	8.6	1,234	37	23	439	2,880	41,671	3,523
Clay	1,296.4	5,696	31.9	48.7	2.3	0.0	1.9	934.2	4,105	1,314	866	14,626	115,410	63,142	7,506
Clinton	50.6	2,467	62.4	1.9	7.3	0.0	8.9	42.6	2,078	84	68	998	9,700	55,217	5,333
Cole	222.3	2,911	50.1	2.6	10.7	0.0	10.0	194.9	2,552	623	264	19,230	36,320	57,988	6,938
Cooper	65.2	3,719	36.8	19.0	3.7	4.9	5.9	51.2	2,925	47	55	1,263	7,510	44,532	4,099
Crawford	44.2	1,780	63.0	8.1	3.6	0.0	5.8	29.0	1,169	33	81	928	10,160	41,584	4,165
Dade	20.9	2,758	51.9	1.1	3.6	23.8	6.9	4.0	526	31	25	526	3,180	39,985	3,329
Dallas	39.6	2,358	42.6	3.7	4.9	0.0	39.8	4.3	254	34	55	573	6,480	37,172	2,969
Daviess	19.9	2,419	62.2	3.1	3.1	0.1	12.4	10.1	1,231	31	27	480	3,520	40,665	3,731
DeKalb	17.0	1,315	62.4	3.4	4.1	0.0	6.0	6.2	478	30	31	1,255	4,110	44,974	4,045
Dent	47.9	3,058	43.1	38.7	4.1	0.0	4.2	2.6	166	54	52	904	5,880	38,379	3,320
Douglas	34.6	2,550	64.0	1.9	3.6	0.0	13.6	7.5	553	50	45	392	4,910	33,378	2,413
Dunklin	76.5	2,405	65.8	1.0	6.7	0.0	5.4	33.5	1,052	95	101	1,553	11,510	37,456	3,284
Franklin	286.0	2,820	58.5	2.0	6.4	0.0	9.3	497.8	4,909	221	346	4,292	49,610	54,853	6,295
Gasconade	55.7	3,719	45.7	31.4	2.9	0.5	4.5	60.7	4,054	51	49	1,019	7,090	42,470	3,780
Gentry	20.3	2,997	59.9	3.6	3.3	0.0	10.5	8.2	1,217	39	22	398	2,810	40,486	3,320
Greene	855.2	3,047	50.1	1.1	8.7	0.2	6.0	1,601.3	5,706	2,175	960	18,824	130,380	55,105	7,254
Grundy	48.8	4,722	61.4	3.0	2.3	10.7	6.0	28.4	2,746	61	33	955	4,270	42,650	3,972
Harrison	40.5	4,640	35.7	40.6	3.2	0.0	7.4	11.6	1,333	42	29	781	3,770	36,188	2,838
Henry	113.3	5,114	25.1	59.5	2.3	0.1	3.3	36.1	1,629	77	73	1,636	9,390	43,972	4,001
Hickory	21.4	2,275	79.2	1.5	2.4	0.0	5.9	11.7	1,244	39	31	287	3,490	35,160	2,641
Holt	15.2	3,273	49.5	0.6	2.4	0.0	13.7	0.8	182	33	15	295	2,130	47,015	5,328
Howard	22.1	2,174	53.2	3.8	5.5	0.3	6.2	33.3	3,276	36	32	466	4,340	43,927	4,075
Howell	94.2	2,317	67.7	2.1	5.1	0.0	5.1	39.4	970	127	134	2,177	16,090	41,586	4,138
Iron	27.4	2,641	71.9	1.5	3.9	0.0	5.6	10.9	1,046	14	63	642	3,850	37,018	2,782
Jackson	3,093.9	4,567	37.7	2.6	9.6	0.3	7.4	6,245.9	9,221	16,635	2,474	42,529	331,110	55,209	6,681

1. Based on the resident population estimated as of July 1 of the year shown.

Table B. States and Counties — Land Area and Population

State / county code	CBSA code[1]	County code[2]	STATE County	Land area[3] (sq. mi)	Population, 2017			Population and population characteristics, 2017										
								Race alone or in combination, not Hispanic or Latino (percent)					Age (percent)					
					Total persons 2017	Rank	Per square mile	White	Black	American Indian, Alaska Native	Asian and Pacific Islancer	Percent Hispanic or Latino[4]	Under 5 years	5 to 17 years	18 to 24 years	25 to 34 years	35 to 44 years	45 to 54 years
				1	2	3	4	5	6	7	8	9	10	11	12	13	14	15
			MISSOURI— Cont'd															
29,097	27,900	3	Jasper	638.5	120,217	521	188.3	86.9	3.1	3.0	1.9	8.1	6.9	18.2	9.1	14.2	12.5	11.8
29,099	41,180	1	Jefferson	656.6	223,810	301	340.9	95.9	1.6	0.8	1.2	2.0	6.0	17.4	7.5	13.0	13.0	14.1
29,101	47,660	4	Johnson	829.3	53,897	939	65.0	88.2	6.1	1.3	2.9	4.4	6.3	15.1	20.4	14.7	10.4	10.0
29,103		9	Knox	504.0	3,977	2,904	7.9	97.8	1.0	1.0	0.7	1.0	6.2	17.6	8.0	9.6	9.1	12.6
29,105	30,060	6	Laclede	764.7	35,443	1,290	46.3	95.3	1.5	1.6	1.1	2.5	6.8	17.9	7.5	11.7	11.6	13.3
29,107	28,140	1	Lafayette	628.4	32,641	1,366	51.9	93.9	3.0	1.3	0.9	2.8	5.8	17.1	7.8	11.6	11.1	13.5
29,109		6	Lawrence	611.7	38,434	1,218	62.8	90.8	0.9	1.8	0.7	7.4	6.6	17.8	7.9	10.9	11.6	12.8
29,111	39,500	9	Lewis	505.0	9,967	2,432	19.7	94.2	4.1	0.9	0.8	1.8	5.7	16.8	12.5	10.3	10.7	12.1
29,113	41,180	1	Lincoln	626.6	56,183	909	89.7	94.7	2.7	0.9	0.9	2.5	6.8	18.6	8.0	13.4	12.4	13.8
29,115		7	Linn	615.6	12,194	2,279	19.8	96.1	1.7	0.7	0.4	2.4	6.2	17.7	7.7	10.5	10.8	11.4
29,117		6	Livingston	532.3	15,173	2,086	28.5	93.4	4.4	0.9	0.8	2.0	5.6	15.3	7.7	13.8	13.4	12.5
29,119	22,220	2	McDonald	539.5	22,828	1,683	42.3	80.7	2.5	4.5	3.7	11.8	7.2	18.5	8.1	11.7	12.0	13.8
29,121		7	Macon	801.2	15,251	2,082	19.0	95.5	3.1	0.9	0.7	1.5	5.8	17.4	7.1	10.1	11.0	12.2
29,123		6	Madison	494.4	12,243	2,274	24.8	96.0	0.9	1.0	1.0	2.3	6.0	17.2	7.3	11.9	11.4	13.0
29,125		8	Maries	527.0	8,867	2,515	16.8	96.7	1.3	1.6	0.8	1.3	4.9	16.1	7.6	10.0	11.0	13.8
29,127	25,300	5	Marion	436.9	28,634	1,466	65.5	92.4	6.3	0.8	1.1	1.7	6.5	16.8	9.2	12.2	11.5	12.4
29,129		9	Mercer	453.8	3,678	2,926	8.1	95.7	0.7	1.2	1.0	2.6	6.2	17.6	8.1	9.0	10.1	12.1
29,131		6	Miller	592.6	25,228	1,598	42.6	96.3	1.1	1.4	0.8	1.9	6.4	17.1	7.6	11.8	11.2	13.1
29,133		6	Mississippi	411.6	13,586	2,191	33.0	72.5	25.5	0.7	0.4	2.2	5.1	16.0	8.1	14.1	13.1	13.8
29,135	27,620	3	Moniteau	415.0	16,063	2,034	38.7	90.6	4.3	1.0	0.6	4.7	6.6	18.2	7.9	13.5	13.3	13.1
29,137		9	Monroe	647.7	8,612	2,535	13.3	94.6	3.8	1.0	0.7	1.8	5.7	16.3	6.4	10.2	10.3	12.1
29,139		6	Montgomery	535.0	11,438	2,326	21.4	95.5	2.3	1.0	0.8	2.0	5.7	16.5	6.7	10.9	10.9	13.2
29,141		8	Morgan	597.6	20,145	1,817	33.7	95.7	1.3	1.7	0.8	2.3	6.4	16.3	6.4	10.3	9.4	12.1
29,143		7	New Madrid	674.8	17,582	1,943	26.1	81.5	16.7	0.8	0.6	2.0	6.3	16.7	7.3	11.8	11.7	13.0
29,145	27,900	3	Newton	624.8	58,290	884	93.3	89.0	1.7	4.3	2.7	5.5	6.1	17.9	8.3	11.8	11.5	13.1
29,147	32,340	6	Nodaway	877.0	22,472	1,707	25.6	93.4	3.3	0.6	2.0	1.8	4.7	11.5	28.6	10.8	9.2	9.7
29,149		9	OREGON	789.8	10,558	2,389	13.4	96.0	0.9	2.9	0.6	1.9	5.9	16.5	6.7	9.7	9.7	12.6
29,151	27,620	3	Osage	606.6	13,662	2,187	22.5	98.2	0.7	0.6	0.3	0.9	5.8	17.1	8.6	11.4	11.7	13.7
29,153		9	Ozark	745.0	9,186	2,489	12.3	97.0	0.7	1.9	0.5	1.7	4.3	14.8	5.4	8.4	9.8	11.9
29,155		7	Pemiscot	492.5	16,826	1,987	34.2	70.3	27.5	0.7	0.6	2.6	7.4	18.6	8.4	11.9	11.5	12.3
29,157		6	Perry	474.4	19,225	1,864	40.5	96.1	1.0	0.7	0.8	2.4	6.0	17.5	7.9	11.7	11.9	13.4
29,159	42,740	4	Pettis	682.2	42,558	1,123	62.4	86.5	4.1	0.9	1.3	9.1	6.8	18.1	8.3	13.4	11.6	12.1
29,161	40,620	5	Phelps	671.8	44,744	1,078	66.6	90.7	3.1	1.5	4.3	2.5	5.7	15.3	16.6	12.0	10.6	11.2
29,163		6	Pike	670.4	18,567	1,891	27.7	89.4	8.6	0.6	0.6	2.3	6.1	16.0	8.2	14.1	12.2	13.0
29,165	28,140	1	Platte	420.2	101,187	595	240.8	83.2	7.7	1.0	4.2	6.2	6.2	17.6	8.1	13.4	13.9	13.6
29,167	44,180	2	Polk	635.5	31,794	1,382	50.0	95.0	1.4	1.5	1.2	2.5	6.0	16.9	12.9	10.7	10.8	12.0
29,169	22,780	5	Pulaski	547.1	52,059	957	95.2	72.8	13.2	1.9	5.4	11.1	6.7	15.3	22.1	18.1	11.9	9.1
29,171		9	Putnam	517.3	4,811	2,846	9.3	96.9	0.7	0.7	1.0	2.0	6.2	16.3	6.5	9.9	10.0	12.3
29,173	25,300	9	Ralls	469.8	10,224	2,410	21.8	96.7	1.9	0.8	0.5	1.3	4.9	16.8	6.7	10.0	11.6	13.4
29,175	33,620	6	Randolph	482.7	24,945	1,612	51.7	91.0	7.2	1.1	1.1	2.0	5.6	15.9	9.3	13.9	12.8	13.7
29,177	28,140	1	Ray	568.8	22,855	1,682	40.2	95.4	2.0	1.2	0.6	2.4	5.6	17.0	7.7	11.0	11.6	13.8
29,179		9	Reynolds	808.5	6,275	2,731	7.8	96.2	1.8	2.6	0.5	1.6	4.5	15.6	6.7	9.6	11.1	13.3
29,181		9	Ripley	629.5	13,564	2,193	21.5	96.6	1.0	1.8	0.6	1.6	6.3	16.6	6.7	11.3	11.7	12.7
29,183	41,180	1	St. Charles	560.4	395,504	177	705.8	89.0	5.8	0.6	3.3	3.3	6.1	17.5	8.5	13.1	13.2	13.5
29,185		8	St. Clair	675.0	9,362	2,476	13.9	96.0	1.0	1.8	0.5	2.4	5.4	14.1	6.4	9.7	9.2	12.3
29,186		6	Ste. Genevieve	499.2	17,843	1,925	35.7	96.3	1.2	0.8	1.5	1.2	5.7	16.1	7.5	10.7	11.0	13.4
29,187	22,100	4	St. Francois	451.9	66,705	797	147.6	93.0	5.1	0.9	0.7	1.6	5.5	15.9	8.1	14.7	13.4	13.5
29,189	41,180	1	St. Louis	507.6	996,726	45	1,963.6	67.9	25.6	0.6	5.2	2.9	5.8	16.2	8.6	12.8	11.8	12.8
29,195	32,180	6	Saline	755.5	22,660	1,694	30.0	82.8	6.3	1.0	2.0	10.1	6.0	16.9	11.3	11.8	11.3	11.6
29,197	28,860	9	Schuyler	307.3	4,508	2,860	14.7	97.7	0.5	0.6	0.5	1.6	7.4	18.2	8.1	10.8	10.0	12.0
29,199		9	Scotland	436.6	4,963	2,833	11.4	98.3	0.6	0.7	0.4	1.0	9.1	20.0	8.6	11.1	10.6	10.8
29,201	43,460	4	Scott	420.0	38,541	1,214	91.8	85.2	12.8	0.9	0.7	2.3	6.4	17.4	7.9	12.6	11.5	13.0
29,203		9	Shannon	1,003.8	8,249	2,572	8.2	96.2	1.0	2.9	0.5	1.9	5.0	16.5	7.0	10.9	9.4	13.1
29,205		9	Shelby	500.9	6,021	2,747	12.0	96.5	1.9	0.7	0.4	2.1	6.0	18.3	7.0	10.1	11.6	11.2
29,207		6	Stoddard	823.2	29,369	1,446	35.7	96.4	1.5	0.9	0.5	1.8	5.8	16.1	7.6	11.8	12.1	13.1
29,209	14,700	6	Stone	464.0	31,699	1,384	68.3	96.1	0.8	1.6	0.6	2.4	3.9	12.8	5.8	7.9	9.1	12.2
29,211		9	Sullivan	648.0	6,229	2,734	9.6	78.1	3.1	0.8	0.6	18.2	6.1	16.6	7.7	10.0	11.5	14.3
29,213	14,700	4	Taney	632.4	55,355	915	87.5	90.6	2.0	1.8	1.7	5.9	5.7	15.4	9.9	11.5	10.9	12.1
29,215		9	Texas	1,177.3	25,735	1,574	21.9	93.0	4.1	2.1	0.7	2.1	5.6	15.9	7.7	11.7	11.3	12.6
29,217		7	Vernon	826.4	20,437	1,803	24.7	95.6	1.3	1.7	1.0	2.1	6.3	17.8	9.0	10.6	11.0	12.8
29,219	41,180	1	Warren	428.6	34,373	1,315	80.2	93.5	3.2	0.9	0.8	3.3	6.5	17.7	7.3	11.9	11.2	13.2
29,221		6	Washington	759.9	25,022	1,608	32.9	95.4	2.8	1.1	0.5	1.4	5.9	17.2	7.4	12.1	12.5	14.3
29,223		9	Wayne	759.2	13,296	2,214	17.5	96.5	1.2	1.6	0.6	1.9	5.7	14.9	6.2	10.3	9.9	13.7
29,225	44,180	2	Webster	592.6	38,665	1,211	65.2	95.8	1.5	1.5	0.6	2.1	7.5	19.8	7.7	12.1	11.9	13.2
29,227		9	Worth	266.6	2,057	3,045	7.7	97.1	1.0	0.5	0.4	1.4	5.0	15.4	7.0	10.5	9.0	12.3
29,229		6	Wright	681.8	18,331	1,903	26.9	96.4	0.9	1.4	0.7	1.9	7.1	18.3	7.2	10.6	10.7	12.4

1. CBSA = Core Based Statistical Area. See Appendix A for explanation. See Appendix B for list of metropolitan areas with component counties.   2. County type code from the Economic Research Service of USDA Rural-Urban Continuum Codes. See Appendix A for definition.   3. Dry land or land partially or temporarily covered by water.   4. May be of any race.

Items 1—15

STATE County	55 to 64 years	65 to 74 years	75 years and over	Percent female	2000	2010	2000-2010	2010-2017	Births	Deaths	Net Migration	Number	Persons per household	Family households	Female family householder[1]	One person
	16	17	18	19	20	21	22	23	24	25	26	27	28	29	30	31
MISSOURI— Cont'd																
Jasper	12.1	8.7	6.6	51.3	104,686	117,404	12.1	2.4	12,269	8,376	-1,077	45,731	2.51	65.4	11.4	27.9
Jefferson	14.6	9.1	5.4	50.3	198,099	218,728	10.4	2.3	19,054	13,908	100	82,308	2.68	73.8	11.3	20.8
Johnson	10.9	7.2	5.1	48.4	48,258	52,595	9.0	2.5	5,202	2,896	-1,025	19,934	2.49	65.8	9.2	23.5
Knox	15.3	11.6	10.1	49.9	4,361	4,131	-5.3	-3.7	354	360	-150	1,653	2.37	67.8	9.0	28.9
Laclede	13.5	10.3	7.4	50.8	32,513	35,571	9.4	-0.4	3,417	2,789	-751	13,740	2.56	70.9	11.8	23.7
Lafayette	14.4	9.9	8.7	50.4	32,960	33,381	1.3	-2.2	2,694	2,673	-758	13,301	2.41	70.6	10.8	25.8
Lawrence	13.4	9.8	8.4	50.4	35,204	38,634	9.7	-0.5	3,576	3,202	-565	14,574	2.58	69.6	9.3	26.1
Lewis	13.6	9.8	8.4	50.0	10,494	10,209	-2.7	-2.4	822	792	-274	3,807	2.46	63.9	7.4	30.0
Lincoln	13.8	8.0	5.2	49.9	38,944	52,560	35.0	6.9	5,280	3,192	1,571	18,415	2.91	73.3	12.0	22.6
Linn	15.0	11.3	9.2	51.2	13,754	12,761	-7.2	-4.4	1,014	1,231	-347	4,936	2.46	65.7	10.3	30.5
Livingston	12.5	9.9	9.2	56.1	14,558	15,195	4.4	-0.1	1,177	1,405	197	5,737	2.39	66.1	8.8	29.3
McDonald	13.3	9.3	6.0	49.4	21,681	23,083	6.5	-1.1	2,310	1,563	-1,017	8,294	2.72	72.4	11.3	24.2
Macon	14.0	12.0	10.2	50.8	15,762	15,566	-1.2	-2.0	1,256	1,386	-179	6,097	2.48	60.8	9.3	34.8
Madison	14.7	10.2	8.4	51.0	11,800	12,226	3.6	0.1	1,014	1,185	190	4,685	2.61	69.4	11.8	25.1
Maries	15.6	11.7	9.3	49.9	8,903	9,178	3.1	-3.4	614	724	-198	3,642	2.44	66.8	9.1	26.7
Marion	13.8	9.7	7.9	51.3	28,289	28,781	1.7	-0.5	2,687	2,329	-483	11,286	2.42	65.1	11.6	29.0
Mercer	15.7	10.6	10.6	49.5	3,757	3,785	0.7	-2.8	315	318	-104	1,425	2.55	67.0	9.1	30.9
Miller	14.2	10.9	7.7	50.1	23,564	24,747	5.0	1.9	2,172	2,005	332	9,408	2.62	66.8	9.2	30.4
Mississippi	12.5	10.0	7.3	46.0	13,427	14,358	6.9	-5.4	1,166	1,277	-661	5,125	2.41	68.2	18.4	27.7
Moniteau	12.0	8.5	6.9	46.8	14,827	15,607	5.3	2.9	1,496	1,041	11	5,492	2.64	70.5	7.7	25.4
Monroe	16.2	12.6	10.3	49.2	9,311	8,840	-5.1	-2.6	685	666	-251	3,524	2.41	65.9	9.1	28.4
Montgomery	15.5	11.0	9.6	50.0	12,136	12,234	0.8	-6.5	979	1,146	-632	4,876	2.35	65.7	10.3	29.8
Morgan	15.5	13.7	9.9	49.7	19,309	20,565	6.5	-2.0	1,878	2,168	-122	7,883	2.52	62.2	8.9	31.3
New Madrid	14.6	10.8	7.8	52.0	19,760	18,960	-4.0	-7.3	1,661	1,724	-1,317	7,305	2.45	67.4	18.1	27.0
Newton	13.7	10.3	7.5	50.2	52,636	58,112	10.4	0.3	5,215	4,457	-551	22,023	2.62	70.0	9.0	25.4
Nodaway	10.6	7.7	7.1	49.8	21,912	23,370	6.7	-3.8	1,674	1,372	-1,212	8,465	2.33	58.5	7.8	29.6
OREGON	16.0	12.8	10.1	51.0	10,344	10,881	5.2	-3.0	931	1,011	-240	4,339	2.48	64.0	8.0	30.9
Osage	14.5	9.3	7.9	48.4	13,062	13,885	6.3	-1.6	1,104	913	-415	5,046	2.66	70.2	5.9	24.7
Ozark	17.4	16.1	12.0	50.0	9,542	9,719	1.9	-5.5	608	896	-243	4,267	2.18	67.8	11.1	27.8
Pemiscot	13.4	9.3	7.1	52.7	20,047	18,296	-8.7	-8.0	1,994	1,690	-1,784	6,939	2.51	62.7	19.8	31.9
Perry	14.0	9.7	7.9	50.2	18,132	18,971	4.6	1.3	1,607	1,455	116	7,438	2.53	71.6	9.0	24.7
Pettis	13.4	8.9	7.4	50.5	39,403	42,201	7.1	0.8	4,208	3,067	-764	16,004	2.58	67.0	11.3	27.9
Phelps	12.6	8.9	7.0	47.7	39,825	45,154	13.4	-0.9	3,820	3,172	-1,084	16,838	2.48	61.4	8.9	29.6
Pike	13.2	9.7	7.6	45.0	18,351	18,516	0.9	0.3	1,589	1,423	-116	6,653	2.43	65.6	10.6	28.3
Platte	12.9	8.7	5.4	50.6	73,781	89,318	21.1	13.3	8,445	4,512	7,949	37,699	2.50	66.6	9.4	28.0
Polk	12.6	10.0	8.0	51.0	26,992	31,137	15.4	2.1	2,740	2,474	407	11,864	2.50	66.5	8.9	24.8
Pulaski	8.0	5.2	3.6	43.4	41,165	52,274	27.0	-0.4	5,954	2,116	-4,147	15,298	2.86	67.5	11.3	26.5
Putnam	15.0	12.8	11.1	49.6	5,223	4,979	-4.7	-3.4	422	455	-131	2,121	2.27	65.9	11.7	30.1
Ralls	15.7	13.0	7.9	49.7	9,626	10,167	5.6	0.6	700	693	51	3,967	2.56	74.2	8.2	21.9
Randolph	12.5	9.3	7.0	47.6	24,663	25,414	3.0	-1.8	2,039	1,961	-546	8,471	2.69	65.7	8.8	30.1
Ray	15.1	10.3	7.8	50.1	23,354	23,494	0.6	-2.7	1,808	1,793	-658	8,670	2.61	69.4	10.4	25.0
Reynolds	16.5	12.2	10.5	48.5	6,689	6,694	0.1	-6.3	428	621	-226	2,652	2.38	67.8	7.4	27.7
Ripley	14.7	11.3	8.8	50.8	13,509	14,100	4.4	-3.8	1,279	1,357	-451	5,353	2.59	69.1	11.3	25.6
St. Charles	13.5	8.7	6.0	50.8	283,883	360,495	27.0	9.7	32,887	18,383	20,626	140,664	2.65	72.7	9.5	22.8
St. Clair	15.8	14.5	12.6	49.7	9,652	9,805	1.6	-4.5	681	1,056	-66	3,990	2.31	66.5	8.3	29.1
Ste. Genevieve	16.6	10.8	8.1	49.2	17,842	18,139	1.7	-1.6	1,279	1,390	-182	7,176	2.46	70.2	8.6	27.6
St. Francois	12.9	9.1	6.9	46.5	55,641	65,370	17.5	2.0	5,287	5,494	1,553	24,759	2.40	65.0	10.2	28.9
St. Louis	14.2	9.9	7.8	52.5	1,016,315	998,882	-1.7	-0.2	84,311	69,625	-16,601	401,716	2.44	64.6	14.1	30.3
Saline	13.4	9.8	8.0	50.1	23,756	23,370	-1.6	-3.0	2,080	1,803	-989	8,785	2.49	65.9	12.6	29.3
Schuyler	13.7	10.6	9.3	50.4	4,170	4,431	6.3	1.7	461	364	-22	1,726	2.52	68.8	11.2	26.3
Scotland	11.8	9.4	8.6	50.5	4,983	4,853	-2.6	2.3	597	430	-59	1,786	2.69	62.3	10.2	29.5
Scott	13.5	10.2	7.6	51.3	40,422	39,187	-3.1	-1.6	3,641	3,106	-1,160	15,267	2.52	68.0	15.1	26.9
Shannon	16.2	12.7	9.1	50.4	8,324	8,441	1.4	-2.3	647	638	-198	3,176	2.56	64.3	9.7	29.7
Shelby	14.8	11.2	9.8	50.4	6,799	6,373	-6.3	-5.5	532	591	-294	2,480	2.37	65.2	7.3	31.3
Stoddard	13.8	10.6	9.1	50.7	29,705	29,968	0.9	-2.0	2,550	2,777	-350	11,855	2.47	63.9	9.5	30.5
Stone	18.0	18.5	11.8	51.2	28,658	32,208	12.4	-1.6	1,818	2,701	397	12,667	2.43	70.6	7.1	24.3
Sullivan	13.9	11.2	8.7	48.8	7,219	6,714	-7.0	-7.2	615	530	-577	2,384	2.64	63.2	11.0	31.6
Taney	13.3	12.4	8.8	51.7	39,703	51,674	30.2	7.1	4,579	3,874	2,975	21,769	2.39	67.3	11.6	26.1
Texas	14.7	11.4	9.2	47.6	23,003	26,008	13.1	-1.0	2,132	2,114	-278	9,239	2.63	65.7	9.2	30.0
Vernon	13.8	10.6	8.0	51.1	20,454	21,159	3.4	-3.4	1,856	1,799	-775	8,204	2.44	67.4	10.4	27.5
Warren	15.0	10.1	7.2	50.0	24,525	32,518	32.6	5.7	2,995	2,014	893	11,823	2.79	75.6	11.3	21.0
Washington	14.3	9.8	6.5	48.6	23,344	25,199	7.9	-0.7	2,158	1,973	-351	9,045	2.64	70.9	11.4	22.8
Wayne	16.2	12.9	10.1	50.5	13,259	13,523	2.0	-1.7	1,033	1,415	160	5,612	2.35	67.8	13.0	26.3
Webster	12.6	8.8	6.3	48.9	31,045	36,202	16.6	6.8	3,885	2,312	910	13,122	2.75	73.8	9.6	21.7
Worth	17.3	11.5	12.2	50.6	2,382	2,171	-8.9	-5.3	163	215	-64	917	2.19	69.4	6.7	24.8
Wright	14.4	10.7	8.6	50.8	17,955	18,815	4.8	-2.6	1,745	1,630	-601	7,395	2.46	65.9	12.8	30.2

1. No spouse present.

Table B. States and Counties — **Agriculture**

STATE County	Land in farms					Value of land and buildings (dollars)		Value of machinery and equiopmnet, average per farm (dollars)	Value of products sold:				Percent of farms with sales of:		Government payments	
	Acreage (1,000)	Percent change, 2007-2012	Acres			Average per farm	Average per acre		Total (mil dol)	Average per farm (acres)	Percent from:		$10,000 or more	$100,000 or more	Total ($1,000)	Percent of farms
			Average size of farm	Total irrigated (1,000)	Total cropland (1,000)						Crops	Livestock and poultry products				
	117	118	119	120	121	122	123	124	125	126	127	128	129	130	131	132
MISSOURI— Cont'd																
Jasper	247	-4.7	190	3.5	127.7	443,779	2,337	62,487	100.5	77,336	32.5	67.5	41.6	8.9	2,322	37.0
Jefferson	98	5.7	138	0.3	36.3	471,186	3,407	53,340	13.6	19,325	51.0	49.0	28.9	3.3	255	12.3
Johnson	391	-7.9	236	1.9	219.9	624,016	2,645	95,386	119.9	72,340	38.5	61.5	47.1	9.3	2,968	40.3
Knox	281	10.8	404	D	193.3	1,205,037	2,981	147,283	76.3	109,799	49.5	50.5	53.8	21.2	5,347	73.4
Laclede	320	10.9	229	0.2	89.6	503,814	2,200	50,168	50.4	36,045	15.1	84.9	46.4	7.4	526	10.8
Lafayette	327	-7.4	278	1.8	244.5	1,176,566	4,225	133,569	143.2	122,010	80.6	19.4	57.8	20.8	4,495	57.0
Lawrence	311	-3.6	168	2.3	118.1	431,114	2,562	62,340	204.9	110,819	7.4	92.6	45.3	10.8	1,959	18.6
Lewis	284	8.8	390	2.0	201.3	1,128,680	2,894	139,615	81.2	111,418	64.0	36.0	51.7	19.3	4,159	71.1
Lincoln	281	13.0	242	1.3	191.8	943,589	3,900	91,473	85.6	73,707	55.9	44.1	44.8	12.0	3,161	55.4
Linn	336	1.7	323	0.3	209.0	780,366	2,416	78,069	66.6	64,131	59.0	41.0	48.7	15.5	6,639	67.9
Livingston	284	-8.2	335	0.4	200.5	976,103	2,916	104,609	72.5	85,636	68.9	31.1	49.8	15.6	6,044	70.0
McDonald	187	-6.6	202	0.3	49.5	466,203	2,314	79,172	175.8	189,865	2.1	97.9	44.0	10.9	630	9.9
Macon	386	-2.1	299	0.3	214.7	740,631	2,477	78,400	66.8	51,777	53.6	46.4	41.6	10.1	6,172	58.1
Madison	107	9.0	287	D	24.1	528,405	1,840	54,603	18.4	49,201	9.8	90.2	41.8	6.7	102	13.1
Maries	241	0.4	289	0.2	59.4	563,396	1,951	60,886	35.3	42,176	13.0	87.0	53.8	6.8	435	16.1
Marion	221	-6.6	315	3.0	157.5	1,120,118	3,561	118,102	87.1	123,751	61.6	38.4	48.0	18.2	3,060	71.2
Mercer	227	12.6	400	D	119.4	887,578	2,219	93,078	102.7	181,146	18.6	81.4	40.9	12.5	3,303	67.4
Miller	248	1.2	245	1.4	62.0	544,853	2,221	58,525	103.0	101,659	4.7	95.3	51.2	11.1	549	13.7
Mississippi	245	-5.2	1,195	86.5	232.3	4,962,234	4,153	473,244	157.0	766,000	97.9	2.1	81.5	55.6	3,759	87.8
Moniteau	235	-3.2	216	0.2	99.9	582,663	2,698	67,761	173.5	159,302	9.4	90.6	57.0	13.5	2,018	37.6
Monroe	356	23.4	335	1.1	237.9	1,047,572	3,125	121,686	86.2	81,207	58.0	42.0	40.8	13.2	7,034	75.6
Montgomery	279	12.5	351	3.2	194.0	1,212,507	3,453	132,268	64.0	80,541	73.9	26.1	50.9	20.5	4,635	65.9
Morgan	198	-8.5	215	0.2	77.6	569,115	2,646	63,366	144.8	157,103	8.6	91.4	56.6	21.3	768	17.5
New Madrid	345	-9.5	1,087	196.5	332.5	4,819,981	4,435	524,943	217.1	684,994	99.9	0.1	84.2	65.6	8,243	90.9
Newton	248	0.8	157	0.3	93.4	404,596	2,577	60,035	251.5	159,393	6.0	94.0	44.3	9.5	1,034	17.3
Nodaway	424	-22.0	338	0.3	293.3	1,100,251	3,251	116,792	141.6	113,082	81.0	19.0	58.3	21.6	7,586	72.6
OREGON	254	6.0	338	0.4	35.9	525,161	1,556	53,593	34.5	45,934	3.4	96.6	45.3	6.8	955	26.7
Osage	283	-4.8	254	2.3	82.4	520,062	2,047	73,506	78.7	70,544	17.7	82.3	55.0	9.7	1,003	30.9
Ozark	229	-7.6	358	0.1	29.1	581,482	1,624	60,313	39.2	61,365	5.3	94.7	54.0	10.6	597	8.6
Pemiscot	305	-1.7	1,344	122.7	287.5	4,861,687	3,618	516,802	186.1	819,758	99.9	0.1	79.3	61.7	7,220	80.6
Perry	226	-5.2	238	D	122.0	636,469	2,673	82,989	63.4	66,614	50.1	49.9	52.2	13.4	2,226	64.9
Pettis	420	2.6	320	0.4	263.2	876,005	2,736	116,004	177.0	135,019	30.8	69.2	52.6	19.0	5,117	51.0
Phelps	157	-10.5	219	0.1	27.2	504,223	2,301	51,199	11.7	16,320	15.8	84.2	34.1	2.6	225	12.0
Pike	362	-3.1	361	3.7	226.0	1,247,957	3,461	127,424	87.4	87,094	62.9	37.1	51.7	15.3	4,506	65.7
Platte	153	-14.4	255	1.7	100.7	992,603	3,888	94,775	44.9	74,917	83.7	16.3	41.9	12.0	1,720	48.2
Polk	336	-4.0	223	1.3	102.6	461,553	2,066	49,912	85.2	56,613	10.6	89.4	49.2	10.0	859	15.3
Pulaski	112	-8.6	216	0.1	20.9	421,379	1,948	50,873	12.9	24,752	15.6	84.4	42.1	4.2	110	6.5
Putnam	293	7.3	451	D	124.7	930,538	2,063	91,116	86.1	132,669	19.3	80.7	49.3	18.3	3,373	59.5
Ralls	283	15.5	392	1.1	196.9	1,258,679	3,210	138,203	54.8	75,806	76.5	23.5	39.0	16.7	4,168	76.3
Randolph	209	-5.5	256	1.1	109.1	673,561	2,630	65,106	36.7	44,873	58.5	41.5	35.5	6.2	2,820	54.8
Ray	273	-6.4	235	7.7	174.7	641,818	2,730	86,155	74.5	64,122	71.7	28.3	41.8	10.1	3,721	53.8
Reynolds	97	-9.5	268	0.0	16.5	391,482	1,463	44,970	4.8	13,284	25.3	74.7	35.5	1.1	79	7.4
Ripley	138	0.4	314	12.1	45.1	563,134	1,794	65,385	19.1	43,583	55.8	44.2	40.5	7.3	777	26.7
St. Charles	158	1.3	279	1.1	121.0	1,184,827	4,240	119,919	62.5	110,417	84.8	15.2	53.0	20.7	1,607	55.5
St. Clair	239	-10.0	328	0.5	99.3	542,646	1,656	69,935	33.8	46,482	42.4	57.6	50.7	9.9	1,115	36.4
Ste. Genevieve	163	-13.9	267	0.2	72.3	616,641	2,305	76,181	26.6	43,755	58.6	41.4	46.9	8.7	1,492	46.4
St. Francois	116	3.4	186	0.1	32.0	466,490	2,513	46,496	14.0	22,332	32.9	67.1	36.8	2.6	343	13.1
St. Louis	30	-8.0	137	0.5	15.4	565,189	4,128	69,313	19.1	87,807	97.3	2.7	37.3	11.1	279	20.7
Saline	461	2.6	481	3.5	362.9	1,934,485	4,023	199,556	212.0	221,075	73.3	26.7	66.1	28.7	5,961	79.7
Schuyler	159	4.6	309	D	83.8	687,409	2,226	76,853	30.4	58,917	48.8	51.2	50.2	12.4	2,272	61.8
Scotland	244	5.4	362	D	158.4	1,063,616	2,936	106,022	82.2	121,938	44.7	55.3	53.9	21.5	4,627	70.0
Scott	223	-2.4	461	72.4	192.8	1,878,114	4,077	237,058	188.8	390,035	69.0	31.0	48.6	26.9	4,263	63.8
Shannon	124	11.8	274	0.0	23.0	458,142	1,670	50,407	10.5	23,197	11.5	88.5	37.4	5.8	171	6.6
Shelby	299	3.5	422	1.6	211.0	1,499,389	3,552	149,536	83.0	117,100	71.2	28.8	59.0	24.0	5,033	75.6
Stoddard	448	-2.8	494	226.7	396.3	2,169,982	4,392	245,480	315.0	347,277	81.3	18.7	49.9	26.1	11,137	73.4
Stone	118	-3.1	196	0.1	32.1	465,231	2,369	50,319	14.0	16,510	10.6	89.4	45.3	7.0	368	10.0
Sullivan	323	-3.3	405	D	158.8	751,872	1,858	87,835	149.6	187,526	12.2	87.8	46.5	14.7	5,745	61.3
Taney	116	8.8	280	0.1	18.8	549,092	1,961	49,271	11.7	28,259	10.8	89.2	38.2	4.3	209	10.1
Texas	392	10.4	303	0.1	68.0	496,529	1,641	48,862	42.0	32,416	8.8	91.2	44.7	7.5	565	10.3
Vernon	419	-8.2	309	5.4	244.4	665,520	2,156	99,091	209.0	154,128	29.8	70.2	51.6	13.6	4,561	44.8
Warren	136	-7.3	219	1.1	85.3	850,634	3,880	94,071	31.4	50,589	78.6	21.4	43.3	11.6	1,941	51.2
Washington	124	-9.7	233	0.0	24.3	447,979	1,919	44,347	11.1	20,846	20.8	79.2	37.9	4.7	106	3.6
Wayne	117	10.0	284	D	28.0	433,238	1,527	59,358	7.8	18,949	20.0	80.0	33.8	2.9	356	24.3
Webster	272	0.3	148	0.2	82.9	386,911	2,612	45,690	76.1	41,450	8.4	91.6	45.5	9.0	1,345	8.9
Worth	125	-17.6	326	D	70.0	733,870	2,254	84,737	37.1	96,646	37.1	62.9	43.2	14.1	2,824	84.1
Wright	294	3.4	236	0.2	67.2	424,095	1,797	48,860	47.2	37,913	6.9	93.1	45.8	8.7	1,041	14.4

Items 117—132

Table B. States and Counties — Water Use, Wholesale Trade, Retail Trade, and Real Estate

STATE County	Water use, 2015		Wholesale Trade[1], 2012				Retail Trade[2], 2012				Real estate and rental and leasing,[2] 2012			
	Public supply water withdrawn (mil gal/day)	Public supply gallons withdrawn per person per day	Number of establishments	Number of employees	Sales (mil dol)	Annual payroll (mil dol)	Number of establishments	Number of employees	Sales (mil dol)	Annual payroll (mil dol)	Number of establishments	Number of employees	Sales (mil dol)	Annual payroll (mil dol)
	133	134	135	136	137	138	139	140	141	142	143	144	145	146
MISSOURI— Cont'd														
Jasper	18.54	156.3	143	1,695	972.5	70.6	514	7,769	1,987.5	166.1	114	506	75.5	13.2
Jefferson	28.68	128.0	132	1,302	798.0	65.5	484	6,756	1,952.6	162.7	143	465	62.2	14.1
Johnson	5.14	95.3	20	108	45.6	4.0	148	1,827	508.2	40.2	36	129	25.1	3.4
Knox	0.00	0.0	8	42	61.2	0.8	16	113	38.1	2.1	NA	NA	NA	NA
Laclede	3.79	106.8	27	305	196.2	11.3	174	1,813	502.4	42.1	28	72	10.9	1.6
Lafayette	2.31	70.6	34	319	184.0	11.6	106	1,055	375.5	20.5	16	D	D	D
Lawrence	2.77	72.6	26	239	92.5	7.1	122	1,320	449.0	31.3	20	48	4.2	0.8
Lewis	0.69	67.6	8	D	D	D	32	288	85.7	6.1	3	D	D	D
Lincoln	2.51	45.9	34	245	91.1	9.8	144	1,473	447.8	34.5	28	71	9.0	1.3
Linn	2.10	170.6	8	50	51.1	1.9	56	535	150.0	11.8	9	D	D	D
Livingston	1.89	125.8	22	272	126.7	11.4	76	1,167	359.1	26.5	11	37	9.8	0.7
McDonald	1.86	82.1	10	D	D	D	65	933	221.2	18.6	8	9	2.0	0.3
Macon	1.86	121.3	14	111	65.7	5.2	67	631	146.5	11.5	12	38	3.5	0.7
Madison	0.62	50.0	11	185	28.7	6.1	38	505	138.0	11.8	6	23	1.1	0.4
Maries	0.30	33.5	8	D	D	D	25	222	50.1	3.4	2	D	D	D
Marion	3.66	126.7	26	321	479.7	14.1	143	1,797	508.5	38.3	27	D	D	D
Mercer	0.13	35.2	1	D	D	D	13	64	25.0	1.1	1	D	D	D
Miller	0.78	31.1	13	167	94.6	5.7	119	1,651	377.4	38.8	51	203	30.1	5.3
Mississippi	1.90	135.4	18	191	256.2	6.9	52	474	182.1	9.5	2	D	D	D
Moniteau	1.47	92.1	10	173	69.8	5.0	55	457	136.2	8.5	5	8	0.5	0.1
Monroe	4.71	548.8	9	67	78.7	2.2	35	277	80.0	4.8	3	10	1.3	0.2
Montgomery	0.44	37.6	19	135	110.7	4.8	36	315	98.1	6.1	8	10	1.7	0.2
Morgan	0.70	34.7	17	56	22.2	1.9	91	762	195.1	16.3	19	39	4.8	0.8
New Madrid	1.95	107.1	32	428	436.0	18.3	77	1,319	495.7	28.0	9	21	3.2	0.5
Newton	4.33	73.9	41	1,200	1,674.4	48.3	196	2,090	853.8	49.2	29	77	10.5	1.7
Nodaway	1.88	82.4	17	221	181.4	8.9	72	1,122	260.0	21.2	20	35	5.7	0.6
OREGON	0.88	80.3	6	D	D	D	44	419	98.8	8.3	7	14	1.5	0.2
Osage	0.55	40.4	6	24	9.3	0.8	49	423	152.5	10.3	5	6	0.5	0.1
Ozark	0.24	25.5	6	32	17.3	0.7	33	214	49.6	3.4	9	16	1.0	0.2
Pemiscot	2.13	121.8	21	233	550.6	10.3	70	688	274.3	13.2	10	D	D	D
Perry	1.48	77.2	12	348	174.5	15.2	75	978	270.2	23.0	12	19	5.0	0.4
Pettis	3.55	84.0	35	350	175.4	15.7	174	2,323	615.1	54.4	44	358	37.0	9.4
Phelps	2.83	63.2	36	365	108.9	13.7	190	2,401	689.2	53.0	40	146	20.0	4.0
Pike	1.13	61.6	25	314	312.7	11.7	66	686	191.0	15.0	3	8	0.6	0.1
Platte	2.42	25.2	103	1,288	4,053.0	85.4	313	6,054	1,986.7	144.3	126	1,164	178.1	41.4
Polk	1.31	41.9	23	531	63.0	9.3	110	1,099	299.5	26.3	14	69	6.2	1.3
Pulaski	5.85	109.9	6	D	D	D	138	1,655	455.2	36.4	46	167	40.6	4.1
Putnam	0.25	51.5	3	D	D	D	24	176	50.3	3.1	4	14	0.8	0.2
Ralls	0.00	0.0	16	168	153.4	7.2	34	185	52.4	3.8	2	D	D	D
Randolph	1.12	44.6	17	D	D	D	97	1,118	296.7	25.3	19	63	9.9	1.6
Ray	2.36	103.5	9	114	186.2	5.7	56	607	138.7	12.6	9	21	1.7	0.4
Reynolds	0.13	20.2	4	D	D	D	20	122	29.6	2.0	4	9	0.4	0.1
Ripley	0.63	45.6	5	D	D	D	43	435	120.2	8.1	11	136	4.6	1.8
St. Charles	17.94	46.5	336	4,305	9,006.9	246.4	1,085	18,318	4,971.7	437.2	350	1,398	438.4	53.2
St. Clair	0.32	33.9	4	9	0.6	0.1	33	317	87.9	5.8	3	4	0.2	0.0
Ste. Genevieve	1.43	79.8	12	133	137.0	6.1	49	462	103.4	10.1	9	27	3.5	0.6
St. Francois	5.07	76.2	32	657	285.0	24.2	229	3,421	882.8	84.5	61	229	24.4	5.4
St. Louis	226.20	225.4	1,587	30,594	32,424.2	1,822.0	3,826	67,577	25,262.7	1,882.4	1,309	10,461	2,048.1	504.3
Saline	2.88	123.8	31	358	382.5	16.0	97	981	253.0	19.1	12	D	D	D
Schuyler	0.00	0.0	2	D	D	D	24	165	48.4	2.7	NA	NA	NA	NA
Scotland	0.15	30.9	6	D	D	D	28	162	39.8	3.0	2	D	D	D
Scott	5.94	152.3	53	823	717.9	30.8	181	1,555	415.7	33.2	40	141	17.5	4.0
Shannon	0.44	53.3	7	D	D	D	19	125	28.4	2.0	7	D	D	D
Shelby	0.23	37.5	15	97	69.7	3.5	35	223	58.9	4.4	4	5	0.5	0.1
Stoddard	3.23	108.2	37	366	428.5	13.4	118	1,277	424.0	29.6	26	51	6.7	1.2
Stone	3.15	101.8	17	D	D	D	99	795	216.8	18.9	38	164	19.0	5.8
Sullivan	0.65	102.3	2	D	D	D	27	184	50.4	3.4	5	4	0.5	0.1
Taney	8.29	151.9	32	D	D	D	414	4,936	939.9	88.7	116	1,023	152.0	35.8
Texas	1.72	67.0	22	102	36.7	2.8	83	742	172.5	14.3	10	33	2.7	0.7
Vernon	2.02	97.0	18	180	80.3	5.7	85	897	238.6	19.1	12	37	6.3	0.8
Warren	1.63	48.6	25	279	153.3	14.6	88	879	298.0	18.8	25	74	13.8	1.7
Washington	0.66	26.6	15	46	15.2	1.3	49	510	122.3	9.9	7	16	1.9	0.5
Wayne	1.33	99.2	11	D	D	D	36	319	72.3	6.3	3	3	0.4	0.0
Webster	1.11	29.6	32	134	69.6	5.0	109	1,123	376.7	23.8	26	50	4.0	0.9
Worth	0.01	4.9	4	D	D	D	12	68	18.2	1.2	2	D	D	D
Wright	0.97	53.1	17	223	89.9	6.9	83	952	245.6	20.0	15	41	3.6	0.6

1. Merchant wholesalers, except manufacturers' sales branches and offices.   2. Employer establishments.

Table B. States and Counties — Professional Services, Manufacturing, and Accommodation and Food Services

STATE County	Professional, scientific, and technical services, 2012				Manufacturing, 2012				Accommodation and food services, 2012			
	Number of establishments	Number of employees	Sales (mil dol)	Annual payroll (mil dol)	Number of establishments	Number of employees	Receipts (mil dol)	Annual payroll (mil dol)	Number of establishments	Number of employees	Receipts (mil dol)	Annual payroll (mil dol)
	147	148	149	150	151	152	153	154	155	156	157	158
MISSOURI— Cont'd												
Jasper	180	D	D	D	171	9,161	3,558.8	397.3	261	4,960	214.4	60.2
Jefferson	245	941	88.6	32.7	173	4,369	1,420.5	224.6	279	5,461	228.4	66.2
Johnson	66	D	D	D	30	1,252	D	43.0	100	1,672	66.3	16.4
Knox	4	D	D	D	NA	NA	NA	NA	6	D	D	D
Laclede	41	169	14.0	4.6	59	4,120	1,327.5	139.4	79	1,099	47.9	12.7
Lafayette	47	D	D	D	40	793	D	28.5	61	696	24.2	6.4
Lawrence	44	123	10.7	3.3	47	1,357	629.9	53.6	50	676	24.9	7.2
Lewis	13	D	D	D	6	104	D	3.9	14	113	4.1	1.2
Lincoln	51	184	15.4	5.5	49	981	387.2	51.3	58	D	D	D
Linn	22	98	9.7	3.1	15	1,003	207.5	27.4	20	226	7.8	2.2
Livingston	31	133	10.5	3.4	16	554	152.7	21.4	25	D	D	D
McDonald	13	44	2.6	0.9	23	2,974	611.6	81.9	33	264	13.3	3.3
Macon	23	D	D	D	9	472	D	15.9	32	366	18.4	5.2
Madison	13	74	5.2	1.5	14	281	D	10.2	22	D	D	D
Maries	6	D	D	D	9	165	D	8.4	11	41	1.5	0.4
Marion	45	258	24.9	8.6	39	1,475	1,488.5	72.2	74	1,115	47.0	12.7
Mercer	3	D	D	D	NA	NA	NA	NA	7	D	D	D
Miller	38	274	20.9	10.3	21	488	D	14.5	54	634	31.9	10.0
Mississippi	9	71	7.7	4.3	6	126	D	6.2	20	267	11.5	3.0
Moniteau	15	65	4.8	1.7	28	677	D	28.1	21	D	D	D
Monroe	10	D	D	D	9	218	D	D	18	141	4.7	1.3
Montgomery	8	D	D	D	19	499	154.8	17.1	21	194	6.7	1.9
Morgan	27	86	6.4	2.0	21	609	D	18.1	53	453	19.0	5.3
New Madrid	15	63	5.0	1.9	15	1,561	883.0	89.5	34	474	26.8	5.5
Newton	70	375	38.0	14.8	72	2,499	724.0	89.2	97	1,684	82.8	21.3
Nodaway	27	124	13.3	4.1	22	1,675	D	69.5	45	1,074	36.7	10.5
OREGON	10	D	D	D	11	137	24.0	3.6	14	171	5.8	1.5
Osage	9	17	1.7	0.4	29	988	D	40.1	20	D	D	D
Ozark	9	D	D	D	8	70	D	1.9	22	187	7.5	2.3
Pemiscot	11	44	3.5	0.9	12	825	D	37.0	29	311	15.1	3.3
Perry	27	118	8.8	4.2	37	3,627	1,142.3	115.6	39	618	20.9	5.8
Pettis	67	1,532	101.8	40.6	49	3,955	1,522.4	152.5	80	1,475	59.4	16.6
Phelps	77	327	35.9	11.5	50	912	484.4	43.1	114	1,810	78.1	21.6
Pike	18	522	43.8	11.5	21	555	324.3	22.8	25	D	D	D
Platte	260	D	D	D	49	2,644	1,870.0	127.4	202	5,779	394.3	101.0
Polk	43	D	D	D	22	343	D	12.1	44	780	27.0	7.3
Pulaski	58	639	99.0	45.5	15	123	24.5	D	99	2,280	91.8	39.3
Putnam	3	D	D	D	5	72	D	2.2	4	D	D	D
Ralls	5	19	1.9	0.5	15	1,272	1,405.4	66.2	11	87	3.0	1.0
Randolph	25	106	5.4	1.7	30	1,128	219.0	40.9	51	582	26.5	6.6
Ray	30	D	D	D	14	305	D	16.7	21	229	9.0	2.2
Reynolds	4	D	D	D	26	259	44.2	8.0	15	D	D	D
Ripley	10	D	D	D	30	446	D	11.6	15	195	7.7	1.9
St. Charles	765	6,210	720.9	239.7	256	10,982	6,851.7	614.3	712	16,108	918.4	227.3
St. Clair	9	25	3.3	1.0	8	28	4.9	1.2	16	78	5.4	0.8
Ste. Genevieve	23	81	6.1	2.5	30	1,467	400.4	74.7	29	D	D	D
St. Francois	79	300	33.6	8.7	49	1,474	272.2	55.7	115	1,802	76.3	21.6
St. Louis	3,618	46,440	8,274.0	3,139.6	950	35,884	15,922.9	2,621.7	2,219	47,895	2,628.8	713.8
Saline	29	D	D	D	21	1,948	747.5	68.9	43	522	17.5	5.3
Schuyler	1	D	D	D	3	9	2.9	0.4	3	D	D	D
Scotland	8	D	D	D	9	49	D	1.5	10	60	1.9	0.6
Scott	66	360	47.3	21.5	54	2,412	847.7	94.9	69	1,189	52.8	15.7
Shannon	4	D	D	D	24	372	51.1	8.9	15	64	3.4	0.8
Shelby	11	45	4.7	1.1	8	239	D	8.9	12	85	2.3	0.7
Stoddard	30	157	17.4	5.5	36	2,506	1,242.8	111.5	42	585	24.5	6.9
Stone	34	76	5.6	1.7	22	108	11.6	3.4	92	584	48.9	10.0
Sullivan	4	D	D	D	4	D	D	D	6	D	D	D
Taney	101	413	31.2	12.3	40	360	84.2	14.8	302	7,039	553.0	144.2
Texas	25	80	5.4	1.8	45	698	157.8	24.1	41	D	D	D
Vernon	34	120	11.1	2.9	20	894	D	46.8	36	456	22.3	4.8
Warren	38	145	14.4	4.9	34	1,383	453.2	58.7	49	D	D	D
Washington	13	35	2.0	0.7	19	533	290.1	17.6	22	D	D	D
Wayne	9	D	D	D	25	335	63.1	11.7	20	166	8.9	2.9
Webster	42	D	D	D	45	696	206.2	24.9	35	526	23.5	5.9
Worth	4	D	D	D	3	D	D	0.4	3	D	D	D
Wright	21	51	5.4	1.2	26	381	D	13.8	23	307	10.8	3.0

Items 147—158

STATE County	Health care and social assistance, 2012				Other services, 2012				Nonemployer businesses, 2015		Value of residential construction authorized by building permits, 2017	
	Number of establish-ments	Number of employees	Receipts (mil dol)	Annual payroll (mil dol)	Number of establis-hments	Number of employees	Receipts (mil dol)	Annual payroll (mil dol)	Number	Receipts (mil dol)	New construction ($1,000)	Number of housing units
	159	160	161	162	163	164	165	166	167	168	169	170
MISSOURI— Cont'd												
Jasper	333	6,521	629.5	315.1	225	1,277	99.9	29.8	6,614	265.7	81,110	724
Jefferson	381	6,119	478.7	186.3	334	1,558	143.2	42.4	12,864	509.1	124,088	744
Johnson	100	2,309	200.4	78.6	62	D	D	D	2,903	106.9	9,762	89
Knox	8	38	2.3	0.8	9	D	D	D	340	15.8	0	0
Laclede	78	1,475	135.0	55.4	49	D	D	D	2,593	119.4	10,172	83
Lafayette	62	D	D	D	46	135	11.3	3.0	2,055	88.2	7,286	36
Lawrence	71	1,279	99.0	46.0	38	109	9.2	2.8	2,629	101.1	1,693	9
Lewis	24	311	12.4	5.9	12	D	D	D	606	27.0	310	3
Lincoln	73	D	D	D	61	D	D	D	3,310	127.5	26,775	149
Linn	24	523	37.9	15.2	27	90	9.6	1.9	921	35.3	180	1
Livingston	43	861	74.4	27.8	22	D	D	D	946	40.3	3,323	25
McDonald	26	296	16.7	7.3	17	D	D	D	1,357	53.9	690	5
Macon	31	550	40.5	15.4	26	D	D	D	1,088	41.9	3,269	13
Madison	29	886	38.9	20.7	16	43	3.4	0.8	700	24.0	652	6
Maries	12	138	8.6	3.0	4	15	2.0	0.2	573	22.3	423	2
Marion	136	2,858	286.2	109.4	57	332	18.2	5.2	1,649	65.6	8,324	48
Mercer	7	D	D	D	8	D	D	D	270	10.3	0	0
Miller	37	495	33.0	13.3	41	D	D	D	1,686	73.5	3,255	13
Mississippi	25	409	19.9	8.0	19	56	4.3	1.1	614	32.8	865	10
Moniteau	32	D	D	D	18	53	3.2	0.8	944	35.7	520	3
Monroe	29	D	D	D	13	D	D	D	593	26.1	0	0
Montgomery	17	382	19.7	8.2	17	D	D	D	860	37.9	4,529	28
Morgan	28	256	13.9	5.2	29	D	D	D	1,602	64.7	82	2
New Madrid	52	886	48.4	17.6	22	58	5.7	1.0	758	25.0	685	3
Newton	141	6,401	607.1	273.5	63	219	19.1	5.1	3,730	168.2	5,124	41
Nodaway	51	1,239	94.2	39.5	40	163	10.6	3.1	1,404	45.8	5,140	43
OREGON	38	458	18.1	8.9	15	D	D	D	726	25.5	100	1
Osage	22	D	D	D	14	37	4.2	0.6	971	36.9	7,300	57
Ozark	10	100	5.8	2.4	13	42	2.7	0.6	738	23.5	68	5
Pemiscot	75	1,276	74.9	32.8	14	45	3.9	1.1	825	26.5	696	13
Perry	51	1,164	86.5	31.9	38	570	17.9	22.3	1,239	47.4	8,092	43
Pettis	136	3,111	229.9	97.5	91	482	34.5	11.2	2,666	112.0	2,193	16
Phelps	148	3,820	343.0	120.7	71	323	24.2	8.3	2,620	97.0	13,505	105
Pike	52	802	49.6	21.5	21	39	5.2	1.2	1,155	50.5	710	13
Platte	201	3,319	354.3	139.8	163	877	94.7	27.0	7,371	361.5	87,283	326
Polk	74	1,924	159.2	63.7	42	218	9.8	2.5	2,391	93.8	2,750	24
Pulaski	62	1,773	158.5	62.7	58	248	19.2	5.9	1,926	68.9	8,194	54
Putnam	10	94	10.1	3.1	6	17	2.0	0.4	417	18.6	50	1
Ralls	13	162	10.0	4.5	12	52	4.9	1.2	723	27.1	195	2
Randolph	72	1,504	128.3	48.0	45	140	10.6	2.5	1,321	55.1	3,140	22
Ray	36	D	D	D	24	D	D	D	1,209	44.6	6,805	42
Reynolds	29	158	7.0	3.0	6	D	D	D	458	18.6	0	0
Ripley	69	796	36.3	16.8	16	46	4.2	0.8	823	34.4	425	14
St. Charles	939	15,694	1,482.9	576.5	592	3,967	336.9	102.9	24,960	1,088.1	478,179	1,998
St. Clair	28	486	22.3	10.4	13	44	4.7	1.0	681	26.4	60	1
Ste. Genevieve	46	815	59.5	23.8	34	138	9.8	2.4	1,129	34.2	665	3
St. Francois	244	5,279	379.4	164.4	99	441	32.0	8.9	3,127	120.4	25,801	289
St. Louis	4,190	86,410	9,445.2	3,803.8	1,961	15,935	1,682.2	529.5	74,431	3,874.6	479,346	1,484
Saline	73	1,618	110.8	47.6	35	152	16.8	4.1	1,192	41.9	1,485	13
Schuyler	3	20	1.2	0.7	7	D	D	D	341	17.4	852	4
Scotland	7	D	D	D	15	D	D	D	520	31.5	255	2
Scott	139	2,990	200.0	90.4	61	322	25.5	6.9	2,211	95.9	5,929	54
Shannon	19	215	13.0	4.7	6	15	1.7	0.4	745	29.9	0	0
Shelby	7	102	5.1	2.1	15	38	4.8	0.9	493	18.1	200	1
Stoddard	90	1,499	84.2	36.2	41	137	9.7	3.0	1,998	105.4	2,981	40
Stone	45	458	39.5	12.1	52	273	21.8	6.5	2,727	120.3	31,210	163
Sullivan	10	254	13.9	6.1	10	21	2.8	0.5	376	12.2	0	0
Taney	125	2,363	247.5	91.8	101	556	49.6	12.9	4,336	178.7	36,682	209
Texas	52	968	70.6	28.2	34	69	6.5	1.4	1,719	67.3	742	11
Vernon	71	1,468	91.0	38.0	34	122	7.5	1.8	1,363	58.7	906	12
Warren	56	D	D	D	36	D	D	D	2,060	75.3	61,372	282
Washington	76	776	66.3	22.9	16	56	4.2	1.1	1,013	35.0	0	0
Wayne	40	379	18.1	7.5	10	48	2.1	0.6	683	27.7	0	0
Webster	56	500	26.9	12.2	35	D	D	D	3,017	114.6	9,476	76
Worth	2	D	D	D	5	D	D	D	198	6.7	0	0
Wright	43	492	30.5	11.7	23	77	6.4	1.5	1,329	56.9	1,033	8

Table B. States and Counties — Government Employment and Payroll, and Local Government Finances

	Government employment and payroll, 2012		March payroll (percent of total)							Local government finances — General revenue				
STATE County	Full-time equivalent employees	March payroll (dollars)	Administration, judicial, and legal	Police and corrections	Fire protection	Highways and transportation	Health and welfare	Natural resources and utilities	Education and libraries	Total (mil dol)	Inter-govern-mental (mil dol)	Taxes Total (mil dol)	Per capita[1] (dollars) Total	Per capita[1] (dollars) Property
	171	172	173	174	175	176	177	178	179	180	181	182	183	184
MISSOURI— Cont'd														
Jasper	4,406	12,579,406	4.8	9.9	4.0	3.6	1.3	3.8	71.5	389.2	139.5	146.6	1,272	589
Jefferson	6,669	24,871,942	2.8	6.2	4.1	2.5	3.8	3.1	76.7	560.9	238.8	255.4	1,160	796
Johnson	2,208	7,565,488	3.1	4.7	2.1	2.3	37.3	2.7	47.4	195.3	49.7	52.6	967	584
Knox	221	492,621	7.9	5.4	0.0	7.2	22.0	5.2	52.2	12.1	5.9	4.4	1,068	756
Laclede	1,413	3,701,221	5.5	5.9	1.6	12.4	1.2	6.8	65.2	72.4	35.3	26.3	742	477
Lafayette	1,188	3,488,934	7.8	8.3	0.6	3.5	2.3	9.3	67.9	88.1	38.4	34.2	1,034	710
Lawrence	1,155	3,231,901	5.5	6.1	0.7	2.7	6.5	2.7	75.5	76.5	38.1	27.2	706	425
Lewis	450	1,137,169	6.6	5.6	0.1	4.4	19.6	4.3	58.6	29.3	13.4	9.1	892	661
Lincoln	1,917	6,064,837	5.5	7.0	1.3	2.6	24.9	0.7	57.6	159.5	58.6	49.5	928	677
Linn	590	1,568,941	6.7	5.1	0.0	4.8	4.2	7.5	69.7	39.5	19.0	13.4	1,074	641
Livingston	654	1,837,354	4.6	6.8	5.3	2.6	13.9	14.2	51.7	49.5	19.1	16.1	1,073	702
McDonald	606	1,598,982	8.5	7.8	0.1	4.5	1.5	6.0	70.3	51.8	29.8	17.6	770	427
Macon	1,039	2,633,830	3.7	3.4	0.8	3.2	42.4	2.9	43.4	92.8	45.8	29.8	1,914	1,610
Madison	682	1,827,224	2.1	3.5	0.1	2.1	44.4	2.8	42.9	25.4	13.9	8.3	667	425
Maries	323	761,125	7.6	6.0	0.0	6.9	9.4	3.4	66.1	18.2	8.6	7.6	847	638
Marion	1,348	3,816,108	4.3	7.2	3.7	3.7	10.5	8.5	58.2	94.9	33.0	39.1	1,361	752
Mercer	176	501,591	15.9	5.2	0.1	7.0	6.8	4.3	59.8	9.5	4.4	3.9	1,038	887
Miller	1,205	3,202,179	4.4	4.5	1.6	2.3	11.6	1.8	73.2	80.0	30.4	36.5	1,472	1,081
Mississippi	496	1,277,944	12.1	11.0	0.1	3.6	4.4	7.4	61.1	39.2	20.9	12.9	904	600
Moniteau	498	1,342,360	7.0	4.0	0.2	3.3	8.9	4.9	70.4	34.2	15.0	12.7	813	528
Monroe	490	1,220,603	5.4	5.4	0.3	4.2	22.2	8.5	53.6	28.8	12.5	9.7	1,109	878
Montgomery	414	1,189,713	7.9	12.4	0.0	5.3	4.0	3.0	66.0	27.1	9.4	13.0	1,088	730
Morgan	588	1,595,566	8.3	9.3	0.7	4.5	8.1	2.2	61.6	37.0	13.2	17.9	892	558
New Madrid	720	1,973,525	9.1	7.8	0.4	5.1	5.0	6.0	65.2	48.9	21.7	21.3	1,153	837
Newton	1,886	5,757,934	4.6	4.8	2.8	1.7	3.3	2.2	80.6	121.7	59.7	39.0	661	405
Nodaway	726	2,001,480	9.5	5.9	0.8	3.6	4.2	6.4	68.6	62.2	22.3	27.8	1,186	755
OREGON	416	986,254	6.1	4.7	0.0	3.9	0.0	4.8	79.9	22.3	13.8	6.1	554	379
Osage	364	958,029	5.9	4.6	2.7	4.1	8.7	5.2	68.3	23.3	8.9	9.6	696	471
Ozark	375	902,737	3.5	3.0	0.0	3.7	2.8	1.2	83.1	20.2	12.4	5.9	612	453
Pemiscot	869	2,608,472	5.8	7.8	0.7	1.4	2.9	7.8	73.3	61.3	38.4	13.9	770	506
Perry	569	1,561,790	6.3	12.2	0.0	3.8	5.0	9.4	63.2	42.8	15.7	20.2	1,064	628
Pettis	2,440	8,051,066	2.4	3.6	1.7	1.5	41.8	2.5	45.8	222.9	54.6	51.1	1,207	624
Phelps	2,804	9,025,924	2.3	3.7	1.2	1.5	51.9	4.5	33.4	301.2	46.2	39.1	869	478
Pike	681	2,031,713	2.7	3.7	0.2	0.7	28.4	3.3	60.9	45.8	18.4	20.6	1,109	754
Platte	2,626	11,215,330	4.0	6.6	2.9	2.1	4.0	1.9	78.0	290.1	82.7	172.3	1,871	1,274
Polk	1,882	6,311,305	2.0	2.0	0.1	1.6	60.7	1.1	32.3	164.9	36.7	18.1	584	439
Pulaski	1,731	5,423,451	3.5	3.9	1.1	2.3	7.4	5.5	75.3	125.6	76.5	29.6	556	371
Putnam	314	940,189	4.5	2.1	0.0	2.4	55.0	5.9	29.6	17.4	5.2	7.7	1,554	1,199
Ralls	284	692,452	21.1	12.6	0.0	13.9	2.2	4.0	41.7	13.1	5.3	6.2	600	404
Randolph	1,211	3,641,751	3.9	5.9	1.9	2.1	2.9	4.9	77.8	104.1	32.8	33.6	1,328	821
Ray	1,243	21,423,521	0.8	0.5	0.3	0.3	89.8	0.8	7.3	87.1	25.3	21.5	933	704
Reynolds	325	775,935	7.0	5.6	0.0	5.7	4.1	1.6	75.1	20.4	10.7	7.5	1,131	997
Ripley	665	1,587,309	4.3	3.8	0.5	1.9	28.8	2.6	58.2	27.1	17.6	6.3	449	337
St. Charles	12,474	44,955,774	5.7	9.4	5.0	2.8	3.2	4.3	66.6	1,191.7	344.4	666.4	1,808	1,183
St. Clair	558	1,434,103	4.2	10.9	0.0	2.8	35.5	3.2	42.1	48.9	23.1	6.2	654	535
Ste. Genevieve	472	1,571,579	6.8	13.6	0.1	3.5	5.8	7.1	62.2	37.1	12.7	20.0	1,125	724
St. Francois	2,385	7,190,551	2.7	4.3	0.6	1.6	5.1	5.3	80.0	178.1	78.4	65.4	993	571
St. Louis	35,141	147,062,201	4.5	10.0	7.3	2.5	1.6	2.8	69.6	3,629.3	1,051.6	2,133.5	2,133	1,497
Saline	749	2,090,138	7.0	10.8	3.2	5.2	6.6	26.6	39.7	61.0	25.6	21.0	898	647
Schuyler	276	469,325	6.5	3.5	0.0	3.7	25.1	6.2	54.3	12.0	5.3	3.2	735	541
Scotland	479	1,508,783	7.5	3.0	0.0	5.6	60.2	4.1	19.3	31.5	5.9	4.5	918	718
Scott	1,609	5,229,887	4.1	7.7	1.4	1.8	4.2	23.8	53.9	108.4	50.7	38.1	973	559
Shannon	529	555,611	8.1	5.1	0.0	7.2	7.0	5.1	67.1	13.2	8.0	2.9	343	223
Shelby	432	1,223,611	12.6	7.4	0.3	6.2	25.9	5.7	38.5	23.5	9.7	6.6	1,064	756
Stoddard	1,139	2,920,419	5.2	6.2	0.8	8.7	6.5	5.3	66.9	72.2	30.2	21.0	704	560
Stone	846	2,351,044	6.0	5.6	1.1	2.7	0.1	2.1	82.4	74.2	35.5	30.6	969	612
Sullivan	370	985,283	6.2	4.1	0.2	3.8	27.9	5.8	50.1	23.6	9.0	6.6	1,012	748
Taney	1,787	5,327,466	7.7	9.1	3.9	4.1	8.3	6.6	58.2	198.6	59.2	103.3	1,952	978
Texas	1,227	3,278,813	3.7	3.2	0.1	3.2	31.5	5.3	50.4	84.8	28.4	20.4	791	654
Vernon	1,038	3,438,287	4.3	4.0	1.4	1.5	36.6	4.4	47.6	48.3	21.1	19.4	934	559
Warren	943	2,742,942	5.8	9.6	2.2	1.6	5.8	4.1	68.2	70.7	27.9	32.8	1,001	734
Washington	953	2,869,920	3.5	2.5	0.3	2.7	34.5	4.9	50.7	69.6	27.6	13.6	541	368
Wayne	459	1,011,584	9.4	3.6	0.0	7.6	5.0	3.2	71.2	25.2	14.3	7.7	573	378
Webster	946	2,669,213	5.5	5.0	0.3	2.8	11.0	3.5	71.2	63.4	29.0	20.2	556	309
Worth	134	294,433	8.2	2.8	0.0	3.4	21.0	5.8	57.6	6.8	2.2	2.2	1,037	834
Wright	792	2,007,501	4.3	3.8	0.3	2.7	11.1	4.2	73.0	47.2	25.3	12.2	656	392

1. Based on the resident population estimated as of July 1 of the year shown.

Table B. States and Counties — **Local Government Finances, Government Employment, and Income Taxes**

	Local government finances (cont.)							Debt outstanding		Government employment, 2016			Individual income tax returns, 2015		
	Direct general expenditure														
			Percent of total for:												
STATE County	Total (mil dol)	Per capita[1] (dollars)	Education	Health and hospitals	Police protection	Public welfare	Highways	Total (mil dol)	Per capita[1] (dollars)	Federal civilian	Federal military	State and local	Number of returns	Mean adjusted gross income	Mean income tax
	185	186	187	188	189	190	191	192	193	194	195	196	197	198	199

MISSOURI— Cont'd

Jasper	396.9	3,443	54.1	10.7	5.4	0.1	5.6	243.6	2,113	289	425	6,468	51,380	46,571	4,808
Jefferson	583.0	2,648	64.1	2.8	6.2	0.0	7.7	577.7	2,623	292	755	8,373	105,460	53,236	5,422
Johnson	233.9	4,299	31.0	47.8	3.5	0.0	4.6	246.2	4,525	1,323	3,783	5,880	22,360	48,111	4,471
Knox	10.9	2,667	49.1	8.8	4.0	18.8	5.9	0.6	147	30	13	276	1,670	33,306	2,759
Laclede	68.0	1,919	74.1	0.0	4.7	0.0	6.3	34.1	962	83	119	1,450	15,120	40,089	3,594
Lafayette	87.7	2,650	57.3	1.7	5.6	0.1	7.0	105.1	3,177	109	114	2,170	14,850	47,886	4,415
Lawrence	78.1	2,031	67.8	0.8	3.9	5.7	6.5	98.6	2,562	249	128	1,773	16,170	41,619	3,656
Lewis	26.7	2,624	50.7	1.4	3.7	15.5	8.9	11.0	1,085	46	33	569	4,270	42,101	3,722
Lincoln	153.2	2,871	47.7	26.4	4.4	0.0	4.4	139.5	2,615	111	186	2,112	25,110	50,671	4,871
Linn	37.6	3,014	60.3	3.0	4.4	0.0	11.3	26.2	2,102	56	41	792	5,450	43,334	4,025
Livingston	59.6	3,966	50.2	2.8	4.8	8.2	7.4	28.8	1,918	75	45	1,346	6,400	43,777	4,432
McDonald	44.0	1,922	69.8	0.0	4.1	0.0	8.0	31.9	1,393	88	76	893	9,110	37,238	2,800
Macon	48.3	3,102	46.4	1.1	3.5	22.2	8.9	21.2	1,363	70	51	1,578	6,940	40,634	3,614
Madison	30.2	2,426	68.9	0.0	6.2	0.0	6.2	3.9	310	38	42	838	4,980	39,963	3,531
Maries	18.1	2,013	61.7	4.7	4.0	0.0	9.9	10.7	1,187	10	30	344	3,750	40,159	3,195
Marion	99.0	3,444	54.3	3.1	3.7	6.3	4.7	133.0	4,628	106	93	1,841	12,810	46,924	4,838
Mercer	9.9	2,650	69.6	5.6	1.5	0.0	12.0	8.6	2,310	29	12	223	1,550	39,682	3,646
Miller	78.5	3,161	59.5	4.2	3.5	6.0	5.7	46.2	1,860	47	85	1,433	10,440	38,928	3,405
Mississippi	35.3	2,466	49.4	5.6	5.4	0.6	6.5	20.3	1,418	16	40	1,044	5,020	40,894	4,217
Moniteau	32.1	2,054	63.0	5.8	3.2	0.0	6.8	31.2	1,994	48	50	1,047	6,610	44,920	3,866
Monroe	28.8	3,309	49.1	3.2	3.9	16.0	10.7	54.4	6,255	76	29	623	3,880	42,063	3,491
Montgomery	28.9	2,411	56.1	3.6	5.3	0.0	7.9	11.0	913	49	38	610	5,150	42,241	3,514
Morgan	40.7	2,025	46.7	0.1	7.7	7.9	8.7	22.0	1,093	40	68	967	8,450	37,119	2,882
New Madrid	46.5	2,517	59.4	2.4	6.4	0.0	7.6	18.4	995	45	60	924	7,050	43,484	4,443
Newton	127.6	2,161	69.8	3.0	3.0	0.5	3.4	106.0	1,794	143	196	2,466	24,640	50,311	5,498
Nodaway	59.7	2,551	52.7	3.7	4.8	0.0	11.8	64.8	2,766	85	65	2,580	8,630	46,862	4,507
OREGON	21.9	1,990	73.6	1.6	2.2	0.0	5.3	3.9	358	34	36	497	3,800	34,120	2,630
Osage	23.1	1,669	59.8	6.0	2.4	0.0	5.6	11.0	794	30	45	804	6,090	47,129	4,041
Ozark	20.7	2,155	78.4	2.7	3.2	0.1	6.5	0.7	69	12	31	433	3,560	33,023	2,836
Pemiscot	61.8	3,411	67.4	1.6	4.6	0.0	5.4	11.3	624	48	57	1,489	6,450	38,672	3,529
Perry	43.0	2,261	53.4	1.8	6.3	0.0	8.0	19.0	1,001	49	65	1,204	9,060	45,599	4,053
Pettis	213.3	5,041	37.6	44.8	2.5	0.0	4.2	106.8	2,524	137	142	3,165	18,000	43,763	4,050
Phelps	295.8	6,576	23.7	59.1	2.1	0.3	2.9	165.9	3,688	340	243	5,956	18,060	46,123	4,834
Pike	43.7	2,354	53.0	1.6	7.4	0.0	9.9	24.3	1,308	62	55	1,671	7,370	43,355	3,882
Platte	285.1	3,097	65.5	0.9	4.8	0.2	5.0	434.8	4,724	743	355	3,894	47,800	78,844	11,465
Polk	168.1	5,419	28.7	60.0	1.0	0.0	3.1	55.0	1,774	69	101	2,386	12,080	42,772	3,816
Pulaski	139.6	2,621	69.4	2.9	2.8	0.0	4.4	141.0	2,648	3,588	10,344	2,078	18,430	43,871	3,334
Putnam	17.9	3,623	40.9	1.9	1.7	18.6	8.7	7.6	1,551	19	16	423	2,060	36,384	2,722
Ralls	12.4	1,207	50.3	3.6	5.3	0.0	17.2	14.9	1,451	29	35	347	4,720	47,885	4,815
Randolph	103.6	4,090	59.4	15.6	4.7	0.0	3.9	94.5	3,731	70	77	2,094	10,360	45,549	4,509
Ray	82.9	3,594	35.4	24.2	3.6	15.3	8.2	32.9	1,426	51	76	1,396	10,530	51,013	5,012
Reynolds	20.8	3,118	70.7	4.1	2.1	0.5	3.4	4.8	719	15	22	399	2,450	36,665	2,838
Ripley	26.6	1,894	72.9	5.2	4.9	0.0	4.4	1.2	88	53	47	584	5,050	33,248	2,826
St. Charles	1,188.4	3,223	54.5	2.1	6.5	0.1	9.4	1,722.2	4,671	732	1,313	15,774	191,540	70,231	8,919
St. Clair	44.1	4,651	28.5	34.9	1.9	0.0	5.3	16.1	1,703	42	31	480	3,620	37,124	3,047
Ste. Genevieve	38.8	2,184	67.5	3.0	6.6	0.0	7.8	28.1	1,581	28	60	971	8,280	50,635	4,869
St. Francois	177.6	2,694	64.6	4.1	6.8	0.1	6.3	112.4	1,705	137	202	5,805	25,750	43,247	4,019
St. Louis	3,854.3	3,853	55.7	1.6	7.0	0.9	5.2	4,175.7	4,174	5,750	3,378	48,868	504,870	85,590	14,162
Saline	61.1	2,617	55.2	5.4	6.9	0.3	7.5	7.5	323	82	74	1,647	9,800	42,758	3,933
Schuyler	11.1	2,542	46.7	3.1	1.3	22.3	14.5	7.8	1,793	31	15	295	1,730	32,496	2,450
Scotland	35.5	7,289	17.7	58.8	1.2	11.4	5.9	18.8	3,848	21	16	570	2,100	39,039	4,286
Scott	109.3	2,794	52.1	2.0	13.1	0.0	3.9	182.4	4,661	104	130	2,115	17,320	48,459	5,396
Shannon	12.9	1,551	60.4	0.2	2.3	0.0	12.2	2.7	326	20	27	327	3,050	31,392	2,359
Shelby	24.1	3,872	42.9	4.0	2.6	27.1	7.7	6.0	969	33	20	594	2,920	39,447	3,219
Stoddard	67.4	2,263	63.7	5.5	2.6	0.0	6.1	41.2	1,384	160	98	1,317	12,370	44,808	4,819
Stone	68.6	2,173	57.5	0.0	4.0	0.0	7.1	49.4	1,566	41	104	1,121	13,970	44,492	4,493
Sullivan	22.7	3,475	48.2	30.8	2.2	0.1	5.6	9.1	1,389	45	21	417	2,750	34,449	2,406
Taney	188.6	3,561	41.8	3.4	3.9	0.0	6.1	593.9	11,215	179	180	2,263	24,660	38,562	4,286
Texas	72.4	2,804	46.8	37.3	2.0	0.1	3.4	30.6	1,185	70	81	1,911	9,300	35,628	2,765
Vernon	45.8	2,207	64.9	3.0	3.5	0.0	7.3	60.2	2,903	94	68	1,639	8,460	39,630	3,374
Warren	69.9	2,135	57.6	4.6	6.2	0.0	5.1	59.4	1,815	44	115	1,273	15,500	50,817	5,081
Washington	67.9	2,707	49.1	31.2	3.2	0.0	3.5	32.5	1,294	55	81	1,489	8,790	35,765	2,565
Wayne	23.2	1,734	66.5	1.8	4.6	0.0	10.8	24.4	1,824	75	44	526	4,520	32,781	2,247
Webster	62.8	1,727	65.3	0.3	4.1	9.7	6.4	23.5	648	87	126	1,362	15,010	44,500	4,071
Worth	7.6	3,657	53.1	2.9	3.3	20.3	3.2	1.0	466	24	0	147	930	38,534	2,901
Wright	48.4	2,598	61.6	0.2	2.3	10.5	5.3	14.9	799	45	61	872	6,940	33,912	2,486

1. Based on the resident population estimated as of July 1 of the year shown.

Table B. States and Counties — **Personal Income and Earnings**

STATE County	Personal income, 2016										Earnings, 2016		
	Total (mil dol)	Percent change 2015-2016	Per capita[1]		Wages and salaries (mil dol)	Supplements to wages and salaries, employer contributions (mil dol)		Proprietors' income (mil dol)	Dividends, interest, and rent (mil dol)	Personal transfer reecipts (mil dol)	Total (mil dol)	Contributions for government social insurance (mil dol)	
			Dollars	Rank		Pension and insurance	Government social insurance					From employee and self-employed	From employer
	62	63	64	65	66	67	68	69	70	71	72	73	74
MISSOURI— Cont'd													
St. Louis city	12,787	-1.2	41,061	1,225	14,415	2,163	1,052	1,332	2,049	3,100	18,962	2,151	1,052
MONTANA	44,773	2.1	43,107	X	19,854	3,087	1,759	4,524	10,471	8,662	29,224	1,939	1,759
Beaverhead	386	-3.4	41,054	1,226	150	27	13	41	102	89	230	26	13
Big Horn	394	2.3	29,532	2,889	196	40	16	9	69	126	261	33	16
Blaine	189	-2.4	28,671	2,943	58	13	5	16	49	59	92	11	5
Broadwater	211	3.8	36,705	1,878	53	9	5	11	44	51	77	11	5
Carbon	441	0.1	42,153	1,084	94	16	8	27	121	90	145	20	8
Carter	61	-5.8	50,296	402	13	2	1	22	13	9	39	2	1
Cascade	3,546	2.4	43,375	958	1,663	289	151	246	780	749	2,349	303	151
Chouteau	180	-1.8	31,202	2,716	48	9	4	2	62	42	63	9	4
Custer	486	-3.6	40,763	1,263	210	33	19	68	98	97	329	41	19
Daniels	68	-4.9	38,811	1,534	29	5	2	2	20	16	38	6	2
Dawson	367	-5.3	39,379	1,440	175	25	17	19	65	72	236	34	17
Deer Lodge	338	3.7	37,184	1,796	125	22	11	13	65	98	171	24	11
Fallon	137	-10.1	43,814	896	75	11	6	18	30	21	110	13	6
Fergus	459	1.8	40,197	1,338	175	29	16	53	116	102	272	35	16
Flathead	4,149	4.8	42,302	1,059	1,784	242	167	459	1,017	831	2,653	351	167
Gallatin	5,012	5.9	47,959	541	2,394	333	211	711	1,294	534	3,650	437	211
Garfield	53	-11.6	40,763	1,263	11	3	1	16	15	9	31	2	1
Glacier	436	0.9	31,869	2,635	166	38	14	28	80	136	245	29	14
Golden Valley	41	-9.4	49,017	465	7	2	1	7	14	9	16	2	1
Granite	124	1.5	36,868	1,844	32	5	3	8	40	29	49	7	3
Hill	684	-1.8	41,321	1,196	324	54	32	40	161	150	450	61	32
Jefferson	516	2.3	43,540	931	116	19	10	31	103	96	175	23	10
Judith Basin	95	-4.5	48,981	469	19	4	2	28	28	16	53	4	2
Lake	1,017	5.8	34,183	2,293	320	57	28	75	261	306	480	63	28
Lewis and Clark	3,010	3.6	44,733	799	1,663	289	142	221	641	553	2,314	288	142
Liberty	82	-6.1	34,038	2,322	22	4	2	14	30	17	41	4	2
Lincoln	644	3.8	33,464	2,399	193	37	18	42	147	236	291	44	18
McCone	75	-10.1	43,988	881	25	4	2	10	19	11	41	5	2
Madison	386	3.5	48,748	484	165	20	16	43	110	72	244	32	16
Meagher	77	-9.2	42,170	1,081	18	3	2	12	23	21	34	4	2
Mineral	141	1.8	33,617	2,380	35	7	3	8	26	49	53	8	3
Missoula	5,125	4.2	44,134	864	2,513	377	225	441	1,434	865	3,555	457	225
Musselshell	176	-1.5	38,443	1,577	59	9	5	10	42	52	83	11	5
Park	736	3.4	45,647	728	215	29	20	63	223	139	327	44	20
Petroleum	24	-12.5	49,505	440	4	1	0	9	5	3	15	1	0
Phillips	154	-6.0	37,247	1,782	49	9	4	16	41	39	78	10	4
Pondera	237	-0.8	39,017	1,493	67	11	6	15	73	59	100	13	6
Powder River	63	-8.2	36,066	1,996	20	4	2	11	16	11	37	4	2
Powell	253	-0.9	36,959	1,826	96	21	8	15	77	61	140	18	8
Prairie	45	-5.4	38,146	1,631	13	3	1	5	13	12	22	3	1
Ravalli	1,638	4.2	38,919	1,509	435	71	40	112	446	415	658	93	40
Richland	608	-12.8	52,929	308	307	43	26	94	123	69	469	55	26
Roosevelt	383	-3.8	33,914	2,336	146	28	12	17	68	113	203	26	12
Rosebud	340	-1.5	36,626	1,893	212	42	18	5	54	84	278	36	18
Sanders	382	4.3	33,125	2,451	95	19	9	36	89	140	159	23	9
Sheridan	178	-9.7	48,864	477	63	11	5	27	50	30	106	12	5
Silver Bow	1,603	1.2	46,395	657	677	111	59	277	299	331	1,124	134	59
Stillwater	417	-0.8	44,314	846	183	27	14	29	97	78	253	31	14
Sweet Grass	160	0.2	44,264	853	78	12	6	7	53	30	103	13	6
Teton	264	-4.2	43,548	928	67	12	5	32	82	55	117	14	5
Toole	187	-5.9	37,476	1,742	90	17	8	18	58	35	133	16	8
Treasure	36	-13.1	52,325	325	7	1	1	7	8	7	16	1	1
Valley	319	-2.7	42,343	1,053	138	23	14	15	80	74	189	27	14
Wheatland	74	-4.0	35,138	2,143	22	4	2	12	21	21	41	4	2
Wibaux	43	-9.2	39,643	1,406	11	3	1	9	6	8	24	3	1
Yellowstone	7,521	1.7	47,467	566	3,927	547	343	943	1,368	1,236	5,760	719	343
NEBRASKA	95,411	1.6	50,016	X	47,003	7,788	3,532	14,032	17,729	13,932	72,355	4,058	3,532
Adams	1,401	0.5	44,216	856	643	115	48	140	315	271	946	104	48
Antelope	324	-1.8	51,137	369	88	16	6	86	61	59	197	14	6
Arthur	20	-12.5	42,994	996	6	1	0	4	4	4	11	1	0
Banner	49	-1.8	61,317	133	9	1	1	26	6	6	37	1	1

1. Based on the resident population estimated as of July 1 of the year shown.

Table B. States and Counties — **Earnings, Social Security, and Housing**

STATE County	Earnings, 2016 (cont.) Percent by selected industries									Social Security beneficiaries, December 2016			Housing units, 2017	
	Farm	Mining, quarrying, and extracting	Construction	Manu- facturing	Information; professional, scientific, technical services	Retail trade	Finance, insurance, real estate, and leasing	Health care and social assistance	Govern- ment	Number	Rate[1]	Supple- mental Security Income recipients, 2016	Total	Percent change, 2010-2017
	75	76	77	78	79	80	81	82	83	84	85	86	87	88
MISSOURI— Cont'd														
St. Louis city	0.0	D	D	8.2	16.3	1.7	9.0	15.9	15.1	53,630	171	16,004	176,846	0.5
MONTANA	1.5	3.8	8.7	4.2	8.0	8.4	7.1	14.2	20.0	223,401	215	18,276	510,389	5.7
Beaverhead	14.1	D	6.0	1.0	4.2	7.9	5.8	12.4	27.0	2,255	239	130	5,338	1.2
Big Horn	2.2	20.6	1.8	-0.7	1.9	4.3	2.1	D	47.3	2,160	162	332	4,734	0.8
Blaine	11.6	D	3.0	0.7	D	9.4	D	D	45.6	1,210	182	197	2,850	0.2
Broadwater	3.9	D	D	D	D	7.5	6.8	7.4	19.1	1,450	251	68	2,742	1.7
Carbon	-2.0	4.2	14.8	1.6	6.9	5.5	6.8	9.7	22.5	2,755	262	112	6,565	2.0
Carter	58.2	0.2	D	0.2	D	5.3	D	D	13.0	305	259	0	827	2.1
Cascade	0.2	0.1	7.7	3.7	6.0	8.7	7.8	17.2	27.3	18,265	224	1,909	38,845	4.2
Chouteau	7.6	0.2	5.0	1.5	D	8.9	5.8	7.0	32.1	1,200	207	68	2,916	1.3
Custer	2.2	1.7	7.4	1.0	3.6	12.9	7.5	D	20.7	2,615	221	249	5,698	2.5
Daniels	-18.9	D	6.8	D	D	D	D	15.5	15.8	470	271	10	1,127	1.4
Dawson	-1.3	6.8	4.4	1.0	5.3	8.9	4.4	D	16.7	1,725	187	104	4,442	5.0
Deer Lodge	0.3	0.1	6.8	D	6.2	5.3	2.5	30.0	30.6	2,625	289	266	5,207	1.7
Fallon	2.5	25.5	10.3	0.7	2.3	4.8	4.0	8.5	15.9	590	191	12	1,639	11.5
Fergus	3.8	D	16.6	6.8	3.4	7.8	7.2	D	20.0	3,045	269	189	5,899	1.1
Flathead	0.2	0.8	10.8	6.8	7.2	9.0	8.7	18.4	12.4	22,750	233	1,343	48,741	3.8
Gallatin	1.9	0.5	13.7	5.1	12.9	11.3	7.3	9.4	15.4	14,440	139	596	49,444	16.9
Garfield	47.1	0.5	D	D	D	7.9	D	D	21.2	300	229	14	864	2.4
Glacier	5.5	3.2	D	D	2.1	7.7	1.2	D	54.2	2,120	155	593	5,391	0.8
Golden Valley	6.0	D	D	D	D	D	2.1	D	19.6	280	344	19	484	1.7
Granite	6.4	0.7	6.0	4.3	D	5.0	D	D	26.3	1,000	304	42	2,836	0.5
Hill	4.6	0.1	5.0	0.4	6.8	7.6	4.8	D	30.0	2,705	164	425	7,343	1.3
Jefferson	1.9	13.9	10.7	6.6	D	3.3	4.7	8.5	26.5	2,920	248	142	5,109	1.1
Judith Basin	51.0	0.3	6.2	0.0	D	3.1	D	D	16.1	545	280	26	1,357	1.6
Lake	3.3	0.7	8.5	5.1	5.9	8.7	3.7	13.7	33.2	7,285	245	728	16,878	1.7
Lewis and Clark	0.5	0.7	5.4	2.3	10.2	6.6	9.0	12.7	35.6	14,925	223	1,091	31,649	4.9
Liberty	32.5	D	3.7	-0.1	D	6.5	D	D	15.3	405	167	51	1,046	0.3
Lincoln	-0.4	0.9	10.8	2.8	4.0	10.6	2.8	15.7	29.1	6,835	355	564	11,664	2.2
McCone	5.9	0.2	4.8	0.5	D	9.0	D	D	16.6	345	198	0	1,022	1.3
Madison	6.7	5.6	10.4	1.9	3.8	4.5	4.0	D	11.5	2,310	290	66	7,011	1.1
Meagher	17.7	D	D	D	D	5.8	D	D	20.0	565	307	49	1,448	1.1
Mineral	-1.0	0.6	10.7	D	D	13.2	D	D	33.4	1,465	355	142	2,500	2.2
Missoula	-0.1	0.0	6.6	3.1	9.3	8.7	7.5	18.5	19.6	21,170	183	2,138	53,982	7.7
Musselshell	-1.6	40.5	8.7	0.5	2.8	4.1	D	9.6	15.6	1,385	299	110	2,702	1.8
Park	1.7	0.2	10.6	7.0	7.1	6.8	6.8	12.3	13.1	3,730	232	241	9,607	2.5
Petroleum	54.8	D	D	0.0	D	D	0.6	D	15.9	110	221	7	334	3.1
Phillips	7.8	D	7.5	1.5	D	8.6	7.1	D	27.0	1,050	255	84	2,352	0.7
Pondera	5.2	1.3	13.5	1.5	4.0	8.5	D	13.0	19.9	1,310	217	192	2,674	0.5
Powder River	23.2	D	D	D	D	9.3	D	D	26.6	375	214	0	1,032	1.0
Powell	2.2	D	D	D	2.3	3.4	2.6	9.6	50.2	1,555	227	111	3,216	3.6
Prairie	0.4	0.7	D	D	D	10.4	D	D	46.6	360	309	14	679	0.9
Ravalli	-0.6	D	13.0	5.9	9.6	7.4	6.6	13.1	19.6	12,570	300	750	19,821	1.2
Richland	2.5	18.7	12.0	4.8	3.2	7.3	8.1	D	9.9	1,860	163	104	5,243	15.2
Roosevelt	-1.2	3.1	3.3	0.4	D	8.9	2.4	D	46.3	1,745	156	372	4,134	1.7
Rosebud	0.7	18.7	D	D	D	3.1	D	D	33.6	1,805	195	225	4,181	3.0
Sanders	0.1	2.6	13.7	5.9	D	7.0	4.1	13.0	24.7	4,205	367	308	6,763	1.3
Sheridan	17.1	3.9	D	D	3.7	5.8	D	D	19.7	920	256	35	2,166	3.7
Silver Bow	0.0	12.9	3.3	4.1	4.8	11.7	6.9	16.4	15.7	8,325	242	977	17,225	3.0
Stillwater	1.7	D	D	5.1	3.5	4.1	1.7	4.0	10.0	2,345	250	80	4,885	1.7
Sweet Grass	-3.0	D	10.7	3.0	1.8	4.7	3.7	2.5	13.7	940	259	22	2,166	0.8
Teton	6.8	D	12.0	1.3	D	6.6	D	6.9	19.7	1,505	250	118	2,920	1.0
Toole	10.1	6.2	D	D	D	4.7	4.4	5.3	30.3	900	181	102	2,381	1.9
Treasure	50.8	0.0	D	0.0	D	D	D	D	14.6	210	307	0	432	2.4
Valley	0.0	0.1	7.4	1.1	5.6	6.7	D	D	23.8	1,830	243	125	4,893	0.3
Wheatland	22.2	D	D	D	D	7.3	2.8	D	18.4	515	244	54	1,210	1.1
Wibaux	6.3	D	D	D	D	12.5	3.0	D	27.8	260	248	6	562	4.5
Yellowstone	0.3	5.9	8.8	5.9	9.6	7.7	8.0	16.5	11.2	30,555	194	2,539	71,213	11.4
NEBRASKA	6.3	0.1	6.1	9.0	7.6	5.6	8.2	10.5	15.8	335,361	176	27,893	837,568	5.1
Adams	8.3	0.0	7.0	15.3	3.6	6.2	3.6	D	15.3	6,760	214	524	13,921	4.3
Antelope	38.6	D	6.6	4.2	1.3	4.8	5.7	7.6	12.2	1,545	243	83	3,321	1.1
Arthur	43.5	0.0	D	0.0	D	D	0.0	D	21.9	105	223	0	254	0.0
Banner	71.5	0.0	D	1.8	0.0	0.6	D	D	8.8	230	318	0	368	-0.3

1. Per 1,000 resident population estimated as of July 1 of the year shown.

Table B. States and Counties — **Professional Services, Manufacturing, and Accommodation and Food Services**

STATE County	Professional, scientific, and technical services, 2012				Manufacturing, 2012				Accommodation and food services, 2012			
	Number of establishments	Number of employees	Sales (mil dol)	Annual payroll (mil dol)	Number of establishments	Number of employees	Receipts (mil dol)	Annual payroll (mil dol)	Number of establishments	Number of employees	Receipts (mil dol)	Annual payroll (mil dol)
	147	148	149	150	151	152	153	154	155	156	157	158
MISSOURI— Cont'd												
St. Louis city......................	1,009	17,461	3,015.1	1,200.0	484	17,422	10,737.0	975.2	1,036	22,069	1,255.7	371.4
MONTANA...................	3,545	16,660	2,191.9	798.8	1,237	15,729	11,535.2	714.5	3,458	46,251	2,420.5	649.5
Beaverhead......................	25	72	5.3	1.5	13	37	6.8	1.2	48	425	18.3	5.0
Big Horn.......................	15	39	3.0	1.2	3	15	D	D	27	234	17.2	3.5
Blaine...........................	13	26	4.8	1.6	5	13	3.4	0.5	12	56	2.6	0.6
Broadwater....................	9	28	2.5	0.7	6	159	D	6.8	21	118	5.4	1.4
Carbon..........................	28	D	D	D	10	D	D	D	51	490	24.8	7.4
Carter...........................	5	9	0.6	0.1	NA	NA	NA	NA	2	D	D	D
Cascade........................	202	1,159	131.8	50.3	62	964	955.3	45.0	240	3,887	194.7	51.5
Chouteau.......................	9	27	2.2	0.6	7	17	5.9	0.7	18	D	D	D
Custer	28	99	7.9	3.1	13	79	D	2.2	39	543	28.5	6.8
Daniels.........................	3	D	D	D	NA	NA	NA	NA	9	D	D	D
Dawson........................	24	71	6.5	2.3	4	37	D	1.6	34	502	25.7	6.4
Deer Lodge	26	112	15.6	4.9	4	87	D	D	30	275	10.9	2.6
Fallon	9	16	2.3	0.5	3	9	D	D	18	104	6.9	1.4
Fergus	34	82	7.8	2.0	26	273	60.6	11.9	47	413	18.5	4.9
Flathead........................	375	1,347	184.6	56.1	182	2,367	620.8	105.3	363	4,362	247.9	67.7
Gallatin.........................	655	2,415	298.0	113.5	188	2,363	491.0	99.5	410	7,193	348.1	96.5
Garfield	NA	NA	NA	NA	NA	NA	NA	NA	5	28	1.1	0.2
Glacier..........................	11	64	6.8	1.8	4	20	2.3	0.5	51	335	38.3	8.7
Golden Valley	1	D	D	D	NA	NA	NA	NA	4	13	0.5	0.1
Granite	5	3	0.7	0.2	5	15	2.2	0.5	16	101	8.3	2.9
Hill..............................	30	206	20.6	10.4	7	18	2.9	0.7	56	758	35.0	9.2
Jefferson.......................	25	36	5.2	1.7	12	234	D	14.6	21	191	7.1	2.1
Judith Basin	4	11	2.1	0.3	NA	NA	NA	NA	10	27	1.4	0.3
Lake............................	52	352	71.8	20.2	35	497	72.4	15.4	76	630	33.5	8.6
Lewis and Clark	250	1,661	209.8	84.0	58	525	D	22.1	198	3,083	142.0	39.6
Liberty	4	10	0.6	0.2	NA	NA	NA	NA	5	32	0.7	0.2
Lincoln.........................	35	84	8.2	2.5	24	137	16.8	4.0	64	488	26.4	7.3
McCone........................	1	D	D	D	NA	NA	NA	NA	5	18	0.6	0.1
Madison	28	60	5.5	1.9	11	69	D	1.8	55	220	15.8	4.0
Meagher........................	3	3	0.2	0.1	NA	NA	NA	NA	15	52	2.2	0.5
Mineral	6	37	2.7	1.1	7	200	D	7.6	19	120	4.8	1.4
Missoula.......................	501	2,865	325.4	137.2	102	1,351	310.6	49.1	342	6,106	317.4	84.0
Musselshell	8	15	1.5	0.5	3	6	1.7	0.3	13	D	D	D
Park............................	74	181	23.7	7.6	29	338	58.9	14.1	118	1,130	75.2	22.3
Petroleum......................	1	D	D	D	NA	NA	NA	NA	2	D	D	D
Phillips.........................	9	28	2.4	0.7	5	13	1.9	0.5	16	109	4.7	1.2
Pondera	10	36	3.0	1.2	8	89	D	3.1	16	141	4.8	1.2
Powder River	4	D	D	D	NA	NA	NA	NA	12	57	2.9	0.6
Powell..........................	9	32	3.3	0.9	8	185	D	D	22	D	D	D
Prairie..........................	4	5	0.8	0.3	NA	NA	NA	NA	6	19	0.6	0.1
Ravalli..........................	122	514	27.3	25.5	84	703	132.4	25.7	96	841	38.4	11.6
Richland........................	40	228	46.6	13.6	12	371	D	14.6	44	569	38.4	8.9
Roosevelt......................	11	21	2.0	0.8	NA	NA	NA	NA	24	256	13.7	3.1
Rosebud........................	5	15	1.4	0.3	3	7	D	D	33	247	10.8	2.6
Sanders........................	24	35	3.5	0.9	20	185	37.6	6.4	39	320	12.5	3.6
Sheridan.......................	11	28	3.3	1.1	NA	NA	NA	NA	15	137	6.9	1.7
Silver Bow.....................	107	654	73.9	30.8	35	492	D	31.5	147	2,244	102.4	28.7
Stillwater	24	55	6.0	1.7	11	441	D	25.6	25	174	11.0	2.6
Sweet Grass	12	28	4.4	1.0	10	53	D	2.0	16	140	6.4	2.0
Teton	10	36	3.7	1.0	7	15	3.0	0.5	19	107	5.2	1.2
Toole	12	36	5.0	1.5	4	30	7.0	1.3	27	202	12.0	2.7
Treasure........................	2	D	D	D	NA	NA	NA	NA	4	13	0.4	0.1
Valley	19	75	6.5	2.5	6	39	D	1.0	34	367	16.4	4.4
Wheatland......................	3	7	1.4	0.2	NA	NA	NA	NA	11	54	3.5	0.6
Wibaux.........................	4	8	0.8	0.4	NA	NA	NA	NA	4	37	1.5	0.5
Yellowstone....................	604	3,578	618.7	198.5	183	3,185	6,880.3	185.8	404	7,935	452.2	121.3
NEBRASKA...................	4,448	74,514	5,726.7	3,639.3	1,844	92,409	57,499.2	4,002.8	4,326	70,128	3,094.5	855.4
Adams..........................	62	306	31.4	12.2	57	2,448	1,858.9	101.8	81	1,354	53.0	13.7
Antelope........................	12	29	4.6	1.1	9	85	D	4.1	15	D	D	D
Arthur	1	D	D	D	NA	NA	NA	NA	1	D	D	D
Banner	NA	NA	NA	NA	NA	NA	NA	NA	NA	NA	NA	NA

Table B. States and Counties — Health Care and Social Assistance, Other Services, Nonemployer Businesses, and Residential Construction

STATE County	Health care and social assistance, 2012				Other services, 2012				Nonemployer businesses, 2015		Value of residential construction authorized by building permits, 2017	
	Number of establishments	Number of employees	Receipts (mil dol)	Annual payroll (mil dol)	Number of establishments	Number of employees	Receipts (mil dol)	Annual payroll (mil dol)	Number	Receipts (mil dol)	New construction ($1,000)	Number of housing units
	159	160	161	162	163	164	165	166	167	168	169	170
MISSOURI— Cont'd												
St. Louis city	1,219	35,572	4,162.1	1,389.0	629	4,529	647.7	151.1	21,107	817.2	79,672	785
MONTANA	3,512	65,657	6,469.5	2,555.4	2,278	10,917	1,222.0	302.8	86,969	3,933.1	847,390	4,932
Beaverhead	40	487	41.1	19.0	21	58	4.0	1.0	878	35.8	700	10
Big Horn	21	D	D	D	9	22	2.3	0.6	509	18.5	162	1
Blaine	15	366	31.1	12.7	10	D	D	D	329	8.6	315	3
Broadwater	7	106	7.0	3.0	9	D	D	D	500	24.3	0	0
Carbon	32	D	D	D	20	D	D	D	1,126	48.6	1,062	7
Carter	2	D	D	D	2	D	D	D	114	6.0	355	7
Cascade	262	6,363	711.9	269.1	155	871	76.6	21.7	4,680	199.2	53,883	205
Chouteau	11	130	9.5	4.9	6	9	0.3	0.1	356	14.3	3,482	13
Custer	49	978	67.2	31.3	27	123	14.2	3.2	867	39.9	490	2
Daniels	4	D	D	D	5	D	D	D	145	6.9	0	0
Dawson	29	631	45.0	20.7	30	97	9.4	2.3	628	25.4	127	1
Deer Lodge	52	1,278	110.6	51.7	12	45	5.0	1.3	462	17.2	1,985	12
Fallon	5	D	D	D	9	21	3.6	0.7	347	14.4	5,066	47
Fergus	47	855	52.9	25.3	32	122	11.1	2.1	993	40.3	565	3
Flathead	339	5,537	572.5	232.6	227	937	87.1	22.7	10,306	495.9	72,599	361
Gallatin	385	4,387	437.5	173.1	269	1,314	155.9	40.3	12,078	586.0	350,787	1,612
Garfield	1	D	D	D	2	D	D	D	132	5.2	0	0
Glacier	18	962	55.3	22.5	17	85	28.6	2.7	740	27.2	0	0
Golden Valley	2	D	D	D	1	D	D	D	81	4.3	NA	NA
Granite	4	D	D	D	3	6	0.3	0.1	323	11.8	NA	NA
Hill	58	1,374	102.1	44.4	37	173	18.3	3.9	938	29.2	238	1
Jefferson	22	225	13.9	5.3	10	34	4.1	1.3	1,024	42.1	1,656	6
Judith Basin	3	6	0.1	0.0	1	D	D	D	182	7.4	NA	NA
Lake	77	1,182	98.1	43.7	50	141	11.0	2.9	2,321	89.3	7,981	61
Lewis and Clark	271	5,376	610.0	219.5	200	1,156	126.8	41.6	5,409	248.4	26,875	146
Liberty	3	D	D	D	3	D	D	D	143	5.2	NA	NA
Lincoln	56	866	60.1	27.3	36	114	10.5	2.5	1,565	60.8	1,150	10
McCone	3	D	D	D	2	D	D	D	170	5.8	0	0
Madison	19	141	12.3	5.2	15	D	D	D	997	39.5	1,276	5
Meagher	7	D	D	D	2	D	D	D	190	7.4	NA	NA
Mineral	13	145	8.7	4.9	7	4	1.4	0.3	325	9.8	0	0
Missoula	489	9,292	965.9	351.1	287	1,889	258.2	56.0	9,848	453.1	139,190	972
Musselshell	9	178	11.1	3.8	8	17	1.7	0.3	340	14.0	300	2
Park	55	850	60.0	27.7	49	181	16.3	4.8	2,115	84.1	9,336	59
Petroleum	1	D	D	D	1	D	D	D	38	1.6	NA	NA
Phillips	9	184	9.5	4.8	13	37	3.9	0.9	354	11.6	238	2
Pondera	18	317	20.9	9.1	12	28	3.1	0.5	447	15.3	0	0
Powder River	1	D	D	D	7	D	D	D	178	6.2	NA	NA
Powell	16	184	14.7	5.6	5	18	1.9	0.5	496	19.9	9,620	36
Prairie	3	D	D	D	2	D	D	D	81	3.1	NA	NA
Ravalli	133	1,459	103.3	46.0	81	246	22.3	5.2	4,324	184.2	3,222	25
Richland	32	676	59.1	21.2	30	117	12.6	3.4	917	48.0	2,500	14
Roosevelt	12	D	D	D	11	58	3.1	0.6	538	21.5	896	4
Rosebud	17	300	13.0	6.1	14	77	5.3	1.9	492	14.8	0	0
Sanders	39	407	28.1	12.0	14	60	5.4	1.2	1,065	42.4	0	0
Sheridan	12	366	18.0	7.9	9	20	3.2	0.6	333	14.7	0	0
Silver Bow	159	3,303	287.5	127.1	72	289	34.1	7.2	2,138	93.1	7,549	70
Stillwater	24	259	14.5	5.4	10	18	3.0	0.5	806	38.0	0	0
Sweet Grass	6	24	1.1	0.3	10	28	2.1	0.5	453	20.5	300	2
Teton	18	238	11.8	5.6	11	14	2.8	0.6	574	25.2	158	1
Toole	12	D	D	D	11	25	2.2	0.4	319	13.4	0	0
Treasure	1	D	D	D	1	D	D	D	53	1.2	NA	NA
Valley	24	603	43.1	19.5	20	63	6.9	1.5	522	18.6	983	5
Wheatland	4	D	D	D	3	5	0.3	0.1	163	5.5	NA	NA
Wibaux	3	D	D	D	NA	NA	NA	NA	76	2.8	1,237	9
Yellowstone	558	12,676	1,527.6	583.0	368	2,134	234.8	58.7	11,441	605.6	141,107	1,218
NEBRASKA	5,410	125,469	12,869.4	4,907.3	3,989	21,832	2,841.3	612.5	131,518	5,743.9	1,446,057	8,863
Adams	116	2,495	247.7	103.7	55	307	33.0	6.8	2,135	93.5	14,522	57
Antelope	15	305	22.9	8.8	20	40	4.5	0.8	654	25.7	3,088	24
Arthur	NA	NA	NA	NA	2	D	D	D	45	3.6	NA	NA
Banner	NA	NA	NA	NA	1	D	D	D	41	1.6	NA	NA

Table B. States and Counties — Government Employment and Payroll, and Local Government Finances

STATE County	Government employment and payroll, 2012									Local government finances				
			March payroll (percent of total)							General revenue				
												Taxes		
													Per capita[1] (dollars)	
	Full-time equivalent employees	March payroll (dollars)	Adminis-tration, judicial, and legal	Police and corrections	Fire protection	Highways and transpor-tation	Health and welfare	Natural resources and utilities	Education and libraries	Total (mil dol)	Inter-govern-mental (mil dol)	Total (mil dol)	Total	Property
	171	172	173	174	175	176	177	178	179	180	181	182	183	184
MISSOURI— Cont'd														
St. Louis city......................	15,033	62,103,817	5.6	17.2	5.7	20.6	1.5	12.9	34.1	2,385.3	762.8	924.8	2,907	1,228
MONTANA...................	X	X	X	X	X	X	X	X	X	X	X	X	X	X
Beaverhead......................	518	1,862,160	5.1	4.6	0.4	2.9	54.8	1.7	29.5	66.4	12.9	10.3	1,104	1,099
Big Horn..........................	748	2,839,698	3.5	4.0	0.0	3.4	4.1	1.1	82.8	62.2	38.7	13.7	1,049	1,040
Blaine..............................	358	1,163,514	11.3	3.8	0.0	6.0	0.6	3.7	73.6	31.5	20.8	7.2	1,083	1,053
Broadwater......................	160	477,725	12.8	12.5	0.0	5.0	4.9	1.1	62.3	14.4	6.3	5.4	935	924
Carbon............................	377	1,229,196	11.7	8.3	1.5	6.6	1.7	4.4	62.9	33.2	13.2	15.7	1,547	1,457
Carter..............................	67	178,052	5.5	6.2	0.0	11.1	1.6	2.3	58.2	7.1	3.5	2.6	2,229	2,201
Cascade...........................	2,704	9,771,107	6.8	13.0	3.8	5.6	3.7	6.9	59.0	238.3	103.2	77.2	944	913
Chouteau	318	956,267	6.0	6.6	0.0	4.7	29.2	2.6	49.0	26.4	10.3	9.2	1,565	1,560
Custer..............................	539	1,661,688	7.8	7.4	3.4	4.8	3.2	3.6	68.6	42.2	19.5	9.9	832	817
Daniels............................	99	271,126	13.7	7.5	0.1	5.3	5.9	3.5	61.2	10.7	3.8	5.1	2,865	1,845
Dawson............................	486	1,501,541	7.2	15.3	1.5	5.5	7.5	3.6	57.4	42.3	16.8	12.8	1,387	1,374
Deer Lodge......................	264	898,579	8.3	14.8	4.3	3.9	1.1	6.9	59.7	28.1	15.5	7.9	855	847
Fallon..............................	190	709,670	11.6	5.6	3.4	9.5	5.9	6.1	55.5	33.9	25.4	5.0	1,645	1,614
Fergus.............................	520	1,621,405	6.8	8.4	2.1	15.7	1.2	2.9	61.6	43.5	22.6	14.7	1,286	1,268
Flathead..........................	2,820	10,913,778	6.6	7.4	3.2	3.5	3.5	3.7	70.8	292.8	116.8	111.5	1,216	1,179
Gallatin...........................	2,434	9,405,208	8.1	11.0	3.8	2.9	5.0	5.6	60.7	253.4	77.2	121.2	1,309	1,215
Garfield...........................	115	230,472	8.7	3.3	2.9	6.0	24.2	7.0	41.9	7.0	2.6	2.3	1,862	1,861
Glacier............................	700	2,311,773	4.2	4.6	0.0	3.2	3.2	2.5	81.1	52.7	34.1	13.8	1,008	1,004
Golden Valley...................	58	147,171	10.6	3.5	0.0	4.0	0.0	0.3	80.9	4.9	2.7	1.9	2,302	2,299
Granite............................	179	573,451	9.2	4.8	0.0	3.8	33.5	2.9	44.5	15.4	5.5	4.2	1,364	1,358
Hill.................................	793	2,599,436	4.3	6.6	2.9	3.9	3.3	3.7	74.5	62.6	35.3	17.8	1,085	1,070
Jefferson	303	957,909	14.8	9.2	0.0	4.0	5.0	1.6	64.0	29.3	15.5	10.6	927	924
Judith Basin.....................	121	355,407	6.9	3.6	0.0	13.7	0.1	1.1	72.7	9.7	4.7	3.9	1,915	1,915
Lake...............................	962	3,993,744	4.2	5.9	0.2	1.6	3.5	2.9	80.7	85.3	44.4	27.2	940	933
Lewis and Clark	1,872	7,755,463	7.5	9.0	2.6	3.9	8.6	5.4	59.9	213.1	82.3	69.8	1,076	1,054
Liberty.............................	111	316,696	12.4	8.7	0.0	7.1	6.6	4.8	58.9	8.2	3.8	3.3	1,372	1,372
Lincoln............................	599	1,992,630	12.4	7.4	0.5	3.8	2.7	4.3	65.2	57.6	31.7	14.9	766	754
McCone...........................	168	326,681	15.1	4.8	0.1	1.2	1.9	4.1	42.3	8.6	3.2	4.3	2,540	2,486
Madison...........................	459	1,488,288	7.5	4.1	0.2	3.8	40.5	2.0	39.5	41.8	10.9	17.1	2,205	2,194
Meagher...........................	122	326,266	10.3	7.3	0.0	3.7	0.0	4.5	46.8	8.8	3.1	3.4	1,746	1,742
Mineral............................	297	957,709	7.9	6.9	0.3	1.9	33.5	1.3	47.5	23.2	8.6	6.0	1,442	1,403
Missoula..........................	3,035	11,623,602	8.8	11.6	6.2	6.3	5.7	3.6	55.2	333.0	140.7	131.9	1,189	1,156
Musselshell......................	259	845,308	4.5	3.3	0.0	3.2	25.2	1.6	61.7	22.2	9.1	7.4	1,596	1,532
Park...............................	528	1,727,963	10.9	8.8	4.3	3.9	4.6	4.7	62.0	50.7	22.2	18.0	1,154	1,123
Petroleum........................	36	121,984	11.4	0.0	0.0	5.5	0.0	6.6	74.9	4.7	3.4	0.9	1,705	1,703
Phillips............................	229	653,111	10.8	5.9	0.1	6.4	3.3	8.6	61.5	21.3	11.3	6.4	1,542	1,503
Pondera...........................	212	607,909	10.4	10.1	0.2	5.9	1.8	7.3	62.5	34.1	12.3	7.0	1,132	1,127
Powder River	137	334,388	14.5	7.2	0.0	8.8	27.7	1.7	37.3	12.1	5.0	3.7	2,074	1,968
Powell.............................	199	625,409	10.4	7.0	0.5	5.1	2.6	2.8	69.0	21.5	10.6	6.4	906	902
Prairie.............................	95	225,508	8.2	3.7	0.0	5.1	32.5	1.7	42.7	7.5	2.4	1.9	1,617	1,608
Ravalli.............................	1,130	3,297,468	9.0	9.9	0.2	2.5	1.0	3.9	72.3	96.2	49.5	36.0	885	874
Richland...........................	560	1,708,152	7.9	8.6	0.2	7.8	4.4	8.1	58.4	72.7	47.2	9.4	866	853
Roosevelt.........................	704	2,186,188	5.4	5.6	0.2	3.3	10.8	2.9	70.0	63.5	42.5	12.7	1,161	1,154
Rosebud...........................	641	1,932,124	5.8	8.0	0.0	6.1	4.9	5.7	68.6	65.9	31.0	16.0	1,705	1,689
Sanders...........................	390	1,112,745	8.1	9.8	0.3	5.2	3.6	1.9	69.3	33.6	16.5	12.8	1,123	1,122
Sheridan..........................	333	1,098,598	7.7	3.6	1.6	5.2	44.9	1.5	34.4	19.8	10.2	5.6	1,551	1,542
Silver Bow........................	995	3,780,881	7.3	11.3	8.8	7.4	1.2	11.1	51.5	120.3	54.8	39.2	1,139	1,112
Stillwater.........................	340	1,123,218	10.5	6.8	1.0	7.0	2.4	1.8	70.1	29.0	12.6	12.5	1,360	1,350
Sweet Grass	197	563,456	9.7	3.8	0.0	3.5	28.6	2.5	49.1	22.0	6.9	6.1	1,698	1,696
Teton..............................	434	1,416,652	5.6	3.0	0.1	2.9	31.7	6.4	49.4	34.6	11.1	9.4	1,552	1,512
Toole..............................	386	1,266,882	7.5	5.0	0.0	3.8	44.2	2.8	34.4	36.1	9.0	7.8	1,492	1,473
Treasure..........................	44	114,460	17.8	4.4	0.0	4.5	6.2	7.2	53.1	3.7	1.5	1.7	2,261	2,258
Valley..............................	402	1,205,227	6.6	9.6	0.0	6.9	3.9	4.9	66.3	36.1	17.0	11.6	1,551	1,486
Wheatland........................	160	440,257	19.4	6.3	0.0	12.1	3.4	4.6	49.3	9.4	4.2	4.2	1,974	1,965
Wibaux............................	61	199,748	22.1	5.7	0.0	16.7	2.2	0.8	52.4	6.8	4.9	1.2	1,174	1,124
Yellowstone......................	4,840	19,590,185	5.0	8.6	4.7	4.9	8.9	6.0	55.1	469.5	175.3	161.7	1,065	989
NEBRASKA..................	X	X	X	X	X	X	X	X	X	X	X	X	X	X
Adams............................	2,340	8,844,524	2.4	3.7	1.5	2.0	0.5	13.9	70.2	174.2	49.6	89.6	2,849	2,506
Antelope..........................	558	1,836,977	2.9	2.2	0.0	3.6	29.5	1.6	60.0	30.0	8.2	17.8	2,718	2,366
Arthur.............................	35	130,066	6.4	2.0	0.0	4.7	0.0	27.0	59.3	5.8	0.9	4.6	9,488	9,335
Banner	61	179,960	9.3	1.7	0.0	7.8	0.0	0.0	79.6	4.4	1.3	2.8	3,726	3,499

1. Based on the resident population estimated as of July 1 of the year shown.

Table B. States and Counties — Local Government Finances, Government Employment, and Income Taxes

STATE County	Local government finances (cont.)							Debt outstanding		Government employment, 2016			Individual income tax returns, 2015		
	Direct general expenditure														
			Percent of total for:												
	Total (mil dol)	Per capita¹ (dollars)	Education	Health and hospitals	Police protection	Public welfare	Highways	Total (mil dol)	Per capita¹ (dollars)	Federal civilian	Federal military	State and local	Number of returns	Mean adjusted gross income	Mean income tax
	185	186	187	188	189	190	191	192	193	194	195	196	197	198	199
MISSOURI— Cont'd															
St. Louis city	2,326.2	7,311	33.4	1.7	10.8	0.0	1.1	3,993.6	12,552	14,101	1,548	20,479	146,340	44,738	5,347
MONTANA	X	X	X	X	X	X	X	X	X	13,326	7,836	75,220	498,450	55,928	6,701
Beaverhead	83.3	8,915	24.9	55.9	2.2	0.0	3.8	91.0	9,739	198	41	856	4,460	47,276	5,033
Big Horn	70.6	5,404	65.3	1.6	3.9	0.0	4.8	34.0	2,603	402	60	2,019	4,680	39,521	3,144
Blaine	33.0	4,932	63.3	2.3	5.1	0.0	8.2	3.4	513	183	29	484	2,670	32,131	3,009
Broadwater	14.1	2,447	49.7	2.6	9.1	0.2	5.3	4.7	809	43	26	208	2,570	50,578	4,847
Carbon	34.2	3,380	55.4	0.7	7.0	0.2	11.0	23.7	2,339	79	47	496	5,030	53,240	5,901
Carter	7.6	6,469	34.7	9.5	5.5	0.1	25.5	0.4	371	13	0	102	570	55,200	5,260
Cascade	242.5	2,968	53.0	1.0	9.7	1.4	5.2	90.0	1,101	1,712	3,476	4,045	40,100	51,053	5,580
Chouteau	26.7	4,530	44.1	21.5	3.3	0.0	8.4	4.1	697	37	26	421	2,280	43,314	4,319
Custer	40.6	3,415	62.2	2.4	7.6	0.1	8.1	9.5	801	200	52	873	5,630	56,800	7,542
Daniels	9.9	5,552	39.1	7.1	5.2	0.0	8.9	3.2	1,792	14	0	115	880	53,164	5,867
Dawson	38.5	4,159	54.9	3.1	5.4	1.0	7.1	8.2	884	35	40	719	4,380	57,290	6,137
Deer Lodge	30.1	3,259	41.6	2.0	6.6	2.8	4.8	4.9	531	82	38	949	4,190	45,221	4,303
Fallon	38.0	12,574	45.8	4.0	2.8	0.0	17.5	0.2	57	12	14	283	1,470	69,221	9,382
Fergus	44.0	3,847	53.6	2.3	4.8	0.0	11.5	9.5	831	133	50	891	5,630	48,908	4,969
Flathead	299.8	3,272	56.2	3.9	5.8	1.2	5.0	178.9	1,952	769	442	4,249	47,940	55,893	6,870
Gallatin	262.4	2,834	48.1	1.3	10.1	4.2	4.1	247.8	2,676	588	470	9,228	53,360	65,961	9,165
Garfield	7.3	5,772	36.8	2.4	2.5	23.3	14.2	0.6	450	26	0	122	570	46,633	4,696
Glacier	51.7	3,768	77.0	2.8	4.0	0.1	4.7	22.4	1,630	459	59	1,987	5,080	35,971	2,951
Golden Valley	4.5	5,323	65.4	0.9	4.3	0.5	4.7	0.0	5	0	0	69	450	42,442	4,451
Granite	15.6	5,012	35.1	0.6	6.3	26.8	7.6	2.0	654	39	15	212	1,430	49,174	5,576
Hill	62.8	3,840	76.1	0.8	4.8	0.0	3.2	16.7	1,020	164	73	1,969	7,730	46,909	4,540
Jefferson	31.9	2,799	57.0	3.8	8.3	0.0	5.0	4.6	400	42	53	703	5,420	62,988	7,134
Judith Basin	9.6	4,741	53.8	0.9	3.4	0.0	18.1	3.4	1,658	33	0	145	990	44,013	4,127
Lake	86.4	2,980	61.8	0.9	5.2	0.3	4.0	23.2	799	106	133	2,919	12,530	43,634	4,144
Lewis and Clark	212.2	3,270	47.9	4.1	8.6	3.1	5.3	156.7	2,415	1,953	309	8,910	33,710	57,709	6,388
Liberty	7.9	3,293	47.0	5.3	10.3	0.0	12.1	1.8	772	17	0	129	960	39,123	3,248
Lincoln	58.1	2,979	51.4	6.8	7.7	0.1	7.8	18.2	932	427	87	744	7,890	44,122	4,388
McCone	8.6	5,082	52.1	3.7	4.1	0.8	13.0	2.4	1,422	19	0	131	880	39,232	3,634
Madison	42.1	5,447	35.2	13.7	4.0	18.5	7.6	7.0	907	61	35	475	3,770	58,768	7,092
Meagher	10.9	5,666	29.5	3.3	0.7	0.0	6.7	0.3	179	29	0	109	950	41,395	3,835
Mineral	24.9	5,975	42.3	33.5	3.9	0.0	3.9	5.6	1,346	57	19	276	1,850	43,661	4,269
Missoula	338.7	3,052	44.0	5.5	7.0	0.8	5.2	188.8	1,701	1,355	539	9,350	56,950	60,472	7,806
Musselshell	23.0	4,926	37.1	29.7	2.1	0.0	4.3	1.8	390	14	21	261	1,960	46,807	4,930
Park	60.3	3,873	58.7	2.2	5.8	0.5	3.5	26.2	1,681	72	73	650	8,540	49,646	5,396
Petroleum	4.6	8,926	53.5	1.5	1.5	0.0	8.0	0.4	812	0	0	54	200	38,450	2,725
Phillips	22.5	5,449	53.5	1.7	4.2	0.0	11.5	7.9	1,903	77	18	304	1,980	40,424	3,707
Pondera	34.1	5,531	42.2	35.4	3.5	1.5	3.2	14.5	2,348	33	25	391	2,990	39,135	3,547
Powder River	12.1	6,877	33.4	1.6	5.0	22.2	16.5	0.1	69	12	0	199	810	53,907	5,207
Powell	23.3	3,289	58.1	0.9	6.4	0.4	8.2	1.7	234	80	24	1,033	2,700	43,501	3,990
Prairie	7.4	6,390	28.9	2.4	3.9	29.4	8.6	2.0	1,732	35	0	148	570	49,830	4,568
Ravalli	99.9	2,460	64.0	1.1	7.3	0.5	5.0	31.4	773	529	190	1,418	19,550	50,445	5,521
Richland	76.0	7,032	41.5	1.4	4.3	0.9	22.5	6.1	568	80	52	726	6,000	78,903	12,376
Roosevelt	58.9	5,389	63.9	10.7	5.5	0.5	4.5	9.1	836	179	51	1,599	4,160	44,523	4,287
Rosebud	68.3	7,269	51.2	7.9	4.8	0.3	4.7	257.2	27,372	241	42	1,491	4,040	53,371	5,539
Sanders	36.1	3,162	60.5	4.1	6.1	0.0	8.2	4.9	428	142	52	511	4,870	40,676	3,869
Sheridan	21.8	6,087	50.6	2.2	6.1	1.6	16.8	1.9	517	70	16	250	1,970	55,903	6,355
Silver Bow	113.4	3,297	39.5	4.4	5.9	0.1	4.1	60.4	1,757	216	169	2,241	16,440	52,761	6,487
Stillwater	30.5	3,315	64.5	0.6	4.5	0.1	6.8	2.6	287	33	42	457	4,370	61,139	6,893
Sweet Grass	22.6	6,259	30.6	0.8	5.2	32.8	6.0	1.4	398	31	16	256	1,770	52,363	5,359
Teton	35.3	5,826	43.7	23.0	0.8	4.8	5.1	8.3	1,372	55	25	455	2,990	52,530	6,007
Toole	36.4	6,970	29.7	40.6	6.4	0.0	6.6	14.4	2,766	153	19	444	2,310	44,917	4,785
Treasure	3.8	5,182	44.6	5.5	3.4	0.1	10.4	0.5	679	0	0	57	390	49,000	4,403
Valley	35.4	4,717	51.9	2.2	5.0	0.1	10.3	8.7	1,160	156	34	608	3,710	50,221	5,589
Wheatland	8.9	4,252	54.8	5.6	6.4	0.1	6.6	3.2	1,505	18	0	133	940	43,243	4,269
Wibaux	6.5	6,114	36.4	10.7	5.5	0.0	16.1	1.2	1,157	0	0	144	470	46,717	3,740
Yellowstone	506.3	3,333	47.8	7.1	5.8	0.2	6.1	224.5	1,478	1,790	746	7,202	77,930	62,341	7,928
NEBRASKA	X	X	X	X	X	X	X	X	X	16,803	12,643	146,708	899,280	61,384	7,566
Adams	180.4	5,735	72.7	0.4	3.1	0.2	6.2	136.0	4,322	105	107	2,266	14,580	57,568	6,774
Antelope	34.5	5,275	71.6	0.0	2.2	0.0	12.9	7.4	1,136	29	22	459	2,970	51,466	6,361
Arthur	4.1	8,356	45.4	0.2	0.8	0.0	11.7	0.0	0	0	0	51	200	42,085	2,830
Banner	4.4	5,725	68.1	0.3	1.3	0.0	14.7	0.0	0	0	0	66	290	42,097	3,097

1. Based on the resident population estimated as of July 1 of the year shown.

Table B. States and Counties — Personal Income and Earnings

STATE County	Personal income, 2016										Earnings, 2016		
			Per capita[1]			Supplements to wages and salaries, employer contributions (mil dol)						Contributions for government social insurance (mil dol)	
	Total (mil dol)	Percent change 2015-2016	Dollars	Rank	Wages and salaries (mil dol)	Pension and insurance	Government social insurance	Proprietors' income (mil dol)	Dividends, interest, and rent (mil dol)	Personal transfer reecipts (mil dol)	Total (mil dol)	From employee and self-employed	From employer
	62	63	64	65	66	67	68	69	70	71	72	73	74
NEBRASKA— Cont'd													
Blaine	27	-16.5	56,531	197	6	1	0	8	8	4	16	1	0
Boone	317	0.1	59,530	157	90	18	6	113	60	43	227	14	6
Box Butte	500	2.5	44,699	807	252	39	30	73	80	107	393	54	30
Boyd	93	-2.8	46,673	640	19	5	1	25	17	23	50	4	1
Brown	166	-3.2	56,162	207	45	10	3	64	28	30	122	7	3
Buffalo	2,372	0.5	48,026	534	1,132	198	83	190	666	317	1,604	177	83
Burt	320	-4.6	48,886	476	75	15	5	68	50	66	164	13	5
Butler	364	-5.9	45,213	760	110	21	8	51	69	67	190	19	8
Cass	1,201	2.2	46,609	647	233	43	17	91	208	198	384	41	17
Cedar	444	1.0	51,207	360	105	21	7	145	80	62	279	18	7
Chase	211	9.1	53,606	277	73	13	5	64	43	33	155	11	5
Cherry	294	-9.1	50,438	396	86	16	6	89	61	45	197	14	6
Cheyenne	526	-1.6	52,314	328	309	45	22	61	89	76	436	46	22
Clay	276	4.0	44,731	801	110	23	8	31	56	53	171	17	8
Colfax	456	2.5	43,834	895	233	38	16	92	68	59	380	34	16
Cuming	636	-8.2	70,495	67	155	27	11	287	89	74	479	25	11
Custer	572	-1.8	52,938	307	176	36	13	168	97	95	393	29	13
Dakota	796	3.9	38,911	1,512	558	92	40	96	92	140	786	86	40
Dawes	305	-0.3	33,976	2,327	126	29	10	38	61	66	204	22	10
Dawson	939	0.2	39,718	1,397	454	86	32	169	142	171	741	70	32
Deuel	85	-2.0	45,160	769	21	4	1	10	24	18	37	4	1
Dixon	265	-2.0	46,012	689	68	13	5	56	42	39	142	11	5
Dodge	1,620	0.8	44,081	871	694	125	51	196	325	325	1,065	115	51
Douglas	32,779	3.2	59,061	162	19,013	2,717	1,419	6,058	6,291	3,736	29,207	3,086	1,419
Dundy	119	1.9	64,873	95	26	5	2	32	33	20	65	4	2
Fillmore	336	-0.9	58,725	170	95	19	7	77	70	56	198	16	7
Franklin	126	-3.9	41,723	1,138	29	6	2	7	37	33	44	5	2
Frontier	114	-10.3	43,379	957	34	7	3	22	20	20	66	6	3
Furnas	216	-6.5	45,177	767	79	16	6	30	39	52	131	13	6
Gage	1,032	0.8	47,342	583	358	73	27	130	175	244	587	61	27
Garden	85	0.1	44,259	854	23	4	2	15	19	22	45	4	2
Garfield	94	-2.9	46,755	629	27	6	2	26	22	19	61	5	2
Gosper	92	-2.9	46,652	643	20	4	1	8	25	18	32	3	1
Grant	31	-14.1	48,006	536	7	1	1	9	10	5	18	1	1
Greeley	109	-6.3	45,604	733	24	5	2	30	26	21	61	4	2
Hall	2,468	2.8	39,994	1,365	1,454	253	107	194	470	446	2,009	226	107
Hamilton	463	-0.9	50,416	399	164	27	12	71	94	71	274	27	12
Harlan	144	-5.3	41,364	1,187	32	7	2	26	29	33	67	6	2
Hayes	54	-13.3	60,719	140	9	2	1	21	9	6	33	1	1
Hitchcock	111	-3.4	39,289	1,455	33	8	2	11	24	31	55	6	2
Holt	577	-1.0	56,290	201	183	33	13	190	91	101	419	34	13
Hooker	35	-8.6	48,804	481	10	2	1	11	6	7	25	2	1
Howard	288	0.2	44,828	789	60	13	4	55	48	51	132	10	4
Jefferson	357	1.0	49,774	424	135	24	11	61	75	71	230	23	11
Johnson	201	-0.1	38,867	1,522	66	17	5	40	30	35	128	11	5
Kearney	499	-14.1	76,225	41	88	17	6	236	71	59	348	20	6
Keith	362	0.8	45,190	763	128	23	9	60	69	75	220	22	9
Keya Paha	56	-7.4	70,751	65	7	1	0	29	10	8	37	1	0
Kimball	161	-2.9	43,846	893	58	11	5	18	36	36	91	10	5
Knox	380	-4.4	44,368	842	107	23	7	85	71	80	223	19	7
Lancaster	14,084	2.8	45,484	741	8,068	1,442	604	848	2,738	2,004	10,962	1,254	604
Lincoln	1,675	0.6	47,120	596	788	126	78	267	245	348	1,258	154	78
Logan	37	-4.5	47,649	556	7	2	0	13	5	7	22	1	0
Loup	35	-8.7	59,289	159	4	1	0	12	6	6	17	1	0
McPherson	26	-12.5	53,349	290	4	1	0	11	5	3	16	1	0
Madison	1,599	0.8	45,673	726	905	162	65	207	279	282	1,339	142	65
Merrick	418	4.5	53,353	289	95	18	7	143	57	68	263	19	7
Morrill	261	-0.3	54,533	252	66	13	5	92	36	43	176	11	5
Nance	155	-2.6	43,479	939	44	9	3	20	27	31	76	7	3
Nemaha	329	3.4	47,179	593	167	36	11	45	57	66	259	25	11
Nuckolls	185	-0.7	43,362	961	52	11	4	34	36	48	100	9	4
Otoe	720	1.8	44,797	791	255	49	19	79	138	135	402	42	19
Pawnee	122	-0.7	46,089	682	33	7	2	31	21	23	74	6	2
Perkins	145	4.6	50,035	413	56	11	4	39	29	24	109	9	4
Phelps	552	-0.5	59,553	156	209	41	15	182	88	84	447	33	15
Pierce	394	-8.1	54,999	240	81	16	6	127	56	51	229	16	6

1. Based on the resident population estimated as of July 1 of the year shown.

Table B. States and Counties — **Earnings, Social Security, and Housing**

STATE County	Earnings, 2016 (cont.)									Social Security beneficiaries, December 2016			Housing units, 2017	
	Percent by selected industries											Supplemental Security Income recipients, 2016		
	Farm	Mining, quarrying, and extracting	Construction	Manufacturing	Information; professional, scientific, technical services	Retail trade	Finance, insurance, real estate, and leasing	Health care and social assistance	Government	Number	Rate[1]		Total	Percent change, 2010-2017
	75	76	77	78	79	80	81	82	83	84	85	86	87	88
NEBRASKA— Cont'd														
Blaine	63.7	0.0	D	0.0	0.0	D	D	0.5	25.0	125	267	5	325	-0.3
Boone	47.5	0.0	3.9	6.0	D	3.5	D	3.6	15.8	1,225	229	44	2,638	-0.4
Box Butte	15.0	0.0	2.9	4.6	2.8	4.0	2.7	D	15.5	1,855	166	176	5,456	-0.4
Boyd	32.9	D	3.2	1.2	D	3.4	5.5	4.6	20.8	615	311	31	1,376	-1.0
Brown	45.7	0.1	4.9	4.1	D	5.9	D	1.7	20.9	775	260	53	1,846	-0.9
Buffalo	3.3	0.2	6.7	13.0	5.2	8.0	4.7	17.7	16.1	7,830	159	446	20,501	7.5
Burt	37.7	0.0	5.2	5.8	D	3.2	D	4.2	17.7	1,795	274	115	3,489	0.6
Butler	19.2	D	4.5	19.0	D	2.8	D	D	20.0	1,850	231	84	4,069	0.4
Cass	13.3	D	7.4	9.7	3.2	6.8	5.2	D	20.2	5,040	197	212	11,544	3.8
Cedar	42.0	D	5.5	5.3	2.2	3.2	6.8	D	13.9	1,890	220	59	4,164	0.4
Chase	33.6	0.0	5.3	1.4	3.2	7.2	5.9	1.5	16.6	860	218	39	1,952	0.3
Cherry	37.2	D	5.7	1.3	3.2	7.5	2.0	5.0	16.8	1,285	220	68	3,250	2.9
Cheyenne	8.6	D	3.0	3.9	2.3	7.6	2.0	8.3	10.4	2,000	199	122	5,015	2.6
Clay	13.1	D	9.0	12.2	D	4.4	D	4.0	26.5	1,490	242	69	3,010	0.3
Colfax	20.5	D	D	D	1.2	2.2	1.9	D	10.3	1,425	134	69	4,204	2.6
Cuming	54.2	D	3.2	6.1	2.3	2.6	4.9	D	8.1	2,145	238	65	4,250	1.1
Custer	37.8	0.0	5.2	12.3	2.5	4.1	4.4	D	12.3	2,530	233	127	5,664	1.5
Dakota	4.0	0.2	4.7	39.8	D	4.2	8.6	3.6	9.6	3,520	173	274	7,845	2.8
Dawes	10.1	D	3.6	0.4	2.8	11.4	3.3	11.0	34.1	1,730	194	90	4,250	0.0
Dawson	18.9	D	3.0	24.0	2.7	5.3	4.0	D	18.7	4,315	181	307	10,244	1.2
Deuel	8.1	0.3	D	4.8	D	7.6	D	5.0	25.7	510	273	26	1,028	-1.4
Dixon	36.7	0.0	6.9	D	D	0.9	1.9	2.3	13.5	1,145	199	48	2,708	0.7
Dodge	6.8	0.1	5.0	20.5	4.1	8.8	4.1	D	18.6	8,370	229	571	16,755	1.0
Douglas	0.0	D	6.3	4.9	11.0	4.7	10.9	11.9	10.5	83,945	151	10,319	234,326	6.7
Dundy	40.9	0.2	2.1	1.3	D	3.6	1.7	3.0	20.7	510	281	25	1,123	-0.2
Fillmore	25.9	0.2	8.5	8.7	D	3.8	8.8	3.8	19.2	1,520	270	48	2,930	0.6
Franklin	5.3	0.1	D	D	D	7.8	D	D	35.7	915	304	49	1,718	-0.9
Frontier	24.2	D	8.3	3.0	D	2.4	10.2	1.1	25.1	570	215	27	1,583	0.6
Furnas	15.6	0.0	4.7	6.6	6.7	6.0	D	10.1	20.6	1,375	288	80	2,715	-0.2
Gage	14.4	D	4.9	20.6	2.3	6.1	3.0	D	20.0	5,450	252	399	10,427	-0.2
Garden	29.7	0.0	D	D	D	8.6	D	11.6	17.7	620	324	36	1,302	-0.9
Garfield	26.8	D	4.2	5.8	D	5.9	D	D	14.1	510	255	17	1,203	2.1
Gosper	18.1	0.0	D	D	D	1.8	D	D	24.0	520	257	14	1,307	3.2
Grant	37.4	0.3	4.0	0.0	D	9.9	1.4	D	18.8	175	264	0	389	-0.5
Greeley	35.6	0.1	2.7	3.1	D	D	5.8	0.6	19.3	595	247	28	1,307	0.5
Hall	2.6	0.1	6.5	20.3	3.5	9.0	5.9	11.5	16.7	10,740	175	943	24,904	5.8
Hamilton	19.1	0.3	5.2	14.6	6.3	5.5	2.9	D	10.2	2,060	225	64	4,118	3.9
Harlan	28.7	D	3.6	D	D	5.1	D	D	23.7	915	264	40	2,389	0.6
Hayes	62.5	D	D	D	D	D	D	0.0	11.9	170	191	10	511	0.6
Hitchcock	0.6	D	13.8	22.7	D	3.7	1.4	0.6	26.7	790	278	41	1,742	-1.2
Holt	13.9	0.3	4.5	2.6	1.8	25.0	6.2	D	10.7	2,585	253	146	5,267	1.0
Hooker	29.3	0.2	D	D	D	3.6	D	D	16.2	225	326	0	442	2.6
Howard	37.2	D	4.4	1.8	1.9	4.8	3.8	4.6	25.2	1,450	226	52	3,096	4.9
Jefferson	21.5	D	7.2	14.8	3.0	6.6	3.2	D	13.0	1,920	267	141	3,910	-0.2
Johnson	25.0	0.0	5.7	D	D	3.5	D	4.5	40.1	910	175	38	2,173	-0.8
Kearney	19.3	1.3	2.4	45.3	1.9	2.7	D	D	7.5	1,200	183	81	2,967	2.8
Keith	17.7	D	7.2	5.6	3.8	9.5	5.2	9.0	13.7	2,190	270	112	5,458	0.6
Keya Paha	70.8	0.0	D	D	D	D	D	D	8.1	250	314	10	546	-0.5
Kimball	5.4	12.0	4.0	9.9	D	5.7	D	1.0	23.3	970	263	54	1,950	-0.7
Knox	27.8	0.0	5.3	4.1	D	5.3	3.8	D	24.7	2,300	271	138	4,969	3.8
Lancaster	0.6	D	5.7	7.9	9.8	6.2	9.6	13.4	22.3	46,720	150	4,842	131,256	8.6
Lincoln	10.9	D	4.6	3.5	3.3	6.8	4.1	15.3	15.6	6,485	183	697	16,822	1.4
Logan	26.8	0.0	D	D	D	4.4	1.9	0.7	18.1	155	194	0	394	-0.3
Loup	67.6	0.0	0.5	1.8	0.0	D	D	D	15.6	160	260	8	457	7.5
McPherson	64.7	0.0	0.5	D	D	D	D	0.0	13.6	70	139	0	282	-0.4
Madison	7.1	D	5.3	14.9	3.9	8.0	7.2	15.1	16.7	7,080	203	538	15,282	1.8
Merrick	21.2	D	30.5	10.2	1.5	3.3	3.7	D	12.4	1,860	237	146	3,828	3.4
Morrill	40.8	D	3.3	5.5	D	3.5	3.9	D	18.1	995	203	93	2,440	-0.1
Nance	23.5	D	D	D	1.4	3.6	4.6	7.4	26.6	735	205	58	1,868	3.7
Nemaha	11.7	0.0	2.5	5.9	D	2.7	D	4.6	57.4	1,580	226	116	3,504	0.2
Nuckolls	22.9	0.1	3.7	D	D	6.4	5.0	16.0	17.9	1,270	298	63	2,452	-0.5
Otoe	10.9	0.0	6.4	20.1	D	6.6	3.8	8.3	22.4	3,475	217	178	7,192	2.4
Pawnee	34.2	D	D	12.3	0.5	3.1	D	3.2	21.1	660	243	41	1,621	2.1
Perkins	24.0	0.0	10.0	4.5	D	3.1	D	3.0	19.9	690	237	22	1,449	-0.1
Phelps	37.4	D	D	D	2.0	4.9	3.8	D	10.3	2,110	230	133	4,260	2.0
Pierce	18.0	1.2	6.3	27.3	D	3.4	D	5.9	9.1	1,435	201	57	3,274	1.6

1. Per 1,000 resident population estimated as of July 1 of the year shown.

Table B. States and Counties — Housing, Labor Force, and Employment

STATE County	Housing units, 2017 (cont.)								Civilian labor force, 2017				Civilian employment[6], 2012-2016		
	Occupied units														
	Owner-occupied					Renter-occupied					Unemployment			Percent	
				Median owner cost as a percent of income											
	Total	Percent	Median value[1]	With a mortgage	Without a mortgage[2]	Median rent[3]	Median rent as a percent of income[2]	Sub-standard units[4] (percent)	Total	Percent change, 2016-2017	Total	Rate[5]	Total	Management, business, science, and arts	Construction, production, and maintenance occupations
	89	90	91	92	93	94	95	96	97	98	99	100	101	102	103
NEBRASKA— Cont'd															
Blaine	251	57.8	106,500	22.3	10.0	600	14.5	4.0	262	-1.1	11	4.2	298	42.3	33.6
Boone	2,236	78.4	104,400	19.1	10.8	593	19.9	1.9	2,914	-2.8	72	2.5	2,814	34.0	31.4
Box Butte	4,722	69.3	99,500	17.1	10.6	549	23.5	2.0	5,566	-1.2	182	3.3	5,721	30.7	37.1
Boyd	909	81.4	56,200	18.2	11.7	466	26.9	0.9	1,078	-1.7	36	3.3	979	44.7	28.8
Brown	1,498	72.6	80,100	16.2	15.4	489	18.3	1.9	1,387	0.7	45	3.2	1,610	42.5	21.8
Buffalo	18,512	63.7	155,900	20.4	10.9	727	26.9	1.6	27,050	-0.4	658	2.4	27,343	32.1	23.1
Burt	2,823	76.7	90,500	19.7	13.5	581	23.1	1.6	3,477	-1.8	129	3.7	2,997	33.6	26.1
Butler	3,479	79.0	108,200	21.2	11.2	663	25.2	2.6	4,544	-1.6	126	2.8	4,197	28.0	35.4
Cass	9,706	81.7	160,900	21.2	14.0	769	26.3	2.2	13,144	0.2	415	3.2	12,980	31.8	25.6
Cedar	3,571	80.3	110,500	18.9	10.8	603	22.4	1.0	4,452	-2.4	101	2.3	4,584	34.0	28.6
Chase	1,693	79.1	95,900	19.3	10.8	590	21.1	0.6	2,287	0.0	43	1.9	2,043	35.6	31.1
Cherry	2,691	61.9	122,300	21.1	10.0	574	19.8	1.1	3,381	-2.5	79	2.3	3,377	38.8	27.9
Cheyenne	4,462	69.5	114,300	18.4	11.4	633	23.2	1.4	5,127	-5.8	150	2.9	5,617	36.4	21.0
Clay	2,600	76.7	82,100	18.9	10.0	557	21.3	2.3	3,259	-1.7	101	3.1	3,128	31.9	34.3
Colfax	3,659	72.3	93,100	19.3	10.0	538	18.5	8.4	5,546	0.1	133	2.4	5,305	23.3	47.8
Cuming	3,783	68.6	109,200	17.8	10.7	623	24.3	1.6	4,714	0.1	128	2.7	4,716	32.6	34.9
Custer	4,781	72.0	93,000	19.2	12.8	583	24.0	2.4	6,335	-0.1	137	2.2	5,629	32.6	30.2
Dakota	7,314	66.7	108,400	19.7	12.1	685	22.4	6.5	10,648	-2.2	433	4.1	10,196	20.8	41.8
Dawes	3,676	61.7	104,200	20.1	14.0	590	26.5	2.3	5,158	-0.9	142	2.8	4,681	37.6	17.3
Dawson	8,791	67.4	95,600	19.1	11.9	671	24.6	4.3	12,855	-0.7	367	2.9	12,282	23.5	42.9
Deuel	850	77.4	72,900	19.0	10.6	621	18.2	1.5	1,034	-2.5	27	2.6	1,035	31.2	26.0
Dixon	2,290	76.9	86,200	18.8	11.4	654	25.0	1.7	2,989	-2.4	95	3.2	2,929	28.8	33.6
Dodge	15,063	65.7	114,700	19.5	12.4	711	24.6	2.2	19,279	1.0	542	2.8	18,603	26.8	29.0
Douglas	210,931	61.4	149,300	20.6	12.5	833	29.2	2.6	288,566	0.4	9,171	3.2	280,910	40.3	17.7
Dundy	815	69.3	70,700	17.1	11.0	513	18.6	0.5	1,185	-0.8	28	2.4	868	48.2	23.6
Fillmore	2,460	74.1	75,000	17.2	10.3	564	19.9	1.0	3,120	-1.8	79	2.5	2,920	33.9	29.6
Franklin	1,389	83.5	60,400	19.2	10.0	556	23.8	1.7	1,476	-1.5	45	3.0	1,543	33.0	31.7
Frontier	1,097	75.9	95,000	18.3	11.9	620	21.3	0.3	1,555	-0.8	40	2.6	1,250	34.2	26.9
Furnas	2,227	68.9	62,500	23.1	11.9	538	21.6	2.8	2,662	-1.8	65	2.4	2,329	36.9	27.6
Gage	9,251	69.5	108,000	19.7	11.5	634	24.2	1.1	10,886	-1.3	383	3.5	10,977	32.8	29.9
Garden	867	79.4	83,100	20.1	10.3	577	21.6	1.8	1,190	0.4	33	2.8	930	35.5	25.8
Garfield	920	75.8	92,400	21.9	10.7	377	24.8	0.5	1,150	-0.3	29	2.5	1,048	31.7	30.2
Gosper	811	69.7	113,000	19.8	10.1	678	17.8	0.0	1,037	-1.6	27	2.6	1,108	29.2	28.8
Grant	272	77.6	52,500	27.5	11.3	450	16.3	0.0	438	-3.1	10	2.3	331	41.4	31.1
Greeley	1,025	80.4	65,600	20.6	11.1	502	17.5	2.4	1,214	-1.5	38	3.1	1,170	35.6	30.5
Hall	22,572	61.4	128,200	20.8	11.2	696	26.9	4.3	31,452	0.3	1,084	3.4	31,485	25.4	34.2
Hamilton	3,705	80.8	123,200	18.7	10.9	651	24.3	1.2	4,638	-0.2	117	2.5	4,745	35.8	26.5
Harlan	1,590	76.0	84,400	19.9	12.4	529	22.5	0.9	1,751	-0.2	45	2.6	1,628	34.0	28.6
Hayes	441	66.2	80,500	22.5	12.1	463	20.0	0.5	569	-3.4	14	2.5	514	47.9	30.7
Hitchcock	1,288	75.2	59,000	18.0	13.7	661	27.3	1.4	1,225	-6.0	42	3.4	1,359	26.0	31.2
Holt	4,569	73.8	96,900	18.6	11.4	557	22.2	0.9	5,738	-1.9	141	2.5	5,583	35.0	25.6
Hooker	301	76.4	77,900	21.6	12.9	636	29.8	0.7	399	2.0	15	3.8	313	36.7	21.7
Howard	2,601	77.8	115,100	20.2	13.6	574	25.9	0.2	3,291	-0.1	101	3.1	3,318	34.6	29.2
Jefferson	3,303	75.7	76,900	18.5	12.2	524	22.2	0.2	4,166	-1.1	102	2.4	3,700	28.6	27.7
Johnson	1,880	73.9	80,900	20.0	12.3	599	24.8	1.6	2,060	-1.3	70	3.4	2,072	33.0	27.6
Kearney	2,752	69.3	119,000	18.3	10.5	704	24.5	1.4	3,740	0.2	83	2.2	3,459	30.0	33.3
Keith	3,926	65.8	104,600	20.3	13.1	598	26.5	0.2	4,553	-1.2	138	3.0	4,003	31.6	28.0
Keya Paha	338	70.4	79,000	22.8	12.2	540	12.5	1.2	605	-2.3	15	2.5	426	50.9	24.9
Kimball	1,591	67.5	83,000	22.6	14.1	684	22.6	0.9	1,957	-0.6	56	2.9	1,719	29.8	30.4
Knox	3,648	74.4	84,500	18.3	11.7	474	20.5	2.5	4,691	-0.4	163	3.5	4,255	36.5	26.3
Lancaster	119,254	59.2	157,000	19.8	10.7	750	29.7	2.2	168,999	0.2	4,461	2.6	163,942	38.8	19.1
Lincoln	14,965	65.6	119,600	20.2	12.3	651	24.3	2.2	18,518	-0.9	561	3.0	17,810	28.8	29.1
Logan	352	67.3	116,500	26.1	10.8	544	17.1	3.7	469	-2.9	13	2.8	430	27.0	35.1
Loup	248	81.0	119,500	23.9	10.0	490	14.5	0.0	392	-0.8	12	3.1	297	48.1	26.6
McPherson	195	67.2	147,900	20.4	13.4	642	14.4	4.1	447	-3.5	10	2.2	213	29.6	30.0
Madison	14,056	65.2	121,900	19.3	12.1	621	25.0	3.3	19,116	-0.1	504	2.6	18,416	28.7	30.6
Merrick	3,311	73.6	88,300	18.7	10.9	569	23.5	0.2	3,998	-0.7	112	2.8	4,065	30.8	28.9
Morrill	2,008	67.5	84,700	19.9	11.6	668	26.5	1.7	2,608	-1.3	76	2.9	2,418	28.4	32.3
Nance	1,568	77.7	81,600	18.7	12.0	519	26.6	0.5	2,011	0.8	50	2.5	1,822	35.6	25.8
Nemaha	2,873	70.6	109,200	19.1	12.2	618	22.5	2.2	3,579	-0.9	140	3.9	3,545	31.6	24.4
Nuckolls	2,042	73.5	56,700	16.8	10.6	479	25.9	2.1	2,348	-0.6	62	2.6	2,236	34.7	25.8
Otoe	6,463	73.7	124,100	19.9	12.2	655	25.3	1.5	8,110	-1.7	272	3.4	8,149	28.1	31.2
Pawnee	1,249	77.1	65,900	17.6	12.4	484	24.9	1.7	1,497	-9.3	46	3.1	1,213	38.6	28.5
Perkins	1,241	76.3	99,400	17.1	11.4	652	24.8	0.1	1,794	-1.2	35	2.0	1,470	44.8	25.9
Phelps	3,773	69.6	114,300	19.4	10.6	582	24.2	0.4	4,908	-0.3	115	2.3	4,702	31.3	33.1
Pierce	2,949	79.5	96,900	18.8	11.2	573	20.4	1.2	4,104	-0.8	111	2.7	3,666	34.3	31.9

1. Specified owner-occupied units. lacking complete plumbing facilities.   2. A value of 10.0 represents 10 percent or less; a value of 50.0 represents 50 percent or more.   3. Specified renter-occupied units.   4. Overcrowded or
5. Percent of civilian labor force.   6. Civilian employed persons 16 years old and over.

Table B. States and Counties — **Nonfarm Employment and Agriculture**

STATE County	Private nonfarm establishments, employment and payroll, 2016									Agriculture, 2012			
	Number of establishments	Employment						Annual payroll		Farms			Farm operators whose principal occupation is farming (percent)
		Total	Health care and social assistance	Manufacturing	Retail trade	Finance and insurance	Professional, scientific, and technical services	Total (mil dol)	Average per employee (dollars)	Number	Percent with:		
											Fewer than 50 acres	500 acres or more	
	104	105	106	107	108	109	110	111	112	113	114	115	116

NEBRASKA— Cont'd													
Blaine	9	11	NA	NA	D	D	NA	0	30,545	117	14.5	66.7	76.1
Boone	203	1,471	316	133	277	85	31	49	33,560	646	12.7	42.4	68.3
Box Butte	315	2,791	592	295	432	124	103	94	33,810	466	17.8	48.7	59.9
Boyd	70	397	116	14	77	39	D	11	27,990	266	14.7	56.0	59.4
Brown	131	842	141	D	270	42	19	27	32,024	328	24.1	51.2	68.3
Buffalo	1,633	23,040	4,232	3,187	4,270	707	841	804	34,913	1,046	29.4	31.4	53.2
Burt	206	1,166	170	40	198	62	69	42	36,154	560	22.9	35.0	63.0
Butler	206	2,083	399	672	259	129	40	76	36,723	840	23.8	32.5	58.2
Cass	551	3,853	409	490	612	234	157	148	38,480	731	34.1	31.1	54.2
Cedar	303	1,888	160	222	350	131	88	64	34,113	939	20.8	29.9	58.7
Chase	164	1,107	129	15	324	71	20	39	35,336	342	11.7	54.1	64.9
Cherry	227	1,574	282	46	383	47	77	42	26,995	566	14.8	70.8	80.4
Cheyenne	295	4,687	510	279	819	147	61	231	49,209	555	10.6	54.1	58.9
Clay	185	1,118	93	46	211	76	32	40	35,584	457	25.2	42.5	67.0
Colfax	264	3,712	249	D	339	88	51	149	40,034	554	22.6	30.3	66.1
Cuming	358	2,603	350	356	367	201	129	95	36,414	918	26.1	25.1	61.2
Custer	387	2,954	625	D	589	178	98	100	33,906	1,352	21.1	43.3	62.9
Dakota	437	11,397	538	5,113	1,064	673	100	453	39,706	243	35.0	28.0	42.4
Dawes	262	2,155	528	19	638	77	63	64	29,871	493	11.8	52.7	53.5
Dawson	698	9,800	1,183	3,501	1,802	242	188	335	34,215	806	24.9	39.0	64.6
Deuel	56	312	52	NA	108	26	NA	8	26,708	237	14.3	51.1	58.2
Dixon	107	1,065	94	D	69	41	D	36	33,869	570	24.9	31.1	60.5
Dodge	1,027	15,878	2,892	3,374	2,747	428	210	559	35,230	767	29.6	28.3	68.3
Douglas	15,610	311,016	48,539	20,156	36,201	37,284	19,738	15,439	49,641	396	58.3	13.6	44.4
Dundy	59	315	96	19	31	14	23	13	40,410	251	8.0	59.0	55.0
Fillmore	223	1,758	302	284	223	132	27	61	34,772	472	13.1	48.5	72.5
Franklin	75	411	117	NA	104	41	21	13	31,616	338	11.2	47.9	67.8
Frontier	72	428	45	D	71	63	15	14	32,960	317	15.8	51.1	60.6
Furnas	164	1,347	317	138	211	73	14	47	34,924	389	16.7	48.3	67.1
Gage	665	7,514	1,812	1,714	1,088	224	149	242	32,176	1,263	26.6	27.4	49.6
Garden	53	249	D	D	57	20	D	5	21,353	261	20.3	51.7	69.7
Garfield	94	601	117	109	115	21	22	16	26,829	226	16.8	41.2	58.0
Gosper	61	195	12	D	24	27	D	7	34,687	260	13.1	55.0	63.1
Grant	30	108	NA	D	25	D	D	2	22,778	80	13.8	65.0	75.0
Greeley	67	316	9	17	104	34	NA	9	29,345	389	9.0	47.8	68.9
Hall	1,881	30,454	4,300	6,814	5,105	1,241	621	1,103	36,214	593	29.3	34.2	59.9
Hamilton	311	2,820	336	628	305	123	108	113	39,999	572	22.7	40.2	72.0
Harlan	105	609	155	D	101	37	37	19	31,067	360	19.7	40.6	60.6
Hayes	17	53	D	NA	12	D	D	2	29,264	235	8.1	60.0	67.7
Hitchcock	66	440	D	95	75	27	D	18	41,211	299	10.4	50.8	59.5
Holt	427	3,451	832	187	558	181	77	112	32,505	1,279	14.3	49.4	64.4
Hooker	32	95	D	D	28	9	D	4	40,979	82	11.0	76.8	54.9
Howard	170	1,068	340	26	208	111	33	32	30,264	682	26.1	29.0	59.1
Jefferson	238	2,656	442	685	419	81	65	88	33,280	627	21.9	33.2	55.5
Johnson	113	862	254	D	153	46	12	28	31,958	587	22.7	25.0	49.1
Kearney	170	1,710	550	289	166	73	19	58	34,169	344	15.1	56.1	78.5
Keith	344	2,640	256	225	690	190	118	81	30,666	388	14.7	46.4	72.2
Keya Paha	22	55	NA	NA	14	D	7	1	24,618	244	11.9	66.0	73.0
Kimball	124	949	D	213	157	45	9	41	43,157	402	9.0	52.5	52.5
Knox	257	1,621	263	42	333	157	65	46	28,387	1,080	17.5	38.1	68.3
Lancaster	8,427	136,325	25,404	12,557	18,835	10,127	8,471	5,595	41,043	1,836	51.1	14.9	34.2
Lincoln	1,054	11,970	2,938	291	2,127	478	389	417	34,826	1,168	29.8	39.2	59.2
Logan	22	58	D	NA	D	NA	D	2	26,862	149	22.8	46.3	63.8
Loup	11	24	NA	D	D	D	NA	0	19,167	138	12.3	49.3	62.3
McPherson	7	22	NA	NA	D	D	NA	1	24,136	118	11.9	71.2	59.3
Madison	1,322	18,045	2,800	2,825	3,012	716	587	669	37,076	753	25.9	29.9	59.2
Merrick	233	1,660	300	220	187	87	32	63	37,933	492	27.8	33.7	57.1
Morrill	106	632	75	D	198	46	8	23	35,877	512	19.3	42.6	61.1
Nance	101	496	149	NA	104	44	18	13	26,617	355	22.8	34.9	64.2
Nemaha	183	1,502	341	D	249	110	49	46	30,348	451	16.0	33.3	57.6
Nuckolls	180	1,130	353	9	237	80	30	32	28,692	435	16.3	43.7	55.2
Otoe	467	5,031	818	1,414	786	152	80	157	31,201	897	29.8	29.7	49.3
Pawnee	64	506	108	D	69	51	11	18	34,678	540	12.4	34.1	52.0
Perkins	126	887	232	50	146	37	22	34	38,545	394	8.6	57.1	65.7
Phelps	330	3,913	861	D	447	123	87	144	36,684	405	16.3	54.1	72.3
Pierce	234	1,538	296	105	223	111	49	52	33,939	677	21.1	30.9	60.4

Table B. States and Counties — Agriculture

STATE County	Land in farms Acreage (1,000) [117]	Percent change, 2007-2012 [118]	Average size of farm [119]	Total irrigated (1,000) [120]	Total cropland (1,000) [121]	Value of land and buildings (dollars) Average per farm [122]	Average per acre [123]	Value of machinery and equipment, average per farm (dollars) [124]	Value of products sold: Total (mil dol) [125]	Average per farm (acres) [126]	Percent from: Crops [127]	Livestock and poultry products [128]	Percent of farms with sales of: $10,000 or more [129]	$100,000 or more [130]	Government payments Total ($1,000) [131]	Percent of farms [132]
NEBRASKA— Cont'd																
Blaine	403	-9.2	3,440	7.0	32.6	1,760,274	512	95,709	34.7	296,214	16.3	83.7	76.9	39.3	293	32.5
Boone	434	7.2	672	184.7	326.9	2,964,181	4,408	289,596	453.4	701,850	42.9	57.1	83.4	59.0	5,870	78.8
Box Butte	675	0.7	1,449	141.6	337.5	1,547,721	1,068	292,384	299.3	642,170	56.3	43.7	65.2	43.3	4,279	68.2
Boyd	291	15.6	1,094	5.2	98.0	1,504,169	1,375	147,015	62.9	236,477	30.2	69.8	72.9	32.3	913	75.9
Brown	725	9.6	2,212	40.2	109.4	1,584,393	716	138,912	195.4	595,826	20.1	79.9	66.5	43.3	1,694	38.4
Buffalo	581	-5.2	555	240.8	342.3	2,074,083	3,737	226,212	395.1	377,751	68.9	31.1	67.5	40.6	8,102	64.9
Burt	310	12.7	553	37.6	278.5	2,886,561	5,216	245,725	226.9	405,252	66.2	33.8	72.3	50.4	4,598	77.0
Butler	370	3.9	441	110.8	306.6	2,179,969	4,948	258,019	276.4	329,043	66.9	33.1	67.0	42.9	6,657	78.6
Cass	345	22.8	472	3.5	304.3	2,732,765	5,792	210,464	149.3	204,291	93.9	6.1	60.7	41.6	4,746	66.5
Cedar	466	-1.7	497	139.0	371.7	2,189,874	4,408	211,296	388.7	413,987	42.0	58.0	75.6	45.4	6,256	73.7
Chase	541	-2.6	1,583	159.7	290.6	3,112,181	1,966	393,310	414.9	1,213,085	44.2	55.8	65.2	52.6	6,032	76.9
Cherry	3,757	-0.1	6,637	50.9	358.5	3,521,118	531	181,652	246.8	435,974	32.4	67.6	78.3	55.7	3,354	27.2
Cheyenne	703	-6.8	1,267	48.7	499.3	1,131,528	893	203,490	205.7	370,593	43.6	56.4	65.0	38.6	7,026	85.4
Clay	331	-9.5	723	191.7	259.1	3,712,295	5,133	386,182	355.1	776,978	59.6	40.4	77.9	58.4	5,141	73.7
Colfax	258	20.8	465	66.8	224.9	2,460,460	5,291	266,197	337.9	609,935	34.2	65.8	77.8	45.5	5,060	75.8
Cuming	363	0.8	395	52.4	312.6	2,120,511	5,364	285,514	1,081.3	1,177,889	12.9	87.1	79.3	49.3	6,797	76.8
Custer	1,504	-6.9	1,112	261.5	484.9	2,110,533	1,898	187,440	845.3	625,226	34.7	65.3	70.6	40.8	7,479	55.4
Dakota	158	-5.2	650	29.3	136.0	3,120,123	4,799	228,041	73.0	300,317	89.4	10.6	56.4	28.8	2,079	68.3
Dawes	824	-2.9	1,671	21.4	172.7	1,243,284	744	109,030	75.6	153,410	27.8	72.2	62.1	37.9	2,428	67.5
Dawson	630	-1.6	782	248.5	321.8	2,429,274	3,106	263,305	826.3	1,025,163	34.3	65.7	71.3	48.9	6,166	55.2
Deuel	277	-0.8	1,168	17.4	216.1	1,167,042	999	226,080	70.6	297,971	57.3	42.7	69.2	43.9	2,383	69.6
Dixon	299	20.3	525	24.0	226.3	2,176,037	4,148	211,812	169.1	296,716	42.0	58.0	63.0	35.4	4,695	73.7
Dodge	330	-2.5	430	118.0	305.0	2,414,327	5,611	281,532	326.0	425,043	60.7	39.3	72.2	48.9	5,602	74.3
Douglas	86	2.1	217	19.8	76.3	1,352,033	6,217	152,404	58.0	146,513	93.4	6.6	47.0	23.7	1,378	40.9
Dundy	521	-12.4	2,075	94.8	208.6	2,820,614	1,359	377,386	195.6	779,363	54.1	45.9	69.3	51.8	3,944	73.3
Fillmore	328	-9.3	696	211.0	296.4	3,835,816	5,513	473,146	334.8	709,335	78.0	22.0	84.1	68.9	5,465	81.4
Franklin	288	-1.3	851	85.8	166.2	2,527,118	2,969	260,417	119.1	352,447	87.0	13.0	78.4	48.2	3,802	81.1
Frontier	452	-4.9	1,426	53.3	174.7	2,093,385	1,468	232,278	124.6	393,145	53.1	46.9	70.7	41.0	3,205	74.4
Furnas	436	-2.3	1,120	66.4	282.7	2,622,414	2,341	282,820	181.6	466,720	54.2	45.8	69.9	44.2	5,719	82.3
Gage	534	-1.1	423	63.8	422.0	1,477,063	3,491	156,753	244.5	193,561	71.5	28.5	60.9	35.7	9,908	75.5
Garden	1,026	-2.1	3,932	35.7	149.4	2,403,636	611	180,276	113.6	435,341	33.3	66.7	65.5	44.1	1,714	70.1
Garfield	346	-5.4	1,531	22.5	70.7	1,517,035	991	146,903	64.8	286,597	34.9	65.1	74.3	42.9	1,373	48.7
Gosper	290	28.5	1,115	98.8	171.8	3,529,077	3,165	330,900	139.1	534,885	79.2	20.8	76.5	55.8	3,628	73.5
Grant	493	-0.4	6,167	1.7	41.0	3,407,063	552	136,288	29.0	362,063	D	D	71.3	53.8	226	8.8
Greeley	338	19.8	870	88.2	154.4	2,807,974	3,229	210,997	187.6	482,134	45.5	54.5	75.1	47.0	3,064	74.0
Hall	330	0.4	556	207.6	245.4	2,484,954	4,470	292,526	353.1	595,405	65.9	34.1	69.5	52.1	4,755	64.6
Hamilton	304	-4.6	532	235.5	273.2	3,430,491	6,446	346,014	353.2	617,547	77.1	22.9	77.4	62.4	5,705	77.6
Harlan	313	-10.9	869	93.3	211.8	2,677,533	3,082	261,208	223.5	620,828	56.6	43.4	67.8	44.2	2,989	68.1
Hayes	385	-15.1	1,639	57.1	186.1	2,121,255	1,294	253,677	163.4	695,383	44.9	55.1	70.2	50.2	4,320	92.8
Hitchcock	399	14.8	1,335	21.5	207.4	1,723,151	1,290	204,060	63.6	212,803	67.4	32.6	71.2	42.1	3,553	79.9
Holt	1,414	-7.7	1,106	280.2	600.5	2,314,973	2,093	217,735	636.4	497,540	51.7	48.3	77.2	43.2	7,584	53.2
Hooker	437	-4.4	5,327	3.1	15.7	2,361,890	443	104,793	17.3	210,500	10.9	89.1	81.7	35.4	897	34.1
Howard	312	12.0	458	115.4	182.5	1,350,003	2,949	186,560	246.3	361,128	45.5	54.5	71.7	39.9	3,603	70.1
Jefferson	352	8.2	562	92.8	270.7	2,206,616	3,928	230,150	219.6	500,234	62.2	37.8	66.3	39.4	5,179	74.8
Johnson	198	12.6	337	14.3	132.9	856,930	2,545	107,278	74.6	127,112	58.7	41.3	54.7	26.7	3,405	79.9
Kearney	294	-9.4	854	194.5	242.8	4,508,817	5,283	440,390	407.4	1,184,375	56.9	43.1	84.0	72.4	5,065	80.2
Keith	541	-6.9	1,395	115.3	253.9	2,593,289	1,859	276,216	228.3	588,492	60.7	39.3	65.7	44.3	3,371	67.0
Keya Paha	466	-3.7	1,909	20.1	98.0	1,480,037	775	148,684	107.1	438,848	27.2	72.8	77.9	43.0	733	40.6
Kimball	598	13.3	1,487	34.4	384.8	1,289,806	868	160,933	60.8	151,256	83.5	16.5	51.0	30.6	5,236	87.3
Knox	628	17.0	581	63.9	326.6	1,612,287	2,774	174,033	312.8	289,671	29.9	70.1	69.4	35.1	7,276	74.4
Lancaster	489	16.0	266	21.4	402.6	1,219,781	4,580	123,412	177.8	96,822	82.5	17.5	42.8	18.1	8,810	59.5
Lincoln	1,423	-11.1	1,219	239.8	432.3	1,749,910	1,436	196,783	782.7	670,087	33.8	66.2	62.2	33.0	5,832	45.5
Logan	330	-9.2	2,216	23.0	61.4	2,518,114	1,136	213,148	42.0	281,846	62.5	37.5	63.1	39.6	1,180	53.0
Loup	283	-20.2	2,051	8.2	29.3	1,519,891	741	106,181	32.1	232,406	24.2	75.8	68.8	37.7	772	58.7
McPherson	471	-13.2	3,990	7.1	20.2	1,789,517	449	88,102	30.1	255,144	19.5	80.5	70.3	39.8	167	18.6
Madison	352	11.6	467	122.0	291.0	2,250,416	4,817	236,368	303.7	403,263	49.2	50.8	71.8	40.2	7,057	69.5
Merrick	235	-5.2	478	167.4	200.2	1,833,841	3,838	280,335	275.2	559,394	58.6	41.4	66.1	47.8	4,182	72.6
Morrill	799	-11.4	1,561	128.6	240.5	1,440,148	923	169,750	345.2	674,223	33.1	66.9	68.9	45.1	3,595	69.7
Nance	208	-8.0	586	63.3	133.7	2,003,290	3,417	204,239	145.9	410,927	49.3	50.7	70.4	46.8	3,285	73.5
Nemaha	253	19.1	562	11.4	211.4	2,284,878	4,068	234,035	108.1	239,772	89.3	10.7	67.4	42.4	4,984	80.9
Nuckolls	350	13.9	804	65.2	230.4	3,033,191	3,773	259,074	168.4	387,140	81.8	18.2	82.8	54.7	4,756	79.3
Otoe	388	20.4	432	8.4	321.9	1,856,521	4,295	174,511	158.5	176,670	84.1	15.9	61.3	36.8	5,428	69.3
Pawnee	269	23.5	498	7.3	180.1	1,288,361	2,588	153,443	75.7	140,241	75.7	24.3	58.7	29.6	4,461	78.3
Perkins	557	-0.3	1,413	127.9	432.1	3,208,183	2,271	350,124	233.1	591,713	78.2	21.8	76.9	56.3	7,804	85.8
Phelps	331	-2.6	818	231.9	265.0	3,684,978	4,504	546,160	738.8	1,824,185	35.7	64.3	85.7	76.3	6,054	77.3
Pierce	329	3.9	486	130.0	260.6	2,102,468	4,324	270,908	261.2	385,832	56.4	43.6	72.8	41.1	5,154	70.3

Table B. States and Counties — Water Use, Wholesale Trade, Retail Trade, and Real Estate

STATE County	Water use, 2015		Wholesale Trade[1], 2012				Retail Trade[2], 2012				Real estate and rental and leasing,[2] 2012			
	Public supply water withdrawn (mil gal/day)	Public supply gallons withdrawn per person per day	Number of establish-ments	Number of employees	Sales (mil dol)	Annual payroll (mil dol)	Number of establish-ments	Number of employees	Sales (mil dol)	Annual payroll (mil dol)	Number of establish-ments	Number of employees	Sales (mil dol)	Annual payroll (mil dol)
	133	134	135	136	137	138	139	140	141	142	143	144	145	146
NEBRASKA— Cont'd														
Blaine	0.02	41.1	NA	NA	NA	NA	2	D	D	D	NA	NA	NA	NA
Boone	0.63	118.5	16	213	518.4	10.3	38	257	85.8	4.6	5	D	D	D
Box Butte	1.58	139.4	20	196	173.0	8.2	47	412	96.5	7.8	10	16	2.8	0.3
Boyd	0.15	74.8	3	16	8.4	0.5	11	74	14.4	1.0	1	D	D	D
Brown	0.49	166.3	4	D	D	D	31	259	68.1	5.3	2	D	D	D
Buffalo	6.45	132.0	77	902	1,254.5	43.0	236	3,677	967.0	78.9	55	156	39.0	4.4
Burt	0.85	129.1	16	180	128.0	6.2	29	179	33.8	2.5	4	5	0.3	0.0
Butler	0.68	83.8	14	129	216.5	6.9	27	298	64.2	4.8	4	3	0.3	0.1
Cass	13.53	530.3	17	D	D	D	70	627	177.8	13.2	20	21	3.3	0.5
Cedar	0.65	75.9	24	161	120.3	7.2	46	377	111.0	8.0	8	14	1.4	0.3
Chase	0.91	230.0	16	222	536.5	10.0	30	260	92.3	7.4	4	7	0.2	0.1
Cherry	0.61	104.3	7	102	222.5	2.3	38	422	87.3	7.6	9	7	1.4	0.2
Cheyenne	2.16	212.5	13	113	194.6	5.6	52	1,508	1,081.6	46.1	7	9	1.5	0.2
Clay	1.25	198.1	24	174	289.5	8.6	25	200	135.9	4.1	2	D	D	D
Colfax	1.11	105.5	17	131	214.2	7.6	43	342	106.0	7.6	6	14	1.4	0.2
Cuming	1.61	176.4	24	163	220.5	7.4	50	378	206.0	7.5	4	5	0.9	0.1
Custer	1.18	109.2	15	120	77.8	5.4	63	483	143.4	10.6	7	10	0.7	0.1
Dakota	2.02	97.2	15	249	219.1	12.3	68	897	198.7	18.5	13	D	D	D
Dawes	1.18	130.3	4	23	10.4	0.7	58	581	169.9	13.8	10	10	1.1	0.2
Dawson	5.97	249.9	34	433	680.1	19.5	107	1,398	423.4	34.4	19	D	D	D
Deuel	0.50	260.3	3	D	D	D	11	118	94.8	2.1	1	D	D	D
Dixon	0.75	129.4	8	35	93.3	1.7	9	61	11.7	0.8	1	D	D	D
Dodge	0.70	19.1	63	640	1,127.7	31.8	162	2,427	1,097.3	59.0	36	172	24.1	4.2
Douglas	56.63	103.0	750	10,775	12,685.1	594.8	1,749	34,754	8,586.0	839.3	713	5,700	977.6	258.1
Dundy	0.28	155.6	5	D	D	D	10	46	12.3	1.1	1	D	D	D
Fillmore	0.78	138.8	24	199	281.1	8.1	30	234	65.0	3.9	5	4	0.4	0.0
Franklin	0.67	224.5	9	68	90.2	2.2	12	102	20.4	2.0	1	D	D	D
Frontier	0.27	102.9	6	D	D	D	12	65	19.2	1.2	1	D	D	D
Furnas	0.58	119.3	10	D	D	D	33	204	52.9	3.8	1	D	D	D
Gage	3.60	164.4	36	349	369.5	15.5	112	1,036	262.4	23.0	14	23	3.7	0.6
Garden	0.22	114.7	3	D	D	D	12	65	11.9	0.9	NA	NA	NA	NA
Garfield	0.18	88.8	3	D	D	D	22	138	29.6	2.1	1	D	D	D
Gosper	0.28	141.9	6	41	101.4	1.6	5	24	3.7	0.3	4	D	D	D
Grant	0.05	78.0	3	D	D	D	4	20	3.3	0.2	NA	NA	NA	NA
Greeley	0.23	94.7	4	49	50.4	2.4	15	92	41.6	1.9	2	D	D	D
Hall	11.94	193.6	98	1,296	910.4	66.9	297	4,864	1,256.3	110.1	77	296	54.3	9.0
Hamilton	1.24	134.9	14	284	545.3	14.7	40	309	116.5	6.1	7	9	3.1	0.7
Harlan	0.45	130.4	10	46	63.2	2.0	18	97	34.4	2.0	1	D	D	D
Hayes	0.09	96.6	NA	NA	NA	NA	2	D	D	D	NA	NA	NA	NA
Hitchcock	0.37	128.3	5	D	D	D	13	71	15.8	1.4	NA	NA	NA	NA
Holt	1.15	111.5	30	374	424.0	16.2	80	615	159.9	11.2	13	17	4.2	0.4
Hooker	0.18	245.9	NA	NA	NA	NA	5	34	7.2	0.6	NA	NA	NA	NA
Howard	0.56	87.4	8	55	43.7	1.9	27	212	52.9	3.8	NA	NA	NA	NA
Jefferson	1.11	152.8	13	D	D	D	33	570	176.9	10.1	4	15	0.7	0.3
Johnson	1.00	193.3	4	D	D	D	26	144	44.8	2.9	4	23	3.6	0.3
Kearney	0.86	130.6	14	182	246.1	8.5	20	160	33.4	3.0	3	3	0.6	0.1
Keith	1.08	133.9	19	154	135.2	6.7	63	560	241.5	12.3	17	44	3.9	0.7
Keya Paha	0.05	62.2	2	D	D	D	3	9	5.0	0.2	NA	NA	NA	NA
Kimball	0.52	141.0	4	D	D	D	22	173	50.3	4.2	3	D	D	D
Knox	0.97	113.5	13	118	151.0	4.4	54	384	82.2	6.5	7	29	1.7	0.6
Lancaster	1.52	5.0	278	4,169	3,139.7	169.3	1,016	17,165	4,322.6	388.1	344	1,715	255.1	56.5
Lincoln	5.63	157.9	46	D	D	D	194	2,180	728.8	49.2	43	104	17.8	2.6
Logan	0.05	64.4	2	D	D	D	2	D	D	D	NA	NA	NA	NA
Loup	0.00	0.0	1	D	D	D	1	D	D	D	NA	NA	NA	NA
McPherson	0.00	0.0	NA	NA	NA	NA	2	D	D	D	NA	NA	NA	NA
Madison	4.94	141.0	64	1,730	2,252.8	78.7	212	3,061	815.2	67.6	59	172	24.8	4.2
Merrick	0.80	102.7	24	198	369.2	9.5	33	204	72.1	3.7	5	10	1.1	0.5
Morrill	0.43	88.6	12	120	71.0	5.9	20	163	37.2	2.9	3	3	0.4	0.0
Nance	0.37	102.9	5	23	52.0	0.9	16	100	25.4	2.0	1	D	D	D
Nemaha	0.89	126.3	9	57	69.5	2.5	37	235	57.7	4.6	5	10	0.8	0.1
Nuckolls	0.55	127.1	16	114	172.0	5.4	26	231	73.8	4.8	1	D	D	D
Otoe	2.54	158.9	21	171	239.4	8.0	80	833	202.5	16.9	15	63	11.9	1.9
Pawnee	0.37	139.2	1	D	D	D	10	76	15.7	1.4	NA	NA	NA	NA
Perkins	0.68	231.0	14	121	218.7	6.0	19	120	56.8	3.5	3	15	1.0	0.1
Phelps	1.62	174.3	28	378	851.6	17.3	48	404	116.5	9.3	9	13	2.7	0.2
Pierce	0.69	95.7	14	D	D	D	36	200	69.6	3.5	3	3	0.5	0.1

1. Merchant wholesalers, except manufacturers' sales branches and offices. 2. Employer establishments.

Table B. States and Counties — Professional Services, Manufacturing, and Accommodation and Food Services

STATE County	Professional, scientific, and technical services, 2012				Manufacturing, 2012				Accommodation and food services, 2012			
	Number of establishments	Number of employees	Sales (mil dol)	Annual payroll (mil dol)	Number of establishments	Number of employees	Receipts (mil dol)	Annual payroll (mil dol)	Number of establishments	Number of employees	Receipts (mil dol)	Annual payroll (mil dol)
	147	148	149	150	151	152	153	154	155	156	157	158
NEBRASKA— Cont'd												
Blaine	NA	NA	NA	NA	NA	NA	NA	NA	1	D	D	D
Boone	8	25	5.5	0.9	11	112	D	5.4	11	94	3.2	0.8
Box Butte	22	93	8.8	2.6	8	328	D	16.2	32	339	14.7	3.9
Boyd	1	D	D	D	5	16	D	0.3	6	20	0.6	0.1
Brown	6	19	1.5	0.4	3	24	D	D	10	87	2.9	0.7
Buffalo	104	630	77.1	27.0	58	3,306	1,785.0	147.3	143	3,084	121.7	33.9
Burt	8	72	20.8	3.8	8	76	22.2	2.8	15	67	2.8	0.6
Butler	9	D	D	D	10	571	D	23.9	15	D	D	D
Cass	37	127	10.3	5.2	19	381	170.5	19.2	41	D	D	D
Cedar	13	D	D	D	12	198	D	9.3	12	87	2.2	0.5
Chase	8	D	D	D	4	22	D	D	9	D	D	D
Cherry	18	62	7.4	1.7	8	23	5.1	0.9	23	300	14.0	3.8
Cheyenne	15	D	D	D	8	273	120.8	15.0	35	520	28.1	6.9
Clay	7	D	D	D	7	67	D	2.5	8	31	1.0	0.3
Colfax	11	58	8.0	1.6	3	D	D	D	19	D	D	D
Cuming	22	104	15.7	3.3	14	323	245.8	14.3	25	290	15.4	2.6
Custer	27	96	9.9	2.6	9	D	D	D	31	313	10.7	3.1
Dakota	25	D	D	D	36	D	D	D	40	526	25.1	7.2
Dawes	18	D	D	D	4	10	1.5	0.3	37	457	17.4	4.9
Dawson	57	D	D	D	26	D	D	D	61	D	D	D
Deuel	3	4	0.3	0.1	NA	NA	NA	NA	5	D	D	D
Dixon	1	D	D	D	NA	NA	NA	NA	6	17	1.1	0.1
Dodge	49	183	20.6	7.0	60	3,402	1,955.3	140.1	97	1,476	56.3	15.8
Douglas	1,742	55,558	3,260.3	2,757.2	431	20,560	10,990.1	904.0	1,258	24,758	1,170.2	342.9
Dundy	5	D	D	D	5	15	2.7	0.4	4	27	1.2	0.3
Fillmore	10	24	2.5	0.7	13	221	415.1	8.7	13	81	2.7	0.6
Franklin	4	15	1.5	0.4	NA	NA	NA	NA	6	33	1.3	0.3
Frontier	3	15	0.9	0.3	NA	NA	NA	NA	3	D	D	D
Furnas	5	18	1.2	0.4	7	98	D	4.4	12	D	D	D
Gage	33	125	10.6	3.8	40	1,252	727.0	56.1	49	628	27.4	6.7
Garden	3	D	D	D	NA	NA	NA	NA	3	32	1.0	0.2
Garfield	7	D	D	D	8	117	D	3.7	9	63	1.8	0.3
Gosper	3	D	D	D	NA	NA	NA	NA	3	D	D	D
Grant	2	D	D	D	NA	NA	NA	NA	5	12	0.1	0.0
Greeley	NA	NA	NA	NA	3	9	D	D	4	9	0.6	0.1
Hall	109	638	69.7	25.2	74	7,241	6,021.9	280.1	156	2,515	114.9	33.0
Hamilton	16	69	13.0	2.7	19	443	D	21.7	19	169	6.8	2.0
Harlan	8	D	D	D	5	37	D	D	14	91	3.6	0.8
Hayes	2	D	D	D	NA	NA	NA	NA	2	D	D	D
Hitchcock	NA	NA	NA	NA	3	85	188.0	3.6	5	17	0.6	0.1
Holt	21	63	7.7	2.8	20	190	D	6.8	41	386	12.8	3.2
Hooker	1	D	D	D	NA	NA	NA	NA	4	7	0.3	0.0
Howard	10	26	3.5	0.9	5	10	2.1	0.3	10	69	2.5	0.5
Jefferson	11	D	D	D	16	572	178.4	20.6	19	160	6.7	1.5
Johnson	4	11	0.7	0.2	4	D	D	D	10	57	2.0	0.5
Kearney	10	27	2.0	0.6	9	260	209.2	12.2	12	118	3.1	1.0
Keith	28	119	9.9	3.6	15	254	D	8.0	46	514	22.9	6.1
Keya Paha	4	5	0.2	0.0	NA	NA	NA	NA	NA	NA	NA	NA
Kimball	9	20	1.5	0.3	8	263	38.7	8.9	16	110	4.0	0.9
Knox	17	D	D	D	6	23	6.4	0.9	22	98	3.5	0.7
Lancaster	842	9,135	1,292.4	460.9	235	12,011	5,963.3	596.5	672	13,483	598.3	156.9
Lincoln	78	D	D	D	17	D	200.8	D	94	D	D	D
Logan	1	D	D	D	NA	NA	NA	NA	1	D	D	D
Loup	NA	NA	NA	NA	NA	NA	NA	NA	1	D	D	D
McPherson	NA	NA	NA	NA	NA	NA	NA	NA	1	D	D	D
Madison	88	702	51.5	20.6	55	3,092	D	132.6	101	1,644	64.6	17.8
Merrick	8	34	4.2	1.4	16	254	D	11.8	13	99	4.4	1.0
Morrill	1	D	D	D	3	36	D	1.4	18	147	4.2	1.1
Nance	5	D	D	D	NA	NA	NA	NA	14	D	D	D
Nemaha	8	36	2.1	0.7	3	D	D	D	20	253	7.0	2.5
Nuckolls	14	31	2.6	0.7	3	6	D	D	9	D	D	D
Otoe	26	85	7.3	2.1	17	1,512	D	66.9	40	398	13.9	4.4
Pawnee	4	D	D	D	5	D	D	D	5	33	0.8	0.2
Perkins	7	25	1.6	0.5	3	10	D	D	3	7	0.6	0.1
Phelps	25	89	11.2	3.6	7	D	D	D	22	316	11.3	3.1
Pierce	11	D	D	D	11	D	D	D	10	99	2.2	0.6

Table B. States and Counties — Health Care and Social Assistance, Other Services, Nonemployer Businesses, and Residential Construction

STATE County	Health care and social assistance, 2012				Other services, 2012				Nonemployer businesses, 2015		Value of residential construction authorized by building permits, 2017	
	Number of establish-ments	Number of employees	Receipts (mil dol)	Annual payroll (mil dol)	Number of establis-hments	Number of employees	Receipts (mil dol)	Annual payroll (mil dol)	Number	Receipts (mil dol)	New construction ($1,000)	Number of housing units
	159	160	161	162	163	164	165	166	167	168	169	170
NEBRASKA— Cont'd												
Blaine	NA	NA	NA	NA	NA	NA	NA	NA	47	1.7	NA	NA
Boone	19	244	14.0	4.7	10	26	3.1	0.8	534	20.6	0	0
Box Butte	29	607	50.5	20.0	31	105	11.7	2.3	708	26.5	0	0
Boyd	9	108	5.2	2.1	4	11	1.6	0.2	204	8.9	423	2
Brown	11	181	11.5	4.8	11	28	3.1	0.8	298	10.0	0	0
Buffalo	177	4,012	453.6	165.4	112	D	D	D	3,731	181.9	36,915	165
Burt	17	227	12.5	5.6	13	72	8.5	2.4	494	21.7	1,028	4
Butler	15	373	28.3	13.0	15	D	D	D	689	28.7	3,861	26
Cass	29	423	26.6	9.8	35	120	9.0	2.4	1,854	80.0	22,527	133
Cedar	13	191	10.2	4.2	25	D	D	D	756	38.4	2,077	13
Chase	10	142	11.6	5.2	12	D	D	D	435	24.8	3,195	10
Cherry	19	345	23.9	9.5	18	36	4.8	0.8	607	24.4	2,904	18
Cheyenne	19	510	45.6	16.9	23	67	6.6	1.8	682	31.2	429	2
Clay	16	154	5.4	2.6	8	D	D	D	540	24.9	3,671	16
Colfax	15	344	36.0	8.6	27	76	8.1	1.9	579	27.6	4,486	18
Cuming	26	385	40.9	14.6	33	132	21.1	3.8	730	36.8	4,765	16
Custer	41	713	44.0	19.8	28	59	7.2	1.2	1,120	41.7	848	6
Dakota	32	520	33.7	12.2	36	240	54.8	14.1	1,028	54.4	6,792	35
Dawes	33	630	44.1	21.3	19	51	3.1	0.8	650	21.8	1,432	13
Dawson	73	1,143	92.1	34.5	62	D	D	D	1,459	64.4	10,530	75
Deuel	3	19	1.0	0.4	3	D	D	D	165	8.7	0	0
Dixon	11	99	4.6	1.8	11	D	D	D	478	20.7	1,020	5
Dodge	114	2,662	231.7	85.4	92	377	36.4	8.9	2,271	101.8	17,082	70
Douglas	1,742	47,573	5,673.5	2,121.5	1,067	8,179	1,287.2	251.7	36,272	1,779.5	426,147	3,402
Dundy	8	D	D	D	3	D	D	D	169	7.3	0	0
Fillmore	14	288	20.5	8.7	22	63	9.4	1.4	501	21.0	2,196	10
Franklin	7	166	9.1	3.6	7	19	1.4	0.2	254	9.6	0	0
Frontier	8	40	1.0	0.5	4	D	D	D	245	12.0	220	2
Furnas	20	359	24.6	10.9	14	D	D	D	424	21.1	389	1
Gage	58	1,780	114.4	48.2	66	242	21.6	5.6	1,566	60.4	13,182	84
Garden	4	D	D	D	4	9	0.5	0.1	191	7.6	710	4
Garfield	7	D	D	D	8	17	1.7	0.4	225	8.8	788	7
Gosper	7	9	0.4	0.2	1	D	D	D	193	9.6	660	3
Grant	NA	NA	NA	NA	2	D	D	D	81	3.8	0	0
Greeley	3	10	0.1	0.1	2	D	D	D	266	12.9	1,008	7
Hall	185	D	D	D	145	987	92.7	21.6	3,832	170.7	27,166	213
Hamilton	19	D	D	D	23	D	D	D	837	32.4	6,709	32
Harlan	8	172	11.2	5.0	6	D	D	D	329	12.6	1,430	10
Hayes	1	D	D	D	NA	NA	NA	NA	80	3.4	295	2
Hitchcock	2	D	D	D	2	D	D	D	225	11.3	0	0
Holt	33	870	75.4	29.2	37	D	D	D	1,282	73.4	1,471	10
Hooker	1	D	D	D	4	4	0.5	0.1	109	4.6	212	1
Howard	10	D	D	D	12	D	D	D	517	23.4	5,477	29
Jefferson	16	411	28.1	11.9	17	D	D	D	465	18.7	1,152	8
Johnson	14	274	22.3	9.4	8	21	1.8	0.3	306	10.7	625	3
Kearney	14	604	27.7	13.2	13	D	D	D	485	22.3	2,270	13
Keith	23	339	32.1	10.6	24	94	8.7	2.2	745	35.4	2,475	15
Keya Paha	NA	NA	NA	NA	3	D	D	D	113	4.5	180	1
Kimball	7	97	9.1	4.0	10	D	D	D	287	12.4	544	2
Knox	19	375	24.2	9.1	12	29	3.3	0.6	659	26.3	4,036	22
Lancaster	971	23,204	2,364.8	939.4	667	4,152	578.3	130.7	20,614	817.8	389,688	2,450
Lincoln	140	D	D	D	79	398	38.3	10.1	2,272	89.7	10,015	61
Logan	1	D	D	D	3	15	0.3	0.2	74	3.2	NA	NA
Loup	NA	NA	NA	NA	1	D	D	D	78	2.2	445	5
McPherson	NA	NA	NA	NA	NA	NA	NA	NA	40	1.8	0	0
Madison	164	D	D	D	106	542	44.3	14.0	2,637	113.4	13,420	78
Merrick	17	343	24.3	9.1	22	48	7.3	1.2	643	27.1	1,385	8
Morrill	8	135	12.6	4.3	6	D	D	D	381	14.4	534	2
Nance	10	165	7.4	3.5	13	D	D	D	272	10.3	1,009	5
Nemaha	21	369	30.8	13.6	17	73	4.5	1.1	499	19.6	35	1
Nuckolls	15	385	28.3	11.4	23	48	4.4	0.8	345	12.4	450	3
Otoe	42	853	66.9	26.5	36	129	11.4	2.9	1,177	45.8	8,509	37
Pawnee	7	116	8.8	3.9	5	14	0.9	0.2	257	10.5	3,300	26
Perkins	7	230	16.5	6.2	10	D	D	D	300	18.6	700	3
Phelps	21	813	59.7	24.7	30	104	21.1	2.9	853	35.1	5,029	31
Pierce	17	D	D	D	13	22	2.6	0.6	647	27.0	4,613	15

Table B. States and Counties — **Personal Income and Earnings**

STATE County	Personal income, 2016										Earnings, 2016		
	Total (mil dol)	Percent change 2015-2016	Per capita[1]		Wages and salaries (mil dol)	Supplements to wages and salaries, employer contributions (mil dol)		Proprietors' income (mil dol)	Dividends, interest, and rent (mil dol)	Personal transfer receipts (mil dol)		Contributions for government social insurance (mil dol)	
			Dollars	Rank		Pension and insurance	Government social insurance				Total (mil dol)	From employee and self-employed	From employer
	62	63	64	65	66	67	68	69	70	71	72	73	74
NEBRASKA— Cont'd													
Platte	1,501	0.2	45,692	723	816	160	61	223	264	228	1,261	128	61
Polk	257	-5.6	49,469	445	56	12	4	67	47	43	138	10	4
Red Willow	471	-2.8	43,936	884	211	39	17	45	99	102	312	36	17
Richardson	369	2.2	45,841	708	96	20	8	64	68	83	187	18	8
Rock	90	-5.3	64,463	98	21	4	1	37	17	9	64	3	1
Saline	595	3.6	41,485	1,169	319	58	23	75	94	105	475	49	23
Sarpy	8,223	2.9	45,934	695	3,783	674	297	240	1,311	1,057	4,993	586	297
Saunders	991	1.5	47,125	595	217	42	15	122	162	163	396	37	15
Scotts Bluff	1,555	2.9	42,706	1,024	782	131	65	170	240	327	1,147	135	65
Seward	795	1.8	45,989	692	269	48	20	102	140	126	440	45	20
Sheridan	255	-0.2	48,745	485	61	13	4	57	50	47	136	10	4
Sherman	120	-7.1	39,350	1,445	30	6	2	19	23	29	58	6	2
Sioux	78	-2.1	62,909	112	9	2	1	44	10	7	55	1	1
Stanton	282	1.1	47,375	576	78	13	5	63	43	35	160	12	5
Thayer	272	-1.1	53,386	286	96	20	7	57	62	52	180	16	7
Thomas	40	-8.5	55,825	217	10	2	1	12	9	6	25	2	1
Thurston	352	-1.8	49,448	446	131	29	9	119	42	60	288	21	9
Valley	180	-0.2	43,014	995	69	15	5	32	37	41	121	11	5
Washington	1,040	1.2	50,465	395	442	77	32	71	193	151	622	69	32
Wayne	404	0.6	43,134	984	159	34	11	74	81	63	278	25	11
Webster	169	-3.5	46,939	616	36	8	3	49	27	38	96	7	3
Wheeler	88	-12.0	113,939	6	11	2	1	64	9	5	77	1	1
York	675	-0.6	48,944	474	324	55	24	82	140	121	485	51	24
NEVADA	128,090	3.0	43,579	X	64,404	10,568	4,752	6,737	29,827	21,652	86,462	5,124	4,752
Churchill	914	1.2	37,770	1,698	399	93	30	51	168	243	572	63	30
Clark	91,150	3.1	42,284	1,061	47,329	7,273	3,540	4,701	20,435	15,267	62,842	7,242	3,540
Douglas	3,145	2.5	65,495	91	872	144	65	253	1,196	454	1,334	153	65
Elko	2,393	5.3	45,866	704	1,099	198	76	203	265	282	1,576	162	76
Esmeralda	33	-4.8	42,147	1,085	20	4	1	-6	7	7	20	3	1
Eureka	65	-6.8	34,159	2,296	436	63	28	2	12	10	528	58	28
Humboldt	739	-1.8	43,884	886	436	89	28	32	100	111	585	60	28
Lander	304	-2.1	53,264	297	254	45	16	1	28	39	316	34	16
Lincoln	150	1.2	29,698	2,872	64	22	4	2	27	51	91	9	4
Lyon	1,788	3.8	33,621	2,379	467	109	34	59	269	477	669	81	34
Mineral	180	5.0	40,494	1,299	78	18	6	5	30	58	107	12	6
Nye	1,550	2.5	35,694	2,046	577	104	41	84	268	538	806	101	41
Pershing	202	-3.1	30,763	2,763	102	30	5	6	27	46	143	12	5
Storey	174	5.2	43,069	990	341	55	29	14	35	32	439	54	29
Washoe	22,550	3.4	49,711	427	10,312	1,851	753	1,152	6,387	3,394	14,068	1,616	753
White Pine	400	-2.6	41,336	1,192	218	61	13	3	56	88	295	28	13
Carson City	2,351	-0.5	42,955	999	1,400	413	83	176	516	554	2,071	188	83
NEW HAMPSHIRE	74,687	2.9	55,945	X	35,731	5,435	2,440	6,552	12,955	11,322	50,158	3,058	2,440
Belknap	3,369	2.9	55,431	226	1,160	199	81	332	697	627	1,772	196	81
Carroll	2,528	3.6	53,462	282	782	133	56	311	695	542	1,283	142	56
Cheshire	3,662	1.5	48,329	509	1,496	267	104	315	757	699	2,182	245	104
Coos	1,306	3.6	40,776	1,261	471	104	34	75	233	421	684	82	34
Grafton	4,999	2.2	56,235	203	3,124	476	223	500	1,153	814	4,322	479	223
Hillsborough	23,051	3.0	56,531	197	12,768	1,767	857	1,890	3,555	3,189	17,282	1,895	857
Merrimack	7,928	3.4	53,359	288	4,068	725	279	719	1,366	1,373	5,792	623	279
Rockingham	19,831	2.9	65,396	94	8,595	1,159	583	1,819	3,213	2,261	12,156	1,326	583
Strafford	5,954	3.3	46,727	636	2,630	485	177	426	907	980	3,719	401	177
Sullivan	2,058	3.2	47,845	548	637	120	46	165	380	416	967	109	46
NEW JERSEY	549,836	2.2	61,240	X	256,478	38,404	19,058	50,440	100,930	79,080	364,381	21,726	19,058
Atlantic	11,992	2.2	44,254	855	6,128	1,099	496	959	2,073	2,807	8,683	1,034	496
Bergen	72,491	1.4	77,187	36	30,664	4,132	2,320	7,346	16,598	7,522	44,462	4,935	2,320
Burlington	25,525	2.6	56,812	189	12,356	1,973	983	1,864	4,079	3,950	17,176	2,013	983
Camden	25,197	2.6	49,392	449	11,204	1,842	893	1,554	3,890	5,201	15,492	1,860	893
Cape May	5,181	2.7	54,865	242	1,695	351	149	505	1,367	1,222	2,699	329	149
Cumberland	5,746	1.9	37,363	1,752	2,887	597	239	431	826	1,630	4,154	496	239
Essex	48,522	2.0	60,887	138	24,101	4,020	1,751	3,871	10,369	7,896	33,743	3,717	1,751
Gloucester	14,618	2.2	50,006	416	5,200	1,002	422	860	1,899	2,485	7,484	889	422
Hudson	37,957	2.9	55,986	212	19,859	2,841	1,373	4,367	4,964	5,470	28,440	3,027	1,373
Hunterdon	10,237	1.3	82,109	26	3,241	468	231	889	1,892	959	4,830	524	231

1. Based on the resident population estimated as of July 1 of the year shown.

Table B. States and Counties — **Earnings, Social Security, and Housing**

STATE County	Earnings, 2016 (cont.) Percent by selected industries									Social Security beneficiaries, December 2016		Supplemental Security Income recipients, 2016	Housing units, 2017	
	Farm	Mining, quarrying, and extracting	Construction	Manufacturing	Information; professional, scientific, technical services	Retail trade	Finance, insurance, real estate, and leasing	Health care and social assistance	Government	Number	Rate[1]		Total	Percent change, 2010-2017
	75	76	77	78	79	80	81	82	83	84	85	86	87	88
NEBRASKA— Cont'd														
Platte	12.8	0.0	5.9	30.0	2.8	5.9	4.5	7.5	13.6	6,390	194	289	13,813	3.3
Polk	40.3	D	3.7	1.2	D	4.8	D	5.4	20.6	1,230	236	36	2,728	-0.1
Red Willow	6.3	1.2	5.4	7.9	3.5	9.3	5.8	13.7	19.4	2,460	228	148	5,330	1.2
Richardson	22.9	D	5.2	10.3	3.2	5.2	3.4	D	16.3	2,205	276	153	4,419	0.6
Rock	49.6	0.1	D	D	D	2.0	D	0.8	16.6	200	142	10	913	-0.1
Saline	10.1	0.0	2.0	39.4	D	4.2	2.6	D	16.8	2,520	176	174	5,840	1.4
Sarpy	0.3	0.0	8.5	4.1	8.4	5.7	8.7	5.3	26.3	23,995	135	1,285	69,023	11.4
Saunders	21.6	D	10.0	6.0	5.5	5.7	5.0	D	21.4	4,115	196	182	9,681	5.0
Scotts Bluff	6.5	D	8.2	5.3	3.9	7.0	4.9	16.0	17.3	8,255	226	851	16,391	-0.1
Seward	12.8	0.0	8.0	16.8	2.7	4.6	4.8	D	15.8	3,275	192	129	7,167	4.2
Sheridan	33.5	D	2.2	8.1	1.8	8.2	D	2.2	23.1	1,390	265	65	2,913	-0.8
Sherman	17.6	0.0	3.7	5.2	D	8.3	3.7	5.5	23.3	830	274	33	1,948	0.4
Sioux	77.9	0.0	0.4	1.6	D	1.3	D	D	7.7	230	182	5	829	1.7
Stanton	31.2	D	D	D	D	0.9	2.2	0.5	9.8	980	164	21	2,693	2.3
Thayer	26.9	0.0	3.9	17.0	1.0	3.2	D	3.7	19.9	1,350	265	81	2,752	0.8
Thomas	34.2	D	D	D	D	D	D	D	16.9	170	235	0	406	1.0
Thurston	32.4	0.1	1.5	6.8	D	4.6	2.0	5.5	33.7	1,120	157	228	2,450	1.7
Valley	17.8	D	5.5	5.0	D	7.5	D	5.1	27.0	1,065	255	56	2,300	1.2
Washington	5.9	D	9.6	18.4	4.8	9.2	4.2	D	23.6	4,015	195	160	8,621	3.9
Wayne	23.6	0.0	1.3	14.6	2.0	4.4	7.2	8.2	24.6	1,500	159	82	3,933	4.2
Webster	42.6	D	D	D	D	3.4	D	4.7	16.8	1,015	283	108	1,913	0.1
Wheeler	84.0	0.0	D	D	0.1	D	D	0.0	4.1	150	187	0	577	0.2
York	12.1	D	5.2	12.0	4.2	5.6	6.2	D	15.0	3,075	223	155	6,328	1.6
NEVADA	0.1	1.8	7.2	3.5	8.8	6.9	4.6	9.4	17.0	506,324	172	55,549	1,249,648	6.5
Churchill	0.9	0.4	9.5	6.5	3.8	5.7	2.0	9.2	34.7	5,625	234	521	10,930	1.0
Clark	0.0	0.0	6.1	2.4	8.6	7.2	5.9	9.3	15.8	343,055	159	42,984	899,686	7.1
Douglas	-0.1	D	14.2	9.7	9.1	5.0	5.8	7.5	13.8	14,160	295	389	24,353	2.9
Elko	1.7	14.6	15.3	0.8	2.8	6.5	2.0	5.8	18.4	6,280	120	497	21,583	10.3
Esmeralda	-26.0	D	D	D	D	D	0.0	0.0	26.2	265	320	23	850	-0.2
Eureka	0.0	D	D	0.0	D	0.2	D	D	3.0	340	175	19	1,078	0.7
Humboldt	1.5	37.2	5.5	2.7	D	5.5	1.0	D	20.7	2,600	154	221	7,527	5.7
Lander	-0.5	73.7	D	D	D	2.3	D	0.2	13.4	895	155	71	2,713	5.4
Lincoln	-0.8	1.0	D	D	D	4.6	2.0	D	50.8	1,085	210	67	2,805	2.7
Lyon	1.4	3.0	11.1	20.8	4.9	6.3	2.4	D	22.9	14,200	269	962	23,343	3.5
Mineral	-1.2	D	D	D	D	D	D	0.7	34.6	1,310	298	136	2,839	0.4
Nye	3.5	14.6	4.9	1.4	18.8	6.8	1.4	7.0	16.6	15,875	366	1,127	22,357	0.0
Pershing	7.8	38.7	D	D	D	3.5	0.4	D	39.5	1,005	152	64	2,480	0.6
Storey	0.0	D	13.8	26.3	3.7	D	D	D	4.8	1,235	310	11	2,040	2.5
Washoe	0.1	0.1	11.3	6.5	11.0	6.8	0.5	11.6	18.1	83,580	185	7,270	196,658	6.4
White Pine	-1.0	38.3	1.7	0.3	D	3.4	1.3	D	38.8	1,810	186	153	4,516	0.4
Carson City	0.1	D	3.2	8.6	8.7	6.4	2.5	14.6	40.1	13,005	240	1,034	23,890	1.5
NEW HAMPSHIRE	0.1	0.1	7.3	11.6	12.2	8.2	9.0	12.5	12.8	294,322	220	19,246	634,666	3.2
Belknap	0.1	0.3	12.1	9.1	7.4	11.3	4.2	13.3	15.1	17,715	292	1,081	38,616	3.3
Carroll	0.2	D	13.0	4.1	10.5	10.9	6.5	10.9	14.1	15,095	318	720	41,192	3.4
Cheshire	0.3	0.1	9.8	14.8	6.4	10.6	7.0	11.0	15.3	18,840	249	1,238	35,631	2.5
Coos	0.5	0.2	6.8	5.2	2.8	9.0	4.1	18.3	27.5	10,640	333	940	21,567	1.2
Grafton	0.4	0.1	4.7	8.8	10.2	6.4	4.3	24.6	10.8	20,635	231	993	52,866	3.4
Hillsborough	0.0	0.0	6.4	14.2	15.3	7.8	11.1	11.3	10.0	79,080	194	7,128	171,096	3.0
Merrimack	0.2	0.2	7.4	7.8	8.6	7.7	9.0	14.3	21.5	33,670	227	2,118	64,977	2.3
Rockingham	0.0	0.1	8.1	10.8	14.7	8.5	8.2	9.2	8.7	62,305	205	2,234	132,260	4.4
Strafford	0.1	D	6.1	10.8	7.3	7.7	13.9	13.4	21.7	25,320	199	2,005	53,802	4.1
Sullivan	0.2	D	9.8	25.4	6.5	9.4	4.7	8.0	14.9	11,020	256	789	22,659	1.4
NEW JERSEY	0.1	0.5	5.5	7.6	15.1	6.0	10.0	11.3	15.1	1,597,052	178	182,022	3,615,817	1.8
Atlantic	0.5	D	7.0	D	6.3	8.0	4.3	15.8	24.4	58,145	215	7,054	128,178	1.2
Bergen	0.0	D	5.4	6.9	15.7	7.4	7.7	14.7	10.0	162,400	172	12,307	357,520	1.5
Burlington	0.1	D	5.3	8.5	11.8	8.1	11.7	13.4	17.9	89,620	200	5,990	179,537	2.2
Camden	0.0	0.2	5.9	7.2	10.3	7.4	5.2	18.7	18.3	98,325	193	16,860	205,957	0.5
Cape May	0.2	D	11.2	D	4.9	9.8	7.2	10.3	27.4	28,415	303	1,740	99,245	1.0
Cumberland	1.4	0.3	6.7	14.6	2.7	7.6	3.0	15.3	27.6	30,755	200	6,024	56,435	1.0
Essex	0.0	0.2	3.5	4.7	13.4	4.4	13.1	10.8	21.5	118,865	148	28,853	317,549	1.5
Gloucester	0.7	D	9.3	9.7	6.0	11.2	3.6	10.4	22.3	57,075	196	4,483	113,410	3.2
Hudson	0.0	D	2.7	2.3	13.3	4.9	28.3	6.1	14.3	81,830	119	21,425	281,637	4.2
Hunterdon	0.2	0.2	10.7	4.3	16.5	7.6	11.4	9.8	14.9	23,725	190	841	50,206	1.4

1. Per 1,000 resident population estimated as of July 1 of the year shown.

STATE County	Housing units, 2017 (cont.)								Civilian labor force, 2017				Civilian employment[6], 2012-2016		
	Occupied units										Unemployment		Percent		
	Owner-occupied					Renter-occupied									
				Median owner cost as a percent of income			Median rent as a percent of income[2]	Sub-standard units[4] (percent)		Percent change, 2016-2017				Management, business, science, and arts	Construction, production, and maintenance occupations
	Total	Percent	Median value[1]	With a mort-gage	Without a mort-gage[2]	Median rent[3]			Total		Total	Rate[5]	Total		
	89	90	91	92	93	94	95	96	97	98	99	100	101	102	103
NEBRASKA— Cont'd															
Platte	12,737	71.8	131,200	18.9	11.3	674	20.8	2.9	17,160	1.3	493	2.9	17,477	29.5	37.6
Polk	2,112	78.1	102,300	18.4	10.0	626	19.5	1.8	2,864	-0.4	68	2.4	2,766	35.1	31.1
Red Willow	4,572	76.4	88,400	18.8	14.1	578	28.7	1.5	5,805	-2.7	147	2.5	5,550	27.0	26.6
Richardson	3,768	75.0	71,300	16.3	12.3	498	19.7	2.3	4,203	-0.6	138	3.3	3,982	32.8	32.0
Rock	695	71.7	67,100	19.8	10.5	521	14.6	0.3	887	-0.2	23	2.6	783	35.6	29.6
Saline	5,119	64.8	99,100	19.4	11.8	714	23.2	2.2	7,333	-0.1	226	3.1	7,012	28.6	38.3
Sarpy	62,907	69.9	167,600	20.1	11.2	899	25.6	2.5	92,240	0.4	2,565	2.8	90,249	42.3	17.4
Saunders	7,991	79.2	155,700	20.4	12.4	740	22.2	1.4	10,858	0.0	304	2.8	10,782	36.1	25.1
Scotts Bluff	14,544	68.3	111,200	22.2	13.1	708	28.2	2.6	18,352	-2.5	628	3.4	18,034	30.2	26.0
Seward	6,348	72.1	154,200	19.1	11.9	710	24.5	1.5	8,719	-0.2	232	2.7	8,627	35.7	27.4
Sheridan	2,227	71.3	78,900	19.7	13.6	592	20.8	2.5	2,685	-1.8	71	2.6	2,566	39.8	23.0
Sherman	1,367	76.9	84,900	21.2	11.5	536	17.2	1.5	1,668	-2.7	48	2.9	1,529	39.0	31.1
Sioux	544	71.5	97,500	27.5	10.7	615	19.9	0.0	765	-2.2	23	3.0	665	55.6	16.7
Stanton	2,342	84.5	111,200	19.1	10.0	750	19.7	1.8	3,445	0.3	97	2.8	3,147	27.5	36.4
Thayer	2,375	77.1	68,900	18.5	10.7	529	19.5	1.8	2,848	-1.7	64	2.2	2,534	33.7	27.9
Thomas	298	70.8	103,700	17.9	10.0	530	20.5	0.7	441	-1.6	14	3.2	377	41.4	28.9
Thurston	2,096	60.6	75,600	17.1	10.0	549	25.1	10.9	2,988	0.4	149	5.0	2,488	37.1	25.4
Valley	1,916	70.6	89,900	17.8	11.8	571	27.7	0.6	2,100	0.5	56	2.7	2,290	38.7	24.8
Washington	8,022	78.3	178,000	22.0	11.8	696	24.5	0.9	11,113	0.2	343	3.1	10,811	37.3	22.7
Wayne	3,567	62.8	129,100	16.9	10.0	546	24.9	3.1	5,635	0.4	138	2.4	5,177	34.8	23.0
Webster	1,551	78.4	77,900	20.3	12.0	450	19.1	0.5	1,669	-2.3	50	3.0	1,750	32.6	30.3
Wheeler	373	75.1	100,500	22.7	11.1	496	13.7	3.5	565	0.0	13	2.3	477	35.6	32.7
York	5,670	70.5	120,800	19.6	10.2	625	26.8	0.4	7,281	-0.4	187	2.6	7,227	39.3	23.1
NEVADA	103,0,701	54.8	191,600	23.4	10.0	984	29.9	4.6	1,462,952	2.3	73,582	5.0	1,302,162	28.0	18.7
Churchill	9,491	60.7	157,800	22.3	10.4	826	28.4	4.3	10,782	0.3	476	4.4	9,094	28.3	28.5
Clark	735,475	52.3	186,700	23.6	10.0	1,013	30.4	4.6	1,072,593	2.1	56,197	5.2	951,652	26.7	17.3
Douglas	19,928	69.2	282,500	25.8	10.0	1,031	29.4	1.9	22,769	1.5	1,093	4.8	20,388	35.1	18.5
Elko	17,618	70.3	197,500	18.9	10.0	886	21.3	4.1	27,304	0.5	1,009	3.7	26,277	25.1	32.6
Esmeralda	454	55.9	77,900	18.7	10.6	471	17.7	6.6	524	-0.4	20	3.8	420	30.5	41.7
Eureka	766	69.8	93,800	15.2	10.0	752	20.3	4.3	1,049	5.4	32	3.1	897	35.0	35.0
Humboldt	6,174	75.3	165,100	18.1	10.0	788	22.6	3.9	8,303	-0.8	347	4.2	8,265	20.6	40.1
Lander	2,102	80.4	128,200	17.0	10.0	616	23.8	4.9	3,171	-0.1	144	4.5	2,779	24.8	49.4
Lincoln	1,835	68.3	130,700	21.4	10.0	585	18.9	1.6	2,053	0.7	96	4.7	1,820	40.4	19.2
Lyon	19,586	68.7	143,200	24.1	10.7	886	27.6	2.8	22,090	1.0	1,316	6.0	20,136	24.5	30.9
Mineral	2,065	65.5	85,200	18.3	10.0	505	21.9	7.3	1,996	0.2	109	5.5	1,849	26.0	30.0
Nye	17,464	69.0	109,100	22.5	11.2	787	29.4	2.9	16,403	1.0	1,047	6.4	14,446	25.3	26.3
Pershing	2,016	67.2	105,100	23.9	10.0	591	24.2	8.0	2,645	4.1	119	4.5	2,120	39.1	31.1
Storey	1,752	84.5	192,700	21.2	10.0	759	22.4	0.0	1,969	3.1	98	5.0	1,828	30.0	22.2
Washoe	169,015	56.8	236,900	23.7	10.0	918	29.7	5.0	239,119	3.8	10,001	4.2	212,755	33.8	19.0
White Pine	3,158	73.1	127,100	18.0	10.0	758	22.6	2.7	4,572	-0.3	184	4.0	3,524	35.6	27.2
Carson City	21,802	55.5	199,500	24.0	12.0	827	27.8	4.1	25,610	3.3	1,294	5.1	23,912	30.9	22.5
NEW HAMPSHIRE	521,373	70.7	239,700	23.8	15.9	1,021	29.0	1.9	746,551	0.0	19,943	2.7	706,801	39.8	20.0
Belknap	24,464	75.6	219,200	24.2	16.8	913	29.1	1.8	30,857	-1.0	813	2.6	30,741	36.9	22.6
Carroll	20,783	79.5	227,300	24.4	14.8	903	29.8	2.6	23,352	-0.7	615	2.6	23,076	31.4	21.2
Cheshire	30,473	70.2	187,300	24.0	17.8	925	30.5	2.2	40,461	-1.6	1,045	2.6	39,932	36.7	23.0
Coos	13,917	71.2	122,000	22.7	16.1	713	28.4	1.8	14,376	-1.2	493	3.4	14,974	30.3	24.9
Grafton	34,903	68.5	214,100	23.1	15.4	892	28.3	2.2	48,495	0.2	1,058	2.2	45,593	42.3	18.8
Hillsborough	156,114	66.1	248,500	23.5	15.1	1,099	29.1	2.1	231,152	0.3	6,555	2.8	217,886	41.1	19.1
Merrimack	56,790	70.9	225,200	23.9	16.2	962	29.5	1.7	81,116	-0.3	1,913	2.4	76,569	39.5	19.6
Rockingham	118,672	76.6	288,300	23.8	15.7	1,134	28.2	1.2	181,322	0.5	5,241	2.9	168,798	42.7	18.8
Strafford	47,779	65.1	214,000	24.3	15.9	982	29.5	3.0	72,363	0.6	1,703	2.4	67,640	36.8	21.0
Sullivan	17,478	74.5	171,800	24.2	16.9	875	28.5	1.4	23,057	-1.6	507	2.2	21,592	35.7	26.7
NEW JERSEY	319,5,014	64.1	316,400	26.0	17.7	1,213	31.8	3.4	4,518,837	-0.3	209,127	4.6	4,322,619	41.2	17.7
Atlantic	101,083	67.1	222,200	28.5	18.8	1,054	35.7	3.8	121,102	-2.6	8,703	7.2	127,703	29.9	16.5
Bergen	337,069	64.7	443,400	26.9	18.6	1,380	30.1	2.3	483,324	-0.2	18,797	3.9	465,821	47.6	14.1
Burlington	164,623	76.3	245,000	24.3	16.4	1,219	30.8	1.5	234,179	0.4	9,597	4.1	221,827	43.3	16.2
Camden	185,722	67.2	193,500	24.8	18.3	991	32.8	2.2	256,929	0.4	13,094	5.1	244,943	39.1	17.7
Cape May	40,073	76.4	296,100	27.7	18.0	1,045	35.7	1.5	47,088	-0.3	4,308	9.1	42,837	34.5	18.4
Cumberland	50,718	64.3	161,900	25.4	17.0	999	36.9	4.1	66,406	-1.1	4,617	7.0	62,195	25.9	29.6
Essex	279,480	44.1	356,000	27.9	19.6	1,077	33.2	4.6	370,503	-0.5	21,014	5.7	361,748	37.6	18.6
Gloucester	104,762	79.4	213,200	24.1	17.3	1,101	33.6	1.3	151,568	0.4	7,156	4.7	144,242	41.2	18.4
Hudson	251,693	30.8	341,300	28.4	19.7	1,247	29.0	7.3	362,646	-0.2	15,869	4.4	345,658	39.7	19.4
Hunterdon	46,935	83.4	389,500	23.7	15.0	1,320	30.5	0.8	64,722	-0.5	2,285	3.5	66,233	51.5	12.5

1. Specified owner-occupied units.   2. A value of 10.0 represents 10 percent or less; a value of 50.0 represents 50 percent or more.   3. Specified renter-occupied units.   4. Overcrowded or lacking complete plumbing facilities.   5. Percent of civilian labor force.   6. Civilian employed persons 16 years old and over.

Table B. States and Counties — Nonfarm Employment and Agriculture

STATE County	Number of establish-ments	Total	Health care and social assistance	Manufac-turing	Retail trade	Finance and insurance	Professional, scientific, and technical services	Total (mil dol)	Average per employee (dollars)	Number	Fewer than 50 acres	500 acres or more	Farm operators whose principal occupation is farming (percent)
	104	105	106	107	108	109	110	111	112	113	114	115	116
NEBRASKA— Cont'd													
Platte	1,016	15,936	1,877	4,985	2,257	502	379	624	39,153	942	24.3	31.0	64.9
Polk	151	1,023	236	49	203	53	26	28	27,322	466	23.2	39.7	66.1
Red Willow	415	3,778	629	313	906	235	111	121	32,042	405	26.7	39.0	47.4
Richardson	268	1,877	419	298	296	57	69	54	28,885	736	21.6	28.7	55.7
Rock	53	333	D	D	38	D	D	12	36,787	247	14.2	68.0	61.1
Saline	303	6,005	505	2,958	537	157	47	247	41,126	756	22.9	32.3	56.6
Sarpy	3,598	52,676	5,539	2,613	9,426	1,738	4,096	2,133	40,493	396	57.6	15.4	39.4
Saunders	537	3,993	746	405	625	215	132	132	32,963	1,204	30.4	25.1	55.8
Scotts Bluff	1,082	13,095	2,549	835	2,547	849	339	462	35,261	966	30.6	22.7	49.7
Seward	463	5,669	886	1,097	518	217	126	191	33,604	992	36.4	23.3	47.0
Sheridan	169	951	190	13	226	80	32	26	27,162	536	16.2	50.9	68.5
Sherman	89	561	179	D	129	18	10	16	27,904	414	12.1	38.9	60.9
Sioux	17	32	D	NA	D	D	D	1	36,344	354	8.2	63.6	71.2
Stanton	115	1,967	D	D	89	32	8	115	58,682	619	20.8	29.9	64.6
Thayer	212	1,974	367	D	244	112	34	68	34,644	432	15.7	44.9	63.9
Thomas	23	220	NA	D	9	D	D	7	33,545	87	14.9	70.1	66.7
Thurston	118	1,425	173	241	162	64	D	67	46,744	367	25.3	45.2	65.7
Valley	182	1,306	360	81	298	67	67	41	31,598	402	13.9	49.3	73.1
Washington	591	6,807	885	1,273	1,057	253	217	307	45,041	821	40.0	21.4	58.0
Wayne	241	3,194	499	834	369	330	142	94	29,564	518	24.7	33.0	67.0
Webster	96	638	167	NA	148	40	3	19	30,301	423	21.5	42.6	53.9
Wheeler	24	134	NA	D	D	D	NA	2	16,485	198	17.2	56.6	67.7
York	518	6,381	1,133	847	932	373	126	224	35,152	541	21.1	43.4	70.6
NEVADA	64,815	1,165,298	121,037	43,023	146,445	36,955	59,623	49,208	42,228	4,137	53.2	18.9	53.0
Churchill	479	5,518	776	416	895	145	352	201	36,379	672	63.1	7.6	54.3
Clark	44,564	847,203	86,056	19,629	108,100	26,494	44,256	34,904	41,199	252	78.6	2.0	46.8
Douglas	1,612	16,841	1,492	1,638	2,051	352	751	627	37,256	255	65.1	7.5	62.4
Elko	1,110	20,350	1,560	233	2,564	283	450	1,097	53,906	552	37.0	31.5	53.4
Esmeralda	12	201	NA	D	D	NA	NA	11	53,990	38	23.7	31.6	63.2
Eureka	33	D	D	D	31	D	D	D	D	101	8.9	49.5	68.3
Humboldt	392	5,611	421	240	964	81	65	315	56,128	359	36.2	38.2	54.6
Lander	94	1,413	D	D	210	13	D	90	63,951	124	37.1	47.6	62.1
Lincoln	83	618	124	D	204	31	14	17	28,265	185	35.7	20.5	43.8
Lyon	806	10,218	552	2,213	1,325	143	380	391	38,227	462	60.0	15.4	56.1
Mineral	60	1,009	117	D	85	D	10	44	43,425	119	67.2	1.7	27.7
Nye	662	8,752	755	87	1,634	145	D	378	43,192	198	63.6	15.2	51.0
Pershing	72	1,071	D	D	140	14	14	55	51,226	154	29.2	37.7	81.8
Storey	88	653	D	95	76	NA	19	19	29,505	6	100.0	0.0	0.0
Washoe	12,170	186,628	24,429	15,585	24,117	5,947	10,164	8,172	43,786	479	69.3	7.1	44.1
White Pine	185	2,728	291	16	353	39	22	148	54,148	160	40.6	26.3	43.8
Carson City	1,916	21,862	3,730	2,586	3,523	1,125	1,188	935	42,754	21	81.0	4.8	47.6
NEW HAMPSHIRE	37,868	594,243	91,765	68,645	100,563	28,757	32,287	29,193	49,127	4,391	55.5	3.5	48.0
Belknap	1,805	21,310	3,969	2,704	5,085	627	627	899	42,168	302	55.6	1.7	42.4
Carroll	1,877	16,502	2,534	807	3,764	382	524	574	34,761	291	53.6	3.4	52.6
Cheshire	1,899	27,234	3,701	4,498	5,750	1,346	628	1,119	41,077	407	53.6	5.7	47.4
Coos	853	9,053	2,137	633	1,852	257	124	308	33,987	293	38.2	6.5	50.2
Grafton	2,845	49,080	11,637	5,203	7,506	887	1,626	2,489	50,710	500	38.0	7.2	45.2
Hillsborough	10,944	184,677	30,117	26,458	29,088	9,189	11,802	10,001	54,153	688	64.0	1.5	50.0
Merrimack	4,050	64,576	12,558	5,644	10,454	3,404	2,802	2,924	45,283	600	55.7	3.8	49.2
Rockingham	9,667	139,449	16,380	14,537	28,176	7,030	10,065	6,886	49,381	658	69.6	0.8	48.8
Strafford	2,620	38,715	7,316	5,240	6,442	3,647	1,312	1,776	45,864	354	58.2	1.1	48.6
Sullivan	915	11,804	1,249	2,921	2,431	430	202	493	41,742	298	51.3	5.7	43.0
NEW JERSEY	231,974	3,636,293	584,649	218,742	464,603	198,374	328,347	214,758	59,060	9,071	71.2	3.1	49.5
Atlantic	6,302	105,922	19,072	1,800	15,978	2,377	4,368	4,072	38,442	402	69.4	2.2	61.4
Bergen	31,645	437,598	74,952	29,407	59,519	15,805	35,178	25,995	59,404	60	88.3	0.0	48.3
Burlington	10,440	182,219	27,533	14,104	25,043	19,076	12,808	9,495	52,110	838	69.5	5.0	56.4
Camden	11,417	178,732	41,541	12,134	24,605	4,828	14,919	8,756	48,987	175	81.1	1.1	50.3
Cape May	3,841	27,491	4,326	577	7,032	1,104	976	1,073	39,031	152	75.7	1.3	48.0
Cumberland	2,815	46,097	9,750	7,815	7,412	1,071	1,005	1,818	39,439	583	61.7	5.3	55.2
Essex	18,763	289,030	55,798	18,994	26,939	19,919	22,356	17,434	60,320	13	100.0	0.0	53.8
Gloucester	5,958	93,340	15,080	8,037	17,466	1,799	3,718	3,885	41,622	584	74.3	2.6	45.0
Hudson	13,389	219,848	28,683	8,101	26,679	35,922	12,358	15,385	69,982	0	0.0	0.0	0.0
Hunterdon	3,769	43,742	7,155	3,535	7,035	3,137	5,190	2,781	63,586	1,447	71.9	1.9	43.7

Table B. States and Counties — **Agriculture**

STATE County	Land in farms Acreage (1,000)	Percent change, 2007-2012	Acres Average size of farm	Total irrigated (1,000)	Total cropland (1,000)	Value of land and buildings (dollars) Average per farm	Average per acre	Value of machinery and equiopmnet, average per farm (dollars)	Value of products sold: Total (mil dol)	Average per farm (acres)	Percent from: Crops	Livestock and poultry products	Percent of farms with sales of: $10,000 or more	$100,000 or more	Government payments Total ($1,000)	Percent of farms
	117	118	119	120	121	122	123	124	125	126	127	128	129	130	131	132
NEBRASKA— Cont'd																
Platte	426	0.1	453	194.0	351.5	2,302,510	5,088	284,312	652.1	692,256	36.3	63.7	75.7	53.7	6,298	74.1
Polk	245	-8.9	526	151.0	212.2	3,128,150	5,943	329,976	326.2	700,084	51.2	48.8	80.3	64.4	3,710	79.2
Red Willow	420	-6.0	1,036	53.1	241.6	1,651,696	1,594	224,978	180.5	445,701	45.7	54.3	64.4	37.5	3,807	61.5
Richardson	319	14.3	434	4.7	245.8	1,653,332	3,812	171,026	162.0	220,139	71.0	29.0	65.4	38.2	6,434	82.2
Rock	645	2.0	2,610	36.3	146.9	2,813,632	1,078	195,603	97.8	395,903	40.2	59.8	82.6	53.8	1,332	36.0
Saline	362	21.3	479	108.1	296.7	2,306,246	4,818	261,522	208.8	276,152	82.3	17.7	65.9	41.4	5,966	80.8
Sarpy	92	-9.0	232	10.4	82.2	1,380,134	5,959	127,424	63.6	160,553	75.4	24.6	45.5	24.5	1,340	58.1
Saunders	469	9.8	390	105.6	412.0	2,054,154	5,268	198,767	380.5	316,033	59.0	41.0	65.2	37.4	7,393	72.3
Scotts Bluff	445	23.6	461	199.2	239.7	860,445	1,867	172,940	390.1	403,791	41.2	58.8	62.1	31.2	3,579	62.3
Seward	355	6.7	358	129.9	294.3	1,799,861	5,031	216,676	308.5	311,017	59.7	40.3	59.3	34.5	6,718	71.2
Sheridan	1,534	-0.4	2,863	60.7	275.5	1,983,683	693	201,590	167.5	312,541	50.0	50.0	62.5	35.1	3,179	57.3
Sherman	281	4.1	679	71.1	127.7	1,609,171	2,369	172,713	114.2	275,754	68.3	31.7	78.7	42.8	2,093	70.5
Sioux	1,224	-5.2	3,459	39.5	94.0	1,981,486	573	151,356	146.0	412,446	20.3	79.7	74.6	44.1	1,338	46.0
Stanton	254	7.9	411	28.4	195.1	1,798,275	4,375	202,628	182.1	294,158	35.1	64.9	67.7	35.4	3,656	77.9
Thayer	326	-7.1	755	135.5	254.0	3,114,514	4,123	323,176	249.4	577,278	74.7	25.3	78.7	56.9	4,259	81.5
Thomas	368	-13.5	4,225	2.9	8.0	2,125,345	503	114,736	22.4	257,770	D	D	73.6	37.9	438	18.4
Thurston	248	24.0	675	11.9	215.9	3,406,256	5,049	284,038	197.7	538,651	47.3	52.7	72.2	57.8	3,744	80.1
Valley	349	-1.9	869	93.1	150.7	1,919,602	2,209	248,953	205.1	510,179	46.5	53.5	76.9	52.2	2,783	75.1
Washington	248	14.2	302	17.3	209.8	1,820,340	6,024	180,247	163.5	199,117	62.8	37.2	54.9	32.6	4,069	59.3
Wayne	280	1.2	540	49.8	238.4	2,363,431	4,373	235,147	203.3	392,380	45.7	54.3	75.5	43.8	3,410	77.4
Webster	302	-1.1	715	55.0	177.8	2,021,950	2,830	228,965	226.9	536,404	40.4	59.6	76.8	45.2	3,545	71.6
Wheeler	357	-0.9	1,804	39.4	90.9	2,208,793	1,225	254,586	259.8	1,312,323	13.6	86.4	74.7	51.5	1,407	52.5
York	340	-1.9	628	252.4	313.1	3,534,628	5,631	429,436	415.4	767,861	72.9	27.1	81.0	65.1	6,039	74.5
NEVADA	5,914	0.8	1,429	687.8	756.9	1,324,673	927	134,626	764.1	184,710	47.9	52.1	42.0	21.2	3,253	8.2
Churchill	197	50.0	294	53.6	56.3	713,604	2,431	110,594	89.9	133,833	34.5	65.5	44.6	18.3	414	7.3
Clark	16	-82.3	62	3.7	4.4	347,790	5,611	66,325	6.8	27,083	48.2	51.8	33.7	4.4	34	3.6
Douglas	101	10.9	396	25.6	18.6	1,141,780	2,884	76,525	D	D	D	D	36.9	12.2	D	0.8
Elko	2,127	2.0	3,853	132.2	170.4	1,908,208	495	122,257	95.6	173,221	15.3	84.7	42.4	23.6	398	6.5
Esmeralda	35	38.7	911	17.5	19.2	1,631,211	1,791	350,737	13.1	345,974	98.2	1.8	60.5	60.5	0	0.0
Eureka	639	-18.5	6,325	46.7	49.1	4,087,158	646	288,782	36.0	356,634	81.2	18.8	72.3	59.4	D	3.0
Humboldt	809	6.9	2,253	137.5	165.3	2,233,571	991	271,593	135.3	376,983	75.7	24.3	48.7	37.9	703	26.7
Lander	314	-7.4	2,532	37.2	44.6	1,880,298	743	211,121	39.3	316,581	68.9	31.1	55.6	46.8	132	15.3
Lincoln	D	D	D	22.0	22.4	1,074,735	D	145,276	23.2	125,487	60.2	39.8	41.6	21.6	34	5.9
Lyon	366	40.4	792	87.7	78.3	1,738,119	2,194	137,630	133.0	287,959	43.8	56.2	44.2	21.4	485	5.8
Mineral	D	D	D	D	D	863,597	D	38,882	0.9	7,429	56.4	43.6	25.2	0.8	0	0.0
Nye	65	-28.3	329	20.0	26.4	703,429	2,139	127,217	70.5	356,035	D	D	36.9	12.6	62	6.1
Pershing	299	22.5	1,943	52.8	57.4	1,813,416	933	262,714	62.8	407,474	52.5	47.5	63.6	42.9	779	29.2
Storey	0	D	14	D	D	550,167	38,384	29,833	D	D	D	D	0.0	0.0	0	0.0
Washoe	443	-8.9	924	15.4	13.7	752,190	814	53,073	16.5	34,543	49.6	50.4	27.8	6.7	75	4.0
White Pine	193	D	1,208	32.7	24.3	987,431	817	150,775	20.7	129,069	43.9	56.1	40.6	22.5	120	7.5
Carson City	D	D	D	D	D	665,048	D	108,429	5.8	275,476	D	D	23.8	19.0	0	0.0
NEW HAMPSHIRE	474	0.5	108	2.6	98.3	449,848	4,167	56,426	190.9	43,477	52.8	47.2	26.6	6.0	3,472	10.6
Belknap	24	2.2	79	0.3	5.7	431,990	5,462	54,798	7.8	25,712	61.2	38.8	22.2	5.0	194	7.3
Carroll	29	-8.4	101	0.2	3.9	479,337	4,751	50,859	5.5	18,801	63.2	36.8	24.1	2.7	203	9.6
Cheshire	63	31.2	156	0.1	9.2	455,386	2,928	52,337	17.3	42,582	39.6	60.4	31.4	6.9	231	7.9
Coos	57	11.6	194	0.0	12.5	462,461	2,386	65,020	14.2	48,461	34.6	65.4	28.7	6.5	200	14.7
Grafton	82	-17.6	165	0.1	17.2	489,910	2,974	61,806	29.8	59,662	19.5	80.5	28.8	8.0	753	19.8
Hillsborough	48	-5.0	69	0.7	11.1	450,385	6,495	52,282	22.5	32,759	69.8	30.2	22.8	7.0	261	6.8
Merrimack	65	0.5	108	0.6	13.7	430,238	3,974	58,167	45.3	75,443	77.7	22.3	30.5	6.8	686	13.0
Rockingham	36	7.2	55	0.3	9.0	406,448	7,428	49,995	18.4	27,964	68.9	31.1	23.7	4.6	352	7.9
Strafford	31	19.2	87	0.3	7.7	425,040	4,904	61,031	12.8	36,144	47.0	53.0	30.5	3.1	295	10.7
Sullivan	39	-9.7	131	0.1	8.3	515,507	3,937	66,409	17.3	58,091	30.8	69.2	23.5	8.1	296	9.4
NEW JERSEY	715	-2.5	79	88.4	456.8	1,008,402	12,792	81,470	1,006.9	111,006	88.5	11.5	36.1	12.3	7,596	11.4
Atlantic	29	-2.9	73	11.3	18.9	903,438	12,320	135,682	125.4	312,040	98.2	1.8	51.7	25.4	247	8.2
Bergen	1	21.7	24	0.1	0.5	1,005,933	42,148	74,700	5.2	86,600	96.3	3.7	60.0	20.0	D	1.7
Burlington	96	11.8	114	13.1	52.3	1,108,438	9,686	98,032	100.9	120,390	95.4	4.6	45.3	14.4	1,939	13.4
Camden	7	-18.5	41	2.5	4.7	513,600	12,583	67,920	16.0	91,526	99.2	0.8	32.6	12.0	20	5.7
Cape May	7	-7.8	48	2.2	4.3	557,868	11,534	51,809	8.0	52,809	93.4	6.6	40.1	10.5	D	2.0
Cumberland	65	-7.1	111	19.3	49.7	889,362	8,035	130,184	170.4	292,216	97.2	2.8	50.9	22.1	520	14.9
Essex	0	-30.4	10	0.0	0.0	624,923	63,469	61,769	1.9	148,462	D	D	69.2	38.5	0	0.0
Gloucester	43	-7.3	74	9.0	32.0	882,231	11,909	93,639	87.7	150,154	93.9	6.1	33.6	15.6	700	13.0
Hudson	0	0.0	0	0.0	0.0	0	0	0	0.0	0	0.0	0.0	0.0	0.0	0	0.0
Hunterdon	96	-4.0	66	1.2	58.3	1,088,382	16,401	59,249	67.2	46,445	85.3	14.7	26.3	5.1	724	10.8

Table B. States and Counties — Water Use, Wholesale Trade, Retail Trade, and Real Estate

STATE County	Water use, 2015 — Public supply water withdrawn (mil gal/day)	Public supply gallons withdrawn per person per day	Wholesale Trade[1], 2012 — Number of establishments	Number of employees	Sales (mil dol)	Annual payroll (mil dol)	Retail Trade[2], 2012 — Number of establishments	Number of employees	Sales (mil dol)	Annual payroll (mil dol)	Real estate and rental and leasing,[2] 2012 — Number of establishments	Number of employees	Sales (mil dol)	Annual payroll (mil dol)
	133	134	135	136	137	138	139	140	141	142	143	144	145	146
NEBRASKA— Cont'd														
Platte	4.96	151.0	51	543	851.1	26.9	161	2,112	541.2	45.6	38	120	21.7	2.8
Polk	0.39	75.0	8	115	211.9	6.2	24	128	50.2	2.8	1	D	D	D
Red Willow	2.34	216.1	22	246	193.8	12.5	80	929	329.2	21.6	15	37	2.7	0.4
Richardson	0.74	91.4	26	137	473.1	5.0	44	331	94.1	7.2	6	16	1.7	0.5
Rock	0.16	115.9	4	D	D	D	7	44	6.8	0.7	NA	NA	NA	NA
Saline	1.36	95.2	21	175	316.6	9.1	43	536	129.2	11.1	8	18	2.6	0.3
Sarpy	30.65	174.5	183	2,932	4,040.2	161.1	367	7,301	2,926.4	174.8	146	580	163.2	22.0
Saunders	49.56	2,358.2	31	193	235.6	9.0	67	566	161.7	12.3	17	22	1.8	0.4
Scotts Bluff	5.66	156.1	56	D	D	D	178	D	D	D	46	116	19.8	3.0
Seward	1.39	81.2	27	258	528.2	14.1	47	521	105.6	10.7	9	11	2.6	0.3
Sheridan	0.59	113.0	12	206	104.3	4.8	42	236	55.7	3.8	2	D	D	D
Sherman	0.23	74.4	3	32	15.2	1.2	17	134	59.1	3.0	1	D	D	D
Sioux	0.08	63.5	1	D	D	D	3	D	D	D	NA	NA	NA	NA
Stanton	0.36	60.6	3	D	D	D	13	83	17.9	1.4	NA	NA	NA	NA
Thayer	0.81	156.9	25	215	524.6	12.3	31	173	56.1	3.4	3	D	D	D
Thomas	0.11	160.8	1	D	D	D	4	25	8.0	0.4	NA	NA	NA	NA
Thurston	0.60	84.9	8	99	103.3	3.5	24	219	73.0	4.7	4	D	D	D
Valley	1.25	300.9	8	76	225.5	3.3	33	267	116.5	6.0	2	D	D	D
Washington	12.18	601.5	18	D	D	D	56	1,106	747.4	42.4	15	20	2.6	0.5
Wayne	0.87	92.9	12	122	63.4	3.2	40	352	69.6	5.9	7	16	1.2	0.5
Webster	0.39	107.6	13	D	D	D	19	163	29.3	2.4	NA	NA	NA	NA
Wheeler	0.04	53.3	3	D	D	D	2	D	D	D	NA	NA	NA	NA
York	1.87	135.4	37	390	427.0	17.6	70	979	290.2	20.9	19	47	5.6	0.9
NEVADA	558.26	193.1	2,501	27,649	19,841.7	1,516.2	8,135	129,977	38,234.2	3,454.1	3,866	22,412	4,981.2	814.7
Churchill	3.38	139.7	15	78	39.1	2.9	69	966	235.1	23.4	32	113	12.5	2.6
Clark	432.47	204.5	1,630	16,747	11,597.1	958.8	5,712	95,369	27,971.7	2,531.6	2,794	17,855	3,700.3	647.4
Douglas	14.08	295.1	41	341	211.6	18.3	172	1,793	516.6	46.8	126	249	35.0	7.3
Elko	12.61	242.8	57	D	D	D	161	2,359	946.5	63.8	41	D	D	D
Esmeralda	0.11	132.7	1	D	D	D	1	D	D	D	NA	NA	NA	NA
Eureka	0.32	158.7	2	D	D	D	7	29	10.2	0.6	NA	NA	NA	NA
Humboldt	3.68	216.2	18	122	71.4	8.1	78	989	325.3	25.6	9	D	D	D
Lander	1.56	264.3	4	34	38.4	2.2	20	235	52.0	6.0	3	4	0.8	0.1
Lincoln	1.16	230.3	2	D	D	D	16	D	D	D	3	D	D	D
Lyon	9.39	178.6	38	749	206.4	24.6	97	1,188	465.5	29.1	33	D	D	D
Mineral	1.05	234.5	2	D	D	D	15	95	31.3	3.0	NA	NA	NA	NA
Nye	6.29	148.1	9	96	55.4	4.5	117	1,404	397.1	34.1	34	79	7.7	1.8
Pershing	1.27	191.4	2	D	D	D	16	131	48.4	3.3	1	D	D	D
Storey	0.53	132.9	NA	NA	NA	NA	20	41	6.0	0.9	1	D	D	D
Washoe	57.68	129.1	584	8,064	6,401.9	414.6	1,391	21,603	6,167.0	580.0	671	D	D	D
White Pine	1.18	120.3	7	64	33.7	2.2	31	408	111.0	9.6	7	D	D	D
Carson City	11.50	210.9	89	519	276.4	25.2	212	3,139	918.2	92.6	111	304	51.7	9.5
NEW HAMPSHIRE	95.52	71.8	1,543	21,140	18,029.2	1,307.9	6,127	95,660	26,018.2	2,403.6	1,338	7,044	1,593.1	309.7
Belknap	3.12	51.5	50	447	214.2	23.9	342	4,907	1,357.5	127.0	78	420	62.0	12.3
Carroll	3.45	73.0	39	310	99.2	14.5	363	3,558	877.7	88.9	69	237	36.1	8.6
Cheshire	4.12	54.3	59	1,151	637.4	47.0	368	5,839	1,692.5	150.1	60	229	45.1	8.0
Coos	4.20	134.6	21	295	89.3	7.5	182	1,800	566.6	45.2	25	68	11.9	2.5
Grafton	7.57	84.8	78	713	487.9	42.6	519	7,712	2,034.2	199.5	144	454	70.5	15.3
Hillsborough	38.74	95.3	537	6,822	4,749.3	470.5	1,584	26,984	7,724.7	700.9	387	2,697	565.9	123.8
Merrimack	8.26	55.8	148	3,176	2,823.3	162.5	624	10,124	2,819.7	243.0	143	848	319.9	41.4
Rockingham	15.35	50.9	487	6,804	8,203.7	455.3	1,587	26,066	6,764.5	625.5	303	1,286	316.8	55.9
Strafford	8.00	63.1	85	1,037	385.9	58.1	385	6,378	1,619.4	166.9	93	560	78.1	22.7
Sullivan	2.71	63.1	39	385	339.1	26.0	173	2,292	561.2	56.5	36	245	86.7	19.2
NEW JERSEY	1,175.42	131.2	12,760	208,830	288,467.8	14,976.8	31,722	436,299	133,665.7	12,676.0	8,749	53,751	17,327.6	2,813.1
Atlantic	30.20	110.1	188	D	D	D	1,227	16,099	4,292.7	394.9	227	1,383	351.1	52.0
Bergen	127.42	135.8	2,720	36,346	77,906.6	2,730.3	3,807	56,423	20,349.2	2,662.1	1,357	7,550	2,481.5	417.9
Burlington	54.20	120.4	492	10,202	14,927.4	618.5	1,428	23,654	6,868.6	645.4	364	3,340	886.7	201.7
Camden	42.83	83.8	572	8,133	4,906.7	442.3	1,730	23,577	6,445.8	593.9	398	2,660	601.1	116.3
Cape May	13.61	143.7	60	D	D	D	669	5,803	1,639.4	166.2	218	681	148.7	26.0
Cumberland	15.72	100.9	152	3,223	2,422.4	133.6	512	7,201	2,049.0	175.0	120	471	96.2	15.8
Essex	31.22	39.2	987	14,029	13,657.7	913.7	2,710	26,114	9,204.6	720.2	879	5,267	1,258.8	214.8
Gloucester	17.52	60.1	296	7,307	16,524.4	437.2	954	16,728	4,452.9	398.7	171	1,228	256.1	63.9
Hudson	0.00	0.0	757	15,906	26,043.1	1,009.8	2,118	23,126	6,647.6	611.5	636	3,698	1,238.8	199.0
Hunterdon	119.90	955.5	143	1,868	1,030.6	150.0	493	6,561	2,350.0	190.2	104	415	123.8	25.3

1. Merchant wholesalers, except manufacturers' sales branches and offices. 2. Employer establishments.

Table B. States and Counties — Professional Services, Manufacturing, and Accommodation and Food Services

STATE County	Professional, scientific, and technical services, 2012				Manufacturing, 2012				Accommodation and food services, 2012			
	Number of establishments	Number of employees	Sales (mil dol)	Annual payroll (mil dol)	Number of establishments	Number of employees	Receipts (mil dol)	Annual payroll (mil dol)	Number of establishments	Number of employees	Receipts (mil dol)	Annual payroll (mil dol)
	147	148	149	150	151	152	153	154	155	156	157	158
NEBRASKA— Cont'd												
Platte	65	465	55.7	23.1	74	5,492	4,438.5	261.6	75	968	40.9	10.5
Polk	12	18	1.9	0.4	6	53	D	1.6	6	37	1.4	0.2
Red Willow	28	123	13.9	4.4	14	293	D	14.3	30	524	21.5	6.0
Richardson	13	63	4.2	1.5	14	193	40.4	7.1	21	193	6.1	1.7
Rock	2	D	D	D	NA	NA	NA	NA	4	15	0.4	0.1
Saline	16	43	4.6	1.2	19	2,654	2,175.0	125.9	27	309	10.6	2.6
Sarpy	297	2,588	354.6	156.8	76	2,699	791.9	139.3	255	4,718	224.7	62.7
Saunders	45	119	15.0	4.9	22	288	104.6	9.5	42	D	D	D
Scotts Bluff	68	D	D	D	39	847	270.7	33.7	100	D	D	D
Seward	29	106	21.4	3.3	20	1,197	576.8	57.3	30	453	18.6	4.4
Sheridan	8	29	3.8	0.7	NA	NA	NA	NA	21	133	4.8	1.3
Sherman	6	13	0.9	0.3	3	10	D	D	8	61	2.5	0.6
Sioux	1	D	D	D	NA	NA	NA	NA	2	D	D	D
Stanton	2	D	D	D	NA	NA	NA	NA	5	60	1.7	0.4
Thayer	9	18	2.3	0.6	11	524	D	15.3	12	115	7.6	1.1
Thomas	1	D	D	D	NA	NA	NA	NA	NA	NA	NA	NA
Thurston	9	D	D	D	6	246	D	10.1	8	65	2.5	0.5
Valley	14	D	D	D	9	74	D	3.2	9	D	D	D
Washington	47	163	20.1	6.5	26	1,134	1,549.7	69.9	52	441	16.1	4.4
Wayne	16	56	10.7	2.7	12	893	217.6	28.6	23	393	11.5	2.5
Webster	2	D	D	D	NA	NA	NA	NA	4	24	0.6	0.2
Wheeler	NA	NA	NA	NA	NA	NA	NA	NA	5	8	0.2	0.1
York	29	122	14.5	4.8	28	777	359.3	34.9	39	710	32.2	8.7
NEVADA	8,102	47,934	7,758.5	2,832.1	1,706	38,123	14,719.1	1,979.3	5,815	296,762	27,481.5	8,555.6
Churchill	43	354	23.4	10.4	18	248	D	12.8	50	586	35.9	9.4
Clark	5,645	35,253	5,825.0	2,128.2	894	17,390	5,673.8	782.0	4,050	250,601	24,283.8	7,612.3
Douglas	238	786	115.6	37.2	74	1,129	713.0	55.1	126	5,326	445.8	125.1
Elko	98	666	123.7	32.7	24	D	D	D	138	5,036	442.7	121.4
Esmeralda	1	D	D	D	NA	NA	NA	NA	1	D	D	D
Eureka	4	D	D	D	NA	NA	NA	NA	5	34	1.5	0.4
Humboldt	19	96	10.3	3.6	13	241	120.0	12.0	62	1,161	84.1	15.7
Lander	1	D	D	D	NA	NA	NA	NA	14	145	6.2	1.6
Lincoln	6	20	2.4	0.6	NA	NA	NA	NA	19	D	D	D
Lyon	62	324	34.8	13.1	81	1,708	729.9	85.9	67	613	31.2	7.9
Mineral	5	22	1.5	0.6	NA	NA	NA	NA	10	D	D	D
Nye	50	155	12.5	4.3	14	60	D	1.7	81	1,401	96.5	22.5
Pershing	2	D	D	D	6	128	D	3.1	13	113	5.8	1.8
Storey	6	7	0.5	0.2	6	91	17.3	3.1	14	71	9.4	2.4
Washoe	1,619	9,029	1,435.4	539.9	442	13,974	6,427.4	840.4	973	28,138	1,860.8	580.8
White Pine	8	25	2.1	0.9	6	23	D	0.8	33	553	31.2	9.4
Carson City	295	1,180	170.1	60.0	122	2,798	634.0	162.7	159	2,740	133.4	41.2
NEW HAMPSHIRE	3,825	30,159	3,947.8	1,697.5	1,851	66,636	18,895.6	3,923.8	3,606	54,047	2,942.3	890.9
Belknap	147	D	D	D	86	2,483	673.3	117.2	223	2,603	157.9	50.7
Carroll	133	D	D	D	74	1,069	225.8	41.2	313	4,034	247.0	70.6
Cheshire	147	628	69.2	30.0	127	4,719	1,101.6	230.1	172	2,543	128.7	40.0
Coos	37	114	11.3	4.3	37	731	189.3	31.0	111	1,747	81.0	31.2
Grafton	254	1,537	210.1	98.4	115	5,758	1,593.9	300.2	378	5,112	296.7	92.2
Hillsborough	1,335	10,986	1,721.0	737.1	554	25,287	7,450.8	1,732.0	897	14,781	762.2	229.8
Merrimack	433	2,850	402.7	171.8	206	5,548	1,577.3	291.1	307	4,965	238.7	75.2
Rockingham	1,049	8,202	1,109.2	462.4	425	14,055	4,580.4	824.8	853	13,804	810.2	237.3
Strafford	235	1,720	217.6	95.3	137	4,428	924.4	228.1	282	3,676	182.8	52.2
Sullivan	55	180	21.1	9.0	90	2,559	578.8	128.0	70	782	37.1	11.8
NEW JERSEY	29,390	307,549	58,738.2	24,013.0	7,758	230,697	108,855.0	14,094.8	20,127	291,933	19,673.6	5,386.8
Atlantic	579	D	D	D	96	1,730	285.4	72.3	860	46,661	4,008.5	1,282.5
Bergen	4,067	37,178	6,945.7	2,557.1	1,107	33,434	12,577.6	2,133.9	2,331	28,682	2,016.7	518.2
Burlington	1,323	D	D	D	343	15,380	5,496.6	1,046.9	914	14,391	771.4	206.5
Camden	1,444	D	D	D	389	11,340	D	613.9	998	14,598	789.4	210.9
Cape May	214	D	D	D	66	615	98.2	21.5	903	5,888	593.0	160.0
Cumberland	207	D	D	D	162	8,055	2,812.0	351.2	265	3,555	173.7	43.6
Essex	2,213	28,745	6,117.7	2,678.1	720	17,556	5,942.0	921.7	1,550	20,633	1,378.7	368.3
Gloucester	514	D	D	D	235	8,056	12,683.6	440.2	483	7,832	406.6	108.0
Hudson	1,335	11,261	1,961.4	898.8	378	7,865	2,682.9	363.9	1,381	15,540	1,214.5	287.1
Hunterdon	561	4,111	888.9	350.4	141	3,485	1,400.2	198.5	312	3,518	206.3	54.9

Table B. States and Counties — Health Care and Social Assistance, Other Services, Nonemployer Businesses, and Residential Construction

STATE County	Health care and social assistance, 2012				Other services, 2012				Nonemployer businesses, 2015		Value of residential construction authorized by building permits, 2017	
	Number of establish-ments	Number of employees	Receipts (mil dol)	Annual payroll (mil dol)	Number of establish-ments	Number of employees	Receipts (mil dol)	Annual payroll (mil dol)	Number	Receipts (mil dol)	New construction ($1,000)	Number of housing units
	159	160	161	162	163	164	165	166	167	168	169	170
NEBRASKA— Cont'd												
Platte	82	1,551	179.9	55.9	78	360	26.7	8.4	2,205	93.9	15,669	72
Polk	9	273	17.4	7.2	9	17	2.8	0.5	446	14.6	1,837	10
Red Willow	50	604	60.9	22.5	33	90	10.1	2.4	881	35.0	649	5
Richardson	26	D	D	D	22	66	4.8	0.8	570	19.2	285	1
Rock	4	D	D	D	5	7	0.9	0.2	216	10.7	350	3
Saline	26	525	37.9	16.4	26	96	6.2	1.8	826	32.6	5,317	33
Sarpy	302	4,733	387.5	146.4	225	1,219	110.5	30.3	9,990	374.8	253,899	1,016
Saunders	31	672	38.8	17.6	27	D	D	D	1,796	67.7	26,900	130
Scotts Bluff	128	D	D	D	76	D	D	D	2,469	107.3	2,817	19
Seward	36	761	53.7	24.0	38	134	15.4	3.5	1,328	43.0	12,322	58
Sheridan	17	208	12.2	6.4	18	42	3.1	0.6	445	17.9	212	3
Sherman	6	D	D	D	6	11	0.9	0.1	269	10.5	200	1
Sioux	1	D	D	D	1	D	D	D	103	3.6	300	2
Stanton	7	D	D	D	4	23	2.7	0.4	497	21.7	2,800	11
Thayer	11	416	25.8	11.1	21	60	16.3	1.4	415	20.0	2,626	9
Thomas	NA	NA	NA	NA	1	D	D	D	87	3.5	0	0
Thurston	9	277	32.6	14.7	8	24	3.2	0.8	262	11.0	0	0
Valley	18	111	5.9	2.5	14	67	6.0	1.3	411	16.7	1,490	6
Washington	40	926	67.4	31.7	41	D	D	D	1,566	68.4	25,349	85
Wayne	24	458	31.7	14.2	20	D	D	D	627	26.5	9,233	65
Webster	9	189	10.7	4.7	5	17	2.1	0.3	293	8.3	80	2
Wheeler	NA	NA	NA	NA	1	D	D	D	84	4.6	1,110	7
York	41	1,063	79.9	35.5	57	253	20.6	5.0	1,051	41.9	2,545	11
NEVADA	6,308	108,585	13,928.5	5,094.7	3,538	25,386	2,608.9	706.5	205,980	10,838.5	2,845,798	19,544
Churchill	41	714	81.1	30.6	42	171	12.2	3.5	1,184	46.6	6,974	32
Clark	4,426	75,019	9,714.9	3,493.8	2,344	17,926	1,602.8	476.8	154,711	7,851.8	1,844,987	14,073
Douglas	121	1,310	165.9	59.1	69	514	41.2	15.1	5,187	345.8	71,307	197
Elko	125	D	D	D	70	D	D	D	2,308	104.9	24,303	161
Esmeralda	NA	NA	NA	NA	1	D	D	D	62	1.4	NA	NA
Eureka	1	D	D	D	1	D	D	D	119	5.6	NA	NA
Humboldt	37	628	55.0	22.2	36	D	D	D	840	33.3	2,031	17
Lander	9	D	D	D	4	D	D	D	265	7.3	0	0
Lincoln	6	128	7.4	3.3	2	D	D	D	285	8.7	2,458	9
Lyon	38	D	D	D	42	202	20.7	5.3	2,536	120.8	82,531	346
Mineral	6	D	D	D	4	D	D	D	150	5.4	0	0
Nye	61	821	82.6	24.3	49	203	16.8	4.4	2,170	80.9	NA	NA
Pershing	6	107	9.0	3.6	4	D	D	D	200	4.4	263	4
Storey	1	D	D	D	3	D	D	D	286	12.7	2,019	10
Washoe	1,190	D	D	D	728	D	D	D	30,391	1,779.4	772,118	4,554
White Pine	16	301	44.6	16.7	13	D	D	D	469	17.0	1,068	3
Carson City	224	3,744	510.8	182.9	126	660	62.8	19.0	4,817	412.4	35,738	138
NEW HAMPSHIRE	3,578	87,099	9,616.5	4,086.4	2,879	16,603	1,554.9	473.3	104,437	5,912.8	758,295	3,625
Belknap	137	3,536	358.6	148.0	147	626	49.1	13.8	5,609	307.3	45,251	182
Carroll	142	2,693	267.9	100.4	111	432	39.6	11.1	5,566	295.2	72,289	215
Cheshire	157	3,954	334.7	156.5	144	938	77.2	22.6	5,892	305.2	22,646	104
Coos	102	2,469	214.2	91.1	68	377	40.5	12.6	2,207	96.5	8,532	50
Grafton	273	10,236	1,482.4	659.8	207	D	D	D	8,108	441.9	51,890	193
Hillsborough	1,094	28,561	3,089.1	1,339.9	824	5,516	490.3	160.3	28,477	1,657.8	184,019	1,033
Merrimack	410	12,310	1,239.7	550.0	411	1,995	257.0	68.2	10,989	589.3	76,141	289
Rockingham	866	15,640	1,697.7	671.8	676	3,639	335.9	104.1	26,488	1,682.6	209,857	979
Strafford	302	6,486	834.3	327.4	204	1,192	111.9	32.9	7,920	392.8	74,498	520
Sullivan	95	1,214	97.8	41.4	87	D	D	D	3,181	144.2	13,172	60
NEW JERSEY	26,935	540,875	60,375.2	24,325.0	18,327	108,216	11,607.8	3,150.1	670,765	39,455.4	4,141,681	28,501
Atlantic	846	17,487	1,969.3	780.4	563	3,588	293.9	85.2	16,682	831.5	154,399	1,090
Bergen	3,664	70,990	9,303.0	3,642.8	2,423	12,297	1,376.8	366.9	92,417	6,364.4	489,329	3,001
Burlington	1,215	25,242	2,710.6	1,006.5	778	4,560	363.7	118.9	27,596	1,601.4	135,558	1,133
Camden	1,535	38,296	4,238.4	1,821.5	920	5,873	478.1	149.4	29,654	1,553.2	104,355	1,400
Cape May	278	4,767	443.7	186.8	296	1,237	96.3	32.4	8,066	492.5	236,490	809
Cumberland	417	8,593	872.1	338.7	240	1,253	97.1	27.3	5,918	277.7	7,490	88
Essex	2,534	53,168	6,274.3	2,462.1	1,639	12,502	1,220.6	360.6	64,781	3,405.1	327,512	2,317
Gloucester	689	13,076	1,298.2	541.2	502	2,838	223.8	66.5	15,905	775.5	91,378	736
Hudson	1,412	26,740	2,397.6	1,000.5	1,092	5,024	439.1	125.3	53,140	2,552.6	700,292	5,073
Hunterdon	363	7,216	794.4	323.9	272	1,466	120.6	38.5	11,934	802.4	41,431	287

Table B. States and Counties — Government Employment and Payroll, and Local Government Finances

	Government employment and payroll, 2012									Local government finances				
			March payroll (percent of total)							General revenue				
													Taxes	
													Per capita[1] (dollars)	
STATE County	Full-time equivalent employees	March payroll (dollars)	Adminis-tration, judicial, and legal	Police and corrections	Fire protection	Highways and transpor-tation	Health and welfare	Natural resources and utilities	Education and libraries	Total (mil dol)	Inter-govern-mental (mil dol)	Total (mil dol)	Total	Property
	171	172	173	174	175	176	177	178	179	180	181	182	183	184
NEBRASKA— Cont'd														
Platte	3,477	20,266,212	1.3	2.8	0.3	1.8	0.3	79.5	13.4	163.8	34.4	61.8	1,892	1,373
Polk	420	1,380,326	5.6	2.1	0.0	3.0	15.0	11.8	58.7	37.3	5.7	21.1	3,974	3,451
Red Willow	459	1,542,403	5.5	7.0	2.8	3.6	3.4	14.8	59.2	39.4	13.2	18.3	1,666	1,234
Richardson	419	1,193,885	9.7	4.8	0.6	7.6	0.0	12.0	63.6	30.7	8.7	18.1	2,182	1,949
Rock	140	411,891	13.3	2.7	0.0	6.6	35.8	2.2	35.4	13.0	2.1	4.8	3,482	3,134
Saline	632	2,291,344	7.0	11.3	0.3	4.0	0.9	7.0	67.4	70.4	19.1	28.7	1,969	1,723
Sarpy	5,078	18,211,968	6.6	10.7	1.5	2.7	1.0	2.9	72.0	450.7	142.5	250.1	1,508	1,248
Saunders	810	2,374,236	6.4	9.1	0.3	4.5	15.3	6.0	56.4	83.3	19.9	36.4	1,747	1,563
Scotts Bluff	2,061	7,164,008	4.8	7.4	1.1	2.8	2.5	7.6	73.3	182.1	72.1	64.7	1,751	1,338
Seward	680	2,373,107	7.0	6.7	0.0	6.0	0.7	9.6	68.9	55.3	12.4	35.6	2,103	1,821
Sheridan	512	1,548,088	13.3	3.5	0.0	6.0	29.3	9.8	37.6	40.3	9.6	11.2	2,111	1,872
Sherman	144	428,471	12.6	3.9	0.0	9.3	0.2	2.5	70.1	13.6	4.9	7.3	2,338	2,074
Sioux	56	132,554	19.8	4.1	0.0	17.1	0.0	2.1	56.8	4.9	1.0	3.0	2,305	2,122
Stanton	142	497,786	10.8	7.3	0.0	12.3	0.9	19.3	48.7	13.2	4.4	6.8	1,111	1,047
Thayer	412	1,461,621	5.5	2.0	0.0	5.1	41.8	4.4	38.2	41.8	5.4	16.6	3,236	3,029
Thomas	60	133,894	17.6	0.2	0.0	4.3	2.3	11.2	63.8	4.0	0.7	2.8	4,143	3,988
Thurston	545	1,799,779	5.2	2.2	0.0	2.7	22.5	1.8	65.3	52.7	28.4	8.7	1,244	1,115
Valley	518	1,666,812	3.3	2.5	0.0	3.6	47.1	17.8	25.3	53.3	10.2	13.7	3,233	2,920
Washington	750	2,779,921	6.4	9.0	0.0	4.2	8.1	3.5	68.0	69.7	16.2	43.5	2,146	1,843
Wayne	341	1,199,613	9.9	5.1	0.0	9.4	0.0	6.2	69.3	36.1	12.9	18.5	1,940	1,746
Webster	258	1,370,728	10.8	2.2	0.0	8.5	14.9	37.0	25.2	25.0	5.9	8.3	2,228	1,836
Wheeler	43	129,479	13.7	4.4	0.0	13.0	0.0	0.4	68.2	4.3	0.9	3.2	3,984	3,805
York	557	2,016,974	7.4	11.4	2.9	4.0	1.6	20.2	51.6	58.5	16.3	32.4	2,356	1,736
NEVADA	X	X	X	X	X	X	X	X	X	X	X	X	X	X
Churchill	944	3,773,220	10.4	12.8	0.4	2.3	1.9	7.4	51.3	114.7	52.6	27.8	1,142	921
Clark	51,796	300,546,553	8.1	16.4	5.9	3.4	8.6	10.1	45.3	8,606.7	3,678.4	2,735.1	1,367	869
Douglas	1,543	6,734,261	11.5	13.8	10.6	2.6	1.1	9.0	47.4	190.9	73.5	79.1	1,682	1,414
Elko	1,843	7,360,751	11.7	10.6	2.2	3.0	2.9	4.9	62.8	202.1	112.9	62.5	1,220	871
Esmeralda	82	243,932	21.0	20.4	0.0	9.4	1.5	2.3	37.8	7.7	4.9	1.6	2,030	2,012
Eureka	151	777,513	15.5	14.0	0.0	9.5	5.9	8.6	42.4	52.6	15.1	33.5	16,737	16,592
Humboldt	805	3,278,576	10.2	13.2	0.3	2.8	19.5	2.9	48.7	119.3	53.7	33.6	1,972	1,745
Lander	301	1,258,391	12.7	11.1	0.0	4.5	25.4	3.4	42.8	97.8	10.8	72.9	12,271	11,925
Lincoln	324	1,339,919	8.9	8.4	0.1	6.3	17.9	11.0	44.6	43.9	32.2	5.0	930	812
Lyon	1,568	6,140,208	8.1	8.1	3.5	1.3	1.3	10.4	64.0	160.6	98.5	45.8	892	708
Mineral	326	1,115,225	7.2	7.3	1.2	2.2	44.5	6.8	29.7	44.0	21.3	4.5	977	861
Nye	1,197	5,104,254	15.1	13.0	3.6	2.6	5.5	2.8	53.7	149.5	78.9	54.1	1,259	1,117
Pershing	319	1,109,998	11.6	9.0	0.3	4.2	22.5	5.0	44.3	34.1	14.3	8.8	1,300	1,263
Storey	188	901,189	19.1	15.5	16.1	3.8	0.0	4.0	34.8	29.3	7.0	16.6	4,219	4,028
Washoe	13,423	56,391,305	10.3	14.1	5.5	4.2	4.2	8.5	50.6	1,707.2	748.2	591.5	1,376	997
White Pine	513	2,356,531	8.8	7.1	1.5	3.7	40.7	2.2	32.8	71.2	22.1	18.0	1,791	1,611
Carson City	1,396	6,652,347	9.5	13.4	7.3	4.2	3.5	6.4	53.3	189.1	96.1	54.9	1,001	717
NEW HAMPSHIRE	X	X	X	X	X	X	X	X	X	X	X	X	X	X
Belknap	2,709	10,085,919	5.6	9.4	4.9	3.9	5.2	2.9	67.2	286.0	77.2	174.6	2,894	2,867
Carroll	2,191	7,449,385	6.3	9.2	2.5	4.0	7.7	3.0	65.3	220.7	71.1	131.4	2,763	2,740
Cheshire	3,313	11,134,351	6.0	8.9	2.9	3.9	7.7	4.1	65.0	326.6	110.7	178.9	2,328	2,314
Coos	1,565	5,117,863	3.6	6.6	2.3	4.9	20.1	3.2	58.8	159.6	71.8	67.1	2,091	2,079
Grafton	4,014	15,506,186	5.7	9.6	3.8	4.9	5.6	2.9	66.7	413.3	113.5	253.8	2,845	2,823
Hillsborough	13,991	56,054,764	4.1	10.8	6.0	4.5	3.9	3.8	65.8	1,458.9	470.6	808.2	2,006	1,981
Merrimack	5,875	21,465,982	6.0	10.6	5.3	4.2	7.6	3.1	61.7	555.7	176.5	328.2	2,236	2,219
Rockingham	10,620	43,247,180	4.5	10.2	6.0	2.4	3.9	2.7	68.4	1,174.1	314.0	771.3	2,590	2,568
Strafford	4,327	16,109,116	5.0	11.0	4.3	2.9	5.3	4.6	64.6	465.8	153.2	257.6	2,076	2,027
Sullivan	1,670	6,151,956	5.3	6.7	2.1	4.8	8.2	3.5	67.8	169.0	64.2	91.6	2,126	2,114
NEW JERSEY	X	X	X	X	X	X	X	X	X	X	X	X	X	X
Atlantic	14,001	71,971,044	5.3	13.7	4.7	1.7	5.3	3.8	63.4	1,749.6	507.4	1,016.6	3,691	3,639
Bergen	32,531	187,619,946	3.6	14.1	2.2	2.4	3.4	3.1	69.8	4,811.6	664.9	3,480.7	3,788	3,728
Burlington	17,657	91,624,216	4.0	9.2	2.6	2.9	2.3	3.0	75.0	2,079.2	596.9	1,183.3	2,622	2,584
Camden	20,756	110,518,829	3.6	10.7	3.0	3.5	5.8	2.8	67.4	3,281.1	1,305.1	1,230.4	2,396	2,359
Cape May	5,885	27,086,618	8.8	13.8	3.3	3.6	9.4	7.3	49.4	701.1	152.6	449.5	4,667	4,561
Cumberland	7,697	36,180,326	5.2	9.1	0.8	1.2	4.3	5.3	72.5	886.9	544.0	234.1	1,483	1,435
Essex	27,848	164,987,769	6.6	19.3	7.5	1.4	6.3	6.8	50.7	4,140.4	1,433.6	2,242.3	2,846	2,712
Gloucester	12,453	61,264,381	3.9	10.6	0.6	1.8	6.9	3.4	70.7	1,465.5	472.5	747.5	2,581	2,536
Hudson	18,627	101,485,405	7.4	23.1	8.9	1.9	5.7	4.8	45.5	2,886.1	1,144.0	1,243.6	1,906	1,849
Hunterdon	5,140	25,927,699	5.8	5.6	0.8	4.7	2.2	2.5	77.1	623.8	82.1	477.9	3,762	3,722

1. Based on the resident population estimated as of July 1 of the year shown.

Table B. States and Counties — Local Government Finances, Government Employment, and Income Taxes

STATE County	Local government finances (cont.)									Government employment, 2016			Individual income tax returns, 2015		
	Direct general expenditure							Debt outstanding							
	Total (mil dol)	Per capita[1] (dollars)	Percent of total for:					Total (mil dol)	Per capita[1] (dollars)	Federal civilian	Federal military	State and local	Number of returns	Mean adjusted gross income	Mean income tax
			Education	Health and hospitals	Police protection	Public welfare	Highways								
	185	186	187	188	189	190	191	192	193	194	195	196	197	198	199
NEBRASKA— Cont'd															
Platte	113.1	3,461	56.1	0.4	3.7	0.6	15.1	2,372.1	72,585	87	115	2,576	16,600	56,825	6,138
Polk	34.4	6,457	55.6	18.0	1.4	0.1	7.2	36.4	6,843	27	18	523	2,590	55,388	5,947
Red Willow	41.1	3,746	48.6	0.9	4.2	0.6	6.1	41.9	3,815	72	37	1,037	5,080	49,479	5,375
Richardson	30.5	3,684	56.0	0.2	3.6	0.5	13.4	14.8	1,787	33	28	584	3,810	48,965	4,783
Rock	12.2	8,902	28.5	45.3	2.3	0.2	9.0	0.5	363	0	0	222	670	43,785	4,888
Saline	69.9	4,800	47.6	15.1	3.0	5.7	7.4	56.7	3,893	60	47	1,478	6,410	50,434	4,618
Sarpy	475.3	2,866	55.1	0.8	7.4	0.2	4.2	984.0	5,933	3,165	6,360	6,748	84,490	68,047	7,795
Saunders	75.5	3,628	42.1	21.4	3.2	0.2	8.3	105.7	5,074	98	73	1,529	10,030	63,496	7,367
Scotts Bluff	188.1	5,089	58.5	0.3	4.2	1.6	3.8	124.2	3,361	157	126	3,207	16,710	49,350	5,076
Seward	66.4	3,923	62.3	0.1	3.8	0.8	11.4	73.7	4,351	48	56	1,109	7,550	62,491	6,786
Sheridan	37.7	7,085	31.7	24.7	2.1	9.8	6.1	9.5	1,782	25	18	595	2,400	40,523	3,784
Sherman	13.4	4,324	49.2	0.3	3.1	0.3	17.7	6.5	2,098	14	11	282	1,420	39,515	3,387
Sioux	4.8	3,666	52.8	0.0	2.8	0.0	23.8	0.0	0	0	0	77	540	37,822	3,191
Stanton	13.6	2,232	42.0	0.7	4.3	0.5	31.8	14.5	2,388	19	21	277	2,780	55,018	5,714
Thayer	43.3	8,429	33.8	38.7	2.7	0.2	7.2	11.5	2,243	29	18	656	2,420	53,462	6,140
Thomas	4.0	5,904	53.0	0.5	3.1	0.0	7.9	0.8	1,214	10	0	93	330	48,952	5,124
Thurston	60.1	8,565	48.8	36.6	1.1	0.1	3.6	70.6	10,050	213	25	1,493	2,760	43,933	4,839
Valley	51.9	12,276	20.8	38.7	0.9	0.1	4.8	58.0	13,716	30	15	584	1,960	41,118	4,357
Washington	65.2	3,221	57.9	0.1	4.7	0.2	11.9	202.8	10,013	50	71	1,561	9,710	71,753	8,956
Wayne	43.1	4,516	51.6	0.3	2.5	0.4	9.5	23.9	2,503	36	29	995	3,760	54,681	5,790
Webster	23.9	6,404	33.4	19.3	2.3	5.0	13.2	9.5	2,548	24	12	313	1,620	43,915	3,866
Wheeler	4.1	5,045	61.1	0.0	2.5	0.0	23.7	0.6	806	0	0	63	380	41,187	3,739
York	55.4	4,034	45.6	2.4	5.0	0.3	13.4	105.0	7,641	56	46	1,143	6,700	58,160	6,782
NEVADA	X	X	X	X	X	X	X	X	X	18,935	17,920	135,048	1,350,680	60,993	8,679
Churchill	117.7	4,831	40.0	0.3	7.9	1.8	3.2	48.9	2,005	601	673	1,263	10,860	48,768	5,044
Clark	9,171.7	4,584	29.1	8.3	9.6	2.7	7.2	21,727.8	10,860	12,977	15,143	85,834	980,020	59,719	8,486
Douglas	187.5	3,990	36.5	0.3	5.7	2.5	2.5	82.9	1,764	88	131	2,215	25,550	77,826	13,803
Elko	209.5	4,091	47.0	0.9	7.2	0.7	5.0	51.6	1,008	348	141	3,462	23,330	66,721	8,065
Esmeralda	8.2	10,566	34.9	3.8	14.2	0.4	10.2	1.0	1,279	0	0	96	400	45,185	4,423
Eureka	40.5	20,245	25.6	2.0	4.9	0.3	18.1	0.0	0	0	0	183	750	61,496	7,497
Humboldt	102.4	6,005	35.6	26.8	6.8	1.0	6.9	5.9	344	163	46	1,338	7,780	61,119	6,989
Lander	42.2	7,095	31.4	24.0	6.2	2.0	4.2	0.0	0	68	16	472	2,540	67,750	9,049
Lincoln	42.9	7,928	28.0	0.6	5.4	1.6	11.1	9.9	1,834	51	13	597	1,690	51,498	4,714
Lyon	173.5	3,380	52.1	0.6	14.8	3.1	4.1	198.7	3,872	73	145	2,087	24,870	44,153	4,212
Mineral	39.6	8,513	17.4	39.2	5.2	0.6	3.6	14.3	3,064	61	13	464	1,880	42,668	3,770
Nye	174.9	4,071	43.6	4.0	14.2	1.5	4.9	134.2	3,123	124	118	1,651	17,930	48,376	5,008
Pershing	35.1	5,199	33.9	28.5	4.8	1.5	1.5	18.6	2,751	17	13	716	2,000	51,924	5,371
Storey	27.2	6,900	26.2	0.0	10.5	0.8	8.2	58.6	14,880	0	11	251	1,890	60,623	7,238
Washoe	1,673.2	3,892	35.9	1.1	6.6	4.3	3.3	4,470.2	10,398	3,657	1,281	24,314	218,390	69,200	10,509
White Pine	67.7	6,746	27.2	38.8	5.4	1.6	6.0	14.1	1,407	171	23	1,165	4,010	53,547	5,999
Carson City	205.0	3,738	48.3	2.1	8.1	1.2	5.3	391.1	7,131	519	146	8,940	26,910	51,688	6,420
NEW HAMPSHIRE	X	X	X	X	X	X	X	X	X	7,672	4,710	82,737	693,070	71,673	10,119
Belknap	273.9	4,541	53.3	0.3	6.3	6.1	4.4	96.2	1,595	142	204	4,120	33,040	65,632	8,927
Carroll	240.5	5,057	57.3	1.0	4.6	7.3	6.0	161.9	3,404	130	159	2,850	25,710	78,370	12,911
Cheshire	326.5	4,248	59.3	0.8	4.3	5.5	5.6	178.9	2,328	160	242	5,359	37,180	64,025	8,551
Coos	150.6	4,691	46.4	1.2	3.9	16.3	6.1	37.2	1,158	418	100	2,659	15,000	44,033	4,355
Grafton	440.6	4,940	56.2	0.8	4.4	4.8	5.7	258.1	2,895	525	282	6,821	44,250	73,895	11,197
Hillsborough	1,496.1	3,713	52.0	0.6	6.1	3.8	4.7	1,157.0	2,872	4,022	1,428	17,449	212,770	71,083	9,859
Merrimack	608.7	4,147	55.4	0.5	5.3	7.4	4.5	341.5	2,327	816	488	16,119	75,090	66,789	8,704
Rockingham	1,129.6	3,793	60.9	0.4	6.4	4.0	3.7	523.7	1,758	1,066	1,247	13,263	166,720	83,550	12,655
Strafford	444.5	3,582	51.7	0.1	5.7	7.3	4.8	294.8	2,375	304	416	11,619	61,960	61,805	7,730
Sullivan	166.1	3,857	51.2	0.5	4.3	11.4	5.9	81.8	1,900	89	144	2,478	21,410	59,874	7,829
NEW JERSEY	X	X	X	X	X	X	X	X	X	49,520	25,197	533,081	4,385,490	83,650	13,240
Atlantic	1,718.6	6,240	52.7	0.6	6.1	2.1	1.7	1,314.6	4,773	2,627	987	19,690	133,990	52,471	5,921
Bergen	4,857.2	5,286	54.3	5.8	7.0	1.3	2.6	3,581.0	3,897	2,614	1,892	45,056	464,930	108,360	19,750
Burlington	2,064.4	4,574	62.3	1.5	4.2	2.2	3.1	2,370.1	5,251	5,029	5,914	23,987	225,530	76,455	10,601
Camden	3,129.5	6,094	51.5	4.2	4.5	3.4	4.0	3,660.4	7,128	2,299	1,062	28,335	246,100	63,785	8,134
Cape May	808.9	8,400	33.8	1.5	5.3	4.4	4.9	673.4	6,992	445	1,173	8,206	49,820	59,979	7,487
Cumberland	880.4	5,580	60.1	2.7	3.8	3.4	2.5	354.4	2,246	644	292	12,371	67,190	47,187	4,601
Essex	4,300.2	5,459	38.9	3.3	8.3	2.9	1.3	3,851.1	4,889	8,965	1,640	62,950	370,380	88,564	15,922
Gloucester	1,410.5	4,871	58.9	0.8	4.6	2.2	1.9	1,385.8	4,785	508	588	19,765	140,590	69,887	8,635
Hudson	2,833.2	4,343	33.2	3.1	8.5	2.8	1.8	3,638.2	5,577	5,554	1,505	37,203	331,950	67,697	10,182
Hunterdon	605.4	4,765	66.0	1.2	3.5	0.8	6.1	565.1	4,448	256	252	7,862	64,620	118,999	21,019

1. Based on the resident population estimated as of July 1 of the year shown.

Table B. States and Counties — **Personal Income and Earnings**

STATE County	Personal income, 2016										Earnings, 2016		
	Total (mil dol)	Percent change 2015-2016	Per capita[1] Dollars	Per capita[1] Rank	Wages and salaries (mil dol)	Supplements to wages and salaries, employer contributions (mil dol) Pension and insurance	Supplements to wages and salaries, employer contributions (mil dol) Government social insurance	Proprietors' income (mil dol)	Dividends, interest, and rent (mil dol)	Personal transfer receipts (mil dol)	Total (mil dol)	Contributions for government social insurance (mil dol) From employee and self-employed	Contributions for government social insurance (mil dol) From employer
	62	63	64	65	66	67	68	69	70	71	72	73	74
NEW JERSEY— Cont'd													
Mercer	23,462	1.1	63,237	108	16,217	2,450	1,164	1,541	4,849	3,317	21,372	2,400	1,164
Middlesex	46,859	3.6	55,980	213	28,340	4,068	2,142	4,318	7,238	6,334	38,868	4,404	2,142
Monmouth	44,583	1.9	71,237	61	14,748	2,296	1,161	3,763	8,716	5,539	21,968	2,500	1,161
Morris	44,392	1.3	89,065	20	24,949	2,978	1,724	4,883	9,008	3,688	34,533	3,713	1,724
Ocean	28,092	2.9	47,413	572	7,609	1,447	632	2,420	5,171	6,594	12,107	1,498	632
Passaic	24,151	1.4	47,547	563	9,244	1,619	733	2,516	3,710	4,821	14,112	1,601	733
Salem	2,866	1.3	45,187	764	1,232	263	95	132	421	708	1,723	205	95
Somerset	30,127	2.9	90,268	19	17,138	1,942	1,146	4,045	5,744	2,309	24,270	2,528	1,146
Sussex	8,007	1.5	56,183	206	1,898	365	154	602	1,212	1,150	3,018	352	154
Union	34,342	2.8	61,808	127	16,016	2,341	1,112	3,199	6,055	4,522	22,668	2,452	1,112
Warren	5,486	1.7	51,454	348	1,753	312	140	374	848	954	2,579	307	140
NEW MEXICO	80,065	1.4	38,393	X	37,640	6,913	3,108	4,501	14,984	19,367	52,163	3,395	3,108
Bernalillo	27,781	3.1	41,038	1,227	16,483	2,851	1,382	1,305	5,249	5,814	22,022	2,771	1,382
Catron	115	0.1	32,683	2,530	23	6	2	6	32	42	37	5	2
Chaves	2,357	-1.4	36,108	1,988	798	154	65	324	391	668	1,340	151	65
Cibola	740	2.7	26,919	3,028	311	68	26	23	106	266	428	54	26
Colfax	455	-0.8	37,097	1,806	166	35	13	30	95	151	244	31	13
Curry	2,113	0.5	42,034	1,098	991	220	93	226	370	460	1,530	169	93
De Baca	72	-0.6	40,269	1,328	19	4	1	11	15	26	36	4	1
Dona Ana	7,037	1.7	32,852	2,509	2,915	620	244	630	1,167	1,985	4,409	526	244
Eddy	2,770	-7.0	48,077	527	1,528	263	116	318	468	521	2,225	254	116
Grant	1,020	-0.8	36,068	1,994	389	89	30	27	200	383	535	69	30
Guadalupe	141	2.0	32,121	2,594	53	10	4	2	23	57	70	9	4
Harding	28	1.0	42,720	1,022	7	2	1	5	8	7	14	1	1
Hidalgo	154	-3.0	35,831	2,029	65	17	5	13	28	54	100	12	5
Lea	2,328	-8.7	33,371	2,415	1,412	238	108	59	302	552	1,817	247	108
Lincoln	807	2.5	41,532	1,159	219	41	18	56	256	234	334	44	18
Los Alamos	1,189	2.8	65,494	92	1,365	129	111	45	224	85	1,651	213	111
Luna	752	1.6	30,751	2,765	290	67	26	51	111	290	434	57	26
McKinley	1,925	2.0	25,688	3,063	761	191	65	82	274	702	1,099	136	65
Mora	182	-8.1	40,421	1,311	25	7	2	36	28	67	70	8	2
Otero	2,269	3.4	34,686	2,210	938	224	84	74	471	581	1,320	163	84
Quay	302	1.8	36,063	1,998	100	21	8	12	54	127	140	19	8
Rio Arriba	1,307	2.9	32,639	2,535	361	78	29	28	184	469	496	67	29
Roosevelt	690	-0.1	36,156	1,981	218	49	17	56	106	186	340	36	17
Sandoval	5,493	4.4	38,677	1,548	1,363	224	110	235	793	1,119	1,932	253	110
San Juan	4,374	-2.2	38,007	1,658	2,265	425	179	178	626	1,031	3,047	372	179
San Miguel	918	1.5	33,062	2,463	280	74	23	20	158	404	397	52	23
Santa Fe	7,650	1.8	51,461	347	2,893	509	224	450	2,362	1,335	4,077	500	224
Sierra	416	1.5	37,162	1,798	111	25	9	21	88	192	167	23	9
Socorro	555	-0.5	32,608	2,536	216	54	17	27	89	190	315	36	17
Taos	1,166	2.4	35,270	2,128	372	70	32	67	290	382	541	74	32
Torrance	446	0.1	29,158	2,920	125	26	10	19	62	175	180	24	10
Union	144	1.8	34,429	2,256	53	10	4	5	27	45	72	9	4
Valencia	2,371	2.3	31,349	2,697	525	109	49	63	328	766	746	111	49
NEW YORK	117,6,080	1.7	59,289	X	639,448	108,255	46,000	95,934	241,061	205,912	889,637	48,416	46,000
Albany	17,588	2.7	56,948	187	13,521	3,503	1,094	1,223	3,229	3,229	19,341	2,079	1,094
Allegany	1,602	0.5	34,021	2,323	536	184	47	78	216	452	845	97	47
Bronx	48,263	2.2	33,154	2,446	15,829	3,768	1,330	2,560	5,560	16,294	23,487	2,728	1,330
Broome	7,839	1.1	40,133	1,350	3,745	1,019	315	457	1,264	1,997	5,537	633	315
Cattaraugus	2,912	1.6	37,493	1,739	1,186	365	100	180	416	803	1,830	207	100
Cayuga	3,006	0.9	38,609	1,557	1,138	309	98	127	450	722	1,672	194	98
Chautauqua	4,737	0.4	36,577	1,903	1,909	516	168	331	686	1,434	2,925	343	168
Chemung	3,446	0.3	39,926	1,374	1,661	402	140	162	480	925	2,365	277	140
Chenango	1,864	1.2	38,366	1,594	821	224	69	96	262	498	1,211	141	69
Clinton	3,321	1.6	40,965	1,240	1,471	427	127	314	444	805	2,338	255	127
Columbia	3,107	1.0	50,935	376	904	241	78	286	632	669	1,508	166	78
Cortland	1,811	0.1	37,670	1,714	715	213	62	101	268	430	1,091	123	62
Delaware	1,658	0.4	36,422	1,927	625	196	54	84	307	482	958	112	54
Dutchess	14,763	1.6	50,132	409	5,877	1,314	488	717	2,571	2,714	8,397	960	488
Erie	43,804	1.8	47,559	562	23,115	5,065	1,929	2,776	7,058	9,251	32,884	3,756	1,929
Essex	1,575	1.7	41,327	1,193	595	182	51	84	298	405	912	107	51
Franklin	1,839	1.4	36,488	1,918	765	286	63	89	269	494	1,203	131	63
Fulton	2,108	1.3	39,159	1,476	685	188	59	107	299	605	1,039	126	59

1. Based on the resident population estimated as of July 1 of the year shown.

STATE County	Earnings, 2016 (cont.) Percent by selected industries									Social Security beneficiaries, December 2016			Housing units, 2017	
	Farm	Mining, quarrying, and extracting	Construction	Manu-facturing	Information; professional, scientific, technical services	Retail trade	Finance, insurance, real estate, and leasing	Health care and social assistance	Govern-ment	Number	Rate[1]	Supple-mental Security Income recipients, 2016	Total	Percent change, 2010-2017
	75	76	77	78	79	80	81	82	83	84	85	86	87	88
NEW JERSEY— Cont'd														
Mercer	0.0	D	2.9	5.7	20.2	4.0	11.2	9.1	19.0	65,055	174	9,665	144,892	1.2
Middlesex	0.0	2.8	4.4	8.3	17.7	5.0	7.7	8.8	13.6	131,195	156	13,316	301,501	2.3
Monmouth	0.1	0.0	9.8	3.8	17.3	7.6	8.3	15.5	14.4	121,790	194	8,012	261,461	1.2
Morris	0.0	D	4.2	8.5	22.0	4.7	11.2	9.0	9.2	84,705	170	4,351	192,996	1.7
Ocean	0.0	1.1	10.0	3.3	8.1	10.4	5.6	17.8	20.9	155,950	263	7,397	283,695	2.0
Passaic	0.0	0.2	7.7	14.4	7.2	7.9	5.9	13.0	19.1	83,800	164	14,750	177,172	0.6
Salem	1.2	0.1	D	13.2	5.0	4.6	2.4	10.5	20.3	15,400	244	1,691	27,612	0.7
Somerset	0.0	0.2	3.9	17.9	20.1	4.4	8.0	6.4	6.9	51,795	155	3,080	126,693	2.9
Sussex	-0.1	0.4	11.0	6.0	8.6	8.2	4.1	13.9	22.1	28,620	201	1,628	62,374	0.7
Union	0.0	D	6.3	11.2	17.6	5.1	7.1	10.1	13.7	86,985	155	11,044	202,232	1.4
Warren	0.4	0.3	D	11.8	6.1	8.9	2.8	13.1	18.4	22,605	212	1,511	45,515	1.3
NEW MEXICO	1.3	4.8	6.1	3.0	12.5	6.9	5.1	12.5	27.1	416,674	200	63,596	937,926	4.1
Bernalillo	0.0	0.2	6.2	3.9	16.9	6.6	6.5	13.5	25.6	125,100	185	17,995	293,858	3.4
Catron	5.7	D	5.3	1.9	D	D	D	D	48.8	1,470	416	73	3,373	2.5
Chaves	6.1	13.8	3.9	4.0	4.8	9.7	4.4	13.3	20.6	12,940	198	2,189	27,348	2.4
Cibola	0.0	D	2.0	1.0	D	7.1	1.9	D	40.0	5,120	190	977	11,367	2.3
Colfax	3.1	2.3	6.5	2.1	3.3	10.3	4.1	D	33.2	3,675	300	399	10,260	2.4
Curry	12.6	D	3.5	2.7	3.3	5.4	2.8	9.7	40.8	7,530	150	1,540	21,294	6.1
De Baca	3.5	16.3	D	D	D	9.8	D	6.5	25.0	555	301	78	1,373	2.2
Dona Ana	3.5	0.1	6.5	3.4	7.8	6.2	4.6	15.9	31.4	40,015	187	8,185	87,838	7.8
Eddy	1.0	33.7	7.6	4.6	3.5	5.0	3.4	7.2	13.7	10,590	184	1,255	24,622	9.0
Grant	0.7	D	4.0	0.7	D	6.4	2.7	9.2	36.4	8,770	313	867	15,031	2.3
Guadalupe	3.0	0.0	2.1	D	D	12.6	D	15.2	30.1	1,105	253	246	2,441	2.0
Harding	13.8	19.6	D	D	D	D	D	D	34.8	210	303	13	538	1.7
Hidalgo	5.8	3.4	D	D	D	6.6	D	D	53.8	1,170	270	172	2,452	2.4
Lea	3.3	34.4	13.7	-19.7	3.8	7.6	5.8	7.4	13.7	9,655	138	1,540	26,653	7.0
Lincoln	0.7	D	7.8	0.6	D	12.0	5.9	13.5	22.0	5,970	309	362	18,164	3.7
Los Alamos	0.0	D	1.1	D	D	1.2	2.1	3.6	7.7	2,010	111	86	8,380	0.3
Luna	6.3	0.6	5.9	9.8	D	8.2	2.3	D	35.1	6,925	285	1,454	11,269	2.4
McKinley	-0.7	D	3.5	3.3	2.1	10.7	3.4	12.4	45.7	11,115	152	4,578	26,280	1.8
Mora	3.1	D	D	D	D	11.0	4.6	D	21.2	1,535	338	299	3,306	2.3
Otero	0.3	0.3	5.4	0.3	4.3	5.9	2.4	11.1	54.8	12,950	199	1,441	31,734	2.4
Quay	0.2	D	4.9	D	2.6	7.5	4.9	12.5	32.0	2,625	313	397	5,684	2.1
Rio Arriba	0.1	0.2	4.1	1.1	3.3	7.1	2.3	17.0	45.8	9,900	253	1,761	20,109	2.4
Roosevelt	15.5	D	4.3	6.7	2.3	6.3	2.5	5.5	35.3	3,120	164	581	8,493	4.1
Sandoval	0.1	0.8	6.7	20.0	6.7	6.8	3.5	8.8	22.5	28,900	206	2,728	56,586	8.2
San Juan	0.0	19.2	7.3	2.0	D	8.6	3.6	13.7	22.7	21,965	172	3,975	51,099	3.6
San Miguel	0.9	0.3	3.6	0.8	2.7	6.8	3.6	D	50.4	7,280	260	1,841	15,931	2.2
Santa Fe	-0.1	0.4	5.1	1.2	11.2	9.1	6.2	14.6	28.4	35,945	243	2,634	73,146	2.6
Sierra	8.9	D	7.7	2.3	2.7	7.5	2.5	D	32.2	4,450	400	607	8,542	2.2
Socorro	6.9	D	1.5	2.6	8.6	4.8	1.6	D	48.1	3,785	224	1,050	8,218	2.0
Taos	-0.4	1.0	7.2	1.4	8.2	9.3	4.2	16.9	22.1	9,420	287	1,137	20,919	3.2
Torrance	3.8	D	3.9	4.5	D	9.5	1.6	7.4	29.8	3,690	239	561	8,061	3.4
Union	-0.5	2.1	D	D	D	8.9	D	D	23.9	1,005	242	114	2,348	1.8
Valencia	-0.6	0.4	9.2	5.1	3.5	10.0	3.5	9.7	30.7	16,180	214	2,461	31,209	3.7
NEW YORK	0.1	0.1	4.7	4.4	17.4	5.0	16.9	11.1	16.3	3,546,954	179	644,377	8,327,388	2.7
Albany	0.0	D	4.5	3.6	13.0	5.5	8.9	11.2	33.5	60,765	197	7,270	141,627	2.8
Allegany	1.0	0.3	6.9	17.2	D	5.3	1.7	8.3	36.9	11,230	238	1,383	26,362	0.9
Bronx	0.0	D	5.8	1.7	2.7	6.1	3.6	26.4	27.4	197,670	135	106,296	528,806	3.3
Broome	0.0	0.1	5.8	11.5	6.4	6.9	5.0	17.0	26.8	47,250	243	6,856	90,934	0.4
Cattaraugus	0.3	0.4	4.5	14.9	3.3	8.5	3.0	D	37.2	19,435	250	2,463	41,581	1.1
Cayuga	1.8	D	6.8	14.4	5.6	6.8	2.9	13.6	30.1	17,475	225	1,792	37,078	1.6
Chautauqua	1.6	0.2	5.1	22.6	3.4	7.9	2.4	13.1	25.1	33,525	259	4,531	67,590	1.0
Chemung	0.0	1.0	5.3	16.6	3.7	7.3	5.5	16.5	24.4	21,555	251	3,077	38,836	1.2
Chenango	0.9	0.0	5.2	27.8	4.4	5.5	9.4	6.2	25.9	12,955	268	1,616	25,627	3.7
Clinton	1.6	D	5.4	9.5	3.4	8.2	2.1	16.6	31.9	19,680	243	2,843	36,594	2.0
Columbia	0.9	D	8.1	6.2	6.4	7.3	3.8	16.4	25.4	15,675	257	1,389	33,533	2.3
Cortland	0.8	0.1	5.0	16.0	5.2	7.4	4.1	D	29.5	9,920	207	1,117	20,793	1.2
Delaware	0.5	1.2	6.2	27.3	3.5	5.2	3.3	9.3	30.8	12,150	267	1,114	31,608	1.3
Dutchess	0.0	D	6.4	12.1	6.9	7.3	3.5	15.8	24.1	59,505	202	5,301	120,740	1.8
Erie	0.1	0.2	4.7	11.1	9.0	6.2	8.6	12.9	21.2	204,290	221	27,635	428,547	2.0
Essex	0.1	1.1	6.5	8.5	3.5	7.4	2.3	11.5	37.1	9,870	260	826	26,291	2.7
Franklin	0.9	D	3.2	D	3.5	6.3	1.7	18.5	51.5	11,820	231	1,817	25,735	1.7
Fulton	0.0	D	4.3	9.4	4.2	12.2	3.1	17.5	27.6	14,065	262	1,871	29,099	1.9

1. Per 1,000 resident population estimated as of July 1 of the year shown.

STATE County	Professional, scientific, and technical services, 2012				Manufacturing, 2012				Accommodation and food services, 2012			
	Number of establish- ments	Number of employees	Sales (mil dol)	Annual payroll (mil dol)	Number of establishments	Number of employees	Receipts (mil dol)	Annual payroll (mil dol)	Number of establishments	Number of employees	Receipts (mil dol)	Annual payroll (mil dol)
	147	148	149	150	151	152	153	154	155	156	157	158
NEW JERSEY— Cont'd												
Mercer	1,591	21,394	5,318.1	2,127.7	246	7,070	2,220.3	378.2	812	11,894	731.4	201.0
Middlesex	4,053	50,970	10,318.6	3,919.9	742	28,277	15,784.9	1,765.7	1,685	21,988	1,387.2	361.2
Monmouth	2,621	20,213	3,516.5	1,446.3	426	8,551	3,053.1	440.2	1,652	23,082	1,318.9	356.7
Morris	2,665	36,232	8,207.1	3,128.9	529	14,358	5,178.0	835.8	1,284	18,783	1,235.0	337.9
Ocean	1,091	5,988	839.5	301.7	278	5,069	1,400.0	231.1	1,145	12,911	801.5	203.7
Passaic	1,051	7,060	1,023.8	413.3	716	18,337	5,214.5	1,030.3	975	10,172	648.0	156.1
Salem	80	D	D	D	38	2,617	D	187.3	106	1,691	89.2	22.8
Somerset	1,827	25,815	5,063.6	2,307.5	300	12,329	4,974.7	1,007.3	798	11,509	739.9	210.9
Sussex	335	1,357	181.3	67.8	119	1,932	465.8	100.1	294	3,455	222.3	52.7
Union	1,389	16,181	1,875.4	1,171.6	619	20,790	20,139.4	1,727.9	1,134	12,856	819.1	211.9
Warren	230	D	D	D	108	3,854	2,050.3	227.0	245	2,294	122.2	32.1
NEW MEXICO	4,687	44,175	7,618.8	2,771.8	1,389	26,731	29,102.4	1,349.2	4,177	82,601	4,349.7	1,250.4
Bernalillo	2,261	18,714	3,488.9	1,101.8	575	11,976	D	569.9	1,394	31,736	1,702.6	495.5
Catron	4	D	D	D	4	13	D	0.6	12	38	1.7	0.4
Chaves	108	994	172.6	64.1	37	877	770.2	37.5	128	2,300	107.8	28.5
Cibola	17	D	D	D	6	38	D	1.1	36	584	27.5	7.7
Colfax	23	D	D	D	13	98	D	3.7	64	1,091	67.0	21.9
Curry	88	535	49.7	19.0	25	534	D	28.5	83	1,949	78.2	22.3
De Baca	1	D	D	D	NA	NA	NA	NA	5	D	D	D
Dona Ana	339	D	D	D	128	2,520	D	87.1	319	6,813	285.2	80.7
Eddy	77	593	54.1	33.5	35	1,459	D	112.1	111	2,083	118.0	31.0
Grant	47	D	D	D	14	121	D	3.6	78	862	33.1	9.6
Guadalupe	2	D	D	D	NA	NA	NA	NA	23	302	15.4	4.3
Harding	NA	NA	NA	NA	NA	NA	NA	NA	1	D	D	D
Hidalgo	4	D	D	D	NA	NA	NA	NA	16	207	9.6	2.7
Lea	82	569	82.1	30.8	37	854	D	68.0	138	2,261	132.1	30.2
Lincoln	53	D	D	D	17	67	D	2.6	99	1,185	60.5	18.0
Los Alamos	65	D	D	D	8	47	D	2.0	37	450	23.8	6.3
Luna	20	D	D	D	12	287	D	9.0	56	770	32.4	8.7
McKinley	43	D	D	D	24	383	D	26.7	143	2,508	119.4	31.5
Mora	NA	NA	NA	NA	NA	NA	NA	NA	3	D	D	D
Otero	71	D	D	D	28	190	D	5.1	108	2,422	164.7	45.1
Quay	12	D	D	D	4	24	D	1.3	33	536	22.9	6.0
Rio Arriba	35	D	D	D	22	95	D	2.9	66	1,089	70.7	20.3
Roosevelt	16	D	D	D	14	329	449.8	14.6	30	587	20.5	6.2
Sandoval	172	760	94.1	39.6	60	3,747	D	243.4	156	3,482	161.0	50.9
San Juan	256	D	D	D	85	1,318	268.6	62.8	197	4,253	201.8	56.3
San Miguel	35	D	D	D	9	48	9.1	1.5	58	719	34.4	8.9
Santa Fe	625	2,604	356.9	151.5	138	719	131.0	27.5	421	9,049	592.4	179.9
Sierra	15	D	D	D	5	121	D	3.0	39	390	15.8	4.7
Socorro	24	D	D	D	5	64	D	2.2	41	621	24.8	6.8
Taos	97	D	D	D	39	104	D	2.6	151	1,974	92.2	31.5
Torrance	13	D	D	D	11	132	D	4.5	26	D	D	D
Union	7	D	D	D	NA	NA	NA	NA	14	171	6.3	1.8
Valencia	75	D	D	D	27	523	D	23.6	91	D	D	D
NEW YORK	59,302	588,820	133,638.8	49,200.3	16,475	426,621	148,879.9	22,073.3	49,731	679,146	49,285.5	13,734.3
Albany	1,116	14,737	3,110.3	1,023.3	231	7,327	3,547.4	423.5	1,011	15,417	866.6	240.8
Allegany	49	199	20.4	7.2	46	2,433	841.8	108.8	92	1,175	50.0	12.4
Bronx	671	3,704	376.9	147.0	323	6,197	1,477.9	251.5	1,735	15,924	1,005.1	250.4
Broome	312	D	D	D	173	7,718	2,200.8	403.1	522	7,985	387.4	104.5
Cattaraugus	96	518	67.8	23.8	74	4,669	1,558.6	286.0	213	2,835	128.6	36.4
Cayuga	92	477	44.4	19.9	88	3,143	1,065.7	155.1	182	1,977	89.5	25.5
Chautauqua	194	1,108	87.5	33.3	197	9,474	5,107.5	428.6	347	4,735	208.7	57.7
Chemung	111	774	83.5	36.1	85	5,495	1,247.0	278.8	202	3,534	154.5	43.3
Chenango	64	316	26.3	8.8	74	3,443	1,661.4	165.3	94	769	34.7	10.0
Clinton	128	734	67.1	26.7	78	3,161	1,279.4	138.5	187	2,648	139.2	38.3
Columbia	175	562	73.5	27.5	73	1,290	462.6	53.7	161	1,419	72.7	20.8
Cortland	82	1,036	99.7	51.1	66	3,163	711.4	146.5	134	2,574	101.0	28.7
Delaware	75	219	21.2	5.8	36	3,593	1,557.2	195.7	124	1,060	44.6	12.4
Dutchess	775	4,010	624.7	224.1	198	8,544	2,481.9	668.2	784	9,107	499.5	136.0
Erie	2,138	28,912	3,598.2	1,656.1	1,008	42,606	15,835.4	2,250.2	2,279	41,143	1,871.9	551.5
Essex	71	D	D	D	28	782	213.1	56.6	201	2,360	150.3	47.2
Franklin	65	410	33.4	17.3	28	460	250.2	19.9	115	846	51.2	13.0
Fulton	77	300	26.2	8.9	71	1,724	712.2	66.3	131	1,209	56.1	15.8

Table B. States and Counties — Health Care and Social Assistance, Other Services, Nonemployer Businesses, and Residential Construction

STATE County	Health care and social assistance, 2012				Other services, 2012				Nonemployer businesses, 2015		Value of residential construction authorized by building permits, 2017	
	Number of establish- ments	Number of employees	Receipts (mil dol)	Annual payroll (mil dol)	Number of establis- hments	Number of employees	Receipts (mil dol)	Annual payroll (mil dol)	Number	Receipts (mil dol)	New construction ($1,000)	Number of housing units
	159	160	161	162	163	164	165	166	167	168	169	170
NEW JERSEY— Cont'd												
Mercer	1,165	28,970	2,981.0	1,326.6	815	6,403	1,245.5	239.1	24,347	1,353.3	84,977	605
Middlesex	2,195	46,302	5,084.5	2,039.8	1,569	10,342	1,635.7	398.2	55,578	3,209.4	326,119	2,730
Monmouth	2,382	40,905	4,809.5	1,842.3	1,477	8,532	738.0	223.9	53,781	3,584.1	311,250	1,474
Morris	1,727	34,457	4,235.4	1,784.5	1,200	7,548	802.0	232.2	42,528	3,040.9	237,322	1,648
Ocean	1,537	30,984	3,185.9	1,246.7	1,061	5,433	489.4	129.6	40,028	2,309.4	539,207	3,427
Passaic	1,431	25,884	2,516.8	1,059.9	956	4,962	443.6	118.5	38,429	1,994.6	66,887	568
Salem	165	3,312	319.9	122.3	100	386	29.1	7.5	2,799	126.0	6,780	40
Somerset	1,173	21,653	2,475.7	980.8	714	4,882	643.1	156.7	26,811	1,799.2	114,222	730
Sussex	361	6,319	551.2	232.3	300	1,285	112.4	33.1	10,927	608.4	17,530	106
Union	1,551	31,943	3,370.8	1,367.2	1,188	6,710	646.0	211.4	42,364	2,406.0	135,399	1,085
Warren	295	4,571	543.1	218.3	222	1,095	112.9	29.0	7,080	367.7	13,754	154
NEW MEXICO	4,967	116,557	11,236.6	4,588.0	2,962	17,464	1,798.6	501.4	121,279	4,788.6	941,816	4,741
Bernalillo	1,893	48,404	5,278.0	2,143.7	1,096	7,326	750.0	217.2	40,022	1,661.8	290,221	1,422
Catron	7	120	2.7	1.7	5	D	D	D	345	12.5	NA	NA
Chaves	176	3,778	331.1	133.6	79	396	33.7	9.6	2,986	135.0	11,718	70
Cibola	49	1,532	150.8	53.9	23	85	7.3	2.0	1,117	31.6	NA	NA
Colfax	39	593	52.5	25.4	28	87	8.6	2.1	769	25.6	8,163	18
Curry	118	2,829	225.6	87.1	76	468	40.0	9.4	1,942	82.3	16,217	84
De Baca	5	D	D	D	3	D	D	D	102	3.6	NA	NA
Dona Ana	496	12,122	1,010.7	418.4	234	1,124	86.4	26.3	12,253	465.5	188,407	1,126
Eddy	114	2,875	275.8	112.9	85	501	48.4	12.5	2,528	124.0	28,807	150
Grant	81	1,645	139.1	58.5	45	172	10.9	2.9	1,550	43.2	1,788	11
Guadalupe	9	D	D	D	9	D	D	D	161	4.6	NA	NA
Harding	1	D	D	D	NA	NA	NA	NA	56	3.4	NA	NA
Hidalgo	10	133	7.6	3.3	3	D	D	D	207	6.3	NA	NA
Lea	112	2,329	207.9	78.7	105	800	122.2	31.3	3,005	179.1	16,851	82
Lincoln	47	598	63.8	25.4	40	204	14.8	3.9	1,867	74.3	19,695	78
Los Alamos	67	1,095	102.6	41.2	24	203	11.2	2.8	1,101	37.4	5,555	24
Luna	50	855	76.3	30.1	28	83	6.6	1.6	979	30.4	3,329	18
McKinley	107	4,407	374.3	155.3	78	469	55.3	10.8	3,721	79.0	1,940	10
Mora	5	119	4.3	2.5	4	D	D	D	291	7.0	NA	NA
Otero	101	2,241	210.4	81.4	67	357	21.3	6.3	3,273	110.2	1,027	4
Quay	26	406	37.9	11.9	23	112	13.1	2.8	365	12.5	NA	NA
Rio Arriba	84	1,878	141.5	63.0	23	115	12.2	3.3	1,873	56.8	0	0
Roosevelt	32	752	57.3	23.2	17	69	8.1	1.7	842	32.9	2,718	18
Sandoval	201	3,058	284.8	107.2	109	583	45.2	16.1	7,865	277.2	146,592	724
San Juan	275	6,819	682.5	291.7	226	1,571	164.1	54.5	5,198	214.9	21,035	91
San Miguel	73	2,950	178.1	80.2	28	150	7.5	2.1	1,378	40.0	140	1
Santa Fe	513	8,697	961.0	384.4	335	1,892	268.6	66.4	16,363	752.4	50,801	221
Sierra	20	784	40.2	19.4	19	106	10.1	2.1	720	22.3	95	1
Socorro	29	736	48.7	24.6	12	D	D	D	754	18.9	538	3
Taos	103	1,476	120.9	53.7	57	229	18.3	5.3	3,301	108.0	10,403	92
Torrance	21	273	10.0	5.1	8	D	D	D	798	25.4	NA	NA
Union	13	D	D	D	10	34	2.9	0.6	297	7.3	NA	NA
Valencia	90	2,685	117.5	57.7	63	D	D	D	3,250	103.2	11,925	110
NEW YORK	56,734	1,468,987	155,666.1	65,180.0	45,646	271,689	39,709.2	9,395.1	1,685,636	86,950.0	6,955,500	39,350
Albany	1,017	33,297	3,522.5	1,396.7	810	5,994	691.9	220.5	17,829	944.8	120,684	761
Allegany	100	1,793	119.8	50.7	75	263	20.0	4.4	2,451	87.9	4,539	44
Bronx	2,145	98,945	10,001.3	4,584.1	1,757	8,242	782.4	224.0	114,788	3,397.5	714,972	5,401
Broome	435	14,852	1,527.8	612.6	341	1,937	151.1	43.6	10,019	418.8	40,385	358
Cattaraugus	175	3,585	324.5	123.1	123	666	53.8	13.7	3,831	146.1	11,882	88
Cayuga	198	4,036	302.4	136.8	131	518	41.1	9.8	4,243	168.8	14,506	97
Chautauqua	279	8,791	623.9	263.5	253	1,448	105.7	24.1	6,997	264.0	21,507	122
Chemung	211	6,421	621.6	294.0	128	670	57.3	15.6	3,875	141.9	16,779	101
Chenango	107	2,025	158.6	65.3	77	256	22.5	6.4	2,758	106.8	9,202	179
Clinton	239	5,147	499.7	231.6	116	560	50.1	13.0	3,942	163.2	26,171	164
Columbia	153	3,929	330.5	150.5	99	335	35.2	9.5	6,005	267.2	29,058	98
Cortland	127	3,591	231.6	106.1	93	401	35.2	9.0	2,353	94.3	2,416	24
Delaware	114	2,167	152.1	63.3	83	417	75.1	10.5	3,624	144.6	6,405	49
Dutchess	901	18,607	2,004.6	847.0	591	2,592	279.2	73.3	21,343	1,003.2	165,668	489
Erie	2,675	74,944	7,532.5	3,154.4	1,752	11,023	1,059.9	283.5	47,593	2,164.7	330,737	1,419
Essex	151	1,978	140.3	61.6	67	282	29.4	7.4	3,092	113.9	21,304	107
Franklin	170	3,276	285.0	126.0	72	225	19.5	5.0	2,781	104.5	17,430	107
Fulton	182	4,128	260.4	113.7	85	486	38.5	11.5	2,813	105.8	7,312	48

Table B. States and Counties — Government Employment and Payroll, and Local Government Finances

	Government employment and payroll, 2012									Local government finances				
			March payroll (percent of total)							General revenue				
												Taxes		
													Per capita[1] (dollars)	
STATE County	Full-time equivalent employees	March payroll (dollars)	Administration, judicial, and legal	Police and corrections	Fire protection	Highways and transportation	Health and welfare	Natural resources and utilities	Education and libraries	Total (mil dol)	Intergovernmental (mil dol)	Total (mil dol)	Total	Property
	171	172	173	174	175	176	177	178	179	180	181	182	183	184
NEW JERSEY— Cont'd														
Mercer	15,352	84,285,619	4.4	12.4	3.3	2.0	4.4	4.9	64.8	2,164.5	711.0	1,168.1	3,172	3,117
Middlesex	26,592	147,425,663	4.2	13.0	2.6	1.8	4.3	3.9	68.2	3,819.6	965.9	2,247.0	2,730	2,672
Monmouth	27,427	142,190,760	5.3	14.3	0.7	3.0	5.2	3.7	66.3	3,459.7	822.0	2,117.8	3,365	3,308
Morris	19,889	108,738,326	4.6	10.9	0.8	2.8	3.7	5.8	68.0	2,618.5	372.1	1,893.1	3,801	3,744
Ocean	20,430	99,202,051	5.5	14.5	0.4	3.0	4.9	5.2	63.9	2,394.3	580.3	1,531.1	2,638	2,603
Passaic	15,817	88,473,333	5.1	16.3	5.0	2.0	8.1	4.7	57.7	2,251.4	742.8	1,305.1	2,595	2,566
Salem	3,305	15,720,003	5.8	12.2	0.0	2.4	4.8	2.4	69.6	394.8	172.3	152.1	2,313	2,287
Somerset	13,026	68,430,732	3.9	11.5	0.6	3.4	3.0	2.1	73.5	1,611.4	277.0	1,174.0	3,583	3,530
Sussex	5,561	30,640,722	5.9	8.8	0.2	3.9	3.0	1.3	75.3	772.0	189.2	484.5	3,286	3,255
Union	23,222	130,750,946	5.8	13.4	5.4	2.2	5.9	2.3	63.3	3,230.4	1,130.6	1,723.2	3,168	3,100
Warren	4,346	20,547,388	6.3	9.9	0.9	3.6	6.8	2.0	68.4	536.8	183.8	292.4	2,716	2,688
NEW MEXICO	X	X	X	X	X	X	X	X	X	X	X	X	X	X
Bernalillo	22,833	89,838,327	6.2	16.3	6.5	6.3	5.2	6.3	51.7	2,451.4	1,173.3	882.0	1,310	743
Catron	146	386,239	12.7	8.6	0.0	7.4	4.7	1.5	64.1	15.7	10.9	2.6	698	511
Chaves	2,443	7,710,245	4.6	11.3	4.7	3.4	1.7	6.7	65.0	249.1	177.0	44.9	682	436
Cibola	909	2,491,571	7.4	11.5	1.3	2.3	1.9	3.3	70.0	97.5	46.9	12.3	451	248
Colfax	652	2,023,377	9.7	9.4	4.3	3.0	9.7	10.8	51.3	63.7	33.7	19.3	1,463	839
Curry	2,120	6,374,697	3.9	9.1	4.6	2.6	2.3	2.7	74.0	176.6	105.3	49.5	991	345
De Baca	134	371,334	8.8	11.3	0.0	8.7	3.7	10.9	56.5	13.8	7.8	2.5	1,319	841
Dona Ana	7,916	26,726,295	5.8	10.4	2.7	2.6	2.1	5.9	66.7	732.8	425.3	209.7	978	447
Eddy	2,143	8,178,370	5.4	14.2	5.2	4.3	2.1	6.4	59.3	275.0	129.3	115.7	2,126	1,225
Grant	1,747	5,905,715	4.3	7.8	1.4	2.5	44.2	2.7	35.9	187.1	80.4	29.7	1,009	473
Guadalupe	390	1,120,471	7.2	4.4	2.0	4.0	2.5	2.3	74.8	29.2	18.8	6.1	1,319	617
Harding	70	190,631	18.3	3.6	0.0	12.0	4.9	3.4	55.3	10.0	6.0	3.0	4,246	2,506
Hidalgo	293	795,504	9.1	17.5	0.0	4.5	3.0	5.4	58.2	28.3	19.6	4.7	976	778
Lea	3,191	11,349,323	4.4	10.8	3.6	2.9	15.4	4.7	55.7	413.1	170.9	153.5	2,314	1,380
Lincoln	853	2,783,245	8.5	11.0	3.3	4.9	5.2	9.6	53.8	99.8	41.5	37.7	1,857	1,135
Los Alamos	1,400	5,075,436	10.8	6.3	17.0	4.7	1.3	11.9	40.5	138.8	77.2	49.3	2,712	875
Luna	1,233	3,637,272	6.8	12.9	1.8	1.9	2.6	2.4	66.6	103.9	67.8	23.4	936	513
McKinley	3,373	9,383,425	3.6	7.5	2.2	1.6	1.9	3.4	78.5	249.0	155.9	62.8	861	271
Mora	208	516,517	10.0	3.6	0.0	4.3	0.8	0.5	79.2	16.8	10.9	2.4	506	430
Otero	1,662	5,122,202	6.3	14.5	0.3	2.5	2.3	4.7	67.9	147.4	86.7	40.4	612	307
Quay	563	1,605,317	7.9	9.3	0.4	3.2	4.0	8.7	65.3	54.3	38.6	8.0	912	461
Rio Arriba	1,378	4,062,743	9.2	7.6	1.7	2.7	5.6	3.5	67.3	133.9	69.5	50.2	1,244	819
Roosevelt	849	2,598,517	4.7	9.9	3.2	3.4	1.0	3.2	73.2	65.0	40.9	14.6	714	505
Sandoval	3,959	13,152,644	7.2	11.4	4.7	3.3	1.2	5.4	66.3	399.2	201.9	135.8	1,002	605
San Juan	5,857	21,149,302	4.2	11.0	2.6	2.0	1.9	8.4	68.4	491.8	290.9	126.9	987	702
San Miguel	1,294	3,946,008	6.9	7.5	1.7	1.8	1.8	6.1	72.8	102.3	63.7	27.0	933	408
Santa Fe	4,848	18,022,225	9.3	12.0	6.4	3.8	4.1	9.6	48.1	527.4	253.9	199.3	1,361	807
Sierra	644	2,455,286	6.7	6.0	0.0	1.9	22.5	6.1	54.0	49.9	22.0	12.6	1,060	582
Socorro	721	1,882,356	6.5	9.1	3.0	3.6	4.4	6.7	63.5	61.4	43.7	9.7	551	305
Taos	1,245	3,508,311	12.0	9.6	1.7	3.3	3.5	5.5	61.6	118.8	59.8	45.9	1,400	624
Torrance	904	2,576,995	5.9	5.6	0.5	2.0	1.4	1.7	82.4	69.5	50.0	14.8	923	704
Union	203	666,897	11.2	10.4	3.2	8.9	2.6	4.7	56.6	23.5	13.2	5.9	1,327	768
Valencia	2,378	6,663,270	5.6	7.4	1.3	1.2	2.2	2.4	79.8	195.8	120.3	56.4	736	383
NEW YORK	X	X	X	X	X	X	X	X	X	X	X	X	X	X
Albany	12,459	58,755,137	5.6	15.4	3.5	2.8	8.7	5.3	57.2	1,776.2	540.6	885.9	2,900	2,024
Allegany	2,326	8,539,230	7.1	8.0	0.7	8.2	7.3	2.7	64.1	300.9	162.2	113.9	2,356	1,929
Bronx	(2)	(2)	(2)	(2)	(2)	(2)	(2)	(2)	(2)	(2)	(2)	(2)	(2)	(2)
Broome	9,618	36,733,525	4.9	8.4	2.7	4.4	10.5	3.0	64.3	1,182.8	494.6	520.5	2,628	1,756
Cattaraugus	4,623	18,563,190	6.2	8.6	1.7	8.0	12.2	3.6	59.1	526.9	273.4	184.2	2,318	1,675
Cayuga	3,237	14,564,325	6.1	8.2	3.3	5.0	9.9	3.2	63.1	427.9	185.0	169.5	2,131	1,441
Chautauqua	6,787	27,243,053	4.8	7.7	2.9	6.8	9.0	2.9	65.0	772.7	364.8	268.8	2,013	1,539
Chemung	3,853	14,858,292	5.0	9.7	2.9	4.0	13.2	3.8	59.7	476.3	219.3	175.3	1,971	1,236
Chenango	2,731	10,005,930	6.4	7.7	1.8	9.2	7.9	1.6	64.4	295.2	157.3	105.1	2,106	1,541
Clinton	3,949	16,260,748	5.3	6.0	0.9	6.0	11.3	2.6	65.0	458.8	198.9	190.2	2,329	1,643
Columbia	3,025	13,243,189	8.0	8.1	0.4	9.6	12.9	2.0	57.7	374.6	114.6	212.1	3,394	2,596
Cortland	2,146	9,594,343	7.0	14.5	2.0	8.9	10.2	5.2	50.7	258.6	118.1	110.0	2,223	1,645
Delaware	2,262	8,403,397	8.5	6.5	0.1	11.8	10.9	1.5	59.1	286.6	118.1	136.3	2,883	2,410
Dutchess	12,054	60,953,575	5.6	9.6	3.0	3.7	5.7	1.9	69.4	1,683.1	521.2	964.5	3,244	2,611
Erie	35,259	161,616,876	3.7	12.8	3.3	2.9	5.3	5.1	65.4	5,298.2	2,255.2	2,176.7	2,368	1,547
Essex	1,990	7,313,826	9.9	6.1	1.3	9.8	14.0	4.4	53.3	255.8	76.1	132.5	3,401	2,621
Franklin	2,713	9,538,618	5.8	5.4	0.9	6.2	10.0	2.2	68.0	305.3	153.8	104.0	2,008	1,575
Fulton	2,664	9,331,227	4.7	7.9	2.7	4.8	13.2	1.3	64.4	301.1	138.4	121.2	2,207	1,595

1. Based on the resident population estimated as of July 1 of the year shown.   2. Bronx, Kings, Queens, and Richmond counties are included with New York county

Table B. States and Counties — Local Government Finances, Government Employment, and Income Taxes

STATE County	Total (mil dol)	Per capita[1] (dollars)	Education	Health and hospitals	Police protection	Public welfare	Highways	Total (mil dol)	Per capita[1] (dollars)	Federal civilian	Federal military	State and local	Number of returns	Mean adjusted gross income	Mean income tax
	185	186	187	188	189	190	191	192	193	194	195	196	197	198	199
NEW JERSEY— Cont'd															
Mercer	2,145.5	5,825	52.3	0.9	5.3	4.3	1.4	1,928.9	5,237	2,340	733	38,323	175,890	91,851	15,121
Middlesex	3,874.0	4,707	54.1	1.1	5.8	2.4	1.7	4,163.4	5,059	2,475	1,775	52,927	405,530	75,789	10,321
Monmouth	3,411.5	5,420	54.8	1.1	6.0	2.1	2.9	2,733.3	4,343	2,044	1,419	33,092	321,780	100,075	17,232
Morris	2,580.5	5,182	55.7	1.5	5.7	1.5	3.1	2,056.9	4,130	5,515	1,128	26,120	254,130	124,405	23,308
Ocean	2,437.7	4,200	51.2	0.6	6.8	3.2	3.4	2,209.0	3,805	3,157	1,397	24,956	283,620	63,328	7,554
Passaic	2,262.2	4,499	45.8	2.5	6.7	5.0	2.2	1,387.8	2,760	1,066	1,013	28,102	249,540	57,433	6,916
Salem	408.1	6,204	53.4	1.9	3.9	2.2	4.2	399.9	6,081	158	127	4,061	30,720	57,965	6,388
Somerset	1,638.3	4,999	58.6	2.0	5.3	1.0	4.6	1,441.4	4,399	1,763	672	16,037	168,590	122,437	23,153
Sussex	733.7	4,976	63.4	1.4	3.9	2.2	4.2	551.0	3,737	339	289	7,494	72,900	77,626	10,475
Union	3,281.6	6,033	53.5	2.9	6.2	1.6	1.8	2,546.6	4,681	1,500	1,126	31,112	274,180	83,187	13,408
Warren	573.8	5,330	58.0	1.8	4.0	3.5	3.9	237.2	2,203	222	213	5,432	53,550	68,313	8,288
NEW MEXICO	X	X	X	X	X	X	X	X	X	29,438	17,159	162,324	917,220	50,879	5,830
Bernalillo	2,337.5	3,471	48.0	2.0	9.0	1.6	5.0	3,333.0	4,949	13,982	5,096	55,842	309,130	55,158	6,586
Catron	17.1	4,674	36.7	2.0	4.1	0.6	7.9	9.9	2,693	97	0	194	1,360	38,590	3,840
Chaves	248.0	3,771	52.6	0.0	6.6	2.3	4.4	107.2	1,630	242	177	4,145	25,780	43,569	4,975
Cibola	102.5	3,749	38.6	30.4	2.4	3.0	2.9	41.6	1,521	316	65	2,876	9,440	36,935	2,981
Colfax	65.2	4,931	40.3	5.9	6.4	0.7	7.3	52.6	3,979	48	31	1,266	5,450	41,401	4,212
Curry	185.3	3,711	57.6	0.2	5.2	0.7	4.3	71.0	1,422	871	4,732	2,462	21,150	40,864	3,825
De Baca	13.6	7,072	35.8	17.8	4.5	0.1	4.9	5.2	2,717	12	0	173	820	32,816	2,706
Dona Ana	719.6	3,356	57.5	1.3	6.7	1.9	4.1	440.1	2,052	3,472	558	16,955	90,980	42,451	4,294
Eddy	252.5	4,640	47.2	2.8	8.5	1.6	5.2	120.4	2,213	683	148	3,318	24,500	67,120	9,592
Grant	196.6	6,690	26.5	40.7	4.6	2.8	2.6	102.5	3,489	199	72	3,195	12,320	45,469	4,618
Guadalupe	26.2	5,682	37.7	0.7	4.4	6.5	5.2	22.0	4,789	22	10	383	1,820	31,473	2,559
Harding	10.9	15,478	46.4	1.6	4.0	0.1	7.1	5.9	8,396	13	0	82	310	41,645	3,935
Hidalgo	27.3	5,693	43.1	2.0	15.9	0.6	2.6	9.5	1,987	250	11	380	1,750	37,938	3,073
Lea	416.5	6,278	45.5	12.6	5.6	1.1	7.8	219.2	3,304	91	177	3,710	28,690	58,214	7,285
Lincoln	102.5	5,048	37.3	4.2	6.6	0.5	5.9	89.0	4,382	94	50	1,075	9,110	44,274	4,623
Los Alamos	168.1	9,258	31.9	0.0	4.1	1.6	6.7	190.8	10,505	233	49	1,627	8,900	101,518	14,783
Luna	99.5	3,974	55.3	2.0	7.7	1.0	3.5	25.7	1,027	435	62	1,659	10,560	31,798	2,248
McKinley	255.3	3,497	63.0	1.1	4.0	1.8	3.8	145.8	1,997	2,483	193	4,836	32,200	32,680	2,549
Mora	17.2	3,658	55.5	0.3	2.6	0.0	3.0	10.3	2,189	39	12	243	1,980	32,829	2,357
Otero	149.2	2,258	50.7	0.5	8.4	3.1	9.6	138.3	2,094	1,761	4,005	4,636	26,830	40,265	3,546
Quay	53.7	6,124	48.7	5.9	4.7	3.6	4.1	28.0	3,197	31	22	816	3,640	31,400	2,377
Rio Arriba	130.8	3,245	54.4	0.5	4.5	1.1	2.9	101.6	2,519	293	103	4,472	16,680	40,569	3,709
Roosevelt	64.4	3,152	61.8	0.1	6.6	2.2	4.8	18.8	922	42	47	2,037	7,810	35,403	3,098
Sandoval	384.6	2,836	51.6	0.1	6.8	1.0	6.1	599.5	4,422	367	368	7,458	63,130	56,124	6,110
San Juan	551.0	4,287	55.6	3.3	6.3	1.2	4.3	2,140.3	16,652	1,508	299	9,823	50,540	51,778	5,704
San Miguel	108.9	3,769	60.5	0.3	4.2	0.7	4.8	73.4	2,539	130	69	3,495	11,710	34,820	2,958
Santa Fe	578.2	3,950	45.8	1.3	6.0	2.2	3.5	916.2	6,259	981	386	14,963	75,540	66,427	9,536
Sierra	50.5	4,245	27.8	29.9	10.1	1.0	8.1	29.4	2,475	86	29	795	4,810	32,427	2,790
Socorro	72.0	4,091	47.8	0.2	3.8	0.0	4.6	25.8	1,466	183	47	2,484	6,830	36,155	3,088
Taos	129.6	3,953	49.9	1.4	3.2	2.6	3.3	125.3	3,823	270	85	1,830	15,670	39,671	4,119
Torrance	69.7	4,348	66.8	0.8	2.8	0.8	2.9	231.1	14,425	66	38	932	5,710	36,005	2,939
Union	21.1	4,754	42.4	8.0	5.7	1.5	6.6	13.0	2,941	42	0	274	1,660	42,155	4,227
Valencia	184.9	2,413	64.8	0.5	5.8	0.6	3.4	196.9	2,570	96	193	3,888	30,460	42,930	3,766
NEW YORK	X	X	X	X	X	X	X	X	X	116,717	55,158	1,275,405	9,614,110	81,419	13,521
Albany	1,817.9	5,952	40.0	3.9	5.2	11.2	3.9	2,211.1	7,239	5,042	682	56,763	153,040	73,361	10,492
Allegany	309.4	6,398	47.0	2.5	1.8	9.8	11.7	294.0	6,080	119	67	3,924	18,910	46,586	4,558
Bronx	(2)	(2)	(2)	(2)	(2)	(2)	(2)	(2)	(2)	4,057	2,321	57,745	654,280	36,210	3,086
Broome	1,232.1	6,221	48.7	3.4	2.9	12.0	3.8	1,229.8	6,209	532	294	18,154	88,970	52,673	6,026
Cattaraugus	550.0	6,922	49.6	5.9	2.3	13.2	7.5	308.3	3,875	143	115	5,623	35,430	52,298	5,803
Cayuga	442.3	5,560	52.0	4.7	3.2	9.3	6.8	665.7	4,985	308	194	8,580	57,310	45,230	4,368
Chautauqua	806.8	6,042	50.1	3.0	2.9	12.8	6.0	490.6	5,518	215	129	5,782	39,370	52,751	5,838
Chemung	467.0	5,252	42.9	3.0	3.0	18.1	8.9	216.1	4,329	86	75	4,134	22,650	46,340	4,581
Chenango	297.2	5,953	57.1	3.1	1.6	8.2	7.3	401.8	4,921	710	118	7,123	36,490	50,920	5,266
Clinton	495.0	6,062	54.0	4.9	1.9	11.3	5.6	225.4	3,607	160	92	4,456	30,070	64,636	8,537
Columbia	381.3	6,100	48.0	4.5	2.2	13.2	9.0	199.2	4,027	112	69	4,065	20,750	49,441	5,045
Cortland	277.6	5,611	47.3	4.6	3.0	10.4	8.5	208.3	4,406	122	68	4,230	19,910	46,584	4,654
Delaware	281.8	5,961	44.9	3.5	1.5	9.4	12.5	1,417.6	4,768	1,269	431	18,362	141,320	72,917	9,809
Dutchess	1,642.8	5,525	55.5	3.6	3.3	7.6	4.0	5,158.7	5,613	8,305	1,640	64,823	449,410	59,367	7,541
Erie	5,644.5	6,141	44.0	10.5	3.7	9.5	3.2	306.9	7,877	340	56	3,888	17,720	50,422	5,548
Essex	273.6	7,022	36.7	6.8	1.3	10.7	9.0	277.2	5,352	163	70	7,291	20,250	46,795	4,863
Franklin	335.9	6,486	56.1	3.6	1.2	11.1	5.6	192.0	3,496	80	83	3,474	24,990	46,962	4,547

1. Based on the resident population estimated as of July 1 of the year shown. 2. Bronx, Kings, Queens, and Richmond counties are included with New York county.

Table B. States and Counties — Land Area and Population

State / county code	CBSA code[1]	County code[2]	STATE County	Land area[3] (sq. mi)	Total persons 2017	Rank	Per square mile	White	Black	American Indian, Alaska Native	Asian and Pacific Islander	Percent Hispanic or Latino[4]	Under 5 years	5 to 17 years	18 to 24 years	25 to 34 years	35 to 44 years	45 to 54 years
				1	2	3	4	5	6	7	8	9	10	11	12	13	14	15
			NEW YORK— Cont'd															
36,037	12,860	4	Genesee	492.9	57,956	890	117.6	92.0	3.8	1.5	1.1	3.4	5.2	15.2	8.6	12.2	11.0	14.2
36,039		6	Greene	647.2	47,470	1,026	73.3	86.9	6.6	0.8	1.8	5.7	4.2	12.4	9.2	11.7	10.8	14.2
36,041		8	Hamilton	1,717.4	4,485	2,861	2.6	96.2	1.5	0.9	1.0	1.6	3.2	10.6	5.9	7.3	8.4	13.6
36,043	46,540	2	Herkimer	1,411.5	62,240	845	44.1	95.6	1.9	0.6	0.9	2.3	5.2	15.7	8.4	11.4	10.7	13.5
36,045	48,060	3	Jefferson	1,268.7	114,187	540	90.0	83.6	7.5	1.0	2.8	7.6	7.8	16.2	12.9	17.1	11.5	10.7
36,047	35,620	1	Kings	69.4	2,648,771	8	38,166.7	37.4	31.1	0.6	13.7	19.1	7.3	15.6	8.4	18.5	13.9	11.9
36,049		6	Lewis	1,274.6	26,551	1,545	20.8	96.5	1.1	0.6	0.8	1.9	6.2	16.8	7.8	11.7	11.3	13.2
36,051	40,380	1	Livingston	631.8	63,799	835	101.0	92.0	3.2	0.7	2.0	3.6	4.2	13.5	15.4	10.8	10.3	13.6
36,053	45,060	2	Madison	654.9	70,965	760	108.4	94.4	2.4	1.0	1.4	2.2	4.6	14.7	13.0	10.6	10.4	13.8
36,055	40,380	1	Monroe	657.2	747,642	87	1,137.6	72.3	15.9	0.6	4.6	8.8	5.5	15.4	10.2	14.1	11.2	13.1
36,057	11,220	4	Montgomery	403.1	49,258	997	122.2	82.6	2.9	0.6	1.2	14.2	6.4	16.5	7.8	12.5	11.2	12.8
36,059	35,620	1	Nassau	284.6	1,369,514	29	4,812.1	60.9	12.1	0.4	10.8	17.2	5.4	16.1	8.9	11.7	11.9	14.3
36,061	35,620	1	New York	22.7	1,664,727	20	73,336.0	48.3	13.3	0.5	13.8	26.1	4.8	9.6	9.1	22.5	14.3	12.4
36,063	15,380	1	Niagara	522.4	211,328	315	404.5	87.7	8.5	1.6	1.6	2.9	5.2	14.9	8.4	12.5	11.0	13.7
36,065	46,540	2	Oneida	1,212.3	231,332	285	190.8	83.4	7.2	0.6	4.9	5.8	5.7	15.6	9.5	12.6	11.0	13.4
36,067	45,060	2	Onondaga	778.4	465,398	148	597.9	79.1	12.6	1.4	4.9	4.9	5.7	15.7	10.4	13.4	11.0	13.2
36,069	40,380	1	Ontario	644.1	109,899	550	170.6	91.4	3.0	0.5	1.8	4.8	5.0	15.5	9.2	11.0	10.7	14.1
36,071	35,620	1	Orange	812.3	382,226	182	470.5	65.9	11.4	0.7	3.5	20.6	6.6	18.9	10.6	11.7	11.8	14.2
36,073	40,380	1	Orleans	391.3	40,983	1,154	104.7	87.9	7.1	1.0	0.9	4.8	5.2	14.6	8.7	12.7	11.3	14.7
36,075	45,060	2	Oswego	951.6	118,478	524	124.5	95.3	1.5	0.9	1.1	2.6	5.3	15.8	11.0	12.3	10.8	14.3
36,077	36,580	7	Otsego	1,001.7	60,094	870	60.0	92.5	2.6	0.6	2.1	3.7	4.3	11.8	17.2	9.7	9.4	12.3
36,079	35,620	1	Putnam	230.3	99,323	601	431.3	79.7	3.2	0.4	2.8	15.1	4.4	15.6	8.6	10.8	11.6	16.5
36,081	35,620	1	Queens	108.8	2,358,582	11	21,678.1	26.2	18.9	0.8	28.3	28.0	6.2	13.9	8.0	16.4	13.8	13.7
36,083	10,580	2	Rensselaer	652.4	159,722	408	244.8	85.0	8.1	0.6	3.5	5.0	5.2	14.5	10.1	14.2	11.6	13.5
36,085	35,620	1	Richmond	57.5	479,458	145	8,338.4	62.1	10.4	0.5	10.1	18.6	5.7	16.1	8.5	13.6	12.5	14.1
36,087	35,620	1	Rockland	173.4	328,868	211	1,896.6	63.8	12.3	0.4	7.0	18.0	7.9	20.0	9.4	11.6	11.0	12.5
36,089	36,300	4	St. Lawrence	2,679.3	109,623	551	40.9	93.2	2.8	1.4	1.6	2.4	5.2	15.0	13.8	12.0	10.8	12.8
36,091	10,580	2	Saratoga	810.0	229,869	287	283.8	91.9	2.4	0.5	3.7	3.2	5.2	15.2	8.2	12.1	12.4	15.1
36,093	10,580	2	Schenectady	204.6	155,565	423	760.3	76.6	12.5	1.1	6.3	7.0	5.9	15.6	9.1	13.1	12.1	13.5
36,095	10,580	2	Schoharie	621.8	31,420	1,396	50.5	94.3	1.9	0.7	1.2	3.2	4.0	13.6	11.0	10.5	10.3	13.7
36,097		6	Schuyler	328.3	18,000	1,919	54.8	96.3	1.5	0.7	1.0	1.8	5.1	14.2	7.1	11.0	10.8	14.5
36,099	42,900	6	Seneca	323.7	34,498	1,310	106.6	90.4	5.8	0.8	1.0	3.4	5.3	14.7	8.8	13.6	10.9	13.0
36,101	18,500	4	Steuben	1,390.5	96,281	617	69.2	95.0	2.2	0.7	1.9	1.7	5.5	16.2	7.7	11.6	11.3	13.7
36,103	35,620	1	Suffolk	911.5	1,492,953	25	1,637.9	68.6	8.0	0.5	4.7	19.5	5.3	16.1	9.2	11.8	11.8	15.2
36,105		1	Sullivan	968.1	75,485	733	78.0	73.5	9.3	0.8	2.2	16.2	5.6	15.6	8.1	11.9	11.4	14.2
36,107	13,780	2	Tioga	518.6	48,578	1,011	93.7	96.0	1.4	0.6	1.2	2.0	5.1	16.1	7.4	10.8	11.0	13.7
36,109	27,060	3	Tompkins	474.6	104,802	574	220.8	79.3	5.0	0.8	12.8	5.0	4.0	10.8	26.8	13.0	10.4	10.2
36,111	28,740	3	Ulster	1,124.2	179,417	364	159.6	81.1	7.3	0.8	2.9	10.3	4.4	13.5	9.3	12.4	11.5	14.4
36,113	24,020	3	Warren	867.2	64,532	821	74.4	94.9	1.8	0.7	1.4	2.6	4.4	13.9	7.4	11.8	10.7	14.2
36,115	24,020	3	Washington	831.2	61,620	846	74.1	93.4	3.4	0.6	0.9	2.8	4.9	14.3	8.0	12.4	11.6	14.6
36,117	40,380	1	Wayne	603.8	90,670	647	150.2	91.6	3.9	0.6	1.2	4.5	5.5	16.0	7.7	11.3	10.9	14.6
36,119	35,620	1	Westchester	430.5	980,244	48	2,277.0	54.7	14.5	0.4	7.1	24.9	5.6	16.5	8.9	11.5	12.7	14.6
36,121		6	Wyoming	592.8	40,493	1,166	68.3	90.5	5.7	0.5	0.8	3.4	4.8	14.1	7.7	14.1	12.4	14.9
36,123	40,380	1	Yates	338.1	24,955	1,611	73.8	95.7	1.5	0.5	0.9	2.3	6.2	15.9	10.9	10.8	9.4	11.4
37,000		0	NORTH CAROLINA	48,617.9	10,273,419	X	211.3	64.8	22.5	1.7	3.6	9.5	5.9	16.5	9.5	13.3	12.6	13.5
37,001	15,500	3	Alamance	423.4	162,391	400	383.5	65.3	20.8	0.8	2.1	12.9	5.8	16.7	9.6	12.4	11.6	13.9
37,003	25,860	2	Alexander	260.0	37,286	1,243	143.4	87.9	6.7	0.7	1.3	4.8	4.9	15.5	7.4	11.4	12.2	14.7
37,005		9	Alleghany	234.4	11,031	2,352	47.1	87.8	2.1	0.8	0.9	9.6	4.5	12.9	6.6	9.2	10.4	13.2
37,007		6	Anson	531.5	24,991	1,609	47.0	45.6	49.1	1.0	1.4	4.1	5.0	14.7	8.4	14.3	12.4	13.4
37,009		7	Ashe	425.1	26,957	1,527	63.4	93.0	1.2	0.7	0.7	5.3	4.2	13.6	6.4	9.7	11.4	13.3
37,011		8	Avery	247.3	17,536	1,949	70.9	89.2	4.8	0.9	0.7	5.4	3.8	11.5	9.6	12.7	13.0	14.0
37,013	47,820	6	Beaufort	832.0	47,088	1,031	56.6	66.8	25.3	0.6	0.6	7.8	4.9	15.6	7.0	9.9	11.0	12.8
37,015		7	Bertie	699.2	19,224	1,865	27.5	35.3	61.6	1.0	0.8	2.3	4.4	13.6	7.8	12.4	10.8	12.8
37,017		6	Bladen	874.9	33,478	1,340	38.3	55.6	34.5	2.9	0.6	7.9	5.0	15.9	7.6	10.6	11.7	13.0
37,019	34,820	2	Brunswick	849.2	130,897	487	154.1	83.4	11.1	1.3	1.1	4.8	4.1	11.6	5.5	9.1	9.6	11.5
37,021	11,700	2	Buncombe	656.4	257,607	264	392.5	85.3	7.1	1.0	1.9	6.6	5.1	13.7	7.7	13.9	13.3	12.9
37,023	25,860	2	Burke	506.2	89,293	652	176.4	83.4	7.0	0.8	4.2	6.3	4.9	14.3	8.2	11.5	11.4	14.7
37,025	16,740	1	Cabarrus	361.2	206,872	322	572.7	67.6	18.8	0.8	4.5	10.4	6.4	19.4	7.9	12.5	14.3	14.8
37,027	25,860	2	Caldwell	471.9	81,981	690	173.7	88.9	6.7	0.7	0.9	5.5	5.0	15.5	7.5	11.2	11.6	15.2
37,029	21,020	8	Camden	240.3	10,581	2,386	44.0	82.5	13.1	1.2	2.8	2.8	5.4	17.9	6.7	10.9	13.5	15.2
37,031	33,980	4	Carteret	507.6	68,881	775	135.7	88.2	6.5	1.1	2.0	4.2	4.3	13.6	6.4	10.3	10.8	13.5
37,033		8	Caswell	425.4	22,646	1,696	53.2	62.5	33.4	1.0	0.9	4.0	4.7	14.1	7.2	11.6	11.3	14.4
37,035	25,860	2	Catawba	401.4	157,974	415	393.6	77.0	9.6	0.6	4.6	9.8	5.7	16.8	8.4	11.7	11.9	14.4
37,037	20,500	2	Chatham	681.5	71,472	758	104.9	73.0	13.0	0.8	2.3	12.5	5.0	15.4	6.3	9.1	11.5	13.9
37,039		9	Cherokee	455.4	28,087	1,491	61.7	93.3	2.0	2.8	0.9	3.2	4.3	13.0	5.9	8.9	9.9	12.6

1. CBSA = Core Based Statistical Area. See Appendix A for explanation. See Appendix B for list of metropolitan areas with component counties.   2. County type code from the Economic Research Service of USDA Rural-Urban Continuum Codes. See Appendix A for definition.   3. Dry land or land partially or temporarily covered by water.   4. May be of any race.

Table B. States and Counties — **Population and Households**

STATE County	Age (percent) (cont.) 55 to 64 years	65 to 74 years	75 years and over	Percent female	Population change, 2000-2017 Total persons 2000	2010	Percent change 2000-2010	2010-2017	Components of change, 2010-2017 Births	Deaths	Net Migration	Households, 2012-2016 Number	Persons per household	Family households	Percent Female family householder[1]	One person
	16	17	18	19	20	21	22	23	24	25	26	27	28	29	30	31
NEW YORK— Cont'd																
Genesee	15.4	10.0	8.2	50.2	60,370	59,944	-0.7	-3.3	4,305	4,476	-1,813	23,825	2.44	65.7	9.5	28.4
Greene	15.8	12.9	8.7	47.8	48,195	49,218	2.1	-3.6	2,955	3,749	-939	17,125	2.61	63.2	9.7	31.9
Hamilton	20.7	18.8	11.5	49.7	5,379	4,843	-10.0	-7.4	234	428	-162	1,239	3.70	66.3	8.2	29.0
Herkimer	15.2	11.5	8.5	50.6	64,427	64,463	0.1	-3.4	4,663	4,956	-1,918	25,670	2.43	64.2	10.9	29.6
Jefferson	10.7	7.7	5.4	47.1	111,738	116,232	4.0	-1.8	15,196	6,527	-10,901	43,428	2.57	68.4	10.9	26.1
Kings	11.0	7.6	5.9	52.6	2,465,326	2,504,706	1.6	5.8	302,186	116,777	-40,797	938,803	2.73	62.6	19.1	28.9
Lewis	15.7	9.8	7.7	49.3	26,944	27,074	0.5	-1.9	2,361	1,822	-1,064	10,307	2.59	69.4	9.2	24.2
Livingston	14.9	10.1	7.1	49.7	64,328	65,214	1.4	-2.2	3,852	3,856	-1,401	24,217	2.41	63.8	11.2	28.0
Madison	15.3	10.3	7.3	50.6	69,441	73,452	5.8	-3.4	4,811	4,435	-2,874	26,121	2.56	65.6	9.9	27.7
Monroe	13.7	9.5	7.2	51.7	735,343	744,402	1.2	0.4	60,464	47,470	-9,641	300,289	2.41	60.4	14.1	32.2
Montgomery	14.4	10.3	8.0	50.7	49,708	50,256	1.1	-2.0	4,369	4,185	-1,177	19,540	2.49	63.7	15.0	30.3
Nassau	14.2	9.6	7.8	51.4	1,334,544	1,339,866	0.4	2.2	102,984	79,453	6,741	440,230	3.04	76.7	11.7	20.0
New York	11.2	8.8	7.2	52.6	1,537,195	1,586,184	3.2	5.0	135,623	74,017	17,213	753,385	2.09	41.3	11.1	47.2
Niagara	15.8	10.6	7.9	51.2	219,846	216,487	-1.5	-2.4	15,635	17,040	-3,645	87,638	2.39	62.4	12.6	32.3
Oneida	14.0	10.1	8.2	50.2	235,469	234,885	-0.2	-1.5	18,681	18,151	-4,082	90,260	2.44	62.0	13.3	31.8
Onondaga	14.0	9.3	7.3	51.8	458,336	467,069	1.9	-0.4	38,394	30,425	-9,638	184,925	2.43	60.5	13.0	31.8
Ontario	15.2	11.5	7.8	50.9	100,224	108,085	7.8	1.7	7,548	7,618	1,980	44,180	2.39	64.7	10.3	28.9
Orange	12.6	8.1	5.6	49.8	341,367	372,827	9.2	2.5	35,259	18,979	-6,977	125,144	2.92	70.6	11.7	24.5
Orleans	15.4	10.3	7.1	50.3	44,171	42,876	-2.9	-4.4	3,084	3,046	-1,944	16,132	2.40	66.2	12.0	27.0
Oswego	14.7	9.6	6.2	49.8	122,377	122,104	-0.2	-3.0	9,230	7,675	-5,205	45,374	2.55	67.2	11.8	24.8
Otsego	14.8	11.8	8.7	51.5	61,676	62,272	1.0	-3.5	3,801	4,350	-1,616	23,539	2.35	62.3	9.2	28.7
Putnam	15.8	10.1	6.6	50.0	95,745	99,648	4.1	-0.3	6,089	5,032	-1,377	34,102	2.84	76.0	8.8	20.3
Queens	12.9	8.4	6.6	51.5	2,229,379	2,230,545	0.1	5.7	220,014	104,872	12,550	779,304	2.93	67.4	16.1	26.2
Rensselaer	14.4	9.8	6.7	50.6	152,538	159,443	4.5	0.2	12,060	10,938	-761	63,553	2.42	62.0	12.0	29.9
Richmond	13.7	9.3	6.5	51.5	443,728	468,730	5.6	2.3	39,185	25,921	-2,412	166,014	2.81	74.0	14.7	22.7
Rockland	12.1	8.4	7.0	51.0	286,753	311,690	8.7	5.5	35,697	15,248	-3,306	99,038	3.19	74.7	10.2	21.4
St. Lawrence	13.7	9.7	7.0	48.9	111,931	111,941	0.0	-2.1	8,689	7,266	-3,750	41,466	2.40	63.4	11.9	28.7
Saratoga	14.3	10.6	6.9	50.5	200,635	219,591	9.4	4.7	16,049	12,686	7,052	90,896	2.43	66.1	9.2	27.0
Schenectady	13.7	9.3	7.5	51.3	146,555	154,751	5.6	0.5	13,122	10,986	-1,238	55,027	2.73	60.4	11.1	34.0
Schoharie	15.9	12.6	8.4	49.9	31,582	32,739	3.7	-4.0	1,868	2,038	-1,158	12,373	2.44	63.7	9.6	28.9
Schuyler	16.8	12.2	8.4	50.2	19,224	18,350	-4.5	-1.9	1,273	1,398	-225	7,376	2.44	65.0	9.6	28.7
Seneca	15.0	11.0	7.7	47.5	33,342	35,244	5.7	-2.1	2,721	2,410	-1,046	13,672	2.33	60.9	10.0	30.4
Steuben	14.9	11.0	8.1	50.2	98,726	98,986	0.3	-2.7	7,898	7,137	-3,451	40,438	2.38	64.2	11.3	29.3
Suffolk	14.2	9.3	7.1	50.7	1,419,369	1,493,200	5.2	0.0	115,108	86,552	-28,710	489,758	2.99	73.8	11.8	21.8
Sullivan	14.8	11.3	7.2	48.6	73,966	77,520	4.8	-2.6	5,989	5,225	-2,835	28,007	2.56	63.1	11.7	30.8
Tioga	16.3	11.1	8.6	50.3	51,784	51,048	-1.4	-4.8	3,537	3,168	-2,855	19,705	2.49	68.2	11.0	26.8
Tompkins	11.1	8.4	5.4	50.8	96,501	101,594	5.3	3.2	6,255	4,792	1,691	38,269	2.36	52.6	8.9	32.7
Ulster	15.3	11.4	7.8	50.5	177,749	182,512	2.7	-1.7	11,535	11,964	-2,619	69,335	2.43	62.1	10.6	30.6
Warren	16.0	12.6	9.0	50.9	63,303	65,698	3.8	-1.8	4,193	4,881	-433	26,944	2.38	61.7	11.4	31.4
Washington	15.3	11.0	7.8	48.2	61,042	63,238	3.6	-2.6	4,386	4,434	-1,548	24,027	2.47	67.9	11.9	25.4
Wayne	15.7	10.9	7.3	50.4	93,765	93,751	0.0	-3.3	7,109	6,126	-4,085	36,576	2.46	67.7	10.8	25.8
Westchester	13.4	8.9	7.7	51.5	923,459	949,201	2.8	3.3	77,370	51,395	5,440	341,762	2.76	69.2	12.9	26.6
Wyoming	14.8	10.5	6.7	45.7	43,424	42,162	-2.9	-4.0	2,747	2,635	-1,791	15,780	2.38	65.4	9.6	28.4
Yates	15.3	11.9	8.2	51.3	24,621	25,363	3.0	-1.6	2,260	1,822	-843	9,532	2.50	68.0	8.7	25.7
NORTH CAROLINA	12.9	9.6	6.3	51.3	8,049,313	9,535,721	18.5	7.7	872,453	614,104	474,259	3,815,392	2.54	65.9	13.4	28.2
Alamance	13.1	9.5	7.3	52.4	130,800	151,198	15.6	7.4	12,916	11,389	9,709	62,053	2.45	66.2	14.2	28.8
Alexander	14.0	11.8	8.1	49.2	33,603	37,192	10.7	0.3	2,552	2,616	179	13,796	2.61	67.8	9.9	28.2
Alleghany	16.4	15.6	11.3	50.2	10,677	11,154	4.5	-1.1	684	937	137	4,798	2.23	72.3	9.3	25.2
Anson	13.9	10.6	7.2	47.8	25,275	26,928	6.5	-7.2	1,833	2,219	-1,577	9,511	2.53	64.5	17.8	30.0
Ashe	16.3	14.6	10.4	50.7	24,384	27,238	11.7	-1.0	1,676	2,439	507	11,905	2.23	69.4	11.7	26.0
Avery	14.1	12.4	8.8	45.5	17,167	17,806	3.7	-1.5	1,045	1,386	77	6,756	2.21	65.4	7.1	28.2
Beaufort	15.5	14.2	9.1	52.3	44,958	47,763	6.2	-1.4	3,508	4,158	11	19,021	2.47	65.1	12.0	31.0
Bertie	16.4	12.1	9.7	49.8	19,773	21,280	7.6	-9.7	1,305	1,786	-1,589	7,673	2.48	62.8	20.2	33.8
Bladen	15.4	12.6	8.1	52.3	32,278	35,182	9.0	-4.8	2,551	2,955	-1,300	14,110	2.40	65.1	18.8	32.1
Brunswick	18.1	20.9	9.6	52.1	73,143	107,431	46.9	21.8	7,505	9,128	24,619	50,562	2.34	68.6	10.2	27.3
Buncombe	14.0	11.5	7.9	52.0	206,330	238,328	15.5	8.1	18,829	17,971	18,206	102,118	2.38	59.0	9.6	33.1
Burke	15.0	11.5	8.4	50.5	89,148	90,838	1.9	-1.7	6,320	7,374	-469	34,199	2.52	66.1	13.0	29.4
Cabarrus	11.6	7.9	5.1	51.3	131,063	178,086	35.9	16.2	17,181	10,728	22,188	68,289	2.79	73.7	12.0	22.4
Caldwell	14.7	11.6	7.8	50.6	77,415	83,047	7.3	-1.3	5,812	6,674	-148	31,912	2.53	66.4	12.1	30.1
Camden	14.6	9.5	6.2	49.9	6,885	9,980	45.0	6.0	642	531	493	3,804	2.68	78.8	14.3	19.4
Carteret	16.8	14.8	9.5	50.9	59,383	66,463	11.9	3.6	4,369	5,554	3,604	29,563	2.28	65.0	11.2	29.6
Caswell	16.0	12.7	8.2	49.0	23,501	23,748	1.1	-4.6	1,478	1,934	-652	8,874	2.49	69.5	13.5	26.7
Catawba	13.8	10.5	6.8	51.1	141,685	154,758	9.2	2.1	12,720	11,536	2,136	59,710	2.56	68.8	11.9	25.9
Chatham	15.1	13.9	9.9	52.0	49,329	63,479	28.7	12.6	4,605	4,659	7,978	27,397	2.48	68.7	8.3	27.3
Cherokee	16.5	17.4	11.4	51.3	24,298	27,441	12.9	2.4	1,620	2,588	1,623	10,857	2.47	66.1	11.1	29.7

1. No spouse present.

Table B. States and Counties — Population, Vital Statistics, Health, and Crime

STATE County	Persons in group quarters, 2017	Daytime Population, 2012-2016		Births, 2017		Deaths, 2017		Persons under 65 with no health insurance, 2016		Medicare, 2017			Serious crimes known to police[2], 2016 Total	
		Number	Employment/ residence ratio	Total	Rate[1]	Number	Rate[1]	Number	Percent	Total beneficiaries	Enrolled in Original Medicare	Enrolled in Medicare Advantage	Number	Rate[3]
	32	33	34	35	36	37	38	39	40	41	42	43	44	45
NEW YORK— Cont'd														
Genesee	1,968	55,202	0.87	559	9.6	624	10.8	2,472	5.3	13,321	6,102	7,219	1,263	2,165
Greene	3,216	44,508	0.81	379	8.0	526	11.1	2,001	5.7	11,223	7,132	4,090	540	1,189
Hamilton	80	4,339	0.80	29	6.5	67	14.9	217	6.7	1,504	1,032	471	54	1,160
Herkimer	1,388	53,731	0.65	599	9.6	656	10.5	2,585	5.2	13,352	8,008	5,344	1,059	1,771
Jefferson	7,118	121,467	1.06	1,869	16.4	936	8.2	5,656	6.1	19,649	13,613	6,037	2,362	2,017
Kings	35,814	2,296,989	0.73	40,752	15.4	17,398	6.6	198,931	8.8	359,709	200,305	159,404	NA	NA
Lewis	313	23,646	0.70	305	11.5	271	10.2	1,307	5.9	5,365	3,698	1,667	236	882
Livingston	6,076	58,111	0.78	503	7.9	534	8.4	2,210	4.6	13,098	5,374	7,725	882	1,374
Madison	4,595	63,079	0.72	633	8.9	597	8.4	2,682	4.9	14,158	8,576	5,582	1,022	1,438
Monroe	26,324	780,432	1.09	8,065	10.8	6,657	8.9	29,587	4.9	150,878	53,266	97,612	18,755	2,515
Montgomery	895	48,042	0.92	629	12.8	551	11.2	2,372	6.0	12,202	6,478	5,724	1,024	2,082
Nassau	20,677	1,269,962	0.87	14,176	10.4	11,218	8.2	56,454	5.0	258,433	196,880	61,554	15,144	1,117
New York	66,711	3,255,760	2.85	17,724	10.6	11,380	6.8	85,635	6.3	276,765	172,828	103,937	175,814	2,052
Niagara	4,060	190,920	0.77	2,102	9.9	2,321	11.0	8,540	5.0	48,145	21,774	26,371	6,092	2,894
Oneida	12,870	240,356	1.07	2,463	10.6	2,474	10.7	8,892	5.0	52,193	32,196	19,997	5,222	2,266
Onondaga	17,131	497,804	1.14	5,157	11.1	4,188	9.0	19,703	5.2	91,689	51,961	39,728	11,133	2,391
Ontario	3,339	109,682	1.00	1,023	9.3	1,067	9.7	3,911	4.5	24,799	10,559	14,239	1,866	1,776
Orange	11,447	350,391	0.85	4,883	12.8	2,783	7.3	19,544	6.1	61,273	48,909	12,364	7,328	1,952
Orleans	2,730	37,926	0.77	431	10.5	411	10.0	2,053	6.4	8,239	3,798	4,441	748	1,822
Oswego	4,939	106,859	0.73	1,150	9.7	1,060	8.9	5,083	5.3	24,502	14,951	9,551	2,310	1,942
Otsego	5,364	62,076	1.04	507	8.4	623	10.4	2,670	6.1	14,279	10,742	3,537	777	1,297
Putnam	2,568	77,236	0.56	819	8.2	739	7.4	3,959	4.8	17,470	13,913	3,557	591	614
Queens	27,504	1,941,171	0.66	29,706	12.6	15,638	6.6	225,096	11.3	342,699	182,253	160,446	NA	NA
Rensselaer	5,880	138,352	0.73	1,600	10.0	1,567	9.8	6,332	4.9	31,175	18,002	13,173	3,655	2,293
Richmond	7,023	397,462	0.63	5,331	11.1	3,976	8.3	21,728	5.4	85,525	51,165	34,360	NA	NA
Rockland	7,004	296,016	0.82	5,262	16.0	2,428	7.4	17,759	6.5	55,426	43,646	11,780	3,542	1,084
St. Lawrence	11,327	109,734	0.96	1,127	10.3	1,066	9.7	5,360	6.6	23,260	17,492	5,767	1,729	1,626
Saratoga	3,428	199,721	0.78	2,160	9.4	1,943	8.5	8,005	4.3	44,356	24,385	19,971	2,816	1,246
Schenectady	4,543	149,508	0.93	1,782	11.5	1,463	9.4	6,130	4.8	35,301	18,629	16,672	4,681	3,049
Schoharie	1,419	28,724	0.78	228	7.3	280	8.9	1,353	5.7	7,009	4,765	2,244	385	1,248
Schuyler	215	16,192	0.74	183	10.2	185	10.3	804	5.6	4,012	2,469	1,543	114	632
Seneca	2,849	33,163	0.88	356	10.3	319	9.2	1,649	6.3	6,621	3,816	2,805	635	1,839
Steuben	1,741	97,204	0.98	1,033	10.7	1,003	10.4	4,594	5.9	21,991	14,406	7,585	1,519	1,571
Suffolk	28,656	1,411,986	0.88	15,513	10.4	12,780	8.6	74,327	6.0	279,865	226,019	53,846	22,237	1,491
Sullivan	3,806	71,680	0.87	778	10.3	738	9.8	4,087	6.9	16,393	13,812	2,581	1,225	1,658
Tioga	504	41,663	0.64	459	9.4	444	9.1	1,869	4.7	10,504	6,429	4,075	462	947
Tompkins	13,229	115,806	1.24	806	7.7	621	5.9	4,429	5.6	16,024	11,899	4,125	1,805	1,721
Ulster	11,636	165,312	0.82	1,518	8.5	1,698	9.5	9,049	6.5	38,382	28,790	9,593	2,633	1,475
Warren	665	71,156	1.20	543	8.4	653	10.1	2,623	5.2	17,443	10,140	7,303	1,195	1,865
Washington	3,103	52,261	0.64	575	9.3	655	10.6	2,636	5.5	14,002	8,071	5,931	574	932
Wayne	1,107	80,196	0.72	962	10.6	839	9.3	3,992	5.3	20,968	8,829	12,139	1,614	1,786
Westchester	27,712	950,167	0.96	10,469	10.7	7,386	7.5	61,342	7.7	170,189	124,592	45,597	12,431	1,275
Wyoming	3,578	38,360	0.84	353	8.7	332	8.2	1,632	5.4	8,173	3,708	4,465	324	799
Yates	1,249	23,025	0.81	326	13.1	258	10.3	1,816	9.5	5,930	2,773	3,156	320	1,289
NORTH CAROLINA	266,771	9,940,621	1.00	120,525	11.7	90,129	8.8	1,023,107	12.2	1,877,989	1,267,739	610,250	315,534	3,110
Alamance	4,468	147,613	0.88	1,823	11.2	1,604	9.9	17,976	13.9	32,123	14,846	17,278	4,369	2,736
Alexander	1,567	31,387	0.62	344	9.2	378	10.1	3,705	12.9	7,656	5,003	2,653	747	2,000
Alleghany	112	10,555	0.93	96	8.7	135	12.2	1,339	16.8	3,322	2,201	1,122	102	1,126
Anson	2,245	24,252	0.84	246	9.8	290	11.6	2,437	13.2	5,193	3,857	1,335	700	3,324
Ashe	320	24,652	0.80	206	7.6	335	12.4	3,251	16.1	7,254	5,283	1,971	327	1,212
Avery	2,521	18,629	1.16	145	8.3	199	11.3	2,126	18.5	4,897	3,595	1,302	229	1,330
Beaufort	504	47,018	0.97	457	9.7	597	12.7	4,734	13.0	12,994	10,678	2,316	1,194	2,535
Bertie	1,260	19,600	0.90	171	8.9	248	12.9	1,797	12.8	5,100	4,483	617	364	1,867
Bladen	316	35,939	1.12	328	9.8	446	13.3	4,408	16.6	6,894	5,090	1,803	NA	NA
Brunswick	842	110,077	0.80	1,011	7.7	1,482	11.3	13,022	14.6	41,407	32,774	8,633	1,607	1,393
Buncombe	7,852	267,175	1.15	2,620	10.2	2,639	10.2	22,904	11.3	57,626	41,752	15,874	7,235	2,832
Burke	2,445	84,853	0.88	886	9.9	1,006	11.3	9,950	14.2	18,645	12,064	6,581	2,104	2,438
Cabarrus	1,320	175,802	0.82	2,522	12.2	1,547	7.5	17,123	9.8	32,767	20,085	12,681	3,939	1,966
Caldwell	953	74,240	0.78	795	9.7	935	11.4	9,097	13.9	18,148	10,937	7,210	2,665	3,306
Camden	17	7,125	0.30	84	7.9	65	6.1	909	10.3	1,719	1,511	207	77	742
Carteret	975	65,631	0.90	563	8.2	824	12.0	6,452	12.3	16,295	13,854	2,441	1,039	1,499
Caswell	1,332	17,555	0.38	197	8.7	256	11.3	2,227	13.2	4,833	2,584	2,249	454	1,991
Catawba	2,364	167,984	1.18	1,707	10.8	1,637	10.4	16,641	13.0	35,438	22,822	12,616	4,716	3,046
Chatham	784	57,270	0.60	662	9.3	742	10.4	7,245	13.5	11,212	6,362	4,850	1,214	1,675
Cherokee	439	27,288	1.01	241	8.6	330	11.7	3,073	15.4	8,999	6,715	2,284	854	3,148

1. Per 1,000 estimated resident population.   2. Data for serious crimes have not been adjusted for underreporting; this may affect comparability between geographic areas and over time.
3. Per 100,000 population estimated by the FBI.

Table B. States and Counties — Crime, Education, Money Income, and Poverty

	Serious crimes known to police, 2016 (cont.)[1]		Education						Money income, 2012-2016				Income and poverty, 2016			
	Rate		School enrollment and attainment, 2012-2016				Local government expenditures,[5] 2013-2014			Households				Percent below poverty level		
			Enrollment[3]		Attainment[4] (percent)							Percent					
STATE County	Violent	Property	Total	Percent private	High school graduate or less	Bachelor's degree or more	Total current spending (mil dol)	Current spending per student (dollars)	Per capita income[6]	Median income (dollars)	with income of less than $50,000	with income of $200,000 or more	Median household income (dollars)	All persons	Children under 18 years	Children 5 to 17 years in families
	46	47	48	49	50	51	52	53	54	55	56	57	58	59	60	61
NEW YORK— Cont'd																
Genesee	218	1,947	13,372	12.5	44.9	21.2	149.9	17,521	26,381	52,641	47.1	1.7	54,211	11.4	16.2	14.3
Greene	227	962	7,867	12.4	50.8	20.3	128.5	20,571	26,307	51,013	48.9	2.9	49,860	16.4	21.3	20.5
Hamilton	107	1,052	785	11.3	44.4	21.6	18.4	38,010	27,371	52,708	48.3	2.3	52,134	10.2	18.4	16.1
Herkimer	201	1,570	14,033	12.0	45.3	21.5	127.4	13,298	24,678	48,893	51.1	1.7	49,633	16.3	23.7	21.5
Jefferson	240	1,777	28,781	12.6	43.9	20.8	284.1	15,191	24,172	49,911	50.1	2.0	46,206	15.3	21.5	21.3
Kings	NA	NA	666,851	29.1	45.8	34.1	(7)	(7)	28,134	50,640	49.4	6.2	54,793	20.6	28.4	28.5
Lewis	112	770	6,009	12.7	55.7	15.5	74.6	17,589	25,230	49,976	50.0	2.3	48,314	15.8	24.3	23.2
Livingston	142	1,232	17,426	9.4	44.9	24.5	138.9	17,099	24,596	52,724	47.3	2.0	54,256	13.9	16.4	14.5
Madison	172	1,266	18,461	25.7	43.4	26.7	170.7	16,739	26,824	55,858	44.6	3.4	57,703	11.1	15.9	13.9
Monroe	333	2,183	195,184	25.0	34.1	36.7	1,967.7	17,891	30,194	53,568	46.8	4.1	54,684	14.7	21.0	19.6
Montgomery	169	1,913	11,310	15.1	52.4	16.0	114.0	14,700	23,885	44,455	55.0	1.6	42,193	19.9	31.9	30.5
Nassau	133	983	348,640	26.1	32.9	43.5	5,054.5	24,889	44,548	102,044	24.1	17.7	105,486	6.1	8.1	7.4
New York	575	1,477	335,196	45.0	25.5	60.4	(7)20,921.7	(7) 20,740	66,522	75,513	37.2	18.9	77,214	17.2	23.6	24.9
Niagara	399	2,495	48,796	16.3	44.0	23.5	476.4	15,927	27,487	50,094	49.9	2.2	50,328	12.6	18.4	15.4
Oneida	286	1,980	54,130	14.0	45.4	23.8	555.1	16,304	26,577	49,838	50.1	2.8	52,404	16.3	25.9	23.3
Onondaga	304	2,087	124,905	26.7	35.3	34.3	1,198.2	16,732	30,225	55,717	45.2	4.3	56,853	14.6	19.9	18.1
Ontario	156	1,620	26,768	22.2	35.8	32.1	278.2	16,961	31,524	58,070	42.5	4.4	58,320	9.6	14.0	13.0
Orange	248	1,704	107,112	24.2	40.4	28.7	1,236.6	20,336	31,272	71,910	35.8	7.2	71,963	12.6	19.3	16.8
Orleans	190	1,632	8,302	10.7	53.2	15.9	100.3	15,895	23,332	48,731	51.0	1.7	50,750	15.2	22.2	19.1
Oswego	223	1,719	30,861	8.4	52.4	18.0	376.6	18,373	24,284	49,571	50.4	2.1	52,621	17.2	23.1	21.4
Otsego	150	1,146	17,016	16.0	42.7	28.5	141.8	19,300	24,989	49,689	50.3	2.3	50,034	14.7	19.3	18.0
Putnam	38	575	24,330	18.1	34.3	38.9	368.0	24,194	41,993	97,606	23.1	13.9	96,267	6.0	6.4	5.6
Queens	NA	NA	552,334	20.9	46.6	30.6	(7)	(7)	27,631	59,758	42.5	4.9	61,844	13.3	18.2	18.3
Rensselaer	296	1,998	39,641	30.4	37.3	29.3	352.5	16,732	31,529	61,754	41.1	3.8	63,174	11.6	17.6	15.5
Richmond	NA	NA	121,105	23.2	42.6	31.4	(7)	(7)	32,678	74,021	35.4	7.8	75,524	13.2	18.6	18.3
Rockland	117	968	95,708	43.4	35.2	40.4	965.2	23,957	35,557	86,134	31.0	13.7	84,358	14.4	25.4	23.8
St. Lawrence	163	1,463	30,797	22.8	47.9	22.8	285.0	18,381	23,313	46,313	52.8	2.3	50,897	17.5	22.8	21.1
Saratoga	112	1,135	52,382	20.7	31.3	39.6	487.3	15,686	37,583	74,080	32.0	6.6	75,904	6.3	7.7	6.3
Schenectady	454	2,595	37,815	19.4	39.4	30.6	416.0	16,472	29,212	59,959	42.4	3.8	57,923	11.4	18.2	16.9
Schoharie	117	1,131	7,594	9.2	49.5	20.5	91.3	20,623	25,638	50,607	49.4	1.6	50,244	12.7	17.9	15.9
Schuyler	72	560	3,710	12.6	49.9	20.8	40.3	18,413	25,004	47,229	52.3	1.1	48,109	15.0	22.1	20.4
Seneca	194	1,645	6,894	18.5	50.1	20.0	78.1	18,973	25,680	50,073	49.9	2.2	48,998	13.5	21.1	20.5
Steuben	193	1,377	21,360	12.5	47.7	22.3	279.9	18,417	26,830	48,823	50.9	2.4	50,190	13.2	21.4	19.2
Suffolk	121	1,369	381,140	15.2	38.9	34.4	5,561.2	22,482	38,779	90,128	27.2	12.7	92,310	7.6	10.5	9.8
Sullivan	268	1,390	16,783	14.5	47.2	22.4	244.5	25,222	27,068	52,027	48.4	3.6	49,016	16.9	25.4	24.1
Tioga	129	817	11,160	12.8	45.0	25.0	131.5	16,752	29,654	58,115	43.3	4.0	55,643	12.7	19.2	16.5
Tompkins	139	1,582	41,980	50.7	25.4	51.6	221.8	19,906	28,888	54,133	46.9	5.8	55,778	18.5	15.4	14.1
Ulster	164	1,311	40,604	14.7	40.5	31.0	516.5	21,740	31,760	60,393	42.4	5.1	61,421	13.9	17.6	15.9
Warren	173	1,692	13,494	9.7	42.2	28.4	170.3	18,485	31,652	57,174	44.0	3.6	55,769	11.7	18.3	16.0
Washington	154	777	12,738	12.5	51.1	20.2	156.3	17,531	25,200	51,449	48.6	2.0	51,052	11.1	17.0	16.0
Wayne	175	1,611	20,414	11.4	46.1	21.2	267.4	18,417	26,209	51,627	48.0	2.1	58,521	10.4	16.4	15.4
Westchester	215	1,060	254,141	25.4	32.1	47.3	3,634.7	24,141	49,938	86,226	31.1	18.3	89,380	10.0	11.5	10.7
Wyoming	113	686	8,147	12.6	53.1	15.0	75.1	17,840	24,610	53,612	46.4	1.3	56,089	10.0	14.4	13.4
Yates	68	1,221	5,556	36.1	48.9	23.2	42.2	18,820	26,001	50,105	49.9	3.4	48,820	14.1	23.5	22.5
NORTH CAROLINA	372	2,737	2,533,803	14.4	40.1	29.0	12,689.0	8,460	26,779	48,256	51.5	3.9	50,595	15.4	21.7	20.3
Alamance	391	2,345	40,058	21.3	43.4	22.1	189.9	7,933	23,989	43,209	56.9	2.1	46,060	16.1	23.8	21.7
Alexander	228	1,773	8,023	15.4	59.0	13.3	43.7	8,264	20,567	40,404	58.6	0.8	46,385	15.0	23.0	21.4
Alleghany	143	982	1,935	7.2	51.2	18.6	16.3	11,062	21,059	38,352	63.9	1.4	35,965	20.6	34.7	31.8
Anson	451	2,873	5,538	5.9	60.7	9.5	35.7	9,948	17,548	34,656	65.9	0.9	35,809	25.1	35.8	33.3
Ashe	107	1,105	5,217	7.5	48.2	19.5	30.7	9,658	22,343	37,360	63.2	1.2	39,709	16.1	25.8	24.6
Avery	215	1,115	3,819	25.6	50.8	19.8	24.7	10,990	21,548	35,891	63.4	4.1	38,098	19.7	30.2	27.6
Beaufort	295	2,240	10,392	7.0	48.2	18.6	64.0	8,761	23,716	40,906	59.0	1.9	41,431	19.0	30.8	29.0
Bertie	190	1,677	4,261	13.2	63.3	11.5	29.9	11,385	17,244	31,129	69.9	0.4	33,809	24.4	34.9	33.8
Bladen	NA	NA	7,839	12.1	53.5	14.8	47.4	9,846	19,510	30,408	69.4	1.3	33,621	26.4	35.3	33.5
Brunswick	91	1,302	20,684	12.6	39.5	27.0	121.4	9,102	28,694	49,356	50.6	2.9	51,457	13.8	23.2	21.4
Buncombe	281	2,551	55,557	16.0	34.6	36.6	270.1	8,804	28,087	46,902	52.8	3.2	50,538	13.5	19.4	19.0
Burke	202	2,236	19,348	10.3	50.4	16.9	108.9	8,348	20,775	39,759	60.9	1.2	41,383	17.7	26.6	24.1
Cabarrus	128	1,838	52,076	13.2	37.3	28.6	278.7	7,609	27,728	58,970	41.6	4.3	63,059	11.0	16.1	13.9
Caldwell	201	3,105	17,465	6.9	54.3	13.8	102.1	8,437	20,587	37,118	62.5	1.5	39,166	17.1	22.7	20.9
Camden	96	646	2,702	7.6	40.2	20.4	16.6	8,699	26,420	60,714	42.4	2.5	65,415	8.7	10.9	9.8
Carteret	120	1,379	14,155	10.5	36.6	25.9	79.0	9,119	29,349	50,599	49.4	3.1	51,557	12.3	17.9	17.0
Caswell	320	1,671	4,854	10.3	58.3	13.2	25.7	9,356	20,235	38,310	62.6	1.2	40,570	19.7	29.5	26.6
Catawba	280	2,766	36,774	13.7	47.1	21.6	198.7	8,202	24,220	45,450	54.3	2.5	49,475	12.7	18.1	17.2
Chatham	152	1,524	13,959	14.8	34.9	38.8	85.8	9,253	35,109	58,555	42.8	7.6	63,303	11.7	17.4	16.4
Cherokee	203	2,945	5,281	11.6	49.6	19.2	33.4	9,510	19,285	35,284	65.5	0.5	37,237	18.4	31.4	28.8

1. Data for serious crimes have not been adjusted for underreporting; this may affect comparability between geographic areas and over time.   2. Per 100,000 population estimated by the FBI.
3. All persons 3 years old and over enrolled in nursery school through college.   4. Persons 25 years old and over.   5. Elementary and secondary education expenditures.
6. Based on population estimated by the American Community Survey, 2011–2015.   7. Bronx, Kings, Queens, and Richmond counties are included with New York county

Table B. States and Counties — Personal Income and Earnings

STATE County	Personal income, 2016 Total (mil dol)	Percent change 2015-2016	Per capita Dollars	Per capita Rank	Wages and salaries (mil dol)	Supplements — Pension and insurance	Supplements — Government social insurance	Proprietors' income (mil dol)	Dividends, interest, and rent (mil dol)	Personal transfer receipts (mil dol)	Earnings, 2016 Total (mil dol)	Contributions — From employee and self-employed	Contributions — From employer
	62	63	64	65	66	67	68	69	70	71	72	73	74
NEW YORK— Cont'd													
Genesee	2,350	-0.1	40,175	1,343	942	269	82	113	351	549	1,405	162	82
Greene	2,008	0.7	42,275	1,064	627	203	53	166	324	508	1,049	116	53
Hamilton	239	1.5	52,576	319	63	30	6	10	58	56	109	12	6
Herkimer	2,353	1.1	37,587	1,723	647	192	57	108	327	666	1,002	122	57
Jefferson	4,983	-1.0	43,711	904	2,605	774	244	197	929	1,002	3,820	426	244
Kings	117,003	2.2	44,502	831	32,067	7,093	2,719	7,065	16,644	28,884	48,944	5,524	2,719
Lewis	1,080	0.1	40,185	1,341	253	95	22	64	144	233	434	46	22
Livingston	2,460	0.9	38,284	1,604	775	261	67	185	339	558	1,288	141	67
Madison	2,859	1.2	40,086	1,356	863	235	75	162	448	599	1,335	154	75
Monroe	36,058	0.6	48,223	516	19,975	3,868	1,665	2,462	5,771	7,497	27,970	3,215	1,665
Montgomery	1,915	1.2	38,853	1,526	768	177	69	90	264	580	1,104	138	69
Nassau	107,986	2.0	79,314	31	39,342	7,087	3,144	9,125	25,099	13,128	58,698	6,319	3,144
New York	256,501	1.8	156,048	3	286,795	32,090	16,990	36,118	83,209	19,772	371,994	36,523	16,990
Niagara	8,884	1.7	41,954	1,109	3,127	761	271	343	1,194	2,209	4,501	548	271
Oneida	9,302	1.7	40,236	1,334	4,498	1,223	379	444	1,459	2,460	6,544	751	379
Onondaga	22,315	1.6	47,865	546	12,538	2,732	1,043	1,685	3,488	4,550	17,997	2,014	1,043
Ontario	5,434	0.9	49,477	444	2,569	535	207	224	874	1,028	3,536	407	207
Orange	17,931	2.2	47,284	589	6,878	1,676	586	901	2,511	3,435	10,041	1,130	586
Orleans	1,449	0.3	35,039	2,157	525	180	45	99	185	400	850	99	45
Oswego	4,386	1.4	36,865	1,845	1,554	464	130	125	519	1,176	2,273	266	130
Otsego	2,327	1.3	38,727	1,545	1,017	268	86	143	386	575	1,514	174	86
Putnam	5,904	1.4	59,693	152	1,400	316	118	277	956	822	2,112	241	118
Queens	101,410	2.1	43,467	945	34,933	7,247	2,922	7,492	13,733	25,650	52,595	5,897	2,922
Rensselaer	7,237	1.6	45,212	761	2,713	685	228	297	1,033	1,485	3,922	452	228
Richmond	24,480	2.5	51,427	350	5,746	1,287	488	1,201	3,251	5,900	8,721	1,012	488
Rockland	18,106	2.2	55,407	227	6,612	1,384	545	1,227	3,102	3,218	9,768	1,084	545
St. Lawrence	3,781	1.4	34,364	2,271	1,556	494	134	145	530	1,072	2,329	267	134
Saratoga	14,144	1.7	62,295	122	4,406	885	368	592	2,979	1,810	6,250	723	368
Schenectady	7,259	0.3	46,967	613	3,735	709	304	283	1,156	1,542	5,031	590	304
Schoharie	1,150	2.2	36,723	1,875	351	111	30	64	158	281	556	63	30
Schuyler	721	1.4	39,821	1,389	190	53	17	72	96	194	332	38	17
Seneca	1,216	0.2	34,967	2,168	531	156	45	65	189	321	797	91	45
Steuben	3,923	0.0	40,467	1,303	2,054	421	161	156	597	964	2,794	323	161
Suffolk	90,832	1.7	60,856	139	39,432	7,757	3,136	6,006	15,643	14,620	56,331	6,214	3,136
Sullivan	3,181	2.0	42,528	1,039	1,054	306	92	136	516	897	1,588	186	92
Tioga	1,985	1.2	40,714	1,276	680	155	55	112	276	460	1,002	117	55
Tompkins	4,275	0.3	40,763	1,263	2,661	523	230	283	849	678	3,697	424	230
Ulster	8,071	1.5	45,030	777	2,666	735	227	548	1,439	1,864	4,177	470	227
Warren	3,121	2.9	48,339	507	1,664	341	143	257	545	689	2,406	280	143
Washington	2,267	1.1	36,684	1,883	676	223	59	101	315	581	1,059	123	59
Wayne	3,788	0.9	41,722	1,139	1,207	364	103	280	458	919	1,953	218	103
Westchester	91,744	1.2	94,140	15	30,832	5,226	2,312	6,534	23,637	9,286	44,903	4,732	2,312
Wyoming	1,525	-1.2	37,396	1,750	570	190	49	99	206	352	908	99	49
Yates	894	1.0	35,856	2,020	255	73	22	104	163	234	454	49	22
NORTH CAROLINA	428,639	3.2	42,203	X	221,504	34,160	16,749	32,069	76,951	84,955	304,482	19,009	16,749
Alamance	5,788	1.8	36,246	1,966	2,561	379	198	314	955	1,345	3,453	434	198
Alexander	1,274	0.6	34,041	2,321	322	59	25	117	175	337	524	62	25
Alleghany	376	1.0	34,655	2,214	106	21	8	42	90	127	177	22	8
Anson	832	-0.5	32,676	2,531	268	57	20	79	99	262	425	47	20
Ashe	887	2.9	32,934	2,487	270	48	21	87	161	290	425	53	21
Avery	569	2.5	32,500	2,550	235	43	19	40	138	167	336	42	19
Beaufort	1,842	2.2	38,758	1,541	646	116	49	119	337	551	930	117	49
Bertie	646	0.7	32,516	2,546	219	46	16	37	80	249	319	39	16
Bladen	1,131	0.4	33,508	2,392	496	90	37	107	142	384	730	83	37
Brunswick	4,821	4.7	37,971	1,663	1,288	227	101	312	1,058	1,491	1,928	256	101
Buncombe	11,071	3.5	43,232	974	5,691	883	440	966	2,637	2,278	7,980	954	440
Burke	2,891	2.5	32,538	2,544	1,147	221	90	138	456	845	1,596	203	90
Cabarrus	8,286	5.2	41,103	1,220	3,259	513	243	525	1,067	1,406	4,539	534	243
Caldwell	2,648	2.4	32,508	2,548	956	164	74	116	404	780	1,309	172	74
Camden	436	2.1	41,865	1,115	59	11	4	17	71	85	91	12	4
Carteret	3,173	2.8	46,056	686	844	152	65	201	781	720	1,263	156	65
Caswell	733	1.7	32,011	2,614	110	25	8	61	96	237	205	26	8
Catawba	6,489	2.8	41,477	1,170	3,790	590	298	484	1,086	1,424	5,162	628	298
Chatham	3,854	2.7	53,342	291	580	93	44	176	1,004	645	894	116	44
Cherokee	824	2.3	29,512	2,892	280	51	22	64	142	342	417	56	22

1. Based on the resident population estimated as of July 1 of the year shown.

Table B. States and Counties — Earnings, Social Security, and Housing

STATE County	Earnings, 2016 (cont.) Percent by selected industries									Social Security beneficiaries, December 2016		Supplemental Security Income recipients, 2016	Housing units, 2017	
	Farm	Mining, quarrying, and extracting	Construction	Manufacturing	Information; professional, scientific, technical services	Retail trade	Finance, insurance, real estate, and leasing	Health care and social assistance	Government	Number	Rate[1]		Total	Percent change, 2010-2017
	75	76	77	78	79	80	81	82	83	84	85	86	87	88
NEW YORK— Cont'd														
Genesee	2.5	0.5	5.8	15.3	3.0	7.1	3.1	9.6	31.9	13,780	237	1,109	25,819	1.1
Greene	0.3	D	5.3	6.8	4.2	7.1	3.3	5.8	36.6	12,410	261	1,312	29,767	1.9
Hamilton	0.0	D	6.1	D	D	6.7	D	D	59.6	1,645	360	68	8,941	2.8
Herkimer	1.1	0.7	7.0	16.4	2.4	7.6	2.1	9.9	30.8	16,130	258	1,613	33,832	1.4
Jefferson	0.9	0.1	4.7	4.2	2.6	6.1	2.0	10.5	57.6	21,895	192	2,689	59,942	3.4
Kings	0.0	D	6.1	2.4	8.9	7.1	6.1	21.6	21.3	335,610	127	132,078	1,044,337	4.4
Lewis	6.0	D	5.9	15.4	2.4	5.8	1.8	D	40.8	5,820	218	561	15,690	3.8
Livingston	2.1	D	7.4	9.2	2.6	6.4	2.1	9.0	36.2	14,095	220	1,244	27,526	1.8
Madison	1.1	D	6.4	13.9	4.8	7.7	2.9	D	24.6	14,720	206	1,252	32,312	1.7
Monroe	0.0	0.0	4.8	12.1	12.6	5.2	6.5	14.5	15.0	158,965	213	25,605	328,321	2.4
Montgomery	0.7	0.4	5.5	16.8	3.3	9.2	2.4	22.7	19.7	13,435	273	1,982	23,506	1.9
Nassau	0.0	0.0	5.9	3.3	13.3	8.0	9.7	18.6	16.8	257,010	188	16,792	472,291	0.8
New York	0.0	0.0	1.6	0.7	28.8	2.8	30.5	5.0	8.0	254,740	153	69,438	886,408	4.6
Niagara	0.6	D	5.5	15.7	4.4	8.4	3.3	13.2	26.8	52,790	249	5,743	100,431	1.3
Oneida	0.2	0.2	3.4	8.6	6.5	6.3	7.7	17.2	31.7	55,120	238	8,132	105,232	1.0
Onondaga	0.1	0.0	4.9	9.4	11.0	6.1	7.8	13.6	20.4	97,445	209	14,262	208,526	3.0
Ontario	0.6	0.1	7.2	14.2	5.5	8.4	3.7	12.1	20.0	26,160	239	1,815	50,917	5.5
Orange	0.2	0.2	5.6	6.1	7.5	8.8	3.5	14.7	30.8	65,435	172	6,811	143,310	4.6
Orleans	3.0	1.3	4.5	20.8	D	5.1	3.8	D	39.9	9,610	233	954	18,589	0.9
Oswego	0.2	0.1	8.7	11.7	D	7.6	2.3	10.7	29.7	27,250	229	3,298	54,523	1.7
Otsego	0.4	D	4.2	4.9	3.4	8.8	6.7	27.6	23.9	14,675	243	1,356	31,322	1.7
Putnam	0.0	0.0	12.7	D	8.9	5.0	3.4	17.4	25.4	18,555	187	801	38,645	1.2
Queens	0.0	D	12.5	2.9	4.4	5.6	7.2	14.4	19.9	333,420	142	71,962	857,157	2.6
Rensselaer	0.1	0.2	8.2	11.2	8.1	5.8	3.8	12.2	26.0	33,595	210	4,089	73,130	2.3
Richmond	0.0	0.0	11.5	D	5.8	7.6	4.6	22.8	22.5	89,470	187	14,906	180,599	2.2
Rockland	0.0	D	7.9	8.6	10.8	7.0	4.3	15.4	21.2	55,625	170	5,063	106,216	2.1
St. Lawrence	1.5	0.1	4.4	8.3	3.1	7.0	2.3	D	38.6	25,710	234	3,668	53,290	2.2
Saratoga	0.2	D	8.0	13.7	10.4	6.6	9.3	10.2	18.1	47,685	210	2,745	106,328	7.8
Schenectady	0.0	D	4.4	13.4	19.3	5.5	4.4	13.8	18.3	33,195	214	5,328	69,739	2.2
Schoharie	0.4	D	11.2	3.7	3.3	7.4	5.5	9.5	35.1	7,100	226	649	17,552	1.9
Schuyler	3.2	D	9.8	19.2	3.2	7.4	D	11.3	23.7	4,900	272	396	9,793	3.6
Seneca	1.2	D	4.1	26.4	D	8.7	2.1	D	33.0	8,115	233	784	16,423	2.4
Steuben	0.9	0.2	2.5	15.0	16.6	5.1	3.1	9.5	22.0	23,785	246	2,840	49,497	1.3
Suffolk	0.2	0.1	8.6	8.1	10.4	6.7	9.2	11.8	21.0	291,760	195	20,359	576,047	1.1
Sullivan	0.1	0.6	5.6	4.6	3.4	6.3	4.2	19.8	34.8	17,855	237	2,677	50,693	3.1
Tioga	0.3	1.1	4.4	40.8	D	5.5	2.1	5.2	19.8	12,120	248	1,111	22,566	1.8
Tompkins	0.3	0.9	2.6	7.5	8.6	5.0	3.6	D	13.9	15,985	153	1,517	43,453	4.2
Ulster	0.4	0.2	6.6	6.4	5.7	8.3	4.1	13.3	30.8	41,170	229	4,110	85,131	1.8
Warren	0.0	0.4	6.9	12.3	8.2	8.9	5.7	15.9	15.3	18,405	285	1,565	40,049	3.4
Washington	2.4	0.6	7.2	19.0	D	7.0	1.7	7.9	39.2	14,655	237	1,597	29,515	2.3
Wayne	2.9	0.3	7.5	23.6	2.8	6.4	2.3	7.2	28.6	22,890	252	2,210	41,758	1.7
Westchester	0.0	D	7.3	5.6	14.5	4.9	11.7	13.7	17.3	167,970	172	17,550	374,901	1.1
Wyoming	5.5	D	4.4	13.0	D	6.7	2.4	D	41.5	9,220	228	666	18,136	0.9
Yates	6.7	D	8.7	15.6	D	7.9	3.1	D	20.8	6,195	248	473	13,847	2.6
NORTH CAROLINA	1.1	0.1	6.0	11.7	10.9	6.1	8.1	10.2	19.0	2,020,386	199	233,432	4,622,575	6.8
Alamance	0.1	0.1	6.1	16.2	4.4	8.6	5.6	20.4	11.3	34,065	214	3,465	70,665	6.1
Alexander	12.0	D	4.7	32.1	D	4.5	2.9	D	20.2	9,330	250	639	16,432	1.5
Alleghany	7.8	D	9.3	16.0	2.6	7.8	3.5	D	17.4	3,475	317	336	8,170	1.3
Anson	12.8	D	3.5	18.4	D	4.6	1.5	D	27.8	5,925	236	1,004	11,606	0.3
Ashe	8.0	D	14.8	9.6	D	8.1	4.2	11.7	14.5	8,030	300	803	17,718	2.5
Avery	3.2	D	8.4	1.1	D	7.4	4.2	D	24.2	4,500	257	404	14,204	2.2
Beaufort	2.2	0.0	4.6	21.6	4.7	7.8	4.3	8.4	17.1	14,155	299	1,873	26,118	5.8
Bertie	10.0	D	D	D	D	2.8	D	D	26.1	5,925	305	1,216	9,873	0.5
Bladen	11.8	0.0	2.9	40.5	D	3.7	1.8	D	17.8	8,540	253	1,519	17,907	1.1
Brunswick	1.7	D	10.0	4.7	7.8	8.5	5.4	10.9	16.6	42,870	339	2,274	88,977	14.8
Buncombe	0.5	0.1	5.9	11.1	8.5	8.0	5.9	21.2	13.8	59,155	232	5,659	124,112	9.5
Burke	1.1	D	3.5	26.5	2.8	5.4	3.5	17.2	24.7	22,085	249	2,021	41,191	0.8
Cabarrus	0.6	D	7.0	9.0	5.7	8.4	4.1	6.6	21.8	34,285	170	3,187	79,443	10.5
Caldwell	0.4	D	4.9	24.7	2.7	7.0	2.3	11.5	16.8	20,585	252	1,959	38,022	0.9
Camden	3.7	0.1	9.6	4.1	D	4.2	D	D	27.6	2,110	202	127	4,257	3.7
Carteret	0.2	D	7.0	4.3	6.2	12.9	6.7	10.9	24.2	18,920	275	1,212	50,146	4.1
Caswell	15.0	D	9.1	8.9	D	3.6	D	D	32.5	6,420	282	723	10,832	1.9
Catawba	0.6	D	3.6	27.8	4.8	8.1	3.3	9.9	11.7	37,505	239	3,062	68,885	1.2
Chatham	3.3	D	6.8	12.1	10.8	7.6	0.0	13.2	16.5	17,865	256	909	32,043	11.5
Cherokee	3.4	D	9.0	9.6	7.4	9.8	5.3	D	20.7	9,925	356	847	18,261	4.3

1. Per 1,000 resident population estimated as of July 1 of the year shown.

Table B. States and Counties — **Housing, Labor Force, and Employment**

	Housing units, 2017 (cont.)								Civilian labor force, 2017				Civilian employment[6], 2012-2016		
	Occupied units										Unemployment		Percent		
		Owner-occupied				Renter-occupied									
				Median owner cost as a percent of income											
STATE County	Total	Percent	Median value[1]	With a mortgage	Without a mortgage[2]	Median rent[3]	Median rent as a percent of income[2]	Sub-standard units[4] (percent)	Total	Percent change, 2016-2017	Total	Rate[5]	Total	Management, business, science, and arts	Construction, production, and maintenance occupations
	89	90	91	92	93	94	95	96	97	98	99	100	101	102	103
NEW YORK— Cont'd															
Genesee	23,825	73.3	108,700	19.9	13.3	716	28.3	1.5	29,723	-0.7	1,448	4.9	29,799	30.7	28.2
Greene	17,125	75.3	175,900	24.5	14.5	856	35.8	2.1	20,757	0.3	1,092	5.3	19,600	34.1	23.9
Hamilton	1,239	85.1	165,500	22.3	13.0	733	22.1	2.5	2,328	-2.1	176	7.6	1,889	29.8	26.6
Herkimer	25,670	70.4	97,300	19.4	12.9	636	25.9	2.0	28,294	-0.2	1,634	5.8	28,992	31.9	23.9
Jefferson	43,428	56.0	144,400	20.5	12.7	943	28.7	2.3	45,455	-1.1	2,978	6.6	45,323	31.6	21.4
Kings	938,803	29.4	590,500	31.5	15.1	1,262	32.7	11.1	1,245,943	0.6	57,829	4.6	1,192,489	39.6	14.8
Lewis	10,307	76.2	122,000	19.7	12.0	708	31.3	1.6	11,727	-0.8	788	6.7	11,818	30.1	35.3
Livingston	24,217	73.3	123,000	20.8	13.7	722	32.0	2.0	31,071	-0.6	1,579	5.1	29,711	36.1	25.3
Madison	26,121	75.4	128,000	21.3	13.2	728	27.0	1.5	32,802	-0.4	1,830	5.6	33,289	36.4	22.4
Monroe	300,289	63.8	140,200	20.9	13.2	843	32.7	1.4	364,394	-0.4	18,193	5.0	364,564	42.5	16.1
Montgomery	19,540	66.7	99,100	21.9	16.3	721	31.3	2.6	22,656	0.9	1,313	5.8	21,845	28.4	28.9
Nassau	440,230	80.3	451,700	27.7	18.4	1,603	33.6	2.7	707,997	0.5	29,365	4.1	672,155	43.8	13.9
New York	753,385	23.1	871,500	18.7	10.0	1,575	28.4	5.9	939,689	0.8	37,956	4.0	892,817	59.8	5.9
Niagara	87,638	71.1	111,500	19.9	13.7	657	29.7	1.2	101,134	0.2	6,284	6.2	100,521	32.4	23.2
Oneida	90,260	66.6	117,600	20.4	13.0	712	29.9	1.7	102,069	-0.3	5,194	5.1	103,299	34.7	21.0
Onondaga	184,925	65.0	137,000	19.9	12.7	797	29.7	1.9	221,699	-0.4	10,500	4.7	222,809	40.6	16.3
Ontario	44,180	72.6	148,400	20.0	13.5	821	30.5	1.3	55,175	-0.5	2,507	4.5	54,018	39.7	19.8
Orange	125,144	68.2	258,700	26.5	17.0	1,157	35.7	4.0	181,557	0.8	8,344	4.6	172,106	35.2	19.5
Orleans	16,132	75.5	92,000	22.5	15.6	658	31.8	2.5	17,796	-0.4	1,058	5.9	18,024	28.5	32.6
Oswego	45,374	72.4	96,000	20.3	13.1	725	31.5	2.6	53,334	-0.6	3,484	6.5	52,399	29.4	28.2
Otsego	23,539	73.7	140,600	21.8	12.9	775	33.9	3.2	28,231	-0.6	1,435	5.1	28,287	36.0	21.0
Putnam	34,102	82.0	354,800	26.8	16.2	1,307	32.5	2.1	51,333	0.6	2,183	4.3	51,246	41.7	16.8
Queens	779,304	43.8	462,300	30.6	14.4	1,401	33.5	9.7	1,190,292	0.8	47,267	4.0	1,120,583	32.9	18.9
Rensselaer	63,553	64.1	180,700	22.0	13.1	883	29.4	1.7	82,277	0.2	3,669	4.5	80,239	39.5	19.2
Richmond	166,014	69.0	448,000	27.6	15.2	1,191	32.8	4.2	226,924	0.8	10,416	4.6	209,754	39.7	17.0
Rockland	99,038	68.9	420,700	28.3	18.2	1,367	37.7	6.6	154,508	0.6	6,788	4.4	147,646	44.2	13.3
St. Lawrence	41,466	71.4	87,400	19.7	12.7	698	30.7	2.9	43,612	-0.1	2,951	6.8	44,102	33.2	21.6
Saratoga	90,896	71.6	238,600	21.0	12.6	1,026	26.1	0.8	118,482	0.2	4,762	4.0	114,846	44.8	16.2
Schenectady	55,027	67.2	165,000	22.1	13.2	857	32.1	1.3	76,475	0.2	3,467	4.5	73,817	38.4	16.7
Schoharie	12,373	75.1	143,700	23.5	14.7	741	28.8	1.7	14,823	0.0	818	5.5	14,016	32.9	25.8
Schuyler	7,376	78.2	111,300	20.3	13.0	708	28.5	2.7	8,291	-0.5	487	5.9	8,243	34.2	25.7
Seneca	13,672	72.6	98,200	20.2	13.6	735	30.2	1.9	16,266	4.3	748	4.6	15,435	31.1	26.7
Steuben	40,438	70.6	94,300	19.8	12.5	675	26.3	2.2	43,104	-0.8	2,501	5.8	43,222	34.0	26.9
Suffolk	489,758	79.5	376,000	28.1	18.9	1,589	35.8	3.0	782,689	0.4	35,544	4.5	737,128	38.1	18.8
Sullivan	28,007	67.0	165,900	25.8	16.1	862	31.8	2.1	34,590	1.0	1,705	4.9	32,596	30.0	24.1
Tioga	19,705	78.2	112,300	19.2	12.4	661	29.5	1.4	22,978	-0.8	1,190	5.2	22,943	36.2	23.4
Tompkins	38,269	55.3	182,600	21.2	12.6	1,011	34.3	2.4	50,395	-0.6	2,211	4.4	49,581	52.3	12.1
Ulster	69,335	69.7	219,800	25.8	16.6	1,022	35.3	2.1	88,895	0.2	4,097	4.6	85,679	39.6	18.9
Warren	26,944	70.7	191,500	23.0	12.9	879	31.1	1.5	32,188	0.0	1,712	5.3	32,246	34.9	20.2
Washington	24,027	72.3	143,900	23.1	13.8	819	30.8	1.9	28,504	-0.1	1,338	4.7	28,849	27.9	29.0
Wayne	36,576	76.7	115,100	20.9	14.3	716	30.4	1.8	44,024	-0.6	2,221	5.0	43,244	32.7	28.1
Westchester	341,762	61.4	507,300	25.5	17.5	1,394	32.9	4.6	484,107	0.6	22,053	4.6	470,856	46.6	12.8
Wyoming	15,780	75.6	104,200	19.9	12.0	614	27.1	1.1	18,086	-0.8	1,029	5.7	18,490	27.9	31.4
Yates	9,532	77.1	126,900	21.6	12.1	701	31.3	3.1	11,702	-0.8	523	4.5	11,327	31.1	28.0
NORTH CAROLINA	381,5,392	64.8	157,100	21.3	11.3	816	29.7	2.7	4,941,702	1.8	224,868	4.6	4,460,824	36.5	22.6
Alamance	62,053	64.9	143,500	21.3	11.6	757	31.0	3.0	79,767	1.1	3,433	4.3	72,546	32.7	25.9
Alexander	13,796	74.4	125,500	19.7	10.0	595	30.5	4.3	18,159	1.9	667	3.7	15,745	26.0	40.0
Alleghany	4,798	75.6	140,700	24.5	11.9	617	31.3	1.5	4,324	-2.2	223	5.2	4,486	29.0	28.4
Anson	9,511	65.0	79,900	21.5	14.0	659	29.0	4.1	10,545	-1.0	560	5.3	10,151	20.9	40.6
Ashe	11,905	74.0	143,700	23.4	10.7	636	32.3	0.8	12,709	1.7	531	4.2	11,740	26.2	29.8
Avery	6,756	75.7	130,900	24.8	11.5	696	32.6	3.2	7,697	1.7	335	4.4	6,502	29.4	23.4
Beaufort	19,021	69.4	122,100	23.7	13.7	652	29.8	1.7	20,100	-0.9	1,032	5.1	18,983	30.3	30.3
Bertie	7,673	73.6	79,900	23.1	18.8	633	32.0	2.2	8,177	-3.0	497	6.1	7,102	23.7	41.8
Bladen	14,110	68.5	85,700	25.3	14.9	615	34.3	2.8	14,462	-0.6	863	6.0	12,652	24.7	40.1
Brunswick	50,562	75.9	189,500	24.7	12.2	866	32.8	1.9	51,242	3.2	2,901	5.7	46,618	28.5	23.6
Buncombe	102,118	64.2	198,100	22.4	11.3	859	30.7	3.4	136,994	2.1	4,778	3.5	119,156	38.7	19.0
Burke	34,199	70.3	113,600	21.8	10.1	614	28.8	3.3	40,584	1.9	1,736	4.3	36,878	28.2	31.1
Cabarrus	68,289	71.2	171,000	19.9	10.7	837	26.8	3.9	104,403	3.3	4,339	4.2	92,139	37.3	21.7
Caldwell	31,912	70.6	108,900	20.2	11.9	618	29.9	1.8	36,528	1.9	1,651	4.5	34,181	23.7	35.7
Camden	3,804	80.4	216,600	24.6	12.4	1,136	36.4	2.2	4,680	0.6	209	4.5	4,345	37.4	22.0
Carteret	29,563	72.5	197,600	24.0	12.0	847	28.4	1.6	32,040	1.6	1,441	4.5	29,981	35.2	22.2
Caswell	8,874	76.1	99,500	23.3	11.5	535	33.2	2.4	9,731	0.5	473	4.9	9,151	26.1	30.8
Catawba	59,710	68.6	137,600	19.9	10.0	680	28.3	3.2	78,425	2.1	3,302	4.2	70,983	30.6	29.6
Chatham	27,397	77.3	243,900	21.7	11.1	803	29.7	2.1	35,166	2.0	1,365	3.9	29,698	40.5	21.8
Cherokee	10,857	79.7	140,700	24.3	11.1	678	29.2	3.2	11,157	0.2	566	5.1	9,455	27.8	26.3

1. Specified owner-occupied units. 2. A value of 10.0 represents 10 percent or less; a value of 50.0 represents 50 percent or more. 3. Specified renter-occupied units.
4. Overcrowded or lacking complete plumbing facilities. 5. Percent of civilian labor force. 6. Civilian employed persons 16 years old and over.

Table B. States and Counties — Nonfarm Employment and Agriculture

STATE County	Private nonfarm establishments, employment and payroll, 2016									Agriculture, 2012			
	Number of establish-ments	Employment						Annual payroll		Farms			Farm operators whose principal occupation is farming (percent)
		Total	Health care and social assistance	Manufac-turing	Retail trade	Finance and insurance	Professional, scientific, and technical services	Total (mil dol)	Average per employee (dollars)	Number	Percent with:		
											Fewer than 50 acres	500 acres or more	
	104	105	106	107	108	109	110	111	112	113	114	115	116
NEW YORK— Cont'd													
Genesee	1,294	16,567	2,772	3,091	2,846	371	309	582	35,121	549	35.3	12.0	56.5
Greene	1,147	10,475	1,167	852	2,220	336	215	348	33,227	273	31.9	5.9	51.3
Hamilton	199	861	30	D	170	14	4	27	31,455	26	34.6	0.0	42.3
Herkimer	1,112	12,489	2,330	3,130	2,041	315	156	434	34,750	687	21.0	7.9	59.7
Jefferson	2,443	30,183	6,395	2,339	6,710	686	931	1,085	35,961	876	20.5	17.2	57.4
Kings	57,621	606,738	198,133	20,927	75,955	18,402	21,266	24,612	40,564	10	100.0	0.0	60.0
Lewis	532	4,812	1,119	1,138	848	85	85	191	39,794	634	18.3	12.5	60.4
Livingston	1,234	14,046	2,185	2,066	2,544	255	410	454	32,315	661	34.2	14.7	55.8
Madison	1,411	17,284	3,079	2,775	2,554	390	654	610	35,318	838	27.3	10.6	58.2
Monroe	17,744	358,650	67,599	35,726	41,706	13,273	25,746	16,016	44,657	475	54.5	10.1	66.7
Montgomery	1,081	15,201	4,055	3,391	2,611	280	270	550	36,197	659	23.2	9.3	67.2
Nassau	48,260	557,159	119,768	15,892	79,399	33,675	42,030	29,787	53,462	55	90.9	1.8	47.3
New York	104,691	2,245,903	240,993	17,702	149,397	301,457	326,941	241,159	107,377	6	100.0	0.0	0.0
Niagara	4,584	60,907	11,184	8,619	11,307	1,320	1,498	2,170	35,635	760	47.2	7.0	52.9
Oneida	4,902	87,875	19,318	9,595	12,205	6,630	3,695	3,456	39,332	1,066	25.7	8.3	56.7
Onondaga	11,709	218,730	41,919	17,112	29,584	10,782	14,180	9,614	43,956	681	44.1	8.8	54.9
Ontario	2,920	46,743	8,473	6,557	9,349	906	1,405	2,180	46,634	853	40.9	10.6	58.0
Orange	9,456	117,570	23,294	7,822	24,283	2,996	4,470	4,597	39,098	658	42.1	4.6	60.6
Orleans	650	8,144	1,454	2,339	1,113	581	107	274	33,701	487	41.9	9.2	55.2
Oswego	2,138	24,454	4,782	3,081	4,514	615	925	1,021	41,748	657	32.6	5.3	54.5
Otsego	1,409	19,436	5,949	935	3,127	1,136	589	770	39,640	995	26.2	6.8	57.3
Putnam	2,875	20,972	4,951	1,349	3,252	554	1,084	908	43,313	72	72.2	4.2	50.0
Queens	49,597	563,339	127,918	20,396	65,305	22,839	16,748	26,655	47,316	6	66.7	0.0	16.7
Rensselaer	2,997	43,574	8,843	3,501	5,738	1,430	3,576	2,005	46,003	495	34.1	8.7	52.3
Richmond	9,240	101,055	31,303	1,169	16,432	2,578	3,811	4,199	41,547	8	100.0	0.0	50.0
Rockland	10,023	110,957	25,303	7,324	14,436	3,128	5,972	5,112	46,074	23	82.6	0.0	65.2
St. Lawrence	1,921	26,637	6,345	2,048	5,161	662	602	988	37,098	1,303	13.7	10.8	60.2
Saratoga	5,278	69,665	9,801	6,259	11,400	3,795	4,542	3,281	47,094	583	46.5	4.5	61.9
Schenectady	3,060	52,478	11,930	4,256	7,249	2,128	3,953	2,366	45,090	169	41.4	3.6	46.2
Schoharie	578	5,411	947	293	1,078	248	191	193	35,664	532	22.0	6.8	62.0
Schuyler	383	3,604	794	632	652	56	58	134	37,297	393	30.8	5.3	50.4
Seneca	717	8,697	1,216	1,501	2,303	173	102	288	33,081	584	30.5	9.1	69.3
Steuben	1,806	25,943	6,938	3,926	4,067	1,030	1,083	1,269	48,919	1,667	19.3	11.4	51.4
Suffolk	49,149	578,418	98,447	51,925	83,692	22,673	45,817	31,145	53,846	604	70.4	1.5	69.2
Sullivan	1,899	20,221	6,491	970	2,829	624	586	676	33,413	321	38.6	7.2	59.5
Tioga	787	7,691	1,130	1,170	1,217	224	229	265	34,400	536	22.9	8.8	54.1
Tompkins	2,370	49,767	5,710	2,954	4,991	1,119	1,947	1,833	36,841	558	43.9	6.8	50.5
Ulster	4,814	46,586	9,586	3,530	9,247	2,040	1,640	1,649	35,405	486	48.4	5.1	67.3
Warren	2,317	31,682	6,666	3,330	6,050	1,291	856	1,248	39,383	117	60.7	0.0	54.7
Washington	1,052	10,292	1,778	2,932	1,785	207	232	411	39,928	851	31.1	11.6	55.6
Wayne	1,726	19,996	3,060	5,993	3,415	517	701	785	39,246	873	38.3	8.6	62.2
Westchester	31,941	389,632	81,294	12,031	51,054	21,030	25,573	25,047	64,284	131	74.8	1.5	58.8
Wyoming	779	8,752	1,222	1,819	1,432	362	327	302	34,488	713	33.0	14.9	62.8
Yates	518	5,016	907	914	746	90	111	157	31,275	919	27.1	3.6	66.6
NORTH CAROLINA	227,347	3,794,926	582,346	432,538	496,375	182,063	220,467	170,980	45,055	50,218	48.1	6.8	48.9
Alamance	3,215	59,118	12,604	9,922	9,079	1,430	1,320	2,308	39,047	732	42.5	4.6	41.7
Alexander	553	7,620	630	3,737	795	167	244	235	30,786	603	55.4	5.0	53.2
Alleghany	245	2,185	398	496	340	63	37	62	28,311	567	43.0	4.6	49.7
Anson	379	5,274	770	1,698	735	81	92	158	29,930	429	26.8	9.3	55.7
Ashe	540	5,663	1,212	841	1,122	214	68	182	32,121	1,140	47.6	2.1	46.4
Avery	474	4,565	847	107	852	101	76	132	28,994	483	63.1	0.8	46.2
Beaufort	1,099	13,552	2,137	2,397	2,321	406	254	462	34,075	364	39.8	21.7	50.5
Bertie	303	4,473	944	1,663	365	73	33	125	27,919	325	30.8	23.1	64.0
Bladen	509	10,307	1,161	5,872	880	141	136	344	33,398	492	42.3	12.4	53.3
Brunswick	2,448	25,315	3,819	1,409	5,051	635	756	898	35,483	254	52.8	7.1	42.9
Buncombe	8,252	116,660	24,852	11,950	18,956	2,745	4,579	4,564	39,120	1,060	64.8	0.9	51.0
Burke	1,403	22,598	4,476	7,381	3,089	379	401	770	34,060	486	58.8	1.6	50.6
Cabarrus	4,234	61,850	9,030	5,975	12,603	916	1,669	2,350	37,988	589	52.0	4.2	50.1
Caldwell	1,309	19,092	3,668	6,661	2,892	342	313	631	33,047	411	56.9	1.7	44.8
Camden	121	622	43	D	94	14	28	16	25,712	60	41.7	36.7	65.0
Carteret	1,931	18,618	3,301	1,011	4,311	530	532	585	31,408	125	64.8	7.2	48.8
Caswell	235	1,549	369	160	309	47	38	42	27,191	543	32.2	6.6	49.9
Catawba	4,090	82,642	11,950	22,806	10,098	1,281	1,904	3,336	40,368	698	55.6	1.7	41.8
Chatham	1,405	14,023	2,640	2,088	2,253	255	573	469	33,464	1,138	47.0	1.9	45.2
Cherokee	579	6,486	1,093	1,324	1,438	189	319	194	29,964	255	54.1	3.9	54.5

Table B. States and Counties — **Agriculture**

	Agriculture, 2012 (cont.)															
	Land in farms					Value of land and buildings (dollars)			Value of products sold:				Percent of farms with sales of:		Government payments	
			Acres								Percent from:					
STATE County	Acreage (1,000)	Percent change, 2007-2012	Average size of farm	Total irrigated (1,000)	Total cropland (1,000)	Average per farm	Average per acre	Value of machinery and equiopmnet, average per farm (dollars)	Total (mil dol)	Average per farm (acres)	Crops	Livestock and poultry products	$10,000 or more	$100,000 or more	Total ($1,000)	Percent of farms
	117	118	119	120	121	122	123	124	125	126	127	128	129	130	131	132
NEW YORK— Cont'd																
Genesee	187	2.1	341	6.3	143.3	898,004	2,632	213,681	237.0	431,607	36.0	64.0	48.1	25.9	2,111	45.5
Greene	43	-3.0	157	0.7	18.7	588,198	3,736	65,901	22.4	82,022	43.5	56.5	40.3	6.2	911	23.8
Hamilton	2	361.8	80	D	0.3	145,692	1,823	28,538	0.3	13,385	D	D	19.2	7.7	0	0.0
Herkimer	140	0.2	204	0.1	76.4	393,428	1,927	92,482	70.4	102,536	25.1	74.9	57.9	21.0	1,414	32.0
Jefferson	291	10.9	332	0.3	173.5	544,535	1,640	133,429	183.6	209,551	24.7	75.3	51.6	24.1	2,974	31.5
Kings	D	D	D	0.0	D	951,000	D	15,000	2.0	199,300	D	D	60.0	40.0	0	0.0
Lewis	182	8.7	287	0.1	97.2	478,692	1,670	145,063	137.0	216,151	17.2	82.8	64.0	35.3	2,400	37.7
Livingston	195	-12.4	295	0.2	149.6	854,528	2,897	176,086	186.8	282,614	43.2	56.8	44.3	22.5	2,425	41.9
Madison	187	-0.4	224	0.8	111.0	456,792	2,042	116,047	117.7	140,489	26.4	73.6	52.0	24.7	2,231	29.2
Monroe	99	-25.8	208	0.9	79.5	737,682	3,551	142,223	90.6	190,695	89.8	10.2	46.1	19.2	1,331	21.7
Montgomery	131	5.5	199	0.2	85.9	458,426	2,299	108,599	86.8	131,701	24.8	75.2	60.8	22.8	1,523	32.0
Nassau	3	108.2	49	0.1	0.3	894,000	18,333	51,509	6.2	113,546	47.9	52.1	47.3	21.8	0	0.0
New York	D	D	D	0.0	0.0	D	D	47,000	D	D	D	D	16.7	0.0	0	0.0
Niagara	143	0.1	188	3.0	118.5	430,664	2,292	136,736	122.7	161,415	62.2	37.8	45.1	14.9	1,684	27.1
Oneida	205	6.7	192	0.2	118.7	383,145	1,991	109,238	113.2	106,181	37.3	62.7	48.2	21.7	2,155	31.5
Onondaga	150	-0.2	221	1.3	101.8	696,072	3,155	166,094	152.1	223,275	31.8	68.2	50.2	19.2	1,688	32.5
Ontario	193	-3.2	226	0.9	148.2	727,475	3,222	149,744	180.3	211,402	42.8	57.2	53.0	25.2	2,675	32.8
Orange	88	8.7	134	2.7	45.8	740,827	5,537	116,939	100.7	153,035	71.5	28.5	59.3	22.9	2,006	27.8
Orleans	135	-3.3	277	4.6	109.5	720,725	2,598	232,292	150.3	308,672	92.1	7.9	46.0	25.5	1,883	39.4
Oswego	94	-6.0	143	0.6	45.4	289,994	2,022	85,426	47.6	72,454	47.3	52.7	39.7	11.6	555	17.8
Otsego	181	2.4	182	0.2	85.5	407,769	2,245	80,409	66.8	67,096	35.6	64.4	42.7	15.8	1,391	21.8
Putnam	6	4.8	82	D	1.6	448,681	5,468	42,181	3.3	45,222	92.2	7.8	29.2	13.9	24	6.9
Queens	0	D	74	0.0	0.4	377,833	5,129	82,333	0.2	26,833	95.7	5.0	100.0	0.0	0	0.0
Rensselaer	89	4.4	179	0.6	50.6	616,113	3,436	104,002	53.1	107,204	52.9	47.1	48.3	16.0	733	30.5
Richmond	D	D	D	0.0	D	440,750	D	D	1.0	120,125	100.0	0.0	50.0	50.0	0	0.0
Rockland	1	D	23	0.1	0.2	1,980,870	86,616	71,913	1.7	75,391	96.5	3.5	56.5	21.7	0	0.0
St. Lawrence	357	2.8	274	0.6	172.1	388,063	1,417	95,682	187.4	143,794	20.7	79.3	48.3	16.7	2,569	20.7
Saratoga	79	4.2	135	0.3	43.8	647,986	4,791	109,096	80.0	137,166	24.3	75.7	43.2	12.9	613	14.2
Schenectady	20	3.9	118	0.1	9.1	406,036	3,454	77,172	4.2	24,621	70.7	29.3	36.7	5.3	101	7.1
Schoharie	98	3.0	185	0.7	55.0	421,389	2,279	86,735	39.5	74,248	39.0	61.0	49.1	13.9	1,105	31.0
Schuyler	69	4.3	176	0.2	38.0	503,155	2,857	92,982	44.5	113,160	29.1	70.9	47.6	17.6	375	16.0
Seneca	130	1.7	223	0.4	98.0	656,699	2,945	168,820	118.9	203,640	44.2	55.8	67.1	39.4	1,017	28.9
Steuben	406	9.1	243	1.2	221.7	446,421	1,834	105,887	187.2	112,301	43.4	56.6	44.6	16.4	3,112	29.8
Suffolk	36	4.6	60	11.8	23.2	696,702	11,697	138,692	239.8	397,050	85.3	14.7	63.7	32.0	790	7.1
Sullivan	54	6.8	168	0.1	22.8	617,897	3,683	74,601	27.1	84,424	15.0	85.0	44.5	13.1	274	18.1
Tioga	108	1.0	201	0.7	50.7	396,076	1,968	83,879	36.7	68,560	30.8	69.2	42.2	14.6	1,112	36.9
Tompkins	91	-16.5	163	0.3	54.4	448,507	2,757	113,717	67.4	120,772	33.7	66.3	43.7	16.1	900	25.8
Ulster	71	-5.3	147	4.2	26.1	738,835	5,042	103,237	55.9	115,019	83.0	17.0	43.0	12.6	328	10.1
Warren	10	11.4	81	0.1	1.5	325,487	3,997	58,376	D	D	D	D	28.2	11.1	D	0.9
Washington	189	-6.6	223	0.6	101.9	539,925	2,426	111,270	139.1	163,510	19.4	80.6	53.3	21.0	2,914	28.6
Wayne	179	6.3	205	1.9	126.3	508,517	2,479	166,179	205.6	235,517	72.7	27.3	60.5	31.2	2,084	27.5
Westchester	8	-9.0	59	0.1	1.5	952,855	16,102	104,863	8.8	67,176	47.6	52.4	46.6	17.6	D	2.3
Wyoming	226	3.6	317	3.4	159.5	828,938	2,617	216,229	318.5	446,711	24.5	75.5	52.7	29.3	3,057	35.1
Yates	127	0.7	138	0.6	88.1	546,444	3,956	115,875	117.0	127,336	37.6	62.4	75.1	45.8	1,081	17.1
NORTH CAROLINA	8,415	-0.7	168	174.5	4,745.0	726,944	4,338	92,882	12,588.1	250,670	34.2	65.8	37.3	16.6	120,129	28.7
Alamance	84	-4.9	114	0.9	31.8	538,171	4,715	60,452	32.9	44,986	46.8	53.2	30.3	9.2	470	17.5
Alexander	59	6.7	97	0.6	20.9	578,788	5,949	70,687	187.7	311,227	5.8	94.2	45.6	28.9	177	6.8
Alleghany	91	18.6	160	D	32.9	770,166	4,803	70,547	36.3	64,092	56.6	43.4	44.1	11.5	590	23.1
Anson	84	-7.9	195	1.1	28.3	725,956	3,725	97,247	193.9	451,900	8.7	91.3	49.4	30.3	551	36.6
Ashe	112	3.7	99	0.2	33.1	561,065	5,687	54,833	54.5	47,790	74.4	25.6	38.1	7.9	216	10.4
Avery	28	1.5	58	0.4	11.6	407,195	6,968	55,195	17.2	35,607	96.1	3.9	44.5	8.1	71	4.8
Beaufort	148	-7.5	407	2.6	129.3	1,244,750	3,056	218,201	121.6	334,074	84.7	15.3	49.2	34.6	3,011	71.7
Bertie	147	-0.4	452	4.2	95.4	1,220,674	2,703	219,246	225.2	692,822	37.4	62.6	68.9	49.2	3,200	74.8
Bladen	117	-7.7	238	4.6	52.9	784,878	3,291	106,965	308.5	627,110	19.3	80.7	46.7	26.2	1,102	38.8
Brunswick	45	3.1	179	1.2	27.4	769,642	4,302	92,492	58.2	229,197	48.0	52.0	34.3	12.6	427	24.8
Buncombe	71	-0.8	67	0.9	17.2	580,025	8,601	48,772	54.4	51,333	72.1	27.9	22.0	4.1	1,481	17.4
Burke	34	18.3	71	1.8	12.9	376,290	5,318	50,689	45.4	93,364	25.0	75.0	30.5	9.9	70	4.5
Cabarrus	66	-0.8	112	0.3	29.9	823,779	7,325	65,380	55.9	94,829	24.8	75.2	25.3	6.3	427	14.3
Caldwell	32	-1.6	78	0.4	11.8	430,625	5,521	45,667	17.8	43,294	53.7	46.3	26.0	7.3	145	6.6
Camden	49	-10.6	822	0.0	46.8	2,334,567	2,841	450,750	48.9	815,217	D	D	56.7	40.0	603	40.0
Carteret	63	13.4	503	0.2	45.5	1,653,072	3,288	92,024	29.2	233,656	98.9	1.2	33.6	15.2	363	18.4
Caswell	97	-5.1	179	1.7	24.8	514,319	2,877	64,361	34.2	63,063	51.7	48.3	29.3	8.5	946	35.4
Catawba	67	-6.7	96	0.7	29.3	519,109	5,400	59,158	67.3	96,430	29.4	70.6	32.2	9.6	447	16.0
Chatham	112	7.3	98	1.2	26.7	487,262	4,961	47,006	163.9	144,033	5.5	94.5	40.3	11.0	546	11.6
Cherokee	21	5.0	84	D	7.6	483,376	5,746	59,451	D	D	D	D	23.1	5.5	232	14.1

Table B. States and Counties — Water Use, Wholesale Trade, Retail Trade, and Real Estate

STATE County	Water use, 2015		Wholesale Trade[1], 2012				Retail Trade[2], 2012				Real estate and rental and leasing,[2] 2012			
	Public supply water withdrawn (mil gal/day)	Public supply gallons withdrawn per person per day	Number of establishments	Number of employees	Sales (mil dol)	Annual payroll (mil dol)	Number of establishments	Number of employees	Sales (mil dol)	Annual payroll (mil dol)	Number of establishments	Number of employees	Sales (mil dol)	Annual payroll (mil dol)
	133	134	135	136	137	138	139	140	141	142	143	144	145	146
NEW YORK— Cont'd														
Genesee	3.74	63.5	76	1,165	1,187.1	51.6	219	2,561	785.8	59.1	29	150	25.2	5.1
Greene	3.07	64.5	27	1,007	724.6	63.0	198	2,329	610.4	53.8	43	181	27.1	7.7
Hamilton	0.75	159.2	NA	NA	NA	NA	33	169	41.6	4.3	7	8	0.9	0.2
Herkimer	28.84	457.1	30	545	162.1	25.3	187	2,016	543.9	44.9	34	113	15.0	2.4
Jefferson	9.29	79.0	67	870	345.2	34.7	476	6,849	1,937.9	161.4	119	588	103.9	17.8
Kings	0.00	0.0	3,457	28,586	16,522.9	1,176.8	9,931	65,979	20,533.1	1,623.7	4,327	15,248	3,765.5	530.6
Lewis	1.81	67.1	7	D	D	D	74	792	258.7	19.8	12	D	D	D
Livingston	3.78	58.4	51	560	458.9	24.0	219	2,501	633.6	55.0	40	206	22.9	5.8
Madison	1.22	17.0	36	434	151.0	16.9	222	2,688	745.5	61.9	43	148	12.1	3.5
Monroe	53.54	71.4	788	10,459	6,131.6	562.0	2,349	40,491	9,494.1	902.0	835	6,237	1,091.2	233.4
Montgomery	2.61	52.6	44	D	D	D	179	2,461	673.3	55.4	22	80	10.2	1.9
Nassau	194.47	142.9	2,856	28,767	27,959.1	1,860.3	6,145	77,488	24,105.6	2,206.3	2,331	9,580	3,054.1	532.1
New York	0.00	0.0	7,678	84,273	128,760.9	6,385.0	11,691	148,493	44,040.0	5,027.8	9,627	70,399	33,323.0	4,826.9
Niagara	49.46	232.6	179	2,187	1,506.4	95.0	735	10,233	2,521.6	212.7	144	563	81.8	16.1
Oneida	32.82	141.2	175	2,081	1,087.5	90.9	830	11,889	3,012.2	263.6	170	686	111.9	20.0
Onondaga	58.04	123.9	591	10,750	17,113.3	559.0	1,682	28,932	6,916.0	639.1	588	3,756	662.3	150.5
Ontario	46.53	424.7	113	1,285	660.2	65.9	527	9,194	2,021.4	193.8	94	423	53.8	10.1
Orange	33.04	87.5	455	6,661	8,298.4	304.8	1,512	23,117	6,221.1	530.6	374	1,407	407.3	51.5
Orleans	1.64	39.4	17	281	130.4	14.3	95	1,097	252.4	22.6	20	61	9.4	1.3
Oswego	34.87	290.2	58	504	368.3	21.8	353	4,392	1,258.4	101.6	69	205	29.6	5.0
Otsego	3.10	51.1	46	460	308.8	19.6	290	3,373	917.0	78.7	53	215	32.7	6.9
Putnam	2.82	28.5	101	905	516.3	50.3	329	3,037	952.2	79.7	89	209	33.9	7.9
Queens	0.00	0.0	2,971	24,171	16,059.4	1,250.3	7,388	59,829	17,003.2	1,542.4	2,840	11,679	3,100.3	509.9
Rensselaer	21.61	134.8	101	1,200	2,270.2	67.3	424	5,814	1,572.2	138.4	101	464	103.0	15.5
Richmond	0.00	0.0	342	1,416	1,460.0	75.0	1,273	15,926	3,816.0	353.5	312	1,151	377.5	43.8
Rockland	33.18	101.8	504	4,697	3,892.0	282.0	1,154	14,253	4,153.7	382.2	443	1,498	281.1	55.0
St. Lawrence	6.95	62.6	46	446	175.0	19.9	414	5,139	1,446.6	116.3	57	167	32.7	5.0
Saratoga	26.12	115.4	176	3,133	2,332.0	181.5	724	10,871	2,980.0	250.5	213	975	233.2	33.5
Schenectady	23.51	152.1	78	774	519.3	37.3	480	7,256	1,821.1	167.3	111	510	112.4	19.5
Schoharie	173.82	5,548.0	19	118	54.9	4.4	95	1,049	319.0	23.9	15	46	7.2	1.5
Schuyler	0.83	45.6	3	D	D	D	59	633	141.4	12.9	5	D	D	D
Seneca	4.41	126.6	27	410	202.5	13.1	183	2,360	489.9	43.9	19	77	26.0	1.9
Steuben	7.50	76.8	40	277	122.4	9.3	326	4,238	1,074.0	95.9	51	232	32.5	8.7
Suffolk	246.12	163.9	2,838	37,819	32,383.0	2,260.5	6,524	79,498	23,693.4	2,182.4	1,677	6,519	1,868.5	303.8
Sullivan	89.77	1,198.9	43	584	363.6	21.5	291	2,673	771.5	66.5	111	398	55.5	9.6
Tioga	3.45	69.8	25	331	396.9	14.3	132	1,367	372.9	32.4	12	23	3.3	0.6
Tompkins	7.87	75.0	36	454	259.0	21.6	349	5,071	1,112.0	105.5	112	609	121.6	20.5
Ulster	394.23	2,188.4	159	1,504	810.4	71.3	733	8,606	2,324.9	211.8	195	732	116.6	22.0
Warren	11.56	178.7	59	575	190.4	21.0	447	6,436	1,549.1	149.5	74	240	45.0	8.9
Washington	2.59	41.6	30	D	D	D	186	1,759	498.8	42.4	17	46	4.8	1.0
Wayne	7.84	85.7	62	607	245.7	22.7	267	3,276	822.6	75.5	58	223	24.7	4.2
Westchester	65.43	67.0	1,286	16,494	20,313.9	1,493.5	3,802	48,739	14,514.2	1,395.5	1,966	8,041	2,436.5	399.2
Wyoming	3.26	79.5	26	219	121.9	9.8	128	1,479	376.0	33.0	18	99	11.3	2.8
Yates	1.10	43.9	10	127	41.0	3.4	92	814	208.9	17.8	22	79	10.2	2.5
NORTH CAROLINA	938.01	93.4	9,713	136,174	105,275.6	7,853.7	34,288	446,373	120,691.0	10,421.2	10,140	47,155	9,301.7	1,942.6
Alamance	15.35	97.0	143	1,642	627.2	70.0	624	8,756	2,108.4	178.0	119	607	142.0	24.4
Alexander	0.03	0.8	17	111	47.8	4.5	86	834	194.8	17.6	10	18	1.6	0.3
Alleghany	0.31	28.6	3	4	1.1	0.7	41	296	67.9	5.9	10	19	1.7	0.3
Anson	8.80	341.6	11	203	109.4	10.3	73	726	181.3	14.7	9	D	D	D
Ashe	0.67	24.8	22	214	101.9	7.0	106	1,020	273.0	22.4	24	48	7.9	1.8
Avery	1.57	88.8	18	D	D	D	82	742	195.5	15.6	32	D	D	D
Beaufort	4.31	90.4	51	477	360.7	20.7	189	2,300	548.4	51.4	36	133	16.6	2.8
Bertie	1.68	83.2	14	126	145.6	4.7	50	357	95.9	6.7	4	5	0.2	0.1
Bladen	37.35	1,088.4	22	174	226.7	6.9	91	823	199.5	15.9	14	27	5.2	0.7
Brunswick	2.80	22.8	69	544	237.1	21.6	371	4,423	1,125.8	100.7	128	556	85.0	20.2
Buncombe	21.12	83.4	265	2,532	1,286.7	110.6	1,135	16,104	3,884.2	381.4	393	1,287	238.0	43.0
Burke	23.00	258.9	48	431	226.2	17.4	260	2,541	680.5	54.9	50	128	15.0	3.0
Cabarrus	17.54	89.1	191	2,454	1,600.3	115.7	708	11,637	2,920.3	247.7	171	645	115.6	18.8
Caldwell	7.16	88.1	64	411	202.3	16.4	256	2,740	701.0	58.2	58	137	16.7	3.4
Camden	0.71	68.9	3	17	4.1	0.4	17	94	24.9	1.7	4	4	1.2	0.1
Carteret	6.97	101.2	47	272	85.7	9.8	363	3,885	972.8	89.3	118	529	63.7	13.5
Caswell	0.43	18.7	5	D	D	D	49	309	63.9	6.5	1	D	D	D
Catawba	4.29	27.7	238	5,320	4,053.8	244.5	715	9,502	2,607.3	222.3	187	534	130.5	17.0
Chatham	25.42	358.4	52	311	115.0	12.6	175	2,089	583.0	43.6	36	80	15.0	2.5
Cherokee	1.73	63.7	15	149	84.4	4.4	130	1,302	363.6	28.6	26	67	15.4	1.8

1. Merchant wholesalers, except manufacturers' sales branches and offices.   2. Employer establishments.

Table B. States and Counties — Professional Services, Manufacturing, and Accommodation and Food Services

STATE County	Professional, scientific, and technical services, 2012				Manufacturing, 2012				Accommodation and food services, 2012			
	Number of establishments	Number of employees	Sales (mil dol)	Annual payroll (mil dol)	Number of establishments	Number of employees	Receipts (mil dol)	Annual payroll (mil dol)	Number of establishments	Number of employees	Receipts (mil dol)	Annual payroll (mil dol)
	147	148	149	150	151	152	153	154	155	156	157	158
NEW YORK— Cont'd												
Genesee	76	322	28.3	11.5	95	2,632	983.0	125.8	144	1,910	89.9	25.2
Greene	76	258	27.5	9.9	29	735	339.8	D	191	2,675	99.2	29.4
Hamilton	2	D	D	D	3	8	D	D	57	234	22.8	4.8
Herkimer	61	184	18.3	5.9	60	2,561	666.2	119.4	168	1,469	71.3	19.9
Jefferson	142	1,092	115.9	45.4	66	2,247	770.5	102.6	335	4,117	198.8	57.0
Kings	4,346	23,391	3,467.9	1,312.8	1,756	18,296	3,644.1	731.0	4,809	34,099	2,453.4	615.5
Lewis	23	82	9.5	2.5	25	1,371	532.7	58.1	64	480	19.1	5.5
Livingston	98	374	31.7	10.9	55	2,106	635.9	91.1	142	2,123	80.4	23.4
Madison	121	681	66.5	27.7	58	2,407	885.5	109.2	164	2,024	86.4	23.8
Monroe	1,973	21,387	3,187.1	1,263.9	887	38,958	14,610.3	2,315.5	1,662	26,555	1,300.3	370.6
Montgomery	61	252	25.1	7.5	74	3,578	839.0	134.3	117	948	49.2	12.0
Nassau	6,835	43,568	6,915.5	2,542.9	1,043	16,580	5,196.7	893.7	3,483	43,996	2,938.8	818.0
New York	17,504	289,103	88,609.6	31,491.6	2,063	21,220	4,970.9	899.1	9,634	206,517	20,382.6	6,032.2
Niagara	325	1,810	234.9	86.1	273	7,987	3,134.9	463.1	521	9,841	1,055.9	183.3
Oneida	408	3,645	555.6	210.0	236	9,807	3,481.3	462.0	559	10,870	791.3	199.6
Onondaga	1,179	13,456	2,065.5	767.9	436	18,565	7,576.0	1,034.6	1,146	18,791	918.7	265.5
Ontario	239	1,469	195.5	79.9	167	6,718	2,671.0	332.4	302	4,879	237.3	72.3
Orange	872	5,909	648.5	248.4	318	7,105	2,592.4	336.9	847	9,601	575.2	150.4
Orleans	35	168	15.0	5.2	36	2,026	764.6	96.5	57	692	28.4	7.9
Oswego	135	546	55.0	19.7	85	2,669	2,131.1	139.6	290	3,599	153.2	41.2
Otsego	116	623	54.1	19.6	58	877	203.8	37.7	210	2,560	148.5	37.6
Putnam	311	1,246	208.6	74.9	87	1,478	308.6	74.3	195	1,604	100.4	26.3
Queens	3,248	13,293	1,585.1	669.1	1,294	22,240	4,438.1	972.5	4,558	40,510	3,139.1	749.9
Rensselaer	280	3,464	460.4	193.0	95	3,383	D	176.2	348	4,009	209.2	58.6
Richmond	873	3,535	663.0	169.2	136	999	285.3	44.8	770	7,805	472.6	109.8
Rockland	1,272	5,270	1,616.3	341.6	251	8,416	9,613.2	601.3	769	7,762	501.2	140.1
St. Lawrence	107	611	55.8	21.1	77	2,639	1,302.9	149.6	256	2,904	131.6	34.0
Saratoga	605	3,852	608.6	210.2	138	5,259	1,977.4	331.6	524	8,089	446.4	128.6
Schenectady	276	3,772	207.5	284.3	110	4,490	1,709.3	283.0	339	3,846	191.7	54.9
Schoharie	36	208	18.4	6.5	21	239	D	9.5	62	459	23.1	6.5
Schuyler	15	38	2.5	0.7	35	574	D	30.4	62	572	34.9	9.2
Seneca	35	139	14.4	3.8	40	1,318	674.2	68.8	72	744	35.3	11.0
Steuben	133	1,707	89.4	157.7	77	4,314	1,237.0	212.9	223	2,562	132.2	34.0
Suffolk	5,622	43,771	6,531.9	2,657.2	2,067	51,967	15,887.4	2,800.5	3,624	45,646	2,990.4	810.8
Sullivan	167	D	D	D	51	1,224	354.0	41.0	243	1,572	139.6	34.7
Tioga	55	D	D	D	44	1,228	438.2	48.6	89	829	36.2	10.6
Tompkins	274	2,312	356.6	124.1	93	2,766	861.1	150.4	334	4,408	231.7	65.4
Ulster	443	1,601	189.3	69.1	170	3,518	D	170.2	546	6,655	367.3	117.4
Warren	168	876	106.7	40.0	76	3,767	928.9	206.4	413	3,992	306.1	85.9
Washington	61	235	35.1	9.2	87	2,942	1,206.2	152.3	127	758	38.0	9.7
Wayne	105	589	116.2	26.9	137	5,702	1,656.8	241.8	165	1,732	71.7	19.1
Westchester	4,205	28,162	4,976.7	2,187.8	601	11,776	4,492.9	584.9	2,460	26,862	2,020.0	562.8
Wyoming	62	351	41.9	10.8	44	1,878	473.7	76.3	81	747	31.7	9.0
Yates	31	118	10.6	3.9	44	836	188.5	33.3	55	382	22.7	6.4
NORTH CAROLINA	22,855	196,287	31,947.9	12,940.3	8,953	403,593	202,344.6	18,191.2	19,496	358,602	18,622.3	5,040.6
Alamance	218	1,375	133.0	55.8	200	9,268	3,138.4	399.3	293	5,761	254.4	71.8
Alexander	37	123	11.5	4.2	69	3,284	591.5	107.7	38	D	D	D
Alleghany	12	40	3.1	0.9	17	444	D	15.6	22	211	10.8	3.3
Anson	27	116	10.0	3.2	20	1,428	393.3	54.5	29	401	16.8	4.7
Ashe	24	58	3.5	1.3	20	1,122	232.7	36.1	46	573	23.7	6.7
Avery	29	66	7.2	2.1	13	174	20.5	5.2	59	593	45.6	12.9
Beaufort	88	341	26.2	9.5	64	2,661	1,462.1	152.1	73	1,141	50.1	12.5
Bertie	11	51	4.9	1.5	11	D	D	42.4	15	166	6.5	1.6
Bladen	33	143	17.7	5.0	28	5,565	1,904.3	178.5	46	448	25.6	6.3
Brunswick	196	637	57.7	22.2	71	1,520	1,983.0	101.4	271	3,436	180.8	48.7
Buncombe	873	4,336	473.4	206.2	287	13,805	2,839.5	590.9	735	14,976	880.1	254.3
Burke	110	464	44.3	16.3	126	7,475	2,804.6	288.8	127	2,102	97.2	25.2
Cabarrus	338	1,505	193.8	73.3	162	5,427	1,757.9	237.4	346	8,214	428.0	113.7
Caldwell	79	324	31.9	10.5	121	6,098	1,158.1	197.1	117	D	D	D
Camden	7	28	3.0	1.5	NA	NA	NA	NA	3	28	1.5	0.4
Carteret	122	447	49.2	18.9	61	981	343.7	32.9	229	3,318	164.4	48.3
Caswell	13	37	3.5	1.4	9	172	33.3	5.6	13	D	D	D
Catawba	322	1,627	654.5	71.2	411	20,830	5,850.9	809.8	342	6,737	290.7	83.7
Chatham	145	468	59.6	22.2	72	1,538	487.4	66.7	103	1,674	91.3	25.5
Cherokee	37	250	15.7	8.3	26	1,168	317.1	41.8	61	817	41.0	11.3

Table B. States and Counties — Health Care and Social Assistance, Other Services, Nonemployer Businesses, and Residential Construction

STATE County	Health care and social assistance, 2012				Other services, 2012				Nonemployer businesses, 2015		Value of residential construction authorized by building permits, 2017	
	Number of establishments	Number of employees	Receipts (mil dol)	Annual payroll (mil dol)	Number of establishments	Number of employees	Receipts (mil dol)	Annual payroll (mil dol)	Number	Receipts (mil dol)	New construction ($1,000)	Number of housing units
	159	160	161	162	163	164	165	166	167	168	169	170
NEW YORK— Cont'd												
Genesee	141	3,053	221.6	98.7	100	626	51.8	15.0	2,924	126.3	7,660	36
Greene	94	1,254	88.1	38.8	83	373	32.7	8.2	3,417	139.8	17,488	83
Hamilton	6	25	1.7	0.8	7	D	D	D	479	19.9	5,756	35
Herkimer	109	2,334	184.1	70.5	94	552	32.1	8.3	3,294	133.4	13,766	56
Jefferson	277	6,183	536.8	247.5	187	912	83.3	21.0	5,164	206.7	14,576	141
Kings	6,394	184,851	16,419.6	7,123.6	4,675	18,153	1,622.5	431.4	263,777	11,593.7	822,800	6,130
Lewis	49	1,071	83.2	41.4	43	164	21.1	4.7	1,676	73.0	8,535	59
Livingston	143	2,019	140.2	61.2	88	337	39.3	8.6	3,552	147.3	15,556	137
Madison	166	3,027	272.9	110.7	98	349	30.6	7.1	4,274	167.0	18,695	99
Monroe	1,949	63,159	5,819.8	2,425.3	1,151	7,580	772.3	209.4	44,438	2,054.7	190,990	1,097
Montgomery	177	3,970	356.9	149.6	87	558	57.5	15.4	2,409	87.4	9,264	49
Nassau	5,771	111,832	13,166.2	5,522.1	4,068	21,377	2,140.6	587.0	136,547	9,394.4	468,220	1,487
New York	8,106	251,513	34,680.5	13,322.5	9,778	92,777	21,846.1	4,572.6	225,955	18,263.9	632,871	4,781
Niagara	512	10,096	789.4	345.9	341	1,593	109.0	31.0	9,638	378.2	51,929	238
Oneida	615	19,043	1,636.6	730.7	407	3,677	219.0	74.3	12,141	486.1	48,095	291
Onondaga	1,294	38,389	4,379.2	1,717.8	876	5,965	613.6	178.1	27,513	1,292.0	153,041	943
Ontario	274	8,001	685.0	340.7	211	1,252	98.6	30.5	6,872	304.9	86,493	383
Orange	961	20,593	2,176.8	957.3	749	3,963	460.3	108.4	24,613	1,149.2	178,613	1,021
Orleans	78	1,544	96.0	46.2	63	209	20.6	4.7	1,775	70.3	2,880	17
Oswego	206	4,897	347.9	156.5	183	699	57.4	13.7	5,441	189.3	20,031	117
Otsego	170	6,049	675.4	281.4	103	617	51.3	11.6	4,321	167.4	6,527	37
Putnam	261	5,055	559.1	239.5	233	1,035	118.0	32.3	9,048	454.6	15,553	51
Queens	5,047	122,646	12,103.5	5,098.2	4,645	19,428	1,863.4	500.0	243,480	9,284.7	690,157	5,104
Rensselaer	354	9,708	732.3	349.1	244	1,361	122.5	48.0	8,769	349.8	35,055	175
Richmond	1,308	30,614	2,960.7	1,274.1	869	3,779	342.3	85.5	35,265	1,602.7	128,136	685
Rockland	1,164	22,289	2,083.5	900.8	731	4,364	350.9	106.5	27,296	1,662.6	116,497	592
St. Lawrence	260	6,640	581.7	259.6	170	706	64.8	14.5	4,942	183.0	16,066	128
Saratoga	544	8,412	761.2	317.9	321	1,668	145.3	45.5	15,563	764.3	254,084	1,122
Schenectady	435	11,854	1,005.7	439.2	205	D	D	D	8,481	337.4	30,438	260
Schoharie	62	1,039	69.9	30.7	31	D	D	D	1,840	69.0	4,115	28
Schuyler	39	836	57.5	27.4	34	D	D	D	1,177	38.4	7,834	56
Seneca	63	1,335	82.0	40.4	49	233	19.1	4.6	1,810	74.8	4,450	26
Steuben	238	5,701	488.2	227.8	148	663	59.6	14.5	5,222	206.3	21,538	222
Suffolk	4,736	95,248	10,416.2	4,491.2	3,945	19,049	2,048.8	520.1	127,010	7,166.4	639,240	1,138
Sullivan	250	5,491	412.0	186.4	160	456	66.6	12.0	5,649	235.9	50,749	293
Tioga	68	1,045	54.3	26.7	65	205	20.3	4.8	2,766	105.1	5,755	46
Tompkins	271	5,283	483.0	199.8	152	966	122.9	23.9	7,389	276.1	70,361	468
Ulster	514	8,991	741.4	312.4	322	1,229	114.9	28.6	16,327	691.2	81,827	336
Warren	283	6,574	569.0	261.1	140	817	84.1	26.0	4,727	225.9	45,848	174
Washington	105	1,535	96.2	44.5	78	271	28.6	7.7	3,714	148.8	23,536	90
Wayne	151	3,061	215.0	102.9	133	434	36.2	9.0	4,759	193.5	14,991	84
Westchester	3,592	79,057	9,638.2	4,111.1	2,819	15,205	2,013.8	539.3	95,840	6,412.8	327,888	1,167
Wyoming	68	1,183	94.2	40.9	62	246	21.7	5.7	2,054	89.5	20,014	152
Yates	50	975	64.1	28.0	45	147	12.3	2.7	1,951	94.1	16,626	60
NORTH CAROLINA	22,977	529,570	55,227.5	21,757.0	13,716	80,710	9,141.5	2,321.3	722,639	30,019.8	12,693,597	67,047
Alamance	379	8,367	801.9	369.4	190	1,097	100.7	29.2	9,727	371.5	166,356	1,223
Alexander	43	559	33.5	14.6	36	139	9.8	2.1	2,254	81.3	22,392	87
Alleghany	27	517	31.1	13.8	10	D	D	D	899	36.2	4,743	18
Anson	45	826	50.7	24.7	21	D	D	D	1,252	42.3	6,444	43
Ashe	51	1,136	73.3	35.1	32	118	10.4	2.8	2,425	96.6	22,880	95
Avery	41	746	72.2	25.4	25	180	20.4	5.1	1,668	60.8	40,684	92
Beaufort	120	2,392	186.5	77.6	80	384	32.1	8.6	3,259	125.4	21,533	179
Bertie	57	1,344	63.4	28.5	18	62	5.3	1.4	890	25.2	1,572	12
Bladen	56	998	52.7	19.8	29	D	D	D	1,734	55.3	8,673	41
Brunswick	221	3,576	326.6	127.5	119	463	45.3	12.0	10,217	421.7	750,548	3,342
Buncombe	844	20,510	2,518.2	1,012.7	456	2,461	261.7	69.8	26,258	1,110.9	419,846	1,900
Burke	187	4,495	461.5	183.6	99	434	41.1	11.1	5,238	195.8	33,405	187
Cabarrus	343	6,008	568.1	244.2	266	1,435	119.0	31.6	14,505	543.7	252,955	1,657
Caldwell	132	2,924	234.4	88.5	79	397	39.0	10.9	4,961	185.9	26,236	108
Camden	5	24	1.4	0.6	7	D	D	D	671	19.8	13,426	52
Carteret	191	3,165	283.7	120.4	143	598	51.3	15.5	6,408	275.9	126,720	631
Caswell	29	467	23.7	11.6	14	D	D	D	1,081	36.0	7,046	38
Catawba	382	11,445	1,153.6	446.6	223	1,410	109.8	31.8	10,603	505.0	87,925	498
Chatham	127	2,581	179.1	67.4	83	306	36.8	8.7	5,895	265.3	202,317	748
Cherokee	76	1,217	96.7	41.9	35	103	7.6	2.2	2,227	78.9	23,414	164

Table B. States and Counties — **Land Area and Population**

State / county code	CBSA code[1]	County code[2]	STATE County	Population, 2017				Population and population characteristics, 2017										
								Race alone or in combination, not Hispanic or Latino (percent)					Age (percent)					
				Land area[3] (sq. mi)	Total persons 2017	Rank	Per square mile	White	Black	American Indian, Alaska Native	Asian and Pacific Islancer	Percent Hispanic or Latino[4]	Under 5 years	5 to 17 years	18 to 24 years	25 to 34 years	35 to 44 years	45 to 54 years
				1	2	3	4	5	6	7	8	9	10	11	12	13	14	15
			NORTH CAROLINA— Cont'd															
37,173		8	Swain	527.7	14,294	2,143	27.1	65.8	1.9	30.5	1.0	5.1	7.0	15.3	8.4	12.5	11.3	13.1
37,175	14,820	6	Transylvania	378.4	33,956	1,328	89.7	91.7	4.6	1.1	1.0	3.4	4.2	11.5	7.9	9.6	9.6	11.4
37,177	28,620	9	Tyrrell	390.8	4,052	2,896	10.4	52.3	36.9	0.6	2.7	9.2	5.2	13.8	7.5	13.9	12.7	12.6
37,179	16,740	1	Union	631.8	231,366	284	366.2	73.6	12.5	0.7	3.6	11.3	5.7	21.5	8.7	9.8	13.8	16.5
37,181	25,780	4	Vance	252.4	44,211	1,086	175.2	40.8	51.3	0.6	0.9	7.7	6.3	17.6	8.7	11.6	10.6	13.3
37,183	39,580	1	Wake	834.8	1,072,203	41	1,284.4	62.0	21.2	0.8	8.1	10.2	6.3	17.9	9.1	14.8	15.0	14.4
37,185		8	Warren	429.1	19,883	1,830	46.3	39.8	51.6	5.8	0.7	3.9	4.8	13.5	7.3	10.7	10.2	12.2
37,187		7	Washington	346.5	12,012	2,292	34.7	45.8	48.6	0.6	0.6	5.6	5.3	15.1	7.8	10.0	9.2	12.6
37,189	14,380	5	Watauga	312.4	55,121	920	176.4	93.1	2.2	0.9	1.7	3.6	3.3	9.7	28.6	11.2	9.2	10.4
37,191	24,140	3	Wayne	553.9	124,172	509	224.2	55.1	32.2	0.9	2.0	12.0	6.6	16.9	9.8	13.6	11.4	12.5
37,193	35,900	6	Wilkes	754.5	68,576	778	90.9	88.4	5.0	0.6	0.8	6.5	5.2	15.6	7.4	10.6	11.4	13.9
37,195	48,980	4	Wilson	367.6	81,671	692	222.2	48.2	40.5	0.7	1.6	10.5	5.8	17.4	8.6	12.0	11.6	13.1
37,197	49,180	2	Yadkin	334.9	37,774	1,229	112.8	85.0	3.7	0.6	0.5	11.4	5.3	15.9	7.9	10.6	11.0	15.4
37,199		8	Yancey	312.6	17,744	1,931	56.8	93.3	1.2	0.7	0.5	5.2	4.8	13.8	6.9	10.1	10.8	13.6
38,000		0	NORTH DAKOTA	69,000.5	755,393	X	10.9	86.4	3.6	6.1	2.2	3.7	7.2	16.1	11.4	15.1	11.7	10.9
38,001		9	Adams	987.6	2,318	3,020	2.3	94.3	1.3	1.6	3.0	1.6	5.2	13.8	5.6	10.1	10.4	11.2
38,003		6	Barnes	1,491.6	10,734	2,370	7.2	93.7	2.2	1.8	1.6	2.0	5.4	14.9	9.9	10.9	10.3	11.5
38,005		9	Benson	1,388.6	6,936	2,678	5.0	42.6	0.7	54.9	0.5	3.1	10.8	23.7	8.2	12.3	8.8	10.2
38,007		9	Billings	1,148.8	940	3,108	0.8	92.0	0.0	0.6	6.6	1.4	7.4	11.9	6.1	13.2	13.8	11.4
38,009		9	Bottineau	1,668.4	6,530	2,710	3.9	93.1	1.3	4.5	1.0	2.3	5.6	16.0	8.4	10.1	9.8	11.1
38,011		9	Bowman	1,161.9	3,166	2,957	2.7	92.8	0.4	1.7	0.2	5.7	6.8	17.6	7.2	10.6	11.2	10.3
38,013		9	Burke	1,103.6	2,131	3,036	1.9	95.3	0.9	2.1	1.1	2.2	8.1	16.8	5.8	12.0	10.2	11.1
38,015	13,900	3	Burleigh	1,632.5	95,030	620	58.2	90.5	2.7	4.7	1.3	2.6	6.9	16.3	9.0	15.0	12.8	11.5
38,017	22,020	3	Cass	1,764.9	177,787	371	100.7	87.1	6.2	1.9	4.0	2.7	7.1	15.2	14.5	17.5	12.9	10.6
38,019		9	Cavalier	1,488.8	3,762	2,918	2.5	96.5	0.6	2.6	0.8	1.0	6.2	15.3	6.2	9.3	8.7	11.0
38,021		9	Dickey	1,131.5	4,861	2,842	4.3	94.8	0.9	1.4	0.9	3.4	6.7	17.6	8.1	10.2	10.1	11.4
38,023		9	Divide	1,260.7	2,288	3,022	1.8	93.6	1.8	1.9	1.7	2.7	6.2	15.2	4.9	10.7	9.7	11.6
38,025		9	Dunn	2,008.5	4,289	2,878	2.1	83.2	1.3	10.4	2.1	5.2	7.1	16.0	6.9	14.5	11.5	12.0
38,027		9	Eddy	630.2	2,316	3,021	3.7	91.7	0.6	5.1	0.8	3.6	7.0	16.3	6.6	10.3	9.6	11.2
38,029		8	Emmons	1,510.4	3,301	2,951	2.2	96.8	0.9	1.4	1.0	1.1	4.8	15.0	7.9	7.3	8.2	12.4
38,031		9	Foster	635.5	3,257	2,955	5.1	96.1	0.6	1.8	0.9	1.6	6.3	15.4	7.0	10.6	10.3	12.2
38,033		9	Golden Valley	1,001.5	1,789	3,069	1.8	94.9	0.8	1.8	0.6	3.1	5.8	16.5	6.4	9.3	12.4	10.3
38,035	24,220	3	Grand Forks	1,436.4	70,795	761	49.3	86.0	5.1	3.5	3.7	4.2	6.8	13.9	20.7	16.2	10.1	9.1
38,037		8	Grant	1,659.2	2,376	3,015	1.4	96.6	0.7	2.5	0.8	1.6	6.4	13.9	6.1	8.7	8.6	11.0
38,039		9	Griggs	708.8	2,258	3,024	3.2	97.5	0.6	0.7	0.2	1.3	5.0	14.0	7.4	7.7	9.5	10.3
38,041		9	Hettinger	1,132.2	2,483	3,007	2.2	93.9	1.3	3.6	0.7	2.5	6.0	17.1	6.4	11.8	10.3	10.8
38,043		8	Kidder	1,351.2	2,482	3,008	1.8	94.7	0.6	0.6	0.8	4.1	6.6	15.4	5.6	10.1	10.0	11.2
38,045		9	LaMoure	1,145.9	4,087	2,894	3.6	97.4	0.8	0.9	0.2	1.6	5.7	15.8	6.0	8.9	9.5	10.9
38,047		9	Logan	992.8	1,918	3,057	1.9	97.1	0.5	1.4	0.7	1.8	5.7	16.0	7.4	8.7	8.2	11.4
38,049	33,500	9	McHenry	1,874.0	5,900	2,760	3.1	96.3	0.6	1.6	0.6	2.1	6.1	17.8	5.6	11.3	11.4	12.5
38,051		9	McIntosh	974.7	2,606	2,997	2.7	95.5	1.1	0.9	1.2	2.2	4.9	13.5	6.0	9.1	7.7	10.7
38,053		9	McKenzie	2,760.5	12,724	2,243	4.6	80.6	1.8	10.8	1.2	8.0	9.5	21.3	8.4	16.6	12.3	11.2
38,055		8	McLean	2,110.6	9,685	2,452	4.6	90.7	0.8	7.4	0.5	2.3	6.2	15.1	6.4	10.7	10.9	11.1
38,057		7	Mercer	1,043.0	8,465	2,550	8.1	94.0	0.9	2.9	0.8	2.9	6.4	16.2	6.6	11.1	11.1	12.2
38,059	13,900	3	Morton	1,926.1	30,796	1,411	16.0	92.0	1.6	4.4	0.8	3.0	7.4	15.8	7.7	15.1	12.7	11.8
38,061		9	Mountrail	1,825.3	10,265	2,408	5.6	63.6	1.4	29.1	0.6	7.8	8.6	18.4	9.0	16.4	12.1	11.6
38,063		8	Nelson	981.8	2,937	2,974	3.0	94.1	2.3	2.4	0.3	2.5	5.3	13.9	6.1	9.8	8.7	10.9
38,065	13,900	3	Oliver	722.5	1,940	3,056	2.7	94.6	1.1	3.4	0.5	2.1	6.9	18.0	4.6	10.6	9.7	12.1
38,067		9	Pembina	1,118.7	6,972	2,675	6.2	93.3	1.2	4.1	0.8	3.4	5.6	14.8	6.0	11.2	11.1	11.3
38,069		7	Pierce	1,018.5	4,099	2,893	4.0	93.5	1.0	4.9	0.2	1.6	5.7	16.2	7.5	9.6	11.1	11.7
38,071		7	Ramsey	1,186.9	11,519	2,321	9.7	86.6	1.2	11.6	1.0	2.8	6.8	16.7	8.2	12.1	10.4	11.7
38,073		8	Ransom	862.4	5,297	2,815	6.1	95.9	1.2	1.4	1.1	1.8	6.0	16.7	7.6	9.4	11.6	13.0
38,075	33,500	9	Renville	877.1	2,463	3,009	2.8	95.7	1.1	1.0	0.5	2.9	6.4	16.3	6.9	11.8	10.1	12.5
38,077	47,420	6	Richland	1,435.8	16,351	2,021	11.4	93.1	1.5	3.1	0.9	3.1	6.2	15.3	14.1	11.2	10.2	10.9
38,079		9	Rolette	903.1	14,531	2,126	16.1	20.8	0.7	78.9	0.4	2.0	9.4	24.2	9.0	12.2	10.9	11.2
38,081		9	Sargent	858.5	3,858	2,914	4.5	93.7	1.4	1.9	1.3	3.2	5.9	15.3	7.0	10.3	11.1	12.2
38,083		9	Sheridan	972.4	1,353	3,090	1.4	96.7	0.8	2.7	0.5	1.3	5.2	13.6	5.5	7.9	7.5	12.0
38,085	13,900	3	Sioux	1,094.1	4,376	2,871	4.0	15.7	1.2	81.8	0.6	4.3	10.7	26.4	9.4	13.5	10.9	12.0
38,087		9	Slope	1,214.9	771	3,121	0.6	93.9	1.8	1.9	0.0	3.2	5.7	14.5	7.1	9.7	8.8	11.4
38,089	19,860	7	Stark	1,334.8	30,209	1,426	22.6	89.4	3.4	2.1	1.7	5.1	8.3	17.5	8.0	17.6	12.0	11.0
38,091		8	Steele	712.2	1,917	3,058	2.7	95.9	0.5	1.8	0.5	2.0	7.3	14.7	6.9	10.1	8.9	12.1
38,093	27,420	7	Stutsman	2,221.7	21,087	1,769	9.5	93.4	1.9	2.3	1.2	2.6	5.4	14.7	10.8	12.3	11.3	11.7
38,095		9	Towner	1,024.6	2,253	3,025	2.2	94.1	0.8	5.8	0.3	0.8	5.8	15.4	6.8	9.3	7.1	13.4
38,097		8	Traill	861.9	8,013	2,592	9.3	93.4	1.3	2.3	1.0	3.8	6.3	16.5	9.1	11.1	10.9	12.4
38,099		6	Walsh	1,281.7	10,855	2,360	8.5	84.8	0.8	2.3	1.4	11.9	6.8	15.9	7.3	11.1	10.4	12.3

1. CBSA = Core Based Statistical Area. See Appendix A for explanation. See Appendix B for list of metropolitan areas with component counties. 2. County type code from the Economic Research Service of USDA Rural-Urban Continuum Codes. See Appendix A for definition. 3. Dry land or land partially or temporarily covered by water. 4. May be of any race.

Table B. States and Counties — **Population and Households**

STATE County	55 to 64 years	65 to 74 years	75 years and over	Percent female	Total persons 2000	Total persons 2010	Percent change 2000-2010	Percent change 2010-2017	Births	Deaths	Net Migration	Number	Persons per household	Family households	Percent Female family householder[1]	One person
	16	17	18	19	20	21	22	23	24	25	26	27	28	29	30	31
NORTH CAROLINA— Cont'd																
Swain	13.6	11.1	7.8	51.8	12,968	13,981	7.8	2.2	1,426	1,325	215	5,425	2.57	64.0	12.0	33.0
Transylvania	15.8	16.3	13.6	51.6	29,334	33,087	12.8	2.6	1,946	2,903	1,835	13,841	2.30	67.6	9.9	28.1
Tyrrell	14.2	10.5	9.6	46.2	4,149	4,407	6.2	-8.1	313	303	-374	1,457	2.45	68.2	14.0	30.3
Union	11.6	7.8	4.6	50.8	123,677	201,349	62.8	14.9	17,192	9,414	22,129	72,304	2.98	79.6	10.4	16.7
Vance	13.9	10.7	7.3	53.5	42,954	45,419	5.7	-2.7	4,067	3,608	-1,665	16,653	2.62	62.6	21.1	31.8
Wake	11.3	7.0	4.2	51.3	627,846	901,059	43.5	19.0	91,720	36,065	114,278	373,245	2.61	66.8	11.4	26.0
Warren	16.6	14.3	10.4	50.4	19,972	21,024	5.3	-5.4	1,338	1,712	-758	7,753	2.49	61.3	15.0	34.1
Washington	16.3	13.8	9.9	52.7	13,723	13,214	-3.7	-9.1	907	1,116	-1,004	5,203	2.37	62.7	19.7	32.7
Watauga	11.9	9.6	6.1	50.1	42,695	51,064	19.6	7.9	2,583	2,422	3,859	20,320	2.32	52.9	6.3	27.8
Wayne	13.1	9.4	6.7	50.9	113,329	122,646	8.2	1.2	12,202	8,354	-2,311	47,013	2.59	66.5	16.7	28.4
Wilkes	14.9	12.2	8.8	50.7	65,632	69,303	5.6	-1.0	4,981	5,653	-1	27,583	2.46	67.7	9.6	28.9
Wilson	13.8	10.5	7.2	52.6	73,814	81,230	10.0	0.5	6,957	5,991	-474	31,942	2.51	64.9	18.5	30.2
Yadkin	14.3	11.3	8.4	50.6	36,348	38,409	5.7	-1.7	2,846	2,970	-490	15,287	2.45	68.5	11.4	29.1
Yancey	14.8	14.5	10.7	50.9	17,774	17,817	0.2	-0.4	1,231	1,582	291	7,479	2.33	68.3	10.2	27.7
NORTH DAKOTA	12.6	8.2	6.8	48.7	642,200	672,585	4.7	12.3	76,402	44,256	49,131	305,163	2.33	60.1	7.7	31.3
Adams	17.0	12.9	13.8	50.3	2,593	2,343	-9.6	-1.1	169	210	15	1,030	2.22	67.4	3.6	26.0
Barnes	15.2	11.6	10.4	49.7	11,775	11,066	-6.0	-3.0	828	940	-217	5,070	2.06	59.7	5.9	31.5
Benson	12.3	8.2	5.5	49.3	6,964	6,660	-4.4	4.1	1,116	540	-301	2,257	3.01	71.1	18.9	24.6
Billings	15.0	11.6	9.6	44.3	888	783	-11.8	20.1	100	24	77	405	2.23	69.4	3.7	28.4
Bottineau	15.8	13.2	10.0	48.3	7,149	6,429	-10.1	1.6	505	561	149	3,047	2.08	60.5	4.9	32.5
Bowman	15.9	10.2	10.3	49.3	3,242	3,151	-2.8	0.5	306	305	14	1,404	2.25	64.6	3.8	31.4
Burke	15.9	12.1	8.1	47.7	2,242	1,968	-12.2	8.3	244	160	66	1,001	2.23	61.8	4.0	34.7
Burleigh	13.0	8.5	6.9	49.8	69,416	81,308	17.1	16.9	9,181	4,981	9,349	38,005	2.30	62.3	9.2	29.5
Cass	10.6	6.7	5.0	49.3	123,138	149,778	21.6	18.7	17,805	7,146	17,126	70,841	2.28	55.5	8.8	32.9
Cavalier	16.0	13.6	13.7	48.9	4,831	3,993	-17.3	-5.8	329	346	-215	1,788	2.11	64.5	2.9	31.5
Dickey	14.7	10.2	10.9	50.6	5,757	5,289	-8.1	-0.8	430	512	-345	2,192	2.22	64.9	5.3	28.1
Divide	16.8	13.1	11.8	48.5	2,283	2,071	-9.3	10.5	196	197	208	1,059	2.15	59.3	2.8	38.6
Dunn	16.4	8.3	7.3	46.1	3,600	3,536	-1.8	21.3	421	245	548	1,548	2.68	69.4	6.3	25.0
Eddy	17.0	10.7	11.3	50.5	2,757	2,385	-13.5	-2.9	202	335	61	1,043	2.19	58.2	8.4	33.3
Emmons	17.3	12.8	14.2	48.8	4,331	3,550	-18.0	-7.0	206	369	-85	1,520	2.22	60.9	3.3	34.0
Foster	16.0	10.6	11.6	50.5	3,759	3,338	-11.2	-2.4	252	309	-23	1,500	2.18	67.5	6.1	29.5
Golden Valley	16.0	12.6	10.6	49.9	1,924	1,680	-12.7	6.5	157	120	68	836	2.18	51.8	3.9	43.9
Grand Forks	10.9	7.0	5.2	48.4	66,109	66,864	1.1	5.9	7,271	3,452	94	28,991	2.24	56.1	7.5	32.4
Grant	16.2	15.7	13.4	50.0	2,841	2,394	-15.7	-0.8	190	205	-5	1,108	2.10	60.8	2.3	35.0
Griggs	16.3	16.7	13.1	48.7	2,754	2,420	-12.1	-6.7	144	279	-25	1,045	2.12	65.6	3.6	34.0
Hettinger	14.7	11.2	11.8	51.7	2,715	2,477	-8.8	0.2	230	245	18	1,109	2.24	69.9	6.6	28.0
Kidder	17.6	12.0	11.5	47.8	2,753	2,435	-11.6	1.9	200	119	-33	1,083	2.23	72.3	2.7	25.7
LaMoure	17.3	12.3	13.5	48.3	4,701	4,139	-12.0	-1.3	302	322	-31	1,810	2.23	62.9	2.4	33.5
Logan	15.6	12.0	15.0	48.1	2,308	1,990	-13.8	-3.6	145	195	-20	878	2.12	63.4	2.4	31.8
McHenry	15.2	11.1	9.2	48.7	5,987	5,394	-9.9	9.4	490	424	432	2,614	2.23	61.4	5.7	32.2
McIntosh	17.1	12.0	19.0	51.0	3,390	2,809	-17.1	-7.2	171	359	-19	1,303	2.02	62.9	5.8	34.2
McKenzie	11.3	5.6	3.8	47.2	5,737	6,359	10.8	100.1	1,246	440	5,394	3,617	2.91	62.5	8.7	27.7
McLean	16.8	13.6	9.2	48.8	9,311	8,962	-3.7	8.1	835	748	623	4,292	2.19	66.4	5.1	29.8
Mercer	17.8	10.3	8.2	48.1	8,644	8,424	-2.5	0.5	734	588	-109	3,675	2.32	68.8	6.4	27.6
Morton	13.6	8.9	7.1	49.4	25,303	27,471	8.6	12.1	3,264	1,965	1,980	12,673	2.29	64.3	6.2	27.0
Mountrail	12.6	7.0	4.3	46.2	6,631	7,673	15.7	33.8	1,140	585	1,961	3,161	3.01	67.4	11.0	29.5
Nelson	18.6	13.6	13.1	47.9	3,715	3,126	-15.9	-6.0	219	415	8	1,517	1.95	57.7	5.3	39.7
Oliver	16.6	14.2	7.3	48.5	2,065	1,846	-10.6	5.1	158	87	23	760	2.33	72.5	2.9	25.4
Pembina	17.0	12.4	10.6	47.3	8,585	7,404	-13.8	-5.8	577	583	-431	3,273	2.12	62.3	5.7	31.6
Pierce	15.1	11.2	11.9	49.2	4,675	4,357	-6.8	-5.9	330	452	-137	2,032	2.06	56.5	6.8	35.0
Ramsey	14.9	10.2	9.1	50.0	12,066	11,451	-5.1	0.6	1,148	967	-107	5,004	2.21	56.2	7.0	37.9
Ransom	15.2	9.9	10.5	48.2	5,890	5,457	-7.4	-2.9	451	567	-46	2,350	2.26	61.1	4.5	33.4
Renville	16.6	10.1	9.3	47.7	2,610	2,470	-5.4	-0.3	228	194	-43	1,011	2.49	65.3	4.3	29.4
Richland	15.1	8.7	8.4	48.4	17,998	16,321	-9.3	0.2	1,307	974	-294	6,677	2.25	63.5	6.7	29.1
Rolette	11.9	6.8	4.3	50.3	13,674	13,937	1.9	4.3	2,115	1,058	-462	4,786	3.02	69.1	22.5	26.5
Sargent	15.7	13.0	9.3	46.9	4,366	3,829	-12.3	0.8	282	241	-17	1,775	2.17	61.6	5.6	30.4
Sheridan	17.1	14.4	16.7	49.5	1,710	1,321	-22.7	2.4	87	79	24	686	2.03	64.1	4.7	32.8
Sioux	9.6	4.4	3.2	50.5	4,044	4,153	2.7	5.4	701	371	-108	1,101	3.96	77.9	32.9	18.3
Slope	19.6	12.8	10.2	47.5	767	727	-5.2	6.1	62	22	6	306	2.17	64.1	4.2	34.6
Stark	12.0	6.7	6.8	48.1	22,636	24,199	6.9	24.8	3,335	1,655	4,147	11,570	2.50	60.1	6.7	30.9
Steele	16.6	13.1	10.3	48.0	2,258	1,975	-12.5	-2.9	162	131	-91	943	2.09	58.7	2.4	37.5
Stutsman	15.2	9.9	8.6	48.9	21,908	21,100	-3.7	-0.1	1,680	1,729	47	9,146	2.13	56.8	7.0	36.9
Towner	18.2	11.9	11.9	49.5	2,876	2,246	-21.9	0.3	172	194	28	982	2.30	62.0	6.3	36.3
Traill	14.4	9.7	9.7	49.4	8,477	8,121	-4.2	-1.3	696	675	-134	3,310	2.32	61.3	6.3	34.6
Walsh	15.4	10.6	10.2	49.0	12,389	11,125	-10.2	-2.4	1,018	1,023	-265	4,841	2.19	62.5	6.3	33.8

1. No spouse present.

STATE County	Housing units, 2017 (cont.)								Civilian labor force, 2017				Civilian employment[6], 2012-2016		
	Occupied units										Unemployment			Percent	
	Owner-occupied					Renter-occupied									
				Median owner cost as a percent of income											
	Total	Percent	Median value[1]	With a mortgage	Without a mortgage[2]	Median rent[3]	Median rent as a percent of income[2]	Sub-standard units[4] (percent)	Total	Percent change, 2016-2017	Total	Rate[5]	Total	Management, business, science, and arts	Construction, production, and maintenance occupations
	89	90	91	92	93	94	95	96	97	98	99	100	101	102	103
NORTH CAROLINA— Cont'd															
Swain	5,425	69.9	121,900	22.2	10.0	597	26.5	2.9	6,941	-2.4	354	5.1	5,560	28.8	21.8
Transylvania	13,841	76.0	203,100	21.1	10.0	670	33.0	2.0	14,217	2.0	620	4.4	13,476	29.8	23.6
Tyrrell	1,457	75.3	112,400	25.3	17.6	759	27.6	2.3	1,534	0.4	117	7.6	1,393	15.9	34.6
Union	72,304	79.5	206,000	20.9	10.5	911	29.2	2.5	119,334	3.2	4,777	4.0	103,107	39.1	21.3
Vance	16,653	59.9	96,700	23.7	13.1	650	31.8	3.6	17,897	-0.5	1,122	6.3	17,440	22.5	31.1
Wake	373,245	63.4	241,600	19.5	10.0	989	28.0	2.7	572,771	3.0	22,450	3.9	517,827	49.8	12.5
Warren	7,753	70.0	95,100	27.3	14.3	622	28.1	1.3	6,872	-3.7	477	6.9	7,031	29.0	27.6
Washington	5,203	64.8	82,400	23.7	14.1	679	34.4	2.1	4,805	-1.2	325	6.8	4,452	18.0	38.9
Watauga	20,320	58.8	230,700	23.6	10.3	832	50.0	2.1	28,574	2.3	1,173	4.1	23,844	35.8	14.9
Wayne	47,013	59.7	114,200	21.1	12.2	727	30.3	3.0	53,488	0.0	2,736	5.1	50,104	29.3	30.4
Wilkes	27,583	74.8	119,100	22.3	12.2	593	30.6	2.1	31,187	3.4	1,342	4.3	27,746	26.0	33.6
Wilson	31,942	59.9	117,100	22.4	13.6	711	31.6	3.2	36,056	-1.1	2,637	7.3	34,973	30.9	29.0
Yadkin	15,287	76.3	126,900	22.1	11.2	593	28.8	3.8	17,756	0.9	713	4.0	15,581	27.1	35.9
Yancey	7,479	75.2	140,500	23.1	10.7	598	31.9	2.4	7,452	-0.3	343	4.6	6,873	30.4	30.0
NORTH DAKOTA	305,163	63.5	164,000	18.4	10.0	736	24.7	2.2	414,405	0.0	10,791	2.6	395,584	35.3	25.5
Adams	1,030	75.3	124,000	16.0	11.3	455	16.0	0.5	1,122	-1.4	27	2.4	1,239	47.1	27.0
Barnes	5,070	67.7	96,700	17.0	10.0	671	20.4	0.9	5,519	-2.2	151	2.7	5,782	33.1	27.8
Benson	2,257	62.9	65,400	15.6	10.0	443	20.8	9.5	2,400	-1.8	85	3.5	2,435	36.3	26.7
Billings	405	69.1	167,200	21.2	10.0	845	13.6	1.5	437	-0.7	13	3.0	519	34.3	33.7
Bottineau	3,047	75.4	128,000	18.4	10.0	634	23.6	0.9	3,147	-3.0	103	3.3	3,335	36.0	26.9
Bowman	1,404	75.8	145,700	15.8	10.0	607	18.1	1.6	1,793	-2.8	31	1.7	1,732	33.4	32.9
Burke	1,001	71.5	116,400	13.5	10.0	792	21.8	2.9	1,104	-4.0	34	3.1	1,111	34.6	34.2
Burleigh	38,005	69.0	220,800	18.9	10.0	798	24.5	2.6	50,739	-0.2	1,224	2.4	50,674	39.2	21.7
Cass	70,841	51.8	183,800	19.5	10.0	731	25.8	1.9	102,364	1.7	2,130	2.1	96,873	38.3	21.3
Cavalier	1,788	82.8	90,500	14.7	10.0	505	18.8	1.0	2,101	-1.1	55	2.6	1,971	42.1	29.2
Dickey	2,192	72.2	105,500	17.7	10.0	601	20.9	2.1	2,552	-0.2	45	1.8	2,790	35.3	27.7
Divide	1,059	81.2	115,800	13.9	10.0	709	20.4	0.5	1,623	-4.0	27	1.7	1,262	38.6	26.7
Dunn	1,548	77.9	162,700	14.2	10.0	900	21.8	2.6	3,211	-1.6	68	2.1	2,050	30.4	34.5
Eddy	1,043	72.5	70,900	15.7	10.0	443	19.3	0.7	1,301	1.3	60	4.6	1,204	37.0	28.3
Emmons	1,520	83.9	84,900	18.3	11.1	440	24.6	1.1	1,580	-0.7	63	4.0	1,516	40.2	22.7
Foster	1,500	70.9	110,400	17.0	10.0	527	22.9	1.2	1,675	-1.1	41	2.4	1,752	34.9	29.3
Golden Valley	836	66.5	115,700	17.4	10.0	588	25.3	1.3	955	-2.1	19	2.0	1,022	32.3	25.1
Grand Forks	28,991	50.2	168,900	18.9	10.0	779	30.4	2.0	39,203	0.6	856	2.2	38,295	34.3	20.2
Grant	1,108	83.8	80,600	19.9	10.7	482	26.6	2.9	1,289	-1.1	37	2.9	1,196	47.6	24.4
Griggs	1,045	71.0	85,800	15.4	10.0	413	21.8	0.0	1,137	-2.4	33	2.9	1,229	32.4	27.0
Hettinger	1,109	83.6	106,000	13.9	10.0	593	27.6	2.1	1,528	-1.2	29	1.9	1,197	36.6	26.9
Kidder	1,083	77.1	100,100	17.5	10.0	509	21.6	1.2	1,355	-1.9	48	3.5	1,355	41.8	23.8
LaMoure	1,810	79.2	87,300	16.8	10.0	569	19.8	0.7	2,298	-1.2	43	1.9	2,011	41.5	28.6
Logan	878	83.6	72,300	17.2	10.0	597	19.2	2.1	958	-0.6	24	2.5	983	36.6	30.2
McHenry	2,614	82.0	118,100	17.8	10.0	486	19.8	0.8	3,339	-1.5	140	4.2	2,948	34.9	33.0
McIntosh	1,303	79.1	67,900	17.7	10.0	518	24.3	0.9	1,249	0.2	32	2.6	1,381	36.3	26.8
McKenzie	3,617	59.1	202,800	13.4	10.0	895	16.9	5.1	8,198	2.7	201	2.5	5,383	31.8	35.6
McLean	4,292	79.5	150,300	16.6	10.0	598	20.8	1.8	5,103	0.3	158	3.1	4,583	35.2	31.5
Mercer	3,675	82.8	152,200	16.5	10.0	710	19.0	2.0	4,520	-3.3	179	4.0	4,375	27.6	36.3
Morton	12,673	73.4	173,400	19.7	10.0	763	24.4	1.2	16,805	-0.4	511	3.0	17,023	32.9	27.2
Mountrail	3,161	69.2	161,400	17.1	10.0	723	18.2	4.7	7,088	-1.0	143	2.0	4,774	34.7	28.8
Nelson	1,517	75.8	77,500	16.0	10.0	476	16.3	1.2	1,503	-2.5	46	3.1	1,542	36.6	23.3
Oliver	760	85.1	125,600	17.1	10.0	543	18.5	1.3	887	-1.7	37	4.2	895	37.3	29.1
Pembina	3,273	76.5	80,200	15.6	10.0	527	20.2	0.8	3,575	-2.7	147	4.1	3,585	32.4	30.1
Pierce	2,032	72.8	102,900	18.7	11.2	625	24.9	1.9	1,922	0.8	61	3.2	2,062	34.7	24.1
Ramsey	5,004	62.8	112,100	17.3	10.0	530	20.1	2.7	5,872	-4.9	157	2.7	6,071	34.5	19.3
Ransom	2,350	67.5	113,600	18.4	10.0	591	20.7	0.6	2,852	0.1	55	1.9	2,840	29.4	37.4
Renville	1,011	76.3	120,400	18.2	10.0	679	19.1	1.2	1,305	-0.6	33	2.5	1,279	34.9	29.2
Richland	6,677	71.2	109,000	17.7	10.0	542	22.9	1.2	8,882	-0.7	209	2.4	8,846	32.4	33.2
Rolette	4,786	67.9	73,900	16.9	10.0	345	24.7	6.4	4,883	-2.4	496	10.2	5,230	37.4	21.8
Sargent	1,775	73.9	83,000	16.7	10.0	578	17.9	1.6	2,399	2.4	49	2.0	2,149	29.9	43.0
Sheridan	686	78.9	71,800	18.3	10.0	300	32.0	0.9	728	-1.5	33	4.5	633	38.9	30.2
Sioux	1,101	41.6	74,300	16.6	10.0	450	14.9	13.4	1,333	-0.9	48	3.6	1,316	39.1	10.3
Slope	306	84.0	117,800	14.5	10.0	675	18.3	0.0	427	-2.5	8	1.9	325	54.5	21.8
Stark	11,570	66.1	222,200	17.3	10.0	898	23.6	3.4	18,283	0.7	489	2.7	16,576	30.0	32.6
Steele	943	78.2	73,600	13.4	10.0	520	14.9	0.8	1,082	0.3	18	1.7	1,004	36.8	30.3
Stutsman	9,146	65.4	120,500	17.6	10.0	631	23.8	0.5	11,074	-0.5	257	2.3	10,944	35.0	25.0
Towner	982	76.9	70,300	14.4	10.0	475	23.3	3.1	1,237	-7.5	31	2.5	976	42.2	20.4
Traill	3,310	74.0	115,300	18.2	10.0	534	23.8	1.2	4,654	0.8	112	2.4	4,173	34.2	30.3
Walsh	4,841	74.2	81,300	17.2	10.0	547	24.1	1.4	5,647	-0.7	186	3.3	5,572	31.4	33.9

1. Specified owner-occupied units.   2. A value of 10.0 represents 10 percent or less; a value of 50.0 represents 50 percent or more.   3. Specified renter-occupied units.
4. Overcrowded or lacking complete plumbing facilities.   5. Percent of civilian labor force.   6. Civilian employed persons 16 years old and over.

Table B. States and Counties — Nonfarm Employment and Agriculture

	Private nonfarm establishments, employment and payroll, 2016									Agriculture, 2012			
		Employment						Annual payroll		Farms			
												Percent with:	
STATE County	Number of establishments	Total	Health care and social assistance	Manufacturing	Retail trade	Finance and insurance	Professional, scientific, and technical services	Total (mil dol)	Average per employee (dollars)	Number	Fewer than 50 acres	500 acres or more	Farm operators whose principal occupation is farming (percent)
	104	105	106	107	108	109	110	111	112	113	114	115	116
NORTH CAROLINA— Cont'd													
Swain	354	3,681	917	D	585	83	46	115	31,323	94	62.8	1.1	26.6
Transylvania	798	7,598	1,509	618	1,543	175	272	235	30,865	221	63.8	2.3	46.6
Tyrrell	77	462	21	41	156	29	D	14	29,877	78	21.8	28.2	57.7
Union	4,526	53,792	5,649	11,572	7,560	927	1,571	2,108	39,192	1,059	55.6	6.8	53.0
Vance	832	13,025	2,404	1,500	2,312	238	309	438	33,648	242	36.4	10.7	36.8
Wake	28,325	453,333	60,406	13,731	59,262	24,689	53,509	23,438	51,701	783	57.0	4.5	49.0
Warren	258	2,217	540	374	369	44	41	59	26,754	256	34.0	11.7	42.6
Washington	228	2,931	611	842	417	60	53	110	37,651	156	25.6	30.1	59.0
Watauga	1,603	17,694	2,768	717	3,704	382	701	556	31,408	609	49.4	2.0	44.7
Wayne	2,137	34,226	7,229	5,688	6,276	1,111	830	1,155	33,733	563	40.1	18.1	60.9
Wilkes	1,163	18,842	3,153	4,527	2,552	357	496	770	40,869	972	44.9	3.9	50.6
Wilson	1,750	31,868	5,219	7,332	3,748	2,993	777	1,263	39,635	297	42.4	17.8	61.3
Yadkin	593	8,630	1,015	2,525	818	192	188	270	31,253	952	55.6	2.7	44.9
Yancey	313	3,427	490	1,033	565	81	104	115	33,498	450	57.3	0.7	31.1
NORTH DAKOTA	24,601	346,947	61,322	23,984	50,760	17,843	15,817	15,817	45,588	30,961	11.0	48.8	56.6
Adams	99	803	328	D	164	38	23	28	35,192	392	12.8	48.7	60.2
Barnes	366	3,956	1,140	531	491	142	78	130	32,750	855	11.6	40.6	52.4
Benson	88	1,043	25	55	56	54	D	34	32,891	563	6.9	54.2	64.5
Billings	62	285	NA	NA	15	D	D	18	62,912	197	4.6	68.5	68.0
Bottineau	261	1,742	265	84	375	123	80	72	41,424	863	8.5	41.7	48.8
Bowman	160	1,200	257	34	229	94	47	46	38,565	348	8.6	55.5	54.3
Burke	81	411	10	NA	87	36	49	18	43,754	488	6.4	47.3	54.3
Burleigh	3,011	47,091	10,705	1,141	7,551	1,898	2,544	2,057	43,671	1,014	23.1	34.7	42.3
Cass	5,523	103,392	17,951	8,595	13,488	8,272	6,030	4,692	45,383	968	21.0	49.8	66.3
Cavalier	158	1,186	220	23	201	92	14	48	40,420	667	7.5	57.1	63.4
Dickey	215	1,749	400	183	316	53	32	53	30,575	543	11.0	45.7	53.8
Divide	97	544	D	D	68	24	11	21	38,441	452	5.5	54.4	54.6
Dunn	164	2,584	D	402	153	32	123	142	54,827	628	13.1	56.5	66.1
Eddy	78	530	204	D	62	21	11	17	32,634	331	8.8	50.2	46.2
Emmons	125	707	184	D	100	51	12	23	32,669	609	6.6	58.1	55.2
Foster	150	1,419	254	D	278	62	8	56	39,485	310	10.3	49.7	61.0
Golden Valley	73	442	128	D	92	32	18	16	35,676	251	7.2	58.6	62.2
Grand Forks	1,918	34,179	7,350	2,337	6,312	900	1,611	1,333	39,003	970	12.3	35.8	62.7
Grant	74	418	189	17	34	31	D	12	29,761	508	8.3	59.4	65.2
Griggs	90	636	D	135	57	24	34	21	33,311	456	6.6	45.8	52.9
Hettinger	95	459	92	D	67	49	15	18	38,259	494	5.9	50.4	54.9
Kidder	68	537	90	D	78	35	26	18	34,361	559	6.4	54.2	49.7
LaMoure	151	1,021	186	83	125	116	NA	36	34,981	642	8.6	49.2	59.0
Logan	67	461	118	D	61	34	D	13	28,694	379	7.4	56.2	58.3
McHenry	123	779	121	D	206	43	14	32	40,673	911	9.2	48.8	64.8
McIntosh	113	817	343	36	131	49	21	25	30,864	471	7.4	51.4	59.7
McKenzie	492	5,435	343	D	458	124	224	372	68,481	574	10.5	59.4	61.1
McLean	256	2,589	447	69	346	116	19	150	57,842	868	7.3	51.6	51.6
Mercer	248	4,349	491	24	480	115	50	294	67,504	422	12.3	46.2	54.3
Morton	838	10,111	1,881	873	1,408	416	1,302	448	44,351	887	20.3	47.9	55.2
Mountrail	389	4,111	242	126	704	113	219	233	56,792	670	4.6	57.9	66.4
Nelson	122	779	274	D	88	64	7	24	30,669	603	6.8	35.8	36.5
Oliver	42	547	17	19	D	D	D	43	79,185	290	13.4	48.3	53.4
Pembina	272	2,396	362	642	356	112	34	100	41,940	584	12.3	45.0	62.3
Pierce	171	1,484	D	D	256	87	54	56	37,455	521	7.5	53.7	58.3
Ramsey	434	4,668	816	88	1,056	300	57	164	35,079	573	11.0	48.5	51.5
Ransom	199	1,493	394	224	179	78	56	51	34,478	548	11.7	36.3	48.7
Renville	113	552	97	22	114	34	10	20	35,527	304	8.2	68.1	73.4
Richland	533	6,087	623	1,809	804	182	158	224	36,857	854	15.6	47.9	64.3
Rolette	195	2,375	563	79	472	99	38	71	29,710	649	9.1	38.8	48.8
Sargent	113	2,339	74	D	144	44	19	117	50,195	537	6.5	45.4	55.9
Sheridan	39	155	28	D	18	10	D	4	27,865	370	7.8	53.5	54.6
Sioux	29	668	D	D	63	D	D	17	25,876	176	10.8	67.0	66.5
Slope	18	76	D	NA	D	NA	NA	4	47,368	221	9.5	62.4	62.0
Stark	1,202	14,757	2,171	1,049	2,295	421	553	745	50,506	837	20.2	39.1	48.6
Steele	60	479	D	126	66	48	5	22	45,537	355	8.7	52.4	63.1
Stutsman	690	9,659	2,772	865	1,530	451	224	357	36,934	1,028	10.1	49.8	55.2
Towner	78	520	D	D	39	56	24	16	30,292	529	7.2	62.4	61.1
Traill	299	2,778	623	415	348	158	40	111	40,064	468	17.3	48.3	63.7
Walsh	400	3,311	649	575	465	167	94	120	36,277	962	13.7	38.9	47.3

Table B. States and Counties — **Agriculture**

	Agriculture, 2012 (cont.)															
	Land in farms					Value of land and buildings (dollars)			Value of products sold:				Percent of farms with sales of:		Government payments	
		Acres									Percent from:					
STATE County	Acreage (1,000)	Percent change, 2007-2012	Average size of farm	Total irrigated (1,000)	Total cropland (1,000)	Average per farm	Average per acre	Value of machinery and equipment, average per farm (dollars)	Total (mil dol)	Average per farm (acres)	Crops	Livestock and poultry products	$10,000 or more	$100,000 or more	Total ($1,000)	Percent of farms
	117	118	119	120	121	122	123	124	125	126	127	128	129	130	131	132
NORTH CAROLINA— Cont'd																
Swain	D	D	D	0.0	D	349,085	D	37,309	0.7	7,202	48.3	51.7	16.0	1.1	17	10.6
Transylvania	18	11.7	81	0.4	6.6	716,964	8,838	43,715	20.4	92,131	81.5	18.5	34.8	11.3	200	12.7
Tyrrell	65	19.9	828	0.0	57.8	2,107,192	2,545	343,936	59.6	763,474	D	D	62.8	42.3	772	83.3
Union	202	13.2	190	0.4	148.3	1,075,361	5,647	112,638	535.8	505,977	24.0	76.0	43.6	25.9	1,807	17.4
Vance	55	-0.4	227	1.6	19.5	784,640	3,460	79,628	17.3	71,463	97.7	2.3	26.4	11.2	446	45.9
Wake	84	-0.9	108	3.2	44.4	1,029,967	9,575	68,049	65.2	83,324	94.1	5.9	33.0	9.6	848	24.8
Warren	66	-9.6	257	0.8	26.0	657,488	2,562	60,867	25.6	100,156	53.7	46.3	37.9	14.5	678	57.4
Washington	91	-5.7	586	4.4	75.9	1,767,526	3,017	301,814	68.4	438,237	95.5	4.5	52.6	35.9	1,639	76.3
Watauga	56	21.8	92	0.0	14.5	684,361	7,474	51,750	15.3	25,108	38.4	61.6	34.5	5.1	222	22.5
Wayne	191	9.1	340	4.8	146.8	1,400,607	4,124	199,504	577.2	1,025,265	27.4	72.6	61.5	44.8	2,943	56.5
Wilkes	111	1.0	114	0.1	36.2	553,577	4,842	80,330	284.9	293,140	6.6	93.4	42.1	19.1	329	6.6
Wilson	111	6.4	375	1.4	86.4	1,431,529	3,817	266,391	179.6	604,822	84.3	15.7	46.5	30.6	1,876	62.3
Yadkin	100	-4.5	106	0.5	53.5	555,887	5,267	68,082	124.7	130,956	26.8	73.2	33.8	12.3	921	25.7
Yancey	31	-7.3	69	0.1	6.2	446,533	6,482	28,402	5.7	12,758	71.8	28.2	23.8	2.7	532	23.3
NORTH DAKOTA	39,263	-1.0	1,268	218.4	27,147.2	1,808,801	1,426	300,285	10,950.7	353,693	88.3	11.7	59.0	40.6	381,710	80.1
Adams	601	-4.1	1,534	D	380.0	1,236,143	806	192,020	107.5	274,329	77.3	22.7	54.1	36.7	4,734	81.9
Barnes	937	3.3	1,096	1.7	836.5	2,449,174	2,235	342,849	376.4	440,175	97.5	2.5	54.9	39.5	11,719	83.6
Benson	802	5.6	1,425	1.2	644.4	1,841,764	1,293	354,654	240.6	427,405	92.7	7.3	62.0	46.0	7,551	83.5
Billings	722	-0.3	3,666	0.0	131.3	2,888,964	788	226,416	36.7	186,127	48.1	51.9	78.7	41.1	1,365	68.5
Bottineau	899	-12.6	1,042	D	773.0	1,408,030	1,351	275,319	254.0	294,359	95.1	4.9	53.3	34.9	9,818	83.4
Bowman	730	1.3	2,099	1.5	372.6	1,577,514	752	251,733	111.4	320,164	54.1	45.9	61.5	41.4	4,005	80.2
Burke	595	4.3	1,219	D	434.6	1,023,576	839	247,330	105.1	215,455	91.7	8.3	50.4	32.4	5,413	86.9
Burleigh	951	8.1	938	4.6	494.7	1,320,447	1,408	162,938	179.6	177,132	72.9	27.1	50.2	23.6	5,300	53.9
Cass	1,107	6.6	1,144	9.3	1,044.5	3,277,384	2,865	455,639	567.1	585,855	96.8	3.2	68.0	54.3	14,691	78.3
Cavalier	940	7.7	1,410	0.0	871.5	2,681,525	1,902	456,447	334.5	501,547	98.2	1.8	65.1	54.4	15,805	92.2
Dickey	633	-9.2	1,166	16.3	481.1	2,629,105	2,254	359,029	266.8	491,398	88.2	11.8	57.8	43.1	10,047	79.4
Divide	565	-20.2	1,250	2.4	419.2	807,018	646	241,810	93.8	207,496	90.9	9.1	55.1	38.3	4,848	90.5
Dunn	1,031	-1.2	1,642	0.4	374.3	1,498,726	913	250,261	124.8	198,707	60.6	39.4	72.3	39.3	3,189	70.9
Eddy	396	5.1	1,196	0.2	288.7	1,600,341	1,338	283,166	105.1	317,538	90.2	9.8	52.0	37.2	4,596	87.9
Emmons	744	-14.7	1,222	3.9	443.9	1,439,232	1,178	269,821	171.3	281,255	80.9	19.1	62.7	47.0	5,117	87.8
Foster	374	-6.5	1,206	2.6	314.3	2,254,016	1,868	422,081	169.4	546,484	80.4	19.6	65.5	51.3	4,700	78.4
Golden Valley	562	-1.4	2,241	D	242.6	1,887,992	843	258,785	59.6	237,327	73.3	26.7	63.3	38.2	4,251	79.7
Grand Forks	816	-1.1	842	18.9	749.2	1,768,300	2,101	322,178	428.8	442,023	94.8	5.2	51.3	39.3	11,254	90.9
Grant	1,050	-0.8	2,067	2.4	504.0	1,904,955	922	235,537	157.1	309,232	70.3	29.7	68.1	45.9	5,753	84.8
Griggs	445	9.7	977	2.8	342.4	1,781,884	1,824	254,471	127.8	280,325	91.5	8.5	53.7	35.5	8,891	88.4
Hettinger	716	1.1	1,449	0.0	558.5	1,624,585	1,121	263,455	159.0	321,927	91.4	8.6	49.4	34.4	8,615	88.7
Kidder	780	3.6	1,396	15.0	429.8	1,290,878	925	198,445	148.3	265,326	72.2	27.8	59.9	40.4	4,079	84.6
LaMoure	726	5.5	1,131	7.4	611.3	2,445,422	2,163	342,617	292.4	455,500	88.9	11.1	63.6	50.9	7,967	85.7
Logan	572	-1.0	1,508	1.5	333.3	1,541,950	1,022	285,359	172.1	454,087	50.0	50.0	63.1	48.3	3,296	90.0
McHenry	1,061	-2.0	1,165	1.2	624.8	1,047,299	899	161,514	198.2	217,581	72.3	27.7	56.4	34.7	8,289	77.9
McIntosh	590	7.3	1,252	D	397.2	1,472,964	1,176	214,769	139.8	296,754	75.3	24.7	66.7	42.7	3,350	79.6
McKenzie	1,064	-1.0	1,854	19.9	425.6	1,366,373	737	246,225	114.4	199,387	69.0	31.0	62.9	38.5	4,116	70.0
McLean	1,113	-4.3	1,282	7.4	838.7	1,681,880	1,312	307,744	293.4	338,025	92.3	7.7	62.2	41.6	11,766	82.8
Mercer	503	-1.3	1,192	1.4	231.0	1,135,981	953	188,306	76.7	181,765	73.3	26.7	65.6	32.5	2,572	70.9
Morton	1,220	4.7	1,375	7.6	549.1	1,405,868	1,022	208,989	225.2	253,934	67.6	32.4	62.8	34.6	5,558	62.0
Mountrail	964	-7.0	1,438	0.2	578.8	1,308,849	910	278,960	154.9	231,166	86.8	13.2	60.3	37.0	7,195	77.0
Nelson	560	1.9	929	2.1	474.9	1,092,551	1,175	230,488	145.8	241,725	93.3	6.7	37.3	24.5	9,207	95.5
Oliver	395	4.4	1,360	5.9	165.1	1,388,955	1,021	192,590	85.5	294,810	60.2	39.8	74.8	39.3	2,057	75.2
Pembina	692	6.6	1,185	5.7	632.8	3,054,467	2,577	574,476	406.0	695,164	98.7	1.3	60.3	44.9	8,554	77.7
Pierce	598	2.9	1,148	1.0	479.8	1,180,380	1,028	257,340	142.1	272,649	90.5	9.5	55.9	41.8	6,473	90.6
Ramsey	698	-2.3	1,219	D	622.7	1,696,558	1,392	394,349	236.1	412,005	96.7	3.3	51.0	41.2	10,448	85.3
Ransom	502	-4.9	915	14.8	339.3	1,673,436	1,828	213,192	179.3	327,126	85.4	14.6	50.2	32.5	9,311	81.6
Renville	500	-9.8	1,645	0.0	445.8	2,659,974	1,617	536,164	156.4	514,605	97.8	2.2	80.6	66.1	6,902	84.2
Richland	869	-4.1	1,017	3.7	788.5	3,021,842	2,970	437,697	535.7	627,234	95.1	4.9	67.7	54.3	15,676	82.2
Rolette	534	-5.9	823	D	365.5	925,470	1,124	187,112	107.9	166,301	90.8	9.2	50.7	24.8	5,631	68.1
Sargent	513	1.5	955	13.7	432.5	2,265,119	2,372	338,054	243.4	453,311	90.3	9.7	55.5	45.8	9,185	87.2
Sheridan	514	2.7	1,388	D	347.3	1,297,773	935	230,697	107.8	291,295	91.1	8.9	53.8	38.9	4,293	82.7
Sioux	573	-21.5	3,256	D	155.9	2,912,585	894	265,188	62.7	356,421	47.1	52.9	71.6	52.3	1,476	58.5
Slope	674	-12.3	3,051	D	245.0	2,603,290	853	329,502	67.6	305,688	72.0	28.0	64.3	41.6	3,166	72.4
Stark	830	-0.9	991	0.8	498.8	1,345,419	1,358	207,119	152.6	182,298	77.8	22.2	52.9	27.4	4,741	66.3
Steele	426	5.9	1,200	6.0	397.0	2,218,885	1,850	483,662	210.6	593,158	98.3	1.7	63.7	57.2	6,646	94.6
Stutsman	1,303	9.2	1,267	8.2	1,030.6	2,212,500	1,746	385,059	464.6	451,941	90.0	10.0	60.1	41.3	13,278	78.3
Towner	645	6.3	1,220	0.4	573.3	1,565,902	1,283	320,216	196.8	372,049	91.2	8.8	60.5	53.1	7,528	87.1
Traill	548	0.8	1,170	2.0	526.2	3,395,635	2,901	477,162	308.8	659,887	99.3	0.7	68.2	54.9	8,804	80.6
Walsh	802	0.9	834	3.4	714.5	1,982,913	2,377	308,740	424.0	440,783	98.3	1.7	49.7	37.8	14,445	87.1

Table B. States and Counties — Water Use, Wholesale Trade, Retail Trade, and Real Estate

STATE County	Water use, 2015 — Public supply water withdrawn (mil gal/ day)	Public supply gallons withdrawn per person per day	Wholesale Trade[1], 2012 — Number of establish-ments	Number of employees	Sales (mil dol)	Annual payroll (mil dol)	Retail Trade[2], 2012 — Number of establish-ments	Number of employees	Sales (mil dol)	Annual payroll (mil dol)	Real estate and rental and leasing,[2] 2012 — Number of establish-ments	Number of employees	Sales (mil dol)	Annual payroll (mil dol)
	133	134	135	136	137	138	139	140	141	142	143	144	145	146
NORTH CAROLINA— Cont'd														
Swain	0.50	34.6	4	D	D	D	96	472	107.1	9.1	7	23	2.0	0.4
Transylvania	1.81	54.5	15	D	D	D	125	1,352	311.3	30.2	48	91	13.4	2.7
Tyrrell	0.48	117.9	1	D	D	D	20	135	36.0	2.3	2	D	D	D
Union	6.57	29.5	266	2,658	1,449.1	126.9	492	6,803	1,943.6	156.4	144	304	60.2	11.2
Vance	5.95	133.5	31	D	D	D	179	2,186	527.9	49.0	51	211	27.5	5.1
Wake	56.66	55.3	1,082	18,108	18,602.6	1,401.0	3,161	51,026	14,359.3	1,264.2	1,320	7,360	1,683.3	391.9
Warren	0.05	2.5	9	21	10.2	0.6	44	314	72.4	6.0	9	D	D	D
Washington	0.79	63.8	12	185	174.1	4.1	48	465	127.7	8.7	4	D	D	D
Watauga	3.30	62.4	37	299	140.2	14.7	318	3,471	762.9	70.2	100	382	55.2	10.0
Wayne	11.27	90.8	95	1,822	1,244.8	74.4	464	5,709	1,557.5	125.8	63	257	29.3	7.1
Wilkes	6.61	96.5	47	D	D	D	223	2,500	1,365.2	53.5	44	185	46.8	7.0
Wilson	9.62	117.7	99	D	D	D	319	3,606	992.7	83.6	76	247	43.1	6.3
Yadkin	1.36	36.2	29	222	87.7	7.8	108	760	242.9	16.0	14	D	D	D
Yancey	0.70	39.8	7	24	3.7	0.4	61	522	144.9	12.3	17	D	D	D
NORTH DAKOTA	84.18	111.2	1,430	18,880	28,150.8	1,078.2	3,185	47,186	15,519.8	1,204.4	912	5,157	1,445.1	247.5
Adams	0.00	0.0	10	49	120.6	1.7	16	169	43.1	4.1	2	D	D	D
Barnes	1.15	103.6	22	192	329.6	9.2	48	479	121.7	10.3	11	86	4.5	1.8
Benson	0.07	10.4	14	86	228.9	4.1	9	55	12.3	1.4	2	D	D	D
Billings	0.00	0.0	1	D	D	D	10	D	D	D	1	D	D	D
Bottineau	0.48	71.5	16	120	99.0	5.6	34	337	95.5	6.8	8	16	1.1	0.1
Bowman	0.22	66.8	13	123	96.6	7.6	19	251	93.2	5.5	3	2	0.2	0.0
Burke	0.26	112.7	6	60	454.5	3.6	10	96	38.5	2.5	3	2	0.7	0.1
Burleigh	11.90	128.0	132	2,094	1,483.2	113.2	373	6,905	1,995.1	177.7	132	404	107.3	13.9
Cass	14.11	82.3	333	6,020	5,497.7	335.9	645	12,500	3,790.4	302.8	277	1,716	302.9	64.8
Cavalier	0.50	130.6	15	D	D	D	29	213	125.7	5.2	1	D	D	D
Dickey	0.83	162.6	16	152	450.1	7.0	41	324	96.3	7.2	1	D	D	D
Divide	0.00	0.0	2	D	D	D	9	86	21.1	1.8	1	D	D	D
Dunn	0.00	0.0	8	50	86.8	2.7	13	161	69.1	3.5	1	D	D	D
Eddy	0.98	414.4	4	D	D	D	10	72	16.7	1.7	2	D	D	D
Emmons	0.43	126.4	14	95	236.9	3.5	20	106	30.7	2.3	NA	NA	NA	NA
Foster	0.43	128.1	19	119	210.8	6.6	28	247	133.0	7.2	2	D	D	D
Golden Valley	0.00	0.0	5	68	87.3	3.2	15	134	72.7	2.8	NA	NA	NA	NA
Grand Forks	8.78	123.8	92	1,235	1,214.9	65.6	314	5,860	1,562.2	130.9	79	504	86.1	14.7
Grant	0.00	0.0	8	50	98.4	2.4	10	31	7.2	0.7	1	D	D	D
Griggs	0.38	164.2	6	104	66.5	5.2	12	60	18.1	1.4	1	D	D	D
Hettinger	0.00	0.0	4	D	D	D	14	87	128.6	2.7	2	D	D	D
Kidder	0.09	37.2	6	17	27.9	0.7	8	66	48.4	1.7	2	D	D	D
LaMoure	0.01	2.4	23	213	391.6	9.9	16	142	133.1	3.8	2	D	D	D
Logan	0.09	46.5	6	D	D	D	11	46	30.5	1.7	1	D	D	D
McHenry	0.97	162.5	5	D	D	D	17	122	26.5	2.5	5	D	D	D
McIntosh	0.26	94.2	11	103	277.1	3.5	19	140	52.1	3.6	3	9	0.8	0.1
McKenzie	0.79	61.6	14	172	263.6	25.7	24	301	166.1	10.6	15	69	27.6	5.0
McLean	0.61	62.6	20	216	528.9	9.4	38	293	132.5	7.2	2	D	D	D
Mercer	6.67	753.4	6	28	21.5	1.5	39	420	125.2	9.6	5	5	0.3	0.1
Morton	2.80	92.4	34	D	D	D	99	1,230	586.1	40.3	43	118	16.8	3.3
Mountrail	0.52	50.3	12	140	406.4	9.1	41	475	274.0	15.4	6	16	1.1	0.3
Nelson	1.33	448.1	13	107	449.2	6.2	19	103	31.5	1.6	4	4	0.1	0.0
Oliver	0.00	0.0	1	D	D	D	2	D	D	D	NA	NA	NA	NA
Pembina	1.10	155.1	35	352	847.9	13.4	45	403	82.9	7.8	3	1	0.3	0.0
Pierce	0.75	173.9	11	112	201.5	5.3	22	263	92.6	6.2	2	D	D	D
Ramsey	0.00	0.0	29	207	622.1	11.0	80	962	311.7	27.1	6	192	7.4	4.6
Ransom	1.02	187.2	13	187	292.1	10.4	30	252	66.2	4.8	4	4	0.7	0.1
Renville	0.00	0.0	12	89	250.5	4.3	13	142	81.1	3.7	2	D	D	D
Richland	2.08	126.8	34	D	D	D	75	899	277.3	19.6	18	50	5.6	1.1
Rolette	1.59	108.5	7	48	103.6	2.9	45	496	132.9	9.7	2	D	D	D
Sargent	0.28	72.2	12	74	145.1	2.9	17	124	20.9	1.8	4	D	D	D
Sheridan	0.01	7.6	3	D	D	D	6	20	5.5	0.2	2	D	D	D
Sioux	0.02	4.6	NA	NA	NA	NA	8	D	D	D	NA	NA	NA	NA
Slope	0.03	39.1	NA	NA	NA	NA	1	D	D	D	NA	NA	NA	NA
Stark	0.00	0.0	53	745	1,186.8	44.7	160	2,050	883.4	62.8	43	211	72.4	12.0
Steele	0.67	342.5	6	D	D	D	10	61	34.4	1.7	1	D	D	D
Stutsman	3.32	157.3	39	470	875.5	24.3	101	1,328	379.1	32.3	28	79	20.9	2.0
Towner	0.19	83.6	8	64	193.8	3.4	13	51	30.4	1.3	2	D	D	D
Traill	0.92	114.8	30	334	1,733.4	16.3	42	313	97.2	7.1	7	9	0.7	0.2
Walsh	1.14	104.6	35	374	599.7	18.9	58	535	123.1	10.4	11	13	1.0	0.3

1. Merchant wholesalers, except manufacturers' sales branches and offices.   2. Employer establishments.

516   NC(Swain)—ND(Walsh)

Items 133–146

Table B. States and Counties — Professional Services, Manufacturing, and Accommodation and Food Services

STATE County	Professional, scientific, and technical services, 2012				Manufacturing, 2012				Accommodation and food services, 2012			
	Number of establishments	Number of employees	Sales (mil dol)	Annual payroll (mil dol)	Number of establishments	Number of employees	Receipts (mil dol)	Annual payroll (mil dol)	Number of establishments	Number of employees	Receipts (mil dol)	Annual payroll (mil dol)
	147	148	149	150	151	152	153	154	155	156	157	158
NORTH CAROLINA— Cont'd												
Swain	11	D	D	D	11	414	D	17.1	82	765	50.0	12.4
Transylvania	67	D	D	D	24	440	61.1	18.3	83	1,106	68.5	21.3
Tyrrell	3	D	D	D	3	105	9.6	2.3	6	D	D	D
Union	395	1,221	156.5	54.2	231	9,760	3,645.4	444.3	264	4,159	192.9	50.8
Vance	46	196	16.4	6.9	41	1,581	756.2	66.1	67	1,239	57.0	15.0
Wake	4,332	40,850	7,315.9	3,072.9	576	12,902	13,105.2	696.6	2,102	42,326	2,165.2	606.3
Warren	14	52	3.8	0.9	9	494	128.9	14.7	23	207	8.9	2.3
Washington	12	66	7.5	1.8	12	780	394.6	47.0	27	D	D	D
Watauga	149	723	47.9	20.0	47	667	108.0	23.6	174	3,416	142.1	43.2
Wayne	147	816	76.0	27.4	83	5,833	1,691.3	243.8	186	3,284	161.7	42.0
Wilkes	83	418	36.5	15.0	73	4,288	1,156.1	138.7	105	1,568	65.7	17.9
Wilson	112	769	95.4	36.3	91	7,809	13,159.9	393.6	138	2,749	139.3	34.2
Yadkin	41	230	20.6	8.1	41	2,064	748.3	79.1	58	875	34.4	9.6
Yancey	17	75	5.0	1.5	12	686	145.0	28.9	21	282	11.6	3.4
NORTH DAKOTA	1,722	13,715	1,846.9	735.7	745	23,541	14,427.4	1,042.8	1,935	35,698	2,045.1	521.3
Adams	4	D	D	D	NA	NA	NA	NA	11	D	D	D
Barnes	15	79	9.6	3.6	10	500	D	23.1	31	356	14.1	3.4
Benson	6	14	1.9	0.9	4	102	D	D	16	D	D	D
Billings	3	5	1.0	0.3	3	13	D	D	14	131	19.0	5.4
Bottineau	20	67	6.4	2.9	10	92	D	4.6	28	237	11.0	2.7
Bowman	4	D	D	D	7	35	D	1.0	17	118	5.1	1.2
Burke	4	D	D	D	NA	NA	NA	NA	12	48	4.4	0.5
Burleigh	308	1,969	314.8	118.4	68	900	D	39.3	173	4,980	242.1	70.7
Cass	481	D	D	D	186	8,566	3,451.1	395.7	388	9,671	446.8	130.9
Cavalier	6	16	1.3	0.6	5	14	3.1	0.6	18	D	D	D
Dickey	9	37	2.6	0.9	13	225	60.0	9.4	19	145	4.6	1.1
Divide	6	15	1.6	0.4	3	6	D	D	7	D	D	D
Dunn	4	16	2.2	0.9	5	D	D	D	9	165	24.6	3.5
Eddy	4	10	1.1	0.2	NA	NA	NA	NA	11	30	1.4	0.3
Emmons	9	12	0.9	0.3	3	6	D	D	10	88	2.8	0.8
Foster	7	10	3.4	0.5	3	D	D	D	10	125	5.2	1.5
Golden Valley	5	18	1.8	0.5	NA	NA	NA	NA	4	D	D	D
Grand Forks	130	1,473	167.2	79.1	55	2,166	590.7	78.4	196	4,191	177.6	52.5
Grant	3	7	0.6	0.1	3	27	D	D	6	D	D	D
Griggs	9	43	4.7	1.6	5	155	21.4	5.1	11	D	D	D
Hettinger	5	15	0.9	0.4	3	5	D	D	5	35	1.3	0.2
Kidder	4	D	D	D	3	6	D	D	8	43	2.0	0.6
LaMoure	2	D	D	D	7	52	D	1.9	16	D	D	D
Logan	2	D	D	D	NA	NA	NA	NA	9	57	1.3	0.3
McHenry	6	14	2.1	0.6	4	D	D	D	7	24	1.3	0.3
McIntosh	6	24	1.6	0.6	4	109	D	3.3	10	D	D	D
McKenzie	32	134	46.7	13.9	5	17	1.6	0.4	28	460	31.8	6.5
McLean	7	20	1.6	0.5	5	67	D	3.2	28	181	9.8	2.1
Mercer	11	69	7.2	2.2	7	35	5.7	0.9	30	348	12.4	3.5
Morton	61	D	D	D	36	913	D	56.0	52	D	D	D
Mountrail	18	44	8.9	2.3	3	D	D	D	30	167	18.8	3.1
Nelson	5	12	0.8	0.3	3	57	D	1.4	15	106	3.4	0.8
Oliver	3	D	D	D	5	D	D	0.7	3	9	0.3	0.1
Pembina	14	27	2.8	0.6	15	520	477.1	22.5	20	D	D	D
Pierce	13	58	4.4	1.1	NA	NA	NA	NA	12	171	5.6	1.5
Ramsey	19	61	7.9	2.4	9	219	D	9.8	47	681	29.6	7.9
Ransom	15	52	4.7	1.3	8	405	D	12.3	19	129	4.8	1.2
Renville	7	14	1.1	0.3	NA	NA	NA	NA	10	30	1.4	0.2
Richland	32	D	D	D	35	1,871	1,276.7	87.2	47	821	89.6	16.1
Rolette	6	8	0.9	0.3	8	231	D	7.4	25	582	43.1	12.5
Sargent	9	34	3.5	1.5	6	D	D	D	14	D	D	D
Sheridan	4	D	D	D	3	43	D	D	2	D	D	D
Sioux	2	D	D	D	NA	NA	NA	NA	6	D	D	D
Slope	NA	NA	NA	NA	NA	NA	NA	NA	1	D	D	D
Stark	71	430	75.9	23.3	28	898	431.8	44.6	80	1,431	111.6	25.8
Steele	3	3	0.3	0.1	8	158	D	4.9	5	20	1.0	0.1
Stutsman	34	174	16.4	6.4	24	902	500.6	37.7	60	926	40.2	11.9
Towner	8	21	1.9	0.5	4	49	D	1.0	9	32	1.3	0.3
Traill	10	31	3.1	1.4	15	311	D	12.3	26	203	7.7	2.0
Walsh	24	88	8.5	3.0	10	522	111.2	17.8	36	259	12.0	2.7

STATE County	Health care and social assistance, 2012				Other services, 2012				Nonemployer businesses, 2015		Value of residential construction authorized by building permits, 2017	
	Number of establish-ments	Number of employees	Receipts (mil dol)	Annual payroll (mil dol)	Number of establis-hments	Number of employees	Receipts (mil dol)	Annual payroll (mil dol)	Number	Receipts (mil dol)	New construction ($1,000)	Number of housing units
	159	160	161	162	163	164	165	166	167	168	169	170
NORTH CAROLINA— Cont'd												
Swain	31	736	89.3	26.7	18	D	D	D	1,346	45.4	7,984	56
Transylvania	70	1,589	148.7	57.5	46	248	21.0	6.0	3,113	128.8	39,912	112
Tyrrell	8	D	D	D	7	44	4.2	1.4	298	10.5	429	3
Union	292	5,038	533.9	201.5	281	1,255	109.2	32.8	17,148	776.7	354,173	1,537
Vance	101	2,512	205.0	83.0	48	225	22.7	6.1	2,500	94.1	9,744	60
Wake	2,688	47,097	5,110.4	2,066.2	1,699	12,705	1,463.3	420.1	84,397	3,906.3	2,147,746	11,335
Warren	23	446	20.0	9.7	12	D	D	D	1,004	34.2	12,339	41
Washington	34	665	34.7	15.0	11	D	D	D	638	18.8	804	6
Watauga	140	3,419	624.9	144.3	82	349	28.4	7.6	4,774	205.3	85,881	325
Wayne	254	6,896	606.6	265.8	142	939	69.3	20.3	6,147	229.8	48,373	280
Wilkes	147	2,783	233.7	91.5	72	338	23.2	8.4	4,460	184.2	24,877	120
Wilson	200	5,103	408.7	169.3	114	619	54.4	15.0	4,650	170.9	52,467	348
Yadkin	52	982	60.4	24.8	35	D	D	D	2,414	91.8	3,266	6
Yancey	32	D	D	D	24	86	7.5	2.2	1,606	53.9	4,591	16
NORTH DAKOTA	1,856	56,639	5,418.4	2,414.4	1,716	9,232	1,064.0	253.7	53,263	2,746.0	606,686	3,411
Adams	13	D	D	D	9	D	D	D	208	8.3	0	0
Barnes	37	1,156	53.4	26.8	28	147	10.5	2.9	881	45.6	12,449	105
Benson	6	50	1.5	0.8	3	10	1.8	0.2	298	11.3	310	1
Billings	NA	NA	NA	NA	4	14	1.7	0.4	102	7.1	1,645	6
Bottineau	6	256	14.3	6.8	9	D	D	D	654	27.2	1,869	5
Bowman	11	226	16.7	8.3	14	D	D	D	272	11.6	1,884	5
Burke	5	D	D	D	2	D	D	D	214	11.5	560	3
Burleigh	271	10,591	1,080.5	488.2	254	1,691	208.8	53.8	7,132	399.6	85,457	433
Cass	439	15,347	1,909.7	815.0	380	2,549	278.0	71.4	11,937	719.3	266,398	1,682
Cavalier	10	242	15.7	5.7	11	D	D	D	390	14.1	995	3
Dickey	23	409	31.5	13.0	20	67	5.9	1.6	441	14.9	1,030	2
Divide	6	D	D	D	5	D	D	D	214	9.3	82	1
Dunn	4	D	D	D	11	D	D	D	334	22.7	5,167	15
Eddy	9	223	11.3	6.5	7	D	D	D	197	7.5	350	2
Emmons	11	213	10.1	5.7	7	12	0.7	0.1	270	8.3	970	4
Foster	11	302	22.9	10.1	7	17	1.2	0.3	287	13.7	1,478	6
Golden Valley	5	114	7.0	3.3	7	28	1.2	0.4	191	7.1	1,000	4
Grand Forks	160	6,865	668.9	301.2	148	827	103.2	21.7	4,000	196.3	51,521	321
Grant	7	224	12.1	5.3	5	D	D	D	220	7.8	898	7
Griggs	5	D	D	D	7	D	D	D	211	8.9	340	3
Hettinger	10	110	5.1	2.6	8	D	D	D	213	8.2	75	1
Kidder	6	47	1.7	0.8	3	D	D	D	241	10.9	425	2
LaMoure	13	D	D	D	13	49	4.4	0.9	342	13.8	703	3
Logan	7	148	4.6	2.5	7	D	D	D	182	7.6	500	1
McHenry	6	D	D	D	7	D	D	D	425	17.6	1,283	7
McIntosh	10	308	17.0	8.9	7	19	1.0	0.2	239	10.6	0	0
McKenzie	9	184	15.1	6.1	27	112	10.6	2.6	769	48.5	15,287	121
McLean	19	443	23.8	12.0	19	D	D	D	701	30.4	9,587	45
Mercer	18	445	26.7	12.7	16	44	4.0	0.9	635	17.8	1,494	5
Morton	64	1,627	99.3	48.3	58	D	D	D	2,320	125.4	45,318	196
Mountrail	13	196	12.5	6.2	19	83	10.1	2.5	711	39.6	3,338	27
Nelson	10	256	11.5	5.6	12	D	D	D	292	10.3	630	1
Oliver	4	D	D	D	2	D	D	D	129	5.6	943	3
Pembina	16	336	19.1	7.2	18	D	D	D	558	22.9	376	2
Pierce	9	D	D	D	14	D	D	D	356	14.4	2,270	9
Ramsey	41	888	56.7	26.1	28	131	10.9	2.2	891	37.2	468	4
Ransom	25	420	26.5	11.9	22	75	6.5	1.3	365	16.2	950	4
Renville	7	D	D	D	3	D	D	D	180	8.0	0	0
Richland	45	578	35.6	18.7	38	143	11.2	3.0	1,148	55.7	6,851	34
Rolette	25	549	54.7	24.7	9	D	D	D	662	17.2	300	1
Sargent	7	65	3.0	1.8	8	31	5.1	0.8	294	13.1	3,390	18
Sheridan	2	D	D	D	5	D	D	D	109	4.1	197	5
Sioux	1	D	D	D	2	D	D	D	94	3.9	0	0
Slope	NA	NA	NA	NA	1	D	D	D	59	4.1	0	0
Stark	91	1,927	131.4	60.4	79	585	78.6	16.0	2,542	139.0	23,210	90
Steele	1	D	D	D	4	7	1.2	0.2	153	9.2	360	2
Stutsman	62	2,423	154.8	88.7	54	299	23.6	6.9	1,347	59.0	6,807	23
Towner	3	D	D	D	6	30	2.5	0.4	246	8.5	0	0
Traill	20	595	34.4	17.5	23	80	15.9	2.2	578	25.3	3,208	12
Walsh	39	726	45.8	21.7	38	101	7.0	1.9	786	33.4	400	1

Table B. States and Counties — Government Employment and Payroll, and Local Government Finances

STATE County	Government employment and payroll, 2012									Local government finances				
			March payroll (percent of total)							General revenue				
												Taxes		
													Per capita[1] (dollars)	
	Full-time equivalent employees	March payroll (dollars)	Adminis-tration, judicial, and legal	Police and corrections	Fire protection	Highways and transpor-tation	Health and welfare	Natural resources and utilities	Education and libraries	Total (mil dol)	Inter-govern-mental (mil dol)	Total (mil dol)	Total	Property
	171	172	173	174	175	176	177	178	179	180	181	182	183	184
NORTH CAROLINA— Cont'd														
Swain	570	1,634,935	2.8	6.9	0.0	0.2	15.2	3.5	58.7	39.0	24.0	8.3	586	366
Transylvania	1,211	3,349,488	5.1	9.9	0.5	1.7	16.3	4.8	52.7	82.0	34.9	38.2	1,162	930
Tyrrell	212	788,126	5.4	5.1	0.0	0.3	6.1	4.4	76.8	19.0	12.0	4.7	1,091	930
Union	6,960	22,437,486	4.7	8.5	1.4	0.7	5.2	5.8	72.3	593.9	274.3	239.3	1,148	942
Vance	2,151	6,716,262	3.1	6.3	2.9	1.8	9.0	3.0	71.8	166.4	101.2	37.4	828	618
Wake	31,235	120,436,016	3.6	9.3	3.7	3.7	7.3	6.6	61.6	3,180.9	1,227.2	1,366.9	1,436	1,077
Warren	682	2,143,055	2.8	7.9	0.0	0.0	10.7	3.8	61.2	57.4	29.8	20.1	976	845
Washington	551	1,546,357	6.0	8.2	0.0	0.4	15.3	5.7	59.9	40.0	25.2	10.3	805	588
Watauga	1,481	4,632,704	6.0	11.0	2.1	4.5	13.2	7.1	47.6	137.3	56.5	63.0	1,214	855
Wayne	5,237	14,176,474	3.0	6.2	2.1	1.3	9.2	6.0	66.2	346.7	199.6	101.5	817	585
Wilkes	3,431	10,259,077	2.0	4.8	0.3	0.9	32.4	1.6	56.6	184.5	95.3	58.2	840	635
Wilson	3,417	11,244,041	5.5	9.5	3.3	2.4	11.6	11.2	53.8	288.2	140.0	90.5	1,105	863
Yadkin	1,268	3,737,818	3.9	5.9	0.1	0.5	11.5	3.0	70.9	88.3	50.5	29.0	763	624
Yancey	773	2,283,963	4.6	6.2	0.2	1.0	23.0	3.1	60.9	45.5	25.0	17.2	973	798
NORTH DAKOTA	X	X	X	X	X	X	X	X	X	X	X	X	X	X
Adams	92	255,672	10.2	8.6	0.0	6.4	7.5	3.3	62.1	8.2	3.6	3.0	1,313	1,054
Barnes	418	1,392,699	15.6	9.1	0.5	3.9	5.1	9.8	55.6	66.9	40.2	17.6	1,597	1,448
Benson	305	941,315	6.1	1.3	0.6	5.7	5.8	1.7	78.6	27.9	19.5	4.6	683	672
Billings	71	278,902	16.6	9.9	1.1	28.8	4.2	4.9	31.5	14.4	10.4	1.7	1,884	1,457
Bottineau	258	801,858	8.7	5.1	0.1	7.5	5.5	8.6	64.2	29.2	15.4	8.8	1,337	1,194
Bowman	154	498,076	10.9	6.0	0.1	7.5	7.8	4.7	63.1	25.9	15.6	5.2	1,630	1,395
Burke	132	476,712	12.0	4.9	0.0	8.5	2.8	2.4	67.3	11.4	4.8	4.3	2,215	1,096
Burleigh	2,640	9,881,026	4.2	8.2	4.2	3.6	6.6	9.1	61.0	347.2	171.6	100.7	1,174	925
Cass	4,659	18,693,995	4.8	9.4	2.9	4.9	9.6	7.5	60.1	694.2	293.1	246.4	1,578	1,145
Cavalier	150	482,792	10.3	7.1	0.0	7.2	5.9	7.5	58.4	17.1	7.4	6.7	1,688	1,662
Dickey	177	602,013	11.3	6.4	0.0	5.8	12.2	3.2	59.7	28.7	12.8	9.2	1,751	1,617
Divide	112	399,142	14.1	7.5	0.0	19.6	4.6	5.6	47.0	17.6	9.2	3.7	1,673	1,505
Dunn	163	514,670	8.7	4.7	0.8	11.8	6.5	2.4	65.0	27.2	19.0	3.9	992	865
Eddy	101	291,076	9.8	5.2	0.0	6.4	5.8	4.1	67.8	12.9	6.6	3.2	1,370	1,257
Emmons	160	461,725	8.9	3.7	0.1	7.4	1.9	9.4	68.6	16.2	7.3	6.2	1,777	1,711
Foster	109	345,480	14.5	2.4	0.1	5.2	6.9	1.6	67.7	14.4	6.3	5.0	1,462	1,302
Golden Valley	168	598,525	4.4	2.4	0.0	4.3	3.1	1.4	83.6	12.6	6.8	3.5	1,923	1,846
Grand Forks	2,414	9,092,121	5.6	9.8	3.4	6.3	6.5	11.9	54.2	280.6	106.1	94.4	1,399	1,054
Grant	103	251,784	10.0	5.5	0.0	9.2	10.7	3.2	60.2	8.5	3.8	3.4	1,448	1,414
Griggs	112	363,293	9.3	4.3	0.0	8.1	9.0	2.0	65.6	13.5	5.4	5.3	2,241	2,176
Hettinger	147	439,881	7.5	2.1	0.1	8.1	4.0	22.4	54.8	15.0	6.5	5.4	2,133	1,985
Kidder	100	305,849	4.8	4.8	0.0	1.6	8.6	4.8	75.3	16.0	7.8	3.7	1,533	1,484
LaMoure	228	740,715	7.4	3.3	0.0	6.3	2.2	19.6	60.3	63.8	47.3	9.5	2,316	2,252
Logan	83	243,512	4.2	4.7	0.0	5.7	6.1	5.0	73.3	10.5	5.6	3.9	2,040	2,023
McHenry	239	766,397	8.6	2.6	0.1	4.2	4.4	4.0	74.9	20.6	10.3	7.3	1,263	1,225
McIntosh	139	432,649	7.6	5.1	0.1	10.8	4.4	16.0	55.9	10.7	5.5	3.7	1,328	1,289
McKenzie	313	1,128,904	9.9	9.8	0.0	9.8	6.5	4.0	57.4	54.1	24.6	7.4	930	751
McLean	438	1,374,148	6.7	7.0	0.0	5.7	12.1	3.3	64.5	43.6	23.1	11.4	1,229	1,093
Mercer	347	1,135,199	9.4	9.5	0.0	9.4	2.8	4.7	62.2	34.8	17.4	9.3	1,093	917
Morton	946	3,200,962	5.4	9.1	1.2	7.7	8.1	5.9	61.5	106.1	48.2	35.2	1,253	1,139
Mountrail	385	1,261,569	8.3	7.4	0.0	8.6	6.2	3.5	65.1	85.8	57.9	12.5	1,434	1,307
Nelson	146	457,045	9.7	3.0	0.0	8.5	4.7	8.9	63.6	17.3	8.0	6.7	2,183	2,144
Oliver	76	233,042	14.9	6.8	0.0	9.6	2.9	7.5	56.4	9.0	3.8	3.7	2,018	1,749
Pembina	393	1,633,628	6.4	4.3	0.0	3.1	4.1	45.4	36.2	40.0	15.7	16.1	2,221	2,125
Pierce	154	464,990	7.2	8.4	0.0	4.1	5.0	3.6	69.5	21.3	8.8	5.5	1,245	1,151
Ramsey	543	1,755,199	7.3	12.7	1.3	4.3	10.4	5.8	57.4	84.1	57.8	15.4	1,331	1,034
Ransom	223	692,010	8.7	4.1	0.8	4.5	6.6	5.2	68.5	23.4	12.3	7.8	1,436	1,220
Renville	140	452,741	8.2	6.0	0.0	8.7	3.5	2.3	70.0	19.2	9.5	5.9	2,288	2,255
Richland	582	2,019,868	4.8	9.7	0.0	6.5	9.5	7.4	61.0	75.6	33.2	29.0	1,787	1,613
Rolette	726	2,856,302	1.9	2.3	0.2	1.2	3.8	2.8	87.6	53.9	43.3	5.9	409	382
Sargent	167	536,100	9.7	3.9	0.0	3.3	5.4	6.8	70.4	21.4	9.5	8.1	2,073	2,002
Sheridan	59	160,666	12.8	0.0	0.0	8.5	0.2	3.7	73.9	5.6	2.2	2.9	2,255	2,229
Sioux	129	394,909	4.4	0.8	1.7	4.0	0.3	1.7	86.3	11.5	9.3	1.5	349	348
Slope	36	114,876	15.1	4.2	0.0	6.9	0.2	2.1	68.6	5.2	3.3	1.0	1,297	1,208
Stark	970	3,430,314	4.3	17.8	1.0	4.4	10.3	9.5	51.8	103.5	43.2	33.0	1,232	836
Steele	76	279,013	12.8	4.5	0.1	2.6	1.4	2.1	76.4	12.4	4.6	4.9	2,441	2,369
Stutsman	738	2,551,998	5.2	10.8	0.9	5.8	9.7	7.6	58.2	88.6	38.8	29.6	1,413	1,195
Towner	120	341,158	12.4	5.1	0.0	10.5	3.7	3.7	63.4	10.1	3.9	3.9	1,695	1,626
Traill	299	1,042,936	6.6	4.5	0.0	5.7	5.6	2.7	74.1	35.7	16.3	11.8	1,468	1,367
Walsh	425	1,396,845	7.5	5.6	0.0	5.1	6.2	9.3	63.8	46.8	22.8	16.0	1,451	1,295

1. Based on the resident population estimated as of July 1 of the year shown.

Table B. States and Counties — Local Government Finances, Government Employment, and Income Taxes

STATE County	Total (mil dol)	Per capita[1] (dollars)	Education	Health and hospitals	Police protection	Public welfare	Highways	Total (mil dol)	Per capita[1] (dollars)	Federal civilian	Federal military	State and local	Number of returns	Mean adjusted gross income	Mean income tax
	185	186	187	188	189	190	191	192	193	194	195	196	197	198	199
NORTH CAROLINA— Cont'd															
Swain	40.3	2,852	47.4	5.4	7.2	14.3	0.2	10.7	758	155	33	2,489	7,670	40,103	3,623
Transylvania	80.6	2,453	45.7	4.8	9.9	7.4	1.1	13.0	395	127	75	1,371	14,190	52,210	5,684
Tyrrell	18.9	4,355	54.4	1.2	9.5	7.3	0.7	10.3	2,385	22	0	444	1,680	32,920	2,646
Union	614.4	2,946	53.1	2.0	6.1	4.7	1.0	748.0	3,587	279	520	9,059	95,300	80,765	11,321
Vance	164.7	3,650	56.0	9.8	6.5	7.1	0.6	48.5	1,074	96	101	2,675	18,730	38,774	3,120
Wake	3,282.9	3,448	42.3	4.0	6.5	3.3	2.2	9,085.4	9,542	5,394	2,969	79,680	480,890	79,902	11,450
Warren	54.2	2,635	50.1	5.1	10.5	10.6	0.3	7.2	348	32	44	1,299	7,650	37,051	2,862
Washington	43.9	3,443	43.6	0.4	7.2	13.8	1.5	7.6	594	30	28	791	5,190	37,464	3,098
Watauga	128.3	2,473	32.3	4.5	9.1	5.1	3.7	134.7	2,596	112	116	6,439	19,530	52,249	6,142
Wayne	344.7	2,774	55.1	4.8	6.3	6.3	1.4	151.3	1,217	1,232	4,320	8,007	52,160	45,402	4,625
Wilkes	183.3	2,645	60.4	4.2	5.5	7.8	0.6	49.6	715	186	157	4,252	27,450	44,796	4,570
Wilson	278.4	3,401	41.7	5.4	8.2	8.1	1.5	192.4	2,351	130	186	5,028	35,750	45,155	4,571
Yadkin	87.9	2,308	57.4	4.6	6.9	10.0	0.9	50.3	1,322	73	86	1,438	16,270	45,322	4,094
Yancey	44.5	2,522	51.4	2.5	6.4	10.3	0.6	14.3	810	45	41	850	7,300	40,083	3,347
NORTH DAKOTA	X	X	X	X	X	X	X	X	X	9,450	11,567	68,278	369,350	69,134	9,803
Adams	8.2	3,529	45.9	0.0	4.8	3.9	18.8	0.1	33	18	14	126	1,130	52,942	6,266
Barnes	64.0	5,811	34.3	4.3	8.8	3.5	21.8	18.2	1,650	79	66	1,066	5,410	56,516	6,492
Benson	27.4	4,053	65.7	0.2	1.4	3.3	17.2	0.6	85	135	42	1,405	2,560	47,262	5,603
Billings	17.0	18,828	14.4	6.5	9.0	0.0	56.2	0.1	133	35	0	126	490	87,629	14,022
Bottineau	32.3	4,914	41.2	2.2	4.2	0.0	32.5	11.5	1,748	70	40	622	3,270	65,682	9,007
Bowman	21.3	6,655	38.7	2.4	2.9	1.6	30.5	1.3	409	25	20	251	1,620	70,241	10,578
Burke	10.7	4,949	47.9	0.4	2.6	2.0	26.1	0.1	67	88	14	181	1,210	72,319	9,833
Burleigh	313.0	3,649	41.6	1.2	5.7	1.7	12.7	181.5	2,116	1,133	580	10,743	46,940	77,122	11,297
Cass	703.9	4,508	39.9	0.1	5.6	3.0	13.2	1,204.5	7,713	2,369	1,095	12,601	85,900	71,327	10,507
Cavalier	16.8	4,263	40.9	2.0	4.3	4.3	23.7	11.4	2,878	42	24	214	1,970	64,358	8,572
Dickey	36.5	6,935	38.3	1.4	3.0	1.6	13.3	34.3	6,520	26	31	304	2,510	51,295	6,010
Divide	23.6	10,577	21.6	1.5	4.6	0.7	33.8	0.9	389	36	15	157	1,210	87,936	11,865
Dunn	24.7	6,221	37.5	0.0	3.7	1.5	33.1	0.3	74	16	27	305	2,160	89,505	15,558
Eddy	13.4	5,660	43.4	0.1	4.4	2.5	14.8	1.6	686	22	14	160	1,160	50,009	5,619
Emmons	14.9	4,274	52.4	1.3	1.9	2.0	14.2	3.8	1,081	23	21	240	1,630	46,896	5,769
Foster	13.8	4,065	45.3	1.9	3.7	2.8	14.1	10.6	3,116	26	21	219	1,720	66,293	9,468
Golden Valley	12.7	7,062	41.7	1.5	3.3	2.2	17.1	4.6	2,568	10	11	174	880	64,327	7,716
Grand Forks	251.5	3,728	47.0	1.0	5.1	1.4	4.7	705.5	10,456	1,032	1,934	9,494	33,760	61,969	8,355
Grant	8.1	3,453	49.5	18.0	2.5	2.6	12.7	1.2	524	24	15	133	1,080	42,149	5,098
Griggs	13.1	5,527	43.9	3.5	2.8	2.9	21.9	3.7	1,562	21	14	172	1,170	54,468	5,894
Hettinger	16.2	6,357	49.8	0.0	2.6	2.3	14.4	1.9	738	19	16	194	1,240	58,929	7,677
Kidder	15.9	6,560	32.7	24.9	1.7	1.4	20.1	2.4	973	21	15	161	1,170	50,482	5,748
LaMoure	23.0	5,581	54.0	0.0	2.5	2.6	15.6	7.0	1,691	41	26	302	2,010	54,262	7,087
Logan	8.8	4,566	63.4	1.0	2.8	0.2	13.9	1.7	867	18	12	138	930	38,669	4,411
McHenry	20.8	3,592	61.0	0.0	2.3	2.7	13.3	1.0	180	45	37	331	2,870	54,732	6,023
McIntosh	10.1	3,663	56.1	1.5	2.9	2.7	15.9	1.7	619	18	16	185	1,330	47,792	5,759
McKenzie	61.8	7,738	29.9	3.0	3.5	1.3	31.4	15.2	1,897	70	79	2,082	4,800	135,533	27,313
McLean	38.0	4,086	53.6	1.4	4.7	3.8	12.0	18.4	1,973	119	61	741	4,710	61,640	7,512
Mercer	37.5	4,418	49.3	0.5	5.7	1.3	17.4	59.3	6,990	38	54	557	4,330	72,727	9,052
Morton	106.7	3,797	49.8	2.5	5.2	2.3	6.9	103.5	3,685	106	190	1,671	15,650	64,841	8,328
Mountrail	86.5	9,907	36.3	0.5	1.9	1.2	37.1	26.9	3,081	48	61	744	4,700	93,921	15,856
Nelson	16.3	5,277	44.9	2.6	2.2	1.3	18.7	14.3	4,644	20	18	230	1,540	53,882	5,893
Oliver	7.8	4,256	42.5	0.0	3.8	0.0	8.3	20.2	10,993	0	12	108	900	65,791	7,552
Pembina	37.7	5,190	45.2	0.5	3.9	2.4	8.5	14.9	2,043	233	80	556	3,600	62,763	8,517
Pierce	24.3	5,462	53.5	2.7	4.5	1.9	9.5	4.3	974	21	25	255	2,060	52,682	5,819
Ramsey	75.8	6,569	35.0	0.9	2.9	2.1	20.4	33.0	2,865	149	70	1,383	5,750	55,779	6,690
Ransom	25.2	4,634	45.6	1.6	2.9	1.7	12.3	21.6	3,965	40	33	491	2,830	54,021	5,832
Renville	20.6	8,041	40.3	0.1	2.1	0.0	28.2	3.6	1,387	25	16	206	1,260	61,060	7,344
Richland	75.3	4,645	43.3	4.4	4.5	1.9	13.1	88.9	5,482	65	102	1,907	7,800	60,298	7,275
Rolette	53.3	3,703	79.0	1.4	2.2	2.2	5.1	6.0	419	935	92	2,036	5,420	42,689	3,924
Sargent	19.0	4,886	48.6	1.5	1.7	2.4	13.8	11.5	2,940	42	24	264	2,050	55,889	6,623
Sheridan	5.5	4,306	39.7	1.2	1.7	1.0	20.2	0.2	179	10	0	106	650	42,989	4,514
Sioux	11.0	2,521	85.3	0.0	0.5	4.1	5.3	3.0	686	230	28	1,257	1,300	31,448	2,365
Slope	3.6	4,734	14.2	2.9	4.4	0.0	33.2	0.4	538	0	0	37	350	65,689	6,829
Stark	96.5	3,605	41.6	0.9	4.4	3.4	11.2	19.1	712	203	193	2,275	16,010	80,041	11,932
Steele	11.3	5,664	42.7	0.0	2.8	4.2	26.4	5.7	2,876	13	12	107	990	57,015	6,994
Stutsman	83.3	3,978	42.4	3.2	5.0	2.2	13.9	57.9	2,766	176	123	1,891	10,410	58,762	7,452
Towner	8.9	3,844	45.7	5.0	3.3	2.3	18.6	2.2	931	20	14	130	1,140	48,038	5,632
Traill	35.4	4,390	54.9	0.9	3.8	2.9	12.5	42.5	5,269	36	49	860	3,730	63,020	7,668
Walsh	51.9	4,703	54.4	1.3	4.4	2.5	9.7	23.8	2,156	56	67	1,113	5,450	54,507	6,372

1. Based on the resident population estimated as of July 1 of the year shown.

State / county code	CBSA code[1]	County code[2]	STATE County	Land area[3] (sq. mi)	Total persons 2017	Rank	Per square mile	White	Black	American Indian, Alaska Native	Asian and Pacific Islander	Percent Hispanic or Latino[4]	Under 5 years	5 to 17 years	18 to 24 years	25 to 34 years	35 to 44 years	45 to 54 years
				1	2	3	4	5	6	7	8	9	10	11	12	13	14	15
			NORTH DAKOTA— Cont'd															
38,101	33,500	5	Ward	2,013.2	68,946	773	34.2	85.2	5.5	3.1	2.7	6.3	7.7	15.6	13.6	18.4	11.8	9.9
38,103		9	Wells	1,270.7	4,022	2,901	3.2	97.3	0.9	1.2	0.5	1.2	5.6	14.8	5.7	9.2	8.2	12.4
38,105	48,780	7	Williams	2,077.7	33,349	1,344	16.1	84.1	4.6	6.0	1.6	7.0	9.3	18.7	8.6	18.9	12.6	10.9
39,000		0	OHIO	40,862.5	11,658,609	X	285.3	81.0	13.9	0.7	2.8	3.8	6.0	16.4	9.2	13.1	11.8	13.0
39,001		6	Adams	583.9	27,726	1,505	47.5	97.8	1.0	1.2	0.4	1.0	6.0	18.1	7.3	11.0	11.9	13.8
39,003	30,620	3	Allen	402.5	103,198	583	256.4	83.4	14.4	0.7	1.3	3.1	6.2	17.0	9.7	12.3	11.6	12.3
39,005	11,740	4	Ashland	423.0	53,628	942	126.8	96.9	1.4	0.6	1.0	1.4	5.9	16.9	10.9	11.0	10.8	12.4
39,007	11,780	4	Ashtabula	702.1	97,807	607	139.3	91.5	4.9	0.8	0.8	4.2	5.6	16.6	7.6	11.5	11.3	13.8
39,009	11,900	4	Athens	503.6	66,597	799	132.2	91.3	3.7	1.0	4.3	1.9	3.9	10.7	29.2	12.6	9.9	10.3
39,011	47,540	4	Auglaize	401.4	45,778	1,057	114.0	96.9	1.2	0.5	1.0	1.7	6.3	18.0	7.9	11.2	11.4	13.0
39,013	48,540	3	Belmont	532.1	68,029	782	127.9	94.2	5.0	0.6	0.7	1.0	5.0	14.0	7.5	12.6	11.7	13.1
39,015	17,140	1	Brown	490.0	43,576	1,099	88.9	97.6	1.3	0.8	0.5	1.0	5.7	17.3	7.5	11.1	11.9	13.9
39,017	17,140	1	Butler	467.0	380,604	183	815.0	83.2	9.7	0.6	4.0	4.7	6.2	17.5	12.3	11.7	12.0	13.0
39,019	15,940	2	Carroll	394.6	27,385	1,513	69.4	97.2	1.1	0.9	0.6	1.4	5.0	16.0	7.3	10.3	10.9	13.6
39,021	46,500	6	Champaign	428.4	38,840	1,209	90.7	95.4	3.4	1.0	0.8	1.6	5.3	17.2	8.4	11.3	11.4	14.2
39,023	44,220	3	Clark	397.5	134,557	471	338.5	86.8	10.7	0.9	1.2	3.3	5.9	16.7	9.0	11.6	10.8	13.0
39,025	17,140	1	Clermont	452.1	204,214	325	451.7	95.0	2.2	0.7	1.7	2.0	5.8	17.5	7.6	12.5	12.4	13.8
39,027	48,940	6	Clinton	408.7	42,009	1,131	102.8	95.3	3.4	0.8	0.8	1.6	6.1	17.2	9.6	11.4	11.6	13.2
39,029	41,400	4	Columbiana	531.9	103,077	585	193.8	95.4	3.1	0.6	0.6	1.7	5.2	15.3	7.3	11.3	11.8	13.4
39,031	18,740	6	Coshocton	563.9	36,544	1,262	64.8	97.1	1.9	0.7	0.6	1.1	6.4	17.3	7.3	11.4	11.3	12.9
39,033	15,340	4	Crawford	401.8	41,746	1,137	103.9	96.5	1.7	0.6	0.8	1.7	5.7	16.0	7.7	11.1	11.4	13.2
39,035	17,460	1	Cuyahoga	457.2	1,248,514	34	2,730.8	60.9	30.9	0.6	3.8	5.9	5.8	15.1	8.9	13.8	11.4	12.8
39,037	24,820	6	Darke	598.1	51,536	967	86.2	97.2	1.2	0.6	0.7	1.6	6.0	17.8	7.8	10.6	11.2	13.2
39,039	19,580	4	Defiance	411.5	38,156	1,222	92.7	87.8	2.3	0.7	0.7	9.9	5.7	17.3	9.0	11.6	11.8	12.2
39,041	18,140	1	Delaware	443.2	200,464	330	452.3	87.1	4.4	0.5	7.4	2.6	6.2	20.6	7.7	9.7	15.1	15.3
39,043	41,780	4	Erie	251.5	74,817	741	297.5	85.9	10.6	0.8	1.0	4.4	5.3	15.2	8.0	11.2	10.4	13.0
39,045	18,140	1	Fairfield	504.4	154,733	425	306.8	88.0	9.0	0.8	2.1	2.1	5.9	18.1	8.4	11.9	12.8	14.2
39,047	47,920	6	Fayette	406.4	28,752	1,463	70.7	94.5	3.6	0.8	1.2	2.1	6.2	17.4	7.7	12.0	12.0	13.4
39,049	18,140	1	Franklin	532.4	1,291,981	31	2,426.7	66.1	24.6	0.9	6.2	5.5	7.2	16.2	9.9	18.2	13.3	12.1
39,051	45,780	2	Fulton	405.4	42,289	1,127	104.3	90.0	1.1	0.6	0.7	8.8	6.1	17.7	8.1	11.1	11.7	13.1
39,053	38,580	6	Gallia	466.5	29,973	1,433	64.3	95.1	3.4	1.0	0.9	1.5	6.3	16.8	8.4	11.7	11.4	12.8
39,055	17,460	1	Geauga	400.2	93,918	627	234.7	96.4	1.7	0.4	1.0	1.5	5.2	17.9	8.4	8.5	10.3	14.2
39,057	19,380	2	Greene	413.7	166,752	387	403.1	86.5	8.5	1.0	4.2	2.8	5.7	15.0	12.0	13.4	11.2	12.3
39,059	15,740	6	Guernsey	522.3	39,093	1,202	74.8	96.6	2.6	0.9	0.7	1.1	5.9	16.4	7.8	11.6	11.0	13.3
39,061	17,140	1	Hamilton	405.9	813,822	75	2,005.0	67.4	27.7	0.7	3.4	3.3	6.6	16.5	9.3	15.2	11.7	12.4
39,063	22,300	4	Hancock	531.4	75,754	731	142.6	90.8	2.6	0.6	2.3	5.4	6.1	16.3	9.1	13.5	11.6	12.8
39,065		6	Hardin	470.4	31,364	1,398	66.7	96.4	1.6	0.7	1.0	1.7	6.2	16.9	15.4	10.4	10.8	12.0
39,067		6	Harrison	402.3	15,216	2,084	37.8	96.4	3.0	0.6	0.5	1.1	5.4	15.7	6.8	10.3	10.7	13.6
39,069		6	Henry	416.0	27,185	1,517	65.3	90.7	1.1	0.7	0.7	7.7	5.7	17.6	7.8	11.4	11.9	12.8
39,071		6	Highland	553.1	42,971	1,115	77.7	96.7	2.4	0.8	0.6	1.1	6.4	17.6	7.5	11.3	11.9	13.3
39,073	18,140	1	Hocking	421.3	28,474	1,471	67.6	97.7	1.2	1.0	0.5	0.9	5.7	16.4	7.6	11.2	11.6	13.8
39,075		7	Holmes	422.5	43,957	1,094	104.0	98.4	0.6	0.3	0.4	0.9	8.5	23.2	9.8	12.6	10.9	10.7
39,077	35,940	4	Huron	491.5	58,494	882	119.0	91.6	2.0	0.8	0.6	6.6	6.4	17.9	8.4	11.6	11.6	13.5
39,079	27,160	7	Jackson	420.3	32,449	1,371	77.2	97.4	1.3	1.2	0.5	1.1	6.7	17.2	7.5	12.4	12.3	13.2
39,081	48,260	3	Jefferson	408.2	66,359	805	162.6	92.5	6.8	0.7	0.8	1.4	5.0	14.3	9.4	10.9	10.5	13.0
39,083	34,540	4	Knox	525.5	61,261	854	116.6	96.6	1.6	0.6	1.0	1.5	6.0	16.8	11.5	10.9	10.7	12.4
39,085	17,460	1	Lake	229.3	230,117	286	1,003.6	89.9	5.1	0.5	1.9	4.3	5.0	15.3	7.8	11.8	11.3	13.8
39,087	26,580	2	Lawrence	453.4	60,249	867	132.9	96.1	3.1	0.7	0.7	1.0	5.7	16.2	7.5	11.9	12.2	13.9
39,089	18,140	1	Licking	682.4	173,448	377	254.2	92.4	5.1	0.8	1.8	1.9	6.1	17.2	9.0	11.8	12.0	13.9
39,091	13,340	6	Logan	458.4	45,325	1,067	98.9	95.5	3.2	0.8	1.2	1.5	6.1	17.2	7.8	11.2	11.9	13.4
39,093	17,460	1	Lorain	491.2	307,924	226	626.9	80.6	9.5	0.8	1.7	10.0	5.7	16.6	8.6	11.2	12.1	13.7
39,095	45,780	2	Lucas	341.0	430,887	163	1,263.6	71.4	21.3	0.8	2.3	7.1	6.4	16.7	9.0	14.1	11.5	12.6
39,097	18,140	1	Madison	465.9	44,036	1,091	94.5	89.9	7.4	0.8	1.6	2.0	5.0	15.6	8.0	13.6	14.2	15.1
39,099	49,660	2	Mahoning	411.5	229,796	288	558.4	77.9	16.3	0.7	1.3	5.9	5.3	14.8	8.6	11.7	11.1	12.7
39,101	32,020	4	Marion	403.8	64,967	819	160.9	90.1	7.6	0.7	0.9	2.6	5.8	15.1	8.2	13.2	12.4	13.9
39,103	17,460	1	Medina	421.4	178,371	368	423.3	95.1	1.9	0.5	1.6	2.1	5.4	17.3	7.6	10.7	12.4	14.9
39,105		6	Meigs	430.1	23,080	1,678	53.7	97.8	1.5	0.8	0.4	0.8	5.2	16.3	6.7	11.1	12.1	13.9
39,107	16,380	7	Mercer	462.4	40,873	1,158	88.4	96.5	1.0	0.5	1.3	1.9	7.3	18.3	8.1	11.6	10.8	11.9
39,109	19,380	2	Miami	406.6	105,122	571	258.5	94.3	3.5	0.6	1.9	1.7	6.0	17.1	7.2	11.9	11.9	13.5
39,111		8	Monroe	455.7	13,946	2,167	30.6	98.4	1.2	0.9	0.4	0.6	5.3	15.3	7.0	10.1	10.7	13.4
39,113	19,380	2	Montgomery	461.8	531,542	130	1,151.0	73.2	22.7	0.9	3.0	2.9	6.2	16.0	9.2	13.5	11.3	12.6
39,115		6	Morgan	416.4	14,709	2,116	35.3	95.2	5.3	1.5	0.8	0.9	4.8	16.2	7.5	10.6	11.1	13.2
39,117	18,140	1	Morrow	406.1	34,994	1,303	86.2	97.3	1.2	0.8	0.7	1.4	5.5	18.0	7.2	10.8	12.3	14.2
39,119	49,780	4	Muskingum	664.6	86,149	667	129.6	94.2	5.8	0.9	0.9	1.1	6.2	16.6	9.0	12.1	11.5	13.1
39,121		7	Noble	398.0	14,406	2,136	36.2	96.1	3.1	0.7	0.5	0.6	4.8	13.6	6.0	9.2	8.2	11.8

1. CBSA = Core Based Statistical Area. See Appendix A for explanation. See Appendix B for list of metropolitan areas with component counties. 2. County type code from the Economic Research Service of USDA Rural-Urban Continuum Codes. See Appendix A for definition. 3. Dry land or land partially or temporarily covered by water. 4. May be of any race.

Table B. States and Counties — **Population and Households**

STATE County	55 to 64 years	65 to 74 years	75 years and over	Percent female	2000	2010	2000-2010	2010-2017	Births	Deaths	Net Migration	Number	Persons per house-hold	Family house-holds	Female family house-holder[1]	One person
	16	17	18	19	20	21	22	23	24	25	26	27	28	29	30	31
NORTH DAKOTA— Cont'd																
Ward	10.6	6.6	5.8	47.1	58,795	61,675	4.9	11.8	8,485	3,487	2,081	26,772	2.48	60.9	6.7	30.2
Wells	16.3	13.3	14.4	49.0	5,102	4,207	-17.5	-4.4	295	478	-4	2,026	2.01	62.5	3.8	35.5
Williams	11.4	5.4	4.4	46.4	19,761	22,399	13.3	48.9	4,085	1,648	8,151	12,390	2.50	60.7	6.5	27.1
OHIO	13.8	9.6	7.1	51.0	11,353,140	11,536,730	1.6	1.1	1,004,081	824,167	-54,642	4,601,449	2.45	63.9	12.8	30.1
Adams	14.5	10.3	7.1	50.2	27,330	28,552	4.5	-2.9	2,431	2,411	-841	10,885	2.55	68.5	12.9	27.4
Allen	13.7	9.7	7.5	49.5	108,473	106,326	-2.0	-2.9	9,240	7,868	-4,504	40,039	2.51	65.0	14.1	29.2
Ashland	13.9	10.2	8.0	50.9	52,523	53,139	1.2	0.9	4,475	3,998	20	20,391	2.51	68.0	10.5	26.5
Ashtabula	15.0	10.8	7.8	49.6	102,728	101,488	-1.2	-3.6	8,029	8,383	-3,327	38,800	2.47	64.3	12.5	29.7
Athens	11.0	7.6	4.9	50.3	62,223	64,764	4.1	2.8	3,927	3,474	1,285	22,328	2.48	54.3	9.7	33.3
Auglaize	14.3	10.0	7.9	50.2	46,611	45,949	-1.4	-0.4	3,961	3,489	-639	18,231	2.49	68.4	8.7	26.4
Belmont	15.8	11.5	8.8	48.8	70,226	70,402	0.3	-3.4	5,041	6,411	-943	27,732	2.35	64.4	10.8	31.4
Brown	14.8	10.3	7.5	50.3	42,285	44,843	6.0	-2.8	3,633	3,528	-1,368	17,047	2.55	70.6	12.5	24.4
Butler	12.9	8.5	5.8	51.0	332,807	368,130	10.6	3.4	32,888	22,747	2,527	135,100	2.68	69.0	12.0	24.7
Carroll	16.1	12.1	8.7	50.0	28,836	28,836	0.0	-5.0	2,011	2,191	-1,271	10,871	2.54	71.9	8.7	23.3
Champaign	14.3	10.4	7.4	50.2	38,890	40,093	3.1	-3.1	2,903	2,820	-1,339	15,162	2.53	70.5	11.8	24.0
Clark	14.0	10.9	8.2	51.6	144,742	138,347	-4.4	-2.7	11,573	12,267	-3,032	54,681	2.43	65.1	14.5	28.7
Clermont	14.5	9.6	6.2	50.8	177,977	197,352	10.9	3.5	16,980	11,924	1,975	75,236	2.65	71.0	10.5	23.8
Clinton	14.2	9.8	6.9	50.6	40,543	42,037	3.7	-0.1	3,664	3,121	-566	16,077	2.53	67.9	11.3	27.1
Columbiana	15.8	11.5	8.5	49.5	112,075	107,841	-3.8	-4.4	7,904	8,795	-3,846	41,782	2.43	68.9	12.7	26.5
Coshocton	14.5	10.6	8.4	50.5	36,655	36,898	0.7	-1.0	3,305	2,862	-785	14,397	2.51	68.3	9.2	27.4
Crawford	14.4	11.4	9.2	51.2	46,966	43,785	-6.8	-4.7	3,464	3,827	-1,675	17,657	2.38	64.7	10.7	30.6
Cuyahoga	14.4	9.8	8.0	52.3	1,393,978	1,280,109	-8.2	-2.5	107,949	98,692	-40,873	534,559	2.30	57.0	15.9	37.3
Darke	14.1	10.6	8.7	50.5	53,309	52,969	-0.6	-2.7	4,454	4,206	-1,677	20,831	2.47	68.5	9.3	27.1
Defiance	14.3	10.3	7.8	50.4	39,500	39,031	-1.2	-2.2	3,171	2,775	-1,277	15,378	2.46	69.4	11.6	24.4
Delaware	12.1	8.3	4.9	50.5	109,989	174,189	58.4	15.1	15,662	7,323	17,849	66,544	2.80	76.1	7.3	20.1
Erie	15.6	12.2	9.1	51.1	79,551	77,066	-3.1	-2.9	5,692	6,682	-1,224	31,731	2.35	63.4	13.4	30.5
Fairfield	13.1	9.3	6.2	50.2	122,759	146,177	19.1	5.9	12,113	8,733	5,274	55,138	2.67	72.7	11.0	23.0
Fayette	13.8	10.3	7.3	50.6	28,433	29,025	2.1	-0.9	2,549	2,534	-276	11,666	2.42	67.2	13.9	27.4
Franklin	11.4	7.1	4.6	51.2	1,068,978	1,163,529	8.8	11.0	134,958	65,458	59,184	489,010	2.46	58.6	14.2	32.1
Fulton	14.8	9.9	7.4	50.3	42,084	42,698	1.5	-1.0	3,553	2,926	-1,041	16,240	2.59	71.9	9.2	24.1
Gallia	14.4	10.5	7.8	50.8	31,069	30,946	-0.4	-3.1	2,729	2,638	-1,077	11,495	2.57	69.7	11.4	26.6
Geauga	15.7	11.5	8.2	50.5	90,895	93,410	2.8	0.5	6,609	5,768	-320	34,890	2.67	75.5	8.2	20.1
Greene	13.7	9.8	7.0	50.8	147,886	161,574	9.3	3.2	13,060	9,912	2,038	64,279	2.41	65.6	10.3	28.5
Guernsey	14.9	11.1	8.0	50.2	40,792	40,091	-1.7	-2.5	3,343	3,264	-1,059	15,863	2.45	65.3	11.9	28.4
Hamilton	13.4	8.6	6.5	51.7	845,303	802,387	-5.1	1.4	79,087	56,157	-11,229	335,334	2.35	58.1	15.1	34.8
Hancock	13.8	9.6	7.3	50.7	71,295	74,789	4.9	1.3	6,593	5,163	-433	31,549	2.34	63.2	9.4	29.5
Hardin	12.6	9.1	6.6	50.3	31,945	32,060	0.4	-2.2	2,730	2,284	-1,147	11,588	2.53	66.6	9.4	27.6
Harrison	16.7	12.0	8.8	50.5	15,856	15,862	0.0	-4.1	1,150	1,449	-336	6,242	2.44	69.5	10.2	25.7
Henry	14.7	9.8	8.3	50.5	29,210	28,215	-3.4	-3.7	2,295	2,007	-1,330	11,035	2.49	71.3	10.0	24.5
Highland	13.9	10.4	7.6	51.0	40,875	43,600	6.7	-1.4	3,937	3,452	-1,105	16,635	2.56	66.9	12.0	27.1
Hocking	15.0	11.0	7.7	50.5	28,241	29,373	4.0	-3.1	2,282	2,131	-1,051	11,326	2.47	70.4	11.4	25.2
Holmes	10.9	7.5	5.9	50.0	38,943	42,364	8.8	3.8	5,601	2,191	-1,811	12,500	3.43	81.0	7.0	16.4
Huron	13.9	9.9	6.8	50.6	59,487	59,625	0.2	-1.9	5,369	4,158	-2,359	22,521	2.57	69.0	12.6	25.6
Jackson	13.9	10.3	6.6	51.1	32,641	33,226	1.8	-2.3	3,077	2,906	-945	12,814	2.53	66.8	12.8	29.2
Jefferson	15.8	11.9	9.2	51.5	73,894	69,709	-5.7	-4.8	4,789	6,886	-1,198	27,776	2.35	64.2	12.6	30.4
Knox	14.0	10.3	7.4	51.0	54,500	60,930	11.8	0.5	5,280	4,414	-509	23,029	2.49	66.1	9.6	27.1
Lake	15.5	11.1	8.4	51.1	227,511	230,050	1.1	0.0	16,465	17,265	1,045	95,249	2.37	65.3	10.7	29.2
Lawrence	14.0	10.8	7.7	51.2	62,319	62,448	0.2	-3.5	5,060	5,345	-1,883	23,243	2.62	66.7	12.6	28.6
Licking	14.0	9.7	6.5	50.9	145,491	166,492	14.4	4.2	14,278	11,105	3,928	64,034	2.59	70.0	12.0	24.8
Logan	15.0	10.4	7.0	50.5	46,005	45,854	-0.3	-1.2	3,958	3,478	-993	18,720	2.40	69.0	12.0	24.8
Lorain	14.3	10.4	7.4	50.8	284,664	301,369	5.9	2.2	24,497	21,265	3,539	117,609	2.50	67.7	13.9	27.4
Lucas	13.8	9.3	6.5	51.6	455,054	441,815	-2.9	-2.5	40,874	31,778	-20,154	178,477	2.38	59.3	15.3	33.7
Madison	13.5	8.8	6.2	45.6	40,213	43,438	8.0	1.4	3,025	2,903	459	14,809	2.60	69.5	11.9	24.8
Mahoning	15.4	11.3	9.3	51.2	257,555	238,807	-7.3	-3.8	17,312	22,021	-4,196	97,484	2.32	61.9	14.4	33.3
Marion	14.1	10.2	7.3	46.8	66,217	66,501	0.4	-2.3	5,496	5,140	-1,872	24,418	2.43	67.3	13.8	28.3
Medina	14.4	10.4	6.9	50.6	151,095	172,333	14.1	3.5	12,841	10,148	3,492	66,465	2.62	71.9	8.6	24.2
Meigs	15.3	11.3	8.0	50.7	23,072	23,767	3.0	-2.9	1,762	2,004	-434	9,204	2.51	68.7	11.5	26.4
Mercer	14.7	9.6	7.7	49.5	40,924	40,814	-0.3	0.1	4,074	2,971	-1,038	16,109	2.51	71.2	7.3	25.3
Miami	14.1	10.7	7.6	50.8	98,868	102,501	3.7	2.6	8,520	7,471	1,662	41,106	2.50	66.3	9.3	27.6
Monroe	15.5	12.9	9.9	49.8	15,180	14,642	-3.5	-4.8	1,083	1,260	-517	5,986	2.39	71.2	10.4	25.4
Montgomery	13.6	9.9	7.7	51.8	559,062	535,176	-4.3	-0.7	48,275	42,353	-9,334	222,677	2.32	60.2	15.3	33.9
Morgan	15.7	11.6	9.3	50.1	14,897	15,056	1.1	-2.3	1,050	1,215	-176	5,932	2.47	69.4	10.0	26.3
Morrow	15.3	9.9	6.9	50.0	31,628	34,827	10.1	0.5	2,773	2,284	-308	12,606	2.75	74.3	10.0	21.4
Muskingum	14.0	9.9	7.6	51.5	84,585	86,086	1.8	0.1	7,483	6,931	-434	34,178	2.46	66.4	12.9	28.3
Noble	19.7	16.1	10.4	41.8	14,058	14,645	4.2	-1.6	1,020	916	-336	4,863	2.43	66.1	6.3	31.7

1. No spouse present.

Table B. States and Counties — **Population, Vital Statistics, Health, and Crime**

STATE County	Persons in group quarters, 2017	Daytime Population, 2012-2016 Number	Employment/ residence ratio	Births, 2017 Total	Rate[1]	Deaths, 2017 Number	Rate[1]	Persons under 65 with no health insurance, 2016 Number	Percent	Medicare, 2017 Total beneficiaries	Enrolled in Original Medicare	Enrolled in Medicare Advantage	Serious crimes known to police[2], 2016 Total Number	Rate[3]
	32	33	34	35	36	37	38	39	40	41	42	43	44	45
NORTH DAKOTA— Cont'd														
Ward	3,131	70,532	1.04	1,164	16.9	480	7.0	4,641	7.8	9,741	8,227	1,514	1,800	2,515
Wells	92	4,365	1.09	43	10.7	49	12.2	236	8.0	1,197	1,100	97	45	1,107
Williams	488	40,750	1.55	651	19.5	213	6.4	2,354	7.6	3,575	3,303	272	1,041	2,762
OHIO	317,470	11,605,082	1.00	137,396	11.8	114,938	9.9	632,536	6.7	2,251,255	1,358,699	892,557	334,234	2,878
Adams	338	25,370	0.73	322	11.6	341	12.3	1,979	8.7	6,946	5,047	1,899	280	1,004
Allen	5,994	110,623	1.13	1,242	12.0	1,074	10.4	5,868	7.2	21,054	15,595	5,459	4,050	4,031
Ashland	2,392	49,342	0.83	620	11.6	580	10.8	3,064	7.3	10,619	6,828	3,791	710	1,358
Ashtabula	3,467	91,911	0.82	1,088	11.1	1,112	11.4	6,682	8.6	22,634	16,920	5,715	NA	NA
Athens	10,112	66,020	1.03	519	7.8	461	6.9	4,492	9.3	11,063	8,244	2,819	1,425	2,212
Auglaize	525	43,813	0.91	565	12.3	493	10.8	2,002	5.3	11,251	8,467	2,784	427	1,000
Belmont	3,805	64,174	0.83	638	9.4	835	12.3	3,383	6.5	14,892	8,212	6,680	662	1,125
Brown	575	34,485	0.49	491	11.3	493	11.3	2,695	7.6	8,403	5,156	3,247	570	1,347
Butler	11,946	350,743	0.87	4,531	11.9	3,347	8.8	18,734	5.9	63,571	36,849	26,722	12,685	3,498
Carroll	405	23,727	0.64	271	9.9	289	10.6	1,719	7.9	4,622	2,621	2,001	NA	NA
Champaign	681	33,864	0.70	396	10.2	396	10.2	2,059	6.5	7,463	4,285	3,178	863	2,228
Clark	3,478	126,667	0.84	1,561	11.6	1,680	12.5	7,244	6.8	30,325	15,725	14,600	5,724	4,480
Clermont	1,718	165,855	0.64	2,307	11.3	1,706	8.4	10,133	5.9	29,852	16,388	13,464	4,114	2,031
Clinton	1,110	42,435	1.03	492	11.7	425	10.1	2,118	6.2	9,285	6,016	3,269	778	1,858
Columbiana	3,959	92,268	0.72	1,057	10.3	1,187	11.5	5,671	7.0	24,835	14,426	10,409	602	775
Coshocton	428	34,250	0.84	467	12.8	374	10.2	2,369	8.0	7,507	5,567	1,940	564	1,547
Crawford	579	39,345	0.83	474	11.4	498	11.9	2,217	6.7	10,514	8,036	2,478	1,124	2,739
Cuyahoga	30,059	1,392,204	1.23	14,637	11.7	13,439	10.8	64,178	6.3	252,587	145,700	106,887	40,035	3,740
Darke	606	47,421	0.80	594	11.5	592	11.5	2,868	6.9	10,389	7,585	2,803	417	874
Defiance	763	37,024	0.92	413	10.8	386	10.1	2,059	6.7	8,886	7,029	1,857	534	1,538
Delaware	2,222	173,258	0.84	2,146	10.7	1,133	5.7	6,603	3.9	22,010	13,465	8,545	2,921	1,717
Erie	1,679	76,441	1.02	782	10.5	914	12.2	3,704	6.3	19,598	15,026	4,572	1,748	2,603
Fairfield	3,337	123,677	0.61	1,689	10.9	1,311	8.5	7,744	6.1	26,442	14,304	12,138	3,972	2,617
Fayette	593	28,743	1.00	346	12.0	318	11.1	1,657	7.1	5,582	3,614	1,968	1,192	4,171
Franklin	30,940	1,341,935	1.18	19,039	14.7	9,542	7.4	86,877	7.9	183,394	103,176	80,219	49,905	4,032
Fulton	391	40,230	0.89	483	11.4	412	9.7	2,036	5.8	9,372	6,530	2,842	593	1,507
Gallia	763	30,849	1.04	363	12.1	357	11.9	1,852	7.7	7,292	5,687	1,605	802	2,692
Geauga	864	84,309	0.79	904	9.6	819	8.7	6,357	8.4	17,687	11,157	6,530	674	717
Greene	8,275	168,310	1.05	1,842	11.0	1,428	8.6	7,088	5.4	22,593	13,723	8,870	3,948	2,459
Guernsey	510	39,655	1.01	462	11.8	451	11.5	2,250	7.1	9,284	6,856	2,429	NA	NA
Hamilton	21,962	928,199	1.32	10,787	13.3	7,768	9.5	42,157	6.2	155,269	91,194	64,074	31,649	4,174
Hancock	1,587	85,245	1.26	895	11.8	699	9.2	3,732	6.0	13,784	10,261	3,524	1,667	2,252
Hardin	1,959	28,356	0.76	360	11.5	328	10.5	1,824	7.4	6,012	4,715	1,296	650	2,060
Harrison	232	14,112	0.79	149	9.8	186	12.2	873	7.2	3,856	2,565	1,291	167	1,147
Henry	346	25,659	0.83	291	10.7	249	9.2	1,365	6.1	5,838	4,658	1,180	394	1,490
Highland	484	38,434	0.72	559	13.0	466	10.8	2,848	8.1	8,075	5,766	2,309	802	1,882
Hocking	307	24,704	0.67	309	10.9	294	10.3	1,563	6.8	5,997	4,300	1,697	641	2,311
Holmes	765	47,009	1.17	771	17.5	326	7.4	7,458	19.8	4,131	2,623	1,508	304	693
Huron	578	54,973	0.86	760	13.0	559	9.6	3,931	8.1	14,117	11,148	2,969	NA	NA
Jackson	325	30,781	0.85	415	12.8	385	11.9	1,985	7.4	6,707	5,181	1,526	639	1,999
Jefferson	2,420	63,643	0.85	657	9.9	933	14.1	3,011	5.9	17,204	11,489	5,715	1,385	2,374
Knox	3,510	56,870	0.85	741	12.1	625	10.2	3,441	7.3	12,176	8,417	3,759	1,295	2,124
Lake	2,802	209,742	0.83	2,244	9.8	2,444	10.6	10,392	5.6	50,481	30,512	19,969	3,183	1,734
Lawrence	669	51,795	0.60	661	11.0	728	12.1	3,464	7.0	14,455	11,534	2,921	1,071	1,833
Licking	3,535	152,798	0.79	1,970	11.4	1,562	9.0	8,426	5.9	31,005	18,386	12,620	2,604	1,792
Logan	450	44,459	0.95	532	11.7	484	10.7	2,462	6.6	9,909	7,442	2,467	863	2,005
Lorain	8,751	273,083	0.77	3,329	10.8	2,947	9.6	15,807	6.4	60,818	38,298	22,521	4,076	1,530
Lucas	9,661	452,767	1.09	5,494	12.8	4,465	10.4	23,468	6.6	81,469	46,993	34,476	17,927	4,347
Madison	4,946	42,712	0.95	405	9.2	404	9.2	1,937	5.9	8,534	4,766	3,768	883	2,015
Mahoning	8,394	233,900	1.01	2,382	10.4	2,920	12.7	11,111	6.2	54,597	27,462	27,135	6,425	2,842
Marion	6,024	65,895	1.01	729	11.2	716	11.0	3,068	6.3	14,448	9,616	4,832	2,647	4,069
Medina	1,199	149,625	0.71	1,759	9.9	1,419	8.0	7,175	4.9	33,886	19,733	14,153	1,476	845
Meigs	212	19,091	0.51	228	9.9	290	12.6	1,512	8.1	4,761	3,715	1,046	299	1,293
Mercer	439	38,791	0.90	596	14.6	394	9.6	1,891	5.6	7,920	6,040	1,880	NA	NA
Miami	1,056	96,966	0.86	1,197	11.4	1,048	10.0	5,873	6.9	22,744	14,061	8,683	2,339	2,346
Monroe	165	13,758	0.87	135	9.7	189	13.6	843	7.8	3,454	1,931	1,523	73	508
Montgomery	14,951	554,366	1.09	6,576	12.4	5,883	11.1	31,824	7.5	117,429	62,735	54,694	19,199	3,726
Morgan	188	12,712	0.60	139	9.4	152	10.3	816	7.0	2,940	2,021	919	231	1,571
Morrow	366	26,048	0.45	379	10.8	308	8.8	2,058	7.1	5,273	3,542	1,731	NA	NA
Muskingum	1,675	85,014	0.97	1,009	11.7	955	11.1	4,538	6.5	20,496	14,159	6,337	2,585	2,999
Noble	2,653	14,157	0.93	131	9.1	131	9.1	684	7.4	1,908	1,412	496	88	700

1. Per 1,000 estimated resident population.   2.   Data for serious crimes have not been adjusted for underreporting; this may affect comparability between geographic areas and over time.
3.   Per 100,000 population estimated by the FBI.

Table B. States and Counties — **Crime, Education, Money Income, and Poverty**

STATE County	Serious crimes known to police, 2016 (cont.)[1] — Rate		Education — School enrollment and attainment, 2012-2016				Education — Local government expenditures,[5] 2013-2014		Money income, 2012-2016				Income and poverty, 2016			
			Enrollment[3]		Attainment[4] (percent)						Households			Percent below poverty level		
												Percent				
	Violent	Property	Total	Percent private	High school graduate or less	Bachelor's degree or more	Total current spending (mil dol)	Current spending per student (dollars)	Per capita income[6]	Median income (dollars)	with income of less than $50,000	with income of $200,000 or more	Median household income (dollars)	All persons	Children under 18 years	Children 5 to 17 years in families
	46	47	48	49	50	51	52	53	54	55	56	57	58	59	60	61
NORTH DAKOTA— Cont'd																
Ward	242	2,274	16,592	8.7	36.6	26.4	118.1	11,692	32,395	63,037	39.2	3.9	61,089	8.8	9.3	8.9
Wells	221	886	638	6.0	48.2	21.3	7.5	13,600	30,260	50,685	49.2	1.9	51,677	10.5	13.2	11.6
Williams	252	2,510	7,124	13.1	36.1	22.5	56.9	12,240	45,442	90,080	27.0	10.6	81,719	6.8	7.8	7.6
OHIO	300	2,577	2,922,228	18.2	44.3	26.7	19,266.6	11,175	27,800	50,674	49.3	3.7	52,357	14.5	20.4	18.7
Adams	61	943	6,069	9.8	67.4	10.9	46.5	9,692	18,901	34,709	65.6	0.7	38,302	20.2	29.6	28.1
Allen	398	3,633	27,882	20.7	49.6	17.4	156.2	10,384	23,600	45,575	53.4	2.2	47,924	15.5	21.9	20.3
Ashland	132	1,226	13,811	29.4	55.7	19.6	88.6	10,393	22,604	48,509	51.7	1.4	50,612	12.2	17.4	16.3
Ashtabula	NA	NA	22,112	13.6	58.9	13.1	147.3	10,530	20,978	41,158	58.4	0.9	43,668	18.2	26.5	24.5
Athens	116	2,096	27,529	4.1	43.2	29.1	95.2	12,991	18,602	34,221	64.1	1.7	38,131	28.8	24.5	23.5
Auglaize	52	949	10,891	9.6	51.8	17.8	77.7	9,962	26,690	55,914	44.8	1.9	59,543	9.2	11.5	9.8
Belmont	129	995	13,502	11.6	52.5	16.4	81.9	9,439	24,533	44,719	55.5	2.1	45,661	15.7	21.5	20.2
Brown	71	1,276	9,341	6.9	62.5	12.4	72.6	10,121	23,776	47,999	51.8	2.1	51,504	16.7	24.3	22.2
Butler	249	3,250	105,059	14.5	43.6	29.1	578.0	10,113	28,556	59,652	42.4	4.7	63,094	12.4	15.8	14.9
Carroll	NA	NA	5,956	13.1	60.7	11.4	31.3	9,527	25,093	48,545	51.2	2.5	48,616	12.8	18.9	17.0
Champaign	90	2,138	9,577	17.0	56.2	16.5	77.7	10,566	24,715	53,673	46.7	1.2	54,037	11.1	16.0	13.9
Clark	360	4,120	32,573	17.2	49.9	18.0	218.7	10,468	23,992	44,154	55.5	1.8	47,410	15.7	22.4	21.2
Clermont	109	1,922	48,130	19.7	43.9	27.6	260.6	9,640	30,060	61,265	40.6	4.6	61,203	10.6	12.9	11.4
Clinton	67	1,791	10,284	16.9	53.8	16.5	70.7	8,854	23,612	48,675	51.2	1.7	53,234	13.4	19.2	17.8
Columbiana	50	725	21,878	10.7	57.7	13.9	162.4	10,629	23,785	45,389	54.4	1.8	46,873	17.2	26.5	25.0
Coshocton	115	1,432	7,846	17.6	63.6	12.1	53.0	10,825	21,521	43,380	56.3	0.7	45,777	12.7	20.7	19.7
Crawford	136	2,603	9,029	15.2	57.3	12.7	65.1	9,788	22,631	40,563	59.5	1.2	44,336	13.9	22.1	20.8
Cuyahoga	721	3,020	312,901	26.3	39.8	30.9	2,365.5	13,483	29,143	45,289	53.7	4.3	46,703	18.3	26.4	25.1
Darke	105	769	12,286	8.9	59.6	13.1	80.1	9,449	23,589	47,043	53.0	1.2	52,771	10.7	14.8	13.0
Defiance	141	1,397	9,765	22.2	54.7	15.8	58.8	9,256	24,703	50,822	49.2	1.8	52,210	10.4	15.1	13.3
Delaware	109	1,608	54,732	20.1	23.9	52.5	287.8	10,027	42,985	94,234	24.6	13.3	102,990	4.7	4.7	4.1
Erie	98	2,504	16,940	16.1	47.7	21.6	160.2	13,393	28,684	48,276	51.6	2.8	51,354	12.5	20.1	17.9
Fairfield	170	2,447	38,884	15.3	42.1	26.4	240.0	9,759	28,746	61,473	40.9	3.7	65,198	9.7	13.0	11.3
Fayette	220	3,951	6,646	6.3	62.0	14.5	41.3	8,636	22,728	41,954	57.8	2.2	44,257	16.0	23.0	20.7
Franklin	416	3,617	333,977	16.7	34.6	38.4	2,370.7	11,706	30,098	54,037	46.2	4.6	56,090	16.6	23.9	21.5
Fulton	94	1,413	10,579	14.1	51.5	17.0	101.4	13,355	27,010	55,860	44.5	2.1	56,504	8.9	11.7	10.6
Gallia	118	2,575	7,074	11.7	59.9	15.4	57.9	13,647	20,914	39,423	59.0	1.3	42,074	20.6	29.8	28.4
Geauga	35	682	22,142	27.9	35.9	37.3	139.3	12,523	37,537	74,165	32.3	8.4	77,938	5.8	8.3	7.3
Greene	126	2,333	48,561	21.2	32.6	37.6	231.2	10,798	31,877	61,116	41.2	5.2	62,751	12.1	14.5	13.2
Guernsey	NA	NA	8,718	12.3	57.9	13.6	58.0	12,303	22,280	41,566	57.8	1.3	43,519	18.6	25.4	22.5
Hamilton	471	3,703	209,850	24.4	36.9	35.6	1,286.7	11,794	31,303	50,399	49.6	5.5	53,344	16.0	23.2	21.1
Hancock	176	2,077	19,340	26.6	43.9	25.8	121.8	10,099	28,244	51,604	48.0	3.3	56,406	10.0	13.1	12.7
Hardin	92	1,968	9,044	33.0	59.4	14.4	43.8	10,203	20,994	44,842	55.6	0.8	46,969	13.3	17.2	15.9
Harrison	89	1,057	2,994	7.6	61.3	9.7	15.3	9,444	22,639	44,000	56.8	1.2	44,274	16.8	23.9	21.8
Henry	121	1,369	6,587	13.7	53.0	16.0	62.3	14,213	26,288	54,941	45.3	2.4	57,752	8.3	11.3	10.4
Highland	103	1,779	9,964	8.0	59.3	12.0	67.0	9,003	21,134	40,593	58.5	1.5	44,729	19.8	28.4	23.7
Hocking	108	2,203	6,797	7.8	56.9	14.1	39.2	9,922	22,091	43,382	56.3	1.3	47,799	14.5	22.4	20.3
Holmes	18	675	9,488	40.7	77.8	7.7	41.4	9,951	19,517	53,619	46.3	2.6	58,783	11.7	16.4	14.9
Huron	NA	NA	14,067	14.5	59.3	13.5	102.4	9,385	23,698	48,838	51.3	1.7	51,278	12.2	17.9	16.4
Jackson	175	1,824	7,689	9.1	58.5	16.9	49.7	9,506	20,583	40,300	61.3	0.8	45,168	18.1	27.2	26.3
Jefferson	156	2,218	15,540	26.1	52.4	15.4	90.9	10,100	23,356	42,327	58.2	1.7	43,558	16.3	24.0	22.8
Knox	108	2,015	15,620	33.1	51.5	21.9	85.8	11,081	23,426	48,619	51.4	1.9	53,375	12.7	17.5	16.5
Lake	214	1,520	52,543	18.7	41.5	27.0	361.5	11,202	31,053	59,958	42.3	3.5	61,946	8.6	12.5	11.6
Lawrence	171	1,662	14,097	9.3	56.0	14.1	122.4	12,694	22,567	44,256	54.8	1.1	42,132	17.9	26.5	25.9
Licking	65	1,727	43,795	19.3	46.0	23.3	266.9	10,029	27,934	57,571	43.8	3.4	58,902	11.7	17.1	16.7
Logan	93	1,912	9,897	14.3	59.6	15.6	79.2	11,972	25,877	51,136	48.5	1.8	53,760	12.2	17.5	15.8
Lorain	151	1,379	77,031	19.8	43.0	23.5	467.0	10,582	27,537	53,459	46.3	3.5	54,951	12.4	17.9	15.0
Lucas	859	3,488	112,555	17.9	41.6	25.1	784.1	10,335	25,977	42,917	55.5	3.0	45,251	19.8	27.9	24.8
Madison	71	1,944	10,119	15.7	55.2	16.4	56.2	12,177	25,687	58,326	41.0	3.8	60,039	11.8	16.0	14.1
Mahoning	265	2,577	54,778	14.9	47.8	22.8	376.8	11,499	24,651	41,872	57.2	2.4	42,839	18.7	27.2	26.1
Marion	224	3,844	14,206	6.6	56.5	12.3	115.8	10,283	21,177	43,567	56.0	1.2	44,783	14.8	22.7	21.8
Medina	53	793	43,656	16.4	38.2	31.5	263.6	9,763	32,911	69,319	34.8	5.0	73,148	6.5	8.1	7.5
Meigs	177	1,115	4,852	11.5	59.2	13.4	35.4	10,594	21,317	39,640	59.2	0.8	39,070	21.1	28.2	25.1
Mercer	NA	NA	9,788	5.2	56.0	16.8	95.4	11,812	26,236	55,220	45.0	2.2	57,577	8.2	10.3	9.2
Miami	106	2,240	24,931	10.4	47.0	21.1	171.6	11,181	27,247	53,432	46.9	2.5	59,591	9.5	13.3	12.6
Monroe	77	432	2,751	16.8	63.6	10.7	23.9	10,118	22,100	41,368	59.2	1.3	44,062	15.2	22.4	20.9
Montgomery	430	3,296	139,113	23.2	38.7	26.1	891.7	11,610	26,392	45,394	54.1	2.8	47,239	18.2	27.2	26.8
Morgan	197	1,374	2,947	9.8	59.0	12.2	20.9	10,357	20,301	38,941	62.8	1.9	40,680	18.7	27.6	24.5
Morrow	NA	NA	8,491	7.4	59.4	13.5	50.2	9,325	23,630	53,032	46.2	1.0	52,953	12.9	19.4	17.4
Muskingum	175	2,824	20,775	13.0	54.9	15.1	177.0	11,997	21,945	42,464	57.8	1.3	44,871	14.8	22.7	20.9
Noble	0	700	2,657	4.1	65.8	9.5	18.6	11,047	21,188	41,398	57.1	1.5	48,836	15.1	18.1	17.0

1. Data for serious crimes have not been adjusted for underreporting; this may affect comparability between geographic areas and over time.   2. Per 100,000 population estimated by the FBI.
3. All persons 3 years old and over enrolled in nursery school through college.   4. Persons 25 years old and over.   5. Elementary and secondary education expenditures.
6. Based on population estimated by the American Community Survey, 2011–2015.

Table B. States and Counties — Personal Income and Earnings

STATE County	Personal income, 2016										Earnings, 2016		
	Total (mil dol)	Percent change 2015-2016	Per capita[1] Dollars	Rank	Wages and salaries (mil dol)	Supplements to wages and salaries, employer contributions (mil dol) Pension and insurance	Government social insurance	Proprietors' income (mil dol)	Dividends, interest, and rent (mil dol)	Personal transfer receipts (mil dol)	Total (mil dol)	Contributions for government social insurance (mil dol) From employee and self-employed	From employer
	62	63	64	65	66	67	68	69	70	71	72	73	74
NORTH DAKOTA— Cont'd													
Ward	3,759	-4.3	53,545	280	1,939	340	186	402	751	457	2,867	347	186
Wells	220	8.8	53,652	274	65	11	7	39	65	48	122	14	7
Williams	2,673	-23.8	77,847	34	1,898	218	169	238	495	188	2,523	316	169
OHIO	517,918	1.9	44,561	X	270,999	46,776	19,011	38,388	81,772	104,012	375,174	21,648	19,011
Adams	852	3.0	30,515	2,787	248	60	16	78	100	313	402	43	16
Allen	4,033	2.1	38,872	1,519	2,331	439	170	274	571	998	3,213	358	170
Ashland	1,877	1.5	34,985	2,167	765	144	56	127	256	436	1,091	124	56
Ashtabula	3,502	1.6	35,654	2,053	1,200	249	89	212	427	1,107	1,750	203	89
Athens	2,130	2.7	32,183	2,582	950	302	47	125	334	535	1,424	107	47
Auglaize	1,995	2.1	43,476	940	951	173	69	121	330	361	1,313	147	69
Belmont	2,562	-1.3	37,311	1,765	968	183	67	116	379	694	1,335	154	67
Brown	1,469	2.2	33,576	2,388	317	82	21	85	170	428	505	57	21
Butler	16,090	2.9	42,620	1,030	7,872	1,307	553	1,173	2,172	3,000	10,905	1,185	553
Carroll	1,001	1.3	36,171	1,979	285	54	22	89	134	259	450	52	22
Champaign	1,462	1.8	37,734	1,701	463	93	32	79	183	339	668	75	32
Clark	5,104	1.7	37,866	1,687	2,022	382	144	218	742	1,437	2,766	322	144
Clermont	9,992	4.1	49,215	456	2,777	451	199	1,537	1,135	1,625	4,965	495	199
Clinton	1,704	3.2	40,673	1,281	795	153	57	276	235	375	1,282	131	57
Columbiana	3,688	-0.1	35,574	2,067	1,171	242	84	231	483	1,073	1,729	199	84
Coshocton	1,206	-6.2	32,939	2,485	425	93	31	89	158	366	638	73	31
Crawford	1,483	1.4	35,242	2,130	536	112	39	61	212	443	749	90	39
Cuyahoga	62,496	1.7	50,023	415	42,743	6,661	2,998	4,898	11,911	12,545	57,301	6,274	2,998
Darke	1,931	-4.3	37,299	1,772	773	146	57	96	298	446	1,073	126	57
Defiance	1,438	1.9	37,687	1,709	724	126	53	113	181	351	1,017	115	53
Delaware	13,071	3.3	66,532	80	4,956	694	338	832	1,981	1,068	6,820	731	338
Erie	3,472	-0.9	46,222	671	1,514	293	109	487	534	759	2,404	249	109
Fairfield	6,416	2.7	42,049	1,096	1,724	328	120	329	842	1,181	2,501	275	120
Fayette	1,010	2.9	35,222	2,132	448	82	32	48	137	293	610	70	32
Franklin	60,887	2.9	48,150	520	43,588	7,504	2,875	4,972	9,670	9,473	58,939	5,952	2,875
Fulton	1,758	2.4	41,358	1,188	796	148	59	153	226	349	1,156	127	59
Gallia	1,070	1.3	35,640	2,058	426	107	30	85	153	368	648	69	30
Geauga	5,781	1.0	61,456	128	1,544	261	115	653	1,127	702	2,574	268	115
Greene	7,597	2.5	46,106	680	4,328	980	323	338	1,384	1,322	5,970	645	323
Guernsey	1,448	0.8	37,069	1,814	639	127	45	107	186	433	919	102	45
Hamilton	43,252	1.4	53,456	283	31,642	4,659	2,225	2,963	9,709	7,138	41,490	4,593	2,225
Hancock	4,563	8.9	60,143	147	2,317	372	165	1,435	493	575	4,289	406	165
Hardin	1,005	-1.5	31,940	2,626	341	75	25	51	125	259	491	56	25
Harrison	539	-2.9	35,205	2,133	153	37	10	29	63	161	230	26	10
Henry	1,129	3.9	40,880	1,247	482	95	35	97	156	249	709	76	35
Highland	1,400	2.6	32,541	2,543	370	90	26	127	168	431	612	65	26
Hocking	983	1.8	34,692	2,209	245	60	16	61	116	294	382	41	16
Holmes	1,716	2.0	39,056	1,489	782	132	59	602	204	215	1,575	144	59
Huron	2,175	1.3	37,220	1,788	981	174	82	112	296	532	1,348	166	82
Jackson	1,098	1.1	33,786	2,354	383	78	27	73	144	353	562	64	27
Jefferson	2,357	0.0	35,342	2,108	890	186	66	93	301	774	1,235	149	66
Knox	2,411	1.7	39,641	1,407	874	167	65	193	380	576	1,299	146	65
Lake	10,560	1.2	46,192	673	4,490	810	323	455	1,502	2,050	6,078	689	323
Lawrence	2,130	0.7	34,996	2,163	480	111	33	96	234	716	721	84	33
Licking	7,270	2.0	42,217	1,074	2,391	436	168	454	970	1,393	3,449	378	168
Logan	1,753	1.4	38,815	1,532	942	157	68	117	223	401	1,285	147	68
Lorain	12,895	2.1	42,089	1,091	4,469	850	322	620	1,767	2,772	6,261	705	322
Lucas	18,810	2.5	43,493	937	10,641	1,889	756	1,565	2,646	4,362	14,851	1,598	756
Madison	1,659	2.6	38,211	1,617	787	164	53	130	216	318	1,134	114	53
Mahoning	9,305	0.2	40,456	1,307	4,033	764	290	640	1,498	2,551	5,727	643	290
Marion	2,193	2.5	33,688	2,365	1,051	225	75	111	282	640	1,463	162	75
Medina	8,927	2.6	50,373	400	2,749	476	195	617	1,182	1,308	4,037	441	195
Meigs	705	1.0	30,472	2,794	123	33	8	35	79	247	199	24	8
Mercer	1,806	-5.1	44,139	862	814	158	57	188	285	307	1,217	128	57
Miami	4,500	3.0	42,985	997	1,797	321	130	231	657	892	2,480	282	130
Monroe	425	-3.3	29,925	2,854	97	26	6	23	69	152	152	18	6
Montgomery	22,870	1.7	43,051	993	12,783	2,174	928	1,363	4,049	5,165	17,248	1,938	928
Morgan	445	0.5	30,061	2,838	105	24	7	26	54	146	163	19	7
Morrow	1,212	1.2	34,591	2,229	260	57	17	66	134	296	400	44	17
Muskingum	3,265	1.3	37,931	1,674	1,428	271	101	205	422	885	2,005	225	101
Noble	424	1.1	29,673	2,876	121	35	7	33	54	104	195	18	7

1. Based on the resident population estimated as of July 1 of the year shown.

Table B. States and Counties — **Earnings, Social Security, and Housing**

STATE County	Earnings, 2016 (cont.) Percent by selected industries									Social Security beneficiaries, December 2016		Supplemental Security Income recipients, 2016	Housing units, 2017	
	Farm	Mining, quarrying, and extracting	Construction	Manu-facturing	Information; professional, scientific, technical services	Retail trade	Finance, insurance, real estate, and leasing	Health care and social assistance	Govern-ment	Number	Rate[1]		Total	Percent change, 2010-2017
	75	76	77	78	79	80	81	82	83	84	85	86	87	88
NORTH DAKOTA— Cont'd														
Ward	0.4	7.6	8.4	1.0	4.1	7.1	8.6	12.6	28.5	9,545	136	612	33,103	23.8
Wells	20.7	D	5.8	2.0	1.4	6.7	5.1	D	11.5	1,175	290	50	2,516	1.4
Williams	0.5	33.2	15.0	1.6	3.9	4.4	6.0	4.3	6.6	3,595	105	202	19,608	87.4
OHIO	0.2	0.6	5.6	14.6	9.0	5.9	7.2	13.1	15.4	2,311,984	199	310,474	5,201,485	1.4
Adams	0.1	D	9.4	17.7	D	9.0	3.4	9.2	21.8	6,710	241	1,774	12,919	-0.5
Allen	0.2	D	4.9	24.8	3.7	6.5	3.3	19.8	13.1	22,695	219	3,025	45,034	0.1
Ashland	0.1	0.2	7.6	20.8	8.9	6.7	2.9	D	14.3	11,550	216	781	22,303	0.7
Ashtabula	-0.1	0.2	9.0	26.4	4.1	6.2	2.9	14.9	15.9	23,345	238	3,094	46,152	0.1
Athens	0.0	D	3.8	1.9	4.6	6.4	3.3	12.3	51.7	9,755	147	2,637	26,665	1.0
Auglaize	1.1	D	5.5	45.9	3.0	5.2	3.7	8.4	10.9	9,335	204	491	19,921	1.7
Belmont	0.1	14.0	6.9	4.3	5.1	10.4	6.2	13.3	17.4	16,890	246	2,009	32,191	-0.8
Brown	-2.0	D	9.4	9.8	2.8	7.1	3.1	11.0	24.5	10,290	236	1,168	20,170	4.5
Butler	0.0	0.1	6.9	20.3	4.2	7.5	9.2	9.8	13.0	67,180	178	7,277	152,100	2.6
Carroll	1.8	2.1	24.9	18.3	2.3	6.2	3.2	6.3	12.7	6,665	241	435	13,630	-0.5
Champaign	2.7	D	4.9	39.1	D	5.0	2.8	D	17.2	8,275	214	656	16,809	0.3
Clark	-0.1	0.5	4.2	16.5	3.2	6.8	8.2	15.4	16.5	31,015	230	4,072	61,269	-0.3
Clermont	0.0	D	7.4	9.5	8.5	7.1	7.6	6.9	10.5	39,330	194	3,419	83,046	3.0
Clinton	0.0	D	3.7	19.3	3.3	4.8	4.6	D	11.9	8,960	214	1,057	18,187	0.3
Columbiana	0.8	0.8	6.5	20.0	2.8	9.1	2.9	14.1	18.8	25,535	246	3,073	46,822	-0.6
Coshocton	0.6	0.9	6.6	27.3	D	6.6	2.9	12.0	14.6	8,740	239	890	16,442	-0.6
Crawford	0.0	D	4.8	21.6	4.2	6.7	7.6	D	15.7	11,060	263	1,171	20,047	-0.6
Cuyahoga	0.0	1.7	3.7	9.8	12.8	4.2	9.4	16.0	14.0	252,580	202	50,421	618,368	-0.5
Darke	-2.4	D	9.2	27.3	D	6.6	4.8	11.4	12.5	11,990	232	793	22,889	0.7
Defiance	1.3	0.0	3.8	32.5	3.6	10.0	5.6	D	12.8	9,155	240	795	16,803	0.4
Delaware	0.1	D	4.1	7.6	12.3	6.8	12.8	7.3	8.7	26,790	136	1,265	73,193	10.3
Erie	0.7	D	3.4	17.6	2.9	6.6	3.4	12.5	15.2	18,815	251	1,627	37,877	0.1
Fairfield	0.2	0.1	8.6	10.7	4.3	9.1	3.9	17.1	19.0	28,340	186	2,454	60,909	3.8
Fayette	0.7	0.0	4.9	17.5	2.0	11.8	6.0	D	17.1	6,580	230	955	12,770	0.6
Franklin	0.0	D	4.3	5.7	12.3	4.9	10.1	11.6	19.6	172,810	136	33,304	555,131	5.3
Fulton	0.7	D	8.6	38.4	D	5.8	3.1	D	12.8	9,075	214	558	17,549	0.8
Gallia	-0.1	D	5.3	6.4	D	7.7	5.4	D	16.8	7,180	239	1,642	13,890	-0.3
Geauga	0.2	D	15.9	20.6	5.4	7.3	3.5	9.6	10.2	18,945	202	709	37,132	1.5
Greene	0.0	D	3.0	4.4	16.2	5.3	2.9	7.1	47.1	29,605	179	2,604	70,336	3.1
Guernsey	-0.1	3.3	9.6	22.9	4.6	6.8	3.1	14.7	16.1	9,670	247	1,495	19,322	0.7
Hamilton	0.0	0.1	5.3	11.8	13.5	4.1	10.0	14.4	10.4	145,185	179	24,288	379,233	0.5
Hancock	0.0	D	2.6	20.4	3.5	3.9	2.0	8.4	5.2	15,135	200	1,077	34,216	3.1
Hardin	1.3	0.0	3.8	26.6	2.1	6.7	4.0	D	17.1	6,405	204	660	13,217	0.9
Harrison	0.7	D	8.8	9.2	D	3.7	3.5	8.7	18.9	3,845	252	534	8,089	-1.0
Henry	2.5	D	9.9	33.4	2.4	5.1	3.4	9.0	17.4	6,155	226	364	12,098	1.1
Highland	1.2	0.4	9.9	17.9	2.1	9.5	5.1	10.9	22.3	10,145	236	1,494	19,329	-0.3
Hocking	0.0	D	10.4	14.1	2.5	8.3	4.5	9.4	29.4	6,820	240	1,010	13,410	0.0
Holmes	0.8	0.6	16.8	37.6	D	10.3	2.7	D	6.3	4,845	111	401	13,617	-0.4
Huron	1.9	D	11.6	27.1	2.2	5.6	3.8	11.2	11.7	12,695	217	1,252	25,293	0.4
Jackson	-0.1	0.7	7.3	29.0	2.2	8.8	3.3	11.7	17.5	7,685	236	1,531	14,841	1.7
Jefferson	0.0	0.4	6.6	8.3	3.8	7.8	2.7	D	15.5	17,795	266	2,503	32,511	-1.0
Knox	-0.1	0.5	11.0	27.4	3.2	6.4	2.9	12.1	12.1	12,875	212	1,171	25,823	2.8
Lake	0.7	0.3	6.1	28.4	5.5	7.4	2.9	9.8	13.1	50,950	222	2,897	102,954	1.7
Lawrence	0.1	D	10.2	D	3.1	8.6	3.2	17.6	25.5	15,095	249	3,550	27,500	-0.4
Licking	0.2	0.3	9.2	14.9	6.1	9.6	8.0	11.5	16.3	34,125	199	3,211	70,852	2.3
Logan	0.7	0.3	5.4	34.5	D	4.7	2.8	8.3	10.6	9,990	221	874	23,446	1.1
Lorain	0.8	0.0	5.7	22.4	4.4	7.1	4.0	11.9	17.8	64,735	211	7,061	131,157	3.2
Lucas	0.1	0.1	5.9	15.7	7.6	6.5	7.1	16.8	15.4	85,495	198	17,613	203,197	0.3
Madison	1.7	0.0	6.0	25.8	D	7.0	1.8	D	21.4	7,700	178	714	16,092	1.0
Mahoning	0.1	0.6	7.2	10.4	5.8	7.9	4.7	18.4	17.3	57,140	248	8,863	111,382	-0.4
Marion	0.8	0.5	4.1	28.0	3.0	6.4	2.1	16.3	18.9	14,455	221	2,266	27,899	0.2
Medina	0.2	0.1	12.3	16.1	5.5	8.1	4.3	8.3	11.9	34,530	195	1,477	72,459	4.7
Meigs	0.3	2.1	9.3	4.0	D	11.1	4.1	D	31.2	5,610	242	1,157	11,168	-0.2
Mercer	-1.2	D	9.3	34.3	3.4	6.3	6.1	D	13.7	8,365	205	415	18,010	2.1
Miami	0.1	D	6.5	29.7	3.8	7.4	3.5	9.4	13.1	22,865	219	1,753	44,324	0.2
Monroe	1.0	D	7.8	D	D	6.6	5.9	D	28.1	4,035	286	410	7,505	-0.8
Montgomery	0.1	0.0	4.8	12.3	11.3	5.2	6.7	19.4	15.7	111,435	210	16,080	254,800	0.0
Morgan	0.0	D	8.6	17.3	3.2	6.8	2.7	9.1	23.2	3,515	238	535	7,980	1.1
Morrow	0.2	0.3	24.6	16.5	D	5.6	2.5	D	23.5	7,185	206	589	14,275	0.8
Muskingum	0.2	1.6	5.7	10.4	4.9	9.6	3.9	D	15.8	20,720	241	3,434	37,922	-0.4
Noble	0.4	10.3	6.1	4.8	4.0	4.5	4.6	6.0	34.6	2,715	188	275	6,167	1.9

1. Per 1,000 resident population estimated as of July 1 of the year shown.

Table B. States and Counties — Housing, Labor Force, and Employment

STATE County	Housing units, 2017 (cont.)								Civilian labor force, 2017				Civilian employment[6], 2012-2016		
	Occupied units										Unemployment			Percent	
	Owner-occupied					Renter-occupied									
				Median owner cost as a percent of income											
	Total	Percent	Median value[1]	With a mortgage	Without a mortgage[2]	Median rent[3]	Median rent as a percent of income[2]	Sub-standard units[4] (percent)	Total	Percent change, 2016-2017	Total	Rate[5]	Total	Management, business, science, and arts	Construction, production, and maintenance occupations
	89	90	91	92	93	94	95	96	97	98	99	100	101	102	103

STATE County	89	90	91	92	93	94	95	96	97	98	99	100	101	102	103
NORTH DAKOTA— Cont'd															
Ward	26,772	60.5	207,600	18.9	10.0	961	26.6	2.0	32,971	-2.1	1,062	3.2	36,479	31.2	27.0
Wells	2,026	80.4	74,900	16.3	10.0	422	18.7	1.4	2,183	-0.8	70	3.2	2,018	32.3	29.0
Williams	12,390	64.4	224,000	15.1	10.0	915	20.2	5.0	23,013	1.3	577	2.5	17,069	29.5	37.6
OHIO	460,1,449	66.0	131,900	20.4	12.0	743	29.0	1.7	5,780,032	0.7	288,853	5.0	5,425,647	35.4	23.4
Adams	10,885	68.6	94,300	21.4	12.7	575	35.2	3.3	10,996	0.4	788	7.2	10,184	28.4	35.5
Allen	40,039	66.4	107,500	19.7	11.6	660	30.7	1.7	48,897	1.2	2,444	5.0	48,117	27.1	31.3
Ashland	20,391	71.5	120,700	20.6	12.4	682	23.3	3.1	26,366	0.3	1,293	4.9	24,465	29.0	32.9
Ashtabula	38,800	71.5	104,700	21.1	12.5	637	31.9	2.3	44,321	0.1	2,625	5.9	40,294	25.0	34.1
Athens	22,328	56.1	113,900	20.8	12.5	726	35.4	2.9	28,594	1.9	1,731	6.1	27,165	37.3	16.9
Auglaize	18,231	75.2	138,700	18.9	10.8	651	23.9	1.9	24,734	0.3	921	3.7	23,101	30.2	34.9
Belmont	27,732	74.0	94,300	18.8	10.9	564	27.0	0.8	30,705	-1.1	1,941	6.3	29,736	27.5	29.5
Brown	17,047	75.0	116,500	21.0	12.7	640	27.0	2.0	19,726	1.1	1,126	5.7	19,036	26.4	32.4
Butler	135,100	68.7	159,800	20.2	11.3	823	28.9	1.6	192,374	1.4	8,534	4.4	178,571	37.8	21.4
Carroll	10,871	79.6	113,300	20.3	11.3	633	25.6	2.2	13,376	-0.6	784	5.9	12,481	25.6	34.9
Champaign	15,162	73.1	124,400	19.7	11.8	687	25.1	1.7	19,859	-0.3	827	4.2	18,234	26.6	37.1
Clark	54,681	65.4	103,200	20.1	11.4	691	30.2	1.8	63,813	0.2	3,092	4.8	59,843	28.6	29.4
Clermont	75,236	73.6	159,100	20.3	11.7	774	28.0	1.3	105,450	1.3	4,615	4.4	98,083	35.6	22.8
Clinton	16,077	64.1	121,700	20.8	10.9	696	26.6	2.2	17,593	2.3	957	5.4	18,952	27.1	30.5
Columbiana	41,782	71.7	104,100	19.3	11.2	621	26.3	1.9	48,018	-0.9	2,867	6.0	46,979	25.7	33.5
Coshocton	14,397	74.7	97,100	20.2	10.7	574	25.4	2.7	14,775	-1.6	1,007	6.8	15,888	22.4	41.8
Crawford	17,657	69.8	85,200	20.4	11.6	633	26.4	1.1	19,020	-0.9	1,093	5.7	18,161	26.6	34.3
Cuyahoga	534,559	58.9	122,200	21.5	13.5	742	30.6	1.4	610,874	0.1	35,755	5.9	582,148	39.0	18.1
Darke	20,831	72.2	112,100	20.2	11.6	624	26.7	1.4	26,452	0.2	1,112	4.2	24,342	24.8	39.6
Defiance	15,378	74.7	109,400	20.0	11.9	669	27.2	1.8	18,498	0.5	902	4.9	18,162	25.7	35.1
Delaware	66,544	81.2	267,600	20.9	11.4	969	26.1	0.9	106,926	1.8	3,758	3.5	96,527	52.3	11.4
Erie	31,731	69.3	130,900	20.1	12.8	708	27.4	0.9	37,920	1.2	2,349	6.2	35,401	30.1	26.1
Fairfield	55,138	71.2	164,400	20.0	11.0	814	29.8	1.7	77,449	1.8	3,300	4.3	70,031	36.3	21.4
Fayette	11,666	61.5	107,100	22.3	11.8	691	28.4	1.9	14,479	-0.2	613	4.2	12,460	25.3	32.8
Franklin	489,010	53.3	153,100	21.0	12.3	869	28.4	2.5	680,584	1.9	27,375	4.0	632,952	42.1	16.2
Fulton	16,240	78.0	131,100	19.7	11.0	647	27.1	1.8	22,640	-0.3	1,107	4.9	20,433	26.4	35.6
Gallia	11,495	74.8	101,200	20.9	12.4	642	26.9	3.7	12,174	0.3	818	6.7	11,525	28.0	30.2
Geauga	34,890	85.4	221,500	20.7	10.9	815	27.4	2.5	48,802	-0.2	2,326	4.8	46,497	40.1	21.3
Greene	64,279	66.8	161,600	19.8	11.0	853	27.7	1.2	82,142	1.1	3,506	4.3	76,492	44.2	16.3
Guernsey	15,863	72.5	98,600	19.7	11.1	595	31.7	2.2	18,907	0.0	1,149	6.1	16,516	26.2	33.3
Hamilton	335,334	57.7	143,700	20.5	12.4	725	29.8	1.9	411,260	1.4	18,001	4.4	388,662	40.6	17.1
Hancock	31,549	69.4	130,700	19.1	11.0	711	26.0	0.8	41,822	0.7	1,515	3.6	37,663	32.5	31.1
Hardin	11,588	72.1	93,500	19.8	12.3	635	25.6	3.5	14,371	-0.2	713	5.0	14,239	26.6	34.1
Harrison	6,242	80.8	85,300	19.4	11.5	598	25.9	2.9	7,116	2.0	427	6.0	6,667	23.3	39.0
Henry	11,035	79.6	113,600	19.2	12.0	693	25.0	1.2	13,655	0.2	709	5.2	13,469	29.1	38.3
Highland	16,635	70.3	102,300	22.3	12.5	664	31.5	2.0	17,154	1.2	1,028	6.0	17,119	26.5	38.7
Hocking	11,326	73.7	114,400	20.5	11.8	569	26.6	2.3	13,251	1.7	713	5.4	12,289	28.1	29.7
Holmes	12,500	76.0	170,500	20.8	10.0	577	23.8	5.4	20,813	-1.0	739	3.6	19,525	20.0	46.7
Huron	22,521	70.7	117,000	20.2	11.3	634	27.0	1.7	28,075	-0.3	1,816	6.5	27,165	24.0	40.3
Jackson	12,814	66.5	90,800	21.4	12.7	675	29.4	2.1	12,956	1.1	926	7.1	13,258	31.7	32.6
Jefferson	27,776	69.6	87,100	18.7	12.3	612	28.5	1.5	28,373	-2.0	2,060	7.3	27,591	29.5	26.5
Knox	23,029	70.7	135,600	22.1	12.6	692	29.4	2.3	31,269	0.0	1,409	4.5	27,924	31.4	28.7
Lake	95,249	73.8	149,300	20.7	11.7	844	27.7	1.2	124,193	0.0	6,409	5.2	117,498	36.5	22.4
Lawrence	23,243	73.6	101,600	19.8	12.2	664	29.9	2.1	24,732	-0.2	1,444	5.8	24,541	30.2	25.9
Licking	64,034	71.6	153,900	20.4	12.2	784	29.4	1.7	89,801	1.6	3,758	4.2	82,701	35.2	23.1
Logan	18,720	73.4	124,400	19.1	12.5	704	26.9	2.2	23,540	0.8	969	4.1	21,142	26.8	40.9
Lorain	117,609	71.3	138,600	20.8	12.3	748	30.5	1.3	151,638	-0.1	9,361	6.2	139,444	33.2	24.8
Lucas	178,477	60.2	105,500	20.6	12.7	674	30.4	1.4	211,724	0.5	12,468	5.9	196,527	33.1	23.8
Madison	14,809	70.0	150,900	20.4	12.2	739	24.3	2.3	20,674	1.5	794	3.8	18,500	30.2	31.2
Mahoning	97,484	68.3	98,300	20.3	12.0	637	30.4	1.1	105,154	-0.9	7,264	6.9	103,000	31.6	24.5
Marion	24,418	68.4	93,400	19.7	11.3	700	30.0	1.5	28,031	0.9	1,427	5.1	25,922	26.3	34.7
Medina	66,465	79.7	182,100	20.4	11.3	833	26.7	1.6	95,615	0.0	4,526	4.7	90,341	38.7	20.9
Meigs	9,204	77.6	86,300	21.4	11.5	585	30.5	2.5	8,970	0.1	731	8.1	8,823	28.2	31.7
Mercer	16,109	76.0	134,800	19.0	10.9	647	24.3	1.0	23,707	1.1	729	3.1	20,711	27.1	39.8
Miami	41,106	69.9	137,600	19.7	10.0	734	26.1	1.2	53,691	1.1	2,280	4.2	49,939	31.1	30.2
Monroe	5,986	75.7	93,200	20.1	10.0	558	29.4	1.6	5,152	-3.3	439	8.5	5,437	24.4	38.8
Montgomery	222,677	60.8	109,600	21.0	13.1	740	30.1	1.5	253,576	1.3	12,365	4.9	238,964	36.0	20.9
Morgan	5,932	76.7	91,400	21.8	12.3	536	29.6	3.2	6,675	-1.3	457	6.8	5,439	31.7	36.6
Morrow	12,606	81.4	137,800	20.8	12.0	639	29.1	2.4	17,053	1.6	831	4.9	16,596	27.7	35.5
Muskingum	34,178	67.0	110,500	20.0	12.7	645	29.7	1.8	39,699	-0.2	2,273	5.7	37,925	25.6	28.9
Noble	4,863	83.4	88,100	22.6	10.0	607	26.5	1.9	4,806	-1.9	346	7.2	3,932	21.6	34.8

1. Specified owner-occupied units.   2. A value of 10.0 represents 10 percent or less; a value of 50.0 represents 50 percent or more.   3. Specified renter-occupied units.
4. Overcrowded or lacking complete plumbing facilities.   5. Percent of civilian labor force.   6. Civilian employed persons 16 years old and over.

Table B. States and Counties — Nonfarm Employment and Agriculture

STATE County	Private nonfarm establishments, employment and payroll, 2016									Agriculture, 2012			
		Employment						Annual payroll		Farms		Percent with:	Farm operators whose principal occupation is farming (percent)
	Number of establishments	Total	Health care and social assistance	Manufac-turing	Retail trade	Finance and insurance	Professional, scientific, and technical services	Total (mil dol)	Average per employee (dollars)	Number	Fewer than 50 acres	500 acres or more	
	104	105	106	107	108	109	110	111	112	113	114	115	116
NORTH DAKOTA— Cont'd													
Ward	2,089	27,110	4,672	490	5,841	1,054	938	1,211	44,664	961	15.3	47.9	60.1
Wells	184	1,285	407	50	243	74	18	42	32,896	543	8.1	50.8	56.9
Williams	1,491	20,466	1,319	333	2,165	404	614	1,349	65,906	758	8.8	52.1	52.4
OHIO	252,201	4,790,178	840,716	662,428	573,837	255,131	250,766	218,467	45,607	75,462	41.1	8.3	43.9
Adams	393	4,354	1,114	683	906	104	88	147	33,728	1,351	38.0	4.2	37.2
Allen	2,412	46,975	12,050	7,882	5,880	1,173	943	1,917	40,801	904	38.8	11.8	42.9
Ashland	1,031	16,447	2,968	3,987	2,098	313	1,064	585	35,548	1,034	36.4	5.4	46.8
Ashtabula	1,914	24,841	5,141	6,515	3,594	575	728	878	35,333	1,099	41.6	6.7	46.8
Athens	1,054	12,856	3,102	283	2,772	398	583	390	30,350	722	31.2	3.3	37.8
Auglaize	975	20,464	2,618	9,353	2,114	338	454	822	40,191	1,040	34.6	9.8	42.5
Belmont	1,445	19,935	4,780	840	4,411	904	582	669	33,534	700	27.1	4.9	42.1
Brown	531	6,051	1,313	864	951	184	117	190	31,376	1,379	40.4	5.7	39.7
Butler	7,111	134,993	17,026	18,979	18,649	8,092	3,740	5,969	44,216	865	51.0	6.6	43.9
Carroll	465	5,454	787	1,471	751	81	103	173	31,776	733	33.2	5.5	40.9
Champaign	566	9,619	1,016	4,073	948	212	252	382	39,741	873	46.0	11.6	46.2
Clark	2,287	41,915	8,325	6,070	5,144	2,583	1,167	1,493	35,621	785	53.2	11.3	49.6
Clermont	3,585	51,395	6,333	5,441	9,565	2,441	2,959	2,100	40,851	822	60.1	5.0	38.6
Clinton	732	14,678	1,760	3,109	1,620	454	648	643	43,810	759	42.2	15.5	53.1
Columbiana	2,036	26,666	5,504	6,043	4,027	538	426	865	32,454	1,045	44.7	4.5	42.0
Coshocton	632	8,786	2,044	2,192	1,343	204	154	297	33,819	1,122	32.6	5.4	40.6
Crawford	802	12,389	2,694	3,550	1,387	599	530	427	34,437	634	33.1	18.6	50.9
Cuyahoga	32,984	666,446	139,174	66,858	62,576	44,565	43,120	34,524	51,803	114	87.7	0.0	40.4
Darke	1,151	16,443	2,201	5,787	2,021	582	293	631	38,400	1,693	41.8	10.8	41.2
Defiance	803	13,765	2,261	3,203	2,350	664	227	575	41,754	1,030	37.5	12.1	38.5
Delaware	4,447	79,055	7,900	5,680	12,355	14,701	3,887	4,066	51,438	755	56.4	9.9	43.8
Erie	1,851	31,553	4,841	6,923	5,226	633	679	1,179	37,361	345	42.9	12.2	48.1
Fairfield	2,649	35,298	7,205	4,135	7,082	838	1,014	1,220	34,549	1,184	51.2	8.2	43.2
Fayette	599	9,784	1,152	1,559	2,535	159	59	315	32,192	504	35.5	24.2	56.5
Franklin	28,237	632,751	115,540	32,342	67,000	57,615	42,234	31,889	50,398	388	62.9	8.2	40.5
Fulton	949	15,587	1,990	7,188	1,762	367	244	642	41,202	825	42.4	13.3	42.8
Gallia	555	9,487	2,683	520	1,511	345	76	367	38,706	957	34.6	2.7	39.0
Geauga	2,712	29,890	4,623	7,982	3,894	680	1,082	1,276	42,696	959	55.2	2.2	49.8
Greene	3,097	52,846	6,887	3,568	9,627	1,344	10,702	2,138	40,461	800	61.6	9.0	39.4
Guernsey	867	13,748	3,056	3,076	1,927	254	300	506	36,836	1,228	36.6	1.6	34.6
Hamilton	21,003	472,410	87,766	39,510	46,064	33,429	40,255	26,762	56,651	295	67.1	3.1	42.4
Hancock	1,709	43,153	5,494	12,117	4,333	691	1,116	1,979	45,855	831	32.7	15.4	45.5
Hardin	451	7,233	664	2,104	869	207	81	235	32,424	793	31.3	14.1	52.2
Harrison	267	3,171	533	380	343	55	30	116	36,558	444	26.6	6.8	46.2
Henry	561	8,363	1,327	3,001	914	240	196	351	41,915	848	33.1	15.7	47.9
Highland	682	8,544	1,637	1,767	1,656	573	115	290	33,982	1,412	38.3	7.9	45.1
Hocking	490	5,309	1,080	851	849	129	101	152	28,682	367	38.4	3.0	40.9
Holmes	1,244	18,650	1,529	6,856	2,170	388	274	638	34,199	1,969	36.7	2.4	50.0
Huron	1,131	17,302	2,785	5,018	2,240	421	411	687	39,723	865	38.7	12.7	47.1
Jackson	611	8,446	1,276	3,004	1,454	269	164	265	31,430	526	32.3	4.9	41.8
Jefferson	1,257	18,853	4,162	1,235	3,189	341	317	681	36,108	493	26.0	4.1	39.4
Knox	1,072	19,198	3,103	4,498	2,299	447	351	738	38,423	1,374	45.8	5.5	44.6
Lake	5,986	86,697	11,106	19,472	13,258	1,878	3,128	3,999	46,130	214	70.6	1.4	55.6
Lawrence	793	10,533	2,885	758	1,989	280	305	327	31,073	592	26.2	1.9	41.9
Licking	3,001	49,497	7,743	9,012	6,807	3,449	1,816	1,933	39,054	1,484	51.1	5.7	39.8
Logan	853	16,253	2,008	4,383	1,781	310	818	687	42,278	868	40.4	12.3	39.2
Lorain	5,598	86,528	15,925	15,522	13,364	1,885	3,396	3,505	40,503	768	52.7	6.0	46.4
Lucas	9,583	207,410	40,867	22,670	24,460	6,142	10,135	8,794	42,401	330	52.7	12.4	58.2
Madison	683	14,224	1,334	3,949	1,890	148	592	573	40,273	699	40.1	21.9	53.2
Mahoning	5,455	87,023	22,138	8,443	12,843	2,387	2,410	3,100	35,618	578	44.5	4.2	48.3
Marion	1,140	21,324	4,326	5,891	2,806	388	275	801	37,569	578	34.1	16.6	41.9
Medina	3,967	52,677	7,003	8,947	8,738	2,524	2,020	2,173	41,256	920	63.0	4.0	50.2
Meigs	306	2,592	589	66	653	130	55	69	26,499	588	27.0	3.2	53.2
Mercer	997	16,439	2,153	4,454	2,074	588	312	604	36,731	1,208	35.3	12.0	45.0
Miami	2,093	35,614	4,533	10,921	4,873	684	939	1,402	39,372	1,068	54.6	10.0	41.8
Monroe	243	2,315	309	80	357	160	46	96	41,648	823	26.5	2.8	41.9
Montgomery	11,338	234,459	51,940	28,704	26,913	10,932	13,366	11,094	47,319	770	63.8	6.6	42.7
Morgan	156	2,146	438	730	315	92	53	68	31,548	510	22.2	5.5	39.4
Morrow	380	3,931	1,022	914	475	61	171	132	33,646	824	43.9	8.7	43.0
Muskingum	1,727	28,579	6,516	2,822	4,704	762	444	1,136	39,765	1,259	35.3	4.8	38.4
Noble	221	1,966	354	227	303	89	84	53	26,744	595	27.2	4.2	33.3

Table B. States and Counties — Agriculture

	Agriculture, 2012 (cont.)															
	Land in farms					Value of land and buildings (dollars)			Value of products sold:				Percent of farms with sales of:		Government payments	
			Acres								Percent from:					
STATE County	Acreage (1,000)	Percent change, 2007-2012	Average size of farm	Total irrigated (1,000)	Total cropland (1,000)	Average per farm	Average per acre	Value of machinery and equipmnet, average per farm (dollars)	Total (mil dol)	Average per farm (acres)	Crops	Livestock and poultry products	$10,000 or more	$100,000 or more	Total ($1,000)	Percent of farms
	117	118	119	120	121	122	123	124	125	126	127	128	129	130	131	132
NORTH DAKOTA— Cont'd																
Ward	1,073	0.7	1,117	0.2	829.4	1,716,400	1,537	298,381	274.5	285,596	93.3	6.7	62.7	39.2	9,875	71.4
Wells	738	-2.5	1,359	0.8	622.3	2,198,269	1,617	364,245	272.0	500,842	95.1	4.9	58.2	44.6	7,746	85.6
Williams	1,063	-7.1	1,403	15.6	739.1	1,044,598	745	289,881	178.7	235,756	93.8	6.2	59.4	36.7	6,315	72.2
OHIO	13,961	0.0	185	46.6	10,748.6	894,933	4,837	116,896	10,064.1	133,366	65.6	34.4	47.4	20.3	228,858	45.9
Adams	172	-6.3	128	0.2	84.4	365,260	2,862	59,237	38.9	28,798	68.6	31.4	33.6	6.6	2,316	55.4
Allen	183	-2.2	203	D	163.0	1,070,715	5,284	144,872	144.1	159,393	76.2	23.8	61.7	30.3	3,593	74.4
Ashland	153	1.6	148	0.2	110.9	677,328	4,578	93,800	103.6	100,214	53.0	47.0	52.5	17.5	2,061	45.4
Ashtabula	166	2.6	151	0.2	109.0	494,527	3,275	114,303	82.3	74,846	74.4	25.6	38.8	13.2	1,609	28.7
Athens	90	10.1	125	0.1	28.0	348,506	2,781	47,575	9.5	13,224	57.2	42.8	21.3	2.1	320	16.8
Auglaize	210	-1.5	202	0.0	191.5	1,220,936	6,044	176,234	190.6	183,235	60.6	39.4	66.1	34.0	5,338	77.1
Belmont	113	-12.3	162	0.0	35.0	540,911	3,344	59,970	20.1	28,764	21.9	78.1	37.4	4.1	613	9.7
Brown	206	-14.1	150	0.1	139.3	539,260	3,602	89,819	82.6	59,891	88.5	11.5	41.8	12.2	3,795	57.9
Butler	146	14.8	169	0.3	116.4	986,918	5,845	107,817	65.0	75,191	80.4	19.6	36.6	12.4	2,379	32.4
Carroll	106	-9.1	145	0.4	58.4	539,031	3,718	86,621	39.2	53,478	51.6	48.4	40.5	10.2	989	28.0
Champaign	190	-7.2	218	3.7	164.9	1,166,636	5,359	147,490	130.4	149,386	86.6	13.4	49.7	24.6	3,854	56.2
Clark	174	-1.7	222	1.6	149.8	1,141,031	5,138	147,288	145.1	184,896	80.4	19.6	45.1	23.8	2,754	47.6
Clermont	121	15.7	147	0.2	88.5	752,370	5,106	83,123	58.0	70,583	93.3	6.7	25.5	8.4	1,264	29.7
Clinton	208	-4.7	274	0.1	187.7	1,360,628	4,962	172,278	163.8	215,867	90.5	9.5	60.1	34.8	3,825	63.8
Columbiana	128	-2.4	122	0.3	81.7	594,740	4,861	98,871	99.3	95,020	38.4	61.6	45.0	15.4	1,509	24.8
Coshocton	170	-0.8	151	0.6	88.7	518,983	3,430	87,948	81.7	72,781	39.9	60.1	39.2	13.4	1,530	30.7
Crawford	240	9.3	379	0.1	221.9	1,772,235	4,681	250,994	193.1	304,645	74.0	26.0	67.2	43.7	4,734	75.6
Cuyahoga	3	-10.4	23	0.1	0.6	391,509	17,113	56,079	10.2	89,605	98.5	1.5	25.4	8.8	12	3.5
Darke	340	-3.0	201	1.1	311.6	1,425,144	7,097	175,760	559.5	330,475	32.2	67.8	65.2	32.9	6,902	69.5
Defiance	225	-3.4	219	0.0	198.1	980,354	4,483	116,630	113.5	110,232	75.9	24.1	48.4	21.8	6,297	85.8
Delaware	141	2.0	187	0.8	123.4	1,108,061	5,937	144,164	121.9	161,464	88.5	11.5	45.0	20.5	2,396	45.2
Erie	83	-0.9	242	0.4	71.9	1,137,035	4,708	184,907	88.2	255,583	92.2	7.8	56.8	31.6	1,343	55.1
Fairfield	207	16.3	175	0.3	162.9	833,232	4,773	114,217	105.8	89,394	79.4	20.6	36.5	15.8	3,782	48.0
Fayette	197	-10.0	390	0.0	180.6	2,134,145	5,473	226,067	143.5	284,808	87.9	12.1	59.9	39.3	4,144	73.0
Franklin	62	4.1	160	0.3	53.5	983,101	6,151	118,101	48.2	124,299	96.2	3.8	44.8	17.5	853	37.9
Fulton	195	6.2	237	0.5	179.6	1,315,518	5,556	166,076	175.7	213,023	69.4	30.6	60.7	35.4	4,204	67.3
Gallia	116	-0.9	121	0.2	34.6	393,862	3,254	51,183	15.1	15,827	51.6	48.4	22.6	2.9	734	23.6
Geauga	67	18.1	70	0.3	32.7	494,216	7,094	47,118	43.6	45,477	41.0	59.0	40.0	9.1	345	5.6
Greene	146	-10.3	182	0.6	124.7	1,095,626	6,012	120,653	95.9	119,883	90.7	9.3	39.6	17.1	2,173	46.6
Guernsey	144	4.5	117	0.0	51.7	336,147	2,871	49,570	21.5	17,502	36.6	63.4	24.9	2.9	291	10.2
Hamilton	22	1.5	73	0.2	10.0	533,654	7,282	73,278	23.6	80,153	61.3	38.7	32.5	10.5	257	13.2
Hancock	230	-7.1	277	0.0	212.8	1,310,924	4,731	164,752	160.2	192,834	91.7	8.3	71.2	41.2	4,142	77.1
Hardin	248	-3.5	313	0.4	222.6	1,527,226	4,887	171,834	272.5	343,571	53.8	46.2	61.9	34.6	4,779	72.1
Harrison	95	2.2	215	0.0	38.1	645,957	3,007	68,225	18.2	41,081	42.6	57.4	32.9	7.9	245	14.4
Henry	236	1.6	278	0.6	221.4	1,570,350	5,645	170,375	155.5	183,383	91.6	8.4	72.3	36.0	4,449	85.6
Highland	265	-2.0	187	0.2	197.7	677,928	3,619	97,353	128.6	91,069	82.6	17.4	43.9	16.3	6,128	62.6
Hocking	38	-9.3	104	0.0	14.0	372,025	3,585	44,937	5.3	14,450	80.2	19.8	22.9	2.7	212	19.3
Holmes	221	17.7	112	0.3	124.1	653,282	5,822	64,655	204.9	104,045	20.9	79.1	59.6	24.3	1,796	12.9
Huron	238	8.6	275	3.2	208.7	1,235,467	4,485	165,143	190.7	220,421	81.0	19.0	55.8	32.1	3,680	57.9
Jackson	72	-0.3	136	0.1	27.2	321,939	2,362	58,485	10.7	20,293	44.2	55.8	29.3	5.9	525	32.3
Jefferson	68	-1.6	139	0.0	25.9	381,974	2,755	68,801	7.8	15,880	48.4	51.6	30.2	3.4	218	19.9
Knox	186	-6.2	135	0.1	128.7	647,124	4,779	91,124	121.4	88,386	66.0	34.0	42.4	15.0	2,491	35.7
Lake	17	6.6	80	1.9	8.6	604,140	7,550	111,075	81.8	382,351	99.4	0.6	48.1	17.8	23	8.9
Lawrence	65	-1.8	109	0.1	17.0	266,258	2,441	50,843	4.8	8,189	57.3	42.7	15.7	1.5	366	18.2
Licking	224	-0.8	151	0.2	161.4	738,829	4,894	103,000	194.8	131,270	52.2	47.8	36.8	12.1	2,331	25.5
Logan	213	5.8	245	0.3	177.7	1,221,374	4,979	135,014	147.9	170,409	82.6	17.4	49.5	23.4	4,046	58.8
Lorain	123	-1.1	160	1.4	102.7	750,453	4,698	125,251	179.1	233,203	89.7	10.3	51.8	20.6	1,519	41.5
Lucas	63	0.2	191	1.5	59.7	1,103,406	5,778	138,709	66.2	200,521	95.2	4.8	58.2	31.8	964	55.2
Madison	263	6.2	377	0.1	244.2	1,917,923	5,092	202,773	193.8	277,230	79.4	20.6	58.4	39.9	5,148	66.0
Mahoning	75	17.0	130	0.9	54.5	644,289	4,968	119,341	65.4	113,234	45.9	54.1	48.1	19.9	847	32.9
Marion	189	-8.5	327	D	174.8	1,562,507	4,773	199,900	151.4	261,990	74.2	25.8	55.0	32.0	4,497	73.5
Medina	95	-0.5	103	0.6	72.4	656,848	6,363	94,628	60.5	65,797	70.1	29.9	37.1	11.6	1,274	20.8
Meigs	76	-2.5	129	0.3	24.6	312,980	2,428	53,207	14.5	24,622	66.8	33.2	29.1	4.3	748	17.9
Mercer	273	-6.8	226	0.1	248.7	1,775,939	7,854	213,011	596.4	493,681	25.7	74.3	76.3	49.7	7,650	79.1
Miami	184	-6.5	173	2.3	164.8	983,794	5,703	103,808	110.0	102,998	91.9	8.1	51.2	21.7	3,147	59.2
Monroe	111	11.9	135	0.0	29.7	311,759	2,308	58,011	13.7	16,612	32.4	67.6	23.2	2.6	264	6.3
Montgomery	124	11.8	161	1.2	104.7	944,147	5,858	111,271	76.8	99,695	84.6	15.4	38.8	13.0	1,656	44.4
Morgan	95	-6.9	187	0.0	30.0	448,463	2,403	64,149	12.2	23,975	41.5	58.5	34.1	5.1	370	22.7
Morrow	168	1.6	204	0.2	139.2	952,987	4,682	131,218	131.7	159,848	70.9	29.1	50.7	20.0	2,689	43.8
Muskingum	173	4.1	138	0.1	79.2	449,031	3,263	70,551	58.1	46,149	51.8	48.2	34.4	7.8	1,298	24.1
Noble	86	-3.6	145	0.1	28.8	368,677	2,547	55,652	9.8	16,403	37.1	62.9	31.9	2.2	78	4.9

Table B. States and Counties — Water Use, Wholesale Trade, Retail Trade, and Real Estate

STATE County	Water use, 2015		Wholesale Trade[1], 2012				Retail Trade[2], 2012				Real estate and rental and leasing,[2] 2012			
	Public supply water withdrawn (mil gal/day)	Public supply gallons withdrawn per person per day	Number of establishments	Number of employees	Sales (mil dol)	Annual payroll (mil dol)	Number of establishments	Number of employees	Sales (mil dol)	Annual payroll (mil dol)	Number of establishments	Number of employees	Sales (mil dol)	Annual payroll (mil dol)
	133	134	135	136	137	138	139	140	141	142	143	144	145	146
NORTH DAKOTA— Cont'd														
Ward	6.87	96.4	102	1,621	2,898.0	100.1	297	5,634	1,902.3	162.9	79	735	195.1	37.9
Wells	0.36	86.4	19	D	D	D	36	209	80.4	4.5	3	D	D	D
Williams	9.17	259.8	91	1,527	1,868.5	119.2	114	1,833	797.5	62.2	77	819	573.6	82.4
OHIO	1,306.28	112.5	11,744	182,791	155,426.0	9,627.2	36,531	549,152	153,554.0	13,099.3	9,932	60,966	16,132.7	2,441.8
Adams	2.05	73.2	9	114	77.9	3.9	77	853	224.9	18.0	8	27	3.0	0.8
Allen	18.17	174.0	124	2,287	1,388.8	91.6	417	6,072	1,641.5	134.3	85	376	55.2	11.0
Ashland	2.99	56.2	39	D	D	D	156	2,036	486.1	46.1	31	156	12.8	3.4
Ashtabula	7.20	73.0	48	385	220.1	14.2	327	3,635	1,081.1	80.6	70	199	26.7	5.3
Athens	7.51	114.0	28	D	D	D	192	2,783	695.1	58.7	61	213	24.8	4.5
Auglaize	5.27	114.9	35	D	D	D	165	2,096	491.8	43.1	31	193	14.4	5.9
Belmont	7.61	110.0	38	D	D	D	299	3,837	1,042.5	82.2	54	320	44.1	8.0
Brown	3.06	69.8	23	138	72.3	4.5	102	979	256.4	21.6	14	51	6.0	1.0
Butler	50.69	134.7	435	9,727	8,239.8	545.4	1,011	17,718	7,072.0	482.8	264	1,283	289.6	45.7
Carroll	0.84	30.2	17	D	D	D	65	671	204.9	16.8	12	57	6.7	1.5
Champaign	2.49	63.9	25	D	D	D	95	980	271.3	21.4	22	56	10.3	1.5
Clark	16.17	118.9	88	2,274	2,697.8	111.4	403	5,708	1,541.5	128.0	95	468	56.8	12.5
Clermont	18.46	91.4	148	1,560	1,051.1	83.5	520	9,185	2,659.3	227.7	140	608	105.3	19.7
Clinton	0.88	21.0	29	383	425.2	17.4	127	1,531	443.1	37.0	27	186	37.4	5.4
Columbiana	9.18	87.6	88	1,108	584.6	49.7	338	3,922	1,126.4	88.9	55	215	25.7	5.9
Coshocton	6.59	180.2	16	D	D	D	107	1,219	307.3	25.5	18	D	D	D
Crawford	2.41	57.0	35	D	D	D	135	1,330	348.9	30.4	27	64	7.3	1.3
Cuyahoga	222.45	177.1	1,930	31,718	21,584.9	1,742.5	4,302	59,458	15,072.5	1,412.8	1,534	13,977	4,931.1	691.5
Darke	3.00	57.6	56	628	528.3	25.4	170	1,956	480.6	43.3	36	131	14.3	3.9
Defiance	3.40	88.7	33	445	422.8	19.7	150	2,344	593.9	54.0	25	95	13.5	2.2
Delaware	19.66	101.9	151	D	D	D	587	11,363	3,178.6	273.5	162	697	146.6	28.0
Erie	11.99	158.7	65	743	1,145.5	35.5	309	4,531	1,072.4	96.7	74	282	41.0	9.2
Fairfield	9.20	60.8	75	D	D	D	412	6,930	1,678.8	151.1	130	491	63.7	10.5
Fayette	1.99	69.4	25	D	D	D	183	2,411	675.2	44.9	15	58	20.8	1.5
Franklin	155.82	124.5	1,274	25,263	20,890.3	1,441.5	3,613	65,130	21,384.9	1,810.6	1,394	9,626	2,688.7	420.3
Fulton	2.54	59.7	42	429	382.8	15.7	157	1,651	433.7	37.4	19	70	6.1	1.6
Gallia	3.47	115.1	17	209	68.3	6.3	120	1,320	336.3	28.7	22	65	9.0	1.6
Geauga	1.45	15.4	135	1,382	592.0	74.1	283	3,696	1,007.8	87.6	65	299	30.3	10.1
Greene	8.98	54.6	79	979	1,101.9	46.9	505	9,080	2,121.3	192.5	128	472	96.7	13.6
Guernsey	5.45	138.8	23	D	D	D	144	1,667	547.0	37.8	34	99	25.3	2.6
Hamilton	114.75	142.1	1,112	18,946	15,311.6	1,065.9	2,821	44,091	11,558.5	1,077.1	979	6,913	1,634.4	313.1
Hancock	11.28	149.3	72	964	953.4	47.8	263	4,090	1,103.7	90.6	60	432	55.4	14.2
Hardin	2.23	70.4	16	115	216.4	4.8	90	930	200.0	18.0	13	49	8.0	0.8
Harrison	0.60	38.8	8	D	D	D	33	281	70.9	5.1	5	D	D	D
Henry	2.96	106.4	26	221	305.7	9.6	79	943	290.7	19.0	19	75	24.6	2.2
Highland	2.30	53.5	14	131	95.8	4.4	139	1,532	393.0	34.1	26	65	10.1	1.7
Hocking	1.67	58.6	5	D	D	D	67	799	213.2	17.5	28	110	10.2	2.5
Holmes	1.80	41.0	60	631	332.2	22.7	157	1,976	456.7	45.1	15	40	10.3	1.2
Huron	5.54	94.8	46	607	601.6	27.7	174	1,993	538.4	43.5	47	151	23.3	4.0
Jackson	1.47	45.1	20	123	60.4	4.3	117	1,410	339.5	29.9	24	79	10.4	2.1
Jefferson	8.77	130.2	45	D	D	D	216	3,082	723.2	65.7	43	196	23.1	6.0
Knox	5.47	89.6	43	D	D	D	177	2,051	585.2	47.6	38	137	16.7	3.2
Lake	22.82	99.5	296	2,993	1,406.6	149.5	789	12,537	3,505.0	293.4	189	711	150.6	23.6
Lawrence	5.43	88.9	20	180	100.3	6.3	154	1,870	553.8	42.4	22	59	8.1	1.5
Licking	12.57	73.7	96	1,574	1,634.8	76.6	444	6,954	2,454.9	167.9	110	357	69.0	10.3
Logan	2.80	61.7	28	1,381	748.8	63.3	148	1,685	442.3	38.2	32	153	28.4	4.0
Lorain	42.42	139.0	246	2,943	1,826.6	130.4	814	12,995	3,707.3	310.4	192	1,116	116.2	26.5
Lucas	81.45	187.8	440	6,310	5,058.6	327.0	1,459	23,721	5,977.9	561.0	411	2,688	2,530.9	161.2
Madison	2.05	46.5	23	D	D	D	103	1,719	1,116.1	44.8	30	87	13.6	1.9
Mahoning	4.30	18.5	279	3,666	1,814.7	178.6	893	12,319	3,104.3	262.6	177	2,348	184.5	59.3
Marion	6.14	93.9	36	541	620.1	25.7	181	2,822	745.3	69.5	44	191	28.9	6.0
Medina	3.01	17.1	233	3,012	1,536.8	162.5	486	8,741	2,651.4	199.7	131	487	85.4	13.7
Meigs	1.75	75.2	7	68	13.2	1.7	63	510	155.5	10.1	8	16	1.8	0.2
Mercer	2.88	70.3	49	1,039	790.3	39.4	168	1,930	496.5	46.4	28	69	10.2	1.7
Miami	10.89	104.5	84	820	740.7	35.7	307	4,558	1,239.3	108.0	73	300	44.1	8.8
Monroe	1.07	74.3	6	D	D	D	47	360	74.4	6.5	1	D	D	D
Montgomery	81.14	152.4	521	7,997	15,523.2	450.6	1,675	26,113	6,490.7	605.1	534	3,167	524.5	110.7
Morgan	0.64	43.3	6	D	D	D	26	268	54.5	4.8	3	D	D	D
Morrow	0.55	15.7	14	D	D	D	51	475	164.1	9.7	6	11	2.2	0.2
Muskingum	9.89	114.6	54	868	707.1	33.6	338	4,448	1,117.8	94.1	56	265	41.2	8.3
Noble	1.04	72.6	5	28	16.7	1.1	34	327	105.0	6.7	3	2	0.7	0.1

1. Merchant wholesalers, except manufacturers' sales branches and offices. 2. Employer establishments.

STATE County	Professional, scientific, and technical services, 2012				Manufacturing, 2012				Accommodation and food services, 2012			
	Number of establish-ments	Number of employees	Sales (mil dol)	Annual payroll (mil dol)	Number of establishments	Number of employees	Receipts (mil dol)	Annual payroll (mil dol)	Number of establishments	Number of employees	Receipts (mil dol)	Annual payroll (mil dol)
	147	148	149	150	151	152	153	154	155	156	157	158
NORTH DAKOTA— Cont'd												
Ward	144	763	116.9	49.4	54	561	D	21.8	173	3,932	211.6	59.1
Wells	9	25	2.0	0.8	7	51	30.0	1.9	17	114	4.8	1.0
Williams	99	558	123.8	37.5	33	250	125.1	12.4	94	2,152	259.1	44.0
OHIO	23,961	233,876	35,970.8	14,219.9	14,482	627,124	313,630.0	33,135.4	23,432	437,293	20,652.8	5,742.7
Adams	26	D	D	D	24	542	103.7	29.8	35	508	21.4	5.8
Allen	164	952	75.8	33.0	124	7,318	15,270.4	448.1	234	4,521	211.3	54.3
Ashland	69	962	127.1	42.8	83	3,655	1,069.9	156.6	91	1,500	61.9	17.2
Ashtabula	118	D	D	D	147	6,167	2,449.5	313.9	229	2,706	121.5	30.8
Athens	71	580	86.0	23.6	38	176	D	6.4	143	2,860	107.2	29.1
Auglaize	70	434	56.8	17.2	83	7,339	2,961.6	363.5	90	1,341	50.5	14.2
Belmont	81	551	55.9	20.1	45	893	D	37.5	127	2,374	112.2	31.4
Brown	28	131	9.2	3.5	32	526	95.1	21.4	67	825	33.0	9.3
Butler	590	3,574	441.6	174.1	402	17,369	10,342.8	997.0	640	12,799	611.8	166.0
Carroll	25	118	9.6	3.5	40	1,366	368.6	55.1	41	485	17.9	5.3
Champaign	47	271	14.6	14.2	41	3,393	1,387.0	170.0	48	701	29.9	7.6
Clark	166	1,172	141.2	58.3	158	6,116	2,832.4	275.0	235	4,288	197.0	53.2
Clermont	385	2,826	469.6	154.5	169	5,182	1,248.5	262.3	280	6,030	285.3	81.9
Clinton	49	D	D	D	41	2,604	1,029.1	128.4	74	1,371	75.2	17.6
Columbiana	106	435	36.3	13.8	171	5,294	1,443.2	213.0	174	2,587	102.9	28.0
Coshocton	29	132	10.8	3.1	52	2,358	1,195.1	113.0	51	717	32.8	9.2
Crawford	45	357	74.1	13.2	80	3,374	1,045.9	149.9	84	987	41.6	10.9
Cuyahoga	4,016	41,345	6,848.8	2,750.9	1,890	69,606	24,399.4	4,048.8	2,959	53,954	2,738.6	758.7
Darke	69	280	30.3	8.8	72	4,475	1,855.5	216.8	88	1,015	43.0	11.0
Defiance	45	221	20.5	7.4	43	3,278	1,018.0	203.5	81	1,228	50.1	13.2
Delaware	534	3,692	667.1	222.2	135	5,463	3,012.0	303.4	421	9,496	460.2	134.1
Erie	117	D	D	D	103	5,465	2,021.6	291.7	263	5,848	305.9	77.6
Fairfield	196	910	76.3	28.9	107	4,219	1,277.9	207.0	244	4,767	203.0	59.6
Fayette	21	72	8.3	2.1	25	1,670	1,343.7	75.9	59	1,053	46.9	12.5
Franklin	3,472	40,628	7,092.6	2,737.0	814	28,991	12,574.1	1,461.7	2,797	57,229	2,980.8	843.3
Fulton	47	D	D	D	93	6,102	3,394.5	290.9	73	936	35.3	10.3
Gallia	29	87	8.7	2.4	22	452	D	22.4	53	886	43.4	11.5
Geauga	349	1,109	207.7	58.4	195	7,259	2,787.3	353.1	171	2,404	98.7	28.5
Greene	437	8,729	1,756.2	651.4	102	3,221	877.9	170.4	311	6,674	319.9	86.5
Guernsey	43	235	30.7	11.1	55	2,634	1,562.7	120.8	89	1,465	71.0	18.0
Hamilton	2,536	40,955	6,599.1	2,839.3	990	45,901	23,167.3	2,800.1	1,853	39,506	2,004.4	569.6
Hancock	136	758	97.8	38.6	94	9,903	4,821.3	491.4	181	4,063	169.8	48.3
Hardin	25	85	7.0	2.4	30	1,722	475.3	73.3	51	868	37.2	12.1
Harrison	13	27	2.4	0.7	12	368	92.3	13.6	27	198	7.9	2.3
Henry	24	91	9.8	3.3	45	3,100	2,313.6	158.0	49	D	D	D
Highland	40	132	11.0	2.9	27	1,698	585.9	68.6	63	878	36.4	9.6
Hocking	26	D	D	D	24	847	287.1	39.3	57	885	45.8	12.6
Holmes	30	267	35.1	11.2	253	6,028	1,483.4	200.9	67	1,374	61.0	17.9
Huron	80	410	33.1	14.4	87	5,436	2,336.8	232.4	107	1,474	60.9	15.5
Jackson	36	153	11.6	3.3	32	3,492	D	117.6	53	884	35.8	9.8
Jefferson	87	D	D	D	35	1,333	D	76.0	142	1,808	76.2	20.0
Knox	54	335	33.4	12.1	69	4,976	2,166.3	300.4	91	1,438	60.7	16.5
Lake	555	3,056	413.5	170.9	617	19,183	6,045.2	970.0	529	9,279	406.8	111.6
Lawrence	42	271	18.0	7.8	34	915	D	30.6	66	1,124	58.9	14.3
Licking	229	1,795	144.3	114.4	151	7,809	2,958.9	358.2	280	4,975	212.7	61.7
Logan	54	766	62.7	27.2	48	4,584	6,790.1	305.7	98	1,214	56.5	15.0
Lorain	448	3,297	276.1	111.4	379	16,010	7,328.0	892.4	514	8,536	397.0	104.6
Lucas	864	8,875	1,182.6	474.5	460	18,286	27,736.6	1,154.6	1,025	19,099	823.0	237.3
Madison	42	D	D	D	44	2,895	1,157.9	135.8	46	844	36.0	10.6
Mahoning	447	3,570	307.8	142.2	326	8,756	1,978.7	398.9	490	9,022	397.2	105.6
Marion	71	303	29.8	9.6	71	5,966	3,681.7	276.5	106	1,893	86.9	22.1
Medina	407	2,028	230.8	83.7	277	8,543	2,970.4	405.6	288	4,897	223.0	61.9
Meigs	11	D	D	D	7	D	D	1.6	28	372	16.4	4.6
Mercer	44	295	31.7	10.6	82	3,807	1,136.9	172.5	85	1,192	44.8	11.9
Miami	159	1,000	112.6	41.6	216	10,888	3,923.9	542.3	188	3,816	159.8	45.7
Monroe	11	D	D	D	9	D	D	D	18	163	5.9	1.6
Montgomery	1,121	12,095	1,713.7	727.6	730	26,188	8,239.2	1,466.6	1,112	22,321	1,028.7	296.6
Morgan	8	D	D	D	9	582	D	27.8	16	159	5.1	1.5
Morrow	33	D	D	D	26	844	D	45.6	29	350	17.6	4.6
Muskingum	106	452	55.6	17.1	72	2,699	867.7	126.2	167	3,102	139.5	39.7
Noble	12	D	D	D	13	299	101.9	D	17	D	D	D

Table B. States and Counties — Health Care and Social Assistance, Other Services, Nonemployer Businesses, and Residential Construction

STATE County	Health care and social assistance, 2012				Other services, 2012				Nonemployer businesses, 2015		Value of residential construction authorized by building permits, 2017	
	Number of establishments	Number of employees	Receipts (mil dol)	Annual payroll (mil dol)	Number of establishments	Number of employees	Receipts (mil dol)	Annual payroll (mil dol)	Number	Receipts (mil dol)	New construction ($1,000)	Number of housing units
	159	160	161	162	163	164	165	166	167	168	169	170
NORTH DAKOTA— Cont'd												
Ward	152	D	D	D	134	751	69.7	19.7	4,303	212.2	30,063	129
Wells	17	461	21.8	10.8	16	D	D	D	378	17.1	0	0
Williams	65	1,485	131.6	57.6	78	467	82.0	17.0	2,562	147.1	13,851	57
OHIO	28,237	798,770	80,915.7	33,141.0	18,851	127,366	13,221.5	3,491.3	763,418	33,534.4	5,020,991	23,917
Adams	48	1,057	67.1	28.3	25	64	26.1	2.2	1,928	74.2	1,111	10
Allen	307	11,307	1,256.5	501.7	197	1,264	92.0	25.5	5,366	211.5	23,767	224
Ashland	112	2,220	188.6	71.4	91	563	44.3	14.7	3,413	150.1	8,975	61
Ashtabula	217	5,453	420.3	171.9	158	646	47.5	10.9	6,141	248.2	16,442	102
Athens	144	3,058	287.7	101.6	80	417	27.6	7.5	3,238	113.7	5,842	26
Auglaize	97	2,259	169.4	60.0	89	529	38.2	11.9	2,732	107.3	33,509	193
Belmont	208	4,715	311.7	127.6	124	654	41.0	12.0	3,232	133.3	818	6
Brown	58	1,461	112.6	42.2	42	180	13.1	3.8	2,734	106.3	18,368	71
Butler	730	15,022	1,491.8	566.6	520	4,178	373.1	108.0	21,945	955.4	165,822	817
Carroll	39	753	41.6	17.4	46	224	16.8	4.0	1,917	83.9	0	0
Champaign	49	1,362	89.1	35.5	48	165	14.0	3.1	2,208	92.4	6,854	39
Clark	313	10,029	912.0	334.8	212	1,363	134.3	40.5	6,681	244.8	19,397	121
Clermont	291	5,950	527.0	211.9	289	1,688	147.8	43.8	13,258	573.1	128,222	952
Clinton	90	1,751	176.2	64.2	60	260	21.5	6.2	2,711	108.7	9,347	47
Columbiana	291	5,444	415.4	161.9	184	857	69.0	18.4	5,919	242.8	10,879	80
Coshocton	84	1,783	143.5	56.0	60	267	22.0	5.0	2,312	92.7	909	3
Crawford	98	2,313	176.8	70.1	73	310	27.1	6.3	2,170	83.4	420	3
Cuyahoga	3,593	137,744	14,792.8	6,409.1	2,495	18,586	2,072.3	568.0	91,324	4,111.1	221,135	827
Darke	77	2,284	186.6	74.3	106	405	24.9	7.0	3,520	146.4	9,965	45
Defiance	85	2,403	194.0	80.8	70	386	31.2	7.1	2,164	87.7	7,119	38
Delaware	395	6,795	541.6	243.4	270	2,266	458.8	94.2	16,658	931.7	332,326	1,319
Erie	208	5,406	489.8	224.1	138	710	47.5	14.3	4,733	186.0	22,689	96
Fairfield	303	6,114	564.4	241.0	171	1,031	101.5	30.4	10,466	453.1	133,189	671
Fayette	53	1,432	114.4	45.8	40	193	10.7	3.2	1,509	59.3	8,041	38
Franklin	3,325	104,976	11,693.1	4,509.2	1,912	17,718	2,309.3	597.1	93,514	4,263.2	1,054,351	5,854
Fulton	93	2,330	197.1	76.4	71	254	25.9	6.0	2,952	128.0	9,669	45
Gallia	70	2,473	227.0	97.3	37	241	17.9	5.4	1,766	75.1	515	5
Geauga	237	3,833	360.2	157.2	176	1,179	108.6	36.7	10,873	624.3	74,639	253
Greene	341	5,861	608.5	219.4	212	1,244	99.7	27.9	9,864	395.1	201,868	616
Guernsey	123	2,653	221.2	74.6	60	276	31.0	6.1	2,249	100.9	6,707	35
Hamilton	2,371	80,058	10,054.4	4,272.5	1,488	11,624	1,292.3	344.2	57,438	2,662.5	280,935	1,618
Hancock	183	5,107	523.6	192.3	137	892	99.6	22.9	4,349	192.4	27,859	104
Hardin	48	645	48.9	18.9	32	117	8.9	2.3	1,509	59.2	10,648	54
Harrison	27	513	39.9	15.0	19	61	5.7	1.2	869	44.3	0	0
Henry	52	1,371	81.3	36.0	42	304	19.7	5.2	1,640	68.5	4,805	24
Highland	97	1,650	128.4	50.9	42	154	13.1	2.9	2,946	126.5	1,165	12
Hocking	47	1,075	74.7	29.9	35	199	22.2	4.2	1,898	72.1	750	6
Holmes	60	1,397	153.1	41.2	53	184	21.5	5.0	5,263	332.8	860	5
Huron	102	2,711	269.6	111.4	105	544	41.3	11.6	3,112	132.6	8,656	39
Jackson	74	1,372	120.4	42.5	40	157	16.7	3.6	1,682	64.9	13,961	62
Jefferson	155	4,577	438.1	164.5	101	590	41.0	11.9	3,074	104.3	1,186	4
Knox	130	2,971	231.6	93.2	77	499	42.7	11.7	4,822	208.5	28,133	132
Lake	608	11,077	944.7	408.2	470	2,718	214.6	66.8	15,490	693.6	93,723	491
Lawrence	123	D	D	D	55	281	28.2	6.3	2,773	100.4	2,305	15
Licking	262	7,491	625.0	254.5	203	1,190	103.1	27.8	11,823	505.1	69,424	263
Logan	94	2,122	180.1	69.5	67	505	79.3	13.1	2,821	118.4	12,046	65
Lorain	616	13,559	1,290.7	534.4	454	2,641	260.3	62.6	17,147	687.3	193,254	964
Lucas	1,275	38,102	4,107.7	1,677.1	731	5,136	444.5	130.0	24,644	1,073.9	126,409	647
Madison	73	D	D	D	46	159	11.9	3.3	2,709	111.0	10,821	43
Mahoning	767	19,562	1,823.7	717.0	382	2,612	216.7	58.4	15,421	646.7	32,376	139
Marion	157	4,315	369.2	151.5	95	648	40.1	11.0	2,997	108.5	8,554	49
Medina	369	7,484	580.7	238.2	300	1,639	128.9	41.0	13,229	632.4	177,634	692
Meigs	41	473	30.4	11.9	17	53	6.7	1.4	1,143	38.1	1,921	14
Mercer	76	2,104	132.6	57.7	86	436	43.3	10.9	2,718	126.5	21,807	94
Miami	197	4,449	374.8	135.0	178	900	81.3	20.7	6,715	263.2	59,521	186
Monroe	18	D	D	D	23	D	D	D	1,063	34.0	0	0
Montgomery	1,466	48,822	5,573.6	2,243.7	852	6,243	682.6	157.5	31,435	1,304.4	107,696	449
Morgan	16	340	20.2	7.7	13	D	D	D	808	26.2	8,042	36
Morrow	47	D	D	D	24	80	7.3	2.0	2,608	121.0	4,433	69
Muskingum	194	6,011	603.1	266.2	159	1,093	86.6	23.9	5,060	202.9	6,238	64
Noble	20	D	D	D	20	D	D	D	737	29.8	4,688	27

STATE County	Full-time equivalent employees	March payroll (dollars)	Adminis-tration, judicial, and legal	Police and corrections	Fire protection	Highways and transpor-tation	Health and welfare	Natural resources and utilities	Education and libraries	Total (mil dol)	Inter-govern-mental (mil dol)	Total (mil dol)	Total	Property
	171	172	173	174	175	176	177	178	179	180	181	182	183	184
NORTH DAKOTA— Cont'd														
Ward	2,136	7,851,589	4.3	7.5	2.8	4.2	5.4	5.7	68.4	241.7	117.3	80.2	1,238	819
Wells	201	657,258	11.8	3.8	0.0	9.3	11.4	5.1	54.7	18.7	8.8	6.5	1,519	1,436
Williams	864	3,064,820	7.6	11.5	0.1	4.9	6.8	4.6	59.1	140.3	49.9	59.7	2,236	1,126
OHIO	X	X	X	X	X	X	X	X	X	X	X	X	X	X
Adams	1,309	4,554,288	8.6	6.3	1.2	4.8	20.7	12.5	44.5	95.0	57.8	28.2	996	856
Allen	4,029	14,917,726	8.3	9.1	4.8	3.4	9.8	5.8	55.9	394.8	197.5	125.6	1,195	774
Ashland	1,952	6,407,247	7.9	9.8	3.4	8.4	11.1	4.1	54.7	148.8	65.0	62.1	1,172	812
Ashtabula	3,445	13,283,345	8.6	8.3	6.3	6.3	10.0	5.8	52.9	379.5	210.8	114.5	1,141	880
Athens	2,322	8,135,468	7.7	8.6	2.5	4.0	14.9	8.3	53.4	218.6	106.3	74.7	1,161	793
Auglaize	1,848	6,837,964	8.1	11.1	3.6	6.2	9.8	11.2	48.9	165.8	68.7	63.4	1,383	791
Belmont	2,607	9,128,313	8.1	10.6	2.1	10.5	11.9	10.3	46.0	191.0	101.3	63.6	913	616
Brown	1,467	5,037,757	10.7	6.4	1.0	3.0	3.9	4.5	68.2	139.2	79.2	35.6	803	573
Butler	12,086	48,616,602	7.6	9.8	5.5	2.6	6.4	6.6	59.8	1,333.8	510.2	553.1	1,493	1,108
Carroll	814	2,533,284	12.9	4.6	0.1	10.7	12.6	3.6	53.6	67.3	39.5	18.9	663	541
Champaign	1,507	5,457,874	8.0	11.9	3.0	4.5	7.3	4.2	60.0	133.3	67.8	46.2	1,167	749
Clark	5,386	19,627,638	7.6	10.0	4.2	2.3	8.2	4.4	57.6	501.3	270.1	168.3	1,227	774
Clermont	5,289	20,437,759	7.0	10.5	7.4	2.9	8.3	2.8	59.9	577.6	246.3	251.2	1,262	1,074
Clinton	1,809	5,888,599	9.0	8.5	2.2	3.7	8.2	6.6	60.3	157.7	71.7	54.0	1,288	849
Columbiana	3,495	11,243,471	8.0	8.4	2.1	5.7	10.5	5.6	58.7	309.6	171.8	94.5	887	570
Coshocton	1,280	4,337,624	6.8	5.0	9.6	5.4	10.8	3.0	57.6	122.4	67.8	38.8	1,056	791
Crawford	1,254	4,325,266	5.9	4.7	3.6	1.8	1.1	5.5	77.2	151.9	72.7	51.8	1,209	747
Cuyahoga	62,490	287,120,691	6.2	10.3	5.0	6.7	17.9	8.2	44.0	8,188.0	2,777.4	3,498.3	2,765	1,595
Darke	1,735	6,310,491	7.2	9.5	3.5	3.8	9.0	4.8	60.8	161.4	77.3	60.1	1,145	652
Defiance	1,658	5,904,403	6.0	5.9	1.8	3.6	22.5	5.1	51.1	159.4	60.4	46.4	1,200	722
Delaware	5,621	21,810,855	6.5	8.3	8.6	3.5	6.9	3.8	60.6	594.5	125.1	379.4	2,096	1,582
Erie	3,210	12,237,910	9.9	7.7	6.1	3.6	6.5	6.6	58.0	347.1	131.6	140.7	1,841	1,302
Fairfield	4,930	17,614,468	7.6	7.4	6.0	3.4	7.0	5.5	62.0	533.2	218.0	227.0	1,539	972
Fayette	1,569	5,994,441	8.4	7.6	3.1	4.0	30.8	6.0	35.4	151.4	51.3	42.0	1,454	900
Franklin	43,936	204,420,126	7.5	12.0	8.0	4.8	6.8	5.9	53.0	6,852.6	2,645.8	3,248.5	2,717	1,632
Fulton	1,714	6,275,872	9.2	6.4	2.8	7.9	4.5	5.4	60.4	175.3	77.4	66.6	1,566	1,017
Gallia	1,230	4,310,190	10.5	5.0	0.3	10.5	8.6	3.8	60.0	121.8	67.0	35.1	1,144	879
Geauga	2,853	10,934,381	6.8	10.3	1.9	6.2	6.6	5.0	60.8	321.0	103.8	177.1	1,890	1,605
Greene	5,165	20,150,214	7.8	10.0	5.1	2.9	8.5	4.8	58.8	586.4	206.6	277.8	1,698	1,294
Guernsey	1,477	4,435,295	10.2	6.1	1.9	6.0	6.7	6.6	52.4	132.8	73.2	38.5	968	624
Hamilton	30,330	130,350,382	7.8	13.0	8.0	5.1	7.5	8.7	47.8	4,236.2	1,499.4	1,927.5	2,403	1,479
Hancock	2,432	8,819,684	8.0	8.9	4.5	4.6	9.6	8.0	55.4	271.6	110.7	109.9	1,453	890
Hardin	1,423	4,258,899	9.1	8.7	1.2	4.7	11.9	3.6	57.1	110.9	55.5	32.7	1,034	564
Harrison	710	1,856,484	14.6	4.5	0.0	15.6	8.0	4.7	51.0	49.7	28.0	13.6	864	670
Henry	1,481	5,408,211	10.0	3.9	0.9	3.5	8.5	11.1	57.7	117.5	56.0	44.6	1,592	1,074
Highland	2,293	6,286,414	5.2	4.7	1.8	3.3	31.1	2.7	50.4	172.7	76.0	41.2	959	563
Hocking	914	2,885,727	10.2	5.6	1.4	5.5	5.2	3.2	67.0	114.8	42.6	28.6	978	747
Holmes	1,321	4,844,879	5.9	5.2	1.1	8.0	34.0	1.8	43.4	120.7	39.0	36.0	838	671
Huron	2,467	10,437,634	6.6	7.8	2.4	4.1	4.3	21.4	48.4	200.0	86.9	77.4	1,306	715
Jackson	1,363	4,190,837	9.9	7.6	2.0	7.6	8.5	6.5	56.1	108.3	64.9	23.7	718	505
Jefferson	2,754	8,388,400	8.2	12.7	2.8	7.2	11.7	7.8	48.7	279.5	143.1	76.7	1,121	730
Knox	2,080	6,852,809	7.4	6.9	4.1	5.9	8.2	4.9	60.0	183.1	81.3	75.5	1,244	918
Lake	9,604	40,201,055	7.4	10.0	6.0	4.6	9.6	6.7	54.4	980.1	328.7	481.4	2,097	1,489
Lawrence	2,540	8,380,560	7.9	7.5	1.5	3.4	6.7	4.8	67.2	216.7	128.7	37.7	607	431
Licking	5,717	20,737,584	8.7	10.0	5.7	3.6	5.5	4.6	60.9	579.7	236.0	255.6	1,525	1,041
Logan	1,959	6,311,962	5.8	5.7	2.0	5.4	16.7	4.0	58.9	181.6	83.8	65.2	1,434	1,028
Lorain	11,564	45,174,817	6.2	9.7	3.8	2.9	8.7	7.0	60.5	1,201.2	540.9	467.7	1,551	1,088
Lucas	14,739	62,111,336	9.0	11.4	8.7	4.8	10.1	5.0	50.5	2,086.3	910.4	780.9	1,783	1,087
Madison	1,659	6,453,004	10.2	8.0	6.0	3.9	8.2	4.3	57.6	145.7	58.9	62.4	1,448	1,020
Mahoning	8,773	31,345,985	6.1	10.6	3.5	4.0	7.9	7.9	58.9	868.3	433.7	320.4	1,363	887
Marion	2,295	8,158,244	7.0	10.0	5.7	2.9	9.1	2.6	60.7	238.0	129.7	65.6	990	651
Medina	5,924	23,018,921	7.1	9.8	2.3	4.3	7.5	6.6	61.1	592.1	209.5	282.6	1,627	1,274
Meigs	1,067	3,103,267	7.9	7.6	0.0	6.4	10.2	11.3	53.7	74.8	52.2	14.0	593	473
Mercer	1,924	6,814,130	6.9	4.9	1.1	2.5	23.6	3.3	56.9	205.3	75.3	58.0	1,418	907
Miami	3,473	13,601,040	7.3	8.3	2.8	3.5	7.7	7.6	59.9	385.2	159.1	157.7	1,531	850
Monroe	802	1,932,268	10.9	3.9	0.2	9.0	13.4	7.6	53.8	74.7	47.7	17.9	1,229	1,062
Montgomery	22,502	93,151,363	7.9	9.7	4.7	6.0	8.0	8.2	54.1	2,605.5	1,042.9	1,055.0	1,974	1,302
Morgan	442	1,318,311	13.5	4.8	0.0	6.2	1.1	3.1	69.8	48.1	33.5	10.1	676	539
Morrow	1,452	4,922,890	11.2	5.3	0.3	5.8	24.4	1.2	49.4	129.7	48.6	32.8	939	663
Muskingum	3,889	12,275,435	6.0	8.2	2.0	4.2	10.5	5.2	60.2	370.0	202.8	113.8	1,324	918
Noble	445	1,384,468	17.5	1.9	0.0	7.5	11.4	15.2	45.8	48.2	22.3	17.2	1,183	1,099

1. Based on the resident population estimated as of July 1 of the year shown.

Table B. States and Counties — Local Government Finances, Government Employment, and Income Taxes

STATE County	Total (mil dol) 185	Per capita[1] (dollars) 186	Education 187	Health and hospitals 188	Police protection 189	Public welfare 190	Highways 191	Total (mil dol) 192	Per capita[1] (dollars) 193	Federal civilian 194	Federal military 195	State and local 196	Number of returns 197	Mean adjusted gross income 198	Mean income tax 199
NORTH DAKOTA— Cont'd															
Ward	230.0	3,550	57.5	0.3	5.1	2.2	10.8	95.7	1,477	1,271	5,787	4,577	34,970	65,312	8,762
Wells	18.0	4,209	46.4	1.9	3.5	4.3	18.7	9.3	2,176	26	25	258	2,140	57,183	7,260
Williams	130.1	4,872	37.2	3.2	4.7	0.9	16.5	127.0	4,757	101	213	2,432	17,810	95,033	16,435
OHIO	X	X	X	X	X	X	X	X	X	77,791	35,432	688,476	5,591,870	57,786	7,262
Adams	85.9	3,030	56.6	4.4	3.7	6.7	8.9	48.9	1,726	65	70	1,464	10,930	41,150	3,494
Allen	385.4	3,665	49.5	5.4	6.9	4.3	6.7	180.7	1,719	327	254	5,795	48,020	50,985	5,823
Ashland	147.7	2,789	50.7	9.1	6.1	3.4	7.9	51.1	966	93	131	2,315	24,640	47,206	4,695
Ashtabula	389.2	3,877	53.0	7.0	3.8	6.1	7.1	243.8	2,429	196	260	4,320	44,750	42,457	3,877
Athens	231.8	3,605	47.4	7.2	2.6	14.9	4.9	68.3	1,062	230	155	11,380	22,230	48,213	5,232
Auglaize	176.4	3,848	52.8	1.4	5.8	4.8	6.3	154.1	3,362	96	116	2,288	23,580	53,942	5,792
Belmont	186.0	2,669	48.0	6.2	2.5	6.5	6.8	55.5	797	164	165	3,649	31,050	54,017	6,571
Brown	134.7	3,035	63.4	3.5	6.0	3.2	5.5	58.8	1,325	89	110	1,957	19,300	43,907	3,877
Butler	1,326.8	3,580	50.2	3.7	7.9	4.7	5.8	1,987.8	5,364	561	945	20,488	175,040	59,486	7,124
Carroll	59.8	2,092	47.0	8.7	3.5	6.9	10.6	17.3	605	48	69	979	12,910	49,909	5,232
Champaign	144.3	3,648	59.7	3.7	3.5	3.9	6.6	60.2	1,522	69	97	1,847	18,450	48,264	4,671
Clark	474.6	3,459	49.3	5.8	5.9	6.2	3.3	206.0	1,502	565	338	6,385	63,560	46,487	4,594
Clermont	582.2	2,924	49.6	6.2	6.8	6.0	5.4	332.6	1,671	364	513	7,346	98,050	61,949	7,564
Clinton	150.9	3,602	49.6	3.5	5.9	5.2	7.7	60.1	1,434	135	104	2,266	19,410	50,272	5,868
Columbiana	314.7	2,954	56.2	3.2	5.1	8.9	6.3	123.5	1,160	618	254	4,404	47,440	44,969	4,387
Coshocton	116.3	3,163	50.7	9.0	6.0	6.2	9.6	60.1	1,634	77	92	1,471	16,260	42,516	3,827
Crawford	163.0	3,804	50.5	4.3	4.1	5.0	8.0	99.7	2,328	83	106	1,782	20,530	40,891	3,439
Cuyahoga	8,005.7	6,328	36.6	14.5	5.9	3.6	2.9	11,286.9	8,922	16,458	3,525	78,902	627,700	60,621	8,498
Darke	165.9	3,160	56.8	4.8	5.9	4.6	7.2	76.5	1,457	106	130	2,114	25,260	47,222	4,728
Defiance	164.9	4,263	38.1	17.8	4.2	3.1	5.7	96.2	2,486	85	95	1,989	18,990	48,787	4,956
Delaware	580.7	3,207	51.8	3.6	4.6	2.2	6.9	734.5	4,057	234	525	7,477	91,960	102,331	16,896
Erie	360.9	4,724	52.1	2.5	5.2	3.9	4.2	232.7	3,046	220	188	5,114	39,610	50,820	5,908
Fairfield	537.8	3,647	55.2	5.3	4.9	3.9	3.7	791.1	5,364	236	402	6,718	71,040	58,803	6,609
Fayette	143.4	4,966	32.8	26.1	3.8	3.7	4.5	83.9	2,906	50	72	1,642	13,350	42,441	4,270
Franklin	6,511.1	5,446	38.1	3.0	6.3	6.0	4.2	8,029.0	6,716	13,244	3,624	119,703	622,650	60,975	8,116
Fulton	197.2	4,637	67.2	2.5	4.2	2.4	4.5	104.1	2,450	92	107	2,463	21,280	50,984	5,115
Gallia	123.5	4,023	57.7	2.3	5.6	5.4	6.2	74.2	2,416	68	74	1,792	12,050	46,226	4,544
Geauga	314.3	3,355	48.5	9.3	6.8	2.6	8.8	302.2	3,225	102	237	3,939	47,630	86,857	14,055
Greene	655.1	4,004	53.0	4.0	6.4	4.0	4.8	524.5	3,206	14,283	3,080	10,922	76,950	65,341	8,313
Guernsey	125.8	3,159	48.1	3.5	4.9	8.6	7.9	38.7	973	119	98	2,209	18,160	45,706	4,845
Hamilton	4,409.2	5,497	37.9	6.8	6.8	4.4	3.4	5,717.7	7,129	8,420	2,119	48,894	403,560	69,978	10,549
Hancock	295.5	3,905	53.3	7.9	3.8	2.7	4.3	240.6	3,180	152	189	3,179	37,430	60,170	7,815
Hardin	110.3	3,489	43.3	1.9	7.5	10.6	8.3	59.1	1,869	72	75	1,401	13,250	44,160	4,006
Harrison	46.0	2,927	48.6	1.1	3.7	9.2	14.1	4.8	305	53	38	744	6,610	53,718	6,115
Henry	116.8	4,166	57.4	9.8	4.3	0.3	7.0	51.0	1,819	69	69	1,950	14,140	51,340	5,615
Highland	157.5	3,663	45.3	24.8	5.4	4.0	5.4	55.6	1,293	98	108	2,195	18,370	41,203	3,520
Hocking	118.1	4,036	34.2	34.9	4.9	5.2	5.5	21.9	748	47	71	1,734	12,480	44,738	4,330
Holmes	122.6	2,851	35.9	29.5	3.5	5.1	8.0	35.7	830	65	110	1,566	28,930	46,109	4,495
Huron	227.6	3,839	59.2	1.8	3.8	5.5	5.6	177.4	2,992	143	147	2,362	13,550	42,677	3,672
Jackson	103.5	3,142	55.6	4.5	4.9	6.5	7.1	74.9	2,274	68	82	1,499	30,590	45,611	4,519
Jefferson	274.2	4,010	48.3	6.7	5.3	3.8	7.4	154.1	2,253	169	164	3,110	27,220	51,112	5,351
Knox	190.4	3,137	48.2	3.8	2.8	3.7	12.6	94.4	1,554	105	146	2,642	27,220	51,112	5,351
Lake	960.6	4,184	51.1	7.4	6.8	2.5	5.5	411.1	1,790	471	599	11,001	123,310	57,963	6,962
Lawrence	214.4	3,452	60.9	5.7	3.5	4.9	4.0	51.1	822	130	153	2,945	25,540	45,569	4,370
Licking	578.6	3,453	56.4	0.8	6.3	6.5	4.5	386.9	2,309	369	440	7,719	81,650	56,935	6,560
Logan	185.1	4,071	51.9	5.6	4.3	4.6	6.6	117.8	2,592	123	118	2,036	22,400	48,316	5,009
Lorain	1,206.9	4,003	55.2	4.3	5.8	3.9	4.7	1,730.7	5,741	1,085	778	14,288	148,450	56,125	6,590
Lucas	1,896.4	4,330	37.6	9.4	7.1	4.9	3.8	2,289.2	5,226	1,847	1,168	28,649	203,390	52,736	6,338
Madison	152.8	3,549	60.2	4.9	4.6	3.8	5.7	137.1	3,184	77	99	3,178	19,210	54,753	6,140
Mahoning	851.8	3,622	47.9	5.8	7.8	3.8	4.3	531.9	2,262	1,182	578	13,551	112,200	49,920	5,885
Marion	232.6	3,512	58.7	1.2	4.1	2.2	4.0	316.2	4,773	114	175	4,017	27,910	44,174	4,146
Medina	715.8	4,121	54.5	3.6	4.6	2.1	11.9	431.2	2,483	340	475	6,804	91,480	67,402	8,688
Meigs	70.8	3,002	53.3	2.8	2.8	10.1	10.2	25.4	1,075	60	58	1,056	9,170	42,552	3,644
Mercer	196.0	4,794	46.2	26.1	3.3	3.1	7.9	89.2	2,183	94	103	2,732	21,110	57,270	7,187
Miami	405.1	3,930	56.7	3.4	6.0	3.1	5.3	280.3	2,720	191	265	4,646	51,300	57,327	6,763
Monroe	83.7	5,754	66.8	2.8	2.6	8.8	8.9	2.9	200	49	36	736	6,270	56,456	6,766
Montgomery	2,652.7	4,965	44.5	3.0	6.4	8.6	5.3	2,338.6	4,377	4,276	3,797	27,066	256,730	52,772	6,191
Morgan	43.8	2,938	48.1	4.6	5.2	8.6	11.1	11.3	760	44	37	618	6,030	40,026	3,270
Morrow	139.5	3,994	47.5	22.8	1.4	3.0	5.3	60.5	1,733	46	88	1,583	15,480	48,455	4,592
Muskingum	340.0	3,956	54.4	3.3	4.9	6.1	6.4	122.4	1,424	218	215	5,070	39,550	46,024	4,691
Noble	36.8	2,523	50.8	2.9	4.1	7.6	14.3	3.0	208	23	30	968	5,400	55,837	6,834

1. Based on the resident population estimated as of July 1 of the year shown.

Table B. States and Counties — Land Area and Population

State / county code	CBSA code[1]	County code[2]	STATE County	Land area[3] (sq. mi)	Total persons 2017	Rank	Per square mile	White	Black	American Indian, Alaska Native	Asian and Pacific Islander	Percent Hispanic or Latino[4]	Under 5 years	5 to 17 years	18 to 24 years	25 to 34 years	35 to 44 years	45 to 54 years
				1	2	3	4	5	6	7	8	9	10	11	12	13	14	15
			OHIO— Cont'd															
39,123	38,840	4	Ottawa	254.9	40,657	1,163	159.5	93.4	1.5	0.5	0.6	5.1	4.4	14.5	6.7	9.5	10.1	13.1
39,125		6	Paulding	416.4	18,845	1,877	45.3	93.7	1.6	0.7	0.5	4.6	5.9	17.9	7.7	10.9	11.5	13.3
39,127	18,140	1	Perry	408.0	36,024	1,274	88.3	98.1	1.0	1.1	0.4	0.9	6.2	17.5	7.7	11.9	12.0	13.9
39,129	18,140	1	Pickaway	501.1	57,830	891	115.4	94.1	4.5	0.7	0.8	1.4	5.7	15.9	9.1	13.2	13.4	14.4
39,131		7	Pike	440.3	28,270	1,482	64.2	97.0	1.8	1.4	0.6	1.1	6.1	17.7	7.6	11.4	12.3	13.3
39,133	10,420	2	Portage	487.4	162,277	403	332.9	91.3	5.5	0.7	2.6	1.8	4.7	14.3	16.3	11.4	10.6	12.9
39,135		6	Preble	424.2	41,120	1,149	96.9	97.6	1.1	0.8	0.8	0.8	5.4	17.2	7.3	11.1	11.8	13.6
39,137		6	Putnam	482.5	33,878	1,330	70.2	93.1	0.7	0.3	0.4	6.2	6.7	18.8	8.0	10.9	11.2	12.8
39,139	31,900	3	Richland	495.3	120,589	519	243.5	87.7	10.6	0.7	1.2	1.9	5.8	15.9	8.3	12.3	11.7	12.6
39,141	17,060	4	Ross	689.2	77,313	717	112.2	91.8	7.4	1.1	1.0	1.2	5.4	15.8	7.8	12.6	13.3	14.6
39,143	23,380	4	Sandusky	408.5	59,195	874	144.9	86.4	4.4	0.6	0.7	9.9	5.7	17.0	7.7	11.3	11.9	13.3
39,145	39,020	4	Scioto	610.2	75,929	730	124.4	95.1	3.5	1.3	0.7	1.3	5.7	15.9	8.8	12.7	12.2	12.9
39,147	45,660	4	Seneca	551.0	55,243	918	100.3	91.5	3.5	0.6	1.0	5.1	5.4	16.7	10.5	11.4	11.6	12.3
39,149	43,380	4	Shelby	407.7	48,759	1,008	119.6	94.8	3.6	0.5	1.5	1.5	6.5	18.7	8.2	11.5	11.5	13.5
39,151	15,940	2	Stark	575.3	372,542	189	647.6	88.8	9.5	0.8	1.4	2.1	5.7	16.0	8.6	11.8	11.2	13.2
39,153	10,420	2	Summit	412.8	541,228	126	1,311.1	79.2	16.2	0.8	4.2	2.1	5.6	15.5	8.6	13.3	11.6	13.4
39,155	49,660	2	Trumbull	618.1	200,380	332	324.2	89.0	9.7	0.7	0.9	1.8	5.3	15.3	7.8	11.4	10.9	13.1
39,157	35,420	4	Tuscarawas	567.4	92,297	635	162.7	95.8	1.5	0.6	0.7	2.6	6.2	16.8	7.7	11.6	11.5	12.6
39,159	18,140	1	Union	431.7	56,741	902	131.4	91.3	3.3	0.6	4.6	1.7	6.4	18.6	8.0	13.1	14.9	15.0
39,161	46,780	6	Van Wert	409.2	28,217	1,484	69.0	95.3	1.8	0.5	0.5	3.2	6.1	17.2	7.8	11.4	11.7	12.8
39,163		8	Vinton	412.4	13,092	2,226	31.7	98.0	1.0	1.1	0.5	0.8	5.3	16.9	7.6	10.7	12.6	13.8
39,165	17,140	1	Warren	401.3	228,882	290	570.4	87.8	4.1	0.5	6.5	2.7	5.9	19.2	7.9	11.0	13.5	15.2
39,167	31,930	4	Washington	632.0	60,418	865	95.6	96.7	2.0	1.0	1.1	1.1	5.0	14.8	8.8	11.2	11.2	12.9
39,169	49,300	4	Wayne	554.9	116,038	532	209.1	95.2	2.4	0.6	1.4	2.0	6.7	17.7	9.7	11.8	11.0	12.1
39,171		6	Williams	421.0	36,784	1,256	87.4	93.5	1.6	0.6	0.7	4.5	5.9	17.0	7.8	11.4	11.7	12.7
39,173	45,780	2	Wood	617.2	130,492	489	211.4	89.7	3.4	0.6	2.2	5.6	5.3	15.0	17.7	12.2	11.1	11.5
39,175		7	Wyandot	406.9	22,029	1,722	54.1	96.0	0.7	0.5	0.8	2.9	5.7	17.0	7.7	11.2	12.1	13.2
40,000		0	**OKLAHOMA**	68,596.6	3,930,864	X	57.3	70.8	8.9	12.4	3.1	10.6	6.7	17.7	9.7	13.9	12.3	11.9
40,001		6	Adair	573.5	21,909	1,729	38.2	50.1	1.1	51.6	1.0	6.6	7.1	19.0	8.7	11.9	12.0	13.0
40,003		9	Alfalfa	866.5	5,907	2,759	6.8	86.2	5.2	5.2	0.5	5.3	5.8	14.6	6.1	10.6	14.8	15.6
40,005		9	Atoka	975.5	13,887	2,172	14.2	78.2	5.0	19.9	1.2	3.4	6.0	16.3	7.8	13.3	11.7	12.1
40,007		9	Beaver	1,814.7	5,315	2,811	2.9	74.1	1.3	2.5	0.6	23.5	5.3	20.6	7.4	10.1	11.3	12.1
40,009	21,120	7	Beckham	901.8	21,793	1,736	24.2	77.4	4.6	4.0	1.3	14.7	7.1	17.3	8.7	15.9	13.1	11.6
40,011		6	Blaine	928.4	9,498	2,465	10.2	77.4	4.6	11.4	0.9	10.3	7.3	18.7	7.2	10.6	10.5	11.9
40,013	20,460	6	Bryan	904.5	46,319	1,042	51.2	78.0	2.7	19.8	0.9	5.8	6.4	17.0	9.6	14.0	11.4	11.9
40,015		6	Caddo	1,278.3	29,173	1,455	22.8	61.9	4.1	26.1	0.9	12.7	6.7	18.4	8.3	13.5	11.8	12.2
40,017	36,420	1	Canadian	896.6	139,926	461	156.1	80.3	4.1	7.2	3.9	8.8	6.8	19.3	7.6	14.8	14.3	12.6
40,019	11,620	5	Carter	822.2	48,190	1,017	58.6	75.1	8.5	13.8	1.7	7.3	7.1	18.4	8.1	12.5	12.3	12.2
40,021	45,140	6	Cherokee	749.4	48,888	1,007	65.2	56.3	2.2	42.7	1.1	7.1	6.1	16.5	14.9	12.3	11.0	12.2
40,023		7	Choctaw	770.4	14,863	2,107	19.3	66.9	12.4	22.3	1.0	4.4	6.8	17.4	7.3	11.1	10.8	11.9
40,025		9	Cimarron	1,834.8	2,154	3,032	1.2	75.6	1.5	3.1	0.9	22.0	6.8	17.8	6.3	9.2	9.8	12.0
40,027	36,420	1	Cleveland	538.8	279,641	246	519.0	76.7	6.4	7.8	5.9	8.7	5.5	16.4	14.5	15.0	13.0	11.4
40,029		9	Coal	516.7	5,642	2,784	10.9	76.2	1.7	24.6	0.8	4.7	6.6	17.3	8.5	10.3	11.3	11.8
40,031	30,020	3	Comanche	1,069.3	121,526	517	113.7	60.9	19.6	7.9	5.0	13.1	7.0	16.7	12.7	16.7	12.1	11.1
40,033	30,020	3	Cotton	632.7	5,823	2,770	9.2	80.6	3.1	12.5	1.2	8.0	5.3	17.0	7.7	11.4	10.8	13.8
40,035		6	Craig	761.4	14,327	2,140	18.8	71.7	4.2	28.2	1.3	3.7	5.8	16.5	7.9	12.0	11.5	13.3
40,037	46,140	2	Creek	950.2	71,704	754	75.5	82.4	3.4	15.9	1.1	4.2	6.2	17.9	7.8	12.0	12.0	13.0
40,039	48,220	7	Custer	988.8	28,800	1,460	29.1	71.2	3.7	8.4	1.6	18.3	7.4	17.5	16.6	13.5	10.6	9.8
40,041		6	Delaware	738.2	42,602	1,121	57.7	71.6	0.8	30.2	1.5	3.8	5.1	15.3	7.4	10.0	10.1	12.4
40,043		9	Dewey	999.5	4,878	2,840	4.9	85.6	1.3	7.9	1.7	6.9	7.5	19.9	6.8	11.4	11.0	11.1
40,045		9	Ellis	1,231.5	3,966	2,906	3.2	89.2	1.3	4.1	0.8	7.0	6.0	17.1	7.3	9.2	12.1	11.2
40,047	21,420	5	Garfield	1,058.5	61,581	848	58.2	77.9	4.3	4.2	4.8	12.4	7.4	18.7	8.6	14.0	11.8	10.8
40,049		6	Garvin	802.1	27,909	1,498	34.8	80.2	3.1	12.0	0.9	8.9	6.9	18.3	7.7	12.3	12.2	11.7
40,051	36,420	1	Grady	1,100.5	54,943	924	49.9	85.7	3.1	9.0	0.9	5.8	5.7	18.4	7.9	12.1	12.8	13.1
40,053		9	Grant	1,000.9	4,395	2,870	4.4	90.6	2.5	4.3	0.5	5.0	6.0	17.9	6.9	10.8	10.1	12.1
40,055		7	Greer	639.3	5,843	2,766	9.1	77.3	9.0	4.3	0.6	11.5	5.9	14.8	7.7	16.0	13.5	13.1
40,057		9	Harmon	537.2	2,689	2,990	5.0	60.1	9.1	3.7	1.6	29.5	6.6	18.4	7.7	11.5	11.1	12.2
40,059		9	Harper	1,039.0	3,808	2,915	3.7	74.3	0.8	1.9	0.6	24.1	7.5	20.0	6.9	11.3	11.4	11.0
40,061		6	Haskell	576.5	12,763	2,242	22.1	77.1	1.3	23.2	1.3	4.4	6.3	17.7	7.4	11.6	11.7	11.8
40,063		7	Hughes	804.6	13,302	2,212	16.5	69.3	6.8	24.8	0.8	5.5	5.7	15.7	8.6	13.7	12.3	12.5
40,065	11,060	7	Jackson	802.7	25,125	1,603	31.3	65.7	8.1	3.3	2.1	24.0	7.7	17.9	10.3	15.0	11.9	10.9
40,067		8	Jefferson	758.8	6,183	2,737	8.1	81.8	2.1	9.0	1.1	10.6	6.7	17.2	6.7	11.4	11.0	11.4
40,069		9	Johnston	642.9	11,060	2,350	17.2	76.9	3.3	20.7	1.2	5.4	5.9	17.5	9.3	11.9	11.2	11.9
40,071	38,620	5	Kay	919.7	44,544	1,083	48.4	79.3	2.9	13.5	1.3	8.1	7.0	18.2	8.5	11.9	11.3	11.1
40,073		6	Kingfisher	898.2	15,669	2,058	17.4	79.1	1.9	5.5	0.6	15.7	6.9	20.2	8.1	11.5	12.0	12.2

1. CBSA = Core Based Statistical Area. See Appendix A for explanation. See Appendix B for list of metropolitan areas with component counties. Service of USDA Rural-Urban Continuum Codes. See Appendix A for definition.   3. Dry land or land partially or temporarily covered by water.   2. County type code from the Economic Research   4. May be of any race.

Table B. States and Counties — **Population and Households**

STATE County	Age (percent) (cont.) 55 to 64 years	65 to 74 years	75 years and over	Percent female	Total persons 2000	Total persons 2010	Percent change 2000-2010	Percent change 2010-2017	Components of change, 2010-2017 Births	Deaths	Net Migration	Households 2012-2016 Number	Persons per house-hold	Percent Family house-holds	Female family house-holder[1]	One person
	16	17	18	19	20	21	22	23	24	25	26	27	28	29	30	31
OHIO— Cont'd																
Ottawa	17.4	14.3	10.0	50.3	40,985	41,434	1.1	-1.9	2,489	3,466	235	17,384	2.31	67.5	9.5	27.7
Paulding	14.8	10.8	7.4	50.2	20,293	19,615	-3.3	-3.9	1,595	1,405	-971	7,659	2.48	69.9	8.6	26.9
Perry	14.6	10.0	6.1	49.9	34,078	36,039	5.8	0.0	3,125	2,498	-630	13,535	2.63	74.2	12.6	21.2
Pickaway	13.0	8.9	6.5	47.4	52,727	55,678	5.6	3.9	4,409	3,781	1,556	19,173	2.72	73.0	10.9	22.3
Pike	14.0	10.0	7.6	50.2	27,695	28,702	3.6	-1.5	2,504	2,401	-525	10,908	2.55	67.6	13.1	28.2
Portage	14.0	9.6	6.4	51.0	152,061	161,421	6.2	0.5	10,493	10,053	484	61,585	2.52	64.5	11.0	27.0
Preble	14.8	11.1	7.7	50.5	42,337	42,259	-0.2	-2.7	3,159	3,329	-961	16,048	2.56	71.8	10.9	23.2
Putnam	14.7	9.2	7.7	49.8	34,726	34,496	-0.7	-1.8	3,246	2,153	-1,732	13,092	2.58	73.5	6.5	22.8
Richland	14.1	10.6	8.6	49.4	128,852	124,476	-3.4	-3.1	10,113	9,900	-4,087	47,935	2.39	64.1	12.6	31.0
Ross	14.4	9.5	6.7	47.3	73,345	78,065	6.4	-1.0	6,071	5,943	-854	28,308	2.52	69.5	14.6	25.5
Sandusky	14.9	10.4	7.8	50.6	61,792	60,946	-1.4	-2.9	4,909	4,576	-2,084	23,666	2.48	67.5	11.5	26.8
Scioto	13.8	10.1	7.8	50.6	79,195	79,497	0.4	-4.5	6,416	6,909	-3,064	29,778	2.48	63.6	11.8	30.2
Seneca	14.4	10.0	7.7	50.1	58,683	56,742	-3.3	-2.6	4,235	4,215	-1,516	21,349	2.47	67.3	11.8	27.2
Shelby	14.0	9.3	6.8	49.8	47,910	49,418	3.1	-1.3	4,428	3,134	-1,974	18,428	2.63	72.4	10.7	23.0
Stark	14.6	10.7	8.3	51.4	378,098	375,592	-0.7	-0.8	30,188	29,531	-3,408	151,101	2.42	65.8	12.2	28.6
Summit	14.6	10.1	7.3	51.5	542,899	541,782	-0.2	-0.1	44,151	40,895	-3,498	221,887	2.40	62.3	13.1	31.7
Trumbull	15.2	11.9	9.0	51.2	225,116	210,318	-6.6	-4.7	15,153	18,189	-6,850	86,508	2.32	63.8	13.2	31.7
Tuscarawas	14.5	10.7	8.5	50.6	90,914	92,582	1.8	-0.3	8,215	7,276	-1,171	36,325	2.52	67.9	10.3	27.0
Union	12.0	7.3	4.7	52.2	40,909	52,259	27.7	8.6	4,560	2,488	2,415	18,798	2.70	73.8	8.0	20.6
Van Wert	14.3	10.4	8.2	50.9	29,659	28,743	-3.1	-1.8	2,373	2,275	-619	11,427	2.47	69.2	9.8	26.5
Vinton	15.8	10.6	6.7	49.8	12,806	13,430	4.9	-2.5	1,051	1,025	-363	4,942	2.64	68.3	11.7	27.4
Warren	13.1	8.4	5.7	49.8	158,383	212,833	34.4	7.5	17,492	11,411	10,136	79,466	2.71	74.8	7.9	21.2
Washington	15.6	11.6	9.0	50.9	63,251	61,778	-2.3	-2.2	4,415	5,244	-481	25,306	2.35	65.8	9.4	29.4
Wayne	13.6	9.8	7.6	50.3	111,564	114,516	2.6	1.3	11,123	7,810	-1,738	43,037	2.60	70.7	9.5	25.5
Williams	14.9	10.2	8.4	50.3	39,188	37,648	-3.9	-2.3	3,130	2,817	-1,177	15,077	2.39	64.3	10.0	30.7
Wood	12.4	8.8	6.1	50.7	121,065	125,489	3.7	4.0	9,882	7,609	2,720	50,025	2.45	62.0	8.1	28.9
Wyandot	14.3	10.2	8.6	50.4	22,908	22,615	-1.3	-2.6	1,849	1,756	-674	9,144	2.41	67.0	9.6	25.9
OKLAHOMA	12.5	8.9	6.4	50.5	3,450,654	3,751,598	8.7	4.8	383,013	278,633	74,597	1,461,500	2.58	66.2	12.3	28.2
Adair	12.5	9.5	6.4	50.0	21,038	22,683	7.8	-3.4	2,151	1,751	-1,179	7,876	2.80	72.4	15.6	23.5
Alfalfa	13.6	9.8	9.3	40.6	6,105	5,642	-7.6	4.7	436	467	292	2,028	2.34	67.1	7.4	27.9
Atoka	13.1	11.4	8.3	48.0	13,879	14,166	2.1	-2.0	1,171	1,078	-373	5,198	2.36	69.9	14.5	26.1
Beaver	13.7	10.8	8.7	50.1	5,857	5,636	-3.8	-5.7	388	324	-391	2,087	2.59	72.2	7.1	23.8
Beckham	12.5	7.8	5.9	46.1	19,799	22,119	11.7	-1.5	2,549	1,744	-1,160	7,508	2.89	69.8	14.1	24.7
Blaine	14.5	10.6	8.8	51.4	11,976	11,943	-0.3	-20.5	1,075	873	-2,928	3,709	2.18	64.7	11.3	31.0
Bryan	11.9	10.3	7.5	51.2	36,534	42,416	16.1	9.2	4,198	3,513	3,198	16,633	2.61	64.0	12.1	30.4
Caddo	12.6	9.4	7.1	47.5	30,150	29,600	-1.8	-1.4	2,954	2,584	-790	10,368	2.74	67.3	13.8	28.5
Canadian	11.8	7.9	4.9	50.4	87,697	115,541	31.8	21.1	12,300	6,605	18,423	43,247	2.95	73.9	10.0	22.3
Carter	13.1	9.1	7.1	51.3	45,621	47,726	4.6	1.0	4,886	4,513	122	18,071	2.64	65.8	11.1	30.0
Cherokee	11.9	9.6	6.6	51.1	42,521	46,985	10.5	4.1	4,452	3,582	1,047	16,386	2.81	65.1	12.1	29.7
Choctaw	14.4	11.6	8.7	52.0	15,342	15,205	-0.9	-2.2	1,444	1,543	-237	5,927	2.51	64.2	16.8	32.2
Cimarron	12.7	14.2	11.2	49.4	3,148	2,475	-21.4	-13.0	180	206	-300	971	2.31	66.5	9.1	30.8
Cleveland	11.4	7.8	5.0	50.0	208,016	256,011	23.1	9.2	21,832	13,800	15,474	101,112	2.57	66.2	10.8	25.4
Coal	14.5	11.1	8.6	50.6	6,031	5,925	-1.8	-4.8	505	595	-196	2,252	2.53	67.9	12.1	28.8
Comanche	11.4	7.0	5.3	48.2	114,996	124,098	7.9	-2.1	13,904	7,267	-9,403	42,929	2.69	65.9	14.9	28.3
Cotton	15.0	10.9	8.2	50.3	6,614	6,193	-6.4	-6.0	451	581	-238	2,368	2.51	72.3	12.0	25.1
Craig	13.6	10.6	8.8	48.5	14,950	15,025	0.5	-4.6	1,188	1,516	-365	5,380	2.53	68.1	11.2	28.9
Creek	13.7	10.0	7.3	50.5	67,367	69,967	3.9	2.5	6,282	6,151	1,644	26,264	2.67	71.2	11.5	24.7
Custer	11.2	7.4	6.1	50.2	26,142	27,469	5.1	4.8	3,287	2,140	165	10,457	2.64	69.0	11.3	22.5
Delaware	15.2	14.7	9.9	50.8	37,077	41,489	11.9	2.7	2,913	3,811	2,031	16,502	2.48	68.1	11.1	27.9
Dewey	13.1	10.3	8.9	50.6	4,743	4,810	1.4	1.4	455	505	117	1,811	2.63	69.4	7.0	27.7
Ellis	15.5	12.1	9.6	51.3	4,075	4,151	1.9	-4.5	317	393	-112	1,626	2.50	65.0	8.1	32.6
Garfield	12.5	8.7	7.4	50.3	57,813	60,580	4.8	1.7	7,019	4,942	-1,056	23,981	2.53	69.9	11.1	26.1
Garvin	13.4	9.7	7.8	50.6	27,210	27,576	1.3	1.2	2,724	2,657	278	10,447	2.61	66.1	9.7	29.8
Grady	14.1	9.4	6.4	50.0	45,516	52,430	15.2	4.8	4,388	3,869	2,025	19,554	2.72	73.4	10.3	22.3
Grant	14.6	11.1	10.5	50.2	5,144	4,527	-12.0	-2.9	374	435	-71	1,967	2.25	65.6	7.4	31.3
Greer	11.5	8.5	9.1	43.0	6,061	6,239	2.9	-6.3	525	566	-356	2,107	2.38	60.5	13.0	35.4
Harmon	13.4	10.3	8.7	51.5	3,283	2,922	-11.0	-8.0	245	238	-246	1,170	2.32	64.8	12.6	27.1
Harper	14.5	8.9	8.4	50.0	3,562	3,685	3.5	3.3	387	337	71	1,361	2.74	66.9	6.5	31.8
Haskell	13.6	11.7	8.2	49.9	11,792	12,769	8.3	0.0	1,112	1,090	-22	4,785	2.66	70.8	11.2	24.5
Hughes	12.7	10.6	8.2	46.1	14,154	14,003	-1.1	-5.0	1,074	1,358	-417	4,224	2.83	68.5	11.8	29.1
Jackson	11.8	7.9	6.6	50.0	28,439	26,446	-7.0	-5.0	3,049	1,816	-2,593	10,151	2.48	66.3	12.1	29.5
Jefferson	14.9	11.9	8.8	49.9	6,818	6,472	-5.1	-4.5	527	678	-141	2,424	2.52	65.0	10.2	30.8
Johnston	13.3	11.0	7.8	50.5	10,513	10,957	4.2	0.9	902	1,014	214	4,157	2.59	66.3	13.1	31.0
Kay	13.1	10.3	8.6	50.4	48,080	46,562	-3.2	-4.3	4,555	4,141	-2,441	18,132	2.45	63.0	12.2	32.0
Kingfisher	13.4	8.4	7.3	50.2	13,926	15,029	7.9	4.3	1,446	1,073	270	5,645	2.70	72.9	10.7	24.5

1. No spouse present.

Table B. States and Counties — Population, Vital Statistics, Health, and Crime

STATE County	Persons in group quarters, 2017	Daytime Population, 2012-2016		Births, 2017		Deaths, 2017		Persons under 65 with no health insurance, 2016		Medicare, 2017			Serious crimes known to police[2], 2016 Total	
		Number	Employment/ residence ratio	Total	Rate[1]	Number	Rate[1]	Number	Percent	Total beneficiaries	Enrolled in Original Medicare	Enrolled in Medicare Advantage	Number	Rate[3]
	32	33	34	35	36	37	38	39	40	41	42	43	44	45
OHIO— Cont'd														
Ottawa	495	37,280	0.80	334	8.2	505	12.4	2,009	6.5	11,296	7,795	3,501	517	1,530
Paulding	85	15,489	0.59	213	11.3	186	9.9	1,028	6.7	3,796	2,953	843	156	1,083
Perry	307	28,964	0.50	428	11.9	361	10.0	2,282	7.6	7,909	5,388	2,521	409	1,181
Pickaway	4,864	48,861	0.67	620	10.7	574	9.9	2,746	6.2	10,054	5,461	4,593	1,562	2,732
Pike	496	29,310	1.10	328	11.6	348	12.3	1,810	7.8	5,320	3,955	1,365	457	1,628
Portage	7,808	144,394	0.78	1,397	8.6	1,403	8.6	9,091	7.0	28,558	15,498	13,060	2,638	1,751
Preble	386	34,847	0.65	422	10.3	447	10.9	2,439	7.3	8,623	5,385	3,238	357	1,146
Putnam	303	28,757	0.69	423	12.5	303	8.9	1,512	5.3	6,516	5,286	1,231	142	437
Richland	6,931	124,628	1.06	1,374	11.4	1,364	11.3	6,481	7.1	28,328	21,048	7,279	4,747	3,951
Ross	6,210	77,229	1.00	821	10.6	824	10.7	3,898	6.6	17,200	11,674	5,527	3,289	4,278
Sandusky	901	59,079	0.97	683	11.5	613	10.4	2,660	5.5	11,348	8,443	2,904	1,297	2,401
Scioto	3,373	75,047	0.92	858	11.3	926	12.2	3,933	6.6	17,051	13,817	3,234	2,442	3,298
Seneca	2,548	50,350	0.79	582	10.5	556	10.1	2,857	6.5	12,782	10,237	2,546	856	1,662
Shelby	589	53,767	1.20	591	12.1	440	9.0	2,180	5.3	8,475	6,304	2,170	1,244	2,650
Stark	9,043	367,419	0.96	4,163	11.2	4,077	10.9	17,591	5.9	88,009	42,349	45,659	9,985	2,932
Summit	10,350	559,777	1.07	5,945	11.0	5,735	10.6	30,012	6.8	106,375	52,004	54,371	16,657	3,157
Trumbull	3,970	196,097	0.90	2,059	10.3	2,459	12.3	10,524	6.7	48,331	25,832	22,499	4,250	2,551
Tuscarawas	1,251	87,730	0.88	1,141	12.4	1,002	10.9	5,969	8.0	20,367	11,931	8,436	892	992
Union	2,893	61,232	1.29	678	11.9	344	6.1	2,229	4.8	6,269	3,821	2,448	433	828
Van Wert	396	26,701	0.86	328	11.6	306	10.8	1,349	5.9	5,205	3,800	1,405	599	2,101
Vinton	68	10,655	0.52	144	11.0	147	11.2	850	8.0	2,493	1,934	559	159	1,227
Warren	5,390	208,220	0.87	2,376	10.4	1,785	7.8	8,753	4.6	32,795	18,821	13,974	2,924	1,309
Washington	1,722	60,911	0.99	594	9.8	728	12.0	3,478	7.4	15,038	11,853	3,185	736	1,265
Wayne	3,566	113,045	0.95	1,524	13.1	1,118	9.6	8,758	9.4	23,665	14,103	9,562	1,675	1,561
Williams	990	37,621	1.02	432	11.7	400	10.9	1,880	6.4	8,257	6,080	2,177	NA	NA
Wood	7,159	132,861	1.05	1,368	10.5	1,091	8.4	5,861	5.6	22,555	14,091	8,464	1,754	1,585
Wyandot	251	20,199	0.80	240	10.9	246	11.2	1,117	6.2	4,917	3,877	1,040	190	891
OKLAHOMA	109,498	3,869,484	1.00	52,280	13.3	39,416	10.0	517,631	16.0	707,093	575,978	131,115	134,685	3,433
Adair	92	20,140	0.75	295	13.5	267	12.2	4,176	22.5	4,365	4,109	256	591	2,717
Alfalfa	1,053	5,906	1.06	63	10.7	47	8.0	547	14.4	1,130	1,084	46	45	764
Atoka	750	13,186	0.85	153	11.0	117	8.4	2,238	21.3	2,669	2,488	181	208	1,523
Beaver	43	5,062	0.84	46	8.7	48	9.0	814	18.6	938	913	25	43	802
Beckham	1,928	26,169	1.31	294	13.5	260	11.9	2,823	16.0	3,321	3,103	218	553	2,303
Blaine	107	9,894	1.03	131	13.8	104	10.9	1,270	16.3	2,107	1,983	124	113	1,234
Bryan	1,134	43,853	0.96	573	12.4	532	11.5	6,457	17.6	9,344	8,575	769	NA	NA
Caddo	1,933	26,987	0.78	373	12.8	367	12.6	4,712	20.6	6,069	5,667	402	613	2,104
Canadian	2,485	102,249	0.57	1,775	12.7	998	7.1	13,452	11.4	18,410	13,499	4,910	4,026	2,952
Carter	913	51,690	1.15	702	14.6	662	13.7	6,530	16.3	10,771	10,048	723	1,912	3,932
Cherokee	2,013	46,037	0.88	624	12.8	496	10.1	8,465	21.5	8,265	7,426	839	912	1,881
Choctaw	172	14,831	0.96	213	14.3	215	14.5	2,457	20.9	3,724	3,431	293	175	1,176
Cimarron	7	2,218	0.95	23	10.7	18	8.4	378	23.2	559	545	14	11	509
Cleveland	10,544	228,405	0.68	2,919	10.4	2,035	7.3	27,064	11.5	32,545	26,261	6,284	9,898	3,577
Coal	61	5,186	0.74	80	14.2	76	13.5	874	19.6	1,214	1,144	70	65	1,166
Comanche	9,956	127,087	1.04	1,699	14.0	1,064	8.8	14,345	14.7	18,232	16,907	1,325	4,867	3,966
Cotton	48	5,544	0.79	50	8.6	85	14.6	787	16.4	1,246	1,173	73	79	1,332
Craig	1,050	15,055	1.07	152	10.6	227	15.8	2,077	18.8	5,250	4,611	639	186	1,266
Creek	1,062	61,283	0.68	846	11.8	909	12.7	9,309	16.0	14,128	9,745	4,383	1,468	2,077
Custer	1,520	29,719	1.03	418	14.5	279	9.7	4,861	20.2	4,629	4,282	346	519	1,726
Delaware	356	37,994	0.78	439	10.3	549	12.9	6,743	21.6	9,408	8,053	1,355	629	1,525
Dewey	93	4,771	0.96	70	14.4	76	15.6	654	17.0	1,132	1,078	54	42	839
Ellis	46	3,840	0.84	43	10.8	53	13.4	486	15.1	884	842	42	48	1,136
Garfield	1,816	63,411	1.03	952	15.5	648	10.5	8,114	15.7	11,767	10,935	832	2,455	3,846
Garvin	317	29,098	1.14	363	13.0	323	11.6	4,081	17.9	6,442	5,769	673	846	3,059
Grady	1,076	45,658	0.66	585	10.6	502	9.1	6,426	14.1	8,872	7,466	1,407	1,212	2,211
Grant	73	4,334	0.92	51	11.6	53	12.1	478	13.7	1,009	965	43	47	1,045
Greer	1,138	5,509	0.74	79	13.5	62	10.6	561	14.6	1,195	1,158	37	46	765
Harmon	100	2,736	0.93	31	11.5	36	13.4	425	20.5	590	567	24	98	3,565
Harper	41	3,539	0.86	53	13.9	69	18.1	672	22.3	795	763	33	9	240
Haskell	78	12,493	0.92	155	12.1	141	11.0	2,122	21.1	3,042	2,739	303	183	1,429
Hughes	1,559	13,163	0.87	154	11.6	175	13.2	1,828	19.2	2,785	2,483	302	270	1,984
Jackson	692	26,425	1.05	380	15.1	197	7.8	3,430	16.2	4,131	3,950	181	766	3,031
Jefferson	144	5,572	0.69	68	11.0	79	12.8	856	17.6	1,562	1,458	104	89	1,433
Johnston	292	10,218	0.79	108	9.8	164	14.8	1,545	17.7	2,337	2,195	142	194	1,776
Kay	1,273	45,975	1.03	614	13.8	551	12.4	5,844	16.4	10,361	9,310	1,051	1,504	3,347
Kingfisher	155	15,201	0.97	186	11.9	136	8.7	2,116	16.1	2,843	2,566	277	163	1,044

1. Per 1,000 estimated resident population. 2. Data for serious crimes have not been adjusted for underreporting; this may affect comparability between geographic areas and over time.
3. Per 100,000 population estimated by the FBI.

Items 32—45

Table B. States and Counties — **Crime, Education, Money Income, and Poverty**

STATE County	Serious crimes known to police, 2016 (cont.)[1] Rate		Education						Money income, 2012-2016				Income and poverty, 2016			
			School enrollment and attainment, 2012-2016				Local government expenditures,[5] 2013-2014			Households				Percent below poverty level		
			Enrollment[3]		Attainment[4] (percent)						Percent					
	Violent	Property	Total	Percent private	High school graduate or less	Bachelor's degree or more	Total current spending (mil dol)	Current spending per student (dollars)	Per capita income[6]	Median income (dollars)	with income of less than $50,000	with income of $200,000 or more	Median household income (dollars)	All persons	Children under 18 years	Children 5 to 17 years in families
	46	47	48	49	50	51	52	53	54	55	56	57	58	59	60	61
OHIO— Cont'd																
Ottawa	98	1,432	8,327	9.4	45.4	21.3	70.7	11,238	30,403	54,580	46.1	3.6	56,569	10.4	15.0	13.4
Paulding	97	986	4,346	12.5	59.5	13.0	35.8	11,744	24,174	48,003	52.5	2.4	51,020	10.7	15.4	14.3
Perry	92	1,088	8,436	9.4	60.4	12.0	63.4	10,873	20,852	43,674	56.4	1.3	47,543	17.0	23.9	22.8
Pickaway	122	2,609	13,202	10.8	56.2	17.3	94.7	10,241	24,779	58,706	42.6	2.2	60,051	13.2	17.8	16.3
Pike	89	1,539	6,391	4.3	62.5	12.3	52.3	10,982	21,375	41,128	58.0	1.6	42,869	20.5	29.7	27.4
Portage	102	1,650	47,222	10.9	45.3	27.3	249.9	11,087	26,769	52,427	47.6	2.9	52,947	13.5	15.0	13.8
Preble	61	1,085	9,771	10.0	56.0	13.5	65.0	10,166	24,605	51,356	48.3	1.6	57,896	11.0	16.8	14.8
Putnam	59	379	8,758	11.9	49.5	19.4	62.5	10,637	27,367	60,245	40.2	2.3	61,069	8.3	9.5	8.1
Richland	248	3,703	27,596	19.7	53.7	16.4	199.9	12,135	22,520	42,849	56.9	1.4	44,835	15.8	22.1	20.2
Ross	278	3,999	17,504	9.6	57.9	15.3	125.4	11,250	22,158	44,587	54.9	2.4	47,507	18.6	24.9	22.5
Sandusky	165	2,236	14,189	14.9	53.0	14.8	91.4	10,836	24,467	49,032	51.1	1.4	52,452	11.6	16.2	13.7
Scioto	182	3,116	18,682	8.4	56.5	15.0	130.5	10,744	20,728	37,936	61.0	1.5	39,245	22.1	31.6	29.9
Seneca	175	1,487	14,689	27.2	54.7	14.7	68.8	11,746	23,900	48,415	51.1	1.6	49,546	12.9	17.7	15.5
Shelby	130	2,520	12,092	13.3	52.7	17.1	81.2	9,580	27,330	56,169	44.8	2.4	59,604	9.4	12.1	10.7
Stark	328	2,604	91,780	17.2	47.5	22.6	577.0	10,005	26,442	48,714	51.3	2.5	51,036	13.2	19.4	16.9
Summit	314	2,842	134,622	15.4	41.2	30.7	842.7	11,325	29,643	51,562	48.4	4.3	52,226	13.7	19.7	19.0
Trumbull	243	2,309	42,908	10.5	56.3	18.0	315.4	10,932	24,445	43,811	56.2	1.9	45,929	17.6	29.2	25.3
Tuscarawas	43	949	20,623	12.9	60.5	15.0	166.9	10,404	24,173	46,992	52.5	1.9	50,273	12.7	16.6	14.1
Union	50	778	14,167	14.1	43.7	29.1	93.1	9,493	30,431	71,282	35.1	6.0	78,796	6.1	7.2	6.3
Van Wert	133	1,968	6,839	15.2	56.1	17.2	54.6	11,191	25,316	50,547	49.4	1.6	52,610	8.9	13.1	11.9
Vinton	170	1,057	2,810	7.8	65.5	9.6	24.0	10,429	19,431	41,080	58.3	0.3	41,522	20.8	31.8	28.6
Warren	69	1,239	59,316	17.4	33.2	41.0	362.8	9,977	36,057	76,200	30.2	9.5	81,543	5.4	6.1	5.3
Washington	105	1,160	13,020	20.2	51.1	18.4	83.4	10,432	25,462	44,763	55.1	2.1	47,802	13.7	19.2	18.0
Wayne	121	1,440	28,596	21.0	55.1	21.5	170.9	10,954	24,311	51,363	48.5	2.3	53,605	11.9	16.2	15.4
Williams	NA	NA	8,701	15.9	56.4	14.2	56.4	10,115	22,757	45,044	56.0	1.4	50,770	9.7	14.3	12.8
Wood	77	1,509	41,786	11.6	37.3	31.7	234.9	12,758	28,843	55,985	44.9	3.8	60,347	11.4	10.9	10.1
Wyandot	66	826	5,219	10.3	57.7	14.6	32.6	9,496	25,064	50,723	49.5	2.3	55,590	8.6	11.3	10.4
OKLAHOMA	450	2,983	999,903	10.7	44.4	24.5	5,254.2	7,681	25,628	48,038	51.6	3.3	49,204	16.1	22.5	21.1
Adair	519	2,197	5,658	3.1	63.5	13.4	40.2	8,849	16,018	33,184	67.9	0.6	33,632	29.0	38.1	36.2
Alfalfa	153	611	1,119	7.8	51.5	20.9	11.3	11,919	27,807	52,226	46.4	3.9	53,695	15.8	19.1	18.5
Atoka	95	1,428	3,017	5.5	58.8	14.7	21.2	9,188	19,159	36,528	65.1	2.3	36,766	19.9	29.9	28.8
Beaver	19	784	1,284	2.6	53.6	21.5	12.2	11,100	26,738	52,908	45.4	3.0	53,493	11.6	15.7	14.4
Beckham	196	2,108	4,974	6.6	55.3	18.3	32.4	7,508	25,269	48,851	50.7	5.4	47,407	17.1	20.8	20.4
Blaine	98	1,135	1,887	4.1	53.0	17.0	22.5	9,579	20,848	44,216	54.7	1.9	44,229	17.7	26.6	26.7
Bryan	NA	NA	11,247	7.9	48.1	22.1	64.6	8,572	21,273	39,936	60.5	1.8	39,219	16.9	24.4	24.6
Caddo	268	1,837	7,038	2.9	55.5	16.1	45.1	8,183	20,499	40,199	59.5	1.9	40,296	21.3	28.0	25.9
Canadian	446	2,506	34,832	9.5	37.8	25.8	177.0	7,036	28,724	66,664	35.0	4.3	68,291	8.4	10.6	9.5
Carter	409	3,523	12,593	8.3	51.5	19.5	73.1	7,795	24,272	46,913	52.8	2.7	47,966	16.4	22.6	21.3
Cherokee	212	1,669	13,945	5.0	46.3	24.1	67.8	8,618	19,627	38,585	60.3	1.3	36,297	23.2	30.7	29.0
Choctaw	188	988	3,276	2.3	59.1	13.0	22.7	8,385	19,085	30,870	67.1	1.8	32,458	26.8	36.7	35.2
Cimarron	139	370	463	9.3	53.3	19.8	5.3	12,164	26,309	44,511	54.0	3.7	44,000	17.7	33.1	32.1
Cleveland	371	3,205	84,562	9.7	34.2	31.8	316.1	7,160	28,378	58,488	42.0	3.9	61,275	12.4	12.5	12.2
Coal	108	1,058	1,302	6.7	57.0	17.0	12.9	11,033	23,716	39,231	58.4	2.7	41,111	21.9	28.9	26.9
Comanche	663	3,303	32,401	7.5	44.0	20.7	168.1	7,672	23,925	47,238	52.6	2.1	48,493	16.2	23.4	23.3
Cotton	34	1,298	1,432	5.6	52.9	16.4	8.7	7,742	22,411	48,732	51.5	0.6	43,019	16.9	22.9	21.8
Craig	109	1,157	3,343	6.4	54.7	14.3	24.4	8,475	20,130	40,036	61.8	1.0	42,781	17.5	23.8	23.0
Creek	218	1,859	16,146	8.2	54.7	15.6	99.5	7,676	23,336	46,517	52.5	2.2	45,630	15.5	21.6	20.6
Custer	143	1,583	9,160	2.8	46.5	27.8	40.9	7,618	23,540	47,250	52.3	2.0	43,247	18.0	20.3	20.5
Delaware	179	1,346	8,572	8.9	52.4	16.7	54.6	8,113	22,267	38,438	61.3	2.1	39,144	17.7	28.0	26.8
Dewey	60	779	1,122	14.6	53.6	22.0	12.4	12,143	25,708	51,654	48.8	4.4	49,398	13.2	18.7	16.6
Ellis	95	1,041	883	5.3	48.2	21.9	12.2	13,925	28,610	52,222	47.0	4.0	51,745	13.0	18.3	17.0
Garfield	367	3,480	14,591	9.9	49.2	21.4	86.2	7,607	24,968	49,675	50.3	2.5	49,841	14.6	21.5	21.0
Garvin	315	2,744	5,533	3.6	58.7	15.4	43.2	7,910	22,208	41,250	57.9	2.9	40,978	17.5	24.2	21.5
Grady	332	1,879	13,375	6.5	51.6	17.8	66.2	7,064	26,250	54,043	46.5	3.7	55,552	13.2	17.1	16.1
Grant	67	978	958	7.0	44.1	24.3	9.5	11,942	29,559	54,040	45.8	1.9	48,118	13.3	19.6	17.6
Greer	116	648	1,280	1.6	51.7	14.4	8.2	8,097	20,147	36,891	64.3	3.5	35,231	26.7	30.3	30.0
Harmon	364	3,201	744	2.6	49.7	21.5	4.8	8,829	21,227	35,676	64.9	0.3	36,703	26.1	36.0	35.5
Harper	0	240	907	5.2	53.7	24.1	7.6	9,764	24,948	48,173	52.1	1.7	48,559	10.6	14.7	13.9
Haskell	172	1,258	2,906	3.6	58.8	12.1	19.2	8,070	18,981	36,067	62.9	0.9	36,418	21.1	30.1	31.1
Hughes	162	1,822	2,931	3.5	60.4	10.9	20.1	8,493	16,672	35,257	64.1	1.4	33,578	24.7	33.6	31.7
Jackson	301	2,730	6,376	5.8	44.1	20.6	38.1	7,623	23,616	44,331	55.2	1.9	44,211	19.2	27.9	28.6
Jefferson	193	1,240	1,375	4.3	58.2	13.3	11.0	9,023	19,651	35,063	66.0	1.9	37,105	22.2	29.9	30.2
Johnston	165	1,611	2,743	3.4	55.7	15.8	16.6	8,531	19,602	38,155	63.2	2.0	38,080	21.9	29.5	28.8
Kay	619	2,729	10,956	9.8	46.3	19.5	69.1	8,189	23,514	42,831	57.2	2.3	44,391	16.6	22.9	21.9
Kingfisher	109	935	4,043	8.7	47.5	22.0	29.1	8,222	30,011	62,912	39.4	4.5	60,814	10.4	14.2	13.2

1. Data for serious crimes have not been adjusted for underreporting; this may affect comparability between geographic areas and over time.   2. Per 100,000 population estimated by the FBI.
3. All persons 3 years old and over enrolled in nursery school through college.   4. Persons 25 years old and over.   5. Elementary and secondary education expenditures.
6. Based on population estimated by the American Community Survey, 2011–2015.

Table B. States and Counties — Personal Income and Earnings

| | Personal income, 2016 | | | | | | | | | | Earnings, 2016 | | |
STATE County	Total (mil dol)	Percent change 2015-2016	Per capita[1] Dollars	Rank	Wages and salaries (mil dol)	Supplements to wages and salaries, employer contributions (mil dol) Pension and insurance	Government social insurance	Proprietors' income (mil dol)	Dividends, interest, and rent (mil dol)	Personal transfer receipts (mil dol)	Total (mil dol)	Contributions for government social insurance (mil dol) From employee and self-employed	From employer
	62	63	64	65	66	67	68	69	70	71	72	73	74
OHIO— Cont'd													
Ottawa	1,894	2.2	46,610	646	620	131	45	102	325	446	897	103	45
Paulding	689	-1.4	36,545	1,910	190	43	12	37	111	169	282	29	12
Perry	1,232	2.7	34,299	2,280	216	53	14	89	120	350	372	41	14
Pickaway	2,121	2.2	36,839	1,846	623	154	38	164	254	471	979	91	38
Pike	929	0.0	32,985	2,472	492	75	34	83	108	333	685	78	34
Portage	6,595	1.5	40,730	1,272	2,559	568	166	382	965	1,300	3,675	368	166
Preble	1,530	1.9	37,099	1,804	419	85	30	106	201	374	640	71	30
Putnam	1,531	1.2	44,953	782	468	93	34	151	218	257	746	78	34
Richland	4,412	1.5	36,434	1,925	2,051	415	149	249	662	1,192	2,864	323	149
Ross	2,651	2.0	34,435	2,254	1,266	279	90	126	332	751	1,760	191	90
Sandusky	2,305	2.4	38,843	1,528	1,100	230	84	127	294	544	1,542	176	84
Scioto	2,537	0.0	33,339	2,421	971	227	68	97	311	946	1,363	152	68
Seneca	2,115	2.1	38,203	1,619	768	159	57	190	277	530	1,175	130	57
Shelby	2,034	0.6	41,829	1,118	1,417	238	104	198	271	372	1,957	216	104
Stark	15,595	1.0	41,741	1,135	6,894	1,232	503	902	2,380	3,589	9,531	1,089	503
Summit	25,060	1.0	46,382	659	14,011	2,266	983	1,450	3,999	4,875	18,710	2,083	983
Trumbull	7,625	1.0	37,781	1,695	3,056	565	228	621	1,110	2,186	4,470	516	228
Tuscarawas	3,722	1.0	40,268	1,329	1,502	293	108	424	504	831	2,327	248	108
Union	2,581	3.1	46,547	652	1,951	293	135	125	297	330	2,505	275	135
Van Wert	1,092	3.2	38,494	1,571	432	88	31	103	139	252	654	69	31
Vinton	403	1.0	31,177	2,721	88	24	6	15	49	138	133	15	6
Warren	12,025	3.1	52,957	306	4,898	739	339	629	1,563	1,474	6,605	725	339
Washington	2,372	0.3	39,140	1,477	1,196	224	88	161	363	605	1,668	191	88
Wayne	4,532	1.0	38,908	1,513	2,220	407	155	522	666	900	3,304	348	155
Williams	1,436	1.4	38,784	1,537	720	143	53	108	193	330	1,025	115	53
Wood	5,733	3.1	44,029	876	3,162	591	230	363	814	940	4,347	471	230
Wyandot	860	-0.1	38,872	1,519	402	78	28	52	117	185	560	61	28
OKLAHOMA	167,503	-2.5	42,717	X	75,614	13,235	5,801	21,658	30,305	32,324	116,307	6,384	5,801
Adair	602	-0.1	27,245	3,019	165	39	14	61	81	215	279	31	14
Alfalfa	255	-9.4	43,791	898	69	16	5	33	81	41	123	11	5
Atoka	419	1.1	30,357	2,810	114	25	9	61	55	135	209	22	9
Beaver	238	-11.0	44,277	850	66	14	5	58	44	38	143	11	5
Beckham	804	-9.6	35,687	2,048	449	68	34	109	153	163	660	71	34
Blaine	403	-2.5	41,818	1,120	124	24	9	62	81	88	220	21	9
Bryan	1,454	4.2	31,902	2,632	655	123	50	115	223	421	942	107	50
Caddo	875	-2.3	29,591	2,881	298	68	23	65	149	262	454	52	23
Canadian	5,724	0.5	41,922	1,111	1,395	237	108	450	779	841	2,190	235	108
Carter	2,011	-1.5	41,406	1,183	1,059	188	81	154	370	462	1,482	169	81
Cherokee	1,442	0.9	29,609	2,880	564	118	42	102	236	426	826	91	42
Choctaw	458	-1.9	30,767	2,762	145	32	12	43	55	179	232	27	12
Cimarron	130	-10.0	60,101	148	27	6	2	54	18	22	89	5	2
Cleveland	11,759	0.6	42,201	1,076	3,442	668	262	969	2,145	1,887	5,340	560	262
Coal	194	-1.6	34,392	2,265	41	9	3	17	33	55	71	8	3
Comanche	4,763	0.0	39,001	1,497	2,393	561	205	262	882	1,036	3,421	379	205
Cotton	220	-3.0	37,103	1,803	53	13	4	12	36	54	82	9	4
Craig	499	-2.8	34,139	2,300	209	46	16	43	75	163	314	36	16
Creek	2,712	-0.1	38,034	1,653	813	141	64	195	448	673	1,212	144	64
Custer	1,050	-5.1	35,834	2,027	514	97	39	95	210	207	745	81	39
Delaware	1,281	-1.0	30,806	2,756	312	59	25	101	244	405	498	61	25
Dewey	211	-0.7	43,849	892	75	14	6	27	47	39	123	13	6
Ellis	208	-16.3	50,893	378	50	10	4	63	44	31	127	9	4
Garfield	2,803	-1.2	44,782	792	1,420	241	111	226	553	528	1,999	226	111
Garvin	1,084	-2.3	38,949	1,503	438	87	34	99	178	275	658	74	34
Grady	2,036	-1.1	37,249	1,781	491	91	38	181	307	424	800	87	38
Grant	219	-3.6	48,955	472	80	14	6	28	55	41	128	13	6
Greer	139	-4.2	23,191	3,097	41	11	3	1	28	58	55	8	3
Harmon	97	4.1	35,784	2,037	26	6	2	21	15	27	55	5	2
Harper	167	-13.5	45,026	778	38	9	3	43	30	27	93	6	3
Haskell	419	-5.0	32,903	2,495	114	22	9	67	56	142	213	22	9
Hughes	419	-4.0	30,857	2,750	98	22	8	44	69	139	171	19	8
Jackson	983	2.4	38,555	1,567	463	115	39	49	191	217	666	75	39
Jefferson	210	-3.8	33,711	2,362	45	9	3	31	30	65	89	9	3
Johnston	352	2.1	31,731	2,655	117	27	9	24	46	118	178	21	9
Kay	1,745	0.4	38,816	1,530	784	132	60	158	328	439	1,134	130	60
Kingfisher	721	0.2	46,079	683	296	49	22	98	156	118	466	48	22

1. Based on the resident population estimated as of July 1 of the year shown.

Table B. States and Counties — Earnings, Social Security, and Housing

STATE County	Earnings, 2016 (cont.) Percent by selected industries									Social Security beneficiaries, December 2016		Supple-mental Security Income recipients, 2016	Housing units, 2017	
	Farm	Mining, quarrying, and extracting	Construction	Manu-facturing	Information; professional, scientific, technical services	Retail trade	Finance, insurance, real estate, and leasing	Health care and social assistance	Govern-ment	Number	Rate[1]		Total	Percent change, 2010-2017
	75	76	77	78	79	80	81	82	83	84	85	86	87	88
OHIO— Cont'd														
Ottawa	0.4	D	6.3	16.1	3.1	6.0	4.2	8.9	18.1	11,355	280	585	28,508	2.1
Paulding	9.1	0.5	6.0	27.7	2.8	5.6	3.0	D	22.5	4,475	238	333	8,766	0.2
Perry	-0.2	2.9	14.3	12.7	2.6	6.0	3.1	D	24.3	7,970	221	1,283	15,321	0.7
Pickaway	3.2	D	9.5	19.4	D	5.7	2.7	8.2	29.9	11,045	192	1,148	21,382	0.5
Pike	0.4	D	9.0	7.2	D	5.0	2.8	9.7	13.0	6,660	236	1,555	12,864	3.1
Portage	0.1	0.8	6.6	21.4	5.2	6.3	2.4	7.2	25.8	30,235	186	2,463	69,098	2.4
Preble	3.1	D	7.6	33.2	D	7.1	2.9	6.9	16.3	9,300	226	722	17,906	0.1
Putnam	2.5	D	10.0	34.4	3.4	6.0	4.0	6.2	12.7	6,780	199	330	13,933	1.5
Richland	0.3	D	7.1	21.7	4.3	8.1	3.4	14.2	18.3	29,100	240	3,464	54,211	-0.7
Ross	0.2	0.1	4.2	18.5	2.3	7.7	2.2	18.5	28.6	16,360	213	2,939	32,066	-0.3
Sandusky	0.1	D	5.3	41.9	2.0	6.3	3.8	D	12.8	13,495	228	1,075	26,359	-0.1
Scioto	-0.2	0.1	3.0	7.4	3.8	7.5	4.0	30.3	24.9	16,990	223	5,434	34,551	1.2
Seneca	-0.1	0.8	6.8	29.6	D	6.9	3.5	9.3	13.8	12,495	226	1,170	24,159	0.2
Shelby	0.7	0.0	8.6	51.1	D	3.7	2.6	5.4	8.5	9,675	199	788	20,440	1.3
Stark	0.3	0.4	7.0	18.7	5.9	7.4	6.2	16.5	13.0	86,395	231	9,774	166,760	0.9
Summit	0.0	0.3	4.4	11.4	9.0	8.0	6.4	15.2	11.8	109,145	202	14,787	245,989	0.4
Trumbull	-0.1	0.1	6.4	24.9	2.7	8.0	5.3	12.7	14.4	52,995	263	6,099	95,746	-0.4
Tuscarawas	0.2	5.3	9.3	23.2	3.8	7.8	3.7	10.8	13.6	20,945	226	1,953	40,192	0.0
Union	-0.1	0.5	4.2	34.6	D	3.9	2.0	3.2	10.6	8,005	144	453	21,153	8.9
Van Wert	7.0	D	5.9	25.0	D	5.6	9.6	12.2	13.2	6,625	235	425	12,713	0.8
Vinton	0.5	D	3.5	25.7	D	2.9	4.8	9.1	29.8	2,785	214	630	6,266	-0.4
Warren	0.0	0.0	6.4	15.6	8.9	7.7	6.7	9.1	10.7	36,035	159	1,848	87,012	7.8
Washington	0.2	2.7	8.7	19.2	4.0	6.1	5.7	20.7	11.3	15,345	253	1,857	28,240	-0.4
Wayne	0.3	2.5	7.5	33.3	3.2	6.7	4.3	7.1	12.9	22,825	196	1,912	46,626	1.7
Williams	0.8	D	4.3	41.9	D	8.5	2.7	10.1	12.4	8,540	231	587	16,666	0.0
Wood	0.3	0.1	9.6	25.7	4.5	4.8	3.5	6.9	16.8	22,335	172	1,410	53,966	1.1
Wyandot	1.1	1.9	12.4	37.3	D	5.3	3.9	D	15.9	4,965	225	340	9,950	0.8
OKLAHOMA	1.0	6.6	6.4	8.2	7.4	6.2	5.3	10.7	19.7	768,889	196	96,315	1,734,066	4.2
Adair	8.7	D	9.4	20.5	1.7	5.7	2.4	9.8	24.4	5,030	227	945	9,363	2.4
Alfalfa	18.9	7.6	7.0	1.8	D	4.2	D	4.6	25.5	1,195	202	93	2,728	-1.3
Atoka	-0.3	4.5	4.2	2.3	D	10.5	6.3	D	28.5	3,375	242	540	6,430	2.0
Beaver	30.5	9.8	D	D	D	1.7	D	0.5	17.4	1,065	197	45	2,676	0.2
Beckham	-0.3	25.5	11.8	3.9	D	8.0	5.9	D	9.8	4,095	183	524	10,024	3.9
Blaine	10.6	4.4	9.3	16.2	3.5	3.5	D	4.6	17.5	2,245	235	235	5,195	0.0
Bryan	0.3	D	5.5	6.6	4.5	6.4	2.4	11.7	39.0	9,920	218	1,636	20,305	3.7
Caddo	4.1	5.0	7.8	1.1	8.4	6.4	D	D	32.2	6,520	221	1,010	13,232	0.7
Canadian	0.9	8.4	8.8	13.0	4.1	7.2	6.1	6.6	17.5	20,990	154	1,116	48,521	5.9
Carter	-0.1	9.0	7.9	18.5	4.7	6.2	4.6	12.5	12.6	11,540	239	1,569	21,681	2.5
Cherokee	2.6	0.4	4.8	1.3	2.5	7.2	3.6	7.0	54.0	10,105	207	1,544	22,170	3.3
Choctaw	2.8	D	4.3	2.7	4.2	5.9	3.0	11.3	28.1	4,080	274	853	7,597	1.0
Cimarron	47.7	D	1.2	D	D	4.7	2.3	D	12.8	635	293	26	1,577	-0.6
Cleveland	0.0	1.1	9.2	5.0	8.8	9.1	5.0	9.3	30.2	44,020	159	3,480	116,042	10.5
Coal	0.9	11.9	8.2	4.2	D	5.1	D	14.0	26.0	1,275	226	216	2,809	0.0
Comanche	-0.1	D	3.7	8.4	7.2	5.5	3.6	5.5	52.4	20,175	166	3,208	51,693	1.9
Cotton	5.3	0.6	4.0	D	D	3.9	0.0	3.5	53.6	1,390	235	145	3,004	-0.4
Craig	3.2	D	3.5	3.7	D	8.7	4.5	10.2	29.3	4,090	283	695	6,751	0.1
Creek	0.0	4.5	12.9	21.2	D	6.1	3.4	9.4	15.5	16,700	235	1,695	30,676	3.1
Custer	0.4	10.2	6.5	6.5	5.1	7.4	5.2	D	20.5	4,855	167	548	12,539	2.7
Delaware	10.0	D	7.8	8.0	D	8.5	3.8	D	24.1	11,265	269	1,224	25,564	3.0
Dewey	-5.1	10.2	18.3	4.7	1.9	5.5	D	3.0	17.8	1,170	239	63	2,442	-0.1
Ellis	34.6	8.6	3.5	0.5	D	3.9	D	3.8	15.8	925	227	58	2,272	-0.6
Garfield	0.5	13.8	12.9	7.2	5.7	5.9	4.5	10.9	16.9	12,430	199	1,291	26,775	-0.2
Garvin	-0.1	11.4	11.0	15.4	3.4	7.4	3.3	D	13.7	6,790	243	853	12,858	0.2
Grady	4.1	6.1	11.7	9.7	4.7	7.9	5.4	7.6	18.3	10,775	197	1,214	22,917	3.1
Grant	11.6	25.3	12.1	0.7	D	3.2	D	D	13.4	1,070	240	71	2,467	-0.8
Greer	-6.6	D	2.5	D	D	6.9	D	18.9	52.1	1,390	233	195	2,710	-1.0
Harmon	24.5	0.6	D	D	D	3.2	D	3.8	25.6	695	258	140	1,534	-0.6
Harper	39.4	6.0	D	D	D	3.6	D	2.5	23.1	780	206	40	1,887	-1.1
Haskell	13.2	6.0	6.3	3.5	D	7.1	1.4	24.5	14.8	3,515	278	521	6,158	2.2
Hughes	16.0	4.8	4.5	2.8	D	7.1	D	D	28.7	3,500	261	433	6,245	1.0
Jackson	-0.4	D	2.2	7.3	D	6.2	4.2	4.6	53.4	4,600	181	656	12,154	0.6
Jefferson	20.0	1.0	D	D	D	6.9	D	D	22.5	1,640	262	235	3,393	0.4
Johnston	0.7	8.9	4.3	14.8	D	3.9	1.6	D	26.6	2,770	250	442	5,189	1.2
Kay	1.1	2.7	9.1	10.2	D	6.9	3.6	9.7	18.6	11,210	249	1,158	21,472	-1.1
Kingfisher	2.2	16.2	8.8	7.9	9.1	9.3	4.8	5.7	9.6	3,010	193	201	6,537	2.0

1. Per 1,000 resident population estimated as of July 1 of the year shown.

STATE County	Housing units, 2017 (cont.)								Civilian labor force, 2017				Civilian employment[6], 2012-2016		
	Occupied units										Unemployment		Percent		
	Owner-occupied					Renter-occupied									
				Median owner cost as a percent of income			Median rent as a percent of income[5]	Sub-standard units[4] (percent)		Percent change, 2016-2017				Management, business, science, and arts	Construction, production, and maintenance occupations
	Total	Percent	Median value[1]	With a mort-gage	Without a mort-gage[2]	Median rent[3]			Total		Total	Rate[5]	Total		
	89	90	91	92	93	94	95	96	97	98	99	100	101	102	103
OHIO— Cont'd															
Ottawa	17,384	78.2	144,200	19.7	12.0	687	27.2	0.8	21,350	1.4	1,428	6.7	19,496	31.2	30.1
Paulding	7,659	77.9	91,100	18.1	12.3	619	24.2	2.4	8,862	-0.3	394	4.4	8,873	24.6	39.9
Perry	13,535	73.3	96,100	21.1	12.9	605	29.5	2.0	16,137	1.4	966	6.0	14,517	27.1	34.6
Pickaway	19,173	74.3	150,100	21.1	12.2	755	26.5	1.5	26,635	1.5	1,223	4.6	25,070	32.8	26.7
Pike	10,908	68.3	97,800	19.9	12.3	662	31.8	4.0	10,880	0.5	756	6.9	10,018	30.9	33.0
Portage	61,585	68.7	150,400	20.8	12.2	813	32.3	1.0	87,688	0.5	4,421	5.0	82,009	32.1	25.0
Preble	16,048	76.5	116,600	21.3	11.7	705	27.7	1.7	21,150	0.5	951	4.5	19,414	27.1	33.6
Putnam	13,092	80.3	143,200	18.2	10.3	674	24.5	0.6	19,006	0.4	677	3.6	17,723	30.9	36.3
Richland	47,935	67.8	102,600	20.5	11.3	639	28.5	1.5	53,228	-0.5	2,931	5.5	50,168	26.7	29.2
Ross	28,308	70.9	111,700	20.4	11.2	685	29.6	2.4	34,130	0.7	1,753	5.1	30,088	28.1	29.1
Sandusky	23,666	73.6	111,300	20.2	12.0	646	27.8	0.9	31,354	0.9	1,488	4.7	28,410	24.8	39.6
Scioto	29,778	68.4	92,000	19.6	12.7	571	31.2	1.9	29,715	-0.7	2,109	7.1	28,086	33.4	23.8
Seneca	21,349	72.2	97,000	19.2	11.4	646	26.7	0.8	27,323	0.5	1,303	4.8	25,681	26.4	37.3
Shelby	18,428	70.8	134,400	19.5	10.7	699	22.9	1.9	24,143	0.1	995	4.1	24,059	27.7	36.9
Stark	151,101	68.7	124,000	19.7	11.3	689	27.5	1.4	187,574	0.5	9,809	5.2	176,807	32.0	25.1
Summit	221,887	65.6	134,300	20.2	11.9	760	29.4	1.0	274,131	0.5	13,884	5.1	260,568	37.5	19.4
Trumbull	86,508	70.3	99,400	20.0	11.5	638	29.4	1.4	89,686	-1.0	6,479	7.2	88,005	27.2	30.0
Tuscarawas	36,325	70.2	114,400	20.0	11.6	694	26.8	1.7	45,706	1.4	2,290	5.0	43,066	25.7	34.3
Union	18,798	77.5	174,300	20.8	13.1	830	25.2	1.3	28,240	1.5	1,051	3.7	25,923	38.1	26.1
Van Wert	11,427	76.0	98,900	18.3	10.3	653	27.0	1.2	14,436	0.8	574	4.0	13,433	25.2	39.6
Vinton	4,942	76.4	84,100	20.9	13.3	620	32.0	3.4	5,464	0.0	373	6.8	5,227	22.2	39.5
Warren	79,466	76.9	196,200	19.9	11.6	957	26.1	0.8	116,363	1.4	4,782	4.1	106,860	47.3	17.4
Washington	25,306	74.6	114,000	19.8	10.5	625	28.3	1.4	27,626	-0.7	1,716	6.2	26,846	30.2	27.6
Wayne	43,037	72.2	136,400	20.4	10.6	690	27.0	3.2	61,709	0.7	2,435	3.9	54,971	31.2	31.7
Williams	15,077	74.5	95,200	20.6	11.7	645	29.1	1.7	19,061	0.0	839	4.4	17,228	24.5	40.5
Wood	50,025	66.5	149,100	19.9	12.1	747	28.2	1.2	70,693	-0.1	3,112	4.4	66,479	35.6	23.8
Wyandot	9,144	73.2	111,500	19.0	10.5	636	23.3	1.2	12,732	0.3	472	3.7	10,893	25.2	41.8
OKLAHOMA	146,1,500	65.7	121,300	20.0	10.4	742	27.8	3.2	1,834,320	0.3	78,714	4.3	1,733,000	33.5	24.8
Adair	7,876	70.0	77,100	20.5	10.3	532	25.9	6.2	8,272	1.5	415	5.0	8,127	24.3	39.0
Alfalfa	2,028	73.9	67,600	15.0	10.0	674	22.4	1.2	2,947	-0.6	79	2.7	2,225	31.0	36.0
Atoka	5,198	72.7	93,200	19.6	11.8	556	28.9	2.6	5,211	3.0	277	5.3	4,490	29.0	29.1
Beaver	2,087	77.2	97,000	18.6	10.0	668	18.2	1.2	3,046	5.6	79	2.6	2,575	33.4	35.7
Beckham	7,508	63.8	123,200	20.0	10.8	724	24.0	1.9	11,364	3.0	449	4.0	9,556	26.7	31.7
Blaine	3,709	75.2	82,900	17.9	10.0	533	22.7	1.9	4,585	4.5	132	2.9	3,442	36.6	24.4
Bryan	16,633	64.6	96,100	19.6	11.3	691	28.6	3.7	20,496	5.1	784	3.8	18,354	29.8	27.6
Caddo	10,368	69.8	79,400	18.0	10.3	547	22.7	3.4	12,367	3.8	555	4.5	11,377	29.0	32.5
Canadian	43,247	76.8	148,800	20.5	10.0	920	24.7	2.5	69,836	0.7	2,489	3.6	65,041	36.0	22.4
Carter	18,071	69.3	102,200	19.4	10.5	698	26.0	3.8	22,511	-0.9	1,035	4.6	20,867	28.2	29.7
Cherokee	16,386	66.8	108,700	20.8	10.2	597	29.8	4.0	19,082	-1.0	1,042	5.5	19,367	31.7	22.5
Choctaw	5,927	70.3	84,200	22.1	11.4	538	34.4	3.2	5,731	-0.4	356	6.2	5,060	28.4	29.6
Cimarron	971	72.9	57,100	21.8	10.0	474	15.0	4.9	1,414	-0.1	34	2.4	1,076	34.1	34.2
Cleveland	101,112	65.2	150,400	20.0	10.1	848	28.3	2.7	140,218	0.8	4,940	3.5	135,757	40.4	17.5
Coal	2,252	71.5	85,200	19.2	10.0	585	26.7	2.8	2,292	-1.2	124	5.4	2,242	33.6	31.9
Comanche	42,929	54.4	118,700	20.3	10.0	793	26.7	2.2	49,246	-0.4	2,185	4.4	49,119	32.6	22.8
Cotton	2,368	76.0	79,300	17.9	11.6	596	23.7	3.3	2,858	-1.0	115	4.0	2,546	32.8	25.3
Craig	5,380	74.9	91,400	20.8	10.0	632	28.7	2.5	6,082	-2.7	272	4.5	5,841	28.0	27.7
Creek	26,264	74.8	106,600	20.0	10.8	715	27.0	4.3	31,523	0.1	1,582	5.0	29,986	29.0	31.3
Custer	10,457	59.1	125,100	18.0	10.0	669	24.5	4.0	15,362	1.1	510	3.3	14,189	30.1	30.1
Delaware	16,502	75.5	110,500	24.3	11.6	654	28.3	3.8	18,488	2.9	814	4.4	15,968	27.6	29.4
Dewey	1,811	72.4	85,600	18.2	10.0	636	19.9	1.1	2,490	-6.9	74	3.0	2,081	31.2	33.8
Ellis	1,626	77.9	79,900	15.0	10.0	650	19.4	0.6	2,236	-0.8	73	3.3	1,800	32.7	33.1
Garfield	23,981	65.2	100,800	19.6	10.2	758	22.1	3.6	27,936	-3.6	1,098	3.9	27,784	27.2	33.5
Garvin	10,447	69.1	89,100	18.5	10.8	601	23.4	3.3	12,630	-0.6	529	4.2	10,669	28.7	33.5
Grady	19,554	76.3	114,900	18.8	10.0	676	26.8	2.4	26,098	0.1	1,063	4.1	24,297	30.2	29.5
Grant	1,967	74.6	78,400	16.6	10.0	650	19.0	1.1	2,909	-3.1	76	2.6	2,133	37.6	30.6
Greer	2,107	69.3	73,800	18.8	12.2	587	27.1	2.2	2,081	-4.9	111	5.3	2,220	27.3	26.8
Harmon	1,170	70.6	50,000	18.4	11.4	496	19.0	2.8	1,288	-0.2	49	3.8	1,152	31.7	27.6
Harper	1,361	79.8	73,700	14.6	10.0	516	21.3	1.9	1,849	-3.1	58	3.1	1,734	29.2	31.4
Haskell	4,785	74.1	84,500	22.8	10.0	571	31.5	3.5	4,372	-2.9	290	6.6	4,552	28.2	34.5
Hughes	4,224	74.9	68,500	19.9	12.2	536	25.8	2.1	5,435	-1.4	307	5.6	4,319	27.7	31.4
Jackson	10,151	58.8	89,100	19.0	10.6	688	25.2	3.2	10,898	-0.9	418	3.8	10,794	27.6	30.5
Jefferson	2,424	71.8	60,000	18.9	11.7	493	24.3	2.0	2,506	-7.5	140	5.6	2,349	23.9	35.9
Johnston	4,157	71.3	76,600	18.9	11.6	589	28.4	2.8	4,986	14.0	202	4.1	3,903	31.0	34.2
Kay	18,132	68.2	80,700	19.2	11.5	633	24.9	3.1	19,236	1.6	1,059	5.5	19,507	27.6	29.9
Kingfisher	5,645	79.0	126,100	18.3	10.0	728	22.5	2.1	8,662	2.6	242	2.8	7,379	32.2	31.8

1. Specified owner-occupied units.   2. A value of 10.0 represents 10 percent or less; a value of 50.0 represents 50 percent or more.   3. Specified renter-occupied units.
4. Overcrowded or lacking complete plumbing facilities.   5. Percent of civilian labor force.   6. Civilian employed persons 16 years old and over.

Table B. States and Counties — Nonfarm Employment and Agriculture

	Private nonfarm establishments, employment and payroll, 2016									Agriculture, 2012			
		Employment						Annual payroll		Farms			
												Percent with:	
STATE County	Number of establishments	Total	Health care and social assistance	Manufacturing	Retail trade	Finance and insurance	Professional, scientific, and technical services	Total (mil dol)	Average per employee (dollars)	Number	Fewer than 50 acres	500 acres or more	Farm operators whose principal occupation is farming (percent)
	104	105	106	107	108	109	110	111	112	113	114	115	116
OHIO— Cont'd													
Ottawa	1,030	10,295	1,795	2,101	1,379	289	179	448	43,488	620	45.2	8.4	40.5
Paulding	297	3,554	565	1,231	368	107	72	117	32,982	676	34.8	18.2	39.8
Perry	421	4,175	878	720	691	137	166	137	32,766	699	39.1	4.9	29.3
Pickaway	781	10,804	1,971	2,261	1,526	302	204	424	39,208	803	39.6	18.3	52.3
Pike	418	7,735	1,593	758	1,027	223	2,047	359	46,387	490	27.6	5.3	38.0
Portage	2,999	46,810	6,049	10,051	8,365	722	1,387	1,758	37,558	847	56.6	3.0	42.9
Preble	655	8,985	1,080	3,310	1,236	244	253	321	35,678	1,088	45.9	11.9	41.8
Putnam	723	10,082	1,076	3,705	1,059	241	222	370	36,690	1,272	27.6	12.2	40.8
Richland	2,597	40,569	5,551	8,493	6,538	1,068	910	1,359	33,495	1,010	37.2	5.0	52.0
Ross	1,213	22,985	6,346	3,925	3,887	449	394	1,033	44,951	980	35.1	9.0	48.1
Sandusky	1,307	23,452	3,146	9,673	2,573	460	432	861	36,696	737	36.9	14.8	47.2
Scioto	1,286	19,155	7,450	1,445	3,122	502	661	624	32,557	689	39.2	4.9	40.3
Seneca	1,106	17,058	2,402	4,192	2,200	401	360	577	33,805	1,113	28.4	14.7	41.3
Shelby	970	24,701	2,098	12,483	1,969	318	372	1,167	47,229	986	32.4	11.1	41.3
Stark	8,183	142,975	28,749	24,632	19,922	5,650	4,191	5,500	38,466	1,168	56.1	3.3	46.5
Summit	13,391	251,233	47,528	29,016	31,039	11,093	14,617	11,624	46,269	304	72.4	1.6	41.4
Trumbull	4,043	67,053	10,522	17,486	9,903	1,612	1,354	2,640	39,372	888	41.6	4.2	46.7
Tuscarawas	2,175	31,127	5,269	7,494	4,472	647	935	1,119	35,938	1,014	39.2	4.7	41.3
Union	1,017	24,207	1,587	6,429	2,274	368	3,651	1,407	58,127	995	48.2	11.1	44.5
Van Wert	544	9,868	1,385	3,225	1,151	796	372	353	35,736	655	29.2	23.1	55.7
Vinton	137	1,704	350	592	161	86	12	50	29,516	226	25.7	3.5	36.3
Warren	4,219	78,842	10,424	11,266	10,149	4,425	5,101	4,036	51,195	942	67.3	4.7	42.3
Washington	1,393	22,761	5,458	3,302	2,990	776	629	962	42,260	1,122	31.0	2.7	48.7
Wayne	2,483	40,184	5,813	12,782	5,039	1,058	1,304	1,641	40,834	1,928	41.7	5.2	52.0
Williams	806	16,035	1,862	7,284	1,345	276	246	585	36,511	984	35.6	9.8	37.5
Wood	2,744	54,283	4,971	12,644	6,582	848	2,055	2,330	42,930	1,091	42.4	13.7	44.6
Wyandot	518	8,264	792	3,466	809	273	84	321	38,883	593	32.2	21.2	42.2
OKLAHOMA	93,232	1,360,379	221,349	129,975	186,499	60,301	73,514	57,194	42,042	80,245	25.0	19.0	42.1
Adair	226	3,102	515	1,020	550	131	75	93	30,070	1,129	26.5	10.5	43.8
Alfalfa	146	1,215	144	24	183	82	28	53	43,525	645	6.8	41.4	55.5
Atoka	280	2,224	340	138	534	146	52	65	29,348	1,103	17.9	16.1	37.0
Beaver	154	1,283	78	D	117	48	30	54	41,719	965	6.1	40.3	32.7
Beckham	795	8,460	1,057	289	1,590	346	248	359	42,412	1,016	15.0	28.0	33.0
Blaine	269	2,204	364	403	320	155	54	81	36,971	798	8.5	35.5	54.1
Bryan	763	10,542	2,155	1,299	1,662	490	491	325	30,837	1,484	23.9	13.9	40.9
Caddo	449	4,402	619	70	819	167	399	150	33,998	1,461	12.3	26.7	46.5
Canadian	2,593	26,056	2,848	2,996	4,311	825	1,453	904	34,690	1,307	32.8	19.3	47.1
Carter	1,618	20,982	3,632	3,330	3,095	679	678	835	39,783	1,321	22.6	15.7	34.1
Cherokee	741	9,297	2,706	129	1,762	341	119	277	29,767	1,233	29.4	8.5	38.8
Choctaw	282	3,084	1,160	91	493	110	85	92	29,690	965	18.4	18.7	50.3
Cimarron	72	340	D	D	80	39	10	10	28,929	554	3.4	52.0	49.6
Cleveland	5,757	69,262	13,179	3,026	12,714	2,655	3,236	2,384	34,414	1,081	53.6	4.8	45.1
Coal	88	812	213	75	169	53	13	25	31,216	571	16.5	23.1	43.1
Comanche	2,197	32,846	6,156	3,412	5,456	1,523	1,390	1,093	33,284	1,107	22.6	23.7	43.8
Cotton	76	1,228	92	D	100	44	20	38	31,254	500	11.4	37.0	51.4
Craig	346	4,028	1,361	180	680	210	90	136	33,770	1,263	21.9	13.9	43.9
Creek	1,361	16,450	2,181	4,008	2,042	426	331	629	38,226	1,777	39.0	6.9	31.6
Custer	921	10,000	1,482	1,106	1,790	375	291	378	37,795	877	15.7	36.7	41.7
Delaware	745	7,580	1,229	632	1,524	331	189	226	29,814	1,345	27.7	8.0	46.4
Dewey	149	1,022	100	68	245	66	18	38	37,662	743	7.1	41.6	40.5
Ellis	125	846	146	D	127	54	26	30	35,668	760	5.3	39.7	42.2
Garfield	1,657	21,265	4,015	2,111	3,619	800	589	790	37,147	1,098	16.8	31.5	46.8
Garvin	708	7,936	951	1,121	1,344	265	164	323	40,728	1,498	25.3	15.3	36.5
Grady	1,124	11,093	1,817	1,672	1,578	406	372	368	33,192	1,666	26.8	17.6	45.3
Grant	127	919	127	11	171	48	14	42	46,223	801	8.1	36.6	50.1
Greer	84	657	242	D	135	43	10	19	28,216	498	5.4	38.6	40.2
Harmon	57	442	123	D	90	39	4	15	33,007	366	4.6	43.7	44.3
Harper	91	523	128	NA	118	41	33	17	32,172	532	4.7	49.1	46.1
Haskell	213	2,468	796	D	481	63	49	72	29,031	864	19.8	14.5	46.9
Hughes	224	2,273	744	93	391	70	32	58	25,621	921	15.4	20.7	47.8
Jackson	513	6,463	1,246	931	1,253	364	120	211	32,656	694	16.7	34.6	44.2
Jefferson	97	778	105	24	142	107	35	29	37,744	417	8.4	42.0	48.2
Johnston	181	2,042	513	499	284	36	29	75	36,968	645	18.0	16.3	42.6
Kay	1,102	14,892	2,307	2,560	2,235	426	543	564	37,897	993	22.7	25.0	43.5
Kingfisher	484	5,297	528	347	637	199	183	247	46,706	1,021	13.0	33.7	49.8

Table B. States and Counties — Agriculture

STATE County	Acreage (1,000) 117	Percent change, 2007-2012 118	Average size of farm 119	Total irrigated (1,000) 120	Total cropland (1,000) 121	Value of land and buildings — Average per farm 122	Average per acre 123	Value of machinery and equipment, average per farm (dollars) 124	Total (mil dol) 125	Average per farm (acres) 126	Crops 127	Livestock and poultry products 128	$10,000 or more 129	$100,000 or more 130	Total ($1,000) 131	Percent of farms 132
OHIO— Cont'd																
Ottawa	113	-2.1	182	1.5	103.6	863,753	4,753	119,450	79.1	127,503	98.5	1.5	59.5	26.8	2,390	74.0
Paulding	221	-13.6	327	0.0	205.3	1,583,920	4,848	188,343	187.2	276,864	55.0	45.0	57.8	27.5	5,581	86.1
Perry	107	9.5	153	0.0	67.8	556,103	3,625	82,957	37.1	53,074	82.3	17.7	31.3	7.2	866	21.3
Pickaway	294	1.7	366	0.8	265.8	1,752,654	4,792	200,377	172.3	214,609	78.8	21.2	51.4	28.0	6,106	64.8
Pike	97	20.8	199	0.7	53.2	631,647	3,176	71,429	26.9	54,855	85.3	14.7	35.5	8.4	992	35.7
Portage	83	0.7	98	0.4	58.7	511,001	5,195	78,929	43.7	51,571	73.7	26.3	32.9	7.8	618	18.5
Preble	224	-2.8	206	0.2	195.1	1,083,226	5,256	148,121	154.8	142,302	65.9	34.1	50.6	24.9	4,689	55.9
Putnam	306	0.6	240	0.6	287.2	1,208,173	5,029	175,040	243.2	191,203	74.8	25.2	78.0	41.4	5,606	84.4
Richland	161	9.6	159	0.1	120.3	789,172	4,962	110,557	128.7	127,408	51.7	48.3	55.0	29.5	1,806	32.5
Ross	222	-0.9	226	D	153.7	816,043	3,607	92,039	79.8	81,432	87.5	12.5	35.5	14.3	6,567	57.1
Sandusky	181	0.1	246	0.8	166.3	1,159,189	4,709	160,579	135.3	183,525	93.5	6.5	65.9	37.9	3,636	76.5
Scioto	94	-7.5	137	0.1	42.0	385,210	2,813	67,393	22.2	32,229	63.5	36.5	25.5	6.1	995	25.5
Seneca	291	7.8	261	0.2	258.1	1,272,024	4,873	163,428	174.6	156,848	85.0	15.0	69.7	33.2	4,919	80.8
Shelby	206	-5.4	209	0.0	183.2	1,245,277	5,952	149,865	207.9	210,807	59.5	40.5	68.6	37.9	3,948	77.1
Stark	136	-1.7	116	0.5	105.4	640,866	5,514	101,840	130.7	111,895	50.6	49.4	46.0	16.5	1,693	26.5
Summit	17	9.1	54	0.3	9.6	459,954	8,451	59,490	11.3	37,118	86.7	13.3	32.2	7.6	112	8.2
Trumbull	114	-9.0	128	0.1	77.5	514,001	4,007	112,287	66.5	74,841	72.0	28.0	44.7	14.8	1,117	30.4
Tuscarawas	138	-3.2	136	0.0	78.4	521,749	3,831	95,939	92.3	91,066	25.6	74.4	38.4	12.5	1,562	25.1
Union	242	10.6	243	0.2	216.6	1,248,834	5,136	151,144	169.0	169,875	84.5	15.5	48.0	22.9	4,372	58.6
Van Wert	227	-7.8	347	0.8	214.8	2,177,867	6,276	212,111	209.7	320,087	73.0	27.0	78.0	43.7	5,103	85.0
Vinton	33	-9.3	148	0.0	11.8	358,668	2,427	42,867	4.7	20,805	82.4	17.6	27.9	2.7	195	35.8
Warren	107	13.0	113	0.7	80.2	809,270	7,150	85,670	66.7	70,815	91.1	8.9	30.7	10.1	1,061	24.3
Washington	139	12.0	124	1.8	49.5	331,367	2,676	58,988	30.5	27,165	59.2	40.8	30.7	5.4	1,152	22.1
Wayne	272	9.4	141	0.8	209.6	878,912	6,238	113,697	381.0	197,614	27.2	72.8	64.0	28.8	4,320	29.2
Williams	208	-2.1	211	1.3	181.6	809,134	3,828	101,897	126.0	128,026	66.2	33.8	44.0	20.6	5,771	79.3
Wood	268	-2.8	246	1.0	252.2	1,429,592	5,821	162,243	227.7	208,712	85.0	15.0	63.2	34.8	5,520	80.8
Wyandot	221	0.6	372	0.0	202.0	1,872,809	5,029	211,556	196.7	331,749	66.8	33.2	63.1	38.1	4,364	86.0
OKLAHOMA	34,356	-2.1	428	479.8	11,279.0	573,858	1,340	74,209	7,129.6	88,848	26.3	73.7	40.8	10.0	256,845	37.1
Adair	252	1.1	223	0.2	44.5	441,987	1,979	56,876	164.2	145,455	1.5	98.5	41.5	10.7	1,278	20.4
Alfalfa	545	0.4	845	1.3	326.6	1,201,132	1,421	186,451	168.5	261,298	36.7	63.3	72.1	34.3	5,814	82.8
Atoka	353	-13.5	320	0.1	59.9	447,024	1,396	52,142	24.5	22,249	17.1	82.9	35.4	2.8	1,311	23.5
Beaver	1,116	-1.2	1,156	24.6	351.9	772,084	668	100,918	187.0	193,772	17.6	82.4	37.8	15.8	7,765	74.1
Beckham	568	9.3	559	6.2	159.8	617,433	1,105	74,880	44.3	43,574	43.5	56.5	35.2	9.1	5,558	66.4
Blaine	522	-10.9	654	3.1	247.1	778,357	1,190	124,377	138.2	173,231	30.2	69.8	65.3	21.2	4,901	77.8
Bryan	441	-10.1	297	8.1	111.8	526,677	1,771	56,929	60.9	41,060	31.9	68.1	40.2	6.3	1,971	26.3
Caddo	708	-5.6	484	30.3	276.1	647,626	1,337	93,927	128.9	88,215	46.9	53.1	54.2	15.2	9,454	61.7
Canadian	501	-1.6	383	10.0	253.8	737,861	1,926	107,595	145.8	111,524	35.7	64.3	44.0	16.1	4,250	42.1
Carter	457	13.3	346	1.1	79.5	545,662	1,579	53,157	33.0	24,953	17.0	83.0	30.2	4.6	1,055	14.8
Cherokee	236	-4.2	191	1.1	46.0	453,732	2,370	56,633	138.7	112,483	75.8	24.2	33.4	3.6	1,083	15.0
Choctaw	330	1.3	342	1.1	63.2	503,597	1,471	63,712	47.5	49,178	13.2	86.8	44.7	8.1	1,810	29.3
Cimarron	1,157	10.8	2,089	39.4	426.9	1,055,505	505	132,971	376.7	679,890	17.4	82.6	46.8	29.8	9,997	86.6
Cleveland	134	-16.3	124	1.4	36.1	386,582	3,125	42,396	14.9	13,764	44.7	55.3	19.7	2.2	585	12.1
Coal	274	1.6	479	0.4	45.1	603,704	1,260	65,790	22.4	39,282	18.5	81.5	43.8	8.4	856	20.0
Comanche	463	-6.9	418	0.7	137.1	577,613	1,381	62,284	47.4	42,794	35.9	64.1	40.3	9.5	2,995	43.9
Cotton	400	9.0	800	0.1	185.5	900,322	1,126	122,376	64.4	128,862	46.0	54.0	61.0	24.2	5,699	79.0
Craig	462	1.1	366	D	110.9	582,744	1,592	61,639	97.3	77,075	11.9	88.1	51.1	8.4	1,725	33.9
Creek	347	-8.1	195	0.4	71.1	349,067	1,788	43,752	23.5	13,238	19.0	81.0	23.5	2.1	384	8.3
Custer	623	9.5	710	8.2	254.9	951,593	1,340	134,592	103.2	117,636	48.3	51.7	58.6	20.4	6,729	69.3
Delaware	283	-8.3	211	0.1	62.4	488,390	2,319	62,352	254.4	189,144	1.8	98.2	48.9	13.8	1,183	27.9
Dewey	625	6.1	841	2.4	165.1	852,131	1,013	90,935	42.0	56,580	49.7	50.3	51.4	13.3	5,420	76.6
Ellis	758	5.6	998	8.7	168.7	796,726	798	83,476	119.8	157,616	11.0	89.0	45.5	15.3	4,705	74.5
Garfield	666	0.4	607	8.4	433.0	870,574	1,434	146,813	151.8	138,239	61.8	38.2	64.4	24.7	9,317	69.1
Garvin	463	-7.5	309	1.1	111.0	488,585	1,580	72,700	44.9	29,975	38.2	61.8	39.6	6.3	2,210	32.0
Grady	583	-4.1	350	14.3	182.7	563,619	1,610	77,691	138.9	83,344	21.0	79.0	40.3	9.8	3,014	33.0
Grant	582	-8.0	727	1.3	409.2	992,482	1,365	152,116	96.9	120,953	73.4	26.6	58.9	24.2	8,734	87.3
Greer	402	7.0	806	3.7	142.9	690,175	856	99,878	32.7	65,681	61.5	38.5	54.0	17.1	4,991	84.5
Harmon	341	5.7	931	25.2	167.1	886,842	953	143,131	53.6	146,579	51.7	48.3	48.1	20.8	4,837	86.6
Harper	618	0.1	1,161	5.9	201.9	884,026	761	78,647	148.7	279,560	9.4	90.6	47.4	20.1	5,563	82.0
Haskell	256	-11.8	296	0.5	46.7	448,627	1,514	60,922	98.8	114,407	2.5	97.5	45.7	10.6	810	23.4
Hughes	436	-1.1	474	1.8	64.0	590,418	1,247	68,746	90.2	97,958	6.1	93.9	41.4	7.5	2,392	36.4
Jackson	479	0.9	690	14.1	295.6	690,865	1,001	154,581	53.2	76,591	78.7	21.3	45.5	20.3	7,021	77.2
Jefferson	475	3.3	1,140	0.1	79.3	1,153,223	1,011	87,902	82.4	197,511	7.5	92.5	63.3	24.0	1,921	59.7
Johnston	284	-15.1	440	0.5	40.9	591,054	1,344	55,721	21.6	33,541	17.6	82.4	42.5	4.8	766	33.6
Kay	484	-1.6	488	1.8	307.1	659,226	1,352	109,617	86.7	87,312	66.5	33.5	54.7	17.3	8,096	67.4
Kingfisher	568	0.2	556	9.1	327.5	757,269	1,362	135,742	161.8	158,497	39.2	60.8	65.2	27.9	4,945	69.9

Table B. States and Counties — Water Use, Wholesale Trade, Retail Trade, and Real Estate

STATE County	Water use, 2015 Public supply water withdrawn (mil gal/ day)	Public supply gallons withdrawn per person per day	Wholesale Trade[1], 2012 Number of establish-ments	Number of employees	Sales (mil dol)	Annual payroll (mil dol)	Retail Trade[2], 2012 Number of establish-ments	Number of employees	Sales (mil dol)	Annual payroll (mil dol)	Real estate and rental and leasing,[2] 2012 Number of establish-ments	Number of employees	Sales (mil dol)	Annual payroll (mil dol)
	133	134	135	136	137	138	139	140	141	142	143	144	145	146
OHIO— Cont'd														
Ottawa	4.58	112.0	27	156	127.5	6.4	144	1,433	427.7	38.2	44	120	15.1	3.4
Paulding	1.31	69.0	15	201	120.1	7.7	48	385	113.0	7.6	6	D	D	D
Perry	0.96	26.7	15	D	D	D	70	626	173.4	13.1	10	16	2.7	0.4
Pickaway	3.66	64.2	38	D	D	D	124	1,402	437.9	32.6	25	85	12.7	2.1
Pike	2.58	91.4	14	133	46.9	4.5	79	890	219.1	18.4	10	71	11.1	2.1
Portage	43.85	270.2	138	2,930	2,204.2	174.6	438	7,363	1,944.3	159.4	105	621	108.5	25.6
Preble	2.56	61.9	26	221	159.9	8.8	106	1,319	415.5	29.3	13	70	13.3	2.3
Putnam	2.52	74.0	35	354	297.1	13.6	110	1,054	274.8	21.6	10	28	2.5	0.8
Richland	14.45	118.7	104	1,993	939.2	78.9	438	6,528	1,501.2	139.9	102	417	49.2	9.1
Ross	9.48	122.8	44	D	D	D	236	3,582	938.9	77.8	51	198	34.7	6.2
Sandusky	7.89	132.2	47	662	764.0	28.1	199	2,366	629.2	54.7	34	172	17.8	3.5
Scioto	8.60	111.9	25	D	D	D	253	3,085	784.0	70.0	45	246	30.4	5.6
Seneca	1.85	33.3	49	646	504.3	27.0	159	2,064	586.5	49.8	29	71	10.6	1.6
Shelby	3.49	71.4	43	979	543.0	35.6	142	1,754	490.0	39.2	37	132	15.4	3.6
Stark	30.44	81.1	329	4,584	2,551.8	212.6	1,261	19,983	5,330.3	453.5	284	1,295	215.7	41.5
Summit	11.08	20.4	821	13,158	7,841.2	752.5	1,755	29,142	8,439.7	745.7	476	2,570	473.6	92.7
Trumbull	33.85	166.1	170	2,528	2,288.6	124.1	685	9,608	2,495.3	201.1	135	1,323	200.4	47.1
Tuscarawas	17.67	190.2	81	758	321.3	28.6	361	4,334	1,180.3	95.1	61	267	38.0	7.4
Union	1.17	21.6	55	689	2,150.6	38.2	121	1,911	631.1	50.4	42	158	24.2	4.2
Van Wert	1.87	65.5	28	D	D	D	87	1,202	282.7	24.6	13	56	16.5	3.1
Vinton	0.18	13.8	1	D	D	D	30	209	43.7	3.4	1	D	D	D
Warren	15.07	67.1	167	3,371	3,109.6	221.0	532	9,726	2,924.2	246.2	151	664	124.7	20.3
Washington	7.63	124.9	68	D	D	D	227	2,724	756.3	62.9	39	D	D	D
Wayne	8.06	69.4	124	D	D	D	366	4,524	1,060.0	100.6	62	217	46.9	7.0
Williams	2.67	71.9	46	680	413.0	25.1	125	1,266	326.6	25.4	23	80	13.3	2.5
Wood	5.21	40.2	167	2,958	2,057.6	137.0	385	6,264	1,813.4	134.2	117	527	127.2	20.7
Wyandot	0.95	42.7	27	342	270.2	13.8	66	786	228.8	16.2	8	D	D	D
OKLAHOMA	611.24	156.3	3,909	50,660	71,892.9	2,718.6	13,051	168,839	50,256.2	4,055.1	4,000	21,261	4,269.6	898.0
Adair	6.91	314.0	8	63	27.9	1.7	58	549	123.4	9.4	7	12	1.4	0.4
Alfalfa	0.70	119.3	9	D	D	D	24	163	57.1	3.4	1	D	D	D
Atoka	40.42	2,930.5	9	35	34.0	1.2	45	438	129.8	9.8	7	D	D	D
Beaver	0.48	88.4	6	D	D	D	19	106	37.5	1.8	5	5	1.6	0.1
Beckham	3.25	136.7	36	547	305.4	29.2	141	1,657	715.4	41.0	40	421	138.4	27.2
Blaine	1.07	108.8	13	D	D	D	47	272	89.7	4.5	4	D	D	D
Bryan	5.53	123.2	28	D	D	D	124	1,441	432.8	31.5	26	70	12.2	2.4
Caddo	7.15	243.7	17	237	191.5	9.4	89	767	283.9	19.1	9	39	12.1	1.4
Canadian	4.24	31.8	102	877	512.8	42.6	255	3,567	1,306.8	88.1	123	721	212.0	41.9
Carter	5.08	104.3	64	866	872.1	32.3	247	2,700	889.7	65.6	70	345	83.0	16.6
Cherokee	7.40	152.7	16	738	111.3	16.4	143	1,710	390.6	33.7	35	146	25.8	3.5
Choctaw	2.69	179.4	6	31	27.6	1.1	43	481	118.8	9.5	3	8	0.5	0.1
Cimarron	0.34	153.4	6	17	30.3	1.0	11	81	38.5	1.7	NA	NA	NA	NA
Cleveland	23.37	85.1	140	1,360	737.9	70.9	710	10,983	3,168.9	262.2	335	1,479	231.0	52.6
Coal	0.46	81.4	2	D	D	D	20	153	41.9	3.1	1	D	D	D
Comanche	20.98	168.3	62	D	D	D	409	5,286	1,407.8	117.9	125	D	D	D
Cotton	0.51	85.1	2	D	D	D	15	124	36.9	1.6	1	D	D	D
Craig	0.10	6.7	16	135	73.4	5.8	62	720	204.9	15.7	5	9	1.3	0.2
Creek	5.89	83.1	64	1,061	579.7	49.4	181	1,877	570.5	43.7	34	103	14.2	2.9
Custer	3.65	122.7	36	338	442.9	21.7	149	1,655	530.9	37.2	45	383	96.6	34.7
Delaware	35.69	860.9	19	100	26.0	3.4	141	1,428	369.2	30.7	36	279	45.2	11.6
Dewey	0.11	22.0	8	25	17.5	1.0	33	246	74.9	3.8	2	D	D	D
Ellis	0.65	153.6	5	69	39.6	3.9	25	269	53.0	3.0	1	D	D	D
Garfield	2.87	45.1	73	D	D	D	267	3,387	926.8	84.3	80	328	57.5	12.4
Garvin	1.99	71.7	25	177	105.5	7.2	110	1,117	433.7	30.3	12	36	15.6	2.2
Grady	2.40	43.9	42	525	324.9	25.9	152	1,602	491.7	34.7	33	164	38.8	8.1
Grant	1.26	278.6	10	40	69.6	1.5	19	D	D	D	1	D	D	D
Greer	1.46	240.5	4	26	7.8	0.7	13	145	30.2	2.7	2	D	D	D
Harmon	0.73	261.8	1	D	D	D	13	D	D	D	1	D	D	D
Harper	0.60	159.8	3	D	D	D	17	127	26.5	2.4	3	D	D	D
Haskell	1.17	91.1	4	60	18.9	1.5	33	473	142.9	10.2	4	6	0.7	0.1
Hughes	2.57	187.1	5	D	D	D	47	427	111.5	7.8	8	34	3.2	1.2
Jackson	0.21	8.2	24	D	D	D	99	1,241	358.3	27.0	20	146	20.1	3.1
Jefferson	13.79	2,197.3	3	D	D	D	25	149	46.0	2.4	1	D	D	D
Johnston	1.98	180.3	9	68	36.1	2.3	34	229	61.1	4.7	3	5	0.4	0.1
Kay	18.13	399.6	43	D	D	D	183	2,126	631.8	48.2	40	132	22.6	4.0
Kingfisher	1.66	106.5	22	331	450.2	16.1	53	556	198.9	14.1	4	4	2.3	0.5

1. Merchant wholesalers, except manufacturers' sales branches and offices.   2. Employer establishments.

Table B. States and Counties — Professional Services, Manufacturing, and Accommodation and Food Services

STATE County	Professional, scientific, and technical services, 2012				Manufacturing, 2012				Accommodation and food services, 2012			
	Number of establish-ments	Number of employees	Sales (mil dol)	Annual payroll (mil dol)	Number of establishments	Number of employees	Receipts (mil dol)	Annual payroll (mil dol)	Number of establishments	Number of employees	Receipts (mil dol)	Annual payroll (mil dol)
	147	148	149	150	151	152	153	154	155	156	157	158
OHIO— Cont'd												
Ottawa	54	D	D	D	53	2,150	811.8	117.7	165	1,703	115.1	30.4
Paulding	12	52	3.2	1.2	38	1,132	282.8	44.9	25	296	11.0	2.7
Perry	21	D	D	D	22	738	D	28.4	47	355	16.6	4.1
Pickaway	56	429	28.7	9.9	35	2,221	900.0	125.1	70	1,254	51.4	14.0
Pike	21	D	D	D	22	1,388	D	88.8	36	597	28.7	7.2
Portage	224	D	D	D	244	9,585	3,010.8	468.2	304	4,925	250.5	61.7
Preble	38	188	11.4	4.9	55	2,761	1,141.7	148.9	56	882	37.4	10.6
Putnam	35	171	18.0	6.0	53	3,209	2,677.9	145.8	60	D	D	D
Richland	187	925	113.1	36.0	168	8,064	3,122.7	385.9	239	4,556	190.1	54.1
Ross	74	645	37.1	15.7	33	4,270	3,928.5	276.6	123	2,486	115.2	30.7
Sandusky	85	431	39.1	12.2	108	8,458	3,878.0	388.4	117	1,844	76.4	19.8
Scioto	80	792	74.0	37.4	43	1,439	1,190.6	64.3	142	2,485	112.8	29.9
Seneca	69	377	29.3	11.9	79	3,498	1,262.6	152.8	106	1,481	53.4	14.5
Shelby	52	364	48.0	18.6	122	10,052	7,166.1	536.9	80	1,300	58.2	14.4
Stark	675	D	D	D	506	22,667	12,182.9	1,061.2	769	13,844	630.1	174.7
Summit	1,500	14,776	2,443.4	856.7	837	27,965	9,557.1	1,402.7	1,195	21,494	974.7	268.9
Trumbull	306	1,436	175.5	49.5	218	15,764	9,668.4	1,095.3	396	11,386	516.3	156.0
Tuscarawas	140	D	D	D	211	7,401	2,276.1	346.3	194	2,700	112.1	30.6
Union	93	2,362	706.6	211.2	53	6,143	10,102.7	424.9	80	1,335	63.9	17.5
Van Wert	36	141	14.7	6.3	39	3,323	1,505.7	130.2	45	798	31.2	7.8
Vinton	7	D	D	D	15	453	98.2	27.5	13	D	D	D
Warren	473	3,934	567.7	234.9	198	9,523	3,803.4	493.3	350	7,767	386.6	107.1
Washington	96	D	D	D	88	3,628	D	222.3	112	D	D	D
Wayne	153	1,668	117.3	88.3	254	10,257	3,203.8	471.4	171	2,937	125.6	36.6
Williams	40	301	23.3	11.2	113	6,337	2,466.3	274.4	71	927	35.0	9.7
Wood	216	1,658	195.1	93.1	179	11,030	4,256.0	623.3	322	6,468	263.9	73.2
Wyandot	23	76	7.9	2.0	41	3,055	958.8	130.8	49	568	22.6	5.5
OKLAHOMA	9,470	71,997	10,991.3	4,115.2	3,610	133,064	74,295.4	6,416.0	7,403	143,561	7,121.2	1,908.3
Adair	17	D	D	D	16	1,075	485.0	38.3	20	198	7.2	2.2
Alfalfa	9	D	D	D	NA	NA	NA	NA	8	44	3.1	0.7
Atoka	10	D	D	D	17	178	47.0	6.6	25	D	D	D
Beaver	18	D	D	D	3	29	D	D	9	D	D	D
Beckham	80	273	47.2	14.3	17	D	D	D	72	999	51.9	10.7
Blaine	21	183	17.1	7.0	7	391	D	16.8	16	129	6.0	1.5
Bryan	63	382	39.7	15.0	35	1,076	243.2	35.3	76	1,573	73.5	21.1
Caddo	34	D	D	D	10	46	D	1.6	36	339	14.1	3.6
Canadian	232	846	172.5	59.6	79	2,979	1,035.6	114.1	171	3,310	160.6	41.7
Carter	134	722	61.5	33.7	43	2,984	4,853.5	178.2	116	2,397	106.7	29.4
Cherokee	45	129	10.4	2.8	21	107	15.1	3.5	88	1,226	53.1	13.5
Choctaw	18	D	D	D	11	133	D	2.7	24	542	18.1	8.1
Cimarron	4	D	D	D	NA	NA	NA	NA	10	82	4.1	1.0
Cleveland	676	3,166	396.5	131.5	132	3,659	1,495.7	158.7	506	11,290	512.4	140.7
Coal	2	D	D	D	5	73	D	2.9	6	D	D	D
Comanche	162	1,129	114.8	49.8	45	3,487	D	183.7	227	4,863	220.5	66.2
Cotton	6	14	1.0	0.4	4	8	D	D	7	64	2.7	0.6
Craig	24	D	D	D	14	440	89.9	16.8	25	345	14.4	3.7
Creek	104	299	35.1	10.4	124	4,057	1,649.9	212.4	90	D	D	D
Custer	74	D	D	D	32	1,184	429.8	57.3	68	1,284	61.3	14.4
Delaware	54	D	D	D	27	693	87.1	22.0	63	1,816	165.8	40.2
Dewey	4	D	D	D	4	28	D	1.4	6	64	1.9	0.6
Ellis	9	29	6.1	0.8	NA	NA	NA	NA	8	D	D	D
Garfield	118	D	D	D	61	2,451	1,668.7	96.5	125	2,198	112.7	26.8
Garvin	61	D	D	D	31	1,067	2,819.8	53.9	49	660	33.1	7.9
Grady	105	300	35.7	11.5	64	1,505	564.1	57.0	62	1,240	53.2	13.6
Grant	6	D	D	D	3	12	2.1	0.3	5	D	D	D
Greer	9	D	D	D	NA	NA	NA	NA	6	55	1.8	0.5
Harmon	4	D	D	D	NA	NA	NA	NA	2	D	D	D
Harper	7	D	D	D	NA	NA	NA	NA	6	D	D	D
Haskell	23	D	D	D	7	70	D	D	13	D	D	D
Hughes	9	D	D	D	6	29	D	1.0	19	202	7.2	2.1
Jackson	41	D	D	D	13	821	225.6	D	56	1,103	42.0	11.4
Jefferson	5	D	D	D	7	28	D	0.9	8	78	3.0	0.8
Johnston	12	D	D	D	9	285	D	9.4	9	D	D	D
Kay	90	509	52.8	21.7	65	2,983	D	171.0	90	1,350	65.2	15.9
Kingfisher	27	277	41.3	18.4	18	470	130.2	22.5	34	370	16.7	4.4

STATE County	Health care and social assistance, 2012				Other services, 2012				Nonemployer businesses, 2015		Value of residential construction authorized by building permits, 2017	
	Number of establishments	Number of employees	Receipts (mil dol)	Annual payroll (mil dol)	Number of establishments	Number of employees	Receipts (mil dol)	Annual payroll (mil dol)	Number	Receipts (mil dol)	New construction ($1,000)	Number of housing units
	159	160	161	162	163	164	165	166	167	168	169	170
OHIO— Cont'd												
Ottawa	76	1,771	123.0	49.8	79	311	28.6	8.4	2,938	120.8	35,785	114
Paulding	32	604	36.0	15.8	17	61	6.0	1.2	1,037	36.3	7,991	40
Perry	61	709	40.0	18.5	28	158	11.4	2.4	2,057	69.5	6,651	38
Pickaway	86	2,266	189.6	73.5	51	179	18.2	4.3	3,336	135.9	33,316	202
Pike	60	1,610	118.0	44.4	21	69	6.6	1.4	1,525	60.8	22,933	89
Portage	267	5,974	418.5	181.0	227	1,518	120.6	40.8	10,202	445.0	66,226	297
Preble	61	975	60.4	21.6	59	235	20.8	5.4	2,442	99.4	6,690	35
Putnam	54	990	49.0	20.9	55	274	30.3	6.4	1,991	82.5	13,313	52
Richland	316	7,570	674.5	274.6	209	1,186	108.4	25.3	6,844	281.9	18,285	77
Ross	158	6,268	754.2	373.1	85	490	35.3	9.7	3,843	147.6	1,445	16
Sandusky	160	3,660	283.4	113.3	99	635	42.3	14.1	3,153	111.8	10,300	48
Scioto	214	6,155	591.9	206.7	89	336	30.4	6.8	3,830	124.1	380	4
Seneca	145	2,536	180.6	69.9	104	505	32.0	8.2	2,903	109.6	5,558	28
Shelby	98	1,929	169.1	64.1	69	342	36.3	9.7	2,730	114.5	23,038	81
Stark	996	28,010	2,455.5	1,090.0	694	4,770	460.7	131.2	23,344	964.4	108,513	525
Summit	1,519	45,181	4,649.6	1,869.0	1,084	7,398	853.5	202.2	37,373	1,665.0	160,875	623
Trumbull	578	10,720	991.1	378.8	313	1,771	128.1	36.8	12,603	533.9	16,022	98
Tuscarawas	200	5,156	397.5	157.3	190	1,096	125.2	27.8	5,953	267.6	12,978	90
Union	78	1,732	166.1	63.3	68	354	29.6	8.9	3,566	164.2	113,278	427
Van Wert	60	1,505	113.3	41.8	45	234	20.2	3.6	1,649	72.0	3,808	20
Vinton	22	D	D	D	8	D	D	D	678	23.3	0	0
Warren	433	9,527	853.7	325.5	244	1,944	175.3	56.3	16,024	786.5	385,016	1,539
Washington	139	5,586	453.2	195.2	110	D	D	D	3,753	155.3	1,363	15
Wayne	235	5,274	415.5	178.6	169	891	97.0	20.4	9,040	415.9	37,362	174
Williams	65	2,006	169.7	71.6	66	372	30.3	7.1	2,227	89.6	5,541	23
Wood	243	4,906	384.2	164.5	210	1,433	126.7	38.6	7,604	328.0	67,297	279
Wyandot	37	772	55.6	21.1	56	240	21.5	5.6	1,333	52.9	4,280	19
OKLAHOMA	10,654	213,226	22,795.4	8,289.9	5,411	32,388	4,037.3	939.7	276,218	12,862.1	2,191,631	11,092
Adair	17	562	33.0	16.5	11	28	1.9	0.4	1,456	49.9	2,306	13
Alfalfa	11	111	6.6	2.9	6	D	D	D	411	14.7	0	0
Atoka	22	466	26.2	9.8	15	D	D	D	950	48.1	3,000	43
Beaver	6	75	7.1	2.3	11	D	D	D	466	19.7	0	0
Beckham	87	1,235	111.5	39.4	39	247	33.4	7.6	1,848	98.2	8,228	28
Blaine	27	365	21.3	10.0	14	28	3.5	0.4	716	30.0	30	1
Bryan	124	2,092	204.5	66.4	34	159	12.8	3.6	2,885	135.0	10,949	101
Caddo	34	618	29.7	13.1	19	88	12.4	3.3	1,536	65.9	1,412	6
Canadian	233	2,849	228.1	88.7	159	1,006	184.0	32.9	10,084	450.3	62,593	318
Carter	217	3,790	323.6	121.1	93	974	148.1	46.4	2,857	121.0	9,125	84
Cherokee	114	2,633	244.7	106.7	41	279	20.4	5.8	912	42.7	0	0
Choctaw	40	975	59.7	27.0	13	D	D	D	205	10.4	0	0
Cimarron	4	D	D	D	4	D	D	D	20,619	947.9	164,901	738
Cleveland	755	12,359	1,158.1	435.8	308	1,761	301.9	44.6	451	42.6	0	0
Coal	11	242	10.4	5.5	4	D	D	D	4,735	208.7	16,496	83
Comanche	275	6,918	704.6	271.8	136	830	69.0	20.9	328	11.2	80	1
Cotton	7	42	5.1	1.4	5	16	1.6	0.3	934	41.8	800	11
Craig	74	1,329	83.1	43.5	16	43	4.4	1.2	4,812	198.8	17,305	87
Creek	113	2,166	147.1	56.4	82	306	35.9	8.1	2,190	105.8	17,112	113
Custer	92	1,668	158.5	59.7	51	302	30.3	8.3	2,751	121.9	4,533	32
Delaware	84	1,440	133.1	47.2	54	241	21.8	5.3	489	21.1	NA	NA
Dewey	9	D	D	D	9	42	8.4	1.1	345	13.2	0	0
Ellis	10	192	15.5	6.9	5	D	D	D	4,267	183.3	13,523	95
Garfield	208	4,158	427.0	151.8	118	586	58.8	14.5	2,107	100.9	1,342	13
Garvin	64	1,277	78.3	30.7	26	129	23.9	4.8	3,707	176.4	18,028	92
Grady	87	D	D	D	65	328	37.1	8.2	366	15.7	500	2
Grant	7	119	5.1	2.5	4	D	D	D	291	11.3	1,050	4
Greer	17	D	D	D	7	15	1.5	0.2	161	6.5	NA	NA
Harmon	6	122	8.5	3.8	2	D	D	D	327	13.4	0	0
Harper	9	127	7.5	3.5	6	D	D	D	1,012	46.0	626	4
Haskell	29	819	53.7	22.3	11	31	2.4	0.4	733	29.8	290	2
Hughes	40	D	D	D	10	D	D	D	1,406	57.8	3,533	21
Jackson	48	1,389	111.1	47.6	34	151	10.6	2.7	435	16.6	NA	NA
Jefferson	7	D	D	D	3	D	D	D	618	27.8	583	3
Johnston	30	586	31.8	15.3	10	32	3.3	0.8	2,578	101.3	6,607	60
Kay	143	2,252	176.8	65.7	75	335	31.6	8.3	1,566	83.2	4,216	16
Kingfisher	39	479	33.3	13.6	29	D	D	D				

Table B. States and Counties — Government Employment and Payroll, and Local Government Finances

	Government employment and payroll, 2012									Local government finances				
			March payroll (percent of total)							General revenue				
												Taxes		
													Per capita[1] (dollars)	
STATE County	Full-time equivalent employees	March payroll (dollars)	Adminis-tration, judicial, and legal	Police and corrections	Fire protection	Highways and transpor-tation	Health and welfare	Natural resources and utilities	Education and libraries	Total (mil dol)	Inter-govern-mental (mil dol)	Total (mil dol)	Total	Property
	171	172	173	174	175	176	177	178	179	180	181	182	183	184
OHIO— Cont'd														
Ottawa	1,807	6,970,433	8.9	9.2	2.9	11.6	10.2	7.2	48.1	169.9	58.3	72.2	1,746	1,408
Paulding	840	2,899,437	7.0	5.4	0.3	5.0	30.9	2.1	47.9	78.4	30.7	20.4	1,057	705
Perry	1,584	4,562,693	8.5	5.7	0.8	9.1	10.2	4.3	60.2	119.5	77.0	27.9	775	640
Pickaway	2,330	14,643,979	43.7	3.1	0.9	1.5	14.8	1.6	34.2	261.8	90.0	68.3	1,211	848
Pike	1,231	4,378,557	9.2	6.9	1.1	6.4	9.9	6.4	59.2	142.7	70.7	26.2	920	694
Portage	6,776	25,510,983	5.9	7.0	4.0	6.3	23.8	3.4	48.7	675.5	218.5	230.1	1,425	1,010
Preble	1,714	6,190,256	11.3	8.4	1.2	8.8	6.9	4.8	52.3	137.6	66.2	50.4	1,204	713
Putnam	1,034	3,725,218	9.3	7.5	0.0	5.3	1.5	3.8	72.3	126.1	61.7	46.9	1,371	814
Richland	5,091	18,513,991	8.5	9.4	5.0	4.1	11.2	8.3	52.0	473.0	237.7	163.9	1,336	864
Ross	2,848	9,604,595	8.8	6.4	2.9	4.7	10.0	4.2	62.4	240.8	134.0	79.9	1,032	625
Sandusky	2,171	7,625,048	7.2	8.4	1.7	3.5	12.3	6.5	58.8	231.5	116.4	82.4	1,362	773
Scioto	2,809	9,457,558	7.1	6.9	2.7	3.9	7.6	6.7	64.1	259.9	167.7	61.3	781	581
Seneca	1,825	6,110,506	9.4	11.2	4.5	4.6	9.9	4.4	55.0	195.7	93.8	60.1	1,073	657
Shelby	1,460	5,397,171	6.3	6.1	4.3	3.0	5.5	5.6	68.3	184.8	82.0	67.4	1,370	761
Stark	11,531	42,201,589	4.3	6.8	4.8	4.1	1.9	6.1	71.3	1,313.7	628.2	474.7	1,266	949
Summit	20,065	81,863,137	7.5	10.7	5.8	4.7	7.7	7.2	54.5	2,401.2	877.7	1,094.2	2,023	1,303
Trumbull	7,911	27,957,859	8.3	9.9	5.3	3.3	10.3	6.6	55.2	724.1	366.6	245.2	1,182	844
Tuscarawas	3,307	11,310,698	8.3	7.0	2.8	5.4	6.0	9.0	58.9	309.5	126.6	106.5	1,152	825
Union	2,131	8,121,953	6.0	5.6	3.5	2.1	30.6	3.2	47.7	262.5	68.5	90.7	1,720	1,149
Van Wert	1,050	4,217,502	8.6	7.4	2.1	8.6	3.4	13.7	52.1	118.7	67.2	36.2	1,260	753
Vinton	591	1,697,854	7.1	2.3	0.0	6.1	13.7	1.9	66.2	47.0	34.8	7.8	590	511
Warren	5,863	22,314,741	4.2	7.3	6.2	2.1	0.6	3.3	75.2	748.9	233.0	383.6	1,766	1,359
Washington	2,326	7,490,510	7.9	9.4	3.2	6.0	8.9	3.7	59.9	189.5	93.8	66.4	1,080	769
Wayne	4,495	16,994,820	7.3	7.8	2.6	5.0	22.5	5.7	48.6	484.9	177.5	144.9	1,261	926
Williams	1,758	5,321,575	7.9	5.7	0.7	4.6	15.8	10.1	54.0	135.0	55.5	50.2	1,339	733
Wood	4,470	17,275,956	8.6	10.8	3.6	3.3	9.2	6.1	56.1	532.6	184.0	232.7	1,815	1,163
Wyandot	1,084	3,936,981	8.9	7.2	0.8	3.5	33.2	5.1	40.6	97.2	30.4	25.4	1,124	531
OKLAHOMA	X	X	X	X	X	X	X	X	X	X	X	X	X	X
Adair	986	2,539,434	3.7	4.1	0.2	2.8	2.6	7.8	77.6	58.2	42.9	7.8	352	205
Alfalfa	248	605,307	12.0	6.9	0.5	12.8	1.7	4.7	59.3	13.7	4.5	6.9	1,225	981
Atoka	901	3,031,357	2.1	2.9	0.0	0.7	13.5	14.8	65.5	69.1	37.2	9.2	658	295
Beaver	349	1,030,481	7.5	3.5	0.0	11.8	12.7	7.2	56.4	23.3	11.7	9.1	1,626	1,124
Beckham	996	2,808,433	5.1	8.4	3.6	5.8	2.7	8.0	63.2	78.3	28.3	36.4	1,577	607
Blaine	619	1,556,580	6.7	6.5	0.9	6.6	23.9	4.9	49.9	45.9	14.5	14.0	1,429	639
Bryan	1,434	4,012,582	7.3	9.9	3.7	4.8	3.9	6.2	62.9	108.1	53.8	36.2	833	407
Caddo	1,563	4,548,760	3.7	5.7	1.7	6.2	8.5	8.8	64.8	96.6	61.1	21.0	708	392
Canadian	3,819	11,398,884	4.8	10.1	3.4	2.2	6.5	2.2	69.3	291.7	123.9	127.1	1,037	614
Carter	1,811	5,386,589	5.3	10.5	3.1	4.9	1.1	6.3	67.9	152.0	61.4	59.3	1,233	591
Cherokee	2,005	6,302,718	3.9	5.1	1.3	3.4	35.5	5.3	44.2	165.4	56.2	22.0	457	230
Choctaw	795	2,289,614	6.3	3.7	1.7	3.9	19.7	5.9	57.8	37.7	23.4	8.9	588	233
Cimarron	196	450,099	9.5	5.4	0.0	14.3	1.7	5.6	54.3	9.9	3.7	3.1	1,291	950
Cleveland	9,950	35,955,536	3.3	6.4	4.0	1.7	32.0	2.8	48.9	893.3	214.7	278.1	1,047	619
Coal	319	840,600	8.4	5.3	4.4	7.5	6.5	3.4	64.6	24.3	13.0	8.5	1,425	897
Comanche	6,240	22,060,234	3.6	5.7	3.0	2.1	37.2	3.2	44.6	505.2	159.3	103.2	817	354
Cotton	263	656,798	7.9	5.3	1.5	6.9	1.4	7.9	66.9	18.1	12.3	3.0	492	352
Craig	859	2,734,367	4.9	5.6	1.6	5.0	35.0	3.8	42.2	46.2	23.2	13.9	943	509
Creek	2,475	7,871,373	5.1	6.6	4.0	2.5	1.9	5.1	74.1	169.5	81.2	61.8	874	489
Custer	1,316	3,555,785	5.3	7.5	2.4	3.8	17.0	5.5	56.6	88.8	32.3	37.3	1,306	656
Delaware	1,264	3,298,724	6.6	7.0	0.4	4.1	1.2	4.6	74.6	80.2	42.1	28.6	690	467
Dewey	334	940,532	8.5	5.7	0.5	11.7	14.3	4.1	54.3	35.1	7.3	21.9	4,581	2,207
Ellis	243	705,922	9.0	9.1	0.0	18.9	2.9	2.2	56.6	31.4	7.5	8.4	2,051	1,616
Garfield	2,242	6,971,075	5.4	9.4	5.9	4.5	1.4	5.0	66.7	176.9	68.5	75.4	1,232	577
Garvin	1,260	3,212,232	6.5	6.6	2.1	5.0	14.9	6.4	57.8	92.3	43.7	25.1	920	451
Grady	1,921	5,776,643	3.4	5.2	3.6	3.2	26.9	2.4	54.3	157.9	56.1	41.4	779	442
Grant	233	634,768	12.0	7.0	0.1	21.2	0.0	6.1	53.1	15.2	6.4	5.9	1,313	1,043
Greer	288	950,821	5.8	5.3	2.0	1.0	29.5	6.4	48.4	16.6	9.5	2.9	481	285
Harmon	242	611,023	7.5	4.4	0.0	5.4	40.8	2.6	38.3	7.4	4.3	1.9	648	388
Harper	266	708,452	8.7	5.5	0.0	9.6	26.4	4.5	45.3	14.8	7.0	5.9	1,592	1,096
Haskell	614	1,704,293	4.5	5.0	0.0	5.1	27.6	1.6	53.4	31.8	20.1	7.0	543	274
Hughes	768	2,037,752	4.4	2.9	0.8	3.3	28.1	3.9	55.8	38.4	20.3	12.6	908	604
Jackson	1,759	6,015,452	3.3	4.6	2.2	1.8	47.3	5.6	33.9	146.2	38.1	20.7	788	304
Jefferson	350	958,729	7.0	3.6	0.7	3.6	15.4	11.0	58.0	49.9	41.2	3.0	470	281
Johnston	410	1,050,719	7.1	6.5	0.6	3.4	2.9	5.1	73.6	22.7	13.6	6.2	561	357
Kay	2,026	5,686,908	6.0	8.0	6.7	4.3	2.5	9.9	60.6	149.2	58.1	50.8	1,108	557
Kingfisher	634	1,825,978	7.8	7.8	3.3	9.1	1.5	4.9	65.1	48.4	22.2	18.8	1,254	825

1. Based on the resident population estimated as of July 1 of the year shown.

Table B. States and Counties — Local Government Finances, Government Employment, and Income Taxes

STATE County	Local government finances (cont.) Direct general expenditure — Total (mil dol)	Per capita¹ (dollars)	Percent of total for: Education	Health and hospitals	Police protection	Public welfare	Highways	Debt outstanding — Total (mil dol)	Per capita¹ (dollars)	Government employment, 2016 — Federal civilian	Federal military	State and local	Individual income tax returns, 2015 — Number of returns	Mean adjusted gross income	Mean income tax
	185	186	187	188	189	190	191	192	193	194	195	196	197	198	199
OHIO— Cont'd															
Ottawa	183.7	4,444	50.5	4.7	6.9	9.8	7.3	162.5	3,930	269	138	2,110	21,570	54,862	6,121
Paulding	83.9	4,350	53.2	21.6	2.3	1.9	7.4	20.8	1,079	49	48	1,059	9,020	44,872	4,084
Perry	127.1	3,530	59.9	5.5	4.7	7.4	7.0	19.6	543	62	91	1,503	15,250	44,526	4,012
Pickaway	245.9	4,360	42.1	29.7	3.7	2.8	4.2	155.1	2,750	92	134	3,873	24,740	52,031	5,287
Pike	136.0	4,775	54.3	20.5	2.3	3.4	5.2	25.3	889	67	70	1,406	11,180	43,671	3,953
Portage	676.4	4,190	37.6	28.6	4.0	3.4	4.1	295.0	1,827	342	401	14,716	76,330	57,581	6,974
Preble	135.2	3,229	56.4	4.3	5.3	6.0	7.0	22.8	546	71	104	1,769	19,550	45,487	4,079
Putnam	148.9	4,353	62.5	3.1	4.2	4.4	6.0	72.4	2,117	65	86	1,543	17,430	56,447	6,587
Richland	480.9	3,920	52.3	8.7	5.0	4.8	5.5	209.0	1,703	639	291	7,052	56,890	45,199	4,535
Ross	234.3	3,026	58.4	0.5	5.1	7.8	4.6	264.6	3,418	1,643	182	5,144	32,790	46,215	4,561
Sandusky	231.1	3,819	59.9	4.6	7.5	4.6	4.8	105.5	1,744	111	149	2,966	30,140	46,685	4,534
Scioto	262.2	3,341	61.1	5.0	1.9	4.1	4.6	211.5	2,694	169	186	5,253	29,080	45,577	4,510
Seneca	196.2	3,502	52.9	6.1	6.7	3.7	7.6	729.9	13,029	128	134	2,492	26,620	44,379	4,103
Shelby	185.3	3,769	51.8	0.7	3.4	11.7	9.7	191.1	3,887	73	122	2,488	23,910	51,963	5,655
Stark	1,278.7	3,411	55.1	4.6	5.7	5.0	5.4	444.1	1,185	963	958	17,992	183,970	53,266	6,277
Summit	2,276.4	4,209	43.9	4.8	5.6	4.3	3.4	4,224.1	7,811	1,707	1,368	28,424	269,210	59,567	7,805
Trumbull	736.8	3,552	53.3	5.9	6.4	5.6	3.7	248.1	1,196	537	532	9,166	99,840	45,294	4,645
Tuscarawas	292.0	3,160	50.0	4.4	5.1	6.3	5.1	119.9	1,297	261	232	4,964	45,040	50,267	5,445
Union	256.7	4,870	31.4	31.2	3.9	1.4	6.7	364.0	6,906	71	134	3,487	25,240	70,931	9,108
Van Wert	130.4	4,536	67.9	0.9	3.8	2.9	7.3	64.6	2,247	51	71	1,399	14,050	46,808	4,447
Vinton	47.0	3,548	53.9	4.2	3.0	10.0	10.2	7.8	588	15	33	656	5,120	40,791	3,323
Warren	743.8	3,424	50.7	0.4	7.2	6.1	4.8	599.3	2,759	305	585	9,718	107,970	81,096	11,751
Washington	192.0	3,124	48.4	9.0	6.4	6.0	9.1	94.7	1,541	213	150	2,804	29,090	50,393	5,577
Wayne	466.4	4,061	44.9	24.0	3.9	6.3	4.1	103.7	903	267	287	6,600	54,260	52,429	5,670
Williams	124.0	3,304	51.6	1.0	5.4	10.9	7.1	67.6	1,801	85	92	2,065	18,460	45,295	4,324
Wood	538.0	4,197	50.7	2.8	4.6	11.9	5.6	402.7	3,142	203	332	11,296	61,380	60,584	7,338
Wyandot	101.5	4,489	33.1	34.8	4.5	8.4	7.7	18.8	830	56	56	1,472	11,120	48,872	5,139
OKLAHOMA	X	X	X	X	X	X	X	X	X	48,263	33,005	289,623	1,641,910	59,002	7,385
Adair	58.1	2,606	75.3	1.7	3.3	0.0	6.3	8.0	359	43	82	1,331	7,860	35,490	2,477
Alfalfa	13.7	2,424	57.6	1.3	4.0	0.0	1.2	6.6	1,158	35	18	559	2,150	78,183	12,959
Atoka	56.5	4,036	38.0	13.0	4.0	0.0	9.5	27.1	1,931	37	49	1,128	5,180	41,028	3,505
Beaver	21.3	3,811	59.5	6.4	2.9	0.1	14.8	3.5	632	29	20	478	2,290	54,570	6,153
Beckham	65.5	2,839	44.5	3.2	6.9	0.0	8.4	42.2	1,830	52	77	1,161	8,870	57,453	6,739
Blaine	43.3	4,420	45.4	22.1	2.7	0.0	10.7	12.1	1,232	52	36	785	4,020	55,027	6,250
Bryan	107.3	2,473	57.5	3.2	6.5	0.0	4.5	150.1	3,458	94	166	7,185	17,320	45,461	4,602
Caddo	102.4	3,449	54.1	1.6	3.8	0.0	12.2	21.8	736	511	103	2,268	10,820	43,426	3,901
Canadian	275.3	2,246	65.8	0.4	5.8	0.0	4.1	217.3	1,773	587	541	5,802	58,940	65,939	7,538
Carter	138.7	2,885	55.4	3.2	6.9	0.0	8.9	72.9	1,517	108	178	3,359	21,160	53,838	6,150
Cherokee	168.8	3,505	38.7	45.6	2.0	0.0	2.6	38.5	800	227	174	8,107	17,960	43,051	3,793
Choctaw	38.5	2,537	57.0	7.0	5.1	0.5	14.4	11.0	728	43	55	1,369	5,630	38,240	3,170
Cimarron	9.8	4,126	56.2	20.2	2.6	0.0	5.2	1.3	527	14	0	250	1,110	39,878	3,827
Cleveland	909.8	3,425	38.7	32.5	4.4	0.0	4.9	703.2	2,647	697	1,050	23,119	121,190	62,353	7,718
Coal	24.2	4,050	54.5	2.2	3.3	0.0	16.0	1.2	199	15	21	369	2,080	42,937	3,583
Comanche	515.7	4,080	36.9	40.3	4.3	0.0	3.0	244.6	1,935	4,021	11,012	10,231	48,780	47,490	4,606
Cotton	18.1	2,940	59.1	0.3	2.7	0.0	14.7	9.2	1,490	26	22	941	2,350	43,587	3,855
Craig	47.8	3,238	66.7	1.2	4.4	0.0	10.2	13.5	915	56	51	1,629	5,580	43,908	4,055
Creek	169.8	2,404	59.1	3.0	5.7	0.0	7.1	161.0	2,279	266	262	3,072	29,270	54,037	5,738
Custer	81.3	2,850	57.0	0.1	7.9	0.0	10.2	57.0	1,999	192	104	2,636	11,920	53,396	5,898
Delaware	80.1	1,934	71.5	1.7	5.9	0.0	2.4	56.3	1,357	74	154	2,450	15,600	44,448	4,230
Dewey	31.7	6,636	49.7	0.2	2.9	9.2	14.3	8.2	1,718	30	18	410	2,130	57,194	6,315
Ellis	30.2	7,367	36.1	47.3	0.6	0.0	4.4	13.0	3,179	22	15	361	1,760	59,351	7,300
Garfield	196.4	3,209	47.9	2.4	5.3	0.1	7.4	189.6	3,098	489	1,386	3,284	27,650	59,540	7,474
Garvin	89.3	3,271	48.3	13.4	4.7	0.0	8.8	23.0	841	80	103	1,670	10,970	48,994	5,079
Grady	154.9	2,916	45.5	28.8	4.1	0.0	7.2	30.5	575	92	200	2,661	21,620	59,044	6,587
Grant	14.3	3,176	61.0	1.3	3.6	0.0	8.2	4.8	1,069	26	16	325	1,960	62,780	9,453
Greer	17.2	2,824	46.1	10.9	6.9	0.0	14.6	3.8	617	26	18	565	1,940	39,165	3,291
Harmon	8.0	2,738	65.6	4.3	8.1	0.0	0.4	0.3	109	21	10	281	970	41,497	4,582
Harper	17.7	4,809	42.7	7.9	3.9	0.0	26.2	2.4	653	23	14	423	1,600	48,622	4,576
Haskell	31.5	2,434	63.9	0.9	4.0	0.2	11.6	2.2	171	57	47	565	4,560	37,370	3,037
Hughes	38.5	2,780	61.1	4.7	3.7	0.0	13.2	24.3	1,755	35	45	977	4,660	38,828	3,444
Jackson	175.1	6,672	28.3	40.8	3.6	0.0	5.4	32.6	1,243	1,396	1,354	2,294	10,790	46,575	4,291
Jefferson	21.5	3,367	52.8	2.1	2.8	0.0	12.1	30.4	4,768	28	23	360	2,230	39,053	3,587
Johnston	21.5	1,952	72.5	4.2	4.8	0.0	3.1	3.8	343	46	40	932	4,220	41,436	3,400
Kay	166.0	3,621	41.7	1.9	7.4	0.0	9.5	127.9	2,790	105	163	4,313	19,000	52,656	5,952
Kingfisher	52.9	3,526	63.6	1.6	4.5	0.0	9.8	16.6	1,106	45	58	889	6,810	69,932	9,084

1. Based on the resident population estimated as of July 1 of the year shown.

Table B. States and Counties — **Land Area and Population**

State / county code	CBSA code[1]	County code[2]	STATE County	Land area[3] (sq. mi)	Total persons 2017	Rank	Per square mile	White	Black	American Indian, Alaska Native	Asian and Pacific Islander	Percent Hispanic or Latino[4]	Under 5 years	5 to 17 years	18 to 24 years	25 to 34 years	35 to 44 years	45 to 54 years
				1	2	3	4	5	6	7	8	9	10	11	12	13	14	15
			OKLAHOMA— Cont'd															
40,075		6	Kiowa	1,015.1	8,893	2,512	8.8	77.7	5.2	8.3	0.9	11.7	6.7	17.0	8.0	10.7	10.8	12.1
40,077		7	Latimer	722.1	10,411	2,396	14.4	72.8	2.0	28.8	1.0	3.6	5.8	15.9	10.0	10.8	10.3	12.1
40,079	22,900	2	Le Flore	1,589.3	49,731	993	31.3	77.1	2.8	17.8	1.2	6.9	6.3	17.6	8.3	12.2	12.0	12.7
40,081	36,420	1	Lincoln	952.3	35,142	1,298	36.9	87.3	2.7	11.2	0.8	3.4	6.3	18.1	7.5	11.5	11.2	13.1
40,083	36,420	1	Logan	743.8	46,784	1,036	62.9	81.2	9.6	6.2	1.2	6.2	6.0	17.6	10.6	11.4	12.7	12.6
40,085		9	Love	514.0	10,034	2,430	19.5	75.1	3.2	9.6	0.9	15.7	6.6	18.1	7.9	12.6	11.4	11.9
40,087	36,420	1	McClain	570.7	39,343	1,194	68.9	84.2	1.4	10.7	1.0	8.0	6.2	19.5	7.7	12.0	13.5	12.9
40,089		7	McCurtain	1,850.6	32,808	1,363	17.7	68.7	9.6	20.8	1.8	5.9	7.0	18.2	8.2	12.1	11.3	12.5
40,091		6	McIntosh	618.5	19,742	1,839	31.9	75.0	4.5	24.7	1.0	2.7	5.6	14.6	7.0	9.9	10.1	12.1
40,093		9	Major	955.0	7,693	2,616	8.1	87.3	1.3	3.5	0.7	9.5	6.7	18.6	6.4	10.6	11.5	11.3
40,095		6	Marshall	371.6	16,434	2,016	44.2	70.5	2.3	14.4	0.7	17.8	5.7	17.1	7.8	10.2	11.0	11.9
40,097		6	Mayes	655.4	40,921	1,157	62.4	73.7	1.1	30.0	0.8	3.6	6.0	17.6	8.1	11.8	11.8	12.5
40,099		7	Murray	416.5	13,853	2,176	33.3	78.3	2.3	18.3	0.9	6.6	5.9	17.4	7.4	11.4	11.7	12.5
40,101	34,780	4	Muskogee	810.4	69,086	772	85.2	63.2	12.8	25.2	1.1	6.2	6.6	17.8	9.2	12.9	12.1	12.0
40,103		6	Noble	731.9	11,277	2,336	15.4	85.3	2.7	11.6	1.0	3.8	5.7	17.8	7.3	11.6	10.9	13.4
40,105		6	Nowata	565.8	10,306	2,403	18.2	75.7	3.5	26.3	0.8	3.0	5.8	17.0	7.5	11.8	11.4	12.8
40,107		6	Okfuskee	618.6	12,140	2,282	19.6	67.6	8.6	25.5	0.9	3.9	5.9	17.3	8.0	12.5	12.4	13.4
40,109	36,420	1	Oklahoma	708.8	787,958	80	1,111.7	59.9	17.2	5.7	4.6	17.5	7.7	18.1	9.0	15.8	12.8	11.5
40,111	46,140	2	Okmulgee	697.3	38,930	1,207	55.8	69.8	10.4	23.5	0.9	4.2	6.2	17.9	9.5	11.8	11.2	11.9
40,113	46,140	2	Osage	2,246.6	47,233	1,030	21.0	69.9	12.5	20.7	0.7	3.6	5.2	17.1	7.6	11.5	11.5	13.0
40,115	33,060	6	Ottawa	470.8	31,312	1,399	66.5	72.3	1.6	25.9	2.1	5.7	7.1	17.9	9.7	11.6	11.2	11.7
40,117	46,140	2	Pawnee	568.2	16,472	2,012	29.0	82.2	1.7	18.0	0.8	3.0	5.9	17.9	7.4	10.8	11.5	13.1
40,119	44,660	4	Payne	684.7	81,575	694	119.1	81.7	5.1	8.3	5.6	4.7	5.5	13.9	26.8	13.8	9.9	8.5
40,121	32,540	5	Pittsburg	1,305.5	44,184	1,089	33.8	76.6	4.3	20.8	0.9	5.0	5.9	16.3	7.5	13.2	11.9	12.3
40,123	10,220	7	Pontotoc	720.4	38,224	1,220	53.1	72.5	3.8	24.7	1.5	5.3	6.6	17.4	11.1	14.2	11.3	11.2
40,125	43,060	4	Pottawatomie	787.7	72,226	750	91.7	78.3	4.4	17.5	1.4	5.1	6.1	17.7	9.6	12.9	12.4	12.6
40,127		9	Pushmataha	1,395.8	11,173	2,342	8.0	76.3	1.8	23.0	0.6	4.0	6.5	16.1	6.9	11.1	10.4	12.4
40,129		9	Roger Mills	1,141.1	3,716	2,921	3.3	85.4	1.9	6.9	0.7	7.5	6.9	19.1	6.5	10.0	11.2	12.0
40,131	46,140	2	Rogers	675.7	91,444	643	135.3	79.6	1.8	20.2	1.9	4.7	5.9	17.9	8.8	12.3	12.0	13.5
40,133		7	Seminole	632.8	24,878	1,615	39.3	70.9	6.3	24.4	0.9	5.2	6.6	18.5	8.9	11.1	11.6	12.3
40,135	22,900	2	Sequoyah	673.3	41,252	1,147	61.3	71.9	2.6	29.7	1.1	4.2	6.0	16.8	8.4	11.7	11.9	13.4
40,137	20,340	4	Stephens	870.2	43,332	1,108	49.8	84.3	2.9	8.8	1.0	7.7	5.9	17.4	7.4	11.8	11.7	12.0
40,139	25,100	7	Texas	2,041.3	20,900	1,781	10.2	45.8	5.3	1.6	3.2	45.7	8.1	19.8	10.9	14.7	12.8	11.6
40,141		6	Tillman	871.1	7,433	2,632	8.5	62.2	8.5	5.1	0.8	26.5	6.1	17.6	7.7	11.0	11.0	12.8
40,143	46,140	2	Tulsa	570.3	646,266	103	1,133.2	66.9	12.1	9.9	4.2	12.7	7.2	18.2	8.9	14.8	12.8	12.1
40,145	46,140	2	Wagoner	561.6	78,657	708	140.1	78.4	4.7	16.0	2.3	6.1	6.0	18.5	7.5	12.9	13.0	13.1
40,147	12,780	4	Washington	415.5	51,932	960	125.0	78.9	3.8	15.2	2.7	5.9	6.3	17.6	7.8	12.7	11.2	11.5
40,149		7	Washita	1,003.2	11,134	2,344	11.1	85.8	1.9	4.8	0.6	9.8	6.7	18.3	7.1	12.2	11.4	11.3
40,151		7	Woods	1,286.5	9,031	2,500	7.0	85.3	4.4	4.1	1.6	7.3	6.7	14.1	16.8	14.7	10.3	9.8
40,153	49,260	7	Woodward	1,242.4	20,459	1,799	16.5	81.8	2.4	4.2	1.0	12.6	7.0	18.0	8.6	14.0	13.2	11.6
41,000		0	OREGON	95,986.7	4,142,776	X	43.2	78.8	2.7	2.4	6.5	13.1	5.7	15.4	8.8	14.2	13.2	12.4
41,001		7	Baker	3,068.0	16,054	2,035	5.2	93.0	1.3	2.5	1.7	4.2	5.2	14.4	6.5	10.9	10.0	11.4
41,003	18,700	3	Benton	675.2	90,951	645	134.7	83.9	1.8	1.6	9.1	7.5	4.2	12.4	22.7	13.3	10.0	9.9
41,005	38,900	1	Clackamas	1,870.7	412,672	170	220.6	84.9	1.6	1.6	6.5	8.7	5.5	16.3	7.6	12.3	13.1	13.6
41,007	11,820	4	Clatsop	828.3	39,182	1,198	47.3	87.9	1.2	2.1	2.9	8.6	5.4	13.8	7.7	12.2	11.6	11.6
41,009	38,900	1	Columbia	658.0	51,782	963	78.7	91.5	1.2	2.9	2.6	5.2	5.4	16.0	7.2	11.4	12.2	13.9
41,011	18,300	5	Coos	1,596.0	63,888	831	40.0	88.9	1.0	5.2	2.5	6.5	5.1	13.5	6.6	11.1	10.4	11.5
41,013	39,260	6	Crook	2,978.9	23,123	1,676	7.8	89.7	0.7	2.5	1.2	7.8	5.4	14.2	6.6	10.2	11.0	11.5
41,015	15,060	7	Curry	1,628.4	22,669	1,691	13.9	89.3	0.9	4.4	1.7	7.1	4.0	10.6	4.9	8.8	8.4	11.1
41,017	13,460	3	Deschutes	3,017.6	186,875	350	61.9	89.5	0.9	1.7	2.3	8.0	5.2	15.3	6.9	12.9	13.0	12.8
41,019	40,700	4	Douglas	5,035.7	109,405	553	21.7	90.7	0.9	3.6	2.1	5.9	5.2	14.1	6.7	11.0	10.4	11.7
41,021		9	Gilliam	1,204.7	1,855	3,062	1.5	90.8	0.8	2.6	1.6	6.3	4.8	14.9	5.7	7.6	10.4	11.5
41,023		9	Grant	4,527.8	7,190	2,652	1.6	93.8	0.8	2.9	1.3	3.7	4.7	13.3	5.5	9.4	10.1	10.6
41,025		7	Harney	10,134.4	7,289	2,642	0.7	89.4	1.5	5.4	1.4	5.3	6.0	15.2	6.9	10.5	11.0	11.2
41,027	26,220	6	Hood River	522.1	23,377	1,664	44.8	65.7	0.8	1.6	2.7	31.3	6.6	17.9	7.9	12.7	13.0	13.2
41,029	32,780	3	Jackson	2,783.2	217,479	307	78.1	83.6	1.3	2.4	2.8	12.9	5.6	15.1	7.5	12.7	11.5	11.7
41,031		6	Jefferson	1,782.2	23,758	1,651	13.3	62.2	1.4	17.3	1.7	19.8	6.6	17.0	7.8	12.7	11.0	12.3
41,033	24,420	3	Josephine	1,638.7	86,352	665	52.7	89.5	0.9	2.9	2.1	7.5	5.2	14.4	6.6	10.6	10.3	11.7
41,035	28,900	5	Klamath	5,942.7	66,935	794	11.3	81.1	1.4	5.9	2.1	13.1	6.2	15.4	8.2	12.5	10.6	11.8
41,037		7	Lake	8,138.6	7,863	2,606	1.0	87.8	1.3	4.2	1.7	8.5	5.6	14.0	6.4	9.7	11.2	12.5
41,039	21,660	2	Lane	4,555.7	374,748	185	82.3	85.6	1.9	2.8	4.9	8.9	5.0	13.7	12.7	13.0	11.9	11.4
41,041	35,440	5	Lincoln	980.4	48,920	1,005	49.9	85.3	1.1	5.2	2.3	9.3	4.7	12.5	5.8	9.8	10.1	11.3
41,043	10,540	3	Linn	2,287.1	125,047	506	54.7	87.8	1.1	2.7	2.3	9.1	6.2	16.6	7.8	13.5	11.8	12.1
41,045	36,620	6	Malheur	9,887.6	30,480	1,421	3.1	62.3	1.6	1.6	2.1	34.0	7.2	18.4	9.7	13.1	12.1	11.4
41,047	41,420	2	Marion	1,180.6	341,286	205	289.1	68.0	1.8	2.1	4.3	26.7	6.7	18.1	9.3	13.9	12.7	11.8

1. CBSA = Core Based Statistical Area. See Appendix A for explanation. See Appendix B for list of metropolitan areas with component counties. Service of USDA Rural-Urban Continuum Codes. See Appendix A for definition. 3. Dry land or land partially or temporarily covered by water.
2. County type code from the Economic Research Service of USDA.
4. May be of any race.

Table B. States and Counties — Population and Households

| | Population, 2017 (cont.) | | | | Population change, 2000-2017 | | | | | | | Households, 2012-2016 | | | | |
| | Age (percent) (cont.) | | | | Total persons | | Percent change | | Components of change, 2010-2017 | | | | | Percent | | |
STATE County	55 to 64 years	65 to 74 years	75 years and over	Percent female	2000	2010	2000-2010	2010-2017	Births	Deaths	Net Migration	Number	Persons per house-hold	Family house-holds	Female family house-holder[1]	One person
	16	17	18	19	20	21	22	23	24	25	26	27	28	29	30	31
OKLAHOMA— Cont'd																
Kiowa	15.3	11.0	8.4	50.3	10,227	9,446	-7.6	-5.9	856	968	-441	3,956	2.29	66.5	11.5	28.2
Latimer	13.3	11.4	10.5	49.1	10,692	11,154	4.3	-6.7	906	882	-772	4,041	2.54	71.3	14.7	24.6
Le Flore	13.3	10.4	7.3	49.8	48,109	50,384	4.7	-1.3	4,264	4,346	-554	18,313	2.65	70.3	12.1	24.8
Lincoln	14.4	10.4	7.5	50.1	32,080	34,273	6.8	2.5	2,934	2,662	611	13,047	2.62	71.0	9.4	25.9
Logan	14.0	9.2	5.9	50.5	33,924	41,853	23.4	11.8	3,661	2,610	3,848	15,273	2.84	72.4	10.1	24.1
Love	12.6	11.2	7.6	50.2	8,831	9,421	6.7	6.5	887	832	560	3,113	3.10	74.9	11.1	22.9
McClain	13.1	9.2	6.1	50.6	27,740	34,506	24.4	14.0	3,100	2,416	4,119	13,532	2.73	75.3	8.6	21.9
McCurtain	12.9	10.2	7.7	50.9	34,402	33,154	-3.6	-1.0	3,299	2,908	-717	12,973	2.51	70.0	15.1	26.6
McIntosh	15.8	13.9	11.1	50.3	19,456	20,252	4.1	-2.5	1,567	2,295	229	8,302	2.39	68.1	10.4	28.4
Major	14.6	10.4	9.8	51.3	7,545	7,527	-0.2	2.2	759	608	19	2,975	2.56	71.5	7.8	23.6
Marshall	14.2	12.4	9.7	50.7	13,184	15,836	20.1	3.8	1,342	1,372	630	5,969	2.65	69.0	10.1	27.2
Mayes	14.1	10.8	7.3	50.2	38,369	41,264	7.5	-0.8	3,582	3,574	-324	15,735	2.56	71.3	10.9	24.9
Murray	14.6	10.9	8.2	49.9	12,623	13,488	6.9	2.7	1,156	1,370	578	5,387	2.49	68.3	9.9	25.8
Muskogee	13.0	9.5	6.9	51.2	69,451	70,988	2.2	-2.7	6,790	6,671	-2,008	26,168	2.53	66.9	14.4	28.6
Noble	13.8	10.8	8.7	50.4	11,411	11,561	1.3	-2.5	930	964	-247	4,699	2.39	72.8	8.9	24.6
Nowata	14.5	10.5	8.7	50.3	10,569	10,536	-0.3	-2.2	843	1,006	-61	4,087	2.52	70.3	12.9	26.7
Okfuskee	13.2	9.8	7.5	46.1	11,814	12,191	3.2	-0.4	1,187	1,219	-9	3,959	2.77	69.0	12.2	27.6
Oklahoma	11.9	7.9	5.4	51.0	660,448	718,377	8.8	9.7	89,494	50,269	30,318	294,672	2.54	62.0	13.9	31.3
Okmulgee	13.3	10.3	7.9	50.7	39,685	40,069	1.0	-2.8	3,682	3,723	-1,091	14,835	2.56	64.4	14.7	30.8
Osage	15.0	11.4	7.7	50.0	44,437	47,485	6.9	-0.5	3,277	3,452	-59	18,218	2.55	70.0	10.3	26.9
Ottawa	12.6	10.3	7.9	50.9	33,194	31,848	-4.1	-1.7	3,184	3,202	-511	11,982	2.59	68.1	13.0	27.5
Pawnee	14.2	10.9	8.1	50.3	16,612	16,579	-0.2	-0.6	1,430	1,499	-37	6,238	2.60	72.9	11.5	23.5
Payne	9.4	6.8	5.3	48.8	68,190	77,350	13.4	5.5	6,723	4,020	1,549	30,164	2.38	54.1	8.2	31.8
Pittsburg	13.2	11.1	8.6	49.0	43,953	45,837	4.3	-3.6	3,797	4,374	-1,045	17,903	2.37	66.4	11.7	28.5
Pontotoc	11.9	9.0	7.4	51.4	35,143	37,492	6.7	2.0	3,897	3,199	60	14,625	2.52	64.7	13.1	28.3
Pottawatomie	12.7	9.4	6.6	52.2	65,521	69,442	6.0	4.0	6,616	5,759	1,958	25,938	2.63	68.8	13.1	26.9
Pushmataha	14.0	12.8	9.8	50.9	11,667	11,572	-0.8	-3.4	1,008	1,191	-218	4,655	2.37	62.4	9.8	33.9
Roger Mills	13.9	11.2	9.3	50.2	3,436	3,647	6.1	1.9	378	240	-69	1,324	2.80	64.4	10.2	29.5
Rogers	13.6	9.4	6.5	50.2	70,641	86,911	23.0	5.2	7,285	5,964	3,280	33,570	2.64	74.8	10.2	21.6
Seminole	13.3	10.0	7.7	51.0	24,894	25,482	2.4	-2.4	2,435	2,472	-552	9,162	2.70	68.6	14.6	26.8
Sequoyah	13.3	10.8	7.7	50.6	38,972	42,439	8.9	-2.8	3,168	3,629	-712	15,467	2.65	71.6	14.6	24.7
Stephens	14.4	10.8	8.6	51.6	43,182	45,048	4.3	-3.8	3,918	4,035	-1,576	17,527	2.51	65.9	10.5	29.9
Texas	10.6	6.7	4.9	46.4	20,107	20,640	2.7	1.3	2,570	1,042	-1,310	7,038	2.98	69.7	9.1	26.3
Tillman	14.1	11.2	8.6	49.5	9,287	7,992	-13.9	-7.0	709	658	-616	3,159	2.29	67.3	14.7	27.9
Tulsa	12.1	8.2	5.8	51.2	563,299	603,433	7.1	7.1	68,606	41,297	15,817	248,811	2.50	63.4	13.5	30.4
Wagoner	13.2	9.8	6.0	50.4	57,491	73,087	27.1	7.6	6,314	4,578	3,841	27,871	2.72	74.9	11.1	20.8
Washington	13.6	10.0	9.1	51.2	48,996	50,974	4.0	-1.3	4,708	4,423	712	20,810	2.46	66.5	11.2	28.9
Washita	14.8	9.6	8.4	50.3	11,508	11,629	1.1	-4.3	1,105	1,019	-583	4,539	2.51	72.8	11.4	23.7
Woods	11.5	8.2	8.0	46.4	9,089	8,878	-2.3	1.7	768	720	93	3,347	2.47	61.1	8.6	29.6
Woodward	12.4	8.4	6.8	47.6	18,486	20,081	8.6	1.9	2,233	1,409	-469	7,301	2.74	70.0	11.1	24.7
OREGON	13.2	10.4	6.7	50.4	3,421,399	3,831,072	12.0	8.1	330,894	246,980	227,565	1,545,745	2.52	63.4	10.6	27.8
Baker	15.9	14.7	11.1	49.2	16,741	16,138	-3.6	-0.5	1,188	1,467	210	7,011	2.20	61.1	7.6	33.8
Benton	12.0	9.6	6.0	49.9	78,153	85,592	9.5	6.3	5,368	4,058	4,036	34,193	2.39	55.7	6.5	28.6
Clackamas	14.3	10.8	6.7	50.8	338,391	375,994	11.1	9.8	29,454	23,435	30,661	151,150	2.59	68.6	9.5	24.4
Clatsop	16.2	13.9	7.8	50.6	35,630	37,029	3.9	5.8	3,060	2,808	1,899	15,876	2.32	61.1	10.9	31.4
Columbia	15.5	11.5	6.8	50.1	43,560	49,353	13.3	4.9	3,650	3,086	1,868	18,941	2.60	64.3	9.6	25.9
Coos	16.4	14.8	10.5	50.7	62,779	63,043	0.4	1.3	4,504	6,316	2,694	25,755	2.40	61.2	9.2	32.6
Crook	16.4	15.3	9.2	50.3	19,182	20,978	9.4	10.2	1,459	1,729	2,394	9,155	2.32	64.7	8.3	29.1
Curry	19.0	19.9	13.3	50.8	21,137	22,364	5.8	1.4	1,304	2,667	1,661	10,396	2.12	56.8	7.2	35.2
Deschutes	14.4	12.4	7.0	50.6	115,367	157,733	36.7	18.5	12,707	9,904	26,052	67,880	2.50	66.2	9.4	25.3
Douglas	15.7	14.5	10.6	50.7	100,399	107,667	7.2	1.6	7,916	10,174	4,086	43,937	2.40	65.7	11.6	26.7
Gilliam	18.1	14.7	12.4	48.6	1,915	1,873	-2.2	-1.0	134	140	-16	788	2.41	65.5	10.2	28.8
Grant	16.7	16.5	13.1	49.7	7,935	7,445	-6.2	-3.4	449	584	-121	3,151	2.24	65.6	8.1	29.5
Harney	15.8	13.4	10.0	49.5	7,609	7,422	-2.5	-1.8	597	608	-123	3,059	2.30	68.4	8.3	25.9
Hood River	13.5	8.9	6.3	50.1	20,411	22,346	9.5	4.6	2,070	1,267	234	8,213	2.66	63.4	6.3	28.2
Jackson	14.3	12.8	8.7	51.1	181,269	203,206	12.1	7.0	16,965	16,473	13,778	83,969	2.47	64.3	11.5	28.4
Jefferson	13.6	11.9	7.1	48.4	19,009	21,719	14.3	9.4	2,099	1,493	1,427	7,577	2.84	71.1	14.4	23.2
Josephine	15.8	14.9	10.5	51.3	75,726	82,713	9.2	4.4	6,081	8,558	6,119	34,778	2.38	63.9	11.1	29.1
Klamath	14.5	12.7	8.1	50.3	63,775	66,380	4.1	0.8	5,857	5,418	149	27,084	2.39	64.8	11.7	26.9
Lake	16.3	14.4	9.8	46.5	7,422	7,886	6.3	-0.3	560	638	57	3,409	2.13	56.0	7.1	37.6
Lane	13.6	11.4	7.3	50.7	322,959	351,713	8.9	6.5	25,933	24,506	21,788	146,692	2.40	59.3	10.8	29.1
Lincoln	18.4	17.6	9.8	51.8	44,479	46,032	3.5	6.3	3,146	4,165	3,888	20,434	2.26	60.3	8.9	31.7
Linn	13.8	10.9	7.3	50.5	103,069	116,672	13.2	7.2	10,685	8,773	6,504	45,378	2.61	67.9	11.3	25.0
Malheur	11.6	9.1	7.3	45.7	31,615	31,312	-1.0	-2.7	3,156	2,136	-1,873	10,294	2.61	67.1	13.4	28.6
Marion	12.2	9.0	6.2	50.1	284,834	315,343	10.7	8.2	32,146	19,480	13,470	115,196	2.75	68.8	13.7	25.3

1. No spouse present.

Table B. States and Counties — Population, Vital Statistics, Health, and Crime

STATE County	Persons in group quarters, 2017	Daytime Population, 2012-2016 Number	Daytime Population Employment/ residence ratio	Births, 2017 Total	Births Rate[1]	Deaths, 2017 Number	Deaths Rate[1]	Persons under 65 with no health insurance, 2016 Number	Percent	Medicare, 2017 Total beneficiaries	Enrolled in Original Medicare	Enrolled in Medicare Advantage	Serious crimes known to police[2], 2016 Total Number	Rate[3]
	32	33	34	35	36	37	38	39	40	41	42	43	44	45
OKLAHOMA— Cont'd														
Kiowa	171	8,693	0.86	123	13.8	112	12.6	1,191	16.7	2,151	1,983	168	140	1,548
Latimer	575	10,566	0.98	134	12.9	100	9.6	1,421	17.9	1,701	1,532	169	126	1,223
Le Flore	1,614	45,922	0.78	579	11.6	667	13.4	8,839	22.3	11,591	10,072	1,520	1,290	2,623
Lincoln	386	29,038	0.61	414	11.8	351	10.0	4,865	17.0	6,548	5,295	1,253	569	1,625
Logan	2,176	34,555	0.48	553	11.8	391	8.4	5,238	13.9	5,781	4,523	1,258	925	1,985
Love	88	11,499	1.43	122	12.2	121	12.1	1,329	16.4	2,071	1,923	147	109	1,100
McClain	194	31,252	0.64	452	11.5	352	8.9	4,775	14.6	7,537	6,458	1,080	902	2,338
McCurtain	454	32,880	0.98	432	13.2	438	13.4	5,532	20.8	7,215	6,609	606	1,110	3,378
McIntosh	345	18,338	0.74	235	11.9	310	15.7	3,029	20.7	5,676	5,089	587	495	2,496
Major	77	7,445	0.92	101	13.1	74	9.6	964	15.5	1,558	1,485	73	81	1,040
Marshall	329	15,142	0.85	187	11.4	151	9.2	2,751	21.9	3,736	3,406	330	364	2,243
Mayes	565	39,412	0.91	466	11.4	548	13.4	5,665	17.0	8,737	7,315	1,421	680	1,675
Murray	313	12,962	0.86	167	12.1	199	14.4	1,770	16.0	2,954	2,760	194	265	1,899
Muskogee	3,504	73,414	1.13	887	12.8	897	13.0	10,496	19.2	16,487	14,425	2,062	2,320	3,359
Noble	273	11,306	0.97	113	10.0	127	11.3	1,334	14.5	2,226	2,085	141	216	1,879
Nowata	157	8,668	0.56	122	11.8	146	14.2	1,535	18.6	2,330	2,100	230	165	1,573
Okfuskee	1,227	11,221	0.74	144	11.9	152	12.5	1,707	18.7	2,578	2,359	220	298	2,460
Oklahoma	14,761	872,763	1.30	12,381	15.7	6,986	8.9	105,836	15.8	135,073	102,551	32,521	32,112	4,093
Okmulgee	1,375	36,471	0.81	497	12.8	524	13.5	5,418	17.5	8,345	7,010	1,335	1,188	3,061
Osage	1,501	38,710	0.52	456	9.7	554	11.7	5,536	15.0	3,951	3,341	610	1,243	2,604
Ottawa	968	31,936	0.99	430	13.7	501	16.0	4,639	18.5	7,219	6,491	728	NA	NA
Pawnee	194	14,053	0.63	193	11.7	184	11.2	2,214	16.6	3,682	3,210	472	217	1,329
Payne	7,781	82,162	1.06	958	11.7	576	7.1	10,092	15.7	12,171	11,238	933	2,757	3,398
Pittsburg	2,419	45,117	1.03	488	11.0	560	12.7	5,580	16.5	9,926	9,030	896	1,444	3,270
Pontotoc	1,700	39,919	1.10	502	13.1	510	13.3	5,423	17.6	7,814	7,370	444	930	2,439
Pottawatomie	3,047	68,784	0.90	847	11.7	809	11.2	9,558	16.5	14,657	11,623	3,034	2,487	3,456
Pushmataha	110	10,214	0.77	154	13.8	150	13.4	1,681	19.9	2,844	2,667	177	115	1,041
Roger Mills	11	3,736	1.00	57	15.3	20	5.4	450	15.4	715	690	25	59	1,553
Rogers	1,216	76,997	0.69	1,034	11.3	846	9.3	9,881	12.9	14,441	10,116	4,325	1,822	2,000
Seminole	581	24,639	0.92	329	13.2	329	13.2	3,814	18.9	5,376	4,672	704	653	2,567
Sequoyah	464	36,460	0.68	459	11.1	538	13.0	6,673	19.9	9,270	7,840	1,431	1,205	2,961
Stephens	540	44,469	0.99	494	11.4	538	12.4	5,740	16.2	9,398	8,271	1,127	1,407	3,179
Texas	572	20,865	0.94	346	16.6	134	6.4	3,950	21.8	2,432	2,344	88	319	1,482
Tillman	267	7,051	0.82	84	11.3	72	9.7	1,105	19.0	1,635	1,560	74	222	3,005
Tulsa	9,863	693,077	1.21	9,555	14.8	5,986	9.3	87,035	15.9	122,922	84,414	38,508	34,067	5,298
Wagoner	319	54,092	0.36	831	10.6	685	8.7	9,236	14.1	6,840	4,812	2,028	1,798	2,341
Washington	798	53,387	1.07	663	12.8	652	12.6	6,350	15.2	12,005	10,993	1,012	1,352	3,358
Washita	206	9,784	0.62	149	13.4	146	13.1	1,602	17.0	2,422	2,272	149	196	1,688
Woods	1,001	10,152	1.23	101	11.2	105	11.6	919	13.6	1,586	1,525	61	114	1,220
Woodward	1,236	21,895	1.08	281	13.7	255	12.5	2,441	14.7	3,402	3,213	190	497	2,282
OREGON	89,553	4,029,437	1.03	46,551	11.2	35,527	8.6	248,573	7.4	809,108	446,274	362,834	132,175	3,229
Baker	428	15,692	0.94	149	9.3	193	12.0	920	8.0	4,754	4,421	333	430	2,674
Benton	5,142	88,797	1.03	760	8.4	582	6.4	4,728	6.6	13,634	7,241	6,393	2,376	2,684
Clackamas	2,956	360,858	0.82	4,290	10.4	3,506	8.5	19,633	5.8	79,122	30,862	48,261	8,815	2,272
Clatsop	908	38,967	1.08	427	10.9	391	10.0	2,296	7.6	10,212	7,835	2,376	1,423	3,724
Columbia	476	40,268	0.53	552	10.7	472	9.1	2,622	6.3	10,731	5,334	5,397	684	1,369
Coos	1,219	63,060	1.01	629	9.8	882	13.8	3,878	8.3	19,328	17,085	2,243	2,681	4,394
Crook	246	20,445	0.89	240	10.4	248	10.7	1,281	7.7	6,386	4,916	1,470	588	2,683
Curry	303	22,137	0.97	181	8.0	362	16.0	1,319	8.8	8,431	7,412	1,019	NA	NA
Deschutes	1,318	171,005	1.00	1,869	10.0	1,478	7.9	11,449	7.9	40,965	29,157	11,809	4,217	2,342
Douglas	1,878	106,375	0.97	1,108	10.1	1,402	12.8	6,018	7.5	32,143	21,318	10,825	3,103	2,864
Gilliam	21	2,021	1.15	18	9.7	25	13.5	72	5.4	588	546	41	NA	NA
Grant	109	7,060	0.94	59	8.2	81	11.3	433	8.6	2,169	1,814	356	136	1,895
Harney	141	7,191	0.99	83	11.4	77	10.6	443	8.1	1,917	1,755	162	228	3,165
Hood River	794	24,238	1.13	281	12.0	163	7.0	2,084	10.6	3,982	3,080	901	273	1,166
Jackson	4,283	211,477	1.01	2,389	11.0	2,307	10.6	13,352	8.0	53,998	36,981	17,017	9,958	4,616
Jefferson	946	21,608	0.91	291	12.2	221	9.3	2,101	11.9	5,406	3,991	1,415	461	2,004
Josephine	1,481	82,695	0.95	879	10.2	1,183	13.7	4,947	7.9	25,547	16,024	9,523	2,671	3,119
Klamath	1,040	65,524	0.98	829	12.4	787	11.8	4,867	9.5	15,913	12,081	3,831	NA	NA
Lake	454	7,851	1.02	85	10.8	102	13.0	486	8.9	2,137	1,964	173	NA	NA
Lane	8,355	361,603	1.01	3,685	9.8	3,481	9.3	23,734	8.1	82,159	40,587	41,572	13,360	3,669
Lincoln	806	47,018	1.02	435	8.9	582	11.9	3,371	9.8	14,473	11,687	2,787	585	1,572
Linn	1,209	116,342	0.93	1,555	12.4	1,301	10.4	7,159	7.2	29,928	14,636	15,291	3,429	2,810
Malheur	3,263	34,181	1.35	443	14.5	257	8.4	2,220	10.1	5,971	5,239	732	932	3,068
Marion	10,972	332,051	1.04	4,583	13.4	2,840	8.3	25,002	9.1	60,392	25,513	34,879	10,709	3,189

1. Per 1,000 estimated resident population.   2. Data for serious crimes have not been adjusted for underreporting; this may affect comparability between geographic areas and over time.
3. Per 100,000 population estimated by the FBI.

Items 32—45

Table B. States and Counties — Crime, Education, Money Income, and Poverty

STATE County	Serious crimes known to police, 2016 (cont.)[1] Rate Violent	Property	Enrollment[3] Total	Percent private	High school graduate or less	Bachelor's degree or more	Total current spending (mil dol)	Current spending per student (dollars)	Per capita income[6]	Median income (dollars)	with income of less than $50,000	with income of $200,000 or more	Median household income (dollars)	All persons	Children under 18 years	Children 5 to 17 years in families
	46	47	48	49	50	51	52	53	54	55	56	57	58	59	60	61
OKLAHOMA— Cont'd																
Kiowa	66	1,482	2,062	3.9	52.7	17.6	14.4	8,619	22,857	38,853	61.6	1.2	36,069	22.3	32.3	31.3
Latimer	136	1,087	2,566	5.8	50.6	15.9	13.1	8,623	22,560	39,701	60.8	2.6	35,942	21.0	28.7	25.0
Le Flore	297	2,326	11,545	4.7	59.0	14.5	78.9	7,915	19,138	37,548	62.9	1.2	37,005	21.6	28.4	27.9
Lincoln	228	1,397	8,208	9.7	53.7	14.3	41.3	7,349	23,878	46,592	53.3	2.1	44,914	15.8	23.2	21.9
Logan	200	1,786	12,023	12.8	42.9	26.6	35.5	7,466	27,483	55,698	45.2	5.3	54,305	14.5	19.8	19.1
Love	121	979	2,398	9.6	60.2	13.4	14.0	7,802	20,440	46,646	52.2	1.3	45,200	13.9	21.6	20.0
McClain	163	2,175	9,827	8.5	46.4	22.9	50.4	6,648	27,217	58,673	43.4	3.8	61,730	10.8	15.0	13.6
McCurtain	262	3,117	7,789	6.8	60.2	13.8	56.2	8,122	18,507	33,439	66.9	1.1	32,664	25.7	37.0	36.8
McIntosh	328	2,168	3,993	7.4	56.0	13.8	25.4	8,094	21,456	36,878	63.4	1.8	36,903	21.2	34.1	32.7
Major	51	989	1,777	6.0	53.4	16.9	9.3	8,246	27,797	51,602	47.1	3.2	51,607	12.1	16.2	15.2
Marshall	154	2,089	3,669	4.7	54.5	13.6	23.7	7,861	21,394	42,886	57.7	1.6	41,669	15.7	24.9	23.2
Mayes	229	1,446	9,732	7.9	52.1	15.3	58.2	7,984	21,756	43,302	55.7	1.5	45,922	17.5	24.8	22.5
Murray	265	1,634	2,940	2.5	55.2	20.2	18.1	6,735	24,454	51,752	48.0	2.4	48,008	13.4	17.9	16.5
Muskogee	698	2,661	17,327	7.8	50.4	19.2	105.5	7,633	21,109	41,117	57.8	1.5	40,581	21.4	29.9	28.3
Noble	165	1,714	2,689	2.4	46.7	22.7	18.4	8,513	26,701	49,367	50.8	2.9	50,316	13.4	17.4	15.8
Nowata	181	1,392	2,373	8.1	57.7	12.6	15.3	8,019	21,085	40,302	61.6	0.8	41,800	17.4	26.1	24.6
Okfuskee	281	2,180	2,723	6.6	58.5	12.1	17.2	8,794	17,381	36,044	62.8	1.1	35,106	25.1	29.7	27.2
Oklahoma	601	3,492	200,808	13.8	38.9	30.8	957.6	7,232	28,059	48,987	50.7	4.5	51,082	16.3	24.3	22.1
Okmulgee	371	2,690	9,667	5.4	49.4	15.6	70.5	7,600	20,721	38,712	61.2	1.4	38,446	20.7	28.3	27.0
Osage	320	2,283	11,090	11.1	53.5	16.9	33.1	8,480	23,416	46,342	52.9	1.5	46,074	15.5	21.7	19.7
Ottawa	NA	NA	7,854	6.7	52.4	13.9	47.5	7,813	18,616	37,139	63.8	1.1	39,210	19.1	27.1	27.4
Pawnee	300	1,029	3,702	7.9	55.4	16.5	20.2	7,617	22,750	45,902	53.7	1.7	44,619	16.6	21.9	20.2
Payne	296	3,102	32,055	3.7	35.2	37.1	83.6	7,717	22,409	38,085	61.3	3.4	42,035	25.1	18.9	18.0
Pittsburg	303	2,966	9,456	7.9	50.4	16.1	66.7	8,423	23,339	43,601	56.1	1.7	44,520	14.4	20.2	20.2
Pontotoc	212	2,227	10,216	4.9	45.4	27.0	58.3	8,139	22,710	44,041	54.8	1.8	44,212	16.3	20.6	19.4
Pottawatomie	488	2,968	18,040	12.9	48.9	17.7	98.3	7,305	21,422	44,351	55.8	2.0	42,453	18.0	24.8	23.5
Pushmataha	172	869	2,311	3.5	57.0	14.4	20.8	9,224	22,207	33,784	65.4	2.6	34,222	22.0	33.9	31.8
Roger Mills	211	1,342	896	7.4	46.6	21.2	11.0	14,199	27,869	48,462	51.2	5.9	54,629	13.0	19.3	17.8
Rogers	210	1,790	23,392	14.0	41.6	23.2	104.4	7,443	28,938	59,828	41.1	3.7	62,622	9.1	12.8	11.7
Seminole	326	2,241	6,389	4.7	52.0	13.9	43.1	8,281	19,374	36,870	63.4	2.2	36,671	22.6	32.9	28.7
Sequoyah	354	2,607	9,619	5.2	56.8	14.1	66.3	7,804	18,698	36,301	63.3	0.9	39,629	19.6	31.1	30.1
Stephens	192	2,987	10,064	6.9	53.1	18.0	62.0	7,543	24,555	43,493	55.0	2.6	44,505	16.7	25.4	24.2
Texas	177	1,306	5,582	4.3	57.8	20.1	37.2	8,148	22,923	51,503	48.5	1.8	50,993	13.9	19.2	17.8
Tillman	244	2,762	1,698	4.5	58.6	16.1	15.1	9,600	20,549	37,880	62.0	1.6	36,350	23.6	32.3	31.9
Tulsa	777	4,521	163,616	17.8	37.0	30.7	915.4	7,712	28,970	50,654	49.3	4.5	51,476	15.7	23.5	21.8
Wagoner	212	2,128	19,100	12.3	45.2	21.8	45.7	6,888	26,159	57,590	42.6	2.9	61,882	11.3	15.6	14.9
Washington	301	3,058	11,942	11.5	44.3	26.3	64.0	7,149	28,528	50,038	50.0	4.3	52,283	14.3	20.8	19.5
Washita	353	1,335	2,568	3.6	52.9	21.4	18.8	8,485	25,032	48,715	51.2	2.6	45,642	16.0	23.6	23.2
Woods	86	1,135	2,329	8.7	45.5	26.7	14.6	10,398	27,464	57,079	43.7	3.0	50,441	13.5	17.2	17.4
Woodward	188	2,093	4,894	4.5	50.8	20.9	31.2	7,871	27,308	58,569	44.0	3.1	57,403	12.5	17.6	17.6
OREGON	265	2,964	960,816	15.1	33.9	31.4	5,634.0	9,760	28,822	53,270	47.0	4.3	57,379	13.4	17.2	15.8
Baker	75	2,599	3,213	21.8	41.2	23.0	22.3	8,867	24,776	41,722	59.7	1.8	42,177	17.6	26.2	25.1
Benton	129	2,555	32,591	6.5	19.3	53.7	84.8	9,763	28,986	52,015	48.4	4.9	56,167	18.4	13.0	11.7
Clackamas	160	2,112	94,964	15.6	29.2	34.1	532.4	9,134	35,506	68,915	35.3	7.3	74,460	8.7	10.7	9.2
Clatsop	141	3,582	7,716	10.9	33.7	24.1	51.3	10,300	27,071	47,492	52.5	2.1	49,898	12.9	18.5	17.3
Columbia	164	1,205	10,884	12.6	42.2	19.2	68.5	8,767	27,449	55,146	45.0	2.7	63,055	11.0	13.3	12.2
Coos	197	4,197	11,514	9.2	43.5	18.4	87.6	9,176	24,261	39,110	62.4	2.0	41,403	17.5	25.5	24.5
Crook	488	2,195	3,754	12.9	48.8	16.1	27.8	8,293	22,346	39,583	59.6	0.9	45,350	14.2	22.9	20.6
Curry	NA	NA	3,259	10.4	38.0	23.6	23.4	10,116	24,908	38,661	60.6	0.9	40,682	14.1	24.5	23.7
Deschutes	156	2,186	39,360	12.4	30.6	33.3	245.9	9,802	30,177	54,211	46.6	4.3	61,248	10.6	14.2	13.2
Douglas	226	2,638	20,656	11.7	43.3	16.3	145.9	10,204	23,608	42,052	57.3	1.9	43,202	15.6	23.2	20.7
Gilliam	NA	NA	418	7.2	47.9	17.1	6.5	22,604	23,360	40,556	59.0	1.4	45,728	12.2	20.5	20.2
Grant	98	1,798	1,251	7.4	42.2	21.7	14.0	15,720	23,960	40,193	59.7	1.2	44,309	16.0	24.6	22.5
Harney	389	2,777	1,574	18.3	45.9	17.3	16.3	15,520	22,795	38,431	60.5	2.0	41,846	16.4	23.6	23.1
Hood River	111	1,055	5,183	9.0	44.6	30.1	44.1	10,725	28,347	56,581	42.8	4.7	53,941	10.7	16.8	15.5
Jackson	349	4,266	45,115	12.5	38.2	26.1	282.0	9,745	25,612	46,343	53.6	2.6	48,538	14.6	19.0	17.0
Jefferson	252	1,752	5,247	3.8	45.7	16.1	43.3	11,849	21,630	47,063	52.7	1.2	44,943	17.3	24.7	24.1
Josephine	223	2,896	16,456	11.8	43.6	17.3	102.5	9,557	23,004	37,867	61.3	2.5	38,921	18.0	24.3	22.3
Klamath	NA	NA	15,126	9.7	43.1	18.9	94.4	9,973	23,071	41,951	59.0	1.7	44,678	19.0	27.7	26.2
Lake	NA	NA	1,431	6.8	49.5	17.3	14.5	11,906	20,327	33,453	67.2	0.6	40,095	15.2	25.4	24.5
Lane	325	3,344	93,334	10.1	33.6	28.7	445.8	9,901	25,612	45,222	54.0	2.6	47,933	18.3	19.9	18.1
Lincoln	161	1,411	7,662	10.6	40.5	23.0	50.2	9,690	24,593	41,303	59.0	1.9	41,791	19.6	30.0	27.5
Linn	115	2,695	28,617	10.4	40.8	18.1	185.7	8,265	22,934	46,782	52.7	1.4	50,876	13.1	17.5	17.0
Malheur	155	2,914	7,746	12.3	49.9	13.3	58.6	11,312	17,150	34,720	61.1	1.8	38,130	22.9	31.0	28.8
Marion	226	2,963	84,561	15.8	42.0	22.4	622.5	8,848	23,348	50,775	49.3	2.1	55,954	13.6	19.6	17.9

1. Data for serious crimes have not been adjusted for underreporting; this may affect comparability between geographic areas and over time.   2. Per 100,000 population estimated by the FBI.
3. All persons 3 years old and over enrolled in nursery school through college.   4. Persons 25 years old and over.   5. Elementary and secondary education expenditures.
6. Based on population estimated by the American Community Survey, 2011–2015.

Table B. States and Counties — **Personal Income and Earnings**

STATE County	Personal income, 2016										Earnings, 2016		
			Per capita[1]			Supplements to wages and salaries, employer contributions (mil dol)						Contributions for government social insurance (mil dol)	
	Total (mil dol)	Percent change 2015-2016	Dollars	Rank	Wages and salaries (mil dol)	Pension and insurance	Government social insurance	Proprietors' income (mil dol)	Dividends, interest, and rent (mil dol)	Personal transfer receipts (mil dol)	Total (mil dol)	From employee and self-employed	From employer
	62	63	64	65	66	67	68	69	70	71	72	73	74
OKLAHOMA— Cont'd													
Kiowa	289	-0.2	31,786	2,646	84	19	6	27	50	94	137	16	6
Latimer	336	-2.7	32,302	2,567	132	31	10	17	52	118	191	23	10
Le Flore	1,548	1.3	31,029	2,735	497	99	40	158	198	510	793	89	40
Lincoln	1,189	0.4	33,855	2,342	251	48	19	124	169	303	443	48	19
Logan	1,748	-0.9	37,519	1,734	276	48	22	99	266	337	445	52	22
Love	363	2.2	36,337	1,945	212	56	16	25	51	95	310	34	16
McClain	1,596	0.7	41,257	1,204	353	61	27	129	223	304	570	62	27
McCurtain	997	-1.1	30,366	2,809	416	80	34	74	126	346	603	73	34
McIntosh	636	-0.5	32,093	2,599	132	26	10	44	100	252	212	28	10
Major	287	-9.5	36,927	1,834	93	18	7	36	54	60	154	16	7
Marshall	558	2.5	34,453	2,249	158	30	13	35	81	166	236	30	13
Mayes	1,467	0.0	35,855	2,022	563	99	44	117	192	400	823	95	44
Murray	535	-6.1	38,462	1,576	200	47	15	44	82	134	307	33	15
Muskogee	2,391	-0.2	34,415	2,258	1,270	267	102	176	407	748	1,815	212	102
Noble	448	-0.7	39,370	1,442	213	43	16	28	89	101	300	34	16
Nowata	352	-5.0	33,749	2,357	61	13	5	26	54	100	105	13	5
Okfuskee	346	-0.4	28,405	2,957	81	20	6	37	57	120	145	16	6
Oklahoma	37,256	0.0	47,583	561	24,545	4,088	1,857	5,012	7,235	6,004	35,502	3,761	1,857
Okmulgee	1,246	-0.4	31,787	2,644	376	78	29	65	180	413	547	67	29
Osage	1,539	-2.7	32,184	2,581	274	56	21	133	233	371	484	54	21
Ottawa	1,087	0.3	34,289	2,283	414	86	32	99	169	346	630	71	32
Pawnee	546	-0.3	33,107	2,454	137	30	11	36	75	165	214	26	11
Payne	2,912	0.3	35,896	2,016	1,434	328	106	225	556	523	2,093	220	106
Pittsburg	1,592	2.0	36,040	2,002	737	158	58	90	297	431	1,043	122	58
Pontotoc	1,557	2.5	40,622	1,286	795	166	61	104	260	360	1,126	126	61
Pottawatomie	2,543	-0.5	35,179	2,135	850	158	66	276	401	651	1,349	146	66
Pushmataha	336	0.9	30,380	2,807	96	22	7	28	48	131	152	19	7
Roger Mills	175	-2.8	47,956	542	37	9	3	39	52	26	88	7	3
Rogers	3,775	0.1	41,134	1,217	1,258	214	98	224	565	724	1,793	209	98
Seminole	788	-3.4	31,272	2,707	270	57	21	71	123	262	419	47	21
Sequoyah	1,300	2.4	31,490	2,676	276	63	22	87	206	428	447	55	22
Stephens	1,773	-9.0	40,212	1,336	619	101	48	231	360	428	998	107	48
Texas	875	-11.2	41,455	1,173	378	69	28	228	112	111	702	57	28
Tillman	333	27.1	44,552	822	77	17	6	115	38	70	215	13	6
Tulsa	36,832	-8.3	57,286	184	18,416	2,729	1,409	8,519	7,431	4,907	31,073	2,953	1,409
Wagoner	2,827	1.0	36,388	1,933	387	69	31	179	340	562	666	78	31
Washington	2,375	-10.6	45,593	736	1,103	195	79	256	478	463	1,633	175	79
Washita	357	-6.4	31,150	2,723	75	17	6	25	67	92	123	14	6
Woods	381	-5.9	41,440	1,176	167	37	12	26	138	64	241	26	12
Woodward	909	-6.7	43,650	910	415	72	31	175	161	142	693	66	31
OREGON	185,840	4.2	45,482	X	96,026	13,948	8,223	14,845	36,783	36,636	133,041	8,473	8,223
Baker	585	2.7	36,412	1,929	207	42	19	29	147	188	297	40	19
Benton	3,776	4.0	42,245	1,069	1,916	331	161	269	953	562	2,676	327	161
Clackamas	20,966	4.2	51,379	353	8,405	1,089	734	1,256	4,276	2,931	11,483	1,487	734
Clatsop	1,600	4.6	41,410	1,181	719	118	66	154	314	409	1,057	136	66
Columbia	2,035	4.8	40,080	1,357	447	78	40	86	296	501	651	91	40
Coos	2,536	3.4	39,769	1,394	917	170	85	208	482	852	1,379	183	85
Crook	828	6.1	36,684	1,883	294	47	25	62	170	262	428	57	25
Curry	898	2.4	39,555	1,417	249	45	23	62	219	314	379	54	23
Deschutes	8,668	7.7	47,809	551	3,551	587	322	1,174	2,057	1,689	5,635	690	322
Douglas	4,021	3.9	37,077	1,810	1,563	276	144	232	755	1,351	2,215	307	144
Gilliam	82	1.2	44,085	870	37	7	3	9	17	21	56	6	3
Grant	278	0.4	38,888	1,518	97	25	9	21	63	81	151	19	9
Harney	275	-0.6	37,685	1,710	94	23	8	32	55	79	157	18	8
Hood River	1,127	4.7	48,498	501	513	75	47	123	267	177	757	91	47
Jackson	9,062	4.2	41,852	1,117	3,693	581	334	898	1,975	2,323	5,506	711	334
Jefferson	754	3.5	32,670	2,532	262	54	23	26	122	259	365	49	23
Josephine	3,188	4.1	37,109	1,802	978	160	91	304	628	1,115	1,533	211	91
Klamath	2,395	2.9	36,043	2,001	923	167	86	158	429	787	1,334	179	86
Lake	294	2.5	37,571	1,727	101	25	9	29	68	86	163	18	9
Lane	15,160	3.9	41,027	1,230	6,784	1,080	606	1,271	3,142	3,627	9,741	1,256	606
Lincoln	1,896	3.3	39,665	1,404	708	120	65	175	428	552	1,067	143	65
Linn	4,713	4.3	38,365	1,595	1,972	312	181	334	754	1,396	2,800	372	181
Malheur	904	-0.7	29,714	2,870	481	99	43	74	163	322	696	86	43
Marion	12,836	4.1	38,168	1,626	6,798	1,209	592	967	2,198	3,327	9,567	1,188	592

1. Based on the resident population estimated as of July 1 of the year shown.

Table B. States and Counties — **Earnings, Social Security, and Housing**

STATE County	Earnings, 2016 (cont.) Percent by selected industries									Social Security beneficiaries, December 2016		Supple-mental Security Income recipients, 2016	Housing units, 2017	
	Farm	Mining, quarrying, and extracting	Construction	Manu-facturing	Information; professional, scientific, technical services	Retail trade	Finance, insurance, real estate, and leasing	Health care and social assistance	Govern-ment	Number	Rate[1]		Total	Percent change, 2010-2017
	75	76	77	78	79	80	81	82	83	84	85	86	87	88
OKLAHOMA— Cont'd														
Kiowa	3.1	11.0	D	D	D	5.3	5.1	9.4	26.1	2,425	269	349	5,153	-1.2
Latimer	1.2	12.4	8.9	D	D	3.8	1.6	3.6	28.4	2,850	270	402	5,012	0.7
Le Flore	10.0	5.0	5.6	7.6	D	6.5	3.1	D	33.9	12,000	241	1,930	22,091	3.0
Lincoln	-1.7	D	15.1	6.4	2.8	6.9	9.9	D	19.4	8,210	235	787	15,390	1.2
Logan	0.8	5.0	13.7	4.9	D	8.4	3.6	11.2	16.5	8,355	182	653	17,566	2.2
Love	0.7	0.9	2.5	1.7	D	3.6	1.0	D	57.8	2,470	248	227	4,577	0.9
McClain	1.0	5.3	17.8	4.0	5.3	9.4	3.8	6.7	17.2	7,675	199	622	15,616	11.6
McCurtain	5.6	D	5.2	23.8	D	7.8	2.4	6.2	20.7	8,215	250	1,508	15,689	1.0
McIntosh	-0.6	D	8.1	1.0	D	15.2	4.8	11.9	26.2	6,355	322	770	13,756	3.0
Major	10.0	20.4	13.1	3.0	D	5.3	0.0	7.2	11.9	1,765	228	95	3,685	0.4
Marshall	1.0	0.7	3.7	33.2	D	8.1	4.7	9.1	16.9	4,170	257	464	10,287	2.8
Mayes	0.4	2.8	14.2	23.8	D	8.6	2.5	D	20.1	9,870	241	1,148	19,529	1.5
Murray	1.4	3.1	7.1	7.9	D	7.7	2.2	D	41.7	3,390	245	334	6,872	1.9
Muskogee	0.2	0.1	5.6	13.7	3.5	6.6	3.9	D	34.1	17,005	246	2,982	30,984	0.2
Noble	2.5	1.2	2.8	D	D	3.4	D	D	21.5	2,710	238	245	5,338	-0.1
Nowata	2.8	2.3	6.6	11.5	D	5.5	5.8	9.8	26.8	2,745	264	282	4,878	1.0
Okfuskee	1.3	2.6	10.6	4.6	D	4.7	3.7	8.8	39.2	2,875	237	587	5,318	0.7
Oklahoma	0.0	5.6	5.4	5.1	9.5	5.7	6.5	13.5	20.1	129,395	165	19,382	338,987	6.1
Okmulgee	0.1	1.3	4.2	18.2	3.2	9.3	3.6	D	35.1	10,035	257	1,506	17,854	-0.2
Osage	9.1	4.9	11.8	6.5	D	4.7	2.9	D	31.3	10,390	220	780	21,823	3.2
Ottawa	4.7	0.9	4.2	11.6	1.8	6.3	2.8	10.8	39.9	8,755	278	1,464	14,069	0.1
Pawnee	1.0	D	8.2	2.6	D	7.6	D	8.5	29.0	4,265	258	430	7,829	1.1
Payne	-0.2	2.2	5.8	5.6	5.5	6.3	4.3	5.6	44.9	12,365	152	1,353	36,414	7.1
Pittsburg	-0.3	8.2	6.6	9.2	D	6.4	3.3	7.1	37.9	11,080	250	1,498	23,171	2.4
Pontotoc	0.3	1.8	5.3	7.8	6.2	5.0	4.2	10.8	41.6	8,510	221	1,222	16,884	1.7
Pottawatomie	0.2	2.1	5.0	12.3	D	7.1	3.7	12.1	22.9	15,950	222	1,952	29,930	2.7
Pushmataha	0.5	D	8.8	5.4	D	7.3	4.7	20.1	32.2	3,420	309	569	6,161	0.8
Roger Mills	-5.8	6.5	D	D	D	2.3	D	0.5	28.9	715	194	71	1,902	-0.2
Rogers	0.2	0.6	14.4	19.2	D	7.0	3.3	7.0	22.5	18,615	205	1,238	38,100	8.4
Seminole	3.9	11.1	4.9	15.0	2.4	8.1	3.2	D	24.3	6,090	242	1,040	11,698	0.5
Sequoyah	0.3	1.0	7.1	2.1	D	10.5	4.9	D	35.5	10,730	259	1,918	19,243	3.1
Stephens	-0.2	D	5.9	11.4	D	7.4	5.2	D	11.3	11,055	251	1,055	20,701	0.2
Texas	22.9	2.8	5.3	20.1	D	4.2	2.5	2.6	11.7	2,775	131	154	8,232	0.3
Tillman	49.0	0.4	D	D	D	1.6	D	1.8	16.8	1,800	239	305	4,007	-1.7
Tulsa	0.0	8.8	5.0	9.1	8.7	5.6	5.8	11.4	7.0	113,450	176	15,161	282,942	5.4
Wagoner	0.7	0.3	16.6	19.9	D	7.2	2.3	D	15.8	14,930	193	1,206	32,289	8.7
Washington	0.4	35.3	3.9	6.6	5.1	5.6	4.7	9.0	7.8	12,625	243	1,098	23,666	0.9
Washita	-3.7	8.2	9.7	3.1	D	5.8	5.1	5.8	31.9	2,485	217	256	5,432	-0.9
Woods	2.0	27.7	3.5	5.7	D	7.1	5.9	D	23.7	1,685	184	98	4,418	-1.3
Woodward	6.1	18.9	6.7	6.9	3.2	5.9	5.0	6.2	12.6	3,850	184	256	8,986	1.7
OREGON	1.2	0.1	6.4	12.2	10.3	6.6	6.5	12.7	16.2	836,215	205	87,402	1,768,494	5.5
Baker	5.5	0.2	4.6	10.6	5.0	8.0	4.1	D	24.5	5,060	317	444	9,034	2.3
Benton	1.2	0.1	3.7	11.4	10.9	5.0	4.4	16.8	29.3	15,400	172	994	38,287	5.6
Clackamas	1.4	0.0	9.4	12.8	11.4	7.6	6.1	13.5	10.2	80,595	198	5,258	167,535	6.7
Clatsop	0.2	D	6.3	12.8	3.6	10.1	4.3	14.4	19.1	10,215	264	786	22,473	4.3
Columbia	1.2	D	7.7	16.9	4.2	8.4	5.2	9.7	19.9	12,235	240	998	21,224	2.5
Coos	1.7	0.1	5.8	7.6	3.8	8.6	4.4	13.1	28.0	20,665	326	2,377	31,065	1.5
Crook	2.5	D	9.1	6.8	9.5	4.4	3.3	9.2	20.0	6,960	311	499	10,783	5.7
Curry	2.4	D	7.4	9.7	6.4	9.9	4.4	9.2	22.5	9,060	401	665	12,959	2.7
Deschutes	0.0	D	11.9	6.0	11.2	8.7	7.4	17.4	14.4	42,600	236	2,374	88,988	11.0
Douglas	0.8	0.5	5.9	12.6	3.6	7.0	4.5	14.7	22.6	34,455	319	3,440	50,261	2.8
Gilliam	18.3	0.0	D	D	D	D	D	2.9	22.0	535	288	48	1,176	1.6
Grant	7.3	0.1	3.1	4.7	5.0	5.7	D	D	46.1	2,300	320	173	4,410	1.5
Harney	14.1	0.0	D	D	D	7.3	1.8	6.2	43.0	2,060	284	229	3,890	1.4
Hood River	7.9	0.0	4.7	13.2	13.0	6.2	4.1	13.4	11.2	4,195	182	270	9,900	6.8
Jackson	0.6	0.1	6.6	8.9	6.5	10.6	6.3	19.4	14.2	55,955	261	4,748	95,387	4.9
Jefferson	1.2	D	4.1	16.0	D	5.9	2.6	D	39.2	5,550	240	601	10,061	2.5
Josephine	0.3	D	6.4	10.4	4.5	12.6	6.6	20.2	13.6	27,230	319	2,842	39,062	2.8
Klamath	2.9	D	5.4	8.4	4.2	8.5	5.0	16.2	24.4	17,685	267	2,082	33,513	2.2
Lake	15.9	D	4.2	5.8	2.9	4.8	2.4	D	45.5	2,300	294	241	4,519	1.9
Lane	0.5	0.2	5.8	9.7	8.2	8.3	6.8	16.5	18.2	84,475	229	9,456	162,591	4.2
Lincoln	1.0	D	6.5	7.3	3.7	9.8	4.0	12.7	24.1	15,910	332	1,292	31,511	2.9
Linn	1.7	D	7.5	21.7	3.6	8.9	3.9	11.7	14.9	29,610	241	3,566	50,344	3.1
Malheur	6.5	D	2.4	6.7	3.5	9.7	3.3	12.3	31.3	6,430	212	982	11,873	1.6
Marion	2.4	0.2	7.5	6.4	5.0	6.9	5.3	15.8	30.0	64,290	191	7,527	126,133	4.3

1. Per 1,000 resident population estimated as of July 1 of the year shown.

Table B. States and Counties — Housing, Labor Force, and Employment

STATE County	Total	Percent	Median value[1]	With a mortgage	Without a mortgage[2]	Median rent[3]	Median rent as a percent of income[2]	Sub-standard units[4] (percent)	Total	Percent change, 2016-2017	Total	Rate[5]	Total	Management, business, science, and arts	Construction, production, and maintenance occupations
	89	90	91	92	93	94	95	96	97	98	99	100	101	102	103
OKLAHOMA— Cont'd															
Kiowa	3,956	68.6	59,600	17.5	10.0	545	24.6	3.5	3,948	-3.9	212	5.4	3,991	30.1	32.1
Latimer	4,041	68.1	81,000	19.3	10.0	529	27.0	3.8	3,419	-8.2	257	7.5	3,908	33.3	32.7
Le Flore	18,313	72.9	83,400	20.3	11.1	581	28.0	3.2	19,373	-1.9	1,126	5.8	18,504	26.0	33.5
Lincoln	13,047	78.5	99,900	19.9	10.0	640	26.5	3.2	15,870	0.0	694	4.4	14,544	28.6	31.9
Logan	15,273	78.8	151,100	19.6	10.0	686	26.8	4.1	21,719	0.7	806	3.7	20,814	34.1	24.0
Love	3,113	79.3	90,900	18.6	10.0	682	23.1	3.3	6,607	0.6	197	3.0	4,092	23.4	31.2
McClain	13,532	79.2	158,600	21.9	10.7	681	23.8	2.0	19,030	0.4	682	3.6	17,038	35.2	24.9
McCurtain	12,973	70.3	74,700	21.1	11.2	575	26.4	5.1	14,830	0.2	938	6.3	12,420	23.2	37.6
McIntosh	8,302	77.4	96,000	21.3	10.6	568	27.8	5.6	6,934	-1.8	542	7.8	6,971	26.6	31.6
Major	2,975	75.3	91,700	15.6	10.0	595	19.2	3.6	4,011	0.5	129	3.2	3,421	28.4	35.5
Marshall	5,969	76.1	85,300	19.5	10.0	632	23.5	4.6	6,548	-1.0	308	4.7	6,189	23.3	35.8
Mayes	15,735	74.3	106,200	20.8	10.5	660	25.2	3.7	19,145	-1.5	920	4.8	16,878	27.7	31.8
Murray	5,387	66.7	99,300	18.3	10.0	648	20.2	5.4	6,428	1.4	240	3.7	6,150	28.4	25.9
Muskogee	26,168	66.8	94,800	19.9	10.6	651	30.5	2.5	29,534	-0.3	1,527	5.2	27,299	28.5	27.5
Noble	4,699	73.7	92,800	18.3	10.0	662	23.0	2.6	5,784	0.5	192	3.3	5,226	35.0	29.8
Nowata	4,087	75.9	78,700	18.7	11.2	658	27.1	2.7	4,618	-1.5	253	5.5	4,217	24.3	35.4
Okfuskee	3,959	72.8	79,300	21.0	10.0	533	26.9	4.1	4,473	-1.7	272	6.1	3,927	27.3	33.5
Oklahoma	294,672	58.7	137,500	20.8	10.8	794	29.3	3.1	378,076	0.8	15,219	4.0	358,667	35.9	21.4
Okmulgee	14,835	70.5	80,600	19.7	11.7	613	28.0	2.4	16,147	0.0	1,016	6.3	14,976	28.6	28.6
Osage	18,218	77.8	105,100	20.5	10.5	648	26.7	3.2	21,127	0.3	1,084	5.1	19,319	31.1	29.7
Ottawa	11,982	69.5	82,300	21.6	10.9	647	28.8	4.9	14,461	0.0	642	4.4	12,913	26.9	29.4
Pawnee	6,238	76.1	87,000	19.6	10.5	647	23.7	4.2	7,453	-0.5	400	5.4	6,674	28.9	35.0
Payne	30,164	49.2	142,800	20.9	10.3	742	39.4	3.7	38,565	-0.8	1,401	3.6	36,187	39.0	19.4
Pittsburg	17,903	71.8	96,700	19.9	10.0	680	27.2	3.0	17,645	0.1	946	5.4	18,439	28.5	28.4
Pontotoc	14,625	64.2	113,100	20.1	10.0	633	27.2	3.1	18,730	1.5	711	3.8	17,466	33.3	23.3
Pottawatomie	25,938	68.4	105,800	19.9	10.0	663	27.9	3.0	33,062	0.0	1,377	4.2	29,227	31.0	26.0
Pushmataha	4,655	76.0	71,600	19.2	10.8	497	27.9	4.3	4,774	-2.1	295	6.2	4,209	30.1	32.7
Roger Mills	1,324	72.7	93,300	17.2	10.0	475	21.0	0.6	1,872	3.4	61	3.3	1,737	29.8	29.9
Rogers	33,570	78.5	148,600	20.1	10.0	799	26.3	3.1	45,043	0.4	1,990	4.4	42,772	34.3	25.9
Seminole	9,162	70.5	70,200	20.0	10.0	582	26.3	4.2	9,338	-1.1	547	5.9	9,355	26.4	32.0
Sequoyah	15,467	71.2	90,900	21.4	11.4	639	30.5	5.4	16,575	-1.6	913	5.5	15,593	27.7	29.6
Stephens	17,527	70.8	100,400	19.1	10.8	655	27.0	2.5	18,256	-4.0	1,141	6.3	18,731	26.5	31.2
Texas	7,038	63.9	98,600	19.4	10.0	671	23.0	7.9	9,385	-0.1	295	3.1	11,257	25.5	40.9
Tillman	3,159	73.9	55,300	20.2	10.9	614	20.9	3.4	3,263	-1.4	140	4.3	3,178	30.6	33.7
Tulsa	248,811	59.1	141,700	20.0	10.7	790	28.0	3.0	319,989	0.6	13,728	4.3	305,406	36.6	21.1
Wagoner	27,871	79.3	144,900	19.9	10.5	815	26.2	2.9	36,823	0.6	1,623	4.4	35,412	32.3	26.6
Washington	20,810	70.1	111,900	18.4	10.0	686	27.0	2.2	23,143	-3.3	1,064	4.6	23,118	35.8	22.0
Washita	4,539	72.1	80,800	17.0	10.0	651	19.1	2.7	5,437	2.2	242	4.5	4,948	31.7	31.4
Woods	3,347	68.4	92,700	16.4	10.0	644	20.1	0.9	4,928	-5.5	131	2.7	4,442	27.1	26.6
Woodward	7,301	71.6	122,200	15.3	10.0	702	23.6	1.9	9,414	-1.1	396	4.2	9,507	27.3	36.9
OREGON	154,5,745	61.4	247,200	23.9	12.2	941	31.6	3.5	2,104,086	2.7	86,789	4.1	1,832,620	37.5	20.6
Baker	7,011	67.5	147,100	21.4	12.2	636	27.2	2.8	7,070	1.6	386	5.5	6,265	34.9	28.6
Benton	34,193	57.2	276,900	21.5	10.9	893	38.0	2.7	48,126	2.8	1,570	3.3	40,655	49.6	13.5
Clackamas	151,150	68.9	319,100	23.8	12.3	1,091	29.8	2.5	218,947	2.9	8,191	3.7	192,469	38.3	20.2
Clatsop	15,876	60.3	245,400	23.0	13.0	872	31.6	2.9	19,248	1.1	795	4.1	16,840	30.5	22.1
Columbia	18,941	71.8	213,200	22.8	11.6	831	32.4	2.0	24,224	2.5	1,253	5.2	20,840	28.4	30.3
Coos	25,755	64.8	169,900	24.8	13.0	727	31.6	3.1	26,645	0.7	1,471	5.5	23,537	28.2	26.2
Crook	9,155	69.0	172,600	25.9	11.6	793	30.6	4.4	9,563	2.3	599	6.3	8,310	23.1	25.9
Curry	10,396	66.0	222,100	28.4	12.5	846	34.5	3.0	9,049	0.0	551	6.1	7,626	32.6	19.8
Deschutes	67,880	65.3	275,300	24.6	12.2	981	32.2	2.5	93,470	3.9	3,937	4.2	78,810	36.4	19.0
Douglas	43,937	67.6	170,000	25.2	12.5	763	31.1	3.1	46,572	1.8	2,492	5.4	39,904	28.9	27.8
Gilliam	788	63.6	112,800	26.2	11.7	796	26.2	2.9	865	3.2	36	4.2	717	31.1	34.0
Grant	3,151	72.8	158,800	23.2	12.1	671	26.4	3.8	3,162	1.7	216	6.8	2,959	39.1	24.3
Harney	3,059	70.6	104,300	20.2	10.4	569	25.9	3.0	3,438	0.4	215	6.3	2,930	33.1	25.1
Hood River	8,213	64.6	325,900	24.6	10.0	1,000	29.4	4.2	14,359	3.2	518	3.6	10,994	36.5	30.8
Jackson	83,969	62.9	224,500	25.5	13.7	895	34.5	3.1	103,952	2.4	4,959	4.8	90,184	31.8	21.7
Jefferson	7,577	68.8	159,400	23.0	11.0	793	26.5	4.2	10,041	1.8	560	5.6	8,128	28.2	30.5
Josephine	34,778	66.0	225,100	27.0	12.4	834	36.3	3.7	35,392	3.2	1,905	5.4	29,477	29.5	25.4
Klamath	27,084	64.1	148,100	22.5	10.9	728	31.2	3.6	29,880	2.2	1,760	5.9	25,576	29.4	26.4
Lake	3,409	61.7	116,600	24.4	11.5	610	29.1	3.4	3,545	2.6	202	5.7	2,909	28.8	32.7
Lane	146,692	58.8	221,000	24.7	12.3	885	34.3	2.7	182,399	2.1	8,118	4.5	162,190	34.6	19.8
Lincoln	20,434	63.1	216,300	26.5	13.3	825	31.1	3.4	21,197	1.4	1,006	4.7	19,068	26.9	21.2
Linn	45,378	64.5	173,100	23.8	12.6	850	32.3	3.1	57,998	2.0	2,763	4.8	49,508	29.6	29.3
Malheur	10,294	59.3	123,400	23.1	11.0	637	35.8	5.0	12,618	1.0	590	4.7	10,722	27.7	31.9
Marion	115,196	59.7	192,900	24.2	12.0	828	30.6	5.2	162,450	3.1	6,991	4.3	142,144	30.4	25.8

1. Specified owner-occupied units.   2. A value of 10.0 represents 10 percent or less; a value of 50.0 represents 50 percent or more.   3. Specified renter-occupied units.
4. Overcrowded or lacking complete plumbing facilities.   5. Percent of civilian labor force.   6. Civilian employed persons 16 years old and over.

Items 89—103

Table B. States and Counties — Nonfarm Employment and Agriculture

STATE County	Private nonfarm establishments, employment and payroll, 2016									Agriculture, 2012			
		Employment						Annual payroll		Farms			
												Percent with:	Farm operators whose principal occupation is farming (percent)
	Number of establishments	Total	Health care and social assistance	Manufacturing	Retail trade	Finance and insurance	Professional, scientific, and technical services	Total (mil dol)	Average per employee (dollars)	Number	Fewer than 50 acres	500 acres or more	
	104	105	106	107	108	109	110	111	112	113	114	115	116
OKLAHOMA— Cont'd													
Kiowa	178	1,427	505	4	282	111	33	40	28,179	667	9.0	44.8	53.2
Latimer	167	1,644	327	D	248	70	63	62	37,521	691	27.2	13.9	36.3
Le Flore	751	8,236	2,771	350	1,558	395	284	269	32,691	1,843	32.2	8.4	48.0
Lincoln	562	5,048	484	652	770	427	128	179	35,440	2,121	26.0	10.6	43.9
Logan	842	6,312	941	414	1,151	258	197	208	32,940	1,203	27.2	14.8	37.1
Love	138	5,333	124	171	115	54	47	164	30,686	621	22.9	15.5	45.7
McClain	843	7,975	1,306	395	1,541	247	283	255	32,018	1,239	39.9	12.2	38.7
McCurtain	603	8,957	1,466	2,522	1,316	248	87	287	32,081	1,577	28.0	8.1	39.9
McIntosh	346	3,130	807	48	946	157	127	101	32,224	1,018	25.8	9.4	36.7
Major	262	1,873	237	58	270	74	62	74	39,584	901	13.7	32.6	45.3
Marshall	272	3,791	618	1,331	635	171	90	126	33,232	525	26.5	15.6	40.8
Mayes	785	10,181	1,049	2,865	1,832	313	409	402	39,495	1,551	36.6	7.7	42.5
Murray	284	3,556	563	326	647	141	71	121	33,941	470	22.1	17.0	37.4
Muskogee	1,419	23,234	5,675	3,340	3,501	578	549	864	37,199	1,735	34.2	8.4	46.0
Noble	212	3,883	361	D	324	171	47	172	44,353	828	15.5	27.5	39.4
Nowata	150	1,317	334	198	161	74	24	36	27,546	889	22.5	14.3	44.2
Okfuskee	165	2,543	1,687	119	226	79	20	82	32,127	881	18.5	15.7	39.5
Oklahoma	23,805	374,642	59,486	19,452	46,956	20,270	25,445	17,249	46,042	1,180	56.6	5.7	44.4
Okmulgee	668	6,795	1,505	1,357	1,290	325	195	211	31,057	1,329	32.3	10.8	44.6
Osage	572	5,397	733	315	821	163	147	184	34,000	1,325	28.5	25.6	47.8
Ottawa	596	9,493	1,466	1,614	1,029	347	318	286	30,144	1,020	36.4	7.9	38.6
Pawnee	257	2,642	476	209	461	86	D	121	45,661	813	21.4	18.2	31.5
Payne	1,837	22,905	3,510	1,513	4,306	904	1,086	725	31,657	1,466	34.9	10.5	34.1
Pittsburg	939	10,878	2,516	1,006	2,102	394	386	371	34,124	1,567	27.1	15.8	39.8
Pontotoc	951	12,525	3,445	1,240	1,700	465	856	444	35,464	1,313	26.9	10.1	38.2
Pottawatomie	1,328	18,613	3,039	2,801	3,044	666	665	571	30,672	1,643	32.0	9.6	39.6
Pushmataha	198	2,175	908	186	375	117	113	57	26,148	732	15.4	15.8	47.0
Roger Mills	86	462	D	D	84	D	12	16	35,364	678	9.9	42.6	49.6
Rogers	1,733	27,747	2,903	6,725	3,044	825	919	1,207	43,512	1,733	47.8	8.1	33.8
Seminole	442	5,219	950	824	796	217	186	175	33,581	1,054	20.7	10.5	36.2
Sequoyah	578	7,324	2,410	310	1,247	382	117	176	24,035	1,204	37.7	6.9	42.6
Stephens	1,070	11,904	2,300	1,182	2,019	677	504	424	35,591	1,286	23.6	17.1	33.0
Texas	497	8,076	452	D	910	256	101	362	44,850	1,024	8.4	42.6	38.7
Tillman	140	1,097	204	D	133	80	18	35	32,061	556	8.1	44.4	52.2
Tulsa	18,879	335,082	53,965	38,037	41,617	15,470	20,437	15,609	46,582	1,036	57.6	3.8	40.0
Wagoner	933	8,548	833	1,912	1,514	286	271	302	35,349	1,090	44.7	7.5	35.0
Washington	1,159	20,107	2,886	1,028	2,567	738	1,622	995	49,508	811	37.5	9.5	41.2
Washita	253	1,389	257	97	278	100	29	44	31,734	973	12.3	36.2	50.5
Woods	283	2,898	363	40	492	153	49	140	48,445	751	13.6	41.9	52.2
Woodward	753	7,242	1,092	499	1,336	298	164	318	43,890	882	15.3	33.9	39.1
OREGON	114,551	1,551,192	245,776	163,707	208,523	60,828	91,071	74,063	47,746	35,439	61.5	10.6	49.9
Baker	526	4,208	646	513	801	114	228	141	33,541	645	31.0	28.7	60.5
Benton	2,119	27,066	6,058	2,870	3,857	611	1,814	1,263	46,651	886	71.4	5.6	46.3
Clackamas	11,799	142,880	20,846	18,178	19,873	5,789	8,347	6,898	48,281	3,745	81.4	1.1	41.1
Clatsop	1,434	14,797	2,173	1,818	2,733	257	380	520	35,128	199	55.3	2.5	45.7
Columbia	904	8,237	1,439	1,482	1,513	286	276	283	34,384	751	69.9	2.4	45.7
Coos	1,557	17,908	3,960	1,435	2,907	417	420	658	36,769	654	41.4	9.5	56.9
Crook	514	4,037	516	726	607	98	119	138	34,302	551	49.9	16.7	51.0
Curry	687	5,235	1,056	716	1,034	163	121	169	32,311	197	37.6	21.3	60.4
Deschutes	6,889	64,536	10,752	4,739	10,796	2,123	3,179	2,617	40,554	1,283	78.9	3.0	44.0
Douglas	2,500	29,777	5,772	3,848	4,958	1,089	797	1,157	38,862	1,927	50.9	8.1	48.3
Gilliam	71	791	65	NA	109	14	D	33	41,650	170	4.1	77.6	63.5
Grant	228	1,482	408	D	229	88	69	52	35,230	398	28.1	36.9	54.3
Harney	198	1,419	402	9	294	36	71	45	31,952	497	21.5	42.3	57.1
Hood River	1,041	10,388	1,544	1,591	1,418	177	453	354	34,046	554	74.9	0.5	56.7
Jackson	6,107	72,083	13,909	6,515	12,152	2,074	2,323	2,741	38,033	1,722	72.1	2.4	56.2
Jefferson	383	4,017	589	1,191	533	62	71	136	33,898	474	42.2	18.4	53.2
Josephine	1,934	22,347	4,685	2,869	4,386	623	846	759	33,948	617	76.3	0.6	55.8
Klamath	1,507	17,435	3,210	2,107	3,027	1,023	687	683	39,158	955	38.7	19.4	63.7
Lake	190	1,175	286	206	155	34	56	45	38,340	373	21.4	40.2	70.2
Lane	9,819	125,284	23,710	14,334	20,136	4,732	5,472	4,998	39,890	2,660	73.9	2.9	44.5
Lincoln	1,536	14,146	1,784	948	2,862	284	314	469	33,178	362	63.3	3.9	48.3
Linn	2,564	36,488	5,526	7,367	5,427	941	909	1,429	39,153	2,083	64.8	6.7	48.7
Malheur	704	8,535	1,635	1,086	1,981	205	225	259	30,318	1,113	33.9	20.8	64.1
Marion	8,023	104,786	19,451	10,586	17,312	3,026	3,687	3,975	37,933	2,567	72.5	5.6	47.1

Table B. States and Counties — **Agriculture**

	Agriculture, 2012 (cont.)														
	Land in farms				Value of land and buildings (dollars)			Value of products sold:				Percent of farms with sales of:		Government payments	
			Acres							Percent from:					
STATE County	Acreage (1,000)	Percent change, 2007-2012	Average size of farm	Total irrigated (1,000)	Total cropland (1,000)	Average per farm	Average per acre	Value of machinery and equiopmnet, average per farm (dollars)	Total (mil dol)	Average per farm (acres)	Crops	Livestock and poultry products	$10,000 or more	$100,000 or more	Total ($1,000)	Percent of farms
	117	118	119	120	121	122	123	124	125	126	127	128	129	130	131	132
OKLAHOMA— Cont'd																
Kiowa	593	5.1	890	2.7	302.3	854,510	961	144,499	107.8	161,627	59.1	40.9	61.3	28.0	8,081	79.2
Latimer	221	3.3	319	0.1	38.2	425,538	1,333	56,986	24.6	35,570	8.5	91.5	34.6	4.6	1,268	15.8
Le Flore	395	-15.3	214	6.1	103.7	425,397	1,985	57,896	287.3	155,883	6.6	93.4	38.0	12.0	2,522	25.6
Lincoln	454	-6.9	214	0.8	106.5	369,323	1,724	54,060	38.7	18,260	26.8	73.2	31.7	3.2	1,147	16.3
Logan	367	-9.0	305	1.1	133.7	575,341	1,884	63,051	44.0	36,563	47.2	52.8	37.2	5.5	2,181	38.3
Love	219	-16.2	353	1.1	48.8	611,282	1,730	56,594	23.9	38,472	19.5	80.5	40.7	7.4	1,234	29.0
McClain	283	-16.1	228	1.7	78.9	466,267	2,043	61,161	48.5	39,117	26.2	73.8	32.6	7.7	1,349	24.8
McCurtain	317	-6.8	201	1.5	70.3	349,785	1,742	57,386	163.1	103,452	7.2	92.8	36.6	7.8	1,573	24.0
McIntosh	236	-4.4	232	0.2	58.1	357,114	1,541	52,882	22.3	21,872	13.1	86.9	37.7	3.6	672	23.3
Major	537	3.8	596	10.1	217.0	668,974	1,122	95,212	105.4	116,986	39.2	60.8	59.4	20.3	3,795	65.7
Marshall	192	21.6	365	0.7	41.8	610,888	1,672	64,185	18.4	34,983	20.8	79.2	37.0	5.3	830	24.0
Mayes	285	-9.0	184	0.4	85.2	388,246	2,112	56,484	76.0	48,985	8.0	92.0	37.0	6.8	1,628	24.2
Murray	208	5.6	443	0.0	24.3	613,813	1,386	65,602	28.0	59,557	8.2	91.8	36.6	4.9	709	33.0
Muskogee	350	-6.5	202	7.3	120.2	356,096	1,765	55,445	50.6	29,140	42.3	57.7	33.9	4.0	2,161	29.6
Noble	443	-5.2	535	1.9	193.3	762,217	1,425	79,824	61.3	73,995	48.4	51.6	51.1	16.2	4,809	64.4
Nowata	292	-17.6	329	0.1	64.8	544,327	1,657	53,998	40.0	45,009	12.3	87.7	46.1	5.5	1,267	31.7
Okfuskee	320	7.0	363	0.7	60.1	463,053	1,276	57,190	34.7	39,373	13.3	86.7	39.7	5.3	922	26.4
Oklahoma	144	-9.8	122	2.3	47.9	378,664	3,099	43,969	20.4	17,300	71.0	29.0	19.7	3.6	502	14.4
Okmulgee	300	2.0	226	0.7	78.0	406,784	1,801	51,241	27.1	20,421	27.7	72.3	30.5	3.8	908	21.6
Osage	1,217	-5.7	918	1.3	131.4	968,906	1,055	58,483	121.5	91,682	6.2	93.8	42.9	11.2	4,433	23.2
Ottawa	193	-18.8	189	0.2	87.9	436,945	2,306	76,215	117.6	115,291	43.1	56.9	39.0	7.8	1,622	25.5
Pawnee	286	-3.9	352	0.0	52.2	468,352	1,331	55,888	26.7	32,864	14.6	85.4	37.8	7.4	1,400	30.3
Payne	350	-2.0	239	0.4	105.1	451,118	1,891	52,108	34.1	23,231	26.5	73.5	33.4	4.1	1,737	23.5
Pittsburg	524	-4.3	334	1.8	95.6	454,824	1,361	54,429	41.6	26,535	15.7	84.3	35.4	4.8	1,898	16.1
Pontotoc	325	-14.4	247	0.9	69.0	434,772	1,759	49,674	36.0	27,438	17.6	82.3	34.4	2.4	1,242	16.4
Pottawatomie	335	-15.1	204	0.9	86.9	358,388	1,756	52,875	35.4	21,523	24.0	76.0	26.0	2.7	1,346	14.2
Pushmataha	297	2.4	406	D	37.9	462,504	1,138	44,060	14.6	19,939	9.7	90.3	36.9	4.4	2,454	23.9
Roger Mills	719	0.0	1,061	5.3	117.5	1,093,820	1,031	96,844	46.0	67,827	28.1	71.9	47.8	14.0	4,532	58.1
Rogers	302	-18.7	174	1.0	71.8	429,069	2,464	44,947	66.4	38,290	11.7	88.3	31.2	4.5	1,186	15.5
Seminole	243	-3.0	231	0.2	48.0	325,581	1,411	46,705	38.1	36,162	10.4	89.6	29.9	2.2	875	20.8
Sequoyah	215	-7.3	179	3.3	63.8	357,679	2,002	52,061	55.5	46,084	23.0	77.0	31.2	3.9	1,620	9.1
Stephens	481	2.3	374	0.1	75.9	474,056	1,268	58,719	42.2	32,782	12.5	87.5	35.1	5.8	2,539	29.9
Texas	1,287	6.7	1,257	153.0	678.8	1,005,370	800	180,940	1,013.9	990,175	15.0	85.0	42.1	19.9	12,943	78.5
Tillman	541	16.7	974	10.6	290.0	977,950	1,004	163,739	102.4	184,257	53.7	46.3	62.4	25.7	6,753	79.0
Tulsa	106	-19.0	103	4.7	42.7	372,738	3,635	35,707	21.0	20,313	70.3	29.7	23.9	2.9	692	10.0
Wagoner	199	-24.3	182	4.0	78.6	443,074	2,428	53,862	33.8	31,050	57.8	42.2	31.1	4.7	1,257	26.2
Washington	231	1.9	285	D	55.6	476,007	1,672	50,665	37.4	46,086	19.2	80.8	35.4	7.5	590	22.3
Washita	633	7.2	651	7.0	343.6	780,371	1,199	136,291	114.7	117,867	54.3	45.7	64.5	23.2	10,153	80.5
Woods	808	-3.0	1,077	2.8	231.1	1,167,659	1,085	114,887	82.5	109,875	43.0	57.0	55.7	23.7	4,609	71.0
Woodward	715	-8.7	810	4.6	149.9	898,007	1,108	85,655	116.5	132,078	13.4	86.6	46.1	13.4	4,264	56.5
OREGON	16,302	-0.6	460	1,629.7	4,690.4	865,613	1,882	90,222	4,883.7	137,805	66.5	33.5	35.6	13.1	85,840	15.1
Baker	711	-0.1	1,102	100.9	107.5	1,117,372	1,014	118,667	93.3	144,583	49.4	50.6	52.2	21.6	1,883	25.7
Benton	124	8.2	140	11.3	68.2	830,059	5,932	68,867	103.3	116,597	78.2	21.8	28.6	10.4	486	6.4
Clackamas	163	-11.0	43	22.2	84.0	585,754	13,486	53,573	325.2	86,833	76.7	23.3	27.5	7.1	607	3.8
Clatsop	16	-22.7	82	0.7	5.3	456,739	5,548	53,940	11.5	58,010	12.3	87.7	22.1	6.0	50	6.0
Columbia	57	-1.9	75	1.9	18.0	414,475	5,493	41,466	39.4	52,413	D	D	17.6	1.6	232	4.1
Coos	157	8.1	241	11.2	20.9	776,687	3,225	60,953	50.4	77,018	21.5	78.6	43.6	12.2	678	10.7
Crook	823	8.0	1,493	61.9	57.0	1,357,530	909	76,437	42.3	76,766	32.1	67.9	38.3	9.4	554	9.3
Curry	63	-14.8	322	3.2	5.2	1,095,939	3,408	71,112	21.4	108,411	44.9	55.1	53.8	19.3	524	17.3
Deschutes	131	1.3	102	34.0	28.9	716,430	7,015	52,158	20.6	16,033	54.1	45.9	22.1	2.4	241	3.4
Douglas	382	-3.7	198	14.6	49.2	611,961	3,084	44,231	64.8	33,629	36.3	63.7	27.3	4.7	730	5.3
Gilliam	723	-1.4	4,255	6.5	331.7	2,117,900	498	293,047	44.1	259,141	84.6	15.4	50.6	40.0	7,931	90.0
Grant	656	-13.8	1,649	31.6	96.4	1,326,967	805	79,166	25.4	63,719	22.3	77.7	50.8	14.8	900	14.8
Harney	1,505	3.0	3,029	165.7	223.0	1,660,966	548	163,302	88.9	178,966	41.7	58.3	55.7	30.0	1,414	24.9
Hood River	26	-4.2	47	14.1	16.3	885,421	19,000	90,121	77.1	139,200	D	D	49.8	26.9	777	13.4
Jackson	214	-12.3	124	36.5	32.8	582,023	4,682	40,415	64.1	37,240	57.6	42.4	25.7	3.4	252	3.8
Jefferson	817	15.2	1,724	41.1	62.9	1,104,840	641	154,973	65.0	137,198	72.7	27.3	40.7	19.4	1,182	32.7
Josephine	28	-25.1	46	9.0	8.4	460,319	10,052	35,806	18.8	30,481	D	D	25.0	4.7	129	2.9
Klamath	650	-3.7	681	159.9	205.2	1,004,853	1,475	136,301	181.5	190,037	56.5	43.5	48.7	21.8	1,951	21.4
Lake	657	-5.2	1,762	148.9	131.1	1,791,244	1,017	171,150	85.6	229,614	52.6	47.4	61.7	33.8	716	20.6
Lane	220	-10.6	83	19.3	100.0	563,427	6,824	49,734	142.5	53,574	74.6	25.4	23.5	5.6	575	5.1
Lincoln	30	-3.1	83	0.4	5.1	400,392	4,795	35,680	5.5	15,293	30.6	69.4	22.7	1.7	93	3.6
Linn	331	-12.0	159	28.7	227.5	769,891	4,840	89,696	241.2	115,812	77.1	22.9	31.3	11.7	882	6.8
Malheur	1,077	-8.0	967	183.0	204.8	1,136,094	1,174	174,964	359.3	322,829	50.7	49.3	68.3	32.6	2,574	40.2
Marion	286	-7.0	111	84.9	213.8	885,406	7,942	130,593	592.9	230,953	81.5	18.5	41.0	17.7	1,583	9.8

Items 117—132   **OK(Kiowa)—OR(Marion) 557**

Table B. States and Counties — Water Use, Wholesale Trade, Retail Trade, and Real Estate

STATE County	Water use, 2015		Wholesale Trade[1], 2012				Retail Trade[2], 2012				Real estate and rental and leasing,[2] 2012			
	Public supply water withdrawn (mil gal/ day)	Public supply gallons withdrawn per person per day	Number of establish- ments	Number of employees	Sales (mil dol)	Annual payroll (mil dol)	Number of establish- ments	Number of employees	Sales (mil dol)	Annual payroll (mil dol)	Number of establish- ments	Number of employees	Sales (mil dol)	Annual payroll (mil dol)
	133	134	135	136	137	138	139	140	141	142	143	144	145	146
OKLAHOMA— Cont'd														
Kiowa	6.38	697.7	8	D	D	D	40	286	58.3	5.5	4	11	1.1	0.2
Latimer	1.40	133.5	5	54	73.5	3.9	24	259	52.5	5.1	4	D	D	D
Le Flore	7.10	143.1	21	D	D	D	145	1,490	406.8	30.3	22	44	5.9	0.9
Lincoln	1.03	29.4	27	183	117.3	8.1	87	814	239.1	17.3	19	69	9.9	2.1
Logan	2.61	56.7	15	63	26.3	2.4	87	1,001	343.9	22.2	40	155	30.2	4.5
Love	0.83	84.1	5	12	9.4	0.5	26	176	77.4	3.8	6	D	D	D
McClain	1.38	36.3	18	103	38.7	3.8	118	1,389	463.6	37.5	27	66	39.7	4.5
McCurtain	5.60	169.5	27	97	86.7	3.7	100	1,156	275.2	24.4	19	78	8.0	1.8
McIntosh	4.59	229.6	6	28	14.6	1.6	68	847	289.7	18.7	12	D	D	D
Major	5.52	710.3	16	100	55.5	3.9	32	264	93.7	5.3	6	D	D	D
Marshall	2.29	141.1	5	64	19.0	4.0	52	542	159.8	12.2	9	31	2.5	0.6
Mayes	47.12	1,152.4	34	344	382.6	18.1	137	1,663	466.8	35.2	20	41	5.4	0.7
Murray	7.77	557.5	7	D	D	D	48	578	196.9	14.2	11	D	D	D
Muskogee	1.15	16.5	57	1,022	509.1	45.7	258	3,194	927.9	75.8	56	211	29.6	5.7
Noble	0.28	24.2	8	81	30.9	2.3	32	326	127.6	7.5	7	17	2.1	0.2
Nowata	1.16	110.1	9	79	33.6	2.1	18	129	36.8	2.7	7	22	1.3	0.5
Okfuskee	0.99	81.3	4	15	2.3	0.2	28	210	88.7	4.8	2	D	D	D
Oklahoma	104.31	134.3	1,128	18,305	43,903.7	1,065.3	2,909	42,001	13,117.1	1,116.5	1,136	6,497	1,502.8	293.8
Okmulgee	5.82	148.5	21	D	D	D	123	1,315	341.0	26.3	16	36	4.7	0.9
Osage	16.58	346.2	15	D	D	D	88	869	216.3	16.8	17	95	21.2	4.7
Ottawa	2.70	84.4	21	180	44.6	6.4	100	993	232.9	20.8	19	46	6.8	1.2
Pawnee	1.02	62.1	5	D	D	D	39	423	115.7	8.8	6	37	8.9	1.9
Payne	2.64	32.7	50	D	D	D	297	4,027	1,021.0	84.7	85	298	53.0	8.3
Pittsburg	5.90	132.3	39	D	D	D	176	2,047	603.8	46.3	44	181	34.5	6.8
Pontotoc	4.35	113.9	41	407	438.3	18.7	167	1,809	437.4	37.8	42	293	65.5	12.6
Pottawatomie	7.51	104.5	38	305	180.3	12.6	238	2,904	755.0	63.6	47	162	23.5	4.5
Pushmataha	0.53	47.4	2	D	D	D	36	328	70.6	5.0	7	22	6.2	0.7
Roger Mills	0.56	147.8	2	D	D	D	16	92	31.6	1.7	1	D	D	D
Rogers	72.73	801.0	73	957	1,885.4	53.1	205	2,530	777.3	62.6	77	222	48.4	7.5
Seminole	3.20	125.3	23	386	161.7	14.2	75	862	233.5	17.6	14	31	6.7	1.4
Sequoyah	4.46	108.4	14	D	D	D	118	1,179	387.7	24.9	14	37	3.8	0.6
Stephens	1.08	24.2	48	D	D	D	194	1,961	550.4	43.9	26	106	23.9	3.8
Texas	4.75	221.0	33	D	D	D	76	890	226.5	18.4	15	42	4.3	0.8
Tillman	1.11	147.7	11	100	83.8	3.7	21	177	27.8	2.7	NA	NA	NA	NA
Tulsa	0.00	0.0	996	14,271	13,182.2	854.3	2,315	36,091	10,454.5	894.5	919	6,119	981.5	242.8
Wagoner	31.31	409.0	36	244	117.8	11.4	115	1,360	389.7	29.0	28	41	4.3	1.0
Washington	1.85	35.6	29	173	194.6	7.4	181	2,270	652.2	53.8	42	195	29.5	5.9
Washita	7.10	608.9	7	131	49.9	5.6	46	283	86.0	5.5	8	69	9.5	2.3
Woods	0.74	79.5	21	186	218.8	9.0	46	465	168.6	10.2	6	10	2.0	0.2
Woodward	6.30	292.2	42	D	D	D	114	1,224	435.2	30.3	33	148	31.4	7.2
OREGON	567.04	140.7	4,393	59,523	48,325.3	3,233.0	13,879	187,402	49,481.1	4,831.5	5,644	26,016	4,649.6	902.8
Baker	3.27	204.3	15	84	30.5	3.0	86	797	198.9	17.6	10	39	4.1	1.7
Benton	11.95	136.5	44	346	452.5	22.6	262	3,455	731.0	82.5	105	453	53.3	10.2
Clackamas	134.35	334.6	563	8,015	5,388.6	456.3	1,188	18,541	5,125.3	486.9	564	2,440	451.9	96.8
Clatsop	10.00	264.3	22	210	110.4	9.1	284	2,756	704.1	67.4	75	239	30.4	6.0
Columbia	4.70	94.8	16	D	D	D	120	1,349	318.1	31.5	37	108	12.8	2.6
Coos	5.05	80.0	42	399	287.8	15.3	262	2,930	745.8	73.8	58	215	26.4	5.1
Crook	2.11	97.5	13	D	D	D	70	583	184.2	14.6	24	33	6.5	0.8
Curry	2.85	126.8	12	35	14.6	0.7	97	988	244.6	23.8	45	81	10.1	1.5
Deschutes	38.00	216.8	215	1,262	794.9	57.1	755	9,365	2,476.6	244.0	388	1,252	186.1	40.0
Douglas	14.20	131.9	54	D	D	D	378	4,419	1,103.4	102.1	120	329	43.4	7.6
Gilliam	0.55	295.9	5	D	D	D	11	52	10.5	1.1	NA	NA	NA	NA
Grant	0.97	135.0	7	D	D	D	38	241	67.4	5.6	10	20	1.2	0.4
Harney	1.72	238.9	3	D	D	D	27	279	107.3	7.2	8	22	2.1	0.4
Hood River	6.30	272.3	24	360	110.5	14.7	157	1,287	315.4	33.5	31	71	10.0	2.0
Jackson	39.04	183.7	206	1,771	828.4	76.8	865	11,223	3,202.7	297.5	306	1,043	164.1	26.3
Jefferson	4.38	193.2	20	194	156.4	9.5	47	506	133.1	11.3	24	65	6.0	1.6
Josephine	7.18	84.7	49	D	D	D	312	4,150	987.9	105.1	106	354	44.8	8.5
Klamath	9.45	143.1	49	533	210.9	21.0	237	2,902	757.5	69.9	72	199	23.5	5.2
Lake	1.56	199.3	8	D	D	D	30	200	74.9	4.8	5	D	D	D
Lane	43.68	120.4	384	4,860	2,852.0	229.0	1,270	18,265	4,291.5	449.9	505	2,115	314.3	58.4
Lincoln	8.65	183.9	27	D	D	D	307	2,758	580.8	62.2	74	320	40.2	7.0
Linn	9.57	79.4	110	1,396	1,066.7	61.3	343	4,753	1,181.6	112.6	112	360	48.5	10.2
Malheur	6.76	222.5	36	584	340.7	17.6	120	1,834	534.5	45.8	29	55	9.0	1.4
Marion	71.92	217.5	264	3,694	3,190.0	177.6	1,103	15,497	3,862.2	377.0	417	1,991	269.7	58.6

1. Merchant wholesalers, except manufacturers' sales branches and offices.   2. Employer establishments.

Table B. States and Counties — **Professional Services, Manufacturing, and Accommodation and Food Services**

STATE County	Professional, scientific, and technical services, 2012				Manufacturing, 2012				Accommodation and food services, 2012			
	Number of establish-ments	Number of employees	Sales (mil dol)	Annual payroll (mil dol)	Number of establishments	Number of employees	Receipts (mil dol)	Annual payroll (mil dol)	Number of establishments	Number of employees	Receipts (mil dol)	Annual payroll (mil dol)
	147	148	149	150	151	152	153	154	155	156	157	158
OKLAHOMA— Cont'd												
Kiowa	16	D	D	D	5	D	D	D	15	D	D	D
Latimer	17	D	D	D	NA	NA	NA	NA	8	D	D	D
Le Flore	86	307	22.1	6.9	30	492	D	17.9	47	D	D	D
Lincoln	40	129	16.7	4.0	29	790	231.5	31.3	44	564	22.6	6.2
Logan	60	160	18.5	5.2	23	363	97.6	14.7	60	837	37.3	9.8
Love	14	D	D	D	5	111	D	4.6	29	579	53.8	10.4
McClain	72	269	40.4	10.4	22	385	103.5	13.9	62	1,110	46.3	12.8
McCurtain	34	D	D	D	29	2,477	1,342.0	91.7	53	691	37.0	7.5
McIntosh	37	D	D	D	14	62	9.5	2.2	34	465	20.8	5.4
Major	17	D	D	D	8	44	D	1.5	11	D	D	D
Marshall	23	D	D	D	20	1,097	245.2	43.8	28	289	17.4	4.1
Mayes	60	D	D	D	58	2,608	1,224.7	130.6	72	940	40.2	10.4
Murray	27	D	D	D	16	451	D	21.5	30	339	17.6	4.8
Muskogee	93	D	D	D	55	3,660	1,489.7	181.3	133	2,384	104.4	27.7
Noble	14	D	D	D	9	1,451	D	80.4	22	D	D	D
Nowata	8	D	D	D	11	254	D	11.3	9	D	D	D
Okfuskee	6	D	D	D	7	132	D	4.5	7	D	D	D
Oklahoma	2,947	22,906	3,372.4	1,360.6	701	21,353	7,681.0	948.9	1,780	39,515	1,909.4	525.0
Okmulgee	44	192	15.1	4.9	34	1,438	533.8	66.3	49	737	32.1	8.0
Osage	45	D	D	D	28	270	D	11.7	43	554	24.7	7.6
Ottawa	50	333	32.3	11.5	43	1,495	D	57.2	58	2,101	228.3	40.2
Pawnee	26	124	36.3	5.4	17	250	D	10.5	22	D	D	D
Payne	150	1,195	131.6	50.4	64	1,538	473.0	62.3	181	3,661	155.0	41.9
Pittsburg	98	422	46.8	18.0	31	999	332.7	50.2	96	1,560	74.2	18.2
Pontotoc	80	342	35.6	12.4	32	1,114	270.3	41.1	69	1,374	62.1	16.7
Pottawatomie	106	681	95.3	29.4	57	2,911	1,112.5	134.5	120	2,528	107.9	29.7
Pushmataha	14	D	D	D	7	85	D	2.7	15	124	4.4	1.2
Roger Mills	6	D	D	D	NA	NA	NA	NA	4	D	D	D
Rogers	135	782	110.8	44.2	150	6,775	3,040.1	365.1	109	3,258	308.2	77.7
Seminole	27	D	D	D	24	738	129.7	29.1	35	553	23.6	6.0
Sequoyah	41	126	10.5	3.2	22	104	D	4.4	59	D	D	D
Stephens	82	427	49.8	15.7	62	2,512	1,935.5	132.0	77	1,098	50.1	12.8
Texas	31	D	D	D	11	D	D	D	50	670	29.2	7.2
Tillman	8	D	D	D	5	D	D	D	10	86	3.5	0.9
Tulsa	2,382	19,526	3,446.4	1,198.9	903	37,197	18,770.2	1,997.1	1,519	30,477	1,425.3	414.5
Wagoner	72	199	18.0	6.1	61	2,163	746.5	111.5	69	D	D	D
Washington	89	D	D	D	36	965	253.2	53.4	111	1,831	91.0	23.2
Washita	20	D	D	D	10	39	D	1.4	14	D	D	D
Woods	23	D	D	D	5	40	D	1.9	33	332	19.2	3.8
Woodward	53	D	D	D	24	498	448.4	32.2	55	862	50.9	11.6
OREGON	11,663	84,493	11,386.1	5,841.1	5,289	D	D	D	10,610	150,482	8,466.8	2,438.5
Baker	40	172	18.4	5.4	29	494	105.1	18.0	56	557	27.5	8.2
Benton	284	1,996	332.6	125.1	93	1,613	412.7	71.4	209	3,087	142.8	41.6
Clackamas	1,231	7,805	1,215.9	525.9	553	15,789	5,371.5	901.1	777	11,638	637.5	188.3
Clatsop	87	326	22.1	7.2	47	1,671	905.8	103.1	248	3,138	210.1	59.7
Columbia	78	275	23.3	8.6	52	1,350	458.3	64.6	85	964	42.9	12.3
Coos	115	439	44.3	16.2	70	1,352	315.7	48.4	165	2,129	126.2	34.9
Crook	34	109	12.2	3.7	30	728	150.8	25.4	44	479	23.7	8.0
Curry	36	105	16.6	2.8	20	578	176.0	27.4	107	880	46.5	12.2
Deschutes	708	2,631	332.0	120.7	279	3,672	801.8	165.8	498	7,635	435.6	133.5
Douglas	157	777	64.4	26.5	126	3,640	1,017.3	158.4	262	3,391	217.2	57.2
Gilliam	3	D	D	D	NA	NA	NA	NA	9	68	1.5	0.6
Grant	18	D	D	D	4	D	D	D	24	135	6.0	1.8
Harney	11	45	2.8	1.2	4	D	D	D	32	186	11.5	2.9
Hood River	125	423	84.4	18.2	63	1,055	304.3	44.5	96	1,306	62.1	19.3
Jackson	506	D	D	D	308	5,370	1,624.6	217.4	586	7,381	382.2	112.5
Jefferson	21	55	3.8	1.3	19	838	168.3	32.4	45	404	21.3	5.9
Josephine	140	563	40.6	13.5	106	2,190	434.8	89.6	199	2,483	124.5	35.8
Klamath	125	625	107.1	24.7	56	1,662	449.9	63.8	171	1,978	110.7	30.1
Lake	12	D	D	D	11	190	34.5	7.2	31	144	6.6	1.6
Lane	948	5,301	583.9	226.2	529	12,345	4,039.3	581.3	937	13,627	711.8	203.7
Lincoln	95	289	27.6	9.8	50	965	579.4	61.0	274	3,593	216.4	63.4
Linn	164	802	84.8	27.8	181	6,318	2,253.6	355.2	216	2,796	130.4	35.5
Malheur	46	185	17.2	7.1	35	1,078	D	34.2	84	1,008	50.8	13.6
Marion	664	3,815	448.4	170.5	352	9,155	2,540.3	347.6	667	D	D	D

STATE County	Health care and social assistance, 2012				Other services, 2012				Nonemployer businesses, 2015		Value of residential construction authorized by building permits, 2017	
	Number of establishments	Number of employees	Receipts (mil dol)	Annual payroll (mil dol)	Number of establishments	Number of employees	Receipts (mil dol)	Annual payroll (mil dol)	Number	Receipts (mil dol)	New construction ($1,000)	Number of housing units
	159	160	161	162	163	164	165	166	167	168	169	170
OKLAHOMA— Cont'd												
Kiowa	24	577	30.6	13.8	8	28	3.5	0.8	606	27.1	215	1
Latimer	25	357	23.0	9.2	8	D	D	D	762	30.1	22	1
Le Flore	95	2,706	202.8	86.1	44	D	D	D	3,042	129.8	5,561	48
Lincoln	57	D	D	D	21	D	D	D	2,478	111.0	819	6
Logan	61	D	D	D	52	176	19.8	3.9	3,673	170.9	2,800	18
Love	10	133	5.5	2.6	6	62	3.1	1.3	630	28.8	0	0
McClain	68	D	D	D	48	D	D	D	3,308	151.8	73,751	359
McCurtain	60	1,634	79.5	37.0	37	146	11.1	3.8	2,241	97.1	700	4
McIntosh	49	916	71.0	25.3	23	102	13.1	3.1	1,412	58.2	710	12
Major	14	231	13.3	6.4	11	D	D	D	701	28.2	1,333	6
Marshall	26	590	70.0	23.2	14	50	4.2	1.1	1,054	46.8	1,700	20
Mayes	86	955	101.6	35.3	46	132	10.6	2.6	2,595	104.9	2,072	14
Murray	31	595	42.3	16.4	11	32	2.8	0.6	882	34.7	2,824	30
Muskogee	230	5,700	616.6	250.4	84	587	57.9	14.6	3,859	171.4	2,875	18
Noble	18	395	24.3	9.8	13	66	5.4	1.2	824	30.3	0	0
Nowata	16	D	D	D	10	30	2.2	0.6	670	24.7	257	4
Okfuskee	43	1,619	104.4	30.0	10	9	3.0	0.7	730	30.0	0	0
Oklahoma	2,873	56,884	7,921.4	2,618.1	1,414	9,503	1,063.4	285.5	61,687	3,142.2	876,625	3,888
Okmulgee	124	2,032	117.5	50.5	39	174	12.7	2.9	2,306	86.1	657	2
Osage	42	732	37.4	15.8	24	76	9.5	1.9	2,923	119.6	25,356	151
Ottawa	72	1,402	110.0	47.6	33	138	12.5	2.8	1,771	70.7	644	11
Pawnee	29	459	27.8	11.4	9	29	2.8	0.8	1,025	41.6	455	2
Payne	160	3,570	305.4	118.4	109	763	167.3	20.9	5,203	224.7	54,999	432
Pittsburg	116	2,560	218.9	87.2	54	340	24.5	7.3	2,659	111.9	2,125	19
Pontotoc	130	3,418	350.1	128.5	46	194	18.0	4.5	2,800	114.3	2,778	25
Pottawatomie	167	2,451	257.4	100.5	72	350	27.9	8.2	4,314	200.4	15,332	100
Pushmataha	24	732	43.3	16.6	7	28	2.5	0.7	800	36.0	0	0
Roger Mills	5	D	D	D	3	D	D	D	359	18.2	0	0
Rogers	193	2,953	268.3	108.2	83	392	43.2	11.7	6,563	288.4	76,627	459
Seminole	43	1,079	81.4	28.1	21	D	D	D	1,362	55.0	1,493	9
Sequoyah	79	2,345	105.4	46.6	29	D	D	D	2,733	116.9	9,439	89
Stephens	101	2,121	177.1	63.3	69	361	68.5	11.3	3,069	145.0	1,572	8
Texas	39	500	44.8	18.0	28	110	12.3	2.2	1,149	54.2	796	7
Tillman	18	298	18.3	7.2	7	D	D	D	442	15.7	500	2
Tulsa	2,063	48,166	5,808.5	2,135.3	1,184	8,068	1,123.9	251.1	49,147	2,414.4	526,379	2,443
Wagoner	76	816	52.8	21.9	58	172	25.9	4.9	5,338	241.2	86,953	500
Washington	172	3,091	284.1	113.0	78	473	38.5	11.9	3,135	135.7	22,386	249
Washita	14	297	13.9	7.4	10	27	3.3	0.6	800	31.3	0	0
Woods	20	D	D	D	18	D	D	D	783	31.1	300	2
Woodward	81	1,029	96.4	34.9	41	262	34.3	8.7	1,477	74.9	5,124	58
OREGON	12,475	217,584	24,956.8	9,689.3	6,894	37,941	4,435.0	1,149.1	278,839	13,308.1	4,153,707	20,053
Baker	53	664	54.6	22.9	37	D	D	D	1,136	39.9	5,104	22
Benton	271	5,258	588.1	258.8	147	891	153.8	30.3	5,783	238.1	36,396	136
Clackamas	1,136	17,962	2,424.2	896.7	677	D	D	D	30,579	1,680.3	464,060	1,702
Clatsop	137	2,163	213.9	89.8	91	D	D	D	2,935	132.9	40,716	168
Columbia	114	1,239	62.2	25.8	64	D	D	D	2,678	108.6	42,937	172
Coos	193	3,539	350.3	143.7	86	D	D	D	3,647	153.5	8,223	32
Crook	35	D	D	D	41	D	D	D	1,447	62.6	37,706	128
Curry	89	885	79.9	31.4	28	D	D	D	1,860	78.8	11,279	43
Deschutes	608	9,398	1,114.0	442.5	329	1,526	156.8	41.9	16,935	880.3	509,349	2,055
Douglas	312	4,830	544.3	244.2	135	657	134.1	17.3	5,739	244.6	58,675	244
Gilliam	9	D	D	D	5	D	D	D	110	3.1	NA	NA
Grant	22	D	D	D	14	D	D	D	475	16.8	NA	NA
Harney	22	309	29.8	10.8	14	D	D	D	517	16.9	2,702	12
Hood River	96	1,759	130.8	59.4	55	244	20.7	6.1	1,878	99.9	28,773	107
Jackson	674	12,116	1,443.8	510.7	315	1,836	157.3	51.0	16,786	753.1	186,575	805
Jefferson	40	622	51.2	24.1	22	D	D	D	1,003	42.1	28,708	112
Josephine	269	4,376	418.5	151.1	103	D	D	D	5,738	251.2	56,781	250
Klamath	203	3,067	323.5	122.2	102	D	D	D	3,350	150.4	27,322	133
Lake	21	292	28.6	12.1	10	D	D	D	481	17.2	3,468	13
Lane	1,135	20,576	2,247.4	828.6	611	3,480	443.9	97.7	23,337	1,040.8	193,504	842
Lincoln	119	1,657	169.4	73.8	111	D	D	D	3,442	175.5	34,712	167
Linn	216	4,660	422.3	174.0	142	D	D	D	5,859	241.4	123,986	539
Malheur	112	1,563	133.1	53.6	57	D	D	D	1,361	56.8	6,388	23
Marion	971	17,456	1,787.0	758.3	484	2,394	215.7	66.8	16,362	790.2	251,017	1,346

Table B. States and Counties — Government Employment and Payroll, and Local Government Finances

STATE County	Full-time equivalent employees	March payroll (dollars)	Administration, judicial, and legal	Police and corrections	Fire protection	Highways and transportation	Health and welfare	Natural resources and utilities	Education and libraries	Total (mil dol)	Inter-governmental (mil dol)	Taxes Total (mil dol)	Per capita Total	Per capita Property
	171	172	173	174	175	176	177	178	179	180	181	182	183	184
OKLAHOMA— Cont'd														
Kiowa	554	1,581,546	4.8	5.3	0.8	4.5	36.0	6.1	41.7	28.0	15.7	7.6	812	529
Latimer	754	2,593,866	3.2	2.1	0.0	3.7	15.7	2.1	72.9	31.9	13.6	7.0	636	318
Le Flore	1,864	5,014,735	3.3	6.0	0.4	3.5	3.6	5.5	75.8	125.0	71.3	28.8	578	300
Lincoln	1,059	2,802,834	6.5	7.7	1.4	5.3	0.3	7.8	70.0	71.7	38.3	21.4	627	358
Logan	875	2,347,456	7.2	7.5	3.8	5.0	0.6	6.6	67.9	60.0	30.1	18.4	421	259
Love	481	1,481,165	6.9	3.8	0.0	3.5	40.8	1.2	43.6	19.3	11.3	5.6	581	387
McClain	1,466	3,975,638	5.5	7.7	3.1	4.0	13.2	3.3	60.7	113.4	39.8	57.3	1,609	1,149
McCurtain	1,454	3,983,530	2.5	5.7	1.1	5.2	4.9	5.0	74.7	93.6	55.4	21.0	632	354
McIntosh	617	1,761,398	8.2	6.9	0.0	2.0	1.7	6.5	74.4	51.2	28.1	16.0	778	358
Major	407	1,118,428	9.8	3.5	0.5	9.3	27.6	2.4	45.6	26.8	10.8	7.7	1,002	610
Marshall	530	1,477,680	5.8	6.2	1.0	4.3	3.0	4.0	74.8	36.0	20.4	10.5	660	446
Mayes	1,472	4,043,970	8.9	5.6	0.7	3.0	3.2	7.1	70.0	95.9	51.9	32.6	792	421
Murray	655	1,707,493	6.8	7.5	3.1	2.3	19.7	11.8	48.5	44.1	24.1	10.4	762	306
Muskogee	3,141	8,727,804	4.0	8.5	4.5	4.3	6.8	5.1	65.6	275.3	85.7	75.6	1,071	547
Noble	622	1,661,200	5.9	6.7	2.5	6.0	18.5	6.1	53.2	44.6	16.7	14.0	1,213	863
Nowata	422	1,000,994	6.4	5.5	1.0	6.4	3.0	5.6	71.4	24.0	14.4	5.9	556	321
Okfuskee	460	1,098,562	3.9	6.1	0.0	6.2	0.9	3.6	76.5	34.2	24.4	6.6	531	326
Oklahoma	24,286	88,713,472	5.8	14.1	10.2	3.4	2.9	6.5	56.5	2,544.3	761.2	1,182.3	1,594	722
Okmulgee	1,552	4,277,777	5.1	5.1	2.9	3.2	3.2	5.9	73.4	89.1	52.5	23.2	586	272
Osage	1,130	2,941,818	9.3	7.0	1.1	14.2	11.3	6.8	48.8	74.5	39.5	19.7	410	229
Ottawa	1,421	4,097,793	5.8	5.3	2.3	2.7	1.7	8.0	73.0	80.7	44.3	21.1	654	269
Pawnee	597	1,604,091	5.8	5.4	1.0	3.9	18.9	7.0	56.7	35.2	20.6	8.5	514	277
Payne	3,634	11,234,115	4.8	7.5	4.2	1.9	31.7	8.2	40.1	192.3	66.9	89.1	1,137	592
Pittsburg	2,380	5,927,369	5.7	11.0	5.4	4.2	4.8	9.9	55.6	254.4	76.4	76.1	1,689	1,039
Pontotoc	1,436	4,130,846	4.3	6.5	3.1	5.4	2.1	5.4	70.4	103.9	50.5	34.4	905	337
Pottawatomie	2,336	6,720,266	6.0	7.2	4.0	2.8	0.1	7.4	71.9	167.8	93.6	52.1	737	301
Pushmataha	607	1,521,960	2.8	3.2	1.8	5.1	17.4	5.2	63.2	38.1	21.2	5.6	504	248
Roger Mills	256	746,029	12.5	6.7	0.0	25.4	12.9	5.1	34.8	20.6	10.5	6.4	1,687	1,138
Rogers	2,835	7,580,674	6.2	6.2	5.0	5.0	1.0	15.1	60.3	197.1	79.1	87.2	986	621
Seminole	1,164	2,881,448	5.7	5.9	2.6	4.0	1.0	5.8	73.2	80.4	47.5	19.7	772	340
Sequoyah	1,722	4,751,418	4.1	6.5	0.8	2.8	13.0	2.9	69.8	115.2	65.1	22.1	534	266
Stephens	1,530	4,875,145	5.7	8.9	3.8	3.6	0.3	5.9	70.1	109.2	51.3	39.9	891	426
Texas	1,138	3,387,767	5.5	7.8	2.0	6.4	23.7	3.4	50.3	93.1	28.0	34.4	1,601	1,035
Tillman	545	1,405,251	6.0	9.3	2.4	4.7	24.1	6.9	45.0	21.8	14.4	3.8	490	335
Tulsa	23,532	78,482,436	5.7	10.6	6.5	3.9	2.1	5.2	62.5	2,206.7	679.3	1,020.7	1,663	890
Wagoner	1,330	3,590,004	7.0	7.2	2.6	4.0	2.4	9.2	64.5	85.8	39.9	34.9	465	232
Washington	1,747	5,123,970	4.5	9.2	5.9	3.5	2.6	6.6	65.7	123.9	52.2	47.3	915	518
Washita	621	1,807,048	6.4	5.9	0.7	7.4	8.9	3.3	66.3	43.9	25.8	12.0	1,030	518
Woods	575	1,537,398	8.0	4.6	2.6	8.1	31.6	4.9	39.0	38.5	13.1	16.6	1,883	804
Woodward	891	2,568,486	5.9	8.6	3.5	5.0	7.2	4.7	61.8	69.5	25.7	32.5	1,583	708
OREGON	X	X	X	X	X	X	X	X	X	X	X	X	X	X
Baker	487	1,718,138	10.0	12.3	6.0	4.4	2.9	7.2	54.6	56.2	31.8	15.5	977	900
Benton	1,834	7,923,562	9.3	13.4	6.2	3.8	7.4	9.4	45.7	259.6	93.0	115.4	1,335	1,185
Clackamas	10,411	44,609,746	8.2	11.7	6.1	3.3	4.7	6.1	57.9	1,431.7	520.8	623.0	1,623	1,458
Clatsop	1,540	5,672,121	8.9	12.5	2.7	5.7	8.3	8.9	49.7	172.7	53.4	71.3	1,912	1,596
Columbia	1,444	6,022,192	7.2	9.3	8.1	2.1	0.4	16.3	52.3	192.4	87.9	59.7	1,211	1,123
Coos	3,079	13,113,856	2.7	5.5	1.8	2.4	45.7	3.7	37.5	386.2	116.4	74.2	1,187	1,048
Crook	584	2,274,092	9.3	15.0	2.6	3.8	3.7	7.2	51.7	72.1	28.3	22.8	1,099	940
Curry	803	3,143,734	7.1	10.1	0.4	5.5	38.6	5.6	31.1	90.5	25.4	26.9	1,211	1,076
Deschutes	4,773	21,188,503	8.1	12.1	5.4	2.6	5.0	7.0	55.3	649.0	217.1	283.8	1,749	1,579
Douglas	3,555	13,196,754	6.3	8.9	6.6	3.1	10.3	6.1	57.1	374.6	196.1	94.6	883	829
Gilliam	145	510,580	18.3	7.1	1.3	10.8	8.3	8.3	45.2	24.4	3.8	15.2	7,770	6,077
Grant	485	1,961,339	5.0	4.3	0.1	3.5	41.5	3.5	38.1	55.0	23.8	7.9	1,083	1,049
Harney	427	1,530,704	6.7	5.9	0.4	3.5	37.4	2.0	42.0	51.3	21.5	7.2	998	925
Hood River	639	2,757,629	6.9	8.8	4.6	6.5	3.0	12.1	54.2	95.2	38.6	26.4	1,171	1,023
Jackson	4,931	20,369,335	9.1	14.6	6.5	6.1	5.2	6.8	50.0	668.0	291.3	260.8	1,263	1,068
Jefferson	1,028	3,923,905	4.1	6.5	1.3	1.7	29.3	8.4	46.4	112.4	50.4	24.0	1,101	997
Josephine	2,192	8,995,230	6.6	12.9	2.5	3.4	1.3	3.1	68.4	243.6	119.9	70.8	854	781
Klamath	1,819	7,192,100	5.9	8.2	6.2	6.2	7.0	7.1	56.2	234.1	125.3	59.4	901	796
Lake	460	1,602,079	5.2	5.5	1.6	6.9	38.3	7.3	33.1	51.6	18.7	10.7	1,372	1,263
Lane	11,647	50,155,119	7.2	10.9	5.2	6.9	4.1	11.4	48.1	1,390.4	585.1	463.2	1,306	1,120
Lincoln	1,465	6,826,571	10.2	14.7	2.9	4.9	8.2	27.9	29.0	200.9	55.6	104.1	2,255	1,881
Linn	3,984	16,207,525	6.1	11.2	5.6	4.0	5.1	4.9	61.9	447.9	223.4	146.4	1,237	1,133
Malheur	1,459	4,992,780	4.9	8.6	1.3	2.7	8.2	7.2	66.0	146.8	85.7	25.2	821	712
Marion	12,046	53,396,211	5.2	8.9	3.6	3.2	3.6	3.7	69.6	1,311.4	678.7	400.1	1,250	1,131

1. Based on the resident population estimated as of July 1 of the year shown.

Table B. States and Counties — Local Government Finances, Government Employment, and Income Taxes

STATE County	Total (mil dol)	Per capita[1] (dollars)	Education	Health and hospitals	Police protection	Public welfare	Highways	Total (mil dol)	Per capita[1] (dollars)	Federal civilian	Federal military	State and local	Number of returns	Mean adjusted gross income	Mean income tax
	185	186	187	188	189	190	191	192	193	194	195	196	197	198	199
OKLAHOMA— Cont'd															
Kiowa	28.9	3,103	50.8	1.7	5.1	0.0	11.2	18.6	1,994	45	33	680	3,550	39,012	3,295
Latimer	33.5	3,038	45.3	21.6	2.5	0.0	11.1	4.0	365	28	37	1,053	4,160	43,882	3,941
Le Flore	128.2	2,571	63.3	5.2	3.9	0.1	7.2	41.9	840	154	180	4,761	17,830	41,745	3,397
Lincoln	69.8	2,043	62.1	1.0	6.3	0.0	9.1	22.4	656	79	130	1,632	13,640	46,904	4,387
Logan	60.7	1,390	56.3	2.5	8.0	0.0	8.8	34.1	782	59	166	1,286	18,160	62,611	7,550
Love	22.3	2,329	73.8	2.7	1.9	0.0	7.2	4.8	506	24	37	3,510	4,280	43,697	3,880
McClain	115.0	3,229	69.2	1.7	5.3	0.0	6.8	54.5	1,531	68	144	1,645	16,620	62,371	7,364
McCurtain	89.7	2,703	65.8	3.0	3.2	0.0	7.5	40.6	1,222	132	121	2,346	12,620	37,746	3,089
McIntosh	48.8	2,370	65.3	1.5	5.7	0.0	9.6	27.7	1,344	36	73	1,109	7,500	41,716	3,664
Major	27.0	3,519	43.6	21.9	3.4	0.2	15.4	8.4	1,096	29	29	373	3,430	55,576	5,746
Marshall	35.6	2,234	67.7	3.5	3.9	0.0	4.1	8.2	513	22	59	752	6,190	42,857	3,786
Mayes	94.4	2,293	68.5	1.3	6.4	0.0	6.3	46.9	1,140	66	151	2,463	16,020	49,175	4,852
Murray	43.2	3,162	41.5	28.0	3.6	0.0	4.3	20.9	1,532	69	51	2,556	5,790	47,843	4,784
Muskogee	284.3	4,027	38.4	31.9	3.5	0.0	3.0	95.6	1,354	2,973	247	6,335	27,040	46,766	4,648
Noble	44.7	3,877	46.3	20.3	3.8	0.0	12.0	32.4	2,812	34	41	1,289	4,830	53,688	5,553
Nowata	24.4	2,295	64.3	0.0	4.0	0.0	11.1	7.8	734	32	38	571	4,190	45,645	4,069
Okfuskee	34.0	2,753	77.0	0.0	2.3	0.0	10.3	17.9	1,449	25	41	1,118	4,020	40,323	3,088
Oklahoma	2,264.8	3,053	44.4	0.4	10.3	0.2	5.6	2,878.7	3,881	26,954	8,407	57,673	342,350	68,402	10,147
Okmulgee	89.9	2,270	65.7	0.5	4.7	0.0	7.2	96.2	2,428	126	141	3,475	15,150	44,035	4,012
Osage	73.9	1,543	50.5	8.5	2.4	0.8	12.7	17.6	367	163	181	2,646	17,790	53,363	5,682
Ottawa	87.3	2,709	53.9	2.6	5.3	0.0	11.8	33.9	1,051	102	115	5,573	12,800	38,895	3,258
Pawnee	33.0	2,003	61.8	3.2	3.7	0.0	10.4	20.5	1,247	216	61	966	6,350	47,527	4,435
Payne	185.3	2,363	48.5	0.4	11.8	0.1	8.4	115.8	1,477	229	285	14,832	29,920	56,223	6,594
Pittsburg	209.1	4,642	32.4	36.3	4.6	0.0	4.1	129.8	2,882	1,852	158	3,896	17,860	48,198	4,764
Pontotoc	100.3	2,643	61.6	0.6	5.6	0.0	7.3	22.3	586	164	137	6,735	16,250	49,734	5,353
Pottawatomie	171.7	2,427	59.2	0.4	6.1	0.0	8.2	62.2	879	147	260	6,278	28,850	47,589	4,660
Pushmataha	38.0	3,395	55.0	22.5	3.5	0.2	8.3	9.5	847	25	41	933	4,190	39,173	3,205
Roger Mills	21.1	5,590	33.6	1.3	3.6	0.0	42.2	0.7	196	37	14	359	1,580	68,253	7,801
Rogers	198.7	2,249	54.8	0.9	4.1	0.0	9.8	136.5	1,544	473	337	6,253	39,830	65,683	7,991
Seminole	79.1	3,109	54.5	1.3	3.6	0.0	6.2	27.2	1,070	156	92	1,873	9,140	42,046	3,761
Sequoyah	115.1	2,781	61.2	12.8	4.0	0.7	4.6	67.9	1,639	129	168	3,089	15,700	41,163	3,645
Stephens	108.9	2,432	55.9	0.5	5.5	0.0	9.4	48.1	1,074	81	163	1,987	18,050	56,492	6,377
Texas	98.3	4,570	36.3	26.0	2.2	0.1	7.6	39.3	1,829	74	77	1,589	9,750	47,199	4,161
Tillman	23.0	2,944	65.1	1.9	5.6	0.0	12.8	6.9	884	34	49	653	2,910	37,308	2,844
Tulsa	2,175.2	3,544	44.8	4.4	6.3	0.8	7.9	3,349.0	5,456	3,404	2,408	31,212	288,580	67,987	9,690
Wagoner	88.4	1,178	62.5	2.4	6.7	0.0	8.5	84.6	1,128	70	303	1,823	31,990	58,170	6,257
Washington	127.7	2,473	49.2	0.7	6.0	0.0	8.3	98.7	1,911	91	191	2,319	23,120	62,508	7,681
Washita	39.5	3,402	50.0	0.3	4.5	0.0	20.5	17.5	1,502	45	42	713	4,630	48,021	4,299
Woods	34.4	3,894	39.3	5.7	3.4	0.0	14.9	7.3	829	28	31	1,115	3,820	70,465	11,148
Woodward	71.3	3,469	43.9	1.0	6.2	0.0	7.9	53.7	2,613	88	73	1,613	8,770	56,053	7,050
OREGON	X	X	X	X	X	X	X	X	X	28,391	11,582	248,090	1,874,420	62,956	7,839
Baker	54.2	3,408	42.8	7.5	5.5	1.6	8.5	12.0	754	215	39	897	6,880	43,570	3,897
Benton	259.2	2,999	46.3	7.4	9.6	0.0	4.2	233.8	2,705	520	248	8,970	38,850	65,967	8,139
Clackamas	1,519.2	3,958	45.7	4.4	7.2	1.0	4.3	2,524.7	6,577	1,089	1,101	14,548	193,730	79,934	11,363
Clatsop	169.8	4,551	35.4	2.0	7.8	5.6	4.9	220.8	5,921	197	499	2,604	18,210	50,123	5,120
Columbia	192.3	3,902	51.6	1.9	4.3	0.2	3.0	214.6	4,353	71	126	1,807	22,600	57,524	5,810
Coos	396.6	6,341	32.9	41.8	2.9	0.1	2.5	240.2	3,841	327	371	4,994	27,290	45,962	4,550
Crook	64.9	3,132	41.4	3.3	7.3	0.2	6.7	59.1	2,852	292	56	879	9,640	47,436	4,525
Curry	101.4	4,557	23.1	33.1	4.3	2.7	5.0	92.8	4,173	85	99	1,118	10,500	46,634	4,949
Deschutes	663.5	4,089	49.1	3.5	7.4	0.4	5.0	1,093.2	6,736	913	453	13,507	87,380	65,753	8,510
Douglas	388.7	3,627	47.5	11.2	5.7	0.2	5.6	258.0	2,407	1,470	308	5,786	45,440	46,878	4,572
Gilliam	26.0	13,296	30.4	4.8	3.1	0.9	11.5	17.9	2,444	13	0	225	830	51,025	4,931
Grant	58.7	8,019	29.3	28.9	3.0	0.6	14.1	34.0	4,719	292	18	710	3,060	42,429	4,179
Harney	51.9	7,203	32.1	38.3	1.6	0.5	8.2	98.9	4,381	238	18	760	3,020	40,487	3,531
Hood River	99.3	4,399	46.3	2.2	2.8	0.6	8.1	887.0	4,297	110	56	1,120	11,650	59,245	6,926
Jackson	678.0	3,285	42.6	5.3	8.6	0.0	6.1	71.9	3,306	1,807	532	8,922	99,240	53,792	6,045
Jefferson	108.0	4,966	39.6	27.4	3.8	0.4	3.9	145.0	1,748	126	56	2,225	9,400	41,312	3,619
Josephine	253.3	3,055	59.6	2.9	7.1	0.1	5.0	72.7	1,103	270	211	2,834	36,270	47,023	4,960
Klamath	233.2	3,538	47.7	4.6	6.8	0.2	7.6	72.7	1,103	876	261	3,743	27,770	44,498	4,288
Lake	52.0	6,689	27.7	39.5	2.5	0.3	10.2	44.6	5,745	261	18	801	3,160	43,409	4,164
Lane	1,390.2	3,921	44.2	5.1	6.9	2.2	4.3	1,580.1	4,457	1,730	1,000	22,034	165,950	56,885	6,798
Lincoln	229.9	4,981	36.4	6.6	7.4	0.1	6.6	316.8	6,864	328	212	3,305	21,990	48,298	4,884
Linn	449.1	3,794	51.6	3.6	6.2	0.4	4.4	449.9	3,801	322	304	6,195	53,260	49,218	4,593
Malheur	157.2	5,132	62.3	4.3	3.4	0.2	3.8	62.8	2,050	222	68	3,024	10,690	40,658	3,493
Marion	1,325.2	4,141	57.0	3.6	5.0	0.2	4.6	1,931.4	6,036	1,317	828	34,325	144,660	52,692	5,430

1. Based on the resident population estimated as of July 1 of the year shown.

Table B. States and Counties — Land Area and Population

				Population, 2017				Population and population characteristics, 2017										
								Race alone or in combination, not Hispanic or Latino (percent)					Age (percent)					
State / county code	CBSA code¹	County code²	STATE County	Land area³ (sq. mi)	Total persons 2017	Rank	Per square mile	White	Black	American Indian, Alaska Native	Asian and Pacific Islander	Percent Hispanic or Latino⁴	Under 5 years	5 to 17 years	18 to 24 years	25 to 34 years	35 to 44 years	45 to 54 years
				1	2	3	4	5	6	7	8	9	10	11	12	13	14	15

State/county code	CBSA	County	STATE County	1	2	3	4	5	6	7	8	9	10	11	12	13	14	15
			OREGON— Cont'd															
41,049	25,840	6	Morrow	2,030.5	11,166	2,343	5.5	61.2	1.1	2.2	1.3	36.2	7.3	19.9	9.0	10.5	12.1	11.1
41,051	38,900	1	Multnomah	431.1	807,555	77	1,873.2	73.4	7.0	1.9	10.4	11.6	5.6	13.5	8.0	18.7	16.4	13.2
41,053	41,420	2	Polk	740.9	83,696	679	113.0	80.9	1.6	3.1	3.6	14.0	5.9	17.1	12.4	12.2	11.5	11.4
41,055		9	Sherman	823.6	1,758	3,070	2.1	90.0	1.5	2.7	1.1	7.1	5.1	14.0	5.9	10.6	11.2	11.7
41,057		6	Tillamook	1,102.4	26,690	1,540	24.2	86.4	0.9	2.3	2.3	10.7	5.1	13.9	6.3	11.0	10.3	11.6
41,059	25,840	4	Umatilla	3,215.4	76,985	722	23.9	67.9	1.3	4.4	1.7	26.8	6.8	18.6	8.9	13.9	12.4	12.1
41,061	29,260	7	Union	2,036.9	26,222	1,557	12.9	91.0	1.3	2.2	3.4	4.8	6.1	16.5	11.3	11.7	11.0	10.1
41,063		9	Wallowa	3,145.9	7,051	2,667	2.2	95.1	1.0	1.8	1.3	3.0	4.8	13.9	4.8	9.6	10.2	10.4
41,065	45,520	6	Wasco	2,381.1	26,437	1,550	11.1	76.1	0.9	4.0	2.6	18.4	6.5	15.9	7.7	13.2	11.1	11.1
41,067	38,900	1	Washington	724.3	588,957	113	813.1	69.3	2.9	1.3	13.7	16.8	6.2	17.1	8.1	15.6	15.0	13.4
41,069		9	Wheeler	1,716.0	1,357	3,089	0.8	91.1	1.7	3.6	2.1	5.6	4.5	10.5	6.0	7.8	8.5	10.0
41,071	38,900	1	Yamhill	715.9	105,722	569	147.7	79.5	1.5	2.4	3.3	16.0	5.8	16.7	10.4	12.6	12.7	12.3
42,000		0	PENNSYLVANIA	44,742.1	12,805,537	X	286.2	78.0	11.8	0.5	4.1	7.3	5.5	15.3	9.2	13.2	11.6	13.3
42,001	23,900	3	Adams	518.7	102,336	593	197.3	90.2	2.3	0.5	1.2	7.1	5.1	15.1	9.4	10.9	10.6	14.2
42,003	38,300	1	Allegheny	730.1	1,223,048	36	1,675.2	80.5	14.5	0.5	4.5	2.1	5.3	13.5	8.9	15.3	11.5	12.4
42,005	38,300	1	Armstrong	653.2	65,642	814	100.5	97.9	1.4	0.4	0.5	0.8	4.7	14.5	7.0	10.7	11.2	13.9
42,007	38,300	1	Beaver	434.7	166,140	390	382.2	91.3	7.7	0.5	0.9	1.6	5.2	14.3	7.5	11.6	11.1	13.3
42,009		6	Bedford	1,012.3	48,480	1,012	47.9	97.6	1.0	0.4	0.6	1.2	4.8	14.7	7.2	10.2	10.7	14.1
42,011	39,740	2	Berks	856.4	417,854	168	487.9	73.0	5.1	0.4	1.9	21.0	5.8	16.7	9.6	12.2	11.5	13.7
42,013	11,020	3	Blair	525.8	123,457	512	234.8	96.0	2.7	0.4	1.0	1.3	5.4	15.3	7.8	12.3	11.3	13.7
42,015	42,380	6	Bradford	1,147.4	60,853	859	53.0	97.1	1.0	0.7	0.9	1.4	5.8	16.1	7.3	10.7	10.4	13.3
42,017	37,980	1	Bucks	604.4	628,341	106	1,039.6	85.5	4.6	0.5	5.6	5.4	4.9	15.7	8.0	11.1	11.6	14.8
42,019	38,300	1	Butler	788.6	187,108	349	237.3	95.7	1.6	0.4	1.8	1.5	5.2	15.1	8.7	11.3	11.6	14.5
42,021	27,780	3	Cambria	688.3	133,054	477	193.3	94.2	4.4	0.3	0.9	1.6	4.9	14.3	9.1	10.4	10.8	12.9
42,023		7	Cameron	396.2	4,592	2,856	11.6	97.2	1.5	0.7	0.7	1.2	4.9	12.8	6.8	9.0	8.9	13.4
42,025	10,900	2	Carbon	381.5	63,853	832	167.4	92.7	2.1	0.6	0.9	4.7	4.8	14.6	6.8	11.0	11.3	14.7
42,027	44,300	3	Centre	1,109.9	162,660	399	146.6	86.8	4.1	0.4	7.2	3.0	4.1	11.2	24.0	14.1	10.5	11.2
42,029	37,980	1	Chester	750.5	519,293	133	691.9	81.0	6.6	0.5	6.1	7.6	5.6	17.3	9.1	11.5	12.2	14.4
42,031		6	Clarion	600.8	38,458	1,217	64.0	97.0	1.6	0.5	1.1	0.9	5.2	13.6	12.3	11.9	10.2	12.9
42,033	20,180	4	Clearfield	1,144.7	79,685	702	69.6	93.8	2.8	0.4	0.9	3.0	4.7	13.6	7.8	12.0	12.1	14.8
42,035	30,820	4	Clinton	888.0	38,998	1,206	43.9	96.1	2.0	0.5	1.0	1.5	5.5	14.8	14.6	11.2	10.0	11.9
42,037	14,100	3	Columbia	483.1	65,932	811	136.5	94.1	2.3	0.5	1.4	2.8	4.5	13.2	15.7	10.7	10.1	12.7
42,039	32,740	4	Crawford	1,012.3	86,159	666	85.1	96.0	2.5	0.5	0.9	1.3	5.5	15.5	9.2	10.9	10.6	13.3
42,041	25,420	2	Cumberland	545.5	250,066	273	458.4	87.7	4.8	0.5	5.1	3.9	5.5	14.9	9.7	13.0	12.1	13.2
42,043	25,420	2	Dauphin	525.1	275,710	248	525.1	68.4	19.4	0.7	5.2	9.2	6.2	16.2	8.2	13.8	11.8	13.1
42,045	37,980	1	Delaware	183.8	564,696	117	3,072.3	68.5	22.6	0.6	6.6	3.8	5.9	16.1	10.0	13.0	11.9	13.2
42,047	41,260	7	Elk	827.4	30,197	1,427	36.5	98.1	0.8	0.5	0.6	0.8	4.9	14.5	7.2	9.6	10.2	15.2
42,049	21,500	2	Erie	799.1	274,541	250	343.6	86.4	8.8	0.5	2.2	4.3	5.6	15.9	10.0	13.2	11.1	12.7
42,051	38,300	1	Fayette	790.3	131,504	485	166.4	93.4	5.8	0.5	0.9	1.2	5.2	14.1	7.4	11.9	11.3	13.9
42,053		9	Forest	427.3	7,297	2,640	17.1	72.8	20.7	0.6	0.3	6.4	1.9	7.8	11.2	17.7	11.7	13.0
42,055	16,540	3	Franklin	772.2	154,234	428	199.7	89.5	4.5	0.5	1.5	5.8	5.9	16.5	7.6	12.1	11.7	13.5
42,057		8	Fulton	437.6	14,590	2,123	33.3	97.1	1.7	0.7	0.4	1.3	5.0	15.1	7.5	10.5	11.4	14.8
42,059		6	Greene	575.9	36,770	1,258	63.8	94.6	3.7	0.7	0.6	1.5	5.3	14.1	9.3	12.3	12.2	13.7
42,061	26,500	6	Huntingdon	874.7	45,491	1,065	52.0	91.7	6.1	0.4	0.9	2.0	4.9	13.8	9.3	12.4	11.8	13.7
42,063	26,860	4	Indiana	827.0	84,953	675	102.7	94.8	2.9	0.4	1.5	1.3	4.7	13.5	16.0	10.9	10.9	13.6
42,065		7	Jefferson	652.4	43,804	1,097	67.1	98.1	0.9	0.6	0.5	0.9	5.7	15.5	7.5	11.5	10.9	13.1
42,067		6	Juniata	391.4	24,514	1,626	62.6	95.1	1.1	0.4	0.6	3.6	5.5	16.9	7.5	11.0	11.2	13.7
42,069	42,540	2	Lackawanna	458.8	210,761	316	459.4	86.7	3.6	0.4	3.3	7.5	5.3	15.1	8.9	12.5	11.1	13.3
42,071	29,540	2	Lancaster	943.9	542,903	125	575.2	83.3	4.5	0.4	2.8	10.5	6.7	17.1	9.0	13.1	11.3	12.3
42,073	35,260	4	Lawrence	358.2	87,069	663	243.1	93.9	5.3	0.4	0.8	1.4	5.4	14.6	8.3	10.7	10.7	13.0
42,075	30,140	3	Lebanon	361.8	139,754	462	386.3	83.2	2.6	0.4	1.7	13.3	5.9	16.9	8.5	11.6	11.7	12.7
42,077	10,900	2	Lehigh	345.2	366,494	191	1,061.7	65.9	6.8	0.4	4.1	24.6	6.0	16.8	9.1	13.1	12.4	13.2
42,079	42,540	2	Luzerne	890.3	317,343	217	356.4	82.8	4.7	0.4	1.6	11.8	5.1	14.5	8.8	12.6	11.4	13.8
42,081	48,700	3	Lycoming	1,228.6	113,841	541	92.7	92.5	5.9	0.6	1.0	2.0	5.5	15.1	9.0	13.1	10.9	12.9
42,083	14,620	7	McKean	979.2	41,330	1,144	42.2	94.5	2.9	0.7	0.9	2.2	4.8	14.9	9.4	11.9	11.5	13.4
42,085	49,660	2	Mercer	672.6	111,750	545	166.1	91.7	6.9	0.5	1.1	1.5	5.0	14.7	9.9	10.4	10.5	13.6
42,087	30,380	4	Mifflin	411.0	46,388	1,041	112.9	96.8	1.3	0.4	0.9	1.7	6.3	16.2	7.3	11.1	10.5	13.5
42,089	20,700	3	Monroe	608.3	168,046	384	276.3	67.9	14.5	0.8	3.0	15.9	4.5	15.3	10.8	11.1	10.6	15.1
42,091	37,980	1	Montgomery	482.9	826,075	74	1,710.7	77.4	10.3	0.4	8.6	5.2	5.5	16.1	8.1	12.5	12.4	13.9
42,093	14,100	3	Montour	130.2	18,272	1,907	140.3	92.3	2.2	0.4	3.4	2.8	5.6	14.6	6.7	13.8	11.1	12.4
42,095	10,900	2	Northampton	369.6	303,405	231	820.9	78.3	6.3	0.5	3.5	13.2	4.9	15.2	9.9	11.9	11.5	13.7
42,097	44,300	4	Northumberland	458.0	92,029	639	200.9	93.6	2.9	0.4	0.7	3.5	5.2	14.5	7.2	12.2	11.5	13.6
42,099	25,420	2	Perry	551.4	46,127	1,050	83.7	96.4	1.4	0.6	0.8	2.0	5.8	15.7	7.2	11.1	11.6	14.6
42,101	37,980	1	Philadelphia	134.2	1,580,863	23	11,779.9	36.1	42.3	0.8	8.2	14.8	6.7	15.1	10.1	19.0	12.4	11.7
42,103	35,620	1	Pike	545.0	55,691	912	102.2	81.8	6.1	0.8	1.8	11.0	3.9	14.7	8.0	9.1	10.3	15.6

1. CBSA = Core Based Statistical Area. See Appendix A for explanation. See Appendix B for list of metropolitan areas with component counties. See Appendix A for definition. Service of USDA Rural-Urban Continuum Codes.   2. County type code from the Economic Research Service of USDA Rural-Urban Continuum Codes. See Appendix A for definition.   3. Dry land or land partially or temporarily covered by water.   4. May be of any race.

Table B. States and Counties — Population and Households

STATE County	55 to 64 years (16)	65 to 74 years (17)	75 years and over (18)	Percent female (19)	Total persons 2000 (20)	Total persons 2010 (21)	Pct change 2000-2010 (22)	Pct change 2010-2017 (23)	Births (24)	Deaths (25)	Net Migration (26)	Number (27)	Persons per household (28)	Family households (29)	Female family householder[1] (30)	One person (31)
OREGON— Cont'd																
Morrow	13.9	9.8	6.3	48.7	10,995	11,177	1.7	-0.1	1,179	559	-644	3,848	2.90	76.1	10.6	19.7
Multnomah	11.6	8.2	4.8	50.5	660,486	735,169	11.3	9.8	68,323	40,681	44,121	313,181	2.43	54.8	10.6	32.5
Polk	12.1	10.4	7.1	51.2	62,380	75,411	20.9	11.0	6,420	4,800	6,676	28,725	2.67	68.5	9.6	23.2
Sherman	16.2	13.1	12.2	49.3	1,934	1,766	-8.7	-0.5	124	117	-16	804	2.11	57.2	7.1	32.8
Tillamook	16.7	15.9	9.2	49.6	24,262	25,254	4.1	5.7	1,823	2,107	1,721	10,154	2.45	62.8	8.1	30.9
Umatilla	12.1	8.9	6.3	47.8	70,548	75,885	7.6	1.4	7,689	4,620	-1,946	26,669	2.69	68.3	13.7	25.7
Union	13.7	11.2	8.4	50.3	24,530	25,744	4.9	1.9	2,202	1,912	202	10,119	2.47	64.3	8.6	26.6
Wallowa	18.3	16.4	11.6	50.9	7,226	7,008	-3.0	0.6	434	602	212	3,039	2.21	63.1	9.4	34.4
Wasco	14.4	11.9	8.2	50.1	23,791	25,211	6.0	4.9	2,249	2,227	1,210	9,883	2.48	65.8	10.3	27.6
Washington	11.7	7.9	5.0	50.5	445,342	529,864	19.0	11.2	51,682	23,004	30,520	209,309	2.66	67.7	10.0	24.7
Wheeler	17.8	18.3	16.5	49.6	1,547	1,439	-7.0	-5.7	75	135	-25	696	1.94	63.5	4.6	32.5
Yamhill	12.9	9.8	6.9	50.0	84,992	99,191	16.7	6.6	8,206	6,333	4,692	35,002	2.77	71.3	11.7	22.5
PENNSYLVANIA	14.1	10.0	7.8	51.0	12,281,054	12,702,857	3.4	0.8	1,025,691	935,944	20,444	4,961,929	2.49	64.4	11.9	29.6
Adams	15.0	11.4	8.3	50.7	91,292	101,417	11.1	0.9	7,337	7,100	748	38,269	2.55	71.4	9.9	24.0
Allegheny	14.6	10.1	8.3	51.7	1,281,666	1,223,338	-4.6	0.0	95,890	99,154	3,758	531,075	2.25	57.2	11.4	35.5
Armstrong	16.5	11.9	9.4	50.3	72,392	68,938	-4.8	-4.8	4,644	6,186	-1,716	28,250	2.36	66.9	10.0	28.8
Beaver	16.0	11.4	9.5	51.4	181,412	170,539	-6.0	-2.6	12,417	15,117	-1,516	69,921	2.38	65.6	11.6	29.9
Bedford	15.8	11.9	10.5	50.1	49,984	49,768	-0.4	-2.6	3,392	3,925	-722	19,757	2.44	68.8	8.2	26.3
Berks	13.5	9.5	7.4	50.8	373,638	411,538	10.1	1.5	35,030	27,320	-1,269	152,451	2.63	69.0	12.8	25.1
Blair	14.8	11.1	9.1	51.0	129,144	127,076	-1.6	-2.8	9,758	11,602	-1,671	50,954	2.41	63.5	11.0	31.3
Bradford	15.4	11.8	9.1	50.5	62,761	62,709	-0.1	-3.0	5,157	4,945	-2,064	24,483	2.49	68.1	9.2	26.4
Bucks	15.7	10.3	7.8	50.9	597,635	625,238	4.6	0.5	42,733	41,153	1,822	233,517	2.64	71.3	9.4	24.1
Butler	15.4	10.4	7.9	50.5	174,083	183,862	5.6	1.8	13,164	13,768	3,999	74,762	2.41	68.1	7.9	26.5
Cambria	15.7	12.1	9.9	50.8	152,598	143,674	-5.8	-7.4	9,624	13,203	-7,070	57,214	2.27	63.6	11.6	32.2
Cameron	18.2	14.6	11.3	50.0	5,974	5,085	-14.9	-9.7	334	466	-362	2,187	2.16	59.1	10.2	36.4
Carbon	16.1	12.1	8.6	50.4	58,802	65,248	11.0	-2.1	4,276	5,790	173	25,813	2.46	65.5	10.5	27.0
Centre	11.3	7.8	5.9	47.4	135,758	154,030	13.5	5.6	9,342	6,945	6,250	57,037	2.49	57.6	6.8	28.1
Chester	14.1	9.2	6.6	50.7	433,501	499,175	15.1	4.0	39,889	27,624	8,240	186,721	2.67	70.3	8.7	23.4
Clarion	14.6	10.6	8.7	51.1	41,765	39,991	-4.2	-3.8	2,892	3,068	-1,364	15,848	2.36	62.8	8.3	28.0
Clearfield	15.0	11.0	9.1	47.6	83,382	81,594	-2.1	-2.3	5,349	6,745	-456	31,303	2.42	66.0	9.1	29.5
Clinton	13.5	9.9	8.3	51.0	37,914	39,241	3.5	-0.6	3,074	2,881	-425	14,710	2.54	66.5	10.0	26.4
Columbia	14.2	10.7	8.2	51.8	64,151	67,296	4.9	-2.0	4,382	4,980	-721	26,356	2.37	63.6	9.9	27.0
Crawford	15.0	11.9	8.1	51.1	90,366	88,761	-1.8	-2.9	6,845	7,119	-2,298	34,522	2.42	67.0	10.7	27.1
Cumberland	13.4	10.2	7.9	50.5	213,674	235,408	10.2	6.2	18,795	16,224	12,234	96,501	2.39	64.3	8.7	29.7
Dauphin	14.1	9.7	6.8	51.5	251,798	268,100	6.5	2.8	24,835	17,819	718	110,211	2.40	63.2	13.9	30.7
Delaware	14.0	8.9	7.2	51.9	550,864	558,979	1.4	1.1	48,271	39,345	-2,762	203,610	2.65	66.9	14.6	28.7
Elk	16.8	11.6	10.0	49.9	35,112	31,946	-9.0	-5.5	2,136	2,830	-1,049	13,362	2.30	63.9	9.1	32.6
Erie	14.2	9.9	7.5	50.6	280,843	280,564	-0.1	-2.1	22,920	20,396	-8,511	110,047	2.42	63.8	13.2	30.0
Fayette	15.6	11.6	8.9	50.5	148,644	136,602	-8.1	-3.7	10,105	13,036	-2,057	53,654	2.41	62.4	12.2	32.6
Forest	14.2	13.2	9.2	31.5	4,946	7,716	56.0	-5.4	234	618	-35	1,816	1.68	58.4	5.7	37.3
Franklin	13.6	10.6	8.6	50.9	129,313	149,618	15.7	3.1	13,207	10,626	2,191	59,392	2.53	69.1	9.8	26.2
Fulton	14.8	12.1	9.0	49.2	14,261	14,844	4.1	-1.7	1,031	1,070	-206	5,989	2.44	69.5	8.4	26.2
Greene	14.7	11.0	7.3	48.2	40,672	38,686	-4.9	-5.0	2,799	3,147	-1,565	14,400	2.34	64.3	12.3	28.1
Huntingdon	14.1	11.5	8.5	46.9	45,586	46,031	1.0	-1.2	3,086	3,336	-256	16,975	2.40	67.6	8.3	28.1
Indiana	14.3	10.6	8.3	49.9	89,605	88,893	-0.8	-4.4	6,025	6,474	-3,481	34,059	2.40	62.7	8.0	28.4
Jefferson	15.4	11.1	9.3	50.3	45,932	45,196	-1.6	-3.1	3,614	4,089	-893	18,360	2.39	68.9	9.0	28.6
Juniata	14.4	11.1	8.7	49.8	22,821	24,636	8.0	-0.5	1,943	1,852	-198	9,326	2.63	68.9	7.6	25.3
Lackawanna	14.2	10.8	8.8	51.6	213,295	214,440	0.5	-1.7	15,905	19,326	-131	85,174	2.40	60.9	12.0	33.0
Lancaster	13.0	9.5	8.0	51.0	470,658	519,447	10.4	4.5	51,722	34,713	6,859	196,171	2.65	70.4	9.5	23.8
Lawrence	15.7	11.6	10.0	51.6	94,643	91,140	-3.7	-4.5	6,660	8,049	-2,647	36,302	2.37	68.6	12.8	29.3
Lebanon	13.5	10.4	8.7	50.9	120,327	133,577	11.0	4.6	11,744	10,346	4,898	52,247	2.56	68.6	11.1	26.9
Lehigh	13.1	9.1	7.2	51.1	312,090	349,673	12.0	4.8	30,226	24,201	11,013	135,363	2.58	66.7	13.5	27.1
Luzerne	14.2	10.8	8.8	50.6	319,250	320,916	0.5	-1.1	22,877	28,829	2,643	127,514	2.40	63.3	13.4	32.1
Lycoming	14.8	10.5	8.3	51.0	120,044	116,108	-3.3	-2.0	9,090	9,218	-2,110	45,587	2.42	65.0	10.7	29.2
McKean	15.1	10.4	8.4	48.5	45,936	43,450	-5.4	-4.9	3,010	3,823	-1,289	17,259	2.29	64.0	12.4	29.7
Mercer	15.2	11.3	9.7	50.6	120,293	116,674	-3.0	-4.2	8,231	10,092	-3,011	45,350	2.36	66.4	11.8	29.5
Mifflin	13.9	11.3	9.9	51.1	46,486	46,682	0.4	-0.6	4,169	3,836	-589	18,695	2.46	67.0	11.1	26.7
Monroe	15.8	10.3	6.4	50.6	138,687	169,838	22.5	-1.1	10,283	10,085	-2,016	57,127	2.88	71.2	11.7	22.5
Montgomery	14.1	9.5	7.8	51.3	750,097	799,930	6.6	3.3	64,701	53,583	15,726	309,884	2.56	68.5	9.4	26.2
Montour	15.2	10.5	10.1	52.0	18,236	18,267	0.2	0.0	1,542	1,576	52	7,361	2.40	61.9	10.2	31.7
Northampton	14.3	10.3	8.3	50.8	267,066	297,696	11.5	1.9	20,831	20,900	6,034	112,819	2.57	69.2	11.4	24.9
Northumberland	15.0	11.4	9.4	49.8	94,556	94,514	0.0	-2.6	6,909	8,348	-984	39,192	2.27	63.5	10.7	31.3
Perry	15.2	11.2	6.9	49.4	43,602	45,965	5.4	0.4	3,944	3,144	-620	17,883	2.52	70.7	9.4	24.4
Philadelphia	11.6	7.7	5.7	52.7	1,517,550	1,526,006	0.6	3.6	163,510	104,570	-3,187	582,594	2.59	53.3	20.4	38.7
Pike	16.5	13.1	8.8	49.6	46,302	57,353	23.9	-2.9	2,745	3,224	-1,190	21,135	2.64	72.1	8.9	23.4

1. No spouse present.

Table B. States and Counties — Population, Vital Statistics, Health, and Crime

STATE County	Daytime Population, 2012-2016			Births, 2017		Deaths, 2017		Persons under 65 with no health insurance, 2016		Medicare, 2017			Serious crimes known to police[2], 2016 Total	
	Persons in group quarters, 2017	Number	Employment/ residence ratio	Total	Rate[1]	Number	Rate[1]	Number	Percent	Total beneficiaries	Enrolled in Original Medicare	Enrolled in Medicare Advantage	Number	Rate[3]
	32	33	34	35	36	37	38	39	40	41	42	43	44	45
OREGON— Cont'd														
Morrow	23	12,138	1.20	174	15.6	79	7.1	1,028	10.9	1,965	1,766	199	310	2,754
Multnomah	19,968	878,433	1.25	9,378	11.6	5,885	7.3	49,888	7.3	125,064	51,667	73,397	42,504	5,384
Polk	1,836	66,497	0.64	943	11.3	682	8.1	4,627	7.0	18,226	7,719	10,507	2,212	2,742
Sherman	0	1,803	1.13	19	10.8	14	8.0	106	8.3	511	420	91	NA	NA
Tillamook	480	25,540	1.00	259	9.7	303	11.4	1,637	8.5	7,558	5,704	1,854	449	1,734
Umatilla	4,179	75,389	0.96	987	12.8	651	8.5	6,166	10.1	13,612	12,379	1,233	1,869	2,425
Union	661	25,711	1.00	315	12.0	275	10.5	1,481	7.3	6,226	5,536	690	640	2,466
Wallowa	105	6,824	1.00	62	8.8	65	9.2	339	6.9	2,289	2,140	149	NA	NA
Wasco	741	25,646	1.00	333	12.6	297	11.2	2,160	10.7	6,275	4,966	1,309	638	2,451
Washington	7,205	566,696	1.01	7,066	12.0	3,448	5.9	30,568	6.0	77,133	32,464	44,669	9,957	1,703
Wheeler	24	1,308	0.88	10	7.4	14	10.3	81	9.5	391	329	62	7	519
Yamhill	5,583	94,988	0.84	1,185	11.2	891	8.4	6,077	7.4	19,518	9,673	9,846	1,951	1,876
PENNSYLVANIA	423,488	12,723,938	0.99	138,818	10.8	131,458	10.3	691,654	6.8	2,635,113	1,546,488	1,088,625	263,242	2,059
Adams	3,966	87,283	0.71	1,016	9.9	998	9.8	5,625	7.1	21,425	14,936	6,489	1,004	983
Allegheny	35,431	1,317,271	1.14	13,149	10.8	13,699	11.2	48,393	4.9	254,712	96,406	158,307	28,974	2,359
Armstrong	650	57,429	0.65	564	8.6	887	13.5	3,147	6.1	18,307	6,544	11,764	515	788
Beaver	3,212	148,014	0.74	1,639	9.9	2,089	12.6	7,330	5.6	40,151	14,333	25,818	3,541	2,163
Bedford	551	44,506	0.80	445	9.2	529	10.9	2,857	7.6	12,011	6,157	5,855	417	889
Berks	11,553	393,891	0.90	4,696	11.2	3,774	9.0	25,190	7.5	81,599	53,246	28,352	7,910	1,907
Blair	3,752	131,296	1.10	1,285	10.4	1,649	13.4	5,664	5.8	31,540	15,711	15,829	1,964	1,572
Bradford	666	62,709	1.03	694	11.4	706	11.6	3,514	7.3	14,491	10,761	3,729	1,025	1,685
Bucks	8,094	571,617	0.83	5,960	9.5	5,981	9.5	25,077	4.9	126,048	83,803	42,245	9,583	1,531
Butler	5,464	186,929	1.01	1,838	9.8	1,969	10.5	6,485	4.3	40,509	15,955	24,554	2,419	1,295
Cambria	6,037	134,602	0.94	1,276	9.6	1,745	13.1	6,099	6.0	35,812	13,471	22,341	2,122	1,576
Cameron	92	4,892	1.04	41	8.9	67	14.6	213	6.1	1,429	980	449	78	1,676
Carbon	699	52,544	0.59	580	9.1	775	12.1	3,165	6.3	15,446	12,050	3,396	1,357	2,136
Centre	19,777	166,713	1.10	1,265	7.8	1,043	6.4	8,764	7.2	23,292	12,307	10,985	1,872	1,160
Chester	13,518	505,439	0.97	5,438	10.5	4,072	7.8	27,100	6.3	86,194	65,344	20,849	6,859	1,329
Clarion	1,379	36,622	0.86	410	10.7	428	11.1	2,225	7.4	8,645	5,475	3,170	489	1,244
Clearfield	5,510	80,383	0.98	710	8.9	946	11.9	4,035	6.8	19,111	11,422	7,689	1,429	1,772
Clinton	2,177	37,553	0.89	416	10.7	392	10.1	2,392	8.0	7,764	4,451	3,313	495	1,257
Columbia	3,944	64,644	0.93	564	8.6	702	10.6	3,553	7.0	15,220	9,293	5,926	993	1,514
Crawford	3,931	84,277	0.93	916	10.6	942	10.9	5,369	8.1	20,832	13,749	7,083	1,192	1,389
Cumberland	12,407	252,988	1.08	2,638	10.5	2,274	9.1	11,365	5.9	53,675	32,654	21,021	2,974	1,200
Dauphin	6,786	321,721	1.38	3,331	12.1	2,518	9.1	15,431	6.8	52,652	27,061	25,591	6,311	2,324
Delaware	22,633	512,217	0.81	6,473	11.5	5,480	9.7	27,150	5.9	104,119	74,763	29,356	12,383	2,199
Elk	355	30,704	0.97	286	9.5	366	12.1	1,241	5.2	7,688	5,957	1,732	532	1,739
Erie	12,534	283,728	1.04	3,031	11.0	2,756	10.0	13,605	6.2	57,875	31,137	26,738	5,924	2,141
Fayette	4,338	121,217	0.75	1,388	10.6	1,835	14.0	6,867	6.7	32,578	14,176	18,401	2,958	2,244
Forest	2,628	8,600	2.12	32	4.4	85	11.6	225	7.1	1,724	1,050	674	97	1,323
Franklin	2,559	143,976	0.88	1,810	11.7	1,587	10.3	11,636	9.4	33,103	25,048	8,055	2,502	1,625
Fulton	122	13,574	0.84	123	8.4	139	9.5	909	7.9	3,590	2,731	858	181	1,245
Greene	2,953	39,713	1.14	387	10.5	433	11.8	1,564	5.6	8,172	3,666	4,506	591	1,589
Huntingdon	4,847	42,494	0.82	393	8.6	511	11.2	2,078	6.5	10,463	6,462	4,001	496	1,161
Indiana	4,827	87,497	1.00	749	8.8	889	10.5	5,084	7.7	18,947	7,300	11,647	1,364	1,580
Jefferson	774	42,638	0.90	483	11.0	517	11.8	2,561	7.4	10,837	6,417	4,420	385	872
Juniata	292	21,350	0.69	260	10.6	260	10.6	1,618	8.2	4,994	2,694	2,299	196	814
Lackawanna	7,837	215,021	1.02	2,157	10.2	2,557	12.1	10,242	6.2	48,627	34,775	13,852	3,839	1,874
Lancaster	12,762	520,928	0.95	7,206	13.3	5,008	9.2	47,029	10.7	106,172	64,995	41,177	8,354	1,552
Lawrence	2,090	81,945	0.83	929	10.7	1,086	12.5	4,129	6.1	23,321	9,563	13,758	1,511	1,745
Lebanon	3,670	127,303	0.85	1,583	11.3	1,484	10.6	8,168	7.4	30,801	18,369	12,432	2,151	1,633
Lehigh	9,077	375,004	1.10	4,194	11.4	3,329	9.1	21,100	7.1	73,553	48,764	24,790	8,313	2,298
Luzerne	11,868	320,892	1.01	3,104	9.8	3,959	12.5	15,920	6.5	73,002	53,686	19,317	6,574	2,089
Lycoming	5,266	118,830	1.05	1,167	10.3	1,320	11.6	5,161	5.8	26,197	17,491	8,706	1,991	1,721
McKean	3,159	41,408	0.93	394	9.5	515	12.5	1,873	6.0	9,683	7,371	2,312	626	1,519
Mercer	6,536	116,864	1.05	1,110	9.9	1,442	12.9	5,851	7.0	27,899	14,665	13,234	2,094	1,870
Mifflin	559	44,143	0.88	590	12.7	517	11.1	3,098	8.5	10,870	6,267	4,603	739	1,595
Monroe	4,443	154,766	0.84	1,408	8.4	1,517	9.0	10,153	7.5	32,007	24,756	7,250	3,546	2,146
Montgomery	21,728	884,540	1.17	8,814	10.7	7,803	9.4	31,145	4.6	162,451	115,798	46,653	13,585	1,656
Montour	844	26,104	1.92	213	11.7	219	12.0	700	4.9	4,302	2,104	2,198	249	1,342
Northampton	11,196	277,200	0.84	2,795	9.2	2,914	9.6	16,104	6.7	64,600	45,705	18,895	5,098	1,697
Northumberland	3,711	84,346	0.77	911	9.9	1,079	11.7	4,456	6.3	22,550	14,503	8,047	1,421	1,532
Perry	659	33,002	0.44	527	11.4	428	9.3	3,077	8.2	9,905	5,311	4,594	495	1,136
Philadelphia	56,406	1,662,101	1.16	21,776	13.8	15,026	9.5	126,800	9.7	253,719	143,175	110,544	64,761	4,123
Pike	478	45,527	0.55	396	7.1	498	8.9	3,315	7.7	9,644	8,164	1,480	678	1,221

1. Per 1,000 estimated resident population.   2. Data for serious crimes have not been adjusted for underreporting; this may affect comparability between geographic areas and over time.
3. Per 100,000 population estimated by the FBI.

Table B. States and Counties — Crime, Education, Money Income, and Poverty

STATE County	Serious crimes known to police, 2016 (cont.)[1] Rate — Violent	Property	Education — School enrollment and attainment, 2012-2016 — Enrollment[3] Total	Percent private	Attainment[4] (percent) High school graduate or less	Bachelor's degree or more	Local government expenditures,[5] 2013-2014 Total current spending (mil dol)	Current spending per student (dollars)	Money income, 2012-2016 Per capita income[6]	Households Median income (dollars)	Percent with income of less than $50,000	with income of $200,000 or more	Income and poverty, 2016 Median household income (dollars)	Percent below poverty level All persons	Children under 18 years	Children 5 to 17 years in families
	46	47	48	49	50	51	52	53	54	55	56	57	58	59	60	61
OREGON— Cont'd																
Morrow	480	2,275	2,887	5.3	59.5	10.0	25.2	10,616	21,279	54,441	43.8	1.1	53,588	14.8	19.2	17.4
Multnomah	482	4,902	186,484	20.9	27.0	42.7	997.5	10,627	33,255	57,449	44.1	6.1	62,292	14.2	18.7	18.0
Polk	239	2,503	22,201	11.0	34.8	29.8	61.8	9,198	24,827	54,010	45.5	2.4	55,218	12.1	14.0	12.8
Sherman	NA	NA	263	11.4	42.5	17.0	3.7	15,237	32,223	41,389	55.8	5.3	57,216	12.2	18.2	17.3
Tillamook	81	1,653	4,707	14.9	43.9	20.9	39.7	12,493	23,688	43,777	56.5	1.4	46,226	12.9	20.4	18.5
Umatilla	231	2,194	18,993	7.3	46.4	15.6	152.8	11,115	21,528	49,287	50.8	1.8	49,667	15.7	19.1	17.8
Union	146	2,319	6,541	14.6	41.0	23.3	36.5	9,648	25,458	45,564	53.5	3.4	47,309	16.0	19.9	18.0
Wallowa	NA	NA	1,182	12.5	39.3	25.2	14.4	16,403	24,956	42,349	58.4	0.9	46,350	14.6	22.5	19.9
Wasco	188	2,262	5,477	11.6	44.1	18.6	39.1	10,821	22,931	46,814	53.3	1.6	50,562	14.2	21.8	20.4
Washington	183	1,520	143,735	18.4	27.8	41.2	830.7	9,622	33,433	69,743	35.6	6.8	75,577	9.0	11.6	10.1
Wheeler	148	371	193	9.3	46.4	17.0	4.7	14,403	22,723	33,400	65.7	0.7	35,341	19.6	39.9	36.9
Yamhill	133	1,744	26,521	25.3	40.1	24.5	157.6	9,382	26,523	54,951	45.9	3.9	60,643	11.7	15.8	14.5
PENNSYLVANIA	316	1,743	3,031,943	24.0	46.4	29.3	24,037.0	13,860	30,137	54,895	45.7	4.9	56,897	12.9	18.4	17.2
Adams	163	819	23,933	26.0	54.1	21.9	279.1	19,925	28,515	61,927	40.1	3.2	59,645	9.4	14.0	13.0
Allegheny	388	1,971	286,799	25.3	35.1	39.1	2,276.8	15,200	33,830	54,357	46.2	5.3	56,099	11.5	15.2	13.6
Armstrong	112	676	12,785	15.4	59.7	15.5	110.8	14,846	24,634	51,887	48.4	2.4	54,715	9.7	15.5	14.2
Beaver	245	1,918	35,204	17.0	47.2	23.4	413.8	12,312	28,018	53,632	52.8	1.4	44,834	13.7	17.3	16.2
Bedford	70	818	9,364	12.7	64.1	13.8	85.3	11,724	23,632	46,746	54.7	1.4	59,205	13.1	19.9	19.0
Berks	272	1,635	103,356	17.4	52.5	23.6	896.1	13,113	27,844	57,068	43.6	3.8	44,191	13.6	20.7	19.6
Blair	214	1,358	26,496	13.4	57.5	19.5	219.2	12,355	24,466	44,033	49.1	2.3	50,567	11.5	18.0	17.2
Bradford	181	1,504	12,633	13.0	59.4	17.7	125.0	13,119	26,255	51,035		2.7				
Bucks	100	1,431	147,847	24.4	36.6	38.3	1,354.6	15,620	39,958	79,559	30.7	10.4	80,132	6.6	8.0	7.5
Butler	107	1,188	44,076	17.1	40.7	33.3	309.5	11,404	33,406	63,345	39.1	5.9	66,277	7.3	8.9	8.3
Cambria	165	1,411	31,048	22.9	55.1	20.2	220.4	12,020	23,993	42,917	56.4	1.7	43,614	15.6	23.1	21.7
Cameron	150	1,526	793	11.1	58.7	15.6	9.5	15,157	25,716	40,347	61.9	2.0	39,069	14.2	24.3	25.0
Carbon	285	1,851	12,632	13.4	57.5	16.0	111.0	12,806	25,743	50,822	49.1	1.6	51,021	13.1	20.7	17.8
Centre	95	1,064	58,312	8.6	37.8	42.4	186.4	14,094	27,584	54,407	46.4	4.8	59,070	17.0	11.7	10.7
Chester	137	1,191	135,889	23.3	29.5	50.2	1,336.0	14,986	44,299	88,995	27.8	14.6	92,551	7.0	7.5	6.9
Clarion	117	1,127	9,746	8.8	57.6	20.9	88.5	16,985	22,451	42,890	56.9	1.4	44,670	15.2	20.1	19.5
Clearfield	272	1,500	14,914	12.3	63.6	13.2	155.5	13,658	21,650	43,361	56.4	1.3	46,173	14.1	22.0	20.3
Clinton	145	1,113	10,172	12.8	58.4	17.5	59.9	13,005	22,084	47,163	53.1	1.2	46,742	17.8	22.6	20.6
Columbia	168	1,346	18,079	8.8	55.6	21.4	81.3	12,728	24,155	46,952	52.4	2.2	48,821	13.5	17.0	16.1
Crawford	94	1,295	19,203	24.6	56.6	20.6	142.1	12,671	23,578	45,637	54.1	2.1	45,388	14.4	21.8	21.3
Cumberland	75	1,125	58,107	22.3	42.5	33.6	354.8	13,685	33,079	62,640	39.0	4.9	64,116	7.9	10.5	9.9
Dauphin	435	1,888	62,067	18.0	44.9	29.3	537.1	12,551	30,068	54,968	44.8	4.0	59,958	11.3	18.4	17.6
Delaware	377	1,822	150,517	33.2	39.2	36.8	1,110.9	15,242	34,857	66,576	38.3	8.3	67,773	10.8	15.4	14.4
Elk	144	1,595	6,098	24.5	57.2	17.8	43.4	11,908	25,753	47,917	51.7	1.2	49,274	10.1	14.0	12.6
Erie	222	1,919	70,047	24.5	48.7	27.0	497.5	12,584	25,555	47,094	52.5	2.8	48,820	15.7	24.0	22.2
Fayette	226	2,018	25,345	11.5	63.0	14.7	212.4	12,482	22,863	40,511	57.6	1.4	42,056	17.5	28.6	26.6
Forest	477	846	479	55.5	73.9	8.3	16.5	14,942	13,283	36,594	69.6	0.7	38,819	24.6	57.1	50.3
Franklin	144	1,482	32,599	17.7	56.6	20.1	250.3	10,953	27,706	55,751	44.5	2.4	59,474	9.1	14.1	13.3
Fulton	172	1,073	2,960	7.6	65.4	13.4	27.1	12,493	24,327	49,420	50.5	1.3	47,450	10.6	17.1	16.3
Greene	129	1,460	7,724	23.1	61.0	17.3	75.6	14,577	24,389	49,116	50.7	2.0	50,579	15.7	21.2	19.9
Huntingdon	164	997	9,454	25.4	62.6	14.7	63.1	10,942	22,217	45,250	54.9	0.9	46,684	13.6	18.6	17.5
Indiana	268	1,312	24,349	10.8	55.1	22.2	164.6	16,738	23,886	45,118	54.5	2.3	43,171	20.0	24.9	22.9
Jefferson	163	709	8,700	15.8	62.2	14.8	67.0	13,962	22,841	43,913	56.2	1.2	42,670	13.3	19.0	17.4
Juniata	83	731	4,668	26.1	69.0	13.3	28.2	9,508	23,461	49,028	51.1	1.8	49,506	10.2	16.7	15.5
Lackawanna	232	1,642	49,489	32.5	47.6	26.1	346.9	12,369	26,179	46,673	53.1	2.7	47,398	14.1	18.8	18.4
Lancaster	176	1,376	124,790	26.0	52.8	25.7	945.0	14,011	28,152	59,237	41.6	3.7	61,347	10.7	15.8	14.9
Lawrence	247	1,498	18,585	16.7	54.8	20.3	152.7	12,427	25,614	45,764	53.6	2.4	46,727	13.7	20.6	19.4
Lebanon	154	1,479	30,086	24.3	57.3	19.9	215.2	11,310	27,051	56,191	43.1	2.5	56,971	9.9	15.0	13.7
Lehigh	234	2,064	86,860	21.7	45.3	28.9	692.8	13,690	29,587	57,685	43.6	4.6	60,243	13.8	20.4	20.8
Luzerne	265	1,824	69,803	22.2	50.1	22.1	554.5	12,531	25,899	46,577	52.7	2.6	46,452	14.6	23.4	21.7
Lycoming	206	1,515	25,629	16.7	51.4	20.6	221.7	13,785	24,855	48,731	51.3	1.9	48,962	14.6	21.1	20.4
McKean	272	1,247	9,383	13.0	58.3	17.0	97.8	15,597	24,303	44,023	56.2	1.8	43,082	17.4	26.8	24.8
Mercer	210	1,660	25,707	23.3	54.6	21.6	249.8	15,593	24,399	45,831	53.9	2.0	49,187	16.1	26.0	23.3
Mifflin	125	1,470	8,953	20.4	68.1	12.1	91.7	17,398	21,665	42,019	58.4	1.3	43,245	14.7	23.0	22.3
Monroe	252	1,894	42,125	11.7	46.9	23.6	422.8	15,395	26,128	58,980	42.2	3.6	59,574	12.0	17.6	16.1
Montgomery	123	1,533	202,771	30.6	30.7	47.5	1,801.2	16,599	42,995	81,902	30.2	12.1	84,156	6.2	7.8	7.0
Montour	253	1,089	3,665	18.0	51.6	28.5	28.2	12,035	31,293	55,233	46.0	5.6	54,861	11.2	19.0	16.4
Northampton	256	1,440	73,114	28.8	44.7	27.9	631.9	14,277	31,086	62,753	39.4	5.0	65,730	9.3	14.1	12.1
Northumberland	265	1,267	16,853	17.6	64.4	15.0	184.4	15,357	23,512	43,701	56.0	1.4	46,783	14.6	21.5	19.6
Perry	168	969	9,272	19.9	58.0	16.3	72.4	11,702	27,648	58,585	41.2	2.4	59,244	9.1	14.1	13.6
Philadelphia	981	3,142	405,977	33.8	50.9	26.3	2,558.9	12,900	23,696	39,770	59.1	3.0	41,514	25.3	37.2	37.0
Pike	150	1,072	12,427	11.1	44.2	25.3	118.9	14,553	29,695	61,199	40.2	4.3	60,082	9.8	15.7	13.9

1. Data for serious crimes have not been adjusted for underreporting; this may affect comparability between geographic areas and over time.   2. Per 100,000 population estimated by the FBI.
3. All persons 3 years old and over enrolled in nursery school through college.   4. Persons 25 years old and over.   5. Elementary and secondary education expenditures.
6. Based on population estimated by the American Community Survey, 2011–2015.

Table B. States and Counties — Personal Income and Earnings

STATE County	Personal income, 2016										Earnings, 2016		
	Total (mil dol)	Percent change 2015-2016	Per capita[1] Dollars	Rank	Wages and salaries (mil dol)	Supplements to wages and salaries, employer contributions (mil dol) Pension and insurance	Government social insurance	Proprietors' income (mil dol)	Dividends, interest, and rent (mil dol)	Personal transfer receipts (mil dol)	Total (mil dol)	Contributions for government social insurance (mil dol) From employee and self-employed	From employer
	62	63	64	65	66	67	68	69	70	71	72	73	74
OREGON— Cont'd													
Morrow	469	-4.1	41,631	1,149	326	52	28	70	60	97	476	52	28
Multnomah	41,195	4.0	51,508	346	29,283	4,080	2,503	3,589	8,114	6,106	39,455	4,888	2,503
Polk	3,094	5.1	37,818	1,694	756	141	68	169	564	714	1,134	151	68
Sherman	95	0.9	55,846	216	44	9	4	17	16	22	73	8	4
Tillamook	1,023	3.5	39,117	1,481	369	64	33	94	231	302	560	72	33
Umatilla	2,884	3.7	37,715	1,704	1,246	227	118	188	444	727	1,779	229	118
Union	960	1.9	36,785	1,856	405	75	39	51	183	283	570	78	39
Wallowa	303	3.5	43,593	919	94	20	9	30	78	86	152	19	9
Wasco	1,104	4.2	42,287	1,060	479	79	41	121	186	279	719	83	41
Washington	31,588	4.2	54,203	263	19,841	2,229	1,529	2,243	6,144	3,865	25,843	3,122	1,529
Wheeler	47	-1.3	35,070	2,152	11	2	1	2	12	17	16	2	1
Yamhill	4,199	4.0	39,974	1,368	1,465	253	134	319	770	926	2,172	273	134
PENNSYLVANIA	648,694	1.8	50,730	X	312,472	54,598	24,572	58,838	111,266	128,605	450,480	26,731	24,572
Adams	4,685	1.6	45,853	706	1,420	281	119	310	819	899	2,130	253	119
Allegheny	67,145	0.4	54,796	247	42,914	6,554	3,305	5,219	11,714	12,256	57,992	6,706	3,305
Armstrong	2,694	1.1	40,522	1,298	684	157	57	200	380	756	1,097	136	57
Beaver	7,310	0.9	43,659	909	2,327	499	196	395	919	1,927	3,417	427	196
Bedford	1,830	1.4	37,873	1,684	580	124	50	219	248	514	973	115	50
Berks	18,983	1.9	45,763	716	8,645	1,649	701	1,254	3,071	3,954	12,249	1,432	701
Blair	5,205	1.4	41,754	1,133	2,481	517	216	408	820	1,429	3,622	443	216
Bradford	2,384	-0.6	39,237	1,460	1,055	215	85	158	419	610	1,513	182	85
Bucks	41,277	2.1	65,895	83	14,324	2,264	1,144	3,053	7,031	5,655	20,786	2,377	1,144
Butler	9,847	1.4	52,698	315	4,510	819	362	642	1,551	1,681	6,333	740	362
Cambria	5,298	1.2	39,322	1,451	2,091	462	179	262	809	1,715	2,993	383	179
Cameron	205	0.1	43,879	887	79	19	7	13	39	64	118	15	7
Carbon	2,901	2.8	45,622	731	638	147	54	543	378	666	1,383	137	54
Centre	6,625	2.0	41,032	1,229	3,728	1,416	283	397	1,231	1,058	5,824	579	283
Chester	38,868	0.8	75,281	47	18,371	2,564	1,320	3,040	8,095	3,919	25,296	2,751	1,320
Clarion	1,448	0.8	37,592	1,721	495	135	42	135	248	420	808	93	42
Clearfield	3,245	2.4	40,266	1,330	1,166	260	99	194	423	862	1,718	212	99
Clinton	1,419	-1.7	36,168	1,980	573	143	48	90	198	381	853	102	48
Columbia	2,569	3.3	38,671	1,550	1,044	255	87	150	388	628	1,536	183	87
Crawford	3,189	0.7	36,975	1,824	1,224	267	104	322	439	917	1,917	227	104
Cumberland	12,769	2.3	51,384	352	6,942	1,244	567	960	2,334	2,083	9,712	1,131	567
Dauphin	13,101	2.5	47,864	547	10,109	2,116	788	832	1,974	2,660	13,845	1,566	788
Delaware	33,575	2.6	59,594	154	13,610	2,172	1,037	2,283	6,150	5,575	19,102	2,161	1,037
Elk	1,365	1.8	44,772	793	637	134	55	67	208	339	893	111	55
Erie	11,259	0.8	40,764	1,262	5,382	1,113	444	704	1,810	2,924	7,642	908	444
Fayette	5,171	1.6	38,960	1,502	1,582	350	134	341	706	1,656	2,407	305	134
Forest	180	1.5	24,639	3,079	99	35	8	10	43	67	151	17	8
Franklin	6,504	1.8	42,275	1,064	2,526	509	215	429	1,065	1,399	3,678	443	215
Fulton	542	0.7	37,026	1,821	221	50	19	43	81	149	333	40	19
Greene	1,583	-3.5	42,565	1,035	774	153	62	94	236	404	1,083	130	62
Huntingdon	1,692	2.6	37,077	1,810	493	130	41	126	235	454	789	94	41
Indiana	3,064	1.0	35,482	2,084	1,378	358	110	191	497	855	2,038	236	110
Jefferson	1,685	-0.4	38,222	1,614	603	129	52	163	267	487	946	114	52
Juniata	963	0.8	38,715	1,547	229	49	20	138	134	219	436	48	20
Lackawanna	9,217	1.9	43,616	917	4,202	822	351	555	1,574	2,300	5,931	722	351
Lancaster	24,684	2.0	45,839	709	11,164	1,924	906	3,354	4,158	4,508	17,347	1,910	906
Lawrence	3,497	1.1	40,061	1,359	1,182	242	101	220	473	1,045	1,744	221	101
Lebanon	6,051	1.5	43,576	922	2,090	463	176	483	976	1,301	3,212	373	176
Lehigh	17,734	2.5	48,834	480	10,437	1,683	813	1,614	2,778	3,409	14,547	1,661	813
Luzerne	13,228	2.3	41,809	1,123	6,333	1,270	539	637	2,108	3,408	8,779	1,087	539
Lycoming	4,631	-1.3	40,185	1,341	2,239	491	185	222	751	1,152	3,137	379	185
McKean	1,651	-0.8	39,416	1,434	639	158	53	135	293	455	985	115	53
Mercer	4,389	1.2	38,872	1,519	1,981	396	166	292	668	1,297	2,834	350	166
Mifflin	1,655	2.0	35,717	2,041	617	130	52	185	209	494	984	117	52
Monroe	6,495	2.8	39,104	1,484	2,463	555	203	423	916	1,461	3,645	425	203
Montgomery	59,805	1.5	72,780	56	35,446	4,734	2,604	422	16,745	7,132	43,207	5,363	2,604
Montour	952	2.0	51,877	340	1,060	172	68	42	134	188	1,342	146	68
Northampton	14,707	2.6	48,650	488	5,532	1,019	461	979	2,319	2,918	7,991	953	461
Northumberland	3,587	2.0	38,764	1,540	1,157	254	99	156	565	999	1,666	215	99
Perry	1,859	1.7	40,573	1,292	279	74	24	143	254	404	520	61	24
Philadelphia	80,973	3.9	51,645	344	44,822	7,483	3,468	20,486	9,783	19,854	76,259	7,533	3,468
Pike	2,352	2.3	42,332	1,054	409	100	34	150	394	569	694	85	34

1. Based on the resident population estimated as of July 1 of the year shown.

Table B. States and Counties — Earnings, Social Security, and Housing

STATE County	Earnings, 2016 (cont.) — Percent by selected industries									Social Security beneficiaries, December 2016		Supplemental Security Income recipients, 2016	Housing units, 2017	
	Farm	Mining, quarrying, and extracting	Construction	Manu-facturing	Information; professional, scientific, technical services	Retail trade	Finance, insurance, real estate, and leasing	Health care and social assistance	Govern-ment	Number	Rate[1]		Total	Percent change, 2010-2017
	75	76	77	78	79	80	81	82	83	84	85	86	87	88
OREGON— Cont'd														
Morrow	20.9	D	9.8	22.4	D	1.6	1.6	D	12.7	2,120	189	232	4,606	3.6
Multnomah	0.1	0.0	5.4	6.5	15.7	5.2	8.0	11.6	16.8	118,725	148	21,163	347,077	6.9
Polk	3.7	D	7.7	10.5	D	5.3	4.5	12.6	28.0	17,780	218	1,419	32,141	6.1
Sherman	19.1	0.2	D	D	0.3	3.2	D	D	35.2	505	294	41	935	1.7
Tillamook	5.3	0.0	7.7	15.8	3.5	7.1	3.9	12.1	21.7	8,140	311	547	19,017	3.6
Umatilla	4.3	0.1	5.2	9.6	2.9	7.1	3.9	11.7	26.4	14,240	186	1,728	30,459	2.6
Union	1.0	D	6.1	14.1	3.6	8.8	4.1	17.9	23.3	6,265	241	625	11,790	2.6
Wallowa	11.1	0.0	8.4	3.7	4.5	7.1	5.0	9.7	27.5	2,440	353	151	4,197	2.2
Wasco	13.1	D	4.7	5.0	9.0	8.9	2.4	20.0	19.8	6,400	247	695	11,679	1.7
Washington	0.5	0.1	5.8	25.2	9.8	5.4	6.6	8.1	6.6	82,580	142	7,281	229,676	8.1
Wheeler	13.3	0.4	D	D	D	D	D	D	36.9	515	388	33	907	1.5
Yamhill	5.8	0.2	7.0	19.8	5.2	6.6	5.4	12.6	14.2	20,735	199	1,595	39,031	5.2
PENNSYLVANIA	0.1	0.6	6.0	9.8	15.2	5.4	7.5	14.0	13.3	2,768,956	217	363,735	5,694,130	2.3
Adams	2.1	1.0	8.0	19.6	4.9	6.4	3.4	D	15.4	24,345	239	1,078	42,341	3.7
Allegheny	0.0	0.6	5.5	5.1	15.8	4.8	10.7	14.8	10.1	266,650	217	34,427	600,795	2.0
Armstrong	-0.3	11.2	5.8	11.5	4.9	7.1	3.2	15.1	17.6	18,200	275	2,050	32,786	0.8
Beaver	0.0	0.4	7.7	12.7	6.0	7.1	3.6	16.7	15.7	44,085	264	4,635	79,508	1.7
Bedford	0.7	D	12.0	12.0	2.6	9.5	3.7	14.7	13.4	13,650	281	1,287	24,344	1.6
Berks	0.5	0.2	7.2	18.8	7.2	6.1	5.3	14.0	16.0	86,240	207	10,652	167,047	1.4
Blair	0.2	0.4	5.6	12.6	5.4	8.3	4.1	19.7	14.3	30,680	248	4,571	56,856	1.0
Bradford	0.0	5.4	5.7	16.3	D	6.0	3.9	24.0		15,975	262	1,873	30,685	2.4
Bucks	0.0	0.1	10.0	10.6	12.8	7.2	6.1	14.8	10.1	131,855	210	7,068	250,646	1.9
Butler	0.0	1.2	7.3	15.8	8.7	6.7	4.2	12.0	14.1	42,415	228	3,198	83,224	6.5
Cambria	0.1	0.4	5.0	8.8	7.1	7.6	5.6	22.6	18.1	38,425	286	4,961	65,972	0.5
Cameron	-0.2	D	2.4	50.8	D	2.8	D	4.8	20.2	1,595	341	144	4,430	-0.5
Carbon	0.1	0.1	4.6	8.6	37.1	5.7	2.6	12.5	12.9	16,995	268	1,336	34,784	1.4
Centre	0.0	0.2	4.5	4.7	8.1	4.7	4.1	10.2	51.3	24,080	149	1,453	66,729	5.4
Chester	0.6	0.0	5.4	8.0	21.3	5.5	15.8	8.5	8.3	88,570	171	4,131	200,241	4.0
Clarion	-0.1	1.2	8.1	11.6	2.9	8.3	3.9	15.6	26.4	9,910	257	1,262	20,554	3.0
Clearfield	-0.1	2.2	4.3	8.1	3.2	8.4	3.8	21.6	19.4	21,155	264	2,454	39,230	1.6
Clinton	1.8	D	6.9	24.3	2.4	6.8	2.5	D	24.7	9,115	234	1,052	19,244	0.8
Columbia	-0.4	D	5.8	18.6	4.7	7.7	3.7	11.4	21.7	15,635	236	1,423	30,197	2.4
Crawford	0.2	1.2	5.9	25.3	3.9	6.6	3.1	16.2	15.2	22,390	259	2,984	44,907	0.5
Cumberland	0.1	0.1	4.5	5.8	11.6	6.1	9.4	12.7	16.3	51,495	208	2,709	106,022	6.0
Dauphin	0.1	0.0	3.6	7.6	7.8	3.7	8.6	15.8	24.2	55,835	204	7,710	124,361	3.3
Delaware	0.0	D	7.3	9.4	10.1	5.2	11.5	13.6	11.1	105,600	187	12,656	224,406	0.7
Elk	-0.1	0.4	5.2	49.0	2.6	5.0	2.7	10.4	9.4	8,640	284	596	17,788	1.2
Erie	0.1	0.1	4.7	19.3	4.8	7.0	8.0	18.1	16.2	62,650	227	10,745	121,406	1.9
Fayette	0.1	3.7	6.4	10.5	4.0	8.5	2.9	15.8	19.6	37,490	283	8,047	63,763	1.6
Forest	-0.1	7.1	D	D	D	1.6	D	11.1	57.8	1,815	248	166	8,731	-0.3
Franklin	0.7	0.1	5.7	16.6	4.8	7.5	3.4	15.8	17.0	35,840	233	2,497	65,418	3.5
Fulton	0.8	D	11.0	37.5	1.4	3.8	1.8	11.3	14.1	3,930	269	367	7,235	1.6
Greene	-0.6	D	9.6	1.9	5.7	5.4	3.4	D	18.2	8,985	242	1,700	16,713	1.5
Huntingdon	1.6	0.9	6.5	8.5	2.5	5.9	4.4	D	29.2	11,350	249	1,143	22,716	1.6
Indiana	0.1	5.8	6.3	6.2	3.8	6.9	5.0	12.6	26.1	20,285	238	2,656	38,995	2.0
Jefferson	0.3	6.0	6.3	23.8	4.6	5.5	2.3	14.8	13.7	11,935	272	1,372	22,700	1.2
Juniata	0.5	D	8.4	29.5	D	6.2	3.8	5.8	11.7	5,720	234	471	11,183	1.8
Lackawanna	0.0	0.0	5.5	10.1	7.5	7.3	7.9	18.4	14.4	53,645	254	6,725	100,514	3.8
Lancaster	0.4	0.1	11.2	15.9	7.0	7.7	5.8	13.2	9.0	110,220	204	9,557	210,909	3.9
Lawrence	0.2	0.4	10.4	13.2	4.7	7.7	6.4	15.7	15.0	23,955	273	3,406	41,244	0.7
Lebanon	0.9	D	6.4	17.5	5.5	8.0	2.9	12.3	20.2	32,310	233	2,548	57,678	3.7
Lehigh	0.0	D	4.6	12.3	7.9	4.9	5.8	20.5	9.2	75,000	207	9,893	146,242	2.5
Luzerne	0.0	0.3	4.8	11.1	5.8	7.2	5.2	16.3	16.1	78,900	249	9,979	150,097	0.9
Lycoming	-0.1	2.7	6.1	16.8	5.2	7.1	4.1	16.5	19.7	28,040	244	3,242	53,433	1.8
McKean	0.0	7.8	6.4	21.8	2.6	5.7	2.0	13.9	17.5	11,095	267	1,585	21,279	0.3
Mercer	-0.1	0.9	5.5	20.1	3.4	8.0	5.9	18.5	13.0	30,990	275	3,824	52,268	1.0
Mifflin	0.7	0.0	6.1	25.9	2.0	8.0	3.0	17.3	12.2	12,250	264	1,381	21,867	1.5
Monroe	0.0	0.1	5.2	14.1	3.2	8.4	2.8	12.3	25.4	35,275	212	3,096	81,459	1.4
Montgomery	0.0	0.0	7.6	10.2	22.8	5.6	7.5	12.9	7.4	155,490	189	8,424	334,377	2.6
Montour	0.2	D	1.1	2.4	D	1.7	7.4	D	8.1	4,515	248	446	8,211	3.1
Northampton	-0.1	0.0	6.4	14.7	7.4	6.5	6.6	9.6	14.3	69,385	230	6,456	123,141	2.3
Northumberland	0.5	0.6	8.6	16.8	3.5	6.3	2.9	12.7	17.9	24,390	264	2,829	45,450	0.7
Perry	0.7	D	14.7	5.6	4.0	8.3	5.0	7.0	24.5	10,425	227	740	20,863	2.2
Philadelphia	0.0	D	2.1	2.2	33.6	2.3	7.2	13.5	13.6	258,140	164	108,140	685,900	2.3
Pike	0.1	0.5	D	D	6.0	9.0	3.4	8.6	28.4	14,595	264	657	39,059	1.9

1. Per 1,000 resident population estimated as of July 1 of the year shown.

Table B. States and Counties — Housing, Labor Force, and Employment

STATE County	Housing units, 2017 (cont.)								Civilian labor force, 2017				Civilian employment[6], 2012-2016		
	Occupied units										Unemployment			Percent	
	Owner-occupied					Renter-occupied									
				Median owner cost as a percent of income			Median rent as a percent of income[2]	Sub-standard units[4] (percent)		Percent change, 2016-2017				Management, business, science, and arts	Construction, production, and maintenance occupations
	Total	Percent	Median value[1]	With a mortgage	Without a mortgage[2]	Median rent[3]			Total		Total	Rate[5]	Total		
	89	90	91	92	93	94	95	96	97	98	99	100	101	102	103
OREGON— Cont'd															
Morrow	3,848	71.9	124,400	19.1	10.3	733	22.8	10.3	5,856	1.5	259	4.4	4,843	28.6	42.1
Multnomah	313,181	53.8	297,300	24.0	13.1	1,013	32.1	3.9	457,151	2.9	16,606	3.6	405,153	44.4	16.0
Polk	28,725	64.6	215,000	22.9	12.1	828	31.9	2.5	39,548	3.1	1,716	4.3	33,643	36.0	22.2
Sherman	804	61.4	150,600	18.8	12.8	754	30.3	1.7	897	0.2	43	4.8	760	34.2	29.9
Tillamook	10,154	70.3	222,700	24.8	12.2	811	33.5	2.1	11,786	1.2	501	4.3	9,859	26.9	34.0
Umatilla	26,669	63.5	143,400	21.8	10.4	682	26.1	6.1	36,924	2.4	1,785	4.8	31,983	25.5	32.6
Union	10,119	63.8	170,500	19.6	10.5	697	30.2	3.9	12,068	0.7	638	5.3	11,142	29.2	25.1
Wallowa	3,039	67.9	211,200	23.5	13.5	687	30.8	2.7	3,359	1.3	187	5.6	2,869	35.6	23.6
Wasco	9,883	63.8	182,300	24.2	11.7	751	29.7	3.4	13,955	1.8	577	4.1	11,117	27.5	27.6
Washington	209,309	60.1	301,600	22.9	10.7	1,111	29.7	3.9	323,022	3.0	11,304	3.5	283,207	44.6	16.2
Wheeler	696	74.4	114,700	28.9	15.4	562	23.0	1.6	743	8.2	29	3.9	522	39.3	28.2
Yamhill	35,002	67.3	236,300	24.5	12.2	917	32.2	3.7	54,567	2.5	2,060	3.8	44,760	32.6	27.1
PENNSYLVANIA	4,961,929	69.0	167,700	21.6	13.1	859	29.8	1.7	6,427,376	-0.4	315,740	4.9	6,043,693	37.2	21.6
Adams	38,269	77.8	194,800	22.5	13.7	847	30.1	2.0	55,457	0.1	2,038	3.7	50,598	29.9	30.5
Allegheny	531,075	64.7	134,400	19.2	12.5	800	28.3	1.1	645,906	-0.3	30,713	4.8	618,606	44.4	14.4
Armstrong	28,250	75.7	95,700	19.7	12.6	614	24.9	1.4	32,676	-1.3	2,009	6.1	29,647	28.0	30.9
Beaver	69,921	73.2	123,800	19.7	12.6	652	27.3	1.4	84,912	-0.5	4,708	5.5	81,926	33.0	24.0
Bedford	19,757	79.8	125,000	21.1	11.7	632	27.5	2.5	23,757	-1.3	1,230	5.2	22,253	25.6	34.1
Berks	152,451	71.8	169,000	22.7	14.4	870	31.7	1.8	212,082	-0.6	9,773	4.6	199,047	31.7	28.0
Blair	50,954	70.7	112,600	19.2	12.2	658	29.5	1.3	60,219	-1.1	2,919	4.8	56,996	30.8	24.9
Bradford	24,483	74.8	139,200	20.2	11.6	678	27.4	2.0	29,363	-2.7	1,509	5.1	26,684	28.6	35.1
Bucks	233,517	76.5	311,600	23.5	14.4	1,143	30.5	1.3	341,433	0.1	14,473	4.2	323,036	42.6	17.9
Butler	74,762	76.7	183,200	19.7	11.8	771	27.9	1.0	98,326	-0.3	4,525	4.6	92,275	37.7	21.5
Cambria	57,214	74.1	88,200	19.3	12.8	586	27.8	1.1	59,765	-2.6	3,627	6.1	57,641	32.7	24.2
Cameron	2,187	69.0	68,400	19.6	11.6	590	27.6	1.2	2,201	-1.4	152	6.9	2,169	22.2	43.1
Carbon	25,813	78.0	141,300	24.2	14.2	805	30.6	2.1	31,500	-0.2	1,753	5.6	29,249	27.0	32.3
Centre	57,037	61.0	206,000	21.2	11.2	930	34.1	2.5	78,636	-0.4	2,907	3.7	75,670	46.0	15.4
Chester	186,721	75.3	331,000	22.3	13.4	1,222	29.6	1.5	281,136	0.3	10,083	3.6	264,255	49.4	14.9
Clarion	15,848	69.3	108,100	19.5	11.1	610	30.5	2.0	17,723	-1.7	1,001	5.6	16,963	29.4	28.1
Clearfield	31,303	77.4	88,300	20.8	13.0	596	28.9	1.7	35,854	-1.3	2,140	6.0	33,698	25.9	32.6
Clinton	14,710	70.7	119,500	20.7	13.0	675	27.8	1.4	18,317	-1.3	1,135	6.2	17,679	25.8	30.6
Columbia	26,356	69.6	140,100	20.8	13.2	721	29.8	1.0	33,804	-0.3	1,765	5.2	30,288	31.2	28.3
Crawford	34,526	73.5	106,700	20.1	12.6	633	27.0	2.8	39,398	-2.7	2,167	5.5	37,894	30.7	30.9
Cumberland	96,501	70.6	191,700	20.8	11.9	911	27.3	1.1	129,985	-0.1	4,954	3.8	122,473	39.4	19.5
Dauphin	110,211	63.2	161,000	20.8	12.0	863	28.6	1.9	141,982	-0.1	6,404	4.5	133,424	38.4	17.8
Delaware	203,610	69.4	233,300	23.1	14.5	996	31.9	1.5	294,762	0.2	13,338	4.5	271,235	42.3	15.6
Elk	13,362	78.6	92,200	17.8	11.1	529	25.4	0.7	15,996	-2.1	778	4.9	15,039	24.8	42.4
Erie	110,047	65.9	120,300	19.7	12.4	701	29.7	1.8	130,755	-2.1	7,563	5.8	128,087	34.1	22.8
Fayette	53,654	72.7	92,000	19.4	12.8	607	28.1	2.5	57,811	-1.1	4,005	6.9	53,742	27.6	30.3
Forest	1,816	84.7	85,600	22.7	12.7	538	27.2	1.3	1,832	-3.2	123	6.7	1,019	26.9	24.5
Franklin	59,392	78.1	174,400	22.1	11.4	826	27.0	1.7	76,656	-1.1	3,414	4.5	71,726	31.5	29.0
Fulton	5,989	78.3	151,700	21.8	11.4	643	24.3	1.5	7,191	-1.5	370	5.1	6,724	24.0	38.2
Greene	14,400	72.8	102,100	18.4	10.7	628	25.8	1.5	16,835	-2.7	997	5.9	14,696	29.5	30.3
Huntingdon	16,975	75.4	120,600	21.2	11.8	565	26.3	1.4	19,739	0.3	1,187	6.0	18,516	28.2	30.7
Indiana	34,059	70.9	107,600	20.1	12.2	704	32.9	3.2	39,219	-2.5	2,323	5.9	38,587	29.5	28.1
Jefferson	18,360	74.8	94,200	19.9	11.2	593	26.2	2.6	20,572	-0.7	1,154	5.6	19,903	25.4	36.3
Juniata	9,326	75.7	146,200	21.2	10.6	596	24.4	2.5	12,394	1.6	574	4.6	11,178	25.8	40.3
Lackawanna	85,174	65.9	147,100	21.6	14.5	717	28.7	1.5	106,305	-0.5	5,453	5.1	97,157	35.0	22.5
Lancaster	196,171	68.4	191,400	22.3	12.3	932	30.3	2.2	280,293	0.1	10,703	3.8	262,220	33.1	27.6
Lawrence	36,302	73.7	99,300	19.8	13.0	643	29.7	1.8	40,603	-2.2	2,471	6.1	39,185	30.9	27.0
Lebanon	52,247	69.6	164,900	21.7	12.8	785	26.8	2.4	70,550	-0.1	2,915	4.1	65,807	29.6	27.9
Lehigh	135,363	65.8	192,300	22.9	14.3	955	32.3	2.2	188,781	-0.2	9,487	5.0	173,024	34.7	23.1
Luzerne	127,514	68.0	123,500	20.7	14.1	712	28.9	1.4	158,265	-0.3	9,352	5.9	146,759	30.8	24.8
Lycoming	45,587	70.2	141,100	21.1	13.4	750	29.7	1.3	57,623	-1.9	3,254	5.6	53,906	29.9	26.6
McKean	17,259	74.3	76,000	18.7	11.0	622	28.9	1.1	18,148	-1.9	1,119	6.2	18,384	29.6	31.4
Mercer	45,350	73.4	111,000	19.6	12.1	657	28.3	2.1	50,990	-3.0	2,790	5.5	50,124	30.2	25.5
Mifflin	18,695	70.2	99,700	21.9	14.1	635	26.6	3.2	20,630	-0.9	1,103	5.3	20,099	25.0	36.4
Monroe	57,127	77.4	170,600	26.9	16.6	1,040	31.9	1.6	81,955	0.1	4,814	5.9	77,253	33.0	21.8
Montgomery	309,884	72.2	293,800	22.3	13.4	1,181	29.3	1.3	448,710	0.3	17,320	3.9	421,051	49.2	14.2
Montour	7,361	72.6	170,700	20.0	12.0	709	26.9	0.7	9,096	-0.4	352	3.9	8,476	39.0	22.5
Northampton	112,819	71.2	207,700	23.2	14.5	969	31.0	1.5	158,727	-0.1	7,779	4.9	146,620	35.1	22.9
Northumberland	39,192	71.0	109,200	20.8	13.4	631	26.5	1.7	43,683	-0.6	2,482	5.7	41,016	28.2	29.4
Perry	17,883	79.8	161,800	22.5	11.5	735	24.6	1.9	24,239	-0.2	1,041	4.3	23,000	29.0	31.0
Philadelphia	582,594	52.4	147,300	23.9	14.5	943	33.9	2.9	704,053	0.1	43,980	6.2	654,917	36.9	16.5
Pike	21,135	84.2	180,600	24.2	13.8	1,133	36.5	1.4	24,836	-0.3	1,471	5.9	24,434	32.0	22.2

1. Specified owner-occupied units.   2. A value of 10.0 represents 10 percent or less; a value of 50.0 represents 50 percent or more.   3. Specified renter-occupied units.
4. Overcrowded or lacking complete plumbing facilities.   5. Percent of civilian labor force.   6. Civilian employed persons 16 years old and over.

Table B. States and Counties — Nonfarm Employment and Agriculture

STATE County	Private nonfarm establishments, employment and payroll, 2016									Agriculture, 2012			
	Number of establishments	Employment						Annual payroll		Farms			Farm operators whose principal occupation is farming (percent)
		Total	Health care and social assistance	Manufacturing	Retail trade	Finance and insurance	Professional, scientific, and technical services	Total (mil dol)	Average per employee (dollars)	Number	Percent with:		
											Fewer than 50 acres	500 acres or more	
	104	105	106	107	108	109	110	111	112	113	114	115	116
OREGON— Cont'd													
Morrow	193	3,966	348	1,435	134	93	D	177	44,626	401	27.7	51.9	63.1
Multnomah	27,246	434,205	67,739	34,471	43,904	20,972	34,295	22,673	52,217	598	84.8	1.7	44.5
Polk	1,436	14,220	2,811	1,830	1,627	269	417	478	33,597	1,143	66.0	5.2	52.2
Sherman	64	473	9	D	117	D	D	16	33,869	186	5.4	76.3	73.7
Tillamook	731	7,190	973	1,553	1,089	142	114	254	35,264	280	45.4	3.2	68.2
Umatilla	1,550	22,570	3,036	3,151	3,025	461	638	800	35,433	1,603	49.0	25.0	49.0
Union	727	7,197	1,468	1,217	1,420	220	228	256	35,602	829	46.4	18.2	46.9
Wallowa	379	1,886	425	76	317	65	95	63	33,248	522	37.0	27.4	47.9
Wasco	681	6,987	1,887	273	1,538	246	260	255	36,465	670	39.4	24.2	52.1
Washington	15,316	265,790	31,081	28,593	32,410	11,876	22,091	17,178	64,629	1,643	74.4	3.0	44.7
Wheeler	30	140	D	D	38	D	NA	4	26,000	153	10.5	51.0	58.8
Yamhill	2,475	29,340	4,855	5,856	3,794	672	622	1,100	37,489	2,028	73.7	3.8	47.0
PENNSYLVANIA	301,484	5,354,964	1,005,144	540,072	667,206	273,515	324,440	261,082	48,755	59,309	39.3	4.1	51.7
Adams	1,956	30,027	4,608	6,227	3,450	481	600	1,035	34,481	1,188	48.2	6.3	50.9
Allegheny	33,962	695,456	127,772	33,838	73,083	50,114	58,114	36,409	52,352	428	50.7	0.9	41.6
Armstrong	1,322	13,905	3,542	1,352	2,083	656	375	465	33,464	783	25.0	6.1	42.0
Beaver	3,369	47,967	10,232	6,144	7,432	923	2,001	1,877	39,129	646	45.2	1.9	47.5
Bedford	1,074	12,856	1,718	1,878	2,239	323	241	437	34,018	1,210	25.0	6.5	50.6
Berks	8,406	156,856	25,628	31,471	20,744	5,848	6,585	7,191	45,846	2,039	47.8	3.5	61.4
Blair	3,185	53,686	13,387	6,809	8,887	1,544	1,790	1,964	36,589	525	35.8	5.9	58.5
Bradford	1,345	18,343	5,038	3,218	2,932	546	513	760	41,436	1,629	25.8	7.6	45.8
Bucks	19,217	247,491	43,800	24,794	38,596	8,386	16,648	11,366	45,926	827	71.1	2.7	51.3
Butler	4,866	82,520	13,403	11,755	11,551	1,958	6,611	3,608	43,727	1,061	39.9	4.1	45.6
Cambria	3,171	46,970	11,781	4,594	6,871	2,142	2,228	1,645	35,031	551	33.4	5.6	37.4
Cameron	108	1,586	191	937	148	17	14	56	35,253	36	25.0	11.1	50.0
Carbon	1,126	13,977	3,436	1,516	2,133	292	345	419	29,963	195	46.2	2.6	37.4
Centre	3,347	45,292	8,884	3,906	8,030	1,252	2,974	1,733	38,267	1,192	40.1	4.8	57.4
Chester	14,314	248,421	37,180	16,077	28,205	24,500	24,038	17,300	69,642	1,730	57.1	2.5	60.7
Clarion	922	11,237	2,976	1,641	1,780	291	231	349	31,072	652	22.1	6.3	39.3
Clearfield	1,988	26,413	5,810	2,655	4,835	622	549	902	34,163	533	34.3	4.3	45.0
Clinton	761	10,586	1,302	2,939	1,939	186	207	381	35,951	469	37.1	3.8	51.0
Columbia	1,424	22,707	4,096	4,771	3,412	679	819	796	35,039	944	37.3	4.6	39.8
Crawford	1,969	27,681	5,433	7,462	3,680	574	770	957	34,567	1,351	31.1	6.0	51.5
Cumberland	6,051	119,834	17,295	7,930	17,437	7,873	8,637	5,365	44,774	1,415	47.0	3.5	53.1
Dauphin	6,858	146,996	33,097	8,194	15,788	9,627	7,874	7,182	48,862	811	49.0	2.7	44.9
Delaware	12,864	210,978	42,077	12,753	26,530	13,479	11,281	11,295	53,535	76	64.5	0.0	48.7
Elk	889	14,030	1,599	6,931	1,477	240	341	550	39,237	271	45.4	1.5	33.6
Erie	6,191	114,476	24,667	20,308	16,123	5,163	3,819	4,372	38,187	1,422	41.2	4.1	48.7
Fayette	2,604	35,982	7,419	3,064	6,525	587	1,011	1,187	33,002	941	34.0	3.4	47.8
Forest	109	1,099	348	230	108	13	D	35	32,064	56	25.0	3.6	41.1
Franklin	3,091	49,814	8,290	7,984	7,555	1,159	1,919	1,856	37,256	1,596	35.9	6.3	60.8
Fulton	263	5,704	690	D	353	74	32	267	46,837	656	22.6	5.2	38.6
Greene	752	11,721	1,649	305	2,359	321	250	486	41,470	876	27.2	3.3	40.4
Huntingdon	813	9,566	2,000	1,130	1,477	408	349	301	31,504	833	25.1	7.1	45.9
Indiana	1,864	25,543	4,942	2,202	4,401	1,327	1,057	960	37,593	1,166	38.0	3.9	50.2
Jefferson	1,125	13,812	3,011	3,489	1,554	239	419	490	35,463	577	25.0	5.7	51.5
Juniata	477	5,877	808	2,369	598	248	59	187	31,853	737	42.3	3.0	47.6
Lackawanna	5,338	95,435	22,124	8,831	12,823	5,255	3,038	3,474	36,404	303	25.1	1.3	43.6
Lancaster	12,874	228,355	35,600	33,465	31,129	7,496	11,719	9,617	42,116	5,657	44.1	1.3	72.2
Lawrence	1,929	26,381	6,499	3,514	3,671	1,150	751	937	35,515	659	33.4	3.6	50.4
Lebanon	2,709	44,345	8,079	9,310	7,018	932	1,149	1,638	36,944	1,219	48.2	2.3	58.9
Lehigh	8,555	174,230	40,076	18,896	22,291	6,542	6,448	8,991	51,604	486	58.8	5.8	56.2
Luzerne	7,241	133,636	25,168	16,953	18,310	5,285	6,086	5,239	39,203	556	38.8	3.6	42.3
Lycoming	2,745	45,232	8,956	7,543	7,555	1,503	1,419	1,705	37,700	1,207	32.4	3.7	44.0
McKean	1,010	12,600	2,629	2,987	1,793	276	201	460	36,525	290	37.2	3.1	36.9
Mercer	2,763	44,900	9,865	7,790	7,495	1,488	784	1,524	33,940	1,185	32.3	4.1	45.1
Mifflin	963	14,218	3,456	3,916	2,257	388	166	538	37,822	808	35.4	2.1	49.0
Monroe	3,372	47,216	7,039	5,420	9,581	983	1,564	1,687	35,721	283	53.0	2.5	55.1
Montgomery	26,220	494,756	82,115	40,518	59,003	37,018	44,839	31,091	62,841	596	75.2	1.0	55.0
Montour	490	14,333	7,514	579	662	1,364	465	969	67,582	459	43.1	1.5	45.3
Northampton	6,320	103,761	14,670	11,972	13,812	3,935	4,113	4,563	43,980	498	62.9	6.0	50.6
Northumberland	1,667	23,822	4,959	4,166	3,460	635	568	846	35,520	847	43.0	6.5	54.7
Perry	790	6,247	977	624	1,208	258	171	171	27,398	889	32.6	4.8	50.6
Philadelphia	27,929	621,865	153,198	21,116	52,151	30,967	47,937	35,402	56,929	22	81.8	0.0	45.5
Pike	918	8,469	1,091	340	1,877	168	206	241	28,425	50	46.0	14.0	34.0

Table B. States and Counties — Agriculture

	Agriculture, 2012 (cont.)														
STATE County	Land in farms				Value of land and buildings (dollars)		Value of machinery and equipment, average per farm (dollars)	Value of products sold:				Percent of farms with sales of:		Government payments	
	Acreage (1,000)	Percent change, 2007-2012	Acres			Average per farm	Average per acre		Total (mil dol)	Average per farm (acres)	Percent from:		$10,000 or more	$100,000 or more	Total ($1,000)	Percent of farms
			Average size of farm	Total irrigated (1,000)	Total cropland (1,000)						Crops	Livestock and poultry products				
	117	118	119	120	121	122	123	124	125	126	127	128	129	130	131	132
OREGON— Cont'd																
Morrow	1,165	5.5	2,906	65.6	486.4	2,762,863	951	302,516	568.1	1,416,736	34.3	65.7	50.4	34.9	11,900	61.1
Multnomah	30	5.2	50	4.6	17.4	598,075	11,928	72,756	68.9	115,278	D	D	30.1	9.5	242	6.0
Polk	145	-13.1	127	20.4	101.0	777,650	6,141	85,558	149.8	131,099	77.6	22.4	33.3	12.8	912	16.1
Sherman	514	-0.1	2,762	2.2	365.1	1,645,672	596	308,538	54.5	292,914	D	D	61.8	44.6	8,820	93.5
Tillamook	37	-3.3	131	7.1	14.5	817,064	6,259	115,754	117.1	418,361	2.6	97.4	53.6	38.6	1,553	34.3
Umatilla	1,308	-9.6	816	147.8	769.7	1,332,795	1,633	163,995	423.3	264,089	87.9	12.1	42.1	22.2	18,381	40.8
Union	412	-15.6	497	49.0	119.2	768,875	1,548	101,823	68.4	82,473	75.0	25.0	39.0	12.2	2,713	30.0
Wallowa	453	-14.3	867	38.0	88.5	1,094,554	1,263	101,395	46.6	89,310	47.5	52.5	45.8	20.5	2,746	38.5
Wasco	1,427	50.3	2,130	50.6	210.0	1,605,100	753	118,193	89.8	134,005	88.7	11.3	41.3	18.4	6,871	39.3
Washington	136	6.1	83	20.3	82.0	774,189	9,371	81,491	238.0	144,840	94.7	5.3	38.5	12.8	1,544	15.0
Wheeler	649	-14.3	4,242	10.4	24.8	2,749,542	648	97,634	14.2	92,536	22.9	77.1	45.1	19.6	748	26.1
Yamhill	177	-1.9	87	22.1	108.5	801,316	9,162	76,411	280.9	138,487	78.9	21.1	32.8	10.8	2,466	16.2
PENNSYLVANIA	7,704	-1.3	130	39.0	4,546.1	704,712	5,425	89,730	7,400.8	124,783	37.6	62.4	48.1	19.9	86,359	27.0
Adams	171	-1.9	144	2.2	125.6	898,623	6,232	113,572	201.7	169,817	56.5	43.5	48.6	19.2	1,818	28.5
Allegheny	35	-8.4	81	0.2	14.1	428,841	5,269	53,269	10.4	24,292	84.2	15.8	31.3	5.1	41	7.9
Armstrong	129	5.6	165	0.2	66.6	474,018	2,875	83,686	35.9	45,800	56.3	43.7	42.1	9.2	924	24.8
Beaver	56	-16.8	86	0.2	28.5	415,333	4,809	67,373	20.9	32,373	52.0	48.0	32.8	6.0	500	16.1
Bedford	210	-0.6	173	0.1	104.3	640,069	3,692	95,976	122.8	101,504	29.7	70.3	48.1	21.7	1,863	29.4
Berks	234	5.2	115	1.6	182.3	1,015,554	8,859	120,253	528.7	259,299	42.6	57.4	58.5	30.2	3,646	28.3
Blair	90	3.1	172	0.3	63.3	783,611	4,565	106,916	107.7	205,145	16.2	83.8	54.1	29.0	1,416	32.6
Bradford	308	15.5	189	0.2	163.3	700,259	3,704	89,510	128.8	79,063	22.6	77.4	43.1	15.3	6,994	43.0
Bucks	64	-15.6	77	0.8	48.0	950,716	12,280	89,245	62.4	75,475	75.1	24.9	41.0	13.7	579	13.7
Butler	136	4.9	128	0.6	77.1	609,486	4,747	89,819	52.9	49,863	69.6	30.4	41.3	10.0	1,502	26.6
Cambria	77	-12.6	140	0.1	45.4	457,327	3,277	82,508	32.6	59,240	55.5	44.5	42.3	8.5	775	31.9
Cameron	6	22.1	173	0.0	1.6	337,472	1,955	55,528	0.7	19,222	45.4	54.6	44.4	0.0	55	38.9
Carbon	21	5.6	109	0.2	13.4	710,523	6,547	99,005	9.3	47,892	91.4	8.6	46.7	8.2	191	42.1
Centre	162	9.1	136	1.1	84.9	736,207	5,416	86,739	91.6	76,830	34.3	65.7	47.2	20.0	1,985	30.3
Chester	164	-1.4	95	1.2	107.1	1,242,743	13,070	110,712	660.7	381,933	81.0	19.0	52.6	27.7	1,631	15.8
Clarion	116	-12.2	178	0.1	60.5	524,998	2,951	75,406	36.1	55,423	55.7	44.3	41.7	10.3	960	33.3
Clearfield	69	10.4	130	0.1	34.8	344,137	2,649	68,355	13.7	25,687	53.2	46.8	36.4	6.9	392	21.6
Clinton	53	-6.9	112	0.8	29.1	608,542	5,414	85,166	60.6	129,122	20.2	79.8	57.1	31.8	951	29.2
Columbia	123	0.1	130	0.6	85.1	610,161	4,693	89,506	74.4	78,762	65.5	34.5	40.7	13.8	2,088	48.9
Crawford	228	-1.9	169	0.3	130.3	475,734	2,822	91,693	116.1	85,918	44.3	55.7	46.3	15.4	2,095	26.6
Cumberland	155	-1.6	109	1.6	119.7	853,018	7,793	95,594	195.4	138,061	30.4	69.6	55.3	26.6	1,997	28.5
Dauphin	129	44.5	160	0.7	60.0	724,409	4,541	94,716	122.6	151,158	23.4	76.6	49.3	20.1	724	27.1
Delaware	5	8.3	62	0.1	1.2	857,868	13,799	57,684	9.8	128,697	99.0	1.0	32.9	6.6	D	2.6
Elk	23	-29.4	87	0.0	9.7	296,376	3,420	49,461	4.2	15,605	47.6	52.4	30.6	2.2	66	8.5
Erie	169	-2.6	119	0.9	96.2	407,705	3,438	75,158	91.7	64,469	76.5	23.5	41.5	12.8	1,693	20.5
Fayette	113	-19.8	120	0.0	55.2	398,345	3,321	66,763	27.0	28,717	52.6	47.4	31.6	5.3	588	17.7
Forest	8	-22.8	148	0.0	2.5	356,125	2,408	69,071	1.8	32,500	38.8	61.2	35.7	5.4	25	17.9
Franklin	265	9.0	166	2.8	201.8	1,101,504	6,646	133,634	413.8	259,277	21.6	78.4	66.3	40.4	4,302	34.1
Fulton	112	8.4	171	0.1	61.1	622,541	3,639	84,477	53.0	80,755	24.7	75.3	41.9	12.0	1,033	53.5
Greene	112	-25.2	128	D	36.3	385,629	3,007	66,540	14.6	16,637	39.3	60.7	28.3	2.2	189	7.2
Huntingdon	158	6.8	190	0.8	77.2	728,200	3,832	89,801	93.5	112,249	19.5	80.5	42.3	14.4	2,274	35.4
Indiana	154	-18.1	132	D	85.4	369,054	2,799	70,768	67.3	57,725	58.4	41.6	38.3	9.9	1,078	22.7
Jefferson	91	4.9	158	0.1	53.2	410,645	2,596	71,778	27.7	48,057	44.9	55.1	44.5	10.2	436	16.1
Juniata	91	-6.8	124	0.3	53.8	622,389	5,039	92,383	101.4	137,639	14.1	85.9	51.4	24.6	1,913	44.6
Lackawanna	33	-17.6	108	0.1	16.1	529,017	4,894	68,812	13.2	43,687	71.2	28.8	32.0	7.3	127	17.5
Lancaster	439	3.3	78	6.1	332.0	973,388	12,529	101,987	1,475.0	260,731	17.7	82.3	74.2	48.4	5,843	18.4
Lawrence	80	-12.9	122	0.1	46.8	501,196	4,105	84,781	38.5	58,451	53.5	46.5	48.7	10.3	652	25.9
Lebanon	121	7.0	100	1.5	97.4	1,052,028	10,562	122,164	348.9	286,245	13.1	86.9	64.1	37.6	2,250	26.6
Lehigh	76	-9.8	157	0.8	63.2	1,308,144	8,329	109,327	90.8	186,899	69.6	30.4	51.4	14.4	701	25.3
Luzerne	61	-8.5	110	0.3	34.4	491,933	4,489	67,198	21.0	37,757	82.2	17.8	31.7	9.2	970	41.4
Lycoming	158	-1.2	131	0.6	79.7	559,934	4,265	73,065	72.2	59,819	53.8	46.2	41.6	13.2	2,246	39.1
McKean	36	-12.5	125	0.0	13.2	258,072	2,062	49,907	5.0	17,076	49.3	50.7	31.4	4.5	192	24.5
Mercer	163	-5.1	138	0.1	97.7	470,815	3,420	88,056	82.7	69,747	56.5	43.5	47.8	14.8	1,376	29.9
Mifflin	91	-3.8	112	0.1	53.2	550,040	4,908	76,090	94.0	116,365	17.7	82.3	55.6	24.8	1,361	26.6
Monroe	26	-9.2	94	0.1	13.0	735,583	7,861	71,198	11.0	38,777	66.8	33.2	35.7	8.5	174	15.5
Montgomery	31	-26.6	52	0.8	18.7	725,669	14,051	52,896	25.6	42,943	71.9	28.1	39.8	8.1	293	10.6
Montour	43	-13.5	95	0.1	29.6	519,508	5,483	62,275	47.4	103,322	60.1	39.9	44.2	17.6	678	36.4
Northampton	66	-3.7	132	0.3	55.6	1,084,882	8,218	115,108	43.5	87,341	82.9	17.1	44.6	16.9	845	23.3
Northumberland	130	-12.3	153	1.4	92.8	748,819	4,898	101,762	154.3	182,218	37.0	63.0	54.0	24.7	2,014	43.1
Perry	135	-6.4	152	0.3	81.3	767,425	5,051	104,962	140.4	157,931	19.7	80.3	52.2	25.5	1,816	36.2
Philadelphia	0	8.8	13	0.0	0.1	587,318	45,337	29,864	0.8	34,909	94.7	5.2	50.0	9.1	0	0.0
Pike	28	2.5	565	0.0	3.4	1,037,120	1,835	55,680	3.0	59,300	91.3	8.7	40.0	10.0	D	6.0

Table B. States and Counties — Water Use, Wholesale Trade, Retail Trade, and Real Estate

STATE County	Water use, 2015 — Public supply water withdrawn (mil gal/day)	Public supply gallons withdrawn per person per day	Wholesale Trade[1], 2012 — Number of establishments	Number of employees	Sales (mil dol)	Annual payroll (mil dol)	Retail Trade[2], 2012 — Number of establishments	Number of employees	Sales (mil dol)	Annual payroll (mil dol)	Real estate and rental and leasing,[2] 2012 — Number of establishments	Number of employees	Sales (mil dol)	Annual payroll (mil dol)
	133	134	135	136	137	138	139	140	141	142	143	144	145	146
OREGON— Cont'd														
Morrow	5.61	501.3	11	60	51.2	3.8	13	79	19.6	2.1	10	11	1.4	0.2
Multnomah	14.72	18.6	1,233	21,805	21,267.8	1,275.5	2,888	37,805	9,982.9	1,016.1	1,373	8,734	1,569.3	369.5
Polk	4.96	62.5	29	264	100.9	10.4	125	1,546	360.7	36.9	59	167	19.4	3.0
Sherman	0.47	279.8	4	D	D	D	7	D	D	D	NA	NA	NA	NA
Tillamook	4.57	178.1	9	105	42.3	3.2	114	1,032	248.9	24.4	27	91	8.0	1.7
Umatilla	28.17	368.1	65	953	738.7	45.4	224	2,922	802.8	70.8	60	148	21.1	4.0
Union	4.58	177.6	22	209	140.3	8.4	103	1,313	318.5	31.6	17	70	9.6	1.8
Wallowa	1.37	199.8	2	D	D	D	51	284	63.6	7.0	18	D	D	D
Wasco	5.34	207.2	25	628	213.6	14.6	123	1,506	389.4	37.1	42	102	10.9	2.6
Washington	50.04	87.1	734	9,915	8,667.6	618.5	1,573	28,336	8,389.7	790.3	809	4,492	1,207.1	158.0
Wheeler	0.17	125.2	1	D	D	D	6	D	D	D	2	D	D	D
Yamhill	8.83	86.0	70	D	D	D	283	3,325	886.6	84.9	102	263	36.4	6.1
PENNSYLVANIA	1,391.70	108.7	12,568	195,004	191,170.1	11,203.8	43,952	643,903	178,794.9	15,330.6	9,438	58,585	13,364.0	2,617.5
Adams	12.39	121.1	61	D	D	D	333	3,231	801.2	74.4	47	210	35.8	7.0
Allegheny	178.17	144.8	1,497	21,265	27,237.9	1,195.1	4,423	72,737	20,553.7	1,730.3	1,291	9,005	2,208.0	414.5
Armstrong	6.65	99.2	35	525	217.2	24.2	215	2,105	551.2	42.1	27	270	33.8	10.0
Beaver	22.14	131.1	112	1,508	1,179.5	74.3	517	7,307	1,590.2	149.3	92	398	83.2	14.2
Bedford	9.99	205.6	39	382	350.6	21.8	183	2,088	576.2	43.0	11	86	21.2	4.9
Berks	31.85	76.7	354	6,912	4,277.4	362.2	1,256	20,219	5,719.4	494.3	246	1,249	213.0	41.4
Blair	13.07	104.1	119	1,832	2,258.4	80.7	561	8,383	2,286.7	189.4	87	349	72.9	11.3
Bradford	3.02	49.3	49	D	D	D	252	3,127	903.7	72.7	30	223	52.6	9.9
Bucks	98.64	157.2	1,152	14,950	12,999.7	854.9	2,408	38,063	10,185.1	975.9	589	3,494	855.9	147.2
Butler	7.66	41.0	253	4,444	3,353.8	249.0	680	11,085	2,902.2	245.0	148	714	160.4	23.9
Cambria	14.93	109.4	115	1,365	664.9	51.0	561	6,927	1,733.8	148.6	86	408	48.3	12.2
Cameron	0.34	71.9	2	D	D	D	17	174	30.9	3.3	1	D	D	D
Carbon	23.34	364.9	19	D	D	D	194	2,142	562.6	49.3	36	121	21.1	3.4
Centre	17.87	111.3	90	873	538.9	42.5	481	7,570	1,748.7	155.7	133	1,036	255.5	34.7
Chester	42.15	81.7	711	12,642	19,155.1	1,204.8	1,517	27,549	12,474.9	984.2	457	2,360	781.2	143.1
Clarion	2.73	69.1	30	385	167.3	14.2	185	1,879	460.4	40.7	21	104	11.0	3.4
Clearfield	5.84	72.1	68	771	703.6	30.4	350	4,731	1,331.3	105.4	43	344	35.9	8.7
Clinton	4.02	101.9	18	D	D	D	121	1,773	582.6	39.5	37	165	26.6	4.3
Columbia	5.02	75.3	46	419	118.4	15.8	236	3,413	904.8	70.4	43	205	33.9	6.4
Crawford	5.67	65.6	57	372	136.3	12.8	317	3,577	973.5	85.5	51	176	24.5	4.3
Cumberland	13.36	54.2	189	2,607	2,666.3	124.9	858	16,016	4,812.9	376.3	222	1,366	316.8	66.3
Dauphin	31.47	115.3	295	6,839	6,655.5	390.2	981	15,280	3,943.9	348.2	218	1,608	505.1	90.5
Delaware	20.79	36.9	522	6,961	5,482.3	536.3	1,700	24,271	6,468.8	602.2	409	2,945	776.4	169.8
Elk	5.32	172.3	26	D	D	D	124	1,496	314.5	28.8	11	46	6.3	1.2
Erie	33.34	119.9	264	3,127	1,242.5	145.7	958	15,221	3,752.8	326.4	182	1,042	158.5	32.3
Fayette	45.89	343.4	107	1,002	496.6	37.7	487	6,040	1,638.8	129.7	69	299	50.9	9.9
Forest	0.41	55.3	1	D	D	D	18	101	24.8	2.0	1	D	D	D
Franklin	8.47	55.1	108	D	D	D	486	7,106	1,809.5	157.6	87	328	54.9	10.4
Fulton	0.37	25.3	12	142	139.8	4.6	42	374	102.9	7.3	3	12	1.2	0.5
Greene	7.19	191.6	26	350	302.8	17.5	138	2,444	883.7	63.3	12	47	6.7	1.1
Huntingdon	2.85	62.4	29	344	94.9	11.6	141	1,424	354.3	28.8	10	28	9.8	1.0
Indiana	4.11	47.3	67	D	D	D	309	5,016	1,318.8	112.7	45	163	26.2	3.8
Jefferson	2.14	48.2	39	441	245.5	17.9	176	1,857	556.2	37.7	24	128	32.2	4.6
Juniata	0.82	33.1	18	133	54.5	5.0	69	601	204.4	13.1	6	12	1.3	0.2
Lackawanna	38.70	182.6	251	3,800	4,374.5	168.9	916	13,197	3,186.3	278.2	138	690	128.5	21.1
Lancaster	54.45	101.5	582	10,776	8,764.0	496.7	1,917	29,783	6,899.6	669.6	342	2,009	396.6	79.1
Lawrence	10.07	114.3	86	D	D	D	292	3,391	838.7	75.6	44	279	29.7	7.0
Lebanon	3.55	25.9	99	2,679	3,913.7	112.7	431	6,597	1,695.7	158.6	70	309	40.5	7.8
Lehigh	34.58	95.9	408	9,182	8,062.4	577.2	1,239	20,261	5,550.4	467.5	315	1,587	324.0	58.2
Luzerne	22.82	71.7	300	5,656	3,435.9	242.3	1,247	18,177	8,097.0	413.8	210	923	214.7	34.0
Lycoming	8.78	75.7	108	2,110	1,271.2	82.6	503	7,404	1,878.1	154.7	89	618	120.0	24.4
McKean	6.77	159.6	31	D	D	D	158	1,551	401.8	34.7	16	62	6.4	1.4
Mercer	13.74	120.3	89	1,099	644.7	42.4	516	7,109	1,527.3	147.2	72	275	101.6	7.8
Mifflin	2.69	57.8	35	D	D	D	162	2,063	539.4	46.9	23	71	11.0	1.7
Monroe	11.35	68.2	97	D	D	D	634	8,710	2,140.4	187.8	123	507	86.8	15.2
Montgomery	63.31	77.3	1,237	19,422	17,692.1	1,444.8	3,261	56,471	16,036.3	1,489.8	931	7,713	1,767.3	412.8
Montour	0.03	1.6	13	149	190.2	6.1	54	662	167.2	13.6	6	18	2.9	0.6
Northampton	9.53	31.7	250	3,917	9,979.8	192.8	873	13,238	3,627.4	316.9	178	726	260.6	27.4
Northumberland	11.05	118.5	56	945	1,152.0	46.6	280	3,188	909.7	76.7	38	182	37.4	7.7
Perry	0.71	15.5	16	144	81.4	6.1	134	1,166	317.8	25.6	10	23	3.4	0.7
Philadelphia	249.54	159.2	1,047	16,940	13,181.9	973.0	4,506	50,185	12,241.3	1,165.5	1,079	8,856	1,951.0	443.5
Pike	3.05	54.5	15	98	31.8	5.4	134	1,862	471.4	40.0	40	442	41.9	10.9

1. Merchant wholesalers, except manufacturers' sales branches and offices.   2. Employer establishments.

Table B. States and Counties — Government Employment and Payroll, and Local Government Finances

STATE County	Government employment and payroll, 2012									Local government finances				
			March payroll (percent of total)							General revenue				
												Taxes		
													Per capita[1] (dollars)	
	Full-time equivalent employees	March payroll (dollars)	Administration, judicial, and legal	Police and corrections	Fire protection	Highways and transportation	Health and welfare	Natural resources and utilities	Education and libraries	Total (mil dol)	Inter-governmental (mil dol)	Total (mil dol)	Total	Property
	171	172	173	174	175	176	177	178	179	180	181	182	183	184
OREGON— Cont'd														
Morrow	611	2,174,057	7.8	9.3	1.6	5.2	17.4	6.6	45.7	79.1	31.3	21.7	1,928	1,801
Multnomah	29,478	148,927,675	7.5	11.9	4.2	13.6	6.4	9.0	42.8	4,680.8	1,700.4	1,856.1	2,445	1,660
Polk	1,230	4,842,625	12.3	13.6	2.4	1.9	8.6	6.6	52.1	138.5	77.6	42.1	552	500
Sherman	121	446,146	20.7	9.6	8.8	9.9	11.4	7.5	29.5	23.4	4.3	6.6	3,808	3,775
Tillamook	1,081	4,310,792	8.6	7.5	1.5	5.0	4.7	26.1	44.4	116.8	36.6	46.1	1,822	1,701
Umatilla	2,519	9,346,604	6.6	11.0	3.9	3.0	1.9	7.4	65.3	307.6	163.2	86.2	1,122	1,020
Union	750	2,655,712	8.7	12.0	2.8	4.4	0.9	8.8	60.1	87.0	50.9	20.7	802	722
Wallowa	382	1,406,470	6.1	5.5	0.3	3.8	43.8	3.1	36.5	46.2	14.1	8.6	1,262	1,113
Wasco	982	3,676,060	6.9	6.4	4.7	3.8	3.2	15.2	58.1	115.4	52.3	37.4	1,468	1,319
Washington	14,620	63,993,061	6.8	11.2	6.7	2.5	2.0	7.5	60.1	1,882.7	665.8	834.1	1,523	1,366
Wheeler	106	329,289	21.3	2.9	0.0	9.3	0.0	7.4	57.6	8.1	5.1	1.6	1,126	1,092
Yamhill	2,820	11,200,226	7.7	9.1	4.6	1.7	6.0	8.9	59.7	320.3	146.1	104.5	1,043	942
PENNSYLVANIA	X	X	X	X	X	X	X	X	X	X	X	X	X	X
Adams	2,548	9,790,732	7.8	9.5	0.9	2.6	2.1	3.4	73.2	374.0	165.8	167.3	1,648	1,256
Allegheny	43,945	195,375,705	6.5	12.8	2.4	11.5	5.4	5.9	53.8	6,769.1	2,823.5	2,739.2	2,228	1,525
Armstrong	2,222	7,529,691	6.9	7.0	0.0	4.1	6.8	5.5	68.9	227.1	114.7	81.0	1,185	1,004
Beaver	5,422	21,094,763	6.4	10.1	0.3	4.8	6.7	6.8	64.1	785.3	350.5	233.6	1,372	1,124
Bedford	1,369	4,444,835	5.3	5.6	0.8	4.2	1.7	5.0	77.4	128.7	70.2	45.3	918	675
Berks	14,566	69,528,665	6.1	16.3	5.1	2.6	4.7	5.3	58.7	2,039.3	792.5	835.6	2,021	1,642
Blair	4,030	13,533,958	4.8	8.4	2.3	5.0	8.5	7.0	62.6	402.4	214.5	126.2	993	707
Bradford	2,246	8,350,493	7.8	4.9	0.5	5.3	11.4	1.9	67.4	247.1	119.2	78.6	1,252	972
Bucks	18,333	88,124,851	6.0	11.7	0.6	4.0	4.0	3.9	68.9	2,731.2	688.4	1,517.1	2,419	2,074
Butler	4,890	20,031,417	6.5	6.1	0.5	3.3	5.6	4.7	72.2	629.8	252.7	262.6	1,420	1,090
Cambria	4,484	15,273,184	8.2	8.3	1.4	5.9	5.7	6.0	63.9	555.1	293.7	143.3	1,012	781
Cameron	214	664,238	8.3	4.9	0.0	5.0	7.5	2.5	70.2	17.3	9.0	6.0	1,223	1,052
Carbon	2,113	7,282,054	7.7	9.6	0.0	3.5	11.6	5.7	60.5	211.1	71.9	108.6	1,671	1,438
Centre	3,965	14,048,206	7.5	8.6	0.0	7.9	9.9	5.8	58.3	455.2	154.4	216.4	1,394	1,018
Chester	13,231	61,935,244	7.1	9.3	0.2	2.2	4.5	2.8	71.3	2,107.9	567.4	1,254.5	2,476	2,063
Clarion	1,226	4,224,897	6.3	6.9	0.0	3.1	1.8	3.0	78.3	155.3	103.3	39.4	993	773
Clearfield	2,608	9,251,789	4.9	5.4	0.0	3.3	1.6	4.7	78.9	261.5	141.7	88.1	1,086	853
Clinton	1,129	4,364,621	9.8	5.9	2.2	2.6	11.0	7.0	59.8	138.0	54.0	44.3	1,121	835
Columbia	1,917	7,059,353	6.5	11.0	0.0	3.3	2.0	3.1	73.5	197.2	86.4	83.5	1,248	914
Crawford	2,501	8,880,019	8.6	8.3	1.6	5.0	10.3	5.8	59.4	270.2	125.4	98.7	1,127	906
Cumberland	7,023	27,433,306	6.6	8.7	0.0	2.7	6.7	4.9	68.9	914.8	308.3	434.2	1,820	1,330
Dauphin	10,041	42,265,280	7.7	13.4	1.0	4.7	1.7	5.4	64.3	1,441.8	522.5	527.9	1,958	1,407
Delaware	18,047	76,207,314	10.5	9.6	1.0	2.0	6.2	4.1	65.6	2,712.5	932.9	1,199.8	2,138	1,938
Elk	1,009	3,366,414	8.9	6.3	0.0	12.9	2.6	6.2	61.7	108.1	52.0	37.3	1,181	901
Erie	8,523	32,472,819	5.3	9.7	2.6	5.6	3.9	6.0	65.7	1,197.6	616.5	364.0	1,297	1,046
Fayette	3,546	14,568,652	6.8	9.1	0.4	5.2	7.7	9.3	61.2	411.7	262.1	104.7	772	570
Forest	197	632,875	20.3	3.4	0.0	3.6	5.7	3.9	62.0	19.5	9.4	7.5	980	863
Franklin	3,820	13,644,359	7.7	8.8	1.7	2.3	9.1	6.1	63.5	415.1	130.8	191.4	1,265	978
Fulton	454	1,468,178	11.3	2.6	0.0	2.5	0.0	2.1	81.0	47.4	25.7	16.4	1,112	912
Greene	1,301	4,613,569	10.4	5.2	0.0	6.2	4.1	7.8	65.3	144.0	67.6	57.8	1,518	1,258
Huntingdon	1,125	3,453,282	9.3	7.1	0.0	3.2	3.8	5.2	70.1	118.4	66.3	38.4	837	613
Indiana	2,289	9,093,274	6.9	6.4	0.1	4.5	4.9	5.1	70.9	313.8	170.3	97.7	1,107	879
Jefferson	1,211	4,334,856	6.6	7.0	0.0	4.9	1.4	6.4	72.3	125.7	68.4	38.4	858	661
Juniata	563	1,993,044	11.0	5.3	1.3	2.6	0.1	1.9	75.5	49.2	23.8	21.6	867	690
Lackawanna	6,361	25,493,690	6.8	11.8	3.2	4.1	6.5	6.5	59.1	757.3	291.3	324.8	1,515	1,101
Lancaster	12,622	54,624,168	5.9	11.7	0.8	2.8	3.4	3.5	70.9	1,833.2	668.6	843.7	1,601	1,327
Lawrence	2,433	9,509,559	8.0	8.4	1.5	4.9	1.0	3.8	71.8	318.9	174.0	106.5	1,185	905
Lebanon	4,116	14,939,586	6.1	9.0	1.7	2.8	9.0	5.5	65.4	485.8	160.6	191.5	1,416	1,136
Lehigh	11,303	49,829,858	7.3	10.7	1.9	4.5	9.3	4.5	60.4	1,670.5	674.3	669.0	1,883	1,523
Luzerne	9,404	36,055,331	7.5	12.5	3.5	3.7	4.7	5.2	62.1	1,080.5	466.5	439.6	1,369	1,039
Lycoming	3,615	14,906,594	7.7	7.9	1.8	4.3	2.7	6.0	68.7	451.3	198.0	155.7	1,329	953
McKean	1,616	5,647,554	6.9	7.4	1.5	4.5	8.7	8.2	62.2	167.7	97.2	44.6	1,033	829
Mercer	3,570	12,446,506	8.5	9.8	1.2	3.2	1.2	4.2	70.1	402.4	216.5	133.0	1,150	861
Mifflin	1,135	4,324,228	8.8	6.8	1.1	5.0	2.7	9.1	64.8	153.4	81.3	46.8	1,002	733
Monroe	5,957	25,067,544	5.7	4.3	0.0	5.4	1.6	1.5	80.9	719.0	225.3	441.5	2,616	2,404
Montgomery	23,690	112,151,487	6.4	12.2	0.4	2.4	5.0	4.0	68.6	3,430.1	888.0	2,054.1	2,541	2,087
Montour	515	1,746,307	6.4	6.4	0.0	4.4	0.9	6.3	73.4	92.9	26.6	26.3	1,431	915
Northampton	10,782	47,706,434	7.1	11.9	1.8	2.5	7.7	4.9	61.8	1,411.9	496.8	671.7	2,244	1,804
Northumberland	3,162	10,304,053	9.0	7.6	0.0	3.1	16.2	4.4	59.0	273.2	137.2	88.2	934	631
Perry	1,241	4,130,390	6.3	5.0	0.0	3.3	5.0	1.5	77.8	139.6	62.3	60.0	1,312	977
Philadelphia	60,937	311,591,353	8.6	18.6	4.6	16.9	6.0	8.1	36.4	11,133.9	5,530.3	4,080.0	2,636	743
Pike	1,166	4,430,795	9.4	13.5	0.0	2.5	4.3	1.7	67.0	128.4	48.7	71.2	1,252	1,185

1. Based on the resident population estimated as of July 1 of the year shown.

Table B. States and Counties — Local Government Finances, Government Employment, and Income Taxes

STATE County	Total (mil dol)	Per capita[1] (dollars)	Education	Health and hospitals	Police protection	Public welfare	Highways	Total (mil dol)	Per capita[1] (dollars)	Federal civilian	Federal military	State and local	Number of returns	Mean adjusted gross income	Mean income tax
					Direct general expenditure — Percent of total for:			Debt outstanding		Government employment, 2016			Individual income tax returns, 2015		
	185	186	187	188	189	190	191	192	193	194	195	196	197	198	199
OREGON— Cont'd															
Morrow	78.1	6,947	32.8	11.0	4.6	0.3	5.8	136.8	12,168	61	32	841	4,800	47,698	4,064
Multnomah	4,425.0	5,828	31.5	4.6	5.2	4.0	6.5	7,864.7	10,358	12,494	2,339	59,562	394,700	68,331	9,506
Polk	140.8	1,844	43.0	8.4	8.3	1.0	5.6	271.5	3,556	73	200	4,948	34,740	57,205	5,888
Sherman	18.9	10,932	20.7	4.0	4.0	1.4	11.8	3.5	2,023	135	0	184	830	56,233	6,327
Tillamook	118.4	4,684	38.3	7.8	3.6	0.3	5.5	166.8	6,595	107	101	1,682	12,020	49,300	4,831
Umatilla	311.2	4,051	58.5	1.4	4.4	0.0	4.1	422.0	5,493	496	181	6,486	31,710	47,469	4,370
Union	90.0	3,495	44.0	3.4	5.7	0.4	5.1	30.5	1,185	229	63	1,824	11,350	49,830	4,811
Wallowa	44.0	6,453	31.6	33.8	3.6	0.8	8.6	38.3	5,620	102	17	525	3,390	45,901	4,212
Wasco	106.5	4,180	48.5	2.2	4.8	0.4	4.4	159.3	6,251	295	64	1,723	11,440	47,931	4,627
Washington	1,940.6	3,543	44.5	2.9	7.1	0.0	5.6	2,532.1	4,623	814	1,443	21,010	272,690	77,505	10,317
Wheeler	9.5	6,659	0.8	2.6	1.5	12.0		2.0	1,419	0	0	106	560	32,129	2,832
Yamhill	320.3	3,195	49.5	5.9	5.8	0.1	3.1	445.1	4,439	489	248	3,866	44,910	58,895	6,291
PENNSYLVANIA	X	X	X	X	X	X	X	X	X	97,071	35,446	640,913	6,200,330	65,378	9,008
Adams	458.0	4,513	68.9	3.6	1.4	3.2	2.7	405.6	3,997	708	255	3,259	51,420	58,274	6,904
Allegheny	6,640.6	5,402	42.9	7.9	4.6	4.6	3.0	13,494.2	10,977	13,034	3,560	52,005	632,260	71,086	10,599
Armstrong	246.9	3,609	57.6	1.5	1.2	7.5	5.0	239.3	3,498	192	171	2,503	32,350	47,666	4,742
Beaver	789.6	4,638	46.6	3.5	3.0	14.1	3.9	1,928.6	11,328	305	429	7,157	85,970	52,818	5,778
Bedford	155.3	3,148	66.4	0.0	0.4	2.0	4.8	224.7	4,556	107	124	2,101	23,100	45,382	4,274
Berks	2,024.3	4,896	54.5	3.4	4.1	7.2	2.8	3,478.7	8,413	927	1,053	21,460	202,920	58,559	7,151
Blair	409.0	3,217	49.0	3.1	3.0	8.6	3.9	474.2	3,730	1,012	316	7,524	59,440	50,914	5,956
Bradford	244.7	3,898	54.4	2.0	1.6	7.3	6.2	751.2	11,963	212	168	2,841	28,710	51,203	5,656
Bucks	2,875.9	4,586	57.6	0.8	5.5	7.0	4.5	3,960.3	6,316	1,157	1,628	21,369	330,540	87,899	14,034
Butler	656.7	3,550	51.5	4.2	2.4	9.5	4.4	1,305.0	7,055	2,878	478	8,473	94,090	71,009	9,840
Cambria	571.5	4,037	49.2	3.2	5.7	14.0	3.6	641.5	4,531	1,024	358	6,904	64,140	47,258	4,953
Cameron	19.1	3,864	59.4	3.8	1.2	2.5	5.9	30.2	6,117	12	12	359	2,450	41,384	3,722
Carbon	219.0	3,370	60.5	0.1	2.6	4.4	3.4	265.0	4,076	109	171	2,493	30,970	49,164	5,061
Centre	453.5	2,923	51.0	2.2	3.5	7.9	6.1	486.7	3,136	465	443	48,697	60,070	64,956	8,284
Chester	2,204.4	4,352	57.7	5.2	3.8	3.4	3.3	2,995.8	5,914	2,405	1,312	23,105	252,920	110,042	19,484
Clarion	168.8	4,258	67.2	3.0	1.9	2.5	3.4	87.7	2,213	99	102	3,219	17,150	46,102	4,495
Clearfield	261.5	3,221	66.6	0.0	3.5	3.1	4.8	310.5	3,824	241	197	4,435	36,830	45,362	4,541
Clinton	137.3	3,474	41.4	0.3	1.3	4.6	4.0	99.3	2,514	146	98	2,975	16,980	46,985	4,466
Columbia	207.5	3,102	63.6	0.0	3.1	3.7	4.7	212.5	3,176	147	162	5,154	29,720	50,086	5,321
Crawford	281.4	3,212	48.8	2.8	1.9	9.1	5.8	238.2	2,719	251	216	3,762	38,850	46,580	4,816
Cumberland	1,033.3	4,330	58.9	3.0	2.8	6.7	2.5	1,275.7	5,346	4,572	1,355	12,595	124,230	75,908	10,956
Dauphin	1,554.4	5,764	46.5	4.7	3.9	9.1	2.6	2,450.3	9,087	2,688	758	38,594	142,090	58,750	7,443
Delaware	2,744.1	4,891	50.1	2.1	4.9	11.1	2.0	4,601.2	8,200	2,088	1,451	23,400	276,660	82,856	13,162
Elk	92.2	2,921	46.8	0.2	2.8	1.8	8.2	287.8	9,123	83	78	1,168	16,510	49,082	5,255
Erie	1,203.4	4,288	44.0	5.6	2.7	14.2	3.5	1,705.3	6,076	1,543	730	15,480	130,590	51,399	6,021
Fayette	427.6	3,152	56.8	10.4	1.2	3.1	3.6	909.8	6,706	353	334	5,915	61,650	46,444	4,756
Forest	20.2	2,638	52.6	4.6	0.8	4.0	10.1	11.6	1,515	70	12	936	2,220	41,901	3,943
Franklin	452.7	2,992	54.1	4.1	1.9	5.5	4.8	619.1	4,092	2,197	397	5,737	76,500	52,722	5,415
Fulton	47.5	3,214	61.6	0.0	3.7	4.3	4.1	65.3	4,419	26	38	691	7,070	46,554	4,295
Greene	138.0	3,624	59.6	4.6	1.0	1.6	6.1	149.4	3,923	119	89	2,407	15,990	61,704	7,954
Huntingdon	134.9	2,937	57.1	1.3	1.8	2.3	5.0	147.7	3,216	112	106	2,936	19,140	46,573	4,398
Indiana	303.7	3,442	61.2	0.1	1.0	6.1	4.2	387.8	4,396	196	216	7,318	36,190	50,498	5,501
Jefferson	139.0	3,104	60.2	0.0	1.5	3.9	5.0	213.5	4,770	111	113	1,805	21,280	45,557	4,574
Juniata	46.0	1,848	65.2	0.1	0.9	2.6	5.4	13.7	550	65	64	703	11,210	46,930	4,399
Lackawanna	820.1	3,824	47.2	0.3	3.9	6.6	3.0	968.6	4,516	940	536	9,743	102,950	51,847	6,135
Lancaster	2,018.4	3,831	55.1	5.4	4.3	5.1	3.3	3,447.0	6,543	1,255	1,369	19,456	264,590	60,257	7,370
Lawrence	334.2	3,719	50.8	2.1	3.0	11.6	4.1	469.7	5,226	204	229	3,319	41,870	48,662	5,183
Lebanon	507.4	3,752	47.7	2.2	2.9	15.0	5.1	705.4	5,215	3,136	353	4,955	68,660	53,625	5,758
Lehigh	1,756.6	4,945	46.2	3.6	3.3	11.2	2.9	1,386.1	4,318	3,275	812	14,728	156,990	49,484	5,566
Luzerne	1,193.5	3,718	54.0	0.4	3.0	3.8	4.4	997.6	8,514	363	288	8,763	54,510	49,756	5,254
Lycoming	560.5	4,783	43.8	0.0	2.2	3.1	3.6	130.5	3,026	439	100	1,959	18,990	48,639	5,217
McKean	182.4	4,229	57.8	3.7	2.0	4.1	3.9	444.6	3,844	249	287	4,831	53,440	47,703	5,044
Mercer	435.3	3,764	63.5	2.3	3.0	2.6	3.1	218.1	4,664	87	119	1,668	21,070	43,564	3,966
Mifflin	166.3	3,555	61.5	4.0	1.7	0.4									
Monroe	739.9	4,384	67.9	0.1	3.0	3.9	2.5	1,201.0	7,115	3,208	446	8,182	78,420	52,881	5,787
Montgomery	3,494.4	4,322	56.9	1.9	5.0	6.2	3.6	4,364.3	5,398	2,568	2,279	32,628	418,810	106,723	18,645
Montour	79.5	4,333	44.5	0.0	1.9	1.3	3.9	895.8	48,800	38	47	1,478	9,130	66,468	9,199
Northampton	1,501.3	5,017	49.8	3.1	4.0	11.6	2.7	2,550.6	8,523	1,089	772	13,682	151,800	63,502	8,114
Northumberland	266.3	2,820	54.3	3.8	5.1	7.1	3.9	255.4	2,704	162	231	4,038	43,530	47,104	4,804
Perry	128.6	2,813	61.7	2.5	0.8	7.4	4.3	107.1	2,343	81	118	1,808	22,600	50,955	4,931
Philadelphia	9,802.9	6,334	34.2	13.8	6.2	5.8	1.1	18,737.5	12,107	30,108	5,156	72,846	673,370	49,070	5,944
Pike	135.9	2,388	49.0	0.4	1.9	5.8	3.9	42.8	752	211	143	2,321	26,800	57,195	6,493

1. Based on the resident population estimated as of July 1 of the year shown.

Table B. States and Counties — **Land Area and Population**

State / county code	CBSA code[1]	County code[2]	STATE County	Land area[3] (sq. mi)	Total persons 2017	Rank	Per square mile	White	Black	American Indian, Alaska Native	Asian and Pacific Islander	Percent Hispanic or Latino[4]	Under 5 years	5 to 17 years	18 to 24 years	25 to 34 years	35 to 44 years	45 to 54 years
				1	2	3	4	5	6	7	8	9	10	11	12	13	14	15
			PENNSYLVANIA— Cont'd															
42,105		9	Potter	1,081.3	16,802	1,989	15.5	97.3	0.9	0.7	0.6	1.4	5.4	15.2	7.0	10.0	9.8	13.3
42,107	39,060	4	Schuylkill	778.6	142,569	453	183.1	92.0	3.4	0.4	0.8	4.4	4.7	14.8	7.2	11.9	11.9	14.4
42,109	42,780	7	Snyder	328.8	40,801	1,160	124.1	95.7	1.5	0.4	1.0	2.4	5.7	15.7	11.5	11.4	10.8	13.1
42,111	43,740	4	Somerset	1,074.4	74,501	742	69.3	95.0	3.1	0.4	0.7	1.5	4.6	13.6	7.2	11.4	11.7	13.9
42,113		8	Sullivan	449.9	6,089	2,742	13.5	93.4	4.1	0.8	0.7	1.9	2.7	8.3	9.0	10.0	9.6	13.3
42,115		6	Susquehanna	823.5	40,985	1,153	49.8	97.2	0.8	0.6	0.7	1.7	4.4	14.3	7.0	10.0	10.0	14.1
42,117		6	Tioga	1,133.8	40,793	1,161	36.0	97.1	1.3	0.6	0.8	1.3	5.3	14.6	9.0	11.1	10.3	13.0
42,119	30,260	4	Union	316.0	44,595	1,081	141.1	86.0	6.7	0.6	2.4	5.6	4.5	13.4	13.5	13.3	12.6	12.7
42,121	36,340	4	Venango	674.3	51,762	964	76.8	97.0	1.8	0.5	0.7	1.1	5.0	14.7	6.9	10.4	10.8	13.3
42,123	47,620	6	Warren	884.1	39,659	1,184	44.9	97.6	0.8	0.6	0.7	1.1	4.9	14.5	6.9	10.5	10.1	13.9
42,125	38,300	1	Washington	857.0	207,298	320	241.9	93.9	4.3	0.5	1.4	1.7	5.0	14.5	8.5	11.1	11.4	13.8
42,127		6	Wayne	725.6	51,205	974	70.6	91.6	3.6	0.5	0.9	4.4	4.1	12.6	7.1	11.0	10.9	14.1
42,129	38,300	1	Westmoreland	1,027.6	352,627	197	343.2	95.2	3.4	0.4	1.3	1.2	4.6	13.9	7.7	10.5	10.8	14.1
42,131	42,540	2	Wyoming	397.3	27,322	1,515	68.8	96.4	1.4	0.5	0.8	1.9	4.9	14.8	8.5	11.1	10.8	13.8
42,133	49,620	2	York	904.2	446,078	159	493.3	85.1	6.8	0.5	1.9	7.5	5.7	16.5	8.2	12.3	12.0	14.1
44,000		0	**RHODE ISLAND**	1,034.0	1,059,639	X	1,024.8	74.3	7.1	1.1	4.3	15.5	5.2	14.4	10.7	13.7	11.7	13.5
44,001	39,300	1	Bristol	24.1	48,912	1,006	2,029.5	93.4	1.8	0.6	2.9	3.1	4.1	14.8	11.1	10.0	10.8	14.3
44,003	39,300	1	Kent	168.6	163,760	396	971.3	90.3	2.5	0.8	3.3	5.0	5.0	14.0	7.2	13.1	12.0	14.8
44,005	39,300	1	Newport	102.4	83,460	682	815.0	87.7	5.1	1.0	2.8	6.0	4.3	12.9	9.6	12.3	11.0	13.5
44,007	39,300	1	Providence	409.6	637,357	105	1,556.0	63.4	10.0	1.1	5.2	22.8	5.7	14.9	10.9	15.2	12.1	13.1
44,009	39,300	1	Washington	329.3	126,150	502	383.1	92.5	2.0	1.5	2.7	3.2	3.7	13.2	14.9	9.2	9.5	13.7
45,000		0	**SOUTH CAROLINA**	30,063.0	5,024,369	X	167.1	65.2	27.8	0.9	2.2	5.7	5.8	16.1	9.3	13.2	12.0	12.9
45,001	24,940	6	Abbeville	490.5	24,722	1,619	50.4	70.1	28.4	0.7	0.6	1.5	5.1	15.6	9.4	10.8	10.3	13.2
45,003	12,260	2	Aiken	1,071.1	168,179	383	157.0	67.8	25.9	1.1	1.5	5.8	5.8	16.2	8.0	12.7	11.4	12.7
45,005		6	Allendale	408.1	9,002	2,502	22.1	23.0	73.2	0.6	0.8	3.3	4.4	14.6	8.6	14.0	11.0	14.3
45,007	24,860	2	Anderson	715.5	198,759	336	277.8	78.9	17.0	0.6	1.3	3.8	6.0	17.0	8.2	12.2	11.8	13.6
45,009		7	Bamberg	393.4	14,381	2,137	36.6	36.9	60.5	0.7	0.7	2.2	4.7	14.8	12.3	10.1	9.8	12.6
45,011		6	Barnwell	548.4	21,345	1,760	38.9	52.4	44.5	1.0	1.0	2.5	6.2	17.8	8.4	11.3	11.3	13.0
45,013	25,940	3	Beaufort	576.4	186,844	351	324.2	69.3	18.8	0.6	1.9	11.1	5.3	13.7	9.4	11.3	10.0	10.5
45,015	16,700	2	Berkeley	1,098.7	217,937	306	198.4	66.1	25.2	1.2	3.7	6.6	6.5	17.5	9.4	14.7	13.1	12.9
45,017	17,900	2	Calhoun	381.2	14,704	2,117	38.6	54.8	41.1	0.9	0.6	3.9	4.8	14.8	7.3	10.6	10.5	13.7
45,019	16,700	2	Charleston	917.5	401,438	174	437.5	65.9	27.6	0.7	2.3	5.1	6.0	13.9	8.8	17.2	12.8	12.4
45,021	23,500	4	Cherokee	392.8	57,105	896	145.4	74.2	21.4	0.7	0.9	4.4	5.9	17.5	9.3	12.7	11.8	13.7
45,023	16,740	1	Chester	580.7	32,301	1,374	55.6	60.3	37.6	1.0	0.7	2.1	5.8	16.8	7.5	12.1	11.0	13.9
45,025		6	Chesterfield	799.0	45,948	1,052	57.5	61.6	33.7	1.0	0.9	4.4	5.7	16.8	8.2	11.5	11.7	14.5
45,027		6	Clarendon	606.9	34,057	1,325	56.1	48.3	47.8	0.6	0.9	3.2	4.9	14.6	9.1	11.4	10.0	12.5
45,029		6	Colleton	1,056.5	37,611	1,233	35.6	58.0	38.1	1.3	0.7	3.4	6.0	16.5	7.8	11.5	10.8	13.1
45,031	22,500	3	Darlington	561.2	67,265	791	119.9	55.8	42.1	0.7	0.7	2.0	6.0	16.4	8.7	11.4	11.4	13.2
45,033		6	Dillon	405.1	30,666	1,415	75.7	47.2	48.1	3.2	0.6	2.6	6.6	18.8	8.2	12.3	11.9	12.3
45,035	16,700	2	Dorchester	573.2	156,456	421	273.0	66.4	26.7	1.2	3.0	5.4	6.2	18.6	8.1	14.1	13.4	13.9
45,037	12,260	2	Edgefield	500.4	26,693	1,539	53.3	57.7	36.2	0.8	0.8	5.9	4.1	14.4	8.3	13.0	12.9	14.3
45,039	17,900	2	Fairfield	686.3	22,607	1,699	32.9	39.4	58.2	0.8	0.9	2.2	4.6	14.8	7.8	10.7	10.4	14.0
45,041	22,500	3	Florence	800.0	138,566	463	173.2	52.9	43.2	0.7	1.8	2.7	6.1	17.8	8.7	12.7	12.3	13.0
45,043	23,860	4	Georgetown	813.6	61,607	847	75.7	64.8	31.7	0.6	0.8	3.0	4.6	14.2	6.8	9.3	9.8	12.3
45,045	24,860	2	Greenville	785.2	506,837	138	645.5	70.0	19.0	0.6	3.0	9.1	6.3	16.9	8.8	13.9	12.8	13.3
45,047	24,940	4	Greenwood	454.7	70,355	765	154.7	60.5	32.5	0.5	1.5	6.1	6.0	16.7	9.3	12.6	11.5	12.9
45,049		6	Hampton	559.9	19,602	1,846	35.0	41.8	53.8	0.7	0.8	4.2	5.3	16.1	8.2	12.9	13.3	12.9
45,051	34,820	2	Horry	1,134.0	333,268	209	293.9	79.1	14.0	1.0	1.9	6.0	4.8	13.6	7.4	11.9	11.2	12.7
45,053	25,940	3	Jasper	655.1	28,458	1,474	43.4	43.6	42.7	0.7	1.0	13.2	5.8	14.8	8.7	13.6	11.5	12.9
45,055	17,900	2	Kershaw	726.6	65,036	818	89.5	70.3	25.2	0.7	1.0	4.3	5.9	17.5	7.4	11.7	11.9	13.4
45,057	16,740	1	Lancaster	549.1	92,550	632	168.5	71.5	22.3	0.6	1.6	5.3	6.1	15.8	6.6	12.1	13.2	13.0
45,059	24,860	2	Laurens	713.8	66,848	796	93.7	69.2	26.0	0.6	0.7	4.9	5.7	16.3	9.1	12.2	11.1	13.4
45,061		6	Lee	410.2	17,350	1,956	42.3	33.2	64.1	0.6	0.7	2.5	5.1	15.5	9.1	13.8	11.2	12.6
45,063	17,900	2	Lexington	699.1	290,642	236	415.7	76.4	15.8	0.9	2.5	6.1	5.9	17.4	7.7	13.5	12.9	13.8
45,065		8	McCormick	359.1	9,545	2,464	26.6	51.7	46.8	0.5	0.7	1.5	3.0	9.1	5.3	10.4	9.4	12.8
45,067		6	Marion	489.3	31,293	1,400	64.0	39.4	57.1	0.9	1.0	2.9	5.9	17.3	8.0	11.3	11.5	12.4
45,069	13,500	6	Marlboro	479.9	26,825	1,532	55.9	41.0	51.6	5.3	0.8	3.2	5.5	14.8	8.2	14.3	12.8	13.4
45,071	35,140	6	Newberry	630.0	38,488	1,216	61.1	60.9	31.2	0.6	1.1	7.5	6.2	15.9	9.6	11.4	10.8	12.8
45,073	42,860	4	Oconee	626.3	77,270	718	123.4	85.8	8.4	0.7	1.2	5.5	5.1	15.0	7.1	11.4	10.5	12.6
45,075	36,700	4	Orangeburg	1,106.1	87,476	661	79.1	34.2	62.6	1.1	1.3	2.2	5.7	16.6	10.0	12.1	10.2	12.3
45,077	24,860	2	Pickens	496.3	123,479	511	248.8	87.2	7.7	0.7	2.4	3.7	5.1	14.0	17.6	11.9	10.6	12.1
45,079	17,900	2	Richland	757.1	411,592	171	543.6	44.2	48.3	0.8	3.8	5.2	5.9	15.6	15.8	14.9	12.2	11.8
45,081	17,900	2	Saluda	452.8	20,452	1,800	45.2	58.9	25.0	0.7	0.5	16.0	6.1	15.7	7.7	12.3	11.5	13.4
45,083	43,900	2	Spartanburg	808.0	306,854	227	379.8	69.8	21.6	0.7	2.8	6.8	6.0	17.1	9.1	13.4	12.0	13.6

1. CBSA = Core Based Statistical Area. See Appendix A for explanation. See Appendix B for list of metropolitan areas with component counties.
Service of USDA Rural-Urban Continuum Codes. See Appendix A for definition.   3. Dry land or land partially or temporarily covered by water.   2. County type code from the Economic Research
4. May be of any race.

Table B. States and Counties — **Population and Households**

STATE County	55 to 64 years	65 to 74 years	75 years and over	Percent female	Total persons 2000	2010	Percent change 2000-2010	2010-2017	Births	Deaths	Net Migration	Number	Persons per house-hold	Family house-holds	Female family house-holder[1]	One person
	16	17	18	19	20	21	22	23	24	25	26	27	28	29	30	31
PENNSYLVANIA— Cont'd																
Potter	15.9	13.2	10.3	50.0	18,080	17,458	-3.4	-3.8	1,349	1,484	-517	6,623	2.56	64.5	8.9	30.7
Schuylkill	14.9	11.2	8.9	48.8	150,336	148,289	-1.4	-3.9	9,823	13,865	-1,594	58,341	2.37	64.8	11.2	30.3
Snyder	13.5	10.0	8.2	50.5	37,546	39,709	5.8	2.8	3,252	2,536	409	14,528	2.62	72.4	9.6	23.3
Somerset	15.7	12.0	9.9	47.9	80,023	77,746	-2.8	-4.2	4,988	6,852	-1,327	29,630	2.40	68.9	8.4	27.6
Sullivan	20.0	15.5	11.6	47.4	6,556	6,428	-2.0	-5.3	332	793	124	2,647	2.21	61.4	6.0	33.9
Susquehanna	17.3	13.3	9.7	49.6	42,238	43,352	2.6	-5.5	2,683	3,272	-1,765	17,368	2.39	67.5	8.6	26.6
Tioga	15.3	12.0	9.4	50.3	41,373	41,896	1.3	-2.6	3,179	3,225	-1,056	16,340	2.51	67.3	8.4	26.7
Union	12.2	9.2	8.4	45.8	41,624	44,949	8.0	-0.8	2,930	2,738	-552	14,649	2.43	67.7	8.2	26.5
Venango	17.2	12.4	9.3	50.6	57,565	54,983	-4.5	-5.9	3,985	4,770	-2,425	21,962	2.38	67.9	11.2	27.8
Warren	16.7	12.5	9.8	49.9	43,863	41,815	-4.7	-5.2	2,849	3,647	-1,345	16,904	2.36	64.1	8.1	31.3
Washington	15.6	11.4	8.7	50.9	202,897	207,848	2.4	-0.3	14,357	18,188	3,478	83,745	2.42	66.2	9.8	28.5
Wayne	16.5	14.1	9.6	47.1	47,722	52,820	10.7	-3.1	2,931	4,292	-219	19,173	2.47	67.5	9.4	27.1
Westmoreland	16.4	12.4	9.8	51.1	369,993	365,164	-1.3	-3.4	22,895	32,103	-3,043	150,697	2.33	66.6	9.9	28.9
Wyoming	15.7	12.5	8.1	49.9	28,080	28,269	0.7	-3.3	2,008	2,178	-769	10,801	2.52	67.4	10.6	26.2
York	14.2	9.9	7.2	50.6	381,751	434,998	13.9	2.5	35,501	28,165	4,128	168,008	2.57	69.4	11.1	24.6
RHODE ISLAND	14.0	9.5	7.3	51.4	1,048,319	1,052,945	0.4	0.6	79,313	70,559	-1,819	410,240	2.47	62.5	13.9	30.4
Bristol	15.5	10.4	9.0	51.6	50,648	49,847	-1.6	-1.9	2,537	3,670	202	19,299	2.37	65.4	8.8	28.6
Kent	15.6	10.6	7.8	51.7	167,090	166,153	-0.6	-1.4	11,611	12,597	-1,307	68,661	2.38	62.9	10.4	30.4
Newport	15.1	12.1	9.1	50.4	85,433	83,141	-2.7	0.4	5,149	5,196	388	35,268	2.24	60.3	10.6	31.3
Providence	13.0	8.3	6.7	51.4	621,602	626,710	0.8	1.7	53,454	40,960	-1,813	237,459	2.55	61.8	16.6	31.4
Washington	16.0	11.9	8.0	51.6	123,546	127,094	2.9	-0.7	6,562	8,136	711	49,553	2.41	65.9	9.8	26.2
SOUTH CAROLINA	13.3	10.6	6.6	51.5	4,012,012	4,625,381	15.3	8.6	417,195	325,675	304,789	1,839,041	2.55	66.4	14.9	28.3
Abbeville	14.6	12.6	8.6	51.6	26,167	25,416	-2.9	-2.7	1,783	2,008	-460	9,499	2.53	65.9	14.9	31.0
Aiken	14.3	11.4	7.5	51.7	142,552	160,106	12.3	5.0	13,887	12,074	6,324	64,455	2.52	67.8	14.2	28.3
Allendale	13.6	12.6	6.9	47.1	11,211	10,419	-7.1	-13.6	675	801	-1,308	3,357	2.49	61.8	23.8	36.3
Anderson	13.4	10.6	7.3	51.9	165,740	187,123	12.9	6.2	16,359	14,746	10,105	74,814	2.54	69.2	13.8	26.7
Bamberg	14.5	12.3	9.0	52.2	16,658	15,987	-4.0	-10.0	1,060	1,287	-1,394	5,732	2.42	62.5	17.8	34.7
Barnwell	14.3	10.9	6.9	52.1	23,478	22,621	-3.7	-5.6	2,028	1,869	-1,444	8,206	2.63	69.1	22.1	28.1
Beaufort	13.5	16.1	10.3	50.7	120,937	162,231	34.1	15.2	14,809	10,499	20,057	67,345	2.52	68.0	10.5	26.6
Berkeley	12.3	8.9	4.8	50.4	142,651	177,867	24.7	22.5	19,209	9,457	29,980	70,482	2.78	70.3	14.7	24.3
Calhoun	16.1	13.7	8.5	52.0	15,185	15,176	-0.1	-3.1	1,030	1,240	-264	6,102	2.41	64.2	14.7	31.7
Charleston	13.1	9.9	5.9	51.5	309,969	350,199	13.0	14.6	35,270	22,258	37,453	150,921	2.44	58.7	13.1	32.3
Cherokee	12.9	9.9	6.4	51.3	52,537	55,467	5.6	3.0	4,922	4,385	1,142	20,353	2.72	64.2	14.6	32.7
Chester	14.4	11.0	7.4	51.6	34,068	33,140	-2.7	-2.5	2,825	2,812	-843	12,265	2.63	64.6	17.8	32.7
Chesterfield	14.1	11.0	6.6	51.3	42,768	46,734	9.3	-1.7	3,705	3,682	-796	18,172	2.49	69.6	16.5	27.1
Clarendon	14.8	13.7	9.0	50.9	32,502	34,966	7.6	-2.6	2,477	2,724	-653	13,282	2.44	67.1	19.0	29.5
Colleton	14.6	12.1	7.5	51.9	38,264	38,892	1.6	-3.3	3,311	3,665	-924	14,865	2.51	65.5	19.2	31.0
Darlington	14.3	11.3	7.3	52.8	67,394	68,692	1.9	-2.1	5,770	5,870	-1,288	26,407	2.51	65.2	19.1	29.9
Dillon	13.5	9.9	6.5	52.4	30,722	32,062	4.4	-4.4	3,063	2,671	-1,801	11,133	2.77	67.2	21.5	30.0
Dorchester	12.5	8.5	4.7	51.4	96,413	136,584	41.7	14.6	13,200	7,136	13,622	53,005	2.77	70.7	15.7	24.7
Edgefield	14.8	11.1	7.0	46.3	24,595	26,978	9.7	-1.1	1,439	1,572	-152	9,084	2.59	72.2	16.3	25.4
Fairfield	17.2	12.9	7.7	52.3	23,454	23,956	2.1	-5.6	1,590	2,102	-838	8,878	2.55	65.8	18.0	31.9
Florence	13.0	10.1	6.3	53.4	125,761	136,879	8.8	1.2	12,666	10,685	-169	51,749	2.62	68.4	18.7	28.1
Georgetown	16.0	16.9	10.0	52.6	55,797	60,158	7.8	2.4	4,187	5,279	2,565	24,379	2.47	70.0	14.6	26.5
Greenville	12.6	9.3	6.1	51.5	379,616	451,221	18.9	12.3	45,227	28,984	39,103	182,466	2.58	67.0	13.0	28.1
Greenwood	12.9	10.1	8.0	53.3	66,271	69,661	5.1	1.0	6,281	5,194	-357	26,806	2.52	65.0	17.7	30.1
Hampton	13.5	10.7	7.0	48.7	21,386	21,090	-1.4	-7.1	1,602	1,566	-1,538	7,290	2.59	62.6	17.4	35.5
Horry	15.4	15.2	7.8	51.7	196,629	269,291	37.0	23.8	22,507	22,095	62,575	122,125	2.43	64.4	11.9	28.6
Jasper	14.4	12.3	6.1	49.3	20,678	24,779	19.8	14.8	2,458	1,712	2,875	9,298	2.87	72.0	18.9	24.4
Kershaw	14.2	11.0	7.0	51.6	52,647	61,570	16.9	5.6	5,336	4,739	2,896	24,106	2.60	70.5	15.4	25.3
Lancaster	12.6	12.9	7.8	51.4	61,351	76,654	24.9	20.7	7,041	5,984	14,647	30,270	2.70	69.2	16.2	27.3
Laurens	14.2	10.6	7.4	51.5	69,567	66,539	-4.4	0.5	5,570	5,827	606	25,465	2.51	70.3	17.3	24.7
Lee	14.5	11.2	7.1	49.2	20,119	19,222	-4.5	-9.7	1,293	1,676	-1,509	6,400	2.58	65.8	22.0	31.8
Lexington	13.3	9.5	5.9	51.3	216,014	262,396	21.5	10.8	23,601	16,565	21,162	107,527	2.55	67.9	12.9	26.1
McCormick	16.8	20.8	12.4	46.0	9,958	10,233	2.8	-6.7	415	926	-172	3,980	2.14	69.0	15.7	26.5
Marion	14.4	12.1	7.2	54.1	35,466	33,062	-6.8	-5.4	2,858	3,108	-1,522	12,090	2.63	66.8	24.4	29.6
Marlboro	13.5	11.1	6.5	47.7	28,818	28,933	0.4	-7.3	2,212	2,385	-1,946	9,736	2.52	67.9	20.1	29.3
Newberry	14.2	11.5	7.7	51.2	36,108	37,508	3.9	2.6	3,251	3,109	863	14,504	2.52	68.1	16.8	28.1
Oconee	15.5	13.9	8.9	50.9	66,215	74,275	12.2	4.0	5,699	6,243	3,558	30,867	2.42	67.8	12.1	28.0
Orangeburg	14.0	11.4	7.7	53.2	91,582	92,495	1.0	-5.4	7,697	7,656	-5,087	33,361	2.61	62.2	18.7	35.2
Pickens	12.4	9.4	6.7	50.1	110,757	119,226	7.6	3.6	8,859	8,179	3,600	45,622	2.49	64.4	9.6	26.2
Richland	11.4	7.7	4.6	51.5	320,677	384,507	19.9	7.0	35,237	21,050	13,089	147,329	2.52	60.5	17.1	31.8
Saluda	14.2	10.9	8.3	49.4	19,181	19,871	3.6	2.9	1,791	1,473	273	7,106	2.78	73.1	13.3	23.3
Spartanburg	12.7	9.6	6.4	51.4	253,791	284,301	12.0	7.9	26,090	21,055	17,601	111,462	2.57	68.4	15.4	27.0

1. No spouse present.

Table B. States and Counties — Population, Vital Statistics, Health, and Crime

STATE County	Persons in group quarters, 2017	Daytime Population, 2012-2016		Births, 2017		Deaths, 2017		Persons under 65 with no health insurance, 2016		Medicare, 2017			Serious crimes known to police[2], 2016 Total	
		Number	Employment/ residence ratio	Total	Rate[1]	Number	Rate[1]	Number	Percent	Total beneficiaries	Enrolled in Original Medicare	Enrolled in Medicare Advantage	Number	Rate[3]
	32	33	34	35	36	37	38	39	40	41	42	43	44	45
PENNSYLVANIA— Cont'd														
Potter	217	17,034	0.97	180	10.7	209	12.4	1,072	8.3	4,435	3,080	1,354	203	1,236
Schuylkill	6,731	135,105	0.83	1,288	9.0	1,805	12.7	6,672	6.1	34,424	24,326	10,098	2,628	1,867
Snyder	2,603	39,018	0.94	445	10.9	353	8.7	2,800	9.0	8,094	4,646	3,448	586	1,509
Somerset	4,922	71,022	0.84	671	9.0	937	12.6	4,238	7.7	18,704	7,956	10,748	840	1,140
Sullivan	441	5,801	0.81	39	6.4	99	16.3	364	8.3	1,771	1,257	514	59	937
Susquehanna	282	36,022	0.68	357	8.7	430	10.5	2,422	7.6	9,397	7,180	2,217	500	1,286
Tioga	1,417	41,153	0.95	427	10.5	465	11.4	2,378	7.6	10,216	7,443	2,774	460	1,102
Union	8,415	47,627	1.14	397	8.9	410	9.2	2,261	7.7	8,334	5,319	3,015	360	803
Venango	1,300	51,613	0.92	510	9.9	672	13.0	2,950	7.2	13,572	8,115	5,457	672	1,277
Warren	760	39,649	0.94	377	9.5	516	13.0	2,007	6.5	9,693	7,193	2,500	656	1,727
Washington	5,536	202,466	0.94	1,944	9.4	2,500	12.1	8,473	5.2	50,180	19,311	30,869	3,528	1,727
Wayne	3,771	48,367	0.86	392	7.7	555	10.8	2,589	7.2	17,981	14,419	3,562	631	1,244
Westmoreland	7,011	335,159	0.86	3,092	8.8	4,460	12.6	13,023	4.7	88,677	31,658	57,019	5,065	1,442
Wyoming	592	27,797	0.99	248	9.1	315	11.5	1,309	6.1	6,957	4,869	2,088	368	1,349
York	8,743	405,150	0.83	4,891	11.0	3,988	8.9	23,244	6.4	88,279	56,652	31,627	8,051	1,817
RHODE ISLAND	41,924	1,032,521	0.96	10,915	10.3	9,760	9.2	43,275	5.1	212,105	120,387	91,718	22,582	2,138
Bristol	2,811	40,008	0.62	351	7.2	529	10.8	1,348	3.5	10,541	5,949	4,592	478	977
Kent	1,163	153,025	0.86	1,634	10.0	1,709	10.4	4,674	3.5	37,722	20,745	16,978	2,486	1,511
Newport	3,912	85,208	1.06	736	8.8	751	9.0	2,438	3.9	19,050	13,097	5,953	1,358	1,651
Providence	26,878	634,479	1.01	7,322	11.5	5,563	8.7	31,511	6.1	116,855	62,244	54,611	15,492	2,442
Washington	7,160	119,801	0.90	872	6.9	1,208	9.6	3,304	3.4	27,916	18,342	9,574	1,480	1,171
SOUTH CAROLINA	136,487	4,796,553	0.98	57,996	11.5	48,071	9.6	484,799	12.1	1,006,760	739,837	266,923	185,824	3,746
Abbeville	961	21,736	0.66	225	9.1	261	10.6	2,295	12.1	4,938	3,335	1,603	642	2,798
Aiken	2,329	160,569	0.93	1,980	11.8	1,777	10.6	15,802	11.8	36,686	27,871	8,815	6,984	4,176
Allendale	1,137	9,907	1.12	68	7.6	104	11.6	689	11.2	1,990	1,203	787	NA	NA
Anderson	2,784	180,144	0.85	2,303	11.6	2,118	10.7	18,515	11.6	40,799	26,605	14,194	10,564	5,374
Bamberg	954	14,381	0.88	118	8.2	179	12.4	1,335	12.4	3,120	2,052	1,069	505	3,491
Barnwell	285	20,718	0.85	247	11.6	274	12.8	1,904	10.9	4,674	3,264	1,410	863	3,996
Beaufort	5,693	178,137	1.04	1,998	10.7	1,600	8.6	18,431	14.1	48,372	39,186	9,186	4,363	2,378
Berkeley	3,601	168,142	0.66	2,834	13.0	1,496	6.9	20,180	11.2	25,831	19,510	6,321	5,927	2,852
Calhoun	158	11,841	0.51	138	9.4	186	12.6	1,433	12.5	2,455	1,732	723	337	2,285
Charleston	10,922	442,121	1.33	5,038	12.5	3,463	8.6	40,835	12.5	80,140	63,238	16,902	13,569	3,418
Cherokee	1,242	53,764	0.88	663	11.6	589	10.3	5,518	11.9	10,941	7,099	3,842	2,194	3,888
Chester	218	28,917	0.72	361	11.2	405	12.5	3,076	11.8	7,456	5,371	2,085	1,220	3,793
Chesterfield	874	45,007	0.94	497	10.8	551	12.0	5,224	13.9	8,827	6,897	1,931	1,692	3,679
Clarendon	1,604	30,852	0.71	317	9.3	372	10.9	3,477	14.0	7,994	5,753	2,241	1,161	3,454
Colleton	389	35,515	0.84	464	12.3	580	15.4	4,016	13.4	8,788	6,164	2,624	1,602	4,264
Darlington	1,395	64,449	0.87	795	11.8	816	12.1	6,656	12.4	13,971	11,183	2,788	3,622	5,368
Dillon	471	30,360	0.92	388	12.7	366	11.9	3,647	14.5	6,146	4,490	1,657	1,918	6,163
Dorchester	1,848	119,439	0.58	1,803	11.5	1,121	7.2	13,211	10.0	22,398	17,152	5,246	5,686	3,688
Edgefield	2,752	23,145	0.69	199	7.5	268	10.0	2,424	12.6	3,596	2,432	1,164	274	1,042
Fairfield	397	22,413	0.93	205	9.1	290	12.8	2,171	12.2	5,093	3,499	1,594	919	4,070
Florence	3,230	147,876	1.16	1,653	11.9	1,529	11.0	11,668	10.3	30,666	24,930	5,736	6,492	4,695
Georgetown	554	61,288	1.02	554	9.0	824	13.4	6,228	13.9	19,442	14,770	4,672	2,150	3,487
Greenville	10,958	515,923	1.15	6,428	12.7	4,268	8.4	51,503	12.4	91,579	60,304	31,275	16,942	3,381
Greenwood	2,525	71,040	1.04	806	11.5	780	11.1	7,474	13.5	16,535	12,138	4,397	3,136	4,480
Hampton	1,476	19,604	0.91	203	10.4	234	11.9	1,752	11.8	4,974	3,438	1,536	662	3,710
Horry	3,764	301,384	1.01	3,202	9.6	3,443	10.3	39,291	16.0	85,709	68,380	17,328	16,328	5,131
Jasper	1,489	23,784	0.72	351	12.3	272	9.6	3,895	18.1	4,099	2,785	1,314	958	3,361
Kershaw	402	56,369	0.74	773	11.9	747	11.5	6,276	11.9	14,505	11,275	3,230	1,662	2,592
Lancaster	1,930	74,742	0.73	1,086	11.7	915	9.9	7,205	10.3	13,287	10,572	2,715	1,966	2,493
Laurens	2,338	61,705	0.83	775	11.6	836	12.5	6,315	12.0	13,750	9,292	4,458	2,152	3,223
Lee	1,599	16,078	0.64	173	10.0	287	16.5	1,619	12.7	3,434	2,461	973	577	3,264
Lexington	2,263	261,253	0.88	3,244	11.2	2,411	8.3	26,350	10.9	50,745	39,535	11,210	8,346	2,916
McCormick	1,109	9,236	0.79	50	5.2	149	15.6	604	11.2	3,625	2,362	1,263	200	2,078
Marion	204	28,421	0.70	369	11.8	442	14.1	3,347	13.2	8,018	6,146	1,871	1,848	5,893
Marlboro	2,765	25,807	0.80	302	11.3	304	11.3	2,678	13.8	6,332	4,631	1,700	1,276	4,678
Newberry	1,194	36,572	0.93	455	11.8	439	11.4	4,003	13.5	9,047	6,556	2,491	908	2,379
Oconee	792	73,615	0.94	780	10.1	900	11.6	8,331	14.2	20,296	14,895	5,401	2,218	2,913
Orangeburg	2,979	89,514	0.99	955	10.9	1,104	12.6	8,866	13.0	20,487	13,469	7,018	3,223	3,683
Pickens	7,083	110,914	0.81	1,244	10.1	1,145	9.3	12,359	12.8	26,566	17,179	9,387	4,491	3,668
Richland	31,258	439,556	1.19	4,922	12.0	3,126	7.6	31,317	9.5	62,008	48,398	13,610	21,715	5,268
Saluda	273	17,850	0.73	241	11.8	199	9.7	2,805	17.4	3,078	2,132	946	334	1,660
Spartanburg	8,169	301,950	1.06	3,661	11.9	3,025	9.9	31,050	12.6	66,980	41,116	25,865	10,270	3,418

1. Per 1,000 estimated resident population. 2. Data for serious crimes have not been adjusted for underreporting; this may affect comparability between geographic areas and over time.
3. Per 100,000 population estimated by the FBI.

Table B. States and Counties — Crime, Education, Money Income, and Poverty

STATE County	Serious crimes known to police, 2016 (cont.)[1] Rate		Education School enrollment and attainment, 2012-2016				Local government expenditures,[5] 2013-2014		Money income, 2012-2016		Households Percent		Income and poverty, 2016		Percent below poverty level	
	Violent	Property	Enrollment[3] Total	Percent private	Attainment[4] (percent) High school graduate or less	Bachelor's degree or more	Total current spending (mil dol)	Current spending per student (dollars)	Per capita income[6]	Median income (dollars)	with income of less than $50,000	with income of $200,000 or more	Median household income (dollars)	All persons	Children under 18 years	Children 5 to 17 years in families
	46	47	48	49	50	51	52	53	54	55	56	57	58	59	60	61
PENNSYLVANIA— Cont'd																
Potter	262	974	3,447	11.3	60.4	15.0	32.8	13,456	22,929	40,921	58.1	1.3	44,267	14.0	24.1	22.1
Schuylkill	483	1,384	28,641	13.7	59.8	15.3	242.4	13,055	24,275	46,573	52.7	1.6	50,299	12.8	17.6	16.4
Snyder	209	1,300	9,513	34.1	62.6	16.7	54.9	11,224	24,708	51,110	48.9	3.4	52,487	12.7	19.8	17.5
Somerset	125	1,016	13,388	15.4	62.0	15.5	120.6	12,666	23,402	45,424	54.2	1.7	43,938	14.1	22.6	21.0
Sullivan	79	858	896	10.8	60.2	15.5	11.7	19,429	26,154	44,926	55.5	1.7	43,426	12.8	22.2	21.0
Susquehanna	157	1,129	7,885	16.7	57.7	16.7	96.2	15,019	26,551	50,160	49.8	2.4	47,518	12.7	19.8	17.7
Tioga	139	963	8,638	13.3	55.0	20.5	71.3	14,626	24,626	48,449	51.5	1.8	49,004	13.3	18.5	17.2
Union	60	743	11,500	50.2	55.8	22.1	51.4	12,932	23,316	51,349	48.4	3.9	57,013	11.8	13.5	11.8
Venango	144	1,133	10,471	13.5	60.4	16.5	81.0	13,127	24,257	43,885	56.0	1.5	41,395	14.6	21.7	19.0
Warren	221	1,506	7,825	13.6	55.4	18.4	61.0	12,525	25,414	44,977	55.7	1.4	43,896	15.3	26.1	25.1
Washington	184	1,543	45,925	17.9	47.1	28.1	378.2	13,538	31,561	57,534	43.5	4.9	58,068	9.7	11.5	10.6
Wayne	120	1,124	9,311	14.8	53.2	20.5	77.0	15,830	24,962	50,595	49.3	2.3	49,357	13.7	18.7	17.9
Westmoreland	172	1,270	74,458	18.6	45.5	26.9	589.2	12,210	30,153	54,142	45.7	3.6	56,544	9.8	14.1	13.0
Wyoming	194	1,155	5,782	21.4	56.2	18.6	54.6	14,902	26,823	53,397	46.9	2.7	55,836	11.3	17.1	15.6
York	234	1,583	102,379	19.8	52.1	23.1	818.4	12,189	28,975	59,853	41.3	3.3	62,305	9.8	13.6	12.3
RHODE ISLAND	239	1,899	266,870	26.5	40.7	32.5	2,138.1	15,071	31,904	58,387	43.9	5.5	60,046	13.3	18.7	17.0
Bristol	70	908	13,399	39.7	30.5	46.4	96.1	14,209	40,998	73,096	34.8	10.7	70,697	8.2	9.2	7.8
Kent	103	1,409	35,905	21.4	37.1	31.8	347.4	15,773	35,323	65,592	38.6	5.1	63,762	9.6	12.8	12.0
Newport	141	1,510	19,087	31.6	29.8	45.5	151.6	15,875	42,086	71,347	36.1	8.6	72,776	9.0	13.1	11.6
Providence	328	2,114	163,594	28.7	46.4	27.3	1,282.9	14,615	27,809	50,637	49.4	4.2	52,011	15.8	22.8	21.0
Washington	71	1,100	34,885	13.9	29.4	44.6	260.1	16,511	37,692	74,302	33.6	8.2	77,000	9.8	10.5	9.4
SOUTH CAROLINA	502	3,244	1,202,103	14.5	43.4	26.5	7,211.5	9,671	25,521	46,898	52.7	3.2	49,587	15.3	23.0	21.8
Abbeville	340	2,458	5,802	19.6	56.9	13.7	28.7	9,170	18,460	34,652	66.5	0.8	40,211	15.3	24.6	23.2
Aiken	536	3,641	38,237	13.7	45.5	25.3	203.3	8,226	25,602	46,454	53.2	2.5	47,394	17.0	26.1	25.1
Allendale	NA	NA	2,064	8.9	66.1	9.8	19.0	14,435	12,649	24,817	77.2	0.1	26,864	38.2	51.7	49.6
Anderson	653	4,721	46,070	14.6	48.0	20.0	286.3	9,092	23,341	43,518	56.3	2.1	45,821	15.4	22.1	20.7
Bamberg	422	3,070	4,230	12.6	51.0	19.1	26.0	12,022	18,260	32,321	69.2	0.9	32,245	28.4	42.7	39.5
Barnwell	722	3,274	5,633	9.8	55.8	13.2	42.2	10,093	19,652	34,787	62.5	0.9	41,803	22.6	35.9	34.7
Beaufort	312	2,066	35,643	17.6	30.3	39.6	223.7	10,792	33,877	59,227	42.0	6.2	65,354	10.3	19.2	18.6
Berkeley	367	2,485	49,846	15.7	42.3	23.0	275.5	8,672	25,992	54,484	45.1	3.1	58,690	12.3	18.4	16.0
Calhoun	258	2,028	3,134	21.9	54.7	17.0	18.8	10,668	22,964	42,779	59.4	2.0	41,786	16.2	26.3	24.5
Charleston	434	2,985	92,434	16.7	31.5	41.1	507.1	11,107	33,700	54,931	45.7	6.7	56,564	15.0	20.8	20.4
Cherokee	416	3,471	13,701	13.4	58.2	16.0	83.4	9,133	19,940	35,719	64.5	1.3	38,273	18.6	27.7	24.3
Chester	672	3,122	7,628	10.5	57.5	14.4	52.9	9,721	19,858	34,319	63.6	1.0	39,972	19.8	30.3	29.0
Chesterfield	478	3,201	10,432	8.1	64.5	11.5	69.2	9,332	19,088	35,733	63.7	0.9	39,869	20.5	31.1	29.1
Clarendon	396	3,059	7,344	12.7	57.0	15.0	48.1	9,580	18,765	34,106	65.7	1.3	34,541	24.9	39.4	38.8
Colleton	751	3,513	8,446	7.1	54.2	15.3	55.9	9,145	20,297	33,918	66.7	1.7	35,760	23.4	38.7	36.6
Darlington	676	4,692	16,699	15.1	55.0	17.1	97.8	9,437	20,144	34,773	64.2	1.4	37,711	21.1	32.3	31.1
Dillon	951	5,212	7,928	8.0	63.4	9.6	48.8	8,158	15,729	30,955	68.2	0.6	31,761	25.6	38.2	35.7
Dorchester	508	3,181	39,986	15.2	38.2	26.4	230.8	8,681	26,288	56,345	43.4	2.8	58,167	9.5	14.2	13.6
Edgefield	80	962	5,780	15.2	55.2	18.6	35.9	10,495	22,695	48,114	52.3	1.6	46,816	17.7	25.8	23.8
Fairfield	775	3,295	4,593	13.0	56.6	17.4	42.0	14,185	20,762	33,798	64.7	1.8	36,715	21.2	32.3	30.6
Florence	620	4,074	37,080	12.5	48.5	22.4	219.4	9,375	23,420	42,523	55.8	2.7	45,044	18.3	27.8	25.7
Georgetown	496	2,991	12,846	9.8	43.4	26.1	101.1	10,413	26,601	45,299	53.5	4.1	47,842	15.2	30.0	28.1
Greenville	483	2,898	119,832	23.1	38.4	32.9	622.9	8,363	28,065	51,595	48.2	4.3	55,452	10.9	15.3	13.8
Greenwood	649	3,832	18,173	11.0	46.9	23.5	103.1	8,741	21,887	37,631	61.7	2.6	40,599	21.7	35.1	33.6
Hampton	829	2,881	4,154	7.6	62.3	11.1	37.0	11,047	20,291	31,734	66.7	1.4	35,667	22.3	32.1	30.1
Horry	600	4,531	62,876	9.6	43.3	22.6	418.1	10,213	24,986	44,746	55.4	2.2	45,608	15.0	27.6	26.8
Jasper	358	3,004	5,988	22.5	57.6	14.5	35.8	12,569	18,921	38,991	65.2	0.7	41,902	20.7	34.9	33.8
Kershaw	379	2,213	14,462	10.6	50.0	20.6	93.4	8,901	23,149	46,328	53.3	2.1	48,824	15.6	21.5	20.4
Lancaster	320	2,173	18,436	10.3	49.1	23.3	104.5	8,736	24,528	46,852	53.0	2.8	53,421	13.0	20.5	20.4
Laurens	518	2,705	15,518	14.6	55.3	14.2	85.0	9,294	20,417	39,848	61.5	1.2	43,191	18.2	27.8	26.9
Lee	566	2,698	4,053	11.3	64.8	10.5	22.3	9,956	15,545	31,169	71.1	1.2	32,015	27.7	40.6	38.5
Lexington	351	2,564	68,550	12.1	39.5	29.9	390.3	10,097	28,141	55,412	44.8	3.5	57,623	11.7	16.7	15.4
McCormick	364	1,714	1,478	14.6	49.7	18.6	10.6	12,419	22,454	41,029	58.3	2.1	43,262	18.1	33.6	32.4
Marion	784	5,108	8,174	15.3	56.8	16.3	49.1	9,496	18,373	30,562	70.2	0.8	31,556	25.2	41.3	40.1
Marlboro	876	3,802	5,925	6.0	66.2	8.4	40.2	9,441	15,849	32,601	69.9	1.0	32,991	28.1	40.8	37.4
Newberry	291	2,088	8,793	16.7	57.5	16.3	61.6	10,140	21,883	39,841	58.4	1.5	42,128	18.9	28.4	26.5
Oconee	293	2,620	16,534	9.7	47.7	23.5	111.4	10,559	25,944	41,818	57.0	3.4	46,996	14.6	24.3	22.6
Orangeburg	468	3,214	24,156	14.1	49.7	20.0	158.3	11,414	18,490	34,763	66.2	1.1	34,557	22.7	36.0	33.3
Pickens	368	3,301	38,399	9.5	47.2	23.6	131.4	7,858	22,258	43,531	56.8	1.7	46,154	14.9	17.9	17.7
Richland	788	4,480	123,332	15.5	31.8	37.5	913.0	10,945	26,852	50,899	49.1	3.6	51,973	16.4	22.0	21.2
Saluda	383	1,277	4,148	7.8	58.7	16.6	20.9	9,583	21,468	41,458	57.9	1.8	43,685	16.7	27.5	25.0
Spartanburg	458	2,961	75,258	15.3	46.2	22.8	463.9	9,782	23,277	45,219	54.4	2.2	47,706	15.6	24.3	22.3

1. Data for serious crimes have not been adjusted for underreporting; this may affect comparability between geographic areas and over time.   2. Per 100,000 population estimated by the FBI.
3. All persons 3 years old and over enrolled in nursery school through college.   4. Persons 25 years old and over.   5. Elementary and secondary education expenditures.
6. Based on population estimated by the American Community Survey, 2011–2015.

Table B. States and Counties — **Personal Income and Earnings**

STATE County	Personal income, 2016										Earnings, 2016		
			Per capita[1]			Supplements to wages and salaries, employer contributions (mil dol)						Contributions for government social insurance (mil dol)	
	Total (mil dol)	Percent change 2015-2016	Dollars	Rank	Wages and salaries (mil dol)	Pension and insurance	Government social insurance	Proprietors' income (mil dol)	Dividends, interest, and rent (mil dol)	Personal transfer receipts (mil dol)	Total (mil dol)	From employee and self-employed	From employer
	62	63	64	65	66	67	68	69	70	71	72	73	74
PENNSYLVANIA— Cont'd													
Potter	614	2.4	36,338	1,944	221	54	18	70	97	191	363	42	18
Schuylkill	5,790	0.9	40,325	1,324	2,056	448	177	335	892	1,554	3,017	377	177
Snyder	1,548	-0.2	38,247	1,610	601	127	52	131	232	423	911	110	52
Somerset	2,796	1.1	37,250	1,780	936	224	79	227	470	795	1,465	178	79
Sullivan	247	-1.6	40,211	1,337	59	16	5	17	64	76	98	12	5
Susquehanna	1,665	0.4	40,747	1,268	358	89	29	163	341	397	640	74	29
Tioga	1,514	-0.1	36,499	1,916	525	131	44	115	274	423	816	97	44
Union	1,652	1.5	36,251	1,965	798	171	67	167	270	324	1,203	138	67
Venango	2,007	-0.2	38,174	1,623	718	179	60	104	303	684	1,061	132	60
Warren	1,587	-1.0	39,645	1,405	604	140	50	136	264	436	929	110	50
Washington	10,988	1.3	52,834	312	4,912	812	375	1,135	1,704	2,197	7,233	814	375
Wayne	1,976	3.0	38,965	1,500	607	142	50	179	382	547	979	116	50
Westmoreland	16,741	0.9	47,096	599	6,011	1,126	501	1,009	2,633	3,883	8,647	1,068	501
Wyoming	1,146	0.8	41,633	1,148	465	87	39	102	190	264	692	82	39
York	20,376	2.5	45,918	700	8,618	1,596	711	1,063	3,091	3,933	11,988	1,441	711
RHODE ISLAND	53,272	1.4	50,373	X	26,197	4,210	2,156	3,566	9,631	10,649	36,130	2,436	2,156
Bristol	3,459	1.3	70,504	66	653	118	55	202	945	427	1,029	134	55
Kent	9,026	2.1	54,832	244	3,807	583	324	534	1,398	1,660	5,248	691	324
Newport	5,080	0.9	61,367	131	2,337	445	204	374	1,350	801	3,359	419	204
Providence	28,281	1.2	44,630	816	16,757	2,535	1,352	1,744	4,372	6,593	22,389	2,856	1,352
Washington	7,426	2.1	58,801	169	2,643	530	220	712	1,566	1,168	4,105	493	220
SOUTH CAROLINA	196,049	3.3	39,527	X	94,249	15,672	7,200	12,597	33,795	44,246	129,718	8,416	7,200
Abbeville	780	2.5	31,374	2,694	234	49	20	50	101	258	352	48	20
Aiken	6,536	2.8	39,030	1,492	3,127	423	231	264	1,074	1,557	4,045	508	231
Allendale	276	4.0	30,507	2,789	118	27	9	14	40	100	169	20	9
Anderson	7,105	2.7	36,147	1,984	2,717	480	209	315	994	1,846	3,720	473	209
Bamberg	454	3.0	31,457	2,682	148	33	11	17	60	171	210	27	11
Barnwell	611	1.1	28,457	2,952	191	40	15	20	98	221	265	36	15
Beaufort	9,172	2.2	50,078	411	3,279	582	266	576	3,187	1,768	4,704	572	266
Berkeley	7,522	6.2	35,667	2,050	2,692	406	197	366	1,042	1,496	3,661	439	197
Calhoun	524	3.5	35,435	2,094	215	41	17	20	84	150	292	37	17
Charleston	21,122	4.0	53,272	296	13,334	2,213	1,021	2,527	4,928	3,082	19,096	2,141	1,021
Cherokee	1,701	2.2	30,026	2,842	756	127	60	63	214	533	1,005	133	60
Chester	1,001	1.9	31,096	2,730	377	68	29	37	127	337	511	67	29
Chesterfield	1,416	2.7	30,783	2,760	598	105	46	57	160	434	807	104	46
Clarendon	953	1.3	28,063	2,975	239	53	18	46	145	381	356	49	18
Colleton	1,303	3.8	34,362	2,272	396	73	30	63	190	430	563	74	30
Darlington	2,346	1.9	34,890	2,183	992	173	75	58	326	713	1,299	168	75
Dillon	825	4.0	26,747	3,035	319	57	26	7	94	319	409	59	26
Dorchester	5,607	3.7	36,460	1,922	1,360	239	103	224	785	1,203	1,926	239	103
Edgefield	868	3.0	32,921	2,492	226	48	17	52	118	227	344	42	17
Fairfield	788	1.7	34,801	2,193	744	118	55	25	108	246	941	114	55
Florence	5,308	1.6	38,258	1,608	2,916	496	219	255	769	1,402	3,886	472	219
Georgetown	2,591	2.2	42,195	1,077	974	162	74	152	670	744	1,362	174	74
Greenville	22,094	3.1	44,298	848	13,649	1,916	1,032	1,629	3,411	3,916	18,226	2,175	1,032
Greenwood	2,418	2.5	34,478	2,245	1,232	243	94	99	401	711	1,667	205	94
Hampton	572	3.9	28,723	2,938	206	42	15	14	85	201	277	37	15
Horry	10,902	4.9	33,820	2,346	4,613	710	364	794	2,131	3,254	6,481	828	364
Jasper	748	4.3	26,274	3,050	361	58	27	55	100	243	501	62	27
Kershaw	2,462	2.5	38,417	1,583	802	140	62	133	335	626	1,136	141	62
Lancaster	3,668	6.4	40,941	1,243	1,203	188	88	497	478	847	1,976	224	88
Laurens	2,137	2.3	32,000	2,616	943	166	73	68	272	735	1,250	164	73
Lee	497	5.5	28,172	2,968	139	28	10	20	62	198	198	26	10
Lexington	12,262	3.3	42,843	1,008	5,325	886	401	824	1,744	2,240	7,435	876	401
McCormick	337	2.6	34,967	2,168	65	17	5	13	73	131	100	15	5
Marion	930	2.5	29,319	2,907	235	47	18	25	113	358	325	47	18
Marlboro	705	2.9	26,175	3,051	315	59	24	9	90	280	407	56	24
Newberry	1,360	1.8	35,718	2,040	530	100	42	34	199	379	705	92	42
Oconee	2,967	2.7	38,863	1,523	1,201	231	90	139	568	796	1,661	209	90
Orangeburg	2,776	2.1	31,575	2,666	1,174	222	92	80	374	954	1,568	205	92
Pickens	4,280	3.1	34,835	2,189	1,520	299	113	208	692	1,051	2,141	264	113
Richland	17,301	2.7	42,245	1,069	11,235	2,059	857	1,237	2,894	3,246	15,389	1,759	857
Saluda	662	1.5	32,793	2,520	156	33	13	32	85	186	234	30	13
Spartanburg	11,874	3.0	39,386	1,438	6,593	1,021	498	777	2,201	2,655	8,888	1,077	498

1. Based on the resident population estimated as of July 1 of the year shown.

Table B. States and Counties — Earnings, Social Security, and Housing

	Earnings, 2016 (cont.) — Percent by selected industries									Social Security beneficiaries, December 2016		Supplemental Security Income recipients, 2016	Housing units, 2017	
STATE County	Farm	Mining, quarrying, and extracting	Construction	Manu-facturing	Information; professional, scientific, technical services	Retail trade	Finance, insurance, real estate, and leasing	Health care and social assistance	Govern-ment	Number	Rate[1]		Total	Percent change, 2010-2017
	75	76	77	78	79	80	81	82	83	84	85	86	87	88
PENNSYLVANIA— Cont'd														
Potter	0.7	0.5	7.0	10.4	13.6	4.7	2.6	14.6	18.0	4,940	292	483	12,980	0.4
Schuylkill	0.3	1.2	4.7	23.0	4.0	6.1	3.3	D	13.1	38,225	267	3,823	69,874	0.8
Snyder	0.0	D	10.5	24.2	3.6	10.9	3.0	D	17.0	8,910	219	621	16,432	2.5
Somerset	0.3	2.9	6.9	10.8	4.0	7.1	4.3	13.4	21.7	20,450	272	2,189	38,458	0.9
Sullivan	0.2	D	10.9	D	D	6.1	D	D	26.5	1,945	319	133	6,375	1.1
Susquehanna	-0.4	12.3	13.0	4.5	4.7	7.5	3.5	D	20.1	10,945	265	840	23,371	1.8
Tioga	0.1	3.7	6.5	14.9	5.8	7.6	4.3	D	21.7	11,145	270	1,087	21,804	2.1
Union	1.1	D	5.8	7.5	2.6	6.2	3.3	D	22.5	8,640	190	545	17,376	2.2
Venango	-0.4	0.9	4.8	22.4	2.7	7.4	3.6	15.5	21.8	15,525	296	2,048	27,591	0.5
Warren	-0.2	3.1	4.2	18.7	3.6	7.5	6.7	13.5	15.8	11,305	283	947	23,615	0.2
Washington	-0.1	6.9	10.3	10.3	8.9	5.2	7.3	11.0	10.0	53,280	257	4,920	95,896	3.1
Wayne	0.1	0.2	12.4	3.1	4.6	9.6	5.1	14.7	25.7	14,600	285	1,130	32,300	2.1
Westmoreland	0.0	0.9	8.4	14.5	7.2	8.6	4.6	13.1	13.4	95,600	269	8,252	170,475	1.4
Wyoming	0.9	7.0	7.1	27.6	D	6.4	2.4	6.5	11.3	7,105	258	600	13,507	1.9
York	-0.1	0.2	9.5	18.8	5.7	6.1	4.0	13.7	13.9	94,185	212	8,315	184,128	3.1
RHODE ISLAND	0.0	D	5.6	8.5	9.6	6.3	9.9	14.1	17.0	220,420	208	33,215	468,251	1.0
Bristol	0.0	0.0	D	D	8.8	4.9	5.9	11.5	17.9	11,070	226	696	21,025	0.9
Kent	0.0	D	6.0	10.4	10.4	8.9	8.6	13.9	13.1	39,185	239	3,605	74,389	0.9
Newport	0.1	D	D	D	12.0	6.1	5.9	6.8	34.9	18,855	226	1,379	42,535	1.8
Providence	0.0	0.0	5.2	6.8	9.6	5.0	11.9	15.9	14.3	122,320	192	25,915	266,296	0.5
Washington	0.2	0.1	6.6	16.2	6.9	10.3	4.4	11.0	21.4	28,990	230	1,620	64,006	2.9
SOUTH CAROLINA	0.1	0.1	6.2	14.0	9.1	7.0	7.4	9.4	20.7	1,089,728	220	117,325	2,284,722	6.9
Abbeville	0.7	0.0	10.0	31.6	3.4	3.6	D	3.0	24.0	6,590	267	601	12,156	0.6
Aiken	-0.3	0.2	9.1	14.7	11.2	6.1	5.0	7.5	12.4	39,370	236	3,973	76,597	6.0
Allendale	4.2	0.0	1.0	34.5	D	2.6	1.2	5.1	32.7	2,330	257	602	4,484	0.0
Anderson	0.1	0.2	5.1	25.8	4.0	8.4	3.4	8.1	21.4	47,490	242	4,279	88,212	4.1
Bamberg	2.2	0.0	2.0	22.5	D	6.8	D	8.6	23.8	3,745	258	715	7,704	-0.2
Barnwell	-0.9	D	4.6	29.2	D	8.8	2.3	D	28.5	5,030	233	1,099	10,569	0.8
Beaufort	0.1	0.0	6.9	0.9	9.3	7.6	7.7	9.3	32.6	47,335	258	2,025	99,275	6.7
Berkeley	0.0	D	8.6	13.8	22.0	6.7	4.9	3.4	18.1	36,050	170	3,151	83,911	14.4
Calhoun	0.5	0.1	10.2	38.6	D	2.5	D	D	13.8	3,935	267	413	7,470	1.8
Charleston	0.0	0.0	6.5	8.0	11.0	6.4	9.9	10.7	24.1	71,430	180	7,216	187,833	10.5
Cherokee	0.4	D	D	36.3	1.9	6.9	3.3	D	13.8	13,930	246	1,646	24,446	1.9
Chester	1.0	0.0	7.7	33.3	D	4.7	D	7.8	18.4	8,440	261	1,147	14,769	0.5
Chesterfield	0.5	D	5.2	38.5	D	4.8	1.8	7.9	13.8	10,905	236	1,534	21,623	0.7
Clarendon	0.7	0.0	4.5	5.3	D	12.8	D	15.0	36.4	9,430	275	1,578	17,793	1.9
Colleton	-0.3	D	7.0	8.5	D	8.2	4.2	13.5	20.3	10,575	281	1,676	20,044	0.7
Darlington	-0.5	0.0	6.6	26.7	2.1	5.6	2.5	10.4	19.6	16,925	251	2,832	30,810	1.7
Dillon	-5.5	0.0	1.1	22.8	D	10.5	3.6	D	19.6	7,225	234	1,562	13,754	0.1
Dorchester	-0.1	D	9.8	18.4	5.9	8.1	4.2	7.5	19.6	27,685	180	2,889	60,915	10.4
Edgefield	2.5	D	8.8	18.2	D	5.0	2.2	D	32.0	5,795	218	832	10,942	3.7
Fairfield	0.7	D	1.4	44.5	D	3.2	0.5	D	8.6	5,820	257	850	11,889	1.8
Florence	0.0	D	3.5	11.2	7.5	7.9	12.8	13.9	21.4	31,405	227	5,861	60,213	2.6
Georgetown	0.2	D	6.1	13.5	6.1	7.5	8.0	11.5	23.2	20,320	331	1,836	35,238	4.7
Greenville	0.0	0.0	7.1	13.4	12.0	6.2	8.7	10.0	11.8	97,675	196	9,633	211,181	8.0
Greenwood	-0.1	D	4.6	25.2	2.9	7.0	3.3	12.3	25.6	16,950	242	1,779	31,439	1.2
Hampton	-2.5	0.0	4.5	8.1	D	8.6	D	D	33.8	4,880	246	991	9,159	0.2
Horry	0.1	0.1	7.6	2.9	6.9	12.3	10.3	11.5	16.3	91,840	286	5,748	205,625	10.6
Jasper	0.4	0.0	15.0	3.6	D	17.8	1.5	13.9	15.6	6,050	216	682	11,816	14.7
Kershaw	2.4	2.3	6.8	20.7	5.3	8.8	5.9	7.2	16.7	15,220	237	1,530	29,118	6.0
Lancaster	0.7	D	3.0	11.5	34.0	5.4	6.2	9.6	10.9	22,280	248	1,705	37,607	15.0
Laurens	0.0	D	4.1	40.3	3.3	4.3	1.9	D	17.2	17,640	265	2,141	31,248	1.8
Lee	5.4	0.0	3.3	15.0	D	7.1	D	14.7	28.9	4,600	261	887	7,769	-0.1
Lexington	-0.1	0.1	7.3	12.7	6.4	8.2	5.1	6.7	19.8	54,445	190	4,528	124,374	9.1
McCormick	0.5	0.0	D	12.3	D	3.7	D	D	47.4	3,700	387	305	5,622	3.1
Marion	0.0	D	3.5	12.2	D	12.4	6.3	D	23.7	8,600	271	1,660	14,917	-0.2
Marlboro	-1.9	D	1.0	38.4	D	7.4	2.5	D	27.6	7,040	260	1,460	12,004	-0.6
Newberry	0.0	D	6.9	39.0	D	6.0	1.6	D	19.7	9,670	254	1,001	18,234	1.7
Oconee	0.0	D	6.1	26.9	D	6.7	3.2	7.2	15.4	22,245	291	1,513	40,316	4.0
Orangeburg	-0.4	0.0	4.0	21.9	2.9	8.9	3.3	7.9	28.2	22,205	251	4,019	42,722	0.5
Pickens	-0.1	D	5.5	17.3	4.0	8.3	3.7	8.0	34.7	27,300	222	2,287	54,368	6.1
Richland	0.0	D	4.0	5.2	10.9	5.3	11.7	11.6	30.4	66,620	163	8,534	173,041	7.0
Saluda	7.4	D	4.4	35.0	D	4.0	0.7	D	23.4	4,745	234	454	9,402	1.2
Spartanburg	0.0	0.1	6.5	24.9	5.3	6.4	5.0	6.7	16.8	67,275	223	7,320	129,209	5.4

1. Per 1,000 resident population estimated as of July 1 of the year shown.

Table B. States and Counties — Housing, Labor Force, and Employment

STATE County	Total	Percent	Median value[1]	With a mortgage	Without a mortgage[2]	Median rent[3]	Median rent as a percent of income[2]	Sub-standard units[4] (percent)	Total	Percent change, 2016-2017	Total	Rate[5]	Total	Management, business, science, and arts	Construction, production, and maintenance occupations
	89	90	91	92	93	94	95	96	97	98	99	100	101	102	103
PENNSYLVANIA— Cont'd															
Potter	6,623	76.8	101,300	21.5	13.7	635	28.8	1.3	7,228	-2.1	474	6.6	7,013	28.9	35.9
Schuylkill	58,341	74.5	95,200	20.5	14.1	650	26.9	1.3	66,298	-1.9	3,886	5.9	63,039	28.1	33.3
Snyder	14,528	73.0	152,500	20.6	11.5	677	26.0	2.8	20,541	0.2	911	4.4	19,637	26.0	32.4
Somerset	29,630	78.3	100,000	20.0	13.3	585	26.7	1.3	33,582	-1.8	2,046	6.1	32,847	28.4	31.0
Sullivan	2,647	82.6	145,800	22.1	13.9	569	23.5	1.4	2,783	-2.8	161	5.8	2,653	24.2	40.6
Susquehanna	17,368	76.8	154,100	22.0	13.2	718	29.4	1.8	20,651	-1.0	977	4.7	18,686	26.5	34.9
Tioga	16,340	74.4	129,900	21.2	13.2	685	27.6	1.5	19,220	-3.2	1,151	6.0	18,326	29.3	32.2
Union	14,649	71.0	164,900	20.1	12.3	695	27.6	1.7	19,834	0.2	868	4.4	18,488	32.9	25.9
Venango	21,962	75.6	82,700	19.1	11.0	585	28.1	1.4	23,056	-2.8	1,411	6.1	23,022	28.7	29.4
Warren	16,904	76.6	90,900	18.7	11.6	571	26.4	1.9	19,337	-2.2	1,022	5.3	18,282	30.1	32.9
Washington	83,745	75.5	156,000	18.9	10.7	687	25.9	1.2	106,484	-0.8	5,588	5.2	99,326	35.3	23.5
Wayne	19,173	79.1	174,500	25.2	12.7	812	33.2	1.0	22,528	0.0	1,144	5.1	20,940	28.3	28.4
Westmoreland	150,697	77.4	140,600	19.4	11.8	664	27.0	0.9	181,839	-0.6	9,422	5.2	173,090	35.0	23.8
Wyoming	10,801	78.8	162,400	21.4	13.1	726	28.7	1.7	13,958	-0.9	734	5.3	13,035	25.2	33.5
York	168,008	74.5	168,300	22.6	13.8	871	30.3	1.4	234,356	-0.3	10,248	4.4	218,951	32.8	27.2
RHODE ISLAND	410,240	59.7	238,200	24.2	14.8	938	30.4	2.0	554,658	0.2	24,791	4.5	520,482	37.5	18.8
Bristol	19,299	70.3	330,000	23.4	15.4	1,017	32.2	0.9	26,179	0.1	1,003	3.8	25,028	48.0	13.3
Kent	68,661	70.1	208,400	24.0	15.1	988	29.8	1.3	91,029	0.3	3,723	4.1	86,828	37.6	18.4
Newport	35,268	60.9	352,900	24.3	14.4	1,133	29.0	1.2	44,318	0.1	1,738	3.9	41,194	42.8	14.9
Providence	237,459	52.9	209,800	24.5	15.0	900	30.6	2.6	323,988	0.2	15,552	4.8	303,186	34.5	20.6
Washington	49,553	72.4	315,100	23.6	14.0	1,062	30.1	1.1	69,144	0.2	2,775	4.0	64,246	44.4	15.3
SOUTH CAROLINA	1,839,041	68.4	143,600	21.3	10.7	811	30.5	2.1	2,312,655	0.8	98,757	4.3	2,129,323	33.5	23.8
Abbeville	9,499	77.6	88,100	23.2	12.8	611	36.3	0.8	10,103	-1.8	463	4.6	9,624	26.6	34.3
Aiken	64,455	73.1	134,000	20.0	10.8	733	30.6	2.0	74,442	0.4	3,056	4.1	69,706	33.6	26.5
Allendale	3,357	64.7	53,700	27.1	15.4	581	33.7	2.9	2,741	3.0	188	6.9	2,776	16.6	34.0
Anderson	74,814	70.8	130,300	20.5	10.0	688	30.1	2.0	89,559	0.7	3,514	3.9	83,276	31.5	27.5
Bamberg	5,732	74.4	65,200	20.0	12.9	655	40.9	4.2	5,230	-1.6	388	7.4	5,697	30.6	30.8
Barnwell	8,206	71.4	76,600	20.0	12.5	591	33.1	3.1	8,082	0.1	488	6.0	8,213	24.9	31.0
Beaufort	67,345	70.5	273,000	26.7	11.4	1,060	30.0	2.4	74,104	2.2	2,991	4.0	72,457	35.0	17.4
Berkeley	70,482	69.8	160,900	22.0	10.6	996	29.9	2.0	98,452	1.5	3,761	3.8	89,136	33.2	25.4
Calhoun	6,102	76.1	98,500	22.8	11.4	711	32.6	2.0	6,848	-0.8	355	5.2	6,343	26.2	36.2
Charleston	150,921	60.5	252,700	23.4	12.5	1,030	32.1	1.9	204,937	1.5	7,135	3.5	189,477	40.7	16.4
Cherokee	20,353	69.6	90,400	19.5	10.7	646	29.9	2.0	24,094	2.4	1,185	4.9	21,473	26.7	32.7
Chester	12,265	73.3	89,300	19.7	10.0	595	33.3	1.8	13,592	1.5	816	6.0	12,547	22.7	35.5
Chesterfield	18,172	71.2	79,100	20.2	10.9	564	30.4	4.0	21,621	-0.1	941	4.4	18,646	23.5	38.1
Clarendon	13,282	74.3	87,200	24.0	12.1	584	29.5	3.4	12,425	-2.3	742	6.0	11,327	29.0	31.1
Colleton	14,865	72.3	85,800	24.1	12.4	710	31.9	2.2	16,844	0.5	808	4.8	15,182	25.8	30.3
Darlington	26,407	68.3	84,700	19.8	10.8	615	31.4	2.3	29,830	-0.3	1,583	5.3	26,096	29.4	27.9
Dillon	11,133	64.9	65,800	19.7	12.9	524	30.8	3.9	12,574	-0.9	717	5.7	11,507	20.3	35.3
Dorchester	53,005	69.7	169,700	22.9	11.2	967	30.5	1.6	74,263	1.5	2,850	3.8	68,884	35.7	21.6
Edgefield	9,084	75.9	119,300	20.3	10.7	601	29.3	2.9	10,557	0.1	482	4.6	10,671	28.1	36.6
Fairfield	8,878	73.9	96,300	19.8	13.5	698	46.5	1.2	10,045	0.5	740	7.4	8,806	23.8	31.7
Florence	51,749	66.4	126,100	20.0	10.4	701	28.9	2.6	65,368	0.0	2,989	4.6	58,873	35.0	21.9
Georgetown	24,379	76.3	165,400	26.6	11.9	830	30.2	1.8	25,289	1.3	1,396	5.5	23,717	31.8	21.7
Greenville	182,466	65.7	160,900	19.5	10.0	798	28.5	2.0	247,585	0.8	9,061	3.7	226,228	37.7	21.6
Greenwood	26,806	63.0	109,700	20.3	10.0	659	31.7	2.5	30,880	-1.5	1,398	4.5	29,014	29.6	28.3
Hampton	7,290	74.5	75,500	23.5	13.1	611	25.3	1.9	8,210	-0.3	367	4.5	7,740	24.3	29.2
Horry	122,125	69.1	162,100	24.3	11.2	859	32.3	2.0	143,389	2.3	7,106	5.0	133,862	28.0	17.9
Jasper	9,298	69.0	112,100	27.2	11.9	816	30.7	3.4	12,228	1.9	445	3.6	12,125	18.4	33.1
Kershaw	24,106	80.7	120,600	22.1	10.5	727	24.6	1.1	29,130	-0.4	1,320	4.5	26,549	32.0	28.8
Lancaster	30,270	78.7	157,700	21.2	10.9	692	32.1	1.6	39,127	2.0	1,819	4.6	33,819	31.2	25.8
Laurens	25,465	70.1	86,500	19.7	10.0	688	29.5	2.2	30,194	0.5	1,325	4.4	28,136	25.2	34.3
Lee	6,400	76.3	68,100	21.7	12.3	659	41.1	2.8	6,414	-0.4	387	6.0	5,930	22.3	34.2
Lexington	107,527	73.6	143,900	19.5	10.0	855	29.1	2.2	147,870	-0.2	5,354	3.6	134,494	36.9	22.1
McCormick	3,980	76.9	120,800	25.4	11.6	491	27.8	0.6	3,385	-0.2	155	4.6	2,833	28.0	30.1
Marion	12,090	70.0	73,400	23.3	12.7	509	35.1	1.5	12,541	-1.1	930	7.4	12,207	27.1	33.0
Marlboro	9,736	67.4	63,300	20.4	11.9	559	28.4	3.3	9,257	-0.6	607	6.6	9,756	24.5	36.4
Newberry	14,504	72.8	100,600	20.6	10.9	691	28.7	3.0	18,491	-3.7	771	4.2	16,246	25.9	34.9
Oconee	30,867	72.9	151,100	21.1	10.1	698	31.5	2.4	34,315	0.2	1,498	4.4	29,823	30.8	29.4
Orangeburg	33,361	68.6	91,200	22.9	13.0	650	32.8	2.3	35,174	-1.3	2,505	7.1	34,563	27.8	30.4
Pickens	45,622	68.3	124,900	20.1	10.3	722	32.2	2.3	56,658	0.5	2,338	4.1	52,111	34.1	25.7
Richland	147,329	59.0	151,500	21.3	10.0	892	31.4	2.1	199,987	-0.3	8,525	4.3	187,553	39.2	15.5
Saluda	7,106	72.8	93,300	22.5	10.0	653	26.2	1.5	8,854	-0.5	347	3.9	8,394	24.1	37.8
Spartanburg	111,462	68.6	124,900	19.7	10.0	721	29.5	2.5	146,296	2.7	5,876	4.0	131,171	30.8	29.9

1. Specified owner-occupied units.   2. A value of 10.0 represents 10 percent or less; a value of 50.0 represents 50 percent or more.   3. Specified renter-occupied units.
4. Overcrowded or lacking complete plumbing facilities.   5. Percent of civilian labor force.   6. Civilian employed persons 16 years old and over.

Table B. States and Counties — Nonfarm Employment and Agriculture

	Private nonfarm establishments, employment and payroll, 2016									Agriculture, 2012			
	Employment						Annual payroll		Farms			
											Percent with:		
STATE County	Number of establish-ments	Total	Health care and social assistance	Manufac-turing	Retail trade	Finance and insurance	Professional, scientific, and technical services	Total (mil dol)	Average per employee (dollars)	Number	Fewer than 50 acres	500 acres or more	Farm operators whose principal occupation is farming (percent)
	104	105	106	107	108	109	110	111	112	113	114	115	116
PENNSYLVANIA— Cont'd													
Potter	365	4,308	932	590	554	69	129	158	36,712	442	23.8	9.3	55.9
Schuylkill	2,738	41,126	7,501	10,019	5,741	885	990	1,524	37,065	791	41.5	5.4	49.7
Snyder	870	15,282	1,704	4,150	2,941	286	179	438	28,655	933	46.7	2.9	47.9
Somerset	1,686	18,295	3,597	2,745	2,728	744	609	623	34,053	1,140	22.5	7.2	48.3
Sullivan	155	1,204	438	72	220	28	21	31	25,974	179	24.6	8.9	50.3
Susquehanna	876	6,997	1,203	573	1,206	176	302	218	31,167	1,005	29.7	5.5	51.0
Tioga	875	10,619	1,829	2,146	1,922	392	237	383	36,048	1,125	21.0	7.0	49.5
Union	925	16,689	4,115	1,592	1,761	446	450	606	36,331	613	37.8	2.3	61.5
Venango	1,172	15,564	3,270	3,803	2,668	317	299	527	33,853	464	33.0	5.4	48.1
Warren	913	14,063	2,944	3,013	2,386	892	244	505	35,907	602	34.7	4.5	39.0
Washington	5,127	82,440	13,712	8,457	8,768	1,521	3,730	4,364	52,934	1,915	36.1	1.8	44.6
Wayne	1,321	12,420	2,431	615	2,861	441	292	429	34,508	711	24.9	4.1	50.4
Westmoreland	8,600	125,776	20,661	17,374	19,344	2,783	6,454	5,037	40,046	1,274	37.3	3.1	46.2
Wyoming	654	10,490	551	2,252	1,307	195	450	534	50,868	508	30.9	3.1	46.1
York	8,646	164,632	25,020	30,464	22,078	3,726	5,947	6,975	42,367	2,171	56.6	4.4	48.9
RHODE ISLAND	28,685	435,148	88,587	40,132	48,978	27,255	23,771	20,151	46,308	1,243	71.1	0.9	49.8
Bristol	1,254	14,525	2,648	2,147	1,403	244	428	487	33,498	42	73.8	0.0	57.1
Kent	4,694	70,605	12,616	5,688	11,529	4,891	4,354	3,077	43,582	126	65.9	1.6	41.3
Newport	2,745	31,346	4,930	1,825	4,303	1,343	3,297	1,340	42,760	214	72.4	0.9	55.6
Providence	15,908	269,673	59,768	22,992	24,943	18,891	12,954	12,971	48,100	425	73.2	0.2	45.6
Washington	3,794	43,531	8,452	7,479	6,795	1,002	1,607	1,974	45,343	436	69.7	1.4	52.8
SOUTH CAROLINA	105,959	1,716,496	230,608	228,268	244,946	69,856	89,194	69,051	40,228	25,266	44.1	8.1	41.0
Abbeville	334	4,772	543	2,064	464	140	44	151	31,644	574	32.2	5.9	34.1
Aiken	2,732	50,307	6,377	7,851	7,513	1,203	1,878	2,115	42,036	1,102	46.5	4.6	33.9
Allendale	122	1,671	300	781	162	54	30	73	43,550	141	22.0	27.0	54.6
Anderson	3,694	57,568	8,773	11,923	9,347	1,139	2,210	2,172	37,721	1,498	50.9	2.9	35.6
Bamberg	261	3,105	530	979	497	91	56	94	30,400	315	19.4	15.6	40.3
Barnwell	354	4,162	440	1,539	728	125	89	134	32,150	397	36.5	11.8	44.6
Beaufort	5,154	54,701	8,209	600	10,121	1,886	2,482	1,855	33,905	137	56.9	16.1	39.4
Berkeley	2,980	46,709	2,684	4,699	7,355	976	3,589	2,258	48,339	373	57.4	9.7	45.8
Calhoun	237	3,694	420	1,365	342	33	18	145	39,239	412	31.1	14.3	45.4
Charleston	13,321	202,114	31,767	15,573	28,565	6,226	15,626	8,777	43,424	359	64.1	3.6	42.9
Cherokee	950	17,671	1,272	5,907	2,927	327	211	591	33,456	490	43.1	3.9	31.4
Chester	511	7,000	615	2,486	943	143	136	280	40,059	477	33.5	8.6	39.8
Chesterfield	684	13,219	1,597	5,771	1,310	206	85	499	37,745	717	36.8	7.9	34.0
Clarendon	465	5,544	1,531	674	1,212	232	76	160	28,844	422	29.6	17.1	55.2
Colleton	738	7,808	1,397	899	1,570	250	211	250	32,068	530	40.4	13.0	42.1
Darlington	1,075	17,022	2,432	2,886	2,482	404	235	755	44,338	385	36.9	20.0	46.2
Dillon	482	7,264	1,160	1,764	1,347	184	392	196	27,030	228	21.1	24.6	46.5
Dorchester	2,282	26,739	3,165	4,426	4,546	693	1,067	950	35,523	411	48.7	7.5	46.7
Edgefield	322	4,962	522	1,011	501	57	63	177	35,753	389	40.1	9.0	36.2
Fairfield	313	7,790	612	1,102	565	57	D	536	68,769	194	32.5	10.3	40.2
Florence	3,136	57,006	13,403	7,075	9,239	3,641	2,372	2,128	37,336	632	33.4	11.1	44.3
Georgetown	1,800	19,471	3,743	2,029	3,180	464	770	717	36,816	209	39.7	13.9	44.0
Greenville	12,909	224,945	27,336	28,166	27,213	9,256	17,050	9,941	44,193	1,101	62.7	1.4	33.9
Greenwood	1,311	22,493	4,478	5,537	3,762	501	714	809	35,983	476	44.1	4.6	49.6
Hampton	325	3,228	670	393	541	128	99	117	36,295	323	28.5	18.6	46.1
Horry	8,629	107,915	11,133	2,819	23,452	3,570	3,641	3,239	30,018	938	44.1	9.8	50.5
Jasper	615	7,512	887	292	2,029	95	190	297	39,576	115	40.9	23.5	65.2
Kershaw	1,109	15,568	2,007	3,514	2,368	515	417	559	35,885	483	44.7	6.8	39.3
Lancaster	1,359	19,564	2,486	2,096	3,151	1,168	930	864	44,140	577	47.1	4.0	47.1
Laurens	927	17,026	2,032	6,545	1,692	295	396	632	37,142	826	40.0	5.3	35.4
Lee	185	1,618	214	117	387	62	40	46	28,639	386	26.2	16.8	45.3
Lexington	6,389	100,083	13,359	9,227	16,935	3,087	3,321	3,788	37,850	1,011	56.2	3.8	42.0
McCormick	84	908	200	269	108	14	17	27	29,254	93	24.7	21.5	35.5
Marion	486	5,081	589	783	1,131	305	87	141	27,708	275	40.7	17.1	41.8
Marlboro	319	4,984	1,080	2,095	749	115	44	167	33,424	224	26.8	20.1	44.6
Newberry	725	12,191	1,423	4,931	1,471	177	152	414	33,953	594	36.2	7.7	38.9
Oconee	1,497	20,436	2,161	5,339	3,116	478	526	852	41,671	884	60.7	1.7	39.3
Orangeburg	1,593	25,314	4,186	6,431	4,003	611	459	887	35,047	1,056	34.2	12.7	42.2
Pickens	1,990	27,859	3,548	5,235	5,321	612	782	875	31,425	727	69.6	1.1	44.0
Richland	8,918	161,532	27,806	9,041	19,808	18,143	11,455	6,923	42,859	398	52.0	4.5	38.9
Saluda	241	3,829	418	2,133	311	39	122	115	30,141	587	30.7	9.2	44.6
Spartanburg	6,225	126,940	16,246	29,203	14,622	2,017	3,737	5,554	43,750	1,338	57.6	1.4	43.7

Table B. States and Counties — **Agriculture**

STATE County	Acreage (1,000)	Percent change, 2007-2012	Average size of farm	Total irrigated (1,000)	Total cropland (1,000)	Average per farm	Average per acre	Value of machinery and equiopmnet, average per farm (dollars)	Total (mil dol)	Average per farm (acres)	Crops	Livestock and poultry products	$10,000 or more	$100,000 or more	Total ($1,000)	Percent of farms
	117	118	119	120	121	122	123	124	125	126	127	128	129	130	131	132
PENNSYLVANIA— Cont'd																
Potter	97	9.3	219	0.0	42.0	601,247	2,749	87,593	35.5	80,204	31.7	68.3	36.2	12.9	1,364	52.0
Schuylkill	106	-10.8	134	1.7	72.1	860,377	6,436	105,598	165.9	209,675	46.3	53.7	47.0	21.0	1,486	42.7
Snyder	91	-9.0	98	0.8	59.7	568,781	5,820	67,891	165.5	177,377	16.4	83.6	56.2	24.9	1,273	25.3
Somerset	215	3.8	188	0.1	119.4	495,161	2,631	91,144	104.2	91,411	26.0	74.0	52.8	21.1	1,602	30.9
Sullivan	37	34.7	209	0.0	15.4	645,698	3,084	97,117	9.5	53,168	26.7	73.3	33.5	8.9	461	43.6
Susquehanna	166	5.2	166	0.1	73.7	675,315	4,079	80,360	43.3	43,106	20.7	79.3	35.2	11.3	1,585	35.2
Tioga	205	11.4	182	0.2	109.0	626,933	3,438	78,940	80.3	71,340	26.5	73.5	43.6	13.3	2,590	42.0
Union	93	46.2	152	0.1	52.7	820,065	5,391	101,024	136.0	221,811	19.1	80.9	73.2	45.0	713	27.2
Venango	62	-5.0	133	0.0	29.0	410,136	3,093	81,901	15.8	33,998	64.5	35.5	39.2	6.7	489	22.8
Warren	82	-17.2	137	0.1	27.6	321,166	2,346	63,495	20.7	34,464	32.9	67.1	28.9	6.6	464	15.9
Washington	206	-2.5	107	0.8	86.4	489,897	4,558	68,244	35.4	18,492	53.1	46.9	28.1	2.7	841	10.9
Wayne	113	21.6	159	0.1	43.2	592,875	3,730	76,821	32.4	45,502	21.0	79.0	43.5	11.4	696	20.0
Westmoreland	143	-14.6	112	0.4	81.9	534,291	4,758	92,900	48.6	38,155	55.6	44.4	37.1	7.1	1,118	25.3
Wyoming	69	-11.8	135	0.1	32.4	542,844	4,011	79,911	14.6	28,772	57.3	42.7	32.7	7.7	633	31.7
York	262	-10.4	121	0.8	195.0	910,957	7,547	87,005	234.1	107,814	62.9	37.1	45.3	16.5	2,746	22.2
RHODE ISLAND	70	2.6	56	4.0	22.6	786,093	14,041	56,065	59.7	47,990	82.1	17.9	35.7	8.7	2,345	15.3
Bristol	D	D	D	0.1	1.1	977,024	D	52,190	2.7	63,548	80.4	19.5	47.6	16.7	D	2.4
Kent	D	D	D	0.2	1.9	790,095	D	39,087	4.4	34,548	80.4	19.6	38.1	7.9	D	7.9
Newport	12	13.9	54	0.5	6.5	1,201,720	22,248	63,850	14.6	68,365	83.1	16.9	47.2	12.6	390	22.4
Providence	D	D	D	0.6	4.9	600,586	D	41,569	14.1	33,127	77.8	22.2	31.3	5.2	949	17.9
Washington	27	10.8	63	2.6	8.2	743,369	11,870	71,654	23.9	54,865	84.6	15.4	32.6	9.6	936	12.6
SOUTH CAROLINA	4,971	1.7	197	159.2	1,967.3	586,518	2,981	72,400	3,040.1	120,323	42.6	57.4	27.0	8.6	46,616	26.9
Abbeville	92	0.9	160	D	23.7	444,972	2,775	52,261	9.6	16,786	31.0	69.0	26.1	1.2	631	19.9
Aiken	154	-3.1	140	1.3	55.8	532,257	3,800	54,850	96.3	87,426	16.3	83.7	26.9	7.1	892	16.1
Allendale	124	-0.7	882	6.5	39.1	1,949,496	2,211	94,773	25.6	181,532	89.3	10.7	27.0	12.8	946	68.8
Anderson	159	-8.1	106	0.6	46.5	463,880	4,367	51,636	62.8	41,918	D	D	23.5	4.3	779	12.3
Bamberg	93	-25.9	294	7.4	36.6	650,460	2,215	93,587	37.2	118,187	69.9	30.1	36.5	15.6	1,408	67.9
Barnwell	88	-5.2	221	4.4	37.5	539,234	2,437	79,058	48.4	121,867	D	D	29.5	13.9	1,091	48.9
Beaufort	42	-14.6	308	3.2	6.4	1,041,226	3,382	99,153	D	D	D	D	32.1	6.6	51	10.9
Berkeley	75	42.4	201	0.4	19.5	718,094	3,568	54,810	6.9	18,413	87.5	12.5	27.1	4.3	388	18.8
Calhoun	118	7.1	287	14.9	64.5	802,779	2,794	154,303	79.7	193,354	69.6	30.4	40.0	19.4	1,632	45.9
Charleston	35	-15.0	99	1.6	8.8	615,329	6,234	49,072	D	D	D	D	28.1	5.8	76	4.7
Cherokee	65	3.0	132	D	16.6	399,810	3,033	43,643	24.0	49,078	40.7	59.3	20.8	2.0	625	15.9
Chester	96	-14.6	200	0.5	19.0	564,608	2,820	65,338	42.6	89,329	D	D	29.8	6.1	376	10.3
Chesterfield	131	-6.8	183	1.2	42.4	500,552	2,739	59,743	121.2	169,050	77.0	23.0	23.2	7.8	1,047	37.1
Clarendon	174	12.3	412	8.5	98.1	758,033	1,840	152,725	139.6	330,829	53.2	46.8	42.2	20.1	1,972	68.7
Colleton	188	7.4	354	2.8	45.9	955,200	2,697	90,266	33.6	63,330	95.4	4.6	28.7	6.6	707	36.2
Darlington	177	2.4	459	7.3	113.7	1,132,418	2,465	182,395	129.2	335,509	58.4	41.6	45.7	26.5	2,806	47.3
Dillon	107	1.7	468	1.3	75.2	1,218,289	2,602	169,167	132.2	579,724	38.6	61.4	43.4	28.1	2,245	69.3
Dorchester	75	14.6	181	2.1	34.5	623,706	3,440	74,095	50.0	121,572	47.1	52.9	28.5	10.7	853	29.2
Edgefield	81	6.4	210	6.0	20.9	619,203	2,955	80,298	44.7	114,854	73.3	26.7	23.7	5.1	540	24.2
Fairfield	45	-14.2	229	D	7.3	640,268	2,791	51,732	30.9	159,237	5.0	95.0	26.8	6.7	137	9.8
Florence	156	-1.7	247	1.8	94.3	546,794	2,215	91,321	54.0	85,517	98.4	1.6	35.1	11.6	2,303	49.8
Georgetown	66	15.1	318	0.5	12.4	747,407	2,354	71,541	12.8	61,287	98.3	1.7	23.0	8.6	313	56.5
Greenville	73	0.3	66	1.6	20.6	430,060	6,498	38,996	16.6	15,044	81.7	18.4	15.8	1.7	180	5.3
Greenwood	86	21.0	180	0.2	12.7	432,540	2,407	46,794	6.7	14,023	33.3	66.7	23.3	1.7	311	11.1
Hampton	139	9.7	431	6.3	51.7	1,032,814	2,398	85,718	34.6	107,266	98.8	1.2	31.6	13.3	1,584	64.4
Horry	178	8.5	189	5.6	108.0	571,035	3,016	93,665	101.3	107,988	78.6	21.4	31.4	14.0	2,149	45.7
Jasper	69	31.6	597	D	8.7	1,620,974	2,717	69,043	6.4	55,626	93.5	6.5	26.1	5.2	60	17.4
Kershaw	83	-3.1	172	1.1	16.7	524,702	3,058	60,770	147.2	304,687	3.3	96.7	23.6	10.8	499	16.6
Lancaster	65	-0.2	113	0.3	14.0	443,986	3,936	45,899	78.0	135,208	4.5	95.5	24.4	7.5	86	8.8
Laurens	123	-5.7	148	0.7	35.0	503,297	3,389	47,098	40.9	49,530	D	D	28.8	4.8	1,085	15.0
Lee	142	1.0	369	7.4	93.2	835,806	2,265	151,886	118.6	307,225	51.3	48.7	31.6	18.9	2,289	66.8
Lexington	108	19.2	107	10.7	49.0	424,407	3,984	64,111	164.6	162,818	25.9	74.1	27.2	10.1	660	13.2
McCormick	30	20.5	323	D	3.6	570,806	1,767	42,785	5.2	55,946	22.6	77.4	21.5	5.4	155	32.3
Marion	80	15.4	292	1.1	44.5	679,087	2,328	107,269	40.6	147,815	69.8	30.2	29.5	14.2	931	66.5
Marlboro	113	-7.5	506	2.7	71.1	1,096,866	2,169	123,723	61.8	276,063	73.5	26.5	33.0	23.2	2,154	62.5
Newberry	104	3.7	176	0.8	31.7	476,949	2,711	66,958	139.5	234,891	D	D	31.1	7.2	1,004	22.2
Oconee	68	-4.0	77	0.3	15.4	407,562	5,308	49,633	121.4	137,313	5.0	95.0	21.4	7.9	382	6.3
Orangeburg	283	-1.5	268	25.4	152.9	677,763	2,528	124,560	231.5	219,264	53.8	46.2	33.3	16.3	3,506	43.9
Pickens	45	-12.3	62	0.8	13.0	344,880	5,575	41,396	8.4	11,611	66.3	33.7	12.5	1.0	167	4.0
Richland	61	3.5	153	2.0	31.1	536,626	3,511	68,653	30.0	75,472	76.9	23.1	24.6	5.8	507	10.1
Saluda	108	-1.7	184	4.4	29.6	524,673	2,853	81,700	126.3	215,130	21.8	78.2	37.0	11.6	750	25.6
Spartanburg	102	-7.3	76	1.9	37.7	377,862	4,964	38,547	34.6	25,829	56.6	43.4	18.1	2.2	833	8.1

Table B. States and Counties — Water Use, Wholesale Trade, Retail Trade, and Real Estate

STATE County	Water use, 2015		Wholesale Trade[1], 2012				Retail Trade[2], 2012				Real estate and rental and leasing,[2] 2012			
	Public supply water withdrawn (mil gal/day)	Public supply gallons withdrawn per person per day	Number of establishments	Number of employees	Sales (mil dol)	Annual payroll (mil dol)	Number of establishments	Number of employees	Sales (mil dol)	Annual payroll (mil dol)	Number of establishments	Number of employees	Sales (mil dol)	Annual payroll (mil dol)
	133	134	135	136	137	138	139	140	141	142	143	144	145	146
PENNSYLVANIA— Cont'd														
Potter	0.91	53.2	6	D	D	D	68	546	152.7	13.6	5	16	1.0	0.2
Schuylkill	23.38	161.7	99	1,562	916.6	55.0	504	5,677	1,381.9	119.1	60	240	40.7	6.6
Snyder	1.60	39.6	26	D	D	D	198	2,867	630.2	54.9	13	47	11.1	1.7
Somerset	22.61	299.4	65	894	443.1	34.6	253	2,643	781.1	60.2	46	151	43.6	5.8
Sullivan	0.65	102.7	2	D	D	D	30	279	64.7	4.5	4	D	D	D
Susquehanna	1.41	33.8	34	267	569.9	8.6	146	1,269	533.6	28.0	15	88	24.5	4.7
Tioga	2.03	48.5	28	394	237.7	17.5	155	2,002	563.9	44.5	23	56	8.9	1.6
Union	2.87	63.8	30	D	D	D	130	1,561	479.2	37.0	28	158	19.0	3.4
Venango	4.68	88.1	43	D	D	D	204	2,565	636.9	53.9	26	79	12.6	1.9
Warren	3.07	76.0	27	211	142.0	8.8	130	2,394	674.6	55.4	18	71	7.3	1.4
Washington	39.71	190.7	227	3,257	2,869.3	186.9	691	8,657	2,342.1	194.5	145	772	221.8	38.3
Wayne	2.38	46.5	24	D	D	D	223	2,560	711.1	60.4	27	62	11.5	2.0
Westmoreland	24.18	67.6	330	5,958	7,333.3	308.5	1,258	18,183	4,671.7	416.7	262	1,106	240.4	38.0
Wyoming	0.66	23.7	18	389	106.5	14.5	114	1,334	393.5	28.0	9	27	10.4	2.0
York	34.82	78.6	359	6,685	4,340.8	301.4	1,297	21,024	5,192.4	463.9	258	1,470	263.7	51.8
RHODE ISLAND	97.46	92.3	1,158	15,697	22,310.4	1,000.2	3,795	47,688	12,063.9	1,206.6	1,058	5,615	1,119.8	218.5
Bristol	0.01	0.2	48	385	204.9	21.5	145	1,355	288.1	32.2	43	127	24.2	3.8
Kent	1.04	6.3	213	2,683	1,670.6	156.9	676	11,126	2,984.2	285.3	177	1,298	261.8	49.5
Newport	7.20	87.4	69	390	331.1	22.0	430	4,211	1,116.5	116.3	112	769	100.9	23.1
Providence	80.06	126.4	701	11,014	19,000.6	720.6	1,996	24,365	5,999.4	594.4	598	3,063	659.5	130.0
Washington	9.15	72.3	127	1,225	1,103.3	79.3	548	6,631	1,675.7	178.4	128	358	73.5	12.2
SOUTH CAROLINA	633.39	129.4	4,337	54,949	45,520.9	2,806.2	17,586	220,438	58,093.8	4,954.6	4,692	23,189	4,334.4	825.9
Abbeville	1.97	79.0	6	52	22.1	2.1	62	439	91.4	7.6	2	D	D	D
Aiken	32.01	193.0	69	505	399.4	20.0	508	6,601	1,749.5	139.6	106	331	53.6	9.8
Allendale	1.19	126.2	8	46	55.2	1.8	26	136	33.9	2.7	4	D	D	D
Anderson	19.00	97.6	167	2,514	2,641.3	105.6	697	8,472	2,189.6	188.1	125	422	91.7	13.1
Bamberg	0.92	61.8	6	D	D	D	56	462	95.3	9.6	2	D	D	D
Barnwell	1.54	70.9	4	D	D	D	74	782	167.1	14.9	10	18	2.2	0.4
Beaufort	12.76	71.1	113	470	295.6	21.4	734	9,080	2,090.5	203.1	379	1,718	267.1	62.8
Berkeley	70.34	346.9	151	2,343	3,248.3	125.6	396	6,173	1,730.6	141.6	130	699	132.4	26.1
Calhoun	1.11	75.1	9	D	D	D	35	224	65.9	3.6	3	D	D	D
Charleston	4.52	11.6	468	5,049	2,875.4	264.4	1,935	26,034	6,707.7	628.9	695	3,295	599.2	118.4
Cherokee	8.98	159.8	22	432	131.6	14.6	235	2,648	800.6	49.4	39	153	24.2	2.6
Chester	3.18	98.6	12	175	302.1	10.0	100	828	234.1	17.1	14	D	D	D
Chesterfield	5.83	126.7	27	305	96.4	10.0	135	1,271	317.7	22.8	16	37	4.1	0.8
Clarendon	2.31	68.4	16	113	74.2	3.8	124	1,247	336.3	24.9	16	34	3.9	1.0
Colleton	2.07	54.9	28	195	107.2	7.3	157	1,635	408.3	32.5	44	144	22.5	3.7
Darlington	6.41	94.9	73	592	859.7	25.3	235	2,246	536.6	45.2	37	102	46.5	2.7
Dillon	4.56	146.0	20	443	391.7	15.4	121	1,159	394.2	22.2	21	62	4.9	1.1
Dorchester	33.04	216.7	73	562	215.3	27.5	297	3,697	973.2	78.7	104	332	65.0	11.3
Edgefield	4.54	171.2	8	125	62.7	6.1	54	405	152.1	9.5	8	22	1.7	0.5
Fairfield	1.88	82.6	10	D	D	D	54	539	224.9	12.1	11	D	D	D
Florence	15.70	113.0	158	2,493	1,585.7	105.5	701	8,277	2,149.6	178.9	130	555	104.3	19.7
Georgetown	8.91	145.4	40	280	135.3	10.2	303	2,776	703.3	62.9	86	417	54.8	13.0
Greenville	45.87	93.3	711	9,278	10,153.0	521.9	1,757	24,790	6,380.5	593.2	534	2,681	838.1	113.6
Greenwood	4.85	69.4	49	421	837.9	19.1	275	3,224	758.9	67.6	44	D	D	D
Hampton	1.47	73.3	10	182	118.2	10.0	92	678	164.8	13.2	7	23	2.1	0.8
Horry	50.13	162.1	238	1,605	734.3	65.4	1,666	20,687	5,240.2	455.3	590	4,496	506.6	131.1
Jasper	27.30	981.2	27	258	146.8	12.6	104	1,425	574.8	40.5	18	69	13.6	3.2
Kershaw	5.33	83.8	16	70	43.5	4.8	178	2,122	586.3	44.0	32	83	14.0	3.2
Lancaster	20.99	244.5	47	1,106	719.7	38.8	238	2,673	732.9	60.3	43	D	D	D
Laurens	4.91	73.7	32	227	115.2	10.6	180	1,680	412.1	32.8	20	50	6.3	1.0
Lee	2.54	141.9	11	80	138.2	3.8	42	381	86.0	7.3	2	D	D	D
Lexington	52.21	185.3	302	5,744	3,889.3	292.0	1,046	15,123	3,974.5	338.3	243	1,277	227.9	43.8
McCormick	0.96	98.9	1	D	D	D	22	122	31.9	2.1	2	D	D	D
Marion	3.41	107.4	21	338	208.4	16.5	128	1,042	239.0	21.0	10	30	3.5	0.9
Marlboro	3.90	141.8	13	114	43.5	4.2	98	704	185.5	14.9	13	29	4.3	0.6
Newberry	6.58	173.1	26	238	160.5	10.0	133	1,389	428.1	29.2	17	65	14.9	2.2
Oconee	10.82	142.9	39	388	201.2	13.4	254	2,920	741.0	63.9	64	153	26.0	5.5
Orangeburg	8.96	100.4	66	529	387.8	21.6	370	4,070	1,016.6	80.2	53	241	25.7	7.9
Pickens	33.01	271.3	66	403	301.3	21.5	324	4,215	1,163.1	97.9	68	345	44.5	9.4
Richland	31.44	77.2	417	5,489	4,191.3	303.2	1,254	18,443	4,780.7	433.4	408	2,792	736.4	133.1
Saluda	0.03	1.5	8	45	14.4	1.4	49	414	115.1	8.5	4	D	D	D
Spartanburg	34.72	116.8	414	5,813	5,340.5	297.1	1,069	13,459	3,966.7	316.7	227	999	180.6	37.3

1. Merchant wholesalers, except manufacturers' sales branches and offices.   2. Employer establishments.

Table B. States and Counties — **Agriculture**

STATE County	Land in farms Acreage (1,000)	Percent change, 2007-2012	Acres Average size of farm	Total irrigated (1,000)	Total cropland (1,000)	Value of land and buildings (dollars) Average per farm	Average per acre	Value of machinery and equipment, average per farm (dollars)	Value of products sold: Total (mil dol)	Average per farm (acres)	Percent from: Crops	Livestock and poultry products	Percent of farms with sales of: $10,000 or more	$100,000 or more	Government payments Total ($1,000)	Percent of farms
	117	118	119	120	121	122	123	124	125	126	127	128	129	130	131	132
SOUTH CAROLINA— Cont'd																
Sumter	176	14.7	342	8.9	69.5	792,967	2,320	105,033	130.5	253,379	36.9	63.1	27.2	10.9	1,870	57.3
Union	47	4.0	179	0.1	9.0	394,534	2,201	43,322	15.3	58,121	12.3	87.7	29.5	1.9	303	14.4
Williamsburg	224	7.2	331	0.8	91.8	689,383	2,086	83,346	61.8	91,032	83.2	16.8	29.9	12.8	2,763	60.1
York	124	-0.2	123	0.7	38.1	621,009	5,031	48,627	96.8	96,452	D	D	23.4	4.1	572	14.6
SOUTH DAKOTA	43,257	-0.9	1,352	378.7	19,147.3	2,281,027	1,687	241,373	10,170.2	317,929	59.7	40.3	65.0	40.7	283,797	71.3
Aurora	442	21.2	1,000	D	267.7	2,361,032	2,361	226,367	127.3	287,910	53.6	46.4	71.7	45.5	3,875	81.4
Beadle	794	3.1	1,053	11.2	576.9	3,014,625	2,864	295,423	300.2	398,088	63.3	36.7	66.3	46.9	7,071	74.9
Bennett	606	-19.5	2,769	6.6	178.6	1,564,995	565	198,361	62.2	283,799	35.8	64.2	76.7	51.1	2,139	73.5
Bon Homme	352	13.9	524	6.6	277.2	1,529,963	2,920	189,478	107.9	160,744	38.3	61.7	66.0	30.3	4,954	86.3
Brookings	449	-2.9	439	16.9	327.4	1,870,065	4,261	195,803	312.5	305,506	51.9	48.1	52.9	29.9	7,038	68.3
Brown	1,079	-0.6	1,022	6.4	854.5	2,980,409	2,917	318,692	520.6	493,029	88.9	11.1	56.9	40.7	17,500	66.3
Brule	514	-0.9	1,263	3.7	263.9	2,876,440	2,278	244,592	150.9	370,715	51.0	49.0	70.0	42.8	2,702	68.8
Buffalo	296	-5.1	3,797	6.3	87.0	4,488,474	1,182	380,705	45.7	585,256	50.3	49.7	70.5	50.0	912	78.2
Butte	1,135	-0.5	1,722	45.4	116.8	1,066,480	619	99,675	75.4	114,340	23.0	77.0	67.2	26.1	3,255	46.7
Campbell	360	-10.1	1,489	2.3	211.0	1,898,711	1,275	321,665	98.9	408,607	62.8	37.2	71.1	51.7	2,928	85.5
Charles Mix	692	4.8	912	15.3	448.9	2,146,680	2,353	264,441	227.9	300,271	45.2	54.8	70.2	44.9	5,433	87.7
Clark	609	19.7	1,020	7.3	401.3	2,584,074	2,534	297,191	249.4	417,714	64.0	36.0	66.2	51.1	5,326	83.9
Clay	259	-3.0	561	20.8	237.6	2,481,560	4,422	279,267	96.8	210,037	82.3	17.7	64.2	46.6	4,323	79.4
Codington	369	0.6	518	4.3	255.9	1,389,913	2,684	168,854	172.4	241,811	62.8	37.2	56.2	33.4	3,757	62.6
Corson	1,242	-3.2	3,846	D	346.4	2,514,418	654	240,712	117.1	362,492	50.9	49.1	86.4	60.4	3,165	66.3
Custer	623	3.7	1,397	3.1	46.9	1,600,944	1,146	76,119	26.0	58,325	11.0	89.0	47.8	15.7	1,285	19.7
Davison	275	-1.5	645	1.7	210.2	2,187,288	3,393	215,440	78.8	184,515	63.7	36.3	55.7	31.4	2,594	65.6
Day	570	0.5	823	0.3	395.0	1,571,924	1,911	211,440	189.7	273,775	83.5	16.5	51.7	32.5	6,718	78.6
Deuel	342	7.8	515	1.1	207.6	1,519,508	2,951	183,530	177.8	267,700	52.5	47.5	54.2	32.2	4,206	78.2
Dewey	1,182	-18.5	3,455	0.0	214.4	1,979,599	573	171,526	69.3	202,535	42.2	57.8	76.9	44.7	4,224	64.9
Douglas	270	19.8	622	2.1	192.3	1,774,048	2,854	210,823	117.5	270,668	35.4	64.6	81.1	50.5	2,807	79.3
Edmunds	697	6.1	1,652	1.0	492.8	3,620,645	2,192	451,389	271.4	643,123	68.7	31.3	74.2	58.3	5,097	81.5
Fall River	1,089	14.6	3,330	7.5	63.8	1,714,394	515	112,138	116.9	357,364	5.5	94.5	59.3	30.3	1,885	40.4
Faulk	616	0.2	2,199	0.5	382.8	4,275,536	1,945	559,368	216.3	772,596	72.3	27.7	83.9	66.4	5,575	87.9
Grant	429	17.9	694	3.4	290.7	2,075,218	2,992	261,960	240.8	389,675	56.4	43.6	66.0	48.1	4,517	70.6
Gregory	635	-3.0	1,257	0.5	239.1	1,534,659	1,221	156,531	94.1	186,410	42.4	57.6	73.5	37.4	2,245	79.4
Haakon	1,133	-1.5	3,949	0.1	324.6	2,375,324	601	186,188	77.1	268,700	43.0	57.0	75.6	50.2	4,539	73.5
Hamlin	311	0.4	636	7.9	241.7	2,272,331	3,572	285,902	188.2	384,920	66.3	33.7	59.1	39.9	4,136	74.8
Hand	905	0.7	2,181	4.5	565.6	4,161,320	1,908	431,607	284.4	685,390	69.6	30.4	77.1	58.1	5,362	85.3
Hanson	274	25.1	741	1.1	212.2	2,773,749	3,745	316,603	110.7	299,054	60.7	39.3	67.6	46.8	2,701	75.1
Harding	1,467	-8.1	5,869	0.7	179.7	2,465,216	420	212,876	70.4	281,628	24.3	75.7	80.0	55.6	2,729	61.6
Hughes	431	4.8	1,275	9.8	269.5	2,502,944	1,963	213,530	107.3	317,577	81.2	18.8	54.7	32.8	3,532	62.1
Hutchinson	513	0.7	640	4.0	409.7	2,103,788	3,287	263,249	186.2	232,226	38.3	61.7	69.1	38.4	7,192	85.2
Hyde	515	7.0	2,486	0.3	216.3	3,454,498	1,390	317,135	94.3	455,705	66.9	33.1	80.7	57.5	2,441	75.4
Jackson	1,158	-2.2	3,873	0.6	176.6	3,077,278	795	179,492	51.9	173,619	34.6	65.4	71.2	41.8	2,083	58.2
Jerauld	333	1.3	1,428	1.4	181.6	2,811,747	1,968	300,974	99.3	426,206	62.4	37.6	67.8	40.8	2,191	73.4
Jones	612	17.9	3,757	0.7	210.1	2,730,785	727	235,785	65.3	400,319	61.5	38.5	74.8	58.3	2,535	81.0
Kingsbury	521	9.1	1,006	2.1	382.3	3,338,884	3,319	324,201	278.3	537,182	63.0	37.0	75.3	55.8	5,135	74.9
Lake	262	-16.9	521	1.8	207.3	2,128,008	4,081	237,606	168.8	336,323	66.6	33.4	56.6	41.8	3,352	75.5
Lawrence	159	18.9	509	2.7	29.7	722,071	1,419	76,962	19.1	61,064	12.7	87.3	41.0	11.9	315	22.1
Lincoln	366	9.8	407	2.9	329.9	2,211,686	5,440	198,632	172.3	191,619	60.0	40.0	61.4	33.1	6,946	71.4
Lyman	1,029	5.3	2,392	8.7	456.4	2,398,733	1,003	253,705	136.8	318,044	69.5	30.5	65.6	47.0	6,670	81.6
McCook	363	-0.1	639	D	299.5	2,713,745	4,248	278,900	157.0	276,347	61.6	38.4	65.0	40.1	3,979	72.9
McPherson	573	10.5	1,439	1.3	286.8	2,201,472	1,530	274,035	159.4	400,425	53.1	46.9	71.4	42.0	3,081	76.9
Marshall	532	-0.4	1,027	D	316.0	2,296,672	2,235	328,147	306.8	592,357	47.6	52.4	58.7	39.6	8,084	82.2
Meade	2,033	-8.0	2,281	4.0	349.8	1,537,875	674	117,736	116.4	130,688	21.8	78.2	60.3	28.5	4,935	42.4
Mellette	699	-4.2	3,051	D	117.4	2,181,253	715	174,258	46.2	201,799	30.1	69.9	82.5	52.8	1,048	65.1
Miner	357	19.1	735	D	231.5	2,361,718	3,212	260,222	123.7	254,517	60.6	39.4	57.4	40.1	4,341	82.5
Minnehaha	408	-3.2	353	1.7	322.4	1,814,344	5,146	191,197	270.2	233,576	60.8	39.2	56.3	34.4	5,753	67.2
Moody	254	-13.3	496	3.2	208.8	2,525,815	5,094	216,696	215.0	419,047	61.1	38.9	59.8	40.7	4,100	76.2
Oglala Lakota	1,101	-17.4	6,329	0.5	97.8	2,910,178	460	155,874	32.3	185,563	27.0	73.0	77.0	36.8	1,772	45.4
Pennington	1,074	-9.4	1,793	5.8	222.8	1,253,793	699	110,694	65.7	109,760	45.0	55.0	55.9	23.7	2,942	30.7
Perkins	1,631	-10.8	3,732	0.2	393.2	2,007,828	538	177,826	125.0	286,087	34.6	65.4	77.6	51.5	4,913	77.1
Potter	538	4.1	2,178	D	357.3	4,354,235	1,999	489,332	157.0	635,684	89.5	10.5	70.9	54.7	3,783	78.1
Roberts	623	5.1	711	2.3	429.3	1,800,643	2,531	225,765	251.2	286,725	79.7	20.3	57.1	36.6	9,142	79.2
Sanborn	360	13.2	896	D	221.8	2,130,490	2,377	270,057	118.8	295,401	58.4	41.6	60.9	39.8	3,561	78.1
Spink	945	4.1	1,400	19.2	714.7	4,166,481	2,976	425,689	447.6	663,096	74.7	25.3	72.3	56.4	12,003	87.4
Stanley	791	-14.1	4,323	0.2	219.4	3,968,497	918	248,842	64.0	349,896	63.7	36.3	77.6	50.3	2,309	62.3
Sully	628	3.2	3,289	24.6	501.0	5,131,304	1,560	595,026	225.6	1,181,042	82.7	17.3	77.5	61.3	3,981	77.0
Todd	860	-1.1	3,723	7.2	125.2	1,902,965	511	163,303	59.7	258,268	26.7	73.3	72.3	42.4	398	37.2

Table B. States and Counties — Water Use, Wholesale Trade, Retail Trade, and Real Estate

STATE County	Water use, 2015		Wholesale Trade[1], 2012				Retail Trade[2], 2012				Real estate and rental and leasing,[2] 2012			
	Public supply water withdrawn (mil gal/ day)	Public supply gallons withdrawn per person per day	Number of establish-ments	Number of employees	Sales (mil dol)	Annual payroll (mil dol)	Number of establish-ments	Number of employees	Sales (mil dol)	Annual payroll (mil dol)	Number of establish-ments	Number of employees	Sales (mil dol)	Annual payroll (mil dol)
	133	134	135	136	137	138	139	140	141	142	143	144	145	146
SOUTH CAROLINA— Cont'd														
Sumter	14.60	135.8	69	635	342.0	28.8	398	4,416	1,096.8	85.4	78	258	28.9	6.4
Union	2.94	105.8	14	102	43.4	4.4	99	905	195.7	16.9	14	134	8.2	3.1
Williamsburg	3.02	92.8	19	249	145.1	8.6	115	927	225.2	18.0	17	45	4.5	1.0
York	20.63	82.1	233	4,335	3,237.0	292.2	656	9,498	2,845.2	218.4	202	717	125.3	25.3
SOUTH DAKOTA	71.95	81.7	1,317	15,827	20,411.1	756.9	3,843	49,867	13,791.8	1,127.3	962	3,526	582.8	105.7
Aurora	0.19	69.5	6	48	65.4	1.5	8	59	10.8	1.1	2	D	D	D
Beadle	2.29	124.6	28	351	615.6	17.8	79	1,084	257.8	23.7	31	155	14.0	2.5
Bennett	0.17	49.7	NA	NA	NA	NA	15	126	32.3	2.4	NA	NA	NA	NA
Bon Homme	0.56	80.2	11	101	76.2	2.9	32	206	47.1	3.7	4	7	0.4	0.1
Brookings	2.77	81.7	29	252	451.6	12.5	121	1,679	375.9	34.7	45	169	21.1	4.4
Brown	3.47	89.5	80	1,048	1,914.6	48.7	201	2,956	809.5	75.0	57	251	31.3	7.0
Brule	0.52	98.5	12	104	102.0	4.3	41	299	99.1	6.4	4	4	0.2	0.1
Buffalo	0.10	47.7	NA	NA	NA	NA	2	D	D	D	NA	NA	NA	NA
Butte	0.52	50.6	6	D	D	D	49	429	157.4	11.4	8	16	1.2	0.4
Campbell	0.08	57.3	5	D	D	D	6	25	10.9	0.4	1	D	D	D
Charles Mix	0.55	58.6	14	182	180.8	5.8	52	445	99.8	7.5	3	D	D	D
Clark	0.16	43.7	8	D	D	D	14	91	34.8	2.0	1	D	D	D
Clay	1.02	73.0	8	44	30.2	1.8	45	665	122.8	11.3	11	20	3.2	0.4
Codington	3.74	133.9	58	773	580.6	36.0	184	2,667	649.1	56.0	50	126	20.3	3.1
Corson	0.18	42.9	4	D	D	D	6	43	15.1	1.1	NA	NA	NA	NA
Custer	0.28	33.2	1	D	D	D	31	261	68.1	4.8	9	16	6.3	0.3
Davison	1.92	96.7	35	D	D	D	130	2,030	530.4	47.3	26	D	D	D
Day	0.44	79.4	9	139	212.7	4.8	29	264	62.2	4.6	2	D	D	D
Deuel	0.17	39.2	6	30	37.6	1.1	23	116	46.1	3.0	1	D	D	D
Dewey	0.33	58.0	5	73	50.1	2.0	14	97	22.0	1.2	4	22	0.9	0.2
Douglas	0.18	60.5	6	D	D	D	18	119	36.4	1.9	2	D	D	D
Edmunds	0.26	65.0	13	202	472.5	8.8	16	126	44.4	2.7	4	6	0.2	0.0
Fall River	0.66	96.1	3	D	D	D	31	239	68.5	4.1	7	11	1.1	0.2
Faulk	0.15	64.2	10	48	113.5	2.4	13	95	29.6	2.2	1	D	D	D
Grant	0.63	88.2	13	129	193.2	6.2	46	501	127.5	10.9	9	18	2.2	0.3
Gregory	0.26	61.9	6	27	39.7	1.0	29	221	67.0	4.5	2	D	D	D
Haakon	0.11	59.1	8	102	232.1	2.7	16	99	29.0	2.0	1	D	D	D
Hamlin	0.41	67.8	11	142	149.8	7.7	18	117	38.5	2.6	2	D	D	D
Hand	0.21	62.7	11	158	89.1	5.0	21	186	36.2	2.8	1	D	D	D
Hanson	0.09	26.6	7	D	D	D	4	32	6.2	0.5	1	D	D	D
Harding	0.03	23.7	NA	NA	NA	NA	7	33	11.4	0.6	NA	NA	NA	NA
Hughes	2.67	152.1	23	D	D	D	105	1,393	347.2	30.6	30	D	D	D
Hutchinson	0.39	53.4	28	336	480.0	12.5	41	321	81.1	6.2	2	D	D	D
Hyde	0.11	78.7	5	58	173.1	2.9	8	97	21.3	1.3	1	D	D	D
Jackson	0.13	39.1	2	D	D	D	14	118	33.6	1.8	NA	NA	NA	NA
Jerauld	0.54	270.4	5	D	D	D	9	65	21.3	1.5	2	D	D	D
Jones	0.05	54.1	2	D	D	D	12	87	32.8	2.0	NA	NA	NA	NA
Kingsbury	0.22	44.1	8	112	240.5	5.2	23	141	34.1	2.5	2	D	D	D
Lake	0.81	64.2	17	198	371.4	11.5	46	491	162.3	12.2	12	28	2.3	0.4
Lawrence	2.35	94.7	19	52	38.8	2.1	142	1,380	434.0	35.2	63	184	22.2	4.6
Lincoln	1.02	19.3	55	390	667.6	19.5	126	1,571	490.6	45.9	54	268	39.2	8.8
Lyman	0.22	56.8	4	D	D	D	16	301	54.5	5.0	1	D	D	D
McCook	0.71	126.8	10	73	100.0	3.4	24	161	52.1	2.9	6	D	D	D
McPherson	0.13	53.8	2	D	D	D	10	61	14.2	1.1	1	D	D	D
Marshall	0.22	46.1	10	60	69.1	2.5	24	194	74.3	4.6	1	D	D	D
Meade	1.42	52.6	21	D	D	D	78	615	211.0	16.2	23	75	11.6	1.9
Mellette	0.09	43.9	NA	NA	NA	NA	7	56	11.6	0.8	1	D	D	D
Miner	0.11	49.2	4	D	D	D	13	65	17.8	1.3	2	D	D	D
Minnehaha	19.65	94.7	359	5,704	3,841.7	291.7	798	14,467	4,264.7	332.8	229	1,189	254.0	44.9
Moody	0.49	76.2	4	31	18.8	1.6	20	188	50.5	3.0	5	5	0.5	0.1
Oglala Lakota	1.10	76.5	1	D	D	D	10	189	51.4	3.2	NA	NA	NA	NA
Pennington	10.62	97.7	158	1,858	1,248.7	83.0	574	8,278	2,250.8	198.6	160	554	97.2	15.8
Perkins	0.16	53.0	5	D	D	D	19	108	24.8	2.2	3	D	D	D
Potter	0.20	86.2	7	94	577.3	5.3	17	123	21.8	1.6	2	D	D	D
Roberts	0.58	56.3	14	101	421.8	4.8	41	359	112.5	6.6	2	D	D	D
Sanborn	0.13	55.2	4	19	25.5	0.8	5	D	D	D	NA	NA	NA	NA
Spink	0.52	79.7	18	202	491.8	11.6	23	184	46.1	3.6	3	4	0.6	0.1
Stanley	0.32	108.3	3	D	D	D	15	133	53.2	3.8	4	D	D	D
Sully	0.00	0.0	5	D	D	D	11	88	42.6	2.4	3	D	D	D
Todd	0.42	42.2	1	D	D	D	15	196	43.0	3.0	3	D	D	D

1. Merchant wholesalers, except manufacturers' sales branches and offices.   2. Employer establishments.

600 SC(Sumter)—SD(Todd)   Items 133—146

Table B. States and Counties — Professional Services, Manufacturing, and Accommodation and Food Services

STATE County	Professional, scientific, and technical services, 2012				Manufacturing, 2012				Accommodation and food services, 2012			
	Number of establishments	Number of employees	Sales (mil dol)	Annual payroll (mil dol)	Number of establishments	Number of employees	Receipts (mil dol)	Annual payroll (mil dol)	Number of establishments	Number of employees	Receipts (mil dol)	Annual payroll (mil dol)
	147	148	149	150	151	152	153	154	155	156	157	158
SOUTH CAROLINA— Cont'd												
Sumter	126	714	75.8	23.2	71	5,524	1,817.5	214.6	158	2,951	127.0	34.9
Union	22	100	5.7	1.8	28	1,483	524.5	63.7	36	485	21.0	6.0
Williamsburg	26	95	10.5	2.8	35	2,110	1,778.0	97.2	27	D	D	D
York	455	2,240	297.2	102.9	213	8,310	3,111.1	439.6	392	7,094	336.9	89.6
SOUTH DAKOTA	1,822	11,144	1,315.4	482.3	1,025	41,931	16,882.6	1,764.7	2,363	37,974	1,873.7	514.2
Aurora	8	D	D	D	5	44	D	1.5	14	35	1.6	0.4
Beadle	28	114	11.0	4.0	31	1,646	495.1	55.7	48	525	21.7	5.4
Bennett	4	5	0.3	0.1	NA	NA	NA	NA	5	46	1.6	0.4
Bon Homme	6	20	1.8	0.5	13	320	D	11.6	14	65	2.4	0.5
Brookings	71	348	43.3	16.2	40	4,565	2,282.1	206.1	84	1,540	55.9	16.0
Brown	80	430	54.7	18.4	40	2,827	D	114.8	108	1,951	81.1	23.8
Brule	22	41	3.3	1.2	3	12	4.6	0.5	24	209	11.4	2.7
Buffalo	1	D	D	D	NA	NA	NA	NA	1	D	D	D
Butte	21	84	6.5	2.5	16	123	60.9	5.2	30	257	11.4	3.3
Campbell	4	7	0.3	0.1	3	48	D	D	7	D	D	D
Charles Mix	10	52	4.5	1.4	8	86	D	3.1	21	438	19.8	7.2
Clark	6	18	2.4	0.4	8	121	D	3.6	9	20	1.3	0.4
Clay	14	50	2.8	1.1	10	275	D	11.5	43	837	28.4	7.5
Codington	72	294	46.2	10.6	78	3,388	1,029.9	140.7	92	1,884	82.6	22.6
Corson	NA	NA	NA	NA	NA	NA	NA	NA	3	D	D	D
Custer	19	D	D	D	12	43	D	1.2	54	366	31.1	7.9
Davison	48	D	D	D	39	1,676	D	75.4	67	1,365	55.9	15.2
Day	5	24	2.2	0.7	13	219	61.5	9.4	17	168	5.2	1.4
Deuel	5	D	D	D	4	D	D	D	13	88	4.3	1.0
Dewey	4	11	0.4	0.1	NA	NA	NA	NA	6	18	1.7	0.2
Douglas	5	10	0.8	0.2	9	105	14.4	3.1	5	D	D	D
Edmunds	6	21	2.6	0.7	5	63	D	2.5	9	72	2.3	0.7
Fall River	13	49	3.1	1.1	8	24	5.5	0.8	37	336	13.5	3.5
Faulk	3	D	D	D	3	13	D	D	13	49	2.5	0.3
Grant	14	46	4.7	1.6	14	580	844.6	25.9	25	286	10.5	2.3
Gregory	8	26	2.3	0.6	6	59	D	D	19	95	3.8	0.8
Haakon	5	14	1.7	0.5	4	62	D	D	7	36	1.6	0.3
Hamlin	3	D	D	D	8	233	D	8.9	11	33	1.4	0.2
Hand	9	30	3.5	1.1	6	40	D	1.6	13	95	3.0	0.6
Hanson	2	D	D	D	3	54	D	D	4	15	0.7	0.1
Harding	NA	NA	NA	NA	NA	NA	NA	NA	3	23	1.0	0.2
Hughes	53	279	35.9	12.3	6	44	D	2.1	51	984	40.9	11.7
Hutchinson	11	30	2.8	1.0	11	214	76.8	8.2	18	D	D	D
Hyde	2	D	D	D	NA	NA	NA	NA	1	D	D	D
Jackson	1	D	D	D	NA	NA	NA	NA	10	39	4.5	1.0
Jerauld	6	8	1.9	0.2	NA	NA	NA	NA	6	42	2.6	0.7
Jones	2	D	D	D	NA	NA	NA	NA	14	78	4.3	1.2
Kingsbury	7	20	2.2	0.5	12	401	75.1	14.3	13	101	3.5	0.9
Lake	29	126	18.1	4.6	21	872	374.0	32.1	36	463	14.3	4.0
Lawrence	69	263	24.8	8.5	41	445	130.9	17.1	137	2,704	197.1	46.4
Lincoln	82	D	D	D	69	2,313	D	97.6	53	D	D	D
Lyman	1	D	D	D	NA	NA	NA	NA	14	173	9.7	2.5
McCook	10	D	D	D	4	8	D	0.2	18	D	D	D
McPherson	4	D	D	D	7	47	4.7	1.6	5	20	0.7	0.2
Marshall	11	21	2.1	0.6	8	355	174.7	16.3	13	115	3.7	1.0
Meade	50	D	D	D	35	225	D	8.3	74	671	43.6	10.9
Mellette	1	D	D	D	NA	NA	NA	NA	4	10	0.4	0.1
Miner	3	16	1.1	0.4	4	32	D	1.3	8	D	D	D
Minnehaha	480	4,148	476.7	201.5	176	10,763	3,612.6	479.0	444	10,517	493.8	147.2
Moody	9	16	1.1	0.4	11	326	88.5	14.1	15	D	D	D
Oglala Lakota	2	D	D	D	NA	NA	NA	NA	10	305	20.3	5.9
Pennington	303	1,928	223.8	76.8	117	2,115	524.3	85.9	352	6,418	351.8	98.3
Perkins	5	11	0.8	0.2	4	D	D	D	8	D	D	D
Potter	3	D	D	D	4	44	D	1.6	12	65	4.8	1.0
Roberts	15	31	3.7	1.0	11	272	D	7.3	18	171	4.6	1.0
Sanborn	7	20	1.9	0.4	NA	NA	NA	NA	6	25	1.2	0.2
Spink	8	36	4.8	1.4	7	72	D	3.3	13	126	4.8	1.2
Stanley	4	D	D	D	3	D	D	D	13	D	D	D
Sully	2	D	D	D	NA	NA	NA	NA	8	D	D	D
Todd	2	D	D	D	3	37	7.0	1.4	3	19	0.6	0.2

STATE County	Health care and social assistance, 2012				Other services, 2012				Nonemployer businesses, 2015		Value of residential construction authorized by building permits, 2017	
	Number of establishments	Number of employees	Receipts (mil dol)	Annual payroll (mil dol)	Number of establishments	Number of employees	Receipts (mil dol)	Annual payroll (mil dol)	Number	Receipts (mil dol)	New construction ($1,000)	Number of housing units
	159	160	161	162	163	164	165	166	167	168	169	170
SOUTH CAROLINA— Cont'd												
Sumter	188	5,504	471.1	184.1	130	996	77.4	27.8	6,120	215.8	30,100	222
Union	30	D	D	D	30	132	8.0	2.3	1,115	32.1	4,540	23
Williamsburg	55	797	55.3	22.5	35	D	D	D	1,748	48.3	5,259	35
York	445	8,980	897.0	307.6	283	2,070	188.3	61.7	16,343	640.1	834,503	3,033
SOUTH DAKOTA	2,298	63,494	6,211.7	2,558.4	1,805	8,371	939.5	214.1	64,006	3,046.1	894,334	5,407
Aurora	10	D	D	D	6	D	D	D	236	8.8	1,763	11
Beadle	50	1,409	87.8	40.4	51	175	16.5	4.2	1,054	48.4	10,274	107
Bennett	5	156	9.1	5.1	2	D	D	D	162	5.3	120	1
Bon Homme	21	367	22.0	9.1	14	D	D	D	466	18.9	2,297	13
Brookings	75	1,396	99.0	43.4	66	354	64.9	9.1	2,050	95.8	32,863	182
Brown	112	2,867	240.5	116.1	79	D	D	D	2,881	141.8	11,103	148
Brule	24	457	24.7	10.8	17	69	8.8	1.9	474	20.7	2,030	16
Buffalo	3	D	D	D	1	D	D	D	31	0.4	0	0
Butte	31	282	18.8	8.1	22	D	D	D	898	36.8	8,609	47
Campbell	4	25	0.8	0.5	2	D	D	D	136	5.7	0	0
Charles Mix	22	524	31.9	14.5	26	D	D	D	683	25.8	5,913	28
Clark	10	140	6.1	2.4	11	D	D	D	271	11.3	3,736	11
Clay	30	721	50.5	17.8	24	113	12.1	2.5	887	39.1	8,879	40
Codington	89	1,691	191.5	65.1	79	327	31.2	7.8	2,136	86.5	19,162	129
Corson	6	19	1.0	0.6	NA	NA	NA	NA	144	5.8	0	0
Custer	20	D	D	D	16	78	6.6	2.1	902	41.6	15,011	66
Davison	79	D	D	D	52	D	D	D	1,449	66.4	11,053	58
Day	19	291	18.1	6.3	14	D	D	D	488	17.6	4,076	22
Deuel	5	161	10.6	4.2	5	D	D	D	376	15.7	585	2
Dewey	9	149	18.7	7.2	6	D	D	D	235	10.5	0	0
Douglas	7	265	13.6	6.7	11	28	4.3	0.7	255	11.7	1,626	10
Edmunds	11	197	8.8	3.8	6	D	D	D	374	21.7	1,885	8
Fall River	22	D	D	D	16	67	4.5	1.1	602	22.8	1,109	10
Faulk	4	D	D	D	5	D	D	D	203	9.9	2,335	9
Grant	24	415	30.1	11.4	18	72	7.3	1.5	645	25.5	5,174	25
Gregory	15	317	18.1	7.4	12	D	D	D	475	18.2	1,362	7
Haakon	7	D	D	D	4	17	1.6	0.5	230	11.5	0	0
Hamlin	12	198	6.5	2.9	7	16	2.3	0.4	444	19.3	8,598	49
Hand	8	229	13.5	6.8	11	19	1.5	0.2	329	15.9	1,650	6
Hanson	2	D	D	D	1	D	D	D	308	11.4	1,714	12
Harding	4	D	D	D	1	D	D	D	169	5.7	350	3
Hughes	58	1,269	110.1	45.7	76	347	50.8	11.6	1,451	62.6	7,396	40
Hutchinson	17	651	40.2	18.8	14	D	D	D	578	20.9	1,328	5
Hyde	3	D	D	D	2	D	D	D	113	5.8	0	0
Jackson	1	D	D	D	5	10	0.8	0.1	186	6.0	212	1
Jerauld	4	131	9.6	3.8	7	16	1.4	0.3	154	6.7	296	1
Jones	2	D	D	D	2	D	D	D	116	4.5	370	9
Kingsbury	14	240	13.2	5.3	13	33	3.0	0.6	494	21.8	4,624	26
Lake	33	694	40.7	18.5	20	D	D	D	1,098	54.9	9,464	38
Lawrence	87	1,401	126.3	54.9	58	233	21.0	5.3	2,407	111.4	67,928	193
Lincoln	132	3,237	232.2	96.7	80	D	D	D	4,607	259.1	43,967	285
Lyman	2	D	D	D	3	D	D	D	253	10.6	2,062	11
McCook	17	251	13.5	5.2	13	D	D	D	494	22.7	4,699	21
McPherson	7	53	3.2	1.1	6	D	D	D	188	9.1	230	1
Marshall	13	175	10.7	4.0	7	27	3.7	0.8	352	16.4	4,424	18
Meade	45	D	D	D	50	151	20.8	4.1	2,160	90.8	27,129	153
Mellette	2	D	D	D	1	D	D	D	99	3.8	254	2
Miner	9	156	7.2	3.3	4	12	1.3	0.4	196	8.3	400	3
Minnehaha	462	20,372	2,348.8	970.6	375	2,326	256.5	67.7	13,120	714.0	375,710	2,586
Moody	15	203	13.9	6.0	6	D	D	D	438	19.0	4,047	18
Oglala Lakota	13	285	30.3	10.4	3	11	0.8	0.2	323	6.4	NA	NA
Pennington	343	D	D	D	268	1,572	193.3	39.2	7,947	375.2	92,684	560
Perkins	16	142	7.8	3.4	16	38	3.3	0.9	275	11.0	0	0
Potter	13	70	6.4	2.8	8	D	D	D	246	13.8	0	0
Roberts	23	532	32.7	14.8	16	42	3.2	0.8	613	21.8	7,310	34
Sanborn	4	D	D	D	4	D	D	D	184	7.4	1,475	7
Spink	17	359	18.3	8.3	12	D	D	D	514	25.1	3,023	14
Stanley	3	D	D	D	11	D	D	D	301	14.5	4,544	16
Sully	3	D	D	D	2	D	D	D	180	7.9	1,267	6
Todd	7	283	37.6	16.2	3	7	0.4	0.1	202	3.5	0	0

Table B. States and Counties — Land Area and Population

State / county code	CBSA code[1]	County code[2]	STATE County	Land area[3] (sq. mi)	Total persons 2017	Rank	Per square mile	White	Black	American Indian, Alaska Native	Asian and Pacific Islander	Percent Hispanic or Latino[4]	Under 5 years	5 to 17 years	18 to 24 years	25 to 34 years	35 to 44 years	45 to 54 years
				1	2	3	4	5	6	7	8	9	10	11	12	13	14	15
			TENNESSEE— Cont'd															
47,117	30,280	6	Marshall	375.5	32,931	1,359	87.7	87.3	7.6	0.9	0.9	5.1	6.1	17.3	7.7	12.7	12.6	14.0
47,119	34,980	1	Maury	613.1	92,163	636	150.3	81.1	12.9	0.8	1.3	5.8	6.7	16.9	7.4	13.9	13.0	12.7
47,121		8	Meigs	195.1	12,068	2,286	61.9	95.5	1.9	1.3	0.6	2.0	5.6	15.3	7.0	10.4	12.0	14.5
47,123		6	Monroe	635.7	46,240	1,045	72.7	92.4	2.6	1.4	0.7	4.6	5.5	16.1	7.6	11.2	11.0	13.7
47,125	17,300	2	Montgomery	539.2	200,182	333	371.3	66.9	21.8	1.3	4.2	10.1	8.4	18.5	11.2	19.2	13.3	11.0
47,127	46,100	9	Moore	129.2	6,384	2,723	49.4	94.4	3.1	0.9	1.0	2.0	4.2	15.1	7.8	10.4	11.9	13.6
47,129	28,940	2	Morgan	522.2	21,636	1,747	41.4	94.3	4.1	1.2	0.4	1.3	4.9	14.6	8.2	13.0	13.2	15.0
47,131	46,460	7	Obion	544.9	30,385	1,423	55.8	84.4	11.6	0.6	0.6	4.3	5.7	16.2	7.6	11.4	11.7	13.1
47,133	18,260	7	Overton	433.5	22,012	1,724	50.8	97.3	1.0	0.9	0.5	1.4	5.2	16.4	7.5	11.0	12.0	13.7
47,135		8	Perry	414.7	7,975	2,594	19.2	93.8	3.5	1.6	0.7	2.6	6.3	15.5	8.1	11.1	10.7	12.6
47,137		9	Pickett	163.0	5,073	2,826	31.1	97.4	0.5	0.9	0.2	2.0	4.7	13.4	6.3	8.5	10.5	13.7
47,139	17,420	3	Polk	434.6	16,757	1,993	38.6	96.4	1.2	1.4	0.4	2.1	5.0	14.7	7.0	10.8	11.7	15.3
47,141	18,260	4	Putnam	401.1	77,674	714	193.7	89.7	2.9	0.8	1.7	6.4	5.9	15.4	14.5	13.0	11.1	11.9
47,143	19,420	6	Rhea	315.4	32,691	1,365	103.6	91.9	2.9	1.0	0.7	5.0	5.9	16.8	9.0	11.6	11.4	13.4
47,145	28,940	2	Roane	360.7	53,036	947	147.0	94.4	3.3	1.2	0.9	1.9	4.5	14.4	7.0	10.2	10.8	14.2
47,147	34,980	1	Robertson	476.3	70,177	766	147.3	84.8	8.1	0.8	0.9	7.0	6.3	18.0	7.6	12.7	13.0	14.1
47,149	34,980	1	Rutherford	619.4	317,157	218	512.0	73.0	16.4	0.8	4.2	8.0	6.7	18.1	12.4	14.8	14.1	13.1
47,151		6	Scott	532.3	21,989	1,725	41.3	98.3	0.5	0.9	0.4	0.9	6.4	18.0	7.6	12.1	12.9	13.7
47,153	16,860	2	Sequatchie	265.9	14,736	2,113	55.4	94.8	1.1	1.1	0.7	3.6	4.9	16.2	7.4	10.8	12.1	13.8
47,155	42,940	4	Sevier	592.5	97,638	609	164.8	91.1	1.6	0.9	1.6	6.0	5.5	15.3	7.7	12.1	11.5	14.2
47,157	32,820	1	Shelby	763.6	936,961	56	1,227.0	37.0	54.4	0.6	3.2	6.4	7.0	18.0	9.4	14.7	12.5	12.7
47,159	34,980	1	Smith	314.3	19,636	1,843	62.5	94.4	2.9	1.0	0.5	2.7	6.0	17.0	7.9	11.9	12.0	14.4
47,161		8	Stewart	459.3	13,355	2,205	29.1	93.7	2.4	1.5	1.4	2.8	5.2	15.5	7.5	10.5	11.7	14.6
47,163	28,700	2	Sullivan	413.4	157,158	418	380.2	94.8	2.9	0.8	1.0	1.9	5.0	14.5	7.5	11.4	11.4	14.2
47,165	34,980	1	Sumner	529.4	183,545	355	346.7	85.9	8.3	0.7	1.9	4.9	6.1	17.7	7.7	12.4	13.2	14.3
47,167	32,820	1	Tipton	458.4	61,366	853	133.9	77.5	19.3	1.0	1.3	2.8	6.1	18.7	8.5	12.7	12.6	14.0
47,169	34,980	1	Trousdale	114.3	10,083	2,423	88.2	85.8	11.8	0.8	0.8	2.6	5.3	13.8	10.3	19.5	12.4	13.3
47,171	27,740	3	Unicoi	186.1	17,759	1,929	95.4	94.2	0.8	0.8	0.4	4.8	4.4	14.4	6.9	10.5	11.4	14.1
47,173	28,940	2	Union	223.6	19,442	1,853	86.9	97.5	0.6	1.1	0.4	1.6	5.6	16.4	7.2	11.8	11.8	14.1
47,175		9	Van Buren	273.4	5,742	2,778	21.0	97.1	1.3	1.0	0.3	1.5	5.5	13.9	6.7	9.6	11.6	13.1
47,177	32,660	6	Warren	432.7	40,651	1,164	93.9	86.6	4.0	0.8	0.9	9.1	6.1	17.6	7.5	11.9	12.8	13.1
47,179	27,740	3	Washington	326.5	127,806	496	391.4	90.4	5.2	0.8	2.0	3.5	5.1	14.1	12.2	12.5	11.7	13.1
47,181		8	Wayne	734.1	16,583	2,003	22.6	90.9	6.7	0.8	0.5	2.1	4.2	13.1	7.9	14.2	13.0	14.7
47,183	32,280	7	Weakley	580.4	33,337	1,345	57.4	88.4	8.4	0.7	1.5	2.5	5.2	14.3	15.9	11.1	10.2	12.4
47,185		7	White	376.7	26,753	1,535	71.0	94.8	2.5	1.0	0.7	2.6	5.8	16.1	7.1	12.1	11.5	13.6
47,187	34,980	1	Williamson	582.6	226,257	297	388.4	86.2	4.9	0.5	5.2	4.8	6.0	21.5	7.6	9.4	14.4	15.6
47,189	34,980	1	Wilson	571.1	136,442	466	238.9	86.8	7.8	0.9	2.1	4.2	6.0	17.9	7.4	11.9	13.6	14.5
48,000		0	TEXAS	261,252.9	28,304,596	X	108.3	43.3	12.6	0.7	5.5	39.4	7.2	18.8	9.8	14.7	13.4	12.5
48,001	37,300	7	Anderson	1,062.6	57,741	892	54.3	60.3	21.5	0.8	1.0	17.8	5.3	14.3	7.9	16.0	15.8	14.5
48,003	11,380	6	Andrews	1,500.7	17,722	1,934	11.8	41.1	1.9	1.0	0.8	56.2	8.9	22.0	9.0	14.9	12.9	11.3
48,005	31,260	5	Angelina	797.8	87,805	659	110.1	61.6	15.4	0.6	1.3	22.2	7.0	18.8	8.7	12.9	11.9	12.6
48,007	18,580	2	Aransas	252.0	25,572	1,582	101.5	68.4	1.8	1.4	2.1	27.7	5.1	13.6	6.9	10.1	9.4	11.8
48,009	48,660	3	Archer	903.1	8,809	2,519	9.8	89.2	1.4	1.4	0.7	8.7	5.4	16.3	7.7	10.7	10.7	13.9
48,011	11,100	2	Armstrong	909.1	1,879	3,061	2.1	90.3	1.2	1.4	0.4	7.5	5.5	16.9	6.2	9.7	11.5	10.7
48,013	41,700	1	Atascosa	1,219.5	48,981	1,004	40.2	34.0	0.9	0.7	0.6	64.5	7.4	20.0	9.0	12.9	12.5	12.1
48,015	26,420	1	Austin	646.5	29,786	1,438	46.1	63.0	9.4	0.7	0.9	27.1	6.2	17.9	8.1	10.9	11.2	12.5
48,017		7	Bailey	827.0	7,077	2,662	8.6	33.6	1.4	0.7	0.7	64.3	8.2	23.3	9.2	11.6	12.0	10.1
48,019	41,700	1	Bandera	791.0	22,351	1,710	28.3	79.0	1.2	1.4	0.9	18.8	4.1	12.7	6.2	8.7	9.2	13.3
48,021	12,420	1	Bastrop	888.2	84,761	678	95.4	54.0	7.5	1.0	1.2	37.8	6.8	18.8	8.3	11.9	12.2	13.1
48,023		8	Baylor	867.5	3,581	2,934	4.1	83.5	3.2	0.9	0.8	13.2	6.1	16.1	6.2	10.6	10.4	12.0
48,025	13,300	6	Bee	880.2	32,563	1,367	37.0	31.8	8.5	0.5	0.8	59.1	6.1	15.4	11.2	17.5	14.7	12.7
48,027	28,660	2	Bell	1,050.9	347,833	200	331.0	48.5	24.1	1.1	5.3	24.8	8.7	19.2	11.4	16.7	12.9	10.8
48,029	41,700	1	Bexar	1,239.9	1,958,578	16	1,579.6	29.0	8.0	0.6	3.7	60.3	7.2	18.6	10.4	15.9	13.4	12.1
48,031		8	Blanco	709.3	11,626	2,319	16.4	77.7	1.4	1.1	1.2	19.7	4.3	14.5	6.8	8.7	10.4	13.2
48,033		8	Borden	897.4	673	3,131	0.7	78.0	1.6	1.2	0.6	19.5	5.9	15.8	6.8	7.7	11.4	14.9
48,035		6	Bosque	983.0	18,326	1,904	18.6	78.6	2.2	0.9	0.7	18.7	5.6	15.9	7.0	9.5	10.3	12.1
48,037	45,500	3	Bowie	885.0	94,012	625	106.2	65.5	25.8	1.3	1.8	7.8	6.4	17.2	8.6	13.7	12.8	12.5
48,039	26,420	1	Brazoria	1,362.3	362,457	192	266.1	48.7	14.2	0.7	7.3	30.6	7.1	19.6	8.1	14.1	14.5	13.4
48,041	17,780	3	Brazos	585.5	222,830	302	380.6	57.2	11.0	0.6	7.0	25.8	6.2	14.5	26.1	16.1	10.9	9.1
48,043		7	Brewster	6,183.8	9,337	2,479	1.5	51.5	1.6	1.4	1.5	45.4	5.6	13.8	7.1	13.8	12.2	11.4
48,045		9	Briscoe	900.0	1,528	3,077	1.7	70.6	3.9	1.1	0.9	25.4	4.7	14.9	7.0	10.7	11.8	11.8
48,047		7	Brooks	943.4	7,235	2,647	7.7	7.2	0.6	0.2	2.4	89.8	8.6	20.0	9.1	12.5	11.0	9.8
48,049	15,220	5	Brown	944.4	38,053	1,223	40.3	72.9	4.1	1.1	1.0	22.4	5.5	16.8	8.9	12.0	11.3	12.3
48,051	17,780	3	Burleson	659.0	18,011	1,918	27.3	66.3	13.0	0.8	0.7	20.6	6.3	16.1	7.2	10.9	10.4	13.2
48,053		6	Burnet	994.3	46,804	1,035	47.1	74.5	2.1	1.1	0.9	22.5	5.7	15.9	7.5	10.8	10.8	12.0

1. CBSA = Core Based Statistical Area. See Appendix A for explanation. See Appendix B for list of metropolitan areas with component counties. 2. County type code from the Economic Research Service of USDA-Rural-Urban Continuum Codes. See Appendix A for definition. 3. Dry land or land partially or temporarily covered by water. 4. May be of any race.

Table B. States and Counties — Population and Households

STATE County	55 to 64 years	65 to 74 years	75 years and over	Percent female	2000	2010	2000-2010	2010-2017	Births	Deaths	Net Migration	Number	Persons per house-hold	Family house-holds	Female family house-holder[1]	One person
	16	17	18	19	20	21	22	23	24	25	26	27	28	29	30	31
TENNESSEE— Cont'd																
Marshall	13.6	9.9	6.0	50.8	26,767	30,606	14.3	7.6	2,679	2,269	1,931	12,044	2.57	70.2	13.4	25.2
Maury	14.0	9.5	6.0	51.8	69,498	80,930	16.4	13.9	8,153	6,061	9,066	32,889	2.57	69.6	13.9	25.4
Meigs	14.5	13.5	7.2	50.3	11,086	11,768	6.2	2.5	870	1,096	529	4,675	2.50	69.3	12.3	27.1
Monroe	14.2	12.9	7.8	50.3	38,961	44,505	14.2	3.9	3,586	3,739	1,908	17,311	2.60	73.4	10.5	24.4
Montgomery	9.4	5.6	3.5	50.1	134,768	172,362	27.9	16.1	24,350	8,350	11,521	67,090	2.78	72.3	14.2	21.6
Moore	15.8	11.8	9.3	50.1	5,740	6,345	10.5	0.6	366	460	136	2,560	2.43	72.4	8.8	23.9
Morgan	13.6	10.6	6.8	45.3	19,757	21,986	11.3	-1.6	1,470	1,641	-178	7,221	2.61	74.0	11.5	21.3
Obion	14.2	11.7	8.4	51.6	32,450	31,807	-2.0	-4.5	2,550	2,772	-1,193	12,719	2.39	69.5	15.2	25.0
Overton	14.1	12.2	8.0	50.7	20,118	22,084	9.8	-0.3	1,700	2,093	335	8,881	2.45	68.9	10.4	28.3
Perry	14.6	12.4	8.7	49.5	7,631	7,928	3.9	0.6	713	794	131	3,209	2.41	69.8	10.1	26.4
Pickett	15.5	16.1	11.2	50.1	4,945	5,077	2.7	-0.1	306	487	175	2,128	2.35	77.2	11.6	21.4
Polk	14.6	12.4	8.4	50.5	16,050	16,826	4.8	-0.4	1,136	1,569	367	6,766	2.43	72.0	11.1	24.3
Putnam	11.8	9.6	6.8	50.2	62,315	72,347	16.1	7.4	6,470	5,582	4,470	30,100	2.38	62.9	12.1	29.0
Rhea	13.5	11.2	7.3	50.5	28,400	31,802	12.0	2.8	2,780	2,729	851	12,408	2.54	68.3	13.9	27.1
Roane	16.4	13.1	9.4	51.2	51,910	54,193	4.4	-2.1	3,438	5,054	500	21,532	2.43	65.2	9.4	30.4
Robertson	13.9	8.9	5.5	50.7	54,433	66,349	21.9	5.8	6,428	4,607	2,039	24,730	2.71	75.2	13.4	20.8
Rutherford	10.6	6.4	3.7	50.7	182,023	262,592	44.3	20.8	28,067	12,420	38,492	103,562	2.76	69.4	12.6	22.5
Scott	12.8	10.0	6.5	50.7	21,127	22,232	5.2	-1.1	1,966	1,955	-244	8,368	2.59	65.7	11.8	29.2
Sequatchie	14.9	12.4	7.5	50.6	11,370	14,121	24.2	4.4	1,105	1,130	642	5,549	2.61	75.6	11.8	21.5
Sevier	14.5	12.0	7.2	51.0	71,170	89,725	26.1	8.8	7,596	7,006	7,284	36,982	2.53	70.1	11.9	24.6
Shelby	12.5	8.1	5.1	52.4	897,472	927,683	3.4	1.0	98,945	56,887	-32,751	349,956	2.63	63.4	20.4	30.9
Smith	14.3	10.5	6.1	50.3	17,712	19,149	8.1	2.5	1,641	1,540	389	7,555	2.51	70.9	11.0	26.2
Stewart	15.1	12.1	7.8	50.0	12,370	13,313	7.6	0.3	956	1,146	233	5,187	2.53	69.8	10.0	27.6
Sullivan	14.5	12.2	9.3	51.4	153,048	156,806	2.5	0.2	11,243	14,481	3,731	65,896	2.34	65.7	11.0	30.1
Sumner	13.1	9.4	6.0	51.1	130,449	160,617	23.1	14.3	14,656	10,276	18,415	63,240	2.71	73.0	12.0	23.2
Tipton	13.3	8.7	5.4	50.7	51,271	61,006	19.0	0.6	5,350	4,046	-937	21,355	2.85	76.3	16.6	19.9
Trousdale	11.6	8.5	5.2	43.5	7,259	7,864	8.3	28.2	697	652	2,166	2,958	2.65	68.0	11.6	26.4
Unicoi	15.5	12.8	10.1	50.8	17,667	18,311	3.6	-3.0	1,138	1,906	231	7,628	2.28	63.3	8.9	32.4
Union	15.2	11.2	6.8	50.6	17,808	19,109	7.3	1.7	1,516	1,518	342	7,271	2.60	73.3	12.2	22.2
Van Buren	16.5	14.9	8.3	49.6	5,508	5,558	0.9	3.3	443	461	198	2,141	2.59	74.0	11.1	22.7
Warren	13.4	10.1	7.2	50.7	38,276	39,824	4.0	2.1	3,435	3,454	879	15,584	2.53	66.6	12.5	29.6
Washington	13.4	10.5	7.4	51.1	107,198	123,065	14.8	3.9	9,678	9,697	4,782	52,409	2.31	63.3	12.1	29.9
Wayne	13.8	11.1	7.9	44.9	16,842	17,027	1.1	-2.6	1,025	1,447	-10	6,020	2.46	71.2	11.0	26.7
Weakley	12.6	10.4	7.9	51.1	34,895	35,015	0.3	-4.8	2,557	2,681	-1,561	13,459	2.33	66.4	10.0	28.2
White	13.8	11.8	8.3	51.1	23,102	25,836	11.8	3.5	2,166	2,613	1,369	9,677	2.68	70.6	9.6	26.7
Williamson	12.7	8.0	4.8	51.1	126,638	183,252	44.7	23.5	15,426	7,685	35,034	71,043	2.89	80.3	7.6	16.5
Wilson	13.3	9.8	5.6	50.9	88,809	114,057	28.4	19.6	10,321	7,141	18,996	45,431	2.73	74.6	11.0	21.5
TEXAS	11.3	7.4	4.9	50.3	20,851,820	25,146,100	20.6	12.6	2,842,169	1,312,326	1,616,768	9,289,554	2.84	69.4	14.2	25.1
Anderson	11.7	8.6	5.9	39.1	55,109	58,458	6.1	-1.2	4,316	4,628	-369	16,572	2.68	69.8	10.6	27.3
Andrews	10.6	5.9	4.6	49.0	13,004	14,786	13.7	19.9	2,221	837	1,508	5,392	3.17	77.4	9.3	19.0
Angelina	12.3	9.0	6.8	51.3	80,130	86,771	8.3	1.2	8,759	6,310	-1,353	30,495	2.77	72.7	16.3	24.4
Aransas	15.7	15.8	11.5	50.5	22,497	23,158	2.9	10.4	1,864	2,479	2,982	9,552	2.54	67.1	5.8	28.3
Archer	15.4	10.8	9.1	50.4	8,854	9,055	2.3	-2.7	550	560	-246	3,331	2.60	73.6	4.9	22.8
Armstrong	16.6	13.1	9.8	51.3	2,148	1,901	-11.5	-1.2	145	200	34	702	2.63	73.4	5.8	22.2
Atascosa	11.8	8.5	5.9	50.2	38,628	44,911	16.3	9.1	4,826	2,871	2,110	15,343	3.08	74.7	15.2	21.6
Austin	14.5	11.2	7.5	50.4	23,590	28,411	20.4	4.8	2,489	1,958	857	11,222	2.57	73.6	11.3	23.5
Bailey	11.3	7.4	6.7	49.8	6,594	7,165	8.7	-1.2	892	424	-567	2,317	3.01	76.3	16.9	21.8
Bandera	19.3	16.5	10.0	50.5	17,645	20,485	16.1	9.1	1,193	1,474	2,143	8,256	2.48	66.5	7.9	28.9
Bastrop	14.0	9.6	5.2	49.2	57,733	74,159	28.5	14.3	7,066	4,629	8,092	25,822	2.95	72.3	11.3	23.2
Baylor	13.9	12.3	12.3	50.9	4,093	3,726	-9.0	-3.9	286	437	4	1,703	2.09	58.6	6.6	38.7
Bee	10.3	7.1	5.0	39.3	32,359	31,861	-1.5	2.2	2,772	1,781	-294	8,698	2.88	71.2	17.5	24.2
Bell	9.7	6.4	4.2	50.2	237,974	310,158	30.3	12.1	45,892	14,759	6,340	113,027	2.84	71.4	14.8	24.5
Bexar	10.6	7.1	4.8	50.6	1,392,931	1,714,774	23.1	14.2	196,888	90,333	136,358	623,321	2.93	67.6	16.5	26.6
Blanco	18.1	15.0	8.9	50.2	8,418	10,499	24.7	10.7	690	841	1,273	4,174	2.59	72.4	8.3	25.0
Borden	14.0	11.3	12.2	48.0	729	641	-12.1	5.0	49	34	14	251	2.78	75.3	6.8	21.5
Bosque	15.2	13.7	10.6	50.5	17,204	18,217	5.9	0.6	1,364	1,775	523	7,098	2.48	70.9	8.5	25.5
Bowie	12.5	9.4	6.9	49.6	89,306	92,565	3.6	1.6	8,892	7,183	-200	33,586	2.62	68.1	16.9	27.7
Brazoria	11.7	7.1	4.4	49.4	241,767	313,127	29.5	15.8	34,496	15,834	30,518	114,290	2.87	73.9	10.9	22.2
Brazos	8.3	5.2	3.7	49.4	152,415	194,861	27.8	14.4	19,875	6,907	14,912	75,797	2.57	55.3	10.9	27.1
Brewster	14.4	13.2	8.6	49.3	8,866	9,232	4.1	1.1	786	548	-142	4,014	2.26	56.7	7.2	36.9
Briscoe	13.6	13.7	11.6	50.1	1,790	1,637	-8.5	-6.7	93	128	-75	698	2.40	71.5	10.5	25.2
Brooks	11.5	9.4	8.1	49.1	7,976	7,223	-9.4	0.2	878	577	-297	2,031	3.34	72.5	21.8	26.0
Brown	13.4	11.1	8.6	50.6	37,674	38,106	1.1	-0.1	3,056	3,541	458	13,361	2.70	67.1	8.3	28.6
Burleson	15.7	11.5	8.7	50.5	16,470	17,187	4.4	4.8	1,459	1,473	842	6,385	2.70	71.0	12.0	26.4
Burnet	15.5	12.9	8.9	51.1	34,147	42,707	25.1	9.6	3,529	3,377	3,931	16,299	2.71	72.4	10.6	24.6

1. No spouse present.

Table B. States and Counties — Population, Vital Statistics, Health, and Crime

STATE County	Persons in group quarters, 2017	Daytime Population, 2012-2016 Number	Employment/ residence ratio	Births, 2017 Total	Births Rate[1]	Deaths, 2017 Number	Deaths Rate[1]	Persons under 65 with no health insurance, 2016 Number	Percent	Medicare, 2017 Total beneficiaries	Enrolled in Original Medicare	Enrolled in Medicare Advantage	Serious crimes known to police[2], 2016 Total Number	Rate[3]
	32	33	34	35	36	37	38	39	40	41	42	43	44	45
TENNESSEE— Cont'd														
Marshall	359	28,153	0.76	377	11.4	324	9.8	3,028	11.4	6,277	4,074	2,204	507	1,598
Maury	1,009	80,662	0.87	1,181	12.8	939	10.2	7,117	9.4	19,828	13,640	6,188	2,128	2,388
Meigs	128	9,898	0.51	133	11.0	155	12.8	1,123	11.9	3,074	1,924	1,149	373	3,151
Monroe	549	43,984	0.91	474	10.3	539	11.7	4,468	12.4	11,596	6,596	4,999	1,946	4,231
Montgomery	3,712	166,472	0.73	3,455	17.3	1,255	6.3	15,343	8.8	23,244	17,638	5,605	5,615	2,838
Moore	104	5,382	0.67	48	7.5	45	7.0	454	9.1	800	635	165	74	1,172
Morgan	2,374	18,173	0.48	215	9.9	231	10.7	1,839	11.7	3,662	1,807	1,855	398	1,860
Obion	461	30,388	0.96	371	12.2	378	12.4	2,681	11.1	8,379	5,870	2,509	1,119	3,680
Overton	286	19,324	0.68	225	10.2	309	14.0	2,074	12.0	4,988	3,955	1,033	334	1,509
Perry	123	7,734	0.94	94	11.8	104	13.0	716	11.7	2,029	1,365	664	163	2,056
Pickett	74	4,691	0.79	43	8.5	57	11.2	396	10.6	1,202	967	235	68	1,318
Polk	244	13,693	0.53	164	9.8	214	12.8	1,428	10.8	4,702	3,225	1,476	472	2,816
Putnam	2,524	81,051	1.21	906	11.7	771	9.9	7,444	12.2	19,182	14,613	4,568	2,541	3,391
Rhea	829	34,756	1.17	380	11.6	379	11.6	3,210	12.5	8,075	5,517	2,558	701	2,147
Roane	646	47,909	0.75	468	8.8	700	13.2	4,027	9.9	14,110	7,934	6,176	1,403	2,674
Robertson	703	58,157	0.69	881	12.6	655	9.3	6,192	10.5	12,572	7,210	5,362	1,253	1,815
Rutherford	4,962	277,398	0.91	4,173	13.2	1,922	6.1	24,067	8.8	38,492	23,641	14,852	9,081	2,967
Scott	264	20,703	0.83	268	12.2	268	12.2	2,017	11.2	4,717	2,721	1,997	366	1,672
Sequatchie	188	12,187	0.56	154	10.5	167	11.3	1,224	10.4	3,197	2,095	1,102	411	2,749
Sevier	981	95,252	1.02	1,066	10.9	1,008	10.3	11,903	15.4	22,640	12,547	10,092	3,195	3,289
Shelby	18,454	1,012,479	1.18	13,196	14.1	8,200	8.8	92,483	11.6	147,908	104,562	43,346	55,631	5,919
Smith	159	16,806	0.71	231	11.8	207	10.5	1,668	10.3	3,798	2,575	1,223	300	1,552
Stewart	92	11,874	0.71	133	10.0	162	12.1	1,178	11.2	3,146	2,449	697	241	1,820
Sullivan	2,632	166,200	1.15	1,498	9.5	1,900	12.1	12,070	9.9	42,381	17,938	24,443	5,325	3,397
Sumner	1,249	148,045	0.70	2,128	11.6	1,604	8.7	13,249	8.7	31,216	17,539	13,678	2,768	1,601
Tipton	962	47,268	0.47	717	11.7	607	9.9	5,161	9.9	10,427	7,889	2,538	1,834	2,958
Trousdale	1,796	6,851	0.68	107	10.6	84	8.3	846	12.2	1,504	943	561	240	2,971
Unicoi	405	17,521	0.94	155	8.7	266	15.0	1,582	11.7	5,072	2,611	2,462	315	1,772
Union	152	15,322	0.44	218	11.2	200	10.3	1,956	12.5	3,581	1,549	2,032	507	2,652
Van Buren	94	4,830	0.62	70	12.2	55	9.6	511	11.8	1,085	806	279	85	1,491
Warren	580	39,583	0.97	454	11.2	473	11.6	4,490	13.6	9,976	7,097	2,879	1,104	2,723
Washington	4,230	133,361	1.13	1,324	10.4	1,315	10.3	9,940	9.8	30,838	16,338	14,500	3,765	2,967
Wayne	2,156	15,618	0.79	131	7.9	200	12.1	1,404	12.2	3,295	2,344	951	150	898
Weakley	1,615	31,773	0.84	343	10.3	357	10.7	2,501	9.6	6,523	5,009	1,514	646	1,914
White	382	24,119	0.76	295	11.0	351	13.1	2,325	11.1	7,132	5,074	2,058	661	2,480
Williamson	1,153	228,291	1.23	2,337	10.3	1,202	5.3	11,006	5.7	30,565	19,771	10,794	2,683	1,233
Wilson	1,359	110,792	0.75	1,549	11.4	1,086	8.0	8,508	7.6	22,200	13,708	8,493	2,568	1,946
TEXAS	606,511	26,954,688	1.00	404,311	14.3	194,621	6.9	4,444,791	18.6	3,886,487	2,495,056	1,391,431	889,989	3,194
Anderson	13,842	58,673	1.05	620	10.7	663	11.5	6,394	17.6	10,659	7,602	3,057	1,145	2,001
Andrews	80	17,417	1.03	304	17.2	95	5.4	2,897	18.2	2,011	1,521	490	485	2,582
Angelina	2,903	88,989	1.04	1,189	13.5	935	10.6	14,196	19.8	17,917	13,078	4,839	2,445	2,770
Aransas	459	22,830	0.80	266	10.4	357	14.0	3,902	21.3	6,509	4,050	2,459	1,120	4,353
Archer	55	6,357	0.44	83	9.4	75	8.5	1,263	17.9	1,250	1,043	206	NA	NA
Armstrong	53	1,520	0.57	18	9.6	21	11.2	229	15.6	427	337	91	13	666
Atascosa	357	45,371	0.88	684	14.0	412	8.4	7,590	18.3	7,443	4,170	3,273	1,401	2,858
Austin	209	26,237	0.78	351	11.8	277	9.3	4,429	18.3	6,304	4,642	1,662	466	1,568
Bailey	107	6,776	0.89	133	18.8	46	6.5	1,596	26.4	1,086	912	174	129	1,791
Bandera	317	17,277	0.56	171	7.7	204	9.1	2,865	18.0	5,785	4,195	1,590	284	1,330
Bastrop	2,354	64,893	0.58	1,134	13.4	697	8.2	14,519	21.1	14,161	9,948	4,213	2,101	2,575
Baylor	69	3,644	1.00	43	12.0	53	14.8	461	16.8	1,016	853	163	68	1,895
Bee	7,650	32,374	0.97	384	11.8	216	6.6	3,916	18.2	4,379	2,638	1,741	576	1,747
Bell	9,406	343,567	1.09	6,314	18.2	2,183	6.3	40,741	13.7	46,674	31,481	15,193	10,265	3,043
Bexar	42,779	1,901,771	1.05	28,376	14.5	13,647	7.0	276,390	16.6	276,334	151,983	124,351	101,848	5,280
Blanco	101	9,864	0.77	111	9.5	126	10.8	1,935	22.4	3,022	2,315	707	95	858
Borden	0	619	0.72	8	11.9	3	4.5	69	13.6	54	D	D	11	1,700
Bosque	323	15,316	0.63	200	10.9	239	13.0	3,068	22.7	4,807	3,135	1,673	152	1,000
Bowie	6,333	99,954	1.18	1,244	13.2	981	10.4	11,463	15.7	19,257	14,950	4,307	3,193	3,424
Brazoria	10,182	292,421	0.70	4,982	13.7	2,459	6.8	45,562	15.0	47,802	29,911	17,891	6,370	1,810
Brazos	14,192	215,071	1.05	2,910	13.1	1,039	4.7	30,850	16.5	22,198	17,479	4,719	6,373	2,917
Brewster	44	9,181	1.00	99	10.6	76	8.1	1,276	17.7	2,083	1,536	547	131	1,441
Briscoe	0	1,472	0.73	12	7.9	9	5.9	345	31.1	408	322	87	13	880
Brooks	58	7,394	1.07	111	15.3	72	10.0	1,045	18.0	1,537	975	562	166	2,301
Brown	1,789	38,411	1.03	417	11.0	466	12.2	5,028	17.1	8,859	6,961	1,898	959	2,541
Burleson	180	14,565	0.60	218	12.1	216	12.0	2,713	19.1	3,973	2,856	1,117	189	1,176
Burnet	1,249	41,656	0.85	542	11.6	484	10.3	6,937	19.8	13,604	9,783	3,821	851	1,903

1. Per 1,000 estimated resident population.   2. Data for serious crimes have not been adjusted for underreporting; this may affect comparability between geographic areas and over time.
3. Per 100,000 population estimated by the FBI.

Table B. States and Counties — Crime, Education, Money Income, and Poverty

STATE County	Serious crimes known to police, 2016 (cont.)[1] Rate Violent	Property	School enrollment and attainment, 2012-2016 Enrollment[3] Total	Percent private	Attainment[4] (percent) High school graduate or less	Bachelor's degree or more	Local government expenditures,[5] 2013-2014 Total current spending (mil dol)	Current spending per student (dollars)	Money income, 2012-2016 Per capita income[6]	Median income (dollars)	Households Percent with income of less than $50,000	with income of $200,000 or more	Income and poverty, 2016 Median household income (dollars)	Percent below poverty level All persons	Children under 18 years	Children 5 to 17 years in families
	46	47	48	49	50	51	52	53	54	55	56	57	58	59	60	61
TENNESSEE— Cont'd																
Marshall	451	1,147	7,040	13.2	58.0	14.0	43.0	8,021	23,407	44,900	54.6	2.2	50,014	13.2	18.8	17.6
Maury	482	1,905	18,966	19.2	47.9	19.6	96.8	8,056	24,986	49,597	50.5	2.7	51,202	11.5	17.5	16.7
Meigs	473	2,678	2,329	8.4	65.3	8.8	15.2	8,384	19,976	35,209	66.2	1.2	40,238	18.3	27.4	25.3
Monroe	580	3,650	8,317	8.4	63.9	12.2	58.2	8,127	19,840	37,054	62.9	0.9	38,265	19.3	26.1	23.9
Montgomery	535	2,304	56,149	11.2	38.3	25.3	258.7	8,274	23,384	51,528	47.8	1.9	55,351	12.9	16.9	17.4
Moore	111	1,061	1,260	11.6	54.4	17.2	8.7	8,992	30,126	49,496	51.0	3.4	54,922	10.9	17.7	15.9
Morgan	229	1,631	3,998	9.9	68.7	7.5	26.4	8,112	18,281	39,728	60.2	1.7	38,069	22.7	28.6	27.0
Obion	490	3,190	7,175	7.9	59.0	16.6	43.8	8,427	21,650	38,933	61.9	1.7	37,437	18.6	27.6	26.3
Overton	181	1,328	4,837	7.8	66.0	13.8	25.7	7,584	19,827	35,065	63.4	1.0	35,273	18.7	25.6	23.2
Perry	290	1,766	1,535	18.0	66.1	9.8	10.4	8,971	18,611	31,274	66.9	0.5	35,140	22.1	32.6	30.9
Pickett	329	988	833	1.1	64.8	9.2	6.2	7,963	20,664	39,014	63.7	0.0	36,595	17.0	27.3	24.6
Polk	251	2,565	3,253	11.1	62.8	9.7	21.0	7,990	22,768	41,520	59.6	1.7	41,984	16.2	25.3	23.2
Putnam	420	2,970	19,720	7.5	53.0	24.4	89.7	8,055	22,555	36,350	61.5	2.4	40,479	19.2	24.0	22.4
Rhea	276	1,871	7,394	10.3	61.0	13.2	41.6	7,830	20,888	38,355	60.8	1.9	42,137	18.2	25.8	24.2
Roane	326	2,348	10,604	14.1	51.6	18.8	61.6	8,685	23,942	42,299	57.1	1.7	47,088	14.2	22.1	21.5
Robertson	372	1,443	16,418	18.3	52.6	18.1	89.6	7,847	25,534	56,331	43.9	2.5	58,487	10.3	16.0	14.9
Rutherford	585	2,382	83,871	10.8	39.4	30.2	403.1	8,286	26,373	58,032	42.2	2.9	61,232	10.3	13.1	11.5
Scott	242	1,430	5,222	5.3	69.4	8.9	34.2	7,774	21,011	30,897	68.8	1.3	34,196	22.0	28.5	27.5
Sequatchie	408	2,341	3,276	11.6	57.2	13.2	16.7	7,143	21,605	46,541	52.9	0.6	43,367	17.7	27.3	26.6
Sevier	318	2,971	18,948	11.8	53.6	17.5	130.1	8,931	22,773	42,586	57.3	2.3	45,251	15.1	24.6	22.9
Shelby	1,384	4,535	253,382	20.0	39.7	30.2	1,381.5	9,221	26,963	46,854	52.3	4.5	47,639	20.8	33.0	29.5
Smith	202	1,351	4,423	10.0	64.1	10.7	25.5	7,932	23,108	44,272	54.7	1.6	46,977	14.6	20.6	18.5
Stewart	476	1,344	3,166	7.7	55.3	13.0	17.2	7,979	21,652	41,835	57.7	0.9	44,605	16.4	25.4	23.4
Sullivan	536	2,861	32,945	14.1	49.7	21.4	196.0	8,912	24,680	40,983	58.1	2.4	43,211	16.4	24.0	23.4
Sumner	247	1,354	42,346	15.0	42.9	25.6	226.1	7,874	29,313	58,972	42.1	4.5	61,134	9.7	13.2	12.3
Tipton	610	2,348	15,735	8.5	54.0	15.6	90.0	7,763	24,969	54,650	45.6	2.6	54,748	16.1	23.3	21.0
Trousdale	508	2,464	1,905	4.4	60.1	14.8	9.5	7,513	23,319	47,667	50.9	0.6	44,971	15.3	24.6	22.1
Unicoi	225	1,547	3,664	8.6	59.9	12.6	21.0	8,174	20,958	35,390	65.5	1.0	39,755	17.3	27.0	24.4
Union	277	2,374	4,039	11.6	67.8	10.0	40.2	6,875	19,030	38,540	62.4	1.3	37,955	22.2	32.4	29.9
Van Buren	316	1,175	1,095	15.9	67.6	11.7	7.1	9,188	21,348	42,813	60.0	2.4	38,123	19.1	31.9	31.4
Warren	481	2,242	8,887	7.5	64.6	13.2	52.6	7,983	20,749	36,245	62.3	1.8	37,682	19.4	31.7	26.5
Washington	348	2,620	32,929	11.3	42.1	30.9	141.7	8,418	26,662	44,444	55.8	3.1	46,316	14.8	20.5	19.1
Wayne	317	581	3,122	9.4	64.9	10.6	21.0	8,521	17,735	34,008	65.8	1.1	37,672	20.9	28.2	25.8
Weakley	204	1,710	10,443	6.6	55.4	21.1	34.6	7,624	19,847	38,040	62.6	1.0	38,214	20.8	26.3	25.5
White	266	2,213	5,416	10.7	64.1	11.8	31.1	7,603	18,785	35,989	66.9	0.9	39,818	17.7	26.1	24.5
Williamson	158	1,075	60,245	23.3	20.1	56.6	333.1	8,732	46,494	100,140	22.7	17.6	107,942	5.2	5.2	4.5
Wilson	282	1,664	30,784	18.5	40.6	28.9	155.8	7,592	29,762	63,426	38.5	4.7	70,955	8.1	10.9	9.9
TEXAS	434	2,760	7,488,362	11.0	42.7	28.1	44,179.3	8,572	27,828	54,727	45.8	5.7	56,583	15.6	22.4	21.4
Anderson	536	1,464	12,932	5.4	56.4	11.8	76.3	9,315	18,087	42,146	56.8	2.4	43,967	20.5	24.4	24.1
Andrews	452	2,129	4,300	4.6	61.8	10.6	35.7	9,471	29,240	70,121	37.3	5.4	60,644	11.7	15.4	14.8
Angelina	283	2,487	22,405	5.1	51.6	15.7	125.3	8,421	21,486	44,185	55.9	2.2	43,658	19.0	26.7	26.2
Aransas	525	3,829	4,324	10.4	45.2	20.2	31.1	9,661	29,426	44,851	54.0	5.4	44,866	18.8	32.9	31.8
Archer	NA	NA	2,011	7.9	44.5	21.8	17.3	9,379	29,086	62,407	41.4	3.3	58,928	10.5	14.2	12.7
Armstrong	154	513	397	4.3	37.1	23.1	3.9	10,466	28,542	65,000	37.6	1.1	54,868	10.8	15.7	15.1
Atascosa	222	2,636	12,328	7.0	60.8	14.3	84.4	9,236	23,416	53,181	46.1	2.4	53,622	16.3	24.8	23.4
Austin	202	1,366	6,618	12.1	46.8	21.0	51.1	8,938	28,351	56,681	45.0	3.6	55,973	14.3	22.0	21.7
Bailey	153	1,638	1,976	4.8	60.9	10.7	13.8	9,366	17,710	40,589	67.5	1.3	40,536	16.6	26.5	24.3
Bandera	178	1,152	4,028	16.5	44.1	24.0	24.3	9,177	28,547	55,434	46.8	4.0	55,885	14.6	24.3	22.3
Bastrop	491	2,084	19,722	9.7	49.2	18.4	137.1	8,691	25,242	55,808	44.5	2.6	56,449	13.2	19.1	18.7
Baylor	223	1,672	775	3.1	44.0	26.6	6.1	10,760	30,495	34,382	65.1	5.5	36,616	17.6	28.5	26.4
Bee	321	1,425	6,774	7.6	62.5	8.9	45.7	8,732	17,504	44,005	57.7	3.9	40,753	27.0	32.9	31.2
Bell	430	2,612	97,351	10.3	37.0	23.2	555.9	8,222	24,213	51,529	47.9	3.0	51,993	12.9	19.6	19.2
Bexar	609	4,671	529,219	13.2	41.9	26.9	2,998.4	8,702	25,317	52,353	47.6	4.3	53,170	16.3	22.0	20.9
Blanco	181	677	2,379	15.2	42.0	28.8	19.0	11,289	30,982	56,573	45.9	5.0	57,634	10.7	17.6	16.2
Borden	618	1,082	93	3.2	30.0	36.5	4.5	17,677	42,236	77,569	25.9	8.4	60,306	10.6	16.7	15.9
Bosque	46	954	3,650	5.6	52.6	17.7	24.4	10,434	24,815	45,419	54.6	3.1	47,636	15.8	26.2	23.6
Bowie	475	2,949	22,210	7.9	48.1	18.8	157.0	8,728	23,705	42,683	57.0	3.4	45,455	19.3	30.1	28.5
Brazoria	187	1,623	91,852	11.2	39.5	28.7	508.5	7,858	31,180	72,006	34.1	7.0	74,510	9.9	13.1	12.7
Brazos	347	2,570	88,942	5.9	34.0	39.8	241.0	8,350	24,157	41,654	55.8	4.3	42,279	24.9	22.5	20.6
Brewster	154	1,287	2,194	10.4	36.8	36.0	15.6	12,846	26,156	38,440	62.1	4.3	43,055	14.9	22.2	21.5
Briscoe	0	880	395	3.0	49.1	23.0	4.6	12,044	22,906	40,385	57.3	2.9	43,376	15.4	25.5	22.2
Brooks	208	2,093	1,781	2.9	59.9	14.6	16.7	10,844	14,885	24,913	70.1	0.8	27,703	32.2	48.7	48.6
Brown	329	2,213	9,070	11.4	51.5	18.5	60.1	9,089	22,090	43,235	56.9	2.5	43,770	17.1	25.4	23.8
Burleson	205	971	3,731	11.6	58.8	14.8	25.9	9,297	25,833	52,513	46.1	3.8	48,533	14.4	24.4	23.2
Burnet	235	1,668	9,327	9.1	45.2	23.0	65.8	9,098	27,434	54,259	47.8	4.3	55,919	11.5	20.4	19.5

1. Data for serious crimes have not been adjusted for underreporting; this may affect comparability between geographic areas and over time.　2. Per 100,000 population estimated by the FBI.
3. All persons 3 years old and over enrolled in nursery school through college.　4. Persons 25 years old and over.　5. Elementary and secondary education expenditures.
6. Based on population estimated by the American Community Survey, 2011–2015.

Table B. States and Counties — Personal Income and Earnings

STATE County	Personal income, 2016										Earnings, 2016		
			Per capita[1]			Supplements to wages and salaries, employer contributions (mil dol)						Contributions for government social insurance (mil dol)	
	Total (mil dol)	Percent change 2015-2016	Dollars	Rank	Wages and salaries (mil dol)	Pension and insurance	Government social insurance	Proprietors' income (mil dol)	Dividends, interest, and rent (mil dol)	Personal transfer receipts (mil dol)	Total (mil dol)	From employee and self-employed	From employer
	62	63	64	65	66	67	68	69	70	71	72	73	74
TENNESSEE— Cont'd													
Marshall	1,087	3.0	34,075	2,309	359	75	26	75	142	269	536	62	26
Maury	3,438	4.8	38,207	1,618	1,561	280	112	329	408	788	2,282	254	112
Meigs	369	2.1	30,712	2,767	78	21	6	20	52	128	126	17	6
Monroe	1,449	3.8	31,512	2,674	563	115	41	99	180	468	819	100	41
Montgomery	7,668	1.0	39,176	1,473	2,031	412	145	513	1,235	1,494	3,101	329	145
Moore	237	-0.4	37,415	1,749	91	26	6	12	30	63	136	15	6
Morgan	603	2.5	27,978	2,981	100	31	7	36	64	207	174	23	7
Obion	1,123	0.8	36,729	1,874	375	72	27	88	207	339	562	66	27
Overton	666	1.4	30,197	2,825	174	42	12	71	78	220	299	35	12
Perry	234	3.2	29,390	2,903	65	16	5	21	37	99	107	13	5
Pickett	193	4.6	37,567	1,728	36	8	3	42	23	64	89	9	3
Polk	538	1.6	32,101	2,597	87	22	6	31	61	166	146	19	6
Putnam	2,826	4.0	37,218	1,790	1,380	299	97	381	500	690	2,157	227	97
Rhea	1,088	2.2	33,551	2,390	507	116	39	49	124	340	711	87	39
Roane	2,022	3.2	38,234	1,612	1,163	156	75	102	272	618	1,496	177	75
Robertson	2,631	3.1	38,033	1,654	931	199	69	239	281	566	1,438	158	69
Rutherford	11,744	5.6	38,098	1,640	6,003	1,020	421	1,313	1,287	1,765	8,756	922	421
Scott	602	1.4	27,435	3,006	180	47	14	38	66	246	279	36	14
Sequatchie	516	3.1	34,671	2,213	105	26	8	33	70	165	173	22	8
Sevier	3,508	4.6	36,285	1,956	1,505	241	114	511	497	860	2,370	266	114
Shelby	43,210	2.6	46,234	668	27,981	4,155	1,874	4,287	6,617	7,740	38,296	4,088	1,874
Smith	674	1.2	34,653	2,215	199	44	14	48	101	173	305	35	14
Stewart	507	0.2	38,469	1,574	132	35	10	29	78	147	206	25	10
Sullivan	6,164	1.9	39,345	1,447	3,310	600	231	493	937	1,672	4,634	531	231
Sumner	7,914	4.7	43,951	882	2,315	396	163	935	951	1,393	3,810	401	163
Tipton	2,219	3.1	36,192	1,976	449	94	32	134	245	511	708	81	32
Trousdale	291	3.7	35,177	2,136	55	14	4	28	31	82	101	11	4
Unicoi	629	1.1	35,499	2,080	244	49	20	31	80	237	344	46	20
Union	560	3.0	29,283	2,909	90	22	6	47	62	183	164	21	6
Van Buren	155	2.2	27,268	3,017	30	9	2	15	20	65	55	7	2
Warren	1,334	3.6	32,930	2,489	555	107	39	94	173	411	795	92	39
Washington	5,086	2.5	39,909	1,378	2,555	513	179	449	745	1,179	3,697	406	179
Wayne	460	-1.9	27,520	2,999	135	34	10	25	57	171	204	26	10
Weakley	1,122	1.1	33,491	2,395	452	116	32	100	167	346	700	75	32
White	846	3.0	31,752	2,651	264	53	19	68	116	281	404	49	19
Williamson	19,934	7.6	90,979	18	8,198	969	532	5,979	2,476	1,109	15,678	1,372	532
Wilson	5,929	5.9	44,650	814	1,960	302	135	566	715	985	2,964	321	135
TEXAS	1,289,310	0.4	46,204	X	670,659	96,253	46,012	154,222	221,051	199,477	967,145	51,051	46,012
Anderson	1,904	3.9	32,978	2,473	917	167	65	104	262	510	1,253	137	65
Andrews	818	-12.0	46,078	684	410	64	27	137	74	108	638	59	27
Angelina	3,424	-1.0	39,002	1,495	1,459	251	103	354	564	905	2,167	226	103
Aransas	1,159	2.4	45,064	773	253	40	18	83	281	299	393	46	18
Archer	395	-4.9	45,387	747	68	14	5	47	68	74	134	12	5
Armstrong	72	-10.1	38,356	1,597	16	3	1	-2	15	21	18	3	1
Atascosa	1,742	-0.3	35,697	2,044	556	96	38	103	307	410	793	86	38
Austin	1,475	-1.4	49,559	437	485	72	34	164	322	260	755	77	34
Bailey	283	-12.1	39,395	1,437	96	19	6	65	42	59	187	14	6
Bandera	889	0.7	40,818	1,259	122	23	8	60	202	212	213	24	8
Bastrop	2,768	4.4	33,453	2,401	681	131	47	223	421	602	1,083	113	47
Baylor	144	-6.5	38,923	1,508	44	9	3	15	25	49	71	8	3
Bee	867	-1.8	26,466	3,044	347	80	22	44	147	260	492	49	22
Bell	14,086	1.2	41,380	1,186	7,715	1,698	642	782	2,378	2,845	10,838	1,162	642
Bexar	84,122	2.2	43,617	916	45,408	7,263	3,265	10,088	15,514	14,610	66,024	6,721	3,265
Blanco	540	1.2	47,365	579	137	23	9	49	156	99	218	22	9
Borden	29	-15.4	46,359	660	9	2	0	2	11	4	13	1	0
Bosque	709	0.4	39,190	1,470	148	33	9	56	129	200	246	25	9
Bowie	3,557	2.1	37,899	1,678	1,770	347	131	224	651	918	2,473	272	131
Brazoria	15,529	-0.7	43,842	894	6,075	971	410	914	1,724	2,283	8,370	869	410
Brazos	7,665	1.6	34,776	2,195	4,125	881	261	748	1,451	1,109	6,016	540	261
Brewster	401	1.6	43,579	921	156	34	10	29	114	79	230	23	10
Briscoe	52	-8.3	35,305	2,119	12	3	1	3	13	15	18	2	1
Brooks	241	-3.8	33,436	2,404	99	24	7	5	28	109	135	16	7
Brown	1,300	0.8	33,973	2,328	599	115	43	80	195	444	836	95	43
Burleson	718	-0.5	40,421	1,311	173	30	12	57	125	176	271	30	12
Burnet	2,019	1.2	43,667	908	604	98	41	169	570	451	912	99	41

1. Based on the resident population estimated as of July 1 of the year shown.

Table B. States and Counties — Earnings, Social Security, and Housing

STATE County	Farm	Mining, quarrying, and extracting	Construction	Manu-facturing	Information; professional, scientific, technical services	Retail trade	Finance, insurance, real estate, and leasing	Health care and social assistance	Govern-ment	Number	Rate[1]	Supple-mental Security Income recipients, 2016	Total	Percent change, 2010-2017
	75	76	77	78	79	80	81	82	83	84	85	86	87	88
TENNESSEE— Cont'd														
Marshall	-1.7	D	7.1	35.3	3.3	8.9	3.2	4.4	18.9	7,205	225	691	13,638	4.0
Maury	-0.4	D	8.2	22.2	4.8	6.5	10.2	9.5	18.0	19,810	221	1,895	37,470	6.3
Meigs	-2.4	0.1	7.1	35.8	D	3.4	D	8.4	23.7	3,435	287	510	5,883	4.4
Monroe	-1.0	D	4.7	39.2	2.6	8.5	3.6	8.5	13.3	13,155	286	1,693	21,218	2.1
Montgomery	-0.1	0.8	8.0	9.3	5.7	11.1	5.4	12.8	23.9	27,285	140	3,433	81,005	15.5
Moore	-1.3	D	5.6	D	D	1.7	0.7	D	30.3	1,470	234	75	3,052	4.8
Morgan	-0.4	D	10.1	8.3	D	4.9	D	6.0	43.6	5,800	267	875	9,004	1.0
Obion	2.2	D	7.5	15.6	D	13.2	5.6	9.6	17.3	8,785	288	1,095	14,638	-0.2
Overton	-2.5	0.9	9.8	17.5	3.6	10.4	5.4	14.7	20.6	6,270	285	680	10,390	0.9
Perry	-2.5	D	6.0	24.1	D	7.2	D	D	23.8	2,370	300	258	4,656	1.2
Pickett	-1.4	0.6	12.2	D	2.5	13.4	3.6	8.6	16.0	1,710	336	150	3,493	1.0
Polk	3.1	D	5.8	7.8	D	7.9	D	D	31.7	4,640	277	500	8,875	11.0
Putnam	-0.5	0.1	6.8	13.4	5.4	9.5	5.1	11.2	25.4	17,710	233	2,142	34,475	8.1
Rhea	-0.6	D	3.9	29.6	D	4.6	1.9	D	40.3	8,255	255	1,222	14,678	2.2
Roane	-0.4	D	D	4.1	D	4.2	1.6	6.9	15.0	15,660	296	1,560	25,617	-0.4
Robertson	0.1	D	11.2	30.5	2.7	6.9	3.6	6.2	14.8	13,875	201	1,251	27,267	4.4
Rutherford	-0.1	D	6.5	25.0	5.9	7.2	6.4	9.5	14.6	42,440	138	3,886	118,422	15.0
Scott	-0.9	0.3	8.6	22.0	1.9	8.5	2.6	D	27.4	5,875	268	1,441	10,005	0.9
Sequatchie	-0.2	3.6	5.0	11.9	D	8.8	7.1	D	29.2	4,160	282	508	6,487	1.8
Sevier	-0.2	D	5.8	3.9	3.5	12.9	6.6	5.8	13.8	24,600	255	1,940	57,507	3.0
Shelby	0.0	D	4.7	10.0	5.7	6.5	8.3	13.7	13.4	156,135	167	33,683	405,571	1.8
Smith	-2.4	D	11.7	28.1	2.2	7.4	4.4	7.9	19.2	4,525	232	524	8,749	2.6
Stewart	-0.7	0.1	12.6	14.8	D	4.7	D	3.7	48.1	3,745	284	416	6,875	1.5
Sullivan	-0.2	0.0	8.1	25.5	5.1	7.2	3.8	18.1	10.4	45,805	293	4,816	75,321	2.1
Sumner	-0.1	D	12.1	13.3	8.8	8.7	6.0	11.7	12.4	35,135	196	2,547	71,262	8.0
Tipton	-1.3	D	13.0	15.5	D	7.3	3.3	D	23.4	12,025	197	1,468	23,833	2.8
Trousdale	-1.0	0.0	D	12.7	4.3	11.1	D	D	27.3	1,930	194	247	3,583	6.4
Unicoi	0.3	D	5.2	37.8	D	4.4	1.7	8.1	15.5	5,265	298	619	8,903	0.8
Union	-2.6	D	D	16.7	D	7.6	D	D	26.2	5,060	263	737	9,373	4.6
Van Buren	-2.5	D	5.8	21.9	D	4.0	D	D	37.6	1,760	308	177	2,686	0.8
Warren	0.3	0.0	5.7	33.0	D	7.0	3.5	12.8	14.2	10,345	256	1,606	17,957	0.8
Washington	-0.2	D	3.4	8.4	6.5	8.4	6.9	22.6	22.4	30,655	241	3,367	60,372	5.4
Wayne	-1.5	D	3.9	9.5	D	5.1	5.0	13.0	36.0	4,350	261	429	7,345	0.8
Weakley	3.8	1.6	3.0	11.6	D	5.9	13.7	D	28.3	7,950	237	877	15,610	0.8
White	-2.7	D	6.3	24.5	2.8	7.3	3.2	10.8	15.0	7,660	290	948	11,885	3.2
Williamson	0.0	D	5.6	1.8	15.0	5.8	11.4	30.0	4.9	30,505	139	1,036	81,756	19.3
Wilson	-0.4	D	10.2	10.5	6.2	12.2	5.8	8.5	11.0	25,800	195	1,559	53,012	16.3
TEXAS	0.3	6.6	8.0	8.5	11.7	6.1	8.4	9.5	14.8	4,024,516	144	657,899	10,932,870	9.6
Anderson	-0.1	5.3	4.3	5.3	7.6	6.0	4.6	10.8	26.5	10,480	182	1,498	20,398	1.4
Andrews	0.3	36.2	12.0	2.4	4.3	3.8	4.9	D	14.6	2,250	126	268	6,250	7.5
Angelina	0.2	5.4	5.2	9.3	4.4	7.3	4.3	20.1	17.9	18,415	210	3,143	36,820	3.5
Aransas	-0.5	4.4	11.6	1.3	8.2	12.9	6.8	D	15.9	7,750	307	627	16,381	6.7
Archer	3.9	16.4	8.1	4.0	D	9.7	D	3.4	21.1	1,895	216	122	4,162	1.3
Armstrong	-38.0	2.6	28.2	D	10.1	D	D	13.1	36.7	440	237	24	906	0.2
Atascosa	0.0	15.3	10.3	3.7	D	8.1	7.0	8.1	18.4	8,855	182	1,408	18,352	4.1
Austin	1.3	6.4	14.0	12.6	7.0	11.9	5.6	4.4	11.1	6,125	207	559	13,222	2.3
Bailey	35.3	0.2	2.3	5.1	3.9	3.7	D	D	11.9	1,125	157	140	2,773	-0.4
Bandera	-1.0	D	18.2	1.5	7.0	6.4	4.1	D	24.1	6,145	283	361	11,907	3.0
Bastrop	-0.8	3.6	15.3	6.0	5.4	10.5	3.9	7.7	17.7	14,685	177	1,837	30,712	4.8
Baylor	1.6	D	D	D	D	5.8	D	D	39.8	1,085	298	129	2,647	-0.7
Bee	-1.1	11.8	2.3	2.1	5.5	8.0	4.4	D	48.3	4,800	146	995	10,711	0.6
Bell	0.1	D	5.6	4.1	3.9	5.5	3.6	14.0	48.3	50,445	148	8,144	140,157	11.7
Bexar	0.0	7.6	5.3	4.1	9.6	6.2	12.2	11.4	21.7	291,870	151	54,525	693,707	4.7
Blanco	1.9	D	21.2	5.6	4.8	4.9	D	D	15.2	2,810	248	134	5,825	5.2
Borden	15.0	D	D	1.6	D	12.0	D	D	40.2	125	189	0	389	1.0
Bosque	10.2	D	10.5	11.9	4.8	5.2	3.7	D	26.5	4,885	271	410	9,730	1.1
Bowie	0.3	0.3	4.5	4.2	3.7	8.9	7.3	18.5	28.7	19,800	211	3,997	39,818	3.4
Brazoria	0.2	2.8	17.3	22.7	5.5	6.1	3.9	8.2	14.3	48,445	137	5,533	136,364	15.2
Brazos	0.1	2.9	7.4	4.3	9.1	6.5	5.2	10.0	37.1	21,870	100	3,439	89,749	15.5
Brewster	-0.2	0.8	10.3	0.7	8.8	4.8	4.0	D	39.2	2,105	229	200	5,520	2.5
Briscoe	15.5	0.6	D	D	D	D	8.3	D	31.4	410	276	36	954	0.1
Brooks	2.5	8.0	2.5	0.0	0.9	4.6	D	7.4	53.9	1,770	244	510	3,239	0.0
Brown	-1.6	1.6	6.3	24.7	D	9.0	4.3	D	20.0	9,395	247	1,229	18,795	2.8
Burleson	1.0	8.3	11.5	5.7	4.0	9.7	5.3	D	15.8	4,200	236	498	9,145	3.6
Burnet	-0.9	1.3	14.6	8.4	7.8	9.7	4.9	13.8	16.3	11,935	260	698	22,686	8.8

1. Per 1,000 resident population estimated as of July 1 of the year shown.

Table B. States and Counties — Housing, Labor Force, and Employment

STATE County	Housing units, 2017 (cont.) Occupied units — Owner-occupied Total	Percent	Median value[1]	With a mortgage	Without a mortgage[2]	Renter-occupied Median rent[3]	Median rent as a percent of income[2]	Sub-standard units[4] (percent)	Civilian labor force, 2017 Total	Percent change, 2016-2017	Unemployment Total	Rate[5]	Civilian employment[6], 2012-2016 Total	Percent Management, business, science, and arts	Construction, production, and maintenance occupations
	89	90	91	92	93	94	95	96	97	98	99	100	101	102	103
TENNESSEE— Cont'd															
Marshall	12,044	71.2	114,700	19.7	11.0	663	27.4	2.6	15,535	3.0	517	3.3	13,699	26.3	35.1
Maury	32,889	67.7	146,000	21.1	10.3	752	28.9	2.6	45,784	3.8	1,472	3.2	39,000	32.2	24.7
Meigs	4,675	78.4	103,900	22.9	11.3	606	34.1	2.9	5,007	2.2	260	5.2	3,960	20.5	45.1
Monroe	17,311	75.8	113,600	21.4	10.4	593	29.6	2.8	19,734	1.7	784	4.0	16,539	24.9	37.2
Montgomery	67,090	59.1	148,600	21.5	10.0	899	28.4	2.6	80,988	1.3	3,302	4.1	75,002	31.9	24.9
Moore	2,560	80.0	161,800	21.6	10.0	615	20.0	2.9	3,484	2.9	108	3.1	2,897	23.3	38.4
Morgan	7,221	81.1	94,300	21.0	11.6	653	29.6	3.8	7,871	0.8	382	4.9	6,925	22.9	31.1
Obion	12,719	66.7	87,200	19.1	12.0	580	28.0	1.6	12,273	-2.4	673	5.5	12,367	28.7	31.7
Overton	8,881	78.2	107,200	22.8	10.3	518	26.7	3.0	9,590	4.0	395	4.1	8,789	28.1	34.7
Perry	3,209	82.0	81,900	25.1	10.3	505	28.3	4.4	3,242	1.6	156	4.8	2,776	18.4	45.2
Pickett	2,128	84.9	118,300	18.3	10.0	445	26.0	2.4	2,454	5.5	108	4.4	2,055	31.5	27.5
Polk	6,766	76.1	109,600	20.4	10.0	654	26.1	3.3	7,372	-0.3	336	4.6	6,474	27.4	35.8
Putnam	30,100	61.8	150,100	22.5	11.0	632	33.6	2.5	34,084	2.5	1,277	3.7	31,520	33.0	23.9
Rhea	12,408	70.2	108,100	19.5	10.0	618	33.3	2.7	13,275	-1.5	852	6.4	13,453	26.2	34.7
Roane	21,532	74.6	127,900	21.3	10.7	672	31.5	2.2	23,150	1.3	1,010	4.4	20,792	32.9	26.0
Robertson	24,730	75.2	158,800	21.4	11.1	831	27.6	2.6	36,117	3.9	1,216	3.4	32,331	31.7	30.6
Rutherford	103,562	65.4	164,800	20.7	10.0	925	28.7	2.9	169,956	3.9	4,896	2.9	147,579	34.3	24.0
Scott	8,368	70.5	86,700	22.1	13.2	524	28.1	0.8	8,171	1.8	415	5.1	7,879	22.7	41.4
Sequatchie	5,549	75.3	135,000	21.1	10.0	655	29.0	5.6	6,087	2.8	300	4.9	5,737	27.3	29.6
Sevier	36,982	67.7	158,200	22.1	10.0	724	29.4	3.2	52,301	2.1	2,086	4.0	45,413	26.4	19.9
Shelby	349,956	56.2	132,200	22.8	11.9	873	32.9	2.9	439,415	1.2	18,976	4.3	427,281	35.2	22.1
Smith	7,555	73.6	118,100	22.3	10.0	554	28.2	2.6	8,996	3.6	318	3.5	8,281	26.6	35.3
Stewart	5,187	76.0	125,200	22.0	12.3	607	26.4	0.7	5,203	0.7	277	5.3	4,814	30.3	29.3
Sullivan	65,896	72.9	125,200	20.3	10.0	613	28.4	1.9	70,193	0.6	2,823	4.0	66,361	32.6	23.0
Sumner	63,240	73.0	184,900	21.7	10.0	900	29.1	1.7	95,769	3.7	2,830	3.0	84,387	35.1	22.6
Tipton	21,355	70.4	140,400	19.9	10.0	766	28.1	1.8	27,774	1.0	1,221	4.4	27,388	29.3	30.4
Trousdale	2,958	76.6	129,100	21.3	12.2	592	28.4	0.1	3,971	3.3	137	3.5	3,530	23.7	27.6
Unicoi	7,628	73.0	112,300	23.5	11.0	619	31.5	2.5	7,044	0.4	377	5.4	6,811	22.9	36.5
Union	7,271	75.7	112,500	22.7	10.5	563	30.6	4.8	7,359	1.1	321	4.4	6,823	22.6	37.4
Van Buren	2,141	88.3	95,200	21.4	10.0	422	26.0	1.8	2,099	3.0	91	4.3	2,189	28.3	28.0
Warren	15,584	69.2	101,800	19.9	10.0	597	27.4	1.6	17,195	-2.7	674	3.9	16,636	25.4	38.2
Washington	52,409	65.7	149,200	20.7	10.0	706	29.4	1.6	59,402	1.1	2,250	3.8	58,605	37.8	19.5
Wayne	6,020	83.0	87,600	21.5	11.2	506	23.5	1.4	6,157	1.1	319	5.2	6,027	24.1	33.1
Weakley	13,459	68.0	98,200	19.2	11.0	575	29.7	0.7	15,897	0.2	772	4.9	14,299	31.8	27.7
White	9,677	77.6	96,400	23.2	10.5	637	33.3	2.2	11,965	1.7	473	4.0	9,674	24.4	34.9
Williamson	71,043	80.5	368,100	19.5	10.0	1,270	27.9	1.4	118,004	3.9	3,150	2.7	102,285	54.9	9.7
Wilson	45,431	77.0	211,700	21.4	10.0	903	29.0	1.6	70,373	3.7	2,058	2.9	61,027	36.6	19.6
TEXAS	9,289,554	61.9	142,700	21.3	11.5	911	29.1	5.3	13,538,411	1.7	577,800	4.3	12,371,392	35.4	22.8
Anderson	16,572	71.8	85,800	22.5	12.7	731	28.4	4.8	23,262	-0.9	843	3.6	19,577	22.4	28.2
Andrews	5,392	72.2	122,000	16.3	10.0	960	23.2	8.3	9,011	3.9	276	3.1	7,887	20.7	42.3
Angelina	30,495	65.0	89,300	19.9	11.6	765	29.1	5.5	36,614	-1.0	1,857	5.1	35,356	27.5	28.7
Aransas	9,552	74.8	154,500	21.4	14.3	827	32.7	2.7	10,366	1.4	701	6.8	9,870	28.8	25.8
Archer	3,331	81.9	113,300	18.9	10.8	633	24.1	2.4	4,093	0.3	140	3.4	4,290	35.9	28.9
Armstrong	702	79.9	113,100	18.9	10.0	733	18.0	1.1	920	-1.3	23	2.5	920	36.1	30.7
Atascosa	15,343	73.8	93,000	18.1	10.6	763	24.3	7.4	21,181	0.9	886	4.2	19,860	25.5	32.5
Austin	11,222	73.6	164,300	21.7	11.1	852	30.1	4.8	13,997	0.0	606	4.3	13,410	31.3	30.1
Bailey	2,317	74.8	62,700	30.9	11.6	695	23.1	9.4	2,670	-1.6	114	4.3	3,202	23.6	40.3
Bandera	8,256	83.1	159,200	20.6	11.0	842	29.0	2.7	9,639	1.6	346	3.6	8,744	38.2	21.9
Bastrop	25,822	77.9	142,100	21.9	11.5	909	28.3	5.4	40,124	3.0	1,415	3.5	32,589	31.9	28.2
Baylor	1,703	77.0	72,600	22.8	14.7	453	16.2	1.8	1,599	-0.2	55	3.4	1,432	39.0	25.2
Bee	8,698	61.2	76,400	19.7	11.9	867	28.4	6.7	9,938	-3.4	641	6.4	10,253	20.1	29.7
Bell	113,027	55.1	130,900	20.9	10.8	869	27.9	3.5	141,233	1.4	5,928	4.2	130,349	32.2	21.3
Bexar	623,321	58.3	134,400	21.5	11.1	902	29.4	4.9	924,590	2.3	32,313	3.5	847,842	34.5	19.6
Blanco	4,174	75.3	192,000	23.3	11.0	748	25.5	3.4	6,217	4.9	169	2.7	4,812	36.0	23.8
Borden	251	70.1	103,800	10.2	10.0	1,188	24.0	0.0	318	-12.9	11	3.5	281	51.6	18.9
Bosque	7,098	77.1	95,000	19.2	11.8	622	25.3	3.8	8,176	0.0	326	4.0	7,230	27.6	32.1
Bowie	33,586	65.3	103,900	20.9	11.4	722	31.6	3.2	39,326	-0.6	1,789	4.5	36,356	30.3	24.9
Brazoria	114,290	71.4	157,100	19.7	10.2	951	25.6	4.6	171,954	1.4	9,053	5.3	157,500	41.1	23.8
Brazos	75,797	45.0	164,600	21.1	10.7	870	37.7	3.8	113,424	2.1	3,476	3.1	101,149	41.0	18.0
Brewster	4,014	57.1	117,500	20.3	10.0	643	25.4	5.1	3,921	-0.9	137	3.5	4,326	38.8	19.9
Briscoe	698	75.1	63,800	19.0	10.0	612	25.5	2.4	556	1.6	24	4.3	755	31.8	35.4
Brooks	2,031	65.8	57,000	26.7	13.8	546	34.6	6.3	2,425	-0.4	199	8.2	2,609	24.6	21.9
Brown	13,361	71.1	91,000	20.9	12.4	659	29.0	1.6	16,183	0.3	621	3.8	14,982	33.2	26.8
Burleson	6,385	79.9	98,500	20.4	10.0	750	22.9	5.7	7,987	1.6	329	4.1	7,499	26.9	34.8
Burnet	16,299	74.4	163,800	23.0	12.5	835	27.2	3.0	22,153	0.9	702	3.2	19,236	30.5	27.1

1. Specified owner-occupied units.   2. A value of 10.0 represents 10 percent or less; a value of 50.0 represents 50 percent or more.   3. Specified renter-occupied units.
4. Overcrowded or lacking complete plumbing facilities.   5. Percent of civilian labor force.   6. Civilian employed persons 16 years old and over.

— **Nonfarm Employment and Agriculture**

STATE County	Private nonfarm establishments, employment and payroll, 2016									Agriculture, 2012			
	Number of establish-ments	Employment						Annual payroll		Farms			
		Total	Health care and social assistance	Manufac-turing	Retail trade	Finance and insurance	Professional, scientific, and technical services	Total (mil dol)	Average per employee (dollars)	Number	Percent with:		Farm operators whose principal occupation is farming (percent)
											Fewer than 50 acres	500 acres or more	
	104	105	106	107	108	109	110	111	112	113	114	115	116
TENNESSEE— Cont'd													
Marshall	475	8,248	725	3,662	1,103	198	119	317	38,475	1,025	34.4	5.4	50.4
Maury	1,746	27,893	5,199	4,756	4,550	1,741	665	1,248	44,743	1,513	39.4	6.3	40.0
Meigs	107	1,500	125	839	243	23	D	53	35,045	317	28.7	5.4	39.1
Monroe	702	11,580	1,320	4,953	1,758	351	170	404	34,862	872	42.0	4.0	48.2
Montgomery	2,827	43,389	7,868	5,415	8,964	1,285	1,819	1,429	32,937	783	38.6	7.8	34.4
Moore	74	1,110	120	D	118	9	16	59	52,852	358	32.1	7.8	45.3
Morgan	158	1,334	299	233	265	48	17	43	31,894	413	32.9	4.4	48.9
Obion	641	9,135	1,107	2,585	1,744	392	121	297	32,485	568	32.6	16.5	57.0
Overton	318	3,621	622	781	534	142	94	124	34,221	922	39.6	4.1	32.9
Perry	112	1,670	422	748	222	56	9	50	29,911	246	19.5	6.1	40.2
Pickett	81	720	133	51	91	45	8	23	32,188	316	34.2	3.5	30.4
Polk	212	1,334	287	125	292	62	10	41	30,723	255	45.5	6.7	58.0
Putnam	1,780	29,439	5,776	4,462	5,001	1,035	550	1,012	34,371	898	46.1	3.1	33.9
Rhea	481	8,269	1,076	3,557	1,179	220	80	262	31,705	411	40.1	5.6	44.8
Roane	720	8,546	2,139	1,013	1,705	222	505	248	29,002	519	45.9	1.2	34.9
Robertson	1,155	18,705	2,045	6,393	2,468	378	243	716	38,277	1,180	46.6	6.6	45.3
Rutherford	5,103	106,987	12,783	17,722	14,401	4,167	2,914	4,595	42,947	1,327	46.5	4.6	41.8
Scott	322	3,637	695	1,074	726	137	27	104	28,537	302	30.8	3.0	43.4
Sequatchie	178	2,031	528	150	458	190	53	57	28,171	188	39.4	8.5	38.8
Sevier	2,748	39,789	2,523	1,602	8,728	910	777	1,091	27,413	603	40.1	1.3	41.3
Shelby	19,463	435,457	71,358	26,674	48,373	16,164	18,117	21,959	50,427	411	53.3	7.8	42.1
Smith	266	3,811	485	1,347	676	111	65	137	35,935	850	24.4	4.4	45.1
Stewart	146	1,253	194	323	257	56	D	37	29,193	350	28.0	7.1	38.6
Sullivan	3,371	62,013	11,718	12,314	8,901	1,974	2,570	2,912	46,964	1,074	58.0	1.8	34.8
Sumner	3,132	46,408	7,003	8,854	6,422	1,700	1,767	1,837	39,578	1,355	48.6	4.1	40.7
Tipton	699	8,734	1,404	1,532	1,669	303	166	307	35,145	520	44.6	10.6	42.9
Trousdale	113	1,234	199	185	214	64	48	38	30,982	290	32.8	4.5	37.6
Unicoi	240	3,777	422	1,731	502	81	15	155	41,144	93	60.2	0.0	31.2
Union	193	1,708	138	564	365	39	41	52	30,520	408	38.0	1.5	42.4
Van Buren	33	438	D	D	39	D	D	15	34,596	245	42.0	5.7	55.1
Warren	720	11,198	1,542	4,204	1,578	317	151	388	34,675	1,122	41.5	6.3	50.4
Washington	2,836	52,484	13,991	4,557	8,891	3,037	1,497	2,035	38,771	1,312	55.6	2.1	49.0
Wayne	209	2,541	594	578	321	145	18	79	30,922	664	19.4	7.7	35.2
Weakley	568	7,763	1,498	1,632	1,194	328	88	233	30,021	861	33.7	12.8	45.5
White	395	5,428	812	2,104	801	128	49	189	34,884	927	38.9	5.0	38.9
Williamson	6,821	118,657	15,882	2,255	14,075	12,188	9,787	7,097	59,813	1,160	46.5	3.5	43.6
Wilson	2,620	39,311	3,900	4,092	6,129	1,004	1,638	1,536	39,066	1,473	37.4	3.7	41.8
TEXAS	579,168	10,429,924	1,509,548	768,921	1,304,467	535,456	708,331	526,783	50,507	248,809	37.7	15.8	42.1
Anderson	919	11,120	2,265	304	2,069	274	174	409	36,784	2,001	38.3	6.5	39.4
Andrews	401	5,228	582	287	546	115	112	268	51,291	169	37.3	39.1	30.8
Angelina	1,876	29,773	7,828	3,731	4,877	861	821	1,024	34,394	975	47.5	3.3	39.8
Aransas	517	4,237	512	56	1,043	163	109	127	29,922	100	49.0	8.0	34.0
Archer	215	1,161	50	94	110	23	41	44	37,546	531	17.1	36.2	47.1
Armstrong	37	279	65	NA	D	D	5	9	31,473	281	5.7	55.5	45.9
Atascosa	780	10,399	1,314	232	1,882	270	281	437	41,978	1,987	29.8	15.0	37.4
Austin	610	7,553	648	938	1,081	277	241	298	39,496	2,098	38.5	7.2	36.1
Bailey	148	1,521	222	381	185	77	38	42	27,529	494	9.5	39.3	46.6
Bandera	387	3,175	339	35	313	79	87	92	28,932	1,002	36.3	17.9	45.7
Bastrop	1,294	14,402	2,007	1,150	3,489	445	399	461	32,013	2,083	40.2	6.7	49.0
Baylor	115	962	495	D	108	42	28	22	22,405	277	7.6	38.3	58.1
Bee	485	4,980	944	142	1,161	185	124	163	32,770	974	31.6	16.9	45.2
Bell	5,043	92,113	24,863	6,198	15,194	3,380	3,186	3,593	39,009	2,533	50.8	6.3	34.2
Bexar	35,653	741,051	117,976	32,950	93,175	67,664	44,071	32,751	44,195	2,457	56.8	4.8	41.4
Blanco	289	2,123	169	229	252	104	86	91	42,960	792	29.8	24.6	41.7
Borden	7	19	NA	NA	D	NA	D	1	28,474	114	7.0	58.8	50.9
Bosque	273	2,433	505	531	386	122	59	83	34,244	1,265	26.1	17.9	41.6
Bowie	2,215	32,982	7,494	2,035	6,605	1,361	1,682	1,134	34,381	1,619	44.4	6.9	40.4
Brazoria	5,518	87,449	9,255	12,921	15,701	2,100	3,316	4,373	50,009	3,091	61.8	8.6	36.4
Brazos	4,251	66,287	9,258	5,496	11,119	1,672	3,338	2,312	34,883	1,412	46.0	7.5	34.7
Brewster	282	2,648	501	47	442	184	40	69	25,924	202	17.3	52.5	51.0
Briscoe	36	103	D	D	21	23	D	3	33,243	282	5.0	44.7	46.5
Brooks	120	1,463	485	NA	238	85	11	36	24,541	374	19.5	21.7	43.3
Brown	882	13,201	3,475	2,660	2,037	453	188	419	31,704	1,918	33.7	13.5	36.5
Burleson	332	3,066	348	368	656	104	142	117	38,015	1,429	30.9	10.6	49.1
Burnet	1,210	11,422	2,132	807	2,140	367	442	419	36,691	1,481	36.5	12.5	35.6

Items 104—116

Table B. States and Counties — **Agriculture**

STATE County	Agriculture, 2012 (cont.)															
	Land in farms				Value of land and buildings (dollars)			Value of products sold:				Percent of farms with sales of:		Government payments	
			Acres								Percent from:					
	Acreage (1,000)	Percent change, 2007-2012	Average size of farm	Total irrigated (1,000)	Total cropland (1,000)	Average per farm	Average per acre	Value of machinery and equiopmnet, average per farm (dollars)	Total (mil dol)	Average per farm (acres)	Crops	Livestock and poultry products	$10,000 or more	$100,000 or more	Total ($1,000)	Percent of farms
	117	118	119	120	121	122	123	124	125	126	127	128	129	130	131	132
TENNESSEE— Cont'd																
Marshall	162	6.9	158	0.0	62.5	477,125	3,017	54,191	38.7	37,764	12.0	88.0	32.5	6.8	534	20.7
Maury	242	7.1	160	0.5	90.1	584,794	3,649	59,194	43.3	28,632	36.7	63.3	29.1	4.0	886	16.1
Meigs	53	7.7	167	0.1	20.0	587,246	3,520	57,767	6.9	21,647	19.3	80.7	30.9	3.8	153	19.6
Monroe	111	19.5	127	0.1	48.1	571,742	4,507	62,169	33.1	37,969	22.4	77.6	26.3	6.4	282	13.9
Montgomery	147	-2.7	188	0.7	77.1	811,156	4,310	79,954	47.3	60,350	77.0	23.0	35.0	8.9	1,031	31.5
Moore	59	13.3	164	0.0	14.8	578,542	3,528	69,791	22.6	63,045	D	D	38.0	9.8	128	13.4
Morgan	55	4.0	134	0.0	19.5	460,262	3,427	57,613	15.1	36,567	7.8	92.2	24.9	3.9	70	6.3
Obion	253	0.4	445	6.1	211.8	1,418,014	3,186	191,794	141.0	248,166	72.5	27.5	48.9	23.1	3,270	65.7
Overton	123	7.2	133	0.1	36.1	433,815	3,250	49,648	16.4	17,787	19.3	80.7	31.0	2.9	345	17.8
Perry	48	-6.3	194	0.0	13.8	384,012	1,981	41,463	2.4	9,951	33.9	66.1	26.0	1.6	155	31.3
Pickett	42	10.2	132	0.0	14.5	384,127	2,905	53,035	12.0	37,842	9.2	90.8	36.7	3.8	144	23.4
Polk	36	9.8	139	0.1	16.3	623,392	4,470	73,286	38.0	149,188	9.0	91.0	35.7	16.1	180	11.8
Putnam	96	-7.7	107	D	31.4	461,269	4,329	51,198	11.5	12,845	23.2	76.8	24.9	2.3	236	13.6
Rhea	58	2.7	140	0.8	24.4	490,925	3,499	56,000	16.8	40,886	55.2	44.8	28.5	4.4	194	16.3
Roane	47	-10.7	90	0.0	14.0	460,058	5,085	48,503	4.9	9,357	21.0	79.0	21.0	0.8	70	9.2
Robertson	209	-8.0	177	2.3	140.7	862,760	4,869	106,988	134.9	114,306	83.8	16.2	37.9	13.5	1,789	31.5
Rutherford	176	7.2	133	0.7	70.4	647,736	4,878	58,704	28.4	21,424	54.3	45.7	26.5	3.1	691	11.8
Scott	39	25.9	130	D	14.9	366,026	2,824	54,722	4.3	14,189	10.1	89.9	11.3	0.7	56	9.3
Sequatchie	31	7.0	163	D	10.0	528,037	3,236	72,968	7.0	37,404	15.1	84.9	31.9	8.0	66	17.0
Sevier	56	-1.6	92	0.0	17.1	545,836	5,926	48,391	5.3	8,713	22.1	77.9	24.0	0.7	61	13.8
Shelby	82	-11.3	199	4.3	60.4	913,324	4,586	77,803	31.8	77,387	94.2	5.8	26.3	8.0	733	22.9
Smith	130	2.0	153	0.2	36.8	405,628	2,658	52,353	18.9	22,205	40.3	59.7	32.2	3.3	507	19.5
Stewart	61	9.5	173	0.2	20.7	455,657	2,629	73,034	8.2	23,537	68.6	31.4	27.4	3.4	176	22.6
Sullivan	85	3.4	79	0.1	31.7	436,682	5,526	46,955	17.8	16,535	9.8	90.2	20.5	2.2	254	16.3
Sumner	167	-8.9	123	0.2	68.7	600,046	4,864	57,937	47.2	34,830	51.7	48.3	27.4	5.4	1,321	22.0
Tipton	155	-8.7	299	5.7	127.3	887,075	2,967	121,448	67.6	130,064	96.8	3.2	33.1	13.3	2,213	44.0
Trousdale	41	-6.2	142	0.1	13.9	548,321	3,854	65,507	8.2	28,259	36.4	63.6	41.4	4.5	90	24.1
Unicoi	5	14.4	58	D	1.9	321,409	5,511	32,602	D	D	D	D	9.7	2.2	7	7.5
Union	45	-1.5	111	0.0	12.8	320,044	2,887	57,931	3.3	8,039	14.1	85.9	20.8	0.7	183	17.6
Van Buren	37	6.1	151	D	11.0	561,576	3,721	60,033	5.6	22,727	17.5	82.5	29.4	3.3	221	20.0
Warren	163	1.7	146	5.4	83.7	519,646	3,569	73,327	88.2	78,595	79.6	20.4	48.1	13.3	531	13.9
Washington	112	-5.8	85	0.9	49.4	546,271	6,417	67,845	38.6	29,405	33.5	66.5	28.3	5.3	381	22.4
Wayne	133	15.7	201	0.2	36.7	404,798	2,014	52,301	22.3	33,581	15.1	84.9	39.8	4.7	533	20.3
Weakley	254	-0.6	295	3.2	203.8	878,358	2,976	140,220	129.6	150,479	66.0	34.0	42.5	19.0	2,897	51.8
White	122	-7.6	131	0.1	39.6	494,409	3,766	60,759	25.4	27,435	14.9	85.1	41.3	2.7	344	16.5
Williamson	139	-14.3	120	0.5	52.4	882,452	7,376	54,664	23.6	20,338	46.1	53.9	24.7	3.8	254	12.2
Wilson	188	-2.4	128	0.2	57.2	566,389	4,432	47,804	18.4	12,470	16.5	83.5	27.6	1.5	423	11.3
TEXAS	130,153	-0.2	523	4,489.2	29,147.5	876,614	1,676	72,180	25,375.6	101,988	29.0	71.0	29.7	7.0	643,993	21.1
Anderson	375	8.4	187	0.9	70.3	458,514	2,446	50,885	44.6	22,278	30.6	69.4	24.5	2.6	835	5.3
Andrews	752	-7.0	4,450	5.0	71.5	1,459,077	328	91,710	12.6	74,426	46.3	53.7	24.3	12.4	1,436	34.9
Angelina	117	1.5	120	0.2	21.7	378,739	3,157	45,106	46.4	47,639	9.2	90.8	24.3	3.3	168	2.6
Aransas	40	-21.8	398	0.0	2.6	679,110	1,704	43,180	1.1	10,750	18.4	81.6	14.0	2.0	93	24.0
Archer	541	6.7	1,020	0.2	115.6	1,002,917	984	87,567	76.8	144,674	16.6	83.4	53.5	21.8	2,480	40.7
Armstrong	434	-15.9	1,545	4.6	143.0	1,623,819	1,051	116,189	19.2	68,349	42.1	57.9	38.8	16.7	2,637	76.2
Atascosa	665	3.4	335	26.7	108.1	655,914	1,959	57,840	85.0	42,778	32.7	67.3	25.2	4.1	1,512	16.8
Austin	370	10.8	176	4.3	71.2	720,469	4,086	48,374	43.5	20,754	40.1	59.9	32.1	3.1	1,256	12.1
Bailey	472	-1.0	955	48.5	307.7	768,374	805	162,789	292.4	592,000	10.9	89.1	38.3	21.9	8,049	80.4
Bandera	402	22.2	402	0.6	34.1	1,082,003	2,694	42,303	11.2	11,166	11.3	88.7	16.3	0.8	455	7.1
Bastrop	388	-3.6	186	2.9	60.3	695,536	3,738	49,157	35.3	16,955	33.7	66.3	26.0	2.7	1,678	12.0
Baylor	544	-0.6	1,963	1.9	146.8	2,039,458	1,039	143,347	44.7	161,509	33.2	66.8	57.0	24.2	2,780	77.6
Bee	539	-1.7	553	5.1	70.4	1,032,344	1,866	56,745	26.0	26,739	38.2	61.8	25.6	4.4	1,051	17.9
Bell	421	-2.5	166	3.1	170.5	509,341	3,062	64,187	84.9	33,510	69.0	31.0	22.5	3.8	2,125	16.3
Bexar	343	-19.5	140	8.3	89.1	597,423	4,281	44,547	72.4	29,462	75.6	24.4	17.1	2.7	706	10.0
Blanco	364	-8.0	460	0.5	22.1	2,172,696	4,728	46,035	19.1	24,172	47.3	52.7	27.4	1.8	481	9.3
Borden	464	6.7	4,073	5.0	63.1	2,381,579	585	242,132	9.4	82,781	56.6	43.4	36.8	16.7	1,527	74.6
Bosque	570	3.4	450	0.7	70.3	1,089,916	2,420	55,434	78.3	61,894	64.1	35.9	31.9	5.2	466	11.2
Bowie	273	-6.4	169	5.9	77.8	382,695	2,269	51,216	66.0	40,780	21.2	78.8	29.4	5.4	1,209	13.1
Brazoria	631	19.3	204	20.4	175.9	619,773	3,036	59,444	118.2	38,252	60.5	39.5	21.8	3.5	4,831	9.4
Brazos	299	8.5	212	7.3	41.9	798,834	3,771	53,654	95.0	67,278	13.1	86.9	26.3	4.2	1,409	8.6
Brewster	1,913	9.5	9,469	0.5	47.1	4,436,252	469	85,431	9.9	49,025	10.5	89.5	31.2	12.4	1,041	15.8
Briscoe	524	-4.1	1,859	22.8	139.6	1,550,957	834	128,057	20.4	72,465	62.6	37.4	36.5	20.2	3,481	84.4
Brooks	573	4.4	1,532	1.1	26.0	1,628,016	1,063	53,329	50.8	135,743	1.1	98.9	26.7	2.9	320	25.4
Brown	595	6.3	310	3.5	84.6	635,187	2,046	45,413	40.7	21,209	18.5	81.5	22.1	2.1	1,191	18.0
Burleson	335	-7.1	235	19.6	81.2	674,186	2,873	67,470	90.1	63,022	38.1	61.9	32.7	5.6	1,432	10.9
Burnet	485	0.6	328	1.7	44.7	1,089,307	3,324	42,226	14.7	9,935	25.3	74.7	19.4	1.6	588	6.6

Table B. States and Counties — Water Use, Wholesale Trade, Retail Trade, and Real Estate

	Water use, 2015		Wholesale Trade[1], 2012				Retail Trade[2], 2012				Real estate and rental and leasing,[2] 2012			
STATE County	Public supply water withdrawn (mil gal/ day)	Public supply gallons withdrawn per person per day	Number of establish-ments	Number of employees	Sales (mil dol)	Annual payroll (mil dol)	Number of establish-ments	Number of employees	Sales (mil dol)	Annual payroll (mil dol)	Number of establish-ments	Number of employees	Sales (mil dol)	Annual payroll (mil dol)
	133	134	135	136	137	138	139	140	141	142	143	144	145	146
TENNESSEE— Cont'd														
Marshall	2.69	85.3	14	D	D	D	102	1,033	289.1	23.3	16	35	4.7	0.8
Maury	12.33	140.5	61	977	474.0	46.8	327	4,023	1,132.0	94.1	68	238	46.4	7.6
Meigs	0.66	55.8	1	D	D	D	29	198	51.9	3.9	4	6	0.3	0.1
Monroe	5.62	122.8	23	133	36.7	4.6	141	1,630	412.1	36.4	27	44	6.6	1.0
Montgomery	22.40	115.8	77	1,020	587.5	46.0	533	8,205	2,146.2	199.1	145	623	103.9	19.2
Moore	0.54	85.4	2	D	D	D	15	80	16.3	1.3	1	D	D	D
Morgan	1.35	62.8	3	D	D	D	33	253	54.2	4.2	1	D	D	D
Obion	4.62	150.8	33	423	301.5	14.5	142	1,826	457.7	40.1	22	60	7.3	1.3
Overton	2.33	105.3	8	D	D	D	63	498	164.1	10.9	8	D	D	D
Perry	0.91	114.8	1	D	D	D	29	188	40.2	3.6	3	3	0.4	0.1
Pickett	0.81	157.4	1	D	D	D	26	121	30.0	2.7	1	D	D	D
Polk	0.87	51.9	5	D	D	D	46	370	84.3	7.1	4	D	D	D
Putnam	12.46	167.1	65	1,150	427.2	52.2	349	4,782	1,282.9	104.4	63	172	34.2	4.5
Rhea	3.91	120.2	7	D	D	D	107	1,150	281.1	22.7	21	97	8.4	1.7
Roane	4.86	92.1	20	D	D	D	151	1,746	472.3	39.4	20	65	11.1	1.9
Robertson	4.83	70.4	39	739	724.1	23.5	172	2,313	675.2	58.2	35	95	12.2	2.1
Rutherford	32.98	110.4	219	6,361	14,847.0	287.0	829	12,376	3,515.3	281.7	188	990	314.0	44.2
Scott	2.53	115.3	4	15	9.8	0.6	67	633	153.3	13.8	10	13	2.5	0.4
Sequatchie	0.81	54.7	9	55	83.4	1.4	37	391	104.0	9.1	7	21	4.1	0.5
Sevier	11.48	119.7	38	D	D	D	645	7,349	1,561.1	150.9	146	1,185	143.2	32.0
Shelby	142.33	151.7	1,180	24,270	35,454.3	1,374.8	3,056	46,778	22,058.5	1,261.1	923	6,988	1,437.0	306.3
Smith	0.57	29.5	7	D	D	D	60	579	158.9	14.4	9	21	2.6	0.5
Stewart	0.71	53.5	3	8	1.4	0.2	37	289	86.6	6.3	4	18	1.3	0.2
Sullivan	23.76	151.5	174	1,733	1,006.2	67.9	547	8,149	2,095.9	187.4	110	443	77.7	13.2
Sumner	24.90	141.5	117	1,572	2,117.7	72.8	449	5,756	1,503.6	136.8	131	785	152.0	41.4
Tipton	3.35	54.1	18	D	D	D	145	1,667	393.6	33.3	25	80	10.5	2.2
Trousdale	0.93	115.6	3	D	D	D	30	234	56.2	4.4	1	D	D	D
Unicoi	1.46	81.7	8	D	D	D	37	505	129.5	11.1	6	19	2.4	0.7
Union	0.78	40.8	7	D	D	D	40	346	87.6	6.8	4	D	D	D
Van Buren	0.00	0.0	1	D	D	D	10	60	9.4	0.8	2	D	D	D
Warren	4.77	118.0	26	D	D	D	157	1,618	376.4	34.6	22	51	11.8	1.5
Washington	19.08	151.1	118	1,259	791.3	52.2	520	8,260	2,011.5	174.7	114	588	91.7	18.0
Wayne	1.07	63.9	5	D	D	D	45	335	65.0	5.8	5	D	D	D
Weakley	2.26	66.5	27	295	243.0	13.6	123	1,178	297.4	24.5	20	57	9.3	1.1
White	2.81	106.0	15	D	D	D	82	811	209.4	18.6	14	32	2.4	0.6
Williamson	1.42	6.7	237	2,762	10,285.7	186.4	766	12,866	3,968.6	354.4	249	1,397	500.8	77.0
Wilson	15.58	120.9	88	1,646	1,362.9	88.5	403	5,471	1,432.6	123.7	106	542	94.8	18.5
TEXAS	2,885.33	105.0	27,752	408,692	691,242.6	24,826.1	78,281	1,150,148	356,116.4	28,835.5	26,639	169,941	38,757.4	7,751.8
Anderson	9.06	157.3	33	D	D	D	164	1,913	572.1	47.1	34	124	34.7	5.8
Andrews	2.36	130.4	15	D	D	D	30	344	169.8	12.5	15	114	26.7	8.5
Angelina	11.30	128.0	62	808	360.6	35.2	324	4,580	1,274.7	109.4	79	329	54.4	10.8
Aransas	0.21	8.3	8	63	10.5	1.1	73	920	288.9	25.0	36	79	13.3	1.9
Archer	4.59	526.7	13	D	D	D	14	102	25.5	1.8	3	D	D	D
Armstrong	0.23	118.1	3	D	D	D	4	D	D	D	1	D	D	D
Atascosa	5.34	110.3	38	D	D	D	115	1,709	564.7	38.8	35	226	66.5	11.6
Austin	2.03	68.7	23	679	728.8	34.1	83	939	272.4	22.4	20	47	9.5	1.5
Bailey	6.18	857.1	19	D	D	D	21	229	49.0	4.3	NA	NA	NA	NA
Bandera	0.63	29.6	5	28	8.1	1.1	49	299	81.2	5.7	8	18	2.8	0.6
Bastrop	10.60	131.6	34	D	D	D	175	2,462	867.8	59.6	44	132	24.8	3.7
Baylor	2.47	682.7	6	35	30.9	1.4	16	99	24.0	1.7	1	D	D	D
Bee	1.07	32.5	12	D	D	D	78	1,050	330.6	26.1	27	98	17.8	3.7
Bell	16.31	48.7	126	2,616	3,630.5	135.2	922	13,098	3,626.1	293.2	299	1,486	217.9	50.4
Bexar	212.33	111.9	1,464	D	D	D	4,845	80,840	26,480.6	1,994.5	1,718	13,472	3,054.2	601.3
Blanco	0.78	70.9	8	D	D	D	32	209	68.7	4.7	4	9	1.1	0.2
Borden	0.06	92.6	NA	NA	NA	NA	1	D	D	D	NA	NA	NA	NA
Bosque	2.33	130.2	10	77	22.0	2.9	53	417	90.7	8.1	10	23	2.1	0.5
Bowie	16.94	181.4	90	D	D	D	413	6,170	1,611.3	146.2	102	455	93.3	17.3
Brazoria	21.13	61.0	228	1,865	1,636.4	102.3	797	13,282	3,686.3	314.0	248	1,566	392.8	77.3
Brazos	31.46	146.3	140	1,704	1,191.8	86.6	629	9,807	2,672.0	207.8	231	1,299	260.8	43.5
Brewster	1.02	111.5	11	D	D	D	49	405	87.7	8.0	21	148	5.4	1.2
Briscoe	0.19	126.2	4	D	D	D	6	23	6.3	0.4	1	D	D	D
Brooks	1.10	152.1	2	D	D	D	18	297	85.8	6.7	4	10	2.1	0.3
Brown	0.06	1.6	35	D	D	D	181	1,872	509.0	41.5	36	132	20.0	3.9
Burleson	1.76	100.8	18	D	D	D	58	653	293.2	17.9	6	14	3.1	0.6
Burnet	4.09	90.0	41	336	163.1	14.8	182	2,015	617.7	52.1	46	148	25.8	5.2

1. Merchant wholesalers, except manufacturers' sales branches and offices.   2. Employer establishments.

Table B. States and Counties — Professional Services, Manufacturing, and Accommodation and Food Services

STATE County	Professional, scientific, and technical services, 2012				Manufacturing, 2012				Accommodation and food services, 2012			
	Number of establish-ments	Number of employees	Sales (mil dol)	Annual payroll (mil dol)	Number of establishments	Number of employees	Receipts (mil dol)	Annual payroll (mil dol)	Number of establishments	Number of employees	Receipts (mil dol)	Annual payroll (mil dol)
	147	148	149	150	151	152	153	154	155	156	157	158
TENNESSEE— Cont'd												
Marshall	30	88	7.7	2.2	45	2,656	1,085.2	128.0	45	512	25.5	6.4
Maury	104	620	57.8	23.4	76	3,582	1,902.1	201.5	158	2,859	123.1	35.4
Meigs	3	D	D	D	11	753	233.0	28.2	15	D	D	D
Monroe	42	197	16.2	6.1	60	4,333	1,509.3	171.6	82	918	41.7	10.6
Montgomery	177	1,677	235.5	78.7	68	5,519	2,256.0	258.2	338	6,157	296.8	81.1
Moore	4	D	D	D	5	D	D	D	8	D	D	D
Morgan	6	D	D	D	20	330	63.3	12.8	8	D	D	D
Obion	32	119	14.1	4.3	39	2,439	1,195.0	82.2	57	822	33.4	8.4
Overton	22	D	D	D	28	D	D	D	25	D	D	D
Perry	4	D	D	D	11	515	D	17.2	8	D	D	D
Pickett	3	5	0.4	0.1	8	86	14.8	2.2	12	D	D	D
Polk	8	14	2.2	0.5	9	108	D	5.4	18	296	9.3	2.5
Putnam	141	584	70.8	25.4	99	4,301	1,214.4	162.2	159	3,666	158.8	45.1
Rhea	29	79	6.0	2.0	29	3,544	848.6	121.0	48	792	30.7	8.0
Roane	56	D	D	D	23	1,096	270.1	40.5	68	1,359	52.0	15.1
Robertson	64	208	21.2	7.3	78	5,788	1,793.0	218.1	91	1,536	65.6	18.4
Rutherford	340	2,304	265.6	117.2	200	14,761	11,539.0	818.0	469	11,020	502.7	146.5
Scott	13	41	3.8	2.1	31	738	113.7	22.2	24	387	14.4	3.9
Sequatchie	13	42	4.0	1.7	8	111	D	5.1	15	D	D	D
Sevier	151	779	69.9	25.3	69	939	263.2	41.2	508	11,751	832.7	221.2
Shelby	1,762	17,349	2,496.2	1,055.5	580	24,360	22,412.7	1,417.0	1,659	36,739	1,889.7	529.1
Smith	16	D	D	D	17	959	D	41.9	21	D	D	D
Stewart	4	D	D	D	9	194	37.1	6.2	19	D	D	D
Sullivan	266	1,875	232.4	89.4	143	15,287	6,361.4	1,030.5	317	6,340	286.4	82.4
Sumner	210	1,837	213.7	92.7	173	6,127	2,158.4	271.7	231	4,416	195.6	58.1
Tipton	33	131	11.1	3.3	26	1,591	446.3	56.2	63	882	39.5	10.1
Trousdale	8	35	2.5	0.8	6	195	D	6.8	9	108	4.3	1.1
Unicoi	7	16	2.0	0.6	19	1,698	440.7	90.4	32	344	15.9	4.1
Union	11	D	D	D	14	544	125.9	19.2	9	161	7.4	2.0
Van Buren	1	D	D	D	6	D	D	D	1	D	D	D
Warren	40	117	10.4	3.4	57	3,276	1,311.7	141.4	51	770	32.3	8.2
Washington	222	2,751	218.3	102.0	116	4,536	1,503.7	179.2	283	6,344	278.5	80.8
Wayne	10	19	1.4	0.4	21	530	79.9	16.4	17	170	7.1	2.0
Weakley	23	91	8.3	2.4	25	1,033	D	34.7	58	816	35.5	8.8
White	18	32	3.4	0.7	40	1,910	561.1	82.2	28	D	D	D
Williamson	792	7,610	1,465.0	580.1	119	2,237	558.3	92.9	437	9,418	485.2	138.0
Wilson	185	D	D	D	108	2,851	1,281.6	143.6	212	4,345	190.0	56.8
TEXAS	62,322	639,561	122,086.2	47,256.4	19,782	767,024	702,603.1	42,529.8	48,721	976,390	54,480.8	14,743.8
Anderson	81	238	32.0	10.6	24	245	D	10.8	68	D	D	D
Andrews	24	D	D	D	7	387	135.9	15.3	26	372	21.4	5.1
Angelina	147	768	91.7	33.6	65	4,602	1,451.6	177.8	144	3,162	141.5	40.1
Aransas	37	153	20.8	4.9	7	26	D	0.8	74	1,032	50.5	13.4
Archer	9	D	D	D	11	D	D	D	8	D	D	D
Armstrong	1	D	D	D	NA	NA	NA	NA	1	D	D	D
Atascosa	44	240	34.2	10.8	21	216	D	8.3	62	951	52.3	13.6
Austin	49	235	23.8	10.9	33	2,085	D	117.2	49	521	28.7	7.5
Bailey	12	38	4.2	1.5	7	148	D	5.2	14	212	7.9	2.3
Bandera	35	104	10.5	3.4	11	35	D	1.0	49	559	26.6	8.6
Bastrop	101	416	46.1	14.6	59	990	284.4	42.0	109	2,273	138.0	39.8
Baylor	7	24	1.4	0.8	4	44	D	1.1	9	71	5.5	0.7
Bee	38	D	D	D	9	92	D	4.3	56	725	40.5	10.5
Bell	365	3,505	407.6	164.2	136	5,724	1,962.5	237.3	584	11,467	552.0	149.9
Bexar	3,963	40,811	6,684.3	2,557.1	873	30,474	14,766.1	1,478.3	3,612	88,432	5,006.7	1,365.3
Blanco	26	D	D	D	13	109	26.4	4.6	27	277	11.5	3.6
Borden	1	D	D	D	NA	NA	NA	NA	NA	NA	NA	NA
Bosque	22	48	5.7	2.3	16	431	115.2	19.2	22	172	10.1	2.3
Bowie	156	846	86.5	29.2	56	1,840	462.7	78.9	184	4,141	193.8	55.7
Brazoria	456	2,433	316.1	126.5	212	12,119	32,864.6	1,016.8	474	9,303	462.5	127.2
Brazos	401	2,690	523.0	134.3	100	4,480	1,063.6	178.3	436	9,491	446.5	121.5
Brewster	17	49	5.6	1.6	11	27	5.9	0.9	40	617	31.5	8.5
Briscoe	1	D	D	D	NA	NA	NA	NA	3	10	0.3	0.1
Brooks	9	25	2.3	0.5	NA	NA	NA	NA	21	289	15.6	4.3
Brown	54	D	D	D	31	2,292	1,222.0	107.5	81	1,270	59.9	16.4
Burleson	23	149	12.4	4.2	15	353	D	16.9	40	266	14.1	3.3
Burnet	84	473	33.5	14.6	52	687	259.9	33.2	110	1,545	89.0	25.6

Table B. States and Counties — Health Care and Social Assistance, Other Services, Nonemployer Businesses, and Residential Construction

STATE County	Health care and social assistance, 2012				Other services, 2012				Nonemployer businesses, 2015		Value of residential construction authorized by building permits, 2017	
	Number of establishments	Number of employees	Receipts (mil dol)	Annual payroll (mil dol)	Number of establishments	Number of employees	Receipts (mil dol)	Annual payroll (mil dol)	Number	Receipts (mil dol)	New construction ($1,000)	Number of housing units
	159	160	161	162	163	164	165	166	167	168	169	170
TENNESSEE— Cont'd												
Marshall	56	724	57.3	19.8	25	111	11.9	2.8	2,020	88.5	27,258	143
Maury	213	5,384	539.7	208.3	107	661	60.5	18.1	6,193	268.9	309,796	1,512
Meigs	10	D	D	D	7	D	D	D	651	28.7	5,400	36
Monroe	72	1,480	118.5	42.1	40	D	D	D	2,736	120.2	16,591	95
Montgomery	331	7,170	662.2	251.9	184	975	76.1	21.2	9,927	434.7	231,931	1,716
Moore	6	187	12.5	7.5	5	9	0.6	0.1	420	20.0	4,610	19
Morgan	15	370	33.2	13.1	7	D	D	D	1,849	71.9	1,915	12
Obion	86	D	D	D	39	D	D	D				
Overton	35	D	D	D	18	D	D	D	1,765	69.1	393	2
Perry	14	396	26.1	10.8	8	D	D	D	609	27.0	1,171	6
Pickett	5	D	D	D	4	D	D	D	477	23.9	NA	NA
Polk	18	395	30.9	12.7	8	22	2.0	0.4	1,046	37.7	33,143	184
Putnam	228	5,719	511.9	214.5	115	D	D	D	5,937	273.3	83,066	543
Rhea	68	968	68.2	28.4	26	89	7.6	2.1	1,595	59.9	16,423	97
Roane	91	1,892	128.8	53.5	46	192	20.3	5.0	3,064	116.0	598	8
Robertson	122	1,908	176.3	70.4	69	209	21.7	5.5	5,048	239.9	94,588	718
Rutherford	524	13,614	1,376.6	586.1	301	2,632	282.7	78.4	20,563	967.9	689,545	3,569
Scott	41	1,002	65.2	23.7	16	D	D	D	1,336	62.6	245	3
Sequatchie	22	D	D	D	8	21	1.8	0.4	1,056	36.7	665	6
Sevier	150	2,281	198.9	67.3	144	846	78.6	22.3	7,864	383.1	145,375	801
Shelby	2,338	68,016	8,166.7	3,140.9	1,202	10,502	1,938.8	366.1	78,921	2,943.8	341,147	1,692
Smith	26	D	D	D	12	D	D	D	1,363	53.7	12,647	69
Stewart	15	195	18.2	8.1	11	D	D	D	810	27.3	846	4
Sullivan	444	12,341	1,521.5	567.3	220	D	D	D	9,746	411.3	82,434	571
Sumner	334	5,369	599.5	219.1	197	944	98.6	24.6	14,653	738.5	354,291	2,368
Tipton	84	1,314	141.3	45.5	41	160	20.1	4.9	3,823	128.4	26,227	159
Trousdale	23	233	19.3	6.1	6	D	D	D	566	23.9	10,416	88
Unicoi	26	747	44.7	18.3	19	D	D	D	799	28.9	746	9
Union	20	177	11.6	4.8	15	47	4.9	1.3	1,239	45.3	13,175	97
Van Buren	2	D	D	D	2	D	D	D	377	15.1	377	2
Warren	98	1,428	114.7	43.6	48	D	D	D	2,972	122.8	11,160	77
Washington	351	14,010	1,641.3	737.0	175	910	69.9	22.6	8,037	372.7	92,666	574
Wayne	31	402	34.3	12.7	12	39	4.7	1.0	874	36.2	165	1
Weakley	81	1,582	134.6	50.9	37	168	15.2	4.2	1,670	71.7	5,714	41
White	38	856	68.3	24.3	27	D	D	D	1,879	77.4	11,459	114
Williamson	634	11,192	1,456.1	591.2	323	2,109	200.2	60.5	25,285	1,704.8	882,193	2,859
Wilson	268	3,941	392.5	151.2	149	1,091	95.2	31.3	10,834	531.9	401,821	2,236
TEXAS	61,342	1,345,664	145,035.1	54,570.6	34,116	259,128	30,172.2	8,454.5	2,205,149	108,490.6	32,513,965	175,112
Anderson	141	2,214	216.2	78.4	60	308	22.3	7.8	2,938	126.9	2,081	14
Andrews	26	475	64.0	22.8	23	D	D	D	1,333	82.1	4,445	18
Angelina	285	7,839	588.4	240.8	119	818	152.6	32.8	5,332	258.0	8,091	53
Aransas	44	518	46.2	14.8	47	150	14.1	3.4	2,650	124.7	32,271	157
Archer	12	D	D	D	10	D	D	D	901	46.9	1,078	7
Armstrong	4	93	3.1	1.6	2	D	D	D	174	7.7	1,605	8
Atascosa	80	1,309	115.4	43.0	48	217	23.8	5.2	3,381	142.9	6,555	36
Austin	44	D	D	D	31	114	11.6	2.8	2,729	134.4	6,559	34
Bailey	15	251	16.9	6.6	12	37	3.9	0.8	383	22.4	0	0
Bandera	24	339	21.4	8.4	32	105	11.4	2.8	2,299	107.1	210	1
Bastrop	108	1,983	155.1	62.7	78	330	31.1	8.6	6,110	286.9	22,753	176
Baylor	13	511	19.3	8.6	15	D	D	D	282	11.9	0	0
Bee	50	D	D	D	38	187	18.3	4.7	1,507	52.2	793	8
Bell	524	22,484	2,849.6	1,245.3	409	2,898	202.5	72.7	16,877	698.9	337,813	2,247
Bexar	4,314	110,407	12,143.6	4,363.8	2,461	17,571	1,645.4	478.9	131,716	6,106.2	1,126,679	7,497
Blanco	18	159	7.8	3.6	15	44	7.4	1.4	1,358	63.9	2,310	12
Borden	NA	NA	NA	NA	NA	NA	NA	NA	55	2.2	NA	NA
Bosque	20	606	42.2	16.4	21	69	5.4	1.4	1,500	64.7	623	8
Bowie	289	7,151	798.4	295.4	154	979	87.0	26.4	5,194	232.8	11,527	153
Brazoria	627	8,038	646.5	273.7	369	2,558	237.6	75.3	23,910	1,037.9	686,234	3,138
Brazos	399	8,166	1,040.0	376.0	266	1,939	374.6	53.6	13,193	608.9	344,442	2,987
Brewster	24	548	30.0	12.1	20	D	D	D	998	34.0	1,632	13
Briscoe	3	4	0.2	0.1	1	D	D	D	128	4.2	NA	NA
Brooks	20	339	10.7	5.3	11	31	3.3	0.7	612	12.7	210	2
Brown	136	3,126	206.2	77.2	69	381	24.3	6.9	2,508	103.9	28,129	280
Burleson	16	D	D	D	26	115	11.4	3.7	1,453	63.9	2,122	16
Burnet	106	1,302	145.3	51.5	71	303	24.0	6.9	5,113	294.2	99,192	592

Table B. States and Counties — Population, Vital Statistics, Health, and Crime

STATE County	Persons in group quarters, 2017	Daytime Population, 2012-2016 Number	Daytime Population, 2012-2016 Employment/ residence ratio	Births, 2017 Total	Births, 2017 Rate[1]	Deaths, 2017 Number	Deaths, 2017 Rate[1]	Persons under 65 with no health insurance, 2016 Number	Persons under 65 with no health insurance, 2016 Percent	Medicare, 2017 Total beneficiaries	Medicare, 2017 Enrolled in Original Medicare	Medicare, 2017 Enrolled in Medicare Advantage	Serious crimes known to police[2], 2016 Total Number	Serious crimes known to police[2], 2016 Total Rate[3]
	32	33	34	35	36	37	38	39	40	41	42	43	44	45
TEXAS— Cont'd														
Caldwell	3,339	32,632	0.58	561	13.3	312	7.4	7,105	20.9	6,923	4,821	2,102	674	1,648
Calhoun	253	25,060	1.34	302	13.9	213	9.8	3,335	18.4	3,938	3,301	637	728	3,690
Callahan	75	11,097	0.51	157	11.3	181	13.0	2,088	18.9	2,863	2,164	699	165	1,220
Cameron	3,354	414,371	0.97	7,047	16.6	2,739	6.5	106,485	29.5	60,072	34,158	25,914	13,708	3,234
Camp	67	10,983	0.68	174	13.5	130	10.1	2,168	20.6	3,017	2,127	890	257	2,024
Carson	25	5,607	0.85	61	10.1	53	8.8	761	15.0	1,088	874	214	82	1,387
Cass	355	27,703	0.78	353	11.8	437	14.6	3,637	15.5	7,813	5,537	2,275	747	2,506
Castro	63	7,565	0.90	118	15.0	36	4.6	1,792	27.6	1,097	947	150	171	2,266
Chambers	228	36,269	0.89	538	13.0	259	6.2	5,524	15.7	3,188	2,191	997	1,168	2,959
Cherokee	2,870	47,818	0.82	777	14.9	523	10.0	9,108	22.5	8,486	5,904	2,581	1,236	2,706
Childress	1,455	7,254	1.08	75	10.6	68	9.6	766	16.7	1,245	937	308	NA	NA
Clay	63	7,758	0.41	87	8.3	123	11.8	1,411	17.5	1,754	1,421	332	114	1,112
Cochran	78	2,759	0.83	37	13.0	9	3.2	686	28.4	538	418	120	83	2,853
Coke	35	2,802	0.71	43	13.0	49	14.8	414	17.2	845	638	207	30	934
Coleman	49	7,665	0.76	73	8.7	115	13.6	1,303	20.4	2,369	1,954	415	NA	NA
Collin	5,074	840,105	0.90	11,158	11.5	4,529	4.7	90,995	10.8	101,322	72,634	28,688	16,097	1,715
Collingsworth	51	2,811	0.83	30	10.0	28	9.4	726	29.7	629	555	74	21	692
Colorado	352	20,239	0.94	262	12.3	265	12.5	3,218	19.6	4,521	3,757	765	279	1,341
Comal	1,241	122,919	0.98	1,627	11.5	1,120	7.9	15,496	14.1	30,524	21,481	9,043	2,674	2,010
Comanche	169	12,169	0.75	166	12.2	174	12.8	2,493	24.5	3,239	2,526	713	307	2,311
Concho	39	4,306	1.16	28	10.3	26	9.6	372	18.4	645	491	155	15	369
Cooke	641	38,333	0.97	569	14.3	407	10.2	6,491	20.4	7,164	5,427	1,737	844	2,192
Coryell	12,082	64,954	0.65	962	12.8	443	5.9	7,510	13.4	8,949	6,357	2,592	1,403	1,864
Cottle	0	1,529	0.95	13	9.4	17	12.3	280	26.3	406	307	99	11	782
Crane	87	5,004	1.09	72	15.2	15	3.2	834	19.8	621	444	177	38	734
Crockett	39	4,179	1.20	45	12.6	28	7.9	633	20.7	666	558	108	40	1,081
Crosby	63	5,220	0.68	82	13.9	59	10.0	1,041	21.6	1,169	802	367	30	629
Culberson	12	2,232	0.97	29	13.0	15	6.7	447	25.3	475	383	92	0	0
Dallam	40	7,692	1.19	163	22.6	30	4.2	1,659	26.0	1,447	1,204	243	260	3,622
Dallas	33,440	2,835,857	1.27	40,530	15.5	16,520	6.3	492,034	21.6	332,353	213,071	119,282	94,170	3,645
Dawson	1,366	13,300	1.00	191	14.9	127	9.9	2,131	21.8	2,265	1,748	517	478	3,593
Deaf Smith	341	19,310	1.03	340	18.1	162	8.6	3,901	24.0	2,652	2,110	541	511	2,718
Delta	55	4,301	0.51	67	12.6	59	11.1	739	18.2	1,268	1,001	268	28	539
Denton	11,930	619,042	0.66	10,371	12.4	3,893	4.7	83,638	11.6	69,626	48,046	21,580	14,351	1,787
DeWitt	1,831	21,730	1.14	266	13.2	233	11.5	2,576	16.9	3,697	3,017	681	452	2,164
Dickens	315	2,259	1.03	21	9.5	16	7.2	337	24.0	561	440	121	37	1,717
Dimmit	82	15,630	2.23	163	15.6	94	9.0	1,650	18.2	1,797	1,167	630	185	1,659
Donley	188	3,218	0.80	31	9.4	44	13.3	536	22.2	858	696	162	48	1,394
Duval	641	11,047	0.88	163	14.5	132	11.7	1,654	18.7	2,292	1,499	793	286	2,533
Eastland	850	18,054	0.97	214	11.6	252	13.7	2,837	20.8	4,556	3,426	1,130	344	1,999
Ector	2,861	153,930	1.01	2,797	17.8	1,220	7.8	29,226	20.9	19,730	15,148	4,582	7,306	4,459
Edwards	5	1,998	0.97	23	11.8	12	6.1	344	24.5	673	523	150	22	1,178
Ellis	1,776	138,100	0.70	2,245	12.9	1,263	7.3	25,255	17.3	27,730	19,157	8,573	3,043	1,834
El Paso	15,268	830,967	0.99	13,224	15.7	5,384	6.4	152,482	21.2	121,822	52,724	69,098	17,420	2,078
Erath	3,931	39,560	0.94	468	11.2	341	8.1	7,032	21.8	6,099	4,588	1,511	777	1,864
Falls	1,913	15,206	0.65	226	13.0	158	9.1	2,429	19.7	2,940	1,899	1,041	129	868
Fannin	3,075	30,226	0.73	370	10.7	447	13.0	5,286	21.1	7,278	5,726	1,551	379	1,224
Fayette	406	24,256	0.94	260	10.3	286	11.3	3,651	19.3	6,618	5,279	1,338	353	1,403
Fisher	22	3,393	0.73	43	11.1	47	12.1	524	17.7	830	647	183	66	1,741
Floyd	35	5,877	0.91	75	12.8	55	9.4	1,087	22.8	1,193	877	316	128	2,211
Foard	32	1,239	0.85	11	9.0	12	9.8	212	24.1	372	314	58	0	0
Fort Bend	5,382	542,263	0.56	10,214	13.4	3,497	4.6	79,016	12.0	65,922	40,381	25,540	12,644	1,705
Franklin	75	10,517	0.99	110	10.2	123	11.4	1,477	17.7	1,868	1,396	472	136	1,280
Freestone	1,631	17,952	0.78	206	10.5	195	9.9	2,926	20.3	3,797	2,866	931	261	1,331
Frio	3,367	21,197	1.40	244	12.4	134	6.8	2,674	20.1	2,529	1,673	856	376	1,973
Gaines	71	18,680	0.90	456	22.1	123	6.0	5,733	30.9	1,878	1,531	347	255	1,242
Galveston	5,225	278,525	0.75	4,269	12.7	2,857	8.5	43,977	15.7	54,087	36,061	18,026	9,711	2,965
Garza	2,129	6,813	1.09	72	11.0	24	3.7	797	22.3	852	606	246	63	987
Gillespie	330	25,799	1.01	262	9.8	366	13.7	4,392	23.6	7,814	6,355	1,459	284	1,088
Glasscock	0	1,551	1.56	15	11.1	7	5.2	232	20.2	158	133	24	17	1,279
Goliad	85	6,380	0.62	78	10.3	78	10.3	835	14.2	1,405	1,065	340	108	1,426
Gonzales	311	21,009	1.07	323	15.5	203	9.7	4,298	24.9	3,872	3,010	862	463	2,240
Gray	2,014	22,769	0.97	305	13.6	240	10.7	3,881	22.4	4,216	3,420	796	1,068	4,585
Grayson	2,275	119,139	0.91	1,610	12.3	1,353	10.3	20,325	19.4	27,790	21,105	6,685	2,752	2,221
Gregg	4,164	143,771	1.38	1,769	14.3	1,265	10.3	19,949	19.5	27,712	20,245	7,468	5,083	4,094
Grimes	2,914	24,883	0.78	343	12.2	252	9.0	4,279	21.0	5,402	3,804	1,598	541	1,959

1. Per 1,000 estimated resident population.   2. Data for serious crimes have not been adjusted for underreporting; this may affect comparability between geographic areas and over time.
3. Per 100,000 population estimated by the FBI.

Table B. States and Counties — Crime, Education, Money Income, and Poverty

STATE County	Serious crimes known to police, 2016 (cont.)[1] Rate Violent	Property	Education — School enrollment and attainment, 2012-2016 — Enrollment[3] Total	Percent private	Attainment[4] (percent) High school graduate or less	Bachelor's degree or more	Local government expenditures,[5] 2013-2014 Total current spending (mil dol)	Current spending per student (dollars)	Money income, 2012-2016 Per capita income[6]	Households Median income (dollars)	Percent with income of less than $50,000	with income of $200,000 or more	Income and poverty, 2016 Median household income (dollars)	Percent below poverty level All persons	Children under 18 years	Children 5 to 17 years in families
	46	47	48	49	50	51	52	53	54	55	56	57	58	59	60	61
TEXAS— Cont'd																
Caldwell	237	1,411	9,810	5.9	57.0	14.7	55.3	8,215	21,485	49,533	50.7	2.1	49,598	16.6	24.0	23.7
Calhoun	654	3,036	5,178	3.7	53.0	15.4	35.5	8,283	25,181	54,167	47.0	2.8	52,916	15.7	25.1	23.3
Callahan	67	1,153	3,020	11.5	52.7	14.7	22.4	9,134	22,557	40,568	57.1	2.5	45,727	14.9	24.7	23.3
Cameron	379	2,855	127,111	4.2	59.4	16.8	931.6	9,168	15,457	34,578	64.0	1.8	36,587	29.1	40.4	37.8
Camp	244	1,780	3,030	8.0	56.9	15.0	28.1	11,442	20,034	40,045	59.7	1.0	41,937	19.2	31.6	30.6
Carson	490	896	1,528	8.4	35.8	26.4	13.7	10,640	28,943	64,554	35.9	2.2	62,573	8.6	12.0	11.0
Cass	376	2,131	6,209	5.1	59.1	14.4	51.1	9,078	21,608	39,366	60.7	1.5	40,597	17.4	26.4	24.8
Castro	93	2,173	2,103	1.8	61.3	13.1	18.8	11,025	21,230	42,733	60.0	1.2	45,229	18.1	25.6	23.8
Chambers	415	2,543	10,235	7.6	45.4	21.1	72.5	9,887	29,729	70,396	39.3	6.2	80,279	9.2	12.6	11.8
Cherokee	412	2,294	12,664	9.8	54.2	17.4	89.4	8,155	19,871	40,769	59.3	2.1	39,407	19.4	28.0	27.2
Childress	NA	NA	1,278	9.5	55.3	15.6	10.2	8,996	18,745	37,125	62.2	0.8	39,140	21.5	27.7	24.9
Clay	137	975	2,281	12.0	52.6	16.3	17.7	10,341	26,696	45,341	53.2	3.2	49,171	13.3	18.8	16.6
Cochran	241	2,613	758	6.2	61.8	9.5	12.3	15,028	20,408	38,625	60.1	1.6	39,900	23.5	38.6	36.8
Coke	31	903	723	6.6	49.5	20.5	5.9	11,383	27,755	41,756	58.7	1.9	41,529	15.6	22.0	19.9
Coleman	NA	NA	1,578	7.7	57.6	14.2	13.4	10,506	25,178	42,049	64.6	4.4	42,258	20.1	33.3	30.6
Collin	154	1,561	255,045	12.9	21.8	50.2	1,477.8	7,998	39,933	86,188	27.2	11.6	90,382	6.3	7.2	6.5
Collingsworth	297	396	741	4.2	51.1	17.0	5.9	9,631	21,116	40,257	60.3	2.2	37,389	19.7	30.7	28.3
Colorado	255	1,086	4,232	12.1	55.7	18.4	32.0	9,049	26,161	45,398	55.4	3.1	48,161	14.5	23.0	22.3
Comal	250	1,760	28,141	12.7	34.1	34.5	199.9	7,190	33,872	69,666	36.3	7.4	76,296	8.6	13.0	12.0
Comanche	196	2,115	2,741	7.2	56.7	17.0	21.3	9,362	21,681	39,054	61.7	1.3	40,052	17.1	28.1	25.2
Concho	25	344	766	1.6	66.1	11.5	5.1	10,925	16,599	48,516	52.4	3.5	39,622	25.8	26.9	24.0
Cooke	343	1,849	9,041	14.7	43.6	21.6	56.2	8,895	28,045	56,269	45.7	3.8	59,243	13.8	21.5	19.9
Coryell	279	1,585	21,810	8.4	40.6	15.1	95.9	8,344	20,555	49,275	50.9	1.8	50,122	14.2	19.2	18.1
Cottle	71	711	368	8.7	58.1	16.2	2.8	13,352	20,397	33,750	64.1	1.2	34,605	21.4	36.5	33.2
Crane	77	656	1,426	3.1	58.2	12.9	14.4	12,545	25,367	60,133	40.4	4.8	57,408	10.3	14.0	13.4
Crockett	81	1,000	771	1.9	60.6	11.0	10.2	12,556	23,861	50,646	48.9	0.9	46,556	16.9	28.5	26.1
Crosby	63	566	1,489	7.2	61.1	12.1	15.7	13,167	19,651	39,026	63.6	1.8	35,136	24.1	38.3	37.0
Culberson	0	0	487	2.9	70.0	7.7	5.2	11,220	18,862	33,981	66.3	2.5	36,663	23.6	38.0	35.5
Dallam	669	2,953	1,954	12.2	56.9	11.8	16.8	8,663	19,908	43,897	54.7	1.8	48,470	11.3	17.9	17.4
Dallas	515	3,130	677,594	12.7	44.5	29.7	4,093.6	8,412	28,552	51,411	48.5	5.8	54,429	16.3	24.9	24.0
Dawson	466	3,127	3,119	6.7	62.2	12.6	29.7	11,058	21,193	42,354	55.6	3.3	41,073	21.4	28.7	26.9
Deaf Smith	319	2,399	5,789	5.3	59.3	14.2	36.3	8,281	19,823	47,219	51.9	1.5	43,944	17.1	27.1	26.0
Delta	0	539	1,167	6.4	49.5	18.6	7.4	9,313	20,822	40,529	57.6	2.1	41,266	18.5	27.9	26.9
Denton	173	1,614	224,226	12.0	26.9	42.2	1,114.7	8,131	36,238	76,678	31.3	9.4	80,841	8.2	9.3	8.8
DeWitt	464	1,700	4,219	8.9	58.5	14.6	34.4	11,569	27,370	50,582	49.4	7.2	46,915	18.2	26.8	26.8
Dickens	557	1,160	410	1.5	52.7	14.3	5.5	13,696	22,526	42,118	58.1	2.0	38,239	21.8	29.0	24.8
Dimmit	27	1,633	3,045	3.7	64.8	10.5	23.0	9,350	19,528	32,204	63.4	3.3	38,275	27.6	38.1	38.6
Donley	87	1,307	949	8.2	46.6	16.5	6.8	11,986	22,454	40,560	58.7	2.4	38,777	18.6	33.6	30.7
Duval	585	1,949	2,498	3.8	66.0	8.9	25.4	9,872	19,853	33,115	66.1	2.3	34,777	26.3	38.4	37.8
Eastland	227	1,772	4,158	7.9	51.0	14.6	27.6	9,424	21,577	34,434	68.1	2.6	37,789	20.0	29.9	28.8
Ector	713	3,746	43,410	10.0	53.9	15.2	236.0	7,368	27,295	58,335	43.5	4.7	53,474	13.9	19.4	19.2
Edwards	214	964	238	0.0	53.9	24.0	7.1	12,490	27,333	39,457	57.7	1.3	36,539	23.3	39.3	40.1
Ellis	168	1,666	44,701	11.8	43.9	21.9	263.4	8,083	27,313	64,382	37.8	4.6	69,448	9.7	14.3	12.3
El Paso	364	1,713	260,231	7.4	47.9	21.7	1,569.7	8,824	19,145	42,075	57.9	2.0	42,048	22.7	31.4	31.1
Erath	151	1,713	14,190	8.4	40.2	28.2	48.9	8,453	22,781	42,492	57.7	2.2	43,787	19.5	20.8	20.4
Falls	128	740	3,785	4.6	60.7	11.9	25.0	11,019	17,257	38,547	60.7	0.8	38,559	25.6	33.8	32.7
Fannin	142	1,082	7,491	9.1	51.7	15.6	51.8	9,321	21,429	45,471	53.4	1.5	46,347	16.1	22.0	19.8
Fayette	258	1,145	5,068	11.5	55.5	17.1	36.9	9,886	28,665	51,290	49.0	4.8	53,776	11.1	16.1	15.4
Fisher	343	1,398	708	7.9	49.2	18.4	6.1	11,285	26,796	41,531	59.3	1.4	46,247	15.6	23.1	22.3
Floyd	466	1,745	1,487	7.0	55.2	16.4	14.4	11,483	23,133	43,070	57.0	1.7	40,536	22.8	37.3	33.1
Foard	0	0	278	1.4	53.1	16.0	3.0	13,399	23,323	48,068	53.2	1.0	36,056	18.0	28.2	25.8
Fort Bend	225	1,480	209,536	13.4	28.3	44.6	1,381.4	7,921	37,134	91,152	25.6	14.2	90,972	8.3	11.0	10.2
Franklin	273	1,007	2,354	17.6	45.1	19.0	14.8	8,969	25,250	42,652	55.9	3.8	44,202	15.8	25.8	22.7
Freestone	143	1,188	4,270	4.9	52.9	11.5	39.5	10,749	23,370	45,134	53.7	2.2	45,681	19.1	26.2	21.8
Frio	178	1,794	4,439	8.9	71.5	7.3	33.4	10,005	17,547	37,163	61.0	2.0	39,193	25.8	33.3	32.2
Gaines	97	1,145	4,988	24.3	68.5	10.5	45.0	13,078	22,837	58,788	42.2	3.1	51,910	14.6	21.2	20.9
Galveston	304	2,661	85,201	11.1	37.3	28.9	647.8	8,080	32,756	63,064	40.7	7.9	64,155	12.9	18.1	17.4
Garza	157	830	1,220	8.8	69.9	8.8	10.0	10,499	19,043	52,708	48.6	4.2	44,210	30.0	31.6	30.3
Gillespie	50	1,038	4,820	19.1	38.7	34.1	35.5	10,939	30,939	55,850	45.3	4.4	58,787	9.8	16.8	15.6
Glasscock	0	1,279	409	2.9	48.0	25.2	6.1	20,545	34,834	62,159	40.9	11.9	71,360	8.7	11.7	10.9
Goliad	211	1,215	1,547	0.3	48.8	16.0	14.0	10,255	30,581	54,375	46.5	5.5	55,264	14.3	24.9	22.6
Gonzales	542	1,698	4,846	10.5	61.3	13.7	40.4	9,783	22,631	46,630	52.7	3.7	45,491	17.1	25.6	24.9
Gray	502	4,082	5,318	9.4	52.0	13.6	37.5	8,971	22,409	45,264	53.6	1.4	47,828	19.4	24.1	21.6
Grayson	270	1,950	30,790	11.1	43.3	20.2	190.8	8,828	25,541	50,212	49.8	2.9	51,808	13.2	19.2	18.0
Gregg	466	3,628	31,380	12.3	44.8	20.7	217.7	9,089	24,386	47,140	52.6	2.8	45,594	17.4	25.0	23.6
Grimes	290	1,669	6,262	6.5	57.3	13.2	41.6	9,358	21,173	47,839	51.5	2.6	50,891	16.7	24.9	24.3

1. Data for serious crimes have not been adjusted for underreporting; this may affect comparability between geographic areas and over time.   2. Per 100,000 population estimated by the FBI.
3. All persons 3 years old and over enrolled in nursery school through college.   4. Persons 25 years old and over.   5. Elementary and secondary education expenditures.
6. Based on population estimated by the American Community Survey, 2011–2015.

Table B. States and Counties — **Personal Income and Earnings**

	Personal income, 2016										Earnings, 2016		
			Per capita[1]			Supplements to wages and salaries, employer contributions (mil dol)						Contributions for government social insurance (mil dol)		
STATE County	Total (mil dol)	Percent change 2015-2016	Dollars	Rank	Wages and salaries (mil dol)	Pension and insurance	Government social insurance	Proprietors' income (mil dol)	Dividends, interest, and rent (mil dol)	Personal transfer reecipts (mil dol)	Total (mil dol)	From employee and self-employed	From employer
	62	63	64	65	66	67	68	69	70	71	72	73	74
TEXAS— Cont'd													
Caldwell	1,294	3.0	31,429	2,685	320	58	23	99	194	341	500	54	23
Calhoun	798	-4.6	36,332	1,946	706	121	49	29	112	209	905	99	49
Callahan	502	-1.5	36,353	1,941	88	17	6	23	84	139	135	16	6
Cameron	11,421	2.3	27,055	3,025	4,769	998	345	911	1,397	3,731	7,023	740	345
Camp	475	-1.9	36,948	1,831	148	28	10	64	74	135	250	24	10
Carson	273	5.6	45,119	770	376	38	27	38	37	47	479	52	27
Cass	1,022	-0.5	33,642	2,374	291	57	21	68	149	383	437	51	21
Castro	359	-30.2	46,835	624	110	18	6	111	46	67	245	13	6
Chambers	1,994	-0.2	49,970	417	858	133	59	102	212	263	1,152	122	59
Cherokee	1,674	0.1	32,404	2,558	568	122	37	131	245	529	857	87	37
Childress	208	8.3	29,459	2,895	103	25	6	11	34	63	146	14	6
Clay	415	-3.9	40,714	1,276	53	12	3	24	70	102	93	10	3
Cochran	127	6.0	44,064	872	31	7	2	38	16	30	78	4	2
Coke	109	-1.2	33,374	2,414	26	7	2	7	20	40	41	5	2
Coleman	300	-4.3	35,608	2,064	72	16	5	21	64	116	114	13	5
Collin	57,483	4.4	61,179	135	25,653	2,919	1,715	6,528	7,830	4,276	36,815	3,642	1,715
Collingsworth	118	13.1	39,032	1,491	41	8	3	15	20	35	67	6	3
Colorado	968	-1.0	46,072	685	292	49	20	96	189	237	456	48	20
Comal	7,189	3.8	53,333	292	2,328	321	164	706	1,275	1,169	3,518	365	164
Comanche	493	-1.5	36,554	1,907	127	26	8	58	88	153	219	22	8
Concho	96	-2.3	22,477	3,105	37	6	3	0	23	33	46	6	3
Cooke	1,880	-6.4	47,889	545	665	114	47	299	358	353	1,125	107	47
Coryell	2,418	-0.5	32,376	2,559	711	153	47	71	477	557	981	99	47
Cottle	81	2.8	58,009	176	19	4	1	5	31	19	29	3	1
Crane	185	-7.4	38,322	1,601	77	14	5	29	18	33	125	11	5
Crockett	125	-10.2	34,063	2,315	60	12	4	6	29	30	82	9	4
Crosby	210	12.4	34,986	2,166	57	11	4	21	31	77	93	9	4
Culberson	95	5.4	43,072	989	55	10	4	1	11	25	70	8	4
Dallam	387	-16.8	54,826	245	174	23	13	121	42	54	331	27	13
Dallas	135,917	0.6	52,784	314	114,427	13,235	7,801	20,588	27,704	16,659	156,051	16,012	7,801
Dawson	446	1.4	34,055	2,317	166	35	11	59	73	127	271	24	11
Deaf Smith	715	-23.0	37,947	1,666	295	50	19	145	98	161	509	41	19
Delta	194	1.3	37,273	1,776	31	10	2	10	22	62	53	6	2
Denton	41,383	4.3	51,332	355	12,006	1,652	833	3,127	4,840	3,880	17,618	1,768	833
DeWitt	1,168	-2.5	55,956	214	326	64	21	127	436	234	537	50	21
Dickens	70	3.0	31,954	2,623	21	5	1	3	15	25	31	3	1
Dimmit	446	-12.8	41,310	1,198	243	44	18	55	57	112	360	37	18
Donley	138	-7.5	40,549	1,295	34	8	2	22	24	38	66	5	2
Duval	404	-8.0	35,308	2,115	128	29	9	4	49	164	170	20	9
Eastland	935	-3.5	51,152	367	304	58	22	86	307	229	471	50	22
Ector	6,538	-7.7	41,522	1,160	3,729	516	255	768	779	1,039	5,268	532	255
Edwards	62	-18.0	32,575	2,540	16	4	1	-6	22	23	15	3	1
Ellis	6,756	4.0	40,094	1,355	2,181	342	159	431	750	1,165	3,113	338	159
El Paso	27,613	2.4	32,954	2,481	13,462	2,842	1,026	1,774	4,360	6,600	19,105	2,036	1,026
Erath	1,379	0.1	33,107	2,454	576	115	39	170	235	322	900	84	39
Falls	560	0.3	32,442	2,554	135	35	9	36	80	193	215	22	9
Fannin	1,234	2.4	36,265	1,963	303	69	21	58	170	366	451	51	21
Fayette	1,212	-1.4	48,197	518	362	64	25	91	315	279	541	58	25
Fisher	176	-4.5	45,679	725	39	9	2	17	27	45	66	6	2
Floyd	226	-9.4	38,116	1,637	64	13	4	40	33	67	121	10	4
Foard	44	-12.1	37,381	1,751	11	2	1	0	9	19	14	2	1
Fort Bend	40,030	0.1	54,005	269	9,289	1,258	628	3,013	5,017	3,444	14,188	1,388	628
Franklin	370	-4.3	34,850	2,188	122	19	9	45	64	105	196	21	9
Freestone	641	-3.4	32,667	2,533	243	49	17	32	125	185	341	39	17
Frio	642	-5.1	33,854	2,343	301	51	21	67	86	157	440	44	21
Gaines	731	-2.9	35,690	2,047	310	55	20	169	79	113	555	46	20
Galveston	15,683	0.1	47,605	559	5,435	1,087	356	823	2,445	2,616	7,701	762	356
Garza	232	5.4	36,064	1,997	72	13	5	69	40	46	160	12	5
Gillespie	1,476	1.8	55,644	220	415	65	29	133	551	294	643	70	29
Glasscock	121	13.4	91,765	17	26	5	2	32	51	6	64	4	2
Goliad	318	-2.7	42,320	1,058	51	12	3	21	72	76	86	9	3
Gonzales	886	-10.7	42,456	1,044	282	54	18	143	212	196	497	41	18
Gray	949	-6.1	41,772	1,131	377	68	25	111	201	197	581	56	25
Grayson	4,993	2.4	38,932	1,505	1,990	317	142	281	745	1,293	2,730	309	142
Gregg	5,517	-3.6	44,580	819	3,511	492	261	589	940	1,255	4,852	531	261
Grimes	987	-0.3	35,677	2,049	340	65	23	54	161	237	482	52	23

1. Based on the resident population estimated as of July 1 of the year shown.

Table B. States and Counties — Earnings, Social Security, and Housing

STATE County	Farm	Mining, quarrying, and extracting	Construction	Manufacturing	Information; professional, scientific, technical services	Retail trade	Finance, insurance, real estate, and leasing	Health care and social assistance	Government	Social Security beneficiaries, December 2016 Number	Rate[1]	Supplemental Security Income recipients, 2016	Housing units, 2017 Total	Percent change, 2010-2017
	75	76	77	78	79	80	81	82	83	84	85	86	87	88
TEXAS— Cont'd														
Caldwell	-0.3	2.9	12.9	5.1	D	9.9	4.2	13.1	19.9	7,325	178	1,064	14,816	7.7
Calhoun	0.0	1.7	19.2	44.5	5.3	4.5	2.4	3.5	9.3	4,365	199	551	11,989	5.1
Callahan	-6.3	4.1	19.1	5.4	4.0	12.6	4.7	6.0	26.1	3,350	243	312	6,679	2.0
Cameron	0.5	0.2	4.5	4.8	3.5	9.1	4.6	20.3	27.8	64,180	152	22,780	151,023	6.4
Camp	7.2	D	16.4	D	D	7.3	6.1	9.0	12.7	2,975	233	494	5,765	1.9
Carson	6.0	D	3.8	D	0.7	1.8	D	D	4.7	1,195	196	46	2,797	0.5
Cass	2.3	2.2	9.2	22.9	D	5.6	3.7	D	19.9	8,240	274	1,139	14,573	1.3
Castro	49.8	1.1	0.8	1.0	3.7	2.7	6.2	0.9	12.7	1,225	157	135	3,175	0.3
Chambers	1.5	7.5	14.8	26.9	D	4.2	2.1	D	11.8	6,280	156	510	15,598	17.3
Cherokee	7.3	1.6	6.8	12.2	D	5.9	4.5	D	27.5	10,815	208	1,435	21,255	1.9
Childress	-0.1	D	D	D	6.8	7.0	5.2	4.8	46.2	1,335	188	167	2,843	-1.4
Clay	0.7	8.7	7.2	4.1	D	9.3	D	D	29.3	2,585	252	170	5,246	1.9
Cochran	47.1	D	D	D	D	2.9	1.8	2.5	22.4	580	199	113	1,359	-0.1
Coke	-8.6	14.1	11.1	D	D	8.0	D	2.4	34.2	945	290	69	2,710	1.8
Coleman	-6.8	1.7	14.4	3.5	D	7.8	10.3	D	26.2	2,480	295	251	5,520	-0.4
Collin	0.0	1.5	6.1	7.8	19.2	7.9	13.4	10.0	8.9	101,935	108	7,734	363,568	20.8
Collingsworth	17.1	D	D	D	D	4.4	4.3	D	16.8	620	205	69	1,597	-1.2
Colorado	1.8	2.5	17.2	16.6	4.2	7.0	4.9	D	13.6	5,125	244	476	10,667	1.3
Comal	-0.2	1.9	15.7	5.3	7.7	10.3	6.0	10.0	11.3	29,250	218	1,427	57,937	23.0
Comanche	11.3	2.3	6.5	3.7	D	8.9	4.8	9.8	18.0	3,660	271	347	7,340	1.7
Concho	-6.5	D	D	D	D	3.1	D	11.6	29.5	705	165	63	1,655	1.1
Cooke	-0.3	11.4	5.4	25.3	3.7	5.9	6.8	D	15.3	7,965	203	593	16,929	2.0
Coryell	-0.7	1.0	8.6	2.2	9.7	6.3	6.6	6.5	41.0	10,435	139	1,249	26,678	5.8
Cottle	11.9	1.1	8.4	0.3	D	8.6	9.3	D	23.4	435	310	50	948	-2.1
Crane	0.2	45.3	D	D	D	3.3	D	3.9	19.4	715	149	87	1,676	2.7
Crockett	-7.2	31.2	D	D	D	7.4	11.2	0.6	25.1	725	198	53	1,887	1.1
Crosby	22.2	D	D	D	D	12.6	D	7.1	24.8	1,320	223	170	2,906	0.2
Culberson	1.8	5.1	D	D	D	15.2	D	D	31.1	530	239	115	1,167	2.6
Dallam	18.7	0.1	10.1	13.7	4.2	5.2	6.6	1.4	4.9	985	136	97	2,944	4.2
Dallas	0.0	3.8	6.4	6.9	17.7	5.0	12.7	9.6	9.3	313,220	121	64,497	1,012,992	7.4
Dawson	12.7	9.3	4.8	1.4	2.3	14.4	4.0	D	29.5	2,445	187	406	5,172	-0.9
Deaf Smith	25.6	D	3.8	16.3	2.5	7.5	3.3	2.5	14.3	2,875	153	410	7,048	-0.4
Delta	7.2	0.7	9.6	D	D	1.9	2.7	27.9	28.9	1,385	269	186	2,480	0.9
Denton	0.1	1.5	8.8	7.5	11.8	7.5	9.0	10.0	14.3	85,995	106	6,852	309,325	20.7
DeWitt	-1.1	16.6	10.4	10.7	D	5.9	6.2	4.2	23.8	4,580	222	492	9,227	0.6
Dickens	6.6	D	D	D	D	7.2	4.0	0.9	26.2	575	261	44	1,280	-0.1
Dimmit	0.4	23.3	11.3	0.5	D	4.0	6.7	D	25.8	1,980	184	572	4,416	1.5
Donley	22.1	D	D	D	D	5.0	9.8	2.7	30.0	880	259	80	2,148	0.4
Duval	-6.0	19.6	D	D	D	3.1	2.4	10.2	37.5	2,535	221	648	5,607	1.5
Eastland	-0.8	23.3	8.4	6.5	2.9	5.6	0.0	D	23.4	4,690	256	604	10,286	0.3
Ector	-0.1	19.4	13.6	7.5	3.9	7.0	5.4	6.0	13.4	20,015	127	3,418	58,175	9.7
Edwards	-66.7	D	D	D	D	16.5	D	2.6	58.2	550	287	78	1,622	1.0
Ellis	0.3	0.6	11.1	24.7	D	7.3	4.1	7.1	14.3	26,595	158	2,890	61,214	12.6
El Paso	0.0	0.0	4.5	5.7	5.1	8.0	5.2	10.5	37.2	127,150	152	29,543	296,585	9.7
Erath	7.6	1.7	9.5	10.9	D	8.1	4.8	9.4	22.6	6,450	156	568	18,157	6.9
Falls	4.0	D	6.1	4.1	4.9	7.1	D	8.8	40.7	3,495	202	714	7,749	0.3
Fannin	-0.8	2.3	8.2	8.9	2.8	9.4	5.8	D	37.6	7,890	233	862	14,430	1.7
Fayette	-0.8	6.8	9.3	7.9	5.5	10.3	7.7	9.7	18.1	6,610	264	412	13,970	0.7
Fisher	6.5	2.3	D	D	D	5.2	D	4.6	25.7	965	249	103	2,205	-0.3
Floyd	29.5	D	2.1	2.3	D	4.7	D	3.9	22.7	1,230	209	160	2,974	-1.0
Foard	-8.5	2.1	D	D	D	7.0	D	D	33.7	350	289	38	784	-0.6
Fort Bend	0.0	4.5	13.7	9.3	10.8	8.9	6.3	9.8	11.9	78,920	106	10,684	252,998	28.6
Franklin	10.5	D	6.0	D	D	3.0	3.9	21.1	12.4	2,445	229	183	5,849	1.4
Freestone	-0.6	20.5	5.2	2.7	5.0	6.7	3.4	D	22.1	4,120	210	449	9,436	1.9
Frio	8.2	14.7	8.9	2.8	2.7	4.3	2.5	D	20.4	2,795	144	714	5,963	2.0
Gaines	3.9	20.5	20.0	1.8	1.4	8.6	2.7	D	14.7	2,090	102	299	6,458	2.5
Galveston	0.0	1.6	8.9	12.2	6.6	6.8	6.9	6.9	28.7	54,130	164	6,718	146,439	10.5
Garza	12.5	34.4	D	D	D	3.2	1.5	D	12.7	865	134	104	2,204	-1.5
Gillespie	-2.2	3.0	15.4	8.3	7.0	10.1	6.6	17.8	11.4	8,035	305	291	13,149	2.9
Glasscock	13.4	D	D	D	2.1	D	D	1.2	11.5	195	144	7	585	0.9
Goliad	-10.1	19.9	D	D	D	4.4	3.9	5.3	29.1	1,670	222	181	3,781	1.9
Gonzales	18.5	6.1	3.6	12.4	3.5	5.4	3.5	D	18.1	4,050	194	509	8,946	1.7
Gray	6.2	14.2	4.3	20.0	D	7.2	3.1	8.5	15.3	4,345	191	346	10,005	-1.5
Grayson	0.3	0.8	9.9	15.2	4.6	8.7	7.7	17.8	14.3	27,765	217	3,047	55,868	4.0
Gregg	-0.1	9.7	12.8	10.2	6.3	8.1	5.2	14.5	9.2	24,830	201	4,658	51,963	4.9
Grimes	-2.4	1.2	9.7	22.0	D	5.2	4.8	D	24.1	5,600	203	750	11,255	3.2

1. Per 1,000 resident population estimated as of July 1 of the year shown.

Table B. States and Counties — Housing, Labor Force, and Employment

	Housing units, 2017 (cont.)								Civilian labor force, 2017				Civilian employment[6], 2012-2016		
	Occupied units										Unemployment			Percent	
	Owner-occupied					Renter-occupied									
				Median owner cost as a percent of income											
STATE County	Total	Percent	Median value[1]	With a mortgage	Without a mortgage[2]	Median rent[3]	Median rent as a percent of income[2]	Sub-standard units[4] (percent)	Total	Percent change, 2016-2017	Total	Rate[5]	Total	Management, business, science, and arts	Construction, production, and maintenance occupations
	89	90	91	92	93	94	95	96	97	98	99	100	101	102	103
TEXAS— Cont'd															
Caldwell	12,664	66.2	119,400	20.6	12.2	772	28.5	6.1	18,406	2.8	712	3.9	17,438	24.2	31.4
Calhoun	7,800	69.2	111,500	19.9	10.0	735	31.3	7.2	10,424	-3.1	606	5.8	9,734	27.1	37.5
Callahan	5,239	81.3	73,200	19.2	12.0	690	22.9	2.5	5,843	0.8	215	3.7	5,162	25.6	33.6
Cameron	121,290	66.8	79,900	23.2	12.5	653	32.5	12.7	166,268	0.3	11,431	6.9	149,676	27.5	21.6
Camp	4,544	70.4	80,300	19.1	12.2	690	27.4	4.5	5,040	-0.2	284	5.6	5,223	22.5	36.9
Carson	2,324	86.0	99,200	17.9	10.0	700	23.2	0.6	3,060	-1.0	97	3.2	2,923	37.5	28.4
Cass	11,770	76.9	65,400	21.8	12.1	570	27.2	4.0	12,198	-0.4	726	6.0	11,952	21.7	35.3
Castro	2,490	66.6	70,400	18.8	10.9	653	25.2	7.8	3,358	-3.8	110	3.3	3,274	23.3	37.4
Chambers	12,967	80.5	158,700	18.1	13.0	867	22.5	2.5	18,511	1.8	1,205	6.5	15,947	35.9	35.0
Cherokee	17,683	73.8	89,300	22.5	12.7	660	28.3	6.1	20,659	-2.4	936	4.5	19,899	28.6	30.2
Childress	2,356	58.2	73,200	22.3	15.2	741	26.1	0.3	2,910	-1.5	86	3.0	2,491	31.5	30.8
Clay	4,106	84.2	82,300	19.4	11.4	634	28.7	3.2	4,797	0.2	171	3.6	4,524	28.9	27.8
Cochran	1,007	78.9	33,000	16.9	10.0	453	20.0	9.7	1,133	-3.3	52	4.6	1,203	24.6	48.9
Coke	1,567	71.1	74,000	18.7	11.5	531	27.7	1.4	1,396	-1.6	51	3.7	1,529	40.9	28.1
Coleman	3,407	72.2	63,800	19.4	11.8	603	25.0	2.1	3,070	0.3	136	4.4	3,339	31.0	33.6
Collin	314,918	66.1	240,700	20.6	11.2	1,168	26.5	2.4	527,317	3.0	17,970	3.4	458,288	52.4	10.8
Collingsworth	1,097	76.4	57,600	16.9	10.7	583	23.8	3.5	1,159	-4.5	42	3.6	1,345	25.9	40.7
Colorado	7,624	81.5	106,200	19.9	11.5	646	23.9	5.4	10,080	3.1	387	3.8	9,067	29.7	30.9
Comal	45,338	74.9	227,000	20.8	10.0	1,018	28.1	3.4	66,826	2.2	2,246	3.4	56,681	38.4	18.8
Comanche	5,079	78.5	79,400	20.3	12.4	496	25.7	5.1	5,288	-1.1	195	3.7	5,341	29.3	34.5
Concho	790	73.7	100,800	19.7	11.9	618	27.1	0.1	1,207	-9.2	51	4.2	1,056	34.2	29.0
Cooke	14,896	69.9	134,000	19.5	11.6	740	27.7	4.3	18,826	-0.3	671	3.6	18,459	29.1	28.3
Coryell	22,791	56.5	103,400	19.7	10.5	917	27.2	2.8	24,691	1.3	1,057	4.3	22,967	30.8	20.0
Cottle	679	66.9	42,600	21.1	13.3	0	23.5	1.6	517	-1.5	22	4.3	653	29.7	23.0
Crane	1,543	78.7	77,800	13.8	10.0	690	24.2	5.4	1,588	-6.8	84	5.3	2,023	17.0	45.2
Crockett	1,431	75.7	76,600	18.1	10.8	554	22.1	5.3	1,689	-2.5	69	4.1	1,752	22.3	36.9
Crosby	2,110	67.7	56,100	18.0	11.6	589	23.7	6.0	2,603	-0.5	108	4.1	2,477	30.2	29.5
Culberson	762	66.3	60,100	18.0	13.2	531	31.2	3.5	913	-8.5	33	3.6	1,047	19.3	28.7
Dallam	2,360	57.7	79,000	20.9	10.1	704	20.9	3.4	4,056	1.6	86	2.1	3,468	20.3	38.6
Dallas	894,542	50.6	138,600	23.0	12.3	935	29.0	7.1	1,333,933	2.9	51,148	3.8	1,219,400	33.6	24.1
Dawson	4,329	71.5	62,200	17.5	11.3	586	24.0	2.8	4,656	0.5	227	4.9	4,870	25.3	34.8
Deaf Smith	6,081	66.1	87,400	19.9	10.5	732	23.1	4.9	8,339	-3.0	255	3.1	8,612	26.4	41.1
Delta	1,971	73.6	71,200	19.8	13.0	558	32.5	2.6	2,609	0.3	85	3.3	1,929	30.8	30.3
Denton	265,790	64.1	212,200	20.7	11.5	1,051	28.2	2.8	464,581	3.0	15,318	3.3	402,523	44.8	14.8
DeWitt	7,105	75.7	104,300	18.0	10.0	694	28.0	4.1	9,586	1.1	426	4.4	7,827	30.9	29.4
Dickens	869	72.6	50,700	17.8	12.7	472	15.0	3.3	682	-1.2	32	4.7	750	37.1	26.4
Dimmit	3,457	73.0	61,300	19.4	12.2	738	21.5	12.7	6,480	4.1	330	5.1	3,972	19.2	22.5
Donley	1,287	75.2	66,400	17.9	12.8	570	24.4	2.4	1,507	-3.0	55	3.6	1,467	31.9	25.2
Duval	3,892	67.8	48,400	18.4	12.2	705	23.1	12.8	4,803	-1.5	368	7.7	4,060	17.6	36.1
Eastland	6,752	73.3	58,800	26.1	12.0	531	20.7	2.8	7,852	6.0	339	4.3	6,842	31.7	27.8
Ector	50,950	66.3	112,300	18.8	10.0	934	24.7	6.6	78,116	2.7	3,212	4.1	71,470	23.1	35.5
Edwards	718	88.6	73,100	16.1	15.5	482	18.9	5.7	904	4.5	29	3.2	958	13.3	33.9
Ellis	53,803	72.2	150,300	20.9	11.5	932	29.8	3.8	87,132	2.7	2,991	3.4	76,262	32.4	27.7
El Paso	261,415	61.4	114,700	22.9	11.2	765	29.6	6.3	353,387	1.2	16,275	4.6	334,280	29.6	22.3
Erath	14,197	60.9	127,100	22.5	10.9	747	33.1	4.2	20,586	1.9	703	3.4	19,362	30.9	29.4
Falls	5,447	72.2	65,200	18.6	12.3	553	26.2	4.4	6,669	1.1	280	4.2	5,897	23.6	35.2
Fannin	12,022	75.0	94,500	20.3	12.7	709	29.3	3.2	15,937	1.3	530	3.3	13,104	30.4	30.0
Fayette	9,553	77.6	154,700	18.0	12.1	733	22.9	1.8	12,623	1.2	399	3.2	11,484	23.6	31.8
Fisher	1,650	72.8	62,700	18.6	10.0	553	21.8	4.0	1,722	-1.9	61	3.5	1,693	30.8	28.6
Floyd	2,444	70.3	57,900	16.9	10.9	658	28.0	7.1	2,694	-1.4	148	5.5	2,505	32.1	37.1
Foard	526	78.5	48,600	24.2	11.1	438	15.7	0.0	595	10.4	20	3.4	537	25.1	28.7
Fort Bend	214,126	78.0	217,600	21.2	11.0	1,252	27.3	3.6	369,788	1.0	17,129	4.6	325,326	49.6	14.7
Franklin	4,114	72.9	116,600	26.0	10.5	707	28.1	2.4	4,533	0.7	208	4.6	4,482	22.6	34.3
Freestone	7,339	75.9	82,500	19.9	12.0	667	24.0	2.8	6,738	-1.7	425	6.3	7,595	24.5	30.8
Frio	4,660	69.2	71,900	23.7	12.6	685	22.9	11.4	9,300	6.1	358	3.8	6,747	18.0	39.3
Gaines	5,630	75.7	102,400	18.3	10.0	752	18.6	5.7	9,239	0.8	280	3.0	8,017	25.2	43.4
Galveston	115,685	66.2	161,500	20.0	11.4	941	29.7	3.3	161,703	1.2	8,412	5.2	146,243	40.3	19.9
Garza	1,625	67.4	83,300	18.6	10.0	734	25.6	3.4	2,117	-0.5	70	3.3	2,257	28.3	31.6
Gillespie	10,498	77.0	254,500	25.1	11.9	893	29.3	4.8	13,193	1.7	340	2.6	11,319	34.8	22.6
Glasscock	438	67.1	191,500	17.3	10.0	1,048	24.4	2.3	689	-7.8	18	2.6	536	44.8	30.8
Goliad	2,798	82.0	124,700	15.0	10.0	686	25.4	3.3	3,244	-2.1	160	4.9	2,954	29.7	31.2
Gonzales	6,611	67.9	98,800	20.9	10.0	618	26.6	11.5	9,361	-2.0	326	3.5	8,783	20.1	38.8
Gray	8,201	72.8	73,700	17.6	10.6	707	26.8	3.3	8,216	-3.0	434	5.3	9,396	24.1	35.3
Grayson	47,161	67.4	110,000	20.5	12.3	785	27.2	3.3	62,020	1.5	2,163	3.5	55,571	31.3	25.1
Gregg	45,446	59.3	125,700	20.3	10.9	787	30.3	3.6	57,632	-1.1	2,954	5.1	54,723	27.6	29.1
Grimes	9,000	77.2	105,800	21.7	10.9	634	26.5	5.7	10,842	-1.7	572	5.3	10,246	24.1	35.4

1. Specified owner-occupied units. 2. A value of 10.0 represents 10 percent or less; a value of 50.0 represents 50 percent or more. 3. Specified renter-occupied units.
4. Overcrowded or lacking complete plumbing facilities. 5. Percent of civilian labor force. 6. Civilian employed persons 16 years old and over.

Table B. States and Counties — Nonfarm Employment and Agriculture

	Private nonfarm establishments, employment and payroll, 2016									Agriculture, 2012			
		Employment						Annual payroll		Farms			
												Percent with:	
STATE County	Number of establish-ments	Total	Health care and social assistance	Manufac-turing	Retail trade	Finance and insurance	Professional, scientific, and technical services	Total (mil dol)	Average per employee (dollars)	Number	Fewer than 50 acres	500 acres or more	Farm operators whose principal occupation is farming (percent)
	104	105	106	107	108	109	110	111	112	113	114	115	116
TEXAS— Cont'd													
Caldwell	604	6,878	1,969	723	1,058	189	114	203	29,502	1,623	42.7	8.3	40.1
Calhoun	453	8,339	806	3,079	1,061	176	586	510	61,128	264	29.2	31.4	46.6
Callahan	211	1,462	137	140	362	56	51	51	34,600	992	27.6	21.3	43.3
Cameron	6,376	108,580	35,817	4,259	18,647	3,399	3,413	2,906	26,761	1,305	66.3	11.5	45.4
Camp	222	2,521	388	198	437	114	30	106	41,964	487	40.0	6.2	41.3
Carson	127	781	23	D	184	37	23	30	38,312	386	15.5	46.6	51.0
Cass	502	5,770	854	1,666	824	226	110	210	36,480	1,024	29.6	5.2	43.1
Castro	159	1,043	D	44	176	57	89	36	34,730	532	9.0	51.5	54.3
Chambers	612	12,115	747	2,347	1,160	119	272	751	62,022	734	56.0	17.7	39.6
Cherokee	746	10,890	2,285	2,384	1,432	357	205	370	33,937	1,574	34.2	6.5	46.9
Childress	155	1,339	113	D	428	56	36	36	27,243	383	5.2	34.5	41.3
Clay	125	695	94	D	213	42	9	21	29,837	861	16.4	27.1	43.4
Cochran	46	254	101	D	61	D	D	8	30,756	288	4.9	47.6	51.7
Coke	55	262	NA	D	88	29	D	6	21,538	443	9.3	40.6	44.9
Coleman	201	1,451	345	100	262	84	35	40	27,467	906	10.9	36.5	46.7
Collin	22,620	388,842	50,360	18,243	51,551	48,319	39,109	23,771	61,134	2,264	64.9	4.4	33.0
Collingsworth	60	498	128	D	78	D	18	18	36,773	383	6.3	41.3	45.2
Colorado	544	5,956	850	1,552	946	179	139	228	38,281	1,575	28.3	13.0	48.6
Comal	3,475	46,645	5,954	3,030	7,113	965	1,825	1,832	39,272	1,104	44.8	9.3	36.9
Comanche	249	2,306	494	119	513	150	60	73	31,798	1,435	26.8	18.6	50.6
Concho	51	708	175	D	73	D	D	26	36,218	401	5.7	51.4	56.9
Cooke	900	12,684	1,040	3,116	1,982	412	236	535	42,185	1,946	40.0	10.9	42.2
Coryell	720	9,764	1,176	508	1,887	409	750	256	26,235	1,308	31.3	16.8	42.3
Cottle	26	109	D	D	51	21	D	3	28,679	264	6.4	44.7	32.2
Crane	86	970	150	D	122	12	11	53	54,991	27	29.6	66.7	51.9
Crockett	129	1,142	21	D	166	D	12	60	52,412	216	4.2	68.1	63.4
Crosby	97	615	161	D	125	26	8	30	48,205	431	8.6	43.4	51.0
Culberson	54	629	84	D	175	D	D	26	41,304	77	9.1	75.3	68.8
Dallam	220	1,809	43	61	282	79	67	63	34,826	371	5.9	62.3	59.0
Dallas	65,781	1,456,092	178,969	96,299	127,241	96,627	140,389	88,127	60,523	839	68.2	5.0	39.7
Dawson	274	2,475	268	112	674	125	64	89	35,965	596	7.2	42.8	55.0
Deaf Smith	395	5,467	528	1,648	844	198	187	221	40,340	621	11.3	55.2	64.6
Delta	54	788	632	NA	41	17	9	11	13,591	529	33.1	10.2	41.2
Denton	14,284	211,883	26,462	14,553	32,205	14,382	9,783	9,210	43,469	3,203	73.2	3.8	34.9
DeWitt	448	5,364	985	624	831	255	108	207	38,598	1,711	24.1	14.0	45.7
Dickens	42	243	15	NA	60	D	10	9	35,453	437	4.8	34.3	35.5
Dimmit	246	4,509	451	49	492	32	31	205	45,368	367	23.2	35.7	36.8
Donley	81	425	43	D	108	18	26	9	22,344	380	8.9	29.7	44.5
Duval	151	2,045	386	D	182	54	30	78	38,303	1,436	11.0	25.0	45.5
Eastland	425	5,476	784	579	831	147	1,039	221	40,424	1,174	17.3	18.6	33.6
Ector	3,584	57,465	6,976	3,311	8,324	1,506	1,389	2,780	48,383	264	70.5	14.4	28.8
Edwards	38	184	13	D	79	D	D	5	27,245	419	6.4	50.6	51.1
Ellis	2,825	42,063	4,061	9,938	6,008	910	890	1,660	39,458	2,264	48.4	8.2	40.8
El Paso	14,393	235,714	45,424	13,758	39,863	6,680	10,889	7,494	31,793	657	81.6	7.6	39.7
Erath	957	11,860	1,584	2,031	2,062	318	368	396	33,370	2,161	30.2	13.7	44.6
Falls	222	1,711	330	131	468	71	53	52	30,143	1,263	26.5	13.2	53.4
Fannin	470	4,992	1,263	622	964	163	112	175	35,149	2,515	41.4	8.5	43.2
Fayette	768	7,370	1,078	1,137	1,406	295	201	252	34,228	2,822	30.8	6.7	41.5
Fisher	72	541	111	D	73	46	18	22	41,030	588	8.5	38.4	38.6
Floyd	150	949	229	40	110	53	7	32	33,358	589	7.3	39.4	39.9
Foard	25	129	D	D	28	D	D	3	26,922	194	8.8	42.3	46.4
Fort Bend	12,668	160,048	26,424	13,004	27,699	5,186	10,273	6,902	43,127	1,286	46.6	9.7	47.1
Franklin	158	5,732	3,582	71	276	97	31	105	18,266	520	28.1	12.1	47.5
Freestone	341	3,504	580	174	469	127	90	140	39,851	1,517	30.3	11.8	45.6
Frio	320	5,340	634	63	722	153	63	232	43,410	651	20.0	35.3	50.8
Gaines	418	3,909	319	194	490	94	60	206	52,765	644	10.6	50.2	55.9
Galveston	5,761	85,769	15,271	6,006	13,750	4,097	4,548	3,397	39,612	612	63.2	8.7	45.4
Garza	125	1,237	164	D	184	27	8	44	35,491	277	8.7	46.9	43.7
Gillespie	977	9,292	1,691	728	1,612	314	352	310	33,322	1,847	30.5	19.9	41.5
Glasscock	30	206	NA	D	D	D	D	12	58,471	186	4.3	70.4	59.7
Goliad	117	755	93	D	87	22	28	31	41,121	1,175	27.9	17.2	44.4
Gonzales	408	4,999	739	1,277	757	170	102	188	37,627	1,674	23.1	18.9	46.1
Gray	567	5,965	821	649	1,048	186	193	245	41,118	417	15.3	47.7	35.7
Grayson	2,526	38,357	8,095	7,031	6,279	1,810	988	1,389	36,220	2,562	50.8	5.6	44.1
Gregg	4,057	64,947	10,903	8,735	9,509	2,108	2,722	2,680	41,270	527	59.0	4.2	42.9
Grimes	417	5,286	323	1,698	666	137	137	227	42,924	1,683	37.3	10.5	39.7

Table B. States and Counties — Agriculture

STATE County	Acreage (1,000)	Percent change, 2007-2012	Average size of farm	Total irrigated (1,000)	Total cropland (1,000)	Average per farm	Average per acre	Value of machinery and equipment, average per farm (dollars)	Total (mil dol)	Average per farm (acres)	Crops	Livestock and poultry products	$10,000 or more	$100,000 or more	Total ($1,000)	Percent of farms
	117	118	119	120	121	122	123	124	125	126	127	128	129	130	131	132
TEXAS— Cont'd																
Caldwell	310	1.9	191	0.6	55.9	632,375	3,306	45,283	62.9	38,779	17.8	82.2	22.2	2.7	1,076	10.2
Calhoun	184	-20.1	697	5.8	60.5	1,223,477	1,755	114,295	42.1	159,489	67.2	32.8	49.2	20.5	1,664	46.2
Callahan	563	5.7	568	0.7	87.2	857,079	1,510	49,690	29.9	30,142	19.5	80.5	28.7	4.9	1,943	26.1
Cameron	310	-11.4	237	112.3	209.2	697,056	2,937	84,762	160.4	122,916	91.9	8.1	32.1	13.3	4,851	45.4
Camp	78	14.1	161	0.7	20.4	418,072	2,602	73,626	137.7	282,686	2.2	97.8	37.8	9.0	118	5.5
Carson	485	-9.8	1,256	49.4	269.8	1,156,262	920	200,505	83.0	214,990	61.0	39.0	44.8	23.8	5,875	75.1
Cass	168	-5.1	164	0.2	38.9	337,149	2,060	50,023	67.6	66,010	7.8	92.2	27.3	5.1	128	4.1
Castro	548	-3.4	1,030	154.9	411.0	1,131,530	1,098	323,836	1,312.1	2,466,429	11.9	88.1	62.0	45.5	10,759	80.5
Chambers	254	-5.1	346	15.2	92.8	690,097	1,996	80,785	25.6	34,868	58.8	41.2	27.1	7.9	3,018	17.2
Cherokee	301	2.4	191	1.4	67.8	472,935	2,470	58,168	134.0	85,123	66.9	33.1	34.1	5.7	736	3.9
Childress	444	11.1	1,159	9.2	142.1	891,243	769	90,394	19.9	51,883	65.5	34.5	38.6	11.2	3,104	80.4
Clay	633	-4.4	735	1.7	99.2	1,158,323	1,577	71,052	79.8	92,695	15.6	84.4	48.0	13.0	2,098	34.5
Cochran	449	-8.2	1,558	67.8	268.5	1,048,688	673	204,642	100.8	349,955	D	D	35.8	25.3	7,287	87.2
Coke	484	-1.4	1,093	1.0	49.0	1,141,964	1,045	62,172	7.0	15,826	29.4	70.6	26.0	3.4	967	34.5
Coleman	726	3.8	801	1.0	135.5	1,210,947	1,512	68,786	28.4	31,320	40.1	59.9	41.3	7.5	2,499	49.2
Collin	313	7.6	138	6.2	136.6	732,661	5,303	45,315	77.8	34,369	65.3	34.7	19.2	3.4	1,307	7.2
Collingsworth	495	-3.5	1,292	27.3	164.1	1,075,068	832	152,681	43.1	112,556	69.4	30.6	47.3	18.8	4,307	79.6
Colorado	485	-8.0	308	20.1	136.2	1,019,175	3,309	68,878	68.0	43,162	65.4	34.6	35.9	7.6	4,361	17.0
Comal	205	6.5	186	0.4	14.1	974,562	5,248	42,853	D	D	D	D	14.5	0.5	131	5.2
Comanche	517	-10.7	360	18.1	133.8	865,152	2,401	69,521	158.1	110,199	16.9	83.1	42.4	8.4	1,563	21.0
Concho	502	-9.0	1,251	2.1	106.6	1,979,873	1,583	117,608	22.8	56,933	62.3	37.7	54.6	13.2	3,244	67.8
Cooke	504	10.6	259	0.4	132.4	845,941	3,267	60,599	63.3	32,538	29.2	70.8	36.9	7.1	1,361	19.2
Coryell	463	-5.2	354	0.4	85.8	861,112	2,432	52,811	68.6	52,408	23.6	76.4	30.2	5.0	959	16.1
Cottle	565	5.6	2,139	2.9	98.4	1,323,023	619	96,019	15.9	60,246	33.5	66.5	33.3	9.1	2,297	81.4
Crane	239	-36.3	8,858	D	D	5,228,185	590	51,926	1.4	52,222	1.6	98.4	55.6	14.8	56	14.8
Crockett	1,546	-3.5	7,158	0.1	8.0	4,508,931	630	78,523	13.9	64,324	0.3	99.7	46.3	16.7	2,214	33.3
Crosby	558	1.0	1,296	111.7	299.6	1,107,218	855	231,005	71.6	166,100	93.9	6.1	53.1	36.2	7,549	88.6
Culberson	1,618	17.8	21,013	6.0	64.5	7,180,273	342	134,844	13.7	178,364	48.1	51.9	57.1	28.6	680	27.3
Dallam	852	-9.1	2,296	175.6	388.4	2,164,833	943	330,364	651.7	1,756,642	25.5	74.5	55.3	40.7	7,262	76.8
Dallas	84	-4.8	100	1.4	35.9	460,257	4,611	52,857	44.5	53,026	85.9	14.1	17.8	4.4	280	6.9
Dawson	558	-1.8	936	61.2	481.2	738,569	789	188,577	73.1	122,700	97.0	3.0	38.9	23.0	11,185	91.9
Deaf Smith	924	-2.4	1,487	119.9	606.7	1,470,176	989	259,588	1,379.1	2,220,734	5.8	94.2	50.4	37.5	13,023	78.9
Delta	131	-1.2	248	D	65.0	452,815	1,826	60,987	29.3	55,475	53.6	46.4	40.8	5.3	801	33.8
Denton	384	9.5	120	3.3	131.9	731,687	6,111	52,478	137.0	42,771	25.8	74.2	18.1	3.2	1,210	7.6
DeWitt	536	-2.3	314	0.6	49.7	819,210	2,613	61,814	61.4	35,856	12.4	87.6	40.9	4.7	1,068	10.0
Dickens	573	-0.3	1,310	13.4	128.3	958,899	732	87,062	18.5	42,394	43.7	56.3	31.1	8.5	3,468	78.9
Dimmit	677	-4.4	1,845	4.8	44.3	2,875,932	1,559	62,379	35.2	95,956	24.3	75.7	25.9	6.5	730	14.4
Donley	585	-0.7	1,540	14.9	68.0	1,659,213	1,078	89,887	95.1	250,337	14.1	85.9	36.3	12.9	2,000	63.4
Duval	960	-6.0	668	D	60.0	872,009	1,305	38,103	14.8	10,309	6.5	93.5	20.5	1.3	2,814	37.0
Eastland	504	-3.2	429	8.9	91.5	852,450	1,987	56,647	27.9	23,744	30.5	69.5	36.4	4.5	1,428	24.0
Ector	429	1.2	1,624	0.8	3.6	786,019	484	48,008	2.2	8,296	28.9	71.1	16.3	1.5	211	5.3
Edwards	970	-2.7	2,315	1.1	13.0	2,907,783	1,256	48,630	8.2	19,485	7.4	92.6	28.9	5.5	2,070	25.8
Ellis	474	7.0	209	0.4	224.4	665,859	3,181	73,345	91.4	40,367	73.7	26.3	24.1	4.5	2,825	24.3
El Paso	209	24.2	319	24.9	53.3	617,767	1,938	93,251	45.5	69,308	87.0	13.0	25.7	9.4	768	9.3
Erath	608	-2.5	281	12.3	124.4	903,801	3,215	72,397	256.4	118,670	7.2	92.8	32.2	7.2	1,814	8.5
Falls	383	-14.1	303	5.1	174.3	589,978	1,947	82,715	135.3	107,123	40.7	59.3	41.3	12.2	4,706	29.1
Fannin	514	8.4	204	1.2	200.0	523,141	2,561	54,400	71.1	28,287	56.0	44.0	28.2	4.9	2,381	20.3
Fayette	492	-13.0	174	1.1	95.4	738,387	4,235	49,415	66.4	23,515	20.8	79.2	32.0	4.9	2,265	15.1
Fisher	495	-9.2	842	2.6	210.1	911,269	1,083	109,594	31.1	52,872	64.8	35.2	36.6	2.3	1,428	15.1
Floyd	582	-7.3	988	96.7	392.9	1,131,611	1,145	188,253	282.7	480,039	D	D	37.0	21.2	9,002	78.7
Foard	368	-2.0	1,898	1.9	98.2	1,401,794	739	100,098	13.8	71,273	44.8	55.2	47.4	22.7	4,632	89.8
Fort Bend	339	-11.4	264	10.3	135.9	1,080,498	4,095	75,835	103.8	80,705	88.5	11.5	36.2	10.7	1,505	69.6
Franklin	113	-15.4	217	0.8	27.9	623,454	2,869	67,423	86.0	165,339	4.4	95.6	48.1	14.6	4,101	29.2
Freestone	421	5.4	278	0.4	47.1	583,104	2,100	56,028	44.1	29,059	13.1	86.9	30.5	4.1	171	7.3
Frio	713	10.5	1,096	60.5	152.9	2,238,931	2,043	113,647	183.7	282,138	59.4	40.6	35.9	16.0	433	6.7
Gaines	775	-18.2	1,203	227.0	570.6	1,167,174	970	255,823	180.5	280,233	97.2	2.8	53.4	38.4	2,765	26.3
Galveston	90	-13.4	146	0.4	17.6	527,309	3,604	49,598	D	D	D	D	24.3	1.0	17,390	83.5
Garza	456	-11.1	1,645	8.1	82.1	1,141,856	694	92,982	12.4	44,711	70.4	29.6	35.7	13.4	756	8.3
Gillespie	652	-0.1	353	1.9	66.4	1,504,356	4,260	41,480	46.1	24,981	24.5	75.5	28.0	3.1	2,696	74.4
Glasscock	434	-9.6	2,332	25.3	134.7	2,086,946	895	302,559	25.9	139,129	89.3	10.7	51.1	30.6	1,901	20.8
Goliad	495	5.4	421	0.7	33.0	871,038	2,068	55,077	19.4	16,549	19.6	80.4	29.7	3.8	5,362	69.4
Gonzales	610	-6.8	364	7.8	69.0	1,176,904	3,231	69,381	517.8	309,295	4.5	95.5	44.0	11.6	751	9.4
Gray	515	1.1	1,235	21.6	161.2	1,096,012	888	129,902	207.7	498,026	11.7	88.3	42.9	16.1	1,202	12.7
Grayson	431	7.7	168	3.5	176.4	632,363	3,757	58,110	91.9	35,889	72.7	27.3	24.6	4.3	3,299	61.4
Gregg	48	6.3	91	0.4	8.2	353,905	3,881	45,812	3.6	6,844	37.3	62.7	15.7	0.8	1,948	14.2
Grimes	417	-4.6	248	1.6	56.7	957,864	3,865	59,447	48.1	28,551	23.0	77.0	31.0	3.7	755	5.8

Table B. States and Counties — Water Use, Wholesale Trade, Retail Trade, and Real Estate

STATE County	Water use, 2015 Public supply water withdrawn (mil gal/day)	Public supply gallons withdrawn per person per day	Wholesale Trade[1], 2012 Number of establishments	Number of employees	Sales (mil dol)	Annual payroll (mil dol)	Retail Trade[2], 2012 Number of establishments	Number of employees	Sales (mil dol)	Annual payroll (mil dol)	Real estate and rental and leasing,[2] 2012 Number of establishments	Number of employees	Sales (mil dol)	Annual payroll (mil dol)
	133	134	135	136	137	138	139	140	141	142	143	144	145	146
TEXAS— Cont'd														
Caldwell	3.70	91.3	18	D	D	D	81	1,035	345.2	26.7	21	55	7.4	1.3
Calhoun	0.25	11.4	16	D	D	D	63	927	435.3	31.4	20	146	35.2	5.9
Callahan	0.25	18.4	7	32	11.7	1.0	38	330	157.0	10.5	8	D	D	D
Cameron	24.18	57.3	317	D	D	D	1,119	16,624	4,124.8	353.2	312	1,338	185.5	32.2
Camp	1.10	86.7	9	82	34.0	2.9	50	371	111.2	8.4	7	D	D	D
Carson	9.00	1,507.8	7	D	D	D	20	150	57.4	2.7	1	D	D	D
Cass	1.05	34.6	18	D	D	D	88	883	218.4	18.4	18	33	5.0	0.7
Castro	1.06	138.5	12	142	117.2	6.2	33	185	55.0	3.6	8	16	2.9	0.3
Chambers	1.59	40.9	32	407	138.9	18.5	85	588	283.2	13.7	22	68	37.5	3.4
Cherokee	6.31	122.4	31	D	D	D	132	1,438	383.2	31.8	29	60	8.8	1.6
Childress	0.00	0.0	3	D	D	D	29	370	90.4	7.3	4	D	D	D
Clay	6.30	608.1	3	D	D	D	28	226	88.8	6.4	5	D	D	D
Cochran	0.40	135.5	3	D	D	D	12	68	50.2	1.7	NA	NA	NA	NA
Coke	0.37	114.3	2	D	D	D	14	66	32.4	1.6	NA	NA	NA	NA
Coleman	1.31	157.1	7	48	23.3	2.1	32	259	68.2	5.0	10	15	1.6	0.4
Collin	3.04	3.3	817	13,530	18,366.8	1,074.2	2,433	44,931	14,623.9	1,209.9	928	6,910	1,363.0	316.6
Collingsworth	0.52	170.8	5	D	D	D	14	74	15.8	1.6	NA	NA	NA	NA
Colorado	2.94	140.9	32	262	151.7	9.7	101	905	256.5	21.3	18	194	49.0	7.9
Comal	16.70	129.4	123	D	D	D	380	5,498	1,894.5	147.7	165	800	131.4	29.0
Comanche	0.04	3.0	22	D	D	D	49	430	138.1	10.2	9	27	1.9	0.7
Concho	0.33	80.9	1	D	D	D	12	73	17.1	1.1	1	D	D	D
Cooke	4.19	106.8	46	D	D	D	145	1,787	543.4	43.4	30	102	21.5	3.1
Coryell	0.21	2.8	11	D	D	D	120	1,704	493.6	36.2	37	112	14.3	3.0
Cottle	0.21	147.3	NA	NA	NA	NA	5	44	11.6	1.0	NA	NA	NA	NA
Crane	1.41	279.3	4	23	16.9	1.3	12	109	30.2	2.0	2	D	D	D
Crockett	0.96	258.8	4	36	36.3	2.3	19	181	72.9	4.7	3	D	D	D
Crosby	1.51	252.6	8	D	D	D	19	133	35.8	2.8	2	D	D	D
Culberson	0.81	362.3	1	D	D	D	17	247	136.7	4.1	2	D	D	D
Dallam	2.05	287.9	20	354	394.1	14.3	23	203	89.8	5.8	5	D	D	D
Dallas	334.54	131.0	3,657	67,700	80,605.0	4,255.0	7,518	112,656	35,957.9	3,151.9	3,490	32,478	7,691.3	1,679.2
Dawson	0.51	37.7	21	104	78.5	4.8	43	659	316.8	19.0	7	D	D	D
Deaf Smith	4.25	224.3	34	D	D	D	66	747	275.8	17.7	14	53	4.5	1.0
Delta	5.37	1,029.3	3	17	16.3	0.6	14	33	11.7	0.6	2	D	D	D
Denton	31.52	40.4	513	8,395	16,900.0	539.7	1,625	26,041	8,274.0	645.1	582	3,180	655.5	129.7
DeWitt	2.81	135.1	14	213	124.9	11.4	61	667	220.2	16.2	13	195	52.1	10.3
Dickens	0.10	45.3	NA	NA	NA	NA	9	57	11.9	1.0	2	D	D	D
Dimmit	1.69	153.9	6	191	174.6	13.1	28	446	142.6	11.2	9	35	3.5	0.9
Donley	0.38	108.6	1	D	D	D	20	113	27.9	1.9	6	9	1.7	0.4
Duval	1.21	106.3	9	74	24.8	2.5	29	240	78.6	4.7	3	29	6.0	1.0
Eastland	0.68	37.4	12	D	D	D	81	807	314.0	19.2	19	34	4.6	0.9
Ector	0.64	4.0	298	4,659	3,608.8	330.5	451	7,286	2,711.7	218.7	176	1,482	604.9	101.9
Edwards	0.20	105.6	NA	NA	NA	NA	7	83	21.7	2.2	2	D	D	D
Ellis	15.24	93.1	113	D	D	D	360	5,007	1,459.4	115.4	122	381	66.0	10.7
El Paso	114.33	136.8	952	D	D	D	2,322	34,934	9,180.6	753.5	699	3,143	617.3	108.0
Erath	2.21	53.7	35	D	D	D	172	1,831	535.2	41.5	40	111	15.8	2.8
Falls	2.29	133.6	9	D	D	D	52	419	97.5	8.4	5	19	3.9	0.9
Fannin	2.60	77.2	11	D	D	D	80	924	281.9	24.3	12	121	8.9	3.1
Fayette	2.56	102.0	34	D	D	D	125	1,134	368.6	28.5	32	109	20.4	3.3
Fisher	0.02	5.2	2	D	D	D	13	70	15.6	1.4	1	D	D	D
Floyd	0.41	69.5	12	D	D	D	22	131	31.5	2.5	1	D	D	D
Foard	0.01	8.2	1	D	D	D	7	31	7.4	0.5	NA	NA	NA	NA
Fort Bend	55.86	78.0	579	5,593	6,110.2	302.2	1,423	23,132	7,147.2	561.9	457	1,521	428.0	61.4
Franklin	2.77	260.1	4	16	5.1	0.7	27	269	105.9	6.1	9	16	2.1	0.3
Freestone	2.10	106.6	13	168	127.5	9.6	63	498	221.3	11.3	12	102	22.6	5.2
Frio	2.72	144.7	13	D	D	D	54	619	250.4	12.7	11	30	6.4	1.2
Gaines	8.21	409.5	27	374	362.2	25.9	45	498	108.9	10.3	12	22	3.8	0.7
Galveston	0.23	0.7	197	1,701	1,933.8	83.5	876	11,165	3,523.0	294.5	283	1,422	252.3	50.3
Garza	4.70	732.7	4	D	D	D	21	203	58.5	3.4	5	13	4.1	0.6
Gillespie	2.13	82.0	33	D	D	D	167	1,490	327.8	33.7	39	182	24.1	6.5
Glasscock	0.00	0.0	2	D	D	D	1	D	D	D	NA	NA	NA	NA
Goliad	0.34	45.1	3	13	3.3	0.3	15	128	41.0	2.0	2	D	D	D
Gonzales	29.05	1,412.0	20	277	228.2	13.1	72	770	238.6	15.7	9	15	3.4	0.5
Gray	1.24	53.4	31	447	1,065.5	31.3	100	1,082	314.8	25.0	30	118	23.7	4.8
Grayson	21.61	172.2	100	905	906.6	36.6	417	5,685	1,620.2	137.9	199	1,220	411.8	62.5
Gregg	7.13	57.4	252	3,592	2,395.6	194.3	664	9,190	2,639.8	233.0	199	1,220	411.8	62.5
Grimes	2.22	80.7	19	195	189.0	9.5	67	713	213.1	16.7	14	44	5.1	1.2

1. Merchant wholesalers, except manufacturers' sales branches and offices. 2. Employer establishments.

Table B. States and Counties — **Personal Income and Earnings**

STATE County	Personal income, 2016										Earnings, 2016		
	Total (mil dol)	Percent change 2015-2016	Per capita¹ Dollars	Per capita¹ Rank	Wages and salaries (mil dol)	Supplements to wages and salaries, employer contributions (mil dol) — Pension and insurance	Government social insurance	Proprietors' income (mil dol)	Dividends, interest, and rent (mil dol)	Personal transfer receipts (mil dol)	Total (mil dol)	Contributions for government social insurance (mil dol) — From employee and self-employed	From employer
	62	63	64	65	66	67	68	69	70	71	72	73	74
TEXAS— Cont'd													
Guadalupe	6,547	3.9	42,164	1,082	1,674	277	118	466	1,023	1,187	2,534	262	118
Hale	1,099	2.2	32,061	2,608	445	83	32	145	160	302	704	67	32
Hall	109	1.6	34,752	2,198	27	6	2	11	19	39	46	5	2
Hamilton	459	0.1	55,320	230	93	19	6	21	205	101	140	16	6
Hansford	357	-27.4	64,374	99	115	22	7	113	45	40	258	15	7
Hardeman	143	-2.0	36,699	1,880	44	10	3	6	28	50	63	7	3
Hardin	2,407	1.6	42,744	1,018	572	90	42	82	271	538	787	96	42
Harris	240,752	-2.3	52,452	322	163,010	20,274	10,726	35,982	46,033	28,891	229,993	22,656	10,726
Harrison	2,738	-0.9	41,146	1,214	1,179	208	84	295	414	620	1,765	183	84
Hartley	308	-33.3	53,566	279	111	21	6	123	51	23	260	13	6
Haskell	198	1.0	34,858	2,187	59	12	4	19	32	67	93	10	4
Hays	7,956	6.4	38,912	1,511	2,627	453	180	728	1,311	1,137	3,988	389	180
Hemphill	304	-13.5	73,671	52	127	21	8	100	84	23	256	19	8
Henderson	3,032	2.1	37,941	1,668	609	120	42	342	457	924	1,114	117	42
Hidalgo	21,081	2.8	24,805	3,074	8,839	1,825	620	2,414	2,276	6,441	13,698	1,349	620
Hill	1,313	0.9	37,444	1,746	358	67	25	106	191	378	555	61	25
Hockley	977	3.3	41,958	1,107	451	78	30	174	121	224	733	68	30
Hood	2,709	4.2	47,654	555	680	100	49	328	507	589	1,157	122	49
Hopkins	1,330	0.5	36,530	1,911	509	87	35	132	200	354	763	79	35
Houston	851	3.4	37,420	1,748	346	61	22	35	142	265	463	51	22
Howard	1,229	-1.3	33,483	2,396	610	135	43	70	203	292	858	90	43
Hudspeth	132	12.5	32,506	2,549	68	17	5	9	16	26	100	11	5
Hunt	3,230	3.3	35,083	2,148	1,553	292	106	177	381	850	2,128	227	106
Hutchinson	891	-0.2	41,422	1,180	560	109	38	52	110	191	760	80	38
Irion	100	-5.5	63,937	102	68	11	4	15	28	12	98	10	4
Jack	320	-11.1	36,585	1,901	155	26	10	21	78	72	213	23	10
Jackson	585	-4.7	39,344	1,448	245	42	17	37	88	146	341	36	17
Jasper	1,330	1.8	37,322	1,760	406	74	29	61	170	414	570	67	29
Jeff Davis	81	-1.0	36,885	1,839	26	6	2	9	24	19	42	4	2
Jefferson	10,649	0.7	41,813	1,121	7,136	1,284	499	847	1,559	2,526	9,767	1,031	499
Jim Hogg	141	-2.9	27,317	3,016	71	18	5	1	20	57	95	11	5
Jim Wells	1,640	1.6	39,858	1,383	671	106	47	142	209	501	966	104	47
Johnson	6,245	3.3	38,247	1,610	1,947	322	138	372	749	1,333	2,779	306	138
Jones	594	2.7	29,703	2,871	172	46	10	57	88	180	285	25	10
Karnes	744	-1.7	48,791	482	299	58	19	65	237	146	441	43	19
Kaufman	4,576	4.2	38,661	1,551	1,294	222	91	230	495	841	1,836	199	91
Kendall	3,276	3.7	77,002	37	737	101	50	412	857	352	1,300	120	50
Kenedy	17	-40.8	41,349	1,189	28	4	2	4	4	2	39	4	2
Kent	32	-7.7	41,662	1,147	11	3	1	1	6	10	16	2	1
Kerr	2,328	0.6	45,196	762	776	129	55	241	722	560	1,201	130	55
Kimble	182	-4.8	41,201	1,207	49	10	3	10	49	52	72	8	3
King	12	-19.4	41,779	1,129	4	1	0	5	2	1	11	1	0
Kinney	105	-5.0	29,350	2,904	38	12	3	-2	24	34	51	6	3
Kleberg	1,111	-1.8	35,066	2,153	482	124	35	59	179	294	700	71	35
Knox	129	-10.0	33,784	2,355	50	11	3	2	19	48	66	7	3
Lamar	1,918	2.9	38,518	1,569	906	149	66	124	259	575	1,245	142	66
Lamb	498	-6.9	37,483	1,740	154	30	10	107	53	134	300	22	10
Lampasas	972	0.6	46,808	627	160	31	11	64	205	252	266	29	11
La Salle	348	-7.2	45,720	720	190	29	13	23	131	57	256	27	13
Lavaca	916	-2.2	46,227	670	235	42	16	106	225	235	399	41	16
Lee	772	-0.4	45,276	755	343	55	24	59	136	159	481	51	24
Leon	683	-4.4	39,459	1,426	255	40	18	74	132	203	387	42	18
Liberty	2,829	0.6	34,631	2,222	720	133	50	170	295	729	1,072	115	50
Limestone	778	-0.5	33,135	2,449	313	76	20	32	109	284	441	46	20
Lipscomb	192	6.0	55,113	238	61	12	4	59	39	22	135	10	4
Live Oak	493	-3.9	40,899	1,246	198	42	14	27	122	99	281	30	14
Llano	924	0.9	45,385	748	183	31	12	98	284	247	324	36	12
Loving	4	9.4	39,221	1,465	2	0	0	0	2	0	3	0	0
Lubbock	11,749	1.8	38,757	1,542	6,012	1,047	405	1,035	1,887	2,296	8,499	852	405
Lynn	213	4.5	37,224	1,787	62	14	4	24	27	54	104	9	4
McCulloch	293	-6.4	35,871	2,019	111	22	7	13	56	100	153	18	7
McLennan	9,453	3.3	38,125	1,635	5,121	836	366	667	1,473	2,084	6,990	759	366
McMullen	84	-7.2	104,531	13	35	6	2	8	52	6	51	5	2
Madison	421	-5.8	30,114	2,832	163	32	11	21	86	129	227	24	11
Marion	335	-1.2	33,010	2,468	69	14	5	16	52	137	105	14	5
Martin	272	-1.4	47,612	558	100	19	7	34	60	45	160	14	7

1. Based on the resident population estimated as of July 1 of the year shown.

Table B. States and Counties — **Earnings, Social Security, and Housing**

STATE County	Earnings, 2016 (cont.) Percent by selected industries									Social Security beneficiaries, December 2016			Housing units, 2017	
	Farm	Mining, quarrying, and extracting	Construction	Manu-facturing	Information; professional, scientific, technical services	Retail trade	Finance, insurance, real estate, and leasing	Health care and social assistance	Govern-ment	Number	Rate[1]	Supple-mental Security Income recipients, 2016	Total	Percent change, 2010-2017
	75	76	77	78	79	80	81	82	83	84	85	86	87	88
TEXAS— Cont'd														
Guadalupe	-0.1	1.3	9.5	25.0	3.9	7.4	4.0	6.1	16.0	25,350	164	1,900	58,427	16.8
Hale	11.6	D	4.5	5.1	2.5	10.6	3.8	D	19.2	5,770	169	945	13,392	-1.0
Hall	16.8	1.1	3.4	2.7	D	4.5	5.7	6.5	27.4	825	265	86	1,918	-1.3
Hamilton	-1.3	D	11.6	6.5	5.8	9.2	4.0	9.4	28.5	2,350	286	165	4,564	0.0
Hansford	41.4	19.6	2.6	1.0	D	1.8	3.3	0.6	12.8	925	167	38	2,344	0.3
Hardeman	5.9	1.6	D	D	D	5.3	4.3	4.2	35.0	1,010	253	133	2,383	-1.4
Hardin	-0.4	4.0	14.1	8.2	5.7	10.7	2.8	15.0	15.4	11,760	209	1,241	24,608	8.9
Harris	0.0	7.8	8.9	9.1	13.8	4.7	7.9	7.7	9.8	518,290	112	105,867	1,768,827	10.6
Harrison	-0.1	14.9	7.4	25.8	D	4.6	5.9	D	10.2	13,480	202	1,910	28,569	3.1
Hartley	47.8	D	D	D	D	2.9	D	D	17.8	585	103	0	2,014	3.5
Haskell	5.0	9.5	5.4	1.8	D	14.4	D	7.5	25.5	1,395	242	165	3,442	-0.1
Hays	-0.1	0.8	14.0	8.6	7.8	9.7	5.1	8.6	21.1	26,105	128	2,250	78,509	32.2
Hemphill	5.6	36.0	10.0	2.2	1.7	2.2	5.8	0.5	11.1	565	137	20	1,689	3.7
Henderson	0.2	14.7	9.1	10.1	5.1	8.8	3.7	11.0	17.0	21,105	264	2,089	41,129	3.9
Hidalgo	0.9	1.1	4.8	2.6	4.2	10.8	4.8	18.7	27.0	105,465	124	41,937	276,743	11.5
Hill	-0.5	3.0	22.4	9.0	4.1	10.3	3.3	D	20.0	8,720	248	965	16,331	1.3
Hockley	3.9	42.6	5.2	1.7	D	3.6	3.1	D	14.0	4,050	175	523	9,353	0.7
Hood	-0.3	24.1	9.1	4.5	5.4	8.4	8.3	10.6	10.3	15,475	273	794	26,485	6.2
Hopkins	4.8	D	6.8	12.4	D	10.2	5.4	6.0	17.1	8,080	223	945	15,387	2.4
Houston	-1.6	8.2	5.8	13.2	D	5.2	9.9	7.1	20.7	5,490	240	888	11,679	1.3
Howard	-1.0	8.5	6.7	13.0	4.0	5.9	3.9	D	29.1	5,690	155	834	13,189	0.5
Hudspeth	5.2	1.0	D	D	D	0.8	D	1.7	60.5	730	179	180	1,570	2.8
Hunt	0.2	D	5.6	39.8	4.3	6.2	2.4	6.6	20.3	18,510	201	2,416	37,766	2.9
Hutchinson	0.7	26.3	19.5	17.8	D	4.5	2.0	D	11.5	4,285	199	350	10,669	0.4
Irion	-1.4	74.8	D	D	D	D	D	D	6.3	345	197	21	860	0.6
Jack	-4.6	32.9	16.8	3.5	D	2.0	3.1	D	16.3	1,730	197	110	4,151	1.4
Jackson	1.2	7.8	15.8	D	4.8	4.2	2.9	D	18.2	3,065	206	314	6,666	1.2
Jasper	0.0	2.5	11.1	20.8	4.4	7.5	3.6	D	19.4	8,670	245	1,295	17,205	2.4
Jeff Davis	-1.7	D	D	D	D	3.5	D	9.3	36.3	655	292	41	1,636	1.4
Jefferson	0.0	0.7	12.1	23.5	7.8	6.0	3.8	11.2	12.7	46,245	181	8,913	108,582	4.0
Jim Hogg	-3.5	8.3	3.7	3.1	D	6.1	D	D	53.0	1,035	197	295	2,469	1.1
Jim Wells	-0.5	31.5	4.0	2.4	3.2	5.6	7.6	D	12.7	8,410	205	1,772	16,375	1.4
Johnson	-0.1	3.6	12.0	16.8	4.1	8.7	3.9	9.1	16.3	29,030	178	2,971	61,982	9.3
Jones	5.7	6.1	5.3	4.0	2.3	4.5	4.8	3.8	45.0	3,540	177	392	7,429	0.2
Karnes	-2.7	32.6	3.7	4.3	D	4.8	3.9	D	24.1	2,760	181	434	5,991	6.0
Kaufman	-0.3	0.3	14.4	14.2	D	8.4	4.1	7.0	21.2	19,670	167	2,489	41,119	7.3
Kendall	-0.5	3.9	17.1	4.6	12.9	16.4	8.5	8.3	9.4	9,175	219	316	16,187	15.1
Kenedy	16.1	D	1.7	0.0	D	D	D	D	12.1	60	140	9	233	0.4
Kent	-4.3	D	D	2.2	D	5.3	D	10.2	55.2	195	259	17	557	0.9
Kerr	-0.6	1.3	11.3	6.5	7.0	9.9	6.6	16.8	17.4	15,595	304	978	24,500	2.8
Kimble	-7.8	3.0	15.5	5.4	D	10.0	11.6	3.4	27.2	1,315	297	118	3,389	0.6
King	10.2	7.6	9.4	0.0	D	6.9	5.1	1.2	35.3	30	102	0	188	1.1
Kinney	-4.4	D	D	D	0.0	2.5	D	1.2	65.3	925	254	120	1,961	1.1
Kleberg	0.7	3.6	3.6	3.0	D	6.6	3.5	D	48.8	5,105	163	1,087	13,301	4.0
Knox	-0.1	23.8	D	D	D	7.3	D	2.6	33.5	860	230	130	2,037	-0.3
Lamar	-0.4	D	8.9	27.7	D	8.1	4.0	15.2	13.6	12,115	244	1,959	22,733	1.1
Lamb	35.3	0.0	2.9	1.0	D	5.4	D	3.5	17.5	2,720	206	432	6,067	-1.0
Lampasas	-4.4	D	12.7	10.2	4.1	23.8	6.2	D	21.1	5,130	248	468	9,394	7.8
La Salle	0.8	51.8	4.8	0.4	D	1.7	D	1.8	22.8	1,215	159	320	2,958	7.7
Lavaca	-1.6	7.8	15.6	18.3	4.1	6.0	5.6	D	13.2	5,135	258	404	10,443	1.0
Lee	-0.2	6.6	39.6	5.6	4.2	3.8	4.5	D	15.7	3,555	209	302	7,752	3.4
Leon	1.3	16.4	21.3	17.9	2.6	4.0	6.0	1.4	12.6	5,220	304	455	9,757	2.6
Liberty	0.0	8.3	12.3	6.5	4.3	9.1	3.6	D	24.8	14,390	177	2,614	31,101	8.2
Limestone	-1.5	10.8	3.9	4.8	D	6.6	3.1	8.3	37.1	5,215	222	755	10,660	1.2
Lipscomb	2.2	11.8	D	D	D	4.0	D	1.6	14.6	595	170	30	1,509	-0.2
Live Oak	-4.5	20.5	D	D	6.5	4.1	6.2	2.3	22.1	2,065	172	193	6,228	2.7
Llano	-2.6	0.4	11.9	4.1	5.8	5.4	9.2	D	15.1	6,730	327	341	15,304	7.2
Loving	-3.2	D	D	D	D	0.0	0.0	0.0	29.6	15	130	0	51	2.0
Lubbock	0.5	0.5	6.7	3.2	7.6	8.8	7.7	15.9	24.8	45,415	150	6,407	127,393	10.7
Lynn	19.9	5.3	D	D	D	2.3	D	D	27.5	1,120	193	156	2,671	-0.2
McCulloch	-7.9	22.8	8.3	5.6	2.1	9.4	4.1	4.9	22.8	2,125	262	303	4,342	0.9
McLennan	0.0	0.4	8.3	18.3	5.4	6.4	8.5	10.8	15.8	43,990	178	7,316	101,621	6.8
McMullen	-6.2	43.8	D	D	D	4.3	D	D	18.0	180	221	12	494	1.9
Madison	0.5	D	13.2	3.7	5.4	13.0	3.9	6.0	31.3	2,540	180	295	5,277	3.5
Marion	-1.0	D	D	18.9	D	7.5	3.2	14.9	19.8	3,045	302	413	6,387	2.8
Martin	6.3	D	17.2	D	D	5.2	D	3.2	21.7	795	140	107	1,888	1.9

1. Per 1,000 resident population estimated as of July 1 of the year shown.

Table B. States and Counties — Housing, Labor Force, and Employment

STATE County	Housing units, 2017 (cont.)								Civilian labor force, 2017				Civilian employment[6], 2012-2016		
	Occupied units										Unemployment		Percent		
	Owner-occupied					Renter-occupied									
				Median owner cost as a percent of income											
	Total	Percent	Median value[1]	With a mortgage	Without a mortgage[2]	Median rent[3]	Median rent as a percent of income[2]	Sub-standard units[4] (percent)	Total	Percent change, 2016-2017	Total	Rate[5]	Total	Management, business, science, and arts	Construction, production, and maintenance occupations
	89	90	91	92	93	94	95	96	97	98	99	100	101	102	103

STATE County	89	90	91	92	93	94	95	96	97	98	99	100	101	102	103
TEXAS— Cont'd															
Guadalupe	49,930	75.4	169,200	20.8	11.1	966	25.8	3.4	77,510	2.2	2,564	3.3	68,376	33.5	25.8
Hale	11,335	61.2	77,700	18.0	10.0	611	24.6	7.0	12,418	-1.2	637	5.1	14,543	25.7	32.9
Hall	1,235	61.9	47,800	23.0	13.1	539	28.9	1.8	1,129	-3.0	70	6.2	1,165	22.1	28.2
Hamilton	3,231	73.3	102,300	19.2	12.6	606	28.2	4.1	3,607	0.4	142	3.9	3,443	28.9	29.7
Hansford	1,979	72.6	89,400	17.0	11.8	673	26.7	3.9	2,856	-2.9	72	2.5	2,587	28.7	41.2
Hardeman	1,590	72.6	38,400	17.9	13.9	517	22.9	2.5	1,654	2.0	64	3.9	1,614	27.8	35.3
Hardin	20,408	79.5	105,100	18.8	10.0	813	25.7	2.8	25,045	-0.3	1,534	6.1	24,149	30.9	30.8
Harris	1,536,259	54.5	145,600	21.5	11.0	937	29.7	6.0	2,268,944	1.0	113,459	5.0	2,130,543	35.0	24.3
Harrison	23,473	73.1	110,100	19.6	11.6	727	25.8	4.4	29,410	-1.6	1,530	5.2	27,895	30.9	31.7
Hartley	1,812	61.7	148,200	18.5	10.0	715	24.5	6.1	2,947	-0.2	58	2.0	2,148	43.7	24.3
Haskell	2,193	75.5	49,200	19.2	10.6	469	29.8	4.2	2,432	-2.9	115	4.7	2,253	26.5	30.2
Hays	64,324	63.0	195,800	23.0	12.1	992	36.1	4.5	108,012	3.2	3,378	3.1	92,791	38.2	17.6
Hemphill	1,374	68.4	127,600	16.0	10.0	775	21.8	5.0	2,335	10.6	58	2.5	1,895	30.2	29.4
Henderson	29,785	74.8	94,100	21.9	13.2	759	30.2	3.0	35,566	0.7	1,476	4.2	30,660	27.6	29.7
Hidalgo	227,477	67.8	81,400	23.7	12.8	677	32.3	14.0	341,602	1.5	25,255	7.4	303,214	27.0	24.0
Hill	12,806	73.0	89,100	20.7	12.2	660	28.1	5.6	16,142	2.3	626	3.9	14,368	26.3	32.1
Hockley	8,103	67.4	80,800	18.5	10.0	656	26.3	5.0	11,270	1.1	419	3.7	10,661	27.0	33.1
Hood	21,040	76.5	162,600	21.4	10.9	868	31.1	3.4	25,691	1.9	1,075	4.2	22,464	31.6	27.7
Hopkins	13,259	71.3	96,300	19.5	11.1	692	29.1	4.7	17,145	-0.9	612	3.6	15,302	28.3	30.6
Houston	8,221	70.4	77,400	23.2	13.9	633	38.9	2.9	10,556	5.1	447	4.2	8,031	23.1	30.5
Howard	11,229	66.4	81,800	17.5	10.0	827	26.6	4.2	13,197	0.1	568	4.3	14,473	27.9	30.6
Hudspeth	940	81.2	44,300	22.7	15.3	624	17.4	10.9	1,537	-0.1	92	6.0	1,121	23.2	31.1
Hunt	31,154	69.2	96,400	21.9	11.9	765	32.9	4.0	41,487	2.6	1,627	3.9	36,775	29.5	28.4
Hutchinson	7,910	76.6	72,800	18.0	10.0	690	24.3	4.2	9,392	-2.3	565	6.0	9,434	23.3	35.5
Irion	632	76.4	153,000	19.1	10.0	859	19.8	3.6	774	-0.5	23	3.0	754	40.1	31.8
Jack	3,066	79.8	77,700	15.8	10.7	733	23.9	5.0	3,930	2.1	147	3.7	3,177	23.6	41.2
Jackson	5,164	72.1	89,900	18.1	10.5	808	21.8	5.9	7,366	1.4	294	4.0	6,524	26.2	39.8
Jasper	11,910	75.6	89,300	19.3	11.2	681	30.7	2.8	13,380	-0.5	996	7.4	12,626	23.1	33.3
Jeff Davis	1,013	75.8	112,100	19.3	11.6	646	17.4	5.9	1,052	-1.8	33	3.1	937	38.6	28.7
Jefferson	94,097	62.4	99,500	21.0	11.3	777	30.2	3.2	107,321	0.0	7,854	7.3	104,648	28.8	28.4
Jim Hogg	1,592	76.3	65,500	20.6	10.1	556	30.6	6.7	1,894	-2.4	137	7.2	1,548	24.9	39.4
Jim Wells	13,557	69.8	73,300	18.0	11.9	721	29.7	7.7	16,709	-4.1	1,259	7.5	16,308	28.1	30.1
Johnson	53,880	73.7	124,500	19.8	11.6	907	28.1	3.8	77,413	2.0	2,915	3.8	70,442	30.4	31.3
Jones	5,580	74.6	73,200	16.9	12.6	699	21.9	1.9	5,635	0.4	300	5.3	5,380	30.6	26.3
Karnes	4,288	74.6	90,000	17.1	10.0	662	28.5	8.9	6,424	2.5	224	3.5	5,344	28.7	29.8
Kaufman	35,739	76.3	141,500	22.8	12.9	916	28.6	3.7	59,437	2.8	2,091	3.5	51,114	32.5	24.9
Kendall	13,390	72.7	285,900	22.5	11.7	1,098	27.9	2.5	20,705	1.9	635	3.1	17,528	44.4	16.6
Kenedy	170	37.1	0	0.0	17.3	471	28.5	4.7	246	13.4	8	3.3	183	25.1	16.9
Kent	284	71.1	72,900	13.8	10.1	492	19.6	4.6	460	-1.9	12	2.6	319	43.3	26.0
Kerr	20,476	69.1	162,600	22.4	12.0	783	28.5	5.3	21,290	-0.1	726	3.4	20,873	31.3	22.2
Kimble	2,119	74.3	114,900	24.6	13.3	618	30.5	1.4	1,897	-2.7	67	3.5	2,127	26.4	26.8
King	114	26.3	72,200	0.0	16.1	729	18.1	8.8	163	-7.9	6	3.7	164	38.4	37.8
Kinney	1,139	80.0	72,700	24.4	12.3	515	26.0	2.7	1,150	-0.3	63	5.5	1,170	27.5	28.2
Kleberg	10,777	54.7	86,600	18.6	11.3	782	29.8	5.8	13,367	-5.1	795	5.9	14,002	29.5	28.3
Knox	1,374	74.7	43,300	13.6	10.0	426	25.0	4.1	1,493	-4.0	59	4.0	1,492	31.8	38.1
Lamar	19,077	64.5	86,300	19.4	11.7	662	29.1	3.8	23,680	2.1	995	4.2	20,717	26.8	30.3
Lamb	4,817	70.3	65,700	20.1	12.3	616	22.7	5.5	5,194	-0.8	268	5.2	5,784	30.3	34.4
Lampasas	7,583	72.4	138,700	21.3	12.6	789	28.7	2.8	9,235	1.0	339	3.7	8,274	29.9	29.3
La Salle	2,101	69.2	63,500	16.8	12.3	384	26.6	14.2	4,203	8.4	155	3.7	2,355	30.4	37.9
Lavaca	7,741	76.5	131,000	18.5	10.2	664	21.6	7.6	8,712	-0.2	312	3.6	8,880	31.3	34.3
Lee	6,014	75.6	127,000	21.9	11.4	779	31.8	4.2	9,625	3.9	314	3.3	7,645	24.1	29.3
Leon	6,279	80.0	99,600	19.2	10.0	635	27.3	3.5	6,160	-5.2	390	6.3	6,707	30.8	33.4
Liberty	25,611	74.9	89,100	20.4	11.9	801	27.0	4.6	31,713	0.7	2,247	7.1	28,442	24.6	38.1
Limestone	8,046	73.5	83,200	23.5	12.4	673	30.2	3.1	8,315	0.0	460	5.5	8,894	27.1	31.2
Lipscomb	1,235	75.1	95,300	16.0	10.0	675	16.2	1.9	1,633	-1.0	53	3.2	1,636	32.6	42.4
Live Oak	3,670	79.2	84,900	16.6	10.0	700	27.0	5.1	5,376	3.5	250	4.7	4,263	25.8	34.2
Llano	8,796	76.2	169,200	21.5	12.2	741	28.6	2.9	8,319	0.5	310	3.7	7,199	31.8	20.7
Loving	37	45.9	0	0.0	10.0	850	46.3	0.0	100	16.3	5	5.0	39	28.2	56.4
Lubbock	109,024	56.3	117,100	20.9	11.1	844	31.8	3.5	155,834	1.7	4,938	3.2	142,209	34.7	20.0
Lynn	2,157	71.0	70,600	23.0	10.0	652	29.8	2.4	2,720	-0.2	102	3.8	2,369	31.2	29.4
McCulloch	3,101	74.5	75,800	19.1	13.0	685	29.7	4.0	3,703	0.0	133	3.6	3,574	25.7	28.4
McLennan	87,185	58.2	118,200	21.8	12.5	789	31.5	3.2	118,021	1.8	4,543	3.8	109,906	32.4	24.2
McMullen	233	74.7	78,100	31.1	10.0	523	10.0	9.0	740	-14.0	14	1.9	280	25.7	25.0
Madison	4,121	68.1	103,900	26.5	10.0	779	25.2	9.0	4,669	-1.9	217	4.6	4,469	28.1	31.1
Marion	4,387	78.5	89,600	19.6	10.5	654	36.1	3.1	4,350	0.4	246	5.7	3,714	26.9	31.5
Martin	1,629	75.1	108,900	18.2	10.0	841	30.4	8.5	2,568	3.6	82	3.2	2,467	26.7	38.0

1. Specified owner-occupied units. 2. A value of 10.0 represents 10 percent or less; a value of 50.0 represents 50 percent or more. 3. Specified renter-occupied units.
4. Overcrowded or lacking complete plumbing facilities. 5. Percent of civilian labor force. 6. Civilian employed persons 16 years old and over.

Table B. States and Counties — Nonfarm Employment and Agriculture

	Private nonfarm establishments, employment and payroll, 2016									Agriculture, 2012			
	Employment							Annual payroll		Farms			
											Percent with:		
STATE County	Number of establishments	Total	Health care and social assistance	Manufacturing	Retail trade	Finance and insurance	Professional, scientific, and technical services	Total (mil dol)	Average per employee (dollars)	Number	Fewer than 50 acres	500 acres or more	Farm operators whose principal occupation is farming (percent)
	104	105	106	107	108	109	110	111	112	113	114	115	116
TEXAS— Cont'd													
Guadalupe	2,026	32,126	3,166	6,804	5,048	631	864	1,272	39,590	2,241	48.3	6.1	35.7
Hale	689	9,036	1,091	604	1,401	243	162	311	34,409	899	11.7	39.6	48.8
Hall	66	646	72	24	91	57	D	21	32,850	390	3.8	44.1	39.5
Hamilton	201	1,585	241	195	392	32	51	52	32,601	1,001	17.1	21.8	42.2
Hansford	146	1,174	288	19	165	91	37	46	39,420	263	5.7	62.7	70.0
Hardeman	83	705	142	D	108	D	D	28	39,321	357	8.4	42.0	37.5
Hardin	803	9,270	1,024	830	2,326	223	306	350	37,768	660	64.8	4.1	33.2
Harris	100,884	2,045,435	262,449	151,272	213,643	79,522	174,681	129,246	63,188	2,207	70.1	4.5	35.0
Harrison	1,286	19,404	1,610	4,837	2,031	833	1,019	776	39,993	1,298	43.4	7.1	41.1
Hartley	115	1,309	328	NA	196	30	14	48	36,851	255	6.7	65.5	64.7
Haskell	139	1,114	149	D	394	49	37	34	30,181	503	8.7	40.4	50.1
Hays	4,034	53,431	7,241	4,140	12,280	1,010	2,188	1,784	33,384	1,439	52.1	6.5	34.3
Hemphill	145	1,383	203	24	204	21	23	64	46,491	232	12.1	58.6	55.6
Henderson	1,295	13,096	2,137	1,485	2,732	413	693	432	32,957	1,961	45.2	6.2	42.4
Hidalgo	11,937	194,826	62,411	6,296	38,238	6,786	6,155	5,356	27,490	2,161	57.9	14.7	51.4
Hill	639	7,337	1,122	1,107	1,526	198	142	237	32,277	1,884	34.6	11.0	43.6
Hockley	504	6,520	878	207	885	243	92	298	45,774	781	14.7	34.1	45.6
Hood	1,282	14,301	2,182	483	3,079	467	392	546	38,209	1,286	57.1	6.8	42.8
Hopkins	750	10,743	1,432	1,774	1,671	498	245	371	34,561	2,113	31.5	8.8	42.0
Houston	343	3,278	322	552	665	144	101	119	36,450	1,505	23.3	13.2	49.9
Howard	725	8,951	1,677	699	1,483	270	186	346	38,606	475	21.3	34.3	48.8
Hudspeth	31	323	D	D	56	D	D	15	46,207	167	13.2	53.9	60.5
Hunt	1,414	23,535	3,102	8,430	3,710	379	600	1,168	49,616	4,206	58.7	3.6	31.9
Hutchinson	464	6,470	575	1,542	939	187	202	352	54,459	247	27.1	38.9	44.1
Irion	58	465	D	NA	24	D	12	21	44,542	155	22.6	52.3	43.9
Jack	222	2,057	72	48	152	32	56	85	41,513	864	17.1	23.8	42.0
Jackson	304	4,621	309	D	528	133	152	202	43,816	811	23.7	25.2	45.3
Jasper	605	8,434	2,273	1,391	1,529	253	187	301	35,678	894	59.5	2.0	36.9
Jeff Davis	63	388	80	NA	63	30	28	11	28,822	84	16.7	69.0	57.1
Jefferson	5,652	103,217	17,467	14,629	14,284	2,687	5,071	5,265	51,005	764	48.0	18.3	45.5
Jim Hogg	84	1,035	542	60	193	45	D	25	24,359	263	15.2	45.2	39.2
Jim Wells	875	13,161	4,423	429	1,658	333	296	443	33,627	1,047	32.7	16.0	33.5
Johnson	2,742	36,603	3,698	5,718	5,974	761	893	1,427	38,978	3,023	61.4	4.3	35.6
Jones	294	2,258	434	211	245	106	45	93	41,089	1,014	25.0	20.9	37.6
Karnes	334	4,766	449	265	554	109	56	260	54,646	1,288	17.5	13.1	45.6
Kaufman	1,856	24,260	3,409	3,599	4,261	646	583	906	37,333	3,041	59.3	4.2	38.5
Kendall	1,269	12,356	1,764	858	2,680	432	1,021	517	41,810	1,387	42.4	13.6	39.3
Kenedy	20	173	NA	NA	NA	NA	NA	13	73,179	28	0.0	89.3	67.9
Kent	12	78	D	NA	18	D	NA	6	71,179	194	8.8	44.3	31.4
Kerr	1,394	16,027	3,747	755	2,987	483	732	591	36,872	1,034	28.9	20.6	38.9
Kimble	131	937	144	66	296	41	11	26	27,556	602	15.4	48.2	46.7
King	1	D	NA	NA	NA	NA	NA	D	D	59	0.0	59.3	23.7
Kinney	38	510	13	NA	30	NA	NA	15	29,769	196	12.8	57.1	43.4
Kleberg	571	6,976	1,732	101	1,614	308	151	213	30,474	401	50.9	10.2	37.7
Knox	87	625	121	NA	121	47	2	22	34,984	228	8.8	47.4	56.1
Lamar	1,180	17,023	3,491	4,582	2,570	498	378	629	36,964	1,843	32.0	11.7	34.6
Lamb	240	2,106	409	73	357	141	61	80	38,204	933	10.1	37.3	52.3
Lampasas	400	3,717	511	644	651	102	106	108	28,997	1,017	37.0	17.2	46.3
La Salle	147	2,782	136	NA	356	D	D	151	54,269	446	11.9	44.6	42.2
Lavaca	483	5,541	1,225	1,233	814	271	136	202	36,478	2,617	29.8	7.7	40.7
Lee	408	5,654	266	404	661	244	164	266	47,034	1,807	33.8	7.2	35.0
Leon	334	4,408	77	681	590	112	49	225	51,070	1,962	30.3	11.6	52.2
Liberty	1,057	12,556	1,651	798	2,693	324	752	472	37,588	1,470	50.7	7.6	46.0
Limestone	388	5,046	1,198	779	961	266	60	179	35,542	1,526	24.1	14.2	50.4
Lipscomb	89	829	D	D	117	65	28	35	42,730	277	6.5	56.0	46.2
Live Oak	279	3,009	139	D	422	96	103	161	53,484	892	13.5	28.5	42.3
Llano	462	3,673	503	82	562	169	150	106	28,791	740	25.8	31.6	42.7
Loving	4	10	NA	NA	NA	D	NA	1	62,700	10	0.0	100.0	80.0
Lubbock	7,120	113,615	24,285	5,094	18,172	5,755	4,350	4,040	35,562	1,116	36.0	26.8	45.6
Lynn	87	678	D	78	67	64	D	29	43,316	455	8.6	49.5	60.4
McCulloch	205	2,225	149	152	480	96	133	86	38,430	619	13.1	36.0	46.2
McLennan	5,169	104,732	18,119	13,986	12,074	5,210	5,125	3,850	36,760	3,278	55.3	5.8	38.8
McMullen	45	632	D	D	73	D	D	59	93,242	238	7.1	64.3	50.4
Madison	252	2,920	262	31	727	93	70	89	30,409	970	28.8	10.4	45.8
Marion	153	1,703	481	362	214	34	19	49	28,956	247	34.8	6.1	34.8
Martin	109	1,225	258	D	154	32	D	63	51,444	414	13.5	42.3	57.0

Table B. States and Counties — **Agriculture**

STATE County	Land in farms		Acres			Value of land and buildings (dollars)		Value of machinery and equiopmnet, average per farm (dollars)	Value of products sold:		Percent from:		Percent of farms with sales of:		Government payments	
	Acreage (1,000)	Percent change, 2007-2012	Average size of farm	Total irrigated (1,000)	Total cropland (1,000)	Average per farm	Average per acre		Total (mil dol)	Average per farm (acres)	Crops	Livestock and poultry products	$10,000 or more	$100,000 or more	Total ($1,000)	Percent of farms
	117	118	119	120	121	122	123	124	125	126	127	128	129	130	131	132
TEXAS— Cont'd																
Guadalupe	383	-0.5	171	1.9	112.1	614,506	3,595	50,088	61.6	27,484	49.2	50.8	25.0	4.0	2,230	12.2
Hale	641	8.8	713	202.2	479.7	844,726	1,185	232,068	409.9	455,984	31.5	68.5	47.2	30.4	15,250	85.4
Hall	509	-4.6	1,305	27.8	186.3	1,006,900	771	121,005	24.8	63,464	74.3	25.7	36.2	13.3	4,834	83.8
Hamilton	446	-5.3	445	0.6	75.6	1,105,527	2,482	58,377	55.8	55,772	19.2	80.8	40.4	6.8	1,233	23.7
Hansford	567	-3.2	2,155	98.1	294.4	1,994,289	925	403,190	783.2	2,977,973	14.1	85.9	74.1	50.2	4,906	81.7
Hardeman	355	-4.2	993	4.5	130.9	869,655	875	82,580	25.4	71,042	36.1	63.9	45.7	8.7	2,043	80.1
Hardin	69	-24.9	104	1.7	22.7	320,964	3,092	62,642	D	D	D	D	18.0	2.0	414	2.1
Harris	236	-8.7	107	5.9	59.9	572,259	5,342	45,283	65.2	29,538	72.8	27.2	20.8	3.4	1,072	6.2
Harrison	200	-0.6	154	0.5	40.9	437,530	2,845	50,800	19.0	14,631	26.2	73.8	23.5	1.9	274	3.3
Hartley	903	-0.9	3,541	155.5	270.3	3,557,855	1,005	348,706	1,180.9	4,630,969	16.4	83.6	68.2	60.0	4,317	72.5
Haskell	567	14.6	1,128	27.5	298.5	834,078	740	144,797	38.7	76,881	74.0	26.0	42.1	16.5	5,201	84.9
Hays	245	4.0	170	1.0	30.3	1,055,578	6,200	33,647	15.0	10,403	48.9	51.1	12.7	1.5	469	4.5
Hemphill	576	4.9	2,482	3.2	39.8	1,837,310	740	115,043	110.6	476,517	2.7	97.3	46.1	19.8	1,293	50.4
Henderson	346	8.5	176	1.4	81.9	525,054	2,979	50,080	49.5	25,253	35.0	65.0	26.8	3.0	193	1.8
Hidalgo	795	10.0	368	183.6	465.6	1,117,900	3,038	115,296	452.8	209,517	91.7	8.3	33.2	14.2	9,106	20.0
Hill	504	-4.0	268	0.9	231.9	602,704	2,252	72,047	119.9	63,662	67.1	32.9	33.4	8.1	3,921	28.7
Hockley	484	-0.1	619	106.9	400.1	643,108	1,038	182,472	78.7	100,790	89.1	10.9	37.5	20.0	10,093	81.6
Hood	224	9.0	174	2.8	43.3	712,228	4,085	52,253	18.7	14,574	45.7	54.3	20.5	2.2	162	5.8
Hopkins	423	8.2	200	1.3	127.7	442,861	2,214	64,010	205.9	97,466	6.3	93.7	40.3	9.8	1,817	9.2
Houston	468	6.2	311	6.0	83.6	697,706	2,244	55,639	49.6	32,944	28.1	71.9	34.7	4.9	1,461	14.6
Howard	498	-4.7	1,049	4.2	161.9	796,236	759	88,682	13.9	29,187	33.5	66.5	18.7	4.8	4,460	62.1
Hudspeth	2,251	-0.3	13,480	18.1	48.3	7,586,677	563	134,042	34.5	206,455	71.7	28.3	65.3	22.2	1,323	35.9
Hunt	455	17.0	108	5.4	180.3	330,262	3,056	41,054	69.3	16,485	64.6	35.4	18.7	1.9	1,324	8.4
Hutchinson	521	-6.5	2,109	35.1	97.8	1,606,478	762	154,777	55.9	226,219	57.5	42.5	39.3	21.9	1,984	30.4
Irion	496	-20.6	3,201	0.7	10.7	3,005,394	939	70,394	7.5	48,148	10.3	89.7	47.1	9.7	904	25.8
Jack	528	-8.4	611	0.4	35.8	1,195,220	1,956	55,066	22.5	26,042	10.1	89.9	35.3	5.9	751	11.9
Jackson	442	-10.3	545	13.1	151.8	1,151,591	2,114	118,181	101.8	125,568	72.7	27.3	48.3	16.5	6,538	36.6
Jasper	88	-8.1	99	0.4	16.3	310,437	3,149	49,808	10.1	11,263	55.8	44.2	18.2	0.7	26	1.3
Jeff Davis	1,255	-9.8	14,941	0.1	3.6	7,177,381	480	76,583	D	D	D	D	38.1	23.8	792	26.2
Jefferson	354	6.2	463	22.4	112.7	767,829	1,657	88,914	38.0	49,778	56.8	43.2	31.8	10.1	3,631	22.3
Jim Hogg	645	0.7	2,452	D	9.6	3,272,540	1,335	58,118	11.1	42,323	D	D	36.1	6.1	1,349	33.1
Jim Wells	504	8.9	481	4.8	192.0	878,878	1,827	85,848	82.9	79,137	42.5	57.5	25.5	4.8	2,904	22.5
Johnson	429	29.5	142	2.4	119.9	578,482	4,077	50,827	78.9	26,083	25.3	74.7	20.4	2.8	834	6.3
Jones	563	-1.8	555	3.6	301.9	617,260	1,112	88,348	43.3	42,685	68.6	31.4	29.2	8.4	5,627	53.7
Karnes	465	11.3	361	0.9	82.7	937,215	2,598	66,483	27.6	21,428	38.8	61.2	32.2	3.4	1,683	18.9
Kaufman	449	6.5	148	1.4	130.5	502,007	3,399	42,963	59.0	19,395	34.4	65.6	19.8	2.3	637	2.8
Kendall	370	8.0	267	0.9	27.5	1,277,133	4,788	32,921	12.5	9,034	16.9	83.1	19.3	1.2	835	6.3
Kenedy	916	0.8	32,728	0.7	3.1	21,522,643	658	288,179	23.7	845,964	D	D	75.0	28.6	44	10.7
Kent	563	-0.8	2,903	1.1	39.3	2,479,716	854	68,263	D	D	D	D	31.4	10.8	1,687	74.2
Kerr	582	-5.1	563	1.9	44.2	1,483,207	2,634	38,048	10.8	10,448	12.2	87.8	18.3	1.6	597	7.6
Kimble	694	12.0	1,153	8.5	15.5	2,044,718	1,773	53,435	D	D	D	D	23.8	2.8	2,269	26.4
King	418	-23.0	7,078	D	23.4	4,304,051	608	122,169	6.6	111,661	D	D	37.3	15.3	748	78.0
Kinney	577	-4.1	2,943	1.2	16.6	3,539,699	1,203	48,612	4.7	24,031	24.7	75.3	32.1	5.1	903	20.9
Kleberg	484	-2.9	1,207	0.1	71.2	2,274,983	1,884	79,327	61.8	154,157	D	D	25.4	4.7	1,570	27.9
Knox	451	-8.7	1,976	21.6	189.7	1,528,439	773	192,219	59.0	258,829	32.4	67.6	64.5	27.2	3,240	82.0
Lamar	497	-4.7	269	7.0	175.8	582,745	2,163	67,187	84.9	46,058	47.7	52.3	36.2	6.5	5,129	25.7
Lamb	616	-2.9	661	179.5	469.1	764,255	1,157	226,869	575.3	616,598	20.3	79.7	46.5	30.3	14,489	85.7
Lampasas	445	6.9	437	0.2	50.3	1,097,964	2,511	49,163	16.1	15,867	18.1	81.9	25.6	3.0	530	11.1
La Salle	635	-2.2	1,423	7.0	44.0	2,777,861	1,952	69,648	18.7	41,890	63.9	36.1	28.0	6.5	1,007	15.9
Lavaca	547	-3.5	209	4.3	80.8	612,201	2,931	46,957	61.9	23,655	20.3	79.7	36.4	3.3	1,440	10.4
Lee	318	-2.3	176	0.9	44.1	563,382	3,199	42,538	38.6	21,340	33.4	66.6	31.0	1.8	935	11.9
Leon	594	4.4	303	0.8	74.0	759,197	2,506	63,997	148.7	75,810	6.7	93.3	32.8	4.6	1,172	6.9
Liberty	287	-3.7	195	5.2	101.1	488,804	2,505	70,376	34.9	23,768	42.1	57.9	22.9	3.3	1,494	6.1
Limestone	487	-3.8	319	0.3	80.9	603,233	1,891	55,660	48.3	31,641	25.6	74.4	38.2	5.0	2,192	15.3
Lipscomb	591	3.5	2,135	23.3	118.4	1,725,505	808	137,588	52.7	190,188	16.9	83.1	44.8	23.5	2,756	75.1
Live Oak	541	7.9	606	0.7	55.7	1,161,267	1,916	63,307	17.9	20,082	15.8	84.2	34.9	4.5	1,774	26.2
Llano	528	-2.0	714	0.8	21.3	1,930,442	2,705	51,043	13.8	18,600	10.4	89.6	32.2	3.2	890	12.3
Loving	380	-11.1	37,952	0.0	0.6	7,543,900	199	74,000	0.9	91,200	0.0	100.0	90.0	30.0	136	60.0
Lubbock	503	-2.6	450	155.5	423.8	834,394	1,853	174,972	174.8	156,631	54.8	45.2	39.0	22.0	10,896	61.6
Lynn	472	-4.4	1,038	71.6	406.7	933,648	900	261,402	67.6	148,560	97.3	2.7	55.6	32.3	9,808	90.1
McCulloch	614	0.3	992	0.9	90.1	1,838,354	1,852	79,971	22.6	36,454	38.2	61.8	36.7	9.5	3,014	39.9
McLennan	554	4.5	169	3.5	244.0	437,533	2,591	54,417	183.1	55,852	40.9	59.1	21.2	4.5	3,662	17.3
McMullen	517	2.2	2,174	D	19.3	3,055,197	1,405	85,521	8.3	35,025	5.2	94.8	31.5	7.6	239	8.0
Madison	291	6.7	300	2.3	35.3	840,584	2,799	79,825	82.9	85,085	D	D	33.5	4.4	1,087	10.6
Marion	40	-5.1	162	0.2	8.3	361,308	2,224	40,939	3.4	13,563	16.5	83.5	16.6	0.8	62	4.9
Martin	454	-0.9	1,096	17.1	279.6	1,130,809	1,032	160,903	20.3	48,949	88.8	11.2	26.1	13.8	5,158	80.9

Table B. States and Counties — Water Use, Wholesale Trade, Retail Trade, and Real Estate

STATE County	Water use, 2015 Public supply water withdrawn (mil gal/day)	Public supply gallons withdrawn per person per day	Wholesale Trade[1], 2012 Number of establish-ments	Number of employees	Sales (mil dol)	Annual payroll (mil dol)	Retail Trade[2], 2012 Number of establish-ments	Number of employees	Sales (mil dol)	Annual payroll (mil dol)	Real estate and rental and leasing,[2] 2012 Number of establish-ments	Number of employees	Sales (mil dol)	Annual payroll (mil dol)
	133	134	135	136	137	138	139	140	141	142	143	144	145	146
TEXAS— Cont'd														
Guadalupe	6.85	45.3	92	D	D	D	270	3,756	1,166.8	90.5	89	373	70.1	14.2
Hale	1.44	41.9	45	D	D	D	114	1,464	346.9	29.0	31	103	15.9	2.4
Hall	0.04	12.7	2	D	D	D	15	94	48.3	1.7	1	D	D	D
Hamilton	0.16	19.6	6	85	32.9	3.7	52	366	87.1	7.8	1	D	D	0.1
Hansford	0.96	171.1	18	98	148.0	3.7	24	213	74.2	5.3	4	4	0.9	0.1
Hardeman	0.07	18.2	7	D	D	D	15	135	33.4	2.3	NA	NA	NA	NA
Hardin	4.03	72.1	19	D	D	D	155	2,033	712.6	51.4	26	54	7.3	1.4
Harris	287.29	63.3	6,363	100,988	340,775.7	6,909.3	12,644	189,299	61,669.4	4,940.5	4,930	37,842	9,174.7	1,850.8
Harrison	8.53	127.8	58	D	D	D	192	2,069	647.6	49.5	62	288	45.3	10.9
Hartley	1.02	164.7	10	78	85.2	4.2	13	D	D	D	5	13	4.2	1.0
Haskell	0.14	24.4	1	D	D	D	27	298	89.8	7.0	NA	NA	NA	NA
Hays	8.21	42.2	117	D	D	D	619	10,400	2,471.3	208.4	177	680	161.8	21.6
Hemphill	0.50	117.3	13	D	D	D	23	148	64.8	3.9	9	96	24.4	5.6
Henderson	4.55	57.2	34	D	D	D	230	2,599	671.8	58.0	56	201	26.4	5.8
Hidalgo	64.64	76.7	841	D	D	D	2,219	33,566	9,296.8	733.9	497	2,209	445.0	61.9
Hill	2.97	85.2	21	D	D	D	151	1,427	409.7	28.1	28	86	12.0	2.1
Hockley	0.50	21.3	23	D	D	D	61	850	221.0	18.8	12	63	13.4	4.7
Hood	4.85	87.5	55	396	222.5	19.5	195	2,394	747.6	60.6	70	376	50.0	11.9
Hopkins	11.05	305.1	31	904	1,176.6	42.2	147	1,659	496.7	37.5	28	116	15.8	2.7
Houston	2.34	102.7	11	D	D	D	60	640	160.7	13.6	9	45	4.8	1.2
Howard	0.03	0.8	27	D	D	D	108	D	D	D	41	156	30.1	4.5
Hudspeth	0.24	71.0	NA	NA	NA	NA	10	41	11.3	0.6	NA	NA	NA	NA
Hunt	4.87	54.2	51	D	D	D	247	3,428	966.3	90.9	66	182	28.5	4.8
Hutchinson	5.30	243.9	19	D	D	D	79	867	205.2	17.7	11	93	17.0	2.2
Irion	0.08	51.5	2	D	D	D	4	17	1.6	0.2	NA	NA	NA	NA
Jack	0.55	62.0	7	D	D	D	26	187	38.7	3.9	7	12	2.4	0.3
Jackson	0.90	60.7	15	124	230.1	7.4	38	511	165.6	10.8	10	D	D	D
Jasper	2.97	83.6	29	D	D	D	127	1,457	425.7	32.5	23	78	14.0	2.3
Jeff Davis	1.12	519.5	1	D	D	D	6	51	7.9	0.8	4	9	2.4	0.4
Jefferson	23.95	94.2	273	2,964	2,451.0	156.3	992	13,877	3,968.3	348.1	264	1,759	372.3	73.9
Jim Hogg	0.67	128.8	4	D	D	D	20	209	72.8	4.6	3	D	D	D
Jim Wells	3.95	95.5	39	D	D	D	142	1,708	641.6	43.8	46	527	128.1	30.9
Johnson	10.33	64.6	124	1,160	604.6	52.8	381	4,843	1,513.4	119.0	108	610	125.6	28.9
Jones	8.07	404.1	23	108	538.5	4.4	34	216	158.4	5.9	6	D	D	D
Karnes	2.75	183.6	13	69	45.3	2.7	39	479	192.0	11.9	11	8	2.1	0.5
Kaufman	0.85	7.4	62	D	D	D	291	3,480	1,021.0	84.9	50	150	27.6	4.8
Kendall	1.66	41.1	51	D	D	D	152	2,107	941.0	66.1	47	116	24.3	4.2
Kenedy	0.07	172.0	NA	NA	NA	NA	NA	NA	NA	NA	1	D	D	D
Kent	0.08	104.7	NA	NA	NA	NA	3	D	D	D	NA	NA	NA	NA
Kerr	5.58	109.5	44	D	D	D	215	3,006	791.7	72.0	84	229	31.7	8.2
Kimble	0.45	102.6	NA	NA	NA	NA	34	239	97.5	6.0	3	7	1.6	0.4
King	0.19	673.8	NA	NA	NA	NA	NA	NA	NA	NA	NA	NA	NA	NA
Kinney	0.82	231.1	2	D	D	D	8	58	9.8	0.8	2	D	D	D
Kleberg	3.31	103.9	5	D	D	D	110	1,490	524.3	33.8	27	D	D	D
Knox	0.14	36.3	11	D	D	D	15	139	31.6	2.1	3	4	0.2	0.1
Lamar	14.84	300.2	43	D	D	D	212	2,426	678.6	57.3	48	161	22.4	4.9
Lamb	1.35	100.9	19	172	123.6	8.4	40	374	93.0	7.8	1	D	D	D
Lampasas	2.71	131.6	6	D	D	D	51	604	208.9	15.1	14	42	9.5	2.0
La Salle	1.36	178.2	6	72	33.9	3.3	22	238	134.4	4.9	5	D	D	D
Lavaca	1.44	72.6	15	D	D	D	90	772	178.8	15.3	12	39	8.5	1.2
Lee	3.97	234.9	19	D	D	D	62	618	151.6	12.8	14	111	39.9	5.5
Leon	1.90	111.2	13	D	D	D	66	558	156.8	10.9	13	51	9.3	2.4
Liberty	6.42	80.6	45	500	239.1	25.8	197	2,468	796.6	60.9	32	192	33.0	8.3
Limestone	1.95	83.6	10	D	D	D	93	966	263.8	20.6	14	47	6.1	1.1
Lipscomb	0.81	227.0	4	D	D	D	20	120	98.1	3.6	1	D	D	D
Live Oak	2.76	225.7	15	D	D	D	39	347	263.0	9.5	10	40	20.1	1.8
Llano	2.87	145.0	15	236	79.0	10.1	68	480	135.3	11.0	22	39	9.1	1.4
Loving	0.01	89.3	NA	NA	NA	NA	NA	NA	NA	NA	NA	NA	NA	NA
Lubbock	1.32	4.4	377	5,273	4,815.9	259.1	1,046	16,460	4,796.6	405.0	394	1,559	270.4	49.7
Lynn	0.15	26.2	4	D	D	D	8	76	18.5	1.7	3	D	D	0.2
McCulloch	2.69	322.5	9	180	57.7	10.5	39	481	139.0	10.6	5	8	0.9	0.2
McLennan	41.41	168.6	239	2,976	1,634.7	123.0	846	11,099	3,223.8	250.4	223	1,512	286.8	63.8
McMullen	0.10	122.0	NA	NA	NA	NA	4	D	D	D	2	D	D	D
Madison	2.37	168.5	6	D	D	D	37	655	244.8	17.9	13	47	14.6	1.2
Marion	0.35	34.4	2	D	D	D	28	192	61.3	4.6	7	8	1.4	0.2
Martin	1.48	262.4	7	D	D	D	12	144	88.7	4.6	1	D	D	D

1. Merchant wholesalers, except manufacturers' sales branches and offices.   2. Employer establishments.

State / county code	CBSA code[1]	County code[2]	STATE County	Land area[3] (sq. mi)	Total persons 2017	Rank	Per square mile	White	Black	American Indian, Alaska Native	Asian and Pacific Islander	Percent Hispanic or Latino[4]	Under 5 years	5 to 17 years	18 to 24 years	25 to 34 years	35 to 44 years	45 to 54 years
				1	2	3	4	5	6	7	8	9	10	11	12	13	14	15
			TEXAS— Cont'd															
48,319		9	Mason	928.8	4,222	2,885	4.5	73.4	0.8	0.7	0.4	25.4	5.2	15.6	7.2	8.0	9.3	11.3
48,321	13,060	4	Matagorda	1,092.9	36,840	1,255	33.7	44.8	10.8	0.7	2.1	42.7	7.2	18.4	8.5	12.5	11.1	11.8
48,323	20,580	5	Maverick	1,279.5	58,216	888	45.5	2.9	0.3	1.1	0.7	95.1	9.4	22.3	11.8	13.1	11.7	11.0
48,325	41,700	1	Medina	1,325.4	50,066	987	37.8	44.5	2.7	0.8	0.9	51.9	5.9	17.5	9.6	12.4	11.4	13.4
48,327		9	Menard	902.0	2,124	3,038	2.4	61.9	1.5	0.6	0.3	36.1	4.1	13.1	6.9	8.9	8.2	10.8
48,329	33,260	3	Midland	900.3	165,049	395	183.3	46.6	6.5	0.8	2.3	45.0	8.8	19.5	8.9	17.8	12.9	10.6
48,331		6	Milam	1,016.9	25,053	1,605	24.6	63.2	9.5	0.8	1.2	26.6	6.4	18.5	7.8	10.8	10.7	12.2
48,333		9	Mills	748.2	4,921	2,838	6.6	80.0	1.2	0.7	0.6	18.6	4.6	16.5	7.0	7.9	9.8	12.0
48,335		7	Mitchell	911.1	8,468	2,549	9.3	49.5	10.3	1.2	0.7	39.5	5.7	15.4	11.7	17.0	12.9	12.1
48,337		6	Montague	930.9	19,539	1,850	21.0	87.0	1.0	1.6	0.6	11.3	6.0	16.7	7.2	11.1	10.5	12.1
48,339	26,420	1	Montgomery	1,042.6	570,934	116	547.6	67.6	5.4	0.8	3.7	24.1	6.9	19.6	8.2	12.7	13.6	13.7
48,341	20,300	7	Moore	899.7	22,097	1,721	24.6	33.1	3.7	0.9	7.9	55.3	9.9	22.1	9.7	13.7	12.7	11.0
48,343		6	Morris	252.0	12,467	2,261	49.5	66.1	24.0	1.4	0.9	10.0	6.3	16.8	7.5	11.0	11.0	11.3
48,345		9	Motley	989.6	1,230	3,098	1.2	79.8	2.8	1.1	0.0	16.8	4.0	14.5	7.6	10.2	8.3	10.7
48,347	34,860	5	Nacogdoches	946.6	65,580	815	69.3	60.7	18.6	0.8	1.8	19.5	6.6	16.8	19.2	11.7	10.1	10.2
48,349	18,620	4	Navarro	1,009.6	48,701	1,010	48.2	57.6	13.6	0.8	2.2	27.3	7.3	18.9	8.6	11.6	11.3	12.4
48,351	13,140	2	Newton	933.7	13,952	2,166	14.9	74.6	21.0	1.4	1.1	3.6	4.8	15.4	8.7	11.7	11.0	13.5
48,353	45,020	6	Nolan	912.0	14,770	2,111	16.2	56.4	5.3	0.8	0.9	37.9	7.2	18.9	8.5	11.9	11.1	11.6
48,355	18,580	2	Nueces	838.3	361,221	194	430.9	30.2	3.8	0.5	2.5	63.9	6.9	17.9	10.0	14.5	12.6	11.9
48,357		7	Ochiltree	917.7	10,073	2,427	11.0	43.8	1.0	1.0	0.7	54.5	8.7	23.3	8.9	13.0	12.7	11.2
48,359	11,100	2	Oldham	1,500.5	2,114	3,039	1.4	79.0	3.9	1.1	1.7	15.6	4.1	21.3	6.8	10.7	14.5	13.5
48,361	13,140	2	Orange	333.8	85,047	674	254.8	82.1	9.1	1.1	1.5	7.7	7.0	17.9	8.2	13.2	12.1	12.7
48,363	33,420	6	Palo Pinto	952.2	28,570	1,468	30.0	76.3	3.0	1.0	1.0	19.9	6.3	17.3	8.1	11.7	10.5	12.4
48,365		6	Panola	811.4	23,243	1,669	28.6	74.5	16.2	1.0	1.0	8.8	6.0	17.6	8.3	11.4	11.9	12.2
48,367	19,100	1	Parker	903.5	133,463	476	147.7	85.0	1.8	1.4	1.0	12.2	6.2	18.5	7.9	11.7	12.4	14.0
48,369		7	Parmer	880.8	9,842	2,441	11.2	34.6	1.4	0.5	0.6	63.5	8.5	20.6	9.3	12.4	11.5	12.4
48,371		7	Pecos	4,763.8	15,634	2,061	3.3	26.2	4.0	0.7	0.9	68.8	6.6	17.6	8.6	15.6	14.1	12.9
48,373		6	Polk	1,057.0	49,162	1,000	46.5	72.1	10.6	2.3	1.0	15.3	5.5	15.0	7.6	12.1	11.7	12.9
48,375	11,100	2	Potter	908.4	120,458	520	132.6	45.5	10.7	0.9	6.1	38.3	8.1	19.5	9.1	15.3	13.0	11.8
48,377		7	Presidio	3,855.3	7,156	2,656	1.9	12.5	1.3	0.6	2.7	83.6	8.1	18.6	8.5	10.6	10.6	10.8
48,379		8	Rains	229.5	11,762	2,307	51.3	86.7	2.8	1.5	1.2	9.1	4.7	14.8	6.7	10.1	10.4	12.4
48,381	11,100	2	Randall	911.9	134,442	472	147.4	73.1	3.7	1.0	2.1	21.8	6.6	17.5	9.9	14.9	12.8	11.5
48,383		6	Reagan	1,175.3	3,710	2,922	3.2	28.4	3.3	0.5	0.6	68.5	8.3	21.2	10.0	12.8	14.1	11.5
48,385		9	Real	699.2	3,429	2,941	4.9	70.4	1.4	1.4	0.8	27.6	4.1	12.9	6.5	9.1	8.7	12.2
48,387		6	Red River	1,043.9	12,229	2,277	11.7	74.6	17.0	1.9	0.5	7.6	5.2	14.6	6.8	10.2	10.6	12.9
48,389	37,780	7	Reeves	2,635.4	15,281	2,080	5.8	18.4	5.0	0.4	1.4	75.3	6.7	15.7	12.2	17.1	15.2	12.1
48,391		6	Refugio	770.5	7,224	2,648	9.4	43.1	6.4	0.8	0.9	50.0	6.3	17.2	7.6	11.4	10.4	12.2
48,393		9	Roberts	924.1	938	3,109	1.0	87.5	0.9	1.6	0.5	11.3	6.0	19.8	4.9	11.6	12.8	11.6
48,395	17,780	3	Robertson	855.1	17,203	1,962	20.1	58.6	20.0	0.8	0.9	20.9	6.6	17.6	7.7	12.0	11.1	12.5
48,397	19,100	1	Rockwall	127.1	96,788	615	761.5	72.7	6.9	0.9	3.5	17.7	6.3	20.9	8.1	11.0	14.7	14.6
48,399		6	Runnels	1,050.9	10,266	2,407	9.8	62.3	2.4	0.9	0.9	34.3	5.4	17.9	7.9	11.6	10.0	12.3
48,401	30,980	3	Rusk	924.0	52,833	950	57.2	65.4	17.5	0.9	0.7	16.9	5.9	17.2	8.6	13.0	12.9	12.8
48,403		8	Sabine	491.4	10,461	2,391	21.3	87.6	7.7	1.1	0.6	4.5	4.8	14.1	6.1	8.7	8.3	11.2
48,405		9	San Augustine	530.7	8,253	2,571	15.6	70.4	22.5	0.8	0.6	7.1	5.1	14.6	6.7	10.1	9.1	12.7
48,407		8	San Jacinto	569.2	28,270	1,482	49.7	76.4	10.1	1.3	0.9	13.1	5.5	16.2	7.5	10.2	10.5	12.2
48,409	18,580	2	San Patricio	693.4	67,215	792	96.9	39.1	1.8	0.7	1.4	57.9	7.5	19.6	8.9	13.3	12.6	12.0
48,411		7	San Saba County	1,135.3	5,959	2,752	5.2	65.4	3.6	1.0	0.8	30.3	5.7	14.9	9.5	14.1	8.7	11.2
48,413		8	Schleicher	1,310.6	3,001	2,968	2.3	45.3	1.6	0.4	0.3	53.1	5.6	21.0	7.5	12.5	11.7	12.0
48,415	43,660	7	Scurry	905.4	17,050	1,977	18.8	53.8	5.2	0.6	0.8	40.6	7.0	18.5	9.7	13.3	12.8	12.2
48,417		8	Shackelford	914.3	3,328	2,947	3.6	86.7	1.7	0.5	0.7	11.6	5.6	18.2	7.0	10.6	10.8	11.7
48,419		7	Shelby	795.6	25,513	1,583	32.1	62.1	18.3	0.6	1.5	18.5	7.3	19.2	8.4	11.7	11.4	12.1
48,421		9	Sherman	923.0	3,067	2,962	3.3	53.9	1.5	0.6	0.5	44.2	6.9	21.3	8.1	11.4	11.0	13.9
48,423	46,340	3	Smith	921.5	227,727	293	247.1	60.9	18.1	0.7	2.1	19.6	6.9	17.7	9.7	13.7	11.7	11.9
48,425	19,100	1	Somervell	186.5	8,845	2,517	47.4	78.6	1.8	1.3	1.2	18.7	5.0	17.6	7.9	11.0	11.8	13.8
48,427	40,100	4	Starr	1,223.2	64,454	822	52.7	3.4	0.1	0.0	0.2	96.3	10.0	23.1	11.3	13.2	11.8	10.9
48,429		7	Stephens	896.7	9,337	2,479	10.4	72.2	2.9	1.0	0.9	24.0	5.4	16.3	9.6	12.4	11.8	11.3
48,431		8	Sterling	923.4	1,295	3,094	1.4	56.7	2.9	1.4	0.7	40.0	6.8	20.8	7.3	11.7	13.1	11.4
48,433		9	Stonewall	916.3	1,388	3,084	1.5	76.1	4.1	0.9	1.6	18.4	6.5	15.6	6.4	8.8	9.9	12.3
48,435		7	Sutton	1,453.9	3,767	2,917	2.6	36.4	0.7	0.2	0.3	62.6	6.7	17.7	7.8	11.8	11.2	12.8
48,437		6	Swisher	890.2	7,515	2,627	8.4	47.4	8.0	0.9	0.5	44.1	6.6	18.9	9.4	14.1	10.8	11.5
48,439	19,100	1	Tarrant	863.7	2,054,475	15	2,378.7	48.6	17.2	0.9	6.5	28.9	7.1	19.4	9.3	14.9	13.6	13.2
48,441	10,180	3	Taylor	915.6	136,290	467	148.9	65.4	8.4	0.9	3.0	24.5	7.3	17.4	14.3	14.7	11.0	10.1
48,443		9	Terrell	2,358.0	810	3,117	0.3	44.3	2.3	1.7	0.6	52.7	5.4	16.4	5.4	8.5	12.5	11.4
48,445		6	Terry	888.8	12,715	2,244	14.3	39.9	4.7	0.5	0.5	55.1	7.5	19.8	9.2	14.5	11.5	11.5
48,447		9	Throckmorton	912.6	1,527	3,078	1.7	83.3	1.4	1.2	0.5	14.4	5.2	15.7	6.7	9.0	9.8	11.7
48,449	34,420	7	Titus	406.1	32,904	1,361	81.0	46.0	9.7	0.7	1.3	43.3	7.6	21.3	9.8	12.2	12.0	12.3

1. CBSA = Core Based Statistical Area. See Appendix A for explanation. See Appendix B for list of metropolitan areas with component counties. Service of USDA Rural-Urban Continuum Codes. See Appendix A for definition. 3. Dry land or land partially or temporarily covered by water. 2. County type code from the Economic Research Service. 4. May be of any race.

Table B. States and Counties — **Population and Households**

STATE County	Population, 2017 (cont.) Age (percent) (cont.)				Population change, 2000-2017							Households, 2012-2016		Percent		
					Total persons		Percent change		Components of change, 2010-2017							
	55 to 64 years	65 to 74 years	75 years and over	Percent female	2000	2010	2000-2010	2010-2017	Births	Deaths	Net Migration	Number	Persons per house-hold	Family house-holds	Female family house-holder[1]	One person
	16	17	18	19	20	21	22	23	24	25	26	27	28	29	30	31
TEXAS— Cont'd																
Mason	14.9	15.6	13.1	49.3	3,738	4,012	7.3	5.2	280	314	244	1,688	2.40	65.2	10.2	31.4
Matagorda	13.9	9.7	6.8	49.9	37,957	36,702	-3.3	0.4	3,884	2,696	-1,046	13,666	2.66	66.9	13.5	30.4
Maverick	9.2	6.7	4.8	50.1	47,297	54,258	14.7	7.3	7,944	2,679	-1,298	16,221	3.47	81.7	19.0	16.9
Medina	13.5	9.9	6.5	48.3	39,304	46,006	17.1	8.8	4,008	2,861	2,923	15,104	3.01	75.2	11.1	20.1
Menard	17.7	16.4	13.8	50.0	2,360	2,242	-5.0	-5.3	129	244	-7	936	2.25	65.6	11.2	31.6
Midland	11.0	5.8	4.6	49.7	116,009	136,872	18.0	20.6	19,495	7,614	15,894	53,960	2.85	70.1	12.6	23.9
Milam	13.8	11.3	8.6	50.9	24,238	24,753	2.1	1.2	2,260	2,091	128	9,423	2.54	64.1	11.4	32.4
Mills	15.0	14.9	12.3	50.5	5,151	4,941	-4.1	-0.4	305	457	132	1,875	2.51	69.0	8.1	30.3
Mitchell	10.2	8.5	6.3	41.0	9,698	9,403	-3.0	-9.9	701	699	-954	2,660	2.45	70.4	8.7	24.5
Montague	14.3	12.7	9.4	50.7	19,117	19,720	3.2	-0.9	1,698	1,920	52	8,083	2.36	67.7	9.3	28.9
Montgomery	12.4	8.1	4.7	50.4	293,768	455,752	55.1	25.3	49,732	24,212	88,572	179,587	2.87	74.3	10.4	21.3
Moore	10.4	5.9	4.6	48.0	20,121	21,904	8.9	0.9	3,097	998	-1,948	6,772	3.25	79.1	10.8	16.8
Morris	14.7	11.6	9.8	52.0	13,048	12,934	-0.9	-3.6	1,121	1,198	-387	5,015	2.49	72.2	14.2	27.1
Motley	15.0	17.6	12.3	48.7	1,426	1,205	-15.5	2.1	59	119	83	475	2.15	58.1	7.8	39.6
Nacogdoches	11.2	8.5	5.8	52.1	59,203	64,524	9.0	1.6	6,403	4,070	-1,299	23,942	2.51	63.2	12.3	29.6
Navarro	13.0	9.8	7.0	50.9	45,124	47,840	6.0	1.8	5,046	3,746	-415	17,409	2.72	74.3	14.8	22.7
Newton	14.7	11.7	8.4	48.2	15,072	14,445	-4.2	-3.4	1,012	1,143	-362	4,629	3.02	61.5	10.6	34.7
Nolan	12.7	10.0	7.9	50.2	15,802	15,217	-3.7	-2.9	1,481	1,292	-639	5,625	2.60	67.4	14.6	28.7
Nueces	12.2	8.3	5.8	50.6	313,645	340,223	8.5	6.2	35,414	20,270	5,937	128,133	2.72	68.3	16.1	24.8
Ochiltree	11.2	6.6	4.3	49.2	9,006	10,223	13.5	-1.5	1,323	602	-882	3,587	2.93	73.3	9.8	22.6
Oldham	14.4	9.3	5.5	48.0	2,185	2,052	-6.1	3.0	157	105	5	616	2.59	75.2	6.7	22.2
Orange	13.3	9.0	6.6	50.5	84,966	81,837	-3.7	3.9	8,201	6,750	1,825	32,269	2.57	70.7	13.3	25.5
Palo Pinto	14.4	11.4	7.8	50.8	27,026	28,122	4.1	1.6	2,599	2,338	200	10,416	2.65	67.7	11.8	25.9
Panola	14.3	11.0	7.5	50.7	22,756	23,796	4.6	-2.3	2,102	2,000	-647	8,905	2.62	69.7	12.8	25.6
Parker	14.0	9.5	5.8	50.2	88,495	116,948	32.2	14.1	10,143	7,461	13,765	43,270	2.80	75.9	8.9	20.7
Parmer	11.7	7.4	6.3	48.2	10,016	10,269	2.5	-4.2	1,135	516	-1,066	3,219	3.06	77.1	12.1	16.9
Pecos	11.2	7.4	5.8	43.2	16,809	15,507	-7.7	0.8	1,567	813	-618	4,334	3.17	66.3	7.5	30.4
Polk	16.5	12.7	5.9	46.1	41,133	45,414	10.4	8.3	3,727	4,519	4,463	17,790	2.39	70.4	15.1	25.9
Potter	11.1	7.0	5.2	48.4	113,546	121,078	6.6	-0.5	14,616	8,646	-6,652	43,154	2.66	64.5	16.2	30.3
Presidio	10.2	11.1	11.5	49.1	7,304	7,817	7.0	-8.5	881	312	-1,259	2,565	2.78	67.1	14.6	31.5
Rains	16.6	14.9	9.4	50.3	9,139	10,914	19.4	7.8	704	974	1,111	4,252	2.59	70.8	11.5	26.4
Randall	12.2	8.5	6.1	50.8	104,312	120,720	15.7	11.4	12,072	7,316	8,933	48,893	2.58	68.3	11.5	25.2
Reagan	11.0	6.4	4.9	46.5	3,326	3,367	1.2	10.2	436	175	76	1,190	3.02	73.0	7.6	22.9
Real	17.8	17.1	11.8	50.0	3,047	3,309	8.6	3.6	255	367	227	1,192	2.71	64.5	14.1	34.3
Red River	15.5	13.4	10.9	51.2	14,314	12,864	-10.1	-4.9	934	1,265	-299	5,163	2.37	63.9	14.4	33.0
Reeves	8.9	6.6	5.5	38.9	13,137	13,783	4.9	10.9	1,356	750	883	3,764	3.08	66.7	9.5	28.8
Refugio	13.4	12.2	9.3	51.1	7,828	7,383	-5.7	-2.2	639	651	-150	2,761	2.59	69.6	13.9	27.6
Roberts	14.1	12.4	6.8	49.9	887	929	4.7	1.0	70	62	1	342	2.75	82.7	13.7	15.2
Robertson	13.6	10.8	8.1	50.6	16,000	16,620	3.9	3.5	1,528	1,344	402	6,366	2.57	70.1	14.9	24.5
Rockwall	12.0	7.5	4.8	50.6	43,080	78,324	81.8	23.6	7,263	3,766	14,821	29,392	2.97	80.9	10.1	15.4
Runnels	13.5	11.3	9.4	49.2	11,495	10,501	-8.6	-2.2	787	998	-24	3,792	2.69	72.3	11.3	25.5
Rusk	13.2	9.7	6.8	47.4	47,372	53,304	12.5	-0.9	4,627	3,927	-1,155	17,795	2.72	72.7	14.3	23.9
Sabine	16.1	17.6	13.1	50.8	10,469	10,835	3.5	-3.5	689	1,226	165	3,682	2.79	64.0	9.8	35.1
San Augustine	16.3	13.8	11.6	50.7	8,946	8,864	-0.9	-6.9	685	990	-307	2,972	2.79	65.6	13.1	32.0
San Jacinto	16.4	13.0	8.4	50.0	22,246	26,377	18.6	7.2	2,049	2,105	1,942	9,631	2.81	72.9	8.0	22.9
San Patricio	11.7	8.7	5.8	49.8	67,138	64,807	-3.5	3.7	7,096	4,490	-210	23,237	2.84	74.8	15.1	21.2
San Saba	13.3	12.8	9.9	45.9	6,186	6,131	-0.9	-2.8	481	486	-185	2,110	2.45	62.4	7.1	31.2
Schleicher	11.6	11.5	6.7	50.0	2,935	3,461	17.9	-13.3	247	168	-549	1,091	2.91	77.5	12.4	19.3
Scurry	11.7	7.9	6.9	46.1	16,361	16,921	3.4	0.8	1,839	1,248	-465	5,908	2.62	66.9	8.1	29.6
Shackelford	16.2	10.5	9.5	51.9	3,302	3,379	2.3	-1.5	242	214	-81	1,317	2.51	68.3	9.5	27.5
Shelby	12.6	9.7	7.5	50.2	25,224	25,448	0.9	0.3	2,691	2,079	-556	9,120	2.80	67.5	16.4	30.2
Sherman	12.4	8.1	7.0	48.3	3,186	3,034	-4.8	1.1	279	192	-56	1,017	2.98	76.0	8.6	20.0
Smith	12.2	9.1	7.1	51.7	174,706	209,721	20.0	8.6	22,297	14,573	10,320	78,040	2.75	68.5	13.0	26.7
Somervell	14.3	11.0	7.7	50.9	6,809	8,491	24.7	4.2	611	606	351	3,241	2.58	76.1	14.2	20.0
Starr	8.4	6.4	4.9	51.3	53,597	60,968	13.8	5.7	9,707	2,838	-3,417	16,219	3.85	82.4	25.0	16.7
Stephens	13.9	10.8	8.5	47.2	9,674	9,630	-0.5	-3.0	744	805	-240	3,338	2.75	68.2	9.6	28.0
Sterling	13.3	8.2	7.6	49.2	1,393	1,143	-17.9	13.3	111	89	125	453	2.63	78.4	9.7	19.4
Stonewall	14.3	13.3	12.8	51.6	1,693	1,490	-12.0	-6.8	100	155	-53	501	2.35	64.1	5.8	33.9
Sutton	14.3	10.3	7.4	49.3	4,077	4,128	1.3	-8.7	386	234	-524	1,481	2.64	72.8	9.3	23.8
Swisher	10.9	9.3	8.5	46.8	8,378	7,854	-6.3	-4.3	759	558	-546	2,630	2.66	72.1	15.5	25.4
Tarrant	11.4	6.8	4.3	51.0	1,446,219	1,810,614	25.2	13.5	203,813	86,920	127,080	682,967	2.82	69.4	14.2	25.2
Taylor	10.9	7.8	6.5	51.1	126,555	131,511	3.9	3.6	14,925	9,324	-758	49,489	2.60	65.9	13.1	26.4
Terrell	12.2	16.8	11.4	50.1	1,081	984	-9.0	-17.7	82	85	-176	396	1.96	50.3	12.9	42.2
Terry	11.2	7.9	6.8	46.8	12,761	12,651	-0.9	0.5	1,411	885	-462	4,214	2.75	71.6	15.8	25.7
Throckmorton	14.5	12.9	14.4	52.3	1,850	1,641	-11.3	-6.9	107	137	-87	725	2.07	63.4	10.6	35.3
Titus	10.8	8.2	5.9	50.9	28,118	32,334	15.0	1.8	3,659	1,947	-1,145	10,573	3.05	78.6	13.3	18.0

1. No spouse present.

Table B. States and Counties — Population, Vital Statistics, Health, and Crime

STATE County	Persons in group quarters, 2017	Daytime Population, 2012-2016		Births, 2017		Deaths, 2017		Persons under 65 with no health insurance, 2016		Medicare, 2017			Serious crimes known to police[2], 2016 Total	
		Number	Employment/ residence ratio	Total	Rate[1]	Number	Rate[1]	Number	Percent	Total beneficiaries	Enrolled in Original Medicare	Enrolled in Medicare Advantage	Number	Rate[3]
	32	33	34	35	36	37	38	39	40	41	42	43	44	45
TEXAS— Cont'd														
Mason	3	3,967	0.95	45	10.7	42	9.9	781	26.7	1,175	922	254	45	1,118
Matagorda	366	35,061	0.89	552	15.0	389	10.6	6,171	20.0	6,871	4,999	1,873	1,363	3,717
Maverick	1,012	53,470	0.84	1,113	19.1	385	6.6	13,611	27.5	9,845	6,722	3,123	1,276	2,192
Medina	2,341	40,051	0.61	595	11.9	431	8.6	6,524	16.6	8,093	5,074	3,019	1,048	2,204
Menard	37	1,952	0.75	15	7.1	27	12.7	385	26.3	622	505	117	4	187
Midland	1,653	171,026	1.20	2,955	17.9	1,083	6.6	25,409	17.5	17,692	14,023	3,669	4,676	2,819
Milam	416	22,305	0.77	321	12.8	282	11.3	3,828	19.5	5,582	3,460	2,122	502	2,057
Mills	138	4,796	0.96	35	7.1	66	13.4	846	24.0	1,306	895	411	28	574
Mitchell	1,668	8,679	0.89	92	10.9	78	9.2	1,134	20.1	1,407	1,080	327	117	1,304
Montague	217	17,851	0.81	251	12.8	258	13.2	3,251	21.5	5,076	4,216	860	436	2,407
Montgomery	3,542	473,519	0.81	7,612	13.3	3,889	6.8	81,793	16.9	78,484	48,154	30,330	9,259	1,674
Moore	153	22,983	1.08	449	20.3	125	5.7	5,063	25.8	2,371	2,006	364	384	1,727
Morris	144	12,038	0.87	155	12.4	155	12.4	1,942	19.8	3,398	2,276	1,122	345	2,782
Motley	0	954	0.84	8	6.5	14	11.4	210	25.7	357	276	81	14	1,236
Nacogdoches	5,019	64,216	0.95	833	12.7	564	8.6	11,001	21.2	11,122	8,447	2,675	1,391	2,118
Navarro	721	47,067	0.94	690	14.2	560	11.5	8,612	21.5	10,104	7,789	2,315	1,254	2,685
Newton	726	12,154	0.55	129	9.2	172	12.3	1,827	17.0	2,509	1,753	756	NA	NA
Nolan	353	15,638	1.10	199	13.5	181	12.3	2,097	17.4	3,121	2,389	732	676	4,930
Nueces	6,723	364,963	1.06	4,887	13.5	2,924	8.1	55,992	18.3	56,649	27,875	28,774	16,004	4,413
Ochiltree	20	11,600	1.22	178	17.7	73	7.2	2,438	26.6	1,210	1,071	139	145	1,338
Oldham	278	2,492	1.58	24	11.4	8	3.8	229	15.0	436	354	82	11	532
Orange	680	75,805	0.78	1,179	13.9	962	11.3	9,875	13.8	16,383	10,248	6,134	2,185	2,603
Palo Pinto	289	26,047	0.84	347	12.1	349	12.2	4,851	21.5	5,615	4,609	1,006	797	2,869
Panola	381	23,440	0.97	269	11.6	275	11.8	3,283	17.3	4,659	3,532	1,126	661	2,790
Parker	1,237	103,783	0.65	1,549	11.6	1,138	8.5	17,019	15.7	20,588	15,220	5,369	1,804	1,415
Parmer	70	11,046	1.25	174	17.7	43	4.4	2,121	25.1	1,362	1,231	130	99	1,029
Pecos	2,056	16,068	1.04	197	12.6	104	6.7	2,577	21.6	2,212	1,708	503	335	2,056
Polk	4,417	45,436	0.93	554	11.3	629	12.8	7,577	21.9	17,513	12,316	5,197	911	1,933
Potter	6,964	146,708	1.47	1,870	15.5	1,164	9.7	23,015	23.1	34,545	26,726	7,819	6,120	5,036
Presidio	0	7,043	0.96	119	16.6	45	6.3	1,568	28.9	1,768	1,391	377	48	719
Rains	56	9,386	0.61	100	8.5	127	10.8	1,817	21.2	2,811	2,166	645	131	1,172
Randall	2,514	101,660	0.59	1,689	12.6	1,069	8.0	14,461	12.9	4,827	3,787	1,040	5,752	4,365
Reagan	27	4,422	1.47	70	18.9	17	4.6	696	21.7	409	332	77	71	1,832
Real	71	3,295	0.95	42	12.2	56	16.3	578	24.5	1,155	905	250	45	1,366
Red River	186	10,438	0.58	115	9.4	169	13.8	1,887	20.5	3,357	2,734	623	125	1,013
Reeves	3,141	16,811	1.49	207	13.5	104	6.8	2,088	20.8	2,065	1,746	319	361	2,426
Refugio	126	6,987	0.89	88	12.2	66	9.1	977	17.0	1,693	1,247	446	97	1,337
Roberts	0	813	0.69	10	10.7	6	6.4	76	10.2	151	112	39	8	878
Robertson	196	15,166	0.80	214	12.4	168	9.8	2,653	19.6	3,222	2,377	845	240	1,443
Rockwall	807	76,397	0.72	1,082	11.2	552	5.7	10,894	13.3	13,045	9,471	3,574	1,251	1,343
Runnels	175	9,859	0.87	108	10.5	125	12.2	1,624	20.0	2,585	2,226	358	246	2,336
Rusk	4,844	47,829	0.74	612	11.6	534	10.1	8,256	20.7	8,060	5,787	2,274	1,571	2,972
Sabine	101	9,899	0.83	108	10.3	158	15.1	1,389	19.2	3,944	3,045	898	195	2,066
San Augustine	174	8,472	0.96	82	9.9	131	15.9	1,122	18.4	2,170	1,652	517	130	1,552
San Jacinto	128	20,806	0.38	299	10.6	303	10.7	4,689	21.5	4,402	2,648	1,754	409	1,486
San Patricio	606	60,373	0.78	1,027	15.3	583	8.7	10,600	18.5	13,066	6,395	6,671	1,966	2,902
San Saba	620	5,658	0.90	64	10.7	69	11.6	1,044	26.4	1,379	1,023	357	32	548
Schleicher	1	3,044	0.92	26	8.7	17	5.7	577	22.7	525	433	91	54	1,715
Scurry	1,715	18,081	1.11	246	14.4	166	9.7	2,342	17.6	2,793	2,151	643	392	2,215
Shackelford	11	3,201	0.92	34	10.2	30	9.0	557	20.7	666	542	124	34	1,019
Shelby	164	24,444	0.87	390	15.3	295	11.6	5,362	25.2	5,126	3,893	1,233	492	2,035
Sherman	29	2,683	0.75	37	12.1	10	3.3	719	27.6	500	443	57	14	456
Smith	5,032	226,311	1.07	3,159	13.9	2,064	9.1	33,998	18.4	44,303	32,225	12,078	7,207	3,233
Somervell	284	9,738	1.30	80	9.0	92	10.4	1,323	18.7	1,593	1,134	459	83	947
Starr	843	60,016	0.85	1,266	19.6	400	6.2	15,589	28.2	9,089	6,358	2,731	900	1,403
Stephens	695	9,369	0.89	96	10.3	96	10.3	1,588	22.8	1,832	1,438	394	180	1,919
Sterling	36	1,416	1.31	16	12.4	13	10.0	216	19.0	227	184	44	1	72
Stonewall	24	1,172	0.88	15	10.8	9	6.5	195	18.4	367	318	48	7	504
Sutton	13	4,092	1.09	55	14.6	25	6.6	656	20.7	720	661	59	46	1,188
Swisher	642	7,043	0.77	95	12.6	68	8.4	1,258	22.9	1,521	1,292	228	169	2,271
Tarrant	25,740	1,939,126	0.99	28,961	14.1	13,274	6.5	303,048	17.0	248,829	141,864	106,965	65,230	3,243
Taylor	5,002	138,460	1.05	2,057	15.1	1,371	10.1	18,571	16.4	24,692	18,917	5,775	4,948	3,625
Terrell	0	774	0.99	8	9.9	10	12.3	130	21.6	246	180	65	14	1,739
Terry	1,159	12,608	0.97	188	14.8	121	9.5	2,378	24.2	2,028	1,401	627	262	2,060
Throckmorton	13	1,543	1.03	14	9.2	12	7.9	239	21.0	356	309	47	0	0
Titus	536	35,789	1.23	502	15.3	254	7.7	6,705	24.3	5,262	3,888	1,373	882	2,708

1. Per 1,000 estimated resident population.   2. Data for serious crimes have not been adjusted for underreporting; this may affect comparability between geographic areas and over time.
3. Per 100,000 population estimated by the FBI.

Table B. States and Counties — Crime, Education, Money Income, and Poverty

STATE County	Serious crimes known to police, 2016 (cont.)[1] Rate Violent	Property	Education — School enrollment and attainment, 2012-2016 Enrollment[3] Total	Percent private	Attainment[4] (percent) High school graduate or less	Bachelor's degree or more	Local government expenditures,[5] 2013-2014 Total current spending (mil dol)	Current spending per student (dollars)	Money income, 2012-2016 Per capita income[6]	Households Median income (dollars)	Percent with income of less than $50,000	Percent with income of $200,000 or more	Income and poverty, 2016 Median household income (dollars)	Percent below poverty level All persons	Children under 18 years	Children 5 to 17 years in families
	46	47	48	49	50	51	52	53	54	55	56	57	58	59	60	61
TEXAS— Cont'd																
Mason	50	1,069	559	13.1	44.6	23.7	7.4	10,472	25,834	38,496	62.3	3.6	44,818	13.2	23.6	21.6
Matagorda	368	3,348	8,522	8.3	55.7	15.2	70.9	10,101	22,939	41,253	58.1	2.5	46,324	17.4	26.4	26.3
Maverick	180	2,012	17,050	5.5	62.3	11.7	125.8	8,319	16,086	37,155	61.1	1.5	35,654	24.3	34.8	33.8
Medina	278	1,926	12,400	11.1	49.2	19.4	80.5	8,505	24,731	58,333	43.2	4.2	51,304	14.4	20.5	19.2
Menard	0	187	534	0.0	57.1	15.1	4.6	14,454	23,331	37,917	63.8	3.3	34,839	21.4	38.9	38.1
Midland	303	2,516	40,549	15.1	41.0	26.2	232.7	8,941	36,869	71,424	34.7	10.3	68,729	9.7	13.2	13.3
Milam	225	1,831	5,552	7.6	56.4	15.7	41.6	8,915	22,132	39,213	59.0	1.6	42,302	16.3	26.5	26.2
Mills	41	533	1,316	5.2	44.0	22.8	12.7	14,585	24,099	44,375	56.2	3.0	43,540	15.8	21.3	18.7
Mitchell	100	1,204	2,120	7.1	59.1	11.1	16.7	11,494	19,334	51,555	46.2	3.3	41,262	21.6	26.8	26.1
Montague	171	2,236	4,201	8.6	53.4	14.8	31.6	9,354	25,403	46,383	55.0	2.2	46,237	16.5	23.7	21.5
Montgomery	172	1,502	137,748	13.1	37.3	33.0	748.1	7,678	35,912	70,805	35.2	10.8	72,506	10.9	14.2	12.9
Moore	175	1,551	6,450	3.1	61.3	13.5	45.3	8,822	20,159	50,552	49.3	2.1	52,344	11.8	17.0	16.9
Morris	306	2,476	2,836	6.1	51.0	16.5	20.2	9,486	21,616	37,902	61.8	2.0	38,255	20.0	31.2	30.7
Motley	0	1,236	225	2.2	46.4	17.4	2.7	16,579	23,131	35,433	68.0	1.5	37,464	18.2	31.6	27.8
Nacogdoches	294	1,824	22,348	5.1	46.8	25.2	94.9	8,430	21,343	38,915	59.9	2.8	38,099	25.4	32.5	34.4
Navarro	381	2,304	11,692	4.4	53.4	15.7	83.4	8,393	21,347	43,388	56.8	2.1	44,111	17.8	27.1	25.2
Newton	NA	NA	3,184	4.8	63.2	7.5	21.5	10,657	19,293	36,829	62.0	1.4	41,388	22.8	31.9	27.9
Nolan	394	4,536	3,794	7.6	53.6	12.7	35.0	10,564	22,240	38,411	60.5	1.9	40,969	18.4	29.9	29.0
Nueces	723	3,690	92,256	7.1	47.1	20.5	541.5	8,597	25,826	51,882	48.2	3.5	53,562	15.1	23.3	21.6
Ochiltree	388	951	2,963	4.3	54.2	16.4	20.1	8,260	24,997	50,011	50.0	3.8	61,194	11.4	16.6	15.8
Oldham	145	387	660	2.3	40.6	25.9	13.2	15,108	23,644	52,292	48.2	6.7	54,212	14.3	32.5	26.5
Orange	342	2,261	20,551	9.0	50.1	15.2	128.4	8,445	26,611	51,443	48.6	2.5	53,611	14.0	20.2	20.0
Palo Pinto	209	2,660	5,696	7.9	52.7	15.8	42.4	9,011	24,891	42,824	56.4	3.2	43,589	16.4	26.0	25.2
Panola	215	2,575	5,493	7.0	47.9	14.2	42.0	10,371	25,345	50,712	49.1	3.7	47,780	15.6	22.0	20.4
Parker	136	1,279	29,872	13.9	38.3	27.0	164.2	8,309	32,274	67,979	36.9	6.9	67,735	9.3	13.0	12.1
Parmer	83	946	2,680	13.8	62.4	16.0	24.3	10,207	21,655	48,589	51.2	2.4	48,344	15.5	21.6	20.8
Pecos	331	1,725	3,639	5.6	65.6	9.6	32.4	10,328	19,738	51,735	47.6	1.2	45,414	17.1	25.3	24.5
Polk	242	1,691	9,135	8.3	58.0	12.0	64.4	9,359	21,411	40,864	57.7	2.5	43,014	20.3	33.0	33.7
Potter	658	4,379	32,900	7.7	52.4	14.6	310.2	8,235	20,984	40,340	59.5	2.2	41,563	22.0	28.7	26.6
Presidio	60	659	1,688	1.0	61.9	25.0	21.0	11,936	16,326	33,453	68.3	0.3	32,742	24.1	37.9	39.2
Rains	125	1,047	2,221	9.2	59.1	9.5	14.4	8,906	23,577	50,405	49.6	1.2	47,354	14.8	26.4	24.8
Randall	560	3,805	35,179	8.6	31.1	30.4	92.3	9,577	31,383	62,635	39.0	4.2	65,795	9.1	11.4	9.9
Reagan	103	1,729	921	5.8	64.2	11.5	10.8	11,731	25,754	59,257	38.3	4.6	67,308	11.8	18.5	18.4
Real	182	1,184	552	4.3	45.9	23.2	6.4	13,967	21,135	37,059	61.7	0.8	36,744	18.4	36.0	36.4
Red River	89	924	2,458	8.0	58.4	13.4	23.2	10,600	20,798	35,016	66.7	1.6	36,352	17.1	28.3	26.7
Reeves	423	2,003	2,843	4.8	65.4	11.2	28.8	11,567	18,458	46,464	52.1	2.0	40,092	25.0	28.6	27.6
Refugio	427	910	1,534	2.7	56.8	10.8	18.4	13,067	24,776	50,145	49.8	2.6	45,366	15.7	24.3	23.7
Roberts	0	878	256	4.7	35.2	31.5	3.2	15,028	31,655	72,500	28.7	1.8	75,816	6.6	7.9	7.2
Robertson	247	1,197	3,918	5.9	52.7	17.4	38.2	11,855	22,980	49,142	50.7	1.6	42,680	18.7	29.4	28.4
Rockwall	104	1,239	25,144	12.7	30.3	38.0	157.9	8,039	37,231	89,161	26.2	11.0	97,484	5.2	7.3	6.5
Runnels	209	2,127	2,274	4.1	57.5	18.1	21.2	10,186	22,856	41,339	59.5	2.1	40,112	17.2	26.8	24.8
Rusk	460	2,512	11,251	7.5	52.8	14.7	72.1	8,739	22,704	47,424	51.9	3.2	46,421	15.6	22.2	21.8
Sabine	307	1,759	1,894	3.3	59.4	12.9	14.7	9,275	20,120	32,500	68.9	2.6	38,451	17.5	29.7	27.6
San Augustine	466	1,086	1,514	2.6	62.9	11.5	8.6	10,806	19,251	29,426	70.5	1.6	36,426	23.8	38.7	36.6
San Jacinto	171	1,315	5,835	3.3	62.8	10.0	32.0	9,328	22,563	44,878	54.4	2.6	45,794	17.7	26.7	25.5
San Patricio	332	2,570	16,547	5.8	53.5	14.5	130.5	8,880	24,008	52,659	46.9	2.2	51,667	15.8	25.6	25.2
San Saba	68	479	1,302	6.7	57.2	14.5	10.1	10,478	19,583	40,718	61.0	1.4	39,995	20.1	33.2	30.4
Schleicher	0	1,715	826	2.4	48.3	19.1	6.5	10,932	26,408	59,766	40.7	4.9	47,258	16.6	25.6	22.6
Scurry	113	2,102	4,729	8.7	52.2	15.4	32.2	9,895	23,758	55,661	44.6	2.4	50,316	15.2	21.6	20.9
Shackelford	60	959	856	9.5	44.7	25.2	7.0	11,623	24,190	50,285	49.5	2.2	55,403	14.8	22.6	20.9
Shelby	244	1,791	6,307	5.8	60.3	15.3	54.4	9,607	20,233	36,312	63.7	2.5	37,410	21.1	30.8	28.8
Sherman	195	260	719	5.3	52.0	21.6	8.1	8,095	23,863	52,969	43.8	2.2	55,761	13.1	17.6	16.4
Smith	328	2,905	58,449	11.6	40.5	24.7	289.8	8,419	25,299	48,683	51.0	3.9	52,520	15.7	21.7	20.1
Somervell	148	799	2,187	3.8	47.7	19.2	21.3	11,443	26,547	50,562	49.5	5.0	56,944	10.8	17.8	15.5
Starr	254	1,149	19,421	1.8	75.4	9.3	173.3	9,815	12,663	26,682	72.7	1.0	26,691	39.9	54.8	51.1
Stephens	203	1,716	1,997	10.1	56.6	16.9	12.6	8,326	22,307	45,217	56.2	2.8	42,831	21.4	30.3	27.6
Sterling	0	72	222	0.0	51.2	23.7	3.7	11,895	25,104	50,156	49.9	3.5	60,577	12.7	21.2	20.0
Stonewall	144	360	312	1.0	60.7	13.5	2.8	11,772	24,285	47,969	51.3	3.2	44,225	15.6	22.4	22.1
Sutton	52	1,136	925	0.5	51.6	16.8	11.8	12,494	28,140	54,547	47.3	4.7	54,760	14.1	23.2	21.4
Swisher	672	1,599	1,832	5.3	56.6	14.8	16.2	10,360	18,699	35,167	63.0	1.6	38,790	22.2	33.0	30.7
Tarrant	405	2,838	550,299	13.1	38.5	30.7	2,920.9	8,174	29,791	60,373	41.3	6.1	61,553	13.6	19.6	19.1
Taylor	411	3,214	38,611	26.7	43.1	24.1	198.8	8,499	24,328	47,044	52.4	2.9	48,215	16.8	20.7	20.3
Terrell	248	1,491	113	12.4	55.4	17.0	2.7	19,086	25,147	24,821	72.2	1.8	41,114	18.7	29.6	28.1
Terry	252	1,809	3,445	8.6	61.9	12.1	25.1	10,606	21,936	40,407	57.6	2.1	38,910	21.8	30.9	29.4
Throckmorton	0	0	251	2.8	50.8	19.9	3.9	13,353	28,860	39,438	56.0	2.8	42,876	14.9	21.2	18.9
Titus	362	2,346	9,031	4.1	57.0	15.2	58.9	8,295	20,043	45,026	55.5	2.5	45,324	14.9	23.4	22.6

1. Data for serious crimes have not been adjusted for underreporting; this may affect comparability between geographic areas and over time. 2. Per 100,000 population estimated by the FBI.
3. All persons 3 years old and over enrolled in nursery school through college. 4. Persons 25 years old and over. 5. Elementary and secondary education expenditures.
6. Based on population estimated by the American Community Survey, 2011–2015.

Table B. States and Counties — **Personal Income and Earnings**

STATE County	Personal income, 2016 Total (mil dol)	Percent change 2015-2016	Per capita¹ Dollars	Per capita¹ Rank	Supplements to wages and salaries, employer contributions (mil dol) Wages and salaries (mil dol)	Pension and insurance	Government social insurance	Proprietors' income (mil dol)	Dividends, interest, and rent (mil dol)	Personal transfer receipts (mil dol)	Earnings, 2016 Total (mil dol)	Contributions for government social insurance (mil dol) From employee and self-employed	From employer
	62	63	64	65	66	67	68	69	70	71	72	73	74
TEXAS— Cont'd													
Mason	155	-10.6	37,632	1,719	38	8	2	19	46	42	68	7	2
Matagorda	1,454	-1.9	39,090	1,485	575	114	39	99	198	363	826	85	39
Maverick	1,571	1.9	27,228	3,021	602	148	43	129	143	537	922	95	43
Medina	1,833	2.3	37,190	1,795	356	76	23	120	301	429	574	58	23
Menard	72	-6.9	33,907	2,338	13	4	1	7	18	27	24	3	1
Midland	17,148	-6.8	105,486	12	5,649	759	374	8,180	2,382	946	14,963	1,004	374
Milam	900	-1.5	36,201	1,973	280	47	19	60	135	288	406	45	19
Mills	177	-4.5	36,072	1,993	47	10	3	7	46	60	67	8	3
Mitchell	269	-5.7	30,812	2,754	94	25	6	13	42	80	138	13	6
Montague	841	-5.6	43,320	966	192	36	13	95	157	231	336	34	13
Montgomery	31,553	-2.3	56,730	193	9,509	1,271	640	2,937	4,980	3,459	14,357	1,417	640
Moore	807	-6.9	36,467	1,920	489	97	33	98	89	135	717	67	33
Morris	503	-4.5	39,979	1,366	153	32	12	87	66	173	284	29	12
Motley	35	-10.9	30,558	2,781	12	3	1	-1	8	13	15	2	1
Nacogdoches	2,225	-0.7	33,812	2,347	866	169	59	271	361	605	1,365	131	59
Navarro	1,720	0.9	35,443	2,092	615	117	43	81	272	519	857	97	43
Newton	429	1.0	30,643	2,776	48	13	3	11	46	137	75	10	3
Nolan	566	1.5	37,774	1,696	261	49	18	42	93	168	370	39	18
Nueces	14,743	-1.1	40,800	1,260	7,993	1,404	577	1,372	2,530	3,233	11,345	1,187	577
Ochiltree	610	-21.0	59,176	160	236	37	15	252	83	60	540	37	15
Oldham	93	-20.1	44,717	805	55	9	4	20	14	15	88	8	4
Orange	3,527	1.7	41,509	1,167	1,170	196	82	129	378	898	1,577	182	82
Palo Pinto	1,048	1.2	37,361	1,753	359	64	24	60	203	285	507	55	24
Panola	891	-6.9	37,930	1,675	376	61	27	81	144	247	545	59	27
Parker	6,303	2.5	48,692	486	1,425	223	100	470	1,013	942	2,219	230	100
Parmer	406	-30.4	41,577	1,157	220	35	16	100	44	70	371	30	16
Pecos	509	-2.8	31,851	2,637	259	53	16	30	70	126	359	35	16
Polk	1,736	1.9	36,231	1,970	437	83	30	86	387	727	636	83	30
Potter	5,059	0.0	41,868	1,114	3,649	622	265	1,051	748	1,098	5,588	548	265
Presidio	243	3.5	34,960	2,173	87	22	6	31	54	66	146	14	6
Rains	372	2.5	32,899	2,498	62	13	4	23	54	120	102	13	4
Randall	6,001	1.0	45,294	754	1,368	194	89	597	941	821	2,248	218	89
Reagan	172	-9.2	47,649	556	92	17	6	20	24	22	134	13	6
Real	102	-3.8	30,105	2,835	21	5	1	8	30	47	35	4	1
Red River	457	0.7	37,454	1,743	90	21	6	13	69	177	130	17	6
Reeves	449	-1.9	30,106	2,834	196	40	12	48	73	113	297	28	12
Refugio	308	-8.3	42,014	1,102	92	18	6	12	70	88	128	14	6
Roberts	37	-14.0	40,354	1,317	10	3	1	-2	12	6	12	2	1
Robertson	642	-2.6	38,305	1,603	183	37	12	42	112	182	274	29	12
Rockwall	5,113	4.9	54,406	256	1,222	177	87	459	682	534	1,944	192	87
Runnels	383	-0.9	36,696	1,881	106	23	7	29	62	122	166	18	7
Rusk	1,874	-2.3	35,532	2,077	629	108	43	152	283	484	931	98	43
Sabine	374	0.3	36,277	1,958	84	18	6	22	69	160	130	16	6
San Augustine	290	-2.3	34,908	2,181	63	15	4	23	45	133	106	12	4
San Jacinto	875	0.3	31,569	2,667	81	20	5	39	124	278	145	19	5
San Patricio	2,765	1.7	40,868	1,249	1,040	185	77	137	379	666	1,439	160	77
San Saba	219	6.9	36,772	1,862	70	18	5	15	46	64	108	11	5
Schleicher	107	-18.1	34,963	2,172	40	8	2	9	18	26	59	6	2
Scurry	784	-12.0	45,218	759	364	64	24	166	111	147	617	55	24
Shackelford	538	1.4	162,378	2	62	11	4	390	53	33	467	21	4
Shelby	953	-8.3	37,254	1,778	323	57	23	140	136	281	542	51	23
Sherman	170	-32.6	55,319	231	39	7	2	80	16	16	129	5	2
Smith	11,232	-0.9	49,857	420	4,672	721	331	2,897	1,746	2,035	8,622	766	331
Somervell	360	-0.3	41,000	1,235	234	50	15	19	57	78	318	32	15
Starr	1,548	1.8	24,140	3,087	491	145	33	102	132	611	771	78	33
Stephens	361	-18.4	36,446	1,924	117	26	8	69	63	104	220	20	8
Sterling	71	-1.7	52,067	335	25	6	2	9	23	11	41	4	2
Stonewall	65	-18.1	45,778	713	25	5	1	-3	20	20	28	3	1
Sutton	178	-14.7	45,911	701	119	17	7	10	38	36	154	16	7
Swisher	307	-15.0	41,073	1,222	73	17	5	97	40	70	191	10	5
Tarrant	96,910	1.4	48,050	531	48,085	6,843	3,470	10,649	16,370	12,667	69,047	7,128	3,470
Taylor	5,841	-1.3	42,783	1,014	2,730	488	203	668	1,143	1,248	4,089	419	203
Terrell	37	-11.4	45,983	693	14	4	1	-2	13	10	17	2	1
Terry	456	3.0	35,617	2,063	169	30	11	66	52	127	276	25	11
Throckmorton	70	-14.7	45,369	749	19	5	1	6	15	20	30	3	1
Titus	1,062	-1.9	32,571	2,541	589	116	41	77	159	277	823	85	41

1. Based on the resident population estimated as of July 1 of the year shown.

STATE County	Earnings, 2016 (cont.) Percent by selected industries									Social Security beneficiaries, December 2016		Supplemental Security Income recipients, 2016	Housing units, 2017	
	Farm	Mining, quarrying, and extracting	Construction	Manufacturing	Information; professional, scientific, technical services	Retail trade	Finance, insurance, real estate, and leasing	Health care and social assistance	Government	Number	Rate[1]		Total	Percent change, 2010-2017
	75	76	77	78	79	80	81	82	83	84	85	86	87	88
TEXAS— Cont'd														
Mason	2.8	D	10.2	2.5	D	5.2	11.4	3.9	20.9	1,200	288	79	2,760	1.0
Matagorda	3.1	1.9	10.8	2.0	5.1	5.6	3.1	D	17.2	7,270	196	1,093	19,400	3.2
Maverick	0.3	1.9	5.6	3.5	2.5	9.6	3.2	D	41.1	10,480	181	3,472	18,477	5.8
Medina	0.8	8.3	13.0	0.9	5.0	8.9	6.2	D	30.3	9,255	188	1,109	18,579	3.3
Menard	-5.7	D	D	D	D	7.3	12.7	D	35.8	640	304	58	1,721	1.1
Midland	0.0	63.0	2.5	4.5	3.4	2.5	4.3	3.1	4.4	18,780	115	2,022	61,132	12.5
Milam	0.9	2.3	18.8	9.1	D	5.3	4.6	D	16.2	6,040	244	812	11,459	1.4
Mills	-5.5	D	8.1	6.0	D	14.4	5.9	7.1	29.6	1,370	280	117	2,865	0.6
Mitchell	-2.0	20.2	D	D	D	5.9	D	2.3	49.0	1,495	176	207	4,070	0.1
Montague	-2.0	27.7	7.9	6.1	7.4	6.2	5.0	D	18.4	5,200	268	461	10,279	1.5
Montgomery	0.0	10.8	13.2	6.2	10.9	6.8	6.5	8.2	11.9	80,825	146	7,280	217,051	22.2
Moore	10.2	4.5	D	D	D	4.5	2.0	D	14.2	2,600	119	267	8,041	2.0
Morris	4.3	D	2.0	33.1	D	4.1	D	3.0	11.6	3,845	308	547	6,052	0.5
Motley	-6.6	0.6	D	D	D	12.7	D	7.5	34.7	360	307	30	773	-0.6
Nacogdoches	4.4	1.4	9.0	10.8	3.7	8.5	5.3	13.1	25.0	11,830	180	2,025	28,399	3.6
Navarro	-1.5	1.4	8.2	18.4	3.5	7.7	5.6	12.5	21.1	10,610	219	1,657	20,848	3.0
Newton	-4.3	D	4.9	9.3	D	6.8	D	9.5	39.0	2,790	197	556	7,309	2.3
Nolan	-0.9	7.1	8.0	15.0	2.8	8.3	3.9	D	25.9	3,265	218	506	7,050	-1.4
Nueces	0.5	3.1	14.3	8.5	7.6	6.2	5.1	14.3	19.1	60,050	166	12,159	149,500	6.0
Ochiltree	10.1	49.3	8.8	1.2	1.6	3.2	2.2	1.2	8.4	1,340	130	101	4,108	1.1
Oldham	22.7	D	24.9	D	D	1.3	D	D	19.6	430	207	30	857	1.9
Orange	-0.4	0.7	14.1	31.0	3.8	6.4	4.3	5.4	15.4	18,535	219	2,443	37,264	5.5
Palo Pinto	-0.1	9.8	8.1	22.6	D	8.3	2.9	D	20.8	6,340	225	745	15,479	1.7
Panola	1.0	D	22.1	8.2	4.2	4.9	3.2	5.7	14.5	5,320	227	649	11,182	2.4
Parker	-0.2	6.7	13.0	8.6	6.4	10.5	4.8	8.6	14.4	23,610	183	1,326	50,049	7.3
Parmer	33.0	D	D	D	D	1.9	D	2.5	11.3	1,465	149	136	3,789	-0.3
Pecos	0.2	13.1	6.2	4.6	D	6.7	3.9	2.9	32.9	2,345	148	353	5,741	2.8
Polk	-1.3	1.3	8.0	11.8	D	9.6	5.4	10.1	26.0	18,840	395	1,729	25,675	13.2
Potter	0.0	8.3	4.8	9.0	7.0	6.6	7.3	15.8	18.4	18,915	157	3,045	49,989	5.7
Presidio	14.2	0.6	D	D	D	5.1	D	D	48.4	1,770	247	608	3,881	1.5
Rains	-3.9	D	14.8	5.2	D	11.6	D	D	23.3	3,010	266	258	5,382	2.1
Randall	3.6	2.0	12.0	4.1	6.4	13.0	6.1	9.4	11.2	20,925	158	1,320	54,749	6.1
Reagan	-2.2	39.4	4.3	0.6	D	2.7	D	D	18.7	445	119	49	1,414	3.1
Real	-8.0	0.3	13.5	6.8	D	8.8	D	12.3	26.1	1,190	350	125	2,639	1.6
Red River	-1.8	D	10.2	14.6	4.8	5.8	4.1	11.5	26.0	3,670	300	498	6,927	1.5
Reeves	1.4	9.6	12.7	0.5	D	8.0	6.4	1.5	34.6	2,260	150	420	4,623	-0.4
Refugio	-7.6	23.5	D	D	0.0	7.0	6.0	4.4	30.8	1,830	251	239	3,743	0.5
Roberts	-23.9	D	D	1.8	D	D	D	D	46.9	180	197	0	438	-0.2
Robertson	4.0	8.8	8.2	2.8	3.9	4.8	3.5	D	20.8	3,775	224	614	8,828	4.1
Rockwall	-0.1	0.8	11.6	7.2	10.4	9.8	6.3	16.8	12.1	13,320	143	767	33,992	21.7
Runnels	-1.7	5.2	8.8	15.2	D	11.5	D	7.5	25.7	2,645	258	298	5,248	-0.9
Rusk	2.2	17.0	9.5	9.2	5.3	4.5	4.3	7.0	14.5	10,435	197	1,198	21,548	1.7
Sabine	2.2	9.2	5.6	18.7	D	6.3	D	12.3	21.7	3,690	355	312	8,257	3.4
San Augustine	13.4	0.9	10.2	3.0	D	5.6	D	14.4	19.9	2,565	310	428	5,449	2.0
San Jacinto	-5.1	D	18.0	5.5	6.8	4.4	3.7	5.2	33.1	6,345	229	739	13,828	4.9
San Patricio	0.4	6.1	24.5	8.6	5.2	6.3	3.1	4.5	24.9	13,620	202	2,302	28,419	7.2
San Saba	-5.4	4.6	5.4	4.2	D	4.3	D	3.8	25.6	1,520	259	145	3,187	0.3
Schleicher	-4.3	19.7	26.2	D	D	2.4	D	5.3	22.3	570	186	57	1,502	0.9
Scurry	-0.8	45.0	5.0	2.2	2.1	4.5	2.8	D	16.5	3,000	172	331	7,184	3.2
Shackelford	-0.1	89.2	0.6	1.2	D	0.5	0.8	D	2.7	715	213	63	1,763	0.5
Shelby	15.2	10.2	4.5	17.9	3.1	7.2	4.5	D	14.1	5,470	212	1,008	12,175	2.5
Sherman	64.1	D	D	D	D	2.9	D	D	11.2	370	120	28	1,318	5.3
Smith	0.2	22.9	4.7	6.2	6.3	9.9	6.0	17.2	10.3	44,410	197	5,396	90,327	3.5
Somervell	0.1	D	4.0	1.6	1.9	2.0	2.1	D	15.0	1,755	202	112	3,852	4.8
Starr	0.7	2.7	2.7	0.4	2.4	8.9	2.0	D	48.9	9,855	154	4,885	19,799	1.4
Stephens	-2.0	35.7	8.7	11.6	D	5.2	5.0	5.9	17.4	2,140	227	236	4,946	0.2
Sterling	-5.9	40.1	4.7	1.2	D	3.3	D	D	20.3	235	174	24	622	1.1
Stonewall	-28.1	20.6	19.9	4.0	D	8.1	D	D	44.9	385	275	21	932	0.4
Sutton	-1.3	27.9	6.2	5.3	D	3.4	2.7	D	16.8	760	197	62	2,059	1.4
Swisher	51.7	D	1.5	2.3	D	2.7	D	D	21.4	1,560	210	165	3,181	-1.2
Tarrant	0.0	5.6	8.3	11.3	7.5	6.4	8.1	10.1	12.4	258,860	128	36,534	766,952	7.2
Taylor	0.6	7.3	6.7	3.8	5.8	7.3	6.4	15.7	23.2	24,780	182	3,858	57,547	3.2
Terrell	-13.1	0.7	4.8	0.0	D	5.5	D	D	76.3	225	275	23	703	0.4
Terry	12.6	15.4	4.0	4.0	2.4	13.6	D	D	22.1	2,225	173	344	4,849	0.4
Throckmorton	-11.2	38.3	D	D	D	2.8	D	2.7	27.0	400	258	24	1,079	0.0
Titus	1.7	3.1	4.0	32.6	2.1	7.2	4.0	7.1	19.9	5,535	170	803	12,365	2.6

1. Per 1,000 resident population estimated as of July 1 of the year shown.

Table B. States and Counties — Housing, Labor Force, and Employment

	Housing units, 2017 (cont.)								Civilian labor force, 2017				Civilian employment[6], 2012-2016		
	Occupied units														
	Owner-occupied					Renter-occupied					Unemployment			Percent	
STATE County				Median owner cost as a percent of income			Median rent as a percent of income[2]	Sub-standard units[4] (percent)		Percent change, 2016-2017				Management, business, science, and arts	Construction, production, and maintenance occupations
	Total	Percent	Median value[1]	With a mortgage	Without a mortgage[2]	Median rent[3]			Total		Total	Rate[5]	Total		
	89	90	91	92	93	94	95	96	97	98	99	100	101	102	103
TEXAS— Cont'd															
Mason	1,688	76.2	136,600	30.2	12.1	811	32.6	1.1	1,799	0.7	60	3.3	2,167	25.0	29.3
Matagorda	13,666	67.1	98,700	19.1	12.7	695	24.5	5.4	16,930	0.5	1,227	7.2	16,151	23.3	34.6
Maverick	16,221	68.7	93,100	23.4	12.8	602	24.0	14.3	23,860	-1.4	2,209	9.3	21,058	21.9	29.1
Medina	15,104	80.9	126,000	20.0	10.2	709	24.5	4.9	21,273	1.5	814	3.8	20,410	32.1	26.5
Menard	936	64.0	56,300	17.7	12.7	623	23.9	5.7	807	-1.1	39	4.8	833	27.1	39.5
Midland	53,960	66.5	175,700	19.1	10.0	1,148	27.2	6.6	89,359	5.3	2,686	3.0	78,827	33.9	28.1
Milam	9,423	66.7	82,400	19.3	11.2	594	27.6	3.8	10,057	-1.9	506	5.0	9,260	29.3	30.6
Mills	1,875	84.0	123,100	24.2	11.6	506	30.6	2.7	1,917	-0.2	67	3.5	1,931	29.2	28.9
Mitchell	2,660	75.5	60,800	17.6	10.0	615	20.2	2.3	2,531	-2.8	139	5.5	3,041	29.6	28.9
Montague	8,083	71.6	93,000	19.8	12.6	731	31.8	3.4	9,083	0.8	365	4.0	8,150	25.8	35.3
Montgomery	179,587	71.7	190,000	20.9	11.2	1,077	27.2	4.3	267,342	0.7	11,577	4.3	238,277	39.0	21.4
Moore	6,772	66.2	98,200	19.4	10.0	706	22.2	11.3	11,012	-1.4	319	2.9	10,581	21.2	45.8
Morris	5,015	73.8	77,000	20.8	11.8	645	28.8	4.6	4,653	-4.7	402	8.6	4,752	25.8	33.7
Motley	475	69.3	55,200	22.1	11.7	575	29.2	4.0	490	-3.4	18	3.7	448	38.6	33.9
Nacogdoches	23,942	56.5	114,300	20.9	10.4	745	32.1	3.4	28,538	-0.4	1,213	4.3	27,989	31.1	26.8
Navarro	17,409	67.6	83,800	22.2	11.8	738	29.9	5.5	22,752	0.1	895	3.9	20,074	26.8	31.9
Newton	4,629	77.6	72,300	22.2	10.8	661	25.9	0.8	5,312	-0.6	418	7.9	4,451	20.0	38.6
Nolan	5,625	68.1	65,400	19.0	11.5	596	26.3	4.0	6,778	-1.1	275	4.1	6,454	26.5	33.6
Nueces	128,133	57.4	116,600	21.3	11.5	912	29.0	5.4	167,523	0.0	9,028	5.4	164,799	29.1	25.2
Ochiltree	3,587	71.1	91,800	19.5	10.7	728	20.1	7.1	4,504	-3.2	166	3.7	4,910	20.8	38.4
Oldham	616	75.6	81,100	21.9	10.0	818	38.8	3.9	890	-1.9	22	2.5	738	38.1	23.7
Orange	32,269	75.1	101,500	19.4	10.0	770	26.7	3.4	37,246	-0.1	2,554	6.9	36,060	29.8	30.7
Palo Pinto	10,416	68.2	87,000	19.9	11.8	724	32.5	5.7	13,403	1.3	544	4.1	11,928	22.5	34.0
Panola	8,905	77.6	92,900	18.9	10.3	706	21.6	3.3	10,320	1.1	564	5.5	10,179	21.7	36.9
Parker	43,270	77.4	170,100	19.6	10.9	901	27.7	2.9	62,302	1.9	2,150	3.5	57,784	38.4	22.7
Parmer	3,219	69.3	83,600	21.4	10.0	643	22.4	9.9	4,913	-0.5	122	2.5	4,608	25.3	43.1
Pecos	4,334	71.4	69,800	16.9	10.0	784	22.7	6.2	6,515	0.5	294	4.5	6,238	19.6	38.2
Polk	17,790	76.4	84,600	21.9	11.5	658	27.5	4.6	17,435	0.5	1,049	6.0	16,777	23.1	29.3
Potter	43,154	57.2	88,700	21.2	11.3	720	29.2	6.5	55,923	-0.2	1,786	3.2	53,402	24.5	29.4
Presidio	2,565	65.0	61,600	19.9	11.3	431	21.4	6.9	3,024	-1.6	283	9.4	2,453	35.0	21.4
Rains	4,252	78.3	95,500	21.9	12.4	645	25.9	4.3	5,666	2.2	200	3.5	4,462	30.7	31.8
Randall	48,893	68.8	151,800	19.2	10.8	863	27.0	2.4	70,283	-0.4	1,980	2.8	66,927	37.0	19.3
Reagan	1,190	70.0	85,000	20.4	10.0	637	20.0	2.6	1,772	4.4	68	3.8	1,732	20.6	48.2
Real	1,192	76.5	110,600	22.2	13.2	806	27.5	2.5	1,049	1.0	60	5.7	1,133	31.8	18.7
Red River	5,163	74.1	62,700	23.3	12.5	575	26.5	1.8	5,215	3.8	270	5.2	4,832	22.0	35.9
Reeves	3,764	70.7	44,400	15.5	10.2	787	22.6	4.9	6,917	14.8	245	3.5	4,953	26.0	30.3
Refugio	2,761	72.9	77,100	17.5	10.0	652	26.1	4.2	3,112	-0.6	180	5.8	3,060	24.1	33.5
Roberts	342	78.9	119,500	18.2	10.0	872	14.9	0.6	437	-0.9	16	3.7	427	43.6	23.4
Robertson	6,366	72.6	99,900	19.0	10.2	632	29.9	2.7	7,351	1.5	344	4.7	7,190	31.1	31.0
Rockwall	29,392	80.2	206,700	20.8	13.2	1,262	28.2	2.0	48,621	2.9	1,610	3.3	42,738	45.3	16.1
Runnels	3,792	74.3	75,600	17.5	13.2	564	22.4	1.8	4,563	-1.6	172	3.8	4,293	31.5	30.9
Rusk	17,795	74.0	107,800	18.6	10.7	700	24.6	2.9	22,113	-1.0	1,118	5.1	20,771	26.1	35.4
Sabine	3,682	87.2	80,700	20.4	13.3	545	35.9	2.1	3,538	1.8	303	8.6	2,988	24.3	31.3
San Augustine	2,972	80.5	80,200	21.9	15.0	601	26.2	5.1	2,872	2.6	214	7.5	2,255	23.3	36.5
San Jacinto	9,631	85.7	88,000	22.3	12.1	697	31.7	3.8	11,436	0.3	644	5.6	10,514	22.2	36.6
San Patricio	23,237	68.3	97,800	20.2	12.3	854	26.8	6.5	30,647	0.3	2,333	7.6	29,384	26.5	31.8
San Saba	2,110	67.4	80,500	23.3	12.4	632	34.6	2.6	2,411	-1.3	77	3.2	2,345	26.5	39.7
Schleicher	1,091	77.5	72,300	14.4	10.0	518	19.2	10.1	1,338	-5.6	49	3.7	1,510	30.4	37.6
Scurry	5,908	73.0	89,400	21.5	10.0	751	23.8	4.0	6,982	-5.6	305	4.4	7,132	22.5	36.7
Shackelford	1,317	79.3	76,400	21.7	13.2	595	30.0	2.3	1,875	0.1	56	3.0	1,485	33.1	23.1
Shelby	9,120	71.2	74,900	22.4	10.9	562	32.2	2.7	10,781	-1.4	552	5.1	9,480	27.8	41.4
Sherman	1,017	77.4	82,900	20.0	10.0	603	21.0	1.3	1,289	-4.4	40	3.1	1,589	29.4	41.3
Smith	78,040	65.2	137,600	21.3	11.9	849	30.3	3.8	105,896	0.6	4,297	4.1	97,098	33.8	24.2
Somervell	3,241	71.1	158,900	21.6	10.7	823	25.8	7.0	4,218	2.3	190	4.5	3,672	32.7	32.8
Starr	16,219	73.8	66,600	24.8	12.1	522	34.1	13.7	26,049	-1.0	3,040	11.7	21,225	21.8	29.3
Stephens	3,338	77.6	77,500	21.9	11.2	553	30.1	4.6	4,030	0.5	189	4.7	3,849	24.9	38.3
Sterling	453	79.0	95,100	17.8	10.0	817	21.1	2.6	607	-9.3	23	3.8	591	30.3	27.6
Stonewall	501	76.0	53,900	15.5	10.3	407	28.4	5.8	621	-2.8	21	3.4	498	35.7	35.5
Sutton	1,481	66.2	92,100	21.7	11.9	636	19.0	5.9	1,514	-4.7	77	5.1	1,749	28.8	42.6
Swisher	2,630	70.8	71,900	18.6	12.7	663	26.0	5.7	2,687	-0.8	109	4.1	2,761	30.0	30.4
Tarrant	682,967	60.4	148,100	21.3	11.7	944	29.2	4.8	1,033,317	2.4	37,978	3.7	948,205	36.3	22.1
Taylor	49,489	58.1	107,600	19.5	11.0	814	29.3	3.0	64,051	1.4	2,267	3.5	61,348	30.4	22.6
Terrell	396	67.9	64,600	18.4	15.2	737	15.8	0.0	391	-3.5	19	4.9	338	31.7	27.5
Terry	4,214	71.8	65,900	18.1	10.3	688	26.4	5.6	5,245	-1.8	262	5.0	4,637	32.0	34.5
Throckmorton	725	72.7	64,100	12.4	12.6	439	22.0	2.8	692	-6.7	30	4.3	680	29.6	31.0
Titus	10,573	67.3	97,200	20.5	10.5	643	25.3	8.4	12,954	0.8	692	5.3	13,954	22.6	39.4

1. Specified owner-occupied units. 2. A value of 10.0 represents 10 percent or less; a value of 50.0 represents 50 percent or more. 3. Specified renter-occupied units.
4. Overcrowded or lacking complete plumbing facilities. 5. Percent of civilian labor force. 6. Civilian employed persons 16 years old and over.

Table B. States and Counties — Nonfarm Employment and Agriculture

STATE County	Private nonfarm establishments, employment and payroll, 2016									Agriculture, 2012			
	Number of establishments	Employment						Annual payroll		Farms			Farm operators whose principal occupation is farming (percent)
		Total	Health care and social assistance	Manufacturing	Retail trade	Finance and insurance	Professional, scientific, and technical services	Total (mil dol)	Average per employee (dollars)	Number	Percent with:		
											Fewer than 50 acres	500 acres or more	
	104	105	106	107	108	109	110	111	112	113	114	115	116

TEXAS— Cont'd													
Mason	141	821	130	44	155	55	37	22	26,408	640	11.1	43.4	48.9
Matagorda	722	8,100	1,309	633	1,396	201	291	455	56,116	856	28.5	27.9	47.7
Maverick	791	12,636	4,195	593	2,781	379	209	308	24,409	294	53.4	20.4	34.4
Medina	724	7,196	946	329	1,452	310	426	228	31,623	1,976	31.9	15.9	50.2
Menard	47	192	D	D	47	23	7	5	25,313	325	14.5	45.2	48.6
Midland	5,195	81,103	7,340	2,595	9,279	1,991	2,773	4,953	61,065	540	47.6	19.8	24.3
Milam	412	4,579	1,320	188	627	213	124	216	47,217	1,909	32.6	12.2	44.9
Mills	107	840	143	83	195	59	17	24	28,581	870	20.3	26.0	43.1
Mitchell	125	1,236	D	D	257	39	27	41	33,366	482	12.2	25.9	32.2
Montague	426	3,743	401	261	638	199	114	164	43,693	1,454	26.2	15.3	39.8
Montgomery	11,152	155,450	20,652	8,658	25,039	5,582	9,488	8,526	54,845	1,601	63.1	3.7	30.7
Moore	441	7,656	609	3,509	897	136	95	322	42,122	261	10.0	58.2	64.8
Morris	223	3,286	180	1,687	329	127	73	106	32,226	412	34.7	8.7	50.0
Motley	26	188	D	D	D	D	D	4	23,707	224	3.6	53.1	39.3
Nacogdoches	1,280	17,923	3,158	3,582	2,899	550	479	581	32,421	1,196	28.6	7.6	43.0
Navarro	959	13,374	2,452	2,944	2,303	370	264	421	31,499	2,573	41.0	9.2	47.6
Newton	124	984	278	73	162	21	97	25	25,763	450	57.8	2.2	31.3
Nolan	359	4,365	589	859	828	135	93	164	37,459	478	15.1	32.4	39.7
Nueces	7,974	146,343	29,955	7,187	19,073	4,015	6,778	5,849	39,965	754	43.4	21.1	36.3
Ochiltree	362	3,701	317	34	418	134	124	176	47,565	348	8.3	54.3	51.1
Oldham	45	590	D	D	72	D	D	19	32,122	159	7.5	64.8	46.5
Orange	1,317	19,316	1,517	4,704	3,199	561	484	944	48,892	671	79.7	3.9	43.7
Palo Pinto	605	5,879	775	1,152	1,063	147	144	214	36,374	1,329	42.2	15.6	32.7
Panola	467	6,761	682	1,023	857	177	229	288	42,608	1,079	34.6	10.1	43.4
Parker	2,590	28,520	3,462	2,863	5,672	672	959	1,055	37,003	4,370	66.1	3.5	35.3
Parmer	193	3,452	183	D	174	78	44	134	38,832	570	8.6	47.9	59.3
Pecos	344	3,896	568	28	752	152	58	157	40,381	291	13.1	67.7	45.0
Polk	756	8,422	1,334	1,262	1,858	347	217	288	34,244	738	40.2	8.5	48.6
Potter	3,579	61,381	12,598	6,505	8,603	4,147	2,228	2,492	40,593	258	35.3	31.4	38.0
Presidio	118	934	46	D	270	57	D	21	22,961	162	8.6	63.6	45.1
Rains	163	1,334	104	70	419	53	218	36	26,963	682	47.5	7.9	44.7
Randall	2,560	32,352	3,403	4,824	5,845	1,308	868	1,352	41,805	892	30.5	27.4	36.4
Reagan	130	1,505	113	D	133	11	18	71	47,148	135	5.2	71.9	51.1
Real	77	717	121	31	93	D	7	18	24,676	241	19.9	40.7	44.4
Red River	160	1,280	146	362	275	86	20	42	32,682	1,139	22.3	17.1	45.7
Reeves	275	3,468	398	9	472	37	56	170	49,080	240	11.7	51.7	43.3
Refugio	155	1,742	243	D	287	40	24	70	40,296	259	31.3	35.9	43.2
Roberts	17	138	NA	NA	D	D	D	6	45,174	107	2.8	73.8	58.9
Robertson	277	2,796	339	166	395	84	290	111	39,786	1,520	28.7	12.0	49.5
Rockwall	2,103	25,646	4,397	1,442	5,405	743	1,357	925	36,054	440	71.8	6.4	35.7
Runnels	216	2,173	277	457	404	127	33	75	34,593	925	12.4	29.6	45.8
Rusk	813	10,430	1,331	1,278	1,393	470	387	416	39,869	1,390	30.9	7.8	35.1
Sabine	155	1,528	301	D	323	54	34	49	32,266	201	36.3	4.5	46.8
San Augustine	120	1,151	366	51	193	42	7	40	34,784	305	23.3	9.8	52.5
San Jacinto	192	1,080	108	127	217	36	34	32	29,961	791	48.5	2.8	44.6
San Patricio	1,052	15,696	1,623	3,409	2,636	382	1,247	720	45,866	701	47.9	21.8	41.8
San Saba	165	893	156	46	210	22	39	24	27,274	744	19.9	33.7	48.8
Schleicher	55	439	D	D	60	25	16	19	42,975	310	10.6	60.6	44.8
Scurry	416	4,919	569	65	750	124	102	250	50,826	677	16.4	32.9	39.0
Shackelford	123	1,038	43	162	95	50	5	44	42,803	233	7.7	47.6	43.3
Shelby	484	6,244	475	2,123	994	588	117	209	33,541	1,048	26.4	8.3	53.3
Sherman	63	370	D	D	120	27	D	15	39,692	313	5.8	59.1	48.6
Smith	5,775	91,444	22,480	6,924	13,229	4,603	4,959	3,780	41,337	2,961	54.8	3.0	45.3
Somervell	215	3,356	499	48	198	43	91	192	57,114	350	38.6	14.0	37.7
Starr	553	8,781	4,597	53	1,811	318	144	185	21,026	1,165	16.8	26.3	39.5
Stephens	243	2,019	232	188	354	136	41	78	38,818	452	7.3	40.9	30.3
Sterling	54	333	D	NA	45	14	14	15	44,631	73	4.1	80.8	56.2
Stonewall	48	422	D	NA	48	D	7	17	40,912	356	5.3	45.5	34.0
Sutton	130	1,042	68	D	141	33	25	50	48,299	218	6.9	71.1	54.1
Swisher	141	1,013	190	121	145	42	25	29	29,080	565	9.6	46.5	54.2
Tarrant	41,261	771,088	101,940	76,574	102,779	46,884	38,138	37,257	48,317	1,278	74.0	3.6	28.7
Taylor	3,445	55,579	12,482	2,489	8,370	2,439	1,789	1,896	34,111	1,149	29.8	19.1	38.7
Terrell	13	45	D	NA	17	D	D	2	39,156	86	0.0	86.0	57.0
Terry	227	2,469	448	59	445	100	57	90	36,615	630	11.4	37.5	55.7
Throckmorton	51	269	D	D	20	D	8	8	27,911	275	5.5	49.1	49.1
Titus	625	13,634	2,037	5,906	1,788	489	90	473	34,710	801	35.8	5.7	37.5

Table B. States and Counties — **Agriculture**

		Land in farms				Value of land and buildings (dollars)			Value of products sold:				Percent of farms with sales of:		Government payments	
STATE County	Acreage (1,000)	Percent change, 2007-2012	Acres					Value of machinery and equiopmnet, average per farm (dollars)			Percent from:						
			Average size of farm	Total irrigated (1,000)	Total cropland (1,000)	Average per farm	Average per acre		Total (mil dol)	Average per farm (acres)	Crops	Livestock and poultry products	$10,000 or more	$100,000 or more	Total ($1,000)	Percent of farms
	117	118	119	120	121	122	123	124	125	126	127	128	129	130	131	132

TEXAS— Cont'd

STATE County	117	118	119	120	121	122	123	124	125	126	127	128	129	130	131	132
Mason	551	2.8	861	3.0	28.9	2,039,833	2,368	59,491	51.4	80,389	9.7	90.3	43.8	8.4	1,749	32.5
Matagorda	568	-1.7	664	32.7	177.0	1,315,683	1,983	126,209	129.7	151,522	59.4	40.6	48.7	16.2	5,271	34.6
Maverick	541	14.2	1,840	13.0	13.8	2,169,796	1,179	59,840	32.6	110,912	8.0	92.0	24.1	8.5	410	7.5
Medina	834	11.4	422	51.4	141.4	1,095,775	2,598	66,329	115.5	58,461	56.2	43.8	28.5	7.2	3,298	19.4
Menard	537	9.2	1,651	1.5	20.7	2,408,895	1,459	54,991	9.6	29,646	13.0	87.0	42.8	7.1	1,249	30.8
Midland	404	-11.4	749	10.7	62.4	1,072,641	1,432	83,080	17.2	31,876	65.7	34.3	17.6	5.0	1,866	23.5
Milam	528	-2.0	277	2.5	143.0	990,114	3,581	65,371	144.7	75,814	26.6	73.4	33.1	7.2	3,451	22.0
Mills	471	-0.6	542	3.3	57.5	1,204,675	2,223	58,645	43.0	49,462	12.6	87.4	40.9	4.8	1,277	22.2
Mitchell	573	-0.3	1,189	4.2	146.7	938,568	789	84,627	21.2	43,956	61.0	39.0	24.1	8.7	7,078	77.8
Montague	489	-3.7	336	0.6	74.0	840,349	2,500	59,290	44.9	30,902	18.7	81.3	32.9	5.7	1,034	14.4
Montgomery	155	-8.6	97	1.2	31.6	573,034	5,905	48,231	23.8	14,888	48.2	51.8	18.4	2.4	227	3.4
Moore	524	-5.4	2,006	122.4	263.6	1,884,521	939	303,854	605.0	2,318,107	19.4	80.6	57.1	39.8	6,010	68.6
Morris	92	7.2	223	0.0	18.1	468,248	2,100	55,663	46.9	113,922	4.9	95.1	41.3	10.4	99	9.2
Motley	595	3.6	2,658	4.2	65.8	1,960,781	738	69,571	12.8	57,143	24.5	75.5	42.0	15.2	1,767	74.6
Nacogdoches	265	-0.1	221	0.3	43.7	558,234	2,521	73,452	322.4	269,544	1.8	98.2	37.0	11.8	595	7.3
Navarro	558	-4.9	217	0.9	146.1	445,243	2,053	57,970	66.4	25,798	47.3	52.7	27.4	3.5	2,633	13.6
Newton	59	-0.8	131	0.0	8.9	261,813	2,004	54,300	2.9	6,551	35.4	64.7	17.1	0.7	D	0.7
Nolan	465	-13.9	973	3.3	118.2	1,093,607	1,124	81,916	23.8	49,847	52.0	48.0	26.2	7.5	3,074	57.3
Nueces	524	2.9	695	0.4	362.6	1,076,476	1,549	160,967	84.9	112,557	92.2	7.8	33.2	12.9	5,340	34.7
Ochiltree	545	-6.0	1,565	48.2	304.6	1,566,761	1,001	223,842	424.6	1,220,129	14.6	85.4	59.2	33.0	6,098	77.3
Oldham	830	-5.7	5,223	3.4	94.8	3,082,126	590	134,522	113.0	710,415	2.4	97.6	45.9	27.0	2,473	81.8
Orange	53	-17.2	79	0.4	6.7	261,493	3,323	47,335	4.3	6,461	44.2	55.8	11.3	0.9	112	1.5
Palo Pinto	593	7.6	446	0.7	55.4	1,074,703	2,407	51,951	53.8	40,472	18.4	81.6	24.8	4.0	489	6.5
Panola	227	4.4	211	0.7	38.6	442,762	2,101	66,066	93.3	86,466	6.0	94.0	34.5	5.8	156	4.7
Parker	494	12.0	113	2.2	93.9	567,100	5,012	49,848	74.3	17,000	20.8	79.2	17.3	2.5	294	2.4
Parmer	554	-1.3	971	163.0	444.7	1,010,667	1,040	277,575	1,329.5	2,332,523	9.9	90.1	59.3	42.1	11,381	83.3
Pecos	2,948	1.4	10,130	13.9	63.7	5,133,601	507	136,553	47.5	163,127	58.1	41.9	47.1	17.5	2,077	33.3
Polk	139	5.7	189	0.4	23.2	515,232	2,732	57,919	7.8	10,618	30.7	69.3	25.2	1.5	106	2.4
Potter	569	-0.8	2,204	3.1	54.2	1,208,547	548	66,465	21.0	81,287	7.7	92.3	29.5	12.0	1,092	22.1
Presidio	1,656	6.1	10,219	0.6	24.5	4,712,426	461	101,093	D	D	D	D	34.6	13.6	555	21.6
Rains	117	19.7	171	0.2	34.3	432,129	2,522	43,035	15.3	22,361	31.2	68.8	26.5	4.7	329	6.5
Randall	571	-0.7	640	15.9	250.8	642,873	1,004	77,600	540.3	605,734	2.9	97.1	29.8	10.0	5,003	42.9
Reagan	699	2.2	5,174	12.1	46.7	2,516,941	486	233,267	11.1	82,259	64.3	35.7	50.4	22.2	1,681	63.0
Real	321	-13.9	1,330	0.5	5.5	1,966,274	1,478	38,465	1.6	6,842	12.2	87.8	14.5	0.4	270	15.8
Red River	449	-0.2	394	2.8	94.7	654,453	1,662	73,917	53.5	46,997	26.5	73.5	42.0	7.5	1,949	18.9
Reeves	1,236	18.8	5,149	10.6	98.2	1,384,817	269	85,475	54.2	225,858	20.0	80.0	33.8	15.4	2,698	58.3
Refugio	475	-3.2	1,833	1.2	86.5	1,673,463	913	151,490	43.0	166,201	76.1	23.9	46.3	18.1	1,669	33.6
Roberts	562	15.9	5,257	6.3	49.3	3,455,290	657	143,140	16.4	153,271	31.5	68.5	57.0	31.8	1,122	57.9
Robertson	468	2.7	308	19.7	107.9	736,551	2,394	70,166	136.4	89,766	24.3	75.7	37.0	6.3	2,945	13.7
Rockwall	45	21.3	103	0.1	14.1	602,114	5,836	38,743	4.1	9,348	48.8	51.2	14.3	1.1	63	2.7
Runnels	666	1.5	720	4.5	247.9	931,382	1,294	89,466	47.4	51,272	62.3	37.7	42.8	10.9	6,002	68.8
Rusk	274	-8.8	197	0.4	47.5	431,437	2,186	58,886	75.3	54,175	25.6	74.4	24.7	3.3	295	2.4
Sabine	29	-8.5	144	0.2	4.6	392,557	2,718	84,005	14.7	73,274	3.8	96.2	31.3	3.0	22	9.0
San Augustine	73	0.3	239	0.0	8.9	552,167	2,310	122,351	63.2	207,262	2.0	98.0	42.6	11.1	25	6.2
San Jacinto	112	17.2	141	0.5	24.3	400,991	2,835	54,541	8.5	10,783	27.9	72.1	19.3	1.4	110	1.6
San Patricio	374	1.2	534	5.6	247.7	852,438	1,597	189,071	86.2	122,989	79.2	20.8	32.5	14.6	3,794	36.9
San Saba	671	-6.5	902	3.6	53.2	2,198,733	2,438	66,862	30.0	40,351	31.1	68.9	43.1	8.9	1,166	18.8
Schleicher	834	4.1	2,689	1.4	32.5	2,490,152	926	79,410	13.6	43,903	20.6	79.4	46.1	10.6	2,325	46.8
Scurry	494	-4.8	730	3.7	206.4	620,700	850	98,991	29.0	42,876	44.9	55.1	23.3	7.4	4,295	69.3
Shackelford	505	-8.5	2,168	D	55.0	2,371,000	1,093	83,609	22.3	95,854	11.6	88.4	54.5	15.9	1,604	53.2
Shelby	197	-0.3	188	1.8	36.4	550,712	2,927	92,111	473.3	451,610	2.1	97.9	46.6	21.6	334	3.9
Sherman	583	-0.2	1,863	126.6	339.1	2,006,652	1,077	378,847	590.4	1,886,121	21.9	78.1	46.3	37.7	6,153	83.1
Smith	302	0.0	102	2.5	77.1	386,589	3,786	43,300	76.8	25,934	77.5	22.5	18.6	2.6	189	1.8
Somervell	91	10.6	261	0.1	12.3	1,016,549	3,894	47,343	4.3	12,294	27.5	72.5	22.0	2.3	42	5.4
Starr	669	2.4	574	8.6	131.3	1,015,723	1,770	66,303	108.5	93,173	25.0	75.0	23.5	4.4	4,099	40.3
Stephens	517	20.4	1,143	D	54.4	1,599,708	1,399	58,681	9.2	20,392	11.6	88.4	37.6	3.1	777	30.3
Sterling	585	1.2	8,015	0.6	12.7	4,225,370	527	140,699	D	D	D	D	71.2	27.4	712	39.7
Stonewall	473	-2.6	1,328	0.7	79.5	955,171	719	52,202	47.4	133,275	5.3	94.7	35.4	6.2	2,288	80.9
Sutton	911	1.8	4,179	1.3	11.0	3,946,307	944	77,894	10.9	49,872	4.6	95.5	45.9	15.1	1,066	26.6
Swisher	546	-3.1	966	65.3	351.1	888,986	921	164,150	586.8	1,038,602	7.6	92.4	45.7	21.2	10,082	86.9
Tarrant	146	-5.6	114	0.9	38.0	722,473	6,339	54,282	34.6	27,076	72.8	27.2	18.0	4.1	109	2.8
Taylor	579	-0.1	504	1.1	158.9	570,210	1,132	55,372	37.6	32,746	27.7	72.3	23.8	4.1	3,600	37.7
Terrell	1,101	-15.5	12,800	0.3	2.0	4,976,860	389	57,116	3.1	35,686	D	D	39.5	9.3	507	22.1
Terry	442	-11.0	702	98.2	377.0	799,537	1,139	189,140	125.8	199,687	70.2	29.8	46.2	27.9	13,162	88.6
Throckmorton	508	-11.5	1,847	D	107.6	2,215,240	1,199	84,844	24.8	90,316	35.1	64.9	54.2	11.6	1,749	60.0
Titus	147	-11.9	183	D	31.1	471,061	2,575	53,954	81.2	101,401	4.5	95.5	35.3	6.1	112	7.6

Items 117—132

Table B. States and Counties — Water Use, Wholesale Trade, Retail Trade, and Real Estate

STATE County	Water use, 2015		Wholesale Trade[1], 2012				Retail Trade[2], 2012				Real estate and rental and leasing,[2] 2012			
	Public supply water withdrawn (mil gal/ day)	Public supply gallons withdrawn per person per day	Number of establish-ments	Number of employees	Sales (mil dol)	Annual payroll (mil dol)	Number of establish-ments	Number of employees	Sales (mil dol)	Annual payroll (mil dol)	Number of establish-ments	Number of employees	Sales (mil dol)	Annual payroll (mil dol)
	133	134	135	136	137	138	139	140	141	142	143	144	145	146
TEXAS— Cont'd														
Mason	0.44	109.1	8	D	D	D	25	140	36.4	2.6	4	5	2.0	0.2
Matagorda	4.44	120.8	31	123	104.9	4.5	128	1,241	324.6	25.7	33	170	32.1	7.5
Maverick	6.95	120.4	44	D	D	D	166	2,511	585.6	49.4	26	71	12.5	1.9
Medina	6.65	137.3	24	D	D	D	100	1,112	436.7	30.3	25	42	5.3	0.9
Menard	0.37	171.0	4	D	D	D	9	49	11.9	0.8	NA	NA	NA	NA
Midland	1.04	6.5	265	4,659	3,749.7	289.5	503	7,463	2,930.6	216.9	266	D	D	D
Milam	10.89	444.3	16	138	110.5	5.3	64	681	186.9	14.6	16	38	5.0	0.9
Mills	0.28	57.1	1	D	D	D	23	203	65.2	5.3	2	D	D	D
Mitchell	1.28	141.2	4	10	4.3	0.6	30	284	71.3	6.2	2	D	D	D
Montague	1.07	55.5	22	68	35.2	3.0	69	686	192.6	15.3	9	12	3.1	0.4
Montgomery	57.29	106.6	501	4,711	9,996.3	290.2	1,313	21,292	6,297.8	535.2	482	2,134	489.6	108.6
Moore	5.07	227.8	29	D	D	D	75	898	276.4	19.4	13	31	5.0	0.8
Morris	0.23	18.4	12	631	212.7	35.0	39	316	63.6	6.1	7	33	4.8	0.8
Motley	0.15	130.7	3	D	D	D	4	24	3.3	0.4	NA	NA	NA	NA
Nacogdoches	11.20	170.6	45	D	D	D	241	2,944	880.8	70.7	54	168	29.3	4.5
Navarro	2.33	48.2	29	D	D	D	163	2,039	539.2	46.1	48	136	19.4	3.3
Newton	0.97	69.4	4	D	D	D	32	177	73.3	3.5	NA	NA	NA	NA
Nolan	2.28	150.9	19	D	D	D	53	691	210.1	14.5	10	47	5.3	0.7
Nueces	72.38	201.2	361	4,987	5,153.6	264.8	1,128	17,030	5,138.3	418.1	414	2,868	667.2	132.2
Ochiltree	1.76	163.8	30	D	D	D	37	448	127.2	11.0	16	90	44.2	5.5
Oldham	0.56	270.7	2	D	D	D	7	D	D	D	NA	NA	NA	NA
Orange	8.40	99.7	36	D	D	D	269	3,130	909.6	71.8	59	272	58.3	8.7
Palo Pinto	1.98	71.0	23	267	121.4	11.8	118	1,089	281.8	23.1	28	91	16.9	3.2
Panola	1.15	48.4	23	D	D	D	81	939	228.7	20.7	26	155	24.8	6.1
Parker	7.51	59.6	97	1,053	779.1	41.6	316	4,515	1,772.7	128.0	88	302	55.0	9.5
Parmer	0.86	88.2	26	201	426.9	6.7	25	167	43.9	3.3	4	4	0.6	0.1
Pecos	4.33	267.2	16	166	135.6	8.0	58	645	185.9	14.4	9	64	11.8	2.2
Polk	561.79	11,960.1	19	99	45.9	4.3	128	1,738	474.6	40.9	30	87	17.6	3.0
Potter	5.46	44.8	169	D	D	D	555	D	D	D	167	827	162.2	29.0
Presidio	2.54	369.4	2	D	D	D	27	212	51.3	3.6	2	D	D	D
Rains	1.25	112.0	5	D	D	D	27	408	149.0	11.2	5	10	1.5	0.2
Randall	2.23	17.1	79	D	D	D	352	5,343	1,805.1	142.0	142	D	D	D
Reagan	0.00	0.0	5	D	D	D	9	60	29.2	1.6	1	D	D	D
Real	0.35	105.8	3	4	1.0	0.1	12	45	14.6	1.0	4	6	0.9	0.1
Red River	0.92	73.9	5	D	D	D	40	249	54.8	4.2	5	5	0.7	0.1
Reeves	3.65	247.8	7	D	D	D	29	425	162.0	9.0	8	29	8.1	1.1
Refugio	0.65	89.2	5	D	D	D	22	252	101.1	5.0	7	29	3.9	0.7
Roberts	0.13	141.9	NA	NA	NA	NA	2	D	D	D	NA	NA	NA	NA
Robertson	2.25	135.1	2	D	D	D	49	370	148.6	8.1	7	39	7.7	2.1
Rockwall	0.00	0.0	66	D	D	D	251	4,179	1,444.8	108.4	76	289	56.0	9.1
Runnels	3.82	362.1	5	D	D	D	47	473	139.8	10.3	2	D	D	D
Rusk	5.77	108.7	27	255	152.4	11.8	126	1,410	442.1	34.2	22	68	12.7	2.7
Sabine	0.76	73.3	1	D	D	D	31	310	65.6	5.4	4	2	0.1	0.0
San Augustine	0.81	95.6	4	12	2.9	0.4	24	215	58.2	4.8	6	10	0.6	0.2
San Jacinto	2.13	77.7	7	D	D	D	29	229	59.6	4.5	13	D	D	D
San Patricio	1.25	18.6	38	D	D	D	150	2,298	712.2	52.4	54	162	26.4	4.2
San Saba	1.43	242.3	9	61	14.1	1.1	35	198	45.3	3.7	3	3	0.2	0.1
Schleicher	0.38	118.3	3	D	D	D	10	56	12.3	1.2	NA	NA	NA	NA
Scurry	0.13	7.4	25	D	D	D	63	739	242.3	18.1	14	88	16.6	4.4
Shackelford	0.00	0.0	8	53	24.1	2.8	14	100	16.1	2.0	5	8	0.7	0.2
Shelby	4.78	188.2	10	D	D	D	93	1,087	302.1	24.3	22	91	9.8	2.5
Sherman	0.44	143.2	6	D	D	D	10	92	28.5	2.7	1	D	D	D
Smith	42.89	192.4	215	D	D	D	829	11,883	3,388.9	293.6	281	1,477	301.0	61.6
Somervell	1.18	135.0	6	46	25.8	1.9	30	218	47.8	4.3	10	17	2.4	0.3
Starr	7.81	122.4	24	D	D	D	135	1,735	435.4	33.6	14	45	5.6	0.9
Stephens	9.32	987.3	6	D	D	D	36	380	84.0	8.4	6	D	D	D
Sterling	0.19	140.5	2	D	D	D	3	D	D	D	1	D	D	D
Stonewall	0.00	0.0	2	D	D	D	6	35	8.9	0.6	1	D	D	D
Sutton	0.81	207.0	8	D	D	D	20	139	49.5	3.0	3	D	D	D
Swisher	0.59	78.3	13	55	23.4	1.8	20	152	51.5	2.9	3	6	0.4	0.1
Tarrant	26.52	13.4	1,944	34,600	30,173.3	1,974.7	5,705	91,200	28,908.8	2,381.7	1,826	12,190	2,647.1	528.7
Taylor	0.46	3.4	146	1,803	2,007.0	90.0	563	7,825	2,223.5	185.7	166	885	150.3	27.1
Terrell	0.13	155.3	NA	NA	NA	NA	4	19	5.0	0.4	NA	NA	NA	NA
Terry	0.17	13.3	18	D	D	D	43	453	131.5	10.1	8	D	D	D
Throckmorton	0.05	31.7	6	17	5.9	0.5	5	19	7.1	0.4	NA	NA	NA	NA
Titus	5.35	164.0	31	D	D	D	133	1,732	477.8	41.7	25	65	10.4	1.6

1. Merchant wholesalers, except manufacturers' sales branches and offices.   2. Employer establishments.

Table B. States and Counties — Professional Services, Manufacturing, and Accommodation and Food Services

STATE County	Professional, scientific, and technical services, 2012				Manufacturing, 2012				Accommodation and food services, 2012			
	Number of establish-ments	Number of employees	Sales (mil dol)	Annual payroll (mil dol)	Number of establishments	Number of employees	Receipts (mil dol)	Annual payroll (mil dol)	Number of establishments	Number of employees	Receipts (mil dol)	Annual payroll (mil dol)
	147	148	149	150	151	152	153	154	155	156	157	158
TEXAS— Cont'd												
Mason	14	D	D	D	6	29	5.3	1.2	14	D	D	D
Matagorda	43	162	11.8	4.2	28	513	1,657.5	41.4	84	1,045	51.5	14.0
Maverick	40	D	D	D	14	339	49.0	9.0	72	2,103	211.4	34.6
Medina	62	380	32.8	11.7	21	247	D	9.2	73	872	41.7	11.1
Menard	2	D	D	D	NA	NA	NA	NA	3	24	1.1	0.3
Midland	495	4,727	1,004.8	266.6	142	D	D	D	298	D	D	D
Milam	41	117	9.1	3.3	14	278	D	14.9	44	381	16.7	4.1
Mills	7	D	D	D	8	59	D	1.6	10	100	4.0	1.1
Mitchell	10	35	4.6	1.2	NA	NA	NA	NA	15	D	D	D
Montague	39	112	18.6	4.6	15	270	D	8.2	30	418	16.2	4.5
Montgomery	1,341	8,823	1,351.7	629.7	407	10,599	D	571.8	782	16,697	944.9	253.2
Moore	21	D	D	D	14	D	D	165.0	47	685	32.6	8.7
Morris	15	D	D	D	15	1,945	1,327.1	136.4	20	275	12.1	3.1
Motley	1	D	D	D	NA	NA	NA	NA	3	10	0.3	0.1
Nacogdoches	94	D	D	D	59	3,883	1,258.7	113.2	115	2,516	99.7	27.7
Navarro	59	298	24.0	8.0	55	2,834	1,046.9	115.2	63	1,017	50.7	13.0
Newton	9	58	4.1	1.5	6	81	D	1.3	3	27	0.4	0.2
Nolan	28	D	D	D	11	665	203.7	38.3	39	506	26.2	6.2
Nueces	812	5,789	849.1	309.6	193	7,063	41,840.9	514.2	849	17,049	892.8	242.4
Ochiltree	23	167	30.6	11.5	9	40	7.3	1.3	19	270	16.3	3.6
Oldham	NA	NA	NA	NA	NA	NA	NA	NA	9	54	2.0	0.5
Orange	92	501	57.9	23.0	74	5,287	6,340.3	426.6	140	2,002	101.2	25.5
Palo Pinto	39	211	33.7	8.6	33	1,325	460.4	55.2	73	1,023	47.1	13.2
Panola	39	206	25.3	8.0	16	905	281.9	29.6	30	419	17.8	4.8
Parker	208	892	115.3	37.7	127	2,360	582.9	109.6	190	3,237	152.0	42.0
Parmer	9	23	1.8	0.4	6	D	D	D	6	D	D	D
Pecos	16	60	2.4	1.8	4	14	D	D	43	627	36.6	7.8
Polk	73	340	30.5	10.1	25	1,227	362.5	58.1	57	940	44.5	11.9
Potter	322	1,967	414.6	115.3	125	11,535	D	716.9	366	D	D	D
Presidio	5	14	0.5	0.2	3	13	D	D	23	185	9.5	2.5
Rains	13	D	D	D	7	85	D	3.0	20	154	7.1	1.8
Randall	199	2,294	123.3	66.7	72	1,297	D	65.8	184	3,387	164.3	43.0
Reagan	7	26	1.8	0.6	NA	NA	NA	NA	7	D	D	D
Real	5	D	D	D	5	23	D	0.9	13	74	4.9	1.1
Red River	8	25	3.2	1.1	14	242	D	8.6	15	D	D	D
Reeves	16	D	D	D	3	6	2.0	D	32	434	33.9	6.4
Refugio	4	20	2.1	0.8	4	5	0.3	0.1	21	D	D	D
Roberts	1	D	D	D	NA	NA	NA	NA	1	D	D	D
Robertson	17	38	4.4	1.0	8	70	D	3.0	26	327	15.8	4.9
Rockwall	226	D	D	D	55	1,081	285.0	56.3	169	3,686	194.1	56.5
Runnels	13	D	D	D	14	505	297.9	18.8	17	D	D	D
Rusk	75	793	150.0	53.9	34	1,297	333.1	51.7	67	D	D	D
Sabine	16	D	D	D	4	309	D	D	15	77	3.9	0.7
San Augustine	7	D	D	D	5	85	D	2.3	7	D	D	D
San Jacinto	22	D	D	D	14	137	D	7.4	11	111	4.4	1.4
San Patricio	78	436	58.0	23.8	38	3,861	D	260.3	125	2,052	103.0	24.1
San Saba	16	39	4.2	1.2	7	30	D	1.4	18	D	D	D
Schleicher	4	D	D	D	NA	NA	NA	NA	1	D	D	D
Scurry	23	D	D	D	16	119	43.0	5.1	49	591	29.4	7.1
Shackelford	5	D	D	D	6	148	D	6.6	9	D	D	D
Shelby	32	133	19.7	4.5	23	2,465	577.3	72.1	34	D	D	D
Sherman	1	D	D	D	NA	NA	NA	NA	2	D	D	D
Smith	596	4,265	689.9	244.8	189	6,739	5,066.1	318.0	405	9,236	427.1	124.3
Somervell	14	59	9.7	3.8	6	33	D	1.1	28	455	23.0	7.4
Starr	30	D	D	D	6	29	2.3	0.6	51	648	35.5	8.2
Stephens	20	92	8.2	2.6	15	348	D	13.7	18	D	D	D
Sterling	2	D	D	D	NA	NA	NA	NA	3	D	D	D
Stonewall	3	D	D	D	NA	NA	NA	NA	5	22	0.8	0.2
Sutton	10	21	1.6	0.4	4	D	D	D	15	203	12.0	2.7
Swisher	7	25	1.5	0.7	8	75	D	3.1	13	D	D	D
Tarrant	4,314	39,363	6,258.9	2,258.2	1,568	70,421	45,771.0	3,894.9	3,474	77,362	4,483.6	1,188.2
Taylor	274	1,775	183.3	72.7	95	2,098	913.9	87.8	301	6,435	303.2	85.3
Terrell	2	D	D	D	NA	NA	NA	NA	5	11	0.4	0.0
Terry	15	61	4.7	1.2	5	22	D	0.8	23	280	15.4	3.4
Throckmorton	2	D	D	D	NA	NA	NA	NA	4	D	D	D
Titus	29	D	D	D	40	5,865	1,341.0	162.5	62	1,229	54.8	15.2

	Health care and social assistance, 2012				Other services, 2012				Nonemployer businesses, 2015		Value of residential construction authorized by building permits, 2017	
STATE County	Number of establishments	Number of employees	Receipts (mil dol)	Annual payroll (mil dol)	Number of establishments	Number of employees	Receipts (mil dol)	Annual payroll (mil dol)	Number	Receipts (mil dol)	New construction ($1,000)	Number of housing units
	159	160	161	162	163	164	165	166	167	168	169	170
TEXAS— Cont'd												
Mason	11	98	5.1	2.7	8	19	2.5	0.4	604	24.2	0	0
Matagorda	79	1,418	151.0	48.1	60	282	31.9	9.3	2,706	118.3	22,843	153
Maverick	96	4,039	213.0	84.4	37	145	9.5	2.5	4,394	157.5	15,941	75
Medina	69	935	55.0	25.4	40	200	18.0	4.4	3,300	146.0	5,829	30
Menard	2	D	D	D	2	D	D	D	291	10.8	NA	NA
Midland	398	7,196	817.7	299.7	264	2,138	337.4	73.6	16,137	1,114.6	159,671	761
Milam	38	791	51.8	22.9	32	117	10.7	2.6	1,614	67.2	1,448	8
Mills	13	156	7.9	3.7	7	D	D	D	452	16.0	NA	NA
Mitchell	8	D	D	D	5	17	1.2	0.3	468	16.1	0	0
Montague	40	643	46.1	19.4	37	122	11.1	2.7	1,918	91.5	0	0
Montgomery	1,015	15,877	2,147.8	724.1	579	4,253	353.2	111.7	45,630	2,624.9	1,205,140	5,294
Moore	43	680	49.6	21.7	27	109	11.9	2.6	1,109	57.5	992	4
Morris	23	257	11.9	5.8	17	78	9.9	2.0	834	30.2	190	2
Motley	1	D	D	D	2	D	D	D	116	3.4	NA	NA
Nacogdoches	202	3,339	353.7	119.6	85	427	37.1	9.6	4,003	173.6	170	4
Navarro	130	2,338	163.0	65.3	63	214	21.0	5.1	3,257	135.0	20,414	256
Newton	9	D	D	D	5	D	D	D	611	21.3	NA	NA
Nolan	32	D	D	D	15	D	D	D	1,037	36.7	715	4
Nueces	1,045	28,174	2,640.5	984.5	522	4,501	525.5	143.9	23,811	1,070.6	148,969	820
Ochiltree	20	D	D	D	24	101	11.6	2.8	804	43.0	4,395	49
Oldham	2	D	D	D	2	D	D	D	204	8.1	172	1
Orange	141	1,419	119.6	43.3	85	D	D	D	4,861	180.1	33,293	501
Palo Pinto	49	670	89.0	31.5	37	145	16.9	3.9	2,167	107.2	777	4
Panola	43	653	56.1	19.7	27	126	12.7	3.2	1,670	76.5	400	3
Parker	207	D	D	D	150	914	79.0	23.9	12,490	698.5	99,711	465
Parmer	9	140	14.3	4.9	19	D	D	D	512	27.5	250	3
Pecos	17	470	51.9	17.6	23	114	10.6	3.1	939	37.2	80	1
Polk	72	1,413	121.7	45.6	43	268	19.6	5.5	3,748	172.1	57,985	295
Potter	460	D	D	D	237	1,916	253.5	60.9	8,268	444.3	124,518	487
Presidio	4	41	2.6	1.3	4	14	0.5	0.2	836	28.7	2,729	14
Rains	12	144	7.8	3.1	12	D	D	D	846	38.4	550	4
Randall	235	D	D	D	162	D	D	D	10,470	484.9	37,165	278
Reagan	5	D	D	D	8	D	D	D	398	14.9	0	0
Real	10	199	8.5	4.3	2	D	D	D	454	21.4	0	0
Red River	16	395	29.8	12.2	7	D	D	D	896	42.9	0	0
Reeves	10	D	D	D	11	D	D	D	701	38.5	720	4
Refugio	8	257	23.0	7.3	7	23	1.9	0.6	505	25.3	938	10
Roberts	NA	NA	NA	NA	NA	NA	NA	NA	97	3.4	NA	NA
Robertson	18	D	D	D	24	139	19.2	5.5	1,235	54.6	17,955	80
Rockwall	234	3,578	472.7	146.0	96	741	53.4	16.9	9,063	534.9	458,725	1,698
Runnels	19	387	24.8	12.0	14	D	D	D	886	33.1	642	4
Rusk	73	1,596	104.0	41.2	41	275	23.2	7.6	3,170	136.0	581	2
Sabine	14	320	12.7	6.3	14	45	3.7	0.9	715	28.0	375	2
San Augustine	17	393	20.8	8.4	5	D	D	D	518	18.8	0	0
San Jacinto	11	138	7.4	3.1	12	40	4.6	1.0	1,905	79.1	80,309	368
San Patricio	97	1,722	113.9	50.0	64	342	42.4	11.4	4,623	178.4	41,873	209
San Saba	17	194	15.3	4.6	6	D	D	D	576	22.7	80	2
Schleicher	3	D	D	D	1	D	D	D	322	12.4	0	0
Scurry	22	538	60.3	19.5	29	251	38.3	9.4	1,153	46.9	1,546	8
Shackelford	4	D	D	D	7	8	1.0	0.2	477	24.8	NA	NA
Shelby	40	820	49.2	19.4	30	D	D	D	1,656	77.7	0	0
Sherman	2	D	D	D	4	7	0.5	0.1	231	11.1	1,273	15
Smith	640	21,211	2,527.9	969.6	347	2,613	252.8	87.5	18,125	911.4	160,809	678
Somervell	15	D	D	D	12	D	D	D	730	34.7	2,930	14
Starr	100	5,009	170.5	85.9	21	D	D	D	6,653	175.0	157	2
Stephens	19	314	19.5	9.6	17	56	4.5	1.1	891	49.3	0	0
Sterling	2	D	D	D	2	D	D	D	170	6.7	NA	NA
Stonewall	6	D	D	D	3	6	0.5	0.1	142	6.8	NA	NA
Sutton	4	61	7.4	2.9	9	13	2.1	0.5	414	14.2	0	0
Swisher	10	206	15.7	5.9	15	D	D	D	485	15.2	0	0
Tarrant	4,575	91,404	11,276.2	4,009.1	2,390	19,504	2,118.4	563.0	162,998	7,691.1	2,382,333	13,252
Taylor	389	11,883	1,026.5	403.9	224	1,763	145.6	40.3	9,861	468.8	63,121	318
Terrell	1	D	D	D	2	D	D	D	91	2.2	NA	NA
Terry	21	446	31.9	12.1	22	63	5.1	1.6	615	24.3	340	4
Throckmorton	3	D	D	D	4	8	0.6	0.1	223	8.4	NA	NA
Titus	88	D	D	D	41	204	19.9	4.8	1,754	77.9	3,130	26

Table B. States and Counties — **Agriculture**

STATE County	Land in farms — Acreage (1,000) [117]	Percent change, 2007-2012 [118]	Acres — Average size of farm [119]	Acres — Total irrigated (1,000) [120]	Acres — Total cropland (1,000) [121]	Value of land and buildings — Average per farm [122]	Value of land and buildings — Average per acre [123]	Value of machinery and equipment, average per farm (dollars) [124]	Value of products sold — Total (mil dol) [125]	Value of products sold — Average per farm (acres) [126]	Percent from: Crops [127]	Percent from: Livestock and poultry products [128]	Percent of farms with sales of: $10,000 or more [129]	Percent of farms with sales of: $100,000 or more [130]	Government payments — Total ($1,000) [131]	Government payments — Percent of farms [132]
TEXAS— Cont'd																
Tom Green	957	3.6	795	31.1	168.2	906,863	1,140	87,951	131.4	109,257	24.8	75.2	26.9	9.4	5,161	25.4
Travis	253	-3.7	223	1.8	61.2	856,591	3,837	55,964	41.7	36,809	82.0	18.0	24.6	6.6	1,130	16.8
Trinity	111	2.1	184	0.2	17.9	427,030	2,318	57,775	7.1	11,672	24.1	75.9	31.1	1.3	161	7.3
Tyler	91	7.6	125	0.6	16.4	364,713	2,924	58,297	19.1	26,333	74.7	25.3	21.7	1.1	43	2.9
Upshur	202	2.1	115	0.4	43.1	330,283	2,863	43,263	60.6	34,526	7.6	92.4	21.8	3.2	298	2.7
Upton	686	8.2	6,794	8.9	46.1	3,991,644	587	142,505	12.7	125,584	63.6	36.4	54.5	34.7	1,495	41.6
Uvalde	977	-1.3	1,527	49.5	139.8	3,052,314	1,999	102,739	112.5	175,742	55.0	45.0	33.6	14.1	2,447	28.1
Val Verde	1,497	0.2	3,556	0.4	8.1	2,028,570	570	39,625	10.7	25,297	3.8	96.2	20.9	6.9	1,146	10.0
Van Zandt	371	-10.9	127	2.4	100.6	405,667	3,191	47,770	94.3	32,360	50.1	49.9	25.7	3.2	887	2.9
Victoria	438	-11.3	286	3.3	80.2	654,921	2,293	54,768	47.6	31,020	58.4	41.6	27.5	4.3	2,451	18.2
Walker	281	25.2	180	0.5	38.6	598,604	3,329	52,780	34.5	22,124	53.8	46.2	16.9	2.1	533	2.8
Waller	315	16.2	163	10.1	79.9	1,020,860	6,245	64,387	91.7	47,575	76.8	23.2	25.1	4.5	2,172	14.7
Ward	392	-9.5	4,211	0.2	5.9	1,560,022	370	53,290	1.8	19,054	6.5	93.5	19.4	3.2	214	18.3
Washington	369	9.0	137	1.4	89.4	758,889	5,549	51,747	45.7	16,955	24.9	75.1	25.9	1.9	914	8.4
Webb	2,098	13.1	3,015	2.6	25.2	3,265,045	1,083	57,487	30.3	43,476	2.8	97.2	31.2	7.0	1,169	14.1
Wharton	661	7.3	425	71.6	391.6	1,080,889	2,541	159,701	373.6	240,591	72.5	27.5	49.5	22.0	13,724	52.9
Wheeler	519	-11.0	942	11.2	99.6	773,481	821	83,860	111.2	201,826	8.2	91.8	40.8	10.2	2,651	61.0
Wichita	367	10.9	574	3.0	117.1	684,844	1,193	80,674	37.9	59,362	51.6	48.4	35.1	9.5	2,069	33.5
Wilbarger	587	-4.3	1,385	15.7	196.6	1,384,455	1,000	143,679	47.2	111,425	66.5	33.5	50.2	18.9	3,593	71.9
Willacy	336	-0.6	1,047	21.1	192.1	1,913,025	1,827	165,358	82.6	257,215	94.9	5.1	40.8	23.1	3,370	60.7
Williamson	559	3.1	220	1.3	211.6	853,775	3,885	61,058	129.6	51,002	57.8	42.2	25.5	6.7	3,659	26.2
Wilson	440	-5.9	180	12.4	103.3	537,404	2,987	50,097	102.1	41,775	27.3	72.7	27.5	3.0	1,988	20.7
Winkler	533	0.1	12,406	D	D	4,500,116	363	95,000	3.4	79,907	D	D	41.9	18.6	D	7.0
Wise	487	10.0	157	2.8	114.3	600,404	3,815	52,997	49.9	16,112	32.9	67.1	23.1	2.6	1,079	7.5
Wood	227	-2.8	155	1.6	52.5	442,703	2,853	57,063	105.9	72,270	6.2	93.8	27.2	5.3	267	3.3
Yoakum	488	10.1	1,441	90.4	265.9	1,166,307	809	247,257	80.0	236,012	91.6	8.4	47.2	32.4	7,563	81.7
Young	524	-0.7	659	0.2	97.8	911,345	1,384	68,309	23.7	29,801	33.8	66.2	33.8	5.2	1,385	30.1
Zapata	563	22.6	1,254	1.8	13.0	1,465,744	1,169	50,205	11.8	26,238	38.7	61.3	32.7	4.2	932	17.4
Zavala	693	-7.9	2,414	29.4	96.0	3,705,300	1,535	109,195	72.7	253,359	39.9	60.1	32.8	18.5	1,427	31.4
UTAH	10,974	-1.1	609	1,104.3	1,645.9	888,886	1,460	84,528	1,816.1	100,746	31.6	68.4	37.2	11.0	23,898	15.4
Beaver	190	20.0	686	37.6	37.1	1,370,004	1,997	140,502	288.5	1,041,520	7.5	92.5	57.8	33.6	419	31.4
Box Elder	1,171	-11.3	948	102.9	328.6	1,140,029	1,203	129,594	169.5	137,284	45.0	55.0	47.4	21.0	7,453	40.5
Cache	269	6.7	221	76.3	137.2	778,555	3,529	96,619	142.9	117,407	26.3	73.7	43.9	14.9	2,456	33.7
Carbon	241	11.6	754	11.1	20.9	918,621	1,218	59,596	9.0	28,248	27.0	73.0	31.3	5.3	239	5.6
Daggett	D	D	D	7.3	6.9	824,255	D	91,882	2.3	45,529	33.5	66.5	45.1	13.7	44	7.8
Davis	55	11.6	112	13.8	13.0	723,596	6,484	66,773	36.8	74,564	85.9	14.1	29.8	8.3	178	7.3
Duchesne	1,089	1.1	1,029	100.9	78.2	856,720	833	92,628	57.1	53,992	33.2	66.8	47.0	11.2	455	8.4
Emery	156	-23.7	266	51.7	41.6	452,336	1,700	65,775	14.1	23,978	36.2	63.8	37.8	6.0	306	16.7
Garfield	92	11.8	328	19.6	17.6	746,086	2,274	57,297	12.0	43,165	30.0	70.0	47.7	8.2	113	7.9
Grand	D	D	D	4.2	6.3	1,571,889	D	100,469	3.9	47,815	58.5	41.5	45.7	14.8	28	11.1
Iron	532	8.2	1,046	61.6	77.6	1,973,149	1,886	141,428	136.7	268,658	39.1	60.9	47.9	21.2	714	12.8
Juab	243	-6.7	688	20.5	47.9	825,640	1,200	86,938	28.4	80,331	40.7	59.3	45.6	11.6	997	35.4
Kane	125	10.6	685	4.0	4.5	966,694	1,410	50,333	4.7	25,590	16.8	83.2	43.2	2.7	214	10.4
Millard	577	1.9	793	115.2	151.6	1,114,356	1,405	200,816	180.6	248,110	41.4	58.6	64.3	27.6	2,312	38.3
Morgan	229	-24.1	760	9.0	15.8	1,196,671	1,575	63,116	20.4	67,648	16.7	83.3	36.5	12.6	71	10.0
Piute	38	-10.7	308	13.9	15.0	901,667	2,931	124,073	16.9	137,797	10.9	89.1	52.8	15.4	101	11.4
Rich	409	12.6	2,591	66.0	77.2	2,606,139	1,006	155,513	32.8	207,753	13.6	86.4	65.2	40.5	597	18.4
Salt Lake	78	-27.3	124	6.8	13.5	586,952	4,731	55,016	21.5	34,160	65.3	34.7	21.3	5.9	80	2.4
San Juan	1,609	4.0	2,157	4.3	113.0	805,649	374	43,488	13.4	17,906	32.6	67.4	16.6	5.2	1,543	23.9
Sanpete	284	-8.7	316	68.9	74.9	679,514	2,153	95,179	147.4	163,604	14.8	85.2	41.6	15.0	1,682	15.5
Sevier	122	-34.1	181	40.2	44.6	548,010	3,019	79,190	63.0	93,399	31.6	68.4	37.1	10.5	452	12.9
Summit	270	-34.9	437	20.8	25.2	996,972	2,281	51,511	24.2	39,079	13.0	87.0	34.0	7.0	154	2.4
Tooele	347	37.2	729	23.0	40.2	870,779	1,194	80,141	40.4	84,845	28.2	71.8	33.8	8.6	170	6.9
Uintah	D	D	D	69.0	62.5	930,444	D	75,442	46.6	37,877	45.7	54.3	33.5	6.3	653	6.6
Utah	343	-0.7	139	75.2	109.5	742,896	5,331	68,401	222.6	90,427	44.1	55.9	29.4	6.2	1,123	7.6
Wasatch	149	126.3	332	12.4	17.4	1,266,053	3,818	53,662	12.2	27,069	26.0	74.0	21.3	3.6	200	3.1
Washington	148	-15.0	256	14.8	20.2	934,487	3,656	50,485	12.6	21,843	51.1	48.9	29.2	5.5	210	7.8
Wayne	42	-6.3	227	15.7	15.3	914,588	4,037	78,561	15.7	84,144	19.3	80.7	62.6	14.4	500	35.3
Weber	117	10.5	105	37.7	32.9	609,955	5,823	60,135	39.9	35,568	41.9	58.1	23.5	4.4	436	8.0
VERMONT	1,252	1.5	171	3.6	488.3	546,627	3,205	86,935	776.1	105,765	22.9	77.1	40.6	15.1	13,930	21.3
Addison	208	11.1	256	0.3	126.8	779,307	3,044	130,227	185.5	227,928	15.3	84.7	47.1	21.4	3,796	32.7
Bennington	41	13.1	136	0.3	11.2	566,646	4,176	81,639	15.1	49,420	52.4	47.6	34.1	7.5	261	10.5
Caledonia	82	-0.1	146	0.1	29.1	464,918	3,182	76,234	37.2	66,509	18.1	81.9	40.4	13.6	628	15.7

Table B. States and Counties — Water Use, Wholesale Trade, Retail Trade, and Real Estate

STATE County	Water use, 2015 Public supply water withdrawn (mil gal/day)	Public supply gallons withdrawn per person per day	Wholesale Trade[1], 2012 Number of establish-ments	Number of employees	Sales (mil dol)	Annual payroll (mil dol)	Retail Trade[2], 2012 Number of establish-ments	Number of employees	Sales (mil dol)	Annual payroll (mil dol)	Real estate and rental and leasing,[2] 2012 Number of establish-ments	Number of employees	Sales (mil dol)	Annual payroll (mil dol)
	133	134	135	136	137	138	139	140	141	142	143	144	145	146
TEXAS— Cont'd														
Tom Green	1.16	9.8	113	D	D	D	418	5,963	1,821.7	149.8	134	595	92.7	16.5
Travis	122.10	103.8	1,166	21,735	56,614.8	1,470.9	3,469	54,094	15,583.7	1,443.3	1,771	10,798	2,455.1	539.0
Trinity	0.96	66.7	3	D	D	D	38	291	62.0	4.9	2	D	D	D
Tyler	2.84	133.0	7	47	39.7	3.6	53	531	115.8	10.0	4	21	1.0	0.2
Upshur	4.29	105.7	11	103	54.1	3.7	76	763	203.4	16.6	10	15	2.6	0.4
Upton	0.00	0.0	6	D	D	D	8	73	22.3	1.4	1	D	D	D
Uvalde	3.63	133.2	29	D	D	D	105	1,249	424.2	27.6	32	97	15.5	2.9
Val Verde	7.18	146.6	24	D	D	D	148	2,019	583.5	44.1	35	122	17.5	2.8
Van Zandt	3.38	63.1	29	263	72.3	11.3	147	1,406	430.7	31.2	29	83	6.2	1.4
Victoria	12.06	130.5	112	1,703	1,247.7	91.4	382	5,501	1,657.7	141.3	127	D	D	D
Walker	2.67	37.8	25	D	D	D	165	2,397	759.7	51.0	57	D	D	D
Waller	4.82	99.1	51	1,043	684.4	47.2	90	934	303.5	21.3	23	104	10.7	2.4
Ward	5.20	443.6	8	116	36.6	4.6	30	359	105.4	7.5	10	151	55.2	16.0
Washington	0.89	25.6	35	508	516.6	24.2	140	1,945	569.2	46.4	48	160	47.0	8.9
Webb	36.08	133.8	357	2,839	2,410.1	97.0	784	12,356	3,217.6	257.8	199	692	132.4	22.0
Wharton	3.69	88.9	49	890	572.2	37.2	163	1,999	563.8	49.1	39	168	29.4	7.5
Wheeler	1.14	201.5	9	D	D	D	33	239	71.6	5.1	6	8	1.1	0.2
Wichita	0.81	6.2	147	1,191	660.1	55.3	502	7,397	1,991.0	166.2	162	807	167.8	29.9
Wilbarger	1.85	142.0	12	D	D	D	48	664	254.6	14.3	10	22	2.7	0.6
Willacy	0.43	19.6	7	D	D	D	32	420	118.4	9.4	9	17	3.5	0.4
Williamson	35.49	69.8	306	D	D	D	1,277	21,844	8,585.0	593.3	408	1,550	348.9	65.5
Wilson	5.69	119.7	19	D	D	D	73	1,151	452.4	25.3	15	28	4.9	0.7
Winkler	1.45	181.1	7	D	D	D	20	195	53.6	4.4	7	D	D	D
Wise	2.23	35.4	57	609	658.0	31.9	154	2,174	757.1	62.1	46	291	61.3	13.8
Wood	4.21	97.1	31	257	169.8	7.6	129	1,345	393.7	33.4	30	133	31.0	4.9
Yoakum	0.97	113.5	11	135	43.6	8.9	28	211	61.6	5.2	6	D	D	D
Young	2.76	151.1	28	D	D	D	68	827	215.5	18.4	20	51	43.4	2.1
Zapata	2.20	153.1	1	D	D	D	32	263	75.7	5.3	4	26	5.7	0.7
Zavala	2.27	185.5	2	D	D	D	17	181	45.6	3.8	NA	NA	NA	NA
UTAH	785.91	262.3	3,015	43,523	30,927.9	2,364.4	9,095	133,535	38,024.5	3,334.9	4,446	16,197	3,226.1	604.8
Beaver	2.25	354.1	1	D	D	D	38	383	115.5	6.6	1	D	D	D
Box Elder	11.70	224.6	32	D	D	D	134	1,605	482.7	33.4	41	43	6.4	0.9
Cache	25.91	214.5	109	D	D	D	402	5,469	1,154.2	108.7	181	483	69.1	16.5
Carbon	4.35	212.4	30	D	D	D	86	1,084	311.3	26.0	15	57	17.9	1.9
Daggett	0.18	162.3	NA	NA	NA	NA	3	D	D	D	2	D	D	D
Davis	46.73	139.1	241	2,363	1,300.8	94.8	827	12,937	3,448.8	309.8	396	1,002	220.0	35.1
Duchesne	7.03	337.0	18	198	90.3	8.2	66	758	264.9	18.2	34	116	76.8	6.9
Emery	1.73	166.8	5	D	D	D	36	478	105.1	10.2	NA	NA	NA	NA
Garfield	1.42	283.5	4	D	D	D	23	116	29.9	2.2	2	D	D	D
Grand	6.05	635.8	13	D	D	D	79	678	170.1	16.0	31	131	14.0	2.7
Iron	10.64	220.0	33	261	246.0	9.7	172	1,892	567.8	43.3	72	165	28.7	4.8
Juab	4.59	433.3	9	62	36.3	2.2	33	313	114.5	5.0	2	D	D	D
Kane	2.33	326.7	4	7	1.3	0.2	41	337	77.1	6.4	16	26	3.6	0.7
Millard	3.91	309.2	13	D	D	D	61	549	122.1	9.1	3	4	0.3	0.1
Morgan	5.37	485.3	4	D	D	D	26	213	52.1	4.6	9	15	1.9	0.3
Piute	0.77	507.6	1	D	D	D	7	D	D	D	NA	NA	NA	NA
Rich	1.22	527.9	1	D	D	D	10	49	9.6	0.7	10	23	5.1	1.1
Salt Lake	394.81	356.5	1,653	27,748	19,734.9	1,640.3	3,395	55,808	17,178.4	1,536.0	1,931	8,980	1,927.6	378.3
San Juan	1.03	65.3	4	D	D	D	36	291	68.7	4.7	2	D	D	D
Sanpete	6.37	221.3	9	45	35.0	1.2	80	861	169.5	15.8	15	42	4.6	0.7
Sevier	5.19	247.3	13	90	211.9	3.4	88	1,255	331.8	29.2	14	85	17.7	2.9
Summit	8.80	222.0	43	551	378.7	32.0	295	4,105	1,013.6	101.5	245	900	124.1	27.6
Tooele	18.35	291.5	13	63	31.9	2.9	104	1,688	496.8	37.1	30	76	10.3	1.6
Uintah	4.93	130.0	45	D	D	D	135	1,575	503.2	43.4	79	453	104.1	21.8
Utah	127.67	222.0	368	5,770	3,112.6	298.4	1,520	22,096	6,039.4	529.6	684	D	D	D
Wasatch	4.34	148.8	17	35	11.0	1.0	88	1,021	267.4	20.7	44	105	27.3	3.4
Washington	49.38	317.3	149	1,284	1,514.7	47.4	574	7,375	1,900.8	168.4	306	702	95.2	18.7
Wayne	1.18	438.3	NA	NA	NA	NA	15	104	32.1	1.9	1	D	D	D
Weber	27.68	113.6	183	2,924	2,655.6	129.1	721	10,462	2,991.6	245.8	280	905	130.9	24.9
VERMONT	42.66	68.1	696	9,464	6,450.1	464.4	3,509	38,910	9,933.8	967.1	741	3,092	509.9	103.6
Addison	3.45	93.2	31	D	D	D	184	1,886	536.9	51.6	37	94	11.0	2.4
Bennington	3.30	90.9	27	D	D	D	271	3,051	806.2	79.8	53	222	29.9	6.7
Caledonia	1.77	57.5	29	D	D	D	173	1,687	451.4	43.1	30	D	D	D

1. Merchant wholesalers, except manufacturers' sales branches and offices. 2. Employer establishments.

Table B. States and Counties — **Land Area and Population**

State / county code	CBSA code[1]	County code[2]	STATE County	Population, 2017				Population and population characteristics, 2017										
								Race alone or in combination, not Hispanic or Latino (percent)					Age (percent)					
				Land area[3] (sq. mi)	Total persons 2017	Rank	Per square mile	White	Black	American Indian, Alaska Native	Asian and Pacific Islander	Percent Hispanic or Latino[4]	Under 5 years	5 to 17 years	18 to 24 years	25 to 34 years	35 to 44 years	45 to 54 years
				1	2	3	4	5	6	7	8	9	10	11	12	13	14	15
			VERMONT— Cont'd															
50,007	15,540	3	Chittenden	536.6	162,372	401	302.6	90.7	3.2	0.8	5.1	2.3	4.9	13.1	16.1	14.1	11.5	12.5
50,009	13,620	9	Essex	663.6	6,230	2,733	9.4	96.8	1.1	1.5	0.8	1.5	4.8	13.0	6.3	8.3	9.8	14.6
50,011	15,540	3	Franklin	633.8	49,025	1,003	77.4	96.0	1.1	2.4	1.1	1.6	6.0	16.4	7.8	12.4	12.4	14.5
50,013	15,540	3	Grand Isle	81.8	6,998	2,672	85.6	95.5	1.2	3.1	0.9	2.1	4.4	14.0	6.6	10.6	10.6	14.6
50,015		8	Lamoille	458.9	25,337	1,590	55.2	96.1	1.5	1.3	1.1	1.9	5.2	15.3	9.4	12.2	12.8	13.9
50,017	17,200	9	Orange	687.0	28,974	1,458	42.2	96.9	1.0	1.3	0.8	1.5	4.6	14.0	8.2	10.7	11.1	13.8
50,019		7	Orleans	693.6	26,841	1,531	38.7	96.9	1.2	1.5	0.7	1.4	5.0	14.5	7.5	10.7	11.2	13.3
50,021	40,860	4	Rutland	929.8	59,087	877	63.5	96.6	1.1	0.9	1.3	1.5	4.6	13.3	9.4	10.7	10.0	13.9
50,023	12,740	4	Washington	687.0	58,290	884	84.8	96.0	1.5	1.0	1.4	2.0	4.8	14.3	9.4	11.1	12.0	14.0
50,025		7	Windham	785.5	42,869	1,117	54.6	94.8	2.0	1.2	1.7	2.3	4.5	13.5	8.0	10.8	10.5	13.1
50,027	17,200	7	Windsor	969.6	55,100	921	56.8	96.3	1.2	1.1	1.4	1.6	4.4	13.8	6.7	10.9	10.9	13.5
51,000		0	VIRGINIA	39,480.6	8,470,020	X	214.5	64.2	20.4	0.8	8.0	9.4	6.0	16.0	9.5	14.0	12.9	13.6
51,001		8	Accomack	449.3	32,545	1,369	72.4	61.6	29.0	0.9	1.1	9.1	5.6	15.1	6.3	11.1	10.3	12.4
51,003	16,820	3	Albemarle	720.5	107,702	559	149.5	78.9	10.7	0.6	6.4	5.8	5.3	14.8	12.1	13.0	11.5	12.2
51,005		6	Alleghany	446.4	15,122	2,089	33.9	93.1	5.7	0.6	0.6	1.5	4.6	14.4	7.3	9.5	10.1	14.4
51,007	40,060	1	Amelia	355.3	13,020	2,227	36.6	75.2	22.0	0.9	0.8	3.0	5.5	15.3	6.9	11.5	10.5	14.5
51,009	31,340	2	Amherst	474.0	31,594	1,390	66.7	77.3	20.1	1.4	1.1	2.4	5.5	14.6	8.0	11.3	10.7	14.2
51,011	31,340	2	Appomattox	334.2	15,681	2,057	46.9	78.8	20.6	0.6	0.6	1.4	5.6	15.9	7.2	11.9	11.3	12.9
51,013	47,900	1	Arlington	26.0	234,965	282	9,037.1	64.3	9.8	0.7	12.7	15.6	6.0	11.9	8.0	24.6	16.7	12.7
51,015	44,420	3	Augusta	966.9	75,144	737	77.7	92.1	5.0	0.6	1.0	2.7	4.7	14.6	7.6	11.4	11.6	14.5
51,017		8	Bath	529.2	4,297	2,876	8.1	92.9	5.1	0.6	0.7	2.0	4.5	10.8	6.6	9.7	9.1	15.2
51,019	31,340	2	Bedford	760.1	77,974	712	102.6	89.2	7.8	0.7	1.7	2.2	4.7	15.3	7.3	10.1	10.5	14.9
51,021		8	Bland	357.6	6,350	2,726	17.8	94.7	4.2	0.6	0.7	0.7	3.8	12.2	6.3	12.2	13.3	15.2
51,023	40,220	2	Botetourt	541.3	33,192	1,351	61.3	93.9	3.8	0.7	1.0	1.8	4.1	14.8	7.1	9.5	10.4	15.5
51,025		6	Brunswick	566.2	16,244	2,026	28.7	42.2	55.1	0.5	0.9	2.4	4.5	12.9	8.8	13.3	11.6	13.1
51,027		9	Buchanan	502.9	21,514	1,756	42.8	95.9	3.1	0.4	0.6	0.7	4.3	13.3	6.7	11.1	11.7	14.9
51,029	16,820	3	Buckingham	579.6	17,065	1,974	29.4	62.7	35.1	0.7	0.7	2.6	4.4	13.5	7.4	13.8	12.8	14.6
51,031	31,340	2	Campbell	503.2	55,010	923	109.3	81.7	15.5	0.8	1.5	2.5	4.9	14.8	7.9	13.1	11.3	13.8
51,033	40,060	1	Caroline	527.6	30,461	1,422	57.7	66.5	29.0	1.5	1.8	4.8	6.9	16.5	6.9	13.7	12.6	13.5
51,035		7	Carroll	474.7	29,708	1,439	62.6	95.6	1.1	0.5	0.3	3.2	4.5	14.1	6.6	9.9	11.0	14.4
51,036	40,060	1	Charles City	182.8	7,004	2,670	38.3	44.6	47.3	7.9	1.6	1.9	4.3	11.3	6.6	10.1	9.5	16.0
51,037		8	Charlotte	475.3	12,119	2,284	25.5	69.2	29.0	0.8	0.6	2.1	5.8	15.6	7.6	10.3	10.0	13.4
51,041	40,060	1	Chesterfield	423.4	343,599	204	811.5	63.9	24.4	0.8	4.6	8.8	5.9	17.9	8.8	11.9	13.4	14.3
51,043	47,900	1	Clarke	175.9	14,508	2,128	82.5	87.7	5.8	1.1	1.9	5.8	4.6	15.7	7.3	9.1	10.3	15.7
51,045	40,220	2	Craig	328.1	5,062	2,827	15.4	97.6	0.7	0.6	0.4	1.5	4.5	14.0	6.7	9.9	10.5	15.0
51,047	47,900	1	Culpeper	379.2	51,282	971	135.2	73.1	15.9	0.8	2.2	10.7	6.8	18.3	7.6	12.0	12.8	14.1
51,049		8	Cumberland	297.5	9,811	2,443	33.0	65.2	32.3	1.1	0.9	2.7	4.9	14.9	7.7	11.5	10.3	14.2
51,051	13,720	9	Dickenson	330.4	14,782	2,110	44.7	98.2	0.7	0.5	0.4	0.9	5.1	14.9	6.5	11.3	12.7	13.0
51,053	40,060	1	Dinwiddie	503.9	28,208	1,485	56.0	63.3	32.7	0.8	1.2	3.5	4.8	15.2	8.8	12.3	11.2	15.1
51,057		6	Essex	257.1	11,028	2,353	42.9	56.8	39.3	1.2	1.5	3.5	5.5	13.9	7.2	11.2	10.0	13.7
51,059	47,900	1	Fairfax	391.0	1,148,433	37	2,937.2	53.8	10.7	0.6	22.2	16.2	6.3	17.1	8.3	13.4	14.4	14.6
51,061	47,900	1	Fauquier	648.0	69,465	770	107.2	82.1	8.8	0.8	2.4	8.3	5.8	17.6	7.9	10.9	11.6	15.4
51,063	13,980	3	Floyd	380.9	15,755	2,053	41.4	94.3	2.4	0.6	0.9	3.0	4.8	15.3	6.5	9.9	11.4	14.1
51,065	16,820	3	Fluvanna	287.1	26,452	1,548	92.1	80.5	16.2	0.9	1.4	3.4	4.7	15.4	7.2	11.3	12.9	14.2
51,067	40,220	2	Franklin	690.5	56,445	906	81.7	88.5	8.8	0.5	0.7	2.8	4.7	14.6	7.9	9.9	9.8	13.9
51,069	49,020	3	Frederick	413.0	86,484	664	209.4	85.3	5.4	0.7	2.3	8.5	6.1	17.1	7.7	12.0	12.3	14.5
51,071	13,980	3	Giles	357.2	16,837	1,986	47.1	95.9	2.1	0.6	1.0	1.6	5.4	15.4	6.9	10.8	11.5	14.5
51,073	47,260	1	Gloucester	217.8	37,292	1,242	171.2	86.9	9.1	1.2	1.7	3.6	5.2	14.9	7.4	11.8	11.4	14.2
51,075	40,060	1	Goochland	280.6	22,685	1,689	80.8	79.3	16.6	0.7	2.0	2.8	3.9	14.0	6.8	9.5	10.9	15.6
51,077		9	Grayson	441.8	15,665	2,059	35.5	90.7	6.1	0.7	0.4	3.3	4.6	12.3	6.9	10.6	11.1	14.5
51,079	16,820	3	Greene	155.9	19,612	1,845	125.8	85.0	8.3	0.7	2.3	6.1	6.0	18.3	6.6	12.1	12.4	14.2
51,081		6	Greensville	295.2	11,679	2,314	39.6	37.5	59.4	0.5	1.1	2.4	5.0	12.2	8.4	15.9	14.8	16.1
51,083		6	Halifax	817.7	34,563	1,308	42.3	60.9	36.8	0.7	0.8	2.1	5.6	15.1	7.5	10.1	10.0	12.9
51,085	40,060	1	Hanover	467.9	105,923	567	226.4	85.4	10.1	0.8	2.4	3.1	5.1	17.1	8.7	10.2	11.7	14.9
51,087	40,060	1	Henrico	233.7	327,898	212	1,403.1	55.1	31.2	0.8	9.6	5.6	6.1	16.8	7.8	14.2	13.3	13.8
51,089	32,300	4	Henry	382.3	51,227	972	134.0	71.5	23.3	0.6	0.9	5.4	4.6	14.9	6.8	10.4	10.2	14.2
51,091		8	Highland	415.2	2,212	3,029	5.3	97.1	0.9	0.3	0.6	1.4	3.8	9.8	4.2	8.7	8.1	10.4
51,093	47,260	1	Isle of Wight	315.6	36,552	1,261	115.8	72.3	24.0	0.9	1.8	3.1	5.3	15.7	7.4	10.9	11.3	14.5
51,095	47,260	1	James City	142.4	75,524	732	530.4	77.8	14.3	0.9	3.9	5.7	4.8	15.3	6.9	10.3	10.8	13.0
51,097		8	King and Queen	315.2	7,003	2,671	22.2	68.5	27.7	2.2	1.0	3.1	4.5	13.7	6.9	11.0	9.8	14.7
51,099		6	King George	179.6	26,337	1,554	146.6	76.4	17.9	1.3	2.8	5.1	6.4	19.0	8.6	12.6	13.3	14.5
51,101	40,060	1	King William	273.9	16,708	1,996	61.0	78.7	17.1	2.2	1.8	2.6	6.0	17.2	7.4	13.0	12.2	14.5
51,103		9	Lancaster	133.3	10,788	2,363	80.9	69.2	28.7	0.6	0.9	1.9	4.2	11.1	5.3	8.6	7.1	10.4
51,105		8	Lee	435.4	23,758	1,651	54.6	93.9	3.9	0.8	0.6	1.9	4.7	14.2	6.7	12.5	12.6	13.9
51,107	47,900	1	Loudoun	515.7	398,080	176	771.9	59.2	8.5	0.6	21.4	13.9	7.2	21.3	7.2	12.1	17.1	15.9

1. CBSA = Core Based Statistical Area. See Appendix A for explanation. See Appendix B for list of metropolitan areas with component counties. 2. County type code from the Economic Research Service of USDA Rural-Urban Continuum Codes. See Appendix A for definition. 3. Dry land or land partially or temporarily covered by water. 4. May be of any race.

Table B. States and Counties — Population and Households

STATE County	55 to 64 years	65 to 74 years	75 years and over	Percent female	2000	2010	2000-2010	2010-2017	Births	Deaths	Net Migration	Number	Persons per house-hold	Family house-holds	Female family house-holder[1]	One person
	16	17	18	19	20	21	22	23	24	25	26	27	28	29	30	31
VERMONT— Cont'd																
Chittenden	13.3	8.5	6.0	50.9	146,571	156,540	6.8	3.7	11,412	7,607	2,158	64,012	2.35	57.5	8.3	28.2
Essex	17.9	15.2	10.1	49.7	6,459	6,306	-2.4	-1.2	396	423	-48	2,691	2.28	65.4	10.7	29.0
Franklin	15.0	9.6	6.0	50.2	45,417	47,752	5.1	2.7	4,220	2,846	-64	18,472	2.61	68.7	9.5	24.2
Grand Isle	18.9	14.1	6.2	49.8	6,901	6,970	1.0	0.4	420	418	30	2,905	2.39	70.6	8.4	24.3
Lamoille	14.5	10.2	6.5	50.0	23,233	24,475	5.3	3.5	1,899	1,423	397	10,342	2.37	60.9	8.0	31.6
Orange	17.4	12.8	7.4	49.8	28,226	28,937	2.5	0.1	1,948	1,841	-47	12,306	2.29	64.8	9.8	27.6
Orleans	15.7	13.3	8.7	49.7	26,277	27,234	3.6	-1.4	1,965	2,214	-117	11,360	2.31	64.2	9.7	28.8
Rutland	16.7	13.0	8.4	50.6	63,400	61,649	-2.8	-4.2	3,904	4,797	-1,658	25,317	2.28	60.5	8.5	32.1
Washington	15.4	11.5	7.5	50.6	58,039	59,526	2.6	-2.1	4,151	3,839	-1,524	24,581	2.31	61.9	10.4	30.3
Windham	17.5	13.7	8.3	51.0	44,216	44,513	0.7	-3.7	2,884	3,180	-1,341	19,011	2.20	59.1	9.1	32.0
Windsor	17.4	13.5	9.0	51.1	57,418	56,661	-1.3	-2.8	3,530	4,201	-857	24,184	2.27	61.4	8.4	30.7
VIRGINIA	12.9	9.0	6.0	50.8	7,078,515	8,001,043	13.0	5.9	743,716	459,403	183,742	3,090,178	2.61	66.9	12.2	26.8
Accomack	16.4	13.4	9.4	51.2	38,305	33,164	-13.4	-1.9	2,879	3,237	-231	13,819	2.31	64.7	12.8	29.4
Albemarle	13.3	10.1	7.6	52.2	79,236	98,990	24.9	8.8	7,933	5,794	6,619	39,431	2.44	64.3	9.0	28.3
Alleghany	15.5	13.8	10.3	51.1	17,215	16,261	-5.5	-7.0	1,054	1,670	-520	6,845	2.28	63.4	8.3	31.5
Amelia	16.7	11.3	7.8	50.6	11,400	12,695	11.4	2.6	1,004	957	279	4,540	2.79	76.1	14.0	20.1
Amherst	15.2	11.8	8.8	51.8	31,894	32,354	1.4	-2.3	2,443	2,479	-727	12,306	2.51	69.6	14.0	26.7
Appomattox	14.8	11.7	8.7	51.4	13,705	15,025	9.6	4.4	1,239	1,177	598	5,972	2.55	76.8	14.8	20.6
Arlington	9.9	6.4	3.9	50.1	189,453	207,684	9.6	13.1	22,727	6,956	11,193	100,707	2.21	46.6	5.9	39.1
Augusta	15.1	11.9	8.6	49.3	65,615	73,751	12.4	1.9	4,940	5,066	1,550	28,425	2.49	72.7	9.3	23.3
Bath	16.8	15.5	11.8	49.4	5,048	4,727	-6.4	-9.1	267	447	-249	2,104	2.11	54.7	2.5	35.8
Bedford	16.5	12.6	8.2	50.7	60,371	74,929	24.1	4.1	5,140	5,456	3,397	30,821	2.48	70.8	8.2	25.2
Bland	14.4	13.5	9.1	45.1	6,871	6,824	-0.7	-6.9	341	630	-182	2,561	2.24	70.7	8.2	27.7
Botetourt	16.4	13.4	8.7	50.5	30,496	33,148	8.7	0.1	1,762	2,330	630	13,305	2.47	73.0	7.8	22.6
Brunswick	15.0	12.0	8.9	47.5	18,419	17,425	-5.4	-6.8	1,049	1,438	-794	6,148	2.37	64.9	19.8	31.8
Buchanan	16.2	13.0	8.7	49.5	26,978	24,100	-10.7	-10.7	1,452	2,138	-1,917	9,124	2.43	68.9	12.4	26.9
Buckingham	14.6	11.5	7.5	44.8	15,623	17,140	9.7	-0.4	1,111	1,128	-64	5,689	2.64	68.3	13.7	27.5
Campbell	14.8	11.1	8.2	51.4	51,078	54,820	7.3	0.5	4,051	3,841	15	22,294	2.45	68.8	12.0	27.2
Caroline	13.8	9.8	6.2	50.8	22,121	28,558	29.1	6.7	2,880	1,875	899	10,965	2.51	72.1	16.6	21.6
Carroll	15.7	13.9	9.9	50.6	29,245	30,076	2.8	-1.2	1,886	2,655	423	12,642	2.34	68.0	10.4	27.6
Charles City	18.7	14.8	8.6	51.6	6,926	7,256	4.8	-3.5	412	574	-87	2,854	2.48	65.0	14.8	29.3
Charlotte	15.5	12.2	9.6	50.6	12,472	12,591	1.0	-3.7	1,010	1,107	-367	4,594	2.63	65.0	14.3	29.7
Chesterfield	13.4	9.3	5.2	51.8	259,903	316,239	21.7	8.7	27,403	16,017	16,223	118,908	2.76	72.1	12.3	23.2
Clarke	16.7	12.4	8.1	50.2	12,652	14,025	10.9	3.4	928	1,082	638	5,591	2.52	65.3	12.4	28.5
Craig	16.9	13.8	8.7	50.4	5,091	5,175	1.6	-2.2	294	377	-29	2,314	2.24	57.2	7.8	37.4
Culpeper	13.2	9.3	5.9	49.9	34,262	46,691	36.3	9.8	4,680	2,839	2,759	16,904	2.81	74.4	11.2	20.9
Cumberland	14.7	13.0	8.8	51.7	9,017	10,039	11.3	-2.3	732	668	-293	4,085	2.38	67.0	16.5	29.0
Dickenson	15.3	12.8	8.5	49.3	16,395	15,882	-3.1	-6.9	1,173	1,515	-756	6,055	2.46	68.9	10.0	29.1
Dinwiddie	15.3	10.2	6.9	51.3	24,533	28,014	14.2	0.7	1,956	1,822	72	10,344	2.65	70.7	16.6	25.3
Essex	16.2	13.3	8.9	52.8	9,989	11,149	11.6	-1.1	902	913	-102	4,447	2.46	62.6	10.9	31.7
Fairfax	12.7	8.1	5.0	50.4	969,749	1,081,682	11.5	6.2	108,013	36,225	-5,419	393,358	2.86	71.4	9.3	22.4
Fauquier	14.8	9.8	6.3	50.5	55,139	65,263	18.4	6.4	5,518	3,886	2,609	23,890	2.83	72.3	7.8	22.4
Floyd	15.7	13.2	8.9	49.6	13,874	15,292	10.2	3.0	1,054	1,114	529	6,303	2.46	68.4	8.3	26.9
Fluvanna	14.7	11.6	7.9	54.3	20,047	25,741	28.4	2.8	1,871	1,493	345	9,829	2.53	74.4	8.7	20.8
Franklin	16.0	14.1	8.9	50.7	47,286	56,139	18.7	0.5	3,703	4,220	874	22,976	2.38	71.7	10.8	24.8
Frederick	13.4	9.9	6.9	50.3	59,209	78,287	32.2	10.5	6,960	4,585	5,827	29,914	2.71	74.3	9.7	20.6
Giles	13.8	12.8	8.8	50.8	16,657	17,286	3.8	-2.6	1,312	1,565	-185	7,290	2.30	67.2	11.9	26.5
Gloucester	16.7	11.0	7.5	50.6	34,780	36,858	6.0	1.2	2,635	2,634	455	14,511	2.53	70.3	8.9	25.2
Goochland	17.8	13.8	7.8	50.9	16,863	21,694	28.6	4.6	1,178	1,287	1,071	8,177	2.54	77.2	6.7	20.3
Grayson	15.9	13.7	10.3	48.4	17,917	15,554	-13.2	0.7	1,031	1,528	575	6,710	2.18	62.9	10.2	33.4
Greene	13.9	10.3	6.3	51.1	15,244	18,393	20.7	6.6	1,555	1,096	769	7,107	2.66	71.6	10.6	21.4
Greensville	12.8	9.4	5.5	37.4	11,560	12,245	5.9	-4.6	848	951	-493	3,705	2.32	69.0	14.2	27.8
Halifax	15.1	13.5	10.2	52.0	37,355	36,241	-3.0	-4.6	2,677	3,406	-925	14,264	2.42	65.5	13.9	31.1
Hanover	14.9	10.3	6.9	51.0	86,320	99,846	15.7	6.1	6,701	6,135	5,559	37,724	2.66	75.3	9.7	19.9
Henrico	13.0	8.8	6.2	52.6	262,300	306,868	17.0	6.9	29,112	18,920	11,054	125,478	2.55	63.7	14.5	29.9
Henry	15.4	12.8	10.7	51.9	57,930	54,185	-6.5	-5.5	3,473	4,991	-1,424	22,136	2.33	66.1	14.6	30.6
Highland	22.3	20.0	12.7	50.4	2,536	2,319	-8.6	-4.6	119	201	-24	1,121	1.99	62.4	7.5	32.8
Isle of Wight	16.4	11.2	7.3	51.1	29,728	35,274	18.7	3.6	2,493	2,499	1,306	13,902	2.57	72.8	9.8	22.3
James City	14.2	13.8	10.9	51.8	48,102	67,383	40.1	12.1	4,871	4,762	7,993	28,352	2.50	70.9	9.6	24.1
King and Queen	16.9	13.4	9.0	49.4	6,630	6,942	4.7	0.9	448	526	140	2,807	2.54	64.9	10.8	29.2
King George	12.8	7.9	4.8	49.3	16,803	23,584	40.4	11.7	2,276	1,145	1,613	8,669	2.90	73.5	9.6	21.5
King William	13.9	9.9	5.8	51.0	13,146	15,927	21.2	4.9	1,385	1,008	410	6,066	2.65	78.0	12.2	19.1
Lancaster	17.7	18.5	17.0	53.0	11,567	11,390	-1.5	-5.3	634	1,454	232	5,097	2.15	59.2	8.8	36.8
Lee	15.0	12.3	8.2	48.1	23,589	25,583	8.5	-7.1	1,719	2,148	-1,394	9,282	2.52	67.3	10.6	29.1
Loudoun	10.2	5.4	3.5	50.4	169,599	312,347	84.2	27.4	37,183	8,636	56,561	117,073	3.08	78.1	8.8	17.1

1. No spouse present.

Table B. States and Counties — Population, Vital Statistics, Health, and Crime

STATE County	Persons in group quarters, 2017	Daytime Population, 2012-2016		Births, 2017		Deaths, 2017		Persons under 65 with no health insurance, 2016		Medicare, 2017			Serious crimes known to police[2], 2016 Total	
		Number	Employment/ residence ratio	Total	Rate[1]	Number	Rate[1]	Number	Percent	Total beneficiaries	Enrolled in Original Medicare	Enrolled in Medicare Advantage	Number	Rate[3]
	32	33	34	35	36	37	38	39	40	41	42	43	44	45
VERMONT— Cont'd														
Chittenden	9,599	174,554	1.16	1,561	9.6	1,081	6.7	5,451	4.2	22,192	19,824	2,368	3,666	2,264
Essex	16	4,898	0.52	58	9.3	62	10.0	307	6.6	1,894	1,752	142	15	245
Franklin	573	42,756	0.76	560	11.4	376	7.7	1,793	4.3	8,937	8,069	868	824	1,686
Grand Isle	0	4,825	0.42	53	7.6	53	7.6	274	4.9	1,828	1,616	213	45	659
Lamoille	726	24,268	0.93	258	10.2	193	7.6	1,143	5.5	11,211	10,154	1,057	189	747
Orange	722	23,847	0.66	254	8.8	258	8.9	1,139	5.0	6,565	6,146	419	83	288
Orleans	778	26,791	0.98	269	10.0	292	10.9	1,217	5.9	7,026	6,440	587	353	1,307
Rutland	2,364	59,771	0.99	499	8.4	629	10.6	2,081	4.6	16,622	15,086	1,536	840	1,418
Washington	2,401	62,159	1.10	537	9.2	517	8.9	1,979	4.3	13,938	12,878	1,060	1,085	1,862
Windham	1,498	45,930	1.11	371	8.7	438	10.2	1,810	5.5	10,746	9,753	993	799	1,855
Windsor	851	53,644	0.92	469	8.5	546	9.9	2,098	4.9	14,581	13,069	1,512	573	1,034
VIRGINIA	242,294	8,213,519	0.98	101,515	12.0	66,786	7.9	692,343	9.9	1,429,188	1,133,212	295,976	174,714	2,077
Accomack	428	32,327	0.95	371	11.4	473	14.5	4,488	17.9	8,719	7,303	1,416	568	1,755
Albemarle	6,701	111,987	1.16	1,050	9.7	884	8.2	8,710	10.6	10,771	9,421	1,350	1,580	1,484
Alleghany	281	15,615	0.95	140	9.3	263	17.4	1,137	9.8	2,100	1,627	473	168	1,085
Amelia	128	9,680	0.47	142	10.9	138	10.6	1,332	12.9	2,812	2,123	689	149	1,158
Amherst	1,162	26,468	0.62	358	11.3	372	11.8	2,764	11.4	7,294	6,000	1,294	332	1,049
Appomattox	56	12,302	0.54	161	10.3	163	10.4	1,457	11.8	3,052	2,554	498	153	993
Arlington	2,984	270,388	1.31	3,074	13.1	1,063	4.5	14,916	7.2	23,628	20,209	3,418	4,071	1,754
Augusta	2,881	69,047	0.84	691	9.2	757	10.1	6,123	10.7	10,788	9,086	1,701	808	1,091
Bath	53	4,629	1.03	33	7.7	46	10.7	351	10.7	1,424	1,283	142	29	659
Bedford	545	61,541	0.57	630	8.1	836	10.7	5,609	9.1	20,841	16,731	4,110	827	1,062
Bland	686	6,101	0.80	46	7.2	84	13.2	426	9.6	1,688	1,293	396	61	942
Botetourt	279	27,627	0.65	228	6.9	345	10.4	2,128	8.2	7,478	5,703	1,776	274	825
Brunswick	1,859	14,555	0.69	134	8.2	222	13.7	1,456	13.2	3,741	2,920	821	117	711
Buchanan	1,007	23,774	1.09	168	7.8	298	13.9	2,099	12.7	6,081	3,515	2,567	404	1,803
Buckingham	2,224	14,566	0.62	125	7.3	152	8.9	1,597	13.4	2,712	2,155	557	165	975
Campbell	439	49,115	0.77	524	9.5	539	9.8	4,788	10.8	11,212	9,197	2,016	871	1,589
Caroline	513	22,336	0.50	388	12.7	277	9.1	2,698	10.9	5,269	4,267	1,003	368	1,223
Carroll	337	25,869	0.70	256	8.6	382	12.9	3,009	13.3	6,103	5,129	973	458	1,553
Charles City	0	5,644	0.56	51	7.3	100	14.3	883	16.3	2,420	1,866	554	49	704
Charlotte	175	10,314	0.61	144	11.9	150	12.4	1,377	14.7	4,079	3,376	703	135	1,119
Chesterfield	4,295	287,378	0.73	3,797	11.1	2,407	7.0	23,422	8.1	49,367	37,246	12,121	7,072	2,095
Clarke	180	11,864	0.65	131	9.0	146	10.1	1,179	10.3	2,943	2,595	348	156	1,087
Craig	9	3,693	0.23	41	8.1	68	13.4	385	9.6	1,122	862	260	27	520
Culpeper	1,470	43,731	0.76	679	13.2	414	8.1	5,280	12.8	8,894	7,367	1,527	590	1,187
Cumberland	37	6,813	0.34	86	8.8	106	10.8	939	12.4	1,469	1,089	380	86	896
Dickenson	511	14,224	0.78	145	9.8	189	12.8	1,319	11.5	4,418	2,578	1,840	180	1,209
Dinwiddie	734	23,490	0.63	202	7.2	272	9.6	2,558	11.3	3,939	3,081	858	385	1,392
Essex	190	10,092	0.80	119	10.8	111	10.1	1,009	11.6	2,784	2,223	562	166	1,500
Fairfax	10,331	1,152,549	1.03	13,949	12.1	5,671	4.9	92,410	9.3	125,918	107,800	18,117	16,466	1,435
Fauquier	389	58,594	0.72	781	11.2	621	8.9	5,409	9.3	11,582	10,179	1,404	711	1,029
Floyd	85	12,684	0.58	131	8.3	157	10.0	1,572	12.8	3,495	2,747	748	133	851
Fluvanna	1,236	18,634	0.37	243	9.2	207	7.8	2,221	11.1	5,644	4,795	849	218	833
Franklin	1,308	48,241	0.68	512	9.1	632	11.2	5,114	12.0	10,743	7,526	3,217	817	1,460
Frederick	1,172	72,489	0.76	1,001	11.6	677	7.8	7,053	10.1	9,716	8,610	1,106	1,148	1,372
Giles	136	14,827	0.73	187	11.1	202	12.0	1,479	11.1	4,617	3,472	1,145	222	1,346
Gloucester	359	30,505	0.63	357	9.6	435	11.7	2,876	9.5	7,849	6,417	1,432	549	1,485
Goochland	877	25,155	1.31	143	6.3	172	7.6	1,080	6.3	3,680	2,875	805	196	881
Grayson	1,103	13,187	0.68	133	8.5	188	12.0	1,435	12.7	3,500	2,957	543	186	1,160
Greene	137	14,088	0.44	197	10.0	148	7.5	2,061	12.8	3,429	2,912	517	206	1,073
Greensville	3,416	11,860	1.04	141	12.1	117	10.0	644	9.8	D	D	D	109	927
Halifax	757	34,563	0.95	393	11.4	491	14.2	3,100	11.8	9,632	8,215	1,417	700	2,016
Hanover	2,029	95,122	0.87	988	9.3	821	7.8	6,029	7.1	22,922	17,618	5,304	1,407	1,362
Henrico	2,807	328,926	1.04	3,915	11.9	2,693	8.2	26,793	9.7	32,631	24,411	8,221	8,865	2,711
Henry	561	48,112	0.80	417	8.1	708	13.8	5,108	13.0	10,896	7,698	3,199	1,416	2,768
Highland	0	1,980	0.74	17	7.7	26	11.8	263	17.2	712	638	74	28	1,281
Isle of Wight	310	29,373	0.61	359	9.8	381	10.4	2,614	8.8	7,516	5,828	1,688	525	1,446
James City	1,085	68,295	0.89	696	9.2	669	8.9	4,420	7.9	5,593	4,778	815	1,237	1,675
King and Queen	0	5,336	0.42	58	8.3	84	12.0	788	14.2	1,590	1,272	318	71	992
King George	301	25,859	1.05	328	12.5	166	6.3	1,564	7.0	3,651	3,240	412	285	1,107
King William	72	12,687	0.56	196	11.7	131	7.8	1,343	9.8	3,138	2,615	522	115	708
Lancaster	185	11,286	1.05	100	9.3	204	18.9	764	11.1	4,613	3,901	713	163	1,506
Lee	1,492	22,290	0.65	223	9.4	320	13.5	2,363	13.4	5,910	3,537	2,374	360	1,472
Loudoun	1,352	332,288	0.84	5,339	13.4	1,475	3.7	24,460	6.9	34,192	28,519	5,673	4,054	1,048

1. Per 1,000 estimated resident population.   2. Data for serious crimes have not been adjusted for underreporting; this may affect comparability between geographic areas and over time.
3. Per 100,000 population estimated by the FBI.

Items 32—45

Table B. States and Counties — Crime, Education, Money Income, and Poverty

STATE County	Serious crimes known to police, 2016 (cont.)[1] Rate		Education						Money income, 2012-2016				Income and poverty, 2016			
			School enrollment and attainment, 2012-2016				Local government expenditures,[5] 2013-2014			Households			Percent below poverty level			
			Enrollment[3]		Attainment[4] (percent)							Percent					
	Violent	Property	Total	Percent private	High school graduate or less	Bachelor's degree or more	Total current spending (mil dol)	Current spending per student (dollars)	Per capita income[6]	Median income (dollars)	with income of less than $50,000	with income of $200,000 or more	Median household income (dollars)	All persons	Children under 18 years	Children 5 to 17 years in families
	46	47	48	49	50	51	52	53	54	55	56	57	58	59	60	61
VERMONT— Cont'd																
Chittenden	163	2,101	46,416	22.0	26.4	49.4	383.9	17,782	34,658	66,414	37.5	6.0	67,833	9.6	8.8	8.1
Essex	16	229	1,159	12.8	59.9	15.9	13.7	20,344	22,191	39,467	59.2	0.8	40,813	15.7	24.5	23.1
Franklin	147	1,538	10,534	8.1	48.1	23.5	122.8	14,747	28,892	58,884	42.0	3.1	59,418	10.5	12.7	11.9
Grand Isle	15	644	1,407	15.8	34.7	34.9	12.1	12,514	35,613	64,295	37.5	5.3	65,601	8.8	13.4	12.1
Lamoille	63	683	5,834	11.2	34.8	36.4	61.6	16,381	29,180	53,316	47.7	4.6	56,207	12.1	14.1	12.3
Orange	14	274	6,072	16.1	43.6	30.2	65.9	16,278	28,691	54,263	45.4	2.4	54,272	10.6	13.6	12.5
Orleans	193	1,115	5,509	14.6	51.6	22.1	73.7	18,702	24,204	43,959	54.2	2.4	43,107	15.5	18.9	17.3
Rutland	162	1,256	13,703	15.0	43.7	29.2	150.5	19,619	27,795	50,029	50.0	2.3	50,569	13.3	16.5	14.9
Washington	127	1,735	13,536	27.8	35.0	40.5	145.1	16,816	31,464	58,171	42.9	3.6	55,803	10.8	13.0	11.5
Windham	111	1,744	9,089	26.3	39.1	35.3	107.5	17,838	28,923	50,917	49.0	3.3	47,074	12.7	17.9	16.7
Windsor	88	945	11,161	17.9	39.0	35.2	141.4	18,394	33,257	54,763	45.6	4.8	58,123	10.0	12.8	11.1
VIRGINIA	218	1,859	2,155,541	17.1	35.9	36.9	13,970.7	10,968	34,967	66,149	38.1	8.5	68,127	11.0	14.3	13.6
Accomack	204	1,551	5,981	13.5	60.0	18.3	51.1	9,731	23,337	38,503	60.4	2.3	39,040	20.0	31.8	29.4
Albemarle	101	1,384	30,134	15.8	26.4	51.5	(7)	(7)	38,039	70,342	35.2	10.3	73,132	8.5	9.4	8.9
Alleghany	265	820	3,068	16.5	53.5	16.3	26.3	10,648	25,220	45,538	54.1	1.4	47,037	14.9	21.7	18.6
Amelia	163	995	2,775	16.1	55.6	14.1	17.1	9,555	25,335	58,269	42.0	0.8	56,172	10.4	15.5	14.8
Amherst	133	916	7,035	27.0	52.2	18.9	43.4	10,115	23,372	47,002	52.4	1.4	46,497	14.3	20.9	18.3
Appomattox	123	870	3,527	13.9	51.8	19.6	19.9	8,505	24,902	52,134	48.2	1.6	51,431	13.9	19.6	19.0
Arlington	161	1,594	47,386	29.1	14.4	73.7	423.0	17,999	64,746	108,706	20.0	20.3	108,635	7.5	8.4	8.7
Augusta	100	991	14,615	20.4	52.0	23.3	98.5	9,234	28,601	56,802	42.9	3.3	56,784	9.2	12.4	11.4
Bath	227	432	853	21.7	53.9	15.4	9.9	15,608	28,210	44,985	61.4	0.5	47,059	11.7	17.7	17.6
Bedford	68	994	17,654	23.2	41.7	27.8	114.1	11,080	29,561	56,725	43.6	3.5	55,708	9.6	12.7	11.4
Bland	31	911	1,214	10.1	48.5	16.2	8.8	10,221	22,249	47,800	54.4	1.5	44,827	13.8	16.7	15.2
Botetourt	111	714	7,465	16.3	42.2	27.3	50.3	10,359	32,518	61,470	40.1	4.1	68,390	7.8	9.4	8.3
Brunswick	128	583	3,770	16.7	60.6	12.4	20.8	10,845	19,461	38,858	58.9	1.7	39,433	22.8	30.0	29.7
Buchanan	254	1,549	4,443	14.6	65.2	9.9	34.9	10,893	18,160	30,335	68.6	1.1	31,763	25.1	30.7	29.3
Buckingham	118	857	3,634	19.6	64.5	11.9	22.1	10,241	19,264	43,514	55.1	0.5	42,455	17.6	24.3	23.2
Campbell	224	1,365	12,296	26.7	48.6	20.4	73.4	8,801	25,219	47,005	52.0	2.2	49,935	13.3	18.4	16.0
Caroline	150	1,073	6,303	16.7	54.1	18.8	39.5	9,003	26,577	57,294	42.0	1.8	55,423	9.9	15.0	14.9
Carroll	85	1,468	5,479	10.1	54.5	12.8	40.0	9,972	21,484	37,048	62.8	0.8	40,390	16.3	22.6	21.0
Charles City	58	647	1,161	13.3	63.4	12.7	9.8	13,332	30,477	54,167	46.4	2.5	56,907	12.4	20.0	20.0
Charlotte	232	887	2,498	5.0	61.1	13.0	22.4	11,185	18,150	33,837	69.9	2.0	38,557	20.8	29.3	29.1
Chesterfield	143	1,951	91,335	15.3	32.3	37.7	524.1	8,855	33,848	73,869	31.6	6.7	76,260	7.0	9.3	8.8
Clarke	118	969	3,130	18.1	41.5	30.0	21.0	10,446	37,630	71,986	33.9	7.6	76,753	7.9	9.1	8.0
Craig	58	463	1,079	5.9	59.1	13.0	7.1	10,164	22,371	40,500	59.0	0.0	48,221	12.6	22.3	20.6
Culpeper	171	1,016	11,829	15.7	48.6	22.3	74.7	9,242	28,969	66,160	36.9	4.8	67,023	9.8	13.4	12.9
Cumberland	219	677	2,033	15.2	56.3	15.1	14.6	10,175	22,126	37,489	60.6	0.2	42,692	18.2	26.4	25.2
Dickenson	228	981	2,803	8.9	60.1	10.7	24.0	10,257	20,757	31,226	66.9	0.6	32,795	25.6	29.9	27.3
Dinwiddie	235	1,157	6,207	10.9	55.4	16.9	41.3	9,343	24,001	51,579	48.0	1.9	54,805	13.0	18.4	16.9
Essex	208	1,292	2,244	11.6	55.3	16.7	16.0	10,271	25,477	47,527	53.1	2.0	50,033	13.1	24.0	25.0
Fairfax	100	1,335	308,624	19.4	21.0	60.3	2,515.4	13,710	51,851	114,329	17.5	21.5	115,518	6.0	7.2	6.7
Fauquier	75	954	17,074	18.1	36.7	33.5	128.4	11,524	41,921	91,221	25.7	12.1	91,372	5.8	7.2	6.4
Floyd	192	659	2,849	26.9	51.9	17.7	19.1	9,133	24,121	47,288	53.4	2.7	42,670	13.7	17.2	15.9
Fluvanna	122	710	5,905	17.2	37.2	31.0	34.5	9,340	30,230	66,425	37.1	3.8	70,005	7.5	9.8	8.8
Franklin	172	1,288	12,047	25.0	48.0	20.6	72.5	9,794	26,188	48,720	50.9	2.6	52,424	13.2	18.4	16.3
Frederick	102	1,270	19,827	18.7	43.1	28.8	NA	NA	31,555	68,929	34.0	4.9	69,346	6.8	9.9	9.3
Giles	115	1,231	3,307	12.8	54.1	15.9	23.0	9,388	25,333	47,675	52.9	2.6	51,780	12.2	17.7	16.1
Gloucester	114	1,371	8,230	16.0	43.3	22.6	54.4	9,652	31,072	62,878	38.8	4.1	64,296	9.4	13.7	12.9
Goochland	103	778	4,756	32.1	37.2	36.1	26.9	10,971	45,995	82,326	28.2	14.5	88,815	6.4	8.6	7.9
Grayson	119	1,042	2,626	5.3	61.0	10.7	22.0	12,149	20,190	31,002	69.0	0.8	36,113	17.4	25.9	25.8
Greene	120	953	4,595	19.5	48.9	24.4	28.9	9,328	28,647	61,615	38.0	3.0	66,170	8.4	12.8	12.2
Greensville	85	842	2,311	10.4	65.3	8.5	NA	NA	15,988	40,559	60.5	0.6	41,539	25.4	26.6	26.8
Halifax	216	1,800	7,219	10.2	56.2	15.8	53.5	9,596	20,706	37,001	61.4	1.3	39,859	18.7	25.8	23.7
Hanover	128	1,234	26,960	17.9	34.1	36.7	164.1	8,984	35,881	81,170	29.0	7.0	83,405	5.8	6.5	6.0
Henrico	193	2,518	81,499	16.7	31.7	40.8	449.6	8,890	34,993	63,699	38.7	7.4	66,524	9.2	11.8	11.3
Henry	225	2,543	10,454	9.0	54.2	11.6	67.3	9,104	20,645	34,992	65.9	1.3	36,703	18.4	28.3	24.6
Highland	183	1,098	278	37.4	55.7	22.4	3.6	17,182	28,736	44,877	56.3	3.2	42,837	13.3	19.2	17.7
Isle of Wight	132	1,313	8,793	21.4	40.6	27.4	51.9	9,426	32,090	66,835	36.3	4.3	70,982	9.5	12.4	11.7
James City	120	1,554	17,260	14.6	25.7	47.8	(8)	(8)	41,314	80,226	29.5	9.1	84,035	6.5	9.4	8.8
King and Queen	252	741	1,347	18.6	55.7	19.2	10.4	12,657	25,392	48,852	51.4	1.4	52,115	13.4	18.7	17.8
King George	97	1,009	6,617	18.9	34.1	34.5	37.0	8,547	35,201	84,342	26.4	7.3	80,664	6.8	8.9	8.2
King William	99	610	4,049	14.8	49.8	18.6	30.7	10,089	29,311	64,297	34.5	3.0	68,053	7.7	11.5	10.6
Lancaster	185	1,321	1,838	7.1	41.5	29.7	14.7	11,704	32,013	50,118	49.9	4.5	44,941	14.0	27.0	27.1
Lee	78	1,395	4,857	9.0	59.3	11.6	33.8	9,941	17,820	31,577	67.3	1.2	32,466	29.9	37.5	33.6
Loudoun	119	929	109,768	17.4	19.7	58.8	883.4	12,485	48,578	125,672	14.8	23.1	134,609	3.5	3.5	3.2

1. Data for serious crimes have not been adjusted for underreporting; this may affect comparability between geographic areas and over time.   2. Per 100,000 population estimated by the FBI.
3. All persons 3 years old and over enrolled in nursery school through college.   4. Persons 25 years old and over.   5. Elementary and secondary education expenditures.
6. Based on population estimated by the American Community Survey, 2011–2015.   7. Charlottesville city is included with Albemarle county.   8. James City country is included with Williamsburg city.

Table B. States and Counties — Personal Income and Earnings

STATE County	Personal income, 2016										Earnings, 2016		
	Total (mil dol)	Percent change 2015-2016	Per capita[1] Dollars	Per capita[1] Rank	Wages and salaries (mil dol)	Supplements to wages and salaries, employer contributions (mil dol): Pension and insurance	Supplements: Government social insurance	Proprietors' income (mil dol)	Dividends, interest, and rent (mil dol)	Personal transfer receipts (mil dol)	Total (mil dol)	Contributions for government social insurance (mil dol): From employee and self-employed	Contributions: From employer
	62	63	64	65	66	67	68	69	70	71	72	73	74
VERMONT— Cont'd													
Chittenden	9,127	2.4	56,501	199	5,505	967	456	643	1,908	1,364	7,572	936	456
Essex	214	1.2	34,708	2,206	37	11	3	14	38	63	65	9	3
Franklin	2,063	2.3	42,178	1,079	829	184	71	114	304	404	1,197	149	71
Grand Isle	376	1.8	54,335	259	42	10	4	27	86	62	83	11	4
Lamoille	1,256	2.4	49,571	435	493	89	43	120	305	224	744	93	43
Orange	1,259	2.1	43,531	933	313	69	27	101	230	270	510	63	27
Orleans	1,110	1.1	41,324	1,194	406	90	37	88	193	333	621	81	37
Rutland	2,928	2.1	49,375	451	1,186	240	103	148	483	943	1,678	222	103
Washington	3,183	2.7	54,404	257	1,696	328	138	231	592	678	2,393	294	138
Windham	2,074	0.0	48,065	529	954	180	83	192	462	484	1,408	179	83
Windsor	2,952	1.9	53,186	299	1,076	217	93	214	716	597	1,599	204	93
VIRGINIA	445,462	2.0	52,941	X	230,876	37,393	16,796	24,091	90,057	61,446	309,156	18,691	16,796
Accomack	1,305	1.9	39,596	1,413	528	112	39	76	276	349	755	90	39
Albemarle	[2] 9,376	[2] 1.8	[2] 60,964	[2] 137	[2] 5,351	[2] 1,071	[2] 380	[2] 624	[2] 3,065	[2] 996	[2] 7,426	[2] 807	[2] 380
Alleghany	[3] 790	[3] 0.9	[3] 37,436	[3] 1,747	[3] 365	[3] 65	[3] 28	[3] 20	[3] 130	[3] 247	[3] 477	[3] 63	[3] 28
Amelia	523	0.9	40,530	1,297	99	19	7	48	75	119	173	20	7
Amherst	1,087	0.6	34,351	2,274	336	72	24	29	176	300	462	60	24
Appomattox	547	0.6	35,344	2,107	110	24	8	17	81	156	159	22	8
Arlington	20,241	3.1	87,986	22	16,952	2,507	1,233	1,180	4,232	953	21,872	2,457	1,233
Augusta	[4] 4,832	[4] 1.6	[4] 39,856	[4] 1,384	[4] 2,070	[4] 388	[4] 151	[4] 251	[4] 931	[4] 1,069	[4] 2,861	[4] 344	[4] 151
Bath	231	0.9	51,519	345	101	17	7	6	79	48	131	16	7
Bedford	3,281	0.9	42,082	1,093	787	135	58	132	631	699	1,112	146	58
Bland	217	-0.1	33,354	2,418	88	23	7	7	38	66	124	16	7
Botetourt	1,553	0.0	46,748	631	448	76	33	55	275	301	612	78	33
Brunswick	535	2.8	32,958	2,480	159	33	12	9	81	179	213	29	12
Buchanan	703	-3.1	31,677	2,659	296	62	22	26	98	302	406	56	22
Buckingham	471	0.9	27,637	2,996	138	35	10	20	72	142	203	25	10
Campbell	[5] 4,841	[5] 1.5	[5] 35,818	[5] 2,030	[5] 3,271	[5] 506	[5] 239	[5] 170	[5] 898	[5] 1,366	[5] 4,185	[5] 508	[5] 239
Caroline	1,247	2.1	41,318	1,197	247	56	18	20	179	235	342	44	18
Carroll	[6] 1,213	[6] 1.5	[6] 33,418	[6] 2,407	[6] 425	[6] 87	[6] 32	[6] 58	[6] 189	[6] 414	[6] 601	[6] 78	[6] 32
Charles City	286	0.4	40,464	1,304	73	13	5	7	53	67	98	13	5
Charlotte	403	2.3	33,255	2,435	116	26	8	16	71	127	166	22	8
Chesterfield	16,797	2.7	49,546	438	6,748	1,076	491	740	2,717	2,378	9,055	1,057	491
Clarke	850	2.6	59,162	161	185	29	13	46	222	108	273	32	13
Craig	179	-1.1	34,705	2,207	28	7	2	3	33	48	40	6	2
Culpeper	2,148	3.6	42,889	1,005	708	129	51	139	373	364	1,027	118	51
Cumberland	338	1.1	34,967	2,168	51	12	4	18	50	92	85	11	4
Dickenson	416	-1.9	27,807	2,987	138	31	10	10	55	191	190	28	10
Dinwiddie	[7] 2,984	[7] 1.5	[7] 38,356	[7] 1,597	[7] 1,316	[7] 246	[7] 98	[7] 84	[7] 545	[7] 857	[7] 1,745	[7] 215	[7] 98
Essex	438	1.6	39,383	1,439	143	26	11	11	84	113	190	25	11
Fairfax	[8] 89,413	[8] 1.3	[8] 75,978	[8] 44	[8] 57,980	[8] 6,777	[8] 3,949	[8] 4,778	[8] 20,578	[8] 6,052	[8] 73,485	[8] 8,360	[8] 3,949
Fauquier	4,410	2.2	63,854	104	1,164	188	82	250	1,094	461	1,684	189	82
Floyd	545	0.6	34,622	2,224	106	22	8	22	97	143	158	22	8
Fluvanna	1,073	1.9	40,825	1,256	182	42	13	34	220	199	271	35	13
Franklin	2,091	-0.1	37,300	1,771	543	100	41	102	430	525	786	104	41
Frederick	[9] 5,189	[9] 3.4	[9] 46,356	[9] 661	[9] 2,666	[9] 442	[9] 195	[9] 351	[9] 897	[9] 800	[9] 3,655	[9] 420	[9] 195
Giles	623	1.3	36,957	1,827	204	41	15	19	95	175	280	37	15
Gloucester	1,709	1.5	45,923	699	345	72	25	55	329	327	497	62	25
Goochland	1,974	1.0	87,084	23	1,445	150	89	61	577	191	1,745	196	89
Grayson	477	0.5	31,556	2,671	92	26	7	13	85	164	137	21	7
Greene	778	2.8	40,175	1,343	144	27	11	51	125	143	233	28	11
Greensville	[10] 532	[10] 1.9	[10] 31,247	[10] 2,712	[10] 300	[10] 65	[10] 22	[10] 6	[10] 77	[10] 169	[10] 392	[10] 48	[10] 22
Halifax	1,208	1.1	34,527	2,239	480	100	36	37	204	388	653	84	36
Hanover	5,788	2.7	55,447	225	2,370	339	172	430	961	749	3,311	381	172
Henrico	19,223	1.9	58,876	165	11,024	1,449	785	2,897	3,426	2,299	16,156	1,753	785
Henry	[11] 2,329	[11] 1.5	[11] 35,899	[11] 2,014	[11] 899	[11] 170	[11] 68	[11] 107	[11] 433	[11] 791	[11] 1,244	[11] 165	[11] 68
Highland	99	1.2	44,881	786	18	5	1	9	37	24	33	4	1
Isle of Wight	1,874	1.6	51,213	359	531	82	37	59	303	318	709	86	37
James City	[12] 5,344	[12] 2.0	[12] 59,632	[12] 153	[12] 1,806	[12] 325	[12] 131	[12] 279	[12] 1,440	[12] 799	[12] 2,541	[12] 295	[12] 131
King and Queen	284	10.5	39,615	1,410	42	9	3	10	41	67	63	9	3
King George	1,357	4.4	52,212	332	920	226	75	99	247	159	1,320	147	75
King William	712	2.4	43,562	924	183	30	13	32	102	131	259	32	13
Lancaster	569	1.8	51,821	341	179	30	13	32	213	143	254	33	13
Lee	677	0.6	28,013	2,979	169	46	13	14	103	277	241	35	13
Loudoun	27,486	4.8	71,218	62	10,824	1,425	747	1,256	3,625	1,407	14,252	1,583	747

1. Based on the resident population estimated as of July 1 of the year shown.   2. Charlottesville city is included with Albemarle county.   3. Covington city is included with Alleghany county.   4. Staunton and Waynesboro cities are included with Augusta county.   5. Lynchburg city is included with Campbell county.   6. Galax city is included with Carroll county.   7. Petersburg and Colonial Heights cities are included with Dinwiddie county.   8. Fairfax city and Falls Church city are included with Fairfax county.   9. Winchester city is included with Frederick county.   10. Emporia city is included with Greensville county.   11. Martinsville city is included with Henry county.   12. Williamsburg city is included with James City county.

Table B. States and Counties — Earnings, Social Security, and Housing

STATE County	Earnings, 2016 (cont.) — Percent by selected industries									Social Security beneficiaries, December 2016		Supplemental Security Income recipients, 2016	Housing units, 2017	
	Farm	Mining, quarrying, and extracting	Construction	Manufacturing	Information; professional, scientific, technical services	Retail trade	Finance, insurance, real estate, and leasing	Health care and social assistance	Government	Number	Rate[1]		Total	Percent change, 2010-2017
	75	76	77	78	79	80	81	82	83	84	85	86	87	88
VERMONT— Cont'd														
Chittenden	0.1	0.0	6.2	10.6	14.8	6.8	6.0	15.6	18.4	29,070	180	3,176	69,710	6.1
Essex	3.1	D	12.5	9.5	D	D	D	D	38.8	2,100	337	219	5,177	3.1
Franklin	1.4	0.2	5.8	17.1	D	7.8	2.0	13.1	29.9	8,970	183	1,236	22,588	4.6
Grand Isle	2.7	D	19.1	2.5	D	D	4.9	D	20.4	1,915	276	136	5,287	4.7
Lamoille	0.0	D	11.1	4.8	7.9	8.0	3.4	15.2	15.0	5,225	207	481	13,715	5.8
Orange	1.7	0.1	14.5	7.0	D	6.4	D	D	22.6	6,890	238	672	15,457	4.1
Orleans	1.7	D	10.1	12.5	D	9.8	3.5	16.4	21.4	7,560	283	986	17,567	8.7
Rutland	0.1	1.8	8.5	13.2	4.7	8.2	3.2	18.2	16.6	17,030	288	2,002	34,459	2.0
Washington	0.1	0.2	6.2	6.2	7.5	6.8	12.0	12.7	25.1	13,810	237	1,396	30,756	2.7
Windham	0.3	D	9.6	11.0	D	7.8	4.1	14.7	12.8	11,450	265	1,250	30,600	2.9
Windsor	0.1	0.2	9.3	6.9	10.9	6.9	3.8	12.1	25.2	15,275	277	1,261	34,910	2.3
VIRGINIA	0.0	0.1	5.6	5.7	19.7	5.1	6.7	9.2	24.2	1,471,294	175	156,608	3,512,877	4.4
Accomack	2.8	0.0	4.6	18.3	13.3	5.4	3.0	D	28.2	9,430	287	1,141	21,267	1.3
Albemarle	(2) -0.1	(2) 0.0	(2) 4.0	(2) 3.4	(2) 13.2	(2) 4.7	(2) 6.8	(2) 10.4	(2) 36.9	19,045	179	966	45,356	7.7
Alleghany	(3) -0.6	(3) D	(3) 6.6	(3) D	(3) D	5.2	2.0	D	17.1	4,630	301	303	8,025	-0.7
Amelia	11.6	D	14.7	9.1	D	5.2	2.0	D	29.9	3,245	253	303	5,572	3.9
Amherst	-1.0	0.0	8.3	21.5	3.2	7.8	2.2	D	28.1	8,330	263	839	14,182	1.5
Appomattox	-3.5	D	10.4	4.1	D	14.6	2.2	D	30.7	4,140	267	538	7,312	5.3
Arlington	0.0	D	1.4	D	33.9	1.7	4.6	3.6	18.8	19,620	85	2,246	114,026	8.2
Augusta	(4) 0.9	(4) D	(4) D	(4) 17.9	(4) 3.8	(4) 6.9	(4) 3.7	(4) D	(4) 18.8	18,445	247	661	32,552	4.4
Bath	-1.2	0.0	5.8	1.8	11.7	1.8	1.7	D	16.2	1,370	310	85	3,298	0.9
Bedford	-1.0	0.0	9.1	13.2	9.6	7.0	5.3	11.1	15.6	20,130	259	1,193	36,863	5.7
Bland	-3.4	D	3.0	33.9	0.0	D	D	D	28.9	1,915	296	122	3,315	1.5
Botetourt	-0.7	D	8.7	19.7	4.4	4.0	3.0	6.5	14.2	8,625	260	734	14,875	2.1
Brunswick	0.4	D	6.9	7.5	D	4.4	2.8	D	27.0	4,410	271	674	8,228	0.8
Buchanan	-0.1	26.5	6.6	4.9	D	5.6	2.9	8.3	21.0	8,455	383	1,658	11,564	-0.1
Buckingham	0.7	D	10.1	3.1	3.3	4.5	1.6	10.4	39.4	3,790	222	431	7,422	2.5
Campbell	(5) -0.1	(5) D	(5) D	(5) 20.3	(5) 10.0	(5) 6.4	(5) 6.2	(5) 17.2	(5) 10.8	13,660	248	1,117	25,829	4.3
Caroline	-2.5	D	7.0	5.9	D	4.5	1.6	D	34.5	6,065	202	473	12,253	4.4
Carroll	(6) 0.6	(6) D	(6) D	(6) 17.0	(6) 4.3	(6) 10.1	(6) 2.6	(6) D	(6) 22.3	8,705	293	558	16,742	0.9
Charles City	-2.1	D	16.1	18.0	D	D	D	D	20.2	2,010	286	122	3,358	4.0
Charlotte	-3.3	0.0	5.3	14.8	D	4.5	2.0	D	29.5	3,675	303	569	6,333	0.9
Chesterfield	0.0	D	8.5	8.5	10.1	8.3	6.7	10.3	16.9	59,150	175	4,334	130,375	6.4
Clarke	0.9	D	9.9	14.1	15.0	3.5	4.9	D	14.8	3,175	222	147	6,347	1.9
Craig	-7.5	0.0	6.6	D	D	6.8	6.3	D	33.0	1,455	283	109	2,903	3.5
Culpeper	-0.5	0.5	10.3	8.3	12.5	8.6	3.8	13.1	21.8	9,455	188	881	18,656	5.7
Cumberland	9.2	0.0	17.0	8.6	D	6.4	D	D	29.6	2,435	250	227	4,716	1.9
Dickenson	-1.3	32.4	7.0	1.0	D	6.3	D	7.3	23.7	5,410	360	881	7,569	-0.1
Dinwiddie	(7) -0.1	(7) D	(7) 6.7	(7) 7.9	(7) D	(7) 8.3	(7) 4.7	(7) D	(7) 23.4	6,230	222	470	11,741	2.7
Essex	-2.7	0.0	5.1	9.3	D	14.4	6.9	20.2	16.9	3,040	274	356	5,850	1.6
Fairfax	(8) 0.0	(8) 0.0	(8) 4.6	(8) 0.6	(8) 38.1	(8) 4.0	(8) 7.8	(8) 6.5	(8) 16.9	125,710	110	10,959	414,436	1.6
Fauquier	-1.0	0.3	13.7	3.2	16.6	7.8	7.1	9.8	21.1	11,950	174	579	26,832	4.7
Floyd	-1.8	D	10.0	13.2	D	6.2	5.5	12.7	22.7	4,215	269	289	8,046	3.2
Fluvanna	-1.3	D	13.1	2.5	5.1	3.7	2.7	D	31.6	5,850	224	235	10,937	5.1
Franklin	0.0	D	12.5	18.0	4.0	9.0	3.2	9.6	17.1	15,110	269	1,206	29,936	2.1
Frederick	(9) 0.0	(9) D	(9) D	(9) 13.7	(9) 8.6	(9) 7.1	(9) 2.0	(9) 17.6	17.9	16,325	193	910	34,241	9.3
Giles	-1.2	0.0	D	26.5	10.0	8.1	2.0	D	16.6	4,940	293	601	8,356	0.4
Gloucester	0.1	D	9.2	2.5	5.0	12.7	4.1	15.8	27.8	8,675	234	623	16,591	4.7
Goochland	-0.4	0.4	5.4	2.3	3.2	1.3	D	1.7	5.2	5,465	243	234	9,271	7.7
Grayson	-5.8	D	5.6	15.5	D	3.2	7.6	D	39.7	5,000	315	336	9,229	0.7
Greene	-0.6	D	13.3	1.4	13.1	10.5	2.4	D	22.3	3,855	199	245	8,289	10.4
Greensville	(10) 0.6	(10) D	(10) D	(10) D	(10) D	(10) 5.3	(10) D	(10) 14.5	(10) 29.2	2,555	221	55	4,189	2.5
Halifax	-0.7	D	6.6	17.8	3.0	6.1	2.4	17.6	18.9	10,635	304	1,533	18,188	1.0
Hanover	-0.1	0.1	12.0	7.2	6.2	8.9	3.9	12.1	9.8	20,590	197	951	41,356	7.8
Henrico	0.0	0.0	4.1	3.6	13.2	5.4	15.4	14.0	8.6	56,030	172	5,039	136,912	3.1
Henry	(11) 0.0	(11) 0.2	(11) D	(11) 20.5	(11) D	(11) 10.5	(11) 3.6	(11) D	(11) 18.3	17,090	331	2,406	26,204	-0.3
Highland	18.2	0.0	8.7	3.8	D	4.5	D	D	26.8	810	366	27	1,875	2.2
Isle of Wight	0.0	0.0	5.2	26.2	D	3.2	3.4	D	13.3	8,335	229	524	15,715	7.4
James City	(12) -0.1	(12) D	(12) 5.0	(12) 6.3	(12) 8.2	(12) 6.5	(12) 11.4	(12) 23.9	24.6	19,245	260	778	33,299	10.8
King and Queen	-1.1	D	13.2	11.4	D	D	D	D	24.6	1,900	269	160	3,499	2.5
King George	-0.2	D	1.9	5.6	19.5	1.9	1.3	1.3	62.0	3,815	147	264	10,092	6.5
King William	-1.2	D	7.7	27.8	4.6	6.4	4.0	D	17.1	3,525	215	202	6,943	6.5
Lancaster	-0.5	D	8.8	1.8	9.1	9.9	12.0	21.3	12.6	4,320	401	283	7,627	3.1
Lee	-3.1	3.4	7.0	2.0	1.7	9.2	2.8	13.1	44.3	7,235	301	1,604	11,776	0.3
Loudoun	0.0	D	10.0	5.8	29.3	5.0	5.4	5.8	14.5	32,370	84	2,014	132,965	21.5

1. Per 1,000 resident population estimated as of July 1 of the year shown. 2. Charlottesville city is included with Albemarle county. 3. Covington city is included with Alleghany county. 4. Staunton and Waynesboro cities are included with Augusta county. 5. Lynchburg city is included with Campbell county. 6. Galax city is included with Carroll county. 7. Petersburg and Colonial Heights cities are included with Dinwiddie county. 8. Fairfax city and Falls Church city are included with Fairfax county. 9. Winchester city is included with Frederick county. 10. Emporia city is included with Greensville county. 11. Martinsville city is included with Henry county. 12. Williamsburg city is included with James City county.

Table B. States and Counties — **Land Area and Population**

State / county code	CBSA code[1]	County code[2]	STATE County	Land area[3] (sq. mi)	Total persons 2017	Rank	Per square mile	White	Black	American Indian, Alaska Native	Asian and Pacific Islancer	Percent Hispanic or Latino[4]	Under 5 years	5 to 17 years	18 to 24 years	25 to 34 years	35 to 44 years	45 to 54 years
				1	2	3	4	5	6	7	8	9	10	11	12	13	14	15
			VIRGINIA— Cont'd															
51,109		8	Louisa	496.1	35,860	1,279	72.3	79.9	17.4	1.0	1.1	2.9	5.4	15.0	6.6	11.4	11.2	14.4
51,111		9	Lunenburg	431.7	12,235	2,276	28.3	61.3	34.3	0.9	0.7	4.5	5.1	13.7	6.7	12.0	12.2	13.3
51,113		8	Madison	320.6	13,277	2,216	41.4	87.3	10.6	0.9	1.1	2.7	5.1	15.3	6.9	10.7	10.5	13.4
51,115	47,260	1	Mathews	85.9	8,779	2,525	102.2	87.2	9.6	1.3	1.7	2.6	3.8	12.0	6.7	8.4	8.6	13.0
51,117		7	Mecklenburg	625.5	30,686	1,413	49.1	61.7	35.1	0.8	1.3	2.9	4.5	14.1	7.1	9.9	10.0	12.9
51,119		8	Middlesex	130.3	10,679	2,379	82.0	79.5	17.8	1.1	0.8	2.6	4.3	11.6	5.7	8.8	8.0	12.2
51,121	13,980	3	Montgomery	386.8	98,559	604	254.8	85.9	4.9	0.6	7.7	3.2	4.4	11.2	27.0	14.7	10.0	10.4
51,125	16,820	3	Nelson	470.8	14,943	2,101	31.7	82.9	12.5	0.9	1.0	4.3	4.1	14.2	6.1	9.3	10.0	12.9
51,127	40,060	1	New Kent	210.0	21,682	1,745	103.2	81.0	14.1	2.0	1.9	3.5	4.9	15.2	7.2	12.4	12.3	15.2
51,131		8	Northampton	211.7	11,846	2,303	56.0	55.6	35.3	0.9	1.2	8.8	5.2	14.6	6.3	10.4	9.3	11.5
51,133		9	Northumberland	191.4	12,275	2,272	64.1	70.5	25.8	0.8	0.7	3.7	3.7	11.3	5.3	8.1	7.6	10.6
51,135		6	Nottoway	314.4	15,434	2,070	49.1	55.5	39.8	1.0	1.0	4.3	5.3	14.2	8.2	14.3	11.7	13.6
51,137		6	Orange	341.1	36,073	1,271	105.8	80.3	14.5	1.0	1.8	4.9	5.5	15.7	7.1	11.7	11.3	13.9
51,139		6	Page	310.0	23,731	1,653	76.6	95.2	2.5	0.6	0.8	2.0	5.1	14.9	6.8	11.2	11.4	14.5
51,141		8	Patrick	483.0	17,665	1,938	36.6	90.7	6.3	0.6	0.5	3.0	3.7	13.6	6.4	8.8	10.4	14.6
51,143	19,260	4	Pittsylvania	969.0	61,258	855	63.2	75.2	22.1	0.6	0.8	2.6	4.2	15.0	7.1	10.3	10.7	14.6
51,145	40,060	1	Powhatan	260.2	28,601	1,467	109.9	86.9	10.4	0.7	1.0	2.2	4.2	14.2	7.6	10.5	12.6	17.0
51,147		6	Prince Edward	350.0	22,703	1,688	64.9	62.8	33.7	0.7	2.0	2.5	5.0	11.6	25.5	10.8	8.7	10.4
51,149	40,060	1	Prince George	265.2	37,809	1,228	142.6	57.4	33.2	1.2	3.4	7.9	5.4	16.0	8.9	16.0	14.7	13.2
51,153	47,900	1	Prince William	335.8	463,023	150	1,378.9	46.2	22.6	0.9	10.8	23.6	7.5	19.8	8.7	13.7	15.3	14.6
51,155	13,980	3	Pulaski	319.8	34,184	1,320	106.9	92.3	6.0	0.6	0.8	1.8	4.7	13.1	7.1	11.3	11.3	14.9
51,157	47,900	1	Rappahannock	266.4	7,321	2,638	27.5	90.7	5.4	1.0	1.4	3.8	3.9	13.1	6.6	9.4	9.1	13.7
51,159		9	Richmond	191.5	8,939	2,510	46.7	62.3	30.5	0.9	1.1	7.3	4.0	12.9	7.1	13.8	13.1	14.1
51,161	40,220	2	Roanoke	250.5	93,730	629	374.2	87.3	6.8	0.6	4.0	3.1	4.7	15.5	7.9	11.1	11.7	14.1
51,163		6	Rockbridge	596.5	22,659	1,695	38.0	93.5	4.1	1.3	0.9	1.8	4.5	12.9	7.7	10.4	9.8	13.2
51,165	25,500	3	Rockingham	849.7	80,227	700	94.4	90.0	2.6	0.5	1.1	7.0	5.6	16.5	9.0	11.6	11.6	13.2
51,167		7	Russell	473.5	27,048	1,524	57.1	97.2	1.1	0.5	0.3	1.4	4.7	14.2	6.9	10.8	12.0	13.9
51,169	28,700	2	Scott	535.8	21,865	1,731	40.8	97.4	1.1	0.6	0.4	1.3	4.1	13.9	6.8	10.7	11.5	14.1
51,171		6	Shenandoah	508.0	43,225	1,110	85.1	89.1	3.1	0.7	1.2	7.4	5.5	15.6	7.2	11.4	10.9	13.8
51,173		7	Smyth	451.4	30,656	1,416	67.9	95.0	2.7	0.6	0.6	2.1	4.7	14.7	7.3	11.0	11.7	14.4
51,175		6	Southampton	599.1	17,750	1,930	29.6	62.6	35.6	0.9	0.7	1.8	4.3	14.5	7.2	10.5	10.7	16.4
51,177	47,900	1	Spotsylvania	401.5	133,033	478	331.3	71.0	17.5	0.9	3.9	9.8	6.2	18.7	8.5	12.5	12.7	14.8
51,179	47,900	1	Stafford	269.2	146,649	445	544.8	65.0	19.9	1.1	5.1	12.8	6.4	19.9	9.8	13.4	13.6	15.3
51,181		8	Surry	278.9	6,540	2,708	23.4	54.1	43.6	0.9	0.9	2.3	4.2	13.1	7.1	10.7	9.0	15.1
51,183	40,060	1	Sussex	490.2	11,373	2,328	23.2	39.9	57.1	0.6	0.6	3.0	4.3	11.3	9.4	18.1	12.2	14.1
51,185	14,140	5	Tazewell	518.8	41,095	1,151	79.2	95.0	3.8	0.5	0.9	1.0	5.0	14.3	6.9	11.1	12.3	13.3
51,187	47,900	1	Warren	214.5	39,563	1,188	184.4	89.1	5.9	1.0	1.8	4.5	6.0	16.1	8.3	12.8	11.6	14.8
51,191	28,700	2	Washington	561.2	54,387	931	96.9	96.1	1.9	0.5	0.8	1.6	4.6	14.0	8.1	10.3	11.6	13.8
51,193		6	Westmoreland	229.4	17,780	1,927	77.5	66.2	27.3	1.2	1.3	6.5	5.5	13.4	6.5	11.5	9.6	12.3
51,195	13,720	7	Wise	403.4	38,586	1,213	95.7	92.2	6.5	0.5	0.6	1.3	5.2	14.5	9.4	13.7	12.4	13.3
51,197		6	Wythe	461.9	28,882	1,459	62.5	95.0	3.7	0.6	0.8	1.3	4.9	15.0	6.7	11.0	11.6	14.9
51,199	47,260	1	York	104.7	67,739	786	647.0	73.8	14.6	0.9	7.6	6.5	5.5	18.3	8.8	12.0	12.6	13.7
			Independent cities															
51,510	47,900	1	Alexandria city	14.9	160,035	406	10,740.6	53.8	23.5	0.7	8.0	16.6	7.2	10.9	5.9	22.1	18.6	13.5
51,520	28,700	2	Bristol city	12.9	16,790	1,991	1,301.6	90.2	7.1	0.7	1.6	2.4	5.2	15.2	7.0	13.4	11.8	13.1
51,530		6	Buena Vista city	6.4	6,327	2,728	988.6	89.7	6.4	1.6	1.5	2.8	3.5	15.3	14.2	12.5	10.3	12.6
51,540	16,820	3	Charlottesville city	10.2	48,019	1,020	4,707.7	68.0	19.6	0.6	9.0	5.6	5.7	10.3	19.8	20.5	12.0	10.3
51,550	47,260	1	Chesapeake city	338.5	240,397	280	710.2	60.1	31.2	1.0	5.0	6.2	6.4	17.9	8.6	14.2	13.4	13.5
51,570	40,060	1	Colonial Heights city	7.5	17,830	1,926	2,377.3	74.0	16.7	1.0	5.0	5.9	7.3	16.6	8.0	12.4	11.3	12.2
51,580		6	Covington city	5.5	5,531	2,793	1,005.6	83.3	14.5	0.9	1.4	2.2	3.2	15.4	8.0	11.7	11.3	14.1
51,590	19,260	4	Danville city	42.8	41,130	1,148	961.0	43.7	51.2	0.6	1.5	4.4	6.4	15.7	8.5	12.7	10.0	11.9
51,595		6	Emporia city	6.9	5,282	2,817	765.5	29.1	63.0	0.6	1.4	6.8	3.8	19.3	7.3	13.1	11.0	12.7
51,600	47,900	1	Fairfax city	6.2	24,097	1,639	3,886.6	58.6	6.5	0.8	19.6	17.2	9.6	14.2	8.9	13.3	12.9	14.0
51,610	47,900	1	Falls Church city	2.0	14,583	2,124	7,291.5	74.6	5.2	0.8	11.6	11.3	7.0	18.3	7.4	11.9	14.1	15.2
51,620		6	Franklin city	8.2	8,176	2,582	997.1	38.7	58.4	0.8	1.2	2.6	6.0	17.9	7.0	13.2	9.6	12.4
51,630	47,900	1	Fredericksburg city	10.5	28,360	1,480	2,701.0	62.7	25.2	1.0	4.3	10.6	6.8	14.0	19.9	15.5	11.8	11.2
51,640		7	Galax city	8.2	6,625	2,702	807.9	77.7	7.2	0.6	1.1	15.3	5.6	16.2	8.6	11.0	10.7	13.5
51,650	47,260	1	Hampton city	51.5	134,669	470	2,614.9	41.2	51.9	1.5	3.7	5.7	5.9	15.1	11.9	15.8	11.0	11.7
51,660	25,500	3	Harrisonburg city	17.3	54,215	934	3,133.8	68.2	8.4	0.5	5.4	19.8	5.6	11.2	31.9	15.1	10.6	8.7
51,670	40,060	1	Hopewell city	10.3	22,621	1,697	2,196.2	49.1	43.0	1.1	2.1	7.7	7.8	18.1	8.2	14.4	11.6	12.1
51,678		6	Lexington city	2.5	7,106	2,660	2,842.4	83.9	9.8	0.9	4.6	3.5	1.6	7.9	45.4	8.4	6.1	6.8
51,680	31,340	2	Lynchburg city	49.0	80,995	697	1,653.0	64.4	29.5	0.7	3.5	4.0	6.2	13.2	25.0	13.8	8.6	9.1
51,683	47,900	1	Manassas city	9.8	41,501	1,141	4,234.8	43.1	15.0	0.7	6.8	37.0	8.5	18.3	9.1	15.2	14.4	13.3
51,685	47,900	1	Manassas Park city	2.5	16,591	2,002	6,636.4	35.3	14.4	0.7	12.3	39.6	4.8	19.4	9.0	17.2	16.2	15.4

1. CBSA = Core Based Statistical Area. See Appendix A for explanation. See Appendix B for list of metropolitan areas with component counties.   2. County type code from the Economic Research Service of USDA Rural-Urban Continuum Codes. See Appendix A for definition.   3. Dry land or land partially or temporarily covered by water.   4. May be of any race.

Table B. States and Counties — **Population and Households**

| | Population, 2017 (cont.) | | | | Population change, 2000-2017 | | | | | | | Households, 2012-2016 | | | | |
| | Age (percent) (cont.) | | | | Total persons | | Percent change | | Components of change, 2010-2017 | | | | | Percent | | |
STATE County	55 to 64 years	65 to 74 years	75 years and over	Percent female	2000	2010	2000-2010	2010-2017	Births	Deaths	Net Migration	Number	Persons per house-hold	Family house-holds	Female family house-holder[1]	One person
	16	17	18	19	20	21	22	23	24	25	26	27	28	29	30	31
VIRGINIA— Cont'd																
Louisa	16.6	12.2	7.1	50.6	25,627	33,168	29.4	8.1	2,711	2,178	2,151	13,146	2.60	72.0	9.8	22.5
Lunenburg	15.5	12.8	8.7	47.1	13,146	12,916	-1.7	-5.3	873	1,085	-474	4,670	2.46	68.4	14.9	28.2
Madison	16.4	12.6	9.1	51.6	12,520	13,309	6.3	-0.2	918	965	22	5,042	2.56	70.5	12.8	25.1
Mathews	16.7	17.4	13.4	51.7	9,207	8,976	-2.5	-2.2	438	845	218	3,837	2.28	70.6	7.4	25.3
Mecklenburg	16.3	14.5	10.7	51.5	32,380	32,721	1.1	-6.2	2,050	3,185	-904	12,066	2.49	63.6	14.5	33.0
Middlesex	18.3	17.8	13.3	51.4	9,932	10,959	10.3	-2.6	635	1,062	156	4,474	2.31	67.2	9.5	28.8
Montgomery	10.1	7.1	5.1	48.1	83,629	94,421	12.9	4.4	6,390	4,389	2,148	35,701	2.47	54.4	6.6	27.5
Nelson	16.9	16.6	9.8	51.3	14,445	15,015	3.9	-0.5	954	1,284	266	6,378	2.31	64.0	15.0	28.1
New Kent	16.1	11.7	5.1	48.9	13,462	18,432	36.9	17.6	1,382	1,061	2,893	7,537	2.59	76.3	10.6	20.5
Northampton	17.0	14.8	10.9	51.9	13,093	12,389	-5.4	-4.4	954	1,390	-103	5,075	2.32	61.8	18.1	32.2
Northumberland	17.5	20.5	15.5	50.8	12,259	12,331	0.6	-0.5	654	1,237	532	5,776	2.12	68.3	8.7	27.8
Nottoway	13.8	10.4	8.3	45.8	15,725	15,852	0.8	-2.6	1,210	1,450	-176	5,676	2.46	64.4	18.4	33.0
Orange	14.4	11.6	8.7	51.3	25,881	33,554	29.6	7.5	2,754	2,568	2,331	13,245	2.59	72.3	11.6	24.6
Page	15.0	12.2	8.8	50.7	23,177	24,050	3.8	-1.3	1,700	2,067	69	9,523	2.47	69.1	12.0	23.8
Patrick	16.5	14.6	11.3	50.6	19,407	18,495	-4.7	-4.5	977	1,863	73	7,805	2.29	66.0	9.9	30.2
Pittsylvania	16.1	13.0	9.0	50.8	61,745	63,476	2.8	-3.5	3,787	5,098	-894	26,327	2.33	69.1	13.5	28.1
Powhatan	16.1	11.6	6.2	48.3	22,377	28,062	25.4	1.9	1,691	1,469	319	9,866	2.60	78.8	9.0	18.1
Prince Edward	11.8	8.8	7.5	50.4	19,720	23,357	18.4	-2.8	1,594	1,616	-648	7,294	2.54	63.4	13.6	29.2
Prince George	12.1	8.4	5.3	45.9	33,047	35,706	8.0	5.9	2,781	1,665	952	11,191	3.01	77.3	11.1	19.6
Prince William	11.1	6.2	3.3	50.0	280,813	401,994	43.2	15.2	48,519	12,488	24,755	138,102	3.18	77.2	11.4	18.4
Pulaski	15.3	13.4	9.0	50.0	35,127	34,859	-0.8	-1.9	2,292	3,079	138	14,553	2.30	68.2	11.7	27.2
Rappahannock	17.6	16.3	10.2	50.6	6,983	7,503	7.4	-2.4	423	520	-84	3,247	2.28	69.4	5.7	26.6
Richmond	13.6	10.8	10.5	44.4	8,809	9,254	5.1	-3.4	499	753	-70	3,084	2.28	68.9	15.0	25.4
Roanoke	14.3	11.8	9.0	51.9	85,778	92,474	7.8	1.4	5,863	7,055	2,514	38,322	2.39	67.6	10.7	28.2
Rockbridge	16.2	14.1	11.2	50.5	20,808	22,349	7.4	1.4	1,303	1,758	781	9,277	2.40	66.5	8.2	27.0
Rockingham	13.9	10.3	8.3	50.9	67,725	76,314	12.7	5.1	6,074	5,111	3,024	29,883	2.57	71.5	9.5	23.4
Russell	16.5	12.2	8.6	50.8	30,308	28,899	-4.6	-6.4	1,859	2,586	-1,120	10,937	2.51	64.5	8.7	32.8
Scott	15.4	13.2	10.3	49.7	23,403	23,174	-1.0	-5.6	1,342	2,218	-424	9,104	2.38	69.7	9.5	27.8
Shenandoah	14.4	12.0	9.2	51.1	35,075	41,996	19.7	2.9	3,336	3,402	1,321	17,222	2.46	67.8	9.8	28.1
Smyth	14.6	12.0	9.5	51.1	33,081	32,213	-2.6	-4.8	2,171	3,121	-584	12,930	2.38	67.1	11.6	28.9
Southampton	16.9	11.4	8.2	48.0	17,482	18,570	6.2	-4.4	1,133	1,345	-615	6,727	2.50	73.4	16.8	23.0
Spotsylvania	12.9	8.5	5.2	50.9	90,395	122,449	35.5	8.6	11,503	5,936	5,078	43,105	2.99	77.0	11.9	18.5
Stafford	11.7	6.5	3.6	49.6	92,446	128,965	39.5	13.7	12,237	4,880	10,326	44,311	3.07	81.2	11.7	15.0
Surry	19.2	13.1	8.5	50.6	6,829	7,065	3.5	-7.4	433	523	-438	2,707	2.49	74.8	15.6	20.0
Sussex	13.6	9.8	7.2	40.3	12,504	12,070	-3.5	-5.8	718	975	-448	3,793	1.75	64.0	19.8	31.7
Tazewell	15.4	12.9	8.8	50.3	44,598	45,073	1.1	-8.8	3,165	4,519	-2,626	17,595	2.38	68.2	10.3	28.3
Warren	14.9	9.6	5.9	49.9	31,584	37,430	18.5	5.7	3,360	2,601	1,367	14,174	2.68	72.3	13.8	22.7
Washington	15.5	12.8	9.3	50.9	51,103	54,959	7.5	-1.0	3,627	4,430	254	22,512	2.35	66.1	10.7	30.2
Westmoreland	16.3	14.7	10.2	51.3	16,718	17,454	4.4	1.9	1,388	1,540	484	7,124	2.44	62.1	9.5	31.0
Wise	14.0	10.7	6.8	47.8	40,123	41,428	3.3	-6.9	3,094	3,606	-2,354	15,225	2.44	67.4	15.1	27.9
Wythe	14.7	12.1	9.0	51.2	27,599	29,235	5.9	-1.2	2,039	2,640	274	12,039	2.40	66.0	8.3	29.8
York	13.4	9.1	6.5	50.9	56,297	65,263	15.9	3.8	4,640	3,038	861	23,872	2.76	78.4	11.1	17.5
Independent cities																
Alexandria city	10.8	7.0	4.1	51.8	128,283	140,006	9.1	14.3	20,089	5,372	5,286	68,063	2.20	48.5	8.6	41.6
Bristol city	13.3	11.4	9.4	52.7	17,367	17,744	2.2	-5.4	1,299	1,882	-368	7,671	2.21	63.3	16.2	32.3
Buena Vista city	12.4	10.6	8.4	53.4	6,349	6,617	4.2	-4.4	411	537	-173	2,709	2.27	65.7	11.0	29.3
Charlottesville city	10.2	6.9	4.3	51.5	45,049	43,428	-3.6	10.6	3,925	1,965	2,636	17,980	2.39	46.7	10.8	34.4
Chesapeake city	13.1	7.9	4.9	51.3	199,184	222,306	11.6	8.1	20,967	12,251	9,441	82,573	2.74	74.7	15.1	21.1
Colonial Heights city	12.5	10.1	9.7	53.6	16,897	17,410	3.0	2.4	1,689	1,607	345	7,206	2.41	63.6	15.7	31.3
Covington city	14.7	12.3	9.4	51.5	6,303	5,954	-5.5	-7.1	298	558	-159	2,472	2.25	58.7	14.5	36.5
Danville city	14.3	11.1	9.4	53.7	48,411	43,074	-11.0	-4.5	3,845	4,922	-843	18,653	2.19	58.0	19.9	37.1
Emporia city	13.4	9.4	10.0	54.3	5,665	5,925	4.6	-10.9	338	566	-416	2,210	2.41	65.5	27.7	32.4
Fairfax city	12.5	8.5	6.1	50.5	21,498	22,542	4.9	6.9	2,963	1,457	30	8,476	2.72	70.0	10.0	19.8
Falls Church city	13.5	8.0	4.7	50.5	10,377	12,282	18.4	18.7	1,296	502	1,481	5,301	2.56	61.6	9.8	33.2
Franklin city	14.6	11.0	8.4	54.6	8,346	8,580	2.8	-4.7	722	880	-246	3,424	2.42	64.3	25.9	33.4
Fredericksburg city	10.1	6.4	4.5	53.8	19,279	24,178	25.4	17.3	2,975	1,363	2,474	10,271	2.45	53.5	18.5	37.6
Galax city	13.5	10.5	10.5	53.7	6,837	6,989	2.2	-5.2	615	823	-157	2,767	2.33	62.7	15.3	34.9
Hampton city	13.6	8.8	6.2	52.0	146,437	137,384	-6.2	-2.0	12,874	8,733	-6,881	53,656	2.47	61.0	18.6	31.7
Harrisonburg city	7.8	5.0	4.2	52.1	40,468	48,909	20.9	10.8	4,268	1,867	2,859	16,626	2.68	51.3	11.9	28.9
Hopewell city	12.4	8.7	6.6	53.4	22,354	22,602	1.1	0.1	2,524	2,034	-472	8,866	2.49	61.9	22.0	32.6
Lexington city	7.5	8.4	7.9	43.6	6,867	7,033	2.4	1.0	186	452	335	1,856	1.91	42.7	8.4	49.2
Lynchburg city	9.7	7.6	6.8	53.1	65,269	75,532	15.7	7.2	7,728	5,655	3,387	28,282	2.41	57.6	16.4	33.0
Manassas city	11.6	6.2	3.4	49.9	35,135	37,819	7.6	9.7	5,044	1,378	-34	12,430	3.31	76.2	11.8	19.3
Manassas Park city	10.2	4.8	2.9	48.6	10,290	14,241	38.4	16.5	1,235	252	1,324	4,730	3.35	72.3	11.9	20.8

1. No spouse present.

Table B. States and Counties — Housing, Labor Force, and Employment

STATE County	Housing units, 2017 (cont.) Occupied units Owner-occupied Total	Percent	Median value[1]	Median owner cost as a percent of income With a mortgage	Without a mortgage[2]	Renter-occupied Median rent[3]	Median rent as a percent of income[2]	Sub-standard units[4] (percent)	Civilian labor force, 2017 Total	Percent change, 2016-2017	Unemployment Total	Rate[5]	Civilian employment[6], 2012-2016 Total	Percent Management, business, science, and arts	Construction, production, and maintenance occupations
	89	90	91	92	93	94	95	96	97	98	99	100	101	102	103
VIRGINIA— Cont'd															
Louisa	13,146	78.3	202,100	22.2	12.4	940	29.2	2.1	19,087	2.9	667	3.5	15,886	34.5	26.0
Lunenburg	4,670	71.1	109,200	24.2	10.5	680	28.2	3.5	5,198	-0.9	227	4.4	4,517	24.9	34.5
Madison	5,042	72.5	241,300	26.0	12.2	752	29.2	4.4	7,290	1.8	215	2.9	5,976	33.7	25.6
Mathews	3,837	84.6	232,000	19.8	11.1	928	29.7	0.3	4,093	1.5	155	3.8	4,077	34.8	27.1
Mecklenburg	12,066	71.8	123,300	23.5	12.0	702	26.6	1.4	12,150	-2.4	638	5.3	12,547	32.5	24.8
Middlesex	4,474	82.2	248,800	26.7	10.0	776	25.1	1.6	5,194	3.4	177	3.4	4,384	30.8	23.7
Montgomery	35,701	53.6	202,900	19.7	10.0	885	33.8	1.8	49,863	0.4	1,911	3.8	46,610	45.4	13.4
Nelson	6,378	72.9	231,500	23.8	10.4	669	25.2	2.4	7,354	1.8	257	3.5	6,778	33.1	25.7
New Kent	7,537	84.1	249,100	20.4	10.0	889	26.3	1.6	11,857	1.7	382	3.2	10,099	36.0	22.2
Northampton	5,075	67.2	164,600	21.5	14.3	729	32.7	1.7	5,403	-7.9	316	5.8	4,741	31.3	26.3
Northumberland	5,776	86.4	256,400	23.8	10.9	675	31.6	2.8	5,364	-1.4	292	5.4	4,933	34.3	22.7
Nottoway	5,676	63.0	125,500	22.2	11.6	770	34.7	5.2	6,985	-0.6	277	4.0	5,732	24.2	30.7
Orange	13,245	78.0	236,100	22.6	10.9	877	31.4	2.9	16,539	1.2	636	3.8	15,787	34.1	26.0
Page	9,523	70.5	171,300	22.9	10.7	700	28.3	2.3	11,640	0.5	617	5.3	10,543	25.7	28.6
Patrick	7,805	77.1	115,300	22.3	10.4	556	31.5	2.7	7,429	-6.5	335	4.5	7,367	26.7	40.5
Pittsylvania	26,327	76.3	114,400	21.4	10.2	652	27.5	1.6	29,542	-0.4	1,341	4.5	27,639	26.3	33.2
Powhatan	9,866	88.6	254,200	21.7	10.0	937	23.1	1.3	13,858	1.8	464	3.3	13,285	40.2	21.4
Prince Edward	7,294	64.6	151,200	23.6	10.0	743	27.5	2.2	10,306	1.6	514	5.0	9,183	29.2	19.9
Prince George	11,191	68.5	205,400	20.6	10.0	1,263	31.5	1.5	15,149	1.6	672	4.4	14,498	37.0	23.1
Prince William	138,102	71.2	345,900	22.5	10.0	1,581	31.1	3.6	239,833	2.2	8,166	3.4	225,941	43.4	16.3
Pulaski	14,553	71.8	136,700	19.5	10.3	620	24.5	1.2	16,260	0.1	870	5.4	15,467	30.0	31.7
Rappahannock	3,247	74.3	362,100	22.7	12.5	1,046	31.2	1.1	3,745	1.1	130	3.5	3,554	37.8	19.2
Richmond	3,084	73.2	153,300	23.0	11.0	815	31.5	1.8	3,893	-0.3	147	3.8	3,134	30.4	29.5
Roanoke	38,322	74.3	189,800	20.7	10.1	894	24.5	1.1	49,144	0.2	1,695	3.4	45,611	40.2	17.3
Rockbridge	9,277	77.4	193,300	23.1	10.0	685	30.9	1.8	10,588	1.3	433	4.1	10,184	33.3	28.1
Rockingham	29,883	74.1	200,900	22.0	10.0	826	27.4	2.6	40,837	0.8	1,336	3.3	38,083	31.7	28.4
Russell	10,937	77.8	94,100	23.7	10.0	544	30.7	1.3	11,056	-1.5	609	5.5	10,527	31.1	29.3
Scott	9,104	76.7	92,200	19.1	10.5	517	33.0	2.2	9,393	-0.2	384	4.1	8,391	23.8	32.6
Shenandoah	17,222	70.8	200,100	22.8	10.5	770	30.6	3.0	21,027	1.1	745	3.5	20,212	29.0	32.9
Smyth	12,930	70.1	91,100	18.8	11.1	572	27.5	1.4	13,117	-4.0	706	5.4	12,870	28.1	32.6
Southampton	6,727	68.5	161,500	22.3	10.3	741	32.6	2.2	8,845	-2.0	333	3.8	7,805	30.6	29.5
Spotsylvania	43,105	77.1	252,900	22.1	10.0	1,368	32.1	1.8	66,131	2.0	2,466	3.7	63,469	39.2	18.8
Stafford	44,311	75.2	314,800	21.1	10.0	1,466	32.0	1.3	69,689	2.2	2,524	3.6	65,669	47.2	14.1
Surry	2,707	81.7	166,600	21.7	11.7	829	30.4	2.3	3,708	1.5	168	4.5	3,165	26.1	39.7
Sussex	3,793	64.8	128,300	23.1	12.7	736	30.0	0.8	3,917	-0.7	233	5.9	2,941	26.1	29.5
Tazewell	17,595	75.1	94,400	19.9	11.8	610	26.7	1.2	15,866	-0.4	939	5.9	16,179	30.1	29.1
Warren	14,174	75.8	223,300	22.2	10.0	939	29.3	1.4	20,033	1.8	743	3.7	18,623	32.7	27.6
Washington	22,512	76.3	136,600	20.6	10.3	626	27.6	1.1	26,908	0.4	1,104	4.1	24,377	35.7	23.3
Westmoreland	7,124	77.3	198,300	24.7	11.4	1,012	31.9	1.2	9,004	0.4	423	4.7	7,543	33.1	22.9
Wise	15,225	68.6	86,000	18.7	11.3	634	36.1	1.5	12,986	-1.5	880	6.8	13,661	34.1	27.7
Wythe	12,039	71.8	128,200	21.1	10.0	617	29.0	1.4	13,646	0.0	711	5.2	12,719	27.1	27.3
York	23,872	72.1	314,400	21.5	10.0	1,403	28.8	1.1	32,591	1.6	1,161	3.6	30,075	49.0	15.2
Independent cities															
Alexandria city	68,063	42.2	520,700	21.8	11.0	1,611	28.2	4.1	98,590	2.4	2,829	2.9	93,357	58.3	8.6
Bristol city	7,671	57.7	109,100	20.4	14.0	669	31.0	2.3	7,471	0.4	341	4.6	7,490	33.6	21.1
Buena Vista city	2,709	59.4	112,400	28.3	15.4	709	36.5	2.7	3,316	1.4	145	4.4	2,842	17.0	38.1
Charlottesville city	17,980	42.2	280,100	21.1	10.0	1,030	31.7	1.4	25,558	2.9	791	3.1	24,137	48.9	9.7
Chesapeake city	82,573	70.1	256,500	24.3	11.8	1,180	31.6	1.4	119,577	1.5	4,624	3.9	107,985	39.3	20.3
Colonial Heights city	7,206	60.4	166,800	23.4	10.0	965	32.3	1.7	8,849	1.7	361	4.1	7,790	34.3	19.7
Covington city	2,472	75.1	70,900	18.2	12.6	590	28.4	3.4	2,379	0.0	149	6.3	2,211	17.5	32.3
Danville city	18,653	54.0	90,800	20.9	11.6	602	28.1	2.8	19,140	0.3	1,151	6.0	16,797	30.5	25.2
Emporia city	2,210	39.5	122,600	25.3	13.6	705	34.2	4.4	2,278	1.6	125	5.5	1,917	30.6	27.8
Fairfax city	8,476	70.7	487,700	21.2	10.3	1,750	30.4	2.9	13,251	2.3	387	2.9	12,509	51.9	9.9
Falls Church city	5,301	59.6	724,000	21.8	10.0	1,569	29.1	2.4	8,160	2.4	219	2.7	7,682	69.5	3.8
Franklin city	3,424	49.7	171,700	26.0	17.4	850	32.4	1.2	3,484	-1.4	193	5.5	3,488	30.4	22.8
Fredericksburg city	10,271	34.8	321,500	19.6	10.0	1,096	30.3	2.2	13,823	2.1	601	4.3	13,919	46.4	9.3
Galax city	2,767	56.5	101,600	24.3	11.5	542	29.3	3.8	2,879	-0.7	130	4.5	2,881	21.3	35.1
Hampton city	53,656	56.2	187,700	24.3	12.3	1,032	33.6	5.1	64,727	1.3	3,292	5.1	61,278	33.1	23.8
Harrisonburg city	16,626	37.4	197,400	21.8	10.0	834	32.6	4.9	24,559	1.5	1,097	4.5	25,148	32.6	19.7
Hopewell city	8,866	50.1	125,400	19.4	14.4	820	29.2	3.1	9,931	1.7	605	6.1	9,362	23.5	31.0
Lexington city	1,856	56.1	230,500	27.5	13.8	765	33.9	0.0	2,265	0.1	128	5.7	2,251	52.2	9.9
Lynchburg city	28,282	50.5	149,600	21.0	11.3	782	33.1	1.5	35,820	1.0	1,777	5.0	35,295	38.6	17.1
Manassas city	12,430	62.2	293,500	23.2	11.6	1,376	31.7	6.8	22,051	2.3	749	3.4	21,842	31.5	23.7
Manassas Park city	4,730	65.8	257,800	26.9	15.0	1,551	27.7	4.6	8,644	2.1	290	3.4	8,120	35.3	27.1

1. Specified owner-occupied units.   2. A value of 10.0 represents 10 percent or less; a value of 50.0 represents 50 percent or more.   3. Specified renter-occupied units.
4. Overcrowded or lacking complete plumbing facilities. 5. Percent of civilian labor force.   6. Civilian employed persons 16 years old and over.

	Private nonfarm establishments, employment and payroll, 2016									Agriculture, 2012			
	Employment						Annual payroll		Farms			
											Percent with:		
STATE County	Number of establish-ments	Total	Health care and social assistance	Manufac-turing	Retail trade	Finance and insurance	Professional, scientific, and technical services	Total (mil dol)	Average per employee (dollars)	Number	Fewer than 50 acres	500 acres or more	Farm operators whose principal occupation is farming (percent)
	104	105	106	107	108	109	110	111	112	113	114	115	116
VIRGINIA— Cont'd													
Louisa	541	6,815	318	1,130	1,202	90	143	320	47,000	485	39.6	8.2	40.6
Lunenburg	173	1,799	186	534	425	71	53	53	29,282	371	20.2	9.7	46.9
Madison	274	2,525	330	267	665	23	80	91	35,891	522	36.2	10.3	49.6
Mathews	174	1,086	222	49	222	19	44	26	24,018	55	72.7	5.5	47.3
Mecklenburg	789	9,872	1,697	1,400	1,789	280	796	343	34,787	527	20.5	12.0	44.8
Middlesex	334	2,195	376	127	474	59	149	65	29,804	73	43.8	12.3	61.6
Montgomery	1,966	29,453	4,515	4,918	5,284	676	2,194	1,150	39,054	603	39.5	6.6	39.6
Nelson	367	3,124	220	489	266	35	191	90	28,717	455	29.0	5.9	36.0
New Kent	360	2,896	586	132	447	33	116	97	33,458	137	52.6	5.1	49.6
Northampton	313	3,060	856	331	458	47	67	102	33,319	147	40.8	24.5	57.1
Northumberland	314	1,631	114	290	329	64	87	60	36,925	98	39.8	27.6	64.3
Nottoway	317	3,425	1,034	373	648	106	99	108	31,488	356	31.2	6.5	56.2
Orange	645	6,875	409	1,404	1,363	134	264	256	37,169	547	35.5	7.5	47.5
Page	400	4,063	505	547	735	170	245	125	30,868	545	45.0	5.3	56.7
Patrick	284	4,334	608	1,360	527	82	100	116	26,738	566	35.5	3.7	40.6
Pittsylvania	833	8,432	1,232	1,865	874	144	176	278	32,962	1,354	25.2	10.1	56.6
Powhatan	683	4,975	295	139	871	118	222	191	38,390	250	42.0	5.2	48.4
Prince Edward	526	6,579	1,818	122	1,384	171	101	212	32,264	413	28.8	8.5	32.4
Prince George	480	10,821	481	1,099	938	92	971	342	31,625	167	32.9	9.6	59.3
Prince William	8,036	98,094	10,030	1,481	22,591	2,122	10,165	4,196	42,772	330	68.2	4.8	53.0
Pulaski	592	11,262	1,193	4,894	1,623	153	222	425	37,777	445	38.7	11.5	42.2
Rappahannock	201	1,100	42	74	167	14	76	38	34,116	397	46.6	7.3	51.9
Richmond	177	2,031	732	142	228	44	45	59	28,961	90	34.4	21.1	54.4
Roanoke	1,987	28,036	4,414	3,391	3,789	3,268	1,758	1,070	38,180	280	52.9	4.3	44.3
Rockbridge	429	5,214	316	1,050	1,478	92	232	152	29,078	833	28.3	8.5	42.4
Rockingham	1,445	27,349	3,937	7,115	1,950	381	493	1,125	41,119	1,902	43.2	2.8	54.6
Russell	450	5,649	1,163	512	900	219	724	203	35,905	995	34.8	7.1	41.5
Scott	275	3,560	705	853	676	85	109	115	32,247	1,292	33.7	3.0	41.4
Shenandoah	881	12,113	1,501	3,666	1,736	264	324	430	35,528	980	45.7	4.9	50.1
Smyth	511	8,777	1,758	3,210	1,232	209	150	332	37,853	792	40.8	9.2	41.2
Southampton	221	2,126	121	741	265	20	61	83	38,999	335	26.3	31.6	60.0
Spotsylvania	2,443	31,225	4,215	1,260	7,827	501	2,749	1,172	37,528	369	56.9	5.4	43.6
Stafford	2,278	31,902	3,402	878	4,794	4,550	4,204	1,343	42,102	215	62.3	1.4	41.9
Surry	74	1,345	D	92	57	D	19	106	78,895	127	43.3	21.3	50.4
Sussex	182	1,961	336	224	331	28	23	61	31,321	123	29.3	26.8	61.8
Tazewell	1,012	12,724	2,465	1,122	3,078	637	352	411	32,298	584	31.8	15.6	43.5
Warren	790	10,438	1,353	1,024	1,751	231	323	364	34,911	346	58.1	5.8	43.1
Washington	1,152	18,034	2,776	3,801	3,211	495	653	665	36,892	1,602	48.3	4.2	39.7
Westmoreland	315	2,539	224	613	453	77	172	70	27,668	152	18.4	21.7	50.7
Wise	731	8,214	1,693	216	1,989	215	376	255	31,051	165	49.7	6.1	32.7
Wythe	680	9,530	1,209	2,038	2,048	262	170	316	33,209	952	34.2	8.3	47.8
York	1,400	18,284	1,811	279	3,793	440	2,061	621	33,957	47	63.8	2.1	70.2
Independent cities													
Alexandria city	4,711	84,594	7,433	1,207	7,587	3,080	19,115	5,145	60,815	NA	NA	NA	NA
Bristol city	619	10,576	891	1,340	1,842	344	183	367	34,662	NA	NA	NA	NA
Buena Vista city	106	1,834	140	837	87	30	14	64	34,784	NA	NA	NA	NA
Charlottesville city	2,062	33,985	9,432	638	3,771	862	2,489	1,805	53,126	NA	NA	NA	NA
Chesapeake city	5,375	89,955	9,794	4,271	16,169	3,576	8,565	3,762	41,826	253	71.1	8.7	44.7
Colonial Heights city	669	9,665	1,679	D	3,383	268	352	244	25,294	NA	NA	NA	NA
Covington city	219	3,938	168	D	728	94	46	177	45,009	NA	NA	NA	NA
Danville city	1,286	23,789	5,164	4,736	4,327	804	407	803	33,743	NA	NA	NA	NA
Emporia city	235	4,008	1,155	858	662	85	54	136	34,002	NA	NA	NA	NA
Fairfax city	2,280	33,021	4,092	156	6,684	1,279	7,348	1,822	55,180	NA	NA	NA	NA
Falls Church city	875	10,060	2,010	74	1,054	194	1,675	510	50,653	NA	NA	NA	NA
Franklin city	270	3,499	1,261	32	1,008	178	109	99	28,380	NA	NA	NA	NA
Fredericksburg city	1,373	19,093	4,577	275	4,166	629	1,340	801	41,959	NA	NA	NA	NA
Galax city	301	5,088	1,438	799	1,247	123	135	156	30,745	NA	NA	NA	NA
Hampton city	2,371	42,353	7,552	2,120	7,226	836	4,473	1,718	40,557	NA	NA	NA	NA
Harrisonburg city	1,593	25,301	3,054	2,861	5,238	863	1,215	804	31,772	NA	NA	NA	NA
Hopewell city	407	6,237	1,144	1,807	659	109	257	323	51,746	NA	NA	NA	NA
Lexington city	278	3,832	675	23	399	104	150	152	39,670	NA	NA	NA	NA
Lynchburg city	2,199	57,209	9,810	6,481	7,779	2,727	3,630	2,231	39,000	NA	NA	NA	NA
Manassas city	1,501	19,240	3,403	3,513	2,421	482	1,381	1,061	55,164	NA	NA	NA	NA
Manassas Park city	330	3,472	123	299	182	24	140	159	45,887	NA	NA	NA	NA

Table B. States and Counties — Government Employment and Payroll, and Local Government Finances

STATE County	Full-time equivalent employees	March payroll (dollars)	Government employment and payroll, 2012 — March payroll (percent of total) — Administration, judicial, and legal	Police and corrections	Fire protection	Highways and transportation	Health and welfare	Natural resources and utilities	Education and libraries	Local government finances — General revenue — Total (mil dol)	Intergovernmental (mil dol)	Taxes — Total (mil dol)	Per capita[1] (dollars) — Total	Property
	171	172	173	174	175	176	177	178	179	180	181	182	183	184
VIRGINIA— Cont'd														
Louisa	1,124	3,411,101	8.2	6.8	4.2	0.0	1.1	4.9	73.3	96.7	33.7	53.8	1,609	1,418
Lunenburg	403	1,190,954	9.0	11.5	0.0	0.0	2.3	2.4	72.9	33.1	20.6	9.9	790	676
Madison	403	1,326,277	10.7	6.4	0.0	0.0	5.8	0.3	69.8	34.3	15.7	16.2	1,227	1,036
Mathews	358	848,780	8.9	7.2	0.0	0.0	5.4	0.0	74.9	23.0	9.7	12.1	1,364	1,166
Mecklenburg	1,375	3,603,811	7.0	12.8	0.2	1.1	10.7	2.6	62.8	94.5	47.2	37.6	1,185	856
Middlesex	280	843,355	10.1	15.3	0.0	0.0	3.5	0.8	70.3	25.5	8.9	15.3	1,409	1,212
Montgomery	2,699	8,781,181	9.0	11.9	0.5	4.6	2.7	5.5	61.5	255.0	103.6	112.5	1,182	829
Nelson	457	1,391,646	8.9	4.1	0.0	0.0	1.6	0.5	80.1	45.2	17.7	23.6	1,590	1,346
New Kent	638	2,123,526	10.3	8.3	5.3	0.3	4.1	7.3	63.1	52.7	21.7	26.8	1,400	1,195
Northampton	850	3,278,000	5.0	9.0	0.0	20.1	6.5	3.2	55.2	101.7	23.0	21.3	1,740	1,417
Northumberland	358	1,244,110	8.2	7.7	0.0	0.0	4.8	0.9	77.1	28.9	10.2	17.4	1,407	1,269
Nottoway	548	1,646,561	8.1	8.7	0.0	2.8	5.9	4.4	67.2	39.4	23.9	10.3	650	454
Orange	1,173	3,380,570	7.0	14.3	3.2	1.7	2.2	2.9	67.7	89.1	37.1	42.7	1,247	997
Page	878	2,456,816	8.1	13.4	0.0	0.6	1.8	3.8	71.0	65.3	32.2	27.2	1,138	890
Patrick	695	1,689,450	5.6	12.0	0.0	0.0	4.5	0.8	75.3	43.9	24.0	14.5	784	617
Pittsylvania	1,563	4,924,209	5.8	7.5	0.1	0.5	1.4	1.2	80.6	127.9	84.1	37.6	599	478
Powhatan	855	2,784,066	7.2	7.7	0.5	0.0	3.4	1.3	77.9	69.7	28.5	38.3	1,361	1,230
Prince Edward	701	2,116,144	10.4	10.6	0.3	3.1	2.0	3.4	66.4	54.6	29.8	19.8	852	490
Prince George	1,519	5,308,620	5.9	28.6	0.9	0.0	2.5	1.5	58.6	118.9	72.6	36.1	976	765
Prince William	15,485	68,447,361	3.7	8.8	4.5	3.3	4.4	3.5	69.0	1,578.6	659.7	752.7	1,749	1,412
Pulaski	1,288	4,175,730	6.1	8.3	0.9	1.1	3.6	5.9	68.5	117.9	56.3	35.2	1,013	707
Rappahannock	256	760,848	9.7	11.1	0.0	0.0	6.5	0.8	68.9	20.6	4.6	14.7	1,978	1,804
Richmond	326	1,099,371	6.8	32.6	0.0	0.0	0.6	2.6	56.3	32.9	20.4	11.5	1,002	790
Roanoke	3,729	13,158,244	7.7	7.6	6.2	0.3	4.8	9.4	62.7	353.7	116.0	158.3	1,704	1,275
Rockbridge	661	1,852,653	7.0	8.7	0.0	0.3	5.5	2.1	74.0	71.1	30.7	29.1	1,299	943
Rockingham	2,706	8,346,966	7.1	8.4	3.0	0.8	4.8	4.5	70.2	227.8	108.4	83.5	1,079	895
Russell	1,094	4,018,658	3.7	6.4	0.2	1.1	0.2	2.5	83.0	73.8	48.1	20.2	710	482
Scott	721	2,170,415	5.9	6.0	0.0	0.8	3.3	2.2	79.1	62.5	41.3	16.4	722	496
Shenandoah	1,504	4,472,709	7.1	9.2	3.6	1.5	4.6	6.2	65.6	123.4	60.3	48.9	1,149	882
Smyth	1,259	3,570,921	6.6	8.1	0.4	1.0	11.3	5.6	65.4	92.2	58.8	22.8	718	494
Southampton	717	2,092,925	8.4	10.2	0.0	0.2	6.0	3.3	70.4	53.2	26.3	21.4	1,162	1,013
Spotsylvania	3,637	13,506,224	7.0	5.7	4.9	0.0	3.5	3.8	72.0	382.7	163.4	188.0	1,496	1,158
Stafford	4,475	17,648,377	6.1	5.1	2.8	0.2	2.7	4.7	77.1	448.6	192.3	213.9	1,592	1,307
Surry	386	1,034,084	6.2	6.4	0.0	0.0	0.8	3.6	77.4	29.5	7.5	21.1	3,078	2,927
Sussex	423	1,312,782	12.9	14.1	0.0	0.2	7.5	2.3	61.1	40.7	22.0	10.1	843	685
Tazewell	1,644	4,416,984	7.8	8.5	0.4	2.1	7.4	4.0	67.6	142.1	75.0	40.0	903	580
Warren	1,201	3,547,039	8.8	13.4	0.9	2.4	2.5	5.2	65.3	103.2	45.3	48.1	1,264	942
Washington	2,294	6,382,778	4.2	19.7	0.0	2.6	2.7	7.4	62.3	154.9	83.7	51.1	926	645
Westmoreland	590	1,733,294	11.3	10.8	0.0	0.5	7.2	2.7	66.0	47.8	21.1	21.6	1,230	999
Wise	1,524	4,814,554	7.6	7.5	0.1	1.5	2.6	6.1	72.2	146.0	82.3	52.0	1,271	712
Wythe	1,424	3,649,638	5.6	26.2	0.3	2.6	1.1	5.5	55.4	100.6	52.2	30.2	1,032	628
York	2,630	9,095,299	7.9	5.3	7.7	0.0	3.3	2.6	66.6	226.0	92.7	107.0	1,618	1,182
Independent cities														
Alexandria city	5,221	27,072,935	10.0	12.5	7.7	2.6	11.9	7.2	44.7	658.7	76.2	498.6	3,408	2,503
Bristol city	765	2,448,312	7.6	15.4	6.1	3.8	8.9	3.5	53.6	72.5	36.3	26.8	1,519	788
Buena Vista city	329	965,276	10.8	5.3	0.0	3.3	1.3	7.0	71.5	22.5	12.2	6.9	1,023	765
Charlottesville city	2,284	8,528,975	9.8	5.8	3.3	6.0	4.6	8.3	55.8	212.5	76.7	93.0	2,116	1,314
Chesapeake city	11,013	41,054,055	4.1	9.2	5.0	1.7	24.6	3.7	49.6	1,127.4	370.1	422.6	1,850	1,301
Colonial Heights city	802	3,016,516	7.0	9.3	9.1	2.9	0.6	5.1	64.2	74.5	26.0	40.1	2,297	1,225
Covington city	279	921,554	6.6	10.3	0.0	0.0	7.9	9.3	65.9	26.1	10.0	11.0	1,904	1,291
Danville city	2,451	7,816,325	9.2	11.3	5.7	3.0	4.1	10.7	51.6	173.3	85.4	50.7	1,180	635
Emporia city	121	358,410	26.1	32.7	0.8	10.3	9.0	14.9	0.0	22.4	7.1	10.4	1,814	786
Fairfax city	414	2,320,342	17.7	23.1	21.4	10.9	3.8	13.9	0.0	121.0	20.6	87.1	3,711	2,469
Falls Church city	720	3,347,248	12.1	9.0	0.2	2.9	0.5	11.6	62.0	84.9	11.0	58.9	4,454	3,374
Franklin city	602	1,874,981	4.7	34.1	3.4	2.6	4.5	7.4	40.0	43.1	23.9	11.8	1,389	766
Fredericksburg city	1,610	5,694,248	7.8	27.8	4.3	5.6	3.2	3.1	44.2	149.0	48.1	67.8	2,483	1,244
Galax city	414	1,172,160	3.5	10.4	0.0	4.3	9.1	11.5	57.5	25.9	13.1	8.9	1,283	595
Hampton city	6,125	20,173,326	6.9	11.1	6.0	1.0	6.7	5.9	61.4	526.3	220.7	218.7	1,599	1,068
Harrisonburg city	1,474	5,157,943	4.1	7.6	6.7	5.8	3.6	11.7	53.6	162.1	48.7	63.4	1,244	631
Hopewell city	1,107	3,758,446	8.1	8.6	4.7	2.5	4.1	11.7	58.7	102.8	47.0	32.3	1,448	1,059
Lexington city	273	881,406	8.8	24.4	4.0	7.7	2.1	13.4	30.0	22.6	6.6	7.8	1,109	687
Lynchburg city	3,057	9,313,489	8.7	9.6	8.0	2.9	7.1	8.5	52.5	265.1	109.0	117.5	1,524	905
Manassas city	1,551	7,149,920	5.0	8.7	4.1	2.5	2.9	8.2	67.1	180.9	61.7	83.5	2,055	1,564
Manassas Park city	547	2,174,966	6.3	8.6	5.6	0.7	1.8	6.3	67.3	58.7	24.8	25.4	1,608	1,293

1. Based on the resident population estimated as of July 1 of the year shown.

Table B. States and Counties — Local Government Finances, Government Employment, and Income Taxes

STATE County	Local government finances (cont.) Direct general expenditure Total (mil dol)	Per capita¹ (dollars)	Percent of total for: Education	Health and hospitals	Police protection	Public welfare	Highways	Debt outstanding Total (mil dol)	Per capita¹ (dollars)	Government employment, 2016 Federal civilian	Federal military	State and local	Individual income tax returns, 2015 Number of returns	Mean adjusted gross income	Mean income tax
	185	186	187	188	189	190	191	192	193	194	195	196	197	198	199
VIRGINIA— Cont'd															
Louisa	99.6	2,980	58.3	1.2	5.3	6.6	0.3	25.5	763	59	111	1,539	15,860	57,416	6,150
Lunenburg	35.6	2,826	62.6	1.1	5.0	6.7	2.1	26.9	2,134	19	36	777	4,820	40,448	3,292
Madison	32.1	2,431	58.6	4.5	8.2	11.2	0.0	15.3	1,157	64	41	542	6,050	58,286	6,299
Mathews	20.3	2,283	58.0	0.8	7.8	7.9	0.7	9.8	1,108	16	65	359	4,240	59,367	6,891
Mecklenburg	89.8	2,829	48.3	6.5	7.0	4.6	2.7	33.6	1,059	118	95	1,793	13,470	44,230	4,376
Middlesex	23.8	2,198	52.5	2.0	5.6	6.1	0.0	22.7	2,100	21	33	1,025	5,260	57,426	6,789
Montgomery	258.1	2,711	48.5	0.4	8.4	3.5	4.9	475.3	4,993	(2) 333	(2) 400	(2) 17,582	35,000	60,134	7,309
Nelson	40.8	2,750	59.8	0.5	7.1	4.4	0.7	45.5	3,068	47	47	686	7,250	58,443	6,649
New Kent	49.4	2,579	54.5	1.0	4.6	4.2	0.0	60.4	3,152	42	66	925	10,180	83,483	12,224
Northampton	81.1	6,632	27.6	1.0	3.1	3.3	15.7	159.5	13,045	33	67	910	5,960	47,864	5,345
Northumberland	27.3	2,213	57.8	1.2	7.1	6.9	1.7	42.0	3,401	30	39	455	5,990	61,014	7,179
Nottoway	38.9	2,460	57.3	0.4	7.7	6.1	2.3	16.5	1,044	338	55	2,506	6,120	41,678	3,525
Orange	87.3	2,548	55.7	0.6	6.4	3.0	2.0	124.0	3,620	61	111	2,248	16,460	58,582	6,303
Page	66.1	2,765	55.3	0.9	7.9	5.0	2.0	77.1	3,228	195	75	1,127	10,690	43,645	3,887
Patrick	36.7	1,989	67.6	1.0	5.6	2.7	0.2	44.5	2,411	43	56	810	7,320	40,880	3,437
Pittsylvania	127.3	2,026	65.4	0.5	5.2	7.6	0.3	112.9	1,797	(3) 201	(3) 323	(3) 6,500	26,790	45,435	4,166
Powhatan	65.5	2,328	65.3	0.3	6.2	5.1	0.0	103.3	3,675	50	86	2,087	13,200	76,544	9,896
Prince Edward	54.4	2,342	50.0	0.5	7.0	7.1	5.6	67.7	2,914	71	60	2,371	7,940	43,809	4,083
Prince George	134.6	3,644	45.1	2.0	4.5	2.6	0.3	173.0	4,684	(4) 4,888	(4) 9,146	(4) 3,177	15,480	57,276	5,609
Prince William	1,678.9	3,902	57.5	1.9	5.9	2.5	1.6	1,440.8	3,349	(5) 7,181	(5) 8,877	(5) 23,715	214,250	75,732	9,290
Pulaski	110.5	3,181	43.4	0.7	5.8	9.2	2.0	71.9	2,069	34	105	2,363	14,700	46,833	4,404
Rappahannock	21.0	2,817	57.1	0.7	5.0	4.4	0.0	10.8	1,446	16	23	305	3,610	72,108	10,181
Richmond	32.3	3,565	42.0	0.6	4.9	5.4	0.1	11.6	1,280	27	25	1,069	3,450	47,412	4,338
Roanoke	397.1	4,275	42.0	6.5	5.5	3.6	0.2	497.3	5,353	(6) 2,174	(6) 370	(6) 6,807	46,040	65,632	8,089
Rockbridge	69.2	3,088	45.1	10.9	3.4	9.5	0.0	67.1	2,995	(7) 145	(7) 145	(7) 2,602	10,060	53,843	5,697
Rockingham	234.6	3,031	52.1	2.8	3.5	11.4	1.3	200.1	2,585	(8) 354	(8) 399	(8) 11,282	36,710	56,137	5,981
Russell	71.0	2,495	57.5	0.7	4.1	8.4	6.4	22.5	790	66	86	1,395	9,980	43,813	3,877
Scott	60.2	2,640	60.3	0.7	6.9	7.1	1.4	30.5	1,339	55	67	1,173	8,170	42,233	3,553
Shenandoah	116.2	2,729	54.8	0.6	6.7	6.1	3.0	146.9	3,449	131	136	1,980	20,600	50,583	5,063
Smyth	94.6	2,984	50.5	0.9	6.6	10.5	2.3	141.0	4,444	73	96	2,918	12,660	40,205	3,135
Southampton	56.0	3,044	56.1	0.8	3.6	3.8	0.2	67.3	3,657	(9) 78	(9) 78	(9) 2,445	7,610	49,588	4,508
Spotsylvania	378.7	3,013	60.7	0.4	4.3	4.3	2.1	483.9	3,850	(10) 445	(10) 502	(10) 9,892	60,960	66,881	7,820
Stafford	443.1	3,298	62.9	0.3	5.0	3.4	1.5	601.1	4,474	4,630	627	6,350	64,270	78,048	9,401
Surry	27.8	4,061	61.1	1.2	4.9	7.5	0.0	16.2	2,369	0	21	568	3,330	47,788	4,613
Sussex	39.1	3,269	58.6	0.5	7.2	7.5	0.1	26.7	2,229	47	28	1,287	4,580	39,058	3,363
Tazewell	136.7	3,088	44.7	17.2	6.0	6.5	4.1	52.5	1,186	71	129	3,369	15,940	48,875	5,126
Warren	120.1	3,155	38.6	12.5	13.4	5.4	1.5	214.6	5,637	186	122	1,836	18,450	57,440	6,184
Washington	172.4	3,125	41.6	10.5	5.9	3.9	1.1	101.3	1,835	(11) 220	(11) 224	(11) 4,761	22,590	52,951	6,036
Westmoreland	49.6	2,832	53.8	0.8	8.0	6.1	1.5	23.2	1,322	52	56	855	8,420	51,078	5,453
Wise	142.7	3,487	49.3	6.0	6.1	9.8	4.4	186.8	4,565	(12) 226	(12) 127	(12) 4,042	13,710	42,699	3,909
Wythe	103.2	3,530	39.8	0.1	5.8	6.6	2.0	150.9	5,159	86	91	2,355	12,640	43,625	3,991
York	226.9	3,430	55.6	0.6	4.0	2.9	0.0	176.3	2,665	(13) 1,045	(13) 1,846	(13) 3,689	31,900	74,525	9,190
Independent cities															
Alexandria city	692.1	4,731	34.7	6.0	9.7	6.4	3.7	714.3	4,882	14,461	1,427	8,236	84,860	101,862	17,306
Bristol city	80.9	4,578	41.9	3.1	10.9	5.1	11.6	60.4	3,418	(11)	(11)	(11)	7,220	41,605	3,933
Buena Vista city	21.2	3,164	51.2	2.1	6.2	6.2	4.2	43.1	6,424	(7)	(7)	(7)	2,820	35,886	2,469
Charlottesville city	227.5	5,176	31.3	8.0	7.2	11.1	6.4	151.8	3,454	(14)	(14)	(14)	20,490	90,885	16,595
Chesapeake city	1,112.4	4,870	42.2	24.6	3.6	2.6	4.4	886.9	3,883	1,091	1,501	14,469	111,850	62,129	6,817
Colonial Heights city	69.5	3,974	51.8	0.0	5.3	0.6	4.6	61.6	3,526	(15)	(15)	(15)	9,040	47,891	4,381
Covington city	33.2	5,752	46.0	0.3	7.1	5.4	4.1	55.3	9,583	(16)	(16)	(16)	2,790	39,505	3,374
Danville city	179.2	4,169	41.3	2.3	5.5	4.2	5.7	156.0	3,628	(3)	(3)	(3)	18,560	39,337	3,949
Emporia city	22.3	3,882	17.9	1.2	14.0	1.4	4.2	14.6	2,551	(17)	(17)	(17)	2,670	32,730	2,533
Fairfax city	112.7	4,804	34.1	0.9	9.6	1.5	4.8	321.3	13,695	(18)	(18)	(18)	12,460	90,082	13,217
Falls Church city	76.6	5,787	47.6	0.3	8.2	2.3	6.9	97.9	7,399	(18)	(18)	(18)	6,360	141,476	25,480
Franklin city	51.8	6,072	32.0	0.5	5.3	3.8	4.2	22.8	2,673	(9)	(9)	(9)	3,880	43,753	3,849
Fredericksburg city	158.1	5,789	24.4	0.5	4.5	4.2	4.1	451.1	16,521	(10)	(10)	(10)	12,650	64,827	8,793
Galax city	28.7	4,153	45.2	0.7	8.9	5.8	7.1	10.9	1,575	(19)	(19)	(19)	2,940	38,549	3,317
Hampton city	524.9	3,836	44.8	0.8	5.1	5.6	1.2	438.4	3,204	7,170	7,304	8,450	46,420	46,427	4,284
Harrisonburg city	165.9	3,255	39.0	0.7	4.7	1.8	11.4	529.2	10,380	(8)	(8)	(8)	17,990	43,956	4,178
Hopewell city	116.0	5,192	43.8	0.5	4.4	5.9	3.4	114.6	5,128	(4)	(4)	(4)	10,620	37,321	2,914
Lexington city	28.1	4,013	24.4	2.6	5.2	2.6	4.3	34.5	4,926	(7)	(7)	(7)	2,370	69,688	9,370
Lynchburg city	262.8	3,408	36.6	0.8	6.5	7.2	2.8	337.4	4,375	(20)	(20)	(20)	32,050	51,166	6,155
Manassas city	169.8	4,182	54.0	2.2	7.8	0.7	6.2	130.5	3,213	(5)	(5)	(5)	20,530	58,638	6,270
Manassas Park city	60.1	3,803	52.0	0.2	7.5	2.3	0.9	123.4	7,811	(5)	(5)	(5)	7,690	53,886	5,255

1. Based on the resident population estimated as of July 1 of the year shown.   2. Radford city is included with Montgomery county.   3. Danville city is included with Pittsylvania county.
4. Hopewell city is included with Prince George county.   5. Manassas and Manassas Park cities are included with Prince William county.   6. Salem city is included with Roanoke county.
7. Buena Vista and Lexington cities are included with Rockbridge county.   8. Harrisonburg city is included with Rockingham county.   9. Franklin city is included with Southampton county.
10. Fredericksburg city is included with Spotsylvania county.   11. Bristol city is included with Washington county.   12. Norton city is included with Wise county.   13. Poquoson city is
included with York county.   14. Charlottesville city is included with Albemarle county.   15. Petersburg and Colonial Heights cities are included with Dinwiddie county.   16. Covington city is
included with Alleghany county.   17. Emporia city is included with Greensville county.   18. Fairfax city and Falls Church city are included with Fairfax county   19. Galax city is included with
Carroll county.   20. Lynchburg city is included with Campbell county.

Table B. States and Counties — Land Area and Population

State / county code	CBSA code[1]	County code[2]	STATE County	Land area[3] (sq. mi)	Total persons 2017	Rank	Per square mile	White	Black	American Indian, Alaska Native	Asian and Pacific Islancer	Percent Hispanic or Latino[4]	Under 5 years	5 to 17 years	18 to 24 years	25 to 34 years	35 to 44 years	45 to 54 years
				1	2	3	4	5	6	7	8	9	10	11	12	13	14	15
			VIRGINIA— Cont'd															
51,690	32,300	4	Martinsville city................	11.0	13,142	2,223	1,194.7	46.7	47.9	0.6	1.3	5.7	7.9	16.8	7.4	11.3	10.3	13.4
51,700	47,260	1	Newport News city	69.1	179,388	365	2,596.1	45.9	43.0	1.3	4.8	9.1	7.3	15.9	11.9	16.9	11.9	11.5
51,710	47,260	1	Norfolk city....................	53.3	244,703	276	4,591.1	46.2	42.9	1.3	5.2	8.0	6.6	13.2	17.8	19.4	11.3	10.1
51,720	13,720	7	Norton city......................	7.5	3,936	2,908	524.8	86.9	7.3	0.8	3.0	4.2	4.9	15.9	8.6	14.5	12.0	11.9
51,730	40,060	1	Petersburg city................	22.7	31,750	1,383	1,398.7	16.5	77.8	1.0	1.9	5.2	8.1	13.9	9.4	15.4	9.7	13.1
51,735	47,260	1	Poquoson city	15.4	12,053	2,288	782.7	93.5	1.7	0.8	3.4	2.6	4.4	17.4	7.8	10.1	12.2	14.6
51,740	47,260	1	Portsmouth city	33.3	94,572	622	2,840.0	39.6	55.3	1.2	2.3	4.4	7.5	16.0	9.0	16.8	12.0	11.4
51,750	13,980	3	Radford city....................	9.7	17,658	1,939	1,820.4	85.3	10.7	0.7	2.8	2.8	3.6	9.1	38.2	12.7	8.6	9.6
51,760	40,060	1	Richmond city	59.9	227,032	295	3,790.2	42.5	49.0	0.8	3.1	6.7	6.0	11.8	12.3	22.0	11.7	11.2
51,770	40,220	2	Roanoke city	42.5	99,837	598	2,349.1	61.0	30.9	0.8	3.8	6.4	7.2	15.3	7.6	15.4	12.2	12.8
51,775	40,220	2	Salem city	14.5	25,862	1,569	1,783.6	86.8	8.4	0.6	2.5	3.4	5.8	14.3	12.5	11.6	10.7	12.7
51,790	44,420	3	Staunton city	19.9	24,528	1,623	1,232.6	83.8	13.1	0.7	2.0	3.2	6.2	13.0	8.3	13.8	12.0	12.0
51,800	47,260	1	Suffolk city.....................	399.2	90,237	649	226.0	51.4	43.1	0.8	2.9	4.4	6.8	17.8	7.9	13.5	12.7	14.2
51,810	47,260	1	Virginia Beach city	244.7	450,435	155	1,840.8	64.9	21.0	1.0	9.1	8.2	6.4	15.9	9.5	16.6	13.0	12.7
51,820	44,420	3	Waynesboro city	15.0	22,327	1,714	1,488.5	78.2	14.4	0.9	1.9	7.7	7.3	16.2	7.4	14.4	11.8	12.1
51,830	47,260	1	Williamsburg city.............	8.9	15,031	2,095	1,688.9	70.1	16.2	0.9	7.9	7.9	3.5	7.7	35.9	13.0	7.1	7.5
51,840	49,020	3	Winchester city................	9.2	27,932	1,496	3,036.1	68.9	13.1	0.7	3.1	17.3	6.6	16.2	10.8	14.2	12.2	12.5
53,000		0	WASHINGTON...........	66,452.7	7,405,743	X	111.4	72.4	5.1	2.5	11.7	12.7	6.2	16.0	8.8	15.1	13.1	12.8
53,001	36,830	6	Adams............................	1,925.0	19,506	1,851	10.1	34.9	0.8	0.7	1.2	63.3	9.6	25.8	10.0	12.4	11.4	10.4
53,003	30,300	3	Asotin............................	636.1	22,535	1,703	35.4	92.5	1.3	2.6	1.9	4.0	5.2	15.2	6.6	11.6	11.0	11.9
53,005	28,420	2	Benton............................	1,700.0	198,171	337	116.6	72.8	2.3	1.5	4.2	21.9	7.2	19.6	8.4	13.7	12.4	11.7
53,007	48,300	3	Chelan............................	2,921.2	76,533	724	26.2	69.1	1.0	1.6	1.8	28.1	6.5	17.4	8.0	12.5	11.5	11.6
53,009	38,820	5	Clallam............................	1,738.7	75,474	734	43.4	85.9	1.5	6.6	3.3	6.3	4.7	12.6	6.3	10.8	9.9	10.3
53,011	38,900	1	Clark............................	628.5	474,643	146	755.2	81.9	3.1	1.8	7.5	9.7	6.2	18.1	8.0	13.2	13.3	13.3
53,013	47,460	3	Columbia........................	868.6	4,047	2,897	4.7	87.1	1.4	2.2	3.2	8.3	5.0	13.8	6.0	10.2	9.4	12.5
53,015	31,020	3	Cowlitz..........................	1,140.4	106,910	563	93.7	86.7	1.6	3.1	2.9	9.0	6.1	16.8	7.6	12.1	11.6	12.7
53,017	48,300	3	Douglas..........................	1,819.3	41,945	1,134	23.1	65.8	0.9	1.6	1.7	31.8	6.4	19.4	8.6	12.0	11.9	11.6
53,019		9	Ferry..............................	2,203.2	7,594	2,619	3.4	77.4	1.5	19.3	2.2	4.6	4.8	12.5	7.7	8.9	10.2	12.0
53,021	28,420	2	Franklin..........................	1,241.6	92,125	637	74.2	41.7	2.6	1.0	3.0	53.3	9.0	23.5	9.6	15.5	13.8	10.6
53,023		8	Garfield..........................	710.8	2,210	3,030	3.1	91.4	0.8	1.2	2.7	5.7	6.2	14.0	5.8	8.3	11.0	10.9
53,025	34,180	5	Grant..............................	2,679.5	95,158	619	35.5	55.5	1.4	1.7	1.5	41.7	8.0	21.7	9.5	13.3	11.8	11.0
53,027	10,140	4	Grays Harbor	1,901.3	72,697	747	38.2	82.6	1.9	6.2	2.8	10.0	5.5	15.1	7.1	11.9	11.3	12.4
53,029	36,020	4	Island............................	208.4	83,159	684	399.0	83.0	3.9	2.0	7.7	7.9	5.7	12.6	9.1	13.9	10.0	10.5
53,031		6	Jefferson........................	1,803.8	31,234	1,402	17.3	91.2	1.4	3.6	3.0	3.6	3.0	9.3	4.8	8.3	8.4	10.6
53,033	42,660	1	King................................	2,115.2	2,188,649	13	1,034.7	64.0	7.8	1.6	21.7	9.7	5.9	14.5	8.1	17.9	14.9	13.6
53,035	14,740	2	Kitsap............................	395.1	266,414	257	674.3	81.5	4.2	2.9	9.5	7.8	5.9	14.8	9.9	14.5	11.5	12.2
53,037	21,260	4	Kittitas............................	2,297.3	46,205	1,048	20.1	86.6	1.6	2.1	3.7	8.9	4.7	12.5	21.6	12.6	9.8	10.5
53,039		6	Klickitat..........................	1,871.6	21,811	1,734	11.7	84.2	0.9	3.4	1.6	12.3	4.8	14.6	6.3	9.9	11.7	12.6
53,041	16,500	4	Lewis..............................	2,402.8	78,200	710	32.5	86.3	1.3	2.9	2.2	10.1	5.8	15.7	7.5	11.8	11.3	12.2
53,043		8	Lincoln............................	2,310.5	10,579	2,387	4.6	93.7	1.1	3.1	1.3	3.4	5.1	16.6	6.3	8.4	10.1	11.4
53,045	43,220	4	Mason............................	959.4	63,710	836	66.4	83.9	1.9	5.0	3.1	9.9	5.3	14.1	7.1	11.6	10.8	12.1
53,047		6	Okanogan	5,266.2	41,742	1,138	7.9	67.4	1.2	12.4	1.6	20.0	6.2	17.0	7.0	10.6	11.1	11.3
53,049		7	Pacific............................	932.8	21,626	1,748	23.2	84.9	1.4	4.2	3.1	9.7	4.2	12.2	5.5	9.3	9.4	11.5
53,051	44,060	2	Pend Oreille	1,400.3	13,354	2,206	9.5	90.6	1.2	4.9	1.7	4.0	4.8	14.4	6.2	8.8	9.5	12.8
53,053	42,660	1	Pierce............................	1,668.1	876,764	64	525.6	72.4	9.5	2.6	11.5	10.9	6.8	16.8	9.0	15.6	13.0	12.8
53,055		9	San Juan........................	173.9	16,715	1,995	96.1	90.8	1.0	1.9	2.1	6.4	2.7	10.4	5.3	7.9	9.3	11.9
53,057	34,580	3	Skagit............................	1,730.1	125,619	503	72.6	76.7	1.4	2.8	3.4	18.3	6.0	15.9	7.8	12.5	11.6	11.7
53,059	38,900	1	Skamania........................	1,658.3	11,837	2,304	7.1	90.6	1.1	2.9	1.9	6.0	4.3	14.4	6.5	10.1	11.9	13.8
53,061	42,660	1	Snohomish......................	2,086.5	801,633	78	384.2	73.6	4.4	2.2	14.1	10.2	6.4	16.3	7.8	14.8	14.0	14.1
53,063	44,060	2	Spokane..........................	1,763.9	506,152	139	287.0	87.9	3.1	2.6	4.5	5.7	6.1	16.1	9.5	15.0	12.1	12.3
53,065	44,060	2	Stevens..........................	2,477.4	44,730	1,079	18.1	89.3	0.9	7.3	1.8	3.8	5.5	16.3	6.9	9.0	10.1	12.3
53,067	36,500	2	Thurston..........................	722.5	280,588	245	388.4	79.4	4.6	2.7	9.6	9.0	5.9	15.8	8.1	14.5	13.3	12.5
53,069		8	Wahkiakum	262.9	4,264	2,881	16.2	91.2	1.2	3.2	2.6	5.0	3.8	13.6	5.9	7.7	8.0	11.4
53,071	47,460	3	Walla Walla	1,270.0	60,567	863	47.7	73.9	2.6	1.6	2.9	21.3	5.6	15.6	13.0	12.8	11.4	11.4
53,073	13,380	3	Whatcom........................	2,107.9	221,404	303	105.0	82.2	1.9	3.8	6.5	9.4	5.5	14.1	14.1	13.5	11.7	11.7
53,075	39,420	4	Whitman..........................	2,159.2	49,046	1,002	22.7	82.1	3.0	1.6	10.9	6.4	4.4	10.7	34.5	14.8	8.9	7.7
53,077	49,420	3	Yakima............................	4,294.5	250,193	272	58.3	44.8	1.2	4.5	1.9	49.4	8.1	21.6	9.6	13.3	11.8	11.2
54,000		0	WEST VIRGINIA	24,040.9	1,815,857	X	75.5	93.8	4.4	0.7	1.2	1.6	5.4	14.9	8.7	11.9	12.1	13.2
54,001		6	Barbour..........................	341.1	16,497	2,010	48.4	97.2	1.8	1.3	0.5	1.0	5.0	14.7	11.6	10.8	11.2	12.9
54,003	25,180	2	Berkeley........................	321.1	114,920	537	357.9	87.0	9.1	0.7	1.7	4.3	6.2	17.4	7.5	13.8	13.2	14.3
54,005	16,620	3	Boone............................	501.5	22,349	1,711	44.6	98.3	1.1	0.4	0.2	0.7	5.1	16.4	7.0	10.1	13.2	13.7
54,007		8	Braxton..........................	510.8	14,237	2,147	27.9	97.9	1.2	0.8	0.4	0.7	5.6	14.5	6.9	11.1	11.3	13.7
54,009	48,260	3	Brooke............................	89.2	22,443	1,708	251.6	97.0	2.2	0.6	0.7	0.9	4.4	13.3	9.2	10.3	10.8	12.8
54,011	26,580	2	Cabell............................	281.0	94,958	621	337.9	92.2	6.1	0.8	1.8	1.4	5.6	14.2	13.5	12.4	11.7	11.7

1. CBSA = Core Based Statistical Area. See Appendix A for explanation. See Appendix B for list of metropolitan areas with component counties.   2.   County type code from the Economic Research Service of USDA Rural-Urban Continuum Codes. See Appendix A for definition.   3.   Dry land or land partially or temporarily covered by water.   4.   May be of any race.

Table B. States and Counties — Population and Households

STATE County	Age (percent) (cont.) 55 to 64 years	65 to 74 years	75 years and over	Percent female	Population change, 2000-2017 Total persons 2000	2010	Percent change 2000-2010	2010-2017	Components of change, 2010-2017 Births	Deaths	Net Migration	Households, 2012-2016 Number	Persons per house-hold	Percent Family house-holds	Female family house-holder[1]	One person
	16	17	18	19	20	21	22	23	24	25	26	27	28	29	30	31
VIRGINIA— Cont'd																
Martinsville city..............	13.7	10.5	8.7	53.9	15,416	13,811	-10.4	-4.8	1,483	1,691	-461	5,787	2.28	57.6	19.6	37.6
Newport News city............	11.9	7.3	5.3	51.6	180,150	180,963	0.5	-0.9	20,452	10,598	-11,537	69,247	2.50	61.2	17.9	32.4
Norfolk city.....................	10.8	6.5	4.4	47.8	234,403	242,823	3.6	0.8	26,819	14,083	-10,781	87,367	2.52	58.0	18.1	32.8
Norton city.......................	13.6	10.5	8.2	52.7	3,904	4,002	2.5	-1.6	292	277	-84	1,858	2.11	50.6	12.5	43.2
Petersburg city................	13.9	9.5	7.0	54.0	33,740	32,437	-3.9	-2.1	4,024	3,135	-1,585	13,175	2.36	55.5	25.0	37.8
Poquoson city..................	14.2	11.1	8.1	50.4	11,566	12,157	5.1	-0.9	668	744	-34	4,610	2.61	72.0	9.4	23.3
Portsmouth city...............	12.7	8.5	6.2	52.1	100,565	95,527	-5.0	-1.0	11,092	7,532	-4,490	36,840	2.53	62.5	21.7	31.6
Radford city....................	9.0	5.1	4.0	52.5	15,859	16,395	3.4	7.7	949	695	981	5,604	2.53	43.7	10.7	32.7
Richmond city..................	12.3	7.7	5.1	52.5	197,790	204,271	3.3	11.1	21,473	13,714	14,659	88,958	2.31	45.7	17.9	42.6
Roanoke city....................	13.4	9.5	6.6	52.2	94,911	96,917	2.1	3.0	10,824	8,407	526	42,541	2.28	55.5	17.0	36.8
Salem city.......................	13.8	10.3	8.3	52.3	24,747	24,817	0.3	4.2	2,014	2,184	1,222	10,060	2.29	62.1	13.8	32.4
Staunton city...................	13.7	11.9	9.2	54.2	23,853	23,745	-0.5	3.3	2,243	2,525	1,049	10,383	2.21	56.3	11.8	37.0
Suffolk city......................	13.2	8.4	5.5	51.6	63,677	84,570	32.8	6.7	8,337	5,363	2,707	31,741	2.72	73.9	17.4	21.7
Virginia Beach city	12.3	8.1	5.5	50.9	425,257	437,994	3.0	2.9	44,188	21,721	-9,824	167,509	2.62	68.9	14.3	24.5
Waynesboro city...............	12.8	9.9	8.3	51.8	19,520	21,000	7.6	6.3	2,244	1,802	891	9,044	2.34	60.8	14.8	33.8
Williamsburg city..............	10.0	8.6	6.7	53.4	11,998	13,693	14.1	9.8	746	726	1,309	4,627	2.36	46.7	6.8	41.7
Winchester city................	12.1	9.0	6.4	51.0	23,585	26,219	11.2	6.5	2,689	1,946	965	10,596	2.49	58.3	13.4	34.2
WASHINGTON.............	12.9	9.2	5.9	50.0	5,894,121	6,724,545	14.1	10.1	639,401	379,922	421,907	2,696,606	2.57	64.5	10.1	27.5
Adams...........................	9.5	6.6	4.3	49.1	16,428	18,728	14.0	4.2	2,849	898	-1,190	5,733	3.28	77.3	13.3	18.6
Asotin...........................	15.8	12.6	9.9	51.3	20,551	21,623	5.2	4.2	1,729	1,750	932	9,297	2.36	62.1	11.4	31.0
Benton...........................	12.5	8.8	5.7	49.9	142,475	175,171	22.9	13.1	19,033	9,569	13,506	68,418	2.71	69.1	11.0	26.0
Chelan...........................	14.1	10.8	7.6	50.1	66,616	72,464	8.8	5.6	6,829	4,944	2,233	27,200	2.70	67.0	9.0	28.3
Clallam...........................	16.6	16.9	11.9	50.6	64,525	71,404	10.7	5.7	4,849	6,892	6,105	31,438	2.28	60.1	9.6	32.8
Clark..............................	12.9	9.4	5.5	50.5	345,238	425,360	23.2	11.6	39,853	23,469	32,876	164,354	2.72	69.8	10.7	23.8
Columbia.........................	15.2	15.9	12.0	51.1	4,064	4,078	0.3	-0.8	252	379	94	1,689	2.29	62.8	9.0	30.7
Cowlitz...........................	14.4	11.2	7.5	50.5	92,948	102,408	10.2	4.4	8,795	7,884	3,615	39,671	2.56	65.8	11.2	27.5
Douglas..........................	12.8	10.1	7.0	49.6	32,603	38,431	17.9	9.1	3,834	2,249	1,945	14,348	2.77	74.3	10.7	20.6
Ferry.............................	17.6	17.1	9.2	48.7	7,260	7,554	4.0	0.5	495	603	149	3,039	2.44	62.6	10.1	31.5
Franklin..........................	9.0	5.8	3.2	48.3	49,347	78,163	58.4	17.9	12,059	2,708	4,462	25,157	3.40	77.0	16.9	18.6
Garfield..........................	17.6	15.0	11.1	51.1	2,397	2,266	-5.5	-2.5	168	176	-50	952	2.31	68.5	5.9	27.8
Grant.............................	11.1	8.2	5.3	49.3	74,698	89,120	19.3	6.8	11,096	4,885	-127	29,783	3.07	72.4	12.8	22.4
Grays Harbor..................	15.8	12.9	8.0	48.7	67,194	72,804	8.3	-0.1	5,702	5,905	99	27,472	2.48	63.7	12.1	28.7
Island............................	14.5	14.7	9.1	50.1	71,558	78,506	9.7	5.9	6,644	4,899	2,902	33,388	2.34	68.2	8.3	26.3
Jefferson........................	20.0	22.8	12.8	50.8	25,953	29,872	15.1	4.6	1,391	2,552	2,509	13,561	2.18	61.7	5.9	30.9
King...............................	12.1	7.8	5.1	49.9	1,737,034	1,931,281	11.2	13.3	182,736	91,699	166,046	831,995	2.46	59.7	8.8	30.2
Kitsap............................	14.0	10.9	6.4	48.9	231,969	251,137	8.3	6.1	21,880	15,302	8,614	98,250	2.55	67.0	9.4	26.1
Kittitas..........................	12.6	9.6	6.1	49.6	33,362	40,906	22.6	13.0	2,972	2,089	4,392	17,164	2.35	54.5	8.1	30.7
Klickitat.........................	16.9	14.7	8.5	49.5	19,161	20,317	6.0	7.4	1,470	1,299	1,317	8,069	2.56	65.4	7.8	27.3
Lewis............................	14.9	12.4	8.3	50.0	68,600	75,457	10.0	3.6	6,497	6,065	2,331	29,426	2.53	66.5	10.8	26.9
Lincoln...........................	16.9	14.5	10.6	49.2	10,184	10,570	3.8	0.1	704	803	109	4,337	2.35	66.7	7.5	27.1
Mason............................	16.4	14.1	8.5	48.3	49,405	60,696	22.9	5.0	4,603	4,647	3,092	22,454	2.67	66.3	9.7	27.1
Okanogan	15.6	13.2	8.0	49.6	39,564	41,117	3.9	1.5	3,805	3,175	14	16,804	2.39	67.4	10.0	26.9
Pacific...........................	18.1	18.6	11.1	49.9	20,984	20,919	-0.3	3.4	1,414	2,257	1,543	8,986	2.28	61.3	8.3	31.6
Pend Oreille	18.3	16.4	8.9	48.9	11,732	13,001	10.8	2.7	845	1,048	561	5,409	2.38	68.4	10.4	26.4
Pierce............................	12.6	8.2	5.2	50.2	700,820	795,217	13.5	10.3	82,453	44,845	44,187	307,106	2.66	66.3	11.6	26.6
San Juan........................	19.8	21.1	11.6	51.7	14,077	15,769	12.0	6.0	615	991	1,321	7,623	2.08	59.3	6.8	32.4
Skagit............................	14.3	12.1	8.1	50.5	102,979	116,896	13.5	7.5	10,556	8,267	6,478	46,108	2.57	68.1	10.0	24.9
Skamania........................	18.9	12.8	7.3	49.0	9,872	11,070	12.1	6.9	704	582	643	4,577	2.46	65.7	8.6	27.6
Snohomish......................	13.5	8.1	4.9	49.8	606,024	713,308	17.7	12.4	68,692	36,438	56,117	278,626	2.69	66.8	10.0	24.4
Spokane..........................	13.2	9.5	6.2	50.4	417,939	471,225	12.7	7.4	43,432	31,089	22,832	191,222	2.46	62.9	10.9	29.5
Stevens..........................	17.4	14.3	8.2	50.1	40,066	43,527	8.6	2.8	3,197	3,258	1,289	17,442	2.49	69.7	9.2	24.9
Thurston.........................	13.3	10.4	6.2	51.1	207,355	252,260	21.7	11.2	22,550	14,971	20,793	103,468	2.54	66.3	10.9	26.4
Wahkiakum	17.4	19.9	12.3	49.6	3,824	3,979	4.1	7.2	201	329	415	1,789	2.23	68.0	8.6	28.2
Walla Walla	12.8	9.8	7.6	48.8	55,180	58,781	6.5	3.0	4,890	4,084	998	21,851	2.49	62.8	10.3	31.1
Whatcom.........................	12.6	10.5	6.4	50.5	166,814	201,145	20.6	10.1	16,704	11,200	14,793	81,019	2.52	60.7	9.0	28.0
Whitman.........................	8.8	5.9	4.3	49.2	40,740	44,778	9.9	9.5	3,222	1,911	2,878	17,185	2.37	49.4	6.3	30.1
Yakima...........................	10.9	7.8	5.6	50.0	222,581	243,237	9.3	2.9	29,681	13,811	-8,916	80,196	3.04	71.6	15.1	23.2
WEST VIRGINIA	14.4	11.5	7.9	50.5	1,808,344	1,853,006	2.5	-2.0	146,363	159,967	-23,089	739,397	2.43	64.8	11.4	29.9
Barbour..........................	14.2	11.7	8.0	51.0	15,557	16,589	6.6	-0.6	1,217	1,406	94	6,169	2.65	67.7	10.7	25.2
Berkeley.........................	13.1	9.4	5.1	50.4	75,905	104,172	37.2	10.3	9,886	6,860	7,641	41,720	2.62	70.0	12.6	24.5
Boone............................	15.4	12.1	6.9	50.3	25,535	24,627	-3.6	-9.3	1,860	2,311	-1,837	9,466	2.48	69.6	13.6	25.6
Braxton..........................	15.0	13.3	8.6	49.5	14,702	14,519	-1.2	-1.9	1,177	1,251	-197	5,417	2.60	69.6	9.1	26.5
Brooke...........................	16.0	13.3	9.9	50.9	25,447	24,071	-5.4	-6.8	1,389	2,421	-577	9,934	2.26	63.1	10.2	31.9
Cabell............................	12.5	10.4	7.8	51.1	96,784	96,316	-0.5	-1.4	8,290	8,468	-1,105	39,954	2.32	55.9	11.8	35.9

1. No spouse present.

Table B. States and Counties — Population, Vital Statistics, Health, and Crime

STATE County	Persons in group quarters, 2017	Daytime Population, 2012-2016		Births, 2017		Deaths, 2017		Persons under 65 with no health insurance, 2016		Medicare, 2017			Serious crimes known to police[2], 2016 — Total	
		Number	Employment/ residence ratio	Total	Rate[1]	Number	Rate[1]	Number	Percent	Total beneficiaries	Enrolled in Original Medicare	Enrolled in Medicare Advantage	Number	Rate[3]
	32	33	34	35	36	37	38	39	40	41	42	43	44	45
VIRGINIA— Cont'd														
Martinsville city..............	377	17,231	1.70	255	19.4	200	15.2	1,097	10.6	8,727	6,060	2,667	392	2,892
Newport News city	7,593	206,826	1.29	2,719	15.2	1,500	8.4	16,931	11.2	28,283	20,630	7,653	6,454	3,552
Norfolk city	33,808	303,561	1.46	3,611	14.8	2,067	8.4	21,989	11.8	32,803	23,768	9,035	11,261	4,583
Norton city.......................	68	3,751	0.86	20	5.1	26	6.6	323	10.1	1,621	1,025	596	160	4,091
Petersburg city	887	33,710	1.13	651	20.5	435	13.7	3,141	12.0	8,989	6,812	2,177	1,312	4,063
Poquoson city	51	8,572	0.44	98	8.1	106	8.8	617	6.3	1,592	1,393	199	191	1,595
Portsmouth city	2,954	105,951	1.23	1,470	15.5	1,031	10.9	7,963	10.2	18,114	13,084	5,030	6,226	6,498
Radford city.....................	2,916	17,045	0.98	132	7.5	67	3.8	1,172	8.9	3,422	2,669	754	400	2,285
Richmond city	12,911	286,184	1.66	3,155	13.9	2,064	9.1	22,098	12.0	64,213	43,370	20,843	9,343	4,200
Roanoke city....................	2,113	124,257	1.54	1,578	15.8	1,150	11.5	10,943	13.3	32,760	23,487	9,273	4,615	4,616
Salem city	1,959	36,183	1.89	355	13.7	298	11.5	1,601	8.3	8,768	6,891	1,877	552	2,174
Staunton city	1,087	24,493	1.02	368	15.0	315	12.8	1,761	9.5	9,474	7,948	1,526	576	2,361
Suffolk city......................	1,040	79,617	0.82	1,239	13.7	809	9.0	6,705	8.8	15,789	12,211	3,579	2,398	2,714
Virginia Beach city	9,632	417,589	0.86	5,935	13.2	3,280	7.3	33,040	8.6	68,289	55,701	12,588	10,590	2,338
Waynesboro city	192	21,100	0.97	346	15.5	214	9.6	2,153	12.2	7,367	6,139	1,229	528	2,460
Williamsburg city	4,376	22,893	2.37	96	6.4	111	7.4	1,011	12.1	6,940	5,995	945	255	1,671
Winchester city................	1,001	40,452	2.05	354	12.7	257	9.2	3,237	14.5	11,431	10,071	1,361	NA	NA
WASHINGTON.............	142,990	7,025,388	0.99	90,459	12.2	56,457	7.6	420,125	6.9	1,277,289	881,553	395,737	276,676	3,796
Adams.............................	162	18,970	0.98	357	18.3	123	6.3	2,111	12.6	1,677	1,479	198	576	2,966
Asotin..............................	174	18,866	0.65	224	9.9	263	11.7	1,134	6.6	5,921	5,002	919	792	3,556
Benton.............................	1,424	189,186	1.02	2,742	13.8	1,444	7.3	12,075	7.3	33,088	32,353	736	4,748	2,448
Chelan.............................	931	79,310	1.14	955	12.5	683	8.9	5,961	9.7	11,720	9,259	2,462	1,909	2,494
Clallam............................	1,888	72,054	0.97	661	8.8	989	13.1	4,592	8.9	25,307	24,611	696	2,141	2,887
Clark................................	3,425	404,409	0.77	5,652	11.9	3,584	7.6	25,879	6.5	84,549	37,551	46,998	10,346	2,210
Columbia.........................	75	4,017	1.03	35	8.6	45	11.1	193	6.9	1,170	1,138	31	137	3,488
Cowlitz............................	1,207	102,190	0.98	1,278	12.0	1,129	10.6	6,018	7.2	22,977	11,977	11,000	3,735	3,588
Douglas...........................	190	34,057	0.66	536	12.8	311	7.4	3,332	9.8	12,548	9,700	2,848	889	2,163
Ferry...............................	252	7,381	0.89	64	8.4	78	10.3	625	11.1	1,890	1,849	41	28	428
Franklin...........................	2,901	82,920	0.87	1,642	17.8	416	4.5	9,282	11.8	9,392	9,199	193	2,014	2,207
Garfield............................	36	2,066	0.81	29	13.1	26	11.8	80	4.8	677	654	22	66	2,974
Grant...............................	1,244	94,586	1.05	1,486	15.6	685	7.2	9,137	11.5	15,653	13,271	2,383	3,956	4,192
Grays Harbor	2,703	69,532	0.93	764	10.5	817	11.2	4,357	8.0	19,221	18,198	1,023	2,016	2,903
Island..............................	1,897	70,753	0.74	970	11.7	738	8.9	3,839	6.3	22,586	16,387	6,200	1,034	1,289
Jefferson..........................	631	29,762	0.95	191	6.1	376	12.0	1,477	7.5	11,844	11,455	389	536	1,746
King.................................	38,699	2,254,543	1.16	25,950	11.9	13,433	6.1	104,849	5.6	310,557	197,138	113,418	99,598	4,604
Kitsap..............................	9,433	246,774	0.91	3,127	11.7	2,297	8.6	13,378	6.3	52,338	42,506	9,831	7,664	2,915
Kittitas............................	2,531	41,140	0.92	436	9.4	298	6.4	2,769	7.8	7,545	6,985	561	1,059	2,412
Klickitat...........................	198	20,369	0.93	188	8.6	180	8.3	1,363	8.4	5,628	5,469	159	263	1,238
Lewis...............................	920	72,946	0.90	934	11.9	883	11.3	4,671	7.8	20,090	13,872	6,218	2,373	3,138
Lincoln.............................	94	9,811	0.88	94	8.9	108	10.2	521	6.8	2,972	2,856	116	175	1,697
Mason	2,535	55,589	0.75	649	10.2	661	10.4	4,503	9.9	15,806	12,699	3,107	1,755	2,862
Okanogan.........................	640	41,667	1.02	498	11.9	483	11.6	4,434	13.8	10,172	9,093	1,079	691	1,656
Pacific.............................	289	20,318	0.94	198	9.2	321	14.8	1,419	9.6	7,369	7,063	306	314	1,501
Pend Oreille	98	12,551	0.89	129	9.7	141	10.6	705	7.2	3,680	3,544	136	308	2,340
Pierce..............................	17,413	781,787	0.87	11,778	13.4	6,936	7.9	47,893	6.5	141,747	97,045	44,702	37,711	4,399
San Juan..........................	187	16,103	1.01	74	4.4	132	7.9	974	8.8	5,435	4,364	1,071	187	1,139
Skagit..............................	1,626	121,274	1.02	1,475	11.7	1,213	9.7	8,328	8.5	29,442	21,985	7,457	4,590	3,722
Skamania	25	9,312	0.56	97	8.2	89	7.5	651	7.0	1,888	1,786	102	78	682
Snohomish	9,818	679,337	0.79	10,064	12.6	5,612	7.0	43,348	6.4	112,585	61,190	51,396	23,553	2,991
Spokane...........................	14,593	495,137	1.04	6,122	12.1	4,663	9.2	25,701	6.3	100,032	64,212	35,820	28,297	5,697
Stevens............................	266	40,452	0.79	446	10.0	477	10.7	2,677	7.8	10,703	10,171	531	806	1,842
Thurston..........................	4,061	254,626	0.90	3,171	11.3	2,256	8.0	12,634	5.6	55,498	35,861	19,637	8,757	3,196
Wahkiakum	48	3,902	0.88	23	5.4	44	10.3	222	7.9	1,387	1,002	386	51	1,252
Walla Walla	4,769	63,891	1.16	662	10.9	604	10.0	3,719	8.2	12,476	11,205	1,271	2,078	3,414
Whatcom..........................	5,895	206,371	0.97	2,373	10.7	1,636	7.4	15,140	8.6	42,816	27,591	15,224	7,159	3,325
Whitman...........................	6,211	50,386	1.14	443	9.0	256	5.2	2,397	6.4	5,679	5,484	195	997	2,083
Yakima	3,501	247,043	0.99	3,942	15.8	2,027	8.1	27,737	13.2	41,160	34,306	6,854	9,833	3,922
WEST VIRGINIA	47,432	1,829,434	0.98	19,098	10.5	22,227	12.2	94,163	6.5	428,870	299,514	129,356	44,044	2,405
Barbour............................	940	14,287	0.59	158	9.6	199	12.1	912	7.2	3,664	2,735	929	240	1,444
Berkeley...........................	889	93,748	0.67	1,388	12.1	1,013	8.8	6,179	6.4	20,590	16,434	4,155	2,567	2,277
Boone..............................	131	24,384	1.11	220	9.8	298	13.3	1,176	6.4	5,234	3,010	2,224	391	1,800
Braxton............................	358	13,794	0.87	166	11.7	176	12.4	787	7.2	3,154	2,128	1,026	189	1,473
Brooke.............................	750	21,359	0.79	190	8.5	323	14.4	889	5.2	4,975	3,081	1,893	191	1,017
Cabell..............................	4,078	109,763	1.34	1,084	11.4	1,092	11.5	4,763	6.3	24,360	16,576	7,784	4,056	4,210

1. Per 1,000 estimated resident population.　　2. Data for serious crimes have not been adjusted for underreporting; this may affect comparability between geographic areas and over time.
3. Per 100,000 population estimated by the FBI.

Table B. States and Counties — Crime, Education, Money Income, and Poverty

STATE County	Serious crimes known to police, 2016 (cont.)[1] Rate		Education School enrollment and attainment, 2012-2016				Local government expenditures,[5] 2013-2014		Money income, 2012-2016		Households Percent		Income and poverty, 2016	Percent below poverty level		
			Enrollment[3]		Attainment[4] (percent)											
	Violent	Property	Total	Percent private	High school graduate or less	Bachelor's degree or more	Total current spending (mil dol)	Current spending per student (dollars)	Per capita income[6]	Median income (dollars)	with income of less than $50,000	with income of $200,000 or more	Median household income (dollars)	All persons	Children under 18 years	Children 5 to 17 years in families
	46	47	48	49	50	51	52	53	54	55	56	57	58	59	60	61
VIRGINIA— Cont'd																
Martinsville city	207	2,686	3,111	10.3	50.1	18.3	24.4	10,801	22,221	31,719	65.0	2.5	34,262	23.2	34.8	34.0
Newport News city	472	3,080	50,337	13.5	38.6	24.7	299.9	10,071	25,520	50,089	49.9	2.5	50,149	14.7	21.1	22.8
Norfolk city	659	3,923	68,248	12.3	39.0	26.6	342.6	10,509	25,450	45,268	54.6	3.0	45,809	21.3	31.2	31.7
Norton city	409	3,682	764	2.9	40.4	17.3	7.6	8,988	19,522	26,000	72.0	1.2	30,587	23.0	33.8	30.9
Petersburg city	740	3,323	6,426	10.5	54.3	16.6	47.3	10,600	20,464	32,169	67.9	0.8	34,238	25.2	36.7	42.6
Poquoson city	167	1,428	3,177	10.3	30.2	39.8	19.9	9,388	39,020	84,643	29.4	8.5	90,119	5.4	6.7	5.8
Portsmouth city	796	5,702	24,627	12.8	44.6	21.1	148.5	9,922	23,878	47,050	52.5	1.7	46,617	18.2	30.1	30.5
Radford city	474	1,811	9,329	3.4	34.0	34.1	14.9	9,213	18,108	31,457	68.5	1.8	35,655	27.2	19.1	18.2
Richmond city	569	3,632	55,733	18.2	38.8	36.7	299.4	12,328	29,011	41,187	58.0	4.6	42,336	26.2	38.9	40.3
Roanoke city	412	4,204	21,907	13.6	46.6	22.9	157.6	11,642	23,611	39,201	60.0	1.9	38,238	22.3	30.6	31.6
Salem city	95	2,079	6,868	25.4	40.7	26.9	40.6	10,570	28,892	52,351	46.6	4.0	57,897	9.2	12.4	12.2
Staunton city	168	2,193	5,273	28.6	40.6	33.7	30.1	10,683	26,678	42,948	56.7	2.1	46,237	12.8	20.8	21.5
Suffolk city	281	2,434	24,274	19.2	40.0	26.6	135.1	9,334	30,331	65,435	38.2	4.4	65,025	11.7	16.8	16.1
Virginia Beach city	155	2,183	118,611	17.8	29.1	34.2	734.7	10,413	33,250	67,719	34.7	5.2	70,596	8.3	11.5	10.9
Waynesboro city	186	2,274	4,565	11.0	48.6	22.6	32.4	10,183	22,967	45,097	55.3	0.9	41,255	14.6	24.1	24.3
Williamsburg city	164	1,508	7,536	4.7	19.8	56.7	122.2	10,832	25,548	50,091	49.9	7.2	49,231	21.1	23.1	22.5
Winchester city	NA	NA	7,038	27.9	44.5	31.3	186.1	10,708	26,984	46,466	53.3	5.3	46,093	15.0	22.0	20.3
WASHINGTON	302	3,494	1,724,293	15.0	32.3	33.6	10,791.3	10,194	32,999	62,848	39.7	6.3	67,064	11.3	13.9	12.8
Adams	206	2,760	5,457	5.0	60.4	13.8	46.9	10,178	17,781	47,554	52.8	1.1	48,698	19.5	25.1	24.3
Asotin	184	3,372	4,807	7.4	39.1	21.0	34.1	10,252	25,760	45,550	55.2	1.6	46,121	14.6	20.6	18.4
Benton	196	2,252	49,291	11.8	34.9	29.4	324.1	9,413	29,529	61,147	40.7	5.1	63,474	10.5	13.9	12.4
Chelan	161	2,334	17,182	10.3	46.0	25.3	137.4	10,443	26,109	51,845	48.2	3.4	51,930	11.5	16.4	15.0
Clallam	302	2,585	14,119	11.0	34.9	24.3	102.6	9,842	26,967	47,180	53.0	1.8	49,502	15.3	22.2	18.8
Clark	231	1,979	116,198	12.7	33.5	27.9	757.7	9,668	30,207	62,879	38.9	4.8	68,937	9.0	10.9	9.3
Columbia	76	3,411	752	10.5	36.0	25.4	5.9	12,558	26,536	42,083	58.0	3.3	47,894	14.0	23.8	21.8
Cowlitz	269	3,319	23,254	9.9	43.0	15.9	166.3	9,935	24,756	49,127	50.9	1.9	51,772	16.3	20.2	18.4
Douglas	112	2,051	9,755	6.4	47.7	17.7	80.4	10,321	23,966	53,758	46.0	1.6	52,363	12.8	17.8	15.7
Ferry	107	321	1,614	17.8	44.1	18.1	13.3	14,390	21,146	39,555	61.1	0.8	40,581	21.3	28.2	26.6
Franklin	189	2,019	26,101	7.6	52.4	15.8	185.6	9,830	20,997	58,284	41.9	2.7	56,940	14.9	21.0	19.6
Garfield	90	2,884	433	2.5	35.3	24.2	4.3	13,098	23,313	51,395	47.5	0.4	51,922	13.9	18.9	17.5
Grant	268	3,924	25,217	6.1	51.3	15.6	191.6	10,097	20,409	50,145	49.8	1.8	48,997	16.1	20.9	19.1
Grays Harbor	212	2,691	14,831	7.0	45.2	15.3	116.1	11,225	23,799	44,521	55.3	2.1	48,210	15.2	22.8	21.3
Island	112	1,177	15,865	15.4	28.1	31.7	77.6	9,626	32,503	60,261	41.3	3.9	64,475	9.4	12.4	11.8
Jefferson	134	1,612	4,351	16.7	27.6	38.8	31.5	10,623	30,871	50,928	48.9	3.2	53,345	12.0	20.6	19.0
King	347	4,257	492,042	19.2	23.5	49.1	2,665.7	10,504	43,629	78,800	32.2	11.8	85,907	9.3	10.6	10.0
Kitsap	260	2,656	58,400	13.3	28.3	31.2	360.4	10,047	32,801	65,017	37.3	4.7	68,706	10.1	11.6	10.5
Kittitas	112	2,300	14,140	9.3	34.3	34.7	48.9	9,909	25,147	47,898	51.6	1.7	50,410	18.2	14.7	13.4
Klickitat	104	1,135	4,333	16.7	41.2	24.4	36.0	11,389	23,227	49,633	50.4	1.0	50,691	15.5	21.0	19.6
Lewis	180	2,958	16,531	12.8	43.8	15.5	120.9	10,219	22,947	42,546	54.6	1.5	47,127	14.7	19.8	18.4
Lincoln	116	1,581	2,193	9.3	39.9	22.0	29.1	14,404	25,382	47,676	52.6	1.5	53,886	12.5	17.3	15.7
Mason	207	2,655	11,428	6.6	44.3	18.6	83.3	10,520	25,628	51,764	48.5	2.5	52,758	14.9	22.6	21.7
Okanogan	177	1,478	8,450	12.7	47.9	18.4	90.5	9,166	22,544	41,581	59.5	1.5	41,726	19.7	26.3	25.0
Pacific	158	1,343	3,624	6.1	44.1	17.0	35.4	11,118	22,187	38,387	62.2	0.9	43,168	17.0	23.7	22.8
Pend Oreille	198	2,142	2,622	18.4	41.3	18.7	19.6	12,544	24,163	46,036	55.1	1.9	48,706	16.2	26.7	24.2
Pierce	483	3,916	204,641	15.1	37.2	25.4	1,312.7	10,199	29,750	61,468	39.6	4.2	64,312	12.1	15.3	14.0
San Juan	61	1,078	2,437	24.0	21.9	47.0	21.0	10,765	40,327	58,029	44.2	6.7	59,658	9.9	15.3	13.6
Skagit	185	3,537	26,291	10.9	37.7	24.7	204.5	10,784	28,586	56,433	44.1	3.5	60,442	11.3	12.0	12.1
Skamania	70	612	2,282	16.3	38.1	22.7	12.5	11,026	28,556	53,082	48.2	2.7	55,802	13.5	18.1	15.8
Snohomish	225	2,765	183,766	15.2	32.4	30.6	1,287.3	9,904	33,883	73,528	32.7	6.2	78,582	8.0	9.1	8.6
Spokane	360	5,337	124,070	17.9	32.1	28.7	752.5	10,235	26,860	50,550	49.4	3.0	52,933	13.3	15.8	14.1
Stevens	112	1,730	9,073	13.3	43.4	18.0	68.9	11,022	22,745	44,115	55.3	1.7	51,303	14.3	20.8	19.4
Thurston	246	2,949	63,698	13.5	29.0	33.3	408.8	9,926	30,583	62,854	38.1	4.0	65,684	10.4	12.0	11.4
Wahkiakum	221	1,031	742	15.4	37.5	15.1	4.5	10,835	27,619	48,116	52.8	2.3	54,162	12.8	24.7	22.2
Walla Walla	261	3,153	16,154	30.6	33.8	28.6	94.1	10,536	24,736	48,705	51.1	3.0	53,598	14.2	17.0	15.7
Whatcom	199	3,126	57,283	12.4	32.6	32.6	267.5	10,162	27,810	54,207	45.8	3.1	56,636	15.2	12.3	11.5
Whitman	176	1,908	24,105	4.5	20.9	49.8	54.4	11,892	20,957	38,636	59.6	2.7	42,693	25.9	14.7	12.9
Yakima	302	3,620	66,719	8.4	55.8	15.3	537.7	10,201	20,653	45,700	54.5	2.3	48,232	18.2	25.5	23.5
WEST VIRGINIA	358	2,047	405,213	10.1	55.1	19.6	3,116.3	11,092	24,002	42,644	56.8	2.3	43,175	17.9	23.9	22.2
Barbour	451	993	4,037	20.9	62.7	12.8	24.7	10,078	18,602	36,733	66.0	0.5	36,485	22.4	30.5	27.0
Berkeley	179	2,098	27,419	12.8	50.4	20.3	199.9	10,973	27,015	57,148	43.1	2.3	56,966	12.9	17.8	16.4
Boone	207	1,593	4,917	7.1	71.3	8.7	57.4	12,645	20,711	37,820	60.9	1.2	36,313	24.2	30.2	27.7
Braxton	281	1,193	2,714	9.4	70.1	12.2	22.1	10,408	20,178	38,092	60.3	1.3	36,612	21.3	31.1	30.1
Brooke	149	868	5,194	25.1	49.9	19.8	38.1	11,741	24,428	46,265	53.3	1.5	46,020	13.4	20.7	18.2
Cabell	461	3,749	24,679	8.7	44.8	26.1	143.6	11,641	23,853	37,760	60.8	2.7	39,462	21.9	25.3	24.7

1. Data for serious crimes have not been adjusted for underreporting; this may affect comparability between geographic areas and over time.   2. Per 100,000 population estimated by the FBI.
3. All persons 3 years old and over enrolled in nursery school through college.   4. Persons 25 years old and over.   5. Elementary and secondary education expenditures.
6. Based on population estimated by the American Community Survey, 2011–2015.

Table B. States and Counties — Personal Income and Earnings

STATE County	Personal income, 2016										Earnings, 2016		
			Per capita[1]			Supplements to wages and salaries, employer contributions (mil dol)						Contributions for government social insurance (mil dol)	
	Total (mil dol)	Percent change 2015-2016	Dollars	Rank	Wages and salaries (mil dol)	Pension and insurance	Government social insurance	Proprietors' income (mil dol)	Dividends, interest, and rent (mil dol)	Personal transfer receipts (mil dol)	Total (mil dol)	From employee and self-employed	From employer
	62	63	64	65	66	67	68	69	70	71	72	73	74
VIRGINIA— Cont'd													
Martinsville city.................	(2)	(2)	(2)	(2)	(2)	(2)	(2)	(2)	(2)	(2)	(2)	(2)	(2)
Newport News city............	7,449	0.9	40,967	1,239	5,752	1,125	437	270	1,485	1,450	7,585	864	437
Norfolk city.......................	9,433	0.1	38,484	1,572	10,833	2,489	911	134	2,455	1,890	14,367	1,650	911
Norton city........................	(3)	(3)	(3)	(3)	(3)	(3)	(3)	(3)	(3)	(3)	(3)	(3)	(3)
Petersburg city..................	(4)	(4)	(4)	(4)	(4)	(4)	(4)	(4)	(4)	(4)	(4)	(4)	(4)
Poquoson city....................	(5)	(5)	(5)	(5)	(5)	(5)	(5)	(5)	(5)	(5)	(5)	(5)	(5)
Portsmouth city.................	3,731	-0.1	39,170	1,475	2,809	765	236	50	754	939	3,860	446	236
Radford city.......................	(6)	(6)	(6)	(6)	(6)	(6)	(6)	(6)	(6)	(6)	(6)	(6)	(6)
Richmond city....................	11,417	2.8	51,160	366	9,771	1,740	689	1,156	2,962	1,865	13,356	1,464	689
Roanoke city......................	4,212	1.2	42,263	1,066	3,476	544	266	317	939	1,014	4,604	550	266
Salem city	(7)	(7)	(7)	(7)	(7)	(7)	(7)	(7)	(7)	(7)	(7)	(7)	(7)
Staunton city.....................	(8)	(8)	(8)	(8)	(8)	(8)	(8)	(8)	(8)	(8)	(8)	(8)	(8)
Suffolk city........................	4,327	2.5	48,467	503	1,544	277	115	159	779	750	2,094	246	115
Virginia Beach city	24,183	1.5	53,432	284	9,157	1,671	705	1,381	5,578	3,258	12,915	1,456	705
Waynesboro city................	(8)	(8)	(8)	(8)	(8)	(8)	(8)	(8)	(8)	(8)	(8)	(8)	(8)
Williamsburg city...............	(9)	(9)	(9)	(9)	(9)	(9)	(9)	(9)	(9)	(9)	(9)	(9)	(9)
Winchester city..................	(10)	(10)	(10)	(10)	(10)	(10)	(10)	(10)	(10)	(10)	(10)	(10)	(10)
WASHINGTON..............	397,772	4.7	54,632	X	203,613	29,174	17,320	29,803	88,021	59,662	279,909	16,216	17,320
Adams..............................	854	-0.3	44,393	839	291	53	28	177	181	174	550	51	28
Asotin...............................	958	5.1	42,940	1,000	235	43	23	67	198	264	369	50	23
Benton..............................	8,780	5.5	45,329	752	4,737	642	428	994	1,377	1,566	6,801	805	428
Chelan..............................	3,621	4.4	47,428	571	1,746	290	168	350	840	762	2,554	310	168
Clallam.............................	3,056	3.8	40,985	1,237	970	203	92	169	834	935	1,434	196	92
Clark................................	21,986	5.2	47,078	603	7,876	1,218	718	1,425	4,360	3,735	11,236	1,418	718
Columbia..........................	190	-1.1	48,136	522	54	13	5	29	39	52	101	11	5
Cowlitz.............................	4,359	4.9	41,449	1,174	1,882	296	180	399	694	1,179	2,757	358	180
Douglas............................	1,527	4.2	36,951	1,829	455	79	42	97	298	349	673	81	42
Ferry................................	250	3.6	32,876	2,502	72	19	7	10	53	93	108	14	7
Franklin	3,186	4.3	35,339	2,109	1,388	242	139	448	410	645	2,218	247	139
Garfield............................	98	0.2	43,447	949	32	10	3	7	22	27	53	6	3
Grant...............................	3,824	5.9	40,879	1,248	1,590	292	151	701	580	835	2,734	271	151
Grays Harbor....................	2,638	3.9	36,824	1,850	932	183	89	131	486	863	1,335	181	89
Island..............................	4,110	4.9	49,741	426	1,065	267	105	258	1,184	824	1,694	207	105
Jefferson..........................	1,514	3.6	48,625	490	344	71	32	108	509	402	556	75	32
King.................................	166,006	4.0	77,213	35	106,180	12,120	8,312	12,836	43,229	14,431	139,448	16,320	8,312
Kitsap..............................	13,164	5.1	49,709	428	5,176	1,226	482	592	3,290	2,235	7,476	907	482
Kittitas.............................	1,802	6.5	40,161	1,347	621	125	59	148	388	359	953	114	59
Klickitat............................	971	5.0	45,595	735	355	66	34	83	220	256	537	66	34
Lewis...............................	2,974	3.7	38,586	1,560	1,071	194	104	173	514	897	1,543	208	104
Lincoln.............................	477	-2.3	46,053	687	112	27	10	77	105	117	226	22	10
Mason..............................	2,363	5.6	37,986	1,662	587	127	54	105	500	679	874	118	54
Okanogan	1,659	5.3	39,912	1,377	601	129	56	165	335	481	951	110	56
Pacific.............................	893	4.3	42,039	1,097	256	53	25	44	193	302	379	53	25
Pend Oreille	484	4.3	36,911	1,836	151	33	13	22	100	164	219	29	13
Pierce..............................	40,228	6.0	46,706	637	17,230	3,087	1,625	2,783	7,150	7,310	24,725	3,035	1,625
San Juan..........................	1,130	2.4	69,155	70	220	36	21	102	613	170	380	48	21
Skagit..............................	5,759	5.3	46,565	651	2,361	449	219	442	1,313	1,238	3,471	428	219
Skamania.........................	464	4.0	40,338	1,321	85	17	8	17	102	101	127	18	8
Snohomish........................	38,996	6.1	49,511	439	17,532	2,685	1,550	2,486	5,856	5,331	24,252	2,971	1,550
Spokane...........................	20,975	4.8	42,028	1,099	10,759	1,756	996	1,213	4,171	4,697	14,723	1,890	996
Stevens............................	1,593	4.5	35,855	2,022	418	89	40	93	301	505	640	86	40
Thurston...........................	12,642	5.7	45,932	696	5,665	1,091	509	710	2,632	2,427	7,974	979	509
Wahkiakum	153	2.8	36,990	1,823	28	7	3	8	42	51	45	7	3
Walla Walla	2,622	3.4	43,459	946	1,198	225	110	279	536	565	1,813	206	110
Whatcom..........................	9,598	4.4	44,273	852	4,142	741	387	857	2,154	1,801	6,127	749	387
Whitman...........................	1,744	1.6	35,697	2,044	891	251	79	155	371	303	1,377	149	79
Yakima.............................	10,125	4.5	40,558	1,294	4,303	717	413	1,042	1,842	2,535	6,475	743	413
WEST VIRGINIA	67,062	-0.3	36,673	X	29,771	5,384	2,383	3,653	9,846	19,477	41,190	2,882	2,383
Barbour............................	494	-0.9	29,329	2,906	124	25	10	20	61	166	178	25	10
Berkeley...........................	4,266	3.5	37,576	1,726	1,433	290	119	185	516	814	2,028	253	119
Boone...............................	708	-0.1	31,026	2,736	232	42	19	22	73	272	315	44	19
Braxton............................	413	-2.0	28,548	2,948	140	27	11	24	61	150	202	27	11
Brooke.............................	858	-0.4	37,320	1,762	334	61	27	45	126	252	467	61	27
Cabell..............................	3,712	0.2	38,676	1,549	2,338	389	191	218	597	1,067	3,116	396	191

1. Based on the resident population estimated as of July 1 of the year shown.   2. Martinsville city is included with Henry county.   3. Norton city is included with Wise county.   4. Petersburg and Colonial Heights cities are included with Dinwiddie county.   5. Poquoson city is included with York county.   6. Radford city is included with Montgomery county.   7. Salem city is included with Roanoke county.   8. Staunton and Waynesboro cities are included with Augusta county.   9. Williamsburg city is included with James City county.   10. Winchester city is included with Frederick county.

Table B. States and Counties — Earnings, Social Security, and Housing

STATE County	Earnings, 2016 (cont.) Percent by selected industries									Social Security beneficiaries, December 2016		Supplemental Security Income recipients, 2016	Housing units, 2017	
	Farm	Mining, quarrying, and extracting	Construction	Manufacturing	Information; professional, scientific, technical services	Retail trade	Finance, insurance, real estate, and leasing	Health care and social assistance	Government	Number	Rate[1]		Total	Percent change, 2010-2017
	75	76	77	78	79	80	81	82	83	84	85	86	87	88
VIRGINIA— Cont'd														
Martinsville city	(2)	(2)	(2)	(2)	(2)	(2)	(2)	(2)	(2)	4,145	316	43	7,063	-1.9
Newport News city	0.0	D	2.5	28.8	8.0	4.3	3.2	10.6	25.2	29,650	164	4,826	77,761	1.8
Norfolk city	0.0	D	D	2.8	7.4	2.7	3.9	10.1	53.1	34,520	141	7,673	97,926	3.1
Norton city	(3)	(3)	(3)	(3)	(3)	(3)	(3)	(3)	(3)	1,405	352	376	1,965	-0.3
Petersburg city	(4)	(4)	(4)	(4)	(4)	(4)	(4)	(4)	(4)	8,085	254	3,081	16,402	0.4
Poquoson city	(5)	(5)	(5)	(5)	(5)	(5)	(5)	(5)	(5)	2,510	210	63	4,799	1.5
Portsmouth city	0.0	0.0	3.9	D	3.9	2.4	1.2	10.3	63.2	18,860	199	3,909	40,879	0.2
Radford city	(6)	(6)	(6)	(6)	(6)	(6)	(6)	(6)	(6)	2,305	132	384	6,511	1.4
Richmond city	0.0	D	3.5	4.6	16.4	2.2	8.7	11.9	27.3	34,775	154	9,581	100,116	1.8
Roanoke city	0.0	D	7.7	D	8.8	6.2	7.6	20.3	13.0	21,575	216	4,732	47,011	-0.8
Salem city	(7)	(7)	(7)	(7)	(7)	(7)	(7)	(7)	(7)	6,310	247	555	10,849	0.1
Staunton city	(8)	(8)	(8)	(8)	(8)	(8)	(8)	(8)	(8)	6,750	278	813	11,841	0.9
Suffolk city	0.5	0.0	5.7	7.5	15.4	5.6	3.3	12.8	27.2	16,555	185	2,304	36,851	11.6
Virginia Beach city	0.0	D	8.5	3.1	11.2	6.7	9.7	11.8	27.8	71,415	158	5,587	184,993	4.0
Waynesboro city	(8)	(8)	(8)	(8)	(8)	(8)	(8)	(8)	(8)	5,365	246	761	10,021	3.1
Williamsburg city	(9)	(9)	(9)	(9)	(9)	(9)	(9)	(9)	(9)	2,510	168	12	5,269	7.0
Winchester city	(10)	(10)	(10)	(10)	(10)	(10)	(10)	(10)	(10)	5,390	196	737	11,844	-0.3
WASHINGTON	1.6	0.2	6.5	9.9	16.8	7.9	6.0	10.3	18.5	1,291,198	177	150,658	3,103,117	7.5
Adams	31.3	0.1	2.7	12.7	1.2	3.8	3.5	D	17.8	2,580	134	341	6,630	6.2
Asotin	0.8	D	13.7	6.8	4.6	13.6	5.0	18.8	18.8	6,490	291	755	10,045	1.8
Benton	7.3	D	7.1	4.7	17.8	5.6	3.7	10.6	16.5	34,210	177	3,829	76,283	11.2
Chelan	8.5	0.0	6.3	4.4	D	9.5	4.2	17.5	20.0	17,045	224	1,494	37,644	6.1
Clallam	0.2	0.1	7.3	5.5	4.7	9.6	3.5	9.7	38.9	25,545	345	1,971	36,912	3.7
Clark	0.2	D	9.5	8.7	11.4	7.6	7.1	12.9	17.5	83,365	179	8,250	182,500	9.0
Columbia	19.0	D	10.5	2.3	1.9	3.0	1.3	9.5	33.2	1,330	333	145	2,169	1.5
Cowlitz	0.6	0.8	14.6	20.4	3.4	6.4	3.6	14.0	15.0	27,185	260	3,836	44,661	2.8
Douglas	15.7	0.0	6.9	4.6	D	9.4	3.7	5.6	25.7	7,880	191	574	16,985	6.1
Ferry	1.9	D	D	D	2.7	3.6	D	D	53.6	2,340	310	254	4,524	2.7
Franklin	16.9	0.2	7.2	8.9	1.8	7.8	3.0	6.5	20.3	10,230	113	1,776	27,958	14.5
Garfield	5.1	0.5	D	0.6	D	4.5	3.0	3.2	63.9	660	292	44	1,246	1.1
Grant	27.6	D	4.2	11.7	2.4	5.3	3.0	5.0	22.6	15,870	169	2,132	37,464	6.8
Grays Harbor	0.8	D	7.2	12.5	3.1	8.2	3.4	10.7	32.2	20,150	281	3,024	36,185	2.9
Island	0.3	D	7.0	3.4	D	5.9	4.0	5.1	53.6	21,785	267	1,029	41,876	4.1
Jefferson	0.7	D	11.2	7.8	7.6	7.9	4.9	7.0	31.1	11,990	388	611	18,643	4.9
King	0.0	0.2	5.3	8.3	26.9	8.6	6.7	8.3	11.8	288,475	134	37,715	934,552	9.8
Kitsap	0.0	D	5.1	2.1	8.0	5.8	3.5	9.9	53.6	51,370	195	5,027	112,667	4.9
Kittitas	4.7	D	9.7	3.2	D	8.4	4.9	6.2	35.3	8,350	186	576	23,666	8.1
Klickitat	9.8	D	4.5	25.1	D	3.3	2.7	2.9	21.0	6,160	289	618	10,432	6.6
Lewis	3.4	0.6	5.9	14.1	3.1	9.8	3.1	14.1	21.2	21,600	282	2,706	35,101	3.1
Lincoln	26.8	D	8.2	D	4.4	3.8	4.2	D	31.1	3,105	300	263	6,039	4.6
Mason	1.4	D	6.8	8.0	3.1	8.4	3.9	5.1	43.7	17,450	281	1,587	33,451	2.9
Okanogan	14.1	1.9	5.7	3.1	D	8.8	2.1	8.2	34.0	10,805	260	1,299	23,206	4.3
Pacific	3.8	0.5	6.3	6.3	D	5.9	2.4	D	35.1	8,005	377	674	16,174	4.0
Pend Oreille	0.9	D	6.8	9.0	4.6	3.3	2.2	D	47.1	4,125	314	514	8,263	4.1
Pierce	0.2	0.1	8.0	5.6	4.8	7.2	5.3	16.2	31.1	148,600	173	19,757	346,026	6.3
San Juan	0.5	D	17.6	2.8	D	10.0	6.2	5.5	14.8	5,230	321	128	14,128	6.1
Skagit	4.3	0.1	9.8	14.9	5.9	8.8	6.1	7.7	24.0	29,615	240	2,453	53,800	4.5
Skamania	-0.1	D	7.7	14.0	D	4.0	D	D	33.2	2,500	216	201	5,864	4.1
Snohomish	0.2	0.1	9.5	30.2	8.0	6.9	6.0	8.7	14.4	119,060	151	12,298	310,084	8.2
Spokane	0.2	0.1	6.3	7.1	7.2	7.5	8.9	17.7	19.7	101,100	203	14,338	216,536	7.5
Stevens	2.1	0.8	7.5	12.5	3.8	7.3	3.1	14.2	28.3	12,695	287	1,346	21,701	2.6
Thurston	0.8	0.1	5.3	3.0	6.3	6.4	4.4	12.7	39.3	57,625	210	5,307	116,820	8.0
Wahkiakum	2.3	0.3	12.2	5.4	D	3.0	D	D	32.3	1,500	359	106	2,150	3.9
Walla Walla	13.3	D	4.0	14.2	3.7	4.8	4.1	15.3	23.2	12,575	210	1,405	24,762	5.6
Whatcom	2.8	D	9.8	13.8	6.9	9.0	5.1	12.6	18.7	43,060	199	4,401	96,619	6.6
Whitman	5.1	D	2.6	17.6	2.2	5.1	2.4	5.4	48.4	5,795	119	457	20,740	7.3
Yakima	17.2	0.0	5.1	8.0	3.0	7.1	2.8	13.9	18.3	43,745	175	7,417	88,611	3.7
WEST VIRGINIA	-0.2	4.6	6.5	8.3	7.5	7.2	4.5	16.5	22.2	470,240	257	74,665	892,226	1.2
Barbour	-1.0	D	9.0	D	D	5.5	2.9	D	21.2	4,200	251	733	7,923	1.0
Berkeley	0.2	D	5.4	4.5	10.0	6.9	3.5	13.8	32.9	21,880	193	2,321	48,524	8.4
Boone	0.0	D	1.4	0.8	D	6.7	D	D	26.9	6,860	301	1,353	11,163	0.8
Braxton	-0.6	2.2	10.8	9.4	2.9	15.7	2.5	12.7	22.0	3,870	270	653	7,434	0.3
Brooke	-0.1	D	D	26.0	D	7.6	3.5	D	10.3	6,460	284	506	10,822	-1.3
Cabell	0.0	0.5	5.7	10.2	6.0	8.1	4.6	27.2	16.5	22,570	236	4,474	46,364	0.4

1. Per 1,000 resident population estimated as of July 1 of the year shown.   2. Martinsville city is included with Henry county.   3. Norton city is included with Wise county.   4. Petersburg and Colonial Heights cities are included with Dinwiddie county.   5. Poquoson city is included with York county.   6. Radford city is included with Montgomery county.   7. Salem city is included with Roanoke county.   8. Staunton and Waynesboro cities are included with Augusta county.   9. Williamsburg city is included with James City county.   10. Winchester city is included with Frederick county.

Table B. States and Counties — Housing, Labor Force, and Employment

STATE County	Housing units, 2017 (cont.) — Occupied units — Owner-occupied					Renter-occupied		Sub-standard units⁴ (percent)	Civilian labor force, 2017		Unemployment		Civilian employment⁶, 2012-2016	Percent	
	Total	Percent	Median value¹	Median owner cost as a percent of income — With a mortgage	Without a mortgage²	Median rent³	Median rent as a percent of income²		Total	Percent change, 2016-2017	Total	Rate⁵	Total	Management, business, science, and arts	Construction, production, and maintenance occupations
	89	90	91	92	93	94	95	96	97	98	99	100	101	102	103
VIRGINIA— Cont'd															
Martinsville city	5,787	52.9	88,700	20.6	12.9	629	29.6	1.1	5,235	1.5	356	6.8	5,363	25.4	29.2
Newport News city	69,247	49.4	189,000	23.6	12.1	972	31.5	2.8	90,074	1.5	4,191	4.7	82,379	33.9	22.4
Norfolk city	87,367	42.8	193,100	25.9	13.9	980	33.5	2.8	111,699	1.4	5,197	4.7	102,488	32.9	22.3
Norton city	1,858	45.3	92,500	22.7	12.2	574	32.1	1.2	1,628	-1.9	90	5.5	1,720	29.1	18.4
Petersburg city	13,175	41.2	111,300	24.7	14.4	857	35.1	3.3	13,392	1.5	978	7.3	12,961	23.7	24.4
Poquoson city	4,610	83.1	301,800	22.5	14.9	1,140	27.8	0.4	6,247	1.4	218	3.5	6,130	51.0	17.0
Portsmouth city	36,840	53.8	169,400	25.4	15.8	977	33.9	2.3	44,552	1.2	2,418	5.4	41,660	30.1	25.1
Radford city	5,604	43.7	153,900	22.7	12.5	762	38.1	1.2	8,285	0.5	418	5.0	7,139	32.2	15.2
Richmond city	88,958	41.4	199,300	23.6	14.1	916	33.5	2.4	116,588	1.8	5,089	4.4	107,261	40.8	15.1
Roanoke city	42,541	52.1	133,000	23.1	12.6	748	30.4	2.0	48,976	0.2	2,066	4.2	47,019	31.2	22.0
Salem city	10,060	64.3	173,800	21.5	11.5	842	28.0	2.0	12,907	0.3	494	3.8	12,357	37.4	19.1
Staunton city	10,383	58.1	163,000	22.2	10.8	799	29.4	1.8	11,848	0.6	433	3.7	11,404	36.5	19.6
Suffolk city	31,741	69.3	236,600	24.5	11.9	1,052	31.5	1.4	43,492	1.4	1,808	4.2	40,152	37.8	22.5
Virginia Beach city	167,509	63.2	262,200	24.7	11.1	1,258	31.2	1.6	232,521	1.6	8,373	3.6	217,132	39.5	17.3
Waynesboro city	9,044	57.9	158,800	24.0	12.9	801	28.7	1.9	10,272	0.9	419	4.1	9,815	28.7	25.6
Williamsburg city	4,627	46.6	319,500	24.3	10.0	1,093	34.8	3.0	6,820	1.7	360	5.3	6,058	52.3	9.1
Winchester city	10,596	45.5	218,600	20.5	12.0	937	32.4	5.0	14,570	1.9	527	3.6	12,814	35.3	21.1
WASHINGTON	2,696,606	62.4	269,300	23.5	11.5	1,056	29.8	3.5	3,724,721	2.5	177,292	4.8	3,331,321	39.5	21.0
Adams	5,733	67.7	146,400	23.2	10.0	697	26.9	13.1	8,918	2.3	514	5.8	7,847	23.7	49.2
Asotin	9,297	66.9	177,600	21.8	10.6	708	26.5	2.2	10,262	3.0	429	4.2	9,577	30.3	23.9
Benton	68,418	68.4	188,300	19.6	10.0	855	28.7	4.1	97,430	3.3	5,360	5.5	83,962	38.4	23.6
Chelan	27,200	65.7	246,100	24.5	10.1	792	24.8	4.1	44,518	2.8	2,169	4.9	33,389	30.9	29.4
Clallam	31,438	69.8	220,200	25.3	11.2	854	32.1	2.6	27,927	2.2	1,904	6.8	27,888	29.4	22.7
Clark	164,354	64.7	249,400	23.3	10.7	1,022	29.9	3.2	227,382	3.0	11,600	5.1	207,100	35.3	23.1
Columbia	1,689	71.8	162,200	26.0	12.9	745	28.5	2.7	1,766	2.7	99	5.6	1,609	34.7	25.2
Cowlitz	39,671	65.8	180,000	22.9	11.8	785	32.8	2.5	46,010	2.6	2,786	6.1	41,357	27.5	30.9
Douglas	14,348	71.1	214,900	23.4	10.0	800	26.1	7.8	21,012	2.3	1,200	5.7	18,126	25.0	34.3
Ferry	3,039	70.7	164,400	26.6	10.0	629	30.7	5.3	2,539	1.9	280	11.0	2,462	39.9	29.8
Franklin	25,157	67.9	169,700	21.1	10.0	829	28.6	10.6	40,873	2.6	2,579	6.3	37,445	24.1	39.9
Garfield	952	70.8	138,500	19.0	12.2	586	28.9	0.7	916	-0.3	50	5.5	910	35.6	25.2
Grant	29,783	61.3	153,800	21.7	10.0	717	24.6	7.3	45,310	1.7	2,835	6.3	38,144	26.5	40.1
Grays Harbor	27,472	67.1	159,400	22.9	11.6	750	29.6	3.3	27,971	2.7	1,978	7.1	26,525	26.5	26.1
Island	33,388	66.6	295,800	24.7	11.5	1,085	29.9	1.7	34,259	4.6	1,784	5.2	32,007	34.8	23.9
Jefferson	13,561	73.9	291,200	26.0	12.4	862	33.0	1.1	12,021	4.5	736	6.1	11,797	33.4	21.0
King	831,995	57.3	407,400	23.3	12.2	1,273	28.5	3.6	1,230,208	2.1	45,500	3.7	1,107,880	50.1	14.2
Kitsap	98,250	67.4	262,400	23.9	11.3	1,081	30.1	2.2	121,104	2.5	5,938	4.9	109,377	38.5	21.3
Kittitas	17,164	55.5	246,300	24.6	10.0	857	37.2	3.3	22,228	3.2	1,180	5.3	20,121	33.2	22.4
Klickitat	8,069	67.4	197,500	25.4	10.0	787	30.5	5.5	10,051	4.2	586	5.8	7,832	34.5	28.4
Lewis	29,426	68.2	174,800	23.8	12.8	822	32.5	3.3	33,151	3.9	2,203	6.6	29,433	26.5	29.8
Lincoln	4,337	78.2	145,300	21.8	11.9	662	24.3	2.8	4,955	1.3	245	4.9	4,188	35.1	26.7
Mason	22,454	77.1	201,800	25.5	11.0	897	32.4	3.1	23,843	1.5	1,571	6.6	22,478	27.3	28.5
Okanogan	16,804	67.0	165,300	21.7	10.0	630	28.1	6.8	20,930	-2.2	1,438	6.9	16,850	29.9	30.7
Pacific	8,986	73.7	159,200	23.4	13.9	703	29.9	1.0	8,410	1.5	592	7.0	7,095	27.1	31.3
Pend Oreille	5,409	76.9	181,700	23.1	10.0	768	30.0	4.3	4,734	1.6	353	7.5	4,262	34.1	29.6
Pierce	307,106	60.8	239,400	24.3	12.4	1,068	31.2	2.9	417,219	3.1	22,377	5.4	374,321	33.3	23.9
San Juan	7,623	72.6	456,800	27.8	11.1	955	29.4	5.9	8,235	4.6	324	3.9	7,629	38.2	21.5
Skagit	46,108	67.5	255,100	24.7	12.4	970	32.4	5.9	59,436	2.5	3,269	5.5	52,621	31.4	27.1
Skamania	4,577	69.3	243,000	23.7	12.4	723	28.7	2.8	5,218	2.8	322	6.2	4,776	35.3	27.9
Snohomish	278,626	66.1	309,800	24.1	12.0	1,197	29.8	3.3	421,369	2.2	17,380	4.1	378,916	38.0	22.1
Spokane	191,222	62.4	186,500	22.9	10.7	805	31.3	2.1	240,421	2.5	12,995	5.4	215,413	35.2	19.3
Stevens	17,442	75.9	174,800	23.6	10.7	674	30.6	4.3	18,284	2.2	1,328	7.3	16,204	29.1	29.5
Thurston	103,468	63.8	242,900	23.6	10.6	1,089	30.6	2.6	134,847	3.9	6,697	5.0	120,004	40.9	17.7
Wahkiakum	1,789	80.7	197,000	21.0	11.9	665	43.0	0.8	1,307	1.5	93	7.1	1,241	30.8	34.0
Walla Walla	21,851	64.8	191,700	23.0	11.7	775	31.2	3.1	29,304	2.1	1,443	4.9	26,294	36.0	21.4
Whatcom	81,019	62.2	283,000	24.6	12.1	938	34.1	2.9	110,074	2.8	5,514	5.0	99,796	34.0	22.2
Whitman	17,185	44.6	188,100	21.2	10.0	719	38.3	1.2	23,465	1.5	1,039	4.4	21,834	47.3	15.1
Yakima	80,196	62.7	160,700	23.6	11.1	776	29.7	8.7	126,814	0.8	8,602	6.8	102,611	24.2	38.3
WEST VIRGINIA	739,397	72.5	107,400	18.8	10.0	658	28.8	1.9	778,832	-0.4	40,515	5.2	750,412	32.3	24.5
Barbour	6,169	71.2	99,600	18.3	10.0	534	29.7	1.2	6,927	-0.4	401	5.8	6,568	22.5	29.8
Berkeley	41,720	73.5	163,800	21.7	10.0	936	28.1	3.0	54,471	0.8	2,009	3.7	50,807	32.9	25.5
Boone	9,466	76.0	72,900	20.4	10.0	582	32.7	2.4	7,692	-3.6	483	6.3	7,163	25.2	30.8
Braxton	5,417	75.6	84,500	16.1	10.0	506	27.3	2.3	5,366	-2.2	395	7.4	5,352	24.7	30.0
Brooke	9,934	73.0	89,200	16.5	10.0	590	26.2	2.0	9,850	-1.2	598	6.1	10,449	30.9	24.9
Cabell	39,954	60.9	114,000	19.2	10.0	688	31.8	1.3	41,479	0.8	1,880	4.5	40,124	36.4	15.9

1. Specified owner-occupied units. 2. A value of 10.0 represents 10 percent or less; a value of 50.0 represents 50 percent or more. 3. Specified renter-occupied units.
4. Overcrowded or lacking complete plumbing facilities. 5. Percent of civilian labor force. 6. Civilian employed persons 16 years old and over.

Items 89—103

Table B. States and Counties — **Nonfarm Employment and Agriculture**

STATE County	Private nonfarm establishments, employment and payroll, 2016									Agriculture, 2012			
		Employment						Annual payroll		Farms			Farm operators whose principal occupation is farming (percent)
												Percent with:	
	Number of establish-ments	Total	Health care and social assistance	Manufac-turing	Retail trade	Finance and insurance	Professional, scientific, and technical services	Total (mil dol)	Average per employee (dollars)	Number	Fewer than 50 acres	500 acres or more	
	104	105	106	107	108	109	110	111	112	113	114	115	116
VIRGINIA— Cont'd													
Martinsville city................	529	9,203	2,092	1,512	1,454	207	307	282	30,672	NA	NA	NA	NA
Newport News city............	3,782	90,485	14,491	29,760	10,461	1,718	5,381	4,510	49,844	NA	NA	NA	NA
Norfolk city......................	5,341	101,136	18,921	6,568	11,948	4,142	10,614	4,662	46,100	NA	NA	NA	NA
Norton city.......................	234	4,928	1,359	D	790	84	81	199	40,366	NA	NA	NA	NA
Petersburg city.................	723	12,639	5,116	1,129	1,420	195	219	467	36,976	NA	NA	NA	NA
Poquoson city	199	1,260	181	7	298	41	77	34	27,002	NA	NA	NA	NA
Portsmouth city................	1,660	27,032	7,824	1,311	3,179	467	1,477	1,034	38,263	NA	NA	NA	NA
Radford city.....................	311	4,280	513	1,188	594	130	144	155	36,206	NA	NA	NA	NA
Richmond city	6,129	120,124	26,688	4,813	9,168	10,953	11,736	7,099	59,100	NA	NA	NA	NA
Roanoke city	3,112	68,516	14,482	4,324	9,783	3,258	2,741	2,997	43,743	NA	NA	NA	NA
Salem city	1,004	18,508	4,728	3,132	1,999	522	583	871	47,059	NA	NA	NA	NA
Staunton city....................	748	10,308	2,248	512	1,936	308	290	313	30,358	NA	NA	NA	NA
Suffolk city.......................	1,588	21,887	4,681	1,892	3,931	712	1,014	859	39,263	308	57.8	10.7	56.2
Virginia Beach city	11,095	158,104	20,235	5,601	24,435	11,714	15,992	6,271	39,661	187	64.7	7.0	48.1
Waynesboro city	628	9,588	697	1,622	2,272	395	296	332	34,640	NA	NA	NA	NA
Williamsburg city..............	543	9,525	820	25	1,789	185	147	274	28,773	NA	NA	NA	NA
Winchester city.................	1,361	25,540	7,332	2,040	4,273	626	914	987	38,631	NA	NA	NA	NA
WASHINGTON.............	186,164	2,685,355	407,355	265,401	336,572	98,196	201,766	156,915	58,434	37,249	63.2	11.0	47.4
Adams.............................	367	4,516	803	1,056	710	84	53	184	40,684	713	17.8	46.6	54.8
Asotin.............................	441	4,740	1,008	362	1,097	141	261	170	35,881	185	35.1	40.0	60.5
Benton............................	4,274	64,268	11,117	3,773	10,296	1,610	7,891	3,234	50,320	1,509	76.0	7.8	44.8
Chelan............................	2,533	28,923	5,942	1,725	4,620	669	1,237	1,250	43,230	890	72.2	2.9	55.7
Clallam...........................	2,032	17,428	4,043	1,046	3,599	481	644	621	35,605	536	79.7	0.6	45.9
Clark..............................	10,614	131,177	21,777	14,181	18,373	5,439	9,174	6,396	48,757	1,929	86.3	0.5	35.4
Columbia.........................	122	790	164	D	103	19	20	29	37,213	308	23.1	37.7	42.5
Cowlitz...........................	2,150	30,646	5,688	6,213	5,083	763	730	1,391	45,389	492	72.4	2.8	46.7
Douglas..........................	745	6,852	834	399	1,741	189	180	231	33,734	849	43.0	25.9	55.9
Ferry..............................	140	1,097	153	177	126	19	27	61	55,763	255	27.8	16.1	52.2
Franklin	1,523	20,033	1,700	3,136	3,332	355	531	837	41,773	883	37.5	27.2	62.7
Garfield	46	310	108	NA	48	11	6	11	36,832	211	15.6	51.2	56.9
Grant..............................	1,846	21,473	2,967	4,142	3,591	536	477	857	39,902	1,552	31.2	25.9	66.6
Grays Harbor	1,622	15,540	2,808	1,945	2,947	557	395	581	37,382	557	63.9	4.7	44.7
Island	1,735	12,552	2,571	824	2,429	368	715	452	36,039	377	80.6	0.8	46.7
Jefferson	1,037	6,860	1,434	676	1,094	122	312	248	36,184	221	64.7	0.9	49.3
King...............................	68,079	1,167,201	149,502	87,277	107,472	42,299	110,197	87,676	75,116	1,837	90.5	0.4	44.3
Kitsap............................	5,795	59,446	12,707	2,273	11,273	1,769	4,212	2,291	38,546	706	94.9	0.1	44.6
Kittitas...........................	1,220	11,102	1,625	556	1,832	207	287	358	32,290	1,006	66.4	6.7	48.9
Klickitat...........................	524	4,036	843	599	443	68	273	159	39,374	760	44.5	22.8	51.7
Lewis.............................	1,849	20,391	3,546	3,251	3,876	361	535	766	37,553	1,647	63.8	2.1	41.0
Lincoln...........................	246	1,567	414	54	292	58	95	67	42,869	897	16.7	48.6	54.3
Mason............................	1,037	10,023	1,892	1,177	1,725	298	257	368	36,754	377	83.8	1.9	40.6
Okanogan........................	1,152	8,610	1,719	643	1,933	215	279	273	31,729	1,449	52.3	11.5	48.5
Pacific	561	4,058	649	578	543	161	108	132	32,481	330	61.8	6.1	45.8
Pend Oreille	216	1,579	385	262	232	48	68	67	42,706	288	45.5	4.2	37.8
Pierce............................	17,409	251,689	47,628	17,868	36,591	9,625	9,547	11,327	45,006	1,478	85.3	0.3	47.0
San Juan.........................	1,019	4,632	353	210	659	129	248	180	38,881	274	73.0	1.5	52.9
Skagit............................	3,457	41,928	7,619	5,809	7,553	1,493	1,833	1,874	44,704	1,074	73.0	4.4	48.0
Skamania.........................	196	1,536	138	364	160	21	42	49	31,870	144	75.0	0.0	45.8
Snohomish.......................	18,253	251,289	30,078	60,299	36,416	8,775	11,777	13,530	53,843	1,438	82.3	1.2	35.5
Spokane..........................	12,823	187,843	38,221	15,030	26,697	11,003	9,023	8,221	43,764	2,501	59.7	9.2	41.5
Stevens...........................	887	7,207	1,659	1,111	1,289	207	208	267	37,062	1,148	44.3	11.1	46.7
Thurston..........................	6,092	71,359	14,503	2,778	12,566	2,753	4,689	2,856	40,028	1,336	79.3	2.0	30.7
Wahkiakum	76	394	45	50	32	9	18	14	35,376	109	50.5	1.8	50.5
Walla Walla	1,364	19,821	4,113	3,488	2,307	657	479	753	38,000	943	53.0	24.0	48.4
Whatcom.........................	6,550	74,548	10,368	10,326	11,683	2,348	3,460	3,132	42,014	1,702	74.7	2.5	45.4
Whitman..........................	826	10,438	1,846	D	1,371	200	328	420	40,225	1,195	21.5	45.4	59.5
Yakima...........................	4,674	68,496	13,849	9,237	10,404	1,497	1,736	2,677	39,080	3,143	73.9	5.5	51.9
WEST VIRGINIA	36,607	558,905	134,188	47,274	86,580	17,092	25,026	21,638	38,715	21,489	28.3	5.8	42.6
Barbour...........................	213	3,092	790	106	336	72	75	89	28,827	513	22.4	6.0	41.1
Berkeley..........................	1,629	24,785	5,958	2,559	4,385	587	910	958	38,662	676	57.5	3.7	34.5
Boone............................	263	3,811	825	115	631	120	78	165	43,373	19	21.1	0.0	73.7
Braxton...........................	254	3,578	867	299	784	83	45	119	33,199	386	16.6	12.2	50.3
Brooke............................	375	6,955	2,293	1,591	903	112	74	264	38,006	96	29.2	8.3	45.8
Cabell............................	2,391	46,924	13,868	4,430	7,039	1,274	1,988	1,804	38,456	383	33.2	2.9	31.6

Table B. States and Counties — Agriculture

STATE County	Acreage (1,000) [117]	Percent change, 2007-2012 [118]	Average size of farm [119]	Total irrigated (1,000) [120]	Total cropland (1,000) [121]	Average per farm [122]	Average per acre [123]	Value of machinery and equipment, average per farm (dollars) [124]	Total (mil dol) [125]	Average per farm (acres) [126]	Crops [127]	Livestock and poultry products [128]	$10,000 or more [129]	$100,000 or more [130]	Total ($1,000) [131]	Percent of farms [132]
VIRGINIA— Cont'd																
Martinsville city	NA	NA	NA	NA	NA	NA	NA	NA	NA	NA	NA	NA	NA	NA	NA	NA
Newport News city	NA	NA	NA	NA	NA	NA	NA	NA	NA	NA	NA	NA	NA	NA	NA	NA
Norfolk city	NA	NA	NA	NA	NA	NA	NA	NA	NA	NA	NA	NA	NA	NA	NA	NA
Norton city	NA	NA	NA	NA	NA	NA	NA	NA	NA	NA	NA	NA	NA	NA	NA	NA
Petersburg city	NA	NA	NA	NA	NA	NA	NA	NA	NA	NA	NA	NA	NA	NA	NA	NA
Poquoson city	NA	NA	NA	NA	NA	NA	NA	NA	NA	NA	NA	NA	NA	NA	NA	NA
Portsmouth city	NA	NA	NA	NA	NA	NA	NA	NA	NA	NA	NA	NA	NA	NA	NA	NA
Radford city	NA	NA	NA	NA	NA	NA	NA	NA	NA	NA	NA	NA	NA	NA	NA	NA
Richmond city	NA	NA	NA	NA	NA	NA	NA	NA	NA	NA	NA	NA	NA	NA	NA	NA
Roanoke city	NA	NA	NA	NA	NA	NA	NA	NA	NA	NA	NA	NA	NA	NA	NA	NA
Salem city	NA	NA	NA	NA	NA	NA	NA	NA	NA	NA	NA	NA	NA	NA	NA	NA
Staunton city	NA	NA	NA	NA	NA	NA	NA	NA	NA	NA	NA	NA	NA	NA	NA	NA
Suffolk city	69	-3.0	225	0.4	50.9	1,016,494	4,521	155,899	62.5	202,760	94.4	5.6	37.3	15.6	2,466	47.4
Virginia Beach city	26	-1.8	140	0.2	21.2	744,428	5,317	93,203	17.7	94,631	95.0	5.0	36.9	13.9	373	23.0
Waynesboro city	NA	NA	NA	NA	NA	NA	NA	NA	NA	NA	NA	NA	NA	NA	NA	NA
Williamsburg city	NA	NA	NA	NA	NA	NA	NA	NA	NA	NA	NA	NA	NA	NA	NA	NA
Winchester city	NA	NA	NA	NA	NA	NA	NA	NA	NA	NA	NA	NA	NA	NA	NA	NA
WASHINGTON	14,748	-1.5	396	1,633.6	7,526.7	910,249	2,299	98,588	9,120.7	244,859	71.2	28.8	34.2	16.4	159,269	19.4
Adams	1,037	-5.6	1,454	127.0	815.0	1,790,387	1,231	252,728	430.2	603,303	79.0	21.0	50.5	39.4	15,567	68.2
Asotin	263	-3.9	1,423	0.5	84.3	1,210,465	851	103,357	20.5	110,854	79.9	20.2	40.5	25.4	2,504	49.2
Benton	704	11.2	466	197.3	519.1	1,276,306	2,738	127,966	923.2	611,771	D	D	34.5	15.0	6,225	10.9
Chelan	76	-19.2	85	22.8	31.5	746,306	8,760	64,446	206.5	231,999	98.2	1.8	65.6	33.7	658	7.0
Clallam	24	3.6	44	4.2	8.1	549,722	12,464	36,032	10.6	19,866	38.8	61.1	16.6	3.9	47	2.2
Clark	75	-4.6	39	3.7	29.0	490,328	12,652	38,798	50.9	26,367	37.1	62.9	16.4	2.6	293	2.4
Columbia	297	-5.1	966	4.1	184.5	1,038,701	1,076	177,896	57.7	187,442	93.4	6.6	39.3	24.0	5,273	73.4
Cowlitz	39	27.1	79	7.6	18.6	689,236	8,693	67,535	28.8	58,482	D	D	19.5	6.9	44	1.6
Douglas	814	-7.8	959	18.3	545.4	976,847	1,019	130,582	199.0	234,442	98.4	1.6	55.2	35.7	12,940	48.5
Ferry	792	5.7	3,107	2.8	19.4	1,320,859	425	55,478	5.3	20,906	54.0	46.0	28.2	7.5	159	13.3
Franklin	625	2.6	708	207.2	452.2	2,071,813	2,927	302,318	740.0	838,068	68.0	32.0	60.6	46.2	8,142	38.7
Garfield	308	0.1	1,462	0.8	187.5	1,384,441	947	153,076	48.2	228,474	92.0	8.0	50.7	37.0	4,878	80.6
Grant	964	-11.4	621	428.2	720.0	2,128,600	3,428	291,085	1,762.3	1,135,499	75.6	24.4	63.0	47.1	11,429	38.5
Grays Harbor	119	0.1	214	8.6	22.8	450,820	2,102	66,575	31.4	56,289	53.3	46.7	22.6	6.8	186	5.4
Island	15	-13.8	40	1.6	7.4	575,838	14,236	41,111	11.5	30,416	28.6	71.4	24.1	3.4	56	4.2
Jefferson	16	22.3	70	1.2	4.2	643,059	9,136	36,900	7.7	34,647	22.7	77.3	33.0	7.2	94	9.0
King	47	-5.2	25	4.1	19.7	545,036	21,432	39,027	120.7	65,732	36.4	63.6	22.8	4.6	791	4.0
Kitsap	10	-34.2	14	0.5	2.5	377,215	26,446	27,010	5.3	7,513	70.0	30.0	14.3	1.4	30	2.5
Kittitas	183	-4.2	182	66.9	68.3	804,841	4,421	77,593	68.9	68,500	68.4	31.6	35.5	12.2	875	10.3
Klickitat	551	-8.3	725	21.7	192.3	1,033,424	1,425	83,599	72.4	95,246	80.3	19.7	31.6	11.4	4,275	37.8
Lewis	133	1.0	81	8.2	54.3	507,676	6,294	48,523	132.3	80,345	22.0	78.0	24.0	6.3	879	6.8
Lincoln	1,115	2.3	1,243	34.7	808.5	1,383,491	1,113	173,996	183.2	204,285	94.7	5.3	46.5	33.8	20,307	77.6
Mason	24	-5.7	63	0.8	4.8	522,432	8,295	40,891	40.8	108,247	6.2	93.8	24.7	8.8	57	2.1
Okanogan	1,205	0.0	832	51.7	129.2	1,103,226	1,326	73,568	287.1	198,150	87.0	13.0	42.1	21.0	2,383	9.5
Pacific	52	-15.5	158	2.5	13.0	546,279	3,456	60,573	36.8	111,461	20.2	79.8	43.3	16.1	305	9.4
Pend Oreille	44	-20.8	151	0.9	15.3	462,514	3,054	45,521	4.0	13,729	58.5	41.5	15.3	2.4	27	2.8
Pierce	49	3.8	33	2.8	11.5	476,152	14,222	35,548	90.9	61,524	26.3	73.7	17.9	3.0	96	1.3
San Juan	16	-27.0	57	0.3	5.5	756,471	13,228	28,427	4.2	15,493	60.8	39.2	33.9	2.9	41	3.6
Skagit	107	-1.8	99	19.2	66.8	752,365	7,585	118,998	272.3	253,515	73.8	26.2	29.1	12.2	1,442	11.1
Skamania	6	18.3	45	0.4	1.3	456,965	10,166	36,611	5.5	38,458	27.7	72.3	25.0	6.9	0	0.0
Snohomish	71	-7.8	49	5.3	29.1	791,114	16,054	40,122	139.5	97,000	45.3	54.7	21.8	6.5	620	4.9
Spokane	537	-14.2	215	10.3	369.6	611,087	2,844	72,631	149.8	59,880	88.7	11.3	25.6	9.3	7,355	24.7
Stevens	527	-0.7	459	6.7	88.8	722,020	1,572	49,637	36.3	31,660	47.9	52.1	32.3	7.3	926	12.6
Thurston	77	-4.9	57	5.3	23.1	498,439	8,689	40,468	122.4	91,634	39.9	60.1	19.5	5.2	267	2.4
Wahkiakum	10	-20.5	88	0.0	2.7	411,376	4,692	38,826	3.5	31,991	8.3	91.7	31.2	7.3	92	11.9
Walla Walla	645	-5.5	684	91.1	565.8	1,426,922	2,086	175,634	437.4	463,795	D	D	42.2	23.5	12,372	45.2
Whatcom	116	12.9	68	35.5	78.7	786,343	11,554	80,437	357.3	209,937	33.5	66.5	31.2	15.5	3,425	17.6
Whitman	1,275	0.3	1,067	4.3	1,020.0	1,490,631	1,397	214,180	370.8	310,294	95.0	5.0	50.5	40.4	28,405	77.9
Yakima	1,780	8.0	566	224.4	306.9	1,021,212	1,803	118,874	1,645.5	523,548	65.0	35.0	45.7	22.4	5,804	11.5
WEST VIRGINIA	3,607	-2.5	168	2.1	804.0	413,407	2,463	50,020	806.8	37,544	17.2	82.8	25.3	4.0	7,034	10.2
Barbour	85	-6.9	165	0.0	19.2	323,021	1,955	52,060	6.6	12,930	17.5	82.5	28.8	1.9	109	8.2
Berkeley	70	-6.7	104	0.1	33.3	596,855	5,757	53,351	30.5	45,185	78.5	21.5	25.7	4.7	374	14.5
Boone	2	-2.9	117	0.0	0.1	203,895	1,736	26,526	0.0	2,526	43.8	56.3	5.3	0.0	D	10.5
Braxton	89	11.9	230	0.0	14.7	376,614	1,635	40,829	4.9	12,586	20.0	80.0	27.7	1.3	147	9.3
Brooke	15	-4.5	153	D	4.3	298,448	1,948	68,323	1.4	14,406	20.4	79.5	30.2	3.1	D	3.1
Cabell	42	-10.9	111	0.0	6.3	332,266	2,998	42,608	2.0	5,198	50.3	49.7	9.4	0.5	60	16.2

Table B. States and Counties — Water Use, Wholesale Trade, Retail Trade, and Real Estate

STATE County	Water use, 2015		Wholesale Trade[1], 2012				Retail Trade[2], 2012				Real estate and rental and leasing,[2] 2012			
	Public supply water withdrawn (mil gal/day)	Public supply gallons withdrawn per person per day	Number of establishments	Number of employees	Sales (mil dol)	Annual payroll (mil dol)	Number of establishments	Number of employees	Sales (mil dol)	Annual payroll (mil dol)	Number of establishments	Number of employees	Sales (mil dol)	Annual payroll (mil dol)
	133	134	135	136	137	138	139	140	141	142	143	144	145	146
VIRGINIA— Cont'd														
Martinsville city..............	2.00	146.6	16	D	D	D	111	1,578	317.8	34.4	31	104	14.3	2.3
Newport News city	22.20	121.7	110	1,438	851.3	72.7	686	9,879	2,480.8	229.7	254	1,672	276.5	60.3
Norfolk city	0.28	1.1	209	3,287	3,195.3	161.6	867	12,440	2,683.2	281.6	291	2,496	430.8	127.7
Norton city.......................	0.53	134.6	8	123	78.3	7.1	48	786	219.7	19.3	11	42	5.0	1.0
Petersburg city	0.00	0.0	21	570	560.1	16.2	145	1,426	334.5	33.0	32	223	27.2	5.8
Poquoson city	0.00	0.0	4	D	D	D	28	305	63.8	6.1	12	20	3.2	0.6
Portsmouth city	60.83	632.3	48	688	249.5	32.0	273	3,081	699.5	71.1	71	332	52.6	9.7
Radford city......................	2.48	142.5	8	51	84.6	2.3	39	537	105.8	11.8	21	83	12.5	2.5
Richmond city	70.23	318.8	269	3,767	3,288.5	201.3	808	8,666	1,955.2	206.1	258	1,539	304.3	67.1
Roanoke city	4.99	50.0	180	2,727	1,398.0	130.3	535	9,912	2,461.0	230.1	155	950	141.8	31.0
Salem city........................	3.84	151.0	77	1,567	1,228.3	89.3	145	1,995	507.8	48.3	35	176	50.4	7.2
Staunton city....................	0.00	0.0	22	200	76.0	7.1	134	1,862	432.7	42.6	43	D	D	D
Suffolk city.......................	44.45	504.2	54	961	666.0	49.8	226	3,536	958.9	79.1	67	243	37.5	8.1
Virginia Beach city	1.76	3.9	391	6,893	8,187.6	477.1	1,500	22,723	5,671.5	521.6	649	6,165	902.5	210.7
Waynesboro city	0.78	36.3	16	253	113.3	12.7	123	2,123	474.3	45.2	30	D	D	D
Williamsburg city	0.00	0.0	7	49	31.9	3.2	119	1,931	348.7	37.9	24	D	D	D
Winchester city.................	0.00	0.0	39	677	286.8	26.1	283	4,126	888.5	94.4	59	260	56.4	8.0
WASHINGTON............	866.53	120.8	7,733	103,307	83,313.4	5,789.8	21,588	307,089	118,924.0	8,722.5	9,913	45,209	9,695.5	1,895.1
Adams............................	5.58	289.8	26	D	D	D	51	548	157.8	13.1	10	21	3.4	0.4
Asotin.............................	5.21	235.7	13	D	D	D	59	1,094	285.9	30.3	21	143	11.8	3.1
Benton............................	34.48	181.2	109	999	1,230.3	44.5	583	9,216	2,463.5	222.7	244	1,004	179.4	30.2
Chelan............................	11.29	149.3	89	2,118	1,018.7	76.5	379	4,154	1,004.5	106.7	118	399	51.9	11.3
Clallam...........................	6.16	83.8	38	D	D	D	287	3,476	812.0	92.1	87	246	35.3	7.0
Clark..............................	46.57	101.4	414	4,410	4,395.4	253.2	1,011	15,547	4,276.5	419.9	465	D	D	D
Columbia........................	1.00	253.5	18	D	D	D	18	111	30.5	2.6	7	12	0.8	0.2
Cowlitz...........................	10.31	99.6	85	1,036	2,021.4	53.2	333	4,644	1,188.3	113.8	104	337	50.7	8.5
Douglas..........................	5.45	134.5	38	D	D	D	98	1,547	430.0	40.2	27	76	11.1	2.2
Ferry..............................	0.58	76.5	1	D	D	D	27	167	45.4	3.8	6	20	0.7	0.3
Franklin..........................	16.30	183.5	113	1,513	1,741.6	67.8	189	2,719	918.9	84.7	56	240	41.0	7.1
Garfield	0.57	256.9	9	D	D	D	11	55	10.4	1.0	NA	NA	NA	NA
Grant.............................	23.52	252.2	117	D	D	D	287	3,160	825.6	77.4	81	203	28.2	5.1
Grays Harbor	7.63	107.3	52	D	D	D	264	2,871	761.5	73.3	82	246	24.5	5.6
Island	6.49	80.5	36	145	57.5	6.3	212	2,181	456.3	52.5	82	238	36.8	6.6
Jefferson	2.25	73.9	20	D	D	D	144	1,012	209.9	26.0	49	116	14.5	2.6
King...............................	197.62	93.3	3,235	49,268	42,092.5	3,183.4	6,524	97,959	61,598.2	3,159.8	4,186	23,233	5,825.0	1,180.7
Kitsap............................	19.63	75.5	147	953	407.9	43.7	731	10,343	2,674.2	276.3	338	979	198.5	32.7
Kittitas	6.90	159.5	41	442	398.7	23.6	159	1,646	516.0	39.0	54	140	25.6	4.1
Klickitat..........................	3.09	147.0	16	D	D	D	47	330	64.5	7.0	21	23	3.6	0.4
Lewis.............................	5.95	78.4	60	D	D	D	314	3,521	912.2	87.0	75	251	34.4	7.7
Lincoln...........................	2.03	196.7	27	D	D	D	46	292	106.9	8.1	5	6	0.5	0.1
Mason............................	4.96	81.3	33	D	D	D	134	1,557	404.3	40.4	44	233	17.6	5.1
Okanogan	6.05	145.7	39	D	D	D	199	1,836	447.0	44.5	60	154	11.5	2.3
Pacific	2.73	130.9	6	D	D	D	89	555	107.9	14.2	22	52	4.5	1.0
Pend Oreille	0.99	75.6	4	D	D	D	32	249	58.3	5.0	7	14	0.8	0.2
Pierce............................	110.41	130.8	686	9,171	7,705.6	449.9	2,154	33,111	10,114.4	944.9	947	4,673	837.6	158.6
San Juan.........................	0.88	54.1	14	61	12.7	2.0	111	608	150.6	19.6	52	92	12.9	2.0
Skagit............................	20.31	166.7	104	1,277	793.5	58.2	553	6,801	1,999.2	186.8	158	467	81.8	14.4
Skamania........................	1.06	93.5	5	24	10.7	1.0	21	134	25.2	2.7	3	D	D	D
Snohomish......................	65.52	84.8	731	7,287	5,652.7	407.7	2,184	32,776	9,130.8	903.2	863	3,131	710.2	122.0
Spokane.........................	138.81	282.7	561	8,334	4,946.9	400.8	1,617	24,749	6,560.8	668.0	614	3,053	518.3	102.2
Stevens..........................	6.19	141.4	21	D	D	D	128	1,214	283.2	27.5	23	76	12.1	2.0
Thurston.........................	22.58	83.8	169	1,824	1,252.0	90.8	769	12,317	3,330.8	324.6	325	994	202.1	31.3
Wahkiakum......................	0.32	79.2	2	D	D	D	9	51	10.1	1.0	6	9	0.4	0.1
Walla Walla	12.72	210.8	70	D	D	D	183	2,322	555.5	56.5	55	175	22.2	5.0
Whatcom.........................	18.13	85.4	289	D	D	D	818	11,310	3,103.6	272.4	317	1,131	230.9	34.3
Whitman..........................	6.26	129.9	61	D	D	D	100	1,331	333.6	28.0	50	194	21.5	4.6
Yakima	30.00	120.6	234	4,373	3,335.1	198.3	713	9,575	2,560.2	246.1	249	974	132.0	26.7
WEST VIRGINIA	184.96	100.3	1,334	16,906	14,295.4	761.9	6,393	85,305	22,637.9	1,908.5	1,405	6,011	1,255.8	203.8
Barbour...........................	1.45	86.8	4	8	1.3	0.2	37	378	89.6	7.0	6	13	0.8	0.3
Berkeley..........................	5.97	53.4	40	840	709.5	39.3	247	3,879	939.2	82.4	67	264	32.9	6.6
Boone.............................	0.19	8.1	10	D	D	D	63	790	227.4	17.7	5	D	D	D
Braxton...........................	1.09	75.6	8	59	23.3	2.1	67	572	171.1	13.5	8	26	3.4	0.6
Brooke............................	5.21	223.1	13	D	D	D	63	931	236.8	20.4	2	D	D	D
Cabell.............................	12.17	125.7	106	1,754	873.6	82.4	439	6,687	1,570.9	145.2	97	362	69.0	12.4

1. Merchant wholesalers, except manufacturers' sales branches and offices.   2. Employer establishments.

Table B. States and Counties — **Land Area and Population**

State / county code	CBSA code[1]	County code[2]	STATE County	Land area[3] (sq. mi)	Total persons 2017	Rank	Per square mile	White	Black	American Indian, Alaska Native	Asian and Pacific Islancer	Percent Hispanic or Latino[4]	Under 5 years	5 to 17 years	18 to 24 years	25 to 34 years	35 to 44 years	45 to 54 years
				1	**2**	**3**	**4**	**5**	**6**	**7**	**8**	**9**	**10**	**11**	**12**	**13**	**14**	**15**
			WEST VIRGINIA— Cont'd															
54,013		8	Calhoun............	279.2	7,307	2,639	26.2	98.0	0.5	0.8	0.4	1.2	4.5	14.2	5.9	9.7	11.4	14.0
54,015	16,620	3	Clay.............	341.9	8,764	2,528	25.6	98.5	0.5	0.9	0.3	0.8	6.1	16.9	6.8	9.8	11.7	13.4
54,017	17,220	9	Doddridge	319.7	8,560	2,540	26.8	96.5	2.4	1.0	0.5	0.8	4.1	12.4	9.3	11.5	12.2	14.8
54,019	13,220	3	Fayette.................	661.6	43,521	1,102	65.8	93.9	5.3	0.8	0.4	1.1	5.8	15.1	7.4	11.1	12.3	13.0
54,021		7	Gilmer............	338.5	8,005	2,593	23.6	82.5	11.0	1.3	1.2	5.6	3.6	10.5	15.2	14.9	13.6	13.2
54,023		7	Grant.............	477.4	11,670	2,316	24.4	97.5	1.3	0.6	0.3	1.3	5.8	14.1	6.8	10.2	10.9	13.8
54,025		6	Greenbrier............	1,019.7	35,287	1,293	34.6	94.1	3.8	1.0	0.8	2.0	5.2	14.4	7.0	10.9	11.6	12.9
54,027	49,020	3	Hampshire.............	640.4	23,471	1,662	36.7	96.8	1.6	0.7	0.6	1.4	4.9	14.5	6.9	10.4	11.2	14.7
54,029	48,260	3	Hancock............	82.6	29,448	1,444	356.5	95.1	3.5	0.6	0.7	1.7	4.4	14.5	6.6	10.4	11.7	13.7
54,031		6	Hardy............	582.3	13,717	2,183	23.6	91.6	3.4	0.8	0.9	4.6	5.0	15.4	6.6	10.6	11.6	14.2
54,033	17,220	5	Harrison	416.0	67,811	784	163.0	95.8	2.5	0.8	0.9	1.6	5.8	15.7	7.3	11.9	12.4	13.5
54,035		6	Jackson...........	464.4	28,976	1,457	62.4	97.9	1.1	0.7	0.5	0.8	5.8	15.8	7.3	10.9	11.6	13.9
54,037	47,900	1	Jefferson...........	209.7	56,338	907	268.7	86.2	7.5	1.0	2.3	5.7	5.5	17.1	8.0	11.4	12.9	15.5
54,039	16,620	3	Kanawha..........	901.6	183,293	356	203.3	90.0	9.1	0.8	1.6	1.1	5.5	14.7	7.7	12.2	12.1	12.7
54,041		7	Lewis............	386.9	16,226	2,027	41.9	97.5	1.1	0.7	0.6	1.2	6.0	15.4	6.7	11.3	12.1	13.9
54,043	26,580	2	Lincoln............	437.0	20,825	1,784	47.7	98.7	0.7	0.6	0.3	0.7	6.0	16.5	6.8	10.6	12.6	14.1
54,045	30,880	6	Logan............	453.8	32,925	1,360	72.6	96.8	2.3	0.5	0.4	0.9	5.4	15.0	7.0	11.1	13.0	13.2
54,047		7	McDowell	533.5	18,456	1,898	34.6	90.0	9.1	0.6	0.3	1.2	5.5	14.9	6.2	10.6	11.7	12.9
54,049	21,900	4	Marion	308.7	56,337	908	182.5	94.6	4.2	0.7	0.8	1.4	5.6	14.6	11.2	11.7	11.9	12.5
54,051	48,540	3	Marshall	305.4	31,190	1,404	102.1	97.7	1.2	0.6	0.5	1.0	5.1	14.5	7.0	11.2	11.3	13.4
54,053	38,580	6	Mason	430.7	26,801	1,534	62.2	97.9	1.4	0.7	0.4	0.7	5.4	15.7	6.9	11.1	12.2	12.8
54,055	14,140	4	Mercer............	419.0	59,753	872	142.6	92.0	7.1	0.7	0.8	1.1	5.9	14.8	8.2	11.6	11.6	12.3
54,057	19,060	3	Mineral	327.9	27,222	1,516	83.0	95.4	3.8	0.6	0.8	0.9	5.4	14.8	8.5	11.4	10.9	13.9
54,059		7	Mingo	423.1	24,127	1,636	57.0	97.1	2.5	0.5	0.4	0.7	6.2	16.1	6.5	11.2	12.7	13.6
54,061	34,060	3	Monongalia	360.1	105,030	573	291.7	90.4	5.0	0.6	4.2	2.2	5.1	11.2	21.2	17.3	11.8	10.6
54,063		8	Monroe............	472.8	13,402	2,200	28.3	97.7	1.4	1.2	0.5	0.9	4.8	15.2	6.2	10.0	10.7	13.8
54,065		8	Morgan............	229.1	17,686	1,936	77.2	96.8	1.4	1.0	0.8	1.6	4.2	13.8	7.3	9.6	10.9	14.7
54,067		6	Nicholas	646.8	25,043	1,607	38.7	98.2	0.6	1.0	0.5	0.8	5.4	15.1	6.5	11.2	11.4	13.4
54,069	48,540	3	Ohio	105.8	42,035	1,130	397.3	94.3	4.9	0.6	1.1	1.1	5.2	14.0	10.1	11.4	10.9	12.0
54,071		8	Pendleton	696.0	6,996	2,673	10.1	96.3	2.6	0.8	0.4	1.1	4.4	13.3	6.2	9.4	10.0	12.5
54,073		6	Pleasants	130.1	7,512	2,628	57.7	96.9	2.0	0.8	0.4	1.1	5.1	14.0	8.0	12.1	13.2	14.7
54,075		9	Pocahontas	940.3	8,456	2,551	9.0	96.9	1.5	1.0	0.5	1.5	4.8	12.6	6.2	11.1	10.7	13.3
54,077	34,060	3	Preston..........	648.8	33,679	1,337	51.9	97.2	1.5	0.7	0.4	1.1	5.0	14.2	6.8	13.4	12.9	13.8
54,079	26,580	2	Putnam............	345.7	56,792	901	164.3	96.7	1.7	0.6	1.1	1.1	5.6	17.1	6.9	11.2	13.4	14.0
54,081	13,220	3	Raleigh............	605.4	75,022	738	123.9	89.1	8.9	0.9	1.4	1.6	5.4	15.5	7.4	12.3	13.0	12.2
54,083	21,180	7	Randolph...........	1,039.7	28,785	1,462	27.7	96.8	2.0	0.6	0.7	1.0	5.2	13.8	8.1	12.2	11.5	13.4
54,085		8	Ritchie	452.0	9,774	2,447	21.6	98.5	0.8	0.6	0.3	0.9	5.0	14.8	6.6	10.0	11.2	14.3
54,087		6	Roane	483.6	14,043	2,161	29.0	98.0	0.7	0.7	0.6	1.1	4.9	16.2	6.4	10.0	11.8	13.2
54,089		6	Summers............	360.6	12,993	2,229	36.0	93.2	5.2	1.0	0.7	1.7	4.0	12.8	5.8	10.7	12.5	13.6
54,091	17,220	6	Taylor.............	172.8	16,930	1,983	98.0	97.1	1.6	0.7	0.7	1.0	5.3	15.0	6.6	12.3	12.6	14.2
54,093		8	Tucker............	419.0	6,915	2,680	16.5	98.2	0.9	0.6	0.6	0.8	4.7	12.3	7.1	9.8	10.8	14.3
54,095		9	Tyler............	256.3	8,795	2,524	34.3	98.5	0.7	0.6	0.4	0.8	5.3	14.6	6.7	9.7	10.9	14.4
54,097		7	Upshur	354.6	24,465	1,627	69.0	97.1	1.4	0.7	0.6	1.4	5.4	15.2	10.9	11.3	11.1	12.6
54,099	26,580	2	Wayne............	506.0	40,153	1,173	79.4	98.3	0.8	0.8	0.5	0.6	5.1	15.5	7.4	10.9	12.2	13.8
54,101		9	Webster............	553.5	8,372	2,557	15.1	98.1	1.0	0.7	0.7	0.8	4.9	15.3	6.6	9.5	11.0	14.0
54,103		6	Wetzel..........	358.1	15,437	2,069	43.1	98.3	0.9	0.5	0.5	0.8	5.4	14.5	7.7	10.3	10.7	13.8
54,105	37,620	3	Wirt.............	232.5	5,794	2,773	24.9	98.3	0.9	0.7	0.5	0.8	4.8	16.3	6.6	10.4	11.4	13.8
54,107	37,620	3	Wood............	366.3	85,104	673	232.3	96.7	2.1	0.7	1.0	1.1	5.8	15.3	7.4	11.5	11.9	13.6
54,109		6	Wyoming............	499.5	21,210	1,765	42.5	98.3	1.2	0.7	0.3	0.7	4.9	15.8	6.9	10.6	12.6	13.0
55,000		0	WISCONSIN................	54,160.7	5,795,483	X	107.0	82.9	7.2	1.4	3.4	6.9	5.8	16.3	9.6	12.6	12.0	13.1
55,001		8	Adams............	645.6	19,973	1,829	30.9	91.7	3.2	1.3	0.8	4.0	3.4	10.9	5.4	9.6	9.6	12.8
55,003		7	Ashland............	1,045.0	15,500	2,067	14.8	85.5	1.0	13.0	1.1	2.8	5.6	16.3	9.2	10.7	11.0	12.4
55,005		6	Barron............	862.7	45,251	1,068	52.5	94.5	1.8	1.4	1.0	2.6	5.5	16.2	7.1	10.8	10.9	12.6
55,007		8	Bayfield............	1,477.9	15,008	2,098	10.2	87.4	1.0	11.5	0.9	2.0	4.2	13.2	6.2	8.2	9.2	13.1
55,009	24,580	2	Brown............	530.1	262,052	262	494.3	82.8	3.5	3.2	3.7	8.7	6.5	17.5	9.2	13.5	12.5	13.3
55,011		8	Buffalo............	671.6	13,167	2,221	19.6	96.4	0.8	0.9	0.6	2.3	5.5	15.4	7.0	10.2	10.4	13.7
55,013		8	Burnett............	821.6	15,352	2,073	18.7	92.6	1.3	5.8	0.8	1.9	4.4	13.4	5.8	7.8	9.2	12.6
55,015	11,540	3	Calumet............	318.2	50,067	986	157.3	92.1	1.2	0.9	2.7	4.4	5.4	18.8	7.6	11.0	13.1	15.2
55,017	20,740	3	Chippewa............	1,008.4	63,813	834	63.3	94.5	2.1	0.9	1.7	1.9	5.6	16.7	7.2	12.4	12.3	13.6
55,019		6	Clark............	1,209.7	34,679	1,306	28.7	93.7	0.9	0.8	0.7	4.8	8.3	21.1	8.0	9.7	10.7	12.1
55,021	31,540	2	Columbia............	765.5	57,248	894	74.8	93.6	2.0	0.9	1.1	3.4	5.4	16.2	7.4	11.8	12.3	14.4
55,023		7	Crawford............	570.7	16,214	2,028	28.4	95.3	2.5	0.7	0.9	1.6	4.8	15.6	7.5	10.3	10.4	13.0
55,025	31,540	2	Dane	1,196.4	536,416	128	448.4	81.8	6.4	0.7	7.1	6.5	5.8	14.3	13.7	15.6	13.0	12.0
55,027	13,180	4	Dodge	875.7	87,786	660	100.2	90.7	3.6	0.8	1.0	4.9	4.8	15.4	7.9	12.6	12.6	14.4
55,029		6	Door	482.0	27,483	1,509	57.0	95.2	1.1	1.1	0.8	3.1	3.9	12.6	6.1	8.3	9.8	12.0

1. CBSA = Core Based Statistical Area. See Appendix A for explanation. See Appendix B for list of metropolitan areas with component counties.   2. County type code from the Economic Research Service of USDA Rural-Urban Continuum Codes. See Appendix A for definition.   3. Dry land or land partially or temporarily covered by water.   4. May be of any race.

Table B. States and Counties — Population and Households

STATE County	55 to 64 years (16)	65 to 74 years (17)	75 years and over (18)	Percent female (19)	2000 (20)	2010 (21)	2000-2010 (22)	2010-2017 (23)	Births (24)	Deaths (25)	Net Migration (26)	Number (27)	Persons per house-hold (28)	Family house-holds (29)	Female family house-holder[1] (30)	One person (31)
WEST VIRGINIA— Cont'd																
Calhoun	16.6	14.3	9.4	50.2	7,582	7,627	0.6	-4.2	527	655	-190	2,913	2.56	67.7	7.8	26.4
Clay	15.4	11.7	8.3	49.5	10,330	9,386	-9.1	-6.6	805	788	-646	3,375	2.66	69.0	9.2	22.9
Doddridge	15.2	12.3	8.2	45.0	7,403	8,198	10.7	4.4	523	601	428	2,625	2.95	64.0	7.3	31.1
Fayette	15.3	11.9	8.2	49.6	47,579	46,049	-3.2	-5.5	3,836	4,772	-1,569	17,845	2.43	67.9	12.5	28.6
Gilmer	11.7	9.1	8.0	40.6	7,160	8,697	21.5	-8.0	471	537	-636	2,709	2.46	64.3	6.9	27.4
Grant	14.6	13.9	9.8	50.1	11,299	11,937	5.6	-2.2	898	962	-200	4,158	2.80	67.4	6.5	26.4
Greenbrier	15.3	13.3	9.3	51.0	34,453	35,480	3.0	-0.5	2,672	3,471	613	14,944	2.34	64.1	11.0	30.8
Hampshire	15.6	13.8	8.0	49.0	20,203	23,969	18.6	-2.1	1,676	1,890	-274	9,977	2.29	51.0	10.2	46.2
Hancock	16.1	12.6	9.6	51.2	32,667	30,675	-6.1	-4.0	2,035	2,922	-311	12,844	2.32	63.2	12.8	32.5
Hardy	15.2	12.9	8.5	49.7	12,669	14,025	10.7	-2.2	1,047	1,098	-259	5,350	2.59	70.1	9.7	26.6
Harrison	14.5	10.9	8.0	50.9	68,652	69,110	0.7	-1.9	5,797	6,225	-820	27,652	2.46	63.9	12.0	31.5
Jackson	15.0	10.9	9.0	50.4	28,000	29,211	4.3	-0.8	2,381	2,508	-86	11,190	2.59	70.6	10.3	26.0
Jefferson	13.9	10.0	5.7	50.4	42,190	53,488	26.8	5.3	4,257	3,266	1,874	20,634	2.62	70.3	10.7	22.3
Kanawha	15.2	11.7	8.3	51.8	200,073	193,048	-3.5	-5.1	15,413	17,757	-7,289	81,708	2.28	61.4	13.0	33.1
Lewis	14.5	12.0	8.1	50.5	16,919	16,372	-3.2	-0.9	1,450	1,592	8	6,541	2.47	68.8	11.5	25.1
Lincoln	14.9	11.2	7.4	50.4	22,108	21,720	-1.8	-4.1	1,879	2,013	-751	7,965	2.69	67.4	12.2	28.3
Logan	15.4	12.5	7.4	50.8	37,710	36,745	-2.6	-10.4	2,878	3,849	-2,868	13,976	2.47	69.3	11.8	26.4
McDowell	17.1	12.5	8.5	51.2	27,329	22,111	-19.1	-16.5	1,750	2,544	-2,900	7,963	2.36	67.5	16.1	27.5
Marion	13.5	11.0	8.0	50.7	56,598	56,418	-0.3	-0.1	4,685	4,786	65	22,427	2.47	66.0	11.3	28.4
Marshall	15.9	12.9	8.7	50.6	35,519	33,107	-6.8	-5.8	2,306	2,958	-1,242	13,306	2.39	67.9	10.7	27.0
Mason	15.6	11.7	8.5	51.7	25,957	27,326	5.3	-1.9	2,050	2,458	-96	10,901	2.42	68.2	11.3	28.2
Mercer	14.2	12.6	8.8	52.1	62,980	62,265	-1.1	-4.0	5,375	6,503	-1,345	25,062	2.41	66.0	13.0	29.2
Mineral	14.0	12.6	8.5	50.1	27,078	28,203	4.2	-3.5	2,084	2,367	-684	11,289	2.37	60.0	10.9	36.3
Mingo	15.5	11.8	6.3	51.0	28,253	26,834	-5.0	-10.1	2,419	2,642	-2,504	10,853	2.35	68.8	14.0	28.2
Monongalia	10.7	7.4	4.7	48.5	81,866	96,189	17.5	9.2	7,843	4,825	5,719	37,820	2.54	53.0	8.2	35.3
Monroe	14.6	14.2	10.4	50.1	14,583	13,498	-7.4	-0.7	949	1,233	193	5,932	2.25	70.3	13.0	26.4
Morgan	16.6	13.8	9.1	50.2	14,943	17,541	17.4	0.8	1,013	1,540	679	7,207	2.41	59.6	6.4	34.5
Nicholas	15.3	13.0	8.6	50.7	26,562	26,233	-1.2	-4.5	2,029	2,429	-779	10,752	2.38	70.8	9.6	24.6
Ohio	15.2	11.7	9.5	51.8	47,427	44,442	-6.3	-5.4	3,382	4,200	-1,576	18,519	2.21	58.2	12.2	36.5
Pendleton	17.4	14.1	12.8	49.4	8,196	7,695	-6.1	-9.1	489	663	-528	3,133	2.28	65.0	7.9	31.9
Pleasants	14.2	11.0	7.7	45.8	7,514	7,604	1.2	-1.2	527	658	39	2,863	2.46	74.5	10.8	20.4
Pocahontas	17.0	14.3	10.0	48.3	9,131	8,722	-4.5	-3.0	615	778	-103	3,646	2.28	67.2	6.9	30.9
Preston	14.3	11.8	7.8	48.6	29,334	33,520	14.3	0.5	2,465	2,559	260	12,441	2.51	69.7	9.2	25.1
Putnam	14.1	10.7	7.1	50.7	51,589	55,508	7.6	2.3	4,360	4,041	995	21,780	2.59	72.0	11.1	24.3
Raleigh	14.1	12.0	8.0	50.0	79,220	78,864	-0.4	-4.9	6,501	7,391	-2,934	30,880	2.42	67.0	13.1	28.1
Randolph	14.5	12.5	8.9	48.4	28,262	29,405	4.0	-2.1	2,199	2,648	-157	11,626	2.33	65.5	8.8	29.4
Ritchie	16.1	13.1	9.0	49.9	10,343	10,449	1.0	-6.5	694	933	-434	3,967	2.51	69.8	10.2	31.1
Roane	16.2	12.7	8.6	50.5	15,446	14,926	-3.4	-5.9	1,064	1,362	-580	5,672	2.54	67.5	9.2	27.0
Summers	16.2	14.1	10.3	54.8	12,999	13,927	7.1	-6.7	821	1,336	-419	5,497	2.23	66.3	10.7	31.3
Taylor	14.5	11.5	8.0	49.3	16,089	16,888	5.0	0.2	1,293	1,427	183	6,732	2.45	66.0	12.2	28.4
Tucker	15.8	14.6	10.5	48.9	7,321	7,141	-2.5	-3.2	462	674	-11	2,924	2.31	67.5	5.4	27.2
Tyler	16.4	13.0	9.0	49.8	9,592	9,211	-4.0	-4.5	636	854	-200	3,518	2.53	64.8	11.1	31.8
Upshur	13.7	11.6	8.3	50.5	23,404	24,254	3.6	0.9	1,928	1,934	232	9,105	2.57	63.9	9.6	27.0
Wayne	14.5	11.9	8.7	51.1	42,903	42,484	-1.0	-5.5	3,007	3,557	-1,773	16,447	2.50	66.7	12.6	30.5
Webster	16.2	14.1	8.4	50.0	9,719	9,154	-5.8	-8.5	665	890	-560	3,952	2.22	67.9	14.5	27.1
Wetzel	15.0	12.4	10.3	50.9	17,693	16,580	-6.3	-6.9	1,246	1,631	-759	6,238	2.55	64.0	10.4	31.5
Wirt	17.3	11.8	7.6	48.9	5,873	5,717	-2.7	1.3	424	437	93	2,432	2.40	61.6	9.5	30.0
Wood	14.6	11.5	8.4	51.5	87,986	86,957	-1.2	-2.1	7,076	7,612	-1,235	36,225	2.36	64.5	11.5	30.7
Wyoming	16.1	12.9	7.2	50.7	25,708	23,802	-7.4	-10.9	1,642	2,474	-1,771	9,222	2.44	71.2	11.7	26.0
WISCONSIN	14.1	9.5	6.9	50.3	5,363,675	5,687,288	6.0	1.9	486,526	358,238	-17,782	2,310,246	2.43	63.7	10.0	29.1
Adams	19.4	17.4	11.5	46.4	18,643	20,875	12.0	-4.3	954	1,824	-31	7,950	2.40	63.9	6.2	30.2
Ashland	15.7	11.3	7.7	49.7	16,866	16,157	-4.2	-4.1	1,297	1,343	-615	6,670	2.30	60.0	10.5	32.4
Barron	15.5	12.3	9.1	49.9	44,963	45,870	2.0	-1.3	3,699	3,588	-704	19,017	2.36	65.5	7.7	28.6
Bayfield	19.3	16.7	10.1	49.0	15,013	15,014	0.0	0.0	876	1,160	288	6,798	2.19	63.8	6.5	30.7
Brown	13.1	8.5	5.9	50.4	226,778	248,007	9.4	5.7	24,600	13,474	3,137	101,888	2.45	64.3	10.0	28.6
Buffalo	15.9	12.5	9.4	49.1	13,804	13,587	-1.6	-3.1	1,039	926	-532	5,707	2.30	66.5	6.4	28.2
Burnett	18.8	16.4	11.5	49.0	15,674	15,457	-1.4	-0.7	976	1,251	177	7,308	2.07	63.9	8.2	29.9
Calumet	14.2	8.8	5.9	49.7	40,631	48,971	20.5	2.2	3,922	2,293	-523	18,839	2.62	74.7	8.2	20.6
Chippewa	14.7	10.3	7.2	48.1	55,195	62,505	13.2	2.1	5,216	4,046	192	24,973	2.43	67.7	8.1	26.3
Clark	13.7	8.8	7.6	49.5	33,557	34,691	3.4	0.0	4,150	2,435	-1,745	12,732	2.66	69.2	7.4	26.0
Columbia	15.1	10.3	7.0	48.9	52,468	56,824	8.3	0.7	4,389	3,841	-96	23,019	2.40	67.6	8.9	26.5
Crawford	15.7	12.9	9.7	48.1	17,243	16,644	-3.5	-2.6	1,186	1,254	-356	6,652	2.35	62.9	8.0	31.8
Dane	11.8	8.1	5.1	50.3	426,526	488,075	14.4	9.9	44,585	22,551	26,370	213,519	2.35	57.6	8.4	30.4
Dodge	15.2	9.4	7.6	47.1	85,897	88,770	3.3	-1.1	6,029	6,409	-553	33,627	2.49	65.7	8.0	28.9
Door	18.4	17.5	11.4	50.5	27,961	27,785	-0.6	-1.1	1,537	2,370	552	13,023	2.10	65.8	5.9	28.1

1. No spouse present.

Table B. States and Counties — Housing, Labor Force, and Employment

STATE County	Total	Percent	Median value[1]	With a mortgage	Without a mortgage[2]	Median rent[3]	Median rent as a percent of income[2]	Sub-standard units[4] (percent)	Total	Percent change, 2016-2017	Total	Rate[5]	Total	Management, business, science, and arts	Construction, production, and maintenance occupations
	89	90	91	92	93	94	95	96	97	98	99	100	101	102	103
WEST VIRGINIA— Cont'd															
Calhoun	2,913	82.4	80,000	18.4	10.0	570	29.0	1.5	2,478	-5.3	259	10.5	2,549	28.6	36.7
Clay	3,375	81.0	77,700	22.8	10.0	461	32.3	2.2	3,175	-2.4	272	8.6	2,693	26.4	36.3
Doddridge	2,625	85.8	95,700	19.3	10.0	545	34.0	1.2	3,894	3.1	162	4.2	2,708	24.7	34.7
Fayette	17,845	77.7	81,300	18.8	10.0	560	28.8	2.2	15,757	-1.2	1,007	6.4	16,362	28.5	26.6
Gilmer	2,709	75.2	84,500	16.2	10.0	549	28.8	1.7	2,435	-4.0	174	7.1	2,696	31.5	25.7
Grant	4,158	79.0	130,700	20.0	10.0	557	24.2	1.1	5,873	-1.3	330	5.6	4,866	22.9	40.9
Greenbrier	14,944	73.8	110,000	19.4	10.0	638	29.1	2.2	15,723	0.4	760	4.8	13,887	32.4	24.7
Hampshire	9,977	59.5	125,600	21.6	10.0	543	27.2	2.2	10,144	2.6	399	3.9	8,963	23.2	38.7
Hancock	12,844	71.8	86,600	17.9	10.2	632	28.1	1.3	12,687	-1.2	773	6.1	13,477	26.2	28.6
Hardy	5,350	73.5	121,100	23.0	10.0	613	23.8	2.7	5,828	2.1	289	5.0	6,096	20.4	40.6
Harrison	27,652	73.1	102,900	17.1	10.0	667	28.5	1.8	32,872	1.7	1,594	4.8	29,946	33.3	22.9
Jackson	11,190	79.2	113,400	18.1	10.0	588	24.6	2.6	11,930	-0.5	683	5.7	11,148	31.4	28.0
Jefferson	20,634	74.3	215,300	20.6	10.0	891	29.5	1.9	28,661	0.5	902	3.1	27,134	40.7	19.9
Kanawha	81,708	69.1	107,100	18.1	10.0	703	26.2	1.6	84,245	-1.1	4,216	5.0	83,440	37.9	17.3
Lewis	6,541	71.0	105,900	19.4	10.0	549	25.5	2.5	6,508	-4.6	430	6.6	6,142	24.2	30.8
Lincoln	7,965	75.6	82,400	16.7	10.0	492	36.6	2.8	7,214	-0.9	491	6.8	7,413	22.5	30.7
Logan	13,976	75.6	85,600	19.0	10.0	581	31.2	1.4	10,757	-3.5	807	7.5	11,271	25.6	32.1
McDowell	7,963	78.2	33,600	21.0	10.7	516	41.5	3.4	4,997	-1.6	423	8.5	4,298	23.2	29.0
Marion	22,427	76.5	107,100	17.3	10.0	715	28.9	2.0	25,559	-0.3	1,333	5.2	25,271	33.5	24.8
Marshall	13,306	76.4	98,100	16.8	10.3	600	25.9	1.1	13,841	-1.5	832	6.0	13,441	26.0	30.1
Mason	10,901	78.8	76,900	18.7	10.0	532	31.2	2.2	9,985	-0.3	669	6.7	9,038	26.0	34.8
Mercer	25,062	72.6	87,400	19.1	10.3	598	29.3	1.1	21,365	-1.4	1,246	5.8	23,412	30.6	21.2
Mineral	11,289	61.1	128,300	19.8	10.0	557	28.9	1.3	11,914	0.2	642	5.4	10,907	24.1	34.4
Mingo	10,853	74.9	70,600	19.2	11.7	592	30.6	1.8	6,755	0.2	584	8.6	7,602	26.8	35.9
Monongalia	37,820	57.6	170,700	17.6	10.0	764	32.9	3.3	52,106	1.7	1,934	3.7	49,200	43.8	16.3
Monroe	5,932	78.7	102,500	19.2	10.1	579	26.4	3.3	6,029	1.0	257	4.3	5,056	28.3	34.0
Morgan	7,207	75.3	168,900	23.7	10.5	763	26.6	2.5	7,715	0.9	306	4.0	7,325	29.7	30.4
Nicholas	10,752	79.6	87,300	18.7	10.0	551	28.9	2.7	9,351	-2.3	661	7.1	9,797	24.4	31.7
Ohio	18,519	67.2	110,000	17.4	10.0	592	31.7	1.6	20,565	-0.2	983	4.8	20,124	34.3	19.3
Pendleton	3,133	78.2	106,400	23.1	10.0	582	21.0	3.0	3,672	0.6	134	3.6	2,719	24.9	36.5
Pleasants	2,863	83.4	104,300	17.7	10.0	628	23.8	1.7	2,856	-3.2	199	7.0	2,934	28.7	33.1
Pocahontas	3,646	80.3	113,000	18.9	10.0	578	26.7	1.7	3,742	0.5	223	6.0	3,633	28.7	31.1
Preston	12,441	81.0	105,900	18.1	10.0	586	27.2	1.4	15,074	1.6	748	5.0	13,627	26.0	33.2
Putnam	21,780	82.0	151,800	18.4	10.0	765	25.6	1.1	26,006	1.0	1,223	4.7	25,573	38.4	20.0
Raleigh	30,880	72.6	105,500	18.3	10.0	659	27.5	1.7	29,526	-1.2	1,584	5.4	28,899	29.6	22.7
Randolph	11,626	71.5	99,300	20.3	10.0	567	27.3	2.1	12,099	-0.7	651	5.4	11,644	28.0	24.9
Ritchie	3,967	77.3	80,400	18.0	10.0	532	25.4	1.3	4,419	-3.0	242	5.5	3,759	22.4	36.5
Roane	5,672	78.4	88,000	20.1	10.0	500	31.2	2.2	5,117	-1.5	437	8.5	4,561	28.4	31.0
Summers	5,497	76.8	88,900	18.7	10.0	561	29.6	3.8	4,537	-0.6	254	5.6	4,751	30.1	30.0
Taylor	6,732	79.0	97,800	19.7	10.0	586	26.7	0.8	7,839	0.4	381	4.9	6,947	32.7	27.9
Tucker	2,924	80.4	105,800	19.7	10.0	524	25.1	1.1	3,396	-2.2	174	5.1	2,993	32.6	29.2
Tyler	3,518	76.5	88,400	18.6	10.0	599	30.6	1.8	3,442	-2.9	248	7.2	3,290	26.9	30.9
Upshur	9,105	75.8	111,200	19.2	10.0	644	24.4	1.5	9,521	-2.8	573	6.0	9,996	34.5	28.7
Wayne	16,447	76.5	85,000	19.0	10.0	627	31.9	1.9	15,556	0.3	905	5.8	14,425	29.2	24.6
Webster	3,952	72.5	66,700	19.5	10.0	491	43.5	0.9	3,362	-3.5	208	6.2	3,009	19.9	36.0
Wetzel	6,238	79.4	86,500	15.7	10.0	543	32.3	1.5	7,057	-1.9	507	7.2	5,542	22.3	36.0
Wirt	2,432	84.0	78,300	17.1	10.0	587	29.8	3.3	2,196	-1.5	173	7.9	2,201	26.8	37.3
Wood	36,225	70.8	109,100	18.4	10.0	641	30.5	1.4	36,269	-1.4	1,977	5.5	36,778	33.0	21.4
Wyoming	9,222	80.6	66,700	16.1	10.0	613	30.7	3.6	6,998	-5.6	490	7.0	6,406	28.3	29.9
WISCONSIN	2,310,246	67.0	167,000	21.8	13.2	789	28.6	2.1	3,151,915	0.7	103,670	3.3	2,910,339	35.0	25.2
Adams	7,950	85.6	129,100	25.4	14.3	699	29.7	1.7	8,316	0.1	423	5.1	7,411	25.4	31.0
Ashland	6,670	69.1	108,700	21.7	13.8	624	28.0	2.8	8,021	0.5	366	4.6	7,473	30.1	25.7
Barron	19,017	73.1	140,900	22.9	13.7	665	26.8	2.1	24,821	1.6	875	3.5	22,142	27.6	35.4
Bayfield	6,798	82.8	162,800	23.5	13.9	609	26.2	3.5	7,546	-0.2	397	5.3	6,873	34.3	26.8
Brown	101,888	65.2	160,700	20.3	12.1	727	27.5	2.8	143,350	1.2	4,223	2.9	132,226	34.0	24.9
Buffalo	5,707	75.1	151,400	22.4	13.9	651	25.8	1.8	6,626	0.5	248	3.7	6,909	30.6	35.6
Burnett	7,308	80.8	150,300	24.9	14.2	627	27.9	2.4	7,365	2.3	359	4.9	6,497	28.4	29.3
Calumet	18,839	81.1	166,600	19.4	11.2	715	26.1	1.5	28,041	0.8	778	2.8	27,080	34.7	28.8
Chippewa	24,973	72.5	152,400	20.6	12.4	752	27.4	1.7	33,697	0.6	1,182	3.5	31,253	28.7	31.8
Clark	12,732	77.8	115,500	22.0	12.9	585	23.3	5.4	18,013	2.4	552	3.1	15,641	28.4	40.2
Columbia	23,019	74.6	177,200	22.3	12.8	753	26.3	1.6	32,023	1.1	942	2.9	29,739	32.7	28.4
Crawford	6,652	76.1	123,800	22.2	13.2	557	28.7	2.8	8,000	0.6	330	4.1	7,528	25.7	35.7
Dane	213,519	58.3	236,000	22.1	12.2	942	29.5	2.2	322,336	1.1	7,729	2.4	292,242	49.3	13.8
Dodge	33,627	71.3	153,900	22.4	13.7	770	25.9	1.6	48,607	1.2	1,419	2.9	43,677	25.6	36.3
Door	13,023	78.9	201,900	23.6	12.8	720	28.4	1.2	15,682	0.8	605	3.9	13,088	32.9	26.0

1. Specified owner-occupied units.   2. A value of 10.0 represents 10 percent or less; a value of 50.0 represents 50 percent or more.   3. Specified renter-occupied units.
4. Overcrowded or lacking complete plumbing facilities.   5. Percent of civilian labor force.   6. Civilian employed persons 16 years old and over.

STATE County	Private nonfarm establishments, employment and payroll, 2016									Agriculture, 2012			
		Employment						Annual payroll		Farms			
												Percent with:	
	Number of establish-ments	Total	Health care and social assistance	Manufac-turing	Retail trade	Finance and insurance	Professional, scientific, and technical services	Total (mil dol)	Average per employee (dollars)	Number	Fewer than 50 acres	500 acres or more	Farm operators whose principal occupation is farming (percent)
	104	105	106	107	108	109	110	111	112	113	114	115	116
WEST VIRGINIA— Cont'd													
Calhoun	97	798	D	18	100	49	26	35	43,873	227	16.7	8.8	35.7
Clay	85	800	324	D	141	D	D	23	29,260	114	20.2	3.5	34.2
Doddridge	72	1,413	142	D	94	D	D	146	103,110	352	19.6	5.4	49.4
Fayette	735	7,889	2,050	474	1,474	234	162	272	34,436	232	39.7	1.3	40.1
Gilmer	120	1,042	272	193	148	28	12	33	31,697	235	9.4	11.1	46.4
Grant	231	2,663	826	283	398	96	39	103	38,520	486	24.5	12.1	45.7
Greenbrier	916	10,905	2,654	870	2,050	229	230	354	32,437	819	29.9	10.4	40.2
Hampshire	319	2,730	911	108	483	180	86	75	27,374	798	40.6	8.8	43.4
Hancock	570	9,109	1,157	2,706	957	284	433	305	33,476	96	47.9	1.0	30.2
Hardy	256	4,959	481	2,713	612	192	56	147	29,703	494	33.8	13.4	52.8
Harrison	1,800	27,946	6,775	1,478	4,836	627	1,716	1,175	42,056	778	26.2	4.4	34.8
Jackson	480	7,041	1,098	1,647	1,232	214	249	285	40,504	732	24.2	3.6	41.7
Jefferson	859	12,602	1,164	905	1,911	343	385	434	34,411	501	51.7	5.6	50.7
Kanawha	4,880	83,337	20,101	3,114	11,524	3,996	5,307	3,550	42,599	210	34.8	1.0	41.0
Lewis	384	5,289	1,194	68	1,087	101	55	216	40,822	476	20.6	5.5	42.9
Lincoln	187	1,525	584	D	308	56	40	46	30,360	149	14.8	4.0	47.7
Logan	597	8,997	1,927	529	1,807	201	233	360	39,985	11	54.5	9.1	45.5
McDowell	244	2,603	1,110	D	459	116	39	75	28,958	11	72.7	9.1	54.5
Marion	1,183	16,063	2,962	803	2,413	404	1,174	611	38,066	557	34.1	0.9	53.5
Marshall	486	9,096	1,673	566	1,277	218	269	382	41,950	682	23.3	1.6	43.5
Mason	323	3,976	991	485	630	107	67	177	44,636	875	26.2	4.0	38.9
Mercer	1,231	17,084	4,669	1,113	3,180	421	543	557	32,622	400	30.8	3.5	40.8
Mineral	444	5,659	1,452	1,082	948	115	158	228	40,203	429	34.3	7.5	33.3
Mingo	387	2,759	604	75	379	144	365	81	29,288	20	70.0	10.0	55.0
Monongalia	2,337	46,993	14,542	3,849	6,325	769	2,498	2,060	43,830	458	26.4	2.6	34.3
Monroe	175	1,399	304	D	129	50	38	51	36,673	796	27.4	7.8	41.7
Morgan	231	2,009	537	D	397	84	96	66	32,993	196	42.9	2.0	46.9
Nicholas	571	6,150	1,611	690	1,552	129	150	194	31,602	393	31.3	5.1	52.2
Ohio	1,385	27,203	7,179	989	3,304	1,147	1,822	1,023	37,612	197	26.4	5.1	38.1
Pendleton	142	1,126	331	145	178	61	15	33	29,346	556	17.3	16.2	51.8
Pleasants	125	2,045	391	487	144	72	39	96	46,953	150	27.3	5.3	44.0
Pocahontas	210	3,088	417	288	290	44	D	71	22,936	389	18.5	14.7	44.7
Preston	531	5,485	1,147	587	934	160	97	191	34,879	1,084	26.2	3.6	46.1
Putnam	1,216	18,180	2,156	2,281	2,545	574	713	795	43,720	544	28.9	1.5	41.9
Raleigh	1,782	26,162	7,141	682	5,022	536	900	929	35,520	332	44.9	2.4	51.5
Randolph	666	9,391	2,772	1,154	1,551	256	206	272	28,988	405	27.7	10.9	44.2
Ritchie	202	2,554	212	925	248	77	65	106	41,368	428	17.5	7.7	42.1
Roane	229	2,165	676	167	484	104	36	75	34,429	575	15.5	7.1	45.2
Summers	160	1,427	443	23	231	50	49	44	31,013	345	21.4	3.8	43.5
Taylor	222	2,434	561	D	461	35	37	102	41,884	404	36.4	4.2	40.1
Tucker	154	2,079	306	240	235	44	14	60	28,644	162	20.4	9.9	52.5
Tyler	106	1,874	491	769	149	79	18	75	39,877	286	18.9	5.2	44.1
Upshur	519	6,050	1,341	792	821	95	227	218	35,980	456	27.9	4.8	42.3
Wayne	488	6,647	2,220	650	1,035	129	145	274	41,253	197	21.8	4.6	39.1
Webster	137	1,262	469	282	165	36	9	38	30,373	70	28.6	0.0	44.3
Wetzel	334	4,345	791	905	951	123	167	179	41,222	249	13.7	2.0	44.6
Wirt	51	311	D	D	68	12	6	7	23,447	217	19.4	6.0	37.3
Wood	2,028	31,635	7,097	2,110	6,270	999	910	1,061	33,528	816	30.3	1.3	34.1
Wyoming	274	2,721	811	39	561	73	53	87	32,102	27	33.3	3.7	33.3
WISCONSIN	140,859	2,524,329	395,239	452,798	314,425	138,232	107,316	115,817	45,880	69,754	32.2	8.8	49.8
Adams	328	3,201	481	393	489	47	60	98	30,696	313	19.8	16.6	55.3
Ashland	516	6,389	1,283	1,098	972	212	152	237	37,173	187	23.5	13.4	35.3
Barron	1,338	16,800	2,732	5,013	3,054	513	295	643	38,268	1,322	25.3	11.0	54.5
Bayfield	431	2,255	338	177	378	83	33	67	29,901	352	27.3	9.9	51.4
Brown	6,473	143,037	21,347	25,464	15,821	8,417	5,303	6,695	46,804	1,111	52.7	6.0	54.3
Buffalo	305	3,000	279	279	257	125	74	110	36,733	1,061	20.3	14.8	49.8
Burnett	395	3,287	763	744	516	84	83	108	32,813	406	27.1	10.6	42.9
Calumet	883	13,021	1,187	3,557	1,835	659	199	530	40,715	719	36.7	9.2	53.3
Chippewa	1,582	21,930	3,259	6,184	3,857	342	568	876	39,952	1,757	29.5	9.6	47.2
Clark	750	9,176	1,006	3,591	1,020	165	156	326	35,475	2,317	23.3	7.1	64.7
Columbia	1,442	20,517	2,822	5,130	3,012	404	464	760	37,035	1,564	39.5	9.6	52.9
Crawford	378	5,772	906	1,518	1,030	120	115	193	33,411	1,105	24.1	6.9	43.5
Dane	14,093	281,349	46,809	25,340	32,249	23,381	22,836	14,743	52,401	2,749	43.0	7.8	47.3
Dodge	1,734	29,770	4,208	9,605	3,373	650	595	1,505	50,555	2,012	36.9	9.7	47.5
Door	1,269	10,404	1,326	2,367	1,784	300	229	379	36,476	803	40.6	6.2	45.0

Table B. States and Counties — **Agriculture**

STATE County	Land in farms — Acreage (1,000)	Land in farms — Percent change, 2007-2012	Acres — Average size of farm	Acres — Total irrigated (1,000)	Acres — Total cropland (1,000)	Value of land and buildings (dollars) — Average per farm	Value of land and buildings (dollars) — Average per acre	Value of machinery and equiopmnet, average per farm (dollars)	Value of products sold: Total (mil dol)	Value of products sold: Average per farm (acres)	Percent from: Crops	Percent from: Livestock and poultry products	Percent of farms with sales of: $10,000 or more	Percent of farms with sales of: $100,000 or more	Government payments — Total ($1,000)	Government payments — Percent of farms
	117	118	119	120	121	122	123	124	125	126	127	128	129	130	131	132
WEST VIRGINIA— Cont'd																
Calhoun	49	-11.7	218	0.0	7.4	331,432	1,521	38,423	2.1	9,326	17.9	82.1	17.2	2.6	40	6.6
Clay	20	0.6	176	D	2.2	329,789	1,873	34,000	0.5	4,570	30.3	69.7	10.5	0.0	37	6.1
Doddridge	65	-19.6	186	D	10.0	349,517	1,882	41,406	2.3	6,452	33.7	66.3	15.3	0.3	50	4.3
Fayette	23	-13.2	100	0.0	6.1	245,427	2,458	43,509	1.7	7,478	41.5	58.5	18.1	0.9	66	7.3
Gilmer	70	9.9	300	0.0	11.7	440,783	1,472	55,600	8.8	37,634	4.4	95.6	25.1	3.0	139	10.2
Grant	112	3.2	231	0.0	21.3	549,519	2,377	44,138	51.3	105,498	2.4	97.6	37.2	11.7	253	19.1
Greenbrier	190	7.4	232	0.0	35.7	658,885	2,837	71,835	76.8	93,722	2.8	97.2	37.6	8.5	461	15.4
Hampshire	142	10.0	178	0.1	34.8	641,143	3,601	51,271	39.2	49,102	19.3	80.7	26.2	5.5	227	16.9
Hancock	9	-7.9	93	D	3.1	271,469	2,932	59,625	0.6	6,750	53.1	46.9	13.5	1.0	2	5.2
Hardy	155	15.6	314	0.0	29.2	891,816	2,837	87,621	189.0	382,530	2.7	97.3	46.6	27.7	336	15.4
Harrison	117	4.8	150	0.0	25.7	318,695	2,119	45,731	9.5	12,264	25.2	74.8	20.3	2.1	71	3.3
Jackson	105	-19.1	143	0.0	25.8	315,790	2,207	42,680	7.4	10,067	28.8	71.2	20.8	1.2	256	8.9
Jefferson	67	-7.1	134	0.3	41.4	918,731	6,874	74,527	35.5	70,920	45.0	55.0	36.7	9.6	852	24.8
Kanawha	26	9.5	124	0.0	4.1	268,152	2,165	31,386	1.3	6,310	33.3	66.7	18.6	0.5	25	8.1
Lewis	82	-10.5	173	D	16.2	341,069	1,969	42,935	7.0	14,753	14.0	86.0	35.1	1.5	73	3.6
Lincoln	26	-20.8	172	0.0	3.3	348,013	2,021	38,450	0.9	6,087	37.6	62.4	12.8	1.3	63	24.8
Logan	1	-40.3	76	D	0.0	147,273	1,949	34,455	0.1	5,364	89.8	10.2	18.2	0.0	0	0.0
McDowell	1	-29.7	95	0.0	0.2	227,091	2,400	47,091	D	D	D	D	9.1	9.1	0	0.0
Marion	53	-8.0	96	0.0	12.7	206,381	2,155	42,246	2.4	4,370	39.1	60.9	11.8	0.0	49	3.6
Marshall	86	-10.3	126	0.0	22.8	277,150	2,199	46,801	3.3	4,890	40.9	59.1	11.9	0.0	121	7.6
Mason	139	5.0	159	0.3	39.7	335,312	2,114	52,757	34.1	38,965	74.1	25.9	24.1	4.6	465	17.5
Mercer	52	-4.0	129	0.0	9.7	287,660	2,222	45,280	3.9	9,790	33.2	66.8	19.8	1.8	34	2.8
Mineral	76	-2.3	178	0.1	16.7	533,772	3,006	49,399	22.2	51,849	6.9	93.1	22.6	5.6	257	11.7
Mingo	2	-49.2	102	0.0	0.1	143,850	1,417	23,300	0.1	5,300	D	D	10.0	0.0	0	0.0
Monongalia	58	-2.1	127	0.0	14.9	391,255	3,090	48,055	4.0	8,784	27.8	72.2	21.8	0.9	165	6.1
Monroe	145	8.9	182	0.0	29.2	414,754	2,283	52,758	31.4	39,447	9.5	90.5	36.8	7.5	426	15.8
Morgan	18	-18.1	94	0.1	7.8	419,311	4,470	39,770	3.0	15,408	77.2	22.8	19.4	3.1	86	6.6
Nicholas	58	13.2	148	0.0	13.6	377,216	2,552	42,771	4.6	11,649	16.8	83.2	22.9	2.0	37	8.7
Ohio	30	-2.4	153	D	11.9	353,061	2,312	80,888	3.5	17,660	20.5	79.5	28.4	5.6	64	24.4
Pendleton	170	0.1	306	D	24.4	711,710	2,326	68,344	118.8	213,608	2.4	97.6	58.6	21.0	207	17.1
Pleasants	21	-16.6	143	D	4.1	277,013	1,933	55,173	D	D	D	D	14.7	2.7	D	1.3
Pocahontas	118	-2.8	305	0.0	18.7	670,208	2,201	61,131	9.3	23,779	11.3	88.7	40.1	4.4	174	21.9
Preston	161	5.5	148	0.1	44.9	365,799	2,467	55,455	18.2	16,749	28.1	71.9	31.5	2.8	222	8.4
Putnam	60	-9.7	110	0.1	12.2	281,868	2,556	39,509	10.1	18,603	83.1	16.9	14.3	1.1	85	9.6
Raleigh	37	-15.1	111	0.0	8.1	276,123	2,487	47,337	3.0	9,036	24.6	75.4	17.2	0.9	47	6.0
Randolph	94	-9.9	232	D	19.8	422,042	1,815	54,812	9.4	23,173	21.8	78.2	35.1	3.2	147	9.9
Ritchie	89	-2.3	207	0.0	17.6	331,741	1,599	54,668	7.6	17,776	15.1	84.9	21.7	1.2	57	4.0
Roane	111	-5.7	193	D	21.6	330,957	1,716	42,193	5.6	9,781	26.2	73.8	23.1	0.7	209	9.6
Summers	58	-2.8	168	0.0	10.9	369,194	2,198	42,614	5.0	14,365	25.7	74.3	25.2	3.5	45	6.7
Taylor	49	-8.7	122	0.0	10.4	301,597	2,481	50,545	3.7	9,228	19.2	80.8	18.1	1.5	131	4.2
Tucker	34	-2.7	210	D	6.7	641,191	3,059	47,975	2.2	13,580	22.6	77.4	29.0	1.9	37	9.9
Tyler	48	1.4	169	0.0	11.5	309,413	1,836	41,035	2.2	7,829	35.1	64.9	26.2	0.3	34	7.0
Upshur	68	-3.4	150	0.0	15.0	348,270	2,320	46,175	6.8	14,925	18.8	81.3	24.6	2.6	48	3.9
Wayne	30	-24.2	153	0.0	3.7	288,345	1,880	36,102	1.0	5,183	40.7	59.2	12.2	1.0	24	4.1
Webster	8	-31.2	113	0.0	1.8	248,500	2,194	25,086	0.3	4,743	62.7	37.3	15.7	0.0	D	2.9
Wetzel	38	-26.5	153	D	7.6	279,361	1,826	34,867	1.2	4,727	43.9	56.1	6.8	0.4	45	4.4
Wirt	38	-7.8	175	D	7.7	287,650	1,642	42,065	2.2	10,286	28.8	71.2	20.3	1.4	55	8.8
Wood	88	-1.3	108	0.0	21.8	251,165	2,333	34,237	6.1	7,496	30.9	69.1	14.0	0.2	102	3.4
Wyoming	3	-26.5	110	D	0.5	227,889	2,072	42,407	0.1	2,556	15.9	84.1	3.7	0.0	0	0.0
WISCONSIN	14,569	-4.1	209	421.7	9,911.0	819,551	3,924	129,561	11,744.5	168,370	39.2	60.8	52.3	24.6	237,304	55.8
Adams	118	2.6	378	44.3	87.5	1,467,256	3,879	173,677	105.7	337,601	88.5	11.5	52.4	23.0	882	54.3
Ashland	46	-17.3	245	0.0	21.2	450,973	1,841	83,807	12.0	64,364	20.9	79.1	42.2	8.0	214	18.2
Barron	310	-4.5	234	11.7	202.9	655,775	2,799	148,573	343.1	259,503	29.1	70.9	58.5	29.0	4,643	59.5
Bayfield	72	-19.6	204	0.1	36.3	414,466	2,031	70,830	13.9	39,528	35.3	64.7	34.9	10.8	267	19.6
Brown	181	-3.2	163	0.5	151.3	884,833	5,425	149,589	307.5	276,792	17.4	82.6	52.8	27.2	3,585	48.7
Buffalo	305	-0.6	288	4.6	162.7	968,225	3,365	147,399	225.8	212,814	32.1	67.9	58.9	30.3	4,876	68.7
Burnett	84	-13.1	206	0.2	44.4	506,421	2,459	84,613	37.2	91,626	38.8	61.2	39.7	13.5	661	42.4
Calumet	142	-6.1	198	0.0	120.9	1,092,981	5,520	172,268	213.2	296,527	25.5	74.5	64.4	33.1	3,196	64.0
Chippewa	385	8.8	219	5.7	249.9	597,028	2,727	114,201	253.2	144,107	38.1	61.9	51.5	24.6	5,088	54.5
Clark	458	4.1	198	0.6	310.9	618,184	3,126	119,200	401.9	173,441	22.9	77.1	64.2	38.2	5,774	38.1
Columbia	308	-2.6	197	1.6	234.1	993,045	5,043	129,485	214.3	137,021	55.7	44.3	51.0	20.5	5,783	51.3
Crawford	217	-9.1	196	0.2	98.4	530,437	2,706	78,187	74.9	67,783	50.3	49.7	48.1	15.3	2,373	61.3
Dane	504	-5.8	183	4.6	396.3	1,111,346	6,057	145,729	471.6	171,553	39.1	60.9	50.5	23.2	12,023	62.2
Dodge	402	-2.6	200	0.8	332.6	1,069,970	5,355	169,021	373.5	185,612	45.8	54.2	57.6	30.2	7,872	58.2
Door	132	-1.9	164	0.9	94.3	668,813	4,070	99,567	82.6	102,905	46.1	53.9	45.0	16.4	1,826	50.7

Table B. States and Counties — Water Use, Wholesale Trade, Retail Trade, and Real Estate

STATE County	Water use, 2015		Wholesale Trade[1], 2012				Retail Trade[2], 2012				Real estate and rental and leasing,[2] 2012			
	Public supply water withdrawn (mil gal/day)	Public supply gallons withdrawn per person per day	Number of establish-ments	Number of employees	Sales (mil dol)	Annual payroll (mil dol)	Number of establish-ments	Number of employees	Sales (mil dol)	Annual payroll (mil dol)	Number of establish-ments	Number of employees	Sales (mil dol)	Annual payroll (mil dol)
	133	134	135	136	137	138	139	140	141	142	143	144	145	146
WEST VIRGINIA— Cont'd														
Calhoun	0.32	42.8	NA	NA	NA	NA	19	128	27.3	2.4	3	6	0.5	0.1
Clay	0.40	44.9	1	D	D	D	17	134	45.7	2.7	1	D	D	D
Doddridge	0.22	26.9	1	D	D	D	10	90	22.8	1.4	1	D	D	D
Fayette	5.37	119.3	25	D	D	D	134	1,683	413.8	37.0	21	56	8.6	1.2
Gilmer	0.64	75.1	4	D	D	D	22	157	38.3	3.2	2	D	D	D
Grant	0.97	82.4	2	D	D	D	38	377	115.2	7.7	5	10	0.9	0.2
Greenbrier	3.42	96.3	17	D	D	D	173	2,029	543.4	47.6	42	118	23.3	3.7
Hampshire	0.53	22.7	6	D	D	D	57	480	123.6	9.6	14	29	3.6	0.8
Hancock	1.46	49.0	13	154	105.9	4.9	93	1,000	235.3	19.2	22	D	D	D
Hardy	3.01	217.3	4	D	D	D	45	599	133.3	12.2	7	20	2.2	0.4
Harrison	7.91	115.1	74	867	381.8	37.0	327	4,727	1,314.7	104.5	62	508	161.0	24.8
Jackson	1.81	61.9	18	254	191.4	9.9	96	1,138	348.2	25.9	14	49	24.9	2.1
Jefferson	2.70	47.8	14	58	51.0	2.8	142	1,866	451.4	40.8	43	117	18.0	3.4
Kanawha	32.16	170.8	256	3,709	2,518.9	183.3	760	11,292	3,186.6	274.2	238	1,208	278.6	42.3
Lewis	1.08	65.7	14	116	109.9	5.8	75	1,063	301.2	23.6	9	39	5.2	0.8
Lincoln	0.30	14.0	3	D	D	D	38	312	80.3	6.5	2	D	D	D
Logan	4.29	123.6	34	411	138.2	18.1	118	1,726	551.2	42.6	20	86	9.3	2.4
McDowell	2.90	146.2	5	D	D	D	53	650	131.2	12.7	6	29	17.9	3.1
Marion	8.21	144.2	44	D	D	D	189	2,291	743.2	55.4	35	128	24.0	4.4
Marshall	4.67	146.0	16	D	D	D	85	1,224	344.7	27.3	7	D	D	D
Mason	2.33	86.2	5	D	D	D	54	575	143.9	11.9	14	51	6.1	1.2
Mercer	3.58	58.5	52	590	355.8	28.1	251	3,183	929.1	78.2	38	126	61.9	4.6
Mineral	1.57	57.2	12	D	D	D	71	999	237.3	20.4	15	37	4.7	0.8
Mingo	4.02	158.9	14	197	55.0	8.2	62	445	119.7	11.2	15	D	D	D
Monongalia	10.87	104.3	56	401	340.9	14.5	382	6,325	1,608.6	129.8	132	D	D	D
Monroe	0.49	36.3	6	16	3.6	0.4	31	145	26.6	2.7	3	4	0.6	0.1
Morgan	0.55	31.4	3	D	D	D	48	397	90.3	8.2	10	29	3.4	0.6
Nicholas	2.78	108.6	17	149	59.3	6.3	109	1,505	432.5	34.7	18	46	9.0	1.5
Ohio	7.70	178.8	72	D	D	D	201	3,486	896.0	79.7	56	D	D	D
Pendleton	0.31	42.9	3	D	D	D	24	204	37.2	3.5	2	D	D	D
Pleasants	0.57	74.3	NA	NA	NA	NA	16	168	45.7	3.7	2	D	D	D
Pocahontas	0.38	44.2	1	D	D	D	33	327	75.7	6.0	11	47	6.2	1.0
Preston	2.21	65.1	15	85	33.3	2.9	94	854	234.5	16.9	20	D	D	D
Putnam	2.61	45.9	74	D	D	D	174	2,359	748.5	55.8	57	316	112.1	18.1
Raleigh	9.89	127.6	96	D	D	D	346	5,057	1,452.4	124.3	74	287	50.0	9.8
Randolph	2.75	94.4	24	238	368.9	8.9	142	1,477	352.7	32.6	21	100	14.7	3.3
Ritchie	0.48	48.1	5	D	D	D	34	288	73.2	5.6	4	8	0.5	0.1
Roane	0.85	58.9	9	78	50.8	2.2	41	513	132.6	11.3	10	22	1.8	0.4
Summers	2.49	188.1	6	D	D	D	29	259	68.4	5.6	3	6	0.5	0.1
Taylor	1.82	107.6	7	D	D	D	33	448	110.9	10.3	2	D	D	D
Tucker	0.61	87.6	1	D	D	D	28	223	50.1	4.8	10	52	3.8	1.1
Tyler	0.57	63.5	NA	NA	NA	NA	21	139	44.1	2.7	1	D	D	D
Upshur	2.11	85.2	12	154	171.6	6.6	82	874	264.2	20.4	19	65	8.8	1.7
Wayne	2.91	71.0	15	252	140.5	11.4	107	1,048	254.9	20.8	19	D	D	D
Webster	0.49	56.0	3	D	D	D	21	153	42.9	3.2	3	D	D	D
Wetzel	1.78	112.5	12	93	27.6	2.4	77	879	208.7	18.7	13	34	4.4	1.0
Wirt	0.00	0.0	1	D	D	D	13	77	19.8	1.2	1	D	D	D
Wood	7.97	92.2	76	699	332.7	27.9	390	6,018	1,396.6	129.2	84	332	68.8	10.4
Wyoming	1.82	82.2	5	D	D	D	72	677	154.3	12.6	9	28	3.1	0.7
WISCONSIN	479.38	83.1	5,990	97,040	77,066.9	5,253.6	19,272	296,956	78,201.8	6,835.0	4,509	23,762	4,358.9	801.1
Adams	0.81	40.2	6	32	10.3	0.8	44	454	192.3	11.7	13	41	4.8	1.1
Ashland	0.99	62.5	11	90	33.7	3.2	87	897	214.2	20.0	9	38	2.7	0.5
Barron	4.48	98.3	41	319	166.0	11.3	220	3,033	713.3	67.7	33	80	12.8	2.0
Bayfield	0.37	24.7	8	D	D	D	69	391	84.5	6.6	9	18	2.1	0.3
Brown	19.19	74.2	329	6,081	4,360.8	321.1	864	14,521	3,686.2	322.1	203	1,407	203.8	43.4
Buffalo	0.40	30.3	9	117	62.3	5.9	46	281	77.8	5.6	10	24	2.5	0.3
Burnett	0.36	23.7	4	D	D	D	63	588	121.0	10.8	15	18	4.3	0.5
Calumet	10.93	219.6	44	498	222.9	22.9	109	1,796	418.6	37.0	13	50	3.1	0.8
Chippewa	6.96	109.6	62	671	408.4	24.9	213	3,500	1,064.9	82.6	34	95	13.8	2.5
Clark	1.23	35.7	41	331	256.0	16.9	99	820	260.6	18.1	7	15	1.7	0.3
Columbia	3.56	62.7	46	494	342.4	23.0	197	3,292	795.2	76.2	41	D	D	D
Crawford	1.43	87.2	11	D	D	D	78	1,034	216.6	22.0	8	21	2.1	0.3
Dane	43.49	83.1	597	11,599	8,106.6	613.2	1,687	29,330	8,516.2	743.4	620	4,076	952.3	158.3
Dodge	6.30	71.2	71	978	474.7	40.7	234	3,189	833.0	69.8	40	100	18.3	2.9
Door	1.36	49.4	25	144	62.9	6.0	259	1,682	414.1	40.8	46	188	20.7	4.4

1. Merchant wholesalers, except manufacturers' sales branches and offices. 2. Employer establishments.

Table B. States and Counties — Professional Services, Manufacturing, and Accommodation and Food Services

STATE County	Professional, scientific, and technical services, 2012				Manufacturing, 2012				Accommodation and food services, 2012			
	Number of establishments	Number of employees	Sales (mil dol)	Annual payroll (mil dol)	Number of establishments	Number of employees	Receipts (mil dol)	Annual payroll (mil dol)	Number of establishments	Number of employees	Receipts (mil dol)	Annual payroll (mil dol)
	147	148	149	150	151	152	153	154	155	156	157	158
WEST VIRGINIA— Cont'd												
Calhoun	5	21	1.8	0.6	6	33	D	0.7	4	22	1.1	0.4
Clay	2	D	D	D	4	43	D	2.4	5	D	D	D
Doddridge	1	D	D	D	NA	NA	NA	NA	3	D	D	D
Fayette	50	222	25.1	9.9	31	583	275.0	31.0	73	989	58.6	16.9
Gilmer	8	55	5.4	2.0	5	214	D	6.4	11	D	D	D
Grant	12	58	4.2	1.6	7	221	68.9	8.8	21	D	D	D
Greenbrier	75	295	24.0	7.7	35	774	D	30.8	88	2,455	190.7	67.3
Hampshire	24	D	D	D	12	153	66.0	7.7	35	310	18.7	5.2
Hancock	47	487	36.2	13.1	20	2,689	D	136.6	79	D	D	D
Hardy	15	48	4.4	1.3	11	2,575	D	71.4	28	309	13.9	3.9
Harrison	139	1,674	270.5	99.6	52	1,752	D	D	155	3,196	155.3	41.2
Jackson	43	236	29.9	11.9	15	1,188	D	78.3	52	852	39.1	10.4
Jefferson	84	360	48.6	18.6	17	816	206.7	35.2	127	D	D	D
Kanawha	565	5,965	884.4	340.3	121	2,985	2,196.6	185.5	458	9,306	552.9	145.9
Lewis	15	56	5.5	1.6	15	124	D	4.6	37	596	34.3	11.0
Lincoln	9	71	8.0	2.6	4	11	2.2	0.5	15	D	D	D
Logan	39	246	17.7	7.5	36	734	157.8	31.1	62	979	48.3	12.7
McDowell	13	D	D	D	4	26	D	0.8	22	D	D	D
Marion	119	1,060	130.7	59.5	50	1,154	469.5	50.6	113	2,043	93.7	23.7
Marshall	33	173	15.7	5.5	19	473	D	24.3	60	792	32.4	8.5
Mason	25	87	9.1	3.0	19	696	D	41.2	33	344	14.2	4.2
Mercer	92	639	71.4	20.2	57	1,246	241.5	50.6	106	2,177	100.9	27.6
Mineral	27	195	11.2	4.5	16	1,821	D	117.3	50	D	D	D
Mingo	47	D	D	D	13	173	D	4.2	31	322	11.2	3.4
Monongalia	205	2,723	394.9	120.9	53	3,668	2,034.3	256.4	281	5,885	253.5	70.4
Monroe	9	30	2.2	0.6	5	411	D	19.0	11	D	D	D
Morgan	13	79	13.2	6.3	6	140	D	D	27	D	D	D
Nicholas	45	246	14.7	7.7	25	709	212.9	30.6	59	844	36.9	10.3
Ohio	154	1,777	215.8	80.0	42	1,520	337.5	55.6	135	2,984	226.7	45.3
Pendleton	5	D	D	D	5	127	D	5.3	11	D	D	D
Pleasants	4	D	D	D	8	565	305.6	32.5	12	D	D	D
Pocahontas	6	D	D	D	6	261	38.1	7.9	24	1,360	51.4	16.8
Preston	29	111	10.4	3.8	25	465	147.1	17.4	36	280	13.6	3.4
Putnam	105	1,037	117.0	42.1	41	1,989	1,948.4	115.1	91	1,535	74.3	19.6
Raleigh	123	864	107.0	41.2	60	1,058	278.6	48.3	149	3,189	177.8	48.3
Randolph	49	226	17.8	6.8	24	1,069	189.4	37.2	54	776	38.4	10.6
Ritchie	14	51	3.8	1.6	13	741	D	31.8	17	D	D	D
Roane	16	46	4.2	1.4	16	226	45.2	8.1	13	D	D	D
Summers	11	70	6.8	2.5	7	19	3.1	0.7	19	247	9.6	2.5
Taylor	10	D	D	D	8	D	D	D	26	D	D	D
Tucker	7	D	D	D	15	224	D	9.9	32	D	D	D
Tyler	8	19	1.4	0.3	4	514	D	46.2	6	D	D	D
Upshur	37	228	15.8	6.4	18	665	285.3	32.5	48	644	30.0	8.5
Wayne	22	158	17.4	5.7	26	523	446.1	26.7	52	D	D	D
Webster	5	D	D	D	7	114	D	3.1	11	D	D	D
Wetzel	19	117	8.9	3.3	10	850	D	70.5	42	606	28.2	6.6
Wirt	4	D	D	D	4	D	D	2.2	8	D	D	D
Wood	161	986	105.9	42.2	59	D	2,261.9	205.7	210	4,070	181.8	53.1
Wyoming	19	55	4.5	1.4	9	51	D	2.5	21	D	D	D
WISCONSIN	11,301	99,162	15,135.0	5,738.3	8,995	436,777	177,728.9	21,879.3	14,137	221,567	10,303.3	2,764.3
Adams	15	57	4.6	1.6	12	377	D	18.3	60	1,117	55.1	17.9
Ashland	29	161	15.2	7.2	23	1,107	219.8	51.9	62	588	28.9	7.9
Barron	66	317	28.2	12.4	92	4,865	1,520.7	199.1	137	1,474	59.1	15.8
Bayfield	9	28	2.0	0.6	21	170	D	5.5	90	515	31.8	9.0
Brown	526	4,885	709.5	255.6	442	24,628	11,068.4	1,230.8	593	11,889	479.2	141.4
Buffalo	18	63	4.8	1.3	20	386	303.2	17.7	41	286	10.5	2.6
Burnett	22	62	7.1	2.3	25	790	286.6	34.5	65	456	20.9	5.8
Calumet	64	206	18.6	7.8	71	3,827	1,616.8	174.4	95	1,502	47.0	12.7
Chippewa	86	383	48.5	17.9	125	5,030	1,930.5	237.5	165	1,801	70.0	17.0
Clark	33	165	13.4	5.1	77	3,513	2,021.0	136.7	57	508	17.8	4.9
Columbia	80	465	41.3	15.9	94	4,732	2,530.5	220.7	167	3,440	158.0	45.2
Crawford	21	227	10.0	4.7	24	1,534	1,054.2	66.7	55	638	27.6	7.0
Dane	1,741	19,907	3,387.5	1,313.8	521	23,154	7,205.3	1,210.9	1,265	24,284	1,111.2	316.1
Dodge	78	467	52.4	19.0	148	10,011	3,727.6	462.8	155	1,801	69.5	18.2
Door	74	237	28.7	9.4	56	1,968	416.7	88.3	238	1,999	147.6	36.9

Health Care and Social Assistance, Other Services, Nonemployer Businesses, and Residential Construction

STATE County	Health care and social assistance, 2012				Other services, 2012				Nonemployer businesses, 2015		Value of residential construction authorized by building permits, 2017	
	Number of establish-ments	Number of employees	Receipts (mil dol)	Annual payroll (mil dol)	Number of establis-hments	Number of employees	Receipts (mil dol)	Annual payroll (mil dol)	Number	Receipts (mil dol)	New construction ($1,000)	Number of housing units
	159	160	161	162	163	164	165	166	167	168	169	170
WEST VIRGINIA— Cont'd												
Calhoun	9	294	17.0	10.0	5	D	D	D	465	9.9	NA	NA
Clay	12	283	10.6	5.2	5	D	D	D	366	11.5	0	0
Doddridge	11	176	4.2	2.4	2	D	D	D	237	7.4	0	0
Fayette	105	2,040	162.6	65.2	56	372	37.0	9.1	1,749	55.4	3,056	27
Gilmer	13	255	14.2	7.1	9	32	2.6	0.6	354	8.6	3,168	29
Grant	28	738	45.9	19.5	19	D	D	D	689	25.2	3,658	53
Greenbrier	145	3,028	238.4	101.2	55	291	26.7	7.9	2,245	82.7	23,730	112
Hampshire	34	752	52.1	21.9	26	107	9.1	2.3	1,422	57.2	7,913	57
Hancock	75	1,251	73.4	31.6	46	198	13.8	3.4	1,221	43.0	3,489	15
Hardy	30	451	28.4	12.1	19	54	5.6	0.9	875	26.9	7,705	53
Harrison	237	6,341	666.5	275.1	134	D	D	D	3,765	154.7	14,983	96
Jackson	62	1,111	71.6	30.1	27	D	D	D	1,467	59.6	286	3
Jefferson	77	1,217	103.1	41.8	72	541	76.6	15.1	3,572	137.1	68,339	274
Kanawha	746	18,799	2,083.3	768.4	388	D	D	D	9,094	391.6	16,557	125
Lewis	35	1,261	112.6	42.7	30	103	8.6	2.2	830	35.2	142	2
Lincoln	18	D	D	D	15	66	4.4	1.3	760	21.6	2,064	16
Logan	96	1,880	186.3	68.7	60	486	87.4	15.9	1,136	44.1	75	1
McDowell	34	867	58.5	21.8	19	D	D	D	491	13.1	339	3
Marion	163	2,878	259.9	99.2	107	761	59.1	20.2	2,605	88.4	10,515	91
Marshall	79	D	D	D	42	208	16.0	4.2	1,131	36.2	197	1
Mason	38	1,034	93.9	37.5	28	111	9.7	2.5	907	27.8	135	3
Mercer	244	4,629	432.9	161.6	94	831	81.3	25.1	3,001	122.7	650	5
Mineral	64	1,382	70.4	28.4	41	180	14.1	3.8	1,379	44.8	5,479	29
Mingo	48	686	71.0	23.7	21	211	19.8	6.8	914	29.3	0	0
Monongalia	233	13,029	1,513.8	539.2	143	1,104	170.3	29.1	5,447	260.9	6,403	67
Monroe	19	338	18.5	7.2	8	29	1.9	0.5	743	26.8	0	0
Morgan	20	558	44.9	16.3	22	66	4.4	1.1	1,168	44.2	7,316	52
Nicholas	58	1,626	100.1	47.2	35	168	19.3	5.1	1,187	44.7	0	0
Ohio	234	D	D	D	125	1,074	117.3	28.9	2,463	114.4	8,546	13
Pendleton	17	325	18.4	7.9	11	49	5.6	1.3	492	14.3	1,588	10
Pleasants	15	497	21.0	8.8	7	D	D	D	304	8.6	1,799	10
Pocahontas	20	415	24.2	9.9	17	104	7.1	1.8	534	22.1	240	4
Preston	62	1,149	68.3	30.3	34	212	20.4	5.2	1,611	65.2	1,059	10
Putnam	120	D	D	D	64	418	51.5	12.8	2,938	120.8	20,795	93
Raleigh	284	7,414	735.3	289.5	112	796	87.8	23.4	3,432	129.8	11,210	56
Randolph	107	2,872	183.3	82.9	44	217	19.9	5.5	1,476	48.5	268	3
Ritchie	18	208	11.7	5.3	11	D	D	D	656	23.8	7,862	57
Roane	22	665	48.6	20.5	8	D	D	D	857	28.0	0	0
Summers	20	426	33.6	12.7	14	D	D	D	479	13.8	2,103	20
Taylor	27	552	47.1	17.7	23	D	D	D	710	20.3	100	1
Tucker	10	284	12.8	6.4	11	101	9.8	2.5	401	14.0	0	0
Tyler	12	544	26.7	13.1	16	53	2.7	0.8	373	8.7	1,512	9
Upshur	77	1,626	100.5	53.6	30	124	11.7	2.5	1,254	50.3	5,886	49
Wayne	72	2,462	312.9	122.2	32	150	14.5	4.2	1,555	51.0	2,189	25
Webster	13	462	25.8	12.5	2	D	D	D	322	10.1	0	0
Wetzel	41	717	52.7	19.7	32	152	9.5	2.6	561	16.6	3,956	45
Wirt	5	73	4.1	1.5	2	D	D	D	278	8.6	1,216	8
Wood	282	7,096	635.4	247.0	150	859	83.5	20.6	4,134	168.7	16,523	125
Wyoming	27	778	36.1	17.6	13	D	D	D	749	21.3	277	2
WISCONSIN	14,659	386,141	40,680.6	16,257.6	10,210	62,054	6,406.7	1,732.2	341,935	15,999.3	3,910,795	19,545
Adams	30	454	31.0	12.0	25	121	10.9	3.4	1,101	47.1	17,825	85
Ashland	62	1,629	143.1	62.5	36	121	9.1	2.7	1,079	40.4	1,060	9
Barron	127	2,646	282.3	112.2	96	316	27.8	7.1	3,148	141.8	32,643	193
Bayfield	21	248	12.4	6.7	24	41	5.2	1.4	1,570	61.1	14,878	99
Brown	593	19,588	2,446.2	907.0	433	2,833	241.9	67.9	13,616	694.3	198,747	951
Buffalo	23	293	14.0	6.3	19	D	D	D	1,030	49.7	8,424	47
Burnett	30	587	34.7	16.6	22	63	6.4	1.4	1,154	42.7	21,147	83
Calumet	79	1,175	95.3	37.3	58	261	18.5	5.1	2,484	99.3	34,753	165
Chippewa	175	3,185	260.2	110.4	101	545	58.6	15.3	3,992	203.5	49,857	246
Clark	61	904	54.5	26.0	62	D	D	D	2,189	127.0	6,360	66
Columbia	132	2,563	206.1	91.7	91	398	37.1	9.9	3,679	164.7	37,638	146
Crawford	48	1,129	74.6	35.1	34	107	9.5	2.4	1,104	49.0	5,698	36
Dane	1,217	43,351	5,188.2	2,019.6	1,094	8,233	1,237.6	280.6	37,088	1,833.0	826,395	4,336
Dodge	205	4,611	437.1	170.0	133	452	39.3	10.9	4,474	199.1	40,815	226
Door	78	1,630	131.8	61.6	98	472	53.9	11.6	2,866	121.0	41,442	207

Table B. States and Counties — **Population, Vital Statistics, Health, and Crime**

STATE County	Persons in group quarters, 2017	Daytime Population, 2012-2016		Births, 2017		Deaths, 2017		Persons under 65 with no health insurance, 2016		Medicare, 2017			Serious crimes known to police[2], 2016 Total	
		Number	Employment/ residence ratio	Total	Rate[1]	Number	Rate[1]	Number	Percent	Total beneficiaries	Enrolled in Original Medicare	Enrolled in Medicare Advantage	Number	Rate[3]
	32	33	34	35	36	37	38	39	40	41	42	43	44	45
WISCONSIN— Cont'd														
Douglas	1,378	40,166	0.83	410	9.5	420	9.7	2,054	5.9	10,247	5,978	4,269	1,553	3,577
Dunn	3,254	41,344	0.86	446	10.0	321	7.2	2,218	6.4	7,656	5,105	2,551	694	1,558
Eau Claire	4,922	107,952	1.11	1,197	11.5	763	7.4	5,064	6.1	20,313	14,312	6,001	2,239	2,183
Florence	53	3,591	0.54	33	7.5	51	11.7	251	7.8	1,004	728	276	105	2,348
Fond du Lac	3,532	97,749	0.92	1,043	10.2	884	8.6	4,570	5.6	22,334	11,380	10,954	1,563	1,534
Forest	359	8,944	0.95	104	11.6	111	12.4	715	10.4	2,555	1,660	895	147	1,634
Grant	4,881	48,007	0.86	571	11.0	472	9.1	2,712	6.9	11,670	6,834	4,837	722	1,378
Green	343	34,458	0.87	368	10.0	342	9.3	1,735	5.7	7,652	6,220	1,432	398	1,070
Green Lake	155	17,804	0.88	190	10.1	215	11.5	1,293	9.0	4,898	2,306	2,592	215	1,144
Iowa	188	22,799	0.92	279	11.8	204	8.6	1,143	5.9	4,572	3,048	1,525	188	790
Iron	82	5,271	0.77	32	5.6	83	14.6	288	7.2	1,809	1,092	717	112	1,942
Jackson	1,317	19,537	0.89	239	11.6	171	8.3	1,424	9.2	3,977	2,665	1,312	282	1,373
Jefferson	3,168	74,738	0.77	828	9.8	672	7.9	3,983	5.8	16,757	11,733	5,024	1,255	1,483
Juneau	1,689	25,132	0.89	273	10.3	257	9.7	1,643	8.3	6,336	5,084	1,252	437	1,675
Kenosha	4,358	148,676	0.76	1,905	11.3	1,336	7.9	9,148	6.4	26,434	18,864	7,570	3,538	2,099
Kewaunee	177	18,265	0.79	197	9.6	185	9.0	971	6.0	4,413	2,210	2,203	160	788
La Crosse	5,748	126,690	1.15	1,225	10.4	976	8.3	4,732	5.0	22,121	13,813	8,308	3,454	2,910
Lafayette	92	14,171	0.69	223	13.3	143	8.5	1,166	8.5	3,150	2,123	1,027	157	934
Langlade	258	18,596	0.91	193	10.1	230	12.0	996	6.9	5,148	2,992	2,157	628	3,296
Lincoln	656	25,679	0.82	272	9.8	307	11.0	1,312	6.1	7,775	4,644	3,131	518	1,865
Manitowoc	1,037	76,226	0.90	780	9.9	820	10.4	3,618	5.7	18,508	10,082	8,426	1,507	1,898
Marathon	1,588	137,611	1.03	1,605	11.8	1,138	8.4	7,205	6.4	25,160	14,162	10,998	1,968	1,447
Marinette	615	42,563	1.08	367	9.1	465	11.5	2,085	6.8	12,333	7,321	5,011	656	1,613
Marquette	134	12,973	0.69	141	9.2	160	10.5	877	7.7	4,914	3,231	1,683	162	1,081
Menominee	57	5,496	1.71	99	21.5	67	14.5	424	11.2	752	561	192	45	972
Milwaukee	23,404	986,932	1.07	13,448	14.1	8,130	8.5	62,419	7.8	151,985	81,938	70,046	45,881	4,789
Monroe	833	46,602	1.06	616	13.5	416	9.1	3,372	9.0	8,402	6,117	2,285	620	1,359
Oconto	271	28,893	0.54	348	9.3	382	10.2	1,853	6.2	7,758	3,593	4,165	NA	NA
Oneida	506	36,206	1.04	302	8.6	442	12.5	1,802	6.8	11,868	7,952	3,916	542	1,530
Outagamie	3,030	186,895	1.05	2,329	12.5	1,318	7.1	8,669	5.5	34,707	14,076	20,631	2,955	1,604
Ozaukee	2,021	83,760	0.91	831	9.4	773	8.7	2,674	3.8	18,688	11,266	7,423	855	972
Pepin	125	6,528	0.77	79	10.9	85	11.7	417	7.3	1,750	1,477	273	85	1,173
Pierce	2,460	30,178	0.52	388	9.3	273	6.5	1,766	5.3	7,865	4,506	3,358	505	1,380
Polk	426	38,881	0.78	407	9.4	423	9.7	2,426	7.0	9,345	5,268	4,077	580	1,342
Portage	3,507	71,356	1.02	673	9.5	497	7.1	3,163	5.6	12,261	7,342	4,920	875	1,243
Price	163	13,918	1.03	110	8.2	153	11.4	666	6.7	4,011	2,583	1,428	166	1,227
Racine	4,791	182,760	0.87	2,387	12.2	1,686	8.6	10,251	6.4	40,156	24,095	16,061	4,175	2,144
Richland	347	16,293	0.84	173	9.9	184	10.5	981	7.3	3,807	3,297	510	122	702
Rock	2,665	150,052	0.85	1,935	11.9	1,429	8.8	9,002	6.7	32,091	21,655	10,435	3,940	2,441
Rusk	155	14,246	1.00	139	9.8	157	11.1	896	8.4	3,541	2,204	1,337	166	1,187
St. Croix	809	75,175	0.75	989	11.1	601	6.8	3,583	4.7	12,865	7,236	5,628	997	1,169
Sauk	731	66,185	1.09	762	11.9	621	9.7	3,974	7.6	12,996	8,385	4,611	1,564	2,449
Sawyer	314	16,808	1.05	169	10.3	198	12.1	1,231	10.3	4,553	3,072	1,481	297	1,821
Shawano	731	36,196	0.74	405	9.9	418	10.2	2,679	8.4	8,957	4,003	4,953	706	1,717
Sheboygan	2,782	116,145	1.01	1,264	11.0	1,087	9.4	5,179	5.5	23,475	12,807	10,667	1,829	1,585
Taylor	218	20,044	0.95	235	11.6	184	9.1	1,443	8.8	3,728	2,137	1,592	250	1,226
Trempealeau	449	29,524	1.00	407	13.8	261	8.9	1,937	8.0	6,699	4,606	2,093	254	877
Vernon	357	27,539	0.78	412	13.4	319	10.4	2,306	9.4	6,651	3,641	3,010	226	768
Vilas	190	21,127	0.97	169	7.8	299	13.8	1,622	11.0	7,239	5,066	2,173	303	1,420
Walworth	2,679	97,941	0.90	996	9.7	888	8.6	6,540	7.8	19,067	14,656	4,411	1,514	1,473
Washburn	205	15,548	0.98	138	8.8	203	12.9	843	7.3	6,553	4,151	2,402	268	1,734
Washington	1,071	117,249	0.77	1,346	10.0	1,102	8.2	4,727	4.2	26,556	15,807	10,749	1,748	1,306
Waukesha	5,303	423,572	1.14	3,849	9.6	3,394	8.5	11,850	3.6	81,757	47,874	33,884	4,740	1,194
Waupaca	1,529	48,955	0.88	490	9.6	679	13.3	2,732	6.7	13,723	6,198	7,526	1,149	2,220
Waushara	1,224	21,098	0.69	228	9.4	247	10.1	1,587	9.2	5,698	2,842	2,856	314	1,314
Winnebago	7,706	180,200	1.12	1,911	11.2	1,479	8.7	7,527	5.5	30,588	13,501	17,088	3,138	1,848
Wood	796	76,899	1.09	825	11.3	760	10.4	3,320	5.7	20,346	10,469	9,877	1,421	1,945
WYOMING	14,133	589,394	1.02	7,513	13.0	4,847	8.4	65,310	13.4	102,076	97,704	4,372	12,890	2,202
Albany	2,064	37,376	0.98	393	10.3	198	5.2	3,723	11.7	4,675	4,375	301	595	1,568
Big Horn	183	11,677	0.95	149	12.5	125	10.5	1,673	17.7	2,530	2,489	41	NA	NA
Campbell	422	51,839	1.13	747	16.2	292	6.3	5,161	11.6	4,910	4,848	62	1,017	2,058
Carbon	806	15,603	0.99	217	14.2	138	9.0	1,847	14.7	2,625	2,490	135	353	2,362
Converse	103	14,090	0.98	191	13.8	119	8.6	1,400	11.6	2,357	2,330	27	NA	NA
Crook	34	6,502	0.78	119	16.1	65	8.8	823	13.6	1,501	1,407	94	98	1,393
Fremont	1,033	40,279	0.98	545	13.7	475	11.9	6,914	21.2	8,111	7,480	631	1,093	2,734

1. Per 1,000 estimated resident population.   2. Data for serious crimes have not been adjusted for underreporting; this may affect comparability between geographic areas and over time.
3. Per 100,000 population estimated by the FBI.

STATE County	Serious crimes known to police, 2016 (cont.)[1] Rate		Education						Money income, 2012-2016				Income and poverty, 2016			
			School enrollment and attainment, 2012-2016				Local government expenditures,[5] 2013-2014			Households			Percent below poverty level			
			Enrollment[3]		Attainment[4] (percent)						Percent					
	Violent	Property	Total	Percent private	High school graduate or less	Bachelor's degree or more	Total current spending (mil dol)	Current spending per student (dollars)	Per capita income[6]	Median income (dollars)	with income of less than $50,000	with income of $200,000 or more	Median household income (dollars)	All persons	Children under 18 years	Children 5 to 17 years in families
	46	47	48	49	50	51	52	53	54	55	56	57	58	59	60	61
WISCONSIN— Cont'd																
Douglas	175	3,402	10,384	8.9	39.3	22.8	72.8	11,490	26,036	48,190	51.7	1.7	50,340	13.6	16.8	14.8
Dunn	164	1,394	14,577	5.0	41.8	26.6	63.3	10,356	25,120	51,787	48.3	2.5	52,181	12.5	13.3	12.2
Eau Claire	153	2,030	30,496	8.9	33.0	30.8	153.4	10,845	26,795	50,538	49.5	2.6	52,209	13.1	14.0	13.1
Florence	112	2,237	775	9.5	45.4	17.5	6.5	15,936	28,358	46,595	53.3	2.3	47,704	12.3	20.3	17.9
Fond du Lac	183	1,352	23,966	23.8	46.3	21.9	143.9	10,704	28,036	56,376	43.9	2.1	58,920	7.7	11.3	9.9
Forest	289	1,345	1,899	6.7	53.5	14.1	20.1	12,753	22,559	41,378	58.4	1.3	42,072	15.9	22.8	21.0
Grant	170	1,209	15,609	10.7	47.2	21.3	84.1	12,007	23,103	49,077	50.9	1.7	47,512	16.7	17.0	15.2
Green	78	992	8,394	8.1	45.7	22.7	65.5	11,464	28,867	57,416	43.0	2.5	60,846	8.2	10.6	9.3
Green Lake	32	1,112	3,888	17.1	53.5	17.7	35.1	11,126	26,115	47,174	52.5	1.9	50,386	11.6	19.0	17.1
Iowa	113	676	5,438	10.9	42.7	23.0	44.4	12,449	29,610	56,641	43.5	3.3	58,372	8.8	12.0	10.9
Iron	17	1,925	912	6.6	41.3	19.7	10.2	13,118	25,536	41,270	59.6	0.8	41,597	14.4	20.2	16.9
Jackson	97	1,275	4,333	8.9	54.1	13.9	34.5	10,680	24,074	49,608	50.3	2.0	51,024	11.1	16.2	15.8
Jefferson	177	1,306	21,724	18.6	44.6	23.5	149.5	10,982	27,272	57,290	43.0	2.3	60,744	9.3	11.0	9.9
Juneau	268	1,406	5,370	15.8	55.7	12.9	44.7	11,847	23,519	47,243	53.2	1.9	47,938	14.4	20.9	18.3
Kenosha	260	1,839	45,490	15.0	42.3	24.6	333.1	11,213	27,335	56,086	44.5	3.4	59,622	13.0	19.0	17.3
Kewaunee	148	641	4,599	17.4	50.3	16.9	35.6	10,113	27,539	58,152	43.2	1.9	61,074	7.6	9.2	8.2
La Crosse	152	2,758	35,694	13.1	31.9	32.5	196.9	12,191	28,240	51,477	48.5	3.4	55,151	13.3	11.9	10.2
Lafayette	107	827	3,902	11.5	50.6	17.7	34.5	12,008	25,877	53,038	47.3	2.1	56,074	11.7	18.0	15.5
Langlade	63	3,233	3,868	13.7	52.3	16.1	35.4	11,641	24,772	43,501	56.4	1.5	44,522	14.2	23.0	21.1
Lincoln	212	1,652	5,680	16.5	49.3	16.0	48.6	10,097	27,322	52,221	48.0	1.7	54,471	10.0	14.6	13.4
Manitowoc	219	1,679	17,505	19.4	49.6	19.7	116.6	10,800	26,751	49,613	50.4	1.8	53,633	9.2	11.4	10.5
Marathon	132	1,315	32,692	12.8	45.1	23.9	224.6	11,141	28,773	54,227	46.0	3.0	56,223	10.4	14.0	12.8
Marinette	39	1,574	8,689	12.8	51.7	14.5	67.4	10,809	25,231	43,893	55.7	1.5	44,265	12.4	17.0	15.6
Marquette	53	1,027	2,811	15.3	54.3	13.8	20.4	11,435	25,268	48,445	51.7	1.0	50,032	12.0	20.0	18.8
Menominee	0	972	1,334	3.1	52.7	16.5	15.8	18,803	15,171	37,147	66.7	0.2	36,562	27.2	41.1	40.5
Milwaukee	1,037	3,752	263,278	25.4	41.0	29.7	1,559.4	11,080	25,881	45,263	54.0	2.8	47,666	19.8	28.4	27.0
Monroe	149	1,210	10,665	14.0	48.6	18.2	77.2	11,013	24,971	53,394	46.6	1.7	56,400	12.0	19.5	17.7
Oconto	NA	NA	7,619	7.8	53.6	16.2	52.8	12,483	27,623	54,018	46.4	2.2	58,025	9.1	13.1	11.3
Oneida	138	1,391	6,324	15.1	41.2	26.2	57.5	13,512	28,084	49,715	50.2	2.4	50,938	9.6	15.6	14.8
Outagamie	162	1,442	46,733	15.4	40.1	27.8	353.6	10,105	29,663	59,806	40.8	3.0	61,764	8.0	10.3	9.2
Ozaukee	62	909	22,967	25.4	25.6	46.7	136.5	10,752	44,369	78,415	31.2	10.8	85,706	5.4	4.8	4.0
Pepin	124	1,049	1,500	14.5	51.4	18.3	15.5	13,080	26,280	51,346	48.6	2.3	53,262	11.5	18.1	16.6
Pierce	205	1,175	13,044	9.9	39.0	27.8	79.9	10,489	30,009	64,364	38.9	3.7	70,086	8.1	7.8	6.8
Polk	312	1,029	9,157	9.0	46.3	19.6	84.4	11,325	27,066	52,039	47.9	1.9	53,661	9.9	13.0	11.6
Portage	126	1,117	21,488	8.6	39.5	30.3	97.0	10,278	26,832	52,411	47.1	2.5	55,064	11.5	11.6	10.8
Price	37	1,190	2,296	10.5	50.8	16.2	22.9	11,444	27,987	43,547	56.9	1.6	46,414	11.1	16.8	15.1
Racine	219	1,925	49,056	19.2	42.6	24.0	349.9	11,755	28,436	56,359	43.4	3.6	56,246	13.6	20.1	18.4
Richland	6	697	3,843	16.3	52.0	17.8	19.8	11,248	24,961	46,564	53.0	1.7	50,306	13.4	21.2	19.3
Rock	229	2,211	39,910	14.5	47.1	20.8	305.6	10,934	25,884	50,968	49.1	2.3	51,573	12.9	19.3	16.6
Rusk	236	951	2,723	18.5	55.4	14.8	25.1	12,406	22,651	39,904	61.1	1.6	43,075	13.8	21.8	20.2
St. Croix	64	1,104	22,558	13.8	31.1	33.4	142.4	9,917	34,679	73,743	31.1	5.9	75,619	5.6	6.2	5.3
Sauk	127	2,322	13,959	14.2	45.7	22.3	112.3	10,982	26,736	53,225	46.5	2.1	57,647	10.1	14.4	13.0
Sawyer	184	1,637	3,195	7.8	43.7	22.1	26.0	11,408	25,680	41,869	58.6	2.8	44,180	15.2	25.5	23.6
Shawano	102	1,615	8,964	11.9	54.4	15.6	61.3	11,008	25,286	48,773	51.2	1.8	50,203	11.9	18.5	16.2
Sheboygan	155	1,430	27,455	16.9	45.3	23.6	207.8	10,727	27,796	54,392	45.5	2.2	55,594	7.1	10.7	9.6
Taylor	103	1,123	4,460	14.3	58.5	13.5	33.9	10,995	24,907	47,306	53.1	2.2	50,963	11.8	18.3	16.5
Trempealeau	66	811	6,539	10.1	49.9	19.3	66.2	11,361	26,002	52,438	47.7	1.9	53,142	8.2	11.7	11.6
Vernon	41	727	6,608	23.3	49.9	21.2	47.0	11,520	24,414	49,476	50.5	2.3	51,002	16.5	25.9	24.3
Vilas	47	1,373	3,674	8.4	38.7	26.8	43.4	16,368	27,537	41,632	59.2	2.4	45,902	12.6	20.6	18.9
Walworth	99	1,374	28,691	10.9	40.7	27.8	188.6	11,649	28,085	55,575	45.2	3.2	58,904	11.2	12.0	10.9
Washburn	188	1,547	2,778	11.8	46.1	21.6	32.8	12,383	26,570	44,437	54.6	1.9	46,989	12.7	21.2	18.2
Washington	61	1,245	32,115	22.9	36.5	29.4	208.0	10,341	34,722	70,325	33.3	5.0	74,631	5.6	6.1	5.3
Waukesha	69	1,125	99,680	23.0	28.3	41.6	674.2	10,760	40,174	78,268	30.7	8.7	82,080	5.2	5.4	4.7
Waupaca	236	1,984	11,051	14.6	52.2	17.7	94.7	10,730	28,145	52,441	47.3	2.2	52,125	10.7	14.6	12.8
Waushara	113	1,201	4,448	12.1	55.5	15.1	31.9	12,037	24,861	46,581	53.5	2.0	47,596	14.3	23.5	20.4
Winnebago	166	1,683	43,085	11.0	41.9	26.9	235.7	10,430	28,446	53,501	46.0	2.7	57,003	11.7	14.1	11.4
Wood	31	1,914	16,174	12.2	46.5	20.4	139.1	11,150	27,687	49,926	50.1	2.2	52,591	9.8	14.0	12.6
WYOMING	244	1,957	149,521	9.4	36.8	26.0	1,464.9	15,885	30,139	59,143	42.6	3.5	61,686	10.9	11.6	10.0
Albany	124	1,444	16,808	6.6	21.0	47.9	60.9	16,176	25,227	43,043	56.7	2.6	47,355	17.3	12.8	11.7
Big Horn	NA	NA	2,934	7.0	40.3	19.3	42.3	17,050	23,041	50,820	48.4	1.1	49,725	11.4	14.0	11.6
Campbell	381	1,678	12,241	8.9	43.2	19.1	131.8	14,935	33,317	80,822	28.9	4.1	79,148	8.4	7.6	7.6
Carbon	167	2,195	3,744	13.4	44.4	20.3	43.0	17,008	27,399	56,972	44.0	2.5	59,103	12.1	12.4	10.7
Converse	NA	NA	3,268	12.8	47.6	15.5	39.4	16,213	31,470	66,737	39.3	2.3	71,517	9.0	9.9	8.7
Crook	71	1,322	1,549	6.1	38.6	21.4	20.1	18,012	32,817	60,307	39.5	4.5	60,953	8.3	8.8	8.2
Fremont	180	2,553	10,331	8.2	41.1	22.4	127.0	18,860	26,606	53,559	47.0	3.0	49,282	16.8	20.2	17.9

1. Data for serious crimes have not been adjusted for underreporting; this may affect comparability between geographic areas and over time.   2. Per 100,000 population estimated by the FBI.
3. All persons 3 years old and over enrolled in nursery school through college.   4. Persons 25 years old and over.   5. Elementary and secondary education expenditures.
6. Based on population estimated by the American Community Survey, 2011–2015.

Table B. States and Counties — **Personal Income and Earnings**

	Personal income, 2016										Earnings, 2016		
			Per capita[1]			Supplements to wages and salaries, employer contributions (mil dol)						Contributions for government social insurance (mil dol)	
STATE County	Total (mil dol)	Percent change 2015-2016	Dollars	Rank	Wages and salaries (mil dol)	Pension and insurance	Government social insurance	Proprietors' income (mil dol)	Dividends, interest, and rent (mil dol)	Personal transfer receipts (mil dol)	Total (mil dol)	From employee and self-employed	From employer
	62	63	64	65	66	67	68	69	70	71	72	73	74
WISCONSIN— Cont'd													
Douglas	1,691	0.5	38,861	1,524	720	158	64	71	269	431	1,012	133	64
Dunn	1,628	1.4	36,411	1,930	760	171	59	89	268	352	1,079	127	59
Eau Claire	4,483	1.3	43,543	930	2,675	495	203	240	891	782	3,613	424	203
Florence	218	-1.1	48,949	473	30	8	2	22	39	49	63	7	2
Fond du Lac	4,562	1.9	44,665	811	2,188	401	172	337	735	823	3,099	363	172
Forest	320	2.2	35,263	2,129	120	34	9	22	63	101	185	22	9
Grant	2,067	1.0	39,588	1,415	746	188	57	267	353	411	1,258	132	57
Green	1,732	1.5	46,729	635	672	135	52	159	326	276	1,018	113	52
Green Lake	838	-0.9	44,759	795	249	53	20	69	195	174	391	46	20
Iowa	1,052	0.5	44,484	832	437	78	35	101	187	173	651	74	35
Iron	255	2.2	44,542	824	58	14	5	21	61	75	98	13	5
Jackson	816	-0.3	39,690	1,401	377	84	29	49	161	170	538	61	29
Jefferson	3,529	1.8	41,698	1,141	1,415	283	110	194	538	635	2,002	236	110
Juneau	981	1.0	37,345	1,755	384	89	30	49	152	244	552	65	30
Kenosha	7,126	2.4	42,368	1,051	2,890	547	227	371	982	1,282	4,035	480	227
Kewaunee	875	-0.5	42,867	1,007	280	58	21	84	139	158	443	47	21
La Crosse	5,402	2.8	45,731	719	3,256	615	255	362	1,020	923	4,487	526	255
Lafayette	718	-1.3	42,877	1,006	164	38	12	120	126	122	334	30	12
Langlade	787	1.3	40,940	1,244	280	59	22	87	139	212	448	51	22
Lincoln	1,155	2.7	41,410	1,181	499	96	39	70	173	275	704	86	39
Manitowoc	3,614	0.9	45,433	746	1,529	297	120	337	591	700	2,282	262	120
Marathon	6,112	2.3	45,076	771	3,349	607	253	440	983	979	4,650	536	253
Marinette	1,633	0.5	40,338	1,321	803	169	64	89	254	452	1,125	138	64
Marquette	560	2.7	37,159	1,799	140	32	11	32	95	154	214	27	11
Menominee	127	1.0	27,907	2,984	72	31	5	9	18	44	116	11	5
Milwaukee	41,269	0.8	43,375	958	27,213	4,529	2,048	2,726	7,257	8,884	36,517	4,282	2,048
Monroe	1,760	2.6	38,566	1,563	885	209	72	133	324	355	1,299	148	72
Oconto	1,558	1.2	41,614	1,152	329	79	26	128	224	322	562	65	26
Oneida	1,662	1.0	46,675	639	703	130	54	128	354	410	1,016	123	54
Outagamie	8,638	3.3	46,814	626	5,366	880	414	576	1,355	1,191	7,236	850	414
Ozaukee	6,530	1.7	73,944	51	2,134	371	162	319	1,696	654	2,986	347	162
Pepin	328	1.0	44,954	781	93	19	7	26	58	76	145	17	7
Pierce	1,786	2.2	43,314	967	420	118	32	103	291	274	672	75	32
Polk	1,838	2.3	42,276	1,063	651	141	51	101	303	399	944	114	51
Portage	2,986	2.7	42,386	1,048	1,623	306	125	220	498	535	2,275	261	125
Price	596	1.3	44,123	868	233	51	18	59	105	161	360	42	18
Racine	8,745	1.7	44,813	790	3,698	705	284	323	1,630	1,662	5,010	605	284
Richland	680	1.4	38,905	1,514	241	59	18	61	110	161	379	41	18
Rock	6,542	2.2	40,477	1,301	3,087	566	240	331	1,136	1,328	4,223	513	240
Rusk	508	0.5	35,944	2,010	202	48	17	36	86	153	302	37	17
St. Croix	4,357	2.8	49,494	441	1,437	271	112	245	670	537	2,065	241	112
Sauk	2,816	2.0	44,037	874	1,478	268	116	286	475	496	2,148	249	116
Sawyer	681	2.5	41,614	1,152	250	57	20	57	153	196	385	47	20
Shawano	1,562	0.7	38,050	1,649	472	105	37	129	248	359	742	86	37
Sheboygan	5,532	3.3	47,930	543	2,976	504	225	457	1,038	868	4,162	481	225
Taylor	746	1.0	36,503	1,915	326	65	26	88	126	155	504	57	26
Trempealeau	1,254	1.5	42,332	1,054	608	123	47	77	192	254	855	99	47
Vernon	1,141	0.7	37,031	1,820	343	80	26	105	185	255	555	63	26
Vilas	1,081	3.6	50,437	397	267	61	22	205	283	269	556	61	22
Walworth	4,529	2.5	43,989	880	1,736	367	136	299	902	770	2,538	293	136
Washburn	678	0.3	43,323	964	214	51	17	59	138	199	340	41	17
Washington	6,990	2.2	52,051	336	2,583	447	198	401	1,159	939	3,630	428	198
Waukesha	26,105	2.2	65,522	90	13,984	2,060	1,054	1,846	5,200	2,900	18,944	2,207	1,054
Waupaca	2,239	2.0	43,448	948	795	170	63	135	367	511	1,162	140	63
Waushara	962	2.6	39,829	1,387	214	53	17	86	175	227	370	42	17
Winnebago	7,414	2.6	43,641	911	4,985	833	372	410	1,352	1,208	6,599	776	372
Wood	3,158	3.0	43,193	978	1,825	332	137	252	501	667	2,545	296	137
WYOMING	32,270	-2.2	55,172	X	13,444	2,612	1,339	3,419	9,886	4,307	20,815	1,205	1,339
Albany	1,488	1.7	38,898	1,515	692	189	68	83	353	214	1,031	125	68
Big Horn	430	-2.4	35,815	2,031	191	44	19	15	79	98	270	37	19
Campbell	2,367	-9.8	48,507	499	1,486	246	141	366	367	253	2,240	267	141
Carbon	768	-0.6	49,195	458	375	96	38	28	169	111	537	69	38
Converse	726	-7.9	51,182	362	322	65	31	66	143	113	485	60	31
Crook	303	-5.3	40,644	1,283	107	23	10	31	73	52	171	21	10
Fremont	1,583	-2.9	39,326	1,450	673	149	67	81	353	361	969	128	67

1. Based on the resident population estimated as of July 1 of the year shown.

Table B. States and Counties — Earnings, Social Security, and Housing

STATE County	Earnings, 2016 (cont.) Percent by selected industries									Social Security beneficiaries, December 2016		Supple-mental Security Income recipients, 2016	Housing units, 2017	
	Farm	Mining, quarrying, and extracting	Construction	Manu-facturing	Information; professional, scientific, technical services	Retail trade	Finance, insurance, real estate, and leasing	Health care and social assistance	Govern-ment	Number	Rate[1]		Total	Percent change, 2010-2017
	75	76	77	78	79	80	81	82	83	84	85	86	87	88
WISCONSIN— Cont'd														
Douglas	0.0	D	8.3	10.2	3.2	6.9	2.8	8.1	20.8	9,790	226	1,169	23,172	1.5
Dunn	1.7	D	6.5	18.6	4.4	5.8	3.5	D	24.1	9,475	214	720	18,506	3.0
Eau Claire	0.1	D	5.1	8.9	6.1	7.7	6.6	23.4	15.7	20,220	197	1,928	44,149	4.7
Florence	-0.1	0.2	5.8	14.2	D	D	0.0	2.4	23.5	1,500	346	66	4,895	2.4
Fond du Lac	2.9	0.5	8.8	24.4	4.5	6.5	4.7	13.0	12.5	22,040	216	1,537	45,246	3.0
Forest	-0.1	D	3.8	8.4	D	3.8	1.9	D	56.1	2,800	310	221	9,191	2.5
Grant	8.5	D	5.9	11.8	4.3	5.4	4.1	9.2	26.1	11,180	215	809	22,119	2.5
Green	3.9	D	5.3	24.0	D	12.3	3.6	12.8	12.5	8,090	220	418	16,015	1.0
Green Lake	3.7	1.4	10.1	14.9	D	7.5	5.7	15.1	16.4	5,160	277	307	10,721	1.0
Iowa	6.4	D	8.7	10.9	2.6	26.3	2.8	D	13.1	5,195	221	341	10,896	1.7
Iron	1.2	D	12.9	8.3	4.0	8.0	D	14.9	24.8	2,170	383	131	6,094	1.6
Jackson	5.0	2.5	15.5	9.1	1.3	4.4	3.0	D	26.1	4,760	233	394	9,943	2.3
Jefferson	1.6	D	7.5	30.9	3.6	6.3	3.4	9.1	13.1	17,205	204	948	35,836	2.0
Juneau	4.0	0.0	4.5	23.6	2.1	5.7	2.5	D	27.8	6,885	261	669	15,142	3.2
Kenosha	0.3	D	4.5	13.9	3.5	7.5	4.0	13.7	16.9	30,610	182	3,749	70,574	1.9
Kewaunee	16.1	D	7.9	24.0	3.2	4.2	3.3	D	16.2	4,650	228	221	9,436	1.4
La Crosse	0.2	D	5.4	11.5	5.0	6.1	7.7	22.1	14.9	22,775	193	2,125	50,253	3.8
Lafayette	25.6	D	7.8	13.1	D	3.0	D	3.0	18.3	3,645	217	186	7,296	0.9
Langlade	7.6	D	4.4	17.8	D	13.3	5.1	D	15.0	5,870	308	432	12,569	1.7
Lincoln	0.7	D	6.9	23.8	1.6	6.4	17.7	7.3	16.2	7,845	282	445	17,174	2.3
Manitowoc	3.8	0.2	5.6	30.8	3.1	5.3	3.2	10.9	11.9	20,295	256	1,371	37,500	0.8
Marathon	1.6	0.2	5.0	22.9	5.1	6.2	10.2	14.5	11.2	28,240	209	1,965	59,203	2.5
Marinette	2.4	D	4.9	38.0	2.4	5.8	2.9	D	12.4	12,650	314	873	30,790	1.4
Marquette	6.5	0.0	5.2	33.0	2.9	5.1	1.6	D	21.4	4,715	311	339	9,960	0.7
Menominee	0.0	0.0	0.4	D	D	D	D	D	89.4	990	218	227	2,295	1.9
Milwaukee	0.0	0.0	3.2	11.6	10.7	4.6	10.6	15.6	13.2	162,725	170	43,075	418,888	0.2
Monroe	2.5	D	5.2	19.0	D	5.0	2.6	7.3	30.3	9,480	209	807	19,912	3.7
Oconto	9.4	D	9.0	21.5	D	6.1	2.6	10.4	19.6	9,725	260	583	24,170	2.7
Oneida	0.9	0.0	8.5	10.6	4.9	12.3	4.6	20.3	15.9	12,000	339	634	31,077	3.2
Outagamie	0.7	0.1	9.6	20.4	5.7	6.4	9.2	12.2	11.2	34,315	186	2,628	76,955	5.2
Ozaukee	0.5	D	4.6	24.0	10.9	5.6	9.6	13.5	8.8	18,940	215	547	37,476	3.3
Pepin	3.4	0.0	12.2	5.8	4.0	7.9	5.2	9.5	17.8	2,080	286	98	3,678	2.8
Pierce	2.5	D	7.3	14.3	3.3	4.6	4.1	4.8	35.2	7,390	178	376	16,590	2.9
Polk	1.0	D	6.5	22.3	D	6.1	3.3	17.3	17.3	11,140	257	626	24,654	1.7
Portage	4.3	D	3.8	12.5	5.0	6.9	18.7	10.0	15.9	13,905	198	855	30,937	2.9
Price	2.3	D	3.8	35.6	6.4	5.1	2.3	10.6	14.6	4,485	334	290	11,358	2.1
Racine	0.3	0.1	5.4	33.1	4.0	6.1	4.3	12.3	14.1	41,930	215	5,518	82,776	0.7
Richland	8.9	D	5.8	23.5	1.9	7.9	2.6	12.9	22.3	4,350	248	358	8,976	1.2
Rock	1.1	0.3	6.5	16.8	5.3	7.3	3.9	16.4	14.6	34,960	217	3,994	68,961	0.8
Rusk	3.5	D	4.8	29.9	D	5.7	2.5	7.2	22.3	4,255	302	358	9,187	3.4
St. Croix	0.4	D	9.1	21.4	6.8	7.9	4.8	11.9	13.9	14,585	166	588	35,823	5.4
Sauk	1.4	D	10.4	17.8	4.6	8.0	4.9	11.1	15.2	14,095	222	872	30,426	2.4
Sawyer	0.4	0.1	9.1	10.6	3.3	10.7	4.5	D	27.4	5,560	340	368	16,507	3.3
Shawano	7.2	0.0	7.1	16.4	D	7.4	3.4	D	20.3	10,320	252	703	20,893	0.8
Sheboygan	1.1	D	4.9	41.4	2.8	5.5	6.5	11.5	9.1	25,305	220	1,791	51,042	0.5
Taylor	4.9	D	7.4	23.5	D	5.8	3.6	D	12.0	4,410	218	241	10,740	1.5
Trempealeau	2.0	D	4.7	42.4	D	4.0	3.2	D	16.2	6,500	219	426	13,148	4.2
Vernon	6.1	D	8.0	8.4	4.5	7.7	3.2	16.3	18.7	7,475	245	609	14,121	2.9
Vilas	1.0	D	11.9	2.9	2.9	6.5	3.2	5.4	23.1	8,410	392	295	25,994	3.5
Walworth	1.1	D	6.6	23.2	5.2	6.9	4.0	7.4	20.8	21,120	205	1,249	52,338	1.6
Washburn	1.0	D	6.3	16.3	D	8.3	3.4	D	23.9	5,340	342	388	13,305	2.5
Washington	0.5	0.3	7.1	27.7	4.5	6.7	7.7	11.4	10.1	27,490	205	912	56,777	3.8
Waukesha	0.1	0.1	7.9	19.3	11.0	7.0	9.7	9.9	6.8	82,730	208	2,989	165,652	3.0
Waupaca	2.9	0.0	6.3	34.4	3.5	6.8	3.1	9.1	17.8	13,740	268	867	25,760	1.4
Waushara	12.3	D	6.6	13.6	3.0	6.3	2.7	D	22.9	7,065	293	387	15,095	1.7
Winnebago	0.3	D	7.1	27.3	7.2	4.9	5.5	9.1	11.9	34,020	201	2,537	75,619	3.1
Wood	1.2	D	5.9	15.6	6.2	5.6	3.6	25.4	12.8	18,630	255	1,521	35,040	2.8
WYOMING	0.4	11.5	8.4	4.1	5.5	5.9	5.4	7.3	25.9	106,720	182	6,723	276,746	5.7
Albany	1.2	0.8	5.8	2.4	7.3	6.1	5.7	7.9	49.8	4,710	124	298	19,304	7.6
Big Horn	2.0	12.5	8.8	7.5	D	3.2	3.1	D	36.5	2,665	223	163	5,466	1.6
Campbell	-0.6	36.2	7.8	1.7	3.1	5.3	3.7	3.0	17.0	5,490	113	301	20,258	6.9
Carbon	0.5	D	12.2	D	2.8	5.8	2.3	D	26.2	2,770	176	160	8,796	2.6
Converse	0.0	23.9	8.1	2.4	3.0	3.7	6.6	D	25.4	2,535	179	138	6,675	4.2
Crook	1.6	12.5	12.4	7.6	D	4.2	D	D	27.5	1,575	210	40	3,658	1.8
Fremont	0.0	7.5	6.4	1.4	4.7	7.0	4.9	D	38.3	8,795	219	854	18,008	1.2

1. Per 1,000 resident population estimated as of July 1 of the year shown.

STATE County	Housing units, 2017 (cont.)								Civilian labor force, 2017				Civilian employment[6], 2012-2016		
	Occupied units										Unemployment			Percent	
			Owner-occupied			Renter-occupied									
				Median owner cost as a percent of income											
	Total	Percent	Median value[1]	With a mortgage	Without a mortgage[2]	Median rent[3]	Median rent as a percent of income[2]	Sub-standard units[4] (percent)	Total	Percent change, 2016-2017	Total	Rate[5]	Total	Management, business, science, and arts	Construction, production, and maintenance occupations
	89	90	91	92	93	94	95	96	97	98	99	100	101	102	103
WISCONSIN— Cont'd															
Douglas	18,538	67.6	135,600	20.9	13.0	719	28.1	2.2	23,776	0.5	1,064	4.5	21,438	30.8	25.1
Dunn	16,445	68.9	154,500	21.8	13.0	728	28.0	1.9	24,598	0.8	807	3.3	22,783	31.2	28.1
Eau Claire	40,202	62.2	153,200	20.4	13.0	757	29.9	2.0	59,489	0.7	1,731	2.9	55,262	34.4	21.3
Florence	1,958	86.8	136,900	22.6	12.8	510	25.4	3.1	2,309	3.3	109	4.7	1,959	27.7	31.6
Fond du Lac	41,029	71.7	147,000	21.1	12.8	709	27.1	2.0	57,544	0.7	1,629	2.8	52,533	29.9	32.8
Forest	3,940	75.9	129,300	23.6	13.6	472	24.2	2.6	4,063	1.2	206	5.1	3,590	28.3	32.4
Grant	19,353	70.6	135,400	21.4	12.3	656	26.0	2.6	28,404	0.3	898	3.2	26,279	30.3	29.7
Green	14,772	74.2	161,900	22.0	14.4	686	25.5	1.4	21,571	1.3	587	2.7	19,921	33.3	29.2
Green Lake	7,939	73.1	137,800	22.2	13.6	618	24.8	2.0	9,731	-0.7	367	3.8	8,922	25.4	38.0
Iowa	9,692	75.6	166,900	22.8	14.1	703	25.7	1.8	13,969	1.6	410	2.9	12,337	32.9	28.8
Iron	2,954	77.6	107,600	21.1	13.6	493	30.2	2.0	2,626	-0.8	163	6.2	2,550	25.8	29.7
Jackson	8,066	73.6	129,100	22.5	13.4	615	24.2	3.4	10,479	1.1	352	3.4	9,274	26.6	32.4
Jefferson	32,366	70.2	175,500	22.7	13.7	783	27.3	1.8	45,977	0.2	1,461	3.2	44,617	31.4	28.4
Juneau	9,978	75.7	118,800	23.6	14.4	673	26.0	1.9	13,664	0.6	457	3.3	11,748	24.6	32.7
Kenosha	62,994	65.6	162,400	22.8	14.5	865	30.8	2.2	89,921	1.3	3,495	3.9	80,892	33.0	25.3
Kewaunee	8,211	79.8	151,200	21.8	12.5	609	22.6	1.6	11,280	1.9	346	3.1	10,368	30.7	36.0
La Crosse	46,657	64.4	158,700	21.0	12.3	761	29.2	1.5	68,207	0.6	1,991	2.9	62,477	36.0	21.0
Lafayette	6,692	75.9	124,100	22.3	13.1	649	25.3	1.9	10,213	3.4	257	2.5	8,701	30.9	34.6
Langlade	8,521	76.2	108,100	21.6	12.1	613	32.6	2.6	9,726	1.2	412	4.2	8,924	27.7	31.8
Lincoln	12,546	76.0	134,200	19.9	12.7	620	23.0	1.9	15,598	1.8	559	3.6	14,265	26.7	32.9
Manitowoc	33,991	75.5	127,500	20.5	13.2	632	25.1	1.4	41,988	0.0	1,494	3.6	40,907	27.3	34.7
Marathon	54,003	72.7	145,900	20.6	12.5	704	27.0	2.0	74,325	0.6	2,193	3.0	70,254	33.3	28.0
Marinette	18,380	75.0	114,000	20.3	13.4	644	27.5	1.7	20,044	-1.3	889	4.4	18,906	25.9	36.7
Marquette	6,328	80.2	142,500	23.3	14.5	723	23.5	2.5	7,644	0.8	293	3.8	6,903	23.1	37.6
Menominee	1,215	68.3	84,500	19.6	10.0	457	24.4	9.5	1,588	0.5	96	6.0	1,481	22.9	22.6
Milwaukee	382,778	49.4	150,000	23.4	14.8	821	31.6	3.2	478,333	0.0	19,351	4.0	450,441	35.8	21.1
Monroe	17,813	68.4	139,100	21.4	12.0	775	25.3	3.4	23,649	2.3	698	3.0	21,086	28.3	32.2
Oconto	15,440	83.2	153,400	21.8	12.9	617	25.2	1.9	20,793	1.2	735	3.5	19,019	28.5	36.7
Oneida	14,965	83.4	163,800	23.0	13.9	730	28.4	0.8	18,434	-1.2	715	3.9	16,502	31.1	24.1
Outagamie	71,194	70.9	157,200	20.4	12.4	745	25.2	1.8	104,727	0.4	3,142	3.0	97,516	33.6	27.4
Ozaukee	34,763	75.6	248,800	20.9	12.1	869	25.5	1.0	49,473	0.5	1,367	2.8	46,156	47.9	16.9
Pepin	2,948	81.9	141,900	23.0	14.1	585	25.8	1.3	4,260	1.8	152	3.6	3,678	32.4	32.1
Pierce	15,101	73.1	193,000	22.4	12.9	781	28.5	1.3	25,207	1.7	845	3.4	22,939	32.4	29.2
Polk	18,188	77.7	156,000	24.3	14.2	732	27.1	1.7	25,067	0.4	945	3.8	21,224	29.3	33.7
Portage	27,844	68.9	155,900	20.5	11.2	664	29.3	2.0	39,814	0.4	1,225	3.1	36,841	32.8	25.1
Price	6,676	77.4	117,600	22.8	13.9	592	26.6	2.3	6,830	-1.1	257	3.8	6,574	28.4	37.3
Racine	75,291	69.2	163,900	21.8	14.0	808	29.9	1.5	100,142	0.0	4,077	4.1	92,275	32.4	27.6
Richland	7,506	74.1	128,000	23.2	13.3	625	27.3	2.6	9,408	1.2	280	3.0	8,386	26.8	35.8
Rock	63,941	68.9	132,500	22.0	12.6	749	29.0	2.0	85,722	1.5	3,191	3.7	76,738	30.0	29.8
Rusk	6,245	76.8	105,400	24.2	13.1	627	27.5	2.6	7,038	0.1	311	4.4	6,440	24.0	38.9
St. Croix	32,811	75.7	213,100	20.9	11.5	922	27.0	1.9	50,667	1.6	1,567	3.1	46,673	37.4	23.6
Sauk	25,293	68.5	169,500	22.3	13.0	738	27.7	2.3	35,768	1.1	1,042	2.9	33,104	29.0	26.8
Sawyer	7,488	73.8	159,800	24.0	13.0	657	26.3	4.1	8,048	1.3	377	4.7	7,071	31.2	25.5
Shawano	16,940	75.9	132,500	21.8	14.1	602	23.1	1.7	21,624	1.2	699	3.2	20,241	27.5	33.1
Sheboygan	47,152	70.1	148,200	20.4	12.5	663	24.6	1.8	63,073	1.8	1,753	2.8	59,601	29.7	31.7
Taylor	8,751	75.5	129,000	22.9	13.2	595	28.1	3.2	11,277	1.4	389	3.4	10,131	27.2	43.2
Trempealeau	11,840	71.8	145,800	22.1	13.8	670	24.0	2.2	16,611	-0.7	509	3.1	15,184	29.5	37.5
Vernon	11,843	79.0	146,100	23.1	13.3	622	26.8	6.6	16,052	1.5	492	3.1	13,375	30.9	31.6
Vilas	10,648	75.3	201,000	26.1	13.9	677	29.3	2.0	10,188	1.8	444	4.4	8,978	28.6	22.7
Walworth	39,967	67.8	189,500	24.0	14.4	828	30.4	2.2	58,265	0.6	1,909	3.3	52,366	30.6	27.2
Washburn	7,151	77.4	147,300	23.3	13.6	661	27.2	1.7	8,009	0.0	312	3.9	6,981	30.2	30.4
Washington	53,187	77.9	215,700	21.9	13.1	841	25.6	0.9	77,851	0.5	2,167	2.8	72,492	35.9	25.1
Waukesha	155,776	76.2	254,700	21.1	12.8	943	27.0	1.2	226,578	0.4	6,580	2.9	211,181	44.5	17.7
Waupaca	21,412	75.1	137,700	21.2	13.9	685	26.3	1.4	26,715	-1.3	856	3.2	25,950	25.8	36.1
Waushara	9,749	81.3	137,200	23.2	13.7	661	28.9	1.8	11,557	0.3	454	3.9	10,377	24.8	37.9
Winnebago	69,169	64.7	144,300	20.8	12.8	693	26.7	1.2	94,244	0.9	2,807	3.0	87,046	30.6	27.1
Wood	31,884	73.6	124,000	19.7	11.7	634	27.0	1.2	35,313	1.6	1,328	3.8	36,703	31.1	30.2
WYOMING	226,985	68.6	199,900	20.4	10.0	802	25.8	2.4	293,345	-2.5	12,329	4.2	293,598	32.7	28.2
Albany	15,565	48.9	220,900	21.9	10.1	729	35.6	2.7	20,471	-2.6	583	2.8	20,838	41.3	16.4
Big Horn	4,459	73.5	148,200	21.8	10.0	598	21.4	2.3	5,396	-2.7	223	4.1	5,330	29.4	34.4
Campbell	17,534	69.8	214,000	18.9	10.0	947	25.1	2.6	23,083	-5.5	1,138	4.9	25,969	25.7	38.3
Carbon	6,095	70.1	153,700	18.7	10.0	829	20.3	3.0	7,957	-5.0	316	4.0	7,591	29.8	34.8
Converse	5,576	73.4	194,500	19.0	10.0	685	22.7	3.3	7,481	-5.1	330	4.4	7,298	24.8	34.8
Crook	2,976	78.9	217,500	18.9	10.0	736	16.2	3.8	3,679	-1.8	128	3.5	3,612	27.4	40.0
Fremont	15,159	70.7	189,600	20.6	10.0	714	23.5	4.2	19,407	-3.3	1,080	5.6	18,659	32.9	25.2

1. Specified owner-occupied units.   2. A value of 10.0 represents 10 percent or less; a value of 50.0 represents 50 percent or more.   3. Specified renter-occupied units.
4. Overcrowded or lacking complete plumbing facilities.   5. Percent of civilian labor force.   6. Civilian employed persons 16 years old and over.

Table B. States and Counties — Nonfarm Employment and Agriculture

STATE County	Private nonfarm establishments, employment and payroll, 2016									Agriculture, 2012			
	Number of establishments	Employment						Annual payroll		Farms			Farm operators whose principal occupation is farming (percent)
		Total	Health care and social assistance	Manufacturing	Retail trade	Finance and insurance	Professional, scientific, and technical services	Total (mil dol)	Average per employee (dollars)	Number	Percent with:		
											Fewer than 50 acres	500 acres or more	
	104	105	106	107	108	109	110	111	112	113	114	115	116

WISCONSIN— Cont'd													
Douglas	1,030	13,748	1,975	1,642	2,279	329	393	520	37,848	364	29.4	5.8	42.0
Dunn	896	14,447	2,409	2,929	1,960	432	409	554	38,328	1,404	24.0	12.0	45.4
Eau Claire	2,709	51,153	11,109	5,078	7,424	2,620	2,291	2,017	39,440	1,313	31.7	4.0	42.3
Florence	102	581	D	146	68	39	7	17	28,482	90	31.1	0.0	38.9
Fond du Lac	2,358	42,959	6,333	8,569	6,026	1,640	1,386	1,746	40,652	1,399	31.9	10.7	59.0
Forest	237	1,681	218	313	255	68	73	50	29,948	127	21.3	9.4	54.3
Grant	1,231	13,980	2,266	2,274	2,575	713	523	476	34,042	2,436	25.6	10.7	53.8
Green	973	13,594	2,077	3,382	1,716	333	381	527	38,761	1,545	42.0	7.4	45.8
Green Lake	459	5,399	1,072	929	1,032	261	76	196	36,259	608	26.8	13.2	48.4
Iowa	569	9,001	1,076	1,187	4,055	193	134	352	39,073	1,588	25.8	9.9	47.2
Iron	193	1,381	310	164	232	30	36	37	27,140	61	34.4	8.2	32.8
Jackson	421	6,557	1,068	563	856	206	107	285	43,437	864	23.0	11.5	49.4
Jefferson	1,952	30,554	4,129	8,501	4,163	641	591	1,193	39,054	1,225	39.7	6.9	46.1
Juneau	563	6,582	1,099	2,212	1,078	169	53	237	35,960	827	29.7	8.1	39.4
Kenosha	3,174	52,787	8,501	7,094	10,953	876	1,332	2,076	39,335	359	51.5	11.1	46.8
Kewaunee	463	4,977	452	1,927	585	140	164	191	38,419	734	27.9	9.4	49.7
La Crosse	3,053	61,882	11,239	7,901	8,916	2,171	1,880	2,529	40,861	748	23.7	10.0	46.9
Lafayette	376	3,200	271	894	389	147	61	107	33,514	1,252	28.9	13.1	57.1
Langlade	560	6,455	928	1,446	1,411	282	131	233	36,159	396	24.2	14.6	56.3
Lincoln	688	8,794	960	2,377	1,361	1,000	115	376	42,793	449	28.1	6.2	48.8
Manitowoc	1,755	30,100	4,392	10,036	3,771	753	540	1,245	41,359	1,224	39.1	7.9	47.7
Marathon	3,353	64,918	10,357	17,196	7,743	4,457	1,523	2,724	41,954	2,266	23.2	7.5	55.0
Marinette	1,065	15,690	2,572	6,178	2,083	415	251	609	38,801	535	31.2	11.8	51.6
Marquette	274	3,554	313	1,255	309	43	72	118	33,342	478	28.0	9.2	52.1
Menominee	24	703	NA	D	39	NA	D	17	23,509	5	60.0	0.0	0.0
Milwaukee	19,879	445,787	87,838	45,690	44,228	34,152	22,370	23,225	52,098	82	76.8	2.4	59.8
Monroe	954	15,766	2,494	3,811	1,956	423	398	651	41,287	1,926	25.7	6.1	44.3
Oconto	791	6,770	1,355	2,026	928	169	140	229	33,843	929	35.1	9.1	48.1
Oneida	1,378	13,774	2,667	1,361	3,567	321	378	526	38,178	150	43.3	9.3	28.0
Outagamie	5,022	103,022	12,912	18,312	13,048	5,864	3,785	4,554	44,207	1,170	38.7	10.7	56.0
Ozaukee	2,774	40,912	6,238	9,088	5,387	2,239	2,379	1,762	43,057	416	38.5	7.0	53.4
Pepin	223	1,816	261	170	250	89	39	70	38,757	459	22.9	10.0	47.3
Pierce	792	6,967	997	1,431	1,063	281	206	241	34,613	1,259	31.6	7.8	52.2
Polk	1,117	13,229	2,539	4,101	1,951	318	307	448	33,879	1,313	30.1	8.1	47.8
Portage	1,701	30,896	3,741	4,844	3,970	4,953	1,025	1,267	41,001	969	27.1	11.8	51.2
Price	396	4,599	825	1,901	555	141	78	173	37,626	472	26.1	7.8	47.2
Racine	4,024	66,437	11,043	15,606	9,313	2,058	1,996	3,058	46,029	575	51.0	8.2	45.6
Richland	366	4,813	962	1,469	859	149	68	160	33,327	1,260	27.9	6.7	44.4
Rock	3,330	57,883	8,754	10,139	9,147	1,335	2,133	2,451	42,336	1,509	44.1	10.3	50.0
Rusk	321	4,338	826	1,626	633	105	40	149	34,408	529	16.8	10.0	62.9
St. Croix	2,226	29,300	4,253	6,088	4,444	890	1,390	1,158	39,533	1,417	39.0	8.0	41.6
Sauk	1,808	31,298	3,811	6,331	4,267	983	1,008	1,173	37,492	1,665	29.1	8.2	51.2
Sawyer	639	4,974	749	601	1,016	168	153	175	35,276	172	26.7	11.0	47.1
Shawano	872	10,456	1,485	2,176	1,547	285	206	360	34,431	1,278	26.7	8.1	54.4
Sheboygan	2,662	54,987	6,591	17,857	5,997	2,083	1,122	2,430	44,197	986	42.4	10.1	52.7
Taylor	480	7,705	1,065	3,033	909	242	112	298	38,672	967	25.9	8.8	52.7
Trempealeau	639	13,995	1,092	8,106	1,063	302	229	557	39,768	1,436	26.5	9.5	48.7
Vernon	630	7,123	1,774	951	1,218	293	152	242	34,000	2,228	31.7	4.2	49.2
Vilas	940	5,816	581	327	1,084	196	132	169	28,988	47	59.6	6.4	40.4
Walworth	2,668	35,008	3,987	8,357	4,913	655	1,335	1,280	36,561	870	45.3	11.1	51.8
Washburn	516	4,516	975	1,153	734	118	184	137	30,353	405	27.4	7.4	39.8
Washington	3,205	51,435	5,982	14,137	7,111	2,081	1,868	2,171	42,204	712	43.3	8.6	51.4
Waukesha	12,544	239,451	28,207	42,842	26,397	13,370	13,201	12,706	53,061	557	54.0	7.7	51.2
Waupaca	1,211	16,565	2,696	5,987	2,438	511	263	616	37,198	1,145	30.0	7.9	49.8
Waushara	465	4,673	791	888	766	98	159	141	30,114	592	27.2	9.6	44.6
Winnebago	3,564	84,456	12,357	21,609	8,751	3,373	3,021	4,271	50,566	1,117	48.5	6.0	39.2
Wood	1,785	34,647	8,742	6,126	3,943	1,360	710	1,510	43,592	1,067	27.8	9.3	56.7
WYOMING	20,966	208,440	33,429	9,183	31,157	6,668	9,720	9,304	44,636	11,736	28.8	36.3	49.8
Albany	1,041	9,743	2,034	395	1,844	495	775	327	33,532	448	26.8	45.5	40.4
Big Horn	305	2,536	380	208	376	98	55	103	40,800	627	32.1	26.6	54.4
Campbell	1,460	20,636	1,634	539	2,698	372	692	1,159	56,178	744	30.4	44.9	36.4
Carbon	520	4,374	584	D	821	135	86	201	46,051	319	16.3	59.9	60.2
Converse	448	4,811	630	174	464	129	148	252	52,459	410	18.3	51.7	57.8
Crook	237	1,503	174	150	161	62	54	71	47,023	482	10.4	58.5	61.8
Fremont	1,281	10,507	2,001	263	2,059	298	373	383	36,444	1,363	37.0	20.4	55.0

Table B. States and Counties — **Land Area and Population**

State / county code	CBSA code[1]	County code[2]	STATE County	Land area[3] (sq. mi)	Total persons 2017	Rank	Per square mile	White	Black	American Indian, Alaska Native	Asian and Pacific Islander	Percent Hispanic or Latino[4]	Under 5 years	5 to 17 years	18 to 24 years	25 to 34 years	35 to 44 years	45 to 54 years
				1	2	3	4	5	6	7	8	9	10	11	12	13	14	15
			WYOMING— Cont'd															
56,015		7	Goshen	2,225.6	13,378	2,201	6.0	87.0	1.2	1.3	1.0	10.7	5.3	14.8	9.2	11.9	11.1	11.4
56,017		7	Hot Springs	2,004.1	4,696	2,851	2.3	93.5	1.1	2.3	0.8	3.8	5.3	16.0	5.6	10.0	10.3	10.7
56,019		7	Johnson	4,154.2	8,476	2,547	2.0	92.8	1.1	1.9	1.0	4.7	4.8	17.1	6.0	10.0	11.2	11.4
56,021	16,940	3	Laramie	2,685.9	98,327	606	36.6	80.8	3.4	1.4	2.1	14.8	6.4	16.9	9.1	14.8	12.2	11.9
56,023		7	Lincoln...........................	4,075.3	19,265	1,863	4.7	93.6	0.7	1.3	0.8	4.7	6.9	19.9	6.7	10.2	12.7	11.8
56,025	16,220	3	Natrona	5,340.5	79,547	703	14.9	88.6	1.8	1.7	1.4	8.4	6.9	17.4	7.8	15.0	12.9	11.5
56,027		9	Niobrara	2,626.0	2,397	3,013	0.9	93.5	1.4	2.8	0.8	3.6	5.8	11.4	8.0	12.6	12.7	11.1
56,029		7	Park...............................	6,939.9	29,568	1,440	4.3	91.7	1.0	1.3	1.3	6.0	5.5	15.3	7.9	11.1	10.9	11.3
56,031		7	Platte.............................	2,084.2	8,562	2,537	4.1	89.8	0.9	1.2	1.3	8.2	5.1	14.8	6.2	10.6	10.0	12.2
56,033	43,260	7	Sheridan........................	2,523.4	30,210	1,425	12.0	92.5	1.3	1.8	1.3	4.5	5.5	16.1	7.8	11.6	11.7	11.8
56,035		9	Sublette.........................	4,886.5	9,799	2,444	2.0	90.2	1.2	1.3	1.4	7.2	6.1	16.8	5.9	11.5	13.6	13.2
56,037	40,540	5	Sweetwater	10,427.0	43,534	1,101	4.2	81.0	1.6	1.5	1.4	16.2	7.0	19.6	8.3	14.6	14.1	11.6
56,039	27,220	7	Teton.............................	3,996.8	23,265	1,667	5.8	82.9	0.8	0.8	1.9	15.0	5.1	13.7	5.8	18.0	16.2	13.4
56,041	21,740	7	Uinta.............................	2,081.8	20,495	1,798	9.8	88.8	1.0	1.4	1.1	9.2	7.6	21.6	7.5	12.0	13.2	10.8
56,043		7	Washakie	2,238.7	8,064	2,588	3.6	84.0	0.9	1.5	1.1	14.2	5.5	18.3	6.6	9.8	12.1	12.2
56,045		7	Weston..........................	2,398.0	6,927	2,679	2.9	92.7	1.1	2.2	1.6	4.2	5.6	15.3	6.6	12.0	11.8	11.9

1. CBSA = Core Based Statistical Area. See Appendix A for explanation. See Appendix B for list of metropolitan areas with component counties. 2. County type code from the Economic Research Service of USDA Rural-Urban Continuum Codes. See Appendix A for definition. 3. Dry land or land partially or temporarily covered by water. 4. May be of any race.

Table B. States and Counties — **Population and Households**

STATE County	Population, 2017 (cont.)				Population change, 2000-2017							Households, 2012-2016				
	Age (percent) (cont.)				Total persons		Percent change		Components of change, 2010-2017						Percent	
	55 to 64 years	65 to 74 years	75 years and over	Percent female	2000	2010	2000-2010	2010-2017	Births	Deaths	Net Migration	Number	Persons per house-hold	Family house-holds	Female family house-holder[1]	One person
	16	17	18	19	20	21	22	23	24	25	26	27	28	29	30	31
WYOMING— Cont'd																
Goshen	14.7	11.9	9.7	48.0	12,538	13,247	5.7	1.0	1,001	1,005	114	5,350	2.38	65.5	6.9	30.9
Hot Springs	16.7	13.9	11.6	49.3	4,882	4,812	-1.4	-2.4	366	498	16	2,262	2.07	61.5	5.8	35.3
Johnson	16.1	13.8	9.6	49.5	7,075	8,569	21.1	-1.1	653	620	-122	3,668	2.32	64.7	6.7	32.9
Laramie	13.1	9.4	6.2	49.4	81,607	91,881	12.6	7.0	9,318	5,699	2,824	37,362	2.53	67.5	11.4	26.7
Lincoln	15.2	10.8	5.8	49.1	14,573	18,106	24.2	6.4	1,816	912	249	7,002	2.63	70.5	5.4	24.0
Natrona	13.8	8.7	6.0	49.6	66,533	75,450	13.4	5.4	8,110	5,123	1,013	32,422	2.44	63.3	9.9	29.9
Niobrara	16.4	11.7	10.2	53.7	2,407	2,484	3.2	-3.5	187	185	-94	981	2.24	58.3	3.4	35.3
Park	15.8	13.3	9.0	50.1	25,786	28,205	9.4	4.8	2,300	1,952	1,020	11,826	2.39	68.1	6.6	26.0
Platte	16.1	14.4	10.7	49.2	8,807	8,667	-1.6	-1.2	625	710	-16	3,680	2.34	67.4	9.4	28.3
Sheridan	15.5	12.1	7.9	49.7	26,560	29,116	9.6	3.8	2,419	2,264	952	12,697	2.28	63.3	6.3	31.1
Sublette	14.6	11.5	6.8	46.1	5,920	10,247	73.1	-4.4	930	343	-1,059	3,203	3.08	71.2	5.5	24.7
Sweetwater	13.5	7.5	3.9	48.5	37,613	43,806	16.5	-0.6	4,560	2,019	-2,880	16,533	2.67	67.7	9.6	27.4
Teton	13.4	9.5	4.9	48.1	18,251	21,294	16.7	9.3	1,847	590	689	8,576	2.54	58.1	5.3	30.0
Uinta	14.1	8.8	4.4	49.6	19,742	21,118	7.0	-3.0	2,247	1,014	-1,886	7,432	2.78	72.6	11.0	23.0
Washakie	14.7	11.5	9.3	49.5	8,289	8,533	2.9	-5.5	687	629	-528	3,493	2.34	63.6	8.0	30.6
Weston	17.4	11.0	8.4	47.5	6,644	7,208	8.5	-3.9	580	502	-362	3,134	2.18	63.8	7.7	31.8

1. No spouse present.

Table B. States and Counties — **Population, Vital Statistics, Health, and Crime**

STATE County	Persons in group quarters, 2017	Daytime Population, 2012-2016		Births, 2017		Deaths, 2017		Persons under 65 with no health insurance, 2016		Medicare, 2017			Serious crimes known to police[2], 2016	
		Number	Employment/ residence ratio	Total	Rate[1]	Number	Rate[1]	Number	Percent	Total beneficiaries	Enrolled in Original Medicare	Enrolled in Medicare Advantage	Total	
													Number	Rate[3]
	32	33	34	35	36	37	38	39	40	41	42	43	44	45
WYOMING— Cont'd														
Goshen	1,207	13,003	0.91	133	9.9	140	10.5	1,451	15.4	3,017	2,966	51	193	1,455
Hot Springs	86	4,651	0.94	45	9.6	69	14.7	472	13.6	1,324	D	D	56	1,195
Johnson	71	7,903	0.84	77	9.1	83	9.8	1,013	15.4	2,030	1,986	44	128	1,504
Laramie	1,951	98,850	1.05	1,317	13.4	845	8.6	8,707	10.7	17,917	17,166	751	3,184	3,273
Lincoln	71	17,112	0.84	260	13.5	134	7.0	2,128	13.3	3,394	3,302	93	127	722
Natrona	1,721	81,759	1.02	1,094	13.8	721	9.1	9,464	13.8	13,529	12,758	770	2,249	2,714
Niobrara	231	2,504	1.01	31	12.9	16	6.7	274	16.0	582	D	D	NA	NA
Park	834	29,375	1.02	330	11.2	267	9.0	3,289	14.6	7,228	7,047	182	509	1,745
Platte	102	8,720	0.99	85	9.9	85	9.9	857	13.1	2,281	2,233	49	96	1,270
Sheridan	1,020	29,604	0.98	331	11.0	343	11.4	2,861	12.1	7,025	6,668	358	442	1,526
Sublette	550	10,745	1.13	119	12.1	51	5.2	1,144	13.6	1,416	1,377	39	82	841
Sweetwater	680	46,577	1.08	607	13.9	299	6.9	4,975	12.8	5,913	5,785	128	870	1,957
Teton	270	26,142	1.25	262	11.3	82	3.5	3,005	15.0	3,267	3,112	155	NA	NA
Uinta	235	19,917	0.90	295	14.4	140	6.8	2,255	12.6	3,092	2,787	305	426	2,069
Washakie	140	8,536	1.05	86	10.7	85	10.5	1,072	16.7	1,810	1,787	23	82	998
Weston	319	6,630	0.83	80	11.5	75	10.8	802	14.4	1,515	1,424	91	65	1,071

1. Per 1,000 estimated resident population.   2. Data for serious crimes have not been adjusted for underreporting; this may affect comparability between geographic areas and over time.
3. Per 100,000 population estimated by the FBI.

Table B. States and Counties — **Crime, Education, Money Income, and Poverty**

STATE County	Serious crimes known to police, 2016 (cont.)[1] Rate		Education						Money income, 2012-2016				Income and poverty, 2016			
			School enrollment and attainment, 2012-2016				Local government expenditures,[5] 2013-2014			Households				Percent below poverty level		
			Enrollment[3]		Attainment[4] (percent)							Percent					
	Violent	Property	Total	Percent private	High school graduate or less	Bachelor's degree or more	Total current spending (mil dol)	Current spending per student (dollars)	Per capita income[6]	Median income (dollars)	with income of less than $50,000	with income of $200,000 or more	Median household income (dollars)	All persons	Children under 18 years	Children 5 to 17 years in families
	46	47	48	49	50	51	52	53	54	55	56	57	58	59	60	61
WYOMING— Cont'd																
Goshen	392	1,063	3,124	16.1	38.1	23.0	31.6	18,541	25,883	44,883	55.6	1.5	47,715	14.6	16.3	13.3
Hot Springs	171	1,024	894	12.8	36.1	22.3	11.6	18,756	29,499	46,087	53.7	2.3	46,024	13.6	17.5	15.2
Johnson	141	1,363	1,779	20.6	38.3	25.5	22.3	17,442	31,888	54,594	46.0	2.8	56,323	8.8	10.4	8.6
Laramie	252	3,021	24,629	9.3	33.2	27.7	226.0	15,489	30,249	61,201	40.1	2.9	61,124	10.1	11.3	9.4
Lincoln.....................	148	574	4,704	7.7	38.2	20.4	50.3	15,463	29,748	64,579	37.4	3.7	63,907	8.6	9.2	7.7
Natrona	203	2,511	19,786	8.6	37.5	22.2	186.4	14,564	30,902	56,983	43.8	3.8	60,559	10.4	11.3	10.0
Niobrara	NA	NA	544	4.4	38.8	19.0	12.9	12,935	23,356	40,640	56.1	3.0	45,332	14.3	14.6	12.7
Park........................	185	1,560	6,488	8.1	31.2	32.0	62.0	15,615	30,179	61,185	40.5	3.0	60,621	11.1	12.8	11.3
Platte......................	119	1,151	1,645	9.2	42.0	19.7	23.7	18,957	30,054	41,051	56.5	3.5	54,588	12.0	14.9	13.1
Sheridan..................	152	1,374	6,630	12.4	31.0	30.1	67.9	15,509	29,630	53,914	46.7	1.7	53,027	9.2	10.8	9.5
Sublette...................	31	810	2,464	10.4	42.2	24.4	29.1	17,259	30,295	76,004	32.3	1.9	72,198	6.7	6.6	5.8
Sweetwater	306	1,651	12,025	8.2	43.4	21.4	119.8	14,366	30,945	68,233	36.3	3.2	74,546	9.8	9.2	7.2
Teton	NA	NA	4,893	19.9	20.4	53.8	45.7	17,606	46,499	75,594	29.4	14.8	84,118	7.3	6.7	5.5
Uinta.......................	92	1,977	5,752	5.5	47.0	18.2	65.9	15,074	25,636	53,323	47.7	2.8	64,713	10.6	11.3	9.6
Washakie..................	73	925	1,761	7.2	43.4	21.1	26.0	17,595	26,325	46,212	53.5	3.4	49,533	13.1	15.2	12.5
Weston.....................	132	939	1,528	17.6	41.3	18.8	19.4	18,676	29,493	55,640	46.7	3.3	56,582	10.7	14.1	12.2

1. Data for serious crimes have not been adjusted for underreporting; this may affect comparability between geographic areas and over time.   2. Per 100,000 population estimated by the FBI.
3. All persons 3 years old and over enrolled in nursery school through college.   4. Persons 25 years old and over.   5. Elementary and secondary education expenditures.
6. Based on population estimated by the American Community Survey, 2011–2015.

Table B. States and Counties — **Personal Income and Earnings**

STATE County	Personal income, 2016										Earnings, 2016		
	Total (mil dol)	Percent change 2015-2016	Per capita[1]		Wages and salaries (mil dol)	Supplements to wages and salaries, employer contributions (mil dol)		Proprietors' income (mil dol)	Dividends, interest, and rent (mil dol)	Personal transfer receipts (mil dol)	Total (mil dol)	Contributions for government social insurance (mil dol)	
			Dollars	Rank		Pension and insurance	Government social insurance					From employee and self-employed	From employer
	62	63	64	65	66	67	68	69	70	71	72	73	74
WYOMING— Cont'd													
Goshen	545	-0.3	40,675	1,279	178	41	18	50	108	118	288	36	18
Hot Springs	240	-0.4	51,302	357	77	18	8	40	49	56	142	16	8
Johnson	369	-2.0	43,447	949	129	29	13	42	104	69	213	26	13
Laramie..............	4,884	1.2	49,763	425	2,423	525	248	307	1,104	796	3,503	449	248
Lincoln..............	752	2.5	39,357	1,444	298	67	28	29	183	128	421	54	28
Natrona	5,599	-5.4	69,087	71	1,915	299	191	1,385	1,605	598	3,790	394	191
Niobrara	112	-1.9	45,046	776	38	11	4	14	27	23	67	8	4
Park..............	1,474	-0.8	50,212	406	589	118	60	107	486	261	874	115	60
Platte..............	378	-2.4	43,532	932	177	40	18	30	77	86	266	35	18
Sheridan..............	1,579	0.7	52,286	331	595	119	62	120	479	254	896	118	62
Sublette..............	448	-8.0	45,863	705	228	44	20	42	152	51	334	39	20
Sweetwater	2,123	-2.9	48,075	528	1,354	235	125	259	275	270	1,974	239	125
Teton..............	4,630	1.2	199,635	1	977	118	107	236	3,419	122	1,438	192	107
Uinta..............	823	-2.7	39,613	1,411	361	76	36	33	141	146	506	67	36
Washakie	347	-2.2	42,129	1,086	161	33	17	22	82	69	232	31	17
Weston..............	304	-6.4	41,947	1,110	97	27	10	35	57	59	169	20	10

1. Based on the resident population estimated as of July 1 of the year shown.

Table B. States and Counties — **Earnings, Social Security, and Housing**

STATE County	Earnings, 2016 (cont.) Percent by selected industries									Social Security beneficiaries, December 2016		Supple-mental Security Income recipients, 2016	Housing units, 2017	
	Farm	Mining, quarrying, and extracting	Construction	Manu-facturing	Information; professional, scientific, technical services	Retail trade	Finance, insurance, real estate, and leasing	Health care and social assistance	Govern-ment	Number	Rate[1]		Total	Percent change, 2010-2017
	75	76	77	78	79	80	81	82	83	84	85	86	87	88
WYOMING— Cont'd														
Goshen	7.7	0.0	5.4	3.9	2.8	5.0	4.8	14.9	32.6	3,135	235	215	6,032	1.0
Hot Springs	-1.0	D	D	2.8	2.5	D	D	9.0	25.3	1,505	322	89	2,588	0.2
Johnson	2.5	6.8	9.1	0.8	5.1	5.0	9.5	3.6	34.2	2,165	255	47	4,624	1.6
Laramie	0.4	1.1	6.6	4.0	7.2	6.7	6.8	7.9	40.6	18,095	185	1,485	43,341	7.1
Lincoln	-0.5	19.1	13.3	1.9	4.8	5.2	3.3	3.3	30.7	3,605	189	144	9,432	5.4
Natrona	0.0	6.4	8.7	3.0	4.5	6.0	6.2	11.7	12.0	14,250	176	1,223	36,923	9.2
Niobrara	1.6	3.9	D	D	D	D	D	D	45.4	605	245	25	1,370	2.4
Park	0.6	4.9	10.1	4.3	6.3	7.4	4.9	11.5	29.6	7,630	259	290	14,455	6.6
Platte	3.2	2.2	8.3	1.3	4.1	6.1	4.6	D	22.5	2,350	271	72	4,857	4.1
Sheridan	0.6	3.5	10.1	3.1	7.5	7.2	4.2	D	31.3	6,870	229	305	14,902	6.9
Sublette	1.2	34.0	12.0	0.6	3.3	4.0	3.8	D	24.4	1,520	152	40	6,018	4.3
Sweetwater	-0.2	32.7	7.4	9.7	2.4	4.8	3.7	3.1	17.0	6,440	146	383	19,734	5.3
Teton	0.2	0.5	12.1	0.6	13.9	6.5	8.4	4.5	14.7	3,020	130	41	13,852	8.1
Uinta	-0.4	8.4	11.3	3.7	7.5	6.8	5.2	10.3	27.2	3,400	164	278	9,018	3.5
Washakie	0.6	3.9	7.9	13.1	5.0	6.1	4.4	D	25.4	1,945	238	85	3,868	0.9
Weston	1.4	7.1	7.7	9.5	2.8	5.1	4.2	D	32.1	1,645	229	47	3,567	1.0

1. Per 1,000 resident population estimated as of July 1 of the year shown.

Table B. States and Counties — Housing, Labor Force, and Employment

STATE County	Housing units, 2017 (cont.)								Civilian labor force, 2017				Civilian employment[6], 2012-2016		
	Occupied units										Unemployment			Percent	
	Owner-occupied					Renter-occupied									
				Median owner cost as a percent of income											Construction, production, and maintenance occupations
	Total	Percent	Median value[1]	With a mort-gage	Without a mort-gage[2]	Median rent[3]	Median rent as a percent of income[2]	Sub-standard units[4] (percent)	Total	Percent change, 2016-2017	Total	Rate[5]	Total	Management, business, science, and arts	
	89	90	91	92	93	94	95	96	97	98	99	100	101	102	103
WYOMING— Cont'd															
Goshen	5,350	76.3	153,000	20.4	12.8	661	25.3	0.7	6,983	-0.8	197	2.8	6,054	34.5	27.4
Hot Springs	2,262	73.7	147,500	22.0	10.0	690	23.7	4.5	2,329	-4.1	90	3.9	2,271	41.3	22.7
Johnson	3,668	73.3	247,800	21.4	12.4	871	24.2	0.0	4,196	-0.4	174	4.1	4,317	31.4	32.4
Laramie	37,362	68.5	195,900	21.1	10.6	849	27.5	1.4	48,162	-1.5	1,779	3.7	46,597	36.8	23.9
Lincoln	7,002	79.1	204,300	20.6	10.0	813	22.4	2.9	8,727	-0.1	325	3.7	9,055	30.8	33.6
Natrona	32,422	65.7	193,200	20.2	10.0	832	25.7	1.9	39,569	-3.6	2,102	5.3	41,876	30.1	28.0
Niobrara	981	70.2	155,200	21.2	13.8	627	22.8	0.1	1,319	-1.6	36	2.7	1,087	36.3	21.7
Park	11,826	72.0	231,100	20.9	10.0	723	21.7	1.4	15,688	-1.7	664	4.2	14,968	32.7	23.9
Platte	3,680	75.4	164,000	22.3	13.4	632	28.9	0.4	4,783	0.0	178	3.7	4,040	29.4	30.1
Sheridan	12,697	68.4	237,700	22.4	10.6	758	25.6	1.4	15,791	-2.2	627	4.0	14,495	38.9	22.9
Sublette	3,203	71.3	264,700	18.9	10.0	1,066	19.7	0.9	4,252	0.4	186	4.4	5,581	37.7	33.3
Sweetwater	16,533	72.5	190,700	18.5	10.0	891	23.4	3.3	21,581	-2.6	982	4.6	23,057	26.5	37.5
Teton	8,576	59.8	720,000	23.0	10.2	1,187	27.0	4.3	15,467	1.3	462	3.0	14,335	40.3	16.8
Uinta	7,432	70.3	179,500	21.2	10.0	643	25.4	3.5	9,138	-3.2	411	4.5	9,477	29.3	32.0
Washakie	3,493	74.5	156,900	21.5	10.6	601	26.4	2.8	4,115	-2.5	168	4.1	3,781	31.0	33.0
Weston	3,134	76.8	172,300	20.0	10.0	762	20.5	3.4	3,771	-4.9	150	4.0	3,310	32.9	35.5

1. Specified owner-occupied units.   2. A value of 10.0 represents 10 percent or less; a value of 50.0 represents 50 percent or more.   3. Specified renter-occupied units.
4. Overcrowded or lacking complete plumbing facilities. 5. Percent of civilian labor force.   6. Civilian employed persons 16 years old and over.

Table B. States and Counties — **Nonfarm Employment and Agriculture**

STATE County	Private nonfarm establishments, employment and payroll, 2016									Agriculture, 2012			
		Employment						Annual payroll		Farms			
												Percent with:	
	Number of establishments	Total	Health care and social assistance	Manufacturing	Retail trade	Finance and insurance	Professional, scientific, and technical services	Total (mil dol)	Average per employee (dollars)	Number	Fewer than 50 acres	500 acres or more	Farm operators whose principal occupation is farming (percent)
	104	105	106	107	108	109	110	111	112	113	114	115	116
WYOMING— Cont'd													
Goshen	348	2,987	707	209	416	137	128	94	31,442	790	15.4	43.0	59.6
Hot Springs	184	1,587	403	42	182	41	49	55	34,432	178	32.6	31.5	42.7
Johnson	467	2,341	397	67	334	156	172	82	34,877	358	19.0	53.4	51.7
Laramie	3,234	35,366	8,045	1,130	5,765	1,578	2,488	1,413	39,958	1,116	33.5	31.2	37.3
Lincoln	668	4,467	774	357	667	108	110	216	48,451	608	41.0	20.1	46.4
Natrona	2,953	32,937	5,675	1,382	5,082	965	1,428	1,443	43,825	397	31.5	33.5	49.4
Niobrara	89	413	56	D	104	D	8	12	28,695	234	6.0	82.5	80.8
Park	1,188	9,669	1,954	588	1,634	306	395	396	40,995	860	37.4	18.8	47.4
Platte	260	2,191	304	128	434	105	45	94	42,831	505	18.2	46.9	59.4
Sheridan	1,178	10,392	2,175	295	1,694	331	728	372	35,824	702	36.3	31.8	45.9
Sublette	408	2,885	161	49	344	75	92	187	64,932	398	32.4	41.5	51.5
Sweetwater	1,268	16,419	1,456	1,807	2,410	315	469	937	57,083	255	27.8	36.9	30.6
Teton	2,105	17,864	1,316	172	1,925	418	988	781	43,739	154	50.6	12.3	41.6
Uinta	573	6,990	1,410	193	1,095	145	227	339	48,558	315	28.9	33.3	44.1
Washakie	358	2,828	736	316	361	101	113	100	35,519	209	39.2	35.4	52.6
Weston	228	1,621	377	D	286	62	25	59	36,493	264	7.2	50.4	51.1

Table B. States and Counties — **Agriculture**

STATE County	Land in farms Acreage (1,000)	Land in farms Percent change, 2007-2012	Acres Average size of farm	Acres Total irrigated (1,000)	Acres Total cropland (1,000)	Value of land and buildings (dollars) Average per farm	Value of land and buildings (dollars) Average per acre	Value of machinery and equiopmnet, average per farm (dollars)	Value of products sold: Total (mil dol)	Value of products sold: Average per farm (acres)	Percent from: Crops	Percent from: Livestock and poultry products	Percent of farms with sales of: $10,000 or more	Percent of farms with sales of: $100,000 or more	Government payments Total ($1,000)	Government payments Percent of farms
	117	118	119	120	121	122	123	124	125	126	127	128	129	130	131	132
WYOMING— Cont'd																
Goshen	1,370	0.1	1,735	109.2	241.5	1,346,967	777	141,356	246.6	312,103	26.8	73.2	58.1	33.3	4,662	55.6
Hot Springs	517	-5.4	2,906	12.6	28.1	2,030,427	699	84,197	16.4	92,388	12.7	87.3	49.4	17.4	361	10.7
Johnson	2,036	4.6	5,686	40.0	59.8	3,452,782	607	119,444	51.7	144,441	8.9	91.1	57.8	32.4	750	14.5
Laramie	1,676	-0.9	1,502	59.3	338.1	1,079,159	719	110,585	190.7	170,918	24.4	75.6	37.0	17.6	4,938	32.7
Lincoln	344	0.3	565	72.7	98.5	1,017,597	1,800	87,056	40.8	67,153	30.7	69.3	45.6	19.9	732	27.8
Natrona	1,691	-22.5	4,259	28.9	43.3	2,656,418	624	133,912	42.9	108,118	16.5	83.5	49.6	23.7	634	11.3
Niobrara	1,359	-6.2	5,807	14.6	75.4	3,112,043	536	122,726	45.3	193,684	18.0	82.0	78.6	49.6	1,331	39.7
Park	813	-7.8	946	110.3	109.9	1,324,298	1,401	105,421	100.3	116,611	63.4	36.6	42.8	18.3	1,271	27.1
Platte	1,224	-6.4	2,424	72.2	147.9	1,743,954	719	178,135	130.4	258,151	23.3	76.7	61.0	32.3	2,397	40.0
Sheridan	1,305	6.6	1,859	49.8	74.6	1,532,138	824	87,229	59.8	85,190	16.5	83.5	46.0	17.1	537	10.5
Sublette	778	29.7	1,954	143.1	122.6	2,626,852	1,345	104,369	54.2	136,116	14.5	85.5	43.5	24.6	373	5.5
Sweetwater	1,665	12.0	6,531	28.4	36.0	1,321,392	202	106,012	21.1	82,894	35.2	64.8	49.8	14.9	250	16.5
Teton	40	-24.1	261	14.7	10.5	829,494	3,181	69,526	9.0	58,675	24.2	75.8	34.4	7.1	16	1.9
Uinta	650	-12.5	2,064	70.1	68.7	1,518,038	735	99,092	29.9	94,816	10.2	89.8	53.7	21.6	88	3.8
Washakie	341	-27.3	1,633	38.4	39.9	1,450,273	888	172,411	51.9	248,153	51.2	48.8	57.9	29.7	451	20.6
Weston	1,290	-2.9	4,888	4.2	57.0	2,282,818	467	132,371	52.2	197,833	4.3	95.7	45.5	26.9	757	27.3

Table B. States and Counties — Water Use, Wholesale Trade, Retail Trade, and Real Estate

STATE County	Water use, 2015		Wholesale Trade[1], 2012				Retail Trade[2], 2012				Real estate and rental and leasing,[2] 2012			
	Public supply water withdrawn (mil gal/day)	Public supply gallons withdrawn per person per day	Number of establish-ments	Number of employees	Sales (mil dol)	Annual payroll (mil dol)	Number of establish-ments	Number of employees	Sales (mil dol)	Annual payroll (mil dol)	Number of establish-ments	Number of employees	Sales (mil dol)	Annual payroll (mil dol)
	133	134	135	136	137	138	139	140	141	142	143	144	145	146
WYOMING— Cont'd														
Goshen	1.85	138.2	20	156	69.8	5.8	51	402	107.4	8.7	14	25	3.5	0.6
Hot Springs	0.67	141.3	4	30	13.1	2.3	26	195	48.2	3.0	6	D	D	D
Johnson	1.61	187.5	6	27	8.6	0.7	52	359	91.4	8.1	17	46	4.8	1.5
Laramie	14.00	144.2	121	1,105	722.2	67.0	370	5,513	1,896.2	161.3	142	461	99.5	16.5
Lincoln	4.05	216.3	8	55	17.8	1.7	79	659	180.6	13.3	13	17	2.2	0.4
Natrona	12.26	149.2	163	1,890	2,052.7	115.2	363	4,796	1,487.5	132.1	166	1,281	502.0	79.4
Niobrara	1.00	393.4	2	D	D	D	13	110	28.8	2.3	5	3	1.7	0.2
Park	3.17	108.5	40	270	227.9	12.3	185	1,523	417.5	37.1	57	117	15.1	2.3
Platte	1.56	177.0	5	28	22.0	0.8	35	371	87.5	8.0	11	44	15.2	2.2
Sheridan	4.55	151.6	34	187	84.7	6.8	151	1,559	475.9	42.5	60	204	28.6	5.9
Sublette	2.21	223.3	8	46	41.6	2.7	41	401	94.7	9.7	31	151	27.9	6.4
Sweetwater	11.37	254.8	61	D	D	D	199	2,461	921.4	69.9	85	377	115.4	21.0
Teton	7.78	336.4	32	D	D	D	241	1,929	512.6	55.6	146	527	128.8	26.0
Uinta	3.90	187.3	20	216	153.9	11.3	92	1,119	389.9	24.3	39	148	29.8	5.1
Washakie	0.09	10.8	8	42	15.8	1.3	46	334	95.4	10.0	17	D	D	D
Weston	1.02	141.0	5	40	27.6	1.7	31	267	76.5	6.1	4	6	1.1	0.2

1. Merchant wholesalers, except manufacturers' sales branches and offices.   2. Employer establishments.

Table B. States and Counties — Professional Services, Manufacturing, and Accommodation and Food Services

STATE County	Professional, scientific, and technical services, 2012				Manufacturing, 2012				Accommodation and food services, 2012			
	Number of establishments	Number of employees	Sales (mil dol)	Annual payroll (mil dol)	Number of establishments	Number of employees	Receipts (mil dol)	Annual payroll (mil dol)	Number of establishments	Number of employees	Receipts (mil dol)	Annual payroll (mil dol)
	147	148	149	150	151	152	153	154	155	156	157	158
WYOMING— Cont'd												
Goshen	24	158	8.4	4.3	12	308	D	9.9	30	320	15.9	3.8
Hot Springs	15	49	4.2	1.7	4	32	8.0	2.1	26	D	D	D
Johnson	49	149	18.1	6.6	12	64	D	2.8	42	403	23.3	7.2
Laramie	458	1,860	279.8	99.7	67	1,190	2,549.8	76.8	207	3,980	224.8	59.8
Lincoln	62	106	12.6	4.0	18	371	D	22.2	60	406	18.0	4.4
Natrona	278	1,537	222.4	83.2	83	2,428	1,780.3	163.0	200	3,814	198.2	57.4
Niobrara	5	9	0.7	0.1	3	D	D	1.4	13	95	5.1	1.2
Park	99	338	36.9	14.6	44	410	90.4	18.5	124	1,891	170.9	49.7
Platte	16	51	6.2	1.3	14	64	10.8	2.3	36	346	21.3	4.1
Sheridan	127	675	92.3	31.2	28	383	102.3	19.3	92	1,213	68.7	19.2
Sublette	54	139	20.1	6.7	9	31	D	1.5	40	358	24.4	6.9
Sweetwater	121	493	90.2	31.7	35	1,772	1,575.5	148.7	113	1,771	128.9	28.1
Teton	268	744	139.3	46.8	34	254	34.1	8.0	186	4,598	344.0	114.7
Uinta	54	285	33.8	13.8	24	233	204.2	9.8	48	875	35.5	9.9
Washakie	37	104	11.9	4.1	14	387	187.5	18.5	32	284	11.6	3.2
Weston	11	23	2.4	0.7	3	D	D	D	22	190	9.4	2.4

Items 147—158

Table B. States and Counties — Health Care and Social Assistance, Other Services, Nonemployer Businesses, and Residential Construction

STATE County	Health care and social assistance, 2012				Other services, 2012				Nonemployer businesses, 2015		Value of residential construction authorized by building permits, 2017	
	Number of establish-ments	Number of employees	Receipts (mil dol)	Annual payroll (mil dol)	Number of establis-hments	Number of employees	Receipts (mil dol)	Annual payroll (mil dol)	Number	Receipts (mil dol)	New construction ($1,000)	Number of housing units
	159	160	161	162	163	164	165	166	167	168	169	170
WYOMING— Cont'd												
Goshen	27	803	60.5	25.6	28	89	9.3	2.3	914	37.1	252	2
Hot Springs	19	395	34.2	15.5	14	58	3.9	1.1	374	12.4	0	0
Johnson	32	375	32.1	13.2	22	104	7.6	2.8	1,200	63.5	1,746	6
Laramie	323	6,700	647.9	305.2	189	943	93.6	27.1	7,665	480.1	88,101	573
Lincoln	56	643	58.5	24.1	38	77	9.9	2.2	1,916	81.2	39,157	137
Natrona	305	5,141	687.2	266.3	207	1,333	227.6	49.8	5,884	301.6	48,652	273
Niobrara	7	D	D	D	7	28	6.7	1.3	244	10.7	0	0
Park	116	1,399	146.3	55.5	70	248	24.9	6.5	3,077	129.0	30,002	129
Platte	22	325	27.7	10.9	13	50	3.7	0.9	716	26.5	5,421	24
Sheridan	128	2,705	302.2	125.1	74	334	31.1	8.6	2,720	115.4	35,648	161
Sublette	23	207	13.3	6.8	32	162	25.1	6.3	991	41.5	10,964	37
Sweetwater	104	1,285	150.2	51.2	88	464	58.7	16.1	2,139	95.1	21,786	105
Teton	117	1,120	158.9	60.5	113	450	109.0	17.0	4,983	325.2	188,298	190
Uinta	67	1,265	110.3	53.9	35	D	D	D	1,398	63.5	9,325	42
Washakie	29	787	51.6	23.0	28	94	9.7	1.8	681	21.1	884	4
Weston	24	352	25.3	10.5	12	38	3.1	0.8	610	23.1	0	0

Table B. States and Counties — Government Employment and Payroll, and Local Government Finances

	Government employment and payroll, 2012									Local government finances				
			March payroll (percent of total)							General revenue				
												Taxes		
													Per capita[1] (dollars)	
STATE County	Full-time equivalent employees	March payroll (dollars)	Administration, judicial, and legal	Police and corrections	Fire protection	Highways and transportation	Health and welfare	Natural resources and utilities	Education and libraries	Total (mil dol)	Inter-governmental (mil dol)	Total (mil dol)	Total	Property
	171	172	173	174	175	176	177	178	179	180	181	182	183	184
WYOMING— Cont'd														
Goshen	800	2,841,581	5.6	7.0	0.0	2.4	1.3	5.3	77.7	86.6	58.5	10.5	773	552
Hot Springs	363	1,248,475	7.7	7.2	0.0	3.0	30.6	3.5	46.8	44.5	12.8	14.8	3,062	2,366
Johnson	670	2,461,238	5.8	13.9	1.0	2.9	30.1	3.1	42.7	83.0	14.4	44.9	5,208	4,585
Laramie	6,173	27,578,286	2.8	4.6	1.9	1.8	39.8	1.5	46.1	796.0	292.8	103.3	1,094	589
Lincoln	1,211	4,847,475	5.1	5.7	0.0	2.9	30.1	3.4	50.4	146.8	60.4	43.1	2,402	2,075
Natrona	3,954	15,321,295	4.4	7.8	3.5	2.3	2.0	5.1	72.5	442.5	254.7	108.8	1,384	938
Niobrara	300	1,035,735	7.3	4.9	0.0	2.2	34.2	5.3	43.5	21.1	9.3	5.8	2,352	1,687
Park	2,084	8,399,901	4.2	4.7	0.4	2.6	27.2	5.2	52.8	238.1	92.8	47.9	1,668	1,494
Platte	543	2,168,168	5.1	7.9	0.2	2.2	1.5	6.3	74.9	46.5	26.6	13.3	1,519	995
Sheridan	2,207	8,719,701	3.2	4.7	1.0	2.3	30.0	3.0	54.6	234.1	106.6	40.1	1,354	946
Sublette	677	2,840,346	8.1	15.4	0.0	10.5	11.9	4.2	49.3	142.2	33.5	91.3	8,805	8,657
Sweetwater	2,985	12,809,450	6.0	8.4	2.4	2.6	20.2	5.8	52.6	382.6	116.8	165.8	3,662	2,797
Teton	1,475	6,340,874	5.4	7.3	1.5	7.9	37.5	5.7	32.3	225.0	41.2	80.1	3,695	2,344
Uinta	1,240	4,518,508	5.8	7.1	0.8	2.5	1.9	5.2	73.2	117.5	70.3	38.1	1,811	1,505
Washakie	459	1,506,233	5.8	5.8	0.7	2.9	2.6	6.0	75.1	45.2	28.7	12.2	1,442	998
Weston	521	1,865,375	4.5	8.0	0.4	2.9	23.8	5.3	54.7	44.2	22.9	9.7	1,375	1,062

1. Based on the resident population estimated as of July 1 of the year shown.

Table B. States and Counties — Local Government Finances, Government Employment, and Income Taxes

STATE County	Total (mil dol)	Per capita[1] (dollars)	Education	Health and hospitals	Police protection	Public welfare	Highways	Total (mil dol)	Per capita[1] (dollars)	Federal civilian	Federal military	State and local	Number of returns	Mean adjusted gross income	Mean income tax
	185	186	187	188	189	190	191	192	193	194	195	196	197	198	199
WYOMING— Cont'd															
Goshen	86.2	6,325	66.3	1.5	3.7	0.9	7.3	10.3	756	76	64	1,359	5,650	49,269	5,225
Hot Springs	44.9	9,306	33.3	31.7	3.7	0.0	5.2	4.5	931	15	24	552	2,290	48,441	4,978
Johnson	95.5	11,080	33.0	26.7	3.3	0.5	6.3	14.7	1,711	130	44	867	4,220	61,523	7,850
Laramie	781.4	8,270	37.0	40.5	2.5	0.2	3.1	132.4	1,401	2,727	3,449	11,448	48,190	59,192	7,471
Lincoln	144.3	8,033	47.9	26.3	3.6	0.1	4.8	60.9	3,388	113	100	1,709	8,160	65,684	7,962
Natrona	436.0	5,546	59.1	0.4	4.8	0.7	4.1	147.1	1,871	644	417	5,259	39,300	78,531	12,922
Niobrara	27.9	11,371	45.7	24.9	4.4	0.1	4.6	111.4	45,347	11	12	453	1,150	56,668	6,757
Park	277.9	9,682	41.4	36.2	2.5	0.0	2.9	79.0	2,754	777	150	2,829	14,880	64,305	8,408
Platte	48.9	5,582	54.4	2.9	7.4	0.1	4.1	8.7	993	108	94	797	4,340	54,150	6,496
Sheridan	252.8	8,543	49.0	26.5	2.5	0.0	5.2	33.2	1,121	765	153	2,782	15,080	68,234	9,337
Sublette	154.1	14,868	43.1	8.2	4.0	1.8	11.0	9.5	919	121	48	966	4,240	84,749	13,410
Sweetwater	389.7	8,609	48.2	17.5	5.5	0.3	4.3	69.5	1,536	206	228	4,356	20,480	71,028	9,255
Teton	218.0	10,059	24.1	34.3	3.8	0.0	2.4	92.9	4,287	429	120	2,051	14,310	248,351	53,945
Uinta	121.7	5,787	64.9	0.8	5.8	0.9	4.8	14.0	665	74	108	2,150	9,280	63,486	7,252
Washakie	52.1	6,153	68.3	0.8	4.1	0.4	3.0	12.8	1,512	115	42	767	3,770	65,318	9,455
Weston	48.0	6,780	47.5	21.6	4.2	0.6	10.3	2.0	286	56	36	752	3,290	66,909	8,892

1. Based on the resident population estimated as of July 1 of the year shown.

PART C.

Metropolitan Areas

(For explanation of symbols, see page viii)

Page

Metropolitan Area Highlights and Rankings

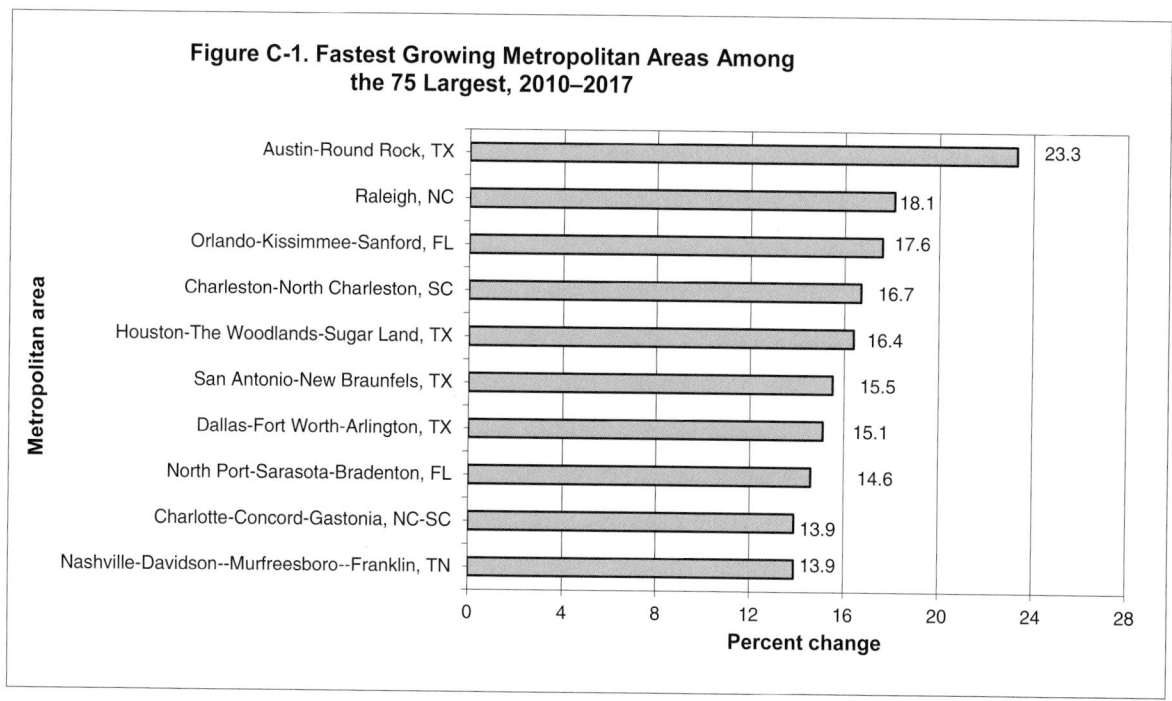

Figure C-1. Fastest Growing Metropolitan Areas Among the 75 Largest, 2010–2017

In 2017, 85.9 percent of Americans lived in metropolitan areas, but these metropolitan areas made up a mere 28 percent of the nation's land area. After nearly a decade of research and development, the Office of Management and Budget (OMB) first established new rules for defining metropolitan areas and issued a completely new list after the 2000 census. This scheme defines a variety of areas called "Core Based Statistical Areas" (CBSAs). Along with the new definition of metropolitan areas, OMB defined a new type of area—called a micropolitan area—that defines the many American communities with population clusters that are too small to meet the 50,000 minimum that defines a metropolitan area. Appendix C lists these micropolitan areas as of August 2017, but because of size constraints, *County and City Extra* continues to include only metropolitan area data in Table C. In 2013, the Census Bureau released data for new metropolitan and micropolitan areas based on the 2010 census, and these were updated in 2015 and again in 2017. This edition of *County and City Extra* uses these 2015 metropolitan area delineations except for Appendix C where one micropolitan area became a metropolitan area (Twin Falls, Idaho). Most of the data producers are now releasing data for the new metropolitan areas. For a few data sources, the counties have been aggregated to the new areas.

With over 20 million people, the New York metropolitan area was the largest, followed by Los Angeles with a population of over 13 million. Chicago ranked third with 9.5 million people. Another 11 metropolitan areas had more than 4

million residents (Dallas, Houston, Washington, Philadelphia, Miami, Atlanta, Boston, San Francisco, Phoenix, Riverside, and Detroit), while 39 other metropolitan areas had between 1 million and 4 million people. Fifty-six percent of the U.S. population lived in these 53 metropolitan areas with one million or more residents.

One hundred seventy-one metropolitan areas grew by 5 percent or more between 2010 and 2017. The Villages, FL had the highest growth rate, increasing by 34.0 percent to a 2017 population of 125,165 residents. Among the 75 largest metropolitan areas, Austin-Round Rock-San Marcos, TX had the largest increase at 23.3 percent followed by Raleigh, NC at 18.1 percent. Five of the most populous metropolitan areas lost population since 2010—Pittsburgh, PA; Cleveland-Elyria, OH, New Haven-Milford, CT; Rochester, NY, and Hartford-West Hartford-East Hartford, CT.

Among metropolitan areas, New York and Los Angeles shared the top spots for density as well as for total population. With 2,753.9 persons per square mile, Los Angeles-Long Beach-Anaheim, CA was the most densely populated metropolitan area in the country. At the other extreme, eight of the largest metropolitan areas had fewer than 200 persons per square mile. These areas typically had large land areas and were located in the west and south.

In 2017, three metropolitan areas had unemployment rates at 10 percent or higher. In contrast, 131 metropolitan areas had unemployment rates at 10 percent or higher in 2010. Topping the list are El Centro, CA and Yuma, AZ, two metropolitan areas with large agricultural workforces and unemployment rates at 19.1 percent and 17.0 percent respectively. Eight of the 10 metropolitan areas with the highest unemployment were in California. Among the 75 most populous metropolitan areas, Bakersfield, CA was the only MSA with an unemployment rate above 9 percent. Two hundred and sixty-seven metropolitan areas had unemployment rates below 5 percent in 2017. Many of them were relatively small areas. Ames, IA and Urban Honolulu, HI had the lowest unemployment rates among all metropolitan areas at 2.0 percent and 2.2 percent respectively followed by Fargo, ND-MN; Fort Collins, CO; and Boulder, CO at 2.4 percent. Twenty-eight of the 75 largest metropolitan areas had unemployment rates below 4 percent. These were metropolitan areas in different regions of the country, and with different employment patterns. Among them was Grand Rapids-Wyoming, MI with an unemployment rate of 3.6 percent. This metropolitan area had the highest level of manufacturing employment of the 75 largest metropolitan areas, with 22.0 percent of the workforce in manufacturing industries.

75 Largest Metropolitan Areas by 2017 Population
Selected Rankings

Population, 2017

Population rank	Metropolitan area	Population [col 2]
1	New York-Newark-Jersey City, NY-NJ-PA	20,320,876
2	Los Angeles-Long Beach-Anaheim, CA	13,353,907
3	Chicago-Naperville-Elgin, IL-IN-WI	9,533,040
4	Dallas-Fort Worth-Arlington, TX	7,399,662
5	Houston-The Woodlands-Sugar Land, TX	6,892,427
6	Washington-Arlington-Alexandria, DC-VA-MD-WV	6,216,589
7	Miami-Fort Lauderdale-West Palm Beach, FL	6,158,824
8	Philadelphia-Camden-Wilmington, PA-NJ-DE-MD	6,096,120
9	Atlanta-Sandy Springs-Roswell, GA	5,884,736
10	Boston-Cambridge-Newton, MA-NH	4,836,531
11	Phoenix-Mesa-Scottsdale, AZ	4,737,270
12	San Francisco-Oakland-Hayward, CA	4,727,357
13	Riverside-San Bernardino-Ontario, CA	4,580,670
14	Detroit-Warren-Dearborn, MI	4,313,002
15	Seattle-Tacoma-Bellevue, WA	3,867,046
16	Minneapolis-St. Paul-Bloomington, MN	3,600,618
17	San Diego-Carlsbad, CA	3,337,685
18	Tampa-St. Petersburg-Clearwater, FL	3,091,399
19	Denver-Aurora-Lakewood, CO	2,888,227
20	Baltimore-Columbia-Towson, MD	2,808,175
21	St. Louis, MO-IL	2,807,338
22	Charlotte-Concord-Gastonia, NC-SC	2,525,305
23	Orlando-Kissimmee-Sanford, FL	2,509,831
24	San Antonio-New Braunfels, TX	2,473,974
25	Portland-Vancouver-Hillsboro, OR-WA	2,453,168
26	Pittsburgh, PA	2,333,367
27	Sacramento-Roseville-Arden-Arcade, CA	2,324,884
28	Las Vegas-Henderson-Paradise, NV	2,204,079
29	Cincinnati, OH-KY-IN	2,179,082
30	Kansas City, MO-KS	2,128,912
31	Austin-Round Rock, TX	2,115,827
32	Columbus, OH	2,078,725
33	Cleveland-Elyria, OH	2,058,844
34	Indianapolis-Carmel-Anderson, IN	2,028,614
35	San Jose-Sunnyvale-Santa Clara, CA	1,998,463
36	Nashville-Davidson— Murfreesboro— Franklin, TN	1,903,045
37	Virginia Beach-Norfolk-Newport News, VA-NC	1,725,246
38	Providence-Warwick, RI-MA	1,621,122
39	Milwaukee-Waukesha-West Allis, WI	1,576,236
40	Jacksonville, FL	1,504,980
41	Oklahoma City, OK	1,383,737
42	Memphis, TN-MS-AR	1,348,260
43	Raleigh, NC	1,335,079
44	Richmond, VA	1,294,204
45	Louisville/Jefferson County, KY-IN	1,293,953
46	New Orleans-Metairie, LA	1,275,762
47	Hartford-West Hartford-East Hartford, CT	1,210,259
48	Salt Lake City, UT	1,203,105
49	Birmingham-Hoover, AL	1,149,807
50	Buffalo-Cheektowaga-Niagara Falls, NY	1,136,856
51	Rochester, NY	1,077,948
52	Grand Rapids-Wyoming, MI	1,059,113
53	Tucson, AZ	1,022,769
54	Tulsa, OK	990,706
55	Fresno, CA	989,255
56	Urban Honolulu, HI	988,650
57	Bridgeport-Stamford-Norwalk, CT	949,921
58	Worcester, MA-CT	942,475
59	Omaha-Council Bluffs, NE-IA	933,316
60	Albuquerque, NM	910,726
61	Greenville-Anderson-Mauldin, SC	895,923
62	Bakersfield, CA	893,119
63	Albany-Schenectady-Troy, NY	886,188
64	Knoxville, TN	877,104
65	McAllen-Edinburg-Mission, TX	860,661
66	New Haven-Milford, CT	860,435
67	Oxnard-Thousand Oaks-Ventura, CA	854,223
68	El Paso, TX	844,818
69	Allentown-Bethlehem-Easton, PA-NJ	840,550
70	Baton Rouge, LA	834,159
71	Columbia, SC	825,033
72	North Port-Sarasota-Bradenton, FL	804,690
73	Dayton, OH	803,416
74	Charleston-North Charleston, SC	775,831
75	Greensboro-High Point, NC	761,184

Total land area, 2017

Population rank	Land area rank	Metropolitan area	Land area (square miles) [col 1]
13	1	Riverside-San Bernardino-Ontario, CA	27,264
11	2	Phoenix-Mesa-Scottsdale, AZ	14,565
60	3	Albuquerque, NM	9,283
4	4	Dallas-Fort Worth-Arlington, TX	9,279
53	5	Tucson, AZ	9,187
9	6	Atlanta-Sandy Springs-Roswell, GA	8,684
19	7	Denver-Aurora-Lakewood, CO	8,346
1	8	New York-Newark-Jersey City, NY-NJ-PA	8,293
5	9	Houston-The Woodlands-Sugar Land, TX	8,266
62	10	Bakersfield, CA	8,132
28	11	Las Vegas-Henderson-Paradise, NV	7,892
21	12	St. Louis, MO-IL	7,863
48	13	Salt Lake City, UT	7,684
16	14	Minneapolis-St. Paul-Bloomington, MN	7,637
24	15	San Antonio-New Braunfels, TX	7,313
30	16	Kansas City, MO-KS	7,256
3	17	Chicago-Naperville-Elgin, IL-IN-WI	7,196
25	18	Portland-Vancouver-Hillsboro, OR-WA	6,687
36	19	Nashville-Davidson— Murfreesboro— Franklin, TN	6,302
54	20	Tulsa, OK	6,270
6	21	Washington-Arlington-Alexandria, DC-VA-MD-WV	6,247
55	22	Fresno, CA	5,958
15	23	Seattle-Tacoma-Bellevue, WA	5,870
68	24	El Paso, TX	5,584
41	25	Oklahoma City, OK	5,512
26	26	Pittsburgh, PA	5,281
49	27	Birmingham-Hoover, AL	5,280
27	28	Sacramento— Roseville— Arden-Arcade, CA	5,095
7	29	Miami-Fort Lauderdale-West Palm Beach, FL	5,070
22	30	Charlotte-Concord-Gastonia, NC-SC	5,064
42	31	Memphis, TN-MS-AR	4,986
2	32	Los Angeles-Long Beach-Anaheim, CA	4,849
32	33	Columbus, OH	4,797
8	34	Philadelphia-Camden-Wilmington, PA-NJ-DE-MD	4,603
44	35	Richmond, VA	4,575
59	36	Omaha-Council Bluffs, NE-IA	4,350
34	37	Indianapolis-Carmel-Anderson, IN	4,307
31	38	Austin-Round Rock, TX	4,222
17	39	San Diego-Carlsbad, CA	4,208
29	40	Cincinnati, OH-KY-IN	4,166
70	41	Baton Rouge, LA	4,027
14	42	Detroit-Warren-Dearborn, MI	3,889
71	43	Columbia, SC	3,703
45	44	Louisville/Jefferson County, KY-IN	3,579
64	45	Knoxville, TN	3,501
10	46	Boston-Cambridge-Newton, MA-NH	3,486
23	47	Orlando-Kissimmee-Sanford, FL	3,481
51	48	Rochester, NY	3,266
40	49	Jacksonville, FL	3,202
46	50	New Orleans-Metairie, LA	3,202
63	51	Albany-Schenectady-Troy, NY	2,812
61	52	Greenville-Anderson-Mauldin, SC	2,711
37	53	Virginia Beach-Norfolk-Newport News, VA-NC	2,683
35	54	San Jose-Sunnyvale-Santa Clara, CA	2,680
52	55	Grand Rapids-Wyoming, MI	2,670
20	56	Baltimore-Columbia-Towson, MD	2,602
74	57	Charleston-North Charleston, SC	2,589
18	58	Tampa-St. Petersburg-Clearwater, FL	2,515
12	59	San Francisco-Oakland-Hayward, CA	2,470
43	60	Raleigh, NC	2,118
58	61	Worcester, MA-CT	2,024
33	62	Cleveland-Elyria, OH	1,999
75	63	Greensboro-High Point, NC	1,994
67	64	Oxnard-Thousand Oaks-Ventura, CA	1,843
38	65	Providence-Warwick, RI-MA	1,587
65	66	McAllen-Edinburg-Mission, TX	1,571
50	67	Buffalo-Cheektowaga-Niagara Falls, NY	1,565
47	68	Hartford-West Hartford-East Hartford, CT	1,515
39	69	Milwaukee-Waukesha-West Allis, WI	1,455
69	70	Allentown-Bethlehem-Easton, PA-NJ	1,453
72	71	North Port-Sarasota-Bradenton, FL	1,299
73	72	Dayton, OH	1,282
57	73	Bridgeport-Stamford-Norwalk, CT	625
66	74	New Haven-Milford, CT	605
56	75	Urban Honolulu, HI	601

75 Largest Metropolitan Areas by 2017 Population
Selected Rankings

Population density, 2017				Percent population change, 2010–2017			
Population rank	Density rank	Metropolitan area	Density (per square kilometer) [col 4]	Population rank	Percent change rank	Metropolitan area	Percent change [col 23]
2	1	Los Angeles-Long Beach-Anaheim, CA	2,753.9	31	1	Austin-Round Rock, TX	23.3
1	2	New York-Newark-Jersey City, NY-NJ-PA	2,450.4	43	2	Raleigh, NC	18.1
12	3	San Francisco-Oakland-Hayward, CA	1,913.7	23	3	Orlando-Kissimmee-Sanford, FL	17.6
56	4	Urban Honolulu, HI	1,646.1	74	4	Charleston-North Charleston, SC	16.7
57	5	Bridgeport-Stamford-Norwalk, CT	1,519.9	5	5	Houston-The Woodlands-Sugar Land, TX	16.4
66	6	New Haven-Milford, CT	1,423.4	24	6	San Antonio-New Braunfels, TX	15.5
10	7	Boston-Cambridge-Newton, MA-NH	1,387.5	4	7	Dallas-Fort Worth-Arlington, TX	15.1
3	8	Chicago-Naperville-Elgin, IL-IN-WI	1,324.8	72	8	North Port-Sarasota-Bradenton, FL	14.6
8	9	Philadelphia-Camden-Wilmington, PA-NJ-DE-MD	1,324.5	22	9	Charlotte-Concord-Gastonia, NC-SC	13.9
18	10	Tampa-St. Petersburg-Clearwater, FL	1,229.3	36	9	Nashville-Davidson— Murfreesboro— Franklin, TN	13.9
7	11	Miami-Fort Lauderdale-West Palm Beach, FL	1,214.9	19	11	Denver-Aurora-Lakewood, CO	13.5
14	12	Detroit-Warren-Dearborn, MI	1,109.0	11	12	Phoenix-Mesa-Scottsdale, AZ	13.0
39	13	Milwaukee-Waukesha-West Allis, WI	1,083.5	28	12	Las Vegas-Henderson-Paradise, NV	13.0
20	14	Baltimore-Columbia-Towson, MD	1,079.4	15	14	Seattle-Tacoma-Bellevue, WA	12.4
33	15	Cleveland-Elyria, OH	1,029.8	40	15	Jacksonville, FL	11.8
38	16	Providence-Warwick, RI-MA	1,021.4	9	16	Atlanta-Sandy Springs-Roswell, GA	11.3
6	17	Washington-Arlington-Alexandria, DC-VA-MD-WV	995.1	18	17	Tampa-St. Petersburg-Clearwater, FL	11.1
5	18	Houston-The Woodlands-Sugar Land, TX	833.8	65	17	McAllen-Edinburg-Mission, TX	11.1
47	19	Hartford-West Hartford-East Hartford, CT	799.0	7	19	Miami-Fort Lauderdale-West Palm Beach, FL	10.6
4	20	Dallas-Fort Worth-Arlington, TX	797.5	48	19	Salt Lake City, UT	10.6
17	21	San Diego-Carlsbad, CA	793.2	41	21	Oklahoma City, OK	10.4
35	22	San Jose-Sunnyvale-Santa Clara, CA	745.7	6	22	Washington-Arlington-Alexandria, DC-VA-MD-WV	10.3
50	23	Buffalo-Cheektowaga-Niagara Falls, NY	726.4	25	23	Portland-Vancouver-Hillsboro, OR-WA	10.2
23	24	Orlando-Kissimmee-Sanford, FL	720.9	32	24	Columbus, OH	9.3
9	25	Atlanta-Sandy Springs-Roswell, GA	677.7	12	25	San Francisco-Oakland-Hayward, CA	9.0
15	26	Seattle-Tacoma-Bellevue, WA	658.8	35	26	San Jose-Sunnyvale-Santa Clara, CA	8.8
37	27	Virginia Beach-Norfolk-Newport News, VA-NC	643.1	61	27	Greenville-Anderson-Mauldin, SC	8.7
43	28	Raleigh, NC	630.4	13	28	Riverside-San Bernardino-Ontario, CA	8.4
73	29	Dayton, OH	626.6	27	29	Sacramento— Roseville— Arden-Arcade, CA	8.2
72	30	North Port-Sarasota-Bradenton, FL	619.5	59	30	Omaha-Council Bluffs, NE-IA	7.9
69	31	Allentown-Bethlehem-Easton, PA-NJ	578.6	17	31	San Diego-Carlsbad, CA	7.8
65	32	McAllen-Edinburg-Mission, TX	547.9	16	32	Minneapolis-St. Paul-Bloomington, MN	7.5
29	33	Cincinnati, OH-KY-IN	523.1	71	32	Columbia, SC	7.5
31	34	Austin-Round Rock, TX	501.2	34	34	Indianapolis-Carmel-Anderson, IN	7.4
22	35	Charlotte-Concord-Gastonia, NC-SC	498.6	46	35	New Orleans-Metairie, LA	7.2
16	36	Minneapolis-St. Paul-Bloomington, MN	471.5	44	36	Richmond, VA	7.1
34	37	Indianapolis-Carmel-Anderson, IN	471.1	52	36	Grand Rapids-Wyoming, MI	7.1
40	38	Jacksonville, FL	470.0	62	38	Bakersfield, CA	6.4
58	39	Worcester, MA-CT	465.8	55	39	Fresno, CA	6.3
67	40	Oxnard-Thousand Oaks-Ventura, CA	463.5	10	40	Boston-Cambridge-Newton, MA-NH	6.2
27	41	Sacramento— Roseville— Arden-Arcade, CA	456.3	30	41	Kansas City, MO-KS	6.0
26	42	Pittsburgh, PA	441.8	54	42	Tulsa, OK	5.7
32	43	Columbus, OH	433.4	75	43	Greensboro-High Point, NC	5.2
46	44	New Orleans-Metairie, LA	398.4	68	44	El Paso, TX	5.1
52	45	Grand Rapids-Wyoming, MI	396.7	45	45	Louisville/Jefferson County, KY-IN	4.7
75	46	Greensboro-High Point, NC	381.8	64	45	Knoxville, TN	4.7
25	47	Portland-Vancouver-Hillsboro, OR-WA	366.9	53	47	Tucson, AZ	4.3
45	48	Louisville/Jefferson County, KY-IN	361.6	2	48	Los Angeles-Long Beach-Anaheim, CA	4.1
21	49	St. Louis, MO-IL	357.0	1	49	New York-Newark-Jersey City, NY-NJ-PA	3.9
19	50	Denver-Aurora-Lakewood, CO	346.1	70	49	Baton Rouge, LA	3.9
24	51	San Antonio-New Braunfels, TX	338.3	56	51	Urban Honolulu, HI	3.7
61	52	Greenville-Anderson-Mauldin, SC	330.5	67	51	Oxnard-Thousand Oaks-Ventura, CA	3.7
51	53	Rochester, NY	330.0	20	53	Baltimore-Columbia-Towson, MD	3.6
11	54	Phoenix-Mesa-Scottsdale, AZ	325.2	57	53	Bridgeport-Stamford-Norwalk, CT	3.6
63	55	Albany-Schenectady-Troy, NY	315.2	29	55	Cincinnati, OH-KY-IN	3.0
36	56	Nashville-Davidson— Murfreesboro— Franklin, TN	302.0	37	56	Virginia Beach-Norfolk-Newport News, VA-NC	2.9
74	57	Charleston-North Charleston, SC	299.6	58	57	Worcester, MA-CT	2.8
30	58	Kansas City, MO-KS	293.4	60	58	Albuquerque, NM	2.7
44	59	Richmond, VA	282.9	69	59	Allentown-Bethlehem-Easton, PA-NJ	2.3
28	60	Las Vegas-Henderson-Paradise, NV	279.3	8	60	Philadelphia-Camden-Wilmington, PA-NJ-DE-MD	2.2
42	61	Memphis, TN-MS-AR	270.4	49	61	Birmingham-Hoover, AL	1.9
41	62	Oklahoma City, OK	251.1	42	62	Memphis, TN-MS-AR	1.8
64	63	Knoxville, TN	250.5	63	62	Albany-Schenectady-Troy, NY	1.8
71	64	Columbia, SC	222.8	39	64	Milwaukee-Waukesha-West Allis, WI	1.3
49	65	Birmingham-Hoover, AL	217.8	38	65	Providence-Warwick, RI-MA	1.2
59	66	Omaha-Council Bluffs, NE-IA	214.6	3	66	Chicago-Naperville-Elgin, IL-IN-WI	0.8
70	67	Baton Rouge, LA	207.1	21	67	St. Louis, MO-IL	0.7
13	68	Riverside-San Bernardino-Ontario, CA	168.0	73	68	Dayton, OH	0.5
55	69	Fresno, CA	166.0	14	69	Detroit-Warren-Dearborn, MI	0.4
54	70	Tulsa, OK	158.0	50	70	Buffalo-Cheektowaga-Niagara Falls, NY	0.1
48	71	Salt Lake City, UT	156.6	47	71	Hartford-West Hartford-East Hartford, CT	-0.2
68	72	El Paso, TX	151.3	51	71	Rochester, NY	-0.2
53	73	Tucson, AZ	111.3	66	71	New Haven-Milford, CT	-0.2
62	74	Bakersfield, CA	109.8	33	74	Cleveland-Elyria, OH	-0.9
60	75	Albuquerque, NM	98.1	26	75	Pittsburgh, PA	-1.0

75 Largest Metropolitan Areas by 2017 Population
Selected Rankings

Percent White, not Hispanic or Latino, alone or in combination, 2017

Population rank	White rank	Metropolitan area	Percent White [col 5]
64	1	Knoxville, TN	88.5
26	2	Pittsburgh, PA	87.1
63	3	Albany-Schenectady-Troy, NY	81.8
29	4	Cincinnati, OH-KY-IN	81.3
52	5	Grand Rapids-Wyoming, MI	80.8
58	6	Worcester, MA-CT	79.2
50	7	Buffalo-Cheektowaga-Niagara Falls, NY	78.9
72	7	North Port-Sarasota-Bradenton, FL	78.9
73	9	Dayton, OH	78.8
45	10	Louisville/Jefferson County, KY-IN	78.2
59	10	Omaha-Council Bluffs, NE-IA	78.2
51	12	Rochester, NY	78.1
16	13	Minneapolis-St. Paul-Bloomington, MN	78.0
38	13	Providence-Warwick, RI-MA	78.0
25	15	Portland-Vancouver-Hillsboro, OR-WA	76.7
21	16	St. Louis, MO-IL	75.5
32	17	Columbus, OH	75.4
30	18	Kansas City, MO-KS	74.8
69	19	Allentown-Bethlehem-Easton, PA-NJ	74.5
34	20	Indianapolis-Carmel-Anderson, IN	74.4
61	21	Greenville-Anderson-Mauldin, SC	74.3
36	22	Nashville-Davidson— Murfreesboro— Franklin, TN	74.2
48	23	Salt Lake City, UT	74.1
10	24	Boston-Cambridge-Newton, MA-NH	72.5
33	25	Cleveland-Elyria, OH	71.6
54	26	Tulsa, OK	70.6
47	27	Hartford-West Hartford-East Hartford, CT	68.8
41	28	Oklahoma City, OK	68.5
14	29	Detroit-Warren-Dearborn, MI	68.4
39	30	Milwaukee-Waukesha-West Allis, WI	68.3
15	31	Seattle-Tacoma-Bellevue, WA	67.9
19	32	Denver-Aurora-Lakewood, CO	66.4
74	33	Charleston-North Charleston, SC	66.0
40	34	Jacksonville, FL	65.2
18	35	Tampa-St. Petersburg-Clearwater, FL	64.8
49	36	Birmingham-Hoover, AL	64.6
66	37	New Haven-Milford, CT	64.5
8	38	Philadelphia-Camden-Wilmington, PA-NJ-DE-MD	63.4
43	39	Raleigh, NC	63.2
57	39	Bridgeport-Stamford-Norwalk, CT	63.2
22	41	Charlotte-Concord-Gastonia, NC-SC	62.8
75	42	Greensboro-High Point, NC	60.1
44	43	Richmond, VA	59.3
20	44	Baltimore-Columbia-Towson, MD	58.6
71	45	Columbia, SC	58.0
37	46	Virginia Beach-Norfolk-Newport News, VA-NC	57.9
70	47	Baton Rouge, LA	57.6
11	48	Phoenix-Mesa-Scottsdale, AZ	57.5
27	49	Sacramento— Roseville— Arden-Arcade, CA	55.9
3	50	Chicago-Naperville-Elgin, IL-IN-WI	54.2
31	51	Austin-Round Rock, TX	54.0
53	52	Tucson, AZ	53.6
46	53	New Orleans-Metairie, LA	52.7
9	54	Atlanta-Sandy Springs-Roswell, GA	48.8
23	55	Orlando-Kissimmee-Sanford, FL	48.6
17	56	San Diego-Carlsbad, CA	48.3
4	57	Dallas-Fort Worth-Arlington, TX	48.0
6	58	Washington-Arlington-Alexandria, DC-VA-MD-WV	47.9
1	59	New York-Newark-Jersey City, NY-NJ-PA	47.5
67	60	Oxnard-Thousand Oaks-Ventura, CA	47.4
28	61	Las Vegas-Henderson-Paradise, NV	45.7
42	62	Memphis, TN-MS-AR	44.8
12	63	San Francisco-Oakland-Hayward, CA	42.9
60	64	Albuquerque, NM	40.9
5	65	Houston-The Woodlands-Sugar Land, TX	37.5
62	66	Bakersfield, CA	35.7
24	67	San Antonio-New Braunfels, TX	35.0
35	68	San Jose-Sunnyvale-Santa Clara, CA	34.4
13	69	Riverside-San Bernardino-Ontario, CA	34.1
56	70	Urban Honolulu, HI	31.9
2	71	Los Angeles-Long Beach-Anaheim, CA	31.6
7	72	Miami-Fort Lauderdale-West Palm Beach, FL	31.3
55	73	Fresno, CA	31.1
68	74	El Paso, TX	12.6
65	75	McAllen-Edinburg-Mission, TX	6.3

Percent Black, not Hispanic or Latino, alone or in combination, 2017

Population rank	Black rank	Metropolitan area	Percent Black [col 6]
42	1	Memphis, TN-MS-AR	48.0
70	2	Baton Rouge, LA	36.3
46	3	New Orleans-Metairie, LA	35.5
9	4	Atlanta-Sandy Springs-Roswell, GA	35.1
71	5	Columbia, SC	34.6
37	6	Virginia Beach-Norfolk-Newport News, VA-NC	32.1
44	7	Richmond, VA	31.0
20	8	Baltimore-Columbia-Towson, MD	30.5
49	9	Birmingham-Hoover, AL	29.6
75	10	Greensboro-High Point, NC	28.1
74	11	Charleston-North Charleston, SC	26.7
6	12	Washington-Arlington-Alexandria, DC-VA-MD-WV	26.5
22	13	Charlotte-Concord-Gastonia, NC-SC	23.6
14	14	Detroit-Warren-Dearborn, MI	23.3
40	15	Jacksonville, FL	22.4
8	16	Philadelphia-Camden-Wilmington, PA-NJ-DE-MD	21.7
7	17	Miami-Fort Lauderdale-West Palm Beach, FL	21.1
33	18	Cleveland-Elyria, OH	21.0
43	19	Raleigh, NC	20.8
21	20	St. Louis, MO-IL	19.4
5	21	Houston-The Woodlands-Sugar Land, TX	17.6
39	22	Milwaukee-Waukesha-West Allis, WI	17.5
61	22	Greenville-Anderson-Mauldin, SC	17.5
73	24	Dayton, OH	17.3
32	25	Columbus, OH	17.2
3	26	Chicago-Naperville-Elgin, IL-IN-WI	17.1
23	27	Orlando-Kissimmee-Sanford, FL	16.8
1	28	New York-Newark-Jersey City, NY-NJ-PA	16.7
34	29	Indianapolis-Carmel-Anderson, IN	16.5
4	30	Dallas-Fort Worth-Arlington, TX	16.4
36	31	Nashville-Davidson— Murfreesboro— Franklin, TN	16.3
45	32	Louisville/Jefferson County, KY-IN	15.8
66	33	New Haven-Milford, CT	13.8
29	34	Cincinnati, OH-KY-IN	13.7
30	35	Kansas City, MO-KS	13.6
50	36	Buffalo-Cheektowaga-Niagara Falls, NY	13.1
18	37	Tampa-St. Petersburg-Clearwater, FL	12.8
28	37	Las Vegas-Henderson-Paradise, NV	12.8
51	39	Rochester, NY	12.2
41	40	Oklahoma City, OK	12.1
47	41	Hartford-West Hartford-East Hartford, CT	11.8
57	42	Bridgeport-Stamford-Norwalk, CT	11.7
16	43	Minneapolis-St. Paul-Bloomington, MN	9.8
54	44	Tulsa, OK	9.7
26	45	Pittsburgh, PA	9.6
63	46	Albany-Schenectady-Troy, NY	9.2
59	47	Omaha-Council Bluffs, NE-IA	8.9
10	48	Boston-Cambridge-Newton, MA-NH	8.6
27	49	Sacramento— Roseville— Arden-Arcade, CA	8.5
12	50	San Francisco-Oakland-Hayward, CA	8.4
13	51	Riverside-San Bernardino-Ontario, CA	8.0
31	52	Austin-Round Rock, TX	7.8
52	53	Grand Rapids-Wyoming, MI	7.7
15	54	Seattle-Tacoma-Bellevue, WA	7.5
2	55	Los Angeles-Long Beach-Anaheim, CA	7.1
24	55	San Antonio-New Braunfels, TX	7.1
72	55	North Port-Sarasota-Bradenton, FL	7.1
64	58	Knoxville, TN	6.6
19	59	Denver-Aurora-Lakewood, CO	6.5
38	59	Providence-Warwick, RI-MA	6.5
11	61	Phoenix-Mesa-Scottsdale, AZ	6.2
69	62	Allentown-Bethlehem-Easton, PA-NJ	6.0
62	63	Bakersfield, CA	5.9
17	64	San Diego-Carlsbad, CA	5.7
55	65	Fresno, CA	5.3
58	66	Worcester, MA-CT	5.1
53	67	Tucson, AZ	4.1
25	68	Portland-Vancouver-Hillsboro, OR-WA	4.0
56	69	Urban Honolulu, HI	3.7
68	70	El Paso, TX	3.4
35	71	San Jose-Sunnyvale-Santa Clara, CA	2.9
60	71	Albuquerque, NM	2.9
67	73	Oxnard-Thousand Oaks-Ventura, CA	2.3
48	74	Salt Lake City, UT	2.2
65	75	McAllen-Edinburg-Mission, TX	0.5

75 Largest Metropolitan Areas by 2017 Population
Selected Rankings

Percent American Indian, Alaska Native, alone or in combination, 2017				Percent Asian and Pacific Islander, alone or in combination, 2017			
Population rank	American Indian Alaska native rank	Metropolitan area	Percent American Indian, Alaska Native [col 7]	Population rank	Asian and Pacific Islander rank	Metropolitan area	Percent Asian and Pacific Islander [col 8]
54	1	Tulsa, OK	13.0	56	1	Urban Honolulu, HI	78.4
41	2	Oklahoma City, OK	6.7	35	2	San Jose-Sunnyvale-Santa Clara, CA	38.7
60	3	Albuquerque, NM	6.0	12	3	San Francisco-Oakland-Hayward, CA	30.2
53	4	Tucson, AZ	3.0	2	4	Los Angeles-Long Beach-Anaheim, CA	18.0
11	5	Phoenix-Mesa-Scottsdale, AZ	2.5	15	5	Seattle-Tacoma-Bellevue, WA	17.8
15	6	Seattle-Tacoma-Bellevue, WA	2.0	27	6	Sacramento— Roseville— Arden-Arcade, CA	17.1
25	7	Portland-Vancouver-Hillsboro, OR-WA	1.7	17	7	San Diego-Carlsbad, CA	14.7
27	8	Sacramento— Roseville— Arden-Arcade, CA	1.5	28	8	Las Vegas-Henderson-Paradise, NV	13.2
56	8	Urban Honolulu, HI	1.5	1	9	New York-Newark-Jersey City, NY-NJ-PA	12.4
16	10	Minneapolis-St. Paul-Bloomington, MN	1.3	6	10	Washington-Arlington-Alexandria, DC-VA-MD-WV	12.1
30	11	Kansas City, MO-KS	1.2	55	11	Fresno, CA	11.4
62	11	Bakersfield, CA	1.2	25	12	Portland-Vancouver-Hillsboro, OR-WA	9.5
19	13	Denver-Aurora-Lakewood, CO	1.1	67	13	Oxnard-Thousand Oaks-Ventura, CA	9.2
28	13	Las Vegas-Henderson-Paradise, NV	1.1	10	14	Boston-Cambridge-Newton, MA-NH	9.1
37	13	Virginia Beach-Norfolk-Newport News, VA-NC	1.1	5	15	Houston-The Woodlands-Sugar Land, TX	8.6
48	13	Salt Lake City, UT	1.1	13	16	Riverside-San Bernardino-Ontario, CA	8.3
50	13	Buffalo-Cheektowaga-Niagara Falls, NY	1.1	16	17	Minneapolis-St. Paul-Bloomington, MN	7.8
55	13	Fresno, CA	1.1	4	18	Dallas-Fort Worth-Arlington, TX	7.7
75	13	Greensboro-High Point, NC	1.1	3	19	Chicago-Naperville-Elgin, IL-IN-WI	7.5
13	20	Riverside-San Bernardino-Ontario, CA	1.0	31	20	Austin-Round Rock, TX	7.0
59	20	Omaha-Council Bluffs, NE-IA	1.0	48	20	Salt Lake City, UT	7.0
4	22	Dallas-Fort Worth-Arlington, TX	0.9	8	22	Philadelphia-Camden-Wilmington, PA-NJ-DE-MD	6.9
14	22	Detroit-Warren-Dearborn, MI	0.9	20	22	Baltimore-Columbia-Towson, MD	6.9
17	22	San Diego-Carlsbad, CA	0.9	9	24	Atlanta-Sandy Springs-Roswell, GA	6.8
22	22	Charlotte-Concord-Gastonia, NC-SC	0.9	43	25	Raleigh, NC	6.7
38	22	Providence-Warwick, RI-MA	0.9	57	26	Bridgeport-Stamford-Norwalk, CT	6.4
39	22	Milwaukee-Waukesha-West Allis, WI	0.9	47	27	Hartford-West Hartford-East Hartford, CT	5.8
43	22	Raleigh, NC	0.9	62	27	Bakersfield, CA	5.8
44	22	Richmond, VA	0.9	19	29	Denver-Aurora-Lakewood, CO	5.5
46	22	New Orleans-Metairie, LA	0.9	37	29	Virginia Beach-Norfolk-Newport News, VA-NC	5.5
52	22	Grand Rapids-Wyoming, MI	0.9	63	29	Albany-Schenectady-Troy, NY	5.5
64	22	Knoxville, TN	0.9	23	32	Orlando-Kissimmee-Sanford, FL	5.4
73	22	Dayton, OH	0.9	58	32	Worcester, MA-CT	5.4
74	22	Charleston-North Charleston, SC	0.9	14	34	Detroit-Warren-Dearborn, MI	5.2
6	35	Washington-Arlington-Alexandria, DC-VA-MD-WV	0.8	40	34	Jacksonville, FL	5.2
12	35	San Francisco-Oakland-Hayward, CA	0.8	11	36	Phoenix-Mesa-Scottsdale, AZ	5.1
20	35	Baltimore-Columbia-Towson, MD	0.8	32	36	Columbus, OH	5.1
31	35	Austin-Round Rock, TX	0.8	44	38	Richmond, VA	4.9
32	35	Columbus, OH	0.8	66	39	New Haven-Milford, CT	4.8
36	35	Nashville-Davidson— Murfreesboro— Franklin, TN	0.8	18	40	Tampa-St. Petersburg-Clearwater, FL	4.4
40	35	Jacksonville, FL	0.8	22	40	Charlotte-Concord-Gastonia, NC-SC	4.4
67	35	Oxnard-Thousand Oaks-Ventura, CA	0.8	39	40	Milwaukee-Waukesha-West Allis, WI	4.4
71	35	Columbia, SC	0.8	75	40	Greensboro-High Point, NC	4.4
9	44	Atlanta-Sandy Springs-Roswell, GA	0.7	41	44	Oklahoma City, OK	4.3
18	44	Tampa-St. Petersburg-Clearwater, FL	0.7	53	45	Tucson, AZ	4.1
21	44	St. Louis, MO-IL	0.7	38	46	Providence-Warwick, RI-MA	3.9
35	44	San Jose-Sunnyvale-Santa Clara, CA	0.7	50	46	Buffalo-Cheektowaga-Niagara Falls, NY	3.9
45	44	Louisville/Jefferson County, KY-IN	0.7	30	48	Kansas City, MO-KS	3.8
49	44	Birmingham-Hoover, AL	0.7	34	48	Indianapolis-Carmel-Anderson, IN	3.8
2	50	Los Angeles-Long Beach-Anaheim, CA	0.6	59	48	Omaha-Council Bluffs, NE-IA	3.8
5	50	Houston-The Woodlands-Sugar Land, TX	0.6	51	51	Rochester, NY	3.7
8	50	Philadelphia-Camden-Wilmington, PA-NJ-DE-MD	0.6	36	52	Nashville-Davidson— Murfreesboro— Franklin, TN	3.5
23	50	Orlando-Kissimmee-Sanford, FL	0.6	69	52	Allentown-Bethlehem-Easton, PA-NJ	3.5
24	50	San Antonio-New Braunfels, TX	0.6	46	54	New Orleans-Metairie, LA	3.4
29	50	Cincinnati, OH-KY-IN	0.6	21	55	St. Louis, MO-IL	3.3
33	50	Cleveland-Elyria, OH	0.6	24	55	San Antonio-New Braunfels, TX	3.3
34	50	Indianapolis-Carmel-Anderson, IN	0.6	52	55	Grand Rapids-Wyoming, MI	3.3
42	50	Memphis, TN-MS-AR	0.6	7	58	Miami-Fort Lauderdale-West Palm Beach, FL	3.2
47	50	Hartford-West Hartford-East Hartford, CT	0.6	29	58	Cincinnati, OH-KY-IN	3.2
51	50	Rochester, NY	0.6	54	58	Tulsa, OK	3.2
58	50	Worcester, MA-CT	0.6	73	61	Dayton, OH	3.1
61	50	Greenville-Anderson-Mauldin, SC	0.6	26	62	Pittsburgh, PA	3.0
63	50	Albany-Schenectady-Troy, NY	0.6	60	62	Albuquerque, NM	3.0
66	50	New Haven-Milford, CT	0.6	33	64	Cleveland-Elyria, OH	2.9
70	50	Baton Rouge, LA	0.6	71	64	Columbia, SC	2.9
72	50	North Port-Sarasota-Bradenton, FL	0.6	74	66	Charleston-North Charleston, SC	2.8
1	67	New York-Newark-Jersey City, NY-NJ-PA	0.5	45	67	Louisville/Jefferson County, KY-IN	2.7
3	67	Chicago-Naperville-Elgin, IL-IN-WI	0.5	42	68	Memphis, TN-MS-AR	2.6
10	67	Boston-Cambridge-Newton, MA-NH	0.5	70	68	Baton Rouge, LA	2.6
26	67	Pittsburgh, PA	0.5	61	70	Greenville-Anderson-Mauldin, SC	2.4
68	67	El Paso, TX	0.5	72	70	North Port-Sarasota-Bradenton, FL	2.4
57	72	Bridgeport-Stamford-Norwalk, CT	0.4	64	72	Knoxville, TN	2.1
69	72	Allentown-Bethlehem-Easton, PA-NJ	0.4	49	73	Birmingham-Hoover, AL	1.9
7	74	Miami-Fort Lauderdale-West Palm Beach, FL	0.3	68	74	El Paso, TX	1.7
65	75	McAllen-Edinburg-Mission, TX	0.1	65	75	McAllen-Edinburg-Mission, TX	1.0

75 Largest Metropolitan Areas by 2017 Population
Selected Rankings

Percent Hispanic or Latino,[1] 2017

Population rank	Hispanic or Latino rank	Metropolitan area	Percent Hispanic or Latino [col 9]
65	1	McAllen-Edinburg-Mission, TX	92.2
68	2	El Paso, TX	82.8
24	3	San Antonio-New Braunfels, TX	55.5
62	4	Bakersfield, CA	53.4
55	5	Fresno, CA	53.2
13	6	Riverside-San Bernardino-Ontario, CA	51.1
60	7	Albuquerque, NM	49.1
7	8	Miami-Fort Lauderdale-West Palm Beach, FL	45.3
2	9	Los Angeles-Long Beach-Anaheim, CA	45.2
67	10	Oxnard-Thousand Oaks-Ventura, CA	42.9
5	11	Houston-The Woodlands-Sugar Land, TX	37.3
53	11	Tucson, AZ	37.3
17	13	San Diego-Carlsbad, CA	33.9
31	14	Austin-Round Rock, TX	32.5
28	15	Las Vegas-Henderson-Paradise, NV	31.3
11	16	Phoenix-Mesa-Scottsdale, AZ	31.0
23	17	Orlando-Kissimmee-Sanford, FL	30.5
4	18	Dallas-Fort Worth-Arlington, TX	28.9
35	19	San Jose-Sunnyvale-Santa Clara, CA	26.6
1	20	New York-Newark-Jersey City, NY-NJ-PA	24.6
19	21	Denver-Aurora-Lakewood, CO	23.1
3	22	Chicago-Naperville-Elgin, IL-IN-WI	22.3
12	23	San Francisco-Oakland-Hayward, CA	21.9
27	24	Sacramento— Roseville— Arden-Arcade, CA	21.7
57	25	Bridgeport-Stamford-Norwalk, CT	19.9
18	26	Tampa-St. Petersburg-Clearwater, FL	19.4
66	27	New Haven-Milford, CT	18.1
48	28	Salt Lake City, UT	17.9
69	29	Allentown-Bethlehem-Easton, PA-NJ	17.1
6	30	Washington-Arlington-Alexandria, DC-VA-MD-WV	15.8
47	31	Hartford-West Hartford-East Hartford, CT	14.9
41	32	Oklahoma City, OK	13.4
38	33	Providence-Warwick, RI-MA	12.9
72	34	North Port-Sarasota-Bradenton, FL	12.6
25	35	Portland-Vancouver-Hillsboro, OR-WA	12.0
58	36	Worcester, MA-CT	11.5
10	37	Boston-Cambridge-Newton, MA-NH	11.2
9	38	Atlanta-Sandy Springs-Roswell, GA	10.8
39	38	Milwaukee-Waukesha-West Allis, WI	10.8
43	40	Raleigh, NC	10.7
59	41	Omaha-Council Bluffs, NE-IA	10.5
22	42	Charlotte-Concord-Gastonia, NC-SC	10.2
15	43	Seattle-Tacoma-Bellevue, WA	10.1
54	44	Tulsa, OK	9.9
56	44	Urban Honolulu, HI	9.9
8	46	Philadelphia-Camden-Wilmington, PA-NJ-DE-MD	9.5
52	46	Grand Rapids-Wyoming, MI	9.5
30	48	Kansas City, MO-KS	9.1
46	49	New Orleans-Metairie, LA	9.0
40	50	Jacksonville, FL	8.8
75	51	Greensboro-High Point, NC	8.5
51	52	Rochester, NY	7.4
36	53	Nashville-Davidson— Murfreesboro— Franklin, TN	7.3
61	54	Greenville-Anderson-Mauldin, SC	6.9
34	55	Indianapolis-Carmel-Anderson, IN	6.8
37	55	Virginia Beach-Norfolk-Newport News, VA-NC	6.8
44	57	Richmond, VA	6.2
16	58	Minneapolis-St. Paul-Bloomington, MN	5.9
20	58	Baltimore-Columbia-Towson, MD	5.9
33	60	Cleveland-Elyria, OH	5.8
71	61	Columbia, SC	5.6
74	61	Charleston-North Charleston, SC	5.6
42	63	Memphis, TN-MS-AR	5.5
63	64	Albany-Schenectady-Troy, NY	5.2
50	65	Buffalo-Cheektowaga-Niagara Falls, NY	5.0
45	66	Louisville/Jefferson County, KY-IN	4.8
49	67	Birmingham-Hoover, AL	4.5
14	68	Detroit-Warren-Dearborn, MI	4.4
32	69	Columbus, OH	4.2
70	70	Baton Rouge, LA	4.1
64	71	Knoxville, TN	3.8
29	72	Cincinnati, OH-KY-IN	3.2
21	73	St. Louis, MO-IL	3.1
73	74	Dayton, OH	2.7
26	75	Pittsburgh, PA	1.8

Percent under 18 years old, 2017

Population rank	Under 18 years old rank	Metropolitan area	Percent Under 18 years old [cols 10 and 11]
65	1	McAllen-Edinburg-Mission, TX	33.0
62	2	Bakersfield, CA	29.0
55	3	Fresno, CA	28.5
48	4	Salt Lake City, UT	27.8
68	5	El Paso, TX	27.5
5	6	Houston-The Woodlands-Sugar Land, TX	26.7
4	7	Dallas-Fort Worth-Arlington, TX	26.2
13	8	Riverside-San Bernardino-Ontario, CA	25.9
59	9	Omaha-Council Bluffs, NE-IA	25.8
24	10	San Antonio-New Braunfels, TX	25.5
42	11	Memphis, TN-MS-AR	24.9
54	11	Tulsa, OK	24.9
9	13	Atlanta-Sandy Springs-Roswell, GA	24.8
34	13	Indianapolis-Carmel-Anderson, IN	24.8
41	13	Oklahoma City, OK	24.8
30	16	Kansas City, MO-KS	24.4
43	16	Raleigh, NC	24.4
11	18	Phoenix-Mesa-Scottsdale, AZ	24.2
52	19	Grand Rapids-Wyoming, MI	24.1
22	20	Charlotte-Concord-Gastonia, NC-SC	24.0
16	21	Minneapolis-St. Paul-Bloomington, MN	23.7
32	21	Columbus, OH	23.7
29	23	Cincinnati, OH-KY-IN	23.6
70	23	Baton Rouge, LA	23.6
31	25	Austin-Round Rock, TX	23.4
28	26	Las Vegas-Henderson-Paradise, NV	23.3
36	26	Nashville-Davidson— Murfreesboro— Franklin, TN	23.3
67	28	Oxnard-Thousand Oaks-Ventura, CA	23.2
39	29	Milwaukee-Waukesha-West Allis, WI	23.1
3	30	Chicago-Naperville-Elgin, IL-IN-WI	23.0
6	30	Washington-Arlington-Alexandria, DC-VA-MD-WV	23.0
27	30	Sacramento— Roseville— Arden-Arcade, CA	23.0
49	30	Birmingham-Hoover, AL	23.0
19	34	Denver-Aurora-Lakewood, CO	22.8
57	35	Bridgeport-Stamford-Norwalk, CT	22.7
45	36	Louisville/Jefferson County, KY-IN	22.6
40	37	Jacksonville, FL	22.5
61	37	Greenville-Anderson-Mauldin, SC	22.5
60	39	Albuquerque, NM	22.4
14	40	Detroit-Warren-Dearborn, MI	22.3
21	40	St. Louis, MO-IL	22.3
35	40	San Jose-Sunnyvale-Santa Clara, CA	22.3
46	40	New Orleans-Metairie, LA	22.3
75	40	Greensboro-High Point, NC	22.3
71	45	Columbia, SC	22.2
23	46	Orlando-Kissimmee-Sanford, FL	22.1
37	46	Virginia Beach-Norfolk-Newport News, VA-NC	22.1
20	48	Baltimore-Columbia-Towson, MD	22.0
73	48	Dayton, OH	22.0
74	48	Charleston-North Charleston, SC	22.0
2	51	Los Angeles-Long Beach-Anaheim, CA	21.9
17	51	San Diego-Carlsbad, CA	21.9
8	53	Philadelphia-Camden-Wilmington, PA-NJ-DE-MD	21.8
44	53	Richmond, VA	21.8
25	55	Portland-Vancouver-Hillsboro, OR-WA	21.7
15	56	Seattle-Tacoma-Bellevue, WA	21.6
1	57	New York-Newark-Jersey City, NY-NJ-PA	21.5
33	58	Cleveland-Elyria, OH	21.3
53	59	Tucson, AZ	21.2
56	59	Urban Honolulu, HI	21.2
69	59	Allentown-Bethlehem-Easton, PA-NJ	21.2
58	62	Worcester, MA-CT	21.0
64	63	Knoxville, TN	20.8
51	64	Rochester, NY	20.7
50	65	Buffalo-Cheektowaga-Niagara Falls, NY	20.4
66	65	New Haven-Milford, CT	20.4
7	67	Miami-Fort Lauderdale-West Palm Beach, FL	20.3
47	68	Hartford-West Hartford-East Hartford, CT	20.2
18	69	Tampa-St. Petersburg-Clearwater, FL	20.1
38	70	Providence-Warwick, RI-MA	20.0
10	71	Boston-Cambridge-Newton, MA-NH	19.9
12	71	San Francisco-Oakland-Hayward, CA	19.9
63	73	Albany-Schenectady-Troy, NY	19.7
26	74	Pittsburgh, PA	19.0
72	75	North Port-Sarasota-Bradenton, FL	16.4

75 Largest Metropolitan Areas by 2017 Population
Selected Rankings

Percent 65 years old and over, 2017				Percent female-headed family households, 2016			
Population rank	65 years old and over rank	Metropolitan area	Percent 65 years old and over [cols 17 + 18]	Population rank	Female households rank	Metropolitan area	Percent female households [col 30]
72	1	North Port-Sarasota-Bradenton, FL	31.7	65	1	McAllen-Edinburg-Mission, TX	22.3
18	2	Tampa-St. Petersburg-Clearwater, FL	19.5	68	2	El Paso, TX	19.7
26	2	Pittsburgh, PA	19.5	42	3	Memphis, TN-MS-AR	18.5
53	4	Tucson, AZ	19.2	55	4	Fresno, CA	17.5
33	5	Cleveland-Elyria, OH	18.1	62	5	Bakersfield, CA	16.2
7	6	Miami-Fort Lauderdale-West Palm Beach, FL	17.9	70	6	Baton Rouge, LA	15.9
64	6	Knoxville, TN	17.9	75	6	Greensboro-High Point, NC	15.9
50	8	Buffalo-Cheektowaga-Niagara Falls, NY	17.7	7	8	Miami-Fort Lauderdale-West Palm Beach, FL	15.8
69	8	Allentown-Bethlehem-Easton, PA-NJ	17.7	46	8	New Orleans-Metairie, LA	15.8
73	10	Dayton, OH	17.6	24	10	San Antonio-New Braunfels, TX	15.3
51	11	Rochester, NY	17.3	71	10	Columbia, SC	15.3
56	12	Urban Honolulu, HI	17.2	13	12	Riverside-San Bernardino-Ontario, CA	15.2
47	13	Hartford-West Hartford-East Hartford, CT	17.0	37	13	Virginia Beach-Norfolk-Newport News, VA-NC	15.1
63	13	Albany-Schenectady-Troy, NY	17.0	49	14	Birmingham-Hoover, AL	15.0
66	15	New Haven-Milford, CT	16.9	9	15	Atlanta-Sandy Springs-Roswell, GA	14.8
38	16	Providence-Warwick, RI-MA	16.7	23	16	Orlando-Kissimmee-Sanford, FL	14.6
61	17	Greenville-Anderson-Mauldin, SC	16.2	20	17	Baltimore-Columbia-Towson, MD	14.5
21	18	St. Louis, MO-IL	16.1	1	18	New York-Newark-Jersey City, NY-NJ-PA	14.4
60	18	Albuquerque, NM	16.1	5	18	Houston-The Woodlands-Sugar Land, TX	14.4
14	20	Detroit-Warren-Dearborn, MI	16.0	14	20	Detroit-Warren-Dearborn, MI	14.2
75	21	Greensboro-High Point, NC	15.9	2	21	Los Angeles-Long Beach-Anaheim, CA	14.1
49	22	Birmingham-Hoover, AL	15.7	28	21	Las Vegas-Henderson-Paradise, NV	14.1
8	23	Philadelphia-Camden-Wilmington, PA-NJ-DE-MD	15.6	8	23	Philadelphia-Camden-Wilmington, PA-NJ-DE-MD	14.0
45	23	Louisville/Jefferson County, KY-IN	15.6	33	23	Cleveland-Elyria, OH	14.0
57	25	Bridgeport-Stamford-Norwalk, CT	15.5	66	23	New Haven-Milford, CT	14.0
40	26	Jacksonville, FL	15.4	60	26	Albuquerque, NM	13.9
58	26	Worcester, MA-CT	15.4	61	26	Greenville-Anderson-Mauldin, SC	13.9
1	28	New York-Newark-Jersey City, NY-NJ-PA	15.3	38	28	Providence-Warwick, RI-MA	13.8
10	28	Boston-Cambridge-Newton, MA-NH	15.3	53	29	Tucson, AZ	13.7
11	28	Phoenix-Mesa-Scottsdale, AZ	15.3	44	30	Richmond, VA	13.6
39	31	Milwaukee-Waukesha-West Allis, WI	15.2	4	31	Dallas-Fort Worth-Arlington, TX	13.5
46	31	New Orleans-Metairie, LA	15.2	51	32	Rochester, NY	13.4
12	33	San Francisco-Oakland-Hayward, CA	15.1	21	33	St. Louis, MO-IL	13.3
20	33	Baltimore-Columbia-Towson, MD	15.1	50	34	Buffalo-Cheektowaga-Niagara Falls, NY	13.2
44	33	Richmond, VA	15.1	3	35	Chicago-Naperville-Elgin, IL-IN-WI	13.1
54	33	Tulsa, OK	15.1	40	35	Jacksonville, FL	13.1
67	37	Oxnard-Thousand Oaks-Ventura, CA	15.0	47	35	Hartford-West Hartford-East Hartford, CT	13.1
27	38	Sacramento— Roseville— Arden-Arcade, CA	14.9	39	38	Milwaukee-Waukesha-West Allis, WI	12.9
29	39	Cincinnati, OH-KY-IN	14.8	73	38	Dayton, OH	12.9
74	40	Charleston-North Charleston, SC	14.7	29	40	Cincinnati, OH-KY-IN	12.8
23	41	Orlando-Kissimmee-Sanford, FL	14.6	54	40	Tulsa, OK	12.8
25	42	Portland-Vancouver-Hillsboro, OR-WA	14.4	22	42	Charlotte-Concord-Gastonia, NC-SC	12.7
28	42	Las Vegas-Henderson-Paradise, NV	14.4	74	42	Charleston-North Charleston, SC	12.7
30	42	Kansas City, MO-KS	14.4	32	44	Columbus, OH	12.6
71	42	Columbia, SC	14.4	45	44	Louisville/Jefferson County, KY-IN	12.6
3	46	Chicago-Naperville-Elgin, IL-IN-WI	14.2	11	46	Phoenix-Mesa-Scottsdale, AZ	12.4
37	46	Virginia Beach-Norfolk-Newport News, VA-NC	14.2	36	46	Nashville-Davidson— Murfreesboro— Franklin, TN	12.4
52	48	Grand Rapids-Wyoming, MI	14.1	58	46	Worcester, MA-CT	12.4
16	49	Minneapolis-St. Paul-Bloomington, MN	13.6	69	46	Allentown-Bethlehem-Easton, PA-NJ	12.4
17	49	San Diego-Carlsbad, CA	13.6	27	50	Sacramento— Roseville— Arden-Arcade, CA	12.3
70	49	Baton Rouge, LA	13.6	34	50	Indianapolis-Carmel-Anderson, IN	12.3
2	52	Los Angeles-Long Beach-Anaheim, CA	13.5	18	52	Tampa-St. Petersburg-Clearwater, FL	12.2
41	52	Oklahoma City, OK	13.5	57	52	Bridgeport-Stamford-Norwalk, CT	12.2
42	52	Memphis, TN-MS-AR	13.5	17	54	San Diego-Carlsbad, CA	12.1
34	55	Indianapolis-Carmel-Anderson, IN	13.4	67	55	Oxnard-Thousand Oaks-Ventura, CA	12.0
59	55	Omaha-Council Bluffs, NE-IA	13.4	6	56	Washington-Arlington-Alexandria, DC-VA-MD-WV	11.9
22	57	Charlotte-Concord-Gastonia, NC-SC	13.3	30	57	Kansas City, MO-KS	11.8
15	58	Seattle-Tacoma-Bellevue, WA	13.1	10	58	Boston-Cambridge-Newton, MA-NH	11.7
35	58	San Jose-Sunnyvale-Santa Clara, CA	13.1	41	58	Oklahoma City, OK	11.7
36	60	Nashville-Davidson— Murfreesboro— Franklin, TN	13.0	43	60	Raleigh, NC	11.6
32	61	Columbus, OH	12.9	59	61	Omaha-Council Bluffs, NE-IA	11.5
24	62	San Antonio-New Braunfels, TX	12.8	48	62	Salt Lake City, UT	11.4
6	63	Washington-Arlington-Alexandria, DC-VA-MD-WV	12.7	56	62	Urban Honolulu, HI	11.4
13	63	Riverside-San Bernardino-Ontario, CA	12.7	63	64	Albany-Schenectady-Troy, NY	11.2
19	65	Denver-Aurora-Lakewood, CO	12.6	12	65	San Francisco-Oakland-Hayward, CA	10.5
55	66	Fresno, CA	12.0	31	66	Austin-Round Rock, TX	10.4
68	66	El Paso, TX	12.0	52	66	Grand Rapids-Wyoming, MI	10.4
9	68	Atlanta-Sandy Springs-Roswell, GA	11.9	26	68	Pittsburgh, PA	10.3
43	69	Raleigh, NC	11.8	35	69	San Jose-Sunnyvale-Santa Clara, CA	10.2
4	70	Dallas-Fort Worth-Arlington, TX	11.1	64	70	Knoxville, TN	10.0
5	71	Houston-The Woodlands-Sugar Land, TX	10.8	19	71	Denver-Aurora-Lakewood, CO	9.7
65	71	McAllen-Edinburg-Mission, TX	10.8	15	72	Seattle-Tacoma-Bellevue, WA	9.6
62	73	Bakersfield, CA	10.7	25	72	Portland-Vancouver-Hillsboro, OR-WA	9.6
31	74	Austin-Round Rock, TX	10.5	72	72	North Port-Sarasota-Bradenton, FL	9.6
48	74	Salt Lake City, UT	10.5	16	75	Minneapolis-St. Paul-Bloomington, MN	9.1

75 Largest Metropolitan Areas by 2017 Population
Selected Rankings

	Birth rate, 2017				Percent under 65 who have no health insurance, 2016		
Population rank	Birth rate rank	Metropolitan area	Births (per 1,000 population) [col 36]	Population rank	No health insurance rank	Metropolitan area	Percent with no health insurance [col 40]
65	1	McAllen-Edinburg-Mission, TX	18.1	65	1	McAllen-Edinburg-Mission, TX	29.7
68	2	El Paso, TX	15.7	68	2	El Paso, TX	21.2
55	3	Fresno, CA	15.4	5	3	Houston-The Woodlands-Sugar Land, TX	18.9
48	4	Salt Lake City, UT	15.3	7	4	Miami-Fort Lauderdale-West Palm Beach, FL	17.4
62	4	Bakersfield, CA	15.3	4	5	Dallas-Fort Worth-Arlington, TX	17.2
5	6	Houston-The Woodlands-Sugar Land, TX	14.9	24	6	San Antonio-New Braunfels, TX	16.4
59	7	Omaha-Council Bluffs, NE-IA	14.4	54	7	Tulsa, OK	15.5
24	8	San Antonio-New Braunfels, TX	13.9	72	8	North Port-Sarasota-Bradenton, FL	15.3
4	9	Dallas-Fort Worth-Arlington, TX	13.8	31	9	Austin-Round Rock, TX	14.5
41	9	Oklahoma City, OK	13.8	9	10	Atlanta-Sandy Springs-Roswell, GA	14.4
42	11	Memphis, TN-MS-AR	13.6	41	10	Oklahoma City, OK	14.4
54	12	Tulsa, OK	13.5	23	12	Orlando-Kissimmee-Sanford, FL	14.3
70	13	Baton Rouge, LA	13.4	18	13	Tampa-St. Petersburg-Clearwater, FL	14.1
13	14	Riverside-San Bernardino-Ontario, CA	13.3	28	14	Las Vegas-Henderson-Paradise, NV	13.5
32	14	Columbus, OH	13.3	75	15	Greensboro-High Point, NC	12.4
34	16	Indianapolis-Carmel-Anderson, IN	13.2	61	16	Greenville-Anderson-Mauldin, SC	12.2
17	17	San Diego-Carlsbad, CA	13.1	40	17	Jacksonville, FL	12.0
56	17	Urban Honolulu, HI	13.1	46	17	New Orleans-Metairie, LA	12.0
31	19	Austin-Round Rock, TX	13.0	11	19	Phoenix-Mesa-Scottsdale, AZ	11.7
36	19	Nashville-Davidson— Murfreesboro— Franklin, TN	13.0	74	20	Charleston-North Charleston, SC	11.6
6	21	Washington-Arlington-Alexandria, DC-VA-MD-WV	12.9	22	21	Charlotte-Concord-Gastonia, NC-SC	11.4
30	21	Kansas City, MO-KS	12.9	42	22	Memphis, TN-MS-AR	11.3
37	21	Virginia Beach-Norfolk-Newport News, VA-NC	12.9	53	23	Tucson, AZ	11.0
46	24	New Orleans-Metairie, LA	12.8	48	24	Salt Lake City, UT	10.7
52	24	Grand Rapids-Wyoming, MI	12.8	71	25	Columbia, SC	10.5
16	26	Minneapolis-St. Paul-Bloomington, MN	12.7	70	26	Baton Rouge, LA	10.2
11	27	Phoenix-Mesa-Scottsdale, AZ	12.6	2	27	Los Angeles-Long Beach-Anaheim, CA	10.1
9	28	Atlanta-Sandy Springs-Roswell, GA	12.5	36	28	Nashville-Davidson— Murfreesboro— Franklin, TN	10.0
28	28	Las Vegas-Henderson-Paradise, NV	12.5	43	29	Raleigh, NC	9.9
40	28	Jacksonville, FL	12.5	64	29	Knoxville, TN	9.9
74	28	Charleston-North Charleston, SC	12.5	60	31	Albuquerque, NM	9.8
15	32	Seattle-Tacoma-Bellevue, WA	12.4	49	32	Birmingham-Hoover, AL	9.7
19	32	Denver-Aurora-Lakewood, CO	12.4	67	32	Oxnard-Thousand Oaks-Ventura, CA	9.7
22	32	Charlotte-Concord-Gastonia, NC-SC	12.4	44	34	Richmond, VA	9.6
39	32	Milwaukee-Waukesha-West Allis, WI	12.4	30	35	Kansas City, MO-KS	9.5
29	36	Cincinnati, OH-KY-IN	12.3	37	35	Virginia Beach-Norfolk-Newport News, VA-NC	9.5
49	36	Birmingham-Hoover, AL	12.3	13	37	Riverside-San Bernardino-Ontario, CA	9.4
3	38	Chicago-Naperville-Elgin, IL-IN-WI	12.2	55	37	Fresno, CA	9.4
45	38	Louisville/Jefferson County, KY-IN	12.2	34	39	Indianapolis-Carmel-Anderson, IN	8.7
1	40	New York-Newark-Jersey City, NY-NJ-PA	12.1	59	40	Omaha-Council Bluffs, NE-IA	8.6
43	40	Raleigh, NC	12.1	1	41	New York-Newark-Jersey City, NY-NJ-PA	8.5
2	42	Los Angeles-Long Beach-Anaheim, CA	12.0	19	41	Denver-Aurora-Lakewood, CO	8.5
61	42	Greenville-Anderson-Mauldin, SC	12.0	3	43	Chicago-Naperville-Elgin, IL-IN-WI	8.3
73	42	Dayton, OH	12.0	6	44	Washington-Arlington-Alexandria, DC-VA-MD-WV	8.2
20	45	Baltimore-Columbia-Towson, MD	11.9	17	45	San Diego-Carlsbad, CA	8.1
35	45	San Jose-Sunnyvale-Santa Clara, CA	11.9	62	45	Bakersfield, CA	8.1
21	47	St. Louis, MO-IL	11.8	21	47	St. Louis, MO-IL	7.9
27	48	Sacramento— Roseville— Arden-Arcade, CA	11.7	57	47	Bridgeport-Stamford-Norwalk, CT	7.9
44	48	Richmond, VA	11.7	32	49	Columbus, OH	7.0
14	50	Detroit-Warren-Dearborn, MI	11.6	69	49	Allentown-Bethlehem-Easton, PA-NJ	7.0
23	50	Orlando-Kissimmee-Sanford, FL	11.6	73	49	Dayton, OH	7.0
67	50	Oxnard-Thousand Oaks-Ventura, CA	11.6	8	52	Philadelphia-Camden-Wilmington, PA-NJ-DE-MD	6.8
8	53	Philadelphia-Camden-Wilmington, PA-NJ-DE-MD	11.5	25	53	Portland-Vancouver-Hillsboro, OR-WA	6.5
25	53	Portland-Vancouver-Hillsboro, OR-WA	11.5	52	54	Grand Rapids-Wyoming, MI	6.4
71	53	Columbia, SC	11.5	14	55	Detroit-Warren-Dearborn, MI	6.2
7	56	Miami-Fort Lauderdale-West Palm Beach, FL	11.3	33	55	Cleveland-Elyria, OH	6.2
75	56	Greensboro-High Point, NC	11.3	39	55	Milwaukee-Waukesha-West Allis, WI	6.2
53	58	Tucson, AZ	11.2	45	58	Louisville/Jefferson County, KY-IN	6.1
60	58	Albuquerque, NM	11.2	15	59	Seattle-Tacoma-Bellevue, WA	6.0
12	60	San Francisco-Oakland-Hayward, CA	11.1	20	59	Baltimore-Columbia-Towson, MD	6.0
33	60	Cleveland-Elyria, OH	11.1	29	61	Cincinnati, OH-KY-IN	5.8
64	62	Knoxville, TN	10.8	27	62	Sacramento— Roseville— Arden-Arcade, CA	5.7
18	63	Tampa-St. Petersburg-Clearwater, FL	10.7	66	63	New Haven-Milford, CT	5.6
50	63	Buffalo-Cheektowaga-Niagara Falls, NY	10.7	12	64	San Francisco-Oakland-Hayward, CA	5.3
10	65	Boston-Cambridge-Newton, MA-NH	10.6	26	65	Pittsburgh, PA	5.1
51	66	Rochester, NY	10.5	35	65	San Jose-Sunnyvale-Santa Clara, CA	5.1
57	67	Bridgeport-Stamford-Norwalk, CT	10.4	51	67	Rochester, NY	5.0
58	68	Worcester, MA-CT	10.3	47	68	Hartford-West Hartford-East Hartford, CT	4.7
38	69	Providence-Warwick, RI-MA	10.2	50	69	Buffalo-Cheektowaga-Niagara Falls, NY	4.6
26	70	Pittsburgh, PA	10.1	63	69	Albany-Schenectady-Troy, NY	4.6
66	70	New Haven-Milford, CT	10.1	16	71	Minneapolis-St. Paul-Bloomington, MN	4.5
69	70	Allentown-Bethlehem-Easton, PA-NJ	10.1	38	71	Providence-Warwick, RI-MA	4.5
63	73	Albany-Schenectady-Troy, NY	10.0	56	73	Urban Honolulu, HI	3.8
47	74	Hartford-West Hartford-East Hartford, CT	9.5	10	74	Boston-Cambridge-Newton, MA-NH	3.2
72	75	North Port-Sarasota-Bradenton, FL	8.0	58	75	Worcester, MA-CT	3.1

75 Largest Metropolitan Areas by 2017 Population
Selected Rankings

	Percent college graduates (bachelor's degree or more), 2,016				Median household income, 2016		
Population rank	Percent college graduates rank	Metropolitan area	Percent college graduates [col 51]	Population rank	Median income rank	Metropolitan area	Median income (dollars) [col 55]
6	1	Washington-Arlington-Alexandria, DC-VA-MD-WV	50.2	35	1	San Jose-Sunnyvale-Santa Clara, CA	145,317
35	2	San Jose-Sunnyvale-Santa Clara, CA	50.1	57	2	Bridgeport-Stamford-Norwalk, CT	143,628
12	3	San Francisco-Oakland-Hayward, CA	48.5	12	3	San Francisco-Oakland-Hayward, CA	132,996
43	4	Raleigh, NC	47.2	6	4	Washington-Arlington-Alexandria, DC-VA-MD-WV	123,186
10	5	Boston-Cambridge-Newton, MA-NH	46.9	10	5	Boston-Cambridge-Newton, MA-NH	111,464
57	6	Bridgeport-Stamford-Norwalk, CT	46.6	1	6	New York-Newark-Jersey City, NY-NJ-PA	105,928
31	7	Austin-Round Rock, TX	42.8	67	7	Oxnard-Thousand Oaks-Ventura, CA	105,609
19	8	Denver-Aurora-Lakewood, CO	42.5	15	8	Seattle-Tacoma-Bellevue, WA	105,124
15	9	Seattle-Tacoma-Bellevue, WA	42.0	56	9	Urban Honolulu, HI	101,034
16	10	Minneapolis-St. Paul-Bloomington, MN	40.5	20	10	Baltimore-Columbia-Towson, MD	99,506
20	11	Baltimore-Columbia-Towson, MD	39.5	19	11	Denver-Aurora-Lakewood, CO	97,108
1	12	New York-Newark-Jersey City, NY-NJ-PA	39.0	31	12	Austin-Round Rock, TX	96,786
25	13	Portland-Vancouver-Hillsboro, OR-WA	38.9	17	13	San Diego-Carlsbad, CA	96,347
47	14	Hartford-West Hartford-East Hartford, CT	38.2	16	14	Minneapolis-St. Paul-Bloomington, MN	96,092
9	15	Atlanta-Sandy Springs-Roswell, GA	37.7	47	15	Hartford-West Hartford-East Hartford, CT	96,040
17	16	San Diego-Carlsbad, CA	37.4	2	16	Los Angeles-Long Beach-Anaheim, CA	95,440
63	16	Albany-Schenectady-Troy, NY	37.4	43	17	Raleigh, NC	93,733
3	18	Chicago-Naperville-Elgin, IL-IN-WI	37.2	8	18	Philadelphia-Camden-Wilmington, PA-NJ-DE-MD	91,914
8	19	Philadelphia-Camden-Wilmington, PA-NJ-DE-MD	36.7	3	19	Chicago-Naperville-Elgin, IL-IN-WI	91,648
30	19	Kansas City, MO-KS	36.7	25	20	Portland-Vancouver-Hillsboro, OR-WA	90,488
44	19	Richmond, VA	36.7	5	21	Houston-The Woodlands-Sugar Land, TX	90,011
32	22	Columbus, OH	36.0	4	22	Dallas-Fort Worth-Arlington, TX	89,027
59	23	Omaha-Council Bluffs, NE-IA	35.4	27	23	Sacramento— Roseville— Arden-Arcade, CA	88,802
66	24	New Haven-Milford, CT	35.1	48	24	Salt Lake City, UT	88,236
39	25	Milwaukee-Waukesha-West Allis, WI	34.9	58	25	Worcester, MA-CT	87,965
74	26	Charleston-North Charleston, SC	34.8	66	26	New Haven-Milford, CT	87,686
26	27	Pittsburgh, PA	34.6	9	27	Atlanta-Sandy Springs-Roswell, GA	86,775
22	28	Charlotte-Concord-Gastonia, NC-SC	34.4	44	28	Richmond, VA	85,866
56	28	Urban Honolulu, HI	34.4	63	29	Albany-Schenectady-Troy, NY	85,684
58	28	Worcester, MA-CT	34.4	69	30	Allentown-Bethlehem-Easton, PA-NJ	82,857
36	31	Nashville-Davidson— Murfreesboro— Franklin, TN	34.2	22	31	Charlotte-Concord-Gastonia, NC-SC	82,776
21	32	St. Louis, MO-IL	34.1	38	32	Providence-Warwick, RI-MA	82,478
4	33	Dallas-Fort Worth-Arlington, TX	33.9	30	33	Kansas City, MO-KS	82,261
34	34	Indianapolis-Carmel-Anderson, IN	33.8	21	34	St. Louis, MO-IL	82,171
51	35	Rochester, NY	33.7	36	35	Nashville-Davidson— Murfreesboro— Franklin, TN	82,049
67	36	Oxnard-Thousand Oaks-Ventura, CA	33.6	59	36	Omaha-Council Bluffs, NE-IA	81,667
2	37	Los Angeles-Long Beach-Anaheim, CA	33.5	39	37	Milwaukee-Waukesha-West Allis, WI	81,614
29	38	Cincinnati, OH-KY-IN	33.1	29	38	Cincinnati, OH-KY-IN	81,041
48	39	Salt Lake City, UT	33.0	32	39	Columbus, OH	80,731
71	40	Columbia, SC	32.9	37	40	Virginia Beach-Norfolk-Newport News, VA-NC	80,622
27	41	Sacramento— Roseville— Arden-Arcade, CA	32.6	11	41	Phoenix-Mesa-Scottsdale, AZ	80,436
38	42	Providence-Warwick, RI-MA	32.4	74	42	Charleston-North Charleston, SC	80,323
5	43	Houston-The Woodlands-Sugar Land, TX	32.0	14	43	Detroit-Warren-Dearborn, MI	78,705
53	44	Tucson, AZ	31.9	34	44	Indianapolis-Carmel-Anderson, IN	78,628
60	45	Albuquerque, NM	31.8	7	45	Miami-Fort Lauderdale-West Palm Beach, FL	78,621
52	46	Grand Rapids-Wyoming, MI	31.7	52	46	Grand Rapids-Wyoming, MI	77,597
50	47	Buffalo-Cheektowaga-Niagara Falls, NY	31.5	72	47	North Port-Sarasota-Bradenton, FL	77,565
37	48	Virginia Beach-Norfolk-Newport News, VA-NC	31.4	40	48	Jacksonville, FL	77,169
23	49	Orlando-Kissimmee-Sanford, FL	30.9	13	49	Riverside-San Bernardino-Ontario, CA	76,397
72	49	North Port-Sarasota-Bradenton, FL	30.9	70	50	Baton Rouge, LA	76,112
11	51	Phoenix-Mesa-Scottsdale, AZ	30.8	24	51	San Antonio-New Braunfels, TX	75,910
40	52	Jacksonville, FL	30.7	26	52	Pittsburgh, PA	75,705
7	53	Miami-Fort Lauderdale-West Palm Beach, FL	30.5	45	53	Louisville/Jefferson County, KY-IN	74,931
14	54	Detroit-Warren-Dearborn, MI	30.4	33	54	Cleveland-Elyria, OH	74,213
33	55	Cleveland-Elyria, OH	30.3	49	55	Birmingham-Hoover, AL	74,082
49	56	Birmingham-Hoover, AL	29.9	41	56	Oklahoma City, OK	73,463
41	57	Oklahoma City, OK	29.8	51	57	Rochester, NY	73,324
46	58	New Orleans-Metairie, LA	29.4	28	58	Las Vegas-Henderson-Paradise, NV	72,277
64	59	Knoxville, TN	29.2	50	59	Buffalo-Cheektowaga-Niagara Falls, NY	72,118
18	60	Tampa-St. Petersburg-Clearwater, FL	28.8	23	60	Orlando-Kissimmee-Sanford, FL	71,881
61	61	Greenville-Anderson-Mauldin, SC	28.7	18	61	Tampa-St. Petersburg-Clearwater, FL	71,830
69	62	Allentown-Bethlehem-Easton, PA-NJ	28.5	46	62	New Orleans-Metairie, LA	71,718
75	63	Greensboro-High Point, NC	28.4	54	63	Tulsa, OK	70,843
45	64	Louisville/Jefferson County, KY-IN	28.3	42	64	Memphis, TN-MS-AR	70,148
24	65	San Antonio-New Braunfels, TX	27.8	71	65	Columbia, SC	69,895
42	66	Memphis, TN-MS-AR	27.5	73	66	Dayton, OH	69,568
73	67	Dayton, OH	27.4	61	67	Greenville-Anderson-Mauldin, SC	69,567
54	68	Tulsa, OK	27.2	55	68	Fresno, CA	68,967
70	69	Baton Rouge, LA	26.9	60	69	Albuquerque, NM	68,558
28	70	Las Vegas-Henderson-Paradise, NV	23.3	64	70	Knoxville, TN	68,038
68	71	El Paso, TX	21.9	62	71	Bakersfield, CA	67,594
13	72	Riverside-San Bernardino-Ontario, CA	21.0	53	72	Tucson, AZ	65,881
55	73	Fresno, CA	20.2	75	73	Greensboro-High Point, NC	64,245
65	74	McAllen-Edinburg-Mission, TX	18.3	68	74	El Paso, TX	57,013
62	75	Bakersfield, CA	16.3	65	75	McAllen-Edinburg-Mission, TX	53,230

75 Metropolitan Areas with Highest Agricultural Sales
Selected Rankings

	Value of agricultural products sold, 2012				Number of farms, 2012	
Value of sales rank	Metropolitan area	Value of sales (millions of dollars) [col 125]	Value of sales rank	Number of farms rank	Metropolitan area	Number of farms [col 113]
1	Fresno, CA	4,973.0	56	1	Dallas-Fort Worth-Arlington, TX	29,659
2	Visalia-Porterville, CA	4,017.1	9	2	Minneapolis-St. Paul-Bloomington, MN	13,251
3	Bakersfield, CA	3,999.0	51	3	Kansas City, MO-KS	12,757
4	Salinas, CA	2,979.7	26	4	St. Louis, MO-IL	11,270
5	Merced, CA	2,967.5	35	5	Portland-Vancouver-Hillsboro, OR-WA	10,838
6	Stockton-Lodi, CA	2,250.2	28	6	Columbus, OH	8,198
7	Modesto, CA	2,228.1	32	7	Madison, WI	7,446
8	Chicago-Naperville-Elgin, IL-IN-WI	2,187.2	8	8	Chicago-Naperville-Elgin, IL-IN-WI	6,841
9	Minneapolis-St. Paul-Bloomington, MN	2,169.8	24	9	Fayetteville-Springdale-Rogers, AR-M	6,835
10	Phoenix-Mesa-Scottsdale, AZ	1,931.2	25	10	Philadelphia-Camden-Wilmington, PA-N	6,543
11	El Centro, CA	1,888.6	36	11	Indianapolis-Carmel-Anderson, IN	6,205
12	Greeley, CO	1,860.7	16	12	Omaha-Council Bluffs, NE-IA	6,055
13	Hanford-Corcoran, CA	1,829.2	58	13	San Diego-Carlsbad, CA	5,732
14	Kennewick-Richland, WA	1,663.2	1	14	Fresno, CA	5,683
15	Miami-Fort Lauderdale-West Palm Beac	1,650.7	21	15	Lancaster, PA	5,657
16	Omaha-Council Bluffs, NE-IA	1,649.3	49	16	Wichita, KS	5,345
17	Yakima, WA	1,645.5	33	17	Boise City, ID	5,077
18	Riverside-San Bernardino-Ontario, CA	1,621.2	42	18	Sacramento— Roseville— Arden-Arcade,	5,076
19	Madera, CA	1,602.8	15	19	Miami-Fort Lauderdale-West Palm Beac	4,978
20	Salisbury, MD-DE	1,575.7	2	20	Visalia-Porterville, CA	4,931
21	Lancaster, PA	1,475.0	48	21	Des Moines-West Des Moines, IA	4,898
22	Sioux City, IA-NE-SD	1,460.1	30	22	Grand Rapids-Wyoming, MI	4,680
23	Oxnard-Thousand Oaks-Ventura, CA	1,440.1	38	23	St. Cloud, MN	4,459
24	Fayetteville-Springdale-Rogers, AR-M	1,356.1	44	24	Rochester, NY	4,268
25	Philadelphia-Camden-Wilmington, PA-N	1,264.9	31	25	Rochester, MN	4,233
26	St. Louis, MO-IL	1,235.6	18	26	Riverside-San Bernardino-Ontario, CA	4,198
27	Grand Island, NE	1,227.8	64	27	Jackson, MS	4,186
28	Columbus, OH	1,180.0	7	28	Modesto, CA	4,143
29	Santa Maria-Santa Barbara, CA	1,177.9	61	29	Memphis, TN-MS-AR	3,934
30	Grand Rapids-Wyoming, MI	1,120.3	57	30	Salem, OR	3,710
31	Rochester, MN	1,111.6	46	31	Cedar Rapids, IA	3,678
32	Madison, WI	1,081.6	22	32	Sioux City, IA-NE-SD	3,644
33	Boise City, ID	1,071.7	43	33	Peoria, IL	3,605
34	Grand Forks, ND-MN	1,023.3	6	34	Stockton-Lodi, CA	3,580
35	Portland-Vancouver-Hillsboro, OR-WA	1,008.7	39	35	Santa Rosa, CA	3,579
36	Indianapolis-Carmel-Anderson, IN	985.1	12	36	Greeley, CO	3,525
37	Yuma, AZ	985.0	41	37	Davenport-Moline-Rock Island, IA-IL	3,513
38	St. Cloud, MN	976.0	53	38	Sioux Falls, SD	3,418
39	Santa Rosa, CA	974.4	10	39	Phoenix-Mesa-Scottsdale, AZ	3,417
40	Fargo, ND-MN	965.2	17	40	Yakima, WA	3,143
41	Davenport-Moline-Rock Island, IA-IL	964.4	73	41	Orlando-Kissimmee-Sanford, FL	3,123
42	Sacramento— Roseville— Arden-Arcade,	961.8	66	42	Columbia, SC	3,085
43	Peoria, IL	960.7	55	43	Green Bay, WI	2,774
44	Rochester, NY	930.7	60	44	San Luis Obispo-Paso Robles-Arroyo G	2,666
45	Waterloo-Cedar Falls, IA	921.7	45	45	Waterloo-Cedar Falls, IA	2,643
46	Cedar Rapids, IA	918.4	5	46	Merced, CA	2,486
47	Mankato-North Mankato, MN	892.1	52	47	Iowa City, IA	2,481
48	Des Moines-West Des Moines, IA	891.6	14	48	Kennewick-Richland, WA	2,392
49	Wichita, KS	864.4	20	49	Salisbury, MD-DE	2,384
50	Champaign-Urbana, IL	802.9	69	50	Bismarck, ND	2,367
51	Kansas City, MO-KS	785.7	27	51	Grand Island, NE	2,339
52	Iowa City, IA	785.1	34	52	Grand Forks, ND-MN	2,292
53	Sioux Falls, SD	781.7	50	53	Champaign-Urbana, IL	2,284
54	Amarillo, TX	776.4	59	54	Yuba City, CA	2,153
55	Green Bay, WI	750.0	23	55	Oxnard-Thousand Oaks-Ventura, CA	2,150
56	Dallas-Fort Worth-Arlington, TX	743.8	71	56	Chico, CA	2,056
57	Salem, OR	742.7	75	57	Reading, PA	2,039
58	San Diego-Carlsbad, CA	726.0	63	58	Bloomington, IL	2,000
59	Yuba City, CA	701.6	54	59	Amarillo, TX	1,976
60	San Luis Obispo-Paso Robles-Arroyo G	665.0	3	60	Bakersfield, CA	1,938
61	Memphis, TN-MS-AR	661.4	62	61	Harrisonburg, VA	1,902
62	Harrisonburg, VA	659.0	47	62	Mankato-North Mankato, MN	1,834
63	Bloomington, IL	655.9	40	63	Fargo, ND-MN	1,772
64	Jackson, MS	633.0	74	64	Napa, CA	1,685
65	Lafayette-West Lafayette, IN	583.0	29	65	Santa Maria-Santa Barbara, CA	1,597
66	Columbia, SC	578.6	65	66	Lafayette-West Lafayette, IN	1,574
67	Goldsboro, NC	577.2	19	67	Madera, CA	1,507
68	Santa Cruz-Watsonville, CA	565.8	4	68	Salinas, CA	1,179
69	Bismarck, ND	553.1	13	69	Hanford-Corcoran, CA	1,056
70	Jonesboro, AR	549.0	72	70	Pine Bluff, AR	1,032
71	Chico, CA	541.3	70	71	Jonesboro, AR	980
72	Pine Bluff, AR	540.5	68	72	Santa Cruz-Watsonville, CA	667
73	Orlando-Kissimmee-Sanford, FL	539.8	67	73	Goldsboro, NC	563
74	Napa, CA	536.1	37	74	Yuma, AZ	562
75	Reading, PA	528.7	11	75	El Centro, CA	421

75 Metropolitan Areas with Highest Agricultural Sales
Selected Rankings

	Land in farms, 2012				Average value of agricultural land and buildings per acre, 2012		
Value of sales rank	Land in farms rank	Metropolitan area	Land in farms (1,000 acres) [col 117]	Value of sales rank	Value per Acre rank	Metropolitan area	Value per acre (1,000 acres) [col 123]
56	1	Dallas-Fort Worth-Arlington, TX	4,075	74	1	Napa, CA	21,801
69	2	Bismarck, ND	3,139	58	2	San Diego-Carlsbad, CA	17,964
51	3	Kansas City, MO-KS	3,124	23	3	Oxnard-Thousand Oaks-Ventura, CA	15,621
26	4	St. Louis, MO-IL	2,912	39	4	Santa Rosa, CA	14,620
54	5	Amarillo, TX	2,889	21	5	Lancaster, PA	12,529
49	6	Wichita, KS	2,856	68	6	Santa Cruz-Watsonville, CA	12,390
9	7	Minneapolis-St. Paul-Bloomington, MN	2,598	18	7	Riverside-San Bernardino-Ontario, CA	10,807
16	8	Omaha-Council Bluffs, NE-IA	2,373	25	8	Philadelphia-Camden-Wilmington, PA-N	10,682
3	9	Bakersfield, CA	2,330	35	9	Portland-Vancouver-Hillsboro, OR-WA	10,520
8	10	Chicago-Naperville-Elgin, IL-IN-WI	2,232	6	10	Stockton-Lodi, CA	10,090
12	11	Greeley, CO	1,956	15	11	Miami-Fort Lauderdale-West Palm Beac	9,911
34	12	Grand Forks, ND-MN	1,911	7	12	Modesto, CA	9,636
17	13	Yakima, WA	1,780	75	13	Reading, PA	8,859
28	14	Columbus, OH	1,746	1	14	Fresno, CA	8,286
22	15	Sioux City, IA-NE-SD	1,733	50	15	Champaign-Urbana, IL	8,014
1	16	Fresno, CA	1,721	63	16	Bloomington, IL	7,961
40	17	Fargo, ND-MN	1,718	45	17	Waterloo-Cedar Falls, IA	7,913
36	18	Indianapolis-Carmel-Anderson, IN	1,689	5	18	Merced, CA	7,737
10	19	Phoenix-Mesa-Scottsdale, AZ	1,651	19	19	Madera, CA	7,614
61	20	Memphis, TN-MS-AR	1,573	71	20	Chico, CA	7,599
53	21	Sioux Falls, SD	1,521	2	21	Visalia-Porterville, CA	7,535
32	22	Madison, WI	1,466	29	22	Santa Maria-Santa Barbara, CA	7,365
33	23	Boise City, ID	1,376	57	23	Salem, OR	7,337
48	24	Des Moines-West Des Moines, IA	1,371	43	24	Peoria, IL	7,332
60	25	San Luis Obispo-Paso Robles-Arroyo G	1,339	8	25	Chicago-Naperville-Elgin, IL-IN-WI	7,285
14	26	Kennewick-Richland, WA	1,329	37	26	Yuma, AZ	7,220
43	27	Peoria, IL	1,288	62	27	Harrisonburg, VA	7,055
4	28	Salinas, CA	1,268	11	28	El Centro, CA	7,002
2	29	Visalia-Porterville, CA	1,239	20	29	Salisbury, MD-DE	6,943
50	30	Champaign-Urbana, IL	1,184	46	30	Cedar Rapids, IA	6,910
27	31	Grand Island, NE	1,181	42	31	Sacramento— Roseville— Arden-Arcade,	6,892
31	32	Rochester, MN	1,158	41	32	Davenport-Moline-Rock Island, IA-IL	6,834
64	33	Jackson, MS	1,156	65	33	Lafayette-West Lafayette, IN	6,657
41	34	Davenport-Moline-Rock Island, IA-IL	1,101	52	34	Iowa City, IA	6,496
46	35	Cedar Rapids, IA	1,075	47	35	Mankato-North Mankato, MN	6,445
24	36	Fayetteville-Springdale-Rogers, AR-M	1,073	59	36	Yuba City, CA	6,343
5	37	Merced, CA	979	16	37	Omaha-Council Bluffs, NE-IA	6,064
38	38	St. Cloud, MN	946	13	38	Hanford-Corcoran, CA	6,031
42	39	Sacramento— Roseville— Arden-Arcade,	927	48	39	Des Moines-West Des Moines, IA	5,875
44	39	Rochester, NY	927	22	40	Sioux City, IA-NE-SD	5,823
63	41	Bloomington, IL	888	36	41	Indianapolis-Carmel-Anderson, IN	5,724
45	42	Waterloo-Cedar Falls, IA	886	73	42	Orlando-Kissimmee-Sanford, FL	5,374
73	43	Orlando-Kissimmee-Sanford, FL	853	26	43	St. Louis, MO-IL	5,260
6	44	Stockton-Lodi, CA	787	9	44	Minneapolis-St. Paul-Bloomington, MN	5,180
7	45	Modesto, CA	768	31	45	Rochester, MN	5,117
30	46	Grand Rapids-Wyoming, MI	746	32	46	Madison, WI	5,002
70	47	Jonesboro, AR	723	28	47	Columbus, OH	4,928
29	48	Santa Maria-Santa Barbara, CA	701	4	48	Salinas, CA	4,893
65	49	Lafayette-West Lafayette, IN	679	53	49	Sioux Falls, SD	4,792
13	50	Hanford-Corcoran, CA	674	30	50	Grand Rapids-Wyoming, MI	4,790
19	51	Madera, CA	654	27	51	Grand Island, NE	4,451
25	52	Philadelphia-Camden-Wilmington, PA-N	653	3	52	Bakersfield, CA	4,435
47	53	Mankato-North Mankato, MN	651	55	53	Green Bay, WI	4,333
35	54	Portland-Vancouver-Hillsboro, OR-WA	644	56	54	Dallas-Fort Worth-Arlington, TX	4,260
52	55	Iowa City, IA	643	60	55	San Luis Obispo-Paso Robles-Arroyo G	4,212
15	56	Miami-Fort Lauderdale-West Palm Beac	610	67	56	Goldsboro, NC	4,124
39	57	Santa Rosa, CA	590	38	57	St. Cloud, MN	3,808
59	58	Yuba City, CA	563	24	58	Fayetteville-Springdale-Rogers, AR-M	3,541
55	59	Green Bay, WI	547	10	59	Phoenix-Mesa-Scottsdale, AZ	3,326
66	60	Columbia, SC	522	66	60	Columbia, SC	3,177
20	61	Salisbury, MD-DE	520	70	61	Jonesboro, AR	3,134
72	62	Pine Bluff, AR	519	40	62	Fargo, ND-MN	3,097
11	63	El Centro, CA	516	51	63	Kansas City, MO-KS	3,062
21	64	Lancaster, PA	439	44	64	Rochester, NY	3,055
57	65	Salem, OR	431	72	65	Pine Bluff, AR	2,912
18	66	Riverside-San Bernardino-Ontario, CA	421	14	66	Kennewick-Richland, WA	2,827
71	67	Chico, CA	381	33	67	Boise City, ID	2,809
23	68	Oxnard-Thousand Oaks-Ventura, CA	281	61	68	Memphis, TN-MS-AR	2,682
74	69	Napa, CA	253	34	69	Grand Forks, ND-MN	2,559
75	70	Reading, PA	234	64	70	Jackson, MS	2,409
58	71	San Diego-Carlsbad, CA	222	12	71	Greeley, CO	1,979
62	71	Harrisonburg, VA	222	49	72	Wichita, KS	1,907
37	73	Yuma, AZ	215	17	73	Yakima, WA	1,803
67	74	Goldsboro, NC	191	69	74	Bismarck, ND	1,116
68	75	Santa Cruz-Watsonville, CA	100	54	75	Amarillo, TX	788

Table C. Metropolitan Areas — **Land Area and Population**

CBSA code[1]	Area name	Population, 2017				Population characteristics, 2017										
						Race alone or in combination, not Hispanic or Latino (percent)					Age (percent)					
		Land area[2] (sq. mi)	Total persons 2017	Rank	Per square mile	White	Black	American Indian, Alaska Native	Asian and Pacific Islander	Percent Hispanic or Latino[3]	Under 5 years	5 to 17 years	18 to 24 years	25 to 34 years	35 to 44 years	45 to 54 years
		1	2	3	4	5	6	7	8	9	10	11	12	13	14	15

1. CBSA = Core Based Statistical Area. DIV = Metropolitan Division. See Appendix A for explanation. See Appendix B for list of metropolitan areas or temporarily covered by water.   2.   Dry land or land partially or temporarily covered by water.   3.   May be of any race.

Table C. Metropolitan Areas — **Population and Households**

Area name	Population, 2017 (cont.)				Population change and components of change, 2000-2017							Households, 2016				
	Age (percent) (cont.)				Total persons		Percent change		Components of change, 2010-2017					Percent		
	55 to 64 years	65 to 74 years	75 years and over	Percent female	2000	2010	2000-2010	2010-2017	Births	Deaths	Net Migration	Number	Persons per house-hold	Family house-holds	Female family house-holder[1]	One person
	16	17	18	19	20	21	22	23	24	25	26	27	28	29	30	31

1. No spouse present.

Table C. Metropolitan Areas — **Population, Vital Statistics, Health, and Crime**

Area name	Daytime Population, 2016		Births, 2017		Deaths, 2017		Persons under 65 with no health insurance, 2016		Medicare, 2017			Serious crimes known to police[2], 2016	
												Total	
	Persons in group quarters, 2017	Number	Employ-ment/ residence ratio	Total	Rate[1]	Number	Rate[1]	Number	Percent	Total benefici-aries	Enrolled in Original Medicare	Enrolled in Medicare Advantage	Number	Rate[3]
	32	33	34	35	36	37	38	39	40	41	42	43	44	45

1. Per 1,000 estimated resident population.   2.   Data for serious crimes have not been adjusted for underreporting; this may affect comparability between geographic areas and over time.
3. Per 100,000 population estimated by the FBI.

Table C. Metropolitan Areas — **Crime, Education, Money Income, and Poverty**

Area name	Serious crimes known to police, 2,016 (cont.)[1]		Education						Income and poverty, 2,016							
	Rate		School enrollment and attainment, 2,016				Local govern-ment expendi-tures,[5]2,013-2,014							Percent below poverty level		
			Enrollment[3]		Attainment[4] (percent)											
	Violent	Property	Total	Percent private	High school grad-uate or less	Bach-elor's degree or more	Total current expendi-tures (mil dol)	Current expendi-tures per student (dollars)	Per capita income[6] (dollars)	Mean house-hold income (dollars)	Median household income	Percent of house-holds with income of less than $50,000	Percent of house-holds with income of $200,000 or more	All persons	Children under 18 years	Age 65 years and over
	46	47	48	49	50	51	52	53	54	55	56	57	58	59	60	61

1. Data for serious crimes have not been adjusted for underreporting; this may affect comparability between geographic areas and over time.   2.   Per 100,000 population estimated by the FBI.
3. All persons 3 years old and over enrolled in nursery school through college.   4.   Persons 25 years old and over.   5.   Elementary and secondary education expenditures.   6.   Based on population estimated by the American Community Survey, 2015.

Table C. Metropolitan Areas — **Personal Income and Earnings**

Area name	Personal income, 2016										Earnings, 2016		
			Per capita[1]		Supplements to wages and salaries, employer contributions (mil dol)							Contributions for government social insurance (mil dol)	
	Total (mil dol)	Percent change, 2015-2016	Dollars	Rank	Wages and salaries (mil dol)	Pension and insurance	Government social insurance	Proprietors' income	Dividends, interest, and rent (mil dol)	Personal transfer reecipts (mil dol)	Total (mil dol)	From employee and self-employed	From employer
	62	63	64	65	66	67	68	69	70	71	72	73	74

1. Based on the resident population estimated as of July 1 of the year shown.

Table C. Metropolitan Areas — **Earnings, Social Security, and Housing**

Area name	Earnings, 2016 (cont.)									Social Security beneficiaries, December 2016			Housing units, 2017	
	Percent by selected industries											Supplemental Security Income recipients, 2016		
	Farm	Mining, quarrying, and extracting	Construction	Manufacturing	Information; professional, scientific, and technical services	Retail trade	Finance, insurance, real estate, rental and leasing	Health care and social assistance	Government	Number	Rate[1]		Total	Percent change, 2010-2017
	75	76	77	78	79	80	81	82	83	84	85	86	87	88

1. Per 1,000 resident population estimated as of July 1 of the year shown.

Table C. Metropolitan Areas — **Housing, Labor Force, and Employment**

Area name	Housing units, 2016									Civilian labor force, 2017				Civilian employment[5], 2016		
	Occupied units											Unemployment			Percent	
		Owner-occupied				Renter-occupied										
				Median owner cost as a percent of income												
	Total	Percent	Median value[1]	With a mortgage	Without a mortgage[2]	Median rent[3]	Median rent as a percent of income	Percent with Internet access		Total	Percent change, 2016-2017	Total	Rate[4]	Total	Management, business, science, and arts	Construction, production, and maintenance occupations
	89	90	91	92	93	94	95	96		97	98	99	100	101	102	103

1. Specified owner-occupied units.   2. A value of 10.0 represents 10 percent or less; a value of 50.0 represents 50 percent or more.   3. Specified renter-occupied units.
4. Overcrowded or lacking complete plumbing facilities.   5. Percent of civilian labor force.   6. Civilian employed persons 16 years old and over.

Table C. Metropolitan Areas — **Nonfarm Employment and Agriculture**

Area name	Private nonfarm establishments, employment and payroll, 2016									Agriculture, 2012			
		Employment						Annual payroll		Farms			
											Percent with:		
	Number of establishments	Total	Health care and social assistance	Manufacturing	Retail trade	Finance and insurance	Professional, scientific, and technical services	Total (mil dol)	Average per employee (dollars)	Number	Fewer than 50 acres	500 acres or more	Farm operators whose principal occupation is farming (percent)
	104	105	106	107	108	109	110	111	112	113	114	115	116

Table C. Metropolitan Areas — Population, Vital Statistics, Health, and Crime

Area name	Daytime Population, 2016			Births, 2017		Deaths, 2017		Persons under 65 with no health insurance, 2016		Medicare, 2017			Serious crimes known to police[2], 2016 — Total	
	Persons in group quarters, 2017	Number	Employment/residence ratio	Total	Rate[1]	Number	Rate[1]	Number	Percent	Total beneficiaries	Enrolled in Original Medicare	Enrolled in Medicare Advantage	Number	Rate[3]
	32	33	34	35	36	37	38	39	40	41	42	43	44	45
Abilene, TX	10,340	172,872	1.03	2,375	14.0	1,717	10.1	23,003	16.8	30,322	23,229	7,094	5,546	3,265
Akron, OH	18,158	705,034	1.01	7,342	10.4	7,138	10.1	39,103	6.8	134,933	67,502	67,431	19,824	2,818
Albany, GA	5,168	151,347	0.98	1,881	12.4	1,492	9.9	18,870	15.2	28,327	18,790	9,536	6,874	4,506
Albany, OR	1,209	120,193	0.95	1,555	12.4	1,301	10.4	7,159	7.2	29,928	14,636	15,291	3,422	2,804
Albany-Schenectady-Troy, NY	32,808	897,744	1.04	8,848	10.0	7,980	9.0	32,561	4.6	172,530	96,600	75,930	20,191	2,299
Albuquerque, NM	14,849	909,689	0.99	10,175	11.2	7,648	8.4	73,842	9.8	167,266	84,265	83,000	56,149	6,190
Alexandria, LA	7,461	156,378	1.03	2,000	13.0	1,611	10.5	15,373	12.3	31,826	25,924	5,902	8,658	5,621
Allentown-Bethlehem-Easton, PA-NJ	22,944	807,617	0.93	8,521	10.1	7,949	9.5	47,377	7.0	175,754	125,085	50,670	D	D
Altoona, PA	3,752	130,631	1.11	1,285	10.4	1,649	13.4	5,664	5.8	31,540	15,711	15,829	1,964	1,572
Amarillo, TX	9,834	262,096	0.99	3,662	13.8	2,315	8.7	38,695	17.6	41,323	32,078	9,246	11,912	4,526
Ames, IA	11,534	101,253	1.08	890	9.1	514	5.3	3,529	4.7	13,151	11,440	1,711	1,798	1,850
Anchorage, AK	10,216	400,237	0.99	6,047	15.1	2,362	5.9	48,246	13.6	49,221	48,342	879	19,145	6,066
Ann Arbor, MI	22,542	404,074	1.22	3,669	10.0	2,349	6.4	14,526	4.9	55,538	38,705	16,833	7,103	1,965
Anniston-Oxford-Jacksonville, AL	2,759	112,159	0.95	1,342	11.7	1,427	12.4	10,386	11.2	28,874	21,358	7,516	4,795	4,177
Appleton, WI	3,209	229,818	0.97	2,814	11.9	1,662	7.0	10,636	5.3	39,738	15,810	23,929	3,464	1,480
Asheville, NC	11,048	459,662	1.04	4,544	10.0	4,991	10.9	42,170	12.1	112,422	80,428	31,993	D	D
Athens-Clarke County, GA	10,825	205,476	0.99	2,219	10.6	1,403	6.7	24,958	14.8	31,812	21,303	10,509	6,457	3,150
Atlanta-Sandy Springs-Roswell, GA	86,256	5,809,080	1.01	73,810	12.5	38,540	6.5	723,573	14.4	785,780	480,231	305,548	196,965	3,402
Atlantic City-Hammonton, NJ	6,222	270,005	0.99	2,862	10.6	2,758	10.2	23,502	10.6	55,255	45,339	9,916	NA	NA
Auburn-Opelika, AL	4,894	145,249	0.82	1,947	12.0	1,048	6.5	14,359	10.5	20,419	14,042	6,377	5,053	3,157
Augusta-Richmond County, GA-SC	18,015	596,386	1.00	7,610	12.7	5,589	9.3	59,988	12.3	108,027	73,451	34,577	20,801	3,495
Austin-Round Rock, TX	42,673	2,069,963	1.01	27,400	13.0	10,609	5.0	262,133	14.5	240,913	167,791	73,122	59,012	2,872
Bakersfield, CA	32,282	892,040	1.02	13,643	15.3	6,050	6.8	61,640	8.1	112,033	70,157	41,876	37,698	4,262
Baltimore-Columbia-Towson, MD	70,742	2,777,480	0.98	33,546	11.9	25,453	9.1	138,738	6.0	470,267	412,605	57,662	97,949	3,501
Bangor, ME	7,733	157,331	1.08	1,379	9.1	1,567	10.3	14,179	12.0	36,210	27,183	9,027	3,110	2,037
Barnstable Town, MA	4,134	210,733	0.96	1,519	7.1	2,832	13.3	4,663	3.1	73,410	63,392	10,018	D	D
Baton Rouge, LA	25,613	844,833	1.03	11,159	13.4	7,077	8.5	71,227	10.2	130,390	67,263	63,129	32,517	3,903
Battle Creek, MI	4,137	142,258	1.14	1,620	12.1	1,397	10.4	7,020	6.5	29,911	20,490	9,421	5,205	3,887
Bay City, MI	1,439	93,565	0.76	1,019	9.8	1,162	11.1	5,048	6.0	25,201	17,342	7,859	2,339	2,223
Beaumont-Port Arthur, TX	18,054	413,702	1.02	5,680	13.8	4,265	10.3	59,600	17.9	72,608	44,270	28,338	13,527	3,314
Beckley, WV	5,524	120,467	0.99	1,254	10.6	1,736	14.6	6,284	6.8	30,654	21,523	9,130	3,829	3,157
Bellingham, WA	5,895	212,541	0.96	2,373	10.7	1,636	7.4	15,140	8.6	42,816	27,591	15,224	7,480	3,474
Bend-Redmond, OR	1,318	183,400	1.02	1,869	10.0	1,478	7.9	11,449	7.9	40,965	29,157	11,809	4,182	2,322
Billings, MT	3,856	170,870	1.01	2,083	12.2	1,576	9.2	11,928	8.6	32,582	24,682	7,901	6,798	3,993
Binghamton, NY	11,413	241,545	0.98	2,386	9.9	2,559	10.6	10,027	5.3	55,007	33,200	21,806	5,881	2,417
Birmingham-Hoover, AL	24,736	1,147,520	1.00	14,188	12.3	12,032	10.5	92,495	9.7	225,325	111,248	114,076	NA	NA
Bismarck, ND	4,377	131,146	0.99	1,964	14.9	1,091	8.3	6,995	6.4	22,503	17,042	5,462	4,056	3,132
Blacksburg-Christiansburg-Radford, VA	13,675	181,879	0.98	1,597	8.7	1,473	8.0	14,305	10.0	32,875	25,886	6,991	3,410	1,880
Bloomington, IL	10,854	191,665	1.04	2,272	12.1	1,392	7.4	6,796	4.4	28,856	20,526	8,328	3,414	1,806
Bloomington, IN	15,269	170,891	1.06	1,588	9.5	1,131	6.7	12,373	9.5	24,832	19,676	5,155	4,727	2,842
Bloomsburg-Berwick, PA	4,788	89,877	1.13	777	9.2	921	10.9	4,253	6.6	19,522	11,397	8,124	NA	NA
Boise City, ID	14,754	686,090	0.99	8,774	12.4	4,679	6.6	65,452	11.2	115,906	61,091	54,814	13,975	2,015
Boston-Cambridge-Newton, MA-NH	167,947	4,968,434	1.07	51,406	10.6	37,620	7.8	126,597	3.2	833,638	652,458	181,181	D	D
Boston, MA Div 14,454	80,109	2,190,194	1.19	21,842	10.8	15,747	7.8	48,069	2.9	332,609	260,027	72,582	D	D
Cambridge-Newton-Framingham, MA Div 15,764	76,222	2,367,099	1.00	25,623	10.7	18,462	7.7	56,269	2.9	416,501	317,724	98,778	34,775	1,465
Rockingham County-Strafford County, NH 40,484	11,616	411,141	0.92	3,941	9.1	3,411	7.8	22,259	6.3	84,528	74,707	9,821	6,439	1,494
Boulder, CO	11,176	358,155	1.21	2,840	8.8	1,853	5.7	19,445	7.2	52,860	31,952	20,908	8,267	2,551
Bowling Green, KY	7,571	177,781	1.04	2,172	12.4	1,457	8.3	9,132	6.5	30,235	22,770	7,467	3,944	2,317
Bremerton-Silverdale, WA	9,433	254,501	0.92	3,127	11.7	2,297	8.6	13,378	6.3	52,338	42,506	9,831	7,673	2,919
Bridgeport-Stamford-Norwalk, CT	19,811	956,523	1.03	9,921	10.4	6,774	7.1	62,457	7.9	151,113	114,757	36,357	15,574	1,664
Brownsville-Harlingen, TX	3,354	417,730	0.97	7,047	16.6	2,739	6.5	106,485	29.5	60,072	34,158	25,914	13,708	3,234
Brunswick, GA	1,588	114,996	0.98	1,283	10.9	1,208	10.2	16,205	17.3	23,976	16,812	7,164	3,954	3,391
Buffalo-Cheektowaga-Niagara Falls, NY	32,340	1,140,112	1.01	12,182	10.7	11,959	10.5	42,343	4.6	240,328	102,308	138,021	31,895	2,828
Burlington, NC	4,468	150,862	0.88	1,823	11.2	1,604	9.9	17,976	13.9	32,123	14,846	17,278	4,369	2,736
Burlington-South Burlington, VT	10,172	222,503	1.04	2,174	10.0	1,510	6.9	7,518	4.2	32,957	29,509	3,449	NA	NA
California-Lexington Park, MD	2,779	104,222	0.85	1,441	12.8	843	7.5	5,412	5.6	15,946	15,199	747	2,302	2,057
Canton-Massillon, OH	9,448	389,152	0.93	4,434	11.1	4,366	10.9	19,310	6.0	92,631	44,970	47,660	NA	NA
Cape Coral-Fort Myers, FL	8,477	711,352	0.96	6,892	9.3	7,417	10.0	88,839	17.2	178,686	119,103	59,584	14,199	1,970
Cape Girardeau, MO-IL	4,131	95,928	1.03	1,084	11.2	978	10.1	8,830	11.3	19,616	17,469	2,147	2,811	2,879
Carbondale-Marion, IL	5,979	130,974	1.09	1,524	12.1	1,232	9.8	6,576	6.5	24,229	19,132	5,097	NA	NA
Carson City, NV	2,866	61,060	1.27	572	10.4	657	12.0	5,238	12.7	15,576	13,364	2,212	1,152	2,110
Casper, WY	1,721	81,111	1.00	1,094	13.8	721	9.1	9,464	13.8	13,529	12,758	770	2,249	2,714

1. Per 1,000 estimated resident population.   2. Data for serious crimes have not been adjusted for underreporting; this may affect comparability between geographic areas and over time.
3. Per 100,000 population estimated by the FBI.

Items 32—45

Table C. Metropolitan Areas — Crime, Education, Money Income, and Poverty

Area name	Serious crimes known to police, 2,016 (cont.)[1] Rate Violent	Property	Education — Enrollment[3] Total	Percent private	High school grad-uate or less	Bach-elor's degree or more	Local govern-ment expendi-tures,[5]2,013-2,014 Total current expendi-tures (mil dol)	Current expendi-tures per student (dollars)	Income and poverty, 2,016 Per capita income[6] (dollars)	Mean house-hold income (dollars)	Median household income	Percent of house-holds with income of less than $50,000	Percent of house-holds with income of $200,000 or more	Percent below poverty level All persons	Children under 18 years	Age 65 years and over
	46	47	48	49	50	51	52	53	54	55	56	57	58	59	60	61
Abilene, TX	361	2,903	44,265	24.7	50.0	20.4	249.7	8,747	22,678	62,145	48,016	51.7	2.3	17.2	19.5	10.3
Akron, OH	253	2,565	176,592	14.5	40.7	31.0	1,092.6	11,269	29,318	70,083	51,598	48.1	4.2	13.8	19.2	5.8
Albany, GA	735	3,771	44,471	7.8	47.4	18.6	264.8	9,721	22,635	57,901	40,667	58.5	2.4	25.0	36.3	10.0
Albany, OR	114	2,690	27,452	11.9	36.1	21.7	185.7	8,265	26,902	69,891	51,310	48.9	2.3	12.4	13.8	7.4
Albany-Schenectady-Troy, NY	290	2,010	218,560	22.4	34.7	37.4	2,003.6	16,280	34,779	85,684	65,855	38.8	6.4	9.9	12.7	5.2
Albuquerque, NM	901	5,289	238,379	11.7	35.9	31.8	1,294.3	9,253	27,324	68,558	50,954	48.9	4.2	16.9	25.6	8.9
Alexandria, LA	923	4,698	38,452	16.3	52.5	19.2	252.3	9,248	23,962	62,594	42,136	55.8	3.5	19.7	26.8	17.9
Allentown-Bethlehem-Easton, PA-NJ	D	D	196,906	24.3	45.3	28.5	1,732.9	14,338	32,265	82,857	63,022	39.4	5.6	11.6	19.2	6.2
Altoona, PA	213	1,359	25,712	13.2	56.4	18.3	219.2	12,355	24,821	58,867	43,443	55.6	1.6	12.9	19.9	9.7
Amarillo, TX	593	3,933	71,166	8.1	41.8	23.7	433.3	8,694	28,376	75,315	54,478	45.0	4.7	15.0	18.4	10.5
Ames, IA	163	1,687	44,208	4.5	21.0	54.8	110.0	9,830	27,937	70,682	53,371	46.8	4.7	21.5	7.5	4.5
Anchorage, AK	1,115	4,951	104,522	11.8	31.4	32.2	1,031.6	15,563	36,479	102,233	82,203	27.7	9.4	7.2	8.6	4.9
Ann Arbor, MI	317	1,648	126,558	8.6	19.5	54.8	507.5	11,550	38,196	94,215	65,601	39.2	9.5	14.8	12.1	7.2
Anniston-Oxford-Jackson-ville, AL	895	3,283	27,731	10.4	49.5	16.5	166.0	9,003	23,818	58,992	41,687	55.7	2.1	16.3	24.9	6.2
Appleton, WI	151	1,329	58,787	12.1	37.7	27.9	394.0	10,142	32,160	79,796	63,902	38.3	3.6	7.6	11.6	4.9
Asheville, NC	D	240	93,273	18.1	36.4	33.4	468.4	8,636	29,029	66,888	50,541	49.3	3.6	13.4	19.2	8.3
Athens-Clarke County, GA	342	2,808	66,464	9.4	37.3	37.0	280.5	10,527	25,980	65,420	43,165	56.2	4.6	20.7	22.0	6.5
Atlanta-Sandy Springs-Roswell, GA	403	2,998	1,571,346	16.3	35.0	37.7	8,844.5	9,022	32,055	86,775	62,613	39.7	7.3	13.1	19.0	8.9
Atlantic City-Hammonton, NJ	NA	NA	70,981	14.7	44.6	27.6	822.8	17,934	29,158	77,520	56,778	45.5	4.9	14.4	24.2	7.3
Auburn-Opelika, AL	572	2,585	54,489	11.8	34.3	35.7	196.8	8,933	25,081	64,562	48,056	52.2	3.0	19.1	17.3	6.9
Augusta-Richmond County, GA-SC	343	3,152	144,503	13.2	45.2	24.6	842.3	8,868	25,058	64,651	48,543	51.2	3.1	18.2	28.7	8.6
Austin-Round Rock, TX	317	2,555	548,299	12.4	29.4	42.8	2,825.9	8,673	36,708	96,786	71,000	33.7	9.1	10.9	13.6	7.0
Bakersfield, CA	580	3,683	253,542	8.2	53.2	16.3	1,735.4	9,658	21,313	67,594	49,903	50.1	3.5	22.7	32.3	12.1
Baltimore-Columbia-Towson, MD	710	2,790	706,556	19.4	34.7	39.5	5,523.4	13,930	38,406	99,506	76,788	33.0	9.9	10.4	13.9	8.5
Bangor, ME	96	1,942	36,895	17.5	42.8	25.0	264.8	11,992	26,306	62,849	47,328	51.5	2.5	15.3	19.8	9.2
Barnstable Town, MA	D	1,562	38,223	15.4	30.1	43.5	441.9	17,258	40,874	91,777	67,898	37.7	7.5	6.5	9.8	3.3
Baton Rouge, LA	505	3,398	226,569	19.0	45.0	26.9	1,365.6	11,042	29,027	76,112	52,487	46.8	5.1	17.2	24.5	9.3
Battle Creek, MI	747	3,140	31,828	15.2	47.3	20.2	246.4	12,173	25,252	61,465	45,902	52.9	2.6	16.9	26.8	6.3
Bay City, MI	370	1,854	22,322	14.5	44.7	17.7	162.7	11,191	25,427	60,261	44,756	55.1	1.9	15.9	26.5	7.8
Beaumont-Port Arthur, TX	574	2,740	98,009	8.3	51.0	17.2	608.5	8,739	26,497	68,907	49,364	50.4	3.8	17.2	25.4	10.3
Beckley, WV	417	2,740	25,176	13.2	54.1	18.1	209.1	10,792	22,869	55,995	44,178	54.4	1.3	15.9	24.5	6.6
Bellingham, WA	224	3,249	60,015	14.1	33.7	32.9	267.5	10,162	28,261	71,154	56,411	44.7	3.5	15.9	10.4	11.8
Bend-Redmond, OR	152	2,171	38,314	11.4	35.8	32.8	245.9	9,802	31,790	78,473	61,870	39.8	4.3	10.7	15.0	6.2
Billings, MT	377	3,616	37,611	20.5	39.0	31.6	238.7	9,717	31,978	74,916	58,037	43.0	4.4	7.3	5.9	6.8
Binghamton, NY	289	2,128	66,170	8.2	41.9	29.0	610.7	17,525	27,610	67,745	51,360	48.5	3.1	16.0	25.1	6.7
Birmingham-Hoover, AL	NA	NA	282,094	15.5	40.2	29.9	1,654.4	9,297	29,265	74,082	52,226	47.5	4.5	13.9	19.5	9.1
Bismarck, ND	294	2,839	28,593	18.5	33.5	30.1	196.4	11,252	36,531	87,226	65,527	36.7	5.9	9.2	10.7	8.6
Blacksburg-Christiansburg-Radford, VA	198	1,682	61,331	8.2	38.4	34.9	199.2	9,787	28,783	72,205	50,950	48.1	4.3	19.3	12.4	8.0
Bloomington, IL	277	1,528	59,141	14.5	29.2	42.2	313.8	10,851	32,178	81,223	61,320	39.7	5.4	12.8	11.3	8.9
Bloomington, IN	313	2,529	62,982	8.9	36.7	38.9	156.2	9,353	26,425	64,315	43,693	54.7	4.2	23.7	21.0	5.4
Bloomsburg-Berwick, PA	NA	NA	20,322	11.4	52.5	23.6	109.5	12,542	26,551	67,173	50,038	50.0	3.7	12.8	17.8	9.4
Boise City, ID	244	1,771	185,743	14.4	34.9	31.3	764.0	6,171	27,789	73,245	55,162	45.4	3.8	12.7	14.4	12.9
Boston-Cambridge-Newton, MA-NH	D	1,399	1,235,762	29.9	31.3	46.9	10,126.4	15,316	43,044	111,464	82,380	31.3	13.1	9.6	11.8	8.8
Boston, MA Div 14,454	D	1,612	524,220	33.9	33.5	45.3	4,228.7	15,800	42,337	108,593	77,847	34.2	12.4	11.8	15.1	10.7
Cambridge-Newton-Framingham, MA Div 15,764	235	1,230	609,121	28.6	29.5	49.7	5,050.5	15,221	44,207	115,482	88,361	29.4	14.4	8.8	10.8	8.1
Rockingham County-Strafford County, NH 40,484	148	1,346	102,421	17.0	31.1	38.9	847.2	13,726	39,926	100,794	77,631	28.1	9.6	4.3	2.5	4.4
Boulder, CO	236	2,314	96,592	10.4	18.1	60.6	571.5	9,409	41,258	105,099	74,615	35.4	12.2	11.0	6.4	6.4
Bowling Green, KY	165	2,153	48,168	8.2	44.8	26.5	213.8	8,277	24,197	62,562	45,649	54.4	3.4	19.7	27.2	11.2
Bremerton-Silverdale, WA	259	2,660	58,668	13.3	29.2	31.9	360.4	10,047	34,035	85,625	69,171	34.8	5.4	10.0	11.9	5.4
Bridgeport-Stamford-Nor-walk, CT	230	1,434	255,201	25.0	32.0	46.6	2,617.7	17,962	52,344	143,628	90,123	29.9	19.2	8.6	9.9	6.3
Brownsville-Harlingen, TX	379	2,855	125,482	4.7	59.5	17.0	931.6	9,168	15,886	51,206	37,061	61.9	1.8	29.3	41.5	25.6
Brunswick, GA	372	3,019	26,585	18.5	46.6	23.1	169.6	9,410	25,684	64,202	46,014	53.4	2.3	20.9	28.1	11.5
Buffalo-Cheektowaga-Niagara Falls, NY	411	2,417	267,185	18.4	37.9	31.5	2,498.1	15,704	30,777	72,118	53,487	46.7	4.0	13.8	19.5	8.2
Burlington, NC	391	2,345	40,835	19.6	39.3	22.4	189.9	7,933	24,888	60,609	45,100	54.0	1.8	16.7	27.5	5.6
Burlington-South Burlington, VT	NA	NA	56,660	21.3	30.9	43.2	518.8	16,799	34,511	86,483	66,367	37.0	6.7	10.3	8.8	9.6
California-Lexington Park, MD	203	1,854	31,185	19.5	43.5	26.1	222.3	12,463	34,694	91,785	78,195	30.5	6.6	10.0	12.1	13.1
Canton-Massillon, OH	NA	NA	91,330	16.6	48.5	23.4	608.3	9,979	27,479	66,227	50,811	49.2	2.4	13.0	19.2	7.4
Cape Coral-Fort Myers, FL	355	1,614	141,077	14.8	43.0	28.3	772.0	8,830	29,775	74,125	52,909	46.6	4.9	12.9	22.8	7.4
Cape Girardeau, MO-IL	480	2,399	26,684	16.3	44.0	26.6	114.2	8,697	26,109	65,422	49,059	51.3	3.5	17.6	15.9	8.7
Carbondale-Marion, IL	NA	NA	34,239	9.4	33.1	30.5	201.1	11,344	24,232	55,799	41,603	57.4	1.3	18.8	19.8	10.7
Carson City, NV	288	1,822	12,265	7.9	42.2	20.4	185.0	7,807	26,358	63,623	52,196	47.5	3.0	11.0	16.0	6.6
Casper, WY	203	2,511	21,627	5.8	39.8	23.5	186.4	14,564	30,288	73,781	59,474	44.3	3.5	9.2	7.7	7.3

1. Data for serious crimes have not been adjusted for underreporting; this may affect comparability between geographic areas and over time.   2. Per 100,000 population estimated by the FBI.
3. All persons 3 years old and over enrolled in nursery school through college.   4. Persons 25 years old and over.   5. Elementary and secondary education expenditures.   6. Based on population estimated by the American Community Survey, 2015.

Table C. Metropolitan Areas — **Land Area and Population**

CBSA/ DIV Code[1]	Area name	Land area[2] 2017 (sq. mi)	Total persons 2017	Rank	Per square mile	White	Black	Amer- ican Indian, Alaska Native	Asian and Pacific Islancer	Percent Hispanic or Latino[3]	Under 5 years	5 to 17 years	18 to 24 years	25 to 34 years	35 to 44 years	45 to 54 years
			Population, 2017			Race alone or in combination, not Hispanic or Latino (percent)					Population characteristics, 2017 — Age (percent)					
		1	2	3	4	5	6	7	8	9	10	11	12	13	14	15
16,300	Cedar Rapids, IA	2,008.8	270,293	178	134.6	89.8	6.1	0.6	2.8	3.0	6.3	17.1	8.8	13.2	12.6	13.0
16,540	Chambersburg-Waynes- boro, PA	772.2	154,234	266	199.7	89.5	4.5	0.5	1.5	5.8	5.9	16.5	7.6	12.1	11.7	13.5
16,580	Champaign-Urbana, IL	1,920.8	239,124	192	124.5	73.1	12.7	0.5	10.7	5.5	5.6	13.8	21.1	14.1	10.9	10.1
16,620	Charleston, WV	1,745.1	214,406	208	122.9	91.2	7.9	0.8	1.4	1.1	5.5	15.0	7.5	11.9	12.2	12.9
16,700	Charleston-North Charles- ton, SC	2,589.4	775,831	74	299.6	66.0	26.7	0.9	2.8	5.6	6.2	15.8	8.8	15.9	13.0	12.8
16,740	Charlotte-Concord-Gastonia, NC-SC	5,064.3	2,525,305	22	498.6	62.8	23.6	0.9	4.4	10.2	6.3	17.7	8.5	14.1	13.8	14.3
16,820	Charlottesville, VA	2,224.1	233,793	194	105.1	76.4	14.8	0.7	5.3	5.2	5.2	14.1	11.9	14.1	11.8	12.4
16,860	Chattanooga, TN-GA	2,088.9	556,548	99	266.4	79.7	14.4	0.8	2.1	4.6	5.7	15.6	8.5	13.5	12.3	13.3
16,940	Cheyenne, WY	2,685.9	98,327	357	36.6	80.8	3.4	1.4	2.1	14.8	6.4	16.9	9.1	14.8	12.2	11.9
16,980	Chicago-Naperville-Elgin, IL-IN-WI	7,196.1	9,533,040	3	1,324.8	54.2	17.1	0.5	7.5	22.3	6.1	16.9	9.2	14.3	13.2	13.4
16,980	Chicago-Naperville-Arling- ton Heights, IL Div 16,974	3,450.4	7,319,978	X	2,121.5	51.1	19.1	0.4	8.4	22.6	6.1	16.5	8.9	15.1	13.4	13.3
16,980	Elgin, IL Div 20,994	1,151.5	639,400	X	555.3	61.5	6.4	0.4	4.5	28.7	6.3	18.9	10.8	12.2	13.0	13.7
16,980	Gary, IN Div 23,844	1,878.3	701,621	X	373.5	64.9	18.0	0.6	1.9	16.1	5.9	17.4	8.9	12.1	12.6	12.9
16,980	Lake County-Kenosha County, IL-WI Div 29,404	715.9	872,041	X	1,218.1	66.0	7.7	0.5	7.5	20.2	5.8	18.4	10.2	11.4	12.4	14.5
17,020	Chico, CA	1,636.5	229,294	196	140.1	75.5	2.6	3.0	6.5	16.4	5.5	14.5	14.4	13.0	10.7	10.8
17,140	Cincinnati, OH-KY-IN	4,165.7	2,179,082	29	523.1	81.3	13.7	0.6	3.2	3.2	6.3	17.3	9.3	13.4	12.2	13.3
17,300	Clarksville, TN-KY	1,698.1	285,042	167	167.9	68.4	21.5	1.2	3.7	9.1	8.5	18.1	12.1	18.1	12.4	10.7
17,420	Cleveland, TN	763.4	122,317	320	160.2	88.7	5.1	1.0	1.3	5.7	5.6	16.1	9.3	12.5	12.4	13.8
17,460	Cleveland-Elyria, OH	1,999.2	2,058,844	33	1,029.8	71.6	21.0	0.6	2.9	5.8	5.6	15.7	8.6	12.7	11.5	13.3
17,660	Coeur d'Alene, ID	1,237.6	157,637	261	127.4	92.8	0.8	2.3	1.9	4.6	6.1	16.9	7.7	12.8	11.8	12.3
17,780	College Station-Bryan, TX	2,099.7	258,044	187	122.9	57.9	11.7	0.6	6.1	25.1	6.3	14.8	23.5	15.5	10.8	9.6
17,820	Colorado Springs, CO	2,683.9	723,878	79	269.7	73.3	7.6	1.5	4.9	16.7	6.7	17.4	10.8	15.6	12.5	12.2
17,860	Columbia, MO	685.5	178,271	237	260.1	81.7	11.0	1.0	5.9	3.4	5.9	14.4	19.6	15.3	11.5	10.7
17,900	Columbia, SC	3,703.0	825,033	71	222.8	58.0	34.6	0.8	2.9	5.6	5.8	16.4	11.7	13.9	12.3	12.8
17,980	Columbus, GA-AL	1,936.2	303,811	163	156.9	48.7	42.7	1.0	3.2	7.0	6.9	17.3	10.1	15.3	12.2	12.2
18,020	Columbus, IN	406.9	82,040	374	201.6	83.8	2.9	0.6	7.6	6.7	6.6	17.2	8.0	14.5	12.4	12.9
18,140	Columbus, OH	4,796.6	2,078,725	32	433.4	75.4	17.2	0.8	5.1	4.2	6.7	17.0	9.3	15.7	13.3	13.0
18,580	Corpus Christi, TX	1,783.8	454,008	118	254.5	33.7	3.4	0.6	2.3	61.0	6.9	17.9	9.7	14.1	12.4	11.9
18,700	Corvallis, OR	675.2	90,951	365	134.7	83.9	1.8	1.6	9.1	7.5	4.2	12.4	22.7	13.3	10.0	9.9
18,880	Crestview-Fort Walton Beach-Destin, FL	1,968.0	271,346	177	137.9	79.4	9.8	1.4	4.5	8.5	6.5	15.3	8.2	15.2	11.9	12.3
19,060	Cumberland, MD-WV	750.0	98,837	355	131.8	90.6	7.9	0.5	1.3	1.6	4.8	13.4	11.2	12.4	11.3	13.0
19,100	Dallas-Fort Worth-Arlington, TX	9,279.1	7,399,662	4	797.5	48.0	16.4	0.9	7.7	28.9	7.0	19.2	9.1	14.8	14.1	13.5
19,100	Dallas-Plano-Irving, TX Div 19,124	5,275.6	4,911,124	X	930.9	45.0	17.3	0.8	8.8	29.9	7.0	19.2	9.1	15.0	14.4	13.6
19,100	Fort Worth-Arlington, TX Div 23,104	4,003.5	2,488,538	X	621.6	54.0	14.7	0.9	5.6	26.8	7.0	19.3	9.0	14.4	13.4	13.2
19,140	Dalton, GA	635.0	144,440	288	227.5	65.8	3.4	0.6	1.4	29.9	6.6	19.3	9.0	13.2	12.6	13.7
19,180	Danville, IL	898.4	77,909	378	86.7	80.2	15.1	0.6	1.3	5.1	6.6	17.3	7.9	12.0	11.4	12.1
19,300	Daphne-Fairhope-Foley, AL	1,589.8	212,628	210	133.7	84.5	9.6	1.4	1.6	4.6	5.6	16.2	7.3	11.4	12.0	13.4
19,340	Davenport-Moline-Rock Island, IA-IL	2,269.7	382,263	140	168.4	81.1	9.0	0.7	2.9	8.8	6.3	16.7	8.3	12.5	12.3	12.5
19,380	Dayton, OH	1,282.1	803,416	73	626.6	78.8	17.3	0.9	3.1	2.7	6.0	16.0	9.5	13.2	11.4	12.6
19,460	Decatur, AL	1,270.1	151,867	270	119.6	78.4	13.0	3.4	0.9	7.0	5.8	16.7	7.8	12.3	12.1	14.1
19,500	Decatur, IL	580.7	105,801	343	182.2	78.9	19.4	0.6	1.7	2.3	6.2	16.1	9.0	11.8	11.5	11.9
19,660	Deltona-Daytona Beach- Ormond Beach, FL	1,586.7	649,202	87	409.2	73.9	11.3	0.8	2.6	13.3	4.6	13.1	7.9	11.1	10.3	12.6
19,740	Denver-Aurora-Lakewood, CO	8,345.8	2,888,227	19	346.1	66.4	6.5	1.1	5.5	23.1	6.1	16.7	8.0	16.6	14.6	13.2
19,780	Des Moines-West Des Moines, IA	2,882.3	645,911	88	224.1	82.5	6.5	0.6	5.0	7.4	7.2	18.2	8.5	14.9	13.7	12.8
19,820	Detroit-Warren-Dearborn, MI	3,889.2	4,313,002	14	1,109.0	68.4	23.3	0.9	5.2	4.4	5.9	16.4	8.5	13.1	12.0	14.1
19,820	Detroit-Dearborn-Livonia, MI Div 19,804	612.0	1,753,616	X	2,865.4	51.5	39.8	1.1	4.2	5.9	6.6	17.2	8.9	13.8	11.8	13.3
19,820	Warren-Troy-Farmington Hills, MI Div 47,664	3,277.2	2,559,386	X	781.0	80.0	12.0	0.9	5.9	3.4	5.4	15.9	8.2	12.7	12.1	14.6
20,020	Dothan, AL	1,716.1	147,914	281	86.2	71.6	24.5	1.1	1.2	3.4	5.8	16.9	7.5	12.5	12.2	13.2
20,100	Dover, DE	586.3	176,824	238	301.6	64.4	27.2	1.3	3.4	7.2	6.3	16.6	10.1	13.6	11.5	12.6
20,220	Dubuque, IA	608.3	97,041	361	159.5	92.1	4.3	0.5	2.2	2.5	6.3	16.7	10.2	12.7	10.9	12.2
20,260	Duluth, MN-WI	8,413.0	278,782	172	33.1	93.1	2.4	3.8	1.6	1.7	5.1	14.6	11.4	11.8	11.4	12.1
20,500	Durham-Chapel Hill, NC	1,757.7	567,428	97	322.8	56.3	27.5	0.9	5.9	11.5	5.8	14.9	11.3	15.0	13.0	12.8
20,700	East Stroudsburg, PA	608.3	168,046	250	276.3	67.9	14.5	0.8	3.0	15.9	4.5	15.3	10.8	11.1	10.6	15.1
20,740	Eau Claire, WI	1,646.3	167,484	252	101.7	92.8	1.9	0.9	3.6	2.2	5.7	15.4	12.9	13.2	11.6	12.1
20,940	El Centro, CA	4,176.6	182,830	230	43.8	11.0	2.7	0.9	1.6	84.3	8.4	20.2	10.3	14.7	12.1	11.3
21,060	Elizabethtown-Fort Knox, KY	1,190.3	150,430	275	126.4	82.7	11.2	1.1	3.0	5.1	6.3	17.7	8.9	13.3	12.8	13.7
21,140	Elkhart-Goshen, IN	463.2	205,032	218	442.6	76.8	7.0	0.7	1.5	16.0	7.6	20.1	8.9	12.7	12.1	12.4
21,300	Elmira, NY	407.4	85,557	368	210.0	88.9	8.0	0.7	2.1	3.1	5.7	15.9	8.7	12.3	11.6	13.1
21,340	El Paso, TX	5,583.7	844,818	68	151.3	12.6	3.4	0.5	1.7	82.8	7.7	19.8	11.3	14.9	12.5	11.5
21,420	Enid, OK	1,058.5	61,581	381	58.2	77.9	4.3	4.2	4.8	12.4	7.4	18.7	8.6	14.0	11.8	10.8
21,500	Erie, PA	799.1	274,541	175	343.6	86.4	8.8	0.5	2.2	4.3	5.6	15.9	10.0	13.2	11.1	12.7
21,660	Eugene, OR	4,555.7	374,748	141	82.3	85.6	1.9	2.8	4.9	8.9	5.0	13.7	12.7	13.0	11.9	11.4

1. CBSA = Core Based Statistical Area. DIV = Metropolitan Division. See Appendix A for explanation. See Appendix B for list of metropolitan areas or temporarily covered by water. 2. Dry land or land partially or temporarily covered by water. 3. May be of any race.

Table C. Metropolitan Areas — **Population and Households**

Area name	Population, 2017 (cont.) Age (percent) (cont.) 55 to 64 years	65 to 74 years	75 years and over	Percent female	Population change and components of change, 2000-2017 Total persons 2000	2010	Percent change 2000-2010	2010-2017	Components of change, 2010-2017 Births	Deaths	Net Migration	Households, 2016 Number	Persons per house-hold	Percent Family house-holds	Female family house-holder[1]	One person
	16	17	18	19	20	21	22	23	24	25	26	27	28	29	30	31
Cedar Rapids, IA...............	13.1	9.0	7.0	50.5	237,230	257,941	8.7	4.8	23,743	15,314	4,099	107,867	2.42	63.7	7.8	28.0
Chambersburg-Waynesboro, PA....................	13.6	10.6	8.6	50.9	129,313	149,618	15.7	3.1	13,207	10,626	2,191	60,492	2.51	68.0	8.9	26.9
Champaign-Urbana, IL...	11.1	7.5	5.6	50.2	210,275	231,889	10.3	3.1	19,582	11,763	-683	94,941	2.35	55.1	10.1	34.2
Charleston, WV............	15.2	11.8	8.1	51.6	235,938	227,061	-3.8	-5.6	18,078	20,856	-9,772	91,529	2.36	60.7	11.8	33.7
Charleston-North Charleston, SC......................	12.8	9.3	5.4	51.2	549,033	664,644	21.1	16.7	67,679	38,851	81,055	287,362	2.59	61.2	12.7	31.9
Charlotte-Concord-Gastonia, NC-SC	12.0	8.2	5.1	51.5	1,717,372	2,216,992	29.1	13.9	217,525	127,523	216,864	917,897	2.66	67.2	12.7	26.8
Charlottesville, VA.......	13.2	10.2	7.0	51.6	189,644	218,707	15.3	6.9	17,349	12,760	10,571	87,091	2.48	60.0	10.5	29.3
Chattanooga, TN-GA..........	13.6	10.3	7.3	51.5	476,531	528,152	10.8	5.4	45,715	39,048	21,764	210,802	2.54	61.3	9.5	34.5
Cheyenne, WY.............	13.1	9.4	6.2	49.4	81,607	91,881	12.6	7.0	9,318	5,699	2,824	38,181	2.52	66.7	9.6	27.7
Chicago-Naperville-Elgin, IL-IN-WI	12.7	8.3	5.9	51.0	9,098,316	9,461,541	4.0	0.8	869,178	501,469	-296,320	3,491,635	2.68	64.7	13.1	29.1
Chicago-Naperville-Arlington Heights, IL Div 16,974......	12.6	8.2	5.9	51.2	7,135,324	7,263,063	1.8	0.8	679,365	384,651	-237,655	2,704,216	2.66	63.2	13.4	30.5
Elgin, IL Div 20,994	12.2	7.9	5.1	50.3	493,088	620,538	25.8	3.0	58,179	27,253	-12,026	212,050	2.95	72.3	11.8	21.5
Gary, IN Div 23,844	14.0	9.4	6.7	51.3	675,971	708,119	4.8	-0.9	60,136	48,012	-18,486	266,593	2.59	67.0	13.8	27.6
Lake County-Kenosha County, IL-WI Div 29,404.........	13.6	8.1	5.6	50.1	793,933	869,821	9.6	0.3	71,498	41,553	-28,153	308,776	2.75	71.0	11.0	23.8
Chico, CA	12.9	10.6	7.5	50.5	203,171	220,002	8.3	4.2	17,691	16,480	8,189	85,531	2.57	59.1	11.8	28.9
Cincinnati, OH-KY-IN	13.4	8.7	6.1	51.0	1,994,830	2,114,686	6.0	3.0	196,146	135,975	5,243	841,382	2.51	65.4	12.8	28.2
Clarksville, TN-KY	9.7	6.3	4.2	49.4	219,630	260,635	18.7	9.4	36,476	13,886	1,425	100,564	2.70	71.5	13.2	22.3
Cleveland, TN...............	13.1	10.2	7.1	51.3	104,015	115,758	11.3	5.7	9,670	8,673	5,584	47,253	2.55	67.5	11.4	26.8
Cleveland-Elyria, OH..........	14.6	10.2	7.9	51.7	2,148,143	2,077,271	-3.3	-0.9	168,361	153,138	-33,117	851,882	2.36	61.0	14.0	33.3
Coeur d'Alene, ID	13.8	11.3	7.1	50.6	108,685	138,464	27.4	13.8	12,815	9,281	15,551	58,875	2.59	67.8	10.4	23.7
College Station-Bryan, TX....	9.2	6.0	4.3	49.6	184,885	228,668	23.7	12.8	22,862	9,724	16,156	91,033	2.62	59.9	12.3	24.7
Colorado Springs, CO	12.1	8.0	4.7	49.5	537,484	645,615	20.1	12.1	68,968	30,704	39,951	267,621	2.59	67.6	9.7	25.5
Columbia, MO	10.8	7.2	4.7	51.5	135,454	162,643	20.1	9.6	15,274	7,406	7,756	68,848	2.43	58.0	10.7	30.8
Columbia, SC	12.6	8.9	5.5	51.4	647,158	767,476	18.6	7.5	68,585	47,169	36,318	309,016	2.53	64.4	15.3	28.5
Columbus, GA-AL	12.2	8.3	5.5	50.7	281,768	295,531	4.9	2.8	33,122	20,065	-5,346	113,256	2.61	65.0	17.0	31.5
Columbus, IN...................	12.3	9.3	6.7	49.8	71,435	76,786	7.5	6.8	7,712	5,243	2,817	31,626	2.55	66.2	9.6	28.9
Columbus, OH.................	12.1	7.8	5.1	50.8	1,675,013	1,902,001	13.6	9.3	197,185	108,704	88,676	779,547	2.55	63.0	12.6	28.9
Corpus Christi, TX..............	12.3	8.8	6.1	50.5	403,280	428,188	6.2	6.0	44,374	27,239	8,709	161,353	2.75	68.8	15.4	24.7
Corvallis, OR	12.0	9.6	6.0	49.9	78,153	85,592	9.5	6.3	5,368	4,058	4,036	34,543	2.41	58.9	6.4	26.3
Crestview-Fort Walton Beach-Destin, FL.......	13.9	10.0	6.7	49.3	211,099	235,865	11.7	15.0	24,958	16,175	26,348	103,309	2.51	65.2	9.3	28.2
Cumberland, MD-WV	13.5	11.3	9.0	48.5	102,008	103,261	1.2	-4.3	7,033	8,870	-2,556	38,956	2.33	62.6	12.0	28.8
Dallas-Fort Worth-Arlington, TX	11.3	6.9	4.2	50.8	5,204,126	6,426,231	23.5	15.1	715,339	299,371	555,586	2,538,547	2.82	69.6	13.5	24.7
Dallas-Plano-Irving, TX Div 19,124...............	11.1	6.6	4.0	50.7	3,445,899	4,228,958	22.7	16.1	476,106	186,458	390,569	1,696,826	2.79	68.7	13.4	25.4
Fort Worth-Arlington, TX Div 23,104.................	11.7	7.3	4.6	50.9	1,758,227	2,197,273	25.0	13.3	239,233	112,913	165,017	841,721	2.86	71.4	13.8	23.4
Dalton, GA......................	11.6	8.3	5.6	50.3	120,031	142,227	18.5	1.6	13,827	8,354	-3,215	49,692	2.86	72.0	13.2	24.0
Danville, IL......................	14.0	10.5	8.2	50.3	83,919	81,625	-2.7	-4.6	7,617	6,925	-4,417	31,928	2.36	63.6	14.1	31.7
Daphne-Fairhope-Foley, AL .	14.2	12.1	7.9	51.5	140,415	182,265	29.8	16.7	16,068	14,356	28,263	76,779	2.68	65.0	10.0	31.1
Davenport-Moline-Rock Island, IA-IL.............	13.8	10.0	7.6	50.7	376,019	379,689	1.0	0.7	34,784	26,581	-5,539	153,275	2.44	65.0	11.6	30.0
Dayton, OH.....................	13.7	10.0	7.6	51.5	805,816	799,251	-0.8	0.5	69,855	59,736	-5,634	328,352	2.36	61.1	12.9	32.2
Decatur, AL	13.8	10.2	7.1	50.9	145,867	153,825	5.5	-1.3	12,896	11,983	-2,802	57,753	2.60	66.1	9.7	32.4
Decatur, IL	14.2	10.8	8.7	52.1	114,706	110,768	-3.4	-4.5	9,821	8,717	-6,090	44,002	2.34	61.1	15.0	34.2
Deltona-Daytona Beach-Ormond Beach, FL	15.4	14.3	10.8	51.4	493,175	590,294	19.7	10.0	40,643	56,277	74,152	255,350	2.46	61.9	10.8	30.9
Denver-Aurora-Lakewood, CO	12.1	7.9	4.7	50.0	2,179,240	2,543,592	16.7	13.5	253,263	121,114	209,394	1,091,571	2.58	63.1	9.7	27.9
Des Moines-West Des Moines, IA................	11.7	7.7	5.3	50.7	481,394	569,633	18.3	13.4	63,958	31,563	43,634	245,643	2.54	64.0	10.5	29.0
Detroit-Warren-Dearborn, MI	14.1	9.4	6.6	51.3	4,452,557	4,296,317	-3.5	0.4	364,121	293,091	-54,640	1,689,859	2.51	63.1	14.2	31.4
Detroit-Dearborn-Livonia, MI Div 19,804..............	13.4	8.8	6.3	51.9	2,061,162	1,820,573	-11.7	-3.7	169,496	130,264	-107,979	677,208	2.55	60.8	19.0	33.8
Warren-Troy-Farmington Hills, MI Div 47,664.....	14.6	9.8	6.8	51.0	2,391,395	2,475,744	3.5	3.4	194,625	162,827	53,339	1,012,651	2.49	64.6	11.0	29.7
Dothan, AL	13.5	10.9	7.5	51.8	130,861	145,643	11.3	1.6	12,831	11,734	1,266	56,133	2.61	65.5	14.0	30.2
Dover, DE.......................	12.6	9.9	6.8	51.8	126,697	162,349	28.1	8.9	16,074	10,887	9,267	64,452	2.63	67.2	19.8	27.7
Dubuque, IA....................	13.6	9.3	8.1	50.6	89,143	93,653	5.1	3.6	8,753	6,419	1,120	37,710	2.46	68.1	8.2	27.2
Duluth, MN-WI..................	15.2	10.7	7.8	49.6	275,486	279,771	1.6	-0.4	20,492	20,721	-533	116,967	2.28	58.2	9.3	33.0
Durham-Chapel Hill, NC.......	12.5	9.0	5.7	52.2	426,493	506,623	18.8	12.0	47,638	26,874	39,686	217,853	2.45	60.8	12.4	31.0
East Stroudsburg, PA..........	15.8	10.3	6.4	50.6	138,687	169,838	22.5	-1.1	10,283	10,085	-2,016	57,284	2.86	65.8	10.5	27.3
Eau Claire, WI	13.0	9.5	6.6	49.7	148,337	161,390	8.8	3.8	13,849	9,844	2,174	66,866	2.39	60.8	7.6	31.5
El Centro, CA	10.4	7.0	5.6	48.7	142,361	174,528	22.6	4.8	22,531	7,106	-7,219	44,855	3.82	77.9	17.2	18.6
Elizabethtown-Fort Knox, KY	13.2	8.4	5.7	50.1	133,896	148,351	10.8	1.4	14,433	9,259	-3,302	56,261	2.62	67.5	12.8	26.3
Elkhart-Goshen, IN.............	11.8	8.2	6.2	50.6	182,791	197,561	8.1	3.8	22,299	11,706	-3,049	72,487	2.76	70.0	10.9	24.3
Elmira, NY	14.5	10.8	8.0	50.4	91,070	88,841	-2.4	-3.7	7,166	6,822	-3,627	34,418	2.36	61.6	10.0	32.8
El Paso, TX	10.4	6.8	5.2	50.8	682,966	804,123	17.7	5.1	98,803	36,570	-21,829	268,172	3.08	73.0	19.7	23.7
Enid, OK........................	12.5	8.7	7.4	50.3	57,813	60,580	4.8	1.7	7,019	4,942	-1,056	24,859	2.45	63.1	10.6	30.7
Erie, PA.........................	14.2	9.9	7.5	50.6	280,843	280,564	-0.1	-2.1	22,920	20,396	-8,511	109,705	2.40	61.9	12.3	30.9
Eugene, OR.....................	13.6	11.4	7.3	50.7	322,959	351,713	8.9	6.5	25,933	24,506	21,788	147,712	2.45	60.2	9.6	27.5

1. No spouse present.

Table C. Metropolitan Areas — Population, Vital Statistics, Health, and Crime

Area name	Daytime Population, 2016 — Persons in group quarters, 2017	Daytime Population, 2016 — Number	Daytime Population, 2016 — Employment/residence ratio	Births, 2017 — Total	Births, 2017 — Rate[1]	Deaths, 2017 — Number	Deaths, 2017 — Rate[1]	Persons under 65 with no health insurance, 2016 — Number	Persons under 65 with no health insurance, 2016 — Percent	Medicare, 2017 — Total beneficiaries	Medicare, 2017 — Enrolled in Original Medicare	Medicare, 2017 — Enrolled in Medicare Advantage	Serious crimes known to police[2], 2016 Total — Number	Serious crimes known to police[2], 2016 Total — Rate[3]
	32	33	34	35	36	37	38	39	40	41	42	43	44	45
Cedar Rapids, IA..............	6,580	268,405	1.00	3,332	12.3	2,167	8.0	8,191	3.7	48,718	35,701	13,017	D	D
Chambersburg-Waynesboro, PA..................	2,559	144,727	0.87	1,810	11.7	1,587	10.3	11,636	9.4	33,103	25,048	8,055	2,502	1,625
Champaign-Urbana, IL........	16,700	242,840	1.02	2,673	11.2	1,703	7.1	11,340	5.9	34,742	20,089	14,655	7,200	3,010
Charleston, WV..............	3,410	236,298	1.19	2,318	10.8	2,873	13.4	10,900	6.3	54,768	35,330	19,438	10,397	4,768
Charleston-North Charleston, SC..............	16,371	758,143	0.99	9,675	12.5	6,080	7.8	74,226	11.6	128,369	99,900	28,469	24,887	3,264
Charlotte-Concord-Gastonia, NC-SC................	36,049	2,498,727	1.02	31,315	12.4	19,009	7.5	242,345	11.4	387,210	256,473	130,737	NA	NA
Charlottesville, VA..........	12,821	237,745	1.08	2,328	10.0	1,829	7.8	20,787	11.4	43,481	37,337	6,143	3,826	1,661
Chattanooga, TN-GA..........	13,113	567,121	1.07	6,423	11.5	5,710	10.3	48,903	10.9	111,348	71,378	39,969	20,908	3,792
Cheyenne, WY................	1,951	99,459	1.03	1,317	13.4	845	8.6	8,707	10.7	17,917	17,166	751	3,184	3,273
Chicago-Naperville-Elgin, IL-IN-WI................	161,820	9,547,879	1.01	115,915	12.2	72,491	7.6	668,032	8.3	1,468,664	1,092,502	376,162	240,415	2,525
Chicago-Naperville-Arlington Heights, IL Div 16,974......................	115,106	7,433,700	1.04	90,690	12.4	55,607	7.6	517,958	8.3	1,109,713	814,322	295,391	196,058	2,679
Elgin, IL Div 20,994..........	12,863	582,395	0.83	7,755	12.1	4,076	6.4	48,928	9.0	97,839	74,116	23,723	10,168	1,601
Gary, IN Div 23,844..........	10,995	663,471	0.88	7,977	11.4	6,893	9.8	48,827	8.4	130,036	96,397	33,639	19,826	2,830
Lake County-Kenosha County, IL-WI Div 29,404......................	22,856	868,313	0.99	9,493	10.9	5,915	6.8	52,319	7.1	131,076	107,667	23,409	14,363	1,653
Chico, CA....................	5,426	226,447	1.00	2,473	10.8	2,373	10.3	12,937	7.1	50,165	47,671	2,494	8,097	3,599
Cincinnati, OH-KY-IN..........	49,617	2,168,509	1.01	26,855	12.3	19,515	9.0	104,771	5.8	377,529	224,015	153,514	62,168	2,874
Clarksville, TN-KY............	9,158	278,377	0.97	5,074	17.8	2,038	7.1	19,860	8.2	38,232	29,278	8,952	7,530	2,641
Cleveland, TN................	2,997	114,430	0.83	1,327	10.8	1,226	10.0	12,465	12.7	26,155	15,917	10,238	4,726	3,878
Cleveland-Elyria, OH..........	43,675	2,100,376	1.05	22,873	11.1	21,068	10.2	103,909	6.2	415,459	245,400	170,060	58,150	2,829
Coeur d'Alene, ID............	1,472	145,132	0.86	1,856	11.8	1,388	8.8	14,012	11.2	35,542	25,230	10,312	3,924	2,553
College Station-Bryan, TX....	14,568	258,607	1.03	3,342	13.0	1,423	5.5	36,216	16.9	29,393	22,712	6,681	6,839	2,708
Colorado Springs, CO........	19,192	704,739	0.98	9,861	13.6	4,776	6.6	42,882	7.1	104,838	71,295	33,542	23,012	3,253
Columbia, MO................	9,016	185,864	1.10	2,073	11.6	1,056	5.9	13,730	9.2	25,405	18,094	7,310	4,904	2,768
Columbia, SC................	34,751	831,013	1.04	9,523	11.5	6,959	8.4	70,352	10.5	137,884	106,571	31,313	33,741	4,115
Columbus, GA-AL..............	10,049	319,196	1.08	4,256	14.0	3,020	9.9	30,680	12.0	55,312	37,090	18,222	13,723	4,329
Columbus, IN................	1,147	89,988	1.22	1,109	13.5	700	8.5	6,720	9.8	15,998	13,010	2,988	2,578	3,148
Columbus, OH................	53,717	2,071,049	1.03	27,663	13.3	15,833	7.6	122,465	7.0	306,887	176,609	130,280	65,296	3,196
Corpus Christi, TX............	7,788	454,520	1.01	6,180	13.6	3,864	8.5	70,494	18.4	76,224	38,320	37,904	19,280	4,227
Corvallis, OR................	5,142	90,655	1.03	760	8.4	582	6.4	4,728	6.6	13,634	7,241	6,393	2,369	2,676
Crestview-Fort Walton Beach-Destin, FL......	6,549	276,383	1.07	3,573	13.2	2,455	9.0	29,025	13.4	50,801	41,044	9,757	7,354	2,741
Cumberland, MD-WV..........	8,199	98,688	0.98	947	9.6	1,200	12.1	4,569	6.3	23,122	21,147	1,975	2,828	2,864
Dallas-Fort Worth-Arlington, TX......................	88,645	7,261,428	1.01	102,423	13.8	45,826	6.2	1,099,068	17.2	909,620	584,160	325,461	204,752	2,836
Dallas-Plano-Irving, TX Div 19,124......................	56,951	4,891,344	1.04	68,210	13.9	28,658	5.8	735,673	17.3	582,307	390,523	191,784	133,044	2,777
Fort Worth-Arlington, TX Div 23,104..............	31,694	2,370,084	0.94	34,213	13.7	17,168	6.9	363,395	17.1	327,313	193,637	133,677	71,708	2,953
Dalton, GA..................	1,343	147,382	1.06	1,886	13.1	1,222	8.5	25,703	20.9	24,263	19,659	4,606	5,896	4,097
Danville, IL..................	2,924	78,260	1.00	1,031	13.2	909	11.7	3,564	5.8	17,589	11,149	6,440	3,375	4,303
Daphne-Fairhope-Foley, AL.	2,278	194,414	0.84	2,325	10.9	2,090	9.8	17,733	10.7	48,928	28,205	20,723	NA	NA
Davenport-Moline-Rock Island, IA-IL..............	8,927	385,890	1.01	4,757	12.4	3,612	9.4	16,520	5.3	76,292	53,408	22,884	D	D
Dayton, OH..................	24,282	820,255	1.05	9,615	12.0	8,359	10.4	44,785	7.0	162,766	90,519	72,247	25,925	3,241
Decatur, AL..................	2,337	149,337	0.95	1,764	11.6	1,683	11.1	14,681	11.8	33,019	24,542	8,477	4,200	2,762
Decatur, IL..................	4,210	114,264	1.17	1,313	12.4	1,156	10.9	4,653	5.6	23,955	20,208	3,747	3,409	3,213
Deltona-Daytona Beach-Ormond Beach, FL.....	14,742	599,138	0.85	5,868	9.0	8,210	12.6	69,598	14.9	174,777	92,494	82,283	20,529	3,252
Denver-Aurora-Lakewood, CO......................	34,420	2,847,006	1.00	35,764	12.4	18,467	6.4	211,278	8.5	393,647	203,112	190,538	95,885	3,343
Des Moines-West Des Moines, IA..............	12,182	648,366	1.04	9,172	14.2	4,631	7.2	25,971	4.7	96,757	76,590	20,168	D	D
Detroit-Warren-Dearborn, MI	48,782	4,314,531	1.01	49,940	11.6	41,075	9.5	222,660	6.2	809,935	498,347	311,587	113,621	2,641
Detroit-Dearborn-Livonia, MI Div 19,804............	22,787	1,810,893	1.09	22,903	13.1	17,881	10.2	103,958	7.1	328,231	192,225	136,005	72,817	4,167
Warren-Troy-Farmington Hills, MI Div 47,664.....	25,995	2,503,638	0.96	27,037	10.6	23,194	9.1	118,702	5.6	481,704	306,122	175,582	40,804	1,597
Dothan, AL..................	1,845	146,892	0.98	1,740	11.8	1,677	11.3	14,035	11.7	33,432	24,349	9,083	D	D
Dover, DE....................	4,697	166,219	0.89	2,172	12.3	1,667	9.4	10,761	7.6	33,500	29,583	3,917	5,228	2,986
Dubuque, IA..................	4,301	105,304	1.16	1,219	12.6	865	8.9	3,175	4.1	20,086	9,429	10,656	2,291	2,347
Duluth, MN-WI................	12,282	280,437	1.01	2,727	9.8	2,831	10.2	10,326	4.7	62,427	29,915	32,512	9,557	3,423
Durham-Chapel Hill, NC......	23,366	602,595	1.16	6,549	11.5	4,019	7.1	56,207	12.2	86,560	56,944	29,615	NA	NA
East Stroudsburg, PA..........	4,443	155,182	0.85	1,408	8.4	1,517	9.0	10,153	7.5	32,007	24,756	7,250	3,546	2,146
Eau Claire, WI................	7,564	168,779	1.03	1,894	11.3	1,330	7.9	7,830	5.9	33,047	22,870	10,117	3,018	1,816
El Centro, CA................	9,471	178,624	0.96	3,106	17.0	1,030	5.6	12,317	8.3	29,532	26,899	2,633	6,073	3,373
Elizabethtown-Fort Knox, KY	3,715	145,859	0.93	1,856	12.3	1,323	8.8	6,512	5.2	28,109	22,354	5,754	1,660	1,120
Elkhart-Goshen, IN............	3,796	231,351	1.29	3,145	15.3	1,621	7.9	25,222	14.7	33,583	23,812	9,770	NA	NA
Elmira, NY..................	4,495	86,712	1.01	937	11.0	932	10.9	3,076	4.6	19,388	11,965	7,423	2,064	2,397
El Paso, TX..................	15,354	844,936	1.01	13,283	15.7	5,399	6.4	153,505	21.2	122,450	53,088	69,362	17,522	2,079
Enid, OK....................	1,816	63,159	1.02	952	15.5	648	10.5	8,114	15.7	11,767	10,935	832	2,453	3,843
Erie, PA....................	12,534	280,644	1.04	3,031	11.0	2,756	10.0	13,605	6.2	57,875	31,137	26,738	5,901	2,133
Eugene, OR..................	8,355	370,682	1.01	3,685	9.8	3,481	9.3	23,734	8.1	82,159	40,587	41,572	13,400	3,648

1. Per 1,000 estimated resident population.   2. Data for serious crimes have not been adjusted for underreporting; this may affect comparability between geographic areas and over time.
3. Per 100,000 population estimated by the FBI.

Items 32—45

Table C. Metropolitan Areas — Crime, Education, Money Income, and Poverty

Area name	Serious crimes known to police, 2,016 (cont.)[1] Rate Violent	Property	School enrollment and attainment, 2,016 Enrollment[3] Total	Percent private	Attainment[4] (percent) High school grad-uate or less	Bachelor's degree or more	Local government expenditures,[5] 2,013-2,014 Total current expenditures (mil dol)	Current expenditures per student (dollars)	Income and poverty, 2,016 Per capita income[6] (dollars)	Mean household income (dollars)	Median household income	Percent of households with income of less than $50,000	Percent of households with income of $200,000 or more	Percent below poverty level All persons	Children under 18 years	Age 65 years and over
	46	47	48	49	50	51	52	53	54	55	56	57	58	59	60	61
Cedar Rapids, IA	220	D	64,052	18.0	34.6	32.7	490.3	11,203	32,957	80,497	63,385	39.3	5.0	9.9	13.2	6.6
Chambersburg-Waynesboro, PA	144	1,482	31,231	17.7	54.2	21.6	250.3	10,953	30,949	77,464	60,559	40.3	3.0	8.0	12.1	4.8
Champaign-Urbana, IL	440	2,570	85,857	11.1	28.4	42.3	370.4	12,012	28,804	70,226	50,564	49.4	4.3	18.1	11.8	7.4
Charleston, WV	615	4,153	46,262	10.8	53.0	22.7	383.2	10,803	26,346	61,337	41,689	55.5	3.6	19.5	24.5	10.5
Charleston-North Charleston, SC	418	2,846	183,438	15.3	35.4	34.8	1,013.4	9,744	32,045	80,323	57,659	43.3	5.9	13.0	17.5	9.1
Charlotte-Concord-Gastonia, NC-SC	NA	NA	627,212	14.5	34.8	34.4	3,155.8	8,185	31,733	82,776	59,979	41.9	6.5	12.3	18.0	8.5
Charlottesville, VA	198	1,462	63,798	16.0	32.1	44.5	332.0	11,576	33,886	85,476	62,523	39.4	7.2	12.3	11.4	6.1
Chattanooga, TN-GA	541	3,251	131,869	19.7	44.9	26.0	668.8	9,018	27,568	68,041	46,537	52.3	4.2	14.3	19.6	9.4
Cheyenne, WY	252	3,021	23,888	6.4	31.4	27.3	226.0	15,489	29,310	73,885	62,221	36.8	2.2	9.7	10.5	7.9
Chicago-Naperville-Elgin, IL-IN-WI	443	2,082	2,469,466	20.0	35.8	37.2	21,342.8	13,593	34,689	91,648	66,020	38.7	8.3	12.4	17.4	9.8
Chicago-Naperville-Arlington Heights, IL Div 16,974	513	2,166	1,877,544	21.2	35.1	38.5	16,166.3	14,142	34,901	91,339	65,750	39.1	8.2	12.7	17.7	10.5
Elgin, IL Div 20,994	193	1,409	184,685	13.9	36.7	33.4	1,661.8	11,848	31,979	93,061	70,493	35.3	8.5	12.0	16.7	7.9
Gary, IN Div 23,844	272	2,558	171,374	17.5	45.9	22.4	1,134.8	9,475	28,048	72,137	56,126	44.3	3.3	13.7	21.2	8.1
Lake County-Kenosha County, IL-WI Div 29,404	175	1,478	235,863	16.8	32.5	40.7	2,379.9	14,254	40,228	110,253	77,331	33.0	12.7	9.6	12.8	6.3
Chico, CA	351	3,248	67,596	6.0	34.9	25.8	316.8	10,197	25,938	65,703	45,177	53.2	3.8	19.9	22.0	9.4
Cincinnati, OH-KY-IN	257	2,617	542,776	19.0	39.0	33.1	3,256.5	10,327	32,229	81,041	60,260	41.8	6.0	12.6	17.5	7.8
Clarksville, TN-KY	428	2,214	81,052	10.9	40.9	22.8	362.2	8,477	23,295	61,242	51,373	48.2	2.4	15.5	18.2	11.3
Cleveland, TN	512	3,366	30,275	18.9	49.3	21.4	150.8	8,139	24,032	60,730	44,881	55.6	1.6	13.0	17.1	6.7
Cleveland-Elyria, OH	446	2,384	486,291	23.8	39.1	30.3	3,596.8	12,404	31,321	74,213	52,131	47.6	4.9	14.5	20.8	8.5
Coeur d'Alene, ID	232	2,321	35,759	14.0	34.7	25.9	140.1	6,163	26,709	66,843	51,765	47.1	2.9	16.3	26.9	8.9
College Station-Bryan, TX	331	2,376	100,693	7.5	36.4	35.3	305.1	8,750	26,025	69,770	42,233	54.9	5.9	24.2	24.2	11.4
Colorado Springs, CO	405	2,848	190,701	11.5	25.6	38.4	999.7	8,348	31,194	80,759	63,651	39.2	5.2	11.5	15.6	6.7
Columbia, MO	380	2,388	59,279	10.2	26.5	43.9	228.1	9,806	29,116	70,450	52,752	46.8	4.3	17.5	16.9	5.6
Columbia, SC	590	3,525	214,713	14.1	37.9	32.9	1,478.3	10,600	27,645	69,895	52,247	47.3	3.6	15.1	19.9	8.5
Columbus, GA-AL	518	3,811	83,322	12.2	40.8	25.6	479.0	9,545	24,231	61,926	43,412	55.5	2.7	18.8	24.9	12.4
Columbus, IN	82	3,067	20,555	12.4	42.2	33.3	115.0	9,146	29,588	73,017	59,102	43.1	3.5	13.6	18.4	8.1
Columbus, OH	285	2,911	529,946	17.0	37.2	36.0	3,562.3	11,088	31,777	80,731	60,294	41.5	5.7	14.2	20.4	8.1
Corpus Christi, TX	659	3,568	113,769	6.1	45.5	21.2	703.1	8,690	25,948	69,942	53,775	46.1	3.7	15.0	23.0	10.5
Corvallis, OR	128	2,549	33,429	7.0	14.7	54.2	84.8	9,763	30,516	77,905	55,459	45.3	6.9	20.5	14.5	5.5
Crestview-Fort Walton Beach-Destin, FL	382	2,359	59,927	11.2	35.3	29.9	337.0	8,800	31,417	77,360	58,624	42.6	5.1	10.5	12.7	6.8
Cumberland, MD-WV	318	2,546	23,227	8.4	52.8	16.4	175.7	13,457	22,014	54,830	45,808	55.3	0.8	16.1	21.6	6.5
Dallas-Fort Worth-Arlington, TX	360	2,476	1,963,059	11.9	37.7	33.9	10,958.3	8,247	32,156	89,027	63,812	38.6	7.7	12.7	18.6	7.9
Dallas-Plano-Irving, TX Div 19,124	357	2,420	1,312,853	11.7	36.1	36.5	7,435.0	8,252	33,387	91,936	65,647	38.1	8.4	12.5	18.2	7.8
Fort Worth-Arlington, TX Div 23,104	366	2,587	650,206	12.3	40.9	28.8	3,523.3	8,237	29,737	83,276	61,132	39.8	6.2	13.2	19.2	8.0
Dalton, GA	689	3,408	37,641	3.5	61.5	11.8	251.9	8,813	21,227	57,870	43,348	56.6	1.9	18.4	26.9	11.7
Danville, IL	808	3,494	18,766	8.2	51.0	14.0	148.2	11,198	23,570	56,819	45,481	54.5	1.2	20.9	30.4	5.0
Daphne-Fairhope-Foley, AL	NA	NA	46,501	22.0	38.5	29.6	267.2	8,824	29,977	74,892	56,732	44.4	4.6	11.4	15.5	7.9
Davenport-Moline-Rock Island, IA-IL	393	D	91,131	16.1	40.0	26.2	683.0	10,831	28,496	69,246	52,590	46.9	3.1	14.5	24.2	7.2
Dayton, OH	311	2,929	208,252	20.5	37.8	27.4	1,294.5	11,399	29,069	69,568	51,427	48.7	3.6	16.1	23.8	8.2
Decatur, AL	232	2,530	34,392	11.1	52.3	18.1	232.8	9,495	23,633	58,555	44,575	53.2	1.3	16.2	21.5	12.0
Decatur, IL	411	2,802	24,471	15.1	44.5	21.6	215.8	13,117	26,729	62,668	46,198	53.4	2.9	17.2	29.4	8.5
Deltona-Daytona Beach-Ormond Beach, FL	391	2,861	135,126	22.2	41.5	23.9	607.9	8,215	25,964	61,275	46,090	53.8	2.6	13.5	17.2	9.9
Denver-Aurora-Lakewood, CO	389	2,954	696,836	13.9	29.7	42.5	4,142.8	9,041	38,106	97,108	71,926	33.4	9.0	9.4	12.1	7.3
Des Moines-West Des Moines, IA	372	D	165,927	17.3	32.3	36.7	1,125.4	10,585	34,043	85,195	65,704	37.8	6.3	9.5	12.9	7.0
Detroit-Warren-Dearborn, MI	556	2,085	1,058,352	12.7	37.4	30.4	7,305.5	10,896	31,574	78,705	56,142	45.0	5.7	14.9	21.9	9.1
Detroit-Dearborn-Livonia, MI Div 19,804	1,034	3,133	443,501	10.8	44.2	23.0	3,134.0	10,969	25,269	63,254	43,464	55.1	3.8	22.7	33.9	12.3
Warren-Troy-Farmington Hills, MI Div 47,664	228	1,369	614,851	14.1	33.0	35.2	4,171.5	10,842	35,902	88,636	65,674	38.2	7.0	9.5	12.8	7.2
Dothan, AL	D	2,865	33,100	14.8	49.5	17.6	193.0	8,657	22,851	56,872	41,040	57.1	2.1	19.5	27.7	13.8
Dover, DE	474	2,512	44,884	13.8	48.8	22.6	329.8	12,828	25,528	66,154	54,140	46.5	3.0	13.8	22.0	6.7
Dubuque, IA	243	2,104	25,254	29.2	40.2	29.1	154.8	10,616	32,588	82,731	60,456	41.3	4.7	10.6	15.6	7.8
Duluth, MN-WI	230	3,193	66,381	12.8	35.7	25.3	411.1	10,882	28,421	66,342	51,294	48.8	3.3	14.4	17.3	7.5
Durham-Chapel Hill, NC	NA	NA	153,659	18.9	29.8	47.0	723.3	9,862	33,909	82,641	56,182	44.1	7.1	14.9	20.4	6.8
East Stroudsburg, PA	252	1,894	39,717	12.9	45.6	25.6	422.8	15,395	28,115	76,141	60,095	39.7	4.7	11.4	17.6	6.9
Eau Claire, WI	138	1,678	43,139	8.8	36.4	25.7	248.9	10,810	27,519	66,019	51,058	49.3	2.5	13.3	16.0	9.2
El Centro, CA	389	2,983	56,865	5.3	54.6	13.9	376.5	10,183	17,180	63,208	49,095	50.2	2.7	24.6	33.7	18.3
Elizabethtown-Fort Knox, KY	122	998	40,817	15.2	40.1	22.0	213.0	8,559	25,795	65,316	51,936	47.4	2.5	14.5	18.5	11.8
Elkhart-Goshen, IN	NA	NA	50,909	16.1	57.4	18.6	340.2	9,409	23,630	65,321	54,216	45.5	2.6	14.3	17.9	7.1
Elmira, NY	200	2,197	20,081	20.5	42.1	27.5	179.0	15,173	27,636	67,332	51,269	48.2	3.4	13.9	20.3	9.3
El Paso, TX	365	1,713	254,609	8.0	46.4	21.9	1,578.6	8,841	19,533	57,013	42,116	57.2	2.1	22.8	32.1	20.3
Enid, OK	365	3,478	14,520	8.4	48.7	22.4	86.2	7,607	24,425	60,299	50,288	49.6	1.9	14.0	22.1	4.7
Erie, PA	215	1,918	66,815	24.1	49.0	28.0	497.5	12,584	25,727	63,819	48,964	51.0	2.9	15.9	24.4	7.8
Eugene, OR	321	3,327	89,466	10.6	33.1	28.8	445.8	9,901	26,418	63,747	47,777	51.9	3.1	19.0	21.2	8.3

1. Data for serious crimes have not been adjusted for underreporting; this may affect comparability between geographic areas and over time.　2. Per 100,000 population estimated by the FBI.
3. All persons 3 years old and over enrolled in nursery school through college.　4. Persons 25 years old and over.　5. Elementary and secondary education expenditures.　6. Based on population estimated by the American Community Survey, 2015.

Table C. Metropolitan Areas — Personal Income and Earnings

| Area name | Personal income, 2016 | | | | | | | | | | Earnings, 2016 | | |
	Total (mil dol)	Percent change, 2015-2016	Per capita[1] Dollars	Rank	Wages and salaries (mil dol)	Supplements to wages and salaries, employer contributions (mil dol) Pension and insurance	Government social insurance	Proprietors' income	Dividends, interest, and rent (mil dol)	Personal transfer receipts (mil dol)	Total (mil dol)	Contributions for government social insurance (mil dol) From employee and self-employed	From employer
	62	63	64	65	66	67	68	69	70	71	72	73	74
Cedar Rapids, IA	12,942	2.2	48,329	83	7,346	1,191	567	687	2,283	2,062	9,791	613	567
Chambersburg-Waynesboro, PA	6,504	1.8	42,275	184	2,526	509	215	429	1,065	1,399	3,678	228	215
Champaign-Urbana, IL	10,358	1.6	43,420	162	5,123	1,259	317	1,193	1,959	1,426	7,891	380	317
Charleston, WV	9,166	0.1	42,063	192	5,339	895	412	740	1,420	2,624	7,386	487	412
Charleston-North Charleston, SC	34,250	4.4	44,998	131	17,386	2,858	1,322	3,116	6,755	5,782	24,682	1,498	1,322
Charlotte-Concord-Gastonia, NC-SC	115,498	4.4	46,679	100	68,027	8,818	4,966	10,793	17,640	17,719	92,605	5,704	4,966
Charlottesville, VA	12,371	1.8	53,475	39	5,964	1,205	424	777	3,653	1,641	8,370	501	424
Chattanooga, TN-GA	23,500	3.0	42,601	178	11,568	1,988	812	2,561	3,596	4,862	16,930	1,031	812
Cheyenne, WY	4,884	1.2	49,763	69	2,423	525	248	307	1,104	796	3,503	201	248
Chicago-Naperville-Elgin, IL-IN-WI	529,122	1.8	55,621	29	292,678	44,038	19,964	39,738	106,000	72,567	396,418	22,029	19,964
Chicago-Naperville-Arlington Heights, IL Div 16,974	412,782	1.8	56,510	X	237,982	34,945	16,218	33,078	84,055	56,767	322,223	17,821	16,218
Elgin, IL Div 20,994	28,409	2.4	44,651	X	12,657	2,355	885	1,439	4,376	3,782	17,336	937	885
Gary, IN Div 23,844	29,513	2.1	42,102	X	12,793	2,193	952	1,616	4,237	6,353	17,554	1,106	952
Lake County-Kenosha County, IL-WI Div 29,404	58,417	1.7	67,051	X	29,247	4,545	1,909	3,606	13,331	5,664	39,305	2,165	1,909
Chico, CA	9,466	4.0	41,725	200	3,505	820	252	845	1,904	2,514	5,422	335	252
Cincinnati, OH-KY-IN	105,372	2.3	48,668	80	57,640	8,852	4,110	7,682	18,474	17,528	78,284	4,581	4,110
Clarksville, TN-KY	10,777	-0.2	38,170	290	5,170	1,227	446	695	1,870	2,239	7,538	388	446
Cleveland, TN	4,503	2.3	37,134	316	1,876	349	137	379	683	1,104	2,741	176	137
Cleveland-Elyria, OH	100,659	1.8	48,968	75	55,996	9,059	3,953	7,242	17,489	19,377	76,250	4,424	3,953
Coeur d'Alene, ID	6,145	4.5	39,820	249	2,336	425	211	452	1,344	1,269	3,424	234	211
College Station-Bryan, TX	9,025	1.1	35,401	348	4,481	948	286	847	1,689	1,466	6,562	313	286
Colorado Springs, CO	31,668	3.2	44,458	140	15,957	2,640	1,263	1,756	6,531	5,507	21,616	1,155	1,263
Columbia, MO	7,645	2.7	43,292	165	4,355	930	296	435	1,406	1,180	6,016	327	296
Columbia, SC	34,000	2.9	41,591	203	18,476	3,277	1,405	2,271	5,250	6,692	25,428	1,552	1,405
Columbus, GA-AL	11,829	1.8	38,313	286	6,376	1,333	482	385	2,777	2,794	8,576	480	482
Columbus, IN	3,857	4.8	47,386	93	2,747	447	197	270	607	642	3,660	217	197
Columbus, OH	97,432	2.8	47,725	87	56,741	9,742	3,775	7,223	14,600	15,174	77,482	4,168	3,775
Corpus Christi, TX	18,667	-0.4	41,052	216	9,286	1,628	671	1,591	3,190	4,198	13,117	722	671
Corvallis, OR	3,776	4.0	42,245	186	1,916	331	161	269	953	562	2,676	166	161
Crestview-Fort Walton Beach-Destin, FL	12,892	3.5	48,274	84	6,061	1,145	476	731	3,793	2,332	8,413	487	476
Cumberland, MD-WV	3,778	2.8	37,949	295	1,596	335	134	155	605	1,211	2,220	152	134
Dallas-Fort Worth-Arlington, TX	369,615	2.1	51,099	59	211,594	26,534	14,624	43,618	61,740	44,290	296,369	15,707	14,624
Dallas-Plano-Irving, TX Div 19,124	254,457	2.3	53,082	X	158,337	18,838	10,792	31,539	42,683	28,205	219,506	11,587	10,792
Fort Worth-Arlington, TX Div 23,104	115,158	1.6	47,202	X	53,257	7,696	3,832	12,079	19,057	16,085	76,863	4,120	3,832
Dalton, GA	4,869	3.6	33,837	368	3,071	481	227	518	831	1,077	4,297	259	227
Danville, IL	2,871	1.5	36,760	323	1,246	275	91	188	442	780	1,800	108	91
Daphne-Fairhope-Foley, AL	8,611	4.0	41,286	215	2,671	421	197	538	1,685	1,858	3,827	276	197
Davenport-Moline-Rock Island, IA-IL	17,246	0.9	45,116	125	8,987	1,596	665	924	3,342	3,294	12,172	738	665
Dayton, OH	34,967	2.1	43,671	156	18,908	3,476	1,382	1,931	6,090	7,378	25,697	1,483	1,382
Decatur, AL	5,412	1.4	35,545	347	2,339	415	173	258	838	1,386	3,185	221	173
Decatur, IL	4,742	0.1	44,507	138	2,672	471	197	333	803	1,051	3,673	215	197
Deltona-Daytona Beach-Ormond Beach, FL	24,924	3.9	39,086	264	8,037	1,242	571	1,062	5,771	6,862	10,911	836	571
Denver-Aurora-Lakewood, CO	162,317	1.2	56,892	22	92,161	11,195	6,584	17,817	31,544	18,370	127,757	7,110	6,584
Des Moines-West Des Moines, IA	32,166	3.8	50,677	61	19,482	2,895	1,471	2,294	5,462	4,226	26,141	1,604	1,471
Detroit-Warren-Dearborn, MI	209,260	2.9	48,692	79	114,911	16,326	8,520	15,317	34,271	40,980	155,074	9,658	8,520
Detroit-Dearborn-Livonia, MI Div 19,804	70,167	2.6	40,110	X	44,889	6,671	3,294	3,871	10,485	19,569	58,726	3,683	3,294
Warren-Troy-Farmington Hills, MI Div 47,664	139,094	3.1	54,584	X	70,022	9,655	5,226	11,446	23,785	21,412	96,348	5,975	5,226
Dothan, AL	5,589	2.2	37,803	300	2,356	423	171	377	929	1,460	3,327	224	171
Dover, DE	6,730	3.4	38,498	281	3,123	739	243	323	1,104	1,722	4,428	264	243
Dubuque, IA	4,372	1.1	45,068	128	2,555	429	199	263	907	788	3,445	223	199
Duluth, MN-WI	11,688	0.7	41,857	196	5,784	1,067	461	547	2,007	2,916	7,858	511	461
Durham-Chapel Hill, NC	27,594	3.4	49,315	74	19,050	2,884	1,371	2,076	5,793	4,039	25,381	1,514	1,371
East Stroudsburg, PA	6,495	2.8	39,104	263	2,463	555	203	423	916	1,461	3,645	221	203
Eau Claire, WI	7,121	0.9	42,737	174	3,709	702	284	464	1,285	1,313	5,158	319	284
El Centro, CA	6,172	0.2	34,122	367	2,526	766	182	764	808	1,675	4,238	211	182
Elizabethtown-Fort Knox, KY	5,827	3.0	38,969	269	2,693	614	225	337	981	1,340	3,868	223	225
Elkhart-Goshen, IN	8,500	4.6	41,712	201	6,362	1,068	486	861	1,241	1,515	8,777	512	486
Elmira, NY	3,446	0.3	39,926	247	1,661	402	140	162	480	925	2,365	137	140
El Paso, TX	27,744	2.5	32,952	373	13,530	2,859	1,032	1,783	4,376	6,627	19,204	1,015	1,032
Enid, OK	2,803	-1.2	44,782	133	1,420	241	111	226	553	528	1,999	115	111
Erie, PA	11,259	0.8	40,764	223	5,382	1,113	444	704	1,810	2,924	7,642	464	444
Eugene, OR	15,160	3.9	41,027	219	6,784	1,080	606	1,271	3,142	3,627	9,741	650	606

1. Based on the resident population estimated as of July 1 of the year shown.

Table C. Metropolitan Areas — Earnings, Social Security, and Housing

Area name	Earnings, 2016 (cont.)									Social Security beneficiaries, December 2016			Housing units, 2017	
	Percent by selected industries											Supplemental Security Income recipients, 2016		
	Farm	Mining, quarrying, and extracting	Construction	Manufacturing	Information; professional, scientific, and technical services	Retail trade	Finance, insurance, real estate, rental and leasing	Health care and social assistance	Government	Number	Rate[1]		Total	Percent change, 2010-2017
	75	76	77	78	79	80	81	82	83	84	85	86	87	88
Cedar Rapids, IA	0.8	0.1	7.6	20.7	D	5.6	9.9	10.9	11.3	51,750	193	4,301	117,383	4.6
Chambersburg-Waynesboro, PA	0.7	0.1	5.7	16.6	4.8	7.5	3.4	15.8	17.0	35,840	233	2,497	65,418	3.5
Champaign-Urbana, IL	0.7	D	4.3	6.4	D	11.7	5.1	D	34.5	33,955	142	3,460	106,496	5.3
Charleston, WV	0.0	D	D	D	D	5.9	D	D	19.8	59,555	274	9,177	108,246	0.0
Charleston-North Charleston, SC	0.0	0.1	7.1	9.7	12.3	6.6	8.7	9.4	22.9	135,165	177	13,256	332,659	11.4
Charlotte-Concord-Gastonia, NC-SC	0.3	0.1	6.8	9.1	D	5.6	D	D	11.6	412,825	167	42,639	1,027,985	9.8
Charlottesville, VA	-0.1	0.2	4.8	3.5	D	4.8	6.4	10.1	35.9	43,390	188	3,280	102,809	6.7
Chattanooga, TN-GA	0.1	0.1	D	13.9	D	6.4	11.5	D	16.6	120,870	219	13,473	244,015	4.1
Cheyenne, WY	0.4	1.1	6.6	4.0	7.2	6.7	6.8	7.9	40.6	18,095	185	1,485	43,341	7.1
Chicago-Naperville-Elgin, IL-IN-WI	0.0	D	5.2	10.1	D	4.9	11.6	9.9	12.0	1,480,175	155	204,156	3,843,027	1.2
Chicago-Naperville-Arlington Heights, IL Div 16,974	0.0	0.1	4.8	7.8	17.2	4.5	12.9	9.9	11.5	1,114,015	152	170,682	2,978,520	1.0
Elgin, IL Div 20,994	-0.1	0.1	7.8	16.2	8.2	5.3	5.7	10.8	19.3	88,805	139	6,065	229,008	2.6
Gary, IN Div 23,844	0.5	0.1	8.7	20.5	4.7	6.7	4.1	15.4	10.9	143,135	204	15,431	301,154	2.4
Lake County-Kenosha County, IL-WI Div 29,404	0.1	0.0	4.9	21.6	9.0	7.3	6.6	7.2	13.0	134,220	154	11,978	334,345	1.5
Chico, CA	3.8	0.0	6.5	5.1	5.7	8.9	5.9	20.4	22.7	51,700	228	11,241	99,404	3.7
Cincinnati, OH-KY-IN	0.0	D	5.9	13.4	D	5.4	D	12.1	11.5	391,335	181	48,164	932,102	2.3
Clarksville, TN-KY	-0.1	D	4.4	9.2	3.8	6.0	3.3	D	48.8	43,660	155	6,166	118,911	10.7
Cleveland, TN	0.7	0.1	6.5	24.9	D	7.7	D	D	12.4	29,025	240	3,116	52,644	6.6
Cleveland-Elyria, OH	0.1	D	4.9	13.0	10.9	5.0	7.9	14.5	14.0	421,740	205	62,565	962,070	0.7
Coeur d'Alene, ID	0.1	0.9	9.4	8.4	7.0	10.7	7.0	12.7	20.9	36,890	241	2,691	70,758	12.0
College Station-Bryan, TX	0.3	3.4	7.6	4.3	8.6	6.5	5.1	9.7	35.6	29,845	117	4,551	107,722	13.4
Colorado Springs, CO	0.0	D	6.5	D	14.8	6.2	6.8	10.2	31.5	108,230	152	9,298	285,038	7.4
Columbia, MO	0.1	0.1	4.5	4.3	7.8	6.8	7.4	11.1	36.7	25,905	147	2,736	77,399	11.3
Columbia, SC	0.2	0.2	5.1	10.2	D	6.2	D	9.5	25.6	150,785	184	16,309	355,294	7.2
Columbus, GA-AL	0.2	D	3.2	D	6.2	5.2	D	10.3	35.7	59,500	194	10,282	134,087	4.6
Columbus, IN	0.6	D	3.7	47.1	4.8	4.2	3.9	7.4	9.3	16,450	201	1,230	34,361	3.8
Columbus, OH	0.1	0.1	4.9	7.9	11.4	5.4	9.5	10.9	18.4	310,790	152	45,431	861,718	5.0
Corpus Christi, TX	0.4	3.5	15.3	8.3	7.3	6.4	4.9	D	19.6	81,420	179	15,088	194,300	6.2
Corvallis, OR	1.2	0.1	3.7	11.4	10.9	5.0	4.4	16.8	29.3	15,400	172	994	38,287	5.6
Crestview-Fort Walton Beach-Destin, FL	0.1	0.1	5.4	3.4	11.7	7.6	5.5	7.9	37.1	55,445	209	4,218	149,075	8.4
Cumberland, MD-WV	-0.2	D	4.3	13.7	D	7.4	4.0	D	24.6	24,260	244	3,081	46,069	-0.6
Dallas-Fort Worth-Arlington, TX	0.0	D	7.2	8.6	14.5	6.0	11.0	D	10.6	919,425	127	130,148	2,794,011	10.5
Dallas-Plano-Irving, TX Div 19,124	0.0	3.1	6.7	7.7	17.0	5.8	12.1	9.7	9.9	579,245	120	87,645	1,859,976	12.2
Fort Worth-Arlington, TX Div 23,104	0.0	6.0	8.6	11.2	7.2	6.7	7.8	10.0	12.7	340,180	139	42,503	934,035	7.2
Dalton, GA	0.5	0.3	1.9	38.1	D	7.2	4.1	D	9.9	26,915	187	3,661	56,029	0.3
Danville, IL	2.8	D	3.7	21.0	2.5	6.7	4.6	9.8	22.1	18,785	239	2,790	36,071	-0.7
Daphne-Fairhope-Foley, AL	0.2	0.2	9.4	6.6	5.7	12.8	7.2	13.0	14.4	52,270	252	3,521	114,162	9.7
Davenport-Moline-Rock Island, IA-IL	0.1	D	7.1	14.5	6.3	6.5	5.4	12.3	16.4	80,250	210	7,516	169,969	1.7
Dayton, OH	0.1	0.1	4.5	12.2	11.7	5.5	5.5	15.6	22.7	163,905	205	20,437	369,460	0.6
Decatur, AL	0.2	D	8.0	30.9	D	6.8	4.0	D	15.0	37,480	246	4,719	67,507	1.6
Decatur, IL	0.7	D	7.0	30.4	4.7	5.1	4.3	13.1	10.4	25,110	235	3,273	50,432	-0.1
Deltona-Daytona Beach-Ormond Beach, FL	0.3	0.0	7.0	7.3	7.7	10.0	6.1	17.6	14.6	184,920	290	14,007	312,058	3.0
Denver-Aurora-Lakewood, CO	0.0	5.9	7.1	4.8	D	D	D	8.7	12.6	381,240	134	36,063	1,173,107	8.7
Des Moines-West Des Moines, IA	0.3	D	7.6	5.7	10.1	5.7	D	10.5	12.8	100,195	158	9,076	270,250	12.5
Detroit-Warren-Dearborn, MI	0.0	D	4.9	14.4	D	5.6	8.4	11.9	10.0	876,955	204	133,853	1,905,942	1.0
Detroit-Dearborn-Livonia, MI Div 19,804	0.0	0.1	3.7	14.4	D	4.5	5.8	13.6	12.3	357,035	203	84,737	814,910	-0.8
Warren-Troy-Farmington Hills, MI Div 47,664	0.0	D	5.6	14.4	19.1	6.3	10.0	10.8	8.5	519,920	204	49,116	1,091,032	2.5
Dothan, AL	2.4	D	5.0	7.7	5.1	9.7	4.2	D	19.4	37,830	256	5,852	69,378	3.7
Dover, DE	2.1	D	5.3	D	4.9	7.3	3.6	12.4	38.3	36,575	209	3,499	71,620	9.6
Dubuque, IA	1.2	D	6.2	19.3	7.7	6.6	10.5	14.6	8.6	20,820	215	1,634	41,334	6.1
Duluth, MN-WI	0.0	4.1	6.6	6.7	5.7	7.1	5.0	D	20.1	64,580	232	6,832	143,891	1.7
Durham-Chapel Hill, NC	0.3	0.0	2.8	14.7	16.0	3.6	6.8	15.8	20.4	92,030	165	9,757	244,300	9.7
East Stroudsburg, PA	0.0	0.1	5.2	14.1	3.2	8.4	2.8	12.3	25.4	35,275	212	3,096	81,459	1.4
Eau Claire, WI	0.5	D	6.5	13.9	5.3	8.3	5.1	19.4	15.5	34,500	207	3,089	72,556	4.6
El Centro, CA	11.8	1.0	2.7	1.7	2.2	7.8	2.4	6.4	39.7	31,630	175	10,381	57,739	3.0
Elizabethtown-Fort Knox, KY	-0.3	D	4.2	15.2	D	6.4	D	D	41.3	30,085	202	4,437	65,561	7.1
Elkhart-Goshen, IN	0.5	D	3.1	50.8	2.4	4.0	2.8	7.7	5.6	35,690	175	3,117	79,004	1.6
Elmira, NY	0.0	1.0	5.3	16.6	3.7	7.3	5.5	16.5	24.4	21,555	251	3,077	38,836	1.2
El Paso, TX	0.1	0.0	D	D	D	7.9	D	10.4	37.3	127,880	152	29,723	298,155	9.7
Enid, OK	0.5	13.8	12.9	7.2	5.7	5.9	4.5	10.9	16.9	12,430	199	1,291	26,775	-0.2
Erie, PA	0.1	0.1	4.7	19.3	4.8	7.0	8.0	18.1	16.2	62,650	227	10,745	121,406	1.9
Eugene, OR	0.5	0.2	5.8	9.7	8.2	8.3	6.8	16.5	18.2	84,475	229	9,456	162,591	4.2

1. Per 1,000 resident population estimated as of July 1 of the year shown.

Table C. Metropolitan Areas — Housing, Labor Force, and Employment

Area name	Housing units, 2016								Civilian labor force, 2017				Civilian employment⁵, 2016		
	Occupied units										Unemployment			Percent	
			Owner-occupied			Renter-occupied									
				Median owner cost as a percent of income											
	Total	Percent	Median value¹	With a mortgage	Without a mortgage²	Median rent³	Median rent as a percent of income	Percent with Internet access	Total	Percent change, 2016-2017	Total	Rate⁴	Total	Management, business, science, and arts	Construction, production, and maintenance occupations
	89	90	91	92	93	94	95	96	97	98	99	100	101	102	103
Cedar Rapids, IA	107,867	74.4	151,100	19.1	11.3	708	25.7	85.5	142,265	-0.7	4,811	3.4	141,067	37.9	22.6
Chambersburg-Waynesboro, PA	60,492	69.9	174,700	20.1	10.8	832	25.2	80.8	76,656	-1.1	3,414	4.5	72,077	31.5	29.9
Champaign-Urbana, IL	94,941	57.0	150,600	18.9	10.4	819	32.3	88.5	119,463	-0.7	5,069	4.2	121,198	45.8	17.8
Charleston, WV	91,529	69.5	111,300	17.9	10.6	685	30.1	79.1	95,112	-1.4	4,971	5.2	89,906	35.8	16.6
Charleston-North Charleston, SC	287,362	65.4	213,200	22.4	11.6	1,051	30.3	85.8	377,652	1.5	13,746	3.6	364,426	39.4	18.7
Charlotte-Concord-Gastonia, NC-SC	917,897	64.8	188,100	19.3	10.0	949	27.5	87.4	1,315,801	3.0	56,515	4.3	1,218,948	38.5	21.5
Charlottesville, VA	87,091	62.2	272,600	20.4	10.4	1,155	30.4	85.4	118,755	2.6	3,960	3.3	110,021	48.3	13.8
Chattanooga, TN-GA	210,802	68.0	160,300	19.7	11.4	765	31.6	80.7	266,950	2.7	10,431	3.9	250,862	34.1	25.6
Cheyenne, WY	38,181	68.1	210,200	20.8	11.4	936	28.7	88.5	48,162	-1.5	1,779	3.7	46,134	37.1	24.5
Chicago-Naperville-Elgin, IL-IN-WI	3,491,635	63.4	229,900	22.4	13.7	1,050	29.6	86.6	4,912,799	-0.5	242,106	4.9	4,724,484	38.7	20.4
Chicago-Naperville-Arlington Heights, IL Div 16,974	2,704,216	61.3	240,800	23.0	14.1	1,076	29.7	86.4	3,791,337	-0.6	190,949	5.0	3,645,338	39.7	19.5
Elgin, IL Div 20,994	212,050	69.3	221,200	22.4	13.1	1,036	30.5	89.3	322,326	-0.6	15,109	4.7	318,106	35.1	24.0
Gary, IN Div 23,844	266,593	71.1	156,100	18.8	10.6	831	28.1	83.2	338,243	-1.1	16,203	4.8	322,337	29.6	28.1
Lake County-Kenosha County, IL-WI Div 29,404	308,776	70.8	239,000	21.7	13.6	1,017	29.7	89.7	460,893	0.1	19,845	4.3	438,703	39.9	19.4
Chico, CA	85,531	59.1	256,500	23.0	13.3	987	38.5	86.4	102,982	1.0	5,916	5.7	93,016	36.3	21.8
Cincinnati, OH-KY-IN	841,382	65.6	165,200	19.1	11.1	793	27.5	86.7	1,107,882	1.6	47,572	4.3	1,068,629	39.8	20.3
Clarksville, TN-KY	100,564	57.6	147,600	20.5	10.6	875	28.2	83.1	111,942	1.4	5,168	4.6	104,540	26.5	28.3
Cleveland, TN	47,253	67.1	146,100	21.3	10.0	699	24.7	76.2	57,544	0.0	2,172	3.8	55,681	30.9	30.2
Cleveland-Elyria, OH	851,882	64.6	146,100	19.9	12.3	776	29.1	83.2	1,031,122	0.0	58,377	5.7	994,426	38.4	20.3
Coeur d'Alene, ID	58,875	65.1	239,600	22.1	10.0	914	30.7	86.5	75,457	2.4	2,900	3.8	68,353	32.0	20.0
College Station-Bryan, TX	91,033	50.5	178,000	21.6	10.0	874	39.8	86.9	128,762	2.0	4,149	3.2	120,601	40.9	19.5
Colorado Springs, CO	267,621	63.1	249,400	21.4	10.0	1,057	29.9	93.0	338,833	3.8	11,060	3.3	326,976	41.6	15.4
Columbia, MO	68,848	51.8	178,500	18.7	10.4	813	28.6	90.1	97,496	-0.8	2,543	2.6	91,624	44.9	15.5
Columbia, SC	309,016	66.8	146,800	20.0	10.0	893	29.9	82.4	402,734	-0.2	16,641	4.1	381,124	38.1	21.0
Columbus, GA-AL	113,256	53.3	153,700	21.7	11.4	833	30.6	79.6	124,870	1.1	6,881	5.5	124,158	32.1	22.7
Columbus, IN	31,626	70.3	147,500	19.0	11.2	878	24.5	84.2	44,516	0.2	1,209	2.7	39,788	43.7	23.4
Columbus, OH	779,547	60.4	172,200	19.7	11.4	877	27.2	88.4	1,076,750	1.8	43,769	4.1	1,034,137	41.3	18.2
Corpus Christi, TX	161,353	60.3	129,000	21.0	12.3	939	28.2	81.2	208,536	0.2	12,062	5.8	205,639	30.4	23.6
Corvallis, OR	34,543	58.5	312,400	20.3	11.7	1,040	41.7	93.2	48,126	2.8	1,570	3.3	41,606	51.4	11.1
Crestview-Fort Walton Beach-Destin, FL	103,309	65.4	213,100	21.0	10.4	1,000	29.9	87.9	125,552	2.7	4,300	3.4	117,295	35.6	20.3
Cumberland, MD-WV	38,956	70.7	120,100	19.1	10.0	704	28.6	80.7	44,428	-0.2	2,516	5.7	39,468	26.2	28.4
Dallas-Fort Worth-Arlington, TX	2,538,547	59.1	189,100	20.8	11.4	1,022	28.1	87.6	3,795,293	2.7	138,248	3.6	3,614,696	38.7	21.4
Dallas-Plano-Irving, TX Div 19,124	1,696,826	57.4	207,100	20.9	11.5	1,050	27.9	87.2	2,562,508	2.9	92,755	3.6	2,432,494	40.4	20.1
Fort Worth-Arlington, TX Div 23,104	841,721	62.5	166,800	20.5	11.2	971	28.6	88.3	1,232,785	2.3	45,493	3.7	1,182,202	35.1	24.0
Dalton, GA	49,692	64.4	117,900	19.5	12.0	671	26.3	80.1	61,112	1.1	3,458	5.7	64,002	22.5	43.7
Danville, IL	31,928	72.5	79,900	18.0	10.4	636	33.8	79.3	34,070	-2.7	2,142	6.3	30,683	26.7	31.5
Daphne-Fairhope-Foley, AL	76,779	73.1	189,100	20.2	10.0	952	29.3	82.1	91,567	1.2	3,652	4.0	90,197	40.1	20.6
Davenport-Moline-Rock Island, IA-IL	153,275	70.9	132,100	19.2	11.6	719	28.1	81.9	189,640	-0.9	8,387	4.4	181,554	33.5	24.4
Dayton, OH	328,352	62.2	129,700	18.9	11.3	761	28.6	86.2	389,409	1.2	18,151	4.7	369,917	37.4	21.4
Decatur, AL	57,753	76.8	120,400	19.8	10.2	572	23.0	72.9	68,480	-0.1	2,918	4.3	61,741	29.9	32.4
Decatur, IL	44,002	67.0	99,300	18.0	10.6	651	31.2	83.1	49,202	-2.0	2,688	5.5	46,658	31.2	25.0
Deltona-Daytona Beach-Ormond Beach, FL	255,350	70.6	171,900	23.6	11.9	988	33.1	81.8	297,886	2.4	13,030	4.4	257,524	32.0	19.7
Denver-Aurora-Lakewood, CO	1,091,571	63.8	349,200	21.0	10.0	1,286	30.8	91.1	1,590,439	3.2	43,443	2.7	1,535,949	43.7	17.4
Des Moines-West Des Moines, IA	245,643	69.4	175,300	19.2	11.1	851	28.4	88.6	346,691	0.6	10,182	2.9	339,224	42.0	18.3
Detroit-Warren-Dearborn, MI	1,689,859	67.6	160,700	19.6	12.7	886	30.1	84.9	2,111,265	1.5	93,706	4.4	2,002,081	38.4	21.3
Detroit-Dearborn-Livonia, MI Div 19,804	677,208	60.4	105,300	19.8	13.9	823	33.0	79.4	789,088	1.4	42,673	5.4	737,706	32.1	24.0
Warren-Troy-Farmington Hills, MI Div 47,664	1,012,651	72.5	187,100	19.4	11.8	955	27.8	88.6	1,322,177	1.5	51,033	3.9	1,264,375	42.1	19.7
Dothan, AL	56,133	69.0	118,200	20.0	10.0	710	28.1	73.1	61,925	-0.2	2,715	4.4	60,053	30.7	25.8
Dover, DE	64,452	67.0	199,000	22.8	10.6	997	30.6	86.6	78,132	0.7	3,886	5.0	77,379	32.7	25.5
Dubuque, IA	37,710	74.1	161,600	18.5	10.6	766	24.8	87.0	54,459	-0.5	1,638	3.0	51,731	34.6	23.2
Duluth, MN-WI	116,967	70.5	156,200	20.1	11.4	735	29.1	81.1	144,328	-0.1	6,682	4.6	136,700	35.1	22.8
Durham-Chapel Hill, NC	217,853	60.0	222,200	19.8	10.1	947	30.5	87.2	295,418	2.1	11,887	4.0	279,409	48.1	15.5
East Stroudsburg, PA	57,284	75.6	164,200	24.8	14.6	982	25.7	85.2	81,955	0.1	4,814	5.9	76,875	33.1	22.4
Eau Claire, WI	66,866	65.8	160,900	19.5	13.2	786	28.4	86.6	93,186	0.7	2,913	3.1	86,570	30.1	25.8
El Centro, CA	44,855	60.8	170,900	23.7	11.1	788	31.8	77.4	73,980	-3.9	14,105	19.1	61,106	23.6	24.5
Elizabethtown-Fort Knox, KY	56,261	65.9	156,700	18.5	10.0	758	25.2	86.4	66,548	2.2	3,154	4.7	67,101	30.8	29.7
Elkhart-Goshen, IN	72,487	66.8	129,300	17.1	10.0	742	25.4	80.0	111,740	3.1	2,825	2.5	97,133	25.4	39.3
Elmira, NY	34,418	64.7	111,600	19.5	10.5	780	30.9	84.3	35,872	-1.6	2,007	5.6	37,717	38.9	19.7
El Paso, TX	268,172	60.1	119,600	23.1	11.8	771	30.4	82.0	354,924	1.2	16,367	4.6	349,249	30.8	21.5
Enid, OK	24,859	62.7	112,800	20.3	10.8	786	24.4	81.5	27,936	-3.6	1,098	3.9	28,348	26.5	34.1
Erie, PA	109,705	66.0	125,700	19.7	12.3	703	28.1	81.5	130,755	-2.1	7,563	5.8	127,683	34.0	21.1
Eugene, OR	147,712	58.9	243,500	23.7	12.0	932	33.0	89.0	182,399	2.1	8,118	4.5	169,464	34.6	18.6

1. Specified owner-occupied units.   2. A value of 10.0 represents 10 percent or less; a value of 50.0 represents 50 percent or more.   3. Specified renter-occupied units.
4. Overcrowded or lacking complete plumbing facilities.   5. Percent of civilian labor force.   6. Civilian employed persons 16 years old and over.

Table C. Metropolitan Areas — **Nonfarm Employment and Agriculture**

Area name	Private nonfarm establishments, employment and payroll, 2016									Agriculture, 2012			
	Number of establishments	Employment						Annual payroll		Farms			Farm operators whose principal occupation is farming (percent)
		Total	Health care and social assistance	Manufacturing	Retail trade	Finance and insurance	Professional, scientific, and technical services	Total (mil dol)	Average per employee (dollars)	Number	Percent with:		
											Fewer than 50 acres	500 acres or more	
	104	105	106	107	108	109	110	111	112	113	114	115	116
Cedar Rapids, IA	6,523	130,819	18,225	17,869	17,400	11,499	6,421	6,103	46,654	3,678	32.5	19.9	55.6
Chambersburg-Waynesboro, PA	3,091	49,814	8,290	7,984	7,555	1,159	1,919	1,856	37,256	1,596	35.9	6.3	60.8
Champaign-Urbana, IL	4,858	75,956	14,411	7,629	10,969	3,399	2,981	3,078	40,527	2,284	28.5	32.7	56.8
Charleston, WV	5,228	87,948	21,250	3,250	12,296	4,148	5,391	3,739	42,511	343	29.2	1.7	40.5
Charleston-North Charleston, SC	18,583	275,562	37,616	24,698	40,466	7,895	20,282	11,984	43,490	1,143	56.3	7.0	45.2
Charlotte-Concord-Gastonia, NC-SC	59,420	1,023,314	128,146	97,757	123,465	80,202	63,900	53,591	52,370	7,328	50.8	4.6	44.6
Charlottesville, VA	6,124	83,950	17,719	4,476	11,714	3,850	6,532	4,066	48,439	2,311	33.3	8.0	43.4
Chattanooga, TN-GA	11,242	217,706	32,085	31,315	28,254	13,559	9,076	8,857	40,684	2,018	44.2	5.0	43.8
Cheyenne, WY	3,234	35,366	8,045	1,130	5,765	1,578	2,488	1,413	39,958	1,116	33.5	31.2	37.3
Chicago-Naperville-Elgin, IL-IN-WI	245,377	4,158,944	597,162	383,614	474,724	269,616	340,278	240,971	57,941	6,841	47.6	18.3	56.1
Chicago-Naperville-Arlington Heights, IL Div 16,974	NA	NA	NA	NA	NA	NA	NA	NA	NA	2,789	48.8	16.7	58.6
Elgin, IL Div 20,994	NA	NA	NA	NA	NA	NA	NA	NA	NA	1,470	40.2	22.6	63.2
Gary, IN Div 23,844	NA	NA	NA	NA	NA	NA	NA	NA	NA	1,874	45.0	21.5	48.8
Lake County-Kenosha County, IL-WI Div 29,404	NA	NA	NA	NA	NA	NA	NA	NA	NA	708	65.4	7.8	51.4
Chico, CA	4,627	60,432	15,032	4,271	10,238	2,564	2,471	2,302	38,087	2,056	66.8	7.0	59.4
Cincinnati, OH-KY-IN	46,150	924,037	145,609	99,514	109,321	58,872	58,052	46,744	50,587	9,242	46.3	4.5	40.7
Clarksville, TN-KY	4,428	69,651	11,264	12,573	12,662	2,020	2,574	2,356	33,826	2,359	31.5	9.6	41.3
Cleveland, TN	2,116	40,526	5,430	8,212	5,440	1,892	754	1,536	37,907	1,062	49.4	4.8	44.9
Cleveland-Elyria, OH	51,247	922,238	177,885	118,781	101,830	51,532	52,746	45,477	49,312	2,975	59.3	3.6	49.1
Coeur d'Alene, ID	4,659	50,135	9,532	5,278	8,929	2,194	2,233	1,915	38,196	824	58.4	6.7	48.1
College Station-Bryan, TX	4,860	72,149	9,945	6,030	12,170	1,860	3,770	2,540	35,206	4,361	35.0	10.1	44.6
Colorado Springs, CO	17,815	241,394	37,593	11,060	33,205	10,800	22,773	10,715	44,390	1,329	45.4	17.6	48.5
Columbia, MO	4,671	77,527	17,549	4,133	12,833	7,279	3,869	2,946	38,005	1,171	39.5	8.6	38.3
Columbia, SC	17,207	292,496	44,622	26,382	40,329	21,874	18,107	12,066	41,252	3,085	44.1	7.2	42.0
Columbus, GA-AL	5,685	96,286	16,791	10,184	14,407	13,035	3,738	3,879	40,287	770	32.2	13.1	42.2
Columbus, IN	1,835	47,791	4,940	13,008	5,023	994	2,923	2,241	46,884	623	44.1	14.4	44.8
Columbus, OH	42,106	859,251	146,260	66,293	100,949	77,748	53,836	41,933	48,802	8,198	47.4	9.9	43.1
Corpus Christi, TX	9,543	166,276	32,090	10,652	22,752	4,560	8,134	6,695	40,266	1,555	45.8	20.6	38.6
Corvallis, OR	2,119	27,066	6,058	2,870	3,857	611	1,814	1,263	46,651	886	71.4	5.6	46.3
Crestview-Fort Walton Beach-Destin, FL	7,437	79,095	10,734	2,046	16,671	2,715	7,067	2,949	37,282	1,147	46.7	5.8	41.9
Cumberland, MD-WV	1,986	30,313	7,449	3,451	4,870	978	1,240	1,088	35,881	720	32.9	5.3	37.2
Dallas-Fort Worth-Arlington, TX	160,269	3,044,254	385,556	240,025	350,393	211,203	233,526	167,046	54,872	29,659	61.7	4.8	35.8
Dallas-Plano-Irving, TX Div 19,124	NA	NA	NA	NA	NA	NA	NA	NA	NA	16,257	61.9	4.6	35.6
Fort Worth-Arlington, TX Div 23,104	NA	NA	NA	NA	NA	NA	NA	NA	NA	13,402	61.5	4.9	36.1
Dalton, GA	2,587	57,127	5,243	21,987	5,868	860	1,413	2,272	39,778	698	46.7	3.2	44.6
Danville, IL	1,411	24,530	5,336	4,861	3,872	1,101	428	973	39,647	956	36.6	29.5	54.5
Daphne-Fairhope-Foley, AL	5,235	61,341	7,858	4,120	13,738	1,607	2,120	1,960	31,955	989	52.6	8.1	45.8
Davenport-Moline-Rock Island, IA-IL	8,873	159,956	24,678	23,582	22,681	6,205	6,449	6,957	43,496	3,513	34.0	19.0	55.7
Dayton, OH	16,528	322,924	63,360	43,193	41,413	12,960	25,007	14,635	45,320	2,638	59.4	8.7	41.3
Decatur, AL	2,960	45,875	6,642	12,092	6,372	1,490	1,602	1,886	41,110	2,788	42.7	4.1	42.7
Decatur, IL	2,441	45,380	8,176	6,330	5,872	1,569	1,086	1,988	43,810	674	35.9	29.5	59.1
Deltona-Daytona Beach-Ormond Beach, FL	14,674	161,757	30,599	9,818	30,724	5,345	7,047	5,563	34,391	1,481	78.8	3.4	55.0
Denver-Aurora-Lakewood, CO	82,462	1,248,441	162,701	55,972	143,912	72,023	108,742	70,125	56,170	4,856	52.4	14.4	43.8
Des Moines-West Des Moines, IA	16,122	314,623	41,679	19,086	40,859	50,044	17,999	15,736	50,015	4,898	41.1	16.0	44.2
Detroit-Warren-Dearborn, MI	99,127	1,741,079	272,645	229,757	208,106	83,748	176,051	94,635	54,354	4,242	56.9	5.8	54.0
Detroit-Dearborn-Livonia, MI Div 19,804	NA	NA	NA	NA	NA	NA	NA	NA	NA	287	77.7	1.4	59.9
Warren-Troy-Farmington Hills, MI Div 47,664	NA	NA	NA	NA	NA	NA	NA	NA	NA	3,955	55.3	6.1	53.5
Dothan, AL	3,409	50,246	10,416	5,382	9,214	1,412	1,399	1,906	37,939	2,331	31.5	12.2	43.5
Dover, DE	3,422	53,196	10,879	4,810	9,317	1,581	2,452	2,040	38,349	863	54.5	9.0	56.8
Dubuque, IA	2,759	55,171	8,317	8,847	7,662	3,948	2,346	2,285	41,419	1,462	28.3	10.3	52.5
Duluth, MN-WI	7,079	110,266	28,830	7,051	16,294	5,169	4,282	4,507	40,874	1,550	25.4	6.1	41.0
Durham-Chapel Hill, NC	12,702	251,653	46,919	17,484	25,779	10,794	33,754	14,782	58,739	2,410	48.6	4.0	46.7
East Stroudsburg, PA	3,372	47,216	7,039	5,420	9,581	983	1,564	1,687	35,721	283	53.0	2.5	55.1
Eau Claire, WI	4,291	73,083	14,368	11,262	11,281	2,962	2,859	2,894	39,594	3,070	30.4	7.2	45.1
El Centro, CA	2,519	33,092	5,105	3,504	8,631	768	854	1,093	33,018	421	29.7	40.6	69.4
Elizabethtown-Fort Knox, KY	2,908	41,533	8,295	7,361	7,098	1,570	1,488	1,486	35,791	2,831	44.0	5.5	44.5
Elkhart-Goshen, IN	4,856	126,911	10,915	68,531	9,552	2,105	2,055	5,716	45,040	1,724	62.8	3.9	38.3
Elmira, NY	1,791	30,971	6,589	5,345	5,300	934	804	1,228	39,640	372	27.2	4.3	53.8
El Paso, TX	14,424	236,037	45,447	13,765	39,919	6,688	10,889	7,509	31,813	824	67.7	17.0	43.9
Enid, OK	NA	NA	NA	NA	NA	NA	NA	NA	NA				
Erie, PA	6,191	114,476	24,667	20,308	16,123	5,163	3,819	4,372	38,187	1,422	41.2	4.1	48.7
Eugene, OR	9,819	125,284	23,710	14,334	20,136	4,732	5,472	4,998	39,890	2,660	73.9	2.9	44.5

Table C. Metropolitan Areas — **Agriculture**

Area name	Land in farms — Acreage (1,000)	Percent change, 2007-2012	Average size of farm	Total irrigated (1,000)	Total cropland (1,000)	Value of land and buildings (dollars) — Average per farm	Average per acre	Value of machinery and equipment, average per farm (dollars)	Value of products sold: Total (mil dol)	Average per farm (acres)	Percent from: Crops	Livestock and poultry products	Percent of farms with sales of: $10,000 or more	$100,000 or more	Government payments Total ($1,000)	Percent of farms
	117	118	119	120	121	122	123	124	125	126	127	128	129	130	131	132
Cedar Rapids, IA	1,075	1.4	292	0.4	930.0	2,020,529	6,910	203,111	918.4	249,694	69.5	30.5	63.3	38.3	28,988	76.7
Chambersburg-Waynesboro, PA	265	9.0	166	2.8	201.8	1,101,504	6,646	133,634	413.8	259,277	21.6	78.4	66.3	40.4	4,302	34.1
Champaign-Urbana, IL	1,184	8.8	518	19.6	1,140.6	4,153,230	8,014	311,067	802.9	351,514	92.5	7.5	73.2	50.6	21,102	84.3
Charleston, WV	48	5.0	141	D	6.4	285,079	2,024	31,985	1.9	5,522	32.7	67.3	15.2	0.3	D	7.6
Charleston-North Charleston, SC	185	16.1	162	4.0	62.8	651,877	4,027	59,942	D	D	D	52.2	27.9	7.1	1,317	18.1
Charlotte-Concord-Gastonia, NC-SC	939	2.4	128	5.0	437.2	717,330	5,599	71,406	D	D	D	D	31.1	10.8	D	13.6
Charlottesville, VA	407	4.8	176	2.5	114.7	1,095,125	6,216	61,828	101.3	43,836	40.3	59.7	35.3	5.0	871	13.3
Chattanooga, TN-GA	267	2.2	132	D	94.7	532,958	4,035	67,110	213.6	105,852	10.7	89.3	31.1	9.0	1,684	11.3
Cheyenne, WY	1,676	-0.9	1,502	59.3	338.1	1,079,159	719	110,585	190.7	170,918	24.4	75.6	37.0	17.6	4,938	32.7
Chicago-Naperville-Elgin, IL-IN-WI	2,232	-2.6	326	D	2,069.2	2,377,211	7,285	210,709	2,187.2	319,717	75.5	24.5	57.9	36.1	44,738	55.3
Chicago-Naperville-Arlington Heights, IL Div 16,974	831	-0.5	298	D	776.8	2,382,011	7,995	200,859	604.2	216,622	89.5	10.5	58.1	33.3	14,208	51.8
Elgin, IL Div 20,994	566	0.6	385	5.1	537.8	3,142,503	8,157	253,384	671.1	456,510	74.7	25.3	66.4	48.0	16,157	63.7
Gary, IN Div 23,844	728	-5.9	389	45.5	664.5	2,295,203	5,904	227,225	807.7	430,977	66.3	33.7	55.1	36.6	12,509	64.2
Lake County-Kenosha County, IL-WI Div 29,404	107	-10.3	151	0.7	90.1	986,410	6,547	117,194	104.3	147,323	70.9	29.1	47.2	21.6	1,864	28.2
Chico, CA	381	1.9	185	199.7	227.3	1,408,199	7,599	135,591	541.3	263,266	97.3	2.7	59.7	26.2	9,386	13.7
Cincinnati, OH-KY-IN	1,216	-5.6	132	D	698.5	582,601	4,427	73,512	418.6	45,298	82.2	17.8	31.2	7.8	14,347	34.1
Clarksville, TN-KY	637	0.5	270	5.5	401.2	958,646	3,552	104,747	280.3	118,814	80.1	19.9	43.1	15.8	9,847	46.5
Cleveland, TN	122	-4.6	115	0.2	44.8	593,111	5,157	61,272	153.7	144,771	6.4	93.6	31.5	12.4	397	11.3
Cleveland-Elyria, OH	304	3.1	102	4.4	217.0	614,628	6,011	86,924	375.3	126,146	83.2	16.8	42.2	13.4	3,173	9.4
Coeur d'Alene, ID	124	-5.1	151	13.8	64.3	624,138	4,139	57,726	23.7	28,750	83.8	16.2	19.5	4.1	1,075	19.7
College Station-Bryan, TX	1,102	0.9	253	46.6	231.0	736,281	2,914	63,936	321.5	73,722	24.9	75.1	32.1	5.4	5,786	20.1
Colorado Springs, CO	720	4.4	542	8.3	57.0	696,877	1,287	43,971	45.2	33,977	46.2	53.8	23.9	4.8	1,334	11.1
Columbia, MO	241	-7.0	206	5.3	144.4	749,119	3,644	69,631	52.2	44,565	66.0	34.0	34.9	8.1	1,837	10.2
Columbia, SC	522	3.0	169	D	198.1	537,771	3,177	78,787	578.6	187,568	26.8	73.2	29.9	11.0	4,185	31.0
Columbus, GA-AL	206	-3.8	267	5.7	51.8	724,603	2,715	63,508	58.6	76,142	D	D	25.8	6.0	1,166	19.8
Columbus, IN	172	3.2	275	13.5	153.4	1,619,191	5,878	151,406	95.6	153,387	89.5	10.5	54.9	27.1	4,647	26.8
Columbus, OH	1,746	5.0	213	2.9	1,448.9	1,049,293	4,928	131,542	1,180.0	143,942	76.3	23.7	42.8	18.9	28,755	63.7
Corpus Christi, TX	938	0.9	603	6.0	612.9	949,925	1,575	166,062	172.2	110,713	85.3	14.8	31.6	12.9	9,227	43.7
Corvallis, OR	124	8.2	140	11.3	68.2	830,059	5,932	68,867	103.3	116,597	78.2	21.8	28.6	10.4	486	35.0
Crestview-Fort Walton Beach-Destin, FL	209	8.7	183	1.5	49.3	565,418	3,097	49,066	38.8	33,870	49.0	51.0	22.1	5.3	1,802	6.4
Cumberland, MD-WV	112	-1.9	156	0.1	28.5	493,965	3,163	50,556	25.4	35,232	13.4	86.6	25.8	3.8	510	27.6
Dallas-Fort Worth-Arlington, TX	4,075	10.8	137	29.3	1,275.6	585,215	4,260	50,241	743.8	25,077	46.4	53.6	19.6	2.8	10,166	19.7
Dallas-Plano-Irving, TX Div 19,124	2,203	9.1	136	18.2	853.9	558,320	4,120	49,299	483.1	29,718	53.6	46.4	19.4	2.9	7,646	7.2
Fort Worth-Arlington, TX Div 23,104	1,872	12.9	140	11.1	421.7	617,838	4,424	51,384	260.7	19,449	33.3	66.7	19.9	2.7	2,520	9.0
Dalton, GA	86	4.1	123	0.6	29.3	560,004	4,542	73,451	222.9	319,338	5.8	94.2	37.8	17.3	358	4.9
Danville, IL	434	-5.0	454	0.2	409.5	3,200,276	7,043	259,283	283.6	296,653	95.7	4.3	60.4	41.8	7,122	11.6
Daphne-Fairhope-Foley, AL	192	1.3	194	7.7	100.9	773,980	3,980	107,905	135.6	137,070	85.3	14.7	35.2	11.7	2,649	76.2
Davenport-Moline-Rock Island, IA-IL	1,101	-10.0	313	21.3	970.1	2,141,963	6,834	206,181	964.4	274,514	77.8	22.2	59.6	39.0	28,824	26.7
Dayton, OH	454	-3.5	172	4.2	394.2	1,006,136	5,845	111,095	282.7	107,154	89.5	10.5	44.1	17.8	6,976	74.8
Decatur, AL	396	3.2	142	5.0	167.3	471,748	3,318	68,907	301.3	108,081	23.3	76.7	32.3	11.8	6,226	51.1
Decatur, IL	337	15.8	499	0.0	321.7	3,911,432	7,833	294,921	211.3	313,540	95.7	4.3	66.0	42.7	5,762	31.2
Deltona-Daytona Beach-Ormond Beach, FL	150	5.6	101	12.9	28.8	564,216	5,584	45,579	128.4	86,726	90.0	10.0	35.0	9.6	D	80.1
Denver-Aurora-Lakewood, CO	2,490	-8.7	513	D	923.4	890,955	1,737	67,853	D	D	D	D	24.4	6.5	D	7.6
Des Moines-West Des Moines, IA	1,371	-3.9	280	D	1,079.5	1,644,653	5,875	143,481	891.6	182,028	70.5	29.5	49.3	22.9	32,090	17.4
Detroit-Warren-Dearborn, MI	557	2.2	131	7.3	437.7	626,459	4,770	106,037	399.2	94,113	83.9	16.1	41.1	14.6	6,302	65.6
Detroit-Dearborn-Livonia, MI Div 19,804	16	-9.6	55	0.3	10.9	408,840	7,442	80,902	26.5	92,456	98.2	1.8	36.9	8.4	102	21.4
Warren-Troy-Farmington Hills, MI Div 47,664	541	2.6	137	7.0	426.9	642,251	4,692	107,860	372.7	94,233	82.9	17.1	41.4	15.1	6,200	9.4
Dothan, AL	587	-0.7	252	20.0	263.4	586,922	2,332	93,694	342.7	147,028	44.1	55.9	34.8	15.3	13,121	22.3
Dover, DE	172	-0.9	200	31.8	147.4	1,596,656	7,999	121,074	277.7	321,816	D	D	53.3	29.8	2,550	60.3
Dubuque, IA	291	-6.2	199	0.0	224.3	1,214,544	6,093	172,274	387.8	265,260	31.0	69.0	67.5	39.7	11,080	37.2
Duluth, MN-WI	290	-9.1	187	D	131.9	345,245	1,843	52,513	35.8	23,111	54.9	45.1	34.8	3.6	2,245	81.2
Durham-Chapel Hill, NC	285	-1.5	118	5.1	104.5	611,832	5,181	58,915	245.0	101,639	28.0	72.0	35.7	9.9	D	7.3
East Stroudsburg, PA	26	-9.2	94	0.1	13.0	735,583	7,861	71,198	11.0	38,777	66.8	33.2	35.7	8.5	174	21.0
Eau Claire, WI	588	5.3	192	8.7	378.7	540,963	2,823	99,430	366.5	119,378	41.7	58.3	47.9	20.6	8,327	15.5
El Centro, CA	516	20.7	1,225	455.0	487.9	8,577,865	7,002	745,304	1,888.6	4,486,078	69.4	30.6	84.3	66.7	2,788	53.8
Elizabethtown-Fort Knox, KY	434	-7.4	153	0.9	245.1	523,605	3,412	77,721	136.4	48,180	66.5	33.5	36.8	7.3	4,749	29.5
Elkhart-Goshen, IN	173	5.8	100	25.5	140.2	808,782	8,067	83,012	296.8	172,178	28.0	72.0	51.8	27.4	2,785	44.3
Elmira, NY	58	-10.8	156	0.2	28.1	376,065	2,407	75,599	16.0	43,143	41.2	58.8	28.5	8.6	482	20.1
El Paso, TX	2,461	1.4	2,986	43.0	101.6	2,030,155	680	101,518	80.0	97,103	80.4	19.6	33.7	12.0	2,091	22.8
Enid, OK																14.7
Erie, PA	169	-2.6	119	0.9	96.2	407,705	3,438	75,158	91.7	64,469	76.5	23.5	41.5	12.8	1,693	20.5
Eugene, OR	220	-10.6	83	19.3	100.0	563,427	6,824	49,734	142.5	53,574	74.6	25.4	23.5	5.6	575	5.1

Table C. Metropolitan Areas — Water Use, Wholesale Trade, Retail Trade, and Real Estate

Area name	Water use, 2015 Public supply water withdrawn (mil gal/day)	Public supply gallons withdrawn per person per day	Wholesale Trade[1], 2012 Number of establishments	Number of employees	Sales (mil dol)	Annual payroll (mil dol)	Retail Trade[2], 2012 Number of establishments	Number of employees	Sales (mil dol)	Annual payroll (mil dol)	Real estate and rental and leasing,[2] 2012 Number of establishments	Number of employees	Sales (mil dol)	Annual payroll (mil dol)
	133	134	135	136	137	138	139	140	141	142	143	144	145	146
Cedar Rapids, IA	44.04	165.5	364	5,483	4,229.0	284.7	882	16,193	4,949.8	393.1	239	1,022	210.4	36.0
Chambersburg-Waynesboro, PA	8.47	55.1	108	D	D	D	486	7,106	1,809.5	157.6	87	328	54.9	10.4
Champaign-Urbana, IL	26.98	112.9	235	3,501	3,586.0	161.9	724	11,239	2,735.2	241.0	213	3,033	562.6	119.0
Charleston, WV	32.75	148.4	267	3,771	2,568.6	186.0	840	12,216	3,459.6	294.5	244	1,220	279.9	42.5
Charleston-North Charleston, SC	107.90	144.9	692	7,954	6,339.0	417.6	2,628	35,904	9,411.5	849.2	929	4,326	796.6	155.8
Charlotte-Concord-Gastonia, NC-SC	234.04	96.5	3,185	46,227	33,695.9	2,696.6	7,467	107,892	29,996.8	2,541.1	2,704	13,096	2,885.5	646.3
Charlottesville, VA	15.25	66.4	146	1,853	868.8	100.8	835	11,100	2,702.8	266.0	289	1,356	248.1	48.0
Chattanooga, TN-GA	77.58	141.6	543	6,354	3,413.3	305.2	1,932	25,651	6,903.8	613.2	445	2,309	453.4	103.9
Cheyenne, WY	14.00	144.2	121	1,105	722.2	67.0	370	5,513	1,896.2	161.3	142	461	99.5	16.5
Chicago-Naperville-Elgin, IL-IN-WI	1,142.97	119.7	12,340	204,598	231,996.5	13,565.0	28,181	437,310	127,688.0	11,090.7	9,629	64,763	21,668.7	3,443.4
Chicago-Naperville-Arlington Heights, IL Div 16,974	905.71	123.4	9,720	158,870	187,061.2	10,316.5	21,489	331,143	93,728.7	8,416.8	7,713	55,585	19,420.2	3,045.0
Elgin, IL Div 20,994	69.39	109.2	801	9,957	9,982.0	598.8	1,767	27,240	6,733.8	599.9	508	2,492	684.0	97.9
Gary, IN Div 23,844	93.36	132.8	612	6,761	6,918.2	335.4	2,125	32,702	10,190.7	748.4	548	2,840	496.9	96.3
Lake County-Kenosha County, IL-WI Div 29,404	74.51	85.4	1,207	29,010	28,035.2	2,314.3	2,800	46,225	17,034.7	1,325.6	860	3,846	1,067.6	204.2
Chico, CA	28.81	127.8	148	D	D	D	725	9,231	2,576.9	240.4	234	1,160	147.6	28.3
Cincinnati, OH-KY-IN	237.83	110.2	2,292	43,770	51,641.2	2,634.6	6,428	104,296	30,586.2	2,564.2	1,911	11,621	2,614.7	482.8
Clarksville, TN-KY	36.68	130.5	147	1,921	1,653.1	79.5	828	11,849	3,261.3	284.6	211	958	146.6	29.3
Cleveland, TN	14.61	120.9	65	D	D	D	409	5,046	1,419.3	118.8	66	294	38.3	8.6
Cleveland-Elyria, OH	292.15	141.8	2,840	42,048	26,946.9	2,259.0	6,674	97,427	25,943.9	2,303.9	2,111	16,590	5,313.5	765.5
Coeur d'Alene, ID	34.69	230.7	132	D	D	D	574	7,996	2,501.7	207.0	201	623	122.6	19.1
College Station-Bryan, TX	35.47	142.4	160	1,805	1,275.7	91.1	736	10,830	3,113.8	233.7	244	1,352	271.6	46.2
Colorado Springs, CO	94.52	135.4	442	4,431	2,576.6	248.6	2,025	29,505	8,137.0	775.0	1,074	3,427	669.1	122.3
Columbia, MO	17.85	102.0	135	1,461	631.4	73.2	627	11,563	3,741.0	287.7	227	920	160.6	28.8
Columbia, SC	92.00	113.6	762	11,901	8,591.9	627.6	2,616	36,865	9,747.3	839.7	701	4,198	985.9	181.5
Columbus, GA-AL	53.20	169.6	182	2,405	1,716.5	95.0	1,034	13,671	3,475.8	300.0	289	1,615	285.7	59.6
Columbus, IN	9.49	116.9	77	998	774.4	52.7	306	4,701	1,113.1	99.4	72	303	57.0	9.4
Columbus, OH	207.31	102.5	1,746	30,642	33,473.9	1,742.1	5,592	97,309	31,432.9	2,571.3	1,937	11,638	3,033.5	480.4
Corpus Christi, TX	73.84	163.2	407				1,351	20,248	6,139.4	495.5	504	3,109	706.8	138.3
Corvallis, OR	11.95	136.5	44	346	452.5	22.6	262	3,455	731.0	82.5	105	453	53.3	10.2
Crestview-Fort Walton Beach-Destin, FL	32.98	125.8	184	1,624	883.8	79.2	1,194	14,773	3,704.0	346.5	528	2,300	404.8	86.3
Cumberland, MD-WV	2.24	22.4	57	596	234.7	25.5	359	4,853	1,160.1	102.0	67	236	34.0	6.4
Dallas-Fort Worth-Arlington, TX	442.68	62.3	7,562	130,067	150,841.7	8,112.6	19,506	305,066	97,494.7	8,162.1	7,462	57,356	12,829.3	2,748.1
Dallas-Plano-Irving, TX Div 19,124	390.06	82.9	5,279	92,203	118,378.4	5,990.3	12,725	199,722	63,747.3	5,406.4	5,314	43,570	9,887.9	2,154.9
Fort Worth-Arlington, TX Div 23,104	52.62	22.0	2,283	37,864	32,463.3	2,122.4	6,781	105,344	33,747.3	2,755.7	2,148	13,786	2,941.5	593.2
Dalton, GA	25.85	179.8	217	3,003	1,320.0	120.1	525	5,401	1,500.4	123.7	75	349	133.7	13.2
Danville, IL	8.95	112.9	77	1,788	3,136.5	84.3	255	3,401	850.3	74.3	45	158	28.7	4.5
Daphne-Fairhope-Foley, AL	23.67	116.2	175	1,868	1,118.2	84.1	950	12,072	3,145.8	280.0	292	1,760	250.3	53.8
Davenport-Moline-Rock Island, IA-IL	40.06	104.4	496	7,650	7,471.4	414.1	1,314	21,284	5,530.5	501.3	326	1,311	309.0	42.9
Dayton, OH	101.01	126.1	684	9,796	17,365.8	533.2	2,487	39,751	9,851.3	905.5	735	3,939	665.2	133.2
Decatur, AL	33.33	218.3	164	2,144	1,455.9	91.4	583	6,300	1,891.5	144.5	87	351	78.8	12.7
Decatur, IL	20.02	186.6	112	D	D	D	395	5,724	1,494.2	133.7	88	471	105.2	13.8
Deltona-Daytona Beach-Ormond Beach, FL	64.62	103.7	474	3,222	1,725.6	154.7	2,104	26,736	6,941.6	642.5	792	2,866	478.1	88.2
Denver-Aurora-Lakewood, CO	453.79	161.2	3,311	48,922	53,628.2	3,061.7	8,302	123,338	35,076.0	3,331.1	4,455	20,864	5,461.1	959.7
Des Moines-West Des Moines, IA	59.77	96.0	795	12,805	10,596.6	699.5	1,966	35,339	9,452.9	842.5	654	3,714	759.0	160.6
Detroit-Warren-Dearborn, MI	634.84	147.6	4,655	66,120	60,968.3	4,010.0	15,127	194,583	54,637.0	4,845.5	3,605	25,561	8,298.0	1,035.2
Detroit-Dearborn-Livonia, MI Div 19,804	466.55	265.2	1,483	23,525	25,358.3	1,417.5	6,091	65,409	17,409.4	1,539.9	1,070	6,044	4,464.6	225.3
Warren-Troy-Farmington Hills, MI Div 47,664	168.29	66.2	3,172	42,595	35,609.9	2,592.5	9,036	129,174	37,227.6	3,305.6	2,535	19,517	3,833.4	810.0
Dothan, AL	22.38	151.0	196	2,986	8,979.2	154.7	716	8,675	2,426.0	204.9	110	440	74.7	16.4
Dover, DE	11.81	68.1	94	D	D	D	561	8,856	2,690.8	214.1	127	459	92.2	17.0
Dubuque, IA	7.71	79.4	158	2,353	2,083.1	107.4	442	7,157	1,659.1	149.1	110	381	72.4	12.2
Duluth, MN-WI	36.82	131.7	267	3,351	2,368.2	158.6	1,168	15,179	3,937.6	340.4	260	1,098	180.2	30.4
Durham-Chapel Hill, NC	64.47	116.7	355	9,817	7,270.2	1,042.0	1,626	23,631	5,748.8	553.7	503	2,351	485.6	94.3
East Stroudsburg, PA	11.35	68.2	97	D	D	D	634	8,710	2,140.4	187.8	123	507	86.8	15.2
Eau Claire, WI	14.36	86.7	157	2,272	1,422.0	94.5	615	10,495	2,723.8	225.7	141	659	91.2	18.5
El Centro, CA	24.47	135.8	197	1,801	1,599.1	72.5	446	7,322	1,676.9	160.3	119	574	92.6	15.9
Elizabethtown-Fort Knox, KY	15.75	106.0	74	D	D	D	501	6,618	1,900.3	154.9	129	543	68.2	12.9
Elkhart-Goshen, IN	12.95	63.6	340	5,803	3,329.9	249.5	678	8,754	2,440.4	206.9	157	768	134.5	25.4
Elmira, NY	8.37	96.1	85	1,193	765.0	51.5	350	5,044	1,174.8	115.8	84	382	106.6	17.0
El Paso, TX	114.57	136.6	952	D	D	D	2,332	34,975	9,192.0	754.1	699	3,143	617.3	108.0
Enid, OK	2.87	45.1					958	15,221	3,752.8	326.4	182	1,042	158.5	32.3
Erie, PA	33.34	119.9	264	3,127	1,242.5	145.7	958	15,221	3,752.8	326.4	182	1,042	158.5	32.3
Eugene, OR	43.68	120.4	384	4,860	2,852.0	229.0	1,270	18,265	4,291.5	449.9	505	2,115	314.3	58.4

1 Merchant wholesalers, except manufacturers' sales branches and offices. 2. Employer establishments.

Table C. Metropolitan Areas — Professional Services, Manufacturing, and Accommodation and Food Services

Area name	Professional, scientific, and technical services, 2012				Manufacturing, 2012				Accommodation and food services, 2012			
	Number of establishments	Number of employees	Sales (mil dol)	Annual payroll (mil dol)	Number of establishments	Number of employees	Sales (mil dol)	Annual payroll (mil dol)	Number of establishments	Number of employees	Sales (mil dol)	Annual payroll (mil dol)
	147	148	149	150	151	152	153	154	155	156	157	158
Cedar Rapids, IA	564	5,682	747.4	328.4	265	19,213	10,486.4	1,348.3	570	9,449	410.9	119.2
Chambersburg-Waynesboro, PA	223	2,067	234.8	100.3	196	8,182	3,180.0	403.9	270	D	D	D
Champaign-Urbana, IL	485	2,967	381.1	144.2	162	7,807	3,700.2	345.5	579	10,454	459.4	126.4
Charleston, WV	585	6,079	898.7	344.1	129	3,062	2,207.6	188.9	483	9,649	568.7	150.6
Charleston-North Charleston, SC	2,001	18,874	3,340.8	1,296.0	465	23,529	13,956.2	1,379.1	1,616	34,059	1,968.3	543.8
Charlotte-Concord-Gastonia, NC-SC	6,214	58,864	10,186.8	3,891.2	2,340	86,773	36,489.5	4,175.6	4,465	87,966	4,719.8	1,269.1
Charlottesville, VA	791	6,406	967.0	401.8	173	3,830	977.5	211.2	551	9,857	561.8	153.9
Chattanooga, TN-GA	942	D	D	D	557	32,303	14,940.6	1,610.2	1,056	21,292	1,089.7	306.5
Cheyenne, WY	458	1,860	279.8	99.7	67	1,190	2,549.8	76.8	207	3,980	224.8	59.8
Chicago-Naperville-Elgin, IL-IN-WI	33,178	323,636	64,623.4	26,279.3	10,473	383,870	194,249.9	21,208.1	19,708	355,344	22,899.9	6,279.1
Chicago-Naperville-Arlington Heights, IL Div 16,974	26,911	277,996	58,343.8	23,040.6	8,005	274,717	127,047.1	14,762.8	15,390	281,814	18,925.7	5,214.3
Elgin, IL Div 20,994	1,690	10,006	1,667.7	598.1	909	33,826	11,678.1	1,702.8	1,064	18,219	856.3	243.1
Gary, IN Div 23,844	1,302	8,302	1,004.9	369.3	545	34,450	41,108.4	2,531.9	1,394	25,099	1,480.8	349.3
Lake County-Kenosha County, IL-WI Div 29,404	3,275	27,332	3,606.9	2,271.3	1,014	40,878	14,416.3	2,210.6	1,860	30,212	1,637.1	472.3
Chico, CA	424	2,394	388.0	97.2	177	4,126	1,341.1	168.3	397	7,091	350.5	96.4
Cincinnati, OH-KY-IN	D	D	D	D	2,239	100,872	47,994.7	5,697.6	4,151	88,347	4,798.4	1,274.3
Clarksville, TN-KY	297	2,668	337.7	120.4	155	10,702	4,287.4	484.5	470	8,759	408.6	113.4
Cleveland, TN	150	867	78.4	32.6	122	8,069	5,718.3	345.2	196	3,834	177.5	47.1
Cleveland-Elyria, OH	5,775	50,835	7,976.9	3,175.2	3,358	120,600	43,530.2	6,669.9	4,461	79,070	3,864.1	1,065.2
Coeur d'Alene, ID	442	D	D	D	241	4,011	D	170.2	362	D	D	D
College Station-Bryan, TX	441	2,877	539.8	139.6	123	4,903	1,180.0	198.2	502	10,084	476.3	129.7
Colorado Springs, CO	2,505	20,151	3,041.6	1,280.6	479	10,471	3,382.5	562.2	1,371	28,383	1,554.0	427.2
Columbia, MO	414	3,570	424.0	156.7	99	3,994	2,042.1	173.3	419	9,006	373.2	104.7
Columbia, SC	1,911	16,971	2,745.8	1,045.8	516	24,989	13,694.4	1,250.5	1,500	29,589	1,391.3	385.3
Columbus, GA-AL	463	3,050	359.1	133.7	186	11,255	3,755.5	471.4	562	12,474	617.9	173.3
Columbus, IN	159	3,550	299.0	234.7	142	11,663	5,636.4	553.6	201	4,243	198.6	54.2
Columbus, OH	4,702	50,668	8,800.6	3,360.9	1,411	60,169	33,070.4	3,129.4	4,071	81,490	4,087.9	1,162.2
Corpus Christi, TX	927	6,378	928.0	338.3	238	10,950	44,697.1	775.4	1,048	20,133	1,046.4	279.9
Corvallis, OR	284	1,996	332.6	125.1	93	1,613	412.7	71.4	209	3,087	142.8	41.6
Crestview-Fort Walton Beach-Destin, FL	811	6,485	975.9	407.7	113	2,832	572.2	139.7	666	16,040	940.1	278.4
Cumberland, MD-WV	123	681	53.9	22.8	68	4,367	1,470.3	236.5	231	D	D	D
Dallas-Fort Worth-Arlington, TX	19,150	210,153	39,787.8	15,548.4	5,481	225,780	109,647.6	12,308.6	12,577	263,818	15,353.0	4,225.5
Dallas-Plano-Irving, TX Div 19,124	14,206	168,149	33,185.1	13,176.9	3,512	145,699	61,179.9	7,948.5	8,449	176,054	10,381.6	2,902.0
Fort Worth-Arlington, TX Div 23,104	4,944	42,004	6,602.7	2,371.5	1,969	80,081	48,467.8	4,360.1	4,128	87,764	4,971.4	1,323.5
Dalton, GA	188	D	D	D	330	17,966	7,111.9	668.8	213	3,781	196.4	50.1
Danville, IL	84	428	46.7	16.6	96	5,168	2,353.2	256.1	143	2,161	86.0	25.4
Daphne-Fairhope-Foley, AL	450	1,899	211.5	86.2	146	3,780	1,438.8	166.8	462	10,726	560.6	161.1
Davenport-Moline-Rock Island, IA-IL	776	5,712	1,007.7	280.0	402	24,533	16,677.3	1,289.9	872	15,809	832.3	208.7
Dayton, OH	1,717	21,824	3,582.6	1,420.6	1,048	40,297	13,041.0	2,179.3	1,611	32,811	1,508.4	428.8
Decatur, AL	230	1,483	167.8	69.3	202	12,048	10,543.3	718.5	243	4,370	197.9	54.9
Decatur, IL	157	1,216	142.7	54.0	109	8,240	13,379.3	435.3	225	4,331	189.8	55.6
Deltona-Daytona Beach-Ormond Beach, FL	1,510	7,316	886.3	301.5	380	8,224	2,024.2	367.4	1,156	22,876	1,134.5	341.5
Denver-Aurora-Lakewood, CO	12,927	108,529	22,675.3	8,365.9	2,237	52,525	24,861.3	2,880.5	5,846	115,312	7,069.5	2,014.3
Des Moines-West Des Moines, IA	1,686	15,965	2,633.1	966.8	427	19,669	11,785.8	953.5	1,354	24,834	1,211.0	348.2
Detroit-Warren-Dearborn, MI	11,419	163,997	24,342.5	12,026.3	5,353	199,394	110,685.0	11,620.7	8,168	153,118	8,567.2	2,275.4
Detroit-Dearborn-Livonia, MI Div 19,804	2,848	46,825	7,135.0	3,444.6	1,483	71,526	56,638.5	4,413.5	3,184	61,446	4,238.8	1,050.2
Warren-Troy-Farmington Hills, MI Div 47,664	8,571	117,172	17,207.5	8,581.7	3,870	127,869	54,046.5	7,207.2	4,984	91,672	4,328.4	1,225.2
Dothan, AL	261	1,359	162.4	59.6	132	4,834	1,646.4	182.8	280	5,084	231.9	61.9
Dover, DE	278	D	D	D	74	4,797	1,930.8	218.9	272	6,183	475.8	101.1
Dubuque, IA	166	2,956	450.9	147.7	144	8,498	6,036.4	434.6	242	4,456	169.5	49.8
Duluth, MN-WI	510	D	D	D	286	6,999	12,135.4	375.2	754	12,463	632.6	155.0
Durham-Chapel Hill, NC	1,838	35,056	6,112.3	2,966.1	350	15,118	10,445.6	957.9	1,179	22,267	1,248.1	344.0
East Stroudsburg, PA	306	D	D	D	111	4,449	D	358.1	387	8,392	724.8	155.1
Eau Claire, WI	265	2,089	252.1	102.8	209	9,968	3,621.4	444.4	440	6,931	276.6	75.5
El Centro, CA	179	787	79.1	30.4	50	2,218	1,466.0	95.4	258	3,516	182.6	47.9
Elizabethtown-Fort Knox, KY	270	1,809	184.5	69.0	88	5,679	2,366.8	262.1	229	5,034	220.3	61.7
Elkhart-Goshen, IN	313	2,004	220.2	81.0	795	53,705	14,833.3	2,288.0	348	6,500	280.7	75.8
Elmira, NY	111	774	83.5	36.1	85	5,495	1,247.0	278.8	202	3,534	154.5	43.3
El Paso, TX	1,202	D	D	D	505	13,129	D	543.2	1,481	28,757	1,385.5	375.5
Enid, OK												
Erie, PA	412	3,028	375.8	135.3	476	21,490	9,437.7	1,179.0	630	10,877	485.4	128.2
Eugene, OR	948	5,301	583.9	226.2	529	12,345	4,039.3	581.3	937	13,627	711.8	203.7

Table C. Metropolitan Areas —

Health Care and Social Assistance, Other Services, Nonemployer Businesses, and Residential Construction

Area name	Health care and social assistance, 2012				Other services, 2012				Nonemployer businesses, 2015		Value of residential construction authorized by building permits, 2017	
	Number of establishments	Number of employees	Receipts (mil dol)	Annual payroll (mil dol)	Number of establishments	Number of employees	Receipts (mil dol)	Annual payroll (mil dol)	Number	Receipts (mil dol)	New construction ($1,000)	Number of housing units
	159	160	161	162	163	164	165	166	167	168	169	170
Cedar Rapids, IA	663	16,556	1,557.5	658.3	469	2,866	281.8	83.6	16,415	714.1	125,366	992
Chambersburg-Waynesboro, PA	305	8,178	820.5	349.3	287	1,558	131.5	32.7	8,947	374.7	63,392	412
Champaign-Urbana, IL	420	13,306	1,770.8	610.5	317	2,293	414.2	69.0	14,015	538.0	137,591	838
Charleston, WV	795	19,917	2,139.0	795.7	416	3,070	299.4	91.1	10,215	423.5	18,130	135
Charleston-North Charleston, SC	1,669	35,964	4,763.9	1,578.2	1,120	7,240	733.9	205.1	58,399	2,762.8	1,606,852	7,267
Charlotte-Concord-Gastonia, NC-SC	5,167	113,438	13,463.8	5,178.0	3,490	22,305	2,609.7	674.3	187,409	8,167.0	4,456,543	22,869
Charlottesville, VA	561	16,296	2,372.6	999.2	381	3,381	666.6	140.0	18,365	841.0	328,951	1,276
Chattanooga, TN-GA	1,275	31,220	3,602.0	1,420.4	716	5,022	569.2	149.4	37,716	1,790.7	440,951	2,631
Cheyenne, WY	323	6,700	647.9	305.2	189	943	93.6	27.1	7,665	480.1	88,101	573
Chicago-Naperville-Elgin, IL-IN-WI	25,714	569,844	63,927.3	24,944.8	17,586	132,350	17,826.4	4,831.8	779,014	35,080.6	4,186,157	22,132
Chicago-Naperville-Arlington Heights, IL Div 16,974	20,277	459,774	51,473.0	20,190.9	13,870	107,796	15,518.3	4,150.1	NA	NA	2,942,953	15,919
Elgin, IL Div 20,994	1,382	26,345	2,910.1	1,147.8	968	6,879	664.2	187.5	NA	NA	318,115	2,088
Gary, IN Div 23,844	1,691	41,436	4,686.3	1,716.8	1,231	8,564	814.5	239.1	NA	NA	504,250	2,212
Lake County-Kenosha County, IL-WI Div 29,404	2,364	42,289	4,858.0	1,889.3	1,517	9,111	829.4	255.1	NA	NA	420,839	1,913
Chico, CA	716	12,868	1,434.5	560.2	321	2,158	190.0	56.0	13,528	626.5	144,287	823
Cincinnati, OH-KY-IN	4,831	134,554	15,421.0	6,374.0	3,255	24,339	2,431.1	681.1	140,795	6,340.4	1,240,838	6,465
Clarksville, TN-KY	510	10,678	986.1	367.7	285	1,577	129.3	36.8	14,072	608.0	241,510	1,813
Cleveland, TN	248	5,054	653.8	200.8	102	873	73.0	21.8	7,844	389.9	102,348	639
Cleveland-Elyria, OH	5,423	173,697	17,969.1	7,747.1	3,895	26,763	2,784.6	775.0	148,063	6,748.7	760,385	3,227
Coeur d'Alene, ID	509	8,630	806.2	308.4	236	D	D	D	11,983	520.3	367,427	1,778
College Station-Bryan, TX	433	8,794	1,080.7	395.8	316	2,193	405.2	62.8	15,881	727.4	364,519	3,083
Colorado Springs, CO	1,955	31,286	3,300.0	1,327.9	1,128	8,548	1,816.7	326.1	50,936	2,028.6	1,651,506	4,965
Columbia, MO	602	16,725	2,033.5	699.4	327	1,985	187.4	53.2	11,463	561.3	289,639	1,634
Columbia, SC	1,637	42,874	4,546.9	1,828.4	1,224	8,398	794.5	241.2	54,051	2,264.5	805,323	4,629
Columbus, GA-AL	691	16,540	1,625.9	635.9	404	2,693	259.9	74.2	19,419	650.9	167,372	917
Columbus, IN	221	4,824	512.8	203.1	111	692	82.5	19.7	4,184	169.7	49,578	204
Columbus, OH	4,677	133,376	14,049.2	5,491.7	2,808	23,334	3,073.2	774.6	148,635	6,826.8	1,758,539	8,892
Corpus Christi, TX	1,186	30,414	2,800.7	1,049.3	633	4,993	581.9	158.7	31,084	1,373.6	223,113	1,186
Corvallis, OR	271	5,258	588.1	258.8	147	891	153.8	30.3	5,783	238.1	36,396	136
Crestview-Fort Walton Beach-Destin, FL	658	11,275	1,378.0	474.1	435	2,145	198.0	56.5	23,311	1,273.6	855,836	2,471
Cumberland, MD-WV	314	7,665	686.5	263.5	180	960	72.1	20.7	4,410	153.8	10,012	50
Dallas-Fort Worth-Arlington, TX	17,015	331,041	40,730.9	15,173.9	8,560	70,090	8,772.4	2,385.7	614,884	32,224.1	13,110,100	62,524
Dallas-Plano-Irving, TX Div 19,124	11,734	226,936	28,266.9	10,701.7	5,677	47,622	6,382.3	1,735.2	NA	NA	10,432,619	47,901
Fort Worth-Arlington, TX Div 23,104	5,281	104,105	12,464.0	4,472.2	2,883	22,468	2,390.1	650.5	NA	NA	2,677,481	14,623
Dalton, GA	225	4,744	525.2	198.0	141	958	85.2	28.7	7,888	375.2	46,580	343
Danville, IL	143	4,736	514.4	235.4	121	540	47.4	13.3	4,239	136.9	13,889	104
Daphne-Fairhope-Foley, AL	444	7,029	622.5	265.3	269	1,203	110.5	31.9	17,876	863.8	460,188	2,417
Davenport-Moline-Rock Island, IA-IL	1,010	22,953	2,081.4	893.8	684	4,209	364.7	106.2	20,884	869.4	127,673	750
Dayton, OH	2,004	59,132	6,556.8	2,598.1	1,242	8,387	863.6	206.1	48,014	1,962.8	369,085	1,251
Decatur, AL	376	6,469	541.2	207.7	180	1,060	103.0	29.5	9,484	370.2	28,314	160
Decatur, IL	291	8,193	886.2	332.1	176	1,170	239.1	37.3	5,713	183.7	8,271	39
Deltona-Daytona Beach-Ormond Beach, FL	1,542	28,190	3,112.5	1,157.7	1,150	5,517	584.5	186.5	48,879	2,051.3	921,105	3,054
Denver-Aurora-Lakewood, CO	7,163	130,863	15,988.2	6,540.4	5,189	35,432	4,395.4	1,161.3	248,548	12,303.7	4,479,714	22,735
Des Moines-West Des Moines, IA	1,414	39,163	4,078.1	1,844.6	1,143	8,007	992.9	271.6	43,795	2,108.2	1,264,250	6,367
Detroit-Warren-Dearborn, MI	12,474	254,643	28,793.7	11,432.0	6,992	44,589	4,734.0	1,273.7	334,728	14,798.5	2,250,302	10,089
Detroit-Dearborn-Livonia, MI Div 19,804	4,091	101,848	12,420.4	4,712.3	2,645	16,865	1,763.8	497.5	NA	NA	487,983	2,529
Warren-Troy-Farmington Hills, MI Div 47,664	8,383	152,795	16,373.3	6,719.7	4,347	27,724	2,970.2	776.2	NA	NA	1,762,319	7,560
Dothan, AL	375	10,243	1,127.1	486.2	221	D	D	D	9,860	433.1	86,669	390
Dover, DE	398	9,405	990.6	379.5	233	1,325	105.5	32.0	9,585	574.1	217,462	1,554
Dubuque, IA	271	7,806	702.0	318.7	201	1,157	109.4	28.1	6,335	278.9	63,698	241
Duluth, MN-WI	931	28,824	2,484.4	1,168.0	525	3,338	297.5	76.6	15,509	613.1	131,658	665
Durham-Chapel Hill, NC	1,373	42,120	5,452.9	1,974.5	755	6,461	1,033.8	248.0	43,648	1,700.7	895,862	4,924
East Stroudsburg, PA	393	7,031	643.1	276.0	309	1,571	115.7	37.0	10,328	473.6	61,286	248
Eau Claire, WI	539	14,294	1,521.9	662.8	302	1,828	162.1	45.1	9,909	512.4	132,246	568
El Centro, CA	268	4,536	511.1	182.9	142	608	53.4	16.5	9,817	338.8	35,674	191
Elizabethtown-Fort Knox, KY	398	8,120	728.7	319.5	182	1,053	95.6	24.0	7,918	317.9	77,794	507
Elkhart-Goshen, IN	362	10,105	1,160.8	413.6	336	2,069	261.0	61.1	12,754	562.7	97,970	560
Elmira, NY	211	6,421	621.6	294.0	128	670	57.3	15.6	3,875	141.9	16,779	101
El Paso, TX	1,525	41,470	4,304.3	1,488.3	910	5,676	464.5	129.4	56,586	2,435.5	601,524	3,277
Enid, OK									NA	NA	13,523	95
Erie, PA	850	24,899	2,216.5	923.1	563	3,591	322.7	80.2	13,841	594.6	49,589	265
Eugene, OR	1,135	20,576	2,247.4	828.6	611	3,480	443.9	97.7	23,337	1,040.8	193,504	842

Table C. Metropolitan Areas — Government Employment and Payroll, and Local Government Finances

Area name	Government employment and payroll, 2012		March payroll (percent of total)							Local government finances, 2012 — General revenue		Taxes	Per capita[1] (dollars)	
	Full-time equivalent employees	March payroll (dollars)	Administration, judicial, and legal	Police and corrections	Fire protection	Highways and transportation	Health and welfare	Natural resources and utilities	Education and libraries	Total (mil dol)	Inter-governmental (mil dol)	Total (mil dol)	Total	Property
	171	172	173	174	175	176	177	178	179	180	181	182	183	184
Cedar Rapids, IA	10,705	42,251,213	4.0	6.0	2.5	6.3	2.3	4.9	72.2	1,343.4	584.3	503.5	1,924	1,486
Chambersburg-Waynesboro, PA	3,820	13,644,359	7.7	8.8	1.7	2.3	9.1	6.1	63.5	415.1	130.8	191.4	1,265	978
Champaign-Urbana, IL	8,553	32,026,460	5.7	8.9	3.4	7.5	6.1	5.5	61.1	891.5	342.7	404.0	1,728	1,506
Charleston, WV	8,227	28,589,774	5.5	6.5	3.8	3.3	7.9	3.1	66.9	735.0	295.9	299.7	1,326	910
Charleston-North Charleston, SC	22,813	76,849,945	8.2	12.8	6.2	2.8	3.9	8.3	55.3	2,449.1	759.7	1,206.4	1,730	1,171
Charlotte-Concord-Gastonia, NC-SC	106,366	436,927,670	3.6	7.0	2.3	1.5	39.9	4.1	40.2	12,067.6	3,110.9	3,416.0	1,487	1,141
Charlottesville, VA	7,679	26,539,813	8.0	9.0	2.3	2.5	3.9	4.9	64.7	782.8	292.5	365.6	1,641	1,221
Chattanooga, TN-GA	19,778	70,912,137	6.7	7.6	2.9	3.3	31.0	10.3	37.0	2,452.8	620.7	669.9	1,245	910
Cheyenne, WY	6,173	27,578,286	2.8	4.6	1.9	1.8	39.8	1.5	46.1	796.0	292.8	103.3	1,094	589
Chicago-Naperville-Elgin, IL-IN-WI	358,119	1,755,095,339	5.6	15.8	4.2	6.1	4.0	6.3	56.6	49,995.8	16,211.6	25,716.1	2,701	2,261
Chicago-Naperville-Arlington Heights, IL Div 16,974	272,297	1,388,594,555	5.4	17.5	4.2	7.0	4.3	6.3	54.0	39,231.9	12,680.6	19,977.9	2,730	2,208
Elgin, IL Div 20,994	25,482	114,832,272	5.3	10.3	5.2	2.2	1.5	6.6	67.5	3,172.7	934.1	1,826.9	2,913	2,670
Gary, IN Div 23,844	25,614	86,646,440	8.5	10.0	3.9	4.2	3.6	7.3	60.8	3,048.3	1,320.8	1,243.6	1,759	1,670
Lake County-Kenosha County, IL-WI Div 29,404	34,726	165,022,072	5.5	8.7	3.9	2.4	4.0	6.2	68.5	4,542.9	1,276.0	2,667.7	3,066	2,896
Chico, CA	8,734	37,694,370	6.4	9.6	2.6	2.0	12.6	5.9	58.9	1,079.1	643.7	243.0	1,097	878
Cincinnati, OH-KY-IN	72,643	287,857,130	6.6	10.8	6.5	4.5	6.9	6.8	56.1	8,861.6	3,178.0	3,802.3	1,786	1,197
Clarksville, TN-KY	8,620	27,138,883	4.3	10.6	3.8	3.1	6.5	6.8	62.4	701.2	298.6	267.5	975	569
Cleveland, TN	4,049	11,684,208	5.5	10.1	5.8	3.7	9.5	2.4	62.1	282.7	134.8	92.6	786	497
Cleveland-Elyria, OH	92,435	406,449,865	6.4	10.2	4.7	5.9	15.2	7.7	48.3	11,282.4	3,960.2	4,907.0	2,378	1,483
Coeur d'Alene, ID	6,580	25,436,541	6.0	8.3	3.6	2.4	37.6	3.3	38.1	678.7	158.8	148.1	1,040	972
College Station-Bryan, TX	8,862	27,409,320	8.4	12.4	4.3	4.5	3.2	11.0	51.4	682.0	173.0	393.1	1,676	1,379
Colorado Springs, CO	25,178	98,225,856	5.3	9.9	3.8	2.2	15.3	15.2	45.7	2,631.8	836.0	850.3	1,272	745
Columbia, MO	6,008	20,052,275	7.9	5.3	3.3	2.8	2.7	11.3	63.5	497.3	161.0	228.2	1,354	805
Columbia, SC	33,084	120,753,751	4.2	6.5	2.3	1.0	25.0	4.6	54.7	3,250.3	958.1	1,087.0	1,385	1,204
Columbus, GA-AL	13,084	41,360,235	6.9	10.8	4.0	2.6	6.1	6.8	60.6	1,009.9	422.9	376.5	1,213	848
Columbus, IN	4,371	15,688,309	3.2	6.6	2.9	1.3	44.5	3.1	37.7	469.7	111.3	106.7	1,348	1,076
Columbus, OH	70,274	306,173,279	9.4	10.4	7.0	4.4	8.1	5.2	53.9	9,594.0	3,610.3	4,421.2	2,274	1,428
Corpus Christi, TX	19,396	62,362,670	4.9	10.1	3.6	4.7	4.1	5.7	63.6	1,651.1	548.8	775.1	1,773	1,396
Corvallis, OR	1,834	7,923,562	9.3	13.4	6.2	3.8	7.4	9.4	45.7	259.6	93.0	115.4	1,335	1,185
Crestview-Fort Walton Beach-Destin, FL	8,719	30,209,052	6.5	11.1	6.5	3.5	2.3	6.1	60.8	813.5	261.8	380.6	1,537	1,209
Cumberland, MD-WV	3,611	14,623,810	4.0	5.7	1.6	3.1	0.5	6.1	76.2	340.7	169.2	105.4	1,034	723
Dallas-Fort Worth-Arlington, TX	263,325	1,034,080,549	5.5	11.1	4.7	4.3	9.8	4.8	58.2	28,591.5	7,248.4	14,334.2	2,139	1,724
Dallas-Plano-Irving, TX Div 19,124	172,608	694,884,179	5.0	10.6	4.8	5.5	10.3	4.8	57.3	19,625.6	4,888.2	9,734.9	2,199	1,766
Fort Worth-Arlington, TX Div 23,104	90,717	339,196,370	6.6	12.1	4.4	1.7	8.6	4.7	60.2	8,965.9	2,360.2	4,599.3	2,022	1,644
Dalton, GA	5,343	18,100,335	4.0	6.7	3.7	3.2	5.9	9.7	65.2	440.0	199.5	149.2	1,045	674
Danville, IL	3,642	12,242,579	7.0	7.8	2.7	3.5	3.6	4.2	67.9	289.5	151.8	91.4	1,132	940
Daphne-Fairhope-Foley, AL	7,374	22,581,577	7.4	8.0	2.9	4.3	20.7	5.6	47.7	640.7	189.9	231.1	1,211	537
Davenport-Moline-Rock Island, IA-IL	14,533	58,873,005	5.4	9.2	3.4	4.7	5.9	5.6	64.3	1,610.6	616.3	675.0	1,764	1,489
Dayton, OH	31,140	126,902,617	7.8	9.6	4.5	5.3	8.1	7.6	55.4	3,577.2	1,408.5	1,490.6	1,861	1,242
Decatur, AL	6,083	20,609,391	3.2	7.4	2.8	2.6	21.3	8.4	53.1	589.6	255.2	134.1	870	438
Decatur, IL	4,204	17,133,160	5.9	11.8	4.5	3.0	2.0	8.2	63.3	407.1	180.7	163.9	1,488	1,260
Deltona-Daytona Beach-Ormond Beach, FL	23,653	83,363,572	6.3	11.3	4.7	2.1	21.7	6.5	45.3	2,404.0	575.9	895.2	1,504	1,170
Denver-Aurora-Lakewood, CO	95,098	432,423,959	6.6	12.7	5.6	6.2	10.7	9.5	46.7	13,355.6	3,846.7	5,924.4	2,240	1,358
Des Moines-West Des Moines, IA	22,853	93,893,961	5.5	8.0	3.0	4.3	8.9	5.3	63.7	2,778.1	968.6	1,212.2	2,058	1,784
Detroit-Warren-Dearborn, MI	115,282	533,695,857	7.4	12.9	5.0	4.6	2.5	4.5	60.8	18,679.3	8,819.4	5,896.0	1,374	1,225
Detroit-Dearborn-Livonia, MI Div 19,804	52,078	243,918,311	7.3	16.2	6.7	6.5	2.2	6.4	52.0	9,260.6	4,384.4	2,686.6	1,499	1,195
Warren-Troy-Farmington Hills, MI Div 47,664	63,204	289,777,546	7.4	10.1	3.5	3.0	2.7	2.9	68.2	9,418.7	4,435.0	3,209.5	1,284	1,246
Dothan, AL	7,365	24,527,281	3.9	6.4	3.0	2.7	40.1	5.5	36.7	730.7	179.2	156.0	1,057	387
Dover, DE	4,210	17,226,252	4.7	6.0	0.1	0.6	1.6	5.6	79.4	494.8	323.1	88.0	525	459
Dubuque, IA	3,261	12,486,456	6.7	9.6	3.9	7.2	5.0	6.0	60.6	400.9	169.8	165.8	1,743	1,320
Duluth, MN-WI	11,586	52,151,960	6.8	9.8	2.9	6.5	13.3	7.0	48.7	1,488.3	728.3	373.6	1,337	1,215
Durham-Chapel Hill, NC	18,475	63,324,374	5.8	6.4	1.4	2.2	10.3	6.8	63.0	1,793.6	701.9	824.7	1,577	1,277
East Stroudsburg, PA	5,957	25,067,544	5.7	4.3	0.0	5.4	1.6	1.5	80.9	719.0	225.3	441.5	2,616	2,404
Eau Claire, WI	5,534	21,894,206	6.1	8.1	3.0	6.4	5.8	4.3	65.0	602.6	268.9	253.5	1,549	1,431
El Centro, CA	10,122	49,143,599	4.2	6.0	1.7	1.1	19.5	16.2	45.5	1,293.3	740.8	180.2	1,019	733
Elizabethtown-Fort Knox, KY	6,654	21,761,001	1.7	4.2	1.5	1.3	37.6	3.5	49.3	547.6	189.2	112.2	746	448
Elkhart-Goshen, IN	6,985	24,411,992	5.4	8.4	4.1	2.5	1.6	3.6	73.6	630.5	315.1	218.4	1,094	907
Elmira, NY	3,853	14,858,297	5.0	9.7	2.9	4.0	13.2	3.8	59.7	476.3	219.3	175.3	1,971	1,236
El Paso, TX	38,548	140,371,856	4.5	10.4	3.7	3.1	8.1	3.1	65.5	3,358.7	1,620.5	1,097.5	1,321	1,022
Enid, OK														
Erie, PA	8,523	32,472,819	5.3	9.7	2.6	5.6	3.9	6.0	65.7	1,197.6	616.5	364.0	1,297	1,046
Eugene, OR	11,647	50,155,119	7.2	10.9	5.2	6.9	4.1	11.4	48.1	1,390.4	585.1	463.2	1,306	1,120

1. Based on the resident population estimated as of July 1 of the year shown.

Area name	Local government finances, 2012 (cont.)							Debt outstanding		Government employment, 2016			Individual income tax returns, 2015		
	Direct general expenditure														
			Percent of total for:												
	Total (mil dol)	Per capita[1] (dollars)	Education	Health and hospitals	Police protection	Public welfare	Highways	Total (mil dol)	Per capita[1] (dollars)	Federal civilian	Federal military	State and local	Number of returns	Mean adjusted gross income	Mean income tax
	185	186	187	188	189	190	191	192	193	194	195	196	197	198	199
Cedar Rapids, IA	1,498.7	5,725	47.4	3.1	3.7	1.0	5.5	1,735.1	6,629	1,169	984	15,506	127,970	65,361	8,045
Chambersburg-Waynesboro, PA	452.7	2,992	54.1	4.1	1.9	5.5	4.8	619.1	4,092	2,197	397	5,737	76,500	52,722	5,415
Champaign-Urbana, IL	941.0	4,025	49.1	2.4	5.0	2.5	6.1	728.3	3,115	1,357	479	36,916	100,470	61,881	7,785
Charleston, WV	776.4	3,436	50.7	3.1	6.2	0.1	2.6	329.2	1,457	2,225	1,024	22,169	98,550	53,492	6,462
Charleston-North Charleston, SC	2,212.6	3,173	45.5	1.1	9.5	0.2	4.7	5,523.5	7,920	10,816	12,595	52,442	350,780	64,945	8,809
Charlotte-Concord-Gastonia, NC-SC	11,496.9	5,006	29.1	35.1	5.3	2.9	2.0	12,295.6	5,354	10,454	6,361	139,727	1,113,370	69,490	9,854
Charlottesville, VA	798.6	3,583	47.8	6.8	5.5	6.6	2.1	859.4	3,856	1,419	1,177	34,271	103,570	86,004	13,461
Chattanooga, TN-GA	2,273.9	4,228	31.4	31.0	4.8	0.8	2.7	1,828.1	3,399	5,517	1,628	31,461	241,440	57,523	7,405
Cheyenne, WY	781.4	8,270	37.0	40.5	2.5	0.2	3.1	132.4	1,401	2,727	3,449	11,448	48,190	59,192	7,471
Chicago-Naperville-Elgin, IL-IN-WI	48,512.9	5,095	44.9	3.1	7.1	1.3	4.3	81,674.3	8,577	54,543	31,142	509,837	4,646,620	76,780	11,980
Chicago-Naperville-Arlington Heights, IL Div 16,974	38,566.5	5,270	42.7	3.4	7.4	1.3	4.3	70,331.4	9,610	45,104	15,232	388,371	NA	NA	NA
Elgin, IL Div 20,994	3,112.0	4,962	53.7	0.6	6.3	0.5	5.5	4,822.0	7,688	1,857	1,278	42,423	NA	NA	NA
Gary, IN Div 23,844	2,464.8	3,487	47.7	2.5	4.8	0.9	2.2	2,682.0	3,795	1,944	2,110	32,614	NA	NA	NA
Lake County-Kenosha County, IL-WI Div 29,404	4,369.5	5,022	56.1	2.3	6.1	1.8	4.4	3,838.9	4,412	5,638	12,522	46,429	NA	NA	NA
Chico, CA	1,098.2	4,957	46.2	6.8	4.4	11.8	3.6	480.5	2,169	557	337	15,908	92,590	53,377	6,061
Cincinnati, OH-KY-IN	9,065.0	4,259	41.6	5.6	6.4	3.8	4.1	13,076.8	6,143	15,339	5,786	112,598	1,040,980	66,741	9,132
Clarksville, TN-KY	654.4	2,385	56.0	3.0	7.0	0.1	4.1	4,800.5	17,498	5,669	27,689	13,694	117,970	45,165	4,274
Cleveland, TN	268.7	2,281	54.1	7.7	7.1	0.1	5.2	242.0	2,054	287	353	5,460	52,490	47,025	4,849
Cleveland-Elyria, OH	11,203.3	5,429	41.3	12.0	5.9	3.4	4.1	14,162.1	6,863	18,456	5,614	114,934	1,038,570	61,463	8,315
Coeur d'Alene, ID	637.0	4,475	29.8	40.2	5.8	0.4	3.9	121.1	851	622	501	10,446	71,980	55,175	6,276
College Station-Bryan, TX	708.6	3,022	50.7	1.9	5.8	0.4	5.6	1,389.0	5,923	822	555	39,161	96,230	58,551	7,780
Colorado Springs, CO	2,586.9	3,871	37.1	21.4	6.1	2.0	8.1	4,453.6	6,663	12,709	37,036	38,952	325,640	60,212	7,084
Columbia, MO	580.4	3,444	44.8	3.1	4.3	0.2	6.2	2,592.5	15,382	2,513	597	28,974	78,330	61,780	8,208
Columbia, SC	3,328.6	4,242	44.0	20.7	4.0	0.1	1.1	7,155.9	9,119	10,295	11,743	73,673	361,720	55,558	6,511
Columbus, GA-AL	1,107.4	3,566	50.3	6.1	5.6	1.9	4.1	1,051.1	3,385	6,844	18,937	17,760	129,630	48,896	5,303
Columbus, IN	465.6	5,883	32.7	40.9	1.8	0.5	0.9	364.3	4,603	169	245	6,263	39,920	62,456	7,509
Columbus, OH	9,248.5	4,757	41.8	5.3	5.8	5.4	4.5	10,699.7	5,504	14,478	5,608	156,975	979,700	63,611	8,449
Corpus Christi, TX	1,702.5	3,895	49.7	4.7	6.4	0.2	3.7	3,153.1	7,214	5,925	4,719	27,278	200,790	54,788	6,903
Corvallis, OR	259.2	2,999	46.3	7.4	9.6	0.0	4.2	233.8	2,705	520	248	8,970	38,850	65,967	8,139
Crestview-Fort Walton Beach-Destin, FL	907.3	3,663	47.7	3.2	7.3	0.3	4.4	501.5	2,025	8,812	15,824	11,118	130,110	64,886	9,772
Cumberland, MD-WV	335.7	3,292	62.0	0.8	3.9	0.5	4.1	213.3	2,092	598	387	7,074	41,630	46,560	4,492
Dallas-Fort Worth-Arlington, TX	28,447.6	4,245	42.1	11.3	5.7	0.4	4.3	75,576.3	11,278	45,174	16,773	370,570	3,259,450	74,072	11,582
Dallas-Plano-Irving, TX Div 19,124	19,555.5	4,418	41.1	11.5	5.2	0.5	4.4	53,566.2	12,101	29,819	10,426	253,839	NA	NA	NA
Fort Worth-Arlington, TX Div 23,104	8,892.1	3,910	44.2	11.0	6.7	0.1	4.1	22,010.2	9,677	15,355	6,347	116,731	NA	NA	NA
Dalton, GA	487.6	3,416	54.9	8.7	3.9	0.4	4.8	143.3	1,004	250	393	6,646	57,710	46,959	5,087
Danville, IL	308.3	3,819	56.4	0.7	6.4	3.5	6.3	102.1	1,265	1,517	154	4,274	34,040	45,644	4,494
Daphne-Fairhope-Foley, AL	700.0	3,669	34.5	19.2	6.1	0.1	7.7	911.0	4,775	345	920	9,048	93,140	59,966	7,644
Davenport-Moline-Rock Island, IA-IL	1,675.1	4,378	48.5	5.0	5.5	1.5	4.6	1,215.2	3,176	5,751	1,470	20,297	184,440	59,550	7,218
Dayton, OH	3,712.9	4,635	47.4	3.3	6.4	7.2	5.2	3,143.4	3,924	18,750	7,142	42,634	384,980	55,891	6,691
Decatur, AL	670.1	4,345	54.9	16.9	4.4	0.3	3.3	924.8	5,996	391	656	7,720	65,870	49,866	5,018
Decatur, IL	452.8	4,112	52.8	2.0	7.8	0.1	8.1	462.5	4,200	323	218	5,330	49,070	55,299	6,619
Deltona-Daytona Beach-Ormond Beach, FL	2,484.9	4,174	30.8	22.3	7.3	0.4	3.9	3,027.1	5,085	1,382	1,204	21,676	295,050	51,320	6,324
Denver-Aurora-Lakewood, CO	12,432.0	4,700	33.7	6.3	6.2	4.2	4.8	24,877.2	9,405	28,898	10,111	175,528	1,386,770	77,883	11,551
Des Moines-West Des Moines, IA	3,004.6	5,101	48.5	8.3	4.2	1.2	5.5	3,647.7	6,193	6,278	2,458	37,803	298,250	71,953	9,675
Detroit-Warren-Dearborn, MI	19,021.2	4,432	43.4	5.7	6.5	3.0	3.8	31,478.0	7,334	28,002	7,848	162,890	2,098,800	63,460	8,881
Detroit-Dearborn-Livonia, MI Div 19,804	9,500.3	5,300	36.3	3.3	7.0	5.2	2.9	21,084.6	11,764	13,988	3,233	73,282	NA	NA	NA
Warren-Troy-Farmington Hills, MI Div 47,664	9,520.9	3,809	50.5	8.0	6.0	0.9	4.7	10,393.4	4,158	14,014	4,615	89,608	NA	NA	NA
Dothan, AL	704.8	4,774	29.3	42.3	4.1	0.1	4.1	485.5	3,289	406	675	10,379	61,710	49,596	5,793
Dover, DE	527.3	3,145	73.4	1.1	4.4	0.0	1.5	478.7	2,856	1,728	4,196	17,318	79,750	50,237	5,031
Dubuque, IA	405.9	4,268	37.6	4.5	4.7	2.0	7.0	372.4	3,916	269	366	4,486	47,450	62,149	7,859
Duluth, MN-WI	1,639.0	5,865	37.0	6.4	5.3	6.4	9.4	1,391.0	4,977	1,613	1,051	23,754	132,090	56,129	6,265
Durham-Chapel Hill, NC	1,919.0	3,670	40.5	5.6	8.2	5.6	2.1	1,899.7	3,633	6,650	1,430	60,341	252,560	70,198	9,769
East Stroudsburg, PA	739.9	4,384	67.9	0.1	3.0	3.9	2.5	1,201.0	7,115	3,208	446	8,182	78,420	52,881	5,787
Eau Claire, WI	676.7	4,137	54.0	4.1	6.5	3.1	11.1	488.8	2,988	534	422	11,664	78,840	58,018	7,446
El Centro, CA	1,172.3	6,625	40.7	23.6	4.1	7.5	2.9	1,408.8	7,962	2,161	367	16,336	78,190	39,845	3,363
Elizabethtown-Fort Knox, KY	515.1	3,425	39.9	37.7	2.7	0.0	2.2	447.0	2,972	5,955	4,847	9,017	66,310	49,496	4,748
Elkhart-Goshen, IN	609.8	3,055	58.2	1.0	3.9	0.2	3.5	758.8	3,801	267	611	8,457	94,480	55,585	6,900
Elmira, NY	467.0	5,252	42.9	3.0	3.0	18.1	8.9	490.6	5,518	215	129	5,782	39,370	52,751	5,838
El Paso, TX	3,277.0	3,945	52.3	15.5	5.0	0.4	1.0	4,036.3	4,859	12,949	27,320	55,851	363,710	41,979	4,056
Enid, OK										489	1,386	3,284	NA	NA	NA
Erie, PA	1,203.4	4,288	44.0	5.6	2.7	14.2	3.5	1,705.3	6,076	1,543	730	15,480	130,590	51,399	6,021
Eugene, OR	1,390.2	3,921	44.2	5.1	6.9	2.2	4.3	1,580.1	4,457	1,730	1,000	22,034	165,950	56,885	6,798

1. Based on the resident population estimated as of July 1 of the year shown.

Table C. Metropolitan Areas — **Personal Income and Earnings**

| | Personal income, 2016 | | | | | | | | | | Earnings, 2016 | | |
| | | | Per capita[1] | | | Supplements to wages and salaries, employer contributions (mil dol) | | | | | | Contributions for government social insurance (mil dol) | |
Area name	Total (mil dol)	Percent change, 2015-2016	Dollars	Rank	Wages and salaries (mil dol)	Pension and insurance	Government social insurance	Proprietors' income	Dividends, interest, and rent (mil dol)	Personal transfer receipts (mil dol)	Total (mil dol)	From employee and self-employed	From employer
	62	63	64	65	66	67	68	69	70	71	72	73	74
Evansville, IN-KY	13,598	2.4	43,038	169	7,142	1,213	535	951	2,304	2,875	9,842	607	535
Fairbanks, AK	5,397	0.6	53,647	36	2,620	736	207	298	988	826	3,861	185	207
Fargo, ND-MN	11,993	2.9	50,364	64	6,692	1,012	579	1,041	2,514	1,505	9,325	554	579
Farmington, NM	4,374	-2.2	38,007	294	2,265	425	179	178	626	1,031	3,047	193	179
Fayetteville, NC	13,933	2.1	36,628	325	8,874	2,150	789	453	3,081	3,551	12,266	624	789
Fayetteville-Springdale-Rogers, AR-MO	29,259	1.5	55,729	28	12,560	1,588	889	1,218	11,726	3,478	16,255	1,029	889
Flagstaff, AZ	5,926	2.8	42,057	193	2,746	577	205	362	1,290	1,139	3,891	231	205
Flint, MI	15,395	2.5	37,675	305	6,366	1,127	487	764	2,129	4,673	8,744	604	487
Florence, SC	7,654	1.7	37,158	315	3,908	669	294	313	1,095	2,115	5,185	345	294
Florence-Muscle Shoals, AL	5,251	1.6	35,832	343	2,182	403	164	295	914	1,418	3,045	216	164
Fond du Lac, WI	4,562	1.9	44,665	136	2,188	401	172	337	735	823	3,099	191	172
Fort Collins, CO	16,019	4.0	47,117	97	7,942	1,146	559	1,024	3,596	2,209	10,671	590	559
Fort Smith, AR-OK	9,779	1.9	34,772	356	4,507	711	351	821	1,547	2,692	6,389	424	351
Fort Wayne, IN	18,251	3.0	42,267	185	9,766	1,642	737	1,464	2,984	3,490	13,609	829	737
Fresno, CA	39,295	3.3	40,101	243	17,025	3,851	1,257	3,620	6,779	9,597	25,753	1,403	1,257
Gadsden, AL	3,583	1.7	34,932	353	1,382	240	103	208	530	1,097	1,934	142	103
Gainesville, FL	11,353	3.4	40,444	235	6,377	1,279	444	366	2,296	2,172	8,466	494	444
Gainesville, GA	7,682	4.5	39,065	265	4,039	663	266	584	1,267	1,416	5,552	335	266
Gettysburg, PA	4,685	1.6	45,853	113	1,420	281	119	310	819	899	2,130	134	119
Glens Falls, NY	5,388	2.1	42,639	177	2,340	565	202	358	860	1,270	3,465	200	202
Goldsboro, NC	4,587	1.6	36,950	319	1,904	388	152	333	797	1,165	2,778	165	152
Grand Forks, ND-MN	4,888	4.2	47,573	89	2,512	464	223	436	996	791	3,636	208	223
Grand Island, NE	3,637	2.3	42,711	175	1,774	311	130	463	668	636	2,678	153	130
Grand Junction, CO	5,871	0.7	39,118	262	2,668	394	205	454	1,152	1,266	3,720	225	205
Grand Rapids-Wyoming, MI	48,710	2.9	46,519	103	26,410	4,287	1,982	3,597	10,370	7,612	36,277	2,190	1,982
Grants Pass, OR	3,188	4.1	37,109	317	978	160	91	304	628	1,115	1,533	120	91
Great Falls, MT	3,546	2.4	43,375	164	1,663	289	151	246	780	749	2,349	152	151
Greeley, CO	12,594	3.2	42,701	176	5,020	700	368	1,575	1,738	1,814	7,663	412	36w8
Green Bay, WI	14,754	1.7	46,362	106	8,573	1,483	641	1,095	2,595	2,229	11,793	708	641
Greensboro-High Point, NC	30,747	2.1	40,663	226	16,897	2,495	1,285	2,566	5,339	6,380	23,243	1,484	1,285
Greenville, NC	6,724	2.8	37,943	296	3,534	693	262	419	1,180	1,440	4,908	294	262
Greenville-Anderson-Mauldin, SC	35,616	3.0	40,246	239	18,829	2,863	1,427	2,220	5,370	7,548	25,337	1,649	1,427
Gulfport-Biloxi-Pascagoula, MS	13,644	2.2	34,872	355	7,359	1,364	576	697	2,584	3,362	9,996	647	576
Hagerstown-Martinsburg, MD-WV	10,799	3.3	40,934	221	4,477	841	352	606	1,577	2,239	6,277	397	352
Hammond, LA	4,684	2.0	35,833	342	1,675	368	104	268	532	1,349	2,414	133	104
Hanford-Corcoran, CA	5,136	2.8	34,287	365	2,321	685	169	319	907	1,145	3,494	167	169
Harrisburg-Carlisle, PA	27,729	2.3	48,816	78	17,330	3,433	1,379	1,935	4,561	5,147	24,076	1,379	1,379
Harrisonburg, VA	4,784	1.5	36,021	340	2,708	499	196	444	903	856	3,847	231	196
Hartford-West Hartford-East Hartford, CT	71,617	0.9	59,343	17	41,257	6,707	2,953	6,372	11,646	11,142	57,289	3,089	2,953
Hattiesburg, MS	5,273	2.7	35,357	350	2,526	417	187	594	873	1,262	3,724	246	187
Hickory-Lenoir-Morganton, NC	13,302	2.4	36,526	326	6,215	1,034	488	854	2,122	3,386	8,591	578	488
Hilton Head Island-Bluffton-Beaufort, NC	9,920	2.4	46,876	99	3,640	641	294	631	3,286	2,010	5,205	340	294
Hinesville, GA	2,569	2.0	31,717	378	1,769	513	161	42	565	574	2,485	108	161
Homosassa Springs, FL	5,199	3.0	36,200	337	1,308	218	93	266	1,264	2,010	1,885	181	93
Hot Springs, AR	3,761	3.3	38,579	279	1,410	203	110	252	745	1,158	1,975	150	110
Houma-Thibodaux, LA	8,924	-6.3	42,190	189	4,600	758	297	467	1,662	1,806	6,122	353	297
Houston-The Woodlands-Sugar Land, TX	351,579	-1.8	51,913	50	196,129	25,332	12,950	44,228	61,256	42,286	278,639	14,559	12,950
Huntington-Ashland, WV-KY-OH	13,128	0.4	36,509	327	5,910	1,042	476	646	1,711	3,835	8,075	556	476
Huntsville, AL	20,328	3.0	45,201	123	12,816	2,132	969	889	3,765	3,404	16,806	1,022	969
Idaho Falls, ID	5,755	4.7	40,365	236	2,820	419	243	885	1,116	957	4,367	270	243
Indianapolis-Carmel-Anderson, IN	99,573	4.0	49,681	71	53,938	8,365	3,934	12,912	14,530	15,354	79,149	4,607	3,934
Iowa City, IA	8,032	2.4	47,574	88	4,530	1,156	341	623	1,669	965	6,650	370	341
Ithaca, NY	4,275	0.3	40,763	224	2,661	523	230	283	849	678	3,697	194	230
Jackson, MI	6,074	3.7	38,331	285	2,786	550	212	301	901	1,548	3,848	248	212
Jackson, MS	24,505	1.0	42,306	182	12,445	1,948	910	2,394	4,182	5,067	17,698	1,152	910
Jackson, TN	4,961	4.0	38,301	287	2,804	551	198	506	677	1,239	4,059	244	198
Jacksonville, FL	67,212	3.5	45,468	121	35,378	5,064	2,509	2,990	14,408	12,451	45,940	2,846	2,509
Jacksonville, NC	8,892	7.2	47,517	90	4,574	1,241	441	343	1,824	1,433	6,599	291	441
Janesville-Beloit, WI	6,542	2.2	40,477	231	3,087	566	240	331	1,136	1,328	4,223	273	240
Jefferson City, MO	6,062	1.5	40,044	245	3,289	738	229	412	996	1,200	4,667	267	229
Johnson City, TN	7,522	2.2	37,298	314	3,204	650	229	613	1,090	2,032	4,696	305	229
Johnstown, PA	5,298	1.2	39,322	258	2,091	462	179	262	809	1,715	2,993	204	179

1. Based on the resident population estimated as of July 1 of the year shown.

Table C. Metropolitan Areas — Earnings, Social Security , and Housing

Area name	Earnings, 2016 (cont.)									Social Security beneficiaries, December 2016			Housing units, 2017	
	Percent by selected industries													
	Farm	Mining, quarrying, and extracting	Construction	Manufacturing	Information; professional, scientific, and technical services	Retail trade	Finance, insurance, real estate, rental and leasing	Health care and social assistance	Government	Number	Rate[1]	Supplemental Security Income recipients, 2016	Total	Percent change, 2010-2017
	75	76	77	78	79	80	81	82	83	84	85	86	87	88
Evansville, IN-KY	0.8	0.4	7.4	20.2	6.2	6.3	4.6	D	9.7	69,025	219	7,278	142,388	2.6
Fairbanks, AK	0.1	3.2	10.2	1.1	4.0	5.4	2.9	9.9	47.3	10,830	108	1,075	44,302	6.0
Fargo, ND-MN	1.1	D	9.7	7.6	9.5	7.1	10.9	D	14.0	33,345	140	3,012	108,963	18.6
Farmington, NM	0.0	19.2	7.3	2.0	D	8.6	3.6	13.7	22.7	21,965	172	3,975	51,099	3.6
Fayetteville, NC	0.4	D	3.1	4.7	D	4.7	2.2	5.9	62.0	63,390	164	11,690	167,536	9.0
Fayetteville-Springdale-Rogers, AR-MO	0.7	D	5.7	9.6	D	5.9	3.7	8.9	11.8	87,525	167	9,060	216,543	9.2
Flagstaff, AZ	0.2	0.2	4.3	10.3	3.5	6.9	4.3	14.9	32.4	19,780	141	2,518	66,071	4.3
Flint, MI	0.1	0.0	5.4	12.0	7.9	8.8	6.0	18.6	16.6	98,970	242	16,819	192,349	0.1
Florence, SC	-0.1	D	4.3	15.1	6.1	7.3	10.2	13.0	19.4	48,330	235	8,693	91,023	2.3
Florence-Muscle Shoals, AL	-0.1	D	8.0	19.8	3.7	9.7	4.4	13.0	20.1	39,080	266	4,666	71,424	2.7
Fond du Lac, WI	2.9	0.5	8.8	24.4	4.5	6.5	4.7	13.0	12.5	22,040	216	1,537	45,246	3.0
Fort Collins, CO	0.2	0.6	8.9	12.8	13.0	6.8	5.9	8.6	22.0	54,520	161	2,530	148,549	11.9
Fort Smith, AR-OK	1.7	1.6	4.9	16.4	4.3	7.1	6.7	14.4	16.0	66,130	235	10,177	125,035	3.4
Fort Wayne, IN	0.6	D	6.7	19.4	D	6.4	7.9	18.7	9.5	82,505	191	8,709	184,608	3.6
Fresno, CA	5.7	0.2	5.6	6.3	5.7	6.9	5.2	14.3	22.8	135,300	138	43,652	330,938	4.9
Gadsden, AL	0.2	0.1	5.2	15.9	3.6	8.5	5.1	22.8	15.2	28,835	281	4,711	47,746	0.6
Gainesville, FL	0.8	D	3.3	3.8	7.9	5.6	5.3	17.6	38.1	47,465	169	6,979	124,481	3.7
Gainesville, GA	0.2	D	6.4	20.2	4.2	6.2	6.0	17.0	11.7	35,530	181	3,129	73,080	6.2
Gettysburg, PA	2.1	1.0	8.0	19.6	4.9	6.4	3.4	D	15.4	24,345	239	1,078	42,341	3.7
Glens Falls, NY	0.8	0.5	7.0	14.4	D	8.3	4.4	13.5	22.6	33,060	262	3,162	69,564	2.9
Goldsboro, NC	5.4	D	4.1	11.8	3.8	8.2	4.0	12.2	32.0	25,910	208	4,399	54,252	2.4
Grand Forks, ND-MN	4.2	0.6	8.8	7.0	4.8	8.0	5.0	D	26.2	17,005	166	1,346	48,078	9.4
Grand Island, NE	7.8	0.1	8.6	17.8	3.5	7.8	5.3	9.8	16.1	16,110	190	1,205	35,946	5.2
Grand Junction, CO	0.2	5.8	10.4	4.3	5.8	7.7	7.1	17.1	17.3	31,720	212	2,525	66,405	6.0
Grand Rapids-Wyoming, MI	0.6	D	6.2	24.1	D	5.7	6.8	D	9.6	190,070	181	19,323	420,246	3.9
Grants Pass, OR	0.3	D	6.4	10.4	4.5	12.6	6.6	20.2	13.6	27,230	319	2,842	39,062	2.8
Great Falls, MT	0.2	0.1	7.7	3.7	6.0	8.7	7.8	17.2	27.3	18,265	224	1,909	38,845	4.2
Greeley, CO	3.6	8.4	14.2	12.2	4.5	6.5	5.6	7.5	12.0	40,730	138	3,308	109,869	14.1
Green Bay, WI	1.8	0.1	5.9	16.9	D	5.1	9.4	D	12.3	61,895	195	5,615	143,209	4.4
Greensboro-High Point, NC	0.6	D	5.6	18.1	8.1	6.2	8.6	11.5	11.7	154,285	204	18,063	334,806	3.7
Greenville, NC	1.4	0.0	5.4	10.4	4.6	6.5	5.0	10.2	37.7	29,915	168	5,908	79,227	5.6
Greenville-Anderson-Mauldin, SC	0.0	0.1	6.5	16.8	9.7	6.6	7.1	D	15.4	190,105	215	18,340	385,009	6.3
Gulfport-Biloxi-Pascagoula, MS	0.0	D	6.3	D	6.4	6.3	3.7	D	29.4	81,090	207	10,846	180,592	8.1
Hagerstown-Martinsburg, MD-WV	0.4	0.1	5.5	9.2	6.3	8.9	9.4	14.4	20.9	53,740	204	5,926	110,012	4.2
Hammond, LA	-0.1	1.0	4.4	5.2	5.6	12.3	5.3	11.9	27.8	23,515	180	5,158	55,288	10.4
Hanford-Corcoran, CA	8.1	D	2.6	8.3	1.8	4.8	2.0	9.3	47.7	17,775	119	4,616	46,398	5.8
Harrisburg-Carlisle, PA	0.1	D	4.2	6.8	9.2	4.8	8.8	14.3	21.0	117,755	207	11,159	251,246	4.3
Harrisonburg, VA	2.7	D	6.9	17.6	6.6	6.3	4.7	12.0	18.2	23,305	175	1,868	53,822	5.3
Hartford-West Hartford-East Hartford, CT	0.1	D	5.1	D	11.7	4.8	18.2	11.9	15.8	231,505	191	23,917	515,787	1.7
Hattiesburg, MS	0.3	1.3	6.3	6.8	D	10.4	D	17.0	22.9	27,880	187	4,705	63,427	2.5
Hickory-Lenoir-Morganton, NC	1.4	0.1	3.8	27.4	D	7.2	3.2	D	15.4	89,505	246	7,681	164,530	1.1
Hilton Head Island-Bluffton-Beaufort, NC	0.2	0.0	7.7	1.1	D	8.6	7.1	9.8	31.0	53,385	252	2,707	111,091	7.5
Hinesville, GA	0.1	D	D	D	D	2.7	1.5	1.9	75.5	9,590	120	1,474	35,086	7.1
Homosassa Springs, FL	0.1	0.2	11.3	1.6	6.8	11.5	4.5	22.3	13.7	59,080	413	3,371	79,489	1.9
Hot Springs, AR	0.2	0.5	8.9	7.4	4.5	10.7	6.1	22.2	13.9	29,990	305	4,012	50,971	0.8
Houma-Thibodaux, LA	0.2	11.9	7.1	9.6	6.5	5.8	4.5	10.2	13.2	41,240	195	7,973	86,859	5.3
Houston-The Woodlands-Sugar Land, TX	0.0	7.4	9.6	9.6	D	5.2	7.6	7.8	10.8	813,905	120	140,683	2,598,634	13.2
Huntington-Ashland, WV-KY-OH	-0.1	0.7	8.8	D	5.6	7.3	4.0	D	17.5	89,220	249	16,704	165,270	0.5
Huntsville, AL	0.0	0.0	4.1	12.2	23.6	5.4	3.4	7.2	29.1	83,245	185	8,945	198,000	9.1
Idaho Falls, ID	2.4	D	5.3	D	D	14.6	D	13.0	10.4	23,730	167	2,682	53,563	7.5
Indianapolis-Carmel-Anderson, IN	0.3	0.1	5.7	11.0	D	6.3	14.8	D	11.3	345,445	172	37,206	860,010	5.3
Iowa City, IA	1.2	0.1	5.4	6.7	4.2	5.4	4.7	7.3	44.1	23,370	138	1,998	73,591	12.4
Ithaca, NY	0.3	0.9	2.6	7.5	8.6	5.0	3.6	D	13.9	15,985	153	1,517	43,453	4.2
Jackson, MI	0.2	0.1	4.8	18.9	4.6	6.1	4.1	15.8	14.9	36,715	232	4,537	69,552	0.1
Jackson, MS	0.5	2.7	5.2	7.9	D	7.7	7.5	13.1	21.8	110,860	191	20,351	242,853	4.4
Jackson, TN	-0.7	D	D	18.0	D	8.1	3.8	13.7	22.7	29,365	227	4,288	56,603	2.4
Jacksonville, FL	0.1	0.0	6.1	5.3	11.3	6.6	13.6	D	14.8	278,895	189	32,573	643,584	7.5
Jacksonville, NC	1.6	D	2.4	0.9	2.0	4.2	2.0	2.9	74.3	25,915	135	3,110	79,305	16.2
Janesville-Beloit, WI	1.1	0.3	6.5	16.8	5.3	7.3	3.9	16.4	14.6	34,960	217	3,994	68,961	0.8
Jefferson City, MO	0.6	D	6.9	9.4	D	6.1	5.0	9.0	33.5	31,855	210	2,475	65,094	2.4
Johnson City, TN	-0.2	D	4.4	10.9	D	8.3	6.3	D	21.8	52,070	259	5,904	97,474	3.9
Johnstown, PA	0.1	0.4	5.0	8.8	7.1	7.6	5.6	22.6	18.1	38,425	286	4,961	65,972	0.5

1. Per 1,000 resident population estimated as of July 1 of the year shown.

Table C. Metropolitan Areas — Professional Services, Manufacturing, and Accommodation and Food Services

Area name	Professional, scientific, and technical services, 2012				Manufacturing, 2012				Accommodation and food services, 2012			
	Number of establish-ments	Number of employees	Sales (mil dol)	Annual payroll (mil dol)	Number of establish-ments	Number of employees	Sales (mil dol)	Annual payroll (mil dol)	Number of establish-ments	Number of employees	Sales (mil dol)	Annual payroll (mil dol)
	147	148	149	150	151	152	153	154	155	156	157	158
Evansville, IN-KY	640	5,050	D	228.1	398	20,872	15,137.5	1,118.6	656	14,254	694.8	185.7
Fairbanks, AK	237	1,683	293.4	86.5	67	641	1,941.2	36.2	213	3,092	255.3	66.4
Fargo, ND-MN	558	D	D	D	224	9,398	3,860.5	D	469	11,495	515.6	151.1
Farmington, NM	256	D	D	D	85	1,318	268.6	62.8	197	4,253	201.8	56.3
Fayetteville, NC	577	6,813	911.9	374.1	115	8,193	5,481.1	379.5	657	13,928	645.9	177.0
Fayetteville-Springdale-Rogers, AR-MO	1,226	9,359	1,413.8	541.7	409	25,466	7,229.0	917.4	950	17,956	786.9	224.0
Flagstaff, AZ	331	1,584	178.5	65.3	90	4,025	2,181.3	312.0	545	11,436	765.7	191.8
Flint, MI	639	3,544	370.3	143.2	273	10,675	9,418.1	684.4	704	13,207	563.9	157.4
Florence, SC	268	2,684	294.3	112.7	148	8,952	4,326.5	479.5	384	6,611	325.8	85.6
Florence-Muscle Shoals, AL	246	1,071	110.4	40.5	181	7,761	3,325.2	322.7	268	5,455	231.8	66.1
Fond du Lac, WI	154	1,337	154.4	76.3	144	9,140	3,989.9	407.6	240	3,872	140.8	39.8
Fort Collins, CO	1,493	8,727	1,031.1	450.9	403	10,163	4,275.7	642.6	847	14,821	756.5	218.0
Fort Smith, AR-OK	534	2,168	304.8	80.0	298	18,435	6,525.7	709.7	458	8,769	433.6	117.5
Fort Wayne, IN	950	5,721	757.5	266.1	621	32,052	19,526.4	1,658.4	817	16,688	703.1	204.7
Fresno, CA	1,522	10,531	1,367.8	474.3	585	25,269	8,658.3	1,052.9	1,450	24,100	1,226.2	333.9
Gadsden, AL	130	1,250	82.2	35.5	96	4,715	1,355.8	194.1	172	3,231	153.0	40.0
Gainesville, FL	841	4,713	553.2	221.0	158	3,270	1,135.7	169.8	578	11,837	553.1	148.7
Gainesville, GA	402	D	D	D	225	17,020	7,629.2	647.1	283	4,742	298.3	67.4
Gettysburg, PA	126	D	D	D	113	5,745	2,148.7	240.8	222	3,521	185.7	53.0
Glens Falls, NY	229	1,111	141.8	49.2	163	6,709	2,135.1	358.7	540	4,750	344.1	95.6
Goldsboro, NC	147	816	76.0	27.4	83	5,833	1,691.3	243.8	186	3,284	161.7	42.0
Grand Forks, ND-MN	178	D	D	D	89	3,692	1,778.5	142.3	257	5,362	226.3	67.4
Grand Island, NE	143	767	90.3	30.2	114	7,947	7,126.4	313.9	198	2,852	128.6	36.5
Grand Junction, CO	561	2,529	289.0	119.8	159	2,388	520.6	95.1	300	6,052	282.6	88.8
Grand Rapids-Wyoming, MI	2,215	17,189	2,524.8	982.1	1,735	94,665	30,246.9	4,672.9	1,735	34,865	1,559.5	448.7
Grants Pass, OR	140	563	40.6	13.5	106	2,190	434.8	89.6	199	2,483	124.5	35.8
Great Falls, MT	202	1,159	131.8	50.3	62	964	955.3	45.0	240	3,887	194.7	51.5
Greeley, CO	533	2,362	311.5	113.7	284	11,102	5,991.4	485.8	400	5,794	273.9	76.2
Green Bay, WI	600	5,179	737.1	266.2	535	28,296	12,057.4	1,384.8	741	13,076	523.8	152.8
Greensboro-High Point, NC	1,717	D	D	D	1,019	53,589	35,757.7	2,468.5	1,494	28,185	1,408.2	385.3
Greenville, NC	311	1,893	247.9	84.4	87	4,905	2,160.8	248.8	362	8,055	357.6	96.7
Greenville-Anderson-Mauldin, SC	2,010	17,391	2,409.8	1,004.5	942	47,115	18,292.1	2,151.2	1,775	31,297	1,515.6	410.8
Gulfport-Biloxi-Pascagoula, MS	692	6,021	792.9	312.5	215	19,150	20,839.8	1,341.7	789	23,827	1,832.9	459.6
Hagerstown-Martinsburg, MD-WV	370	2,689	324.2	120.5	168	7,822	3,601.7	405.2	461	7,743	386.2	110.3
Hammond, LA	208	889	93.5	33.6	79	2,389	681.2	84.4	213	4,285	185.8	50.9
Hanford-Corcoran, CA	85	461	51.0	18.4	60	4,380	2,904.0	180.5	172	2,824	378.6	42.6
Harrisburg-Carlisle, PA	1,411	15,758	2,357.2	1,010.5	408	15,894	7,108.0	779.4	1,256	22,385	1,204.4	333.9
Harrisonburg, VA	215	1,489	174.5	76.4	134	9,603	6,229.7	422.4	277	6,596	298.7	94.5
Hartford-West Hartford-East Hartford, CT	2,801	30,314	5,830.7	2,201.0	1,638	69,502	21,474.5	4,621.6	2,685	42,030	2,453.9	706.2
Hattiesburg, MS	309	1,777	214.9	80.2	91	4,070	1,202.2	170.7	313	6,850	301.0	82.8
Hickory-Lenoir-Morganton, NC	548	2,538	742.2	102.2	727	37,686	10,405.1	1,403.5	624	10,992	481.6	134.1
Hilton Head Island-Bluffton-Beaufort, NC	579	2,999	352.7	150.2	90	713	128.5	27.5	555	11,189	688.9	202.0
Hinesville, GA	76	776	65.5	25.7	19	1,737	767.7	83.4	105	1,680	81.6	19.0
Homosassa Springs, FL	254	891	106.3	35.8	44	203	35.8	7.2	191	2,362	114.6	32.2
Hot Springs, AR	217	1,160	91.1	40.4	90	2,180	476.9	95.1	274	5,162	218.0	63.4
Houma-Thibodaux, LA	447	4,432	492.2	211.9	202	8,876	2,402.4	462.9	394	7,792	410.5	113.8
Houston-The Woodlands-Sugar Land, TX	16,999	221,829	49,233.9	19,369.0	5,365	214,702	290,261.2	13,767.5	10,981	226,927	13,340.3	3,592.4
Huntington-Ashland, WV-KY-OH	507	4,535	452.5	174.0	246	11,611	19,017.6	716.9	649	11,746	561.3	151.9
Huntsville, AL	1,442	33,281	7,765.6	2,691.5	344	20,108	8,833.7	1,121.3	828	16,350	810.1	224.6
Idaho Falls, ID	406	8,460	1,379.8	585.5	158	3,193	845.8	117.1	280	4,757	207.9	59.7
Indianapolis-Carmel-Anderson, IN	5,276	48,613	7,960.5	3,183.3	1,704	72,434	41,533.8	3,938.9	3,983	84,075	4,306.3	1,207.4
Iowa City, IA	328	2,127	314.1	96.7	125	6,061	3,799.2	276.4	419	8,252	436.6	114.4
Ithaca, NY	274	2,312	356.6	124.1	93	2,766	861.1	150.4	334	4,408	231.7	65.4
Jackson, MI	217	2,504	367.1	180.4	268	8,414	2,621.3	409.3	275	4,788	201.5	57.3
Jackson, MS	1,412	9,876	1,571.9	566.0	355	15,987	8,597.5	793.7	1,096	20,707	1,050.9	273.8
Jackson, TN	194	1,874	138.2	72.2	135	9,352	4,578.7	437.0	256	5,191	242.5	68.8
Jacksonville, FL	4,523	35,397	6,308.6	2,429.5	803	25,439	11,888.7	1,444.0	2,849	55,538	2,999.8	853.5
Jacksonville, NC	246	1,748	198.1	69.5	40	1,049	271.0	34.2	347	6,640	353.1	86.9
Janesville-Beloit, WI	208	1,172	129.3	49.5	224	8,850	4,474.2	421.3	363	5,355	236.2	63.7
Jefferson City, MO	290	1,937	279.3	93.1	147	5,562	3,774.8	238.7	279	4,545	185.2	54.0
Johnson City, TN	273	2,908	232.5	106.2	170	7,241	2,132.8	309.7	380	7,891	343.0	100.3
Johnstown, PA	228	3,359	380.3	168.2	127	5,232	1,798.8	241.6	300	4,070	179.0	47.8

Table C. Metropolitan Areas — **Health Care and Social Assistance, Other Services, Nonemployer Businesses, and Residential Construction**

Area name	Health care and social assistance, 2012				Other services, 2012				Nonemployer businesses, 2015		Value of residential construction authorized by building permits, 2017	
	Number of establish-ments	Number of employees	Receipts (mil dol)	Annual payroll (mil dol)	Number of establis-hments	Number of employees	Receipts (mil dol)	Annual payroll (mil dol)	Number	Receipts (mil dol)	New construc-tion ($1,000)	Number of housing units
	159	160	161	162	163	164	165	166	167	168	169	170
Evansville, IN-KY	852	24,213	2,658.0	999.2	548	3,988	441.5	121.4	17,072	694.9	151,582	921
Fairbanks, AK	290	5,748	746.9	305.5	185	842	88.8	25.6	5,587	230.5	2,950	15
Fargo, ND-MN	606	19,302	2,096.3	901.9	485	3,040	316.3	82.2	15,880	866.9	307,216	1,891
Farmington, NM	275	6,819	682.5	291.7	226	1,571	164.1	54.5	5,198	214.9	21,035	91
Fayetteville, NC	843	21,330	2,156.0	978.9	441	2,504	229.0	61.4	19,535	694.1	166,287	935
Fayetteville-Springdale-Rogers, AR-MO	1,084	22,894	2,307.6	908.9	596	3,738	472.9	101.8	35,197	1,561.9	981,573	4,729
Flagstaff, AZ	381	6,995	1,040.7	354.3	230	1,307	105.8	32.7	9,015	375.9	155,762	697
Flint, MI	1,294	25,418	2,787.5	1,148.7	562	3,406	376.2	91.1	27,934	979.0	92,816	434
Florence, SC	450	15,888	1,783.9	668.8	275	1,693	165.6	40.0	12,347	457.0	111,222	1,021
Florence-Muscle Shoals, AL.	382	6,957	731.4	269.8	186	D	D	D	10,153	421.2	50,745	775
Fond du Lac, WI	281	5,764	758.8	248.8	191	1,245	114.4	31.3	4,931	234.3	43,395	185
Fort Collins, CO	1,021	18,142	1,988.2	783.2	658	3,536	374.1	96.2	30,473	1,392.6	660,383	2,935
Fort Smith, AR-OK	681	18,011	1,641.2	658.4	341	1,645	141.9	40.0	18,176	860.3	95,115	721
Fort Wayne, IN	1,069	31,129	3,035.1	1,282.7	791	5,195	491.7	147.2	26,989	1,090.5	335,364	1,722
Fresno, CA	2,204	42,281	5,325.6	1,997.0	1,000	7,367	747.6	200.1	50,405	2,577.2	627,312	2,933
Gadsden, AL	316	7,433	701.9	303.4	125	632	98.9	19.0	7,071	312.8	18,928	112
Gainesville, FL	757	22,437	2,752.6	1,043.5	392	2,664	465.2	93.2	19,003	733.8	208,625	2,269
Gainesville, GA	443	9,275	1,297.8	493.4	246	1,193	123.8	32.4	14,989	667.9	252,064	1,363
Gettysburg, PA	182	4,634	448.2	167.1	150	909	75.1	19.8	6,528	274.8	50,929	249
Glens Falls, NY	388	8,109	665.2	305.5	218	1,088	112.7	33.7	8,441	374.7	69,384	264
Goldsboro, NC	254	6,896	606.6	265.8	142	939	69.3	20.3	6,147	229.8	48,373	280
Grand Forks, ND-MN	250	9,377	823.3	372.6	204	1,128	126.4	27.2	6,206	287.5	71,602	417
Grand Island, NE	231	5,479	552.8	199.0	202	1,161	111.3	25.6	5,829	253.6	40,737	282
Grand Junction, CO	426	10,176	1,029.0	427.2	293	1,883	182.6	47.8	11,373	489.7	142,442	755
Grand Rapids-Wyoming, MI..	2,285	64,137	6,540.1	2,608.2	1,690	11,582	1,100.9	313.1	71,476	3,485.7	930,596	4,839
Grants Pass, OR	269	4,376	418.5	151.1	103	D	D	D	5,738	251.2	56,781	250
Great Falls, MT	262	6,363	711.9	269.1	155	871	76.6	21.7	4,680	199.2	53,883	205
Greeley, CO	435	7,951	893.1	325.4	329	1,537	175.9	44.5	20,948	980.3	794,426	3,646
Green Bay, WI	701	21,661	2,578.4	964.5	505	3,019	261.3	72.2	17,107	852.0	245,179	1,176
Greensboro-High Point, NC..	1,697	41,710	4,164.2	1,648.4	1,095	6,325	947.5	185.8	54,458	2,299.3	603,220	3,055
Greenville, NC	510	16,075	1,880.0	681.9	183	1,104	93.9	25.1	10,307	400.6	198,692	1,137
Greenville-Anderson-Mauldin, SC	1,770	35,622	3,666.0	1,530.0	1,138	9,603	1,165.4	351.8	59,664	2,594.9	1,795,415	5,299
Gulfport-Biloxi-Pascagoula, MS	789	18,643	2,454.1	1,001.3	462	2,663	247.4	73.3	26,655	1,040.7	310,373	1,938
Hagerstown-Martinsburg, MD-WV	637	15,877	1,685.9	725.3	377	2,229	191.8	54.1	14,130	590.7	241,271	1,257
Hammond, LA	301	8,143	655.2	261.4	149	966	98.1	25.5	9,340	324.9	135,452	983
Hanford-Corcoran, CA	231	4,770	587.8	203.5	94	382	37.4	9.9	4,378	196.1	61,658	272
Harrisburg-Carlisle, PA	1,562	42,982	3,882.5	1,598.3	1,285	9,158	1,124.9	310.5	34,213	1,637.2	302,175	1,564
Harrisonburg, VA	263	7,433	708.4	298.6	231	1,164	109.4	31.6	8,057	359.3	90,387	452
Hartford-West Hartford-East Hartford, CT	3,543	99,706	10,449.5	4,596.2	2,462	15,615	1,759.3	537.5	80,958	4,347.1	258,634	1,507
Hattiesburg, MS	368	11,108	1,237.7	562.0	168	943	83.1	22.5	10,465	484.5	25,159	134
Hickory-Lenoir-Morganton, NC	744	19,423	1,882.9	733.3	437	2,380	199.7	55.8	23,056	968.0	169,958	880
Hilton Head Island-Bluffton-Beaufort, NC	470	6,794	751.1	249.6	351	2,862	258.7	86.0	16,879	879.6	745,808	2,275
Hinesville, GA	81	2,055	251.1	101.6	68	435	32.7	9.5	3,442	101.3	97,233	505
Homosassa Springs, FL	390	7,932	819.7	307.1	212	744	53.2	15.5	8,892	346.1	101,124	546
Hot Springs, AR	319	7,374	717.5	275.4	161	766	53.3	16.2	7,961	329.6	8,752	38
Houma-Thibodaux, LA	478	11,115	1,181.6	466.8	285	2,135	304.2	92.7	15,024	688.5	94,606	437
Houston-The Woodlands-Sugar Land, TX	14,336	290,976	35,675.8	13,099.0	7,926	72,280	8,932.1	2,623.8	566,184	28,894.6	7,880,444	42,395
Huntington-Ashland, WV-KY-OH	1,054	28,659	3,170.0	1,241.0	457	3,096	360.0	96.4	17,197	651.9	47,333	264
Huntsville, AL	1,053	23,925	2,645.2	1,060.2	556	4,015	617.2	140.6	29,300	1,162.2	423,532	2,959
Idaho Falls, ID	577	8,114	865.6	297.5	194	892	91.4	22.7	10,566	481.0	165,923	1,185
Indianapolis-Carmel-Anderson, IN	4,724	131,895	15,661.0	6,100.5	3,192	26,908	4,270.6	900.2	137,653	5,891.9	2,190,102	9,079
Iowa City, IA	450	16,991	2,046.3	803.9	270	1,667	207.7	46.4	11,030	520.8	222,189	1,327
Ithaca, NY	271	5,283	483.0	199.8	152	966	122.9	23.9	7,389	276.1	70,361	468
Jackson, MI	351	9,060	936.8	409.4	210	1,361	129.7	37.1	8,894	342.6	39,168	193
Jackson, MS	1,446	44,764	4,786.6	1,894.4	853	5,442	604.1	185.0	48,768	2,124.1	392,449	1,743
Jackson, TN	370	12,812	1,231.3	510.1	151	812	66.4	20.5	8,308	362.4	65,676	440
Jacksonville, FL	3,685	74,724	9,238.6	3,315.2	2,369	13,420	2,219.2	438.7	107,122	4,416.8	2,740,377	12,959
Jacksonville, NC	257	5,765	491.7	197.5	210	1,172	89.9	26.6	9,253	331.3	136,735	1,005
Janesville-Beloit, WI	320	9,667	1,120.9	438.4	268	1,417	105.0	30.8	7,974	342.7	59,459	378
Jefferson City, MO	370	9,486	874.8	358.5	325	1,760	200.3	59.5	9,013	383.3	54,319	322
Johnson City, TN	458	16,539	1,833.8	815.0	234	1,347	100.5	32.1	12,170	523.4	108,445	696
Johnstown, PA	540	11,708	1,047.3	444.7	312	1,690	133.9	34.2	6,206	243.2	17,701	83

Table C. Metropolitan Areas — **Agriculture**

	Agriculture, 2012 (cont.)															
	Land in farms					Value of land and buildings (dollars)			Value of products sold:				Percent of farms with sales of:		Government payments	
			Acres					Value of machinery and equipment, average per farm (dollars)			Percent from:					
Area name	Acreage (1,000)	Percent change, 2007-2012	Average size of farm	Total irrigated (1,000)	Total cropland (1,000)	Average per farm	Average per acre		Total (mil dol)	Average per farm (acres)	Crops	Live-stock and poultry products	$10,000 or more	$100,000 or more	Total ($1,000)	Percent of farms
	117	118	119	120	121	122	123	124	125	126	127	128	129	130	131	132
Jonesboro, AR..................	723	6.7	738	581.6	684.0	2,311,689	3,134	359,641	549.0	560,225	99.4	0.6	60.0	44.9	25,872	68.1
Joplin, MO......................	494	-2.0	172	3.8	221.1	422,288	2,457	61,142	352.0	122,343	13.5	86.5	43.1	9.2	3,356	26.2
Kahului-Wailuku-Lahaina, HI	229	1.6	203	41.5	49.6	1,998,207	9,836	53,229	188.1	166,755	96.5	3.5	37.1	7.1	558	10.5
Kalamazoo-Portage, MI......	319	-3.5	173	73.1	237.9	782,997	4,538	138,933	438.6	237,484	81.1	18.9	47.4	18.5	4,898	23.6
Kankakee, IL....................	343	-11.2	419	14.6	327.9	2,769,373	6,612	264,800	287.5	351,460	90.2	9.8	71.8	48.5	5,827	76.5
Kansas City, MO-KS	3,124	-5.1	245	D	1,916.0	749,999	3,062	83,462	785.7	61,589	68.9	31.1	41.2	10.1	34,070	44.7
Kennewick-Richland, WA	1,329	7.0	555	404.5	971.3	1,569,965	2,827	192,328	1,663.2	695,308	D	D	44.1	26.5	14,367	21.2
Killeen-Temple, TX............	1,329	-0.5	274	3.7	306.5	727,280	2,658	57,979	169.6	34,905	45.8	54.2	25.2	4.0	3,614	15.2
Kingsport-Bristol-Bristol, TN-VA..........................	569	-2.9	105	0.5	161.6	374,389	3,558	48,349	126.4	23,393	15.2	84.8	26.1	3.5	6,226	30.7
Kingston, NY	71	-5.3	147	4.2	26.1	738,835	5,042	103,237	55.9	115,019	83.0	17.0	43.0	12.6	328	10.1
Knoxville, TN	538	-6.7	96	1.6	194.1	495,626	5,174	57,244	158.2	28,176	56.8	43.2	22.7	2.2	1,294	13.0
Kokomo, IN......................	144	-11.1	303	D	134.5	1,924,391	6,353	182,880	140.4	294,874	81.1	18.9	68.1	37.2	2,993	67.0
La Crosse-Onalaska, WI-MN	388	-5.3	233	1.1	216.2	792,875	3,409	126,932	232.8	139,555	48.7	51.3	56.6	25.2	7,429	71.6
Lafayette, LA....................	761	-3.1	232	152.3	537.5	627,401	2,702	115,382	440.9	134,575	84.1	15.9	32.9	11.7	14,740	39.4
Lafayette-West Lafayette, IN	679	-0.4	431	D	638.6	2,869,720	6,657	239,864	583.0	370,363	75.3	24.7	57.4	39.8	12,438	64.2
Lake Charles, LA...............	573	-1.8	461	27.4	141.2	1,029,838	2,235	77,753	52.3	42,007	60.6	39.4	27.3	6.2	3,549	22.7
Lake Havasu City-Kingman, AZ	1,244	45.0	3,714	20.8	29.1	1,792,487	483	75,743	30.2	90,102	68.9	31.1	33.7	11.9	1,242	11.3
Lakeland-Winter Haven, FL..	521	-5.1	216	79.9	125.1	1,182,091	5,480	64,954	350.3	145,042	90.2	9.8	48.1	18.3	419	1.4
Lancaster, PA...................	439	3.3	78	6.1	332.0	973,388	12,529	101,987	1,475.0	260,731	17.7	82.3	74.2	48.4	5,843	18.4
Lansing-East Lansing, MI....	668	-1.8	206	7.4	549.2	837,223	4,057	126,959	513.0	158,584	63.2	36.8	46.4	19.6	9,730	43.6
Laredo, TX.......................	2,098	13.1	3,015	2.6	25.2	3,265,045	1,083	57,487	30.3	43,476	2.8	97.2	31.2	7.0	1,169	14.1
Las Cruces, NM.................	660	12.0	302	76.3	93.8	540,877	1,790	75,238	351.0	160,729	47.5	52.5	23.9	8.1	1,453	9.5
Las Vegas-Henderson-Paradise, NV...............	16	-82.3	62	3.7	4.4	347,790	5,611	66,325	6.8	27,083	48.2	51.8	33.7	4.4	34	3.6
Lawrence, KS...................	211	-4.5	223	3.3	127.3	636,186	2,854	82,519	43.9	46,436	66.2	33.8	37.7	8.4	2,332	46.9
Lawton, OK......................	863	-0.2	537	0.8	322.6	678,021	1,263	80,981	111.8	69,573	41.7	58.3	46.7	14.1	8,694	54.8
Lebanon, PA.....................	121	7.0	100	1.5	97.4	1,052,028	10,562	122,164	348.9	286,245	13.1	86.9	64.1	37.6	2,250	26.6
Lewiston, ID-WA................	585	-6.7	952	1.3	265.7	1,245,914	1,309	136,184	101.7	165,337	87.2	12.8	44.4	26.0	7,534	54.0
Lewiston-Auburn, ME.........	59	16.9	128	0.8	22.0	329,181	2,564	72,955	53.8	116,266	22.1	77.9	32.8	8.0	445	15.6
Lexington-Fayette, KY.........	759	-6.0	161	3.1	281.9	895,506	5,577	77,863	459.8	97,273	19.6	80.4	42.7	11.0	7,009	31.4
Lima, OH	183	-2.2	203	D	163.0	1,070,715	5,284	144,872	144.1	159,393	76.2	23.8	61.7	30.3	3,593	74.4
Lincoln, NE......................	844	11.9	298	151.4	696.9	1,423,260	4,770	156,127	486.3	171,957	68.0	32.0	48.6	23.8	15,528	63.6
Little Rock-North Little Rock-Conway, AR..............	788	-2.6	223	233.1	424.9	654,503	2,936	91,716	348.0	98,485	68.6	31.4	33.2	7.8	16,332	22.1
Logan, UT-ID....................	531	11.5	259	137.5	278.0	718,986	2,776	105,031	249.0	121,400	24.9	75.1	44.4	16.3	5,876	39.8
Longview, TX....................	525	-3.6	143	1.2	98.9	371,975	2,602	49,545	139.5	37,992	18.1	81.9	22.0	2.9	634	2.3
Longview, WA	39	27.1	79	7.6	18.6	689,236	8,693	67,535	28.8	58,482	D	D	19.5	6.9	44	1.6
Los Angeles-Long Beach-Anaheim, CA...............	152	-22.3	95	47.7	74.7	1,534,556	16,194	50,774	351.6	218,935	94.1	5.9	35.6	12.9	290	3.4
Anaheim-Santa Ana-Irvine, CA Div 11,244...............	60	-30.8	194	8.1	15.2	4,237,538	21,854	70,968	158.5	508,055	99.0	1.0	41.3	18.3	43	4.8
Los Angeles-Long Beach-Glendale, CA Div 31,084..	92	-15.5	71	39.7	59.6	882,832	12,459	45,905	193.1	149,225	90.1	9.9	34.2	11.6	247	3.1
Louisville/Jefferson County, KY-IN	1,068	-8.0	141	D	607.7	573,173	4,054	69,317	410.6	54,342	60.1	39.9	33.6	7.7	13,211	37.0
Lubbock, TX.....................	1,533	-1.9	766	338.8	1,130.1	915,687	1,196	206,678	314.0	156,835	72.9	27.1	45.8	27.4	28,253	73.9
Lynchburg, VA...................	552	6.9	186	D	151.2	674,238	3,620	60,278	74.4	25,088	28.4	71.6	35.9	4.1	2,334	18.5
Macon, GA	145	-14.1	197	10.1	46.0	599,775	3,039	77,030	120.5	164,170	31.4	68.6	28.5	10.6	1,459	19.1
Madera, CA......................	654	-3.8	434	292.3	304.2	3,302,033	7,614	182,022	1,602.8	1,063,547	77.4	22.6	70.2	46.8	2,400	11.4
Madison, WI	1,466	-3.8	197	14.2	1,067.2	984,545	5,002	132,972	1,081.6	145,256	40.2	59.8	49.3	22.9	31,173	62.4
Manchester-Nashua, NH......	48	-5.0	69	0.7	11.1	450,385	6,495	52,282	22.5	32,759	69.8	30.2	22.8	7.0	261	6.8
Manhattan, KS..................	628	-5.0	454	26.0	264.3	853,839	1,881	103,492	171.4	123,929	51.7	48.3	54.2	19.6	4,125	59.9
Mankato-North Mankato, MN	651	-5.6	355	1.7	588.8	2,286,660	6,445	257,171	892.1	486,398	49.3	50.7	71.0	49.7	13,782	82.1
Mansfield, OH...................	161	9.6	159	0.1	120.3	789,172	4,962	110,557	128.7	127,408	51.7	48.3	55.0	29.5	1,806	32.5
McAllen-Edinburg-Mission, TX	795	10.0	368	183.6	465.6	1,117,900	3,038	115,296	452.8	209,517	91.7	8.3	33.2	14.2	9,106	20.0
Medford, OR.....................	214	-12.3	124	36.5	32.8	582,023	4,682	40,415	64.1	37,240	57.6	42.4	25.7	3.4	252	3.8
Memphis, TN-MS-AR...........	1,573	-0.6	400	D	1,086.1	1,072,560	2,682	131,704	641.0	168,123	D	D	32.2	13.4	26,335	44.6
Merced, CA......................	979	-6.0	394	468.2	522.6	3,045,778	7,737	236,454	2,967.5	1,193,694	42.9	57.1	76.0	45.7	9,528	20.2
Miami-Fort Lauderdale-West Palm Beach, FL	610	1.4	122	409.8	509.9	1,213,970	9,911	83,861	1,650.7	331,597	98.0	2.0	52.0	15.2	8,726	7.1
Fort Lauderdale-Pompano Beach-Deerfield Beach, FL Div 22,744 .	14	65.9	24	1.8	4.3	540,185	22,916	31,886	47.4	77,099	91.2	8.8	41.0	8.6	246	2.9
Miami-Miami Beach-Kendall, FL Div 33,124........	81	21.3	28	45.2	64.9	699,727	25,423	47,644	604.2	204,549	98.0	2.0	58.5	16.0	6,944	8.5
West Palm Beach-Boca Raton-Delray Beach, FL Div 48,424	514	-2.2	365	362.7	440.7	2,586,187	7,090	182,476	999.0	709,041	98.3	1.7	43.2	16.2	1,536	6.0
Michigan City-La Porte, IN ...	228	-11.0	312	54.4	209.3	1,896,432	6,084	188,253	223.1	305,215	80.5	19.5	55.7	33.8	4,036	58.4
Midland, MI......................	90	-1.2	161	1.0	69.5	580,838	3,600	98,339	70.1	126,285	67.9	32.1	39.1	14.1	2,310	44.3
Midland, TX......................	858	-6.2	899	27.9	342.0	1,097,884	1,221	116,852	37.5	39,285	78.2	21.8	21.3	8.8	7,024	48.4
Milwaukee-Waukesha-West Allis, WI......................	295	0.9	167	2.2	238.1	1,011,705	6,056	128,100	250.1	141,516	49.0	51.0	50.8	22.7	5,478	43.0
Minneapolis-St. Paul-Bloomington, MN...........	2,598	-1.6	196	105.7	2,044.9	1,015,662	5,180	136,564	2,169.8	163,748	66.3	33.7	52.7	22.9	43,747	54.6
Missoula, MT....................	247	-12.3	388	16.8	19.9	1,074,215	2,769	40,830	13.6	21,355	29.8	70.2	22.1	4.6	395	9.4

Area name	Water use, 2015		Wholesale Trade[1], 2012				Retail Trade[2], 2012				Real estate and rental and leasing,[2] 2012			
	Public supply water withdrawn (mil gal/day)	Public supply gallons withdrawn per person per day	Number of establish-ments	Number of employees	Sales (mil dol)	Annual payroll (mil dol)	Number of establishments	Number of employees	Sales (mil dol)	Annual payroll (mil dol)	Number of establish-ments	Number of employees	Sales (mil dol)	Annual payroll (mil dol)
	133	134	135	136	137	138	139	140	141	142	143	144	145	146
Jonesboro, AR..............	16.30	127.0	153	1,899	1,854.8	94.1	524	7,142	1,858.9	156.2	124	509	83.2	13.9
Joplin, MO	22.87	129.1	184	2,895	2,647.0	118.9	710	9,859	2,841.3	215.3	143	583	86.0	14.9
Kahului-Wailuku-Lahaina, HI	42.10	255.6	140	1,141	714.6	50.4	759	9,174	2,461.0	258.2	306	2,022	454.4	70.8
Kalamazoo-Portage, MI.......	27.90	83.2	287	D	D	D	1,115	14,993	3,764.0	338.3	242	2,430	239.0	73.5
Kankakee, IL	13.26	119.6	119	2,196	1,443.3	95.0	370	5,548	1,463.3	120.0	95	371	70.9	10.6
Kansas City, MO-KS	270.80	129.7	2,529	42,419	52,860.3	2,756.7	6,294	104,436	29,998.3	2,579.3	2,430	13,232	3,092.0	568.9
Kennewick-Richland, WA.....	50.78	181.9	222	2,512	2,971.9	112.3	772	11,935	3,382.4	307.4	300	1,244	220.5	37.3
Killeen-Temple, TX..............	19.23	44.6	143	2,717	3,687.0	139.5	1,093	15,406	4,328.6	344.5	350	1,640	241.7	55.4
Kingsport-Bristol-Bristol, TN-VA.........................	40.07	130.5	275	3,317	1,816.0	121.0	1,101	15,030	3,779.9	327.2	208	741	126.5	23.1
Kingston, NY	394.23	2,188.4	159	1,504	810.4	71.3	733	8,606	2,324.9	211.8	195	732	116.6	22.0
Knoxville, TN	112.42	130.5	867	12,090	8,194.7	621.5	2,923	44,783	11,873.6	1,086.3	791	4,105	764.5	149.0
Kokomo, IN........................	8.47	102.6	62	559	512.7	31.6	328	4,927	1,193.3	104.0	71	311	50.4	8.9
La Crosse-Onalaska, WI-MN	15.09	110.2	137	2,724	6,239.4	119.7	491	9,017	2,027.3	185.4	125	801	101.7	20.9
Lafayette, LA	51.43	104.9	708	10,557	5,896.8	547.1	1,856	25,397	7,064.9	625.9	688	6,875	2,269.2	460.8
Lafayette-West Lafayette, IN	14.55	67.9	142	1,637	1,256.9	69.6	611	9,409	2,378.7	200.9	181	892	148.2	30.0
Lake Charles, LA................	29.01	141.1	199	2,196	1,971.0	102.7	772	10,240	3,155.4	241.0	216	1,018	235.6	41.5
Lake Havasu City-Kingman, AZ........................	47.86	233.8	114	816	391.1	30.5	593	8,918	2,712.7	211.4	199	628	83.2	15.6
Lakeland-Winter Haven, FL..	67.54	103.9	544	8,056	10,601.3	394.0	1,756	22,988	6,495.3	558.8	651	2,928	510.6	93.1
Lancaster, PA....................	54.45	101.5	582	10,776	8,764.0	496.7	1,917	29,783	6,899.6	669.6	342	2,009	396.6	79.1
Lansing-East Lansing, MI.....	29.88	63.3	327	5,044	7,143.8	236.0	1,416	20,926	5,462.7	475.9	385	2,530	349.8	88.0
Laredo, TX........................	36.08	133.8	357	2,839	2,410.1	97.0	784	12,356	3,217.6	257.8	199	692	132.4	22.0
Las Cruces, NM.................	33.99	158.6	102	D	D	D	496	7,916	1,965.4	167.7	209	690	116.6	18.9
Las Vegas-Henderson-Paradise, NV..............	432.47	204.5	1,630	16,747	11,597.1	958.8	5,712	95,369	27,971.7	2,531.6	2,794	17,855	3,700.3	647.4
Lawrence, KS	12.67	107.3	71	610	282.9	24.6	373	6,066	1,354.2	122.6	157	761	97.7	20.9
Lawton, OK.......................	21.49	164.5	64	D	D	D	424	5,410	1,444.7	119.5	126	519	90.6	16.5
Lebanon, PA......................	3.55	25.9	99	2,679	3,913.7	112.7	431	6,597	1,695.7	158.6	70	309	40.5	7.8
Lewiston, ID-WA................	15.28	245.8	55	613	497.2	26.3	259	3,343	968.8	87.2	60	280	37.3	7.6
Lewiston-Auburn, ME.........	7.92	73.9	102	1,236	473.9	54.6	439	6,018	1,818.1	138.5	111	376	62.9	11.6
Lexington-Fayette, KY.........	55.56	111.0	473	9,899	9,127.9	669.6	1,734	27,528	7,438.5	652.4	554	2,474	505.0	85.7
Lima, OH	18.17	174.0	124	2,287	1,388.8	91.6	417	6,072	1,641.5	134.3	85	376	55.2	11.0
Lincoln, NE	2.91	9.0	305	4,427	3,667.9	183.4	1,063	17,686	4,428.3	398.8	353	1,726	257.6	56.7
Little Rock-North Little Rock-Conway, AR...............	76.47	104.5	868	12,971	9,583.7	658.8	2,605	37,471	10,847.9	901.3	836	4,140	765.8	147.3
Logan, UT-ID.....................	37.53	280.4	119	978	613.1	37.7	447	5,980	1,270.6	118.4	190	D	D	D
Longview, TX.....................	17.19	78.9	290	3,950	2,602.1	209.8	866	11,363	3,285.3	283.8	231	1,303	427.0	65.6
Longview, WA....................	10.31	99.6	85	1,036	2,021.4	53.2	333	4,644	1,188.3	113.8	104	337	50.7	8.5
Los Angeles-Long Beach-Anaheim, CA..............	1,713.98	128.5	27,704	317,329	297,600.8	18,082.1	37,817	528,453	166,583.0	14,835.1	19,194	120,995	38,846.0	6,397.2
Anaheim-Santa Ana-Irvine, CA Div 11,244.............	457.54	144.3	6,434	79,685	97,796.0	5,200.7	9,390	143,012	45,193.6	4,135.3	5,320	38,952	9,259.7	1,921.2
Los Angeles-Long Beach-Glendale, CA Div 31,084...............	1,256.44	123.5	21,270	237,644	199,804.8	12,881.4	28,427	385,441	121,389.4	10,699.7	13,874	82,043	29,586.3	4,476.1
Louisville/Jefferson County, KY-IN	175.09	137.0	1,322	19,345	15,452.9	992.4	4,011	59,405	16,279.7	1,413.5	1,250	8,356	3,099.2	326.1
Lubbock, TX	2.98	9.6	389	D	D	D	1,073	16,669	4,850.9	409.5	399	D	D	D
Lynchburg, VA...................	18.03	69.4	178	2,025	1,098.8	87.6	939	13,555	3,665.7	315.0	269	773	131.2	23.3
Macon, GA	29.29	127.3	224	2,679	1,666.2	128.0	980	11,588	2,932.4	260.9	225	969	179.2	32.4
Madera, CA	15.63	100.8	76	815	508.9	37.8	326	3,455	1,012.9	84.3	75	336	38.4	8.5
Madison, WI	50.72	79.1	709	13,072	8,970.5	679.2	2,123	38,927	11,740.7	1,042.3	695	4,410	992.1	164.6
Manchester-Nashua, NH......	38.74	95.3	537	6,822	4,749.3	470.5	1,584	26,984	7,724.7	700.9	387	2,697	565.9	123.8
Manhattan, KS	9.25	93.9	56	725	307.1	30.8	353	6,208	1,242.8	130.0	129	511	74.1	13.2
Mankato-North Mankato, MN	10.45	105.4	123	1,798	1,325.4	85.2	395	6,930	1,645.7	151.2	104	692	75.5	16.9
Mansfield, OH....................	14.45	118.7	104	1,993	939.2	78.9	438	6,528	1,501.2	139.9	102	417	49.2	9.1
McAllen-Edinburg-Mission, TX.........................	64.64	76.7	841	D	D	D	2,219	33,566	9,296.8	733.9	497	2,209	445.0	61.9
Medford, OR......................	39.04	183.7	206	1,771	828.4	76.8	865	11,223	3,202.7	297.5	306	1,043	164.1	26.3
Memphis, TN-MS-AR	181.72	135.2	1,435	28,963	41,205.9	1,583.6	4,178	61,787	26,311.6	1,598.5	1,125	7,663	1,573.2	327.6
Merced, CA	50.17	186.9	112	1,635	2,260.2	71.2	528	7,497	1,959.5	173.3	152	532	79.1	14.6
Miami-Fort Lauderdale-West Palm Beach, FL	824.30	137.1	14,077	109,773	124,749.4	5,674.1	22,695	290,852	90,104.2	7,832.7	10,475	48,690	11,005.1	1,996.5
Fort Lauderdale-Pompano Beach-Deerfield Beach, FL Div 22,744 .	233.65	123.2	3,902	33,141	33,606.6	1,781.8	7,070	97,344	32,042.9	2,675.4	3,237	17,682	3,934.9	701.7
Miami-Miami Beach-Kend-all, FL Div 33,124........	351.92	130.7	8,242	61,377	78,985.4	3,003.6	10,389	123,883	38,361.2	3,252.7	4,776	19,563	4,936.4	811.9
West Palm Beach-Boca Raton-Delray Beach, FL Div 48,424	238.73	167.8	1,933	15,255	12,157.3	888.7	5,236	69,625	19,700.1	1,904.6	2,462	11,445	2,133.8	482.9
Michigan City-La Porte, IN ...	9.35	84.3	100	1,161	694.9	46.8	457	5,845	1,367.8	116.2	84	367	95.2	10.6
Midland, MI.......................	0.14	1.7	44	297	703.7	16.7	314	4,050	1,015.7	88.4	63	257	36.8	8.4
Midland, TX	2.52	15.1	272	D	D	D	515	7,607	3,019.3	221.5	267	1,505	491.4	79.1
Milwaukee-Waukesha-West Allis, WI....................	147.00	93.3	1,981	34,545	23,162.4	2,243.4	4,695	77,813	20,086.4	1,806.6	1,354	9,103	1,636.8	343.6
Minneapolis-St. Paul-Bloom-ington, MN	337.29	95.7	4,390	77,536	72,483.1	5,723.3	10,525	179,498	51,537.1	4,494.9	4,636	27,832	6,835.8	1,224.7
Missoula, MT	30.41	266.3	151	1,838	1,220.7	81.5	570	7,931	2,044.0	180.0	206	918	130.6	29.7

1   Merchant wholesalers, except manufacturers' sales branches and offices. 2. Employer establishments.

Table C. Metropolitan Areas — Professional Services, Manufacturing, and Accommodation and Food Services

Area name	Professional, scientific, and technical services, 2012				Manufacturing, 2012				Accommodation and food services, 2012			
	Number of establish-ments	Number of employees	Sales (mil dol)	Annual payroll (mil dol)	Number of establish-ments	Number of employees	Sales (mil dol)	Annual payroll (mil dol)	Number of establish-ments	Number of employees	Sales (mil dol)	Annual payroll (mil dol)
	147	148	149	150	151	152	153	154	155	156	157	158
Jonesboro, AR....................	188	916	129.1	47.1	120	5,910	2,325.7	245.4	248	4,784	213.7	57.5
Joplin, MO	250	D	D	D	243	11,659	4,282.8	486.5	358	6,644	297.2	81.6
Kahului-Wailuku-Lahaina, HI	390	1,381	186.4	67.0	99	997	D	41.1	499	19,943	2,307.5	625.7
Kalamazoo-Portage, MI.......	621	5,037	771.8	268.6	398	18,339	8,609.7	1,051.9	695	13,630	575.0	173.0
Kankakee, IL	152	735	64.1	24.5	100	4,889	4,842.8	269.7	219	3,675	160.3	47.4
Kansas City, MO-KS	6,155	69,705	13,938.8	5,014.4	1,744	74,320	40,520.9	4,025.8	3,910	82,476	4,552.6	1,254.3
Kennewick-Richland, WA	511	9,341	1,701.1	687.2	197	6,764	2,821.7	327.1	492	7,736	405.8	114.5
Killeen-Temple, TX.............	474	4,383	504.2	203.8	180	6,556	2,110.1	268.1	697	13,241	632.5	170.8
Kingsport-Bristol-Bristol, TN-VA	460	2,948	327.7	135.9	282	24,543	9,574.3	1,421.8	586	10,841	488.5	140.0
Kingston, NY	443	1,601	189.3	69.1	170	3,518	D	170.2	546	6,655	367.3	117.4
Knoxville, TN	1,691	21,671	2,523.0	1,399.6	727	33,148	13,060.5	1,823.5	1,507	32,820	1,566.1	466.9
Kokomo, IN	114	631	61.2	22.6	70	7,671	D	593.4	186	3,866	159.9	46.1
La Crosse-Onalaska, WI-MN	274	1,949	185.4	88.2	179	7,092	1,996.6	277.2	365	6,575	252.0	74.4
Lafayette, LA....................	1,761	10,784	1,848.4	631.0	582	19,339	9,405.7	1,128.7	969	19,563	1,026.7	290.3
Lafayette-West Lafayette, IN	331	2,418	345.0	108.9	161	16,598	13,028.7	935.4	446	8,493	383.2	104.9
Lake Charles, LA..............	432	5,212	479.4	222.9	128	8,620	44,186.6	688.2	358	10,817	984.6	210.8
Lake Havasu City-Kingman, AZ	239	931	72.4	30.8	133	2,566	D	109.5	382	5,787	256.7	74.3
Lakeland-Winter Haven, FL..	1,036	6,724	768.7	300.4	401	14,200	9,822.2	681.0	788	15,188	797.9	220.1
Lancaster, PA...................	957	12,486	1,249.1	1,037.2	856	33,212	13,655.7	1,638.7	998	17,833	878.4	246.9
Lansing-East Lansing, MI.....	1,051	7,399	1,210.3	408.7	341	17,312	16,198.9	1,002.6	913	17,000	708.1	201.7
Laredo, TX.......................	317	1,803	186.1	58.6	69	635	339.6	22.0	389	8,216	423.7	106.2
Las Cruces, NM................	339	D	D	D	128	2,520	D	87.1	319	6,813	285.2	80.7
Las Vegas-Henderson-Paradise, NV..............	5,645	35,253	5,825.0	2,128.2	894	17,390	5,673.8	782.0	4,050	250,601	24,283.8	7,612.3
Lawrence, KS	292	D	D	D	69	3,079	1,217.3	136.1	301	6,511	261.1	72.2
Lawton, OK......................	168	1,143	115.7	50.2	49	3,495	1,354.6	D	234	4,927	223.2	66.8
Lebanon, PA.....................	197	1,083	151.2	48.6	205	8,099	2,743.8	336.5	232	3,320	146.1	40.5
Lewiston, ID-WA................	112	D	D	D	60	3,067	1,175.1	144.0	139	2,677	133.7	38.7
Lewiston-Auburn, ME..........	183	1,652	359.2	80.1	150	5,205	1,886.9	251.6	209	3,021	153.3	44.5
Lexington-Fayette, KY.........	1,384	12,042	1,702.3	653.5	423	25,017	17,174.3	1,286.4	1,051	23,086	1,191.8	340.1
Lima, OH	164	952	75.8	33.0	124	7,318	15,270.4	448.1	234	4,521	211.3	54.3
Lincoln, NE	871	9,241	1,313.8	464.2	255	13,208	6,540.1	653.7	702	13,936	616.8	161.3
Little Rock-North Little Rock-Conway, AR..............	2,012	12,058	1,911.2	627.2	540	21,045	9,263.0	990.1	1,461	29,034	1,362.2	386.9
Logan, UT-ID...................	385	2,538	251.4	88.6	226	10,761	4,556.5	443.1	178	3,173	130.7	35.4
Longview, TX....................	508	3,998	554.5	213.9	233	10,657	4,029.0	552.1	426	8,138	374.1	105.1
Longview, WA	140	830	86.5	34.9	116	5,722	3,264.5	385.6	215	2,796	124.2	39.2
Los Angeles-Long Beach-Anaheim, CA..............	45,444	633,648	90,371.7	35,143.8	17,461	509,552	211,129.0	28,731.8	27,439	499,255	32,015.8	8,990.4
Anaheim-Santa Ana-Irvine, CA Div 11,244.	14,120	112,581	24,110.2	8,899.6	4,701	150,020	47,299.4	8,879.0	7,141	143,519	9,050.6	2,599.9
Los Angeles-Long Beach-Glendale, CA Div 31,084.	31,324	521,067	66,261.5	26,244.3	12,760	359,532	163,829.6	19,852.8	20,298	355,736	22,965.1	6,390.6
Louisville/Jefferson County, KY-IN	3,045	26,012	3,734.3	1,286.6	1,223	65,362	37,466.2	3,253.0	2,382	56,076	2,984.5	793.9
Lubbock, TX	640	3,878	483.4	176.3	246	5,075	1,586.2	219.0	638	14,366	721.2	191.8
Lynchburg, VA..................	508	5,203	1,175.9	359.6	276	15,749	6,265.7	883.3	461	8,653	367.3	101.8
Macon, GA	467	2,857	365.3	128.7	154	5,041	1,729.2	234.4	470	8,864	394.7	109.9
Madera, CA	116	493	66.9	21.6	92	3,298	1,441.1	168.0	193	2,461	150.1	37.1
Madison, WI	1,917	20,780	3,515.0	1,348.2	734	31,666	12,491.6	1,595.6	1,567	29,215	1,330.4	378.2
Manchester-Nashua, NH......	1,335	10,986	1,721.0	737.1	554	25,287	7,450.8	1,732.0	897	14,781	762.2	229.8
Manhattan, KS..................	198	D	D	D	60	1,847	472.0	93.5	201	4,325	164.5	46.5
Mankato-North Mankato, MN	189	1,540	173.9	77.6	138	7,573	4,903.6	321.6	208	4,343	170.1	46.8
Mansfield, OH..................	187	925	113.1	36.0	168	8,064	3,122.7	385.9	239	4,556	190.1	54.1
McAllen-Edinburg-Mission, TX	886	5,381	566.0	169.6	268	5,713	1,675.4	216.0	1,014	19,468	985.9	247.1
Medford, OR....................	506	D	D	D	308	5,370	1,624.6	217.4	586	7,381	382.2	112.5
Memphis, TN-MS-AR	2,112	19,494	2,687.2	1,117.7	846	34,515	26,369.2	1,846.8	2,239	55,258	3,253.0	858.2
Merced, CA	142	791	67.1	26.2	116	9,973	4,435.6	405.4	298	4,585	232.9	60.2
Miami-Fort Lauderdale-West Palm Beach, FL..........	28,955	142,450	26,210.5	9,220.5	4,452	63,174	16,753.9	2,987.1	11,402	234,634	16,293.0	4,445.0
Fort Lauderdale-Pompano Beach-Deerfield Beach, FL Div 22,744 .	9,583	46,815	8,286.6	2,833.0	1,454	21,057	6,010.6	1,054.7	3,685	72,428	5,129.2	1,322.2
Miami-Miami Beach-Kend-all, FL Div 33,124........	12,008	58,711	11,734.8	4,018.8	2,070	30,387	7,192.9	1,318.2	5,052	104,467	7,696.6	2,078.4
West Palm Beach-Boca Raton-Delray Beach, FL Div 48,424.	7,364	36,924	6,189.1	2,368.7	928	11,731	3,550.4	614.2	2,665	57,739	3,467.3	1,044.3
Michigan City-La Porte, IN ...	158	1,069	85.0	40.4	172	7,589	2,644.0	350.5	235	4,992	357.0	78.7
Midland, MI......................	154	785	87.9	34.9	62	6,241	3,591.1	466.1	138	2,861	136.2	40.7
Midland, TX.....................	499	4,739	1,006.1	267.4	143	3,296	1,324.8	165.8	304	6,675	477.6	109.6
Milwaukee-Waukesha-West Allis, WI........................	3,841	40,983	6,746.8	2,630.0	2,465	114,114	40,901.0	6,604.8	3,179	59,849	2,856.5	780.7
Minneapolis-St. Paul-Bloom-ington, MN	13,160	111,963	20,342.0	8,273.1	4,641	176,842	71,530.0	10,348.0	6,596	144,111	7,830.5	2,217.4
Missoula, MT....................	501	2,865	325.4	137.2	102	1,351	310.6	49.1	342	6,106	317.4	84.0

Table C. Metropolitan Areas — **Health Care and Social Assistance, Other Services, Nonemployer Businesses, and Residential Construction**

Area name	Health care and social assistance, 2012				Other services, 2012				Nonemployer businesses, 2015		Value of residential construction authorized by building permits, 2017	
	Number of establishments	Number of employees	Receipts (mil dol)	Annual payroll (mil dol)	Number of establishments	Number of employees	Receipts (mil dol)	Annual payroll (mil dol)	Number	Receipts (mil dol)	New construction ($1,000)	Number of housing units
	159	160	161	162	163	164	165	166	167	168	169	170
Jonesboro, AR	405	9,349	958.7	378.4	151	D	D	D	9,048	419.5	97,158	866
Joplin, MO	474	12,922	1,236.6	588.5	288	1,496	119.0	35.0	10,344	433.9	86,234	765
Kahului-Wailuku-Lahaina, HI	393	6,138	741.5	308.2	383	2,185	238.1	62.0	16,174	788.5	209,950	861
Kalamazoo-Portage, MI	760	21,248	2,457.4	946.4	516	3,367	414.5	97.6	20,682	871.0	200,398	1,036
Kankakee, IL	311	7,349	753.9	294.5	180	956	100.3	25.1	6,193	214.8	32,539	198
Kansas City, MO-KS	5,421	133,626	15,085.9	5,992.9	3,361	22,120	3,219.6	701.1	142,397	6,646.3	1,970,930	9,851
Kennewick-Richland, WA	662	11,539	1,309.8	520.5	345	1,968	161.5	50.3	12,154	544.6	457,942	1,809
Killeen-Temple, TX	606	24,367	2,965.3	1,295.4	506	3,411	248.4	84.7	21,167	883.1	365,942	2,456
Kingsport-Bristol-Bristol, TN-VA	733	17,517	1,976.4	754.1	387	2,119	527.7	56.8	18,022	706.1	117,221	788
Kingston, NY	514	8,991	741.4	312.4	322	1,229	114.9	28.6	16,327	691.2	81,827	336
Knoxville, TN	1,987	53,573	5,749.5	2,129.1	1,162	8,068	755.7	251.4	60,935	2,964.3	840,797	4,574
Kokomo, IN	221	5,417	456.4	182.6	129	922	68.2	18.9	4,225	150.6	15,545	92
La Crosse-Onalaska, WI-MN	327	12,270	1,508.1	539.7	274	1,785	157.9	46.8	7,703	342.7	84,997	432
Lafayette, LA	1,533	32,257	3,120.9	1,178.7	715	5,199	674.7	168.1	41,190	1,785.9	362,262	1,771
Lafayette-West Lafayette, IN	424	11,181	1,217.2	433.2	276	1,907	218.4	49.4	11,041	478.2	184,092	976
Lake Charles, LA	521	12,330	1,209.9	457.2	244	1,617	178.0	51.1	14,099	645.2	291,760	1,898
Lake Havasu City-Kingman, AZ	478	8,222	995.0	364.2	290	1,394	110.3	29.4	10,592	461.3	189,366	913
Lakeland-Winter Haven, FL	1,048	27,066	3,015.2	1,109.8	673	3,366	328.5	94.6	41,872	1,618.1	869,723	4,604
Lancaster, PA	1,110	34,977	3,387.5	1,411.1	1,031	6,339	588.6	161.3	41,260	2,188.1	280,779	1,436
Lansing-East Lansing, MI	1,155	27,524	2,988.8	1,167.0	817	6,682	808.3	240.6	31,133	1,359.2	179,150	907
Laredo, TX	536	14,678	926.2	373.6	203	1,129	101.1	27.1	24,479	1,146.6	215,452	1,331
Las Cruces, NM	496	12,122	1,010.7	418.4	234	1,124	86.4	26.3	12,253	465.5	188,407	1,126
Las Vegas-Henderson-Paradise, NV	4,426	75,019	9,714.9	3,493.8	2,344	17,926	1,602.8	476.8	154,711	7,851.8	1,844,987	14,073
Lawrence, KS	289	6,580	545.8	211.1	181	1,423	230.7	37.2	8,004	329.5	84,863	306
Lawton, OK	282	6,960	709.7	273.2	141	846	70.7	21.3	5,063	219.8	16,576	84
Lebanon, PA	279	8,165	772.4	341.9	233	1,086	110.1	27.5	8,125	388.0	61,078	366
Lewiston, ID-WA	192	4,024	440.3	159.8	108	561	39.4	12.2	3,209	129.6	26,017	125
Lewiston-Auburn, ME	385	9,531	947.5	402.8	211	1,024	84.6	23.5	6,137	288.8	38,329	252
Lexington-Fayette, KY	1,524	34,868	4,154.5	1,607.9	792	5,378	821.8	163.5	35,556	1,678.2	352,017	2,326
Lima, OH	307	11,307	1,256.5	501.7	197	1,264	92.0	25.5	5,366	211.5	23,767	224
Lincoln, NE	1,007	23,965	2,418.6	963.5	705	4,286	593.7	134.2	21,942	860.9	402,010	2,508
Little Rock-North Little Rock-Conway, AR	2,067	52,656	5,908.8	2,359.2	1,178	8,198	1,001.5	238.3	50,928	2,245.8	445,378	3,215
Logan, UT-ID	373	5,431	519.3	170.7	191	D	D	D	9,455	368.1	219,879	1,373
Longview, TX	543	12,575	1,468.4	479.6	311	2,349	288.1	91.0	15,380	745.0	29,582	187
Longview, WA	240	5,444	567.0	232.1	148	D	D	D	4,469	182.6	64,616	484
Los Angeles-Long Beach-Anaheim, CA	40,695	651,603	87,943.5	31,496.0	20,823	146,211	17,344.3	4,317.7	1,323,907	71,793.1	7,847,474	31,084
Anaheim-Santa Ana-Irvine, CA Div 11,244	10,873	152,659	20,682.2	7,379.9	4,980	35,537	3,782.2	1,039.3	NA	NA	2,300,253	9,510
Los Angeles-Long Beach-Glendale, CA Div 31,084	29,822	498,944	67,261.3	24,116.1	15,843	110,674	13,562.1	3,278.3	NA	NA	5,547,221	21,574
Louisville/Jefferson County, KY-IN	3,410	86,187	9,206.9	3,559.7	1,965	16,301	1,665.5	481.2	85,248	3,855.9	1,022,768	5,785
Lubbock, TX	864	22,490	2,538.0	873.1	472	3,502	313.4	94.4	21,764	1,105.4	438,840	2,388
Lynchburg, VA	572	13,913	1,313.6	539.9	452	2,320	207.0	60.3	14,632	541.7	119,165	770
Macon, GA	642	16,370	1,869.5	686.3	318	1,831	220.9	58.8	18,146	618.2	60,688	320
Madera, CA	204	5,871	761.0	321.0	112	489	45.2	11.8	7,161	350.2	96,078	415
Madison, WI	1,473	49,078	5,684.6	2,239.3	1,298	9,034	1,314.3	300.0	45,196	2,195.3	901,221	4,632
Manchester-Nashua, NH	1,094	28,561	3,089.1	1,339.9	824	5,516	490.3	160.3	28,477	1,657.8	184,019	1,033
Manhattan, KS	230	4,249	391.3	142.5	172	1,252	223.3	48.7	5,122	224.0	86,084	381
Mankato-North Mankato, MN	301	11,383	823.6	416.8	186	1,230	262.3	31.3	6,242	268.6	82,963	516
Mansfield, OH	316	7,570	674.5	274.6	209	1,186	108.4	25.3	6,844	281.9	18,285	77
McAllen-Edinburg-Mission, TX	2,048	54,356	3,479.0	1,471.2	571	3,701	350.3	84.2	69,823	2,680.3	609,699	4,297
Medford, OR	674	12,116	1,443.8	510.7	315	1,836	157.3	51.0	16,786	753.1	186,575	805
Memphis, TN-MS-AR	2,948	80,010	9,324.5	3,561.1	1,557	12,365	2,119.0	414.4	108,553	4,160.9	724,726	3,860
Merced, CA	427	6,718	788.1	302.8	183	895	72.4	26.3	10,850	545.0	132,371	550
Miami-Fort Lauderdale-West Palm Beach, FL	20,622	297,739	39,497.8	13,743.7	12,231	68,020	7,193.6	1,854.5	885,524	38,524.4	4,566,545	19,723
Fort Lauderdale-Pompano Beach-Deerfield Beach, FL Div 22,744	6,273	89,756	12,193.7	4,272.6	4,124	21,448	2,245.9	602.5	NA	NA	991,062	5,034
Miami-Miami Beach-Kendall, FL Div 33,124	9,030	132,886	17,547.4	6,100.1	4,903	28,561	3,116.7	758.0	NA	NA	2,258,626	10,554
West Palm Beach-Boca Raton-Delray Beach, FL Div 48,424	5,319	75,097	9,756.7	3,371.0	3,204	18,011	1,831.0	493.9	NA	NA	1,316,857	4,135
Michigan City-La Porte, IN	228	5,626	611.2	208.3	194	1,090	79.0	22.5	5,858	206.4	37,400	157
Midland, MI	239	6,268	682.2	242.8	147	882	113.0	23.2	4,899	192.0	22,467	142
Midland, TX	405	7,331	829.3	304.4	272	2,159	340.6	74.2	16,579	1,137.7	160,758	766
Milwaukee-Waukesha-West Allis, WI	4,732	123,973	13,694.3	5,445.8	2,736	20,368	2,267.0	636.2	89,843	4,337.4	760,232	3,693
Minneapolis-St. Paul-Bloomington, MN	9,429	270,065	26,555.5	11,497.3	6,672	51,085	5,701.2	1,543.4	264,395	12,575.8	3,569,215	15,100
Missoula, MT	489	9,292	965.9	351.1	287	1,889	258.2	56.0	9,848	453.1	139,190	972

Table C. Metropolitan Areas — Government Employment and Payroll, and Local Government Finances

Area name	Government employment and payroll, 2012									Local government finances, 2012				
	Full-time equivalent employees	March payroll (dollars)	March payroll (percent of total)							General revenue				
			Administration, judicial, and legal	Police and corrections	Fire protection	Highways and transportation	Health and welfare	Natural resources and utilities	Education and libraries	Total (mil dol)	Intergovernmental (mil dol)	Taxes Total (mil dol)	Per capita[1] (dollars) Total	Per capita[1] (dollars) Property
	171	172	173	174	175	176	177	178	179	180	181	182	183	184
Jonesboro, AR	4,524	13,523,979	4.9	9.6	2.5	3.7	1.1	9.1	68.6	354.5	215.8	87.8	708	311
Joplin, MO	6,292	18,337,340	4.7	8.3	3.6	3.0	2.0	3.3	74.4	510.9	199.2	185.7	1,065	527
Kahului-Wailuku-Lahaina, HI	2,328	11,762,934	19.0	23.7	3.6	6.9	6.2	25.4	0.0	252.6	23.1	224.7	1,419	1,316
Kalamazoo-Portage, MI	9,976	43,436,306	7.0	10.5	12.8	2.9	6.0	3.3	56.6	1,340.8	705.4	408.5	1,238	1,210
Kankakee, IL	4,413	16,356,166	7.8	13.5	3.6	3.7	1.5	3.4	65.4	441.9	208.0	169.2	1,496	1,433
Kansas City, MO-KS	86,196	339,122,341	5.7	9.8	5.2	3.5	13.8	6.1	54.6	9,183.3	2,533.9	4,159.3	2,040	1,219
Kennewick-Richland, WA	10,152	53,295,192	5.2	7.0	3.2	4.4	10.2	28.7	40.3	1,194.4	543.2	325.4	1,213	704
Killeen-Temple, TX	19,513	61,961,488	4.6	8.5	3.2	1.8	4.0	4.2	72.6	1,379.2	598.6	457.1	1,087	854
Kingsport-Bristol-Bristol, TN-VA	11,566	36,313,120	5.1	10.8	2.2	3.5	5.1	5.7	66.0	805.9	377.3	312.3	1,011	695
Kingston, NY	8,282	38,442,668	5.7	7.7	1.3	4.8	8.8	1.7	68.0	1,095.2	330.4	630.3	3,467	2,848
Knoxville, TN	29,145	97,687,242	5.6	9.5	2.6	3.1	10.2	13.4	54.2	2,517.0	845.0	1,010.5	1,191	718
Kokomo, IN	4,091	15,459,399	5.0	6.2	3.5	2.0	35.8	3.0	42.2	435.8	136.7	118.7	1,433	1,170
La Crosse-Onalaska, WI-MN	5,559	21,504,753	6.0	8.2	2.4	4.3	16.8	4.2	57.0	720.4	365.8	237.4	1,755	1,630
Lafayette, LA	17,787	55,296,831	6.7	12.0	3.2	3.4	8.4	8.0	57.3	1,668.5	663.9	685.1	1,444	587
Lafayette-West Lafayette, IN	5,636	18,225,886	7.4	11.9	4.8	5.8	2.8	5.4	60.9	552.8	259.3	207.6	1,006	798
Lake Charles, LA	9,670	30,588,485	5.1	13.5	3.3	5.8	7.9	5.3	57.2	1,055.7	360.2	475.0	2,361	1,046
Lake Havasu City-Kingman, AZ	5,613	20,393,845	13.0	13.4	11.7	4.5	2.0	5.6	47.4	538.5	183.2	229.9	1,131	849
Lakeland-Winter Haven, FL	22,910	75,047,946	7.9	12.5	4.2	2.1	2.6	10.6	56.6	1,844.2	710.5	644.8	1,047	726
Lancaster, PA	12,622	54,624,168	5.9	11.7	0.8	2.8	3.4	3.5	70.9	1,833.0	668.6	843.7	1,601	1,327
Lansing-East Lansing, MI	15,249	64,035,635	8.2	8.0	3.0	4.4	9.2	6.8	56.5	1,895.2	923.3	587.0	1,260	1,174
Laredo, TX	14,741	48,977,584	5.1	9.2	5.1	3.0	3.0	3.7	70.4	1,245.0	614.2	391.8	1,512	1,216
Las Cruces, NM	7,916	26,726,295	5.8	10.4	2.7	2.6	2.1	5.9	66.7	732.8	425.3	209.7	978	447
Las Vegas-Henderson-Paradise, NV	51,796	300,546,553	8.1	16.4	5.9	3.4	8.6	10.1	45.3	8,606.7	3,678.4	2,735.1	1,367	869
Lawrence, KS	4,535	18,551,008	5.6	11.2	5.0	2.9	33.2	7.9	33.4	537.2	114.0	188.6	1,671	1,239
Lawton, OK	6,503	22,717,032	3.8	5.7	3.0	2.2	36.2	3.3	45.2	523.3	171.6	106.3	802	354
Lebanon, PA	4,116	14,939,586	6.1	9.0	1.7	2.8	9.0	5.5	65.4	485.8	160.6	191.5	1,416	1,136
Lewiston, ID-WA	2,076	7,939,079	7.0	11.4	5.6	6.0	7.0	7.6	51.8	188.3	89.3	64.0	1,042	932
Lewiston-Auburn, ME	3,959	13,779,680	4.1	8.3	4.8	4.2	2.0	5.1	70.2	355.6	153.6	163.3	1,517	1,507
Lexington-Fayette, KY	16,579	58,038,313	4.2	11.6	6.9	2.1	7.1	4.3	61.5	1,418.6	398.6	746.8	1,540	758
Lima, OH	4,029	14,917,726	8.3	9.1	4.8	3.4	9.8	5.8	55.9	394.8	197.5	125.6	1,195	774
Lincoln, NE	11,413	48,128,898	5.2	7.7	3.8	4.5	4.1	11.5	61.4	1,034.8	326.0	505.1	1,628	1,186
Little Rock-North Little Rock-Conway, AR	24,915	82,533,612	5.8	10.8	5.3	3.7	2.5	8.9	61.2	2,303.6	1,228.7	601.7	838	423
Logan, UT-ID	3,888	12,693,319	7.2	7.0	2.3	3.6	11.8	5.5	59.8	338.7	155.8	113.9	888	560
Longview, TX	9,132	29,631,047	5.5	10.9	3.9	2.0	4.4	4.8	66.6	721.4	245.0	370.6	1,710	1,319
Longview, WA	3,301	15,112,407	7.8	11.6	3.0	7.2	3.7	14.2	51.3	420.9	170.2	127.1	1,246	848
Los Angeles-Long Beach-Anaheim, CA	471,707	2,757,691,350	8.8	12.1	4.7	5.2	12.5	8.6	45.7	77,422.5	34,902.2	24,415.1	1,870	1,275
Anaheim-Santa Ana-Irvine, CA Div 11,244	85,251	527,595,855	5.4	11.0	4.8	3.1	7.4	5.7	58.4	14,543.9	5,867.6	5,580.4	1,806	1,406
Los Angeles-Long Beach-Glendale, CA Div 31,084	386,456	2,230,095,495	9.6	12.3	4.7	5.7	13.7	9.3	42.7	62,878.6	29,034.6	18,834.7	1,891	1,234
Louisville/Jefferson County, KY-IN	45,148	162,939,795	3.7	9.1	3.7	3.4	14.2	6.3	58.2	4,084.7	1,333.6	1,583.1	1,265	787
Lubbock, TX	13,751	49,840,306	4.7	10.3	4.2	1.2	27.8	5.7	45.1	1,319.2	362.2	422.7	1,420	1,113
Lynchburg, VA	9,196	26,684,206	6.4	11.2	3.2	1.3	7.0	5.1	63.4	712.1	348.1	270.1	1,058	752
Macon, GA	9,317	31,505,415	6.5	10.3	4.0	2.8	5.6	5.3	64.2	803.6	331.4	347.0	1,491	1,002
Madera, CA	4,578	20,019,402	8.1	8.1	0.2	2.2	10.1	5.2	64.4	627.3	366.3	154.2	1,013	706
Madison, WI	23,987	100,319,066	5.9	10.2	2.5	6.5	6.7	6.3	60.2	2,887.9	993.2	1,412.8	2,276	2,136
Manchester-Nashua, NH	13,991	56,054,764	4.1	10.8	6.0	4.5	3.9	3.8	65.8	1,458.9	470.6	808.2	2,006	1,981
Manhattan, KS	3,088	9,783,062	8.5	11.2	3.9	5.6	3.6	7.1	58.8	275.9	79.3	146.5	1,497	1,108
Mankato-North Mankato, MN	3,049	12,248,005	8.1	9.4	1.0	5.0	10.7	5.9	57.5	419.6	200.3	109.1	1,113	999
Mansfield, OH	5,091	18,513,991	8.5	9.4	5.0	4.1	11.2	8.3	52.0	473.0	237.7	163.9	1,336	864
McAllen-Edinburg-Mission, TX	39,042	129,583,687	3.7	6.7	1.7	1.6	2.9	3.9	78.6	3,159.2	1,926.2	864.1	1,071	868
Medford, OR	4,931	20,369,335	9.1	14.6	6.5	6.1	5.2	6.8	50.0	903.9	365.9	258.6	1,263	1,068
Memphis, TN-MS-AR	53,881	181,275,652	6.8	14.3	6.6	4.1	9.1	12.2	45.2	5,455.9	2,056.3	2,087.0	1,555	1,086
Merced, CA	10,959	49,202,192	6.5	7.6	1.6	1.1	10.0	6.7	63.4	1,305.5	840.8	219.3	836	680
Miami-Fort Lauderdale-West Palm Beach, FL	222,370	1,025,593,818	5.5	14.7	6.9	4.6	20.6	7.6	34.5	30,329.9	7,063.4	12,134.4	2,106	1,662
Fort Lauderdale-Pompano Beach-Deerfield Beach, FL Div 22,744	73,864	331,154,408	5.1	13.2	6.2	3.7	29.6	6.0	33.6	9,918.0	2,186.8	3,161.3	1,742	1,392
Miami-Miami Beach-Kendall, FL Div 33,124	102,308	498,941,928	4.9	14.9	6.0	5.9	20.8	6.6	32.3	14,058.6	3,695.7	5,524.1	2,132	1,564
West Palm Beach-Boca Raton-Delray Beach, FL Div 48,424	46,198	195,497,482	7.6	16.4	10.2	2.6	5.1	13.1	41.6	6,353.4	1,180.9	3,449.0	2,542	2,211
Michigan City-La Porte, IN	4,264	12,639,630	5.9	11.9	4.3	3.5	3.5	6.6	63.1	369.8	180.5	137.0	1,231	1,055
Midland, MI	2,175	9,622,686	11.4	7.8	3.3	4.0	3.3	5.7	62.5	271.7	113.5	103.5	1,235	1,220
Midland, TX	7,075	27,853,270	5.2	7.7	3.9	1.9	29.9	1.6	47.9	800.8	131.1	362.9	2,393	1,787
Milwaukee-Waukesha-West Allis, WI	53,007	250,453,387	5.4	13.5	4.4	4.2	8.1	4.6	57.7	7,417.1	2,812.4	3,111.6	1,986	1,860
Minneapolis-St. Paul-Bloomington, MN	104,532	577,809,573	7.1	9.9	1.7	3.7	7.6	5.5	63.0	15,990.0	6,976.7	5,332.5	1,558	1,450
Missoula, MT	3,035	11,623,602	8.8	11.6	6.2	6.3	5.7	3.6	55.2	333.0	140.7	131.9	1,189	1,156

1. Based on the resident population estimated as of July 1 of the year shown.

Table C. Metropolitan Areas — Local Government Finances, Government Employment, and Income Taxes

Area name	Total (mil dol)	Per capita[1] (dollars)	Education	Health and hospitals	Police protection	Public welfare	Highways	Total (mil dol)	Per capita[1] (dollars)	Federal civilian	Federal military	State and local	Number of returns	Mean adjusted gross income	Mean income tax
	Local government finances, 2012 (cont.) — Direct general expenditure — Percent of total for:							Debt outstanding		Government employment, 2016			Individual income tax returns, 2015		
	185	186	187	188	189	190	191	192	193	194	195	196	197	198	199
Jonesboro, AR	344.4	2,776	59.5	0.3	5.9	0.1	5.2	518.7	4,182	383	519	9,285	51,210	50,240	5,784
Joplin, MO	524.5	3,009	58.0	8.8	4.8	0.2	5.1	349.6	2,005	432	621	8,934	76,020	47,783	5,032
Kahului-Wailuku-Lahaina, HI	264.1	1,668	0.0	0.0	15.8	6.0	2.7	281.6	1,779	841	1,153	9,105	79,720	54,463	6,182
Kalamazoo-Portage, MI	1,323.6	4,011	48.7	15.6	6.2	1.0	5.0	1,469.4	4,452	823	532	18,922	155,510	60,318	7,996
Kankakee, IL	442.3	3,912	52.1	0.7	6.1	0.1	5.9	327.2	2,894	238	214	5,758	50,580	53,622	5,762
Kansas City, MO-KS	8,722.0	4,278	43.2	9.9	7.0	0.6	5.4	16,793.0	8,237	27,758	11,045	123,978	998,460	68,564	9,404
Kennewick-Richland, WA	1,130.0	4,213	43.9	21.1	4.0	0.0	3.7	7,044.2	26,261	1,256	759	18,388	122,130	60,848	7,118
Killeen-Temple, TX	1,411.2	3,357	57.9	3.8	4.8	0.5	5.9	2,196.8	5,226	10,731	36,144	27,342	182,680	47,944	4,769
Kingsport-Bristol-Bristol, TN-VA	860.9	2,786	50.0	3.8	6.6	1.8	4.1	782.5	2,532	884	916	15,739	130,750	48,675	5,266
Kingston, NY	1,119.8	6,160	51.1	2.0	2.8	12.1	5.4	695.1	3,823	473	281	12,593	86,590	58,845	7,017
Knoxville, TN	2,428.1	2,862	44.3	9.6	6.5	0.1	3.1	4,983.9	5,875	5,414	2,627	52,768	383,400	60,068	8,139
Kokomo, IN	406.5	4,907	32.7	36.7	3.9	0.3	1.8	200.3	2,417	186	248	11,113	40,320	49,427	5,167
La Crosse-Onalaska, WI-MN	720.8	5,328	43.6	2.8	4.0	21.7	5.6	467.2	3,453	542	367	11,113	65,880	59,726	7,367
Lafayette, LA	1,702.8	3,589	44.6	7.6	6.9	0.4	5.4	2,036.0	4,292	1,387	2,136	24,281	210,340	57,960	7,503
Lafayette-West Lafayette, IN	486.9	2,359	51.4	0.5	5.8	0.7	6.1	413.5	2,003	531	671	24,999	88,700	55,881	6,668
Lake Charles, LA	995.9	4,950	38.4	7.2	6.5	0.4	6.8	2,332.0	11,591	567	956	13,987	91,330	59,027	7,426
Lake Havasu City-Kingman, AZ	555.1	2,730	33.9	2.7	6.9	0.1	8.7	627.7	3,087	449	445	7,090	80,250	41,725	4,049
Lakeland-Winter Haven, FL	1,992.7	3,234	48.6	3.2	8.2	1.6	5.5	2,776.3	4,506	1,089	1,253	27,116	283,800	47,365	5,109
Lancaster, PA	2,018.4	3,831	55.1	5.4	4.3	5.1	3.3	3,447.0	6,543	1,255	1,369	19,456	264,590	60,257	7,370
Lansing-East Lansing, MI	1,885.3	4,048	47.2	10.6	4.5	3.4	4.3	2,304.1	4,947	1,933	913	48,099	214,880	57,657	7,078
Laredo, TX	1,204.4	4,647	58.3	1.3	6.0	0.4	1.5	1,569.6	6,056	3,330	544	19,121	110,420	40,036	3,749
Las Cruces, NM	719.6	3,356	57.5	1.3	6.7	1.9	4.1	440.1	2,052	3,472	558	16,955	90,980	42,451	4,294
Las Vegas-Henderson-Paradise, NV	9,171.7	4,584	29.1	8.3	9.6	2.7	7.2	21,727.8	10,860	12,977	15,143	85,834	980,020	59,719	8,486
Lawrence, KS	474.7	4,206	28.6	35.1	4.9	0.0	3.3	544.9	4,828	443	464	15,310	50,900	61,161	7,784
Lawton, OK	533.8	4,027	37.6	38.9	4.3	0.0	3.4	253.8	1,915	4,047	11,034	11,172	51,130	47,311	4,572
Lebanon, PA	507.4	3,752	47.7	2.2	2.9	15.0	5.1	705.4	5,215	3,136	353	4,955	68,660	53,625	5,758
Lewiston, ID-WA	188.3	3,065	43.4	3.1	7.2	0.1	7.4	47.1	767	253	190	5,185	28,490	52,465	5,540
Lewiston-Auburn, ME	348.5	3,239	53.0	0.2	4.0	0.4	5.6	353.5	3,285	274	329	5,065	49,210	47,646	4,629
Lexington-Fayette, KY	1,363.2	2,811	49.9	3.2	5.3	0.7	2.2	2,544.8	5,247	4,543	1,518	46,751	226,130	60,277	7,936
Lima, OH	385.4	3,665	49.5	5.4	6.9	4.3	6.7	180.7	1,719	327	254	5,795	48,020	50,985	5,823
Lincoln, NE	1,130.3	3,642	53.2	1.9	4.3	0.9	6.9	2,872.1	9,255	3,271	1,135	31,616	150,480	62,257	7,658
Little Rock-North Little Rock-Conway, AR	2,292.8	3,195	53.1	2.7	6.0	0.0	4.2	3,061.0	4,265	9,636	6,810	60,583	322,620	59,932	7,593
Logan, UT-ID	308.4	2,404	52.6	4.4	6.1	0.3	5.4	194.5	1,516	378	534	11,497	52,830	54,501	5,352
Longview, TX	736.4	3,399	58.8	4.2	5.0	0.0	4.6	1,187.1	5,479	487	422	11,375	92,880	55,659	6,850
Longview, WA	424.6	4,163	38.6	3.9	5.4	0.0	4.9	609.4	5,974	222	279	5,884	45,820	53,596	5,782
Los Angeles-Long Beach-Anaheim, CA	74,228.5	5,687	36.2	9.6	7.8	8.4	3.3	106,636.6	8,170	59,766	22,517	688,975	6,145,410	74,683	11,693
Anaheim-Santa Ana-Irvine, CA Div 11,244	13,915.7	4,503	41.4	2.9	7.7	7.3	4.5	22,316.3	7,222	11,413	5,126	146,588	NA	NA	NA
Los Angeles-Long Beach-Glendale, CA Div 31,084	60,312.8	6,054	35.0	11.1	7.8	8.7	3.1	84,320.3	8,464	48,353	17,391	542,387	NA	NA	NA
Louisville/Jefferson County, KY-IN	4,180.4	3,341	44.5	11.9	4.0	0.3	2.5	7,079.6	5,658	8,930	4,018	66,563	614,680	60,102	7,608
Lubbock, TX	1,388.9	4,666	35.4	31.5	4.7	0.1	2.3	2,311.9	7,767	1,343	644	29,412	133,190	55,285	7,159
Lynchburg, VA	701.3	2,747	47.7	1.7	5.7	7.2	1.9	641.2	2,511	556	831	12,957	113,960	52,706	5,708
Macon, GA	816.9	3,510	46.8	7.0	6.4	0.3	2.9	577.8	2,483	1,142	610	13,082	97,780	49,631	5,464
Madera, CA	649.2	4,265	45.6	3.7	3.9	8.8	6.2	475.5	3,124	311	222	10,236	58,560	47,479	4,730
Madison, WI	2,933.1	4,725	47.0	1.8	6.0	8.3	7.1	3,254.4	5,243	5,545	1,775	82,949	328,770	72,001	9,951
Manchester-Nashua, NH	1,496.1	3,713	52.0	0.6	6.1	3.8	4.7	1,157.0	2,872	4,022	1,428	17,449	212,770	71,083	9,859
Manhattan, KS	320.7	3,279	52.2	2.1	6.0	0.0	6.6	601.2	6,146	488	380	12,717	37,690	57,146	6,548
Mankato-North Mankato, MN	409.8	4,181	36.2	5.3	4.8	5.7	13.5	455.8	4,650	290	357	8,253	46,390	58,202	6,894
Mansfield, OH	480.9	3,920	52.3	8.7	5.0	4.8	5.5	209.0	1,703	639	291	7,052	56,890	45,199	4,535
McAllen-Edinburg-Mission, TX	3,161.8	3,920	67.1	2.0	3.8	0.5	2.9	3,738.4	4,635	4,289	1,755	53,619	311,010	37,813	3,310
Medford, OR	678.0	3,285	42.6	5.3	8.6	0.0	6.1	887.0	4,297	1,807	532	8,922	99,240	53,792	6,045
Memphis, TN-MS-AR	5,764.4	4,296	46.3	6.7	8.6	0.9	2.8	6,748.2	5,030	14,083	5,529	67,693	619,600	56,006	7,298
Merced, CA	1,403.1	5,349	48.6	3.6	4.1	10.0	2.7	901.0	3,435	782	396	17,781	101,360	44,913	4,087
Miami-Fort Lauderdale-West Palm Beach, FL	31,257.3	5,424	25.8	15.2	8.8	2.5	2.0	39,629.0	6,877	34,031	14,108	271,733	2,941,120	69,511	11,993
Fort Lauderdale-Pompano Beach-Deerfield Beach, FL Div 22,744	10,214.0	5,627	24.6	26.3	10.2	1.2	1.4	8,639.5	4,760	6,945	3,943	96,891	NA	NA	NA
Miami-Miami Beach-Kendall, FL Div 33,124	14,468.1	5,584	25.8	12.2	7.5	3.5	2.2	23,549.3	9,089	20,205	7,410	119,869	NA	NA	NA
West Palm Beach-Boca Raton-Delray Beach, FL Div 48,424	6,575.2	4,847	27.6	4.7	9.3	2.5	2.5	7,440.3	5,485	6,881	2,755	54,973	NA	NA	NA
Michigan City-La Porte, IN	330.9	2,974	53.0	1.0	4.1	0.3	2.3	311.4	2,799	171	336	6,700	51,640	49,502	5,409
Midland, MI	272.5	3,250	51.0	2.8	4.1	2.1	7.6	318.6	3,800	147	131	3,231	40,240	71,709	10,219
Midland, TX	864.5	5,700	32.3	45.1	3.2	0.0	1.2	654.6	4,316	575	339	9,293	76,670	98,399	17,989
Milwaukee-Waukesha-West Allis, WI	7,419.0	4,735	44.0	7.8	7.8	3.4	5.7	8,456.0	5,396	10,708	4,400	77,722	769,950	68,150	9,538
Minneapolis-St. Paul-Bloomington, MN	16,677.1	4,873	39.7	6.9	5.5	5.4	7.0	24,523.9	7,166	21,126	12,883	227,690	1,779,880	78,938	11,457
Missoula, MT	338.7	3,052	44.0	5.5	7.0	0.8	5.2	188.8	1,701	1,355	539	9,350	56,950	60,472	7,806

1. Based on the resident population estimated as of July 1 of the year shown.

Table C. Metropolitan Areas — Personal Income and Earnings

Area name	Personal income, 2016										Earnings, 2016		
			Per capita[1]			Supplements to wages and salaries, employer contributions (mil dol)						Contributions for government social insurance (mil dol)	
	Total (mil dol)	Percent change, 2015-2016	Dollars	Rank	Wages and salaries (mil dol)	Pension and insurance	Government social insurance	Proprietors' income	Dividends, interest, and rent (mil dol)	Personal transfer receipts (mil dol)	Total (mil dol)	From employee and self-employed	From employer
	62	63	64	65	66	67	68	69	70	71	72	73	74
Mobile, AL	14,914	1.9	35,951	341	8,412	1,369	617	1,023	2,354	3,754	11,423	744	617
Modesto, CA	22,366	3.6	41,299	214	8,878	1,838	653	2,091	3,593	4,908	13,460	763	653
Monroe, LA	6,804	3.3	37,914	297	3,224	592	210	520	1,052	1,838	4,546	257	210
Monroe, MI	6,455	3.3	43,263	166	2,065	375	152	299	817	1,344	2,891	197	152
Montgomery, AL	15,165	2.5	40,558	227	7,871	1,492	587	816	2,820	3,321	10,767	668	587
Morgantown, WV	5,400	-0.3	39,024	268	3,196	594	243	310	855	1,058	4,343	267	243
Morristown, TN	4,045	3.7	34,482	360	1,772	337	126	400	527	1,152	2,635	174	126
Mount Vernon-Anacortes, WA	5,759	5.3	46,565	101	2,361	449	219	442	1,313	1,238	3,471	208	219
Muncie, IN	3,983	3.7	34,452	361	1,905	378	143	217	624	1,161	2,644	171	143
Muskegon, MI	6,180	3.5	35,641	346	2,707	503	208	306	867	1,760	3,724	248	208
Myrtle Beach-Conway-North Myrtle Beach, NC-SC	15,722	4.9	34,993	352	5,901	937	465	1,105	3,189	4,745	8,409	619	465
Napa, CA	9,355	5.0	65,805	11	4,263	829	311	1,550	2,197	1,198	6,952	382	311
Naples-Immokalee-Marco Island, FL	30,708	1.9	84,101	5	7,222	887	489	1,811	17,130	3,346	10,408	716	489
Nashville-Davidson— Murfreesboro— Franklin, TN	97,835	5.4	52,450	45	50,766	7,276	3,442	19,792	12,844	13,107	81,276	4,622	3,442
New Bern, NC	5,216	2.3	41,357	210	2,434	562	204	211	1,161	1,290	3,411	202	204
New Haven-Milford, CT	45,074	1.8	52,603	44	21,311	3,547	1,633	3,546	8,002	8,620	30,037	1,670	1,633
New Orleans-Metairie, LA	59,897	-0.9	47,205	95	30,036	5,034	1,982	5,708	11,528	10,936	42,760	2,362	1,982
New York-Newark-Jersey City, NY-NJ-PA	1,327,036	2.0	65,846	10	703,960	104,861	49,291	121,592	276,987	201,094	979,704	54,411	49,291
Dutchess County-Putnam County, NY Div 20,524	20,666	1.5	52,536	X	7,278	1,630	606	995	3,527	3,535	10,509	595	606
Nassau County-Suffolk County, NY Div 35,004	198,818	1.9	69,661	X	78,774	14,844	6,280	15,131	40,742	27,748	115,029	6,253	6,280
Newark, NJ-PA Div 35,084	177,980	2.1	70,980	X	87,752	12,214	6,151	17,638	34,675	21,092	123,756	7,220	6,151
New York-Jersey City-White Plains, NY-NJ Div 35,614	929,572	2.0	64,559	X	530,156	76,173	36,253	87,828	198,044	148,720	730,410	40,342	36,253
Niles-Benton Harbor, MI	6,777	3.6	44,007	148	3,085	620	235	301	1,198	1,599	4,240	267	235
North Port-Sarasota-Bradenton, FL	40,945	2.6	51,931	49	13,542	1,833	926	2,402	15,609	8,338	18,702	1,348	926
Norwich-New London, CT	14,538	1.2	53,885	34	7,164	1,466	528	938	2,903	2,496	10,095	531	528
Ocala, FL	12,134	4.0	34,765	357	4,188	671	291	446	2,703	4,154	5,597	458	291
Ocean City, NJ	5,181	2.7	54,865	31	1,695	351	149	505	1,367	1,222	2,699	180	149
Odessa, TX	6,538	-7.7	41,522	205	3,729	516	255	768	779	1,039	5,268	277	255
Ogden-Clearfield, UT	25,771	5.3	39,381	257	11,228	2,228	905	1,351	4,446	3,497	15,712	925	905
Oklahoma City, OK	61,308	0.1	44,646	137	30,754	5,241	2,333	6,964	11,125	10,100	45,291	2,472	2,333
Olympia-Tumwater, WA	12,642	5.7	45,932	111	5,665	1,091	509	710	2,632	2,427	7,974	470	509
Omaha-Council Bluffs, NE-IA	49,545	2.8	53,613	37	25,625	3,909	1,933	7,085	8,980	6,483	38,552	2,231	1,933
Orlando-Kissimmee-Sanford, FL	98,062	4.6	40,169	241	58,930	7,658	4,026	5,388	16,234	18,626	76,001	4,734	4,026
Oshkosh-Neenah, WI	7,414	2.6	43,641	158	4,985	833	372	410	1,352	1,208	6,599	405	372
Owensboro, KY	4,604	0.1	39,027	267	2,268	378	175	246	752	1,167	3,068	197	175
Oxnard-Thousand Oaks-Ventura, CA	47,398	2.4	55,779	27	18,757	3,470	1,323	3,993	9,398	6,420	27,544	1,573	1,323
Palm Bay-Melbourne-Titusville, FL	24,141	3.3	41,685	202	10,597	1,600	750	949	5,280	6,023	13,896	950	750
Panama City, FL	8,025	3.0	40,130	242	3,750	657	279	376	1,767	1,864	5,062	318	279
Parkersburg-Vienna, WV	3,439	-1.2	37,608	306	1,558	295	126	202	514	1,005	2,180	155	126
Pensacola-Ferry Pass-Brent, FL	19,420	3.1	39,984	246	8,398	1,495	626	857	4,052	4,424	11,376	714	626
Peoria, IL	17,327	0.6	46,052	108	9,711	1,591	679	739	3,234	3,075	12,720	733	679
Philadelphia-Camden-Wilmington, PA-NJ-DE-MD.	355,663	2.3	58,589	18	176,532	27,585	13,420	35,418	63,907	60,315	252,956	14,784	13,420
Camden, NJ Div 15,804	65,340	2.5	52,199	X	28,760	4,816	2,298	4,279	9,868	11,637	40,152	2,464	2,298
Montgomery County-Bucks County-Chester County, PA Div 33,874	139,950	1.5	71,242	X	68,141	9,563	5,069	6,516	31,871	16,706	89,288	5,422	5,069
Philadelphia, PA Div 37,964	114,549	3.5	53,747	X	58,432	9,656	4,505	22,769	15,933	25,428	95,362	5,189	4,505
Wilmington, DE-MD-NJ Div 48,864	35,823	1.7	49,547	X	21,200	3,551	1,549	1,855	6,235	6,544	28,154	1,709	1,549
Phoenix-Mesa-Scottsdale, AZ	196,801	4.0	42,218	187	105,910	14,554	7,521	13,336	36,284	34,883	141,320	8,831	7,521
Pine Bluff, AR	2,964	1.5	32,227	376	1,397	258	112	188	392	968	1,955	129	112
Pittsburgh, PA	119,896	0.7	51,187	58	62,940	10,317	4,929	8,940	19,607	24,354	87,126	5,265	4,929
Pittsfield, MA	6,635	2.7	52,288	47	2,939	546	211	451	1,370	1,636	4,148	242	211
Pocatello, ID	2,929	4.1	34,709	358	1,313	276	120	155	478	674	1,865	122	120
Portland-South Portland, ME	26,944	3.5	50,871	60	13,925	2,243	1,032	1,940	5,042	4,631	19,140	1,235	1,032
Portland-Vancouver-Hillsboro, OR-WA	122,434	4.3	50,489	62	67,402	8,964	5,667	8,934	24,062	18,165	90,967	5,630	5,667
Port St. Lucie, FL	22,726	2.4	48,852	77	6,208	964	435	954	7,893	4,745	8,561	627	435
Prescott, AZ	8,200	3.9	36,353	332	2,495	433	185	546	2,139	2,566	3,659	296	185
Providence-Warwick, RI-MA	80,641	1.9	49,940	66	37,416	6,327	2,958	5,185	13,214	16,802	51,886	3,330	2,958
Provo-Orem, UT	21,812	7.2	36,154	338	10,403	1,686	800	2,216	3,572	2,699	15,105	877	800
Pueblo, CO	5,969	3.6	36,148	339	2,669	416	208	283	1,005	1,783	3,577	223	208
Punta Gorda, FL	6,866	3.2	38,473	282	1,909	289	134	354	2,013	2,292	2,686	234	134
Racine, WI	8,745	1.7	44,813	132	3,698	705	284	323	1,630	1,662	5,010	320	284
Raleigh, NC	65,726	4.0	50,444	63	34,799	4,597	2,539	4,373	11,439	7,748	46,308	2,808	2,539
Rapid City, SD	6,572	2.2	45,120	124	2,959	547	225	639	1,573	1,177	4,369	269	225

1. Based on the resident population estimated as of July 1 of the year shown.

Table C. Metropolitan Areas — **Earnings, Social Security , and Housing**

Area name	Farm	Mining, quarrying, and extracting	Construction	Manufacturing	Information; professional, scientific, and technical services	Retail trade	Finance, insurance, real estate, rental and leasing	Health care and social assistance	Government	Social Security beneficiaries, December 2016 Number	Rate[1]	Supplemental Security Income recipients, 2016	Housing units, 2017 Total	Percent change, 2010-2017
	75	76	77	78	79	80	81	82	83	84	85	86	87	88
Mobile, AL	0.2	0.4	7.1	15.6	9.0	6.7	7.5	12.5	15.1	90,530	218	15,207	183,897	3.2
Modesto, CA	6.8	0.0	6.3	12.9	4.2	7.5	4.1	16.0	18.6	87,305	161	21,784	181,602	1.2
Monroe, LA	0.6	1.2	5.7	9.5	D	8.1	7.2	18.3	16.3	34,800	194	7,846	80,166	5.7
Monroe, MI	0.7	D	7.6	17.1	D	6.5	3.0	9.4	12.9	34,465	231	2,512	64,306	2.1
Montgomery, AL	0.7	0.1	5.0	12.1	D	6.1	D	D	28.9	79,045	212	14,218	167,794	3.9
Morgantown, WV	-0.3	1.2	7.3	9.6	D	5.5	2.8	D	28.2	22,230	161	2,684	60,156	3.1
Morristown, TN	-0.1	D	D	28.5	3.0	8.4	2.8	D	13.4	30,750	263	3,594	51,333	1.7
Mount Vernon-Anacortes, WA	4.3	0.1	9.8	14.9	5.9	8.8	6.1	7.7	24.0	29,615	240	2,453	53,800	4.5
Muncie, IN	0.4	D	4.5	11.0	6.6	8.3	6.3	19.5	22.5	25,900	224	3,044	52,730	0.7
Muskegon, MI	0.7	0.1	6.2	27.1	4.0	9.6	3.6	17.0	14.1	41,960	242	6,216	74,110	0.7
Myrtle Beach-Conway-North Myrtle Beach, NC-SC	0.5	D	8.2	3.3	7.1	11.4	9.2	11.3	16.4	134,710	301	8,022	294,602	11.8
Napa, CA	1.2	D	7.7	23.8	6.0	4.9	5.9	9.0	15.1	26,815	189	2,252	55,847	2.0
Naples-Immokalee-Marco Island, FL	1.0	0.1	12.2	2.8	12.0	8.7	10.7	12.7	9.6	91,370	250	4,176	214,423	8.7
Nashville-Davidson— Murfreesboro— Franklin, TN	-0.1	0.1	6.6	7.7	11.9	6.5	8.6	20.8	9.5	306,970	164	32,044	780,528	11.0
New Bern, NC	1.0	D	3.5	8.0	4.8	5.7	2.9	9.0	50.1	30,465	243	3,185	59,656	4.0
New Haven-Milford, CT	0.1	0.1	6.1	8.7	10.1	6.5	6.5	15.5	15.1	163,110	190	20,162	367,195	1.4
New Orleans-Metairie, LA	0.0	2.9	6.6	7.7	10.9	D	7.1	11.5	14.7	232,300	183	44,545	558,501	2.2
New York-Newark-Jersey City, NY-NJ-PA	0.0	D	4.8	D	18.7	4.9	17.3	10.6	13.8	3,273,025	161	595,018	7,983,552	2.6
Dutchess County-Putnam County, NY Div 20,524	0.0	D	7.7	D	7.3	6.9	3.4	16.1	24.3	78,060	198	6,102	159,385	1.6
Nassau County-Suffolk County, NY Div 35,004	0.1	0.1	7.2	5.6	11.8	7.4	9.5	15.3	18.9	548,770	192	37,151	1,048,338	1.0
Newark, NJ-PA Div 35,084	0.0	0.3	4.7	9.5	17.9	4.5	10.1	9.3	13.6	409,290	162	50,454	991,109	1.6
New York-Jersey City-White Plains, NY-NJ Div 35,614	0.0	0.2	4.4	2.7	20.1	4.6	19.9	10.0	12.9	2,236,905	154	501,311	5,784,720	3.1
Niles-Benton Harbor, MI	1.2	0.2	4.1	30.1	3.7	5.2	4.3	11.8	14.2	37,415	243	4,699	77,503	0.8
North Port-Sarasota-Bradenton, FL	0.7	D	9.0	6.1	11.7	9.2	8.7	15.9	10.1	230,860	293	10,661	431,041	7.5
Norwich-New London, CT	0.5	0.1	5.5	18.7	7.9	5.9	2.8	11.3	27.6	55,200	205	4,330	123,398	2.0
Ocala, FL	-0.4	0.1	7.2	8.5	7.8	11.1	5.0	19.3	15.9	114,875	330	9,827	168,361	2.6
Ocean City, NJ	0.2	D	11.2	D	4.9	9.8	7.2	10.3	27.4	28,415	303	1,740	99,245	1.0
Odessa, TX	-0.1	19.4	13.6	7.5	3.9	7.0	5.4	6.0	13.4	20,015	127	3,418	58,175	9.7
Ogden-Clearfield, UT	0.2	D	8.7	15.3	D	7.0	5.9	9.5	24.7	82,800	127	6,593	223,069	9.3
Oklahoma City, OK	0.1	D	6.5	5.6	D	6.3	6.3	D	21.0	229,420	167	27,254	575,039	6.7
Olympia-Tumwater, WA	0.8	0.1	5.3	3.0	6.3	6.4	4.4	12.7	39.3	57,625	210	5,307	116,820	8.0
Omaha-Council Bluffs, NE-IA	0.8	0.1	6.8	5.9	D	5.1	9.9	10.8	13.5	147,105	159	14,788	386,106	6.6
Orlando-Kissimmee-Sanford, FL	0.2	0.0	6.8	4.5	12.8	7.2	8.7	11.4	11.2	426,665	174	60,538	1,033,243	9.7
Oshkosh-Neenah, WI	0.3	D	7.1	27.3	7.2	4.9	5.5	9.1	11.9	34,020	201	2,537	75,619	3.1
Owensboro, KY	2.1	0.8	5.9	20.9	D	7.1	D	17.4	12.2	28,120	238	4,109	51,266	3.7
Oxnard-Thousand Oaks-Ventura, CA	3.4	0.7	5.6	14.4	10.2	7.5	8.3	9.3	17.7	136,870	161	16,375	288,813	2.5
Palm Bay-Melbourne-Titusville, FL	0.1	0.0	5.6	17.1	10.8	7.5	4.5	14.0	16.9	157,930	273	12,019	278,104	3.1
Panama City, FL	0.0	D	6.2	5.6	8.9	9.1	5.7	D	26.3	44,260	222	5,085	112,388	3.3
Parkersburg-Vienna, WV	-0.3	1.8	6.8	D	D	9.5	6.2	15.7	22.4	24,995	273	3,848	43,599	0.4
Pensacola-Ferry Pass-Brent, FL	0.2	0.2	5.8	4.4	8.6	7.2	8.1	15.7	26.8	106,575	221	12,591	213,299	5.9
Peoria, IL	0.4	D	5.7	22.7	D	5.2	D	14.3	11.5	79,125	211	7,301	166,896	1.6
Philadelphia-Camden-Wilmington, PA-NJ-DE-MD	0.1	D	D	D	21.0	5.1	9.5	13.2	12.5	1,119,180	184	181,399	2,487,986	2.2
Camden, NJ Div 15,804	0.2	D	6.3	8.2	10.1	8.4	7.7	14.9	18.9	245,020	196	27,333	498,904	1.7
Montgomery County-Bucks County-Chester County, PA Div 33,874	0.2	0.0	7.5	9.7	20.0	5.9	9.5	12.1	8.3	375,915	191	19,623	785,264	2.8
Philadelphia, PA Div 37,964	0.0	0.0	3.1	3.7	28.9	2.9	8.0	13.5	13.1	363,740	170	120,796	910,306	1.9
Wilmington, DE-MD-NJ Div 48,864	0.2	0.3	5.2	D	12.6	5.0	17.1	13.3	14.3	134,505	186	13,647	293,512	2.6
Phoenix-Mesa-Scottsdale, AZ	0.3	0.5	5.9	8.1	11.3	7.4	12.1	12.1	12.7	753,820	162	67,139	1,911,838	6.3
Pine Bluff, AR	5.1	D	3.0	17.4	D	5.6	D	D	29.6	21,160	229	5,235	42,374	1.0
Pittsburgh, PA	0.0	1.4	6.5	7.7	13.0	5.6	8.7	14.2	11.3	557,720	238	65,529	1,126,447	2.2
Pittsfield, MA	0.0	0.1	8.3	10.2	8.7	7.8	5.6	19.1	14.7	34,225	270	4,013	69,246	1.1
Pocatello, ID	0.7	D	6.3	7.9	5.2	8.1	7.1	15.6	25.7	14,650	174	1,971	34,233	3.1
Portland-South Portland, ME	0.1	D	6.6	D	10.5	6.9	9.3	14.6	15.9	118,930	225	9,964	273,376	4.1
Portland-Vancouver-Hillsboro, OR-WA	0.5	0.1	6.6	13.3	D	5.9	D	13.1	13.1	400,735	165	44,746	992,907	7.3
Port St. Lucie, FL	0.6	D	7.4	5.2	9.1	9.3	6.1	17.7	15.3	123,555	266	8,579	221,174	2.8
Prescott, AZ	0.2	2.6	8.2	6.0	5.6	9.5	5.3	16.0	19.6	77,005	343	3,740	116,541	5.5
Providence-Warwick, RI-MA	0.0	D	D	D	8.8	6.9	7.9	14.5	16.6	341,020	211	52,165	703,701	2.3
Provo-Orem, UT	0.2	0.0	10.1	9.4	D	10.3	D	11.2	11.2	56,300	94	4,275	176,557	16.2
Pueblo, CO	0.1	D	8.0	8.2	6.6	8.7	3.5	21.1	21.5	36,370	221	6,279	71,116	2.3
Punta Gorda, FL	1.7	0.3	8.3	1.9	8.4	12.3	6.6	21.8	14.9	66,585	374	2,711	103,996	3.3
Racine, WI	0.3	0.1	5.4	33.1	4.0	6.1	4.3	12.3	14.1	41,930	215	5,518	82,776	0.7
Raleigh, NC	0.3	0.1	7.0	8.6	19.9	5.9	7.8	9.4	14.4	181,680	139	17,440	534,909	14.8
Rapid City, SD	0.2	D	9.1	3.7	D	7.9	7.1	D	23.6	32,360	223	2,354	66,070	9.1

1. Per 1,000 resident population estimated as of July 1 of the year shown.

Table C. Metropolitan Areas — Professional Services, Manufacturing, and Accommodation and Food Services

Area name	Professional, scientific, and technical services, 2012				Manufacturing, 2012				Accommodation and food services, 2012			
	Number of establishments	Number of employees	Sales (mil dol)	Annual payroll (mil dol)	Number of establishments	Number of employees	Sales (mil dol)	Annual payroll (mil dol)	Number of establishments	Number of employees	Sales (mil dol)	Annual payroll (mil dol)
	147	148	149	150	151	152	153	154	155	156	157	158
Mobile, AL	850	9,039	1,175.1	474.0	343	16,063	10,562.7	886.3	671	13,684	617.9	167.9
Modesto, CA	649	5,111	507.5	196.0	395	19,963	11,703.6	1,007.8	813	13,611	705.7	192.6
Monroe, LA	449	2,737	379.1	125.2	136	6,067	2,438.8	286.3	310	6,524	298.1	81.5
Monroe, MI	147	828	129.9	40.6	128	6,591	2,976.5	351.3	259	4,280	179.9	49.6
Montgomery, AL	756	6,906	1,421.8	433.6	287	17,367	14,627.6	896.5	671	13,503	636.6	174.8
Morgantown, WV	234	2,834	405.3	124.7	78	4,133	2,181.4	273.8	317	6,165	267.1	73.8
Morristown, TN	110	438	48.8	14.1	144	10,205	4,224.1	418.1	178	3,065	152.3	40.6
Mount Vernon-Anacortes, WA	300	D	D	D	174	5,269	11,529.4	295.7	330	4,195	291.5	79.1
Muncie, IN	163	1,522	240.5	63.4	130	4,205	1,591.3	191.2	211	4,417	172.7	49.6
Muskegon, MI	223	1,513	182.5	65.7	259	12,483	3,727.0	608.0	335	5,450	236.1	67.6
Myrtle Beach-Conway-North Myrtle Beach, NC-SC	866	3,696	400.6	143.7	216	4,213	2,742.7	222.8	1,489	29,339	1,897.5	499.8
Napa, CA	395	1,801	280.5	101.5	431	10,837	4,623.5	622.5	375	10,466	774.1	247.7
Naples-Immokalee-Marco Island, FL	1,342	4,810	784.7	270.4	197	2,722	607.5	130.0	763	19,624	1,406.5	404.2
Nashville-Davidson— Murfreesboro— Franklin, TN	3,785	38,289	6,215.8	2,520.0	1,488	61,378	28,947.4	2,916.1	3,530	76,659	4,275.8	1,250.6
New Bern, NC	250	1,884	220.7	97.0	85	3,535	1,308.0	164.3	234	4,207	198.3	54.1
New Haven-Milford, CT	1,907	16,222	2,461.1	1,216.8	1,151	31,792	10,818.1	1,879.2	1,969	26,342	1,487.2	411.3
New Orleans-Metairie, LA	3,884	31,419	5,507.7	2,078.7	742	34,170	104,969.4	2,377.1	3,217	69,067	4,502.4	1,259.1
New York-Newark-Jersey City, NY-NJ-PA	69,819	710,316	163,194.8	61,316.7	16,232	346,950	134,229.9	19,621.2	48,312	634,388	49,193.7	13,558.1
Dutchess County-Putnam County, NY Div 20,524	1,086	5,256	833.3	299.0	285	10,022	2,790.6	742.5	979	10,711	599.9	162.2
Nassau County-Suffolk County, NY Div 35,004	12,457	87,339	13,447.4	5,200.1	3,110	68,546	21,084.1	3,694.2	7,107	89,642	5,929.2	1,628.8
Newark, NJ-PA Div 35,084	9,067	112,684	22,364.6	9,712.9	2,448	70,600	38,127.3	4,797.5	5,475	72,580	4,728.5	1,272.8
New York-Jersey City-White Plains, NY-NJ Div 35,614	47,209	505,037	126,549.4	46,104.7	10,389	197,783	72,228.0	10,387.1	34,751	461,455	37,936.1	10,494.2
Niles-Benton Harbor, MI	284	2,149	201.0	108.3	289	8,330	1,962.8	388.9	365	5,323	241.7	69.4
North Port-Sarasota-Bradenton, FL	2,703	20,704	1,945.0	841.3	591	13,680	3,538.1	670.9	1,446	26,437	1,429.1	419.4
Norwich-New London, CT	529	8,100	666.1	862.0	172	12,435	4,693.7	950.2	698	28,347	3,023.8	748.7
Ocala, FL	669	3,676	415.5	157.2	178	4,806	1,471.2	212.9	437	7,369	375.2	102.5
Ocean City, NJ	214	D	D	D	66	615	98.2	21.5	903	5,888	593.0	160.0
Odessa, TX	227	1,832	205.4	80.1	251	4,756	1,706.3	265.7	261	6,150	389.0	94.0
Ogden-Clearfield, UT	1,443	10,848	1,407.6	525.8	596	27,115	14,050.6	1,478.6	855	15,956	671.2	190.6
Oklahoma City, OK	4,132	27,776	4,052.7	1,582.9	1,050	31,032	11,209.0	1,338.6	2,685	57,866	2,741.9	749.8
Olympia-Tumwater, WA	593	D	D	D	168	2,883	910.5	123.8	533	7,785	419.2	120.5
Omaha-Council Bluffs, NE-IA	2,342	59,415	3,755.6	2,966.2	656	30,185	17,651.7	1,361.4	1,901	36,416	1,866.7	512.8
Orlando-Kissimmee-Sanford, FL	7,816	58,862	8,811.8	3,756.9	1,337	32,960	11,209.7	1,917.5	4,484	138,873	10,349.4	2,695.0
Oshkosh-Neenah, WI	247	2,575	514.5	134.8	300	23,892	11,476.5	1,321.6	367	5,963	234.6	65.3
Owensboro, KY	169	1,563	105.3	44.8	125	6,938	5,391.9	357.4	193	4,448	191.8	55.3
Oxnard-Thousand Oaks-Ventura, CA	2,634	22,377	3,185.4	2,063.2	867	23,166	8,334.0	1,295.4	1,598	27,725	1,597.4	442.6
Palm Bay-Melbourne-Titusville, FL	1,669	13,893	2,433.6	981.2	407	19,152	5,441.9	1,311.3	1,042	18,994	902.6	257.7
Panama City, FL	434	3,465	493.8	184.2	110	3,904	1,482.5	197.5	497	10,318	581.6	165.7
Parkersburg-Vienna, WV	165	D	D	D	63	2,882	D	207.9	218	D	D	D
Pensacola-Ferry Pass-Brent, FL	1,063	9,010	1,234.8	486.1	229	4,433	2,552.0	262.3	747	14,767	744.0	203.9
Peoria, IL	676	6,718	865.5	374.9	331	19,563	13,708.7	1,081.5	870	15,632	778.2	212.7
Philadelphia-Camden-Wilmington, PA-NJ-DE-MD	18,064	199,353	37,881.9	16,087.3	5,115	172,790	99,584.5	10,453.8	12,771	198,333	11,474.3	3,164.3
Camden, NJ Div 15,804	3,281	D	D	D	967	34,775	D	2,101.0	2,395	36,821	1,967.4	525.4
Montgomery County-Bucks County-Chester County, PA Div 33,874	8,266	83,896	15,163.1	6,634.4	2,565	82,694	30,889.5	4,823.6	4,218	66,585	3,705.4	1,043.4
Philadelphia, PA Div 37,964	4,370	59,242	12,848.3	5,152.2	1,132	35,487	27,083.4	2,173.3	4,774	69,816	4,429.8	1,218.4
Wilmington, DE-MD-NJ Div 48,864	2,147	D	D	D	451	19,834	D	1,356.0	1,384	25,111	1,371.7	377.1
Phoenix-Mesa-Scottsdale, AZ	11,812	91,918	15,658.8	5,865.3	3,000	94,061	36,827.5	5,560.6	7,121	165,154	9,456.3	2,745.4
Pine Bluff, AR	87	594	66.7	28.3	70	5,532	2,226.6	243.5	134	2,365	93.0	23.1
Pittsburgh, PA	5,871	81,204	15,404.9	5,698.3	2,506	90,107	38,416.1	4,812.4	5,374	92,549	4,548.1	1,266.2
Pittsfield, MA	338	2,688	397.7	162.8	151	5,275	1,288.9	310.7	522	7,006	418.7	124.2
Pocatello, ID	165	1,277	84.2	40.3	44	1,633	916.3	67.7	197	3,199	135.5	37.2
Portland-South Portland, ME	1,923	13,183	2,086.5	801.2	662	21,142	6,501.6	1,099.6	1,823	24,102	1,457.2	436.0
Portland-Vancouver-Hillsboro, OR-WA	8,099	68,556	9,720.6	5,233.3	3,058	D	D	D	5,743	86,242	4,870.0	1,428.9
Port St. Lucie, FL	1,211	5,244	685.0	246.3	296	4,883	1,709.0	237.3	724	12,867	642.0	182.8
Prescott, AZ	522	1,748	190.9	74.3	184	2,765	706.9	130.8	548	8,223	407.5	130.8
Providence-Warwick, RI-MA	4,042	27,215	4,161.4	1,605.4	2,183	66,543	19,277.2	3,628.5	4,214	63,818	3,450.4	982.0
Provo-Orem, UT	1,654	16,956	1,741.7	656.3	525	15,963	6,082.1	807.2	709	13,249	577.3	161.5
Pueblo, CO	238	1,744	435.3	157.3	90	4,221	2,333.3	216.8	356	5,698	236.0	67.8
Punta Gorda, FL	381	1,295	138.5	50.5	69	402	90.4	14.6	261	4,804	219.2	61.7
Racine, WI	310	1,967	234.8	91.7	325	15,444	8,100.1	844.4	382	5,974	251.7	70.5
Raleigh, NC	4,656	41,942	7,437.7	3,117.2	738	21,629	17,865.0	1,146.8	2,415	47,908	2,436.0	675.1
Rapid City, SD	372	2,151	243.7	83.2	164	2,383	570.3	95.4	480	7,455	426.6	117.1

Area name	Health care and social assistance, 2012				Other services, 2012				Nonemployer businesses, 2015		Value of residential construction authorized by building permits, 2017	
	Number of establish-ments	Number of employees	Receipts (mil dol)	Annual payroll (mil dol)	Number of establis-hments	Number of employees	Receipts (mil dol)	Annual payroll (mil dol)	Number	Receipts (mil dol)	New construc-tion ($1,000)	Number of housing units
	159	160	161	162	163	164	165	166	167	168	169	170
Mobile, AL	734	21,863	2,397.2	927.8	570	3,577	334.8	96.2	30,496	1,117.8	166,505	998
Modesto, CA	1,075	24,257	3,635.0	1,274.8	604	3,817	371.6	118.9	27,111	1,418.2	170,165	719
Monroe, LA	661	14,936	1,407.9	504.3	243	1,568	144.3	42.1	14,105	573.4	152,246	752
Monroe, MI	282	5,347	457.9	193.6	156	727	67.6	17.0	8,299	363.4	69,839	450
Montgomery, AL	875	20,240	2,062.6	869.8	569	3,906	468.3	130.1	24,543	1,018.8	154,132	761
Morgantown, WV	295	14,178	1,582.2	569.5	177	1,316	190.7	34.3	7,058	326.1	7,462	77
Morristown, TN	230	5,680	491.1	189.8	114	526	42.4	12.9	6,669	290.2	56,317	268
Mount Vernon-Anacortes, WA	330	7,152	700.3	296.6	252	1,128	106.0	31.3	7,712	369.9	133,298	663
Muncie, IN	313	9,158	873.1	318.7	174	1,043	105.9	26.2	5,649	206.4	15,205	72
Muskegon, MI	369	11,494	982.3	483.8	250	1,315	120.8	29.6	9,379	357.4	54,912	257
Myrtle Beach-Conway-North Myrtle Beach, NC-SC	878	14,479	1,600.7	571.0	623	3,183	324.9	77.9	33,816	1,513.6	1,568,752	8,587
Napa, CA	404	10,222	1,360.7	553.3	241	1,359	127.7	40.0	11,921	730.9	65,750	183
Naples-Immokalee-Marco Island, FL	995	16,310	2,089.4	772.0	850	5,209	474.4	138.1	38,777	2,323.8	1,138,174	4,194
Nashville-Davidson— Mur-freesboro— Franklin, TN	4,208	109,447	13,584.2	5,158.9	2,507	19,844	2,180.7	640.4	164,992	8,687.5	4,082,862	20,631
New Bern, NC	293	8,064	806.0	330.9	167	832	70.7	18.5	7,353	280.8	48,875	295
New Haven-Milford, CT	2,408	73,162	7,788.2	3,238.4	1,717	9,881	977.8	297.8	59,574	3,112.0	124,211	750
New Orleans-Metairie, LA	3,205	67,442	7,698.1	2,899.3	1,850	12,712	1,868.6	426.7	116,471	5,280.2	655,895	2,966
New York-Newark-Jersey City, NY-NJ-PA	60,802	1,438,772	161,273.4	66,480.3	48,848	291,897	42,605.8	10,194.7	1,861,540	103,653.2	8,228,018	50,578
Dutchess County-Putnam County, NY Div 20,524	1,162	23,662	2,563.7	1,086.5	824	3,627	397.2	105.5	NA	NA	181,221	540
Nassau County-Suffolk County, NY Div 35,004	10,507	207,080	23,582.4	10,013.4	8,013	40,426	4,189.4	1,107.1	NA	NA	1,107,460	2,625
Newark, NJ-PA Div 35,084	7,795	155,717	17,765.9	7,176.8	5,410	35,343	3,614.8	1,051.8	NA	NA	894,319	6,259
New York-Jersey City-White Plains, NY-NJ Div 35,614	41,338	1,052,313	117,361.3	48,203.6	34,601	212,501	34,404.4	7,930.2	NA	NA	6,045,018	41,154
Niles-Benton Harbor, MI	399	9,410	816.5	329.2	251	1,199	116.0	32.2	9,842	395.1	75,942	237
North Port-Sarasota-Braden-ton, FL	2,393	40,770	4,488.5	1,669.2	1,448	7,481	648.2	176.8	71,186	3,575.8	1,856,925	8,179
Norwich-New London, CT	734	17,357	1,728.0	751.2	459	2,498	274.7	61.9	16,548	788.9	65,433	295
Ocala, FL	878	15,494	1,874.0	674.9	455	2,315	196.6	54.0	24,391	1,017.0	373,992	2,246
Ocean City, NJ	278	4,767	443.7	186.8	296	1,237	96.3	32.4	8,066	492.5	236,490	809
Odessa, TX	293	7,384	823.7	297.6	250	2,276	340.1	83.5	11,141	612.8	92,739	492
Ogden-Clearfield, UT	1,431	21,624	2,361.9	801.8	809	4,688	374.1	106.9	39,963	1,726.9	744,237	3,534
Oklahoma City, OK	4,134	76,535	9,611.3	3,270.6	2,067	13,049	1,632.8	381.5	105,556	5,150.4	1,199,517	5,419
Olympia-Tumwater, WA	790	13,079	1,584.8	619.1	483	2,769	331.1	98.1	14,707	630.2	269,890	1,067
Omaha-Council Bluffs, NE-IA	2,439	61,248	6,795.6	2,552.5	1,603	10,653	1,536.4	314.5	58,505	2,675.9	797,040	4,955
Orlando-Kissimmee-San-ford, FL	5,726	108,835	13,809.2	4,884.8	3,592	23,294	2,405.8	635.2	221,721	8,815.5	5,043,464	19,065
Oshkosh-Neenah, WI	439	13,580	1,272.0	555.0	257	2,279	221.0	68.1	8,307	383.1	101,146	549
Owensboro, KY	348	7,891	759.3	301.6	167	1,100	83.1	25.8	6,528	275.1	23,606	264
Oxnard-Thousand Oaks-Ventura, CA	2,557	32,438	3,987.6	1,434.5	1,176	7,150	763.3	188.6	67,736	3,653.3	461,558	2,565
Palm Bay-Melbourne-Titus-ville, FL	1,522	31,218	3,727.6	1,387.7	958	4,563	372.7	117.7	42,420	1,698.9	738,164	2,753
Panama City, FL	515	10,051	1,078.2	412.5	321	1,936	160.6	43.4	14,826	721.4	337,739	1,786
Parkersburg-Vienna, WV	287	7,169	639.4	248.5	152	D	D	D	4,412	177.3	17,739	133
Pensacola-Ferry Pass-Brent, FL	1,019	24,040	2,905.3	1,091.4	594	3,417	307.7	88.5	32,054	1,359.9	487,279	2,609
Peoria, IL	840	30,651	3,197.1	1,286.0	613	6,256	590.3	251.2	19,632	734.5	61,553	257
Philadelphia-Camden-Wilm-ington, PA-NJ-DE-MD.	17,408	463,943	51,028.6	20,690.6	11,378	74,202	9,462.5	2,309.9	410,065	21,806.0	2,030,197	13,544
Camden, NJ Div 15,804	3,439	76,614	8,247.2	3,369.2	2,200	13,271	1,065.6	334.8	NA	NA	331,291	3,269
Montgomery County-Bucks County-Chester County, PA Div 33,874	6,477	145,503	15,158.5	6,213.8	4,374	28,315	4,325.0	894.6	NA	NA	841,907	4,297
Philadelphia, PA Div 37,964	5,528	191,974	21,925.2	8,572.2	3,609	24,712	3,271.7	844.7	NA	NA	681,563	3,970
Wilmington, DE-MD-NJ Div 48,864	1,964	49,852	5,697.8	2,535.4	1,195	7,904	800.2	235.9	NA	NA	175,436	2,008
Phoenix-Mesa-Scottsdale, AZ	11,231	207,257	24,523.2	9,574.2	5,505	43,914	4,609.6	1,279.1	316,042	15,396.1	6,502,995	29,312
Pine Bluff, AR	237	4,827	429.9	173.6	105	530	49.1	15.8	4,706	164.3	7,214	74
Pittsburgh, PA	7,942	190,828	18,711.4	7,858.7	5,155	32,089	3,524.7	897.4	144,705	6,683.4	955,403	4,328
Pittsfield, MA	438	11,415	1,091.4	488.4	278	1,675	144.1	39.5	10,183	450.2	60,626	194
Pocatello, ID	335	3,819	314.1	115.4	120	591	61.6	15.7	5,007	198.7	29,436	223
Portland-South Portland, ME	2,038	44,844	4,350.3	1,882.7	1,164	6,448	701.2	179.9	48,294	2,351.1	497,816	2,517
Portland-Vancouver-Hills-boro, OR-WA	7,272	132,399	16,118.5	6,283.0	4,277	25,065	3,122.2	806.2	174,121	8,730.1	3,122,424	15,983
Port St. Lucie, FL	1,191	18,821	2,288.4	829.9	761	3,811	330.2	96.8	40,041	1,810.6	500,457	2,287
Prescott, AZ	759	11,555	1,245.1	517.8	364	1,717	142.9	41.0	18,282	750.9	447,425	1,976
Providence-Warwick, RI-MA	4,650	123,284	11,708.9	5,129.5	3,361	18,660	1,923.7	529.5	108,621	5,062.9	412,316	2,010
Provo-Orem, UT	1,219	21,246	2,228.3	776.1	634	3,398	272.7	73.9	44,439	1,931.7	1,617,431	7,245
Pueblo, CO	419	11,404	1,063.1	458.0	238	1,222	93.1	28.2	8,177	323.3	62,271	368
Punta Gorda, FL	485	8,927	1,119.6	401.0	297	1,326	113.0	33.0	12,899	602.0	315,753	1,297
Racine, WI	459	10,588	764.4	335.7	317	1,839	140.4	44.5	9,535	395.1	67,504	278
Raleigh, NC	3,069	53,424	5,654.4	2,278.0	1,959	13,792	1,557.4	446.6	100,662	4,615.2	2,632,993	14,180
Rapid City, SD	408	11,766	1,318.5	509.7	334	1,801	220.7	45.4	11,009	507.6	134,824	779

Table C. Metropolitan Areas — **Population, Vital Statistics, Health, and Crime**

Area name	Daytime Population, 2016 — Persons in group quarters, 2017	Number	Employ-ment/residence ratio	Births, 2017 — Total	Rate[1]	Deaths, 2017 — Number	Rate[1]	Persons under 65 with no health insurance, 2016 — Number	Percent	Medicare, 2017 — Total benefici-aries	Enrolled in Original Medicare	Enrolled in Medicare Advantage	Serious crimes known to police[2], 2016 Total — Number	Rate[3]
	32	33	34	35	36	37	38	39	40	41	42	43	44	45
Texarkana, TX-AR..............	7,926	154,306	1.08	1,974	13.1	1,603	10.7	15,317	12.9	30,896	24,272	6,624	5,622	3,760
The Villages, FL	8,012	132,612	1.35	494	3.9	1,857	14.8	5,436	11.7	25,834	14,852	10,982	1,385	1,110
Toledo, OH........................	17,211	627,705	1.08	7,345	12.2	5,968	9.9	31,365	6.3	113,396	67,614	45,782	21,268	3,519
Topeka, KS........................	5,046	235,904	1.03	2,806	12.0	2,317	9.9	17,161	9.1	49,303	42,366	6,937	9,894	4,256
Trenton, NJ........................	20,261	426,156	1.31	4,039	10.8	2,941	7.8	26,707	8.9	64,441	45,696	18,745	8,075	2,181
Tucson, AZ........................	25,202	1,016,029	1.00	11,490	11.2	9,881	9.7	88,068	11.0	214,923	115,262	99,661	48,485	4,763
Tulsa, OK	15,530	992,509	1.01	13,412	13.5	9,688	9.8	128,629	15.5	174,309	122,648	51,661	41,467	4,212
Tuscaloosa, AL..................	12,830	243,330	1.04	2,950	12.1	2,245	9.2	18,780	9.5	42,926	30,252	12,674	7,614	3,156
Tyler, TX...........................	5,032	233,566	1.09	3,159	13.9	2,064	9.1	33,998	18.4	44,303	32,225	12,078	736	327
Urban Honolulu, HI.............	36,580	993,055	1.00	12,927	13.1	8,401	8.5	30,330	3.8	175,363	91,340	84,023	33,923	3,407
Utica-Rome, NY	14,258	291,927	0.99	3,062	10.4	3,130	10.7	11,477	5.0	65,545	40,204	25,341	6,313	2,155
Valdosta, GA	6,526	145,114	1.01	1,953	13.4	1,239	8.5	19,416	16.3	22,477	16,695	5,781	5,178	3,613
Vallejo-Fairfield, CA............	11,855	389,622	0.75	5,160	11.6	3,511	7.9	22,453	6.1	74,707	42,947	31,761	13,741	3,140
Victoria, TX.......................	1,992	100,006	1.00	1,398	14.0	913	9.2	15,316	18.5	18,967	13,902	5,065	NA	NA
Vineland-Bridgeton, NJ	10,174	154,740	1.02	1,912	12.5	1,418	9.3	14,695	12.1	28,843	23,114	5,729	6,434	4,156
Virginia Beach-Norfolk-Newport News, VA-NC	71,577	1,731,181	1.01	22,246	12.9	14,484	8.4	134,317	9.5	283,145	222,101	61,044	54,553	3,163
Visalia-Porterville, CA..........	4,796	452,311	0.95	7,292	15.7	2,983	6.4	39,771	9.9	59,684	49,812	9,872	13,232	2,876
Waco, TX..........................	10,490	267,988	1.03	3,726	13.9	2,265	8.4	40,290	18.5	45,665	30,329	15,335	8,470	3,210
Walla Walla, WA.................	4,844	68,019	1.13	697	10.8	649	10.0	3,912	8.1	13,646	12,343	1,302	2,212	3,414
Warner Robins, GA.............	3,943	188,184	0.98	2,431	12.7	1,633	8.5	22,578	14.0	31,664	23,933	7,731	7,568	3,992
Washington-Arlington-Alexandria, DC-VA-MD-WV	106,105	6,286,524	1.05	80,082	12.9	37,466	6.0	437,282	8.2	D	D	D	131,916	2,144
Silver Spring-Frederick-Rockville, MD Div 43,524	13,532	1,245,944	0.93	15,744	12.0	7,888	6.0	77,226	7.0	193,316	171,996	21,320	21,216	1,640
Washington-Arlington-Alexandria, DC-VA-MD-WV Div 47,894	92,573	5,040,580	1.08	64,338	13.1	29,578	6.0	360,056	8.6	D	D	D	110,700	2,278
Waterloo-Cedar Falls, IA......	7,303	176,192	1.07	2,078	12.2	1,549	9.1	6,648	4.9	33,265	23,611	9,653	4,142	2,424
Watertown-Fort Drum, NY....	7,118	117,154	1.06	1,869	16.4	936	8.2	5,656	6.1	19,649	13,613	6,037	2,360	2,016
Wausau, WI.......................	1,588	137,899	1.03	1,605	11.8	1,138	8.4	7,205	6.4	25,160	14,162	10,998	1,967	1,446
Weirton-Steubenville, WV-OH	3,396	113,190	0.85	1,108	9.4	1,676	14.2	5,327	5.8	30,551	20,673	9,877	2,340	1,960
Wenatchee, WA..................	1,121	115,018	0.95	1,491	12.6	994	8.4	9,293	9.8	24,268	18,959	5,310	2,795	2,376
Wheeling, WV-OH	6,681	145,853	1.05	1,395	9.9	1,806	12.8	6,411	5.9	33,023	18,974	14,049	2,723	1,905
Wichita, KS........................	11,479	644,264	1.00	8,694	13.5	5,686	8.8	57,974	10.7	109,594	87,755	21,839	4,563	709
Wichita Falls, TX	12,722	149,903	0.99	1,846	12.2	1,551	10.3	18,582	15.9	28,128	23,535	4,592	5,120	3,410
Williamsport, PA.................	5,266	116,631	1.03	1,167	10.3	1,320	11.6	5,161	5.8	26,197	17,491	8,706	1,990	1,720
Wilmington, NC	7,717	292,923	1.08	2,923	10.1	2,523	8.8	26,182	11.4	56,325	45,496	10,829	9,376	3,317
Winchester, VA-WV.............	2,587	140,777	1.03	1,590	11.5	1,188	8.6	11,859	10.8	26,491	22,911	3,581	2,163	1,613
Winston-Salem, NC.............	13,178	640,589	0.93	7,350	11.0	6,355	9.5	68,276	12.6	130,697	59,135	71,562	NA	NA
Worcester, MA-CT...............	33,280	868,142	0.86	9,688	10.3	8,000	8.5	24,040	3.1	173,247	114,252	58,995	D	D
Yakima, WA.......................	3,501	251,594	1.02	3,942	15.8	2,027	8.1	27,737	13.2	41,160	34,306	6,854	9,818	3,916
York-Hanover, PA	8,743	409,528	0.84	4,891	11.0	3,988	8.9	23,244	6.4	88,279	56,652	31,627	8,068	1,821
Youngstown-Warren-Board-man, OH-PA	18,900	537,925	0.97	5,551	10.2	6,821	12.6	27,486	6.6	130,827	67,959	62,868	NA	NA
Yuba City, CA....................	2,036	160,125	0.83	2,427	14.0	1,316	7.6	12,257	8.4	29,096	27,552	1,544	5,313	3,115
Yuma, AZ	9,207	201,490	0.95	3,014	14.5	1,605	7.7	23,862	15.1	32,992	25,536	7,456	NA	NA

1. Per 1,000 estimated resident population. 2. Data for serious crimes have not been adjusted for underreporting; this may affect comparability between geographic areas and over time.
3. Per 100,000 population estimated by the FBI.

Table C. Metropolitan Areas — Crime, Education, Money Income, and Poverty

Area name	Serious crimes known to police, 2,016 (cont.)[1] Rate Violent	Property	Education — School enrollment and attainment, 2,016 — Enrollment[3] Total	Percent private	Attainment[4] (percent) High school grad-uate or less	Bach-elor's degree or more	Local government expendi-tures,[5] 2,013-2,014 Total current expendi-tures (mil dol)	Current expendi-tures per student (dollars)	Income and poverty, 2,016 Per capita income[6] (dollars)	Mean house-hold income (dollars)	Median household income	Percent of house-holds with income of less than $50,000	Percent of house-holds with income of $200,000 or more	Percent below poverty level All persons	Children under 18 years	Age 65 years and over
	46	47	48	49	50	51	52	53	54	55	56	57	58	59	60	61
Texarkana, TX-AR..............	447	3,312	38,454	8.1	51.1	18.4	240.3	8,989	24,098	61,706	42,513	55.6	3.2	20.6	34.8	7.7
The Villages, FL	234	876	9,611	24.3	40.7	29.0	72.8	8,788	30,697	68,118	54,562	46.4	3.1	9.9	18.0	7.0
Toledo, OH........................	617	2,902	159,288	16.7	39.0	27.1	1,120.4	10,998	28,242	67,246	48,822	50.8	3.6	17.5	23.8	9.3
Topeka, KS........................	392	3,865	54,315	11.4	41.7	28.2	402.6	10,406	29,151	71,877	56,548	44.3	3.3	9.5	10.7	7.0
Trenton, NJ........................	403	1,779	96,703	21.2	36.3	42.7	1,081.6	18,723	40,963	111,623	77,650	32.7	13.4	11.1	15.1	6.9
Tucson, AZ........................	496	4,267	268,380	10.3	34.1	31.9	1,149.6	7,936	26,700	65,881	47,560	51.7	3.6	18.4	27.2	8.6
Tulsa, OK	589	3,623	248,525	14.4	40.4	27.2	1,288.7	7,664	28,151	70,843	51,623	48.4	4.2	15.1	22.7	8.1
Tuscaloosa, AL...................	368	2,788	69,053	10.4	41.2	27.7	306.6	9,122	24,345	63,581	46,086	53.2	3.1	18.8	24.0	7.3
Tyler, TX............................	327	D	58,212	12.8	38.0	24.9	289.8	8,419	24,837	68,343	52,572	47.5	4.0	16.2	21.5	11.1
Urban Honolulu, HI..............	335	3,073	241,926	24.2	34.3	34.4	2,327.5	12,458	33,691	101,034	80,513	29.2	10.1	8.5	9.6	8.9
Utica-Rome, NY	266	1,889	65,082	11.8	46.0	24.7	682.5	15,644	27,110	67,927	52,534	46.9	2.8	16.4	28.1	8.2
Valdosta, GA......................	320	3,293	41,015	9.9	49.6	22.9	208.0	8,904	21,746	57,866	39,734	59.6	2.4	22.6	30.9	17.8
Vallejo-Fairfield, CA............	462	2,678	108,484	11.4	35.7	25.4	576.9	8,725	32,543	93,929	73,900	32.6	7.6	11.6	18.9	8.1
Victoria, TX........................	NA	NA	23,049	8.0	45.4	19.2	153.7	9,076	31,224	84,354	55,228	46.6	5.4	13.6	19.0	8.1
Vineland-Bridgeton, NJ	518	3,638	35,965	8.4	61.6	13.8	485.7	17,611	21,495	61,132	49,110	50.6	2.4	19.2	25.5	11.1
Virginia Beach-Norfolk-Newport News, VA-NC	352	2,811	458,904	15.9	34.0	31.4	2,730.7	10,226	31,622	80,622	61,805	39.8	5.1	11.4	17.5	6.1
Visalia-Porterville, CA..........	353	2,523	139,007	5.7	56.5	13.7	978.7	9,681	18,870	61,897	45,881	55.2	2.6	25.2	33.9	14.2
Waco, TX...........................	424	2,786	80,035	24.0	47.6	21.1	447.8	9,060	24,493	67,246	46,590	53.0	3.7	19.4	26.2	8.9
Walla Walla, WA.................	250	3,164	17,398	34.3	32.8	29.8	99.9	10,636	29,124	76,021	54,655	45.9	4.3	12.1	11.8	8.0
Warner Robins, GA	452	3,540	56,841	11.0	37.1	26.8	306.8	9,264	25,963	69,914	59,409	42.5	3.4	18.7	24.3	13.7
Washington-Arlington-Alexandria, DC-VA-MD-WV	301	1,843	1,613,130	20.2	28.0	50.2	12,697.8	13,817	45,545	123,186	95,843	24.7	16.2	8.4	10.3	8.1
Silver Spring-Frederick-Rockville, MD Div 43,524......................	189	1,452	340,097	19.9	24.4	55.7	2,817.9	14,681	47,827	129,955	97,786	23.7	17.9	6.8	7.9	6.8
Washington-Arlington-Alexandria, DC-VA-MD-WV Div 47,894	331	1,947	1,273,033	20.3	28.9	48.7	9,879.8	13,589	44,936	121,481	95,386	25.0	15.7	8.8	10.9	8.5
Waterloo-Cedar Falls, IA......	442	1,981	46,454	12.9	39.8	27.8	311.8	11,699	29,512	72,333	53,877	46.3	3.4	14.6	18.0	7.4
Watertown-Fort Drum, NY....	240	1,776	25,247	11.0	46.0	20.6	284.1	15,191	23,964	61,225	45,624	53.8	2.0	16.0	23.1	7.2
Wausau, WI........................	132	1,314	31,082	10.4	44.2	24.7	224.6	11,141	29,556	73,258	54,774	45.6	4.2	11.2	17.3	8.4
Weirton-Steubenville, WV-OH	159	1,801	26,289	22.0	52.9	18.4	175.6	10,688	23,883	56,392	44,733	55.3	1.9	13.4	19.9	8.8
Wenatchee, WA...................	144	2,232	27,617	13.0	46.6	23.4	217.7	10,398	26,300	68,430	52,231	47.4	2.8	9.6	10.5	9.4
Wheeling, WV-OH...............	350	1,555	28,453	13.1	49.8	20.3	208.8	11,094	26,016	62,509	44,131	54.1	2.2	17.3	25.2	8.1
Wichita, KS........................	709	D	175,864	16.9	36.9	30.7	1,087.3	9,414	27,146	69,658	53,663	47.0	3.5	14.0	18.4	8.7
Wichita Falls, TX	362	3,047	34,508	6.4	44.8	23.4	214.5	8,595	23,055	58,325	44,951	55.4	2.0	16.6	20.9	14.1
Williamsport, PA	206	1,515	25,621	19.1	46.7	21.2	221.7	13,785	25,222	61,228	49,052	51.6	1.3	15.1	25.0	7.0
Wilmington, NC	364	2,953	65,962	12.6	33.5	36.5	304.1	8,739	29,390	69,977	50,155	49.7	4.8	17.9	21.5	12.8
Winchester, VA-WV.............	139	1,474	29,564	18.7	47.9	26.6	222.6	10,638	30,918	78,433	60,962	37.5	3.9	8.0	10.4	5.0
Winston-Salem, NC.............	NA	NA	159,373	14.3	42.5	26.4	832.6	8,370	26,865	67,076	47,711	52.1	3.8	16.2	23.2	8.8
Worcester, MA-CT...............	D	1,600	236,289	19.1	39.0	34.4	2,037.1	14,018	34,197	87,965	67,763	38.4	7.4	9.9	11.6	7.1
Yakima, WA........................	300	3,616	68,473	8.6	53.8	15.9	537.7	10,201	22,026	65,675	48,965	50.8	2.2	18.0	26.6	7.3
York-Hanover, PA	235	1,587	100,573	18.9	51.2	24.2	818.4	12,189	29,610	75,945	62,462	38.0	3.8	9.9	13.5	7.0
Youngstown-Warren-Boardman, OH-PA	NA	NA	115,504	14.5	50.8	22.5	942.0	12,133	25,818	60,428	44,981	54.8	2.5	18.2	30.6	7.8
Yuba City, CA.....................	398	2,718	48,548	7.3	42.9	17.2	313.9	8,898	23,757	68,476	50,775	49.3	2.4	17.1	25.3	8.4
Yuma, AZ...........................	NA	NA	51,630	5.0	52.4	15.4	251.2	6,748	20,845	56,872	43,518	55.7	1.7	18.0	27.3	12.6

1. Data for serious crimes have not been adjusted for underreporting; this may affect comparability between geographic areas and over time.   2. Per 100,000 population estimated by the FBI.
3. All persons 3 years old and over enrolled in nursery school through college.   4. Persons 25 years old and over.   5. Elementary and secondary education expenditures.   6. Based on population estimated by the American Community Survey, 2015.

Table C. Metropolitan Areas — **Agriculture**

Area name	land in farms					Value of land and buildings (dollars)		Value of machinery and equipment, average per farm (dollars)	Value of products sold:				Percent of farms with sales of:		Government payments	
	Acreage (1,000)	Percent change, 2007-2012	Average size of farm	Total irrigated (1,000)	Total cropland (1,000)	Average per farm	Average per acre		Total (mil dol)	Average per farm (acres)	Crops	Live-stock and poultry products	$10,000 or more	$100,000 or more	Total ($1,000)	Percent of farms
	117	118	119	120	121	122	123	124	125	126	127	128	129	130	131	132
Texarkana, TX-AR	609	0.4	235	21.4	223.1	475,867	2,027	61,443	188.1	72,558	30.0	70.0	34.1	7.9	3,271	16.9
The Villages, FL	183	14.7	134	3.1	20.7	717,143	5,350	45,931	42.1	30,773	58.9	41.1	19.3	5.3	164	2.9
Toledo, OH	526	0.8	234	2.9	491.5	1,339,764	5,717	160,193	469.6	209,092	80.6	19.4	61.5	34.6	10,688	72.1
Topeka, KS	1,606	-4.5	356	30.4	746.2	645,650	1,812	88,309	290.6	64,475	54.1	45.9	44.2	12.8	13,372	51.5
Trenton, NJ	20	-9.1	73	1.1	12.4	1,474,301	20,310	59,195	19.7	72,533	83.1	16.9	43.0	11.0	310	14.3
Tucson, AZ	D	D	D	32.4	36.7	1,651,870	D	64,622	97.3	113,786	76.8	23.2	31.2	10.3	1,085	5.3
Tulsa, OK	2,757	-8.9	303	12.2	525.7	487,549	1,610	48,596	320.1	35,165	20.5	79.5	31.0	5.0	10,260	18.1
Tuscaloosa, AL	349	-15.0	252	D	79.8	579,205	2,299	70,007	203.4	146,773	D	D	35.1	12.3	1,801	22.9
Tyler, TX	302	0.0	102	2.5	77.1	386,589	3,786	43,300	76.8	25,934	77.5	22.5	18.6	2.6	189	1.8
Urban Honolulu, HI	69	14.5	69	10.8	22.2	1,396,597	20,171	56,908	161.5	161,650	90.0	10.0	54.6	12.7	283	6.1
Utica-Rome, NY	345	4.0	197	0.3	195.1	387,175	1,965	102,671	183.6	104,752	32.6	67.4	52.0	21.4	3,569	31.7
Valdosta, GA	268	-17.4	298	37.0	127.0	994,700	3,343	118,135	172.8	191,747	73.9	26.1	35.2	14.1	4,463	47.7
Vallejo-Fairfield, CA	407	13.6	473	130.9	169.6	2,631,010	5,558	146,770	307.4	357,463	79.0	21.0	53.1	22.7	1,911	15.7
Victoria, TX	933	-3.2	344	4.1	113.1	748,694	2,174	54,903	67.0	24,741	47.2	52.8	28.4	4.1	3,202	14.4
Vineland-Bridgeton, NJ	65	-7.1	111	19.3	49.7	889,362	8,035	130,184	170.4	292,216	97.2	2.8	50.9	22.1	520	14.9
Virginia Beach-Norfolk-Newport News, VA-NC	348	-3.4	225	5.6	D	954,757	4,240	128,940	D	D	D	D	39.2	17.0	7,172	37.0
Visalia-Porterville, CA	1,239	6.0	251	557.4	677.5	1,893,271	7,535	144,666	4,017.1	814,657	41.6	58.4	70.2	36.6	12,174	13.5
Waco, TX	936	-4.0	206	8.6	418.3	479,933	2,328	62,287	318.4	70,112	40.8	59.2	26.8	6.6	8,368	20.6
Walla Walla, WA	943	-5.3	753	95.2	750.3	1,331,341	1,767	176,191	495.1	395,756	D	D	41.5	23.7	17,645	52.1
Warner Robins, GA	145	1.2	245	33.2	89.1	763,294	3,110	139,532	129.7	219,166	72.7	27.3	30.7	14.9	2,575	34.1
Washington-Arlington-Alexandria, DC-VA-MD-WV	1,192	-2.8	132	D	D	1,082,771	8,191	74,808	479.4	53,150	D	D	31.3	7.8	9,447	15.6
Silver Spring-Frederick-Rockville, MD Div 43,524	245	-9.2	133	2.4	172.7	1,095,421	8,262	106,409	198.8	107,576	58.6	41.4	37.6	15.7	3,896	28.8
Washington-Arlington-Alexandria, DC-VA-MD-WV Div 47,894	947	-1.0	132	D	D	1,079,511	8,173	66,666	280.6	39,126	D	D	29.7	5.7	5,551	12.2
Waterloo-Cedar Falls, IA	886	5.4	335	0.8	817.5	2,653,546	7,913	260,785	921.7	348,721	69.2	30.8	66.5	46.6	23,091	81.8
Watertown-Fort Drum, NY	291	10.9	332	0.3	173.5	544,535	1,640	133,429	183.6	209,551	24.7	75.3	51.6	24.1	2,974	31.5
Wausau, WI	479	-2.4	211	6.2	320.1	616,429	2,916	136,874	391.1	172,605	24.8	75.2	61.9	32.7	6,615	48.5
Weirton-Steubenville, WV-OH	92	-2.7	134	D	33.3	354,781	2,643	67,448	9.9	14,394	44.8	55.2	27.9	3.1	D	15.5
Wenatchee, WA	890	-8.9	512	41.1	577.0	858,859	1,678	96,734	405.5	233,192	98.3	1.7	60.6	34.7	13,598	27.3
Wheeling, WV-OH	229	-10.3	145	D	69.6	403,551	2,779	56,892	26.9	17,067	24.1	75.9	25.3	2.5	798	10.6
Wichita, KS	2,856	-1.3	534	147.5	1,911.4	1,018,921	1,907	140,007	864.4	161,729	63.3	36.7	54.3	23.6	25,429	62.2
Wichita Falls, TX	1,541	2.7	759	4.8	332.0	968,725	1,277	78,397	194.6	95,797	23.0	77.0	45.3	14.2	6,647	35.8
Williamsport, PA	158	-1.2	131	0.6	79.7	559,934	4,265	73,065	72.2	59,819	53.8	46.2	41.6	13.2	2,246	39.1
Wilmington, NC	59	-11.1	152	1.8	31.7	719,145	4,720	86,745	178.9	464,691	21.8	78.2	41.3	24.4	1,612	31.2
Winchester, VA-WV	243	6.7	164	0.3	74.5	747,885	4,556	53,968	73.5	49,694	44.1	55.9	30.0	5.5	625	11.7
Winston-Salem, NC	379	-5.4	89	2.1	174.8	500,191	5,592	54,495	252.2	59,444	37.1	62.9	26.1	6.9	3,083	19.6
Worcester, MA-CT	160	-3.9	71	1.8	52.3	619,520	8,716	50,890	101.7	45,155	56.7	43.3	27.4	7.0	1,949	11.5
Yakima, WA	1,780	8.0	566	224.4	306.9	1,021,212	1,803	118,874	1,645.5	523,548	65.0	35.0	45.7	22.4	5,804	11.5
York-Hanover, PA	262	-10.4	121	0.8	195.0	910,957	7,547	87,005	234.1	107,814	62.9	37.1	45.3	16.5	2,746	22.2
Youngstown-Warren-Boardman, OH-PA	352	-2.5	133	1.2	229.7	523,104	3,940	102,994	214.6	80,935	58.1	41.9	46.8	15.9	3,340	30.7
Yuba City, CA	563	8.1	261	326.8	365.6	1,658,114	6,343	168,077	701.6	325,882	93.5	6.5	66.0	35.1	14,667	22.8
Yuma, AZ	215	2.0	382	181.4	200.1	2,758,098	7,220	372,064	985.0	1,752,685	D	D	61.7	28.5	1,815	17.1

Area name	Water use, 2015		Wholesale Trade[1], 2012				Retail Trade[2], 2012				Real estate and rental and leasing,[2] 2012			
	Public supply water withdrawn (mil gal/day)	Public supply gallons withdrawn per person per day	Number of establish-ments	Number of employees	Sales (mil dol)	Annual payroll (mil dol)	Number of establishments	Number of employees	Sales (mil dol)	Annual payroll (mil dol)	Number of establish-ments	Number of employees	Sales (mil dol)	Annual payroll (mil dol)
	133	134	135	136	137	138	139	140	141	142	143	144	145	146
Texarkana, TX-AR..............	19.83	132.4	132	1,974	2,955.7	87.5	577	7,946	2,151.3	185.7	131	589	110.1	20.1
The Villages, FL	24.13	203.0	45	D	D	D	217	2,840	908.8	62.1	79	176	25.6	5.7
Toledo, OH..........................	89.20	147.2	649	9,697	7,499.0	479.7	2,001	31,636	8,224.9	732.7	547	3,285	2,664.1	183.5
Topeka, KS..........................	18.66	79.8	192	2,204	1,496.3	107.9	801	10,823	2,632.3	233.1	218	946	138.5	27.3
Trenton, NJ..........................	37.62	101.3	354	D	D	D	1,305	18,794	5,127.4	477.9	347	1,934	729.3	91.8
Tucson, AZ..........................	175.40	173.7	703	6,172	3,099.3	269.6	2,770	43,642	11,377.2	1,094.8	1,250	6,042	973.5	205.5
Tulsa, OK	133.35	135.9	1,210	16,787	15,854.1	976.9	3,066	44,465	12,865.2	1,081.7	1,097	6,653	1,083.1	261.7
Tuscaloosa, AL...................	37.53	156.4	160	1,774	1,240.0	86.6	835	10,366	2,796.3	233.7	192	1,511	166.7	45.0
Tyler, TX.............................	42.89	192.4	215	D	D	D	829	11,883	3,388.9	293.6	281	1,477	301.0	61.6
Urban Honolulu, HI..............	168.78	169.0	1,167	13,446	8,052.8	596.9	2,889	46,165	13,036.4	1,233.1	1,219	7,213	2,553.5	340.7
Utica-Rome, NY	61.66	208.6	205	2,626	1,249.6	116.1	1,017	13,905	3,556.1	308.4	204	799	126.9	22.4
Valdosta, GA	14.47	101.3	128	1,261	1,438.4	48.5	563	6,439	1,880.1	142.3	142	1,467	107.4	26.5
Vallejo-Fairfield, CA............	52.18	119.7	249	4,165	2,803.7	215.6	1,060	17,610	5,106.6	469.9	381	1,629	389.2	59.2
Victoria, TX.........................	12.40	124.1	115	1,716	1,251.0	91.8	397	5,629	1,698.7	143.3	129	1,057	604.9	59.8
Vineland-Bridgeton, NJ	15.72	100.9	152	3,223	2,422.4	133.6	512	7,201	2,049.0	175.0	120	471	96.2	15.8
Virginia Beach-Norfolk-Newport News, VA-NC	167.40	97.1	1,282	18,502	16,160.5	1,040.2	5,848	87,532	21,164.8	1,960.2	2,017	14,556	2,348.7	549.1
Visalia-Porterville, CA..........	70.33	152.9	325	4,564	3,890.5	191.8	1,044	14,210	3,903.5	340.6	306	1,421	249.0	40.9
Waco, TX............................	43.70	166.3	248	D	D	D	898	11,518	3,321.4	258.7	228	1,531	290.6	64.7
Walla Walla, WA..................	13.72	213.4	88	673	602.4	25.8	201	2,433	586.0	59.1	62	187	23.0	5.2
Warner Robins, GA	27.15	144.3	73	D	D	D	581	7,789	2,146.6	179.0	151	519	81.0	14.4
Washington-Arlington-Alexandria, DC-VA-MD-WV	568.53	93.2	3,527	49,567	57,941.8	3,388.0	16,124	264,471	74,306.7	7,157.0	6,881	53,448	15,623.8	3,069.8
Silver Spring-Frederick-Rockville, MD Div 43,524......	368.73	286.9	875	11,325	11,642.7	792.1	3,438	58,054	16,973.9	1,633.0	1,570	13,206	4,741.5	869.1
Washington-Arlington-Alexandria, DC-VA-MD-WV Div 47,894	199.80	41.5	2,652	38,242	46,299.2	2,595.9	12,686	206,417	57,332.8	5,524.0	5,311	40,242	10,882.3	2,200.7
Waterloo-Cedar Falls, IA......	18.33	107.4	197	3,210	2,774.7	154.0	639	10,445	2,555.7	225.1	164	706	141.0	22.9
Watertown-Fort Drum, NY....	9.29	79.0	67	870	345.2	34.7	476	6,849	1,937.9	161.4	119	588	103.9	17.8
Wausau, WI.........................	10.98	80.8	180	2,955	1,276.6	126.2	472	9,545	2,572.4	208.5	83	412	79.2	11.9
Weirton-Steubenville, WV-OH	15.44	128.1	71	D	D	D	372	5,013	1,195.3	105.3	67	306	35.9	8.4
Wenatchee, WA	16.74	144.1	127	D	D	D	477	5,701	1,434.5	146.9	145	475	63.0	13.5
Wheeling, WV-OH................	19.98	138.6	126	D	D	D	585	8,547	2,283.3	189.1	117	601	84.5	16.8
Wichita, KS..........................	73.91	114.7	727	9,369	9,027.7	524.5	2,115	31,655	8,362.2	740.0	650	4,202	610.9	138.1
Wichita Falls, TX	11.70	77.6	163	1,255	715.2	58.5	544	7,725	2,105.4	174.4	170	822	169.1	30.2
Williamsport, PA	8.78	75.7	108	2,110	1,271.2	82.6	503	7,404	1,878.1	154.7	89	618	120.0	24.4
Wilmington, NC	9.02	32.4	315	2,837	1,368.8	136.0	1,174	14,996	4,258.4	367.1	425	2,314	395.5	86.3
Winchester, VA-WV.............	5.80	43.3	129	D	D	D	537	8,118	2,358.1	195.3	127	432	90.4	14.8
Winston-Salem, NC.............	68.60	104.0	608	8,614	5,513.2	389.1	2,151	27,365	7,696.4	651.1	530	2,200	739.1	77.4
Worcester, MA-CT...............	259.35	277.2	827	12,550	7,416.0	685.2	2,928	43,798	12,212.7	1,080.8	643	2,883	651.1	124.6
Yakima, WA.........................	30.00	120.6	234	4,373	3,335.1	198.3	713	9,575	2,560.2	246.1	249	974	132.0	26.7
York-Hanover, PA	34.82	78.6	359	6,685	4,340.8	301.4	1,297	21,024	5,192.4	463.9	258	1,470	263.7	51.8
Youngstown-Warren-Board-man, OH-PA	51.89	94.4	538	7,293	4,748.0	345.2	2,094	29,036	7,127.0	610.9	384	3,946	486.5	114.2
Yuba City, CA.....................	22.56	132.0	96	D	D	D	414	5,557	1,459.7	136.6	134	559	68.5	14.4
Yuma, AZ	36.29	177.7	137	2,433	1,439.8	102.5	449	7,408	1,996.0	171.9	159	639	91.9	18.0

1 Merchant wholesalers, except manufacturers' sales branches and offices. 2. Employer establishments.

Table C. Metropolitan Areas

Professional Services, Manufacturing, and Accommodation and Food Services

Area name	Professional, scientific, and technical services, 2012				Manufacturing, 2012				Accommodation and food services, 2012			
	Number of establishments	Number of employees	Sales (mil dol)	Annual payroll (mil dol)	Number of establishments	Number of employees	Sales (mil dol)	Annual payroll (mil dol)	Number of establishments	Number of employees	Sales (mil dol)	Annual payroll (mil dol)
	147	148	149	150	151	152	153	154	155	156	157	158
Texarkana, TX-AR..............	208	1,126	118.7	38.6	99	5,410	2,601.2	308.5	270	5,616	260.2	74.3
The Villages, FL	128	500	53.9	21.0	36	942	461.9	40.7	106	2,464	117.2	35.9
Toledo, OH........................	1,127	D	D	D	732	35,417	35,387.1	2,068.8	1,420	26,503	1,122.3	320.8
Topeka, KS........................	517	D	D	D	131	5,986	2,893.2	270.6	434	D	D	D
Trenton, NJ........................	1,591	21,394	5,318.1	2,127.7	246	7,070	2,220.3	378.2	812	11,894	731.4	201.0
Tucson, AZ........................	2,531	16,514	2,241.1	940.0	640	24,297	8,686.6	1,906.7	1,787	42,311	2,154.7	637.4
Tulsa, OK..........................	2,808	D	D	D	1,317	52,150	24,817.4	2,774.6	1,901	37,592	1,899.4	537.9
Tuscaloosa, AL...................	357	2,263	328.8	102.3	172	12,576	14,491.5	745.1	418	9,331	443.6	113.5
Tyler, TX...........................	596	4,265	689.9	244.8	189	6,739	5,066.1	318.0	405	9,236	427.1	124.3
Urban Honolulu, HI.............	2,399	18,234	2,895.1	1,105.4	544	9,076	D	370.8	2,355	57,486	5,273.2	1,333.0
Utica-Rome, NY	469	3,829	573.9	215.9	296	12,368	4,147.5	581.4	727	12,339	862.6	219.5
Valdosta, GA......................	239	1,235	144.3	51.3	103	3,263	2,683.6	142.3	322	5,907	255.2	68.6
Vallejo-Fairfield, CA............	547	3,258	415.3	150.6	259	9,266	11,412.2	558.9	711	11,129	625.6	163.2
Victoria, TX........................	173	899	118.4	42.6	77	2,090	2,172.9	136.0	204	3,702	192.7	50.8
Vineland-Bridgeton, NJ	207	D	D	D	162	8,055	2,812.0	351.2	265	3,555	173.7	43.6
Virginia Beach-Norfolk-Newport News, VA-NC	4,187	51,649	9,454.7	3,521.0	847	54,304	15,652.6	2,873.8	3,805	74,606	3,885.1	1,062.9
Visalia-Porterville, CA..........	407	D	D	D	237	11,412	8,362.4	538.0	568	8,540	451.9	118.1
Waco, TX...........................	377	2,607	337.8	140.5	240	14,284	6,478.1	682.2	502	9,682	475.4	130.6
Walla Walla, WA.................	117	459	46.0	17.6	137	3,450	1,773.2	159.6	147	1,998	95.8	28.4
Warner Robins, GA	312	3,445	450.1	174.3	85	5,334	2,785.0	216.8	343	6,719	310.2	80.9
Washington-Arlington-Alexandria, DC-VA-MD-WV	30,747	517,949	125,259.6	49,288.9	2,091	49,219	15,671.4	3,030.8	12,138	247,606	17,932.2	4,868.0
Silver Spring-Frederick-Rockville, MD Div 43,524......	6,546	80,941	15,488.5	7,179.1	544	14,259	5,408.7	974.0	2,259	39,978	2,529.6	701.8
Washington-Arlington-Alexandria, DC-VA-MD-WV Div 47,894	24,201	437,008	109,771.1	42,109.9	1,547	34,961	10,262.7	2,056.8	9,879	207,628	15,402.6	4,166.1
Waterloo-Cedar Falls, IA......	280	3,998	310.2	210.6	213	15,285	10,703.1	762.0	370	7,330	342.8	91.2
Watertown-Fort Drum, NY....	142	1,092	115.9	45.4	66	2,247	770.5	102.6	335	4,117	198.8	57.0
Wausau, WI........................	225	1,943	284.9	113.9	238	14,472	4,306.0	654.1	305	4,458	180.7	51.8
Weirton-Steubenville, WV-OH	155	D	D	D	77	5,822	3,877.9	314.9	276	4,415	375.3	63.3
Wenatchee, WA	217	1,070	116.2	45.4	109	2,005	635.0	99.6	341	4,174	233.2	73.2
Wheeling, WV-OH...............	268	2,501	287.4	105.6	106	2,887	981.8	117.4	322	6,150	371.3	85.2
Wichita, KS........................	1,350	11,334	1,676.4	603.6	687	46,169	23,736.2	2,589.4	1,320	25,323	1,163.6	321.8
Wichita Falls, TX	250	1,551	212.3	72.3	142	5,114	1,434.9	238.1	286	D	D	D
Williamsport, PA.................	200	2,151	184.5	74.5	160	8,162	3,186.7	371.5	296	4,696	237.9	62.6
Wilmington, NC	937	5,852	1,090.5	295.5	207	5,268	2,640.9	349.5	746	13,951	673.8	185.5
Winchester, VA-WV.............	269	1,885	178.2	85.7	119	6,864	3,469.8	346.3	294	5,209	255.3	68.9
Winston-Salem, NC.............	1,288	8,118	1,077.1	446.8	671	26,926	18,915.9	1,212.5	1,133	20,985	989.5	278.5
Worcester, MA-CT...............	1,945	D	D	D	1,132	40,227	12,621.8	2,273.0	1,956	27,526	1,425.5	400.0
Yakima, WA........................	319	2,023	193.3	80.5	232	8,152	2,622.2	327.3	416	5,364	281.5	79.8
York-Hanover, PA	705	5,671	635.2	279.4	568	31,890	11,489.4	1,602.6	791	13,391	593.3	165.9
Youngstown-Warren-Boardman, OH-PA	917	5,807	560.3	218.3	730	31,925	14,956.5	1,845.3	1,140	24,546	1,101.8	309.3
Yuba City, CA.....................	204	978	118.4	46.1	100	2,091	650.7	99.0	224	3,374	171.4	44.9
Yuma, AZ...........................	221	1,364	132.3	68.0	68	2,084	884.3	79.8	329	5,736	307.5	76.2

Table C. Metropolitan Areas

Health Care and Social Assistance, Other Services, Nonemployer Businesses, and Residential Construction

Area name	Health care and social assistance, 2012				Other services, 2012				Nonemployer businesses, 2015		Value of residential construction authorized by building permits, 2017	
	Number of establishments	Number of employees	Receipts (mil dol)	Annual payroll (mil dol)	Number of establishments	Number of employees	Receipts (mil dol)	Annual payroll (mil dol)	Number	Receipts (mil dol)	New construction ($1,000)	Number of housing units
	159	160	161	162	163	164	165	166	167	168	169	170
Texarkana, TX-AR	370	8,528	889.6	333.1	212	1,253	110.7	32.9	8,300	364.9	18,581	185
The Villages, FL	146	2,956	381.2	123.8	64	304	22.2	6.7	6,006	251.6	504,233	1,814
Toledo, OH	1,611	45,338	4,689.0	1,918.0	1,012	6,823	597.0	174.5	35,200	1,529.9	203,375	971
Topeka, KS	609	19,147	1,803.3	791.6	449	3,859	347.5	108.9	13,051	551.7	66,170	335
Trenton, NJ	1,165	28,970	2,981.0	1,326.6	815	6,403	1,245.5	239.1	24,347	1,353.3	84,977	605
Tucson, AZ	2,777	56,539	6,617.5	2,441.8	1,483	10,691	1,008.6	281.2	64,179	2,556.9	1,025,886	4,495
Tulsa, OK	2,640	57,324	6,459.5	2,399.4	1,479	9,217	1,253.9	281.4	72,114	3,390.1	733,732	3,644
Tuscaloosa, AL	479	14,351	1,485.8	644.6	259	1,660	154.9	43.1	13,552	590.5	208,589	1,169
Tyler, TX	640	21,211	2,527.9	969.6	347	2,613	252.8	87.5	18,125	911.4	160,809	678
Urban Honolulu, HI	2,520	50,049	6,302.6	2,481.0	2,012	14,967	1,522.4	411.8	64,258	3,187.6	504,266	1,968
Utica-Rome, NY	724	21,377	1,820.7	801.3	501	4,229	251.1	82.6	15,435	619.5	61,861	347
Valdosta, GA	400	8,078	828.5	305.9	174	1,111	78.5	22.0	8,566	413.2	190,024	1,089
Vallejo-Fairfield, CA	861	21,490	3,241.8	1,204.0	552	3,228	326.8	102.6	23,834	990.2	247,226	907
Victoria, TX	314	6,698	684.2	276.3	158	1,175	163.1	46.9	6,809	312.1	9,519	61
Vineland-Bridgeton, NJ	417	8,593	872.1	338.7	240	1,253	97.1	27.3	5,918	277.7	7,490	88
Virginia Beach-Norfolk-Newport News, VA-NC	3,558	88,360	9,916.7	4,051.8	2,792	18,235	2,070.9	534.5	99,469	3,999.6	1,107,543	6,182
Visalia-Porterville, CA	836	15,488	1,610.2	632.1	383	2,114	219.4	60.0	20,102	979.6	274,753	1,314
Waco, TX	574	17,072	1,527.0	641.3	379	2,408	236.0	65.4	15,865	727.5	187,429	1,007
Walla Walla, WA	171	4,358	455.3	204.5	88	D	D	D	3,465	145.0	37,946	148
Warner Robins, GA	351	7,250	654.0	264.3	181	983	79.5	22.9	12,195	378.9	203,788	1,196
Washington-Arlington-Alexandria, DC-VA-MD-WV	15,282	295,912	36,062.8	14,351.2	12,704	147,087	35,947.3	8,469.9	526,235	24,307.8	4,569,027	27,265
Silver Spring-Frederick-Rockville, MD Div 43,524	4,197	73,187	8,433.4	3,585.4	2,317	21,946	4,674.0	1,095.5	NA	NA	809,972	3,530
Washington-Arlington-Alexandria, DC-VA-MD-WV Div 47,894	11,085	222,725	27,629.4	10,765.8	10,387	125,141	31,273.3	7,374.5	NA	NA	3,759,055	23,735
Waterloo-Cedar Falls, IA	446	12,695	1,142.7	482.3	309	1,779	161.8	43.2	9,882	441.3	91,679	708
Watertown-Fort Drum, NY	277	6,183	536.8	247.5	187	912	83.3	21.0	5,164	206.7	14,576	141
Wausau, WI	367	10,123	1,133.0	459.7	221	1,313	138.5	37.7	7,863	385.9	100,730	611
Weirton-Steubenville, WV-OH	295	7,787	682.8	262.3	179	953	64.5	18.5	5,254	185.5	7,338	29
Wenatchee, WA	285	6,275	701.9	314.4	205	720	79.7	19.0	6,250	273.4	132,515	629
Wheeling, WV-OH	521	12,959	1,076.5	427.5	291	1,936	174.3	45.2	6,826	283.9	9,561	20
Wichita, KS	1,710	42,014	4,111.4	1,693.2	983	6,533	748.0	191.4	40,305	1,792.0	377,317	2,731
Wichita Falls, TX	414	11,201	1,080.1	404.4	242	1,300	124.4	32.5	9,416	442.8	28,265	119
Williamsport, PA	287	8,233	825.8	345.7	240	1,546	152.8	35.4	6,254	281.5	24,378	137
Wilmington, NC	845	13,790	1,374.7	550.2	495	2,759	244.2	70.6	24,089	1,118.9	698,103	2,762
Winchester, VA-WV	383	8,763	1,051.5	423.6	215	1,204	101.6	30.6	8,903	390.2	166,419	888
Winston-Salem, NC	1,155	39,069	3,997.0	1,523.5	848	4,224	485.5	115.3	45,251	1,787.9	679,026	3,765
Worcester, MA-CT	2,274	67,479	6,940.7	3,070.9	1,518	8,318	808.2	227.2	58,294	2,860.9	324,565	1,768
Yakima, WA	557	12,903	1,431.4	574.7	281	1,449	130.9	34.3	9,242	429.4	107,941	434
York-Hanover, PA	924	24,161	2,604.4	1,031.9	783	5,242	651.3	139.7	25,875	1,231.5	167,413	838
Youngstown-Warren-Boardman, OH-PA	1,755	40,695	3,681.2	1,454.5	946	5,527	442.5	117.9	34,325	1,463.8	68,311	324
Yuba City, CA	329	5,566	789.3	253.2	155	724	67.1	20.7	8,862	495.0	75,824	303
Yuma, AZ	359	7,092	794.1	282.4	194	1,099	77.8	25.0	8,910	341.6	176,071	1,101

Table C. Metropolitan Areas — Government Employment and Payroll, and Local Government Finances

	Government employment and payroll, 2012									Local government finances, 2012				
			March payroll (percent of total)							General revenue				
												Taxes		
													Per capita[1] (dollars)	
Area name	Full-time equivalent employees	March payroll (dollars)	Administration, judicial, and legal	Police and corrections	Fire protection	Highways and transportation	Health and welfare	Natural resources and utilities	Education and libraries	Total (mil dol)	Inter-governmental (mil dol)	Total (mil dol)	Total	Property
	171	172	173	174	175	176	177	178	179	180	181	182	183	184
Texarkana, TX-AR..............	6,292	19,132,215	5.6	9.2	3.4	2.8	3.9	5.8	68.2	458.1	217.9	156.0	1,042	715
The Villages, FL	1,509	4,669,736	4.3	3.1	1.1	6.4	1.4	4.3	72.3	251.5	43.7	105.9	1,042	834
Toledo, OH........................	20,923	85,663,164	9.0	10.9	7.2	4.7	9.5	5.3	52.3	2,794.2	1,171.7	1,080.1	1,774	1,098
Topeka, KS........................	10,897	35,463,350	4.3	10.3	3.4	3.2	2.7	5.2	70.1	954.7	354.8	369.2	1,574	1,171
Trenton, NJ........................	15,352	84,285,619	4.4	12.4	3.3	2.0	4.4	4.9	64.8	2,164.5	711.0	1,168.1	3,172	3,117
Tucson, AZ........................	31,634	115,785,276	10.5	14.5	6.6	3.5	2.2	7.1	52.9	3,257.1	1,214.5	1,427.3	1,438	1,057
Tulsa, OK	33,451	106,348,173	5.8	9.5	5.7	4.2	2.6	6.1	63.2	2,858.0	992.1	1,256.0	1,319	714
Tuscaloosa, AL..................	11,519	40,376,521	3.7	7.3	3.3	3.6	45.3	3.8	32.1	1,108.1	293.7	229.4	983	397
Tyler, TX...........................	8,764	29,028,100	7.6	10.8	2.8	1.5	6.8	3.6	65.8	648.3	207.0	325.4	1,515	1,170
Urban Honolulu, HI..............	9,304	47,881,176	14.1	35.4	14.0	2.6	6.8	20.8	0.0	2,232.4	331.8	1,316.4	1,348	833
Utica-Rome, NY	13,622	60,609,793	5.4	11.3	5.5	6.7	5.6	4.7	59.5	1,597.5	779.4	603.1	2,024	1,388
Valdosta, GA.....................	7,094	22,829,566	3.5	7.5	1.9	1.7	36.8	2.6	44.7	654.5	164.9	169.0	1,171	661
Vallejo-Fairfield, CA.............	14,386	72,410,858	7.6	13.9	3.4	2.8	9.9	7.1	53.4	1,896.3	937.5	594.6	1,413	1,051
Victoria, TX........................	5,691	19,191,140	4.0	10.2	2.9	1.9	29.7	3.0	47.2	483.0	112.9	173.9	1,800	1,367
Vineland-Bridgeton, NJ	7,697	36,180,326	5.2	9.1	0.8	1.2	4.3	5.3	72.5	886.9	544.0	234.1	1,483	1,435
Virginia Beach-Norfolk-Newport News, VA-NC	78,042	285,080,100	5.2	9.8	4.7	2.6	8.9	7.9	57.4	7,361.3	2,849.8	2,945.6	1,733	1,190
Visalia-Porterville, CA..........	21,502	97,324,423	4.7	7.2	1.7	1.1	30.4	3.5	50.1	3,132.9	1,499.7	450.9	998	665
Waco, TX...........................	11,156	37,341,296	5.7	11.3	3.0	2.0	4.2	8.5	64.1	1,218.5	462.8	380.3	1,484	1,179
Walla Walla, WA.................	2,119	9,087,256	8.5	10.7	5.3	6.5	9.7	4.4	51.5	269.2	118.5	82.8	1,307	907
Warner Robins, GA..............	6,945	22,535,113	5.6	9.7	2.9	2.1	4.2	3.2	70.2	591.5	229.4	253.3	1,365	800
Washington-Arlington-Alexandria, DC-VA-MD-WV	238,082	1,225,240,040	6.3	10.4	4.1	8.1	7.2	5.9	54.7	35,371.1	10,257.7	19,074.9	3,255	1,833
Silver Spring-Frederick-Rockville, MD Div 43,524.....................	49,143	284,578,074	3.5	7.4	4.0	2.8	6.0	9.5	65.7	6,273.9	1,440.7	3,712.4	2,984	1,415
Washington-Arlington-Alexandria, DC-VA-MD-WV Div 47,894	188,939	940,661,966	7.1	11.3	4.2	9.7	7.5	4.8	51.4	29,097.2	8,817.0	15,362.6	3,328	1,946
Waterloo-Cedar Falls, IA......	5,986	22,105,854	5.2	9.3	3.5	4.9	8.6	9.6	56.3	779.9	309.2	283.0	1,677	1,331
Watertown-Fort Drum, NY....	5,239	20,682,670	6.0	6.1	2.2	6.7	6.7	3.0	66.9	631.5	312.9	217.3	1,807	1,154
Wausau, WI........................	5,721	22,517,091	4.6	6.0	1.9	5.6	19.3	2.6	59.4	701.3	346.1	232.0	1,722	1,622
Weirton-Steubenville, WV-OH	4,496	13,800,652	7.0	10.6	2.3	5.5	8.0	7.2	56.9	422.2	201.3	126.9	1,036	755
Wenatchee, WA..................	4,724	22,972,485	4.8	6.6	2.1	5.8	6.9	31.1	41.1	513.2	239.9	153.9	1,361	918
Wheeling, WV-OH...............	5,774	18,658,082	6.6	9.0	3.0	7.2	6.7	13.1	53.0	499.7	202.4	181.6	1,241	837
Wichita, KS........................	24,964	87,029,872	6.0	10.7	4.3	3.5	5.1	4.4	64.0	2,420.1	936.4	884.7	1,391	1,088
Wichita Falls, TX	6,724	21,253,583	6.4	13.3	6.1	3.0	9.1	5.3	54.1	453.8	154.7	207.0	1,372	1,062
Williamsport, PA.................	3,615	14,906,594	7.7	7.9	1.8	4.3	2.7	6.0	68.7	451.3	198.0	155.7	1,329	953
Wilmington, NC	13,583	50,754,541	2.9	7.0	2.4	1.1	45.2	4.5	33.4	1,618.1	350.1	385.0	1,461	1,059
Winchester, VA-WV.............	5,411	16,715,382	6.8	13.2	4.1	1.2	2.9	3.6	66.6	418.3	170.3	190.4	1,454	1,027
Winston-Salem, NC.............	1,023,990	75,606,649	4.5	8.8	4.0	1.2	8.6	5.0	65.1	1,918.0	964.0	681.2	1,052	828
Worcester, MA-CT...............	32,279	147,826,569	3.6	7.7	4.7	3.3	1.4	4.3	74.0	3,495.3	1,632.4	1,503.7	1,628	1,589
Yakima, WA.......................	8,019	34,900,911	7.0	10.7	3.2	2.8	3.3	5.9	66.0	970.4	601.4	232.4	941	607
York-Hanover, PA	12,293	50,416,660	6.7	12.2	1.5	2.7	6.3	3.6	64.5	1,771.5	572.5	787.5	1,799	1,467
Youngstown-Warren-Boardman, OH-PA	20,254	71,750,350	7.4	10.2	3.8	3.6	7.7	6.8	59.4	1,994.8	1,016.8	698.5	1,251	866
Yuba City, CA.....................	6,669	32,864,622	7.3	8.3	2.0	2.2	10.3	3.3	64.0	941.7	532.4	189.6	1,129	918
Yuma, AZ	7,924	25,609,990	12.0	12.1	3.1	2.2	2.4	7.3	59.9	638.9	314.0	221.6	1,108	716

1. Based on the resident population estimated as of July 1 of the year shown.

Table C. Metropolitan Areas

Local Government Finances, Government Employment, and Income Taxes

Area name	Local government finances, 2012 (cont.)									Government employment, 2016			Individual income tax returns, 2015		
	Direct general expenditure							Debt outstanding							
			Percent of total for:												
	Total (mil dol)	Per capita¹ (dollars)	Education	Health and hospitals	Police protection	Public welfare	Highways	Total (mil dol)	Per capita¹ (dollars)	Federal civilian	Federal military	State and local	Number of returns	Mean adjusted gross income	Mean income tax
	185	186	187	188	189	190	191	192	193	194	195	196	197	198	199
Texarkana, TX-AR...............	437.3	2,921	59.2	2.4	5.9	1.0	4.9	430.1	2,873	4,194	423	9,094	63,080	48,984	5,510
The Villages, FL	263.4	2,592	27.3	1.6	6.0	0.5	7.8	594.1	5,846	1,675	212	2,988	55,010	73,583	10,570
Toledo, OH.........................	2,631.6	4,323	42.5	7.5	6.3	6.1	4.2	2,796.0	4,593	2,142	1,607	42,408	286,050	54,290	6,462
Topeka, KS..........................	921.3	3,928	54.3	2.2	6.2	0.2	4.0	1,441.3	6,144	3,662	988	23,516	110,210	53,809	5,906
Trenton, NJ..........................	2,145.5	5,825	52.3	0.9	5.3	4.3	1.4	1,928.9	5,237	2,340	733	38,323	175,890	91,851	15,121
Tucson, AZ...........................	3,531.8	3,559	37.0	3.1	9.1	2.7	5.3	5,788.9	5,833	12,829	7,908	66,739	439,010	55,216	6,392
Tulsa, OK.............................	2,829.0	2,972	48.0	4.0	5.9	0.6	8.2	3,865.4	4,061	4,718	3,693	49,447	428,960	64,334	8,562
Tuscaloosa, AL.....................	1,116.2	4,783	30.5	41.4	4.7	0.0	5.1	682.1	2,923	1,928	1,005	24,789	96,380	52,675	6,068
Tyler, TX..............................	645.1	3,003	55.0	5.1	5.6	0.2	3.4	1,145.0	5,330	648	481	13,461	98,810	59,735	7,936
Urban Honolulu, HI................	1,596.7	1,635	0.0	1.5	15.2	0.0	7.8	5,300.0	5,428	30,549	53,314	68,647	486,840	63,554	7,636
Utica-Rome, NY	1,653.0	5,546	53.3	2.7	2.8	10.6	6.2	1,633.5	5,480	2,445	498	27,352	133,050	50,693	5,476
Valdosta, GA	724.2	5,017	28.8	47.7	4.1	0.7	2.5	413.2	2,862	1,187	4,559	11,607	56,180	43,715	4,486
Vallejo-Fairfield, CA..............	1,873.8	4,454	35.1	6.1	9.3	7.8	4.2	1,624.0	3,860	3,760	6,774	22,205	205,360	63,502	7,199
Victoria, TX..........................	470.7	4,872	36.4	29.6	5.8	0.0	7.0	443.6	4,591	211	208	6,918	45,530	61,819	8,600
Vineland-Bridgeton, NJ	880.4	5,580	60.1	2.7	3.8	3.4	2.5	354.4	2,246	644	292	12,371	67,190	47,187	4,601
Virginia Beach-Norfolk-Newport News, VA-NC	7,765.7	4,568	42.7	6.6	4.8	4.0	3.4	9,372.3	5,513	57,619	84,089	104,466	813,220	58,778	6,811
Visalia-Porterville, CA..........	3,186.6	7,050	39.0	24.4	3.2	8.0	4.7	1,380.8	3,055	1,061	689	31,246	177,190	43,449	4,249
Waco, TX.............................	1,187.0	4,631	42.3	2.5	5.0	0.6	1.8	11,603.4	45,270	3,075	618	15,757	112,090	51,133	5,917
Walla Walla, WA..................	257.4	4,061	43.0	9.4	5.8	0.0	7.2	267.1	4,213	1,418	166	4,701	27,300	56,100	6,492
Warner Robins, GA...............	571.7	3,082	54.7	6.0	6.4	0.1	5.0	263.3	1,419	14,929	3,766	12,289	83,460	51,363	5,077
Washington-Arlington-Alexandria, DC-VA-MD-WV	35,473.9	6,053	40.6	3.4	5.3	10.4	3.3	44,210.4	7,544	384,338	64,476	324,984	3,051,310	90,688	14,007
Silver Spring-Frederick-Rockville, MD Div 43,524	6,498.3	5,222	51.5	1.7	5.2	3.2	3.5	7,084.9	5,694	51,993	9,625	53,778	NA	NA	NA
Washington-Arlington-Alexandria, DC-VA-MD-WV Div 47,894	28,975.7	6,277	38.1	3.8	5.3	12.0	3.3	37,125.5	8,043	332,345	54,851	271,206	NA	NA	NA
Waterloo-Cedar Falls, IA......	855.9	5,072	49.6	11.0	4.2	0.3	7.5	561.2	3,325	637	633	13,943	76,630	59,035	6,761
Watertown-Fort Drum, NY....	631.0	5,247	49.6	3.4	2.6	9.2	6.9	554.7	4,612	3,112	14,783	8,255	50,890	47,383	4,610
Wausau, WI..........................	710.6	5,274	41.9	10.2	3.9	18.8	7.9	440.9	3,273	411	356	7,631	67,800	60,469	7,750
Weirton-Steubenville, WV-OH	426.7	3,482	52.1	4.9	6.0	2.5	5.9	341.9	2,790	262	403	5,317	56,040	46,648	4,681
Wenatchee, WA....................	488.0	4,317	47.1	12.8	4.5	0.0	5.8	1,944.4	17,202	872	312	8,281	56,330	56,771	6,944
Wheeling, WV-OH................	488.4	3,335	43.9	3.2	5.0	2.6	4.4	552.7	3,775	613	498	9,069	66,450	56,414	7,178
Wichita, KS...........................	2,506.2	3,940	49.5	4.3	5.3	0.1	5.5	6,729.7	10,580	4,909	5,354	36,175	294,850	60,542	7,711
Wichita Falls, TX	440.1	2,918	47.9	5.2	7.0	0.7	4.4	688.7	4,566	1,928	5,752	10,485	62,870	54,475	6,524
Williamsport, PA	560.5	4,783	43.8	0.0	2.2	3.1	4.4	997.6	8,514	363	288	8,763	54,510	49,756	5,254
Wilmington, NC	1,610.9	6,115	23.7	45.2	4.9	2.9	1.0	1,660.3	6,303	1,048	868	22,191	126,390	60,785	8,030
Winchester, VA-WV..............	404.5	3,090	60.9	0.7	5.4	3.3	1.5	564.7	4,314	2,042	473	7,368	63,140	59,503	7,038
Winston-Salem, NC..............	2,021.7	3,121	49.0	5.3	7.8	4.7	1.7	1,785.1	2,756	2,059	1,551	29,752	295,110	56,726	6,942
Worcester, MA-CT...............	3,721.4	4,029	62.3	0.4	3.9	0.2	3.5	2,671.4	2,892	3,285	2,155	55,925	453,000	68,623	9,170
Yakima, WA.........................	1,052.2	4,260	60.9	3.2	4.2	0.8	4.9	606.3	2,455	1,258	779	16,275	110,050	47,273	5,197
York-Hanover, PA	1,790.5	4,089	47.4	3.5	3.3	9.2	2.6	2,454.1	5,605	4,208	1,318	15,981	222,120	58,950	6,823
Youngstown-Warren-Boardman, OH-PA	2,023.9	3,626	53.2	5.1	6.2	4.2	4.0	1,224.6	2,194	1,968	1,397	27,548	265,480	47,734	5,249
Yuba City, CA......................	962.8	5,733	49.2	5.2	4.2	8.2	2.8	640.8	3,816	1,625	4,163	9,607	68,240	49,475	4,792
Yuma, AZ	616.3	3,081	47.8	2.1	6.0	2.5	4.6	668.5	3,342	3,433	4,868	10,948	84,000	40,613	3,708

1. Based on the resident population estimated as of July 1 of the year shown.

75 Largest Cities by 2017 Population
Selected rankings

	Percent population change, 2010–2017				Percent White alone, 2016				Percent Black alone, 2016		
Population rank	Percent change rank	City	Percent change [col 26]	Population rank	White rank	City	Percent White [col 5]	Population rank	Black rank	City	Percent Black [col 6]
73	1	Irvine city, California	30.8	59	1	Corpus Christi city, Texas	89.7	23	1	Detroit city, Michigan	79.1
18	2	Seattle city, Washington	19.1	71	2	Lincoln city, Nebraska	85.5	25	2	Memphis city, Tennessee	64.5
11	3	Austin city, Texas	18.5	22	3	El Paso city, Texas	82.2	30	3	Baltimore city, Maryland	62.5
64	4	Henderson city, Nevada	17.7	36	4	Mesa city, Arizona	81.3	49	4	New Orleans city, Louisiana	59.7
19	5	Denver city, Colorado	17.5	7	5	San Antonio city, Texas	79.4	38	5	Atlanta city, Georgia	50.8
72	6	Orlando city, Florida	17.4	42	6	Colorado Springs city, Colorado	78.8	70	6	Newark city, New Jersey	49.9
15	7	Fort Worth city, Texas	17.3	40	7	Omaha city, Nebraska	78.2	51	7	Cleveland city, Ohio	49.6
17	8	Charlotte city, North Carolina	16.8	43	8	Miami city, Florida	78.1	20	8	Washington city, District of Columbia	47.1
43	9	Miami city, Florida	16.0	26	9	Portland city, Oregon	77.9	62	9	St. Louis city, Missouri	46.8
38	10	Atlanta city, Georgia	15.7	64	10	Henderson city, Nevada	77.6	6	10	Philadelphia city, Pennsylvania	42.2
20	11	Washington city, District of Columbia	15.3	19	11	Denver city, Colorado	75.4	66	11	Cincinnati city, Ohio	41.7
41	12	Raleigh city, North Carolina	15.0	60	12	Lexington-Fayette urban county, Kentucky	75.0	68	12	Greensboro city, North Carolina	40.1
52	13	Tampa city, Florida	14.8	11	13	Austin city, Texas	74.6	31	13	Milwaukee city, Wisconsin	38.6
49	14	New Orleans city, Louisiana	14.4	50	14	Wichita city, Kansas	74.5	17	14	Charlotte city, North Carolina	36.0
7	15	San Antonio city, Texas	13.9	33	15	Tucson city, Arizona	74.0	12	15	Jacksonville city, Florida	30.6
54	16	Aurora city, Colorado	12.9	55	16	Anaheim city, California	70.9	3	16	Chicago city, Illinois	29.7
36	17	Mesa city, Arizona	12.8	32	17	Albuquerque city, New Mexico	70.6	41	17	Raleigh city, North Carolina	29.1
5	18	Phoenix city, Arizona	12.4	29	18	Louisville/Jefferson County	70.2	14	18	Columbus city, Ohio	28.9
9	19	Dallas city, Texas	12.0	27	19	Oklahoma City city, Oklahoma	68.0	37	19	Kansas City city, Missouri	28.5
14	20	Columbus city, Ohio	11.4	5	20	Phoenix city, Arizona	67.8	16	20	Indianapolis city, Indiana	28.0
42	21	Colorado Springs city, Colorado	11.3	65	21	Pittsburgh city, Pennsylvania	67.6	24	21	Nashville-Davidson	27.9
26	22	Portland city, Oregon	11.0	18	22	Seattle city, Washington	67.5	74	22	Toledo city, Ohio	27.5
21	23	Boston city, Massachusetts	10.9	44	23	Virginia Beach city, Virginia	67.0	21	23	Boston city, Massachusetts	25.8
27	23	Oklahoma City city, Oklahoma	10.9	8	24	San Diego city, California	66.5	52	24	Tampa city, Florida	24.9
24	25	Nashville-Davidson	10.6	69	25	Plano city, Texas	65.8	9	25	Dallas city, Texas	24.6
4	26	Houston city, Texas	10.4	52	26	Tampa city, Florida	64.5	1	26	New York city, New York	24.3
46	26	Minneapolis city, Minnesota	10.4	46	27	Minneapolis city, Minnesota	64.3	72	27	Orlando city, Florida	24.1
71	28	Lincoln city, Nebraska	10.2	24	28	Nashville-Davidson	64.0	29	28	Louisville/Jefferson County	23.8
69	29	Plano city, Texas	10.1	15	29	Fort Worth city, Texas	63.7	45	29	Oakland city, California	23.5
13	30	San Francisco city, California	9.8	53	29	Bakersfield city, California	63.7	75	30	Jersey City city, New Jersey	23.2
28	30	Las Vegas city, Nevada	9.8	47	31	Tulsa city, Oklahoma	63.2	65	31	Pittsburgh city, Pennsylvania	22.7
53	32	Bakersfield city, California	9.4	74	32	Toledo city, Ohio	62.9	4	32	Houston city, Texas	22.6
75	33	Jersey City city, New Jersey	9.3	28	33	Las Vegas city, Nevada	62.8	48	33	Arlington city, Texas	21.6
8	34	San Diego city, California	9.0	48	34	Arlington city, Texas	62.7	15	34	Fort Worth city, Texas	19.0
45	35	Oakland city, California	8.8	67	35	Anchorage municipality, Alaska	62.0	44	35	Virginia Beach city, Virginia	18.3
60	35	Lexington-Fayette urban county, Kentucky	8.8	9	36	Dallas city, Texas	61.8	46	36	Minneapolis city, Minnesota	18.1
10	37	San Jose city, California	8.7	72	36	Orlando city, Florida	61.8	43	37	Miami city, Florida	15.7
12	38	Jacksonville city, Florida	8.5	37	37	Kansas City city, Missouri	61.6	47	38	Tulsa city, Oklahoma	15.2
48	38	Arlington city, Texas	8.5	16	38	Indianapolis city, Indiana	60.9	54	38	Aurora city, Colorado	15.2
68	40	Greensboro city, North Carolina	7.9	14	40	Columbus city, Ohio	60.2	63	38	St. Paul city, Minnesota	15.2
58	41	Riverside city, California	7.8	34	41	Fresno city, California	60.0	27	40	Oklahoma City city, Oklahoma	14.5
35	42	Sacramento city, California	7.6	41	41	Raleigh city, North Carolina	59.4	60	41	Lexington-Fayette urban county, Kentucky	14.5
63	42	St. Paul city, Minnesota	7.6	12	43	Jacksonville city, Florida	59.0	28	43	Las Vegas city, Nevada	13.8
59	44	Corpus Christi city, Texas	6.7	54	44	Aurora city, Colorado	58.8	35	44	Sacramento city, California	13.4
61	45	Stockton city, California	6.4	4	45	Houston city, Texas	57.2	61	45	Stockton city, California	12.8
37	46	Kansas City city, Missouri	6.3	63	46	St. Paul city, Minnesota	57.1	39	46	Long Beach city, California	12.6
34	47	Fresno city, California	6.1	58	47	Riverside city, California	56.0	40	47	Omaha city, Nebraska	12.2
1	48	New York city, New York	5.5	21	48	Boston city, Massachusetts	53.2	69	48	Plano city, Texas	10.6
2	48	Los Angeles city, California	5.5	2	49	Los Angeles city, California	52.3	50	49	Wichita city, Kansas	10.4
22	48	El Paso city, Texas	5.5	66	50	Cincinnati city, Ohio	51.1	19	50	Denver city, Colorado	9.8
16	51	Indianapolis city, Indiana	5.2	39	51	Long Beach city, California	50.4	2	51	Los Angeles city, California	8.8
55	52	Anaheim city, California	4.8	35	52	Sacramento city, California	49.5	11	52	Austin city, Texas	7.6
29	53	Louisville/Jefferson County	4.0	17	53	Charlotte city, North Carolina	49.2	34	52	Fresno city, California	7.6
40	54	Omaha city, Nebraska	3.9	68	54	Greensboro city, North Carolina	48.6	7	54	San Antonio city, Texas	7.4
56	55	Urban Honolulu CDP, Hawaii	3.8	3	55	Chicago city, Illinois	48.4	18	55	Seattle city, Washington	7.1
6	56	Philadelphia city, Pennsylvania	3.6	73	56	Irvine city, California	48.2	58	55	Riverside city, California	7.1
44	57	Virginia Beach city, Virginia	2.9	62	57	St. Louis city, Missouri	46.5	42	57	Colorado Springs city, Colorado	6.7
57	57	Santa Ana city, California	2.9	13	58	San Francisco city, California	46.4	5	58	Phoenix city, Arizona	6.5
70	57	Newark city, New Jersey	2.9	57	59	Santa Ana city, California	44.7	53	58	Bakersfield city, California	6.5
47	60	Tulsa city, Oklahoma	2.5	61	60	Stockton city, California	44.4	8	60	San Diego city, California	6.4
32	61	Albuquerque city, New Mexico	2.3	31	61	Milwaukee city, Wisconsin	43.6	26	61	Portland city, Oregon	6.1
33	61	Tucson city, Arizona	2.3	1	62	New York city, New York	42.5	64	62	Henderson city, Nevada	5.4
50	63	Wichita city, Kansas	2.1	20	63	Washington city, District of Columbia	40.7	67	62	Anchorage municipality, Alaska	5.4
39	64	Long Beach city, California	1.6	6	64	Philadelphia city, Pennsylvania	40.4	13	64	San Francisco city, California	5.0
66	65	Cincinnati city, Ohio	1.5	38	64	Atlanta city, Georgia	40.4	33	64	Tucson city, Arizona	5.0
67	66	Anchorage municipality, Alaska	0.9	51	66	Cleveland city, Ohio	40.0	59	66	Corpus Christi city, Texas	4.5
3	67	Chicago city, Illinois	0.8	10	67	San Jose city, California	39.1	71	67	Lincoln city, Nebraska	4.4
25	68	Memphis city, Tennessee	0.1	45	68	Oakland city, California	34.6	22	68	El Paso city, Texas	4.1
31	68	Milwaukee city, Wisconsin	0.1	49	69	New Orleans city, Louisiana	34.1	36	69	Mesa city, Arizona	3.8
65	70	Pittsburgh city, Pennsylvania	-1.0	75	70	Jersey City city, New Jersey	33.7	32	70	Albuquerque city, New Mexico	3.2
30	71	Baltimore city, Maryland	-1.5	30	71	Baltimore city, Maryland	30.8	10	71	San Jose city, California	3.0
51	72	Cleveland city, Ohio	-2.8	70	72	Newark city, New Jersey	30.5	55	72	Anaheim city, California	2.4
62	73	St. Louis city, Missouri	-3.4	25	73	Memphis city, Tennessee	28.0	56	73	Urban Honolulu CDP, Hawaii	1.7
74	74	Toledo city, Ohio	-3.8	56	74	Urban Honolulu CDP, Hawaii	18.1	73	74	Irvine city, California	1.1
23	75	Detroit city, Michigan	-5.7	23	75	Detroit city, Michigan	13.6	57	75	Santa Ana city, California	0.9

75 Largest Cities by 2017 Population
Selected rankings

Percent American Indian, Alaska Native alone, 2016				Percent Asian and Pacific Islander alone, 2016				Percent Hispanic or Latino,[1] 2016			
Population rank	American Indian, Alaska Native rank	City	Percent American Indian, Alaska Native [col 7]	Population rank	Asian and Pacific Islander rank	City	Percent Asian and Pacific Islander [col 8]	Population rank	Hispanic or Latino rank	City	Percent Hispanic or Latino [col 12]
67	1	Anchorage municipality, Alaska	8.0	56	1	Urban Honolulu CDP, Hawaii	52.1	22	1	El Paso, Texas	80.7
32	2	Albuquerque city, New Mexico	5.0	73	2	Irvine, California	43.3	57	2	Santa Ana city, California	77.3
47	3	Tulsa city, Oklahoma	4.8	10	3	San Jose city, California	34.9	43	3	Miami city, Florida	73.6
27	4	Oklahoma City city, Oklahoma	3.4	13	4	San Francisco city, California	34.5	7	4	San Antonio city, Texas	64.0
36	5	Mesa city, Arizona	3.3	75	5	Jersey City city, New Jersey	25.4	59	5	Corpus Christi city, Texas	63.5
33	6	Tucson city, Arizona	2.5	61	6	Stockton city, California	21.7	55	6	Anaheim city, California	54.7
5	7	Phoenix city, Arizona	2.0	35	7	Sacramento city, California	18.4	58	7	Riverside city, California	51.0
46	8	Minneapolis city, Minnesota	1.5	69	7	Plano city, Texas	18.4	53	8	Bakersfield city, California	50.5
53	9	Bakersfield city, California	1.3	63	9	St. Paul city, Minnesota	18.2	34	9	Fresno city, California	49.3
34	10	Fresno city, California	1.1	8	10	San Diego city, California	17.1	2	10	Los Angeles city, California	48.9
45	11	Oakland city, California	1.0	55	11	Anaheim city, California	16.5	32	11	Albuquerque city, New Mexico	47.6
61	11	Stockton city, California	1.0	45	12	Oakland city, California	16.4	4	12	Houston city, Texas	44.8
35	13	Sacramento city, California	0.9	18	13	Seattle city, Washington	14.9	39	13	Long Beach city, California	44.5
7	14	San Antonio city, Texas	0.8	34	14	Fresno city, California	14.7	5	14	Phoenix city, Arizona	43.8
19	14	Denver city, Colorado	0.8	1	15	New York city, New York	14.1	33	15	Tucson city, Arizona	43.3
50	14	Wichita city, Kansas	0.8	39	16	Long Beach city, California	12.5	9	16	Dallas city, Texas	41.4
54	14	Aurora city, Colorado	0.8	57	17	Santa Ana city, California	12.0	61	17	Stockton city, California	40.9
63	14	St. Paul city, Minnesota	0.8	2	18	Los Angeles city, California	11.4	11	18	Austin city, Texas	34.8
64	14	Henderson city, Nevada	0.8	21	19	Boston city, Massachusetts	9.8	15	18	Fort Worth city, Texas	34.8
2	20	Los Angeles city, California	0.7	67	20	Anchorage municipality, Alaska	9.1	70	20	Newark city, New Jersey	34.4
39	20	Long Beach city, California	0.7	53	21	Bakersfield city, California	8.1	10	21	San Jose city, California	32.1
55	20	Anaheim city, California	0.7	26	22	Portland city, Oregon	7.7	28	21	Las Vegas city, Nevada	32.1
58	20	Riverside city, California	0.7	4	23	Houston city, Texas	7.4	72	23	Orlando city, Florida	30.3
71	20	Lincoln city, Nebraska	0.7	6	24	Philadelphia city, Pennsylvania	7.1	19	24	Denver city, Colorado	30.2
22	25	El Paso city, Texas	0.6	11	25	Austin city, Texas	7.0	8	25	San Diego city, California	30.0
26	25	Portland city, Oregon	0.6	64	26	Henderson city, Nevada	6.8	3	26	Chicago city, Illinois	29.7
38	25	Atlanta city, Georgia	0.6	44	27	Virginia Beach city, Virginia	6.7	48	26	Arlington city, Texas	29.7
11	28	Austin city, Texas	0.5	46	28	Minneapolis city, Minnesota	6.6	1	28	New York city, New York	29.2
28	28	Las Vegas city, Nevada	0.5	3	29	Chicago city, Illinois	6.4	54	29	Aurora city, Colorado	28.7
42	28	Colorado Springs city, Colorado	0.5	17	30	Charlotte city, North Carolina	6.3	35	30	Sacramento city, California	28.6
43	28	Miami city, Florida	0.5	28	30	Las Vegas city, Nevada	6.3	75	31	Jersey City city, New Jersey	28.0
48	28	Arlington city, Texas	0.5	58	30	Riverside city, California	6.3	36	32	Mesa city, Arizona	27.0
57	28	Santa Ana city, California	0.5	54	33	Aurora city, Colorado	6.2	45	33	Oakland city, California	26.1
1	34	New York city, New York	0.4	48	34	Arlington city, Texas	6.0	52	34	Tampa city, Florida	24.2
6	34	Philadelphia city, Pennsylvania	0.4	72	34	Orlando city, Florida	6.0	21	35	Boston city, Massachusetts	19.1
8	34	San Diego city, California	0.4	65	36	Pittsburgh city, Pennsylvania	5.6	27	36	Oklahoma City city, Oklahoma	18.7
10	34	San Jose city, California	0.4	14	37	Columbus city, Ohio	5.2	31	36	Milwaukee city, Wisconsin	18.7
13	34	San Francisco city, California	0.4	68	38	Greensboro city, North Carolina	5.0	42	38	Colorado Springs city, Colorado	17.5
15	34	Fort Worth city, Texas	0.4	50	39	Wichita city, Kansas	4.9	50	39	Wichita city, Kansas	16.9
18	34	Seattle city, Washington	0.4	52	39	Tampa city, Florida	4.9	47	40	Tulsa city, Oklahoma	16.1
31	34	Milwaukee city, Wisconsin	0.4	41	41	Raleigh city, North Carolina	4.7	64	41	Henderson city, Nevada	15.9
51	34	Cleveland city, Ohio	0.4	15	42	Fort Worth city, Texas	4.6	69	42	Plano city, Texas	15.5
52	34	Tampa city, Florida	0.4	12	43	Jacksonville city, Florida	4.4	13	43	San Francisco city, California	15.2
59	34	Corpus Christi city, Texas	0.4	31	43	Milwaukee city, Wisconsin	4.4	6	44	Philadelphia city, Pennsylvania	14.4
68	34	Greensboro city, North Carolina	0.4	38	45	Atlanta city, Georgia	4.3	40	45	Omaha city, Nebraska	13.9
69	34	Plano city, Texas	0.4	71	45	Lincoln city, Nebraska	4.3	17	46	Charlotte city, North Carolina	13.8
75	34	Jersey City city, New Jersey	0.4	27	47	Oklahoma City city, Oklahoma	4.0	73	47	Irvine city, California	11.4
3	48	Chicago city, Illinois	0.3	5	48	Phoenix city, Arizona	3.9	51	48	Cleveland city, Ohio	11.0
16	48	Indianapolis city, Indiana	0.3	20	48	Washington city, District of Columbia	3.9	20	49	Washington city, District of Columbia	10.9
17	48	Charlotte city, North Carolina	0.3	24	48	Nashville-Davidson	3.9	37	49	Kansas City city, Missouri	10.9
20	48	Washington city, District of Columbia	0.3	19	51	Denver city, Colorado	3.7	16	51	Indianapolis city, Indiana	10.5
21	48	Boston city, Massachusetts	0.3	40	51	Omaha city, Nebraska	3.7	24	52	Nashville-Davidson	10.4
23	48	Detroit city, Michigan	0.3	60	51	Lexington-Fayette urban county, Kentucky	3.7	26	53	Portland city, Oregon	10.2
25	48	Memphis city, Tennessee	0.3	9	54	Dallas city, Texas	3.6	41	53	Raleigh city, North Carolina	10.2
30	48	Baltimore city, Maryland	0.3	62	55	St. Louis city, Missouri	3.3	63	55	St. Paul city, Minnesota	9.7
37	48	Kansas City city, Missouri	0.3	47	56	Tulsa city, Oklahoma	3.2	12	56	Jacksonville city, Florida	9.4
40	48	Omaha city, Nebraska	0.3	16	57	Indianapolis city, Indiana	3.1	67	57	Anchorage municipality, Alaska	9.0
41	48	Raleigh city, North Carolina	0.3	33	57	Tucson city, Arizona	3.1	46	58	Minneapolis city, Minnesota	8.8
60	48	Lexington-Fayette urban county, Kentucky	0.3	37	57	Kansas City city, Missouri	3.1	74	58	Toledo city, Ohio	8.8
70	48	Newark city, New Jersey	0.3	49	60	New Orleans city, Louisiana	3.0	44	60	Virginia Beach city, Virginia	8.1
74	48	Toledo city, Ohio	0.3	32	61	Albuquerque city, New Mexico	2.9	68	61	Greensboro city, North Carolina	7.6
4	62	Houston city, Texas	0.2	7	62	San Antonio city, Texas	2.8	71	62	Lincoln city, Nebraska	7.4
9	62	Dallas city, Texas	0.2	42	63	Colorado Springs city, Colorado	2.7	56	63	Urban Honolulu CDP, Hawaii	7.2
12	62	Jacksonville city, Florida	0.2	29	64	Louisville/Jefferson County	2.6	25	64	Memphis city, Tennessee	7.1
24	62	Nashville-Davidson	0.2	30	65	Baltimore city, Maryland	2.5	23	65	Detroit city, Michigan	7.0
44	62	Virginia Beach city, Virginia	0.2	51	66	Cleveland city, Ohio	2.1	60	66	Lexington-Fayette urban county, Kentucky	6.9
56	62	Urban Honolulu CDP, Hawaii	0.2	36	67	Mesa city, Arizona	2.0	18	67	Seattle city, Washington	6.4
62	62	St. Louis city, Missouri	0.2	59	67	Corpus Christi city, Texas	2.0	14	68	Columbus city, Ohio	5.8
14	69	Columbus city, Ohio	0.1	70	67	Newark city, New Jersey	2.0	49	69	New Orleans city, Louisiana	5.6
29	69	Louisville/Jefferson County	0.1	23	70	Detroit city, Michigan	1.8	29	70	Louisville/Jefferson County	5.2
49	69	New Orleans city, Louisiana	0.1	66	71	Cincinnati city, Ohio	1.7	30	71	Baltimore city, Maryland	5.1
65	69	Pittsburgh city, Pennsylvania	0.1	22	72	El Paso city, Texas	1.6	38	72	Atlanta city, Georgia	4.9
72	69	Orlando city, Florida	0.1	25	72	Memphis city, Tennessee	1.6	66	73	Cincinnati city, Ohio	4.2
66	74	Cincinnati city, Ohio	0.0	74	74	Toledo city, Ohio	1.0	62	74	St. Louis city, Missouri	4.0
73	74	Irvine city, California	0.0	43	75	Miami city, Florida	0.9	65	75	Pittsburgh city, Pennsylvania	2.8

75 Largest Cities by 2017 Population
Selected rankings

Percent under 18 years old, 2016				Percent 65 years old and over, 2016				Percent high school graduate or less, 2016			
Population rank	Under 18 years old rank	City	Percent under 18 years old [col 14]	Population rank	65 years old and over rank	City	Percent 65 years old and over [col 20]	Population rank	Percent high school graduate or less rank	City	Percent high school graduate or less [col 40]
53	1	Bakersfield city, California	30.0	56	1	Urban Honolulu CDP, Hawaii	19.5	57	1	Santa Ana city, California	65.6
15	2	Fort Worth city, Texas	28.4	64	1	Henderson city, Nevada	19.5	70	2	Newark city, New Jersey	61.0
34	3	Fresno city, California	28.3	43	3	Miami city, Florida	17.6	43	3	Miami city, Florida	55.1
61	4	Stockton city, California	28.1	36	4	Mesa city, Arizona	16.3	51	4	Cleveland city, Ohio	53.6
22	5	El Paso city, Texas	27.3	13	5	San Francisco city, California	14.9	23	5	Detroit city, Michigan	52.2
5	6	Phoenix city, Arizona	27.0	28	6	Las Vegas city, Nevada	14.7	61	6	Stockton city, California	50.9
57	6	Santa Ana city, California	27.0	32	6	Albuquerque city, New Mexico	14.7	6	7	Philadelphia city, Pennsylvania	48.5
31	8	Milwaukee city, Wisconsin	26.3	65	8	Pittsburgh city, Pennsylvania	14.6	55	8	Anaheim city, California	47.8
27	9	Oklahoma City city, Oklahoma	25.8	29	9	Louisville/Jefferson County	14.4	31	9	Milwaukee city, Wisconsin	46.8
23	10	Detroit city, Michigan	25.7	74	10	Toledo city, Ohio	14.0	34	10	Fresno city, California	46.1
48	10	Arlington city, Texas	25.7	33	11	Tucson city, Arizona	13.8	7	11	San Antonio city, Texas	45.8
50	10	Wichita city, Kansas	25.7	59	12	Corpus Christi city, Texas	13.7	53	12	Bakersfield city, California	45.3
54	13	Aurora city, Colorado	25.6	1	13	New York city, New York	13.5	58	13	Riverside city, California	44.8
63	14	St. Paul city, Minnesota	25.4	50	14	Wichita city, Kansas	13.4	4	14	Houston city, Texas	44.7
4	15	Houston city, Texas	25.3	35	15	Sacramento city, California	13.3	30	15	Baltimore city, Maryland	44.6
7	15	San Antonio city, Texas	25.3	52	15	Tampa, Florida	13.3	9	16	Dallas city, Texas	44.3
55	15	Anaheim city, California	25.3	44	17	Virginia Beach city, Virginia	13.2	59	17	Corpus Christi city, Texas	44.2
25	18	Memphis city, Tennessee	25.2	47	17	Tulsa city, Oklahoma	13.2	22	18	El Paso city, Texas	44.1
47	19	Tulsa city, Oklahoma	25.0	51	19	Cleveland city, Ohio	13.1	28	18	Las Vegas city, Nevada	44.1
9	20	Dallas city, Texas	24.9	68	19	Greensboro city, North Carolina	13.1	15	20	Fort Worth city, Texas	44.0
16	21	Indianapolis city, Indiana	24.8	12	21	Jacksonville city, Florida	13.0	74	20	Toledo city, Ohio	44.0
67	21	Anchorage municipality, Alaska	24.8	49	21	New Orleans city, Louisiana	13.0	2	22	Los Angeles city, California	43.1
59	23	Corpus Christi city, Texas	24.7	6	23	Philadelphia city, Pennsylvania	12.9	5	23	Phoenix city, Arizona	42.8
36	24	Mesa city, Arizona	24.5	30	23	Baltimore city, Maryland	12.9	25	23	Memphis city, Tennessee	42.8
17	25	Charlotte city, North Carolina	24.4	42	25	Colorado Springs city, Colorado	12.8	1	25	New York city, New York	42.6
40	25	Omaha city, Nebraska	24.4	71	25	Lincoln city, Nebraska	12.8	54	26	Aurora city, Colorado	42.0
58	27	Riverside city, California	24.3	22	27	El Paso city, Texas	12.7	16	27	Indianapolis city, Indiana	41.2
42	28	Colorado Springs city, Colorado	24.2	23	27	Detroit city, Michigan	12.7	48	28	Arlington city, Texas	41.1
28	29	Las Vegas city, Nevada	23.9	40	27	Omaha city, Nebraska	12.7	39	29	Long Beach city, California	39.5
39	30	Long Beach city, California	23.4	45	27	Oakland city, California	12.7	12	30	Jacksonville city, Florida	39.4
69	30	Plano city, Texas	23.4	26	31	Portland city, Oregon	12.4	27	31	Oklahoma City city, Oklahoma	39.0
74	30	Toledo city, Ohio	23.4	37	31	Kansas City city, Missouri	12.4	29	31	Louisville/Jefferson County	39.0
37	33	Kansas City city, Missouri	23.3	61	31	Stockton city, California	12.4	50	33	Wichita city, Kansas	38.8
70	33	Newark city, New Jersey	23.3	8	34	San Diego city, California	12.3	33	34	Tucson city, Arizona	38.7
12	35	Jacksonville city, Florida	23.1	18	34	Seattle city, Washington	12.3	47	34	Tulsa city, Oklahoma	38.7
10	36	San Jose city, California	23.0	2	36	Los Angeles city, California	12.1	35	36	Sacramento city, California	38.6
14	36	Columbus city, Ohio	23.0	25	36	Memphis city, Tennessee	12.1	52	37	Tampa, Florida	38.5
32	36	Albuquerque city, New Mexico	23.0	60	36	Lexington-Fayette urban county, Kentucky	12.1	3	38	Chicago city, Illinois	38.2
73	39	Irvine city, California	22.7	66	36	Cincinnati city, Ohio	12.1	14	39	Columbus city, Ohio	37.4
35	40	Sacramento city, California	22.5	7	40	San Antonio city, Texas	11.9	36	40	Mesa city, Arizona	37.1
44	40	Virginia Beach city, Virginia	22.5	3	41	Chicago city, Illinois	11.8	66	40	Cincinnati city, Ohio	37.1
71	40	Lincoln city, Nebraska	22.5	62	41	St. Louis city, Missouri	11.8	62	42	St. Louis city, Missouri	36.8
68	43	Greensboro city, North Carolina	22.4	27	43	Oklahoma City city, Oklahoma	11.7	75	43	Jersey City city, New Jersey	36.4
29	44	Louisville/Jefferson County	22.3	16	44	Indianapolis city, Indiana	11.6	37	44	Kansas City city, Missouri	36.1
51	44	Cleveland city, Ohio	22.3	20	44	Washington city, District of Columbia	11.6	49	45	New Orleans city, Louisiana	36.0
66	44	Cincinnati city, Ohio	22.3	55	44	Anaheim city, California	11.6	63	46	St. Paul city, Minnesota	35.7
6	47	Philadelphia city, Pennsylvania	22.1	10	47	San Jose city, California	11.5	40	47	Omaha city, Nebraska	35.6
64	48	Henderson city, Nevada	21.9	69	48	Plano city, Texas	11.4	24	48	Nashville-Davidson	35.5
52	49	Tampa, Florida	21.7	19	49	Denver city, Colorado	11.2	64	49	Henderson city, Nevada	34.9
33	50	Tucson city, Arizona	21.6	24	49	Nashville-Davidson	11.2	56	50	Urban Honolulu CDP, Hawaii	34.5
11	51	Austin city, Texas	21.5	38	51	Atlanta city, Georgia	11.1	21	51	Boston city, Massachusetts	34.3
24	52	Nashville-Davidson	21.4	21	52	Boston city, Massachusetts	11.0	72	51	Orlando city, Florida	34.3
3	53	Chicago city, Illinois	21.2	34	52	Fresno city, California	11.0	10	53	San Jose city, California	34.1
1	54	New York city, New York	21.1	48	54	Arlington city, Texas	10.6	45	54	Oakland city, California	34.0
30	55	Baltimore city, Maryland	21.0	54	54	Aurora city, Colorado	10.6	65	55	Pittsburgh city, Pennsylvania	33.2
60	55	Lexington-Fayette urban county, Kentucky	21.0	39	56	Long Beach city, California	10.5	32	56	Albuquerque city, New Mexico	32.8
2	57	Los Angeles city, California	20.8	5	57	Phoenix city, Arizona	10.4	68	57	Greensboro city, North Carolina	32.5
72	57	Orlando city, Florida	20.8	58	57	Riverside city, California	10.4	19	58	Denver city, Colorado	31.0
75	59	Jersey City city, New Jersey	20.7	4	59	Houston city, Texas	10.2	60	59	Lexington-Fayette urban county, Kentucky	29.7
49	60	New Orleans city, Louisiana	20.4	63	59	St. Paul city, Minnesota	10.2	67	60	Anchorage municipality, Alaska	29.3
19	61	Denver city, Colorado	20.3	41	61	Raleigh city, North Carolina	10.1	71	61	Lincoln city, Nebraska	28.4
41	62	Raleigh city, North Carolina	20.2	9	62	Dallas city, Texas	10.0	38	62	Atlanta city, Georgia	28.3
8	63	San Diego city, California	19.8	70	62	Newark city, New Jersey	10.0	8	63	San Diego city, California	28.1
62	63	St. Louis city, Missouri	19.8	73	64	Irvine city, California	9.9	44	64	Virginia Beach city, Virginia	27.8
45	65	Oakland city, California	19.7	67	65	Anchorage municipality, Alaska	9.8	17	65	Charlotte city, North Carolina	27.4
46	66	Minneapolis city, Minnesota	19.6	72	65	Orlando city, Florida	9.8	20	66	Washington city, District of Columbia	27.3
38	67	Atlanta city, Georgia	19.4	14	67	Columbus city, Ohio	9.7	11	67	Austin city, Texas	26.8
26	68	Portland city, Oregon	18.3	17	68	Charlotte city, North Carolina	9.6	46	68	Minneapolis city, Minnesota	26.6
56	69	Urban Honolulu CDP, Hawaii	18.1	31	68	Milwaukee city, Wisconsin	9.6	42	69	Colorado Springs city, Colorado	25.1
20	70	Washington city, District of Columbia	17.7	75	68	Jersey City city, New Jersey	9.6	13	70	San Francisco city, California	24.4
43	71	Miami city, Florida	17.4	53	71	Bakersfield city, California	9.5	26	71	Portland city, Oregon	23.1
21	72	Boston city, Massachusetts	16.1	15	72	Fort Worth city, Texas	9.4	41	72	Raleigh city, North Carolina	22.3
65	73	Pittsburgh city, Pennsylvania	15.3	46	73	Minneapolis city, Minnesota	9.3	69	73	Plano city, Texas	19.5
18	74	Seattle city, Washington	15.0	11	74	Austin city, Texas	8.5	18	74	Seattle city, Washington	14.9
13	75	San Francisco city, California	13.5	57	75	Santa Ana city, California	8.4	73	75	Irvine city, California	11.3

75 Largest Cities by 2017 Population
Selected rankings

Percent college graduates (bachelor's degree or more), 2016				Percent female-headed family households, 2016				Percent of households composed of one person, 2016			
Population rank	Percent college graduate rank	City	Percent college graduates [col 41]	Population rank	Female households rank	City	Percent female households [col 31]	Population rank	One-person household rank	City	Percent one-person households [col 33]
73	1	Irvine city, California	71.6	23	1	Detroit city, Michigan	28.3	38	1	Atlanta city, Georgia	48.6
18	2	Seattle city, Washington	63.1	70	2	Newark city, New Jersey	24.8	66	2	Cincinnati city, Ohio	44.8
13	3	San Francisco city, California	57.2	25	3	Memphis city, Tennessee	22.7	62	3	St. Louis city, Missouri	44.5
20	4	Washington city, District of Columbia	56.8	51	4	Cleveland city, Ohio	22.5	65	4	Pittsburgh city, Pennsylvania	44.3
69	5	Plano city, Texas	56.6	30	5	Baltimore city, Maryland	21.9	20	5	Washington city, District of Columbia	43.8
41	6	Raleigh city, North Carolina	50.8	31	6	Milwaukee city, Wisconsin	21.6	51	6	Cleveland city, Ohio	43.7
38	7	Atlanta city, Georgia	50.5	34	7	Fresno city, California	20.0	49	7	New Orleans city, Louisiana	43.3
26	8	Portland city, Oregon	49.6	61	8	Stockton city, California	19.8	46	8	Minneapolis city, Minnesota	41.5
11	9	Austin city, Texas	49.2	22	9	El Paso city, Texas	19.6	23	9	Detroit city, Michigan	40.1
21	10	Boston city, Massachusetts	48.4	6	10	Philadelphia city, Pennsylvania	19.5	30	10	Baltimore city, Maryland	39.6
46	10	Minneapolis city, Minnesota	48.4	57	11	Santa Ana city, California	18.2	74	11	Toledo city, Ohio	38.8
19	12	Denver city, Colorado	47.4	68	11	Greensboro city, North Carolina	18.2	18	12	Seattle city, Washington	38.6
75	13	Jersey City city, New Jersey	46.5	49	13	New Orleans city, Louisiana	18.1	70	13	Newark city, New Jersey	38.2
65	14	Pittsburgh city, Pennsylvania	45.7	74	14	Toledo city, Ohio	18.0	6	14	Philadelphia city, Pennsylvania	38.1
8	15	San Diego city, California	44.2	66	15	Cincinnati city, Ohio	17.8	43	14	Miami city, Florida	38.1
17	16	Charlotte city, North Carolina	44.1	75	15	Jersey City city, New Jersey	17.8	19	16	Denver city, Colorado	37.2
60	17	Lexington-Fayette urban county, Kentucky	43.7	62	17	St. Louis city, Missouri	17.6	21	16	Boston city, Massachusetts	37.2
10	18	San Jose city, California	42.6	7	18	San Antonio city, Texas	17.5	3	18	Chicago city, Illinois	37.1
45	19	Oakland city, California	41.1	33	18	Tucson city, Arizona	17.5	25	19	Memphis city, Tennessee	36.8
42	20	Colorado Springs city, Colorado	40.3	1	20	New York city, New York	17.3	16	20	Indianapolis city, Indiana	36.2
71	20	Lincoln city, Nebraska	40.3	55	21	Anaheim city, California	17.1	37	21	Kansas City city, Missouri	36.0
63	22	St. Paul city, Minnesota	39.7	72	22	Orlando city, Florida	16.9	68	22	Greensboro city, North Carolina	35.9
24	23	Nashville-Davidson	39.2	43	23	Miami city, Florida	16.6	31	23	Milwaukee city, Wisconsin	35.8
3	24	Chicago city, Illinois	38.5	48	23	Arlington city, Texas	16.6	52	23	Tampa city, Florida	35.8
49	25	New Orleans city, Louisiana	38.4	53	25	Bakersfield city, California	16.5	14	25	Columbus city, Ohio	35.7
72	26	Orlando city, Florida	37.6	39	26	Long Beach city, California	16.2	47	26	Tulsa city, Oklahoma	35.6
56	27	Urban Honolulu CDP, Hawaii	37.5	4	27	Houston city, Texas	16.1	63	27	St. Paul city, Minnesota	35.5
68	27	Greensboro city, North Carolina	37.5	15	28	Fort Worth city, Texas	15.9	13	28	San Francisco city, California	34.8
52	29	Tampa city, Florida	37.3	21	29	Boston city, Massachusetts	15.8	9	29	Dallas city, Texas	34.6
1	30	New York city, New York	37.0	5	30	Phoenix city, Arizona	15.7	40	29	Omaha city, Nebraska	34.6
66	30	Cincinnati city, Ohio	37.0	58	30	Riverside city, California	15.7	72	31	Orlando city, Florida	34.4
67	32	Anchorage municipality, Alaska	36.5	38	32	Atlanta city, Georgia	15.6	24	32	Nashville-Davidson	34.2
14	33	Columbus city, Ohio	35.3	59	33	Corpus Christi city, Texas	15.5	26	32	Portland city, Oregon	34.2
37	34	Kansas City city, Missouri	35.2	9	34	Dallas city, Texas	15.4	11	34	Austin city, Texas	34.1
40	34	Omaha city, Nebraska	35.2	3	35	Chicago city, Illinois	15.3	29	34	Louisville/Jefferson County	34.1
32	36	Albuquerque city, New Mexico	35.0	12	35	Jacksonville city, Florida	15.3	33	34	Tucson city, Arizona	34.1
44	36	Virginia Beach city, Virginia	35.0	16	35	Indianapolis city, Indiana	15.3	50	37	Wichita city, Kansas	34.0
62	38	St. Louis city, Missouri	34.1	14	38	Columbus city, Ohio	15.1	41	38	Raleigh city, North Carolina	33.5
2	39	Los Angeles city, California	32.8	20	39	Washington city, District of Columbia	15.0	32	39	Albuquerque city, New Mexico	33.1
64	40	Henderson city, Nevada	32.7	44	40	Virginia Beach city, Virginia	14.8	56	40	Urban Honolulu CDP, Hawaii	32.8
4	41	Houston city, Texas	32.5	29	41	Louisville/Jefferson County	14.7	4	41	Houston city, Texas	32.7
9	42	Dallas city, Texas	31.6	47	41	Tulsa city, Oklahoma	14.7	1	42	New York city, New York	32.4
35	43	Sacramento city, California	31.0	32	43	Albuquerque city, New Mexico	14.6	45	42	Oakland city, California	32.4
30	44	Baltimore city, Maryland	30.8	52	43	Tampa city, Florida	14.6	17	44	Charlotte city, North Carolina	32.2
47	45	Tulsa city, Oklahoma	30.7	2	45	Los Angeles city, California	14.3	35	45	Sacramento city, California	31.9
16	46	Indianapolis city, Indiana	30.1	24	46	Nashville-Davidson	14.2	60	46	Lexington-Fayette urban county, Kentucky	31.7
50	46	Wichita city, Kansas	30.1	63	47	St. Paul city, Minnesota	14.0	27	47	Oklahoma City city, Oklahoma	30.6
39	48	Long Beach city, California	30.0	37	48	Kansas City city, Missouri	13.9	28	48	Las Vegas city, Nevada	30.5
27	49	Oklahoma City city, Oklahoma	29.7	28	49	Las Vegas city, Nevada	13.7	2	49	Los Angeles city, California	30.3
6	50	Philadelphia city, Pennsylvania	28.6	17	50	Charlotte city, North Carolina	13.6	71	49	Lincoln city, Nebraska	30.3
29	51	Louisville/Jefferson County	28.4	60	51	Lexington-Fayette urban county, Kentucky	13.4	12	51	Jacksonville city, Florida	29.9
5	52	Phoenix city, Arizona	27.9	41	52	Raleigh city, North Carolina	13.1	39	52	Long Beach city, California	29.8
12	52	Jacksonville city, Florida	27.9	45	53	Oakland city, California	13.0	7	53	San Antonio city, Texas	29.4
48	52	Arlington city, Texas	27.9	27	54	Oklahoma City city, Oklahoma	12.9	42	53	Colorado Springs city, Colorado	29.4
15	55	Fort Worth city, Texas	27.6	35	54	Sacramento city, California	12.9	64	55	Henderson city, Nevada	29.2
54	56	Aurora city, Colorado	27.4	67	56	Anchorage municipality, Alaska	12.3	5	56	Phoenix city, Arizona	28.2
43	57	Miami city, Florida	26.6	40	57	Omaha city, Nebraska	12.0	75	56	Jersey City city, New Jersey	28.2
36	58	Mesa city, Arizona	26.5	36	58	Mesa city, Arizona	11.8	8	58	San Diego city, California	27.8
33	59	Tucson city, Arizona	26.1	54	58	Aurora city, Colorado	11.8	54	59	Aurora city, Colorado	26.9
7	60	San Antonio city, Texas	26.0	50	60	Wichita city, Kansas	11.7	22	60	El Paso city, Texas	25.8
25	61	Memphis city, Tennessee	25.6	10	61	San Jose city, California	11.4	59	61	Corpus Christi city, Texas	25.7
55	62	Anaheim city, California	24.8	8	62	San Diego city, California	11.3	15	62	Fort Worth city, Texas	25.4
58	63	Riverside city, California	24.2	65	62	Pittsburgh city, Pennsylvania	11.3	48	63	Arlington city, Texas	24.7
22	64	El Paso city, Texas	23.8	11	64	Austin city, Texas	11.0	61	64	Stockton city, California	24.4
31	65	Milwaukee city, Wisconsin	23.3	56	64	Urban Honolulu CDP, Hawaii	11.0	44	65	Virginia Beach city, Virginia	24.2
28	66	Las Vegas city, Nevada	23.0	71	66	Lincoln city, Nebraska	10.5	34	66	Fresno city, California	24.1
59	67	Corpus Christi city, Texas	22.4	42	67	Colorado Springs city, Colorado	10.4	36	67	Mesa city, Arizona	24.0
53	68	Bakersfield city, California	22.0	19	68	Denver city, Colorado	10.3	67	67	Anchorage municipality, Alaska	24.0
34	69	Fresno city, California	21.6	69	68	Plano city, Texas	10.3	69	69	Plano city, Texas	23.8
74	70	Toledo city, Ohio	18.7	64	70	Henderson city, Nevada	9.9	53	70	Bakersfield city, California	21.9
61	71	Stockton city, California	16.7	26	71	Portland city, Oregon	9.6	73	71	Irvine city, California	21.7
51	72	Cleveland city, Ohio	16.3	46	72	Minneapolis city, Minnesota	8.7	58	72	Riverside city, California	19.4
23	73	Detroit city, Michigan	14.9	13	73	San Francisco city, California	7.8	10	73	San Jose city, California	19.2
70	74	Newark city, New Jersey	13.8	18	74	Seattle city, Washington	6.6	55	74	Anaheim city, California	16.8
57	75	Santa Ana city, California	13.7	73	75	Irvine city, California	6.2	57	75	Santa Ana city, California	10.2

75 Largest Cities by 2017 Population
Selected rankings

Median household income, 2016				Median value of owner-occupied housing units, 2016				Percent with commutes of 30 minutes or more, 2016			
Population rank	Median income rank	City	Median income (dollars) [col 42]	Population rank	Median value rank	City	Median value (dollars) [col 53]	Population rank	Commutes of 30 minutes or more rank	City	Commutes of 30 minutes or more [col 56]
13	1	San Francisco city, California	103,801	13	1	San Francisco city, California	$1,024,000	1	1	New York city, New York	71.0
10	2	San Jose city, California	101,940	73	2	Irvine city, California	$806,000	75	2	Jersey City city, New Jersey	67.3
73	3	Irvine city, California	97,496	10	3	San Jose city, California	$802,000	3	3	Chicago city, Illinois	62.3
69	4	Plano city, Texas	88,398	56	4	Urban Honolulu CDP, Hawaii	$661,700	13	4	San Francisco city, California	57.9
67	5	Anchorage municipality, Alaska	85,634	45	5	Oakland city, California	$649,700	70	5	Newark city, New Jersey	56.2
18	6	Seattle city, Washington	83,476	18	6	Seattle city, Washington	$606,200	6	6	Philadelphia city, Pennsylvania	54.6
20	7	Washington city, District of Columbia	75,506	2	7	Los Angeles city, California	$593,500	45	7	Oakland city, California	54.0
8	8	San Diego city, California	71,481	20	8	Washington city, District of Columbia	$576,100	20	8	Washington city, District of Columbia	53.1
44	9	Virginia Beach city, Virginia	71,117	1	9	New York city, New York	$569,700	2	9	Los Angeles city, California	52.4
64	10	Henderson city, Nevada	68,191	8	10	San Diego city, California	$567,400	21	10	Boston city, Massachusetts	52.1
45	11	Oakland city, California	68,060	55	11	Anaheim city, California	$548,100	10	11	San Jose city, California	50.1
11	12	Austin city, Texas	66,697	39	12	Long Beach city, California	$518,900	39	12	Long Beach city, California	49.0
56	13	Urban Honolulu CDP, Hawaii	65,155	21	13	Boston city, Massachusetts	$495,400	43	13	Miami city, Florida	48.3
55	14	Anaheim city, California	64,464	57	14	Santa Ana city, California	$461,600	30	14	Baltimore city, Maryland	45.5
41	15	Raleigh city, North Carolina	64,456	26	15	Portland city, Oregon	$395,100	54	15	Aurora city, Colorado	44.5
21	16	Boston city, Massachusetts	63,621	75	16	Jersey City city, New Jersey	$376,300	55	16	Anaheim city, California	44.0
58	17	Riverside city, California	63,548	19	17	Denver city, Colorado	$360,900	18	17	Seattle city, Washington	43.8
75	18	Jersey City city, New Jersey	63,227	58	18	Riverside city, California	$346,900	58	17	Riverside city, California	43.8
26	19	Portland city, Oregon	62,127	67	19	Anchorage municipality, Alaska	$320,800	4	19	Houston city, Texas	43.5
57	20	Santa Ana city, California	61,895	11	20	Austin city, Texas	$308,500	48	20	Arlington city, Texas	42.7
19	21	Denver city, Colorado	61,105	35	21	Sacramento city, California	$306,900	69	21	Plano city, Texas	42.4
17	22	Charlotte city, North Carolina	61,017	64	22	Henderson city, Nevada	$291,100	15	22	Fort Worth city, Texas	41.9
42	23	Colorado Springs city, Colorado	60,308	69	22	Plano city, Texas	$291,100	9	23	Dallas city, Texas	41.7
39	24	Long Beach city, California	60,075	43	24	Miami city, Florida	$277,700	72	24	Orlando city, Florida	40.3
54	25	Aurora city, Colorado	59,467	44	25	Virginia Beach city, Virginia	$271,400	26	25	Portland city, Oregon	40.0
53	26	Bakersfield city, California	59,233	38	26	Atlanta city, Georgia	$262,600	28	26	Las Vegas city, Nevada	39.1
1	27	New York city, New York	58,856	54	27	Aurora city, Colorado	$253,400	5	27	Phoenix city, Arizona	38.7
15	28	Fort Worth city, Texas	56,428	3	28	Chicago city, Illinois	$243,900	19	28	Denver city, Colorado	38.6
46	29	Minneapolis city, Minnesota	56,255	61	29	Stockton city, California	$243,700	24	29	Nashville-Davidson	37.4
71	30	Lincoln city, Nebraska	55,792	42	30	Colorado Springs city, Colorado	$243,600	17	30	Charlotte city, North Carolina	37.1
35	31	Sacramento city, California	55,187	41	31	Raleigh city, North Carolina	$242,500	23	31	Detroit city, Michigan	36.8
2	32	Los Angeles city, California	54,432	53	32	Bakersfield city, California	$236,600	38	32	Atlanta city, Georgia	36.7
59	33	Corpus Christi city, Texas	54,344	46	33	Minneapolis city, Minnesota	$235,200	61	33	Stockton city, California	35.4
24	34	Nashville-Davidson	54,310	70	33	Newark city, New Jersey	$235,200	36	34	Mesa city, Arizona	34.7
48	35	Arlington city, Texas	54,272	28	35	Las Vegas city, Nevada	$228,300	11	35	Austin city, Texas	34.4
63	36	St. Paul city, Minnesota	54,085	34	36	Fresno city, California	$227,500	65	36	Pittsburgh city, Pennsylvania	34.3
38	37	Atlanta city, Georgia	53,843	72	37	Orlando city, Florida	$224,600	12	37	Jacksonville city, Florida	34.0
60	38	Lexington-Fayette urban county, Kentucky	53,178	49	38	New Orleans city, Louisiana	$219,700	7	38	San Antonio city, Texas	33.7
3	39	Chicago city, Illinois	53,006	52	39	Tampa city, Florida	$216,100	52	39	Tampa city, Florida	33.5
27	40	Oklahoma City city, Oklahoma	52,915	5	40	Phoenix city, Arizona	$213,300	57	39	Santa Ana city, California	33.5
40	41	Omaha city, Nebraska	52,672	24	41	Nashville-Davidson	$210,600	35	41	Sacramento city, California	33.4
36	42	Mesa city, Arizona	52,393	36	42	Mesa city, Arizona	$209,000	73	42	Irvine city, California	32.9
5	43	Phoenix city, Arizona	52,062	17	43	Charlotte city, North Carolina	$201,500	62	43	St. Louis city, Missouri	32.5
12	44	Jacksonville city, Florida	51,298	63	44	St. Paul city, Minnesota	$198,500	51	44	Cleveland city, Ohio	32.3
37	45	Kansas City city, Missouri	51,235	32	45	Albuquerque city, New Mexico	$191,600	41	45	Raleigh city, North Carolina	31.9
28	46	Las Vegas city, Nevada	51,115	60	46	Lexington-Fayette urban county, Kentucky	$181,200	56	46	Urban Honolulu CDP, Hawaii	31.8
32	47	Albuquerque city, New Mexico	50,522	4	47	Houston city, Texas	$163,700	63	47	St. Paul city, Minnesota	31.5
52	48	Tampa city, Florida	50,405	71	48	Lincoln city, Nebraska	$160,600	8	48	San Diego city, California	31.3
14	49	Columbus city, Ohio	49,602	12	49	Jacksonville city, Florida	$157,800	44	48	Virginia Beach city, Virginia	31.3
61	50	Stockton city, California	49,271	9	50	Dallas city, Texas	$157,100	64	50	Henderson city, Nevada	30.5
7	51	San Antonio city, Texas	49,268	27	50	Oklahoma City city, Oklahoma	$157,100	49	51	New Orleans city, Louisiana	30.4
50	52	Wichita city, Kansas	49,202	48	52	Arlington city, Texas	$154,900	16	52	Indianapolis city, Indiana	28.5
29	53	Louisville/Jefferson County	48,996	6	53	Philadelphia city, Pennsylvania	$154,000	29	53	Louisville/Jefferson County	28.4
4	54	Houston city, Texas	47,793	30	54	Baltimore city, Maryland	$153,500	25	54	Memphis city, Tennessee	27.8
30	55	Baltimore city, Maryland	47,350	68	55	Greensboro city, North Carolina	$152,100	22	55	El Paso city, Texas	27.5
9	56	Dallas city, Texas	47,243	15	56	Fort Worth city, Texas	$151,000	66	55	Cincinnati city, Ohio	27.5
72	57	Orlando city, Florida	46,761	29	57	Louisville/Jefferson County	$150,900	33	57	Tucson city, Arizona	27.3
68	58	Greensboro city, North Carolina	45,064	40	58	Omaha city, Nebraska	$149,900	37	58	Kansas City city, Missouri	26.6
34	59	Fresno city, California	44,905	37	59	Kansas City city, Missouri	$146,300	46	59	Minneapolis city, Minnesota	26.5
65	60	Pittsburgh city, Pennsylvania	44,707	33	60	Tucson city, Arizona	$144,000	31	60	Milwaukee city, Wisconsin	26.2
16	61	Indianapolis city, Indiana	44,615	14	61	Columbus city, Ohio	$140,700	14	61	Columbus city, Ohio	25.4
22	62	El Paso city, Texas	43,200	66	62	Cincinnati city, Ohio	$134,100	32	62	Albuquerque city, New Mexico	24.6
47	63	Tulsa city, Oklahoma	43,134	7	63	San Antonio city, Texas	$133,900	27	63	Oklahoma City city, Oklahoma	24.2
6	64	Philadelphia city, Pennsylvania	41,449	59	64	Corpus Christi city, Texas	$132,400	53	64	Bakersfield city, California	23.9
62	65	St. Louis city, Missouri	40,346	47	65	Tulsa city, Oklahoma	$130,100	42	65	Colorado Springs city, Colorado	23.4
33	66	Tucson city, Arizona	40,021	16	66	Indianapolis city, Indiana	$128,200	60	66	Lexington-Fayette urban county, Kentucky	22.5
25	67	Memphis city, Tennessee	38,826	62	67	St. Louis city, Missouri	$125,800	74	67	Toledo city, Ohio	19.8
49	68	New Orleans city, Louisiana	38,681	22	68	El Paso city, Texas	$125,300	68	68	Greensboro city, North Carolina	19.3
66	69	Cincinnati city, Ohio	38,539	50	69	Wichita city, Kansas	$123,500	34	69	Fresno city, California	19.2
31	70	Milwaukee city, Wisconsin	38,097	65	70	Pittsburgh city, Pennsylvania	$120,800	71	70	Lincoln city, Nebraska	16.7
74	71	Toledo city, Ohio	35,301	31	71	Milwaukee city, Wisconsin	$114,700	47	71	Tulsa city, Oklahoma	16.1
43	72	Miami city, Florida	34,901	25	72	Memphis city, Tennessee	$96,800	40	72	Omaha city, Nebraska	16.0
70	73	Newark city, New Jersey	31,100	74	73	Toledo city, Ohio	$79,100	59	73	Corpus Christi city, Texas	15.7
23	74	Detroit city, Michigan	28,099	51	74	Cleveland city, Ohio	$66,800	50	74	Wichita city, Kansas	14.3
51	75	Cleveland city, Ohio	27,551	23	75	Detroit city, Michigan	$43,500	67	75	Anchorage municipality, Alaska	13.5

75 Largest Cities by 2017 Population
Selected rankings

Median Non-Family household Income, 2016				Unemployment rate, 2016				Percent change in civilian labor force, 2016-2017			
Population rank	Poverty rate rank	City	Poverty rate [col 46]	Population rank	Unemployment rate rank	City	Unemployment rate [col 64]	Population rank	Percent change rank	City	Percent change [col 62]
13	1	San Francisco city, California	81,776	23	1	Detroit city, Michigan	9.3	42	1	Colorado Springs city, Colorado	3.9
10	2	San Jose city, California	64,349	61	2	Stockton city, California	8.0	24	2	Nashville-Davidson	3.8
20	3	Washington city, District of Columbia	61,948	70	3	Newark city, New Jersey	7.5	43	3	Miami city, Florida	3.7
67	4	Anchorage municipality, Alaska	59,348	51	4	Cleveland city, Ohio	7.4	72	4	Orlando city, Florida	3.5
73	5	Irvine city, California	57,991	34	5	Fresno city, California	6.7	12	5	Jacksonville city, Florida	3.4
18	6	Seattle city, Washington	56,657	74	6	Toledo city, Ohio	6.6	17	6	Charlotte city, North Carolina	3.3
8	7	San Diego city, California	55,059	53	7	Bakersfield city, California	6.5	11	7	Austin city, Texas	3.2
45	8	Oakland city, California	54,956	6	8	Philadelphia city, Pennsylvania	6.2	19	7	Denver city, Colorado	3.2
21	9	Boston city, Massachusetts	53,327	20	9	Washington city, District of Columbia	6.1	54	7	Aurora city, Colorado	3.2
69	10	Plano city, Texas	52,752	30	9	Baltimore city, Maryland	6.1	5	10	Phoenix city, Arizona	3.1
57	11	Santa Ana city, California	51,788	67	11	Anchorage municipality, Alaska	6.0	36	10	Mesa city, Arizona	3.1
11	12	Austin city, Texas	50,991	3	12	Chicago city, Illinois	5.5	26	12	Portland city, Oregon	3.0
75	13	Jersey City city, New Jersey	50,809	32	12	Albuquerque city, New Mexico	5.5	38	12	Atlanta city, Georgia	3.0
44	14	Virginia Beach city, Virginia	49,116	28	14	Las Vegas city, Nevada	5.4	9	14	Dallas city, Texas	2.9
39	15	Long Beach city, California	48,786	59	15	Corpus Christi city, Texas	5.3	41	14	Raleigh city, North Carolina	2.9
41	16	Raleigh city, North Carolina	48,535	38	16	Atlanta city, Georgia	5.2	69	14	Plano city, Texas	2.9
55	17	Anaheim city, California	48,045	49	17	New Orleans city, Louisiana	5.1	29	17	Louisville/Jefferson County	2.8
19	18	Denver city, Colorado	46,593	65	18	Pittsburgh city, Pennsylvania	4.9	60	18	Lexington-Fayette urban county, Kentucky	2.7
38	19	Atlanta city, Georgia	45,708	68	18	Greensboro city, North Carolina	4.9	48	19	Arlington city, Texas	2.5
35	20	Sacramento city, California	45,661	4	20	Houston city, Texas	4.8	7	20	San Antonio city, Texas	2.3
26	21	Portland city, Oregon	45,511	25	20	Memphis city, Tennessee	4.8	15	20	Fort Worth city, Texas	2.3
64	22	Henderson city, Nevada	45,435	39	20	Long Beach city, California	4.8	52	22	Tampa city, Florida	2.2
1	23	New York city, New York	45,345	64	20	Henderson city, Nevada	4.8	18	23	Seattle city, Washington	2.1
54	24	Aurora city, Colorado	44,818	66	20	Cincinnati city, Ohio	4.8	28	23	Las Vegas city, Nevada	2.1
17	25	Charlotte city, North Carolina	44,790	2	25	Los Angeles city, California	4.7	58	23	Riverside city, California	2.1
3	26	Chicago city, Illinois	41,895	33	25	Tucson city, Arizona	4.7	64	23	Henderson city, Nevada	2.1
56	27	Urban Honolulu CDP, Hawaii	41,427	35	25	Sacramento city, California	4.7	14	27	Columbus city, Ohio	1.9
2	28	Los Angeles city, California	41,386	43	25	Miami city, Florida	4.7	33	28	Tucson city, Arizona	1.7
24	29	Nashville-Davidson	41,374	75	25	Jersey City city, New Jersey	4.7	61	28	Stockton city, California	1.7
15	30	Fort Worth city, Texas	40,732	31	30	Milwaukee city, Wisconsin	4.6	10	30	San Jose city, California	1.6
72	31	Orlando city, Florida	40,635	58	30	Riverside city, California	4.6	20	30	Washington city, District of Columbia	1.6
46	32	Minneapolis city, Minnesota	40,481	1	32	New York city, New York	4.5	44	30	Virginia Beach city, Virginia	1.6
53	33	Bakersfield city, California	40,454	47	32	Tulsa city, Oklahoma	4.5	13	33	San Francisco city, California	1.5
63	34	St. Paul city, Minnesota	39,704	17	34	Charlotte city, North Carolina	4.4	21	33	Boston city, Massachusetts	1.5
48	35	Arlington city, Texas	39,591	22	34	El Paso city, Texas	4.4	46	33	Minneapolis city, Minnesota	1.5
14	36	Columbus city, Ohio	39,571	29	34	Louisville/Jefferson County	4.4	2	36	Los Angeles city, California	1.4
9	37	Dallas city, Texas	39,570	50	34	Wichita city, Kansas	4.4	63	36	St. Paul city, Minnesota	1.4
4	38	Houston city, Texas	38,351	62	34	St. Louis city, Missouri	4.4	66	36	Cincinnati city, Ohio	1.4
5	39	Phoenix city, Arizona	38,040	5	39	Phoenix city, Arizona	4.3	22	39	El Paso city, Texas	1.3
42	40	Colorado Springs city, Colorado	37,616	37	39	Kansas City city, Missouri	4.3	39	39	Long Beach city, California	1.3
12	41	Jacksonville city, Florida	36,657	12	41	Jacksonville city, Florida	4.2	45	41	Oakland city, California	1.2
60	42	Lexington-Fayette urban county, Kentucky	36,607	36	41	Mesa city, Arizona	4.2	4	42	Houston city, Texas	1.1
52	43	Tampa city, Florida	35,514	41	41	Raleigh city, North Carolina	4.2	25	42	Memphis city, Tennessee	1.1
30	44	Baltimore city, Maryland	35,342	45	41	Oakland city, California	4.2	27	42	Oklahoma City city, Oklahoma	1.1
37	45	Kansas City city, Missouri	35,341	14	45	Columbus city, Ohio	4.1	73	42	Irvine city, California	1.1
7	46	San Antonio city, Texas	34,729	52	46	Tampa city, Florida	4.0	8	46	San Diego city, California	1.0
36	47	Mesa city, Arizona	34,573	8	47	San Diego city, California	3.9	30	46	Baltimore city, Maryland	1.0
40	48	Omaha city, Nebraska	33,517	27	47	Oklahoma City city, Oklahoma	3.9	35	46	Sacramento city, California	1.0
27	49	Oklahoma City city, Oklahoma	33,460	9	49	Dallas city, Texas	3.8	47	46	Tulsa city, Oklahoma	1.0
28	50	Las Vegas city, Nevada	33,340	15	49	Fort Worth city, Texas	3.8	55	46	Anaheim city, California	1.0
58	51	Riverside city, California	33,021	48	51	Arlington city, Texas	3.7	57	46	Santa Ana city, California	1.0
59	52	Corpus Christi city, Texas	32,351	55	51	Anaheim city, California	3.7	34	52	Fresno city, California	0.9
62	53	St. Louis city, Missouri	32,184	16	53	Indianapolis city, Indiana	3.6	32	53	Albuquerque city, New Mexico	0.8
65	54	Pittsburgh city, Pennsylvania	32,179	26	53	Portland city, Oregon	3.6	1	54	New York city, New York	0.7
68	55	Greensboro city, North Carolina	31,959	44	53	Virginia Beach city, Virginia	3.6	23	54	Detroit city, Michigan	0.7
32	56	Albuquerque city, New Mexico	31,896	57	53	Santa Ana city, California	3.6	68	54	Greensboro city, North Carolina	0.7
16	57	Indianapolis city, Indiana	31,788	60	53	Lexington-Fayette urban county, Kentucky	3.6	74	54	Toledo city, Ohio	0.7
29	58	Louisville/Jefferson County	31,494	7	58	San Antonio city, Texas	3.5	40	58	Omaha city, Nebraska	0.5
50	59	Wichita city, Kansas	31,472	72	58	Orlando city, Florida	3.5	16	59	Indianapolis city, Indiana	0.3
71	60	Lincoln city, Nebraska	30,997	18	60	Seattle city, Washington	3.4	71	60	Lincoln city, Nebraska	0.2
47	61	Tulsa city, Oklahoma	30,738	21	60	Boston city, Massachusetts	3.4	6	61	Philadelphia city, Pennsylvania	0.1
34	62	Fresno city, California	30,656	69	60	Plano city, Texas	3.4	51	62	Cleveland city, Ohio	0.0
6	63	Philadelphia city, Pennsylvania	29,943	73	60	Irvine city, California	3.4	56	62	Urban Honolulu CDP, Hawaii	0.0
66	64	Cincinnati city, Ohio	29,715	10	64	San Jose city, California	3.3	59	62	Corpus Christi city, Texas	0.0
61	65	Stockton city, California	29,522	63	64	St. Paul city, Minnesota	3.3	75	62	Jersey City city, New Jersey	0.0
25	66	Memphis city, Tennessee	29,281	40	66	Omaha city, Nebraska	3.2	37	66	Kansas City city, Missouri	-0.1
22	67	El Paso city, Texas	27,720	42	66	Colorado Springs city, Colorado	3.2	31	67	Milwaukee city, Wisconsin	-0.2
31	68	Milwaukee city, Wisconsin	27,653	46	68	Minneapolis city, Minnesota	3.1	65	67	Pittsburgh city, Pennsylvania	-0.2
43	69	Miami city, Florida	26,523	54	68	Aurora city, Colorado	3.1	67	67	Anchorage municipality, Alaska	-0.2
49	70	New Orleans city, Louisiana	26,414	11	70	Austin city, Texas	2.9	49	70	New Orleans city, Louisiana	-0.5
33	71	Tucson city, Arizona	25,751	13	70	San Francisco city, California	2.9	70	71	Newark city, New Jersey	-0.6
74	72	Toledo city, Ohio	25,402	19	72	Denver city, Colorado	2.8	3	72	Chicago city, Illinois	-0.7
51	73	Cleveland city, Ohio	21,167	24	73	Nashville-Davidson	2.7	53	73	Bakersfield city, California	-1.0
23	74	Detroit city, Michigan	20,170	71	73	Lincoln city, Nebraska	2.7	50	74	Wichita city, Kansas	-1.1
70	75	Newark city, New Jersey	19,164	56	75	Urban Honolulu CDP, Hawaii	NA	62	75	St. Louis city, Missouri	-1.2

Table D. Cities — **Population**

AREANAME	Percent Hispanic or Latino[1], 2016	Percent foreign born, 2016	Age of population (percent), 2016							Median age 2016	Percent female 2016	Population			
			Under 18 years	18 to 24 years	25 to 34 years	35 to 44 years	45 to 54 years	55 to 64 years	65 years and over			Census counts		Percent change	
												2000	2010	2000-2010	2010-2017
	12	13	14	15	16	17	18	19	20	21	22	23	24	25	26
United States...................	17.8	13.5	22.8	9.6	13.7	12.6	13.2	12.8	15.2	37.9	50.8	281,421,906	308,758,105	9.7	5.5
ALABAMA	4.1	3.4	22.6	9.5	12.9	12.3	13.3	13.2	16.1	39.0	51.6	4,447,100	4,780,135	7.5	2.0
Alabaster............................	5.9	6.0	27.1	6.6	11.2	21.3	11.5	10.0	12.2	36.7	49.7	22,619	31,084	37.4	6.8
Auburn...............................	4.5	8.5	16.9	36.3	13.2	9.4	10.0	6.0	8.1	24.2	52.0	42,987	53,404	24.2	19.8
Bessemer............................	3.2	3.2	18.1	10.0	10.2	10.8	12.2	16.1	22.5	46.1	59.5	29,672	27,467	-7.4	-3.9
Birmingham........................	3.6	4.0	21.2	10.3	17.2	12.5	11.9	12.9	14.1	36.0	52.9	242,820	211,984	-12.7	-0.6
Decatur	14.8	6.9	24.0	8.4	11.1	12.8	15.7	11.7	16.1	40.0	50.3	53,929	55,781	3.4	-2.5
Dothan	2.9	2.1	23.5	8.3	13.6	12.2	12.8	12.8	16.9	38.9	52.6	57,737	65,778	13.9	3.7
Enterprise..........................	9.1	1.1	28.8	9.0	14.3	11.4	13.4	10.3	12.9	33.3	52.6	21,178	26,610	25.6	6.2
Florence.............................	3.3	3.9	18.7	14.5	10.5	11.9	10.3	15.4	18.6	40.8	52.7	36,264	39,338	8.5	1.3
Gadsden.............................	7.8	7.0	22.4	8.8	13.6	13.3	13.9	12.7	15.2	38.3	51.9	38,978	36,900	-5.3	-4.0
Homewood..........................	2.4	4.2	17.5	17.9	18.3	11.2	15.0	10.8	9.3	31.5	55.1	25,043	25,183	0.6	1.2
Hoover...............................	7.6	12.1	25.5	6.5	15.3	14.3	13.7	10.0	14.8	36.6	52.1	62,742	80,698	28.6	5.2
Huntsville..........................	6.3	6.6	23.5	11.4	14.3	12.0	12.1	12.1	14.6	35.6	50.8	158,216	180,376	14.0	7.9
Madison.............................	3.4	6.2	22.9	10.0	15.3	13.3	15.4	12.8	10.4	37.7	48.1	29,329	42,955	46.5	13.7
Mobile...............................	2.5	3.5	20.1	11.3	15.8	12.5	11.3	12.3	16.6	36.9	51.9	198,915	194,666	-2.1	-2.3
Montgomery.......................	3.6	5.1	23.5	10.6	15.3	12.4	12.4	12.3	13.6	35.5	53.0	201,568	205,525	2.0	-2.9
Opelika..............................	0.8	3.5	28.4	4.4	16.0	14.0	12.2	10.8	14.2	35.4	49.1	23,498	26,425	12.5	14.4
Phenix City........................	0.8	1.2	25.9	10.4	13.4	14.3	11.3	13.4	11.3	35.4	50.4	28,265	32,979	16.7	9.8
Prattville	4.3	3.2	24.8	6.5	15.0	12.3	16.2	10.5	14.8	37.5	51.0	24,303	34,010	39.9	4.4
Tuscaloosa.........................	2.4	4.3	18.3	26.0	14.7	9.6	10.5	9.8	11.2	27.9	53.1	77,906	90,360	16.0	11.0
Vestavia Hills......................	1.9	4.5	30.3	6.3	12.5	15.3	10.9	10.7	14.0	35.8	50.1	24,476	33,781	38.0	1.5
ALASKA	6.9	7.7	25.2	10.2	16.4	12.5	12.6	12.9	10.2	33.5	47.4	626,932	710,249	13.3	4.2
Anchorage..........................	9.0	10.3	24.8	10.3	17.7	13.2	12.1	12.1	9.8	33.0	48.7	260,283	291,829	12.1	0.9
Fairbanks...........................	11.0	9.5	23.1	20.4	19.9	10.2	11.0	8.5	6.9	28.0	46.8	30,224	31,556	4.4	0.3
Juneau..............................	6.7	8.1	21.9	8.3	14.8	16.4	12.5	14.9	11.2	37.5	47.2	30,711	31,275	1.8	2.6
ARIZONA	30.9	13.5	23.5	9.7	13.4	12.3	12.2	12.0	16.9	37.5	50.3	5,130,632	6,392,309	24.6	9.8
Apache Junction	14.7	8.3	19.6	6.6	5.8	9.7	10.4	12.4	35.5	52.9	50.9	31,814	35,735	12.3	13.4
Avondale............................	50.6	16.8	28.1	8.3	15.5	15.7	13.0	9.4	9.9	34.3	49.4	35,883	76,132	112.2	10.4
Buckeye.............................	35.0	8.7	26.2	8.2	12.5	18.2	11.9	9.8	13.2	36.3	46.1	6,537	50,902	678.7	34.5
Bullhead City.......................	25.4	9.3	19.9	5.6	9.7	8.8	12.4	14.7	28.9	49.1	54.9	33,769	39,540	17.1	1.8
Casa Grande.......................	38.7	10.1	31.1	9.1	12.3	10.9	9.9	10.8	15.9	33.8	52.1	25,224	48,587	92.6	14.2
Chandler............................	20.4	14.9	25.5	7.4	16.7	15.2	13.4	11.3	10.5	35.2	50.2	176,581	236,194	33.8	7.3
El Mirage...........................	47.8	15.9	32.2	11.4	16.0	12.7	11.7	8.0	8.1	29.5	50.7	7,609	31,797	317.9	10.8
Flagstaff............................	19.2	4.6	16.9	35.6	11.7	9.2	9.1	9.2	8.3	23.7	50.0	52,894	66,065	24.9	8.9
Florence.............................	35.9	12.8	6.5	9.3	23.5	21.6	11.3	9.1	18.6	39.5	22.0	17,054	25,559	49.9	2.0
Gilbert...............................	15.7	8.6	31.4	7.6	14.9	14.2	13.9	8.9	9.2	33.1	51.5	109,697	208,401	90.0	16.3
Glendale............................	37.0	17.4	23.8	10.1	15.9	12.2	13.1	13.0	12.0	35.2	50.6	218,812	226,099	3.3	9.1
Goodyear	26.8	10.7	26.7	8.4	11.2	13.8	13.1	12.8	14.1	37.5	51.2	18,911	65,223	244.9	22.4
Kingman............................	15.5	3.0	21.5	7.3	15.1	10.1	13.0	11.2	21.8	39.8	47.5	20,069	28,070	39.9	5.0
Lake Havasu City................	14.5	4.6	14.2	5.1	9.8	9.4	12.1	15.0	34.3	54.5	49.5	41,938	52,531	25.3	3.6
Marana..............................	20.3	10.3	20.3	9.6	9.3	13.5	10.1	12.5	24.9	42.9	52.6	13,556	34,556	154.9	29.6
Maricopa............................	28.8	11.5	27.6	9.9	11.3	17.0	12.4	11.0	10.8	35.3	51.4	1,040	43,482	4,081.0	10.4
Mesa.................................	27.0	12.7	24.5	9.6	14.9	12.6	11.9	10.3	16.3	35.7	50.8	396,375	440,121	11.0	12.8
Oro Valley	12.5	6.5	18.7	9.0	6.0	9.2	10.5	14.6	31.9	49.8	49.9	29,700	41,028	38.1	8.1
Peoria...............................	17.1	9.0	23.7	7.8	11.6	11.6	15.2	12.5	17.4	41.6	51.1	108,364	154,094	42.2	9.1
Phoenix..............................	43.8	19.9	27.0	9.9	15.6	13.8	12.7	10.6	10.4	33.4	50.4	1,321,045	1,446,909	9.5	12.4
Prescott.............................	6.9	3.7	9.8	6.8	8.4	9.4	10.8	17.0	37.8	58.4	52.2	33,938	39,778	17.2	7.4
Prescott Valley....................	20.7	10.5	18.9	10.3	7.4	7.0	14.2	15.4	26.9	49.8	52.4	23,535	38,879	65.2	14.4
Queen Creek.......................	14.9	7.6	33.8	3.6	11.7	21.8	12.7	9.5	6.9	35.4	48.3	4,316	26,326	510.0	48.8
Sahuarita...........................	36.3	9.6	25.4	6.9	11.1	14.2	9.1	8.6	24.7	39.5	52.3	3,242	25,289	680.0	15.9
San Luis	95.6	51.3	29.6	10.1	16.1	13.0	14.8	11.2	5.3	32.6	45.6	15,322	27,909	82.1	16.3
Scottsdale..........................	9.8	12.6	15.7	6.3	11.6	12.3	14.0	15.9	24.2	48.5	51.1	202,705	217,439	7.3	15.0
Sierra Vista	27.0	11.8	21.5	8.6	16.9	10.8	10.8	9.6	21.8	38.5	51.5	37,775	45,265	19.8	-5.2
Surprise.............................	17.7	10.2	25.0	6.6	9.9	12.7	10.4	12.1	23.2	40.9	52.0	30,848	117,511	280.9	14.1
Tempe...............................	18.4	15.7	13.8	23.2	21.9	9.9	10.5	10.2	10.4	29.8	48.4	158,625	161,777	2.0	14.4
Tucson	43.3	15.8	21.6	15.5	14.7	11.5	11.4	11.5	13.8	33.4	50.5	486,699	523,475	7.6	2.3
Yuma................................	58.8	20.5	27.0	13.1	14.8	11.0	10.2	9.2	14.7	31.0	48.7	77,515	90,715	17.0	5.3
ARKANSAS...................	7.2	4.6	23.7	9.7	12.8	12.2	12.7	12.7	16.3	38.0	50.8	2,673,400	2,916,031	9.1	3.0
Bella Vista..........................	2.4	2.1	17.0	5.9	8.1	9.7	10.7	14.0	34.6	54.3	52.4	16,582	26,510	59.9	7.5
Benton...............................	5.8	3.6	27.3	9.5	14.8	14.3	12.2	9.9	11.9	34.0	48.4	21,906	30,703	40.2	16.6
Bentonville	9.0	14.3	25.5	8.1	21.5	18.5	11.0	8.4	6.9	33.0	48.0	19,730	35,299	78.9	39.7
Conway	5.2	3.4	20.3	22.8	16.3	11.9	10.5	8.9	9.4	29.6	51.4	43,167	58,871	36.4	11.7
Fayetteville.........................	9.6	8.1	18.9	29.2	16.4	10.2	10.6	6.8	7.9	25.9	50.4	58,047	73,585	26.8	15.9
Fort Smith	18.9	12.6	24.3	8.1	13.5	12.7	12.4	12.3	16.6	38.1	51.6	80,268	86,270	7.5	2.0
Hot Springs	8.7	8.1	14.7	12.6	11.4	9.7	10.4	17.4	23.7	46.3	52.5	35,750	36,277	1.5	1.8

1. May be of any race.

Table D. Cities — **Households, Group Quarters, Crime, and Education**

	Households, 2016								Serious crimes known to police[2], 2016				Educational attainment, 2016		
				Perecnt					Total		Rate[3]			Attainment[4] (percent)	
AREANAME	Number	Persons per house-hold	Family	Married couple family	Female headed family[1]	Non-family	One person	Persons in group quarters	Number	Rate	Violent	Property	Population age 25 and over	High school graduate or less	Bachelor's degree or more
	27	28	29	30	31	32	33	34	35	36	37	38	39	40	41
United States	118,860,065	2.65	65.4	47.9	12.6	34.6	28.0	8,079,879	9,167,220	2,837	386	2,451	218,475,480	39.7	31.3
ALABAMA	1,852,518	2.56	65.2	46.7	14.2	34.8	30.7	119,659	169,248	3,480	532	2,948	3,300,713	45.5	24.7
Alabaster	11,342	2.88	74.8	60.3	11.3	25.2	23.1	NA	585	1,771	294	1,477	21,843	32.8	31.7
Auburn	21,975	2.63	54.8	42.4	8.1	45.2	29.1	5,296	1,335	2,090	329	1,761	29,550	17.7	59.4
Bessemer	11,420	2.25	57.2	25.7	27.2	42.8	39.3	830	3,166	11,906	2,869	9,037	19,034	52.6	15.5
Birmingham	90,117	2.27	53.7	25.2	22.7	46.3	40.6	8,836	15,890	7,476	1,609	5,867	146,225	43.2	26.8
Decatur	21,119	2.56	64.9	47.9	11.5	35.1	32.3	NA	2,754	4,973	278	4,695	37,123	44.1	23.3
Dothan	26,119	2.56	61.2	40.5	16.5	38.8	34.4	870	3,374	4,885	819	4,065	46,203	41.8	23.3
Enterprise	10,082	2.74	70.6	48.5	14.9	29.4	25.8	NA	881	3,121	347	2,774	17,324	39.8	24.9
Florence	17,874	2.12	51.1	33.8	16.0	48.9	41.1	2,144	1,596	3,974	488	3,486	26,672	43.1	27.9
Gadsden	13,568	2.57	59.7	29.8	24.4	40.3	34.8	1,019	2,985	8,309	1,292	7,017	24,650	53.1	11.7
Homewood	10,772	2.18	57.0	46.7	7.9	43.0	35.2	2,146	1,058	4,097	325	3,772	16,533	12.2	69.2
Hoover	32,110	2.63	71.4	58.7	9.9	28.6	25.2	423	1,266	1,479	121	1,357	57,842	19.4	57.7
Huntsville	80,540	2.34	57.6	39.2	14.3	42.4	37.1	7,622	11,185	5,808	928	4,880	127,670	30.8	42.6
Madison	17,814	2.68	68.6	57.4	8.5	31.4	27.7	NA	1,220	2,556	438	2,118	32,233	12.9	58.7
Mobile	79,188	2.33	55.4	33.0	18.0	44.6	38.7	8,670	13,478	5,393	684	4,709	132,227	40.0	29.0
Montgomery	80,899	2.39	57.7	31.4	19.2	42.3	38.0	6,379	10,204	5,113	609	4,504	131,915	39.4	30.8
Opelika	12,098	2.43	56.8	40.5	15.3	43.2	40.4	513	1,697	5,623	732	4,891	20,068	37.3	30.9
Phenix City	15,113	2.38	56.3	37.3	14.5	43.7	40.5	517	2,144	5,566	849	4,717	23,225	45.1	20.7
Prattville	14,398	2.42	65.9	55.7	7.6	34.1	31.3	NA	1,445	4,048	235	3,813	24,294	45.5	26.2
Tuscaloosa	36,313	2.48	50.8	28.9	15.3	49.2	37.3	9,478	4,212	4,215	480	3,735	55,520	34.9	36.3
Vestavia Hills	12,527	2.76	68.1	56.4	8.2	31.9	29.3	NA	422	1,234	73	1,161	21,987	10.3	71.0
ALASKA	248,468	2.87	66.0	49.2	11.1	34.0	25.1	27,826	30,842	4,157	804	3,353	478,951	34.8	29.6
Anchorage	105,249	2.76	66.5	48.5	12.3	33.5	24.0	7,658	18,071	6,042	1,144	4,898	193,529	29.3	36.5
Fairbanks	10,231	2.95	55.8	43.4	7.2	44.2	29.2	2,603	1,573	4,847	687	4,159	18,506	37.2	26.3
Juneau	12,701	2.51	66.4	53.1	9.3	33.6	22.7	608	1,877	5,694	855	4,839	22,667	21.2	40.8
ARIZONA	2,519,052	2.69	65.5	47.4	12.6	34.5	27.3	156,879	239,015	3,448	470	2,978	4,626,409	37.2	28.9
Apache Junction	16,779	2.38	60.3	51.2	8.5	39.7	34.9	NA	1,038	2,696	280	2,415	29,604	49.9	14.8
Avondale	25,849	3.20	78.4	50.2	17.8	21.6	15.1	NA	3,495	4,283	286	3,997	52,685	43.8	18.3
Buckeye	18,783	3.08	76.3	63.0	10.2	23.7	17.0	6,820	1,060	1,642	54	1,588	42,380	41.7	17.5
Bullhead City	16,665	2.39	61.7	41.5	14.1	38.3	31.2	NA	1,504	3,815	251	3,564	29,808	56.9	9.8
Casa Grande	16,323	3.33	72.5	41.6	21.1	27.5	23.5	229	2,028	3,900	546	3,354	32,600	45.9	17.3
Chandler	90,570	2.72	67.2	51.0	10.8	32.8	24.7	822	6,710	2,523	210	2,313	166,090	25.1	42.1
El Mirage	10,383	3.37	76.6	50.6	20.9	23.4	16.6	NA	1,126	3,276	215	3,060	19,785	53.7	13.2
Flagstaff	22,839	2.54	50.0	38.8	7.7	50.0	28.2	13,412	3,121	4,385	372	4,012	33,937	26.3	45.5
Florence	4,417	2.26	66.4	54.4	8.4	33.6	31.4	15,826	173	556	71	485	21,693	55.0	10.0
Gilbert	74,275	3.19	78.7	63.7	10.0	21.3	15.7	463	3,603	1,408	81	1,327	144,656	19.5	45.4
Glendale	85,557	2.83	65.7	41.2	15.6	34.3	27.3	3,889	14,009	5,766	496	5,271	162,684	45.6	20.8
Goodyear	24,232	3.03	78.5	65.4	10.0	21.5	18.2	3,863	2,373	2,893	378	2,515	50,158	31.8	27.5
Kingman	12,355	2.23	54.9	37.2	14.2	45.1	35.1	1,504	1,581	5,439	347	5,091	20,667	37.2	16.2
Lake Havasu City	23,815	2.25	61.2	51.7	7.4	38.8	28.5	211	1,359	2,529	262	2,266	43,354	46.2	12.3
Marana	15,883	2.70	80.0	69.3	9.6	20.0	14.7	NA	1,085	2,535	93	2,441	30,522	21.9	44.8
Maricopa	14,019	3.35	75.2	57.6	12.7	24.8	17.8	NA	745	1,501	195	1,306	29,350	33.7	21.9
Mesa	173,852	2.77	67.5	49.2	11.8	32.5	24.0	3,791	13,265	2,773	429	2,345	319,479	37.1	26.5
Oro Valley	18,138	2.41	68.6	56.2	8.9	31.4	26.5	NA	682	1,547	66	1,481	31,624	18.2	51.5
Peoria	58,106	2.80	71.1	54.8	10.6	28.9	24.7	1,412	4,059	2,322	200	2,122	112,343	30.8	31.9
Phoenix	555,953	2.87	64.1	41.6	15.7	35.9	28.2	18,374	69,252	4,365	674	3,690	1,018,747	42.8	27.9
Prescott	20,055	2.00	60.6	53.4	6.6	39.4	32.2	2,497	1,094	2,585	402	2,183	35,457	21.2	38.9
Prescott Valley	17,712	2.42	65.2	53.7	7.0	34.8	30.2	208	1,072	2,499	182	2,317	30,547	38.4	21.8
Queen Creek	11,617	3.05	76.5	61.8	6.6	23.5	21.4	NA	NA	NA	NA	NA	22,203	19.7	38.3
Sahuarita	10,507	2.73	81.5	70.3	8.8	18.5	16.5	125	398	1,543	89	1,454	19,468	21.5	41.1
San Luis	8,577	3.56	90.4	67.5	19.2	9.6	6.3	1,618	466	1,446	121	1,325	19,395	62.8	9.4
Scottsdale	112,795	2.17	57.0	46.8	7.1	43.0	34.4	1,639	6,067	2,519	153	2,365	192,504	15.3	58.7
Sierra Vista	18,104	2.25	62.9	44.1	10.7	37.1	30.8	2,534	1,363	3,171	198	2,973	30,205	30.7	28.8
Surprise	46,771	2.83	76.7	63.7	10.3	23.3	18.8	349	2,624	2,008	103	1,905	90,720	33.1	27.8
Tempe	71,710	2.42	49.7	31.9	11.2	50.3	31.2	8,881	9,046	5,063	505	4,559	114,965	21.1	45.5
Tucson	207,065	2.43	55.5	33.3	17.5	44.5	34.1	26,776	35,510	6,654	795	5,859	333,475	38.7	26.1
Yuma	34,416	2.66	68.1	47.9	14.6	31.9	25.0	3,277	3,722	2,388	338	2,051	56,813	46.3	19.1
ARKANSAS	1,142,718	2.54	65.5	48.1	13.2	34.5	29.3	85,075	114,134	3,819	551	3,269	1,990,448	48.3	22.4
Bella Vista	12,381	2.28	72.0	63.4	6.7	28.0	21.8	172	259	916	233	683	21,912	31.4	31.2
Benton	12,936	2.73	69.6	56.7	6.9	30.4	27.8	NA	1,728	4,948	507	4,442	22,610	39.8	28.1
Bentonville	17,553	2.64	68.6	55.3	9.1	31.4	21.3	NA	755	1,625	187	1,438	31,253	27.9	49.9
Conway	23,305	2.58	60.0	47.4	10.6	40.0	28.8	5,177	3,315	5,015	511	4,504	37,139	32.1	38.7
Fayetteville	33,903	2.28	43.5	28.8	7.8	56.5	37.7	6,591	4,194	4,950	542	4,408	43,507	27.0	49.4
Fort Smith	36,368	2.38	59.3	39.8	13.8	40.7	34.2	1,639	5,943	6,710	806	5,904	59,520	49.9	20.0
Hot Springs	16,123	2.18	47.6	34.5	11.6	52.4	45.6	1,777	3,170	8,876	778	8,097	26,786	45.8	18.6

1. No spouse present. 2. Data for serious crimes have not been adjusted for underreporting. This may affect comparability between geographic areas and over time. 3. Per 100,000 population estimated by the FBI. 4. Persons 25 years old and over.

Table D. Cities — **Income and Housing**

AREANAME	Money income, 2016					Median earnings, 2016			Housing units, 2016				
	Households			Median family income	Median non-family household income	All persons	Men	Women	Total	Occupied	Percent owner occupied	Median value[1] (dollars)	Median rent (dollars)
	Median income	Percent with income less than $20,000	Percent with income of $200,000 or more										
	42	43	44	45	46	47	48	49	50	51	52	53	54
United States..............	57,617	16.2	6.4	71,062	34,963	31,986	38,017	27,104	135,702,775	118,860,065	63.1	205,000	981
ALABAMA	46,257	22.4	3.3	59,764	25,741	29,164	35,550	23,511	2,230,180	1,852,518	68.5	136,200	743
Alabaster........................	75,627	5.9	1.7	82,449	41,983	42,571	54,937	31,951	12,259	11,342	80.2	167,700	1,012
Auburn	50,094	29.3	3.7	81,121	19,210	15,737	28,902	11,004	25,979	21,975	43.7	245,600	872
Bessemer........................	35,067	28.4	0.4	48,100	19,859	26,238	29,055	23,574	13,168	11,420	56.2	83,900	684
Birmingham....................	36,241	30.2	2.3	43,062	23,901	25,182	26,170	23,584	114,371	90,117	45.9	88,500	777
Decatur	43,902	23.9	2.3	59,945	27,887	28,643	31,787	25,427	24,218	21,119	67.2	132,800	594
Dothan	42,336	24.8	4.0	56,746	24,706	26,003	32,046	21,591	30,960	26,119	57.9	142,000	720
Enterprise.......................	55,806	20.2	1.9	64,472	26,849	31,314	41,580	17,442	12,476	10,082	55.4	161,500	871
Florence.........................	40,509	27.8	2.0	55,996	22,797	23,957	24,823	23,094	21,252	17,874	59.0	133,900	588
Gadsden	27,610	36.0	1.4	41,218	17,452	20,902	25,923	19,152	17,038	13,568	53.5	85,600	582
Homewood.....................	73,310	10.5	10.6	102,675	42,203	38,996	34,874	40,161	12,672	10,772	58.5	356,400	1,030
Hoover	79,004	9.1	13.7	101,950	41,666	41,638	56,662	32,985	34,976	32,110	67.9	278,600	1,021
Huntsville.......................	51,895	20.0	6.3	71,114	33,097	29,437	36,414	23,054	89,849	80,540	56.7	182,200	766
Madison	100,318	4.9	14.8	121,506	50,725	42,383	62,098	33,135	19,283	17,814	70.6	273,700	863
Mobile............................	39,463	27.7	2.9	49,759	26,587	26,110	30,789	22,472	94,169	79,188	53.7	125,100	804
Montgomery	41,625	24.9	3.3	54,734	26,751	27,290	30,768	24,943	93,476	80,899	55.7	117,200	813
Opelika...........................	47,223	21.5	1.1	63,068	39,561	31,125	32,426	30,496	12,591	12,098	61.0	158,100	734
Phenix City.....................	46,418	23.3	3.0	57,053	36,143	30,825	44,591	22,694	17,622	15,113	53.1	120,900	788
Prattville	54,656	17.7	1.5	73,073	34,964	35,135	50,652	28,208	14,596	14,398	66.8	152,000	1,004
Tuscaloosa.....................	39,298	24.9	4.6	53,151	27,573	20,421	24,675	17,612	47,324	36,313	45.3	173,100	810
Vestavia Hills	97,023	12.2	19.8	139,959	34,714	51,662	71,468	41,034	13,996	12,527	74.4	338,200	1,076
ALASKA	76,440	9.6	7.1	88,604	51,252	36,209	42,368	30,859	310,672	248,468	64.5	267,800	1,208
Anchorage......................	85,634	6.7	10.2	98,717	59,348	41,059	46,817	35,169	115,539	105,249	61.1	320,800	1,296
Fairbanks	64,857	13.1	5.7	72,563	40,009	30,702	32,302	24,889	11,688	10,231	35.9	197,800	1,242
Juneau...........................	80,708	6.3	5.6	98,008	57,459	42,464	47,360	37,853	13,445	12,701	63.0	347,700	1,219
ARIZONA	53,558	16.8	4.8	63,877	34,776	30,675	34,951	26,303	2,961,136	2,519,052	63.2	205,900	976
Apache Junction	42,096	25.5	2.3	56,949	23,925	21,130	23,287	19,616	21,509	16,779	79.0	89,100	902
Avondale........................	58,404	11.7	2.1	63,106	42,197	31,328	36,355	26,657	27,824	25,849	54.6	204,300	1,092
Buckeye.........................	57,482	10.6	1.6	61,087	38,100	31,741	37,479	26,736	20,725	18,783	69.1	193,500	1,133
Bullhead City..................	41,981	19.8	1.2	54,895	23,640	24,033	27,388	20,658	23,358	16,665	54.4	139,400	778
Casa Grande..................	46,917	20.8	1.6	49,793	26,579	25,559	29,690	22,229	20,561	16,323	63.8	137,500	927
Chandler	75,369	8.3	8.5	87,229	50,562	41,005	50,145	35,509	97,246	90,570	60.7	275,400	1,211
El Mirage........................	49,490	11.0	1.9	49,322	43,128	30,228	31,800	25,639	11,439	10,383	63.4	157,100	1,084
Flagstaff.........................	59,658	18.8	4.4	76,020	36,368	19,601	20,948	16,714	26,827	22,839	50.2	331,400	1,125
Florence.........................	48,801	23.7	2.1	54,628	19,415	16,181	9,724	17,512	7,023	4,417	73.5	127,900	726
Gilbert............................	91,576	5.2	9.9	97,693	60,583	42,732	57,125	35,126	78,642	74,275	69.0	307,000	1,382
Glendale.........................	51,022	17.6	2.9	59,305	31,575	30,185	31,153	27,926	92,993	85,557	54.1	200,900	906
Goodyear........................	73,960	6.0	5.2	82,107	49,691	36,504	45,334	29,842	26,608	24,232	73.3	262,600	1,257
Kingman.........................	42,363	27.3	2.0	56,502	19,512	35,239	40,461	31,945	13,908	12,355	66.6	135,600	821
Lake Havasu City............	48,322	15.9	3.7	56,238	32,096	27,060	30,803	23,084	32,247	23,815	69.3	221,700	804
Marana...........................	77,396	6.1	3.6	81,740	53,076	38,175	52,772	27,232	18,557	15,883	77.8	250,100	1,234
Maricopa	62,360	10.4	2.2	71,120	37,601	30,051	40,239	23,701	17,035	14,019	72.0	172,100	1,320
Mesa..............................	52,393	16.0	4.0	59,833	34,573	30,005	32,906	24,886	205,704	173,852	59.3	209,000	960
Oro Valley	68,533	6.9	7.9	85,305	48,159	33,787	42,462	23,799	20,581	18,138	69.6	298,900	1,190
Peoria............................	68,882	9.5	4.2	81,012	39,768	38,853	42,007	32,968	63,821	58,106	70.8	248,700	1,178
Phoenix..........................	52,062	17.0	5.0	59,682	38,040	30,671	32,114	27,244	611,421	555,953	53.0	213,300	960
Prescott..........................	53,662	19.7	3.7	75,703	30,809	24,322	30,724	20,494	22,604	20,055	65.6	325,000	937
Prescott Valley	43,333	18.3	1.7	58,451	23,243	24,377	35,788	20,401	20,486	17,712	69.1	183,800	885
Queen Creek...................	95,712	13.1	14.3	109,361	0	55,633	72,351	29,597	13,295	11,617	86.0	315,300	1,456
Sahuarita.......................	78,549	6.0	2.6	82,779	44,284	40,929	54,193	28,400	11,272	10,507	83.4	205,700	1,260
San Luis.........................	36,890	24.3	2.9	39,078	16,255	15,765	20,917	11,935	8,949	8,577	75.4	116,100	718
Scottsdale......................	81,381	10.7	15.7	108,661	51,474	46,809	56,496	36,661	135,962	112,795	65.4	439,300	1,256
Sierra Vista	49,864	18.1	1.3	51,143	44,456	24,942	29,481	21,705	20,502	18,104	51.4	163,400	899
Surprise..........................	60,521	9.3	2.2	64,432	45,161	35,027	41,754	29,872	55,148	46,771	77.8	225,700	1,269
Tempe............................	56,365	19.6	4.5	74,342	37,856	29,764	31,196	26,922	79,258	71,710	42.6	252,400	1,092
Tucson...........................	40,021	27.0	1.5	48,358	25,751	22,274	23,730	21,419	233,782	207,065	50.5	144,000	783
Yuma.............................	42,731	19.2	2.1	47,030	27,882	26,875	33,128	21,221	41,892	34,416	60.4	134,800	744
ARKANSAS....................	44,334	21.7	2.9	55,484	25,339	27,687	31,890	23,450	1,354,801	1,142,718	64.6	123,300	701
Bella Vista	64,728	8.7	4.2	74,389	47,188	35,575	35,896	33,951	13,142	12,381	82.4	161,200	876
Benton............................	70,130	13.1	5.6	87,511	29,790	33,374	40,510	30,620	14,425	12,936	71.0	146,400	721
Bentonville	79,761	10.8	10.3	98,076	62,105	45,710	52,757	37,335	18,540	17,553	55.7	210,400	875
Conway	49,183	19.0	3.6	64,813	31,608	27,317	30,049	22,192	26,530	23,305	49.3	170,400	787
Fayetteville	38,202	28.2	5.4	66,963	25,901	24,066	26,444	21,229	34,509	33,903	34.6	199,400	766
Fort Smith	38,051	24.4	1.7	46,375	23,177	24,166	26,872	21,364	40,330	36,368	50.8	115,400	651
Hot Springs	37,361	28.0	2.5	48,616	24,167	22,421	25,743	20,852	19,953	16,123	59.2	117,900	617

1. Specified owner-occupied units; $2,000,000 represents $2,000,000 or more.

Table D. Cities — **Commuting, Computer Access, Migration, Labor Force, and Employment**

AREANAME	Commuting[1] 2016 Percent		Computer access[2] Percent		Migration		Civilian labor force, 2016				Civilian employment, 2016			
									Unemployment[3]		Population age 16 and older		Population age 16 to 64	
	Drove alone	With commutes of 30 minutes or more	With a computer in the house	With Internet access	Percent who lived in the same house one year ago	Percent who lived in another state or county one year ago	Total	Percent change 2016-2017	Total	Rate	Number	Percent in labor force	Number	Percent who worked full-year full-time
	55	56	57	58	59	60	61	62	63	64	65	66	67	68
United States..................	76.3	38.0	89.3	81.2	85.4	6.3	160,588,515	1.0	6,994,415	4.4	257,950,721	63.1	208,735,556	49.8
ALABAMA	86.1	34.5	83.9	74.3	86.1	5.9	2,168,444	-0.2	95,338	4.4	3,897,741	57.3	3,113,789	46.7
Alabaster............................	91.7	52.4	95.2	88.9	89.2	4.2	17,559	-0.2	560	3.2	25,117	60.6	21,082	50.9
Auburn................................	79.5	25.0	97.2	89.2	68.9	20.3	29,389	1.5	1,215	4.1	54,101	59.7	48,958	35.3
Bessemer............................	NA	24.3	77.6	66.2	83.9	3.1	9,664	-1.9	582	6.0	22,090	54.9	16,125	37.1
Birmingham.......................	81.5	24.8	83.5	70.8	81.4	5.7	91,670	-0.9	4,817	5.3	173,787	61.6	143,758	44.7
Decatur..............................	91.9	26.8	85.0	73.6	80.2	7.3	26,024	-0.2	1,073	4.1	43,871	56.8	35,005	45.5
Dothan................................	87.3	19.5	83.6	75.5	85.4	4.8	29,149	-0.3	1,274	4.4	53,608	57.9	42,153	47.5
Enterprise..........................	88.8	18.9	88.7	82.0	76.6	10.0	10,839	0.2	468	4.3	20,647	63.0	17,055	45.5
Florence.............................	90.5	23.3	77.5	67.0	71.2	14.9	18,079	-1.5	822	4.5	33,772	52.1	26,325	40.3
Gadsden.............................	77.4	19.3	78.6	67.5	76.0	8.3	13,594	-1.0	737	5.4	28,773	49.8	23,316	39.4
Homewood.........................	80.7	15.8	95.5	90.0	74.9	10.1	13,935	-0.1	416	3.0	21,828	75.9	19,452	53.8
Hoover...............................	82.5	33.0	95.3	91.4	82.2	6.6	44,223	-0.1	1,373	3.1	66,627	69.2	54,067	56.5
Huntsville..........................	87.2	20.3	90.5	83.3	79.2	7.4	94,140	0.9	3,805	4.0	155,191	64.1	126,563	50.3
Madison.............................	91.3	20.0	99.4	95.1	83.9	8.4	24,496	1.1	855	3.5	39,114	74.3	34,111	55.7
Mobile...............................	84.3	26.0	80.3	68.1	85.5	4.1	86,166	-0.9	4,627	5.4	158,492	57.5	126,431	47.5
Montgomery......................	84.3	20.3	85.6	79.0	79.7	7.9	92,498	-0.2	4,081	4.4	157,686	62.7	130,561	48.2
Opelika..............................	77.7	26.1	83.9	76.8	81.7	7.0	13,923	1.6	561	4.0	21,865	67.7	17,615	58.9
Phenix City.......................	89.4	32.2	84.2	71.6	83.9	11.0	15,183	0.0	598	3.9	27,874	65.9	23,748	53.6
Prattville............................	89.7	30.8	89.5	82.3	85.3	9.5	17,063	0.1	628	3.7	27,409	62.2	22,180	54.6
Tuscaloosa........................	81.2	16.3	83.1	72.5	75.4	14.5	45,609	-0.1	2,210	4.8	83,574	60.2	72,447	40.7
Vestavia Hills....................	89.1	20.1	92.2	87.4	82.7	7.4	17,653	0.0	497	2.8	25,124	64.8	20,264	54.6
ALASKA	69.0	15.3	93.9	85.8	81.2	8.0	362,783	-0.1	25,977	7.2	575,088	70.2	499,256	46.5
Anchorage.........................	76.3	13.5	96.0	91.7	79.7	6.3	155,462	-0.2	9,287	6.0	232,183	73.2	203,098	52.9
Fairbanks..........................	73.6	7.1	91.1	79.9	67.7	20.7	12,831	0.6	973	7.6	26,130	74.9	23,881	53.8
Juneau...............................	67.8	10.2	95.3	89.7	77.4	13.3	17,435	0.4	828	4.7	26,074	70.7	22,438	52.3
ARIZONA	76.5	36.2	90.8	82.9	81.5	6.6	3,312,720	2.7	161,315	4.9	5,483,490	59.4	4,313,664	47.7
Apache Junction	77.2	42.7	87.3	76.6	77.4	15.8	14,711	3.0	910	6.2	33,359	43.6	19,104	42.4
Avondale............................	80.0	49.1	92.8	83.1	85.9	3.9	42,780	3.1	1,878	4.4	62,136	67.4	53,943	55.1
Buckeye.............................	75.5	51.2	96.5	89.8	82.8	8.4	26,288	3.1	1,354	5.2	49,466	49.6	40,935	43.5
Bullhead City.....................	73.9	17.1	84.4	80.8	79.6	12.5	16,477	2.6	980	5.9	33,124	45.9	21,553	41.1
Casa Grande......................	74.8	30.1	94.1	86.8	73.1	12.1	24,013	3.5	1,272	5.3	39,592	52.8	30,926	40.8
Chandler............................	81.0	33.8	96.8	89.3	80.1	6.6	142,010	3.2	5,338	3.8	191,336	72.6	165,254	58.3
El Mirage...........................	80.6	51.8	94.9	82.5	92.0	1.1	16,275	3.0	745	4.6	24,828	68.9	21,999	50.6
Flagstaff............................	68.9	9.9	96.1	85.8	63.1	22.3	41,841	2.4	1,665	4.0	61,014	65.3	55,088	37.3
Florence.............................	NA	38.3	86.7	80.1	74.8	20.0	3,390	2.4	179	5.3	24,297	10.3	19,509	8.0
Gilbert................................	79.4	42.5	98.4	95.8	77.3	8.5	131,473	3.2	4,585	3.5	170,580	69.7	148,783	54.7
Glendale............................	75.5	44.6	92.4	77.4	82.3	5.5	121,277	3.1	5,495	4.5	193,895	64.8	164,455	50.9
Goodyear...........................	76.8	48.6	97.9	90.2	83.9	4.6	36,972	3.0	1,586	4.3	59,485	58.8	48,620	51.9
Kingman.............................	86.1	15.4	89.5	80.9	81.7	8.7	12,935	3.0	734	5.7	23,335	51.4	17,013	45.4
Lake Havasu City..............	85.8	23.7	88.8	85.3	75.7	14.2	23,748	2.9	1,292	5.4	47,286	46.5	28,840	41.9
Marana..............................	76.4	49.3	96.6	93.1	83.2	4.5	22,163	2.0	797	3.6	35,350	52.0	24,542	50.0
Maricopa...........................	70.4	61.7	95.0	92.1	77.8	8.4	23,833	3.9	1,141	4.8	35,591	67.7	30,507	47.6
Mesa..................................	76.5	34.7	90.9	86.0	80.6	5.6	239,712	3.1	9,984	4.2	378,327	64.1	299,533	51.9
Oro Valley.........................	77.0	39.0	94.2	91.4	81.3	8.8	19,182	1.9	828	4.3	37,346	49.4	23,373	46.7
Peoria................................	79.7	43.6	94.9	89.2	85.6	5.1	85,252	3.1	3,414	4.0	129,879	62.2	101,254	53.1
Phoenix.............................	73.7	38.7	90.4	81.5	82.4	3.9	811,570	3.1	34,946	4.3	1,226,153	66.9	1,058,372	51.5
Prescott.............................	78.0	14.5	89.1	83.5	79.2	12.3	17,867	2.7	906	5.1	39,461	43.0	23,403	39.4
Prescott Valley..................	74.3	25.1	92.1	82.5	86.8	6.6	20,956	3.0	879	4.2	35,541	47.2	23,958	42.0
Queen Creek......................	74.2	56.2	NA	NA	82.9	10.0	17,775	3.5	622	3.5	24,933	69.2	22,472	56.7
Sahuarita...........................	88.6	44.9	95.8	93.3	86.7	6.2	12,242	1.6	477	3.9	22,145	46.9	15,039	52.8
San Luis............................	75.3	60.5	82.0	79.5	87.1	4.9	17,377	-5.4	6,508	37.5	23,970	62.2	22,276	31.7
Scottsdale.........................	78.0	31.5	95.8	91.4	82.9	6.9	139,861	3.2	4,893	3.5	213,234	60.8	153,545	53.8
Sierra Vista	79.2	14.5	91.2	78.5	78.1	17.0	18,184	0.4	904	5.0	34,472	52.4	25,063	46.5
Surprise.............................	82.2	49.3	96.2	92.3	89.2	4.3	55,570	3.1	2,511	4.5	103,516	52.0	72,730	47.9
Tempe................................	72.3	21.8	96.0	86.5	73.9	9.3	109,401	3.1	4,277	3.9	159,818	69.5	140,846	46.3
Tucson	74.6	27.3	90.0	83.7	74.3	7.6	254,150	1.7	11,913	4.7	428,481	62.2	355,229	41.8
Yuma.................................	80.2	11.8	87.0	81.5	71.8	10.5	43,995	3.0	4,889	11.1	71,277	61.3	57,332	47.4
ARKANSAS....................	83.1	26.1	84.6	70.6	84.2	6.4	1,354,265	0.9	49,831	3.7	2,358,465	57.5	1,872,835	48.1
Bella Vista.........................	90.4	40.5	94.2	76.4	83.6	9.1	12,357	3.5	455	3.7	24,026	50.8	14,187	58.0
Benton...............................	NA	46.7	91.3	84.2	85.5	9.7	17,266	1.4	505	2.9	26,666	71.4	22,402	64.8
Bentonville........................	88.1	10.0	94.1	60.5	84.0	7.9	25,416	3.6	741	2.9	36,363	70.8	33,111	60.4
Conway..............................	79.8	22.6	91.4	82.0	83.8	9.2	33,580	1.2	1,099	3.3	53,045	60.9	46,938	47.5
Fayetteville.......................	76.0	16.6	96.4	81.3	69.6	13.2	47,255	3.2	1,252	2.6	69,308	61.5	62,666	38.0
Fort Smith	82.1	10.7	86.2	73.9	80.8	6.8	39,805	-0.9	1,424	3.6	69,132	55.1	54,464	46.5
Hot Springs	77.4	19.4	83.5	71.6	84.8	6.5	14,557	0.7	639	4.4	31,999	53.7	23,249	47.8

1. Employed persons. 2. Households. 3. Percent of civilian labor force.

Table D. Cities — Construction, Wholesale Trade, and Retail Trade

AREANAME	Value of residential construction authorized by building permits, 2017			Wholesale trade[1], 2012				Retail trade[2], 2012			
	New construction ($1,000)	Number of housing units	Percent single family	Number of establishments	Number of employees	Sales (mil dol)	Annual payroll (mil dol)	Number of establishments	Number of employees	Sales (mil dol)	Annual payroll (mil dol)
	69	70	71	72	73	74	75	76	77	78	79
United States	258,505,416	1,281,977	64.0	355,983	4,880,666	5,208,023.5	287,549.6	1,062,083	14,703,529	4,219,821.9	369,001.4
ALABAMA	2,772,775	14,799	82.7	4,600	60,332	57,746.6	2,894.7	18,211	218,531	58,565.0	5,123.1
Alabaster	NA	NA	NA	44	579	489.1	26.3	92	1,773	388.8	39.2
Auburn	262,022	963	59.5	34	217	235.5	9.0	206	3,180	779.4	70.4
Bessemer	6,330	41	100.0	58	944	417.9	52.0	194	2,746	732.0	70.4
Birmingham	19,355	103	94.2	500	9,168	7,099.9	481.8	943	12,300	3,305.9	318.1
Decatur	10,969	47	100.0	77	1,316	1,022.6	56.7	332	4,256	1,140.4	99.1
Dothan	52,810	186	98.9	148	D	D	D	501	7,114	1,990.0	173.0
Enterprise	11,219	80	88.8	11	38	13.6	1.4	155	1,802	521.3	47.9
Florence	28,475	594	12.8	49	584	209.3	22.4	302	4,139	967.8	88.7
Gadsden	1,364	12	100.0	39	351	293.5	14.5	229	3,037	731.2	60.6
Homewood	16,774	40	100.0	65	775	499.4	42.2	224	3,152	662.1	76.7
Hoover	81,233	284	100.0	80	1,134	2,347.7	102.5	384	7,578	2,425.7	200.6
Huntsville	88,517	1,524	75.1	225	3,051	3,197.3	168.8	999	14,677	3,945.3	360.9
Madison	169,285	558	100.0	52	728	426.2	39.6	131	2,356	550.6	52.7
Mobile	39,373	366	31.1	353	4,191	2,717.6	205.9	968	14,109	3,661.5	339.7
Montgomery	38,872	260	100.0	274	4,739	3,703.7	214.7	874	11,871	3,163.3	294.6
Opelika	53,413	212	100.0	32	373	261.3	18.4	206	2,732	725.2	58.3
Phenix City	19,660	136	38.2	10	D	D	D	125	1,683	413.4	36.8
Prattville	51,711	188	100.0	19	84	33.2	2.7	152	2,669	621.9	60.7
Tuscaloosa	154,069	917	34.9	77	955	638.5	48.4	475	6,821	1,782.8	149.8
Vestavia Hills	46,429	112	100.0	39	220	213.9	14.5	156	1,659	396.1	43.3
ALASKA	395,668	1,539	73.2	638	7,734	5,216.3	440.9	2,508	33,721	10,474.3	977.4
Anchorage	285,957	1,019	78.5	336	5,228	3,147.7	296.6	860	15,253	4,966.8	462.2
Fairbanks	0	0	0.0	47	531	309.2	29.6	208	3,630	1,300.3	116.3
Juneau	NA	NA	NA	36	265	196.9	12.8	142	1,821	491.4	53.0
ARIZONA	8,701,276	39,472	71.1	5,570	73,496	69,437.3	4,144.3	17,479	286,184	84,716.5	7,367.8
Apache Junction	5,950	42	90.5	11	D	D	D	90	1,591	515.0	41.0
Avondale	61,505	252	100.0	15	161	73.6	8.2	113	3,480	1,360.9	107.5
Buckeye	531,670	2,195	100.0	15	106	71.4	4.9	50	597	260.8	14.1
Bullhead City	35,351	143	100.0	9	64	26.3	2.4	119	2,195	552.0	52.5
Casa Grande	27,810	114	100.0	25	403	196.3	17.9	190	3,440	896.6	75.4
Chandler	452,428	2,230	27.6	228	4,007	5,269.8	257.8	658	13,607	4,225.0	382.5
El Mirage	2,466	9	100.0	4	36	16.5	1.3	26	498	117.5	12.0
Flagstaff	110,050	499	47.3	68	554	377.7	26.2	322	5,224	1,383.9	120.5
Florence	74,383	218	100.0	1	D	D	D	12	142	39.9	3.1
Gilbert	288,570	1,709	93.6	143	1,264	666.2	63.7	470	9,470	2,762.7	251.0
Glendale	151,528	643	26.7	118	1,188	834.2	47.7	674	12,710	3,821.3	320.8
Goodyear	363,846	1,434	76.4	23	D	D	D	141	3,318	788.1	74.7
Kingman	46,683	286	95.8	22	211	115.2	7.7	128	2,586	896.1	59.8
Lake Havasu City	68,161	341	96.5	48	223	86.2	9.0	215	2,843	914.5	71.1
Marana	235,677	788	100.0	20	108	41.2	5.1	114	2,868	865.1	73.1
Maricopa	203,524	844	100.0	7	16	4.6	0.6	26	729	213.8	16.1
Mesa	774,940	3,014	74.7	292	3,313	2,705.3	168.9	1,315	22,342	5,819.7	549.5
Oro Valley	96,889	335	100.0	23	57	52.4	3.6	90	2,092	496.7	46.5
Peoria	345,020	2,391	72.4	60	289	266.3	12.7	387	8,515	2,657.7	235.0
Phoenix	1,302,805	6,832	42.9	1,853	30,877	31,193.7	1,638.2	3,712	60,797	18,448.4	1,620.7
Prescott	107,879	335	96.1	62	557	453.8	29.8	279	4,290	1,030.2	102.4
Prescott Valley	174,213	937	53.0	31	430	305.1	15.7	100	1,348	360.2	32.2
Queen Creek	336,002	1,076	100.0	7	14	5.0	0.6	50	973	227.1	20.0
Sahuarita	75,562	287	100.0	3	D	D	D	23	730	192.6	16.4
San Luis	32,903	248	100.0	8	233	36.1	11.0	36	591	136.0	10.2
Scottsdale	292,945	632	88.6	505	4,707	4,011.1	311.5	1,218	18,728	5,848.1	574.5
Sierra Vista	10,629	63	100.0	12	86	25.4	2.4	160	2,810	686.5	63.9
Surprise	265,424	951	85.8	27	401	159.2	16.0	169	4,396	1,137.0	105.7
Tempe	116,744	708	10.2	436	8,635	8,373.2	562.7	755	14,805	7,231.6	431.6
Tucson	369,565	2,047	34.6	446	4,468	2,221.8	192.0	1,883	30,599	7,878.2	774.0
Yuma	104,879	614	85.0	80	1,615	963.8	67.0	302	5,503	1,528.9	132.8
ARKANSAS	1,766,488	10,795	68.3	2,884	34,492	31,256.1	1,630.8	10,923	135,448	36,815.3	3,061.5
Bella Vista	50,328	194	100.0	12	20	21.6	0.9	25	307	60.7	5.8
Benton	30,566	146	100.0	23	138	130.1	5.6	127	1,859	659.5	46.2
Bentonville	183,359	903	50.8	86	1,135	1,338.4	79.1	119	2,488	1,024.2	68.7
Conway	49,075	304	64.1	57	618	460.6	27.8	284	4,730	1,246.1	100.9
Fayetteville	108,874	457	100.0	54	550	372.7	25.1	419	7,043	1,766.8	156.5
Fort Smith	51,229	375	25.3	171	2,184	1,605.2	98.1	521	7,161	1,767.6	157.2
Hot Springs	8,652	36	100.0	43	409	151.5	14.7	364	4,655	1,242.1	108.3

1. Merchant wholesalers except manufacturers' sales branches and offices. 2. Establishments with payroll.

Table D. Cities — Real Estate, Professional Services, and Manufacturing

AREANAME	Real estate and rental and leasing, 2012				Professional, scientific, and technical services[1], 2012				Manufacturing, 2012			
	Number of establishments	Number of employees	Receipts (mil dol)	Annual payroll (mil dol)	Number of establishments	Number of employees	Receipts (mil dol)	Annual payroll (mil dol)	Number of establishments	Number of employees	Receipts (mil dol)	Annual payroll (mil dol)
	80	81	82	83	84	85	86	87	88	89	90	91
United States..................	354,106	1,923,770	487,655.2	85,326.0	851,542	7,997,617	1,440,060.5	566,412.5	297,191	11,214,165	5,696,729.6	593,397.0
ALABAMA	3,858	22,852	3,919.4	819.6	9,062	88,566	16,043.5	5,633.1	4,283	232,650	124,809.8	11,099.5
Alabaster............................	17	54	11.1	1.8	58	528	119.8	20.0	26	1,145	478.6	63.1
Auburn................................	54	299	45.0	8.5	125	1,074	102.4	44.3	60	3,523	D	141.7
Bessemer............................	27	159	26.3	6.6	72	D	D	D	41	1,549	466.6	70.1
Birmingham........................	281	3,076	417.2	129.1	834	D	D	D	249	10,654	4,118.4	568.2
Decatur...............................	57	218	43.9	6.7	139	978	110.2	44.0	82	4,735	4,680.9	284.7
Dothan	94	D	D	D	192	D	D	D	78	D	1,285.1	D
Enterprise..........................	40	198	19.6	4.1	49	425	74.3	21.0	18	844	D	32.6
Florence.............................	77	309	47.2	9.1	134	D	D	D	53	2,616	631.6	82.3
Gadsden.............................	39	182	34.3	5.0	99	1,065	55.2	29.2	48	3,839	1,058.2	162.3
Homewood.........................	59	362	70.9	17.5	157	1,291	225.2	76.1	24	1,121	564.1	55.4
Hoover...............................	95	675	274.1	36.2	281	D	D	D	25	345	49.7	13.1
Huntsville...........................	311	D	D	D	999	28,634	6,933.7	2,324.3	173	13,598	6,213.8	771.4
Madison..............................	56	266	48.8	8.9	150	D	D	D	32	977	D	48.4
Mobile	310	1,554	312.4	60.4	701	D	D	D	152	8,817	3,274.4	471.1
Montgomery........................	219	1,890	339.1	64.8	575	5,871	1,258.6	386.5	172	10,902	9,125.1	528.6
Opelika..............................	40	149	17.8	4.0	62	D	D	D	34	2,067	D	93.7
Phenix City........................	34	95	16.7	2.5	46	170	16.6	4.4	31	D	1,110.6	113.0
Prattville............................	35	138	20.4	3.9	54	276	28.7	10.8	15	839	651.5	54.1
Tuscaloosa.........................	124	1,192	129.1	35.8	232	1,584	260.5	78.4	53	4,454	4,234.8	221.7
Vestavia Hills.....................	81	1,191	389.9	73.2	173	D	D	D	15	47	D	1.9
ALASKA	872	4,212	1,022.7	187.6	1,866	17,328	3,140.3	1,163.5	527	12,450	D	514.5
Anchorage..........................	383	2,403	631.3	112.1	1,128	13,444	2,515.7	954.8	182	2,049	479.8	95.7
Fairbanks	88	468	116.2	25.1	137	D	D	D	37	239	D	10.7
Juneau	61	249	42.2	7.0	86	D	D	D	26	236	75.4	11.7
ARIZONA..........................	8,089	40,479	9,329.7	1,693.2	16,112	119,843	19,041.9	7,272.6	4,269	131,941	51,243.5	8,193.2
Apache Junction	40	141	22.6	2.6	22	76	7.6	2.2	13	85	D	3.5
Avondale............................	42	118	15.7	3.1	47	197	14.8	5.4	9	29	12.9	1.5
Buckeye.............................	19	59	9.6	2.0	37	196	32.4	10.6	11	203	D	6.4
Bullhead City......................	52	187	20.0	4.5	45	D	D	D	6	39	D	1.3
Casa Grande......................	52	198	39.6	5.6	59	D	D	D	37	1,753	1,807.3	96.5
Chandler............................	304	896	252.4	34.7	642	3,678	535.3	203.9	165	7,413	2,535.2	459.9
El Mirage...........................	10	D	D	D	7	18	2.4	0.4	13	251	74.4	12.3
Flagstaff	129	450	101.0	16.3	249	D	D	D	58	3,453	2,006.0	287.8
Florence.............................	4	D	D	D	8	23	1.4	0.8	NA	NA	NA	NA
Gilbert...............................	292	787	170.2	33.4	533	D	D	D	118	1,887	338.2	84.8
Glendale............................	215	820	160.3	26.3	308	D	D	D	134	2,988	829.9	156.5
Goodyear............................	62	136	25.4	4.4	88	480	48.3	24.1	22	1,220	384.0	58.7
Kingman.............................	35	94	14.4	2.6	48	D	D	D	11	133	47.4	5.1
Lake Havasu City................	80	277	38.8	6.6	96	319	26.2	9.5	65	916	217.3	34.4
Marana..............................	31	81	12.7	2.8	57	D	D	D	30	1,028	344.7	59.1
Maricopa...........................	15	29	4.7	0.7	38	94	6.4	4.0	11	148	D	6.4
Mesa.................................	547	2,280	456.6	72.6	1,021	5,199	668.1	255.6	245	7,319	3,353.0	583.2
Oro Valley	60	D	D	D	123	447	49.3	36.5	10	2,279	803.0	215.5
Peoria...............................	156	621	111.0	20.1	219	D	D	D	49	874	177.8	36.4
Phoenix.............................	1,894	13,507	2,965.5	673.8	4,848	43,895	7,794.4	2,992.6	1,338	38,642	12,978.9	2,175.5
Prescott.............................	127	254	52.5	7.3	218	D	D	D	61	1,457	404.8	76.0
Prescott Valley...................	36	99	21.8	4.0	42	336	43.9	21.0	31	603	149.6	24.3
Queen Creek......................	24	D	D	D	52	136	13.3	4.6	5	27	D	1.3
Sahuarita...........................	10	17	2.7	0.4	14	34	3.1	1.2	3	D	D	D
San Luis............................	5	D	D	D	6	D	D	D	5	D	D	D
Scottsdale..........................	983	5,713	2,175.5	276.0	1,986	D	D	D	216	7,082	4,532.5	612.3
Sierra Vista	60	317	42.5	9.0	103	D	D	D	11	57	7.8	1.7
Surprise.............................	63	148	31.2	4.2	81	D	D	D	19	281	143.7	8.9
Tempe...............................	407	3,684	1,027.0	165.6	970	12,464	2,302.8	772.1	373	15,660	5,445.1	914.4
Tucson	735	3,966	628.3	129.9	1,563	10,568	1,457.1	581.5	393	6,648	1,551.5	312.7
Yuma................................	124	513	71.6	14.0	171	D	D	D	42	1,800	785.5	71.2
ARKANSAS....................	2,802	12,867	1,922.7	409.8	5,655	31,871	4,464.9	1,549.2	2,688	153,706	62,712.9	6,290.8
Bella Vista.........................	24	D	D	D	34	65	9.3	2.6	NA	NA	NA	NA
Benton...............................	26	53	14.9	1.3	62	250	26.1	8.8	35	561	133.7	24.4
Bentonville.........................	67	286	68.9	14.3	225	D	D	D	21	304	135.3	12.0
Conway..............................	94	402	98.9	17.6	168	D	D	D	54	3,479	1,156.6	168.0
Fayetteville........................	137	2,012	133.0	52.1	364	1,850	231.9	87.0	57	4,106	1,031.7	156.0
Fort Smith	156	813	124.2	25.5	272	D	D	D	148	13,228	4,983.3	538.8
Hot Springs	73	302	48.2	8.4	147	D	D	D	33	800	147.3	37.0

1. Establishments subject to federal tax.

Accommodation and Food Services, Arts, Entertainment, and Recreation, and Health Care and Social Assistance

AREANAME	Accommodaton and food services, 2012				Arts, entertainment, and recreation[1], 2012				Health care and social assistance,[1] 2012			
	Number of establish-ments	Number of employees	Receipts (mil dol)	Annual payroll (mil dol)	Number of establish-ments	Number of employees	Receipts (mil dol)	Annual payroll (mil dol)	Number of establish-ments	Number of employees	Receipts (mil dol)	Annual payroll (mil dol)
	92	93	94	95	96	97	98	99	100	101	102	103
United States..................	662,489	12,007,689	708,138.6	196,103.3	99,659	1,486,462	161,690.3	50,328.5	690,525	9,542,138	1,008,744.6	409,811.9
ALABAMA	8,339	157,337	7,576.5	2,071.1	782	10,487	885.0	178.3	8,489	142,386	14,627.8	5,995.0
Alabaster......................	48	1,162	60.6	17.0	5	D	D	D	85	D	D	D
Auburn	198	3,581	163.3	41.4	13	D	D	D	103	D	D	D
Bessemer......................	95	1,734	86.8	24.2	7	89	6.5	2.0	85	D	D	D
Birmingham...................	564	11,239	625.3	185.7	38	570	38.8	10.9	615	12,973	1,675.5	690.7
Decatur.........................	140	2,847	134.6	38.0	10	171	6.8	2.2	217	2,511	271.7	95.3
Dothan..........................	223	4,538	209.2	56.1	18	D	D	D	257	D	D	D
Enterprise.....................	73	1,202	58.3	14.4	9	D	D	D	75	D	D	D
Florence.......................	129	3,445	141.4	42.9	10	D	D	D	183	3,575	406.3	142.1
Gadsden.......................	90	2,203	101.3	27.6	6	D	D	D	182	5,271	564.2	244.0
Homewood....................	117	2,294	132.3	35.5	6	D	D	D	182	5,513	800.3	271.4
Hoover..........................	187	4,241	244.5	72.4	20	213	19.4	3.1	219	3,211	266.0	124.0
Huntsville.....................	527	11,685	575.1	162.0	53	831	33.1	12.8	596	9,963	1,301.2	536.7
Madison	109	1,795	93.9	24.8	11	105	3.9	1.2	110	D	D	D
Mobile..........................	488	10,868	488.5	134.3	41	1,339	25.6	7.7	469	10,192	1,150.0	515.1
Montgomery..................	471	9,716	462.3	127.8	28	D	D	D	539	D	D	D
Opelika.........................	98	2,049	94.4	25.6	3	D	D	D	82	D	D	D
Phenix City...................	67	1,285	60.2	14.6	3	D	D	D	53	D	D	D
Prattville......................	85	2,148	103.2	28.2	7	D	D	D	73	D	D	D
Tuscaloosa....................	284	6,941	344.2	86.9	13	157	8.5	3.2	217	D	D	D
Vestavia Hills	77	1,770	83.6	23.4	13	226	19.2	8.0	118	D	D	D
ALASKA	2,126	26,836	2,221.3	626.0	441	4,161	328.4	68.0	1,851	21,389	2,810.2	1,098.5
Anchorage.....................	788	14,957	1,106.2	338.1	108	D	D	D	962	12,792	1,783.5	682.5
Fairbanks......................	138	2,215	177.4	46.9	31	D	D	D	165	2,316	301.7	136.0
Juneau	119	1,329	81.5	24.1	27	D	D	D	92	644	90.1	33.2
ARIZONA	11,669	251,455	13,996.6	4,030.3	1,424	33,881	3,279.3	1,088.3	15,041	184,186	20,221.1	7,974.6
Apache Junction	45	665	28.9	7.9	4	D	D	D	48	1,078	84.4	37.2
Avondale.......................	86	1,658	82.7	22.2	7	D	D	D	104	1,026	109.9	35.9
Buckeye........................	46	798	35.8	9.3	4	163	5.7	2.3	16	D	D	D
Bullhead City.................	85	1,091	54.2	14.5	7	167	4.0	1.5	109	2,009	285.4	97.3
Casa Grande.................	114	D	D	D	7	D	D	D	144	1,810	164.5	71.2
Chandler.......................	474	10,996	559.8	181.3	63	2,325	434.4	62.7	676	7,874	833.7	289.4
El Mirage......................	11	128	7.1	1.6	NA	NA	NA	NA	6	D	D	D
Flagstaff.......................	300	6,034	326.5	86.4	29	440	27.4	9.3	286	2,220	273.8	105.4
Florence	24	D	D	D	2	D	D	D	17	D	D	D
Gilbert..........................	287	6,139	297.6	85.7	48	1,045	48.7	14.8	619	5,146	520.0	191.9
Glendale.......................	381	8,050	387.3	108.4	40	D	D	D	574	7,794	931.5	370.5
Goodyear......................	113	2,899	141.1	39.2	12	D	D	D	129	3,464	369.7	146.7
Kingman........................	92	1,681	74.6	21.2	5	D	D	D	103	D	D	D
Lake Havasu City...........	134	2,333	97.3	29.5	12	D	D	D	165	2,272	263.2	93.2
Marana.........................	96	2,178	121.3	36.3	14	454	19.5	9.8	44	D	D	D
Maricopa.......................	30	479	23.2	5.9	3	D	D	D	33	D	D	D
Mesa............................	733	14,688	685.3	202.1	76	1,920	85.3	29.5	1,135	14,098	1,418.9	568.5
Oro Valley.....................	67	1,998	87.2	30.1	14	D	D	D	117	D	D	D
Peoria...........................	243	5,889	281.9	85.8	31	480	28.5	9.0	368	4,425	462.6	214.7
Phoenix.........................	2,493	57,339	3,479.6	992.4	295	6,038	626.0	312.8	3,435	45,960	5,433.6	2,241.6
Prescott........................	154	2,390	116.7	34.9	17	163	10.3	3.5	323	3,046	292.3	110.1
Prescott Valley..............	75	1,112	49.3	14.8	11	241	7.4	2.9	103	1,203	95.9	41.0
Queen Creek..................	38	698	31.9	9.4	4	109	6.9	1.7	71	D	D	D
Sahuarita......................	19	438	15.1	4.0	2	D	D	D	19	D	D	D
San Luis........................	14	206	9.5	2.2	1	D	D	D	14	123	10.6	4.7
Scottsdale.....................	746	22,062	1,370.6	421.5	145	3,996	294.0	97.4	1,422	13,486	1,598.1	648.8
Sierra Vista...................	100	2,058	91.3	26.4	8	D	D	D	135	1,490	125.8	49.2
Surprise........................	140	3,145	151.8	42.8	11	210	10.9	4.1	165	1,110	119.2	43.1
Tempe..........................	563	12,672	646.1	183.9	60	1,217	267.5	181.7	507	7,866	855.5	321.6
Tucson..........................	1,214	26,136	1,235.4	350.0	117	1,487	61.4	17.9	1,485	19,878	2,194.4	824.6
Yuma............................	227	4,641	254.2	64.1	14	D	D	D	273	D	D	D
ARKANSAS...................	5,473	95,854	4,307.3	1,182.5	563	5,927	499.0	104.3	5,936	86,999	8,540.6	3,495.8
Bella Vista.....................	20	D	D	D	2	D	D	D	26	402	28.6	11.3
Benton..........................	62	1,080	51.2	13.5	9	53	1.6	0.5	80	1,254	91.3	43.5
Bentonville....................	123	2,365	111.2	30.2	10	119	8.0	2.2	99	1,121	120.3	44.2
Conway.........................	172	4,248	177.6	48.5	11	D	D	D	206	2,682	239.8	96.7
Fayetteville...................	326	6,288	270.4	77.3	28	309	13.5	4.3	304	4,648	483.1	202.3
Fort Smith.....................	245	5,188	232.1	67.2	16	D	D	D	299	6,889	843.4	335.9
Hot Springs...................	194	4,178	178.1	52.6	27	D	D	D	199	2,884	369.2	142.9

1. Establishments subject to federal tax.

AREANAME	Other services[1]				Government employment and payroll, 2012								
					Full-time equivalent employees	March payroll	Percent of total for:						
	Number of establishments	Number of employees	Receipts (mil dol)	Annual payroll (mil dol)		Total (dollars)	Administrative, judicial, and legal	Police and corrections	Fire protection	Highways and transportation	Health and welfare	Natural resources and utilities	Education and libraries
	104	105	106	107	108	109	110	111	112	113	114	115	116
United States...............	422,719	2,543,493	230,974.9	69,948.3	X	X	X	X	X	X	X	X	X
ALABAMA	5,009	31,262	3,191.9	893.0	X	X	X	X	X	X	X	X	X
Alabaster........................	36	177	12.5	3.9	226	902,906	9.2	32.9	29.4	6.0	0.0	14.0	4.0
Auburn	70	342	24.8	7.2	541	1,872,172	15.3	25.8	16.5	9.6	0.9	24.2	4.1
Bessemer........................	45	470	67.5	19.5	570	2,109,401	7.5	25.2	23.3	0.5	0.9	32.7	1.8
Birmingham....................	308	3,072	292.1	97.3	4,784	19,867,336	9.5	27.6	17.4	3.5	0.9	29.6	4.1
Decatur	77	654	60.7	18.3	695	2,762,157	6.2	20.0	17.7	5.1	1.4	45.8	0.0
Dothan	145	D	D	D	980	3,540,917	11.7	22.1	20.0	3.1	0.8	33.9	0.0
Enterprise.......................	45	236	21.2	6.5	572	1,406,470	3.3	16.3	8.9	3.8	48.7	17.5	0.8
Florence.........................	70	471	30.4	9.5	814	2,966,594	5.4	16.5	13.1	6.3	0.6	51.8	0.0
Gadsden	51	332	33.7	10.1	813	2,569,152	8.3	19.3	20.9	8.8	0.9	30.2	2.8
Homewood	63	1,403	81.3	31.4	357	1,440,394	4.5	33.6	23.3	6.7	0.0	16.2	7.0
Hoover	79	450	43.0	12.5	663	3,382,691	10.6	31.1	26.9	5.3	0.7	8.2	7.7
Huntsville	269	2,553	476.6	101.5	2,636	11,833,638	8.9	19.0	14.5	7.2	2.2	32.4	0.0
Madison	54	366	30.0	9.7	374	1,553,149	16.6	30.8	22.6	2.6	0.0	24.9	0.0
Mobile	311	2,205	183.3	55.0	2,894	9,605,291	10.7	26.2	21.6	4.7	1.5	25.1	3.9
Montgomery....................	243	1,612	142.5	42.9	2,884	10,068,707	8.1	26.1	17.3	7.2	0.4	29.4	2.1
Opelika..........................	49	232	22.7	6.1	355	1,405,862	10.4	27.1	19.6	3.6	0.5	35.2	2.4
Phenix City.....................	46	253	19.0	6.6	795	2,466,225	53.9	13.6	9.1	2.5	0.4	18.3	0.5
Prattville	44	210	18.2	5.4	328	1,108,761	10.0	29.2	32.0	3.9	0.0	16.8	0.0
Tuscaloosa.....................	103	1,037	83.4	26.8	1,302	4,845,351	13.7	29.6	21.7	13.7	0.3	17.3	0.0
Vestavia Hills	55	493	33.3	12.2	264	1,136,169	7.5	27.3	44.1	1.9	0.0	6.9	5.2
ALASKA	882	4,807	495.9	152.7	X	X	X	X	X	X	X	X	X
Anchorage......................	400	2,688	261.8	87.3	9,819	51,971,256	4.5	7.8	6.6	5.5	1.4	9.1	63.8
Fairbanks	82	408	40.9	12.3	207	1,185,064	19.9	35.9	23.3	6.8	8.7	5.4	0.0
Juneau	45	202	18.7	5.3	1,960	10,163,476	5.6	5.4	3.1	7.4	27.2	8.1	43.2
ARIZONA	7,025	46,847	4,192.9	1,223.9	X	X	X	X	X	X	X	X	X
Apache Junction	31	165	25.8	8.4	234	1,013,473	20.4	42.8	0.0	10.1	7.9	13.1	5.7
Avondale........................	58	399	27.3	8.4	512	2,677,540	26.3	33.3	15.4	3.4	3.4	12.3	1.8
Buckeye	12	37	3.0	0.8	391	1,821,664	27.3	19.8	28.2	3.6	1.6	9.5	2.0
Bullhead City..................	36	207	15.3	4.8	298	1,290,523	21.2	44.5	0.0	12.9	1.8	11.0	0.0
Casa Grande...................	61	361	28.4	8.8	385	1,771,597	18.0	31.5	19.5	7.8	0.7	17.0	3.4
Chandler	257	1,995	169.0	53.6	1,623	9,363,010	16.5	33.2	15.8	6.3	4.4	16.4	3.0
El Mirage	13	58	3.7	1.3	144	789,368	14.2	35.0	17.6	4.7	0.0	9.4	0.0
Flagstaff.........................	123	695	58.4	17.0	767	3,403,748	18.4	24.3	12.4	4.2	3.2	21.7	4.8
Florence.........................	3	D	D	D	163	645,551	22.7	26.9	19.9	12.8	1.7	13.7	2.3
Gilbert	212	1,299	91.0	27.5	1,117	5,590,864	15.8	33.0	20.5	2.9	0.1	18.9	0.0
Glendale.........................	250	1,436	143.9	40.6	1,775	9,436,681	12.7	32.7	19.8	5.2	1.8	16.0	2.7
Goodyear	48	281	17.3	5.6	482	2,715,439	27.9	20.6	25.2	2.4	0.0	14.0	0.0
Kingman	41	257	19.9	6.4	335	1,383,755	16.2	24.7	22.1	11.4	0.0	22.8	0.0
Lake Havasu City............	117	416	37.7	9.5	484	2,122,419	13.0	26.9	20.4	8.0	0.0	20.7	0.0
Marana	69	387	30.7	10.5	306	1,328,433	22.4	36.4	0.0	14.2	1.2	11.8	0.0
Maricopa	23	D	D	D	204	1,087,610	13.2	32.5	35.7	1.6	0.0	5.6	2.4
Mesa..............................	552	3,294	272.4	78.7	3,616	20,622,110	15.1	36.5	16.1	6.6	1.6	17.7	1.6
Oro Valley	49	327	22.6	8.3	311	1,409,218	13.9	47.7	0.0	6.6	0.8	15.0	4.3
Peoria............................	157	942	72.8	23.1	1,162	6,255,922	23.5	26.8	16.6	7.4	0.0	20.3	2.2
Phoenix..........................	1,631	14,684	1,515.2	403.1	13,392	69,633,897	11.5	35.6	16.7	9.5	5.0	18.7	1.5
Prescott..........................	111	551	45.7	13.9	538	2,411,836	19.0	24.9	16.7	6.7	0.0	14.5	3.4
Prescott Valley	54	199	17.3	4.8	189	851,635	20.9	38.1	0.0	4.8	7.5	7.0	8.5
Queen Creek...................	21	101	6.9	2.3	217	1,060,750	23.5	0.0	16.7	8.1	23.4	23.1	0.0
Sahuarita.......................	8	91	4.3	1.9	131	644,309	29.4	41.1	0.0	11.3	0.0	7.5	0.0
San Luis.........................	3	6	0.3	0.1	233	639,318	48.6	5.8	13.3	7.7	0.0	21.5	0.0
Scottsdale.......................	533	3,863	294.6	94.1	2,454	13,029,893	23.6	31.2	13.0	3.8	2.1	18.0	3.7
Sierra Vista.....................	47	253	19.6	6.5	380	1,580,863	16.3	28.2	17.1	6.7	1.2	17.2	2.1
Surprise..........................	87	462	30.5	9.9	738	4,192,160	14.5	25.4	22.6	5.1	6.0	22.1	0.0
Tempe............................	292	2,006	188.3	62.7	1,762	9,492,774	16.0	31.6	13.1	6.2	9.5	18.8	1.5
Tucson...........................	756	4,997	423.7	128.2	4,691	21,780,237	12.6	30.8	18.8	10.4	3.2	19.2	0.0
Yuma..............................	115	709	52.0	16.5	946	3,797,070	16.5	30.3	16.4	7.6	3.3	23.1	0.0
ARKANSAS....................	3,157	17,091	1,427.6	423.7	X	X	X	X	X	X	X	X	X
Bella Vista......................	11	D	D	D	93	498,217	10.0	35.9	53.0	1.1	0.0	0.0	0.0
Benton............................	48	216	21.4	5.5	270	875,166	13.5	25.7	22.5	4.2	2.4	27.6	0.0
Bentonville......................	62	475	27.9	13.7	435	1,712,143	20.1	20.9	18.7	4.1	0.0	33.1	3.1
Conway..........................	100	535	40.7	11.2	474	1,540,085	12.3	31.7	27.5	7.8	0.0	17.9	0.0
Fayetteville.....................	111	661	43.6	14.9	692	2,378,996	14.3	27.3	16.7	11.7	2.3	20.9	0.0
Fort Smith	143	751	62.0	17.6	880	3,505,049	10.2	26.1	17.9	14.1	2.6	29.1	0.0
Hot Springs	82	454	27.2	9.5	597	2,082,915	9.8	24.7	17.9	10.7	1.2	28.2	0.0

1. Establishments subject to federal tax.

Table D. Cities — **City Government Finances**

AREANAME	City government finances, 2012									
	General revenue							General expenditure		
	Intergovernmental			Taxes						
					Per capita[1] (dollars)				Per capita[1] (dollars)	
	Total (mil dol)	Total (mil dol)	Percent from state government	Total (mil dol)	Total	Property	Sales and gross receipts	Total (mil dol)	Total	Capital outlays
	117	118	119	120	121	122	123	124	125	126
United States...............	X	X	X	X	X	X	X	X	X	X
ALABAMA	X	X	X	X	X	X	X	X	X	X
Alabaster...........................	27.6	0.0	0.0	19.2	619	107	511	23.9	773	0
Auburn	94.7	3.9	77.7	64.8	1,135	368	766	67.3	1,180	135
Bessemer	51.9	5.8	81.8	34.8	1,279	240	1,039	52.4	1,924	4
Birmingham	436.4	42.3	52.9	334.4	1,583	243	985	466.4	2,207	235
Decatur	174.2	68.7	100.0	61.6	1,103	209	877	202.0	3,616	209
Dothan	93.4	4.5	88.0	70.5	1,046	66	980	98.8	1,467	83
Enterprise.........................	30.6	1.8	95.9	23.0	826	157	670	32.1	1,155	209
Florence	64.7	4.1	76.8	43.9	1,107	284	821	58.6	1,477	59
Gadsden	64.3	6.9	28.4	44.2	1,206	66	731	60.4	1,647	45
Homewood	54.6	1.8	36.5	50.5	1,996	632	1,363	51.4	2,034	100
Hoover	104.2	6.8	51.4	83.0	998	121	853	95.0	1,143	78
Huntsville	329.0	28.2	93.3	217.9	1,186	320	866	337.4	1,836	440
Madison	51.4	5.9	79.3	34.9	777	291	451	50.2	1,117	123
Mobile	353.3	20.4	65.4	248.6	1,275	83	1,192	344.5	1,767	296
Montgomery	280.1	36.3	46.1	169.8	830	151	679	218.0	1,065	80
Opelika	54.6	2.4	35.3	39.9	1,425	328	810	51.4	1,834	224
Phenix City........................	33.7	1.9	100.0	26.0	717	165	552	36.4	1,007	213
Prattville	35.5	1.0	99.2	26.5	765	71	695	28.2	814	6
Tuscaloosa........................	163.4	34.6	20.3	77.7	834	145	637	163.0	1,750	124
Vestavia Hills	34.2	1.8	33.1	29.1	857	387	470	34.6	1,017	160
ALASKA	X	X	X	X	X	X	X	X	X	X
Anchorage.........................	1,296.8	572.1	91.3	546.6	1,830	1,623	208	1,251.1	4,190	417
Fairbanks	42.7	11.6	100.0	21.4	659	432	227	39.7	1,220	110
Juneau..............................	316.5	94.8	75.9	83.0	2,561	1,130	1,431	302.2	9,325	1,605
ARIZONA	X	X	X	X	X	X	X	X	X	X
Apache Junction	26.7	11.0	100.0	11.6	316	0	316	29.2	793	0
Avondale...........................	84.4	25.7	100.0	40.9	523	67	456	73.8	945	93
Buckeye	61.1	12.9	69.2	27.9	512	172	339	48.2	882	7
Bullhead City.....................	48.4	17.4	91.6	11.3	286	0	285	42.5	1,075	35
Casa Grande.....................	70.3	17.3	83.1	29.4	586	128	458	77.3	1,541	234
Chandler	333.6	72.6	90.2	151.1	617	130	487	266.6	1,089	179
El Mirage	30.1	8.5	100.0	9.5	290	94	196	33.0	1,011	114
Flagstaff	130.0	35.8	90.1	54.3	801	176	624	120.0	1,768	130
Florence	23.1	8.7	80.8	6.8	254	38	210	20.6	772	122
Gilbert	261.7	63.3	83.0	136.2	614	108	503	189.6	854	154
Glendale............................	324.3	103.3	81.2	145.1	625	87	538	226.0	974	13
Goodyear	108.3	19.5	99.3	60.0	864	237	627	78.8	1,135	56
Kingman	39.6	14.2	100.0	12.5	439	0	439	31.4	1,108	1
Lake Havasu City..............	80.6	21.3	85.8	26.9	509	186	322	98.9	1,874	405
Marana	50.4	18.1	58.5	27.9	760	14	742	43.7	1,189	179
Maricopa	36.8	14.6	100.0	19.2	428	242	187	33.5	747	45
Mesa	511.1	172.3	70.6	156.6	346	32	309	601.2	1,330	186
Oro Valley	29.7	10.8	100.0	15.4	373	0	373	29.9	723	49
Peoria...............................	190.2	41.3	95.5	90.5	566	140	418	239.6	1,498	187
Phoenix.............................	2,902.9	848.4	63.4	987.1	663	152	507	2,651.7	1,780	445
Prescott............................	74.7	16.1	77.8	30.5	761	71	684	77.2	1,928	429
Prescott Valley	38.2	14.1	87.4	14.0	357	47	310	41.2	1,051	74
Queen Creek.....................	50.6	8.0	99.8	20.6	739	223	477	52.0	1,861	347
Sahuarita	26.6	12.6	63.4	10.0	379	11	368	22.4	852	221
San Luis	21.1	8.0	87.4	6.9	228	0	228	26.1	861	37
Scottsdale	477.7	126.1	80.7	238.4	1,068	291	776	562.4	2,518	823
Sierra Vista	48.4	13.6	97.0	18.9	407	9	398	48.8	1,052	142
Surprise............................	112.2	31.8	91.0	40.3	332	56	276	106.8	880	55
Tempe...............................	344.4	69.4	71.3	183.5	1,097	215	883	286.8	1,715	177
Tucson	736.3	277.8	53.0	280.3	534	76	458	608.5	1,159	174
Yuma.................................	125.5	30.9	90.5	51.1	545	108	435	125.6	1,341	167
ARKANSAS...................	X	X	X	X	X	X	X	X	X	X
Bella Vista	12.2	6.0	28.9	3.3	122	28	94	12.1	440	15
Benton..............................	23.3	4.6	40.9	12.8	398	73	324	22.8	712	138
Bentonville	57.6	8.2	48.3	30.3	790	159	630	57.0	1,486	389
Conway	95.8	7.8	55.2	33.5	532	61	471	88.6	1,408	244
Fayetteville	107.6	24.4	45.2	48.2	626	53	572	96.7	1,256	246
Fort Smith	133.9	29.8	38.6	61.3	700	146	554	126.0	1,439	456
Hot Springs	69.7	12.2	60.6	26.7	752	1	751	69.2	1,951	328

1. Based on population estimated as of July 1 of the year shown.

AREANAME	Public welfare	Highways	Parking facilities	Education	Health and hospitals	Police protection	Sewerage and sanitation	Parks and recreation	Housing and community development	Interest on debt
	127	128	129	130	131	132	133	134	135	136
United States................	X	X	X	X	X	X	X	X	X	X
ALABAMA	X	X	X	X	X	X	X	X	X	X
Alabaster......................	0.0	6.5	0.0	0.0	0.0	25.9	23.2	8.6	0.0	0.0
Auburn..........................	0.0	5.6	0.0	0.0	2.5	16.6	14.8	7.9	1.4	12.2
Bessemer......................	0.0	6.1	0.0	0.0	0.0	21.1	6.2	3.2	0.0	6.0
Birmingham...................	0.0	12.7	1.3	0.0	0.0	16.8	0.0	4.0	1.4	4.9
Decatur.........................	0.3	5.0	0.0	53.7	2.3	6.1	12.6	3.4	0.9	1.1
Dothan..........................	0.0	10.4	0.0	4.0	2.8	16.8	17.1	8.5	0.5	3.4
Enterprise.....................	0.0	8.4	0.0	16.6	0.7	13.2	23.7	7.3	0.0	8.6
Florence.......................	0.0	9.8	0.0	14.4	0.0	15.5	16.1	11.6	0.3	2.8
Gadsden.......................	0.0	6.2	0.0	0.0	0.0	16.2	16.8	9.0	2.3	4.3
Homewood.....................	0.1	5.6	0.0	28.6	0.0	16.9	4.9	6.2	0.0	4.2
Hoover..........................	0.0	9.1	0.0	2.1	0.3	21.8	8.8	8.6	0.0	4.5
Huntsville	0.2	6.6	0.5	5.6	1.2	12.4	8.8	9.0	2.3	8.1
Madison	0.0	14.5	0.0	0.0	0.0	14.0	12.2	7.0	0.0	6.1
Mobile	0.0	7.7	2.7	0.0	0.4	12.3	20.0	8.1	0.1	4.3
Montgomery...................	0.0	5.6	1.7	0.0	0.0	20.0	7.3	12.6	1.3	6.6
Opelika.........................	0.0	8.4	0.0	14.7	0.6	16.6	11.9	9.8	0.5	6.3
Phenix City....................	0.0	1.8	0.0	5.6	0.3	16.9	14.0	10.2	0.0	3.9
Prattville.......................	0.0	0.0	0.0	0.0	0.0	22.0	13.5	6.2	0.0	8.8
Tuscaloosa....................	0.1	14.2	0.3	7.9	0.1	17.4	9.0	8.0	1.4	2.3
Vestavia Hills	0.0	4.8	0.0	0.7	0.5	12.9	7.4	16.4	0.0	5.5
ALASKA	X	X	X	X	X	X	X	X	X	X
Anchorage......................	0.0	5.9	0.4	53.2	2.1	9.9	5.0	1.7	0.0	2.8
Fairbanks	0.0	33.1	0.6	0.0	0.0	15.6	0.0	0.0	0.0	0.5
Juneau	0.0	4.5	0.0	28.1	32.3	5.7	3.6	4.3	1.4	3.0
ARIZONA	X	X	X	X	X	X	X	X	X	X
Apache Junction	0.0	24.4	0.0	0.0	0.0	30.0	0.0	11.6	6.9	0.0
Avondale.......................	3.8	15.7	0.0	0.0	0.0	31.7	20.3	3.4	0.4	17.7
Buckeye........................	0.0	4.5	0.0	0.0	0.0	19.8	24.3	3.3	0.4	6.7
Bullhead City..................	0.0	20.8	0.0	0.0	4.2	23.1	21.7	7.4	1.4	6.8
Casa Grande..................	0.0	8.0	0.0	0.0	0.0	17.5	17.4	8.7	0.9	4.7
Chandler	0.0	7.7	0.0	0.0	0.0	21.8	19.2	0.9	13.7	1.9
El Mirage.......................	0.0	8.4	0.0	0.0	1.4	31.0	25.8	3.8	0.3	3.7
Flagstaff........................	0.0	14.0	0.0	0.0	0.0	13.5	14.1	0.0	12.3	6.6
Florence........................	0.0	8.9	3.0	0.0	0.0	25.5	11.9	4.9	4.2	8.4
Gilbert...........................	0.0	20.7	0.0	0.0	0.0	19.1	13.1	5.3	0.8	18.5
Glendale........................	0.0	3.3	0.2	0.0	0.0	22.4	12.4	4.5	6.7	13.2
Goodyear.......................	0.0	2.1	0.0	0.0	0.0	16.8	9.8	9.8	5.8	2.3
Kingman........................	0.0	5.6	0.0	0.0	0.0	23.3	22.2	11.9	2.1	10.7
Lake Havasu City.............	0.0	6.5	0.0	0.0	0.0	11.7	38.4	6.7	0.4	10.8
Marana..........................	0.0	15.9	0.0	0.0	0.0	23.0	2.8	3.8	0.9	3.2
Maricopa	0.0	3.8	0.0	0.0	0.0	20.8	0.0	6.7	29.9	6.1
Mesa	0.6	10.4	0.0	0.0	0.0	26.2	11.2	7.4	3.3	0.0
Oro Valley	0.0	14.5	0.0	0.0	0.0	40.4	0.0	9.9	0.0	5.5
Peoria...........................	0.0	9.6	0.0	0.2	0.0	12.3	12.7	11.6	0.7	10.4
Phoenix.........................	0.0	6.6	0.0	0.9	0.0	17.8	11.1	7.4	7.3	3.3
Prescott.........................	0.0	26.8	0.1	0.0	0.0	16.5	17.0	7.8	0.3	11.3
Prescott Valley	0.0	10.3	0.0	0.0	0.0	20.4	14.9	3.7	0.0	8.9
Queen Creek...................	0.0	6.0	0.0	0.0	0.0	3.2	8.0	12.7	1.3	11.5
Sahuarita......................	0.0	27.9	0.0	0.0	0.0	23.8	7.8	5.8	0.0	24.2
San Luis........................	0.5	5.6	0.0	0.0	0.0	14.5	18.2	0.0	0.6	9.3
Scottsdale......................	0.0	5.4	0.0	0.0	0.0	14.2	16.1	6.3	1.5	2.4
Sierra Vista	0.0	26.3	0.0	0.0	0.0	32.3	13.8	9.6	2.6	4.6
Surprise........................	0.0	14.1	0.0	0.0	0.0	19.0	11.3	12.5	5.8	5.2
Tempe...........................	0.0	10.3	0.0	0.0	0.0	21.8	10.9	1.8	14.8	6.0
Tucson	0.0	5.0	0.0	0.0	0.0	21.9	6.7	8.0	12.2	11.1
Yuma	0.0	11.8	0.0	0.0	0.6	17.9	15.0	9.1	1.2	X
ARKANSAS....................	X	X	X	X	X	X	X	X	X	X
Bella Vista......................	0.0	26.0	0.0	0.0	0.0	19.9	13.8	0.0	0.0	0.0
Benton...........................	0.0	22.3	0.0	0.0	1.5	20.7	12.3	6.4	0.0	7.0
Bentonville	0.0	16.9	0.0	0.0	0.0	12.6	25.2	11.3	0.2	5.6
Conway..........................	0.0	14.7	0.0	0.0	0.4	11.7	15.7	4.1	0.0	15.9
Fayetteville....................	0.0	11.2	1.0	0.0	1.0	16.4	26.2	5.7	0.5	5.3
Fort Smith......................	0.0	13.8	0.2	0.0	0.1	12.5	25.6	2.5	1.0	8.9
Hot Springs....................	0.0	6.7	0.2	0.0	0.9	15.8	27.9	2.4	0.4	2.1

AREANAME	Money income, 2016					Median earnings, 2016			Housing units, 2016				
	Households			Median family income	Median non-family household income	All persons	Men	Women	Total	Occupied	Percent owner occupied	Median value[1] (dollars)	Median rent (dollars)
	Median income	Percent with income less than $20,000	Percent with income of $200,000 or more										
	42	43	44	45	46	47	48	49	50	51	52	53	54
ARKANSAS— Cont'd													
Jacksonville	43,414	21.4	0.0	52,109	24,425	27,156	29,439	24,165	12,223	10,443	49.3	123,100	706
Jonesboro	41,434	23.8	3.4	48,589	24,781	23,460	24,805	22,913	32,632	29,449	51.0	143,400	722
Little Rock	45,605	20.4	6.8	62,962	31,919	31,097	36,641	27,268	94,965	83,957	53.7	161,000	834
North Little Rock	40,507	23.5	2.9	43,053	31,003	30,501	29,515	31,098	32,716	28,691	42.4	131,700	791
Paragould	50,146	22.7	4.5	55,235	25,654	27,076	29,232	25,263	11,169	10,184	61.5	116,100	668
Pine Bluff	32,502	35.8	2.8	40,527	19,656	25,282	30,074	21,933	22,456	17,809	49.2	76,900	686
Rogers	53,179	14.7	8.2	62,867	35,819	30,820	37,857	23,550	25,364	23,576	62.0	166,300	826
Russellville	32,188	35.1	3.2	52,144	16,950	18,390	22,283	9,455	12,112	11,349	52.1	137,300	689
Sherwood	54,446	15.9	1.9	61,796	39,565	34,284	41,366	27,474	12,737	11,633	64.2	148,700	829
Springdale	47,523	15.5	4.3	50,443	30,466	27,126	30,170	24,831	29,696	29,019	46.8	160,300	718
Texarkana	35,788	30.0	1.1	50,671	18,902	22,768	24,660	20,079	15,209	12,740	58.2	116,300	680
West Memphis	26,279	36.4	0.5	36,948	20,959	21,422	27,456	18,801	10,967	9,875	50.2	83,600	683
CALIFORNIA	67,739	14.0	10.1	77,359	44,115	32,499	37,947	28,554	14,061,375	12,944,178	53.6	477,500	1,375
Adelanto	34,801	22.0	0.4	39,085	23,571	21,045	26,769	12,449	8,207	7,806	57.3	177,600	1,059
Alameda	92,377	9.0	13.3	117,471	62,086	52,339	60,272	50,030	32,430	30,338	51.5	771,500	1,672
Alhambra	52,819	16.4	4.8	57,495	40,205	30,863	32,348	26,858	30,016	27,960	39.6	585,500	1,323
Aliso Viejo	105,262	5.7	17.6	125,846	78,993	60,058	78,970	42,363	20,589	19,624	64.7	617,200	2,040
Anaheim	64,464	10.6	6.1	67,919	48,045	28,696	31,862	24,278	103,367	99,255	41.5	548,100	1,489
Antioch	81,203	11.1	7.8	85,598	54,806	36,115	48,540	29,652	36,359	34,163	61.5	356,900	1,658
Apple Valley	46,682	12.8	3.3	51,429	32,586	26,877	32,497	22,086	26,074	24,012	58.8	245,000	1,023
Arcadia	89,421	12.9	16.4	101,354	38,759	48,219	61,177	36,903	20,769	19,597	57.4	1,132,200	1,504
Atascadero	71,255	7.4	4.3	78,704	43,426	35,831	43,179	26,806	11,626	11,285	57.6	485,700	1,319
Atwater	50,174	22.0	1.2	56,503	23,972	25,311	31,433	11,745	8,901	8,313	53.4	221,900	935
Azusa	58,196	11.2	1.9	65,161	51,321	22,483	23,868	19,471	14,539	12,939	51.4	384,700	1,333
Bakersfield	59,233	15.1	4.9	65,108	40,454	30,765	37,159	23,088	121,920	116,507	57.3	236,600	1,015
Baldwin Park	63,549	9.1	3.3	62,006	41,744	24,214	27,151	20,852	17,217	16,714	58.4	379,500	1,385
Banning	35,972	25.6	1.9	47,554	24,264	20,538	25,133	17,927	12,375	11,291	60.1	241,600	833
Beaumont	83,330	10.0	5.7	85,855	52,076	40,983	55,947	32,274	13,460	12,849	77.1	312,800	1,519
Bell	41,116	11.9	1.9	39,344	27,500	22,439	24,881	18,707	9,234	8,645	29.2	389,500	1,023
Bellflower	49,750	14.8	4.0	54,262	36,575	31,357	35,751	25,647	25,115	23,038	38.9	415,200	1,206
Bell Gardens	35,088	24.1	0.8	35,522	11,334	19,112	24,114	15,617	10,258	10,069	18.6	310,900	1,129
Belmont	132,259	6.0	31.8	169,137	62,272	70,990	90,404	53,244	10,956	10,253	64.9	1,523,200	2,157
Benicia	83,380	14.2	8.8	105,459	54,961	49,875	56,139	39,053	12,286	11,531	73.6	519,300	1,672
Berkeley	78,121	15.5	19.3	129,371	46,246	31,920	41,422	26,378	49,565	46,078	41.5	930,500	1,657
Beverly Hills	118,594	10.0	25.3	143,384	82,879	68,052	76,625	50,541	17,063	14,758	43.5	2,000,000	2,070
Brea	93,994	7.5	11.9	114,895	49,407	50,020	55,351	46,099	16,463	15,915	63.3	659,900	1,631
Brentwood	82,088	10.9	8.8	94,941	30,181	40,635	41,617	38,588	21,217	20,068	66.9	543,100	2,038
Buena Park	70,224	9.1	6.2	75,972	33,596	25,556	30,271	20,908	24,732	23,555	56.4	542,300	1,455
Burbank	72,618	17.5	9.4	90,908	49,660	41,849	46,850	38,112	42,108	40,724	41.4	691,200	1,459
Burlingame	110,920	6.3	26.0	141,712	77,645	77,448	96,151	60,809	13,257	12,608	46.8	1,702,600	2,074
Calexico	43,011	25.8	0.8	52,675	12,436	19,304	25,974	15,859	11,471	8,822	64.8	175,500	964
Camarillo	79,397	9.0	11.1	103,080	54,454	31,685	36,941	27,188	24,332	23,168	63.2	588,300	1,892
Campbell	119,386	8.2	24.3	136,844	80,763	52,039	62,298	42,280	16,515	14,709	50.0	1,058,500	1,963
Carlsbad	113,217	5.2	24.7	141,282	65,536	63,467	72,204	50,730	46,537	41,640	66.0	804,100	1,869
Carson	80,616	8.9	6.8	85,148	51,432	35,708	36,401	34,875	26,550	25,790	73.8	429,700	1,472
Cathedral City	44,075	20.1	3.3	44,375	29,375	25,565	27,086	24,318	24,014	18,502	57.8	271,100	1,208
Ceres	55,390	15.2	2.8	56,801	17,484	25,819	34,781	19,495	13,120	12,718	63.9	261,100	1,086
Cerritos	101,003	8.8	15.0	114,566	49,012	59,022	62,717	50,870	16,389	15,875	76.0	677,000	2,291
Chico	39,488	29.6	3.4	65,409	25,987	20,868	23,950	16,016	39,317	34,985	43.1	293,200	997
Chino	68,666	10.1	5.1	69,616	60,640	28,600	35,478	23,493	21,005	20,149	57.6	434,100	1,477
Chino Hills	99,324	8.9	15.6	105,368	58,840	44,278	53,906	30,933	25,092	24,026	77.8	596,700	2,031
Chula Vista	68,699	13.2	6.4	75,908	39,687	35,532	38,383	30,624	87,460	79,639	56.4	464,500	1,413
Citrus Heights	59,465	10.4	1.8	67,811	45,575	32,449	36,202	29,775	35,524	34,269	57.5	269,000	1,144
Claremont	95,864	11.8	13.0	120,490	61,603	32,107	53,607	23,561	13,126	11,985	63.7	644,800	1,373
Clovis	65,976	13.1	7.1	78,829	33,609	33,229	39,046	29,571	38,025	35,979	59.1	309,800	1,128
Coachella	31,001	27.4	0.0	40,339	21,241	22,156	25,338	18,760	14,949	14,192	65.0	201,600	935
Colton	51,754	15.9	0.8	64,858	23,325	31,185	33,827	26,142	18,632	17,166	55.4	231,700	1,136
Compton	49,125	20.7	0.9	51,597	20,833	23,698	26,218	20,038	23,374	22,458	53.4	327,900	1,137
Concord	76,335	7.7	9.4	80,475	59,829	39,178	47,205	30,585	47,313	45,848	55.8	530,900	1,569
Corona	71,584	11.9	7.2	81,381	45,547	32,482	41,226	24,152	52,386	50,765	63.8	442,600	1,493
Costa Mesa	81,019	8.1	11.0	80,300	76,870	36,625	39,105	34,741	40,027	38,127	36.8	720,800	1,749
Covina	70,047	12.9	4.9	80,835	24,948	36,767	37,871	35,363	15,811	15,106	54.4	478,500	1,347
Culver City	78,472	9.7	10.7	100,988	52,209	48,658	51,977	39,063	17,832	17,134	52.0	832,300	1,691
Cupertino	161,759	7.1	37.7	187,193	67,611	101,120	125,880	67,745	21,566	20,555	64.2	1,604,700	3,027
Cypress	92,383	7.9	11.7	100,323	52,017	46,613	51,902	39,058	17,377	16,247	69.7	602,800	1,719
Daly City	89,843	8.3	12.0	92,899	64,395	37,933	41,049	32,231	33,998	32,969	56.0	737,500	2,021
Dana Point	89,738	5.0	18.7	120,275	54,559	42,302	47,416	37,054	16,553	14,429	60.5	861,100	1,848
Danville	139,103	3.2	33.9	170,247	67,917	80,808	121,128	51,469	16,646	16,646	83.2	1,038,800	2,141
Davis	64,452	22.1	14.6	118,540	30,403	25,519	31,410	21,350	24,509	23,542	43.8	641,200	1,361

1. Specified owner-occupied units; $2,000,000 represents $2,000,000 or more.

Table D. Cities — Commuting, Computer Access, Migration, Labor Force, and Employment

	Commuting[1] 2016		Computer access[2]		Migration		Civilian labor force, 2016				Civilian employment, 2016			
	Percent		Percent						Unemployment[3]		Population age 16 and older		Population age 16 to 64	
AREANAME	Drove alone	With commutes of 30 minutes or more	With a computer in the house	With Internet access	Percent who lived in the same house one year ago	Percent who lived in another state or county one year ago	Total	Percent change 2016-2017	Total	Rate	Number	Percent in labor force	Number	Percent who worked full-year full-time
	55	56	57	58	59	60	61	62	63	64	65	66	67	68
ARKANSAS— Cont'd														
Jacksonville	83.8	18.8	91.1	84.2	84.9	7.9	11,821	1.4	510	4.3	21,532	54.6	17,573	51.2
Jonesboro	77.2	8.6	88.6	80.0	73.6	10.2	37,752	2.7	1,135	3.0	59,485	62.1	49,160	49.3
Little Rock	82.9	12.7	86.1	77.3	83.5	6.1	97,955	1.4	3,230	3.3	158,683	63.3	130,275	52.3
North Little Rock	85.4	15.8	86.4	74.1	84.8	3.8	30,133	1.4	1,103	3.7	50,849	65.9	43,860	52.2
Paragould	NA	29.8	90.4	80.8	61.3	12.4	12,462	-0.3	497	4.0	22,111	59.5	18,222	49.9
Pine Bluff	89.1	17.7	84.9	59.7	85.1	6.9	16,822	-1.3	962	5.7	34,790	47.2	27,703	35.3
Rogers	81.1	10.4	91.3	53.7	89.0	3.7	35,049	3.3	949	2.7	47,271	67.1	40,865	59.3
Russellville	79.4	7.3	92.9	78.9	79.3	11.9	13,731	0.1	532	3.9	24,951	55.9	21,490	32.7
Sherwood	81.3	32.1	85.0	75.2	84.8	6.4	15,822	1.4	478	3.0	22,908	62.1	17,621	53.3
Springdale	78.1	20.0	91.2	68.9	78.9	8.7	38,989	3.1	969	2.5	57,479	66.9	49,900	55.0
Texarkana	78.3	15.3	85.3	75.4	86.2	5.1	13,775	-0.1	638	4.6	27,365	55.6	21,761	38.4
West Memphis	71.5	24.1	83.3	73.1	60.5	3.8	10,837	0.7	527	4.9	18,706	55.9	14,784	39.9
CALIFORNIA	73.6	43.4	92.2	85.2	86.6	5.0	19,311,958	1.1	918,881	4.8	31,191,530	63.3	25,843,091	46.9
Adelanto	76.3	51.0	94.7	84.4	83.6	8.9	9,492	1.1	846	8.9	22,326	48.9	20,575	27.4
Alameda	58.1	54.3	94.7	88.7	88.4	7.0	42,361	1.4	1,447	3.4	63,244	67.0	51,030	54.3
Alhambra	77.9	53.9	91.9	85.6	90.8	2.6	46,909	1.4	1,887	4.0	71,757	60.7	56,320	52.0
Aliso Viejo	81.8	40.7	98.7	96.3	85.3	4.5	30,362	1.2	955	3.1	40,616	77.6	36,145	57.8
Anaheim	76.6	44.0	94.3	90.3	87.7	3.6	171,817	1.0	6,439	3.7	273,702	65.4	232,893	47.5
Antioch	69.1	67.1	92.4	86.8	87.6	5.0	51,441	1.0	2,445	4.8	86,394	63.8	73,280	44.9
Apple Valley	75.2	42.8	93.2	89.0	89.3	4.8	28,774	1.8	1,609	5.6	56,642	52.2	45,022	34.9
Arcadia	80.8	46.5	95.2	93.1	89.2	4.3	29,843	1.6	1,068	3.6	47,555	58.7	36,197	52.1
Atascadero	83.0	25.4	94.7	89.2	89.7	6.5	15,610	1.2	507	3.2	24,293	67.6	19,336	53.9
Atwater	78.9	30.3	93.1	87.3	78.1	6.7	12,176	1.2	1,055	8.7	21,309	57.7	17,509	38.1
Azusa	71.3	44.2	93.4	79.1	89.3	4.4	25,170	1.5	1,191	4.7	39,969	67.2	35,321	43.8
Bakersfield	81.8	23.9	92.8	87.3	81.1	4.4	174,590	-1.0	11,281	6.5	275,401	64.4	239,791	47.4
Baldwin Park	73.3	48.5	94.6	80.2	92.0	1.5	34,986	1.5	1,772	5.1	59,646	65.3	51,450	50.8
Banning	76.5	32.1	89.1	77.9	88.0	5.2	11,180	2.3	703	6.3	25,737	43.3	17,773	32.7
Beaumont	86.2	58.7	97.0	91.5	86.3	7.6	21,093	2.1	857	4.1	32,560	60.4	27,332	51.6
Bell	77.7	60.4	91.2	75.9	NA	NA	15,282	1.4	809	5.3	27,390	66.1	24,651	45.3
Bellflower	83.6	43.4	90.1	80.2	92.7	1.7	36,831	1.2	1,929	5.2	60,096	59.4	50,778	46.7
Bell Gardens	74.0	59.2	82.3	67.1	NA	NA	18,349	1.1	901	4.9	31,490	58.0	27,667	37.7
Belmont	75.1	53.7	98.1	93.5	85.8	8.1	16,690	1.6	466	2.8	21,806	66.2	16,476	54.4
Benicia	76.9	48.2	94.3	89.3	NA	NA	15,009	1.1	554	3.7	23,918	64.4	18,782	47.5
Berkeley	32.9	44.5	96.0	89.7	70.0	18.1	63,624	1.4	2,227	3.5	106,798	63.3	90,585	37.0
Beverly Hills	69.0	43.7	93.7	88.9	90.7	5.3	18,632	1.2	763	4.1	28,585	61.2	21,268	47.5
Brea	78.0	53.2	94.7	92.3	85.3	4.8	22,634	0.9	739	3.3	34,936	68.2	28,374	52.9
Brentwood	76.7	62.1	93.0	89.5	85.8	5.7	28,533	1.2	1,195	4.2	47,871	60.0	37,966	44.6
Buena Park	81.8	47.7	94.1	90.5	88.8	5.6	40,840	1.0	1,583	3.9	69,509	64.5	58,142	48.5
Burbank	80.9	46.3	89.7	85.5	88.1	4.6	59,564	1.2	3,063	5.1	87,626	63.0	69,123	47.8
Burlingame	67.2	47.8	96.9	93.6	82.8	12.3	18,224	1.5	467	2.6	24,043	70.9	19,190	58.1
Calexico	80.3	25.6	82.6	73.4	NA	NA	18,766	5.7	5,621	30.0	29,218	60.0	23,847	33.4
Camarillo	80.6	29.9	91.9	90.6	86.3	7.2	33,596	0.1	1,222	3.6	56,144	63.0	42,987	44.4
Campbell	79.9	45.9	94.3	87.9	80.5	7.2	25,731	1.6	752	2.9	34,086	68.5	29,216	56.6
Carlsbad	76.9	41.4	97.8	93.4	87.4	7.4	54,721	1.1	2,052	3.7	89,638	66.6	72,996	54.2
Carson	81.1	44.2	90.3	85.7	95.1	1.2	46,530	1.1	2,273	4.9	75,783	66.6	60,455	51.7
Cathedral City	81.4	20.0	86.4	76.5	90.7	3.1	25,913	2.2	1,268	4.9	42,516	59.1	33,792	43.3
Ceres	83.6	29.0	92.7	85.3	86.6	3.0	21,758	-0.5	1,928	8.9	34,783	62.7	31,132	39.6
Cerritos	83.3	50.2	95.2	92.1	87.6	5.0	25,521	1.4	1,044	4.1	42,524	55.6	32,723	47.4
Chico	69.3	17.3	93.2	84.8	73.9	10.8	48,405	1.3	2,168	4.5	75,760	63.2	64,878	33.4
Chino	79.1	55.7	94.7	89.1	78.1	15.5	41,534	2.1	1,696	4.1	72,597	49.3	61,223	35.7
Chino Hills	78.8	66.8	97.7	94.3	88.1	8.0	42,866	2.3	1,423	3.3	63,209	65.3	54,552	45.1
Chula Vista	79.1	43.0	91.7	84.1	88.1	2.7	122,207	0.9	5,389	4.4	208,134	65.1	173,090	43.1
Citrus Heights	78.8	36.3	92.2	87.5	84.5	6.4	43,574	1.0	1,946	4.5	71,295	65.3	57,691	51.2
Claremont	68.0	37.3	95.8	92.9	85.6	7.9	17,054	1.3	730	4.3	30,863	62.0	24,981	40.1
Clovis	84.7	24.1	93.6	88.8	86.9	3.0	52,413	1.1	2,376	4.5	79,865	65.7	67,045	46.7
Coachella	88.3	14.4	75.7	54.6	NA	NA	19,920	1.3	2,429	12.2	32,736	66.6	29,722	44.7
Colton	77.7	30.7	91.0	80.4	89.2	5.4	24,692	1.8	1,301	5.3	40,778	62.3	34,322	47.1
Compton	75.9	54.0	88.4	77.5	91.1	0.5	39,559	1.2	2,462	6.2	72,271	61.1	62,674	43.4
Concord	69.5	49.8	93.5	87.3	82.9	8.1	66,610	1.3	2,353	3.5	103,565	66.5	85,708	49.1
Corona	79.6	61.4	92.5	88.8	89.2	5.4	83,384	2.2	3,338	4.0	134,938	66.4	117,565	45.3
Costa Mesa	76.1	30.8	96.2	90.5	86.9	3.9	65,738	1.2	2,079	3.2	91,737	73.1	81,014	54.4
Covina	77.2	56.8	93.6	85.7	88.6	3.0	24,373	1.3	1,235	5.1	40,836	66.3	34,272	53.0
Culver City	79.9	41.7	91.4	86.1	90.4	4.7	23,153	1.4	1,030	4.4	33,271	67.6	25,641	56.7
Cupertino	76.6	51.6	96.4	93.5	86.7	7.6	29,950	1.7	954	3.2	46,365	61.4	38,386	51.4
Cypress	83.1	48.3	97.2	94.0	93.1	3.8	25,130	1.0	879	3.5	39,865	61.3	32,323	49.8
Daly City	61.0	50.5	93.7	88.7	88.6	5.5	64,636	1.5	1,737	2.7	91,259	69.1	73,892	52.4
Dana Point	80.1	45.3	97.9	94.0	87.8	3.0	18,998	1.0	616	3.2	29,268	69.0	22,958	47.8
Danville	73.7	43.3	94.9	93.9	89.4	4.2	21,125	1.3	718	3.4	34,565	60.2	24,883	55.2
Davis	55.0	24.9	98.4	94.7	69.4	15.4	35,503	1.7	1,178	3.3	58,513	56.9	51,005	32.9

1. Employed persons. 2. Households. 3. Percent of civilian labor force.

Table D. Cities — City Government Finances

AREANAME	City government finances, 2012									
	General revenue							General expenditure		
		Intergovernmental		Taxes					Per capita[1] (dollars)	
					Per capita[1] (dollars)					
	Total (mil dol)	Total (mil dol)	Percent from state government	Total (mil dol)	Total	Property	Sales and gross receipts	Total (mil dol)	Total	Capital outlays
	117	118	119	120	121	122	123	124	125	126
ARKANSAS— Cont'd										
Jacksonville	66.7	10.5	44.6	9.9	344	27	317	75.1	2,619	339
Jonesboro	78.3	23.6	30.3	30.7	435	65	371	71.4	1,014	147
Little Rock	376.0	98.2	37.1	121.4	617	247	370	369.8	1,881	297
North Little Rock	90.5	26.5	30.0	39.2	606	159	447	97.5	1,506	165
Paragould	29.1	6.0	40.6	7.3	270	31	239	27.7	1,027	152
Pine Bluff	45.8	15.6	31.1	17.4	370	78	293	42.9	915	56
Rogers	66.9	18.0	35.4	33.4	565	89	476	49.1	832	178
Russellville	28.8	7.4	31.7	14.0	492	24	468	23.4	820	49
Sherwood	26.4	11.3	17.7	7.8	261	19	243	26.0	868	128
Springdale	72.7	20.3	30.2	29.9	406	72	333	53.9	732	67
Texarkana	31.4	6.9	34.8	13.5	449	104	344	26.4	879	33
West Memphis	33.0	8.5	26.7	13.1	507	50	458	32.5	1,262	139
CALIFORNIA	X	X	X	X	X	X	X	X	X	X
Adelanto	12.0	0.9	64.5	6.2	197	83	105	18.3	586	65
Alameda	117.1	11.9	69.1	72.8	961	544	346	118.5	1,564	250
Alhambra	94.9	11.0	57.2	48.2	570	309	260	85.5	1,012	77
Aliso Viejo	19.0	1.4	100.0	14.0	283	134	120	22.2	448	112
Anaheim	697.7	119.6	21.0	267.6	779	340	436	658.5	1,917	451
Antioch	69.2	16.1	79.1	35.4	336	194	139	57.9	550	87
Apple Valley	55.7	5.3	91.3	27.5	389	258	118	55.8	790	105
Arcadia	68.8	2.9	73.3	48.5	848	441	400	64.5	1,130	99
Atascadero	31.8	7.6	92.3	15.9	555	349	188	28.1	978	301
Atwater	26.6	3.9	48.1	8.3	291	192	93	49.2	1,714	675
Azusa	58.3	7.2	30.8	36.3	767	353	363	55.0	1,161	37
Bakersfield	360.1	84.2	69.9	149.4	417	223	192	382.6	1,069	301
Baldwin Park	50.2	15.9	46.5	25.1	328	172	153	43.8	572	46
Banning	33.1	4.9	90.4	13.0	427	251	175	30.4	1,003	237
Beaumont	83.3	0.7	100.0	14.4	366	160	203	79.5	2,017	1,172
Bell	29.7	1.8	72.8	16.9	471	317	154	30.0	835	223
Bellflower	32.9	3.7	60.2	25.4	328	163	163	34.3	442	71
Bell Gardens	36.8	3.6	71.1	22.7	531	201	329	31.1	726	78
Belmont	43.6	2.2	83.1	25.6	965	712	247	44.8	1,687	160
Benicia	43.3	1.4	100.0	29.1	1,061	603	453	46.0	1,679	414
Berkeley	293.3	31.1	90.2	147.9	1,281	526	494	300.7	2,605	242
Beverly Hills	261.2	5.5	72.9	142.7	4,124	1,370	2,727	226.1	6,532	1,003
Brea	90.0	3.5	86.5	56.2	1,395	893	497	87.6	2,176	593
Brentwood	78.8	1.8	100.0	33.7	628	397	152	88.6	1,654	238
Buena Park	87.0	7.0	64.8	64.8	788	449	336	105.8	1,285	278
Burbank	265.6	36.3	55.0	147.7	1,412	849	560	282.4	2,701	443
Burlingame	72.1	2.7	100.0	42.6	1,436	445	977	70.0	2,356	686
Calexico	34.0	6.5	59.4	15.9	405	203	194	33.5	852	103
Camarillo	73.4	5.0	40.6	40.7	617	335	278	73.6	1,117	261
Campbell	46.2	3.4	53.9	33.2	823	390	428	49.3	1,222	160
Carlsbad	179.5	13.2	50.3	112.9	1,033	528	496	160.2	1,465	200
Carson	105.5	19.8	56.9	74.0	799	340	456	135.1	1,459	403
Cathedral City	70.1	6.3	64.9	52.7	1,002	695	304	69.7	1,324	144
Ceres	34.3	3.7	83.6	18.9	406	213	188	38.7	834	89
Cerritos	96.9	2.0	89.7	65.5	1,320	774	541	96.8	1,950	141
Chico	99.3	7.9	55.7	69.9	799	467	330	91.9	1,050	275
Chino	102.9	7.3	90.6	54.2	677	425	248	109.3	1,365	144
Chino Hills	60.2	3.8	89.2	21.6	283	154	126	65.7	861	137
Chula Vista	240.2	25.5	80.3	126.8	501	240	258	247.0	976	73
Citrus Heights	52.7	10.0	85.5	32.4	382	164	216	48.9	578	136
Claremont	35.2	1.7	82.5	23.2	653	293	356	34.7	978	122
Clovis	110.7	10.2	67.2	46.4	470	218	249	105.9	1,074	201
Coachella	37.8	11.0	71.9	18.0	421	228	167	49.1	1,150	551
Colton	50.0	6.2	92.7	27.9	524	332	190	44.1	829	84
Compton	98.6	17.9	28.9	54.6	558	319	236	114.4	1,170	108
Concord	120.0	9.6	80.8	70.7	566	241	321	128.3	1,026	86
Corona	225.6	16.4	78.9	106.2	672	397	245	219.2	1,388	272
Costa Mesa	117.6	9.7	76.3	92.1	823	381	439	111.9	1,001	113
Covina	49.3	4.1	69.9	32.6	672	369	300	49.1	1,013	132
Culver City	173.5	27.4	43.4	99.6	2,528	1,144	1,336	143.8	3,651	482
Cupertino	60.4	2.0	89.4	42.9	716	306	399	59.2	989	78
Cypress	43.8	2.7	66.2	33.4	683	409	270	44.8	917	226
Daly City	103.9	12.0	48.5	57.4	551	324	225	112.7	1,082	108
Dana Point	29.3	1.6	100.0	25.1	740	287	445	31.5	929	121
Danville	35.0	6.4	100.0	21.8	508	306	190	34.7	809	181
Davis	96.8	18.9	87.5	47.1	714	397	221	90.4	1,372	150

1. Based on population estimated as of July 1 of the year shown.

AREANAME	City government finances, 2012 (cont.)									
	General expenditures (cont.)									
	Percent of total for:									
	Public welfare	Highways	Parking facilities	Education	Health and hospitals	Police protection	Sewerage and sanitation	Parks and recreation	Housing and community development	Interest on debt
	127	128	129	130	131	132	133	134	135	136
ARKANSAS— Cont'd										
Jacksonville	0.0	4.8	0.0	0.0	51.2	10.2	15.6	3.1	0.4	2.2
Jonesboro	0.0	12.4	0.0	0.0	1.1	17.0	17.2	3.4	0.5	15.4
Little Rock	0.0	4.7	0.2	0.0	5.8	15.0	12.9	10.2	2.6	6.0
North Little Rock	0.0	6.2	0.0	0.0	0.4	18.6	16.6	6.3	3.6	5.9
Paragould	0.2	9.6	0.0	0.0	0.5	10.6	23.1	6.0	0.0	2.5
Pine Bluff	0.5	10.5	0.0	0.0	0.1	24.5	18.2	6.0	4.3	1.9
Rogers	0.0	9.9	0.0	0.0	0.8	17.6	15.7	9.0	0.0	5.8
Russellville	0.0	20.6	0.0	0.0	1.1	18.7	18.5	6.1	0.0	0.0
Sherwood	0.0	20.6	0.0	0.0	1.0	23.1	14.0	13.5	0.0	1.2
Springdale	0.0	8.2	0.0	0.0	1.0	20.7	17.2	4.4	1.2	9.5
Texarkana	0.0	5.7	0.0	0.0	1.2	28.6	21.0	1.4	0.8	3.8
West Memphis	0.0	13.7	0.0	0.0	0.5	20.8	16.6	4.2	2.0	3.0
CALIFORNIA	X	X	X	X	X	X	X	X	X	X
Adelanto	0.0	9.8	0.0	0.0	1.4	25.8	0.0	4.3	9.3	0.0
Alameda	0.0	8.5	0.8	0.0	14.8	22.2	8.2	11.0	6.1	3.5
Alhambra	0.0	9.2	2.7	0.0	0.1	28.1	12.5	7.4	4.9	4.2
Aliso Viejo	0.0	15.3	0.0	0.0	1.0	28.2	0.0	7.9	0.5	9.0
Anaheim	0.0	8.5	0.0	0.0	0.1	16.5	8.2	12.1	18.0	10.6
Antioch	0.0	16.1	0.0	0.0	2.4	43.6	4.2	9.6	8.8	3.6
Apple Valley	0.0	8.4	0.0	0.0	2.9	19.9	23.3	8.7	11.7	5.3
Arcadia	0.0	9.9	0.0	0.0	6.9	25.6	2.2	4.2	3.1	1.5
Atascadero	0.0	7.5	0.0	0.0	0.0	21.1	6.6	9.2	20.1	4.0
Atwater	0.0	2.7	0.0	0.0	0.0	14.1	51.3	3.5	5.4	8.0
Azusa	0.0	3.3	0.0	0.0	1.2	30.7	8.1	6.3	8.1	11.6
Bakersfield	0.0	10.0	0.0	0.0	0.0	17.9	17.4	6.8	2.6	3.6
Baldwin Park	0.0	15.9	0.0	0.0	0.0	41.3	0.6	8.7	17.9	3.9
Banning	0.0	11.9	0.0	0.0	0.3	24.5	18.5	2.1	18.5	4.9
Beaumont	0.0	3.8	0.0	0.0	0.6	12.7	7.1	4.6	0.6	0.5
Bell	0.0	6.8	0.0	0.0	0.0	22.5	4.9	3.5	21.8	9.1
Bellflower	0.0	31.2	0.0	0.0	0.0	30.7	0.0	6.3	6.8	6.6
Bell Gardens	0.0	13.1	0.0	0.0	0.0	42.3	7.6	15.9	3.0	3.7
Belmont	0.0	9.5	0.0	0.0	0.0	21.4	17.5	8.4	8.9	2.3
Benicia	0.0	7.0	0.0	0.0	0.0	19.3	14.2	10.6	0.2	3.1
Berkeley	0.0	7.4	2.4	0.0	11.4	18.1	14.2	5.9	6.0	1.9
Beverly Hills	0.0	5.7	21.3	0.0	4.9	17.9	10.5	9.5	0.1	1.7
Brea	0.0	14.6	0.0	0.0	4.1	30.3	6.4	10.8	11.8	1.2
Brentwood	0.0	14.0	0.0	0.0	0.0	18.8	17.9	12.0	9.8	9.7
Buena Park	0.0	12.0	0.0	0.0	0.3	20.3	3.1	4.7	23.0	5.3
Burbank	0.0	7.2	0.3	0.0	4.6	15.9	9.3	5.7	14.2	5.8
Burlingame	0.0	24.2	2.0	0.0	0.0	13.4	14.4	8.0	0.0	2.4
Calexico	0.0	6.0	0.0	0.0	0.9	30.5	16.3	3.8	10.3	0.4
Camarillo	0.0	24.2	0.0	0.0	0.3	20.3	17.6	0.9	6.1	5.0
Campbell	0.0	13.9	0.0	0.0	0.0	26.2	0.0	12.0	10.3	3.4
Carlsbad	0.0	8.7	0.0	0.0	8.2	17.9	8.5	13.4	4.7	1.6
Carson	0.0	13.8	1.0	0.0	0.1	16.4	0.1	13.3	26.3	7.1
Cathedral City	0.0	9.7	0.0	0.0	4.2	22.1	0.6	1.4	22.4	15.6
Ceres	0.0	8.7	0.0	0.0	1.2	28.2	19.7	5.0	9.7	5.6
Cerritos	0.0	10.6	0.0	0.0	0.3	14.0	3.4	14.7	6.5	8.1
Chico	0.0	17.5	1.9	0.0	0.3	23.6	6.6	3.2	11.8	6.1
Chino	0.0	13.4	0.0	0.0	0.0	25.6	18.7	5.2	15.2	6.1
Chino Hills	0.0	20.8	0.0	0.0	0.0	17.3	14.6	6.5	0.4	6.1
Chula Vista	0.0	10.6	0.1	0.0	0.9	20.6	17.6	9.9	2.7	7.6
Citrus Heights	0.0	22.4	0.0	0.0	1.3	38.7	1.2	0.1	14.3	2.1
Claremont	0.0	12.7	0.0	0.0	0.8	28.4	15.5	9.0	4.2	2.9
Clovis	0.0	10.8	0.0	0.0	0.7	21.2	28.1	5.4	3.1	2.4
Coachella	0.0	33.0	0.0	0.0	0.4	12.4	16.2	10.2	4.8	5.7
Colton	0.0	6.2	0.0	0.0	1.3	23.1	11.2	3.9	8.2	9.8
Compton	0.0	8.3	0.0	0.0	0.0	15.0	9.0	2.9	15.0	1.3
Concord	0.0	12.7	0.0	0.0	0.0	33.4	16.2	6.9	3.5	2.3
Corona	0.0	4.4	0.1	0.0	0.5	18.5	23.8	3.9	7.9	9.2
Costa Mesa	0.0	8.7	0.0	0.0	1.0	33.4	0.0	6.1	2.3	2.0
Covina	0.0	5.4	0.2	0.0	0.7	30.8	3.6	5.8	13.9	6.1
Culver City	0.0	5.6	0.2	0.0	3.7	19.6	11.6	4.8	13.5	6.5
Cupertino	0.0	11.9	0.0	0.0	0.3	28.1	2.6	25.6	1.8	3.2
Cypress	0.0	21.7	0.0	0.0	0.5	31.3	3.4	13.1	11.8	1.7
Daly City	0.0	10.1	0.0	0.0	0.5	24.9	20.5	8.8	1.7	0.4
Dana Point	0.0	24.9	0.0	0.0	1.0	30.4	0.0	14.2	0.0	1.4
Danville	0.0	21.8	0.0	0.0	1.0	21.0	0.0	21.4	0.4	1.5
Davis	0.0	8.9	0.0	0.0	0.0	16.4	20.0	26.2	3.7	2.4

Table D. Cities — City Government Finances, City Government Employment, and Climate

AREANAME	City government finances, 2012 (cont.) Debt outstanding Total (mil dol)	Per capita[1] (dollars)	Debt issued during year	Climate[2] Average daily temperature Mean January	July	Limits January[3]	July[4]	Annual precipitation (inches)	Heating degree days	Cooling degree days
	137	138	139	140	141	142	143	144	145	146
ARKANSAS— Cont'd										
Jacksonville	28.9	1,008	1.9	38.2	79.9	27.4	91.1	50.56	3,470	1,699
Jonesboro	298.0	4,230	2.9	35.6	81.6	25.8	92.3	46.18	3,737	1,858
Little Rock	511.4	2,601	23.9	40.1	82.4	30.8	92.8	50.93	3,084	2,086
North Little Rock	204.0	3,152	19.6	40.1	82.4	30.8	92.8	50.93	3,084	2,086
Paragould	25.8	953	7.4	NA	NA	NA	NA	NA	NA	NA
Pine Bluff	29.1	619	9.6	40.8	82.4	31.5	92.4	52.48	2,935	2,099
Rogers	160.5	2,718	85.8	32.9	77.5	22.0	88.8	46.92	4,483	1,269
Russellville	0.0	0	0.0	NA	NA	NA	NA	NA	NA	NA
Sherwood	8.3	277	0.0	NA	NA	NA	NA	NA	NA	NA
Springdale	110.5	1,501	0.0	34.3	78.9	24.2	89.1	46.02	4,166	1,439
Texarkana	34.1	1,136	0.0	44.3	82.7	35.6	92.7	47.38	2,421	2,280
West Memphis	31.2	1,214	0.0	37.5	81.5	28.5	90.9	52.80	3,417	1,903
CALIFORNIA	X	X	X	X	X	X	X	X	X	X
Adelanto	0.0	0	0.0	NA	NA	NA	NA	NA	NA	NA
Alameda	152.6	2,014	3.6	50.9	64.9	44.7	72.7	22.94	2,400	377
Alhambra	70.5	834	0.0	56.3	75.6	42.6	89.0	18.56	1,295	1,575
Aliso Viejo	34.0	686	0.0	56.7	72.4	47.2	82.3	14.03	1,465	1,183
Anaheim	1,822.5	5,304	0.0	56.9	73.2	45.2	84.0	11.23	1,286	1,183
Antioch	41.8	397	0.0	45.7	74.4	37.8	90.7	13.33	2,714	1,294
Apple Valley	63.0	893	0.0	45.5	80.0	31.4	99.1	6.20	2,929	1,179
										1,735
Arcadia	40.4	707	0.0	56.3	75.6	42.6	89.0	18.56	1,295	1,575
Atascadero	27.6	962	0.0	47.3	71.6	33.1	91.3	14.71	2,932	785
Atwater	93.3	3,253	0.0	NA	NA	NA	NA	NA	NA	NA
Azusa	235.4	4,970	0.0	54.6	73.8	41.5	88.7	16.96	1,727	1,191
Bakersfield	345.9	966	49.8	47.8	83.1	39.3	96.9	6.49	2,120	2,286
Baldwin Park	66.8	873	0.0	56.3	75.6	42.6	89.0	18.56	1,295	1,575
Banning	48.2	1,591	0.0	NA	NA	NA	NA	NA	NA	NA
Beaumont	9.6	244	0.4	NA	NA	NA	NA	NA	NA	NA
Bell	55.7	1,550	0.0	58.8	76.6	47.9	88.9	14.44	949	1,837
Bellflower	31.8	410	0.0	57.0	73.8	46.0	82.9	12.94	1,211	1,186
Bell Gardens	36.7	856	0.0	58.8	76.6	47.9	88.9	14.44	949	1,837
Belmont	38.8	1,460	0.0	48.1	69.7	36.4	88.2	28.71	2,769	569
Benicia	55.1	2,008	4.3	46.3	71.2	38.8	87.4	19.58	2,757	786
Berkeley	188.8	1,635	0.0	50.0	62.8	43.6	70.4	25.40	2,857	142
Beverly Hills	142.3	4,111	0.0	57.9	69.5	49.4	76.9	18.68	1,379	893
Brea	39.1	971	0.0	56.9	73.2	45.2	84.0	11.23	1,286	1,294
Brentwood	194.1	3,622	22.4	NA	NA	NA	NA	NA	NA	NA
Buena Park	115.5	1,403	0.0	57.0	73.8	46.0	82.9	12.94	1,211	1,186
Burbank	463.3	4,430	9.8	54.8	75.5	42.0	88.9	17.49	1,575	1,455
Burlingame	33.1	1,114	0.0	50.0	62.7	42.9	70.5	23.35	2,720	184
Calexico	2.8	71	0.0	55.8	91.4	41.3	107.0	2.96	1,080	3,952
Camarillo	90.1	1,367	7.6	55.7	66.0	45.3	74.0	13.61	1,961	389
Campbell	28.0	694	0.1	48.7	70.3	38.8	85.4	22.64	2,641	613
Carlsbad	65.0	594	0.2	54.7	67.6	45.4	72.1	11.13	2,009	505
Carson	217.3	2,347	0.0	56.3	69.4	46.2	77.6	14.79	1,526	742
Cathedral City	271.4	5,160	0.3	57.3	92.1	44.2	108.2	5.23	951	4,224
Ceres	50.3	1,083	0.0	47.2	77.7	40.1	93.6	13.12	2,358	1,570
Cerritos	153.8	3,099	0.0	57.0	73.8	46.0	82.9	12.94	1,211	1,186
Chico	163.2	1,865	0.0	44.5	76.9	35.2	93.0	26.23	2,945	1,334
Chino	211.8	2,645	12.9	54.6	73.8	41.5	88.7	16.96	1,727	1,191
Chino Hills	127.2	1,667	0.0	56.9	73.2	45.2	84.0	11.23	1,286	1,294
Chula Vista	512.8	2,027	4.0	57.3	70.1	46.1	76.1	9.95	1,321	862
Citrus Heights	28.5	337	0.0	46.9	77.7	39.2	94.8	24.61	2,532	1,528
Claremont	26.2	739	0.0	54.6	73.8	41.5	88.7	16.96	1,727	1,191
Clovis	232.4	2,358	0.0	46.0	81.4	38.4	96.6	11.23	2,447	1,963
Coachella	94.7	2,219	2.4	NA	NA	NA	NA	NA	NA	NA
Colton	96.4	1,813	0.0	54.4	79.6	41.8	96.0	16.43	1,599	1,937
Compton	73.6	752	0.0	57.0	73.8	46.0	82.9	12.94	1,211	1,186
Concord	63.7	510	0.0	46.3	71.2	38.8	87.4	19.58	2,757	786
Corona	346.1	2,191	25.3	54.7	75.9	41.5	92.0	12.00	1,599	1,534
Costa Mesa	38.8	347	0.0	55.9	67.3	48.2	71.4	11.65	1,719	543
Covina	86.2	1,779	2.3	54.6	73.8	41.5	88.7	16.96	1,727	1,191
Culver City	206.5	5,244	0.0	56.7	70.8	46.1	80.0	13.32	1,344	959
Cupertino	43.9	734	43.9	48.7	70.3	38.8	85.4	22.64	2,641	613
Cypress	8.8	181	0.0	57.0	73.8	46.0	82.9	12.94	1,211	1,186
Daly City	45.3	435	0.0	50.6	57.3	44.6	61.1	19.77	3,665	17
Dana Point	8.2	241	0.0	55.4	68.7	43.9	77.3	13.56	1,756	666
Danville	12.9	300	0.0	47.5	72.4	39.3	85.2	23.96	3,267	983
Davis	55.0	835	0.0	45.2	74.3	37.1	92.7	19.05	2,853	1,127

1. Based on the population estimated as of July 1 of the year shown. 2. Represents normal values based on the 30-year period, 1971±2000. 3. Average daily minimum. 4. Average daily maximum.

Table D. Cities — **Land Area and Population**

STATE Place code	AREANAME	Land area[1] (sq. mi)	Total persons 2017	Rank	Per square mile	White	Black or African American	American Indian, Alaskan Native	Asian	Hawaiian Pacific Islander	Some other race	Two or more races (percent)
		1	2	3	4	5	6	7	8	9	10	11
	CALIFORNIA— Cont'd											
06 18,394	Delano	14.3	53,138	721	3,715.9	77.1	4.3	0.5	7.2	0.4	8.9	1.7
06 18,996	Desert Hot Springs	30.2	28,757	1,294	952.2	72.9	11.7	0.0	4.3	0.4	9.3	1.3
06 19,192	Diamond Bar	14.9	56,665	663	3,803.0	19.9	4.5	0.5	62.9	0.0	8.6	3.5
06 19,766	Downey	12.4	113,092	255	9,120.3	65.7	2.8	0.3	10.1	0.1	18.8	2.1
06 20,018	Dublin	15.2	60,939	611	4,009.1	40.9	3.6	0.4	45.0	0.0	2.7	7.5
06 20,956	East Palo Alto	2.5	29,765	1,259	11,906.0	29.0	12.0	0.6	2.5	4.6	44.2	7.2
06 21,712	El Cajon	14.5	103,894	295	7,165.1	65.7	6.0	1.7	2.4	0.1	16.1	7.9
06 21,782	El Centro	11.2	44,364	856	3,961.1	32.7	1.2	1.4	4.0	0.6	57.4	2.8
06 22,020	Elk Grove	42.1	171,844	149	4,081.8	47.6	8.5	0.6	28.8	1.8	3.5	9.1
06 22,230	El Monte	9.6	116,109	243	12,094.7	34.3	0.8	0.9	30.7	0.4	31.6	1.4
06 22,300	El Paso de Robles (Paso Robles)	19.4	31,918	1,181	1,645.3	88.7	0.4	0.0	1.1	0.0	7.2	2.6
06 22,678	Encinitas	18.8	63,184	585	3,360.9	94.5	0.0	0.0	2.5	0.1	1.3	1.6
06 22,804	Escondido	37.2	151,969	173	4,085.2	74.5	3.3	1.6	8.1	0.8	8.1	3.7
06 23,042	Eureka	9.4	27,177	1,351	2,891.2	80.6	1.0	2.2	4.9	0.0	4.0	7.2
06 23,182	Fairfield	41.0	116,266	242	2,835.8	46.9	17.1	0.3	14.7	0.8	11.5	8.6
06 24,638	Folsom	27.7	78,038	441	2,817.3	70.5	2.6	0.7	16.1	0.3	3.3	6.4
06 24,680	Fontana	43.0	211,815	105	4,925.9	44.1	6.7	0.7	7.0	0.5	37.1	3.9
06 25,338	Foster City	3.8	34,412	1,104	9,055.8	42.9	3.6	0.1	46.6	0.2	1.0	5.7
06 25,380	Fountain Valley	9.1	56,313	667	6,188.2	64.6	0.2	0.2	29.4	0.3	2.3	3.0
06 26,000	Fremont	77.5	234,962	96	3,031.8	22.8	3.8	0.4	58.4	1.0	9.6	4.1
06 27,000	Fresno	113.6	527,438	34	4,642.9	60.0	7.6	1.1	14.7	0.2	12.6	3.8
06 28,000	Fullerton	22.4	140,392	188	6,267.5	54.6	2.7	0.3	25.0	0.1	11.1	6.2
06 28,168	Gardena	5.8	60,224	618	10,383.4	26.4	19.7	0.3	25.1	2.8	21.4	4.2
06 29,000	Garden Grove	18.0	174,226	148	9,679.2	39.2	1.4	0.5	42.1	0.1	14.1	2.6
06 29,504	Gilroy	16.1	57,664	652	3,581.6	76.2	0.9	1.5	10.3	0.0	7.0	4.1
06 30,000	Glendale	30.4	203,054	112	6,679.4	74.1	1.8	0.0	15.2	0.1	4.8	3.9
06 30,014	Glendora	19.6	52,445	731	2,675.8	64.5	2.5	0.2	13.1	0.2	11.8	7.7
06 30,378	Goleta	7.9	31,116	1,207	3,938.7	76.7	2.0	1.5	11.2	0.0	6.1	2.6
06 31,960	Hanford	16.9	56,499	666	3,343.1	73.7	4.9	0.8	4.1	0.0	13.2	3.4
06 32,548	Hawthorne	6.1	87,854	375	14,402.3	28.5	22.1	0.4	5.7	0.5	38.1	4.7
06 33,000	Hayward	45.5	160,500	159	3,527.5	44.3	7.5	0.7	25.5	3.0	12.8	6.3
06 33,182	Hemet	29.3	85,160	391	2,906.5	71.9	10.0	1.9	4.1	0.8	5.8	5.5
06 33,434	Hesperia	73.1	94,859	329	1,297.7	84.4	3.6	1.3	1.4	0.4	6.7	2.1
06 33,588	Highland	18.8	55,342	682	2,943.7	63.7	6.5	0.2	8.2	0.0	16.1	5.2
06 34,120	Hollister	7.3	38,404	996	5,260.8	79.4	0.3	0.6	1.5	0.0	10.6	7.6
06 36,000	Huntington Beach	26.9	201,874	114	7,504.6	72.7	2.1	0.4	11.3	0.7	8.5	4.4
06 36,056	Huntington Park	3.0	58,822	641	19,607.3	NA	NA	NA	NA	NA	NA	NA
06 36,294	Imperial Beach	4.2	27,418	1,343	6,528.1	71.0	4.4	1.2	10.7	0.0	3.6	9.1
06 36,448	Indio	33.2	89,793	364	2,704.6	49.3	3.5	0.8	3.4	0.0	39.3	3.7
06 36,546	Inglewood	9.1	110,598	268	12,153.6	20.9	45.6	1.1	2.5	0.3	24.9	4.8
06 36,770	Irvine	65.6	277,453	73	4,229.5	48.2	1.1	0.0	43.3	0.5	2.3	4.7
06 39,220	Laguna Hills	6.6	31,318	1,200	4,745.2	68.0	1.6	0.0	18.1	0.1	6.1	6.0
06 39,248	Laguna Niguel	14.7	66,334	550	4,512.5	77.4	1.6	0.0	9.9	0.1	6.6	4.4
06 39,290	La Habra	7.4	62,466	591	8,441.4	57.4	1.3	0.7	14.9	0.0	22.1	3.6
06 39,486	Lake Elsinore	38.0	66,411	548	1,747.7	51.7	4.4	0.6	4.2	0.2	32.2	6.6
06 39,496	Lake Forest	16.6	84,293	400	5,077.9	69.6	2.9	0.9	16.9	0.1	6.1	3.6
06 39,892	Lakewood	9.4	80,967	420	8,613.5	43.4	9.7	0.2	22.4	0.4	17.1	6.7
06 40,004	La Mesa	9.1	60,021	620	6,595.7	66.2	14.3	0.5	7.0	0.5	6.0	5.5
06 40,032	La Mirada	7.8	49,095	779	6,294.2	51.7	2.6	0.1	16.6	0.1	21.5	7.4
06 40,130	Lancaster	94.3	160,316	160	1,700.1	61.8	20.6	0.5	5.5	0.1	5.6	6.0
06 40,340	La Puente	3.5	40,322	943	11,520.6	24.1	0.6	1.8	9.7	0.0	62.7	1.1
06 40,354	La Quinta	35.3	41,304	917	1,170.1	74.3	2.2	0.2	2.6	0.0	16.4	4.3
06 40,830	La Verne	8.4	32,461	1,168	3,864.4	72.0	5.4	0.1	9.8	0.0	5.5	7.2
06 40,886	Lawndale	2.0	33,078	1,148	16,539.0	30.9	7.7	0.3	17.5	4.2	33.7	5.5
06 41,124	Lemon Grove	3.9	27,108	1,357	6,950.8	63.6	17.2	1.0	5.8	0.7	5.3	6.4
06 41,474	Lincoln	23.5	47,674	807	2,028.7	82.1	2.7	0.1	4.5	0.0	5.9	4.7
06 41,992	Livermore	27.0	90,295	360	3,344.3	75.3	0.9	0.2	11.8	0.8	4.1	6.9
06 42,202	Lodi	13.7	65,884	553	4,809.1	60.7	1.0	0.1	8.0	0.0	15.9	14.4
06 42,524	Lompoc	11.6	43,542	869	3,753.6	65.6	4.6	2.0	3.3	0.0	16.2	8.4
06 43,000	Long Beach	50.3	469,450	39	9,333.0	50.4	12.6	0.7	12.5	0.9	17.4	5.4
06 43,280	Los Altos	6.5	30,743	1,223	4,729.7	NA	NA	NA	NA	NA	NA	NA
06 44,000	Los Angeles	468.7	3,999,759	2	8,533.7	52.3	8.8	0.7	11.4	0.1	23.1	3.6
06 44,028	Los Banos	10.0	39,183	978	3,918.3	59.5	1.1	0.2	2.8	0.0	31.9	4.5
06 44,112	Los Gatos	11.2	30,724	1,224	2,743.2	81.5	0.5	0.0	12.9	0.4	0.3	4.4
06 44,574	Lynwood	4.8	71,099	502	14,812.3	64.7	8.3	1.3	0.6	1.2	22.1	1.8
06 45,022	Madera	15.8	65,508	560	4,146.1	62.3	4.3	2.1	1.3	0.0	25.7	4.4
06 45,400	Manhattan Beach	3.9	35,924	1,066	9,211.3	75.9	1.0	0.0	15.1	0.0	2.9	5.1
06 45,484	Manteca	20.5	79,268	434	3,866.7	69.1	4.5	1.2	7.4	0.8	9.8	7.2
06 46,114	Martinez	12.6	38,373	997	3,045.5	69.3	3.8	0.5	12.1	0.0	6.1	8.3
06 46,492	Maywood	1.2	27,586	1,336	22,988.3	NA	NA	NA	NA	NA	NA	NA
06 46,842	Menifee	46.5	90,595	358	1,948.3	60.1	7.7	0.0	8.4	0.0	18.0	5.9

1. Dry land or land partially or temporarily covered by water.   2. Hispanic or Latino persons may be of any race.

AREANAME	Percent Hispanic or Latino[1], 2016	Percent foreign born, 2016	Age of population (percent), 2016							Median age 2016	Percent female 2016	Population			
												Census counts		Percent change	
			Under 18 years	18 to 24 years	25 to 34 years	35 to 44 years	45 to 54 years	55 to 64 years	65 years and over			2000	2010	2000-2010	2010-2017
	12	13	14	15	16	17	18	19	20	21	22	23	24	25	26
CALIFORNIA— Cont'd															
Delano...............	81.8	37.8	29.1	14.5	18.4	14.8	12.0	4.9	6.3	27.4	41.6	38,824	53,041	36.6	0.2
Desert Hot Springs.............	48.9	24.2	23.6	4.0	11.2	13.2	16.0	14.3	17.7	40.8	50.8	16,582	27,052	63.1	6.3
Diamond Bar	14.7	50.0	17.5	7.6	15.9	10.6	14.7	18.6	15.1	44.0	52.7	56,287	55,552	-1.3	2.0
Downey...............	73.5	32.5	26.1	10.0	16.8	13.8	13.9	9.1	10.3	32.9	51.0	107,323	111,770	4.1	1.2
Dublin................	11.0	37.7	26.7	5.0	14.0	19.8	16.4	10.7	7.3	36.7	48.4	29,973	46,036	53.6	32.4
East Palo Alto........	68.0	39.0	29.4	11.4	18.3	16.2	14.1	5.3	5.3	28.2	44.5	29,506	28,155	-4.6	5.7
El Cajon.............	30.4	30.0	30.0	7.5	14.7	11.1	12.0	12.8	11.8	33.4	50.4	94,869	99,514	4.9	4.4
El Centro............	87.5	32.7	28.3	10.1	15.1	10.3	10.5	11.7	14.0	33.5	49.8	37,835	42,583	12.5	4.2
Elk Grove............	18.6	22.9	27.5	9.0	10.7	14.9	13.6	12.4	11.9	36.5	52.9	59,984	153,015	155.1	12.3
El Monte.............	64.2	51.4	24.3	10.3	15.3	12.5	12.4	12.5	12.7	35.1	49.1	115,965	113,484	-2.1	2.3
El Paso de Robles (Paso Robles)...........	31.8	11.7	24.4	9.0	14.8	8.6	15.5	10.9	16.8	37.7	53.4	24,297	29,785	22.6	7.2
Encinitas............	14.1	12.6	21.6	4.6	11.0	13.5	14.9	14.1	20.2	44.1	51.8	58,014	59,519	2.6	6.2
Escondido............	53.2	30.0	25.1	10.7	16.8	12.5	13.6	10.9	10.4	33.7	49.5	133,559	143,976	7.8	5.6
Eureka...............	10.3	7.3	15.7	9.2	10.5	12.9	14.0	17.7	19.9	45.8	48.3	26,128	27,196	4.1	-0.1
Fairfield.............	31.3	22.9	24.7	9.6	15.6	11.3	13.3	12.7	12.8	35.0	51.4	96,178	105,398	9.6	10.3
Folsom...............	13.3	17.1	26.1	5.7	10.9	12.0	20.4	12.0	12.8	41.8	47.0	51,884	72,203	39.2	8.1
Fontana..............	69.3	26.6	28.4	10.5	15.9	14.3	13.0	9.4	8.4	32.0	51.8	128,929	196,468	52.4	7.8
Foster City..........	5.6	46.4	23.3	2.8	14.9	15.8	13.8	14.7	14.8	40.8	48.7	28,803	30,567	6.1	12.6
Fountain Valley.......	16.7	30.8	19.3	6.5	12.4	10.4	17.9	14.5	18.6	45.6	50.3	54,978	55,360	0.7	1.7
Fremont..............	13.7	49.1	24.4	6.0	16.4	17.8	13.1	10.4	11.9	36.8	50.3	203,413	214,079	5.2	9.8
Fresno...............	49.3	21.8	28.3	11.2	16.7	11.9	11.1	9.9	11.0	30.9	51.4	427,652	497,069	16.2	6.1
Fullerton............	35.4	31.7	21.1	12.4	15.7	12.5	13.4	12.1	12.9	35.5	50.0	126,003	135,239	7.3	3.8
Gardena..............	38.8	34.9	23.8	8.9	11.4	13.4	14.7	12.9	14.9	39.2	52.4	57,746	58,829	1.9	2.4
Garden Grove.........	35.7	43.9	23.0	10.1	14.7	13.7	14.8	11.7	11.9	36.3	49.1	165,196	170,960	3.5	1.9
Gilroy...............	57.7	24.8	29.4	7.7	11.7	15.5	13.0	10.7	12.0	35.8	55.6	41,464	48,810	17.7	18.1
Glendale.............	17.8	53.2	18.4	7.0	15.4	14.7	14.4	13.1	17.1	41.6	51.7	194,973	191,670	-1.7	5.9
Glendora.............	29.1	21.3	20.8	5.1	12.6	11.4	14.9	17.3	17.9	45.1	52.7	49,415	50,395	2.0	4.1
Goleta...............	30.3	21.4	21.9	11.9	13.3	12.1	13.9	11.4	15.5	37.9	49.7	55,204	29,914	-45.8	4.0
Hanford..............	51.2	20.0	24.2	10.5	14.3	10.5	15.1	12.4	13.1	35.5	48.9	41,686	54,371	30.4	3.9
Hawthorne............	59.5	36.8	27.0	8.7	18.9	14.9	11.8	9.0	9.6	32.1	51.8	84,112	84,293	0.2	4.2
Hayward..............	41.8	40.9	21.4	11.4	17.1	12.8	14.2	11.7	11.4	35.1	50.6	140,030	144,348	3.1	11.2
Hemet................	37.3	14.6	28.7	7.1	11.2	8.7	11.2	10.4	22.7	38.7	50.6	58,812	78,728	33.9	8.2
Hesperia.............	58.4	19.1	26.7	11.5	13.1	12.8	12.6	12.4	10.9	33.0	48.6	62,582	90,173	44.1	5.2
Highland.............	53.3	23.7	32.0	10.1	11.1	11.7	12.7	13.1	9.3	31.3	51.4	44,605	53,104	19.1	4.2
Hollister............	67.2	18.6	29.9	9.7	15.3	13.8	14.6	8.0	8.6	32.9	50.1	34,413	34,741	1.0	10.5
Huntington Beach......	18.2	16.2	19.3	7.1	12.5	12.2	16.3	14.2	18.3	43.9	49.3	189,594	191,037	0.8	5.7
Huntington Park......	97.0	46.6	31.1	9.6	12.1	14.6	12.7	8.6	11.2	33.0	52.6	61,348	58,118	-5.3	1.2
Imperial Beach	45.0	18.3	24.6	8.4	19.3	12.0	12.1	9.5	14.0	34.0	49.4	26,992	26,324	-2.5	4.2
Indio................	64.6	24.9	23.7	8.8	12.0	12.3	12.7	9.9	20.6	40.5	51.8	49,116	79,116	61.1	13.5
Inglewood............	45.9	29.6	19.9	10.8	15.4	13.9	15.4	12.3	12.4	38.2	52.8	112,580	109,673	-2.6	0.8
Irvine...............	11.4	38.8	22.7	13.4	14.6	15.0	15.3	9.1	9.9	34.6	51.2	143,072	212,043	48.2	30.8
Laguna Hills.........	23.1	25.4	20.7	10.6	10.0	14.1	17.6	13.9	13.1	41.4	46.7	31,178	30,212	-3.1	3.7
Laguna Niguel........	18.8	20.2	20.3	7.2	12.3	9.7	14.4	18.8	17.3	45.3	51.7	61,891	62,985	1.8	5.3
La Habra.............	57.7	30.9	23.8	7.8	17.0	13.6	11.7	13.3	12.8	36.6	48.6	58,974	60,287	2.2	3.6
Lake Elsinore........	56.0	19.6	30.1	7.9	17.4	15.4	11.4	9.9	8.0	32.2	52.3	28,928	53,418	84.7	24.3
Lake Forest..........	20.1	23.4	20.6	8.6	14.3	15.0	15.7	12.3	13.4	38.9	49.9	58,707	77,448	31.9	8.8
Lakewood.............	33.8	25.7	25.0	9.1	13.6	15.2	12.3	12.6	12.2	37.1	51.9	79,345	80,054	0.9	1.1
La Mesa..............	21.2	16.9	18.4	8.5	20.6	10.5	12.7	14.6	14.7	37.3	48.0	54,749	57,013	4.1	5.3
La Mirada............	41.7	22.1	17.6	17.7	13.2	11.6	12.4	13.4	14.1	36.1	48.8	46,783	48,523	3.7	1.2
Lancaster............	39.5	10.7	26.7	10.4	14.7	12.8	13.6	12.1	9.9	33.6	51.0	118,718	156,643	31.9	2.3
La Puente............	83.9	39.8	22.1	11.8	17.9	13.5	13.7	9.0	11.9	33.4	51.7	41,063	39,827	-3.0	1.2
La Quinta............	34.8	19.0	19.3	5.0	10.1	12.8	9.8	16.9	26.1	47.2	49.9	23,694	37,468	58.1	10.2
La Verne.............	35.6	15.4	20.4	10.7	8.3	11.6	13.4	16.7	19.0	44.4	52.5	31,638	31,121	-1.6	4.3
Lawndale.............	54.4	41.0	17.4	15.3	17.1	14.6	13.0	13.1	9.6	35.5	46.6	31,711	32,769	3.3	0.9
Lemon Grove..........	44.5	20.8	24.5	9.8	11.8	15.3	10.4	13.5	14.8	38.4	52.7	24,918	25,318	1.6	7.1
Lincoln..............	19.1	9.8	20.7	6.3	11.9	13.0	12.6	7.9	27.6	43.0	52.3	11,205	42,932	283.2	11.0
Livermore	21.1	15.4	22.5	7.5	13.4	11.6	18.6	13.9	12.5	40.9	50.9	73,345	81,397	11.0	10.9
Lodi.................	39.2	18.8	26.5	7.9	12.6	13.8	11.7	12.7	15.0	37.3	51.2	56,999	62,134	9.0	6.0
Lompoc...............	52.7	17.6	27.3	9.3	14.5	12.1	12.2	12.2	12.4	33.6	44.7	41,103	42,440	3.3	2.6
Long Beach...........	44.5	26.2	23.4	11.0	17.6	13.6	13.6	10.4	10.5	33.6	50.9	461,522	462,235	0.2	1.6
Los Altos............	4.3	28.4	23.8	3.5	5.6	13.3	15.8	17.3	20.7	46.8	53.3	27,693	29,001	4.7	6.0
Los Angeles..........	48.9	37.7	20.8	10.4	17.8	14.2	13.5	11.1	12.1	35.6	50.7	3,694,820	3,792,724	2.6	5.5
Los Banos............	70.8	28.9	31.3	7.6	13.3	13.6	11.7	11.5	11.0	33.6	51.4	25,869	35,967	39.0	8.9
Los Gatos............	5.7	20.0	23.8	3.0	9.3	11.1	18.7	14.1	19.9	46.2	49.1	28,592	29,444	3.0	4.3
Lynwood..............	87.5	39.9	30.1	12.1	16.8	16.3	9.5	8.5	6.8	29.8	51.1	69,845	69,766	-0.1	1.9
Madera...............	73.9	29.5	32.9	9.3	15.0	14.3	11.4	7.8	9.4	30.6	51.2	43,207	61,416	42.1	6.7
Manhattan Beach	7.4	12.3	22.3	3.0	11.4	16.4	18.2	15.7	13.0	43.2	50.7	33,852	35,135	3.8	2.2
Manteca..............	40.6	16.6	26.7	10.0	14.1	11.6	13.6	12.5	11.5	34.5	52.5	49,258	67,276	36.6	17.8
Martinez.............	13.4	11.2	18.5	8.4	11.0	11.8	15.0	17.4	17.8	45.2	52.0	35,866	36,036	0.5	6.5
Maywood..............	97.5	52.3	27.1	12.7	14.3	12.9	12.6	8.2	12.1	31.4	53.7	28,083	27,395	-2.4	0.7
Menifee..............	34.6	16.6	24.8	7.6	13.8	11.1	11.1	11.9	19.8	38.5	51.7	NA	77,519	**********	16.9

1. May be of any race.

Households, Group Quarters, Crime, and Education

AREANAME	Households, 2016								Serious crimes known to police[2], 2016				Educational attainment, 2016		
				Percent					Total		Rate[3]			Attainment[4] (percent)	
	Number	Persons per household	Family	Married couple family	Female headed family[1]	Non-family	One person	Persons in group quarters	Number	Rate	Violent	Property	Population age 25 and over	High school graduate or less	Bachelor's degree or more
	27	28	29	30	31	32	33	34	35	36	37	38	39	40	41
CALIFORNIA— Cont'd															
Delano	10,070	4.28	87.7	65.7	13.8	12.3	8.3	9,565	1,816	3,449	501	2,947	29,733	71.0	8.0
Desert Hot Springs	11,019	2.57	58.3	39.5	16.0	41.7	33.0	NA	1,151	4,028	787	3,241	20,619	56.0	14.6
Diamond Bar	17,788	3.18	81.6	64.1	13.9	18.4	15.7	161	997	1,744	115	1,629	42,541	21.7	53.3
Downey	32,646	3.45	80.1	51.5	21.0	19.9	16.9	642	3,744	3,264	325	2,939	72,353	46.6	23.7
Dublin	19,879	2.94	77.7	62.9	7.5	22.3	18.2	1,226	1,184	1,959	144	1,815	40,675	12.5	65.7
East Palo Alto	7,897	3.74	75.2	45.1	19.3	24.8	14.6	NA	639	2,133	404	1,729	17,585	66.8	14.1
El Cajon	32,447	3.12	70.7	48.3	16.9	29.3	24.1	2,455	2,841	2,719	378	2,341	64,819	46.7	18.2
El Centro	11,716	3.73	80.2	54.4	19.1	19.8	17.2	518	2,519	5,697	464	5,234	27,236	52.6	14.9
Elk Grove	51,695	3.27	81.4	60.7	13.8	18.6	16.8	875	2,889	1,702	322	1,380	107,816	25.8	38.1
El Monte	27,249	4.21	83.6	50.6	22.8	16.4	12.6	1,194	2,949	2,513	382	2,131	75,805	70.8	10.2
El Paso de Robles (Paso Robles)	11,813	2.69	73.9	57.6	10.4	26.1	23.4	NA	1,044	3,269	210	3,059	21,228	31.9	29.5
Encinitas	24,018	2.61	64.3	54.7	6.6	35.7	25.8	357	1,142	1,796	165	1,631	46,574	11.6	59.9
Escondido	45,367	3.29	73.0	52.5	14.0	27.0	19.2	2,195	3,841	2,512	363	2,149	97,314	47.8	22.9
Eureka	11,838	2.20	51.6	31.9	9.1	48.4	34.0	1,232	1,776	6,582	945	5,637	20,445	34.2	29.0
Fairfield	38,027	2.97	76.0	52.3	17.1	24.0	17.9	1,932	3,321	2,900	416	2,484	75,362	37.9	25.4
Folsom	27,417	2.63	70.5	56.8	9.1	29.5	25.9	5,230	1,460	1,890	98	1,792	52,702	21.6	47.6
Fontana	57,868	3.61	81.9	58.5	16.8	18.1	13.7	554	5,266	2,513	415	2,098	128,037	54.3	17.8
Foster City	12,903	2.64	72.8	59.0	10.9	27.2	22.6	NA	375	1,100	94	1,006	25,256	8.3	74.0
Fountain Valley	18,741	2.99	76.9	62.3	9.9	23.1	17.2	491	1,506	2,629	110	2,519	41,957	25.3	42.1
Fremont	71,599	3.23	83.0	71.7	7.1	17.0	13.7	1,611	5,135	2,177	178	1,999	162,316	24.0	56.3
Fresno	166,288	3.09	68.4	40.1	20.0	31.6	24.1	8,127	23,729	4,522	611	3,911	316,019	46.1	21.6
Fullerton	45,635	3.01	68.7	52.4	10.6	31.3	21.7	3,474	3,940	2,775	240	2,535	93,665	31.2	42.6
Gardena	19,844	2.99	66.3	45.7	13.4	33.7	28.0	791	1,820	2,995	556	2,439	40,400	42.8	26.6
Garden Grove	47,718	3.63	78.8	55.9	14.1	21.2	13.4	1,834	4,867	2,762	309	2,452	116,931	46.8	23.6
Gilroy	16,557	3.30	80.9	51.0	21.9	19.1	14.3	467	1,924	3,554	336	3,218	34,641	43.8	24.9
Glendale	75,013	2.65	67.8	49.1	12.6	32.2	27.2	1,740	3,677	1,812	112	1,700	149,782	31.1	42.5
Glendora	17,174	2.96	78.3	58.1	14.6	21.7	16.9	977	1,431	2,732	134	2,598	38,456	33.8	30.8
Goleta	10,232	2.99	72.2	51.9	13.3	27.8	17.9	NA	521	1,673	119	1,554	20,414	26.8	43.0
Hanford	20,068	2.74	69.3	46.6	14.9	30.7	22.6	479	1,762	3,148	475	2,673	36,289	47.2	16.3
Hawthorne	28,870	3.03	67.1	35.5	21.1	32.9	26.7	654	3,187	3,569	732	2,837	56,550	47.6	21.6
Hayward	45,792	3.40	75.8	51.5	15.9	24.2	17.1	3,381	5,272	3,272	392	2,880	106,790	47.7	26.7
Hemet	29,465	2.83	65.9	47.5	12.3	34.1	30.9	764	4,005	4,721	724	3,997	54,128	51.4	11.6
Hesperia	26,802	3.49	80.1	52.1	15.5	19.9	15.5	NA	2,133	2,272	356	1,916	57,877	62.7	9.9
Highland	16,035	3.42	79.1	50.6	18.4	20.9	18.3	NA	1,373	2,488	433	2,055	31,849	45.8	24.1
Hollister	10,424	3.53	80.8	62.4	16.9	19.2	15.6	NA	512	1,349	306	1,043	22,310	48.4	15.4
Huntington Beach	78,998	2.53	64.8	48.3	12.0	35.2	27.1	1,020	4,889	2,396	177	2,218	147,664	22.8	41.4
Huntington Park	15,576	3.77	82.6	49.7	22.4	17.4	12.7	NA	2,451	4,106	776	3,330	34,899	78.1	6.0
Imperial Beach	9,453	2.83	67.8	35.3	23.4	32.2	24.5	929	443	1,604	257	1,347	18,362	44.3	22.5
Indio	30,887	2.83	59.6	43.6	10.9	40.4	35.0	929	2,381	2,669	490	2,179	59,749	59.5	14.4
Inglewood	38,724	2.82	64.3	33.5	26.0	35.7	30.3	1,350	3,286	2,932	741	2,192	76,754	43.5	22.5
Irvine	94,321	2.74	69.2	59.1	6.2	30.8	21.7	7,486	3,889	1,458	57	1,401	170,063	11.3	71.6
Laguna Hills	10,587	2.93	77.5	62.2	11.3	22.5	15.8	NA	570	1,779	106	1,673	21,645	20.7	49.5
Laguna Niguel	24,116	2.69	76.4	64.0	7.1	23.6	20.0	376	816	1,230	98	1,132	47,348	16.2	55.2
La Habra	18,547	3.30	77.6	53.5	15.6	22.4	16.7	467	1,454	2,327	163	2,164	42,136	39.2	29.2
Lake Elsinore	17,692	3.63	82.1	61.9	12.8	17.9	14.4	556	2,020	3,161	243	2,918	39,786	41.0	20.3
Lake Forest	29,496	2.80	75.9	60.2	11.7	24.1	20.3	140	851	1,019	126	893	58,860	21.6	47.7
Lakewood	24,806	3.26	75.2	52.3	17.8	24.8	19.7	777	2,744	3,350	272	3,077	53,413	30.1	29.3
La Mesa	23,594	2.51	58.2	42.8	12.8	41.8	29.4	777	1,866	3,075	325	2,750	43,837	27.0	36.8
La Mirada	13,953	3.29	80.6	61.5	12.6	19.4	13.7	3,251	974	1,959	171	1,788	31,826	35.0	27.7
Lancaster	49,934	3.07	69.4	43.0	18.8	30.6	24.5	6,959	4,591	2,835	681	2,154	100,768	50.3	17.3
La Puente	9,460	4.26	89.4	45.7	28.7	10.6	8.9	NA	691	1,688	320	1,368	26,663	67.4	14.2
La Quinta	16,017	2.55	71.2	57.1	8.5	28.8	25.0	NA	1,171	2,852	209	2,643	30,984	27.0	34.3
La Verne	11,299	2.80	71.4	49.1	14.5	28.6	23.0	772	602	1,824	124	1,699	22,329	25.8	40.0
Lawndale	9,556	3.45	71.8	46.1	15.9	28.2	19.6	NA	722	2,151	578	1,573	22,323	54.1	17.1
Lemon Grove	7,909	3.35	75.6	48.6	20.4	24.4	18.7	NA	648	2,402	515	1,887	17,657	52.0	13.1
Lincoln	18,084	2.59	66.0	59.7	5.1	34.0	27.7	NA	570	1,207	61	1,146	34,305	20.7	40.5
Livermore	30,749	2.89	79.4	66.7	10.2	20.6	16.2	374	2,458	2,745	194	2,550	62,359	25.9	38.5
Lodi	23,014	2.78	68.5	50.3	13.4	31.5	25.4	713	2,286	3,513	539	2,974	42,449	51.8	18.1
Lompoc	13,930	2.94	70.6	50.9	11.5	29.4	25.4	2,816	1,199	2,692	498	2,193	27,685	45.1	12.4
Long Beach	160,769	2.87	60.7	38.2	16.2	39.3	29.8	8,607	17,070	3,583	597	2,985	308,744	39.5	30.0
Los Altos	11,615	2.60	82.7	71.9	8.8	17.3	16.4	336	356	1,148	42	1,106	22,219	7.1	79.6
Los Angeles	1,378,844	2.82	59.7	38.5	14.3	40.3	30.3	85,128	127,968	3,193	719	2,474	2,735,071	43.1	32.8
Los Banos	10,831	3.46	82.7	57.8	19.3	17.3	13.5	123	1,282	3,397	321	3,076	23,009	63.0	9.6
Los Gatos	11,959	2.52	70.3	57.2	8.7	29.7	24.0	393	637	2,058	68	1,990	22,336	14.8	65.8
Lynwood	14,840	4.61	87.1	52.6	22.2	12.9	8.3	2,737	2,182	3,011	647	2,364	41,162	75.5	6.8
Madera	18,471	3.48	76.5	55.2	18.2	23.5	21.1	NA	2,364	3,651	780	2,871	37,251	62.9	7.3
Manhattan Beach	14,693	2.43	65.4	55.4	4.9	34.6	26.2	NA	1,083	3,012	147	2,865	26,680	6.7	78.3
Manteca	24,828	3.07	71.5	50.7	13.6	28.5	20.4	711	2,944	3,818	316	3,502	48,666	53.8	14.0
Martinez	14,770	2.55	68.1	53.5	9.9	31.9	26.3	631	909	2,359	132	2,226	27,970	23.3	39.6
Maywood	7,096	3.88	87.3	56.0	19.7	12.7	9.2	NA	563	2,012	436	1,576	16,643	84.7	4.7
Menifee	29,148	3.03	73.8	56.1	11.8	26.2	23.9	NA	2,254	2,529	151	2,378	59,825	38.8	22.1

1. No spouse present. 2. Data for serious crimes have not been adjusted for underreporting. This may affect comparability between geographic areas and over time. 3. Per 100,000 population estimated by the FBI. 4. Persons 25 years old and over.

AREANAME	Money income, 2016 Households Median income	Percent with income less than $20,000	Percent with income of $200,000 or more	Median family income	Median non-family household income	Median earnings, 2016 All persons	Men	Women	Housing units, 2016 Total	Occupied	Percent owner occupied	Median value[1] (dollars)	Median rent (dollars)
	42	43	44	45	46	47	48	49	50	51	52	53	54
CALIFORNIA— Cont'd													
Delano............................	41,157	20.0	0.2	42,159	21,719	16,627	18,912	14,164	10,945	10,070	55.2	168,800	833
Desert Hot Springs.............	34,037	25.2	0.4	31,390	33,453	20,670	20,511	20,729	14,237	11,019	57.4	177,500	894
Diamond Bar	95,639	7.0	12.7	110,007	38,330	42,006	48,125	40,055	18,542	17,788	72.5	669,900	1,941
Downey............................	65,578	10.2	5.1	72,270	36,179	32,211	35,368	31,408	34,039	32,646	45.4	530,400	1,337
Dublin..............................	140,886	6.0	30.5	152,333	78,772	80,967	99,225	56,218	20,508	19,879	64.5	845,000	2,557
East Palo Alto....................	67,708	15.2	9.7	68,429	47,573	26,915	32,065	22,846	8,293	7,897	35.8	721,500	1,642
El Cajon...........................	45,577	20.6	2.2	55,436	27,341	26,911	29,312	23,861	33,529	32,447	38.3	424,300	1,182
El Centro..........................	47,500	26.0	3.3	53,811	18,971	25,568	27,809	21,778	13,967	11,716	54.9	182,300	770
Elk Grove..........................	91,899	8.0	10.8	98,463	51,135	43,214	51,835	36,907	52,950	51,695	73.6	374,300	1,552
El Monte............................	48,434	19.1	2.7	50,887	20,460	21,647	23,876	19,229	28,428	27,249	40.0	430,600	1,191
El Paso de Robles (Paso Robles).........................	67,573	7.6	6.8	76,086	37,037	36,693	45,920	28,919	12,322	11,813	68.5	461,000	1,095
Encinitas..........................	111,044	9.1	22.4	143,275	54,450	57,246	71,171	47,947	25,952	24,018	64.1	933,900	1,865
Escondido.........................	60,328	14.2	4.4	62,792	38,456	25,786	30,162	22,282	47,043	45,367	48.7	450,300	1,301
Eureka..............................	42,889	18.8	2.9	53,571	28,603	26,836	30,315	23,845	13,093	11,838	48.6	281,600	899
Fairfield...........................	69,235	10.0	8.3	76,290	50,349	33,937	37,144	27,163	39,413	38,027	55.5	376,000	1,361
Folsom.............................	102,460	6.0	15.7	124,284	56,215	61,875	83,216	47,690	28,761	27,417	70.6	482,600	1,525
Fontana............................	66,073	11.9	3.8	67,487	53,233	30,034	36,270	21,452	60,314	57,868	64.5	337,100	1,188
Foster City........................	141,947	3.8	30.4	156,705	97,050	86,404	100,494	62,048	13,670	12,903	59.4	1,199,800	3,182
Fountain Valley...................	88,563	10.5	11.4	95,752	48,688	42,355	51,405	32,872	19,304	18,741	67.7	673,600	2,031
Fremont............................	122,419	4.9	24.6	135,098	56,406	62,341	80,333	51,080	74,967	71,599	58.4	877,700	2,168
Fresno..............................	44,905	24.2	4.3	51,015	30,656	25,960	28,238	22,747	176,898	166,288	46.5	227,500	913
Fullerton	72,656	12.9	11.0	83,812	49,419	31,555	36,343	30,024	48,091	45,635	51.1	607,700	1,473
Gardena............................	55,827	17.4	3.7	64,688	32,052	29,270	31,409	26,495	20,626	19,844	44.2	436,800	1,177
Garden Grove.....................	63,566	11.1	6.3	67,480	45,207	29,876	31,954	25,396	49,013	47,718	51.1	532,700	1,483
Gilroy..............................	88,836	9.9	8.3	87,974	59,709	35,880	40,747	27,270	17,251	16,557	59.4	640,700	1,635
Glendale...........................	64,611	18.8	9.9	72,008	41,491	37,358	41,770	32,324	78,169	75,013	33.5	717,600	1,479
Glendora...........................	81,007	10.3	10.1	89,009	36,188	36,303	45,961	30,975	17,798	17,174	71.0	537,500	1,532
Goleta..............................	91,415	6.4	10.6	94,310	71,493	35,126	40,345	24,145	10,932	10,232	60.3	771,000	2,005
Hanford............................	48,528	17.1	4.1	52,946	35,721	29,560	29,713	27,474	20,834	20,068	50.8	193,200	959
Hawthorne.........................	48,354	16.0	3.1	51,577	30,052	24,830	27,766	21,901	29,657	28,870	26.8	467,700	1,094
Hayward...........................	75,352	11.3	7.6	78,863	50,030	35,327	39,493	31,086	47,076	45,792	50.8	515,600	1,634
Hemet..............................	37,314	27.3	1.0	44,950	21,865	25,916	30,037	19,902	34,307	29,465	54.8	180,500	996
Hesperia...........................	51,255	17.5	2.8	52,397	31,805	29,288	35,845	20,846	27,621	26,802	61.5	215,700	1,148
Highland...........................	51,466	21.5	5.8	51,367	41,449	28,173	31,351	23,826	16,803	16,035	64.3	305,100	1,047
Hollister...........................	70,997	13.6	5.5	80,705	27,428	29,010	36,103	19,847	10,670	10,424	59.0	477,400	1,160
Huntington Beach...............	86,112	9.0	11.6	100,290	61,019	41,747	49,765	36,713	83,580	78,998	59.7	724,800	1,768
Huntington Park..................	35,137	28.9	0.6	38,586	15,756	20,642	23,145	16,925	15,805	15,576	29.3	354,300	1,036
Imperial Beach...................	53,322	13.0	4.7	49,949	38,209	32,931	37,201	28,452	11,043	9,453	30.5	493,500	1,258
Indio................................	40,449	24.4	2.9	54,179	21,894	26,785	30,697	22,332	37,590	30,887	68.6	267,700	977
Inglewood.........................	51,620	17.2	3.3	59,302	32,208	30,346	31,281	27,126	40,272	38,724	36.3	418,900	1,247
Irvine...............................	97,496	11.6	18.4	113,646	57,991	54,247	73,348	41,439	101,592	94,321	48.7	806,000	2,243
Laguna Hills.......................	91,316	3.1	20.0	107,754	52,479	39,733	45,444	35,141	10,804	10,587	69.5	672,600	1,909
Laguna Niguel	107,101	6.0	21.0	136,473	60,406	43,561	54,201	29,528	25,197	24,116	69.9	802,100	1,973
La Habra...........................	72,404	11.4	5.3	73,848	56,033	31,966	35,699	31,099	19,198	18,547	54.9	512,300	1,414
Lake Elsinore......................	63,742	10.7	3.6	65,349	41,573	31,424	38,236	22,930	19,766	17,692	64.6	329,800	1,309
Lake Forest........................	100,557	8.0	14.5	115,335	64,102	51,267	61,398	41,535	30,473	29,496	68.5	608,500	1,954
Lakewood..........................	86,068	11.1	5.4	96,589	47,849	40,317	50,556	35,461	25,583	24,806	72.8	520,600	1,501
La Mesa............................	62,908	13.3	3.7	72,620	50,725	36,651	40,976	29,446	25,317	23,594	37.7	479,000	1,425
La Mirada	93,180	7.5	8.6	96,553	50,695	41,113	45,595	31,576	14,067	13,953	73.9	549,600	1,686
Lancaster..........................	46,910	23.8	3.4	52,954	30,480	33,789	41,622	30,705	55,363	49,934	48.1	239,000	1,114
La Puente..........................	49,661	15.6	0.7	48,139	27,156	22,103	26,354	16,863	9,780	9,460	52.8	398,300	1,351
La Quinta..........................	68,996	9.7	13.4	85,841	40,747	39,386	41,486	31,835	26,749	16,017	68.8	360,800	1,579
La Verne...........................	85,740	9.3	10.6	96,626	51,663	37,161	42,202	32,190	11,410	11,299	78.7	583,700	1,433
Lawndale...........................	58,693	8.5	1.2	65,042	44,200	25,496	30,802	17,348	10,141	9,556	33.0	502,300	1,293
Lemon Grove......................	60,754	18.7	2.3	65,848	34,102	28,454	28,319	28,541	8,233	7,909	49.3	417,700	1,370
Lincoln.............................	87,172	11.7	13.4	103,796	47,532	51,576	67,250	34,000	19,037	18,084	81.4	401,900	1,814
Livermore	111,625	8.3	18.8	129,310	52,018	47,336	70,203	37,087	31,555	30,749	71.2	681,100	1,925
Lodi.................................	55,317	12.2	4.2	61,350	46,334	31,738	37,456	24,768	24,476	23,014	53.0	301,400	1,070
Lompoc............................	52,063	16.5	1.9	61,662	28,182	27,899	30,936	23,705	14,609	13,930	42.4	289,700	1,079
Long Beach	60,075	15.8	6.8	67,534	48,786	31,597	32,460	30,449	168,588	160,769	37.7	518,900	1,194
Los Altos..........................	218,054	6.5	53.1	246,258	77,500	131,030	181,787	91,837	12,162	11,615	77.5	2,000,000	3,115
Los Angeles.......................	54,432	19.3	8.4	61,372	41,386	28,930	31,097	25,742	1,478,666	1,378,844	35.9	593,500	1,315
Los Banos.........................	43,014	13.9	1.6	51,308	23,338	25,410	35,285	19,571	11,919	10,831	54.0	278,400	1,175
Los Gatos.........................	147,468	5.7	37.9	184,730	85,522	87,368	102,145	62,530	12,641	11,959	68.7	1,667,200	2,336
Lynwood...........................	45,201	13.1	2.8	46,184	29,414	22,879	24,719	20,283	15,187	14,840	40.2	346,200	1,072
Madera.............................	38,306	21.4	0.7	40,752	33,031	23,693	24,429	21,912	19,444	18,471	46.0	216,800	950
Manhattan Beach	131,861	5.0	34.3	185,675	75,806	79,825	100,145	70,309	16,580	14,693	62.5	2,000,000	1,975
Manteca............................	62,106	13.6	3.6	73,550	31,026	31,732	40,946	22,365	25,695	24,828	57.7	355,400	1,318
Martinez...........................	99,147	8.5	13.9	120,067	54,315	53,956	62,087	51,181	15,431	14,770	69.2	573,700	1,626
Maywood...........................	37,146	22.0	0.0	42,922	0	21,107	23,376	17,159	7,378	7,096	26.7	358,000	981
Menifee............................	59,895	11.3	4.7	76,749	26,382	34,408	43,874	25,322	31,264	29,148	73.5	311,800	1,487

1. Specified owner-occupied units; $2,000,000 represents $2,000,000 or more.

Table D. Cities — Commuting, Computer Access, Migration, Labor Force, and Employment

AREANAME	Commuting 2016 Percent		Computer access Percent		Migration		Civilian labor force, 2016				Civilian employment, 2016			
									Unemployment[3]		Population age 16 and older		Population age 16 to 64	
	Drove alone	With commutes of 30 minutes or more	With a computer in the house	With Internet access	Percent who lived in the same house one year ago	Percent who lived in another state or county one year ago	Total	Percent change 2016-2017	Total	Rate	Number	Percent in labor force	Number	Percent who worked full-year full-time
	55	56	57	58	59	60	61	62	63	64	65	66	67	68
CALIFORNIA— Cont'd														
Delano	NA	16.9	61.3	54.5	86.2	10.3	22,278	0.4	5,609	25.2	39,038	46.9	35,741	23.9
Desert Hot Springs	84.7	50.2	82.3	74.5	84.1	1.8	11,495	2.2	785	6.8	22,696	56.9	17,656	41.4
Diamond Bar	79.0	66.0	96.3	92.0	90.7	4.8	30,652	1.3	1,133	3.7	48,218	60.6	39,627	49.3
Downey	80.6	50.6	94.7	88.5	91.6	1.5	57,935	1.3	2,561	4.4	87,215	68.3	75,511	55.1
Dublin	60.4	59.1	99.2	97.9	81.1	14.6	31,040	1.5	982	3.2	44,493	72.0	40,121	55.1
East Palo Alto	72.6	30.3	97.8	82.1	91.0	2.9	15,069	1.4	477	3.2	21,581	77.4	20,005	53.3
El Cajon	78.7	39.9	92.2	85.3	80.9	7.1	45,483	0.8	1,987	4.4	75,479	60.1	63,199	42.1
El Centro	80.2	12.5	80.2	74.9	85.8	3.8	19,322	-6.8	2,853	14.8	32,842	51.2	26,640	33.6
Elk Grove	80.5	47.7	97.2	92.7	87.9	3.9	81,656	1.1	3,173	3.9	130,221	64.2	110,041	49.5
El Monte	72.6	44.1	88.8	76.7	93.6	1.5	51,926	1.4	2,418	4.7	91,286	59.7	76,537	43.6
El Paso de Robles (Paso Robles)	68.9	40.4	95.2	85.1	NA	NA	16,429	1.2	610	3.7	24,766	65.3	19,412	51.7
Encinitas	70.9	28.5	94.5	92.7	86.8	3.6	33,524	1.1	1,083	3.2	51,147	65.5	38,427	50.7
Escondido	75.9	47.0	92.3	84.3	86.6	2.6	69,590	1.0	2,713	3.9	117,529	68.3	101,725	48.4
Eureka	75.5	12.0	90.1	84.4	87.3	7.1	12,872	0.6	527	4.1	23,331	61.3	17,905	42.2
Fairfield	79.6	43.8	93.6	89.1	82.0	9.0	53,324	0.7	2,403	4.5	90,049	65.1	75,321	46.3
Folsom	77.6	34.1	96.2	93.7	88.2	6.9	36,796	1.2	1,281	3.5	59,742	61.3	49,813	50.3
Fontana	78.0	45.6	94.8	84.3	91.5	3.6	97,523	2.1	4,591	4.7	157,134	66.6	139,473	47.4
Foster City	72.7	55.2	99.3	97.6	79.1	12.3	20,025	1.6	521	2.6	26,867	66.4	21,812	53.6
Fountain Valley	79.7	49.9	95.7	90.3	86.9	5.1	28,823	1.0	1,048	3.6	47,218	59.8	36,705	48.8
Fremont	72.1	58.8	95.9	91.4	88.9	6.1	120,299	1.3	3,932	3.3	181,200	66.5	153,361	57.2
Fresno	76.4	19.2	88.4	80.1	82.1	3.7	233,354	0.9	15,742	6.7	388,619	61.2	331,042	39.8
Fullerton	79.0	49.6	93.5	89.4	85.2	5.7	71,131	1.1	2,538	3.6	114,429	66.6	96,337	45.6
Gardena	76.2	40.1	86.9	75.7	91.2	1.6	30,497	1.3	1,464	4.8	47,742	60.4	38,792	48.9
Garden Grove	76.9	47.5	94.9	86.1	90.9	2.8	83,156	0.9	3,240	3.9	138,928	65.6	118,109	46.6
Gilroy	77.1	53.7	97.9	90.7	88.4	1.7	28,581	1.5	1,123	3.9	40,379	70.9	33,765	45.5
Glendale	78.6	48.8	88.6	83.6	87.6	3.2	103,362	1.5	4,481	4.3	167,747	64.3	133,420	49.3
Glendora	79.2	53.4	94.9	86.2	89.1	2.8	26,089	1.5	1,127	4.3	42,409	63.0	33,110	44.9
Goleta	77.0	8.6	NA	NA	87.5	4.9	17,093	0.5	514	3.0	24,726	72.1	19,936	53.6
Hanford	79.5	23.1	91.8	82.5	79.9	8.7	24,646	0.6	1,830	7.4	43,446	64.0	36,192	46.8
Hawthorne	73.0	45.5	89.9	72.0	88.1	3.4	45,321	1.3	2,095	4.6	65,709	69.0	57,287	50.4
Hayward	68.1	56.5	92.6	87.3	88.9	5.2	78,926	1.2	3,105	3.9	128,738	66.5	110,564	50.9
Hemet	73.8	47.0	85.0	71.3	81.0	4.4	29,327	1.5	1,986	6.8	61,536	45.3	42,401	33.9
Hesperia	84.7	53.1	91.8	86.0	88.2	2.9	35,315	1.8	2,176	6.2	72,200	53.3	62,001	41.8
Highland	81.8	33.6	84.0	79.4	NA	NA	24,493	2.1	1,216	5.0	39,295	60.5	34,189	42.4
Hollister	80.9	50.8	97.1	94.5	92.8	2.9	19,136	1.6	1,255	6.6	26,979	69.5	23,785	44.9
Huntington Beach	80.6	49.5	93.4	88.1	88.3	4.3	109,334	1.0	3,774	3.5	166,873	65.8	130,102	50.0
Huntington Park	67.9	51.6	82.7	68.0	95.1	0.3	26,925	1.3	1,294	4.8	42,407	63.1	35,810	47.7
Imperial Beach	81.3	48.6	94.4	84.4	NA	NA	12,093	0.6	618	5.1	21,082	65.4	17,237	45.1
Indio	80.5	24.8	84.7	70.9	89.7	2.7	39,912	2.1	2,580	6.5	69,686	54.0	51,471	44.4
Inglewood	72.6	51.4	92.2	80.9	90.0	1.3	53,236	1.1	2,853	5.4	91,735	65.5	78,052	47.8
Irvine	75.9	32.9	97.1	92.4	78.6	11.3	139,933	1.1	4,715	3.4	211,343	64.0	184,890	46.5
Laguna Hills	80.7	25.1	NA	NA	NA	NA	17,388	1.0	562	3.2	25,668	69.1	21,530	54.9
Laguna Niguel	75.6	41.6	97.1	93.6	87.4	2.7	35,228	0.9	1,166	3.3	53,674	66.0	42,354	50.2
La Habra	76.1	50.3	95.2	89.5	90.7	3.6	30,837	0.8	1,107	3.6	48,377	64.5	40,467	46.8
Lake Elsinore	79.0	70.5	96.8	91.6	84.5	5.6	28,889	2.0	1,386	4.8	47,248	66.5	42,114	45.9
Lake Forest	84.9	42.7	94.5	92.1	85.9	2.8	48,005	1.1	1,514	3.2	68,353	71.7	57,240	54.8
Lakewood	85.2	45.8	95.4	90.7	92.0	2.4	43,514	1.3	1,894	4.4	63,135	64.6	53,261	48.9
La Mesa	81.9	36.6	92.1	89.0	83.4	3.8	30,894	1.0	1,230	4.0	49,933	69.1	41,103	53.2
La Mirada	80.5	50.9	94.3	86.5	90.8	4.2	24,546	1.4	1,069	4.4	41,521	59.8	34,591	46.4
Lancaster	84.1	37.4	82.0	75.2	92.7	2.1	65,468	1.5	4,317	6.6	122,190	50.6	106,407	42.6
La Puente	71.7	54.4	93.2	75.3	90.6	1.5	19,294	1.3	925	4.8	32,728	64.0	27,934	42.5
La Quinta	76.5	18.5	94.5	91.5	86.9	5.5	18,861	2.0	969	5.1	33,491	60.4	22,801	49.6
La Verne	71.0	51.8	97.9	93.3	90.8	3.9	16,160	1.4	703	4.4	26,996	62.6	20,849	43.9
Lawndale	73.3	40.5	95.0	86.3	89.5	1.3	16,812	1.3	719	4.3	28,084	71.1	24,903	47.7
Lemon Grove	80.9	40.4	88.9	82.7	84.2	1.7	12,503	0.9	594	4.8	21,041	62.0	17,073	46.4
Lincoln	77.9	44.2	95.1	90.6	83.3	10.4	18,915	1.0	801	4.2	38,152	57.9	25,174	54.7
Livermore	74.4	44.0	96.0	92.8	91.0	3.9	48,581	1.4	1,483	3.1	71,346	71.9	60,239	56.3
Lodi	79.9	33.3	88.3	81.9	83.2	4.1	29,424	1.5	1,963	6.7	49,744	62.0	40,075	46.6
Lompoc	69.7	48.0	87.6	81.6	80.3	4.3	17,662	0.0	1,049	5.9	32,698	60.4	27,283	46.6
Long Beach	73.6	49.0	92.5	83.8	87.5	3.8	240,470	1.3	11,472	4.8	372,374	66.9	323,004	47.3
Los Altos	77.3	29.7	NA	NA	90.8	3.7	14,794	1.5	446	3.0	23,938	57.6	17,600	51.6
Los Angeles	69.7	52.4	90.5	80.5	88.5	3.2	2,068,455	1.4	97,673	4.7	3,241,537	65.8	2,760,333	47.3
Los Banos	82.0	38.8	90.0	72.2	90.7	2.5	16,435	0.7	1,902	11.6	27,442	61.0	23,283	38.8
Los Gatos	85.6	46.3	96.1	95.2	90.2	6.4	16,076	1.5	529	3.3	23,627	62.1	17,540	55.8
Lynwood	74.0	56.0	91.4	81.7	91.8	0.8	28,838	1.2	1,589	5.5	52,210	61.8	47,387	50.0
Madera	78.5	36.1	84.9	73.1	89.9	2.4	27,541	0.3	2,408	8.7	45,898	59.8	39,838	40.0
Manhattan Beach	79.9	44.3	NA	NA	88.2	3.8	19,911	1.4	692	3.5	28,665	67.9	24,007	54.3
Manteca	81.4	40.6	91.5	86.0	83.6	7.0	36,141	2.0	1,966	5.4	58,199	62.8	49,380	43.0
Martinez	73.2	43.3	92.6	89.3	89.3	3.7	20,917	1.3	729	3.5	32,133	65.3	25,327	50.5
Maywood	75.8	48.6	76.8	63.6	NA	NA	12,557	1.2	572	4.6	21,157	63.1	17,800	42.4
Menifee	81.0	58.0	91.9	89.6	88.2	4.3	37,732	2.0	1,891	5.0	69,422	56.4	51,903	44.3

1. Employed persons. 2. Households. 3. Percent of civilian labor force.

AREANAME	Value of residential construction authorized by building permits, 2017			Wholesale trade[1], 2012				Retail trade[2], 2012			
	New construction ($1,000)	Number of housing units	Percent single family	Number of establish-ments	Number of employees	Sales (mil dol)	Annual payroll (mil dol)	Number of establish-ments	Number of employees	Sales (mil dol)	Annual payroll (mil dol)
	69	70	71	72	73	74	75	76	77	78	79
CALIFORNIA— Cont'd											
Delano	11,530	67	100.0	20	180	189.0	7.9	80	1,045	277.3	26.3
Desert Hot Springs	7,930	35	100.0	1	D	D	D	40	549	144.4	13.1
Diamond Bar	35,149	77	100.0	249	634	1,359.9	29.2	113	1,062	311.6	23.4
Downey	38,763	144	95.8	97	813	338.5	37.5	275	4,421	1,163.8	107.2
Dublin	425,890	1,197	80.7	64	323	222.6	20.3	175	3,862	1,329.0	124.1
East Palo Alto	775	2	100.0	5	D	D	D	24	926	270.5	24.8
El Cajon	13,841	50	100.0	134	1,080	556.8	49.7	445	6,280	1,756.0	158.4
El Centro	895	6	100.0	53	433	294.8	15.8	200	4,172	925.9	91.7
Elk Grove	75,250	402	100.0	42	347	83.9	18.9	280	5,913	1,823.8	173.9
El Monte	35,855	179	12.8	294	1,887	808.8	71.4	274	3,254	1,676.8	111.8
El Paso de Robles (Paso Robles)	32,907	244	8.6	47	328	129.7	14.1	151	2,429	625.2	61.4
Encinitas	32,207	115	100.0	96	462	212.1	24.3	282	3,927	1,119.7	110.9
Escondido	83,353	459	51.2	132	1,165	545.8	54.2	541	9,202	2,786.0	263.2
Eureka	480	4	100.0	42	388	134.3	15.8	233	3,186	971.3	84.0
Fairfield	72,748	268	100.0	69	1,393	869.7	72.1	311	5,307	1,398.6	133.8
Folsom	90,837	494	28.1	44	374	788.8	36.4	282	5,534	1,639.5	151.0
Fontana	164,525	663	84.8	145	3,620	1,811.5	165.0	321	5,905	2,145.1	171.5
Foster City	0	0	0.0	60	D	D	D	31	876	305.0	25.3
Fountain Valley	5,034	16	100.0	105	1,076	657.1	60.4	221	3,205	1,298.6	88.7
Fremont	491,566	1,946	16.8	458	9,470	13,487.4	720.4	411	7,229	2,617.9	231.1
Fresno	284,088	1,467	46.4	514	7,741	5,459.8	388.1	1,539	22,005	5,960.2	555.9
Fullerton	29,891	211	10.0	236	2,434	2,539.6	141.5	374	5,211	1,516.4	130.8
Gardena	9,880	49	91.8	164	1,540	642.6	63.2	177	2,197	754.0	66.5
Garden Grove	2,770	11	100.0	232	2,465	1,239.7	113.3	402	5,005	1,656.2	134.7
Gilroy	122,835	518	47.1	41	D	D	D	313	5,155	1,191.9	111.9
Glendale	38,722	230	3.5	254	1,911	1,386.6	97.1	731	11,330	3,138.2	300.7
Glendora	28,788	101	100.0	34	362	162.9	25.1	131	2,471	688.2	64.0
Goleta	9,345	42	100.0	52	999	620.2	95.5	127	2,317	727.7	66.4
Hanford	45,740	183	100.0	26	325	191.2	18.5	168	2,905	741.6	67.5
Hawthorne	3,569	24	50.0	67	1,209	480.3	56.2	183	3,443	1,382.2	101.6
Hayward	141,676	414	100.0	457	6,380	4,546.4	386.7	399	5,840	1,765.7	162.5
Hemet	1,000	5	100.0	21	124	69.1	4.0	203	3,658	845.5	93.6
Hesperia	50,145	232	100.0	42	186	231.4	7.7	173	2,101	615.5	45.9
Highland	18,017	67	100.0	14	D	D	D	59	836	234.9	21.1
Hollister	125,335	521	99.6	20	212	72.2	10.3	88	1,192	318.2	32.5
Huntington Beach	72,603	277	19.1	403	4,714	10,353.7	291.2	556	8,069	2,505.6	233.2
Huntington Park	0	0	0.0	55	740	399.3	28.5	182	2,196	622.7	55.4
Imperial Beach	15,101	110	19.1	6	9	3.3	0.3	30	224	45.3	4.4
Indio	78,630	478	73.2	35	373	166.7	15.3	162	2,624	862.9	79.5
Inglewood	1,440	8	25.0	81	2,277	977.4	76.3	257	3,440	1,219.9	85.6
Irvine	764,433	3,240	52.9	986	18,431	30,339.3	1,395.5	593	9,845	4,254.4	363.2
Laguna Hills	0	0	0.0	94	623	282.3	41.9	186	2,324	452.6	51.3
Laguna Niguel	63,692	235	0.9	63	264	95.4	11.1	133	2,959	1,254.0	107.5
La Habra	23,317	111	100.0	72	416	247.9	22.0	173	3,158	912.1	78.9
Lake Elsinore	163,096	564	100.0	37	272	79.4	10.4	157	2,732	784.9	69.5
Lake Forest	230,226	763	100.0	187	3,004	1,741.4	213.4	205	3,212	1,068.1	116.0
Lakewood	2,442	20	20.0	32	142	38.9	5.3	228	4,820	1,104.4	106.2
La Mesa	624	4	100.0	23	192	66.6	8.5	229	3,846	1,070.3	101.9
La Mirada	15,445	31	100.0	125	3,047	2,257.2	185.6	88	1,375	391.9	40.2
Lancaster	38,855	121	100.0	68	867	887.2	30.5	300	4,983	1,562.3	132.5
La Puente	632	5	100.0	24	110	40.7	3.6	92	1,111	243.8	25.7
La Quinta	32,884	113	100.0	17	33	34.7	3.3	93	2,204	637.4	57.4
La Verne	12,072	25	100.0	66	691	527.1	37.9	74	1,298	355.7	27.2
Lawndale	2,378	11	100.0	15	111	39.2	4.8	87	774	208.4	19.2
Lemon Grove	3,623	26	53.8	9	46	16.7	2.8	77	1,227	411.6	35.5
Lincoln	55,379	181	100.0	16	151	55.5	6.3	52	975	268.0	24.8
Livermore	95,035	390	79.0	162	3,292	2,192.9	228.9	281	3,560	1,212.0	126.4
Lodi	67,264	449	35.0	39	265	639.3	14.3	209	3,353	974.6	93.3
Lompoc	0	0	0.0	9	51	12.6	2.2	111	1,395	371.9	35.3
Long Beach	217,713	1,220	8.5	318	4,469	6,962.3	284.9	957	13,033	3,783.9	334.5
Los Altos	39,803	45	91.1	17	D	D	D	102	D	D	D
Los Angeles	3,554,382	14,846	15.9	8,552	83,938	63,834.9	4,787.1	11,359	133,706	40,156.9	3,735.0
Los Banos	59,224	270	100.0	11	131	122.9	4.9	74	1,197	270.5	26.6
Los Gatos	23,428	23	100.0	28	D	D	D	176	D	D	D
Lynwood	4,490	26	100.0	39	580	312.5	28.8	118	1,386	322.3	27.6
Madera	17,400	116	100.0	22	250	213.0	14.2	173	2,163	556.1	50.7
Manhattan Beach	69,112	106	100.0	40	D	D	D	178	2,924	772.1	69.1
Manteca	206,251	820	80.5	26	393	225.1	13.9	177	3,440	824.0	85.3
Martinez	0	0	0.0	23	D	D	D	57	1,031	309.8	32.5
Maywood	312	3	100.0	20	432	233.0	20.4	54	472	107.1	9.3
Menifee	196,900	717	100.0	14	57	39.8	2.4	87	1,672	417.3	37.9

1. Merchant wholesalers except manufacturers' sales branches and offices.   2.   Establishments with payroll.

AREANAME	Real estate and rental and leasing, 2012				Professional, scientific, and technical services[1], 2012				Manufacturing, 2012			
	Number of establish-ments	Number of employees	Receipts (mil dol)	Annual payroll (mil dol)	Number of establish-ments	Number of employees	Receipts (mil dol)	Annual payroll (mil dol)	Number of establish-ments	Number of employees	Receipts (mil dol)	Annual payroll (mil dol)
	80	81	82	83	84	85	86	87	88	89	90	91
CALIFORNIA— Cont'd												
Delano	19	69	10.6	1.6	20	D	D	D	11	85	38.3	2.9
Desert Hot Springs	10	D	D	D	8	215	4.4	2.9	NA	NA	NA	NA
Diamond Bar	98	D	D	D	234	D	D	D	14	231	D	9.9
Downey	153	1,051	130.9	28.1	145	D	D	D	79	1,968	1,037.0	95.1
Dublin	55	214	73.4	10.1	190	1,452	291.3	124.2	18	1,281	509.7	118.6
East Palo Alto	20	92	48.2	4.5	19	D	D	D	6	D	D	D
El Cajon	158	625	90.8	20.7	199	2,323	151.5	60.1	162	4,472	D	242.7
El Centro	46	207	45.5	6.7	90	D	D	D	16	204	D	7.7
Elk Grove	110	427	68.7	12.9	198	D	D	D	30	532	111.0	22.4
El Monte	72	390	52.0	11.1	105	D	D	D	142	2,558	515.5	113.7
El Paso de Robles (Paso Robles)	55	178	26.8	5.3	77	273	31.3	12.1	67	2,175	524.6	101.9
Encinitas	181	428	86.5	19.1	525	1,658	350.3	110.8	41	186	48.2	10.7
Escondido	180	937	862.9	53.1	337	1,810	230.1	84.0	165	2,794	D	125.1
Eureka	61	263	46.4	8.4	103	D	D	D	29	541	109.6	19.1
Fairfield	99	406	106.4	15.0	156	D	D	D	60	2,638	1,718.9	152.8
Folsom	103	489	95.5	17.6	327	D	D	D	26	674	198.9	49.2
Fontana	88	538	131.0	25.1	89	411	34.7	10.0	105	4,084	1,574.6	197.3
Foster City	50	352	119.1	24.9	151	2,145	485.6	210.3	11	817	D	D
Fountain Valley	106	346	80.4	15.6	231	D	D	D	86	2,752	2,318.1	165.1
Fremont	240	1,052	392.8	54.1	1,047	13,204	2,603.7	1,153.9	328	18,254	5,194.0	1,594.2
Fresno	506	3,269	512.4	105.4	1,121	D	D	D	335	12,295	4,367.7	522.7
Fullerton	172	684	123.9	23.6	378	3,338	471.3	246.0	195	6,326	2,032.2	315.5
Gardena	54	332	27.1	7.8	69	364	27.2	10.6	224	4,643	891.1	222.1
Garden Grove	138	495	125.3	19.1	244	D	D	D	272	7,436	1,533.1	355.2
Gilroy	40	136	48.6	4.7	73	382	51.8	19.1	54	1,346	498.9	68.7
Glendale	310	2,740	1,391.5	162.4	888	D	D	D	198	4,473	842.3	237.4
Glendora	63	256	46.6	7.8	114	692	77.5	31.3	41	827	363.0	37.9
Goleta	52	278	43.8	9.9	158	D	D	D	109	5,347	1,857.5	408.2
Hanford	50	200	34.3	4.8	52	268	30.2	10.9	29	894	D	35.3
Hawthorne	64	427	74.0	13.7	72	514	87.5	23.5	67	3,043	D	209.5
Hayward	171	1,330	279.1	57.6	262	D	D	D	315	10,345	4,108.1	608.5
Hemet	74	345	51.8	8.1	75	333	33.7	11.6	21	748	169.0	36.2
Hesperia	54	187	31.5	5.6	51	450	30.8	8.0	53	392	55.4	16.2
Highland	20	57	10.4	1.4	24	113	16.3	3.4	9	168	D	5.8
Hollister	32	81	20.9	2.8	46	147	15.6	4.6	38	1,274	341.6	D
Huntington Beach	319	1,411	311.7	62.6	769	D	D	D	320	12,880	D	1,221.6
Huntington Park	21	104	13.7	2.4	26	240	16.0	6.1	100	2,565	441.3	99.1
Imperial Beach	20	D	D	D	21	88	9.2	2.5	NA	NA	NA	NA
Indio	45	232	38.4	7.8	73	D	D	D	25	329	48.7	13.1
Inglewood	65	939	147.2	31.8	73	D	D	D	68	2,175	D	99.3
Irvine	647	10,154	2,790.0	512.7	2,768	D	D	D	427	27,718	11,089.1	1,999.5
Laguna Hills	93	631	88.9	28.8	335	1,852	279.2	119.9	49	426	74.9	20.6
Laguna Niguel	108	446	112.4	22.8	298	872	138.3	41.2	24	209	D	12.2
La Habra	48	128	33.4	3.9	80	381	47.0	13.4	57	829	168.9	38.3
Lake Elsinore	39	103	20.6	3.6	55	235	35.7	8.0	65	790	113.3	31.5
Lake Forest	115	1,051	165.2	49.8	412	3,461	683.1	298.9	96	5,765	1,446.9	283.3
Lakewood	36	147	28.9	4.4	67	367	30.4	11.8	10	238	D	8.7
La Mesa	133	884	104.7	26.8	229	1,068	128.8	51.4	21	115	18.7	4.0
La Mirada	56	501	98.5	23.4	67	355	47.1	17.3	58	2,267	590.8	93.1
Lancaster	132	545	134.8	19.0	149	D	D	D	57	983	219.7	36.2
La Puente	19	62	10.5	2.0	15	239	32.2	16.5	13	105	9.3	2.6
La Quinta	87	190	44.5	7.5	89	339	65.4	25.8	4	6	1.1	0.3
La Verne	34	153	21.1	4.6	72	290	37.7	11.8	55	1,093	204.7	53.5
Lawndale	22	295	59.8	9.2	43	D	D	D	18	239	D	10.5
Lemon Grove	16	71	22.3	1.9	23	119	6.7	2.7	9	81	16.3	3.8
Lincoln	38	86	18.0	2.4	44	216	18.0	6.8	10	601	176.9	30.1
Livermore	99	525	173.9	24.0	204	D	D	D	132	3,690	1,339.4	234.4
Lodi	77	403	39.7	10.1	104	656	71.3	25.7	80	2,124	561.9	81.6
Lompoc	31	146	18.8	4.1	35	D	D	D	23	573	108.4	25.5
Long Beach	502	3,660	2,647.9	266.4	1,036	7,701	1,489.9	485.4	234	8,027	4,464.4	758.2
Los Altos	98	304	114.2	21.0	275	D	D	D	23	189	30.0	12.6
Los Angeles	5,948	36,498	14,628.8	2,035.5	14,376	134,211	30,105.0	10,658.0	5,034	101,103	43,502.5	4,752.3
Los Banos	23	59	8.4	1.2	18	86	7.9	3.3	9	553	D	26.3
Los Gatos	105	366	123.7	18.9	277	1,637	303.1	122.9	32	488	169.9	36.6
Lynwood	16	100	10.7	4.5	15	96	7.2	2.2	51	1,057	236.6	42.3
Madera	35	148	19.2	4.0	38	D	D	D	35	1,055	445.4	51.3
Manhattan Beach	127	430	272.3	23.1	308	1,384	312.1	121.5	19	82	D	2.9
Manteca	56	231	50.5	9.3	54	319	23.7	9.4	22	972	D	57.2
Martinez	41	171	35.4	5.8	78	D	D	D	18	907	D	111.5
Maywood	3	4	0.2	0.0	4	D	D	D	16	228	D	6.9
Menifee	50	242	36.5	6.8	52	174	13.4	3.8	16	266	61.8	11.7

1. Establishments subject to federal tax.

Table D. Cities — **Population**

AREANAME	Percent Hispanic or Latino[1], 2016	Percent foreign born, 2016	Age of population (percent), 2016							Median age 2016	Percent female 2016	Population			
			Under 18 years	18 to 24 years	25 to 34 years	35 to 44 years	45 to 54 years	55 to 64 years	65 years and over			Census counts		Percent change	
												2000	2010	2000-2010	2010-2017
	12	13	14	15	16	17	18	19	20	21	22	23	24	25	26
CALIFORNIA— Cont'd															
Menlo Park	11.1	20.7	25.4	9.1	14.7	11.5	13.6	11.0	14.8	35.6	52.2	30,785	32,019	4.0	7.3
Merced	53.2	21.4	31.4	13.1	16.0	12.5	10.3	8.4	8.3	27.7	48.1	63,893	78,957	23.6	5.2
Milpitas	13.3	57.0	21.2	7.3	19.6	13.9	12.6	13.5	11.9	36.2	49.4	62,698	66,815	6.6	16.9
Mission Viejo	16.5	21.1	21.2	6.2	10.5	14.0	15.9	13.7	18.4	43.7	49.4	93,102	93,112	0.0	3.1
Modesto	39.7	16.0	27.2	8.5	14.5	13.2	11.2	12.0	13.4	34.7	50.3	188,856	203,119	7.6	5.5
Monrovia	35.1	26.4	22.9	9.6	9.4	17.8	14.6	11.6	14.1	39.3	50.5	36,929	36,590	-0.9	1.3
Montclair	69.5	35.2	26.3	13.8	15.3	13.6	10.1	10.3	10.6	31.2	49.4	33,049	36,664	10.9	7.1
Montebello	79.0	36.6	26.0	10.5	13.5	13.8	12.1	10.6	13.6	35.0	52.9	62,150	62,490	0.5	1.1
Monterey	15.2	15.4	16.6	13.3	20.3	9.0	9.5	14.1	17.2	34.9	49.9	29,674	27,697	-6.7	3.4
Monterey Park	25.1	55.4	17.2	5.3	15.8	11.4	13.5	15.1	21.6	45.3	50.6	60,051	60,228	0.3	1.4
Moorpark	36.8	19.1	28.1	7.0	10.5	12.3	14.9	17.3	9.8	37.7	53.3	31,415	34,517	9.9	6.6
Moreno Valley	57.9	22.8	29.7	12.7	15.7	13.3	12.5	8.5	7.4	29.7	52.0	142,381	193,312	35.8	7.2
Morgan Hill	32.5	16.7	26.1	7.8	9.9	10.1	17.4	13.1	15.6	39.6	51.0	33,556	37,905	13.0	18.8
Mountain View	19.2	41.2	20.6	7.2	22.6	17.7	10.7	10.2	11.1	34.9	47.7	70,708	74,020	4.7	10.0
Murrieta	30.6	15.3	28.1	10.1	13.8	12.4	12.8	11.4	11.4	33.5	50.1	44,282	103,606	134.0	9.4
Napa	38.4	22.4	23.0	7.2	12.9	13.1	13.2	12.6	18.0	40.2	52.3	72,585	77,117	6.2	3.4
National City	68.0	42.7	23.4	14.5	16.6	12.7	10.1	10.3	12.3	32.5	50.2	54,260	58,560	7.9	4.8
Newark	37.5	31.8	20.1	9.0	16.0	14.7	16.8	11.5	11.9	37.9	47.7	42,471	42,573	0.2	11.6
Newport Beach	7.3	15.1	17.5	6.4	14.9	11.6	12.1	14.8	22.6	44.4	53.6	70,032	85,219	21.7	1.1
Norco	36.7	14.3	17.2	8.1	15.1	14.0	18.5	12.8	14.3	41.1	48.9	24,157	27,063	12.0	-1.1
Norwalk	65.7	33.4	24.5	10.4	15.2	12.9	13.4	11.3	12.2	34.9	50.1	103,298	105,549	2.2	0.5
Novato	18.9	21.5	20.2	6.9	8.0	13.4	15.1	17.0	19.3	46.2	53.7	47,630	51,872	8.9	7.9
Oakland	26.1	27.9	19.7	8.2	19.6	15.8	12.6	11.4	12.7	36.5	50.7	399,484	390,822	-2.2	8.8
Oakley	32.6	16.6	27.7	12.5	13.3	15.2	11.2	11.2	8.9	32.4	51.1	25,619	35,432	38.3	17.7
Oceanside	36.8	19.9	22.2	9.4	15.3	11.5	11.4	13.5	16.7	37.6	51.5	161,029	166,992	3.7	5.5
Ontario	70.4	25.7	26.5	10.1	16.2	14.2	13.7	10.1	9.3	33.5	52.2	158,007	163,921	3.7	7.3
Orange	39.2	22.8	22.4	11.5	15.1	13.8	13.8	11.4	12.0	35.7	50.0	128,821	136,432	5.9	3.0
Oxnard	74.1	35.9	28.5	10.2	14.9	14.3	12.3	9.8	10.0	32.3	50.0	170,358	197,969	16.2	6.1
Pacifica	19.9	20.5	19.2	6.3	14.8	10.9	17.6	15.4	15.7	43.4	50.0	38,390	37,304	-2.8	4.8
Palmdale	59.9	24.6	31.3	10.0	14.4	11.3	14.2	10.0	8.8	31.2	51.1	116,670	152,755	30.9	3.1
Palm Desert	30.5	22.5	14.3	9.8	13.1	8.3	11.7	12.1	30.7	49.2	54.0	41,155	48,450	17.7	9.3
Palm Springs	36.8	21.6	12.8	7.6	7.7	7.5	16.7	18.0	29.6	52.9	41.8	42,807	44,538	4.0	8.1
Palo Alto	5.8	35.6	20.1	6.3	10.9	12.4	15.4	14.0	21.0	45.3	50.1	58,598	64,409	9.9	4.3
Paradise	7.6	1.2	9.8	7.3	7.5	4.7	15.4	21.9	33.4	58.8	52.1	26,408	26,199	-0.8	1.8
Paramount	83.9	36.3	27.1	12.9	13.2	13.6	14.1	9.6	9.6	32.6	49.8	55,266	54,098	-2.1	1.5
Pasadena	35.0	28.5	17.5	8.5	17.9	14.8	12.1	13.6	15.5	38.9	52.5	133,936	137,139	2.4	4.0
Perris	76.7	29.5	32.2	13.9	15.8	11.2	13.1	7.6	6.1	26.2	52.7	36,189	68,550	89.4	13.6
Petaluma	21.9	17.3	19.0	7.7	13.2	12.8	13.8	14.8	18.8	42.9	50.1	54,548	57,941	6.2	5.1
Pico Rivera	87.3	30.2	19.8	10.2	15.8	12.4	13.5	11.4	16.9	38.3	52.7	63,428	62,948	-0.8	0.9
Pittsburg	47.0	32.6	26.9	9.6	15.0	14.1	12.8	10.9	10.8	33.7	49.2	56,769	63,259	11.4	14.0
Placentia	40.1	27.7	24.4	9.5	14.5	12.3	11.8	12.3	15.3	37.3	52.0	46,488	50,917	9.5	2.4
Pleasant Hill	22.0	15.8	20.8	8.0	15.8	10.0	15.0	14.5	15.9	40.8	51.5	32,837	33,102	0.8	5.7
Pleasanton	8.7	31.8	25.7	4.4	9.5	13.7	17.6	14.8	14.4	43.2	52.0	63,654	70,273	10.4	18.1
Pomona	73.6	35.0	25.8	15.7	15.5	12.4	11.6	11.0	8.0	30.2	49.2	149,473	149,030	-0.3	2.6
Porterville	66.8	25.0	29.7	12.4	14.3	11.3	12.3	7.9	12.1	29.9	49.0	39,615	57,323	44.7	3.2
Poway	13.9	17.4	25.4	7.1	9.2	12.7	14.5	14.5	16.6	41.0	52.9	48,044	47,806	-0.5	4.7
Rancho Cordova	21.5	24.1	24.8	8.3	18.3	14.3	12.7	9.2	12.5	34.4	48.6	55,060	64,805	17.7	13.5
Rancho Cucamonga	36.5	20.1	22.9	9.8	15.8	14.5	14.5	12.0	10.5	36.0	50.2	127,743	165,372	29.5	7.3
Rancho Palos Verdes	9.7	28.5	21.5	5.7	5.8	10.1	20.0	13.8	23.0	48.3	52.0	41,145	41,660	1.3	1.7
Rancho Santa Margarita	21.9	14.8	25.3	9.1	13.9	14.2	16.2	15.1	6.4	36.7	50.4	47,214	47,855	1.4	2.0
Redding	9.4	6.7	21.9	10.0	13.8	11.0	11.2	13.3	18.8	38.0	50.8	80,865	89,861	11.1	2.2
Redlands	35.6	16.2	22.9	10.7	17.0	12.6	9.9	11.1	15.9	34.5	56.2	63,591	68,667	8.0	4.2
Redondo Beach	13.7	19.4	18.4	3.8	14.5	14.5	17.5	16.5	15.0	44.5	49.4	63,261	66,921	5.8	1.5
Redwood City	41.2	36.2	20.5	9.1	19.5	13.5	14.8	11.3	11.4	35.7	49.8	75,402	76,827	1.9	12.8
Rialto	77.8	26.7	29.4	13.3	16.7	11.5	11.9	8.9	8.2	29.0	48.3	91,873	99,150	7.9	4.4
Richmond	45.0	35.6	22.6	10.1	15.2	15.0	13.4	10.4	13.3	36.4	50.9	99,216	103,267	4.1	6.6
Ridgecrest	13.2	7.5	21.0	7.7	15.1	14.6	15.1	10.4	16.2	36.8	48.3	24,927	27,616	10.8	4.6
Riverside	51.0	22.4	24.3	14.5	16.0	13.0	11.7	10.2	10.4	31.8	50.4	255,166	303,985	19.1	7.8
Rocklin	11.8	12.8	27.9	8.5	9.3	13.7	17.4	11.9	11.4	38.3	50.3	36,330	57,117	57.2	13.5
Rohnert Park	27.5	15.4	17.9	12.1	20.4	8.6	12.7	17.0	11.2	34.8	52.9	42,236	40,818	-3.4	4.9
Rosemead	33.9	60.1	18.7	9.5	12.5	11.9	14.0	16.2	17.2	43.3	50.6	53,505	53,771	0.5	1.5
Roseville	15.0	12.2	23.7	7.6	11.7	13.4	13.7	12.5	17.4	40.4	52.8	79,921	119,164	49.1	13.6
Sacramento	28.6	22.8	22.5	9.3	18.8	13.0	11.9	11.3	13.3	34.7	50.5	407,018	466,394	14.6	7.6
Salinas	78.4	42.2	30.0	10.3	16.5	15.8	10.0	8.8	8.6	30.7	50.6	151,060	150,498	-0.4	4.7
San Bernardino	65.6	23.2	31.4	12.7	14.5	12.3	11.0	9.7	8.4	28.5	50.9	185,401	209,961	13.2	3.4
San Bruno	26.8	32.4	18.0	8.2	17.4	13.8	16.7	10.6	15.3	39.1	49.6	40,165	41,067	2.2	5.4
San Buenaventura (Ventura)	37.7	14.8	20.5	8.8	13.6	13.5	11.7	14.8	17.0	40.5	49.2	100,916	107,234	6.3	3.3
San Carlos	7.3	16.5	27.4	5.0	7.7	17.3	13.3	16.2	13.1	40.5	54.9	27,718	28,383	2.4	7.5
San Clemente	17.0	12.4	21.9	5.5	10.2	12.6	15.8	15.8	18.3	44.9	53.1	49,936	63,482	27.1	2.8
San Diego	30.0	26.7	19.8	12.1	18.8	14.0	12.3	10.7	12.3	34.6	49.4	1,223,400	1,301,948	6.4	9.0
San Dimas	28.4	27.0	17.1	7.6	14.3	11.8	12.2	15.6	21.4	44.1	54.3	34,980	33,375	-4.6	2.8

1. May be of any race.

Table D. Cities — Households, Group Quarters, Crime, and Education

	Households, 2016								Serious crimes known to police[2], 2016				Educational attainment, 2016		
				Perecnt					Total		Rate[3]			Attainment[4] (percent)	
AREANAME	Number	Persons per house-hold	Family	Married couple family	Female headed family[1]	Non-family	One person	Persons in group quarters	Number	Rate	Violent	Property	Population age 25 and over	High school graduate or less	Bachelor's degree or more
	27	28	29	30	31	32	33	34	35	36	37	38	39	40	41
CALIFORNIA— Cont'd															
Menlo Park	11,460	2.85	72.0	55.5	13.9	28.0	21.7	1,188	653	1,936	89	1,847	22,215	13.0	68.7
Merced	24,221	3.36	69.0	39.5	22.1	31.0	21.7	1,092	3,263	3,926	588	3,338	45,863	49.8	16.4
Milpitas	22,870	3.30	78.2	65.6	10.2	21.8	13.6	2,007	1,887	2,359	120	2,239	55,448	30.4	47.5
Mission Viejo	33,544	2.83	76.1	63.9	8.7	23.9	19.4	1,613	1,058	1,080	77	1,004	69,942	19.5	49.7
Modesto	70,591	2.97	73.8	51.4	15.9	26.2	21.1	2,789	11,428	5,368	988	4,380	136,341	46.8	18.3
Monrovia	13,038	2.83	70.7	45.3	16.4	29.3	24.0	NA	892	2,370	159	2,211	25,080	31.8	34.3
Montclair	10,018	3.86	77.1	51.8	17.3	22.9	13.7	293	1,923	4,920	537	4,383	23,322	53.8	17.4
Montebello	19,027	3.30	75.2	43.3	20.9	24.8	19.5	NA	2,192	3,414	333	3,081	40,208	55.2	18.7
Monterey	12,001	2.16	51.5	41.9	7.1	48.5	40.5	2,519	1,183	4,150	351	3,799	19,943	10.3	56.2
Monterey Park	19,788	3.08	76.6	51.6	19.7	23.4	19.7	225	1,835	2,974	212	2,761	47,312	48.6	27.1
Moorpark	11,144	3.27	84.7	67.6	10.7	15.3	13.2	NA	333	914	102	813	23,670	22.8	48.7
Moreno Valley	49,785	4.11	84.8	53.5	22.5	15.2	10.8	754	6,981	3,385	418	2,967	118,244	50.2	17.3
Morgan Hill	15,118	2.90	75.9	59.8	11.2	24.1	18.4	302	724	1,645	186	1,459	29,194	25.3	44.4
Mountain View	32,696	2.45	57.5	42.3	8.2	42.5	30.9	552	1,652	1,488	44	1,444	69,068	31.3	28.9
Murrieta	31,090	3.57	84.6	66.6	13.1	15.4	12.4	325	1,908	2,335	162	2,173	58,138	19.5	66.9
Napa	30,017	2.64	62.7	48.2	10.9	37.3	32.0	1,087	1,875	2,312	365	1,947	56,168	34.8	34.7
National City	16,398	3.51	74.6	39.5	25.3	25.4	21.6	3,652	1,643	2,669	434	2,236	37,970	53.7	16.1
Newark	14,029	3.25	76.0	57.6	10.1	24.0	17.0	150	1,294	2,820	235	2,584	32,457	38.5	29.6
Newport Beach	37,351	2.31	60.6	53.9	5.1	39.4	29.4	533	2,351	2,687	126	2,562	65,930	7.2	69.3
Norco	7,978	2.98	66.0	47.8	14.4	34.0	28.8	2,972	823	3,149	195	2,954	19,968	39.8	21.3
Norwalk	26,883	3.85	82.0	52.4	20.8	18.0	12.3	2,541	2,382	2,217	390	1,827	69,065	52.8	19.0
Novato	22,779	2.43	61.2	49.2	9.8	38.8	30.7	662	1,118	1,987	142	1,845	40,815	23.2	43.9
Oakland	158,084	2.61	54.4	36.3	13.0	45.6	32.4	6,625	30,011	7,061	1,426	5,636	302,872	34.0	41.1
Oakley	12,130	3.34	79.1	63.6	9.6	20.9	18.1	NA	474	1,165	135	1,030	24,312	37.6	19.7
Oceanside	62,661	2.79	65.4	49.5	11.8	34.6	27.1	789	5,003	2,821	360	2,461	120,045	33.3	30.1
Ontario	49,020	3.52	79.4	50.3	21.1	20.6	15.9	751	5,320	3,082	349	2,733	109,884	56.2	15.0
Orange	43,533	3.06	73.0	58.0	11.1	27.0	19.9	7,312	2,836	1,999	161	1,839	92,856	33.2	35.6
Oxnard	49,895	4.14	80.3	52.0	18.8	19.7	13.9	1,498	7,021	3,359	453	2,905	127,486	55.6	17.0
Pacifica	13,281	2.93	70.5	53.3	9.8	29.5	22.1	199	557	1,405	164	1,241	29,081	25.5	46.7
Palmdale	44,225	3.55	78.8	52.3	19.8	21.2	16.0	234	3,425	2,148	437	1,711	92,441	50.7	16.3
Palm Desert	22,343	2.33	58.3	43.7	8.9	41.7	32.4	263	2,221	4,228	147	4,082	39,650	30.1	32.3
Palm Springs	22,935	2.06	42.9	33.3	4.3	57.1	44.6	497	3,029	6,322	574	5,748	37,935	34.8	36.7
Palo Alto	28,228	2.36	64.9	51.1	9.3	35.1	28.9	525	1,509	2,242	108	2,133	49,358	7.7	81.3
Paradise	12,373	2.10	59.8	45.6	10.3	40.2	34.0	512	547	2,062	170	1,892	22,012	33.2	22.2
Paramount	13,626	4.01	81.7	51.8	22.0	18.3	14.8	295	2,057	3,695	562	3,133	32,953	67.6	11.4
Pasadena	55,291	2.50	53.5	40.1	9.6	46.5	35.6	3,774	3,923	2,738	333	2,405	105,151	26.8	51.8
Perris	17,261	4.41	86.5	50.6	28.4	13.5	10.9	NA	2,383	3,125	295	2,830	41,172	64.6	10.4
Petaluma	22,318	2.68	69.6	54.8	9.7	30.4	25.5	749	1,308	2,147	328	1,818	44,419	31.2	37.5
Pico Rivera	17,883	3.53	77.7	49.1	20.3	22.3	16.2	472	1,841	2,856	341	2,514	44,556	54.1	16.1
Pittsburg	20,509	3.43	79.2	49.6	19.5	20.8	15.4	350	2,253	3,188	393	2,795	44,858	48.2	20.6
Placentia	16,071	3.22	80.5	59.0	14.8	19.5	14.7	533	867	1,642	146	1,496	34,543	27.5	39.9
Pleasant Hill	13,727	2.51	65.8	47.2	14.1	34.2	26.2	360	1,589	4,522	225	4,297	24,831	12.1	51.0
Pleasanton	29,774	2.75	80.1	70.0	7.6	19.9	16.8	306	1,704	2,092	123	1,969	57,453	12.9	66.1
Pomona	35,503	4.15	76.0	47.4	18.4	24.0	15.4	4,967	5,443	3,532	498	3,034	89,209	57.9	16.0
Porterville	17,895	3.22	71.8	43.2	18.7	28.2	22.7	1,339	1,530	2,712	381	2,331	34,152	57.8	9.8
Poway	15,890	3.12	80.2	65.6	12.0	19.8	15.7	549	520	1,028	128	899	33,826	21.8	48.2
Rancho Cordova	24,611	2.92	68.7	47.4	15.2	31.3	24.2	NA	1,680	2,325	339	1,986	48,359	36.6	29.1
Rancho Cucamonga	57,514	3.02	74.4	52.1	15.2	25.6	20.8	NA	4,257	2,404	150	2,254	118,812	28.2	35.2
Rancho Palos Verdes	15,748	2.66	73.9	65.9	5.9	26.1	23.7	498	444	1,034	63	971	30,884	10.6	70.3
Rancho Santa Margarita	18,087	2.71	69.8	55.1	11.0	30.2	25.3	NA	315	635	97	538	32,132	16.5	47.0
Redding	36,472	2.44	61.6	46.9	10.9	38.4	30.7	2,745	4,557	4,958	783	4,174	62,492	29.4	25.4
Redlands	24,217	2.83	70.5	48.5	18.0	29.5	24.8	2,664	3,138	4,390	315	4,075	47,337	29.7	36.1
Redondo Beach	29,688	2.28	59.4	47.4	6.4	40.6	33.7	156	1,902	2,779	234	2,545	52,854	15.8	55.3
Redwood City	30,293	2.75	63.2	50.7	7.9	36.8	26.5	1,577	1,667	1,915	188	1,727	59,851	30.5	48.1
Rialto	26,445	3.88	80.6	49.0	18.7	19.4	16.2	573	2,338	2,250	434	1,816	59,115	61.6	10.7
Richmond	34,949	3.11	68.4	44.9	14.8	31.6	25.2	1,266	4,804	4,333	919	3,414	73,957	45.8	25.3
Ridgecrest	12,391	2.30	61.1	48.6	8.6	38.9	34.6	NA	714	2,462	514	1,948	20,463	25.3	33.1
Riverside	91,360	3.41	73.9	51.3	15.7	26.1	19.4	13,289	12,990	3,986	529	3,457	198,904	44.8	24.2
Rocklin	21,072	2.96	71.2	57.8	10.7	28.8	24.7	435	1,267	2,043	105	1,939	39,931	18.0	46.6
Rohnert Park	15,533	2.74	62.6	48.2	11.3	37.4	23.0	NA	947	2,217	477	1,739	29,811	33.4	23.9
Rosemead	14,513	3.73	80.1	55.7	16.6	19.9	15.8	387	1,416	2,569	303	2,266	39,126	67.1	15.2
Roseville	48,500	2.71	68.6	55.5	10.6	31.4	26.3	1,086	3,515	2,652	150	2,501	91,170	23.0	39.7
Sacramento	183,212	2.65	58.1	38.6	12.9	41.9	31.9	8,887	18,832	3,801	716	3,085	337,717	38.6	31.0
Salinas	39,274	3.96	80.5	54.0	18.3	19.5	14.5	1,531	5,747	3,621	633	2,987	93,809	64.0	12.6
San Bernardino	57,920	3.55	74.4	39.2	26.0	25.6	20.9	10,790	12,056	5,548	1,324	4,224	120,866	59.6	9.1
San Bruno	14,635	2.90	69.4	54.0	7.6	30.6	21.9	NA	1,215	2,786	250	2,536	31,700	29.0	44.2
San Buenaventura (Ventura)	40,630	2.65	65.4	47.5	11.2	34.6	27.2	1,879	4,118	3,736	334	3,402	77,407	25.5	36.9
San Carlos	10,677	2.78	80.4	65.9	8.5	19.6	15.7	NA	NA	NA	NA	NA	20,140	9.7	70.7
San Clemente	27,741	2.34	62.6	52.9	7.2	37.4	31.5	359	874	1,326	114	1,212	47,417	16.4	49.5
San Diego	495,726	2.76	60.6	44.5	11.3	39.4	27.8	38,420	33,956	2,402	377	2,025	957,831	28.1	44.2
San Dimas	11,469	2.91	71.9	60.7	6.4	28.1	24.4	955	846	2,425	235	2,190	25,848	24.8	38.0

1. No spouse present. 2. Data for serious crimes have not been adjusted for underreporting. This may affect comparability between geographic areas and over time. 3. Per 100,000 population estimated by the FBI. 4. Persons 25 years old and over.

Table D. Cities — **Population**

AREANAME	Percent Hispanic or Latino[1], 2016	Percent foreign born, 2016	Age of population (percent), 2016							Median age 2016	Percent female 2016	Population Census counts		Percent change	
			Under 18 years	18 to 24 years	25 to 34 years	35 to 44 years	45 to 54 years	55 to 64 years	65 years and over			2000	2010	2000-2010	2010-2017
	12	13	14	15	16	17	18	19	20	21	22	23	24	25	26
CALIFORNIA— Cont'd															
San Francisco	15.2	35.1	13.5	7.3	23.4	15.8	13.5	11.7	14.9	38.0	49.0	776,733	805,193	3.7	9.8
San Gabriel	32.0	55.1	18.4	9.4	15.1	13.5	14.5	11.7	17.3	40.7	53.5	39,804	39,647	-0.4	2.2
San Jacinto	55.8	21.4	25.4	12.3	12.2	12.8	14.9	11.4	10.9	35.1	51.3	23,779	44,199	85.9	9.2
San Jose	32.1	39.3	23.0	8.9	16.1	14.5	14.1	11.8	11.5	36.3	49.2	894,943	952,574	6.4	8.7
San Juan Capistrano	38.9	19.0	24.4	9.9	11.3	7.5	16.6	12.4	17.9	41.9	50.6	33,826	34,427	1.8	4.8
San Leandro	26.8	36.5	19.3	7.0	13.9	11.4	16.8	14.0	17.7	43.9	52.9	79,452	84,952	6.9	6.6
San Luis Obispo	17.0	9.5	16.4	31.6	13.2	6.9	9.4	10.6	11.9	26.7	49.6	44,174	45,164	2.2	5.3
San Marcos	35.4	23.1	29.4	10.0	11.2	14.2	12.6	10.8	11.7	34.5	50.0	54,977	83,657	52.2	15.0
San Mateo	25.3	34.6	20.5	6.9	16.8	15.5	14.1	10.3	16.0	39.0	50.6	92,482	97,207	5.1	7.8
San Pablo	67.5	48.4	27.5	9.9	13.9	16.4	12.7	7.4	12.1	34.2	50.4	30,215	29,512	-2.3	5.6
San Rafael	35.0	31.2	22.2	7.4	11.3	15.0	14.4	11.1	18.4	40.7	47.9	56,063	57,694	2.9	2.4
San Ramon	7.1	34.6	26.5	6.4	10.3	17.0	19.6	10.4	9.8	40.1	49.5	44,722	71,423	59.7	6.3
Santa Ana	77.3	46.1	27.0	11.2	17.4	13.9	12.7	9.4	8.4	31.5	48.8	337,977	324,796	-3.9	2.9
Santa Barbara	35.8	23.6	18.3	11.5	14.8	11.9	12.8	11.6	19.1	39.6	50.3	92,325	88,375	-4.3	4.2
Santa Clara	16.9	43.8	20.9	12.3	20.6	16.2	11.5	7.7	10.9	33.2	48.4	102,361	116,497	13.8	9.1
Santa Clarita	30.6	20.3	21.7	9.9	12.0	12.8	16.9	13.6	13.1	39.7	49.8	151,088	204,186	35.1	3.3
Santa Cruz	16.0	11.9	12.8	28.0	12.2	10.6	11.6	10.7	14.1	31.8	51.3	54,593	59,945	9.8	8.5
Santa Maria	72.7	37.6	30.2	11.7	15.1	13.4	10.4	8.1	11.1	30.1	50.9	77,423	99,595	28.6	7.4
Santa Monica	18.1	23.9	13.6	5.5	23.6	11.9	13.6	14.1	17.7	40.2	50.0	84,084	89,742	6.7	2.9
Santa Paula	83.1	29.8	29.1	8.7	17.4	11.9	11.0	11.2	10.7	30.9	48.7	28,598	29,270	2.3	3.6
Santa Rosa	30.4	19.2	22.4	7.8	14.0	12.7	13.0	13.1	17.0	39.9	51.8	147,595	167,824	13.7	4.4
Santee	17.4	10.5	18.9	8.2	16.3	13.4	12.9	17.1	13.2	39.3	53.5	52,975	53,416	0.8	8.8
Saratoga	2.7	44.0	20.3	2.7	8.6	11.6	20.0	14.2	22.6	48.8	51.4	29,843	30,004	0.5	3.0
Seaside	44.3	25.9	27.0	13.0	16.7	10.2	12.6	10.7	9.8	31.7	46.3	31,696	33,025	4.2	3.4
Simi Valley	25.1	17.3	21.4	9.1	13.2	13.0	15.4	13.5	14.3	40.1	51.3	111,351	124,243	11.6	2.1
Soledad	70.7	23.9	22.4	7.5	12.0	18.6	26.3	5.6	7.6	40.8	33.3	11,263	25,738	128.5	2.1
South Gate	95.5	41.8	28.0	11.4	14.6	14.4	12.8	8.9	10.0	31.6	51.1	96,375	94,417	-2.0	1.1
South Pasadena	25.3	26.9	25.8	4.8	17.0	19.9	12.5	9.4	10.4	36.3	51.7	24,292	25,627	5.5	1.0
South San Francisco	34.8	40.7	20.1	5.2	19.5	14.7	12.0	14.1	14.4	38.2	49.9	60,552	63,654	5.1	5.9
Stanton	40.7	40.6	23.7	8.0	15.0	14.9	14.5	12.2	11.8	37.5	51.1	37,403	37,827	1.1	1.9
Stockton	40.9	24.6	28.1	10.4	14.9	12.0	12.2	10.2	12.4	32.5	50.7	243,771	291,726	19.7	6.4
Suisun City	26.2	21.8	22.9	11.6	18.8	9.7	10.5	13.5	13.0	34.0	51.0	26,118	28,095	7.6	5.5
Sunnyvale	20.0	48.4	22.2	6.1	20.4	16.8	13.1	9.6	11.7	35.8	48.7	131,760	140,060	6.3	9.7
Temecula	28.8	15.2	28.9	9.4	12.9	12.0	17.0	10.3	9.5	34.4	50.5	57,716	100,048	73.3	14.3
Temple City	19.9	50.5	22.3	7.5	10.0	13.2	15.6	12.6	18.6	42.8	53.6	33,377	35,550	6.5	2.3
Thousand Oaks	16.0	18.6	20.3	7.9	11.2	11.0	16.3	15.4	17.8	44.7	51.0	117,005	126,480	8.1	2.0
Torrance	17.9	31.2	21.2	7.5	12.6	15.1	14.0	14.3	15.3	40.2	51.9	137,946	145,259	5.3	1.0
Tracy	37.8	25.1	27.9	9.5	12.6	13.9	15.0	11.2	10.0	35.1	51.3	56,929	83,353	46.4	9.0
Tulare	58.0	19.0	29.6	12.4	14.5	11.9	10.2	11.3	10.2	30.7	51.4	43,994	59,312	34.8	7.7
Turlock	35.1	28.0	23.3	9.2	17.2	9.4	14.2	11.4	15.4	35.5	52.6	55,810	68,619	23.0	7.2
Tustin	36.4	34.4	23.4	8.6	19.2	15.3	12.9	10.4	10.4	34.1	48.3	67,504	75,316	11.6	6.9
Twentynine Palms	13.6	7.1	21.7	30.4	21.4	7.5	6.4	7.8	4.8	24.5	43.9	14,764	25,048	69.7	6.0
Union City	20.1	43.3	18.5	10.4	19.3	13.2	12.2	12.3	14.1	35.8	48.6	66,869	69,516	4.0	8.4
Upland	38.5	17.8	19.5	13.0	10.7	12.5	14.8	13.1	16.4	41.3	51.7	68,393	73,713	7.8	4.5
Vacaville	22.4	14.2	23.5	8.6	15.1	12.2	15.5	11.7	13.4	37.6	48.1	88,625	92,422	4.3	8.2
Vallejo	25.7	28.0	20.9	9.2	14.0	13.7	12.1	14.7	15.4	38.5	51.0	116,760	115,943	-0.7	5.3
Victorville	51.6	16.1	32.1	8.2	13.9	14.1	13.0	9.2	9.5	31.6	50.6	64,029	115,921	81.0	5.6
Visalia	53.3	13.8	31.3	9.4	13.8	12.1	11.0	10.4	11.9	31.5	53.3	91,565	124,452	35.9	6.9
Vista	54.7	28.2	25.5	12.1	17.2	12.5	12.3	12.3	8.1	31.9	47.9	89,857	93,501	4.1	8.6
Walnut	27.3	50.3	20.5	8.4	12.5	10.3	12.8	17.6	17.9	43.5	50.1	30,004	29,177	-2.8	3.5
Walnut Creek	10.6	24.7	16.2	6.5	13.9	12.4	10.8	11.9	28.3	46.2	54.2	64,296	64,165	-0.2	8.7
Wasco	76.5	26.8	26.1	11.4	21.2	12.6	12.0	12.5	4.1	30.8	40.3	21,263	25,552	20.2	5.6
Watsonville	85.3	35.4	33.1	11.4	12.6	14.9	11.9	8.2	7.9	30.4	50.9	44,265	51,204	15.7	5.7
West Covina	53.6	35.7	23.7	9.6	14.8	13.3	11.6	13.5	13.5	35.8	50.1	105,080	106,113	1.0	1.4
West Hollywood	10.6	23.7	3.9	2.1	39.2	15.7	11.3	12.7	15.2	37.5	43.9	35,716	34,398	-3.7	7.8
Westminster	25.8	44.4	20.6	8.8	13.2	11.2	13.7	15.4	17.1	40.9	50.0	88,207	89,613	1.6	2.2
West Sacramento	28.7	20.2	25.7	11.1	12.7	17.1	10.7	10.8	12.0	35.2	49.8	31,615	48,744	54.2	9.8
Whittier	66.3	16.7	25.1	9.3	13.1	13.4	14.0	11.7	13.4	37.4	51.0	83,680	85,313	2.0	1.8
Wildomar	42.4	15.0	27.9	9.2	12.9	15.3	10.4	13.4	10.8	35.0	51.6	14,064	32,220	129.1	14.6
Windsor	38.8	22.1	24.2	9.4	8.7	12.9	15.8	12.2	16.9	42.6	49.4	22,744	26,795	17.8	2.8
Woodland	50.5	26.9	23.9	8.8	16.2	13.1	13.9	12.1	12.0	35.8	50.1	49,151	55,476	12.9	8.2
Yorba Linda	20.9	21.7	26.4	7.0	9.8	11.4	15.1	12.9	17.4	40.9	51.4	58,918	64,169	8.9	6.3
Yuba City	25.8	24.9	25.8	8.9	13.8	15.1	10.9	11.4	14.1	35.6	50.5	36,758	65,634	78.6	1.9
Yucaipa	29.5	9.5	23.7	10.0	10.2	12.4	13.0	15.7	14.9	40.4	49.9	41,207	51,371	24.7	4.5
COLORADO	21.3	9.8	22.8	9.6	15.1	13.5	13.0	12.6	13.4	36.7	49.6	4,301,261	5,029,325	16.9	11.5
Arvada	14.5	4.6	21.6	8.1	14.6	14.1	13.3	12.5	15.8	38.4	50.2	102,153	106,642	4.4	11.4
Aurora	28.7	19.3	25.6	9.6	16.1	15.0	12.5	10.5	10.6	34.2	50.7	276,393	324,709	17.5	12.9
Boulder	11.1	11.9	12.6	29.3	17.4	10.5	10.6	9.7	9.8	28.5	48.2	94,673	97,705	3.2	9.6
Brighton	24.9	10.7	30.8	6.0	13.3	16.8	13.1	10.1	10.0	34.9	44.5	20,905	33,780	61.6	20.1
Broomfield	12.2	7.3	23.5	8.3	14.3	14.4	15.0	11.6	12.9	38.4	50.9	38,272	55,858	46.0	22.3

1. May be of any race.

Table D. Cities — Households, Group Quarters, Crime, and Education

AREANAME	Households, 2016							Serious crimes known to police[2], 2016				Educational attainment, 2016		
	Number	Persons per household	Family	Married couple family	Female headed family[1]	Non-family	One person	Persons in group quarters	Total Number	Rate	Rate Violent	Rate Property	Population age 25 and over	High school graduate or less	Bachelor's degree or more
	27	28	29	30	31	32	33	34	35	36	37	38	39	40	41
CALIFORNIA— Cont'd															
San Francisco	358,703	2.37	48.5	37.0	7.8	51.5	34.8	20,804	53,592	6,152	711	5,441	689,696	24.4	57.2
San Gabriel	12,591	3.15	74.0	50.3	17.1	26.0	18.6	746	753	1,856	241	1,614	29,176	44.0	33.1
San Jacinto	12,134	3.89	84.2	56.2	24.8	15.8	12.2	185	1,801	3,794	270	3,524	29,529	47.9	19.7
San Jose	320,447	3.15	73.6	56.5	11.4	26.4	19.2	14,626	28,636	2,749	373	2,375	697,641	34.1	42.6
San Juan Capistrano	11,781	3.07	77.9	66.9	8.2	22.1	19.3	NA	523	1,421	236	1,185	23,833	35.2	31.9
San Leandro	34,977	2.57	63.8	47.4	12.3	36.2	30.3	494	4,017	4,372	530	3,842	66,672	41.7	27.8
San Luis Obispo	19,090	2.41	40.8	31.1	6.8	59.2	35.4	1,471	2,254	4,718	373	4,345	24,741	19.0	46.7
San Marcos	28,706	3.28	78.5	60.9	11.6	21.5	14.9	NA	1,342	1,415	208	1,207	57,755	34.6	35.7
San Mateo	38,710	2.64	64.0	49.9	10.8	36.0	28.1	1,579	2,383	2,274	231	2,043	75,494	25.7	52.8
San Pablo	8,716	3.45	77.3	49.0	19.3	22.7	18.9	479	1,427	4,652	694	3,958	19,098	65.4	10.9
San Rafael	23,376	2.43	57.3	44.5	8.5	42.7	34.0	2,057	1,962	3,301	419	2,882	41,451	30.7	51.3
San Ramon	25,847	2.92	78.7	70.1	6.1	21.3	17.6	109	862	1,121	51	1,070	50,779	10.3	70.0
Santa Ana	74,294	4.43	82.1	55.3	18.2	17.9	10.2	4,896	8,592	2,546	478	2,069	206,445	65.6	13.7
Santa Barbara	36,514	2.48	58.4	43.3	11.1	41.6	27.5	1,434	3,457	3,737	429	3,307	64,570	27.8	48.7
Santa Clara	44,392	2.72	68.4	57.0	8.2	31.6	23.1	5,170	2,973	2,319	124	2,195	84,157	19.1	60.7
Santa Clarita	61,687	2.92	73.8	58.6	9.0	26.2	20.4	1,808	3,336	1,519	151	1,368	124,488	28.3	35.7
Santa Cruz	25,275	2.16	46.5	30.7	12.6	53.5	38.0	9,917	4,131	6,358	802	5,556	38,135	15.5	52.3
Santa Maria	27,248	3.86	78.3	51.4	19.5	21.7	15.7	1,101	3,144	2,960	476	2,484	61,775	58.7	15.0
Santa Monica	47,265	1.92	38.4	30.1	5.7	61.6	49.9	1,726	4,514	4,806	506	4,300	74,863	14.0	70.8
Santa Paula	9,615	3.14	68.9	49.7	14.5	31.1	25.6	NA	423	1,374	260	1,114	18,867	54.8	14.4
Santa Rosa	64,202	2.68	61.7	43.1	10.3	38.3	29.4	3,230	3,668	2,080	373	1,707	122,314	31.8	33.1
Santee	18,959	2.92	75.4	60.2	10.7	24.6	17.4	2,486	1,027	1,751	191	1,560	42,130	32.6	29.1
Saratoga	10,653	2.87	86.4	79.3	6.2	13.6	11.9	228	314	1,008	90	918	23,704	9.6	74.5
Seaside	10,904	3.02	63.1	42.3	9.5	36.9	31.0	1,324	735	2,110	368	1,743	20,588	37.7	29.4
Simi Valley	41,020	3.06	74.2	56.8	11.8	25.8	20.3	794	1,740	1,367	137	1,231	87,758	30.3	32.2
Soledad	NA	NA	NA	NA	NA	NA	NA	8,412	288	1,161	306	855	17,960	68.9	10.1
South Gate	23,762	4.02	84.9	47.3	24.9	15.1	11.2	NA	4,095	4,231	682	3,549	57,857	68.5	7.2
South Pasadena	10,076	2.56	62.2	41.5	15.1	37.8	27.6	NA	694	2,643	103	2,540	17,977	11.1	68.9
South San Francisco	20,881	3.17	73.8	52.5	14.3	26.2	17.7	832	1,565	2,302	219	2,083	50,026	35.0	34.4
Stanton	10,822	3.55	71.7	47.4	14.9	28.3	23.0	170	865	2,214	335	1,879	26,408	57.4	21.0
Stockton	95,851	3.13	69.2	40.2	19.8	30.8	24.4	6,607	16,015	5,194	1,421	3,773	189,078	50.9	16.7
Suisun City	9,306	3.16	78.9	49.9	17.0	21.1	16.5	NA	734	2,466	269	2,197	19,329	37.0	19.2
Sunnyvale	56,245	2.70	69.4	60.0	4.8	30.6	21.1	930	2,298	1,491	103	1,389	109,525	20.3	62.8
Temecula	32,551	3.47	82.8	69.3	10.7	17.2	12.2	82	2,732	2,389	127	2,262	69,844	27.9	31.2
Temple City	10,415	3.45	79.8	59.4	12.3	20.2	16.6	NA	629	1,722	134	1,588	25,511	42.3	35.4
Thousand Oaks	46,830	2.71	67.1	54.1	10.5	32.9	25.7	1,993	1,850	1,425	126	1,298	92,443	18.2	52.4
Torrance	53,614	2.72	71.7	55.9	11.2	28.3	23.7	1,439	3,479	2,334	173	2,161	104,979	22.0	49.3
Tracy	26,744	3.33	82.3	61.2	15.7	17.7	14.8	190	2,050	2,334	172	2,162	55,924	41.5	19.4
Tulare	19,606	3.18	78.4	49.8	21.0	21.6	16.2	356	1,988	3,160	356	2,804	36,378	52.9	13.6
Turlock	25,137	2.87	68.7	50.6	9.3	31.3	26.9	635	2,887	3,953	526	3,427	49,188	48.4	20.6
Tustin	27,573	2.88	63.7	44.1	13.8	36.3	25.5	861	1,926	2,359	147	2,212	54,655	29.5	45.2
Twentynine Palms	9,131	2.46	58.5	42.4	11.0	41.5	32.3	3,547	456	1,740	351	1,389	12,461	37.7	15.8
Union City	21,702	3.44	83.4	65.2	12.6	16.6	9.9	746	2,178	2,885	372	2,513	53,533	32.7	40.3
Upland	27,326	2.78	70.8	49.4	15.2	29.2	21.4	637	2,544	3,306	316	2,990	51,774	36.0	29.1
Vacaville	32,697	2.80	72.5	55.3	11.9	27.5	20.9	6,726	2,264	2,318	212	2,106	66,729	32.3	27.2
Vallejo	40,419	2.97	73.4	47.6	17.7	26.6	20.0	1,432	5,863	4,794	861	3,933	84,811	39.5	24.9
Victorville	32,803	3.60	82.5	49.3	23.4	17.5	15.6	4,042	4,276	3,464	606	2,858	73,000	52.9	12.2
Visalia	41,357	3.13	74.9	50.0	18.2	25.1	19.6	1,544	4,676	3,564	366	3,199	77,645	43.4	23.2
Vista	30,416	3.28	70.8	49.4	15.6	29.2	20.3	1,854	1,987	1,942	364	1,579	63,416	47.5	22.0
Walnut	8,570	3.50	88.8	72.8	13.6	11.2	9.2	NA	541	1,777	82	1,695	21,356	22.0	48.5
Walnut Creek	30,542	2.23	57.7	46.8	7.8	42.3	33.7	1,101	2,198	3,146	112	3,035	53,394	13.1	61.5
Wasco	6,466	3.25	84.9	59.5	20.1	15.1	15.1	5,379	NA	NA	NA	NA	16,484	77.8	3.1
Watsonville	14,634	3.65	80.2	51.9	12.8	19.8	16.5	378	1,976	3,652	440	3,212	29,845	65.1	15.5
West Covina	30,803	3.47	77.8	53.0	16.9	22.2	16.9	889	3,076	2,823	243	2,580	71,937	43.8	28.7
West Hollywood	23,033	1.59	18.5	14.5	2.9	81.5	58.1	NA	1,876	5,127	751	4,375	34,500	12.7	60.8
Westminster	27,587	3.31	76.1	56.6	12.2	23.9	19.1	294	3,029	3,272	334	2,938	64,658	45.0	25.3
West Sacramento	18,230	2.87	63.6	40.8	13.9	36.4	26.7	NA	1,452	2,712	435	2,277	33,486	35.5	29.1
Whittier	27,597	3.09	72.2	50.3	15.7	27.8	21.2	1,690	3,048	3,469	294	3,176	56,987	37.1	26.0
Wildomar	9,418	3.82	81.5	60.3	15.0	18.5	10.3	NA	704	1,939	135	1,804	22,669	44.6	16.4
Windsor	9,435	2.91	76.1	59.4	12.4	23.9	21.4	NA	395	1,431	304	1,127	18,311	37.5	29.4
Woodland	20,304	2.86	70.8	49.9	12.3	29.2	24.5	1,102	1,740	2,940	368	2,571	39,721	49.5	23.6
Yorba Linda	21,941	3.09	84.3	73.7	6.4	15.7	12.9	331	766	1,115	60	1,055	45,457	17.7	55.6
Yuba City	22,096	2.98	71.3	52.3	13.3	28.7	23.5	939	2,302	3,426	405	3,021	43,640	45.6	16.4
Yucaipa	18,397	2.87	72.8	56.7	9.4	27.2	21.8	494	1,275	2,374	210	2,164	35,330	42.1	24.7
COLORADO	2,108,992	2.57	63.9	49.9	9.4	36.1	27.3	118,125	170,833	3,083	343	2,741	3,745,506	30.5	39.9
Arvada	45,850	2.55	65.5	51.1	10.3	34.5	25.2	426	3,108	2,652	173	2,479	82,460	29.3	37.2
Aurora	127,661	2.82	64.7	45.8	11.8	35.3	26.9	2,659	13,186	3,598	532	3,066	234,900	42.0	27.4
Boulder	40,031	2.43	45.5	37.1	5.4	54.5	30.1	10,941	3,436	3,147	238	2,909	62,791	11.8	73.0
Brighton	11,365	3.16	77.1	54.2	14.3	22.9	20.0	1,570	1,481	3,860	375	3,485	23,698	46.4	18.5
Broomfield	26,269	2.52	63.1	53.4	6.9	36.9	27.7	NA	1,647	2,460	51	2,409	45,359	18.6	51.9

1. No spouse present.   2. Data for serious crimes have not been adjusted for underreporting. This may affect comparability between geographic areas and over time.   3. Per 100,000 population estimated by the FBI.   4. Persons 25 years old and over.

Table D. Cities — **Income and Housing**

AREANAME	Money income, 2016					Median earnings, 2016			Housing units, 2016				
	Households			Median family income	Median non-family household income	All persons	Men	Women	Total	Occupied	Percent owner occupied	Median value[1] (dollars)	Median rent (dollars)
	Median income	Percent with income less than $20,000	Percent with income of $200,000 or more										
	42	43	44	45	46	47	48	49	50	51	52	53	54
CALIFORNIA— Cont'd													
San Francisco	103,801	13.5	23.3	123,326	81,776	56,678	61,743	51,535	392,823	358,703	37.9	1,024,000	1,784
San Gabriel	60,941	15.9	6.2	62,752	50,270	30,502	31,005	29,681	14,020	12,591	43.7	660,600	1,429
San Jacinto	52,235	15.1	2.5	53,008	21,525	22,182	35,243	16,009	14,056	12,134	68.5	238,300	1,127
San Jose	101,940	10.1	19.4	111,902	64,349	42,508	51,112	35,931	333,355	320,447	56.9	802,000	1,919
San Juan Capistrano	82,987	14.3	16.6	94,561	20,668	40,767	52,191	30,569	12,512	11,781	71.6	679,200	1,965
San Leandro	65,963	10.8	6.5	79,341	50,712	40,165	48,457	32,310	37,323	34,977	57.1	558,100	1,353
San Luis Obispo	49,521	27.4	4.8	85,202	24,342	20,678	26,237	13,595	20,418	19,090	38.8	606,000	1,368
San Marcos	81,709	9.3	7.1	85,897	53,972	34,112	45,950	22,470	30,635	28,706	63.7	508,700	1,600
San Mateo	114,444	7.1	25.7	130,361	80,958	56,768	74,917	42,964	40,811	38,710	54.8	1,038,400	2,242
San Pablo	50,115	15.9	0.0	52,988	32,730	25,134	30,249	17,805	9,074	8,716	33.0	338,200	1,270
San Rafael	73,428	14.3	18.4	100,632	57,850	35,785	36,958	32,423	23,991	23,376	46.1	898,000	1,823
San Ramon	151,327	5.1	37.1	176,953	77,018	86,666	103,136	65,255	27,157	25,847	71.5	924,300	2,348
Santa Ana	61,895	9.4	4.2	58,209	51,788	24,181	27,629	19,540	75,932	74,294	44.6	461,600	1,438
Santa Barbara	67,593	12.1	11.6	74,133	52,854	35,039	41,574	29,026	40,335	36,514	40.6	1,033,700	1,731
Santa Clara	110,110	5.9	18.8	124,196	73,376	55,214	72,074	36,980	46,723	44,392	44.0	956,800	2,280
Santa Clarita	94,649	6.3	13.7	108,401	50,378	41,574	47,319	37,390	63,148	61,687	68.9	490,600	1,761
Santa Cruz	65,198	22.2	11.6	88,962	37,235	22,509	30,134	21,110	26,832	25,275	46.3	826,200	1,680
Santa Maria	55,775	12.3	3.5	57,211	34,856	22,733	24,594	21,242	28,280	27,248	47.7	340,300	1,343
Santa Monica	90,088	15.2	14.9	107,949	74,353	61,168	70,399	51,779	53,714	47,265	27.7	1,241,200	1,572
Santa Paula	49,333	13.9	2.5	57,371	26,613	25,580	30,239	20,625	10,089	9,615	49.2	372,200	1,148
Santa Rosa	71,854	10.9	6.9	84,615	45,173	33,929	38,061	30,493	68,389	64,202	56.3	484,400	1,568
Santee	78,804	5.9	7.5	91,243	47,092	39,539	45,398	34,685	20,078	18,959	73.4	428,800	1,592
Saratoga	173,423	8.3	41.8	188,108	60,739	100,079	125,694	70,318	11,187	10,653	84.6	2,000,000	1,439
Seaside	60,289	11.7	5.7	75,857	33,339	28,485	33,732	25,125	12,048	10,904	34.2	443,700	1,652
Simi Valley	94,363	8.5	12.1	108,558	53,668	41,746	50,553	36,060	42,927	41,020	71.3	546,800	1,878
Soledad	69,795	12.5	4.5	72,279	0	29,583	28,865	40,831	4,298	4,110	71.8	366,500	669
South Gate	46,556	16.1	1.0	47,343	32,132	24,999	30,741	20,048	24,327	23,762	42.4	363,900	1,042
South Pasadena	96,469	15.6	22.8	114,784	82,966	62,024	76,625	50,175	10,979	10,076	41.1	969,200	1,694
South San Francisco	90,545	9.7	17.1	91,403	54,787	41,533	41,578	41,458	21,814	20,881	56.7	801,900	1,840
Stanton	59,426	9.6	3.5	76,399	37,485	29,405	30,622	26,072	11,028	10,822	58.0	413,200	1,430
Stockton	49,271	20.2	4.6	56,991	29,522	30,451	34,895	24,733	101,908	95,851	46.1	243,700	1,024
Suisun City	79,462	12.0	6.9	83,960	45,243	31,991	41,587	22,242	9,306	9,306	56.6	336,900	1,733
Sunnyvale	121,546	7.8	25.4	131,939	93,252	71,442	90,648	50,025	59,408	56,245	45.6	1,152,500	2,331
Temecula	90,179	5.7	8.6	92,166	78,717	39,597	50,221	28,971	34,189	32,551	62.2	411,300	1,762
Temple City	59,502	16.4	2.9	71,033	22,240	31,296	40,852	26,142	10,928	10,415	56.8	705,500	1,505
Thousand Oaks	100,578	7.8	19.5	124,972	64,187	46,426	67,181	31,447	49,261	46,830	70.5	684,500	2,028
Torrance	85,710	9.1	15.1	106,657	51,394	48,883	52,123	41,135	58,284	53,614	54.7	698,800	1,565
Tracy	81,576	4.9	6.7	85,506	45,258	41,022	50,107	32,168	27,585	26,744	58.1	403,300	1,637
Tulare	47,259	17.3	0.9	50,457	31,898	27,474	31,509	22,620	20,556	19,606	59.8	185,200	902
Turlock	50,691	20.3	3.4	58,697	26,766	30,380	37,325	22,004	25,898	25,137	53.2	306,500	962
Tustin	71,601	9.7	12.4	86,897	51,113	36,765	35,673	38,806	29,034	27,573	45.2	570,100	1,747
Twentynine Palms	40,450	26.8	1.3	39,845	40,447	25,079	24,609	26,253	11,600	9,131	32.5	117,800	998
Union City	98,367	5.7	15.7	107,703	56,004	48,002	49,579	40,753	22,609	21,702	62.8	677,900	1,990
Upland	65,578	12.7	5.6	74,823	48,372	31,094	32,729	27,186	27,783	27,326	51.2	505,100	1,434
Vacaville	85,422	8.8	9.1	98,554	56,364	42,393	53,335	28,124	34,219	32,697	61.2	396,400	1,464
Vallejo	65,241	12.9	4.7	68,232	41,145	31,347	32,655	30,681	42,734	40,419	53.3	332,700	1,384
Victorville	48,065	16.8	0.9	51,875	23,284	27,801	34,005	20,716	34,462	32,803	52.0	210,500	1,227
Visalia	55,280	15.2	4.7	60,730	41,814	31,293	33,431	28,307	44,224	41,357	60.3	214,500	951
Vista	61,433	8.5	4.8	64,980	47,281	27,522	31,016	24,007	31,870	30,416	48.0	463,300	1,445
Walnut	100,513	8.7	17.6	101,090	66,371	40,605	50,758	31,764	9,156	8,570	84.0	779,600	2,098
Walnut Creek	89,814	9.6	18.1	127,357	55,042	51,209	69,326	41,313	32,002	30,542	60.5	788,000	1,875
Wasco	41,379	19.6	0.0	47,911	25,484	19,859	24,073	16,054	6,813	6,466	55.2	166,900	694
Watsonville	53,135	14.1	3.2	57,250	22,212	22,049	22,372	20,583	14,806	14,634	40.7	444,300	1,356
West Covina	74,076	10.5	4.7	81,681	32,343	31,993	35,132	30,793	31,649	30,803	57.6	501,800	1,571
West Hollywood	67,736	19.9	11.0	98,490	61,732	50,344	60,169	42,391	25,962	23,033	21.9	672,800	1,502
Westminster	60,426	18.3	5.7	64,682	39,107	28,375	30,695	24,748	28,334	27,587	48.9	598,300	1,414
West Sacramento	62,205	20.5	7.1	76,013	43,186	40,752	48,048	34,225	19,978	18,230	58.3	339,000	939
Whittier	73,866	12.3	6.9	86,380	40,384	37,499	44,786	31,400	28,917	27,597	56.4	509,300	1,176
Wildomar	67,921	6.1	2.0	67,859	62,708	31,061	45,648	24,699	9,935	9,418	70.3	325,200	1,511
Windsor	82,212	7.5	8.3	90,426	40,448	35,390	41,157	30,879	9,856	9,435	80.4	572,900	1,760
Woodland	57,341	14.4	4.5	67,661	32,126	30,602	35,978	23,873	20,665	20,304	47.6	337,100	1,025
Yorba Linda	126,350	5.7	26.6	143,203	59,047	56,723	71,884	48,088	23,006	21,941	81.3	851,100	1,909
Yuba City	50,246	14.5	2.0	58,130	27,444	24,877	28,226	21,382	23,210	22,096	46.3	257,200	941
Yucaipa	64,714	17.8	5.1	87,116	19,583	32,651	48,932	21,019	20,134	18,397	79.7	300,700	1,051
COLORADO	65,685	12.8	7.2	80,761	40,936	35,274	40,637	30,019	2,339,140	2,108,992	64.8	314,200	1,171
Arvada	75,082	8.1	8.4	86,334	51,400	40,421	45,457	35,771	46,847	45,850	73.0	342,700	1,343
Aurora	59,467	10.2	2.8	67,555	44,818	31,475	32,430	30,230	133,083	127,661	57.2	253,400	1,262
Boulder	70,158	18.4	13.7	113,391	40,950	26,473	31,204	22,824	43,542	40,031	52.2	685,500	1,436
Brighton	67,337	10.5	2.0	76,900	34,259	37,052	41,454	32,084	11,653	11,365	58.5	283,500	1,507
Broomfield	84,349	8.9	15.3	105,397	50,690	50,374	58,169	39,735	27,090	26,269	64.7	383,600	1,507

1. Specified owner-occupied units; $2,000,000 represents $2,000,000 or more.

Table D. Cities — Commuting, Computer Access, Migration, Labor Force, and Employment

AREANAME	Commuting[1] 2016 — Percent		Computer access[2] — Percent		Migration		Civilian labor force, 2016				Civilian employment, 2016			
	Drove alone	With commutes of 30 minutes or more	With a computer in the house	With Internet access	Percent who lived in the same house one year ago	Percent who lived in another state or county one year ago	Total	Percent change 2016-2017	Unemployment[3] Total	Rate	Population age 16 and older Number	Percent in labor force	Population age 16 to 64 Number	Percent who worked full-year full-time
	55	56	57	58	59	60	61	62	63	64	65	66	67	68
CALIFORNIA— Cont'd														
San Francisco	33.7	57.9	92.5	87.1	86.8	7.0	568,722	1.5	16,499	2.9	763,084	70.2	633,747	56.2
San Gabriel	77.5	45.8	94.9	87.6	90.0	2.5	21,569	1.5	837	3.9	33,905	63.2	26,909	54.2
San Jacinto	75.8	55.2	87.9	82.2	87.3	5.6	18,434	2.2	1,150	6.2	37,291	59.6	32,113	38.0
San Jose	75.6	50.1	94.6	90.4	86.7	4.8	551,165	1.6	18,402	3.3	816,000	68.4	697,619	51.3
San Juan Capistrano	82.7	36.1	92.1	87.9	NA	NA	17,424	0.8	546	3.1	29,011	59.7	22,515	48.5
San Leandro	72.3	55.6	88.9	81.9	92.6	2.1	47,634	1.2	1,764	3.7	74,551	61.9	58,523	53.0
San Luis Obispo	65.7	11.8	92.9	89.4	69.8	11.2	25,762	1.4	775	3.0	40,700	64.2	35,028	33.7
San Marcos	76.7	43.4	95.4	91.9	80.6	3.8	42,088	0.9	1,579	3.8	69,872	67.6	58,726	49.3
San Mateo	70.5	44.2	95.1	91.1	85.3	8.4	64,225	1.6	1,661	2.6	85,049	70.8	68,448	55.8
San Pablo	57.9	55.9	92.7	88.8	91.7	2.8	13,864	1.0	563	4.1	22,983	64.5	19,285	42.7
San Rafael	67.2	42.1	92.8	88.9	87.5	6.7	32,835	0.7	917	2.8	46,685	64.9	35,814	44.7
San Ramon	72.1	51.6	99.6	97.1	88.5	6.2	40,254	1.3	1,284	3.2	58,223	70.9	50,779	59.1
Santa Ana	73.6	33.5	92.2	83.3	89.6	2.2	159,335	1.0	5,743	3.6	255,427	67.9	227,513	47.8
Santa Barbara	63.9	9.4	93.8	89.1	82.7	6.5	50,589	0.5	1,507	3.0	76,690	65.8	59,087	47.6
Santa Clara	69.3	31.0	95.9	92.9	75.8	14.6	69,700	1.7	2,126	3.1	101,740	68.0	88,075	48.8
Santa Clarita	77.8	54.0	95.6	92.3	86.4	3.7	97,948	1.5	4,221	4.3	148,230	67.1	124,347	50.1
Santa Cruz	57.6	29.0	94.1	88.3	77.0	12.4	33,367	0.5	1,302	3.9	57,377	63.0	48,295	34.0
Santa Maria	62.7	26.9	87.0	81.7	84.8	2.1	49,146	0.5	3,479	7.1	77,535	67.6	65,691	54.0
Santa Monica	67.7	41.4	95.0	89.5	84.4	6.2	57,086	1.3	2,505	4.4	81,228	70.2	64,903	51.2
Santa Paula	78.4	43.0	75.3	70.2	NA	NA	14,191	-1.0	1,219	8.6	22,290	66.7	19,049	47.2
Santa Rosa	75.0	22.8	92.6	85.5	85.6	5.0	89,799	1.1	3,116	3.5	140,005	67.2	110,228	50.1
Santee	79.0	44.0	95.2	91.3	87.9	2.0	29,300	0.9	1,065	3.6	48,097	66.0	40,483	50.7
Saratoga	80.4	45.0	96.3	93.5	96.6	1.7	14,942	1.7	510	3.4	25,427	56.9	18,477	48.8
Seaside	70.7	18.0	94.3	89.0	83.0	9.5	17,455	0.3	565	3.2	26,117	65.5	22,762	46.5
Simi Valley	82.5	44.7	94.5	92.7	92.3	3.5	68,234	0.1	2,568	3.8	102,483	69.6	84,389	53.3
Soledad	NA	34.8	84.7	75.7	87.7	8.6	7,977	-0.1	882	11.1	20,522	34.5	18,577	36.2
South Gate	72.9	55.9	91.8	84.3	94.5	0.6	43,263	1.2	2,201	5.1	71,627	64.2	62,097	45.8
South Pasadena	78.9	56.8	95.1	93.0	NA	NA	15,068	1.5	562	3.7	19,710	72.7	17,008	60.3
South San Francisco	65.9	46.6	92.1	87.5	90.3	6.5	39,095	1.6	1,123	2.9	54,849	70.4	45,187	57.7
Stanton	78.5	50.0	91.6	86.0	88.9	2.3	18,794	1.0	730	3.9	30,811	65.7	26,271	44.5
Stockton	75.0	35.4	85.2	75.3	85.0	4.0	131,386	1.7	10,449	8.0	229,799	60.4	191,751	40.6
Suisun City	72.4	44.5	92.4	86.2	88.7	5.6	14,533	0.3	701	4.8	23,539	63.6	19,709	48.0
Sunnyvale	72.5	31.7	97.0	90.3	79.5	9.9	87,517	1.8	2,436	2.8	121,929	70.2	104,043	57.1
Temecula	77.8	49.4	97.6	94.8	77.7	9.4	54,459	2.2	2,212	4.1	85,014	67.9	74,220	45.7
Temple City	79.3	57.1	89.4	84.2	93.3	3.0	18,434	1.3	707	3.8	29,624	52.7	22,874	49.3
Thousand Oaks	81.3	29.1	95.1	92.3	88.9	6.0	65,730	0.1	2,348	3.6	106,853	63.9	83,884	48.4
Torrance	80.0	43.6	93.9	88.5	87.3	4.2	79,385	1.5	3,037	3.8	119,708	64.8	97,167	52.1
Tracy	70.9	65.0	94.9	90.7	85.1	6.0	43,267	1.9	2,061	4.8	68,450	65.4	59,499	48.1
Tulare	82.4	18.6	92.4	80.0	91.2	0.6	27,620	1.0	1,789	6.5	46,783	60.1	40,396	42.2
Turlock	83.4	25.6	82.3	75.1	91.0	3.1	33,810	0.1	1,874	5.5	58,813	59.5	47,565	41.3
Tustin	74.8	34.2	96.9	91.6	83.9	4.1	43,186	1.0	1,440	3.3	64,603	74.0	56,436	56.8
Twentynine Palms	63.1	18.9	92.8	91.1	57.6	29.0	6,894	1.7	412	6.0	20,584	73.4	19,344	58.0
Union City	70.6	60.8	97.5	92.6	88.6	5.3	37,978	1.2	1,374	3.6	62,644	65.1	52,009	55.2
Upland	73.8	41.3	92.7	87.8	88.1	6.0	39,305	2.1	1,582	4.0	63,442	65.3	50,856	46.2
Vacaville	81.6	33.8	93.9	91.5	83.7	6.8	45,833	0.7	1,915	4.2	78,219	61.4	65,086	48.4
Vallejo	71.7	53.0	93.6	88.1	85.1	6.8	57,309	0.5	3,008	5.2	98,462	63.8	79,811	44.1
Victorville	70.8	48.1	95.7	89.6	79.8	5.6	46,052	1.8	3,121	6.8	88,509	55.5	76,870	36.2
Visalia	83.6	23.3	93.6	87.7	87.7	3.2	61,208	0.8	3,340	5.5	93,623	59.1	78,020	43.4
Vista	80.7	32.2	95.7	89.8	89.3	3.3	45,479	0.9	1,949	4.3	78,765	67.4	70,566	53.4
Walnut	74.4	59.5	NA	NA	95.2	3.1	16,088	1.6	608	3.8	24,651	56.8	19,267	49.3
Walnut Creek	57.7	51.1	95.8	90.9	85.4	9.0	34,683	1.4	1,154	3.3	59,683	60.0	40,104	51.4
Wasco	92.4	35.7	68.0	65.7	85.3	11.8	8,675	-0.8	1,419	16.4	20,275	48.9	19,196	35.0
Watsonville	69.4	32.0	79.7	73.5	NA	NA	26,672	-2.0	3,190	12.0	38,270	67.3	34,023	49.8
West Covina	83.1	57.0	93.7	88.6	86.0	2.8	53,590	1.4	2,470	4.6	84,936	64.2	70,410	50.6
West Hollywood	78.3	57.2	92.4	90.5	83.0	8.2	27,195	1.3	1,450	5.3	35,261	79.2	29,683	56.3
Westminster	77.6	46.1	91.0	86.4	87.4	3.2	42,393	0.8	1,680	4.0	74,755	58.4	59,093	43.8
West Sacramento	80.4	35.5	93.5	86.6	84.8	8.1	25,602	1.3	1,191	4.7	40,508	59.8	34,137	43.9
Whittier	80.8	53.8	89.7	81.4	90.5	2.6	44,263	1.3	2,017	4.6	68,199	64.9	56,567	53.2
Wildomar	78.3	44.6	93.2	86.1	78.7	7.8	17,104	2.1	806	4.7	27,170	63.5	23,276	42.4
Windsor	73.4	25.0	91.4	89.3	NA	NA	14,290	1.0	484	3.4	21,701	65.8	17,053	51.8
Woodland	75.4	32.3	87.8	79.1	85.3	4.7	30,353	1.2	1,900	6.3	46,303	62.4	39,241	45.3
Yorba Linda	83.1	57.6	96.7	94.4	89.6	3.7	35,360	1.1	1,151	3.3	53,293	61.1	41,428	49.8
Yuba City	77.5	32.9	86.9	82.1	84.0	9.6	31,693	2.6	2,754	8.7	51,114	59.6	41,719	43.7
Yucaipa	83.4	50.3	91.6	81.6	88.0	2.9	25,016	2.1	1,077	4.3	41,535	59.4	33,565	43.7
COLORADO	75.0	35.7	93.6	86.9	81.5	9.7	2,992,307	3.4	84,839	2.8	4,417,829	68.0	3,674,773	52.8
Arvada	82.1	45.1	92.7	89.5	80.9	10.5	66,200	3.2	1,763	2.7	94,414	70.6	75,879	56.9
Aurora	74.5	44.5	94.0	84.5	81.6	10.2	189,373	3.2	5,839	3.1	279,162	71.7	240,680	58.4
Boulder	50.3	20.1	98.8	93.8	66.0	17.8	63,787	3.4	1,471	2.3	95,716	66.2	85,090	37.9
Brighton	83.1	53.9	88.6	83.2	89.6	6.2	18,953	3.0	628	3.3	27,325	64.1	23,590	53.1
Broomfield	79.4	40.2	97.7	94.4	78.6	17.4	37,971	3.3	997	2.6	52,782	70.9	44,216	58.4

1. Employed persons. 2. Households. 3. Percent of civilian labor force.

Table D. Cities — **Population**

AREANAME	Percent Hispanic or Latino[1], 2016	Percent foreign born, 2016	Age of population (percent), 2016							Median age 2016	Percent female 2016	Population			
			Under 18 years	18 to 24 years	25 to 34 years	35 to 44 years	45 to 54 years	55 to 64 years	65 years and over			Census counts		Percent change	
												2000	2010	2000-2010	2010-2017
	12	13	14	15	16	17	18	19	20	21	22	23	24	25	26
GEORGIA......................	9.3	10.1	24.4	9.8	13.6	13.4	13.6	12.0	13.2	36.5	51.3	8,186,453	9,688,690	18.4	7.6
Albany..........................	2.5	1.1	25.5	12.9	13.3	12.7	10.6	11.6	13.5	35.1	55.0	76,939	77,434	0.6	-5.5
Alpharetta....................	7.5	29.5	27.7	6.6	10.1	15.0	17.8	12.6	10.2	33.9	47.7	34,854	57,384	64.6	14.7
Athens-Clarke County..........	10.9	10.2	17.1	28.2	17.2	9.7	9.2	8.7	10.0	38.7	51.8	100,266	115,486	15.2	8.8
Atlanta.........................	4.9	7.4	19.4	12.8	21.5	13.7	12.2	9.3	11.1	27.4	50.3	416,474	420,425	0.9	15.7
Augusta-Richmond County..	5.0	3.5	23.2	11.5	16.6	11.4	11.5	12.4	13.5	33.0	51.6	195,182	195,837	2.8	0.7
Columbus......................	7.6	5.3	24.6	10.6	16.4	12.5	11.5	11.6	12.7	31.9	50.9	186,291	190,571	2.3	1.8
Dalton..........................	49.1	26.9	29.7	13.1	13.2	13.6	12.1	9.4	8.9	33.7	50.7	27,912	33,106	18.6	1.9
Douglasville..................	2.2	6.4	25.2	11.0	15.7	14.6	13.2	11.3	9.1	36.3	58.8	20,065	30,946	54.2	8.8
Duluth.........................	12.8	38.2	23.0	12.4	6.7	16.5	18.4	11.7	11.4	33.5	58.1	22,122	26,604	20.3	10.7
Dunwoody.....................	5.1	22.7	25.7	4.4	14.0	16.5	13.5	9.9	15.9	40.3	49.5	32,808	46,282	41.1	7.2
East Point....................	2.9	4.3	19.3	6.0	14.8	15.3	16.1	11.6	17.0	38.0	52.2	39,595	33,722	-14.8	4.6
Gainesville	41.5	30.1	28.2	12.5	10.4	14.9	10.0	9.8	14.2	33.8	52.0	25,578	33,951	32.7	18.9
Hinesville....................	13.2	6.0	29.2	15.5	15.2	12.2	11.8	9.1	7.0	26.9	51.3	30,392	33,434	10.0	-0.9
Johns Creek.................	8.7	29.5	28.2	4.4	7.2	17.7	18.3	15.0	9.1	40.9	52.8	NA	76,639	NA	10.1
Kennesaw....................	14.7	13.5	23.6	13.4	13.3	14.8	18.0	9.4	7.5	34.9	51.8	21,675	30,592	41.1	12.3
LaGrange.....................	3.0	11.1	25.9	12.0	15.2	10.6	10.5	12.7	13.1	32.6	52.6	25,998	29,440	13.2	3.5
Lawrenceville................	25.6	24.2	26.1	11.5	17.1	10.7	12.0	9.7	12.8	32.6	51.9	22,397	27,293	21.9	9.5
Macon-Bibb County	3.2	3.6	25.0	10.2	13.8	11.3	12.3	12.7	14.7	36.1	53.1	NA	155,600	NA	-1.9
Marietta......................	20.5	19.3	25.0	11.5	13.2	15.4	15.4	9.2	10.2	35.2	50.7	58,748	56,595	-3.7	7.9
Milton.........................	3.8	13.6	27.5	6.8	5.4	10.4	25.3	16.4	8.2	44.9	55.4	NA	32,842	NA	18.5
Newnan........................	13.2	9.4	26.0	7.0	13.8	17.4	16.2	9.5	10.1	36.9	50.2	16,242	32,893	102.5	18.3
Peachtree City	8.3	10.1	27.5	3.9	7.0	14.1	16.0	13.5	18.0	43.4	52.2	31,580	34,364	8.8	2.6
Rome..........................	16.6	14.5	21.0	13.3	14.5	14.4	12.6	10.6	13.6	36.4	51.8	34,980	36,370	4.0	0.0
Roswell.......................	15.1	17.9	25.9	7.7	14.7	11.2	15.9	13.2	11.5	36.0	50.5	79,334	88,337	11.3	7.3
Sandy Springs................	16.7	20.9	18.0	10.9	20.0	16.0	12.9	10.3	11.9	35.7	52.0	85,781	93,817	9.4	13.8
Savannah.....................	5.9	5.0	20.6	14.6	17.8	12.5	9.7	11.3	13.5	32.8	51.4	131,510	137,002	4.2	6.9
Smyrna........................	14.3	20.9	22.2	8.5	20.5	17.7	14.2	8.1	8.8	34.6	52.4	40,999	51,202	24.9	10.7
Statesboro...................	7.1	4.0	15.5	45.9	9.9	6.6	6.5	7.0	8.5	21.8	47.3	22,698	28,380	25.0	10.6
Stockbridge..................	1.7	15.9	31.4	9.4	14.4	4.9	20.6	10.7	8.7	31.7	54.7	9,853	26,350	167.4	10.5
Valdosta......................	1.6	2.4	22.6	20.1	15.1	11.9	7.1	11.1	12.1	28.9	52.6	43,724	54,760	25.2	2.4
Warner Robins................	7.7	6.9	23.8	7.4	15.6	15.5	11.0	13.7	13.1	36.0	53.1	48,804	68,944	41.3	8.6
HAWAII.........................	10.4	18.4	21.5	9.1	14.4	12.6	12.4	12.9	17.0	38.9	49.7	1,211,537	1,360,301	12.3	4.9
East Honolulu CDP............	4.1	14.8	18.3	5.3	9.5	11.4	16.5	15.2	23.7	48.3	52.7	NA	NA	NA	NA
Hilo CDP......................	9.0	9.9	19.6	12.6	12.1	10.0	12.7	13.4	19.6	41.2	50.5	40,759	NA	NA	NA
Kahului CDP..................	11.4	35.7	25.8	9.6	13.7	14.4	13.6	9.6	13.4	35.3	49.4	20,146	NA	NA	NA
Kailua CDP (Honolulu County)....................	7.2	8.2	18.5	8.1	13.8	12.4	13.0	14.6	19.6	42.4	50.7	36,513	NA	NA	NA
Kaneohe CDP.................	4.1	9.7	21.0	5.8	15.8	11.9	12.2	14.6	18.8	40.7	49.3	34,970	NA	NA	NA
Mililani Town CDP..............	12.6	9.2	23.8	7.1	17.7	10.6	10.7	13.0	16.9	36.5	48.7	28,608	NA	NA	NA
Pearl City CDP................	13.4	9.7	20.4	10.2	12.9	13.0	10.2	10.7	22.6	38.7	50.0	30,976	NA	NA	NA
Urban Honolulu CDP	7.2	26.1	18.1	8.6	15.0	13.1	12.9	12.8	19.5	41.4	50.6	NA	337,721	NA	3.8
Waipahu CDP..................	7.4	43.7	22.4	9.7	14.2	13.3	11.1	11.3	18.0	38.9	51.7	33,108	NA	NA	NA
IDAHO	12.3	5.8	25.9	9.5	13.1	12.2	11.8	12.3	15.2	36.1	50.0	1,293,953	1,567,650	21.2	9.5
Boise City.....................	9.9	8.1	23.0	9.7	16.9	14.1	12.2	11.2	12.9	35.3	51.8	185,787	208,344	12.1	8.7
Caldwell.......................	29.5	12.3	30.5	10.0	16.8	11.1	12.6	9.0	10.0	29.9	49.7	25,967	46,319	78.4	18.0
Coeur d'Alene................	5.7	2.0	25.4	11.3	14.8	12.0	12.7	8.9	14.9	34.6	52.3	34,514	44,155	27.9	14.7
Idaho Falls	16.5	6.4	27.7	8.5	14.7	13.0	10.7	10.8	14.6	34.3	49.5	50,730	57,098	12.6	7.0
Lewiston......................	4.4	1.6	20.1	10.9	12.8	11.5	11.7	14.3	18.7	38.5	50.8	30,904	31,897	3.2	2.9
Meridian......................	6.8	3.1	28.7	7.5	11.5	14.0	12.4	11.7	14.1	36.5	46.9	34,919	76,258	118.4	31.0
Nampa	27.9	6.5	33.6	9.2	12.7	13.7	9.4	9.9	11.6	31.2	51.7	51,867	81,820	57.7	14.4
Pocatello.....................	8.1	3.9	23.6	12.0	15.3	12.5	11.3	11.4	13.9	34.3	52.6	51,466	54,232	5.4	1.8
Post Falls	4.1	2.1	22.7	9.0	17.7	10.7	10.2	12.3	17.5	35.7	49.2	17,247	27,735	60.8	20.0
Rexburg.......................	9.6	5.5	24.4	41.4	18.8	4.9	4.6	2.4	3.6	22.8	48.7	17,257	25,473	47.6	11.2
Twin Falls	22.0	13.6	29.7	9.2	14.2	11.7	12.5	9.6	13.1	32.8	52.6	34,469	44,329	28.6	11.0
ILLINOIS........................	17.0	13.9	22.8	9.5	13.8	12.9	13.4	12.9	14.6	37.9	50.9	12,419,293	12,831,565	3.3	-0.2
Addison.......................	44.3	40.1	23.1	8.1	14.3	16.3	11.5	14.4	12.3	37.7	47.0	35,914	36,970	2.9	-0.4
Algonquin.....................	6.3	12.3	25.8	6.9	13.2	12.4	16.9	14.1	10.7	38.9	54.3	23,276	30,049	29.1	3.2
Alton..........................	2.3	1.9	28.5	7.8	14.9	10.5	10.4	11.6	16.2	34.2	55.8	30,496	27,918	-8.5	-4.3
Arlington Heights.............	5.1	17.6	22.9	5.5	9.9	13.9	13.9	15.1	18.9	43.1	50.5	76,031	75,188	-1.1	0.6
Aurora.........................	45.5	23.8	29.0	10.8	12.2	16.6	13.0	9.4	9.0	33.5	50.7	142,990	197,948	38.4	1.5
Bartlett.......................	15.3	14.5	29.3	7.2	10.6	12.8	17.8	12.4	10.0	36.8	51.9	36,706	41,159	12.1	0.0
Batavia.......................	12.4	6.9	23.8	10.2	13.3	13.2	17.3	10.9	11.3	37.5	51.1	23,866	26,182	9.7	1.5
Belleville.....................	1.7	2.7	21.5	8.2	19.3	10.0	15.1	14.1	11.8	36.3	54.7	41,410	44,314	7.0	-6.0
Belvidere.....................	34.9	18.3	28.9	8.7	8.8	17.6	13.0	9.4	13.5	36.9	48.9	20,820	25,646	23.2	-1.8
Berwyn........................	67.5	27.9	27.8	10.6	13.6	12.9	13.4	11.9	9.8	34.1	50.8	54,016	56,653	4.9	-1.9
Bloomington...................	6.2	12.0	20.2	12.7	15.6	13.1	13.1	12.3	12.8	36.1	50.5	64,808	76,692	18.3	1.6
Bolingbrook...................	25.5	25.5	25.5	10.1	12.3	14.6	17.7	10.3	9.5	36.6	48.3	56,321	73,365	30.3	2.5
Buffalo Grove.................	9.1	34.9	22.2	7.9	10.6	15.8	15.6	14.6	13.4	42.1	51.1	42,909	41,501	-3.3	-0.7

1. May be of any race.

AREANAME	Households, 2016							Serious crimes known to police[2], 2016				Educational attainment, 2016		
			Perecnt						Total		Rate[3]			Attainment[4] (percent)	
	Number	Persons per house-hold	Family	Married couple family	Female headed family[1]	Non-family	One person	Persons in group quarters	Number	Rate	Violent	Property	Population age 25 and over	High school graduate or less	Bachelor's degree or more
	27	28	29	30	31	32	33	34	35	36	37	38	39	40	41
GEORGIA........................	3,686,135	2.73	67.3	47.4	15.1	32.7	27.2	256,905	350,760	3,402	398	3,004	6,785,395	41.4	30.5
Albany..........................	28,054	2.53	60.8	28.3	27.0	39.2	33.4	4,024	4,493	6,045	1,174	4,870	46,151	45.3	20.1
Alpharetta.....................	23,559	2.76	72.4	57.5	11.7	27.6	22.6	NA	1,343	2,068	54	2,014	42,906	13.9	66.4
Athens-Clarke County..........	47,020	2.41	47.1	30.0	13.1	52.9	37.2	10,228	4,633	3,738	430	3,308	67,534	33.3	41.0
Atlanta........................	193,815	2.27	41.4	22.6	15.6	58.6	48.6	32,325	29,925	6,332	1,084	5,249	320,649	28.3	50.5
Augusta-Richmond County..	73,962	2.52	62.9	36.3	20.5	37.1	31.1	9,603	9,498	4,817	429	4,388	128,071	46.9	22.3
Columbus......................	73,051	2.59	63.1	38.8	18.8	36.9	32.9	8,008	10,803	5,339	598	4,741	127,871	38.6	27.4
Dalton.........................	11,293	2.94	67.9	40.7	20.9	32.1	28.5	845	1,216	3,578	332	3,245	19,494	53.7	18.2
Douglasville...................	11,763	2.72	69.3	39.4	27.7	30.7	23.7	1,207	1,943	5,837	586	5,251	21,233	31.6	32.2
Duluth.........................	11,667	2.51	66.0	45.2	17.0	34.0	29.5	NA	803	2,702	538	2,164	18,973	20.8	49.5
Dunwoody.......................	21,001	2.33	62.0	50.6	10.5	38.0	32.7	NA	2,145	4,357	158	4,198	34,160	12.2	74.5
East Point......................	16,901	2.07	30.9	19.7	9.2	69.1	61.1	555	4,115	11,497	1,179	10,318	26,491	34.3	31.1
Gainesville	12,200	3.19	65.1	41.8	18.4	34.9	29.1	1,108	1,567	3,975	411	3,564	23,717	56.4	22.4
Hinesville......................	12,411	2.66	68.8	40.6	22.3	31.2	25.1	530	1,577	4,711	681	4,030	18,574	35.8	17.5
Johns Creek....................	27,227	3.08	79.2	69.1	7.5	20.8	17.2	NA	714	844	32	812	56,494	20.4	63.3
Kennesaw	12,741	2.63	65.7	43.1	18.3	34.3	28.4	NA	673	1,968	193	1,775	21,199	29.1	41.9
LaGrange.......................	10,919	2.74	65.8	28.1	33.8	34.2	32.7	818	1,790	5,787	508	5,279	19,111	51.7	20.3
Lawrenceville	10,864	2.80	66.7	35.7	26.0	33.3	28.5	1,069	1,069	3,458	291	3,167	19,189	42.0	20.0
Macon-Bibb County	57,642	2.54	57.9	33.6	20.0	42.1	36.9	6,174	NA	NA	NA	NA	98,924	45.6	25.9
Marietta.......................	22,634	2.57	60.9	40.4	15.0	39.1	32.6	2,836	2,515	4,226	391	3,834	38,697	38.1	39.1
Milton	14,918	2.57	77.1	60.3	15.7	22.9	21.4	NA	348	903	26	877	25,240	14.0	65.5
Newnan........................	14,202	2.64	68.6	46.6	20.8	31.4	22.4	NA	1,221	3,202	564	2,638	25,402	40.3	29.9
Peachtree City	13,518	2.59	72.8	60.6	9.6	27.2	22.8	NA	564	1,594	54	1,540	24,139	15.7	59.7
Rome..........................	14,275	2.43	63.4	37.4	21.0	36.6	31.5	1,657	1,665	4,590	593	3,997	23,939	46.8	30.8
Roswell........................	32,537	2.89	71.2	57.1	8.7	28.8	21.3	463	1,845	1,928	149	1,779	62,845	20.6	58.4
Sandy Springs.................	45,183	2.32	52.3	39.8	8.4	47.7	39.0	724	2,954	2,743	109	2,635	75,234	20.5	62.9
Savannah......................	55,363	2.45	56.1	29.9	21.6	43.9	34.7	11,145	9,936	4,118	487	3,631	95,104	39.7	26.6
Smyrna........................	25,693	2.20	52.9	36.9	11.8	47.1	35.6	NA	1,745	3,053	343	2,710	39,303	23.4	53.5
Statesboro.....................	10,134	2.32	44.1	23.0	15.2	55.9	37.7	7,859	1,284	4,119	318	3,801	12,119	51.8	23.7
Stockbridge	9,009	3.18	80.2	50.6	25.4	19.8	17.5	NA	NA	NA	NA	NA	16,977	27.2	32.3
Valdosta.......................	21,712	2.50	55.1	29.9	13.5	44.9	37.2	2,286	3,263	5,839	369	5,471	32,333	49.8	24.9
Warner Robins..................	29,590	2.50	67.4	47.4	12.9	32.6	28.0	311	4,605	6,188	664	5,524	51,214	34.4	31.4
HAWAII.......................	455,868	3.04	69.2	51.8	11.7	30.8	24.5	44,287	47,170	3,302	309	2,993	990,937	36.1	31.9
East Honolulu CDP	15,624	2.93	77.9	65.4	10.2	22.1	17.0	268	NA	NA	NA	NA	35,164	16.4	60.7
Hilo CDP	17,043	2.66	63.3	44.2	14.9	36.7	32.1	1,349	NA	NA	NA	NA	31,659	34.8	35.0
Kahului CDP	7,486	4.34	88.4	61.3	19.5	11.6	10.4	1,521	NA	NA	NA	NA	21,960	52.7	12.4
Kailua CDP (Honolulu County)	12,201	3.06	74.5	58.4	11.3	25.5	18.1	253	NA	NA	NA	NA	27,576	23.0	50.3
Kaneohe CDP	10,890	3.39	78.5	63.5	11.9	21.5	16.5	828	NA	NA	NA	NA	27,646	39.6	38.3
Mililani Town CDP..............	9,136	3.61	80.2	62.6	12.3	19.8	12.5	NA	NA	NA	NA	NA	22,753	21.8	34.7
Pearl City CDP.................	13,807	3.14	77.0	60.0	11.7	23.0	18.2	1,687	NA	NA	NA	NA	31,193	32.7	33.8
Urban Honolulu CDP	128,883	2.63	59.5	43.4	11.0	40.5	32.8	13,343	NA	NA	NA	NA	257,939	34.5	37.5
Waipahu CDP	8,166	4.71	84.5	52.9	18.3	15.5	14.4	1,643	NA	NA	NA	NA	27,205	50.3	16.1
IDAHO.........................	610,872	2.71	67.4	53.8	9.1	32.6	26.6	30,052	33,233	1,974	230	1,744	1,087,265	37.4	27.6
Boise City.....................	89,012	2.47	56.7	44.3	8.9	43.3	34.8	3,071	5,791	2,623	298	2,326	150,245	26.5	41.4
Caldwell.......................	16,553	3.13	66.3	52.4	9.9	33.7	25.3	1,389	1,159	2,195	248	1,947	31,603	53.9	14.0
Coeur d'Alene	19,309	2.54	56.8	38.2	12.0	43.2	30.1	1,315	1,591	3,172	345	2,827	31,848	37.1	29.7
Idaho Falls	22,256	2.65	64.7	50.4	8.0	35.3	27.8	1,224	1,620	2,717	424	2,293	38,418	26.9	35.5
Lewiston.......................	13,315	2.31	61.7	46.0	11.0	38.3	29.1	1,036	1,376	4,212	141	4,072	21,886	44.2	19.8
Meridian.......................	33,458	2.85	74.2	58.2	9.9	25.8	24.0	NA	1,562	1,660	112	1,548	61,038	25.8	36.7
Nampa.........................	30,041	2.98	66.1	49.9	12.4	33.9	28.6	1,980	2,975	3,251	363	2,888	52,238	47.9	21.3
Pocatello......................	20,500	2.58	61.1	45.8	10.9	38.9	31.9	1,925	1,837	3,373	380	2,993	35,236	38.8	29.4
Post Falls	12,267	2.58	68.7	47.0	15.0	31.3	24.1	265	830	2,675	229	2,446	21,761	43.9	16.1
Rexburg	6,937	3.29	81.3	78.0	2.0	18.7	12.0	471	198	704	32	672	7,973	13.0	45.0
Twin Falls.....................	17,072	2.76	70.1	53.7	11.1	29.9	22.8	1,061	1,227	2,552	327	2,225	29,488	40.8	21.5
ILLINOIS.......................	4,822,046	2.59	64.3	47.0	12.6	35.7	29.6	300,819	318,160	2,485	436	2,049	8,665,219	37.1	34.0
Addison........................	12,312	2.86	68.7	52.6	11.7	31.3	26.8	NA	703	1,887	134	1,753	24,318	57.4	22.2
Algonquin......................	10,940	2.94	80.8	67.6	10.7	19.2	14.1	NA	393	1,281	39	1,242	21,632	22.6	45.2
Alton..........................	10,820	2.43	55.0	28.2	22.1	45.0	34.2	554	1,358	5,062	682	4,380	17,114	46.3	17.9
Arlington Heights................	30,610	2.40	63.4	55.0	6.3	36.6	33.8	NA	780	1,025	76	949	53,265	21.3	53.0
Aurora.........................	62,913	3.11	73.2	52.4	15.0	26.8	20.2	1,717	3,498	1,739	314	1,425	118,787	42.4	32.4
Bartlett........................	13,782	3.21	80.3	74.3	5.2	19.7	16.8	NA	282	678	77	601	28,096	25.1	44.2
Batavia........................	11,062	2.73	66.9	58.9	7.9	33.1	26.4	NA	440	1,657	98	1,559	20,024	22.0	51.9
Belleville......................	18,856	2.16	51.1	29.0	18.2	48.9	40.2	1,140	1,930	4,635	610	4,025	29,441	32.5	24.6
Belvidere......................	9,041	2.83	78.8	54.7	20.4	21.2	18.1	NA	345	1,377	259	1,118	16,141	57.7	12.0
Berwyn........................	16,754	3.32	69.1	50.4	15.4	30.9	24.2	NA	1,405	2,495	302	2,193	34,371	55.0	17.8
Bloomington....................	32,784	2.31	57.5	44.6	10.0	42.5	34.3	2,233	1,654	2,104	391	1,714	52,332	26.5	47.0
Bolingbrook....................	22,954	3.18	80.9	61.8	13.3	19.1	16.7	NA	1,102	1,480	212	1,268	47,229	32.1	38.7
Buffalo Grove..................	14,593	2.71	73.2	63.9	7.6	26.8	24.4	NA	222	535	31	503	27,748	18.4	64.0

1. No spouse present.   2. Data for serious crimes have not been adjusted for underreporting. This may affect comparability between geographic areas and over time.   3. Per 100,000 population estimated by the FBI.   4. Persons 25 years old and over.

Table D. Cities — Accommodation and Food Services, Arts, Entertainment, and Recreation, and Health Care and Social Assistance

AREANAME	Accommodaton and food services, 2012				Arts, entertainment, and recreation,[1] 2012				Health care and social assistance,[1] 2012			
	Number of establish-ments	Number of employees	Receipts (mil dol)	Annual payroll (mil dol)	Number of establish-ments	Number of employees	Receipts (mil dol)	Annual payroll (mil dol)	Number of establish-ments	Number of employees	Receipts (mil dol)	Annual payroll (mil dol)
	92	93	94	95	96	97	98	99	100	101	102	103
GEORGIA	18,815	353,638	18,976.6	5,173.4	2,232	28,800	2,877.8	953.0	20,166	256,945	28,196.2	11,171.4
Albany	211	D	D	D	15	D	D	D	238	D	D	D
Alpharetta	286	6,486	342.2	98.9	33	D	D	D	389	3,667	556.5	236.2
Athens-Clarke County	342	6,927	307.6	83.9	27	354	20.5	5.5	394	D	D	D
Atlanta	1,618	42,124	3,023.4	844.6	272	3,724	871.2	309.6	1,336	17,100	2,332.0	908.9
Augusta-Richmond County	424	9,448	447.0	125.6	28	D	D	D	577	9,118	1,230.5	456.4
Columbus	442	10,453	519.3	149.2	30	427	26.0	6.5	520	6,215	649.7	261.6
Dalton	120	D	D	D	7	D	D	D	122	D	D	D
Douglasville	129	2,867	130.6	36.6	4	D	D	D	115	1,033	118.2	46.4
Duluth	144	1,624	82.0	22.3	19	D	D	D	166	D	D	D
Dunwoody	141	3,952	244.2	73.0	17	D	D	D	202	3,057	258.8	98.0
East Point	72	1,504	97.0	26.8	14	D	D	D	83	1,789	177.9	59.5
Gainesville	151	2,837	163.0	43.3	15	D	D	D	271	D	D	D
Hinesville	80	1,307	68.7	14.9	3	D	D	D	49	525	40.8	18.1
Johns Creek	137	2,100	98.6	30.2	20	557	47.0	15.0	158	D	D	D
Kennesaw	111	2,319	109.7	31.5	15	D	D	D	85	D	D	D
LaGrange	86	1,738	76.2	21.7	7	D	D	D	79	D	D	D
Lawrenceville	128	2,022	107.6	29.9	15	D	D	D	262	D	D	D
Macon-Bibb County	266	4,795	207.3	58.8	11	D	D	D	365	D	D	D
Marietta	289	4,708	264.5	74.0	24	174	19.7	3.8	392	D	D	D
Milton	44	635	34.6	9.8	17	171	13.5	3.2	28	D	D	D
Newnan	112	2,784	129.1	37.1	7	189	9.1	2.2	93	D	D	D
Peachtree City	100	2,410	112.6	35.3	20	D	D	D	119	D	D	D
Rome	138	3,070	136.6	40.0	11	D	D	D	215	D	D	D
Roswell	237	4,531	234.3	68.0	51	D	D	D	352	5,025	553.5	202.6
Sandy Springs	266	4,373	280.1	75.7	33	577	39.2	11.4	640	8,319	1,459.9	597.1
Savannah	571	12,766	759.1	203.0	40	D	D	D	486	8,390	1,182.6	453.3
Smyrna	161	2,788	152.3	41.7	19	291	13.0	4.8	208	1,508	188.3	61.4
Statesboro	124	D	D	D	4	D	D	D	148	D	D	D
Stockbridge	83	1,205	57.8	14.1	8	D	D	D	143	D	D	D
Valdosta	214	4,519	199.0	53.2	13	D	D	D	275	D	D	D
Warner Robins	157	3,608	168.4	44.7	11	234	7.1	2.4	179	D	D	D
HAWAII	3,518	98,364	9,536.7	2,536.0	398	7,327	571.1	168.2	2,794	26,788	3,180.4	1,347.2
East Honolulu CDP	65	D	D	D	12	D	D	D	64	548	56.6	19.3
Hilo CDP	146	2,239	133.8	33.2	6	D	D	D	176	2,291	225.8	99.0
Kahului CDP	84	1,703	123.3	31.2	10	D	D	D	75	704	99.2	42.4
Kailua CDP (Honolulu County)	86	1,446	81.3	20.9	9	D	D	D	113	D	D	D
Kaneohe CDP	74	1,140	76.8	17.5	12	D	D	D	81	725	78.1	31.0
Mililani Town CDP	41	1,055	60.1	15.0	3	119	8.8	1.8	19	180	19.9	10.1
Pearl City CDP	74	1,346	79.7	19.3	3	146	11.9	2.5	76	785	82.2	31.8
Urban Honolulu CDP	1,471	38,426	3,944.0	955.4	103	1,558	117.6	31.5	1,262	11,394	1,445.9	615.3
Waipahu CDP	77	1,007	64.5	15.0	3	5	0.7	0.1	86	749	74.2	28.6
IDAHO	3,564	54,257	2,680.2	726.1	573	6,755	355.9	102.6	4,271	49,613	4,281.1	1,636.4
Boise City	617	11,334	523.9	154.0	56	1,166	44.4	12.3	793	D	D	D
Caldwell	65	1,007	46.6	12.2	5	D	D	D	93	1,484	160.5	55.9
Coeur d'Alene	184	3,531	181.2	51.4	28	244	18.5	5.6	274	D	D	D
Idaho Falls	191	3,578	159.1	46.2	13	D	D	D	416	D	D	D
Lewiston	95	D	D	D	13	D	D	D	119	1,820	167.6	56.4
Meridian	178	3,513	161.9	44.2	25	439	19.6	5.9	279	D	D	D
Nampa	159	2,965	122.8	34.2	16	D	D	D	197	3,419	215.1	99.1
Pocatello	151	2,633	111.4	30.7	17	D	D	D	245	D	D	D
Post Falls	57	735	34.0	9.7	8	65	4.8	1.2	83	1,406	124.7	47.3
Rexburg	48	840	30.4	8.5	7	60	1.8	0.5	84	D	D	D
Twin Falls	140	2,486	123.3	32.4	23	D	D	D	235	D	D	D
ILLINOIS	27,117	469,870	27,937.4	7,707.1	3,564	49,286	5,591.9	1,678.3	27,624	383,980	39,270.3	16,150.8
Addison	73	D	D	D	8	D	D	D	50	969	81.3	41.9
Algonquin	82	1,821	81.9	26.2	16	D	D	D	89	733	76.2	36.1
Alton	92	1,842	85.5	26.3	11	D	D	D	92	D	D	D
Arlington Heights	148	2,732	161.0	45.4	29	274	16.7	5.1	351	D	D	D
Aurora	257	4,005	227.2	56.8	34	973	161.4	29.9	304	4,552	575.3	222.8
Bartlett	36	460	24.8	6.5	7	D	D	D	49	D	D	D
Batavia	63	1,094	50.3	15.2	5	D	D	D	57	D	D	D
Belleville	142	D	D	D	14	D	D	D	159	4,006	362.8	191.6
Belvidere	49	D	D	D	5	D	D	D	45	D	D	D
Berwyn	86	D	D	D	6	42	2.7	0.7	130	3,811	433.8	197.0
Bloomington	223	4,927	234.3	67.4	33	601	18.3	6.0	204	2,790	335.9	142.6
Bolingbrook	154	3,230	173.5	49.0	19	569	17.7	8.6	138	D	D	D
Buffalo Grove	101	1,514	92.8	28.1	14	D	D	D	172	1,506	181.5	64.6

1. Establishments subject to federal tax.

AREANAME	Other services[1]				Government employment and payroll, 2012								
						March payroll							
							Percent of total for:						
	Number of establishments	Number of employees	Receipts (mil dol)	Annual payroll (mil dol)	Full-time equivalent employees	Total (dollars)	Administrative, judicial, and legal	Police and corrections	Fire protection	Highways and transportation	Health and welfare	Natural resources and utilities	Education and libraries
	104	105	106	107	108	109	110	111	112	113	114	115	116
GEORGIA......................	11,682	71,989	6,311.9	1,949.9	X	X	X	X	X	X	X	X	X
Albany..............................	113	D	D	D	1,213	4,293,454	11.1	19.0	17.2	7.2	2.0	31.0	0.0
Alpharetta.........................	138	D	D	D	443	2,007,691	5.5	32.0	22.6	9.9	0.0	9.9	0.0
Athens-Clarke County.........	153	929	66.0	21.6	1,759	6,225,567	17.5	31.3	12.0	9.2	0.6	19.8	3.4
Atlanta.............................	879	8,945	574.9	212.4	8,214	31,551,612	15.9	34.2	13.9	16.0	0.2	18.5	0.0
Augusta-Richmond County..	220	1,531	148.4	44.6	2,708	8,108,733	23.7	31.7	13.0	8.3	1.7	16.6	2.0
Columbus..........................	259	1,902	157.2	51.1	3,147	10,081,635	11.8	34.7	14.0	7.5	4.7	18.9	2.8
Dalton..............................	57	D	D	D	692	2,865,431	2.7	12.6	11.3	8.7	0.3	61.7	0.0
Douglasville......................	80	369	35.4	10.7	232	792,422	15.8	53.4	0.0	14.1	0.0	8.0	0.0
Duluth..............................	133	785	73.7	21.0	140	565,431	33.5	44.9	0.0	10.3	0.0	10.1	0.0
Dunwoody..........................	73	435	28.6	8.8	67	294,800	23.0	77.0	0.0	0.0	0.0	0.0	0.0
East Point.........................	38	747	41.5	13.4	535	1,898,606	17.4	33.8	15.0	2.6	0.0	22.3	0.0
Gainesville	86	398	34.2	9.9	670	2,183,927	9.3	16.9	16.0	8.4	2.2	43.8	0.0
Hinesville.........................	39	208	14.9	4.4	201	695,457	7.4	56.2	19.8	0.0	3.5	2.5	0.0
Johns Creek......................	78	D	D	D	8	41,438	87.5	12.5	0.0	0.0	0.0	0.0	0.0
Kennesaw	99	963	111.3	41.3	205	735,014	16.6	34.2	0.0	9.0	2.2	24.9	0.0
LaGrange	45	D	D	D	408	1,594,338	6.9	28.0	14.4	4.1	0.7	29.6	0.0
Lawrenceville.....................	135	767	85.7	27.2	246	987,618	20.7	41.4	0.0	4.4	0.0	30.9	0.0
Macon-Bibb County	145	839	91.3	25.4	1,169	3,501,960	8.9	33.1	34.1	4.1	1.9	14.4	0.0
Marietta............................	220	1,340	152.1	45.4	734	3,368,637	23.6	11.1	12.3	4.3	11.8	24.4	0.0
Milton...............................	30	D	D	D	121	520,911	22.5	27.5	44.2	3.3	0.0	2.5	0.0
Newnan.............................	69	308	24.4	6.4	267	989,419	6.4	31.3	19.7	8.0	0.0	19.0	0.6
Peachtree City	86	758	53.4	17.9	270	1,079,307	11.4	29.0	29.7	14.7	0.0	5.3	3.6
Rome................................	62	429	39.4	10.8	589	1,937,155	8.3	18.6	26.8	11.5	0.6	25.2	0.0
Roswell.............................	200	1,408	111.7	41.6	741	2,812,794	17.5	29.3	11.9	8.4	0.0	29.5	0.0
Sandy Springs....................	170	D	D	D	295	1,455,396	3.8	60.7	34.3	0.0	0.0	0.0	0.0
Savannah..........................	221	1,473	144.6	43.6	2,548	9,836,488	9.9	34.9	11.9	8.9	2.7	25.8	0.0
Smyrna.............................	102	452	41.9	12.4	391	1,523,989	10.9	37.3	23.1	6.6	3.6	14.0	2.3
Statesboro.........................	55	288	21.2	5.4	279	845,101	12.3	28.4	12.3	12.1	0.0	32.0	0.0
Stockbridge.......................	38	175	12.6	3.1	68	227,107	32.1	0.0	0.0	21.8	0.0	33.5	0.0
Valdosta............................	92	512	31.4	8.5	574	1,813,002	8.4	32.3	17.3	9.7	3.4	24.8	0.0
Warner Robins....................	81	473	34.5	10.5	536	1,642,600	10.8	31.9	21.3	10.1	3.3	20.5	0.0
HAWAII............................	1,519	11,014	877.5	279.0	X	X	X	X	X	X	X	X	X
East Honolulu CDP.............	24	101	4.3	1.6	NA	NA	NA	NA	NA	NA	NA	NA	NA
Hilo CDP	68	351	30.2	8.4	NA	NA	NA	NA	NA	NA	NA	NA	NA
Kahului CDP	53	471	34.8	11.6	NA	NA	NA	NA	NA	NA	NA	NA	NA
Kailua CDP (Honolulu County)	47	196	15.1	4.7	NA	NA	NA	NA	NA	NA	NA	NA	NA
Kaneohe CDP.....................	38	268	20.0	7.2	NA	NA	NA	NA	NA	NA	NA	NA	NA
Mililani Town CDP...............	15	93	5.1	2.0	NA	NA	NA	NA	NA	NA	NA	NA	NA
Pearl City CDP....................	43	187	21.3	6.1	NA	NA	NA	NA	NA	NA	NA	NA	NA
Urban Honolulu CDP	721	6,242	481.7	157.1	NA	NA	NA	NA	NA	NA	NA	NA	NA
Waipahu CDP	53	276	23.2	6.9	NA	NA	NA	NA	NA	NA	NA	NA	NA
IDAHO........................	2,055	9,826	849.8	240.9	X	X	X	X	X	X	X	X	X
Boise City..........................	371	2,083	162.4	51.1	1,617	7,522,788	17.0	29.2	23.6	4.2	0.9	17.7	4.2
Caldwell............................	46	290	30.2	8.4	228	861,823	8.7	36.4	24.0	12.2	0.0	13.3	3.2
Coeur d'Alene....................	82	447	32.5	10.0	318	1,619,497	16.8	30.1	21.9	7.8	0.2	19.0	3.2
Idaho Falls	92	448	42.2	11.5	659	2,848,455	10.4	20.7	20.0	4.4	0.0	33.4	2.9
Lewiston	65	381	28.8	8.9	314	1,377,725	8.6	24.1	24.4	12.2	3.9	16.1	2.7
Meridian	90	556	37.4	13.7	343	1,643,338	14.3	34.7	25.5	8.1	0.0	15.4	0.0
Nampa..............................	100	578	47.8	14.8	565	2,435,649	5.6	35.1	21.4	3.5	2.1	14.7	2.4
Pocatello...........................	76	416	39.1	9.5	561	2,333,293	10.6	25.9	18.5	10.3	1.9	26.0	2.6
Post Falls	48	236	18.4	5.5	169	673,051	14.6	40.3	0.0	12.1	1.2	22.8	0.0
Rexburg............................	25	D	D	D	115	440,960	21.3	29.6	8.0	11.5	0.8	17.1	0.0
Twin Falls	87	614	50.1	14.4	284	1,088,260	9.5	36.0	16.2	11.3	4.2	14.9	5.2
ILLINOIS........................	18,681	117,388	10,571.7	3,334.1	X	X	X	X	X	X	X	X	X
Addison............................	113	775	89.8	27.4	245	1,559,535	9.6	44.1	0.0	4.2	9.2	20.0	8.6
Algonquin..........................	66	364	22.1	7.5	143	751,901	11.3	26.1	0.0	11.5	0.3	33.9	0.0
Alton................................	46	251	16.2	5.6	230	1,141,005	7.5	40.6	24.3	8.2	1.8	13.2	0.0
Arlington Heights...............	138	912	99.9	29.3	594	3,727,355	11.4	27.0	22.6	8.1	2.6	6.6	15.0
Aurora..............................	159	1,044	120.6	29.7	1,402	8,465,715	9.4	32.8	18.5	7.5	8.1	14.5	5.4
Bartlett.............................	33	142	18.3	4.9	166	992,280	14.8	48.1	0.0	13.2	11.3	12.4	0.0
Batavia.............................	55	509	52.3	18.0	160	528,428	11.6	29.4	18.9	8.0	7.5	24.3	0.0
Belleville...........................	96	635	49.6	15.9	345	1,469,633	6.3	35.6	25.0	5.2	0.0	14.8	4.1
Belvidere...........................	30	231	17.9	6.1	125	645,335	6.9	38.7	26.4	8.1	0.0	13.1	4.0
Berwyn..............................	53	214	19.6	4.7	402	2,004,230	7.2	46.5	25.8	5.7	1.5	5.4	6.1
Bloomington.......................	127	1,022	74.9	28.0	723	3,168,188	7.2	25.0	19.2	14.3	0.0	27.5	5.8
Bolingbrook........................	79	424	31.8	10.7	391	2,517,306	8.3	44.4	26.4	8.1	0.0	9.5	0.0
Buffalo Grove.....................	77	463	37.9	11.1	255	1,764,688	6.4	35.2	28.3	6.6	3.6	14.2	0.0

1. Establishments subject to federal tax.

Table D. Cities — **Population**

AREANAME	Percent Hispanic or Latino[1], 2016	Percent foreign born, 2016	Age of population (percent), 2016							Median age 2016	Percent female 2016	Population			
												Census counts		Percent change	
			Under 18 years	18 to 24 years	25 to 34 years	35 to 44 years	45 to 54 years	55 to 64 years	65 years and over			2000	2010	2000-2010	2010-2017
	12	13	14	15	16	17	18	19	20	21	22	23	24	25	26
ILLINOIS— Cont'd															
Burbank	27.9	25.0	22.7	8.9	14.1	9.8	13.2	17.0	14.3	40.0	47.7	27,902	28,925	3.7	-0.5
Calumet City	18.1	11.6	23.0	13.6	12.3	9.0	14.0	11.2	16.9	36.5	60.5	39,071	37,116	-5.0	-1.3
Carbondale	4.7	9.3	12.4	37.6	17.4	6.6	8.7	8.4	9.0	25.0	51.9	20,681	26,426	27.8	-2.0
Carol Stream	11.3	22.6	20.4	8.1	15.8	9.8	18.0	15.2	12.7	40.1	53.4	40,438	39,729	-1.8	0.7
Carpentersville	37.1	25.0	31.5	9.4	11.9	18.0	12.7	9.0	7.5	32.8	50.0	30,586	37,691	23.2	1.2
Champaign	6.4	12.5	12.8	30.5	16.1	9.2	9.7	11.4	10.3	28.6	45.7	67,518	81,269	20.4	7.6
Chicago	29.7	20.7	21.2	10.2	19.7	14.1	12.2	10.9	11.8	34.4	51.5	2,896,016	2,695,620	-6.9	0.8
Chicago Heights	39.5	15.0	30.5	11.3	13.2	10.4	12.1	8.8	13.7	32.1	53.6	32,776	30,367	-7.3	-1.5
Cicero	88.7	41.0	31.3	11.8	15.1	14.9	10.9	8.8	7.3	29.7	49.0	85,616	84,241	-1.6	-2.0
Collinsville	3.1	8.7	20.0	6.1	17.9	16.9	11.1	13.3	14.7	39.8	50.1	24,707	25,558	3.4	-3.3
Crystal Lake	15.2	11.3	21.6	8.1	11.6	10.5	20.1	14.4	13.6	43.5	51.1	38,000	40,945	7.8	-1.3
Danville	6.5	3.1	24.8	10.0	12.5	12.0	10.9	13.0	16.8	37.3	49.4	33,904	33,019	-2.6	-4.8
Decatur	3.0	2.2	21.4	10.5	13.4	9.5	11.9	14.2	19.2	41.0	53.4	81,860	76,166	-7.0	-5.2
DeKalb	11.5	7.5	17.1	32.9	11.0	10.3	9.8	8.9	10.1	25.0	51.7	39,018	44,127	13.1	-2.1
Des Plaines	19.4	35.0	15.9	6.5	12.6	11.6	16.1	17.4	20.0	48.2	52.9	58,720	58,385	-0.6	-0.3
Downers Grove	3.5	9.3	19.6	7.3	10.1	11.2	16.0	19.1	16.8	45.9	49.3	48,724	48,874	0.3	1.4
East St. Louis	1.7	1.2	25.8	5.6	15.1	13.6	9.6	13.2	17.0	37.1	55.3	31,542	26,917	-14.7	-0.9
Elgin	48.3	28.7	26.6	9.1	13.8	12.7	13.8	11.4	12.5	35.2	49.1	94,487	108,148	14.5	4.0
Elk Grove Village	11.6	18.4	17.4	8.2	12.4	12.3	17.2	13.2	19.3	44.9	49.2	34,727	33,125	-4.6	-1.1
Elmhurst	5.9	9.2	28.4	7.6	10.1	13.5	12.6	11.3	16.4	38.6	49.7	42,762	44,135	3.2	5.7
Evanston	11.9	18.7	19.5	16.3	13.8	12.0	10.5	13.5	14.4	35.4	54.1	74,239	74,485	0.3	0.4
Freeport	6.1	2.9	19.4	7.9	11.1	11.1	10.9	15.3	24.3	45.9	54.2	26,443	25,637	-3.0	-6.0
Galesburg	7.5	4.6	18.8	13.6	12.0	11.1	10.8	14.5	19.1	39.6	47.9	33,706	32,189	-4.5	-4.4
Glendale Heights	34.3	39.7	25.3	6.9	19.9	13.0	11.2	11.4	12.2	33.8	51.8	31,765	34,212	7.7	-0.5
Glen Ellyn	4.1	13.3	25.3	8.6	11.5	12.9	13.7	11.9	16.2	37.7	53.8	26,999	27,771	2.9	1.0
Glenview	5.8	20.3	27.2	4.7	9.9	12.3	15.0	13.0	17.9	42.3	50.5	41,847	44,719	6.9	6.6
Granite City	10.3	4.0	25.5	3.8	11.5	11.8	11.3	17.6	18.5	41.1	51.2	31,301	29,849	-4.6	-3.7
Gurnee	10.5	12.8	24.6	11.0	12.1	14.7	13.4	12.3	12.0	36.8	50.3	28,834	31,226	8.3	-1.5
Hanover Park	36.9	29.7	26.5	11.4	11.5	15.8	11.8	10.4	12.5	35.3	52.6	38,278	38,022	-0.7	-0.1
Harvey	30.6	14.6	31.2	14.2	9.4	14.4	11.0	11.1	8.6	28.7	50.6	30,000	25,264	-15.8	-1.4
Highland Park	12.4	12.5	24.1	6.7	3.3	12.5	14.3	16.5	22.8	46.5	53.9	31,365	29,745	-5.2	0.1
Hoffman Estates	15.8	32.3	22.4	7.1	13.6	14.3	15.9	12.8	13.7	41.3	49.0	49,495	51,886	4.8	-0.6
Joliet	24.9	12.0	27.6	10.8	12.8	15.2	12.8	9.8	10.9	34.0	51.2	106,221	147,605	39.0	0.6
Kankakee	15.5	9.5	23.6	10.2	14.2	11.4	14.0	12.7	13.9	35.9	51.4	27,491	27,562	0.3	-4.9
Lake in the Hills	10.1	9.9	27.1	14.4	10.6	12.9	18.5	11.0	5.5	33.4	51.2	23,152	29,005	25.3	-0.2
Lansing	12.3	10.7	20.9	9.1	13.4	17.6	10.6	13.6	14.8	38.1	58.8	28,332	28,351	0.1	-1.4
Lombard	16.2	19.9	22.4	10.0	13.4	13.4	12.1	13.0	15.7	36.6	50.6	42,322	43,347	2.4	0.9
McHenry	14.5	14.4	24.4	8.4	9.6	14.0	17.4	13.2	13.0	39.8	50.1	21,501	27,016	25.6	-0.4
Melrose Park	78.9	33.7	29.4	7.0	13.4	19.3	8.7	8.9	13.4	35.1	51.0	23,171	25,414	9.7	-0.9
Moline	17.7	8.3	21.7	6.8	14.8	11.1	10.8	14.9	19.9	40.1	51.8	43,768	43,484	-0.6	-2.9
Mount Prospect	13.6	26.9	26.0	7.0	12.1	14.9	13.1	13.3	13.4	38.2	51.4	56,265	54,177	-3.7	-0.5
Mundelein	30.8	32.6	24.0	9.0	13.4	12.8	15.3	13.8	11.8	38.4	47.0	30,935	30,977	0.1	1.3
Naperville	6.7	19.0	27.2	8.7	10.2	14.9	14.9	13.4	10.7	37.7	50.7	128,358	142,126	10.7	3.9
Niles	4.1	32.6	14.4	9.6	13.4	10.7	10.7	16.3	24.9	46.8	47.3	30,068	29,806	-0.9	-1.1
Normal	5.2	5.5	20.5	29.6	13.4	10.4	8.9	9.8	7.4	24.9	53.0	45,386	52,544	15.8	3.3
Northbrook	3.0	20.2	19.9	3.7	6.9	11.1	14.4	15.2	28.8	50.5	53.4	33,435	33,197	-0.7	0.6
North Chicago	31.6	16.9	14.7	31.3	18.6	7.5	9.4	10.1	8.3	25.7	38.3	35,918	32,577	-9.3	-8.4
Oak Forest	17.8	11.9	20.4	10.0	11.3	8.4	20.3	14.4	15.2	44.8	52.3	28,051	27,954	-0.3	-1.0
Oak Lawn	20.6	19.2	21.0	9.5	13.3	10.4	13.9	17.6	14.3	40.9	53.3	55,245	56,690	2.6	-1.1
Oak Park	8.8	9.5	24.4	6.2	10.1	17.4	14.6	13.6	13.8	40.7	52.8	52,524	51,878	-1.2	0.7
O'Fallon	8.2	4.6	27.0	5.4	15.3	17.7	12.0	10.6	11.9	35.9	48.4	21,910	28,674	30.9	2.1
Orland Park	6.5	16.9	21.4	6.3	11.1	8.8	13.3	13.9	25.2	46.4	52.7	51,077	56,664	10.9	3.7
Oswego	18.2	10.6	28.0	7.2	12.9	15.4	17.3	8.9	10.2	35.5	45.8	13,326	30,431	128.4	14.5
Palatine	12.2	22.5	24.9	5.3	18.6	13.7	14.2	12.6	10.7	35.7	50.9	65,479	68,551	4.7	0.1
Park Ridge	5.7	14.1	23.2	5.1	11.0	9.3	16.8	15.3	19.3	46.5	51.7	37,775	37,479	-0.8	0.0
Pekin	0.7	0.0	19.7	8.8	15.1	9.8	14.5	13.3	18.8	41.0	49.9	33,857	34,097	0.7	-4.0
Peoria	6.3	7.7	23.9	11.2	12.9	13.7	11.2	12.6	14.5	36.0	52.2	112,936	115,105	1.9	-1.9
Plainfield	20.8	10.6	35.4	7.9	9.5	15.4	19.4	6.6	5.8	32.5	53.3	13,038	39,854	205.7	10.2
Quincy	1.6	1.5	21.8	8.8	12.7	12.2	10.7	12.9	21.0	41.3	52.4	40,366	40,636	0.7	-0.8
Rockford	19.5	11.5	24.5	8.6	14.0	11.5	13.2	11.9	16.2	37.5	51.1	150,115	153,301	2.1	-4.1
Rock Island	12.5	7.3	20.2	15.2	13.2	11.4	11.6	14.0	14.4	36.1	49.6	39,684	39,005	-1.7	-2.3
Romeoville	39.5	21.7	27.8	11.9	16.6	13.3	13.1	7.5	9.9	31.4	50.1	21,153	39,621	87.3	0.0
Round Lake Beach	47.1	23.4	32.2	10.6	12.4	13.7	13.5	9.5	8.0	31.5	46.7	25,859	28,101	8.7	-1.8
St. Charles	6.1	6.7	25.8	6.8	18.9	8.0	14.2	11.8	14.5	34.1	50.5	27,896	32,329	15.9	1.2
Schaumburg	12.3	31.8	21.4	5.1	15.7	16.2	13.3	13.2	15.1	38.7	49.4	75,386	74,229	-1.5	-0.1
Skokie	13.8	39.1	24.8	4.9	8.3	16.0	12.0	15.4	18.5	42.1	52.9	63,348	64,845	2.4	-1.3
Springfield	2.9	3.9	21.6	9.1	13.6	12.5	12.2	13.9	17.1	39.4	54.1	111,454	116,463	4.5	-1.4
Streamwood	31.1	29.7	23.0	8.1	15.7	16.0	15.0	14.9	7.3	37.5	46.3	36,407	39,839	9.4	0.3
Tinley Park	9.5	8.3	20.5	8.9	15.6	11.7	12.1	16.9	14.2	38.8	47.0	48,401	56,822	17.4	-0.3
Urbana	5.9	19.2	13.9	40.8	19.9	6.8	6.1	5.5	7.0	24.0	52.6	36,395	41,606	14.3	0.9
Vernon Hills	11.5	34.8	21.6	6.8	9.4	13.8	19.2	15.4	13.9	44.2	51.8	20,120	25,027	24.4	4.9

1. May be of any race.

Table D. Cities — Households, Group Quarters, Crime, and Education

AREANAME	Households, 2016								Serious crimes known to police[2], 2016				Educational attainment, 2016		
			Percent						Total		Rate[3]			Attainment[4] (percent)	
	Number	Persons per house-hold	Family	Married couple family	Female headed family[1]	Non-family	One person	Persons in group quarters	Number	Rate	Violent	Property	Population age 25 and over	High school graduate or less	Bachelor's degree or more
	27	28	29	30	31	32	33	34	35	36	37	38	39	40	41
ILLINOIS— Cont'd															
Burbank	9,829	2.84	67.5	51.2	8.5	32.5	29.7	222	474	1,625	240	1,385	19,276	52.9	14.1
Calumet City	14,767	2.49	55.6	24.8	21.0	44.4	42.2	NA	1,569	4,238	570	3,668	23,289	42.5	17.7
Carbondale	11,578	1.90	36.7	18.7	14.1	63.3	48.7	4,211	984	3,731	523	3,208	13,140	18.1	50.0
Carol Stream	14,111	2.75	66.1	54.2	10.7	33.9	24.3	NA	342	845	89	756	28,002	33.8	37.3
Carpentersville	11,176	3.43	74.9	48.9	16.7	25.1	13.2	NA	699	1,808	80	1,728	22,643	50.2	17.7
Champaign	34,343	2.29	45.8	34.1	7.8	54.2	38.5	7,859	3,655	4,198	773	3,425	49,115	20.6	53.3
Chicago	1,053,986	2.51	53.3	32.7	15.3	46.7	37.1	59,998	117,329	4,305	1,108	3,197	1,855,563	38.2	38.5
Chicago Heights	9,613	3.03	70.8	40.7	15.7	29.2	26.0	861	980	3,237	578	2,659	17,468	51.5	18.2
Cicero	22,495	3.65	79.0	47.5	22.9	21.0	17.5	778	1,975	2,357	314	2,043	47,244	73.6	6.6
Collinsville	11,012	2.51	69.2	43.6	20.1	30.8	23.9	NA	789	3,207	215	2,992	20,479	39.9	21.3
Crystal Lake	15,438	2.54	67.3	54.2	8.7	32.7	29.9	298	668	1,655	109	1,546	27,776	31.4	36.2
Danville	13,226	2.36	62.7	40.5	17.4	37.3	35.7	2,409	2,391	7,488	1,556	5,932	21,933	52.8	15.3
Decatur	30,770	2.21	54.4	31.8	18.3	45.6	40.2	3,544	3,049	4,194	539	3,655	48,679	45.2	20.6
DeKalb	14,118	2.56	55.3	35.7	13.4	44.7	26.9	4,426	1,661	3,860	518	3,342	20,291	28.3	41.8
Des Plaines	22,196	2.52	64.1	50.2	10.2	35.9	29.4	1,064	617	1,051	87	964	44,270	38.0	33.9
Downers Grove	20,496	2.38	59.7	50.1	8.1	40.3	37.4	713	684	1,371	66	1,305	36,158	19.1	55.0
East St. Louis	10,803	2.47	59.5	14.6	40.1	40.5	37.8	226	1,361	5,084	2,828	2,256	18,459	56.9	14.0
Elgin	36,969	3.05	71.1	51.8	13.6	28.9	23.9	1,720	1,801	1,595	209	1,386	73,555	46.8	24.6
Elk Grove Village	14,357	2.35	61.0	48.4	7.4	39.0	34.9	NA	535	1,609	75	1,534	25,254	35.9	36.0
Elmhurst	15,893	2.77	70.6	58.9	8.3	29.4	28.1	1,256	562	1,213	56	1,157	28,968	18.2	59.4
Evanston	29,073	2.35	52.0	37.7	11.3	48.0	39.0	6,701	1,801	2,379	172	2,207	48,089	19.0	65.1
Freeport	11,386	1.99	53.6	31.0	18.2	46.4	44.5	748	700	2,886	198	2,688	17,004	45.4	14.7
Galesburg	12,592	2.17	43.8	30.9	10.0	56.2	47.0	4,067	1,111	3,573	399	3,174	21,207	50.0	17.4
Glendale Heights	11,151	3.02	75.8	51.4	16.8	24.2	21.2	NA	590	1,712	78	1,633	22,865	46.3	24.7
Glen Ellyn	10,993	2.58	63.5	57.9	5.0	36.5	32.9	NA	270	955	92	863	18,776	11.6	70.1
Glenview	17,650	2.76	70.0	62.7	5.8	30.0	28.1	728	652	1,358	85	1,273	33,730	17.6	62.9
Granite City	12,441	2.41	57.1	39.4	13.0	42.9	36.5	243	791	2,737	661	2,076	21,329	46.3	13.5
Gurnee	11,022	2.80	69.0	56.9	9.4	31.0	27.1	NA	1,293	4,169	74	4,095	19,921	19.2	54.3
Hanover Park	10,304	3.37	81.5	60.9	16.9	18.5	15.5	NA	295	768	102	667	21,542	43.4	22.4
Harvey	8,024	3.16	67.1	30.9	26.6	32.9	30.2	NA	734	2,915	743	2,172	13,971	54.1	11.3
Highland Park	11,057	2.55	69.0	60.9	5.1	31.0	27.9	257	286	962	71	891	19,678	14.2	71.4
Hoffman Estates	17,440	2.81	77.7	61.5	10.6	22.3	17.3	NA	484	928	105	822	34,717	28.1	48.1
Joliet	47,921	2.99	70.6	51.1	15.4	29.4	23.4	2,936	3,289	2,224	330	1,894	90,138	44.2	22.6
Kankakee	9,171	2.61	57.0	33.3	17.9	43.0	28.7	1,845	1,233	4,651	698	3,953	17,062	63.5	11.8
Lake in the Hills	9,186	3.15	78.8	56.6	15.1	21.2	15.7	NA	171	589	83	507	16,917	28.1	36.6
Lansing	11,383	2.55	67.5	37.7	25.5	32.5	29.5	NA	1,999	7,052	399	6,653	20,389	41.4	23.8
Lombard	16,299	2.63	67.4	51.9	10.7	32.6	29.3	566	994	2,266	109	2,157	29,324	28.7	47.7
McHenry	11,167	2.82	67.0	54.5	8.1	33.0	23.2	NA	443	1,667	150	1,516	21,286	45.0	25.7
Melrose Park	8,113	3.15	65.1	35.9	22.1	34.9	31.6	NA	372	1,466	201	1,265	16,310	63.7	10.6
Moline	17,486	2.22	56.2	42.2	9.9	43.8	38.4	346	1,655	3,893	461	3,432	28,008	33.7	26.3
Mount Prospect	20,284	2.71	77.9	60.5	11.7	22.1	20.5	NA	590	1,076	47	1,028	36,878	28.6	41.7
Mundelein	10,850	2.83	73.3	63.6	4.1	26.7	21.2	295	322	1,016	85	931	20,775	28.6	50.5
Naperville	50,672	2.87	77.5	65.2	8.5	22.5	19.0	2,846	1,687	1,139	63	1,077	94,862	13.4	69.2
Niles	11,269	2.46	62.8	49.1	10.6	37.2	34.1	1,301	731	2,446	97	2,349	22,015	35.5	33.4
Normal	18,473	2.67	60.6	42.1	12.4	39.4	25.3	4,958	1,224	2,237	263	1,973	27,084	22.7	47.6
Northbrook	13,269	2.35	70.4	61.7	8.1	29.6	27.2	702	393	1,165	33	1,132	24,406	16.3	65.7
North Chicago	7,466	2.60	57.5	36.6	19.7	42.5	33.5	9,865	NA	NA	NA	NA	15,787	45.5	18.3
Oak Forest	9,365	2.96	72.0	54.6	11.0	28.0	24.0	79	342	1,218	150	1,068	19,332	43.5	21.6
Oak Lawn	20,713	2.69	65.1	44.7	12.6	34.9	31.2	526	1,016	1,789	139	1,650	39,106	38.3	30.0
Oak Park	20,777	2.47	61.1	45.8	11.9	38.9	33.6	510	1,603	3,061	206	2,855	35,934	13.6	66.1
O'Fallon	11,890	2.51	69.4	52.0	9.8	30.6	29.0	NA	563	1,937	155	1,782	20,168	19.1	49.6
Orland Park	22,678	2.64	71.6	61.7	8.5	28.4	26.6	649	1,359	2,303	42	2,261	43,777	29.6	41.7
Oswego	10,738	3.08	84.7	71.3	6.3	15.3	13.1	NA	431	1,243	92	1,150	21,477	21.6	45.8
Palatine	26,743	2.56	61.5	47.3	7.7	38.5	28.7	249	637	917	53	864	47,987	18.0	53.0
Park Ridge	14,440	2.53	70.5	58.4	8.9	29.5	25.1	527	387	1,024	32	992	26,497	18.5	61.0
Pekin	14,131	2.22	59.1	36.4	16.7	40.9	34.3	1,765	803	2,430	421	2,009	23,699	44.2	18.9
Peoria	46,774	2.38	58.5	35.9	19.2	41.5	36.4	4,117	5,304	4,608	760	3,848	75,031	33.2	35.2
Plainfield	11,952	3.49	86.1	76.9	7.1	13.9	11.2	NA	367	852	86	766	23,739	18.7	56.5
Quincy	17,097	2.30	62.1	45.7	10.5	37.9	33.6	1,252	1,532	3,755	512	3,243	28,166	45.3	22.7
Rockford	60,659	2.37	58.5	33.7	18.8	41.5	35.3	3,903	8,036	5,453	1,664	3,789	98,597	46.6	22.6
Rock Island	16,066	2.27	65.0	38.6	18.5	35.0	28.8	2,857	1,200	3,113	410	2,703	25,386	39.6	22.9
Romeoville	11,964	3.40	71.5	49.4	14.6	28.5	20.5	1,268	668	1,681	113	1,568	25,292	43.6	20.5
Round Lake Beach	7,983	3.31	75.4	58.6	9.3	24.6	21.6	NA	619	2,227	137	2,090	15,181	47.6	18.2
St. Charles	12,671	2.73	72.9	56.9	12.5	27.1	20.6	463	553	1,648	128	1,520	23,608	18.5	45.8
Schaumburg	29,556	2.48	63.8	49.6	9.3	36.2	30.4	510	1,760	2,354	99	2,255	54,252	26.9	46.8
Skokie	22,461	2.83	71.2	55.3	13.2	28.8	26.3	768	1,715	2,646	244	2,402	45,148	29.2	49.1
Springfield	50,310	2.22	56.4	36.3	15.2	43.6	36.4	3,692	6,459	5,541	1,116	4,425	80,043	31.9	36.8
Streamwood	12,471	3.17	75.3	49.9	15.5	24.7	21.1	NA	614	1,509	118	1,391	27,393	45.8	26.9
Tinley Park	22,633	2.69	69.2	55.8	10.2	30.8	26.5	NA	814	1,423	84	1,339	42,963	29.2	36.9
Urbana	15,884	2.17	40.1	24.3	8.6	59.9	41.2	7,528	1,705	4,015	382	3,634	19,016	21.6	55.8
Vernon Hills	10,008	2.58	76.9	68.7	7.3	23.1	21.9	NA	397	1,494	71	1,422	18,529	22.5	58.3

1. No spouse present. 2. Data for serious crimes have not been adjusted for underreporting. This may affect comparability between geographic areas and over time. 3. Per 100,000 population estimated by the FBI. 4. Persons 25 years old and over.

Table D. Cities — Income and Housing

AREANAME	Money income, 2016					Median earnings, 2016			Housing units, 2016				
	Households												
	Median income	Percent with income less than $20,000	Percent with income of $200,000 or more	Median family income	Median non-family household income	All persons	Men	Women	Total	Occupied	Percent owner occupied	Median value[1] (dollars)	Median rent (dollars)
	42	43	44	45	46	47	48	49	50	51	52	53	54
ILLINOIS— Cont'd													
Burbank	54,382	14.0	2.2	70,879	29,952	31,875	35,650	27,627	10,427	9,829	72.5	180,400	1,005
Calumet City	47,639	26.5	0.3	50,965	25,175	26,472	30,295	23,574	16,801	14,767	52.4	113,900	860
Carbondale	21,990	41.8	0.0	41,007	18,967	14,642	12,344	14,942	14,107	11,578	28.4	113,000	634
Carol Stream	74,292	10.4	5.9	86,778	53,406	36,955	48,694	32,992	15,004	14,111	61.9	250,900	1,164
Carpentersville	62,270	9.9	2.5	60,355	51,604	34,142	40,476	26,922	11,556	11,176	58.9	157,100	1,166
Champaign	45,406	21.9	5.9	74,449	31,173	26,948	28,596	25,923	38,049	34,343	47.3	162,000	868
Chicago	53,006	21.0	7.1	62,960	41,895	35,317	38,209	31,604	1,201,732	1,053,986	43.7	243,900	1,034
Chicago Heights	40,354	27.9	0.9	55,799	20,976	25,420	27,458	21,454	11,257	9,613	61.9	95,700	852
Cicero	41,484	17.3	0.8	42,348	26,149	25,392	28,351	21,289	24,749	22,495	45.9	153,100	855
Collinsville	47,368	16.0	1.5	47,872	40,654	30,252	32,231	26,538	11,991	11,012	69.4	135,300	822
Crystal Lake	76,613	10.6	4.4	85,522	34,929	32,325	45,047	25,126	16,517	15,438	72.3	202,200	1,153
Danville	35,378	29.8	0.4	47,031	24,399	31,147	35,470	28,261	15,111	13,226	61.9	68,100	726
Decatur	38,124	25.4	2.8	51,292	29,163	25,608	31,665	21,639	36,097	30,770	58.6	78,300	650
DeKalb	41,138	23.0	4.8	66,815	26,149	18,446	21,547	13,022	16,776	14,118	39.3	158,700	837
Des Plaines	58,990	15.9	6.5	76,873	29,578	32,658	41,184	30,193	23,072	22,196	72.1	257,700	1,032
Downers Grove	82,009	11.0	13.2	119,625	42,150	46,323	55,788	40,260	21,414	20,496	73.4	336,700	1,278
East St. Louis	23,884	42.5	2.3	29,416	17,040	20,610	19,658	21,134	13,316	10,803	45.0	45,900	429
Elgin	61,070	13.0	5.8	72,101	36,625	28,179	33,344	25,044	39,297	36,969	68.7	179,100	1,040
Elk Grove Village	64,870	10.4	7.1	101,828	47,177	41,731	51,463	36,216	15,117	14,357	68.7	265,000	990
Elmhurst	102,356	5.7	19.4	123,994	48,355	51,235	63,769	36,608	16,805	15,893	77.6	424,000	1,244
Evanston	66,165	16.4	13.4	96,589	45,215	37,319	39,277	36,156	32,346	29,073	56.2	380,300	1,243
Freeport	35,274	29.7	1.6	48,520	21,234	25,739	31,798	21,363	12,483	11,386	55.7	71,700	603
Galesburg	32,101	30.7	1.4	57,259	21,052	25,522	27,741	23,533	14,390	12,592	50.2	70,100	672
Glendale Heights	51,493	11.7	2.3	51,402	50,866	27,668	35,431	22,577	11,964	11,151	59.4	190,500	1,108
Glen Ellyn	91,557	14.0	21.6	148,119	35,402	47,984	66,031	32,451	11,429	10,993	69.9	438,300	1,068
Glenview	111,600	12.2	24.2	156,434	36,709	58,512	82,391	41,523	18,417	17,650	84.1	476,800	1,447
Granite City	46,515	19.1	1.4	57,666	31,255	27,514	33,825	25,063	13,825	12,441	69.7	79,000	719
Gurnee	90,581	10.5	9.0	110,420	42,988	42,431	48,044	39,697	11,310	11,022	70.2	259,500	1,154
Hanover Park	70,628	10.5	1.8	75,320	49,069	33,631	38,011	26,691	10,442	10,304	73.6	171,900	1,348
Harvey	28,295	35.2	0.0	40,347	10,923	21,473	21,107	21,902	10,109	8,024	58.5	72,300	919
Highland Park	125,376	10.3	30.4	166,601	37,493	50,850	92,471	32,385	11,867	11,057	83.8	579,400	1,378
Hoffman Estates	83,658	6.7	11.5	92,335	44,920	41,605	46,454	40,368	17,962	17,440	74.1	260,500	1,297
Joliet	63,864	11.3	2.9	77,979	35,398	32,095	41,351	26,028	51,568	47,921	71.3	174,700	984
Kankakee	40,773	27.4	2.8	47,022	23,588	22,037	25,057	20,686	10,997	9,171	45.5	83,100	773
Lake in the Hills	81,237	6.1	10.4	85,387	56,955	32,291	51,314	26,536	9,523	9,186	72.9	216,800	1,339
Lansing	52,966	20.1	1.1	56,914	30,910	31,807	40,133	30,085	12,017	11,383	63.0	120,300	899
Lombard	79,888	9.0	6.8	97,910	50,375	40,900	51,700	31,389	17,109	16,299	70.2	258,900	1,216
McHenry	76,886	11.4	2.1	86,610	34,853	35,186	36,728	28,915	11,821	11,167	68.3	173,100	1,363
Melrose Park	43,830	21.3	1.0	53,052	21,518	28,058	29,790	26,387	8,288	8,113	50.7	169,800	867
Moline	49,970	17.1	2.2	59,963	37,136	31,619	36,320	26,304	19,114	17,486	66.3	125,700	694
Mount Prospect	71,370	15.2	7.3	89,888	24,723	40,460	51,810	32,018	20,553	20,284	68.4	333,000	1,000
Mundelein	80,769	4.1	10.5	99,629	37,265	37,075	47,232	30,020	11,270	10,850	78.1	239,600	1,192
Naperville	116,482	6.0	22.9	133,293	61,458	56,026	84,976	40,161	52,789	50,672	73.9	421,400	1,471
Niles	52,036	16.2	5.1	75,280	27,283	32,049	37,004	27,403	12,279	11,269	72.9	273,900	1,099
Normal	57,473	12.2	4.1	73,421	40,942	22,633	29,939	16,726	20,275	18,473	58.0	166,900	851
Northbrook	99,243	5.2	21.9	124,982	66,194	70,242	87,240	46,153	13,688	13,269	83.1	531,600	2,086
North Chicago	45,617	19.9	2.2	49,379	35,617	20,416	20,315	20,695	8,310	7,466	37.1	105,100	1,160
Oak Forest	85,104	11.5	4.4	94,961	43,797	32,195	38,095	30,190	9,736	9,365	84.2	186,000	1,097
Oak Lawn	61,993	10.7	3.3	75,850	37,930	36,363	45,798	31,141	21,972	20,713	78.9	185,700	948
Oak Park	99,633	11.5	20.3	134,237	51,432	55,544	69,093	49,833	22,207	20,777	58.7	389,400	1,114
O'Fallon	88,954	9.2	6.6	101,696	49,443	44,178	60,260	31,299	12,631	11,890	72.0	190,300	978
Orland Park	80,828	10.4	11.1	98,324	40,854	40,324	51,697	31,914	24,118	22,678	90.7	290,400	1,134
Oswego	100,473	2.2	12.7	109,884	39,722	50,433	60,861	36,685	10,738	10,738	93.5	241,300	D
Palatine	80,521	7.0	10.0	101,863	59,707	49,246	57,542	40,088	27,544	26,743	71.1	269,100	1,205
Park Ridge	96,500	6.2	19.5	131,462	51,520	49,138	68,125	40,661	15,608	14,440	78.3	445,000	1,166
Pekin	44,578	16.2	2.4	57,477	30,554	27,376	39,411	25,039	15,079	14,131	72.5	101,500	684
Peoria	47,369	24.2	5.2	64,383	26,114	30,403	36,438	26,173	54,037	46,774	55.1	130,500	750
Plainfield	125,154	6.7	21.7	137,650	0	60,289	75,800	41,976	12,313	11,952	85.1	320,600	1,915
Quincy	43,947	19.2	3.7	57,846	26,477	30,476	37,080	23,027	18,732	17,097	65.6	111,800	680
Rockford	39,537	26.1	2.5	50,149	24,264	24,777	29,723	21,814	66,291	60,659	49.7	89,200	712
Rock Island	49,003	18.8	1.3	60,560	36,858	27,376	31,457	24,355	18,150	16,066	65.3	101,300	627
Romeoville	78,831	8.2	2.2	83,781	41,123	32,200	41,242	26,151	12,835	11,964	74.3	186,500	1,541
Round Lake Beach	67,020	8.9	1.6	78,970	32,105	30,787	31,959	25,106	8,864	7,983	73.0	126,800	1,120
St. Charles	101,744	7.0	17.0	116,123	48,018	41,598	75,488	31,225	13,283	12,671	70.1	287,900	1,143
Schaumburg	76,122	7.9	5.2	91,615	52,413	45,255	56,683	34,513	30,915	29,556	68.5	232,500	1,381
Skokie	68,430	13.7	10.4	85,173	37,632	38,304	42,040	30,133	25,003	22,461	67.0	310,900	1,246
Springfield	48,179	20.8	4.2	64,657	36,165	31,096	33,084	30,084	56,060	50,310	64.7	131,800	755
Streamwood	85,758	8.0	3.3	89,572	54,690	35,672	41,543	28,963	12,687	12,471	81.6	172,400	1,663
Tinley Park	76,672	6.9	8.4	100,216	43,198	45,421	52,087	34,161	23,515	22,633	82.9	219,400	1,119
Urbana	32,088	37.7	4.9	58,016	18,926	15,156	20,648	12,077	18,425	15,884	32.4	151,300	804
Vernon Hills	101,151	8.2	18.3	120,649	50,568	44,201	59,896	36,282	10,643	10,008	65.5	354,100	1,253

1. Specified owner-occupied units; $2,000,000 represents $2,000,000 or more.

Table D. Cities — Commuting, Computer Access, Migration, Labor Force, and Employment

	Commuting[1] 2016		Computer access[2]		Migration		Civilian labor force, 2016				Civilian employment, 2016			
	Percent		Percent						Unemployment[3]		Population age 16 and older		Population age 16 to 64	
AREANAME	Drove alone	With commutes of 30 minutes or more	With a computer in the house	With Internet access	Percent who lived in the same house one year ago	Percent who lived in another state or county one year ago	Total	Percent change 2016-2017	Total	Rate	Number	Percent in labor force	Number	Percent who worked full-year full-time
	55	56	57	58	59	60	61	62	63	64	65	66	67	68
ILLINOIS— Cont'd														
Burbank	74.2	57.2	85.0	80.6	NA	NA	14,272	-0.5	740	5.2	22,284	67.1	18,261	52.5
Calumet City	68.1	64.5	82.8	74.8	73.1	5.9	16,460	-0.7	1,354	8.2	29,379	68.1	23,178	46.6
Carbondale	83.5	12.1	97.6	78.5	59.6	22.3	11,614	-2.3	524	4.5	23,468	54.4	21,113	25.2
Carol Stream	84.8	46.1	94.3	90.2	88.7	6.2	24,034	-0.3	975	4.1	31,954	71.3	26,979	58.8
Carpentersville	91.0	59.2	94.6	90.7	83.4	8.2	19,046	-0.7	1,148	6.0	27,618	71.8	24,744	52.1
Champaign	67.6	11.3	95.2	82.9	73.6	14.8	43,504	-0.7	1,815	4.2	76,701	63.8	67,755	43.9
Chicago	49.4	62.3	87.3	77.4	84.7	3.6	1,364,817	-0.7	75,492	5.5	2,191,267	67.0	1,872,511	50.4
Chicago Heights	78.2	32.6	82.9	74.2	NA	NA	13,039	-0.7	1,036	7.9	22,141	61.2	18,031	45.9
Cicero	67.9	56.2	87.9	70.8	91.6	1.1	36,814	-0.7	2,044	5.6	59,610	65.5	53,534	48.5
Collinsville	82.1	29.3	93.6	91.5	82.4	10.4	12,830	-0.8	610	4.8	22,583	65.5	18,509	55.2
Crystal Lake	77.7	45.0	92.7	91.1	86.2	8.0	22,739	-0.5	926	4.1	32,591	69.6	27,209	48.3
Danville	86.6	10.1	79.4	73.6	87.3	4.1	12,626	-2.6	911	7.2	26,437	44.4	20,800	37.5
Decatur	82.7	10.5	83.1	76.6	76.1	6.5	32,139	-2.0	1,972	6.1	57,695	58.5	43,999	45.1
DeKalb	75.6	21.7	93.7	85.9	67.7	12.9	22,260	-0.6	1,025	4.6	34,339	67.4	30,231	36.6
Des Plaines	78.9	44.9	87.3	79.1	94.3	0.9	32,626	-0.6	1,421	4.4	49,877	64.5	38,492	52.6
Downers Grove	74.7	42.8	87.0	85.5	87.0	6.5	27,534	-0.3	1,043	3.8	41,251	66.9	32,958	55.6
East St. Louis	69.9	24.9	70.4	49.6	NA	NA	8,970	-2.1	705	7.9	20,549	54.5	15,974	37.8
Elgin	78.0	43.1	92.2	81.3	88.5	5.5	57,202	-0.7	3,156	5.5	87,998	67.8	73,657	50.8
Elk Grove Village	79.9	41.8	89.9	86.7	89.6	1.4	19,226	-0.5	804	4.2	28,716	68.7	22,176	58.5
Elmhurst	71.1	47.0	93.3	90.5	89.9	5.8	23,747	-0.5	927	3.9	33,707	68.6	26,270	56.8
Evanston	47.2	49.8	94.6	88.0	82.2	7.1	39,540	-0.5	1,621	4.1	62,611	60.4	51,801	42.2
Freeport	71.6	26.6	78.9	71.9	79.9	5.4	10,537	0.7	559	5.3	19,275	59.3	13,598	47.9
Galesburg	80.6	10.5	76.2	65.2	87.9	7.4	12,545	-2.0	661	5.3	25,958	50.7	19,975	36.6
Glendale Heights	72.2	37.7	94.9	85.5	84.7	6.8	19,327	-0.6	869	4.5	25,809	69.6	21,684	55.0
Glen Ellyn	59.2	49.5	89.7	88.2	86.1	9.0	14,298	-0.4	538	3.8	22,171	64.4	17,584	51.5
Glenview	72.6	49.2	91.7	86.2	85.8	3.7	23,304	-0.5	860	3.7	37,858	60.6	28,990	50.6
Granite City	77.4	36.8	88.4	82.4	91.7	2.2	13,166	-2.4	704	5.3	23,189	57.5	17,602	45.2
Gurnee	80.8	46.3	95.5	91.8	84.7	4.7	17,347	-0.1	690	4.0	24,166	74.0	20,456	56.7
Hanover Park	81.1	47.9	95.9	88.5	85.8	6.8	20,811	-0.6	1,097	5.3	26,516	69.9	22,161	52.0
Harvey	73.8	44.9	90.8	71.8	NA	NA	8,280	-1.3	818	9.9	18,653	61.1	16,441	40.0
Highland Park	74.0	40.4	94.1	92.0	87.7	8.3	15,163	-0.2	512	3.4	22,411	67.2	15,938	55.9
Hoffman Estates	80.9	49.2	93.4	91.1	87.2	5.8	30,185	-0.5	1,202	4.0	40,150	71.3	33,398	54.3
Joliet	85.0	45.8	90.5	85.7	90.0	3.2	75,485	-0.7	4,735	6.3	110,252	68.3	94,239	50.4
Kankakee	72.4	29.2	81.5	65.4	90.4	4.4	11,280	-0.1	803	7.1	20,206	59.7	16,628	45.4
Lake in the Hills	83.0	52.7	96.9	95.3	93.9	3.9	16,233	-0.4	720	4.4	21,954	73.3	20,361	51.8
Lansing	80.4	43.2	87.6	80.2	NA	NA	14,426	-0.5	863	6.0	24,239	64.8	19,938	44.5
Lombard	73.7	40.2	92.1	89.9	84.1	4.2	25,343	-0.4	994	3.9	34,746	69.2	27,949	52.3
McHenry	80.2	44.2	89.5	89.2	83.4	3.6	14,144	-0.6	620	4.4	24,768	68.0	20,655	59.1
Melrose Park	75.6	45.8	83.9	66.1	NA	NA	11,986	-0.6	623	5.2	18,691	66.9	15,254	51.5
Moline	87.3	12.7	91.3	84.4	87.2	4.1	21,510	-1.2	1,015	4.7	31,482	62.0	23,684	51.2
Mount Prospect	79.6	44.4	94.3	85.3	91.8	1.1	29,510	-0.6	1,096	3.7	42,095	70.8	34,723	54.6
Mundelein	77.1	47.8	93.1	89.4	89.9	2.3	18,269	-0.1	763	4.2	24,354	75.1	20,707	56.0
Naperville	71.2	51.0	96.3	95.2	86.8	8.4	78,892	-0.3	3,122	4.0	112,643	70.5	96,802	53.7
Niles	81.5	43.3	85.3	73.7	NA	NA	13,896	-0.5	610	4.4	25,573	53.1	18,364	42.5
Normal	78.0	16.6	96.0	81.6	77.4	13.8	28,187	-1.9	1,102	3.9	44,225	70.4	40,203	42.2
Northbrook	79.9	37.6	94.4	88.7	90.2	4.2	16,344	-0.5	627	3.8	26,354	55.5	17,152	57.7
North Chicago	41.3	23.2	91.7	81.6	73.1	22.8	9,067	-0.3	525	5.8	25,674	74.0	23,254	49.2
Oak Forest	81.3	51.2	91.1	89.0	NA	NA	15,204	-0.4	766	5.0	22,530	70.9	18,311	58.7
Oak Lawn	80.7	56.9	86.7	82.8	91.3	1.5	28,728	-0.5	1,428	5.0	45,247	66.0	37,212	53.3
Oak Park	54.8	64.7	93.2	88.1	88.8	3.4	29,605	-0.3	1,210	4.1	40,354	72.2	33,219	58.2
O'Fallon	90.9	29.9	94.3	89.1	82.5	10.6	13,762	-0.5	575	4.2	22,636	72.2	19,083	61.4
Orland Park	83.2	56.0	89.9	85.7	94.9	2.8	30,608	-0.5	1,254	4.1	49,043	59.2	33,794	52.3
Oswego	80.8	45.9	NA	NA	NA	NA	19,043	-0.3	780	4.1	24,851	75.6	21,457	63.7
Palatine	73.4	51.8	93.7	89.1	86.2	8.0	39,531	-0.5	1,606	4.1	53,188	74.3	45,860	59.1
Park Ridge	65.3	51.6	94.2	89.9	91.7	1.8	19,623	-0.7	766	3.9	30,221	64.2	23,087	54.9
Pekin	88.2	23.5	84.5	78.7	87.7	3.3	14,995	-2.4	924	6.2	27,236	64.9	21,014	47.9
Peoria	80.2	10.8	85.0	73.8	85.9	5.1	51,673	-2.4	3,064	5.9	90,862	62.2	74,138	45.1
Plainfield	82.6	55.2	NA	NA	93.2	2.7	22,501	-0.4	900	4.0	29,422	77.3	26,988	58.8
Quincy	87.1	8.5	84.9	73.7	85.7	2.2	19,161	-0.6	770	4.0	32,937	62.3	24,423	57.3
Rockford	76.1	19.7	86.0	77.5	83.0	4.8	65,881	-1.8	4,926	7.5	116,275	61.5	92,369	42.7
Rock Island	71.9	16.8	89.1	79.5	79.8	7.7	17,966	-1.3	926	5.2	32,150	67.9	26,474	47.6
Romeoville	84.1	52.9	89.5	86.6	94.3	2.4	20,079	-0.4	1,110	5.5	31,336	67.5	27,175	53.7
Round Lake Beach	82.3	56.0	93.6	88.7	88.6	3.5	15,007	-0.4	950	6.3	19,186	72.0	17,054	54.9
St. Charles	77.6	43.2	93.7	91.6	82.0	6.1	18,325	-0.4	668	3.6	27,584	66.7	22,519	55.2
Schaumburg	84.3	48.9	95.1	91.4	85.6	5.5	44,371	-0.5	1,725	3.9	60,348	70.9	49,186	60.0
Skokie	74.1	43.8	90.5	87.6	89.0	3.5	32,960	-0.5	1,377	4.2	50,730	61.4	38,804	48.8
Springfield	81.0	12.2	87.2	80.0	80.8	6.6	58,649	-2.4	2,640	4.5	93,903	62.1	74,176	46.6
Streamwood	86.9	49.9	96.0	93.2	93.5	1.6	23,678	-0.4	1,141	4.8	31,066	71.9	28,159	55.6
Tinley Park	79.9	56.6	93.5	92.4	89.2	2.2	32,281	-0.3	1,370	4.2	49,750	71.1	41,110	51.8
Urbana	50.9	8.4	91.4	78.1	67.8	19.6	20,987	-0.7	905	4.3	36,854	58.8	33,910	30.2
Vernon Hills	83.7	41.6	94.0	91.8	87.3	5.2	15,107	-0.2	528	3.5	21,125	71.7	17,539	54.2

1. Employed persons.   2. Households.   3. Percent of civilian labor force.

AREANAME	Money income, 2016					Median earnings, 2016			Housing units, 2016				
	Households			Median family income	Median non-family household income	All persons	Men	Women	Total	Occupied	Percent owner occupied	Median value[1] (dollars)	Median rent (dollars)
	Median income	Percent with income less than $20,000	Percent with income of $200,000 or more										
	42	43	44	45	46	47	48	49	50	51	52	53	54
KANSAS	54,935	15.3	4.4	70,792	31,227	31,098	36,936	25,501	1,259,870	1,110,407	65.7	144,900	789
Dodge City	43,336	19.4	3.5	50,526	26,331	26,060	27,360	22,712	9,703	8,987	60.8	112,000	666
Garden City	49,742	13.6	1.0	60,503	37,930	31,817	40,353	22,835	9,328	8,936	58.3	149,500	771
Hutchinson	40,185	21.6	2.6	53,142	23,911	25,791	28,595	22,472	18,865	16,324	59.7	97,700	714
Kansas City	42,141	21.1	1.1	48,467	28,659	26,105	28,916	23,121	63,564	54,655	54.7	89,600	813
Lawrence	54,243	20.4	3.8	80,042	30,819	21,015	24,471	18,352	39,790	36,506	45.2	191,500	870
Leavenworth	55,092	16.5	1.8	71,139	27,200	30,622	40,540	22,166	14,137	12,800	46.4	122,200	930
Leawood	150,725	3.4	37.2	173,833	56,152	65,133	100,291	45,760	12,937	12,304	88.3	455,300	1,378
Lenexa	77,694	6.0	8.8	91,998	43,610	42,145	51,846	37,103	22,587	20,950	60.8	251,800	1,032
Manhattan	51,571	18.1	5.6	93,097	29,958	19,101	21,706	14,650	23,645	19,648	39.1	200,000	868
Olathe	82,242	8.1	7.2	97,314	39,019	41,035	50,520	34,185	48,673	46,897	70.9	217,300	935
Overland Park	78,602	7.5	11.9	106,511	47,257	42,933	52,372	36,879	81,583	76,554	61.9	264,900	1,134
Salina	44,076	18.0	2.2	58,003	30,033	26,472	35,228	23,604	21,178	19,087	61.6	114,200	700
Shawnee	80,033	9.8	9.6	98,738	37,377	36,521	41,379	30,634	25,475	24,734	74.2	210,300	997
Topeka	45,054	17.8	2.1	61,057	30,908	30,080	31,743	26,315	59,887	51,471	53.5	107,900	730
Wichita	49,202	18.3	3.7	65,721	31,472	30,584	38,061	24,210	170,037	151,885	59.4	123,500	762
KENTUCKY	46,659	22.0	3.4	59,023	27,220	30,070	35,309	24,405	1,965,577	1,717,706	66.8	135,600	707
Bowling Green	37,305	25.1	3.3	45,918	26,065	16,439	19,961	12,110	26,268	24,485	37.6	145,800	711
Covington	41,039	26.2	1.4	46,363	32,496	29,805	31,156	25,749	20,394	17,391	47.3	107,000	640
Elizabethtown	42,327	25.6	4.2	70,784	21,219	30,820	35,363	22,203	14,742	13,011	42.8	186,800	687
Florence	52,488	14.4	5.8	57,467	34,173	31,861	36,206	27,512	14,445	13,677	49.3	148,000	849
Frankfort	46,464	16.6	0.7	61,720	41,892	26,284	26,323	26,237	13,723	11,902	45.1	125,800	684
Georgetown	58,497	18.0	0.7	73,606	34,684	34,746	38,333	26,453	13,323	12,857	56.3	155,200	767
Henderson	37,271	33.9	1.2	51,901	19,884	24,341	37,613	17,427	12,216	11,466	49.7	125,600	614
Hopkinsville	32,792	36.2	4.1	40,786	16,186	25,302	27,199	22,013	14,408	11,941	46.5	120,700	630
Jeffersontown	68,473	3.6	2.1	73,121	51,227	42,724	45,049	40,227	11,831	10,946	76.0	177,600	963
Lexington-Fayette	53,178	18.4	5.9	71,536	36,607	29,333	33,431	24,345	140,976	127,137	55.6	181,200	818
Louisville/Jefferson County	48,996	18.2	4.0	64,256	31,494	31,299	35,326	28,465	277,703	251,788	57.8	150,900	785
Nicholasville	41,898	21.6	0.8	43,677	26,870	26,023	28,115	25,407	11,355	10,099	53.0	137,200	791
Owensboro	43,924	24.2	1.9	60,070	27,864	31,346	41,471	24,542	27,752	25,194	60.8	117,800	732
Paducah	31,368	36.1	4.2	50,764	17,866	24,226	25,789	22,760	13,632	11,621	50.7	124,800	634
Richmond	32,322	36.6	1.2	37,321	25,588	16,698	18,158	16,218	14,403	13,634	45.5	127,300	639
LOUISIANA	45,146	23.6	3.8	57,490	26,826	30,261	38,063	23,485	2,037,067	1,720,801	64.3	158,000	808
Alexandria	39,918	29.6	6.4	50,143	24,608	27,794	28,963	27,288	21,094	17,119	49.8	143,100	763
Baton Rouge	38,470	28.4	5.3	54,726	25,356	23,505	30,715	20,251	98,155	81,939	46.8	166,100	818
Bossier City	46,268	19.7	1.5	56,647	36,814	26,268	27,509	21,525	28,498	24,904	52.5	163,900	959
Central	65,129	5.1	4.8	74,310	48,310	37,303	44,979	36,447	10,692	9,373	84.0	187,700	942
Houma	44,518	26.7	1.7	55,631	21,427	27,756	35,651	23,121	14,842	13,223	60.7	154,700	788
Kenner	52,281	21.0	4.1	59,299	32,091	30,667	35,886	25,951	27,544	24,208	57.6	161,200	993
Lafayette	48,139	23.2	6.2	64,551	35,105	30,564	36,298	26,177	57,470	50,473	57.7	193,900	837
Lake Charles	38,600	30.1	4.2	49,737	21,786	24,615	35,121	18,951	34,405	30,546	53.3	146,100	736
Monroe	24,950	39.3	3.1	30,656	18,250	20,282	25,803	15,896	19,833	15,998	37.2	150,800	656
New Iberia	35,341	34.2	0.3	37,978	27,962	22,356	32,333	14,059	13,223	11,766	60.7	106,800	766
New Orleans	38,681	29.6	5.4	54,315	26,414	30,179	32,208	26,752	193,120	154,355	46.3	219,700	934
Shreveport	34,647	32.9	3.9	43,945	25,145	23,587	27,054	19,677	88,962	75,509	50.8	150,000	743
Slidell	42,771	21.1	2.8	50,343	30,094	27,365	35,404	22,535	11,259	10,508	58.6	153,100	972
MAINE	53,079	17.4	3.7	68,277	31,024	30,594	35,747	26,046	730,786	531,660	71.9	184,700	797
Bangor	44,214	23.7	5.0	79,099	26,865	26,549	25,277	27,112	14,972	13,003	52.2	137,000	759
Lewiston	38,841	26.2	0.3	46,859	27,771	26,503	30,367	22,728	16,938	15,556	46.1	139,800	680
Portland	51,851	19.4	5.8	71,992	42,733	32,849	37,114	27,810	33,081	30,179	39.6	280,600	1,028
South Portland	57,348	15.2	3.3	72,529	41,660	35,912	36,842	33,853	12,675	12,069	57.1	262,100	1,093
MARYLAND	78,945	11.2	10.5	95,336	47,868	41,235	47,434	36,379	2,447,211	2,194,657	65.9	306,900	1,314
Annapolis	78,150	13.0	12.7	93,940	42,367	37,345	40,062	36,247	19,389	17,623	49.3	404,200	1,455
Baltimore	47,350	24.6	5.4	57,669	35,342	33,838	36,292	32,015	297,628	240,761	45.7	153,500	999
Bowie	103,563	5.0	15.4	122,592	79,333	56,343	55,451	56,659	22,029	20,713	78.8	342,200	1,807
College Park	78,728	26.7	12.0	112,932	20,261	15,174	18,764	10,913	8,506	7,421	44.4	326,800	1,558
Frederick	67,352	13.2	5.4	79,167	52,423	35,627	37,066	34,218	29,648	27,035	53.2	269,900	1,204
Gaithersburg	84,312	7.5	10.8	91,128	68,776	35,594	40,372	32,358	25,331	23,759	50.6	362,800	1,714
Hagerstown	37,010	28.9	1.6	41,636	26,558	25,320	26,612	23,516	18,197	15,996	45.2	152,300	784
Laurel	67,912	6.9	7.3	87,118	56,063	44,599	47,411	39,403	11,666	11,226	43.0	254,200	1,354
Rockville	101,814	9.5	19.7	127,511	62,328	50,357	61,801	41,698	25,343	24,370	57.0	523,700	1,780
Salisbury	37,557	19.3	0.9	39,076	29,083	19,157	20,302	16,763	14,826	12,513	33.4	164,200	1,045
MASSACHUSETTS	75,297	14.0	10.8	95,207	42,343	40,557	47,506	33,407	2,858,087	2,579,398	62.0	366,900	1,179
Agawam Town	58,642	11.0	4.0	83,347	40,711	34,490	47,570	30,521	12,488	12,095	79.5	211,900	1,005
Attleboro	82,405	9.5	8.7	98,043	41,585	42,246	49,148	40,820	17,032	16,344	69.6	294,000	991
Barnstable Town	68,184	13.5	7.1	78,081	38,906	32,477	40,315	23,433	25,315	17,972	73.8	335,400	1,345

1. Specified owner-occupied units; $2,000,000 represents $2,000,000 or more.

Table D. Cities — Commuting, Computer Access, Migration, Labor Force, and Employment

AREANAME	Commuting[1] 2016 Percent — Drove alone	With commutes of 30 minutes or more	Computer access[2] Percent — With a computer in the house	With Internet access	Migration — Percent who lived in the same house one year ago	Percent who lived in another state or county one year ago	Civilian labor force, 2016 — Total	Percent change 2016-2017	Unemployment[3] — Total	Rate	Civilian employment, 2016 — Population age 16 and older — Number	Percent in labor force	Population age 16 to 64 — Number	Percent who worked full-year full-time
	55	56	57	58	59	60	61	62	63	64	65	66	67	68
KANSAS	82.2	21.2	88.5	80.0	83.4	7.2	1,478,783	-0.4	53,567	3.6	2,273,338	66.3	1,835,667	53.8
Dodge City	76.8	4.9	74.7	67.2	79.1	12.9	14,176	-0.7	395	2.8	20,882	75.4	18,523	52.9
Garden City	79.9	7.7	90.1	78.6	84.9	4.0	14,898	1.1	405	2.7	18,062	67.5	15,405	56.7
Hutchinson	81.3	10.2	80.4	72.2	81.6	7.4	19,105	-0.4	786	4.1	32,756	58.4	25,445	49.6
Kansas City	83.0	24.2	87.6	72.3	85.8	5.3	70,691	1.0	3,692	5.2	114,707	67.8	97,535	51.6
Lawrence	80.3	25.1	94.3	84.8	69.6	13.3	52,326	-0.1	1,631	3.1	80,404	72.8	71,213	43.6
Leavenworth	80.1	20.6	92.0	78.3	75.0	18.4	14,010	0.9	620	4.4	27,866	57.9	24,261	50.4
Leawood	81.3	29.0	96.9	96.6	87.1	4.2	17,506	1.2	490	2.8	26,381	65.1	20,507	51.2
Lenexa	83.5	26.7	93.6	91.8	77.1	10.1	31,028	1.3	963	3.1	41,754	70.7	34,626	55.7
Manhattan	74.1	8.2	95.7	85.8	64.5	16.9	29,245	0.4	795	2.7	48,612	65.8	43,424	39.5
Olathe	82.8	26.0	95.6	91.2	85.1	5.1	77,431	1.2	2,228	2.9	102,565	72.8	87,122	59.4
Overland Park	83.2	19.6	95.5	93.3	80.7	8.8	108,107	1.1	3,288	3.0	147,786	72.7	120,790	58.9
Salina	74.9	10.8	84.5	78.5	80.2	7.3	26,055	1.8	857	3.3	37,393	65.1	30,041	57.8
Shawnee	87.7	29.9	94.7	89.5	87.4	8.7	36,271	1.1	1,137	3.1	52,007	78.5	44,492	62.9
Topeka	79.5	12.6	81.0	65.6	82.2	6.5	63,176	-0.9	2,475	3.9	99,517	63.2	78,639	52.8
Wichita	83.2	14.3	86.0	80.4	83.6	5.1	185,587	-1.1	8,148	4.4	301,195	67.5	248,890	52.8
KENTUCKY	82.2	30.5	84.8	76.8	84.3	6.8	2,052,368	2.0	100,302	4.9	3,542,057	59.1	2,854,532	47.3
Bowling Green	78.1	20.0	88.8	83.7	66.4	16.8	32,187	3.3	1,390	4.3	53,276	63.4	45,580	34.4
Covington	70.1	27.7	82.2	76.2	79.3	12.2	18,977	2.4	869	4.6	31,762	68.4	26,819	50.2
Elizabethtown	84.8	18.7	79.5	69.5	77.0	11.1	14,067	2.0	611	4.3	24,001	65.0	19,520	50.5
Florence	NA	22.7	91.3	87.3	79.6	10.4	16,568	2.4	692	4.2	26,177	70.1	20,796	54.6
Frankfort	79.7	20.5	89.3	77.7	73.2	10.0	14,108	1.7	599	4.2	21,658	65.1	17,826	48.2
Georgetown	80.8	24.3	88.3	84.7	78.2	9.3	17,684	2.5	700	4.0	25,766	69.7	22,386	57.2
Henderson	87.7	24.5	78.9	70.4	78.8	7.6	13,145	2.2	646	4.9	22,158	56.9	17,604	47.4
Hopkinsville	89.2	17.4	80.0	64.8	80.1	5.6	12,360	2.0	816	6.6	24,242	50.3	19,436	41.2
Jeffersontown	77.1	31.7	87.7	83.5	82.8	9.0	15,851	3.0	600	3.8	21,175	68.9	16,990	58.1
Lexington-Fayette	78.5	22.5	92.6	85.5	76.0	9.1	174,304	2.7	6,360	3.6	257,828	69.1	219,205	50.8
Louisville/Jefferson County	80.5	28.4	88.4	82.4	82.5	4.5	394,248	2.8	17,464	4.4	493,730	65.6	404,939	51.6
Nicholasville	86.3	36.3	89.6	79.0	82.0	5.0	15,032	2.6	600	4.0	21,563	58.5	17,593	47.8
Owensboro	81.8	20.2	86.2	79.5	81.3	6.0	27,003	2.5	1,252	4.6	46,841	58.3	35,800	47.4
Paducah	78.5	19.7	74.4	66.7	78.0	3.8	10,670	1.4	697	6.5	20,293	59.7	15,831	42.3
Richmond	84.5	26.0	87.5	71.3	61.9	17.5	17,798	1.9	817	4.6	29,160	63.5	26,185	37.3
LOUISIANA	82.9	32.7	84.5	73.7	86.4	5.4	2,112,320	-0.6	108,317	5.1	3,690,800	59.3	3,016,621	46.1
Alexandria	82.5	14.2	81.4	66.7	83.0	5.9	19,333	-1.7	1,187	6.1	37,335	57.9	29,850	47.4
Baton Rouge	81.9	23.4	86.4	77.1	79.8	7.1	114,691	0.0	5,534	4.8	182,278	62.6	151,471	42.8
Bossier City	88.1	13.9	89.6	66.8	83.2	10.4	30,142	-1.4	1,390	4.6	53,875	64.3	45,784	52.8
Central	89.8	40.3	92.1	87.2	NA	NA	15,356	0.0	574	3.7	20,726	62.4	15,969	60.3
Houma	NA	24.7	83.0	71.6	80.2	8.0	14,356	-4.6	861	6.0	27,328	52.8	22,412	46.3
Kenner	80.8	29.8	83.4	71.9	89.4	2.4	33,395	-0.5	1,475	4.4	51,366	66.1	41,585	54.6
Lafayette	83.3	18.1	89.1	83.0	81.6	5.4	60,273	-1.2	2,996	5.0	105,067	63.6	86,453	50.8
Lake Charles	85.2	11.8	82.9	69.6	82.6	4.9	41,876	5.6	1,706	4.1	60,921	60.5	49,155	44.2
Monroe	72.1	10.8	75.7	64.4	88.4	3.8	20,269	-0.9	1,282	6.3	36,976	47.7	30,015	32.2
New Iberia	88.3	28.6	77.1	62.7	79.1	5.4	11,351	-2.5	944	8.3	23,123	55.7	18,083	35.5
New Orleans	67.4	30.4	85.3	72.8	84.3	7.2	179,465	-0.5	9,201	5.1	320,306	62.2	269,374	44.2
Shreveport	86.6	13.5	81.6	67.6	85.6	3.3	83,357	-1.3	4,906	5.9	153,101	58.4	124,749	41.9
Slidell	85.1	45.9	86.2	78.6	84.2	6.8	12,583	-0.3	653	5.2	20,596	65.2	17,112	49.1
MAINE	79.3	32.1	88.8	80.9	86.9	6.0	700,099	1.1	22,958	3.3	1,108,711	62.3	852,059	48.5
Bangor	77.3	11.5	89.9	81.4	79.0	11.0	16,783	0.3	557	3.3	26,815	63.7	21,595	46.1
Lewiston	72.0	24.1	88.0	77.3	81.5	8.3	17,310	0.6	586	3.4	28,923	59.5	22,119	41.4
Portland	63.2	20.1	91.9	84.5	78.3	7.6	39,100	2.2	960	2.5	56,901	73.1	47,237	53.5
South Portland	77.6	15.6	93.0	87.7	82.8	5.6	14,875	2.3	377	2.5	22,334	67.2	17,956	51.1
MARYLAND	73.8	51.7	91.8	85.4	86.4	6.3	3,219,455	1.3	133,209	4.1	4,819,956	68.0	3,943,508	55.0
Annapolis	68.1	43.1	92.0	83.8	76.1	5.6	22,503	1.2	758	3.4	33,264	75.5	25,874	65.7
Baltimore	59.5	45.5	84.5	73.5	82.6	7.0	294,248	1.0	18,042	6.1	498,366	62.6	419,118	47.7
Bowie	76.9	63.1	95.6	93.8	90.9	5.5	34,794	1.9	1,204	3.5	47,283	72.8	39,366	60.7
College Park	59.1	56.9	97.1	81.0	62.3	23.6	15,200	1.7	809	5.3	28,800	49.7	26,775	31.1
Frederick	70.9	35.7	87.2	81.9	81.7	8.0	37,616	1.5	1,439	3.8	57,821	69.8	48,281	54.6
Gaithersburg	61.4	50.0	95.0	87.7	83.4	6.9	36,444	1.6	1,165	3.2	54,822	75.8	47,162	56.4
Hagerstown	77.4	42.9	82.1	68.0	80.8	5.2	19,505	0.2	1,084	5.6	31,450	60.8	25,549	46.5
Laurel	66.7	52.1	96.6	86.9	83.7	10.9	15,916	1.8	626	3.9	20,385	76.5	17,307	60.5
Rockville	60.2	50.5	97.0	93.4	84.1	8.1	37,232	1.8	1,145	3.1	53,052	70.7	42,412	54.7
Salisbury	87.8	21.9	90.5	72.6	75.2	7.2	15,603	1.4	995	6.4	26,846	67.3	22,415	37.0
MASSACHUSETTS	70.1	45.7	90.7	85.1	87.0	5.9	3,657,173	1.3	135,691	3.7	5,601,991	67.4	4,527,566	51.0
Agawam Town	91.4	19.7	88.0	82.6	NA	NA	15,978	0.5	617	3.9	24,141	65.2	18,222	57.9
Attleboro	84.8	43.3	93.1	85.2	88.2	6.8	24,532	1.2	972	4.0	36,420	70.2	30,162	58.1
Barnstable Town	80.4	18.6	96.4	88.1	90.6	2.0	23,809	0.9	1,041	4.4	36,994	64.8	27,502	49.1

1. Employed persons. 2. Households. 3. Percent of civilian labor force.

Table D. Cities — Construction, Wholesale Trade, and Retail Trade

AREANAME	Value of residential construction authorized by building permits, 2017			Wholesale trade[1], 2012				Retail trade[2], 2012			
	New construction ($1,000)	Number of housing units	Percent single family	Number of establish-ments	Number of employees	Sales (mil dol)	Annual payroll (mil dol)	Number of establish-ments	Number of employees	Sales (mil dol)	Annual payroll (mil dol)
	69	70	71	72	73	74	75	76	77	78	79
KANSAS	1,781,716	8,984	67.3	3,790	52,168	60,226.3	3,055.4	10,548	145,480	38,276.5	3,325.0
Dodge City	7,742	42	90.5	44	535	470.1	27.0	108	1,697	469.2	38.7
Garden City	4,130	33	87.9	27	199	227.0	9.5	149	2,259	538.9	49.9
Hutchinson	2,655	10	100.0	50	630	742.0	25.0	202	2,967	705.3	66.8
Kansas City	47,565	297	91.2	197	4,909	4,507.3	256.9	405	6,193	1,594.1	155.6
Lawrence	60,504	203	96.1	53	413	168.8	16.7	333	5,800	1,253.6	118.2
Leavenworth	3,050	14	100.0	9	D	D	D	110	1,589	405.0	34.5
Leawood	18,516	54	100.0	34	407	217.0	33.5	137	2,931	520.8	74.5
Lenexa	181,863	836	36.0	289	4,625	2,981.9	267.5	200	3,850	2,504.9	122.2
Manhattan	32,748	154	66.9	31	480	144.0	19.7	260	5,438	1,031.9	111.4
Olathe	229,035	954	60.7	154	3,054	3,163.4	177.9	336	6,935	2,223.4	179.6
Overland Park	202,616	827	61.9	248	7,767	18,445.8	776.3	739	13,517	3,011.8	310.8
Salina	10,660	69	56.5	72	898	704.3	43.4	243	3,949	1,112.7	86.1
Shawnee	55,398	217	69.6	58	805	700.8	45.9	175	3,243	761.8	72.7
Topeka	17,599	85	100.0	120	1,342	845.1	62.1	574	8,921	2,185.9	197.4
Wichita	181,109	1,306	64.5	515	7,443	7,544.6	436.2	1,477	24,136	6,284.9	572.7
KENTUCKY	1,974,160	12,630	63.1	3,690	57,630	71,745.9	3,090.3	15,224	202,615	54,870.0	4,619.2
Bowling Green	73,649	686	30.5	108	1,303	2,669.4	65.2	449	6,831	1,634.5	150.6
Covington	0	0	0.0	26	D	D	D	121	1,297	396.0	33.7
Elizabethtown	18,328	145	51.7	36	319	194.9	14.2	264	4,076	1,089.3	97.1
Florence	NA	NA	NA	40	D	D	D	295	6,297	1,571.5	138.6
Frankfort	1,389	8	100.0	22	D	D	D	137	1,965	476.8	42.0
Georgetown	NA	NA	NA	18	D	D	D	107	1,687	510.4	35.6
Henderson	1,678	9	77.8	34	D	D	D	152	2,089	665.2	51.4
Hopkinsville	6,185	62	61.3	50	739	958.0	28.8	169	2,369	717.7	61.0
Jeffersontown	5,800	32	75.0	163	2,822	1,782.0	150.6	145	2,960	1,005.9	85.4
Lexington-Fayette	164,720	1,348	55.1	352	7,283	4,517.8	527.7	1,192	19,820	4,994.8	466.9
Louisville/Jefferson County	479,528	3,292	37.5	1,006	15,867	13,048.4	836.7	2,659	41,294	10,964.4	1,004.0
Nicholasville	20,002	141	88.7	27	D	D	D	117	1,996	741.7	56.1
Owensboro	22,827	260	94.6	67	943	527.4	41.0	336	4,944	1,209.2	111.0
Paducah	8,306	33	69.7	72	D	D	D	320	5,310	1,415.2	120.6
Richmond	13,945	198	63.1	18	99	134.9	3.7	199	2,976	712.7	59.7
LOUISIANA	2,986,279	15,224	89.1	4,823	64,259	68,012.8	3,260.2	16,743	220,257	61,396.4	5,334.6
Alexandria	NA	NA	NA	73	914	443.7	37.0	385	5,698	1,633.6	142.8
Baton Rouge	74,469	253	100.0	306	3,894	2,296.2	192.8	1,146	16,570	4,262.5	409.4
Bossier City	54,478	322	100.0	77	1,165	822.5	55.7	379	5,660	1,621.7	137.8
Central	23,701	146	100.0	9	33	250.0	3.7	40	867	203.6	18.8
Houma	NA	NA	NA	68	686	325.7	42.9	167	2,292	639.3	51.6
Kenner	16,334	58	82.8	113	883	385.7	48.5	266	4,356	1,554.2	130.9
Lafayette	NA	NA	NA	276	3,728	1,815.8	182.4	808	12,699	3,434.7	316.5
Lake Charles	144,834	1,052	37.7	72	847	764.6	33.7	442	6,000	1,812.8	143.5
Monroe	36,026	211	58.8	81	1,211	1,198.0	53.9	400	5,914	1,452.5	131.1
New Iberia	3,633	29	41.4	54	695	330.9	34.5	208	2,791	743.1	68.9
New Orleans	137,093	660	67.7	256	3,794	2,687.0	191.5	1,275	12,371	3,245.1	337.8
Shreveport	76,600	295	100.0	294	D	D	D	875	12,231	3,645.9	311.7
Slidell	4,421	27	100.0	27	158	337.9	7.3	282	4,263	1,096.7	96.6
MAINE	827,749	4,358	82.2	1,344	14,753	12,961.3	691.5	6,351	80,155	21,521.7	1,884.6
Bangor	18,402	98	55.1	63	849	463.0	41.9	310	6,147	1,819.4	136.7
Lewiston	3,533	18	100.0	37	657	300.1	30.0	157	1,935	710.1	46.6
Portland	9,635	42	64.3	174	2,511	1,899.3	129.6	395	4,893	1,551.1	135.3
South Portland	11,490	136	29.4	50	811	2,204.9	43.1	244	4,606	1,131.5	98.7
MARYLAND	3,257,334	16,224	76.3	4,768	73,369	60,734.2	4,378.5	18,179	281,678	76,379.7	7,168.5
Annapolis	11,867	46	100.0	62	404	423.4	22.4	488	7,230	1,508.1	172.2
Baltimore	70,287	438	38.6	544	8,592	7,954.3	495.2	1,839	15,747	3,647.7	379.0
Bowie	NA	NA	NA	14	168	62.8	11.9	149	3,864	884.7	82.7
College Park	NA	NA	NA	11	55	15.5	4.5	69	1,686	494.9	46.8
Frederick	91,529	497	49.9	78	844	448.2	45.2	320	5,293	1,594.9	145.0
Gaithersburg	8,428	80	40.0	76	1,339	619.5	79.4	337	6,863	2,146.6	197.4
Hagerstown	4,255	26	100.0	51	463	287.1	20.7	207	4,043	1,212.7	101.4
Laurel	13,246	47	83.0	11	195	101.4	9.1	138	2,078	542.5	48.4
Rockville	55,026	146	14.4	74	1,661	4,078.6	182.6	321	5,420	1,877.2	162.5
Salisbury	3,074	19	78.9	58	707	461.6	31.3	234	4,178	987.1	91.9
MASSACHUSETTS	4,092,416	17,728	41.1	6,619	114,195	123,904.4	8,035.1	24,311	351,598	92,915.4	9,161.7
Agawam Town	NA	NA	NA	49	729	819.9	46.1	75	922	262.8	26.5
Attleboro	15,628	98	77.6	32	496	227.5	26.1	134	2,277	638.5	51.3
Barnstable Town	43,565	344	11.9	47	444	185.9	22.3	384	4,724	1,267.9	127.6

1. Merchant wholesalers except manufacturers' sales branches and offices. 2. Establishments with payroll.

Table D. Cities — **Real Estate, Professional Services, and Manufacturing**

AREANAME	Real estate and rental and leasing, 2012				Professional, scientific, and technical services[1], 2012				Manufacturing, 2012			
	Number of establishments	Number of employees	Receipts (mil dol)	Annual payroll (mil dol)	Number of establishments	Number of employees	Receipts (mil dol)	Annual payroll (mil dol)	Number of establishments	Number of employees	Receipts (mil dol)	Annual payroll (mil dol)
	80	81	82	83	84	85	86	87	88	89	90	91
KANSAS	2,999	14,256	2,743.1	507.6	7,071	60,615	8,562.6	3,577.1	2,875	152,423	86,076.3	7,578.3
Dodge City	21	D	D	D	42	D	D	D	17	D	D	D
Garden City	26	69	13.5	2.3	54	D	D	D	12	D	D	7.6
Hutchinson	52	145	22.9	3.9	82	D	D	D	41	1,579	441.5	70.9
Kansas City	128	519	107.4	18.4	173	D	D	D	161	10,043	10,883.2	640.0
Lawrence	141	D	D	D	249	D	D	D	45	2,467	957.6	103.4
Leavenworth	25	130	39.4	3.8	73	D	D	D	17	685	178.8	28.4
Leawood	102	D	D	D	236	D	D	D	14	189	26.4	9.8
Lenexa	105	588	133.8	31.5	319	D	D	D	135	6,020	2,108.2	298.4
Manhattan	102	D	D	D	117	D	D	D	34	673	137.0	28.9
Olathe	131	585	134.3	24.4	342	1,676	199.2	77.5	100	5,995	1,402.8	337.4
Overland Park	362	2,042	672.6	98.2	1,219	D	D	D	84	2,007	667.9	95.7
Salina	59	199	48.3	6.0	101	D	D	D	55	3,944	1,128.0	159.4
Shawnee	77	306	61.9	10.1	168	929	127.9	46.9	46	1,586	D	105.0
Topeka	173	803	124.1	24.6	382	D	D	D	84	4,722	2,456.0	220.0
Wichita	478	3,607	493.4	121.0	1,002	8,827	1,463.6	506.0	442	25,801	10,181.7	1,336.6
KENTUCKY	3,534	18,250	4,845.5	637.3	8,064	62,431	7,746.8	2,799.3	3,782	213,545	129,284.4	10,140.1
Bowling Green	102	363	73.7	10.4	181	D	D	D	95	7,873	5,079.8	402.6
Covington	32	203	62.0	10.6	124	D	D	D	28	746	215.7	33.6
Elizabethtown	61	304	42.3	7.6	110	D	D	D	51	4,727	2,009.7	220.6
Florence	49	260	71.8	7.9	102	1,559	106.1	43.1	38	3,293	1,633.6	176.6
Frankfort	27	154	13.2	3.5	102	714	77.5	30.0	15	550	104.0	23.3
Georgetown	32	D	D	D	53	261	31.3	12.5	22	7,150	D	502.3
Henderson	36	D	D	D	62	364	31.7	11.1	54	2,214	1,110.0	98.3
Hopkinsville	44	124	19.1	3.1	58	D	D	D	49	4,305	D	191.7
Jeffersontown	85	586	185.4	19.1	180	3,598	284.8	154.5	93	3,786	999.1	163.6
Lexington-Fayette	431	2,128	442.3	76.6	1,067	10,048	1,438.1	560.1	224	8,005	2,922.0	351.1
Louisville/Jefferson County	926	7,168	2,895.1	289.1	2,191	21,986	3,257.7	1,129.8	718	40,666	28,642.1	2,159.3
Nicholasville	21	87	10.8	2.2	52	286	63.6	15.3	51	2,245	588.9	79.9
Owensboro	63	427	57.1	11.7	128	D	D	D	64	3,644	2,865.5	159.3
Paducah	58	252	47.8	8.1	140	D	D	D	36	D	D	D
Richmond	42	150	29.2	4.2	77	D	D	D	32	1,896	D	83.4
LOUISIANA	4,500	31,298	7,486.4	1,461.4	11,669	87,367	13,417.4	4,986.5	3,308	136,327	271,191.1	8,489.3
Alexandria	98	472	76.2	15.2	202	1,325	163.5	55.0	37	1,826	753.8	99.6
Baton Rouge	339	1,827	382.5	71.7	1,144	D	D	D	185	4,968	D	343.8
Bossier City	79	508	104.5	16.1	116	D	D	D	47	1,018	D	47.8
Central	15	42	5.7	0.8	25	75	9.7	3.2	21	155	D	5.6
Houma	61	589	138.9	37.8	145	925	121.6	47.4	32	1,045	228.4	59.8
Kenner	86	622	156.8	20.9	159	1,862	349.7	122.5	54	1,074	182.8	43.0
Lafayette	334	2,352	623.9	122.8	1,009	7,293	1,312.5	444.7	129	3,831	1,042.7	171.7
Lake Charles	117	480	85.9	16.5	275	1,775	214.0	77.5	39	1,224	1,251.5	76.1
Monroe	119	811	137.7	26.1	292	D	D	D	41	1,356	455.0	66.4
New Iberia	56	311	60.9	12.3	100	400	51.5	15.9	49	1,703	566.7	100.5
New Orleans	379	2,156	411.6	79.1	1,421	D	D	D	144	6,049	4,352.7	335.6
Shreveport	285	2,266	439.8	90.1	574	D	D	D	145	4,796	3,670.1	251.9
Slidell	37	365	116.2	26.1	139	583	62.2	21.6	26	1,895	D	115.8
MAINE	1,580	6,242	1,100.4	220.6	3,457	21,188	3,061.0	1,134.1	1,650	49,238	16,044.5	2,424.3
Bangor	90	404	80.3	14.5	157	D	D	D	37	775	167.2	34.7
Lewiston	48	222	31.1	6.6	83	D	D	D	65	1,507	430.2	65.7
Portland	226	1,453	291.5	56.6	586	5,193	1,044.1	380.9	101	2,425	747.5	112.2
South Portland	48	459	93.8	16.4	101	686	96.6	37.9	33	1,452	247.9	86.6
MARYLAND	6,001	42,838	13,410.1	2,253.2	19,529	D	D	D	3,096	100,079	39,533.0	5,908.9
Annapolis	98	449	115.3	25.7	371	D	D	D	37	324	65.5	14.9
Baltimore	596	4,055	883.7	187.6	1,524	20,740	4,544.9	1,808.5	409	11,748	5,043.3	574.0
Bowie	28	170	59.1	7.0	167	D	D	D	6	19	2.6	0.7
College Park	19	77	10.8	2.5	75	D	D	D	6	101	D	4.3
Frederick	99	462	123.1	23.3	369	D	D	D	59	2,045	D	129.9
Gaithersburg	95	514	181.9	30.3	415	D	D	D	35	1,039	397.5	72.6
Hagerstown	65	251	58.6	8.6	113	1,009	111.0	43.9	61	3,335	1,870.3	199.2
Laurel	42	655	104.1	25.6	74	930	154.4	60.6	12	115	D	8.2
Rockville	131	1,785	1,087.7	198.4	861	18,500	3,927.4	1,747.3	61	1,516	348.0	107.9
Salisbury	77	478	55.7	16.0	156	D	D	D	46	2,713	882.7	109.7
MASSACHUSETTS	6,485	42,788	13,628.4	2,357.9	21,203	243,993	57,979.0	22,938.7	6,806	234,168	81,927.8	14,395.3
Agawam Town	20	77	20.6	3.4	65	707	80.2	36.0	54	2,280	779.8	112.5
Attleboro	26	115	23.8	5.4	59	342	38.7	16.0	88	3,518	926.6	223.9
Barnstable Town	70	227	72.0	9.2	201	D	D	D	46	897	215.2	51.6

1. Establishments subject to federal tax.

Table D. Cities — Accommodation and Food Services, Arts, Entertainment, and Recreation, and Health Care and Social Assistance

AREANAME	Accommodaton and food services, 2012				Arts, entertainment, and recreation[1], 2012				Health care and social assistance,[1] 2012			
	Number of establish-ments	Number of employees	Receipts (mil dol)	Annual payroll (mil dol)	Number of establish-ments	Number of employees	Receipts (mil dol)	Annual payroll (mil dol)	Number of establish-ments	Number of employees	Receipts (mil dol)	Annual payroll (mil dol)
	92	93	94	95	96	97	98	99	100	101	102	103
KANSAS..................	5,943	106,850	4,873.4	1,342.9	668	9,807	615.7	170.2	5,977	93,121	9,677.8	3,955.4
Dodge City..........................	71	D	D	D	5	D	D	D	53	D	D	D
Garden City........................	66	1,333	67.5	17.5	4	37	0.8	0.3	68	981	66.9	26.7
Hutchinson.........................	99	1,867	82.0	23.3	1	D	D	D	103	1,783	206.1	89.5
Kansas City........................	227	4,773	254.8	69.8	24	D	D	D	224	D	D	D
Lawrence............................	270	6,211	249.2	69.3	22	327	36.2	3.7	203	2,798	242.1	93.0
Leavenworth	59	974	43.6	11.6	6	39	1.0	0.2	65	D	D	D
Leawood	73	2,185	96.2	31.7	14	D	D	D	158	1,906	259.5	108.9
Lenexa	106	1,884	94.5	28.0	18	D	D	D	144	4,505	700.3	214.6
Manhattan	168	3,912	150.0	41.4	8	D	D	D	132	1,402	163.2	57.6
Olathe	234	5,437	245.6	70.9	32	D	D	D	244	D	D	D
Overland Park	456	10,355	538.6	162.8	71	1,583	78.0	25.7	664	12,623	1,736.3	705.9
Salina	132	2,986	115.8	31.0	10	D	D	D	137	2,391	231.7	93.3
Shawnee............................	109	2,166	95.9	27.2	12	D	D	D	121	1,609	123.8	58.3
Topeka	330	6,636	291.1	80.0	32	D	D	D	358	5,825	699.8	308.8
Wichita	962	19,526	918.8	255.2	78	1,300	48.4	18.5	977	18,132	2,250.5	883.1
KENTUCKY	7,678	156,965	7,500.1	2,083.5	931	11,322	862.3	237.6	9,449	127,446	11,985.2	5,178.2
Bowling Green	243	5,498	255.4	68.2	15	425	12.3	4.3	289	D	D	D
Covington...........................	125	1,793	117.0	29.4	9	D	D	D	39	D	D	D
Elizabethtown.....................	112	2,798	132.4	37.0	9	115	5.2	1.4	204	D	D	D
Florence............................	161	3,755	201.4	55.7	21	500	20.0	5.8	136	2,375	210.7	92.3
Frankfort............................	88	1,698	83.5	22.2	6	D	D	D	109	1,198	100.9	45.0
Georgetown	80	D	D	D	5	D	D	D	93	D	D	D
Henderson	81	1,388	64.2	16.5	9	D	D	D	105	D	D	D
Hopkinsville........................	77	1,524	67.6	19.2	5	39	1.9	0.6	120	1,151	111.2	36.4
Jeffersontown....................	108	2,931	141.4	41.9	18	397	13.0	4.8	101	2,692	165.9	77.6
Lexington-Fayette	772	17,490	939.4	270.7	91	1,469	110.6	37.9	895	12,181	1,255.7	587.7
Louisville/Jefferson County.	1,651	39,711	2,006.3	572.1	220	3,486	288.7	88.2	2,072	32,822	3,186.5	1,478.1
Nicholasville......................	53	D	D	D	9	D	D	D	67	551	35.4	17.4
Owensboro.........................	134	3,481	150.9	44.1	13	D	D	D	235	D	D	D
Paducah............................	174	3,615	161.2	46.8	10	D	D	D	187	D	D	D
Richmond...........................	113	2,762	121.8	33.3	11	D	D	D	134	1,421	115.1	50.1
LOUISIANA	9,019	193,928	11,697.9	3,110.7	1,085	18,036	2,224.7	606.4	10,240	167,792	15,869.9	6,156.9
Alexandria	165	3,114	158.9	43.1	11	D	D	D	277	5,734	754.5	262.4
Baton Rouge	699	15,983	881.3	244.6	65	1,706	232.9	31.8	746	12,755	1,183.1	497.2
Bossier City.......................	202	7,287	643.8	129.8	23	935	126.5	17.7	153	2,187	184.1	66.4
Central	15	363	12.6	3.5	4	D	D	D	36	473	33.6	14.0
Houma	90	1,690	114.5	33.7	9	78	3.3	1.2	145	D	D	D
Kenner	184	3,718	210.3	58.3	20	D	D	D	149	1,864	186.3	74.9
Lafayette	542	12,372	689.9	202.6	50	D	D	D	756	14,701	1,619.6	624.3
Lake Charles......................	197	6,132	579.2	125.3	24	D	D	D	314	5,528	599.3	241.0
Monroe..............................	167	3,761	170.7	46.2	17	310	15.7	2.3	346	5,454	463.4	179.3
New Iberia.........................	81	D	D	D	10	D	D	D	157	D	D	D
New Orleans	1,300	35,510	2,765.4	764.7	129	3,024	367.8	140.6	628	8,481	1,013.6	371.5
Shreveport	460	12,644	750.2	196.0	43	D	D	D	687	D	D	D
Slidell	180	3,220	150.4	41.0	4	D	D	D	196	D	D	D
MAINE	3,958	49,672	2,901.3	850.8	585	4,484	368.2	96.3	3,071	41,700	3,486.8	1,613.4
Bangor	139	3,366	222.7	58.4	8	D	D	D	211	4,175	353.1	166.6
Lewiston............................	74	1,015	51.8	14.3	11	D	D	D	98	1,182	131.6	53.6
Portland.............................	330	5,887	312.7	99.7	39	404	34.3	8.7	278	4,363	470.5	216.3
South Portland	124	2,729	137.4	41.5	11	D	D	D	106	1,379	150.4	64.4
MARYLAND	11,344	204,222	12,516.8	3,410.5	1,561	24,878	2,726.9	806.3	13,217	168,241	18,823.4	7,784.6
Annapolis	194	4,975	299.5	91.6	NA	NA	NA	NA	143	1,523	189.2	69.3
Baltimore...........................	1,541	21,832	1,607.8	435.6	NA	NA	NA	NA	1,069	16,427	1,991.0	827.4
Bowie	72	1,969	110.3	30.4	NA	NA	NA	NA	188	1,744	157.8	67.7
College Park	111	1,966	116.5	30.5	NA	NA	NA	NA	29	175	16.3	7.5
Frederick...........................	218	4,153	220.7	64.6	NA	NA	NA	NA	318	4,441	550.3	212.9
Gaithersburg......................	204	3,774	267.0	71.0	NA	NA	NA	NA	170	1,725	182.4	60.5
Hagerstown........................	127	2,416	121.7	34.9	NA	NA	NA	NA	132	1,703	199.8	82.6
Laurel...............................	79	1,725	94.2	26.6	NA	NA	NA	NA	94	1,192	123.7	48.6
Rockville............................	252	4,133	278.5	76.7	NA	NA	NA	NA	278	4,285	845.6	434.3
Salisbury...........................	143	2,552	128.3	31.6	NA	NA	NA	NA	161	2,553	311.6	133.3
MASSACHUSETTS	16,898	273,185	17,509.0	5,019.8	2,277	35,108	3,412.3	1,261.8	13,136	237,631	26,639.0	12,209.0
Agawam Town	58	618	30.0	7.9	9	D	D	D	53	1,341	109.3	47.0
Attleboro...........................	83	D	D	D	9	102	3.7	1.9	90	2,274	169.0	83.7
Barnstable Town.................	196	2,834	192.1	58.4	21	136	11.2	2.6	157	2,523	267.3	130.6

1. Establishments subject to federal tax.

Other Services and Government Employment and Payroll

AREANAME	Other services[1]				Government employment and payroll, 2012								
					Full-time equivalent employees	Total (dollars)	*March payroll — Percent of total for:*						
	Number of establish-ments	Number of employees	Receipts (mil dol)	Annual payroll (mil dol)			Adminis-trative, judicial, and legal	Police and corrections	Fire protection	Highways and trans-portation	Health and welfare	Natural resources and utilities	Education and libraries
	104	105	106	107	108	109	110	111	112	113	114	115	116
KANSAS	3,957	21,148	1,920.4	560.0	X	X	X	X	X	X	X	X	X
Dodge City	37	229	22.9	5.6	249	803,190	14.8	27.3	12.1	6.2	2.3	27.5	6.6
Garden City	35	D	D	D	310	1,086,046	12.7	30.4	12.2	6.7	0.7	30.7	0.0
Hutchinson	66	343	20.9	7.2	392	1,720,937	8.7	26.7	25.6	7.2	2.1	25.6	0.0
Kansas City	157	827	89.5	25.3	2,707	14,492,572	12.6	24.6	15.1	5.6	5.3	29.9	0.0
Lawrence	117	713	43.2	14.4	1,978	10,089,159	4.2	10.8	8.9	2.8	58.2	13.8	0.0
Leavenworth	44	255	17.7	5.7	268	973,969	12.2	33.1	20.9	8.2	4.8	17.2	0.0
Leawood	48	451	48.8	18.0	262	1,218,472	17.8	32.5	22.4	11.6	1.7	11.1	0.0
Lenexa	68	538	49.5	18.3	414	1,898,039	18.6	33.0	22.5	12.1	0.0	11.7	0.0
Manhattan	72	D	D	D	362	1,385,412	18.7	0.0	25.9	14.5	5.9	32.8	0.0
Olathe	158	1,168	93.9	28.8	826	3,674,590	18.5	24.2	20.1	16.9	2.0	17.6	0.0
Overland Park	304	1,696	122.8	39.0	899	4,414,214	19.0	34.6	19.7	13.5	0.9	8.8	0.0
Salina	87	D	D	D	484	1,858,261	10.4	24.5	22.0	12.0	3.3	23.9	0.0
Shawnee	76	534	37.2	13.3	287	1,666,597	13.6	38.1	23.7	12.5	0.8	9.1	0.0
Topeka	190	1,382	108.7	34.1	1,062	3,978,506	7.7	32.8	28.1	11.7	1.6	15.4	0.0
Wichita	560	4,092	364.5	115.2	2,864	12,396,633	10.7	30.7	18.5	13.7	3.8	15.4	2.9
KENTUCKY	4,793	31,452	2,830.7	850.2	X	X	X	X	X	X	X	X	X
Bowling Green	137	784	69.1	19.1	699	2,772,912	7.1	20.2	19.5	5.5	2.9	30.0	0.0
Covington	74	318	25.9	8.4	421	1,788,490	6.5	36.3	30.5	3.6	11.9	5.7	0.0
Elizabethtown	66	436	37.9	11.0	289	996,440	11.3	24.1	21.7	8.8	0.0	27.7	0.0
Florence	67	538	35.4	12.7	198	919,937	6.2	36.7	28.5	4.6	0.0	11.5	0.0
Frankfort	38	233	14.8	4.7	530	2,153,521	5.6	15.6	18.6	4.9	2.2	22.3	0.0
Georgetown	38	166	11.3	3.2	179	621,131	11.9	34.9	35.4	6.1	0.0	6.7	0.0
Henderson	41	D	D	D	454	1,639,406	10.9	14.7	13.1	5.8	6.0	45.6	0.0
Hopkinsville	39	229	21.7	5.9	398	1,517,254	6.4	20.1	21.3	2.1	5.3	33.5	0.0
Jeffersontown	78	735	118.2	28.7	108	518,932	9.2	65.9	0.0	12.9	5.5	1.6	1.2
Lexington-Fayette	393	3,062	238.3	81.6	3,926	16,180,537	10.0	31.5	18.1	5.0	11.0	15.2	3.0
Louisville/Jefferson County	1,023	8,809	890.5	254.0	8,264	32,734,538	10.3	29.9	8.6	12.9	15.7	14.6	2.2
Nicholasville	46	174	21.5	4.3	214	748,387	13.4	32.1	20.0	4.1	0.0	17.4	0.0
Owensboro	90	706	49.6	17.4	840	3,418,017	7.9	17.9	10.1	5.1	3.1	53.8	0.0
Paducah	76	584	48.2	13.4	537	2,054,380	7.5	18.4	12.7	12.4	7.8	37.6	0.0
Richmond	48	242	17.3	4.8	264	708,015	11.1	30.0	21.4	6.8	9.1	12.4	0.0
LOUISIANA	5,092	36,098	3,916.0	1,216.5	X	X	X	X	X	X	X	X	X
Alexandria	89	539	45.5	13.2	858	3,139,622	13.3	29.0	18.9	9.8	0.4	22.4	0.0
Baton Rouge	392	4,825	381.6	214.7	7,745	28,842,476	18.7	20.3	13.5	8.8	15.7	11.6	4.2
Bossier City	98	634	55.2	15.9	738	2,695,669	13.1	32.2	30.2	2.8	1.1	15.5	0.0
Central	24	115	12.9	4.0	11	24,511	92.3	7.7	0.0	0.0	0.0	0.0	0.0
Houma	57	527	77.3	29.1	2,552	9,484,779	6.9	16.5	2.3	2.5	60.4	8.0	3.4
Kenner	107	759	114.6	27.1	633	2,227,138	15.0	42.0	19.4	6.5	3.2	7.8	0.0
Lafayette	232	2,047	253.7	62.1	3,047	10,656,600	18.8	30.9	10.4	8.4	1.8	24.1	2.4
Lake Charles	98	793	74.7	23.3	1,030	3,427,311	10.3	24.5	19.4	6.9	0.4	29.2	0.0
Monroe	65	549	40.9	12.8	1,137	2,092,527	21.1	3.5	2.5	12.5	15.1	42.2	0.0
New Iberia	69	388	35.3	10.7	222	646,974	12.2	1.2	36.3	13.5	4.6	27.2	0.0
New Orleans	364	2,537	210.4	62.9	6,570	26,033,023	13.9	33.2	9.9	2.7	8.0	23.7	1.6
Shreveport	252	2,069	184.1	54.8	2,841	10,287,795	8.1	28.1	26.4	6.9	2.4	18.7	7.2
Slidell	83	392	28.4	8.2	294	1,068,129	19.4	46.5	0.0	11.4	0.0	18.5	0.0
MAINE	2,041	9,424	881.5	242.9	X	X	X	X	X	X	X	X	X
Bangor	71	499	47.6	12.4	1,172	4,803,542	4.3	9.1	8.0	17.8	2.9	5.2	50.9
Lewiston	60	355	30.1	8.5	1,063	4,275,573	4.7	10.1	8.1	4.7	0.9	4.1	64.8
Portland	167	1,005	87.6	26.5	2,667	11,280,661	5.1	9.2	9.4	4.1	13.4	3.5	50.8
South Portland	63	561	29.1	10.6	774	2,806,318	7.4	11.7	11.2	5.1	0.2	9.9	54.4
MARYLAND	7,877	57,077	5,195.8	1,677.9	X	X	X	X	X	X	X	X	X
Annapolis	153	1,410	122.6	50.1	620	3,140,557	12.6	28.5	24.6	16.2	0.0	13.6	0.0
Baltimore	682	6,054	643.0	173.9	26,392	122,552,640	6.0	16.4	7.7	3.4	7.5	8.8	48.9
Bowie	43	274	19.4	6.5	332	1,491,481	15.5	19.2	0.0	6.4	9.8	36.4	0.0
College Park	45	300	26.5	9.3	308	540,180	25.6	19.0	0.0	6.4	12.3	21.9	0.0
Frederick	147	996	81.8	25.1	560	2,537,922	10.7	39.5	0.0	8.4	5.7	23.2	0.0
Gaithersburg	133	875	110.8	28.8	303	1,564,921	28.1	25.0	0.0	16.4	6.3	21.9	0.0
Hagerstown	81	428	34.6	11.4	445	2,038,054	10.3	26.5	16.9	6.9	0.7	32.9	0.0
Laurel	51	465	33.5	12.3	197	975,036	19.1	49.9	0.0	7.4	0.0	18.1	0.0
Rockville	185	1,289	135.0	38.5	652	3,046,807	18.3	18.4	0.0	9.1	8.6	45.6	0.0
Salisbury	83	757	60.2	19.3	375	1,345,111	6.4	35.5	18.2	7.5	4.4	26.4	0.0
MASSACHUSETTS	11,154	67,531	5,985.4	1,892.2	X	X	X	X	X	X	X	X	X
Agawam Town	46	197	22.9	5.6	958	3,825,533	4.3	9.2	8.3	3.0	2.5	2.9	64.5
Attleboro	67	272	24.0	6.7	1,376	5,707,365	4.1	9.4	7.8	1.4	1.4	7.2	68.0
Barnstable Town	119	629	54.1	17.3	1,040	5,101,618	12.3	17.0	0.0	7.1	2.3	6.5	50.4

1. Establishments subject to federal tax.

Table D. Cities — City Government Finances

AREANAME	General revenue Total (mil dol) 117	Intergovernmental Total (mil dol) 118	Intergovernmental Percent from state government 119	Taxes Total (mil dol) 120	Taxes Per capita (dollars) Total 121	Taxes Per capita (dollars) Property 122	Taxes Per capita (dollars) Sales and gross receipts 123	General expenditure Total (mil dol) 124	General expenditure Per capita (dollars) Total 125	General expenditure Capital outlays 126
KANSAS	X	X	X	X	X	X	X	X	X	X
Dodge City	42.1	4.4	73.2	19.0	676	272	403	61.8	2,199	497
Garden City	32.6	5.3	13.6	13.7	508	224	285	32.2	1,196	137
Hutchinson	47.8	10.1	16.6	24.0	572	287	285	36.3	867	15
Kansas City	345.7	20.8	59.0	197.9	1,342	609	724	304.9	2,068	35
Lawrence	300.0	35.4	66.1	51.1	569	251	318	265.3	2,952	315
Leavenworth	35.9	6.9	24.9	18.7	523	329	194	39.7	1,108	180
Leawood	52.4	9.2	26.4	36.5	1,121	518	604	38.2	1,173	233
Lenexa	84.1	15.1	53.5	48.4	979	537	442	101.5	2,056	664
Manhattan	75.3	14.5	19.2	38.3	675	346	329	70.4	1,243	66
Olathe	165.1	23.5	34.3	90.7	697	288	410	149.2	1,147	163
Overland Park	224.8	42.2	25.4	90.5	506	129	377	208.7	1,166	223
Salina	68.5	10.3	26.4	25.7	535	240	295	75.4	1,572	264
Shawnee	54.4	10.0	26.2	38.6	607	330	277	48.9	769	62
Topeka	206.4	27.9	31.8	106.8	835	320	515	153.6	1,201	139
Wichita	562.5	102.8	20.6	167.5	435	306	129	543.6	1,410	223
KENTUCKY	X	X	X	X	X	X	X	X	X	X
Bowling Green	98.4	10.3	24.6	55.7	916	177	90	76.0	1,251	71
Covington	71.2	13.5	27.4	40.2	989	171	183	54.8	1,350	183
Elizabethtown	45.8	8.2	36.9	25.3	863	132	268	37.6	1,280	347
Florence	43.3	5.6	79.1	28.8	928	238	141	28.8	926	346
Frankfort	67.6	2.6	55.3	25.5	937	148	150	57.0	2,091	104
Georgetown	46.6	3.3	36.0	15.8	523	64	100	38.6	1,277	68
Henderson	46.8	13.7	10.5	17.3	597	254	172	40.9	1,415	213
Hopkinsville	42.0	7.0	7.7	23.2	702	139	127	37.4	1,128	88
Jeffersontown	25.4	1.1	76.1	17.1	637	144	99	23.6	876	92
Lexington-Fayette	544.8	60.2	29.6	318.9	1,045	282	143	440.5	1,443	142
Louisville/Jefferson County	935.3	222.4	25.0	456.1	753	225	93	992.9	1,640	335
Nicholasville	20.8	2.5	72.9	13.4	473	139	110	18.1	638	35
Owensboro	98.3	27.0	14.9	35.0	602	166	123	105.2	1,812	630
Paducah	63.2	11.9	37.1	32.6	1,297	237	164	49.1	1,954	263
Richmond	34.6	1.4	35.9	20.5	631	93	132	25.5	785	137
LOUISIANA	X	X	X	X	X	X	X	X	X	X
Alexandria	82.5	13.7	28.9	53.7	1,121	153	967	92.8	1,936	198
Baton Rouge	959.1	199.4	55.2	458.1	1,992	692	1,300	1,203.6	5,233	1,750
Bossier City	108.4	8.2	55.5	71.3	1,090	181	909	129.1	1,975	823
Central	9.1	0.3	100.0	8.6	313	0	313	4.7	169	2
Houma	411.9	103.8	73.9	117.3	3,483	1,624	1,859	430.0	12,764	2,321
Kenner	77.5	40.2	21.3	22.2	332	125	207	70.3	1,050	164
Lafayette	402.4	70.2	47.1	201.1	1,631	828	803	443.4	3,597	882
Lake Charles	116.9	27.3	9.2	70.1	952	108	845	117.0	1,590	348
Monroe	129.3	28.8	34.5	77.5	1,564	218	1,346	140.8	2,843	755
New Iberia	32.2	4.6	29.3	21.4	693	131	562	42.4	1,376	297
New Orleans	1,505.1	535.6	44.1	499.4	1,349	692	647	1,604.4	4,334	1,371
Shreveport	369.6	59.6	35.0	209.5	1,037	312	725	315.2	1,560	169
Slidell	55.2	15.5	65.5	27.4	1,001	202	798	55.1	2,012	612
MAINE	X	X	X	X	X	X	X	X	X	X
Bangor	131.1	38.3	93.4	54.2	1,653	1,624	29	165.2	5,035	1,527
Lewiston	117.7	52.6	84.0	49.4	1,355	1,342	13	112.8	3,095	292
Portland	318.6	71.3	78.7	144.3	2,178	2,129	49	329.4	4,972	746
South Portland	82.8	11.7	92.5	61.0	2,430	2,411	20	82.1	3,270	347
MARYLAND	X	X	X	X	X	X	X	X	X	X
Annapolis	82.8	14.6	35.6	43.3	1,125	985	140	65.6	1,703	14
Baltimore	3,407.6	1,720.1	81.7	1,238.8	1,989	1,226	267	3,659.5	5,874	527
Bowie	46.8	10.8	16.7	27.6	491	444	47	42.1	748	0
College Park	15.3	2.1	19.1	9.8	315	239	76	14.1	451	4
Frederick	90.8	14.2	14.9	46.5	700	655	45	84.6	1,273	9
Gaithersburg	54.0	13.4	7.5	31.2	495	390	104	49.4	783	40
Hagerstown	57.3	7.1	21.8	26.1	645	527	114	50.2	1,239	16
Laurel	29.2	4.0	20.5	20.5	800	757	43	25.4	992	3
Rockville	92.8	17.8	12.0	40.8	644	553	86	94.1	1,486	5
Salisbury	51.7	5.3	32.3	22.5	725	675	49	39.7	1,279	49
MASSACHUSETTS	X	X	X	X	X	X	X	X	X	X
Agawam Town	84.8	27.5	99.5	50.0	1,745	1,720	26	102.8	3,589	65
Attleboro	126.9	47.0	97.8	61.9	1,412	1,380	32	113.5	2,593	116
Barnstable Town	177.7	41.0	87.9	109.9	2,458	2,319	139	175.2	3,917	633

1. Based on population estimated as of July 1 of the year shown.

AREANAME	Public welfare	Highways	Parking facilities	Education	Health and hospitals	Police protection	Sewerage and sanitation	Parks and recreation	Housing and community development	Interest on debt
					City government finances, 2012 (cont.)					
					General expenditures (cont.)					
					Percent of total for:					
	127	128	129	130	131	132	133	134	135	136
KANSAS	X	X	X	X	X	X	X	X	X	X
Dodge City	0.0	1.2	0.0	0.0	0.8	7.8	35.2	17.9	0.0	16.3
Garden City	0.0	11.0	0.0	0.0	0.0	19.9	11.8	14.6	0.0	1.0
Hutchinson	0.0	4.4	0.0	0.0	1.3	22.1	23.3	12.7	0.0	3.8
Kansas City	0.0	2.6	0.2	0.0	3.4	15.9	7.5	2.3	1.5	23.3
Lawrence	0.0	2.7	0.5	0.0	59.4	5.5	8.3	3.1	1.3	2.8
Leavenworth	0.0	10.0	0.0	0.0	0.0	17.1	12.8	5.5	9.0	2.9
Leawood	0.0	22.0	0.0	0.0	0.0	21.4	0.0	17.6	0.0	6.5
Lenexa	0.0	20.0	0.0	0.0	0.0	12.2	3.8	8.5	0.0	16.9
Manhattan	0.0	6.3	0.0	0.0	1.1	17.5	8.4	8.0	1.8	12.6
Olathe	0.0	15.8	0.0	0.0	0.2	13.0	15.5	3.6	0.0	9.4
Overland Park	0.0	21.1	0.0	0.0	0.0	14.4	2.5	5.2	0.0	25.8
Salina	0.0	9.2	0.0	0.0	1.6	11.2	10.5	9.0	5.0	11.5
Shawnee	0.0	12.9	0.0	0.0	0.0	24.3	6.3	9.2	0.0	18.0
Topeka	1.1	9.1	1.4	0.0	0.0	20.4	12.2	10.5	1.5	7.1
Wichita	0.0	13.4	0.0	0.0	0.7	13.7	8.7	4.9	0.0	31.2
KENTUCKY	X	X	X	X	X	X	X	X	X	X
Bowling Green	0.0	9.4	0.0	0.0	0.0	12.0	10.5	10.4	6.4	20.5
Covington	0.0	7.9	3.6	0.0	0.0	19.6	4.0	2.4	21.8	12.5
Elizabethtown	0.0	9.8	0.1	0.0	0.0	10.7	9.3	8.0	0.0	3.4
Florence	0.0	44.2	0.0	0.0	0.0	16.0	5.1	0.0	0.0	10.7
Frankfort	0.0	3.8	0.0	0.0	5.8	7.9	12.9	5.0	0.0	2.6
Georgetown	0.2	3.1	0.0	0.0	0.0	7.8	10.8	2.3	1.1	49.3
Henderson	0.0	5.4	0.0	0.0	0.0	9.2	27.0	2.5	13.3	1.8
Hopkinsville	0.7	5.7	0.0	0.0	0.0	20.8	13.6	1.2	13.7	14.5
Jeffersontown	0.0	9.1	0.0	0.0	0.0	23.5	4.4	2.6	2.8	37.7
Lexington-Fayette	2.0	2.5	0.3	0.0	3.6	10.8	15.8	4.0	1.1	4.1
Louisville/Jefferson County	1.2	6.8	7.9	5.7	3.3	10.2	1.5	5.7	6.5	9.9
Nicholasville	0.0	18.8	0.0	0.0	0.0	22.5	18.6	0.0	0.0	5.0
Owensboro	0.0	5.3	0.2	0.0	0.0	7.1	17.8	7.1	27.9	10.8
Paducah	0.0	8.5	0.0	3.6	0.0	12.3	6.2	4.9	18.9	2.5
Richmond	0.0	3.7	0.0	0.0	0.0	13.5	29.4	8.7	7.4	15.3
LOUISIANA	X	X	X	X	X	X	X	X	X	X
Alexandria	0.0	13.7	0.0	0.0	0.0	18.0	11.3	3.8	8.9	3.0
Baton Rouge	0.2	8.7	0.1	1.3	8.7	10.5	28.4	2.0	5.2	5.2
Bossier City	0.0	1.7	0.0	0.0	0.4	15.1	16.6	5.5	6.7	5.7
Central	0.0	4.9	0.0	0.0	2.1	3.8	0.0	0.0	0.0	0.0
Houma	0.4	4.2	0.0	0.0	41.2	6.3	5.5	2.3	1.7	1.6
Kenner	0.0	19.8	0.0	0.0	0.2	23.7	14.3	6.4	1.0	2.8
Lafayette	0.2	7.6	0.2	0.0	1.4	12.7	9.1	6.0	5.0	8.8
Lake Charles	0.7	13.5	0.0	0.0	0.5	14.4	17.5	8.9	13.5	3.4
Monroe	0.1	4.4	0.0	0.0	0.0	13.1	9.8	5.7	17.4	5.8
New Iberia	0.4	16.2	0.0	0.0	0.0	14.0	25.5	5.1	10.0	4.0
New Orleans	0.2	7.6	0.1	0.0	0.8	8.9	13.7	5.5	15.5	5.9
Shreveport	0.0	4.5	0.2	0.0	0.0	18.2	14.6	9.9	7.6	4.3
Slidell	0.0	11.7	0.0	0.0	0.7	14.9	13.3	2.9	10.4	1.7
MAINE	X	X	X	X	X	X	X	X	X	X
Bangor	0.0	0.0	0.4	26.4	2.3	4.8	3.0	22.8	0.9	2.0
Lewiston	0.9	3.4	0.0	49.5	0.0	5.9	6.7	0.6	1.5	5.2
Portland	7.7	5.4	0.6	30.3	1.3	4.1	8.1	2.0	1.0	5.2
South Portland	0.3	4.6	0.0	52.3	0.0	5.4	11.2	4.3	0.0	1.6
MARYLAND	X	X	X	X	X	X	X	X	X	X
Annapolis	0.0	7.2	2.3	0.0	0.0	25.6	12.0	5.3	0.0	5.0
Baltimore	0.0	5.7	0.8	38.4	3.3	10.2	6.6	1.6	2.1	1.4
Bowie	0.0	11.4	0.0	0.0	0.5	17.6	23.4	16.4	0.1	1.5
College Park	0.0	22.3	1.0	0.0	0.6	7.3	18.8	9.4	1.5	2.1
Frederick	0.0	10.8	3.8	0.0	0.0	30.2	13.3	9.7	0.6	5.8
Gaithersburg	0.0	8.4	0.0	0.0	1.2	15.6	4.7	20.3	1.6	11.6
Hagerstown	0.0	5.9	1.4	0.0	0.0	23.0	29.3	6.2	1.0	2.0
Laurel	0.0	4.9	0.0	0.0	0.0	34.6	4.6	9.1	0.2	1.9
Rockville	0.0	12.9	2.9	0.0	0.4	17.1	13.5	19.7	4.1	4.0
Salisbury	0.0	9.1	1.5	0.0	0.5	25.3	23.5	5.2	2.1	3.6
MASSACHUSETTS	X	X	X	X	X	X	X	X	X	X
Agawam Town	0.1	2.9	0.0	52.9	1.8	4.2	4.3	0.8	0.0	0.8
Attleboro	0.6	3.1	0.0	63.9	0.2	5.5	8.6	1.4	0.5	2.3
Barnstable Town	0.2	2.3	0.0	45.7	0.6	6.2	4.5	2.8	0.2	2.5

AREANAME	City government finances, 2012 (cont.)			Climate[2]						
	Debt outstanding			Average daily temperature						
				Mean		Limits				
	Total (mil dol)	Per capita[1] (dollars)	Debt issued during year	January	July	January[3]	July[4]	Annual precipitation (inches)	Heating degree days	Cooling degree days
	137	138	139	140	141	142	143	144	145	146
KANSAS..........	X	X	X	X	X	X	X	X	X	X
Dodge City......	220.7	7,857	12.2	30.1	79.8	18.7	92.8	22.35	5,037	1,481
Garden City......	42.2	1,564	3.5	28.6	77.8	14.7	92.1	18.77	5,423	1,191
Hutchinson......	54.3	1,294	5.6	28.5	79.9	17.0	92.7	30.32	5,146	1,454
Kansas City......	1,786.2	12,115	126.8	29.1	79.0	19.9	89.4	40.17	4,847	1,406
Lawrence......	287.4	3,197	46.3	29.9	80.2	20.5	90.6	39.78	4,685	1,582
Leavenworth......	32.8	917	10.5	26.6	79.1	16.4	89.8	40.94	5,331	1,356
Leawood......	60.6	1,863	5.3	29.1	79.0	19.9	89.4	40.17	4,847	1,406
Lenexa......	280.1	5,672	46.2	29.1	79.0	19.9	89.4	40.17	4,847	1,406
Manhattan......	344.8	6,084	41.3	27.8	79.9	16.1	92.5	34.80	5,120	1,465
Olathe......	1,141.4	8,779	55.5	29.1	79.0	19.9	89.4	40.17	4,847	1,406
Overland Park......	1,428.3	7,983	15.2	29.1	79.0	19.9	89.4	40.17	4,847	1,406
Salina......	168.5	3,513	22.8	29.0	81.3	18.8	93.3	32.19	4,952	1,600
Shawnee......	215.7	3,390	22.2	29.1	79.0	19.9	89.4	40.17	4,847	1,406
Topeka......	364.4	2,850	72.6	27.2	78.4	17.2	89.1	35.64	5,225	1,357
Wichita......	3,471.3	9,003	335.8	30.2	81.0	20.3	92.9	30.38	4,765	1,658
KENTUCKY..........	X	X	X	X	X	X	X	X	X	X
Bowling Green......	283.6	4,667	7.1	34.2	78.5	25.4	89.2	51.63	4,243	1,413
Covington......	162.2	3,993	3.6	32.0	76.1	24.1	85.9	45.91	4,713	1,154
Elizabethtown......	55.2	1,880	18.5	NA	NA	NA	NA	NA	NA	NA
Florence......	69.3	2,230	3.1	NA	NA	NA	NA	NA	NA	NA
Frankfort......	46.6	1,711	0.0	30.3	75.2	20.8	86.9	43.56	5,129	994
Georgetown......	473.4	15,642	0.0	NA	NA	NA	NA	NA	NA	NA
Henderson......	50.4	1,744	15.8	32.6	77.6	23.6	88.4	44.77	4,374	1,344
Hopkinsville......	170.2	5,136	12.2	33.2	78.2	24.4	88.5	50.92	4,298	1,433
Jeffersontown......	160.3	5,960	0.0	33.0	78.4	24.9	87.0	44.54	4,352	1,443
Lexington-Fayette......	1,000.4	3,277	37.3	31.6	75.9	22.5	86.3	46.39	4,769	1,094
Louisville/Jefferson County.	1,594.3	2,633	310.5	NA	NA	NA	NA	NA	NA	NA
Nicholasville......	32.1	1,130	3.5	NA	NA	NA	NA	NA	NA	NA
Owensboro......	399.8	6,888	55.2	33.5	79.2	24.4	90.7	46.53	4,159	1,565
Paducah......	39.7	1,583	6.6	35.2	79.9	27.2	90.8	46.04	3,893	1,635
Richmond......	104.2	3,208	2.7	34.7	75.8	25.6	87.0	47.33	4,231	1,150
LOUISIANA..........	X	X	X	X	X	X	X	X	X	X
Alexandria......	94.9	1,980	2.6	48.1	83.3	38.0	92.8	61.44	1,908	2,602
Baton Rouge......	1,639.8	7,130	219.4	50.1	81.7	40.2	90.7	63.08	1,689	2,628
Bossier City......	360.5	5,513	5.7	48.3	81.0	37.4	91.0	61.06	1,981	2,220
Central......	0.0	0	0.0	NA	NA	NA	NA	NA	NA	NA
Houma......	213.1	6,326	64.3	53.1	82.5	43.4	90.7	63.67	1,346	2,804
Kenner......	61.5	919	19.6	52.6	82.7	43.4	91.1	64.16	1,417	2,773
Lafayette......	1,132.6	9,186	183.7	51.3	82.2	41.6	91.2	60.54	1,531	2,671
Lake Charles......	92.3	1,253	3.7	50.9	82.6	41.2	91.0	57.19	1,546	2,705
Monroe......	177.3	3,581	34.9	44.6	83.0	33.5	94.1	58.04	2,399	2,311
New Iberia......	38.7	1,257	24.3	51.3	82.3	41.4	91.1	60.89	1,544	2,680
New Orleans......	2,018.9	5,454	51.5	52.7	82.2	43.3	90.9	65.15	1,416	2,686
Shreveport......	540.8	2,676	85.6	46.4	83.4	36.5	93.3	51.30	2,251	2,405
Slidell......	25.1	916	0.0	50.7	82.1	40.2	91.1	62.66	1,652	2,548
MAINE..........	X	X	X	X	X	X	X	X	X	X
Bangor......	109.4	3,335	32.1	18.0	69.2	8.3	79.6	39.57	7,676	313
Lewiston......	152.4	4,182	7.6	20.5	71.4	11.5	81.5	45.79	7,107	465
Portland......	423.0	6,384	38.7	21.7	68.7	12.5	78.8	45.83	7,318	347
South Portland......	50.1	1,994	30.0	NA	NA	NA	NA	NA	NA	NA
MARYLAND..........	X	X	X	X	X	X	X	X	X	X
Annapolis......	96.8	2,513	0.0	32.8	77.5	23.8	87.7	44.78	4,695	1,162
Baltimore......	2,621.6	4,208	13.3	36.8	81.7	29.4	90.6	43.59	4,720	1,147
Bowie......	18.0	320	0.1	31.8	75.2	21.2	87.1	44.66	4,970	917
College Park......	8.4	269	0.0	NA	NA	NA	NA	NA	NA	NA
Frederick......	224.2	3,375	31.4	33.3	77.9	25.1	88.9	40.64	4,430	1,272
Gaithersburg......	142.6	2,261	0.0	31.8	75.3	23.8	85.4	43.08	4,990	983
Hagerstown......	66.0	1,630	7.9	29.3	75.2	20.8	86.1	39.45	5,249	902
Laurel......	10.1	396	0.1	NA	NA	NA	NA	NA	NA	NA
Rockville......	135.9	2,144	40.7	31.8	75.3	23.8	85.4	43.08	4,990	983
Salisbury......	70.9	2,286	15.2	NA	NA	NA	NA	NA	NA	NA
MASSACHUSETTS..........	X	X	X	X	X	X	X	X	X	X
Agawam Town......	25.0	871	6.2	NA	NA	NA	NA	NA	NA	NA
Attleboro......	72.7	1,660	1.5	27.4	72.2	17.8	83.0	48.34	6,012	558
Barnstable Town......	131.5	2,941	18.5	29.2	70.5	21.2	77.8	43.03	6,026	413

1. Based on the population estimated as of July 1 of the year shown.   2. Represents normal values based on the 30-year period, 1971±2000.   3. Average daily minimum.   4. Average daily maximum.

STATE Place code	AREANAME	Land area[1] (sq. mi)	Total persons 2017	Rank	Per square mile	White	Black or African American	American Indian, Alaskan Native	Asian	Hawaiian Pacific Islander	Some other race	Two or more races (percent)
		1	2	3	4	5	6	7	8	9	10	11
	MASSACHUSETTS—Cont'd											
25 05,595	Beverly	15.1	41,816	906	2,769.3	92.7	1.0	0.0	2.7	0.0	0.9	2.8
25 07,000	Boston	48.3	685,094	21	14,184.1	53.2	25.8	0.3	9.8	0.0	5.2	5.7
25 07,740	Braintree Town	13.8	37,156	1,028	2,692.5	84.5	4.1	0.3	8.2	0.0	1.0	1.9
25 09,000	Brockton	21.3	95,672	325	4,491.6	39.0	40.7	0.3	0.9	0.0	16.4	2.7
25 11,000	Cambridge	6.4	113,630	252	17,754.7	63.7	11.4	0.5	17.9	0.0	1.8	4.6
25 13,205	Chelsea	2.2	40,227	948	18,285.0	41.9	5.1	0.0	3.2	0.0	10.9	38.9
25 13,660	Chicopee	22.8	55,515	679	2,434.9	86.1	5.1	0.0	3.1	0.0	4.7	1.0
25 21,990	Everett	3.4	46,324	831	13,624.7	53.9	23.2	0.5	10.6	0.1	9.8	2.0
25 23,000	Fall River	33.1	89,420	365	2,701.5	78.5	5.0	0.0	1.7	0.0	10.4	4.3
25 23,875	Fitchburg	27.8	40,793	929	1,467.4	80.1	3.2	0.0	3.0	0.0	9.7	4.0
25 25,172	Franklin Town	26.6	32,996	1,149	1,240.5	NA	NA	NA	NA	NA	NA	NA
25 26,150	Gloucester	26.2	30,172	1,246	1,151.6	NA	NA	NA	NA	NA	NA	NA
25 29,405	Haverhill	33.0	63,639	579	1,928.5	84.7	2.5	0.1	2.5	0.2	8.3	1.8
25 30,840	Holyoke	21.3	40,341	942	1,893.9	87.0	3.9	0.3	1.7	0.0	5.9	1.3
25 34,550	Lawrence	6.9	80,162	427	11,617.7	68.3	5.7	0.6	1.9	0.0	20.9	2.6
25 35,075	Leominster	28.8	41,615	911	1,445.0	79.8	4.2	0.2	2.3	0.0	10.9	2.6
25 37,000	Lowell	13.6	111,346	262	8,187.2	60.4	8.1	0.6	23.1	0.2	5.4	2.2
25 37,490	Lynn	10.7	94,063	338	8,790.9	45.5	11.7	0.4	7.1	0.2	28.9	6.2
25 37,875	Malden	5.0	61,246	605	12,249.2	60.4	18.9	0.0	15.4	0.0	3.9	1.4
25 38,715	Marlborough	20.9	39,873	954	1,907.8	78.1	3.8	0.0	5.9	0.0	10.5	1.8
25 39,835	Medford	8.1	57,797	651	7,135.4	75.6	9.6	0.0	10.7	0.0	1.4	2.7
25 40,115	Melrose	4.7	28,367	1,309	6,035.5	NA	NA	NA	NA	NA	NA	NA
25 40,710	Methuen Town	22.2	50,259	757	2,263.9	77.4	3.4	0.0	4.8	0.0	11.1	3.3
25 45,000	New Bedford	20.0	95,120	328	4,756.0	64.2	6.8	0.1	1.9	0.1	22.9	4.0
25 45,560	Newton	17.8	88,994	368	4,999.7	76.9	2.2	0.2	13.8	0.0	3.3	3.5
25 46,330	Northampton	34.2	28,593	1,301	836.1	86.2	3.0	0.0	2.9	0.0	1.0	6.9
25 52,490	Peabody	16.2	52,987	724	3,270.8	92.7	3.1	0.0	0.9	0.0	1.9	1.5
25 53,960	Pittsfield	40.5	42,591	893	1,051.6	88.7	4.3	0.0	1.3	0.0	1.4	4.3
25 55,745	Quincy	16.6	94,166	336	5,672.7	59.2	5.1	0.4	30.9	0.0	0.8	3.6
25 56,585	Revere	5.7	53,993	708	9,472.5	75.6	5.8	0.8	2.6	0.0	6.1	9.1
25 59,105	Salem	8.3	43,415	873	5,230.7	75.2	7.3	0.9	0.9	0.0	11.6	4.1
25 62,535	Somerville	4.1	81,360	416	19,843.9	73.1	7.0	0.3	11.0	0.0	6.1	2.5
25 67,000	Springfield	31.9	154,758	165	4,851.3	66.0	21.1	0.2	1.9	0.0	5.8	4.9
25 69,170	Taunton	46.7	57,139	657	1,223.5	81.9	9.4	0.0	1.1	0.0	5.7	1.9
25 72,600	Waltham	12.7	62,442	592	4,916.7	70.6	7.4	0.0	11.2	0.0	6.5	4.3
25 73,440	Watertown Town	4.0	35,756	1,071	8,939.0	79.0	0.5	0.2	10.1	0.0	7.8	2.4
25 76,030	Westfield	46.3	41,700	909	900.6	NA	NA	NA	NA	NA	NA	NA
25 77,890	West Springfield Town	16.7	28,704	1,296	1,718.8	89.0	1.4	0.3	5.7	0.0	2.2	1.4
25 78,972	Weymouth Town	16.8	56,664	664	3,372.9	86.2	6.8	0.0	5.5	0.0	1.2	0.5
25 81,035	Woburn	12.6	39,701	960	3,150.9	80.8	3.8	0.0	9.2	0.0	4.3	2.0
25 82,000	Worcester	37.4	185,677	132	4,964.6	66.4	14.5	0.4	7.8	0.0	7.6	3.3
26 00,000	MICHIGAN	56,559.4	9,962,311	X	176.1	78.5	13.7	0.5	2.9	0.0	1.2	3.1
26 01,380	Allen Park	7.0	27,156	1,352	3,879.4	91.5	2.9	0.2	0.0	0.0	1.6	3.8
26 03,000	Ann Arbor	27.9	121,477	230	4,354.0	71.2	6.3	0.0	15.9	0.1	0.9	5.6
26 05,920	Battle Creek	42.6	51,286	747	1,203.9	70.4	18.0	0.6	1.1	0.0	1.3	8.6
26 06,020	Bay City	10.2	33,188	1,146	3,253.7	NA	NA	NA	NA	NA	NA	NA
26 12,060	Burton	23.4	28,643	1,298	1,224.1	91.7	3.6	0.2	1.5	0.0	0.1	2.9
26 21,000	Dearborn	24.2	94,491	333	3,904.6	84.5	10.5	0.0	1.3	0.0	0.7	3.0
26 21,020	Dearborn Heights	11.7	55,758	677	4,765.6	84.5	10.5	0.0	1.3	0.0	0.7	3.0
26 22,000	Detroit	138.7	673,104	23	4,852.9	13.6	79.1	0.3	1.8	0.0	3.5	1.7
26 24,120	East Lansing	13.4	48,844	783	3,645.1	71.8	8.6	0.3	16.0	0.0	0.4	2.9
26 24,290	Eastpointe	5.2	32,511	1,165	6,252.1	NA	NA	NA	NA	NA	NA	NA
26 27,440	Farmington Hills	33.3	81,050	418	2,433.9	67.2	20.2	0.0	10.0	0.0	0.4	2.2
26 29,000	Flint	33.4	96,448	320	2,887.7	41.5	52.8	0.3	0.3	0.0	0.8	4.3
26 31,420	Garden City	5.9	26,650	1,375	4,516.9	NA	NA	NA	NA	NA	NA	NA
26 34,000	Grand Rapids	44.4	198,829	119	4,478.1	66.8	18.7	0.4	2.2	0.0	5.9	5.9
26 38,640	Holland	16.7	33,366	1,137	1,998.0	83.7	3.5	0.3	3.9	0.0	4.5	4.1
26 40,680	Inkster	6.3	24,453	1,426	3,881.4	16.6	67.8	4.3	1.2	0.0	0.0	10.1
26 41,420	Jackson	10.9	32,704	1,163	3,000.4	70.2	24.2	0.1	0.0	0.1	2.0	3.4
26 42,160	Kalamazoo	24.7	75,807	462	3,069.1	71.3	19.8	0.0	1.7	0.0	0.8	6.4
26 42,820	Kentwood	20.9	51,747	738	2,475.9	60.7	21.7	0.1	11.9	0.0	2.4	3.2
26 46,000	Lansing	39.2	116,986	239	2,984.3	61.0	22.2	0.6	3.7	0.2	2.9	9.4
26 47,800	Lincoln Park	5.9	36,655	1,043	6,212.7	67.3	12.3	0.0	0.8	0.0	13.6	6.0
26 49,000	Livonia	35.7	94,105	337	2,636.0	89.2	5.5	0.0	3.1	0.1	0.1	2.0
26 50,560	Madison Heights	7.1	30,050	1,249	4,232.4	74.7	6.3	1.2	7.1	0.0	4.4	6.4
26 53,780	Midland	34.4	41,950	903	1,219.5	90.5	2.4	0.2	4.0	0.0	0.0	2.9
26 56,020	Mount Pleasant	7.7	25,847	1,399	3,356.8	84.1	2.5	1.6	3.9	0.0	0.1	7.7
26 56,320	Muskegon	14.1	38,131	1,002	2,704.3	55.3	33.7	1.0	0.4	0.0	1.0	8.5
26 59,440	Novi	30.2	59,715	627	1,977.3	64.2	7.4	0.7	23.3	0.0	2.2	2.2

1. Dry land or land partially or temporarily covered by water. 2. Hispanic or Latino persons may be of any race.

Table D. Cities — **Population**

AREANAME	Percent Hispanic or Latino[1], 2016	Percent foreign born, 2016	Age of population (percent), 2016							Median age 2016	Percent female 2016	Population Census counts		Percent change	
			Under 18 years	18 to 24 years	25 to 34 years	35 to 44 years	45 to 54 years	55 to 64 years	65 years and over			2000	2010	2000-2010	2010-2017
	12	13	14	15	16	17	18	19	20	21	22	23	24	25	26
MASSACHUSETTS—Cont'd															
Beverly	4.0	7.9	18.6	14.4	11.1	11.7	15.8	13.8	14.6	40.1	49.3	39,862	39,502	-0.9	5.9
Boston	19.1	28.9	16.1	15.0	24.3	12.5	10.9	10.1	11.0	32.1	52.0	589,141	617,725	4.9	10.9
Braintree Town	2.0	15.4	22.4	7.6	8.8	15.9	13.5	15.8	16.0	42.4	55.8	33,698	35,726	6.0	4.0
Brockton	12.3	34.3	26.3	9.0	13.5	12.4	12.3	12.6	13.8	35.6	52.1	94,304	93,763	-0.6	2.0
Cambridge	9.6	32.5	11.9	21.0	27.9	11.0	7.7	8.3	12.2	30.2	51.2	101,355	105,201	3.8	8.0
Chelsea	68.0	45.3	26.9	6.0	18.2	18.7	13.6	7.7	8.7	34.1	48.5	35,080	35,177	0.3	14.4
Chicopee	22.0	9.8	21.2	8.2	15.0	11.5	12.8	11.8	19.5	39.3	53.3	54,653	55,298	1.2	0.4
Everett	24.1	43.5	22.0	6.7	22.3	13.6	14.4	9.2	11.7	34.5	52.7	38,037	41,664	9.5	11.2
Fall River	11.9	19.6	21.5	8.8	14.3	14.5	11.0	12.1	17.9	39.6	51.6	91,938	88,857	-3.4	0.6
Fitchburg	26.8	11.4	19.6	12.7	12.7	14.0	14.4	13.3	13.3	40.0	49.6	39,102	40,318	3.1	1.2
Franklin Town	2.2	8.1	24.3	10.1	5.9	12.7	19.1	13.2	14.6	43.3	52.2	29,560	31,633	7.0	4.3
Gloucester	1.9	9.0	13.6	5.5	12.6	10.0	14.0	19.6	24.8	51.0	50.8	30,273	28,789	-4.9	4.8
Haverhill	19.7	9.6	20.3	10.5	14.6	11.9	14.9	15.7	12.2	39.1	53.9	58,969	60,879	3.2	4.5
Holyoke	56.3	6.1	25.3	12.1	15.5	12.4	12.6	11.4	10.7	32.8	48.4	39,838	39,880	0.1	1.2
Lawrence	78.7	40.2	27.4	12.1	15.4	14.0	10.2	10.8	10.1	31.2	50.4	72,043	76,381	6.0	5.0
Leominster	20.6	16.7	22.8	6.9	11.5	12.1	14.3	15.4	17.0	42.6	57.0	41,303	40,759	-1.3	2.1
Lowell	17.1	27.8	22.9	14.6	17.4	11.3	13.8	10.2	9.8	31.7	50.3	105,167	106,519	1.3	4.5
Lynn	41.9	35.9	23.2	8.5	16.4	14.5	12.4	11.3	13.7	35.8	48.5	89,050	90,329	1.4	4.1
Malden	11.7	42.8	20.0	6.5	20.5	12.4	15.2	12.1	13.4	36.4	50.3	56,340	59,460	5.5	3.0
Marlborough	16.3	29.6	16.4	9.6	15.3	10.8	16.2	12.9	18.8	42.6	51.8	36,255	38,499	6.2	3.6
Medford	6.3	21.7	11.5	16.0	21.3	10.8	10.6	15.5	14.3	35.6	51.2	55,765	56,212	0.8	2.8
Melrose	2.4	10.4	22.4	7.5	12.2	17.6	13.3	14.9	12.1	38.0	53.0	27,134	26,993	-0.5	5.1
Methuen Town	30.0	19.8	24.5	9.7	10.7	15.4	13.1	11.7	15.0	37.8	53.2	43,789	47,252	7.9	6.4
New Bedford	19.3	19.6	24.4	8.2	15.4	13.7	12.3	12.0	14.0	36.0	52.3	93,768	95,066	1.4	0.1
Newton	7.0	20.0	23.7	12.2	7.8	12.8	13.7	11.7	18.1	41.1	53.3	83,829	85,079	1.5	4.6
Northampton	9.6	5.4	16.1	16.6	12.4	13.8	11.2	13.9	16.0	38.8	57.1	28,978	28,547	-1.5	0.2
Peabody	6.6	14.7	18.8	7.7	12.3	10.8	12.4	15.3	22.7	45.5	52.5	48,129	51,251	6.5	3.4
Pittsfield	6.8	3.1	15.6	8.4	14.5	9.3	14.3	15.4	22.5	46.3	51.1	45,793	44,738	-2.3	-4.8
Quincy	3.3	33.6	16.4	9.5	19.1	12.4	14.9	12.5	15.3	39.4	52.2	88,025	92,266	4.8	2.1
Revere	34.3	43.6	20.7	8.9	13.4	12.5	16.7	12.1	15.7	40.2	47.1	47,283	51,737	9.4	4.4
Salem	17.6	15.1	15.0	14.1	16.2	9.4	17.1	13.2	15.1	40.1	56.0	40,407	41,340	2.3	5.0
Somerville	11.6	24.3	10.9	15.1	34.5	15.8	7.9	8.5	7.3	31.1	50.7	77,478	75,677	-2.3	7.5
Springfield	43.7	9.7	23.7	13.3	13.6	12.9	12.5	11.8	12.2	33.9	52.9	152,082	153,195	0.7	1.0
Taunton	5.8	12.1	20.2	9.1	16.8	10.8	13.5	14.5	15.2	38.3	53.7	55,976	55,874	-0.2	2.3
Waltham	14.6	29.9	14.0	18.0	16.8	13.9	11.4	12.5	13.3	36.1	52.5	59,226	60,628	2.4	3.0
Watertown Town	8.5	17.1	15.5	7.5	19.9	18.2	13.7	10.7	14.6	39.4	53.7	32,986	31,914	-3.2	12.0
Westfield	5.0	5.4	16.7	18.0	7.3	9.8	15.5	15.5	17.3	43.1	47.3	40,072	41,094	2.6	1.5
West Springfield Town	12.3	16.1	26.2	8.0	15.9	11.6	13.9	11.5	12.8	34.9	49.1	27,899	28,391	1.8	1.1
Weymouth Town	4.1	11.7	19.0	9.2	13.7	13.1	12.1	14.5	18.4	41.2	53.8	53,988	53,762	-0.4	5.4
Woburn	7.1	22.8	18.9	7.8	16.4	14.7	14.7	14.0	13.5	39.5	50.4	37,258	38,134	2.4	4.1
Worcester	20.6	19.9	18.1	15.7	16.4	11.2	13.1	12.1	13.4	34.9	50.5	172,648	180,983	4.8	2.6
MICHIGAN	4.9	6.7	22.1	9.8	12.6	11.7	13.6	14.1	16.2	39.7	50.8	9,938,444	9,884,129	-0.5	0.8
Allen Park	12.1	5.0	21.1	7.4	8.9	13.0	17.6	12.0	20.1	44.8	48.2	29,376	28,198	-4.0	-3.7
Ann Arbor	4.7	19.7	12.3	32.4	16.6	9.6	8.8	8.8	11.5	28.0	49.1	114,024	113,939	-0.1	6.6
Battle Creek	6.2	3.6	24.9	9.3	13.9	10.8	11.8	12.5	16.9	36.2	54.0	53,364	52,392	-1.8	-2.1
Bay City	6.9	2.3	22.3	8.6	14.9	13.3	11.3	12.9	16.7	37.0	48.7	36,817	34,932	-5.1	-5.0
Burton	1.5	0.3	22.3	9.6	14.2	11.1	14.5	13.1	15.2	36.8	54.1	30,308	29,999	-1.0	-4.5
Dearborn	2.4	30.4	28.9	11.5	13.7	11.1	11.6	10.6	12.6	31.4	50.8	97,775	98,148	0.4	-3.7
Dearborn Heights	3.2	19.1	27.6	7.4	15.4	12.3	11.5	12.3	13.6	34.8	51.2	58,264	57,774	-0.8	-3.5
Detroit	7.0	5.9	25.7	10.4	15.0	12.0	11.9	12.3	12.7	34.0	52.3	951,270	713,854	-25.0	-5.7
East Lansing	4.7	18.3	7.8	62.6	10.7	6.6	3.0	3.6	5.7	21.2	48.8	46,525	48,586	4.4	0.5
Eastpointe	1.7	2.9	24.2	10.8	14.9	15.1	11.7	13.1	10.2	35.0	54.4	34,077	32,405	-4.9	0.3
Farmington Hills	1.9	16.2	19.3	8.8	10.2	11.7	16.9	14.6	18.6	45.1	52.4	82,111	79,716	-2.9	1.7
Flint	5.8	1.7	27.6	9.4	14.1	11.7	13.2	12.8	11.3	34.1	53.1	124,943	102,260	-18.2	-5.7
Garden City	4.2	5.3	17.7	8.9	13.5	11.4	18.5	13.5	16.5	43.7	51.2	30,047	27,646	-8.0	-3.6
Grand Rapids	15.2	10.3	23.8	13.1	20.3	10.8	10.3	10.3	11.4	31.1	49.3	197,800	188,040	-4.9	5.7
Holland	16.3	8.1	14.5	20.3	15.0	9.5	12.8	15.5	12.4	35.1	49.6	35,048	33,095	-5.6	0.8
Inkster	7.0	5.7	27.7	10.3	14.2	9.7	10.0	14.2	13.9	34.5	52.6	30,115	25,366	-15.8	-3.6
Jackson	7.6	2.2	27.2	10.7	14.9	10.5	13.7	11.8	11.2	33.3	50.5	36,316	33,479	-7.8	-2.3
Kalamazoo	9.9	4.7	22.2	25.4	12.7	12.5	9.1	8.5	9.6	26.4	50.3	77,145	74,271	-3.7	2.1
Kentwood	15.2	18.5	27.0	9.0	17.4	13.1	11.2	10.3	11.8	32.6	51.9	45,255	48,709	7.6	6.2
Lansing	12.3	6.8	23.2	13.7	17.3	12.3	11.5	11.8	10.2	32.7	52.1	119,128	114,246	-4.1	2.4
Lincoln Park	25.0	10.5	27.3	9.7	12.6	14.2	14.5	12.0	9.7	35.6	53.4	40,008	38,100	-4.8	-3.8
Livonia	3.0	8.0	20.1	7.3	12.2	10.8	14.9	16.9	17.8	44.7	51.6	100,545	96,942	-3.6	-2.9
Madison Heights	5.3	22.1	16.8	6.0	16.8	14.9	14.9	14.3	16.4	42.9	49.8	31,101	29,694	-4.5	1.2
Midland	2.9	5.4	21.5	10.6	14.8	13.4	12.5	11.2	16.1	37.6	52.1	41,685	41,875	0.5	0.2
Mount Pleasant	3.3	6.1	11.6	49.3	11.5	6.4	5.3	8.2	7.8	21.9	55.4	25,946	26,016	0.3	-0.6
Muskegon	10.8	2.7	23.9	10.8	13.7	12.8	12.2	12.5	14.1	36.7	48.4	40,105	38,396	-4.3	-0.7
Novi	3.8	28.2	25.2	7.4	13.2	12.6	15.7	13.3	12.6	37.4	51.9	47,386	55,232	16.6	8.1

1. May be of any race.

AREANAME	Households, 2016								Serious crimes known to police[2], 2016				Educational attainment, 2016		
				Perecnt					Total		Rate[3]			Attainment[4] (percent)	
	Number	Persons per house-hold	Family	Married couple family	Female headed family[1]	Non-family	One person	Persons in group quarters	Number	Rate	Violent	Property	Population age 25 and over	High school graduate or less	Bachelor's degree or more
	27	28	29	30	31	32	33	34	35	36	37	38	39	40	41
MASSACHUSETTS— Cont'd															
Beverly	15,898	2.40	59.3	49.0	5.7	40.7	34.8	3,271	395	956	157	799	27,700	28.4	50.5
Boston	267,592	2.33	47.2	26.9	15.8	52.8	37.2	49,351	19,256	2,857	707	2,150	463,337	34.3	48.4
Braintree Town	13,945	2.64	67.1	50.0	13.6	32.9	29.3	526	754	2,001	239	1,763	26,092	30.1	41.9
Brockton	30,572	3.07	70.3	37.6	27.3	29.7	26.0	1,827	3,324	3,492	1,081	2,411	61,818	57.9	16.9
Cambridge	43,973	2.14	41.8	30.7	6.9	58.2	36.3	16,399	2,665	2,400	265	2,135	74,206	16.7	74.1
Chelsea	12,565	3.10	64.6	25.5	27.4	35.4	26.0	769	1,285	3,205	923	2,282	26,612	59.8	18.4
Chicopee	23,753	2.30	60.1	34.2	20.7	39.9	34.6	NA	1,581	2,779	466	2,313	39,521	50.3	16.0
Everett	16,198	2.85	69.3	39.0	21.5	30.7	26.1	NA	819	1,752	334	1,418	33,011	50.3	19.6
Fall River	37,002	2.36	61.8	38.9	17.1	38.2	32.3	1,435	2,633	2,979	1,094	1,885	61,997	57.5	17.6
Fitchburg	14,933	2.58	61.6	39.7	15.5	38.4	29.4	1,808	1,159	2,869	775	2,095	27,382	54.2	21.1
Franklin Town	11,582	2.77	75.0	66.6	5.6	25.0	21.3	1,061	99	298	3	295	21,728	22.0	55.6
Gloucester	13,344	2.20	61.1	52.7	4.8	38.9	33.5	391	302	1,012	245	768	24,116	30.4	42.3
Haverhill	24,539	2.52	58.6	35.8	17.3	41.4	28.7	975	1,355	2,156	593	1,562	43,482	39.1	27.7
Holyoke	14,310	2.73	60.7	29.8	24.2	39.3	32.8	1,246	2,448	6,009	1,070	4,939	25,210	50.9	25.5
Lawrence	24,566	3.21	69.1	28.5	35.0	30.9	27.6	1,248	2,106	2,612	740	1,872	48,485	66.8	10.9
Leominster	16,593	2.49	64.0	42.7	17.6	36.0	33.1	389	1,211	2,915	650	2,265	29,298	42.8	29.2
Lowell	38,046	2.78	64.6	33.2	23.1	35.4	25.9	4,904	2,587	2,330	342	1,988	69,134	49.9	24.8
Lynn	33,635	2.73	62.2	34.6	19.8	37.8	31.5	816	2,636	2,851	772	2,079	63,351	57.6	17.0
Malden	23,661	2.55	61.5	44.2	10.4	38.5	30.2	NA	886	1,450	277	1,173	44,731	45.1	33.2
Marlborough	15,571	2.51	66.3	54.3	10.7	33.7	24.9	582	722	1,810	401	1,409	29,372	39.5	38.2
Medford	22,724	2.41	56.0	41.8	10.9	44.0	28.7	2,365	759	1,323	155	1,168	41,520	28.8	51.7
Melrose	10,652	2.59	64.7	49.2	9.8	35.3	28.4	296	233	830	68	762	19,584	20.3	57.8
Methuen Town	17,328	2.86	74.3	48.1	17.9	25.7	22.9	435	900	1,803	158	1,645	32,887	38.9	29.0
New Bedford	39,425	2.36	59.6	31.4	22.4	40.4	33.1	2,022	3,735	3,951	855	3,097	64,019	57.9	16.3
Newton	30,309	2.68	71.7	59.9	8.6	28.3	23.7	7,751	688	772	52	720	57,121	12.4	76.6
Northampton	11,536	2.14	49.5	36.8	10.2	50.5	38.9	3,739	727	2,549	438	2,111	19,175	25.0	55.7
Peabody	21,633	2.40	54.7	43.0	9.4	45.3	35.9	580	896	1,707	392	1,314	38,601	37.9	34.7
Pittsfield	20,430	2.05	52.7	31.5	16.7	47.3	38.9	1,040	1,359	3,158	792	2,366	32,556	39.6	26.1
Quincy	39,974	2.32	51.9	36.9	8.8	48.1	37.6	1,136	1,914	2,048	437	1,612	69,479	34.2	46.7
Revere	18,650	2.84	65.5	45.7	12.9	34.5	28.2	272	1,405	2,625	490	2,136	37,436	60.3	21.4
Salem	18,550	2.22	53.0	37.8	12.0	47.0	38.3	1,920	1,164	2,714	305	2,409	30,584	39.4	35.9
Somerville	31,495	2.49	42.6	28.5	8.0	57.4	28.3	3,026	1,413	1,747	255	1,492	60,164	24.3	64.9
Springfield	55,894	2.66	64.3	29.5	28.0	35.7	30.9	5,512	6,664	4,324	1,032	3,293	97,063	53.4	18.0
Taunton	22,987	2.44	63.8	41.1	13.5	36.2	31.0	766	952	1,678	358	1,321	40,224	42.3	25.2
Waltham	22,873	2.42	58.3	44.8	10.3	41.7	30.8	7,615	787	1,237	156	1,082	42,808	29.9	50.2
Watertown Town	15,448	2.26	55.4	43.1	9.3	44.6	34.4	NA	438	1,264	110	1,154	26,969	22.7	63.6
Westfield	15,391	2.46	69.4	54.2	10.1	30.6	27.6	3,649	643	1,542	223	1,319	27,174	38.7	32.0
West Springfield Town	11,434	2.48	58.0	37.4	11.9	42.0	36.1	NA	1,394	4,859	655	4,204	18,746	37.5	25.4
Weymouth Town	23,593	2.35	61.5	39.5	13.3	38.5	30.1	470	688	1,225	287	939	40,159	34.2	36.7
Woburn	15,560	2.52	66.7	50.7	12.1	33.3	25.3	317	528	1,332	207	1,125	28,934	27.1	51.9
Worcester	72,092	2.36	48.3	31.3	13.3	51.7	42.9	14,067	7,010	3,798	892	2,906	122,327	44.3	30.0
MICHIGAN	3,884,153	2.50	63.8	46.8	12.3	36.2	29.7	230,466	235,192	2,369	459	1,910	6,760,402	38.8	28.3
Allen Park	11,245	2.41	64.6	49.5	9.6	35.4	33.4	NA	553	2,027	194	1,833	19,465	37.3	25.2
Ann Arbor	48,343	2.25	45.7	37.7	5.2	54.3	35.8	12,026	2,268	1,927	179	1,748	66,898	8.8	76.5
Battle Creek	20,714	2.42	56.7	33.2	18.3	43.3	39.5	1,329	2,929	4,809	979	3,831	33,922	47.8	18.2
Bay City	13,913	2.38	65.6	40.6	19.2	34.4	28.2	438	1,133	3,360	614	2,746	23,153	44.5	14.8
Burton	11,633	2.45	61.8	40.0	15.4	38.2	31.2	NA	871	3,049	382	2,668	19,524	48.8	14.8
Dearborn	31,162	3.02	67.6	48.7	13.0	32.4	28.6	361	3,145	3,323	367	2,956	56,239	43.7	28.5
Dearborn Heights	18,882	2.93	67.6	40.3	16.8	32.4	27.4	495	1,292	2,313	371	1,943	36,248	49.3	16.2
Detroit	259,295	2.54	53.8	18.6	28.3	46.2	40.1	13,826	45,492	6,793	2,049	4,744	429,990	52.2	14.9
East Lansing	12,715	2.52	36.9	29.7	5.3	63.1	32.8	16,358	837	1,728	239	1,488	14,319	9.0	75.8
Eastpointe	12,469	2.61	62.7	33.6	24.0	37.3	34.7	170	1,328	4,061	816	3,245	21,223	47.1	16.5
Farmington Hills	35,360	2.28	59.7	47.8	9.0	40.3	36.6	685	1,134	1,389	98	1,291	58,407	19.3	52.9
Flint	38,859	2.44	58.0	24.2	27.4	42.0	36.0	2,706	4,888	5,011	1,587	3,424	61,407	52.6	10.5
Garden City	10,766	2.48	60.7	40.0	14.6	39.3	34.3	60	562	2,099	265	1,833	19,615	57.4	9.9
Grand Rapids	73,880	2.55	57.1	37.1	13.9	42.9	30.3	7,911	5,661	2,880	675	2,205	124,064	35.9	36.0
Holland	14,275	2.27	56.1	42.6	7.3	43.9	34.5	3,333	966	2,852	348	2,504	23,249	41.0	25.9
Inkster	9,298	2.60	62.6	21.7	30.6	37.4	32.1	327	1,048	4,269	1,316	2,953	15,159	56.8	9.2
Jackson	12,773	2.51	56.1	25.3	23.8	43.9	38.2	846	1,912	5,783	1,234	4,549	20,444	44.7	17.6
Kalamazoo	27,790	2.48	46.6	26.4	14.5	53.4	37.9	7,017	4,152	5,435	1,212	4,223	39,805	34.2	31.3
Kentwood	18,699	2.74	64.3	44.7	14.7	35.7	27.1	483	1,633	3,147	312	2,834	33,051	38.3	28.2
Lansing	49,334	2.36	45.9	27.6	15.2	54.1	39.5	981	4,700	4,080	1,180	2,900	74,038	39.9	23.7
Lincoln Park	13,287	2.76	64.0	39.0	18.9	36.0	31.2	85	1,379	3,746	728	3,018	23,147	60.4	10.7
Livonia	37,441	2.47	66.9	55.8	7.7	33.1	28.3	1,513	1,839	1,952	153	1,799	68,285	29.3	36.8
Madison Heights	13,626	2.20	52.2	34.0	13.2	47.8	41.7	NA	723	2,386	267	2,119	23,234	38.8	23.2
Midland	17,572	2.34	61.5	48.9	9.0	38.5	30.6	1,204	559	1,323	114	1,209	28,700	25.7	43.7
Mount Pleasant	7,735	2.56	40.9	26.0	11.4	59.1	36.9	6,491	422	1,619	257	1,362	10,286	26.4	48.6
Muskegon	13,693	2.40	52.1	23.4	21.9	47.9	40.0	5,500	1,746	4,542	713	3,829	25,031	55.2	9.5
Novi	21,996	2.68	68.5	56.3	9.9	31.5	24.7	348	693	1,166	57	1,109	39,912	16.4	57.2

1. No spouse present. 2. Data for serious crimes have not been adjusted for underreporting. This may affect comparability between geographic areas and over time. 3. Per 100,000 population estimated by the FBI. 4. Persons 25 years old and over.

— **Accommodation and Food Services, Arts, Entertainment, and Recreation, and Health Care and Social Assistance**

AREANAME	Accommodation and food services, 2012				Arts, entertainment, and recreation[1], 2012				Health care and social assistance,[1] 2012			
	Number of establish-ments	Number of employees	Receipts (mil dol)	Annual payroll (mil dol)	Number of establish-ments	Number of employees	Receipts (mil dol)	Annual payroll (mil dol)	Number of establish-ments	Number of employees	Receipts (mil dol)	Annual payroll (mil dol)
	92	93	94	95	96	97	98	99	100	101	102	103
MASSACHUSETTS— Cont'd												
Beverly	115	D	D	D	20	D	D	D	128	D	D	D
Boston	2,276	52,474	4,409.2	1,271.2	215	D	D	D	935	18,605	3,118.9	1,413.4
Braintree Town	124	2,474	142.7	42.4	18	D	D	D	86	2,494	250.8	104.6
Brockton	153	2,206	123.9	36.4	10	166	6.5	1.8	193	5,657	650.7	302.7
Cambridge	466	9,912	784.2	227.4	46	771	164.9	19.5	226	3,649	628.1	254.3
Chelsea	71	746	46.9	11.9	2	D	D	D	35	629	48.9	22.2
Chicopee	115	1,553	79.4	22.2	5	55	4.4	1.1	45	1,055	113.9	43.4
Everett	91	D	D	D	5	109	5.6	1.7	38	D	D	D
Fall River	182	D	D	D	12	120	7.1	1.8	196	5,222	598.4	259.4
Fitchburg	83	1,145	56.0	14.9	3	D	D	D	68	1,217	113.4	45.8
Franklin Town	68	1,532	90.2	24.5	14	D	D	D	54	779	75.9	31.3
Gloucester	117	1,078	72.4	21.0	13	93	12.1	4.1	60	687	65.7	29.6
Haverhill	131	1,829	100.6	28.9	23	551	30.4	10.5	103	2,729	284.2	119.1
Holyoke	92	1,516	77.7	21.2	11	154	5.0	2.0	77	1,518	115.5	58.1
Lawrence	119	D	D	D	4	83	1.9	0.7	82	1,243	149.0	68.2
Leominster	107	2,048	93.9	28.3	16	D	D	D	91	1,667	171.2	69.6
Lowell	218	D	D	D	14	128	8.9	2.5	133	3,122	284.3	143.1
Lynn	140	D	D	D	16	74	3.8	1.2	99	2,137	142.9	73.1
Malden	95	1,129	65.6	19.1	5	D	D	D	81	3,105	759.8	393.0
Marlborough	133	2,397	139.9	39.1	17	374	22.9	6.0	77	1,549	133.4	57.5
Medford	102	1,323	95.0	24.2	12	D	D	D	94	1,788	210.8	94.1
Melrose	40	467	25.4	6.4	6	34	2.2	0.8	74	D	D	D
Methuen Town	104	1,800	96.9	27.4	11	234	10.6	3.6	92	2,434	285.6	124.6
New Bedford	216	D	D	D	17	196	10.9	3.1	137	2,981	245.8	115.8
Newton	191	4,920	381.6	109.6	47	703	86.8	41.7	354	5,904	636.5	291.6
Northampton	105	1,982	92.3	30.0	18	244	11.3	3.2	116	1,464	160.8	76.5
Peabody	141	2,605	154.7	46.5	7	20	2.1	0.4	107	2,241	326.5	148.1
Pittsfield	141	1,849	90.2	26.8	19	236	14.2	3.4	143	1,881	179.7	82.1
Quincy	241	3,168	205.7	55.1	25	252	23.6	6.8	216	5,889	618.3	243.1
Revere	96	1,142	79.0	17.9	8	D	D	D	45	D	D	D
Salem	132	1,707	116.4	31.4	18	D	D	D	101	D	D	D
Somerville	195	2,436	167.1	49.0	16	122	9.6	2.4	83	1,859	219.9	94.5
Springfield	268	4,663	236.2	65.1	15	126	10.0	2.6	301	7,082	910.0	482.5
Taunton	111	D	D	D	6	D	D	D	93	1,312	137.9	60.8
Waltham	304	3,249	244.9	68.9	23	496	33.8	7.2	135	1,854	207.3	102.0
Watertown Town	84	996	61.7	16.6	17	D	D	D	69	764	93.8	34.9
Westfield	78	1,356	61.7	18.4	9	95	3.6	1.1	67	758	74.6	33.8
West Springfield Town	105	2,119	109.8	31.3	9	D	D	D	68	1,694	109.4	58.5
Weymouth Town	102	1,520	73.7	19.1	12	D	D	D	135	D	D	D
Woburn	102	2,048	148.1	39.2	24	346	15.8	4.5	119	3,488	393.7	153.8
Worcester	441	6,201	342.0	95.4	26	420	21.3	7.0	395	12,907	1,671.6	839.6
MICHIGAN	19,491	347,337	17,962.4	4,871.7	2,706	32,268	2,881.5	1,119.9	21,447	270,655	27,434.6	11,943.9
Allen Park	68	1,258	61.4	18.3	8	D	D	D	72	752	78.4	32.4
Ann Arbor	381	8,311	467.1	131.5	37	156	10.6	3.3	307	D	D	D
Battle Creek	140	D	D	D	12	128	4.6	1.3	147	1,939	187.9	82.0
Bay City	102	1,744	59.5	19.7	15	D	D	D	104	1,410	154.2	66.0
Burton	56	1,191	53.5	14.3	8	D	D	D	83	D	D	D
Dearborn	257	4,444	236.5	67.6	18	D	D	D	368	3,186	479.1	179.2
Dearborn Heights	97	1,408	65.6	17.2	5	79	5.2	1.6	94	D	D	D
Detroit	933	20,452	2,237.3	495.8	49	2,577	500.3	295.9	668	21,711	2,848.7	1,101.4
East Lansing	121	2,411	100.0	26.3	5	28	0.9	0.3	109	2,481	410.1	139.5
Eastpointe	47	704	33.1	9.1	5	D	D	D	81	D	D	D
Farmington Hills	175	2,826	137.7	40.1	25	480	16.2	6.2	395	5,861	509.0	236.8
Flint	179	2,260	102.2	25.3	5	D	D	D	148	2,244	254.3	97.4
Garden City	46	740	28.2	7.6	2	D	D	D	73	D	D	D
Grand Rapids	408	8,881	448.6	130.1	56	1,134	38.9	11.2	393	7,651	938.5	470.8
Holland	79	1,893	78.4	24.5	5	178	5.2	1.8	106	1,892	160.2	79.9
Inkster	22	187	13.4	3.1	NA	NA	NA	NA	16	63	4.7	1.5
Jackson	96	1,480	65.6	17.9	9	D	D	D	134	1,613	206.7	111.5
Kalamazoo	210	4,849	194.0	61.6	27	397	17.4	6.2	168	2,775	310.1	160.3
Kentwood	106	2,408	117.2	32.5	16	D	D	D	99	2,708	326.4	158.6
Lansing	233	4,028	181.5	50.1	24	449	82.3	10.9	213	2,226	253.4	123.9
Lincoln Park	67	895	45.1	10.9	4	16	0.8	0.2	45	D	D	D
Livonia	259	5,903	276.8	81.4	23	D	D	D	448	4,931	510.1	217.3
Madison Heights	101	1,743	87.2	23.8	13	116	6.0	1.8	93	1,696	141.7	72.2
Midland	111	2,562	122.9	37.3	14	305	14.1	4.9	166	D	D	D
Mount Pleasant	73	D	D	D	4	D	D	D	103	D	D	D
Muskegon	72	1,276	57.1	16.1	9	201	10.7	3.5	91	D	D	D
Novi	161	3,802	205.2	60.5	20	D	D	D	227	2,509	311.6	114.5

1. Establishments subject to federal tax.

AREANAME	Other services[1]					Government employment and payroll, 2012							
							March payroll						
							Perent of total for:						
	Number of establish-ments	Number of employees	Receipts (mil dol)	Annual payroll (mil dol)	Full-time equivalent employees	Total (dollars)	Adminis-trative, judicial, and legal	Police and corrections	Fire protection	Highways and trans-portation	Health and welfare	Natural resources and utilities	Education and libraries
	104	105	106	107	108	109	110	111	112	113	114	115	116
MASSACHUSETTS—Cont'd													
Beverly	63	329	28.7	8.5	996	4,817,626	4.0	11.2	9.0	4.5	1.8	2.6	66.3
Boston	1,253	9,009	772.9	242.2	19,230	112,444,857	3.5	18.3	12.2	2.2	8.9	3.5	49.1
Braintree Town	91	1,006	75.5	22.8	1,198	6,476,545	2.5	10.2	9.4	2.2	1.8	15.8	58.0
Brockton	146	1,021	74.7	25.7	3,168	15,359,504	2.3	8.6	7.5	1.3	0.8	2.7	75.2
Cambridge	153	1,154	107.3	39.0	5,751	29,806,492	5.4	9.0	6.6	1.8	37.9	3.3	26.6
Chelsea	36	251	36.9	7.1	1,195	6,010,338	2.8	12.8	10.5	1.7	2.0	0.7	68.2
Chicopee	72	406	28.9	9.7	1,968	9,607,115	2.4	8.9	8.8	2.2	1.0	8.2	68.6
Everett	74	439	37.2	11.3	1,148	6,059,197	2.8	14.5	12.3	1.2	2.1	1.4	63.1
Fall River	150	728	56.9	17.6	2,306	10,353,050	2.4	15.4	12.8	3.5	0.6	2.2	61.8
Fitchburg	50	241	23.4	6.3	1,151	5,547,200	3.4	9.4	7.3	2.6	1.4	5.1	70.3
Franklin Town	58	546	44.2	13.5	966	4,884,796	3.9	7.4	6.9	0.9	1.2	3.4	75.4
Gloucester	53	223	18.9	5.7	1,097	5,414,614	3.5	6.3	6.5	1.4	2.1	2.0	78.1
Haverhill	84	417	36.6	12.5	1,832	8,913,896	3.7	7.9	7.8	2.3	3.5	5.7	67.6
Holyoke	46	229	15.1	4.7	1,884	8,334,885	2.7	13.7	8.2	1.9	1.5	16.1	55.4
Lawrence	88	567	48.9	15.2	537	3,239,260	9.3	38.4	19.3	2.8	4.3	18.5	2.0
Leominster	67	278	23.7	6.4	1,158	5,702,455	3.5	8.2	8.6	2.7	4.5	1.1	71.5
Lowell	142	671	60.4	19.1	2,860	17,379,993	21.6	7.8	6.2	1.2	1.9	2.6	57.2
Lynn	98	492	40.5	12.2	3,200	15,232,790	2.0	9.3	9.0	0.6	2.4	2.0	71.9
Malden	96	609	50.6	17.0	1,385	7,796,658	4.0	11.7	8.4	1.5	2.2	1.1	67.0
Marlborough	68	703	100.0	29.9	1,155	5,341,768	2.6	10.8	7.8	2.2	2.8	3.2	68.1
Medford	110	657	57.4	19.1	1,214	5,909,654	4.2	14.6	12.9	2.3	1.5	3.3	61.4
Melrose	42	212	18.3	6.1	763	3,328,642	4.7	9.6	9.5	2.3	3.8	3.1	64.8
Methuen Town	57	326	24.1	8.9	1,087	7,336,774	2.5	10.2	7.0	2.2	1.2	5.3	71.1
New Bedford	137	787	79.6	21.8	2,769	11,838,508	3.4	15.9	8.7	0.5	2.2	2.3	64.5
Newton	178	1,202	106.0	36.3	2,832	16,441,085	4.0	8.3	7.3	3.8	2.0	4.3	68.5
Northampton	60	325	25.5	8.5	1,315	6,640,659	6.9	16.3	15.0	3.3	4.8	8.4	45.1
Peabody	116	626	68.0	15.6	1,445	6,993,068	3.9	10.1	8.5	2.0	3.4	9.6	59.9
Pittsfield	73	363	30.8	10.9	1,418	6,191,800	2.1	11.1	7.7	3.1	2.0	2.3	70.3
Quincy	182	1,019	102.2	29.6	2,107	11,341,562	3.7	14.1	12.3	2.7	1.9	3.4	58.4
Revere	76	312	30.3	7.5	1,148	6,190,389	2.9	10.4	9.9	1.4	2.2	0.9	70.9
Salem	92	548	44.5	13.3	1,293	5,566,047	3.8	10.4	7.7	2.3	1.1	2.1	70.6
Somerville	109	1,376	119.9	44.1	1,637	10,044,072	4.6	10.5	15.6	1.3	3.6	1.4	56.7
Springfield	183	1,829	123.1	43.5	6,400	28,244,315	2.7	10.9	5.2	0.8	1.6	1.8	75.7
Taunton	80	381	28.6	8.7	1,574	7,371,663	2.8	12.1	9.6	1.1	6.5	4.4	62.0
Waltham	135	747	59.8	21.5	1,543	7,799,064	4.9	13.2	11.2	3.6	1.6	2.7	59.4
Watertown Town	77	1,305	112.4	47.4	718	3,483,060	6.4	20.3	14.0	1.6	1.6	4.8	50.1
Westfield	57	288	29.1	10.3	1,493	7,020,504	2.4	7.7	7.1	1.5	0.9	11.5	68.2
West Springfield Town	63	469	44.3	12.1	976	3,909,287	3.2	12.1	9.7	5.8	0.8	0.5	65.8
Weymouth Town	110	532	44.7	13.4	1,151	5,346,322	0.0	0.0	0.0	0.0	0.0	0.0	100.0
Woburn	102	D	D	D	1,052	4,899,436	3.8	10.6	8.5	4.3	1.8	2.5	67.9
Worcester	254	1,668	157.3	46.3	5,736	34,255,682	3.1	10.9	7.3	1.4	1.6	2.9	72.6
MICHIGAN	13,062	75,714	6,509.2	1,982.4	X	X	X	X	X	X	X	X	X
Allen Park	43	278	19.6	4.6	145	695,062	17.1	36.5	23.7	3.5	2.1	12.0	1.1
Ann Arbor	148	945	71.1	25.5	1,014	4,848,561	15.1	39.8	10.1	6.4	0.3	20.8	0.0
Battle Creek	75	D	D	D	520	2,297,856	15.9	27.9	16.4	20.0	2.1	17.3	0.0
Bay City	61	390	30.3	10.7	307	1,423,139	12.6	19.6	15.4	7.2	3.8	41.4	0.0
Burton	55	260	23.3	7.6	88	380,820	19.8	42.5	6.3	13.2	3.7	10.2	0.0
Dearborn	192	864	64.3	17.4	923	3,654,827	12.9	29.4	13.1	4.0	5.7	11.8	4.5
Dearborn Heights	83	282	25.1	6.7	306	1,426,569	13.6	40.6	19.1	3.5	0.6	11.8	3.5
Detroit	609	3,355	261.9	82.4	12,364	57,433,160	8.6	36.8	19.2	8.8	3.7	16.3	1.7
East Lansing	25	167	11.3	3.3	396	1,817,436	16.7	32.0	14.5	2.5	2.2	20.9	4.6
Eastpointe	54	259	22.1	6.3	180	830,736	14.8	39.6	19.5	6.0	0.0	11.0	3.5
Farmington Hills	155	1,573	97.8	33.6	445	2,178,404	16.2	39.5	19.9	10.2	0.0	13.4	0.0
Flint	105	665	52.6	13.9	3,484	16,192,746	3.4	5.1	4.1	1.1	80.7	4.6	0.0
Garden City	51	249	19.2	5.3	125	1,093,459	18.2	37.0	20.6	11.9	0.0	10.8	1.6
Grand Rapids	229	1,640	123.7	40.7	1,502	7,515,829	14.9	31.3	17.1	6.5	4.9	18.7	5.4
Holland	60	528	48.1	16.3	501	2,186,069	19.7	18.0	6.4	11.0	2.5	31.8	8.0
Inkster	15	74	2.7	1.8	210	862,765	16.2	39.6	11.9	3.5	10.7	10.1	0.0
Jackson	55	448	37.4	11.5	317	1,468,468	14.1	26.2	16.9	10.7	9.1	20.9	0.0
Kalamazoo	135	1,028	100.7	33.6	737	3,816,582	9.9	48.7	0.0	14.8	4.0	21.7	0.0
Kentwood	68	759	66.8	26.7	223	1,105,109	17.7	43.8	20.2	4.1	0.4	7.1	0.0
Lansing	145	D	D	D	1,615	8,042,053	9.4	18.0	12.0	4.6	2.5	31.5	0.0
Lincoln Park	60	339	32.7	10.6	136	745,448	11.3	45.2	24.4	3.7	3.5	7.7	0.1
Livonia	212	1,646	201.4	50.7	675	3,250,072	15.0	29.9	18.3	6.5	2.1	12.7	4.9
Madison Heights	86	577	55.1	18.3	168	954,270	18.4	39.5	19.8	4.4	6.9	6.2	3.1
Midland	83	593	47.7	13.7	384	1,817,246	18.5	13.7	13.1	13.3	3.3	24.4	7.5
Mount Pleasant	43	302	15.7	4.7	138	584,882	17.9	28.1	11.5	10.7	3.3	20.6	0.0
Muskegon	43	230	20.5	5.8	249	1,066,412	10.8	37.4	17.3	11.3	4.4	11.2	0.0
Novi	95	941	74.1	26.9	303	1,465,600	14.7	34.8	16.3	10.0	0.9	6.5	8.2

1. Establishments subject to federal tax.

Table D. Cities — City Government Finances, City Government Employment, and Climate

AREANAME	City government finances, 2012 (cont.)			Climate[2]						
	Debt outstanding			Average daily temperature						
				Mean		Limits				
	Total (mil dol)	Per capita[1] (dollars)	Debt issued during year	January	July	January[3]	July[4]	Annual precipitation (inches)	Heating degree days	Cooling degree days
	137	138	139	140	141	142	143	144	145	146

AREANAME	137	138	139	140	141	142	143	144	145	146
MASSACHUSETTS— Cont'd										
Beverly	89.1	2,208	0.0	28.8	72.6	20.4	82.1	45.51	5,704	582
Boston	1,572.5	2,454	245.5	29.3	73.9	22.1	82.2	42.53	5,630	777
Braintree Town	145.9	4,001	8.7	NA	NA	NA	NA	NA	NA	NA
Brockton	242.9	2,583	12.5	27.9	72.1	17.8	83.2	48.25	6,008	529
Cambridge	340.3	3,209	55.5	29.3	73.9	22.1	82.2	42.53	5,630	777
Chelsea	35.1	947	2.0	29.3	73.9	22.1	82.2	42.53	5,630	777
Chicopee	51.4	924	11.0	21.5	68.9	10.4	81.7	48.07	7,312	287
Everett	61.8	1,452	1.4	29.3	73.9	22.1	82.2	42.53	5,630	777
Fall River	271.7	3,064	39.8	28.5	74.2	20.0	83.1	50.77	5,734	740
Fitchburg	74.6	1,846	20.7	24.2	71.9	15.2	81.0	49.13	6,576	548
Franklin Town	55.4	1,710	16.4	NA	NA	NA	NA	NA	NA	NA
Gloucester	137.0	4,689	26.4	28.8	72.6	20.4	82.1	45.51	5,704	582
Haverhill	94.2	1,525	3.0	25.3	72.2	15.6	83.5	46.88	6,435	550
Holyoke	104.5	2,604	16.8	21.5	68.9	10.4	81.7	48.07	7,312	287
Lawrence	148.3	1,917	0.0	24.5	71.8	14.5	82.9	44.09	6,539	510
Leominster	58.1	1,421	13.9	24.2	71.9	15.2	81.0	49.13	6,576	548
Lowell	256.6	2,363	32.8	23.6	72.4	14.1	84.5	43.14	6,575	532
Lynn	67.5	740	0.0	29.3	73.9	22.1	82.2	42.53	5,630	777
Malden	106.3	1,761	5.1	29.3	73.9	22.1	82.2	42.53	5,630	777
Marlborough	60.4	1,537	31.1	25.9	73.4	16.2	84.0	45.87	6,060	651
Medford	45.4	795	34.5	29.3	73.9	22.1	82.2	42.53	5,630	777
Melrose	63.4	2,311	5.5	29.3	73.9	22.1	82.2	42.53	5,630	777
Methuen Town	66.0	1,374	0.5	24.5	71.8	14.5	82.9	44.09	6,539	510
New Bedford	257.5	2,716	19.6	28.5	74.2	20.0	83.1	50.77	5,734	740
Newton	217.6	2,495	9.9	25.9	73.4	16.2	84.0	45.87	6,060	651
Northampton	81.7	2,847	20.6	22.3	71.2	11.2	83.2	45.57	6,856	452
Peabody	45.3	874	10.0	28.8	72.6	20.4	82.1	45.51	5,704	582
Pittsfield	87.1	1,966	7.2	19.9	67.6	11.2	77.5	48.71	7,689	222
Quincy	211.7	2,279	14.8	26.0	71.6	18.1	81.2	51.19	6,371	558
Revere	59.8	1,117	0.2	29.3	73.9	22.1	82.2	42.53	5,630	777
Salem	62.2	1,472	6.0	28.8	72.6	20.4	82.1	45.51	5,704	582
Somerville	99.6	1,281	18.7	29.3	73.9	22.1	82.2	42.53	5,630	777
Springfield	260.5	1,693	0.0	25.7	73.7	17.2	84.9	46.16	6,104	759
Taunton	120.6	2,154	0.7	27.4	72.2	17.8	83.0	48.34	6,012	558
Waltham	106.4	1,717	23.1	25.4	71.5	15.7	82.7	46.95	6,370	485
Watertown Town	44.3	1,348	4.0	29.3	73.9	22.1	82.2	42.53	5,630	777
Westfield	98.9	2,398	0.0	21.5	68.9	10.4	81.7	48.07	7,312	287
West Springfield Town	43.5	1,522	0.0	NA	NA	NA	NA	NA	NA	NA
Weymouth Town	91.2	1,657	25.5	NA	NA	NA	NA	NA	NA	NA
Woburn	86.3	2,221	30.5	25.5	71.5	15.7	82.5	48.31	6,401	472
Worcester	657.7	3,607	57.8	23.6	70.1	15.8	79.3	49.05	6,831	371
MICHIGAN	X	X	X	X	X	X	X	X	X	X
Allen Park	85.9	3,076	3.7	24.5	73.5	17.8	83.4	32.89	6,422	736
Ann Arbor	244.9	2,113	25.9	23.4	72.6	16.6	83.0	35.35	6,503	691
Battle Creek	87.6	1,690	0.0	23.1	71.0	15.3	82.5	35.15	6,742	559
Bay City	72.6	2,101	3.7	21.0	71.5	13.8	81.5	31.25	7,106	545
Burton	12.1	411	3.5	21.3	70.6	13.3	82.0	31.61	7,005	555
Dearborn	274.1	2,831	7.6	24.7	73.7	16.1	85.7	33.58	6,224	788
Dearborn Heights	58.1	1,016	3.6	24.7	73.7	16.1	85.7	33.58	6,224	788
Detroit	8,166.1	11,720	1,166.2	24.7	73.7	16.1	85.7	33.58	6,224	788
East Lansing	60.8	1,250	0.0	21.6	70.3	13.9	82.1	31.53	7,098	558
Eastpointe	15.3	472	0.4	25.3	73.6	18.8	83.3	33.97	6,160	757
Farmington Hills	17.7	219	0.0	24.7	73.7	16.1	85.7	33.58	6,224	788
Flint	170.4	1,696	13.5	21.3	70.6	13.3	82.0	31.61	7,005	555
Garden City	50.5	1,842	12.9	24.7	73.7	16.1	85.7	33.58	6,224	788
Grand Rapids	552.9	2,902	23.4	22.4	71.4	15.6	82.3	37.13	6,896	613
Holland	47.8	1,433	12.8	24.4	71.4	17.6	82.5	36.25	6,589	611
Inkster	48.3	1,924	9.7	24.5	73.5	17.8	83.4	32.89	6,422	736
Jackson	42.3	1,268	13.0	22.2	71.3	14.7	82.7	30.67	6,873	570
Kalamazoo	453.2	6,023	117.6	24.3	73.2	17.0	84.2	37.41	6,235	773
Kentwood	20.1	405	0.0	22.4	71.4	15.6	82.3	37.13	6,896	613
Lansing	693.1	6,066	30.4	21.6	70.3	13.9	82.1	31.53	7,098	558
Lincoln Park	16.7	443	0.0	24.5	73.5	17.8	83.4	32.89	6,422	736
Livonia	52.7	549	0.0	24.7	73.7	16.1	85.7	33.58	6,224	788
Madison Heights	14.5	483	0.0	24.7	73.7	16.1	85.7	33.58	6,224	788
Midland	35.9	855	4.6	22.9	72.7	16.2	83.8	30.69	6,645	679
Mount Pleasant	13.0	496	1.5	20.7	70.6	13.5	82.2	31.57	7,329	492
Muskegon	30.6	826	6.5	23.5	69.9	17.1	80.0	32.88	6,943	487
Novi	48.0	844	0.0	22.1	71.0	14.3	81.7	29.28	6,989	550

1. Based on the population estimated as of July 1 of the year shown.   2. Represents normal values based on the 30-year period, 1971±2000.   3. Average daily minimum.   4. Average daily maximum.

STATE Place code	AREANAME	Land area[1] (sq. mi)	Population, 2017			Race 2016 Race alone[2] (percent)						
			Total persons 2017	Rank	Per square mile	White	Black or African American	American Indian, Alaskan Native	Asian	Hawaiian Pacific Islander	Some other race	Two or more races (percent)
		1	2	3	4	5	6	7	8	9	10	11
	MICHIGAN— Cont'd											
26 59,920	Oak Park	5.2	29,654	1,261	5,702.7	38.4	55.2	0.0	1.2	0.0	3.4	1.9
26 65,440	Pontiac	19.9	59,792	626	3,004.6	33.5	49.8	0.8	2.3	0.0	2.0	11.5
26 65,560	Portage	32.3	48,816	785	1,511.3	83.6	6.5	0.3	4.2	0.0	1.0	4.4
26 65,820	Port Huron	8.1	29,051	1,283	3,586.5	82.7	8.1	0.5	3.4	0.0	0.7	4.8
26 69,035	Rochester Hills	32.8	74,205	476	2,262.3	74.9	6.8	0.2	15.4	0.0	0.7	2.1
26 69,800	Roseville	9.8	47,501	814	4,847.0	72.9	20.5	0.1	2.2	0.0	1.9	2.4
26 70,040	Royal Oak	11.8	59,112	634	5,009.5	91.7	3.0	0.0	4.3	0.0	0.2	0.8
26 70,520	Saginaw	17.1	48,677	791	2,846.6	44.2	45.3	0.4	0.2	0.0	3.9	6.0
26 70,760	St. Clair Shores	11.7	59,635	629	5,097.0	92.1	5.2	0.2	1.0	0.0	0.0	1.4
26 74,900	Southfield	26.3	73,208	481	2,783.6	20.4	70.7	0.3	2.6	0.0	1.5	4.7
26 74,960	Southgate	6.9	29,084	1,282	4,215.1	85.6	9.1	0.8	1.7	0.0	0.8	2.0
26 76,460	Sterling Heights	36.4	132,631	207	3,643.7	83.8	6.0	0.3	7.1	0.0	0.6	2.1
26 79,000	Taylor	23.6	61,276	604	2,596.4	74.3	19.6	0.6	2.0	0.0	0.5	2.9
26 80,700	Troy	33.5	83,813	403	2,501.9	72.3	2.5	0.2	22.6	0.0	0.1	2.3
26 84,000	Warren	34.4	135,022	200	3,925.1	72.0	17.2	0.1	8.3	0.0	0.3	2.0
26 86,000	Westland	20.4	81,747	412	4,007.2	74.8	18.1	0.7	2.7	0.1	1.3	2.2
26 88,900	Wyandotte	5.3	24,977	1,416	4,712.6	NA	NA	NA	NA	NA	NA	NA
26 88,940	Wyoming	24.6	75,938	459	3,086.9	76.8	8.0	0.9	1.8	0.0	5.9	6.7
27 00,000	MINNESOTA	79,625.5	5,576,606	X	70.0	83.3	6.0	1.1	4.7	0.0	2.0	2.8
27 01,486	Andover	33.9	32,902	1,150	970.6	NA	NA	NA	NA	NA	NA	NA
27 01,900	Apple Valley	16.9	52,435	732	3,102.7	79.4	8.8	0.1	7.3	0.0	1.4	3.1
27 06,382	Blaine	33.8	64,557	569	1,910.0	81.1	2.8	0.5	10.3	0.0	2.4	2.9
27 06,616	Bloomington	34.7	85,866	387	2,474.5	74.0	9.9	0.5	3.8	0.1	8.1	3.5
27 07,948	Brooklyn Center	8.0	31,006	1,213	3,875.8	49.0	25.1	0.0	15.7	0.0	6.3	3.9
27 07,966	Brooklyn Park	26.1	80,581	423	3,087.4	46.6	32.2	0.6	15.2	0.3	1.8	3.3
27 08,794	Burnsville	24.9	61,439	602	2,467.4	73.2	11.4	0.0	3.6	0.0	5.4	6.4
27 13,114	Coon Rapids	22.6	62,656	589	2,772.4	85.1	7.6	0.2	3.6	0.0	0.6	2.9
27 13,456	Cottage Grove	33.6	36,793	1,040	1,095.0	83.5	4.2	0.0	5.7	0.0	1.8	4.3
27 17,000	Duluth	71.8	86,066	386	1,198.7	89.1	2.7	3.3	2.0	0.0	0.2	2.6
27 17,288	Eagan	31.2	66,627	545	2,135.5	81.0	8.9	0.8	5.4	0.0	1.4	2.6
27 18,116	Eden Prairie	32.5	64,400	571	1,981.5	78.9	5.9	0.0	10.7	0.0	0.7	3.1
27 18,188	Edina	15.5	51,958	736	3,352.1	85.2	4.0	0.1	7.0	0.0	1.2	2.5
27 22,814	Fridley	10.2	27,853	1,327	2,730.7	NA	NA	NA	NA	NA	NA	NA
27 31,076	Inver Grove Heights	27.9	35,392	1,080	1,268.5	87.8	2.1	0.1	2.5	0.0	6.0	1.4
27 35,180	Lakeville	36.1	63,748	578	1,765.9	85.6	2.0	0.4	6.3	0.2	2.4	3.2
27 39,878	Mankato	19.1	42,264	898	2,212.8	88.6	4.8	0.7	2.9	0.0	0.3	2.8
27 40,166	Maple Grove	32.6	71,066	503	2,179.9	84.0	5.6	0.1	6.9	0.0	0.3	3.1
27 40,382	Maplewood	17.0	40,918	926	2,406.9	63.8	11.1	0.1	13.8	0.0	1.8	9.5
27 43,000	Minneapolis	54.0	422,331	46	7,820.9	64.3	18.1	1.5	6.6	0.0	4.8	4.7
27 43,252	Minnetonka	26.9	53,085	722	1,973.4	88.5	3.2	0.1	5.3	0.0	0.3	2.7
27 43,864	Moorhead	22.3	43,122	877	1,933.7	90.0	3.1	1.8	1.5	0.0	0.2	3.3
27 47,680	Oakdale	11.0	28,083	1,317	2,553.0	80.2	6.1	0.2	8.8	0.0	1.1	3.5
27 49,300	Owatonna	14.5	25,794	1,400	1,778.9	NA	NA	NA	NA	NA	NA	NA
27 51,730	Plymouth	32.7	78,395	438	2,397.4	80.6	3.0	0.7	12.3	0.0	1.1	2.5
27 54,214	Richfield	6.7	36,151	1,058	5,395.7	68.4	9.3	0.9	8.1	0.0	7.9	5.3
27 54,880	Rochester	55.0	115,733	244	2,104.2	79.6	7.7	0.8	7.6	0.0	1.8	2.5
27 55,852	Roseville	13.0	36,314	1,053	2,793.4	76.6	7.9	0.4	8.6	0.0	2.2	4.3
27 56,896	St. Cloud	40.0	67,984	531	1,699.6	77.9	16.0	0.3	3.0	0.0	1.2	1.7
27 57,220	St. Louis Park	10.6	49,029	781	4,625.4	83.4	7.3	1.3	3.6	0.0	2.3	2.2
27 58,000	St. Paul	52.0	306,621	63	5,896.6	57.1	15.2	0.8	18.2	0.0	3.4	5.3
27 58,738	Savage	15.6	31,352	1,199	2,009.7	79.1	2.2	0.0	10.5	0.0	4.6	3.5
27 59,350	Shakopee	28.1	40,893	927	1,455.3	73.3	7.2	0.3	8.0	0.0	5.9	5.3
27 59,998	Shoreview	10.8	26,794	1,368	2,480.9	NA	NA	NA	NA	NA	NA	NA
27 71,032	Winona	18.9	26,928	1,364	1,424.8	NA	NA	NA	NA	NA	NA	NA
27 71,428	Woodbury	34.9	69,756	513	1,998.7	75.9	7.8	0.2	9.2	0.1	1.8	5.1
28 00,000	MISSISSIPPI	46,923.1	2,984,100	X	63.6	58.5	38.0	0.4	0.9	0.0	1.0	1.1
28 06,220	Biloxi	43.0	45,908	836	1,067.6	64.7	25.8	0.3	3.9	0.0	0.8	4.5
28 14,420	Clinton	41.8	25,154	1,413	601.8	48.5	40.1	0.0	4.8	0.0	5.4	1.2
28 29,180	Greenville	26.9	30,686	1,227	1,140.7	NA	NA	NA	NA	NA	NA	NA
28 29,700	Gulfport	55.6	71,822	496	1,291.8	58.9	34.7	1.4	2.2	0.0	0.8	2.0
28 31,020	Hattiesburg	53.2	46,377	830	871.7	NA	NA	NA	NA	NA	NA	NA
28 33,700	Horn Lake	16.0	27,095	1,358	1,693.4	NA	NA	NA	NA	NA	NA	NA
28 36,000	Jackson	111.0	166,965	156	1,504.2	15.8	83.3	0.0	0.3	0.2	0.0	0.4
28 46,640	Meridian	53.7	37,940	1,009	706.5	NA	NA	NA	NA	NA	NA	NA
28 54,040	Olive Branch	36.7	37,435	1,025	1,020.0	NA	NA	NA	NA	NA	NA	NA
28 55,760	Pearl	25.5	26,534	1,381	1,040.5	NA	NA	NA	NA	NA	NA	NA
28 69,280	Southaven	41.3	54,031	707	1,308.3	65.6	28.1	0.0	3.1	0.0	1.5	1.8
28 74,840	Tupelo	64.4	38,114	1,003	591.8	NA	NA	NA	NA	NA	NA	NA

1. Dry land or land partially or temporarily covered by water.   2. Hispanic or Latino persons may be of any race.

Table D. Cities — **Population**

AREANAME	Percent Hispanic or Latino[1], 2016	Percent foreign born, 2016	Age of population (percent), 2016							Median age 2016	Percent female 2016	Population			
												Census counts		Percent change	
			Under 18 years	18 to 24 years	25 to 34 years	35 to 44 years	45 to 54 years	55 to 64 years	65 years and over			2000	2010	2000-2010	2010-2017
	12	13	14	15	16	17	18	19	20	21	22	23	24	25	26
MICHIGAN— Cont'd															
Oak Park	4.2	9.8	18.0	9.0	17.1	13.8	11.2	15.4	15.4	37.8	52.2	29,793	29,408	-1.3	0.8
Pontiac	15.7	7.3	27.8	10.7	14.4	12.4	14.3	9.8	10.6	33.0	51.7	66,337	59,633	-10.1	0.3
Portage	3.9	6.4	21.2	10.9	14.0	11.0	14.2	13.4	15.3	38.8	51.5	44,897	46,307	3.1	5.4
Port Huron	3.5	4.3	18.9	11.3	12.8	11.7	14.8	15.3	15.2	40.4	47.5	32,338	30,178	-6.7	-3.7
Rochester Hills	6.9	22.7	24.2	6.8	11.8	14.7	14.5	12.0	16.0	40.0	51.8	68,825	70,996	3.2	4.5
Roseville	2.9	4.1	23.8	8.3	15.2	12.1	14.6	12.7	13.4	37.4	51.5	48,129	47,336	-1.6	0.3
Royal Oak	3.1	8.8	12.0	8.1	27.5	10.5	12.6	13.3	16.1	36.2	51.5	60,062	57,231	-4.7	3.3
Saginaw	14.5	2.1	26.6	10.2	15.1	11.5	11.4	11.8	13.4	33.6	51.2	61,799	51,496	-16.7	-5.5
St. Clair Shores	2.7	3.5	18.8	6.7	13.8	13.5	12.3	16.7	18.2	43.1	51.4	63,096	59,755	-5.3	-0.2
Southfield	2.4	6.1	19.0	8.3	12.7	13.2	13.7	13.0	20.2	42.5	52.7	78,296	71,724	-8.4	2.1
Southgate	9.7	5.2	18.1	8.4	16.8	11.1	12.6	14.9	18.0	40.6	54.0	30,136	30,047	-0.3	-3.2
Sterling Heights	2.5	26.4	21.5	8.9	14.4	12.1	13.8	13.7	15.7	39.5	51.6	124,471	129,675	4.2	2.3
Taylor	4.1	3.7	20.4	11.3	12.9	12.2	13.7	15.2	14.3	40.1	51.4	65,868	63,131	-4.2	-2.9
Troy	2.0	27.0	20.1	6.9	12.2	12.4	14.7	15.8	17.8	44.2	50.8	80,959	80,976	0.0	3.5
Warren	2.6	14.9	23.5	9.1	14.0	12.0	13.2	12.2	16.1	37.5	50.1	138,247	134,055	-3.0	0.7
Westland	3.8	7.2	19.3	7.5	13.9	13.4	15.3	14.6	16.1	41.9	52.2	86,602	84,143	-2.8	-2.8
Wyandotte	5.1	4.5	19.6	4.8	11.5	11.5	17.1	16.9	18.6	46.0	53.6	28,006	25,883	-7.6	-3.5
Wyoming	21.4	10.8	23.4	11.0	16.7	13.3	14.1	11.1	10.4	34.1	50.2	69,368	72,124	4.0	5.3
MINNESOTA	5.2	8.2	23.3	9.2	13.5	12.3	13.2	13.4	15.0	37.9	50.2	4,919,479	5,303,924	7.8	5.1
Andover	5.4	1.7	27.2	8.0	8.5	14.9	18.9	12.5	10.0	39.9	50.9	26,588	30,590	15.1	7.6
Apple Valley	2.2	10.5	24.0	8.6	13.1	12.6	15.2	14.1	12.4	37.9	52.4	45,527	49,102	7.9	6.8
Blaine	5.1	12.2	24.6	6.5	12.6	15.9	15.1	13.1	12.2	38.5	50.8	44,942	57,179	27.2	12.9
Bloomington	10.4	14.8	18.7	7.2	14.6	12.5	12.6	11.9	22.6	42.6	51.1	85,172	82,893	-2.7	3.6
Brooklyn Center	12.6	18.7	27.5	6.8	19.3	13.1	9.4	9.8	14.0	33.3	54.0	29,172	30,135	3.3	2.9
Brooklyn Park	5.9	24.6	29.5	8.4	14.7	12.2	13.2	11.8	10.1	33.4	53.7	67,388	75,776	12.4	6.3
Burnsville	9.1	12.8	22.8	9.0	15.6	10.9	12.0	14.0	15.7	36.0	54.5	60,220	60,276	0.1	1.9
Coon Rapids	4.7	9.4	22.6	9.7	13.1	11.6	14.5	13.9	14.6	37.7	50.9	61,607	61,480	-0.2	1.9
Cottage Grove	4.3	3.2	27.4	9.3	9.2	14.3	15.4	12.0	12.4	37.0	50.0	30,582	34,594	13.1	6.4
Duluth	1.8	3.9	19.1	19.2	14.2	10.4	11.1	11.6	14.3	32.6	50.7	86,918	86,268	-0.7	-0.2
Eagan	5.5	13.1	21.0	8.5	14.6	12.3	14.8	16.6	12.2	38.6	50.5	63,557	64,150	0.9	3.9
Eden Prairie	6.7	17.2	23.2	6.2	12.2	12.6	17.9	16.6	11.3	41.8	50.7	54,901	60,797	10.7	5.9
Edina	2.2	12.4	25.9	3.2	12.6	11.2	15.5	11.3	20.3	43.0	53.8	47,425	47,980	1.2	8.3
Fridley	11.8	12.9	22.7	6.8	18.1	10.1	9.6	15.4	17.2	37.4	48.3	27,449	27,215	-0.9	2.3
Inver Grove Heights	13.1	10.1	21.9	6.9	9.4	14.2	13.9	13.5	20.1	43.4	47.5	29,751	33,994	14.3	4.1
Lakeville	3.0	8.8	29.9	6.8	10.0	15.6	16.9	13.0	7.9	36.5	49.4	43,128	55,999	29.8	13.8
Mankato	4.2	7.9	16.7	32.9	13.4	8.5	7.7	9.0	11.9	25.3	50.5	32,427	39,857	22.9	6.0
Maple Grove	0.7	7.7	28.5	4.5	10.2	15.4	15.8	14.8	10.7	40.3	50.7	50,365	61,549	22.2	15.5
Maplewood	3.9	11.3	22.8	9.7	17.2	12.5	10.0	11.6	16.2	35.2	54.2	34,947	38,017	8.8	7.6
Minneapolis	8.8	15.4	19.6	14.3	21.8	13.5	11.3	10.3	9.3	32.0	48.4	382,618	382,603	0.0	10.4
Minnetonka	1.0	11.3	20.5	4.4	13.2	11.9	13.0	17.4	19.7	45.1	51.7	51,301	49,735	-3.1	6.7
Moorhead	4.8	5.4	22.1	19.6	14.2	10.6	9.5	10.8	13.2	31.6	52.3	32,177	39,436	22.6	9.3
Oakdale	4.6	9.0	21.0	7.6	9.8	12.7	12.4	16.6	19.9	43.8	54.7	26,653	27,364	2.7	2.6
Owatonna	9.2	4.5	24.9	7.7	11.8	11.8	15.6	11.9	16.3	38.1	53.2	22,434	25,610	14.2	0.7
Plymouth	4.8	15.2	23.5	3.8	15.8	14.3	12.6	15.4	14.5	40.1	49.9	65,894	70,585	7.1	11.1
Richfield	17.8	19.2	25.2	4.4	20.1	12.5	10.6	10.4	16.9	35.2	52.6	34,439	35,094	1.9	3.0
Rochester	6.1	12.2	23.9	9.3	16.0	13.1	11.8	11.4	14.4	35.6	51.3	85,806	106,801	24.5	8.4
Roseville	3.7	13.1	20.5	12.3	14.0	11.3	9.8	15.5	16.5	37.1	51.3	33,690	33,661	-0.1	7.9
St. Cloud	2.1	10.9	18.1	20.6	15.1	12.2	10.4	10.7	12.9	31.8	46.8	59,107	65,928	11.5	3.1
St. Louis Park	3.6	11.7	16.9	6.3	25.0	14.5	11.9	11.6	13.7	35.8	53.5	44,126	45,206	2.4	8.5
St. Paul	9.7	20.1	25.4	11.4	18.3	12.4	11.8	10.4	10.2	31.7	50.6	287,151	285,063	-0.7	7.6
Savage	6.2	12.2	27.0	12.1	12.3	15.0	17.1	9.7	6.9	34.0	52.0	21,115	26,912	27.5	16.5
Shakopee	7.7	11.9	28.4	4.8	11.9	16.2	15.7	12.7	10.3	38.2	49.2	20,568	37,069	80.2	10.3
Shoreview	1.7	9.6	21.0	5.9	14.0	9.0	16.0	15.8	18.2	45.0	53.8	25,924	25,043	-3.4	7.0
Winona	1.7	1.6	13.2	30.4	8.9	7.6	9.2	12.7	17.9	31.3	50.4	27,069	27,586	1.9	-2.4
Woodbury	6.2	13.4	30.1	8.8	13.0	14.4	13.6	10.5	9.5	34.0	50.5	46,463	61,965	33.4	12.6
MISSISSIPPI	2.9	2.0	24.2	10.3	12.7	12.5	12.6	12.7	15.0	37.2	51.8	2,844,658	2,968,103	4.3	0.5
Biloxi	7.2	4.9	26.8	11.5	15.3	11.7	8.8	11.5	14.4	32.2	50.1	50,644	44,249	-12.6	3.7
Clinton	4.6	8.3	23.9	8.5	18.4	12.2	8.9	11.2	16.9	34.3	52.2	23,347	25,215	8.0	-0.2
Greenville	0.9	0.1	27.5	7.7	13.6	11.0	10.7	15.1	14.3	35.7	53.1	41,633	34,410	-17.3	-10.8
Gulfport	8.4	5.2	22.9	11.5	13.9	11.4	12.8	13.7	13.7	36.5	51.9	71,127	67,786	-4.7	6.0
Hattiesburg	1.8	3.8	22.7	18.9	17.6	13.5	8.8	9.3	9.1	28.8	55.2	44,779	45,751	2.2	1.4
Horn Lake	6.0	3.2	25.1	13.0	12.4	15.3	14.7	10.4	9.1	33.9	50.0	14,099	26,068	84.9	3.9
Jackson	1.3	1.7	25.5	11.8	15.3	12.3	11.8	11.8	11.6	33.0	54.1	184,256	173,595	-5.8	-3.8
Meridian	4.0	1.6	28.6	9.4	10.1	14.6	9.6	12.8	14.9	35.8	50.9	39,968	41,149	3.0	-7.8
Olive Branch	4.0	2.8	22.7	6.0	16.3	13.5	16.9	13.0	11.5	39.9	52.3	21,054	33,486	59.0	11.8
Pearl	4.8	1.2	24.9	9.7	13.9	11.7	11.5	11.8	16.6	35.8	53.4	21,961	25,700	17.0	3.2
Southaven	7.2	4.9	27.2	8.4	11.2	15.8	13.1	11.6	12.6	36.6	53.6	28,977	48,976	69.0	10.3
Tupelo	3.6	0.5	24.8	10.8	14.1	10.4	12.7	12.2	15.0	35.1	52.1	34,211	37,680	10.1	1.2

1. May be of any race.

Table D. Cities — Households, Group Quarters, Crime, and Education

	Households, 2016								Serious crimes known to police[2], 2016				Educational attainment, 2016		
			Perecnt						Total		Rate[3]			Attainment[4] (percent)	
AREANAME	Number	Persons per house-hold	Family	Married couple family	Female headed family[1]	Non-family	One person	Persons in group quarters	Number	Rate	Violent	Property	Population age 25 and over	High school graduate or less	Bachelor's degree or more
	27	28	29	30	31	32	33	34	35	36	37	38	39	40	41
MICHIGAN— Cont'd															
Oak Park	12,545	2.36	51.3	30.4	13.0	48.7	40.6	NA	672	2,252	352	1,900	21,629	30.7	29.5
Pontiac	22,432	2.57	54.3	23.1	25.1	45.7	39.0	1,981	NA	NA	NA	NA	36,764	50.5	13.4
Portage	19,379	2.50	60.2	46.3	10.2	39.8	29.0	NA	1,395	2,873	206	2,667	32,900	24.7	44.3
Port Huron	13,040	2.21	52.4	30.0	15.3	47.6	37.8	1,143	1,030	3,530	963	2,567	20,427	49.3	12.8
Rochester Hills	27,843	2.60	67.8	57.8	6.4	32.2	28.7	NA	NA	NA	NA	NA	50,626	19.6	57.3
Roseville	18,965	2.49	62.8	35.5	21.1	37.2	29.5	NA	2,078	4,356	518	3,838	32,361	52.2	13.6
Royal Oak	29,590	1.99	44.6	35.4	6.3	55.4	39.9	266	679	1,144	109	1,034	47,158	16.2	58.3
Saginaw	19,773	2.41	57.3	26.8	25.7	42.7	34.1	1,270	1,645	3,361	1,467	1,894	30,944	53.5	13.9
St. Clair Shores	27,195	2.19	55.5	43.6	8.5	44.5	40.1	930	1,552	1,353	199	1,353	44,557	35.6	25.5
Southfield	33,963	2.11	49.7	29.1	18.5	50.3	46.1	1,444	2,364	3,219	266	2,954	53,144	26.2	38.8
Southgate	12,615	2.30	56.6	38.8	10.9	43.4	36.6	NA	946	3,244	271	2,973	21,365	43.4	17.5
Sterling Heights	48,904	2.69	70.6	53.7	10.8	29.4	25.9	1,017	1,744	1,316	174	1,142	92,205	41.3	28.9
Taylor	24,275	2.49	63.7	35.1	20.1	36.3	30.8	673	1,869	3,049	607	2,442	41,764	58.8	9.3
Troy	32,801	2.54	70.8	63.6	4.4	29.2	26.1	NA	1,416	1,691	93	1,598	61,069	20.0	57.6
Warren	52,164	2.56	65.5	42.2	17.2	34.5	29.6	1,384	4,227	3,117	516	2,601	91,125	51.0	17.5
Westland	36,968	2.18	54.2	36.4	13.2	45.8	39.3	842	2,015	2,469	370	2,099	59,748	42.2	18.9
Wyandotte	11,197	2.22	58.9	44.7	9.6	41.1	34.7	73	434	1,734	196	1,538	18,869	43.0	16.3
Wyoming	27,985	2.68	65.7	44.7	12.9	34.3	24.4	434	2,111	2,781	464	2,317	49,509	48.3	19.8
MINNESOTA	2,148,725	2.51	63.6	50.3	8.9	36.4	29.2	132,543	131,150	2,376	243	2,133	3,725,283	32.3	34.8
Andover	10,740	3.02	82.1	72.8	6.2	17.9	11.7	NA	NA	NA	NA	NA	21,032	28.1	39.3
Apple Valley	19,365	2.66	73.4	59.4	9.3	26.6	23.6	363	1,213	2,349	124	2,225	35,006	25.1	43.7
Blaine	23,628	2.66	75.4	59.6	9.7	24.6	19.0	110	1,791	2,838	124	2,714	43,335	29.6	31.3
Bloomington	36,866	2.29	58.6	43.3	10.6	41.4	36.2	950	2,987	3,428	203	3,225	63,190	27.8	42.1
Brooklyn Center	12,024	2.55	60.9	33.5	17.4	39.1	32.2	NA	1,196	3,871	363	3,509	20,264	44.4	20.6
Brooklyn Park	27,711	2.87	67.1	43.6	17.0	32.9	27.2	258	2,738	3,431	388	3,043	49,485	30.6	33.1
Burnsville	24,126	2.52	67.5	52.9	12.9	32.5	25.8	389	1,778	2,882	203	2,679	41,763	28.0	39.1
Coon Rapids	23,352	2.65	65.9	46.1	13.0	34.1	25.9	402	1,889	3,028	167	2,861	42,216	38.5	21.4
Cottage Grove	12,189	2.95	74.3	61.8	11.2	25.7	19.5	77	585	1,618	47	1,571	22,776	32.2	32.2
Duluth	35,137	2.26	49.5	34.2	11.3	50.5	37.4	6,817	4,139	4,808	362	4,445	53,195	31.6	34.7
Eagan	27,062	2.44	63.7	49.6	8.9	36.3	28.4	320	1,184	1,775	60	1,715	46,840	18.9	51.2
Eden Prairie	25,764	2.47	68.4	57.6	7.3	31.6	27.0	176	765	1,195	56	1,138	45,110	18.1	60.9
Edina	21,591	2.36	60.5	53.0	6.8	39.5	32.3	307	961	1,900	51	1,849	36,396	9.5	70.5
Fridley	11,810	2.31	55.0	34.4	12.1	45.0	37.0	146	1,048	3,768	280	3,488	19,364	37.8	31.1
Inver Grove Heights	14,595	2.39	61.3	48.8	8.4	38.7	26.0	179	879	2,508	240	2,268	24,966	31.6	33.3
Lakeville	21,912	2.83	78.4	65.9	7.9	21.6	16.4	33	656	1,065	68	997	39,205	15.0	49.9
Mankato	15,849	2.41	49.7	34.8	7.2	50.3	26.9	3,557	1,441	3,489	271	3,218	21,040	32.7	36.9
Maple Grove	25,244	2.75	76.1	64.9	7.4	23.9	19.3	60	1,231	1,764	63	1,701	46,605	15.0	54.3
Maplewood	14,899	2.62	65.7	50.1	12.5	34.3	25.5	1,095	1,854	4,514	248	4,266	27,117	30.9	34.3
Minneapolis	171,906	2.30	44.0	31.6	8.7	56.0	41.5	17,620	22,216	5,331	1,109	4,222	273,349	26.6	48.4
Minnetonka	22,423	2.32	62.3	53.6	6.2	37.7	30.1	451	798	1,533	56	1,477	39,372	13.1	63.9
Moorhead	16,792	2.38	59.9	50.1	7.2	40.1	31.2	3,639	1,040	2,447	160	2,287	25,401	26.5	34.9
Oakdale	12,005	2.32	57.3	47.4	6.9	42.7	40.6	282	896	3,176	160	3,017	20,066	39.0	28.8
Owatonna	9,859	2.46	63.8	59.3	3.6	36.2	33.0	499	650	2,523	148	2,376	16,661	41.6	25.2
Plymouth	30,648	2.49	66.7	59.6	5.4	33.3	24.4	1,007	1,057	1,373	62	1,310	56,103	14.8	57.7
Richfield	13,681	2.61	61.6	46.4	10.9	38.4	28.6	304	996	2,736	214	2,521	25,338	33.0	38.7
Rochester	46,478	2.40	59.7	46.3	9.4	40.3	30.8	2,326	2,721	2,401	214	2,188	76,193	25.1	43.7
Roseville	14,493	2.36	55.3	45.7	7.0	44.7	37.4	1,499	1,884	5,240	197	5,043	23,972	28.1	46.5
St. Cloud	26,515	2.35	51.3	36.8	8.4	48.7	36.8	5,181	3,073	4,563	435	4,128	41,329	33.8	28.5
St. Louis Park	23,886	2.01	46.4	35.3	7.0	53.6	42.9	680	1,251	2,565	135	2,430	37,418	19.7	54.1
St. Paul	112,803	2.60	54.4	35.4	14.0	45.6	35.5	8,747	11,781	3,876	648	3,228	191,117	35.7	39.7
Savage	9,940	3.10	82.8	66.6	11.5	17.2	13.7	NA	458	1,472	119	1,353	18,766	22.2	46.7
Shakopee	14,509	2.73	68.8	57.7	5.7	31.2	27.1	1,059	861	2,125	165	1,959	27,129	31.7	35.0
Shoreview	11,351	2.32	62.1	53.4	6.3	37.9	32.8	NA	NA	NA	NA	NA	19,378	19.0	46.0
Winona	10,089	2.23	50.0	40.5	7.7	50.0	38.0	3,552	850	3,148	170	2,978	14,699	35.9	34.2
Woodbury	23,086	2.97	74.7	63.0	7.6	25.3	20.5	NA	1,385	2,006	67	1,940	41,985	16.1	57.6
MISSISSIPPI	1,091,245	2.65	67.0	44.9	17.7	33.0	28.8	93,060	91,115	3,049	280	2,768	1,957,022	46.7	21.8
Biloxi	16,796	2.56	62.2	41.4	16.7	37.8	32.7	2,920	2,875	6,257	396	5,860	28,370	47.4	20.3
Clinton	9,252	2.67	70.5	48.8	18.7	29.5	25.0	473	NA	NA	NA	NA	17,029	27.9	43.7
Greenville	11,710	2.59	58.1	23.9	31.3	41.9	38.2	446	2,057	6,482	277	6,205	19,960	47.3	20.3
Gulfport	27,723	2.55	61.4	37.6	18.0	38.6	33.7	1,417	4,057	5,583	314	5,269	47,310	40.7	22.7
Hattiesburg	17,977	2.63	60.0	30.5	24.2	40.0	32.3	3,827	2,899	6,167	313	5,855	29,838	37.5	25.9
Horn Lake	9,504	2.84	70.7	42.7	19.7	29.3	24.9	NA	721	2,663	74	2,589	16,738	43.9	18.2
Jackson	64,929	2.50	60.9	29.9	27.8	39.1	32.1	6,531	9,335	5,489	853	4,636	106,119	38.1	28.6
Meridian	15,005	2.50	60.0	35.4	23.5	40.0	36.7	1,564	2,047	5,200	594	4,606	24,242	42.7	20.8
Olive Branch	14,121	2.60	69.2	55.8	12.0	30.8	22.6	NA	999	2,736	183	2,553	26,165	36.0	27.8
Pearl	10,792	2.45	67.9	41.1	16.9	32.1	24.2	NA	NA	NA	NA	NA	17,338	52.1	16.4
Southaven	18,348	2.89	76.6	51.3	21.2	23.4	18.6	NA	1,539	2,887	111	2,776	34,253	37.1	24.6
Tupelo	15,823	2.41	65.3	39.9	15.4	34.7	30.4	707	NA	NA	NA	NA	25,003	36.2	27.9

1. No spouse present.   2. Data for serious crimes have not been adjusted for underreporting. This may affect comparability between geographic areas and over time.   3. Per 100,000 population estimated by the FBI.   4. Persons 25 years old and over.

Table D. Cities — Income and Housing

AREANAME	Money income, 2016 — Households			Median family income	Median non-family household income	Median earnings, 2016			Housing units, 2016				
	Median income	Percent with income less than $20,000	Percent with income of $200,000 or more			All persons	Men	Women	Total	Occupied	Percent owner occupied	Median value[1] (dollars)	Median rent (dollars)
	42	43	44	45	46	47	48	49	50	51	52	53	54
MICHIGAN— Cont'd													
Oak Park	51,150	20.8	3.8	69,922	37,413	27,728	30,793	25,178	13,506	12,545	55.5	96,400	1,000
Pontiac	31,387	31.0	0.1	38,540	23,330	22,209	22,031	22,464	27,086	22,432	43.1	56,600	754
Portage	65,814	9.7	3.6	81,558	38,210	32,445	42,024	30,600	20,883	19,379	69.6	165,700	730
Port Huron	36,248	25.6	0.8	44,583	25,747	21,902	26,776	19,036	13,891	13,040	50.5	79,200	762
Rochester Hills	81,195	8.7	11.7	100,647	42,326	45,254	63,582	33,553	28,624	27,843	76.2	294,200	1,243
Roseville	47,285	16.1	1.0	49,714	39,756	30,128	36,134	23,316	20,154	18,965	64.1	81,300	1,000
Royal Oak	74,109	10.9	7.4	101,182	54,111	46,792	56,206	40,372	31,568	29,590	65.1	200,400	1,009
Saginaw	29,901	37.2	0.1	31,742	23,729	17,973	20,864	16,888	24,332	19,773	58.3	34,900	681
St. Clair Shores	56,781	13.8	3.9	75,546	39,631	38,144	46,331	30,192	28,636	27,195	80.5	122,600	904
Southfield	49,664	17.2	1.7	63,100	40,741	36,667	36,699	36,572	36,771	33,963	45.5	147,000	1,051
Southgate	51,013	20.3	0.9	59,432	33,016	31,100	40,949	21,816	13,015	12,615	56.6	103,800	825
Sterling Heights	61,828	11.2	2.9	70,690	36,759	32,063	40,716	25,815	50,131	48,904	73.0	173,400	967
Taylor	45,761	24.1	0.9	55,608	28,456	27,115	31,747	21,816	25,538	24,275	66.7	87,700	863
Troy	95,975	7.2	13.7	116,513	57,771	51,772	74,583	32,031	33,538	32,801	73.2	286,800	1,104
Warren	46,249	18.0	1.3	55,438	30,882	26,851	32,582	22,813	56,330	52,164	68.7	113,500	858
Westland	45,638	18.0	1.2	60,253	33,927	31,158	36,116	25,480	38,981	36,968	58.1	113,200	856
Wyandotte	49,104	15.7	0.8	67,062	30,782	35,775	42,288	28,008	12,414	11,197	68.0	101,900	752
Wyoming	51,886	14.3	1.2	57,002	37,810	27,645	35,024	23,287	28,817	27,985	66.3	112,800	800
MINNESOTA	65,599	12.7	6.4	83,344	37,804	36,219	41,616	30,787	2,409,701	2,148,725	71.3	211,800	912
Andover	108,179	2.4	9.1	117,350	68,464	44,797	55,360	39,574	10,782	10,740	89.5	262,000	1,533
Apple Valley	88,569	5.5	8.2	97,392	46,093	41,883	50,563	35,840	20,383	19,365	84.5	230,500	1,152
Blaine	86,186	8.5	8.0	96,210	40,417	45,183	49,473	40,226	24,384	23,628	85.3	220,600	1,171
Bloomington	68,108	12.3	6.7	88,918	43,197	41,981	45,748	41,102	38,532	36,866	64.8	237,600	1,020
Brooklyn Center	54,225	11.1	2.3	57,842	34,716	31,999	37,868	28,819	12,155	12,024	56.8	161,700	961
Brooklyn Park	61,734	13.9	6.9	78,041	37,280	36,088	41,179	31,766	30,505	27,711	69.2	204,700	989
Burnsville	67,214	8.4	3.7	79,098	46,264	39,008	40,431	38,024	25,148	24,126	65.7	233,900	1,107
Coon Rapids	66,239	9.6	3.0	77,539	43,853	35,964	40,988	30,760	23,819	23,352	72.9	188,100	1,054
Cottage Grove	91,579	1.3	7.7	94,491	57,271	47,204	52,292	36,687	12,600	12,189	91.3	236,900	1,121
Duluth	48,126	19.7	4.4	65,987	32,318	25,082	26,339	24,251	37,126	35,137	60.4	154,500	761
Eagan	81,552	9.4	11.7	110,035	47,428	45,531	54,639	36,953	27,756	27,062	67.3	274,400	1,126
Eden Prairie	99,988	4.7	17.1	127,963	53,148	52,095	61,979	41,658	26,915	25,764	70.8	360,200	1,365
Edina	91,118	9.0	23.9	137,104	46,707	61,688	78,875	47,778	22,268	21,591	69.4	466,500	1,336
Fridley	56,437	11.6	3.6	69,614	36,216	35,621	40,276	31,084	12,179	11,810	65.5	178,700	935
Inver Grove Heights	69,028	9.9	7.7	84,375	48,673	38,844	40,939	36,710	15,170	14,595	67.3	225,000	899
Lakeville	107,207	2.2	13.2	117,593	52,064	50,545	60,365	42,478	22,434	21,912	86.5	300,000	1,429
Mankato	47,350	19.2	3.8	66,415	34,221	21,794	26,765	15,809	16,914	15,849	45.2	165,400	849
Maple Grove	113,957	3.2	15.6	124,818	61,791	60,477	72,844	40,073	25,700	25,244	86.1	284,200	1,458
Maplewood	64,438	10.6	6.2	88,979	36,797	34,852	40,028	31,685	15,691	14,899	69.8	220,100	1,099
Minneapolis	56,255	20.2	6.9	81,568	40,481	31,932	35,125	30,337	182,891	171,906	46.7	235,200	932
Minnetonka	96,417	7.9	16.8	121,327	65,426	57,229	67,200	45,045	23,478	22,423	71.8	347,600	1,284
Moorhead	55,589	17.7	4.3	71,985	30,193	30,102	39,749	22,180	18,016	16,792	60.4	192,900	776
Oakdale	63,616	8.2	3.4	97,788	32,275	43,714	52,317	32,301	12,261	12,005	76.1	223,700	1,080
Owatonna	58,335	14.1	4.6	85,125	38,011	39,298	44,003	32,667	10,484	9,859	74.5	149,900	621
Plymouth	97,940	6.8	17.6	119,920	50,329	51,105	57,424	46,769	32,199	30,648	69.6	335,000	1,309
Richfield	67,127	10.4	3.7	81,393	46,578	35,729	39,229	31,735	14,600	13,681	63.2	215,400	999
Rochester	67,712	11.5	5.9	86,776	41,079	40,070	41,144	35,428	48,500	46,478	69.5	177,300	950
Roseville	65,956	13.8	3.8	83,001	43,152	36,169	39,091	32,484	15,096	14,493	61.2	230,000	990
St. Cloud	43,750	20.2	1.6	64,217	30,165	23,209	26,376	18,496	27,521	26,515	49.9	155,700	735
St. Louis Park	75,672	11.9	7.9	95,938	49,399	48,021	54,611	41,737	24,697	23,886	54.4	261,100	1,140
St. Paul	54,085	18.1	5.1	67,105	39,704	30,964	31,990	28,607	119,785	112,803	49.9	198,500	902
Savage	110,191	4.4	12.0	119,866	53,500	42,267	56,595	32,413	9,940	9,940	83.3	288,900	1,159
Shakopee	76,924	13.3	5.0	99,366	38,824	42,017	52,226	36,549	15,266	14,509	75.2	236,700	1,264
Shoreview	84,431	7.0	10.2	106,803	51,650	42,895	51,295	39,493	11,702	11,351	79.6	257,000	1,058
Winona	45,025	21.0	2.8	69,837	26,529	17,319	23,135	12,101	11,522	10,089	63.5	137,900	630
Woodbury	103,902	3.9	12.1	120,251	59,972	51,598	58,753	41,214	24,291	23,086	78.2	314,700	1,434
MISSISSIPPI	41,754	24.9	2.6	52,672	22,552	27,427	32,514	22,421	1,307,492	1,091,245	67.3	113,900	728
Biloxi	35,906	30.9	0.6	42,876	22,456	21,485	28,750	17,548	20,431	16,796	41.2	124,700	747
Clinton	61,645	13.1	1.9	73,898	32,963	34,814	36,112	32,465	9,726	9,252	62.7	180,700	1,031
Greenville	24,935	39.4	2.4	36,140	20,169	23,598	26,081	22,005	14,377	11,710	51.0	75,300	646
Gulfport	39,320	24.3	1.3	47,970	25,767	23,798	26,456	19,904	33,508	27,723	52.2	118,100	774
Hattiesburg	36,598	25.1	2.8	56,726	22,953	17,663	18,428	17,145	21,378	17,977	35.4	100,700	762
Horn Lake	45,496	20.5	0.9	47,681	28,316	26,846	32,119	24,562	11,044	9,504	64.8	104,700	907
Jackson	39,724	23.8	3.1	46,786	25,884	25,029	25,858	24,512	75,898	64,929	52.4	88,500	813
Meridian	30,773	36.2	2.6	38,148	22,601	27,695	30,974	21,285	18,873	15,005	55.9	81,400	652
Olive Branch	72,379	6.9	2.8	82,260	48,847	35,861	46,732	31,126	14,726	14,121	67.3	170,900	1,076
Pearl	45,270	14.3	0.7	47,487	38,606	27,934	38,407	26,190	11,013	10,792	66.4	133,600	744
Southaven	57,716	14.1	3.1	61,033	32,305	35,797	42,384	30,063	19,581	18,348	68.1	142,700	1,035
Tupelo	41,467	22.9	1.9	51,499	22,430	25,685	36,356	21,233	17,417	15,823	52.0	139,000	691

1. Specified owner-occupied units; $2,000,000 represents $2,000,000 or more.

Table D. Cities — Commuting, Computer Access, Migration, Labor Force, and Employment

AREANAME	Commuting 2016 Percent — Drove alone	With commutes of 30 minutes or more	Computer access Percent — With a computer in the house	With Internet access	Migration — Percent who lived in the same house one year ago	Percent who lived in another state or county one year ago	Civilian labor force 2016 — Total	Percent change 2016-2017	Unemployment — Total	Rate	Civilian employment 2016 — Population age 16 and older Number	Percent in labor force	Population age 16 to 64 Number	Percent who worked full-year full-time
	55	56	57	58	59	60	61	62	63	64	65	66	67	68
MICHIGAN— Cont'd														
Oak Park	83.3	25.9	91.0	78.8	85.9	6.9	14,429	1.2	831	5.8	24,501	66.8	19,923	47.5
Pontiac	74.1	30.2	81.3	73.9	75.9	6.2	25,212	0.6	2,043	8.1	43,754	61.1	37,402	40.1
Portage	88.7	16.5	91.5	89.2	86.8	3.3	25,163	0.4	949	3.8	39,273	67.0	31,844	52.6
Port Huron	71.4	27.0	82.7	75.4	75.4	6.5	12,895	0.7	871	6.8	24,468	59.6	20,028	39.8
Rochester Hills	87.6	38.3	94.8	90.9	86.7	8.0	39,423	1.8	1,118	2.8	58,413	63.8	46,675	51.3
Roseville	86.1	38.7	84.5	74.8	83.0	6.7	23,442	1.2	1,292	5.5	37,337	61.6	30,973	46.6
Royal Oak	86.6	34.4	94.4	91.2	81.4	8.7	38,573	2.0	809	2.1	52,596	71.1	43,105	62.9
Saginaw	76.4	16.0	77.5	68.1	79.4	3.6	19,238	-0.8	1,858	9.7	37,326	55.1	30,758	34.1
St. Clair Shores	88.1	39.3	87.9	83.4	87.7	2.6	31,571	1.5	1,304	4.1	49,860	66.5	38,966	56.7
Southfield	86.2	32.9	90.0	84.2	82.3	8.0	35,110	1.3	1,731	4.9	61,359	63.1	46,623	49.2
Southgate	87.6	25.2	84.9	76.2	79.2	3.0	15,715	1.7	500	3.2	24,241	64.2	18,992	48.3
Sterling Heights	88.0	37.2	91.6	86.6	87.0	4.3	67,600	1.5	2,753	4.1	107,877	61.0	87,078	46.4
Taylor	89.6	28.6	87.0	76.0	89.5	2.1	28,883	1.4	1,553	5.4	50,130	59.6	41,393	44.5
Troy	87.7	35.2	94.8	90.9	87.8	6.3	43,747	1.8	1,233	2.8	69,425	64.4	54,498	52.6
Warren	88.9	38.7	84.1	78.2	86.7	4.6	64,070	1.3	3,307	5.2	107,704	60.4	85,977	45.6
Westland	78.8	38.4	88.4	81.8	84.8	3.1	43,696	1.6	1,650	3.8	67,846	66.0	54,743	51.3
Wyandotte	87.2	35.1	85.1	75.0	NA	NA	13,401	1.7	494	3.7	21,004	62.9	16,371	53.8
Wyoming	83.0	20.3	94.8	88.5	82.7	5.0	44,498	1.4	1,719	3.9	59,744	72.7	51,915	54.5
MINNESOTA	77.8	31.4	90.2	83.4	85.6	7.3	3,063,604	0.9	105,766	3.5	4,375,523	69.5	3,545,188	55.0
Andover	78.2	50.9	93.9	92.2	91.1	3.2	18,788	1.4	528	2.8	25,127	75.0	21,867	58.7
Apple Valley	82.5	38.5	91.4	88.0	86.7	9.1	30,289	1.5	863	2.8	41,038	72.6	34,619	59.4
Blaine	80.3	39.9	93.9	91.3	87.9	7.4	36,258	1.4	1,125	3.1	48,655	75.2	40,951	62.6
Bloomington	78.2	30.3	91.9	82.9	86.8	5.1	46,669	1.4	1,459	3.1	70,861	66.5	51,608	58.8
Brooklyn Center	79.3	34.1	89.3	74.1	87.0	6.9	15,519	1.5	612	3.9	23,081	73.8	18,751	57.2
Brooklyn Park	77.9	33.5	92.3	84.5	91.4	4.5	42,649	1.4	1,480	3.5	58,934	70.8	50,874	57.0
Burnsville	77.1	36.7	95.0	87.4	83.3	6.8	35,968	1.3	1,101	3.1	48,416	75.6	38,801	64.5
Coon Rapids	81.7	38.9	89.3	83.8	87.6	5.9	35,753	1.4	1,192	3.3	49,786	71.1	40,709	59.4
Cottage Grove	83.1	37.0	90.7	86.2	90.4	3.1	20,364	1.5	650	3.2	27,444	70.5	22,982	59.8
Duluth	74.5	9.7	89.9	81.1	75.6	10.0	46,084	0.4	1,620	3.5	71,120	66.8	58,756	44.4
Eagan	80.5	34.4	95.3	92.6	86.8	6.7	40,232	1.4	1,090	2.7	53,655	78.0	45,536	59.9
Eden Prairie	80.9	28.3	95.7	92.5	82.8	7.6	36,693	1.5	971	2.6	50,753	75.6	43,533	60.7
Edina	73.9	25.9	93.3	87.6	88.0	6.1	25,902	1.5	702	2.7	39,649	65.1	29,226	56.5
Fridley	83.1	34.3	86.5	82.1	81.4	15.8	14,867	1.4	553	3.7	21,974	70.4	17,244	63.8
Inver Grove Heights	79.7	23.0	89.4	82.1	83.3	10.2	19,916	1.5	634	3.2	28,833	67.8	21,765	60.8
Lakeville	83.7	37.1	97.8	94.8	87.0	5.7	35,398	1.5	968	2.7	46,878	79.5	41,965	61.4
Mankato	77.2	11.5	95.0	83.8	65.7	19.3	25,832	1.2	735	2.8	35,721	73.3	30,767	40.2
Maple Grove	83.6	45.4	95.9	92.3	89.4	4.3	40,985	1.5	1,104	2.7	52,526	76.8	45,069	63.0
Maplewood	81.5	40.9	89.2	85.2	86.9	4.2	20,731	1.4	739	3.6	32,061	69.4	25,551	51.5
Minneapolis	59.9	26.5	90.5	80.6	76.2	10.2	238,621	1.5	7,437	3.1	339,834	73.8	301,399	49.6
Minnetonka	77.0	29.4	93.0	89.7	84.2	4.7	30,232	1.5	843	2.8	43,240	66.1	32,901	57.8
Moorhead	80.7	11.9	87.3	74.0	80.5	11.5	24,360	0.4	669	2.7	35,282	65.8	29,531	49.9
Oakdale	84.5	31.1	89.7	87.5	89.7	8.7	16,315	1.5	534	3.3	22,887	66.4	17,292	57.2
Owatonna	82.3	15.9	90.0	85.3	86.6	5.1	14,312	-3.5	470	3.3	18,858	71.7	14,823	65.1
Plymouth	78.1	38.2	96.0	92.1	81.7	9.8	44,213	1.6	1,228	2.8	60,651	72.0	49,486	61.5
Richfield	73.7	27.1	89.4	85.2	82.8	6.2	20,228	1.7	607	3.0	28,221	71.8	22,143	60.4
Rochester	70.2	11.9	91.2	86.0	84.2	8.6	63,682	1.0	1,667	2.6	89,321	71.2	72,872	57.9
Roseville	78.2	23.0	90.2	85.9	80.2	10.1	19,369	1.5	564	2.9	28,919	69.1	23,016	56.5
St. Cloud	79.0	11.2	90.2	82.8	71.4	16.9	37,375	1.0	1,358	3.6	56,287	68.5	47,618	41.8
St. Louis Park	76.8	25.5	93.0	87.0	76.7	6.9	30,852	1.5	810	2.6	41,356	75.9	34,679	62.2
St. Paul	68.6	31.5	90.6	83.1	79.5	10.7	157,688	1.4	5,199	3.3	233,665	69.3	202,773	47.3
Savage	85.9	39.8	97.6	93.2	89.6	7.5	18,314	1.6	490	2.7	23,462	81.9	21,350	61.1
Shakopee	85.4	28.5	92.9	91.7	86.1	10.1	23,292	1.4	661	2.8	29,666	75.7	25,471	58.6
Shoreview	85.2	37.3	94.1	90.9	85.0	9.7	15,024	1.4	426	2.8	21,838	73.9	17,015	59.0
Winona	65.0	14.2	88.4	84.7	70.3	14.4	15,660	-1.1	504	3.2	22,929	67.0	18,255	36.8
Woodbury	80.4	34.6	97.7	95.9	84.7	9.1	39,209	1.4	985	2.5	50,079	75.1	43,537	59.4
MISSISSIPPI	84.6	31.7	82.1	70.3	86.6	5.8	1,280,071	0.1	64,956	5.1	2,349,401	57.1	1,899,767	46.1
Biloxi	69.1	20.6	79.3	69.6	67.4	17.7	19,833	-0.2	924	4.7	34,710	59.9	28,106	44.4
Clinton	80.7	33.5	91.3	88.8	85.4	5.3	13,276	0.6	477	3.6	19,693	63.5	15,441	56.4
Greenville	79.1	10.8	79.7	64.9	88.2	4.0	11,579	-3.1	804	6.9	23,373	49.9	18,961	38.2
Gulfport	83.9	24.2	83.8	75.7	80.6	6.4	29,341	-0.7	1,427	4.9	57,406	62.6	47,531	48.8
Hattiesburg	76.7	14.8	87.0	75.4	71.5	14.8	22,172	1.4	1,036	4.7	40,379	66.9	35,711	43.5
Horn Lake	NA	41.0	88.9	82.1	82.4	6.2	12,870	0.3	493	3.8	20,780	65.1	18,323	50.2
Jackson	83.3	24.0	86.0	78.2	80.7	5.0	75,299	0.4	3,777	5.0	130,528	65.1	110,992	46.4
Meridian	88.1	6.7	78.1	65.0	77.3	7.7	15,351	-0.9	868	5.7	28,343	53.5	22,517	47.2
Olive Branch	91.0	31.5	93.8	88.5	85.9	8.2	19,493	0.7	612	3.1	29,623	68.3	25,384	57.1
Pearl	NA	18.6	85.4	76.3	81.5	9.0	12,969	0.7	493	3.8	20,600	62.4	16,198	54.6
Southaven	86.5	32.9	93.6	83.1	85.6	6.7	27,291	0.5	903	3.3	40,603	64.8	33,908	56.4
Tupelo	90.1	15.2	84.8	76.0	81.8	5.8	17,819	-0.2	757	4.2	30,179	64.5	24,368	56.2

1. Employed persons. 2. Households. 3. Percent of civilian labor force.

Table D. Cities — City Government Finances

AREANAME	General revenue Total (mil dol)	Intergovernmental Total (mil dol)	Intergovernmental Percent from state government	Taxes Total (mil dol)	Taxes Per capita (dollars) Total	Taxes Per capita (dollars) Property	Taxes Per capita (dollars) Sales and gross receipts	General expenditure Total (mil dol)	General expenditure Per capita (dollars) Total	General expenditure Per capita (dollars) Capital outlays
	117	118	119	120	121	122	123	124	125	126
MICHIGAN— Cont'd										
Oak Park	34.3	6.1	77.1	15.3	515	501	14	32.4	1,094	25
Pontiac	80.8	29.4	48.1	29.2	491	278	50	91.7	1,541	157
Portage	42.4	7.6	94.6	24.0	508	481	26	39.8	842	89
Port Huron	56.4	17.9	36.7	21.0	712	492	23	60.3	2,048	427
Rochester Hills	71.4	14.4	64.9	31.6	437	403	34	59.2	819	60
Roseville	60.4	8.9	82.4	25.0	527	511	16	53.3	1,126	43
Royal Oak	80.5	15.1	59.4	31.4	537	481	56	82.6	1,412	97
Saginaw	92.8	33.0	36.6	21.3	420	150	24	92.8	1,827	78
St. Clair Shores	68.3	10.3	86.2	32.7	546	515	32	62.0	1,037	61
Southfield	103.2	22.5	49.8	64.7	892	863	29	95.5	1,316	49
Southgate	30.9	6.3	84.0	16.4	550	533	17	30.8	1,034	2
Sterling Heights	116.0	21.5	85.9	55.5	426	408	17	126.6	970	137
Taylor	98.5	28.2	37.2	43.0	688	652	36	96.7	1,549	17
Troy	91.2	12.7	89.5	49.2	600	579	21	79.5	969	131
Warren	142.5	27.4	77.3	78.9	588	570	18	136.7	1,019	40
Westland	82.4	25.5	58.5	27.2	327	312	14	78.6	943	2
Wyandotte	44.6	7.8	56.0	16.7	656	640	16	53.7	2,107	160
Wyoming	74.0	21.7	50.6	26.8	365	333	32	64.1	874	19
MINNESOTA	X	X	X	X	X	X	X	X	X	X
Andover	22.9	1.9	92.9	12.6	406	393	12	18.3	588	147
Apple Valley	46.2	2.4	99.7	25.9	518	476	43	38.3	766	170
Blaine	45.6	3.0	81.8	23.5	396	359	37	44.2	746	172
Bloomington	120.6	11.3	85.5	69.9	812	609	203	137.2	1,595	316
Brooklyn Center	39.3	5.0	72.8	18.2	595	514	59	39.3	1,280	319
Brooklyn Park	79.5	9.0	54.3	44.0	566	543	23	69.8	898	50
Burnsville	55.1	4.0	78.6	33.5	547	501	46	54.1	885	185
Coon Rapids	50.6	4.4	75.2	28.1	453	367	86	69.6	1,124	385
Cottage Grove	32.6	4.1	86.1	13.7	391	358	32	30.2	858	186
Duluth	206.7	90.6	73.8	42.1	488	216	272	223.1	2,586	972
Eagan	55.0	3.8	90.8	28.6	442	413	29	57.4	885	201
Eden Prairie	70.0	5.2	80.2	37.9	610	555	54	67.1	1,079	147
Edina	63.6	3.2	88.7	32.5	663	592	70	63.8	1,301	290
Fridley	25.2	2.5	85.3	13.4	485	445	39	22.0	798	53
Inver Grove Heights	31.7	4.0	89.5	15.9	466	442	24	53.2	1,557	670
Lakeville	38.7	2.8	74.0	25.0	436	404	32	42.0	732	180
Mankato	77.8	20.6	42.2	21.6	539	345	195	74.6	1,863	805
Maple Grove	94.0	6.8	98.0	34.4	534	494	40	87.7	1,362	607
Maplewood	49.5	5.8	59.6	18.9	481	447	34	51.2	1,300	407
Minneapolis	1,017.5	148.8	51.2	459.8	1,170	858	312	1,439.6	3,663	222
Minnetonka	66.8	15.6	62.1	35.1	686	601	85	65.7	1,286	502
Moorhead	71.8	30.0	77.2	8.2	210	171	39	91.5	2,342	1,042
Oakdale	20.9	1.3	73.5	10.5	379	346	33	27.2	981	403
Owatonna	26.3	7.8	88.0	10.8	426	355	71	25.3	995	237
Plymouth	77.8	8.1	86.5	32.3	443	399	45	66.3	909	162
Richfield	43.3	7.0	35.4	22.3	617	560	57	42.6	1,180	117
Rochester	216.6	36.4	96.7	62.4	572	415	158	238.9	2,190	743
Roseville	33.7	3.3	86.1	17.5	506	445	61	34.0	981	217
St. Cloud	89.0	22.7	89.2	36.3	550	348	201	105.0	1,592	659
St. Louis Park	76.4	3.2	86.2	35.3	760	659	101	77.7	1,676	320
St. Paul	510.2	119.9	59.1	175.4	602	412	190	504.8	1,733	219
Savage	32.0	3.4	94.3	16.3	584	537	46	22.4	802	183
Shakopee	36.9	5.1	99.9	15.9	410	373	37	36.0	928	217
Shoreview	25.3	1.3	99.9	11.3	441	424	17	23.1	899	137
Winona	24.8	11.9	97.0	7.9	284	213	71	23.2	837	90
Woodbury	61.1	3.7	75.8	30.7	475	432	44	55.7	863	229
MISSISSIPPI	X	X	X	X	X	X	X	X	X	X
Biloxi	102.9	58.6	70.6	23.1	518	393	125	110.6	2,484	715
Clinton	22.4	8.4	97.4	8.5	332	293	39	20.7	810	145
Greenville	30.6	10.5	67.0	12.3	368	293	75	32.5	970	190
Gulfport	510.2	92.4	40.6	32.6	466	348	117	508.4	7,267	1,373
Hattiesburg	68.9	33.4	74.6	25.2	537	368	168	64.6	1,378	307
Horn Lake	18.5	4.3	95.2	7.0	264	233	31	15.9	598	35
Jackson	222.7	65.9	65.5	79.3	452	389	63	212.1	1,210	208
Meridian	43.9	15.5	100.0	18.6	456	387	69	39.7	973	158
Olive Branch	42.4	15.2	100.0	15.0	434	379	55	33.8	978	185
Pearl	24.5	10.5	91.4	6.9	263	226	37	32.5	1,241	187
Southaven	49.4	12.7	100.0	25.8	512	457	55	48.7	966	118
Tupelo	65.5	32.8	96.4	15.7	442	418	24	62.2	1,751	529

1. Based on population estimated as of July 1 of the year shown.

AREANAME	City government finances, 2012 (cont.)									
	General expenditures (cont.)									
	Percent of total for:									
	Public welfare	Highways	Parking facilities	Education	Health and hospitals	Police protection	Sewerage and sanitation	Parks and recreation	Housing and community development	Interest on debt
	127	128	129	130	131	132	133	134	135	136
MICHIGAN— Cont'd										
Oak Park	0.0	4.6	0.0	0.0	0.0	26.1	25.4	3.4	1.7	4.4
Pontiac	0.0	7.1	0.9	0.0	0.0	12.5	18.4	0.4	15.4	3.8
Portage	0.3	15.3	0.0	0.0	0.0	16.1	25.8	5.4	0.7	6.0
Port Huron	0.0	9.9	0.2	0.0	0.0	12.5	24.6	6.6	19.9	4.4
Rochester Hills	0.0	16.6	0.0	0.0	0.0	14.1	16.0	17.9	0.0	1.7
Roseville	0.0	9.7	0.0	0.0	0.0	22.0	20.2	4.1	2.4	0.9
Royal Oak	0.0	8.3	2.6	0.0	0.9	15.6	28.0	4.9	2.8	4.3
Saginaw	0.0	6.8	0.3	0.0	0.0	19.4	19.6	0.4	17.3	1.0
St. Clair Shores	0.0	8.8	0.0	0.0	0.0	18.5	24.7	7.1	0.1	3.1
Southfield	0.0	8.3	0.0	0.0	0.0	25.8	3.3	9.2	0.8	2.2
Southgate	0.0	10.8	0.0	0.0	0.0	19.5	14.2	3.9	0.7	2.6
Sterling Heights	0.0	9.6	0.0	0.0	0.0	23.7	27.1	2.0	0.7	0.9
Taylor	0.0	6.6	0.0	0.0	0.0	13.8	11.6	3.9	20.5	5.2
Troy	0.0	17.7	0.0	0.0	0.0	27.5	18.5	11.2	0.2	3.2
Warren	0.0	10.2	0.0	0.0	0.0	25.5	15.8	5.4	3.9	3.3
Westland	0.0	7.6	0.0	0.0	0.0	18.9	22.4	3.3	2.0	0.4
Wyandotte	0.0	10.3	0.0	0.0	0.0	12.1	10.3	3.8	0.0	1.2
Wyoming	0.0	10.0	0.0	0.0	0.0	23.8	19.2	7.1	14.4	1.7
MINNESOTA	X	X	X	X	X	X	X	X	X	X
Andover	0.0	21.8	0.0	0.0	0.1	14.3	10.5	11.4	13.2	10.2
Apple Valley	0.0	23.5	0.0	0.0	0.1	20.0	12.9	18.3	1.6	4.4
Blaine	0.0	19.5	0.0	0.0	0.0	20.6	22.6	3.2	4.5	4.2
Bloomington	0.0	15.1	0.0	0.0	4.6	18.4	9.8	10.4	0.3	2.3
Brooklyn Center	0.0	19.6	0.0	0.0	0.0	18.2	16.1	7.6	5.8	2.3
Brooklyn Park	0.0	12.2	0.0	0.0	0.0	24.2	11.5	13.9	1.1	5.9
Burnsville	0.0	20.0	0.0	0.0	0.0	22.5	13.2	12.7	0.0	4.0
Coon Rapids	0.0	11.5	0.9	0.0	0.1	12.5	11.3	29.9	4.5	4.1
Cottage Grove	0.0	33.1	0.0	0.0	3.9	16.5	6.7	11.5	4.3	12.1
Duluth	0.0	10.1	0.4	0.0	0.0	13.3	14.3	13.0	4.6	4.5
Eagan	0.0	20.7	0.0	0.0	0.0	19.5	13.7	14.3	0.0	5.8
Eden Prairie	1.2	12.6	0.0	0.0	0.0	17.7	14.4	15.9	4.9	12.0
Edina	0.0	27.8	0.0	0.0	0.8	13.8	14.5	20.4	1.1	3.7
Fridley	0.0	16.8	0.0	0.0	0.0	23.9	27.0	6.0	5.6	0.1
Inver Grove Heights	0.0	24.4	0.0	0.0	0.0	10.4	20.8	20.6	1.3	4.3
Lakeville	0.0	25.3	0.0	0.0	0.0	21.3	9.7	9.7	1.2	8.8
Mankato	0.0	18.4	5.3	0.0	0.0	11.5	15.6	4.6	16.8	3.8
Maple Grove	0.0	38.8	0.0	0.0	0.0	10.9	8.6	15.2	1.5	5.0
Maplewood	0.0	30.5	0.0	0.0	0.3	15.2	9.0	8.7	0.7	17.9
Minneapolis	0.0	6.6	3.3	0.0	1.1	10.1	41.6	7.3	9.6	8.6
Minnetonka	0.0	31.5	0.0	0.0	0.5	16.6	9.2	10.9	8.2	3.8
Moorhead	0.0	11.8	0.0	0.0	0.4	8.0	8.7	5.0	1.2	11.2
Oakdale	0.0	28.1	0.0	0.0	0.0	15.5	10.8	5.0	0.0	3.0
Owatonna	0.0	25.9	0.0	0.0	0.0	16.3	14.0	13.5	3.4	3.0
Plymouth	0.0	16.9	0.0	0.0	0.0	14.7	11.2	18.8	2.0	8.3
Richfield	0.0	7.8	0.0	0.0	0.3	17.0	11.9	11.5	23.0	12.9
Rochester	0.0	14.1	1.4	0.0	0.1	8.6	5.1	7.5	0.2	27.8
Roseville	0.0	14.4	0.0	0.0	0.0	18.2	17.2	12.1	4.2	1.3
St. Cloud	0.0	11.6	1.2	0.0	0.9	15.3	22.1	22.3	1.4	4.9
St. Louis Park	0.0	9.2	0.0	0.0	0.0	9.0	10.3	10.9	1.1	25.9
St. Paul	0.0	12.4	1.3	0.0	0.7	17.5	8.3	15.6	9.7	6.3
Savage	0.0	30.8	0.0	0.0	0.0	19.3	12.0	7.6	0.9	11.4
Shakopee	0.0	22.2	0.0	0.0	0.0	18.6	16.8	12.4	0.0	13.3
Shoreview	0.0	15.7	0.0	0.0	0.0	7.9	23.0	26.0	3.7	6.4
Winona	0.0	12.5	0.0	0.0	0.5	18.9	18.0	13.8	3.7	0.8
Woodbury	0.0	22.0	2.9	0.0	3.0	20.7	11.9	11.7	3.2	3.7
MISSISSIPPI	X	X	X	X	X	X	X	X	X	X
Biloxi	1.0	7.1	0.0	0.0	0.2	13.5	15.9	12.3	0.7	2.1
Clinton	0.0	13.3	0.0	0.0	0.0	19.0	28.7	7.7	0.0	3.8
Greenville	0.4	16.8	0.0	0.0	0.9	22.4	13.5	2.6	0.0	1.1
Gulfport	0.0	5.6	0.0	0.0	72.1	4.7	4.9	3.1	2.1	1.8
Hattiesburg	0.0	16.5	0.3	0.0	1.6	16.2	16.4	6.6	2.8	2.3
Horn Lake	0.0	6.3	0.0	0.0	0.7	27.6	15.3	6.7	0.7	6.2
Jackson	0.5	9.5	0.0	0.0	0.5	15.4	16.2	6.3	0.9	4.0
Meridian	0.0	13.7	0.4	0.0	0.0	18.3	14.0	5.1	2.6	5.1
Olive Branch	0.0	10.9	0.0	0.0	2.5	22.3	22.4	4.0	0.0	5.9
Pearl	0.0	22.1	0.0	0.0	1.4	19.0	18.3	4.3	0.0	6.3
Southaven	0.0	2.9	0.0	0.0	0.6	21.9	9.2	9.5	0.0	8.5
Tupelo	0.0	24.5	0.0	0.0	0.0	16.4	11.5	9.2	0.1	4.2

Table D. Cities — Income and Housing

AREANAME	Money income, 2016					Median earnings, 2016			Housing units, 2016				
	Households			Median family income	Median non-family household income	All persons	Men	Women	Total	Occupied	Percent owner occupied	Median value[1] (dollars)	Median rent (dollars)
	Median income	Percent with income less than $20,000	Percent with income of $200,000 or more										
	42	43	44	45	46	47	48	49	50	51	52	53	54
MISSOURI	51,746	17.2	3.9	65,058	31,409	30,800	36,375	25,766	2,760,226	2,372,190	66.1	151,400	771
Ballwin..........................	77,458	4.8	7.9	106,783	46,317	41,526	51,663	35,094	12,651	12,233	81.5	238,300	1,131
Blue Springs..................	72,592	7.9	5.3	79,380	45,657	39,440	51,259	30,448	21,104	19,500	74.3	161,800	941
Cape Girardeau..................	41,518	26.3	2.9	56,414	21,083	22,077	30,676	18,158	17,591	15,280	53.0	148,300	813
Chesterfield..................	109,566	9.6	24.1	132,754	48,858	60,204	85,115	34,388	21,096	19,433	78.1	367,700	1,136
Columbia......................	50,044	22.0	4.6	78,277	30,377	26,015	30,799	22,075	53,323	47,982	44.8	187,200	820
Florissant....................	51,118	11.9	1.0	66,394	35,833	31,616	37,138	25,857	20,812	19,527	64.2	94,400	1,031
Gladstone......................	55,252	10.1	1.6	63,889	35,860	30,141	35,289	21,485	11,988	10,775	68.2	140,300	854
Hazelwood......................	51,815	11.1	4.7	71,136	39,469	32,543	40,832	29,058	12,524	11,925	63.3	107,500	827
Independence..................	45,970	16.5	2.2	55,007	35,784	31,112	36,793	26,073	54,850	48,151	58.9	109,600	764
Jefferson City	49,825	17.6	2.3	69,794	31,253	31,622	31,605	31,640	18,694	17,047	61.8	133,400	630
Joplin..........................	40,198	22.2	2.8	60,441	27,432	27,107	33,485	25,281	25,996	21,935	59.6	122,300	769
Kansas City...................	51,235	18.6	3.9	64,095	35,341	31,806	37,270	27,385	228,329	198,202	53.0	146,300	857
Kirkwood......................	76,704	11.1	10.7	103,320	37,097	42,123	52,201	32,457	12,293	11,183	70.4	299,300	1,046
Lee's Summit..................	85,137	10.8	8.3	98,633	40,060	42,342	55,407	37,011	36,566	35,217	76.2	209,100	880
Liberty........................	69,544	8.5	2.6	82,765	40,688	37,152	45,220	32,130	12,171	11,464	79.6	177,000	748
Maryland Heights	59,730	12.4	0.8	70,943	36,867	34,401	35,545	33,556	12,256	11,524	50.0	152,400	942
O'Fallon......................	85,313	6.4	6.9	92,840	46,622	41,511	51,049	32,112	31,923	30,696	83.4	224,400	1,056
Raytown........................	49,438	14.2	0.7	66,036	36,679	30,899	31,748	30,576	14,441	13,228	61.4	104,900	774
St. Charles...................	63,006	10.8	4.2	79,321	42,535	33,358	45,543	21,825	30,810	28,060	66.3	193,200	963
St. Joseph....................	44,528	23.1	2.3	55,585	30,658	27,092	29,747	26,218	33,552	29,434	58.5	113,100	682
St. Louis......................	40,346	26.5	3.8	48,062	32,184	30,013	31,411	27,273	175,710	139,021	43.6	125,800	781
St. Peters....................	74,822	6.8	5.1	87,917	42,134	40,257	47,001	31,835	22,323	21,681	82.8	172,900	959
Springfield	33,286	29.9	1.0	44,495	23,875	20,716	22,542	18,521	81,975	74,126	41.3	115,900	679
University City	61,036	18.2	12.8	82,243	36,349	38,397	52,430	32,142	18,059	15,845	39.8	245,500	977
Wentzville....................	91,670	5.1	4.2	94,574	55,867	47,470	55,686	38,138	12,292	11,396	84.1	222,800	959
Wildwood......................	132,129	2.3	26.9	143,272	53,462	54,714	80,757	38,698	12,276	11,932	93.3	367,700	1,137
MONTANA	50,027	17.7	3.7	66,288	30,181	27,162	32,486	22,375	497,749	416,125	68.0	217,200	741
Billings........................	54,222	14.0	4.0	72,343	35,347	31,836	40,361	26,633	49,914	46,477	63.6	215,500	848
Bozeman........................	58,859	16.5	9.8	98,225	36,212	24,415	30,458	18,142	20,746	17,788	47.7	359,200	959
Butte-Silver Bow............	46,650	25.0	3.3	59,485	25,438	25,532	34,055	20,581	16,481	13,894	72.1	145,900	594
Great Falls....................	43,367	21.5	2.6	61,906	27,209	28,199	32,114	22,367	27,226	25,163	61.6	167,300	691
Helena..........................	61,204	18.4	2.1	80,808	34,252	30,079	32,310	27,083	14,514	13,191	55.6	215,800	780
Missoula	43,527	22.8	4.2	66,686	29,954	21,654	21,453	21,865	32,244	30,350	45.9	276,500	803
NEBRASKA	56,927	14.7	4.2	73,488	31,765	31,448	37,517	26,448	827,191	747,562	65.3	148,100	769
Bellevue......................	60,191	13.6	3.3	70,923	34,796	31,851	37,383	26,613	20,045	19,175	61.3	144,000	905
Fremont........................	43,627	16.6	1.4	56,682	32,058	29,967	35,841	26,059	11,738	10,884	56.6	123,700	723
Grand Island..................	51,497	21.7	3.6	56,366	30,131	28,121	31,389	24,216	20,476	19,205	55.3	125,100	751
Kearney........................	52,839	13.3	2.2	75,116	37,005	26,089	34,469	20,506	12,706	11,803	58.4	181,000	712
Lincoln........................	55,792	15.2	3.7	73,704	30,997	28,279	31,778	24,955	118,654	112,386	56.1	160,600	773
Omaha..........................	52,672	16.7	5.2	72,556	33,517	31,805	36,801	27,588	190,653	175,881	56.6	149,900	860
NEVADA	55,180	15.6	4.3	65,384	35,412	31,132	35,119	27,294	1,221,759	1,055,158	54.9	239,500	1,003
Carson City....................	52,196	17.9	3.0	65,457	31,484	27,937	29,606	24,735	23,436	21,704	54.7	254,600	873
Henderson......................	68,191	12.0	6.2	76,725	45,435	39,348	47,299	31,102	126,349	110,948	64.3	291,100	1,164
Las Vegas......................	51,115	17.6	4.2	61,976	33,340	30,771	32,418	27,165	251,196	223,819	52.7	228,300	996
North Las Vegas............	55,972	13.0	2.3	62,027	39,832	30,235	33,771	25,424	81,353	71,898	54.6	192,600	1,137
Reno............................	51,313	16.9	4.6	64,772	35,458	28,748	30,664	26,436	104,100	96,742	45.7	304,000	908
Sparks..........................	57,444	16.4	3.7	72,644	29,059	31,818	37,008	27,172	39,309	37,218	58.0	275,900	1,031
NEW HAMPSHIRE.........	70,936	10.6	7.5	86,696	38,603	36,144	41,648	30,883	625,337	520,643	70.1	251,100	1,026
Concord........................	66,136	13.0	6.5	79,876	35,921	34,274	37,546	31,465	18,877	17,484	51.8	219,500	1,015
Dover..........................	71,917	7.8	4.4	85,837	51,418	36,572	39,957	32,654	12,963	12,478	60.4	232,100	1,029
Manchester....................	54,664	17.0	2.8	65,798	34,748	32,642	36,544	30,300	49,318	46,141	41.6	219,300	1,058
Nashua........................	69,769	12.1	5.4	81,820	37,230	36,729	43,098	31,175	36,692	35,663	51.5	256,800	1,178
Rochester......................	65,747	11.3	3.1	74,421	35,467	35,544	40,596	30,536	13,659	13,279	67.5	158,900	1,079
NEW JERSEY	76,126	12.9	12.0	94,546	41,163	40,881	49,101	32,614	3,604,688	3,194,519	63.2	328,200	1,244
Atlantic City	24,465	41.2	2.1	32,277	17,574	19,882	22,001	16,553	20,671	15,199	26.7	146,300	823
Bayonne........................	59,628	15.3	7.7	65,739	47,728	41,286	45,889	35,597	28,452	25,222	38.1	298,100	1,167
Bergenfield....................	92,274	6.2	13.2	102,353	51,809	42,642	51,010	36,493	8,304	8,024	66.2	345,900	1,456
Bridgeton......................	35,305	37.1	0.0	41,627	14,033	16,572	16,260	18,200	7,350	6,567	29.8	117,400	888
Camden........................	26,783	40.7	2.0	30,111	15,895	21,826	21,517	22,636	29,460	24,505	37.4	79,300	853
Clifton........................	77,923	10.8	6.4	90,020	41,563	37,617	46,589	26,928	31,885	28,998	57.9	345,100	1,379
East Orange..................	40,561	26.0	2.3	48,614	26,370	27,247	29,692	26,353	27,025	22,751	22.9	213,300	1,011
Elizabeth......................	42,690	20.8	2.2	45,213	26,938	23,916	29,752	19,918	45,066	41,026	25.1	263,800	1,070
Englewood......................	88,176	9.9	21.2	91,656	66,250	49,137	51,623	36,727	11,550	10,602	46.4	404,000	1,412
Fair Lawn......................	122,559	6.7	20.4	131,792	65,498	55,489	75,268	50,049	12,076	11,702	84.7	410,200	1,762
Fort Lee........................	81,405	14.1	11.3	108,402	56,158	57,322	69,528	46,441	18,671	17,513	57.8	291,400	1,733

1. Specified owner-occupied units; $2,000,000 represents $2,000,000 or more.

AREANAME	Commuting[1] 2016 Percent		Computer access[2] Percent		Migration		Civilian labor force, 2016		Unemployment[3]		Civilian employment, 2016 Population age 16 and older		Population age 16 to 64	
	Drove alone	With commutes of 30 minutes or more	With a computer in the house	With Internet access	Percent who lived in the same house one year ago	Percent who lived in another state or county one year ago	Total	Percent change 2016-2017	Total	Rate	Number	Percent in labor force	Number	Percent who worked full-year full-time
	55	56	57	58	59	60	61	62	63	64	65	66	67	68
MISSOURI	81.7	32.3	87.9	79.0	84.3	7.1	3,050,713	-0.9	114,587	3.8	4,865,244	63.0	3,888,265	51.4
Ballwin	91.7	39.0	92.5	87.7	NA	NA	16,911	-0.5	444	2.6	23,501	72.0	17,838	65.2
Blue Springs	92.4	45.5	94.2	87.1	88.8	2.5	30,706	0.0	1,095	3.6	40,680	71.1	34,492	60.2
Cape Girardeau	83.8	6.9	88.0	83.2	64.6	16.3	19,772	-1.8	736	3.7	32,068	55.4	25,419	39.6
Chesterfield	87.9	35.1	96.3	91.2	88.3	5.9	24,797	-0.6	642	2.6	39,093	62.5	28,137	51.7
Columbia	79.8	11.9	94.4	84.4	73.1	12.0	66,645	-0.8	1,760	2.6	100,781	63.2	86,748	45.3
Florissant	84.4	43.8	91.5	87.0	81.0	5.1	28,068	-0.9	1,101	3.9	40,411	63.5	32,050	49.1
Gladstone	81.3	21.3	95.1	88.0	77.8	10.6	14,841	0.1	582	3.9	22,433	62.9	17,197	52.1
Hazelwood	NA	21.4	88.8	86.3	86.7	4.8	13,742	-1.2	528	3.8	22,234	69.1	17,224	62.0
Independence	88.7	36.3	85.9	76.5	90.1	3.9	58,360	-0.3	2,746	4.7	92,346	64.1	72,219	56.6
Jefferson City	87.1	16.0	86.5	67.5	77.3	10.9	20,712	-1.6	663	3.2	35,443	57.2	28,149	49.6
Joplin	82.6	11.4	83.5	73.0	83.1	8.4	25,643	-1.8	869	3.4	42,070	63.1	33,554	48.8
Kansas City	81.6	26.6	89.0	78.9	82.1	8.1	258,629	-0.1	11,008	4.3	381,279	69.5	321,424	55.1
Kirkwood	82.3	34.0	92.8	89.1	91.1	3.7	15,752	-0.6	401	2.5	21,089	64.6	15,246	58.2
Lee's Summit	86.3	45.6	93.7	88.4	86.9	5.7	54,790	0.0	1,603	2.9	71,474	71.6	57,169	60.5
Liberty	80.2	22.7	94.2	92.1	82.7	11.4	16,263	0.2	609	3.7	24,694	70.5	20,364	57.2
Maryland Heights	86.5	26.0	95.9	87.2	80.6	12.4	16,061	-0.9	456	2.8	22,244	76.6	18,797	59.7
O'Fallon	82.7	42.5	94.7	91.7	92.2	4.5	48,388	-0.7	1,332	2.8	66,965	72.8	57,007	59.1
Raytown	87.1	28.7	91.9	86.3	91.4	4.8	15,468	0.0	815	5.3	24,713	70.3	20,085	54.3
St. Charles	85.2	29.3	93.6	86.5	86.2	5.8	38,370	-0.8	1,214	3.2	57,841	68.7	46,992	53.2
St. Joseph	84.6	12.8	83.3	73.0	79.0	7.8	38,912	-1.3	1,379	3.5	61,787	59.9	51,157	48.9
St. Louis	70.6	32.5	83.9	73.1	81.1	8.6	155,752	-1.2	6,871	4.4	256,102	65.7	219,464	49.7
St. Peters	85.7	39.1	94.9	90.3	91.2	4.1	34,085	-0.6	983	2.9	45,883	73.2	36,900	60.3
Springfield	78.9	13.4	89.9	77.1	72.3	12.1	85,786	-0.6	2,766	3.2	140,413	61.9	116,084	43.9
University City	68.4	20.4	88.2	79.7	70.8	8.8	18,675	-0.9	637	3.4	28,381	62.8	22,620	49.0
Wentzville	86.1	40.7	97.1	93.1	88.8	3.1	20,142	-0.6	536	2.7	25,469	73.7	21,956	62.8
Wildwood	90.3	44.1	99.0	97.4	94.1	4.7	19,039	-0.4	516	2.7	28,102	70.2	24,358	54.1
MONTANA	76.0	15.9	87.8	78.9	83.6	7.5	525,453	0.7	21,174	4.0	838,974	63.4	655,093	49.3
Billings	84.4	6.8	91.4	83.9	82.2	4.7	56,807	0.5	1,984	3.5	87,350	66.7	69,761	55.9
Bozeman	71.0	6.2	94.7	86.4	70.9	13.9	28,827	3.8	760	2.6	39,862	74.0	35,050	40.8
Butte-Silver Bow	88.8	13.4	78.0	70.8	84.1	9.6	17,149	-0.2	723	4.2	27,651	60.5	21,595	43.9
Great Falls	86.2	5.9	82.0	72.3	81.6	7.3	28,130	0.3	1,062	3.8	46,952	64.5	36,758	54.0
Helena	73.7	4.0	87.5	83.9	74.4	9.3	16,959	0.1	529	3.1	25,301	64.4	19,018	57.8
Missoula	70.0	11.7	93.0	87.1	72.2	14.0	39,751	1.5	1,364	3.4	61,424	73.7	52,907	47.3
NEBRASKA	82.0	18.9	88.6	81.7	83.5	7.0	1,007,011	-0.2	29,567	2.9	1,484,034	69.5	1,198,744	57.4
Bellevue	83.1	23.9	95.2	86.2	79.8	10.9	26,670	0.5	843	3.2	40,628	68.0	33,719	54.0
Fremont	80.5	24.7	83.9	79.1	83.0	4.6	13,794	1.0	378	2.7	20,214	67.1	15,410	53.5
Grand Island	80.2	13.7	86.2	80.2	77.4	10.3	26,093	0.5	896	3.4	38,962	69.6	31,921	58.8
Kearney	88.2	9.1	91.1	87.7	67.8	13.0	18,784	-0.4	441	2.3	25,283	73.0	21,166	54.6
Lincoln	80.5	16.7	92.2	85.6	77.3	7.8	152,394	0.2	4,039	2.7	224,253	72.2	188,289	54.5
Omaha	82.1	16.0	87.7	80.9	82.1	6.0	229,019	0.5	7,359	3.2	348,663	68.8	291,708	54.1
NEVADA	78.8	32.2	91.0	80.6	82.6	5.4	1,462,955	2.3	73,583	5.0	2,339,612	63.3	1,897,851	49.1
Carson City	81.2	22.3	91.5	85.2	83.2	9.1	25,610	3.3	1,294	5.1	44,265	57.8	33,024	51.0
Henderson	83.0	30.5	93.0	87.1	83.5	5.6	151,068	2.1	7,289	4.8	237,452	59.7	180,220	49.7
Las Vegas	77.1	39.1	90.4	79.8	80.2	5.0	303,891	2.1	16,560	5.4	497,326	62.3	404,558	47.9
North Las Vegas	83.7	44.9	92.9	81.3	83.9	4.3	109,794	2.0	6,317	5.8	180,615	65.5	157,772	48.3
Reno	76.8	18.9	90.5	79.3	77.5	6.7	129,344	3.8	5,373	4.2	198,228	68.0	163,244	49.7
Sparks	79.5	23.7	89.3	79.9	84.3	4.7	51,966	3.8	2,158	4.2	78,120	65.9	63,461	51.2
NEW HAMPSHIRE	79.7	37.1	92.3	86.3	84.9	7.1	746,549	0.0	19,942	2.7	1,108,050	67.6	881,118	54.4
Concord	79.1	28.0	89.1	81.7	85.3	9.4	22,379	-0.4	521	2.3	35,952	60.8	27,561	49.2
Dover	80.3	23.5	95.0	87.9	79.1	9.9	18,198	0.6	400	2.2	25,058	77.2	21,554	59.7
Manchester	74.3	26.0	90.3	85.9	76.6	9.7	62,404	0.3	1,776	2.8	91,194	68.8	76,160	55.3
Nashua	78.8	34.7	91.2	85.0	81.6	9.5	49,146	0.2	1,575	3.2	73,195	67.4	57,787	56.7
Rochester	80.9	41.6	85.8	78.9	81.0	4.7	17,218	0.6	400	2.3	25,984	67.2	19,791	60.7
NEW JERSEY	70.8	46.8	90.7	83.8	89.6	4.8	4,518,832	-0.3	209,126	4.6	7,197,473	65.3	5,825,318	51.7
Atlantic City	40.9	22.8	72.0	57.6	76.8	3.3	14,903	-2.4	1,505	10.1	30,942	58.1	24,723	33.9
Bayonne	47.9	55.0	86.0	75.9	89.6	2.1	33,243	-0.2	1,672	5.0	51,852	61.6	41,698	49.9
Bergenfield	75.5	53.3	92.3	90.9	NA	NA	14,866	-0.1	545	3.7	21,913	68.4	17,600	53.0
Bridgeton	54.3	42.9	77.4	55.0	82.1	6.8	8,313	-1.1	683	8.2	18,287	52.6	16,182	38.0
Camden	54.3	35.0	79.3	61.4	87.5	3.3	26,183	0.2	2,565	9.8	55,033	54.9	47,832	34.4
Clifton	73.9	46.3	89.6	81.4	92.1	4.7	45,016	-0.2	2,115	4.7	70,398	67.2	57,134	53.5
East Orange	57.9	53.9	87.7	79.9	84.6	3.7	29,688	-0.7	2,156	7.3	50,284	63.0	42,806	42.3
Elizabeth	56.3	40.0	84.7	76.3	87.3	4.6	62,610	-0.7	3,600	5.7	97,132	70.5	85,341	50.7
Englewood	60.4	45.9	93.8	88.0	NA	NA	15,056	-0.2	642	4.3	23,250	65.5	18,415	58.8
Fair Lawn	73.0	44.9	94.7	91.9	NA	NA	18,265	-0.3	678	3.7	27,413	72.0	21,900	58.7
Fort Lee	54.1	62.7	91.8	87.5	87.6	7.4	19,471	0.0	611	3.1	32,850	61.2	23,137	57.1

1. Employed persons.   2. Households.   3. Percent of civilian labor force.

AREANAME	General revenue							General expenditure		
	Intergovernmental			Taxes					Per capita[1] (dollars)	
					Per capita[1] (dollars)					
	Total (mil dol)	Total (mil dol)	Percent from state government	Total (mil dol)	Total	Property	Sales and gross receipts	Total (mil dol)	Total	Capital outlays
	117	118	119	120	121	122	123	124	125	126
MISSOURI	X	X	X	X	X	X	X	X	X	X
Ballwin............................	18.7	9.4	1.9	5.3	173	15	159	18.7	613	106
Blue Springs....................	53.1	13.3	54.5	24.5	462	193	260	57.4	1,082	459
Cape Girardeau................	57.8	5.4	100.0	35.6	921	61	860	52.2	1,349	435
Chesterfield	34.7	22.0	9.0	9.6	202	20	182	34.5	723	209
Columbia.........................	138.4	19.3	25.9	63.8	563	95	468	212.6	1,877	640
Florissant........................	33.1	18.3	15.6	8.4	161	11	147	32.8	626	96
Gladstone........................	29.7	4.2	55.7	15.5	597	132	465	27.7	1,069	194
Hazelwood.......................	38.3	16.6	5.6	17.5	683	419	264	41.8	1,627	196
Independence..................	188.3	31.9	65.8	87.8	748	125	624	191.9	1,636	278
Jefferson City	59.3	4.3	100.0	36.2	838	120	718	57.9	1,340	163
Joplin..............................	79.1	7.5	60.0	45.9	914	50	864	75.9	1,511	421
Kansas City	1,256.7	117.6	15.8	742.9	1,599	266	877	1,156.0	2,489	448
Kirkwood..........................	31.5	7.3	39.6	15.7	568	296	272	30.7	1,115	279
Lee's Summit...................	126.6	6.4	34.2	72.9	788	290	499	116.7	1,263	277
Liberty.............................	33.0	1.0	69.8	19.8	663	218	445	32.0	1,073	157
Maryland Heights	47.8	14.1	52.2	24.5	891	113	778	36.8	1,340	394
O'Fallon	65.0	5.7	97.0	39.2	478	97	381	58.2	710	117
Raytown	24.5	1.7	100.0	13.8	468	60	405	23.7	802	108
St. Charles......................	85.0	6.1	40.0	58.8	884	225	659	87.4	1,314	334
St. Joseph.......................	112.7	24.2	75.0	53.0	685	173	513	85.5	1,107	153
St. Louis..........................	986.4	175.2	99.4	544.6	1,706	233	878	1,082.7	3,391	490
St. Peters........................	69.7	8.7	23.6	38.5	712	244	469	72.3	1,337	393
Springfield	302.8	56.5	34.5	151.6	934	123	811	276.2	1,702	333
University City	39.5	14.2	32.7	14.1	401	174	227	40.5	1,149	172
Wentzville........................	32.7	2.6	11.6	20.8	663	174	488	39.1	1,245	374
Wildwood.........................	13.3	6.4	6.0	5.9	164	64	100	11.4	318	100
MONTANA	X	X	X	X	X	X	X	X	X	X
Billings............................	139.3	26.8	53.7	38.1	356	286	52	121.4	1,134	258
Bozeman	47.2	7.7	100.0	17.3	446	415	31	47.1	1,218	295
Butte-Silver Bow..............	75.8	25.6	85.0	27.7	820	793	27	64.6	1,913	455
Great Falls......................	59.8	11.2	86.2	17.7	300	264	36	59.2	1,004	125
Helena.............................	39.8	8.5	54.5	9.3	320	301	19	38.1	1,306	175
Missoula..........................	74.2	24.8	96.6	28.9	422	381	42	74.8	1,093	151
NEBRASKA	X	X	X	X	X	X	X	X	X	X
Bellevue..........................	47.3	5.6	93.3	31.0	589	275	302	46.0	874	117
Fremont...........................	32.4	11.1	42.3	11.6	439	202	237	26.6	1,007	230
Grand Island....................	57.1	7.8	100.0	23.4	468	139	329	52.8	1,053	87
Kearney...........................	41.2	6.7	95.0	15.3	478	83	395	40.5	1,270	296
Lincoln.............................	295.4	84.6	29.9	137.0	516	178	338	277.5	1,045	307
Omaha.............................	610.0	80.9	60.1	392.9	903	317	586	580.3	1,333	325
NEVADA	X	X	X	X	X	X	X	X	X	X
Carson City......................	111.3	36.0	61.3	38.3	701	418	283	103.8	1,902	301
Henderson........................	402.5	181.2	47.5	129.1	487	256	231	422.6	1,594	454
Las Vegas........................	801.6	407.6	63.4	200.6	336	186	150	876.8	1,470	462
North Las Vegas...............	281.9	110.2	80.4	84.1	377	246	131	281.1	1,260	340
Reno................................	315.2	72.0	57.4	121.3	526	255	271	287.2	1,245	153
Sparks.............................	93.5	28.6	69.1	34.8	378	260	118	85.8	933	92
NEW HAMPSHIRE.........	X	X	X	X	X	X	X	X	X	X
Concord............................	62.7	3.7	75.0	39.6	931	895	36	59.6	1,402	31
Dover...............................	105.4	21.2	95.8	64.9	2,139	2,120	18	90.6	2,982	200
Manchester......................	391.9	151.9	74.0	152.0	1,379	1,330	50	436.7	3,964	479
Nashua............................	282.0	81.9	99.2	176.1	2,033	2,010	23	264.6	3,055	177
Rochester	102.0	39.7	96.1	54.8	1,835	1,692	143	100.7	3,371	643
NEW JERSEY	X	X	X	X	X	X	X	X	X	X
Atlantic City	265.6	40.5	25.2	197.6	4,993	4,875	117	225.7	5,703	269
Bayonne	247.8	88.4	85.4	137.0	2,113	2,095	18	277.8	4,287	148
Bergenfield......................	32.3	2.9	94.6	28.1	1,033	1,005	28	28.7	1,057	46
Bridgeton.........................	34.1	9.2	55.7	12.4	491	454	37	34.9	1,382	155
Camden...........................	232.9	174.8	71.9	30.2	391	338	53	160.2	2,073	195
Clifton.............................	115.4	15.5	73.5	84.3	990	936	54	103.5	1,216	37
East Orange	399.7	273.1	95.8	111.4	1,730	1,712	17	362.6	5,630	108
Elizabeth..........................	263.2	59.9	65.7	151.2	1,191	1,058	134	254.8	2,007	251
Englewood........................	130.4	25.5	71.3	98.9	3,607	3,555	52	132.8	4,840	411
Fair Lawn.........................	44.1	4.4	97.6	38.3	1,166	1,116	50	39.3	1,195	65
Fort Lee...........................	75.6	8.8	24.0	61.9	1,726	1,666	61	78.8	2,198	328

1. Based on population estimated as of July 1 of the year shown.

AREANAME	Public welfare	Highways	Parking facilities	Education	Health and hospitals	Police protection	Sewerage and sanitation	Parks and recreation	Housing and community development	Interest on debt
				City government finances, 2012 (cont.)						
				General expenditures (cont.)						
				Percent of total for:						
	127	128	129	130	131	132	133	134	135	136
MISSOURI	X	X	X	X	X	X	X	X	X	X
Ballwin	0.0	26.8	0.0	0.0	0.0	25.3	1.6	20.8	0.0	6.3
Blue Springs	0.0	4.3	0.0	0.0	0.0	16.3	33.2	7.3	0.0	6.1
Cape Girardeau	0.0	23.1	0.0	0.0	0.6	13.1	19.5	15.6	0.7	2.2
Chesterfield	0.0	20.9	0.0	0.0	0.0	22.6	0.8	28.1	0.0	8.7
Columbia	0.3	9.2	2.5	0.0	2.7	7.7	25.4	7.7	0.9	2.5
Florissant	0.0	13.2	0.0	0.0	1.9	30.6	0.5	18.0	2.8	1.4
Gladstone	0.0	11.8	0.0	0.0	0.8	18.2	17.1	13.9	1.8	5.2
Hazelwood	0.0	0.9	0.0	0.0	0.0	19.1	0.3	8.1	0.0	2.2
Independence	1.9	13.2	0.0	0.0	1.6	15.3	15.0	3.9	0.4	8.1
Jefferson City	0.0	20.0	1.2	0.0	1.0	18.7	8.8	13.4	0.7	3.2
Joplin	0.3	11.6	0.1	0.0	3.2	12.8	22.9	7.3	2.2	0.8
Kansas City	0.5	13.1	0.4	0.0	4.6	17.1	7.8	4.6	3.5	8.1
Kirkwood	0.0	5.0	0.0	0.0	0.0	21.3	10.0	12.4	0.0	1.8
Lee's Summit	0.0	15.2	0.0	0.0	0.0	15.6	11.5	6.5	1.2	3.3
Liberty	0.0	13.8	0.0	0.0	0.0	14.6	20.9	11.7	4.7	6.1
Maryland Heights	0.9	36.0	0.0	0.0	0.0	26.9	8.2	10.0	3.4	3.1
O'Fallon	0.0	16.9	0.0	0.0	0.0	20.3	13.7	13.5	0.3	7.4
Raytown	0.0	5.9	0.0	0.0	0.0	28.8	18.1	6.2	2.8	11.3
St. Charles	0.0	22.9	0.1	0.0	0.0	21.1	5.4	10.0	0.6	8.9
St. Joseph	2.1	11.2	0.4	0.0	5.5	11.2	14.3	7.0	1.5	5.9
St. Louis	0.0	2.3	0.9	0.0	3.6	23.2	1.7	2.2	2.7	8.4
St. Peters	0.0	24.8	0.0	0.0	0.7	19.4	20.1	17.9	0.2	4.6
Springfield	0.4	10.7	0.1	0.0	2.9	23.9	12.1	10.6	0.9	5.3
University City	0.0	18.3	0.5	0.0	0.0	18.1	6.7	8.2	3.5	2.0
Wentzville	0.0	14.6	0.0	0.0	0.0	18.0	37.0	7.4	0.0	5.5
Wildwood	0.0	34.1	0.0	0.0	0.0	26.6	0.1	4.4	0.0	1.4
MONTANA	X	X	X	X	X	X	X	X	X	X
Billings	0.0	16.9	1.9	0.0	0.6	16.1	21.3	3.4	2.8	1.8
Bozeman	11.0	10.4	0.8	0.0	0.0	20.0	29.4	0.9	0.2	3.2
Butte-Silver Bow	0.2	7.2	0.2	0.0	7.7	10.3	23.9	4.7	0.4	2.6
Great Falls	0.0	12.3	1.1	0.0	0.0	20.7	22.3	10.6	4.0	2.1
Helena	0.0	10.7	5.1	0.0	0.4	18.4	19.1	15.1	0.1	3.1
Missoula	0.2	13.6	1.8	0.0	1.9	17.8	14.7	6.3	1.4	3.5
NEBRASKA	X	X	X	X	X	X	X	X	X	X
Bellevue	0.0	10.3	0.0	0.0	0.0	34.9	13.4	5.1	0.4	3.6
Fremont	0.0	16.1	0.0	0.0	0.0	16.9	17.3	8.7	9.2	1.3
Grand Island	0.0	12.5	0.1	0.0	0.0	16.4	18.8	8.4	1.9	2.1
Kearney	0.0	21.9	0.1	0.0	0.0	16.5	18.4	15.8	3.0	0.7
Lincoln	2.3	19.2	1.4	0.0	4.4	12.9	12.2	4.2	3.8	1.5
Omaha	0.3	10.5	0.8	0.0	0.0	16.3	19.0	13.1	0.3	7.2
NEVADA	X	X	X	X	X	X	X	X	X	X
Carson City	2.3	10.5	0.0	0.0	4.2	15.9	10.8	10.1	1.5	9.1
Henderson	0.0	1.7	0.0	0.0	0.0	17.2	10.2	28.6	2.7	2.3
Las Vegas	0.1	6.9	0.4	0.0	0.4	14.6	13.4	11.0	2.7	3.5
North Las Vegas	0.0	13.1	0.0	0.0	0.0	26.3	10.0	10.6	2.4	3.8
Reno	0.0	9.4	0.0	0.0	0.0	18.6	14.1	3.8	6.8	15.2
Sparks	0.0	7.6	0.0	0.0	0.0	23.2	17.6	6.4	0.6	13.5
NEW HAMPSHIRE	X	X	X	X	X	X	X	X	X	X
Concord	1.8	11.5	1.5	0.0	0.3	16.9	15.6	4.2	0.0	4.5
Dover	0.9	5.5	0.4	50.9	0.0	7.9	7.8	2.6	0.3	5.1
Manchester	0.3	5.2	0.6	39.2	1.3	7.0	4.3	1.3	0.9	5.3
Nashua	0.3	2.6	0.0	55.6	0.3	6.6	7.7	1.0	0.5	4.0
Rochester	0.6	7.4	0.0	57.0	0.0	6.1	4.6	0.7	0.3	2.9
NEW JERSEY	X	X	X	X	X	X	X	X	X	X
Atlantic City	0.6	1.1	0.0	0.0	1.7	16.6	1.7	3.0	11.8	1.9
Bayonne	0.0	0.6	0.5	41.0	0.0	9.0	4.6	1.2	21.6	4.2
Bergenfield	0.0	7.1	0.0	0.0	1.5	23.3	16.4	2.7	0.0	1.9
Bridgeton	0.0	3.9	0.0	0.0	0.4	15.8	23.3	1.5	13.4	0.5
Camden	0.0	2.8	0.0	0.0	1.1	17.8	5.7	1.0	24.6	2.6
Clifton	0.1	2.8	0.0	0.0	1.0	20.0	12.8	1.5	3.1	2.4
East Orange	0.0	0.5	0.1	63.0	1.4	7.5	2.7	0.7	4.4	0.7
Elizabeth	0.0	2.3	0.8	0.0	2.2	17.0	12.9	4.9	15.8	1.7
Englewood	0.0	2.1	0.0	52.5	0.6	9.2	4.3	0.7	5.2	1.0
Fair Lawn	0.2	2.9	0.0	0.0	1.8	20.0	13.4	4.5	0.0	3.4
Fort Lee	0.3	3.2	1.7	0.0	1.8	18.2	8.2	2.4	8.3	3.6

Accommodation and Food Services, Arts, Entertainment, and Recreation, and Health Care and Social Assistance

AREANAME	Accommodaton and food services, 2012				Arts, entertainment, and recreation[1], 2012				Health care and social assistance,[1] 2012			
	Number of establish-ments	Number of employees	Receipts (mil dol)	Annual payroll (mil dol)	Number of establish-ments	Number of employees	Receipts (mil dol)	Annual payroll (mil dol)	Number of establish-ments	Number of employees	Receipts (mil dol)	Annual payroll (mil dol)
	92	93	94	95	96	97	98	99	100	101	102	103
NEW JERSEY— Cont'd												
Garfield	43	343	28.9	7.8	1	D	D	D	29	313	13.6	6.1
Hackensack	120	D	D	D	12	D	D	D	342	D	D	D
Hoboken	219	D	D	D	24	D	D	D	125	2,091	237.4	98.6
Jersey City	471	4,941	422.5	97.5	47	484	52.6	13.9	439	6,026	521.3	210.3
Kearny	56	532	33.2	8.7	3	D	D	D	68	D	D	D
Linden	95	986	62.1	14.7	6	74	3.8	1.1	63	1,413	115.3	44.9
Long Branch	93	1,567	88.5	25.3	6	137	4.3	1.2	84	D	D	D
Millville	56	673	42.5	8.7	3	D	D	D	59	939	73.2	33.9
Newark	536	7,920	582.4	146.1	15	D	D	D	310	4,836	383.4	162.7
New Brunswick	161	2,009	127.1	35.8	4	D	D	D	80	D	D	D
Paramus	156	3,372	221.9	58.6	22	D	D	D	199	2,320	258.7	100.4
Passaic	115	674	46.1	9.7	12	100	4.7	1.4	103	D	D	D
Paterson	232	D	D	D	12	D	D	D	156	1,927	192.0	71.6
Perth Amboy	102	614	41.5	8.7	3	D	D	D	66	1,254	70.5	30.2
Plainfield	75	613	33.5	7.8	1	D	D	D	71	947	78.0	32.2
Rahway	53	524	34.2	8.4	3	D	D	D	39	D	D	D
Sayreville	82	677	37.9	9.2	10	203	15.2	5.0	50	D	D	D
Trenton	140	D	D	D	6	D	D	D	94	1,646	147.3	64.5
Union City	126	831	53.8	12.9	5	D	D	D	156	1,745	91.7	40.7
Vineland	128	2,165	98.9	26.5	7	D	D	D	164	2,173	268.1	95.2
Westfield	74	D	D	D	11	218	10.1	4.2	150	1,979	178.7	81.2
West New York	87	669	42.8	11.0	9	D	D	D	95	D	D	D
NEW MEXICO	4,177	82,601	4,349.7	1,250.4	488	10,536	1,207.2	219.7	3,970	67,477	6,071.0	2,449.7
Alamogordo	75	D	D	D	7	D	D	D	67	801	75.0	26.8
Albuquerque	1,281	29,238	1,579.0	454.8	138	D	D	D	1,468	25,832	2,659.8	1,045.2
Carlsbad	69	1,320	78.4	20.0	4	D	D	D	52	1,124	152.2	54.9
Clovis	78	1,927	77.4	21.9	7	42	1.6	0.5	94	D	D	D
Farmington	129	3,091	150.4	41.9	11	D	D	D	193	D	D	D
Hobbs	98	1,703	110.1	24.6	7	D	D	D	68	D	D	D
Las Cruces	276	6,189	262.7	72.6	18	383	9.9	2.9	379	8,409	840.8	336.9
Rio Rancho	91	2,066	90.2	26.7	15	D	D	D	122	1,646	119.9	51.6
Roswell	119	2,281	106.2	28.0	5	D	D	D	134	3,029	289.8	111.6
Santa Fe	349	7,896	532.7	158.5	58	186	28.8	8.2	362	3,454	397.5	170.6
NEW YORK	49,731	679,146	49,285.5	13,734.3	9,600	103,072	16,431.7	4,940.4	43,548	540,067	55,599.5	22,400.9
Albany	453	5,990	373.4	98.6	21	730	12.9	4.8	216	3,700	522.7	199.4
Auburn	94	1,291	54.4	15.1	11	61	3.8	1.2	101	1,097	105.3	48.2
Binghamton	171	3,078	154.7	38.0	12	D	D	D	103	1,390	167.0	74.4
Buffalo	660	11,300	510.5	158.3	44	820	185.7	95.7	363	7,108	684.7	361.8
Elmira	63	995	42.7	10.7	7	137	7.2	1.5	70	794	85.7	36.4
Freeport	95	638	48.3	12.2	20	92	18.8	2.7	109	1,395	96.8	41.3
Glen Cove	82	D	D	D	10	135	15.3	3.2	118	D	D	D
Harrison	67	D	D	D	25	197	12.4	4.6	87	D	D	D
Hempstead	121	983	63.5	14.5	5	D	D	D	115	1,342	148.1	53.1
Ithaca	203	2,774	153.0	43.5	10	67	6.9	1.8	68	669	57.7	22.6
Jamestown	72	733	37.0	8.9	10	D	D	D	55	543	54.4	18.6
Lindenhurst	80	893	52.0	12.7	8	D	D	D	52	555	46.4	18.9
Long Beach	91	1,052	61.6	17.7	11	97	8.0	1.8	94	D	D	D
Middletown	67	616	30.1	8.4	5	D	D	D	71	2,591	332.5	147.7
Mount Vernon	104	692	49.5	11.4	15	159	13.2	5.3	111	927	75.2	29.0
Newburgh	87	1,121	79.9	18.1	5	D	D	D	76	887	81.0	32.2
New Rochelle	208	1,949	139.6	37.0	35	D	D	D	234	3,089	327.0	117.8
New York	21,506	304,855	27,452.9	7,757.8	4,956	50,582	11,117.6	3,322.1	18,267	234,221	22,637.1	8,976.3
Niagara Falls	171	5,873	883.7	134.7	13	D	D	D	68	1,178	67.5	32.2
North Tonawanda	55	642	27.4	8.3	7	50	2.7	0.7	53	301	22.2	9.5
Ossining	44	417	28.0	10.4	6	31	4.9	1.4	33	337	27.3	11.1
Port Chester	98	948	70.4	20.3	8	D	D	D	39	469	77.9	30.2
Poughkeepsie	126	D	D	D	5	7	0.7	0.2	103	2,052	299.4	131.4
Rochester	570	7,114	366.7	105.5	64	1,228	62.6	20.8	264	5,172	420.6	192.5
Rome	81	D	D	D	15	66	3.3	1.0	85	1,234	94.7	41.1
Saratoga Springs	170	3,198	196.3	57.3	39	949	162.4	34.0	109	1,410	158.0	74.2
Schenectady	182	1,857	93.1	25.5	8	402	80.7	11.6	138	1,958	182.0	82.2
Spring Valley	46	D	D	D	4	D	D	D	40	509	41.2	14.9
Syracuse	386	6,146	311.3	92.3	29	162	13.8	4.3	316	4,768	625.4	249.8
Troy	146	1,747	95.0	28.2	7	D	D	D	107	1,509	139.2	62.8
Utica	158	D	D	D	8	52	2.6	0.7	143	2,547	301.7	130.7
Valley Stream	82	1,147	66.7	17.9	14	62	7.4	1.9	134	954	157.5	46.6
Watertown	105	2,206	96.5	28.7	10	50	2.6	0.7	96	1,331	140.6	63.4
White Plains	203	3,100	235.8	75.9	31	233	28.3	5.7	348	5,680	639.1	303.9

1. Establishments subject to federal tax.

Table D. Cities — Other Services and Government Employment and Payroll

AREANAME	Other services[1] Number of establishments	Number of employees	Receipts (mil dol)	Annual payroll (mil dol)	Government employment and payroll, 2012 Full-time equivalent employees	Total (dollars)	March payroll Percent of total for: Administrative, judicial, and legal	Police and corrections	Fire protection	Highways and transportation	Health and welfare	Natural resources and utilities	Education and libraries
	104	105	106	107	108	109	110	111	112	113	114	115	116
NEW JERSEY— Cont'd													
Garfield	65	268	29.8	8.1	172	1,065,564	10.9	55.4	1.4	9.0	14.1	5.5	3.1
Hackensack	117	757	63.8	20.3	540	2,983,931	6.1	38.2	33.3	3.4	8.9	5.9	3.9
Hoboken	118	D	D	D	712	4,180,854	7.4	42.5	22.9	2.8	7.1	10.6	3.1
Jersey City	318	1,625	144.0	44.1	2,936	18,762,329	8.1	43.6	27.3	3.2	7.6	6.7	2.0
Kearny	58	241	26.5	6.9	326	2,506,387	6.0	43.9	30.5	0.2	2.6	7.9	1.8
Linden	101	647	63.6	20.9	585	3,237,694	11.7	49.9	25.1	3.6	5.9	2.5	0.8
Long Branch	52	195	11.3	3.2	338	2,021,115	9.6	41.0	10.8	0.7	12.9	21.3	3.7
Millville	32	147	9.8	3.3	210	1,102,759	14.1	44.9	6.7	4.0	8.6	14.2	0.0
Newark	425	4,834	339.5	123.8	3,857	25,580,741	14.8	36.1	19.3	0.6	13.6	10.8	2.2
New Brunswick	74	535	49.5	15.3	1,983	11,480,514	2.4	14.2	6.5	0.7	1.8	3.7	67.3
Paramus	63	494	49.3	22.3	293	1,879,108	9.0	31.6	18.6	10.8	1.2	13.4	8.4
Passaic	90	251	20.0	5.3	563	3,095,395	9.0	45.4	25.9	6.9	9.0	1.7	2.3
Paterson	183	1,164	94.0	28.2	1,472	8,450,610	6.5	42.6	30.2	1.1	8.2	5.3	1.6
Perth Amboy	89	736	67.5	23.4	401	2,317,835	10.2	44.0	15.6	5.1	10.9	6.6	1.8
Plainfield	75	266	22.3	6.6	551	3,548,125	11.6	36.0	23.0	0.9	9.8	7.5	2.9
Rahway	42	162	19.7	5.2	277	1,741,702	7.4	40.4	21.7	9.0	8.1	6.9	4.4
Sayreville	87	372	38.5	11.7	240	1,549,628	10.5	59.2	0.8	2.5	2.2	9.8	4.9
Trenton	83	359	27.6	7.6	2,747	16,968,078	3.1	14.5	9.4	0.5	3.5	5.2	60.7
Union City	105	233	17.4	4.5	2,174	11,223,072	2.5	14.9	0.8	0.1	2.4	3.3	73.7
Vineland	108	538	44.6	12.1	718	3,828,158	13.3	30.7	5.0	1.6	10.8	34.6	2.3
Westfield	83	465	40.5	11.7	238	1,357,302	9.1	33.5	21.3	15.6	9.8	5.2	5.0
West New York	75	228	17.6	4.0	1,416	9,134,998	2.4	10.3	4.4	1.4	1.5	0.3	79.2
NEW MEXICO	2,182	12,810	1,115.9	349.7	X	X	X	X	X	X	X	X	X
Alamogordo	38	202	14.8	4.1	280	741,098	18.0	39.9	1.3	4.0	10.8	22.4	3.5
Albuquerque	718	4,969	379.7	125.0	6,438	33,331,138	10.6	29.5	14.1	15.4	8.8	17.0	1.5
Carlsbad	39	195	24.0	6.2	381	1,625,310	11.0	22.8	19.6	11.1	0.7	23.8	1.9
Clovis	55	332	26.5	7.3	383	1,169,467	11.4	25.1	25.2	9.8	5.3	18.8	2.8
Farmington	116	973	105.0	36.0	882	3,555,193	11.2	22.9	12.7	4.9	2.4	35.0	4.8
Hobbs	62	571	72.3	23.8	403	1,643,293	10.3	27.3	18.4	9.1	3.7	22.7	2.5
Las Cruces	138	753	51.6	16.6	1,337	4,708,150	16.1	21.4	12.0	10.4	4.2	18.4	1.9
Rio Rancho	67	437	31.6	12.0	606	2,382,289	13.5	29.4	20.0	10.8	8.8	12.6	4.3
Roswell	46	222	19.0	5.4	548	1,751,942	8.5	26.4	20.7	10.4	1.6	25.5	3.2
Santa Fe	162	866	71.7	23.4	1,540	6,258,370	13.8	15.1	12.9	7.7	6.4	28.1	2.3
NEW YORK	34,948	168,002	14,493.2	4,209.4	X	X	X	X	X	X	X	X	X
Albany	146	825	81.6	24.9	1,455	6,784,879	6.9	38.4	23.1	4.0	10.7	16.1	0.0
Auburn	53	242	19.2	5.0	306	1,503,241	6.8	27.5	30.2	4.3	6.2	19.5	0.0
Binghamton	81	439	34.3	10.7	581	2,791,570	8.2	32.5	25.6	1.7	4.0	21.6	0.0
Buffalo	301	1,577	149.1	47.0	8,627	45,770,501	2.5	13.0	9.3	1.2	2.8	5.8	63.6
Elmira	29	155	12.6	3.8	297	1,470,047	6.0	34.4	27.9	5.6	6.2	16.6	0.0
Freeport	95	491	40.6	11.1	414	2,410,577	14.5	41.4	0.5	2.6	0.9	35.0	0.0
Glen Cove	71	259	21.8	5.5	313	2,051,266	16.9	46.0	2.4	7.0	7.0	17.7	0.0
Harrison	44	D	D	D	272	1,502,544	14.2	43.3	8.0	7.9	2.8	13.9	7.7
Hempstead	97	562	59.8	16.0	437	2,884,577	9.4	54.8	2.8	5.5	2.5	17.0	3.8
Ithaca	42	274	21.6	6.5	454	2,158,827	9.3	24.0	19.7	8.1	0.9	28.6	0.0
Jamestown	44	211	19.7	5.0	658	3,048,026	3.6	13.9	18.8	8.5	1.7	2.6	51.0
Lindenhurst	102	289	31.4	6.7	72	206,485	20.7	0.0	5.1	24.6	6.2	32.4	0.0
Long Beach	54	178	8.6	2.4	484	2,657,473	9.3	32.7	12.4	11.0	4.5	25.8	0.0
Middletown	54	376	29.6	8.9	283	1,449,586	12.4	41.3	15.8	7.3	3.0	20.2	0.0
Mount Vernon	128	768	87.4	28.0	873	4,489,959	6.4	36.3	23.8	1.9	2.2	13.5	2.9
Newburgh	62	479	52.2	12.3	258	1,411,393	6.5	44.1	27.5	10.5	1.6	9.6	0.0
New Rochelle	157	669	59.3	15.7	652	4,204,505	7.5	35.0	29.4	4.5	9.0	14.1	0.0
New York	15,271	69,456	5,597.1	1,634.2	404,260	2,380,283,176	3.2	19.0	5.4	13.7	18.1	4.4	34.0
Niagara Falls	62	323	23.2	6.3	687	3,126,891	0.0	30.2	23.2	0.0	6.6	0.0	0.0
North Tonawanda	56	153	11.3	3.0	281	1,334,637	8.0	28.4	16.0	17.6	0.8	25.8	0.0
Ossining	38	109	10.2	2.8	186	1,201,283	12.6	41.7	0.4	13.3	0.9	24.9	0.0
Port Chester	73	282	34.4	9.6	227	2,070,548	10.9	52.5	7.8	6.0	2.3	13.1	0.0
Poughkeepsie	71	288	25.8	7.1	365	2,055,377	6.9	43.5	19.1	6.3	5.4	15.8	0.0
Rochester	274	1,741	176.4	53.9	9,049	47,150,145	2.7	13.0	6.6	0.8	3.9	4.3	67.0
Rome	56	208	21.1	5.3	373	1,669,365	8.0	27.2	30.1	12.6	4.5	16.3	0.0
Saratoga Springs	49	232	18.3	5.5	349	1,565,062	9.5	32.3	19.4	23.7	4.3	7.4	0.0
Schenectady	90	526	61.4	17.3	637	3,109,293	5.4	38.3	21.7	5.1	10.0	14.6	0.0
Spring Valley	36	94	11.3	1.8	298	901,316	12.0	64.5	0.6	10.1	7.0	0.4	0.0
Syracuse	198	1,576	131.3	43.9	5,644	31,187,441	1.4	12.0	7.9	4.1	2.4	3.2	68.9
Troy	55	398	31.1	12.3	598	3,268,327	9.0	41.8	17.7	4.1	9.7	13.5	0.0
Utica	75	516	35.6	12.4	614	2,894,903	5.7	39.6	26.6	3.3	11.4	9.1	0.0
Valley Stream	116	1,253	73.5	22.6	225	1,128,453	12.8	3.8	0.6	18.2	0.6	37.3	6.6
Watertown	47	259	24.6	6.6	370	1,573,042	9.1	22.3	27.5	9.6	5.8	20.8	2.5
White Plains	141	958	83.4	26.2	1,041	6,536,682	8.4	25.5	18.2	8.2	6.7	11.5	3.6

1. Establishments subject to federal tax.

Table D. Cities — Population

AREANAME	Percent Hispanic or Latino[1], 2016	Percent foreign born, 2016	Age of population (percent), 2016							Median age 2016	Percent female 2016	Population			
			Under 18 years	18 to 24 years	25 to 34 years	35 to 44 years	45 to 54 years	55 to 64 years	65 years and over			Census counts		Percent change	
												2000	2010	2000-2010	2010-2017
	12	13	14	15	16	17	18	19	20	21	22	23	24	25	26
NEW YORK— Cont'd															
Yonkers	35.0	31.2	20.8	10.7	13.1	12.7	13.4	12.2	17.3	39.5	52.4	196,086	195,993	0.0	3.1
NORTH CAROLINA	9.2	7.8	22.6	9.6	13.0	12.9	13.7	12.8	15.5	38.7	51.4	8,049,313	9,535,721	18.5	7.7
Apex	7.3	12.1	29.5	7.3	12.1	18.9	16.9	8.8	6.6	35.7	52.4	20,212	37,540	85.7	34.4
Asheboro	28.0	15.2	23.0	11.5	11.0	11.9	14.7	10.8	17.2	39.0	53.1	21,672	25,395	17.2	1.8
Asheville	6.3	6.3	16.9	10.6	16.1	13.8	13.8	11.6	17.2	39.8	51.6	68,889	83,365	21.0	10.2
Burlington	18.2	11.3	22.1	7.7	13.6	12.8	13.7	11.5	18.6	40.0	56.0	44,917	50,877	13.3	4.3
Cary	9.3	22.7	26.8	3.9	11.1	16.5	16.2	12.9	12.8	40.5	50.3	94,536	135,698	43.5	22.3
Chapel Hill	6.4	16.0	16.3	32.6	12.1	10.5	9.4	9.1	10.1	25.5	51.3	48,715	57,221	17.5	4.6
Charlotte	13.8	16.4	24.4	9.5	17.7	15.1	13.3	10.4	9.6	34.0	52.1	540,828	735,688	36.0	16.8
Concord	9.9	9.4	25.2	8.0	13.4	13.9	14.7	12.3	12.5	37.3	52.6	55,977	79,288	41.6	16.1
Durham	14.3	15.2	22.6	10.7	19.8	13.8	11.9	10.6	10.7	33.3	53.2	187,035	228,354	22.1	17.2
Fayetteville	11.7	7.0	23.8	14.3	18.2	10.7	10.2	10.0	12.8	30.7	50.8	121,015	200,571	65.7	4.6
Garner	13.9	7.7	29.9	9.3	14.3	9.7	14.7	9.7	12.3	31.7	49.2	17,757	25,774	45.1	12.0
Gastonia	10.4	8.2	24.8	6.6	14.1	11.6	13.9	13.2	15.8	38.4	54.5	66,277	71,736	8.2	6.8
Goldsboro	5.2	8.1	21.2	12.6	15.6	9.0	14.4	9.9	17.3	35.9	49.7	39,043	35,465	-9.2	-0.8
Greensboro	7.6	10.7	22.4	12.5	16.3	12.3	12.3	11.2	13.1	34.3	53.6	223,891	268,926	20.1	7.9
Greenville	7.2	5.9	18.9	26.5	15.8	10.1	10.7	8.8	9.3	27.3	53.8	60,476	84,567	39.8	9.0
Hickory	17.9	12.8	28.3	11.9	11.9	11.9	11.1	12.0	12.9	33.9	51.0	37,222	39,987	7.4	1.6
High Point	13.1	13.8	25.9	9.8	12.4	12.6	14.5	10.9	14.0	36.1	52.6	85,839	104,497	21.7	6.7
Huntersville	6.4	7.2	27.5	5.7	13.2	13.3	17.3	10.7	12.3	37.1	53.2	24,960	46,763	87.4	20.2
Indian Trail	13.4	9.8	28.8	11.4	9.8	12.8	17.9	8.1	11.2	35.0	53.1	11,905	33,583	182.1	16.1
Jacksonville	15.3	3.6	25.7	30.6	16.5	10.2	4.9	5.8	6.4	23.1	42.8	66,715	70,094	5.1	3.4
Kannapolis	17.8	9.5	30.3	7.6	18.9	14.0	10.4	6.2	12.7	31.5	51.1	36,910	42,607	15.4	14.5
Matthews	4.8	13.8	19.2	7.7	12.0	13.5	14.8	15.6	17.2	43.0	50.0	22,127	27,183	22.8	18.2
Monroe	30.5	18.1	24.7	10.9	12.6	16.3	11.8	11.7	12.1	35.7	51.5	26,228	32,783	25.0	7.0
Mooresville	11.9	10.4	30.0	7.1	16.7	14.1	13.1	9.0	10.1	33.1	53.7	18,823	34,303	82.2	10.3
New Bern	12.7	7.2	25.9	8.9	15.0	10.6	12.4	10.3	17.0	35.1	51.2	23,128	29,343	26.9	0.8
Raleigh	10.2	13.0	20.2	13.1	18.7	14.9	12.9	10.2	10.1	33.8	52.3	276,093	404,056	46.3	15.0
Rocky Mount	5.6	5.5	25.0	10.0	12.9	10.7	14.1	12.8	14.4	36.3	54.7	55,893	57,712	3.3	-5.5
Salisbury	14.2	8.8	21.5	13.5	9.2	11.8	13.0	15.5	15.6	38.8	51.5	26,462	33,529	26.7	1.0
Sanford	28.5	17.1	28.5	6.9	15.1	10.5	15.1	11.8	12.1	34.7	56.8	23,220	28,134	21.2	4.2
Thomasville	4.1	2.1	25.3	6.1	13.7	10.8	14.0	12.5	17.5	39.0	50.4	19,788	26,776	35.3	-0.6
Wake Forest	2.7	4.6	30.6	8.4	13.8	13.7	16.3	7.3	9.9	33.0	55.0	12,588	30,096	139.1	40.4
Wilmington	5.9	5.2	18.6	16.9	13.8	12.5	11.2	12.8	14.2	35.7	51.4	75,838	106,419	40.3	11.9
Wilson	8.1	6.2	23.8	10.7	12.4	12.5	10.7	14.0	15.9	37.8	51.5	44,405	49,159	10.7	0.4
Winston-Salem	13.9	9.4	23.9	10.7	13.5	12.5	12.5	12.3	14.6	36.1	53.2	185,776	229,646	23.6	6.5
NORTH DAKOTA	3.5	3.2	23.0	11.7	15.3	11.4	11.5	12.6	14.5	35.0	48.5	642,200	672,585	4.7	12.3
Bismarck	2.4	2.3	21.3	9.1	15.1	11.3	12.3	13.4	17.5	37.9	51.3	55,532	61,303	10.4	18.9
Fargo	3.3	6.6	20.3	17.9	18.7	11.2	10.3	9.5	12.0	31.0	46.6	90,599	105,605	16.6	15.9
Grand Forks	3.7	6.1	18.8	22.9	17.9	9.7	9.4	10.1	11.2	29.1	48.1	49,321	52,918	7.3	7.8
Minot	6.5	5.0	22.7	12.7	21.2	12.7	9.0	9.6	12.2	30.6	46.3	36,567	41,091	12.4	16.4
West Fargo	1.1	3.9	27.5	9.4	16.7	15.6	11.0	11.9	7.8	33.5	50.9	14,940	25,836	72.9	38.2
OHIO	3.6	4.4	22.5	9.3	12.9	11.9	13.3	13.9	16.2	39.3	51.0	11,353,140	11,536,730	1.6	1.1
Akron	2.5	7.3	21.6	11.2	15.1	11.2	13.2	13.0	14.6	36.6	52.8	217,074	199,079	-8.3	-0.6
Barberton	0.5	2.1	19.7	5.3	13.8	10.3	12.4	15.1	23.3	45.6	51.1	27,899	26,570	-4.8	-1.7
Beavercreek	3.7	9.0	19.9	7.9	14.6	11.3	13.5	15.1	17.7	42.5	49.0	37,984	45,174	18.9	3.9
Bowling Green	7.3	4.8	13.9	43.3	13.0	6.5	4.7	7.9	10.7	22.8	56.5	29,636	30,058	1.4	5.9
Brunswick	2.1	4.2	23.2	9.7	13.3	11.8	14.8	14.1	13.2	38.6	51.9	33,388	34,278	2.7	1.7
Canton	5.4	2.9	23.9	10.7	12.0	11.9	12.5	14.5	14.6	37.7	52.3	80,806	73,051	-9.6	-2.9
Cincinnati	4.2	5.2	22.3	13.7	18.3	11.7	10.4	11.5	12.1	32.2	51.9	331,285	296,852	-10.4	1.5
Cleveland	11.0	5.5	22.3	10.8	15.2	11.3	13.4	13.9	13.1	36.4	50.9	478,403	396,682	-17.1	-2.8
Cleveland Heights	2.9	10.5	21.6	13.2	14.2	10.9	10.3	12.4	17.4	35.7	55.5	49,958	46,214	-7.5	-3.6
Columbus	5.8	11.7	23.0	11.1	20.9	12.9	11.8	10.6	9.7	32.3	51.3	711,470	788,877	10.9	11.4
Cuyahoga Falls	2.1	5.7	21.5	7.2	14.8	17.4	11.0	12.9	15.2	38.9	49.6	49,374	49,594	0.4	-0.7
Dayton	4.1	5.0	21.2	14.3	16.3	10.6	10.7	13.6	13.2	33.8	51.1	166,179	141,960	-14.6	-1.1
Delaware	4.0	4.9	26.5	10.7	13.2	17.4	11.9	10.1	10.1	34.6	54.2	25,243	34,756	37.7	13.0
Dublin	7.1	20.1	28.8	5.4	7.1	16.7	17.5	13.9	10.5	40.6	47.6	31,392	41,355	31.7	15.1
Elyria	5.3	1.6	23.7	9.6	10.8	12.3	12.1	16.1	15.4	39.8	51.0	55,953	54,539	-2.5	-1.2
Euclid	1.7	4.7	20.5	9.2	10.3	14.9	12.7	13.7	18.7	41.1	50.8	52,717	48,905	-7.2	-3.5
Fairborn	3.3	4.7	19.4	13.3	19.8	11.0	10.9	9.7	15.8	32.4	54.4	32,052	32,918	2.7	1.9
Fairfield	9.5	10.8	22.4	9.6	15.8	14.0	10.7	13.4	14.1	37.5	49.1	42,097	42,503	1.0	0.1
Findlay	6.6	6.6	14.9	13.4	16.3	11.4	11.4	13.6	19.0	39.1	51.9	38,967	41,185	5.7	0.3
Gahanna	3.3	5.4	23.6	7.5	11.8	13.4	16.2	12.5	15.0	39.9	55.5	32,636	33,233	1.8	6.2
Garfield Heights	4.2	2.5	22.5	7.2	12.4	11.9	13.2	14.3	18.6	41.1	54.8	30,734	28,849	-6.1	-3.5
Green	1.2	4.4	18.7	11.1	8.3	12.1	16.6	14.7	18.6	44.9	49.3	22,817	25,740	12.8	0.0
Grove City	2.1	2.1	27.2	6.0	15.4	13.5	11.8	11.5	14.5	35.6	54.4	27,075	35,617	31.5	15.2

1. May be of any race.

AREANAME	Households, 2016								Serious crimes known to police[2], 2016				Educational attainment, 2016		
			Percent						Total		Rate[3]			Attainment[4] (percent)	
	Number	Persons per house-hold	Family	Married couple family	Female headed family[1]	Non-family	One person	Persons in group quarters	Number	Rate	Violent	Property	Population age 25 and over	High school graduate or less	Bachelor's degree or more
	27	28	29	30	31	32	33	34	35	36	37	38	39	40	41
NEW YORK— Cont'd															
Yonkers	72,040	2.75	66.5	41.6	17.3	33.5	29.1	2,904	3,130	1,549	467	1,082	137,576	43.6	34.2
NORTH CAROLINA	3,882,423	2.55	65.5	48.0	13.1	34.5	28.5	255,962	315,534	3,110	372	2,737	6,877,185	38.5	30.4
Apex	17,020	2.77	73.9	61.4	7.9	26.1	21.1	208	641	1,354	85	1,270	29,936	12.3	68.0
Asheboro	10,729	2.36	53.0	39.3	10.2	47.0	40.5	868	1,605	6,119	396	5,722	17,146	48.2	22.1
Asheville	37,527	2.28	48.3	34.1	11.1	51.7	39.6	3,392	4,894	5,465	600	4,866	64,618	26.2	46.0
Burlington	22,784	2.28	55.0	33.1	20.0	45.0	34.8	970	2,225	4,217	743	3,474	37,140	40.5	22.3
Cary	60,298	2.71	75.5	62.6	8.3	24.5	20.9	350	1,807	1,096	92	1,005	113,803	14.7	67.7
Chapel Hill	18,559	2.58	53.8	41.3	8.6	46.2	32.3	10,355	1,476	2,460	188	2,272	29,760	11.4	75.0
Charlotte	319,816	2.59	59.4	41.1	13.6	40.6	32.2	12,681	43,292	4,830	732	4,098	556,496	27.4	44.1
Concord	31,432	2.82	68.8	51.3	14.4	31.2	26.1	1,290	2,329	2,604	139	2,465	60,040	33.4	35.4
Durham	106,400	2.38	55.9	36.6	14.8	44.1	33.5	10,218	10,623	4,028	747	3,281	175,595	28.7	49.4
Fayetteville	79,645	2.45	59.9	36.8	19.6	40.1	35.5	9,815	10,732	5,308	757	4,550	126,795	33.6	25.9
Garner	10,351	2.76	62.1	41.5	15.5	37.9	23.1	NA	1,079	3,785	302	3,483	17,483	27.2	38.5
Gastonia	29,559	2.51	61.5	41.4	17.0	38.5	31.8	1,376	4,016	5,346	767	4,579	51,842	39.4	28.2
Goldsboro	14,192	2.38	64.5	38.3	22.0	35.5	32.9	1,986	2,388	6,657	1,084	5,573	23,704	45.4	16.6
Greensboro	113,922	2.39	56.7	34.8	18.2	43.3	35.9	14,210	11,132	3,857	643	3,214	187,012	32.5	37.5
Greenville	37,921	2.26	46.6	27.6	14.2	53.4	39.7	5,914	3,834	4,178	508	3,670	49,964	29.5	35.4
Hickory	15,663	2.50	60.1	41.0	15.1	39.9	32.3	1,308	2,118	5,238	408	4,830	24,185	38.6	29.4
High Point	43,265	2.58	64.4	38.2	20.8	35.6	30.0	3,747	4,704	4,221	647	3,574	74,203	45.9	27.9
Huntersville	19,465	2.80	79.7	68.6	8.1	20.3	16.2	NA	1,220	2,262	117	2,145	36,642	15.3	51.6
Indian Trail	13,270	2.88	71.9	60.9	9.0	28.1	22.1	NA	NA	NA	NA	NA	22,862	33.3	33.8
Jacksonville	19,925	2.82	68.2	54.3	12.0	31.8	25.1	11,564	1,246	1,868	162	1,707	29,655	35.4	23.4
Kannapolis	16,066	3.01	72.6	51.6	16.6	27.4	25.4	320	1,054	2,249	252	1,997	30,237	41.4	23.2
Matthews	11,540	2.70	72.6	63.3	9.0	27.4	21.3	326	1,121	3,570	146	3,423	23,047	25.5	49.6
Monroe	11,003	3.11	81.1	49.2	25.7	18.9	12.9	653	2,191	6,264	649	5,615	22,424	56.3	13.6
Mooresville	12,988	2.79	68.7	50.0	11.6	31.3	26.4	303	1,543	4,229	274	3,955	22,968	33.3	31.6
New Bern	11,728	2.53	63.8	41.3	17.2	36.2	30.9	392	1,170	3,882	411	3,471	19,636	39.0	26.7
Raleigh	180,773	2.43	56.0	39.7	13.1	44.0	33.5	20,096	NA	NA	NA	NA	306,244	22.3	50.8
Rocky Mount	20,529	2.65	70.9	42.7	23.8	29.1	26.3	1,079	2,542	4,586	785	3,801	36,010	50.4	20.0
Salisbury	12,170	2.49	58.7	35.9	15.3	41.3	31.9	3,677	1,994	5,844	973	4,871	22,098	40.5	19.7
Sanford	10,398	2.73	62.3	46.6	12.6	37.7	35.4	717	12	41	3	37	18,804	45.0	23.5
Thomasville	10,880	2.49	62.9	42.0	14.1	37.1	32.7	482	1,188	4,381	321	4,060	18,911	50.6	19.1
Wake Forest	14,221	2.78	73.1	56.2	14.5	26.9	21.8	NA	1,008	2,520	135	2,385	24,335	20.6	59.0
Wilmington	50,083	2.24	48.1	33.4	11.3	51.9	38.2	5,166	5,530	4,692	644	4,048	75,848	30.7	40.7
Wilson	18,478	2.60	59.5	32.7	21.3	40.5	37.3	1,560	2,091	4,204	521	3,684	32,472	52.8	22.4
Winston-Salem	95,506	2.43	60.7	39.5	16.4	39.3	34.1	9,774	13,461	5,528	749	4,779	158,309	35.5	34.3
NORTH DAKOTA	315,134	2.32	58.7	47.7	7.2	41.3	32.3	26,100	19,305	2,547	251	2,296	495,015	34.7	29.6
Bismarck	30,628	2.18	55.3	40.6	11.0	44.7	36.3	2,084	2,698	3,683	292	3,391	47,865	31.9	34.6
Fargo	55,368	2.08	47.0	36.0	7.9	53.0	39.3	5,055	4,329	3,571	388	3,184	74,366	25.2	42.2
Grand Forks	25,056	2.14	50.1	36.2	8.4	49.9	38.8	3,907	1,972	3,409	308	3,101	33,467	32.7	34.9
Minot	20,370	2.35	55.1	45.7	3.9	44.9	34.1	1,306	1,517	2,959	273	2,686	31,801	39.1	29.1
West Fargo	13,019	2.67	68.8	58.2	8.8	31.2	19.0	72	560	1,582	186	1,396	21,968	21.5	41.3
OHIO	4,624,669	2.44	63.3	45.9	12.7	36.7	30.3	313,225	334,234	2,878	300	2,577	7,922,061	43.3	27.5
Akron	83,071	2.31	54.9	31.0	17.4	45.1	36.3	5,548	9,934	5,036	654	4,382	132,665	48.6	21.3
Barberton	11,055	2.33	57.4	41.5	14.5	42.6	35.8	386	874	3,339	287	3,053	19,584	68.6	11.6
Beavercreek	19,544	2.35	69.2	56.8	7.7	30.8	26.8	1,101	1,101	2,368	71	2,297	33,381	18.0	51.4
Bowling Green	10,884	2.34	45.4	32.0	8.9	54.6	31.2	6,072	602	1,917	134	1,783	13,529	28.9	40.8
Brunswick	12,775	2.70	65.2	47.4	12.7	34.8	28.5	283	249	716	72	644	23,321	38.5	25.6
Canton	29,592	2.32	54.7	30.3	18.3	45.3	38.6	2,627	4,368	6,096	987	5,109	46,671	54.7	15.0
Cincinnati	135,565	2.11	45.8	23.7	17.8	54.2	44.8	12,699	18,231	6,100	938	5,162	191,240	37.1	37.0
Cleveland	168,306	2.22	49.0	21.0	22.5	51.0	43.7	12,842	27,354	7,082	1,695	5,388	258,281	53.6	16.3
Cleveland Heights	18,738	2.33	55.2	35.0	16.7	44.8	35.4	942	1,142	2,555	324	2,231	29,076	20.6	54.9
Columbus	349,113	2.40	52.9	32.2	15.1	47.1	35.7	23,546	39,967	4,634	544	4,090	568,823	37.4	35.3
Cuyahoga Falls	21,806	2.23	52.8	39.2	10.4	47.2	39.4	506	1,210	2,466	137	2,330	35,091	28.6	37.8
Dayton	58,752	2.19	49.5	24.5	20.2	50.5	42.7	12,118	8,702	6,204	1,041	5,163	90,638	46.0	16.3
Delaware	13,733	2.73	64.3	47.6	14.1	35.7	27.0	2,278	963	2,491	189	2,302	24,994	35.3	38.8
Dublin	16,698	2.68	75.4	69.4	3.2	24.6	21.9	NA	547	1,193	50	1,143	29,551	10.3	73.7
Elyria	21,839	2.43	58.8	33.8	16.4	41.2	34.2	NA	1,645	3,067	300	2,767	35,800	49.3	15.9
Euclid	22,380	2.09	48.1	27.7	16.3	51.9	46.6	637	1,604	3,383	580	2,803	33,294	41.9	21.8
Fairborn	14,647	2.28	49.0	29.4	11.7	51.0	41.3	695	1,002	2,983	253	2,730	22,917	34.9	28.6
Fairfield	16,044	2.62	64.6	45.1	12.1	35.4	28.0	637	1,155	2,698	257	2,441	28,988	46.7	27.5
Findlay	19,311	2.06	48.1	39.8	5.7	51.9	37.5	1,679	1,415	3,438	284	3,154	29,686	41.2	26.4
Gahanna	13,406	2.58	69.3	58.3	6.5	30.7	27.4	NA	809	2,321	57	2,263	23,992	26.0	48.3
Garfield Heights	12,052	2.28	59.8	37.3	19.3	40.2	31.0	472	419	1,500	236	1,264	19,621	49.5	16.6
Green	9,766	2.61	73.7	55.8	14.0	26.3	24.3	NA	NA	NA	NA	NA	18,033	40.7	30.5
Grove City	15,963	2.48	66.1	49.6	14.1	33.9	28.4	NA	1,731	4,310	110	4,201	26,611	38.8	30.7

1. No spouse present.   2. Data for serious crimes have not been adjusted for underreporting. This may affect comparability between geographic areas and over time.   3. Per 100,000 population estimated by the FBI.   4. Persons 25 years old and over.

Table D. Cities — Income and Housing

	Money income, 2016					Median earnings, 2016			Housing units, 2016				
	Households												
AREANAME	Median income	Percent with income less than $20,000	Percent with income of $200,000 or more	Median family income	Median non-family household income	All persons	Men	Women	Total	Occupied	Percent owner occupied	Median value[1] (dollars)	Median rent (dollars)
	42	43	44	45	46	47	48	49	50	51	52	53	54
NEW YORK— Cont'd													
Yonkers	62,049	17.7	7.4	74,091	40,999	34,426	36,883	31,165	79,313	72,040	46.7	402,500	1,287
NORTH CAROLINA	50,584	18.6	4.4	62,289	30,977	30,552	35,022	26,099	4,540,697	3,882,423	64.2	165,400	839
Apex	101,552	4.7	12.1	115,745	65,796	52,354	65,442	41,854	17,166	17,020	75.0	307,800	1,220
Asheboro	33,082	25.4	1.2	48,527	21,654	22,312	27,238	17,057	11,475	10,729	54.9	107,200	607
Asheville	45,814	19.8	3.5	60,575	31,736	24,695	25,807	23,198	41,240	37,527	47.5	251,300	923
Burlington	40,900	26.0	1.5	48,760	25,724	26,335	30,787	23,887	25,232	22,784	46.4	124,900	740
Cary	100,167	5.3	15.6	111,934	51,173	55,599	80,867	41,036	63,497	60,298	71.7	332,800	1,175
Chapel Hill	66,137	20.5	14.3	106,625	37,044	17,631	22,551	15,549	20,857	18,559	51.4	371,500	1,096
Charlotte	61,017	13.7	7.7	72,899	44,790	35,227	40,753	30,938	349,447	319,816	52.2	201,500	1,052
Concord	60,107	13.6	6.9	75,581	40,829	34,065	43,466	26,163	34,453	31,432	67.0	197,200	875
Durham	52,208	16.4	5.3	72,951	38,368	32,402	36,234	31,167	114,984	106,400	47.7	196,100	949
Fayetteville	42,918	20.4	1.6	49,241	33,324	25,595	29,812	21,078	94,365	79,645	46.0	130,900	873
Garner	61,215	13.4	8.2	80,131	44,089	34,003	35,299	31,329	10,893	10,351	61.3	170,400	1,020
Gastonia	48,286	18.0	2.5	54,176	33,182	30,288	35,051	25,648	33,036	29,559	55.6	140,100	803
Goldsboro	28,554	36.5	2.7	45,096	14,348	21,488	23,179	20,538	16,107	14,192	32.3	136,500	707
Greensboro	45,064	23.1	4.5	55,738	31,959	27,086	31,260	23,345	129,716	113,922	48.9	152,100	803
Greenville	36,806	34.1	3.3	54,289	23,188	25,283	31,634	21,247	43,017	37,921	31.1	162,200	727
Hickory	38,128	27.9	4.0	52,544	21,341	22,272	27,089	18,290	17,681	15,663	48.7	158,600	708
High Point	41,250	21.9	3.5	46,692	31,623	27,833	31,678	26,052	49,059	43,265	50.6	147,600	803
Huntersville	92,791	8.4	13.1	111,390	51,401	50,726	61,360	36,929	20,447	19,465	70.6	288,000	1,172
Indian Trail	82,394	9.6	4.0	86,726	42,272	40,669	48,221	32,126	13,441	13,270	85.3	214,800	1,205
Jacksonville	39,604	18.3	1.1	43,457	27,389	24,074	24,499	22,738	22,430	19,925	34.9	159,900	938
Kannapolis	53,255	17.7	2.4	60,210	28,925	27,390	28,743	26,805	18,759	16,066	53.7	124,300	813
Matthews	74,658	5.3	8.0	92,274	37,212	38,426	45,217	31,548	11,837	11,540	72.6	247,100	1,206
Monroe	46,655	15.6	2.3	50,303	30,465	23,692	30,618	17,498	11,912	11,003	62.0	158,300	880
Mooresville	59,474	13.9	3.1	70,499	34,724	36,857	42,763	30,363	13,453	12,988	49.3	202,500	1,005
New Bern	39,947	23.2	3.2	51,269	29,669	23,506	26,860	22,239	13,897	11,728	53.9	157,900	818
Raleigh	64,456	11.4	7.5	81,052	48,535	36,629	40,277	33,833	201,158	180,773	49.1	242,500	1,027
Rocky Mount	37,192	27.2	2.3	48,582	20,114	25,608	30,992	23,032	25,638	20,529	52.2	109,600	672
Salisbury	43,096	22.9	3.5	46,912	30,525	22,771	26,476	21,881	15,285	12,170	47.1	116,600	733
Sanford	39,974	28.3	2.8	56,740	18,258	25,287	31,429	17,706	11,978	10,398	49.3	119,500	679
Thomasville	37,362	20.7	0.4	45,365	30,265	27,212	35,520	21,448	12,137	10,880	57.3	113,700	720
Wake Forest	73,781	6.6	3.5	93,633	49,375	42,917	52,679	38,216	14,848	14,221	67.2	271,700	1,002
Wilmington	38,800	27.4	5.6	65,869	26,237	26,309	35,608	19,975	57,177	50,083	43.3	236,300	873
Wilson	32,450	27.2	4.7	47,314	22,544	23,190	26,663	20,004	21,265	18,478	47.5	140,600	718
Winston-Salem	42,605	23.8	4.9	54,859	26,952	27,045	29,597	24,812	107,837	95,506	54.6	144,500	745
NORTH DAKOTA	60,656	14.8	4.8	79,530	37,158	35,039	41,897	27,452	368,545	315,134	63.2	184,100	776
Bismarck	58,522	11.8	4.9	81,451	42,834	40,293	46,419	32,138	33,271	30,628	64.4	235,900	819
Fargo	52,699	18.1	4.0	71,742	39,808	31,203	36,140	26,358	58,791	55,368	42.7	196,400	771
Grand Forks	45,687	22.1	1.5	73,605	28,589	26,094	29,530	24,483	26,933	25,056	46.4	207,700	763
Minot	62,713	14.2	3.7	81,515	38,212	33,013	37,641	27,125	23,943	20,370	57.5	212,600	908
West Fargo	74,072	4.9	6.3	89,329	47,562	36,743	41,732	32,103	13,320	13,019	66.1	229,000	880
OHIO	52,334	17.9	4.1	66,722	31,164	31,289	37,345	25,921	5,164,400	4,624,669	65.4	140,100	759
Akron	35,184	26.7	1.7	42,974	26,806	25,919	30,112	22,609	95,670	83,071	49.7	78,000	724
Barberton	41,860	23.6	0.0	48,130	25,380	27,463	37,765	23,594	11,982	11,055	57.9	87,400	772
Beavercreek	80,911	8.3	7.7	97,545	53,819	48,354	62,000	40,142	20,272	19,544	72.8	181,000	1,248
Bowling Green	43,151	22.5	3.1	60,501	27,579	11,216	14,395	9,294	11,770	10,884	38.0	169,400	692
Brunswick	70,320	5.5	3.4	81,327	39,855	35,710	41,392	27,763	13,265	12,775	80.0	163,900	852
Canton	31,714	29.0	0.5	40,425	22,479	20,398	22,378	15,573	35,072	29,592	49.5	73,400	630
Cincinnati	38,539	29.3	4.3	52,237	29,715	26,902	30,091	25,018	162,392	135,565	38.0	134,100	684
Cleveland	27,551	38.3	1.5	32,836	21,167	22,240	24,115	21,166	212,568	168,306	41.8	66,800	669
Cleveland Heights	50,833	26.6	6.1	62,457	30,993	36,020	40,606	31,904	21,922	18,738	52.2	121,700	942
Columbus	49,602	19.4	2.4	58,034	39,571	30,566	31,906	28,344	388,841	349,113	44.0	140,700	882
Cuyahoga Falls	52,139	10.4	1.4	73,699	37,475	36,087	43,628	26,782	24,574	21,806	62.1	129,200	861
Dayton	28,894	36.7	0.8	40,680	22,090	19,394	21,664	17,121	74,465	58,722	46.9	66,900	671
Delaware	65,620	14.9	5.0	90,610	38,110	40,156	50,851	30,704	14,365	13,733	60.6	178,000	842
Dublin	129,436	8.2	24.4	152,083	67,325	66,300	90,014	42,279	17,350	16,698	71.8	376,300	1,501
Elyria	41,356	23.3	0.7	53,560	29,497	26,020	31,336	22,717	25,266	21,839	59.0	101,500	724
Euclid	36,974	30.3	0.8	51,016	25,014	31,077	32,420	29,231	26,107	22,380	49.4	81,100	741
Fairborn	37,550	26.0	1.8	53,514	31,449	27,767	31,910	21,690	16,360	14,647	43.0	113,200	748
Fairfield	64,785	10.8	1.4	70,303	40,633	30,467	35,635	27,229	17,007	16,044	56.6	160,300	896
Findlay	45,994	16.0	1.9	61,997	31,440	27,628	35,725	18,723	20,572	19,311	52.6	131,600	730
Gahanna	80,773	8.3	5.8	91,461	51,192	37,443	42,400	32,320	14,183	13,406	68.7	204,800	900
Garfield Heights	46,090	14.3	0.0	56,573	31,105	33,369	36,632	30,863	13,893	12,052	65.4	74,500	892
Green	65,792	15.3	7.6	82,731	37,719	34,780	40,599	22,033	10,468	9,766	75.0	170,900	803
Grove City	59,431	10.3	2.0	65,441	42,642	40,732	44,952	37,244	16,538	15,963	65.7	160,800	895

1. Specified owner-occupied units; $2,000,000 represents $2,000,000 or more.

AREANAME	Commuting[1] 2016 Percent — Drove alone	With commutes of 30 minutes or more	Computer access[2] Percent — With a computer in the house	With Internet access	Migration — Percent who lived in the same house one year ago	Percent who lived in another state or county one year ago	Civilian labor force, 2016 — Total	Percent change 2016-2017	Unemployment[3] — Total	Rate	Civilian employment, 2016 — Population age 16 and older — Number	Percent in labor force	Population age 16 to 64 — Number	Percent who worked full-year full-time
	55	56	57	58	59	60	61	62	63	64	65	66	67	68
NEW YORK— Cont'd														
Yonkers	51.2	56.1	87.8	79.0	92.2	3.7	95,859	0.6	5,143	5.4	164,521	63.1	129,876	48.7
NORTH CAROLINA	81.3	33.2	88.1	78.7	84.3	7.6	4,941,701	1.8	224,869	4.6	8,115,833	62.0	6,547,242	49.5
Apex	81.3	31.8	NA	NA	85.7	6.6	25,897	3.1	891	3.4	34,757	80.5	31,655	61.6
Asheboro	NA	19.7	87.7	76.2	80.9	6.0	11,232	0.5	543	4.8	20,662	60.9	16,163	48.1
Asheville	74.1	13.1	88.2	81.5	82.8	7.1	49,135	2.0	1,733	3.5	76,077	62.9	60,777	47.1
Burlington	88.9	25.9	86.0	71.7	88.4	4.2	25,868	1.1	1,158	4.5	42,437	64.5	32,605	55.6
Cary	78.0	30.8	97.3	95.2	83.7	8.0	91,345	3.1	3,310	3.6	125,300	69.6	104,354	60.0
Chapel Hill	51.7	21.8	96.2	86.0	64.8	21.1	30,111	2.2	1,379	4.6	49,669	61.9	43,815	32.9
Charlotte	77.3	37.1	93.6	85.8	80.5	8.3	479,698	3.3	21,123	4.4	658,524	71.7	578,030	56.2
Concord	82.1	45.0	92.5	86.4	82.9	9.0	46,919	3.3	1,979	4.2	69,454	69.6	58,250	56.8
Durham	75.4	28.7	92.3	84.3	77.1	10.7	143,779	2.2	5,890	4.1	209,193	71.0	181,057	53.3
Fayetteville	80.1	20.8	89.8	81.7	78.4	9.6	76,173	0.4	4,738	6.2	161,120	63.2	134,860	49.0
Garner	80.0	52.5	96.2	90.0	84.6	8.3	16,330	2.7	615	3.8	21,084	71.0	17,537	56.7
Gastonia	83.5	41.5	87.9	81.1	81.4	10.7	36,627	2.8	1,808	4.9	59,185	64.4	47,217	51.5
Goldsboro	77.2	26.0	78.1	72.5	73.9	11.8	12,414	-0.4	844	6.8	29,310	50.4	23,117	34.5
Greensboro	81.0	19.3	88.1	68.9	82.2	7.5	144,426	0.7	7,148	4.9	229,532	64.5	191,822	46.7
Greenville	83.2	16.4	87.8	80.3	64.6	16.7	47,766	1.3	2,520	5.3	75,955	60.1	67,428	41.4
Hickory	80.2	23.7	84.4	77.4	71.5	17.4	20,467	2.1	892	4.4	31,123	62.3	25,916	41.4
High Point	80.5	26.7	87.2	77.1	81.6	7.8	54,282	0.9	2,835	5.2	89,937	60.8	73,817	46.6
Huntersville	79.4	43.4	93.6	89.8	86.1	5.8	32,765	3.5	1,164	3.6	41,500	69.4	34,763	60.8
Indian Trail	85.9	55.7	94.3	91.4	79.6	9.7	20,594	3.2	799	3.9	28,280	73.5	23,995	59.0
Jacksonville	64.8	13.1	93.3	85.7	68.2	20.5	19,100	0.7	1,201	6.3	52,387	71.8	48,068	61.4
Kannapolis	85.0	40.0	92.1	85.5	78.6	11.1	22,979	3.0	1,055	4.6	35,513	69.6	29,351	56.3
Matthews	81.5	53.3	94.9	90.3	87.8	9.1	17,657	3.4	680	3.9	26,137	66.4	20,707	52.9
Monroe	NA	30.9	91.4	85.6	79.7	6.6	17,252	3.2	798	4.6	27,160	67.4	22,942	50.2
Mooresville	82.0	34.4	93.1	84.2	72.6	10.7	19,890	3.1	877	4.4	26,784	66.6	23,096	53.0
New Bern	78.4	29.9	92.1	80.3	88.3	6.5	12,609	0.5	607	4.8	22,800	63.1	17,694	46.0
Raleigh	78.6	31.9	96.1	90.3	77.7	9.2	253,820	2.9	10,570	4.2	375,916	71.8	329,500	54.5
Rocky Mount	85.8	22.8	82.8	69.9	83.3	11.4	23,732	-0.8	1,916	8.1	43,450	60.7	35,465	46.1
Salisbury	79.1	17.2	82.3	69.8	78.1	10.0	14,018	2.2	803	5.7	27,714	57.8	22,419	41.0
Sanford	88.8	24.0	83.5	64.8	83.0	10.0	12,608	1.6	683	5.4	21,663	63.7	18,137	44.6
Thomasville	NA	30.8	82.8	77.8	84.0	5.4	12,360	0.7	621	5.0	21,528	56.6	16,689	42.0
Wake Forest	82.9	49.2	94.8	91.1	77.4	11.4	20,996	3.0	792	3.8	28,664	74.2	24,725	58.4
Wilmington	82.6	16.3	90.0	76.7	83.7	8.6	61,899	2.2	2,706	4.4	97,874	59.6	81,196	43.1
Wilson	68.8	20.6	83.4	72.1	91.2	2.2	21,302	-1.1	1,819	8.5	39,310	59.1	31,422	47.3
Winston-Salem	81.9	19.0	88.7	78.6	82.6	8.2	116,989	0.9	5,528	4.7	190,875	60.8	155,528	45.0
NORTH DAKOTA	80.2	15.4	89.2	80.6	83.2	7.8	414,399	0.0	10,789	2.6	600,126	71.0	490,275	56.9
Bismarck	89.0	7.6	90.7	82.7	84.3	6.3	38,718	-0.1	927	2.4	55,821	70.5	43,752	61.7
Fargo	83.1	5.3	92.4	84.5	76.2	9.6	70,289	1.7	1,469	2.1	97,735	75.5	83,257	53.7
Grand Forks	80.6	8.2	89.6	79.4	75.5	12.2	32,716	0.6	673	2.1	48,054	72.1	41,609	47.2
Minot	81.5	15.0	94.0	88.8	82.7	4.4	24,041	-2.2	745	3.1	39,136	74.3	33,143	61.5
West Fargo	81.0	7.9	96.0	91.2	77.0	6.1	21,146	1.8	420	2.0	25,525	82.1	22,809	60.4
OHIO	83.1	30.7	87.9	80.6	85.0	5.6	5,780,021	0.7	288,847	5.0	9,318,105	63.2	7,433,191	50.1
Akron	82.3	24.4	81.8	74.8	86.4	5.0	91,776	0.4	5,299	5.8	160,178	61.6	131,268	44.6
Barberton	87.0	26.6	72.1	64.7	NA	NA	12,734	0.4	742	5.8	21,230	49.8	15,145	48.7
Beavercreek	92.6	13.4	95.6	93.6	84.3	11.9	23,443	1.2	892	3.8	38,386	60.2	30,185	54.1
Bowling Green	71.6	14.5	94.6	83.9	55.8	21.5	16,925	-0.2	778	4.6	27,710	70.4	24,317	29.8
Brunswick	88.8	42.4	93.0	86.1	92.5	2.7	19,952	-0.1	915	4.6	27,500	76.6	22,907	60.6
Canton	75.9	22.0	84.0	74.5	81.2	3.8	31,787	0.4	1,972	6.2	56,336	61.3	45,951	41.5
Cincinnati	71.1	27.5	86.3	78.0	72.7	8.5	145,152	1.4	6,998	4.8	238,186	66.8	201,906	45.1
Cleveland	68.3	32.3	82.3	66.2	81.1	4.1	159,290	0.0	11,710	7.4	309,115	59.0	258,694	37.9
Cleveland Heights	74.5	30.0	90.7	83.8	82.2	7.4	22,797	0.2	1,174	5.1	36,023	58.8	28,242	42.9
Columbus	80.1	25.4	91.5	84.4	77.6	7.2	463,347	1.9	18,929	4.1	682,539	70.7	598,511	51.6
Cuyahoga Falls	89.7	24.6	86.7	83.8	89.6	4.4	26,737	0.5	1,238	4.6	39,830	68.5	32,353	55.9
Dayton	69.8	21.7	81.6	73.7	76.8	6.0	59,114	1.2	3,425	5.8	113,605	59.1	95,026	36.2
Delaware	83.0	49.6	93.5	87.3	84.9	7.2	21,074	1.6	781	3.7	30,258	68.9	26,222	50.9
Dublin	86.1	41.6	NA	NA	80.1	8.7	25,087	2.0	863	3.4	33,534	72.3	28,801	58.1
Elyria	83.2	31.4	86.0	77.5	83.7	5.0	27,059	-0.1	1,706	6.3	42,108	63.2	33,861	45.6
Euclid	80.8	32.8	79.8	66.0	84.7	3.4	22,702	0.1	1,581	7.0	39,638	58.8	30,797	50.2
Fairborn	83.0	24.0	88.8	79.1	75.9	10.4	17,236	1.1	745	4.3	28,076	62.0	22,697	47.7
Fairfield	88.0	32.1	88.9	84.7	85.8	8.0	24,379	1.5	991	4.1	34,229	71.1	28,201	57.7
Findlay	78.0	15.1	87.5	80.7	74.8	12.1	21,989	0.7	838	3.8	36,119	64.5	28,246	52.9
Gahanna	83.0	22.9	NA	NA	85.0	5.4	20,360	2.1	764	3.8	27,558	74.3	22,346	61.1
Garfield Heights	84.7	33.7	84.5	76.3	87.9	3.0	13,685	0.0	918	6.7	22,350	65.6	17,171	59.2
Green	89.8	17.2	92.7	86.6	88.8	2.9	13,929	0.6	635	4.6	21,922	60.9	17,159	52.0
Grove City	87.7	40.5	95.2	91.8	87.8	1.8	21,797	2.0	842	3.9	30,167	70.1	24,383	69.0

1. Employed persons. 2. Households. 3. Percent of civilian labor force.

Table D. Cities — Construction, Wholesale Trade, and Retail Trade

AREANAME	Value of residential construction authorized by building permits, 2017			Wholesale trade[1], 2012				Retail trade[2], 2012			
	New construction ($1,000)	Number of housing units	Percent single family	Number of establish-ments	Number of employees	Sales (mil dol)	Annual payroll (mil dol)	Number of establish-ments	Number of employees	Sales (mil dol)	Annual payroll (mil dol)
	69	70	71	72	73	74	75	76	77	78	79
NEW YORK— Cont'd											
Yonkers	19,457	361	1.9	161	1,348	852.6	72.2	657	9,473	2,708.5	250.0
NORTH CAROLINA........	12,693,597	67,047	73.6	9,713	136,174	105,275.6	7,853.7	34,288	446,373	120,691.0	10,421.2
Apex............................	283,521	1,388	100.0	44	753	621.3	39.8	131	2,427	657.6	56.1
Asheboro......................	5,607	62	93.5	33	313	180.7	11.8	196	2,375	556.5	48.5
Asheville......................	80,993	381	83.7	155	1,477	883.6	71.4	776	11,310	2,822.0	265.2
Burlington	37,157	286	100.0	81	1,025	423.2	40.9	367	5,655	1,236.2	120.3
Cary............................	259,754	1,307	81.8	144	1,776	2,938.5	134.8	495	9,194	2,877.2	229.4
Chapel Hill	69,578	548	13.0	27	141	176.5	7.7	199	2,833	684.1	72.3
Charlotte......................	NA	NA	NA	1,540	25,446	19,884.6	1,617.4	2,600	39,240	10,901.0	960.8
Concord.......................	NA	NA	NA	113	1,941	1,285.3	92.3	489	9,070	2,228.3	189.2
Durham........................	430,107	2,962	60.2	173	5,168	4,131.5	426.0	871	13,896	3,313.6	317.4
Fayetteville..................	55,529	313	82.1	104	2,032	663.0	79.3	825	12,882	3,625.9	311.0
Garner.........................	70,221	832	24.2	57	1,381	1,135.3	57.4	112	1,911	490.5	42.2
Gastonia......................	90,083	315	100.0	86	848	328.4	34.2	378	5,774	1,341.6	125.3
Goldsboro....................	8,324	47	83.0	56	1,306	1,019.9	54.9	311	4,058	1,143.7	90.6
Greensboro..................	263,463	1,609	45.2	541	7,993	9,675.9	453.6	1,232	19,426	4,950.9	488.9
Greenville....................	129,950	839	36.4	70	700	350.5	35.0	421	6,355	1,589.1	141.5
Hickory	NA	NA	NA	129	4,126	3,196.1	196.6	454	6,897	1,934.2	165.6
High Point....................	38,824	309	95.5	298	4,852	3,737.6	268.8	410	4,792	1,347.0	114.9
Huntersville.................	NA	NA	NA	66	621	341.0	41.8	161	2,686	782.3	65.0
Indian Trail..................	NA	NA	NA	84	838	379.9	44.2	91	1,494	468.6	42.2
Jacksonville.................	5,729	74	24.3	26	109	73.0	4.5	340	5,936	1,691.7	141.4
Kannapolis...................	NA	NA	NA	25	178	118.1	8.3	158	1,596	398.1	36.6
Matthews.....................	NA	NA	NA	53	549	204.2	31.8	170	3,135	1,099.4	85.6
Monroe........................	13,474	84	100.0	76	1,328	647.5	58.3	230	3,076	861.7	68.7
Mooresville..................	NA	NA	NA	81	690	499.8	38.7	226	3,734	1,130.1	84.1
New Bern.....................	19,164	94	100.0	33	D	D	D	248	3,073	834.7	72.9
Raleigh........................	617,209	3,216	42.4	570	8,627	5,399.8	577.4	1,698	27,148	7,268.5	688.9
Rocky Mount................	960	8	100.0	74	1,406	1,071.4	63.1	331	4,143	1,014.0	89.4
Salisbury.....................	NA	NA	NA	47	945	612.8	38.8	203	2,948	832.5	70.1
Sanford.......................	19,139	110	100.0	22	D	D	D	192	2,658	706.4	58.3
Thomasville.................	6,972	40	65.0	30	453	211.9	22.1	128	1,458	354.7	31.5
Wake Forest	132,876	817	100.0	26	139	96.6	7.8	87	1,725	489.2	43.6
Wilmington...................	NA	NA	NA	139	1,191	570.6	58.3	764	10,389	3,009.5	261.3
Wilson.........................	35,641	275	48.4	76	742	444.0	30.7	263	3,268	899.3	76.9
Winston-Salem.............	293,003	1,960	60.4	239	3,943	2,266.4	189.6	1,008	15,129	4,067.8	365.3
NORTH DAKOTA............	606,686	3,411	61.9	1,430	18,880	28,150.8	1,078.2	3,185	47,186	15,519.8	1,204.4
Bismarck......................	68,722	375	84.0	115	1,967	1,346.8	106.9	357	6,779	1,948.7	175.8
Fargo..........................	165,530	1,225	36.2	251	5,114	4,124.9	288.3	518	11,065	3,299.9	266.9
Grand Forks	44,645	291	36.1	59	965	697.8	50.3	279	5,654	1,501.8	126.4
Minot..........................	20,421	92	87.0	68	1,285	2,418.1	80.1	250	5,160	1,686.7	149.6
West Fargo..................	67,082	341	100.0	41	477	194.6	23.5	91	1,133	373.8	27.1
OHIO..........................	5,020,991	23,917	67.5	11,744	182,791	155,426.0	9,627.2	36,531	549,152	153,554.0	13,099.3
Akron..........................	NA	NA	NA	217	2,998	1,695.8	153.6	612	7,731	1,906.6	185.0
Barberton....................	945	7	100.0	22	523	113.2	17.8	71	780	171.4	15.5
Beavercreek.................	NA	NA	NA	23	167	327.3	9.5	216	4,600	941.1	87.2
Bowling Green..............	NA	NA	NA	15	116	109.0	6.5	99	1,599	368.3	34.6
Brunswick....................	15,621	84	100.0	48	532	238.0	27.5	93	1,759	727.5	48.8
Canton........................	1,209	12	100.0	89	1,263	770.9	58.2	249	3,432	823.7	73.9
Cincinnati....................	91,635	716	25.4	358	5,890	6,371.5	337.1	941	13,549	3,977.7	350.4
Cleveland	9,004	180	80.0	577	9,142	5,475.0	465.9	1,206	10,637	2,764.9	244.1
Cleveland Heights	311	1	100.0	8	43	11.8	1.6	97	1,340	294.9	32.8
Columbus.....................	668,600	4,229	15.4	807	17,060	14,346.8	1,005.3	2,566	46,211	13,114.2	1,178.1
Cuyahoga Falls	NA	NA	NA	39	573	243.9	26.5	171	3,313	1,015.8	79.1
Dayton........................	2,888	21	100.0	158	3,063	12,234.4	182.6	375	3,791	870.1	88.8
Delaware.....................	60,942	237	92.8	14	120	40.6	6.4	118	1,738	539.0	44.8
Dublin.........................	103,999	288	89.6	88	1,426	1,730.1	115.1	118	2,215	997.6	79.5
Elyria..........................	4,937	53	41.5	56	309	150.4	12.6	219	3,567	887.5	79.0
Euclid.........................	0	0	0.0	34	533	206.2	25.9	84	993	235.3	22.0
Fairborn......................	18,312	79	100.0	11	330	338.2	17.0	78	1,061	300.0	22.6
Fairfield......................	3,772	23	100.0	72	1,793	1,060.2	92.0	175	3,937	1,355.5	133.3
Findlay........................	6,876	37	94.6	40	638	483.4	29.8	205	3,287	823.7	72.0
Gahanna......................	5,785	26	92.3	38	619	358.8	28.4	87	1,378	475.2	39.6
Garfield Heights............	0	0	0.0	27	404	152.7	15.1	78	960	211.5	18.5
Green	NA	NA	NA	31	457	465.3	45.9	55	1,490	706.3	46.3
Grove City	36,964	176	100.0	32	869	592.4	38.9	121	3,256	1,130.1	76.0

1. Merchant wholesalers except manufacturers' sales branches and offices.   2. Establishments with payroll.

AREANAME	Real estate and rental and leasing, 2012				Professional, scientific, and technical services[1], 2012				Manufacturing, 2012			
	Number of establishments	Number of employees	Receipts (mil dol)	Annual payroll (mil dol)	Number of establishments	Number of employees	Receipts (mil dol)	Annual payroll (mil dol)	Number of establishments	Number of employees	Receipts (mil dol)	Annual payroll (mil dol)
	80	81	82	83	84	85	86	87	88	89	90	91
NEW YORK— Cont'd												
Yonkers	363	1,099	341.3	42.1	254	D	D	D	88	2,755	984.9	141.4
NORTH CAROLINA	10,140	47,155	9,301.7	1,942.6	22,730	190,441	30,520.8	12,461.5	8,953	403,593	202,344.6	18,191.2
Apex	27	74	12.0	2.8	158	611	83.3	27.8	34	1,042	1,399.5	63.7
Asheboro	38	152	34.8	4.5	76	358	28.0	10.0	63	6,915	3,002.3	245.9
Asheville	244	785	163.3	26.3	575	D	D	D	130	4,595	983.8	224.4
Burlington	66	419	106.4	18.7	107	828	75.6	33.9	92	3,671	855.4	141.8
Cary	218	681	151.2	29.9	903	D	D	D	68	1,693	696.0	79.4
Chapel Hill	88	381	67.0	13.7	293	D	D	D	17	D	7.4	D
Charlotte	1,372	8,759	2,045.6	494.7	3,202	D	D	D	643	21,152	9,376.1	1,164.0
Concord	103	464	88.7	13.4	207	D	D	D	87	4,261	1,352.5	190.7
Durham	275	1,601	337.0	66.8	973	D	D	D	144	7,368	4,773.1	499.7
Fayetteville	264	1,622	314.8	54.9	443	D	D	D	63	2,169	616.0	109.6
Garner	33	128	39.8	4.6	76	558	63.6	21.5	22	684	611.1	39.6
Gastonia	90	546	125.8	21.3	170	D	D	D	104	5,248	1,597.3	223.9
Goldsboro	44	216	23.0	6.0	104	614	61.0	22.9	49	3,089	808.7	137.0
Greensboro	455	3,181	525.0	135.4	936	D	D	D	308	16,855	22,411.9	1,025.3
Greenville	125	546	86.3	17.7	228	D	D	D	35	424	84.9	15.1
Hickory	100	324	88.9	9.9	199	1,198	602.5	54.9	161	5,444	1,261.8	195.0
High Point	115	754	127.8	25.4	273	D	D	D	241	12,901	3,676.7	541.1
Huntersville	62	160	42.1	8.0	183	856	120.2	52.3	25	706	209.7	35.8
Indian Trail	21	55	11.9	2.1	59	174	17.3	6.4	53	830	197.3	35.3
Jacksonville	100	390	73.2	12.0	152	D	D	D	12	D	D	D
Kannapolis	33	142	18.6	4.1	56	D	D	D	28	468	101.5	22.4
Matthews	50	236	32.3	7.5	144	690	89.7	35.9	34	713	296.9	38.6
Monroe	43	135	28.6	5.4	90	422	47.5	18.4	89	6,657	2,763.7	321.8
Mooresville	64	191	45.4	7.3	147	1,618	202.9	72.6	73	2,277	825.9	109.7
New Bern	51	223	29.9	7.0	111	D	D	D	34	2,008	683.6	100.2
Raleigh	735	5,229	1,173.6	305.0	2,185	22,893	4,304.5	1,706.4	267	5,229	1,842.0	270.5
Rocky Mount	77	357	54.8	12.0	125	803	83.1	33.8	43	4,002	940.1	217.5
Salisbury	44	205	18.3	4.3	97	529	64.3	20.7	66	1,904	585.2	84.1
Sanford	38	144	26.2	5.2	66	D	D	D	44	4,754	1,224.1	195.9
Thomasville	24	D	D	D	44	141	15.6	3.5	86	2,096	642.1	79.0
Wake Forest	33	76	17.9	3.2	116	D	D	D	14	111	18.0	6.2
Wilmington	249	1,574	260.9	58.6	652	D	D	D	91	3,247	1,623.2	250.0
Wilson	65	229	41.2	5.8	97	D	D	D	59	6,692	12,784.2	334.9
Winston-Salem	293	1,575	276.0	58.3	672	D	D	D	200	8,322	4,017.0	410.7
NORTH DAKOTA	912	5,157	1,445.1	247.5	1,706	13,633	1,836.9	732.4	745	23,541	14,427.4	1,042.8
Bismarck	122	389	101.5	13.2	274	D	D	D	57	824	D	35.8
Fargo	238	1,613	286.7	62.0	411	D	D	D	126	6,087	2,601.4	278.6
Grand Forks	73	481	83.5	14.3	117	D	D	D	42	2,015	564.1	73.6
Minot	68	D	D	D	119	D	D	D	26	346	110.3	13.9
West Fargo	21	D	D	D	38	D	D	D	42	2,294	791.0	109.1
OHIO	9,932	60,966	16,132.7	2,441.8	23,851	228,728	35,259.4	13,870.3	14,482	627,124	313,630.0	33,135.4
Akron	167	1,062	182.7	40.1	449	D	D	D	269	8,672	3,477.8	461.5
Barberton	6	19	1.9	0.4	27	D	D	D	50	1,938	530.0	97.4
Beavercreek	46	176	56.2	4.8	188	D	D	D	28	D	76.3	D
Bowling Green	38	159	21.8	4.3	49	D	D	D	35	1,906	729.3	87.6
Brunswick	22	92	17.7	2.3	56	390	35.0	12.3	49	969	204.1	45.2
Canton	71	248	39.3	8.2	155	D	D	D	136	8,020	6,885.8	429.7
Cincinnati	405	2,489	609.1	120.1	1,118	19,286	3,946.0	1,410.5	363	12,881	7,058.1	760.4
Cleveland	349	3,895	816.6	177.7	1,159	17,004	3,382.2	1,318.3	805	22,075	7,794.7	1,192.0
Cleveland Heights	50	166	27.9	4.4	104	D	D	D	8	46	6.3	1.5
Columbus	904	6,933	1,893.8	317.8	2,055	D	D	D	518	19,881	9,829.7	1,036.6
Cuyahoga Falls	42	197	26.6	5.6	108	867	73.7	33.2	76	2,565	857.7	128.3
Dayton	136	713	118.0	24.4	306	D	D	D	266	9,794	2,940.7	467.6
Delaware	36	117	25.0	5.8	54	355	48.7	14.7	38	2,755	2,055.5	169.2
Dublin	75	673	434.5	29.4	369	3,381	496.2	250.6	33	1,051	404.2	58.3
Elyria	48	223	34.8	7.1	79	D	D	D	100	4,869	1,604.5	260.5
Euclid	49	355	51.3	9.7	42	361	39.4	16.1	75	5,059	1,704.4	368.8
Fairborn	35	161	23.0	4.0	76	D	D	D	12	443	85.9	22.3
Fairfield	50	299	94.5	11.8	82	D	D	D	82	3,088	880.8	140.4
Findlay	50	382	46.4	12.4	108	649	87.7	34.2	56	5,654	2,137.3	287.6
Gahanna	40	159	35.3	6.3	143	973	120.1	46.4	27	754	235.0	32.9
Garfield Heights	20	69	10.8	2.8	48	360	46.8	20.8	18	838	186.7	40.7
Green	22	176	38.5	6.0	77	958	102.9	39.9	37	1,479	458.4	66.2
Grove City	34	164	36.7	6.5	46	389	52.7	14.4	29	1,545	393.2	70.7

1. Establishments subject to federal tax.

Accommodation and Food Services, Arts, Entertainment, and Recreation, and Health Care and Social Assistance

AREANAME	Accommodation and food services, 2012				Arts, entertainment, and recreation[1], 2012				Health care and social assistance,[1] 2012			
	Number of establishments	Number of employees	Receipts (mil dol)	Annual payroll (mil dol)	Number of establishments	Number of employees	Receipts (mil dol)	Annual payroll (mil dol)	Number of establishments	Number of employees	Receipts (mil dol)	Annual payroll (mil dol)
	92	93	94	95	96	97	98	99	100	101	102	103
NEW YORK— Cont'd												
Yonkers	351	3,484	259.8	65.3	46	1,168	286.4	45.1	403	4,301	453.0	184.7
NORTH CAROLINA	19,496	358,602	18,622.3	5,040.6	2,696	37,335	3,805.3	1,167.0	19,152	292,709	27,305.8	11,432.3
Apex	90	1,635	79.2	21.5	10	D	D	D	104	D	D	D
Asheboro	102	1,875	87.1	22.8	8	D	D	D	121	D	D	D
Asheville	541	11,795	698.6	201.3	64	1,459	103.0	35.1	530	7,203	898.5	383.9
Burlington	188	4,010	175.6	50.4	16	D	D	D	208	3,755	374.2	204.6
Cary	372	7,249	386.6	114.4	56	956	57.7	17.6	471	4,842	566.0	221.9
Chapel Hill	220	4,078	221.9	63.0	29	97	12.9	4.1	209	D	D	D
Charlotte	1,888	40,752	2,413.6	659.0	231	5,691	619.8	322.6	1,739	25,574	3,149.2	1,263.4
Concord	233	6,309	337.1	89.4	46	2,034	599.3	132.0	197	3,012	361.3	155.4
Durham	645	12,968	767.1	209.7	64	731	58.8	11.4	604	8,801	935.0	342.0
Fayetteville	480	10,965	516.5	143.3	42	D	D	D	597	9,245	705.4	309.7
Garner	66	1,528	68.1	18.8	4	D	D	D	83	934	84.4	31.8
Gastonia	191	3,998	199.4	51.2	20	224	11.9	2.6	270	D	D	D
Goldsboro	144	2,625	129.6	33.4	13	128	5.8	1.4	156	2,442	232.0	104.5
Greensboro	789	16,835	856.6	237.3	72	1,183	77.5	21.7	723	12,951	1,352.5	583.9
Greenville	288	6,910	313.5	85.4	23	D	D	D	332	D	D	D
Hickory	219	4,748	210.4	59.9	12	130	7.0	2.3	237	D	D	D
High Point	229	D	D	D	20	234	18.3	2.9	235	4,742	580.3	213.0
Huntersville	99	2,246	118.5	33.8	28	703	130.4	49.4	145	D	D	D
Indian Trail	55	887	41.7	10.8	11	114	7.9	1.7	43	337	33.1	11.5
Jacksonville	219	4,593	257.1	60.9	15	203	9.4	2.8	179	D	D	D
Kannapolis	74	D	D	D	10	D	D	D	48	934	81.5	36.3
Matthews	104	2,147	103.8	28.4	22	250	19.1	4.6	129	D	D	D
Monroe	105	1,927	91.2	24.5	8	D	D	D	116	D	D	D
Mooresville	159	2,948	149.8	40.0	44	D	D	D	147	2,454	339.9	123.9
New Bern	123	2,528	108.2	30.7	15	213	8.3	2.6	147	D	D	D
Raleigh	1,145	24,150	1,237.1	348.9	135	4,102	350.3	97.6	1,291	18,328	1,959.5	866.1
Rocky Mount	146	3,442	150.4	41.8	20	D	D	D	192	3,250	310.3	125.0
Salisbury	138	2,714	123.3	34.0	13	85	5.4	1.7	157	D	D	D
Sanford	92	1,665	77.3	20.9	6	D	D	D	123	2,042	213.9	78.1
Thomasville	72	D	D	D	7	D	D	D	35	745	46.6	21.9
Wake Forest	57	1,050	47.5	14.0	17	195	9.0	2.3	93	1,027	78.7	31.8
Wilmington	440	9,326	440.1	124.0	48	544	29.8	8.0	547	8,125	895.9	369.0
Wilson	124	2,521	133.0	32.7	11	D	D	D	151	D	D	D
Winston-Salem	539	11,157	564.9	159.4	56	548	32.9	8.9	510	9,646	868.9	430.6
NORTH DAKOTA	1,935	35,698	2,045.1	521.3	259	2,153	145.3	34.2	1,235	15,038	1,809.1	775.9
Bismarck	162	4,873	236.6	69.4	23	D	D	D	196	D	D	D
Fargo	316	8,386	389.1	114.6	52	662	51.3	10.4	284	5,329	931.1	386.1
Grand Forks	174	4,076	173.4	51.4	24	D	D	D	97	D	D	D
Minot	150	3,741	203.9	56.9	19	D	D	D	102	D	D	D
West Fargo	38	D	D	D	6	D	D	D	39	D	D	D
OHIO	23,432	437,293	20,652.8	5,742.7	2,869	36,390	3,903.5	1,464.8	22,945	393,909	34,637.9	15,470.9
Akron	407	5,634	257.4	69.3	31	310	42.4	9.4	351	7,424	853.5	418.3
Barberton	46	D	D	D	3	D	D	D	75	2,196	237.1	87.3
Beavercreek	105	2,738	140.8	37.8	4	D	D	D	121	D	D	D
Bowling Green	117	2,586	89.2	23.7	10	D	D	D	75	D	D	D
Brunswick	63	1,072	50.8	13.5	9	D	D	D	51	762	51.6	27.8
Canton	170	2,652	119.8	31.6	14	123	7.4	1.6	154	3,277	373.8	185.5
Cincinnati	738	15,321	858.6	247.4	82	1,803	462.6	323.2	652	15,018	2,070.9	917.9
Cleveland	980	16,885	950.9	254.3	63	2,425	509.8	290.4	402	7,946	537.2	237.2
Cleveland Heights	80	1,005	55.6	16.3	9	51	2.1	0.6	85	1,247	77.8	38.2
Columbus	1,959	42,063	2,259.0	637.6	152	3,969	354.9	122.1	1,620	31,398	3,077.4	1,331.6
Cuyahoga Falls	119	2,339	111.2	32.1	9	D	D	D	130	2,582	252.4	100.3
Dayton	276	4,570	206.8	57.9	17	210	23.6	5.6	285	5,572	659.7	342.5
Delaware	87	1,313	62.5	17.1	8	D	D	D	92	1,626	86.5	40.9
Dublin	123	3,294	167.6	52.9	27	D	D	D	195	D	D	D
Elyria	118	2,230	96.8	26.9	8	74	2.5	1.0	115	D	D	D
Euclid	71	D	D	D	7	D	D	D	98	2,556	121.2	62.9
Fairborn	74	1,535	71.9	20.2	7	D	D	D	39	D	D	D
Fairfield	104	1,990	100.4	25.7	9	D	D	D	136	D	D	D
Findlay	147	3,530	146.5	42.1	8	51	1.6	0.4	125	D	D	D
Gahanna	104	1,861	89.4	24.3	12	D	D	D	140	2,473	261.4	110.1
Garfield Heights	46	654	29.6	7.2	4	10	0.8	0.2	62	614	63.7	33.4
Green	54	949	45.3	12.2	10	106	6.9	2.1	67	D	D	D
Grove City	110	2,387	130.7	34.8	14	D	D	D	94	1,147	128.8	47.1

1. Establishments subject to federal tax.

AREANAME	Other services[1]				Government employment and payroll, 2012								
						March payroll							
					Full-time equivalent employees	Total (dollars)	Percent of total for:						
	Number of establishments	Number of employees	Receipts (mil dol)	Annual payroll (mil dol)			Administrative, judicial, and legal	Police and corrections	Fire protection	Highways and transportation	Health and welfare	Natural resources and utilities	Education and libraries
	104	105	106	107	108	109	110	111	112	113	114	115	116
NEW YORK— Cont'd													
Yonkers	305	1,248	129.1	34.1	5,538	39,341,604	3.2	17.5	10.4	1.0	2.7	6.0	58.2
NORTH CAROLINA	11,506	64,643	5,548.4	1,664.9	X	X	X	X	X	X	X	X	X
Apex	64	436	30.8	10.3	344	1,509,120	15.4	23.1	14.9	7.4	4.6	28.3	0.0
Asheboro	43	265	27.2	7.5	349	1,396,592	5.9	23.8	15.1	5.8	2.2	22.5	0.0
Asheville	214	1,148	87.1	27.3	1,057	3,889,185	9.1	23.7	24.5	5.3	3.3	19.0	0.0
Burlington	86	514	39.3	11.9	628	2,130,883	10.7	32.6	15.8	5.7	0.1	29.4	0.0
Cary	196	1,880	141.3	54.1	1,135	5,112,012	14.8	23.3	19.4	15.6	0.0	21.6	0.0
Chapel Hill	59	545	34.2	13.1	840	3,017,788	12.7	26.8	15.1	19.0	2.7	8.1	3.9
Charlotte	1,161	9,188	865.2	265.7	7,449	34,348,745	9.7	36.0	16.2	12.9	2.2	17.0	0.0
Concord	134	672	60.1	15.6	923	3,576,064	7.2	20.8	21.3	7.1	4.4	23.7	0.0
Durham	306	2,624	221.3	72.2	1,086	4,030,398	25.2	0.0	0.0	16.5	6.6	47.8	0.0
Fayetteville	256	1,445	107.3	33.2	1,960	7,748,728	4.9	24.8	14.8	6.6	0.8	30.0	0.0
Garner	52	338	30.0	8.8	177	821,893	16.4	47.7	0.0	3.4	1.0	15.0	0.0
Gastonia	122	742	51.1	16.1	935	3,494,489	15.2	23.5	14.9	10.2	1.1	28.7	0.0
Goldsboro	73	484	38.1	11.4	449	1,502,437	12.1	25.9	19.1	3.7	0.8	27.4	0.0
Greensboro	413	2,580	239.4	71.4	3,098	11,503,988	8.8	28.2	17.9	6.9	2.9	20.8	2.5
Greenville	103	692	52.0	14.4	1,347	5,208,426	6.5	18.6	12.5	6.2	2.4	34.6	0.0
Hickory	105	824	63.2	18.2	636	2,107,555	11.1	23.4	23.3	9.5	0.2	23.5	3.6
High Point	150	1,094	111.3	31.0	1,446	5,797,223	10.4	32.4	13.1	5.0	2.2	31.9	3.2
Huntersville	71	360	27.5	8.2	161	688,375	25.1	57.8	0.0	7.5	0.0	9.6	0.0
Indian Trail	60	283	24.5	6.8	48	144,392	56.2	0.0	0.0	9.0	0.0	9.0	0.0
Jacksonville	109	795	48.3	16.8	542	2,172,480	13.1	25.3	14.1	6.1	0.2	19.4	0.0
Kannapolis	48	D	D	D	289	1,109,005	13.6	30.3	23.4	4.8	0.0	27.8	0.0
Matthews	66	310	21.4	6.9	163	577,637	14.5	49.3	6.0	9.7	1.3	6.1	0.0
Monroe	82	392	37.1	11.2	511	1,971,029	15.1	20.8	15.3	6.0	0.0	37.8	0.0
Mooresville	81	506	50.3	12.2	760	1,406,044	10.4	25.8	21.5	3.5	0.0	23.4	4.8
New Bern	54	280	22.6	6.9	449	1,701,922	12.5	25.9	16.3	4.6	1.3	33.6	0.0
Raleigh	712	5,192	401.9	131.8	3,936	15,850,858	10.6	25.2	16.4	6.4	0.7	28.5	0.0
Rocky Mount	89	D	D	D	1,002	3,610,762	13.3	21.6	15.9	8.8	1.5	39.0	0.0
Salisbury	41	338	22.5	8.0	458	1,569,483	17.2	19.6	16.0	10.0	0.7	25.8	0.0
Sanford	52	284	18.9	6.3	345	1,295,948	13.5	31.2	15.8	6.0	2.5	21.9	0.0
Thomasville	45	207	22.4	5.7	377	1,184,674	5.8	27.3	23.1	5.5	0.0	20.8	0.0
Wake Forest	46	310	31.0	9.2	200	792,417	16.8	36.0	0.0	10.9	6.1	19.0	0.0
Wilmington	240	1,326	102.4	32.2	949	3,706,301	13.1	34.8	22.0	7.7	2.3	17.8	0.0
Wilson	74	D	D	D	776	2,938,961	12.7	19.6	12.6	8.5	5.3	36.1	0.0
Winston-Salem	276	1,682	131.3	43.3	2,489	8,460,457	12.1	31.4	15.9	7.1	5.7	23.1	0.0
NORTH DAKOTA	1,296	6,652	721.6	189.3	X	X	X	X	X	X	X	X	X
Bismarck	138	D	D	D	605	2,280,206	9.2	23.4	16.3	8.9	10.4	15.3	4.2
Fargo	226	1,642	138.6	44.9	836	3,889,052	10.7	22.5	14.1	18.2	12.7	15.1	3.8
Grand Forks	99	642	52.1	15.8	549	2,249,631	11.5	21.4	13.7	14.6	8.9	22.9	0.0
Minot	84	521	48.4	14.6	348	1,359,688	12.5	26.4	15.9	13.9	0.0	20.0	3.8
West Fargo	52	313	35.3	9.8	120	521,710	16.1	47.5	0.0	0.0	0.0	30.4	6.0
OHIO	15,038	99,624	8,638.0	2,607.8	X	X	X	X	X	X	X	X	X
Akron	272	1,576	104.3	34.7	1,872	8,159,087	15.0	31.5	21.9	4.1	0.5	18.7	0.0
Barberton	36	195	19.1	6.4	256	1,078,359	17.1	23.7	20.5	6.9	9.7	22.1	0.0
Beavercreek	54	443	31.1	9.3	144	794,411	6.5	49.4	0.0	17.6	4.9	14.0	0.0
Bowling Green	40	190	9.6	3.5	302	1,389,538	15.6	20.6	19.6	2.1	0.6	31.6	0.0
Brunswick	59	422	39.6	12.5	156	716,777	14.6	38.7	22.6	9.5	2.3	6.8	0.0
Canton	115	597	54.1	15.3	914	3,932,055	14.5	23.0	20.1	7.9	7.6	22.3	0.0
Cincinnati	415	3,189	264.2	77.6	5,222	26,843,252	9.4	25.7	17.7	5.4	8.4	28.9	0.0
Cleveland	546	3,780	261.7	90.6	7,389	33,318,506	12.7	29.1	13.0	9.9	7.8	25.3	0.0
Cleveland Heights	52	306	27.0	8.7	461	2,098,391	11.2	30.1	23.8	3.9	3.6	16.1	0.0
Columbus	916	8,412	668.6	217.0	8,035	42,573,757	14.7	32.2	23.9	4.3	5.7	16.8	0.0
Cuyahoga Falls	92	522	39.1	12.7	489	2,562,538	13.6	24.8	17.8	10.3	2.3	25.4	0.0
Dayton	176	1,277	133.1	38.3	1,940	9,617,585	13.2	22.8	17.4	11.8	4.6	25.3	0.0
Delaware	33	D	D	D	269	1,371,645	23.1	26.5	19.6	10.0	0.0	17.2	0.0
Dublin	34	D	D	D	836	2,882,615	15.9	35.7	0.0	4.5	15.6	11.3	0.0
Elyria	56	340	58.0	8.9	532	2,415,086	14.1	27.3	15.3	5.3	6.2	26.7	0.0
Euclid	50	149	11.5	3.3	454	1,882,329	12.3	36.1	22.3	4.1	5.6	15.3	0.0
Fairborn	38	187	15.5	4.8	222	557,607	20.8	22.1	26.3	4.5	1.3	11.4	0.0
Fairfield	82	590	60.6	17.0	340	1,631,218	20.0	30.2	17.2	8.1	0.0	22.3	0.0
Findlay	81	587	46.9	15.2	325	1,499,497	13.1	24.6	25.6	9.6	3.8	22.6	0.0
Gahanna	58	676	49.3	18.0	274	1,378,735	13.1	50.2	0.0	7.2	1.6	18.8	0.0
Garfield Heights	32	205	11.2	3.5	204	993,260	15.9	40.2	25.6	1.0	4.0	2.4	0.0
Green	41	531	92.4	27.9	131	615,958	19.2	0.0	49.5	27.4	0.0	2.9	0.0
Grove City	57	1,019	73.6	25.3	169	893,462	12.9	61.0	0.0	6.2	0.0	15.6	0.0

1. Establishments subject to federal tax.

Table D. Cities — Population

AREANAME	Percent Hispanic or Latino[1], 2016	Percent foreign born, 2016	Age of population (percent), 2016							Median age 2016	Percent female 2016	Population Census counts		Percent change	
			Under 18 years	18 to 24 years	25 to 34 years	35 to 44 years	45 to 54 years	55 to 64 years	65 years and over			2000	2010	2000-2010	2010-2017
	12	13	14	15	16	17	18	19	20	21	22	23	24	25	26
OHIO— Cont'd															
Hamilton	5.6	2.7	22.3	11.2	14.2	12.1	10.4	14.9	15.0	36.5	51.3	60,690	62,272	2.6	-0.3
Hilliard	5.9	6.3	29.8	7.7	13.1	14.6	13.6	10.5	10.8	34.4	49.9	24,230	28,228	16.5	27.3
Huber Heights	3.9	6.7	24.9	6.4	11.1	12.2	14.2	16.9	14.2	42.0	52.5	38,212	38,101	-0.3	-0.3
Kent	2.7	15.3	16.0	38.2	10.9	8.0	7.8	7.6	11.5	23.5	53.1	27,906	28,906	3.6	3.5
Kettering	3.0	6.0	24.7	5.8	14.2	10.9	13.9	11.5	19.1	39.6	54.9	57,502	56,145	-2.4	-1.7
Lakewood	5.5	6.1	19.6	9.5	21.7	12.7	12.4	12.9	11.2	34.0	52.7	56,646	52,131	-8.0	-3.6
Lancaster	0.7	1.0	23.5	6.8	14.0	10.9	14.0	13.5	17.2	40.5	51.6	35,335	38,762	9.7	3.9
Lima	3.6	2.6	23.4	16.0	13.6	10.4	13.8	12.0	10.7	31.7	49.5	40,081	38,639	-3.6	-3.9
Lorain	29.1	3.6	24.4	11.8	13.1	12.0	11.9	11.9	15.0	35.6	53.0	68,652	64,099	-6.6	-0.4
Mansfield	2.9	2.2	19.8	10.9	18.0	11.2	12.5	11.3	16.2	36.5	45.7	49,346	47,835	-3.1	-3.5
Marion	3.8	1.0	21.7	10.2	14.3	13.8	14.4	11.7	13.9	37.5	44.3	35,318	36,828	4.3	-2.3
Mason	1.6	6.8	25.0	5.2	5.4	14.9	17.1	16.1	16.3	44.8	50.6	22,016	30,859	40.2	7.7
Massillon	1.1	1.0	26.1	6.8	14.3	11.2	10.1	13.4	18.2	37.5	48.5	31,325	32,243	2.9	0.3
Medina	0.7	2.5	22.0	6.5	12.0	15.9	13.1	13.9	16.5	41.4	48.1	25,139	26,663	6.1	-1.8
Mentor	2.3	4.6	18.7	6.6	11.8	11.7	10.6	19.3	21.2	46.2	53.0	50,278	47,159	-6.2	-0.1
Middletown	2.8	2.9	25.0	9.6	12.8	11.0	11.1	12.6	17.8	37.6	49.8	51,605	48,678	-5.7	0.3
Newark	1.0	1.8	25.9	12.1	11.2	10.6	14.3	13.4	12.4	35.4	50.9	46,279	47,562	2.8	3.9
North Olmsted	2.5	12.1	17.6	8.6	12.7	10.7	13.0	16.6	20.7	45.4	50.6	34,113	32,713	-4.1	-3.0
North Ridgeville	2.8	8.9	21.3	4.1	12.9	11.1	14.2	15.1	21.4	45.4	51.9	22,338	29,466	31.9	13.5
North Royalton	3.6	12.4	21.6	8.2	14.2	10.7	15.5	12.5	17.3	42.0	55.0	28,648	30,444	6.3	-0.5
Parma	5.8	10.6	19.2	7.9	13.6	14.4	13.2	14.6	17.2	41.7	51.4	85,655	81,601	-4.7	-3.0
Reynoldsburg	4.1	6.6	24.4	7.3	14.8	16.4	12.0	11.1	13.9	37.1	47.3	32,069	35,911	12.0	5.4
Riverside	5.1	3.5	24.0	9.7	16.6	11.6	10.6	12.2	15.2	34.8	48.9	23,545	25,173	6.9	-0.3
Sandusky	6.5	3.9	20.5	8.5	9.2	8.9	14.4	15.9	22.7	47.7	52.4	27,844	25,919	-6.9	-4.1
Shaker Heights	1.2	8.7	24.3	4.3	12.8	12.6	11.7	14.9	19.5	42.3	56.9	29,405	28,494	-3.1	-3.7
Springfield	3.1	1.5	23.8	11.1	15.0	11.3	9.2	12.9	16.7	35.0	53.2	65,358	60,612	-7.3	-2.3
Stow	3.2	4.2	19.4	6.7	14.0	13.6	13.4	13.0	19.8	42.1	52.6	32,139	34,837	8.4	-0.2
Strongsville	2.7	11.8	17.4	7.1	14.8	7.8	15.2	14.2	23.5	47.0	52.5	43,858	44,750	2.0	0.0
Toledo	8.8	3.2	23.4	10.7	15.4	11.5	12.2	12.9	14.0	35.4	51.4	313,619	287,288	-8.4	-3.8
Troy	1.6	3.3	20.2	9.0	15.1	10.1	18.9	12.6	14.1	40.3	52.6	21,999	25,211	14.6	2.6
Upper Arlington	1.8	9.4	26.3	4.2	11.2	13.2	14.4	14.2	16.5	40.7	50.0	33,686	33,702	0.0	4.9
Warren	3.6	1.6	22.1	10.3	14.3	10.9	10.2	15.2	17.1	37.5	51.4	46,832	41,701	-11.0	-5.1
Westerville	4.1	6.6	18.5	7.2	11.4	12.9	13.4	14.6	21.9	45.0	53.3	35,318	36,267	2.7	9.6
Westlake	5.7	5.1	24.1	5.4	10.2	9.6	10.7	17.9	22.2	46.1	51.2	31,719	32,729	3.2	-1.3
Wooster	1.2	2.9	18.2	13.3	12.4	10.4	11.9	13.9	19.9	39.5	51.8	24,811	26,178	5.5	1.7
Xenia	2.1	0.6	24.4	9.2	14.5	11.8	11.7	13.7	14.7	36.0	52.1	24,164	25,667	6.2	3.5
Youngstown	10.3	1.7	20.4	10.5	11.9	11.2	13.6	16.1	16.4	41.4	52.7	82,026	66,979	-18.3	-3.5
Zanesville	2.7	2.2	23.7	5.7	17.4	11.1	12.6	11.5	18.1	38.5	57.5	25,586	25,472	-0.4	-0.3
OKLAHOMA	10.3	5.8	24.5	9.9	13.7	12.2	12.3	12.4	15.0	36.4	50.5	3,450,654	3,751,598	8.7	4.8
Bartlesville	6.7	7.2	23.9	9.3	13.8	10.8	11.3	12.2	18.7	37.9	54.8	34,748	35,752	2.9	1.8
Broken Arrow	7.8	6.9	25.0	6.8	14.4	12.9	13.0	13.2	14.7	38.0	51.4	74,859	98,843	32.0	9.6
Edmond	6.2	7.5	27.3	11.5	14.8	11.9	10.7	11.3	12.7	33.2	52.2	68,315	81,149	18.8	13.3
Enid	14.9	9.9	24.2	10.3	13.6	12.6	11.2	10.6	17.5	36.8	50.3	47,045	49,379	5.0	1.5
Lawton	14.4	5.6	23.8	15.4	15.8	11.6	11.3	11.3	10.7	31.6	47.6	92,757	96,867	4.4	-3.3
Midwest City	7.8	3.7	24.6	8.6	17.0	11.0	11.6	12.8	14.4	34.9	51.7	54,088	54,371	0.5	5.4
Moore	10.9	4.4	25.9	7.2	16.2	16.0	11.5	12.0	11.2	35.3	52.5	41,138	55,081	33.9	11.7
Muskogee	8.8	3.0	22.4	11.0	13.5	10.1	11.3	15.3	16.3	38.2	52.3	38,310	39,223	2.4	-3.5
Norman	7.6	8.6	18.3	21.7	15.1	10.0	11.0	10.4	13.5	31.1	50.1	95,694	110,925	15.9	10.7
Oklahoma City	18.7	11.0	25.8	9.4	16.1	13.2	12.0	11.8	11.7	34.1	51.1	506,132	580,254	14.6	10.9
Owasso	5.8	3.5	30.6	8.7	17.9	12.0	9.7	11.8	9.3	30.7	49.8	18,502	29,717	60.6	21.9
Ponca City	9.1	2.3	25.1	11.1	12.3	12.4	11.0	11.6	16.6	36.0	50.5	25,919	25,401	-2.0	-4.6
Shawnee	5.3	1.2	22.6	12.8	12.9	12.2	11.1	11.7	16.7	35.9	51.9	28,692	29,857	4.1	4.6
Stillwater	2.7	9.3	13.8	38.2	15.0	8.7	6.2	7.6	10.5	24.2	47.0	39,065	45,688	17.0	9.1
Tulsa	16.1	10.8	25.0	10.2	15.5	12.2	11.5	12.3	13.2	34.5	51.4	393,049	392,012	-0.3	2.5
OREGON	12.8	9.6	21.2	9.0	14.0	13.0	12.6	13.4	16.8	39.2	50.5	3,421,399	3,831,072	12.0	8.1
Albany	11.3	6.9	22.4	8.9	13.5	11.7	14.1	11.4	18.0	39.4	48.8	40,852	50,156	22.8	6.7
Beaverton	18.0	19.5	17.7	10.7	13.6	14.6	15.6	14.0	13.7	40.7	50.9	76,129	89,786	17.9	8.6
Bend	8.8	3.7	20.7	7.5	15.5	14.2	11.9	11.9	18.3	39.3	51.4	52,029	76,639	47.3	23.3
Corvallis	8.1	10.0	13.7	31.8	16.8	8.4	6.8	10.3	12.2	27.1	49.5	49,322	54,501	10.5	6.3
Eugene	9.9	7.4	17.0	19.3	14.6	10.9	10.4	11.6	16.2	34.3	50.4	137,893	156,430	13.4	8.0
Grants Pass	10.8	0.7	22.7	10.4	15.4	12.0	7.7	12.5	19.2	35.6	55.7	23,003	35,908	56.1	4.7
Gresham	17.7	14.8	22.9	10.7	12.2	12.0	14.1	14.6	13.5	37.8	50.2	90,205	105,641	17.1	5.1
Hillsboro	23.8	20.6	26.6	9.3	19.1	15.5	11.8	8.2	9.6	32.3	50.5	70,186	92,251	31.4	15.9
Keizer	21.8	9.7	22.3	10.2	12.7	12.9	13.8	15.3	12.8	38.9	48.7	32,203	36,485	13.3	7.8
Lake Oswego	4.1	11.5	20.6	4.9	10.1	11.5	18.0	14.8	20.0	46.0	51.5	35,278	36,718	4.1	6.7
McMinnville	20.8	11.4	25.3	10.7	12.7	12.0	9.9	11.8	17.6	36.3	50.0	26,499	32,182	21.4	6.7
Medford	13.1	5.6	21.8	6.3	15.7	12.2	11.9	12.3	19.8	39.6	51.0	63,154	74,943	18.7	9.1
Oregon City	8.8	3.7	23.4	7.0	11.5	17.2	13.4	12.8	14.7	39.7	50.4	25,754	32,609	26.6	11.5
Portland	10.2	13.7	18.3	8.0	19.9	17.0	13.0	11.4	12.4	36.7	50.5	529,121	583,799	10.3	11.0

1. May be of any race.

Table D. Cities — Households, Group Quarters, Crime, and Education

AREANAME	Households, 2016								Serious crimes known to police[2], 2016				Educational attainment, 2016		
			Percent						Total		Rate[3]			Attainment[4] (percent)	
	Number	Persons per house-hold	Family	Married couple family	Female headed family[1]	Non-family	One person	Persons in group quarters	Number	Rate	Violent	Property	Population age 25 and over	High school graduate or less	Bachelor's degree or more
	27	28	29	30	31	32	33	34	35	36	37	38	39	40	41
OHIO— Cont'd															
Hamilton	24,997	2.41	61.0	35.6	19.2	39.0	32.4	1,786	3,723	5,964	525	5,439	41,285	54.9	16.6
Hilliard	12,570	2.88	79.1	61.4	14.6	20.9	19.4	NA	407	1,168	106	1,062	22,740	26.6	47.7
Huber Heights	15,359	2.55	68.5	50.1	14.4	31.5	26.5	NA	1,365	3,575	225	3,350	26,999	36.8	23.5
Kent	10,997	2.25	48.6	28.8	16.2	51.4	41.1	5,337	563	1,877	223	1,654	13,759	21.1	51.9
Kettering	23,919	2.28	58.1	41.4	14.0	41.9	37.1	502	1,081	1,952	132	1,820	38,232	29.8	34.0
Lakewood	23,887	2.09	45.4	32.4	9.4	54.6	45.8	303	944	1,875	125	1,750	35,625	24.9	42.2
Lancaster	15,512	2.51	63.0	40.9	13.8	37.0	27.9	901	1,979	4,953	358	4,595	27,740	46.6	14.8
Lima	14,594	2.33	54.2	26.4	26.6	45.8	39.6	3,451	2,615	6,934	944	5,990	22,649	56.3	10.7
Lorain	26,325	2.39	61.7	32.5	22.7	38.3	33.9	753	918	1,444	200	1,244	40,674	49.5	12.8
Mansfield	18,370	2.18	53.1	31.6	14.2	46.9	37.4	6,552	2,825	6,055	461	5,594	32,343	53.4	14.6
Marion	13,740	2.34	53.9	35.1	15.4	46.1	40.6	5,661	1,427	3,934	295	3,639	25,689	62.6	8.0
Mason	12,860	2.54	72.8	66.3	4.0	27.2	25.7	NA	337	1,020	18	1,002	23,066	20.8	61.9
Massillon	13,306	2.36	60.1	38.7	14.4	39.9	34.9	809	784	2,430	310	2,120	21,624	52.0	18.8
Medina	11,067	2.33	61.6	46.2	12.1	38.4	33.0	NA	108	227	4	223	18,733	35.9	35.6
Mentor	19,289	2.40	68.6	54.4	12.5	31.4	27.7	NA	1,094	2,335	109	2,226	34,918	35.6	36.6
Middletown	18,552	2.56	65.8	41.1	18.7	34.2	26.8	710	3,551	7,281	523	6,759	31,512	59.4	16.4
Newark	17,874	2.67	63.0	39.4	20.2	37.0	30.2	1,437	484	1,007	25	982	30,469	46.7	20.1
North Olmsted	12,573	2.50	70.9	58.5	8.3	29.1	21.2	427	645	2,025	82	1,943	23,463	36.7	31.6
North Ridgeville	12,753	2.57	69.0	59.5	3.8	31.0	28.0	NA	205	619	36	583	24,628	37.3	32.8
North Royalton	12,321	2.43	61.0	48.6	7.8	39.0	33.9	NA	NA	NA	NA	NA	21,240	32.0	36.1
Parma	33,376	2.35	62.4	43.8	14.5	37.6	31.8	1,000	1,210	1,521	136	1,385	57,876	44.1	20.6
Reynoldsburg	15,399	2.51	64.6	44.8	12.8	35.4	28.3	31	1,436	3,839	233	3,606	26,395	31.2	37.7
Riverside	10,968	2.28	59.2	39.1	12.3	40.8	34.7	NA	673	2,701	205	2,496	16,540	45.6	18.7
Sandusky	11,775	2.08	52.3	31.8	18.7	47.7	40.5	536	956	3,812	179	3,633	17,772	55.7	13.8
Shaker Heights	11,290	2.42	65.7	46.6	16.1	34.3	29.9	NA	NA	NA	NA	NA	19,598	17.4	63.3
Springfield	23,365	2.40	56.2	30.0	19.9	43.8	32.1	2,981	4,451	7,480	691	6,790	38,438	57.3	15.1
Stow	15,116	2.27	62.4	50.6	7.5	37.6	32.2	399	672	1,931	86	1,845	25,627	29.3	41.2
Strongsville	18,990	2.33	64.4	54.1	6.6	35.6	26.0	NA	901	2,019	43	1,976	33,717	29.6	43.0
Toledo	118,122	2.29	53.6	28.5	18.0	46.4	38.8	7,439	14,510	5,213	1,192	4,020	183,699	44.0	18.7
Troy	10,858	2.32	58.5	48.2	7.7	41.5	30.8	NA	761	2,956	117	2,839	18,128	50.1	15.3
Upper Arlington	13,573	2.57	73.9	65.3	6.1	26.1	23.1	NA	558	1,587	46	1,542	24,326	6.5	77.6
Warren	17,773	2.10	54.0	24.9	22.3	46.0	39.9	2,599	1,744	4,359	577	3,782	26,970	58.6	14.2
Westerville	15,519	2.43	70.5	59.0	8.5	29.5	23.6	2,004	962	2,479	54	2,425	29,547	25.6	51.1
Westlake	12,538	2.50	64.3	54.2	6.3	35.7	30.7	905	475	1,468	43	1,425	22,789	21.2	51.9
Wooster	11,016	2.19	58.5	42.6	10.7	41.5	37.2	2,894	849	3,158	272	2,887	18,517	42.4	26.0
Xenia	10,513	2.39	58.8	38.9	14.2	41.2	31.8	1,121	882	3,387	204	3,184	17,431	50.7	15.7
Youngstown	26,697	2.25	50.6	21.0	23.9	49.4	41.2	4,176	2,862	4,459	662	3,797	44,448	59.6	13.8
Zanesville	11,345	2.19	52.8	30.4	20.0	47.2	42.1	577	1,425	5,590	373	5,217	17,972	61.6	11.5
OKLAHOMA	1,469,342	2.60	65.5	48.3	11.9	34.5	28.7	109,868	134,685	3,433	450	2,983	2,571,636	43.4	25.2
Bartlesville	15,243	2.45	68.1	52.1	11.8	31.9	27.3	624	1,241	3,377	297	3,080	25,372	39.5	31.5
Broken Arrow	40,978	2.66	73.8	58.5	10.8	26.2	21.7	460	2,462	2,278	154	2,124	74,635	29.9	35.3
Edmond	32,433	2.76	72.7	58.7	10.6	27.3	22.9	1,516	1,529	1,664	145	1,520	55,860	17.1	54.7
Enid	20,273	2.36	60.0	44.1	12.1	40.0	33.0	1,713	2,255	4,317	410	3,907	32,514	51.1	21.9
Lawton	33,440	2.57	63.7	41.1	15.1	36.3	31.8	8,870	4,472	4,638	810	3,828	57,477	44.9	20.4
Midwest City	24,341	2.34	57.1	33.7	16.5	42.9	37.2	NA	2,351	4,068	218	3,850	38,305	43.0	20.6
Moore	23,256	2.63	77.3	57.3	15.0	22.7	20.1	371	1,518	2,468	133	2,335	41,084	33.2	24.1
Muskogee	15,425	2.40	66.3	40.1	18.1	33.7	30.8	1,358	1,913	4,996	1,060	3,935	25,525	48.5	19.3
Norman	47,571	2.38	56.9	41.9	8.2	43.1	26.8	8,866	4,326	3,542	277	3,265	73,300	26.0	42.6
Oklahoma City	241,046	2.59	61.9	44.3	12.9	38.1	30.6	14,780	30,059	4,684	783	3,901	413,674	39.0	29.7
Owasso	13,443	2.69	66.8	54.7	7.6	33.2	26.9	219	868	2,442	217	2,225	22,121	31.0	35.5
Ponca City	10,736	2.42	63.7	44.2	14.5	36.3	32.5	524	1,181	4,792	872	3,919	16,886	42.9	24.3
Shawnee	11,826	2.52	56.8	35.9	15.9	43.2	36.6	1,657	1,684	5,336	840	4,496	20,315	46.3	21.0
Stillwater	19,747	2.17	42.1	32.2	7.3	57.9	35.9	6,745	1,729	3,483	290	3,193	23,764	24.8	46.7
Tulsa	165,545	2.40	57.3	37.0	14.7	42.7	35.6	6,855	28,400	6,999	1,095	5,904	261,474	38.7	30.7
OREGON	1,571,678	2.55	63.4	48.7	10.1	36.6	27.4	88,778	132,175	3,229	265	2,964	2,857,952	32.7	32.7
Albany	20,683	2.53	61.9	46.8	10.2	38.1	28.8	842	1,555	2,959	82	2,878	36,510	26.9	32.0
Beaverton	40,190	2.41	61.4	45.5	10.0	38.6	29.5	821	1,614	1,649	147	1,501	69,835	26.6	44.8
Bend	37,021	2.44	60.1	45.9	9.9	39.9	26.5	641	2,124	2,380	112	2,268	65,463	30.1	40.2
Corvallis	22,204	2.30	51.8	39.5	7.5	48.2	29.9	5,938	1,636	2,918	136	2,783	31,160	10.7	58.8
Eugene	67,993	2.35	52.7	38.3	9.4	47.3	31.4	6,726	6,938	4,208	368	3,840	106,139	26.9	38.6
Grants Pass	14,939	2.46	60.8	41.1	14.3	39.2	32.6	994	2,112	5,660	257	5,402	25,296	41.3	13.8
Gresham	39,646	2.77	64.8	45.5	13.9	35.2	25.2	1,883	3,506	3,145	385	2,760	74,114	37.5	21.4
Hillsboro	36,132	2.88	71.0	57.8	8.1	29.0	19.9	956	2,371	2,270	299	1,971	67,503	31.5	39.3
Keizer	14,162	2.73	67.4	53.8	10.5	32.6	20.8	347	840	2,201	173	2,028	26,309	34.8	26.2
Lake Oswego	16,514	2.37	67.8	57.6	6.6	32.2	26.5	181	481	1,238	82	1,155	29,223	9.7	70.8
McMinnville	12,454	2.65	67.8	50.9	10.2	32.2	27.0	1,725	882	2,590	175	2,415	22,212	38.6	25.9
Medford	34,952	2.29	58.0	42.6	11.2	42.0	34.5	1,692	6,114	7,567	505	7,062	58,649	35.3	27.8
Oregon City	13,259	2.67	71.1	57.1	11.5	28.9	22.8	NA	814	2,231	206	2,025	25,288	32.1	24.5
Portland	263,774	2.36	51.5	38.1	9.6	48.5	34.2	16,369	36,544	5,691	502	5,189	471,385	23.1	49.6

1. No spouse present.   2. Data for serious crimes have not been adjusted for underreporting. This may affect comparability between geographic areas and over time.   3. Per 100,000 population estimated by the FBI.   4. Persons 25 years old and over.

AREANAME	Money income, 2016 Households Median income	Percent with income less than $20,000	Percent with income of $200,000 or more	Median family income	Median non-family household income	Median earnings, 2016 All persons	Men	Women	Housing units, 2016 Total	Occupied	Percent owner occupied	Median value[1] (dollars)	Median rent (dollars)
	42	43	44	45	46	47	48	49	50	51	52	53	54
OHIO— Cont'd													
Hamilton	39,748	25.8	2.7	51,883	23,154	25,992	32,407	20,613	28,825	24,997	51.7	105,100	760
Hilliard	92,218	10.9	14.4	101,956	39,541	42,175	50,146	37,455	12,570	12,570	73.1	212,600	1,151
Huber Heights	56,923	15.6	2.7	68,777	30,721	35,259	40,759	30,524	17,299	15,359	71.7	100,500	900
Kent	24,434	39.5	5.0	57,903	18,666	10,306	13,493	9,207	12,769	10,997	36.7	158,900	654
Kettering	51,563	15.5	4.6	66,841	35,301	36,229	40,939	32,136	25,921	23,919	61.5	131,000	805
Lakewood	47,456	17.3	2.7	75,202	34,992	35,640	38,761	32,094	26,361	23,887	41.9	146,200	726
Lancaster	42,166	19.6	0.5	52,475	24,562	27,066	34,154	20,125	17,229	15,512	56.2	116,800	771
Lima	29,305	29.3	2.0	34,895	21,733	22,406	26,787	17,123	17,654	14,594	45.4	64,000	642
Lorain	36,398	28.9	1.2	47,866	22,865	24,258	27,963	21,449	29,781	26,325	58.0	84,200	650
Mansfield	36,972	29.0	0.2	46,539	26,647	22,209	19,644	24,157	22,248	18,370	47.3	72,300	661
Marion	34,212	34.4	0.6	51,630	17,331	25,322	30,581	22,840	15,639	13,740	56.0	70,300	632
Mason	101,865	5.3	22.1	124,299	44,482	52,040	76,346	40,416	12,860	12,860	86.9	259,100	1,177
Massillon	43,654	16.6	0.9	54,387	31,587	28,637	31,822	22,388	14,963	13,306	63.3	104,000	694
Medina	65,111	11.6	4.6	78,634	41,570	36,881	42,001	30,567	11,357	11,067	65.5	166,300	792
Mentor	64,764	9.0	4.7	84,167	34,572	41,181	51,090	32,231	20,317	19,289	86.4	169,500	955
Middletown	36,911	27.2	1.5	44,117	22,603	23,914	30,721	20,336	21,974	18,552	50.0	86,200	760
Newark	44,182	24.3	1.2	55,063	25,301	25,591	30,099	22,520	21,562	17,874	57.1	122,200	719
North Olmsted	69,090	9.6	4.0	80,440	50,146	35,394	39,775	28,256	13,619	12,573	74.9	157,000	891
North Ridgeville	67,283	5.5	3.9	78,004	36,107	40,905	49,613	26,200	13,360	12,753	83.0	166,300	1,269
North Royalton	70,007	7.9	3.4	91,113	41,934	40,345	45,949	32,247	12,898	12,321	64.4	205,300	815
Parma	52,446	13.5	1.0	64,096	32,366	31,919	36,802	26,777	35,837	33,376	70.5	108,100	804
Reynoldsburg	77,817	7.5	2.3	86,609	47,271	36,182	37,853	33,987	15,897	15,399	58.3	151,500	948
Riverside	40,275	19.3	1.4	49,587	30,862	31,473	36,485	26,769	11,823	10,968	49.8	90,600	840
Sandusky	35,706	26.5	0.3	41,776	25,979	24,295	25,641	23,458	14,656	11,775	62.3	87,300	690
Shaker Heights	77,849	12.6	17.5	114,203	45,218	42,170	56,113	36,428	12,654	11,290	57.7	224,300	989
Springfield	36,202	27.1	0.7	42,689	22,897	23,199	26,938	19,690	27,216	23,365	46.1	76,100	739
Stow	65,363	7.2	4.7	82,442	44,878	40,593	46,506	30,199	15,607	15,116	67.7	173,200	982
Strongsville	75,719	7.6	8.9	99,531	45,638	45,047	52,237	33,563	19,496	18,990	79.5	209,000	958
Toledo	35,301	29.2	0.9	46,596	25,402	25,329	30,165	21,435	136,264	118,122	48.2	79,100	650
Troy	55,348	17.3	1.4	72,856	29,665	32,016	41,077	26,442	11,620	10,858	60.0	123,000	696
Upper Arlington	110,271	3.9	23.6	135,283	59,457	57,334	72,412	41,780	13,866	13,573	78.3	389,000	1,246
Warren	23,489	40.4	0.8	33,947	18,865	21,471	25,972	19,275	20,372	17,773	46.0	64,200	572
Westerville	89,835	6.9	8.6	112,731	44,698	47,167	61,601	34,927	15,955	15,519	78.6	214,900	980
Westlake	83,121	7.9	16.9	96,343	56,935	45,501	52,078	32,042	13,609	12,538	78.1	252,100	1,119
Wooster	42,844	20.3	2.8	54,270	26,072	21,125	25,998	18,864	11,904	11,016	61.4	123,800	715
Xenia	40,131	25.6	1.3	51,692	25,646	25,687	30,185	23,829	11,769	10,513	56.0	88,600	679
Youngstown	26,789	38.8	0.8	33,829	21,322	18,281	20,124	17,049	33,505	26,697	58.5	43,000	618
Zanesville	24,412	39.7	0.4	41,616	18,470	18,814	25,116	16,470	13,185	11,345	41.9	81,800	658
OKLAHOMA	49,176	19.3	3.5	61,633	28,564	30,262	35,891	24,542	1,721,072	1,469,342	64.9	132,200	744
Bartlesville	50,868	17.7	5.1	64,215	27,090	27,006	35,442	19,536	17,426	15,243	61.7	128,500	626
Broken Arrow	70,221	9.6	4.1	79,155	40,311	36,219	41,897	31,212	43,574	40,978	74.1	160,900	957
Edmond	79,370	11.5	12.9	103,820	37,093	37,598	51,171	30,587	35,131	32,433	68.3	221,600	967
Enid	45,295	19.6	1.5	53,300	27,247	25,962	31,718	18,993	21,849	20,273	57.6	113,000	790
Lawton	47,036	17.1	1.2	58,880	34,787	25,183	29,340	21,288	40,442	33,440	44.0	116,900	771
Midwest City	47,381	19.0	1.1	56,865	33,235	29,680	35,137	24,723	26,101	24,341	58.9	109,800	769
Moore	65,031	10.5	1.6	73,395	30,577	35,653	43,590	31,531	24,049	23,256	64.3	138,600	1,019
Muskogee	33,609	30.6	1.3	47,300	17,887	25,079	27,454	21,726	18,376	15,425	55.0	86,200	604
Norman	52,041	18.4	5.1	70,984	30,459	26,335	31,281	20,984	52,390	47,571	55.1	172,400	788
Oklahoma City	52,915	17.3	4.8	65,791	33,460	30,867	36,216	25,751	272,749	241,046	59.2	157,100	802
Owasso	65,367	7.3	6.8	83,617	49,390	37,142	50,381	28,116	14,244	13,443	68.7	172,500	933
Ponca City	42,808	22.0	2.2	51,892	27,377	26,156	32,230	20,647	12,051	10,736	57.7	98,700	649
Shawnee	36,810	24.1	2.4	49,848	27,923	22,238	30,319	17,070	13,676	11,826	58.7	113,200	608
Stillwater	28,544	42.4	2.5	72,539	14,677	17,209	20,405	13,771	22,266	19,747	34.9	164,600	744
Tulsa	43,134	22.1	4.4	55,085	30,738	29,553	32,724	24,694	187,765	165,545	49.3	130,100	768
OREGON	57,532	15.0	5.3	70,929	35,305	30,897	36,271	25,768	1,732,887	1,571,678	61.7	287,100	1,015
Albany	58,693	13.7	5.5	71,411	38,725	32,803	35,897	31,131	21,836	20,683	62.2	193,000	872
Beaverton	64,636	10.3	5.7	77,092	45,241	32,409	38,214	29,156	42,130	40,190	49.6	363,100	1,215
Bend	60,784	10.1	3.8	73,299	39,503	31,777	37,284	25,892	40,800	37,021	58.3	347,300	1,209
Corvallis	46,707	25.2	4.6	68,012	27,330	17,067	17,782	15,620	24,203	22,204	45.2	315,100	1,066
Eugene	46,189	21.5	3.4	65,918	27,789	21,992	24,153	20,281	73,090	67,993	48.7	267,300	958
Grants Pass	35,058	27.4	2.0	47,626	18,731	19,911	22,383	16,071	15,557	14,939	44.7	236,500	812
Gresham	58,042	15.4	2.8	71,667	33,812	27,538	32,064	24,360	42,140	39,646	53.5	264,600	1,086
Hillsboro	75,466	8.4	6.3	80,743	58,677	36,773	46,440	27,867	38,127	36,132	53.1	313,400	1,344
Keizer	67,914	11.3	2.2	75,411	49,637	31,126	32,460	28,551	14,682	14,162	60.4	234,300	890
Lake Oswego	109,337	5.9	22.9	144,288	46,711	60,935	90,270	36,257	17,248	16,514	73.1	594,200	1,451
McMinnville	53,206	14.1	4.7	62,500	40,111	28,995	28,121	29,195	13,144	12,454	58.1	252,300	861
Medford	44,697	22.2	3.6	62,607	29,381	27,205	29,458	26,444	37,216	34,952	49.7	238,100	901
Oregon City	69,564	16.9	3.6	85,164	30,671	35,699	42,856	30,176	13,986	13,259	67.3	342,700	1,347
Portland	62,127	15.5	8.0	80,758	45,511	35,699	40,174	31,816	280,479	263,774	52.0	395,100	1,153

1. Specified owner-occupied units; $2,000,000 represents $2,000,000 or more.

Table D. Cities — Commuting, Computer Access, Migration, Labor Force, and Employment

AREANAME	Commuting 2016 Percent — Drove alone (55)	With commutes of 30 minutes or more (56)	Computer access Percent — With a computer in the house (57)	With Internet access (58)	Migration — Percent who lived in the same house one year ago (59)	Percent who lived in another state or county one year ago (60)	Civilian labor force, 2016 — Total (61)	Percent change 2016-2017 (62)	Unemployment Total (63)	Rate (64)	Civilian employment, 2016 Population age 16 and older — Number (65)	Percent in labor force (66)	Population age 16 to 64 — Number (67)	Percent who worked full-year full-time (68)
OHIO— Cont'd														
Hamilton	83.8	36.3	86.8	80.6	83.7	5.1	28,128	1.3	1,373	4.9	49,312	58.6	40,000	45.9
Hilliard	81.0	22.5	95.5	88.6	87.7	6.5	19,245	1.9	647	3.4	27,232	72.1	23,313	55.9
Huber Heights	85.8	29.9	94.3	89.9	85.0	7.1	18,342	1.3	900	4.9	30,588	65.3	25,009	50.0
Kent	77.1	27.7	86.7	72.8	73.0	16.7	17,004	0.4	792	4.7	25,824	60.9	22,360	24.9
Kettering	85.2	21.0	90.9	87.8	84.7	4.0	29,367	1.3	1,237	4.2	42,892	64.4	32,390	57.7
Lakewood	77.6	30.0	92.3	83.1	80.3	4.8	29,798	0.0	1,355	4.5	41,493	76.1	35,875	56.6
Lancaster	79.9	42.8	88.9	78.3	80.1	11.2	18,245	1.9	886	4.9	32,266	55.0	25,421	41.3
Lima	83.9	15.1	81.9	69.1	77.0	6.4	14,900	1.2	918	6.2	29,566	63.0	25,560	42.2
Lorain	80.3	31.3	82.6	72.6	83.3	4.2	27,513	-0.2	2,222	8.1	49,870	61.1	40,339	46.0
Mansfield	82.4	16.6	81.5	69.9	73.1	9.1	17,726	-0.6	1,094	6.2	38,665	50.6	31,088	37.7
Marion	78.9	24.5	81.9	69.7	82.7	8.0	13,791	0.8	781	5.7	30,654	46.5	25,412	35.3
Mason	85.9	34.9	94.5	92.0	89.6	7.8	17,103	1.5	687	4.0	26,214	66.9	20,820	61.9
Massillon	83.2	21.8	84.4	80.4	84.5	2.0	15,361	0.2	835	5.4	24,604	64.4	18,748	52.6
Medina	82.6	47.8	89.0	85.9	87.5	2.5	13,263	0.2	678	5.1	21,192	68.7	16,857	59.3
Mentor	86.6	33.3	90.8	88.7	92.6	1.6	26,270	-0.1	1,237	4.7	38,731	64.2	28,810	55.8
Middletown	83.5	31.9	82.9	74.3	76.9	6.8	21,092	1.3	1,151	5.5	37,215	54.9	28,628	43.7
Newark	82.1	30.5	88.9	82.1	86.3	3.1	24,137	1.6	1,065	4.4	37,597	62.3	31,483	44.8
North Olmsted	82.3	33.1	95.2	90.5	85.2	6.3	17,371	0.1	838	4.8	26,583	68.8	19,987	55.9
North Ridgeville	89.0	48.7	93.8	89.9	87.7	3.7	17,636	0.1	899	5.1	26,836	61.0	19,778	53.4
North Royalton	88.2	39.9	89.5	86.6	87.3	3.6	17,414	0.1	833	4.8	24,469	68.3	19,236	60.7
Parma	86.5	35.3	88.1	82.9	84.5	3.7	42,125	0.0	2,323	5.5	66,240	67.6	52,618	56.3
Reynoldsburg	87.8	34.3	96.5	91.8	78.2	13.0	20,988	1.9	850	4.0	30,393	77.4	25,005	66.3
Riverside	84.7	18.9	89.4	83.6	87.5	8.9	10,870	1.1	559	5.1	19,589	60.3	15,793	51.0
Sandusky	79.3	18.2	81.1	70.9	88.7	3.5	11,946	1.4	830	6.9	21,149	52.2	15,461	39.0
Shaker Heights	72.2	28.5	95.0	87.1	89.4	3.1	14,099	-0.1	647	4.6	22,111	69.3	16,764	55.7
Springfield	79.1	24.2	80.8	74.8	73.7	6.5	25,443	0.0	1,345	5.3	46,503	58.1	36,645	41.2
Stow	89.0	35.3	85.0	84.3	86.2	5.8	18,797	0.5	823	4.4	28,723	66.6	21,864	57.6
Strongsville	83.7	45.3	90.0	87.1	81.7	8.4	24,310	0.0	1,126	4.6	37,547	65.1	27,057	62.3
Toledo	82.7	19.8	87.6	79.7	80.3	5.0	130,164	0.7	8,606	6.6	221,140	62.2	182,253	44.0
Troy	91.7	21.5	92.4	85.7	85.4	6.7	13,771	0.9	544	4.0	21,337	70.2	17,733	57.0
Upper Arlington	88.9	18.3	98.4	96.0	88.8	5.6	18,541	2.0	624	3.4	26,789	68.1	21,030	58.6
Warren	91.6	20.5	77.6	65.8	83.5	5.7	14,384	-0.6	1,242	8.6	31,714	47.6	24,902	34.5
Westerville	83.0	24.1	93.7	91.6	90.8	4.3	22,145	2.0	826	3.7	33,406	66.6	24,683	57.4
Westlake	81.8	36.1	93.3	90.7	90.0	1.4	16,998	0.0	761	4.5	25,677	62.0	18,511	56.3
Wooster	79.4	15.9	89.5	85.2	72.9	9.7	14,214	0.8	577	4.1	22,601	59.1	17,232	41.7
Xenia	76.8	29.4	88.1	75.3	81.8	5.7	11,433	1.1	594	5.2	20,780	54.7	16,912	44.5
Youngstown	74.6	17.3	78.1	67.7	81.8	7.4	22,770	-0.8	1,935	8.5	53,078	50.8	42,540	33.3
Zanesville	80.8	20.3	78.2	64.1	75.9	2.7	9,919	0.1	658	6.6	19,948	53.4	15,346	38.2
OKLAHOMA	82.6	26.3	87.3	76.9	83.3	7.1	1,834,312	0.3	78,708	4.3	3,063,649	61.0	2,475,357	49.8
Bartlesville	78.8	13.1	86.3	78.9	81.2	9.7	16,444	-2.8	743	4.5	29,573	58.2	22,480	45.0
Broken Arrow	85.8	21.4	96.0	91.2	85.2	7.3	56,689	1.2	2,200	3.9	85,350	69.4	69,302	57.5
Edmond	83.0	25.3	95.1	91.0	80.7	8.2	47,177	1.1	1,526	3.2	68,993	65.7	57,446	50.2
Enid	81.3	8.9	85.6	77.1	85.1	7.8	22,158	-3.4	911	4.1	38,464	63.5	29,795	53.2
Lawton	69.8	8.3	89.1	84.5	65.8	13.8	36,944	0.0	1,732	4.7	74,390	63.3	64,246	49.2
Midwest City	89.6	24.4	86.2	77.9	77.5	6.7	26,576	1.1	1,226	4.6	44,555	65.9	36,285	60.7
Moore	86.5	29.5	94.4	89.1	85.2	6.5	31,052	1.0	1,100	3.5	46,406	70.7	39,522	61.1
Muskogee	82.7	13.2	83.0	70.1	77.7	8.3	16,581	0.3	835	5.0	30,722	56.7	24,482	45.0
Norman	81.7	28.3	91.3	85.1	75.4	12.6	61,917	1.1	2,144	3.5	102,810	63.2	86,375	43.2
Oklahoma City	82.5	24.2	90.3	83.1	79.8	7.6	314,088	1.1	12,346	3.9	491,160	66.7	416,210	52.5
Owasso	83.3	25.8	94.5	88.4	78.7	14.3	18,761	1.3	710	3.8	26,184	77.5	22,796	58.9
Ponca City	82.3	15.8	89.6	72.5	73.3	10.7	10,565	2.0	602	5.7	20,612	61.6	16,224	49.5
Shawnee	81.1	29.1	83.3	66.7	79.8	8.5	14,745	0.9	654	4.4	25,011	53.6	19,759	38.5
Stillwater	80.2	10.7	91.5	83.7	62.7	22.6	24,312	-0.5	843	3.5	43,309	57.2	38,132	31.3
Tulsa	80.3	16.1	89.7	80.3	79.2	6.1	197,396	1.0	8,955	4.5	311,844	65.7	258,444	50.1
OREGON	72.4	31.9	91.7	84.9	81.6	8.0	2,104,078	2.7	86,786	4.1	3,327,652	61.9	2,638,764	46.8
Albany	83.9	17.6	90.1	83.3	84.1	6.5	25,680	2.3	1,173	4.6	42,769	59.8	33,194	50.4
Beaverton	64.2	37.3	95.4	91.5	82.4	10.5	56,360	3.2	1,986	3.5	82,883	68.6	69,506	48.8
Bend	74.8	9.0	93.7	87.5	80.6	10.3	51,177	4.5	1,858	3.6	74,620	66.5	57,921	48.0
Corvallis	57.6	11.5	97.3	90.0	64.5	18.1	30,947	2.8	1,022	3.3	50,190	58.4	43,235	33.5
Eugene	67.5	13.6	94.0	84.0	69.7	12.2	84,860	2.2	3,514	4.1	141,772	62.1	114,860	40.9
Grants Pass	83.9	13.7	82.1	72.1	75.6	10.5	16,067	3.9	860	5.4	30,412	57.8	23,152	38.3
Gresham	71.2	41.9	90.8	81.8	86.0	5.0	56,527	2.8	2,209	3.9	88,413	66.0	73,395	47.3
Hillsboro	75.5	27.1	95.9	89.2	79.0	8.6	58,194	3.1	1,982	3.4	80,304	71.3	70,244	55.3
Keizer	84.2	26.9	93.9	89.5	84.0	6.7	19,896	3.2	810	4.1	31,159	65.9	26,163	51.8
Lake Oswego	70.3	38.8	96.8	95.4	88.8	6.9	21,208	2.9	710	3.3	32,052	67.7	24,207	58.6
McMinnville	75.9	31.0	88.9	79.8	82.7	8.2	17,165	2.5	662	3.9	26,509	58.8	20,413	52.3
Medford	77.6	7.8	90.6	84.7	77.6	6.5	40,152	2.8	1,885	4.7	64,707	62.5	48,542	51.0
Oregon City	76.9	58.3	90.7	87.6	82.5	6.1	19,171	3.1	788	4.1	28,688	67.4	23,366	54.2
Portland	58.2	40.0	93.7	87.4	79.1	9.2	375,617	3.0	13,494	3.6	535,200	69.4	455,976	50.4

1. Employed persons. 2. Households. 3. Percent of civilian labor force.

Table D. Cities — City Government Finances

AREANAME	City government finances, 2012									
	General revenue							General expenditure		
	Intergovernmental			Taxes					Per capita[1] (dollars)	
					Per capita[1] (dollars)					
	Total (mil dol)	Total (mil dol)	Percent from state government	Total (mil dol)	Total	Property	Sales and gross receipts	Total (mil dol)	Total	Capital outlays
	117	118	119	120	121	122	123	124	125	126
OHIO— Cont'd										
Hamilton	89.3	12.8	82.9	38.5	618	143	14	83.9	1,348	178
Hilliard	35.0	7.3	60.4	23.3	762	41	50	31.8	1,040	211
Huber Heights	30.3	5.3	52.2	16.8	442	90	32	34.7	911	258
Kent	26.7	4.8	93.2	14.4	488	94	24	31.0	1,046	271
Kettering	81.4	18.4	94.3	48.4	863	160	8	83.8	1,495	462
Lakewood	61.0	11.1	71.9	35.2	685	265	25	53.0	1,032	61
Lancaster	74.4	14.1	95.8	19.9	511	72	1	62.8	1,614	139
Lima	73.9	31.0	93.2	18.5	482	32	28	56.9	1,483	345
Lorain	67.9	22.6	96.7	25.7	402	58	34	56.8	890	61
Mansfield	55.9	12.3	51.1	27.7	588	43	15	51.8	1,101	78
Marion	39.4	10.3	100.0	13.8	375	33	10	36.5	989	43
Mason	54.1	7.0	87.3	29.3	937	192	66	56.2	1,798	343
Massillon	35.7	5.9	26.8	17.4	540	50	45	33.4	1,036	44
Medina	27.0	2.3	92.3	16.9	636	121	21	24.7	931	114
Mentor	61.5	10.0	90.4	40.5	862	94	40	59.9	1,274	0
Middletown	84.2	23.4	47.0	24.4	501	100	5	78.5	1,612	138
Newark	52.3	16.1	92.8	22.0	462	55	6	52.1	1,091	140
North Olmsted	41.3	6.2	95.2	23.4	724	285	44	35.0	1,082	136
North Ridgeville	32.6	5.0	88.6	15.8	516	189	54	29.7	972	100
North Royalton	28.1	4.2	100.0	16.8	554	150	19	25.8	852	47
Parma	80.5	21.4	100.0	48.3	599	109	29	75.6	937	31
Reynoldsburg	27.3	3.4	100.0	14.8	406	60	10	25.5	702	31
Riverside	11.8	3.1	96.7	6.6	263	93	1	11.2	447	11
Sandusky	39.2	10.7	84.2	17.6	686	79	317	32.3	1,262	169
Shaker Heights	52.5	8.5	41.5	33.5	1,195	272	23	57.7	2,057	258
Springfield	86.7	27.8	35.7	38.2	635	49	32	79.9	1,328	177
Stow	35.8	7.4	100.0	21.6	623	215	21	32.9	950	128
Strongsville	63.9	10.5	39.1	39.3	881	209	21	66.8	1,498	383
Toledo	451.3	105.2	62.6	175.0	618	42	23	399.2	1,408	377
Troy	33.3	3.4	70.1	17.1	674	74	29	30.1	1,187	140
Upper Arlington	43.7	6.5	59.0	27.9	815	255	41	52.7	1,538	476
Warren	62.9	13.4	36.4	19.8	486	36	24	56.8	1,394	127
Westerville	85.6	17.7	81.5	50.6	1,359	332	29	96.9	2,605	855
Westlake	58.8	5.1	53.1	39.7	1,222	403	54	49.3	1,518	310
Wooster	134.0	6.0	94.8	14.0	532	83	27	128.8	4,877	371
Xenia	28.5	5.5	95.4	13.4	514	62	40	28.4	1,089	214
Youngstown	104.6	20.7	41.1	54.6	826	37	116	89.8	1,358	37
Zanesville	44.9	17.1	96.5	17.8	701	46	54	34.3	1,347	67
OKLAHOMA	X	X	X	X	X	X	X	X	X	X
Bartlesville	40.2	4.0	79.0	22.5	619	96	523	44.1	1,213	354
Broken Arrow	90.6	4.1	24.8	53.9	528	119	409	91.4	896	239
Edmond	93.1	6.8	73.5	55.3	651	0	651	115.9	1,364	281
Enid	67.3	6.0	81.8	38.4	769	57	712	80.2	1,606	728
Lawton	96.6	12.3	38.3	56.7	575	41	534	92.9	943	108
Midwest City	69.8	4.9	68.6	36.3	646	46	600	62.1	1,107	89
Moore	45.7	1.5	65.9	32.5	561	58	503	41.5	717	95
Muskogee	130.4	3.3	45.2	28.4	729	5	724	134.9	3,462	322
Norman	443.4	6.4	56.7	79.6	687	68	619	422.1	3,646	294
Oklahoma City	1,107.5	90.6	50.5	601.9	1,003	139	865	835.1	1,392	272
Owasso	32.7	0.8	93.6	20.7	658	0	658	29.0	924	98
Ponca City	41.3	2.3	61.5	16.3	655	21	635	56.7	2,278	730
Shawnee	34.1	5.6	40.8	20.1	656	2	653	30.7	1,003	220
Stillwater	49.0	2.9	45.6	29.0	622	29	593	48.2	1,033	155
Tulsa	741.9	77.4	11.3	340.0	862	161	701	712.6	1,806	561
OREGON	X	X	X	X	X	X	X	X	X	X
Albany	59.2	9.0	56.9	32.7	638	505	133	56.1	1,094	127
Beaverton	79.4	16.3	57.8	44.0	475	344	131	78.1	842	126
Bend	88.7	15.0	54.7	44.0	558	331	227	81.1	1,029	162
Corvallis	71.4	12.8	43.7	35.6	647	446	202	62.4	1,135	94
Eugene	265.1	45.3	46.0	119.6	757	620	138	254.5	1,612	275
Grants Pass	36.2	6.8	64.2	20.5	589	453	136	35.8	1,028	164
Gresham	102.2	33.7	52.1	39.5	363	243	120	106.4	979	155
Hillsboro	134.5	12.8	83.8	79.4	832	541	291	124.8	1,309	91
Keizer	21.2	3.3	99.7	10.7	290	216	74	18.1	490	50
Lake Oswego	80.7	14.9	44.5	43.4	1,164	919	245	69.2	1,857	263
McMinnville	37.5	4.1	96.1	15.2	459	360	99	30.1	909	86
Medford	102.4	14.5	49.3	58.0	758	455	303	104.2	1,361	306
Oregon City	52.1	16.8	99.0	19.9	594	337	257	43.8	1,308	472
Portland	1,298.8	266.5	44.2	612.5	1,016	708	308	1,280.8	2,124	548

1. Based on population estimated as of July 1 of the year shown.

Table D. Cities — **City Government Finances**

AREANAME	City government finances, 2012 (cont.)									
	General expenditures (cont.)									
	Percent of total for:									
	Public welfare	Highways	Parking facilities	Education	Health and hospitals	Police protection	Sewerage and sanitation	Parks and recreation	Housing and community development	Interest on debt
	127	128	129	130	131	132	133	134	135	136
OHIO— Cont'd										
Hamilton	0.0	6.1	0.5	0.0	1.5	24.9	20.3	0.9	3.4	4.7
Hilliard	0.0	24.2	0.0	0.0	0.5	19.2	1.2	7.4	0.0	8.3
Huber Heights	0.0	13.8	0.0	0.0	0.0	17.2	7.9	12.9	4.7	5.3
Kent	0.4	5.1	0.0	0.0	3.0	20.7	13.4	5.7	2.8	0.8
Kettering	0.0	11.2	0.0	0.0	0.0	17.2	0.0	14.9	1.4	0.8
Lakewood	3.1	12.4	0.5	0.0	0.8	19.5	15.5	4.3	5.6	4.7
Lancaster	0.0	5.4	0.0	0.0	0.4	12.7	21.9	2.9	0.9	23.9
Lima	0.0	16.0	0.0	0.0	0.0	15.9	21.7	1.8	6.7	2.8
Lorain	1.5	5.3	0.0	0.0	2.1	22.9	25.4	0.6	7.9	2.8
Mansfield	0.0	13.1	0.0	1.8	0.0	16.3	8.4	0.5	3.4	0.6
Marion	0.0	8.9	0.0	0.0	1.3	18.4	33.3	2.5	0.0	2.0
Mason	0.0	17.2	0.0	0.0	0.0	10.0	9.1	17.8	0.0	7.0
Massillon	0.0	11.0	0.1	0.0	1.8	14.9	25.5	10.7	0.9	5.3
Medina	0.0	17.5	8.9	0.0	0.0	17.4	12.9	13.7	0.0	1.6
Mentor	0.0	24.6	0.0	0.0	0.0	19.1	0.0	11.9	0.8	2.7
Middletown	0.0	12.5	0.0	0.0	1.0	10.4	16.2	3.7	18.8	2.3
Newark	0.0	9.2	0.0	0.0	0.0	16.1	17.8	0.0	0.0	2.0
North Olmsted	0.9	13.9	0.0	0.0	0.0	15.9	22.0	12.1	0.5	5.6
North Ridgeville	0.0	12.1	0.0	0.0	8.5	17.4	25.4	1.3	4.6	3.6
North Royalton	0.0	20.6	0.0	0.0	0.7	23.5	21.0	1.5	2.7	1.6
Parma	0.0	5.8	0.0	0.0	0.4	40.5	0.5	5.1	11.3	1.6
Reynoldsburg	0.0	5.9	0.0	0.0	0.8	30.8	31.8	3.9	0.0	1.4
Riverside	0.0	14.6	0.0	0.0	0.0	41.2	0.0	0.4	0.0	0.8
Sandusky	0.0	8.5	0.0	0.0	0.0	15.5	25.9	1.2	2.8	6.9
Shaker Heights	0.0	7.5	0.0	0.0	1.0	20.4	8.3	8.9	8.8	1.6
Springfield	0.0	3.0	0.0	0.0	0.0	15.5	8.1	0.0	5.0	1.9
Stow	0.0	10.2	0.0	0.0	0.9	18.9	2.2	7.6	0.0	3.2
Strongsville	0.0	30.1	0.0	0.0	0.5	17.2	11.8	7.8	0.0	4.3
Toledo	0.4	8.8	0.2	0.0	3.7	23.7	22.4	1.8	3.2	5.8
Troy	0.0	7.4	0.4	0.0	1.1	12.4	14.3	12.0	6.3	2.2
Upper Arlington	0.0	34.9	0.0	0.0	0.4	13.2	6.2	6.9	2.2	3.4
Warren	0.0	8.6	0.2	0.0	1.6	12.9	18.9	4.3	7.2	1.3
Westerville	0.0	2.3	0.0	0.0	0.0	14.8	10.3	17.5	0.0	1.5
Westlake	0.0	17.5	0.0	0.0	0.0	13.8	11.8	6.6	0.0	1.6
Wooster	0.0	1.4	0.0	0.0	76.3	4.9	6.2	1.1	0.2	0.4
Xenia	0.0	1.1	0.3	0.0	0.0	19.2	20.9	0.6	1.7	1.4
Youngstown	0.0	6.3	0.1	0.0	1.5	22.0	27.0	2.7	6.8	1.8
Zanesville	0.0	10.9	0.0	0.0	1.2	22.8	24.7	2.4	0.0	3.0
OKLAHOMA	X	X	X	X	X	X	X	X	X	X
Bartlesville	0.0	15.9	0.0	0.0	0.0	12.6	20.7	12.2	2.0	1.5
Broken Arrow	0.0	7.8	0.0	0.0	0.8	18.6	18.5	7.7	0.8	5.5
Edmond	1.6	24.4	0.0	0.0	1.5	11.6	15.1	8.3	0.6	0.3
Enid	0.3	12.1	0.0	0.0	5.1	10.6	19.3	6.6	17.6	0.7
Lawton	0.0	9.4	0.0	5.7	0.9	21.2	15.2	1.3	1.1	1.4
Midwest City	0.0	8.1	0.0	0.0	0.0	23.9	12.5	4.6	7.6	6.6
Moore	0.0	14.8	0.0	0.0	0.0	23.2	14.3	3.7	3.2	1.9
Muskogee	0.0	3.1	0.0	0.0	65.8	5.4	5.9	4.1	0.6	0.1
Norman	0.0	6.6	0.0	0.0	68.5	5.5	5.8	1.8	0.4	3.1
Oklahoma City	0.0	8.8	0.7	2.5	0.9	18.5	8.3	17.3	3.5	5.8
Owasso	0.0	4.3	0.0	0.0	4.7	22.5	13.0	6.5	1.6	5.2
Ponca City	0.0	7.2	0.0	0.0	1.8	11.7	12.2	6.8	1.4	3.7
Shawnee	0.0	12.2	0.0	0.0	0.0	22.5	9.6	3.8	2.4	0.3
Stillwater	0.4	18.2	0.0	0.0	0.2	21.6	13.9	8.0	0.0	2.1
Tulsa	2.1	19.7	1.1	0.0	8.8	12.2	19.9	4.8	0.0	6.0
OREGON	X	X	X	X	X	X	X	X	X	X
Albany	0.0	7.1	0.0	0.0	3.9	21.6	16.2	10.8	0.1	1.7
Beaverton	0.0	7.6	0.0	0.0	0.0	31.5	10.8	0.2	1.1	0.8
Bend	0.0	12.0	0.8	0.0	0.0	21.4	12.9	0.0	4.1	3.6
Corvallis	0.0	5.9	0.2	0.0	0.0	20.1	18.1	9.1	2.8	3.7
Eugene	0.0	2.5	1.5	0.0	0.0	18.2	14.0	9.7	2.9	0.9
Grants Pass	0.0	8.4	0.0	0.0	0.0	30.5	11.8	5.8	3.1	1.3
Gresham	0.0	10.0	0.0	0.0	0.0	20.1	23.2	3.0	1.4	3.3
Hillsboro	0.0	8.1	0.1	0.0	0.0	20.0	22.0	13.5	1.2	2.5
Keizer	0.0	10.4	0.0	0.0	0.0	28.9	33.1	2.7	4.7	7.4
Lake Oswego	0.0	4.0	0.0	0.0	0.0	13.3	14.8	11.9	0.0	6.6
McMinnville	0.0	5.9	0.0	0.0	10.6	19.5	16.7	11.4	0.0	3.2
Medford	0.0	12.8	0.4	0.0	0.0	19.0	14.3	5.7	5.9	15.0
Oregon City	0.0	35.9	0.8	0.0	0.0	15.8	13.8	8.7	1.1	3.8
Portland	0.0	13.9	0.6	0.0	0.0	13.5	20.3	7.8	7.5	7.6

City Government Finances, City Government Employment, and Climate

AREANAME	City government finances, 2012 (cont.) Debt outstanding Total (mil dol)	Per capita[1] (dollars)	Debt issued during year	Climate[2] Average daily temperature Mean January	July	Limits January[3]	July[4]	Annual precipitation (inches)	Heating degree days	Cooling degree days
	137	138	139	140	141	142	143	144	145	146
OHIO— Cont'd										
Hamilton	315.7	5,070	50.5	28.7	76.6	19.9	88.1	43.36	5,261	1,135
Hilliard	62.6	2,046	8.0	NA	NA	NA	NA	NA	NA	NA
Huber Heights	57.3	1,501	0.6	27.9	77.0	20.6	87.2	39.41	5,343	1,214
Kent	19.1	645	0.0	27.2	74.1	20.1	83.9	36.07	5,752	856
Kettering	18.1	324	0.0	27.9	77.0	20.6	87.2	39.41	5,343	1,214
Lakewood	92.2	1,795	12.3	25.7	71.9	18.8	81.4	38.71	6,121	702
Lancaster	375.7	9,659	0.2	26.5	73.1	17.8	84.4	36.55	5,887	764
Lima	36.5	953	1.1	25.5	73.6	18.1	84.0	37.20	5,932	835
Lorain	48.2	755	6.9	27.1	73.8	19.3	85.0	38.02	5,731	818
Mansfield	9.9	210	0.4	24.3	71.0	16.2	81.8	43.24	6,364	653
Marion	44.8	1,215	0.0	24.5	72.7	16.0	83.7	38.35	6,300	703
Mason	120.3	3,846	16.6	NA	NA	NA	NA	NA	NA	NA
Massillon	22.4	697	0.1	25.2	71.8	17.4	82.3	38.47	6,154	678
Medina	45.6	1,720	0.0	23.7	71.3	16.2	82.0	38.34	6,525	558
Mentor	34.9	742	4.4	23.0	68.8	14.3	80.0	47.33	6,956	372
Middletown	241.5	4,959	0.3	27.5	74.2	18.3	86.3	39.54	5,609	879
Newark	24.5	514	2.9	25.8	72.7	17.3	83.8	41.62	6,084	687
North Olmsted	38.8	1,199	1.4	25.7	71.9	18.8	81.4	38.71	6,121	702
North Ridgeville	34.1	1,115	4.1	NA	NA	NA	NA	NA	NA	NA
North Royalton	40.3	1,328	15.0	25.7	71.9	18.8	81.4	38.71	6,121	702
Parma	37.5	465	0.0	25.7	71.9	18.8	81.4	38.71	6,121	702
Reynoldsburg	22.9	631	0.0	28.3	75.1	20.3	85.3	38.52	5,492	951
Riverside	2.0	79	0.0	NA	NA	NA	NA	NA	NA	NA
Sandusky	27.6	1,078	4.1	25.6	73.8	18.9	81.8	34.46	6,065	785
Shaker Heights	27.3	972	0.3	25.7	71.9	18.8	81.4	38.71	6,121	702
Springfield	42.8	711	0.0	26.1	73.5	18.2	83.8	37.70	5,921	796
Stow	28.9	832	0.0	27.2	74.1	20.1	83.9	36.07	5,752	856
Strongsville	60.3	1,353	10.7	25.7	71.9	18.8	81.4	38.71	6,121	702
Toledo	357.2	1,260	8.3	27.5	77.6	21.7	87.1	33.52	5,464	1,257
Troy	19.5	768	0.0	NA	NA	NA	NA	NA	NA	NA
Upper Arlington	51.9	1,515	6.0	28.3	75.1	20.3	85.3	38.52	5,492	951
Warren	33.9	832	0.0	24.0	70.2	15.3	82.4	37.80	6,678	458
Westerville	75.5	2,027	10.0	27.7	74.4	19.7	85.4	39.35	5,434	924
Westlake	43.8	1,350	7.4	27.1	73.8	19.3	85.0	38.02	5,731	818
Wooster	10.1	381	0.0	NA	NA	NA	NA	NA	NA	NA
Xenia	7.4	286	1.1	NA	NA	NA	NA	NA	NA	NA
Youngstown	32.0	483	0.0	24.9	69.9	17.4	81.0	38.02	6,451	552
Zanesville	6.6	261	0.0	24.3	68.4	16.3	78.7	36.91	6,639	373
OKLAHOMA	X	X	X	X	X	X	X	X	X	X
Bartlesville	60.7	1,673	0.0	35.4	82.2	23.7	94.5	38.99	3,743	1,894
Broken Arrow	183.9	1,802	48.4	34.8	81.3	23.5	92.9	40.46	3,917	1,746
Edmond	136.7	1,609	0.0	36.7	82.0	26.2	93.1	35.85	3,663	1,907
Enid	78.5	1,572	17.0	33.1	82.6	21.9	94.4	34.25	4,269	1,852
Lawton	141.0	1,431	38.0	38.2	84.2	26.4	95.7	31.64	3,326	2,199
Midwest City	106.7	1,901	73.2	36.7	82.0	26.2	93.1	35.85	3,663	1,907
Moore	71.4	1,232	25.2	36.7	82.0	26.2	93.1	35.85	3,663	1,907
Muskogee	44.3	1,136	5.0	36.1	82.1	25.2	93.1	43.77	3,667	1,858
Norman	372.5	3,217	23.4	35.8	82.1	23.2	93.9	41.65	3,713	1,906
Oklahoma City	1,318.9	2,199	185.3	36.7	82.0	26.2	93.1	35.85	3,663	1,907
Owasso	39.4	1,254	0.0	NA	NA	NA	NA	NA	NA	NA
Ponca City	59.4	2,385	24.9	33.8	82.9	23.8	94.1	36.41	4,053	1,964
Shawnee	23.5	767	3.5	37.3	83.0	25.5	94.5	40.87	3,460	2,024
Stillwater	38.1	817	4.6	34.5	82.3	21.9	93.6	36.71	3,899	1,881
Tulsa	1,254.1	3,179	126.1	37.4	81.9	27.1	92.2	45.10	3,413	1,905
OREGON	X	X	X	X	X	X	X	X	X	X
Albany	122.1	2,381	0.0	40.3	66.5	33.6	81.2	43.66	4,715	247
Beaverton	26.4	285	0.0	40.0	66.8	33.8	79.2	39.95	4,723	287
Bend	92.3	1,171	10.9	31.2	63.5	22.6	80.7	11.73	7,042	147
Corvallis	59.4	1,080	0.0	38.1	63.8	31.6	77.4	67.76	5,501	139
Eugene	418.2	2,649	112.5	39.8	66.2	33.0	81.5	50.90	4,786	242
Grants Pass	12.2	350	0.0	NA	NA	NA	NA	NA	NA	NA
Gresham	82.4	758	3.0	40.0	68.3	33.5	81.5	45.70	4,491	450
Hillsboro	62.2	652	0.0	40.5	67.6	35.1	80.4	38.19	4,532	323
Keizer	28.7	779	0.0	40.3	66.8	33.5	81.5	40.00	4,784	257
Lake Oswego	156.3	4,196	37.7	41.8	69.3	35.7	82.6	46.05	4,132	475
McMinnville	22.1	668	5.6	39.6	66.6	33.0	81.9	41.66	4,815	288
Medford	380.1	4,966	26.6	39.1	72.7	30.9	90.2	18.37	4,539	711
Oregon City	33.8	1,009	0.0	41.8	69.3	35.7	82.6	46.05	4,132	475
Portland	3,381.1	5,608	353.6	41.8	69.3	35.7	82.6	46.05	4,132	475

1. Based on the population estimated as of July 1 of the year shown. 2. Represents normal values based on the 30-year period, 1971±2000. 3. Average daily minimum. 4. Average daily maximum.

Table D. Cities — **Land Area and Population**

STATE Place code	AREANAME	Land area[1] (sq. mi)	Total persons 2017	Rank	Per square mile	White	Black or African American	American Indian, Alaskan Native	Asian	Hawaiian Pacific Islander	Some other race	Two or more races (percent)
		1	2	3	4	5	6	7	8	9	10	11
	OREGON— Cont'd											
41 61,200	Redmond	16.8	30,011	1,251	1,786.4	NA	NA	NA	NA	NA	NA	NA
41 64,900	Salem	48.6	169,798	151	3,493.8	82.0	0.9	1.0	3.3	1.2	4.8	6.9
41 69,600	Springfield	15.8	62,353	595	3,946.4	90.4	0.3	0.5	0.8	0.6	1.9	5.5
41 73,650	Tigard	12.7	53,148	720	4,184.9	83.9	0.2	0.2	7.1	0.1	2.0	6.5
41 74,950	Tualatin	8.2	27,478	1,339	3,351.0	81.3	2.1	0.8	4.7	0.5	7.6	3.1
41 80,150	West Linn	7.4	26,703	1,372	3,608.5	NA	NA	NA	NA	NA	NA	NA
42 00,000	PENNSYLVANIA	44,742.1	12,805,537	X	286.2	80.9	11.0	0.2	3.3	0.0	2.1	2.5
42 02,000	Allentown	17.5	121,283	231	6,930.5	61.5	13.8	0.0	2.0	0.0	18.2	4.5
42 02,184	Altoona	9.8	44,098	865	4,499.8	NA	NA	NA	NA	NA	NA	NA
42 06,064	Bethel Park	11.7	32,404	1,170	2,769.6	95.5	0.6	0.0	2.6	0.0	0.1	1.3
42 06,088	Bethlehem	19.1	75,707	464	3,963.7	81.3	7.7	0.4	2.9	0.0	6.2	3.8
42 13,208	Chester	4.8	34,077	1,112	7,099.4	24.5	67.4	0.1	0.0	0.0	1.4	1.7
42 21,648	Easton	4.3	27,109	1,356	6,304.4	82.0	7.3	0.0	5.3	0.0	1.4	4.0
42 24,000	Erie	19.1	97,369	316	5,097.9	75.7	15.8	0.4	3.5	0.2	1.6	2.8
42 32,800	Harrisburg	8.1	49,192	777	6,073.1	30.7	56.0	0.6	5.7	0.0	4.8	2.2
42 33,408	Hazleton	6.0	24,723	1,422	4,120.5	86.6	3.0	0.0	1.0	0.3	7.4	1.7
42 41,216	Lancaster	7.2	59,708	628	8,292.8	63.2	17.9	0.2	5.0	0.0	6.4	7.3
42 42,168	Lebanon	4.2	25,770	1,401	6,135.7	60.3	7.4	0.0	3.0	0.0	24.2	5.1
42 50,528	Monroeville	19.7	27,716	1,331	1,406.9	82.9	10.0	0.0	2.9	0.0	0.4	3.8
42 54,656	Norristown	3.5	34,510	1,102	9,860.0	36.6	44.4	0.3	1.6	0.7	12.7	3.7
42 60,000	Philadelphia	134.2	1,580,863	6	11,779.9	40.4	42.2	0.4	7.1	0.0	6.7	3.3
42 61,000	Pittsburgh	55.4	302,407	65	5,458.6	67.6	22.7	0.1	5.6	0.1	0.4	3.5
42 61,536	Plum	28.6	27,258	1,349	953.1	NA	NA	NA	NA	NA	NA	NA
42 63,624	Reading	9.9	88,423	371	8,931.6	54.0	9.2	3.9	0.9	0.0	9.5	22.5
42 69,000	Scranton	25.3	77,605	446	3,067.4	84.2	6.3	0.2	4.0	0.0	0.7	4.6
42 73,808	State College	4.6	42,430	895	9,223.9	81.9	3.6	0.2	12.3	0.2	0.1	1.8
42 85,152	Wilkes-Barre	7.0	40,806	928	5,829.4	68.3	18.8	0.4	1.7	0.0	6.5	4.3
42 85,312	Williamsport	8.7	28,462	1,306	3,271.5	83.5	10.0	0.0	0.8	0.0	0.9	4.8
42 87,048	York	5.3	44,132	862	8,326.8	55.5	26.3	0.8	2.9	0.0	8.7	5.9
44 00,000	RHODE ISLAND	1,034.0	1,059,639	X	1,024.8	80.5	6.4	0.5	3.5	0.1	5.9	3.1
44 19,180	Cranston	28.4	81,202	417	2,859.2	84.1	4.9	0.4	4.8	0.1	3.5	2.2
44 22,960	East Providence	13.3	47,600	810	3,578.9	79.3	9.6	0.2	2.0	0.5	1.7	6.6
44 54,640	Pawtucket	8.7	72,001	493	8,276.0	65.1	14.9	1.3	3.3	0.2	8.7	6.4
44 59,000	Providence	18.4	180,393	137	9,804.0	52.5	13.4	1.7	5.9	0.1	21.5	4.8
44 74,300	Warwick	35.0	80,871	421	2,310.6	89.9	1.9	0.2	3.3	0.2	1.2	3.3
44 80,780	Woonsocket	7.8	41,759	907	5,353.7	73.9	11.7	0.2	7.1	0.0	5.0	2.1
45 00,000	SOUTH CAROLINA	30,063.0	5,024,369	X	167.1	67.4	27.0	0.3	1.5	0.1	1.6	2.2
45 00,550	Aiken	20.9	30,721	1,225	1,469.9	63.9	29.4	0.0	2.1	0.2	0.2	4.1
45 01,360	Anderson	14.5	27,293	1,347	1,882.3	NA	NA	NA	NA	NA	NA	NA
45 13,330	Charleston	109.0	134,875	201	1,237.4	73.0	23.6	0.1	2.0	0.0	0.1	1.2
45 16,000	Columbia	135.0	133,114	204	986.0	52.5	40.0	0.0	2.8	0.4	1.7	2.6
45 25,810	Florence	21.9	37,778	1,015	1,725.0	67.2	21.9	0.0	8.3	0.0	0.8	1.9
45 29,815	Goose Creek	41.4	42,619	892	1,029.4	68.1	26.4	0.2	2.5	0.0	1.4	1.3
45 30,850	Greenville	29.0	68,219	528	2,352.4	75.6	16.3	0.0	2.2	0.0	3.6	2.4
45 30,985	Greer	21.2	30,899	1,216	1,457.5	90.5	5.4	0.0	1.0	0.0	2.0	1.0
45 34,045	Hilton Head Island	41.4	40,055	950	967.5	92.5	3.7	0.5	1.2	0.0	0.2	1.9
45 48,535	Mount Pleasant	45.1	86,668	382	1,921.7	NA	NA	NA	NA	NA	NA	NA
45 49,075	Myrtle Beach	23.6	32,795	1,156	1,389.6	51.4	42.0	0.1	1.7	0.0	1.7	3.2
45 50,875	North Charleston	73.7	110,861	266	1,504.2	51.0	39.8	0.0	2.7	0.1	4.3	2.2
45 61,405	Rock Hill	38.0	73,068	484	1,922.8	43.5	50.9	0.3	1.1	0.1	0.4	3.7
45 68,290	Spartanburg	19.8	37,498	1,021	1,893.8	67.8	23.3	1.0	1.0	0.0	2.9	4.1
45 70,270	Summerville	19.3	50,388	755	2,610.8	46.3	48.1	0.3	2.5	0.0	0.3	2.5
45 70,405	Sumter	32.5	39,982	952	1,230.2	84.7	1.7	8.9	1.5	0.0	0.7	2.5
46 00,000	SOUTH DAKOTA	75,809.3	869,666	X	11.5	84.7	1.7	8.9	1.5	0.0	0.7	2.5
46 00,100	Aberdeen	16.0	28,388	1,308	1,774.3	87.9	2.3	4.4	1.6	0.0	0.0	3.7
46 52,980	Rapid City	54.5	74,421	475	1,365.5	79.5	0.9	12.5	1.6	0.0	0.2	5.4
46 59,020	Sioux Falls	77.1	176,888	143	2,294.3	84.5	5.3	2.2	3.0	0.0	1.8	3.1
47 00,000	TENNESSEE	41,234.9	6,715,984	X	162.9	77.8	16.8	0.3	1.7	0.1	1.2	2.1
47 03,440	Bartlett	32.3	59,102	636	1,829.8	69.8	23.1	0.1	3.3	0.0	0.8	2.8
47 08,280	Brentwood	41.2	42,667	891	1,035.6	87.3	2.3	0.5	8.1	0.0	0.1	1.8
47 08,540	Bristol	32.6	26,842	1,367	823.4	92.1	3.2	0.0	0.6	0.0	1.4	2.6
47 14,000	Chattanooga	143.0	179,139	140	1,252.7	61.7	32.7	0.1	2.8	0.0	0.3	2.4
47 15,160	Clarksville	98.0	153,205	169	1,563.3	66.8	22.9	0.9	3.1	0.9	1.4	4.0
47 15,400	Cleveland	27.1	44,483	853	1,641.4	88.5	7.3	0.8	0.3	0.1	1.3	1.7
47 16,420	Collierville	36.0	50,286	756	1,396.8	73.2	15.3	1.2	6.9	0.0	0.0	3.4

1. Dry land or land partially or temporarily covered by water.   2. Hispanic or Latino persons may be of any race.

Table D. Cities — **Population**

AREANAME	Percent Hispanic or Latino[1], 2016	Percent foreign born, 2016	Age of population (percent), 2016							Median age 2016	Percent female 2016	Population Census counts		Percent change	
			Under 18 years	18 to 24 years	25 to 34 years	35 to 44 years	45 to 54 years	55 to 64 years	65 years and over			2000	2010	2000-2010	2010-2017
	12	13	14	15	16	17	18	19	20	21	22	23	24	25	26
OREGON— Cont'd															
Redmond	15.3	5.4	24.4	9.8	18.7	11.3	12.6	9.6	13.7	33.3	51.8	13,481	26,212	94.4	14.5
Salem	22.6	11.6	22.5	11.5	14.7	13.5	11.3	11.1	15.3	35.9	52.2	136,924	154,728	13.0	9.7
Springfield	10.0	4.2	24.2	10.4	16.6	11.1	11.4	13.5	12.7	34.1	54.4	52,864	59,388	12.3	5.0
Tigard	9.7	14.4	22.1	6.0	14.5	15.1	12.5	13.0	16.9	39.2	52.1	41,223	48,189	16.9	10.3
Tualatin	20.0	11.2	26.6	8.5	13.1	18.4	12.3	12.3	8.7	36.3	51.2	22,791	26,120	14.6	5.2
West Linn	3.1	12.4	22.4	5.7	8.6	9.8	18.4	18.0	17.1	46.9	52.0	22,261	25,100	12.8	6.4
PENNSYLVANIA	7.0	6.8	20.9	9.3	13.1	11.6	13.6	14.1	17.4	40.6	51.0	12,281,054	12,702,857	3.4	0.8
Allentown	52.7	16.4	27.8	12.9	15.9	11.2	10.8	10.1	11.4	30.5	51.9	106,632	118,093	10.7	2.7
Altoona	2.1	0.7	21.3	9.4	12.9	11.7	12.2	16.7	15.7	40.6	50.6	49,523	45,984	-7.1	-4.1
Bethel Park	1.0	5.5	18.1	7.7	12.5	8.1	13.6	17.0	23.0	47.1	53.1	33,556	32,315	-3.7	0.3
Bethlehem	28.3	7.9	20.1	13.7	14.6	13.3	10.8	12.7	14.8	35.9	50.9	71,329	74,986	5.1	1.0
Chester	12.3	4.2	22.3	18.0	15.5	8.9	12.7	11.0	11.6	30.6	51.8	36,854	33,972	-7.8	0.3
Easton	21.4	15.2	14.6	21.4	14.7	10.6	13.9	13.5	11.4	33.9	47.9	26,263	26,769	1.9	1.3
Erie	8.5	8.9	23.7	10.8	16.8	10.5	12.8	12.1	13.3	34.0	51.8	103,717	101,782	-1.9	-4.3
Harrisburg	18.4	12.8	24.8	11.0	18.6	11.7	11.5	12.7	9.9	31.9	53.9	48,950	49,528	1.2	-0.7
Hazleton	43.0	25.4	18.5	9.3	12.6	10.2	19.1	12.5	17.9	44.5	50.6	23,329	25,340	8.6	-2.4
Lancaster	43.2	11.7	23.2	13.2	17.3	14.6	10.3	11.1	10.2	33.2	50.9	56,348	59,322	5.3	0.7
Lebanon	42.7	8.5	26.8	13.0	13.4	9.7	12.8	11.0	13.3	32.9	53.0	24,461	25,477	4.2	1.2
Monroeville	4.9	5.5	14.8	6.3	16.7	11.3	9.3	17.2	24.4	45.8	54.7	29,349	28,341	-3.4	-2.2
Norristown	27.2	22.5	27.1	5.6	20.7	13.5	10.9	11.1	11.0	32.5	48.2	31,282	34,340	9.8	0.5
Philadelphia	14.4	14.8	22.1	10.5	18.9	12.2	11.9	11.6	12.9	34.1	52.6	1,517,550	1,526,006	0.6	3.6
Pittsburgh	2.8	8.8	15.3	16.3	20.6	9.8	11.0	12.3	14.6	33.5	50.8	334,563	305,391	-8.7	-1.0
Plum	1.0	2.5	22.3	5.0	11.7	11.4	14.8	14.6	20.1	44.8	50.4	26,940	27,124	0.7	0.5
Reading	67.9	18.5	28.4	13.2	13.8	11.7	12.7	9.3	10.9	31.1	50.2	81,207	88,079	8.5	0.4
Scranton	14.1	8.5	20.9	13.1	13.7	10.5	11.4	12.8	17.6	36.4	50.3	76,415	76,089	-0.4	2.0
State College	4.0	17.5	4.3	59.4	14.8	3.6	4.3	6.7	7.0	21.7	48.2	38,420	41,980	9.3	1.1
Wilkes-Barre	23.5	9.0	24.0	15.7	9.8	12.4	10.3	12.9	14.9	35.6	48.7	43,123	41,498	-3.8	-1.7
Williamsport	2.4	2.3	24.2	17.2	17.2	8.3	9.8	9.8	13.5	29.9	50.6	30,706	29,381	-4.3	-3.1
York	35.0	10.3	26.9	14.1	13.8	12.6	11.4	11.2	10.0	32.1	49.7	40,862	43,806	7.2	0.7
RHODE ISLAND	14.9	14.1	19.7	10.8	13.5	11.6	13.9	14.0	16.5	40.2	51.6	1,048,319	1,052,945	0.4	0.6
Cranston	16.9	15.2	17.5	9.7	14.0	12.0	14.3	12.8	19.7	41.9	50.1	79,269	80,396	1.4	1.0
East Providence	4.2	15.8	17.7	6.1	14.7	11.4	11.5	17.4	21.2	45.2	53.4	48,688	47,061	-3.3	1.1
Pawtucket	21.7	25.1	20.7	8.9	19.1	12.3	13.8	13.8	11.4	36.1	48.3	72,958	71,169	-2.5	1.2
Providence	44.8	28.6	23.2	18.0	17.1	13.4	10.5	8.7	9.1	29.5	51.9	173,618	177,997	2.5	1.3
Warwick	5.3	7.9	16.6	6.0	13.8	11.4	16.5	14.4	21.5	46.2	52.4	85,808	82,655	-3.7	-2.2
Woonsocket	14.2	17.2	19.9	5.6	14.9	12.9	13.7	18.9	14.1	41.8	51.8	43,224	41,209	-4.7	1.3
SOUTH CAROLINA	5.5	4.8	22.2	9.5	13.0	12.3	13.0	13.2	16.7	39.1	51.5	4,012,012	4,625,381	15.3	8.6
Aiken	0.9	2.9	22.2	11.2	12.0	10.5	10.0	12.5	21.5	40.1	52.0	25,337	29,566	16.7	3.9
Anderson	3.3	1.6	21.5	13.8	12.7	10.3	10.5	9.0	22.2	37.6	54.5	25,514	26,433	3.6	3.3
Charleston	2.3	4.1	16.1	12.6	20.1	12.7	10.8	13.3	14.4	35.7	53.0	96,650	119,997	24.2	12.4
Columbia	5.7	5.4	15.9	26.9	17.4	11.0	9.5	9.3	10.0	28.5	48.2	116,278	129,819	11.6	2.5
Florence	1.2	5.6	24.3	8.3	13.8	11.8	10.9	13.3	17.6	39.1	55.3	30,248	37,451	23.8	0.9
Goose Creek	8.9	5.7	20.1	14.9	14.5	11.3	13.8	15.9	9.4	36.2	48.0	29,208	36,437	24.8	17.0
Greenville	4.8	5.8	21.1	10.8	19.0	14.7	10.5	9.8	14.0	34.4	53.4	56,002	59,162	5.6	15.3
Greer	16.1	13.5	30.8	5.0	17.3	16.3	12.3	9.2	9.1	34.0	54.6	16,843	25,638	52.2	20.5
Hilton Head Island	14.8	11.6	15.8	2.3	9.7	8.7	14.4	17.2	31.9	54.3	51.9	33,862	37,094	9.5	8.0
Mount Pleasant	4.0	4.2	26.5	4.2	15.5	14.3	13.8	11.3	14.4	37.3	50.1	47,609	67,814	42.4	27.8
Myrtle Beach	12.3	14.1	21.6	7.6	14.7	9.4	11.2	14.6	21.0	42.1	52.0	22,759	27,101	19.1	21.0
North Charleston	10.5	7.1	23.5	10.1	18.7	14.7	11.8	11.0	10.1	33.6	52.6	79,641	97,581	22.5	13.6
Rock Hill	6.9	5.8	24.6	12.7	13.4	15.0	11.4	10.0	13.0	34.5	51.8	49,765	66,558	33.7	9.8
Spartanburg	4.1	3.3	22.0	11.0	16.9	11.7	12.3	10.7	15.4	35.0	53.1	39,673	36,760	-7.3	2.0
Summerville	4.4	2.5	27.3	9.3	14.7	15.4	11.4	10.6	11.4	33.9	52.4	27,752	42,675	53.8	18.1
Sumter	3.5	3.7	24.6	13.9	12.4	10.4	11.8	10.5	16.4	33.8	51.8	39,643	40,541	2.3	-1.4
SOUTH DAKOTA	3.7	3.6	24.7	9.9	12.9	11.4	11.8	13.4	15.9	36.8	49.7	754,844	814,197	7.9	6.8
Aberdeen	NA	1.2	22.6	11.0	14.8	10.3	10.0	14.9	16.5	36.6	50.1	24,658	26,105	5.9	8.7
Rapid City	5.0	2.4	23.4	8.7	15.4	9.8	12.2	12.9	17.5	37.1	49.8	59,607	68,461	14.9	8.7
Sioux Falls	5.2	8.1	25.6	9.5	16.1	13.8	10.5	11.7	12.7	34.4	50.1	123,975	153,967	24.2	14.9
TENNESSEE	5.2	4.8	22.6	9.3	13.3	12.6	13.4	13.0	15.7	38.6	51.2	5,689,283	6,346,295	11.5	5.8
Bartlett	1.7	4.1	26.7	6.1	8.5	13.1	13.0	14.1	18.5	41.6	50.0	40,543	56,920	40.4	3.8
Brentwood	4.3	10.9	32.1	5.8	5.1	13.9	16.2	14.2	12.6	41.6	52.5	23,445	37,084	58.2	15.1
Bristol	1.8	1.5	19.1	7.4	11.9	13.1	14.1	14.5	20.1	44.1	54.1	24,821	26,712	7.6	0.5
Chattanooga	7.1	6.1	20.3	10.3	16.3	13.2	11.9	12.7	15.3	36.7	53.0	155,554	170,315	9.5	5.2
Clarksville	11.6	5.2	26.9	12.4	20.5	10.9	11.3	8.9	9.0	29.8	51.3	103,455	132,906	28.5	15.3
Cleveland	11.0	7.4	21.6	14.2	15.7	12.5	11.8	8.4	15.8	33.3	54.0	37,192	41,264	10.9	7.8
Collierville	1.8	8.6	27.6	6.7	9.0	16.0	16.3	12.4	12.1	40.4	51.0	31,872	45,601	43.1	10.3

1. May be of any race.

Table D. Cities — Households, Group Quarters, Crime, and Education

AREANAME	Number	Persons per house-hold	Family	Married couple family	Female headed family[1]	Non-family	One person	Persons in group quarters	Number	Rate	Violent	Property	Population age 25 and over	High school graduate or less	Bachelor's degree or more
	27	28	29	30	31	32	33	34	35	36	37	38	39	40	41
OREGON— Cont'd															
Redmond	10,101	2.88	71.7	45.4	18.3	28.3	19.0	NA	1,057	3,624	278	3,347	19,309	43.0	17.7
Salem	60,439	2.63	60.1	44.7	11.9	39.9	32.3	8,616	7,202	4,325	321	4,005	110,506	36.0	27.8
Springfield	23,379	2.62	60.5	40.7	13.4	39.5	26.9	726	3,146	5,144	301	4,843	40,485	39.5	18.6
Tigard	20,216	2.55	63.8	51.0	8.8	36.2	27.9	411	1,679	3,236	256	2,980	37,339	23.0	42.4
Tualatin	10,790	2.59	64.7	52.4	11.2	35.3	26.7	NA	781	2,853	190	2,664	18,258	19.4	45.9
West Linn	10,372	2.57	75.1	62.7	7.0	24.9	22.3	NA	256	952	48	904	19,312	11.9	60.1
PENNSYLVANIA	4,937,771	2.50	63.8	47.4	11.7	36.2	30.0	427,424	263,242	2,059	316	1,743	8,921,975	45.0	30.8
Allentown	41,625	2.77	63.7	27.5	26.3	36.3	28.0	5,320	3,889	3,224	458	2,767	71,437	61.4	15.4
Altoona	18,514	2.35	63.6	40.4	18.8	36.4	32.4	1,053	978	2,166	348	1,818	30,881	58.9	15.2
Bethel Park	12,798	2.47	75.8	64.7	11.2	24.2	23.7	276	330	1,029	69	960	23,691	26.1	43.6
Bethlehem	28,912	2.44	60.3	37.1	17.7	39.7	31.1	5,860	2,051	2,739	753	1,986	50,619	43.8	28.9
Chester	10,902	2.78	56.6	16.5	35.0	43.4	34.8	3,654	1,585	4,647	1,571	3,075	20,277	61.5	11.9
Easton	9,289	2.52	62.9	39.8	15.5	37.1	27.3	3,564	519	1,927	275	1,652	17,270	53.4	25.9
Erie	40,028	2.33	53.1	30.5	15.8	46.9	37.6	5,153	2,631	2,657	356	2,301	64,577	55.2	21.2
Harrisburg	20,148	2.31	50.2	21.4	23.8	49.8	43.5	2,285	1,868	3,813	1,074	2,739	31,442	53.3	19.9
Hazleton	10,425	2.34	60.1	42.6	14.4	39.9	35.9	304	454	1,836	380	1,456	17,816	68.3	13.0
Lancaster	21,741	2.57	54.3	30.4	15.9	45.7	33.1	3,364	2,651	4,467	821	3,647	37,658	59.2	19.0
Lebanon	9,536	2.66	57.8	31.3	21.3	42.2	34.4	408	679	2,128	267	1,862	15,486	63.9	7.1
Monroeville	12,253	2.24	59.5	47.7	8.2	40.5	35.8	569	599	2,225	430	1,795	22,063	33.6	36.3
Norristown	12,655	2.65	57.9	26.2	27.2	42.1	28.9	811	766	2,658	235	2,423	23,116	55.8	19.9
Philadelphia	580,205	2.62	53.4	27.6	19.5	46.6	38.1	49,090	64,719	4,120	979	3,141	1,057,805	48.5	28.6
Pittsburgh	136,300	2.05	42.2	27.5	11.3	57.8	44.3	23,996	12,234	4,045	782	3,263	207,677	33.2	45.7
Plum	10,913	2.50	74.6	64.3	6.7	25.4	22.6	NA	176	638	109	529	19,925	33.7	36.7
Reading	26,783	3.16	63.7	27.1	28.9	36.3	29.8	3,008	2,888	3,288	680	2,608	51,187	69.0	9.2
Scranton	30,631	2.35	55.1	36.5	12.8	44.9	37.4	5,362	1,912	2,472	279	2,193	50,999	54.5	22.3
State College	12,657	2.31	27.9	24.1	1.5	72.1	42.9	12,804	530	912	67	845	15,253	14.0	71.4
Wilkes-Barre	13,980	2.66	60.3	33.3	21.4	39.7	35.4	3,434	1,316	3,238	531	2,707	24,487	59.4	16.8
Williamsport	11,308	2.27	56.3	35.4	18.5	43.7	36.6	3,208	896	3,072	357	2,716	16,908	48.0	22.2
York	16,000	2.65	62.0	33.6	22.1	38.1	29.7	1,533	1,824	4,144	945	3,199	25,894	60.8	12.9
RHODE ISLAND	408,239	2.48	60.6	42.3	13.9	39.4	32.3	42,752	22,582	2,138	239	1,899	734,045	39.3	34.1
Cranston	31,154	2.47	58.1	43.1	11.1	41.9	35.4	3,928	1,634	2,013	153	1,860	58,953	41.5	32.4
East Providence	19,805	2.34	62.0	41.2	16.4	38.0	35.7	947	619	1,304	145	1,159	36,061	42.8	27.7
Pawtucket	27,316	2.60	61.9	36.8	18.4	38.1	32.0	511	2,375	3,315	426	2,889	50,285	48.7	22.6
Providence	58,170	2.84	57.9	32.0	20.5	42.1	32.7	14,231	6,432	3,586	577	3,009	105,408	48.0	31.0
Warwick	35,208	2.30	59.0	41.8	11.7	41.0	34.8	623	1,686	2,069	75	1,994	63,199	38.0	31.5
Woonsocket	18,075	2.24	49.0	28.8	16.6	51.0	44.6	879	1,184	2,852	511	2,342	30,847	52.9	19.7
SOUTH CAROLINA	1,877,887	2.57	65.2	46.4	14.2	34.8	29.3	136,582	185,824	3,746	502	3,244	3,388,476	42.4	27.2
Aiken	12,194	2.42	75.0	51.3	18.6	25.0	24.2	1,436	2,063	6,698	844	5,854	20,583	33.1	39.9
Anderson	12,122	2.11	47.1	25.7	18.8	52.9	49.1	1,952	2,491	9,051	1,079	7,972	17,816	45.4	22.0
Charleston	57,854	2.28	48.8	37.8	9.5	51.2	40.5	5,784	3,768	2,788	302	2,486	98,024	21.4	52.8
Columbia	47,289	2.22	49.0	28.7	14.9	51.0	37.1	28,805	8,501	6,321	831	5,490	76,627	32.2	41.5
Florence	14,801	2.55	69.0	40.3	23.7	31.0	28.8	620	2,981	7,767	1,068	6,698	25,832	35.8	27.1
Goose Creek	14,884	2.69	71.4	56.4	10.1	28.6	25.4	2,035	1,075	2,588	380	2,208	27,285	33.0	25.9
Greenville	29,281	2.15	50.5	34.8	14.1	49.5	42.3	4,458	3,219	4,901	606	4,295	45,889	28.3	49.2
Greer	11,998	2.72	65.3	39.3	23.6	34.7	27.0	NA	837	2,893	335	2,558	21,058	38.8	32.6
Hilton Head Island	16,243	2.48	66.9	54.7	10.7	33.1	25.3	190	NA	NA	NA	NA	33,180	21.2	52.0
Mount Pleasant	31,552	2.66	64.4	54.5	7.2	35.6	28.2	386	1,572	1,865	153	1,712	58,355	15.2	57.9
Myrtle Beach	14,105	2.28	49.2	31.7	10.5	50.8	46.5	NA	4,940	15,503	1,692	13,812	22,844	37.6	29.2
North Charleston	43,248	2.46	51.8	31.1	18.3	48.2	40.9	5,600	7,229	6,543	901	5,642	74,437	49.0	22.1
Rock Hill	27,812	2.51	62.4	36.6	18.7	37.6	28.4	3,052	2,993	4,123	616	3,507	45,781	42.2	25.1
Spartanburg	15,193	2.35	53.5	26.8	18.9	46.5	37.5	2,202	2,793	7,334	1,103	6,231	25,352	38.7	32.8
Summerville	18,659	2.78	68.5	50.2	16.0	31.5	26.3	296	2,034	4,056	375	3,681	33,092	30.5	33.6
Sumter	16,591	2.36	59.5	39.2	17.9	40.5	38.4	1,546	1,947	4,765	690	4,074	25,037	40.8	24.6
SOUTH DAKOTA	334,003	2.49	62.9	49.3	9.3	37.1	31.0	34,010	20,762	2,399	418	1,981	565,894	37.8	28.9
Aberdeen	12,377	2.20	53.8	44.9	5.4	46.2	40.4	1,338	756	2,653	470	2,183	18,948	32.0	25.1
Rapid City	29,331	2.40	60.4	42.1	14.8	39.6	34.9	3,573	3,513	4,711	728	3,983	50,243	33.5	33.1
Sioux Falls	69,330	2.43	58.1	44.4	9.1	41.9	34.4	5,895	6,478	3,699	512	3,186	113,159	32.8	36.3
TENNESSEE	2,556,332	2.54	65.4	47.8	13.0	34.6	28.7	152,979	231,932	3,487	633	2,854	4,527,198	45.4	26.1
Bartlett	19,491	2.97	77.1	63.2	7.9	22.9	20.3	799	1,161	1,971	321	1,650	39,366	29.9	32.7
Brentwood	13,501	3.14	87.2	79.5	6.1	12.8	11.3	NA	425	994	58	936	26,420	10.7	74.1
Bristol	12,044	2.20	60.3	42.1	14.6	39.7	34.3	650	1,056	3,962	593	3,369	19,928	47.6	21.1
Chattanooga	72,349	2.34	48.8	34.6	11.3	51.2	45.4	8,606	11,622	6,537	1,023	5,513	123,320	43.1	29.9
Clarksville	54,765	2.68	71.4	50.1	14.9	28.6	22.4	3,243	4,824	3,163	615	2,548	91,172	37.7	25.5
Cleveland	17,620	2.34	54.1	33.8	15.7	45.9	36.4	3,052	3,090	6,956	864	6,091	28,425	44.0	25.8
Collierville	16,242	3.02	87.5	79.1	5.4	12.5	11.2	NA	822	1,660	162	1,498	32,336	17.4	58.6

1. No spouse present. 2. Data for serious crimes have not been adjusted for underreporting. This may affect comparability between geographic areas and over time. 3. Per 100,000 population estimated by the FBI. 4. Persons 25 years old and over.

Table D. Cities — **Income and Housing**

AREANAME	Money income, 2016					Median earnings, 2016			Housing units, 2016				
	Households												
	Median income	Percent with income less than $20,000	Percent with income of $200,000 or more	Median family income	Median non-family household income	All persons	Men	Women	Total	Occupied	Percent owner occupied	Median value[1] (dollars)	Median rent (dollars)
	42	43	44	45	46	47	48	49	50	51	52	53	54
OREGON— Cont'd													
Redmond	62,004	12.6	1.0	63,355	31,684	29,806	28,333	30,404	10,101	10,101	58.8	234,000	909
Salem	51,945	13.9	2.8	62,658	32,323	25,734	27,142	23,089	65,345	60,439	54.6	221,000	891
Springfield	40,360	21.8	2.1	51,254	25,273	25,871	30,012	19,793	24,230	23,379	53.7	178,900	875
Tigard	74,696	14.2	9.8	96,677	36,418	40,406	44,537	36,353	20,846	20,216	62.4	377,600	1,187
Tualatin	76,941	3.7	5.0	88,396	60,390	41,156	56,776	31,872	11,713	10,790	51.3	392,600	1,209
West Linn	118,527	5.4	24.0	128,387	38,719	54,888	80,766	46,524	10,518	10,372	82.0	469,900	1,294
PENNSYLVANIA	56,907	16.1	5.4	72,313	32,488	32,465	40,443	27,415	5,611,995	4,937,771	68.5	174,100	881
Allentown	35,813	25.9	1.2	36,980	26,371	22,173	24,524	20,453	44,991	41,625	42.5	121,800	967
Altoona	36,734	25.7	0.4	48,620	23,666	24,416	27,239	21,775	20,380	18,514	63.4	84,100	667
Bethel Park	73,400	13.4	3.2	83,856	31,533	37,108	47,347	27,008	13,695	12,798	79.1	181,800	962
Bethlehem	52,588	15.9	2.2	61,813	36,067	30,619	33,792	26,300	31,659	28,912	51.1	167,700	994
Chester	29,144	36.1	0.6	41,204	21,056	20,718	21,582	19,590	13,324	10,902	39.7	72,200	837
Easton	50,582	15.9	4.0	65,759	36,098	24,580	30,112	20,267	11,396	9,289	44.4	133,900	872
Erie	36,476	28.4	0.4	47,951	25,011	24,112	26,973	20,760	44,813	40,028	51.7	89,000	658
Harrisburg	34,702	25.4	1.4	38,091	26,941	25,523	27,388	23,197	24,885	20,148	35.0	78,400	820
Hazleton	34,038	27.1	1.8	53,218	23,837	25,441	28,771	22,944	12,437	10,425	54.0	100,700	611
Lancaster	41,099	27.7	1.2	47,359	28,599	22,072	27,545	20,007	23,547	21,741	42.6	102,600	799
Lebanon	35,928	21.8	1.3	36,663	24,388	23,049	30,130	19,256	10,682	9,536	36.2	89,700	767
Monroeville	60,590	18.1	4.4	85,124	31,115	36,662	50,122	31,390	12,983	12,253	68.1	149,600	853
Norristown	44,017	17.8	1.8	46,149	38,426	30,589	31,592	29,237	14,547	12,655	33.7	143,900	1,036
Philadelphia	41,449	27.3	3.5	50,280	29,943	30,678	31,680	29,454	674,504	580,205	52.1	154,000	976
Pittsburgh	44,707	25.0	4.1	62,450	32,179	30,517	32,384	26,645	156,632	136,300	47.2	120,800	874
Plum	73,692	7.8	5.9	86,025	50,500	41,305	50,911	26,438	12,044	10,913	73.8	142,600	932
Reading	25,865	37.9	0.4	30,938	18,734	20,202	23,593	13,443	31,272	26,783	40.8	76,100	784
Scranton	38,807	28.2	1.4	48,699	23,261	24,881	30,469	20,605	35,725	30,631	48.0	109,500	729
State College	35,541	36.4	5.8	108,387	21,008	7,736	10,564	5,740	14,311	12,657	29.7	289,900	947
Wilkes-Barre	35,420	29.1	1.5	43,738	24,372	21,233	26,326	17,606	18,886	13,980	48.7	76,400	668
Williamsport	36,604	24.5	2.0	46,880	26,942	21,610	27,059	16,692	12,958	11,308	40.5	105,800	770
York	30,357	28.3	0.4	32,036	24,539	21,709	25,526	17,107	19,704	16,000	40.7	79,200	774
RHODE ISLAND	60,596	17.2	5.4	77,940	35,174	35,343	41,141	30,492	462,598	408,239	58.0	247,700	948
Cranston	67,275	11.7	3.7	77,696	40,109	37,604	46,633	31,529	34,150	31,154	69.0	224,200	965
East Providence	55,847	18.4	3.3	73,152	25,766	40,416	47,093	32,187	20,808	19,805	60.3	211,000	853
Pawtucket	46,792	21.4	2.4	50,891	32,288	30,505	35,439	26,517	30,808	27,316	42.5	182,000	883
Providence	40,335	28.5	5.2	42,693	29,773	25,962	31,808	20,222	67,393	58,170	33.1	179,400	915
Warwick	59,372	17.1	4.1	77,944	33,057	36,336	40,414	33,343	38,115	35,208	66.5	205,300	1,110
Woonsocket	37,909	31.2	1.4	55,444	26,061	32,333	40,210	27,772	20,634	18,075	34.6	158,500	789
SOUTH CAROLINA	49,501	19.1	3.7	61,535	29,193	29,640	34,430	24,876	2,236,262	1,877,887	68.6	153,900	841
Aiken	50,256	20.6	2.8	58,737	23,854	28,976	38,056	20,968	13,527	12,194	57.3	189,700	869
Anderson	30,663	34.9	0.0	38,912	21,126	22,924	31,371	18,398	13,351	12,122	40.6	122,900	653
Charleston	61,467	20.7	8.1	97,122	37,400	36,591	44,931	31,531	65,690	57,854	56.6	297,700	1,126
Columbia	48,577	22.7	5.0	59,617	32,982	21,584	23,794	19,131	54,438	47,289	46.0	164,600	885
Florence	51,483	23.5	3.4	64,185	20,719	29,322	28,435	29,644	17,129	14,801	61.7	155,400	747
Goose Creek	61,540	6.5	3.9	77,668	47,225	32,636	42,225	26,387	15,707	14,884	71.9	176,800	1,291
Greenville	49,000	19.6	9.1	70,916	35,572	32,316	39,224	30,237	33,294	29,281	43.4	266,400	928
Greer	50,681	13.9	3.7	60,144	41,469	30,277	32,040	29,518	12,990	11,998	57.1	165,800	848
Hilton Head Island	81,599	13.5	16.8	93,355	54,048	35,220	41,544	32,913	34,345	16,243	82.3	463,100	1,239
Mount Pleasant	100,308	7.0	17.6	127,434	64,655	55,648	70,074	44,226	33,725	31,552	70.2	437,000	1,497
Myrtle Beach	38,194	30.4	3.4	58,563	24,132	22,462	22,181	23,183	24,826	14,105	56.8	215,500	784
North Charleston	35,600	29.0	1.3	48,302	27,063	27,025	32,057	22,529	47,743	43,248	44.9	152,000	895
Rock Hill	45,821	23.9	1.9	52,768	31,706	24,811	30,118	19,386	29,540	27,812	47.8	153,500	858
Spartanburg	39,886	27.8	1.8	47,425	28,969	25,076	26,877	21,937	17,415	15,193	42.7	114,600	718
Summerville	58,569	12.4	4.4	71,653	29,951	36,775	41,644	30,554	20,042	18,659	61.0	190,000	1,079
Sumter	35,332	30.8	1.9	46,282	17,702	22,199	26,329	17,573	18,794	16,591	52.9	134,400	706
SOUTH DAKOTA	54,467	15.8	3.7	70,853	32,296	31,032	36,465	26,067	383,827	334,003	67.2	160,700	706
Aberdeen	45,175	19.0	0.7	76,499	31,146	30,859	35,110	25,739	13,370	12,377	58.4	168,900	635
Rapid City	47,813	22.6	3.6	59,317	30,376	26,605	30,398	24,284	31,707	29,331	61.9	177,700	747
Sioux Falls	56,867	13.5	4.9	79,912	35,543	35,038	37,866	30,761	74,469	69,330	60.8	173,400	794
TENNESSEE	48,547	18.9	3.8	60,659	29,670	30,164	34,420	25,436	2,919,698	2,556,332	65.1	157,700	806
Bartlett	80,531	6.1	5.1	86,708	48,660	43,653	52,242	34,568	20,279	19,491	84.9	174,600	1,297
Brentwood	156,936	5.6	32.8	168,310	56,971	70,886	111,563	36,611	14,347	13,501	92.3	617,300	2,931
Bristol	38,333	18.3	2.0	53,793	23,059	25,487	31,181	19,219	13,976	12,044	67.1	132,100	686
Chattanooga	41,226	23.1	3.5	57,476	31,590	29,981	31,517	26,123	83,133	72,349	54.9	164,400	781
Clarksville	51,696	15.1	1.7	56,289	34,195	29,728	38,564	21,109	63,294	54,765	54.9	150,100	919
Cleveland	40,012	21.8	2.5	42,495	29,602	22,748	25,593	21,792	18,732	17,620	47.0	147,500	670
Collierville	111,574	2.9	15.0	123,392	50,387	52,127	69,653	35,572	16,433	16,242	80.0	313,000	1,180

1. Specified owner-occupied units; $2,000,000 represents $2,000,000 or more.

AREANAME	Commuting[1] 2016 Percent		Computer access[2] Percent		Migration		Civilian labor force, 2016				Civilian employment, 2016			
									Unemployment[3]		Population age 16 and older		Population age 16 to 64	
	Drove alone	With commutes of 30 minutes or more	With a computer in the house	With Internet access	Percent who lived in the same house one year ago	Percent who lived in another state or county one year ago	Total	Percent change 2016-2017	Total	Rate	Number	Percent in labor force	Number	Percent who worked full-year full-time
	55	56	57	58	59	60	61	62	63	64	65	66	67	68
OREGON— Cont'd														
Redmond	72.9	33.6	94.6	87.0	72.9	7.6	12,728	4.8	666	5.2	22,801	72.8	18,797	56.5
Salem	74.1	21.4	90.2	84.3	78.8	9.2	81,046	3.3	3,548	4.4	133,923	62.0	108,238	45.7
Springfield	83.0	16.2	92.3	81.8	73.7	2.9	31,468	2.2	1,484	4.7	48,479	62.8	40,598	40.0
Tigard	77.3	35.5	92.2	89.5	83.1	9.9	30,434	3.2	1,030	3.4	41,218	67.2	32,440	54.7
Tualatin	80.0	27.8	95.9	92.0	88.5	7.0	15,535	3.0	529	3.4	21,224	74.8	18,764	59.2
West Linn	70.7	40.4	95.9	91.9	89.2	5.6	15,022	3.1	499	3.3	21,806	63.8	17,224	51.7
PENNSYLVANIA	76.1	38.3	86.9	80.2	87.1	5.3	6,427,370	-0.4	315,737	4.9	10,427,404	62.1	8,205,643	50.4
Allentown	67.5	24.2	86.6	74.9	75.1	8.1	54,912	0.0	3,946	7.2	89,940	62.2	76,183	43.0
Altoona	79.9	13.8	80.8	72.2	86.6	6.7	20,230	-0.9	1,135	5.6	36,294	56.3	29,276	41.5
Bethel Park	71.2	44.5	92.0	88.9	94.3	1.7	17,107	-0.2	695	4.1	26,707	62.0	19,369	51.3
Bethlehem	77.8	25.5	91.2	82.6	81.0	9.9	37,427	0.0	2,079	5.6	63,486	62.2	52,211	47.1
Chester	51.8	32.6	79.6	64.1	81.0	10.4	13,325	0.2	1,132	8.5	26,968	54.5	23,021	35.1
Easton	66.9	33.5	86.7	74.6	78.7	9.3	11,977	-0.1	758	6.3	23,394	62.4	20,325	46.0
Erie	74.9	16.6	82.8	72.9	82.0	5.8	44,198	-2.1	2,838	6.4	77,635	58.9	64,507	41.6
Harrisburg	64.7	17.8	88.1	76.8	68.4	11.3	21,487	0.1	1,492	6.9	37,853	64.4	33,027	42.9
Hazleton	71.3	20.4	80.5	69.0	NA	NA	11,633	0.7	1,119	9.6	20,860	63.4	16,445	41.6
Lancaster	61.6	25.5	83.3	73.1	73.5	8.3	26,937	0.1	1,530	5.7	47,022	66.2	40,976	43.6
Lebanon	75.7	21.5	82.2	78.0	84.2	3.7	11,547	-0.3	684	5.9	19,564	66.5	16,153	45.2
Monroeville	74.7	51.8	91.1	87.9	92.2	3.3	14,583	-0.3	667	4.6	24,566	62.5	17,731	54.8
Norristown	65.2	43.7	83.9	71.6	77.0	7.2	18,138	0.4	890	4.9	25,405	72.2	21,622	51.4
Philadelphia	50.7	54.6	84.1	73.5	84.5	5.6	704,053	0.1	43,980	6.2	1,259,066	59.7	1,057,461	44.9
Pittsburgh	54.4	34.3	87.3	79.4	77.8	9.8	157,058	-0.2	7,740	4.9	262,207	63.6	217,736	46.7
Plum	87.0	46.6	90.5	89.9	NA	NA	14,969	-0.2	667	4.5	21,989	66.1	16,472	57.1
Reading	55.5	29.2	83.1	75.9	82.2	3.5	33,925	-0.3	2,476	7.3	65,697	57.1	56,171	35.3
Scranton	71.5	21.5	81.8	70.7	85.3	8.1	36,801	-0.5	1,984	5.4	62,966	56.3	49,344	41.3
State College	34.5	7.3	94.6	82.3	41.8	37.3	16,398	-0.5	752	4.6	40,761	47.4	37,827	21.8
Wilkes-Barre	71.5	16.9	78.2	68.2	74.9	9.0	18,500	-0.4	1,258	6.8	31,514	56.1	25,458	38.8
Williamsport	68.1	8.8	84.4	78.6	79.2	5.6	13,457	-1.8	866	6.4	22,533	61.5	18,635	40.2
York	74.1	32.5	82.1	72.9	74.0	6.3	17,835	-0.1	1,517	8.5	33,463	59.2	29,087	38.4
RHODE ISLAND	80.3	32.7	88.0	82.3	85.9	5.7	554,658	0.2	24,791	4.5	874,310	63.9	700,255	48.8
Cranston	87.0	23.3	86.9	83.1	88.5	2.9	41,328	0.2	1,777	4.3	68,668	62.9	52,734	53.8
East Providence	87.3	39.5	83.3	75.5	83.8	5.5	24,295	0.3	1,182	4.9	39,861	64.8	29,837	59.9
Pawtucket	81.9	31.1	88.1	79.7	87.7	2.9	36,299	0.3	1,868	5.1	58,640	66.3	50,517	48.7
Providence	63.6	27.2	84.3	74.5	78.4	7.2	86,438	0.1	4,653	5.4	142,773	62.3	126,427	39.7
Warwick	88.6	32.0	86.4	82.8	86.3	7.4	46,040	0.4	1,777	3.9	69,566	63.2	52,061	51.0
Woonsocket	78.5	35.9	86.7	81.7	81.5	7.0	19,032	-0.2	1,146	6.0	33,639	61.7	27,802	45.5
SOUTH CAROLINA	82.5	34.8	87.1	76.7	85.2	7.2	2,312,651	0.8	98,757	4.3	3,986,784	60.5	3,156,637	49.2
Aiken	86.5	39.9	92.9	88.6	70.7	12.2	13,426	0.4	610	4.5	24,590	54.1	17,936	46.5
Anderson	77.4	20.7	77.9	64.8	72.7	12.7	11,684	0.6	509	4.4	22,039	57.8	15,924	47.0
Charleston	74.9	29.4	91.7	77.5	83.8	8.3	73,246	1.6	2,476	3.4	117,783	67.2	97,998	54.3
Columbia	64.7	14.4	91.3	80.1	62.1	25.6	60,272	-0.5	2,817	4.7	115,529	64.6	102,097	40.2
Florence	88.4	19.6	86.4	74.2	84.4	3.7	18,978	0.1	859	4.5	29,677	60.3	22,915	56.7
Goose Creek	81.4	39.2	94.1	92.4	80.6	11.5	19,525	1.4	759	3.9	34,037	69.5	30,097	57.8
Greenville	84.8	13.1	86.2	76.7	72.2	10.2	35,315	0.8	1,263	3.6	54,367	67.5	44,921	52.5
Greer	80.2	34.7	89.8	82.2	88.0	6.5	15,308	1.5	523	3.4	23,525	77.1	20,551	57.6
Hilton Head Island	76.2	21.8	95.7	88.6	87.7	3.7	18,083	2.2	613	3.4	34,966	58.1	22,046	56.5
Mount Pleasant	78.3	27.9	96.2	93.6	84.0	6.1	46,165	1.7	1,359	2.9	64,615	67.3	52,484	61.6
Myrtle Beach	74.2	12.4	91.9	74.4	85.5	9.3	15,405	1.9	861	5.6	25,936	53.4	19,165	47.0
North Charleston	81.6	37.7	86.9	67.7	82.8	8.9	52,508	1.4	2,060	3.9	87,696	62.9	76,375	47.8
Rock Hill	81.8	36.0	90.6	84.0	82.2	10.7	38,679	2.0	1,755	4.5	56,609	67.3	47,118	49.2
Spartanburg	79.8	24.5	77.4	70.8	78.7	6.9	17,209	2.7	836	4.9	30,337	60.0	24,521	47.3
Summerville	83.2	55.7	94.8	87.4	83.3	7.6	23,794	1.6	932	3.9	39,240	69.3	33,296	59.4
Sumter	82.9	17.2	80.6	72.3	77.2	12.4	16,081	-0.2	863	5.4	31,846	62.0	25,176	49.2
SOUTH DAKOTA	79.9	15.2	87.6	79.6	84.4	7.8	455,175	0.7	15,147	3.3	673,517	67.9	535,948	56.0
Aberdeen	78.0	3.3	88.3	80.5	81.7	8.9	15,155	-0.6	470	3.1	22,965	61.6	18,270	50.7
Rapid City	83.2	5.8	89.4	80.6	80.9	6.5	36,573	1.7	1,232	3.4	58,144	63.1	45,198	48.6
Sioux Falls	84.0	9.7	91.1	86.0	80.9	8.4	101,756	1.8	2,902	2.9	133,814	74.4	111,712	63.3
TENNESSEE	83.5	35.5	85.5	76.3	85.8	6.0	3,198,767	2.0	118,557	3.7	5,320,715	60.6	4,275,460	49.3
Bartlett	88.4	41.8	90.8	89.0	85.9	2.9	30,816	1.3	1,001	3.2	44,731	58.1	33,873	53.9
Brentwood	82.8	40.9	98.8	96.8	90.2	5.9	21,724	3.8	618	2.8	30,439	64.2	25,063	50.7
Bristol	82.5	29.6	87.0	80.4	91.4	3.3	11,879	0.1	470	4.0	22,599	62.6	17,158	53.0
Chattanooga	82.5	19.4	82.2	75.0	85.2	5.5	83,614	2.6	3,286	3.9	146,302	59.4	119,086	47.7
Clarksville	89.5	28.5	88.7	79.5	78.5	12.6	60,022	1.3	2,567	4.3	113,692	65.6	100,103	52.9
Cleveland	83.4	25.3	84.0	71.9	73.6	8.5	20,661	-0.1	768	3.7	35,327	59.3	28,352	46.1
Collierville	85.2	37.5	96.3	93.6	88.0	5.3	25,247	1.5	753	3.0	37,401	67.1	31,444	51.4

1. Employed persons.   2. Households.   3. Percent of civilian labor force.

Table D. Cities — City Government Finances

AREANAME	General revenue Total (mil dol) 117	Intergovernmental Total (mil dol) 118	Intergovernmental Percent from state government 119	Taxes Total (mil dol) 120	Taxes Per capita (dollars) Total 121	Taxes Per capita (dollars) Property 122	Taxes Per capita (dollars) Sales and gross receipts 123	General expenditure Total (mil dol) 124	General expenditure Per capita (dollars) Total 125	General expenditure Per capita (dollars) Capital outlays 126
OREGON— Cont'd										
Redmond	35.3	5.9	60.8	13.4	502	328	174	32.9	1,229	258
Salem	251.3	76.0	63.8	101.3	642	489	153	240.9	1,527	209
Springfield	103.6	9.1	99.1	32.9	549	452	97	90.7	1,514	262
Tigard	45.1	9.8	49.5	26.0	522	305	217	43.3	870	90
Tualatin	29.9	5.6	64.3	13.3	498	310	188	27.4	1,025	191
West Linn	24.0	5.0	70.0	11.3	439	271	168	22.2	865	100
PENNSYLVANIA	X	X	X	X	X	X	X	X	X	X
Allentown	129.2	30.4	47.0	56.8	477	247	115	175.0	1,471	88
Altoona	29.3	7.5	47.2	17.6	381	194	73	27.1	587	40
Bethel Park	24.5	2.7	71.8	13.8	427	131	46	25.6	790	60
Bethlehem	101.1	27.5	100.0	47.5	632	280	117	89.6	1,193	0
Chester	47.9	12.2	79.6	19.2	563	252	84	45.6	1,340	83
Easton	52.4	14.3	75.3	14.8	546	331	69	53.4	1,967	129
Erie	113.3	23.8	46.1	46.9	464	337	53	105.0	1,039	74
Harrisburg	93.9	6.2	90.0	30.4	616	345	171	78.7	1,595	121
Hazleton	18.6	7.2	55.0	8.3	329	113	39	13.3	528	65
Lancaster	69.1	11.7	71.8	31.0	522	384	54	87.4	1,472	261
Lebanon	21.7	10.2	34.6	8.3	325	116	37	26.5	1,036	259
Monroeville	23.1	1.7	95.3	19.7	695	159	284	30.1	1,058	116
Norristown	28.2	3.4	47.9	21.6	627	320	95	30.2	875	85
Philadelphia	6,411.8	2,254.7	74.3	3,239.1	2,089	323	474	5,483.2	3,537	209
Pittsburgh	607.0	163.6	87.2	357.2	1,166	443	419	548.9	1,791	25
Plum	13.3	1.8	85.5	9.6	352	192	32	13.6	498	25
Reading	139.8	30.8	89.3	42.9	488	220	111	135.9	1,543	96
Scranton	67.6	10.7	95.5	45.2	593	179	69	70.2	923	3
State College	36.3	5.5	55.6	11.4	272	114	42	35.4	843	78
Wilkes-Barre	52.9	20.4	46.2	24.1	583	208	78	57.3	1,386	201
Williamsport	41.3	20.3	45.8	15.5	526	329	123	30.5	1,035	151
York	68.7	9.7	51.4	24.7	566	395	110	63.2	1,448	39
RHODE ISLAND	X	X	X	X	X	X	X	X	X	X
Cranston	282.2	60.2	92.5	187.4	2,322	2,290	32	256.9	3,184	42
East Providence	148.4	43.6	95.5	91.6	1,942	1,918	24	155.3	3,292	150
Pawtucket	197.7	91.3	77.8	95.5	1,339	1,328	10	192.3	2,697	24
Providence	747.8	292.1	91.6	325.5	1,822	1,765	57	715.3	4,004	160
Warwick	318.8	59.3	98.4	219.5	2,682	2,607	74	303.4	3,707	110
Woonsocket	147.2	67.5	95.5	57.6	1,401	1,352	50	147.3	3,584	80
SOUTH CAROLINA	X	X	X	X	X	X	X	X	X	X
Aiken	42.7	5.6	22.9	23.7	790	330	460	40.3	1,341	206
Anderson	40.2	4.0	38.2	19.7	735	460	275	43.2	1,613	63
Charleston	207.6	27.8	72.1	132.3	1,053	446	607	178.8	1,424	222
Columbia	222.0	28.7	56.5	95.1	721	383	339	189.3	1,435	255
Florence	47.5	3.6	40.8	22.6	603	96	506	40.8	1,086	63
Goose Creek	19.6	0.7	100.0	11.6	298	47	251	20.5	528	67
Greenville	95.3	5.9	100.0	64.6	1,066	598	468	99.6	1,643	290
Greer	28.9	2.8	31.9	15.7	593	370	223	45.5	1,711	36
Hilton Head Island	89.1	35.5	16.2	48.4	1,261	625	586	94.8	2,471	1,299
Mount Pleasant	114.5	34.1	60.2	59.9	833	385	448	106.8	1,486	667
Myrtle Beach	161.3	12.2	83.8	82.5	2,918	878	2,040	123.3	4,360	375
North Charleston	122.2	14.2	23.7	93.4	915	471	408	119.1	1,168	208
Rock Hill	88.3	12.8	15.4	35.8	525	351	174	102.2	1,502	271
Spartanburg	53.3	13.1	6.6	33.4	895	449	446	42.1	1,130	160
Summerville	29.5	3.1	88.8	21.9	494	238	255	26.9	608	53
Sumter	43.8	6.9	24.7	24.0	587	218	369	40.1	980	178
SOUTH DAKOTA	X	X	X	X	X	X	X	X	X	X
Aberdeen	39.6	5.1	70.4	24.2	900	292	609	38.1	1,414	18
Rapid City	138.0	19.9	85.8	75.4	1,077	309	768	126.9	1,813	706
Sioux Falls	226.3	20.3	62.2	149.5	933	282	651	225.7	1,408	474
TENNESSEE	X	X	X	X	X	X	X	X	X	X
Bartlett	55.6	18.3	51.6	21.0	361	305	56	47.7	820	25
Brentwood	49.5	19.7	38.7	18.1	463	278	185	45.0	1,153	330
Bristol	75.0	35.6	60.9	26.6	999	899	101	74.6	2,797	336
Chattanooga	485.4	165.9	19.7	139.3	809	668	141	396.3	2,300	197
Clarksville	137.4	38.8	51.1	37.5	262	197	65	103.9	725	103
Cleveland	109.5	65.6	56.3	19.7	464	400	64	96.6	2,278	237
Collierville	56.6	15.9	37.4	25.4	547	460	87	51.4	1,107	164

1. Based on population estimated as of July 1 of the year shown.

AREANAME	Public welfare	Highways	Parking facilities	Education	Health and hospitals	Police protection	Sewerage and sanitation	Parks and recreation	Housing and community development	Interest on debt
	City government finances, 2012 (cont.)									
	General expenditures (cont.)									
	Percent of total for:									
	127	128	129	130	131	132	133	134	135	136
OREGON— Cont'd										
Redmond	0.0	21.1	0.0	0.0	0.0	15.5	10.0	8.1	3.5	10.2
Salem	0.0	14.5	0.7	0.0	0.5	13.9	12.1	3.7	13.0	8.7
Springfield	0.0	5.4	0.0	0.0	5.6	16.9	38.3	0.0	1.1	4.0
Tigard	0.3	7.7	0.0	0.0	0.0	32.1	6.0	8.9	0.0	3.8
Tualatin	0.0	6.8	0.1	0.0	0.0	16.5	24.6	7.3	13.2	1.4
West Linn	0.0	8.3	0.0	0.0	0.0	26.6	11.1	13.8	0.0	1.9
PENNSYLVANIA	X	X	X	X	X	X	X	X	X	X
Allentown	0.0	8.9	0.0	0.0	3.5	18.4	23.6	4.4	6.1	2.8
Altoona	0.0	14.2	0.0	0.0	0.0	19.2	3.2	1.2	0.4	4.1
Bethel Park	0.0	22.7	0.0	0.0	0.0	23.6	35.2	3.1	0.5	0.9
Bethlehem	0.0	9.0	0.0	0.0	4.0	14.3	14.7	6.1	3.7	7.6
Chester	0.0	7.2	0.0	0.0	1.1	32.8	3.0	11.5	2.2	2.3
Easton	0.0	6.5	0.4	0.0	0.1	15.5	18.0	5.8	18.7	5.4
Erie	0.0	11.3	0.0	0.0	0.0	14.0	14.2	2.1	11.8	7.3
Harrisburg	0.0	7.4	0.0	0.0	0.2	24.9	23.4	3.9	8.6	3.8
Hazleton	0.0	13.4	0.0	0.0	1.1	27.9	2.4	0.8	7.7	3.1
Lancaster	0.0	5.5	0.0	0.0	0.0	20.9	23.8	6.2	5.6	9.3
Lebanon	0.0	53.3	0.1	0.0	0.7	15.7	0.8	1.4	6.1	0.1
Monroeville	0.0	20.1	0.0	0.0	0.3	34.5	4.7	6.1	1.2	3.1
Norristown	0.0	15.4	0.0	0.0	1.6	24.2	5.2	2.1	0.0	4.5
Philadelphia	10.4	2.1	0.0	1.4	24.8	11.1	7.0	1.5	3.5	3.9
Pittsburgh	0.0	0.6	0.0	0.0	2.5	14.1	2.8	3.0	16.9	6.6
Plum	0.0	28.0	0.0	0.0	0.0	29.8	11.8	0.2	0.0	4.0
Reading	0.0	8.0	0.0	0.0	2.7	20.8	21.1	2.8	14.3	8.1
Scranton	0.0	4.2	3.7	0.0	2.3	23.1	4.8	1.1	0.2	11.1
State College	0.0	15.4	4.9	0.0	0.9	24.5	27.4	3.1	3.2	2.6
Wilkes-Barre	0.0	23.8	0.5	0.0	4.6	16.0	7.5	7.7	7.2	7.7
Williamsport	0.0	28.5	0.0	0.0	0.0	21.9	14.1	2.4	3.5	1.1
York	0.0	6.2	0.9	0.0	3.2	15.4	23.5	4.9	6.1	8.0
RHODE ISLAND	X	X	X	X	X	X	X	X	X	X
Cranston	0.0	6.7	0.0	55.8	1.1	9.1	6.7	0.9	0.6	2.1
East Providence	0.0	3.8	0.0	57.0	0.3	7.9	7.4	1.5	0.8	1.9
Pawtucket	0.0	1.0	0.0	62.2	0.0	8.3	1.9	0.8	1.8	1.1
Providence	0.0	1.4	0.0	53.6	0.0	11.5	1.4	1.2	2.1	5.7
Warwick	0.4	2.3	0.0	56.7	0.1	6.4	4.3	0.7	0.4	1.6
Woonsocket	0.2	1.6	0.0	53.4	0.1	6.0	10.2	0.1	1.1	8.0
SOUTH CAROLINA	X	X	X	X	X	X	X	X	X	X
Aiken	0.0	7.0	0.0	0.0	0.0	22.5	13.8	12.3	1.7	0.1
Anderson	0.0	8.9	1.2	0.0	0.0	14.1	22.7	7.2	3.6	9.8
Charleston	0.4	3.1	5.1	0.0	0.0	22.4	4.6	13.3	3.8	1.7
Columbia	0.0	4.0	1.7	0.0	0.7	13.1	43.5	7.0	3.2	2.4
Florence	0.0	6.9	0.0	0.0	0.1	23.0	19.5	15.0	6.8	1.0
Goose Creek	0.0	12.8	0.0	0.0	0.0	27.9	5.4	24.9	0.0	0.3
Greenville	0.0	7.1	3.2	0.0	0.5	18.3	13.4	14.0	4.6	2.4
Greer	0.0	2.8	0.0	0.0	0.0	10.2	60.8	3.3	1.8	7.7
Hilton Head Island	0.0	1.9	0.0	0.0	0.0	6.5	2.0	0.0	30.1	4.5
Mount Pleasant	0.0	41.5	0.0	0.0	0.0	10.2	14.4	4.9	1.7	4.1
Myrtle Beach	0.0	3.8	1.5	0.0	0.0	16.0	11.8	19.5	3.8	7.6
North Charleston	0.0	4.5	0.5	0.0	0.0	25.1	8.9	5.1	1.0	5.2
Rock Hill	0.0	2.7	0.0	0.0	0.0	13.2	22.9	12.5	2.9	3.6
Spartanburg	0.0	6.2	2.3	0.0	0.0	22.3	4.7	7.7	4.1	5.1
Summerville	0.0	11.9	0.0	0.0	0.0	23.8	8.6	7.7	0.1	1.8
Sumter	0.0	1.7	0.0	0.0	0.0	23.3	16.2	12.9	8.3	0.8
SOUTH DAKOTA	X	X	X	X	X	X	X	X	X	X
Aberdeen	0.0	29.4	0.0	0.0	3.2	9.7	7.1	15.7	0.0	2.8
Rapid City	0.6	19.1	0.5	0.0	2.8	10.2	14.4	12.7	1.8	3.0
Sioux Falls	0.0	19.1	0.9	0.0	4.2	12.3	22.3	14.2	2.2	3.2
TENNESSEE	X	X	X	X	X	X	X	X	X	X
Bartlett	0.7	8.5	0.0	0.0	5.6	26.6	15.0	11.0	0.0	2.2
Brentwood	0.0	19.3	0.0	0.5	0.2	13.3	16.6	5.6	0.0	3.8
Bristol	0.0	4.9	0.0	54.1	0.0	9.0	9.0	5.1	0.9	1.0
Chattanooga	3.7	5.6	0.4	0.0	0.6	13.8	18.8	6.1	2.6	4.4
Clarksville	0.0	10.6	0.3	0.0	0.0	22.6	26.1	6.1	1.6	6.6
Cleveland	0.0	6.0	0.0	47.1	0.6	9.4	11.6	2.5	1.3	2.9
Collierville	0.7	12.6	0.0	0.0	1.6	20.1	14.9	7.5	0.0	2.6

Table D. Cities — Accommodation and Food Services, Arts, Entertainment, and Recreation, and Health Care and Social Assistance

AREANAME	Accommodaton and food services, 2012				Arts, entertainment, and recreation[1], 2012				Health care and social assistance,[1] 2012			
	Number of establishments	Number of employees	Receipts (mil dol)	Annual payroll (mil dol)	Number of establishments	Number of employees	Receipts (mil dol)	Annual payroll (mil dol)	Number of establishments	Number of employees	Receipts (mil dol)	Annual payroll (mil dol)
	92	93	94	95	96	97	98	99	100	101	102	103
TENNESSEE— Cont'd												
Columbia	101	1,771	81.2	22.3	7	D	D	D	136	D	D	D
Cookeville	137	D	D	D	10	D	D	D	173	D	D	D
Franklin	281	6,519	337.0	97.6	95	D	D	D	285	4,901	744.3	269.8
Gallatin	58	905	44.3	12.2	6	D	D	D	84	D	D	D
Germantown	70	1,454	82.7	22.4	13	130	5.8	1.9	191	D	D	D
Hendersonville	112	2,638	113.7	34.6	26	D	D	D	142	2,039	249.7	85.2
Jackson	210	4,703	220.3	62.4	17	D	D	D	261	D	D	D
Johnson City	239	5,668	249.2	72.7	16	D	D	D	252	D	D	D
Kingsport	193	4,387	199.6	58.9	19	D	D	D	228	3,761	503.7	220.1
Knoxville	714	17,958	865.1	267.4	47	548	34.6	9.6	755	16,303	2,046.1	772.1
La Vergne	29	412	20.6	5.3	NA	NA	NA	NA	15	143	7.3	3.6
Lebanon	108	2,239	98.8	28.6	8	D	D	D	136	2,476	294.2	114.8
Maryville	94	1,644	75.5	22.0	13	D	D	D	140	1,629	171.3	82.1
Memphis	1,243	28,822	1,503.9	425.7	82	1,976	210.8	102.7	1,415	26,987	2,964.4	1,216.1
Morristown	106	D	D	D	9	D	D	D	123	2,306	227.8	96.0
Murfreesboro	314	7,922	356.0	105.3	21	D	D	D	327	6,004	576.4	262.1
Nashville-Davidson	1,714	40,106	2,573.8	759.3	665	4,720	1,476.9	524.5	1,467	30,924	4,176.2	1,568.7
Oak Ridge	74	1,604	76.3	21.4	6	101	4.6	1.6	101	D	D	D
Smyrna	109	2,367	112.1	32.0	6	D	D	D	117	D	D	D
Spring Hill	57	1,188	45.9	14.2	9	19	3.6	0.5	35	D	D	D
TEXAS	48,721	976,390	54,480.8	14,743.8	4,966	83,587	7,770.7	2,523.6	55,176	945,659	93,988.1	36,493.1
Abilene	284	D	D	D	34	258	21.1	4.0	316	7,710	657.8	271.4
Allen	170	3,771	194.3	56.4	24	462	25.4	8.1	259	D	D	D
Amarillo	500	10,147	514.1	139.7	52	687	38.7	11.3	567	10,579	1,228.0	437.8
Arlington	684	15,492	910.8	233.2	67	3,881	616.2	255.2	865	15,821	1,542.7	638.3
Austin	2,517	55,702	3,474.7	962.5	317	4,559	468.8	144.0	2,329	37,842	4,746.7	1,859.6
Baytown	174	3,836	193.7	52.2	12	D	D	D	213	D	D	D
Beaumont	283	6,727	320.7	88.3	35	D	D	D	501	D	D	D
Bedford	93	1,993	98.5	27.8	9	D	D	D	191	D	D	D
Big Spring	71	1,057	61.0	13.8	3	D	D	D	57	D	D	D
Brownsville	299	5,246	244.3	65.5	26	D	D	D	418	13,860	789.1	346.9
Bryan	139	2,436	115.0	32.5	13	D	D	D	186	2,546	275.6	118.1
Burleson	105	2,511	112.7	31.4	8	D	D	D	95	1,020	82.2	34.5
Carrollton	244	3,204	187.6	49.4	27	D	D	D	328	3,721	410.7	148.7
Cedar Hill	86	2,068	97.8	25.6	6	D	D	D	79	1,220	84.9	30.5
Cedar Park	137	2,517	119.2	31.5	20	D	D	D	163	D	D	D
Cleburne	81	1,365	63.3	18.1	7	68	3.7	0.6	99	D	D	D
College Station	287	6,966	327.7	88.0	21	330	14.7	5.0	136	D	D	D
Conroe	164	3,450	175.2	48.5	10	125	11.6	1.4	200	D	D	D
Coppell	73	1,538	93.3	22.2	9	159	6.8	2.3	106	D	D	D
Copperas Cove	50	934	42.1	10.8	3	D	D	D	27	426	22.3	10.3
Corpus Christi	749	15,806	825.4	223.7	57	D	D	D	907	17,743	1,577.5	620.5
Dallas	2,687	59,649	3,851.5	1,087.3	283	4,840	477.0	208.1	3,535	56,873	8,201.1	3,427.0
Deer Park	44	769	46.6	11.2	2	D	D	D	45	D	D	D
Del Rio	87	1,613	76.2	19.5	7	41	1.1	0.5	84	D	D	D
Denton	283	5,961	277.1	75.9	20	291	15.1	4.0	390	6,232	770.2	285.0
DeSoto	60	1,240	63.9	17.8	5	89	5.7	2.1	165	3,622	236.3	105.8
Duncanville	60	1,406	69.0	19.1	5	101	5.7	1.5	101	2,187	105.2	47.1
Eagle Pass	65	D	D	D	7	D	D	D	81	D	D	D
Edinburg	120	1,970	102.3	25.9	12	D	D	D	331	9,143	433.5	212.2
El Paso	1,362	27,187	1,310.8	354.0	89	D	D	D	1,300	26,860	2,875.1	1,005.3
Euless	89	1,538	76.0	20.2	5	D	D	D	77	D	D	D
Farmers Branch	99	1,493	83.9	25.9	6	D	D	D	136	2,292	285.2	112.7
Flower Mound	118	2,866	157.4	42.2	23	411	26.0	7.3	178	1,971	257.9	91.6
Fort Worth	1,288	28,324	1,609.5	440.5	134	2,108	225.1	46.6	1,602	24,161	2,738.6	1,078.8
Friendswood	70	1,121	55.0	14.1	11	D	D	D	111	D	D	D
Frisco	254	6,182	360.8	100.4	41	1,555	148.3	83.1	394	D	D	D
Galveston	212	6,605	391.2	110.0	22	480	35.2	7.9	85	D	D	D
Garland	309	5,540	286.8	79.7	31	504	40.5	9.4	414	7,134	439.2	187.8
Georgetown	103	2,188	109.6	30.5	14	D	D	D	152	2,278	225.8	90.9
Grand Prairie	216	3,855	221.9	54.6	21	D	D	D	234	2,519	181.0	66.5
Grapevine	175	7,278	628.9	152.0	17	379	26.3	5.7	186	D	D	D
Greenville	68	1,304	65.2	17.1	4	D	D	D	110	D	D	D
Haltom City	72	735	37.6	9.0	7	49	4.1	0.5	35	D	D	D
Harker Heights	63	951	37.1	10.2	15	D	D	D	34	D	D	D
Harlingen	170	3,749	203.8	57.5	16	D	D	D	334	11,017	834.5	354.0
Houston	5,645	122,643	7,746.6	2,082.8	442	10,362	1,681.5	523.7	6,526	105,192	11,479.2	4,372.6
Huntsville	94	D	D	D	3	D	D	D	78	D	D	D
Hurst	103	2,129	126.6	32.5	14	182	9.7	2.5	130	D	D	D

1. Establishments subject to federal tax.

AREANAME	Other services[1]				Government employment and payroll, 2012								
					Full-time equivalent employees	March payroll							
						Total (dollars)	Percent of total for:						
	Number of establish-ments	Number of employees	Receipts (mil dol)	Annual payroll (mil dol)			Adminis-trative, judicial, and legal	Police and corrections	Fire protection	Highways and trans-portation	Health and welfare	Natural resources and utilities	Education and libraries
	104	105	106	107	108	109	110	111	112	113	114	115	116
TENNESSEE—Cont'd													
Columbia	57	381	30.1	9.6	492	1,828,149	7.0	18.8	18.5	8.4	0.0	42.6	0.0
Cookeville	80	413	34.4	9.2	2,260	9,757,664	1.2	3.6	1.9	1.3	85.3	5.8	0.0
Franklin	133	1,096	75.2	26.9	635	2,507,514	14.1	24.5	24.1	7.9	2.9	21.9	0.0
Gallatin	46	230	20.9	6.9	429	1,515,188	8.8	22.7	17.5	5.7	0.0	40.3	0.0
Germantown	51	506	24.7	9.6	286	1,166,262	0.4	46.4	32.0	8.9	0.0	6.3	0.0
Hendersonville	78	421	27.5	8.9	317	1,225,951	9.7	37.8	33.9	3.9	0.4	5.6	0.0
Jackson	91	D	D	D	732	2,706,306	10.3	39.0	26.4	6.9	0.2	15.5	0.0
Johnson City	104	D	D	D	2,069	7,207,080	4.3	9.1	5.7	7.6	0.0	24.2	46.3
Kingsport	83	531	48.6	15.0	2,088	7,112,728	4.6	8.2	5.7	3.4	0.1	9.0	66.2
Knoxville	392	3,196	242.1	83.5	2,544	10,707,196	7.3	20.0	11.8	5.2	1.3	49.6	0.0
La Vergne	24	794	124.4	25.1	165	495,446	15.9	42.8	0.0	4.2	0.0	26.3	4.3
Lebanon	56	657	63.8	20.5	337	1,064,568	9.9	34.9	13.8	8.3	1.8	27.1	0.0
Maryville	50	266	19.8	6.8	929	3,586,065	5.2	6.5	5.0	4.0	0.0	15.5	63.0
Memphis	712	5,678	522.2	172.5	24,196	79,305,378	2.0	15.7	10.1	4.9	0.8	25.5	40.2
Morristown	49	245	21.5	6.7	417	1,625,386	6.0	20.1	18.2	6.1	0.3	38.5	0.0
Murfreesboro	167	1,164	91.2	29.6	2,265	7,333,077	3.8	13.4	9.7	3.3	0.2	20.3	45.7
Nashville-Davidson	868	8,126	726.0	233.6	21,697	83,700,973	6.4	13.3	7.5	1.1	9.0	11.1	49.9
Oak Ridge	44	D	D	D	1,132	4,632,934	5.5	7.1	8.2	4.8	1.0	10.3	62.3
Smyrna	46	442	34.2	16.1	426	1,763,154	14.1	27.9	24.5	2.1	0.0	27.9	0.0
Spring Hill	26	136	10.8	3.2	153	514,319	5.2	29.3	24.9	4.9	0.0	23.4	4.4
TEXAS	28,255	216,219	21,861.4	6,765.6	X	X	X	X	X	X	X	X	X
Abilene	162	1,407	104.9	34.0	1,115	4,154,689	10.5	32.0	23.1	4.8	5.7	16.9	2.3
Allen	81	693	53.5	17.3	662	2,925,255	11.5	28.9	20.0	3.9	2.3	27.3	4.5
Amarillo	296	2,035	192.1	55.1	2,117	7,521,677	9.3	27.1	24.7	8.3	4.8	19.1	2.1
Arlington	374	2,410	207.6	61.6	2,551	12,130,944	13.1	38.1	20.5	5.1	4.7	13.8	2.7
Austin	1,319	11,317	1,060.8	331.5	12,580	64,599,610	10.4	24.1	13.4	7.1	8.1	30.6	1.9
Baytown	87	779	71.7	24.8	748	3,193,832	12.8	28.9	19.0	2.5	7.2	18.6	3.5
Beaumont	178	1,744	180.5	55.1	1,387	7,544,738	11.5	29.5	22.1	6.9	9.1	14.8	1.6
Bedford	55	334	28.4	8.5	396	1,910,062	12.2	44.6	25.8	2.3	0.9	11.0	3.3
Big Spring	28	D	D	D	255	860,648	10.2	23.3	19.7	6.6	10.8	21.6	0.0
Brownsville	98	498	35.4	11.2	1,660	6,576,268	6.3	28.3	16.9	10.1	3.1	22.4	2.2
Bryan	120	727	64.4	18.2	926	4,516,110	3.1	19.6	11.5	1.8	0.7	38.5	3.0
Burleson	66	364	26.8	8.7	314	1,837,857	11.3	27.1	16.3	3.9	5.4	20.8	2.6
Carrollton	168	1,866	164.0	66.9	750	3,791,660	11.3	30.8	28.1	4.7	3.6	12.4	3.2
Cedar Hill	35	227	19.1	5.7	345	1,415,937	9.4	29.5	24.7	6.8	4.1	17.5	2.3
Cedar Park	105	720	53.2	19.3	366	1,608,634	12.6	30.9	18.4	2.3	0.5	20.7	3.2
Cleburne	51	317	28.3	8.6	331	1,384,254	10.9	25.9	23.1	7.1	3.7	23.7	1.6
College Station	75	549	34.1	11.0	818	3,487,614	20.0	22.9	18.5	6.9	0.0	27.4	0.0
Conroe	104	679	59.5	17.1	506	2,148,894	13.0	28.8	20.3	9.4	1.3	18.9	0.0
Coppell	48	964	119.8	36.7	374	2,007,729	18.0	24.0	25.7	6.8	0.9	15.3	4.2
Copperas Cove	42	228	21.2	5.7	265	875,963	7.7	30.2	19.1	1.6	1.2	17.4	2.0
Corpus Christi	358	3,496	346.7	116.1	2,747	10,789,288	5.1	28.6	19.2	4.2	3.3	21.1	1.6
Dallas	1,450	12,565	1,440.8	409.3	14,235	67,511,933	7.3	31.8	17.3	19.3	4.4	14.9	1.2
Deer Park	58	906	130.9	49.5	328	1,382,968	18.7	32.7	5.3	2.7	0.0	31.9	2.9
Del Rio	32	D	D	D	479	1,348,047	13.5	25.7	21.8	5.8	8.4	17.9	0.0
Denton	150	972	89.5	27.1	1,265	6,238,827	15.5	19.1	17.6	2.9	1.6	38.3	2.8
DeSoto	39	154	15.1	4.3	317	1,509,174	9.4	33.2	25.8	4.2	5.1	12.0	3.0
Duncanville	63	321	32.4	8.9	262	1,180,545	13.5	32.0	24.0	4.8	0.9	15.2	3.2
Eagle Pass	29	126	7.5	2.1	351	916,457	7.8	31.5	17.9	15.9	3.9	20.4	1.6
Edinburg	69	313	21.9	6.5	687	2,190,991	12.2	35.3	5.2	5.7	1.0	33.1	3.3
El Paso	714	4,354	334.6	101.8	5,996	23,812,936	7.0	28.9	21.6	16.9	1.4	12.9	2.2
Euless	59	D	D	D	434	2,144,456	12.6	34.2	21.4	3.9	1.0	17.4	4.5
Farmers Branch	53	615	61.6	17.3	372	1,986,448	11.5	30.7	24.2	3.4	5.2	21.2	0.0
Flower Mound	88	931	73.4	25.9	440	1,883,026	25.4	26.1	22.5	3.5	4.1	11.7	3.5
Fort Worth	700	6,296	605.7	172.5	6,536	32,292,472	9.5	36.9	20.2	4.1	1.8	17.7	2.4
Friendswood	57	303	22.4	7.9	194	961,732	21.4	48.5	0.4	6.3	7.0	10.9	5.4
Frisco	142	1,037	80.7	26.6	594	2,715,180	9.9	30.4	23.9	5.3	1.2	19.8	3.8
Galveston	64	301	25.2	8.2	808	3,423,101	7.9	29.1	17.6	21.5	3.7	16.9	0.0
Garland	230	1,159	100.6	32.4	1,920	9,882,194	9.5	22.2	17.3	5.1	4.8	30.5	2.2
Georgetown	75	446	37.7	12.4	540	2,310,226	14.5	21.6	17.8	5.7	3.2	24.6	2.8
Grand Prairie	143	1,111	98.2	32.3	1,169	5,599,824	10.7	29.3	27.8	5.1	5.9	13.3	1.6
Grapevine	69	662	56.1	18.8	572	2,942,808	10.6	24.3	22.7	7.0	1.2	13.7	2.9
Greenville	36	211	16.2	5.5	403	1,671,286	7.6	21.2	16.8	3.9	1.7	41.0	1.8
Haltom City	65	D	D	D	281	1,111,357	13.5	36.6	17.0	6.0	1.5	13.9	4.9
Harker Heights	32	151	9.1	2.7	218	830,939	17.0	29.4	23.6	4.0	1.0	16.2	3.2
Harlingen	91	501	34.2	10.3	751	2,448,262	8.2	27.6	19.8	7.2	2.5	27.1	1.8
Houston	3,244	31,771	3,283.0	1,045.9	21,007	99,616,057	8.7	36.5	20.9	7.6	4.6	8.9	1.5
Huntsville	41	244	21.2	5.3	308	1,115,825	24.2	27.0	5.3	6.6	0.0	23.7	2.4
Hurst	71	450	31.1	10.3	371	1,783,347	13.7	36.1	21.5	5.6	0.0	15.6	6.0

1. Establishments subject to federal tax.

AREANAME	Percent Hispanic or Latino[1], 2016	Percent foreign born, 2016	Age of population (percent), 2016							Median age 2016	Percent female 2016	Population Census counts		Percent change	
			Under 18 years	18 to 24 years	25 to 34 years	35 to 44 years	45 to 54 years	55 to 64 years	65 years and over			2000	2010	2000-2010	2010-2017
	12	13	14	15	16	17	18	19	20	21	22	23	24	25	26
TEXAS— Cont'd															
Irving	43.5	38.5	26.2	10.4	18.9	16.0	12.5	7.9	8.2	32.0	50.8	191,615	216,285	12.9	11.1
Keller	9.8	6.4	28.4	8.0	7.8	13.4	18.6	11.7	12.0	39.3	54.8	27,345	39,627	44.9	19.3
Killeen	24.9	8.8	30.9	12.6	20.3	13.3	10.5	6.8	5.6	27.8	51.2	86,911	127,696	46.9	13.9
Kingsville	72.3	6.4	20.4	24.4	12.6	8.7	9.1	9.3	15.5	28.9	46.5	25,575	26,213	2.5	-2.8
Kyle	51.8	6.7	32.9	7.5	18.7	17.4	7.2	8.0	8.3	28.2	50.4	5,314	28,257	431.7	53.9
Lake Jackson	30.8	15.6	25.9	8.8	13.0	14.1	12.1	15.5	10.6	37.7	52.8	26,386	26,832	1.7	2.4
Lancaster	15.9	6.2	34.4	8.2	11.9	12.5	16.5	9.2	7.3	30.6	56.1	25,894	36,664	41.6	7.4
La Porte	34.0	10.8	23.7	9.2	15.8	11.8	14.4	12.5	12.6	35.6	51.3	31,880	33,806	6.0	4.6
Laredo	95.4	28.3	33.9	11.3	13.6	13.1	10.8	8.3	9.0	28.2	51.5	176,576	236,057	33.7	10.4
League City	22.4	9.0	25.8	9.5	17.0	12.8	13.1	10.9	10.8	33.7	51.7	45,444	83,563	83.9	25.5
Leander	17.2	7.9	34.6	4.3	9.4	16.4	14.3	11.2	9.8	35.8	53.0	7,596	26,697	251.5	84.4
Lewisville	33.5	20.8	25.6	8.8	18.3	15.8	11.9	10.6	9.1	33.3	50.6	77,737	95,393	22.7	11.1
Little Elm	24.4	16.7	34.3	5.0	15.5	20.4	12.8	5.5	6.5	33.8	51.2	3,646	25,877	609.7	79.9
Longview	17.8	11.1	24.6	10.3	12.9	12.9	11.5	12.2	15.6	35.9	50.6	73,344	80,425	9.7	1.4
Lubbock	35.4	5.9	23.0	19.1	15.4	11.3	9.5	9.4	12.2	29.7	50.1	199,564	229,627	15.1	10.6
Lufkin	23.1	8.2	23.6	12.6	10.8	12.4	11.9	12.1	16.7	37.4	54.5	32,709	35,106	7.3	2.1
McAllen	83.9	27.3	29.9	10.1	14.0	11.1	11.3	9.6	13.9	32.6	50.4	106,414	131,029	23.1	8.9
McKinney	19.3	16.3	27.9	7.8	13.2	16.7	13.7	10.2	10.5	35.6	50.3	54,369	131,160	141.2	38.3
Mansfield	17.9	11.8	30.6	6.6	13.3	16.2	14.7	10.0	8.5	34.7	54.2	28,031	56,421	101.3	22.2
Mesquite	39.2	18.9	29.2	10.7	12.7	12.7	13.2	11.7	9.8	32.8	53.6	124,523	139,518	12.0	3.2
Midland	45.2	11.8	27.7	9.3	18.5	13.0	10.6	10.2	10.7	32.0	50.7	94,996	111,190	17.0	22.4
Mission	91.4	27.5	33.9	9.4	12.1	13.1	13.4	7.1	11.1	30.5	50.1	45,408	77,690	71.1	8.7
Missouri City	16.2	19.2	23.2	9.2	10.8	13.4	13.7	15.8	13.8	38.6	54.9	52,913	66,688	26.0	11.7
Nacogdoches	18.8	6.1	20.9	32.2	11.1	8.3	9.0	7.2	11.2	24.1	55.4	29,914	32,934	10.1	2.1
New Braunfels	32.8	8.1	24.5	9.1	12.3	14.6	12.4	11.4	15.8	37.5	52.2	36,494	57,729	58.2	37.1
North Richland Hills	15.8	6.5	23.5	8.3	15.1	10.3	14.1	12.8	15.8	37.2	54.6	55,635	63,343	13.9	11.2
Odessa	57.0	11.9	27.8	11.1	17.0	11.3	10.6	11.6	10.7	31.0	50.2	90,943	99,876	9.8	17.0
Paris	11.6	5.0	22.2	5.4	11.2	12.5	14.2	12.9	21.6	43.6	54.1	25,898	25,251	-2.5	-1.8
Pasadena	65.5	26.0	30.2	12.0	15.0	9.8	13.4	10.1	9.5	30.2	52.7	141,674	149,307	5.4	2.8
Pearland	17.5	15.3	26.7	9.6	12.6	16.5	14.3	10.0	10.3	36.1	51.1	37,640	93,120	147.4	28.8
Pflugerville	24.3	15.9	25.3	6.6	16.5	16.4	15.2	11.6	8.5	35.8	51.8	16,335	48,366	196.1	31.0
Pharr	92.5	32.7	33.7	7.4	14.8	12.4	11.1	6.4	14.3	31.1	55.8	46,660	70,467	51.0	12.8
Plano	15.5	25.4	23.4	8.8	12.5	15.9	15.4	12.5	11.4	38.1	50.7	222,030	259,857	17.0	10.1
Port Arthur	30.7	18.5	29.2	9.3	14.1	11.4	11.1	12.6	12.3	32.6	52.9	57,755	54,376	-5.9	2.1
Richardson	16.7	24.0	24.9	9.3	15.4	13.6	10.5	12.5	13.9	35.2	50.3	91,802	99,228	8.1	17.7
Rockwall	12.5	8.9	23.2	8.1	9.4	16.8	14.0	13.0	15.5	40.7	54.5	17,976	37,556	108.9	17.7
Rosenberg	55.3	19.7	33.3	7.1	15.4	13.5	10.2	9.5	11.1	32.0	52.3	24,043	31,876	32.6	18.1
Round Rock	34.5	14.4	25.4	12.1	13.9	16.0	14.7	9.2	8.8	33.9	50.6	61,136	100,011	63.6	23.7
Rowlett	12.3	13.5	24.3	7.6	11.1	14.9	17.3	14.7	10.2	41.0	49.6	44,503	56,242	26.4	11.8
San Angelo	41.9	6.3	23.7	13.4	15.8	10.9	10.6	10.3	15.3	33.2	51.1	88,439	93,221	5.4	7.4
San Antonio	64.0	14.7	25.3	10.7	16.2	13.2	11.8	10.7	11.9	33.5	50.5	1,144,646	1,327,343	16.0	13.9
San Juan	94.0	27.0	26.8	12.3	11.6	14.2	11.8	10.2	13.1	34.7	56.9	26,229	33,985	29.6	8.8
San Marcos	44.4	11.1	16.9	37.5	16.0	8.1	9.6	5.4	6.5	23.8	54.6	34,733	45,122	29.9	39.8
Schertz	25.0	7.4	24.3	10.0	9.1	14.7	18.9	11.7	11.3	39.7	52.1	18,694	31,797	70.1	26.1
Seguin	56.3	6.2	23.2	11.1	11.8	12.5	12.1	10.7	18.7	38.5	51.1	22,011	25,601	16.3	13.2
Sherman	17.4	7.4	24.3	12.4	12.7	10.3	14.2	10.1	16.1	36.4	51.1	35,082	38,349	9.3	9.3
Socorro	96.3	32.1	29.2	11.5	10.9	12.5	12.9	8.7	14.2	33.3	54.4	27,152	32,052	18.0	6.2
Southlake	8.0	13.1	35.4	4.8	5.0	14.2	21.3	12.8	6.5	39.4	55.8	21,519	26,575	23.5	19.8
Sugar Land	8.3	39.2	22.2	7.6	10.8	13.6	13.7	16.4	15.8	42.0	49.6	63,328	78,600	24.1	12.6
Temple	29.3	8.3	26.5	7.3	12.8	13.1	11.7	10.2	18.6	37.4	51.5	54,514	66,075	21.2	12.8
Texarkana	4.0	3.0	26.8	11.2	12.0	12.5	9.6	13.6	14.3	35.0	53.3	34,782	36,409	4.7	2.5
Texas City	26.5	5.1	25.2	10.3	11.5	11.3	13.2	15.1	13.5	36.2	53.1	41,521	45,091	8.6	7.7
The Colony	24.6	13.1	20.9	10.2	17.4	16.8	16.5	11.7	6.4	35.9	46.3	26,531	36,308	36.9	17.7
Tyler	22.9	10.3	26.0	11.4	17.3	9.6	10.0	11.0	14.8	32.5	53.3	83,650	96,887	15.8	8.4
Victoria	54.0	10.8	25.4	11.6	14.4	12.3	11.1	11.5	13.7	34.0	52.0	60,603	62,624	3.3	7.2
Waco	32.4	10.8	22.8	21.2	13.3	10.5	10.5	9.4	12.2	28.6	51.5	113,726	124,831	9.8	9.3
Waxahachie	27.2	10.9	26.7	12.4	15.2	13.3	11.7	8.9	11.8	32.6	53.2	21,426	29,538	37.9	19.6
Weatherford	16.4	6.8	26.5	9.9	13.1	13.6	10.0	10.4	16.5	35.5	51.5	19,000	25,782	35.7	8.9
Weslaco	88.6	21.5	29.0	9.1	13.0	12.1	10.6	10.0	16.2	34.2	49.5	26,935	36,847	36.8	9.5
Wichita Falls	22.5	7.0	22.5	15.4	17.1	10.6	10.3	10.8	13.3	32.0	47.0	104,197	104,724	0.5	0.0
Wylie	26.0	12.9	39.4	6.3	13.6	16.0	13.2	5.5	5.9	29.0	51.5	15,132	41,671	175.4	19.6
UTAH	13.8	8.3	30.2	11.3	14.7	13.4	10.3	9.6	10.5	30.7	49.6	2,233,169	2,763,889	23.8	12.2
American Fork	5.6	2.9	33.5	10.8	12.9	13.4	9.8	8.3	11.4	29.5	51.2	21,941	26,520	20.9	11.3
Bountiful	6.8	5.6	28.5	8.5	14.6	11.0	11.4	11.0	15.1	33.6	48.0	41,301	42,570	3.1	3.6
Cedar City	10.3	4.0	30.9	12.4	15.0	15.5	4.1	8.1	14.0	28.5	51.8	20,527	28,867	40.6	10.2
Clearfield	17.9	4.5	30.9	14.7	15.0	14.4	11.3	8.7	5.0	29.0	46.8	25,974	29,927	15.2	4.8
Cottonwood Heights	8.7	12.7	21.5	11.4	16.0	11.1	10.4	14.6	15.0	36.1	51.7	27,569	33,585	21.8	1.2
Draper	6.9	8.6	30.7	8.4	13.5	15.7	13.7	9.3	8.6	32.6	49.7	25,220	42,272	67.6	12.9
Holladay	3.4	9.5	23.6	9.3	10.7	11.9	14.5	13.0	17.1	40.1	49.9	14,561	30,127	106.9	1.9

1. May be of any race.

Table D. Cities — Households, Group Quarters, Crime, and Education

AREANAME	Number (27)	Persons per house-hold (28)	Family (29)	Married couple family (30)	Female headed family[1] (31)	Non-family (32)	One person (33)	Persons in group quarters (34)	Number (35)	Rate (36)	Violent (37)	Property (38)	Population age 25 and over (39)	High school graduate or less (40)	Bachelor's degree or more (41)
TEXAS— Cont'd															
Irving	85,407	2.77	64.9	45.9	13.2	35.1	27.5	1,420	7,011	2,912	216	2,696	151,209	40.6	36.2
Keller	15,437	3.00	86.0	75.5	7.6	14.0	12.4	NA	295	627	64	563	29,634	20.9	50.9
Killeen	52,417	2.73	68.9	44.7	17.8	31.1	27.0	NA	4,942	3,450	695	2,755	81,073	33.2	15.4
Kingsville	8,370	2.68	63.3	35.2	13.7	36.7	26.3	1,768	984	3,752	248	3,504	13,368	46.3	16.4
Kyle	11,229	3.43	76.6	52.1	17.1	23.4	17.8	NA	689	1,842	206	1,636	23,288	39.7	26.4
Lake Jackson	10,064	2.73	77.1	70.1	4.4	22.9	20.7	NA	497	1,796	195	1,601	17,993	33.5	34.9
Lancaster	13,547	2.84	74.3	39.1	33.8	25.7	21.8	419	1,501	3,827	574	3,254	22,288	37.5	24.9
La Porte	12,197	2.87	78.8	55.3	18.2	21.2	17.9	NA	675	1,906	206	1,700	23,540	46.2	18.7
Laredo	69,849	3.65	80.1	51.7	21.7	19.9	18.3	3,066	8,830	3,405	362	3,043	141,289	61.1	17.5
League City	35,193	2.87	77.4	64.8	7.1	22.6	20.0	486	2,019	1,990	81	1,910	65,734	22.1	44.1
Leander	13,187	3.34	82.1	61.3	13.5	17.9	16.2	NA	501	1,232	113	1,119	26,953	18.7	44.4
Lewisville	39,805	2.62	62.9	46.5	12.2	37.1	31.3	477	2,811	2,658	208	2,450	68,643	35.8	31.2
Little Elm	13,254	3.21	82.3	67.6	11.3	17.7	13.3	NA	438	1,057	99	958	25,822	21.8	45.6
Longview	30,502	2.55	65.3	42.7	18.2	34.7	30.2	3,940	3,956	4,787	551	4,237	53,150	46.4	21.5
Lubbock	93,891	2.57	59.7	39.5	14.1	40.3	28.5	11,650	15,402	6,090	1,084	5,006	146,100	38.7	31.5
Lufkin	13,525	2.57	54.2	34.2	18.4	45.8	39.1	1,340	1,681	4,595	380	4,215	23,085	42.9	21.2
McAllen	44,903	3.14	74.7	47.6	22.1	25.3	21.6	1,188	4,685	3,294	151	3,143	85,392	43.3	28.9
McKinney	59,705	2.87	76.0	60.8	10.9	24.0	20.9	1,042	2,500	1,473	141	1,332	110,802	26.3	43.6
Mansfield	21,431	3.02	78.4	66.8	9.8	21.6	17.7	NA	844	1,281	102	1,179	40,920	24.0	41.4
Mesquite	46,121	3.10	72.2	48.5	16.9	27.8	24.2	661	6,137	4,210	414	3,796	86,384	47.8	18.2
Midland	46,915	2.83	68.4	48.5	15.7	31.6	25.0	1,746	3,764	2,732	299	2,433	84,823	42.6	27.7
Mission	24,318	3.43	76.7	53.6	16.3	23.3	19.7	NA	2,299	2,725	142	2,582	47,409	51.6	23.9
Missouri City	25,169	2.96	74.3	56.1	13.2	25.7	21.7	NA	1,407	1,861	190	1,670	50,604	28.4	42.2
Nacogdoches	11,263	2.53	51.2	28.5	18.3	48.8	34.7	5,391	988	2,899	349	2,550	15,910	42.6	29.8
New Braunfels	25,887	2.70	69.3	56.0	10.1	30.7	25.4	1,076	1,928	2,629	282	2,347	47,101	35.0	33.5
North Richland Hills	27,115	2.56	69.4	51.0	14.3	30.6	26.8	351	1,499	2,129	183	1,946	47,580	31.8	35.8
Odessa	40,481	2.86	62.8	42.0	15.6	37.2	33.1	1,868	5,114	4,151	808	3,342	71,969	52.2	18.5
Paris	9,968	2.45	61.6	36.8	18.3	38.4	34.9	630	1,159	4,691	684	4,007	18,120	53.5	16.3
Pasadena	47,930	3.18	75.8	49.2	18.1	24.2	18.1	1,001	4,699	3,039	447	2,592	88,691	56.4	16.6
Pearland	38,606	3.02	80.5	65.2	10.4	19.5	18.3	633	2,257	2,001	176	1,824	74,780	23.9	44.3
Pflugerville	19,677	3.00	74.0	58.6	10.4	26.0	17.6	NA	1,092	1,852	244	1,607	40,359	28.0	35.4
Pharr	21,501	3.59	81.6	47.4	31.0	18.4	13.1	NA	2,035	2,618	293	2,324	45,577	62.4	15.6
Plano	106,062	2.69	71.5	57.9	10.3	28.5	23.8	919	5,890	2,043	139	1,904	193,941	19.5	56.6
Port Arthur	21,377	2.56	59.4	30.4	20.9	40.6	35.2	651	2,191	3,947	652	3,295	34,084	60.6	12.2
Richardson	43,095	2.60	68.2	51.6	13.8	31.8	25.5	1,342	2,629	2,322	138	2,184	74,675	21.4	54.7
Rockwall	16,729	2.58	67.9	60.6	3.9	32.1	29.1	NA	849	1,950	92	1,858	29,949	23.4	43.2
Rosenberg	11,326	3.25	72.1	37.2	27.3	27.9	21.7	NA	725	1,994	294	1,700	22,026	56.2	15.6
Round Rock	37,060	3.24	74.4	55.3	12.5	25.6	20.1	515	2,826	2,369	145	2,224	75,360	28.2	40.3
Rowlett	20,341	2.99	82.8	66.6	12.5	17.2	14.5	285	1,023	1,676	151	1,525	41,568	31.4	35.1
San Angelo	37,703	2.59	61.3	42.3	12.2	38.7	31.0	5,839	5,405	5,306	364	4,942	65,112	43.8	25.4
San Antonio	498,154	2.95	64.1	41.6	17.5	35.9	29.4	22,668	88,540	5,908	718	5,190	954,233	45.8	26.0
San Juan	10,440	3.50	88.5	59.4	28.6	11.5	8.1	NA	972	2,622	396	2,225	22,340	66.1	12.7
San Marcos	23,142	2.39	45.2	24.9	15.1	54.8	33.0	6,611	2,231	3,465	353	3,113	28,234	41.6	29.4
Schertz	13,454	2.89	79.9	64.3	13.0	20.1	16.8	289	814	2,075	217	1,859	25,744	32.5	36.8
Seguin	9,479	2.85	64.4	40.2	15.4	35.6	27.1	1,610	1,187	4,192	392	3,800	18,812	66.8	12.4
Sherman	14,779	2.70	64.1	39.6	20.7	35.9	31.3	1,662	1,378	3,350	309	3,041	26,293	38.7	22.4
Socorro	9,308	3.57	86.0	50.3	25.7	14.0	10.5	NA	347	1,037	132	906	19,722	67.5	6.8
Southlake	8,214	3.78	89.1	74.8	13.3	10.9	7.3	NA	415	1,354	62	1,292	18,582	17.5	59.9
Sugar Land	28,690	3.06	81.2	71.6	7.1	18.8	15.2	388	1,537	1,706	85	1,621	61,970	20.4	59.4
Temple	27,942	2.58	65.1	43.0	15.9	34.9	29.8	1,570	2,549	3,472	305	3,167	48,746	41.4	23.0
Texarkana	13,355	2.71	58.7	33.3	24.4	41.3	36.6	1,460	2,189	5,846	839	5,008	23,356	45.1	25.3
Texas City	16,679	2.80	69.5	38.4	22.6	30.5	26.5	1,640	2,008	4,175	518	3,657	31,157	50.4	12.1
The Colony	17,084	2.48	59.7	46.6	10.2	40.3	31.6	NA	555	1,293	154	1,139	29,207	26.3	39.4
Tyler	36,812	2.72	58.6	42.7	13.8	41.4	35.5	4,553	4,177	3,976	409	3,567	65,696	34.7	28.2
Victoria	23,191	2.87	64.8	41.3	17.7	35.2	29.1	1,227	2,584	3,767	392	3,374	42,661	47.5	19.7
Waco	47,966	2.63	56.5	37.3	15.2	43.5	31.9	8,342	5,577	4,168	519	3,649	75,247	48.7	21.1
Waxahachie	11,544	2.86	77.5	56.3	19.1	22.5	19.4	1,375	926	2,711	152	2,559	20,937	33.7	24.4
Weatherford	11,297	2.53	59.1	45.2	7.4	40.9	34.4	1,415	667	2,267	177	2,090	19,063	43.7	18.1
Weslaco	13,038	3.03	74.3	50.9	16.7	25.7	22.8	559	2,109	5,274	430	4,844	24,798	51.4	19.6
Wichita Falls	38,585	2.30	62.6	42.6	14.5	37.4	29.9	15,923	4,179	3,992	425	3,567	64,990	42.3	25.6
Wylie	13,315	3.70	89.1	66.1	16.4	10.9	5.9	NA	467	978	107	871	26,843	32.7	36.3
UTAH	943,147	3.19	75.4	61.3	9.6	24.6	18.7	45,776	97,465	3,194	243	2,952	1,783,244	31.0	32.6
American Fork	7,990	3.56	86.5	66.8	15.6	13.5	12.7	303	882	2,260	61	2,198	16,038	27.3	36.9
Bountiful	14,569	3.00	76.3	63.9	10.4	23.7	20.4	380	793	1,802	107	1,695	27,770	21.5	48.4
Cedar City	10,187	3.11	66.0	51.4	13.2	34.0	26.4	515	702	2,306	220	2,086	18,260	29.3	33.1
Clearfield	9,830	3.11	75.0	58.0	7.8	25.0	18.1	NA	693	2,251	94	2,157	16,780	32.3	21.9
Cottonwood Heights	11,909	2.88	64.1	55.4	6.3	35.9	29.7	NA	958	2,777	116	2,661	23,000	17.0	52.2
Draper	14,967	3.08	80.0	66.1	8.7	20.0	14.0	1,487	1,490	3,124	155	2,969	28,934	15.6	51.0
Holladay	10,937	2.80	74.9	60.3	10.2	25.1	21.8	NA	NA	NA	NA	NA	20,692	13.8	53.0

1. No spouse present.   2. Data for serious crimes have not been adjusted for underreporting. This may affect comparability between geographic areas and over time.   3. Per 100,000 population estimated by the FBI.   4. Persons 25 years old and over.

Table D. Cities — Accommodation and Food Services, Arts, Entertainment, and Recreation, and Health Care and Social Assistance

AREANAME	Accommodation and food services, 2012				Arts, entertainment, and recreation[1], 2012				Health care and social assistance,[1] 2012			
	Number of establishments	Number of employees	Receipts (mil dol)	Annual payroll (mil dol)	Number of establishments	Number of employees	Receipts (mil dol)	Annual payroll (mil dol)	Number of establishments	Number of employees	Receipts (mil dol)	Annual payroll (mil dol)
	92	93	94	95	96	97	98	99	100	101	102	103
TEXAS— Cont'd												
Irving	545	11,557	795.8	219.0	41	882	308.9	194.8	524	9,189	1,018.6	422.2
Keller	81	1,232	64.1	17.2	10	D	D	D	116	D	D	D
Killeen	248	5,406	275.3	73.2	20	D	D	D	162	D	D	D
Kingsville	70	D	D	D	4	27	1.9	0.7	49	D	D	D
Kyle	39	461	26.7	7.0	5	D	D	D	42	D	D	D
Lake Jackson	58	1,421	67.1	18.7	6	180	4.8	2.3	127	D	D	D
Lancaster	32	646	34.6	10.3	2	D	D	D	42	882	44.4	19.0
La Porte	68	1,241	60.2	17.1	4	4	0.1	0.1	39	D	D	D
Laredo	388	D	D	D	29	D	D	D	495	D	D	D
League City	121	2,047	101.4	28.6	19	D	D	D	147	D	D	D
Leander	27	405	20.0	5.0	4	D	D	D	37	D	D	D
Lewisville	232	4,707	268.4	69.0	29	D	D	D	235	4,569	466.8	185.6
Little Elm	23	D	D	D	4	85	4.4	1.3	18	160	9.8	3.7
Longview	239	5,463	255.8	71.5	18	233	14.7	4.0	330	D	D	D
Lubbock	597	13,817	697.7	186.1	56	966	44.5	14.4	681	12,591	1,244.5	475.9
Lufkin	122	2,852	129.3	36.8	11	84	4.1	1.0	206	4,992	368.7	159.6
McAllen	402	8,909	434.2	116.1	27	298	31.6	5.0	737	15,849	1,434.3	538.1
McKinney	229	4,652	233.6	66.7	28	756	34.3	12.7	340	5,253	601.0	220.2
Mansfield	118	D	D	D	16	D	D	D	177	1,699	177.1	68.4
Mesquite	217	5,218	270.6	75.1	22	324	22.3	4.3	309	D	D	D
Midland	279	6,352	431.1	102.8	24	D	D	D	319	D	D	D
Mission	135	2,294	119.2	28.9	11	239	10.1	3.2	262	D	D	D
Missouri City	101	1,540	82.2	20.4	10	D	D	D	163	1,529	104.2	40.9
Nacogdoches	105	2,457	96.1	27.0	9	D	D	D	172	2,233	248.4	76.5
New Braunfels	228	4,685	247.9	66.5	27	D	D	D	214	D	D	D
North Richland Hills	127	2,539	118.8	33.0	20	D	D	D	129	2,717	342.9	117.9
Odessa	230	5,893	377.8	90.6	23	239	15.9	2.6	273	5,379	633.2	215.6
Paris	93	1,462	67.5	18.9	8	D	D	D	153	3,443	310.7	115.6
Pasadena	202	3,882	206.4	54.8	10	D	D	D	307	6,675	807.2	289.9
Pearland	180	4,226	212.0	58.5	15	D	D	D	242	2,374	209.8	83.3
Pflugerville	61	1,266	61.4	17.6	7	100	6.1	1.7	59	D	D	D
Pharr	92	1,721	102.4	22.5	10	95	5.8	1.3	141	3,312	128.5	68.5
Plano	681	14,581	846.9	241.8	63	1,334	112.0	25.0	1,326	16,372	2,368.0	869.3
Port Arthur	102	1,890	86.4	24.4	8	D	D	D	111	D	D	D
Richardson	322	5,202	307.9	82.9	31	427	31.0	10.6	479	5,290	475.4	182.8
Rockwall	124	3,006	154.6	46.0	16	D	D	D	168	2,085	270.0	90.3
Rosenberg	92	1,713	89.5	25.8	2	D	D	D	52	D	D	D
Round Rock	278	6,112	340.4	92.7	29	D	D	D	288	D	D	D
Rowlett	70	990	49.9	14.0	9	D	D	D	100	1,983	246.4	72.1
San Angelo	210	4,220	211.7	57.1	22	264	15.8	3.7	225	3,970	425.1	200.0
San Antonio	3,209	79,964	4,616.3	1,242.7	255	D	D	D	3,448	74,255	8,556.3	3,003.7
San Juan	28	363	19.3	4.6	3	D	D	D	52	942	37.0	17.6
San Marcos	212	4,456	215.6	59.6	6	D	D	D	119	D	D	D
Schertz	58	1,287	62.4	17.5	4	D	D	D	44	681	61.7	24.3
Seguin	81	1,368	73.6	17.3	5	D	D	D	89	D	D	D
Sherman	102	2,593	124.4	35.3	13	171	6.6	1.6	208	4,944	426.2	184.1
Socorro	24	263	12.7	3.0	1	D	D	D	12	303	7.1	3.8
Southlake	111	D	D	D	21	D	D	D	193	2,328	300.7	102.7
Sugar Land	328	7,038	377.8	109.4	27	772	63.8	17.7	563	D	D	D
Temple	170	3,451	159.8	44.4	17	136	8.5	2.0	157	D	D	D
Texarkana	134	3,369	158.4	46.2	18	169	6.4	2.4	215	4,013	462.8	181.8
Texas City	74	1,229	55.7	15.6	3	D	D	D	92	2,400	223.0	86.3
The Colony	47	1,083	50.1	14.3	10	136	11.6	2.8	47	D	D	D
Tyler	310	7,298	339.0	97.3	33	D	D	D	465	11,350	1,145.8	482.2
Victoria	176	3,538	182.8	48.4	27	D	D	D	254	D	D	D
Waco	350	7,672	380.5	106.7	29	338	20.8	5.4	317	6,697	512.1	245.1
Waxahachie	80	1,902	85.0	25.3	3	D	D	D	86	D	D	D
Weatherford	116	2,114	98.8	28.6	6	D	D	D	128	1,988	207.2	79.7
Weslaco	84	1,781	86.0	21.4	10	D	D	D	174	D	D	D
Wichita Falls	236	5,370	249.6	76.2	20	D	D	D	305	5,113	540.1	185.9
Wylie	42	D	D	D	5	42	3.6	0.8	50	D	D	D
UTAH	5,108	95,933	4,789.3	1,362.9	790	17,988	982.5	330.3	6,601	77,036	8,253.6	3,016.8
American Fork	82	1,558	69.8	18.5	7	D	D	D	129	D	D	D
Bountiful	69	D	D	D	10	D	D	D	209	D	D	D
Cedar City	82	1,224	57.5	14.8	9	D	D	D	117	D	D	D
Clearfield	32	611	23.0	6.5	5	D	D	D	44	D	D	D
Cottonwood Heights	54	799	43.5	11.6	13	D	D	D	120	D	D	D
Draper	94	1,494	72.3	21.8	15	D	D	D	132	997	104.1	37.5
Holladay	51	578	30.2	8.2	11	D	D	D	96	972	85.2	33.2

1. Establishments subject to federal tax.

Table D. Cities — Other Services and Government Employment and Payroll

AREANAME	Other services[1]				Government employment and payroll, 2012								
					Full-time equivalent employees	March payroll							
						Total (dollars)	Percent of total for:						
	Number of establish-ments	Number of employees	Receipts (mil dol)	Annual payroll (mil dol)			Adminis-trative, judicial, and legal	Police and corrections	Fire protection	Highways and trans-portation	Health and welfare	Natural resources and utilities	Education and libraries
	104	105	106	107	108	109	110	111	112	113	114	115	116

AREANAME	104	105	106	107	108	109	110	111	112	113	114	115	116
TEXAS— Cont'd													
Irving	239	2,926	307.3	114.7	1,743	8,046,007	11.8	31.8	18.7	7.1	2.9	19.2	3.6
Keller	55	377	31.5	9.8	322	1,442,647	19.7	27.3	24.3	2.1	4.2	18.4	3.8
Killeen	150	974	79.5	24.9	1,394	4,447,306	9.5	31.5	19.2	10.2	0.6	25.4	2.0
Kingsville	31	D	D	D	241	740,345	13.5	34.2	17.7	5.2	3.4	18.4	2.6
Kyle	18	91	7.2	2.0	143	570,004	14.8	39.7	0.0	1.7	5.7	18.1	3.7
Lake Jackson	28	191	12.6	4.6	223	1,137,302	14.0	31.7	0.5	2.3	1.6	37.2	0.0
Lancaster	24	150	17.5	5.4	197	872,132	6.8	31.3	33.7	2.6	3.3	16.0	2.4
La Porte	42	5,934	655.6	342.7	386	1,606,505	14.9	33.6	6.2	5.1	7.8	22.0	0.0
Laredo	175	975	90.0	24.7	2,366	9,931,436	6.8	30.9	24.7	11.9	8.6	14.4	1.1
League City	93	670	50.8	15.5	495	2,096,779	14.9	38.2	2.0	7.5	5.2	20.9	5.0
Leander	26	146	11.5	3.6	176	773,154	15.8	34.3	18.9	9.2	0.8	16.9	0.0
Lewisville	150	1,053	116.4	32.6	702	3,410,758	13.2	32.7	24.8	4.3	1.7	15.0	2.1
Little Elm	12	44	4.1	1.4	174	691,106	17.2	23.6	29.0	9.8	0.8	13.6	2.1
Longview	155	1,278	152.8	44.8	813	3,225,874	7.0	26.2	26.9	3.4	3.3	21.3	2.7
Lubbock	338	2,485	217.7	69.3	2,120	8,958,861	10.0	27.2	23.3	4.5	2.1	29.5	1.5
Lufkin	75	615	135.8	27.5	429	1,543,350	10.3	27.6	23.6	6.7	2.2	23.4	1.9
McAllen	145	1,046	142.4	30.6	1,664	5,174,843	11.6	30.2	15.6	10.8	1.0	24.6	3.0
McKinney	132	1,023	89.8	27.9	813	4,047,327	14.6	26.8	24.0	4.8	0.1	11.7	2.8
Mansfield	67	D	D	D	451	2,111,359	10.1	41.1	18.9	1.8	1.4	11.7	1.5
Mesquite	122	946	102.3	28.3	1,105	5,253,222	10.9	34.0	25.7	3.7	4.0	15.6	2.0
Midland	157	D	D	D	894	4,038,726	12.2	27.1	26.9	7.2	3.1	13.6	0.0
Mission	72	434	36.4	9.7	597	1,943,490	10.4	37.6	17.4	3.6	1.5	22.5	3.1
Missouri City	68	415	28.1	9.5	283	1,318,714	9.4	42.4	22.9	9.3	0.0	4.5	0.0
Nacogdoches	49	298	23.9	7.2	302	1,195,157	10.1	30.1	23.9	1.7	1.3	26.6	1.9
New Braunfels	105	1,334	54.3	37.3	732	3,498,442	7.2	20.5	22.3	4.6	3.6	21.9	2.5
North Richland Hills	73	459	48.3	13.6	574	2,442,427	13.2	35.1	19.1	9.2	9.3	9.3	4.0
Odessa	149	1,399	178.1	47.0	873	3,249,214	13.9	28.3	26.0	7.1	3.0	16.3	0.0
Paris	58	301	28.1	7.8	203	911,303	16.1	38.4	1.6	2.6	5.8	17.2	7.9
Pasadena	135	1,402	179.6	68.1	960	4,082,891	10.8	48.1	2.1	4.7	5.5	18.7	2.8
Pearland	129	906	77.4	25.7	598	2,337,139	14.4	37.4	8.4	4.4	15.8	16.8	0.0
Pflugerville	51	308	28.6	10.5	253	1,010,931	16.1	44.8	0.0	8.0	1.3	21.6	3.5
Pharr	52	340	29.9	8.1	558	1,780,708	10.5	35.0	15.9	8.1	1.9	18.2	3.4
Plano	419	3,683	759.6	161.0	2,089	10,395,648	9.8	32.0	22.2	2.2	0.0	14.1	5.2
Port Arthur	36	162	11.7	3.2	668	2,985,904	7.8	28.2	20.4	6.1	9.3	23.9	1.7
Richardson	146	1,302	141.4	44.2	1,085	4,745,385	14.8	25.0	17.8	5.0	3.3	20.5	3.5
Rockwall	55	559	27.7	10.4	286	1,221,546	32.3	33.7	9.6	3.1	0.0	16.3	0.0
Rosenberg	53	230	30.8	8.3	213	967,179	15.7	34.7	16.7	5.1	5.0	18.2	0.0
Round Rock	147	1,405	151.8	46.8	471	2,565,694	21.2	46.9	28.7	0.0	0.0	0.7	2.5
Rowlett	74	396	34.4	11.4	332	1,590,040	18.8	30.9	25.7	4.7	2.6	10.7	1.9
San Angelo	161	867	85.1	23.1	915	3,145,374	16.7	27.8	25.3	3.8	3.2	19.2	0.0
San Antonio	1,694	12,508	1,000.7	326.7	15,382	70,371,976	6.9	20.9	12.5	5.3	3.5	46.3	2.1
San Juan	14	D	D	D	204	595,583	10.6	35.0	12.1	4.4	4.5	31.9	0.4
San Marcos	73	D	D	D	528	2,976,832	13.7	28.7	14.8	4.1	4.9	21.3	2.7
Schertz	36	342	28.5	9.8	292	1,152,930	17.4	24.7	12.8	2.8	16.4	9.2	3.8
Seguin	47	323	25.3	7.7	907	3,729,350	5.2	8.3	6.1	1.8	68.5	7.0	0.7
Sherman	43	375	37.8	16.0	387	1,528,362	13.7	25.7	23.1	4.3	3.0	22.7	2.2
Socorro	24	112	8.0	1.6	92	274,728	24.8	59.5	0.0	13.4	2.2	0.0	0.0
Southlake	68	D	D	D	274	1,309,065	24.1	24.8	21.4	7.0	0.0	20.0	2.7
Sugar Land	128	947	72.3	23.2	631	3,018,681	23.4	31.1	19.1	10.0	1.3	10.4	0.0
Temple	104	933	55.9	26.2	731	2,585,537	12.4	26.7	22.3	6.4	2.4	25.4	2.6
Texarkana	91	661	56.2	17.8	562	2,018,866	13.1	24.0	17.3	8.1	4.9	29.4	1.7
Texas City	38	241	27.2	9.5	481	1,954,986	8.1	29.3	20.9	5.9	1.6	25.9	2.0
The Colony	32	157	11.7	3.1	311	1,270,659	11.9	29.0	21.2	3.8	7.3	20.1	4.5
Tyler	170	1,478	125.2	57.0	778	3,106,473	9.1	34.9	25.5	3.1	3.1	18.2	1.7
Victoria	103	D	D	D	566	2,159,618	10.1	31.7	22.5	6.4	0.0	22.4	3.2
Waco	177	1,205	90.1	28.9	1,507	5,739,695	9.4	29.8	17.3	5.4	5.9	25.5	2.4
Waxahachie	42	262	29.4	6.8	264	1,145,356	12.3	28.0	25.5	3.4	3.0	21.1	0.0
Weatherford	63	579	42.4	15.3	345	1,550,071	17.4	23.4	20.0	5.7	2.6	21.9	3.2
Weslaco	45	347	28.5	7.3	368	1,252,682	6.2	31.0	27.7	5.1	2.2	17.8	3.2
Wichita Falls	142	835	70.0	20.7	1,213	4,712,736	7.8	25.5	27.3	8.3	5.3	16.8	1.2
Wylie	33	172	13.3	4.5	191	622,464	4.4	29.0	33.5	4.3	0.0	22.4	6.3
UTAH	3,631	21,705	1,875.3	549.2	X	X	X	X	X	X	X	X	X
American Fork	55	448	23.4	5.8	215	711,482	13.8	21.8	14.3	3.1	1.3	25.9	5.2
Bountiful	72	572	38.0	11.3	195	922,673	14.7	32.2	0.0	14.9	0.0	37.8	0.0
Cedar City	43	174	14.8	3.9	172	568,537	11.0	28.7	7.6	11.9	1.2	27.7	2.2
Clearfield	34	194	11.7	4.6	150	543,342	19.4	32.7	17.0	4.0	0.9	22.9	0.0
Cottonwood Heights	25	150	5.7	1.9	68	323,642	24.8	70.5	0.0	4.6	0.0	0.0	0.0
Draper	78	494	43.8	10.8	152	605,204	26.7	28.9	0.0	17.1	3.4	14.1	0.0
Holladay	40	158	11.1	3.1	18	69,533	64.5	0.0	0.0	0.0	22.6	12.9	0.0

1. Establishments subject to federal tax.

AREANAME	Percent Hispanic or Latino[1], 2016	Percent foreign born, 2016	Age of population (percent), 2016							Median age 2016	Percent female 2016	Population			
												Census counts		Percent change	
			Under 18 years	18 to 24 years	25 to 34 years	35 to 44 years	45 to 54 years	55 to 64 years	65 years and over			2000	2010	2000-2010	2010-2017
	12	13	14	15	16	17	18	19	20	21	22	23	24	25	26
UTAH— Cont'd															
Kaysville	2.3	3.9	39.8	9.0	9.8	14.4	12.6	7.2	7.1	26.5	48.9	20,351	27,582	35.5	15.2
Layton	12.1	5.9	33.3	9.0	13.1	16.0	8.1	10.2	10.2	30.9	51.3	58,474	67,539	15.5	13.6
Lehi	6.1	4.2	43.1	6.7	12.8	18.0	8.2	5.3	5.9	25.2	48.2	19,028	47,767	151.0	31.3
Logan	15.4	11.9	25.1	29.2	19.9	8.8	5.3	5.2	6.5	23.7	49.0	42,670	48,215	13.0	6.0
Midvale	32.5	19.7	27.8	7.7	24.8	17.4	8.7	8.2	5.4	29.4	48.5	27,029	27,999	3.6	18.6
Murray	5.5	6.7	21.2	9.0	14.8	15.5	9.9	9.5	20.1	37.0	54.4	34,024	46,685	37.2	5.6
Ogden	34.5	14.7	29.3	9.9	15.2	15.2	10.7	10.3	9.5	31.6	48.0	77,226	82,836	7.3	5.1
Orem	17.0	10.5	28.9	16.5	18.2	12.3	7.3	7.0	9.8	26.7	48.4	84,324	88,328	4.7	10.8
Pleasant Grove	7.3	5.5	29.2	19.2	16.7	10.2	9.6	9.3	5.9	25.8	50.0	23,468	33,547	42.9	15.8
Provo	20.1	12.7	21.6	39.4	16.1	7.2	5.4	4.9	5.3	23.3	50.1	105,166	112,487	7.0	4.3
Riverton	8.0	4.9	38.0	9.7	11.8	15.6	9.6	8.8	6.6	27.5	50.4	25,011	38,832	55.3	11.6
Roy	12.4	4.0	28.2	11.1	17.4	11.6	8.3	12.5	11.0	30.2	48.9	32,885	36,862	12.1	4.7
St. George	15.6	8.0	25.6	12.2	13.8	9.4	9.7	9.8	19.4	34.0	51.0	49,663	72,761	46.5	16.0
Salt Lake City	20.5	17.4	21.0	12.1	21.1	14.5	10.0	10.8	10.5	32.7	48.3	181,743	186,443	2.6	7.6
Sandy	9.2	6.8	26.2	7.2	13.6	12.7	13.6	12.7	14.1	37.2	51.1	88,418	89,950	1.7	6.9
South Jordan	3.8	5.1	31.3	7.6	15.5	15.0	11.4	9.9	9.2	33.0	49.2	29,437	50,473	71.5	40.6
Spanish Fork	10.0	4.2	45.4	8.9	16.8	11.9	7.9	4.8	4.2	20.9	49.9	20,246	34,748	71.6	13.5
Springville	18.6	8.5	38.7	14.6	11.5	14.1	7.4	6.5	7.1	23.1	50.9	20,424	29,584	44.8	12.5
Taylorsville	19.4	12.8	24.8	9.5	21.4	11.0	10.8	9.8	12.7	32.5	49.5	57,439	58,688	2.2	2.2
Tooele	13.4	4.5	33.6	9.3	15.2	12.7	12.4	7.7	9.1	31.2	52.4	22,502	31,603	40.4	9.6
West Jordan	19.3	10.5	32.1	9.9	13.5	14.2	12.4	11.5	6.3	30.6	47.9	68,336	103,601	51.6	9.9
West Valley City	39.8	21.4	31.6	9.8	15.1	13.9	11.8	9.4	8.4	30.8	48.0	108,896	129,465	18.9	5.2
VERMONT	2.0	4.5	19.0	10.6	11.5	11.3	13.9	15.5	18.2	43.1	50.7	608,827	625,741	2.8	-0.3
Burlington	3.4	11.0	16.7	34.0	12.6	9.6	8.2	8.5	10.5	24.7	49.4	38,889	42,417	9.1	-0.4
VIRGINIA	9.0	12.3	22.2	9.8	13.7	13.0	13.8	12.9	14.6	38.2	50.8	7,078,515	8,001,043	13.0	5.9
Alexandria	16.8	28.3	18.3	6.6	21.5	19.1	13.2	11.3	10.1	36.6	52.1	128,283	140,006	9.1	14.3
Blacksburg	4.7	13.4	9.9	55.0	13.4	4.9	7.0	5.2	4.6	21.2	45.7	39,573	42,526	7.5	4.8
Charlottesville	5.3	13.2	16.1	21.6	19.5	11.8	11.1	10.3	9.7	30.8	51.9	45,049	43,428	-3.6	10.6
Chesapeake	5.7	4.7	24.2	8.3	15.0	12.9	14.3	12.9	12.5	36.9	51.2	199,184	222,306	11.6	8.1
Danville	4.1	3.4	21.4	8.7	12.7	11.8	10.7	14.2	20.5	40.0	51.3	48,411	43,074	-11.0	-4.5
Hampton	5.5	3.6	21.0	11.8	16.1	10.8	12.6	13.4	14.2	36.2	52.6	146,437	137,384	-6.2	-2.0
Harrisonburg	18.9	11.8	16.1	36.2	12.3	10.0	8.7	7.1	9.5	23.2	50.3	40,468	48,909	20.9	10.8
Leesburg	11.3	20.1	27.7	7.5	14.0	16.7	16.3	9.6	8.2	35.3	50.3	28,311	42,614	50.5	27.2
Lynchburg	3.5	4.5	19.3	25.8	12.8	7.8	10.2	9.7	14.3	27.7	55.2	65,269	75,532	15.7	7.2
Manassas	30.2	23.5	27.4	10.4	14.3	13.3	14.2	10.7	9.6	32.9	50.4	35,135	37,819	7.6	9.7
Newport News	8.8	5.4	23.1	13.0	16.4	11.1	12.6	11.7	12.2	33.4	51.2	180,150	180,963	0.5	-0.9
Norfolk	7.8	7.6	20.2	17.9	19.2	11.1	10.4	10.9	10.3	30.6	47.9	234,403	242,823	3.6	0.8
Petersburg	4.9	2.7	22.4	11.6	12.8	11.0	12.6	13.6	16.0	36.7	55.4	33,740	32,437	-3.9	-2.1
Portsmouth	4.2	3.3	23.6	10.9	15.5	11.6	11.7	12.7	14.0	35.0	52.1	100,565	95,527	-5.0	-1.0
Richmond	6.5	6.0	17.9	13.1	21.7	11.7	11.5	12.1	11.9	33.4	52.4	197,790	204,271	3.3	11.1
Roanoke	6.2	6.5	22.4	7.5	14.8	13.5	13.3	13.2	15.2	38.7	52.5	94,911	96,917	2.1	3.0
Suffolk	4.1	4.1	24.8	8.6	12.2	13.2	14.6	12.9	13.7	38.2	51.1	63,677	84,570	32.8	6.7
Virginia Beach	8.1	10.1	22.5	9.8	16.7	12.8	13.0	12.1	13.2	35.8	50.9	425,257	437,907	3.0	2.9
Winchester	19.1	15.5	19.9	8.2	16.8	12.5	12.2	11.9	18.5	39.2	49.6	23,585	26,219	11.2	6.5
WASHINGTON	12.4	14.0	22.4	9.1	14.7	13.0	13.1	13.0	14.8	37.7	50.1	5,894,121	6,724,545	14.1	10.1
Auburn	14.0	18.9	26.1	8.2	14.1	13.3	13.0	14.2	11.0	36.5	50.8	40,314	70,162	74.0	15.1
Bellevue	5.9	36.9	21.1	6.0	16.6	15.0	13.7	12.3	15.2	39.1	50.4	109,569	127,887	16.7	12.9
Bellingham	10.3	11.0	16.1	26.9	14.6	10.5	8.5	9.9	13.4	28.9	51.3	67,171	81,252	21.0	9.6
Bothell	10.4	17.7	24.7	9.5	15.7	11.5	12.0	14.8	11.9	35.3	48.3	30,150	39,870	32.2	14.2
Bremerton	10.4	7.4	19.5	15.4	21.2	12.2	10.3	10.9	10.5	32.1	47.5	37,259	37,795	1.4	8.6
Burien	26.2	26.6	19.9	7.1	15.6	13.6	15.6	15.3	12.9	38.9	44.3	31,881	48,072	50.8	7.5
Des Moines	17.6	18.9	19.4	4.6	14.7	14.4	14.1	15.7	17.0	42.9	52.1	29,267	29,655	1.3	5.3
Edmonds	7.5	14.4	18.6	9.4	11.1	9.4	17.3	14.2	20.1	46.3	55.0	39,515	39,744	0.6	6.2
Everett	15.3	18.5	21.0	9.3	17.9	13.7	13.5	12.5	12.1	36.3	47.6	91,488	103,052	12.6	6.8
Federal Way	21.8	29.7	25.4	7.6	16.0	13.2	10.4	13.6	13.8	35.5	52.6	83,259	89,302	7.3	8.3
Issaquah	11.3	22.8	25.1	5.7	15.7	19.6	13.9	9.5	10.5	37.5	51.8	11,212	30,439	171.5	23.2
Kennewick	29.1	14.9	28.7	10.3	12.7	12.8	10.7	11.4	13.4	33.8	49.6	54,693	73,990	35.3	10.3
Kent	18.5	31.3	24.3	9.5	17.7	13.1	13.2	11.4	10.8	34.2	49.5	79,524	118,614	49.2	8.3
Kirkland	7.3	22.3	20.9	6.4	19.3	14.4	13.5	12.2	13.3	36.9	49.9	45,054	80,585	78.9	10.0
Lacey	8.3	8.3	24.2	6.4	18.7	12.8	11.5	8.1	18.3	35.4	55.6	31,226	42,572	36.3	16.9
Lake Stevens	10.5	7.1	28.4	7.8	16.1	16.9	11.9	7.0	11.9	33.3	49.1	6,361	28,060	341.1	16.8
Lakewood	17.7	18.7	20.9	10.7	18.1	11.7	10.0	15.0	13.7	35.2	49.7	58,211	57,527	-1.2	4.8
Longview	11.0	4.9	25.9	9.6	13.0	11.5	10.8	10.4	18.8	36.0	53.8	34,660	36,836	6.3	2.1
Lynnwood	11.4	28.1	14.2	12.2	12.7	12.0	18.4	15.4	15.0	43.8	53.4	33,847	35,881	6.0	6.7
Marysville	8.9	8.5	24.1	9.0	11.8	13.7	13.0	14.1	14.3	38.7	52.4	25,315	60,007	137.0	14.8
Mount Vernon	37.3	19.8	26.2	9.5	10.9	12.2	11.2	12.9	17.0	36.8	50.0	26,232	31,722	20.9	10.5
Olympia	10.9	9.1	17.2	9.0	18.7	12.1	12.0	13.9	17.2	38.6	51.6	42,514	46,777	10.0	10.3

1. May be of any race.

Table D. Cities — Households, Group Quarters, Crime, and Education

AREANAME	Households, 2016 Number	Persons per house-hold	Family	Married couple family	Female headed family[1]	Non-family	One person	Persons in group quarters	Serious crimes known to police[2], 2016 Total Number	Rate	Rate[3] Violent	Property	Educational attainment, 2016 Population age 25 and over	High school graduate or less	Attainment[4] (percent) Bachelor's degree or more
	27	28	29	30	31	32	33	34	35	36	37	38	39	40	41
UTAH— Cont'd															
Kaysville	8,160	3.83	88.6	81.2	6.4	11.4	11.4	NA	289	931	58	873	15,982	11.5	52.1
Layton	24,166	3.13	77.8	65.4	7.5	22.2	19.5	NA	1,825	2,418	172	2,246	43,666	25.7	30.4
Lehi	15,224	4.01	89.2	81.5	5.9	10.8	8.4	NA	846	1,391	127	1,265	30,693	18.0	42.6
Logan	16,977	2.86	65.4	56.1	7.8	34.6	20.1	2,183	906	1,785	102	1,682	23,152	32.6	37.0
Midvale	12,143	2.71	58.9	38.6	12.8	41.1	28.9	NA	NA	NA	NA	NA	21,296	35.8	29.0
Murray	18,871	2.59	64.7	47.6	10.3	35.3	28.4	NA	3,811	7,659	553	7,106	34,368	32.5	33.4
Ogden	28,511	2.95	65.1	44.6	14.3	34.9	27.2	2,638	4,509	5,247	514	4,733	52,785	46.2	17.0
Orem	28,873	3.33	78.6	65.7	8.6	21.4	14.5	1,417	2,512	2,627	68	2,559	53,278	25.2	36.8
Pleasant Grove	11,239	3.44	76.3	63.3	8.7	23.7	16.0	NA	268	687	31	657	20,039	20.5	36.7
Provo	30,531	3.45	68.8	57.7	7.4	31.2	10.9	11,576	2,866	2,476	129	2,348	45,537	22.1	40.7
Riverton	10,802	3.96	88.7	70.8	7.2	11.3	10.6	NA	NA	NA	NA	NA	22,391	29.4	26.3
Roy	12,733	2.99	74.9	63.5	8.8	25.1	18.2	NA	744	1,949	113	1,837	23,193	45.1	18.4
St. George	26,601	3.06	74.1	59.9	10.0	25.9	21.5	858	1,626	1,989	196	1,793	51,150	28.6	29.3
Salt Lake City	76,982	2.43	51.5	37.0	9.0	48.5	35.1	6,505	18,287	9,430	920	8,510	129,735	29.1	45.6
Sandy	31,740	3.00	77.8	64.3	9.4	22.2	17.8	590	3,312	3,501	170	3,331	63,886	24.2	43.1
South Jordan	20,979	3.29	80.1	68.3	9.8	19.9	15.8	NA	1,620	2,307	77	2,230	42,125	21.3	34.1
Spanish Fork	9,136	4.15	86.1	75.1	8.3	13.9	11.4	976	552	1,433	26	1,407	17,746	24.0	35.8
Springville	8,563	3.84	85.2	74.1	8.5	14.8	10.6	NA	695	2,117	85	2,032	15,420	25.9	36.1
Taylorsville	20,450	2.95	75.5	50.2	18.5	24.5	18.9	NA	NA	NA	NA	NA	39,696	45.5	19.0
Tooele	10,658	3.14	75.5	57.4	13.9	24.5	19.5	NA	1,515	4,529	436	4,093	19,297	47.3	14.7
West Jordan	32,556	3.48	80.6	62.3	13.3	19.4	14.1	516	3,963	3,489	275	3,214	65,917	34.9	24.5
West Valley City	37,400	3.64	82.4	56.6	16.8	17.6	12.6	318	7,256	5,275	596	4,679	79,961	56.3	14.5
VERMONT	254,851	2.35	60.6	47.2	9.0	39.4	30.2	25,240	11,591	1,856	158	1,697	439,563	37.2	36.4
Burlington	15,514	2.27	38.1	29.7	5.0	61.9	36.6	7,044	1,505	3,545	344	3,201	20,844	25.3	51.8
VIRGINIA	3,120,692	2.62	66.1	49.9	11.8	33.9	27.4	241,626	174,714	2,077	218	1,859	5,721,173	34.7	38.1
Alexandria	69,875	2.21	46.8	34.7	7.9	53.2	43.5	1,672	3,128	2,014	185	1,828	116,979	19.1	62.6
Blacksburg	14,300	2.55	37.6	29.4	4.2	62.4	20.7	8,515	456	1,024	97	928	15,801	13.1	77.8
Charlottesville	18,443	2.40	51.2	34.3	12.3	48.8	28.8	2,668	1,477	3,144	526	2,618	29,225	30.7	52.1
Chesapeake	83,364	2.79	73.3	52.6	15.2	26.7	22.7	5,519	7,008	2,962	412	2,550	160,682	34.6	31.5
Danville	17,936	2.25	58.5	34.7	21.0	41.5	37.2	1,564	1,872	4,491	804	3,687	29,272	45.1	20.5
Hampton	54,181	2.41	54.4	32.3	15.3	45.6	36.8	4,568	5,099	3,763	323	3,440	90,993	38.5	27.3
Harrisonburg	16,619	2.76	55.9	31.8	15.5	44.1	27.4	7,277	1,217	2,297	219	2,078	25,333	40.2	35.0
Leesburg	17,892	2.93	77.1	65.2	5.4	22.9	19.2	NA	932	1,758	209	1,549	34,108	22.8	56.4
Lynchburg	27,545	2.52	55.0	35.0	14.9	45.0	33.1	10,767	2,114	2,635	375	2,260	44,029	38.9	33.4
Manassas	12,351	3.35	80.1	59.5	13.9	19.9	15.9	NA	938	2,219	291	1,928	25,783	41.3	29.7
Newport News	67,628	2.55	59.5	39.7	15.1	40.5	32.1	9,285	6,454	3,552	472	3,080	116,209	36.0	27.3
Norfolk	87,910	2.49	56.0	33.7	18.7	44.0	34.6	26,519	11,261	4,583	659	3,923	151,771	37.3	28.2
Petersburg	13,493	2.32	48.0	22.6	19.6	52.0	44.1	644	1,312	4,063	740	3,323	21,056	52.3	18.5
Portsmouth	36,615	2.51	59.0	32.0	21.8	41.0	32.2	3,254	6,226	6,498	796	5,702	62,369	43.1	21.2
Richmond	91,704	2.31	43.0	22.5	16.6	57.0	43.9	11,335	9,343	4,200	569	3,632	153,809	35.7	38.8
Roanoke	42,213	2.31	53.3	35.1	13.4	46.7	40.8	2,136	4,615	4,616	412	4,204	69,862	48.1	21.1
Suffolk	33,377	2.66	70.8	49.4	16.7	29.2	23.6	434	2,398	2,714	281	2,434	59,503	38.3	26.5
Virginia Beach	168,061	2.63	69.0	49.5	14.8	31.0	24.2	10,758	10,590	2,338	155	2,183	306,588	27.8	35.0
Winchester	11,563	2.29	59.3	36.9	15.0	40.7	36.3	1,032	842	3,077	223	2,854	19,777	48.3	32.9
WASHINGTON	2,768,076	2.58	64.5	50.2	9.8	35.5	27.0	142,590	276,676	3,796	302	3,494	4,996,555	31.4	35.1
Auburn	29,453	2.56	63.8	44.4	13.8	36.2	27.3	561	3,958	5,048	423	4,625	49,910	40.1	24.0
Bellevue	56,289	2.49	68.0	57.9	7.5	32.0	24.7	1,383	4,787	3,365	98	3,268	103,080	14.5	66.2
Bellingham	34,317	2.41	45.3	35.1	8.8	54.7	32.0	4,728	4,974	5,783	262	5,522	49,891	25.9	42.0
Bothell	17,095	2.67	68.0	55.2	8.7	32.0	23.5	1,059	1,265	2,886	114	2,772	30,757	20.7	48.1
Bremerton	16,066	2.35	52.7	34.8	12.2	47.3	37.3	2,907	1,778	4,460	502	3,959	26,470	34.3	23.6
Burien	20,840	2.43	56.9	39.7	10.6	43.1	34.2	463	2,830	5,556	489	5,067	37,269	45.3	27.6
Des Moines	12,298	2.49	63.2	43.7	13.6	36.8	28.7	597	1,413	4,482	374	4,108	23,690	36.6	22.2
Edmonds	17,063	2.43	61.5	47.6	9.2	38.5	31.3	326	1,229	2,947	177	2,769	30,108	17.7	49.2
Everett	42,175	2.48	56.0	37.0	11.2	44.0	35.6	4,563	6,099	5,596	450	5,146	76,004	39.9	20.7
Federal Way	35,043	2.74	67.8	46.0	15.5	32.2	24.1	876	6,479	6,725	474	6,251	64,813	38.5	28.0
Issaquah	14,913	2.49	68.1	51.5	12.1	31.9	24.1	NA	1,186	3,179	99	3,080	25,838	17.4	64.7
Kennewick	28,558	2.77	63.5	44.6	15.3	36.5	27.4	1,272	2,442	3,059	232	2,827	49,120	40.4	25.6
Kent	44,532	2.82	68.4	46.5	13.4	31.6	24.3	2,011	7,906	6,148	292	5,856	84,425	42.1	26.0
Kirkland	34,997	2.47	65.3	54.4	7.4	34.7	26.2	1,311	2,098	2,367	93	2,275	63,726	14.7	62.3
Lacey	18,539	2.52	64.2	52.9	9.8	35.8	27.7	964	1,833	3,882	231	3,651	33,099	25.4	33.7
Lake Stevens	10,908	2.90	81.6	61.0	14.5	18.4	15.9	NA	565	1,797	213	1,584	20,213	32.1	28.7
Lakewood	25,529	2.32	58.9	39.8	13.3	41.1	32.2	1,341	3,398	5,649	751	4,898	41,502	39.9	23.0
Longview	14,342	2.53	58.0	34.7	12.7	42.0	33.6	990	2,075	5,630	388	5,242	24,094	44.9	16.6
Lynnwood	14,539	2.57	61.0	44.5	11.4	39.0	28.8	772	2,769	7,440	387	7,053	28,022	33.1	32.1
Marysville	24,490	2.74	68.8	56.9	9.4	31.2	25.3	448	2,075	3,044	232	2,812	45,210	38.0	20.5
Mount Vernon	11,623	2.91	63.7	47.3	11.7	36.3	24.1	760	1,412	4,090	255	3,835	22,232	38.6	18.4
Olympia	22,411	2.22	52.0	38.7	10.7	48.0	39.6	1,424	2,699	5,295	394	4,901	37,774	21.2	48.3

1. No spouse present.   2. Data for serious crimes have not been adjusted for underreporting. This may affect comparability between geographic areas and over time.   3. Per 100,000 population estimated by the FBI.   4. Persons 25 years old and over.

Table D. Cities — Income and Housing

AREANAME	Money income, 2016					Median earnings, 2016			Housing units, 2016				
	Households												
	Median income	Percent with income less than $20,000	Percent with income of $200,000 or more	Median family income	Median non-family household income	All persons	Men	Women	Total	Occupied	Percent owner occupied	Median value[1] (dollars)	Median rent (dollars)
	42	43	44	45	46	47	48	49	50	51	52	53	54
UTAH— Cont'd													
Kaysville	94,009	8.6	7.8	104,870	17,457	37,887	65,234	18,687	8,160	8,160	87.4	306,400	763
Layton	68,892	9.6	3.4	80,300	35,630	30,854	40,018	21,951	24,915	24,166	67.2	235,000	943
Lehi	91,129	5.1	5.7	92,349	40,328	38,603	58,165	22,597	15,795	15,224	79.1	314,400	1,526
Logan	40,496	18.7	1.7	43,583	28,674	19,166	23,657	13,520	18,662	16,977	38.7	172,900	690
Midvale	53,512	22.9	2.1	53,707	48,816	33,200	36,499	30,688	13,119	12,143	30.1	235,000	995
Murray	54,484	12.1	2.5	71,531	29,030	27,155	31,383	25,270	19,787	18,871	63.8	262,500	1,026
Ogden	44,381	21.9	2.2	57,282	27,165	27,493	31,812	22,286	31,797	28,511	57.9	143,600	727
Orem	59,776	14.0	4.0	64,173	40,310	22,628	30,874	16,373	30,522	28,873	58.5	238,700	933
Pleasant Grove	69,030	9.2	5.9	77,444	30,148	26,058	37,306	12,723	11,654	11,239	66.2	264,800	882
Provo	46,883	19.5	4.1	50,831	39,297	13,077	16,525	10,663	33,208	30,531	36.6	248,600	785
Riverton	87,126	2.5	8.8	90,510	47,731	30,447	55,042	12,494	11,075	10,802	86.6	315,700	1,738
Roy	65,840	12.2	0.0	70,627	45,231	31,991	43,835	21,361	12,931	12,733	83.2	167,400	916
St. George	52,697	15.2	4.9	62,213	27,500	21,927	30,189	17,441	33,924	26,601	64.7	264,800	934
Salt Lake City	56,994	16.1	5.8	71,679	41,324	31,196	35,022	26,713	83,759	76,982	47.2	285,100	902
Sandy	94,025	8.0	10.6	106,572	43,750	40,165	54,622	30,858	33,297	31,740	84.1	312,600	1,126
South Jordan	95,764	4.5	9.7	110,729	50,290	40,098	51,624	24,959	21,549	20,979	77.7	385,300	1,348
Spanish Fork	70,897	12.8	5.5	76,274	25,519	30,131	46,006	11,404	9,369	9,136	73.6	241,800	1,179
Springville	65,851	4.3	2.8	70,386	40,076	26,397	33,951	20,357	9,073	8,563	68.3	239,100	1,007
Taylorsville	55,359	12.2	1.9	63,005	33,883	29,957	32,477	26,104	21,147	20,450	68.7	219,800	941
Tooele	50,355	10.9	0.8	58,578	26,894	29,146	36,882	17,786	11,007	10,658	75.1	160,000	905
West Jordan	71,517	4.7	2.3	77,287	46,483	30,750	37,101	25,928	33,690	32,556	73.1	252,100	1,160
West Valley City	63,882	9.4	2.0	65,276	41,163	27,494	32,225	24,783	38,506	37,400	68.6	202,200	1,073
VERMONT	57,677	16.2	4.8	74,805	32,445	32,028	36,322	29,214	329,539	254,851	69.8	223,700	925
Burlington	43,838	26.0	2.9	79,401	27,878	16,899	17,592	16,299	16,189	15,514	39.2	269,300	1,080
VIRGINIA	68,114	13.3	9.3	83,306	41,568	36,282	41,905	30,591	3,491,185	3,120,692	65.3	264,000	1,159
Alexandria	87,920	7.6	17.0	120,726	73,872	55,460	66,401	48,221	76,573	69,875	39.7	578,500	1,625
Blacksburg	34,232	39.6	6.7	100,408	15,074	6,832	10,083	6,242	16,056	14,300	30.0	310,200	998
Charlottesville	45,547	25.5	4.4	66,799	27,634	25,000	27,150	20,116	20,603	18,443	37.5	277,400	1,120
Chesapeake	72,928	10.0	6.5	81,981	44,220	36,707	41,488	33,075	90,115	83,364	70.7	267,100	1,184
Danville	36,936	27.5	0.7	46,063	23,054	25,728	26,898	23,254	22,262	17,936	53.4	100,900	628
Hampton	50,435	16.8	2.3	62,418	40,106	30,874	36,263	27,392	60,419	54,181	56.8	194,900	1,057
Harrisonburg	42,521	28.5	1.7	61,748	20,003	15,767	19,027	10,476	18,233	16,619	42.5	187,200	736
Leesburg	108,609	2.8	19.7	126,817	67,376	56,163	80,314	35,039	18,783	17,892	73.5	411,700	1,431
Lynchburg	41,264	20.0	2.3	52,314	27,984	20,076	20,762	18,288	32,591	27,545	48.9	153,600	725
Manassas	70,193	14.0	5.1	79,931	44,125	35,078	37,455	26,259	13,336	12,351	66.0	312,300	1,437
Newport News	50,524	15.3	3.2	63,223	31,164	28,203	32,055	23,726	78,019	67,628	49.4	185,000	991
Norfolk	46,467	21.8	3.1	55,717	36,715	26,402	28,942	23,218	97,865	87,910	41.0	195,500	988
Petersburg	33,850	33.6	1.7	46,122	24,177	25,640	26,968	24,844	16,481	13,493	35.7	101,000	856
Portsmouth	48,516	18.7	1.8	57,065	36,325	29,628	32,980	23,927	41,154	36,615	53.2	174,800	968
Richmond	42,373	26.8	4.9	57,064	32,871	27,068	30,706	25,207	100,671	91,704	41.3	211,400	942
Roanoke	37,044	27.2	1.4	46,710	26,057	26,749	31,340	23,712	47,392	42,213	52.9	125,500	750
Suffolk	66,669	12.3	4.8	76,366	40,414	37,374	47,387	30,736	36,200	33,377	66.3	247,600	1,096
Virginia Beach	71,117	8.9	5.9	81,081	49,116	35,479	39,533	30,698	184,348	168,061	62.2	271,400	1,280
Winchester	43,798	15.0	6.4	41,954	41,321	22,181	23,517	21,399	13,548	11,563	40.5	226,500	933
WASHINGTON	67,106	12.7	7.6	81,234	41,513	36,353	43,776	29,662	3,025,802	2,768,076	62.5	306,400	1,135
Auburn	60,430	13.6	5.5	73,628	37,224	38,238	41,395	35,575	30,495	29,453	59.1	279,800	1,074
Bellevue	113,877	7.4	22.4	130,610	82,490	66,056	81,900	46,826	61,902	56,289	57.6	756,800	1,846
Bellingham	47,652	20.7	3.0	75,180	32,541	21,428	25,918	15,714	35,734	34,317	40.6	352,700	961
Bothell	81,443	6.2	14.7	111,452	45,085	44,782	58,849	31,875	17,990	17,095	59.0	466,500	1,547
Bremerton	50,562	21.3	1.4	56,579	37,839	30,475	33,890	23,243	18,218	16,066	40.0	201,800	960
Burien	55,260	11.5	4.3	69,668	34,647	31,657	32,148	29,936	22,285	20,840	51.2	345,700	1,030
Des Moines	70,155	7.3	4.6	81,128	46,775	32,473	39,378	30,679	12,775	12,298	58.7	314,600	1,202
Edmonds	84,864	6.6	15.3	113,366	52,902	50,051	60,995	39,770	17,788	17,063	75.0	463,300	1,290
Everett	52,626	17.4	4.5	62,331	37,529	33,981	39,822	26,768	45,217	42,175	43.1	293,700	1,078
Federal Way	65,788	11.8	3.9	71,325	51,834	36,426	45,164	30,963	36,258	35,043	55.4	314,700	1,204
Issaquah	100,989	6.9	18.1	122,460	72,272	53,073	76,215	40,848	15,878	14,913	59.2	608,600	1,881
Kennewick	56,483	15.3	3.4	71,433	32,013	31,614	40,139	26,185	30,222	28,558	64.6	194,900	838
Kent	65,423	13.3	4.8	68,597	48,874	35,113	40,793	28,001	46,256	44,532	52.8	320,000	1,180
Kirkland	114,336	8.1	16.3	126,680	73,658	56,930	71,822	44,353	37,661	34,997	65.1	582,100	1,688
Lacey	59,748	11.3	2.3	68,628	41,940	33,194	45,434	26,392	19,267	18,539	55.5	248,200	1,240
Lake Stevens	88,878	5.0	5.3	91,325	61,006	48,449	52,598	41,507	11,180	10,908	77.6	335,900	1,670
Lakewood	47,637	16.4	2.6	52,927	33,450	30,040	35,854	28,050	26,722	25,529	36.8	260,800	951
Longview	37,232	27.1	0.9	51,467	23,758	21,657	21,577	21,689	15,531	14,342	52.4	167,000	795
Lynnwood	60,405	22.3	4.9	78,389	35,934	31,298	42,952	22,385	15,664	14,539	55.1	368,000	1,089
Marysville	73,132	10.8	4.0	85,890	44,419	37,091	49,243	30,275	25,412	24,490	70.7	286,300	1,293
Mount Vernon	59,285	14.9	2.9	70,979	31,346	24,827	30,796	22,718	12,932	11,623	59.6	252,400	918
Olympia	56,061	18.0	4.9	75,975	35,848	34,625	37,952	31,101	23,937	22,411	45.6	261,900	1,051

1. Specified owner-occupied units; $2,000,000 represents $2,000,000 or more.

Table D. Cities — Commuting, Computer Access, Migration, Labor Force, and Employment

AREANAME	Commuting[1] 2016 Percent — Drove alone	With commutes of 30 minutes or more	Computer access[2] Percent — With a computer in the house	With Internet access	Migration — Percent who lived in the same house one year ago	Percent who lived in another state or county one year ago	Civilian labor force, 2016 — Total	Percent change 2016-2017	Unemployment[3] — Total	Rate	Civilian employment, 2016 — Population age 16 and older — Number	Percent in labor force	Population age 16 to 64 — Number	Percent who worked full-year full-time
	55	56	57	58	59	60	61	62	63	64	65	66	67	68
UTAH— Cont'd														
Kaysville	77.2	35.1	NA	NA	NA	NA	14,634	3.2	409	2.8	20,405	60.0	18,192	43.4
Layton	80.0	34.2	94.1	83.9	86.0	7.2	38,867	3.2	1,213	3.1	53,209	67.7	45,500	51.7
Lehi	76.5	31.5	97.3	91.6	81.9	8.3	26,861	4.7	801	3.0	37,953	69.6	34,366	48.4
Logan	69.9	9.6	94.7	83.6	71.0	11.0	27,989	2.5	771	2.8	38,590	72.8	35,289	42.3
Midvale	71.4	29.4	95.3	86.5	70.4	13.1	20,352	3.0	632	3.1	24,376	70.1	22,597	54.6
Murray	73.9	18.4	88.6	77.7	82.0	8.8	29,573	2.8	890	3.0	39,672	68.2	29,796	57.5
Ogden	83.0	19.0	87.2	77.4	83.3	6.0	41,911	2.9	1,706	4.1	63,852	63.3	55,602	51.4
Orem	76.6	17.8	96.7	90.8	75.9	7.4	51,035	4.5	1,516	3.0	71,375	70.0	61,838	45.2
Pleasant Grove	83.2	22.7	96.2	86.0	79.1	8.2	19,225	4.5	567	2.9	28,817	72.2	26,518	47.5
Provo	62.2	16.9	97.8	66.7	60.2	17.9	66,899	4.4	1,859	2.8	94,770	73.1	88,536	32.3
Riverton	75.3	40.0	97.8	92.9	NA	NA	23,783	2.8	626	2.6	28,030	74.1	25,222	50.5
Roy	79.5	26.1	94.6	90.4	81.1	12.0	19,206	3.3	756	3.9	28,209	69.5	24,025	57.0
St. George	73.9	11.1	89.4	80.7	78.4	9.2	36,544	4.9	1,240	3.4	63,871	57.3	47,896	40.8
Salt Lake City	69.0	19.8	93.3	79.9	79.1	9.0	112,853	3.0	3,462	3.1	156,453	72.9	136,178	54.4
Sandy	76.8	32.1	93.8	86.4	85.5	4.7	54,272	2.9	1,609	3.0	73,927	67.3	60,380	54.0
South Jordan	67.9	42.3	97.6	87.4	85.6	7.1	35,656	3.0	1,042	2.9	50,016	70.5	43,647	54.6
Spanish Fork	80.5	21.7	95.6	91.7	81.4	5.6	17,697	4.3	519	2.9	22,770	66.6	21,136	45.3
Springville	80.7	20.3	96.4	91.2	82.4	7.7	16,509	4.5	479	2.9	21,422	69.9	19,069	48.7
Taylorsville	79.8	23.7	93.9	82.3	82.9	5.9	34,526	2.9	1,114	3.2	47,111	71.1	39,465	56.4
Tooele	77.1	43.0	88.5	82.5	81.3	11.7	16,622	2.7	648	3.9	23,909	62.0	20,824	43.5
West Jordan	81.0	33.8	97.3	93.5	85.0	3.2	63,213	2.8	1,862	2.9	81,328	74.8	74,125	56.3
West Valley City	73.8	26.7	94.4	85.9	82.1	7.6	71,943	2.9	2,378	3.3	98,130	73.1	86,626	55.4
VERMONT	75.6	31.1	89.3	81.3	86.4	6.0	344,760	0.1	10,382	3.0	519,521	65.2	405,921	52.0
Burlington	47.9	18.4	90.8	84.1	65.6	14.5	24,084	0.5	595	2.5	35,910	63.6	31,476	35.9
VIRGINIA	76.9	42.1	90.5	83.3	84.3	9.1	4,307,753	1.5	161,619	3.8	6,761,091	65.8	5,533,046	53.2
Alexandria	59.6	55.5	95.6	90.6	77.3	15.8	98,590	2.4	2,829	2.9	129,596	77.1	113,888	65.8
Blacksburg	62.1	10.4	98.2	93.6	59.6	24.5	20,637	0.4	984	4.8	41,317	57.0	39,251	22.1
Charlottesville	57.0	14.0	92.4	78.0	71.2	19.4	25,558	2.9	791	3.1	40,509	59.9	35,973	38.9
Chesapeake	82.9	42.7	92.5	88.6	86.0	9.6	119,577	1.5	4,624	3.9	187,281	66.9	157,564	53.3
Danville	72.0	15.5	83.9	76.6	87.4	4.8	19,140	0.3	1,151	6.0	33,218	55.2	24,648	43.5
Hampton	82.9	26.4	92.6	81.9	84.7	9.3	64,727	1.3	3,292	5.1	109,432	64.4	90,137	51.9
Harrisonburg	66.8	13.5	91.7	78.2	66.4	23.2	24,559	1.5	1,097	4.5	45,367	63.1	40,319	32.6
Leesburg	75.0	58.9	98.2	95.9	91.2	3.3	28,867	2.1	828	2.9	40,086	75.5	35,767	58.5
Lynchburg	71.2	11.0	86.6	76.4	76.8	18.1	35,820	1.0	1,777	5.0	66,551	61.2	55,058	38.1
Manassas	79.1	57.7	92.2	90.1	86.2	7.3	22,051	2.3	749	3.4	31,612	70.3	27,631	48.6
Newport News	78.2	25.3	91.6	83.0	78.2	11.7	90,074	1.5	4,191	4.7	143,398	69.1	121,181	53.5
Norfolk	70.8	24.2	89.4	83.1	72.3	15.2	111,699	1.4	5,197	4.7	200,912	69.7	175,629	53.5
Petersburg	76.3	37.3	80.7	70.9	70.0	18.2	13,392	1.5	978	7.3	25,302	60.2	20,186	46.9
Portsmouth	75.6	33.3	86.4	76.2	79.2	10.7	44,552	1.2	2,418	5.4	75,067	66.3	61,685	54.1
Richmond	74.2	21.8	87.1	71.4	77.5	12.4	116,588	1.8	5,089	4.4	186,086	65.9	159,503	46.4
Roanoke	81.2	41.7	85.5	73.3	82.8	7.8	48,976	0.2	2,066	4.2	79,157	62.7	63,967	52.2
Suffolk	86.1	48.3	90.4	82.8	88.0	7.9	43,492	1.4	1,808	4.2	69,718	64.9	57,498	56.3
Virginia Beach	80.6	31.3	94.7	89.0	80.8	9.0	232,521	1.6	8,373	3.6	362,611	71.5	303,021	56.7
Winchester	69.8	18.9	78.3	73.3	81.6	11.2	14,570	1.9	527	3.6	22,781	59.5	17,697	44.4
WASHINGTON	72.1	40.0	93.0	87.3	82.3	7.6	3,724,722	2.5	177,292	4.8	5,841,524	64.1	4,762,711	49.7
Auburn	76.8	54.4	92.9	88.7	78.9	8.2	40,083	2.6	1,759	4.4	57,691	67.6	49,299	50.9
Bellevue	64.6	37.2	97.9	95.5	78.4	8.6	78,917	2.2	2,710	3.4	115,037	65.8	93,475	57.3
Bellingham	66.6	19.4	91.7	87.1	72.5	10.5	46,386	2.8	2,215	4.8	74,446	64.2	62,722	39.7
Bothell	72.8	51.0	94.4	91.4	80.9	9.5	25,201	2.5	999	4.0	36,825	65.8	31,283	48.5
Bremerton	66.4	31.5	89.1	84.8	75.9	7.8	17,070	2.3	993	5.8	33,516	65.0	29,254	53.0
Burien	68.8	44.0	91.2	86.3	86.9	2.3	27,150	2.1	1,149	4.2	41,935	68.4	35,346	50.3
Des Moines	74.4	49.9	95.2	92.4	83.0	6.5	16,472	2.0	719	4.4	25,919	65.5	20,626	55.2
Edmonds	75.0	53.9	95.5	91.5	82.9	11.1	22,985	2.0	859	3.7	35,491	65.3	27,097	51.3
Everett	67.5	38.5	92.5	80.3	80.5	6.7	56,151	2.2	2,553	4.5	88,922	64.9	75,713	50.5
Federal Way	74.8	60.0	94.0	89.5	76.5	8.4	50,220	2.2	2,162	4.3	74,993	66.7	61,615	49.9
Issaquah	63.1	51.6	99.0	95.7	77.0	7.1	21,009	2.3	712	3.4	28,648	76.9	24,733	56.7
Kennewick	80.3	22.5	92.2	86.2	87.2	5.1	40,470	3.3	2,181	5.4	59,666	59.9	48,850	46.0
Kent	67.0	55.6	94.6	89.8	83.2	4.5	65,216	2.2	2,823	4.3	100,069	68.2	86,324	50.7
Kirkland	70.7	42.8	96.7	93.5	82.0	8.4	52,485	2.6	1,941	3.7	71,525	70.7	59,878	55.2
Lacey	80.8	33.8	91.4	88.8	73.6	14.7	20,714	3.5	1,118	5.4	37,608	58.0	28,869	47.2
Lake Stevens	78.2	53.2	97.7	94.2	83.3	5.2	16,735	4.0	721	4.3	23,069	71.0	19,313	61.0
Lakewood	76.0	36.5	91.6	87.4	77.4	7.6	26,361	3.0	1,539	5.8	49,293	60.4	40,994	50.4
Longview	77.7	22.7	90.7	77.3	80.3	8.2	15,519	2.4	946	6.1	28,870	52.3	21,855	33.6
Lynnwood	69.2	47.9	91.7	87.5	90.1	4.8	20,307	2.0	855	4.2	33,812	63.8	28,089	38.6
Marysville	80.0	43.9	95.2	90.5	85.9	4.7	34,759	2.9	1,509	4.3	53,061	67.0	43,408	51.0
Mount Vernon	80.7	28.7	94.0	91.1	78.3	11.6	15,459	2.5	865	5.6	26,479	61.2	20,602	51.1
Olympia	74.2	22.3	91.5	81.2	72.3	16.7	27,289	4.0	1,302	4.8	44,435	63.9	35,641	47.0

1. Employed persons.   2. Households.   3. Percent of civilian labor force.

Table D. Cities — Construction, Wholesale Trade, and Retail Trade

AREANAME	Value of residential construction authorized by building permits, 2017			Wholesale trade[1], 2012				Retail trade[2], 2012			
	New construction ($1,000)	Number of housing units	Percent single family	Number of establishments	Number of employees	Sales (mil dol)	Annual payroll (mil dol)	Number of establishments	Number of employees	Sales (mil dol)	Annual payroll (mil dol)
	69	70	71	72	73	74	75	76	77	78	79
UTAH— Cont'd											
Kaysville	44,525	123	100.0	22	269	117.4	11.7	62	707	169.1	17.7
Layton	67,897	302	72.8	47	321	117.8	10.7	295	4,761	1,123.0	106.0
Lehi	256,527	934	100.0	22	303	180.4	15.0	144	2,159	637.8	63.4
Logan	39,027	328	58.8	67	606	435.2	23.7	248	3,710	725.7	71.2
Midvale	12,860	55	96.4	48	604	354.9	25.5	149	2,153	554.8	53.1
Murray	21,621	88	100.0	109	1,032	520.2	54.1	353	5,656	1,921.1	161.3
Ogden	14,084	96	87.5	100	1,412	949.3	67.5	344	3,839	1,121.8	93.9
Orem	76,614	414	44.9	102	1,421	658.4	62.1	451	7,296	1,843.7	165.6
Pleasant Grove	25,050	71	93.0	19	75	28.7	2.6	65	675	219.9	21.0
Provo	53,365	240	92.9	55	1,506	1,153.2	99.6	317	4,334	1,205.9	98.9
Riverton	87,233	355	67.6	21	76	42.2	2.7	68	1,184	261.9	25.9
Roy	3,362	32	65.6	7	D	D	D	72	906	236.3	19.3
St. George	214,583	1,595	59.1	106	D	D	D	425	5,477	1,468.9	126.9
Salt Lake City	98,297	630	14.0	603	12,541	10,292.8	748.3	918	14,096	4,071.1	374.7
Sandy	55,116	385	11.7	130	1,173	847.6	59.8	382	6,580	2,199.2	187.0
South Jordan	239,504	1,055	79.9	38	1,231	900.5	73.8	112	2,249	662.1	55.5
Spanish Fork	84,875	341	81.5	19	186	106.2	7.3	88	1,077	204.4	19.6
Springville	33,684	113	100.0	25	639	228.5	25.2	74	1,095	301.6	23.9
Taylorsville	23,853	154	11.0	18	76	41.8	2.9	101	1,695	375.1	36.2
Tooele	14,394	90	100.0	7	D	D	D	75	1,334	361.7	31.4
West Jordan	167,824	799	56.6	76	1,201	1,118.5	66.9	207	3,971	945.0	84.5
West Valley City	29,524	224	100.0	143	2,669	1,906.8	143.3	280	5,549	1,457.0	157.9
VERMONT	326,499	1,749	56.2	696	9,464	6,450.1	464.4	3,509	38,910	9,933.8	967.1
Burlington	6,829	63	12.7	48	539	327.8	37.4	224	3,271	610.2	75.9
VIRGINIA	5,747,050	33,760	66.6	6,232	88,353	86,613.6	4,983.1	27,415	410,918	110,002.4	10,007.9
Alexandria	33,029	149	100.0	82	1,139	502.8	61.6	480	7,180	2,416.0	222.6
Blacksburg	20,279	98	100.0	14	D	D	D	97	1,363	284.4	22.3
Charlottesville	64,041	193	46.1	48	513	183.3	23.7	331	3,925	747.9	82.8
Chesapeake	341,818	1,077	100.0	239	3,447	2,225.2	169.7	789	15,088	4,114.9	336.7
Danville	1,104	4	100.0	50	545	285.2	24.5	306	4,165	965.0	87.2
Hampton	10,621	170	100.0	71	886	344.7	39.3	436	6,791	1,512.5	148.3
Harrisonburg	11,278	61	90.2	57	1,006	405.9	43.2	334	5,664	1,519.8	144.6
Leesburg	5,369	22	100.0	27	366	172.4	19.0	266	5,403	1,388.7	124.5
Lynchburg	21,970	156	69.2	69	877	509.0	39.0	385	7,371	1,995.2	178.2
Manassas	21,324	239	16.7	41	D	D	D	194	2,778	895.3	86.1
Newport News	44,889	441	22.7	110	1,438	851.3	72.7	686	9,879	2,480.8	229.7
Norfolk	68,781	633	67.8	209	3,287	3,195.3	161.6	867	12,440	2,683.2	281.6
Petersburg	194	3	100.0	21	570	560.1	16.2	145	1,426	334.5	33.0
Portsmouth	19,541	158	100.0	48	688	249.5	32.0	273	3,081	699.5	71.1
Richmond	122,715	1,317	24.8	269	3,767	3,288.5	201.3	808	8,666	1,955.2	206.1
Roanoke	24,249	174	10.3	180	2,727	1,398.0	130.3	535	9,912	2,461.0	230.1
Suffolk	91,292	562	91.5	54	961	666.0	49.8	226	3,536	958.9	79.1
Virginia Beach	198,525	1,523	42.4	391	6,893	8,187.6	477.1	1,500	22,723	5,671.5	521.6
Winchester	22,932	170	10.6	39	677	286.8	26.1	283	4,126	888.5	94.4
WASHINGTON	9,912,596	45,794	50.5	7,733	103,307	83,313.4	5,789.8	21,588	307,089	118,924.0	8,722.5
Auburn	45,122	139	100.0	174	3,739	4,631.5	198.0	281	4,676	1,475.0	140.8
Bellevue	291,136	1,308	28.5	324	4,333	5,128.3	368.3	673	12,225	4,113.9	412.6
Bellingham	80,416	571	38.0	147	D	D	D	532	8,805	2,243.5	206.9
Bothell	105,897	519	31.0	63	1,357	1,465.7	112.4	100	1,451	363.3	41.6
Bremerton	27,843	112	100.0	27	191	83.1	9.6	134	1,704	572.5	55.8
Burien	18,045	58	100.0	23	138	33.0	4.7	163	2,013	573.1	58.3
Des Moines	91,490	451	10.0	15	116	91.7	10.1	38	360	93.3	10.2
Edmonds	37,622	184	32.6	39	201	177.8	12.4	133	1,449	448.2	43.9
Everett	66,011	294	88.8	134	2,108	1,355.6	129.1	449	6,782	2,023.4	194.6
Federal Way	24,893	74	70.3	54	450	250.1	22.5	257	4,441	1,184.1	118.0
Issaquah	149,583	831	15.0	44	272	372.7	17.3	136	3,108	2,801.7	110.1
Kennewick	75,487	387	56.1	67	659	927.9	31.5	378	6,113	1,620.4	148.4
Kent	117,496	351	90.9	430	8,772	6,803.7	509.9	340	4,711	1,447.2	137.9
Kirkland	158,674	349	94.0	104	1,023	656.4	81.0	216	4,128	1,776.8	148.9
Lacey	47,088	163	100.0	23	493	421.0	24.6	148	3,567	869.8	92.1
Lake Stevens	54,238	169	98.8	6	40	15.9	1.2	45	848	219.2	20.3
Lakewood	15,056	60	81.7	67	834	1,407.2	41.8	227	2,725	701.2	69.7
Longview	6,710	33	75.8	39	637	712.5	30.9	175	3,043	796.3	78.7
Lynnwood	13,514	43	100.0	95	794	407.1	44.8	425	7,823	2,042.0	210.1
Marysville	35,639	235	32.8	34	236	117.4	12.5	172	3,450	933.4	88.4
Mount Vernon	26,123	159	100.0	32	385	219.6	18.1	135	2,017	491.7	53.0
Olympia	28,508	127	74.0	39	390	461.9	24.3	367	5,515	1,396.7	142.3

1. Merchant wholesalers except manufacturers' sales branches and offices. 2. Establishments with payroll.

AREANAME	Real estate and rental and leasing, 2012				Professional, scientific, and technical services[1], 2012				Manufacturing, 2012			
	Number of establish-ments	Number of employees	Receipts (mil dol)	Annual payroll (mil dol)	Number of establish-ments	Number of employees	Receipts (mil dol)	Annual payroll (mil dol)	Number of establish-ments	Number of employees	Receipts (mil dol)	Annual payroll (mil dol)
	80	81	82	83	84	85	86	87	88	89	90	91
UTAH— Cont'd												
Kaysville	36	77	11.5	2.4	90	647	74.6	35.3	15	180	37.4	7.1
Layton	111	313	69.3	9.9	177	D	D	D	43	870	372.5	39.8
Lehi	58	70	17.2	3.3	173	D	D	D	32	518	198.1	27.0
Logan	108	396	57.3	14.3	179	D	D	D	112	7,049	2,431.3	301.9
Midvale	69	468	105.0	25.5	92	D	D	D	34	435	D	18.9
Murray	134	1,271	154.0	51.4	300	2,624	380.0	136.7	118	1,590	320.6	65.0
Ogden	100	413	51.5	10.6	245	D	D	D	134	7,939	3,135.1	383.0
Orem	185	566	108.3	15.8	358	7,806	401.3	195.9	122	2,729	780.8	124.9
Pleasant Grove	48	98	13.9	3.4	99	670	83.9	32.6	30	238	D	9.1
Provo	120	569	85.7	13.1	346	D	D	D	81	1,908	376.7	96.3
Riverton	41	95	15.9	2.7	89	191	14.6	4.9	8	D	D	0.7
Roy	19	54	5.6	1.0	29	249	16.2	8.5	17	65	8.1	D
St. George	218	541	77.1	14.8	324	D	D	D	87	1,376	322.3	55.1
Salt Lake City	528	3,093	878.2	142.4	1,434	16,666	3,114.5	1,238.7	457	24,316	11,969.2	1,556.7
Sandy	202	654	157.6	28.0	443	2,500	324.0	131.8	103	2,619	891.9	137.8
South Jordan	93	253	42.3	10.3	230	1,478	223.0	60.7	23	D	D	D
Spanish Fork	29	60	12.7	2.1	80	381	36.1	9.2	39	1,771	671.8	94.5
Springville	19	21	2.9	0.6	66	320	29.0	10.5	46	3,092	1,538.7	143.1
Taylorsville	48	157	20.9	4.6	85	D	D	D	17	601	85.8	26.6
Tooele	19	61	8.5	1.3	32	165	13.4	6.1	19	729	343.7	D
West Jordan	82	181	30.4	5.2	153	D	D	D	106	2,439	895.2	116.7
West Valley City	73	525	111.5	24.5	118	D	D	D	156	4,762	2,397.5	240.5
VERMONT	741	3,092	509.9	103.6	2,093	15,781	1,762.8	730.9	1,013	31,487	9,315.5	1,594.3
Burlington	61	347	91.9	15.5	267	D	D	D	24	613	192.2	30.9
VIRGINIA	8,862	54,246	11,758.9	2,378.3	29,176	416,651	90,042.2	35,093.6	5,101	228,197	96,389.9	11,586.1
Alexandria	240	1,475	524.1	76.6	1,228	16,537	3,436.0	1,497.8	72	1,332	273.0	57.9
Blacksburg	50	393	73.4	14.9	153	D	D	D	20	1,473	514.6	99.8
Charlottesville	99	502	107.6	19.7	316	D	D	D	46	455	98.7	21.6
Chesapeake	273	1,227	291.6	52.9	509	7,649	1,029.3	412.6	130	3,965	1,504.2	211.6
Danville	64	339	48.7	9.1	72	D	D	D	46	4,635	1,703.0	223.7
Hampton	114	750	117.3	23.7	273	D	D	D	68	2,189	508.3	114.9
Harrisonburg	72	351	75.9	10.9	137	D	D	D	46	2,556	832.6	99.4
Leesburg	64	288	136.2	14.5	302	D	D	D	11	347	D	D
Lynchburg	109	447	79.9	14.5	199	D	D	D	83	8,339	2,749.6	504.3
Manassas	52	229	64.0	11.4	212	D	D	D	32	4,012	1,365.7	366.4
Newport News	254	1,672	276.5	60.3	361	D	D	D	91	26,503	5,578.9	1,558.5
Norfolk	291	2,496	430.8	127.7	700	D	D	D	130	6,866	1,812.5	328.2
Petersburg	32	223	27.2	5.8	34	D	D	D	28	1,646	D	91.0
Portsmouth	71	332	52.6	9.7	144	D	D	D	56	2,196	447.1	97.6
Richmond	258	1,539	304.3	67.1	844	10,249	2,511.6	888.8	187	5,882	16,885.9	386.3
Roanoke	155	950	141.8	31.0	326	D	D	D	100	3,869	1,629.7	174.8
Suffolk	67	243	37.5	8.1	121	D	D	D	46	1,996	1,521.0	103.6
Virginia Beach	649	6,165	902.5	210.7	1,391	17,195	3,883.4	1,188.8	207	5,616	1,954.2	255.1
Winchester	59	260	56.4	8.0	130	D	D	D	23	2,197	866.2	117.6
WASHINGTON	9,913	45,209	9,695.5	1,895.1	19,882	D	D	D	6,992	248,192	131,530.6	14,461.8
Auburn	86	344	96.7	13.9	120	D	D	D	159	9,859	1,243.4	582.4
Bellevue	517	3,594	974.9	195.2	1,260	14,873	2,735.3	1,204.9	115	1,733	621.1	87.9
Bellingham	199	847	193.4	27.6	432	D	D	D	126	3,061	D	129.2
Bothell	75	269	75.9	9.9	201	D	D	D	38	3,273	1,724.1	260.6
Bremerton	67	218	38.4	6.6	83	D	D	D	21	578	D	27.2
Burien	72	226	38.4	6.5	95	477	40.2	15.8	28	82	D	2.8
Des Moines	16	36	6.0	1.1	32	106	9.0	3.5	6	18	3.2	0.8
Edmonds	76	205	46.1	10.6	174	755	109.3	45.1	19	214	D	9.2
Everett	168	1,056	172.8	36.9	312	D	D	D	134	43,136	D	3,324.1
Federal Way	101	442	92.4	15.2	167	1,491	176.7	97.4	25	347	D	12.5
Issaquah	77	311	89.4	14.5	189	1,046	145.5	96.2	27	1,407	505.4	96.3
Kennewick	117	683	123.7	19.6	202	D	D	D	45	714	293.9	37.4
Kent	155	866	200.1	36.9	217	1,766	282.1	127.2	247	14,012	7,642.4	924.1
Kirkland	182	867	643.3	64.0	457	D	D	D	50	668	146.4	34.4
Lacey	54	210	45.1	6.0	74	2,388	319.2	147.8	17	415	D	19.8
Lake Stevens	30	D	D	D	20	69	7.1	2.5	12	D	5.4	D
Lakewood	102	445	85.3	12.9	111	544	55.3	21.0	36	585	D	24.6
Longview	55	208	34.2	5.8	83	D	D	D	37	2,469	1,391.6	203.7
Lynnwood	90	307	99.0	13.1	155	D	D	D	48	675	213.4	31.0
Marysville	63	218	67.8	9.8	60	336	31.8	8.4	55	1,672	340.2	68.8
Mount Vernon	56	143	24.1	4.4	117	512	64.3	22.6	32	673	328.2	26.9
Olympia	114	428	88.3	14.2	280	1,524	210.6	88.8	32	514	205.9	24.6

1. Establishments subject to federal tax.

Accommodation and Food Services, Arts, Entertainment, and Recreation, and Health Care and Social Assistance

AREANAME	Accommodation and food services, 2012				Arts, entertainment, and recreation[1], 2012				Health care and social assistance,[1] 2012			
	Number of establishments	Number of employees	Receipts (mil dol)	Annual payroll (mil dol)	Number of establishments	Number of employees	Receipts (mil dol)	Annual payroll (mil dol)	Number of establishments	Number of employees	Receipts (mil dol)	Annual payroll (mil dol)
	92	93	94	95	96	97	98	99	100	101	102	103
UTAH— Cont'd												
Kaysville	16	354	11.4	3.4	6	239	14.9	3.3	52	D	D	D
Layton	149	3,414	138.2	40.9	19	D	D	D	156	2,734	304.0	116.0
Lehi	50	1,117	48.2	12.4	17	D	D	D	62	D	D	D
Logan	120	2,287	98.7	26.6	19	244	10.7	1.9	175	D	D	D
Midvale	94	1,572	73.1	21.6	6	D	D	D	53	D	D	D
Murray	113	2,538	120.0	40.6	13	D	D	D	298	D	D	D
Ogden	184	3,206	124.0	36.2	14	D	D	D	270	D	D	D
Orem	152	3,262	148.0	43.6	43	D	D	D	238	4,058	391.5	134.5
Pleasant Grove	29	280	12.9	3.1	11	35	4.6	0.8	60	D	D	D
Provo	186	3,335	143.9	40.6	32	387	25.6	7.2	285	D	D	D
Riverton	48	758	32.8	9.6	5	10	0.8	0.2	79	D	D	D
Roy	40	661	29.6	7.4	5	55	1.5	0.6	53	D	D	D
St. George	216	3,957	197.1	55.1	30	393	13.9	4.6	383	D	D	D
Salt Lake City	735	16,057	961.6	277.0	77	1,617	227.7	90.4	587	5,979	775.9	270.9
Sandy	188	3,696	173.1	49.7	28	D	D	D	272	D	D	D
South Jordan	68	1,569	65.6	20.3	13	D	D	D	123	D	D	D
Spanish Fork	40	664	28.4	7.4	7	D	D	D	59	644	44.7	15.2
Springville	39	D	D	D	7	26	1.6	0.3	63	D	D	D
Taylorsville	83	1,618	80.8	21.1	11	D	D	D	100	1,045	93.1	34.5
Tooele	45	755	33.8	8.9	6	60	3.3	1.1	58	D	D	D
West Jordan	116	2,362	125.2	32.2	13	D	D	D	170	2,883	365.1	92.4
West Valley City	179	2,987	161.6	43.4	18	D	D	D	101	D	D	D
VERMONT	1,920	31,365	1,564.3	494.0	286	5,468	233.6	73.7	1,370	14,976	1,297.2	578.2
Burlington	151	2,846	172.1	51.6	12	107	7.2	2.0	96	1,655	135.2	70.7
VIRGINIA	16,832	320,514	17,795.9	4,908.6	1,970	35,718	2,993.0	875.7	16,070	236,459	25,556.4	10,868.1
Alexandria	387	8,051	647.5	180.7	41	606	45.8	15.2	343	3,739	466.5	194.6
Blacksburg	100	2,054	91.4	25.1	7	D	D	D	93	1,512	197.5	73.2
Charlottesville	293	5,199	293.3	75.9	25	D	D	D	121	D	D	D
Chesapeake	466	10,267	447.6	121.1	42	D	D	D	456	6,275	637.4	290.0
Danville	139	2,850	120.4	33.6	11	D	D	D	175	3,730	374.9	152.4
Hampton	250	5,380	249.0	72.2	23	D	D	D	217	3,137	322.2	134.7
Harrisonburg	186	4,468	216.0	58.8	11	D	D	D	128	2,006	163.9	75.6
Leesburg	118	2,305	135.4	37.9	11	D	D	D	166	1,736	209.9	92.8
Lynchburg	215	5,071	216.4	61.0	21	243	10.2	3.1	205	D	D	D
Manassas	109	1,587	91.4	24.7	10	116	4.8	1.4	157	D	D	D
Newport News	386	6,621	323.8	87.6	28	D	D	D	327	6,977	693.3	380.1
Norfolk	593	11,264	547.1	148.4	41	504	37.2	10.7	422	6,733	776.7	359.3
Petersburg	79	885	39.1	10.2	6	D	D	D	103	3,619	364.2	135.7
Portsmouth	172	2,624	107.1	29.3	17	119	10.7	2.2	166	3,362	274.4	117.8
Richmond	618	11,470	576.5	184.1	53	896	52.7	10.8	441	11,147	1,922.8	628.0
Roanoke	320	6,509	308.1	94.4	17	188	7.9	2.6	228	4,017	462.5	191.5
Suffolk	147	2,477	122.9	30.6	12	D	D	D	155	2,625	273.4	125.1
Virginia Beach	1,153	21,910	1,202.7	324.3	153	1,714	129.4	31.6	919	12,464	1,177.1	571.3
Winchester	130	2,518	119.1	33.1	12	D	D	D	226	D	D	D
WASHINGTON	16,333	234,145	14,297.3	4,159.7	2,029	41,184	4,079.6	1,177.3	16,888	194,136	20,414.0	8,703.2
Auburn	145	1,859	107.0	30.9	28	D	D	D	163	2,421	232.0	100.8
Bellevue	432	8,993	618.4	184.7	63	1,856	151.9	47.0	887	8,423	958.7	398.7
Bellingham	325	5,589	277.4	84.5	50	434	20.2	6.1	423	4,236	422.2	171.3
Bothell	140	1,982	120.6	32.9	7	D	D	D	152	1,457	128.3	50.7
Bremerton	108	1,440	88.2	22.7	6	76	2.2	0.9	110	2,072	208.8	76.9
Burien	103	1,221	61.3	17.6	11	D	D	D	182	1,404	166.8	67.1
Des Moines	55	744	42.8	12.0	2	D	D	D	55	475	34.1	14.8
Edmonds	113	1,426	83.1	23.3	11	346	20.8	6.3	210	D	D	D
Everett	343	4,457	265.2	72.9	27	364	18.6	6.4	362	5,867	622.3	298.1
Federal Way	221	3,085	182.5	51.8	16	325	14.1	6.6	320	4,356	425.8	144.9
Issaquah	109	1,729	107.2	31.5	8	260	12.5	4.3	200	2,294	388.2	126.9
Kennewick	195	3,554	183.4	51.8	17	575	22.9	8.5	246	3,243	314.4	114.6
Kent	272	3,198	179.9	50.2	21	308	22.3	8.6	283	2,592	199.0	79.1
Kirkland	191	2,958	187.3	57.6	44	801	33.4	12.5	324	D	D	D
Lacey	122	1,852	101.8	28.7	11	D	D	D	114	D	D	D
Lake Stevens	42	621	39.4	9.0	4	145	3.7	1.0	39	276	28.1	10.4
Lakewood	179	2,433	132.6	35.9	16	599	28.9	13.6	192	2,524	199.3	92.3
Longview	104	1,490	63.4	19.3	12	D	D	D	131	1,795	161.7	68.4
Lynnwood	204	3,092	189.1	53.0	9	D	D	D	193	2,322	158.2	62.4
Marysville	104	1,365	81.6	21.4	8	D	D	D	118	1,282	114.0	49.3
Mount Vernon	83	915	52.0	14.4	6	167	6.6	2.4	114	D	D	D
Olympia	215	3,316	166.4	52.7	12	152	7.7	2.3	400	4,538	594.5	232.9

1. Establishments subject to federal tax.

AREANAME	Other services[1]				Government employment and payroll, 2012								
						March payroll							
							Percent of total for:						
	Number of establish-ments	Number of employees	Receipts (mil dol)	Annual payroll (mil dol)	Full-time equivalent employees	Total (dollars)	Adminis-trative, judicial, and legal	Police and corrections	Fire protection	Highways and trans-portation	Health and welfare	Natural resources and utilities	Education and libraries
	104	105	106	107	108	109	110	111	112	113	114	115	116
UTAH— Cont'd													
Kaysville	27	134	9.5	2.7	134	462,338	10.8	22.9	9.0	7.6	0.0	39.1	0.0
Layton	108	729	48.9	13.9	349	1,449,599	18.3	33.6	21.9	4.9	0.0	21.4	0.0
Lehi	36	203	13.8	4.1	336	1,214,483	12.5	20.4	13.7	4.2	0.0	36.3	4.1
Logan	86	509	36.2	11.4	471	1,727,277	13.4	20.5	14.4	3.6	0.0	36.1	3.5
Midvale	60	338	31.1	8.2	75	305,262	65.6	0.0	0.0	6.5	2.9	20.3	0.0
Murray	138	886	86.2	27.3	431	1,925,114	16.4	23.1	16.8	2.6	0.0	30.9	3.1
Ogden	134	957	76.3	22.7	634	2,507,571	18.7	28.7	20.1	7.0	5.2	16.9	0.0
Orem	137	740	53.8	15.5	516	2,194,808	19.2	27.2	17.2	4.8	2.4	19.7	7.3
Pleasant Grove	38	138	13.3	3.4	245	686,046	17.4	27.3	9.0	3.6	2.6	26.1	8.0
Provo	118	749	59.2	17.7	702	2,815,201	17.2	23.0	14.4	5.6	1.8	29.5	4.4
Riverton	36	173	15.0	3.8	91	415,613	39.8	2.6	0.0	25.0	0.6	22.8	0.0
Roy	38	172	11.7	3.2	176	633,604	20.3	31.4	22.5	4.2	0.0	16.1	0.0
St. George	118	695	59.3	16.2	700	2,450,568	9.2	24.3	5.4	10.7	2.4	44.2	0.0
Salt Lake City	459	4,071	340.1	115.3	2,853	13,446,478	15.0	21.7	15.0	20.9	2.4	14.9	4.1
Sandy	118	785	56.3	19.2	496	2,122,916	21.0	24.1	15.6	9.8	7.5	20.1	0.0
South Jordan	52	295	22.6	6.9	333	1,224,842	20.3	19.7	17.6	6.1	2.9	18.3	0.0
Spanish Fork	38	236	17.2	5.4	215	776,827	12.0	18.4	0.0	6.4	4.3	34.7	2.8
Springville	33	124	10.2	2.2	213	858,647	17.7	20.4	1.6	8.5	0.6	42.5	4.7
Taylorsville	37	220	19.4	5.4	122	499,977	35.5	62.2	0.0	0.0	0.4	0.3	0.0
Tooele	33	D	D	D	184	603,981	20.7	27.5	3.3	5.6	6.8	29.9	3.6
West Jordan	93	670	67.8	22.8	409	1,901,684	7.2	32.4	23.5	4.1	0.0	8.0	0.0
West Valley City	123	642	71.8	20.9	699	2,859,122	17.7	37.1	17.3	7.1	8.8	9.1	0.0
VERMONT	1,057	4,255	398.4	109.0	X	X	X	X	X	X	X	X	X
Burlington	65	361	25.2	9.7	741	3,858,642	9.5	18.3	12.6	11.2	3.0	32.5	2.0
VIRGINIA	11,654	76,041	6,881.1	2,289.3	X	X	X	X	X	X	X	X	X
Alexandria	241	2,374	213.3	75.6	5,221	27,072,935	10.0	12.5	7.7	2.6	12.6	6.5	44.7
Blacksburg	45	D	D	D	360	1,254,541	15.3	27.9	0.6	24.0	1.6	12.0	0.0
Charlottesville	100	817	69.3	23.2	2,140	8,097,522	10.3	6.1	3.5	6.3	5.6	8.0	55.6
Chesapeake	361	2,768	291.0	89.0	9,069	32,784,817	5.1	11.5	6.3	2.1	5.7	4.5	62.1
Danville	84	466	34.2	8.7	2,451	7,816,325	9.2	11.3	5.7	3.0	5.2	9.6	51.6
Hampton	153	854	66.1	21.4	6,070	20,036,058	6.9	11.2	6.1	1.0	5.7	6.3	61.8
Harrisonburg	101	595	47.0	15.8	1,474	5,157,943	4.1	7.6	6.7	5.8	0.3	15.0	53.6
Leesburg	78	478	39.0	13.4	378	1,973,445	18.8	28.6	0.0	10.5	0.0	34.5	1.1
Lynchburg	130	929	73.3	24.1	3,057	9,313,489	8.7	9.6	8.0	2.9	8.1	7.5	52.5
Manassas	121	713	75.6	20.4	1,551	7,149,920	5.0	8.7	4.1	2.5	3.1	8.0	67.1
Newport News	251	1,757	157.4	53.0	8,390	34,469,339	6.2	10.2	4.6	1.3	4.5	9.2	63.2
Norfolk	287	2,254	192.7	73.6	11,723	42,393,144	6.3	13.5	5.5	3.7	10.1	7.2	51.8
Petersburg	63	508	33.1	13.2	1,422	4,584,024	6.0	20.2	8.9	4.5	6.2	4.0	47.4
Portsmouth	128	1,019	117.8	35.7	4,082	15,197,404	6.6	10.7	7.0	0.8	8.6	5.3	58.8
Richmond	370	2,708	213.2	75.5	8,746	33,243,527	9.0	18.5	6.0	1.8	8.7	7.9	42.5
Roanoke	207	1,415	111.5	37.8	3,839	13,972,707	8.1	12.9	8.3	1.7	8.0	2.4	56.6
Suffolk	84	551	35.7	12.1	3,545	11,901,204	10.3	7.7	9.6	2.9	3.6	6.8	58.2
Virginia Beach	724	4,164	320.0	99.7	18,286	64,539,702	3.7	9.5	3.6	0.3	6.6	7.3	60.5
Winchester	69	422	29.0	9.2	1,441	5,056,458	6.8	23.0	6.6	2.0	4.0	7.0	48.8
WASHINGTON	9,852	54,069	4,710.4	1,503.1	X	X	X	X	X	X	X	X	X
Auburn	143	808	83.2	28.8	428	2,532,346	24.2	34.3	0.0	15.0	4.6	18.9	0.0
Bellevue	332	2,177	173.9	64.4	1,278	8,997,838	17.4	19.2	22.6	7.6	8.6	23.3	0.0
Bellingham	201	1,185	106.1	34.2	813	4,462,504	14.2	23.4	26.3	8.6	0.9	16.4	3.3
Bothell	64	407	39.1	10.4	290	2,203,744	15.3	29.0	30.7	8.0	5.8	5.8	0.0
Bremerton	60	300	27.1	8.7	363	2,283,752	11.7	25.1	21.9	5.4	0.6	29.5	0.0
Burien	98	471	39.1	11.3	70	380,590	32.7	0.0	0.0	22.6	20.3	22.5	0.0
Des Moines	23	D	D	D	130	840,420	26.3	37.5	0.0	7.8	4.0	18.8	0.0
Edmonds	59	325	27.2	9.0	206	1,296,656	16.1	35.4	0.0	8.9	4.8	28.4	0.0
Everett	192	1,194	118.6	38.2	1,193	7,513,828	9.0	22.1	21.2	14.6	2.1	22.6	3.2
Federal Way	136	668	49.6	16.5	338	1,899,108	20.8	52.5	0.0	7.2	0.0	15.6	0.0
Issaquah	76	D	D	D	241	1,458,971	48.2	24.1	0.0	5.7	0.0	22.0	0.0
Kennewick	114	736	52.9	17.4	365	2,339,914	19.2	32.4	27.2	7.2	0.0	14.0	0.0
Kent	221	1,354	135.1	42.8	659	3,957,128	25.4	33.2	0.0	11.4	1.3	24.6	0.0
Kirkland	151	703	57.2	18.9	575	3,364,380	21.8	25.2	24.8	2.6	0.0	12.1	0.0
Lacey	71	423	34.4	11.2	244	1,204,776	6.5	40.8	0.0	5.7	7.4	37.2	0.0
Lake Stevens	27	111	6.8	2.1	60	371,914	10.4	53.2	0.0	21.3	10.4	0.0	0.0
Lakewood	130	607	54.2	18.0	252	1,631,866	29.1	53.0	0.0	11.9	1.0	3.8	0.0
Longview	72	459	34.1	10.9	291	1,531,626	13.5	28.3	20.6	13.2	0.0	18.9	5.5
Lynnwood	134	974	87.8	27.1	514	3,172,400	18.5	30.1	20.2	2.4	0.0	17.3	0.0
Marysville	103	496	52.8	13.3	244	1,573,886	23.0	37.9	0.0	9.3	0.0	24.8	0.0
Mount Vernon	55	271	22.6	7.3	209	1,138,810	14.6	30.5	21.7	3.5	0.0	18.1	5.0
Olympia	130	638	50.1	16.9	524	3,201,082	31.0	21.7	21.0	4.7	0.3	21.2	0.0

1. Establishments subject to federal tax.

Table D. Cities — **City Government Finances**

AREANAME	General revenue Total (mil dol) 117	Intergovernmental Total (mil dol) 118	Percent from state government 119	Taxes Total (mil dol) 120	Per capita (dollars) Total 121	Property 122	Sales and gross receipts 123	General expenditure Total (mil dol) 124	Per capita (dollars) Total 125	Capital outlays 126
UTAH— Cont'd										
Kaysville	15.6	1.7	75.8	6.7	236	50	186	10.3	364	62
Layton	45.3	3.8	61.6	25.7	375	112	263	40.3	587	14
Lehi	47.8	1.8	100.0	28.4	552	308	244	36.9	718	82
Logan	58.6	7.2	21.6	20.1	408	111	297	49.7	1,011	194
Midvale	17.3	1.8	50.9	11.1	368	138	230	17.2	568	9
Murray	52.5	4.5	36.2	29.2	604	209	395	48.5	1,005	89
Ogden	102.4	13.2	30.0	48.5	578	280	298	114.7	1,367	205
Orem	78.3	6.3	49.6	38.7	427	131	296	65.7	725	49
Pleasant Grove	23.6	2.0	81.2	9.0	261	99	162	21.4	621	39
Provo	87.3	11.8	35.6	39.2	339	125	214	98.1	850	250
Riverton	19.6	1.5	82.4	10.7	264	47	217	34.9	864	199
Roy	21.0	1.5	77.3	10.5	279	86	193	16.4	436	23
St. George	76.3	3.8	65.5	38.0	504	165	340	76.8	1,020	221
Salt Lake City	529.4	30.7	31.4	201.1	1,062	642	419	382.9	2,021	145
Sandy	79.3	5.3	56.3	44.9	502	168	334	64.8	724	74
South Jordan	55.2	2.4	79.1	34.3	614	349	265	50.1	895	75
Spanish Fork	37.6	1.4	82.8	10.0	277	75	202	31.9	880	170
Springville	25.9	1.1	90.9	10.0	325	103	223	30.3	989	165
Taylorsville	24.7	2.8	76.1	17.3	287	79	208	28.5	473	69
Tooele	20.4	1.8	85.9	11.5	358	130	227	20.7	645	92
West Jordan	65.0	6.3	62.5	35.7	329	119	210	59.0	544	60
West Valley City	134.8	12.6	33.4	67.2	507	262	245	154.8	1,168	359
VERMONT	X	X	X	X	X	X	X	X	X	X
Burlington	110.0	17.7	38.0	38.4	908	674	234	92.8	2,192	417
VIRGINIA	X	X	X	X	X	X	X	X	X	X
Alexandria	694.5	112.0	62.0	498.6	3,394	2,493	843	697.3	4,746	514
Blacksburg	40.4	14.5	48.6	16.4	382	130	252	36.6	855	218
Charlottesville	233.9	98.5	67.6	93.0	2,089	1,298	743	229.9	5,163	617
Chesapeake	886.7	369.8	97.8	422.6	1,852	1,303	538	865.4	3,792	475
Danville	173.3	85.4	95.4	50.7	1,186	638	544	179.2	4,189	318
Hampton	525.3	220.7	90.2	218.7	1,599	1,068	519	516.8	3,777	217
Harrisonburg	165.0	51.6	74.2	63.4	1,238	628	603	166.3	3,246	275
Leesburg	59.3	13.1	95.3	31.9	693	279	414	58.7	1,273	249
Lynchburg	266.8	110.8	87.0	117.5	1,510	897	597	268.3	3,449	589
Manassas	181.8	62.5	84.3	83.5	2,049	1,559	467	169.8	4,168	200
Newport News	774.9	330.7	85.5	322.2	1,785	1,271	515	806.2	4,467	333
Norfolk	1,105.0	447.5	74.8	416.3	1,691	1,027	664	1,153.5	4,686	548
Petersburg	125.4	70.3	87.3	45.2	1,406	1,038	357	129.9	4,039	140
Portsmouth	430.0	216.4	85.2	161.2	1,669	1,218	439	514.7	5,331	1,170
Richmond	1,063.0	471.0	79.9	412.6	1,951	1,242	709	1,029.3	4,866	638
Roanoke	385.6	172.3	96.1	172.9	1,766	1,081	685	378.3	3,865	222
Suffolk	304.8	145.8	82.7	134.3	1,577	1,160	411	324.3	3,808	436
Virginia Beach	1,602.6	600.6	84.2	810.1	1,817	1,221	583	1,799.1	4,036	628
Winchester	116.1	39.1	89.9	61.6	2,267	1,283	983	112.7	4,147	231
WASHINGTON	X	X	X	X	X	X	X	X	X	X
Auburn	109.0	17.7	41.8	43.9	598	200	378	107.6	1,464	393
Bellevue	284.5	33.1	23.5	153.0	1,157	275	833	257.3	1,947	276
Bellingham	120.9	15.0	39.1	67.7	825	212	593	118.7	1,446	280
Bothell	54.5	14.0	63.8	29.4	848	273	531	61.1	1,763	521
Bremerton	57.7	6.4	49.1	25.4	646	218	419	58.3	1,484	236
Burien	28.1	4.7	75.2	18.7	378	142	222	34.9	705	215
Des Moines	29.2	4.6	73.5	12.6	412	142	257	26.8	881	214
Edmonds	45.6	4.4	75.7	28.0	693	332	334	42.6	1,054	137
Everett	182.2	16.6	67.5	108.1	1,033	367	650	170.4	1,629	324
Federal Way	65.3	12.0	93.7	40.0	435	107	311	59.1	643	167
Issaquah	59.7	10.5	71.1	31.0	949	250	650	53.3	1,633	344
Kennewick	68.6	6.5	69.3	41.7	550	142	391	69.4	914	179
Kent	137.7	20.6	82.9	62.9	511	157	335	140.6	1,143	354
Kirkland	106.7	9.7	53.2	61.0	731	262	428	105.7	1,267	159
Lacey	56.2	9.1	68.1	26.8	611	136	454	60.0	1,365	347
Lake Stevens	14.7	2.9	47.3	9.7	333	139	178	9.2	318	2
Lakewood	45.5	9.7	66.3	28.3	480	104	367	49.0	831	168
Longview	58.1	10.3	61.4	25.0	685	222	460	58.2	1,593	375
Lynnwood	66.8	5.6	76.9	38.6	1,065	319	731	58.4	1,610	230
Marysville	60.6	3.7	74.9	30.1	483	246	222	58.8	943	114
Mount Vernon	38.0	3.3	70.9	17.8	552	222	318	33.3	1,033	107
Olympia	99.6	9.9	54.8	50.0	1,045	267	761	116.3	2,434	673

1. Based on population estimated as of July 1 of the year shown.

AREANAME	Public welfare	Highways	Parking facilities	Education	Health and hospitals	Police protection	Sewerage and sanitation	Parks and recreation	Housing and community development	Interest on debt
	127	128	129	130	131	132	133	134	135	136
UTAH— Cont'd										
Kaysville	0.0	10.3	0.0	0.0	0.0	7.6	51.5	11.5	0.0	0.4
Layton	0.0	16.8	0.0	0.0	0.0	26.0	19.4	9.8	1.1	0.5
Lehi	0.0	39.4	0.0	0.0	0.0	13.0	21.2	1.1	0.0	4.8
Logan	0.0	14.4	0.0	0.0	0.0	16.5	26.1	11.6	5.4	0.7
Midvale	0.0	9.4	0.0	0.0	0.0	30.1	15.3	2.0	3.5	7.1
Murray	0.0	15.6	0.0	0.0	0.0	19.8	13.0	13.4	2.1	1.2
Ogden	0.0	4.7	0.0	0.0	0.0	14.8	16.3	5.7	17.8	2.5
Orem	0.0	11.1	0.0	0.0	0.0	20.7	17.2	10.0	3.7	2.9
Pleasant Grove	0.0	3.1	0.0	0.0	0.0	20.0	22.6	14.2	0.0	8.8
Provo	0.0	10.5	0.0	0.0	0.0	15.5	9.1	27.2	5.6	4.5
Riverton	0.0	25.5	0.0	0.0	0.0	7.2	8.5	5.8	2.0	36.7
Roy	0.0	7.7	0.0	0.0	0.0	26.4	11.6	13.2	2.1	0.2
St. George	0.0	18.8	0.0	0.0	0.0	16.5	19.8	18.3	1.4	6.6
Salt Lake City	0.0	10.9	0.0	0.0	0.0	14.9	5.8	5.6	9.0	3.8
Sandy	0.0	7.4	0.0	0.0	0.0	18.4	13.6	11.7	1.0	5.4
South Jordan	0.0	14.1	0.0	0.0	0.0	10.9	6.1	12.5	9.7	3.6
Spanish Fork	0.0	10.9	0.0	0.0	0.0	11.9	16.0	20.8	0.0	2.7
Springville	0.0	7.8	0.0	0.0	0.9	12.7	15.8	12.5	0.0	5.5
Taylorsville	0.0	10.3	0.0	0.0	0.0	27.4	1.8	1.8	4.8	1.3
Tooele	0.0	12.0	0.0	0.0	0.0	16.2	9.4	17.6	12.8	5.1
West Jordan	0.0	17.8	0.0	0.0	0.0	22.3	18.1	4.0	3.7	2.0
West Valley City	0.0	7.4	0.0	0.0	1.1	13.1	5.3	16.7	25.5	4.1
VERMONT	X	X	X	X	X	X	X	X	X	X
Burlington	0.0	9.2	5.2	0.0	0.0	11.3	8.3	8.8	5.6	3.9
VIRGINIA	X	X	X	X	X	X	X	X	X	X
Alexandria	6.3	3.7	0.0	34.5	6.0	9.6	6.1	3.7	2.0	2.8
Blacksburg	0.0	22.9	0.0	0.0	1.6	19.2	16.1	5.9	6.9	2.2
Charlottesville	11.0	6.3	0.1	31.0	8.0	7.1	5.8	5.3	2.3	1.6
Chesapeake	3.3	5.6	0.0	54.2	3.3	4.6	3.4	2.3	0.4	2.3
Danville	4.2	5.7	0.0	41.3	2.3	5.5	6.6	2.2	2.3	1.7
Hampton	5.7	1.3	0.1	45.5	0.8	5.2	4.9	6.8	8.5	3.2
Harrisonburg	1.8	11.3	0.1	38.9	0.7	4.7	9.4	3.1	0.3	18.0
Leesburg	0.0	9.2	0.0	0.0	0.0	19.2	10.4	11.6	0.0	4.3
Lynchburg	7.1	2.8	0.1	35.8	0.7	6.4	15.5	2.2	2.9	2.8
Manassas	0.7	6.2	0.1	54.0	2.2	7.8	7.8	0.2	2.3	3.2
Newport News	5.1	3.9	0.0	42.3	8.5	5.7	4.8	3.1	5.8	3.6
Norfolk	6.6	4.6	1.0	36.0	3.2	5.9	5.3	4.1	9.5	3.1
Petersburg	11.4	4.7	0.0	40.0	1.0	9.0	4.0	1.3	1.0	1.0
Portsmouth	5.0	1.3	0.2	33.2	2.1	6.8	5.2	2.1	6.8	2.7
Richmond	1.6	2.7	0.0	31.6	4.5	8.9	10.5	2.5	9.1	0.8
Roanoke	15.3	3.5	0.4	39.4	0.9	6.1	2.2	2.5	6.6	3.1
Suffolk	4.4	6.8	0.0	45.2	0.2	6.3	2.0	1.6	1.2	2.8
Virginia Beach	3.8	4.8	0.1	46.8	3.0	5.0	7.1	5.9	1.4	3.0
Winchester	6.4	5.0	0.8	43.4	1.0	6.4	10.1	2.6	1.9	4.9
WASHINGTON	X	X	X	X	X	X	X	X	X	X
Auburn	0.0	19.6	0.0	0.0	0.5	15.0	33.6	9.0	0.2	2.2
Bellevue	0.0	15.0	0.0	0.0	6.3	11.9	18.4	15.2	5.3	2.8
Bellingham	0.0	10.0	1.2	0.0	7.0	13.4	14.1	16.3	1.8	1.6
Bothell	0.0	30.3	0.0	0.0	0.2	16.3	12.8	2.0	1.6	0.9
Bremerton	0.0	5.7	0.8	0.0	4.2	18.7	14.8	21.3	1.8	3.3
Burien	0.0	31.7	0.0	0.0	3.0	27.1	2.7	8.9	2.0	2.6
Des Moines	0.1	19.9	0.0	0.0	0.8	24.9	4.7	24.1	0.0	1.4
Edmonds	0.0	7.5	0.0	0.0	0.1	18.8	16.6	11.8	0.0	2.5
Everett	0.2	7.5	0.1	0.0	4.4	15.4	24.4	7.7	1.3	4.0
Federal Way	0.2	28.9	0.0	0.0	1.1	27.6	4.7	10.0	2.0	1.0
Issaquah	0.0	14.9	0.0	0.0	0.0	8.3	20.1	9.3	2.9	3.0
Kennewick	0.0	11.4	0.0	0.0	5.3	18.7	4.5	20.4	0.8	2.9
Kent	0.2	5.1	0.0	0.0	1.2	15.6	40.1	11.7	2.0	3.1
Kirkland	0.0	10.8	0.1	0.0	0.7	17.1	22.2	8.0	0.0	2.1
Lacey	0.0	19.2	0.0	0.0	2.9	14.1	25.7	13.0	0.0	1.6
Lake Stevens	0.2	13.5	0.0	0.0	0.4	40.6	12.7	1.9	2.0	3.5
Lakewood	1.0	17.8	0.0	0.0	0.6	40.2	7.5	3.3	4.9	0.3
Longview	0.2	8.3	0.0	0.0	0.0	15.9	40.1	5.9	2.7	1.2
Lynnwood	0.0	8.5	0.0	0.0	7.2	19.4	9.5	17.2	1.2	1.4
Marysville	0.0	17.7	0.0	0.0	4.9	14.4	17.3	5.1	0.0	5.8
Mount Vernon	0.0	9.6	0.0	0.0	0.5	19.0	29.6	4.4	0.0	2.1
Olympia	0.0	6.3	0.0	0.0	1.9	9.4	24.8	12.3	0.4	3.4

Construction, Wholesale Trade, and Retail Trade

AREANAME	Value of residential construction authorized by building permits, 2017			Wholesale trade[1], 2012				Retail trade[2], 2012			
	New construction ($1,000)	Number of housing units	Percent single family	Number of establish-ments	Number of employees	Sales (mil dol)	Annual payroll (mil dol)	Number of establish-ments	Number of employees	Sales (mil dol)	Annual payroll (mil dol)
	69	70	71	72	73	74	75	76	77	78	79
WASHINGTON—Cont'd											
Pasco	128,447	557	84.0	77	939	595.5	46.6	157	2,051	722.8	67.7
Pullman	32,328	216	25.0	11	177	182.1	9.0	51	1,027	222.7	20.4
Puyallup	78,649	353	33.1	39	652	343.0	27.6	239	5,078	1,686.5	152.9
Redmond	152,392	1,350	6.9	173	3,101	4,143.8	257.7	251	3,923	947.4	105.4
Renton	62,783	249	49.0	110	3,308	2,769.4	197.3	264	5,284	1,831.9	165.6
Richland	90,880	360	75.3	19	186	192.6	7.6	143	2,531	680.0	60.7
Sammamish	148,545	367	100.0	31	52	46.8	2.9	47	413	129.3	12.6
SeaTac	6,887	18	100.0	19	177	146.3	10.2	71	943	213.9	18.1
Seattle	1,724,516	9,887	6.0	1,093	16,045	12,790.5	1,049.7	2,530	34,652	40,037.9	1,230.2
Shoreline	45,600	204	44.1	33	135	57.2	5.6	121	2,364	835.7	75.9
Spokane	149,075	832	40.0	249	3,330	1,686.8	158.8	862	13,166	3,132.8	341.2
Spokane Valley	94,432	737	17.1	202	2,963	1,772.5	140.6	476	7,626	1,987.3	207.5
Tacoma	160,698	1,127	12.3	210	2,967	2,750.1	151.2	744	11,177	3,036.6	314.9
University Place	34,977	120	98.3	12	75	49.4	4.1	51	728	154.9	19.8
Vancouver	109,038	1,546	11.4	185	2,441	2,580.9	139.4	555	10,131	2,863.9	278.6
Walla Walla	10,783	45	100.0	54	483	437.5	18.3	150	1,667	386.1	40.7
Wenatchee	13,119	69	88.4	52	587	710.1	27.7	185	2,635	615.3	68.3
Yakima	25,965	125	97.6	108	2,196	1,875.8	100.9	346	5,078	1,334.7	134.8
WEST VIRGINIA	463,092	2,719	86.4	1,334	16,906	14,295.4	761.9	6,393	85,305	22,637.9	1,908.5
Charleston	4,597	19	100.0	121	1,588	1,059.8	78.1	358	5,805	1,495.4	134.6
Huntington	590	8	50.0	73	1,250	511.6	62.2	211	2,788	670.4	66.6
Morgantown	5,744	63	17.5	26	142	47.8	5.3	260	4,385	1,081.4	86.6
Parkersburg	842	11	100.0	40	338	134.5	12.1	203	3,074	791.4	68.8
Wheeling	8,438	12	100.0	62	D	D	D	142	1,690	380.3	37.4
WISCONSIN	3,910,795	19,545	60.2	5,990	97,040	77,066.9	5,253.6	19,272	296,956	78,201.8	6,835.0
Appleton	18,679	80	85.0	98	1,432	5,759.6	66.1	291	4,865	1,306.6	111.5
Beloit	6,080	112	10.7	19	456	292.8	25.0	115	1,756	481.9	40.3
Brookfield	63,097	335	11.3	108	1,733	686.6	105.7	301	5,576	1,022.7	117.4
Eau Claire	28,255	145	54.5	79	1,509	961.9	64.8	340	6,565	1,419.6	131.8
Fitchburg	44,014	373	11.5	25	967	1,149.6	59.0	58	614	173.3	16.1
Fond du Lac	11,797	55	100.0	41	812	610.4	46.3	211	3,688	959.5	81.9
Franklin	8,927	23	100.0	35	402	292.7	23.6	75	2,107	614.6	52.0
Green Bay	26,021	98	100.0	106	2,190	1,714.9	122.4	340	5,909	1,595.9	134.6
Greenfield	47,393	396	3.5	14	192	128.7	7.3	149	3,100	932.8	80.5
Janesville	20,595	101	86.1	75	1,941	1,843.2	96.1	276	5,678	1,422.0	144.0
Kenosha	6,207	30	80.0	56	763	769.3	42.7	295	5,162	1,369.5	114.4
La Crosse	11,860	106	25.5	61	1,690	2,434.7	78.4	251	4,879	976.7	97.7
Madison	363,805	2,188	17.3	270	4,849	2,859.6	252.1	972	17,918	4,804.9	409.1
Manitowoc	7,587	64	18.8	27	461	211.0	23.9	146	2,436	555.8	53.0
Menomonee Falls	45,084	139	100.0	89	1,425	651.3	89.4	126	2,741	700.4	63.1
Milwaukee	36,556	715	1.0	485	11,513	8,694.3	908.5	1,368	15,652	3,894.9	360.3
Mount Pleasant	19,945	78	89.7	21	346	145.5	14.4	64	1,331	441.7	31.9
Neenah	15,304	101	43.6	24	278	252.6	13.1	82	1,520	436.6	34.5
New Berlin	11,816	27	85.2	119	2,332	1,178.0	137.1	96	2,375	579.0	64.6
Oak Creek	21,742	150	20.7	32	1,429	891.0	89.5	80	2,059	718.9	43.7
Oshkosh	16,024	168	18.5	50	1,198	517.4	48.5	250	4,856	1,205.0	107.7
Racine	1,134	4	100.0	42	448	225.6	22.3	281	3,410	622.1	61.4
Sheboygan	1,731	9	100.0	41	451	304.5	18.9	197	3,362	758.9	74.1
Stevens Point	NA	NA	NA	32	332	270.7	14.4	120	2,003	470.3	39.3
Sun Prairie	NA	NA	NA	33	822	362.4	38.0	70	1,155	305.8	25.6
Superior	NA	NA	NA	39	669	817.8	31.9	113	1,835	541.2	45.8
Waukesha	NA	NA	NA	115	2,148	1,126.3	119.0	213	4,314	1,601.4	120.4
Wausau	NA	NA	NA	44	817	375.7	36.8	187	4,576	1,239.9	101.2
Wauwatosa	NA	NA	NA	56	1,033	652.0	55.5	293	5,436	1,107.9	113.4
West Allis	NA	NA	NA	107	1,830	975.2	99.4	243	4,249	1,154.4	102.4
West Bend	NA	NA	NA	25	201	93.9	8.1	120	2,163	553.4	46.4
WYOMING	526,251	1,926	76.0	709	7,003	5,597.9	398.7	2,681	30,088	9,446.0	796.0
Casper	33,674	188	35.1	80	841	1,414.8	51.5	299	4,299	1,244.2	116.3
Cheyenne	61,747	408	54.9	93	782	336.4	52.5	321	4,632	1,561.0	112.7
Gillette	4,783	17	100.0	49	813	462.8	41.3	160	2,202	757.5	62.0
Laramie	7,618	48	83.3	19	95	127.6	4.0	131	1,671	470.8	35.7

1. Merchant wholesalers except manufacturers' sales branches and offices. 2. Establishments with payroll.

Table D. Cities — Real Estate, Professional Services, and Manufacturing

AREANAME	Real estate and rental and leasing, 2012				Professional, scientific, and technical services[1], 2012				Manufacturing, 2012			
	Number of establishments	Number of employees	Receipts (mil dol)	Annual payroll (mil dol)	Number of establishments	Number of employees	Receipts (mil dol)	Annual payroll (mil dol)	Number of establishments	Number of employees	Receipts (mil dol)	Annual payroll (mil dol)
	80	81	82	83	84	85	86	87	88	89	90	91
WASHINGTON— Cont'd												
Pasco	46	224	39.2	6.8	61	369	37.2	16.4	37	D	D	59.8
Pullman	40	180	19.4	4.4	36	304	40.0	17.3	12	D	D	D
Puyallup	86	417	83.6	13.0	119	627	65.7	26.1	43	954	240.9	43.2
Redmond	128	1,207	288.5	71.4	385	D	D	D	127	6,634	3,469.5	443.1
Renton	115	610	212.1	29.7	208	2,109	213.2	103.7	71	13,466	D	994.5
Richland	89	268	46.3	9.2	181	D	D	D	39	1,839	D	119.8
Sammamish	41	D	D	D	197	405	85.7	26.5	6	14	2.5	0.6
SeaTac	40	312	71.5	11.6	17	243	32.8	13.3	15	130	D	6.0
Seattle	1,966	11,652	2,431.3	587.9	4,631	50,113	10,321.5	4,432.8	859	20,323	5,200.2	1,054.2
Shoreline	70	282	64.4	11.6	113	D	D	D	17	147	29.9	5.9
Spokane	281	1,580	283.9	57.9	741	D	D	D	200	4,292	1,101.4	202.5
Spokane Valley	147	814	146.0	26.8	189	1,245	123.8	51.5	189	6,500	2,048.1	324.3
Tacoma	297	1,748	304.2	64.2	504	D	D	D	194	6,347	1,923.4	338.4
University Place	55	D	D	D	66	251	29.2	11.6	17	87	D	2.9
Vancouver	273	1,384	225.1	51.1	570	D	D	D	182	6,379	2,585.4	336.6
Walla Walla	42	128	17.4	4.0	79	356	36.7	14.4	83	1,043	221.4	46.9
Wenatchee	61	211	32.7	5.9	101	D	D	D	23	401	71.9	14.9
Yakima	146	587	81.6	16.1	211	D	D	D	99	2,981	838.8	122.6
WEST VIRGINIA	1,405	6,011	1,255.8	203.8	2,918	23,115	2,804.7	1,053.4	1,245	48,686	24,553.1	2,603.9
Charleston	135	663	154.9	22.9	385	D	D	D	39	528	148.4	22.8
Huntington	74	259	50.9	9.4	135	D	D	D	52	3,170	1,697.1	206.5
Morgantown	79	435	64.2	10.7	126	D	D	D	22	446	D	23.3
Parkersburg	53	239	52.6	7.4	89	D	D	D	25	657	134.7	26.1
Wheeling	49	D	D	D	136	D	D	D	37	D	D	D
WISCONSIN	4,509	23,762	4,358.9	801.1	11,253	98,507	15,028.9	5,701.2	8,995	436,777	177,728.9	21,879.3
Appleton	60	D	D	D	193	1,791	315.2	106.8	104	7,600	D	409.2
Beloit	17	88	66.4	4.6	38	212	20.4	9.2	52	2,599	1,801.2	132.8
Brookfield	94	1,075	88.2	31.8	306	3,589	744.8	278.8	56	1,544	368.5	79.4
Eau Claire	94	462	72.5	14.0	145	1,527	188.2	78.6	79	3,823	1,148.1	170.4
Fitchburg	42	247	46.1	7.9	85	556	90.6	34.8	30	3,154	1,287.1	205.2
Fond du Lac	31	144	25.7	3.7	91	1,050	125.8	63.4	72	4,252	1,894.6	202.1
Franklin	25	127	25.8	3.3	58	424	80.7	23.0	52	3,383	1,221.8	176.4
Green Bay	94	610	93.9	21.6	226	D	D	D	130	10,215	6,399.1	513.4
Greenfield	38	182	31.6	6.8	80	589	63.7	26.0	17	106	D	4.8
Janesville	53	260	74.1	12.6	107	624	70.8	24.5	82	3,985	1,600.9	187.1
Kenosha	67	289	44.5	7.3	125	816	73.3	33.0	99	2,044	738.6	95.7
La Crosse	74	475	70.7	12.9	171	D	D	D	93	4,666	1,527.4	195.8
Madison	369	2,871	759.2	115.5	1,019	13,787	2,399.8	978.8	182	8,788	2,798.2	467.9
Manitowoc	19	D	D	D	58	453	68.2	16.7	75	6,299	1,804.1	295.0
Menomonee Falls	20	260	33.5	14.7	91	1,294	253.1	76.0	176	8,361	3,503.9	464.3
Milwaukee	460	3,036	618.5	127.5	1,091	D	D	D	540	22,779	8,678.9	1,199.8
Mount Pleasant	20	80	9.6	2.8	50	387	38.9	19.2	35	2,073	3,299.8	155.3
Neenah	17	142	151.8	6.5	51	476	60.8	31.5	60	5,008	2,079.0	262.2
New Berlin	27	263	44.5	7.7	109	2,193	348.9	102.6	130	6,222	2,305.6	359.7
Oak Creek	38	405	92.1	16.3	35	414	32.6	12.5	55	11,025	6,369.1	607.7
Oshkosh	53	306	43.0	8.3	100	D	D	D	115	11,025	6,369.1	607.7
Racine	37	121	31.0	3.8	118	D	D	D	143	4,602	1,264.5	245.5
Sheboygan	31	181	41.8	8.1	94	D	D	D	89	6,676	2,068.9	311.6
Stevens Point	19	D	D	D	57	635	57.0	23.5	30	1,791	570.9	73.8
Sun Prairie	25	70	13.3	2.1	60	404	50.5	20.4	29	1,020	283.2	48.2
Superior	34	106	14.5	2.4	55	323	35.1	14.3	40	1,200	D	77.6
Waukesha	56	321	69.7	10.8	188	1,794	285.7	100.4	142	9,474	4,144.2	668.2
Wausau	39	D	D	D	130	D	D	D	64	4,486	1,177.6	184.4
Wauwatosa	45	268	89.0	13.0	236	D	D	D	51	3,718	1,267.0	356.5
West Allis	43	293	77.6	14.4	86	925	100.6	52.4	92	3,448	743.0	196.1
West Bend	18	D	D	D	49	D	D	D	52	1,779	409.9	79.6
WYOMING	1,076	4,546	1,259.1	215.6	2,132	D	D	D	553	10,094	10,783.8	630.6
Casper	124	649	182.3	31.4	216	1,146	166.8	64.1	27	471	91.8	25.8
Cheyenne	112	390	89.7	14.4	414	D	D	D	51	1,132	2,542.4	75.4
Gillette	61	265	72.1	9.9	94	D	D	D	27	482	D	30.7
Laramie	50	132	20.2	3.0	95	D	D	D	21	141	D	5.5

1. Establishments subject to federal tax.

AREANAME	City government finances, 2012 (cont.)			Climate[2]						
	Debt outstanding			Average daily temperature						
				Mean		Limits				
	Total (mil dol)	Per capita[1] (dollars)	Debt issued during year	January	July	January[3]	July[4]	Annual precipitation (inches)	Heating degree days	Cooling degree days
	137	138	139	140	141	142	143	144	145	146
WASHINGTON— Cont'd										
Pasco	48.6	727	4.2	34.2	75.2	28.0	89.3	8.01	4,731	909
Pullman	7.0	224	0.3	NA	NA	NA	NA	NA	NA	NA
Puyallup	75.3	1,972	2.6	39.9	64.9	32.9	77.8	40.51	4,991	153
Redmond	82.8	1,463	8.0	25.1	55.0	20.0	65.0	82.86	9,630	12
Renton	184.1	1,921	26.1	40.9	65.3	35.9	75.3	37.07	4,797	173
Richland	147.2	2,861	0.3	33.0	73.2	26.0	87.9	7.55	5,133	739
Sammamish	7.7	157	0.0	40.8	65.2	35.2	75.0	35.96	4,756	174
SeaTac	5.8	208	0.0	40.9	65.3	35.9	75.3	37.07	4,797	173
Seattle	4,163.6	6,556	431.3	41.5	65.5	36.0	74.5	38.25	4,615	192
Shoreline	38.3	704	0.0	40.8	65.2	35.2	75.0	35.96	4,756	174
Spokane	189.9	906	0.0	27.3	68.6	21.7	82.5	16.67	6,820	394
Spokane Valley	7.9	88	0.0	NA	NA	NA	NA	NA	NA	NA
Tacoma	1,587.6	7,849	58.5	41.0	65.6	35.1	76.1	38.95	4,650	167
University Place	55.9	1,770	5.9	41.0	65.6	35.1	76.1	38.95	4,650	167
Vancouver	263.9	1,597	10.6	39.0	65.4	32.4	77.3	41.92	4,990	197
Walla Walla	62.5	1,959	0.0	34.7	75.3	28.8	89.9	20.88	4,882	957
Wenatchee	42.9	1,318	18.9	29.2	74.4	23.2	87.8	9.12	5,533	832
Yakima	60.7	653	2.8	29.1	69.1	20.5	87.2	8.26	6,104	431
WEST VIRGINIA	X	X	X	X	X	X	X	X	X	X
Charleston	118.0	2,315	9.2	33.4	73.9	24.2	84.9	44.05	4,644	978
Huntington	44.1	897	2.3	32.1	76.3	23.5	87.1	41.74	4,737	1,128
Morgantown	120.1	3,972	3.8	30.8	73.5	22.3	83.4	43.30	5,174	815
Parkersburg	67.9	2,176	4.9	30.7	75.4	22.3	85.8	40.69	5,091	1,038
Wheeling	49.6	1,759	8.3	29.6	74.8	21.4	85.2	40.34	5,313	926
WISCONSIN	X	X	X	X	X	X	X	X	X	X
Appleton	159.0	2,176	6.9	16.0	71.6	7.8	81.4	30.16	7,721	572
Beloit	93.8	2,547	28.1	19.1	72.4	11.6	82.5	35.25	6,969	664
Brookfield	66.3	1,745	9.1	20.0	74.3	11.5	85.1	32.09	6,886	791
Eau Claire	99.4	1,476	8.5	11.9	71.4	2.5	82.6	32.12	8,196	554
Fitchburg	29.6	1,143	6.6	NA	NA	NA	NA	NA	NA	NA
Fond du Lac	203.2	4,724	19.8	16.6	71.8	9.1	81.1	30.15	7,534	586
Franklin	32.5	906	0.0	20.7	72.0	13.4	81.1	34.81	7,087	616
Green Bay	209.5	1,998	5.7	15.6	69.9	7.1	81.2	29.19	7,963	463
Greenfield	32.8	886	7.3	19.9	73.8	12.7	81.9	33.86	6,847	764
Janesville	106.9	1,682	22.1	17.7	72.1	8.6	83.8	32.78	7,238	629
Kenosha	179.5	1,797	26.2	20.8	71.3	13.2	78.7	34.74	6,999	549
La Crosse	98.7	1,894	17.8	15.9	74.0	6.3	85.2	32.36	7,340	775
Madison	526.8	2,195	99.4	17.3	71.6	9.3	82.1	32.95	7,493	582
Manitowoc	154.4	4,618	11.6	18.7	69.9	10.8	79.6	30.49	7,563	425
Menomonee Falls	94.1	2,625	18.0	16.5	69.3	8.1	80.2	33.45	7,832	407
Milwaukee	1,306.0	2,181	454.0	20.0	74.3	11.5	85.1	32.09	6,886	791
Mount Pleasant	47.2	1,806	5.6	NA	NA	NA	NA	NA	NA	NA
Neenah	75.6	2,939	5.0	NA	NA	NA	NA	NA	NA	NA
New Berlin	45.0	1,133	6.4	19.9	73.8	12.7	81.9	33.86	6,847	764
Oak Creek	112.6	3,230	18.5	20.7	72.0	13.4	81.1	34.81	7,087	616
Oshkosh	221.7	3,326	42.5	16.1	72.0	7.8	81.8	31.57	7,639	591
Racine	233.6	2,986	30.0	20.7	71.3	13.3	78.6	35.35	7,032	567
Sheboygan	62.5	1,281	1.4	20.9	71.4	13.2	81.4	31.90	7,056	559
Stevens Point	44.4	1,651	18.4	NA	NA	NA	NA	NA	NA	NA
Sun Prairie	70.0	2,289	0.0	NA	NA	NA	NA	NA	NA	NA
Superior	54.2	2,019	18.4	12.1	66.6	3.4	76.2	30.78	9,006	241
Waukesha	127.7	1,793	19.3	19.5	73.8	11.4	84.2	34.64	6,893	784
Wausau	50.1	1,279	7.7	13.0	70.1	3.6	80.8	33.36	8,237	464
Wauwatosa	100.8	2,142	19.5	20.0	74.3	11.5	85.1	32.09	6,886	791
West Allis	78.5	1,294	5.9	19.9	73.8	12.7	81.9	33.86	6,847	764
West Bend	79.7	2,525	6.8	18.4	70.6	10.7	81.3	32.85	7,371	502
WYOMING	X	X	X	X	X	X	X	X	X	X
Casper	19.5	338	0.1	22.3	70.0	12.2	86.8	13.03	7,571	428
Cheyenne	86.1	1,395	14.1	25.9	67.7	14.8	81.9	15.45	7,388	273
Gillette	91.7	2,916	2.2	NA	NA	NA	NA	NA	NA	NA
Laramie	44.3	1,394	0.5	20.3	62.9	7.8	79.4	11.19	9,233	75

1. Based on the population estimated as of July 1 of the year shown.   2. Represents normal values based on the 30-year period, 1971±2000.   3. Average daily minimum.   4. Average daily maximum.

Congressional Districts of the 115th Congress

(For explanation of symbols, see page viii)

Page

Table E. Congressional Districts 115th Congress — **Age and Education**

STATE District	Population and population characteristics, 2016 (cont.)										Education, 2016		
	Age (percent)										Total Enrollment[1]	Attainment[2] (percent)	
	Under 5 years	5 to 17 years	18 to 24 years	25 to 34 years	35 to 44 years	45 to 54 years	55 to 64 years	65 to 74 years	75 years and over	Median age		High school graduate or more	Bachelor's degree or more
	15	16	17	18	19	20	21	22	23	24	25	26	27
UNITED STATES	6.1	16.6	9.6	13.7	12.6	13.3	12.8	8.9	6.3	37.9	81,572,277	87.5	31.3
ALABAMA	5.9	16.7	9.5	12.9	12.3	13.3	13.2	9.5	6.6	39.0	1,186,076	85.1	24.7
District 1	5.9	17.0	8.5	12.8	12.0	13.1	13.6	10.2	6.9	39.6	164,401	87.1	24.0
District 2	6.0	16.6	9.3	13.7	12.0	13.4	12.9	9.6	6.5	38.2	157,639	83.9	21.8
District 3	5.9	16.4	11.2	12.6	12.1	13.2	13.0	9.3	6.2	38.3	183,593	83.6	22.8
District 4	6.0	16.7	8.2	12.0	12.1	13.8	13.4	10.8	7.0	40.7	151,443	80.4	17.0
District 5	5.5	16.6	9.1	12.8	12.7	14.2	13.4	9.2	6.6	40.1	175,896	86.4	30.3
District 6	6.1	17.5	7.9	13.3	13.4	13.4	13.0	9.0	6.4	39.0	176,435	90.1	36.7
District 7	6.0	16.2	12.5	13.5	11.7	11.9	13.3	8.8	6.3	36.5	176,669	83.8	19.4
ALASKA	7.1	18.2	10.2	16.4	12.4	12.5	12.9	7.1	3.2	33.5	187,359	93.1	29.6
At Large	7.1	18.2	10.2	16.4	12.4	12.5	12.9	7.1	3.2	33.5	187,359	93.1	29.6
ARIZONA	6.3	17.2	9.7	13.4	12.3	12.2	12.0	9.8	7.0	37.5	1,761,534	86.7	28.9
District 1	5.8	18.6	10.5	12.0	11.8	10.8	12.7	11.2	6.6	37.5	209,497	85.7	24.5
District 2	5.8	14.5	9.5	13.2	10.9	11.7	13.4	11.8	9.1	40.8	170,792	90.2	34.0
District 3	7.1	19.4	13.7	13.0	12.9	11.9	10.2	7.2	4.6	32.7	223,542	77.0	16.5
District 4	4.7	14.2	7.5	10.1	10.3	11.3	14.4	16.2	11.4	47.9	151,481	88.0	19.2
District 5	7.1	19.2	7.1	13.1	13.4	13.5	10.7	9.1	7.0	37.5	212,718	93.1	36.0
District 6	5.7	14.8	7.3	13.0	12.4	14.6	14.0	11.0	7.2	42.3	165,696	93.0	45.4
District 7	8.6	22.1	11.3	16.4	13.3	12.0	8.9	4.9	2.6	29.7	231,564	67.9	14.0
District 8	5.5	17.0	7.7	11.0	11.8	12.5	12.9	11.7	10.0	42.6	189,776	91.8	29.4
District 9	6.1	15.0	12.8	18.6	13.3	11.8	11.2	6.5	4.8	33.5	206,468	90.1	37.5
ARKANSAS	6.3	17.3	9.7	12.8	12.2	12.7	12.6	9.5	6.8	38.0	739,490	86.0	22.4
District 1	6.1	17.0	8.7	12.2	12.0	12.8	13.1	10.2	7.7	39.9	166,837	83.3	16.5
District 2	6.4	17.1	10.0	13.8	12.3	12.8	12.5	9.0	6.0	36.9	195,735	90.7	30.0
District 3	6.8	18.2	10.7	13.9	13.0	12.0	11.3	8.4	5.8	35.3	209,119	86.2	26.9
District 4	5.9	17.0	9.3	11.0	11.5	13.1	13.9	10.7	7.8	40.8	167,799	83.5	15.8
CALIFORNIA	6.3	16.8	9.8	15.0	13.2	13.3	11.9	7.8	5.7	36.4	10,490,279	82.4	32.9
District 1	5.1	14.6	10.1	11.5	10.7	11.9	15.0	12.6	8.7	43.0	169,406	89.8	23.7
District 2	5.0	14.9	8.2	10.7	12.4	13.9	15.1	12.5	7.4	44.1	170,125	90.1	40.8
District 3	6.2	17.4	12.1	14.3	11.6	12.6	12.1	8.2	5.6	35.0	216,913	83.3	25.1
District 4	5.1	16.5	7.2	10.4	11.7	13.7	15.3	12.0	8.1	44.2	172,511	93.0	33.3
District 5	5.4	15.1	9.0	13.2	12.8	13.4	14.3	9.9	6.8	40.4	178,403	87.3	31.2
District 6	6.9	17.3	9.6	18.1	13.0	11.4	11.5	7.5	4.7	33.9	200,740	83.3	27.5
District 7	6.3	17.6	8.2	12.9	13.2	14.3	12.7	8.2	6.8	38.5	193,451	89.9	32.9
District 8	7.2	20.2	10.1	13.1	11.8	12.2	12.5	8.0	4.9	34.5	198,952	81.7	17.1
District 9	6.8	20.1	9.6	13.4	13.0	12.4	11.7	7.7	5.3	35.1	217,093	79.0	19.1
District 10	7.2	19.8	9.6	14.2	12.5	12.8	11.5	7.2	5.0	34.4	205,653	78.7	16.6
District 11	5.8	16.9	8.1	13.0	12.9	14.2	12.9	9.2	7.0	39.7	192,032	87.9	43.6
District 12	4.6	8.4	6.4	24.8	16.2	13.3	11.5	8.0	6.6	37.8	125,568	88.3	59.5
District 13	6.0	12.8	9.9	18.1	14.7	12.6	12.0	8.2	5.6	37.0	190,261	85.1	47.2
District 14	5.3	14.7	8.0	14.7	14.5	14.4	13.0	8.8	6.5	39.6	185,677	88.4	47.5
District 15	5.7	17.5	7.6	14.1	14.7	15.3	12.5	7.8	5.0	38.6	200,629	90.1	45.0
District 16	8.8	21.4	11.3	15.6	11.9	11.2	9.9	6.0	4.0	30.2	224,429	66.5	12.2
District 17	6.6	15.0	8.0	18.5	16.0	13.7	10.7	6.2	5.2	36.0	193,217	91.1	57.0
District 18	5.6	16.0	7.8	13.5	13.8	15.0	13.0	8.4	7.0	40.2	189,886	93.2	61.5
District 19	6.3	17.9	9.6	14.7	13.6	14.1	11.7	7.1	4.9	36.0	218,600	80.1	35.5
District 20	6.8	17.7	12.2	13.8	12.7	12.1	11.7	7.7	5.3	34.6	217,280	75.3	27.9
District 21	8.5	23.3	11.0	14.7	13.1	11.7	9.0	5.1	3.5	29.3	223,485	59.0	7.9
District 22	7.8	20.6	9.9	14.8	12.5	11.6	10.3	6.9	5.4	32.9	228,377	80.5	24.1
District 23	7.3	19.5	9.7	15.0	12.1	12.1	11.7	7.7	4.9	33.8	199,815	83.4	20.8
District 24	5.8	14.9	15.4	12.7	11.2	11.4	12.3	9.4	6.9	35.8	212,257	85.1	34.0
District 25	6.7	19.1	9.7	12.7	12.3	15.3	12.8	7.1	4.4	36.3	209,633	84.4	27.8
District 26	6.1	17.9	9.7	13.1	12.1	13.5	12.9	8.4	6.2	37.4	197,302	82.7	34.1
District 27	5.6	13.3	8.3	13.5	13.2	14.2	14.2	9.0	8.6	42.2	172,718	84.4	40.5
District 28	4.7	10.6	7.3	19.7	15.4	14.2	12.4	8.6	7.0	39.7	141,608	87.5	46.2
District 29	6.0	17.7	10.2	17.1	14.0	13.7	11.2	6.0	4.2	34.4	197,716	70.3	19.2
District 30	5.5	14.3	8.6	14.9	13.8	14.3	13.2	8.4	7.1	39.9	193,944	88.2	42.4
District 31	8.1	18.7	11.4	15.9	12.9	12.1	10.4	6.2	4.2	32.3	209,625	78.9	22.7
District 32	5.7	16.9	10.4	15.0	12.9	13.2	12.2	7.9	5.6	36.1	193,191	75.4	21.4
District 33	4.4	13.2	8.9	14.7	13.3	14.8	13.6	9.7	7.4	41.7	169,955	95.5	65.4
District 34	6.6	14.7	10.3	19.3	14.7	13.1	10.0	6.7	4.6	34.5	191,061	66.9	25.4
District 35	6.8	19.5	11.9	15.8	13.7	12.7	10.4	5.7	3.4	32.3	219,055	70.9	16.1
District 36	5.6	17.5	7.8	11.9	11.4	12.5	12.2	11.6	9.6	41.1	177,223	79.5	20.6
District 37	5.5	13.5	11.2	18.5	13.9	13.1	11.2	6.9	6.1	35.7	182,732	79.6	36.9
District 38	6.2	17.2	10.2	14.0	13.4	13.5	12.0	7.8	5.6	37.0	193,378	80.8	23.5
District 39	6.0	15.6	9.9	14.4	12.5	13.5	13.4	8.4	6.3	38.2	194,424	88.6	41.6
District 40	7.5	21.4	11.6	15.3	13.8	12.8	8.7	5.6	3.2	30.6	228,912	55.6	9.8
District 41	7.3	20.0	13.3	15.4	12.7	12.1	9.9	5.7	3.6	30.9	236,325	75.6	18.3
District 42	6.8	19.5	9.0	14.3	13.8	13.1	11.5	6.9	5.1	35.2	233,033	86.4	25.0
District 43	7.2	16.2	10.3	15.9	14.1	13.1	11.4	6.2	5.4	35.2	196,934	78.1	26.5
District 44	7.3	20.7	10.8	15.0	13.1	12.9	9.8	6.4	4.2	32.3	214,775	64.0	12.3
District 45	5.8	15.6	9.8	13.0	13.8	15.4	12.1	8.1	6.3	38.9	220,862	94.3	56.0
District 46	7.3	18.9	10.9	17.3	13.5	12.9	9.6	5.2	4.2	32.1	214,676	66.6	18.7
District 47	6.2	16.3	10.1	15.3	13.5	14.5	11.7	7.5	5.0	36.4	193,575	81.6	32.0
District 48	5.1	14.6	8.0	13.9	12.1	15.0	14.4	9.4	7.6	41.8	172,743	89.2	44.6
District 49	6.9	16.7	9.8	13.7	12.0	14.0	12.1	8.9	5.9	37.2	189,512	90.3	44.0
District 50	6.9	17.4	9.2	13.8	12.2	13.6	13.1	8.0	5.9	36.9	202,824	86.3	28.2
District 51	6.8	18.4	12.0	16.5	12.2	12.4	10.4	6.4	4.9	32.5	212,444	68.0	14.1
District 52	5.8	13.8	10.4	17.1	14.3	12.4	11.9	8.1	6.2	36.6	195,744	95.3	57.4
District 53	6.3	13.7	10.9	18.8	14.1	12.5	11.0	7.2	5.5	35.3	209,595	88.7	37.8

1. All persons 3 years old and over enrolled in nursery school through college and graduate or professional school.　　2. Persons 25 years old and over.

STATE District	Households, 2016						Group Quarters, 2010					
	Number	Average household size	Family households (percent)	Married couple family (percent)	Female family house-holder[1]	One person households (percent)	Total in group quarters, 2016	Percent 65 years and over	Persons in correctional institutions	Persons in nursing facilities	Persons in college dormitories	Persons in military quarters
	28	29	30	31	32	33	34	35	36	37	38	39
UNITED STATES.............	11,860,065	2.65	65.4	47.9	12.6	28.0	8,079,879	18.3	2,263,602	1,502,264	2,521,090	338,191
ALABAMA........................	1,852,518	2.56	65.2	46.7	14.2	30.7	119,659	18.7	41,177	22,995	36,341	2,152
District 1............................	264,399	2.60	64.9	46.4	14.6	31.0	16,265	19.1	5,651	2,671	2,579	0
District 2............................	259,766	2.55	63.8	44.7	14.2	32.3	19,684	15.4	13,081	3,727	3,107	1,274
District 3............................	270,850	2.54	67.4	49.9	13.2	28.1	20,245	15.9	7,014	3,016	6,949	0
District 4............................	256,036	2.64	68.8	52.2	12.5	27.9	7,773	39.0	2,922	3,652	791	0
District 5............................	278,329	2.50	63.9	47.8	11.9	32.1	16,167	17.5	5,087	2,879	5,347	823
District 6............................	267,123	2.60	67.7	52.7	11.4	28.5	11,911	23.8	4,884	2,733	2,830	0
District 7............................	256,015	2.49	60.0	32.4	22.1	35.1	27,614	15.1	2,538	4,317	14,738	55
ALASKA........................	248,468	2.87	66.0	49.2	11.1	25.1	27,826	5.9	4,206	1,626	1,872	5,055
At Large........................	248,468	2.87	66.0	49.2	11.1	25.1	27,826	5.9	4,206	1,626	1,872	5,055
ARIZONA........................	2,519,052	2.69	65.5	47.4	12.6	27.3	156,879	12.2	67,767	13,819	27,987	5,172
District 1............................	249,358	2.94	68.6	48.2	14.0	24.9	34,210	4.2	15,071	816	7,630	0
District 2............................	301,297	2.33	59.9	43.1	12.5	32.7	21,284	19.9	7,538	2,914	118	3,352
District 3............................	242,621	2.99	71.5	46.7	18.4	21.8	27,197	5.3	11,711	863	6,913	0
District 4............................	296,652	2.44	64.9	53.5	8.5	28.7	29,358	6.9	19,869	1,431	1,213	1,164
District 5............................	274,044	2.85	72.2	58.8	9.2	21.6	3,482	55.3	11	859	346	0
District 6............................	313,796	2.42	61.4	47.2	10.0	31.2	4,883	53.4	10	1,594	274	0
District 7............................	245,571	3.29	67.9	37.2	20.5	24.5	11,273	5.2	8,915	840	1,162	656
District 8............................	286,511	2.69	70.1	55.8	9.6	25.0	11,843	30.5	4,624	2,809	861	0
District 9............................	309,202	2.49	55.9	36.1	12.9	32.2	13,349	12.2	18	1,693	9,470	0
ARKANSAS	1,142,718	2.54	65.5	48.1	13.2	29.3	85,075	21.7	25,844	18,532	24,144	619
District 1............................	273,559	2.55	65.8	46.8	14.1	29.9	29,156	20.6	15,495	5,770	2,669	0
District 2............................	293,331	2.53	64.3	46.0	14.2	30.0	17,778	20.1	3,461	3,521	6,184	616
District 3............................	303,127	2.56	65.9	51.0	10.9	27.3	17,203	21.3	1,599	3,663	9,499	0
District 4............................	272,701	2.52	65.8	48.6	13.7	30.0	20,938	24.7	5,289	5,578	5,792	3
CALIFORNIA	12,944,178	2.97	68.7	49.5	13.2	23.9	813,569	15.4	256,807	111,884	172,843	57,628
District 1............................	273,669	2.48	61.5	46.6	10.0	30.2	24,797	14.1	11,908	2,834	2,728	5
District 2............................	283,904	2.45	60.3	45.7	10.1	31.2	19,512	13.5	9,975	2,246	2,645	393
District 3............................	251,190	2.86	70.8	51.9	12.8	21.1	22,032	9.1	12,154	1,728	4,981	1,321
District 4............................	274,386	2.64	68.3	55.1	9.2	25.8	12,598	15.3	8,633	1,677	458	0
District 5............................	262,302	2.76	66.4	48.6	11.8	26.3	13,089	22.6	1,940	3,657	3,581	0
District 6............................	271,977	2.77	61.1	39.0	15.1	29.4	11,044	19.4	2,254	1,789	1,493	0
District 7............................	261,127	2.78	69.5	50.6	12.7	24.7	11,867	23.1	6,682	1,704	22	0
District 8............................	232,951	3.04	73.0	49.2	15.9	22.0	15,147	10.8	6,717	1,325	117	4,748
District 9............................	237,359	3.15	73.9	50.7	15.5	20.9	12,648	21.5	1,358	2,403	2,194	0
District 10..........................	235,531	3.13	76.1	54.7	14.3	19.3	8,461	24.1	4,848	2,580	584	0
District 11..........................	266,301	2.81	70.7	52.5	12.2	22.5	8,239	35.3	865	3,004	1,568	0
District 12..........................	324,880	2.28	46.2	35.4	7.2	36.4	17,267	18.3	1,573	2,810	5,993	0
District 13..........................	287,921	2.55	55.6	39.3	11.8	32.1	21,973	13.2	1,044	2,600	11,927	661
District 14..........................	253,163	2.92	70.9	53.4	11.8	22.1	11,015	29.2	1,090	1,939	2,487	0
District 15..........................	250,240	3.04	77.6	62.0	10.7	17.2	9,088	23.6	5,669	2,136	1,076	0
District 16..........................	210,616	3.38	74.3	44.8	20.1	20.6	19,190	11.0	12,113	2,113	1,443	0
District 17..........................	257,515	2.97	73.8	62.4	7.4	18.6	10,902	20.8	2,564	1,666	2,592	0
District 18..........................	268,446	2.69	69.7	56.9	8.4	22.6	17,292	24.9	4	2,889	6,712	5
District 19..........................	226,671	3.31	75.4	55.2	13.3	17.6	12,515	11.7	1,448	916	3,356	0
District 20..........................	227,623	3.14	69.5	50.7	12.5	23.5	30,146	8.9	11,516	2,072	8,411	2,504
District 21..........................	187,890	3.65	82.5	56.9	17.4	13.8	40,096	4.1	44,549	1,252	239	2,038
District 22..........................	241,790	3.09	74.2	51.2	16.4	19.6	7,577	28.5	1,349	1,709	1,566	0
District 23..........................	242,551	2.91	68.9	48.2	15.2	25.6	19,457	9.1	17,160	2,293	560	329
District 24..........................	252,574	2.78	65.6	50.3	10.3	24.1	36,489	7.2	11,387	1,805	15,714	475
District 25..........................	225,209	3.19	75.4	55.2	13.9	18.9	10,079	5.7	7,129	251	1,775	0
District 26..........................	228,178	3.13	71.9	54.3	12.0	22.2	11,660	18.2	1,535	1,644	2,316	1,349
District 27..........................	243,721	2.91	70.1	51.0	13.8	23.2	13,874	25.4	331	3,659	5,809	0
District 28..........................	297,443	2.35	51.9	37.6	9.1	35.9	10,689	32.8	183	3,356	647	0
District 29..........................	211,315	3.41	71.0	46.1	16.5	21.4	6,071	35.7	307	2,842	151	0
District 30..........................	275,641	2.72	64.3	47.1	12.3	26.6	10,496	41.0	20	2,996	2,746	0
District 31..........................	222,147	3.25	74.5	47.0	19.6	20.7	21,241	15.4	5,464	2,391	2,739	0
District 32..........................	191,240	3.70	79.9	53.3	18.0	15.5	11,565	29.1	74	2,895	3,298	0
District 33..........................	301,954	2.29	54.2	44.0	6.6	36.0	20,779	11.2	98	1,851	14,107	0
District 34..........................	255,952	2.87	58.6	32.9	16.5	31.2	22,981	11.7	8,722	3,270	2,438	0
District 35..........................	191,182	3.76	79.4	52.5	18.2	15.0	26,020	11.5	6,996	2,041	1,948	0
District 36..........................	267,899	2.75	61.8	46.4	10.6	31.9	12,787	16.9	9,107	1,504	70	0
District 37..........................	273,317	2.61	54.2	33.8	13.9	35.4	16,899	14.0	155	2,263	7,976	0
District 38..........................	204,335	3.42	78.3	54.0	17.2	16.9	10,375	26.5	156	2,794	3,305	0
District 39..........................	225,793	3.20	78.3	60.5	11.9	16.3	7,576	26.5	2	1,230	2,630	0
District 40..........................	182,996	3.93	82.8	48.6	22.9	13.5	3,267	37.5	7	1,571	5	0
District 41..........................	194,812	3.82	79.1	52.9	18.5	15.9	15,567	11.9	1,171	1,826	7,379	0
District 42..........................	227,143	3.46	78.6	61.5	11.3	17.5	6,206	10.4	5,652	440	161	0
District 43..........................	239,020	2.99	67.4	41.0	19.2	26.7	9,696	27.0	120	2,478	3,293	0
District 44..........................	188,841	3.79	78.6	46.8	22.1	17.3	8,723	16.1	2,843	1,687	587	20
District 45..........................	276,707	2.75	70.8	58.5	8.5	22.9	12,446	22.2	534	789	5,705	0
District 46..........................	185,670	3.87	77.3	52.0	18.6	14.2	16,958	19.0	4,906	2,887	1,967	0
District 47..........................	239,498	2.94	65.3	44.6	14.5	26.0	9,650	31.5	235	2,931	2,040	2
District 48..........................	265,180	2.72	67.2	53.0	9.6	24.2	5,550	30.5	13	1,555	1,249	14
District 49..........................	256,731	2.80	69.2	55.0	10.9	23.7	20,945	6.5	782	1,612	7,910	16,563
District 50..........................	238,443	3.11	74.6	58.6	11.1	18.9	9,828	26.3	889	1,975	757	0
District 51..........................	201,097	3.55	75.6	47.2	20.7	19.2	33,421	4.0	17,756	1,059	0	11,846
District 52..........................	281,618	2.58	61.5	49.7	8.1	27.9	22,709	8.6	2,774	1,881	4,151	15,213
District 53..........................	268,519	2.81	61.4	44.2	12.0	27.2	13,070	28.3	46	3,059	3,237	142

1. No spouse present.

Table E. Congressional Districts 115th Congress — **Housing and Money Income**

STATE District	Housing units, 2016 Total	Occupied units as a percent of all units	Owner-occupied units as a percent of occupied units	Median value¹ (dollars)	Percent valued at $500,000 or more	Median rent²	Per capita income (dollars)	Median income (dollars)	Percent with income of $100,000 or more
	40	41	42	43	44	45	46	47	48
UNITED STATES............	135,702,775	87.6	63.1	205,000	13.6	981	31,128	57,617	26.2
ALABAMA......................	2,230,180	83.1	68.5	136,200	3.8	743	25,810	46,257	18.3
District 1.............................	333,004	79.4	68.1	141,600	3.9	808	25,695	47,083	19.1
District 2.............................	313,602	82.8	65.2	119,900	2.5	748	24,161	42,035	16.0
District 3.............................	325,956	83.1	69.5	132,600	3.7	715	24,132	46,544	16.3
District 4.............................	311,748	82.1	74.5	113,500	2.8	617	22,320	41,110	13.7
District 5.............................	315,647	88.2	70.6	155,100	3.7	723	29,758	51,690	23.2
District 6.............................	303,544	88.0	74.8	174,600	7.1	899	33,383	61,413	27.4
District 7.............................	326,679	78.4	55.9	97,000	2.0	723	20,732	34,664	11.5
ALASKA........................	310,672	80.0	64.5	267,800	9.7	1,208	34,187	76,440	36.5
At Large.............................	310,672	80.0	64.5	267,800	9.7	1,208	34,187	76,440	36.5
ARIZONA.......................	2,961,136	85.1	63.2	205,900	8.6	976	27,997	53,558	22.4
District 1.............................	336,911	74.0	69.9	168,400	6.8	886	22,491	50,537	18.7
District 2.............................	347,680	86.7	61.6	172,700	6.0	839	28,577	49,072	18.7
District 3.............................	271,748	89.3	63.0	142,700	2.3	884	19,232	44,224	12.9
District 4.............................	393,811	75.3	73.8	175,700	5.0	873	26,523	49,466	16.8
District 5.............................	319,978	85.6	71.3	261,800	8.5	1,222	32,918	71,693	33.6
District 6.............................	360,600	87.0	64.9	328,000	26.0	1,110	42,779	67,830	33.2
District 7.............................	265,503	92.5	44.6	154,300	2.0	867	16,959	40,991	12.5
District 8.............................	323,967	88.4	72.7	229,300	5.1	1,170	30,432	61,754	27.7
District 9.............................	340,938	90.7	46.6	251,300	11.8	985	32,415	55,349	24.0
ARKANSAS	1,354,801	84.3	64.6	123,300	2.8	701	24,264	44,334	16.1
District 1.............................	339,214	80.6	65.5	98,000	1.4	635	21,907	40,492	12.0
District 2.............................	338,893	86.6	62.2	148,600	3.8	786	27,592	49,498	19.9
District 3.............................	332,180	91.3	61.0	149,500	3.8	732	25,991	47,903	19.6
District 4.............................	344,514	79.2	70.0	98,400	2.2	620	21,182	39,586	12.4
CALIFORNIA	14,061,375	92.1	53.6	477,500	47.0	1,375	33,389	67,739	33.7
District 1.............................	324,143	84.4	64.7	264,000	14.0	968	26,949	47,488	19.2
District 2.............................	319,437	88.9	62.2	605,500	58.8	1,413	44,818	66,604	35.0
District 3.............................	269,946	93.1	55.9	335,100	21.1	1,155	29,224	61,508	27.8
District 4.............................	357,820	76.7	72.8	394,700	31.5	1,264	38,757	74,074	36.5
District 5.............................	288,708	90.9	60.1	473,100	44.8	1,491	35,209	73,006	35.5
District 6.............................	289,591	93.9	46.1	289,700	13.4	1,069	26,642	51,932	22.3
District 7.............................	274,471	95.1	63.9	353,700	19.9	1,185	34,031	68,735	33.0
District 8.............................	305,097	76.4	59.7	219,600	6.7	1,069	21,809	49,194	20.1
District 9.............................	253,065	93.8	57.3	330,300	20.5	1,098	26,494	61,454	28.9
District 10...........................	246,078	95.7	57.7	304,800	10.7	1,120	25,293	60,235	25.7
District 11...........................	278,373	95.7	61.5	642,600	62.7	1,629	44,515	86,000	43.8
District 12...........................	357,877	90.8	35.2	1,052,200	X	1,788	64,839	105,918	52.8
District 13...........................	305,826	94.1	43.5	687,300	72.3	1,416	41,397	73,601	37.8
District 14...........................	264,892	95.6	59.2	945,200	92.1	2,071	50,487	103,850	52.5
District 15...........................	259,201	96.5	62.6	731,300	79.6	1,875	44,491	106,291	53.2
District 16...........................	227,951	92.4	46.1	201,500	6.8	873	18,362	40,207	15.3
District 17...........................	269,153	95.7	53.4	910,700	88.1	2,331	49,171	121,150	60.0
District 18...........................	284,485	94.4	60.1	1,235,900	93.4	2,040	66,772	125,790	59.5
District 19...........................	234,732	96.6	59.4	722,300	82.5	1,765	36,864	93,139	47.3
District 20...........................	250,659	90.8	51.8	568,300	56.9	1,399	29,672	67,419	31.8
District 21...........................	200,392	93.8	49.8	168,000	3.6	865	15,153	41,174	12.8
District 22...........................	257,241	94.0	59.7	248,700	8.4	984	25,763	56,524	24.5
District 23...........................	269,616	90.0	60.0	228,600	5.6	971	25,392	54,437	24.4
District 24...........................	281,507	89.7	55.6	544,500	54.1	1,442	32,445	68,929	31.4
District 25...........................	238,192	94.5	65.4	435,200	39.5	1,445	31,565	75,367	37.2
District 26...........................	244,372	93.4	61.1	563,600	59.0	1,628	34,606	76,914	39.2
District 27...........................	261,990	93.0	52.4	663,000	76.6	1,426	35,241	71,223	36.0
District 28...........................	324,850	91.6	32.6	757,400	80.6	1,415	41,930	63,940	31.6
District 29...........................	218,659	96.6	40.9	444,900	30.7	1,247	21,309	50,655	21.6
District 30...........................	291,967	94.4	52.0	652,900	72.1	1,609	41,473	76,778	38.8
District 31...........................	235,092	94.5	51.7	336,100	19.5	1,235	23,514	58,668	24.5
District 32...........................	199,697	95.8	58.6	451,800	35.9	1,365	23,237	67,101	29.0
District 33...........................	338,961	89.1	49.0	1,156,900	91.5	1,955	69,375	101,956	51.9
District 34...........................	273,373	93.6	20.9	542,400	55.9	1,105	21,540	40,847	16.3
District 35...........................	199,050	96.0	56.9	338,700	10.1	1,277	19,394	57,159	22.3
District 36...........................	362,087	74.0	65.2	252,500	13.9	1,022	25,180	44,567	19.4
District 37...........................	291,827	93.7	34.6	682,300	66.6	1,388	33,653	55,190	27.0
District 38...........................	212,321	96.2	60.4	467,200	38.8	1,348	25,489	66,421	31.0
District 39...........................	236,139	95.6	65.6	630,800	71.7	1,611	35,092	85,188	42.5
District 40...........................	191,181	95.7	32.8	384,100	22.1	1,129	15,885	42,902	13.8
District 41...........................	204,125	95.4	55.9	318,700	9.0	1,295	21,233	62,069	25.3
District 42...........................	238,368	95.3	69.5	395,100	24.4	1,576	29,264	76,504	36.4
District 43...........................	253,244	94.4	41.0	481,400	46.2	1,223	26,562	54,614	25.3
District 44...........................	196,959	95.9	47.3	368,900	15.5	1,127	19,009	50,890	21.2
District 45...........................	290,404	95.3	62.9	685,800	76.9	2,079	48,000	97,356	49.3
District 46...........................	192,260	96.6	39.2	492,000	47.9	1,459	21,018	61,304	25.8
District 47...........................	250,388	95.7	45.9	570,500	62.6	1,292	30,348	65,450	30.6
District 48...........................	285,805	92.8	58.0	735,900	78.9	1,826	47,277	88,903	44.4
District 49...........................	279,914	91.7	57.5	708,900	71.6	1,756	42,826	80,877	41.7
District 50...........................	255,900	93.2	63.0	460,100	40.5	1,392	30,315	71,692	33.9
District 51...........................	226,274	88.9	43.4	315,800	11.8	1,114	18,206	46,639	16.0
District 52...........................	306,934	91.8	52.7	675,500	74.7	1,809	46,537	90,854	45.4
District 53...........................	290,781	92.3	48.3	486,300	46.6	1,436	33,570	69,314	33.0

1. Specified owner-occupied units.   2. Specified renter-occupied units.

Table E. Congressional Districts 115th Congress — Poverty, Labor Force, Employment, and Social Security

STATE District	Poverty, 2016			Civilian labor force, 2016			Civilian employment,[2] 2016				Persons under 65 years of age with no health insurance, 2016 (percent)	Social Security beneficiaries, December 2016		Supplemental Security Income recipients, December 2016
					Unemployment			Percent						
	Persons below poverty level (percent)	Families below poverty level (percent)	Percent of households receiving food stamps in past 12 months	Total	Total	Rate[1]	Total	Management, business, science, and arts occupations	Service, sales, and office	Construction and production		Number	Rate[3]	
	49	50	51	52	53	54	55	56	57	58	59	60	61	62
UNITED STATES	14.0	10.0	12.4	161,879,627	9,308,586	5.8	152,571,041	37.6	41.4	21.0	10.0	60,018,120	185.7	8,250,117
ALABAMA	17.1	12.7	14.6	2,219,288	140,963	6.4	2,078,325	34.2	40.6	25.2	10.7	1,120,486	230.4	167,349
District 1	17.6	13.5	13.9	310,162	17,567	5.7	292,595	33.7	42.5	23.8	12.5	166,162	235.9	22,448
District 2	19.3	15.2	17.1	304,235	18,432	6.1	285,803	32.0	40.7	27.3	12.0	159,131	233.5	27,019
District 3	16.5	11.0	13.8	322,974	21,347	6.6	301,627	33.4	39.1	27.5	9.8	163,892	231.0	22,994
District 4	17.8	13.5	15.0	294,561	17,966	6.1	276,595	28.0	39.0	33.1	11.4	180,215	263.8	24,818
District 5	14.8	11.6	11.0	343,106	17,818	5.2	325,288	39.1	38.6	22.3	9.6	150,949	211.8	16,662
District 6	9.9	6.8	8.0	346,899	15,368	4.4	331,531	42.6	39.0	18.4	7.8	142,687	202.0	11,454
District 7	24.4	18.5	24.0	297,351	32,465	10.9	264,886	28.2	45.8	26.0	12.2	157,450	236.5	41,954
ALASKA	9.9	6.7	10.5	388,062	30,964	8.0	357,098	37.2	39.9	22.9	15.5	95,500	128.7	12,449
At Large	9.9	6.7	10.5	388,062	30,964	8.0	357,098	37.2	39.9	22.9	15.5	95,500	128.7	12,449
ARIZONA	16.4	11.9	12.4	3,242,632	210,851	6.5	3,031,781	36.1	45.2	18.6	11.9	1,274,815	183.9	119,079
District 1	20.9	14.8	14.5	306,353	27,463	9.0	278,890	33.7	45.7	20.5	13.0	149,896	195.5	18,201
District 2	17.3	12.7	13.1	330,451	21,953	6.6	308,498	39.5	46.0	14.5	9.6	168,409	233.0	13,830
District 3	20.7	16.4	20.4	349,141	33,254	9.5	315,887	25.3	48.2	26.5	14.0	110,836	147.3	18,007
District 4	13.7	9.2	11.3	291,128	20,705	7.1	270,423	29.8	50.5	19.8	11.1	212,968	282.5	12,324
District 5	9.0	6.7	6.5	381,454	19,194	5.0	362,260	44.9	41.0	14.2	7.6	130,266	165.9	6,430
District 6	11.9	8.3	7.8	400,267	20,130	5.0	380,137	45.8	41.5	12.7	10.3	139,237	182.1	8,184
District 7	28.4	24.8	25.5	382,247	24,472	6.4	357,775	21.6	49.0	29.4	19.4	88,680	108.4	23,771
District 8	8.5	5.3	6.4	353,857	18,952	5.4	334,905	40.0	43.5	16.5	8.2	173,601	221.9	8,233
District 9	16.7	12.0	9.8	447,734	24,728	5.5	423,006	40.7	43.9	15.4	11.9	100,922	128.6	10,099
ARKANSAS	17.2	12.4	12.5	1,351,706	69,030	5.1	1,282,676	33.5	40.9	25.6	9.3	685,361	229.4	108,580
District 1	18.9	14.0	16.0	311,166	22,271	7.2	288,895	29.0	40.1	30.9	9.7	182,238	251.1	32,979
District 2	16.2	11.2	10.2	360,210	16,952	4.7	343,258	39.3	41.6	19.0	7.7	159,618	210.3	26,576
District 3	14.7	10.2	10.2	375,631	12,227	3.3	363,404	35.2	40.7	24.1	10.4	161,371	203.2	19,392
District 4	19.5	14.4	14.0	304,699	17,580	5.8	287,119	29.0	41.2	29.8	9.5	182,134	256.8	29,633
CALIFORNIA	14.3	10.5	9.6	19,620,589	1,277,331	6.5	18,343,258	38.3	41.7	20.0	8.3	5,754,771	146.6	1,275,744
District 1	17.3	10.5	10.6	298,622	22,081	7.4	276,541	34.6	43.2	22.2	6.7	182,279	259.2	31,752
District 2	12.7	7.5	7.6	361,084	21,432	5.9	339,652	43.6	41.1	15.3	7.0	151,369	211.3	18,455
District 3	15.2	9.6	11.4	340,397	21,559	6.3	318,838	33.3	42.1	24.6	7.1	124,765	168.5	23,163
District 4	9.2	6.2	6.3	337,515	18,239	5.4	319,276	42.6	42.1	15.3	4.9	166,804	226.3	12,889
District 5	10.2	6.8	7.6	394,127	24,518	6.2	369,609	34.5	46.6	19.0	6.2	137,965	187.5	17,150
District 6	21.5	17.4	14.8	370,024	28,258	7.6	341,766	35.7	45.4	18.8	6.3	109,549	143.4	45,118
District 7	11.6	8.9	7.7	363,019	20,698	5.7	342,321	41.9	42.8	15.2	4.4	126,684	171.5	23,178
District 8	20.4	15.2	19.8	296,223	28,148	9.5	268,075	27.4	47.4	25.2	8.2	122,812	169.7	28,218
District 9	14.2	11.5	15.2	349,565	29,608	8.5	319,957	28.5	44.5	26.9	6.1	115,809	152.2	27,947
District 10	12.7	9.0	13.2	350,240	32,350	9.2	317,890	27.4	41.7	30.9	6.0	115,857	155.5	25,805
District 11	9.4	6.9	7.2	385,292	23,555	6.1	361,737	43.6	41.5	14.8	6.8	124,704	164.9	21,641
District 12	10.3	5.9	4.7	471,797	20,386	4.3	451,411	59.4	33.1	7.5	3.5	104,975	138.7	38,377
District 13	15.5	10.7	8.1	417,180	21,654	5.2	395,526	50.0	36.7	13.3	6.3	104,249	138.0	32,562
District 14	6.7	3.8	4.1	425,359	16,196	3.8	409,163	45.4	40.8	13.7	4.8	112,284	149.9	14,452
District 15	7.2	5.0	4.9	406,651	16,211	4.0	390,440	48.3	36.7	15.0	3.6	94,424	122.7	15,348
District 16	28.1	25.0	27.4	307,886	38,502	12.5	269,384	21.1	44.9	34.0	9.1	93,389	127.9	38,365
District 17	6.5	3.6	2.5	420,696	18,043	4.3	402,653	60.3	27.9	11.9	2.9	88,329	114.0	14,740
District 18	8.1	5.1	3.3	386,348	13,542	3.5	372,806	61.1	29.5	9.3	3.4	100,850	136.5	10,810
District 19	11.3	7.4	9.2	408,869	22,787	5.6	386,082	38.6	42.5	18.9	6.2	89,199	117.1	25,631
District 20	13.2	9.7	8.9	358,622	19,176	5.3	339,446	31.2	40.5	28.3	8.9	107,689	144.8	14,821
District 21	27.2	23.9	24.4	290,123	32,713	11.3	257,410	17.9	37.2	44.9	10.7	79,672	109.7	26,229
District 22	19.4	15.5	17.1	346,063	27,870	8.1	318,193	34.2	41.6	24.3	7.8	111,193	147.2	26,480
District 23	19.8	15.8	14.4	316,145	31,096	9.8	285,049	35.0	40.4	24.7	7.0	114,136	157.4	26,824
District 24	12.7	6.9	6.4	376,162	19,280	5.1	356,882	36.4	42.7	20.9	9.7	132,268	179.1	13,550
District 25	12.7	9.6	7.7	350,747	22,429	6.4	328,318	38.9	41.2	20.0	7.3	98,303	134.9	22,937
District 26	10.2	6.5	7.2	368,896	18,829	5.1	350,067	37.3	38.5	24.2	11.3	117,551	161.8	14,453
District 27	13.3	9.7	4.4	369,435	17,851	4.8	351,584	43.7	42.6	13.8	6.5	111,906	154.5	29,186
District 28	14.0	9.3	5.3	418,270	30,457	7.3	387,813	49.0	38.7	12.3	9.4	91,055	128.3	44,318
District 29	18.9	16.1	13.7	377,007	25,254	6.7	351,753	25.5	47.1	27.4	12.9	77,990	107.4	32,838
District 30	11.9	8.5	5.8	420,992	27,679	6.6	393,313	47.7	39.6	12.7	7.7	108,509	142.8	21,805
District 31	18.8	14.6	18.0	349,533	29,564	8.5	319,969	30.5	44.7	24.7	9.4	93,542	126.0	27,948
District 32	12.3	9.9	8.9	368,518	22,692	6.2	345,826	28.1	46.4	25.6	10.3	102,823	142.9	27,107
District 33	8.7	4.4	2.1	393,125	20,938	5.3	372,187	63.9	29.8	6.3	4.4	113,482	159.2	10,851
District 34	24.6	20.5	12.2	401,900	26,429	6.6	375,471	28.3	48.5	23.2	18.7	77,815	102.6	43,223
District 35	16.0	13.5	14.7	365,307	30,979	8.5	334,328	21.9	45.5	32.5	13.0	79,090	106.2	22,457
District 36	20.1	15.4	10.6	313,511	29,082	9.3	284,429	26.9	47.9	25.2	13.1	157,091	209.5	24,065
District 37	18.9	14.5	10.0	393,398	25,121	6.4	368,277	41.0	44.1	14.8	11.8	93,925	128.8	36,355
District 38	11.8	8.6	7.7	343,080	21,046	6.1	322,034	32.3	44.6	23.1	9.3	108,636	153.2	25,813
District 39	9.6	6.9	5.3	376,907	20,250	5.4	356,657	42.2	42.2	15.6	6.5	105,998	145.2	16,261
District 40	22.4	19.6	17.6	343,929	27,256	7.9	316,673	15.9	46.4	37.7	15.8	70,711	97.8	26,029
District 41	16.3	12.9	14.2	358,392	31,078	8.7	327,314	26.3	42.9	30.8	10.5	94,304	124.1	24,811
District 42	10.8	8.2	7.6	378,356	26,626	7.0	351,730	35.3	44.3	20.4	7.8	106,168	133.9	12,475
District 43	17.9	13.9	11.1	369,746	24,895	6.7	344,851	31.1	48.2	20.7	11.8	94,365	130.3	26,627
District 44	20.9	18.1	17.3	344,745	28,413	8.2	316,332	19.6	45.4	35.1	12.6	86,463	119.5	35,538
District 45	8.8	5.2	2.6	413,296	20,443	4.9	392,853	54.5	36.2	9.4	4.5	108,031	139.6	9,826
District 46	16.0	12.1	14.2	380,589	20,807	5.5	359,782	23.3	49.4	27.2	14.7	74,089	100.7	27,039
District 47	15.5	10.7	10.5	370,657	21,910	5.9	348,747	37.4	42.5	20.1	8.6	96,321	134.8	33,579
District 48	9.3	5.9	4.6	390,554	17,252	4.4	373,302	45.1	41.9	13.0	6.9	120,223	165.3	10,388
District 49	9.3	5.8	4.8	359,773	15,051	4.2	344,722	44.2	40.9	14.9	7.7	113,035	152.8	8,431
District 50	12.5	8.9	9.4	376,402	23,424	6.2	352,978	34.3	44.6	21.1	8.9	119,259	158.7	15,433
District 51	20.7	17.8	17.8	337,739	37,228	11.0	300,511	20.5	53.7	25.8	12.7	111,948	149.8	38,423
District 52	9.4	5.1	2.9	391,720	18,827	4.8	372,893	58.0	33.2	8.8	4.9	106,995	142.6	14,301
District 53	11.3	6.7	6.5	416,056	27,619	6.6	388,437	44.2	42.2	13.6	7.5	103,889	135.5	19,722

1. Percent of civilian labor force.   2. Persons 16 years old and over.   3. Per 1,000 resident population estimated in the 2016 American Community Survey.

STATE District	Number of farms	Acres	Average size of farm (acres)	Irrigated land (acres)	Total ($1,000)	Average per farm (dollars)	Percent from crops	Percent from livestock and poultry products	Total ($1,000)	Average per farm receiving payments (dollars)
			Land in farms			Value of products sold				Government payments
	63	64	65	66	67	68	69	70	71	72
UNITED STATES............	2,109,303	914,527,657	434	55,822,231	394,644,481	187,097	53.8	46.2	8,053,346	9,925
ALABAMA......................	43,223	8,902,654	206	113,008	5,571,173	128,894	23.6	76.4	88,145	6,802
District 1............................	3,041	621,188	204	11,518	337,273	110,909	78.6	21.4	9,284	10,125
District 2............................	8,890	2,339,433	263	40,808	1,477,342	166,180	24.7	75.3	29,691	6,929
District 3............................	5,244	1,101,850	210	15,725	685,901	130,797	22.0	78.0	7,690	7,180
District 4............................	12,450	1,691,155	136	11,693	1,879,383	150,954	9.7	90.3	15,683	5,528
District 5............................	6,283	1,043,516	166	19,334	507,359	80,751	46.8	53.2	12,988	6,559
District 6............................	2,759	414,441	150	2,353	211,764	76,754	16.5	83.5	2,073	5,498
District 7............................	4,556	1,691,071	371	11,577	472,151	103,633	16.9	83.1	10,736	7,201
ALASKA......................	762	833,861	1,094	2,451	58,925	77,329	42.2	57.8	2,432	12,472
At Large	762	833,861	1,094	2,451	58,925	77,329	42.2	57.8	2,432	12,473
ARIZONA......................	20,005	26,249,195	1,312	880,613	3,732,113	186,559	55.6	44.4	31,329	10,245
District 1............................	13,505	20,238,604	1,499	274,134	1,189,607	88,086	41.3	58.7	15,323	6,574
District 2............................	1,452	981,592	676	67,103	170,117	117,161	D	D	2,662	13,513
District 3............................	1,467	3,206,653	2,186	220,098	1,051,870	717,021	57.8	42.2	5,901	23,892
District 4............................	1,851	1,618,174	874	236,656	927,038	500,831	65.5	34.5	4,673	26,551
District 5............................	559	39,587	71	22,692	123,985	221,798	26.0	74.0	945	26,995
District 6............................	459	105,916	231	16,105	77,337	168,490	D	D	295	12,303
District 7............................	173	D	D	22,562	110,396	638,125	D	D	911	70,065
District 8............................	455	D	D	16,399	60,936	133,925	70.4	29.6	541	18,664
District 9............................	84	7,562	90	4,864	20,827	247,937	95.6	4.4	78	12,964
ARKANSAS	45,071	13,810,786	306	4,803,902	9,775,758	216,897	49.5	50.5	262,967	20,013
District 1............................	14,422	7,829,889	543	4,372,332	4,886,232	338,804	87.6	12.4	213,501	29,087
District 2............................	5,715	1,031,106	180	81,263	377,217	66,005	25.3	74.7	10,237	9,418
District 3............................	9,735	1,617,495	166	9,975	1,696,333	174,251	2.7	97.3	12,498	6,975
District 4............................	15,199	3,332,296	219	340,332	2,815,976	185,274	14.7	85.3	26,731	9,151
CALIFORNIA	77,857	25,569,001	328	7,861,964	42,627,472	547,510	71.2	28.8	146,919	19,349
District 1............................	8,970	3,605,203	402	823,662	1,598,258	178,178	80.2	19.8	20,753	19,414
District 2............................	5,047	2,066,839	410	103,785	1,213,224	240,385	57.7	42.3	5,084	16,453
District 3............................	6,350	2,502,923	394	1,126,206	2,636,257	415,159	91.0	9.0	44,654	27,770
District 4............................	5,257	1,451,586	276	204,969	866,959	164,915	81.3	18.7	3,025	15,672
District 5............................	3,592	544,785	152	92,050	851,570	237,074	89.4	10.6	1,043	10,032
District 6............................	171	23,658	138	9,578	16,301	95,328	89.6	10.4	240	21,799
District 7............................	814	154,475	190	34,153	158,078	194,199	55.6	44.4	846	14,582
District 8............................	1,016	451,523	444	63,093	298,555	293,853	16.4	83.6	379	17,209
District 9............................	3,238	689,573	213	404,975	1,895,907	585,518	74.5	25.5	4,447	15,548
District 10..........................	4,768	895,191	188	411,475	2,605,175	546,387	51.5	48.5	8,320	16,030
District 11..........................	327	112,764	345	18,602	54,849	167,734	78.3	21.7	219	10,418
District 12..........................	X	X	X	X	X	X	X	X	X	X
District 13..........................	32	D	D	25	1,386	43,320	34.8	65.2	4	1,300
District 14..........................	180	24,402	136	1,370	59,526	330,702	97.6	2.4	116	12,909
District 15..........................	395	122,196	309	8,413	47,578	120,450	83.5	16.5	44	2,921
District 16..........................	4,025	1,389,192	345	718,961	4,429,651	1,100,534	52.4	47.6	11,620	17,396
District 17..........................	74	13,886	188	993	10,881	147,042	93.7	6.3	4	1,466
District 18..........................	523	80,723	154	10,387	186,955	357,466	96.2	3.8	66	13,263
District 19..........................	736	204,524	278	10,694	176,147	239,330	95.6	4.4	6	802
District 20..........................	2,323	1,938,924	835	309,691	3,603,918	1,551,407	97.3	2.7	822	6,273
District 21..........................	5,300	2,806,804	530	1,670,398	9,238,009	1,743,021	61.6	38.4	22,328	21,449
District 22..........................	3,817	673,040	176	413,405	2,735,381	716,631	50.6	49.4	8,027	19,158
District 23..........................	3,373	2,214,121	656	465,834	2,351,633	697,193	84.5	15.5	4,352	13,068
District 24..........................	4,487	2,092,601	466	195,967	2,176,789	485,132	95.4	4.6	4,079	15,162
District 25..........................	505	58,321	115	29,580	80,815	160,030	D	D	186	5,806
District 26..........................	1,885	231,273	123	69,082	1,105,491	586,467	99.5	0.5	134	3,612
District 27..........................	154	4,357	28	1,448	24,375	158,280	99.0	1.0	7	1,167
District 28..........................	133	3,668	28	46	1,907	14,339	33.0	67.0	47	15,759
District 29..........................	59	1,703	29	245	8,994	152,438	99.1	0.9	0	0
District 30..........................	51	2,077	41	592	3,853	75,553	95.5	4.5	8	2,733
District 31..........................	181	3,547	20	2,222	5,777	31,918	96.2	3.8	10	3,386
District 32..........................	58	767	13	128	13,127	226,320	99.9	0.1	0	0
District 33..........................	133	8,247	62	1,982	6,266	47,110	93.0	7.0	D	D
District 34..........................	X	X	X	X	X	X	X	X	X	X
District 35..........................	195	7,032	36	1,442	311,590	1,597,900	7.8	92.2	569	21,901
District 36..........................	1,148	201,280	175	111,349	734,534	639,838	78.6	21.4	1,447	16,439
District 37..........................	23	448	19	439	2,725	118,471	D	D	0	0
District 38..........................	30	1,770	59	108	6,575	219,161	100.0	0.0	0	0
District 39..........................	115	1,527	13	657	9,804	85,251	96.0	4.0	D	D
District 40..........................	16	128	8	95	1,450	90,631	D	D	0	0
District 41..........................	426	30,431	71	8,036	43,767	102,739	D	D	181	9,037
District 42..........................	1,314	106,046	81	20,049	225,256	171,428	41.9	58.1	548	18,880
District 43..........................	46	712	15	132	8,896	193,384	99.4	0.6	0	0
District 44..........................	56	521	9	152	13,299	237,477	0.0	0.0	0	0
District 45..........................	114	48,582	426	5,163	96,549	846,923	98.7	1.3	10	1,615
District 46..........................	41	1,137	28	111	5,239	127,776	99.1	0.9	24	7,942
District 47..........................	43	D	D	944	3,623	84,263	96.6	3.4	D	D
District 48..........................	37	3,114	84	1,638	39,131	1,057,588	D	D	D	D
District 49..........................	935	D	D	6,737	137,991	147,584	81.4	18.6	71	4,730
District 50..........................	4,302	160,752	37	36,291	529,777	123,147	90.8	9.2	388	4,844
District 51..........................	721	557,584	773	462,112	1,955,250	2,711,858	70.3	29.7	2,789	21,790
District 52..........................	227	6,597	29	2,203	31,502	138,777	98.3	1.7	D	D
District 53..........................	84	1,594	19	290	6,909	82,246	99.2	0.8	0	0

Table E. Congressional Districts 115th Congress — Nonfarm Employment and Payroll

	Private nonfarm employment and payroll, 2016												
STATE District	Employment											Annual payroll	
		Percent by selected industries											
	Number of establishments	Total	Manufacturing	Construction	Wholesale trade	Retail trade	Health care and social assistance	Finance and Insurance	Real estate and rental and leasing	Professional, scientific, and technical services	Information	Total (mil dol)	Average per employee (dollars)
	73	74	75	76	77	78	79	80	81	82	83	84	85
UNITED STATES	7,757,807	126,752,238	9.1	5.0	4.8	12.6	15.6	5.0	1.7	6.9	2.7	6,435,142	50,769
ALABAMA	99,584	1,673,249	15.0	4.9	4.3	14.2	14.7	4.2	1.4	6.0	2.0	68,971	41,220
District 1	15,611	236,720	11.9	6.8	4.1	16.4	13.3	3.4	2.0	5.2	1.7	9,449	39,918
District 2	14,252	215,224	12.9	4.3	4.8	15.7	17.0	3.7	1.3	4.4	1.5	8,267	38,409
District 3	11,510	179,100	21.7	3.9	3.4	16.6	14.6	2.5	1.1	2.9	1.1	6,150	34,339
District 4	12,538	188,796	27.5	3.8	3.4	15.4	15.9	3.1	0.9	2.0	1.1	6,498	34,418
District 5	15,137	255,797	15.4	4.5	3.8	14.2	15.6	2.7	1.1	15.7	2.1	11,466	44,823
District 6	16,197	251,622	6.8	6.1	5.0	16.3	12.3	8.2	1.5	5.2	4.4	11,807	46,922
District 7	13,840	287,267	16.4	5.4	5.8	9.8	17.6	5.2	1.9	3.9	1.8	13,461	46,857
ALASKA	21,077	266,072	4.8	6.4	3.5	13.2	18.7	2.9	1.7	7.3	2.5	15,239	57,275
At Large	21,077	266,072	4.8	6.4	3.5	13.2	18.7	2.9	1.7	7.3	2.5	15,239	57,275
ARIZONA	139,134	2,379,409	6.1	6.0	3.9	13.5	15.1	6.2	2.0	6.2	2.0	106,431	44,730
District 1	11,927	166,416	9.4	4.2	2.0	17.8	17.2	1.7	1.4	2.7	1.6	6,415	38,550
District 2	15,397	217,943	2.7	4.8	1.4	17.6	22.3	5.1	2.2	7.2	1.8	7,972	36,577
District 3	9,888	165,199	9.9	6.8	4.9	15.0	16.3	1.9	1.3	3.7	2.0	6,621	40,078
District 4	12,645	141,929	6.7	7.0	3.1	20.4	19.1	2.1	1.7	2.5	1.3	4,690	33,041
District 5	14,439	187,758	7.4	8.4	2.3	19.4	15.9	5.2	1.9	5.6	1.7	7,590	40,427
District 6	24,973	379,927	3.5	6.8	2.7	12.2	12.6	10.1	2.4	7.4	2.4	19,556	51,472
District 7	14,033	387,001	9.9	6.9	8.9	7.6	13.1	6.6	1.6	4.8	1.3	19,479	50,334
District 8	11,511	152,527	3.0	6.3	1.7	23.4	23.4	3.0	2.0	3.3	1.0	5,319	34,873
District 9	23,646	475,935	5.7	5.3	4.5	10.6	13.3	9.1	2.8	10.9	3.6	24,710	51,918
ARKANSAS	65,611	1,023,854	15.0	4.5	4.6	14.4	16.7	3.6	1.2	3.7	2.5	40,969	40,015
District 1	13,855	192,289	19.1	3.8	5.3	16.9	19.8	3.1	1.1	2.0	3.3	6,526	33,941
District 2	18,848	294,396	7.0	5.3	5.3	14.5	19.6	5.2	1.5	4.8	4.2	12,285	41,728
District 3	18,788	328,502	15.9	4.2	4.8	13.1	13.2	2.8	1.2	4.5	1.4	15,048	45,809
District 4	13,748	186,615	23.7	4.8	2.5	15.6	16.9	3.2	1.1	2.3	1.0	6,504	34,853
CALIFORNIA	922,477	14,600,349	7.9	5.0	5.8	11.7	13.2	4.2	2.0	8.2	4.9	886,644	60,728
District 1	15,365	171,410	6.9	5.4	3.1	17.9	22.1	3.8	1.7	4.6	1.4	6,766	39,471
District 2	21,721	226,752	8.5	6.1	4.2	15.9	15.9	3.9	2.2	6.1	2.9	11,976	52,816
District 3	11,822	165,851	8.9	6.5	5.1	18.1	17.6	3.3	1.6	3.9	1.7	7,446	44,898
District 4	18,692	222,875	4.0	8.4	2.4	15.8	14.8	6.0	2.6	5.5	2.1	10,422	46,761
District 5	17,266	234,849	11.8	7.4	4.1	14.7	17.6	3.1	1.6	4.4	1.2	12,434	52,945
District 6	15,582	263,366	4.3	6.3	6.0	11.8	18.5	3.1	2.2	7.7	2.7	13,492	51,231
District 7	13,795	213,587	4.9	6.2	5.2	15.4	15.4	9.9	1.8	8.0	2.9	11,861	55,532
District 8	9,402	116,450	4.7	5.7	1.2	19.6	18.5	2.1	2.3	3.2	1.4	4,036	34,655
District 9	10,777	159,812	8.0	7.1	5.9	15.0	17.6	3.9	1.6	2.9	1.2	7,215	45,149
District 10	12,185	190,329	13.6	5.4	5.9	16.7	16.0	2.2	1.5	4.0	1.0	8,414	44,209
District 11	16,983	230,676	4.2	6.9	3.3	15.2	18.4	7.7	2.2	7.5	2.2	13,861	60,090
District 12	32,718	613,587	1.3	3.1	2.5	7.0	10.2	8.7	2.5	17.5	9.9	59,999	97,785
District 13	19,174	300,945	6.4	5.7	4.8	10.1	17.1	3.2	1.8	8.4	3.8	19,734	65,573
District 14	19,454	351,648	6.5	4.9	5.4	10.4	9.1	4.3	2.2	9.5	12.2	37,629	107,006
District 15	16,997	289,706	8.1	7.1	9.4	11.2	11.3	4.2	1.7	11.4	5.8	21,236	73,303
District 16	9,102	149,720	16.1	5.0	6.9	13.7	18.9	1.9	1.5	2.6	1.8	6,272	41,890
District 17	21,411	562,051	15.3	4.3	13.4	5.9	6.2	2.0	1.0	14.2	8.1	68,100	121,084
District 18	22,079	404,129	3.1	2.9	2.9	9.6	17.0	3.2	1.5	14.4	15.8	46,637	115,401
District 19	13,930	202,572	7.0	8.2	5.0	11.4	11.2	2.8	1.8	11.4	5.5	13,440	66,346
District 20	16,384	200,289	7.7	5.5	5.5	17.4	15.5	2.4	1.7	5.6	1.3	8,920	44,537
District 21	6,911	105,964	17.3	4.4	9.0	19.6	11.5	1.2	1.4	1.7	0.7	4,211	39,744
District 22	14,384	208,974	7.6	5.9	3.8	18.2	18.1	4.7	1.9	4.4	1.1	8,408	40,232
District 23	12,055	186,208	4.3	6.2	3.9	14.3	19.1	3.4	1.9	5.8	1.6	7,943	42,659
District 24	20,372	242,652	8.6	5.8	3.7	14.3	15.6	2.7	2.1	6.2	3.4	11,375	46,879
District 25	12,375	161,452	9.9	6.4	4.3	17.6	13.0	2.8	1.9	7.5	1.7	6,773	41,897
District 26	18,932	242,372	9.6	5.1	6.1	15.5	14.2	5.1	1.8	9.2	2.5	13,300	54,874
District 27	21,984	254,910	2.4	2.1	3.1	12.2	18.8	7.4	1.9	9.7	1.9	12,958	50,833
District 28	25,077	337,666	5.5	2.5	2.3	10.5	17.3	2.7	2.7	7.1	14.2	18,737	55,489
District 29	12,253	171,756	15.1	7.5	7.8	13.2	19.6	1.6	2.5	3.4	2.0	8,012	46,645
District 30	30,390	391,843	4.9	3.3	2.9	10.2	13.3	6.5	2.3	6.5	21.4	19,320	49,306
District 31	13,186	240,722	8.0	5.1	5.2	14.2	21.0	3.4	1.4	3.8	2.0	10,292	42,753
District 32	15,315	246,743	16.8	4.5	10.4	14.0	14.2	3.3	1.4	4.1	1.3	11,326	45,901
District 33	40,788	508,491	5.9	1.8	2.6	10.3	11.8	4.5	3.4	13.5	10.6	38,147	75,019
District 34	23,945	349,223	5.6	1.4	9.8	7.1	13.9	7.5	2.2	10.6	4.5	22,693	64,982
District 35	13,495	260,410	12.2	6.4	12.1	13.6	11.2	1.7	1.3	2.0	1.3	11,765	45,177
District 36	12,438	169,377	3.1	6.5	1.8	20.4	16.5	1.8	2.5	2.6	1.5	5,989	35,362
District 37	21,475	295,656	3.0	2.0	3.1	8.8	10.7	3.8	3.0	10.3	18.9	19,212	64,979
District 38	14,810	243,609	13.4	5.8	14.5	13.9	13.7	2.6	1.5	3.2	1.4	10,758	44,160
District 39	19,665	257,648	10.5	8.0	11.5	12.7	9.1	5.7	1.7	5.8	1.3	11,941	46,345
District 40	11,400	211,391	21.6	2.4	16.3	11.4	11.5	1.4	1.2	1.9	0.8	9,117	43,128
District 41	10,126	184,914	8.4	9.0	5.3	16.1	15.2	2.3	1.5	3.3	1.2	7,571	40,945
District 42	11,740	155,850	11.7	15.2	6.4	15.2	11.1	1.8	1.6	4.9	1.1	6,340	40,677
District 43	15,217	291,799	10.9	2.9	6.3	10.3	11.5	2.2	2.5	6.4	2.3	15,274	52,344
District 44	8,735	163,841	20.6	6.1	11.6	10.6	8.6	1.1	1.3	1.8	1.2	7,775	47,455
District 45	26,021	413,301	10.1	5.0	8.1	8.3	8.7	8.4	4.0	14.5	4.7	29,008	70,185
District 46	18,049	392,810	10.6	7.0	5.8	7.7	13.3	4.9	2.0	5.0	1.4	18,892	48,095
District 47	15,770	243,080	7.3	5.3	5.3	12.1	15.1	5.3	1.9	5.6	1.9	12,345	50,786
District 48	25,408	327,565	7.6	4.3	5.0	14.3	12.3	6.7	4.1	10.6	1.5	19,508	59,554
District 49	21,754	276,231	11.8	5.5	6.3	12.8	12.4	2.6	2.0	12.1	2.5	15,097	54,655
District 50	16,313	200,829	7.5	12.7	3.2	17.6	11.5	2.0	1.8	3.9	1.0	7,877	39,223
District 51	10,343	141,209	11.7	3.9	6.7	23.7	14.5	2.4	1.7	3.0	1.6	5,175	36,646
District 52	29,498	525,065	7.6	4.8	6.8	8.8	7.7	6.4	2.6	13.4	4.5	36,033	68,626
District 53	16,279	234,195	3.0	4.8	2.0	13.1	28.2	4.6	2.4	6.7	1.0	10,679	45,598

STATE District	Representative, 115th Congress	Land area,[1] 2017 (sq mi)	Total persons	Per square mile	White	Black	American Indian, Alaska Native	Asian and Pacific Islander	Some other race (percent)	Two or more races (percent)	Hispanic or Latino[2] (percent)	Non-Hispanic White alone (percent)	Percent female	Percent foreign-born	Percent born in state of residence
					Race alone (percent)										
		1	2	3	4	5	6	7	8	9	10	11	12	13	14
COLORADO		103,639.8	5,540,545	53.5	84.0	4.2	1.0	3.3	4.1	3.3	21.3	68.5	49.6	9.8	42.8
District 1.................	Diana DeGette (D)	189.9	812,843	4,279.8	77.4	8.6	0.7	3.6	6.3	3.3	27.6	57.9	49.9	13.5	42.2
District 2.................	Jared Polis (D)	7,535.4	803,470	106.6	89.9	1.0	0.5	3.3	2.4	3.0	10.5	82.7	49.0	7.4	35.3
District 3.................	Scott R. Tipton (R)	49,730.5	738,119	14.8	88.8	1.0	2.9	1.0	4.0	2.4	24.3	70.8	49.8	6.0	50.3
District 4.................	Ken Buck (R)	38,102.1	795,836	20.9	92.0	1.4	0.6	2.0	1.8	2.1	22.2	72.4	49.5	8.4	48.4
District 6.................	Mike Coffman (R)	474.0	813,566	1,716.5	71.8	9.4	0.7	6.8	7.5	3.7	19.2	61.6	50.5	14.9	42.3
District 7.................	Ed Perlmutter (D)	342.2	789,772	2,308.2	87.3	1.8	1.1	3.5	3.2	3.1	29.7	63.1	49.9	11.6	49.4
CONNECTICUT....		4,842.7	3,576,452	738.5	76.7	10.6	0.3	4.6	4.8	3.1	15.7	67.4	51.2	14.4	55.2
District 1.................	John B. Larson (D)	675.4	712,461	1,054.9	69.2	15.5	0.3	5.1	6.6	3.3	16.8	60.9	52.1	14.7	58.9
District 2.................	Joe Courtney (D)	1,988.1	705,034	354.6	86.4	4.1	0.3	3.6	2.2	3.4	8.3	81.7	49.9	7.3	57.5
District 3.................	Rosa L. DeLauro (D)	470.3	717,162	1,524.8	72.6	14.0	0.2	5.1	5.2	2.9	15.4	63.9	51.4	13.5	61.2
District 4.................	James A. Himes (D)	460.8	732,469	1,589.4	73.3	12.6	0.3	5.3	5.1	3.4	19.8	61.0	51.4	22.4	42.7
District 5.................	Elizabeth H. Esty (D)	1,248.1	709,326	568.3	82.1	6.6	0.2	3.7	4.8	2.6	18.2	70.0	51.2	13.6	56.1
DELAWARE.........		1,948.8	952,065	488.5	69.2	22.0	0.4	4.0	1.6	2.7	9.2	62.7	51.7	9.4	45.0
At Large.................	Lisa Blunt Rochester (D)	1,948.8	952,065	488.6	69.2	22.0	0.4	4.0	1.6	2.7	9.2	62.7	51.7	9.4	45.0
DISTRICT OF COLUMBIA........		61.1	681,170	11,148.4	40.7	47.1	0.3	3.9	5.5	2.6	10.9	36.3	52.5	13.3	37.2
Delegate District (At Large)............	Eleanor Holmes Norton (D)	61.1	681,170	11,141.2	40.7	47.1	0.3	3.9	5.5	2.6	10.9	36.3	52.5	13.3	37.2
FLORIDA		53,634.0	20,612,439	384.3	75.6	16.1	0.3	2.8	2.8	2.6	24.9	54.7	51.1	20.6	35.8
District 1.................	Matt Gaetz (R)	4,017.4	762,506	189.8	76.8	13.8	0.5	2.7	2.0	4.2	6.4	73.3	49.6	5.4	39.7
District 2.................	Neal P. Dunn (R)	11,003.7	720,418	65.5	81.7	12.7	0.3	2.2	0.7	2.3	6.4	76.3	48.7	5.8	51.1
District 3.................	Ted S. Yoho (R)	3,564.9	732,088	205.4	76.3	15.5	0.2	3.6	1.2	3.2	9.6	68.6	50.3	7.8	50.2
District 4.................	John H. Rutherford (R)	1,569.8	778,620	496.0	82.0	8.8	0.2	4.7	1.2	3.1	8.2	75.6	51.0	9.4	40.6
District 5.................	Al Lawson (D)	3,817.6	728,346	190.8	45.0	47.7	0.3	2.1	1.7	3.2	8.0	39.6	51.6	7.1	59.6
District 6.................	Ron DeSantis (R)	2,171.4	765,005	352.3	84.1	10.3	0.3	1.7	1.4	2.2	12.6	73.7	51.4	7.9	34.5
District 7.................	Stephanie N. Murphy (D)	392.9	762,326	1,940.1	77.9	10.7	0.2	4.3	3.5	3.4	25.3	58.1	51.1	13.3	37.7
District 8.................	Bill Posey (R)	1,751.5	744,430	425.0	83.2	9.3	0.2	2.3	2.0	3.0	10.4	75.1	51.4	9.6	32.5
District 9.................	Darren Soto (D)	2,311.9	832,753	360.2	74.6	14.1	0.2	3.5	4.2	3.5	39.0	42.8	51.4	16.4	29.8
District 10...............	Val Butler Demings (D)	436.5	791,447	1,813.1	57.1	28.2	0.1	5.3	5.8	3.5	27.0	37.4	51.1	15.2	34.5
District 11...............	Daniel Webster (R)	2,390.1	758,331	317.3	86.9	8.4	0.2	1.1	0.9	2.4	9.8	78.8	51.8	25.9	30.0
District 12...............	Gus M. Bilirakis (R)	859.4	760,472	884.9	88.6	4.9	0.3	2.9	1.0	2.4	9.8	78.1	51.6	6.6	32.4
District 13...............	Charlie Crist (D)	181.8	728,996	4,009.7	79.0	12.3	0.3	3.7	1.9	2.8	12.2	71.6	52.0	9.6	34.7
District 14...............	Kathy Castor (D)	275.9	769,968	2,790.8	68.9	19.6	0.4	4.7	2.8	3.6	29.0	44.9	51.8	11.6	38.7
District 15...............	Dennis A. Ross (R)	1,087.4	762,822	701.5	76.1	13.9	0.3	3.3	3.9	2.6	23.0	58.3	50.4	20.3	42.2
District 16...............	Vern Buchanan (R)	1,293.4	803,454	621.2	83.7	7.7	0.3	1.9	4.1	2.1	17.7	70.8	51.7	11.4	31.9
District 17...............	Thomas J. Rooney (R)	5,573.0	768,138	137.8	86.8	7.5	0.2	1.2	2.5	1.8	15.4	74.5	50.5	13.5	32.4
District 18...............	Brian J. Mast (R)	1,511.3	754,652	499.3	81.3	12.4	0.3	2.2	1.9	1.8	16.1	67.7	51.1	11.3	32.5
District 19...............	Francis Rooney (R)	750.0	799,332	1,065.8	86.0	8.0	0.1	1.6	2.8	1.5	19.4	69.9	51.4	15.2	24.2
District 20...............	Alcee L. Hastings (D)	2,159.4	794,621	368.0	39.5	53.0	0.4	2.9	1.5	2.8	24.1	18.5	51.2	16.9	42.2
District 21...............	Lois Frankel (D)	256.1	758,201	2,960.3	76.4	16.2	0.1	2.4	2.4	2.1	23.4	56.6	52.2	35.1	27.6
District 22...............	Theodore E. Deutch (D)	164.9	737,019	4,469.7	75.1	15.8	0.3	3.3	2.7	2.8	20.4	58.3	50.7	26.9	27.8
District 23...............	Debbie Wasserman Schultz (D)	187.8	749,377	3,989.9	74.2	13.4	0.3	4.6	4.2	3.2	37.1	43.3	52.1	27.0	32.8
District 24...............	Frederica S. Wilson (D)	102.4	749,624	7,319.9	42.3	48.7	0.3	1.3	5.9	1.5	39.3	11.2	51.3	35.8	42.1
District 25...............	Mario Diaz-Balart (R)	3,505.5	763,628	217.8	89.6	4.6	0.2	1.1	3.5	1.0	76.1	18.9	51.2	42.5	25.0
District 26...............	Carlos Curbelo (R)	2,184.5	788,816	361.1	81.3	11.2	0.1	1.7	4.0	1.7	69.9	17.1	51.5	58.2	35.8
District 27...............	Ileana Ros-Lehtinen (R)	113.2	747,049	6,597.0	85.5	5.2	0.2	2.4	4.7	2.0	71.5	21.1	50.4	47.8	27.6
GEORGIA		57,597.8	10,310,371	179.0	58.7	31.6	0.4	3.9	2.9	2.5	9.3	53.2	51.3	55.0	54.6
District 1.................	Earl L. "Buddy" Carter (R)	8,062.0	734,172	91.1	63.0	29.7	0.3	1.5	1.8	3.7	6.6	59.1	50.8	10.1	56.0
District 2.................	Sanford D. Bishop Jr. (D)	9,626.3	672,244	69.8	42.2	51.9	0.3	1.4	1.7	2.5	4.9	40.1	51.3	4.7	71.7
District 3.................	A. Drew Ferguson IV (R)	3,836.2	729,810	190.2	68.9	24.7	0.1	1.9	1.6	2.9	5.7	65.0	51.9	3.6	62.7
District 4.................	Henry C. "Hank" Johnson Jr. (D)	497.0	752,273	1,513.6	30.1	59.3	0.3	4.5	4.0	1.9	10.2	24.5	53.1	5.3	46.6
District 5.................	John Lewis (D)	264.9	747,809	2,822.8	31.9	57.7	0.5	4.6	2.3	2.9	6.4	28.7	51.3	16.0	52.9
District 6.................	Karen Handel (R)	298.9	756,004	2,529.1	67.7	14.9	1.2	11.3	1.6	3.3	12.3	58.9	50.9	9.1	32.8
District 7.................	Robert Woodall (R)	392.6	789,864	2,011.7	53.8	21.1	0.2	14.3	8.1	2.5	18.6	44.1	50.8	21.8	34.9
District 8.................	Austin Scott (R)	8,716.9	710,108	81.5	63.5	30.9	0.3	1.3	1.9	2.2	6.1	59.7	51.1	25.2	69.0
District 9.................	Doug Collins (R)	5,211.6	736,075	141.2	87.2	7.2	0.2	1.2	2.2	2.1	12.4	77.4	50.5	4.1	60.8
District 10...............	Jody B. Hice (R)	7,096.9	741,464	104.5	68.7	24.9	0.1	2.3	1.8	2.3	5.9	65.2	51.2	7.6	65.5
District 11...............	Barry Loudermilk (R)	1,070.7	764,184	713.7	72.8	16.5	0.6	3.5	4.0	2.6	12.1	66.0	50.8	6.1	43.7
District 12...............	Rick W. Allen (R)	8,186.2	719,970	87.9	58.2	35.6	0.3	1.9	2.3	1.7	6.2	54.9	50.6	12.3	65.4
District 13...............	David Scott (D)	714.2	746,218	1,044.8	30.5	59.6	0.1	2.9	4.2	2.7	10.3	26.0	53.5	4.6	49.9
District 14...............	Tom Graves (R)	3,623.2	710,176	196.0	84.4	9.5	0.6	1.1	2.5	1.8	11.6	76.6	50.7	10.6	58.4
HAWAII		6,422.5	1,428,557	222.4	25.1	1.8	0.2	48.2	0.9	23.9	10.4	22.1	49.7	7.2	53.3
District 1.................	Colleen Hanbusa (D)	209.0	706,501	3,379.6	17.5	2.1	0.1	57.9	0.8	21.7	8.5	15.4	50.0	18.4	53.5
District 2.................	Tulsi Gabbard (D)	6,213.4	722,056	116.2	32.5	1.5	0.3	38.6	0.9	26.1	12.2	28.6	49.4	22.3	53.1
IDAHO..................		82,644.5	1,683,140	20.4	89.7	0.7	1.6	1.6	3.9	2.5	12.3	82.3	50.0	14.5	48.3
District 1.................	Raul Labrador (R)	39,419.8	864,758	21.9	89.6	0.4	1.7	1.3	4.5	2.4	10.7	84.4	49.4	5.8	44.1
District 2.................	Michael K. Simpson (R)	43,224.6	818,382	18.9	89.8	0.9	1.5	1.9	3.3	2.6	14.0	80.2	50.6	4.1	52.7
ILLINOIS		55,515.4	12,801,539	230.6	71.3	14.2	0.2	5.4	6.4	2.5	17.0	61.6	50.9	7.6	67.1
District 1.................	Bobby L. Rush (D)	258.4	691,474	2,676.1	42.3	50.0	0.1	1.8	3.8	1.9	10.4	36.2	53.4	13.9	75.7
District 2.................	Robin L. Kelly (D)	1,080.7	713,917	660.6	37.1	57.0	0.1	0.8	3.3	1.8	14.0	26.9	53.2	7.5	75.7

1. Dry land or land partially or temporarily covered by water. 2. May be of any race.

STATE District	Population and population characteristics, 2016 (cont.)										Education, 2016		
	Age (percent)											Attainment[2] (percent)	
	Under 5 years	5 to 17 years	18 to 24 years	25 to 34 years	35 to 44 years	45 to 54 years	55 to 64 years	65 to 74 years	75 years and over	Median age	Total Enrollment[1]	High school graduate or more	Bachelor's degree or more
	15	16	17	18	19	20	21	22	23	24	25	26	27
COLORADO	6.0	16.7	9.6	15.2	13.5	13.0	12.6	8.3	5.0	36.7	1,382,107	91.4	39.9
District 1	6.3	14.2	8.4	21.3	15.2	11.9	11.0	7.2	4.6	35.0	183,403	88.4	47.6
District 2	4.9	14.5	13.0	14.1	12.8	13.0	13.7	9.0	5.0	37.7	214,600	96.5	54.3
District 3	5.6	16.3	9.4	12.1	12.0	12.8	14.4	10.7	6.7	40.2	168,435	89.6	29.2
District 4	6.3	19.1	9.0	12.5	13.5	13.6	12.7	8.1	5.1	37.1	209,878	91.1	34.9
District 5	6.5	19.0	8.0	14.2	14.8	14.0	11.7	7.2	4.4	36.6	211,194	92.6	41.8
District 6	6.2	16.8	9.1	16.3	13.3	13.1	12.4	7.7	5.1	35.9	191,073	87.9	32.5
District 7													
CONNECTICUT	5.2	15.9	10.0	12.2	11.8	14.7	14.1	9.0	7.1	40.9	914,755	90.5	38.6
District 1	5.3	16.5	9.2	13.1	12.3	14.0	13.4	8.7	7.4	40.2	181,154	89.4	36.8
District 2	4.7	14.5	12.0	11.5	10.9	15.0	14.7	9.9	6.9	41.9	177,660	92.9	35.1
District 3	4.7	15.0	11.1	13.9	11.5	14.2	13.8	9.0	7.0	39.5	186,184	91.2	36.2
District 4	5.8	17.7	9.2	11.6	12.8	14.9	13.7	7.9	6.5	39.8	202,178	89.5	48.8
District 5	5.4	15.4	8.5	11.0	11.9	15.2	15.1	9.8	7.7	43.2	167,579	89.6	36.3
DELAWARE	5.8	15.7	9.0	13.5	11.5	13.2	13.8	10.6	7.0	40.6	227,224	89.3	31.0
At Large	5.8	15.7	9.0	13.5	11.5	13.2	13.8	10.6	7.0	40.6	227,224	89.3	31.0
DISTRICT OF COLUMBIA	6.4	11.3	11.8	22.7	14.5	11.4	10.3	6.8	4.8	33.9	168,430	90.5	56.8
Delegate District (At Large)	6.4	11.3	11.8	22.7	14.5	11.4	10.3	6.8	4.8	33.9	168,430	90.5	56.8
FLORIDA	5.4	14.7	8.6	12.9	11.9	13.3	13.3	11.1	8.7	42.1	4,718,808	87.4	28.6
District 1	6.1	15.3	10.1	14.0	11.6	13.0	13.5	9.7	6.5	38.7	183,460	90.3	27.9
District 2	4.9	14.8	9.3	12.2	11.2	13.9	14.6	11.5	7.7	43.2	159,021	86.2	23.4
District 3	5.5	15.2	13.1	13.3	11.7	12.5	12.6	9.4	6.8	37.8	200,548	88.2	25.9
District 4	5.7	15.1	8.1	14.8	12.8	13.7	13.7	10.0	6.0	39.8	181,982	93.5	39.2
District 5	6.8	16.6	13.6	15.7	12.3	11.6	11.2	7.4	5.0	33.0	214,527	84.2	21.4
District 6	4.6	13.4	8.0	10.6	10.2	12.9	15.1	14.0	11.1	47.5	160,188	89.6	23.9
District 7	5.4	14.6	12.1	15.6	13.0	13.4	12.1	7.8	5.9	36.5	209,938	91.8	37.8
District 8	4.5	13.6	7.7	10.6	9.6	13.5	15.6	13.4	11.4	48.1	157,027	90.7	29.0
District 9	6.2	18.2	8.7	13.9	13.6	12.7	11.3	9.4	5.9	37.4	208,900	85.9	24.6
District 10	6.5	16.7	8.7	17.3	13.8	14.0	11.6	7.1	4.2	35.5	205,907	85.9	30.3
District 11	3.9	11.5	5.6	8.7	8.3	10.8	14.6	20.6	15.9	55.6	117,838	88.3	20.6
District 12	4.9	14.1	6.7	10.2	11.4	13.8	14.2	13.3	11.2	46.6	151,361	90.0	26.9
District 13	4.7	12.4	6.9	12.7	11.1	14.2	15.6	12.3	9.9	46.5	142,245	89.8	27.8
District 14	6.3	15.6	10.6	15.8	13.3	13.9	11.7	7.7	5.2	36.2	199,357	88.4	35.3
District 15	6.0	16.8	8.3	14.1	13.1	13.0	12.5	9.2	6.9	38.4	183,658	87.6	25.8
District 16	5.1	14.1	7.0	10.4	10.8	12.9	13.9	14.0	11.9	47.0	162,487	89.7	30.7
District 17	4.2	13.1	6.5	9.4	9.4	12.2	14.6	16.9	13.8	51.3	140,383	87.2	21.3
District 18	4.9	14.0	7.3	10.0	10.9	13.2	14.3	13.2	12.0	47.1	154,454	89.6	30.5
District 19	4.4	13.2	6.6	10.2	10.2	11.2	14.4	16.1	13.7	50.2	149,967	88.2	32.3
District 20	6.8	17.1	9.4	14.6	13.9	13.3	11.7	7.4	5.7	36.4	206,196	80.4	19.7
District 21	5.1	14.1	7.2	11.7	11.4	13.0	12.4	12.0	13.2	45.4	161,934	86.7	34.3
District 22	5.1	13.5	6.9	12.4	11.7	15.0	14.6	10.9	9.9	45.2	161,720	90.8	37.9
District 23	5.2	15.0	8.0	13.3	13.1	15.1	13.1	9.6	7.8	41.6	187,699	92.2	38.6
District 24	6.3	15.3	9.6	15.7	13.1	13.6	12.6	7.9	5.8	37.1	184,991	77.9	19.4
District 25	5.4	14.3	7.9	12.3	13.6	15.2	12.0	10.3	8.8	42.5	163,586	77.1	22.7
District 26	6.5	15.6	9.4	13.8	13.7	14.7	11.7	8.3	6.2	38.4	205,889	83.6	27.2
District 27	5.0	12.7	7.9	15.1	13.7	14.8	12.4	9.2	9.0	41.9	163,545	84.2	37.5
GEORGIA	6.4	18.0	9.8	13.6	13.4	13.6	12.0	8.3	4.9	36.5	2,747,236	86.4	30.5
District 1	6.9	16.9	10.5	14.7	12.3	12.5	11.8	8.9	5.4	35.8	192,543	87.4	25.0
District 2	6.4	17.9	10.3	13.8	12.2	11.7	13.0	8.8	5.9	36.1	181,966	82.1	17.6
District 3	5.9	17.9	9.5	12.3	13.2	14.1	12.5	9.1	5.5	38.3	189,750	86.0	26.5
District 4	7.3	18.7	8.7	14.9	13.3	14.1	12.3	7.1	3.7	35.3	209,236	86.9	29.8
District 5	6.3	14.2	12.2	19.2	13.9	12.8	10.0	7.1	4.2	33.8	198,972	88.8	42.0
District 6	6.2	17.8	7.4	13.3	14.7	15.9	12.8	7.7	4.2	38.4	194,160	93.2	60.6
District 7	6.3	21.0	8.8	11.8	16.0	15.3	11.0	6.1	3.7	36.5	229,444	88.1	39.6
District 8	6.2	17.9	10.1	13.3	13.0	12.2	12.6	8.9	5.9	36.7	186,871	84.6	21.8
District 9	5.7	17.3	9.5	11.1	11.9	13.8	13.0	11.2	6.7	40.8	175,867	80.8	21.6
District 10	5.9	17.7	13.3	11.5	12.5	13.3	11.7	9.0	5.0	36.3	210,064	86.9	26.7
District 11	6.2	18.2	9.3	14.3	14.1	14.8	11.5	7.3	4.4	36.3	201,942	89.6	41.0
District 12	6.4	17.2	11.0	14.4	12.6	12.3	12.3	8.3	5.5	35.7	189,405	84.2	20.9
District 13	7.3	20.1	8.7	13.6	14.4	13.6	11.5	6.9	4.1	35.2	206,719	89.5	29.6
District 14	6.0	18.8	8.9	12.2	13.5	13.8	11.8	9.3	5.6	38.1	180,297	80.3	18.1
HAWAII	6.4	15.2	9.1	14.4	12.5	12.4	12.9	9.7	7.4	38.9	331,540	92.0	31.9
District 1	6.2	14.4	8.7	15.3	13.1	12.6	12.1	9.3	8.5	39.2	170,189	91.4	36.0
District 2	6.5	16.0	9.5	13.6	12.1	12.2	13.7	10.1	6.2	38.5	161,351	92.6	27.8
IDAHO	6.8	19.1	9.5	13.1	12.2	11.8	12.3	9.2	6.0	36.1	454,191	90.4	27.6
District 1	6.3	18.5	9.1	11.9	12.2	12.4	13.0	10.2	6.4	38.0	222,377	90.2	25.4
District 2	7.3	19.8	9.8	14.4	12.4	11.0	11.4	8.3	5.6	34.0	231,814	90.7	30.1
ILLINOIS	6.0	16.8	9.5	13.8	12.9	13.4	12.9	8.4	6.2	37.9	3,286,606	88.8	34.0
District 1	5.4	16.3	9.9	13.4	11.6	13.9	13.9	8.8	6.8	39.4	184,500	88.8	28.9
District 2	6.3	18.0	10.7	11.6	12.2	13.3	12.9	8.7	6.2	38.0	192,309	86.9	23.3

1. All persons 3 years old and over enrolled in nursery school through college and graduate or professional school. 2. Persons 25 years old and over.

Table E. Congressional Districts 115th Congress — **Nonfarm Employment and Payroll**

STATE District		Private nonfarm employment and payroll, 2016												
		Employment											Annual payroll	
			Percent by selected industries											
	Number of establishments	Total	Manufac-turing	Construc-tion	Wholesale trade	Retail trade	Health care and social assistance	Finance and Insurance	Real estate and rental and leasing	Professio-nal, scientific, and technical services	Information	Total (mil dol)	Average per employee (dollars)
	73	74	75	76	77	78	79	80	81	82	83	84	85
COLORADO	165,264	2,318,190	5.2	6.6	4.4	12.1	13.3	4.6	2.0	8.4	3.7	120,399	51,937
District 1............................	29,618	496,227	4.1	4.9	5.1	8.5	13.2	5.3	2.4	9.5	3.2	28,878	58,195
District 2............................	30,011	356,951	7.2	5.3	5.1	13.2	12.3	3.0	2.1	11.2	3.6	18,241	51,103
District 3............................	25,551	252,456	4.5	9.2	2.9	15.8	17.3	2.8	2.8	4.3	1.7	9,777	38,729
District 4............................	19,686	241,416	11.4	9.1	3.8	15.1	13.1	4.6	1.3	6.1	4.2	12,339	51,110
District 6............................	20,336	326,513	2.5	5.7	5.9	12.2	14.5	8.2	1.8	7.9	8.1	19,112	58,533
District 7............................	19,500	269,887	6.2	11.1	5.3	14.7	13.0	3.7	1.7	8.2	2.3	12,821	47,504
CONNECTICUT...............	89,416	1,533,879	10.1	3.8	4.8	12.2	18.6	8.2	1.3	6.9	2.5	94,659	61,712
District 1............................	18,540	377,872	11.7	4.2	4.7	10.7	18.0	11.9	1.1	6.6	3.0	22,700	60,073
District 2............................	14,386	215,723	12.9	3.8	4.0	16.4	17.8	3.2	0.9	5.6	1.7	9,872	45,760
District 3............................	16,503	308,835	12.2	4.0	4.9	11.1	20.9	3.2	1.4	4.6	1.8	16,067	52,023
District 4............................	21,896	336,223	4.3	2.7	6.0	10.9	15.7	12.9	1.5	9.9	3.6	30,204	89,834
District 5............................	17,551	267,494	11.7	4.7	3.7	15.1	22.8	5.1	1.7	5.4	1.8	14,078	52,628
DELAWARE....................	25,366	400,069	6.8	5.0	4.2	14.0	16.9	10.6	1.6	7.4	1.7	21,196	52,982
At Large............................	25,366	400,069	6.8	5.0	4.2	14.0	16.9	10.6	1.6	7.4	1.7	21,196	52,982
DISTRICT OF COLUMBIA	23,177	526,879	0.2	1.9	0.9	4.2	13.0	3.4	2.3	19.5	4.3	39,834	75,603
Delegate District (At Large).......................	23,177	526,879	0.2	1.9	0.9	4.2	13.0	3.4	2.3	19.5	4.3	39,834	75,603
FLORIDA	546,218	8,169,642	3.8	4.9	3.9	13.3	13.3	4.4	2.0	6.1	2.1	363,336	44,474
District 1............................	16,955	208,689	3.1	6.5	2.8	18.2	17.2	5.4	2.3	7.7	1.3	8,022	38,442
District 2............................	14,940	173,017	6.6	5.3	3.2	17.7	18.2	3.4	1.8	8.6	2.0	6,191	35,784
District 3............................	16,478	216,562	6.0	5.3	3.1	17.9	24.3	3.4	1.9	5.3	2.0	8,033	37,093
District 4............................	23,983	355,941	4.3	5.2	4.7	12.8	14.6	10.1	1.9	6.8	1.8	16,503	46,364
District 5............................	14,651	231,147	5.7	7.1	4.5	16.2	14.7	5.7	1.7	5.4	3.0	9,979	43,174
District 6............................	16,927	181,257	6.0	6.4	2.7	19.1	18.9	3.3	2.0	4.3	2.1	6,178	34,083
District 7............................	24,259	341,794	2.6	6.3	2.6	13.6	15.3	7.4	2.1	9.9	4.0	16,650	48,712
District 8............................	18,379	219,142	9.1	5.9	2.4	17.6	17.6	2.8	1.8	7.1	1.8	9,227	42,104
District 9............................	13,478	193,190	5.4	5.9	2.7	17.5	13.9	3.6	3.7	2.9	1.7	7,103	36,769
District 10..........................	22,907	479,029	4.1	4.3	4.7	12.8	7.1	2.0	3.5	5.8	1.8	19,619	40,955
District 11..........................	12,340	140,927	4.0	7.3	2.0	20.6	25.8	2.4	2.0	3.5	1.9	4,728	33,552
District 12..........................	16,550	168,479	4.3	6.8	2.5	20.8	20.5	4.5	1.9	7.3	1.3	6,087	36,131
District 13..........................	21,271	301,078	8.3	4.4	4.4	13.0	19.6	6.5	2.2	7.2	3.2	13,730	45,601
District 14..........................	24,612	424,550	2.9	4.6	4.8	10.2	14.8	8.6	2.0	11.8	3.5	22,164	52,206
District 15..........................	16,463	256,097	6.5	7.6	6.6	15.6	13.2	6.8	2.0	5.7	2.2	10,639	41,542
District 16..........................	21,196	229,239	5.8	6.9	3.7	17.6	18.6	3.2	2.6	6.3	1.5	9,283	40,493
District 17..........................	13,760	137,652	6.5	8.2	2.5	21.8	20.7	3.0	1.9	3.6	1.1	4,846	35,208
District 18..........................	21,571	223,989	3.4	6.2	2.9	18.0	16.9	3.3	2.3	7.2	1.7	9,675	43,194
District 19..........................	25,537	300,371	2.5	9.6	3.0	18.7	16.7	2.9	2.7	5.5	1.8	12,246	40,769
District 20..........................	17,351	255,643	5.6	6.7	8.7	14.0	13.8	3.4	1.8	6.7	5.3	12,014	46,997
District 21..........................	21,658	201,112	1.9	5.7	2.6	17.7	20.0	3.4	2.3	6.5	1.6	8,272	41,133
District 22..........................	33,420	351,980	3.0	5.4	5.4	13.9	12.3	6.5	2.7	10.2	2.5	17,617	50,050
District 23..........................	26,148	295,718	1.9	3.6	4.2	20.6	13.2	4.4	3.9	6.6	2.6	13,511	45,690
District 24..........................	16,401	213,698	5.8	3.5	7.8	13.5	22.7	2.9	1.8	4.4	2.2	9,344	43,727
District 25..........................	26,169	333,224	6.0	5.8	12.6	12.9	8.9	3.9	2.5	4.2	3.4	15,038	45,129
District 26..........................	15,223	131,696	2.5	6.3	5.8	21.0	13.9	4.3	2.6	4.5	1.3	4,538	34,461
District 27..........................	32,348	354,819	0.8	2.6	2.4	13.8	15.1	7.6	2.6	12.1	1.7	19,425	54,745
GEORGIA	228,330	3,804,433	9.7	4.5	5.6	12.8	13.1	4.7	1.6	6.9	3.2	182,911	48,078
District 1............................	15,774	230,310	11.4	4.3	3.6	15.8	14.9	2.3	1.5	3.8	1.2	8,922	38,738
District 2............................	12,942	202,809	13.4	3.7	4.8	13.8	18.5	9.6	1.3	4.2	1.3	8,093	39,903
District 3............................	15,035	226,611	16.4	5.0	4.0	17.3	15.2	3.6	1.1	2.9	1.7	8,445	37,265
District 4............................	11,245	150,249	11.1	8.0	5.2	17.5	15.0	2.1	1.7	4.4	2.0	5,811	38,673
District 5............................	22,133	529,484	3.5	2.7	4.3	6.8	12.4	4.2	2.2	9.1	4.9	32,892	62,121
District 6............................	28,524	478,508	1.7	2.8	6.1	9.4	11.0	9.3	2.1	14.3	8.5	32,963	68,887
District 7............................	24,763	359,243	8.1	7.2	11.3	13.7	9.1	4.4	1.4	8.6	3.9	18,218	50,711
District 8............................	13,248	185,537	12.9	3.9	3.6	17.3	17.8	3.7	1.2	4.1	1.1	6,283	33,862
District 9............................	14,712	201,396	24.2	4.8	4.7	15.8	13.7	2.6	0.9	2.6	1.1	7,617	37,819
District 10..........................	13,100	159,169	12.3	5.4	3.7	17.7	16.1	2.7	1.7	3.3	1.3	5,488	34,480
District 11..........................	21,091	362,353	7.1	6.6	7.9	11.8	9.5	5.8	2.6	9.0	3.5	20,588	56,816
District 12..........................	13,169	210,926	12.5	4.4	3.6	15.8	21.2	2.7	1.2	5.4	1.6	8,130	38,542
District 13..........................	11,107	171,442	6.3	6.6	7.5	18.1	16.5	2.3	2.9	2.5	1.3	6,936	40,455
District 14..........................	10,652	175,666	28.5	3.9	5.0	14.7	12.9	1.9	0.8	2.2	1.1	6,472	36,844
HAWAII	32,350	528,415	2.5	6.3	3.7	13.4	13.4	3.6	2.3	4.3	1.6	22,892	43,323
District 1............................	18,230	320,441	3.0	7.1	4.6	12.7	14.1	4.9	2.1	5.1	1.9	14,997	46,800
District 2............................	13,913	185,382	1.9	5.7	2.4	16.2	14.0	1.6	2.8	3.2	1.0	6,974	37,620
IDAHO..........................	45,826	562,282	10.7	6.8	5.6	15.0	16.2	4.0	1.3	5.8	2.3	22,243	39,559
District 1............................	21,696	242,730	11.8	9.1	4.9	16.1	15.1	4.1	1.4	4.4	2.5	9,003	37,089
District 2............................	23,825	309,751	10.2	5.2	6.1	14.5	17.6	3.9	1.3	7.1	2.2	12,870	41,550
ILLINOIS	319,605	5,513,071	9.7	3.8	5.8	11.5	14.6	6.3	1.4	7.1	2.2	295,308	53,565
District 1............................	11,931	191,669	6.0	4.8	3.7	16.6	20.4	2.5	1.4	2.5	1.1	7,874	41,084
District 2............................	10,151	165,045	18.3	4.3	5.2	13.9	20.1	2.1	1.3	2.4	1.8	6,889	41,740

Table E. Congressional Districts 115th Congress — Land Area and Population Characteristics

STATE District	Representative, 115th Congress	Land area,[1] 2017 (sq mi)	Total persons	Per square mile	White	Black	American Indian, Alaska Native	Asian and Pacific Islander	Some other race (percent)	Two or more races (percent)	Hispanic or Latino[2] (percent)	Non-Hispanic White alone (percent)	Percent female	Percent foreign-born	Percent born in state of residence
		1	2	3	4	5	6	7	8	9	10	11	12	13	14
ILLINOIS— Cont'd															
District 3	Daniel Lipinski (D)	237.0	720,930	3,042.2	73.5	5.3	0.3	4.2	14.5	2.2	33.1	56.7	49.8	21.0	70.8
District 4	Luis V. Gutierrez (D)	52.4	695,098	13,260.2	55.4	3.8	0.6	3.7	33.9	2.6	70.1	21.5	49.3	33.5	53.4
District 5	Michael Quigley (D)	95.6	723,373	7,564.1	82.1	2.5	0.2	7.0	4.7	3.5	19.3	69.1	50.7	22.0	55.2
District 6	Peter J. Roskam (R)	378.9	722,323	1,906.5	83.0	2.6	0.1	9.1	2.3	2.9	9.3	77.1	51.1	14.7	65.7
District 7	Danny K. Davis (D)	62.3	723,481	11,606.0	35.5	47.2	0.2	7.5	7.4	2.2	16.6	27.3	52.5	13.8	62.6
District 8	Raja Krishnamoorthi (D)	205.6	717,789	3,490.9	64.9	4.6	0.4	12.9	14.3	2.9	29.4	51.5	49.6	28.2	59.0
District 9	Janice D. Schakowsky (D)	105.4	724,071	6,870.9	71.1	10.0	0.3	13.0	2.5	3.1	10.8	63.3	51.6	25.3	54.6
District 10	Bradley Scott Schneider (D)	300.1	710,610	2,367.8	71.2	6.8	0.2	11.3	7.9	2.6	22.5	57.2	50.5	24.5	56.5
District 11	Bill Foster (D)	280.6	730,480	2,603.7	65.5	10.6	0.4	8.6	11.6	3.3	27.0	51.6	51.0	18.4	65.5
District 12	Mike Bost (R)	5,008.3	693,736	138.5	78.0	17.0	0.2	1.5	0.9	2.5	3.4	75.9	50.5	2.8	68.2
District 13	Rodney Davis (R)	5,793.4	704,699	121.6	81.4	11.1	0.2	3.9	0.5	3.0	3.4	78.8	50.5	5.0	73.8
District 14	Randy Hultgren (R)	1,597.5	736,397	461.0	86.4	3.5	0.2	4.6	3.2	2.2	12.6	77.6	50.0	10.1	70.1
District 15	John Shimkus (R)	14,695.9	700,549	47.7	92.6	4.5	0.2	0.7	0.5	1.4	2.7	90.7	50.4	1.7	76.5
District 16	Adam Kinzinger (R)	7,917.3	687,998	86.9	90.6	3.4	0.1	1.4	2.2	2.2	9.3	83.9	50.1	4.9	76.5
District 17	Cheri Bustos (D)	6,930.2	691,212	99.7	81.8	11.7	0.3	1.5	1.6	3.1	9.4	75.4	50.7	4.5	72.3
District 18	Darin LaHood (R)	10,515.7	713,402	67.8	90.7	4.1	0.2	2.6	0.6	1.8	2.8	88.7	50.7	4.0	77.8
INDIANA		35,825.6	6,633,053	185.1	83.5	9.3	0.3	2.2	2.4	2.4	6.8	79.5	50.7	5.3	68.2
District 1	Peter J. Visclosky (D)	1,156.8	711,958	615.4	69.6	18.7	0.3	1.2	7.2	3.0	15.6	62.5	50.9	5.7	59.5
District 2	Jackie Walorski (R)	3,958.7	724,060	182.9	86.6	7.0	0.6	1.4	2.4	2.0	9.4	79.9	50.8	5.9	68.9
District 3	Jim Banks (R)	4,180.2	740,262	177.1	87.7	6.3	0.2	2.2	0.9	2.7	6.0	82.8	50.7	4.5	69.8
District 4	Todd Rokita (R)	6,351.6	749,049	117.9	88.6	4.5	0.2	2.9	2.2	1.6	6.1	85.3	49.8	5.8	70.0
District 5	Susan W. Brooks (R)	1,924.8	768,412	399.2	84.8	7.4	0.2	3.2	1.4	3.0	5.0	81.6	51.7	6.2	65.0
District 6	Luke Messer (R)	6,206.9	720,656	116.1	92.9	2.7	0.2	1.5	1.3	1.4	2.5	91.6	50.4	2.8	71.7
District 7	André Carson (D)	303.9	751,554	2,473.0	58.2	30.6	0.4	3.1	4.3	3.4	10.6	52.5	51.6	9.7	68.3
District 8	Larry Bucshon (R)	7,255.8	717,028	98.8	91.6	3.9	0.2	1.2	0.7	2.3	2.3	90.2	50.0	2.5	75.0
District 9	Trey Hollingsworth (R)	4,486.8	750,074	167.2	91.5	2.6	0.2	2.6	1.1	2.1	3.4	89.3	50.8	4.0	65.7
IOWA		55,855.1	3,134,693	56.1	90.4	3.6	0.3	2.5	1.3	1.8	5.7	86.4	50.3	5.1	70.5
District 1	Rod Blum (R)	12,048.7	771,008	64.0	91.4	3.8	0.4	1.8	0.9	1.5	3.8	88.7	50.3	3.9	75.4
District 2	David Loebsack (D)	12,261.9	778,964	63.5	89.7	4.5	0.2	2.3	1.5	1.8	5.4	85.9	50.4	4.8	67.8
District 3	David Young (R)	8,788.4	824,082	93.8	88.2	4.3	0.3	3.5	1.4	2.3	6.7	83.5	50.6	6.5	67.9
District 4	Steve King (R)	22,756.1	760,639	33.4	92.5	1.6	0.4	2.3	1.6	1.6	6.9	87.7	50.1	5.1	71.1
KANSAS		81,758.4	2,907,289	35.6	84.6	5.7	0.7	2.8	2.5	3.6	11.6	76.2	50.2	7.1	59.1
District 1	Roger W. Marshall (R)	52,541.8	708,078	13.5	89.1	3.0	0.5	1.9	2.4	3.1	15.8	76.7	49.4	8.0	63.3
District 2	Lynn Jenkins (R)	14,143.4	716,597	50.7	86.3	4.9	1.3	1.7	2.3	3.5	6.4	82.6	50.0	3.1	63.8
District 3	Kevin Yoder (R)	757.3	759,978	1,003.5	80.7	8.3	0.4	4.5	2.8	3.4	11.9	72.1	50.9	10.5	44.3
District 4	Ron Estes (R)	14,315.3	722,636	50.5	82.5	6.5	0.9	3.2	2.7	4.2	12.3	73.7	50.4	6.5	66.1
KENTUCKY		39,485.2	4,436,974	112.4	87.1	8.3	0.3	1.4	0.8	2.1	3.4	84.9	50.9	3.5	68.9
District 1	James Comer (R)	12,082.3	717,739	59.4	89.1	7.6	0.3	0.6	0.7	1.6	2.7	87.5	50.5	1.6	69.7
District 2	Brett Guthrie (R)	7,177.7	754,967	105.2	89.8	5.8	0.4	1.5	0.8	2.4	3.2	87.2	50.8	3.3	69.9
District 3	John A. Yarmuth (D)	319.6	740,860	2,318.2	71.6	22.1	0.2	2.8	0.7	2.6	5.1	67.8	51.7	6.8	68.4
District 4	Thomas Massie (R)	4,376.3	754,502	172.4	91.9	3.4	0.2	1.3	0.8	2.4	3.1	89.7	50.5	2.8	61.1
District 5	Harold Rogers (R)	11,233.9	703,315	62.6	96.8	1.5	0.3	0.3	0.2	0.9	1.5	95.9	50.4	0.9	77.7
District 6	Garland "Andy" Barr (R)	4,295.4	765,591	178.2	84.8	8.8	0.2	2.1	1.8	2.4	4.7	81.8	51.3	5.5	67.3
LOUISIANA		43,206.7	4,681,666	108.4	62.0	32.4	0.5	1.7	1.5	2.0	4.9	58.8	51.0	4.1	78.2
District 1	Steve Scalise (R)	4,030.8	803,427	199.3	78.2	14.0	1.2	2.2	2.1	2.4	8.8	71.8	51.5	6.3	74.9
District 2	Cedric Richmond (D)	1,268.4	792,390	624.7	31.0	61.9	0.3	2.8	2.2	1.8	6.4	27.8	51.5	6.5	77.8
District 3	Clay Higgins (R)	6,984.2	785,686	112.5	70.1	25.1	0.3	1.4	1.0	2.1	3.5	67.7	51.3	2.8	83.5
District 4	Mike Johnson (R)	12,436.2	753,181	60.6	60.3	34.9	0.6	1.0	1.1	2.1	3.8	58.0	50.6	2.4	74.4
District 5	Ralph Lee Abraham (R)	14,453.3	748,306	51.8	62.3	34.6	0.3	0.7	0.7	1.4	2.4	60.8	50.0	1.6	80.3
District 6	Garret Graves (R)	4,033.9	798,676	198.0	69.8	24.1	0.5	2.0	1.5	2.1	4.6	66.8	51.3	4.4	78.4
MAINE		30,844.1	1,331,479	43.2	94.4	1.5	0.6	1.3	0.2	2.0	1.6	93.4	51.1	3.8	62.6
District 1	Chellie Pingree (D)	3,286.4	676,165	205.7	94.1	1.8	0.4	1.8	0.1	1.7	1.7	92.9	51.3	4.6	55.8
District 2	Bruce Poliquin (R)	27,557.7	655,314	23.8	94.7	1.2	0.8	0.8	0.2	2.2	1.4	94.0	51.0	3.0	69.6
MARYLAND		9,710.7	6,016,447	619.6	56.5	29.8	0.3	6.3	3.8	3.3	9.8	51.4	51.5	15.3	47.6
District 1	Andrew Harris (R)	3,977.1	735,590	185.0	81.6	12.1	0.2	2.1	1.0	3.0	3.9	79.3	50.7	5.6	62.2
District 2	C. A. Dutch Ruppersberger (D)	348.7	764,948	2,194.0	55.1	34.2	0.2	5.5	1.4	3.6	7.1	50.3	52.3	12.0	61.3
District 3	John P. Sarbanes (D)	304.5	764,166	2,509.9	62.9	22.2	0.2	7.9	3.4	3.5	8.8	58.2	51.5	16.3	49.8
District 4	Anthony G. Brown (D)	297.9	755,108	2,535.2	30.5	52.3	0.3	3.0	11.6	2.4	17.3	26.0	51.9	19.8	30.7
District 5	Steny H. Hoyer (D)	1,482.6	758,857	511.8	49.0	38.7	0.3	4.3	3.1	4.6	7.9	45.5	51.0	11.1	39.7
District 6	John K. Delaney (D)	1,952.2	757,889	388.2	69.4	14.2	0.2	10.6	1.8	3.7	13.4	58.9	50.7	21.3	44.0
District 7	Elijah E. Cummings (D)	488.2	722,745	1,480.3	35.9	52.9	0.4	7.7	0.7	2.4	4.0	32.9	52.6	11.8	61.0
District 8	Jamie Raskin (D)	859.5	757,144	880.9	67.0	12.5	0.3	9.2	7.5	3.6	15.2	60.0	51.3	24.3	33.2
MASSACHUSETTS		7,800.9	6,811,779	873.2	78.5	7.4	0.2	6.5	4.2	3.1	11.4	72.4	51.5	16.5	60.9
District 1	Richard E. Neal (D)	2,350.2	729,294	310.3	86.2	6.3	0.2	2.1	2.7	2.6	17.7	72.7	51.9	7.0	67.1
District 2	James P. McGovern (D)	1,628.0	749,202	460.2	82.7	5.2	0.2	5.6	3.4	2.9	10.0	77.0	51.2	11.7	66.1
District 3	Niki Tsongas (D)	757.6	761,611	1,005.3	79.3	3.7	0.2	8.5	6.0	2.3	18.8	68.1	50.7	18.3	61.1
District 4	Joseph P. Kennedy III (D)	668.2	753,156	1,127.1	85.8	3.5	0.0	6.2	2.2	2.2	5.0	83.0	50.9	12.9	60.3
District 5	Katherine Clark (D)	265.1	759,165	2,863.9	76.8	5.1	0.1	11.3	3.2	3.4	9.2	71.4	51.3	24.1	52.5
District 6	Seth Moulton (D)	526.7	766,310	1,454.9	84.6	3.8	0.1	4.0	5.1	2.3	9.3	81.2	51.2	13.2	68.6
District 7	Michael E. Capuano (D)	62.7	779,173	12,423.4	49.3	26.5	0.4	10.7	5.9	7.2	21.5	40.6	51.7	32.8	40.6
District 8	Stephen F. Lynch (D)	326.4	773,806	2,371.0	75.6	9.7	0.2	8.2	4.0	2.3	6.1	72.2	52.3	18.5	63.2
District 9	William R. Keating (D)	1,216.1	740,062	608.6	88.0	2.5	0.2	1.6	5.0	2.7	5.2	86.3	52.0	8.9	69.8

1. Dry land or land partially or temporarily covered by water. 2. May be of any race.

Table E. Congressional Districts 115th Congress — **Age and Education**

STATE District	Population and population characteristics, 2016 (cont.)										Education, 2016		
	Age (percent)											Attainment[2] (percent)	
	Under 5 years	5 to 17 years	18 to 24 years	25 to 34 years	35 to 44 years	45 to 54 years	55 to 64 years	65 to 74 years	75 years and over	Median age	Total Enrollment[1]	High school graduate or more	Bachelor's degree or more
	15	16	17	18	19	20	21	22	23	24	25	26	27
ILLINOIS— Cont'd													
District 3	6.1	18.1	8.9	13.3	12.5	14.0	13.4	8.2	5.3	37.7	192,193	85.8	26.9
District 4	7.1	18.4	9.6	17.9	15.2	12.4	10.0	5.8	3.7	33.2	182,935	73.1	24.5
District 5	6.4	12.1	9.4	22.2	14.6	12.0	10.8	7.2	5.4	35.0	159,341	92.2	54.7
District 6	5.6	17.6	8.3	11.8	11.6	15.6	14.7	8.7	6.0	40.5	191,128	94.9	52.2
District 7	6.1	14.1	10.6	20.2	13.7	11.8	11.5	7.4	4.7	34.5	172,521	86.2	40.7
District 8	6.4	17.8	7.9	14.4	14.6	13.5	12.7	7.4	5.3	37.3	180,422	86.0	32.6
District 9	5.8	15.6	7.8	13.8	13.6	13.2	13.6	8.5	8.2	40.1	184,789	90.9	53.2
District 10	6.5	18.0	9.7	12.1	13.2	13.7	12.8	8.1	6.0	38.2	184,296	89.4	44.1
District 11	6.6	19.0	9.8	12.7	14.7	14.1	11.2	7.0	4.8	36.1	203,053	87.5	36.0
District 12	6.1	16.4	8.7	13.3	12.1	13.3	13.8	9.4	6.9	39.4	166,512	90.1	24.0
District 13	5.3	14.2	14.9	13.4	11.2	12.1	13.3	8.6	7.1	36.9	202,318	92.4	30.2
District 14	5.7	20.5	8.6	10.5	13.4	15.6	13.2	7.8	4.9	38.9	210,889	93.3	42.1
District 15	5.9	16.8	8.3	12.2	12.2	12.8	13.8	9.8	8.2	40.5	163,992	89.6	20.2
District 16	5.1	16.9	9.4	11.3	12.2	13.6	13.9	10.0	7.7	41.0	172,537	90.1	22.2
District 17	6.1	16.2	9.5	12.2	11.6	12.7	14.0	9.9	7.9	40.2	162,258	87.3	18.7
District 18	5.6	16.7	8.8	11.6	12.6	13.2	13.6	9.9	7.9	40.6	180,613	93.2	31.7
INDIANA	6.3	17.5	10.0	12.9	12.3	13.0	13.0	8.7	6.3	37.6	1,684,219	88.4	25.6
District 1	5.9	17.4	9.0	12.4	12.9	13.0	13.8	9.1	6.5	38.7	171,210	89.5	22.6
District 2	6.6	18.3	9.6	12.1	12.1	12.6	13.2	8.7	6.7	38.0	180,811	84.3	20.8
District 3	6.9	18.8	9.0	12.6	11.9	12.8	13.0	8.8	6.2	37.2	184,225	87.4	22.9
District 4	6.0	16.9	12.6	12.4	11.8	12.9	12.7	8.6	6.2	36.6	205,746	89.5	26.0
District 5	6.3	17.9	8.3	13.6	13.1	14.0	12.4	8.3	6.0	37.9	194,506	93.4	45.0
District 6	5.7	16.4	10.4	11.6	11.8	13.6	13.5	9.9	7.1	40.1	172,753	88.2	20.7
District 7	7.8	18.3	9.5	16.2	12.9	12.5	11.8	6.6	4.5	33.8	200,779	84.8	23.5
District 8	6.0	16.8	9.6	12.4	11.5	13.0	14.0	9.7	7.0	39.4	170,312	88.6	21.3
District 9	5.7	16.2	12.0	12.7	12.2	13.0	13.0	9.0	6.2	38.0	203,877	89.1	26.3
IOWA	6.3	16.9	10.2	12.6	11.8	12.5	13.3	9.0	7.4	38.0	804,741	91.8	28.4
District 1	6.2	16.6	10.4	12.0	11.4	12.6	13.7	9.2	8.0	38.8	191,587	92.3	27.1
District 2	6.1	16.6	10.7	12.8	11.9	12.2	13.3	9.2	7.2	38.0	202,239	92.1	28.5
District 3	6.9	18.0	8.5	13.9	13.1	13.1	12.6	8.1	6.0	36.9	211,065	92.0	33.1
District 4	5.9	16.3	11.5	11.5	10.7	12.0	13.9	9.4	8.7	39.1	199,850	90.6	24.7
KANSAS	6.8	17.8	10.3	13.0	12.2	12.1	12.8	8.5	6.6	36.5	774,902	90.5	32.8
District 1	7.2	17.1	12.6	12.7	11.3	10.8	12.5	8.4	7.4	35.4	190,293	88.3	23.9
District 2	6.1	16.5	11.6	12.1	11.6	12.0	13.5	9.5	7.1	37.5	190,228	92.2	29.2
District 3	6.9	18.8	8.0	13.6	13.8	13.3	12.4	7.9	5.4	36.8	199,543	92.0	47.4
District 4	6.9	18.8	9.3	13.3	11.8	12.1	13.0	8.3	6.5	36.3	194,838	89.4	29.5
KENTUCKY	6.2	16.7	9.7	12.7	12.5	13.5	13.3	9.3	6.3	38.7	1,085,033	85.7	23.4
District 1	6.0	16.6	9.8	11.7	11.7	12.9	13.8	10.2	7.4	40.2	165,286	83.9	15.7
District 2	6.2	17.2	10.4	12.0	12.7	13.4	13.0	9.1	5.9	38.4	192,545	87.1	20.9
District 3	6.3	15.7	8.7	15.0	12.2	12.9	13.7	8.9	6.5	38.2	172,864	89.9	30.9
District 4	6.2	18.1	8.5	12.2	13.3	14.4	12.9	8.7	5.5	38.5	187,781	89.4	28.3
District 5	5.9	16.3	8.5	11.9	12.5	14.2	13.7	10.4	6.5	41.0	159,103	76.3	12.4
District 6	6.2	16.1	11.9	13.6	12.7	13.0	12.6	8.4	5.6	36.7	207,454	87.2	31.7
LOUISIANA	6.6	17.3	9.6	14.3	12.5	12.5	12.8	8.6	5.8	36.5	1,172,916	84.4	23.4
District 1	6.5	16.9	8.7	13.5	12.6	12.8	13.6	9.2	6.1	38.4	201,104	87.2	30.3
District 2	6.6	16.2	9.3	16.3	12.7	12.6	12.9	8.3	5.1	35.9	199,135	81.4	23.4
District 3	6.9	18.1	9.4	14.2	12.3	12.7	12.7	8.0	5.7	36.0	195,591	83.5	21.0
District 4	6.7	17.9	9.4	13.7	11.9	12.3	12.6	9.1	6.4	36.7	180,914	85.2	19.9
District 5	6.3	17.4	10.0	13.0	12.7	12.1	12.8	9.3	6.4	37.4	182,687	80.9	16.8
District 6	6.3	17.5	10.8	15.2	12.7	12.7	12.0	8.0	4.8	35.2	213,485	87.9	27.9
MAINE	4.8	14.3	8.3	11.8	11.4	14.4	15.7	11.4	7.8	44.5	293,857	92.3	30.1
District 1	4.8	14.2	8.1	12.1	11.8	14.6	15.5	11.2	7.8	44.3	149,556	93.9	36.9
District 2	4.8	14.5	8.5	11.5	10.9	14.1	16.0	11.7	7.9	44.7	144,301	90.7	23.0
MARYLAND	6.0	16.4	9.1	13.9	12.8	14.2	13.2	8.6	6.0	38.5	1,540,625	90.1	39.3
District 1	5.0	16.3	9.3	11.1	11.3	14.6	14.6	10.7	7.1	42.5	180,554	89.8	30.6
District 2	7.0	16.7	8.9	15.9	12.5	13.4	11.9	8.0	5.7	36.2	192,242	89.5	33.4
District 3	5.7	15.0	9.7	15.3	12.8	13.4	13.6	8.0	6.4	38.2	194,776	92.8	47.2
District 4	7.1	16.9	8.2	15.0	13.9	13.6	12.6	7.9	4.8	36.8	191,391	86.6	34.0
District 5	5.6	16.7	10.5	12.8	12.3	15.6	13.2	8.5	4.8	38.3	207,855	91.2	33.7
District 6	5.9	17.2	9.0	13.0	12.9	14.8	13.0	8.3	5.8	38.9	199,313	90.0	41.5
District 7	5.6	15.9	9.7	15.1	12.1	13.6	13.4	8.5	6.2	37.7	186,928	89.1	37.8
District 8	6.4	16.1	7.6	12.6	13.7	14.4	13.2	9.0	6.9	40.4	187,566	91.9	55.6
MASSACHUSETTS	5.3	15.0	10.4	13.9	12.1	14.1	13.5	9.0	6.8	39.5	1,737,713	90.4	42.7
District 1	5.2	15.2	10.6	12.4	11.0	13.7	14.4	10.1	7.4	40.9	175,874	88.0	29.7
District 2	5.0	15.5	12.6	12.2	11.9	14.4	13.5	8.4	6.5	39.0	206,344	91.0	38.4
District 3	5.8	16.7	9.9	12.6	12.4	15.1	13.9	8.3	5.3	39.3	200,589	88.4	37.4
District 4	4.8	17.7	9.4	11.1	11.8	15.9	13.5	9.0	6.8	41.4	208,837	93.4	51.0
District 5	5.4	14.2	9.7	14.8	13.3	14.1	13.1	8.2	7.2	39.4	195,483	93.2	57.4
District 6	5.4	15.7	8.5	11.8	11.6	15.3	14.5	9.6	7.6	42.8	180,837	92.4	44.0
District 7	5.5	11.5	15.7	23.2	13.0	10.9	9.8	6.3	4.2	31.8	233,097	84.3	42.9
District 8	5.5	13.9	8.4	16.4	12.9	13.4	13.4	8.8	7.3	39.3	177,909	91.9	46.8
District 9	4.8	14.4	8.3	10.6	11.2	14.3	15.1	12.3	8.8	45.5	158,743	91.0	35.9

1. All persons 3 years old and over enrolled in nursery school through college and graduate or professional school.   2. Persons 25 years old and over.

STATE District	Number	Average household size	Family households (percent)	Married couple family (percent)	Female family house-holder[1]	One person households (percent)	Total in group quarters, 2016	Percent 65 years and over	Persons in correctional institutions	Persons in nursing facilities	Persons in college dormitories	Persons in military quarters
	28	29	30	31	32	33	34	35	36	37	38	39
ILLINOIS— Cont'd												
District 3	244,418	2.90	70.0	52.6	11.4	25.8	11,007	30.2	3,160	3,740	1,890	0
District 4	223,350	3.10	68.4	44.6	16.5	22.6	3,417	34.4	1	1,268	285	0
District 5	297,889	2.39	52.3	41.5	7.1	35.6	10,932	32.7	0	3,882	4,823	0
District 6	262,303	2.72	71.0	60.3	7.8	24.1	9,271	36.8	786	4,034	3,517	0
District 7	295,886	2.35	50.1	27.2	18.6	41.7	28,956	6.3	11,612	3,240	7,992	16
District 8	253,677	2.81	69.2	51.2	12.4	25.6	5,292	45.7	0	2,564	744	0
District 9	286,837	2.45	58.5	46.2	8.7	34.5	22,139	27.4	31	8,543	8,803	0
District 10	251,252	2.75	70.6	55.9	10.8	24.9	19,894	19.5	704	5,665	2,088	12,155
District 11	251,942	2.87	70.8	52.5	13.6	24.2	7,111	33.9	1,085	2,891	1,495	0
District 12	277,601	2.42	63.0	43.5	14.4	31.1	22,847	22.6	10,700	5,209	3,332	307
District 13	283,971	2.34	58.4	42.6	11.2	32.9	40,411	12.5	5,125	5,481	27,454	0
District 14	250,357	2.92	76.3	62.9	9.5	19.3	4,453	33.0	1,364	1,562	158	0
District 15	275,299	2.45	65.1	50.5	10.5	29.4	26,762	23.2	12,642	6,376	3,900	0
District 16	270,748	2.47	68.7	52.1	11.6	25.5	18,735	26.0	6,821	5,619	6,178	0
District 17	283,430	2.35	61.3	43.0	13.6	32.9	23,818	21.2	8,864	5,921	5,835	5
District 18	283,990	2.43	67.2	53.7	9.8	28.1	22,309	27.7	7,248	6,421	6,455	228
INDIANA	2,533,270	2.54	65.0	48.4	11.8	28.6	187,052	20.5	48,694	41,158	75,434	0
District 1	270,418	2.57	66.7	46.7	14.3	27.8	16,990	19.0	7,380	3,116	3,194	0
District 2	265,086	2.65	67.2	50.7	11.7	27.3	21,980	20.0	5,936	4,482	8,659	0
District 3	282,012	2.58	66.4	50.9	11.1	27.9	13,023	33.2	2,229	4,852	3,948	0
District 4	286,048	2.50	65.3	51.0	9.9	27.2	33,277	15.3	7,233	4,934	15,651	178
District 5	304,370	2.48	64.6	50.2	10.3	28.8	14,407	25.1	4,416	4,444	5,257	0
District 6	280,264	2.50	67.2	51.3	10.5	26.8	21,190	23.8	5,096	5,532	8,541	50
District 7	285,276	2.58	56.1	34.2	17.1	35.8	14,884	18.3	3,216	3,152	5,162	0
District 8	281,301	2.45	65.5	49.3	11.4	28.4	27,336	19.4	10,561	5,980	10,509	3
District 9	278,495	2.61	65.9	51.1	10.2	27.2	23,965	17.9	2,627	4,666	14,513	3
IOWA	1,247,932	2.43	63.7	50.6	9.1	29.4	100,516	26.1	13,309	26,871	44,574	3
District 1	307,410	2.42	64.2	52.9	7.5	28.7	26,445	26.1	2,415	7,519	13,934	0
District 2	308,367	2.44	63.0	49.2	9.8	29.7	25,454	21.8	5,185	5,702	11,804	0
District 3	321,446	2.51	64.2	49.4	10.4	29.2	17,402	27.7	3,690	5,218	5,248	0
District 4	310,709	2.35	63.5	50.8	8.6	30.0	31,215	29.1	2,019	8,432	13,588	3,943
KANSAS	1,110,407	2.55	64.5	50.1	10.0	29.6	79,042	24.4	18,009	20,672	27,754	3,425
District 1	269,153	2.52	63.4	50.3	8.7	30.4	29,938	23.2	5,306	7,084	10,873	192
District 2	277,244	2.48	63.1	48.9	9.6	30.5	28,587	17.4	7,436	5,478	12,652	0
District 3	288,299	2.61	67.5	52.0	10.8	26.9	6,257	49.6	1,355	3,598	544	326
District 4	275,711	2.57	63.8	49.0	10.6	30.6	14,260	29.4	3,912	4,512	3,685	5,856
KENTUCKY	1,717,706	2.51	65.3	47.3	13.2	28.8	131,248	19.2	41,122	26,044	36,340	3,843
District 1	278,896	2.48	65.2	49.0	12.0	30.0	26,650	20.4	7,869	5,548	4,101	2,013
District 2	284,181	2.58	67.0	50.4	11.9	26.5	22,751	21.3	4,501	4,378	7,527	0
District 3	305,947	2.37	58.2	38.8	14.2	34.7	15,566	30.7	2,662	4,723	3,307	0
District 4	280,953	2.63	70.6	52.4	12.5	24.4	16,471	21.9	9,255	3,657	1,768	0
District 5	270,305	2.51	67.8	47.8	14.3	28.4	24,178	15.1	12,451	4,570	5,039	0
District 6	297,424	2.49	63.8	45.9	13.9	28.4	25,632	12.1	4,384	3,168	14,598	0
LOUISIANA	1,720,801	2.65	63.8	42.7	16.0	30.2	128,612	16.7	60,804	24,524	24,891	2,861
District 1	301,862	2.62	65.9	48.3	12.8	28.0	13,562	24.4	1,182	2,957	5,469	57
District 2	295,726	2.60	57.5	32.1	20.3	36.0	23,242	12.0	11,687	3,058	4,007	138
District 3	289,330	2.67	64.0	42.6	15.3	29.6	12,254	26.9	4,329	4,273	2,935	0
District 4	279,395	2.62	63.6	43.4	15.6	31.3	21,802	18.4	13,410	5,425	2,390	2,524
District 5	265,342	2.64	65.5	42.4	17.8	30.0	47,062	11.6	28,559	5,925	6,333	142
District 6	289,146	2.73	66.5	47.6	14.5	26.6	10,690	23.4	1,637	2,886	3,757	0
MAINE	531,660	2.44	62.0	48.2	9.1	30.0	35,892	22.5	3,679	7,878	17,251	131
District 1	276,441	2.38	61.0	48.5	8.4	30.7	17,310	24.5	2,708	4,128	7,433	119
District 2	255,219	2.49	63.1	48.0	10.0	29.2	18,582	20.4	971	3,750	9,818	12
MARYLAND	2,194,657	2.68	66.5	47.4	14.0	27.3	140,535	19.4	35,832	28,001	48,141	7,534
District 1	272,561	2.64	69.0	54.4	10.4	25.2	17,220	20.6	5,648	3,465	5,803	7
District 2	281,015	2.64	66.0	42.6	17.1	27.9	22,759	17.1	7,411	3,533	3,971	2,113
District 3	292,373	2.56	62.7	45.9	11.9	29.1	16,500	19.9	583	3,399	6,910	4,515
District 4	264,065	2.84	65.9	40.5	18.7	28.1	6,048	42.2	1,149	2,597	410	115
District 5	261,844	2.82	70.6	52.1	14.3	24.2	20,097	11.8	1,111	2,598	14,602	387
District 6	270,725	2.72	70.1	52.5	12.6	24.3	22,354	17.6	12,569	3,716	2,766	93
District 7	270,269	2.59	59.3	35.3	19.5	32.6	23,863	14.8	6,305	4,677	10,895	0
District 8	281,805	2.65	68.6	55.6	8.0	26.5	11,694	37.8	1,056	4,016	2,784	304
MASSACHUSETTS	2,579,398	2.54	63.3	46.3	12.5	28.9	252,586	17.7	24,683	43,833	135,773	498
District 1	285,949	2.46	63.0	41.4	16.5	30.6	25,990	20.9	1,897	5,855	13,226	0
District 2	279,000	2.52	61.2	45.6	11.7	31.4	45,215	13.9	1,576	5,572	26,184	0
District 3	270,620	2.75	69.8	49.8	15.2	23.5	18,244	19.7	6,829	3,823	4,944	0
District 4	271,263	2.67	71.1	57.7	9.1	23.5	27,546	19.7	2,520	4,914	15,480	25
District 5	292,625	2.50	63.7	50.8	9.2	28.1	28,336	16.5	771	4,440	18,907	113
District 6	289,280	2.58	66.9	52.5	10.5	27.9	19,220	28.9	2,014	4,919	5,965	73
District 7	292,430	2.47	50.7	27.9	17.1	34.1	56,921	4.7	1,895	2,728	42,309	261
District 8	302,523	2.50	59.9	43.9	11.5	30.9	16,292	35.8	3,879	6,322	3,522	26
District 9	295,708	2.45	64.8	48.3	12.0	29.5	14,822	30.2	3,302	5,260	5,236	

1. No spouse present.

STATE District	Total	Occupied units as a percent of all units	Owner-occupied units as a percent of occupied units	Median value[1] (dollars)	Percent valued at $500,000 or more	Median rent[2]	Per capita income (dollars)	Median income (dollars)	Percent with income of $100,000 or more
	40	41	42	43	44	45	46	47	48
ILLINOIS— Cont'd									
District 3	262,329	93.2	73.3	216,800	7.4	951	29,713	66,270	29.4
District 4	246,720	90.5	45.6	231,000	8.0	944	23,939	51,383	21.1
District 5	323,087	92.2	54.7	337,200	26.6	1,266	48,869	80,269	39.6
District 6	275,030	95.4	78.0	316,000	20.1	1,256	46,654	97,387	48.8
District 7	341,982	86.5	39.9	262,300	18.8	1,116	37,667	54,147	29.4
District 8	265,262	95.6	66.2	216,100	4.0	1,176	30,276	67,745	30.3
District 9	311,711	92.0	59.3	339,400	23.8	1,099	41,955	67,084	34.5
District 10	266,693	94.2	69.5	262,900	22.4	1,113	40,667	74,971	37.6
District 11	265,752	94.8	71.3	207,900	6.8	1,156	32,678	72,198	34.1
District 12	320,440	86.6	66.6	109,100	1.7	746	26,882	47,430	19.7
District 13	319,867	88.8	64.5	122,600	1.7	750	27,673	49,758	20.3
District 14	265,968	94.1	79.7	254,700	7.6	1,163	37,982	90,345	43.7
District 15	314,640	87.5	75.2	102,600	1.4	616	25,860	49,927	17.8
District 16	297,001	91.2	71.5	135,500	1.5	780	28,866	57,182	22.8
District 17	322,755	87.8	65.2	99,300	1.5	671	24,700	45,360	15.4
District 18	314,217	90.4	75.8	146,300	3.1	753	32,668	60,857	26.4
INDIANA	2,854,595	88.7	68.3	134,800	3.0	768	27,464	52,314	20.1
District 1	305,809	88.4	70.7	155,500	3.2	837	28,232	56,370	22.9
District 2	307,094	86.3	69.5	122,200	1.6	706	24,293	51,292	16.1
District 3	317,884	88.7	71.5	121,000	2.8	697	25,709	51,453	17.8
District 4	312,532	91.5	69.5	140,700	2.3	752	27,319	53,996	21.2
District 5	328,974	92.5	69.6	178,400	7.9	904	38,140	67,461	31.7
District 6	314,052	89.2	70.8	121,800	2.2	717	25,803	51,033	17.8
District 7	332,521	85.8	51.4	112,700	1.5	801	23,208	41,429	13.7
District 8	317,897	88.5	72.3	116,800	1.6	675	25,987	50,261	17.5
District 9	317,832	87.6	70.1	145,500	2.8	803	28,010	55,078	21.0
IOWA	1,380,087	90.4	70.6	142,300	3.0	741	30,047	56,247	22.4
District 1	339,871	90.4	73.8	144,100	3.3	693	30,633	57,402	22.0
District 2	342,891	89.9	69.2	136,600	2.6	750	27,917	52,150	20.7
District 3	348,269	92.3	69.6	164,200	4.1	823	33,074	62,323	27.0
District 4	349,056	89.0	70.1	120,700	1.9	668	28,357	53,335	19.6
KANSAS	1,259,870	88.1	65.7	144,900	4.0	789	28,950	54,935	22.5
District 1	319,287	84.3	65.1	111,000	1.8	695	24,350	48,156	14.9
District 2	317,557	87.3	65.8	127,500	2.7	737	26,783	51,778	19.2
District 3	310,534	92.8	65.8	218,400	8.9	974	37,433	71,562	34.3
District 4	312,492	88.2	66.0	125,800	2.5	745	26,686	52,054	20.9
KENTUCKY	1,965,577	87.4	66.8	135,600	3.5	707	26,046	46,659	18.0
District 1	333,801	83.6	68.6	104,700	2.6	626	22,856	40,253	12.3
District 2	324,766	87.5	69.6	142,000	3.2	685	25,750	49,960	18.0
District 3	336,148	91.0	59.3	160,300	4.5	805	30,288	51,070	20.2
District 4	311,200	90.3	71.2	163,400	4.4	781	30,526	60,912	27.1
District 5	328,462	82.3	72.4	81,000	1.5	575	18,575	30,585	9.4
District 6	331,200	89.8	61.0	157,300	4.6	748	27,670	50,659	20.0
LOUISIANA	2,037,067	84.5	64.3	158,000	4.7	808	25,664	45,146	19.4
District 1	335,344	90.0	68.8	199,600	7.5	927	31,238	56,938	25.5
District 2	353,897	83.6	52.4	154,600	5.2	865	23,818	36,798	14.7
District 3	335,929	86.1	67.4	143,100	4.1	769	24,365	44,668	19.2
District 4	344,482	81.1	63.3	128,900	3.4	733	22,832	39,748	15.1
District 5	332,282	79.9	63.6	112,800	2.9	668	20,613	36,718	14.0
District 6	335,133	86.3	70.1	178,800	4.8	900	30,571	59,270	27.4
MAINE	730,786	72.8	71.9	184,700	6.2	797	29,604	53,079	21.2
District 1	352,103	78.5	70.2	238,900	9.0	900	33,540	61,173	26.1
District 2	378,683	67.4	73.7	139,100	3.4	711	25,544	46,638	16.0
MARYLAND	2,447,211	89.7	65.9	306,900	19.6	1,314	38,662	78,945	38.7
District 1	342,000	79.7	74.8	275,600	12.3	1,039	34,345	69,254	33.0
District 2	308,544	91.1	60.7	231,600	7.0	1,223	32,194	69,128	31.0
District 3	315,271	92.7	63.8	327,200	21.9	1,395	43,726	83,620	41.9
District 4	286,317	92.2	61.5	296,300	16.6	1,389	35,970	79,350	37.7
District 5	281,325	93.1	75.3	326,200	12.4	1,493	38,916	95,442	47.1
District 6	297,987	90.9	68.7	296,900	24.2	1,313	37,910	75,774	38.1
District 7	319,686	84.5	55.4	260,000	20.9	1,086	35,078	61,392	30.9
District 8	296,081	95.2	67.2	444,100	40.8	1,609	50,881	98,991	49.5
MASSACHUSETTS	2,858,087	90.2	62.0	366,900	28.2	1,179	39,771	75,297	37.7
District 1	319,368	89.5	65.2	211,300	4.8	849	29,632	55,716	25.2
District 2	301,201	92.6	62.9	271,200	10.4	972	33,892	64,868	32.0
District 3	285,588	94.8	63.5	333,700	21.4	1,109	37,598	77,995	38.8
District 4	285,798	94.9	72.4	397,500	37.2	1,240	49,383	98,530	49.5
District 5	310,494	94.2	58.9	516,700	52.0	1,527	48,695	92,268	46.4
District 6	308,176	93.9	70.8	422,300	33.1	1,202	42,372	84,913	41.7
District 7	314,851	92.9	33.7	465,200	43.7	1,444	35,107	60,873	32.0
District 8	321,126	94.2	60.4	413,000	33.1	1,439	43,213	82,333	41.4
District 9	411,485	71.9	71.2	355,100	25.2	942	37,633	68,173	32.7

1. Specified owner-occupied units.   2. Specified renter-occupied units.

Table E. Congressional Districts 115th Congress — Poverty, Labor Force, Employment, and Social Security

STATE District	Poverty, 2016 — Persons below poverty level (percent)	Poverty, 2016 — Families below poverty level (percent)	Percent of households receiving food stamps in past 12 months	Civilian labor force, 2016 — Total	Unemployment — Total	Unemployment — Rate[1]	Civilian employment[2], 2016 — Total	Percent — Management, business, science, and arts occupations	Percent — Service, sales, and office	Percent — Construction and production	Persons under 65 years of age with no health insurance, 2016 (percent)	Social Security beneficiaries, December 2016 — Number	Social Security beneficiaries — Rate[3]	Supplemental Security Income recipients, December 2016
	49	50	51	52	53	54	55	56	57	58	59	60	61	62
ILLINOIS— Cont'd														
District 3	10.3	8.3	12.2	364,688	26,175	7.2	338,513	31.0	43.2	25.8	9.0	116,277	161.3	12,545
District 4	16.5	14.6	18.3	370,765	23,985	6.5	346,780	27.2	42.8	30.0	17.0	76,115	109.5	18,869
District 5	8.3	5.2	5.6	440,426	16,317	3.7	424,109	50.6	35.9	13.5	6.9	97,139	134.3	11,723
District 6	4.7	3.0	4.8	398,207	15,396	3.9	382,811	47.4	39.1	13.5	5.4	112,950	156.4	4,360
District 7	22.5	18.1	22.4	383,023	35,777	9.3	347,246	44.4	40.9	14.7	8.7	100,072	138.3	34,172
District 8	11.4	8.9	10.9	393,346	19,633	5.0	373,713	34.8	41.9	23.4	9.3	106,151	147.9	9,774
District 9	12.2	7.8	9.3	374,147	15,318	4.1	358,829	50.1	36.8	13.0	7.0	122,274	168.9	18,461
District 10	9.0	6.4	9.0	373,464	19,567	5.2	353,897	41.7	40.3	18.0	9.2	108,518	152.7	9,401
District 11	9.2	6.9	11.5	391,026	19,476	5.0	371,550	36.4	41.1	22.4	7.7	98,637	135.0	8,489
District 12	16.4	11.7	17.8	325,670	22,275	6.8	303,395	31.3	44.0	24.7	6.7	146,654	211.4	20,402
District 13	16.9	10.6	13.0	357,617	20,422	5.7	337,195	38.3	41.8	19.9	4.9	136,900	194.3	15,391
District 14	6.7	5.3	7.2	396,174	19,268	4.9	376,906	42.4	37.5	20.0	4.5	112,205	152.4	4,325
District 15	14.2	10.4	13.9	331,648	18,360	5.5	313,288	31.5	38.8	29.8	6.5	155,333	221.7	14,182
District 16	12.4	8.4	12.7	352,022	22,597	6.4	329,425	30.8	41.6	27.6	5.2	143,900	209.2	8,444
District 17	18.2	13.5	18.5	337,813	26,225	7.8	311,588	27.7	43.5	28.9	6.0	157,484	227.8	18,701
District 18	9.6	6.1	9.2	359,988	18,107	5.0	341,881	38.4	41.2	20.4	3.9	148,041	207.5	8,371
INDIANA	14.1	9.6	10.8	3,332,231	167,215	5.0	3,165,016	33.1	39.6	27.3	9.4	1,318,046	198.7	128,383
District 1	14.3	10.4	12.1	346,004	20,532	5.9	325,472	30.1	42.4	27.6	7.6	145,278	204.1	16,133
District 2	14.5	9.6	10.6	354,288	21,894	6.2	332,394	28.3	39.0	32.8	12.8	144,596	199.7	13,199
District 3	13.5	9.7	10.1	371,521	16,399	4.4	355,122	29.7	37.3	32.9	11.0	146,349	197.7	12,822
District 4	12.8	7.8	9.7	379,225	18,612	4.9	360,613	33.6	37.4	29.0	8.3	145,440	194.2	10,335
District 5	9.8	7.3	6.6	412,268	15,346	3.7	396,922	46.9	36.9	16.2	7.2	135,644	176.5	9,916
District 6	14.7	9.7	11.6	352,789	16,544	4.7	336,245	31.1	38.4	30.5	10.3	165,779	230.0	14,772
District 7	20.8	16.0	17.2	376,283	24,263	6.4	352,020	30.0	45.8	24.2	10.8	123,023	163.7	23,965
District 8	13.8	9.0	10.7	354,823	14,851	4.2	339,972	30.8	38.8	30.4	9.0	159,090	221.9	14,915
District 9	12.7	7.8	8.5	385,030	18,774	4.9	366,256	34.8	41.3	23.9	7.7	152,847	203.8	12,326
IOWA	11.8	7.6	10.9	1,679,847	66,229	3.9	1,613,618	36.1	38.6	25.4	5.0	630,014	201.0	50,942
District 1	11.2	7.5	10.0	418,587	16,188	3.9	402,399	34.1	38.9	27.0	5.0	163,573	212.2	12,841
District 2	13.9	9.2	11.5	403,888	16,314	4.0	387,574	35.1	38.1	26.8	5.2	158,040	202.9	15,000
District 3	9.4	6.1	11.9	453,516	19,209	4.2	434,307	40.2	39.7	20.1	4.9	144,029	174.8	13,125
District 4	12.7	7.5	10.3	403,856	14,518	3.6	389,338	34.4	37.4	28.2	5.1	164,372	216.1	9,976
KANSAS	12.1	7.9	7.9	1,493,137	67,003	4.5	1,426,134	38.1	39.1	22.8	10.1	535,673	184.3	48,072
District 1	13.0	7.5	7.2	351,332	16,336	4.6	334,996	32.2	39.7	28.1	11.1	135,157	190.9	9,842
District 2	13.4	8.3	9.1	360,763	15,543	4.3	345,220	36.1	39.5	24.3	9.2	148,073	206.6	14,914
District 3	8.5	6.4	5.6	416,340	17,127	4.1	399,213	46.6	36.9	16.5	9.3	116,034	152.7	9,159
District 4	13.9	9.5	10.0	364,702	17,997	4.9	346,705	35.8	40.6	23.6	11.1	136,409	188.8	14,157
KENTUCKY	18.5	14.0	14.9	2,079,319	124,677	6.0	1,954,642	33.4	40.0	26.6	6.0	972,352	219.1	180,613
District 1	20.0	14.6	14.3	305,704	17,527	5.7	288,177	26.7	40.0	33.3	8.1	172,853	240.8	26,701
District 2	16.1	11.6	12.6	366,203	19,862	5.4	346,341	29.6	38.8	31.6	4.8	166,895	221.1	24,567
District 3	14.7	9.9	11.4	393,621	22,844	5.8	370,777	36.1	40.6	23.3	5.1	145,971	197.0	24,959
District 4	12.9	9.8	11.1	377,833	17,089	4.5	360,744	37.4	39.8	22.8	4.8	146,016	193.5	19,996
District 5	29.3	24.7	27.6	244,466	23,773	9.7	220,693	29.7	41.6	28.7	6.5	193,283	274.8	60,857
District 6	18.6	13.6	13.4	391,492	23,582	6.0	367,910	38.0	39.6	22.4	6.8	147,334	192.4	23,533
LOUISIANA	20.2	15.4	16.7	2,172,162	151,211	7.0	2,020,951	33.4	43.3	23.3	11.9	882,185	188.4	177,524
District 1	13.8	10.4	11.1	396,096	21,417	5.4	374,679	38.3	40.6	21.2	11.6	152,500	189.8	19,051
District 2	24.9	19.4	22.9	382,184	35,654	9.3	346,530	31.0	46.2	22.8	12.9	140,870	177.8	42,295
District 3	20.5	15.6	15.3	366,854	27,885	7.6	338,969	28.7	44.5	26.7	12.4	146,547	186.5	25,261
District 4	23.4	18.3	18.1	319,738	24,728	7.7	295,010	32.8	43.8	23.4	12.6	151,121	200.6	32,761
District 5	24.8	19.1	20.8	306,026	21,093	6.9	284,933	30.7	45.2	24.1	12.4	159,222	212.8	39,634
District 6	14.6	10.6	12.4	401,264	20,434	5.1	380,830	37.3	40.3	22.4	9.8	131,925	165.2	18,522
MAINE	12.5	7.6	14.2	689,036	30,560	4.4	658,476	37.2	41.3	21.5	9.9	334,291	251.1	37,294
District 1	10.2	6.3	11.3	365,524	11,538	3.2	353,986	41.0	40.1	18.9	7.8	163,495	241.8	15,076
District 2	14.9	9.1	17.4	323,512	19,022	5.9	304,490	32.8	42.6	24.6	12.1	170,796	260.6	22,218
MARYLAND	9.7	6.3	11.0	3,249,158	175,235	5.4	3,073,923	45.1	39.0	15.8	7.0	966,632	160.7	120,710
District 1	10.2	6.4	11.1	384,518	20,538	5.3	363,980	37.8	41.8	20.4	5.4	156,334	212.5	11,425
District 2	10.3	6.9	14.0	397,847	20,813	5.2	377,034	41.0	41.1	17.8	6.8	123,963	162.1	17,851
District 3	8.8	5.9	8.8	430,818	19,673	4.6	411,145	50.4	36.5	13.1	6.1	116,412	152.3	15,477
District 4	8.9	6.5	9.9	428,000	25,029	5.8	402,971	40.0	41.9	18.1	11.6	101,696	134.7	10,885
District 5	7.4	4.3	8.5	411,815	21,138	5.1	390,677	43.3	39.4	17.3	6.0	108,321	156.2	9,858
District 6	9.6	6.3	11.3	399,273	19,996	5.0	379,277	46.2	38.0	15.8	7.1	118,407	156.2	13,862
District 7	16.4	11.4	19.3	371,924	28,641	7.7	343,283	45.7	41.2	13.1	6.1	126,763	175.4	33,487
District 8	6.2	3.7	5.5	424,963	19,407	4.6	405,556	55.6	33.2	11.3	6.8	114,736	151.5	7,865
MASSACHUSETTS	10.4	7.3	12.0	3,769,850	198,840	5.3	3,571,010	45.6	39.1	15.4	2.9	1,246,936	183.1	186,896
District 1	14.0	10.2	16.7	378,613	23,706	6.3	354,907	37.0	42.0	21.1	3.7	165,397	226.8	37,250
District 2	10.5	6.3	12.0	404,840	21,268	5.3	383,572	42.9	39.8	17.3	2.6	134,981	180.2	20,225
District 3	11.0	8.1	14.9	419,765	22,039	5.3	397,726	42.2	40.4	17.4	3.3	129,652	170.2	24,007
District 4	6.2	4.6	7.6	411,779	16,376	4.0	395,403	51.5	35.1	13.5	2.0	131,962	175.2	11,103
District 5	7.8	5.0	7.0	438,286	17,083	3.9	421,203	55.7	34.8	9.6	3.4	120,669	158.9	11,000
District 6	7.2	4.9	9.0	421,881	18,616	4.4	403,265	46.8	38.0	15.2	2.3	151,312	197.5	14,128
District 7	20.4	16.4	19.8	459,899	33,275	7.2	426,624	46.5	41.2	12.2	3.8	90,328	115.9	34,269
District 8	9.1	6.8	9.8	444,626	24,796	5.6	419,830	48.1	37.9	14.0	2.4	135,282	174.8	16,131
District 9	8.0	5.4	11.0	390,161	21,681	5.6	368,480	37.0	43.2	19.8	3.0	187,353	253.2	18,783

1. Percent of civilian labor force. 2. Persons 16 years old and over. 3. Per 1,000 resident population estimated in the 2016 American Community Survey.

STATE District	Number of farms	Land in farms — Acres	Average size of farm (acres)	Irrigated land (acres)	Value of products sold — Total ($1,000)	Average per farm (dollars)	Percent from crops	Percent from livestock and poultry products	Government payments — Total ($1,000)	Average per farm receiving payments (dollars)
	63	64	65	66	67	68	69	70	71	72
ILLINOIS— Cont'd										
District 3	97	13,188	136	326	8,734	90,045	0.0	0.0	212	8,140
District 4	X	X	X	X	X	X	X	X	X	X
District 5	21	349	17	D	X	X	X	X	X	X
District 6	187	17,561	94	462	30,306	162,064	95.9	4.1	D	D
District 7	X	X	X	X	X	X	X	X	420	9,765
District 8	21	4,457	212	D	3,655	174,060	99.7	0.3	X	X
District 9	X	X	X	X	X	X	X	X	D	D
District 10	141	8,223	58	407	13,357	94,727	95.6	4.4	126	8,421
District 11	131	31,383	240	D	23,965	182,943	95.8	4.2	559	9,172
District 12	6,959	1,905,115	274	15,491	688,176	98,890	85.7	14.3	29,651	6,488
District 13	7,760	2,974,971	383	13,854	1,842,362	237,418	88.1	11.9	53,882	9,103
District 14	2,132	625,197	293	18,015	560,569	262,931	83.2	16.8	13,128	13,274
District 15	22,203	7,559,605	340	102,777	3,613,564	162,751	78.7	21.3	155,644	8,968
District 16	10,468	4,292,328	410	48,782	3,466,237	331,127	84.7	15.3	92,879	11,381
District 17	9,730	3,458,529	355	118,763	2,861,291	294,069	75.5	24.5	85,811	11,696
District 18	13,826	5,528,495	400	187,608	3,658,219	264,590	84.0	16.0	112,453	10,343
INDIANA	58,695	14,720,396	251	437,445	11,210,818	191,001	67.2	32.8	267,287	8,331
District 1	1,212	348,046	287	38,398	300,726	248,123	D	D	6,174	9,572
District 2	7,547	1,747,268	232	183,555	1,685,428	223,324	61.1	38.9	32,668	8,128
District 3	11,801	1,957,311	166	53,255	1,877,293	159,079	54.8	45.2	38,957	6,794
District 4	8,570	3,273,095	382	47,054	2,697,593	314,772	72.4	27.6	59,486	10,747
District 5	2,682	803,313	300	5,904	690,258	257,367	89.1	10.9	13,671	8,507
District 6	10,531	2,532,278	240	20,206	1,686,224	160,120	69.8	30.2	50,568	8,006
District 7	185	17,001	92	163	26,173	141,475	D	D	201	6,708
District 8	9,529	2,812,457	295	79,188	1,677,310	176,022	65.2	34.8	45,753	8,707
District 9	6,638	1,229,627	185	9,722	569,814	85,841	61.2	38.8	19,809	6,733
IOWA	88,637	30,622,731	345	171,656	30,821,532	347,728	56.3	43.7	782,290	11,262
District 1	22,478	6,620,256	295	D	6,557,733	291,740	57.8	42.2	197,364	10,957
District 2	20,546	5,960,872	290	24,598	4,317,514	210,139	60.7	39.3	168,748	11,138
District 3	12,191	4,565,364	374	D	2,960,578	242,849	69.2	30.8	94,951	10,699
District 4	33,422	13,476,239	403	125,421	16,980,000	508,219	52.5	47.6	321,228	11,713
KANSAS	61,773	46,137,295	747	2,881,292	18,460,564	298,845	37.8	62.2	442,090	10,426
District 1	30,489	30,369,854	996	2,320,029	14,300,000	469,295	32.3	67.8	306,513	12,602
District 2	19,808	7,356,986	371	50,780	1,835,532	92,666	60.9	39.1	69,467	6,390
District 3	1,013	195,215	193	2,877	47,298	46,691	73.0	27.0	1,567	5,458
District 4	10,463	8,215,240	785	507,606	2,269,393	216,897	53.7	46.3	64,543	9,324
KENTUCKY	77,064	13,049,347	169	73,573	5,067,334	65,755	45.0	55.0	169,821	5,087
District 1	22,897	4,970,288	217	46,542	2,738,196	119,588	47.8	52.2	88,556	6,975
District 2	19,734	3,055,139	155	14,508	1,059,346	53,681	48.6	51.4	44,239	5,052
District 3	223	13,572	61	101	5,973	26,784	82.2	17.8	184	4,611
District 4	11,411	1,595,512	140	6,248	311,349	27,285	62.8	37.2	13,820	3,421
District 5	11,144	1,522,271	137	1,494	277,300	24,883	32.6	67.4	8,668	2,468
District 6	11,655	1,892,565	162	4,680	675,171	57,930	24.4	75.6	14,353	3,310
LOUISIANA	28,093	7,900,864	281	1,092,881	3,809,401	135,600	73.1	26.9	138,164	14,625
District 1	1,386	376,150	271	1,242	101,752	73,414	48.0	52.0	291	4,037
District 2	404	234,194	580	1,175	103,689	256,656	95.7	4.3	277	6,915
District 3	5,363	1,709,327	319	246,622	646,950	120,632	83.8	16.2	23,708	11,824
District 4	7,545	1,535,386	203	104,062	737,447	97,740	29.8	70.2	19,192	11,980
District 5	11,106	3,503,066	315	730,933	1,891,903	170,350	84.7	15.3	90,840	16,970
District 6	2,289	542,736	237	8,847	327,660	143,146	83.0	17.0	3,857	10,285
MAINE	8,173	1,454,104	178	30,887	763,062	93,364	62.1	37.9	10,162	7,629
District 1	2,650	234,530	89	2,884	91,532	34,540	66.5	33.5	1,525	6,809
District 2	5,523	1,219,574	221	28,003	671,531	121,588	61.5	38.5	8,637	7,795
MARYLAND	12,256	2,030,745	166	104,910	2,271,397	185,329	46.3	53.7	36,024	7,784
District 1	5,451	1,180,832	217	97,880	1,731,665	317,678	41.3	58.7	25,698	8,696
District 2	115	7,376	64	182	5,909	51,381	89.3	10.7	304	17,878
District 3	204	20,466	100	112	27,937	136,945	86.8	13.2	118	7,345
District 4	114	7,095	62	628	11,343	99,500	98.2	1.8	38	2,916
District 5	1,850	198,919	108	1,755	70,566	38,144	87.3	12.7	2,074	5,171
District 6	2,360	341,624	145	1,644	199,544	84,552	49.6	50.4	3,123	5,385
District 7	604	69,173	115	305	53,048	87,827	D	D	673	5,342
District 8	1,558	205,260	132	2,404	171,386	110,004	D	D	3,997	7,686
MASSACHUSETTS	7,755	523,517	68	23,433	492,211	63,470	77.8	22.2	8,124	10,415
District 1	2,043	189,425	93	1,513	72,106	35,294	56.3	43.7	2,293	10,059
District 2	1,832	142,899	78	3,554	125,634	68,578	75.5	24.5	1,671	8,033
District 3	936	37,576	40	1,304	40,736	43,522	71.8	28.2	565	8,972
District 4	750	33,528	45	2,149	41,671	55,562	88.0	12.0	467	6,578
District 5	196	6,332	32	700	43,367	221,262	99.3	0.7	D	D
District 6	464	18,673	40	464	20,476	44,129	74.9	25.1	174	9,141
District 7	23	282	12	30	164	7,113	86.0	13.4	D	D
District 8	162	5,471	34	612	9,196	56,763	66.6	33.4	120	7,031
District 9	1,349	89,331	66	13,107	138,861	102,936	84.1	15.9	2,740	18,269

Table E. Congressional Districts 115th Congress — **Nonfarm Employment and Payroll**

STATE District	Number of establish-ments	Total	Manufact-uring	Construc-tion	Wholesale trade	Retail trade	Health care and social assistance	Finance and Insurance	Real estate and rental and leasing	Professio-nal, scientific, and technical services	Information	Total (mil dol)	Average per employee (dollars)
	73	74	75	76	77	78	79	80	81	82	83	84	85
ILLINOIS— Cont'd													
District 3	15,644	227,989	11.9	6.1	4.9	13.9	14.2	2.5	1.3	4.6	0.8	10,218	44,820
District 4	11,019	140,177	15.5	3.7	7.6	17.5	17.0	2.7	1.1	2.4	1.0	5,593	39,897
District 5	23,375	383,537	7.6	3.4	5.0	10.4	13.2	3.7	2.8	5.7	2.4	20,306	52,945
District 6	25,612	390,897	9.3	4.3	6.2	12.4	12.6	7.3	1.1	7.2	2.7	21,477	54,942
District 7	30,036	817,997	2.6	1.5	2.8	4.7	12.9	16.0	2.1	17.9	5.3	67,193	82,143
District 8	23,551	418,644	12.8	6.1	12.0	9.9	8.3	5.0	1.8	6.9	3.2	24,366	58,202
District 9	20,623	299,523	6.8	2.9	4.5	12.0	23.5	2.9	1.8	5.8	2.1	15,337	51,204
District 10	21,561	368,852	10.4	3.2	12.8	10.8	12.1	7.4	1.1	11.0	1.3	27,883	75,595
District 11	16,098	274,618	9.8	4.0	8.6	16.1	14.1	3.1	1.2	4.8	1.4	12,675	46,154
District 12	14,685	217,707	12.0	4.4	3.5	16.2	19.6	3.2	1.1	4.3	1.1	8,363	38,414
District 13	15,495	246,755	7.4	4.8	4.1	13.9	22.4	4.4	1.7	4.5	2.4	9,796	39,701
District 14	17,645	192,487	13.7	7.7	6.0	15.8	11.9	3.0	1.1	5.8	1.0	8,547	44,402
District 15	15,367	202,608	19.3	4.5	5.7	13.2	18.4	3.6	1.0	2.4	1.3	7,472	36,880
District 16	15,063	223,584	19.9	3.5	4.7	14.9	15.3	3.5	1.1	3.4	1.2	9,297	41,581
District 17	14,851	267,932	15.1	3.4	3.9	11.6	19.4	3.5	0.8	3.8	1.4	13,233	49,388
District 18	16,029	253,201	9.8	4.4	6.4	16.5	14.1	12.3	0.9	3.4	1.3	10,842	42,821
INDIANA	146,078	2,720,277	18.4	4.5	4.3	12.0	15.6	3.7	1.3	4.7	1.6	117,009	43,014
District 1	14,793	237,701	15.0	5.6	3.2	15.5	19.3	2.5	1.2	3.4	1.0	10,201	42,916
District 2	15,621	316,002	33.7	3.1	4.8	10.7	13.2	2.5	0.9	2.6	1.3	13,236	41,886
District 3	17,467	320,650	27.0	4.0	5.1	11.8	15.6	3.6	1.1	2.6	1.5	13,236	41,280
District 4	15,058	255,057	22.9	4.8	4.1	14.7	14.7	2.2	1.1	2.5	1.0	9,902	38,823
District 5	21,571	384,196	6.6	4.3	4.7	11.9	16.1	7.5	1.9	8.2	2.6	18,357	47,781
District 6	14,280	239,973	22.1	4.0	2.8	12.5	17.0	3.1	0.8	3.8	1.0	9,481	39,507
District 7	15,162	350,471	9.5	5.6	5.6	8.8	15.8	4.1	2.2	7.2	3.0	17,748	50,639
District 8	16,244	278,663	20.0	5.6	4.7	13.0	17.8	3.3	1.0	3.2	1.4	11,411	40,949
District 9	15,232	239,013	19.1	5.4	3.6	15.3	16.6	3.0	1.2	3.2	1.2	8,904	37,253
IOWA	81,563	1,354,487	15.4	4.9	5.1	13.8	16.5	7.3	1.0	4.1	2.2	56,930	42,031
District 1	19,583	349,963	18.1	4.5	4.6	13.7	16.4	6.3	0.9	4.0	2.2	14,387	41,110
District 2	18,874	314,996	19.6	5.2	3.8	14.5	18.5	3.3	0.9	3.7	2.0	12,471	39,590
District 3	20,647	375,053	8.2	5.0	5.3	13.7	14.4	13.8	1.4	5.1	2.5	17,821	47,517
District 4	22,066	288,970	18.4	5.4	6.9	14.6	18.5	3.6	0.9	3.2	2.0	10,935	37,840
KANSAS	74,884	1,184,710	13.5	5.5	5.3	13.0	16.2	5.1	1.3	5.5	2.6	51,016	43,062
District 1	20,010	241,515	16.6	4.9	5.8	15.4	18.2	4.0	1.1	3.1	1.9	8,403	34,794
District 2	15,898	235,451	14.1	6.2	3.1	13.7	20.2	4.4	1.1	5.4	1.5	8,825	37,480
District 3	21,283	392,420	8.4	5.4	7.1	11.8	13.6	7.5	1.5	8.1	4.3	20,771	52,930
District 4	17,199	282,513	19.0	6.1	4.3	13.5	16.0	3.3	1.4	4.4	1.9	11,914	42,173
KENTUCKY	92,000	1,603,173	14.7	4.4	4.5	13.4	15.9	4.7	1.1	4.7	2.0	65,243	40,696
District 1	14,355	216,646	22.8	4.4	3.6	15.1	16.1	3.0	1.0	2.6	1.2	7,715	35,611
District 2	14,608	233,403	19.7	4.7	3.0	14.5	16.5	3.7	1.1	2.7	2.8	8,515	36,482
District 3	19,425	415,566	11.0	4.3	4.8	10.6	15.3	7.4	1.3	5.4	2.1	20,441	49,188
District 4	14,364	246,768	13.9	4.4	5.7	13.7	14.0	5.4	1.2	3.2	1.2	10,395	42,123
District 5	11,560	161,572	10.4	2.9	3.3	18.6	22.4	3.4	1.0	5.6	2.6	5,242	32,442
District 6	17,215	286,388	15.2	5.4	4.6	13.9	16.5	2.9	1.3	6.3	2.5	11,846	41,365
LOUISIANA	105,732	1,709,226	6.9	7.9	4.4	14.0	17.2	3.8	1.8	5.7	1.8	75,125	43,953
District 1	21,106	322,609	4.9	5.3	5.3	14.8	17.6	4.6	2.1	5.3	3.3	14,633	45,357
District 2	16,070	296,096	8.4	5.1	3.7	11.0	12.7	3.7	1.8	6.9	1.2	14,281	48,232
District 3	19,703	287,295	8.8	6.1	5.3	14.9	17.8	2.9	2.6	5.4	1.3	12,334	42,931
District 4	15,002	216,636	8.6	6.2	4.3	15.9	21.9	3.3	1.5	3.7	1.4	8,162	37,676
District 5	15,112	210,895	8.0	5.3	3.9	16.7	26.3	4.1	1.4	4.2	2.0	7,468	35,409
District 6	18,207	329,060	5.1	17.8	4.1	14.3	14.0	4.1	1.5	7.2	1.5	15,561	47,290
MAINE	41,178	511,936	9.7	5.0	3.6	16.4	21.8	5.5	1.3	4.5	2.3	21,349	41,703
District 1	23,366	300,426	9.0	4.9	3.5	15.6	21.3	6.0	1.4	5.1	2.1	13,280	44,205
District 2	17,522	207,750	10.9	5.1	3.5	17.8	22.8	4.5	1.2	3.5	2.6	7,845	37,760
MARYLAND	138,480	2,282,725	4.3	6.6	4.0	12.9	16.2	4.4	2.0	12.1	2.3	121,952	53,424
District 1	17,649	196,831	8.7	7.4	3.8	17.6	18.1	2.7	1.4	4.4	1.1	7,615	38,690
District 2	16,457	341,450	8.4	6.9	7.1	13.4	11.4	4.5	1.9	12.2	1.9	18,882	55,301
District 3	21,075	382,835	2.8	5.2	4.3	11.6	16.0	4.0	2.0	12.9	3.4	21,094	55,099
District 4	12,929	198,099	2.3	8.6	4.3	16.4	14.0	2.6	2.7	10.1	2.0	8,801	44,428
District 5	14,122	208,343	2.2	12.5	3.2	15.7	12.9	2.0	2.3	15.7	1.6	9,840	47,232
District 6	18,921	290,187	6.4	6.4	3.7	15.5	14.6	5.4	1.5	12.1	2.9	14,573	50,219
District 7	15,662	300,115	2.2	2.8	2.2	8.9	26.7	6.8	2.1	11.1	1.8	18,207	60,668
District 8	21,085	320,828	2.1	6.8	2.3	10.0	17.5	5.1	2.4	14.9	2.9	20,160	62,837
MASSACHUSETTS	177,631	3,254,781	6.8	4.0	4.4	11.5	19.8	5.8	1.4	8.7	3.5	204,747	62,907
District 1	16,248	253,580	11.2	4.2	3.5	14.2	23.0	4.9	1.2	3.9	1.3	11,130	43,892
District 2	16,760	295,089	9.0	3.5	4.2	13.2	26.1	5.4	1.0	5.5	1.4	13,255	44,920
District 3	16,467	279,026	14.5	4.3	6.3	10.8	19.1	3.6	1.0	9.4	3.7	18,174	65,132
District 4	20,832	340,133	8.4	4.0	7.0	13.7	16.6	3.8	1.7	6.3	3.0	19,735	58,020
District 5	21,006	388,851	4.1	4.3	4.1	10.0	13.9	4.2	1.5	11.8	5.3	26,718	68,711
District 6	21,277	354,981	10.2	5.2	4.7	13.8	19.0	3.3	1.1	8.4	5.4	21,354	60,154
District 7	17,095	504,144	2.1	1.8	2.7	6.9	21.3	6.3	1.7	11.0	4.1	40,035	79,411
District 8	24,588	536,974	3.3	4.3	3.7	9.6	21.4	12.6	1.9	11.7	3.8	39,550	73,654
District 9	22,707	248,225	6.8	7.1	3.9	18.8	21.0	3.0	1.3	5.0	1.4	11,241	45,286

Note: Private nonfarm employment and payroll, 2016. Employment — Percent by selected industries. Annual payroll.

Table E. Congressional Districts 115th Congress — Land Area and Population Characteristics

STATE District	Representative, 115th Congress	Land area,[1] 2017 (sq mi)	Total persons	Per square mile	Race alone (percent)						Hispanic or Latino[2] (percent)	Non-Hispanic White alone (percent)	Percent female	Percent foreign-born	Percent born in state of residence
					White	Black	American Indian, Alaska Native	Asian and Pacific Islander	Some other race (percent)	Two or more races (percent)					
		1	2	3	4	5	6	7	8	9	10	11	12	13	14
MICHIGAN		56,559.4	9,928,300	175.5	78.5	13.7	0.5	3.0	1.2	3.1	4.9	75.3	50.8	6.7	76.3
District 1	Jack Bergman (R)	25,028.3	699,621	28.0	92.3	1.4	2.6	0.7	0.2	2.9	1.8	91.0	49.3	2.1	79.4
District 2	Bill Huizenga (R)	3,297.3	734,965	222.9	84.7	6.5	0.5	2.3	2.4	3.7	10.0	78.3	50.8	5.7	78.4
District 3	Justin Amash (R)	2,629.5	733,618	279.0	84.2	8.0	0.3	1.8	2.2	3.6	6.9	80.2	50.1	5.4	76.9
District 4	John L. Moolenar (R)	8,458.0	700,487	82.8	93.9	1.7	0.6	1.1	0.3	2.4	3.1	91.6	50.0	1.9	86.1
District 5	Daniel T. Kildee (D)	2,348.9	681,278	290.0	77.3	17.4	0.4	0.9	0.9	3.1	5.0	73.7	51.4	2.1	84.7
District 6	Fred Upton (R)	3,547.7	716,163	201.9	84.4	8.0	0.5	1.6	1.4	4.1	6.1	80.7	50.8	4.6	69.9
District 7	Tim Walberg (R)	4,227.9	700,983	165.8	91.0	4.4	0.5	1.1	0.5	2.4	4.3	87.6	49.8	2.8	74.0
District 8	Mike Bishop (R)	1,503.1	734,008	488.3	85.0	5.7	0.2	5.0	1.0	3.1	5.3	81.6	50.9	8.4	74.4
District 9	Sander M. Levin (D)	183.7	711,069	3,870.8	77.3	14.2	0.2	4.7	0.7	2.9	2.7	75.4	51.3	11.5	75.9
District 10	Paul Mitchell (R)	4,142.2	714,802	172.6	93.2	2.5	0.2	1.6	0.5	2.1	3.1	90.8	50.4	5.8	83.4
District 11	David A.Trott (R)	419.1	732,690	1,748.2	82.1	5.0	0.2	9.4	0.5	2.7	2.9	79.9	51.0	13.6	70.2
District 12	Debbie Dingell (D)	403.2	708,880	1,758.2	78.6	10.9	0.3	4.9	1.3	4.0	6.2	74.5	51.3	11.9	67.3
District 13	Vacant	184.9	658,383	3,561.2	37.7	54.9	0.5	1.4	2.7	2.9	7.4	33.7	52.4	7.5	76.3
District 14	Brenda L. Lawrence (D)	185.6	701,353	3,779.7	33.4	56.1	0.3	4.8	2.1	3.2	4.6	31.4	52.1	9.6	72.4
MINNESOTA		79,625.5	5,519,952	69.3	83.3	6.0	1.1	4.7	2.0	2.8	5.2	80.5	50.2	8.2	68.0
District 1	Timothy J. Walz (D)	11,974.1	672,415	56.2	90.2	3.0	0.3	2.7	1.9	1.8	6.4	86.0	50.2	6.0	69.0
District 2	Jason Lewis (R)	2,437.9	700,264	287.2	84.5	4.5	0.4	4.5	2.8	3.3	6.0	81.5	50.6	8.2	68.0
District 3	Erik Paulsen (R)	527.0	709,906	1,347.1	80.0	8.2	0.3	7.1	1.7	2.6	4.8	77.2	51.2	12.3	62.6
District 4	Betty McCollum (D)	332.6	702,162	2,111.2	70.3	9.8	0.5	12.3	2.6	4.6	6.7	66.9	51.1	14.3	61.6
District 5	Keith Ellison (D)	135.7	708,082	5,217.3	67.4	16.6	1.2	6.1	4.4	4.2	8.8	63.9	49.8	14.9	56.1
District 6	Tom Emmer (R)	2,881.6	696,720	241.8	90.8	2.9	0.4	2.7	1.0	2.1	2.7	89.4	49.6	4.3	76.6
District 7	Collin C. Peterson (D)	33,429.2	668,049	20.0	91.6	1.1	3.3	1.0	1.3	1.8	4.5	88.8	49.7	2.8	72.4
District 8	Richard M. Nolan (D)	27,907.4	662,354	23.7	92.9	1.0	2.9	0.8	0.3	2.0	1.7	91.9	49.2	1.8	78.5
MISSISSIPPI		46,923.1	2,988,726	63.7	58.5	38.0	0.4	0.9	1.0	1.1	2.9	56.8	51.8	2.0	71.5
District 1	Trent Kelly (R)	10,572.9	764,223	72.3	68.6	28.1	0.2	0.7	1.1	1.3	2.9	66.9	52.1	1.8	64.2
District 2	Bennie G. Thompson (D)	15,551.4	705,911	45.4	30.8	66.6	0.4	0.4	1.1	0.7	1.8	30.4	51.9	1.1	83.7
District 3	Gregg Harper (R)	12,754.2	751,004	58.9	60.9	35.8	0.9	0.8	0.9	0.6	2.7	59.1	51.5	2.2	77.8
District 4	Steven Palazzo (R)	8,044.5	767,588	95.4	71.6	23.6	0.3	1.6	1.0	1.8	4.1	68.9	51.7	2.7	61.7
MISSOURI		68,746.3	6,093,000	88.6	82.3	11.5	0.5	2.1	1.2	2.5	4.0	79.6	50.9	4.1	66.3
District 1	William Lacy Clay (D)	225.2	735,410	3,265.3	43.3	49.0	0.3	3.1	1.3	3.0	3.6	40.9	52.9	5.9	69.6
District 2	Ann Wagner (R)	465.8	763,176	1,638.4	89.4	4.1	0.1	4.4	0.4	1.6	2.6	87.1	51.3	8.1	65.7
District 3	Blaine Luetkemeyer (R)	6,851.5	783,679	114.4	92.5	3.4	0.3	1.1	0.5	2.2	2.4	90.8	50.1	1.8	76.0
District 4	Vicky Hartzler (R)	14,406.0	761,860	52.9	88.9	4.7	0.8	2.0	0.9	2.8	3.6	86.5	49.7	3.5	62.1
District 5	Emanuel Cleaver (D)	2,425.2	763,288	314.7	68.4	22.3	0.5	2.3	3.6	3.0	9.1	63.6	51.9	5.7	60.7
District 6	Sam Graves (R)	18,195.5	767,878	42.2	90.4	3.9	0.3	1.6	1.0	2.8	3.9	87.9	50.0	3.1	64.7
District 7	Bill Long (R)	6,272.8	776,586	123.8	91.7	1.9	1.2	1.5	1.2	2.5	5.0	88.2	50.9	3.3	58.2
District 8	Jason T. Smith (R)	19,901.1	741,123	37.2	91.7	4.7	0.6	0.8	0.3	1.9	1.7	90.6	50.1	1.4	73.4
MONTANA		145,545.4	1,042,520	7.2	89.0	0.4	6.4	0.9	0.4	3.1	3.6	86.4	49.5	2.1	54.7
At Large	Greg Gianforte (R)	145,545.4	1,042,520	7.2	89.0	0.4	6.4	0.9	0.4	3.1	3.6	86.4	49.5	2.1	54.7
NEBRASKA		76,818.1	1,907,116	24.8	87.4	4.7	0.8	2.2	2.0	2.4	10.6	79.7	50.2	7.0	64.7
District 1	Jeff Fortenberry (R)	8,879.0	639,048	72.0	89.2	3.1	1.3	2.4	1.4	2.6	8.7	82.5	49.7	7.0	67.4
District 2	Don Bacon (R)	509.7	661,142	1,297.1	81.9	9.6	0.3	3.5	1.8	2.9	11.1	72.9	50.5	8.6	59.4
District 3	Adrian Smith (R)	67,429.4	606,926	9.0	92.9	1.1	0.9	0.6	2.9	1.5	12.1	84.2	50.3	5.4	67.5
NEVADA		109,780.2	2,940,058	26.8	66.9	8.9	1.2	9.0	9.3	4.7	28.5	49.8	49.9	20.0	26.4
District 1	Dina Titus (D)	104.5	722,331	6,913.0	53.0	11.5	0.7	10.2	20.0	4.6	46.6	29.0	49.0	32.9	24.2
District 2	Mark E. Amodei (R)	55,829.3	713,779	12.8	80.9	1.7	2.5	4.6	6.5	3.7	22.3	66.6	49.5	12.5	31.6
District 3	Jacky Rosen (D)	2,848.9	779,908	273.8	68.0	6.7	0.5	15.2	3.7	5.9	16.6	56.7	50.6	17.9	22.7
District 4	Ruben J. Kihuen (D)	50,997.4	724,040	14.2	65.7	15.6	1.1	5.4	7.6	4.7	29.1	46.4	50.4	16.6	27.7
NEW HAMPSHIRE		8,952.7	1,334,795	149.1	93.4	1.2	0.1	2.5	0.6	2.2	3.5	90.7	50.2	5.7	41.7
District 1	Carol Shea-Porter (D)	2,464.5	671,625	272.5	93.4	1.3	0.1	2.6	0.4	2.2	3.5	90.6	49.7	5.6	41.8
District 2	Ann M. Kuster (D)	6,488.2	663,170	102.2	93.5	1.2	0.2	2.3	0.8	2.1	3.5	90.9	50.8	5.9	41.6
NEW JERSEY		7,355.1	8,944,469	1,216.1	68.1	13.4	0.2	9.6	6.1	2.7	20.0	55.5	51.1	22.5	52.2
District 1	Donald Norcross (D)	350.2	731,932	2,090.0	67.8	17.0	0.1	5.2	6.7	3.1	13.6	62.5	51.7	9.8	54.9
District 2	Frank A. LoBiondo (R)	2,095.0	725,217	346.2	75.4	12.2	0.4	4.0	5.0	3.0	16.4	65.5	50.7	10.5	59.8
District 3	Thomas MacArthur (R)	898.2	739,696	823.5	79.7	10.8	0.1	4.0	2.2	3.2	8.1	74.8	51.1	9.1	61.9
District 4	Christopher H. Smith (R)	691.2	732,142	1,059.2	84.7	6.8	0.1	3.9	3.0	1.5	10.1	78.2	51.8	11.9	59.1
District 5	Josh Gottheimer (D)	991.6	742,865	749.1	79.5	5.4	0.3	11.1	1.5	2.3	14.0	68.2	51.3	20.2	52.3
District 6	Frank Pallone Jr. (D)	215.2	750,419	3,486.4	63.7	10.0	0.2	19.3	4.2	2.5	22.0	47.4	50.6	29.5	49.7
District 7	Leonard Lance (R)	969.9	732,070	754.8	78.8	5.0	0.1	9.5	4.6	2.0	13.0	70.6	50.6	19.1	55.6
District 8	Albio Sires (D)	54.7	778,294	14,232.8	57.4	10.3	0.4	9.5	18.7	3.8	52.1	26.1	50.1	44.5	36.6
District 9	Bill Pascrell, Jr. (D)	95.3	760,005	7,974.2	62.2	10.1	0.2	12.6	11.7	3.2	37.6	38.8	51.6	38.3	42.9
District 10	Donald M. Payne, Jr. (D)	75.8	758,062	9,996.5	29.0	51.5	0.3	7.0	9.1	3.1	21.1	18.7	52.0	29.0	50.1
District 11	Rodney P. Frelinghuysen (R)	505.8	733,706	1,450.5	82.0	3.2	0.0	10.8	1.8	2.2	11.2	73.0	51.1	18.3	58.1
District 12	Bonnie Watson Coleman (D)	412.1	760,061	1,844.4	59.4	17.1	0.4	17.5	3.7	1.9	18.1	46.5	51.3	27.7	46.8
NEW MEXICO		121,310.0	2,081,015	17.2	74.0	2.0	9.3	1.6	9.9	3.2	48.5	37.8	50.5	9.5	52.9
District 1	Michelle Lujan Grisham (D)	4,600.8	702,719	152.7	71.3	2.7	4.9	2.7	14.7	3.6	49.5	39.4	51.3	10.1	53.6
District 2	Steve Pearce (R)	71,745.4	691,695	9.6	85.3	1.9	5.1	0.7	4.7	2.3	54.9	36.7	49.6	12.4	49.3

1. Dry land or land partially or temporarily covered by water.   2. May be of any race.

Items 1—14

STATE District	Under 5 years (15)	5 to 17 years (16)	18 to 24 years (17)	25 to 34 years (18)	35 to 44 years (19)	45 to 54 years (20)	55 to 64 years (21)	65 to 74 years (22)	75 years and over (23)	Median age (24)	Total Enrollment[1] (25)	High school graduate or more (26)	Bachelor's degree or more (27)
MICHIGAN	5.8	16.3	9.8	12.6	11.7	13.6	14.0	9.5	6.7	39.7	2,488,397	90.4	28.3
District 1	4.7	14.1	8.6	10.4	10.5	13.0	16.4	12.9	9.3	46.4	147,418	91.9	24.6
District 2	6.5	17.5	10.9	13.0	11.5	12.7	12.9	8.6	6.3	36.8	184,393	89.8	23.8
District 3	6.4	17.6	9.1	14.0	12.2	13.2	13.4	8.3	5.9	37.2	185,654	90.8	31.4
District 4	5.1	15.6	11.1	11.3	10.9	13.2	14.6	10.5	7.7	41.4	174,883	91.1	21.9
District 5	5.8	16.4	8.8	11.9	11.5	13.4	14.5	10.2	7.5	41.0	163,633	90.1	19.0
District 6	5.9	16.7	10.8	12.1	11.4	12.8	13.8	9.7	6.7	38.8	184,294	90.3	28.0
District 7	5.3	16.7	8.7	11.3	11.9	14.1	14.9	10.1	6.8	41.9	167,911	91.7	24.6
District 8	5.3	16.5	12.9	11.8	11.8	14.3	13.2	8.8	5.4	38.1	215,805	94.2	40.6
District 9	5.6	14.5	7.8	15.4	12.3	13.5	14.6	9.3	7.0	40.5	158,401	90.0	30.3
District 10	4.9	16.4	8.0	10.8	11.5	15.8	15.1	10.3	7.2	43.6	163,919	90.7	23.0
District 11	5.7	16.3	8.0	11.9	12.6	15.0	14.8	9.2	6.4	41.5	185,212	94.6	46.6
District 12	5.8	15.4	14.2	14.2	11.3	12.8	12.4	8.3	5.6	35.3	214,447	89.9	34.0
District 13	6.8	17.6	9.8	14.1	11.6	13.1	13.7	7.7	5.6	36.3	168,164	81.8	14.7
District 14	6.6	17.0	9.0	13.7	12.4	13.3	12.6	8.7	6.8	37.7	174,263	87.6	30.8
MINNESOTA	6.4	17.0	9.2	13.5	12.4	13.2	13.4	8.6	6.5	37.9	1,392,956	92.9	34.8
District 1	6.4	16.7	10.5	12.6	11.4	12.3	13.5	8.9	7.9	38.3	167,492	91.6	28.0
District 2	6.6	18.5	8.5	12.1	13.4	14.6	13.3	7.6	5.5	37.7	179,798	94.6	38.5
District 3	6.0	18.3	6.4	12.9	12.7	14.6	14.3	8.6	6.2	40.1	179,513	95.0	49.0
District 4	6.7	17.1	9.8	15.2	12.0	12.5	12.9	8.0	5.8	36.0	188,379	91.5	42.2
District 5	7.0	13.3	11.0	20.4	13.3	11.6	11.4	6.7	5.2	34.0	176,212	91.2	44.5
District 6	6.4	18.8	9.4	12.3	13.6	14.5	12.7	7.5	4.7	37.1	190,336	94.8	29.5
District 7	6.4	17.2	9.1	11.2	11.0	12.0	14.2	10.0	8.9	40.2	159,478	91.1	21.8
District 8	5.3	15.9	8.8	11.0	11.0	13.1	15.5	11.2	8.4	43.4	151,748	93.3	23.0
MISSISSIPPI	6.3	17.9	10.3	12.7	12.5	12.5	12.6	9.0	6.0	37.2	781,666	84.1	21.8
District 1	5.8	18.0	10.5	12.0	12.7	13.1	12.4	9.3	6.2	37.9	199,345	83.7	20.7
District 2	6.9	18.2	10.2	13.1	12.4	11.8	12.9	9.1	5.7	36.2	190,196	80.6	19.3
District 3	5.9	18.1	10.5	12.5	12.5	12.6	12.7	8.9	6.1	37.1	196,086	85.5	25.9
District 4	6.4	17.6	10.1	13.0	12.5	12.8	12.7	8.9	6.2	37.5	196,039	86.4	21.1
MISSOURI	6.1	16.8	9.6	13.1	12.1	13.0	13.4	9.2	6.8	38.4	1,507,305	89.6	28.5
District 1	6.4	15.4	10.3	17.2	12.4	12.3	13.1	7.7	5.3	35.5	187,516	88.8	31.8
District 2	5.3	16.6	7.3	11.2	12.0	14.0	15.0	9.9	8.5	43.2	181,382	94.8	49.2
District 3	6.2	17.7	8.8	12.5	12.4	13.6	13.7	9.2	6.0	38.7	195,447	90.5	26.4
District 4	6.1	16.4	12.5	12.8	11.3	12.1	12.5	9.3	6.9	36.6	201,757	88.6	23.9
District 5	6.8	16.6	8.6	15.2	12.2	12.8	13.0	8.4	6.4	37.1	175,551	90.1	28.2
District 6	5.9	17.7	9.1	12.1	12.7	13.5	13.1	9.2	6.7	38.7	190,026	91.1	28.6
District 7	6.2	16.8	10.9	12.6	11.7	12.4	12.6	9.7	7.1	37.7	198,781	88.5	23.2
District 8	5.9	16.7	8.9	11.6	11.9	13.2	13.9	10.2	7.7	40.8	176,845	83.7	15.0
MONTANA	5.9	16.1	9.7	12.2	11.5	12.3	14.8	10.5	7.1	40.1	242,914	92.8	31.0
At Large	5.9	16.1	9.7	12.2	11.5	12.3	14.8	10.5	7.1	40.1	242,914	92.8	31.0
NEBRASKA	6.9	17.9	9.9	13.4	12.3	12.0	12.7	8.3	6.6	36.3	505,491	90.9	31.4
District 1	6.6	17.4	12.1	13.5	11.9	11.5	12.5	8.5	6.4	35.4	176,414	92.3	32.5
District 2	7.6	18.6	8.7	15.4	13.4	12.6	11.7	7.1	4.9	34.8	183,149	90.7	39.2
District 3	6.6	17.7	9.0	11.3	11.3	12.0	13.9	9.6	8.9	39.8	145,928	89.6	22.2
NEVADA	6.2	16.8	8.6	14.4	13.3	13.3	12.4	9.4	5.5	37.9	700,680	86.0	23.5
District 1	6.5	16.3	10.3	15.3	13.5	13.5	11.4	8.3	4.8	36.0	161,983	77.3	15.2
District 2	6.0	16.0	9.0	13.5	11.8	13.1	14.0	10.5	6.0	39.5	173,903	87.9	25.5
District 3	6.5	15.9	6.4	15.2	14.4	13.4	12.1	9.9	6.0	39.0	180,643	93.2	31.5
District 4	5.9	18.8	8.8	13.6	13.4	13.2	11.9	8.8	5.6	37.0	184,151	84.6	20.4
NEW HAMPSHIRE	4.8	14.7	9.5	12.0	11.4	15.1	15.4	10.1	6.9	42.7	307,848	92.8	36.6
District 1	4.7	14.5	10.0	12.4	11.8	15.0	15.6	9.6	6.4	41.9	158,449	93.4	37.2
District 2	4.9	14.8	9.0	11.6	11.0	15.3	15.3	10.7	7.3	43.6	149,399	92.3	35.9
NEW JERSEY	5.8	16.4	8.8	12.9	12.9	14.4	13.4	8.8	6.6	39.5	2,239,783	89.3	38.6
District 1	5.9	16.4	8.8	13.7	12.6	13.9	13.4	8.9	6.4	38.8	178,220	90.1	30.4
District 2	5.5	16.1	8.4	12.1	11.5	14.1	14.4	10.6	7.2	41.4	170,942	87.1	25.8
District 3	5.1	15.5	8.5	11.5	11.4	14.6	14.3	10.7	8.3	43.3	174,587	92.8	33.9
District 4	6.6	17.6	8.3	10.4	11.0	14.2	13.7	9.8	8.2	41.3	187,237	92.0	39.6
District 5	5.2	17.3	8.4	10.4	11.9	16.1	14.6	9.0	7.0	42.3	192,609	93.7	47.7
District 6	5.9	15.4	10.5	14.3	13.6	14.0	12.9	7.6	5.8	37.6	198,176	88.7	38.9
District 7	5.0	17.4	7.9	10.1	12.6	16.6	15.0	8.6	6.9	42.7	181,239	93.4	51.3
District 8	6.5	14.9	9.0	19.7	16.1	12.9	10.6	6.3	4.1	35.0	187,960	79.6	33.1
District 9	6.0	16.1	8.8	14.0	14.0	13.9	12.5	8.2	6.5	38.3	185,828	84.5	33.6
District 10	7.3	16.7	10.2	15.4	13.8	13.6	11.5	6.8	4.7	35.3	203,894	85.8	28.3
District 11	5.1	16.0	8.2	10.2	12.6	15.9	14.5	9.8	7.9	43.4	183,764	94.8	54.4
District 12	5.6	17.0	8.7	12.7	13.2	14.3	13.3	8.6	6.5	39.4	195,327	89.6	45.5
NEW MEXICO	6.0	17.5	9.6	13.3	12.0	12.0	13.1	9.8	6.7	37.7	539,773	85.4	27.2
District 1	5.8	16.2	9.1	14.6	12.2	12.8	13.4	9.8	6.2	38.3	177,738	88.4	32.9
District 2	6.3	18.2	10.8	12.8	11.5	11.3	12.6	9.3	7.1	36.6	182,592	80.8	21.0

1. All persons 3 years old and over enrolled in nursery school through college and graduate or professional school.   2. Persons 25 years old and over.

Table E. Congressional Districts 115th Congress — **Age and Education**

STATE District	Under 5 years	5 to 17 years	18 to 24 years	25 to 34 years	35 to 44 years	45 to 54 years	55 to 64 years	65 to 74 years	75 years and over	Median age	Total Enrollment[1]	High school graduate or more	Bachelor's degree or more
	15	16	17	18	19	20	21	22	23	24	25	26	27
NEW MEXICO— Cont'd													
District 3	5.9	18.2	8.9	12.6	12.2	11.9	13.5	10.1	6.7	38.2	179,443	86.8	27.2
NEW YORK	5.9	15.3	9.7	14.6	12.5	13.8	13.0	8.7	6.6	38.4	4,843,659	86.3	35.7
District 1	4.7	16.6	9.7	10.7	12.1	15.5	13.5	10.2	7.2	41.7	181,325	92.3	34.1
District 2	6.0	15.8	9.2	12.9	11.9	16.1	14.1	7.9	6.1	40.3	173,068	88.9	31.2
District 3	5.6	15.3	7.9	10.2	11.5	14.4	15.2	10.2	9.6	44.5	176,178	93.1	51.6
District 4	5.5	17.0	9.4	12.2	12.0	14.4	13.1	9.0	7.4	40.3	190,039	89.6	42.5
District 5	6.2	16.2	10.0	14.2	12.5	14.6	13.1	7.5	5.5	37.3	215,011	82.2	25.5
District 6	5.8	13.4	7.0	15.9	14.0	13.7	14.5	8.9	6.8	40.4	170,622	83.7	35.9
District 7	7.2	16.0	9.1	21.1	14.1	12.2	9.9	5.9	4.4	33.2	185,718	71.9	33.7
District 8	6.2	14.5	9.5	17.9	12.9	12.9	12.1	7.4	6.5	36.2	186,199	84.7	33.7
District 9	6.7	16.7	8.1	16.3	14.0	12.6	12.3	8.2	5.1	36.4	191,703	84.8	37.5
District 10	7.2	12.0	8.8	18.5	15.5	11.5	11.6	8.6	6.2	37.1	159,796	88.7	60.3
District 11	6.3	15.6	8.4	14.2	13.0	13.8	13.0	9.1	6.6	39.0	178,860	86.1	34.4
District 12	4.6	7.4	8.5	28.0	14.8	12.1	10.0	8.0	6.5	35.7	120,260	93.4	72.2
District 13	6.3	14.3	10.2	20.4	13.6	12.8	10.6	6.6	5.2	34.4	204,516	75.3	31.0
District 14	6.7	13.8	8.2	16.8	16.1	13.5	11.0	7.7	6.2	37.6	158,998	77.6	25.6
District 15	7.7	20.5	11.9	16.3	12.2	12.3	9.8	5.6	3.5	30.7	236,117	65.5	12.4
District 16	6.1	15.6	9.5	12.0	12.9	14.2	12.4	8.9	8.2	40.0	185,716	85.0	40.6
District 17	6.3	18.4	9.2	11.3	12.2	14.3	12.9	8.5	6.9	39.1	204,200	86.6	44.5
District 18	5.5	17.7	9.9	11.3	12.1	15.2	13.6	8.6	6.0	39.6	186,624	90.3	35.7
District 19	4.4	14.4	10.4	10.8	10.3	15.1	15.5	11.2	7.8	44.6	151,671	89.3	29.2
District 20	5.4	14.4	12.4	13.4	11.5	13.6	13.3	9.2	6.7	38.9	182,585	91.3	38.7
District 21	5.4	14.9	10.5	12.6	11.2	14.1	14.2	10.0	7.2	40.6	155,650	89.4	23.2
District 22	5.4	15.2	11.4	11.5	10.7	13.7	14.3	9.9	7.8	41.0	173,042	89.2	26.0
District 23	5.3	15.0	12.5	11.8	10.4	12.9	14.7	10.0	7.5	40.2	179,782	89.5	26.1
District 24	5.5	15.7	10.6	12.5	11.2	13.9	14.2	9.3	7.0	39.6	176,336	89.4	30.3
District 25	5.6	15.6	10.5	14.0	11.1	13.3	13.5	9.2	7.2	38.5	186,609	89.8	37.3
District 26	5.8	14.6	10.5	14.7	10.9	12.6	14.1	9.1	7.5	38.4	173,262	89.8	30.8
District 27	4.7	15.6	8.4	11.7	11.4	15.3	15.0	10.4	7.4	43.6	159,772	93.3	30.7
NORTH CAROLINA	5.9	16.7	9.6	13.0	12.9	13.6	12.7	9.3	6.1	38.7	2,523,926	87.3	30.4
District 1	5.6	15.8	11.1	13.7	12.2	12.8	13.1	9.4	6.4	38.0	190,413	83.0	27.7
District 2	6.5	19.9	7.5	12.2	14.0	15.3	11.7	8.0	4.8	37.8	226,248	89.8	36.2
District 3	6.3	16.0	12.2	13.2	11.1	12.0	12.9	9.8	6.5	37.2	179,602	88.4	22.8
District 4	6.0	16.0	11.7	16.5	14.5	13.4	11.4	6.4	4.1	34.9	240,340	92.3	54.5
District 5	5.4	16.0	10.4	11.5	12.0	13.8	13.7	10.1	7.2	40.5	182,296	85.9	26.3
District 6	5.4	17.2	8.3	11.2	12.8	14.4	13.9	10.0	7.0	41.1	185,541	84.8	24.6
District 7	5.4	15.2	9.5	11.5	12.4	13.0	14.3	11.9	6.9	42.1	174,939	87.1	24.9
District 8	6.9	17.4	9.6	14.1	12.7	12.6	11.9	8.9	5.8	36.3	198,447	89.3	26.5
District 9	5.8	19.8	8.0	11.1	13.7	14.7	13.0	8.4	5.3	39.0	205,457	86.9	33.8
District 10	5.2	16.0	8.5	11.9	12.6	14.3	13.9	10.6	7.1	41.8	170,262	86.0	24.6
District 11	4.8	14.5	8.1	11.0	11.2	13.7	14.6	13.1	9.0	45.3	153,435	85.6	24.0
District 12	7.1	17.1	10.0	18.2	15.0	13.1	9.9	6.1	3.6	33.6	224,791	89.0	39.8
District 13	5.6	16.8	9.9	12.5	12.1	14.3	12.8	9.2	6.8	39.5	192,155	86.5	27.0
NORTH DAKOTA	7.2	15.8	11.7	15.3	11.4	11.5	12.6	7.7	6.8	35.0	181,543	92.4	29.6
At Large	7.2	15.8	11.7	15.3	11.4	11.5	12.6	7.7	6.8	35.0	181,543	92.4	29.6
OHIO	6.0	16.5	9.3	12.9	11.9	13.3	13.9	9.3	7.0	39.3	2,830,005	90.0	27.5
District 1	6.8	17.8	9.5	13.7	12.1	13.1	13.3	8.1	5.9	36.8	191,465	90.6	33.8
District 2	5.8	16.6	7.9	13.5	12.2	14.1	13.6	9.2	7.1	40.1	161,682	89.2	32.3
District 3	7.8	17.3	11.2	18.1	13.1	11.9	10.8	6.1	3.6	32.2	218,216	87.6	27.8
District 4	5.8	16.7	9.7	11.4	12.1	13.2	14.2	9.6	7.2	40.7	170,772	89.7	17.9
District 5	5.8	16.4	9.9	12.2	11.6	12.9	14.3	9.5	7.3	39.9	179,085	92.6	26.2
District 6	5.2	15.8	8.4	10.9	11.7	13.6	15.4	10.9	8.1	43.4	150,496	87.2	15.9
District 7	5.9	17.9	8.0	11.0	11.6	13.3	14.7	10.4	7.3	41.0	169,901	88.6	20.9
District 8	6.1	17.5	10.2	11.6	11.7	13.3	13.6	9.3	6.8	38.5	184,589	89.4	23.8
District 9	6.2	16.3	9.9	13.8	11.8	13.0	13.4	9.1	6.5	38.0	168,106	87.2	21.6
District 10	6.0	15.9	9.9	13.4	11.4	12.7	13.7	9.7	7.4	39.2	189,513	90.6	27.9
District 11	6.2	15.6	10.2	13.8	11.2	12.7	14.0	9.1	7.3	38.5	172,769	88.0	26.8
District 12	5.9	17.3	8.5	12.8	13.3	14.2	13.0	8.8	6.3	38.9	191,348	93.0	41.0
District 13	5.3	14.4	10.8	12.8	11.4	13.0	14.5	10.1	7.9	40.6	167,873	90.0	23.7
District 14	4.8	16.6	7.4	10.6	11.0	14.8	15.8	10.7	8.3	44.7	161,543	91.7	34.1
District 15	6.0	15.9	9.4	14.7	12.7	13.5	13.2	8.5	6.0	38.0	184,544	91.0	31.4
District 16	5.6	15.7	8.2	11.9	11.2	14.0	14.7	10.1	8.6	42.9	168,103	93.5	33.3
OKLAHOMA	6.7	17.8	9.9	13.7	12.1	12.2	12.5	8.7	6.2	36.4	1,004,589	87.8	25.2
District 1	7.1	18.1	8.8	14.3	12.7	12.5	12.5	8.2	5.9	36.2	203,425	89.6	30.2
District 2	6.2	17.4	9.2	12.0	11.4	12.5	13.3	10.6	7.5	39.5	177,822	85.4	17.0
District 3	6.5	17.8	11.0	12.8	11.9	12.2	12.4	8.8	6.6	36.6	204,780	88.2	22.9
District 4	6.1	17.5	11.6	13.7	12.2	12.4	12.3	8.6	5.7	35.8	210,411	89.8	25.5
District 5	7.7	18.0	9.2	15.5	12.7	11.8	11.9	7.8	5.6	34.7	208,151	86.3	30.1
OREGON	5.7	15.5	9.0	14.0	13.0	12.5	13.4	10.2	6.7	39.2	960,446	90.3	32.7
District 1	5.9	16.6	8.2	15.0	14.3	13.3	12.5	8.7	5.4	37.7	198,746	91.8	41.1
District 2	5.6	16.1	7.9	12.2	11.6	12.0	14.5	11.9	8.0	41.6	176,093	88.2	23.8

1. All persons 3 years old and over enrolled in nursery school through college and graduate or professional school.   2. Persons 25 years old and over.

STATE District	Households, 2016						Group Quarters, 2010					
	Number	Average household size	Family households (percent)	Married couple family (percent)	Female family house-holder[1]	One person households (percent)	Total in group quarters, 2016	Percent 65 years and over	Persons in correctional institutions	Persons in nursing facilities	Persons in college dormitories	Persons in military quarters
	28	29	30	31	32	33	34	35	36	37	38	39
NEW MEXICO— Cont'd												
District 3	245,991	2.74	62.5	43.9	13.5	31.6	12,632	17.2	3,544	1,465	2,115	444
NEW YORK	7,209,054	2.66	63.0	43.8	14.1	29.9	575,964	19.7	95,306	116,558	218,960	8,100
District 1	237,708	2.94	72.3	57.6	10.7	22.8	20,248	20.6	1,648	4,504	9,203	6
District 2	217,363	3.26	75.4	57.1	12.4	21.2	6,185	46.7	6	2,952	720	4
District 3	247,036	2.91	74.6	63.2	7.8	22.0	13,156	41.2	10	5,607	3,982	4
District 4	230,997	3.08	75.3	58.4	13.0	21.4	11,537	28.5	1,657	4,200	4,748	0
District 5	224,668	3.47	75.5	43.9	24.2	21.1	14,739	30.2	234	5,713	2,367	0
District 6	266,579	2.80	65.2	48.4	12.5	28.5	6,516	62.0	17	4,179	812	0
District 7	256,169	2.93	61.4	39.3	16.3	26.2	13,039	12.2	3,636	1,600	1,803	0
District 8	284,949	2.64	59.5	29.6	22.5	32.0	18,820	26.0	256	4,120	2,056	0
District 9	274,241	2.66	60.6	34.2	20.4	31.3	8,138	27.0	0	2,585	611	0
District 10	302,765	2.27	48.2	39.4	5.8	41.6	20,960	10.2	165	2,076	16,711	0
District 11	257,947	2.82	71.4	53.1	13.6	24.9	7,979	36.4	924	3,540	1,457	60
District 12	358,652	1.92	37.5	30.4	5.3	48.7	27,110	10.4	414	3,896	16,755	0
District 13	292,811	2.72	56.6	24.2	24.5	33.9	14,857	29.6	334	5,101	1,924	0
District 14	234,113	2.89	63.1	39.2	16.3	29.2	14,842	21.9	11,095	5,195	2,355	0
District 15	253,527	2.96	67.5	25.0	34.7	28.5	19,476	8.9	981	2,145	2,352	0
District 16	265,359	2.71	65.6	41.9	17.5	30.2	16,552	41.8	0	7,221	5,113	0
District 17	242,934	2.98	71.1	56.0	10.9	23.5	21,611	23.3	3,245	4,756	8,571	0
District 18	247,953	2.81	69.4	55.1	10.0	24.9	25,804	14.3	8,143	3,627	7,046	4,409
District 19	262,401	2.50	63.3	48.0	9.7	29.4	40,963	13.1	9,986	4,771	12,644	3
District 20	279,485	2.48	57.9	41.7	12.2	33.8	31,309	16.3	1,298	4,651	18,920	0
District 21	277,069	2.41	65.7	48.7	11.2	27.6	43,135	10.4	18,001	3,692	11,032	3,614
District 22	270,214	2.48	62.6	46.4	11.3	30.1	33,208	18.0	6,104	6,243	17,830	0
District 23	272,324	2.43	62.1	46.7	10.7	30.2	42,950	13.9	6,988	5,257	23,896	0
District 24	278,410	2.43	61.7	45.0	11.7	29.8	30,337	17.7	4,484	4,882	14,806	0
District 25	288,805	2.40	59.7	41.1	14.9	32.9	27,131	20.7	1,499	4,931	14,361	0
District 26	298,589	2.31	55.7	36.0	15.1	37.0	20,496	20.0	926	3,778	11,661	0
District 27	285,986	2.43	64.6	50.6	10.0	29.2	24,866	20.3	13,255	5,336	5,224	0
NORTH CAROLINA	3,882,423	2.55	65.5	48.0	13.1	28.5	255,962	16.6	61,680	46,638	89,795	26,326
District 1	294,949	2.43	60.7	37.5	17.9	32.1	33,067	15.6	13,922	6,285	10,496	594
District 2	288,710	2.81	73.2	57.9	12.1	22.7	9,423	21.8	1,132	3,214	1,773	5,949
District 3	285,216	2.55	66.6	51.1	11.3	27.6	27,684	6.2	6,616	2,817	8,725	19,749
District 4	321,545	2.54	61.0	45.8	11.3	30.0	31,740	7.0	5,518	2,406	22,784	0
District 5	299,083	2.43	66.4	49.1	12.6	28.5	23,788	18.3	2,268	3,598	10,492	0
District 6	297,993	2.51	67.9	49.5	14.4	27.5	14,767	23.6	2,493	3,811	6,738	0
District 7	308,011	2.48	63.9	47.1	12.2	29.9	17,073	29.2	5,511	3,495	9	33
District 8	288,388	2.62	66.9	49.1	14.2	28.4	19,334	17.1	8,325	3,469	3,449	0
District 9	278,978	2.74	71.4	53.6	13.3	24.3	13,898	45.8	50	2,736	2,155	1
District 10	297,132	2.51	65.6	48.7	12.3	29.0	14,827	30.8	2,503	4,741	4,033	0
District 11	305,113	2.40	65.0	49.8	10.8	29.3	15,894	23.1	5,915	4,622	4,965	0
District 12	320,462	2.61	60.1	40.9	14.5	31.7	13,495	10.1	4,648	3,049	13,560	0
District 13	296,838	2.52	64.2	45.5	13.8	29.4	20,972	28.6	2,779	2,395	616	0
NORTH DAKOTA	315,134	2.32	58.7	47.7	7.2	32.3	26,100	25.3	2,489	6,433	10,570	1,380
At Large	315,134	2.32	58.7	47.7	7.2	32.3	26,100	25.3	2,489	6,433	10,570	1,380
OHIO	4,624,669	2.44	63.3	45.9	12.7	30.3	313,225	25.3	76,590	83,019	106,042	571
District 1	289,541	2.48	63.5	45.5	14.1	30.3	21,517	17.7	6,431	4,486	7,060	0
District 2	297,079	2.40	63.4	47.4	11.6	30.0	10,201	55.0	880	5,887	712	0
District 3	306,114	2.50	55.7	32.0	17.2	34.4	22,729	10.7	2,353	2,793	11,851	0
District 4	274,691	2.49	67.2	50.1	12.0	26.9	29,329	17.6	15,892	5,563	5,261	0
District 5	288,645	2.43	64.6	50.7	9.1	28.8	17,956	31.9	971	6,014	8,367	0
District 6	276,003	2.47	66.8	50.3	10.9	28.5	22,207	30.8	9,881	6,354	3,595	0
District 7	278,042	2.57	68.9	53.6	10.8	26.4	14,893	35.8	795	6,223	5,129	0
District 8	276,239	2.57	67.1	49.8	12.0	25.6	17,166	24.8	1,369	4,682	8,537	0
District 9	298,778	2.32	56.9	34.1	16.7	36.3	14,209	26.5	1,894	4,930	5,512	0
District 10	297,509	2.33	61.0	42.6	13.7	32.8	25,726	21.5	1,997	5,845	12,267	547
District 11	298,406	2.24	53.7	28.8	20.5	40.3	24,132	21.5	3,906	6,243	7,446	0
District 12	287,747	2.57	67.4	54.2	9.8	26.2	18,686	19.4	6,071	3,929	6,352	0
District 13	298,591	2.31	58.7	39.9	14.4	34.7	20,266	20.6	5,134	5,394	10,204	0
District 14	288,659	2.42	67.2	53.9	9.3	28.2	11,950	40.5	2,076	5,260	1,338	24
District 15	280,339	2.54	65.8	50.4	10.7	26.8	31,041	11.1	16,670	3,476	9,591	0
District 16	288,286	2.48	67.6	53.8	9.0	27.4	11,217	51.7	270	5,940	2,820	0
OKLAHOMA	1,469,342	2.60	65.5	48.3	11.9	28.7	109,868	24.0	40,562	21,678	30,148	7,203
District 1	312,495	2.52	64.5	46.7	12.7	29.6	9,019	28.8	2,371	3,656	2,981	0
District 2	275,946	2.63	68.8	50.3	12.5	27.4	22,970	19.9	9,915	5,506	4,623	0
District 3	281,394	2.66	65.9	51.5	10.2	28.7	29,793	13.8	15,091	4,818	10,089	463
District 4	290,128	2.60	67.3	50.7	10.7	26.1	28,661	12.1	7,991	3,797	7,490	6,740
District 5	309,379	2.57	61.4	43.1	13.5	31.2	19,425	18.8	5,194	3,901	4,965	0
OREGON	1,571,678	2.55	63.4	48.7	10.1	27.4	88,778	18	22,203	11,491	23,704	178
District 1	311,524	2.62	66.5	53.2	9.2	25.5	13,462	20.7	4,641	1,964	3,338	127
District 2	315,374	2.50	65.4	49.4	11.3	26.6	21,757	19.0	8,762	2,660	1,775	13

1. No spouse present.

Table E. Congressional Districts 115th Congress — **Housing and Money Income**

STATE District	Total	Occupied units as a percent of all units	Owner-occupied units as a percent of occupied units	Median value[1] (dollars)	Percent valued at $500,000 or more	Median rent[2]	Per capita income (dollars)	Median income (dollars)	Percent with income of $100,000 or more
	40	41	42	43	44	45	46	47	48
NEW MEXICO— Cont'd									
District 3	308,501	79.7	70.5	179,300	8.4	858	25,561	49,210	20.3
NEW YORK	8,232,039	87.6	53.3	302,400	26.6	1,194	35,534	62,909	31.2
District 1	307,076	77.4	78.2	379,700	25.1	1,698	40,163	90,435	45.0
District 2	235,550	92.3	80.8	372,400	14.6	1,594	36,835	93,362	46.9
District 3	273,740	90.2	82.8	598,000	62.0	1,763	53,684	111,504	55.0
District 4	243,400	94.9	77.2	458,000	39.0	1,581	42,094	100,178	50.1
District 5	241,730	92.9	55.1	439,300	30.7	1,289	26,356	66,529	30.3
District 6	296,048	90.0	45.0	576,900	59.6	1,499	30,194	61,956	28.3
District 7	278,491	92.0	21.6	685,000	71.4	1,362	30,310	55,207	28.6
District 8	313,461	90.9	34.3	570,400	59.0	1,221	29,320	51,634	25.3
District 9	300,923	91.1	28.5	613,300	62.2	1,308	30,897	54,895	25.8
District 10	358,765	84.4	30.2	1,003,100	82.4	1,819	69,523	85,756	45.4
District 11	283,049	91.1	59.6	509,400	51.1	1,333	32,625	71,072	35.8
District 12	429,521	83.5	27.2	1,007,200	X	2,105	83,122	100,281	50.3
District 13	314,990	93.0	9.8	469,600	46.9	1,122	24,876	41,103	17.6
District 14	262,067	89.3	32.0	501,700	50.2	1,392	25,661	53,512	22.3
District 15	268,303	94.5	8.8	388,200	22.1	1,047	14,846	29,234	8.3
District 16	283,565	93.6	50.6	442,400	42.1	1,315	41,543	69,086	35.4
District 17	258,463	94.0	66.5	464,400	43.3	1,525	44,547	94,451	47.7
District 18	277,467	89.4	67.7	296,200	16.8	1,206	38,305	80,493	40.3
District 19	361,494	72.6	72.4	202,900	6.1	886	31,677	59,619	27.3
District 20	325,898	85.8	59.5	211,800	4.8	930	34,756	64,226	29.8
District 21	375,306	73.8	70.5	141,400	3.7	809	27,243	52,350	20.3
District 22	320,632	84.3	69.7	121,100	1.8	715	27,133	52,967	20.1
District 23	338,917	80.4	68.5	103,800	2.4	717	25,547	48,730	17.9
District 24	314,487	88.5	66.9	131,300	2.3	790	29,784	56,388	23.6
District 25	315,009	91.7	62.2	142,500	2.0	856	30,921	53,723	24.0
District 26	337,604	88.4	59.5	125,400	2.1	740	28,141	47,358	19.3
District 27	316,083	90.5	76.7	152,900	3.2	757	33,051	62,698	26.5
NORTH CAROLINA	4,540,697	85.5	64.2	165,400	6.2	839	28,156	50,584	20.2
District 1	338,284	87.2	56.2	133,200	3.1	776	24,035	40,895	15.0
District 2	319,841	90.3	72.4	205,500	6.5	885	31,315	65,792	30.1
District 3	380,142	75.0	63.7	155,900	4.7	828	24,808	47,565	16.7
District 4	353,683	90.9	55.9	259,400	12.3	1,063	37,872	70,587	32.4
District 5	362,542	82.5	67.2	147,100	4.7	713	26,338	45,001	15.4
District 6	329,918	90.3	68.0	143,600	4.2	699	26,311	47,335	18.0
District 7	383,766	80.3	66.3	162,500	5.7	827	26,259	45,002	16.4
District 8	337,184	85.5	63.9	156,000	3.7	831	25,695	50,570	18.4
District 9	310,704	89.8	73.2	187,700	11.4	841	32,597	55,913	26.5
District 10	340,332	87.3	66.0	150,300	5.3	740	25,925	46,508	15.8
District 11	393,863	77.5	71.2	163,500	5.4	697	25,237	43,855	13.6
District 12	351,283	91.2	51.2	183,700	8.4	1,033	30,913	59,268	25.4
District 13	339,155	87.5	61.6	153,800	5.1	776	26,904	47,440	18.5
NORTH DAKOTA	368,545	85.5	63.2	184,100	4.4	776	33,339	60,656	26.1
At Large	368,545	85.5	63.2	184,100	4.4	776	33,339	60,656	26.1
OHIO	5,164,400	89.5	65.4	140,100	3.2	759	29,164	52,334	21.4
District 1	321,738	90.0	60.5	164,700	6.5	766	31,423	55,712	24.9
District 2	326,154	91.1	66.4	152,000	5.4	758	32,935	55,472	24.8
District 3	343,147	89.2	44.4	124,200	3.2	839	24,115	45,860	15.1
District 4	308,885	88.9	70.4	122,800	1.6	689	26,004	52,632	18.8
District 5	311,630	92.6	71.3	141,800	2.7	704	30,424	57,171	23.4
District 6	321,412	85.9	73.4	110,100	1.7	645	24,818	46,839	14.8
District 7	305,372	91.1	74.1	138,200	2.3	690	26,745	53,374	19.4
District 8	302,857	91.2	68.1	147,300	1.7	772	28,539	58,213	23.2
District 9	349,512	85.5	56.7	99,000	2.1	699	25,452	41,417	14.0
District 10	334,796	88.9	61.2	124,700	1.9	765	28,999	49,988	20.4
District 11	365,865	81.6	48.8	90,000	3.5	726	26,140	35,735	14.8
District 12	312,735	92.0	70.5	204,900	6.9	877	36,847	67,415	33.6
District 13	337,749	88.4	62.6	100,900	0.6	703	24,583	42,430	13.4
District 14	310,477	93.0	77.5	173,300	4.6	857	35,365	63,362	28.8
District 15	307,676	91.1	68.8	162,100	4.1	861	30,410	61,514	26.0
District 16	304,395	94.7	74.8	162,700	2.0	824	33,452	64,197	27.1
OKLAHOMA	1,721,072	85.4	64.9	132,200	3.4	744	25,880	49,176	19.1
District 1	346,905	90.1	61.2	150,200	4.0	798	29,587	52,319	23.0
District 2	353,724	78.0	71.3	98,300	2.8	634	20,913	40,770	12.8
District 3	337,006	83.5	69.1	120,000	2.6	702	24,016	47,724	18.0
District 4	332,783	87.2	65.2	143,900	2.7	764	26,796	55,183	19.9
District 5	350,654	88.2	58.9	146,800	5.1	775	27,725	49,616	20.9
OREGON	1,732,887	90.7	61.7	287,100	15.8	1,015	30,822	57,532	24.9
District 1	338,365	92.1	61.9	346,300	20.8	1,192	36,229	72,097	34.1
District 2	363,249	86.8	64.9	233,800	12.4	877	26,409	49,837	18.4

1. Specified owner-occupied units.   2. Specified renter-occupied units.

STATE District	Poverty, 2016			Civilian labor force, 2016			Civilian employment,[2] 2016				Social Security beneficiaries, December 2016		
					Unemployment			Percent					
	Persons below poverty level (percent)	Families below poverty level (percent)	Percent of households receiving food stamps in past 12 months	Total	Total	Rate[1]	Total	Management, business, science, and arts occupations	Service, sales, and office	Construction and production	Persons under 65 years of age with no health insurance, 2016 (percent)	Number	Rate[3]	Supplemental Security Income recipients, December 2016
	49	50	51	52	53	54	55	56	57	58	59	60	61	62
NEW MEXICO— Cont'd														
District 3	19.5	14.8	14.5	305,705	26,156	8.6	279,549	37.6	43.5	18.9	12.3	140,615	204.8	21,242
NEW YORK	14.7	10.9	15.0	10,103,433	599,965	5.9	9,503,468	40.3	43.2	16.5	7.0	3,546,954	179.6	644,377
District 1	7.2	5.3	6.1	370,386	18,371	5.0	352,015	39.6	41.7	18.7	5.8	147,610	205.5	9,796
District 2	7.1	5.1	7.8	390,427	19,449	5.0	370,978	35.4	44.7	19.9	6.4	132,040	184.9	9,828
District 3	5.2	3.3	3.4	369,244	13,570	3.7	355,674	50.2	38.7	11.0	4.1	148,508	202.7	7,014
District 4	6.8	4.7	5.7	374,272	16,066	4.3	358,206	42.9	42.5	14.6	5.8	135,476	187.3	10,145
District 5	12.4	10.3	16.5	415,523	34,116	8.2	381,407	30.1	50.2	19.6	8.5	108,013	136.0	29,233
District 6	14.2	11.4	9.8	391,501	20,871	5.3	370,630	37.3	46.7	16.0	11.7	115,621	153.4	18,472
District 7	23.6	20.0	25.6	390,265	24,329	6.2	365,936	39.1	45.0	15.9	10.1	85,698	112.2	33,784
District 8	20.8	16.7	26.7	388,752	33,432	8.6	355,320	39.3	45.8	14.8	7.8	110,065	142.6	53,010
District 9	17.7	13.9	20.9	373,840	25,368	6.8	348,472	41.4	45.6	13.0	8.1	100,144	135.6	33,648
District 10	16.4	12.3	11.5	395,918	20,048	5.1	375,870	59.4	32.7	7.9	6.5	102,539	144.6	21,965
District 11	14.1	11.0	13.1	351,870	19,807	5.6	332,063	40.6	42.1	17.3	6.3	129,293	175.8	28,764
District 12	9.9	4.9	6.1	457,026	18,857	4.1	438,169	67.2	28.6	4.2	4.5	106,850	149.3	14,192
District 13	27.3	23.9	29.6	422,990	36,696	8.7	386,294	34.6	52.0	13.4	10.2	106,538	131.1	57,523
District 14	15.2	12.1	16.7	359,113	19,347	5.4	339,766	30.4	47.6	22.0	13.9	95,756	138.4	22,463
District 15	36.0	32.5	46.9	336,716	37,519	11.1	299,197	17.9	62.4	19.7	9.9	92,303	120.1	71,889
District 16	13.2	9.7	13.8	374,624	27,689	7.4	346,935	42.5	44.1	13.4	7.3	125,729	170.6	22,225
District 17	11.1	7.7	8.2	377,480	21,008	5.6	356,472	46.4	39.6	14.0	8.6	128,125	172.1	10,227
District 18	10.1	6.6	8.0	365,395	17,755	4.9	347,640	40.3	41.4	18.3	5.4	132,361	183.2	11,744
District 19	13.5	9.0	10.2	350,115	21,145	6.0	328,970	37.1	42.2	20.7	6.2	162,547	232.8	14,823
District 20	11.0	7.1	12.2	387,206	19,977	5.2	367,229	42.9	42.7	14.4	4.1	149,239	206.3	18,799
District 21	13.7	8.9	14.9	333,981	20,070	6.0	313,911	32.4	43.9	23.7	6.1	166,677	234.2	19,122
District 22	15.2	10.1	15.8	337,235	19,542	5.8	317,693	35.8	43.3	20.8	4.3	168,946	240.2	22,095
District 23	16.2	10.0	15.5	331,468	19,731	6.0	311,737	36.9	40.3	22.9	7.1	164,718	234.1	19,304
District 24	14.3	9.6	14.2	360,114	20,939	5.8	339,175	38.3	42.1	19.6	5.1	153,805	217.4	20,431
District 25	15.4	11.2	15.5	374,178	22,001	5.9	352,177	43.6	41.0	15.4	4.3	154,479	214.3	25,509
District 26	17.8	12.7	19.6	347,128	18,552	5.3	328,576	36.4	46.3	17.3	3.9	156,383	220.5	28,467
District 27	8.5	5.6	8.3	376,666	13,710	3.6	362,956	38.0	39.5	22.5	4.2	167,491	232.6	9,905
NORTH CAROLINA	15.4	11.2	13.5	4,955,312	309,063	6.2	4,646,249	37.1	40.4	22.5	12.2	2,020,386	199.1	233,432
District 1	21.1	16.6	19.6	357,806	26,569	7.4	331,237	35.1	40.1	24.8	13.7	163,567	218.0	37,356
District 2	10.5	7.7	10.6	411,999	22,678	5.5	389,321	43.4	37.5	19.1	9.3	143,984	175.6	16,055
District 3	14.8	9.8	14.6	331,276	27,625	8.3	303,651	33.1	41.9	25.0	13.0	153,893	204.0	15,877
District 4	11.1	6.8	7.2	482,269	20,812	4.3	461,457	51.8	36.8	11.4	9.3	113,846	134.4	15,815
District 5	17.7	12.4	12.9	354,715	20,396	5.7	334,319	34.1	41.5	24.4	13.4	168,301	224.0	14,119
District 6	16.0	12.2	15.3	371,687	23,044	6.2	348,643	34.3	38.7	27.0	13.1	172,353	225.7	13,576
District 7	18.6	12.9	16.1	352,350	26,292	7.5	326,058	32.1	42.7	25.1	15.2	182,233	233.5	18,551
District 8	15.3	11.7	13.2	353,956	25,413	7.2	328,543	34.6	41.6	23.8	10.6	159,384	205.7	22,824
District 9	15.1	12.0	14.5	366,446	22,644	6.2	343,802	39.7	37.6	22.6	10.3	120,701	155.0	6,558
District 10	14.6	10.8	14.6	372,347	24,467	6.6	347,880	32.3	42.0	25.7	11.9	174,619	229.9	19,376
District 11	16.3	11.4	12.5	339,431	18,797	5.5	320,634	30.2	43.2	26.6	14.8	210,697	281.1	16,922
District 12	13.7	9.8	10.9	476,778	26,049	5.5	450,729	39.9	41.8	18.3	13.5	117,744	138.6	25,908
District 13	16.5	12.7	14.3	384,252	24,277	6.3	359,975	33.6	41.5	24.8	12.2	139,064	181.0	10,495
NORTH DAKOTA	10.7	6.4	7.2	419,151	11,782	2.8	407,369	36.1	39.1	24.8	8.1	127,962	168.8	8,214
At Large	10.7	6.4	7.2	419,151	11,782	2.8	407,369	36.1	39.1	24.8	8.1	127,962	168.8	8,214
OHIO	14.6	10.5	13.8	5,875,897	332,095	5.7	5,543,802	36.0	40.6	23.4	6.6	2,311,984	199.1	310,474
District 1	14.8	10.4	12.8	378,121	23,965	6.3	354,156	40.5	40.1	19.4	5.9	127,530	172.5	19,900
District 2	14.3	10.5	13.4	371,076	17,765	4.8	353,311	39.5	40.4	20.1	5.7	148,224	204.6	22,671
District 3	22.2	17.5	18.7	420,292	29,897	7.1	390,395	34.5	44.7	20.8	10.6	103,567	131.5	28,768
District 4	12.4	8.7	12.6	352,632	17,277	4.9	335,355	28.7	38.3	33.0	6.3	152,028	212.9	15,014
District 5	10.1	6.2	9.5	380,010	16,720	4.4	363,290	33.8	37.1	29.1	4.8	144,805	200.9	9,451
District 6	15.9	11.3	16.1	322,073	18,766	5.8	303,307	29.3	40.5	30.2	7.1	167,621	238.4	23,204
District 7	11.3	7.7	11.4	363,960	19,360	5.3	344,600	30.0	40.1	29.9	9.3	157,889	216.8	14,412
District 8	12.3	8.2	11.3	366,057	19,005	5.2	347,052	35.1	38.0	26.9	6.2	144,705	198.8	14,687
District 9	20.7	16.6	21.7	357,349	29,004	8.1	328,345	31.8	43.1	25.1	6.8	147,138	208.4	32,323
District 10	17.1	13.3	14.0	351,756	22,220	6.3	329,536	37.5	42.0	20.5	6.6	146,824	203.8	19,649
District 11	26.4	21.2	26.1	333,393	34,559	10.4	298,834	35.0	45.8	19.2	7.1	136,547	197.3	40,727
District 12	9.8	6.8	8.5	397,279	14,424	3.6	382,855	44.8	39.0	16.1	4.8	134,018	176.7	13,718
District 13	18.1	13.8	16.8	353,056	24,218	6.9	328,838	31.5	45.4	23.2	6.8	160,144	225.7	25,364
District 14	8.7	5.9	7.9	365,810	13,783	3.8	352,027	40.6	38.3	21.1	6.4	154,699	217.6	10,100
District 15	12.6	8.4	12.1	376,636	16,191	4.3	360,445	40.8	38.8	20.5	5.4	131,804	177.2	13,658
District 16	6.9	4.7	7.3	386,397	14,941	3.9	371,456	40.1	39.5	20.4	5.3	154,441	212.3	6,828
OKLAHOMA	16.3	11.5	13.3	1,853,639	110,892	6.0	1,742,747	34.1	41.8	24.0	16.1	768,889	196.0	96,315
District 1	15.4	11.2	12.2	405,677	23,800	5.9	381,877	36.4	42.3	21.3	15.3	145,810	183.0	17,752
District 2	18.9	14.0	16.8	314,660	25,017	8.0	289,643	28.7	42.2	29.1	21.6	182,378	243.3	27,109
District 3	16.4	11.5	11.7	360,526	19,571	5.4	340,955	32.6	40.5	26.9	14.9	152,668	195.8	14,366
District 4	13.5	8.6	11.0	375,494	20,261	5.4	355,233	35.0	42.4	22.6	12.6	149,042	190.6	16,048
District 5	17.3	12.3	14.9	397,282	22,243	5.6	375,039	36.5	41.8	21.7	16.3	138,991	170.4	21,040
OREGON	13.3	8.5	16.8	2,058,323	117,641	5.7	1,940,682	38.8	40.7	20.5	7.3	836,215	204.3	87,402
District 1	9.3	6.5	12.0	443,566	19,234	4.3	424,332	44.2	38.0	17.8	5.1	134,610	162.0	11,751
District 2	14.2	9.4	19.2	376,536	26,320	7.0	350,216	30.9	44.3	24.8	9.9	200,602	247.7	18,220

1. Percent of civilian labor force.   2. Persons 16 years old and over.   3. Per 1,000 resident population estimated in the 2016 American Community Survey.

STATE District	Agriculture 2012									
	Land in farms				Value of products sold				Government payments	
	Number of farms	Acres	Average size of farm (acres)	Irrigated land (acres)	Total ($1,000)	Average per farm (dollars)	Percent from crops	Percent from livestock and poultry products	Total ($1,000)	Average per farm receiving payments (dollars)
	63	64	65	66	67	68	69	70	71	72
NEW MEXICO— Cont'd										
District 3	12,723	19,249,622	1,513	277,321	877,541	68,973	16.6	83.4	29,752	10,021
NEW YORK	35,537	7,183,576	202	59,807	5,415,125	152,380	41.5	58.5	74,511	7,955
District 1	499	27,475	55	8,672	196,009	392,803	83.0	17.0	605	15,508
District 2	39	1,088	28	265	4,469	114,580	98.0	2.0	D	D
District 3	112	10,121	90	2,954	45,149	403,114	88.6	11.4	185	61,793
District 4	10	20	2	14	492	49,170	D	D	0	0
District 5	X	X	X	X	X	X	X	X	X	X
District 6	X	X	X	X	X	X	X	X	X	X
District 7	X	X	X	X	X	X	X	X	X	X
District 8	X	X	X	X	X	X	X	X	X	X
District 9	X	X	X	X	X	X	X	X	X	X
District 10	X	X	X	X	X	X	X	X	X	X
District 11	X	X	X	X	X	X	X	X	X	X
District 12	X	X	X	X	X	X	X	X	X	X
District 13	X	X	X	X	X	X	X	X	X	X
District 14	X	X	X	X	X	X	X	X	X	X
District 15	X	X	X	X	X	X	X	X	X	X
District 16	10	1,017	102	9	828	82,774	91.8	8.2	0	0
District 17	70	2,001	29	113	6,584	94,053	62.7	37.3	D	D
District 18	871	110,109	126	3,066	113,514	130,326	71.9	28.1	2,102	10,778
District 19	5,314	957,846	180	8,894	462,961	87,121	44.3	55.7	8,095	6,581
District 20	1,181	161,612	137	804	113,423	96,040	44.2	55.8	1,111	5,142
District 21	6,108	1,496,682	245	2,668	977,396	160,019	23.1	76.9	15,284	9,983
District 22	4,770	941,790	197	2,123	493,919	103,547	26.9	73.1	10,122	7,174
District 23	8,716	1,667,821	191	5,848	1,054,998	121,042	39.1	60.9	14,867	6,541
District 24	2,712	603,589	223	3,754	667,658	246,187	46.4	53.6	6,666	8,199
District 25	364	56,344	155	810	47,235	129,766	88.4	11.6	760	9,266
District 26	58	10,225	176	38	8,791	151,564	99.2	0.8	D	D
District 27	4,674	1,135,393	243	19,756	1,218,619	260,723	46.4	53.6	14,616	9,351
NORTH CAROLINA	50,218	8,414,756	168	174,526	12,588,142	250,670	34.2	65.8	120,129	8,332
District 1	3,457	1,267,552	367	37,421	1,411,910	408,421	48.5	51.5	29,500	13,176
District 2	4,319	540,316	125	9,955	794,538	183,963	20.7	79.3	6,417	7,902
District 3	3,115	1,258,856	404	23,466	1,667,112	535,188	52.2	47.8	25,085	13,663
District 4	1,051	113,099	108	2,044	117,955	112,231	33.8	66.2	1,419	5,609
District 5	7,523	782,829	104	3,009	863,937	114,839	22.6	77.4	4,295	3,873
District 6	6,051	744,474	123	12,316	442,156	73,072	44.1	55.9	6,752	4,271
District 7	5,330	1,205,092	226	46,178	3,720,633	698,055	21.0	79.0	19,390	8,106
District 8	5,065	901,322	178	11,176	1,694,602	334,571	21.9	78.1	9,344	7,205
District 9	1,068	128,936	121	1,065	282,689	264,690	68.8	31.2	819	7,805
District 10	4,082	385,987	95	1,696	307,645	75,366	22.2	77.8	2,462	3,558
District 11	6,428	461,764	72	8,510	305,338	47,501	65.3	34.7	6,241	6,125
District 12	483	49,775	103	918	36,733	76,052	71.7	28.3	289	3,849
District 13	2,246	574,754	256	16,772	942,895	419,811	54.3	45.7	8,114	8,058
NORTH DAKOTA	30,961	39,262,613	1,268	218,407	10,950,680	353,693	88.3	11.7	381,710	15,398
At Large	30,961	39,262,613	1,268	218,407	10,950,000	353,693	88.3	11.7	381,710	15,398
OHIO	75,462	13,960,604	185	46,569	10,064,085	133,366	65.6	34.4	228,858	6,603
District 1	1,200	124,692	104	970	80,571	67,142	89.9	10.1	1,194	4,593
District 2	6,107	983,627	161	1,478	373,277	61,123	82.8	17.2	17,161	5,529
District 3	92	16,593	180	144	19,539	212,376	94.4	5.6	120	4,435
District 4	9,348	2,307,012	247	6,343	1,844,009	197,262	76.8	23.2	45,190	6,949
District 5	10,792	2,847,931	264	6,809	2,386,632	221,148	70.5	29.5	61,441	7,107
District 6	11,766	1,584,934	135	4,365	426,139	36,218	46.0	54.0	10,048	4,426
District 7	9,520	1,354,995	142	6,634	1,072,386	112,646	50.5	49.5	15,873	5,529
District 8	6,055	1,174,229	194	5,577	1,371,101	226,441	43.7	56.3	23,599	6,752
District 9	506	76,485	151	1,354	82,288	162,624	97.9	2.1	1,493	4,993
District 10	1,898	378,015	199	1,868	254,837	134,266	86.2	13.8	6,374	6,612
District 11	81	2,497	31	197	3,575	44,131	94.0	6.0	37	7,391
District 12	4,307	712,235	165	1,331	536,943	124,668	67.4	32.6	9,618	6,438
District 13	1,038	107,448	104	184	57,947	55,825	69.0	31.0	962	4,413
District 14	3,053	342,898	112	2,734	265,078	86,825	77.1	22.9	2,865	4,783
District 15	6,879	1,598,791	232	5,392	850,104	123,580	83.2	16.8	27,660	8,745
District 16	2,820	348,222	123	1,189	439,660	155,908	32.6	67.4	5,223	7,048
OKLAHOMA	80,245	34,356,110	428	479,750	7,129,584	88,848	26.3	73.7	256,845	8,634
District 1	3,160	575,332	182	D	99,709	31,553	42.0	58.0	2,618	4,392
District 2	29,692	8,013,419	270	38,897	2,053,254	69,152	16.2	83.8	37,636	5,317
District 3	30,326	19,992,205	659	395,097	4,172,753	137,597	30.6	69.4	182,507	10,572
District 4	13,283	5,059,287	381	33,614	711,085	53,533	28.0	72.0	31,371	7,483
District 5	3,784	715,867	189	D	92,783	24,520	28.2	71.8	2,714	4,391
OREGON	35,439	16,301,578	460	1,629,735	4,883,674	137,805	66.5	33.5	85,840	16,054
District 1	4,759	400,597	84	46,715	584,568	122,834	84.9	15.1	4,343	6,861
District 2	13,284	13,924,323	1,048	1,349,942	2,419,047	182,102	58.7	41.3	72,580	21,038

Table E. Congressional Districts 115th Congress — Nonfarm Employment and Payroll

STATE District	Number of establish-ments	Employment Total	Manufact-uring	Construc-tion	Wholesale trade	Retail trade	Health care and social assistance	Finance and Insurance	Real estate and rental and leasing	Professio-nal, scientific, and technical services	Information	Annual payroll Total (mil dol)	Average per employee (dollars)
	73	74	75	76	77	78	79	80	81	82	83	84	85
NEW MEXICO— Cont'd													
District 3	14,317	175,940	3.6	5.0	2.5	17.3	20.1	3.2	1.5	9.0	1.6	7,046	40,048
NEW YORK	544,073	8,178,455	5.1	4.4	4.4	11.6	18.9	6.8	2.2	7.9	3.6	521,873	63,811
District 1	23,101	240,530	7.7	8.1	5.9	17.0	20.5	3.0	1.1	6.9	1.6	12,700	52,801
District 2	20,657	248,534	11.3	9.6	8.4	14.7	15.3	2.5	1.3	5.6	2.3	11,724	47,171
District 3	29,761	385,416	3.3	4.4	7.0	10.5	22.7	7.3	2.0	9.6	2.9	24,442	63,418
District 4	24,618	269,755	3.1	6.1	3.3	14.9	22.0	5.5	1.7	7.4	1.7	12,995	48,172
District 5	11,571	159,716	1.9	5.3	2.2	12.7	18.9	1.3	1.9	2.3	0.8	6,967	43,622
District 6	18,756	167,770	2.6	7.8	3.6	14.6	33.9	3.7	2.8	4.1	1.5	6,820	40,654
District 7	22,322	227,425	4.6	6.7	6.0	10.8	22.4	4.2	2.8	5.1	2.6	9,484	41,703
District 8	11,539	136,711	3.3	3.1	3.9	15.7	29.0	3.1	2.5	2.6	1.9	5,347	39,113
District 9	12,771	125,110	0.9	2.7	1.7	12.7	44.8	1.6	3.2	3.1	2.3	4,916	39,296
District 10	40,310	810,907	1.4	2.2	3.2	6.9	12.4	13.6	2.9	12.1	8.5	74,402	91,752
District 11	16,191	154,361	1.1	7.6	2.1	16.5	33.5	2.7	1.7	3.8	1.5	6,232	40,371
District 12	70,310	1,523,839	1.3	2.7	5.0	6.6	9.0	13.3	3.4	15.2	7.3	171,221	112,362
District 13	10,098	146,859	0.3	1.5	0.5	10.1	49.8	1.4	3.6	1.9	1.4	7,175	47,440
District 14	12,251	151,251	3.3	9.9	4.6	11.5	24.2	2.1	2.4	1.9	2.0	5,416	43,169
District 15	9,235	125,450	3.9	4.6	8.3	13.6	31.1	1.4	3.8	1.9	1.4	8,026	45,416
District 16	16,283	176,729	3.5	8.6	2.6	16.6	22.4	2.3	3.6	3.4	2.2	22,442	65,001
District 17	26,445	345,251	3.9	5.6	5.3	11.6	21.8	5.8	2.1	7.2	2.5	9,900	43,963
District 18	19,320	225,181	6.3	5.1	5.1	18.2	20.2	2.8	1.5	5.8	2.3	6,245	37,305
District 19	16,879	167,396	8.2	5.6	3.4	17.3	22.5	3.5	1.2	3.2	1.6	15,952	47,386
District 20	19,043	336,634	7.0	4.3	4.1	13.0	20.1	5.8	1.4	8.5	2.7	6,690	37,153
District 21	15,532	180,068	11.1	4.8	3.0	20.2	21.5	2.5	1.1	2.7	1.9	8,630	38,440
District 22	14,267	224,510	13.5	3.2	3.6	14.8	20.6	4.9	0.9	4.3	2.1	8,294	37,193
District 23	14,500	222,997	15.3	3.5	2.7	15.0	18.4	2.5	1.1	2.9	1.5	11,941	43,048
District 24	16,415	277,393	10.3	4.4	5.6	14.2	19.3	4.4	1.6	5.8	2.0	15,829	44,743
District 25	17,182	353,784	9.7	3.4	4.1	11.6	19.0	3.7	1.8	7.2	3.0	15,392	44,003
District 26	17,567	349,800	8.6	3.4	4.9	12.0	18.9	7.5	1.6	7.7	1.8	8,520	40,475
District 27	16,241	210,491	17.4	6.1	4.8	18.9	15.0	2.6	1.2	3.2	1.3	170,980	45,055
NORTH CAROLINA	227,347	3,794,926	11.4	4.9	5.0	13.1	15.3	4.8	1.4	5.8	2.2	11,118	42,946
District 1	14,142	258,880	12.4	4.1	2.7	11.9	22.0	4.0	1.2	5.0	1.7	7,534	38,892
District 2	15,427	193,725	13.3	7.2	5.1	17.1	13.9	2.4	1.3	4.7	1.7	6,110	32,795
District 3	15,874	186,316	9.6	6.1	2.7	19.4	16.5	3.4	2.4	3.9	1.3	27,890	58,388
District 4	25,357	477,663	3.3	4.7	7.5	11.4	14.3	5.8	1.9	14.8	5.4	11,971	43,666
District 5	16,039	274,151	12.4	5.9	4.5	13.7	18.8	4.5	1.2	3.4	1.3	7,424	37,176
District 6	13,397	199,709	23.5	5.9	4.6	14.2	16.5	2.3	0.8	2.3	1.5	7,897	37,132
District 7	16,804	212,677	12.3	5.7	4.0	17.7	18.0	3.1	1.6	4.0	2.2	7,161	35,031
District 8	13,936	204,415	10.8	5.2	3.0	18.4	19.8	2.0	1.3	3.7	1.4	10,416	43,943
District 9	16,737	237,045	15.1	5.8	4.5	14.7	14.1	5.5	1.4	4.5	1.5	10,851	38,120
District 10	18,158	284,658	19.1	3.9	4.7	14.1	19.8	1.9	1.1	2.9	1.3	7,035	34,515
District 11	15,990	203,831	20.2	5.7	3.7	16.9	16.5	2.2	1.1	2.6	1.3	31,590	61,140
District 12	24,307	516,688	5.0	4.7	7.2	9.2	11.0	11.1	1.8	8.6	3.0	16,240	44,382
District 13	20,391	365,903	15.0	4.2	6.1	11.9	14.9	3.9	1.5	4.0	1.7	15,817	45,588
NORTH DAKOTA	24,601	346,947	6.9	6.7	6.6	14.6	17.7	5.1	1.6	4.6	2.1	15,817	45,588
At Large	24,601	346,947	6.9	6.7	6.6	14.6	17.7	5.1	1.6	4.6	2.1	218,467	45,607
OHIO	252,201	4,790,178	13.8	3.9	4.9	12.0	17.6	5.3	1.4	5.2	1.8	22,596	57,835
District 1	16,813	390,697	9.2	4.5	5.2	9.7	19.1	6.3	1.5	7.6	2.8	12,206	45,759
District 2	15,819	266,754	10.0	4.4	5.4	14.3	16.6	6.5	1.5	8.1	2.5	18,808	50,564
District 3	15,069	371,971	6.5	3.9	5.1	10.4	19.6	8.8	2.0	5.6	1.7	11,248	41,414
District 4	14,458	271,591	28.9	3.9	4.3	11.6	15.7	2.1	0.7	3.9	1.0	12,205	39,601
District 5	16,205	308,203	21.7	3.7	3.8	12.8	14.0	3.0	1.1	3.9	0.9	6,298	35,483
District 6	12,971	177,481	14.5	4.9	3.7	15.5	22.4	2.9	1.1	2.4	0.9	8,119	37,300
District 7	14,281	217,664	22.7	5.9	4.7	14.5	17.2	2.5	0.8	2.5	1.1	10,150	41,219
District 8	13,751	246,245	19.3	4.3	7.0	13.3	14.3	5.0	1.0	2.7	1.0	11,000	43,902
District 9	13,397	250,566	17.1	4.0	4.5	11.5	18.1	2.9	1.7	3.0	1.6	13,481	45,575
District 10	15,005	295,801	11.3	3.5	3.7	13.2	20.0	4.2	1.2	8.2	3.0	23,072	55,244
District 11	18,423	417,631	8.3	3.0	4.7	7.0	27.4	6.0	2.5	7.5	1.7	15,906	49,192
District 12	17,556	323,352	8.1	3.8	2.9	11.3	17.4	11.7	1.1	6.2	2.4	10,070	39,014
District 13	14,797	258,120	17.0	4.6	4.6	15.3	18.1	2.0	1.5	3.2	1.4	15,993	48,794
District 14	20,335	327,767	18.2	3.9	7.8	11.8	12.5	6.7	1.6	5.3	1.5	9,555	40,730
District 15	14,076	234,597	11.2	3.7	5.3	15.5	15.3	4.1	1.5	5.1	2.4	12,130	41,011
District 16	18,370	295,771	13.9	4.1	5.0	16.0	17.2	4.5	1.1	4.2	2.0	57,194	42,042
OKLAHOMA	93,232	1,360,379	9.6	5.3	4.3	13.7	16.3	4.4	1.7	5.4	2.1	17,542	46,505
District 1	21,498	377,201	11.7	5.5	4.6	12.3	15.4	4.5	2.0	6.1	2.9	5,377	33,144
District 2	13,035	162,235	14.4	4.4	3.3	16.9	23.3	3.8	0.9	2.7	1.1	7,041	37,516
District 3	17,236	187,687	12.3	6.7	4.5	16.2	14.2	3.9	1.7	3.6	1.4	7,243	34,877
District 4	16,662	207,679	8.1	5.5	2.7	17.2	18.1	4.0	1.9	4.6	1.6	17,369	45,575
District 5	24,320	381,111	5.9	4.9	5.3	12.2	15.8	5.4	1.7	6.5	2.3	74,063	47,746
OREGON	114,551	1,551,192	10.6	5.6	5.4	13.4	15.8	3.9	1.8	5.9	2.5	22,047	60,012
District 1	23,055	367,384	12.0	5.5	8.0	12.1	12.2	3.9	2.1	7.6	3.5	9,504	37,523
District 2	23,524	253,292	10.8	5.9	3.3	16.8	18.0	3.1	1.6	3.7	1.9		

STATE District	Representative, 115th Congress	Land area,[1] 2017 (sq mi)	Total persons	Per square mile	Population and population characteristics, 2016						Hispanic or Latino[2] (percent)	Non-Hispanic White alone (percent)	Percent female	Percent foreign-born	Percent born in state of residence
					Race alone (percent)										
					White	Black	American Indian, Alaska Native	Asian and Pacific Islander	Some other race (percent)	Two or more races (percent)					
		1	2	3	4	5	6	7	8	9	10	11	12	13	14
OREGON— Cont'd															
District 3	Earl Blumenauer (D)	1,074.5	835,143	777.3	79.2	5.5	0.9	7.4	2.0	5.0	11.4	71.0	50.7	13.2	42.9
District 4	Peter A. DeFazio (D)	17,272.3	795,499	46.1	89.1	0.8	1.2	2.5	1.7	4.7	7.8	83.9	50.4	5.1	48.0
District 5	Kurt Schrader (D)	5,189.1	822,071	158.4	84.7	1.1	0.9	3.1	4.0	6.2	16.4	75.3	50.9	9.5	52.5
PENNSYLVANIA ..		44,742.1	12,784,227	285.7	80.9	11.0	0.2	3.3	2.1	2.5	7.0	76.9	51.0	6.8	72.4
District 1	Robert A. Brady (D)	78.0	721,901	9,255.3	46.5	35.5	0.4	6.9	7.5	3.3	18.0	38.4	51.2	14.0	65.3
District 2	Dwight Evans (D)	74.1	711,404	9,602.5	31.6	56.4	0.2	6.1	2.9	2.7	5.8	29.6	54.0	10.1	65.4
District 3	Mike Kelly (R)	3,850.7	693,850	180.2	91.8	4.6	0.1	1.3	0.4	1.7	2.3	90.2	50.6	3.0	81.2
District 4	Scott Perry (R)	1,517.9	726,738	478.8	84.7	8.0	0.2	2.7	2.2	2.3	7.0	80.8	51.2	5.4	65.2
District 5	Glenn Thompson (R)	10,711.4	700,472	65.4	93.4	2.8	0.1	1.7	0.2	1.8	2.0	92.0	48.7	3.1	79.4
District 6	Ryan A. Costello (R)	860.5	737,397	856.9	86.3	4.1	0.2	5.0	1.7	2.6	5.9	83.0	51.0	6.9	71.7
District 7	Vacant	862.5	712,330	825.9	86.2	5.8	0.1	4.8	0.8	2.2	3.8	83.7	51.2	7.6	72.4
District 8	Brian K. Fitzpatrick (R)	707.0	709,746	1,003.9	87.7	3.5	0.1	5.3	1.3	2.1	5.3	83.9	50.9	10.1	67.2
District 9	Bill Shuster (R)	5,730.1	689,669	120.4	94.2	3.1	0.1	0.7	0.3	1.5	2.2	92.5	50.7	1.6	80.3
District 10	Tom Marino (R)	8,377.6	689,108	82.3	92.5	3.2	0.1	0.9	1.0	2.3	4.4	89.7	50.2	3.1	68.6
District 11	Lou Barletta (R)	3,356.2	707,150	210.7	88.9	5.7	0.1	1.9	1.7	1.7	6.6	85.0	50.3	4.6	78.2
District 12	Keith J. Rothfus (R)	2,163.1	697,773	322.6	92.5	2.8	0.1	2.2	0.3	2.2	1.4	91.5	50.8	3.0	83.2
District 13	Brendan F. Boyle (D)	155.2	731,754	4,715.9	62.0	20.1	0.4	8.5	5.5	3.5	12.3	56.8	52.5	19.1	65.8
District 14	Michael F. Doyle (D)	209.3	696,529	3,328.1	71.9	20.8	0.1	2.9	0.5	3.8	2.7	70.2	52.0	5.4	77.3
District 15	Vacant	1,285.2	725,473	564.5	84.3	5.4	0.2	2.7	4.9	2.6	16.6	74.4	50.8	7.7	65.8
District 16	Lloyd Smucker (R)	997.7	725,915	727.6	83.2	6.5	0.5	1.9	2.9	5.0	18.7	71.7	50.9	7.3	69.0
District 17	Matt Cartwright (D)	1,732.9	699,918	403.9	86.7	6.1	0.2	1.8	1.9	2.4	9.2	81.6	50.3	5.9	66.8
District 18	Conor Lamb(D)	2,072.8	707,100	341.1	93.0	2.6	0.1	2.1	0.3	1.9	1.2	92.3	51.1	3.5	81.1
RHODE ISLAND ...		1,034.0	1,056,426	1,021.7	80.5	6.4	0.5	3.6	5.9	3.1	14.9	72.8	51.6	14.1	56.4
District 1	David Cicilline (D)	268.6	536,871	1,998.6	76.4	9.1	0.6	4.0	6.3	3.6	16.6	67.6	51.4	17.4	50.5
District 2	James R. Langevin (D)	765.4	519,555	678.8	84.7	3.6	0.4	3.2	5.5	2.6	13.2	78.1	51.8	10.6	62.5
SOUTH CAROLINA		30,063.0	4,961,119	165.0	67.4	27.0	0.3	1.6	1.6	2.2	5.5	63.7	51.5	4.8	57.0
District 1	Mark Sanford (R)	1,547.8	761,869	492.2	75.6	18.2	0.3	1.9	1.7	2.5	6.5	71.1	51.8	5.6	43.5
District 2	Joe Wilson (R)	3,022.4	703,246	232.7	70.2	23.5	0.3	1.8	1.4	2.8	5.3	66.4	51.3	4.8	52.4
District 3	Jeff Duncan (R)	5,268.3	684,619	129.9	77.3	18.0	0.2	1.3	1.2	2.1	4.8	74.1	51.2	4.1	64.0
District 4	Trey Gowdy (R)	1,299.4	716,552	551.5	74.1	18.9	0.2	2.5	2.2	2.1	8.4	68.4	51.5	7.2	56.5
District 5	Ralph Norman (R)	5,505.8	704,256	127.9	68.1	26.5	0.6	1.1	1.7	2.0	4.1	65.6	51.1	3.3	56.8
District 6	James E. Clyburn (D)	8,064.1	680,469	84.4	38.1	57.2	0.2	1.3	1.4	1.8	5.1	35.1	51.1	4.1	70.6
District 7	Tom Rice (R)	5,355.1	710,108	132.6	66.8	28.1	0.5	1.3	1.3	2.1	4.2	64.1	52.5	4.3	56.9
SOUTH DAKOTA ..		75,809.3	865,454	11.4	84.7	1.7	8.9	1.5	0.7	2.5	3.7	82.4	49.7	3.6	64.5
At Large	Kristi Noem (R)	75,809.3	865,454	11.4	84.7	1.7	8.9	1.5	0.7	2.5	3.7	82.4	49.7	3.6	64.5
TENNESSEE		41,234.9	6,651,194	161.3	77.8	16.8	0.3	1.8	1.2	2.1	5.2	74.1	51.2	4.8	61.2
District 1	David P. Roe (R)	4,141.9	714,504	172.5	94.0	2.0	0.4	0.8	0.7	2.0	3.8	91.5	50.7	2.7	62.2
District 2	John J. Duncan Jr. (R)	2,321.7	740,182	318.8	88.9	6.3	0.3	1.7	1.0	1.7	4.0	86.0	51.0	4.2	61.0
District 3	Chuck Fleischmann (R)	4,570.3	728,254	159.3	85.2	10.9	0.2	1.5	0.3	1.9	3.6	82.3	50.8	3.4	66.1
District 4	Scott DesJarlais (R)	5,984.8	767,655	128.3	84.9	9.2	0.2	1.6	1.1	2.9	6.2	80.3	50.7	4.8	60.3
District 5	Jim Cooper (D)	1,248.4	762,535	610.8	67.6	24.9	0.2	3.5	1.5	2.3	9.4	59.9	51.9	11.2	52.6
District 6	Diane Black (R)	6,474.9	761,538	117.6	91.8	4.5	0.3	1.1	0.6	1.8	4.3	88.4	51.3	3.2	62.4
District 7	Marsha Blackburn (R)	9,160.3	765,730	83.6	84.5	9.8	0.3	2.2	0.7	2.4	5.3	80.4	50.5	4.1	53.7
District 8	David Kustoff (R)	6,848.9	706,468	103.2	75.2	19.5	0.4	2.1	0.7	2.1	2.9	73.1	51.1	3.6	67.2
District 9	Steve Cohen (D)	483.8	704,328	1,456.0	25.8	66.1	0.3	1.7	4.2	1.7	7.4	23.0	52.7	5.9	66.7
TEXAS		261,252.9	27,862,596	106.6	74.3	12.1	0.5	4.8	5.8	2.6	39.1	42.5	50.4	17.0	59.7
District 1	Louie Gohmert (R)	7,868.6	717,735	91.2	76.4	18.1	0.6	1.2	2.2	1.5	17.4	62.1	51.2	8.0	73.2
District 2	Ted Poe (R)	308.7	779,662	2,525.6	66.6	12.7	0.3	6.8	11.6	2.0	31.3	47.5	50.2	19.4	52.4
District 3	Sam Johnson (R)	480.8	842,800	1,752.9	68.8	9.7	0.4	15.5	2.2	3.5	14.6	57.1	50.9	21.0	43.0
District 4	John Ratcliffe (R)	10,130.5	735,554	72.6	81.7	10.5	0.6	1.2	3.7	2.4	13.3	72.5	50.7	6.0	67.8
District 5	Jeb Hensarling (R)	5,044.2	764,456	151.6	76.1	14.9	0.7	2.3	3.8	2.2	28.8	52.3	50.4	15.4	65.0
District 6	Joe Barton (R)	2,148.6	770,255	358.5	65.8	20.3	0.6	5.1	4.6	3.6	22.2	49.6	50.8	13.5	58.7
District 7	John Abney Culberson (R)	162.1	770,606	4,754.9	67.3	12.8	0.2	10.2	6.4	3.2	31.9	42.9	51.1	29.4	43.7
District 8	Kevin Brady (R)	6,055.0	813,519	134.4	83.0	9.0	0.6	2.8	2.2	2.3	21.6	65.3	49.2	12.5	56.9
District 9	Al Green (D)	165.7	793,923	4,792.3	37.1	37.1	0.2	12.7	11.4	1.4	38.8	10.9	51.7	34.8	49.1
District 10	Michael T. McCaul (R)	5,071.7	823,296	162.3	73.6	10.9	0.6	5.4	6.9	2.6	26.0	55.5	49.8	16.1	56.3
District 11	K. Michael Conaway (R)	27,832.6	759,136	27.3	88.4	4.1	0.4	1.2	3.9	2.0	38.1	55.6	49.6	8.6	70.3
District 12	Kay Granger (R)	1,441.1	770,350	534.5	79.0	8.6	0.6	3.8	4.8	3.2	22.0	63.0	51.2	11.1	60.6
District 13	Mac Thornberry (R)	38,349.5	707,421	18.4	85.6	5.1	0.8	2.2	3.2	3.2	27.0	63.4	49.4	10.2	64.9
District 14	Randy K. Weber Sr. (R)	2,446.6	753,147	307.8	72.4	20.0	0.6	3.2	2.2	1.7	24.8	50.7	49.5	10.4	67.1
District 15	Vicente Gonzalez (D)	7,804.1	776,887	99.5	80.0	1.6	0.3	1.4	15.1	1.6	81.9	14.9	50.7	22.5	64.1
District 16	Beto O'Rourke (D)	710.8	735,784	1,035.1	81.7	4.0	0.5	1.5	9.5	2.7	80.3	13.6	50.7	23.5	57.1
District 17	Bill Flores (R)	7,650.6	761,922	99.6	74.7	13.1	0.5	5.1	3.4	3.2	25.3	54.9	49.8	11.8	66.9
District 18	Sheila Jackson-Lee (D)	235.3	787,352	3,346.5	48.2	36.3	0.1	4.2	8.6	2.6	41.8	17.0	49.2	21.8	58.7
District 19	Jodey C. Arrington (R)	25,835.7	734,532	28.4	83.6	6.1	0.9	1.6	5.2	2.6	37.4	53.3	49.3	7.6	72.5
District 20	Joaquin Castro (D)	199.7	791,141	3,961.6	82.7	5.4	0.6	3.1	5.9	2.3	69.6	21.1	50.5	15.4	66.8
District 21	Lamar Smith (R)	5,920.9	804,470	135.9	86.3	3.7	0.5	3.8	3.0	2.7	30.2	60.4	50.5	10.2	56.8
District 22	Pete Olson (R)	1,033.5	881,407	852.9	60.4	13.3	0.6	19.1	4.0	2.5	25.2	40.2	50.4	25.3	50.4
District 23	Will Hurd (R)	58,058.2	772,944	13.3	80.3	3.9	1.3	1.6	10.7	2.2	68.3	25.0	49.6	16.9	63.3
District 24	Kenny Marchant (R)	262.8	790,319	3,007.3	62.6	11.8	0.6	14.0	7.2	3.8	24.8	46.5	51.1	23.6	45.9
District 25	Roger Williams (R)	7,622.6	762,897	100.1	83.6	7.5	0.5	3.0	1.6	3.7	19.4	68.0	50.2	7.6	58.0

1. Dry land or land partially or temporarily covered by water.   2. May be of any race.

STATE District	Population and population characteristics, 2016 (cont.)										Education, 2016		
	Age (percent)											Attainment[2] (percent)	
	Under 5 years	5 to 17 years	18 to 24 years	25 to 34 years	35 to 44 years	45 to 54 years	55 to 64 years	65 to 74 years	75 years and over	Median age	Total Enrollment[1]	High school graduate or more	Bachelor's degree or more
	15	16	17	18	19	20	21	22	23	24	25	26	27
OREGON— Cont'd													
District 3	6.0	14.1	8.3	17.4	15.9	13.4	12.1	7.9	4.8	37.0	197,165	90.7	41.2
District 4	5.1	13.8	11.5	12.4	11.0	11.6	14.3	12.2	8.2	41.3	187,578	90.9	26.7
District 5	6.0	16.8	9.0	12.7	12.2	12.5	13.5	10.3	6.8	39.5	200,864	89.9	30.0
PENNSYLVANIA	5.6	15.3	9.3	13.1	11.6	13.6	14.2	9.7	7.7	40.6	2,975,685	90.1	30.8
District 1	7.0	16.4	9.1	19.4	13.0	12.4	11.5	6.7	4.5	33.7	176,652	82.3	27.4
District 2	6.2	13.6	13.0	18.7	11.1	11.4	12.0	7.9	6.2	34.1	200,892	87.4	36.7
District 3	5.3	15.0	8.9	12.0	10.8	14.3	15.1	10.5	8.3	43.3	152,354	91.3	26.5
District 4	5.6	16.0	8.7	12.7	11.9	14.2	13.9	9.7	7.4	40.8	163,677	89.2	26.7
District 5	4.7	14.2	12.8	11.8	11.2	13.1	14.3	10.2	7.9	40.6	173,118	90.7	25.1
District 6	5.7	16.6	9.1	12.2	11.6	14.8	14.3	8.8	6.9	40.8	187,249	94.1	43.2
District 7	5.8	16.4	8.3	10.8	11.8	14.5	14.4	9.7	8.3	42.6	175,802	93.0	43.4
District 8	4.8	16.1	7.9	11.0	11.8	15.1	15.5	10.1	7.7	43.6	165,669	93.4	39.7
District 9	5.0	15.2	9.2	11.1	11.3	13.4	15.2	11.0	8.7	43.5	143,382	88.9	18.6
District 10	5.2	15.4	8.8	11.0	10.9	14.1	14.7	11.5	8.3	43.8	146,474	89.2	22.5
District 11	5.6	14.7	9.0	12.1	11.3	14.2	14.8	10.5	7.8	42.5	150,748	90.0	25.1
District 12	5.4	14.8	6.8	11.2	11.4	14.0	15.8	11.1	9.3	45.2	146,951	93.5	33.7
District 13	6.5	16.7	8.4	14.6	12.4	12.9	12.8	8.6	7.0	37.7	177,710	87.9	35.4
District 14	5.1	11.8	11.4	17.7	10.4	12.0	14.4	9.3	7.8	38.4	161,581	92.9	35.4
District 15	5.4	16.3	9.4	12.3	12.3	13.3	13.7	9.7	7.7	40.3	175,431	89.8	29.2
District 16	6.8	17.4	9.6	12.9	11.7	12.9	12.5	8.8	7.1	37.6	173,281	84.1	25.1
District 17	4.7	15.0	9.6	12.4	11.3	14.2	14.5	10.2	8.2	42.2	154,413	89.3	22.7
District 18	5.0	14.9	7.2	11.6	12.1	13.9	15.2	11.0	9.2	44.4	150,301	94.5	36.5
RHODE ISLAND	5.1	14.7	10.8	13.5	11.6	13.9	14.0	9.2	7.2	40.2	264,768	88.5	34.1
District 1	5.4	15.4	10.3	14.4	11.6	13.4	14.0	8.4	7.2	38.9	138,752	86.5	34.2
District 2	4.8	13.9	11.3	12.7	11.7	14.4	13.9	10.0	7.4	41.3	126,016	90.6	34.0
SOUTH CAROLINA	5.8	16.3	9.5	13.0	12.3	13.0	13.2	10.4	6.4	39.1	1,209,286	86.6	27.2
District 1	5.9	15.8	8.4	14.5	13.0	12.6	12.7	11.0	6.1	38.6	180,257	92.3	39.9
District 2	5.8	16.8	9.5	12.9	12.9	13.7	13.4	9.5	5.7	38.9	169,213	89.7	33.5
District 3	5.9	16.2	10.2	12.2	11.5	13.0	13.5	10.6	7.1	39.5	167,782	83.5	22.0
District 4	6.1	16.9	9.2	13.5	12.7	13.5	12.5	9.4	6.4	38.3	177,558	86.7	30.7
District 5	5.7	17.2	8.7	11.9	12.8	14.0	13.4	9.9	6.1	40.3	171,189	86.6	23.0
District 6	6.1	15.8	13.0	14.4	11.4	11.5	12.4	9.6	5.8	35.4	179,496	81.7	19.6
District 7	5.3	15.6	7.9	11.9	11.8	12.7	14.8	12.6	7.5	43.0	163,791	84.8	20.1
SOUTH DAKOTA	7.0	17.6	9.9	12.9	11.4	11.8	13.5	8.9	7.0	36.8	218,239	91.2	28.9
At Large	7.0	17.6	9.9	12.9	11.4	11.8	13.5	8.9	7.0	36.8	218,239	91.2	28.9
TENNESSEE	6.1	16.5	9.3	13.3	12.6	13.4	13.0	9.4	6.2	38.6	1,578,309	87.0	26.1
District 1	4.9	15.4	8.8	11.1	12.0	14.3	14.0	11.5	7.9	43.2	150,814	84.7	19.4
District 2	5.6	15.3	10.4	12.6	12.1	13.6	13.3	10.3	7.0	40.0	172,477	88.4	31.0
District 3	5.3	15.7	8.2	12.4	12.4	13.6	14.3	10.5	7.6	41.7	162,161	86.1	22.7
District 4	6.2	17.0	10.6	13.3	13.0	13.2	12.3	9.0	5.5	37.2	188,806	87.8	22.6
District 5	6.8	14.7	9.9	18.8	13.7	12.5	11.7	7.2	4.7	34.8	181,392	87.4	37.5
District 6	6.1	16.8	8.0	12.1	12.1	13.8	13.3	10.8	6.8	41.1	168,201	86.5	21.9
District 7	6.3	18.8	8.8	12.6	13.2	13.7	12.3	8.7	5.7	37.7	202,131	87.6	28.1
District 8	6.0	17.2	8.5	11.2	12.4	14.0	13.7	10.4	6.9	40.7	168,981	88.2	27.6
District 9	7.6	17.8	10.8	15.6	12.6	12.3	12.1	6.8	4.4	33.6	183,346	85.8	24.1
TEXAS	7.2	19.0	10.0	14.5	13.4	12.6	11.2	7.2	4.8	34.5	7,603,170	82.9	28.9
District 1	6.6	17.8	10.6	12.3	11.8	12.2	12.5	9.2	6.8	36.8	181,506	82.0	20.9
District 2	7.2	17.6	8.5	16.5	15.1	12.7	11.7	6.9	3.5	35.0	208,522	89.0	40.8
District 3	6.3	20.0	8.3	12.5	15.8	12.8	11.0	6.7	3.8	36.7	239,492	93.6	53.5
District 4	6.1	18.3	8.4	11.6	12.8	12.8	13.2	9.8	7.1	39.6	183,617	86.4	22.1
District 5	7.2	19.1	9.0	13.9	13.7	12.6	11.2	7.9	5.5	35.6	196,388	79.7	21.1
District 6	6.5	19.2	10.0	13.9	13.0	13.9	11.7	7.7	4.1	35.2	216,566	88.2	28.7
District 7	7.5	17.9	7.3	17.4	14.6	12.8	11.4	6.4	4.4	34.9	207,928	89.8	50.7
District 8	6.4	18.3	9.5	12.9	13.3	13.7	12.4	8.4	5.0	37.2	207,347	87.1	30.2
District 9	7.3	19.3	11.3	16.7	13.2	12.1	10.7	5.9	3.6	32.0	229,528	79.5	23.8
District 10	6.6	18.7	8.3	15.2	14.7	13.5	11.3	7.2	4.6	35.8	216,021	89.0	38.7
District 11	7.5	18.0	10.5	14.0	11.1	11.4	12.0	8.5	6.9	34.9	191,252	81.7	20.4
District 12	7.0	17.8	8.7	15.3	13.4	12.8	12.3	7.6	5.1	35.7	196,944	88.0	29.9
District 13	6.8	17.8	10.2	13.4	12.5	11.5	12.4	8.8	6.5	36.1	176,177	82.2	20.4
District 14	6.7	18.0	8.9	14.0	13.2	12.8	13.2	8.0	5.1	36.6	188,746	85.8	22.7
District 15	9.0	22.9	10.5	13.7	13.0	10.9	8.8	6.6	4.7	30.7	239,255	70.7	19.8
District 16	7.9	19.5	11.3	15.3	12.4	11.1	10.3	6.7	5.4	32.1	221,463	79.3	23.9
District 17	6.7	16.5	15.1	15.5	12.2	11.3	10.4	7.1	5.0	32.3	235,328	85.4	29.4
District 18	8.0	19.1	10.9	16.4	14.3	12.4	9.6	5.8	3.7	32.4	214,741	76.2	22.4
District 19	6.8	18.1	13.2	14.4	12.2	10.8	10.9	7.5	6.0	33.1	216,092	81.9	22.4
District 20	7.0	18.5	12.0	16.8	13.4	11.7	9.8	6.4	4.3	32.2	225,129	80.3	24.7
District 21	5.5	14.7	10.9	14.5	13.2	12.7	12.9	9.3	6.3	37.8	193,237	92.9	45.1
District 22	7.3	20.2	8.4	12.8	15.4	14.0	11.3	6.7	4.0	35.8	261,864	90.5	45.1
District 23	7.4	20.6	10.3	14.0	13.0	12.1	10.2	7.2	5.3	33.5	215,688	74.3	21.7
District 24	6.1	17.2	8.0	17.9	14.7	14.0	11.9	6.3	4.2	35.6	195,248	89.6	44.7
District 25	6.0	17.7	9.9	13.3	13.5	13.1	12.6	8.6	5.2	37.1	196,687	90.5	37.2

1. All persons 3 years old and over enrolled in nursery school through college and graduate or professional school.   2. Persons 25 years old and over.

Table E. Congressional Districts 115th Congress — **Households and Group Quarters**

STATE District	Households, 2016						Group Quarters, 2010					
	Number	Average household size	Family households (percent)	Married couple family (percent)	Female family house-holder[1]	One person households (percent)	Total in group quarters, 2016	Percent 65 years and over	Persons in correctional institutions	Persons in nursing facilities	Persons in college dormitories	Persons in military quarters
	28	29	30	31	32	33	34	35	36	37	38	39
OREGON— Cont'd												
District 3	324,260	2.52	57.6	42.9	10.3	29.5	18,330	15.5	2,065	2,399	6,604	0
District 4	318,197	2.44	61.5	46.9	9.6	28.5	18,908	16.5	1,354	2,067	8,825	21
District 5	302,323	2.67	66.0	51.7	10.3	26.8	16,321	19.1	5,381	2,401	3,162	17
PENNSYLVANIA	4,937,771	2.50	63.8	47.4	11.7	30.0	427,424	21.0	97,820	87,775	177,332	259
District 1	260,860	2.70	55.4	28.8	20.0	35.1	18,455	9.2	10,896	2,024	7,108	14
District 2	279,336	2.42	49.1	24.8	19.1	42.5	36,094	13.8	680	4,909	23,446	0
District 3	278,846	2.39	64.1	49.0	10.1	29.8	27,892	19.5	6,328	5,188	11,315	11
District 4	281,239	2.50	66.7	50.8	11.5	27.4	22,578	20.4	6,485	3,922	7,205	37
District 5	263,672	2.47	63.1	50.2	8.1	29.5	48,734	11.4	14,533	5,088	23,276	0
District 6	274,134	2.62	69.1	54.4	10.6	25.2	18,530	24.0	3,336	4,461	7,424	0
District 7	258,813	2.66	71.4	58.6	8.8	24.7	24,570	21.2	5,890	5,118	10,160	0
District 8	265,416	2.64	71.0	57.4	8.9	23.8	9,808	46.3	1,039	4,098	1,569	0
District 9	277,770	2.40	63.9	49.3	10.4	30.4	22,479	23.8	6,117	5,134	8,771	0
District 10	256,391	2.58	66.5	52.1	9.5	28.4	28,850	15.5	11,878	4,486	10,876	0
District 11	278,092	2.44	64.6	48.4	11.5	29.5	28,443	22.1	7,333	6,231	9,991	6
District 12	283,824	2.40	66.7	53.6	9.3	29.0	16,441	32.7	4,480	4,694	3,073	6
District 13	268,338	2.68	64.8	44.7	15.1	29.3	11,793	57.8	2	6,384	1,329	121
District 14	317,371	2.11	48.4	31.5	13.2	42.0	27,803	15.0	4,663	4,194	15,905	0
District 15	275,165	2.55	68.2	50.8	12.2	26.0	23,008	21.1	1,424	5,210	13,039	63
District 16	261,448	2.70	68.2	51.2	12.2	25.9	18,712	27.5	1,132	5,327	9,156	0
District 17	270,356	2.50	63.8	47.2	11.7	29.8	24,950	25.7	7,876	6,346	7,783	1
District 18	286,700	2.40	66.6	53.8	8.9	28.5	18,284	30.3	3,728	4,961	5,906	0
RHODE ISLAND	408,239	2.48	60.6	42.3	13.9	32.3	42,752	18.5	3,783	8,420	24,687	1,385
District 1	205,952	2.50	60.2	40.9	14.9	33.2	22,549	21.3	350	4,996	13,035	1,385
District 2	202,287	2.47	61.0	43.6	13.0	31.4	20,203	15.5	3,433	3,424	11,652	0
SOUTH CAROLINA	1,877,887	2.57	65.2	46.4	14.2	29.3	136,582	13.0	41,649	19,020	46,463	19,413
District 1	290,002	2.59	63.7	49.7	11.0	29.7	9,708	15.4	531	1,662	2,560	4,436
District 2	269,439	2.54	68.3	49.9	13.8	25.8	19,348	12.8	1,458	2,391	823	11,567
District 3	258,490	2.57	67.8	48.1	13.6	27.0	21,020	14.3	7,044	3,116	9,817	0
District 4	273,239	2.56	65.4	47.0	14.1	29.0	17,729	14.5	3,776	2,832	9,668	0
District 5	267,518	2.59	67.7	49.4	13.5	28.7	12,426	20.0	5,318	2,792	3,289	611
District 6	248,721	2.56	58.0	33.9	19.0	35.9	42,512	6.5	18,400	3,087	17,383	2,799
District 7	270,478	2.57	65.3	46.1	15.3	29.6	13,839	22.4	5,122	3,140	2,923	0
SOUTH DAKOTA	334,003	2.49	62.9	49.3	9.3	31.0	34,010	21.1	6,327	7,005	10,248	597
At Large	334,003	2.49	62.9	49.3	9.3	31.0	34,010	21.1	6,327	7,005	10,248	597
TENNESSEE	2,556,332	2.54	65.4	47.8	13.0	28.7	152,979	19.8	46,957	33,041	53,136	1,544
District 1	283,213	2.46	65.3	48.5	12.0	29.4	16,617	26.7	4,577	4,466	4,176	0
District 2	294,685	2.45	63.1	49.2	9.2	30.0	17,287	19.1	1,901	3,686	10,443	0
District 3	285,079	2.49	63.1	48.1	10.9	32.4	18,819	23.8	4,913	4,071	4,884	3
District 4	284,054	2.65	68.4	51.4	12.8	25.0	15,060	21.1	3,301	3,584	6,619	0
District 5	311,394	2.38	56.7	38.3	14.2	33.0	22,412	9.0	6,769	2,588	13,660	0
District 6	289,792	2.59	70.6	55.6	10.3	25.2	10,941	36.4	2,385	3,730	2,283	0
District 7	273,435	2.74	73.1	57.7	11.8	22.7	16,792	21.2	8,311	3,918	2,350	1,250
District 8	260,950	2.64	72.7	54.8	13.2	23.5	18,158	21.3	7,494	4,158	4,748	10
District 9	273,730	2.51	56.5	27.9	23.0	36.6	16,893	14.0	7,306	2,840	3,973	281
TEXAS	9,535,612	2.86	69.2	49.9	14.1	25.2	608,204	14.9	267,405	94,278	119,834	35,260
District 1	250,547	2.76	69.0	51.3	14.4	26.6	27,455	17.3	8,132	5,093	9,123	0
District 2	287,714	2.68	65.9	49.6	12.0	28.2	9,909	18.4	2,441	1,873	2,921	0
District 3	304,582	2.76	73.6	60.1	9.6	22.6	2,931	31.9	1,061	1,326	387	0
District 4	262,678	2.73	69.9	53.9	11.8	26.9	18,138	25.8	8,850	5,078	2,237	0
District 5	253,878	2.91	70.7	50.9	13.7	24.1	24,817	14.9	17,768	3,964	938	0
District 6	263,565	2.89	74.0	53.2	14.8	21.4	8,287	32.8	689	2,419	2,137	0
District 7	303,045	2.54	63.2	48.5	10.3	31.9	1,442	58.1	3	774	5	0
District 8	276,789	2.83	73.4	57.7	10.8	21.5	29,537	8.5	23,107	2,021	2,615	0
District 9	267,825	2.95	68.3	40.6	20.6	25.4	3,204	32.7	154	1,629	1,520	0
District 10	289,151	2.80	68.9	53.7	11.2	24.9	14,291	25.7	2,453	3,156	4,344	0
District 11	264,303	2.79	65.5	48.9	11.6	29.0	22,278	18.3	9,050	3,721	3,615	1,924
District 12	280,567	2.70	67.1	50.0	11.8	27.1	14,161	20.3	5,807	3,540	3,405	202
District 13	254,848	2.63	68.6	52.2	12.0	26.4	37,612	11.8	17,511	4,208	2,479	5,487
District 14	271,252	2.65	68.1	48.5	14.1	27.6	33,797	9.5	22,748	2,861	2,869	40
District 15	221,925	3.43	78.2	52.4	20.2	18.0	15,404	14.6	8,632	2,035	1,514	0
District 16	239,593	3.01	71.7	46.4	19.7	24.9	14,472	9.8	6,076	1,482	491	5,683
District 17	278,052	2.63	61.9	43.9	13.2	27.9	31,381	11.1	8,355	3,792	14,831	0
District 18	274,686	2.79	63.5	36.5	20.6	29.3	20,383	3.8	12,624	783	5,661	0
District 19	256,558	2.69	65.2	47.1	13.2	27.0	44,319	10.0	19,845	4,073	10,748	621
District 20	254,256	3.06	66.3	42.8	18.5	26.8	12,396	11.9	4	2,081	4,846	9,322
District 21	315,308	2.50	60.2	47.3	8.9	31.2	17,284	19.9	600	4,024	7,505	3,793
District 22	284,890	3.07	79.5	63.6	10.9	17.1	6,970	21.6	4,494	1,409	4	0
District 23	226,789	3.32	76.0	55.7	15.1	21.2	19,106	7.6	16,613	1,566	193	877
District 24	310,253	2.54	63.2	47.7	10.5	29.8	3,473	65.8	53	1,913	480	0
District 25	266,033	2.74	71.7	58.3	9.3	22.3	35,081	9.6	11,967	3,274	10,926	2,822

1. No spouse present.

Items 28—39

STATE District	Housing units, 2016						Money income, 2016		
		Occupied units						Households	
			Owner-occupied			Renter-occupied			
	Total	Occupied units as a percent of all units	Owner-occupied units as a percent of occupied units	Median value[1] (dollars)	Percent valued at $500,000 or more	Median rent[2]	Per capita income (dollars)	Median income (dollars)	Percent with income of $100,000 or more
	40	41	42	43	44	45	46	47	48
OREGON— Cont'd									
District 3	343,772	94.3	56.0	359,700	24.1	1,136	33,839	63,231	29.2
District 4	349,873	90.9	61.9	227,800	7.2	889	26,405	46,749	17.1
District 5	337,628	89.5	63.9	288,700	15.3	981	30,917	60,395	25.8
PENNSYLVANIA	5,611,995	88.0	68.5	174,100	6.4	881	31,272	56,907	25.1
District 1	299,235	87.2	54.2	137,600	6.5	978	25,346	45,025	18.3
District 2	333,571	83.7	49.3	160,600	14.4	982	29,672	41,320	20.4
District 3	317,724	87.8	72.1	132,500	3.5	691	28,265	51,289	20.1
District 4	304,280	92.4	72.3	179,900	2.8	899	30,393	61,333	25.2
District 5	342,855	76.9	71.4	123,900	2.7	722	25,863	48,410	18.0
District 6	292,116	93.8	73.9	270,200	15.4	1,128	41,560	82,139	40.2
District 7	273,542	94.6	76.9	298,700	17.0	1,191	43,082	85,881	43.4
District 8	280,043	94.8	76.2	317,200	16.5	1,141	40,591	80,199	39.1
District 9	318,698	87.2	71.9	125,700	2.1	684	25,638	47,697	16.0
District 10	342,609	74.8	74.2	160,100	3.5	735	26,909	52,199	19.8
District 11	322,375	86.3	70.5	155,200	2.5	779	28,364	53,833	20.8
District 12	318,254	89.2	78.2	151,300	3.8	728	33,788	60,387	27.3
District 13	288,189	93.1	62.3	225,700	7.2	1,063	30,882	60,105	27.1
District 14	364,557	87.1	54.0	101,700	3.1	772	29,097	44,939	17.2
District 15	291,641	94.4	68.1	200,200	5.1	987	32,510	62,755	27.6
District 16	279,040	93.7	64.9	190,800	5.6	934	28,576	57,144	23.6
District 17	324,494	83.3	68.1	143,500	1.5	779	26,874	51,635	19.9
District 18	318,772	89.9	76.5	170,400	4.2	785	34,727	63,825	29.5
RHODE ISLAND	462,598	88.2	58.0	247,700	10.5	948	33,008	60,596	28.1
District 1	230,632	89.3	52.1	255,400	13.1	918	32,302	56,547	26.2
District 2	231,966	87.2	64.1	242,600	8.2	982	33,739	63,976	30.1
SOUTH CAROLINA	2,236,262	84.0	68.6	153,900	6.5	841	27,016	49,501	19.4
District 1	348,334	83.3	69.9	239,400	17.6	1,120	35,549	64,973	29.2
District 2	299,720	89.9	73.2	155,600	4.8	896	29,799	57,253	24.0
District 3	304,659	84.8	68.9	130,500	4.2	702	24,185	45,042	16.4
District 4	302,372	90.4	65.8	157,400	6.0	822	28,564	51,718	20.7
District 5	302,165	88.5	73.0	139,700	3.9	790	25,936	48,743	18.8
District 6	300,957	82.6	57.4	99,700	3.7	821	20,001	35,296	10.7
District 7	378,055	71.5	71.4	143,500	4.2	766	24,069	43,146	14.6
SOUTH DAKOTA	383,827	87.0	67.2	160,700	4.3	706	28,585	54,467	19.8
At Large	383,827	87.0	67.2	160,700	4.3	706	28,585	54,467	19.8
TENNESSEE	2,919,698	87.6	65.1	157,700	5.8	806	27,087	48,547	18.8
District 1	348,133	81.4	69.2	138,400	3.2	640	23,487	41,006	12.3
District 2	330,653	89.1	67.6	168,900	6.3	777	28,119	50,701	19.3
District 3	327,695	87.0	69.3	153,100	3.4	728	26,075	43,938	17.1
District 4	313,866	90.5	67.3	155,700	2.8	811	25,460	50,598	17.8
District 5	339,150	91.8	55.5	204,400	10.7	968	32,051	54,470	22.2
District 6	321,552	90.1	71.9	165,300	4.4	751	26,712	50,731	19.4
District 7	321,494	85.1	71.5	167,300	13.2	842	29,219	53,276	24.3
District 8	295,175	88.4	69.8	158,600	4.9	738	30,049	54,145	24.8
District 9	321,980	85.0	44.4	98,500	2.3	864	22,217	39,761	12.2
TEXAS	10,754,268	88.7	61.1	161,500	6.8	956	28,714	56,565	25.9
District 1	306,661	81.7	65.5	125,600	2.5	783	22,948	45,313	15.9
District 2	306,712	93.8	61.5	216,400	10.5	1,209	39,593	72,711	36.8
District 3	319,034	95.5	65.1	296,800	12.9	1,240	41,962	88,619	44.3
District 4	308,017	85.3	72.0	122,900	3.7	765	26,686	52,481	22.7
District 5	290,453	87.4	63.0	130,300	5.1	867	24,307	50,536	20.9
District 6	288,838	91.3	65.5	163,800	2.9	1,003	29,087	65,758	28.7
District 7	329,230	92.0	50.2	252,300	25.2	1,177	45,900	71,183	36.7
District 8	314,497	88.0	70.7	198,000	9.3	1,075	32,984	64,861	31.7
District 9	292,333	91.6	46.8	123,700	0.7	921	20,788	46,048	15.4
District 10	321,841	89.8	66.4	228,600	12.5	1,152	36,517	73,476	36.6
District 11	331,335	79.8	67.8	135,900	4.5	885	27,915	50,602	22.2
District 12	307,169	91.3	62.1	167,000	6.3	992	31,952	62,214	28.7
District 13	305,820	83.3	64.6	111,300	2.7	773	25,315	50,150	19.4
District 14	317,734	85.4	63.8	151,500	2.9	884	29,325	58,103	28.8
District 15	254,072	87.3	66.6	96,200	1.4	728	18,423	41,947	16.6
District 16	263,748	90.8	58.7	125,700	2.2	781	20,563	44,045	15.4
District 17	320,751	86.7	55.8	158,500	4.2	927	26,713	50,888	22.0
District 18	305,284	90.0	47.7	130,900	7.0	888	24,132	42,662	18.4
District 19	301,908	85.0	61.2	104,500	2.4	838	23,579	47,875	17.6
District 20	274,530	92.6	54.7	132,400	1.8	915	22,507	49,421	18.3
District 21	359,518	87.7	58.8	271,100	16.0	1,108	38,034	68,987	33.2
District 22	303,476	93.9	71.8	260,200	9.2	1,149	38,041	87,901	44.4
District 23	265,187	85.5	70.5	116,200	5.5	841	23,280	51,293	21.9
District 24	332,586	93.3	47.3	255,000	14.2	1,096	40,379	70,454	34.5
District 25	310,435	85.7	69.2	231,200	18.6	1,010	36,139	69,083	32.8

1. Specified owner-occupied units.   2. Specified renter-occupied units.

Table E. Congressional Districts 115th Congress — **Age and Education**

STATE District	Population and population characteristics, 2016 (cont.)										Education, 2016		
	Age (percent)											Attainment[2] (percent)	
	Under 5 years	5 to 17 years	18 to 24 years	25 to 34 years	35 to 44 years	45 to 54 years	55 to 64 years	65 to 74 years	75 years and over	Median age	Total Enrollment[1]	High school graduate or more	Bachelor's degree or more
	15	16	17	18	19	20	21	22	23	24	25	26	27
TEXAS— Cont'd													
District 26	7.0	20.4	9.1	13.3	15.3	14.9	10.8	6.2	3.2	35.2	253,659	92.5	44.2
District 27	6.8	18.3	9.8	13.1	12.1	12.3	12.4	8.7	6.4	36.4	183,395	82.6	20.3
District 28	8.5	22.6	10.3	13.2	12.8	11.6	9.5	6.7	4.7	31.4	223,425	70.9	17.7
District 29	9.2	21.4	10.4	14.9	13.7	12.0	10.4	5.2	2.6	31.2	217,416	61.9	10.4
District 30	7.5	19.8	10.4	15.2	13.1	12.5	11.4	6.2	4.0	33.0	200,919	77.3	20.5
District 31	7.2	19.4	9.3	14.8	14.8	12.6	10.2	7.3	4.6	34.6	231,263	92.4	34.3
District 32	7.3	17.5	8.6	16.3	13.8	13.5	11.6	6.8	4.6	35.2	196,206	86.8	43.4
District 33	9.1	22.6	11.3	15.2	13.6	11.9	8.6	4.8	3.1	29.7	222,578	58.9	9.3
District 34	8.5	21.0	11.0	12.5	12.1	11.5	9.6	8.1	5.9	32.3	210,418	68.8	15.1
District 35	8.1	18.3	11.8	18.1	13.7	11.1	9.6	5.4	3.9	31.2	224,622	76.9	20.4
District 36	6.9	18.5	9.7	12.9	12.4	13.1	12.7	8.4	5.3	36.5	184,503	84.5	19.4
UTAH	8.3	21.9	11.3	14.7	13.4	10.2	9.6	6.2	4.3	30.7	973,643	91.7	32.6
District 1	8.6	22.9	11.1	13.6	13.6	10.5	10.0	5.9	3.9	30.5	241,635	92.2	28.9
District 2	7.1	20.3	10.4	15.2	13.4	10.3	10.4	7.5	5.6	33.2	224,332	90.0	32.5
District 3	8.3	22.2	15.1	13.7	12.0	9.8	9.2	6.0	3.7	27.7	268,713	94.5	41.6
District 4	9.2	22.3	8.9	16.1	14.8	10.6	9.0	5.6	3.6	31.0	238,963	90.6	28.2
VERMONT	4.9	14.1	10.6	11.5	11.3	13.9	15.5	11.0	7.2	43.1	143,386	92.1	36.4
At Large	4.9	14.1	10.6	11.5	11.3	13.9	15.5	11.0	7.2	43.1	143,386	92.1	36.4
VIRGINIA	6.0	16.2	9.8	13.7	13.0	13.8	12.9	8.7	5.9	38.2	2,146,237	89.3	38.1
District 1	6.0	17.6	9.0	11.9	12.8	14.8	12.9	9.4	5.6	39.3	198,126	91.5	37.5
District 2	6.1	15.9	11.4	15.5	12.5	12.4	12.4	8.1	6.0	35.9	193,554	92.2	34.4
District 3	6.8	15.6	12.1	16.4	11.4	12.6	12.2	7.6	5.3	34.4	201,531	88.8	26.2
District 4	5.8	15.4	10.1	15.4	12.2	13.5	13.8	8.6	5.3	37.5	193,030	87.5	30.1
District 5	4.7	15.2	10.0	11.7	11.0	13.3	14.7	11.4	7.9	42.7	173,736	86.0	27.9
District 6	5.1	15.3	12.5	11.5	11.2	13.4	13.3	10.2	7.7	40.3	194,303	87.2	26.6
District 7	5.8	17.7	7.8	12.3	13.7	14.5	12.9	9.5	5.8	39.9	192,770	90.9	39.0
District 8	7.0	14.0	7.2	19.7	16.5	13.4	11.3	6.6	4.3	36.1	178,763	90.7	61.8
District 9	4.8	13.6	11.4	11.5	11.5	13.5	14.4	11.2	8.1	43.0	167,279	83.6	20.4
District 10	6.7	20.1	7.8	11.2	14.9	15.9	11.8	7.3	4.3	37.9	236,159	92.3	54.3
District 11	6.7	17.7	9.0	13.7	15.1	14.6	12.0	7.1	4.4	36.9	216,986	90.7	55.5
WASHINGTON	6.2	16.2	9.1	14.7	13.0	13.1	13.0	9.0	5.8	37.7	1,744,806	90.8	35.1
District 1	6.7	16.8	7.1	14.3	13.8	14.9	12.9	8.4	5.0	38.5	179,058	93.9	43.4
District 2	5.8	14.7	10.5	14.4	12.9	12.5	13.5	9.5	6.2	38.2	172,375	91.5	30.3
District 3	6.0	17.6	8.0	12.2	12.4	13.2	13.6	10.5	6.5	39.8	170,639	90.9	25.4
District 4	7.7	21.2	9.2	13.2	12.1	11.5	11.7	8.0	5.5	34.0	195,024	80.1	20.1
District 5	5.7	15.7	11.5	13.8	11.3	12.2	13.5	9.6	6.6	37.4	185,686	93.2	30.4
District 6	5.6	14.4	8.5	13.5	11.2	12.6	14.9	11.9	7.3	41.6	147,750	92.0	29.7
District 7	4.5	11.2	10.2	21.0	14.4	12.8	12.4	8.0	5.5	36.6	166,075	94.8	61.0
District 8	7.2	18.0	8.4	12.0	14.3	14.7	13.0	7.8	4.6	38.0	187,201	90.3	34.5
District 9	6.1	15.5	7.9	16.8	14.4	13.6	12.3	7.6	5.6	37.3	168,310	88.6	41.8
District 10	6.5	16.8	9.5	15.6	12.7	12.5	12.4	8.5	5.5	36.1	172,688	91.2	28.7
WEST VIRGINIA	5.6	15.0	8.9	11.8	12.2	13.3	14.5	11.1	7.6	42.3	394,881	86.0	20.8
District 1	5.2	14.3	10.8	12.2	11.8	13.0	13.9	11.0	7.7	41.4	139,979	89.1	23.5
District 2	5.7	15.9	7.5	11.9	11.8	14.1	15.0	10.9	7.1	42.6	133,249	86.1	21.5
District 3	5.8	14.9	8.3	11.2	12.8	12.7	14.7	11.5	8.2	42.9	121,653	82.6	17.4
WISCONSIN	5.8	16.5	9.7	12.6	11.9	13.5	14.0	9.2	6.9	39.4	1,428,041	91.9	29.5
District 1	5.7	17.5	8.2	11.9	12.0	14.8	14.7	8.9	6.3	40.8	173,966	91.5	28.2
District 2	5.9	15.7	12.1	14.2	12.5	12.9	12.8	8.4	5.7	36.6	202,069	94.7	42.6
District 3	5.7	15.3	13.1	12.0	10.7	12.5	13.9	9.5	7.4	38.4	186,610	92.2	25.4
District 4	7.3	18.1	11.1	16.4	12.8	11.7	11.3	6.6	4.7	32.8	202,773	85.4	27.4
District 5	5.4	15.9	8.5	12.2	12.0	14.1	14.5	9.3	8.0	41.4	175,070	94.5	36.9
District 6	5.4	15.9	8.9	11.7	11.6	14.0	14.8	10.0	7.7	41.8	166,083	92.2	26.4
District 7	5.2	16.4	7.2	10.6	11.1	14.1	15.8	11.4	8.2	44.6	148,551	91.5	23.1
District 8	5.8	16.9	8.2	12.1	12.0	14.3	14.4	9.2	6.9	40.5	172,919	92.6	25.4
WYOMING	6.5	17.6	9.2	13.8	12.3	11.8	13.8	9.1	5.8	37.2	151,204	93.2	27.1
At Large	6.5	17.6	9.2	13.8	12.3	11.8	13.8	9.1	5.8	37.2	151,204	93.2	27.1

1. All persons 3 years old and over enrolled in nursery school through college and graduate or professional school.   2. Persons 25 years old and over.

STATE District	Households, 2016					Group Quarters, 2010					
	Number	Average household size	Family households (percent)	Married couple family (percent)	Female family house-holder[1]	One person households (percent)	Total in group quarters, 2016	Percent 65 years and over	Persons in correctional institutions	Persons in nursing facilities	Persons in college dormitories	Persons in military quarters
	28	29	30	31	32	33	34	35	36	37	38	39
TEXAS— Cont'd												
District 26	282,462	2.95	74.9	61.1	10.3	19.1	13,035	14.1	1,179	1,636	6,475	0
District 27	260,365	2.77	68.1	47.3	14.7	26.5	14,971	31.7	3,832	4,197	1,365	103
District 28	212,327	3.44	77.1	52.6	18.9	20.0	6,513	32.3	3,252	2,888	740	146
District 29	234,493	3.25	73.7	46.7	18.4	21.4	2,191	36.1	31	1,008	0	0
District 30	263,998	2.77	65.1	36.5	22.3	29.2	17,441	9.2	11,108	2,286	2,507	0
District 31	280,467	2.91	71.8	55.6	11.6	23.4	14,426	16.1	3,442	2,183	2,041	4,084
District 32	286,210	2.62	62.9	46.7	11.7	28.8	5,174	38.4	22	2,226	2,437	0
District 33	229,843	3.30	73.1	43.7	21.0	21.4	6,437	19.3	2,147	1,389	534	0
District 34	210,523	3.34	76.5	52.1	18.7	20.0	18,964	13.7	13,244	2,881	2,180	41
District 35	264,053	3.04	63.3	39.4	17.6	26.3	20,224	9.9	7,971	2,563	5,761	115
District 36	251,784	2.83	72.2	52.2	13.7	23.8	20,700	16.7	12,140	2,926	0	0
UTAH	943,147	3.19	75.4	61.3	9.6	18.7	45,776	10.4	12,666	5,854	15,666	523
District 1	234,783	3.19	77.5	64.5	8.6	17.6	8,078	10.6	1,892	1,190	3,227	488
District 2	247,006	2.97	70.4	55.9	9.8	22.8	14,730	12.1	3,459	1,763	3,443	35
District 3	219,529	3.35	78.3	66.7	8.0	15.3	15,896	7.5	441	1,279	8,960	0
District 4	241,829	3.25	75.8	58.8	11.7	18.6	7,072	12.4	6,874	1,622	36	0
VERMONT	254,851	2.35	60.6	47.2	9.0	30.2	25,240	15.0	1,592	3,588	16,895	5
At Large	254,851	2.35	60.6	47.2	9.0	30.2	25,240	15.0	1,592	3,588	16,895	5
VIRGINIA	3,120,692	2.62	66.1	49.9	11.8	27.4	241,626	12.0	1,592	30,324	84,048	37,568
District 1	277,101	2.74	72.7	59.2	9.5	22.7	17,199	13.8	4,215	2,568	6,380	3,351
District 2	271,729	2.61	67.4	49.0	14.1	25.2	35,252	11.2	1,685	2,534	7,086	7,370
District 3	281,520	2.53	60.3	37.8	17.5	32.1	27,622	5.4	6,045	3,045	11,014	24,287
District 4	286,585	2.55	61.3	40.4	16.5	31.2	33,025	10.2	19,352	2,662	2,942	316
District 5	283,654	2.49	65.7	49.2	12.5	28.0	29,034	13.8	10,972	4,052	12,206	0
District 6	293,613	2.45	62.9	46.5	11.6	30.6	34,450	12.6	4,623	4,349	19,615	1,398
District 7	286,841	2.66	69.8	54.7	10.9	24.8	11,407	19.8	4,500	2,649	3,721	0
District 8	314,900	2.47	57.1	44.7	8.6	33.0	6,691	28.6	944	2,026	1,084	846
District 9	281,436	2.40	62.4	48.3	10.3	31.4	32,723	13.1	10,091	4,288	14,085	0
District 10	272,000	3.02	78.9	65.6	8.9	17.4	6,153	18.7	1,606	907	1,068	0
District 11	271,313	2.93	70.7	55.3	10.2	23.0	8,070	13.6	1,207	1,244	4,847	0
WASHINGTON	2,768,076	2.58	64.5	50.2	9.8	27.0	142,590	18.6	31,960	22,156	35,534	12,385
District 1	270,730	2.69	70.7	58.9	7.6	22.1	8,947	23.7	2,676	1,313	620	0
District 2	278,780	2.56	63.2	49.5	9.1	26.9	14,203	20.5	1,754	2,323	3,862	2,504
District 3	267,226	2.68	68.8	54.2	9.5	24.2	7,245	35.8	1,539	1,617	0	14
District 4	239,010	2.95	69.9	52.2	13.1	24.4	9,691	25.7	4,028	2,246	382	4
District 5	274,826	2.47	62.2	47.8	10.2	28.4	28,820	11.8	5,656	2,927	13,048	513
District 6	278,664	2.44	62.4	48.3	9.4	29.3	18,745	16	8,063	3,211	1,022	5,694
District 7	344,997	2.16	49.3	39.9	6.3	37.4	20,948	13.6	1,851	2,700	10,456	362
District 8	261,473	2.80	72.9	58.2	9.8	20.8	6,517	24.8	839	1,305	2,155	0
District 9	280,742	2.59	63.3	46.3	11.8	27.0	13,351	26.9	3,031	2,422	1,348	0
District 10	271,628	2.64	67.0	50.3	12.0	26.3	14,123	17.9	2,523	2,092	2,641	3,294
WEST VIRGINIA	722,125	2.47	64.7	48.1	12.1	29.7	48,027	18.9	16,591	9,748	17,113	79
District 1	240,041	2.48	62.5	46.8	11.2	30.6	21,581	15.8	6,965	3,632	10,300	0
District 2	245,164	2.49	65.5	49.0	12.3	29.4	11,221	23.6	2,583	2,791	3,447	79
District 3	236,920	2.43	66.2	48.3	12.7	29.1	15,225	20.1	7,043	3,325	3,366	0
WISCONSIN	2,326,998	2.42	62.8	48.5	9.7	29.8	146,260	23.1	38,102	33,808	56,773	132
District 1	276,902	2.53	67.9	52.6	10.4	26.3	14,412	21.6	6,723	3,632	2,368	0
District 2	306,923	2.41	59.3	47.1	8.5	30.0	17,375	19.7	2,269	2,791	8,805	0
District 3	286,437	2.41	61.7	49.4	8.0	29.6	31,691	15.5	6,311	3,325	18,297	122
District 4	278,710	2.49	55.0	29.6	19.5	36.1	18,140	17.5	2,539	3,173	9,814	0
District 5	294,420	2.41	64.3	52.7	7.9	29.8	13,971	33.1	1,490	4,832	5,703	0
District 6	291,448	2.36	64.5	52.0	7.8	28.9	24,522	20.2	12,174	5,078	6,097	0
District 7	294,702	2.36	64.8	52.3	8.4	29.1	11,864	42.6	3,541	5,073	1,198	0
District 8	297,456	2.40	64.7	51.9	8.0	28.6	14,285	31.5	3,055	4,742	4,491	10
WYOMING	223,619	2.55	65.1	52.3	7.8	27.7	14,290	18.4	3,576	2,450	4,443	503
At Large	223,619	2.55	65.1	52.3	7.8	27.7	14,290	18.4	3,576	2,450	4,443	503

1. No spouse present.

STATE District	Total	Housing units, 2016 Occupied units as a percent of all units	Owner-occupied units as a percent of occupied units	Median value[1] (dollars)	Percent valued at $500,000 or more	Median rent[2]	Money income, 2016 Per capita income (dollars)	Median income (dollars)	Percent with income of $100,000 or more
	40	41	42	43	44	45	46	47	48
TEXAS— Cont'd									
District 26	297,609	94.9	70.8	247,100	9.7	1,183	38,097	87,272	43.9
District 27	315,223	82.6	64.1	133,400	2.9	887	26,761	53,047	22.1
District 28	243,934	87.0	69.5	112,800	1.7	796	18,843	44,021	17.2
District 29	257,812	91.0	51.8	99,800	1.4	851	17,512	41,737	12.6
District 30	289,960	91.0	51.1	113,300	3.0	936	21,974	44,689	15.7
District 31	309,412	90.6	62.5	213,600	4.1	1,054	31,588	69,228	31.5
District 32	307,744	93.0	55.1	220,100	18.9	1,102	42,307	70,119	34.6
District 33	252,362	91.1	46.6	91,300	0.9	836	15,556	38,445	8.4
District 34	260,991	80.7	67.4	80,200	1.6	687	16,944	37,989	12.5
District 35	289,114	91.3	49.3	131,300	1.4	1,000	21,480	48,490	16.3
District 36	298,938	84.2	69.0	132,500	2.5	896	28,675	58,984	27.2
UTAH	1,054,242	89.5	69.9	250,300	9.9	954	26,993	65,977	27.9
District 1	273,648	85.8	73.6	217,500	8.3	854	26,194	65,896	26.9
District 2	286,317	86.3	67.2	239,300	8.6	923	26,807	60,700	23.8
District 3	242,475	90.5	69.4	299,000	17.1	967	28,770	70,763	33.6
District 4	251,802	96.0	69.5	259,600	6.3	1,060	26,246	68,711	28.0
VERMONT	329,539	77.3	69.8	223,700	7.2	925	31,836	57,677	24.3
At Large	329,539	77.3	69.8	223,700	7.2	925	31,836	57,677	24.3
VIRGINIA	3,491,185	89.4	65.3	264,000	19.2	1,159	36,206	68,114	33.1
District 1	307,517	90.1	75.5	296,100	13.6	1,268	37,264	81,338	40.2
District 2	309,617	87.8	61.0	262,400	12.1	1,200	33,688	66,953	30.0
District 3	315,842	89.1	53.6	198,000	5.1	1,005	27,901	51,794	20.2
District 4	314,423	91.1	59.3	202,500	6.2	969	29,971	54,607	23.3
District 5	349,033	81.3	69.5	180,700	10.7	852	28,754	52,237	21.4
District 6	334,040	87.9	66.1	182,600	4.7	764	27,250	50,061	19.1
District 7	308,114	93.1	72.2	252,700	10.4	1,136	35,846	73,580	33.1
District 8	339,759	92.7	50.7	542,700	54.5	1,732	54,612	100,719	50.7
District 9	342,012	82.3	68.9	124,100	3.1	664	24,290	41,698	13.6
District 10	286,461	95.0	78.7	477,400	46.4	1,584	49,981	120,384	59.1
District 11	284,367	95.4	64.9	474,300	45.5	1,750	45,038	106,554	53.9
WASHINGTON	3,025,802	91.5	62.5	306,400	21.8	1,135	35,284	67,106	31.4
District 1	294,552	91.9	71.1	430,400	38.6	1,455	42,593	91,018	45.2
District 2	308,952	90.2	60.2	332,300	16.3	1,148	32,802	65,187	28.7
District 3	294,395	90.8	68.8	264,700	8.8	991	29,968	61,304	26.1
District 4	264,425	90.4	66.1	182,500	3.5	788	23,991	52,484	21.2
District 5	306,397	89.7	63.6	198,500	5.6	819	27,495	51,697	19.7
District 6	319,458	87.2	64.9	263,200	14.9	1,030	32,637	60,616	25.1
District 7	366,008	94.3	50.3	575,300	59.7	1,428	54,859	84,579	42.5
District 8	285,222	91.7	72.5	342,400	25.2	1,159	36,598	79,516	38.6
District 9	297,767	94.3	54.1	400,800	36.3	1,347	40,171	75,407	37.7
District 10	288,626	94.1	57.7	256,500	7.2	1,128	29,976	62,206	25.0
WEST VIRGINIA	886,710	81.4	72.4	117,900	2.2	682	24,769	43,385	15.9
District 1	290,927	82.5	71.8	119,500	2.5	682	26,172	45,611	18.0
District 2	297,359	82.4	73.1	142,600	2.2	731	26,713	48,358	18.0
District 3	298,424	79.4	72.4	94,700	2.0	626	21,256	37,728	11.7
WISCONSIN	2,668,443	87.2	66.7	173,200	4.5	802	30,902	56,811	23.1
District 1	302,912	91.4	68.4	195,300	4.5	861	32,083	61,589	26.9
District 2	328,877	93.3	63.1	226,200	6.9	922	34,919	65,589	29.2
District 3	323,438	88.6	69.4	155,400	3.0	727	27,175	52,154	19.1
District 4	310,678	89.7	44.7	131,600	3.5	814	24,156	41,816	15.4
District 5	312,518	94.2	69.6	224,200	7.1	887	37,330	68,162	30.1
District 6	323,487	90.1	70.6	160,100	4.1	716	31,307	57,129	22.3
District 7	419,132	70.3	74.7	155,000	3.6	693	29,417	51,738	19.0
District 8	347,401	85.6	72.0	160,500	3.0	722	30,536	57,888	22.3
WYOMING	270,625	82.6	68.8	209,500	7.7	840	30,042	59,882	25.0
At Large	270,625	82.6	68.8	209,500	7.7	840	30,042	59,882	25.0

1. Specified owner-occupied units.   2. Specified renter-occupied units.

Poverty, Labor Force, Employment, and Social Security

STATE District	Poverty, 2016			Civilian labor force, 2016			Civilian employment,[2] 2016				Persons under 65 years of age with no health insurance, 2016 (percent)	Social Security beneficiaries, December 2016		Supplemental Security Income recipients, December 2016
	Persons below poverty level (percent)	Families below poverty level (percent)	Percent of households receiving food stamps in past 12 months	Total	Unemployment Total	Rate[1]	Total	Management, business, science, and arts occupations	Service, sales, and office	Construction and production		Number	Rate[3]	
	49	50	51	52	53	54	55	56	57	58	59	60	61	62
TEXAS— Cont'd														
District 26	8.4	5.2	6.2	462,704	18,264	3.9	444,440	47.5	38.3	14.2	9.8	92,044	108.9	6,310
District 27	14.4	10.6	14.4	354,036	19,608	5.5	334,428	29.9	43.2	26.9	19.8	137,533	186.7	21,576
District 28	26.0	21.8	22.7	308,042	23,204	7.5	284,838	27.7	47.9	24.5	26.1	111,560	151.5	30,643
District 29	23.6	21.7	20.2	355,752	23,269	6.5	332,483	17.5	41.2	41.3	31.1	76,361	99.8	22,123
District 30	21.1	17.3	17.8	362,028	21,690	6.0	340,338	30.4	43.4	26.2	21.9	102,890	137.3	31,338
District 31	8.4	6.1	8.7	416,445	24,835	6.0	391,610	40.6	42.6	16.8	11.0	116,349	140.0	11,563
District 32	11.4	8.1	7.0	421,203	18,468	4.4	402,735	44.1	38.7	17.2	16.3	96,959	128.6	11,988
District 33	25.0	22.5	22.4	355,069	19,131	5.4	335,938	13.8	43.9	42.3	32.6	80,984	105.9	24,053
District 34	28.1	23.9	22.4	291,183	21,120	7.3	270,063	26.5	50.5	23.0	30.5	116,007	160.4	40,100
District 35	20.4	16.0	16.4	419,446	20,455	4.9	398,991	28.1	46.4	25.5	21.1	104,060	126.5	24,372
District 36	14.4	11.2	12.5	340,535	24,948	7.3	315,587	30.9	38.4	30.7	19.1	133,074	181.6	16,391
UTAH	10.2	7.2	7.2	1,515,318	61,917	4.1	1,453,401	37.8	41.6	20.6	9.7	385,942	126.5	31,368
District 1	10.0	7.7	8.4	364,236	12,895	3.5	351,341	35.0	39.7	25.3	8.5	93,372	123.3	7,595
District 2	11.9	7.9	6.6	375,841	18,087	4.8	357,754	35.6	42.7	21.7	10.6	113,768	151.8	8,998
District 3	11.1	7.1	6.1	371,957	15,895	4.3	356,062	42.9	42.0	15.1	8.2	89,735	119.4	6,218
District 4	8.0	6.1	7.7	403,284	15,040	3.7	388,244	37.8	42.0	20.2	11.4	89,067	112.4	8,557
VERMONT	11.9	7.7	13.0	338,091	13,267	3.9	324,824	40.6	38.7	20.7	4.5	144,889	232.0	15,574
At Large	11.9	7.7	13.0	338,091	13,267	3.9	324,824	40.6	38.7	20.7	4.5	144,889	232.0	15,574
VIRGINIA	11.0	7.6	8.6	4,333,640	218,154	5.0	4,115,486	43.5	38.6	17.9	10.1	1,471,294	174.9	156,608
District 1	6.9	4.5	5.8	396,783	16,926	4.3	379,857	44.0	38.7	17.3	8.1	131,106	168.8	8,133
District 2	9.6	6.7	7.2	363,064	19,816	5.5	343,248	39.0	41.5	19.5	9.4	122,269	163.9	10,748
District 3	15.6	11.2	13.7	373,984	24,467	6.5	349,517	35.1	42.5	22.4	11.5	135,804	183.7	32,323
District 4	15.9	11.9	13.1	386,085	26,133	6.8	359,952	38.1	42.4	19.5	9.3	139,504	182.5	14,958
District 5	13.8	9.0	10.6	350,826	18,121	5.2	332,705	36.9	40.4	22.7	11.4	178,647	243.0	17,949
District 6	14.4	10.0	10.6	377,998	19,302	5.1	358,696	33.9	42.7	23.4	11.1	168,742	223.5	16,997
District 7	7.7	5.2	6.6	412,804	20,662	5.0	392,142	43.5	40.1	16.4	9.0	140,949	181.8	8,111
District 8	8.9	5.9	4.1	466,853	16,542	3.5	450,311	58.5	30.5	11.0	11.7	76,930	98.2	7,932
District 9	18.8	12.5	14.7	311,483	20,607	6.6	290,876	31.1	43.3	25.6	11.4	198,405	280.6	24,746
District 10	4.9	3.6	3.4	451,638	17,679	3.9	433,959	54.5	32.7	12.8	7.8	96,412	116.5	6,215
District 11	6.6	4.9	4.8	442,122	17,899	4.0	424,223	52.9	34.6	12.6	10.6	82,526	102.8	8,496
WASHINGTON	11.3	7.1	12.6	3,696,275	200,134	5.4	3,496,141	40.6	38.4	21.0	6.9	1,291,198	177.2	150,658
District 1	6.5	3.8	7.8	387,582	19,332	5.0	368,250	48.3	34.1	17.5	4.9	109,496	148.3	6866
District 2	11.6	7.2	12.4	376,012	19,104	5.1	356,908	36.0	41.8	22.2	7.3	136,793	187.8	15,124
District 3	11.1	6.9	16.3	338,247	19,493	5.8	318,754	34.5	40.5	24.9	6.2	150,271	208.1	16,067
District 4	15.7	10.9	18.0	328,233	21,368	6.5	306,865	28.7	37.2	34.1	12.0	123,785	173.1	17,135
District 5	14.0	7.8	15.4	337,226	19,355	5.7	317,871	35.7	43.7	20.6	6.3	148,019	193.7	19,354
District 6	12.2	8.0	13.2	318,441	20,042	6.3	298,399	36.5	41.5	22.0	7.9	158,049	226.0	16,356
District 7	9.2	4.6	7.0	476,764	20,219	4.2	456,545	59.0	31.0	10.0	5.1	106,293	138.7	13,572
District 8	8.4	5.2	9.9	376,308	16,897	4.5	359,411	38.8	37.7	23.5	5.7	112,994	153.1	10,008
District 9	12.0	8.6	14.0	407,802	19,534	4.8	388,268	43.4	38.1	18.5	6.9	101,270	136.9	16,981
District 10	12.4	9.1	13.7	349,660	24,790	7.1	324,870	34.8	42.3	22.9	6.8	144,228	197.0	19,195
WEST VIRGINIA	17.9	12.9	17.9	801,304	60,791	7.6	740,513	33.8	43.1	23.1	6.5	470,240	256.8	74,665
District 1	17.4	11.1	15.1	285,235	19,321	6.8	265,914	35.3	41.6	23.1	6.3	151,296	245.2	20,994
District 2	15.5	10.9	15.2	284,698	19,574	6.9	265,124	35.3	41.9	22.8	7.0	150,464	241.6	19,273
District 3	21.0	16.7	23.5	231,371	21,896	9.5	209,475	30.1	46.3	23.6	6.2	168,480	285.0	34,398
WISCONSIN	11.8	7.7	11.9	3,088,665	125,970	4.1	2,962,695	35.9	39.2	24.9	6.2	1,189,455	205.8	117,813
District 1	10.4	8.1	12.7	375,252	18,722	5.0	356,530	34.3	40.7	25.0	5.9	146,416	204.7	13,687
District 2	11.3	6.4	10.0	437,936	14,087	3.2	423,849	45.1	36.9	18.0	4.7	130,710	172.6	11,327
District 3	12.6	7.1	10.5	381,156	15,355	4.0	365,801	31.9	40.6	27.5	7.6	156,612	217.0	12,426
District 4	23.9	18.8	25.9	361,102	25,634	7.1	335,468	33.2	44.6	22.3	8.5	113,107	158.6	39,467
District 5	7.0	4.0	7.2	398,936	13,731	3.4	385,205	41.9	37.6	20.5	4.0	149,626	207.0	7,452
District 6	9.1	5.5	9.2	375,725	11,873	3.2	363,852	32.7	37.6	29.8	5.1	160,149	225.1	10,386
District 7	10.7	7.4	11.2	364,019	12,760	3.5	351,259	32.5	38.1	29.4	8.2	179,136	252.8	11,640
District 8	9.1	6.2	9.0	394,539	13,808	3.5	380,731	33.3	38.6	28.1	5.6	153,699	211.1	11,428
WYOMING	11.3	6.3	5.9	304,583	17,000	5.6	287,583	33.0	39.2	27.7	13.4	106,720	182.3	6,723
At Large	11.3	6.3	5.9	304,583	17,000	5.6	287,583	33.0	39.2	27.7	13.4	106,720	182.3	6,723

1. Percent of civilian labor force.   2. Persons 16 years old and over.   3. Per 1,000 resident population estimated in the 2016 American Community Survey.

STATE District	Agriculture 2012									
	Land in farms				Value of products sold				Government payments	
	Number of farms	Acres	Average size of farm (acres)	Irrigated land (acres)	Total ($1,000)	Average per farm (dollars)	Percent from crops	Percent from livestock and poultry products	Total ($1,000)	Average per farm receiving payments (dollars)
	63	64	65	66	67	68	69	70	71	72
TEXAS— Cont'd										
District 26............	3,302	378,816	115	3,483	144,039	43,622	28.8	71.2	1,060	4,400
District 27............	12,248	4,802,357	392	136,796	1,227,580	100,227	54.0	46.0	42,540	14,347
District 28............	7,794	5,145,001	660	79,700	406,827	52,197	36.3	63.7	11,471	7,439
District 29............	100	3,742	37	9	1,099	10,995	81.8	18.3	0	0
District 30............	387	38,849	100	1,212	24,876	64,280	95.4	4.6	135	4,657
District 31............	4,996	953,480	191	4,435	212,132	42,460	62.2	37.8	5,772	5,305
District 32............	220	28,677	130	58	9,079	41,269	40.2	59.8	108	6,012
District 33............	107	8,001	75	27	7,499	70,083	96.0	3.9	2	300
District 34............	8,326	4,632,760	556	174,856	931,238	111,847	44.1	55.9	17,803	9,825
District 35............	1,133	250,124	221	1,547	39,002	34,423	73.0	27.0	873	6,616
District 36............	6,888	1,108,089	161	25,421	119,925	17,411	53.7	46.3	5,295	17,534
UTAH	18,027	10,974,396	609	1,104,257	1,816,147	100,746	31.6	68.4	23,898	8,584
District 1............	7,334	5,425,669	740	500,075	568,013	77,449	37.1	62.9	12,472	9,805
District 2............	4,911	2,536,753	517	404,236	897,850	182,824	24.8	75.2	6,598	7,558
District 3............	3,651	2,577,805	706	127,071	205,267	56,222	42.2	57.8	2,877	6,851
District 4............	2,131	434,169	204	72,875	145,017	68,051	37.3	62.7	1,950	8,906
VERMONT	7,338	1,251,713	171	3,565	776,105	105,765	22.9	77.1	13,930	8,929
At Large	7,338	1,251,713	171	3,565	776,105	105,765	22.9	77.1	13,930	8,929
VIRGINIA	46,030	8,302,444	180	68,651	3,753,287	81,540	36.2	63.8	82,318	7,719
District 1............	2,338	522,532	223	10,540	215,529	92,185	87.3	12.7	8,842	14,495
District 2............	567	157,025	277	11,243	280,070	493,951	48.3	51.7	4,246	19,478
District 3............	369	104,848	284	3,470	64,905	175,894	81.9	18.1	2,661	19,423
District 4............	3,003	766,641	255	7,971	473,780	157,769	61.3	38.7	19,465	14,735
District 5............	12,069	2,441,870	202	15,716	613,975	50,872	40.7	59.3	18,392	5,929
District 6............	8,195	1,297,577	158	11,153	1,271,186	155,117	9.9	90.1	7,944	6,576
District 7............	3,265	523,003	160	4,983	242,528	74,281	68.7	31.3	5,367	10,713
District 8............	33	1,227	37	15	1,611	48,818	D	D	D	D
District 9............	13,389	2,166,935	162	2,506	487,735	36,428	17.9	82.1	14,226	4,245
District 10............	2,775	318,962	115	1,050	100,953	36,379	61.2	38.8	1,150	5,478
District 11............	27	1,824	68	4	1,014	37,546	D	D	D	D
WASHINGTON	37,249	14,748,107	396	1,633,571	9,120,749	244,859	71.2	28.8	159,269	22,014
District 1............	3,651	215,635	59	44,402	568,090	155,598	45.9	54.1	4,361	10,794
District 2............	1,660	124,240	75	19,235	251,457	151,480	61.8	38.2	1,391	10,303
District 3............	5,698	888,616	156	53,077	379,033	66,520	44.4	55.6	5,823	11,418
District 4............	10,221	7,236,719	708	1,287,721	6,100,198	596,830	73.0	27.0	64,825	25,302
District 5............	7,733	5,665,632	733	112,588	1,151,558	148,915	92.9	7.1	79,599	24,364
District 6............	2,533	197,926	78	15,406	86,682	34,221	D	D	390	4,432
District 7............	196	2,185	11	195	D	D	D	D	38	5,463
District 8............	3,967	349,188	88	95,859	413,543	104,246	70.5	29.5	2,648	11,220
District 9............	115	1,916	17	282	D	D	D	D	29	4,767
District 10............	1,475	66,050	45	4,806	130,983	88,802	43.3	56.7	166	8,316
WEST VIRGINIA	21,489	3,606,674	168	2,064	806,775	37,544	17.2	82.8	7,034	3,203
District 1............	8,458	1,305,274	154	D	D	D	D	D	1,923	3,162
District 2............	7,563	1,366,085	181	1,238	473,385	62,592	16.2	83.8	3,203	3,632
District 3............	5,468	935,315	171	D	D	D	D	D	1,909	2,703
WISCONSIN	69,754	14,568,926	209	421,721	11,744,476	168,370	39.2	60.8	237,304	6,093
District 1............	2,667	563,204	211	12,892	485,265	181,952	D	D	D	D
District 2............	9,962	2,127,676	214	42,496	1,553,585	155,951	38.1	61.9	44,895	6,876
District 3............	19,895	4,295,732	216	218,340	2,936,452	147,597	45.4	54.6	61,572	5,263
District 4............	37	455	12	23	4,098	110,746	D	D	D	D
District 5............	3,462	635,541	184	11,247	611,624	176,668	43.5	56.5	12,337	6,184
District 6............	8,882	1,813,360	204	52,490	1,824,851	205,455	38.0	62.0	34,602	6,824
District 7............	16,175	3,418,268	211	70,755	2,438,450	150,754	36.2	63.8	39,552	5,465
District 8............	8,674	1,714,690	198	13,478	1,890,152	217,910	28.1	71.9	32,326	6,516
WYOMING	11,736	30,363,641	2,587	1,435,710	1,689,416	143,952	26.0	74.0	28,146	10,027
At Large	11,736	30,363,641	2,587	1,435,710	1,689,416	143,952	26.0	74.0	28,146	10,027

		Private nonfarm employment and payroll, 2016											
		Employment										Annual payroll	
			Percent by selected industries										
STATE District	Number of establishments	Total	Manufacturing	Construction	Wholesale trade	Retail trade	Health care and social assistance	Finance and Insurance	Real estate and rental and leasing	Professional, scientific, and technical services	Information	Total (mil dol)	Average per employee (dollars)
	73	74	75	76	77	78	79	80	81	82	83	84	85
TEXAS— Cont'd													
District 26	15,199	240,064	6.3	5.2	5.0	15.4	11.1	8.9	1.7	4.7	1.8	10,705	44,591
District 27	15,738	249,150	8.8	8.3	4.6	15.0	18.8	2.8	2.0	4.3	1.2	10,180	40,858
District 28	11,101	161,914	2.5	4.3	3.7	18.7	22.8	3.6	1.4	2.4	1.1	4,950	30,572
District 29	10,649	213,699	15.2	13.4	7.3	12.1	5.6	2.3	1.7	4.8	0.8	10,137	47,434
District 30	13,665	343,059	6.3	3.5	4.8	8.8	19.1	5.5	2.7	10.1	3.4	22,453	65,449
District 31	15,228	241,132	5.7	6.4	2.9	16.5	19.2	4.7	1.7	9.3	2.4	10,767	44,653
District 32	21,973	344,278	6.0	4.2	3.2	12.2	17.7	7.4	3.3	9.6	4.0	19,421	56,410
District 33	12,588	273,772	15.3	8.3	11.5	9.6	9.8	1.7	1.6	3.6	1.2	12,634	46,148
District 34	10,816	170,804	4.1	2.9	2.9	17.4	31.9	3.1	1.6	2.7	1.7	4,849	28,390
District 35	15,636	304,332	7.4	7.1	7.2	13.5	11.7	2.9	1.8	4.9	3.8	12,704	41,745
District 36	12,903	244,582	15.8	11.5	3.8	12.0	10.9	2.0	1.5	7.7	0.8	13,545	55,382
UTAH	77,504	1,239,348	9.8	6.3	4.7	12.6	11.2	5.3	1.6	7.2	3.7	54,331	43,839
District 1	17,909	231,999	17.5	6.8	3.3	15.3	12.1	4.1	2.0	6.2	1.3	8,839	38,099
District 2	21,144	373,647	10.1	5.4	5.8	10.8	11.3	5.9	1.5	7.2	3.1	17,898	47,901
District 3	19,109	261,713	5.4	5.8	3.8	13.8	12.7	4.5	2.0	7.0	5.0	10,463	39,978
District 4	18,858	303,855	9.4	9.0	5.8	14.4	11.6	6.1	1.5	8.4	5.9	14,263	46,939
VERMONT	21,174	262,705	11.4	5.3	4.5	15.2	18.6	3.6	1.3	4.9	2.7	10,828	41,219
At Large	21,174	262,705	11.4	5.3	4.5	15.2	18.6	3.6	1.3	4.9	2.7	10,828	41,219
VIRGINIA	199,548	3,254,172	7.4	5.5	3.3	13.2	13.5	4.7	1.7	14.1	2.7	170,160	52,290
District 1	17,052	214,902	5.2	9.9	5.3	18.0	12.8	4.1	1.4	9.2	1.3	8,919	41,500
District 2	16,321	229,214	4.7	5.5	2.2	15.4	12.1	5.7	3.1	10.1	1.9	8,726	38,071
District 3	16,694	334,293	14.1	4.7	3.2	13.8	18.1	3.2	1.7	7.9	2.1	15,125	45,244
District 4	15,673	273,860	9.0	6.8	4.8	11.3	16.2	5.1	1.5	7.5	1.2	13,088	47,791
District 5	16,718	207,989	12.2	6.8	2.9	15.6	17.8	3.4	1.4	5.7	1.9	8,496	40,849
District 6	18,096	308,049	14.1	5.1	3.2	14.4	15.9	4.2	1.3	4.3	1.6	11,922	38,701
District 7	18,985	291,085	3.7	5.8	4.0	15.6	14.2	10.5	1.7	8.3	2.7	14,275	49,040
District 8	20,512	360,285	1.0	4.1	1.6	10.2	9.4	2.8	2.3	26.6	3.0	24,207	67,189
District 9	14,206	208,791	20.2	3.9	4.2	16.9	16.9	2.8	1.0	3.9	1.6	7,614	36,466
District 10	22,539	338,195	5.4	7.7	3.2	11.6	10.2	2.6	1.4	21.4	3.8	19,823	58,614
District 11	22,048	431,483	0.8	2.9	2.0	10.5	10.3	6.1	1.9	30.9	6.0	33,961	78,708
WASHINGTON	186,164	2,685,355	9.9	6.5	5.0	12.5	15.2	3.7	1.8	7.5	4.9	156,915	58,434
District 1	19,264	273,387	10.2	9.5	5.1	9.1	9.3	2.2	1.5	9.1	18.2	23,558	86,171
District 2	19,869	273,601	22.8	7.4	3.0	16.2	13.4	3.7	1.5	4.4	2.3	13,847	50,609
District 3	16,100	194,262	13.0	8.6	4.4	14.7	16.8	3.5	1.7	5.6	2.2	8,965	46,152
District 4	14,187	191,422	12.6	6.2	6.4	15.9	16.8	2.3	1.6	5.8	1.2	8,244	43,066
District 5	17,033	233,124	9.1	5.6	5.6	14.4	20.6	5.3	1.8	4.5	2.0	9,964	42,743
District 6	17,157	194,723	4.8	5.8	2.5	17.0	24.2	3.4	1.7	5.3	1.5	8,173	41,972
District 7	28,807	461,573	3.9	4.4	3.6	8.9	14.4	4.7	2.4	13.0	6.3	34,422	74,575
District 8	15,426	173,457	10.0	9.7	7.2	15.1	13.5	1.8	1.4	3.6	2.9	8,417	48,527
District 9	22,852	447,136	10.2	5.0	6.9	9.1	13.9	3.6	1.9	6.2	5.1	29,862	66,786
District 10	14,837	203,713	7.0	7.9	5.0	16.3	16.0	4.2	1.9	4.4	2.1	8,560	42,022
WEST VIRGINIA	36,607	558,905	8.5	4.3	3.3	15.5	24.0	3.1	1.2	4.5	1.9	21,638	38,715
District 1	12,924	209,694	9.5	4.1	3.0	14.9	24.3	2.6	0.9	4.6	1.7	8,288	39,524
District 2	12,285	185,108	8.8	5.3	3.6	15.3	21.8	3.8	1.3	4.5	2.0	7,307	39,474
District 3	11,077	155,363	7.2	3.6	3.2	17.3	27.5	2.5	1.0	3.4	2.1	5,583	35,935
WISCONSIN	140,859	2,524,329	17.9	4.3	4.8	12.5	15.7	5.5	1.0	4.3	2.2	115,817	45,880
District 1	15,191	245,541	20.0	4.4	5.1	16.8	14.0	2.4	1.0	2.9	1.2	10,267	41,812
District 2	19,233	360,351	11.4	4.8	4.9	12.6	15.9	7.1	1.4	7.2	5.3	17,857	49,554
District 3	17,032	278,726	18.7	3.8	4.0	14.3	16.8	5.0	1.0	3.0	1.8	10,964	39,335
District 4	13,450	306,701	10.4	2.0	4.7	7.6	18.4	9.8	1.3	5.5	2.3	16,757	54,637
District 5	21,300	410,849	16.8	4.7	6.3	12.1	16.0	4.5	1.2	4.8	2.6	20,422	49,708
District 6	16,747	307,770	26.4	4.8	3.6	12.2	14.1	3.7	0.8	3.2	1.0	13,721	44,582
District 7	19,077	249,122	23.3	4.6	4.0	14.8	17.2	4.3	0.8	2.5	1.0	9,669	38,812
District 8	18,287	328,939	21.4	5.1	4.5	12.3	13.8	5.1	0.9	3.2	1.6	14,405	43,791
WYOMING	20,966	208,440	4.4	8.9	3.8	14.9	16.0	3.2	2.2	4.7	1.9	9,304	44,636
At Large	20,966	208,440	4.4	8.9	3.8	14.9	16.0	3.2	2.2	4.7	1.9	9,304	44,636

APPENDIX A
GEOGRAPHIC CONCEPTS AND CODES

GEOGRAPHIC AREAS COVERED

County and City Extra presents data for states (Table A), states and counties (Table B), metropolitan areas (Table C), cities with populations of 25,000 or more in 2010 (Table D), and congressional districts (Table E).

STATES AND COUNTIES

Data are presented for each of the 50 states, the District of Columbia, and the United States as a whole. The states are arranged alphabetically and counties in Table B are arranged alphabetically within each state. Data are presented for 3,142 counties and county equivalents.

County equivalents

In Louisiana, the primary divisions of the state are known as parishes rather than counties. In Alaska, the county equivalents are the organized boroughs, together with the census areas that were developed for general statistical purposes by the state of Alaska and the U.S. Census Bureau. Four states—Maryland, Missouri, Nevada, and Virginia—have one or more incorporated places that are legally independent of any county and thus constitute primary divisions of their states. Within each state, independent cities are listed alphabetically following the list of counties. The District of Columbia is not divided into counties or county equivalents—data for the entire district are presented as a county equivalent. New York City contains five counties: Bronx, Kings, New York, Queens, and Richmond.

County changes since the 2010 census

- The independent city of Bedford, Virginia changed to town status and was added to Bedford County, effective July 1, 2013. In this book, all the data have been updated to reflect this change except the 2012 Census of Governments data in columns 171 through 193, where Bedford county does not include Bedford city.
- Wade Hampton Census Area, AK (02-270) changed its name and FIPS code to Kusilvak Census Area (02-158), effective July 1, 2015.
- Shannon County, SD (46-113) changed its name and FIPS code to Oglala Lakota County (46-102), effective May 1, 2015.
- Petersburg Borough, AK was created from part of Petersburg Census Area and part of Hoonah-Angoon Census Area. Petersburg Borough retains the FIPS code 02-195, formerly used by Petersburg Census Area, effective January 3, 2013.
- Prince of Wales-Hyder Census Area added part of the former Petersburg Census Area, effective January 3, 2013.

County changes since the 2000 census

- Broomfield County, CO, was created from parts of Adams, Boulder, Jefferson, and Weld Counties, effective November 15, 2001. The boundaries of Broomfield County reflect the boundaries of Broomfield city legally in effect on that date.
- Clifton Forge city, VA, formerly an independent city, became a town within Alleghany County, effective July 1, 2001.
- Effective June 20, 2007, the Skagway-Hoonah-Angoon Census Area in Alaska was divided into the Skagway Municipality and the Hoonah-Angoon Census Area.
- In May and June, 2008, the Wrangell-Petersburg and Prince of Wales-Outer Ketchikan Census Areas were dissolved and replaced by Wrangell City and Borough, Petersburg Census Area, and Prince of Wales Census Area. Some territory from the Prince of Wales Outer Ketchikan Census Area became part of the existing Ketchikan Gateway Borough.

METROPOLITAN AREAS

Table C presents data for 382 metropolitan statistical areas and 31 metropolitan divisions, which are located within the 11 largest metropolitan statistical areas. The metropolitan statistical areas are listed alphabetically, and the metropolitan divisions are listed alphabetically under the metropolitan statistical area of which they are components.

The U.S. Office of Management and Budget (OMB) defines metropolitan and micropolitan statistical areas according to published standards. The major purpose of defining these areas is to enable all U.S. government agencies to use the same geographic definitions in tabulating and publishing data. The general concept of a metropolitan or micropolitan statistical area is that of a core area containing a substantial population nucleus, together with adjacent communities that have a high degree of economic and social integration with the core.

New delineations of these Core Based Statistical Areas (CBSAs) based on the 2010 census were released in February 2013 and updated in July 2015. Table C in this book uses these delineations for metropolitan areas and metropolitan divisions. Micropolitan areas are not included in Table C. A few of the data items in Table C were released under the old scheme but have been aggregated from county data to the newly defined metropolitan areas. This results in a higher level of data suppression for those items. New delineations were released in August 2017, designating one new Metropolitan Area: Twin Falls, Idaho, consisting of Twin Falls county and Jerome county. It is not included in Table C because it was not a Metropolitan Area at the time of most of the data in this book.

Appendix B lists the metropolitan areas and metropolitan divisions with their component counties and 2010 census populations. Appendix C lists the metropolitan and micropolitan areas, together with their 2010 census populations and their 2017 estimated populations.

Standard definitions of metropolitan areas were first issued in 1949 by the Bureau of the Budget (the predecessor of OMB), under the designation "standard metropolitan area" (SMA). The term was changed to "standard metropolitan statistical area"

(SMSA) in 1959, and to "metropolitan statistical area" (MSA) in 1983. The term "metropolitan area" (MA) was adopted in 1990 and referred collectively to metropolitan statistical areas (MSAs), consolidated metropolitan statistical areas (CMSAs), and primary metropolitan statistical areas (PMSAs). The term "core based statistical area" (CBSA) became effective in 2000 and refers collectively to metropolitan and micropolitan statistical areas.

The 2010 standards provide that each CBSA must contain at least one urban area of 10,000 or more population. Each metropolitan statistical area must have at least one urbanized area of 50,000 or more inhabitants. Each micropolitan statistical area must have at least one urban cluster of at least 10,000 but less than 50,000 people.

Under the standards, A metro area contains a core urban area of 50,000 or more population, and a micro area contains an urban core of at least 10,000 (but less than 50,000) population. Each metro or micro area consists of one or more counties and includes the counties containing the core urban area, as well as any adjacent counties that have a high degree of social and economic integration (as measured by commuting to work) with the urban core.

If specified criteria are met, a metropolitan statistical area containing a single core with a population of 2.5 million or more may be subdivided to form smaller groupings of counties referred to as "metropolitan divisions."

As of July 15, 2015, there were 382 metropolitan statistical areas and 556 micropolitan statistical areas in the United States. Table C includes the 382 metropolitan statistical areas and the 31 metropolitan divisions. The metropolitan areas and metropolitan divisions are listed in Appendix B with their 2010 census population counts. The metropolitan areas, metropolitan divisions, and micropolitan areas are listed in Appendix C with their 2010 census populations and their 2017 estimated populations.

The largest city in each metropolitan or micropolitan statistical area is designated a "principal city." Additional cities qualify if specified requirements are met concerning population size and employment. The title of each metropolitan or micropolitan statistical area consists of the names of up to three of its principal cities and the name of each state into which the metropolitan or micropolitan statistical area extends. Titles of metropolitan divisions also typically are based on principal city names, but in certain cases consist of county names. The principal city need not be an incorporated place if it meets the requirements of population size and employment. Usually such a principal city is a census designated place in decennial census data, but it is not included in most other data sources and is not in Table D (cities) in this volume.

In view of the importance of cities and towns in New England, the 2010 standards also provide for a set of geographic areas that are defined using cities and towns in the six New England states. These New England city and town areas (NECTAs) are not included in this volume.

Appendix B lists the 382 metropolitan statistical areas, together with their component metropolitan divisions, where appropriate, the component counties of each area, and their 2010 census populations. Appendix C provides the same information for the 382 metropolitan areas and it also includes the 556 micropolitan statistical areas. Maps showing the metropolitan and micropolitan areas within each state can be found in Appendix D.

CITIES

Table D presents data for 1,437 cities with 2010 census populations of 25,000 or more. Corresponding data for states are also provided. The states are arranged alphabetically and the cities are ordered alphabetically within each state.

As used in this volume, the term *city* refers to places that have been incorporated as cities, boroughs, towns, or villages under the laws of their respective states. Towns in the New England states and New York are treated as minor civil divisions (MCDs) and are not included in the cities database. For Hawaii, data for the census designated places (CDPs) are included in the cities table, since the Census Bureau does not recognize any incorporated places in Hawaii. CDPs are delineated by the Census Bureau, in cooperation with states and localities, as statistical counterparts of incorporated places for purposes of the decennial census. CDPs comprise densely settled concentrations of population that are identifiable by name but are not legally incorporated as places.

Appendix E lists the 1,437 cities followed by the county where each city is located. If a city includes portions of more than one county, the population in each part is specified.

A consolidated city is an incorporated place that has combined its government functions with a county or subcounty entity but contains one or more other semi-independent incorporated places that continue to function as local governments within the consolidated government. Each consolidated city contains a core city, the area of a consolidated city not included in another separately incorporated place. The census geographic term for this core is the "balance" of the consolidated city. Thus the "balance" is essentially the core city of the consolidated government. This volume includes the consolidated city data where possible, but some data sources include numbers only for the "balance" and others do not specify which entity is represented.

Consolidated cities included in this volume are Milford, CT; Athens-Clarke County, GA; Augusta-Richmond County, GA; Indianapolis, IN; Louisville-Jefferson County, KY; Butte-Silver Bow, MT; and Nashville-Davidson, TN.

Appendix E lists these seven consolidated cities, followed by the component places and their 2010 census populations.

On January 1, 2014, Macon, Georgia consolidated with Bibb county. A small portion of Macon that was in Jones county was de-annexed. Data from years prior to 2015 represent the smaller Macon city rather than the consolidated Macon-Bibb County.

CONGRESSIONAL DISTRICTS

The congressional districts shown in this volume are the districts used for the election of the 115th Congress, which convened in January 2017. These are the districts that were established following the 2010 Census and are based on population data from that census. Data are shown for the 435 regular districts plus the District of Columbia, which has a non-voting delegate, but no representative. Corresponding data for each state also are

METROPOLITAN STATISTICAL AREAS, METROPOLITAN DIVISIONS, AND COMPONENTS (as defined July 2015)—*Continued*

Core based statistical area	State/ County FIPS code	Title and Geographic Components	2010 Census Population	Core based statistical area	State/ County FIPS code	Title and Geographic Components	2010 Census Population
14540		Bowling Green, KY	158,599	16580		Champaign-Urbana, IL	231,891
14540	21003	Allen County	19,956	16580	17019	Champaign County	201,081
14540	21031	Butler County	12,690	16580	17053	Ford County	14,081
14540	21061	Edmonson County	12,161	16580	17147	Piatt County	16,729
14540	21227	Warren County	113,792				
				16620		Charleston, WV	227,078
14740		Bremerton-Silverdale, WA	251,133	16620	54005	Boone County	24,629
14740	53035	Kitsap County	251,133	16620	54015	Clay County	9,386
				16620	54039	Kanawha County	193,063
14860		Bridgeport-Stamford-Norwalk, CT	916,829				
14860	09001	Fairfield County	916,829	16700		Charleston-North Charleston, SC	664,607
				16700	45015	Berkeley County	177,843
15180		Brownsville-Harlingen, TX	406,220	16700	45019	Charleston County	350,209
15180	48061	Cameron County	406,220	16700	45035	Dorchester County	136,555
15260		Brunswick, GA	112,370	16740		Charlotte-Concord-Gastonia, NC-SC	2,217,012
15260	13025	Brantley County	18,411	16740	37025	Cabarrus County	178,011
15260	13127	Glynn County	79,626	16740	37071	Gaston County	206,086
15260	13191	McIntosh County	14,333	16740	37097	Iredell County	159,437
				16740	37109	Lincoln County	78,265
15380		Buffalo-Cheektowaga-Niagara Falls, NY	1,135,509	16740	37119	Mecklenburg County	919,628
15380	36029	Erie County	919,040	16740	37159	Rowan County	138,428
15380	36063	Niagara County	216,469	16740	37179	Union County	201,292
				16740	45023	Chester County	33,140
15500		Burlington, NC	151,131	16740	45057	Lancaster County	76,652
15500	37001	Alamance County	151,131	16740	45091	York County	226,073
15540		Burlington-South Burlington, VT	211,261	16820		Charlottesville, VA	218,705
15540	50007	Chittenden County	156,545	16820	51003	Albemarle County	98,970
15540	50011	Franklin County	47,746	16820	51029	Buckingham County	17,146
15540	50013	Grand Isle County	6,970	16820	51065	Fluvanna County	25,691
				16820	51079	Greene County	18,403
15680		California-Lexington Park, MD	105,151	16820	51125	Nelson County	15,020
15680	24037	St. Mary's County	105,151	16820	51540	Charlottesville city	43,475
15940		Canton-Massillon, OH	404,422	16860		Chattanooga, TN-GA	528,143
15940	39019	Carroll County	28,836	16860	13047	Catoosa County	63,942
15940	39151	Stark County	375,586	16860	13083	Dade County	16,633
				16860	13295	Walker County	68,756
15980		Cape Coral-Fort Myers, FL	618,754	16860	47065	Hamilton County	336,463
15980	12071	Lee County	618,754	16860	47115	Marion County	28,237
				16860	47153	Sequatchie County	14,112
16020		Cape Girardeau, MO-IL	96,275				
16020	17003	Alexander County	8,238	16940		Cheyenne, WY	91,738
16020	29017	Bollinger County	12,363	16940	56021	Laramie County	91,738
16020	29031	Cape Girardeau County	75,674				
16060		Carbondale-Marion, IL	126,575				
16060	17077	Jackson County	60,218				
16060	17199	Williamson County	66,357				
16180		Carson City, NV	55,274				
16180	32510	Carson City	55,274				
16220		Casper, WY	75,450				
16220	56025	Natrona County	75,450				
16300		Cedar Rapids, IA	257,940				
16300	19011	Benton County	26,076				
16300	19105	Jones County	20,638				
16300	19113	Linn County	211,226				
16540		Chambersburg-Waynesboro, PA	149,618				
16540	42055	Franklin County	149,618				

Core based statistical area	State/ County FIPS code	Title and Geographic Components	2010 Census Population	Core based statistical area	State/ County FIPS code	Title and Geographic Components	2010 Census Population
16980		Chicago-Naperville-Elgin, IL-IN-WI..................	9,461,105	17780		College Station-Bryan, TX.................................	228,660
				17780	48041	Brazos County	194,851
16980		Chicago-Naperville-Arlington Heights, IL Div 16974	7,262,718	17780	48051	Burleson County	17,187
				17780	48395	Robertson County	16,622
16980	17031	Cook County..	5,194,675				
16980	17043	DuPage County	916,924	17820		Colorado Springs, CO.....................................	645,613
16980	17063	Grundy County	50,063	17820	08041	El Paso County	622,263
16980	17093	Kendall County	114,736	17820	08119	Teller County	23,350
16980	17111	McHenry County..	308,760				
16980	17197	Will County	677,560	17860		Columbia, MO...	162,642
16980		Elgin, IL Div 20994	620,429	17860	29019	Boone County	162,642
16980	17037	DeKalb County	105,160				
16980	17089	Kane County...	515,269	17900		Columbia, SC	767,598
16980		Gary, IN Div 23844	708,070	17900	45017	Calhoun County	15,175
16980	18073	Jasper County	33,478	17900	45039	Fairfield County	23,956
16980	18089	Lake County	496,005	17900	45055	Kershaw County	61,697
16980	18111	Newton County	14,244	17900	45063	Lexington County	262,391
16980	18127	Porter County	164,343	17900	45079	Richland County	384,504
16980		Lake County-Kenosha County, IL-WI Div 29404	869,888	17900	45081	Saluda County	19,875
16980	17097	Lake County	703,462	17980		Columbus, GA-AL..	294,865
16980	55059	Kenosha County	166,426	17980	01113	Russell County	52,947
				17980	13053	Chattahoochee County	11,267
17020		Chico, CA...	220,000	17980	13145	Harris County	32,024
17020	06007	Butte County	220,000	17980	13197	Marion County	8,742
				17980	13215	Muscogee County	189,885
17140		Cincinnati, OH-KY-IN..	2,114,580				
17140	18029	Dearborn County	50,047	18020		Columbus, IN..	76,794
17140	18115	Ohio County	6,128	18020	18005	Bartholomew County..	76,794
17140	18161	Union County	7,516				
17140	21015	Boone County	118,811	18140		Columbus, OH..	1,901,974
17140	21023	Bracken County	8,488	18140	39041	Delaware County	174,214
17140	21037	Campbell County	90,336	18140	39045	Fairfield County	146,156
17140	21077	Gallatin County	8,589	18140	39049	Franklin County	1,163,414
17140	21081	Grant County	24,662	18140	39073	Hocking County	29,380
17140	21117	Kenton County	159,720	18140	39089	Licking County	166,492
17140	21191	Pendleton County	14,877	18140	39097	Madison County	43,435
17140	39015	Brown County	44,846	18140	39117	Morrow County	34,827
17140	39017	Butler County	368,130	18140	39127	Perry County	36,058
17140	39025	Clermont County	197,363	18140	39129	Pickaway County	55,698
17140	39061	Hamilton County	802,374	18140	39159	Union County	52,300
17140	39165	Warren County	212,693				
				18580		Corpus Christi, TX	428,185
17300		Clarksville, TN-KY	260,625	18580	48007	Aransas County	23,158
17300	21047	Christian County	73,955	18580	48355	Nueces County	340,223
17300	21221	Trigg County...	14,339	18580	48409	San Patricio County	64,804
17300	47125	Montgomery County..	172,331				
17420		Cleveland, TN...	115,788	18700		Corvallis, OR	85,579
17420	47011	Bradley County	98,963	18700	41003	Benton County	85,579
17420	47139	Polk County	16,825				
				18880		Crestview-Fort Walton Beach-Destin, FL	235,865
17460		Cleveland-Elyria, OH	2,077,240	18880	12091	Okaloosa County	180,822
17460	39035	Cuyahoga County	1,280,122	18880	12131	Walton County	55,043
17460	39055	Geauga County	93,389				
17460	39085	Lake County	230,041	19060		Cumberland, MD-WV	103,299
17460	39093	Lorain County	301,356	19060	24001	Allegany County	75,087
17460	39103	Medina County	172,332	19060	54057	Mineral County	28,212
17660		Coeur d'Alene, ID	138,494				
17660	16055	Kootenai County	138,494				

Core based statistical area	State/ County FIPS code	Title and Geographic Components	2010 Census Population	Core based statistical area	State/ County FIPS code	Title and Geographic Components	2010 Census Population
19100		Dallas-Fort Worth-Arlington, TX	6,426,214	19780		Des Moines-West Des Moines, IA	569,633
19100		Dallas-Plano-Irving, TX Div 19124	4,230,520	19780	19049	Dallas County	66,135
19100	48085	Collin County	782,341	19780	19077	Guthrie County	10,954
19100	48113	Dallas County	2,368,139	19780	19121	Madison County	15,679
19100	48121	Denton County	662,614	19780	19153	Polk County	430,640
19100	48139	Ellis County	149,610	19780	19181	Warren County	46,225
19100	48231	Hunt County	86,129				
19100	48257	Kaufman County	103,350	19820		Detroit-Warren-Dearborn, MI	4,296,250
19100	48397	Rockwall County	78,337	19820		Detroit-Dearborn-Livonia, MI Div 19804	1,820,584
19100		Fort Worth-Arlington, TX Div 23104	2,195,694	19820	26163	Wayne County	1,820,584
19100	48221	Hood County	51,182	19820		Warren-Troy-Farmington Hills, MI 47664	2,475,666
19100	48251	Johnson County	150,934	19820	26087	Lapeer County	88,319
19100	48367	Parker County	116,927	19820	26093	Livingston County	180,967
19100	48425	Somervell County	8,490	19820	26099	Macomb County	840,978
19100	48439	Tarrant County	1,809,034	19820	26125	Oakland County	1,202,362
19100	48497	Wise County	59,127	19820	26147	St. Clair County	163,040
19140		Dalton, GA	142,227	20020		Dothan, AL	145,639
19140	13213	Murray County	39,628	20020	01061	Geneva County	26,790
19140	13313	Whitfield County	102,599	20020	01067	Henry County	17,302
				20020	01069	Houston County	101,547
19180		Danville, IL	81,625				
19180	17183	Vermilion County	81,625	20100		Dover, DE	162,310
				20100	10001	Kent County	162,310
19300		Daphne-Fairhope-Foley, AL	182,265				
19300	01003	Baldwin County	182,265	20220		Dubuque, IA	93,653
				20220	19061	Dubuque County	93,653
19340		Davenport-Moline-Rock Island, IA-IL	379,690				
19340	17073	Henry County	50,486	20260		Duluth, MN-WI	279,771
19340	17131	Mercer County	16,434	20260	27017	Carlton County	35,386
19340	17161	Rock Island County	147,546	20260	27137	St. Louis County	200,226
19340	19163	Scott County	165,224	20260	55031	Douglas County	44,159
19380		Dayton, OH	799,232	20500		Durham-Chapel Hill, NC	504,357
19380	39057	Greene County	161,573	20500	37037	Chatham County	63,505
19380	39109	Miami County	102,506	20500	37063	Durham County	267,587
19380	39113	Montgomery County	535,153	20500	37135	Orange County	133,801
				20500	37145	Person County	39,464
19460		Decatur, AL	153,829				
19460	01079	Lawrence County	34,339	20700		East Stroudsburg, PA	169,842
19460	01103	Morgan County	119,490	20700	42089	Monroe County	169,842
19500		Decatur, IL	110,768	20740		Eau Claire, WI	161,151
19500	17115	Macon County	110,768	20740	55017	Chippewa County	62,415
				20740	55035	Eau Claire County	98,736
19660		Deltona-Daytona Beach-Ormond Beach, FL	590,289				
19660	12035	Flagler County	95,696	20940		El Centro, CA	174,528
19660	12127	Volusia County	494,593	20940	06025	Imperial County	174,528
19740		Denver-Aurora-Lakewood, CO	2,543,482	21060		Elizabethtown-Fort Knox, KY	148,338
19740	08001	Adams County	441,603	21060	21093	Hardin County	105,543
19740	08005	Arapahoe County	572,003	21060	21123	Larue County	14,193
19740	08014	Broomfield County	55,889	21060	21163	Meade County	28,602
19740	08019	Clear Creek County	9,088				
19740	08031	Denver County	600,158	21140		Elkhart-Goshen, IN	197,559
19740	08035	Douglas County	285,465	21140	18039	Elkhart County	197,559
19740	08039	Elbert County	23,086				
19740	08047	Gilpin County	5,441	21300		Elmira, NY	88,830
19740	08059	Jefferson County	534,543	21300	36015	Chemung County	88,830
19740	08093	Park County	16,206				
				21340		El Paso, TX	804,123
				21340	48141	El Paso County	800,647
				21340	48229	Hudspeth County	3,476

Core based statistical area	State/County FIPS code	Title and Geographic Components	2010 Census Population	Core based statistical area	State/County FIPS code	Title and Geographic Components	2010 Census Population
21420		Enid, OK	60,580	23060		Fort Wayne, IN	416,257
21420	40047	Garfield County	60,580	23060	18003	Allen County	355,329
				23060	18179	Wells County	27,636
21500		Erie, PA	280,566	23060	18183	Whitley County	33,292
21500	42049	Erie County	280,566				
				23420		Fresno, CA	930,450
21660		Eugene, OR	351,715	23420	06019	Fresno County	930,450
21660	41039	Lane County	351,715				
				23460		Gadsden, AL	104,430
21780		Evansville, IN-KY	311,552	23460	01055	Etowah County	104,430
21780	18129	Posey County	25,910				
21780	18163	Vanderburgh County	179,703	23540		Gainesville, FL	264,275
21780	18173	Warrick County	59,689	23540	12001	Alachua County	247,336
21780	21101	Henderson County	46,250	23540	12041	Gilchrist County	16,939
21820		Fairbanks, AK	97,581	23580		Gainesville, GA	179,684
21820	02090	Fairbanks North Star Borough	97,581	23580	13139	Hall County	179,684
22020		Fargo, ND-MN	208,777	23900		Gettysburg, PA	101,407
22020	27027	Clay County	58,999	23900	42001	Adams County	101,407
22020	38017	Cass County	149,778				
				24020		Glens Falls, NY	128,923
22140		Farmington, NM	130,044	24020	36113	Warren County	65,707
22140	35045	San Juan County	130,044	24020	36115	Washington County	63,216
22180		Fayetteville, NC	366,383	24140		Goldsboro, NC	122,623
22180	37051	Cumberland County	319,431	24140	37191	Wayne County	122,623
22180	37093	Hoke County	46,952				
				24220		Grand Forks, ND-MN	98,461
22220		Fayetteville-Springdale-Rogers, AR-MO	463,204	24220	27119	Polk County	31,600
22220	05007	Benton County	221,339	24220	38035	Grand Forks County	66,861
22220	05087	Madison County	15,717				
22220	05143	Washington County	203,065	24260		Grand Island, NE	81,850
22220	29119	McDonald County	23,083	24260	31079	Hall County	58,607
				24260	31081	Hamilton County	9,124
22380		Flagstaff, AZ	134,421	24260	31093	Howard County	6,274
22380	04005	Coconino County	134,421	24260	31121	Merrick County	7,845
22420		Flint, MI	425,790	24300		Grand Junction, CO	146,723
22420	26049	Genesee County	425,790	24300	08077	Mesa County	146,723
22500		Florence, SC	205,566	24340		Grand Rapids-Wyoming, MI	988,938
22500	45031	Darlington County	68,681	24340	26015	Barry County	59,173
22500	45041	Florence County	136,885	24340	26081	Kent County	602,622
				24340	26117	Montcalm County	63,342
22520		Florence-Muscle Shoals, AL	147,137	24340	26139	Ottawa County	263,801
22520	01033	Colbert County	54,428				
22520	01077	Lauderdale County	92,709	24420		Grants Pass, OR	82,713
				24420	41033	Josephine County	82,713
22540		Fond du Lac, WI	101,633				
22540	55039	Fond du Lac County	101,633	24500		Great Falls, MT	81,327
				24500	30013	Cascade County	81,327
22660		Fort Collins, CO	299,630				
22660	08069	Larimer County	299,630	24540		Greeley, CO	252,825
				24540	08123	Weld County	252,825
22900		Fort Smith, AR-OK	280,467				
22900	05033	Crawford County	61,948	24580		Green Bay, WI	306,241
22900	05131	Sebastian County	125,744	24580	55009	Brown County	248,007
22900	40079	Le Flore County	50,384	24580	55061	Kewaunee County	20,574
22900	40135	Sequoyah County	42,391	24580	55083	Oconto County	37,660

Core based statistical area	State/County FIPS code	Title and Geographic Components	2010 Census Population	Core based statistical area	State/County FIPS code	Title and Geographic Components	2010 Census Population
24660		Greensboro-High Point, NC	723,801				
24660	37081	Guilford County	488,406	26300		Hot Springs, AR	96,024
24660	37151	Randolph County	141,752	26300	05051	Garland County	96,024
24660	37157	Rockingham County	93,643				
				26380		Houma-Thibodaux, LA	208,178
24780		Greenville, NC	168,148	26380	22057	Lafourche Parish	96,318
24780	37147	Pitt County	168,148	26380	22109	Terrebonne Parish	111,860
24860		Greenville-Anderson-Mauldin, SC	824,112	26420		Houston-The Woodlands-Sugar Land, TX	5,920,416
24860	45007	Anderson County	187,126	26420	48015	Austin County	28,417
24860	45045	Greenville County	451,225	26420	48039	Brazoria County	313,166
24860	45059	Laurens County	66,537	26420	48071	Chambers County	35,096
24860	45077	Pickens County	119,224	26420	48157	Fort Bend County	585,375
				26420	48167	Galveston County	291,309
25060		Gulfport-Biloxi-Pascagoula, MS	370,702	26420	48201	Harris County	4,092,459
25060	28045	Hancock County	43,929	26420	48291	Liberty County	75,643
25060	28047	Harrison County	187,105	26420	48339	Montgomery County	455,746
25060	28059	Jackson County	139,668	26420	48473	Waller County	43,205
25180		Hagerstown-Martinsburg, MD-WV	251,599	26580		Huntington-Ashland, WV-KY-OH	364,908
25180	24043	Washington County	147,430	26580	21019	Boyd County	49,542
25180	54003	Berkeley County	104,169	26580	21089	Greenup County	36,910
				26580	39087	Lawrence County	62,450
25220		Hammond, LA	121,097	26580	54011	Cabell County	96,319
25220	22105	Tangipahoa Parish	121,097	26580	54043	Lincoln County	21,720
				26580	54079	Putnam County	55,486
25260		Hanford-Corcoran, CA	152,982	26580	54099	Wayne County	42,481
25260	06031	Kings County	152,982				
				26620		Huntsville, AL	417,593
25420		Harrisburg-Carlisle, PA	549,475	26620	01083	Limestone County	82,782
25420	42041	Cumberland County	235,406	26620	01089	Madison County	334,811
25420	42043	Dauphin County	268,100				
25420	42099	Perry County	45,969	26820		Idaho Falls, ID	133,265
				26820	16019	Bonneville County	104,234
25500		Harrisonburg, VA	125,228	26820	16023	Butte County	2,891
25500	51165	Rockingham County	76,314	26820	16051	Jefferson County	26,140
25500	51660	Harrisonburg city	48,914				
				26900		Indianapolis-Carmel-Anderson, IN	1,887,877
25540		Hartford-West Hartford-East Hartford, CT	1,212,381	26900	18011	Boone County	56,640
25540	09003	Hartford County	894,014	26900	18013	Brown County	15,242
25540	09007	Middlesex County	165,676	26900	18057	Hamilton County	274,569
25540	09013	Tolland County	152,691	26900	18059	Hancock County	70,002
				26900	18063	Hendricks County	145,448
25620		Hattiesburg, MS	142,842	26900	18081	Johnson County	139,654
25620	28035	Forrest County	74,934	26900	18095	Madison County	131,636
25620	28073	Lamar County	55,658	26900	18097	Marion County	903,393
25620	28111	Perry County	12,250	26900	18109	Morgan County	68,894
				26900	18133	Putnam County	37,963
25860		Hickory-Lenoir-Morganton, NC	365,497	26900	18145	Shelby County	44,436
25860	37003	Alexander County	37,198				
25860	37023	Burke County	90,912	26980		Iowa City, IA	152,586
25860	37027	Caldwell County	83,029	26980	19103	Johnson County	130,882
25860	37035	Catawba County	154,358	26980	19183	Washington County	21,704
25940		Hilton Head Island-Bluffton-Beaufort, NC	187,010	27060		Ithaca, NY	101,564
25940	45013	Beaufort County	162,233	27060	36109	Tompkins County	101,564
25940	45053	Jasper County	24,777				
				27100		Jackson, MI	160,248
25980		Hinesville, GA	77,917	27100	26075	Jackson County	160,248
25980	13179	Liberty County	63,453				
25980	13183	Long County	14,464				
26140		Homosassa Springs, FL	141,236				
26140	12017	Citrus County	141,236				

Core based statistical area	State/ County FIPS code	Title and Geographic Components	2010 Census Population	Core based statistical area	State/ County FIPS code	Title and Geographic Components	2010 Census Population
27140		Jackson, MS	567,122	28140		Kansas City, MO-KS	2,009,342
27140	28029	Copiah County	29,449	28140	20091	Johnson County	544,179
27140	28049	Hinds County	245,285	28140	20103	Leavenworth County	76,227
27140	28089	Madison County	95,203	28140	20107	Linn County	9,656
27140	28121	Rankin County	141,617	28140	20121	Miami County	32,787
27140	28127	Simpson County	27,503	28140	20209	Wyandotte County	157,505
27140	28163	Yazoo County	28,065	28140	29013	Bates County	17,049
				28140	29025	Caldwell County	9,424
27180		Jackson, TN	130,011	28140	29037	Cass County	99,478
27180	47023	Chester County	17,131	28140	29047	Clay County	221,939
27180	47033	Crockett County	14,586	28140	29049	Clinton County	20,743
27180	47113	Madison County	98,294	28140	29095	Jackson County	674,158
				28140	29107	Lafayette County	33,381
27260		Jacksonville, FL	1,345,596	28140	29165	Platte County	89,322
27260	12003	Baker County	27,115	28140	29177	Ray County	23,494
27260	12019	Clay County	190,865				
27260	12031	Duval County	864,263	28420		Kennewick-Richland, WA	253,340
27260	12089	Nassau County	73,314	28420	53005	Benton County	175,177
27260	12109	St. Johns County	190,039	28420	53021	Franklin County	78,163
27340		Jacksonville, NC	177,772	28660		Killeen-Temple, TX	405,300
27340	37133	Onslow County	177,772	28660	48027	Bell County	310,235
				28660	48099	Coryell County	75,388
27500		Janesville-Beloit, WI	160,331	28660	48281	Lampasas County	19,677
27500	55105	Rock County	160,331				
				28700		Kingsport-Bristol-Bristol, TN-VA	309,544
27620		Jefferson City, MO	149,807	28700	47073	Hawkins County	56,833
27620	29027	Callaway County	44,332	28700	47163	Sullivan County	156,823
27620	29051	Cole County	75,990	28700	51169	Scott County	23,177
27620	29135	Moniteau County	15,607	28700	51191	Washington County	54,876
27620	29151	Osage County	13,878	28700	51520	Bristol city	17,835
27740		Johnson City, TN	198,716	28740		Kingston, NY	182,493
27740	47019	Carter County	57,424	28740	36111	Ulster County	182,493
27740	47171	Unicoi County	18,313				
27740	47179	Washington County	122,979	28940		Knoxville, TN	837,571
				28940	47001	Anderson County	75,129
27780		Johnstown, PA	143,679	28940	47009	Blount County	123,010
27780	42021	Cambria County	143,679	28940	47013	Campbell County	40,716
				28940	47057	Grainger County	22,657
27860		Jonesboro, AR	121,026	28940	47093	Knox County	432,226
27860	05031	Craighead County	96,443	28940	47105	Loudon County	48,556
27860	05111	Poinsett County	24,583	28940	47129	Morgan County	21,987
				28940	47145	Roane County	54,181
27900		Joplin, MO	175,518	28940	47173	Union County	19,109
27900	29097	Jasper County	117,404				
27900	29145	Newton County	58,114	29020		Kokomo, IN	82,752
				29020	18067	Howard County	82,752
27980		Kahului-Wailuku-Lahaina, HI	154,924				
27980	15005	Kalawao County	90	29100		La Crosse-Onalaska, WI-MN	133,665
27980	15009	Maui County	154,834	29100	27055	Houston County	19,027
				29100	55063	La Crosse County	114,638
28020		Kalamazoo-Portage, MI	326,589				
28020	26077	Kalamazoo County	250,331	29180		Lafayette, LA	466,750
28020	26159	Van Buren County	76,258	29180	22001	Acadia Parish	61,773
				29180	22045	Iberia Parish	73,240
28100		Kankakee, IL	113,449	29180	22055	Lafayette Parish	221,578
28100	17091	Kankakee County	113,449	29180	22099	St. Martin Parish	52,160
				29180	22113	Vermilion Parish	57,999
				29200		Lafayette-West Lafayette, IN	201,789
				29200	18007	Benton County	8,854
				29200	18015	Carroll County	20,155
				29200	18157	Tippecanoe County	172,780

METROPOLITAN STATISTICAL AREAS, METROPOLITAN DIVISIONS, AND COMPONENTS (as defined July 2015)—*Continued*

Core based statistical area	State/ County FIPS code	Title and Geographic Components	2010 Census Population	Core based statistical area	State/ County FIPS code	Title and Geographic Components	2010 Census Population
29340		Lake Charles, LA	199,607	30780		Little Rock-North Little Rock-Conway, AR	699,757
29340	22019	Calcasieu Parish	192,768	30780	05045	Faulkner County	113,237
29340	22023	Cameron Parish	6,839	30780	05053	Grant County	17,853
				30780	05085	Lonoke County	68,356
29420		Lake Havasu City-Kingman, AZ	200,186	30780	05105	Perry County	10,445
29420	04015	Mohave County	200,186	30780	05119	Pulaski County	382,748
				30780	05125	Saline County	107,118
29460		Lakeland-Winter Haven, FL	602,095				
29460	12105	Polk County	602,095	30860		Logan, UT-ID	125,442
				30860	16041	Franklin County	12,786
29540		Lancaster, PA	519,445	30860	49005	Cache County	112,656
29540	42071	Lancaster County	519,445				
				30980		Longview, TX	214,369
29620		Lansing-East Lansing, MI	464,036	30980	48183	Gregg County	121,730
29620	26037	Clinton County	75,382	30980	48401	Rusk County	53,330
29620	26045	Eaton County	107,759	30980	48459	Upshur County	39,309
29620	26065	Ingham County	280,895				
				31020		Longview, WA	102,410
29700		Laredo, TX	250,304	31020	53015	Cowlitz County	102,410
29700	48479	Webb County	250,304				
				31080		Los Angeles-Long Beach-Anaheim, CA	12,828,837
29740		Las Cruces, NM	209,233	31080		Anaheim-Santa Ana-Irvine, CA Div 11244	3,010,232
29740	35013	Dona Ana County	209,233	31080	06059	Orange County	3,010,232
				31080		Los Angeles-Long Beach-Glendale, CA Div 31084	9,818,605
29820		Las Vegas-Henderson-Paradise, NV	1,951,269				
29820	32003	Clark County	1,951,269	31080	06037	Los Angeles County	9,818,605
29940		Lawrence, KS	110,826	31140		Louisville/Jefferson County, KY-IN	1,235,708
29940	20045	Douglas County	110,826	31140	18019	Clark County	110,232
				31140	18043	Floyd County	74,578
30020		Lawton, OK	130,291	31140	18061	Harrison County	39,364
30020	40031	Comanche County	124,098	31140	18143	Scott County	24,181
30020	40033	Cotton County	6,193	31140	18175	Washington County	28,262
				31140	21029	Bullitt County	74,319
30140		Lebanon, PA	133,568	31140	21103	Henry County	15,416
30140	42075	Lebanon County	133,568	31140	21111	Jefferson County	741,096
				31140	21185	Oldham County	60,316
30300		Lewiston, ID-WA	60,888	31140	21211	Shelby County	42,074
30300	16069	Nez Perce County	39,265	31140	21215	Spencer County	17,061
30300	53003	Asotin County	21,623	31140	21223	Trimble County	8,809
30340		Lewiston-Auburn, ME	107,702	31180		Lubbock, TX	290,805
30340	23001	Androscoggin County	107,702	31180	48107	Crosby County	6,059
				31180	48303	Lubbock County	278,831
30460		Lexington-Fayette, KY	472,099	31180	48305	Lynn County	5,915
30460	21017	Bourbon County	19,985				
30460	21049	Clark County	35,613	31340		Lynchburg, VA	252,634
30460	21067	Fayette County	295,803	31340	51009	Amherst County	32,353
30460	21113	Jessamine County	48,586	31340	51011	Appomattox County	14,973
30460	21209	Scott County	47,173	31340	51019	Bedford County	68,676
30460	21239	Woodford County	24,939	31340	51031	Campbell County	54,842
				31340	51515	Bedford city	6,222
30620		Lima, OH	106,331	31340	51680	Lynchburg city	75,568
30620	39003	Allen County	106,331				
				31420		Macon, GA	232,293
30700		Lincoln, NE	302,157	31420	13021	Bibb County	155,547
30700	31109	Lancaster County	285,407	31420	13079	Crawford County	12,630
30700	31159	Seward County	16,750	31420	13169	Jones County	28,669
				31420	13207	Monroe County	26,424
				31420	13289	Twiggs County	9,023
				31460		Madera, CA	150,865
				31460	06039	Madera County	150,865

Appendix B

B-9

Core based statistical area	State/ County FIPS code	Title and Geographic Components	2010 Census Population	Core based statistical area	State/ County FIPS code	Title and Geographic Components	2010 Census Population
31540		Madison, WI..............................	605,435	33340		Milwaukee-Waukesha-West Allis, WI	1,555,908
31540	55021	Columbia County	56,833	33340	55079	Milwaukee County..............................	947,735
31540	55025	Dane County	488,073	33340	55089	Ozaukee County..............................	86,395
31540	55045	Green County	36,842	33340	55131	Washington County..............................	131,887
31540	55049	Iowa County	23,687	33340	55133	Waukesha County..............................	389,891
31700		Manchester-Nashua, NH	400,721	33460		Minneapolis-St. Paul-Bloomington, MN............	3,348,859
31700	33011	Hillsborough County	400,721	33460	27003	Anoka County..............................	330,844
				33460	27019	Carver County..............................	91,042
31740		Manhattan, KS	92,719	33460	27025	Chisago County	53,887
31740	20149	Pottawatomie County	21,604	33460	27037	Dakota County..............................	398,552
31740	20161	Riley County....................	71,115	33460	27053	Hennepin County..............................	1,152,425
				33460	27059	Isanti County..............................	37,816
31860		Mankato-North Mankato, MN	96,740	33460	27079	Le Sueur County..............................	27,703
31860	27013	Blue Earth County	64,013	33460	27095	Mille Lacs County..............................	26,097
31860	27103	Nicollet County...........	32,727	33460	27123	Ramsey County..............................	508,640
				33460	27139	Scott County..............................	129,928
31900		Mansfield, OH...........	124,475	33460	27141	Sherburne County..............................	88,499
31900	39139	Richland County...........	124,475	33460	27143	Sibley County..............................	15,226
				33460	27163	Washington County..............................	238,136
32580		McAllen-Edinburg-Mission, TX	774,769	33460	27171	Wright County..............................	124,700
32580	48215	Hidalgo County	774,769	33460	55093	Pierce County..............................	41,019
				33460	55109	St. Croix County..............................	84,345
32780		Medford, OR...........	203,206				
32780	41029	Jackson County	203,206	33540		Missoula, MT..............................	109,299
				33540	30063	Missoula County..............................	109,299
32820		Memphis, TN-MS-AR	1,324,829				
32820	05035	Crittenden County	50,902	33660		Mobile, AL..............................	412,992
32820	28009	Benton County	8,729	33660	01097	Mobile County..............................	412,992
32820	28033	DeSoto County...........	161,252				
32820	28093	Marshall County...........	37,144	33700		Modesto, CA..............................	514,453
32820	28137	Tate County...........	28,886	33700	06099	Stanislaus County..............................	514,453
32820	28143	Tunica County...........	10,778				
32820	47047	Fayette County...........	38,413	33740		Monroe, LA..............................	176,441
32820	47157	Shelby County...........	927,644	33740	22073	Ouachita Parish..............................	153,720
32820	47167	Tipton County...........	61,081	33740	22111	Union Parish..............................	22,721
32900		Merced, CA...........	255,793	33780		Monroe, MI..............................	152,021
32900	06047	Merced County...........	255,793	33780	26115	Monroe County..............................	152,021
33100		Miami-Fort Lauderdale-West Palm Beach, FL....	5,564,635	33860		Montgomery, AL..............................	374,536
33100		Fort Lauderdale-Pompano Beach-Deerfield Beach, FL Div 22744	1,748,066	33860	01001	Autauga County	54,571
				33860	01051	Elmore County..............................	79,303
33100	12011	Broward County..............................	1,748,066	33860	01085	Lowndes County..............................	11,299
33100		Miami-Miami Beach-Kendall, FL Div 33124	2,496,435	33860	01101	Montgomery County..............................	229,363
33100	12086	Miami-Dade County..............................	2,496,435				
33100		West Palm Beach-Boca Raton-Delray Beach, FL Div 48424............	1,320,134	34060		Morgantown, WV..............................	129,709
				34060	54061	Monongalia County..............................	96,189
33100	12099	Palm Beach County..............................	1,320,134	34060	54077	Preston County..............................	33,520
33140		Michigan City-La Porte, IN..............................	111,467	34100		Morristown, TN..............................	113,951
33140	18091	LaPorte County..............................	111,467	34100	47063	Hamblen County..............................	62,544
				34100	47089	Jefferson County..............................	51,407
33220		Midland, MI..............................	83,629				
33220	26111	Midland County..............................	83,629	34580		Mount Vernon-Anacortes, WA..............................	116,901
				34580	53057	Skagit County..............................	116,901
33260		Midland, TX	141,671				
33260	48317	Martin County..............................	4,799	34620		Muncie, IN..............................	117,671
33260	48329	Midland County..............................	136,872	34620	18035	Delaware County..............................	117,671
				34740		Muskegon, MI..............................	172,188
				34740	26121	Muskegon County..............................	172,188

Core based statistical area	State/ County FIPS code	Title and Geographic Components	2010 Census Population	Core based statistical area	State/ County FIPS code	Title and Geographic Components	2010 Census Population
34820		Myrtle Beach-Conway-North Myrtle Beach, NC-SC	376,722	35620		New York-Newark-Jersey City, NY-NJ-PA	19,567,410
34820	37019	Brunswick County	107,431	35620		Dutchess County-Putnam County, NY Div 20524	397,198
34820	45051	Horry County	269,291	35620	36027	Dutchess County	297,488
				35620	36079	Putnam County	99,710
34900		Napa, CA	136,484	35620		Nassau County-Suffolk County, NY Div 35004	2,832,882
34900	06055	Napa County	136,484	35620	36059	Nassau County	1,339,532
				35620	36103	Suffolk County	1,493,350
34940		Naples-Immokalee-Marco Island, FL	321,520	35620		Newark, NJ-PA Div 35084	2,471,171
34940	12021	Collier County	321,520	35620	34013	Essex County	783,969
				35620	34019	Hunterdon County	128,349
34980		Nashville-Davidson—Murfreesboro—Franklin, TN	1,670,890	35620	34027	Morris County	492,276
34980	47015	Cannon County	13,801	35620	34035	Somerset County	323,444
34980	47021	Cheatham County	39,105	35620	34037	Sussex County	149,265
34980	47037	Davidson County	626,681	35620	34039	Union County	536,499
34980	47043	Dickson County	49,666	35620	42103	Pike County	57,369
34980	47081	Hickman County	24,690	35620		New York-Jersey City-White Plains, NY-NJ Div 35614	13,866,159
34980	47111	Macon County	22,248	35620	34003	Bergen County	905,116
34980	47119	Maury County	80,956	35620	34017	Hudson County	634,266
34980	47147	Robertson County	66,283	35620	34023	Middlesex County	809,858
34980	47149	Rutherford County	262,604	35620	34025	Monmouth County	630,380
34980	47159	Smith County	19,166	35620	34029	Ocean County	576,567
34980	47165	Sumner County	160,645	35620	34031	Passaic County	501,226
34980	47169	Trousdale County	7,870	35620	36005	Bronx County	1,385,108
34980	47187	Williamson County	183,182	35620	36047	Kings County	2,504,700
34980	47189	Wilson County	113,993	35620	36061	New York County	1,585,873
				35620	36071	Orange County	372,813
35100		New Bern, NC	126,802	35620	36081	Queens County	2,230,722
35100	37049	Craven County	103,505	35620	36085	Richmond County	468,730
35100	37103	Jones County	10,153	35620	36087	Rockland County	311,687
35100	37137	Pamlico County	13,144	35620	36119	Westchester County	949,113
35300		New Haven-Milford, CT	862,477	35660		Niles-Benton Harbor, MI	156,813
35300	09009	New Haven County	862,477	35660	26021	Berrien County	156,813
35380		New Orleans-Metairie, LA	1,189,866	35840		North Port-Sarasota-Bradenton, FL	702,281
35380	22051	Jefferson Parish	432,552	35840	12081	Manatee County	322,833
35380	22071	Orleans Parish	343,829	35840	12115	Sarasota County	379,448
35380	22075	Plaquemines Parish	23,042				
35380	22087	St. Bernard Parish	35,897	35980		Norwich-New London, CT	274,055
35380	22089	St. Charles Parish	52,780	35980	09011	New London County	274,055
35380	22093	St. James Parish	22,102				
35380	22095	St. John the Baptist Parish	45,924	36100		Ocala, FL	331,298
35380	22103	St. Tammany Parish	233,740	36100	12083	Marion County	331,298
				36140		Ocean City, NJ	97,265
				36140	34009	Cape May County	97,265
				36220		Odessa, TX	137,130
				36220	48135	Ector County	137,130
				36260		Ogden-Clearfield, UT	597,159
				36260	49003	Box Elder County	49,975
				36260	49011	Davis County	306,479
				36260	49029	Morgan County	9,469
				36260	49057	Weber County	231,236

Core based statistical area	State/ County FIPS code	Title and Geographic Components	2010 Census Population	Core based statistical area	State/ County FIPS code	Title and Geographic Components	2010 Census Population
36420		Oklahoma City, OK	1,252,987	37980		Philadelphia-Camden-Wilmington, PA-NJ-DE-MD	5,965,343
36420	40017	Canadian County	115,541	37980		Camden, NJ Div 15804	1,250,679
36420	40027	Cleveland County	255,755	37980	34005	Burlington County	448,734
36420	40051	Grady County	52,431	37980	34007	Camden County	513,657
36420	40081	Lincoln County	34,273	37980	34015	Gloucester County	288,288
36420	40083	Logan County	41,848	37980		Montgomery County-Bucks County-Chester County, PA Div 33874	1,924,009
36420	40087	McClain County	34,506				
36420	40109	Oklahoma County	718,633	37980	42017	Bucks County	625,249
				37980	42029	Chester County	498,886
36500		Olympia-Tumwater, WA	252,264	37980	42091	Montgomery County	799,874
36500	53067	Thurston County	252,264	37980		Philadelphia, PA Div 37964	2,084,985
				37980	42045	Delaware County	558,979
36540		Omaha-Council Bluffs, NE-IA	865,350	37980	42101	Philadelphia County	1,526,006
36540	19085	Harrison County	14,928	37980		Wilmington, DE-MD-NJ Div 48864	705,670
36540	19129	Mills County	15,059	37980	10003	New Castle County	538,479
36540	19155	Pottawattamie County	93,158	37980	24015	Cecil County	101,108
36540	31025	Cass County	25,241	37980	34033	Salem County	66,083
36540	31055	Douglas County	517,110				
36540	31153	Sarpy County	158,840	38060		Phoenix-Mesa-Scottsdale, AZ	4,192,887
36540	31155	Saunders County	20,780	38060	04013	Maricopa County	3,817,117
36540	31177	Washington County	20,234	38060	04021	Pinal County	375,770
36740		Orlando-Kissimmee-Sanford, FL	2,134,411	38220		Pine Bluff, AR	100,258
36740	12069	Lake County	297,052	38220	05025	Cleveland County	8,689
36740	12095	Orange County	1,145,956	38220	05069	Jefferson County	77,435
36740	12097	Osceola County	268,685	38220	05079	Lincoln County	14,134
36740	12117	Seminole County	422,718				
				38300		Pittsburgh, PA	2,356,285
36780		Oshkosh-Neenah, WI	166,994	38300	42003	Allegheny County	1,223,348
36780	55139	Winnebago County	166,994	38300	42005	Armstrong County	68,941
				38300	42007	Beaver County	170,539
36980		Owensboro, KY	114,752	38300	42019	Butler County	183,862
36980	21059	Daviess County	96,656	38300	42051	Fayette County	136,606
36980	21091	Hancock County	8,565	38300	42125	Washington County	207,820
36980	21149	McLean County	9,531	38300	42129	Westmoreland County	365,169
37100		Oxnard-Thousand Oaks-Ventura, CA	823,318	38340		Pittsfield, MA	131,219
37100	06111	Ventura County	823,318	38340	25003	Berkshire County	131,219
37340		Palm Bay-Melbourne-Titusville, FL	543,376	38540		Pocatello, ID	82,839
37340	12009	Brevard County	543,376	38540	16005	Bannock County	82,839
37460		Panama City, FL	184,715	38860		Portland-South Portland, ME	514,098
37460	12005	Bay County	168,852	38860	23005	Cumberland County	281,674
37460	12045	Gulf County	15,863	38860	23023	Sagadahoc County	35,293
				38860	23031	York County	197,131
37620		Parkersburg-Vienna, WV	92,673				
37620	54105	Wirt County	5,717	38900		Portland-Vancouver-Hillsboro, OR-WA	2,226,009
37620	54107	Wood County	86,956	38900	41005	Clackamas County	375,992
				38900	41009	Columbia County	49,351
37860		Pensacola-Ferry Pass-Brent, FL	448,991	38900	41051	Multnomah County	735,334
37860	12033	Escambia County	297,619	38900	41067	Washington County	529,710
37860	12113	Santa Rosa County	151,372	38900	41071	Yamhill County	99,193
				38900	53011	Clark County	425,363
37900		Peoria, IL	379,186	38900	53059	Skamania County	11,066
37900	17123	Marshall County	12,640				
37900	17143	Peoria County	186,494	38940		Port St. Lucie, FL	424,107
37900	17175	Stark County	5,994	38940	12085	Martin County	146,318
37900	17179	Tazewell County	135,394	38940	12111	St. Lucie County	277,789
37900	17203	Woodford County	38,664				
				39140		Prescott, AZ	211,033
				39140	04025	Yavapai County	211,033

Core based statistical area	State/County FIPS code	Title and Geographic Components	2010 Census Population	Core based statistical area	State/County FIPS code	Title and Geographic Components	2010 Census Population
39300		Providence-Warwick, RI-MA	1,600,852	40220		Roanoke, VA	308,707
39300	25005	Bristol County	548,285	40220	51023	Botetourt County	33,148
39300	44001	Bristol County	49,875	40220	51045	Craig County	5,190
39300	44003	Kent County	166,158	40220	51067	Franklin County	56,159
39300	44005	Newport County	82,888	40220	51161	Roanoke County	92,376
39300	44007	Providence County	626,667	40220	51770	Roanoke city	97,032
39300	44009	Washington County	126,979	40220	51775	Salem city	24,802
39340		Provo-Orem, UT	526,810	40340		Rochester, MN	206,877
39340	49023	Juab County	10,246	40340	27039	Dodge County	20,087
39340	49049	Utah County	516,564	40340	27045	Fillmore County	20,866
				40340	27109	Olmsted County	144,248
39380		Pueblo, CO	159,063	40340	27157	Wabasha County	21,676
39380	08101	Pueblo County	159,063				
				40380		Rochester, NY	1,079,671
39460		Punta Gorda, FL	159,978	40380	36051	Livingston County	65,393
39460	12015	Charlotte County	159,978	40380	36055	Monroe County	744,344
				40380	36069	Ontario County	107,931
39540		Racine, WI	195,408	40380	36073	Orleans County	42,883
39540	55101	Racine County	195,408	40380	36117	Wayne County	93,772
				40380	36123	Yates County	25,348
39580		Raleigh, NC	1,130,490				
39580	37069	Franklin County	60,619	40420		Rockford, IL	349,431
39580	37101	Johnston County	168,878	40420	17007	Boone County	54,165
39580	37183	Wake County	900,993	40420	17201	Winnebago County	295,266
39660		Rapid City, SD	134,598	40580		Rocky Mount, NC	152,392
39660	46033	Custer County	8,216	40580	37065	Edgecombe County	56,552
39660	46093	Meade County	25,434	40580	37127	Nash County	95,840
39660	46103	Pennington County	100,948				
				40660		Rome, GA	96,317
39740		Reading, PA	411,442	40660	13115	Floyd County	96,317
39740	42011	Berks County	411,442				
				40900		Sacramento—Roseville—Arden-Arcade, CA	2,149,127
39820		Redding, CA	177,223	40900	06017	El Dorado County	181,058
39820	06089	Shasta County	177,223	40900	06061	Placer County	348,432
				40900	06067	Sacramento County	1,418,788
39900		Reno, NV	425,417	40900	06113	Yolo County	200,849
39900	32029	Storey County	4,010				
39900	32031	Washoe County	421,407	40980		Saginaw, MI	200,169
				40980	26145	Saginaw County	200,169
40060		Richmond, VA	1,208,101				
40060	51007	Amelia County	12,690	41060		St. Cloud, MN	189,093
40060	51033	Caroline County	28,545	41060	27009	Benton County	38,451
40060	51036	Charles City County	7,256	41060	27145	Stearns County	150,642
40060	51041	Chesterfield County	316,236				
40060	51053	Dinwiddie County	28,001	41100		St. George, UT	138,115
40060	51075	Goochland County	21,717	41100	49053	Washington County	138,115
40060	51085	Hanover County	99,863				
40060	51087	Henrico County	306,935	41140		St. Joseph, MO-KS	127,329
40060	51101	King William County	15,935	41140	20043	Doniphan County	7,945
40060	51127	New Kent County	18,429	41140	29003	Andrew County	17,291
40060	51145	Powhatan County	28,046	41140	29021	Buchanan County	89,201
40060	51149	Prince George County	35,725	41140	29063	DeKalb County	12,892
40060	51183	Sussex County	12,087				
40060	51570	Colonial Heights city	17,411				
40060	51670	Hopewell city	22,591				
40060	51730	Petersburg city	32,420				
40060	51760	Richmond city	204,214				
40140		Riverside-San Bernardino-Ontario, CA	4,224,851				
40140	06065	Riverside County	2,189,641				
40140	06071	San Bernardino County	2,035,210				

Core based statistical area	State/ County FIPS code	Title and Geographic Components	2010 Census Population	Core based statistical area	State/ County FIPS code	Title and Geographic Components	2010 Census Population
41180		St. Louis, MO-IL............	2,787,701	41940		San Jose-Sunnyvale-Santa Clara, CA...............	1,836,911
41180	17005	Bond County	17,768	41940	06069	San Benito County............................	55,269
41180	17013	Calhoun County	5,089	41940	06085	Santa Clara County...........................	1,781,642
41180	17027	Clinton County	37,762				
41180	17083	Jersey County	22,985	42020		San Luis Obispo-Paso Robles-Arroyo Grande, CA............	269,637
41180	17117	Macoupin County	47,765				
41180	17119	Madison County	269,282	42020	06079	San Luis Obispo County	269,637
41180	17133	Monroe County	32,957				
41180	17163	St. Clair County	270,056	42100		Santa Cruz-Watsonville, CA	262,382
41180	29071	Franklin County	101,492	42100	06087	Santa Cruz County	262,382
41180	29099	Jefferson County	218,733				
41180	29113	Lincoln County	52,566	42140		Santa Fe, NM	144,170
41180	29183	St. Charles County	360,485	42140	35049	Santa Fe County	144,170
41180	29189	St. Louis County	998,954				
41180	29219	Warren County	32,513	42200		Santa Maria-Santa Barbara, CA...............	423,895
41180	29510	St. Louis city	319,294	42200	06083	Santa Barbara County	423,895
41420		Salem, OR............................	390,738	42220		Santa Rosa, CA	483,878
41420	41047	Marion County.......................	315,335	42220	06097	Sonoma County	483,878
41420	41053	Polk County	75,403				
				42340		Savannah, GA	347,611
41500		Salinas, CA............................	415,057	42340	13029	Bryan County	30,233
41500	06053	Monterey County.....................	415,057	42340	13051	Chatham County	265,128
				42340	13103	Effingham County	52,250
41540		Salisbury, MD-DE	373,802				
41540	10005	Sussex County	197,145	42540		Scranton—Wilkes-Barre—Hazleton, PA............	563,631
41540	24039	Somerset County	26,470	42540	42069	Lackawanna County	214,437
41540	24045	Wicomico County	98,733	42540	42079	Luzerne County..............................	320,918
41540	24047	Worcester County	51,454	42540	42131	Wyoming County	28,276
41620		Salt Lake City, UT	1,087,873	42660		Seattle-Tacoma-Bellevue, WA......................	3,439,809
41620	49035	Salt Lake County..................	1,029,655	42660		Seattle-Bellevue-Everett, WA Div 42644	2,644,584
41620	49045	Tooele County	58,218	42660	53033	King County...............................	1,931,249
				42660	53061	Snohomish County	713,335
41660		San Angelo, TX......................	111,823	42660		Tacoma-Lakewood, WA Div 45104	795,225
41660	48235	Irion County........................	1,599	42660	53053	Pierce County...............................	795,225
41660	48451	Tom Green County..................	110,224				
				42680		Sebastian-Vero Beach, FL......................	138,028
41700		San Antonio-New Braunfels, TX	2,142,508	42680	12061	Indian River County	138,028
41700	48013	Atascosa County	44,911				
41700	48019	Bandera County	20,485	42700		Sebring, FL	98,786
41700	48029	Bexar County	1,714,773	42700	12055	Highlands County............................	98,786
41700	48091	Comal County	108,472				
41700	48187	Guadalupe County	131,533	43100		Sheboygan, WI	115,507
41700	48259	Kendall County	33,410	43100	55117	Sheboygan County	115,507
41700	48325	Medina County	46,006				
41700	48493	Wilson County	42,918	43300		Sherman-Denison, TX	120,877
				43300	48181	Grayson County	120,877
41740		San Diego-Carlsbad, CA	3,095,313				
41740	06073	San Diego County	3,095,313	43340		Shreveport-Bossier City, LA....................	439,811
				43340	22015	Bossier Parish..............................	116,979
41860		San Francisco-Oakland-Hayward, CA...............	4,335,391	43340	22017	Caddo Parish...............................	254,969
41860		Oakland-Hayward-Berkeley, CA Div 36084	2,559,296	43340	22031	De Soto Parish..............................	26,656
41860	06001	Alameda County	1,510,271	43340	22119	Webster Parish..............................	41,207
41860	06013	Contra Costa County.............	1,049,025				
41860		San Francisco-Redwood City-South San Francisco, CA Div 41884	1,523,686	43420		Sierra Vista-Douglas, AZ	131,346
				43420	04003	Cochise County	131,346
41860	06075	San Francisco County	805,235				
41860	06081	San Mateo County	718,451	43580		Sioux City, IA-NE-SD	168,563
41860		San Rafael, CA Div 42034	252,409	43580	19149	Plymouth County	24,986
41860	06041	Marin County	252,409	43580	19193	Woodbury County	102,172
				43580	31043	Dakota County	21,006
				43580	31051	Dixon County	6,000
				43580	46127	Union County	14,399

Core based statistical area	State/ County FIPS code	Title and Geographic Components	2010 Census Population	Core based statistical area	State/ County FIPS code	Title and Geographic Components	2010 Census Population
43620		Sioux Falls, SD	228,261	45300		Tampa-St. Petersburg-Clearwater, FL	2,783,243
43620	46083	Lincoln County	44,828	45300	12053	Hernando County	172,778
43620	46087	McCook County	5,618	45300	12057	Hillsborough County	1,229,226
43620	46099	Minnehaha County	169,468	45300	12101	Pasco County	464,697
43620	46125	Turner County	8,347	45300	12103	Pinellas County	916,542
43780		South Bend-Mishawaka, IN-MI	319,224	45460		Terre Haute, IN	172,425
43780	18141	St. Joseph County	266,931	45460	18021	Clay County	26,890
43780	26027	Cass County	52,293	45460	18153	Sullivan County	21,475
				45460	18165	Vermillion County	16,212
43900		Spartanburg, SC	313,268	45460	18167	Vigo County	107,848
43900	45083	Spartanburg County	284,307				
43900	45087	Union County	28,961	45500		Texarkana, TX-AR	149,198
				45500	05081	Little River County	13,171
44060		Spokane-Spokane Valley, WA	527,753	45500	05091	Miller County	43,462
44060	53051	Pend Oreille County	13,001	45500	48037	Bowie County	92,565
44060	53063	Spokane County	471,221				
44060	53065	Stevens County	43,531	45540		The Villages, FL	93,420
				45540	12119	Sumter County	93,420
44100		Springfield, IL	210,170				
44100	17129	Menard County	12,705	45780		Toledo, OH	610,001
44100	17167	Sangamon County	197,465	45780	39051	Fulton County	42,698
				45780	39095	Lucas County	441,815
44140		Springfield, MA	621,570	45780	39173	Wood County	125,488
44140	25013	Hampden County	463,490				
44140	25015	Hampshire County	158,080	45820		Topeka, KS	233,870
				45820	20085	Jackson County	13,462
44180		Springfield, MO	436,712	45820	20087	Jefferson County	19,126
44180	29043	Christian County	77,422	45820	20139	Osage County	16,295
44180	29059	Dallas County	16,777	45820	20177	Shawnee County	177,934
44180	29077	Greene County	275,174	45820	20197	Wabaunsee County	7,053
44180	29167	Polk County	31,137				
44180	29225	Webster County	36,202	45940		Trenton, NJ	366,513
				45940	34021	Mercer County	366,513
44220		Springfield, OH	138,333				
44220	39023	Clark County	138,333	46060		Tucson, AZ	980,263
				46060	04019	Pima County	980,263
44300		State College, PA	153,990				
44300	42027	Centre County	153,990	46140		Tulsa, OK	937,478
				46140	40037	Creek County	69,967
44420		Staunton-Waynesboro, VA	118,502	46140	40111	Okmulgee County	40,069
44420	51015	Augusta County	73,750	46140	40113	Osage County	47,472
44420	51790	Staunton city	23,746	46140	40117	Pawnee County	16,577
44420	51820	Waynesboro city	21,006	46140	40131	Rogers County	86,905
				46140	40143	Tulsa County	603,403
44700		Stockton-Lodi, CA	685,306	46140	40145	Wagoner County	73,085
44700	06077	San Joaquin County	685,306				
				46220		Tuscaloosa, AL	230,162
44940		Sumter, SC	107,456	46220	01065	Hale County	15,760
44940	45085	Sumter County	107,456	46220	01107	Pickens County	19,746
				46220	01125	Tuscaloosa County	194,656
45060		Syracuse, NY	662,577				
45060	36053	Madison County	73,442	46340		Tyler, TX	209,714
45060	36067	Onondaga County	467,026	46340	48423	Smith County	209,714
45060	36075	Oswego County	122,109				
				46520		Urban Honolulu, HI	953,207
45220		Tallahassee, FL	367,413	46520	15003	Honolulu County	953,207
45220	12039	Gadsden County	46,389				
45220	12065	Jefferson County	14,761	46540		Utica-Rome, NY	299,397
45220	12073	Leon County	275,487	46540	36043	Herkimer County	64,519
45220	12129	Wakulla County	30,776	46540	36065	Oneida County	234,878

Core based statistical area	State/ County FIPS code	Title and Geographic Components	2010 Census Population	Core based statistical area	State/ County FIPS code	Title and Geographic Components	2010 Census Population
46660		Valdosta, GA	139,588	47900		Washington-Arlington-Alexandria, DC-VA-MD-WV	5,636,232
46660	13027	Brooks County	16,243				
46660	13101	Echols County	4,034	47900		Silver Spring-Frederick-Rockville, MD Div 43524	1,205,162
46660	13173	Lanier County	10,078				
46660	13185	Lowndes County	109,233	47900	24021	Frederick County	233,385
				47900	24031	Montgomery County	971,777
46700		Vallejo-Fairfield, CA	413,344	47900		Washington-Arlington-Alexandria, DC-VA-MD-WV Div 47894	4,431,070
46700	06095	Solano County	413,344				
				47900	11001	District of Columbia	601,723
47020		Victoria, TX	94,003	47900	24009	Calvert County	88,737
47020	48175	Goliad County	7,210	47900	24017	Charles County	146,551
47020	48469	Victoria County	86,793	47900	24033	Prince George's County	863,420
				47900	51013	Arlington County	207,627
47220		Vineland-Bridgeton, NJ	156,898	47900	51043	Clarke County	14,034
47220	34011	Cumberland County	156,898	47900	51047	Culpeper County	46,689
				47900	51059	Fairfax County	1,081,726
47260		Virginia Beach-Norfolk-Newport News, VA-NC	1,676,822	47900	51061	Fauquier County	65,203
				47900	51107	Loudoun County	312,311
47260	37053	Currituck County	23,547	47900	51153	Prince William County	402,002
47260	37073	Gates County	12,197	47900	51157	Rappahannock County	7,373
47260	51073	Gloucester County	36,858	47900	51177	Spotsylvania County	122,397
47260	51093	Isle of Wight County	35,270	47900	51179	Stafford County	128,961
47260	51095	James City County	67,009	47900	51187	Warren County	37,575
47260	51115	Mathews County	8,978	47900	51510	Alexandria city	139,966
47260	51199	York County	65,464	47900	51600	Fairfax city	22,565
47260	51550	Chesapeake city	222,209	47900	51610	Falls Church city	12,332
47260	51650	Hampton city	137,436	47900	51630	Fredericksburg city	24,286
47260	51700	Newport News city	180,719	47900	51683	Manassas city	37,821
47260	51710	Norfolk city	242,803	47900	51685	Manassas Park city	14,273
47260	51735	Poquoson city	12,150	47900	54037	Jefferson County	53,498
47260	51740	Portsmouth city	95,535				
47260	51800	Suffolk city	84,585	47940		Waterloo-Cedar Falls, IA	167,819
47260	51810	Virginia Beach city	437,994	47940	19013	Black Hawk County	131,090
47260	51830	Williamsburg city	14,068	47940	19017	Bremer County	24,276
				47940	19075	Grundy County	12,453
47300		Visalia-Porterville, CA	442,179				
47300	06107	Tulare County	442,179	48060		Watertown-Fort Drum, NY	116,229
				48060	36045	Jefferson County	116,229
47380		Waco, TX	252,772				
47380	48145	Falls County	17,866	48140		Wausau, WI	134,063
47380	48309	McLennan County	234,906	48140	55073	Marathon County	134,063
47460		Walla Walla, WA	62,859	48260		Weirton-Steubenville, WV-OH	124,454
47460	53013	Columbia County	4,078	48260	39081	Jefferson County	69,709
47460	53071	Walla Walla County	58,781	48260	54009	Brooke County	24,069
				48260	54029	Hancock County	30,676
47580		Warner Robins, GA	179,605				
47580	13153	Houston County	139,900	48300		Wenatchee, WA	110,884
47580	13225	Peach County	27,695	48300	53007	Chelan County	72,453
47580	13235	Pulaski County	12,010	48300	53017	Douglas County	38,431
				48540		Wheeling, WV-OH	147,950
				48540	39013	Belmont County	70,400
				48540	54051	Marshall County	33,107
				48540	54069	Ohio County	44,443
				48620		Wichita, KS	630,919
				48620	20015	Butler County	65,880
				48620	20079	Harvey County	34,684
				48620	20095	Kingman County	7,858
				48620	20173	Sedgwick County	498,365
				48620	20191	Sumner County	24,132

Core based statistical area	State/ County FIPS code	Title and Geographic Components	2010 Census Population	Core based statistical area	State/ County FIPS code	Title and Geographic Components	2010 Census Population
48660		Wichita Falls, TX..............................	151,306	49420		Yakima, WA.......................................	243,231
48660	48009	Archer County	9,054	49420	53077	Yakima County...............................	243,231
48660	48077	Clay County	10,752				
48660	48485	Wichita County	131,500	49620		York-Hanover, PA.............................	434,972
				49620	42133	York County....................................	434,972
48700		Williamsport, PA...............................	116,111				
48700	42081	Lycoming County	116,111	49660		Youngstown-Warren-Boardman, OH-PA	565,773
				49660	39099	Mahoning County.............................	238,823
48900		Wilmington, NC.................................	254,884	49660	39155	Trumbull County..............................	210,312
48900	37129	New Hanover County........................	202,667	49660	42085	Mercer County................................	116,638
48900	37141	Pender County	52,217				
				49700		Yuba City, CA...................................	166,892
49020		Winchester, VA-WV	128,472	49700	06101	Sutter County	94,737
49020	51069	Frederick County.............................	78,305	49700	06115	Yuba County	72,155
49020	51840	Winchester city...............................	26,203				
49020	54027	Hampshire County	23,964	49740		Yuma, AZ...	195,751
				49740	04027	Yuma County.................................	195,751
49180		Winston-Salem, NC...........................	640,595				
49180	37057	Davidson County.............................	162,878				
49180	37059	Davie County	41,240				
49180	37067	Forsyth County...............................	350,670				
49180	37169	Stokes County................................	47,401				
49180	37197	Yadkin County................................	38,406				
49340		Worcester, MA-CT.............................	916,980				
49340	09015	Windham County	118,428				
49340	25027	Worcester County	798,552				

CORE BASED STATISTICAL AREAS
(Metropolitan and Micropolitan),
METROPOLITAN DIVISIONS, AND COMPONENTS
(as defined August, 2017)—*Continued*

Core based statistical area	State/County FIPS code	Title and Geographic Components	2010 Census Population	2017 Estimated Population	Core based statistical area	State/County FIPS code	Title and Geographic Components	2010 Census Population	2017 Estimated Population
15380		Buffalo-Cheektowaga-Niagara Falls, NY Metro area	1,135,509	1,136,856	16060		Carbondale-Marion, IL Metro area	126,575	125,612
	36029	Erie County, NY	919,040	925,528		17077	Jackson County, IL	60,218	58,284
	36063	Niagara County, NY	216,469	211,328		17199	Williamson County, IL	66,357	67,328
15420		Burley, ID Micro area	43,021	44,393	16100		Carlsbad-Artesia, NM Micro area	53,829	56,997
	16031	Cassia County, ID	22,952	23,664		35015	Eddy County, NM	53,829	56,997
	16067	Minidoka County, ID	20,069	20,729	16140		Carroll, IA Micro Area	20,816	20,320
15460		Burlington, IA-IL Micro area	47,656	46,212		19027	Carroll County, IA	20,816	20,320
	17071	Henderson County, IL	7,331	6,795	16180		Carson City, NV Metro area	55,274	54,745
	19057	Des Moines County, IA	40,325	39,417		32510	Carson City, NV Metro area	55,274	54,745
15500		Burlington, NC Metro area	151,131	162,391	16220		Casper, WY Metro area	75,450	79,547
	37001	Alamance County, NC	151,131	162,391		56025	Natrona County, WY	75,450	79,547
15540		Burlington-South Burlington, VT Metro area	211,261	218,395	16260		Cedar City, UT Micro area	46,163	51,001
	50007	Chittenden County, VT	156,545	162,372		49021	Iron County, UT	46,163	51,001
	50011	Franklin County, VT	47,746	49,025	16300		Cedar Rapids, IA Metro area	257,940	270,293
	50013	Grand Isle County, VT	6,970	6,998		19011	Benton County, IA	26,076	25,642
15580		Butte-Silver Bow, MT Micro area	34,200	34,602		19105	Jones County, IA	20,638	20,536
	30093	Silver Bow County, MT	34,200	34,602		19113	Linn County, IA	211,226	224,115
15620		Cadillac, MI Micro area	47,584	48,274	16340		Cedartown, GA Micro area	41,475	42,085
	26113	Missaukee County, MI	14,849	14,998		13233	Polk County, GA	41,475	42,085
	26165	Wexford County, MI	32,735	33,276	16380		Celina, OH Micro area	40,814	40,873
15660		Calhoun, GA Micro area	55,186	57,089		39107	Mercer County, OH	40,814	40,873
	13129	Gordon County, GA	55,186	57,089	16420		Central City, KY Micro Area	31,499	30,816
15680		California-Lexington Park, MD Metro area	105,151	112,667		21177	Muhlenberg County, KY	31,499	30,816
	24037	St. Mary's County, MD	105,151	112,667	16460		Centralia, IL Micro area	39,437	37,902
15700		Cambridge, MD Micro area	32,618	32,162		17121	Marion County, IL	39,437	37,902
	24019	Dorchester County, MD	32,618	32,162	16500		Centralia, WA Micro area	75,455	78,200
15740		Cambridge, OH Micro area	40,087	39,093		53041	Lewis County, WA	75,455	78,200
	39059	Guernsey County, OH	40,087	39,093	16540		Chambersburg-Waynesboro, PA Metro area	149,618	154,234
15780		Camden, AR Micro area	31,488	29,115		42055	Franklin County, PA	149,618	154,234
	05013	Calhoun County, AR	5,368	5,247	16580		Champaign-Urbana, IL Metro area	231,891	239,124
	05103	Ouachita County, AR	26,120	23,868		17019	Champaign County, IL	201,081	209,399
15820		Campbellsville, KY Micro area	24,512	25,472		17053	Ford County, IL	14,081	13,280
	21217	Taylor County, KY	24,512	25,472		17147	Piatt County, IL	16,729	16,445
15860		Cañon City, CO Micro area	46,824	47,559	16620		Charleston, WV Metro area	227,078	214,406
	08043	Fremont County, CO	46,824	47,559		54005	Boone County, WV	24,629	22,349
15900		Canton, IL Micro area	37,069	35,110		54015	Clay County, WV	9,386	8,764
	17057	Fulton County, IL	37,069	35,110		54039	Kanawha County, WV	193,063	183,293
15940		Canton-Massillon, OH Metro area	404,422	399,927	16660		Charleston-Mattoon, IL Micro area	64,921	62,887
	39019	Carroll County, OH	28,836	27,385		17029	Coles County, IL	53,873	51,979
	39151	Stark County, OH	375,586	372,542		17035	Cumberland County, IL	11,048	10,908
15980		Cape Coral-Fort Myers, FL Metro area	618,754	739,224	16700		Charleston-North Charleston, SC Metro area	664,607	775,831
	12071	Lee County, FL	618,754	739,224		45015	Berkeley County, SC	177,843	217,937
16020		Cape Girardeau, MO-IL Metro area	96,275	96,782		45019	Charleston County, SC	350,209	401,438
	17003	Alexander County, IL	8,238	6,315		45035	Dorchester County, SC	136,555	156,456
	29017	Bollinger County, MO	12,363	12,306					
	29031	Cape Girardeau County, MO	75,674	78,161					

Core based statistical area	State/ County FIPS code	Title and Geographic Components	2010 Census Population	2017 Estimated Population	Core based statistical area	State/ County FIPS code	Title and Geographic Components	2010 Census Population	2017 Estimated Population
16740		Charlotte-Concord-Gastonia, NC-SC Metro area	2,217,012	2,525,305	17140		Cincinnati, OH-KY-IN Metro area	2,114,580	2,179,082
	37025	Cabarrus County, NC	178,011	206,872		18029	Dearborn County, IN	50,047	49,741
	37071	Gaston County, NC	206,086	220,182		18115	Ohio County, IN	6,128	5,828
	37097	Iredell County, NC	159,437	175,711		18161	Union County, IN	7,516	7,200
	37109	Lincoln County, NC	78,265	82,403		21015	Boone County, KY	118,811	130,728
	37119	Mecklenburg County, NC	919,628	1,076,837		21023	Bracken County, KY	8,488	8,267
	37159	Rowan County, NC	138,428	140,644		21037	Campbell County, KY	90,336	92,488
	37179	Union County, NC	201,292	231,366		21077	Gallatin County, KY	8,589	8,776
	45023	Chester County, SC	33,140	32,301		21081	Grant County, KY	24,662	24,984
	45057	Lancaster County, SC	76,652	92,550		21117	Kenton County, KY	159,720	165,399
	45091	York County, SC	226,073	266,439		21191	Pendleton County, KY	14,877	14,573
16820		Charlottesville, VA Metro area	218,705	233,793		39015	Brown County, OH	44,846	43,576
	51003	Albemarle County, VA	98,970	107,702		39017	Butler County, OH	368,130	380,604
	51029	Buckingham County, VA	17,146	17,065		39025	Clermont County, OH	197,363	204,214
	51065	Fluvanna County, VA	25,691	26,452		39061	Hamilton County, OH	802,374	813,822
	51079	Greene County, VA	18,403	19,612		39165	Warren County, OH	212,693	228,882
	51125	Nelson County, VA	15,020	14,943	17200		Claremont-Lebanon, NH-VT Micro area	218,466	216,537
	51540	Charlottesville city, VA	43,475	48,019		33009	Grafton County, NH	89,118	89,386
16860		Chattanooga, TN-GA Metro area	528,143	556,548		33019	Sullivan County, NH	43,742	43,077
	13047	Catoosa County, GA	63,942	66,550		50017	Orange County, VT	28,936	28,974
	13083	Dade County, GA	16,633	16,285		50027	Windsor County, VT	56,670	55,100
	13295	Walker County, GA	68,756	68,939	17220		Clarksburg, WV Micro area	94,196	93,301
	47065	Hamilton County, TN	336,463	361,613		54017	Doddridge County, WV	8,202	8,560
	47115	Marion County, TN	28,237	28,425		54033	Harrison County, WV	69,099	67,811
	47153	Sequatchie County, TN	14,112	14,736		54091	Taylor County, WV	16,895	16,930
16940		Cheyenne, WY Metro area	91,738	98,327	17260		Clarksdale, MS Micro area	26,151	23,154
	56021	Laramie County, WY	91,738	98,327		28027	Coahoma County, MS	26,151	23,154
16980		Chicago-Naperville-Elgin, IL-IN-WI Metro area	9,461,105	9,533,040	17300		Clarksville, TN-KY Metro area	260,625	285,042
						21047	Christian County, KY	73,955	70,416
16980		Chicago-Naperville-Arlington Heights, IL Metro Div 16974	7,262,718	7,319,978		21221	Trigg County, KY	14,339	14,444
	17031	Cook County, IL	5,194,675	5,211,263		47125	Montgomery County, TN	172,331	200,182
	17043	DuPage County, IL	916,924	930,128	17340		Clearlake, CA Micro area	64,665	64,246
	17063	Grundy County, IL	50,063	50,586		06033	Lake County, CA	64,665	64,246
	17093	Kendall County, IL	114,736	126,218	17380		Cleveland, MS Micro area	34,145	31,945
	17111	McHenry County, IL	308,760	309,122		28011	Bolivar County, MS	34,145	31,945
	17197	Will County, IL	677,560	692,661	17420		Cleveland, TN Metro area	115,788	122,317
						47011	Bradley County, TN	98,963	105,560
16980		Elgin, IL Metro Div 20994	620,429	639,400		47139	Polk County, TN	16,825	16,757
	17037	DeKalb County, IL	105,160	104,733	17460		Cleveland-Elyria, OH Metro area	2,077,240	2,058,844
	17089	Kane County, IL	515,269	534,667		39035	Cuyahoga County, OH	1,280,122	1,248,514
						39055	Geauga County, OH	93,389	93,918
16980		Gary, IN Metro Div 23844	708,070	701,621		39085	Lake County, OH	230,041	230,117
	18073	Jasper County, IN	33,478	33,447		39093	Lorain County, OH	301,356	307,924
	18089	Lake County, IN	496,005	485,640		39103	Medina County, OH	172,332	178,371
	18111	Newton County, IN	14,244	14,130	17500		Clewiston, FL Micro area	39,140	40,347
	18127	Porter County, IN	164,343	168,404		12051	Hendry County, FL	39,140	40,347
16980		Lake County-Kenosha County, IL-WI Metro Div 29404	869,888	872,041	17540		Clinton, IA Micro area	49,116	47,010
						19045	Clinton County, IA	49,116	47,010
	17097	Lake County, IL	703,462	703,520	17580		Clovis, NM Micro area	48,376	49,812
	55059	Kenosha County, WI	166,426	168,521		35009	Curry County, NM	48,376	49,812
17020		Chico, CA Metro area	220,000	229,294	17660		Coeur d'Alene, ID Metro area	138,494	157,637
	06007	Butte County, CA	220,000	229,294		16055	Kootenai County, ID	138,494	157,637
17060		Chillicothe, OH Micro area	78,064	77,313	17700		Coffeyville, KS Micro area	35,471	32,556
	39141	Ross County, OH	78,064	77,313		20125	Montgomery County, KS	35,471	32,556

Core based statistical area	State/ County FIPS code	Title and Geographic Components	2010 Census Population	2017 Estimated Population	Core based statistical area	State/ County FIPS code	Title and Geographic Components	2010 Census Population	2017 Estimated Population
17740		Coldwater, MI Micro area.....................	45,248	43,410	18420		Corinth, MS Micro area........................	37,057	37,210
	26023	Branch County, MI	45,248	43,410		28003	Alcorn County, MS	37,057	37,210
17780		College Station-Bryan, TX Metro area...	228,660	258,044	18460		Cornelia, GA Micro area	43,041	44,567
	48041	Brazos County, TX.............................	194,851	222,830		13137	Habersham County, GA	43,041	44,567
	48051	Burleson County, TX..........................	17,187	18,011	18500		Corning, NY Micro area.......................	98,990	96,281
	48395	Robertson County, TX........................	16,622	17,203		36101	Steuben County, NY	98,990	96,281
17820		Colorado Springs, CO Metro area........	645,613	723,878	18580		Corpus Christi, TX Metro area..............	428,185	454,008
	08041	El Paso County, CO...........................	622,263	699,232		48007	Aransas County, TX	23,158	25,572
	08119	Teller County, CO	23,350	24,646		48355	Nueces County, TX............................	340,223	361,221
17860		Columbia, MO Metro area....................	162,642	178,271		48409	San Patricio County, TX.....................	64,804	67,215
	29019	Boone County, MO.............................	162,642	178,271	18620		Corsicana, TX Micro area....................	47,735	48,701
17900		Columbia, SC Metro area....................	767,598	825,033		48349	Navarro County, TX	47,735	48,701
	45017	Calhoun County, SC..........................	15,175	14,704	18660		Cortland, NY Micro area	49,336	47,786
	45039	Fairfield County, SC..........................	23,956	22,607		36023	Cortland County, NY	49,336	47,786
	45055	Kershaw County, SC..........................	61,697	65,036	18700		Corvallis, OR Metro area.....................	85,579	90,951
	45063	Lexington County, SC........................	262,391	290,642		41003	Benton County, OR...........................	85,579	90,951
	45079	Richland County, SC.........................	384,504	411,592	18740		Coshocton, OH Micro area..................	36,901	36,544
	45081	Saluda County, SC............................	19,875	20,452		39031	Coshocton County, OH	36,901	36,544
17980		Columbus, GA-AL Metro area	294,865	303,811	18780		Craig, CO Micro area..........................	13,795	13,131
	01113	Russell County, AL............................	52,947	57,045		08081	Moffat County, CO	13,795	13,131
	13053	Chattahoochee County, GA	11,267	10,343	18820		Crawfordsville, IN Micro area	38,124	38,525
	13145	Harris County, GA.............................	32,024	33,915		18107	Montgomery County, IN	38,124	38,525
	13197	Marion County, GA............................	8,742	8,450	18860		Crescent City, CA Micro area	28,610	27,470
	13215	Muscogee County, GA........................	189,885	194,058		06015	Del Norte County, CA.........................	28,610	27,470
18020		Columbus, IN Metro area	76,794	82,040	18880		Crestview-Fort Walton Beach-Destin, FL Metro area	235,865	271,346
	18005	Bartholomew County, IN	76,794	82,040		12091	Okaloosa County, FL.........................	180,822	202,970
18060		Columbus, MS Micro area...................	59,779	59,186		12131	Walton County, FL............................	55,043	68,376
	28087	Lowndes County, MS.........................	59,779	59,186	18900		Crossville, TN Micro area	56,053	59,078
18100		Columbus, NE Micro area...................	32,237	33,175		47035	Cumberland County, TN	56,053	59,078
	31141	Platte County, NE.............................	32,237	33,175	18980		Cullman, AL Micro area	80,406	82,755
18140		Columbus, OH Metro area...................	1,901,974	2,078,725		01043	Cullman County, AL...........................	80,406	82,755
	39041	Delaware County, OH........................	174,214	200,464	19000		Cullowhee, NC Micro area...................	40,271	42,973
	39045	Fairfield County, OH..........................	146,156	154,733		37099	Jackson County, NC	40,271	42,973
	39049	Franklin County, OH..........................	1,163,414	1,291,981	19060		Cumberland, MD-WV Metro area..........	103,299	98,837
	39073	Hocking County, OH	29,380	28,474		24001	Allegany County, MD..........................	75,087	71,615
	39089	Licking County, OH	166,492	173,448		54057	Mineral County, WV	28,212	27,222
	39097	Madison County, OH.........................	43,435	44,036	19100		Dallas-Fort Worth-Arlington, TX Metro area	6,426,214	7,399,662
	39117	Morrow County, OH	34,827	34,994	19100		Dallas-Plano-Irving, TX Metro Div 19124	4,230,520	4,911,124
	39127	Perry County, OH.............................	36,058	36,024		48085	Collin County, TX..............................	782,341	969,603
	39129	Pickaway County, OH........................	55,698	57,830		48113	Dallas County, TX.............................	2,368,139	2,618,148
	39159	Union County, OH	52,300	56,741		48121	Denton County, TX............................	662,614	836,210
18180		Concord, NH Micro area......................	146,445	149,216		48139	Ellis County, TX................................	149,610	173,620
	33013	Merrimack County, NH.......................	146,445	149,216		48231	Hunt County, TX...............................	86,129	93,872
18220		Connersville, IN Micro area.................	24,277	23,209		48257	Kaufman County, TX..........................	103,350	122,883
	18041	Fayette County, IN	24,277	23,209		48397	Rockwall County, TX	78,337	96,788
18260		Cookeville, TN Micro area...................	106,042	111,363					
	47087	Jackson County, TN..........................	11,638	11,677					
	47133	Overton County, TN..........................	22,083	22,012					
	47141	Putnam County, TN...........................	72,321	77,674					
18300		Coos Bay, OR Micro area....................	63,043	63,888					
	41011	Coos County, OR.............................	63,043	63,888					
18380		Cordele, GA Micro area......................	23,439	22,736					
	13081	Crisp County, GA..............................	23,439	22,736					

Core based statistical area	State/County FIPS code	Title and Geographic Components	2010 Census Population	2017 Estimated Population	Core based statistical area	State/County FIPS code	Title and Geographic Components	2010 Census Population	2017 Estimated Population
19100		Fort Worth-Arlington, TX Metro Div 23104............	2,195,694	2,488,538	19740		Denver-Aurora-Lakewood, CO Metro area............	2,543,482	2,888,227
	48221	Hood County, TX............	51,182	58,273		08001	Adams County, CO............	441,603	503,167
	48251	Johnson County, TX............	150,934	167,301		08005	Arapahoe County, CO............	572,003	643,052
	48367	Parker County, TX............	116,927	133,463		08014	Broomfield County, CO............	55,889	68,341
	48425	Somervell County, TX............	8,490	8,845		08019	Clear Creek County, CO............	9,088	9,574
	48439	Tarrant County, TX............	1,809,034	2,054,475		08031	Denver County, CO............	600,158	704,621
	48497	Wise County, TX............	59,127	66,181		08035	Douglas County, CO............	285,465	335,299
19140		Dalton, GA Metro area............	142,227	144,440		08039	Elbert County, CO............	23,086	25,642
	13213	Murray County, GA............	39,628	39,782		08047	Gilpin County, CO............	5,441	6,013
	13313	Whitfield County, GA............	102,599	104,658		08059	Jefferson County, CO............	534,543	574,613
						08093	Park County, CO............	16,206	17,905
19180		Danville, IL Metro area............	81,625	77,909	19760		DeRidder, LA Micro area............	35,654	36,928
	17183	Vermilion County, IL............	81,625	77,909		22011	Beauregard Parish, LA............	35,654	36,928
19220		Danville, KY Micro area............	53,174	54,380	19780		Des Moines-West Des Moines, IA Metro area............	569,633	645,911
	21021	Boyle County, KY............	28,432	29,924		19049	Dallas County, IA............	66,135	87,235
	21137	Lincoln County, KY............	24,742	24,456		19077	Guthrie County, IA............	10,954	10,670
						19121	Madison County, IA............	15,679	16,013
19260		Danville, VA Micro area............	106,561	102,388		19153	Polk County, IA............	430,640	481,830
	51143	Pittsylvania County, VA............	63,506	61,258		19181	Warren County, IA............	46,225	50,163
	51590	Danville city, VA............	43,055	41,130					
19300		Daphne-Fairhope-Foley, AL Metro area............	182,265	212,628	19820		Detroit-Warren-Dearborn, MI Metro area............	4,296,250	4,313,002
	01003	Baldwin County, AL............	182,265	212,628	19820		Detroit-Dearborn-Livonia, MI Metro Div 19804............	1,820,584	1,753,616
19340		Davenport-Moline-Rock Island, IA-IL Metro area............	379,690	382,263		26163	Wayne County, MI............	1,820,584	1,753,616
	17073	Henry County, IL............	50,486	49,328	19820		Warren-Troy-Farmington Hills, MI Metro Div 47664............	2,475,666	2,559,386
	17131	Mercer County, IL............	16,434	15,618		26087	Lapeer County, MI............	88,319	88,174
	17161	Rock Island County, IL............	147,546	144,808		26093	Livingston County, MI............	180,967	189,651
	19163	Scott County, IA............	165,224	172,509		26099	Macomb County, MI............	840,978	871,375
19380		Dayton, OH Metro area............	799,232	803,416		26125	Oakland County, MI............	1,202,362	1,250,836
	39057	Greene County, OH............	161,573	166,752		26147	St. Clair County, MI............	163,040	159,350
	39109	Miami County, OH............	102,506	105,122	19860		Dickinson, ND Micro area............	24,199	30,209
	39113	Montgomery County, OH............	535,153	531,542		38089	Stark County, ND............	24,199	30,209
19420		Dayton, TN Micro area............	31,809	32,691	19940		Dixon, IL Micro area............	36,031	34,406
	47143	Rhea County, TN............	31,809	32,691		17103	Lee County, IL............	36,031	34,406
19460		Decatur, AL Metro area............	153,829	151,867	19980		Dodge City, KS Micro area............	33,848	34,381
	01079	Lawrence County, AL............	34,339	33,049		20057	Ford County, KS............	33,848	34,381
	01103	Morgan County, AL............	119,490	118,818	20020		Dothan, AL Metro area............	145,639	147,914
19500		Decatur, IL Metro area............	110,768	105,801		01061	Geneva County, AL............	26,790	26,421
	17115	Macon County, IL............	110,768	105,801		01067	Henry County, AL............	17,302	17,147
19540		Decatur, IN Micro area............	34,387	35,491		01069	Houston County, AL............	101,547	104,346
	18001	Adams County, IN............	34,387	35,491	20060		Douglas, GA Micro area............	42,356	43,014
19580		Defiance, OH Micro area............	39,037	38,156		13069	Coffee County, GA............	42,356	43,014
	39039	Defiance County, OH............	39,037	38,156	20100		Dover, DE Metro area............	162,310	176,824
19620		Del Rio, TX Micro area............	48,879	49,205		10001	Kent County, Delaware............	162,310	176,824
	48465	Val Verde County, TX............	48,879	49,205	20140		Dublin, GA Micro area............	58,414	57,118
19660		Deltona-Daytona Beach-Ormond Beach, FL Metro area............	590,289	649,202		13167	Johnson County, GA............	9,980	9,788
	12035	Flagler County, FL............	95,696	110,510		13175	Laurens County, GA............	48,434	47,330
	12127	Volusia County, FL............	494,593	538,692	20180		DuBois, PA Micro area............	81,642	79,685
19700		Deming, NM Micro area............	25,095	24,078		42033	Clearfield County, PA............	81,642	79,685
	35029	Luna County, NM............	25,095	24,078	20220		Dubuque, IA Metro area............	93,653	97,041
						19061	Dubuque County, IA............	93,653	97,041

Core based statistical area	State/County FIPS code	Title and Geographic Components	2010 Census Population	2017 Estimated Population	Core based statistical area	State/County FIPS code	Title and Geographic Components	2010 Census Population	2017 Estimated Population
20260		Duluth, MN-WI Metro area......................	279,771	278,782	21120		Elk City, OK Micro area	22,119	21,793
	27017	Carlton County, MN..............................	35,386	35,498		40009	Beckham County, OK............................	22,119	21,793
	27137	St. Louis County, MN	200,226	200,000					
	55031	Douglas County, WI	44,159	43,284	21140		Elkhart-Goshen, IN Metro area..............	197,559	205,032
						18039	Elkhart County, IN................................	197,559	205,032
20300		Dumas, TX Micro area..........................	21,904	22,097					
	48341	Moore County, TX	21,904	22,097	21180		Elkins, WV Micro area	29,405	28,785
						54083	Randolph County, WV...........................	29,405	28,785
20340		Duncan, OK Micro area	45,048	43,332					
	40137	Stephens County, OK	45,048	43,332	21220		Elko, NV Micro area..............................	50,805	54,610
						32007	Elko County, NV...................................	48,818	52,649
20380		Dunn, NC Micro area............................	114,678	132,754		32011	Eureka County, NV	1,987	1,961
	37085	Harnett County, NC..............................	114,678	132,754					
					21260		Ellensburg, WA Micro area....................	40,915	46,205
20420		Durango, CO Micro area	51,334	55,589		53037	Kittitas County, WA..............................	40,915	46,205
	08067	La Plata County, CO	51,334	55,589					
					21300		Elmira, NY Metro area...........................	88,830	85,557
20460		Durant, OK Micro area..........................	42,416	46,319		36015	Chemung County, NY	88,830	85,557
	40013	Bryan County, OK	42,416	46,319					
					21340		El Paso, TX Metro area	804,123	844,818
20500		Durham-Chapel Hill, NC Metro area......	504,357	567,428		48141	El Paso County, TX..............................	800,647	840,410
	37037	Chatham County, NC............................	63,505	71,472		48229	Hudspeth County, TX...........................	3,476	4,408
	37063	Durham County, NC..............................	267,587	311,640					
	37135	Orange County, NC..............................	133,801	144,946	21380		Emporia, KS Micro area	33,690	33,392
	37145	Person County, NC	39,464	39,370		20111	Lyon County, KS..................................	33,690	33,392
20540		Dyersburg, TN Micro area	38,335	37,463	21420		Enid, OK Metro area.............................	60,580	61,581
	47045	Dyer County, TN	38,335	37,463		40047	Garfield County, OK.............................	60,580	61,581
20580		Eagle Pass, TX Micro area...................	54,258	58,216	21460		Enterprise, AL Micro area	49,948	51,874
	48323	Maverick County, TX............................	54,258	58,216		01031	Coffee County, AL	49,948	51,874
20660		Easton, MD Micro area.........................	37,782	37,103	21500		Erie, PA Metro area	280,566	274,541
	24041	Talbot County, MD...............................	37,782	37,103		42049	Erie County, PA...................................	280,566	274,541
20700		East Stroudsburg, PA Metro area..........	169,842	168,046	21540		Escanaba, MI Micro area......................	37,069	35,965
	42089	Monroe County, PA..............................	169,842	168,046		26041	Delta County, MI..................................	37,069	35,965
20740		Eau Claire, WI Metro area....................	161,151	167,484	21580		Española, NM Micro area......................	40,246	39,159
	55017	Chippewa County, WI	62,415	63,813		35039	Rio Arriba County, NM.........................	40,246	39,159
	55035	Eau Claire County, WI..........................	98,736	103,671					
					21640		Eufaula, AL-GA Micro Area...................	29,970	27,628
20780		Edwards, CO Micro area	52,197	54,772		01005	Barbour County, AL..............................	27,457	25,270
	08037	Eagle County, CO	52,197	54,772		13239	Quitman County, GA............................	2,513	2,358
20820		Effingham, IL Micro area	34,242	34,132	21660		Eugene, OR Metro area	351,715	374,748
	17049	Effingham County, IL............................	34,242	34,132		41039	Lane County, OR	351,715	374,748
20900		El Campo, TX Micro area	41,280	41,968	21700		Eureka-Arcata-Fortuna, CA Micro area .	134,623	136,754
	48481	Wharton County, TX	41,280	41,968		06023	Humboldt County, CA...........................	134,623	136,754
20940		El Centro, CA Metro area	174,528	182,830	21740		Evanston, WY Micro area.....................	21,118	20,495
	06025	Imperial County, CA.............................	174,528	182,830		56041	Uinta County, WY................................	21,118	20,495
20980		El Dorado, AR Micro area	41,639	39,449	21780		Evansville, IN-KY Metro area	311,552	315,669
	05139	Union County, AR................................	41,639	39,449		18129	Posey County, IN	25,910	25,595
						18163	Vanderburgh County, IN.......................	179,703	181,616
21020		Elizabeth City, NC Micro area...............	64,094	63,798		18173	Warrick County, IN	59,689	62,530
	37029	Camden County, NC............................	9,980	10,581		21101	Henderson County, KY	46,250	45,928
	37139	Pasquotank County, NC........................	40,661	39,743					
	37143	Perquimans County, NC	13,453	13,474	21820		Fairbanks, AK Metro area.....................	97,581	99,703
						02090	Fairbanks North Star Borough, AK.....	97,581	99,703
21060		Elizabethtown-Fort Knox, KY	148,338	150,430					
		Metro area			21840		Fairfield, IA Micro area.........................	16,843	18,422
	21093	Hardin County, KY	105,543	108,071		19101	Jefferson County, IA............................	16,843	18,422
	21123	Larue County, KY.................................	14,193	14,205					
	21163	Meade County, KY...............................	28,602	28,154					

CORE BASED STATISTICAL AREAS
(Metropolitan and Micropolitan),
METROPOLITAN DIVISIONS, AND COMPONENTS
(as defined August, 2017)—*Continued*

Core based statistical area	State/County FIPS code	Title and Geographic Components	2010 Census Population	2017 Estimated Population	Core based statistical area	State/County FIPS code	Title and Geographic Components	2010 Census Population	2017 Estimated Population
21860		Fairmont, MN Micro Area......................	20,840	19,850	22660		Fort Collins, CO Metro area..................	299,630	343,976
	27091	Martin County, MN	20,840	19,850		08069	Larimer County, CO	299,630	343,976
21900		Fairmont, WV Micro area.....................	56,418	56,337	22700		Fort Dodge, IA Micro area	38,013	36,605
	54049	Marion County, WV	56,418	56,337		19187	Webster County, IA	38,013	36,605
21980		Fallon, NV Micro area.........................	24,877	24,230	22780		Fort Leonard Wood, MO Micro area......	52,274	52,059
	32001	Churchill County, NV	24,877	24,230		29169	Pulaski County, MO	52,274	52,059
22020		Fargo, ND-MN Metro area....................	208,777	241,356	22800		Fort Madison-Keokuk, IA-IL-MO Micro area..................................	62,105	59,038
	27027	Clay County, MN	58,999	63,569		17067	Hancock County, IL........................	19,104	18,020
	38017	Cass County, ND	149,778	177,787		19111	Lee County, IA.............................	35,862	34,295
22060		Faribault-Northfield, MN Micro area	64,142	65,968		29045	Clark County, MO	7,139	6,723
	27131	Rice County, MN	64,142	65,968	22820		Fort Morgan, CO Micro area................	28,159	28,192
22100		Farmington, MO Micro area..................	65,359	66,705		08087	Morgan County, CO	28,159	28,192
	29187	St. Francois County, MO..................	65,359	66,705	22840		Fort Payne, AL Micro Area.................	71,109	71,617
22140		Farmington, NM Metro area	130,044	126,926		01049	DeKalb County, AL	71,109	71,617
	35045	San Juan County, NM	130,044	126,926	22860		Fort Polk South, LA Micro area............	52,334	50,726
22180		Fayetteville, NC Metro area.................	366,383	386,662		22115	Vernon Parish, LA.........................	52,334	50,726
	37051	Cumberland County, NC	319,431	332,546	22900		Fort Smith, AR-OK Metro area	280,467	282,086
	37093	Hoke County, NC	46,952	54,116		05033	Crawford County, AR	61,948	62,996
22220		Fayetteville-Springdale-Rogers, AR-MO Metro area	463,204	537,463		05131	Sebastian County, AR	125,744	128,107
	05007	Benton County, AR..........................	221,339	266,300		40079	Le Flore County, OK	50,384	49,731
	05087	Madison County, AR	15,717	16,339		40135	Sequoyah County, OK	42,391	41,252
	05143	Washington County, AR	203,065	231,996	23060		Fort Wayne, IN Metro area.................	416,257	434,617
	29119	McDonald County, MO	23,083	22,828		18003	Allen County, IN	355,329	372,877
22260		Fergus Falls, MN Micro area	57,303	58,345		18179	Wells County, IN	27,636	27,984
	27111	Otter Tail County, MN	57,303	58,345		18183	Whitley County, IN	33,292	33,756
22280		Fernley, NV Micro area........................	51,980	54,122	23140		Frankfort, IN Micro area....................	33,224	32,317
	32019	Lyon County, NV	51,980	54,122		18023	Clinton County, IN	33,224	32,317
22300		Findlay, OH Micro area.......................	74,782	75,754	23180		Frankfort, KY Micro area	70,706	73,029
	39063	Hancock County, OH	74,782	75,754		21005	Anderson County, KY.......................	21,421	22,544
22340		Fitzgerald, GA Micro area...................	17,634	16,996		21073	Franklin County, KY	49,285	50,485
	13017	Ben Hill County, GA	17,634	16,996	23240		Fredericksburg, TX Micro area.............	24,837	26,646
22380		Flagstaff, AZ Metro area.....................	134,421	140,776		48171	Gillespie County, TX	24,837	26,646
	04005	Coconino County, AZ	134,421	140,776	23300		Freeport, IL Micro area.....................	47,711	45,054
22420		Flint, MI Metro area	425,790	407,385		17177	Stephenson County, IL......................	47,711	45,054
	26049	Genesee County, MI	425,790	407,385	23340		Fremont, NE Micro area	36,691	36,707
22500		Florence, SC Metro area	205,566	205,831		31053	Dodge County, NE	36,691	36,707
	45031	Darlington County, SC	68,681	67,265	23380		Fremont, OH Micro area....................	60,944	59,195
	45041	Florence County, SC........................	136,885	138,566		39143	Sandusky County, OH......................	60,944	59,195
22520		Florence-Muscle Shoals, AL Metro area	147,137	147,038	23420		Fresno, CA Metro area	930,450	989,255
	01033	Colbert County, AL	54,428	54,500		06019	Fresno County, CA..........................	930,450	989,255
	01077	Lauderdale County, AL......................	92,709	92,538	23460		Gadsden, AL Metro area	104,430	102,755
22540		Fond du Lac, WI Metro area................	101,633	102,548		01055	Etowah County, AL.........................	104,430	102,755
	55039	Fond du Lac County, WI	101,633	102,548	23500		Gaffney, SC Micro area	55,342	57,105
22580		Forest City, NC Micro area	67,810	66,551		45021	Cherokee County, SC	55,342	57,105
	37161	Rutherford County, NC......................	67,810	66,551	23540		Gainesville, FL Metro area	264,275	284,687
22620		Forrest City, AR Micro area	28,258	25,930		12001	Alachua County, FL.........................	247,336	266,944
	05123	St. Francis County, AR.....................	28,258	25,930		12041	Gilchrist County, FL........................	16,939	17,743
					23580		Gainesville, GA Metro area.................	179,684	199,335
						13139	Hall County, GA............................	179,684	199,335

Core based statistical area	State/County FIPS code	Title and Geographic Components	2010 Census Population	2017 Estimated Population	Core based statistical area	State/County FIPS code	Title and Geographic Components	2010 Census Population	2017 Estimated Population
23620		Gainesville, TX Micro area	38,437	39,895	24420		Grants Pass, OR Metro area	82,713	86,352
	48097	Cooke County, TX	38,437	39,895		41033	Josephine County, OR	82,713	86,352
23660		Galesburg, IL Micro area	52,919	50,638	24460		Great Bend, KS Micro area	27,674	26,476
	17095	Knox County, IL	52,919	50,638		20009	Barton County, KS	27,674	26,476
23700		Gallup, NM Micro area	71,492	72,564	24500		Great Falls, MT Metro area	81,327	81,654
	35031	McKinley County, NM	71,492	72,564		30013	Cascade County, MT	81,327	81,654
23780		Garden City, KS Micro area	40,753	41,044	24540		Greeley, CO Metro area	252,825	304,633
	20055	Finney County, KS	36,776	37,084		08123	Weld County, CO	252,825	304,633
	20093	Kearny County, KS	3,977	3,960	24580		Green Bay, WI Metro area	306,241	320,050
23820		Gardnerville Ranchos, NV Micro area	46,997	48,309		55009	Brown County, WI	248,007	262,052
	32005	Douglas County, NV	46,997	48,309		55061	Kewaunee County, WI	20,574	20,445
23860		Georgetown, SC Micro area	60,158	61,607		55083	Oconto County, WI	37,660	37,553
	45043	Georgetown County, SC	60,158	61,607	24620		Greeneville, TN Micro area	68,831	68,808
23900		Gettysburg, PA Metro area	101,407	102,336		47059	Greene County, TN	68,831	68,808
	42001	Adams County, PA	101,407	102,336	24640		Greenfield Town, MA Micro area	71,372	70,702
23940		Gillette, WY Micro area	46,133	46,242		25011	Franklin County, MA	71,372	70,702
	56005	Campbell County, WY	46,133	46,242	24660		Greensboro-High Point, NC Metro area	723,801	761,184
23980		Glasgow, KY Micro area	52,272	53,908		37081	Guilford County, NC	488,406	526,953
	21009	Barren County, KY	42,173	43,801		37151	Randolph County, NC	141,752	143,282
	21169	Metcalfe County, KY	10,099	10,107		37157	Rockingham County, NC	93,643	90,949
24020		Glens Falls, NY Metro area	128,923	126,152	24700		Greensburg, IN Micro area	25,740	26,737
	36113	Warren County, NY	65,707	64,532		18031	Decatur County, IN	25,740	26,737
	36115	Washington County, NY	63,216	61,620	24740		Greenville, MS Micro area	51,137	46,221
24060		Glenwood Springs, CO Micro area	73,537	77,008		28151	Washington County, MS	51,137	46,221
	08045	Garfield County, CO	56,389	59,118	24780		Greenville, NC Metro area	168,148	179,042
	08097	Pitkin County, CO	17,148	17,890		37147	Pitt County, NC	168,148	179,042
24100		Gloversville, NY Micro area	55,531	53,877	24820		Greenville, OH Micro area	52,959	51,536
	36035	Fulton County, NY	55,531	53,877		39037	Darke County, OH	52,959	51,536
24140		Goldsboro, NC Metro area	122,623	124,172	24860		Greenville-Anderson-Mauldin, SC Metro area	824,112	895,923
	37191	Wayne County, NC	122,623	124,172		45007	Anderson County, SC	187,126	198,759
24220		Grand Forks, ND-MN Metro area	98,461	102,414		45045	Greenville County, SC	451,225	506,837
	27119	Polk County, MN	31,600	31,619		45059	Laurens County, SC	66,537	66,848
	38035	Grand Forks County, ND	66,861	70,795		45077	Pickens County, SC	119,224	123,479
24260		Grand Island, NE Metro area	81,850	85,045	24900		Greenwood, MS Micro area	42,914	39,362
	31079	Hall County, NE	58,607	61,519		28015	Carroll County, MS	10,597	10,139
	31081	Hamilton County, NE	9,124	9,207		28083	Leflore County, MS	32,317	29,223
	31093	Howard County, NE	6,274	6,437	24940		Greenwood, SC Micro area	95,078	95,077
	31121	Merrick County, NE	7,845	7,882		45001	Abbeville County, SC	25,417	24,722
24300		Grand Junction, CO Metro area	146,723	151,616		45047	Greenwood County, SC	69,661	70,355
	08077	Mesa County, CO	146,723	151,616	24980		Grenada, MS Micro area	21,906	21,087
24330		Grand Rapids, MN Micro Area	45,058	45,137		28043	Grenada County, MS	21,906	21,087
	27061	Itasca County, MN	45,058	45,137	25060		Gulfport-Biloxi-Pascagoula, MS Metro area	370,702	394,232
24340		Grand Rapids-Wyoming, MI Metro area	988,938	1,059,113		28045	Hancock County, MS	43,929	47,053
	26015	Barry County, MI	59,173	60,586		28047	Harrison County, MS	187,105	205,027
	26081	Kent County, MI	602,622	648,594		28059	Jackson County, MS	139,668	142,152
	26117	Montcalm County, MI	63,342	63,550	25100		Guymon, OK Micro area	20,640	20,900
	26139	Ottawa County, MI	263,801	286,383		40139	Texas County, OK	20,640	20,900
24380		Grants, NM Micro area	27,213	26,853					
	35006	Cibola County, NM	27,213	26,853					

CORE BASED STATISTICAL AREAS
(Metropolitan and Micropolitan),
METROPOLITAN DIVISIONS, AND COMPONENTS
(as defined August, 2017)—*Continued*

Core based statistical area	State/ County FIPS code	Title and Geographic Components	2010 Census Population	2017 Estimated Population	Core based statistical area	State/ County FIPS code	Title and Geographic Components	2010 Census Population	2017 Estimated Population
25180		Hagerstown-Martinsburg, MD-WV Metro area	251,599	265,498	25860		Hickory-Lenoir-Morganton, NC Metro area	365,497	366,534
	24043	Washington County, MD	147,430	150,578		37003	Alexander County, NC	37,198	37,286
	54003	Berkeley County, WV	104,169	114,920		37023	Burke County, NC	90,912	89,293
						37027	Caldwell County, NC	83,029	81,981
25200		Hailey, ID Micro area	27,701	28,444		37035	Catawba County, NC	154,358	157,974
	16013	Blaine County, ID	21,376	22,024					
	16025	Camas County, ID	1,117	1,102	25880		Hillsdale, MI Micro area	46,688	45,879
	16063	Lincoln County, ID	5,208	5,318		26059	Hillsdale County, MI	46,688	45,879
25220		Hammond, LA Metro area	121,097	132,497	25900		Hilo, HI Micro area	185,079	200,381
	22105	Tangipahoa Parish, LA	121,097	132,497		15001	Hawaii County, HI	185,079	200,381
25260		Hanford-Corcoran, CA Metro area	152,982	150,101	25940		Hilton Head Island-Bluffton-Beaufort, SC Metro area	187,010	215,302
	06031	Kings County, CA	152,982	150,101		45013	Beaufort County, SC	162,233	186,844
25300		Hannibal, MO Micro area	38,948	38,858		45053	Jasper County, SC	24,777	28,458
	29127	Marion County, MO	28,781	28,634	25980		Hinesville, GA Metro area	77,917	80,400
	29173	Ralls County, MO	10,167	10,224		13179	Liberty County, GA	63,453	61,386
25420		Harrisburg-Carlisle, PA Metro area	549,475	571,903		13183	Long County, GA	14,464	19,014
	42041	Cumberland County, PA	235,406	250,066	26020		Hobbs, NM Micro area	64,727	68,759
	42043	Dauphin County, PA	268,100	275,710		35025	Lea County, NM	64,727	68,759
	42099	Perry County, PA	45,969	46,127	26090		Holland, MI Micro area	111,408	116,447
25460		Harrison, AR Micro area	45,233	45,209		26005	Allegan County, MI	111,408	116,447
	05009	Boone County, AR	36,903	37,381	26140		Homosassa Springs, FL Metro area	141,236	145,647
	05101	Newton County, AR	8,330	7,828		12017	Citrus County, FL	141,236	145,647
25500		Harrisonburg, VA Metro area	125,228	134,442	26220		Hood River, OR Micro area	22,346	23,377
	51165	Rockingham County, VA	76,314	80,227		41027	Hood River County, OR	22,346	23,377
	51660	Harrisonburg city, VA	48,914	54,215	26260		Hope, AR Micro Area	31,606	30,188
25540		Hartford-West Hartford-East Hartford, CT Metro area	1,212,381	1,210,259		05057	Hempstead County, AR	22,609	21,861
	09003	Hartford County, CT	894,014	895,388		05099	Nevada County, AR	8,997	8,327
	09007	Middlesex County, CT	165,676	163,410	26300		Hot Springs, AR Metro area	96,024	98,658
	09013	Tolland County, CT	152,691	151,461		05051	Garland County, AR	96,024	98,658
25580		Hastings, NE Micro area	31,364	31,678	26340		Houghton, MI Micro area	38,784	38,410
	31001	Adams County, NE	31,364	31,678		26061	Houghton County, MI	36,628	36,305
25620		Hattiesburg, MS Metro area	142,842	148,877		26083	Keweenaw County, MI	2,156	2,105
	28035	Forrest County, MS	74,934	75,471	26380		Houma-Thibodaux, LA Metro area	208,178	210,512
	28073	Lamar County, MS	55,658	61,374		22057	Lafourche Parish, LA	96,318	98,426
	28111	Perry County, MS	12,250	12,032		22109	Terrebonne Parish, LA	111,860	112,086
25700		Hays, KS Micro area	28,452	28,689	26420		Houston-The Woodlands-Sugar Land, TX Metro area	5,920,416	6,892,427
	20051	Ellis County, KS	28,452	28,689		48015	Austin County, TX	28,417	29,786
25720		Heber, UT Micro area	23,530	32,106		48039	Brazoria County, TX	313,166	362,457
	49051	Wasatch County, UT	23,530	32,106		48071	Chambers County, TX	35,096	41,441
25740		Helena, MT Micro area	74,801	79,664		48157	Fort Bend County, TX	585,375	764,828
	30043	Jefferson County, MT	11,406	11,891		48167	Galveston County, TX	291,309	335,036
	30049	Lewis and Clark County, MT	63,395	67,773		48201	Harris County, TX	4,092,459	4,652,980
25760		Helena-West Helena, AR Micro area	21,757	18,572		48291	Liberty County, TX	75,643	83,658
	05107	Phillips County, AR	21,757	18,572		48339	Montgomery County, TX	455,746	570,934
25780		Henderson, NC Micro area	45,422	44,211		48473	Waller County, TX	43,205	51,307
	37181	Vance County, NC	45,422	44,211	26460		Hudson, NY Micro area	63,096	60,604
25820		Hereford, TX Micro area	19,372	18,836		36021	Columbia County, NY	63,096	60,604
	48117	Deaf Smith County, TX	19,372	18,836	26500		Huntingdon, PA Micro area	45,913	45,491
25840		Hermiston-Pendleton, OR Micro area	87,062	88,151		42061	Huntingdon County, PA	45,913	45,491
	41049	Morrow County, OR	11,173	11,166					
	41059	Umatilla County, OR	75,889	76,985					

Core based statistical area	State/County FIPS code	Title and Geographic Components	2010 Census Population	2017 Estimated Population	Core based statistical area	State/County FIPS code	Title and Geographic Components	2010 Census Population	2017 Estimated Population
26540		Huntington, IN Micro area	37,124	36,337	27100		Jackson, MI Metro area	160,248	158,640
	18069	Huntington County, IN	37,124	36,337		26075	Jackson County, MI	160,248	158,640
26580		Huntington-Ashland, WV-KY-OH Metro area	364,908	356,474	27140		Jackson, MS Metro area	567,122	578,715
						28029	Copiah County, MS	29,449	28,516
	21019	Boyd County, KY	49,542	47,979		28049	Hinds County, MS	245,285	239,497
	21089	Greenup County, KY	36,910	35,518		28089	Madison County, MS	95,203	104,618
	39087	Lawrence County, OH	62,450	60,249		28121	Rankin County, MS	141,617	152,080
	54011	Cabell County, WV	96,319	94,958		28127	Simpson County, MS	27,503	26,947
	54043	Lincoln County, WV	21,720	20,825		28163	Yazoo County, MS	28,065	27,057
	54079	Putnam County, WV	55,486	56,792	27160		Jackson, OH Micro area	33,225	32,449
	54099	Wayne County, WV	42,481	40,153		39079	Jackson County, OH	33,225	32,449
26620		Huntsville, AL Metro area	417,593	455,448					
	01083	Limestone County, AL	82,782	94,402	27180		Jackson, TN Metro area	130,011	129,235
	01089	Madison County, AL	334,811	361,046		47023	Chester County, TN	17,131	17,119
						47033	Crockett County, TN	14,586	14,473
26660		Huntsville, TX Micro area	82,446	86,912		47113	Madison County, TN	98,294	97,643
	48455	Trinity County, TX	14,585	14,667					
	48471	Walker County, TX	67,861	72,245	27220		Jackson, WY-ID Micro area	31,464	34,646
						16081	Teton County, ID	10,170	11,381
26700		Huron, SD Micro area	17,398	18,157		56039	Teton County, WY	21,294	23,265
	46005	Beadle County, SD	17,398	18,157					
					27260		Jacksonville, FL Metro area	1,345,596	1,504,980
26740		Hutchinson, KS Micro area	64,511	62,510		12003	Baker County, FL	27,115	28,283
	20155	Reno County, KS	64,511	62,510		12019	Clay County, FL	190,865	212,230
						12031	Duval County, FL	864,263	937,934
26780		Hutchinson, MN Micro area	36,651	35,884		12089	Nassau County, FL	73,314	82,721
	27085	McLeod County, MN	36,651	35,884		12109	St. Johns County, FL	190,039	243,812
26820		Idaho Falls, ID Metro area	133,265	145,643	27300		Jacksonville, IL Micro area	40,902	38,800
	16019	Bonneville County, ID	104,234	114,595		17137	Morgan County, IL	35,547	33,798
	16023	Butte County, ID	2,891	2,602		17171	Scott County, IL	5,355	5,002
	16051	Jefferson County, ID	26,140	28,446					
					27340		Jacksonville, NC Metro area	177,772	193,893
26860		Indiana, PA Micro area	88,880	84,953		37133	Onslow County, NC	177,772	193,893
	42063	Indiana County, PA	88,880	84,953					
					27380		Jacksonville, TX Micro area	50,845	52,240
26900		Indianapolis-Carmel-Anderson, IN Metro area	1,887,877	2,028,614		48073	Cherokee County, TX	50,845	52,240
	18011	Boone County, IN	56,640	65,875	27420		Jamestown, ND Micro area	21,100	21,087
	18013	Brown County, IN	15,242	15,035		38093	Stutsman County, ND	21,100	21,087
	18057	Hamilton County, IN	274,569	323,747					
	18059	Hancock County, IN	70,002	74,985	27460		Jamestown-Dunkirk-Fredonia, NY Micro area	134,905	129,046
	18063	Hendricks County, IN	145,448	163,685					
	18081	Johnson County, IN	139,654	153,897		36013	Chautauqua County, NY	134,905	129,046
	18095	Madison County, IN	131,636	129,498					
	18097	Marion County, IN	903,393	950,082	27500		Janesville-Beloit, WI Metro area	160,331	162,309
	18109	Morgan County, IN	68,894	69,713		55105	Rock County, WI	160,331	162,309
	18133	Putnam County, IN	37,963	37,702					
	18145	Shelby County, IN	44,436	44,395	27540		Jasper, IN Micro area	54,734	54,923
						18037	Dubois County, IN	41,889	42,558
26940		Indianola, MS Micro area	29,450	25,981		18125	Pike County, IN	12,845	12,365
	28133	Sunflower County, MS	29,450	25,981					
					27600		Jefferson, GA Micro area	60,485	67,519
26960		Ionia, MI Micro area	63,905	64,291		13157	Jackson County, GA	60,485	67,519
	26067	Ionia County, MI	63,905	64,291					
					27620		Jefferson City, MO Metro area	149,807	151,465
26980		Iowa City, IA Metro area	152,586	171,491		29027	Callaway County, MO	44,332	45,032
	19103	Johnson County, IA	130,882	149,210		29051	Cole County, MO	75,990	76,708
	19183	Washington County, IA	21,704	22,281		29135	Moniteau County, MO	15,607	16,063
						29151	Osage County, MO	13,878	13,662
27020		Iron Mountain, MI-WI Micro area	30,591	29,786					
	26043	Dickinson County, MI	26,168	25,415	27660		Jennings, LA Micro Area	31,594	31,477
	55037	Florence County, WI	4,423	4,371		22053	Jefferson Davis Parish, LA	31,594	31,477
27060		Ithaca, NY Metro area	101,564	104,802	27700		Jesup, GA Micro area	30,099	29,817
	36109	Tompkins County, NY	101,564	104,802		13305	Wayne County, GA	30,099	29,817

CORE BASED STATISTICAL AREAS
(Metropolitan and Micropolitan),
METROPOLITAN DIVISIONS, AND COMPONENTS
(as defined August, 2017)—*Continued*

Core based statistical area	State/County FIPS code	Title and Geographic Components	2010 Census Population	2017 Estimated Population	Core based statistical area	State/County FIPS code	Title and Geographic Components	2010 Census Population	2017 Estimated Population
27740		Johnson City, TN Metro area................	198,716	202,053	28420		Kennewick-Richland, WA Metro area....	253,340	290,296
	47019	Carter County, TN	57,424	56,488		53005	Benton County, WA........................	175,177	198,171
	47171	Unicoi County, TN	18,313	17,759		53021	Franklin County, WA.......................	78,163	92,125
	47179	Washington County, TN.................	122,979	127,806	28500		Kerrville, TX Micro area	49,625	51,720
27780		Johnstown, PA Metro area....................	143,679	133,054		48265	Kerr County, TX	49,625	51,720
	42021	Cambria County, PA.......................	143,679	133,054	28540		Ketchikan, AK Micro area	13,477	13,856
27860		Jonesboro, AR Metro area....................	121,026	131,269		02130	Ketchikan Gateway Borough, AK......	13,477	13,856
	05031	Craighead County, AR	96,443	107,115	28580		Key West, FL Micro area	73,090	77,013
	05111	Poinsett County, AR.......................	24,583	24,154		12087	Monroe County, FL........................	73,090	77,013
27900		Joplin, MO Metro area........................	175,518	178,507	28620		Kill Devil Hills, NC Micro area..............	38,327	40,151
	29097	Jasper County, MO........................	117,404	120,217		37055	Dare County, NC...........................	33,920	36,099
	29145	Newton County, MO.......................	58,114	58,290		37177	Tyrrell County, NC.........................	4,407	4,052
27920		Junction City, KS Micro area	34,362	33,855	28660		Killeen-Temple, TX Metro area............	405,300	443,773
	20061	Geary County, KS	34,362	33,855		48027	Bell County, TX.............................	310,235	347,833
27940		Juneau, AK Micro area	31,275	32,094		48099	Coryell County, TX.........................	75,388	74,913
	02110	Juneau City and Borough, AK...........	31,275	32,094		48281	Lampasas County, TX......................	19,677	21,027
27980		Kahului-Wailuku-Lahaina, HI Metro area	154,924	166,348	28700		Kingsport-Bristol-Bristol, TN-VA Metro area........	309,544	306,659
	15005	Kalawao County, HI	90	88		47073	Hawkins County, TN	56,833	56,459
	15009	Maui County, HI	154,834	166,260		47163	Sullivan County, TN.......................	156,823	157,158
28020		Kalamazoo-Portage, MI Metro area	326,589	338,338		51169	Scott County, VA...........................	23,177	21,865
	26077	Kalamazoo County, MI....................	250,331	262,985		51191	Washington County, VA...................	54,876	54,387
	26159	Van Buren County, MI	76,258	75,353		51520	Bristol city, VA	17,835	16,790
28060		Kalispell, MT Micro area	90,928	100,000	28740		Kingston, NY Metro area	182,493	179,417
	30029	Flathead County, MT.......................	90,928	100,000		36111	Ulster County, NY	182,493	179,417
28100		Kankakee, IL Metro area	113,449	109,605	28780		Kingsville, TX Micro area....................	32,477	31,505
	17091	Kankakee County, IL	113,449	109,605		48261	Kenedy County, TX........................	416	417
28140		Kansas City, MO-KS Metro area	2,009,342	2,128,912		48273	Kleberg County, TX........................	32,061	31,088
	20091	Johnson County, KS	544,179	591,178	28820		Kinston, NC Micro area......................	59,495	56,883
	20103	Leavenworth County, KS	76,227	81,095		37107	Lenoir County, NC.........................	59,495	56,883
	20107	Linn County, KS	9,656	9,726	28860		Kirksville, MO Micro area...................	30,038	29,885
	20121	Miami County, KS	32,787	33,461		29001	Adair County, MO	25,607	25,377
	20209	Wyandotte County, KS....................	157,505	165,288		29197	Schuyler County, MO	4,431	4,508
	29013	Bates County, MO	17,049	16,334	28900		Klamath Falls, OR Micro area	66,380	66,935
	29025	Caldwell County, MO	9,424	9,100		41035	Klamath County, OR	66,380	66,935
	29037	Cass County, MO..........................	99,478	103,724	28940		Knoxville, TN Metro area....................	837,571	877,104
	29047	Clay County, MO...........................	221,939	242,874		47001	Anderson County, TN.....................	75,129	76,257
	29049	Clinton County, MO	20,743	20,554		47009	Blount County, TN.........................	123,010	129,929
	29095	Jackson County, MO.......................	674,158	698,895		47013	Campbell County, TN.....................	40,716	39,648
	29107	Lafayette County, MO	33,381	32,641		47057	Grainger County, TN......................	22,657	23,144
	29165	Platte County, MO.........................	89,322	101,187		47093	Knox County, TN...........................	432,226	461,860
	29177	Ray County, MO............................	23,494	22,855		47105	Loudon County, TN........................	48,556	52,152
28180		Kapaa, HI Micro area........................	67,091	72,159		47129	Morgan County, TN........................	21,987	21,636
	15007	Kauai County, HI	67,091	72,159		47145	Roane County, TN.........................	54,181	53,036
28260		Kearney, NE Micro area	52,591	56,262		47173	Union County, TN..........................	19,109	19,442
	31019	Buffalo County, NE........................	46,102	49,732	29020		Kokomo, IN Metro area	82,752	82,363
	31099	Kearney County, NE.......................	6,489	6,530		18067	Howard County, IN	82,752	82,363
28300		Keene, NH Micro area.......................	77,117	75,960	29060		Laconia, NH Micro area......................	60,088	60,785
	33005	Cheshire County, NH	77,117	75,960		33001	Belknap County, NH.......................	60,088	60,785
28340		Kendallville, IN Micro area..................	47,536	47,452	29100		La Crosse-Onalaska, WI-MN Metro area	133,665	136,934
	18113	Noble County, IN...........................	47,536	47,452		27055	Houston County, MN......................	19,027	18,660
28380		Kennett, MO Micro area	31,953	30,119		55063	La Crosse County, WI	114,638	118,274
	29069	Dunklin County, MO.......................	31,953	30,119					

CORE BASED STATISTICAL AREAS
(Metropolitan and Micropolitan),
METROPOLITAN DIVISIONS, AND COMPONENTS
(as defined August, 2017)—*Continued*

Core based statistical area	State/County FIPS code	Title and Geographic Components	2010 Census Population	2017 Estimated Population	Core based statistical area	State/County FIPS code	Title and Geographic Components	2010 Census Population	2017 Estimated Population
29180		Lafayette, LA Metro area	466,750	491,558	29940		Lawrence, KS Metro area	110,826	120,793
	22001	Acadia Parish, LA	61,773	62,590		20045	Douglas County, KS	110,826	120,793
	22045	Iberia Parish, LA	73,240	72,176					
	22055	Lafayette Parish, LA	221,578	242,485	29980		Lawrenceburg, TN Micro area	41,869	43,396
	22099	St. Martin Parish, LA	52,160	54,171		47099	Lawrence County, TN	41,869	43,396
	22113	Vermilion Parish, LA	57,999	60,136					
					30020		Lawton, OK Metro area	130,291	127,349
29200		Lafayette-West Lafayette, IN Metro area	201,789	219,239		40031	Comanche County, OK	124,098	121,526
						40033	Cotton County, OK	6,193	5,823
	18007	Benton County, IN	8,854	8,613					
	18015	Carroll County, IN	20,155	20,039	30060		Lebanon, MO Micro area	35,571	35,443
	18157	Tippecanoe County, IN	172,780	190,587		29105	Laclede County, MO	35,571	35,443
29260		La Grande, OR Micro area	25,748	26,222	30140		Lebanon, PA Metro area	133,568	139,754
	41061	Union County, OR	25,748	26,222		42075	Lebanon County, PA	133,568	139,754
29300		LaGrange, GA Micro area	67,044	69,786	30220		Levelland, TX Micro area	22,935	23,088
	13285	Troup County, GA	67,044	69,786		48219	Hockley County, TX	22,935	23,088
29340		Lake Charles, LA Metro area	199,607	209,357	30260		Lewisburg, PA Micro area	44,947	44,595
	22019	Calcasieu Parish, LA	192,768	202,445		42119	Union County, PA	44,947	44,595
	22023	Cameron Parish, LA	6,839	6,912					
					30280		Lewisburg, TN Micro area	30,617	32,931
29380		Lake City, FL Micro area	67,531	69,612		47117	Marshall County, TN	30,617	32,931
	12023	Columbia County, FL	67,531	69,612					
					30300		Lewiston, ID-WA Metro area	60,888	62,920
29420		Lake Havasu City-Kingman, AZ Metro area	200,186	207,200		16069	Nez Perce County, ID	39,265	40,385
						53003	Asotin County, WA	21,623	22,535
	04015	Mohave County, AZ	200,186	207,200					
					30340		Lewiston-Auburn, ME Metro area	107,702	107,651
29460		Lakeland-Winter Haven, FL Metro area	602,095	686,483		23001	Androscoggin County, ME	107,702	107,651
	12105	Polk County, FL	602,095	686,483	30380		Lewistown, PA Micro area	46,682	46,388
						42087	Mifflin County, PA	46,682	46,388
29500		Lamesa, TX Micro area	13,833	12,813	30420		Lexington, NE Micro area	26,370	25,737
	48115	Dawson County, TX	13,833	12,813		31047	Dawson County, NE	24,326	23,709
29540		Lancaster, PA Metro area	519,445	542,903		31073	Gosper County, NE	2,044	2,028
	42071	Lancaster County, PA	519,445	542,903					
					30460		Lexington-Fayette, KY Metro area	472,099	512,650
29620		Lansing-East Lansing, MI Metro area	464,036	477,656		21017	Bourbon County, KY	19,985	20,029
						21049	Clark County, KY	35,613	36,046
	26037	Clinton County, MI	75,382	78,443		21067	Fayette County, KY	295,803	321,959
	26045	Eaton County, MI	107,759	109,027		21113	Jessamine County, KY	48,586	53,375
	26065	Ingham County, MI	280,895	290,186		21209	Scott County, KY	47,173	54,873
						21239	Woodford County, KY	24,939	26,368
29660		Laramie, WY Micro area	36,299	38,332					
	56001	Albany County, WY	36,299	38,332	30580		Liberal, KS Micro area	22,952	22,159
						20175	Seward County, KS	22,952	22,159
29700		Laredo, TX Metro area	250,304	274,794					
	48479	Webb County, TX	250,304	274,794	30620		Lima, OH Metro area	106,331	103,198
						39003	Allen County, OH	106,331	103,198
29740		Las Cruces, NM Metro area	209,233	215,579					
	35013	Doña Ana County, NM	209,233	215,579	30660		Lincoln, IL Micro area	30,305	29,245
						17107	Logan County, IL	30,305	29,245
29780		Las Vegas, NM Micro area	29,393	27,748					
	35047	San Miguel County, NM	29,393	27,748	30700		Lincoln, NE Metro area	302,157	331,519
						31109	Lancaster County, NE	285,407	314,358
29820		Las Vegas-Henderson-Paradise, NV Metro area	1,951,269	2,204,079		31159	Seward County, NE	16,750	17,161
	32003	Clark County, NV	1,951,269	2,204,079	30780		Little Rock-North Little Rock-Conway, AR Metro area	699,757	738,344
29860		Laurel, MS Micro area	84,823	84,512		05045	Faulkner County, AR	113,237	123,654
	28061	Jasper County, MS	17,062	16,582		05053	Grant County, AR	17,853	18,165
	28067	Jones County, MS	67,761	67,930		05085	Lonoke County, AR	68,356	72,898
						05105	Perry County, AR	10,445	10,348
29900		Laurinburg, NC Micro area	36,157	35,093		05119	Pulaski County, AR	382,748	393,956
	37165	Scotland County, NC	36,157	35,093		05125	Saline County, AR	107,118	119,323

Core based statistical area	State/ County FIPS code	Title and Geographic Components	2010 Census Population	2017 Estimated Population	Core based statistical area	State/ County FIPS code	Title and Geographic Components	2010 Census Population	2017 Estimated Population
30820		Lock Haven, PA Micro area	39,238	38,998	31340		Lynchburg, VA Metro area	252,634	261,254
	42035	Clinton County, PA	39,238	38,998		51009	Amherst County, VA	32,353	31,594
						51011	Appomattox County, VA	14,973	15,681
30860		Logan, UT-ID Metro area	125,442	138,002		51019	Bedford County, VA	68,676	77,974
	16041	Franklin County, ID	12,786	13,564		51031	Campbell County, VA	54,842	55,010
	49005	Cache County, UT	112,656	124,438		51680	Lynchburg city, VA	75,568	80,995
30880		Logan, WV Micro area	36,743	32,925	31380		Macomb, IL Micro area	32,612	30,823
	54045	Logan County, WV	36,743	32,925		17109	McDonough County, IL	32,612	30,823
30900		Logansport, IN Micro area	38,966	37,994	31420		Macon, GA Metro area	232,293	228,914
	18017	Cass County, IN	38,966	37,994		13021	Bibb County, GA	155,547	152,862
						13079	Crawford County, GA	12,630	12,295
30940		London, KY Micro area	126,369	127,615		13169	Jones County, GA	28,669	28,470
	21121	Knox County, KY	31,883	31,227		13207	Monroe County, GA	26,424	27,113
	21125	Laurel County, KY	58,849	60,174		13289	Twiggs County, GA	9,023	8,174
	21235	Whitley County, KY	35,637	36,214	31460		Madera, CA Metro area	150,865	156,890
30980		Longview, TX Metro area	214,369	217,481		06039	Madera County, CA	150,865	156,890
	48183	Gregg County, TX	121,730	123,367					
	48401	Rusk County, TX	53,330	52,833	31500		Madison, IN Micro area	32,428	32,089
	48459	Upshur County, TX	39,309	41,281		18077	Jefferson County, IN	32,428	32,089
31020		Longview, WA Metro area	102,410	106,910	31540		Madison, WI Metro area	605,435	654,230
	53015	Cowlitz County, WA	102,410	106,910		55021	Columbia County, WI	56,833	57,248
						55025	Dane County, WI	488,073	536,416
31060		Los Alamos, NM Micro area	17,950	18,738		55045	Green County, WI	36,842	36,851
	35028	Los Alamos County, NM	17,950	18,738		55049	Iowa County, WI	23,687	23,715
31080		Los Angeles-Long Beach-Anaheim, CA Metro area	12,828,837	13,353,907	31580		Madisonville, KY Micro area	46,920	45,547
						21107	Hopkins County, KY	46,920	45,547
31080		Anaheim-Santa Ana-Irvine, CA Metro Div 11244	3,010,232	3,190,400	31620		Magnolia, AR Micro area	24,552	23,627
	06059	Orange County, CA	3,010,232	3,190,400		05027	Columbia County, AR	24,552	23,627
					31660		Malone, NY Micro area	51,599	51,116
31080		Los Angeles-Long Beach-Glendale, CA Metro Div 31084	9,818,605	10,163,507		36033	Franklin County, NY	51,599	51,116
	06037	Los Angeles County, CA	9,818,605	10,163,507	31680		Malvern, AR Micro area	32,923	33,574
31140		Louisville/Jefferson County, KY-IN Metro area	1,235,708	1,293,953		05059	Hot Spring County, AR	32,923	33,574
	18019	Clark County, IN	110,232	116,973	31700		Manchester-Nashua, NH Metro area	400,721	409,697
	18043	Floyd County, IN	74,578	77,071		33011	Hillsborough County, NH	400,721	409,697
	18061	Harrison County, IN	39,364	39,898					
	18143	Scott County, IN	24,181	23,870	31740		Manhattan, KS Metro area	92,719	98,080
	18175	Washington County, IN	28,262	27,827		20149	Pottawatomie County, KS	21,604	23,908
	21029	Bullitt County, KY	74,319	80,246		20161	Riley County, KS	71,115	74,172
	21103	Henry County, KY	15,416	16,006	31820		Manitowoc, WI Micro area	81,442	79,175
	21111	Jefferson County, KY	741,096	771,158		55071	Manitowoc County, WI	81,442	79,175
	21185	Oldham County, KY	60,316	66,415	31860		Mankato-North Mankato, MN Metro area	96,740	100,939
	21211	Shelby County, KY	42,074	47,421		27013	Blue Earth County, MN	64,013	66,973
	21215	Spencer County, KY	17,061	18,507		27103	Nicollet County, MN	32,727	33,966
	21223	Trimble County, KY	8,809	8,561					
31180		Lubbock, TX Metro area	290,805	316,983	31900		Mansfield, OH Metro area	124,475	120,589
	48107	Crosby County, TX	6,059	5,899		39139	Richland County, OH	124,475	120,589
	48303	Lubbock County, TX	278,831	305,225					
	48305	Lynn County, TX	5,915	5,859	31930		Marietta, OH Micro area	61,778	60,418
31220		Ludington, MI Micro area	28,705	29,073		39167	Washington County, OH	61,778	60,418
	26105	Mason County, MI	28,705	29,073					
					31940		Marinette, WI-MI Micro area	65,778	63,356
31260		Lufkin, TX Micro area	86,771	87,805		26109	Menominee County, MI	24,029	23,046
	48005	Angelina County, TX	86,771	87,805		55075	Marinette County, WI	41,749	40,310
31300		Lumberton, NC Micro area	134,168	132,606	31980		Marion, IN Micro area	70,061	66,491
	37155	Robeson County, NC	134,168	132,606		18053	Grant County, IN	70,061	66,491

Core based statistical area	State/ County FIPS code	Title and Geographic Components	2010 Census Population	2017 Estimated Population	Core based statistical area	State/ County FIPS code	Title and Geographic Components	2010 Census Population	2017 Estimated Population
37220		Pahrump, NV Micro area	43,946	44,202	37980		Montgomery County-Bucks County-Chester County, PA Metro Div 33874	1,924,009	1,973,709
	32023	Nye County, NV	43,946	44,202		42017	Bucks County, PA	625,249	628,341
37260		Palatka, FL Micro area	74,364	73,464		42029	Chester County, PA	498,886	519,293
	12107	Putnam County, FL	74,364	73,464		42091	Montgomery County, PA	799,874	826,075
37300		Palestine, TX Micro area	58,458	57,741	37980		Philadelphia, PA Metro Div 37964	2,084,985	2,145,559
	48001	Anderson County, TX	58,458	57,741		42045	Delaware County, PA	558,979	564,696
37340		Palm Bay-Melbourne-Titusville, FL Metro area	543,376	589,162		42101	Philadelphia County, PA	1,526,006	1,580,863
	12009	Brevard County, FL	543,376	589,162	37980		Wilmington, DE-MD-NJ Metro Div 48864	705,670	725,331
37420		Pampa, TX Micro area	22,535	22,404		10003	New Castle County, Delaware	538,479	559,793
	48179	Gray County, TX	22,535	22,404		24015	Cecil County, MD	101,108	102,746
37460		Panama City, FL Metro area	184,715	199,723		34033	Salem County, NJ	66,083	62,792
	12005	Bay County, FL	168,852	183,563	38060		Phoenix-Mesa-Scottsdale, AZ Metro area	4,192,887	4,737,270
	12045	Gulf County, FL	15,863	16,160		04013	Maricopa County, AZ	3,817,117	4,307,033
37500		Paragould, AR Micro area	42,090	45,053		04021	Pinal County, AZ	375,770	430,237
	05055	Greene County, AR	42,090	45,053	38100		Picayune, MS Micro area	55,834	55,270
37540		Paris, TN Micro area	32,330	32,450		28109	Pearl River County, MS	55,834	55,270
	47079	Henry County, TN	32,330	32,450	38180		Pierre, SD Micro area	21,361	22,084
37580		Paris, TX Micro area	49,793	49,587		46065	Hughes County, SD	17,022	17,666
	48277	Lamar County, TX	49,793	49,587		46117	Stanley County, SD	2,966	3,011
37620		Parkersburg-Vienna, WV Metro area	92,673	90,898		46119	Sully County, SD	1,373	1,407
	54105	Wirt County, WV	5,717	5,794	38220		Pine Bluff, AR Metro area	100,258	90,963
	54107	Wood County, WV	86,956	85,104		05025	Cleveland County, AR	8,689	8,202
37660		Parsons, KS Micro area	21,607	20,145		05069	Jefferson County, AR	77,435	69,115
	20099	Labette County, KS	21,607	20,145		05079	Lincoln County, AR	14,134	13,646
37740		Payson, AZ Micro area	53,597	53,501	38240		Pinehurst-Southern Pines, NC Micro area	88,247	97,264
	04007	Gila County, AZ	53,597	53,501		37125	Moore County, NC	88,247	97,264
37780		Pecos, TX Micro area	13,783	15,281	38260		Pittsburg, KS Micro area	39,134	39,034
	48389	Reeves County, TX	13,783	15,281		20037	Crawford County, KS	39,134	39,034
37800		Pella, IA Micro Area	33,309	33,105	38300		Pittsburgh, PA Metro area	2,356,285	2,333,367
	19125	Marion County, IA	33,309	33,105		42003	Allegheny County, PA	1,223,348	1,223,048
37860		Pensacola-Ferry Pass-Brent, FL Metro area	448,991	487,784		42005	Armstrong County, PA	68,941	65,642
						42007	Beaver County, PA	170,539	166,140
	12033	Escambia County, FL	297,619	313,512		42019	Butler County, PA	183,862	187,108
	12113	Santa Rosa County, FL	151,372	174,272		42051	Fayette County, PA	136,606	131,504
						42125	Washington County, PA	207,820	207,298
37900		Peoria, IL Metro area	379,186	372,427		42129	Westmoreland County, PA	365,169	352,627
	17123	Marshall County, IL	12,640	11,730	38340		Pittsfield, MA Metro area	131,219	126,313
	17143	Peoria County, IL	186,494	183,011		25003	Berkshire County, MA	131,219	126,313
	17175	Stark County, IL	5,994	5,434	38380		Plainview, TX Micro area	36,273	34,134
	17179	Tazewell County, IL	135,394	133,526		48189	Hale County, TX	36,273	34,134
	17203	Woodford County, IL	38,664	38,726	38420		Platteville, WI Micro area	51,208	51,999
37940		Peru, IN Micro area	36,903	35,845		55043	Grant County, WI	51,208	51,999
	18103	Miami County, IN	36,903	35,845	38460		Plattsburgh, NY Micro area	82,128	80,980
37980		Philadelphia-Camden-Wilmington, PA-NJ-DE-MD Metro area	5,965,343	6,096,120		36019	Clinton County, NY	82,128	80,980
37980		Camden, NJ Metro Div 15804	1,250,679	1,251,521	38500		Plymouth, IN Micro area	47,051	46,498
	34005	Burlington County, NJ	448,734	448,596		18099	Marshall County, IN	47,051	46,498
	34007	Camden County, NJ	513,657	510,719					
	34015	Gloucester County, NJ	288,288	292,206					

CORE BASED STATISTICAL AREAS
(Metropolitan and Micropolitan),
METROPOLITAN DIVISIONS, AND COMPONENTS
(as defined August, 2017)—*Continued*

Core based statistical area	State/ County FIPS code	Title and Geographic Components	2010 Census Population	2017 Estimated Population	Core based statistical area	State/ County FIPS code	Title and Geographic Components	2010 Census Population	2017 Estimated Population
38540		Pocatello, ID Metro area	82,839	85,269		44005	Newport County, RI	82,888	83,460
	16005	Bannock County, ID	82,839	85,269		44007	Providence County, RI	626,667	637,357
38580		Point Pleasant, WV-OH Micro area	58,258	56,774		44009	Washington County, RI	126,979	126,150
	39053	Gallia County, OH	30,934	29,973	39340		Provo-Orem, UT Metro area	526,810	617,675
	54053	Mason County, WV	27,324	26,801		49023	Juab County, UT	10,246	11,250
38620		Ponca City, OK Micro area	46,562	44,544		49049	Utah County, UT	516,564	606,425
	40071	Kay County, OK	46,562	44,544	39380		Pueblo, CO Metro area	159,063	166,475
38700		Pontiac, IL Micro area	38,950	36,518		08101	Pueblo County, CO	159,063	166,475
	17105	Livingston County, IL	38,950	36,518	39420		Pullman, WA Micro area	44,776	49,046
38740		Poplar Bluff, MO Micro area	42,794	42,666		53075	Whitman County, WA	44,776	49,046
	29023	Butler County, MO	42,794	42,666	39460		Punta Gorda, FL Metro area	159,978	182,033
38780		Portales, NM Micro area	19,846	18,847		12015	Charlotte County, FL	159,978	182,033
	35041	Roosevelt County, NM	19,846	18,847	39500		Quincy, IL-MO Micro area	77,314	76,201
38820		Port Angeles, WA Micro area	71,404	75,474		17001	Adams County, IL	67,103	66,234
	53009	Clallam County, WA	71,404	75,474		29111	Lewis County, MO	10,211	9,967
38840		Port Clinton, OH Micro area	41,428	40,657	39540		Racine, WI Metro area	195,408	196,071
	39123	Ottawa County, OH	41,428	40,657		55101	Racine County, WI	195,408	196,071
38860		Portland-South Portland, ME Metro area	514,098	532,083	39580		Raleigh, NC Metro area	1,130,490	1,335,079
	23005	Cumberland County, ME	281,674	292,500		37069	Franklin County, NC	60,619	66,168
	23023	Sagadahoc County, ME	35,293	35,392		37101	Johnston County, NC	168,878	196,708
	23031	York County, ME	197,131	204,191		37183	Wake County, NC	900,993	1,072,203
38900		Portland-Vancouver-Hillsboro, OR-WA Metro area	2,226,009	2,453,168	39660		Rapid City, SD Metro area	134,598	146,850
	41005	Clackamas County, OR	375,992	412,672		46033	Custer County, SD	8,216	8,691
	41009	Columbia County, OR	49,351	51,782		46093	Meade County, SD	25,434	28,018
	41051	Multnomah County, OR	735,334	807,555		46103	Pennington County, SD	100,948	110,141
	41067	Washington County, OR	529,710	588,957	39700		Raymondville, TX Micro area	22,134	21,584
	41071	Yamhill County, OR	99,193	105,722		48489	Willacy County, TX	22,134	21,584
	53011	Clark County, WA	425,363	474,643	39740		Reading, PA Metro area	411,442	417,854
	53059	Skamania County, WA	11,066	11,837		42011	Berks County, PA	411,442	417,854
38920		Port Lavaca, TX Micro area	21,381	21,744	39780		Red Bluff, CA Micro area	63,463	63,926
	48057	Calhoun County, TX	21,381	21,744		06103	Tehama County, CA	63,463	63,926
38940		Port St. Lucie, FL Metro area	424,107	473,429	39820		Redding, CA Metro area	177,223	179,921
	12085	Martin County, FL	146,318	159,923		06089	Shasta County, CA	177,223	179,921
	12111	St. Lucie County, FL	277,789	313,506	39860		Red Wing, MN Micro area	46,183	46,304
39020		Portsmouth, OH Micro area	79,499	75,929		27049	Goodhue County, MN	46,183	46,304
	39145	Scioto County, OH	79,499	75,929	39900		Reno, NV Metro area	425,417	464,593
39060		Pottsville, PA Micro area	148,289	142,569		32029	Storey County, NV	4,010	4,006
	42107	Schuylkill County, PA	148,289	142,569		32031	Washoe County, NV	421,407	460,587
39140		Prescott, AZ Metro area	211,033	228,168	39940		Rexburg, ID Micro area	50,778	52,235
	04025	Yavapai County, AZ	211,033	228,168		16043	Fremont County, ID	13,242	13,094
39220		Price, UT Micro area	21,403	20,295		16065	Madison County, ID	37,536	39,141
	49007	Carbon County, UT	21,403	20,295	39980		Richmond, IN Micro area	68,917	66,185
39260		Prineville, OR Micro area	20,978	23,123		18177	Wayne County, IN	68,917	66,185
	41013	Crook County, OR	20,978	23,123	40060		Richmond, VA Metro area	1,208,101	1,294,204
39300		Providence-Warwick, RI-MA Metro area	1,600,852	1,621,122		51007	Amelia County, VA	12,690	13,020
	25005	Bristol County, MA	548,285	561,483		51033	Caroline County, VA	28,545	30,461
	44001	Bristol County, RI	49,875	48,912		51036	Charles City County, VA	7,256	7,004
	44003	Kent County, RI	166,158	163,760		51041	Chesterfield County, VA	316,236	343,599
						51053	Dinwiddie County, VA	28,001	28,208
						51075	Goochland County, VA	21,717	22,685

Core based statistical area	State/ County FIPS code	Title and Geographic Components	2010 Census Population	2017 Estimated Population	Core based statistical area	State/ County FIPS code	Title and Geographic Components	2010 Census Population	2017 Estimated Population
	51085	Hanover County, VA	99,863	105,923	40580		Rocky Mount, NC Metro area	152,392	146,738
	51087	Henrico County, VA	306,935	327,898		37065	Edgecombe County, NC	56,552	52,747
	51101	King William County, VA	15,935	16,708		37127	Nash County, NC	95,840	93,991
	51127	New Kent County, VA	18,429	21,682					
	51145	Powhatan County, VA	28,046	28,601	40620		Rolla, MO Micro area	45,156	44,744
	51149	Prince George County, VA	35,725	37,809		29161	Phelps County, MO	45,156	44,744
	51183	Sussex County, VA	12,087	11,373					
	51570	Colonial Heights city, VA	17,411	17,830	40660		Rome, GA Metro area	96,317	97,613
	51670	Hopewell city, VA	22,591	22,621		13115	Floyd County, GA	96,317	97,613
	51730	Petersburg city, VA	32,420	31,750					
	51760	Richmond city, VA	204,214	227,032	40700		Roseburg, OR Micro area	107,667	109,405
						41019	Douglas County, OR	107,667	109,405
40080		Richmond-Berea, KY Micro area	99,972	107,924					
	21151	Madison County, KY	82,916	91,226	40740		Roswell, NM Micro area	65,645	64,866
	21203	Rockcastle County, KY	17,056	16,698		35005	Chaves County, NM	65,645	64,866
40100		Rio Grande City, TX Micro area	60,968	64,454	40760		Ruidoso, NM Micro Area	20,497	19,395
	48427	Starr County, TX	60,968	64,454		35027	Lincoln County, NM	20,497	19,395
40140		Riverside-San Bernardino-Ontario, CA	4,224,851	4,580,670	40780		Russellville, AR Micro area	83,939	85,358
	06065	Riverside County, CA	2,189,641	2,423,266		05115	Pope County, AR	61,754	63,835
	06071	San Bernardino County, CA	2,035,210	2,157,404		05149	Yell County, AR	22,185	21,523
40180		Riverton, WY Micro area	40,123	39,803	40820		Ruston, LA Micro area	46,735	47,744
	56013	Fremont County, WY	40,123	39,803		22061	Lincoln Parish, LA	46,735	47,744
40220		Roanoke, VA Metro area	308,707	314,128	40860		Rutland, VT Micro area	61,642	59,087
	51023	Botetourt County, VA	33,148	33,192		50021	Rutland County, VT	61,642	59,087
	51045	Craig County, VA	5,190	5,062					
	51067	Franklin County, VA	56,159	56,445	40900		Sacramento—Roseville—Arden-Arcade, CA Metro area	2,149,127	2,324,884
	51161	Roanoke County, VA	92,376	93,730		06017	El Dorado County, CA	181,058	188,987
	51770	Roanoke city, VA	97,032	99,837		06061	Placer County, CA	348,432	386,166
	51775	Salem city, VA	24,802	25,862		06067	Sacramento County, CA	1,418,788	1,530,615
						06113	Yolo County, CA	200,849	219,116
40260		Roanoke Rapids, NC Micro area	76,790	71,172					
	37083	Halifax County, NC	54,691	51,310	40940		Safford, AZ Micro area	37,220	37,466
	37131	Northampton County, NC	22,099	19,862		04009	Graham County, AZ	37,220	37,466
40300		Rochelle, IL Micro area	53,497	51,063	40980		Saginaw, MI Metro area	200,169	191,934
	17141	Ogle County, IL	53,497	51,063		26145	Saginaw County, MI	200,169	191,934
40340		Rochester, MN Metro area	206,877	218,280	41060		St. Cloud, MN Metro area	189,093	197,759
	27039	Dodge County, MN	20,087	20,762		27009	Benton County, MN	38,451	39,937
	27045	Fillmore County, MN	20,866	20,980		27145	Stearns County, MN	150,642	157,822
	27109	Olmsted County, MN	144,248	154,930					
	27157	Wabasha County, MN	21,676	21,608	41100		St. George, UT Metro area	138,115	165,662
						49053	Washington County, UT	138,115	165,662
40380		Rochester, NY Metro area	1,079,671	1,077,948					
	36051	Livingston County, NY	65,393	63,799	41140		St. Joseph, MO-KS Metro area	127,329	126,935
	36055	Monroe County, NY	744,344	747,642		20043	Doniphan County, KS	7,945	7,727
	36069	Ontario County, NY	107,931	109,899		29003	Andrew County, MO	17,291	17,555
	36073	Orleans County, NY	42,883	40,983		29021	Buchanan County, MO	89,201	89,065
	36117	Wayne County, NY	93,772	90,670		29063	DeKalb County, MO	12,892	12,588
	36123	Yates County, NY	25,348	24,955					
					41180		St. Louis, MO-IL Metro area	2,787,701	2,807,338
40420		Rockford, IL Metro area	349,431	338,291		17005	Bond County, IL	17,768	16,948
	17007	Boone County, IL	54,165	53,513		17013	Calhoun County, IL	5,089	4,833
	17201	Winnebago County, IL	295,266	284,778		17027	Clinton County, IL	37,762	37,614
						17083	Jersey County, IL	22,985	21,941
40460		Rockingham, NC Micro area	46,639	44,798		17117	Macoupin County, IL	47,765	45,446
	37153	Richmond County, NC	46,639	44,798		17119	Madison County, IL	269,282	265,428
						17133	Monroe County, IL	32,957	34,097
40540		Rock Springs, WY Micro area	43,806	43,534		17163	St. Clair County, IL	270,056	262,479
	56037	Sweetwater County, WY	43,806	43,534		29071	Franklin County, MO	101,492	103,330
						29099	Jefferson County, MO	218,733	223,810
						29113	Lincoln County, MO	52,566	56,183

CORE BASED STATISTICAL AREAS
(Metropolitan and Micropolitan),
METROPOLITAN DIVISIONS, AND COMPONENTS
(as defined August, 2017)—*Continued*

Core based statistical area	State/County FIPS code	Title and Geographic Components	2010 Census Population	2017 Estimated Population	Core based statistical area	State/County FIPS code	Title and Geographic Components	2010 Census Population	2017 Estimated Population
	29183	St. Charles County, MO	360,485	395,504	41860		Oakland-Hayward-Berkeley, CA Metro Div 36084..................	2,559,296	2,810,629
	29189	St. Louis County, MO	998,954	996,726		06001	Alameda County, CA	1,510,271	1,663,190
	29219	Warren County, MO	32,513	34,373		06013	Contra Costa County, CA...............	1,049,025	1,147,439
	29510	St. Louis city, MO	319,294	308,626	41860		San Francisco-Redwood City-South San Francisco, CA Metro Div 41884..	1,523,686	1,655,773
41220		St. Marys, GA Micro area	50,513	53,044		06075	San Francisco County, CA	805,235	884,363
	13039	Camden County, GA	50,513	53,044		06081	San Mateo County, CA...................	718,451	771,410
41260		St. Marys, PA Micro Area	31,946	30,197	41860		San Rafael, CA Metropolitan Div 42034.................................	252,409	260,955
	42047	Elk County, PA	31,946	30,197		06041	Marin County, CA	252,409	260,955
41400		Salem, OH Micro area......................	107,841	103,077					
	39029	Columbiana County, OH	107,841	103,077	41940		San Jose-Sunnyvale-Santa Clara, CA Metro area	1,836,911	1,998,463
41420		Salem, OR Metro area......................	390,738	424,982		06069	San Benito County, CA	55,269	60,310
	41047	Marion County, OR	315,335	341,286		06085	Santa Clara County, CA..................	1,781,642	1,938,153
	41053	Polk County, OR	75,403	83,696	42020		San Luis Obispo-Paso Robles-Arroyo Grande, CA Metro area	269,637	283,405
41460		Salina, KS Micro area......................	61,697	60,597		06079	San Luis Obispo County, CA.............	269,637	283,405
	20143	Ottawa County, KS........................	6,091	5,863					
	20169	Saline County, KS	55,606	54,734	42100		Santa Cruz-Watsonville, CA Metro area	262,382	275,897
41500		Salinas, CA Metro area......................	415,057	437,907		06087	Santa Cruz County, CA....................	262,382	275,897
	06053	Monterey County, CA........................	415,057	437,907	42140		Santa Fe, NM Metro area	144,170	148,750
41540		Salisbury, MD-DE Metro area................	373,802	405,853		35049	Santa Fe County, NM......................	144,170	148,750
	10005	Sussex County, DE	197,145	225,322	42200		Santa Maria-Santa Barbara, CA Metro..	423,895	448,150
	24039	Somerset County, MD......................	26,470	25,918		06083	Santa Barbara County, CA...............	423,895	448,150
	24045	Wicomico County, MD......................	98,733	102,923					
	24047	Worcester County, MD.....................	51,454	51,690	42220		Santa Rosa, CA Metro area..................	483,878	504,217
41620		Salt Lake City, UT Metro area	1,087,873	1,203,105		06097	Sonoma County, CA........................	483,878	504,217
	49035	Salt Lake County, UT	1,029,655	1,135,649	42300		Sault Ste. Marie, MI Micro area.............	38,520	37,711
	49045	Tooele County, UT..........................	58,218	67,456		26033	Chippewa County, MI......................	38,520	37,711
41660		San Angelo, TX Metro area	111,823	119,535	42340		Savannah, GA Metro area....................	347,611	387,543
	48235	Irion County, TX	1,599	1,516		13029	Bryan County, GA..........................	30,233	37,060
	48451	Tom Green County, TX....................	110,224	118,019		13051	Chatham County, GA......................	265,128	290,501
41700		San Antonio-New Braunfels, TX Metro..	2,142,508	2,473,974		13103	Effingham County, GA.....................	52,250	59,982
	48013	Atascosa County, TX.......................	44,911	48,981	42380		Sayre, PA Micro area..........................	62,622	60,853
	48019	Bandera County, TX........................	20,485	22,351		42015	Bradford County, PA.......................	62,622	60,853
	48029	Bexar County, TX..........................	1,714,773	1,958,578	42420		Scottsbluff, NE Micro area..................	38,971	38,308
	48091	Comal County, TX..........................	108,472	141,009		31007	Banner County, NE	690	742
	48187	Guadalupe County, TX......................	131,533	159,659		31157	Scotts Bluff County, NE...................	36,970	36,363
	48259	Kendall County, TX.........................	33,410	44,026		31165	Sioux County, NE	1,311	1,203
	48325	Medina County, TX.........................	46,006	50,066	42460		Scottsboro, AL Micro area	53,227	51,909
	48493	Wilson County, TX	42,918	49,304		01071	Jackson County, AL........................	53,227	51,909
41740		San Diego-Carlsbad, CA Metro area.....	3,095,313	3,337,685	42540		Scranton—Wilkes-Barre—Hazleton, PA Metro area	563,631	555,426
	06073	San Diego County, CA	3,095,313	3,337,685		42069	Lackawanna County, PA...................	214,437	210,761
41760		Sandpoint, ID Micro area....................	40,877	43,560		42079	Luzerne County, PA	320,918	317,343
	16017	Bonner County, ID..........................	40,877	43,560		42131	Wyoming County, PA	28,276	27,322
41780		Sandusky, OH Micro area....................	77,079	74,817	42620		Searcy, AR Micro area........................	77,076	79,016
	39043	Erie County, OH	77,079	74,817		05145	White County, AR............................	77,076	79,016
41820		Sanford, NC Micro area......................	57,866	60,430	42660		Seattle-Tacoma-Bellevue, WA Metro area	3,439,809	3,867,046
	37105	Lee County, NC..............................	57,866	60,430					
41860		San Francisco-Oakland-Hayward, CA Metro area	4,335,391	4,727,357					

C-24

Appendix C

Core based statis-tical area	State/ County FIPS code	Title and Geographic Components	2010 Census Population	2017 Estimated Population	Core based statis-tical area	State/ County FIPS code	Title and Geographic Components	2010 Census Population	2017 Estimated Population
42660		Seattle-Bellevue-Everett, WA Metro Div 42644	2,644,584	2,990,282		22031	De Soto Parish, LA	26,656	27,340
	53033	King County, WA	1,931,249	2,188,649		22119	Webster Parish, LA	41,207	39,378
	53061	Snohomish County, WA	713,335	801,633	43380		Sidney, OH Micro area	49,423	48,759
42660		Tacoma-Lakewood, WA Metro Div 45104	795,225	876,764		39149	Shelby County, OH	49,423	48,759
	53053	Pierce County, WA	795,225	876,764	43420		Sierra Vista-Douglas, AZ Metro area	131,346	124,756
42680		Sebastian-Vero Beach, FL Metro area	138,028	154,383		04003	Cochise County, AZ	131,346	124,756
	12061	Indian River County, FL	138,028	154,383	43460		Sikeston, MO Micro area	39,191	38,541
42700		Sebring, FL Metro area	98,786	102,883		29201	Scott County, MO	39,191	38,541
	12055	Highlands County, FL	98,786	102,883	43500		Silver City, NM Micro area	29,514	27,687
42740		Sedalia, MO Micro area	42,201	42,558		35017	Grant County, NM	29,514	27,687
	29159	Pettis County, MO	42,201	42,558	43580		Sioux City, IA-NE-SD Metro area	168,563	168,618
42780		Selinsgrove, PA Micro area	39,702	40,801		19149	Plymouth County, IA	24,986	25,220
	42109	Snyder County, PA	39,702	40,801		19193	Woodbury County, IA	102,172	102,429
42820		Selma, AL Micro area	43,820	39,215		31043	Dakota County, NE	21,006	20,186
	01047	Dallas County, AL	43,820	39,215		31051	Dixon County, NE	6,000	5,754
42860		Seneca, SC Micro area	74,273	77,270		46127	Union County, SD	14,399	15,029
	45073	Oconee County, SC	74,273	77,270	43620		Sioux Falls, SD Metro area	228,261	259,094
42900		Seneca Falls, NY Micro area	35,251	34,498		46083	Lincoln County, SD	44,828	56,664
	36099	Seneca County, NY	35,251	34,498		46087	McCook County, SD	5,618	5,499
42940		Sevierville, TN Micro area	89,889	97,638		46099	Minnehaha County, SD	169,468	188,616
	47155	Sevier County, TN	89,889	97,638		46125	Turner County, SD	8,347	8,315
42980		Seymour, IN Micro area	42,376	43,884	43660		Snyder, TX Micro area	16,921	17,050
	18071	Jackson County, IN	42,376	43,884		48415	Scurry County, TX	16,921	17,050
43020		Shawano, WI Micro area	46,181	45,550	43700		Somerset, KY Micro area	63,063	64,449
	55078	Menominee County, WI	4,232	4,615		21199	Pulaski County, KY	63,063	64,449
	55115	Shawano County, WI	41,949	40,935	43740		Somerset, PA Micro area	77,742	74,501
43060		Shawnee, OK Micro area	69,442	72,226		42111	Somerset County, PA	77,742	74,501
	40125	Pottawatomie County, OK	69,442	72,226	43760		Sonora, CA Micro area	55,365	54,248
43100		Sheboygan, WI Metro area	115,507	115,344		06109	Tuolumne County, CA	55,365	54,248
	55117	Sheboygan County, WI	115,507	115,344	43780		South Bend-Mishawaka, IN-MI Metro area	319,224	321,815
43140		Shelby, NC Micro area	98,078	97,334		18141	St. Joseph County, IN	266,931	270,434
	37045	Cleveland County, NC	98,078	97,334		26027	Cass County, MI	52,293	51,381
43180		Shelbyville, TN Micro area	45,058	48,117	43900		Spartanburg, SC Metro area	313,268	334,391
	47003	Bedford County, TN	45,058	48,117		45083	Spartanburg County, SC	284,307	306,854
43220		Shelton, WA Micro area	60,699	63,710		45087	Union County, SC	28,961	27,537
	53045	Mason County, WA	60,699	63,710	43940		Spearfish, SD Micro area	24,097	25,429
43260		Sheridan, WY Micro area	29,116	30,210		46081	Lawrence County, SD	24,097	25,429
	56033	Sheridan County, WY	29,116	30,210	43980		Spencer, IA Micro area	16,667	16,170
43300		Sherman-Denison, TX Metro area	120,877	131,140		19041	Clay County, IA	16,667	16,170
	48181	Grayson County, TX	120,877	131,140	44020		Spirit Lake, IA Micro area	16,667	17,199
43320		Show Low, AZ Micro area	107,449	108,956		19059	Dickinson County, IA	16,667	17,199
	04017	Navajo County, AZ	107,449	108,956	44060		Spokane-Spokane Valley, WA Metro area	527,753	564,236
43340		Shreveport-Bossier City, LA Metro area	439,811	440,933		53051	Pend Oreille County, WA	13,001	13,354
	22015	Bossier Parish, LA	116,979	127,634		53063	Spokane County, WA	471,221	506,152
	22017	Caddo Parish, LA	254,969	246,581		53065	Stevens County, WA	43,531	44,730
					44100		Springfield, IL Metro area	210,170	208,697
						17129	Menard County, IL	12,705	12,245
						17167	Sangamon County, IL	197,465	196,452

Core based statistical area	State/County FIPS code	Title and Geographic Components	2010 Census Population	2017 Estimated Population	Core based statistical area	State/County FIPS code	Title and Geographic Components	2010 Census Population	2017 Estimated Population
44140		Springfield, MA Metro area	621,570	631,652	44980		Sunbury, PA Micro area	94,528	92,029
	25013	Hampden County, MA	463,490	469,818		42097	Northumberland County, PA	94,528	92,029
	25015	Hampshire County, MA	158,080	161,834	45000		Susanville, CA Micro area	34,895	31,163
44180		Springfield, MO Metro area	436,712	462,369		06035	Lassen County, CA	34,895	31,163
	29043	Christian County, MO	77,422	85,432	45020		Sweetwater, TX Micro area	15,216	14,770
	29059	Dallas County, MO	16,777	16,673		48353	Nolan County, TX	15,216	14,770
	29077	Greene County, MO	275,174	289,805	45060		Syracuse, NY Metro area	662,577	654,841
	29167	Polk County, MO	31,137	31,794		36053	Madison County, NY	73,442	70,965
	29225	Webster County, MO	36,202	38,665		36067	Onondaga County, NY	467,026	465,398
44220		Springfield, OH Metro area	138,333	134,557		36075	Oswego County, NY	122,109	118,478
	39023	Clark County, OH	138,333	134,557	45140		Tahlequah, OK Micro area	46,987	48,888
44260		Starkville, MS Micro area	47,671	49,799		40021	Cherokee County, OK	46,987	48,888
	28105	Oktibbeha County, MS	47,671	49,799	45180		Talladega-Sylacauga, AL Micro area	93,830	90,819
44300		State College, PA Metro area	153,990	162,660		01037	Coosa County, AL	11,539	10,754
	42027	Centre County, PA	153,990	162,660		01121	Talladega County, AL	82,291	80,065
44340		Statesboro, GA Micro area	70,217	76,149	45220		Tallahassee, FL Metro area	367,413	382,627
	13031	Bulloch County, GA	70,217	76,149		12039	Gadsden County, FL	46,389	46,071
44420		Staunton-Waynesboro, VA Metro area	118,502	121,999		12065	Jefferson County, FL	14,761	14,144
	51015	Augusta County, VA	73,750	75,144		12073	Leon County, FL	275,487	290,292
	51790	Staunton city, VA	23,746	24,528		12129	Wakulla County, FL	30,776	32,120
	51820	Waynesboro city, VA	21,006	22,327	45300		Tampa-St. Petersburg-Clearwater, FL Metro area	2,783,243	3,091,399
44460		Steamboat Springs, CO Micro area	23,509	25,220		12053	Hernando County, FL	172,778	186,553
	08107	Routt County, CO	23,509	25,220		12057	Hillsborough County, FL	1,229,226	1,408,566
44500		Stephenville, TX Micro area	37,890	41,969		12101	Pasco County, FL	464,697	525,643
	48143	Erath County, TX	37,890	41,969		12103	Pinellas County, FL	916,542	970,637
44540		Sterling, CO Micro area	22,709	21,896	45340		Taos, NM Micro area	32,937	32,795
	08075	Logan County, CO	22,709	21,896		35055	Taos County, NM	32,937	32,795
44580		Sterling, IL Micro area	58,498	56,118	45380		Taylorville, IL Micro area	34,800	33,102
	17195	Whiteside County, IL	58,498	56,118		17021	Christian County, IL	34,800	33,102
44620		Stevens Point, WI Micro area	70,019	70,474	45460		Terre Haute, IN Metro area	172,425	169,965
	55097	Portage County, WI	70,019	70,474		18021	Clay County, IN	26,890	26,198
44660		Stillwater, OK Micro area	77,350	81,575		18153	Sullivan County, IN	21,475	20,746
	40119	Payne County, OK	77,350	81,575		18165	Vermillion County, IN	16,212	15,505
44700		Stockton-Lodi, CA Metro area	685,306	745,424		18167	Vigo County, IN	107,848	107,516
	06077	San Joaquin County, CA	685,306	745,424	45500		Texarkana, TX-AR Metro area	149,198	150,355
44740		Storm Lake, IA Micro area	20,260	20,110		05081	Little River County, AR	13,171	12,359
	19021	Buena Vista County, IA	20,260	20,110		05091	Miller County, AR	43,462	43,984
44780		Sturgis, MI Micro area	61,295	60,947		48037	Bowie County, TX	92,565	94,012
	26149	St. Joseph County, MI	61,295	60,947	45520		The Dalles, OR Micro area	25,213	26,437
44860		Sulphur Springs, TX Micro area	35,161	36,496		41065	Wasco County, OR	25,213	26,437
	48223	Hopkins County, TX	35,161	36,496	45540		The Villages, FL Metro area	93,420	125,165
44900		Summerville, GA Micro area	26,015	24,770		12119	Sumter County, FL	93,420	125,165
	13055	Chattooga County, GA	26,015	24,770	45580		Thomaston, GA Micro area	27,153	26,135
44920		Summit Park, UT Micro area	36,324	41,106		13293	Upson County, GA	27,153	26,135
	49043	Summit County, UT	36,324	41,106	45620		Thomasville, GA Micro area	44,720	44,779
44940		Sumter, SC Metro area	107,456	106,847		13275	Thomas County, GA	44,720	44,779
	45085	Sumter County, SC	107,456	106,847	45660		Tiffin, OH Micro area	56,745	55,243
						39147	Seneca County, OH	56,745	55,243

CORE BASED STATISTICAL AREAS
(Metropolitan and Micropolitan),
METROPOLITAN DIVISIONS, AND COMPONENTS
(as defined August, 2017)—*Continued*

Core based statistical area	State/County FIPS code	Title and Geographic Components	2010 Census Population	2017 Estimated Population	Core based statistical area	State/County FIPS code	Title and Geographic Components	2010 Census Population	2017 Estimated Population
45700		Tifton, GA Micro area	40,118	40,598	46340		Tyler, TX Metro area	209,714	227,727
	13277	Tift County, GA	40,118	40,598		48423	Smith County, TX	209,714	227,727
45740		Toccoa, GA Micro area	26,175	25,890	46380		Ukiah, CA Micro area	87,841	88,018
	13257	Stephens County, GA	26,175	25,890		06045	Mendocino County, CA	87,841	88,018
45780		Toledo, OH Metro area	610,001	603,668	46460		Union City, TN-KY Micro area	38,620	36,577
	39051	Fulton County, OH	42,698	42,289		21075	Fulton County, KY	6,813	6,192
	39095	Lucas County, OH	441,815	430,887		47131	Obion County, TN	31,807	30,385
	39173	Wood County, OH	125,488	130,492	46500		Urbana, OH Micro area	40,097	38,840
45820		Topeka, KS Metro area	233,870	233,149		39021	Champaign County, OH	40,097	38,840
	20085	Jackson County, KS	13,462	13,318					
	20087	Jefferson County, KS	19,126	18,998	46520		Urban Honolulu, HI Metro area	953,207	988,650
	20139	Osage County, KS	16,295	15,772		15003	Honolulu County, HI	953,207	988,650
	20177	Shawnee County, KS	177,934	178,187	46540		Utica-Rome, NY Metro area	299,397	293,572
	20197	Wabaunsee County, KS	7,053	6,874		36043	Herkimer County, NY	64,519	62,240
45860		Torrington, CT Micro area	189,927	182,177		36065	Oneida County, NY	234,878	231,332
	09005	Litchfield County, CT	189,927	182,177	46620		Uvalde, TX Micro area	26,405	27,132
45900		Traverse City, MI Micro area	143,372	148,671		48463	Uvalde County, TX	26,405	27,132
	26019	Benzie County, MI	17,525	17,573	46660		Valdosta, GA Metro area	139,588	145,437
	26055	Grand Traverse County, MI	86,986	91,807		13027	Brooks County, GA	16,243	15,587
	26079	Kalkaska County, MI	17,153	17,634		13101	Echols County, GA	4,034	3,936
	26089	Leelanau County, MI	21,708	21,657		13173	Lanier County, GA	10,078	10,425
45940		Trenton, NJ Metro area	366,513	374,733		13185	Lowndes County, GA	109,233	115,489
	34021	Mercer County, NJ	366,513	374,733	46700		Vallejo-Fairfield, CA Metro area	413,344	445,458
45980		Troy, AL Micro area	32,899	33,267		06095	Solano County, CA	413,344	445,458
	01109	Pike County, AL	32,899	33,267	46740		Valley, AL Micro area	34,215	33,713
46020		Truckee-Grass Valley, CA Micro area	98,764	99,814		01017	Chambers County, AL	34,215	33,713
	06057	Nevada County, CA	98,764	99,814	46780		Van Wert, OH Micro area	28,744	28,217
46060		Tucson, AZ Metro area	980,263	1,022,769		39161	Van Wert County, OH	28,744	28,217
	04019	Pima County, AZ	980,263	1,022,769	46820		Vermillion, SD Micro area	13,864	13,990
46100		Tullahoma-Manchester, TN Micro area	100,210	103,070		46027	Clay County, SD	13,864	13,990
	47031	Coffee County, TN	52,796	55,034	46860		Vernal, UT Micro area	32,588	35,150
	47051	Franklin County, TN	41,052	41,652		49047	Uintah County, UT	32,588	35,150
	47127	Moore County, TN	6,362	6,384	46900		Vernon, TX Micro area	13,535	12,764
46140		Tulsa, OK Metro area	937,478	990,706		48487	Wilbarger County, TX	13,535	12,764
	40037	Creek County, OK	69,967	71,704	46980		Vicksburg, MS Micro area	58,377	55,718
	40111	Okmulgee County, OK	40,069	38,930		28021	Claiborne County, MS	9,604	8,950
	40113	Osage County, OK	47,472	47,233		28149	Warren County, MS	48,773	46,768
	40117	Pawnee County, OK	16,577	16,472	47020		Victoria, TX Metro area	94,003	99,646
	40131	Rogers County, OK	86,905	91,444		48175	Goliad County, TX	7,210	7,562
	40143	Tulsa County, OK	603,403	646,266		48469	Victoria County, TX	86,793	92,084
	40145	Wagoner County, OK	73,085	78,657	47080		Vidalia, GA Micro area	36,346	36,030
46180		Tupelo, MS Micro area	136,268	140,081		13209	Montgomery County, GA	9,123	9,031
	28057	Itawamba County, MS	23,401	23,508		13279	Toombs County, GA	27,223	26,999
	28081	Lee County, MS	82,910	84,933	47180		Vincennes, IN Micro area	38,440	37,508
	28115	Pontotoc County, MS	29,957	31,640		18083	Knox County, IN	38,440	37,508
46220		Tuscaloosa, AL Metro area	230,162	242,799	47220		Vineland-Bridgeton, NJ Metro area	156,898	152,538
	01065	Hale County, AL	15,760	14,812		34011	Cumberland County, NJ	156,898	152,538
	01107	Pickens County, AL	19,746	20,176	47240		Vineyard Haven, MA Micro area	16,535	17,325
	01125	Tuscaloosa County, AL	194,656	207,811		25007	Dukes County, MA	16,535	17,325
46300		Twin Falls, ID Metro area	99,604	108,751					
	16053	Jerome County, ID	22,374	23,627					
	16083	Twin Falls County, ID	77,230	85,124					

Core based statistical area	State/County FIPS code	Title and Geographic Components	2010 Census Population	2017 Estimated Population	Core based statistical area	State/County FIPS code	Title and Geographic Components	2010 Census Population	2017 Estimated Population
47260		Virginia Beach-Norfolk-Newport News, VA-NC Metro area	1,676,822	1,725,246	47900		Washington-Arlington-Alexandria, DC-VA-MD-WV Metro Div 47894	4,431,070	4,905,757
	37053	Currituck County, NC	23,547	26,331		11001	District of Columbia, DC	601,723	693,972
	37073	Gates County, NC	12,197	11,544		24009	Calvert County, MD	88,737	91,502
	51073	Gloucester County, VA	36,858	37,292		24017	Charles County, MD	146,551	159,700
	51093	Isle of Wight County, VA	35,270	36,552		24033	Prince George's County, MD	863,420	912,756
	51095	James City County, VA	67,009	75,524		51013	Arlington County, VA	207,627	234,965
	51115	Mathews County, VA	8,978	8,779		51043	Clarke County, VA	14,034	14,508
	51199	York County, VA	65,464	67,739		51047	Culpeper County, VA	46,689	51,282
	51550	Chesapeake city, VA	222,209	240,397		51059	Fairfax County, VA	1,081,726	1,148,433
	51650	Hampton city, VA	137,436	134,669		51061	Fauquier County, VA	65,203	69,465
	51700	Newport News city, VA	180,719	179,388		51107	Loudoun County, VA	312,311	398,080
	51710	Norfolk city, VA	242,803	244,703		51153	Prince William County, VA	402,002	463,023
	51735	Poquoson city, VA	12,150	12,053		51157	Rappahannock County, VA	7,373	7,321
	51740	Portsmouth city, VA	95,535	94,572		51177	Spotsylvania County, VA	122,397	133,033
	51800	Suffolk city, VA	84,585	90,237		51179	Stafford County, VA	128,961	146,649
	51810	Virginia Beach city, VA	437,994	450,435		51187	Warren County, VA	37,575	39,563
	51830	Williamsburg city, VA	14,068	15,031		51510	Alexandria city, VA	139,966	160,035
47300		Visalia-Porterville, CA Metro area	442,179	464,493		51600	Fairfax city, VA	22,565	24,097
	06107	Tulare County, CA	442,179	464,493		51610	Falls Church city, VA	12,332	14,583
47340		Wabash, IN Micro area	32,888	31,443		51630	Fredericksburg city, VA	24,286	28,360
	18169	Wabash County, IN	32,888	31,443		51683	Manassas city, VA	37,821	41,501
47380		Waco, TX Metro area	252,772	268,696		51685	Manassas Park city, VA	14,273	16,591
	48145	Falls County, TX	17,866	17,437		54037	Jefferson County, WV	53,498	56,338
	48309	McLennan County, TX	234,906	251,259	47920		Washington Court House, OH Micro area	29,030	28,752
47420		Wahpeton, ND-MN Micro area	22,897	22,675		39047	Fayette County, OH	29,030	28,752
	27167	Wilkin County, MN	6,576	6,324	47940		Waterloo-Cedar Falls, IA Metro area	167,819	169,892
	38077	Richland County, ND	16,321	16,351		19013	Black Hawk County, IA	131,090	132,648
47460		Walla Walla, WA Metro area	62,859	64,614		19017	Bremer County, IA	24,276	24,911
	53013	Columbia County, WA	4,078	4,047		19075	Grundy County, IA	12,453	12,333
	53071	Walla Walla County, WA	58,781	60,567	47980		Watertown, SD Micro area	27,227	28,099
47540		Wapakoneta, OH Micro area	45,949	45,778		46029	Codington County, SD	27,227	28,099
	39011	Auglaize County, OH	45,949	45,778	48020		Watertown-Fort Atkinson, WI Micro area	83,686	84,832
47580		Warner Robins, GA Metro area	179,605	191,779		55055	Jefferson County, WI	83,686	84,832
	13153	Houston County, GA	139,900	153,479	48060		Watertown-Fort Drum, NY Metro area	116,229	114,187
	13225	Peach County, GA	27,695	27,099		36045	Jefferson County, NY	116,229	114,187
	13235	Pulaski County, GA	12,010	11,201	48100		Wauchula, FL Micro area	27,731	27,411
47620		Warren, PA Micro area	41,815	39,659		12049	Hardee County, FL	27,731	27,411
	42123	Warren County, PA	41,815	39,659	48140		Wausau, WI Metro area	134,063	135,732
47660		Warrensburg, MO Micro area	52,595	53,897		55073	Marathon County, WI	134,063	135,732
	29101	Johnson County, MO	52,595	53,897	48180		Waycross, GA Micro area	55,070	55,178
47700		Warsaw, IN Micro area	77,358	79,206		13229	Pierce County, GA	18,758	19,307
	18085	Kosciusko County, IN	77,358	79,206		13299	Ware County, GA	36,312	35,871
47780		Washington, IN Micro area	31,648	33,113	48220		Weatherford, OK Micro area	27,469	28,800
	18027	Daviess County, IN	31,648	33,113		40039	Custer County, OK	27,469	28,800
47820		Washington, NC Micro area	47,759	47,088	48260		Weirton-Steubenville, WV-OH Metro area	124,454	118,250
	37013	Beaufort County, NC	47,759	47,088		39081	Jefferson County, OH	69,709	66,359
47900		Washington-Arlington-Alexandria, DC-VA-MD-WV Metro area	5,636,232	6,216,589		54009	Brooke County, WV	24,069	22,443
						54029	Hancock County, WV	30,676	29,448
47900		Silver Spring-Frederick-Rockville, MD Metro Div 43524	1,205,162	1,310,832	48300		Wenatchee, WA Metro area	110,884	118,478
	24021	Frederick County, MD	233,385	252,022		53007	Chelan County, WA	72,453	76,533
	24031	Montgomery County, MD	971,777	1,058,810		53017	Douglas County, WA	38,431	41,945

ALASKA - Core Based Statistical Areas (CBSAs) and Counties

CANADA

Prince of Wales-Hyder (pt)

Wrangell

Juneau

Juneau

Skagway

Haines

Hoonah-Angoon

Yakutat

Sitka

Petersburg

Prince of Wales-Hyder (pt)

Ketchikan

Ketchikan Gateway

Southeast Fairbanks

Valdez-Cordova

Anchorage

FAIRBANKS

ANCHORAGE

Denali

Fairbanks North Star

Matanuska-Susitna

Kenai Peninsula

Yukon-Koyukuk

North Slope

Northwest Arctic

Nome (pt)

Nome (pt)

Wade Hampton

Bethel

Dillingham

Bristol Bay

Lake and Peninsula

Kodiak Island

Aleutians East

Aleutians West (pt)

Aleutians West (pt)

Arctic Ocean

RUSSIA

CANADA

Pacific Ocean

LEGEND

Metropolitan Statistical Area

Micropolitan Statistical Area

International

County or Statistical Equivalent

Coastline

FAIRBANKS

Juneau

Bethel

Arctic Ocean

CBSA boundaries and names are as of February 2013. All other boundaries and names are as of January 1, 2012.

300 Miles
300 Kilometers
225
225
150
150
75
75
0
0

N

U.S. DEPARTMENT OF COMMERCE Economics and Statistics Administration U.S. Census Bureau

Appendix D

D-5

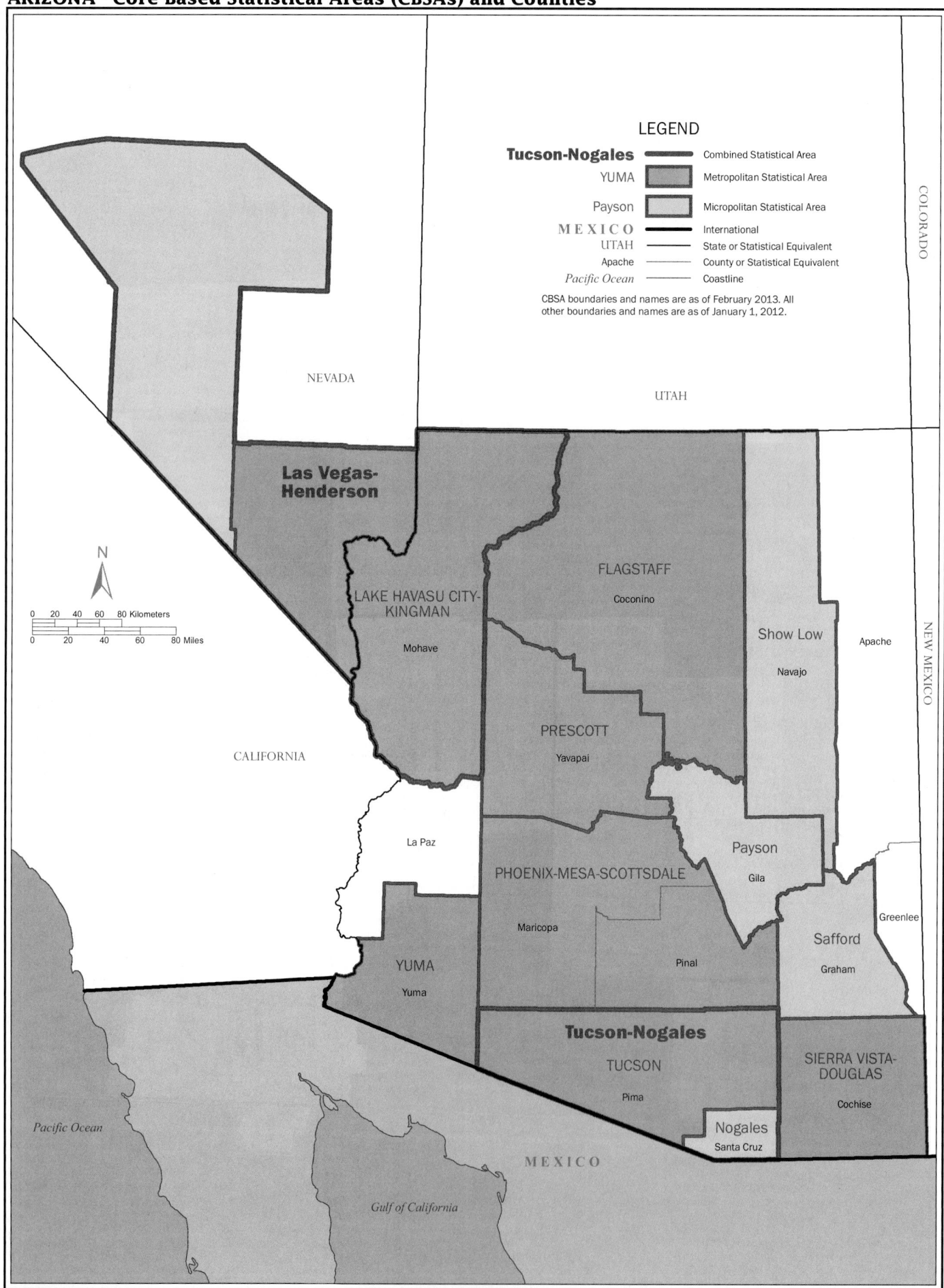

LEGEND

Tucson-Nogales ▬▬▬ Combined Statistical Area

YUMA ▬▬ Metropolitan Statistical Area

Payson ▬▬ Micropolitan Statistical Area

M E X I C O ▬▬ International

UTAH ▬▬ State or Statistical Equivalent

Apache ▬▬ County or Statistical Equivalent

Pacific Ocean ▬▬ Coastline

CBSA boundaries and names are as of February 2013. All other boundaries and names are as of January 1, 2012.

ARKANSAS - Core Based Statistical Areas (CBSAs) and Counties

KENTUCKY

TENNESSEE

MISSOURI

OKLAHOMA

MISSISSIPPI

LOUISIANA

TEXAS

Clay

Randolph

Fulton

Baxter
Mountain
Home

Marion

Boone

Carroll

McDonald

Benton

Madison

Washington
FAYETTEVILLE-
SPRINGDALE-
ROGERS

Sequoyah

Le Flore

FORT SMITH

Crawford

Sebastian

Franklin

Logan

Scott

Polk

Sevier

Little River

Howard

Pike

Hempstead

Miller
TEXARKANA

Bowie

Nevada

Lafayette

Columbia
Magnolia

Union
El Dorado

Ouachita
Camden
Camden

Calhoun

Bradley

Ashley

Drew

Chicot

Desha

Arkansas

Cleveland

Lincoln
PINE BLUFF

Jefferson

Dallas

Clark
Arkadelphia

Hot Spring
Malvern
Hot Springs-
Malvern

Grant

HOT
SPRINGS
Garland

Saline

Pulaski
LITTLE ROCK-NORTH LITTLE ROCK-CONWAY

Perry
Little Rock-North Little Rock

Faulkner

Conway

Van Buren

Searcy

Marion

Stone

Cleburne

White
Searcy

Independence
Batesville

Izard

Sharp

Lawrence

Jackson

Woodruff

Monroe

Lee

Phillips
Helena-
West Helena

St. Francis
Forrest City

Cross

Poinsett
JONESBORO

Craighead
Jonesboro-
Paragould

Greene
Paragould

Mississippi
Blytheville

Crittenden

Tunica

Tate

DeSoto
MEMPHIS

Marshall

Benton

Fayette

Shelby

Tipton
Memphis-Forrest City

Johnson

Pope
Russellville

Newton

Harrison

Yell

Montgomery

Garland

Legend

	Combined Statistical Area
	Metropolitan Statistical Area
	Micropolitan Statistical Area
	State or Statistical Equivalent
	County or Statistical Equivalent

Hot Springs-Malvern

FORT SMITH
TEXAS
Camden
Arkansas

CBSA boundaries and names are as of February 2013. All other boundaries and names are as of January 1, 2012.

N

40 Miles
40 Kilometers

OREGON

IDAHO

LEGEND

Fresno-Madera ——— Combined Statistical Area

NAPA — Metropolitan Statistical Area

Ukiah — Micropolitan Statistical Area

San Rafael •••••• Metropolitan Division

M E X I C O ——— International

NEVADA ——— State or Statistical Equivalent

Alameda ——— County or Statistical Equivalent

Pacific Ocean ——— Coastline

CBSA boundaries and names are as of February 2013. All other boundaries and names are as of January 1, 2012.

Del Norte
Crescent City
Siskiyou
Modoc

Eureka-Arcata-Fortuna

Humboldt
Trinity

REDDING
Shasta
Redding-Red Bluff

Susanville
Lassen

Red Bluff
Tehama

Plumas

CHICO

Ukiah
Mendocino

Glenn
Butte

Colusa
Sierra

Yuba
Nevada

Clear-lake
Lake

Sutter
YUBA CITY

Placer

— Truckee-Grass Valley

Sacramento-Roseville

SACRAMENTO–ROSEVILLE–ARDEN-ARCADE

SANTA ROSA
Sonoma

NAPA
Napa

Yolo

El Dorado

Sacra-mento

Alpine

N

1

Solano

San Rafael —

Amador

0 20 40 60 80 Kilometers

0 20 40 60 80 Miles

SAN FRANCISCO-OAKLAND-HAYWARD

Marin

Contra Costa
2

San Joaquin
STOCKTON-LODI

Calaveras

Sonora
Tuolumne

NEVADA

Mono

San Francisco —
San Francisco-Redwood City-South San Francisco

Alameda

MODESTO
Stanislaus

San Jose-San Francisco-Oakland

Santa Clara
3

Merced
Modesto-Merced

Mariposa

Madera

San Mateo
SANTA CRUZ-WATSONVILLE

Santa Cruz

MERCED

MADERA

Fresno-Madera

SALINAS

San Benito

FRESNO

Fresno

Inyo

Monterey

VISALIA-PORTERVILLE

Kings
HANFORD-CORCORAN

Tulare

Visalia-Porterville-Hanford

KEY
1 VALLEJO-FAIRFIELD
2 Oakland-Hayward-Berkeley
3 SAN JOSE-SUNNYVALE-SANTA CLARA

— SAN LUIS OBISPO-PASO ROBLES-ARROYO GRANDE

San Luis Obispo

BAKERSFIELD

Kern

Los Angeles-Long Beach

RIVERSIDE-SAN BERNARDINO-ONTARIO

San Bernardino

Pacific Ocean

Santa Barbara

Ventura

Los Angeles-Long Beach-Glendale

LOS ANGELES-LONG BEACH-ANAHEIM

SANTA MARIA-SANTA BARBARA

Los Angeles

Anaheim-Santa Ana-Irvine

Riverside

OXNARD-THOUSAND OAKS-VENTURA

Orange

SAN DIEGO-CARLSBAD

EL CENTRO
Imperial

San Diego

ARIZONA

M E X I C O

COLORADO - Core Based Statistical Areas (CBSAs) and Counties

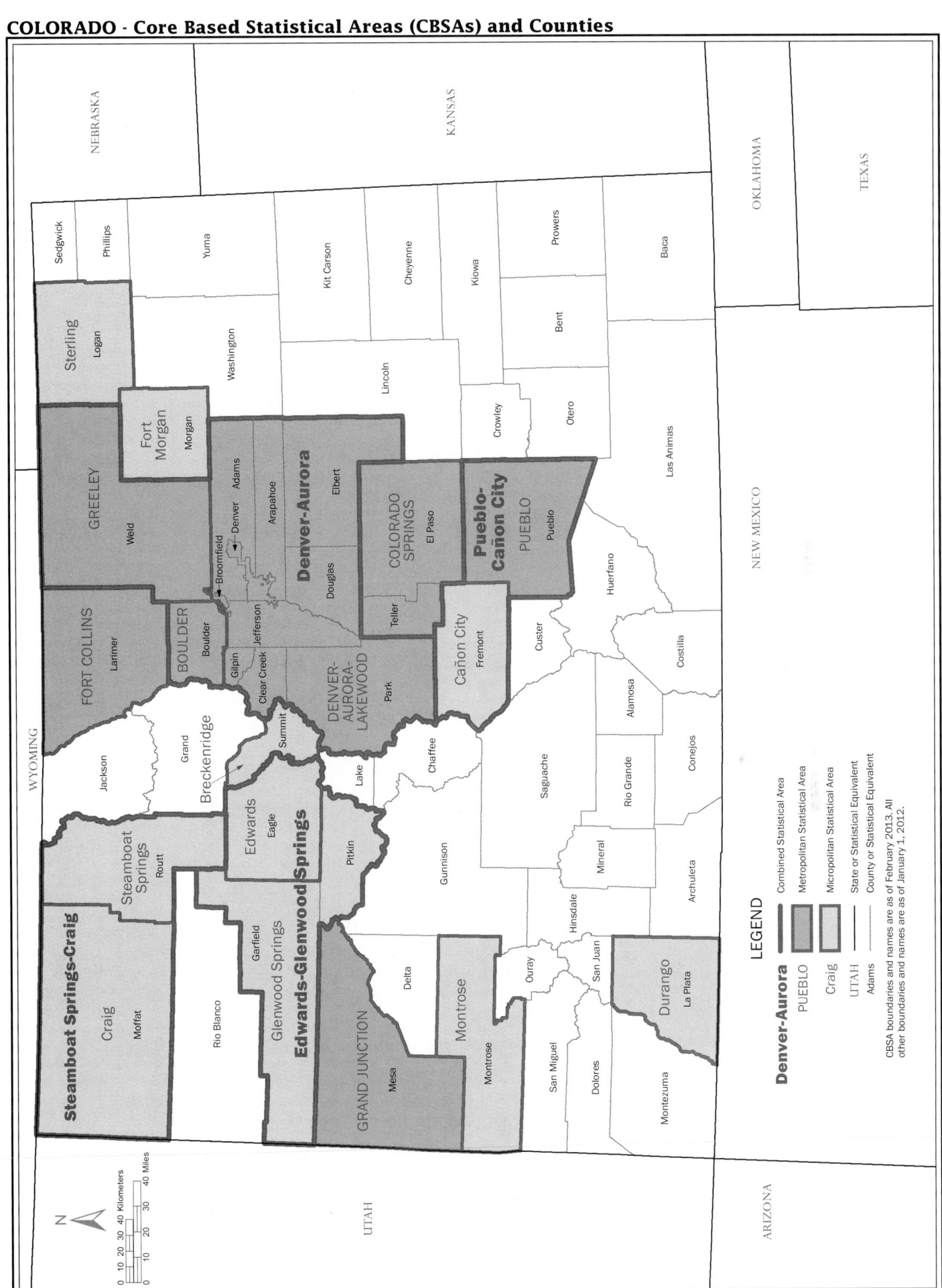

NEBRASKA

KANSAS

OKLAHOMA

TEXAS

Sedgwick

Phillips

Yuma

Kit Carson

Cheyenne

Kiowa

Prowers

Baca

Sterling
Logan

Washington

Lincoln

Bent

GREELEY
Weld

Fort
Morgan
Morgan

Denver-Aurora
Adams
Denver
Arapahoe
Elbert

COLORADO
SPRINGS
El Paso

Pueblo-
Cañon City
PUEBLO
Pueblo

Crowley

Otero

Las Animas

NEW MEXICO

FORT COLLINS
Larimer

BOULDER
Boulder

Broomfield

Jefferson

Douglas

Teller

Gilpin

DENVER-
AURORA-
LAKEWOOD
Park

Cañon City
Fremont

Custer

Huerfano

Costilla

Clear Creek

WYOMING

Jackson

Grand

Breckenridge

Summit

Lake

Chaffee

Saguache

Rio Grande

Conejos

Alamosa

Steamboat
Springs
Routt

Edwards
Eagle

Pitkin

Gunnison

Mineral

Archuleta

Steamboat Springs-Craig

Craig
Moffat

Rio Blanco

Garfield

Glenwood Springs

Edwards-Glenwood Springs

GRAND JUNCTION
Mesa

Delta

Montrose
Montrose

Ouray

Hinsdale

San Juan

San Miguel

Dolores

Montezuma

Durango
La Plata

LEGEND

Denver-Aurora Combined Statistical Area

PUEBLO Metropolitan Statistical Area

Craig Micropolitan Statistical Area

UTAH State or Statistical Equivalent

Adams County or Statistical Equivalent

CBSA boundaries and names are as of February 2013. All other boundaries and names are as of January 1, 2012.

UTAH

ARIZONA

N

0 10 20 30 40 Kilometers
0 10 20 30 40 Miles

CONNECTICUT - Core Based Statistical Areas (CBSAs) and Counties

DELAWARE - Core Based Statistical Areas (CBSAs) and Counties

Chester

PHILADELPHIA-
CAMDEN-
WILMINGTON
(pt)

Delaware

Philadelphia

Camden

Burlington

PENNSYLVANIA

Wilmington

Gloucester

**Philadelphia-Reading-
Camden (pt)**

Cecil

New
Castle

Salem

NEW JERSEY

MARYLAND

DOVER

Kent

Delaware Bay

N

| 0 | 3 | 6 | 9 | 12 Kilometers |
| 0 | 3 | 6 | 9 | 12 Miles |

Atlantic Ocean

Sussex

SALISBURY

Wicomico

Worcester

Philadelphia-Reading-Camden

Somerset

Chesapeake
Bay

VIRGINIA

LEGEND

Philadelphia-Reading-Camden	Combined Statistical Area
DOVER	Metropolitan Statistical Area
Wilmington	Metropolitan Division
MARYLAND	State or Statistical Equivalent
Kent	County or Statistical Equivalent
Atlantic Ocean	Coastline

CBSA boundaries and names are as of February 2013. All
other boundaries and names are as of January 1, 2012.

U.S. DEPARTMENT OF COMMERCE Economics and Statistics Administration U.S. Census Bureau

PENNSYLVANIA

WEST VIRGINIA

Frederick

MARYLAND

Jefferson

VIRGINIA

Montgomery

Clarke

Loudoun

Washington-
Baltimore-
Arlington
(pt)

WASHINGTON-
ARLINGTON-
ALEXANDRIA

DISTRICT OF
COLUMBIA

District of
Columbia

Warren

Falls Church

Arlington

Washington-
Arlington-
Alexandria

Fairfax
city

Manassas

Fairfax

Alexandria

Fauquier

Prince George's

Manassas
Park

Rappahannock

Chesapeake
Bay

Prince William

Culpeper

Charles

Calvert

Stafford

N

0 4 8 12 16 Kilometers
0 4 8 12 16 Miles

Fredericksburg

Spotsylvania

LEGEND

Washington-Baltimore-Arlington ━━━━━ Combined Statistical Area

WASHINGTON-BALTIMORE-ARLINGTON ▭ Metropolitan Statistical Area

Washington-Arlington-Alexandria ••••• Metropolitan Division

VIRGINIA ──── State or Statistical Equivalent

District of Columbia ──── County or Statistical Equivalent

Chesapeake Bay ──── Coastline

CBSA boundaries and names are as of February 2013. All
other boundaries and names are as of January 1, 2012.

U.S. DEPARTMENT OF COMMERCE Economics and Statistics Administration U.S. Census Bureau

FLORIDA - Core Based Statistical Areas (CBSAs) and Counties

Jacksonville-St. Marys-Palatka

Orlando-Deltona-Daytona Beach

Miami-Fort Lauderdale-Port St. Lucie

Gainesville-Lake City

Tallahassee-Bainbridge

North Port-Sarasota

Cape Coral-Fort Myers-Naples

Atlantic Ocean

GEORGIA

ALABAMA

MISSISSIPPI

Gulf of Mexico

Key West

LEGEND

North Port-Sarasota	Combined Statistical Area
OCALA	Metropolitan Statistical Area
Arcadia	Micropolitan Statistical Area
Miami-Miami Beach-Kendall	Metropolitan Division
GEORGIA	State or Statistical Equivalent
Alachua	County or Statistical Equivalent
Gulf of Mexico	Coastline

CBSA boundaries and names are as of February 2013. All other boundaries and names are as of January 1, 2012.

Counties shown on map: Escambia, Santa Rosa, Okaloosa, Walton, Holmes, Washington, Bay, Jackson, Calhoun, Gulf, Liberty, Franklin, Gadsden, Leon, Wakulla, Jefferson, Madison, Taylor, Lafayette, Dixie, Hamilton, Suwannee, Columbia, Baker, Nassau, Duval, Clay, Union, Bradford, Gilchrist, Levy, Alachua, St. Johns, Flagler, Putnam, Marion, Citrus, Sumter, Lake, Hernando, Pasco, Pinellas, Hillsborough, Seminole, Orange, Osceola, Volusia, Brevard, Indian River, St. Lucie, Martin, Okeechobee, Highlands, Polk, Manatee, Hardee, DeSoto, Sarasota, Charlotte, Glades, Hendry, Lee, Collier, Palm Beach, Broward, Miami-Dade, Monroe

CRESTVIEW-FORT WALTON BEACH-DESTIN, PENSACOLA-FERRY PASS-BRENT, PANAMA CITY, TALLAHASSEE, LAKE CITY, GAINESVILLE, OCALA, THE VILLAGES, PALATKA, JACKSONVILLE, DELTONA-DAYTONA BEACH-ORMOND BEACH, ORLANDO-KISSIMMEE-SANFORD, PALM BAY-MELBOURNE-TITUSVILLE, SEBASTIAN-VERO BEACH, PORT ST. LUCIE, LAKELAND-WINTER HAVEN, SEBRING, HOMOSASSA SPRINGS, TAMPA-ST. PETERSBURG-CLEARWATER, NORTH PORT-SARASOTA-BRADENTON, PUNTA GORDA, ARCADIA, CAPE CORAL-FORT MYERS, CLEWISTON, NAPLES-IMMOKALEE-MARCO ISLAND, WEST PALM BEACH-BOCA RATON-DELRAY BEACH, FORT LAUDERDALE-POMPANO BEACH-DEERFIELD BEACH, MIAMI-MIAMI BEACH-KENDALL

GEORGIA - Core Based Statistical Areas (CBSAs) and Counties

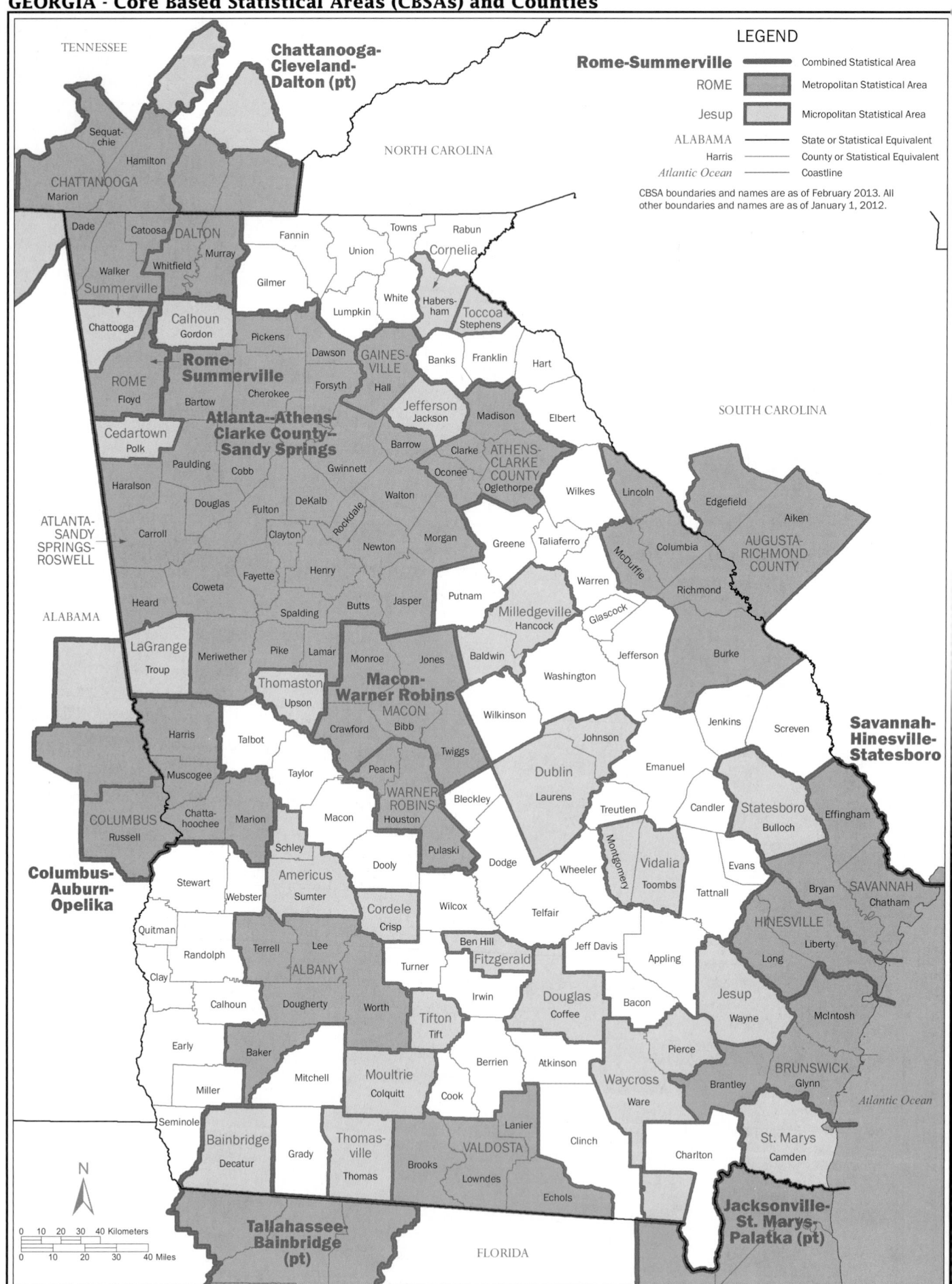

HAWAII - Core Based Statistical Areas (CBSAs) and Counties

Hilo
Hawaii

Kalawao
Maui

KAHULUI-
WAILUKU-
LAHAINA

Honolulu
(pt)

URBAN
HONOLULU
(pt)

Kauai

Kapaa

N

0 40 80 120 160 Kilometers

0 40 80 120 160 Miles

URBAN HONOLULU
(pt)

Honolulu
(pt)

Pacific Ocean

LEGEND

URBAN HONOLULU   Metropolitan Statistical Area

Hilo   Micropolitan Statistical Area

State or Statistical Equivalent

Maui   County or Statistical Equivalent

Coastline

Pacific Ocean

CBSA boundaries and names are as of February 2013. All
other boundaries and names are as of January 1, 2012.

URBAN
HONOLULU
(pt)

Honolulu
(pt)

MIDWAY
ISLANDS
(U.S.
Unincorporated
Territory)

IDAHO - Core Based Statistical Areas (CBSAs) and Counties

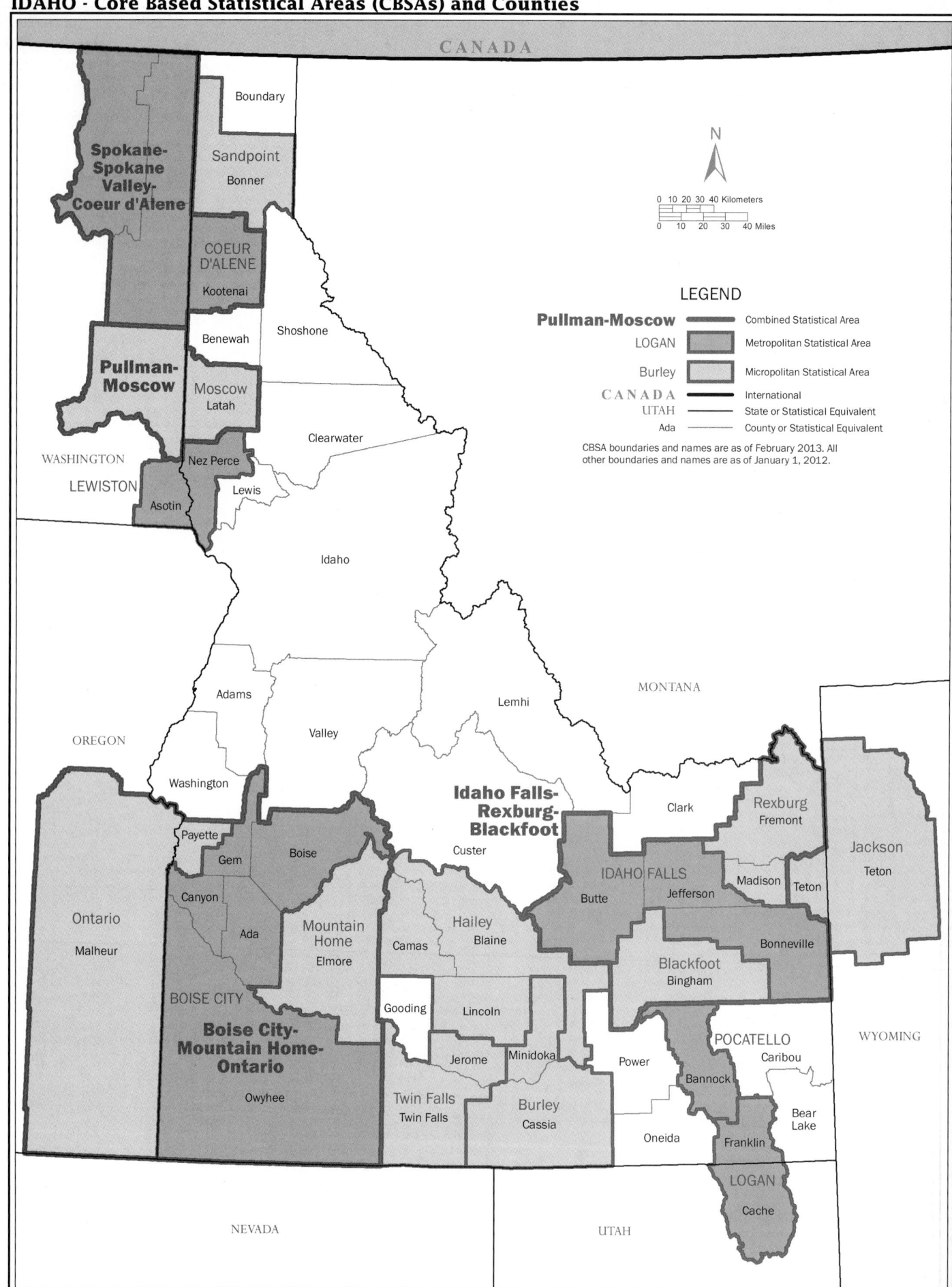

LEGEND

Pullman-Moscow	Combined Statistical Area
LOGAN	Metropolitan Statistical Area
Burley	Micropolitan Statistical Area
CANADA	International
UTAH	State or Statistical Equivalent
Ada	County or Statistical Equivalent

CBSA boundaries and names are as of February 2013. All other boundaries and names are as of January 1, 2012.

U.S. DEPARTMENT OF COMMERCE Economics and Statistics Administration U.S. Census Bureau

ILLINOIS - Core Based Statistical Areas (CBSAs) and Counties

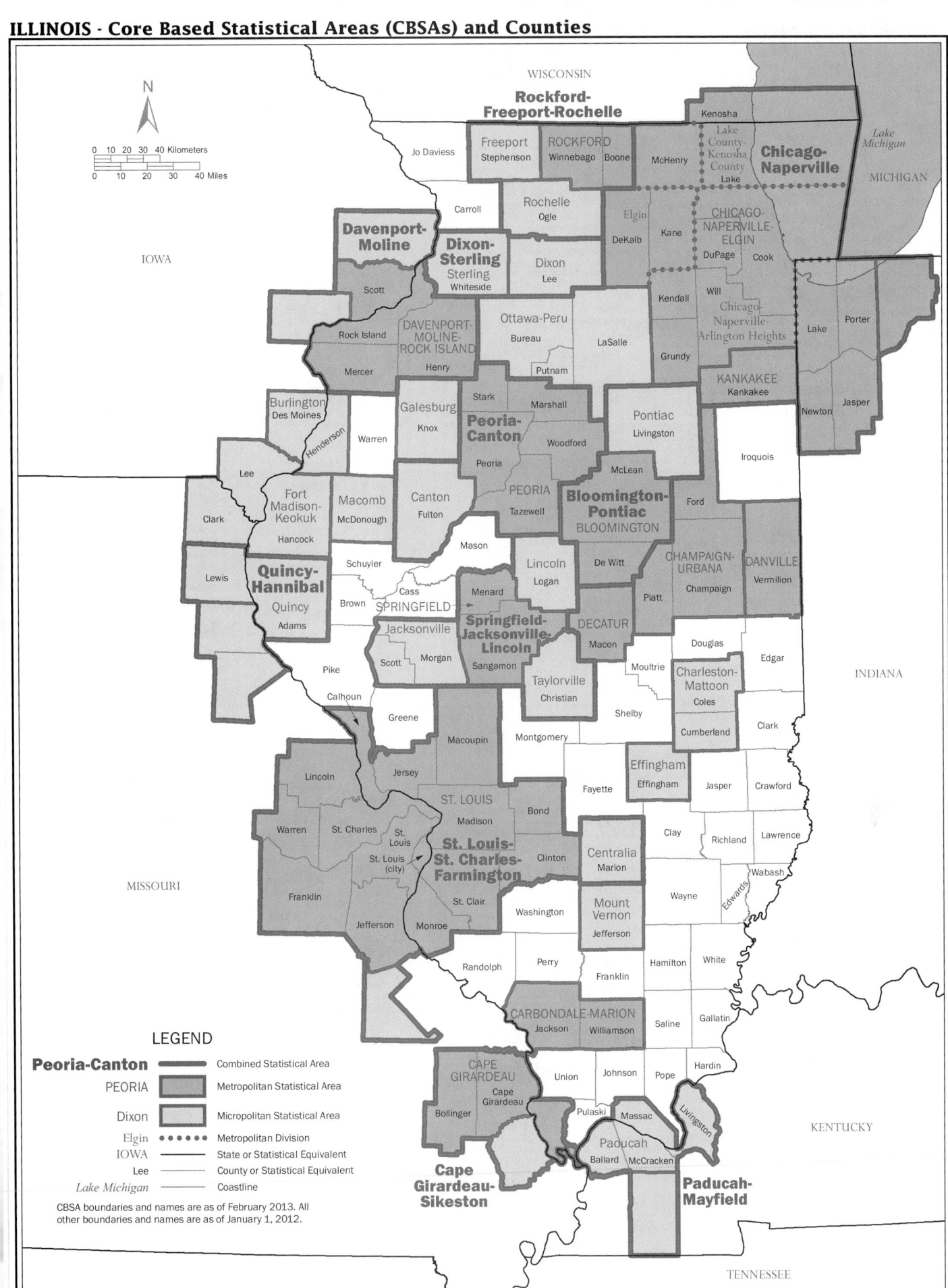

LEGEND

Peoria-Canton	Combined Statistical Area
PEORIA	Metropolitan Statistical Area
Dixon	Micropolitan Statistical Area
Elgin •••••	Metropolitan Division
IOWA	State or Statistical Equivalent
Lee	County or Statistical Equivalent
Lake Michigan	Coastline

CBSA boundaries and names are as of February 2013. All other boundaries and names are as of January 1, 2012.

U.S. DEPARTMENT OF COMMERCE Economics and Statistics Administration U.S. Census Bureau

CHICAGO-NAPERVILLE-ELGIN (pt)

Lake Michigan

DuPage

Cook

SOUTH BEND-MISHAWAKA

Cass

South Bend-Elkhart-Mishawaka (pt)

MICHIGAN

Lake Erie

Chicago-Naperville (pt)

Will

Lake

Porter

Gary

Newton

Jasper

MICHIGAN CITY-LA PORTE

LaPorte

St. Joseph

Starke

Pulaski

Plymouth

Marshall

Fulton

ELKHART-GOSHEN

Elkhart

Warsaw

Kosciusko

LaGrange

Kendallville

Noble

Whitley

Angola

Steuben

Auburn

DeKalb

Fort Wayne-Huntington-Auburn

Allen

FORT WAYNE

Decatur

Adams

Wells

Kokomo-Peru

White

Logans-port

Cass

Peru

Miami

Wabash

Wabash

Hunting-ton

Huntington

Lafayette-West Lafayette-Frankfort

Benton

Warren

Fountain

Carroll

LAFAYETTE-WEST LAFAYETTE

Tippecanoe

KOKOMO

Howard

Frankfort

Clinton

Tipton

Marion

Grant

Black-ford

Jay

OHIO

ILLINOIS

Vermillion

Parke

Crawfords-ville

Mont-gomery

Boone

Hamilton

Madison

MUNCIE

Delaware

Randolph

Indianapolis-Carmel-Muncie

Putnam

Hendricks

Marion

INDIANAPOLIS-CARMEL-ANDERSON

Hancock

New Castle

Henry

Wayne

Richmond

Richmond-Connersville

TERRE HAUTE

Vigo

Clay

Owen

BLOOMINGTON

Morgan

Johnson

Shelby

Rush

Fayette

Union

Connersville

Franklin

Butler

Warren

CINCINNATI

Hamilton

Clermont

Sullivan

Monroe

Brown

COLUMBUS

Bartholomew

Decatur

Greens-burg

Ripley

Dearborn

Ohio

Boone

Kenton

Campbell

Brown

Bloomington-Bedford

Greene

Bedford

Lawrence

Seymour

Jackson

North Vernon

Jennings

Madison

Jefferson

Switzer-land

Gallatin

Grant

Pendle-ton

Bracken

Knox

Vincennes

Daviess

Washington

Martin

Orange

Washington

Scott

Clark

Oldham

Henry

Trimble

Cincinnati-Wilmington-Maysville

Gibson

Pike

Jasper

Dubois

Crawford

Harrison

Floyd

Jefferson

Shelby

Spencer

LOUISVILLE/JEFFERSON COUNTY

Posey

Vander-burgh

Warrick

Spencer

Perry

Bullitt

EVANSVILLE

Henderson

KENTUCKY

Louisville/Jefferson County--Elizabethtown--Madison

N

0 10 20 30 40 Kilometers

0 10 20 30 40 Miles

LEGEND

Kokomo-Peru	Combined Statistical Area
MUNCIE	Metropolitan Statistical Area
Peru	Micropolitan Statistical Area
Gary	Metropolitan Division
OHIO	State or Statistical Equivalent
Jay	County or Statistical Equivalent
Lake Michigan	Coastline

CBSA boundaries and names are as of February 2013. All other boundaries and names are as of January 1, 2012.

IOWA - Core Based Statistical Areas (CBSAs) and Counties

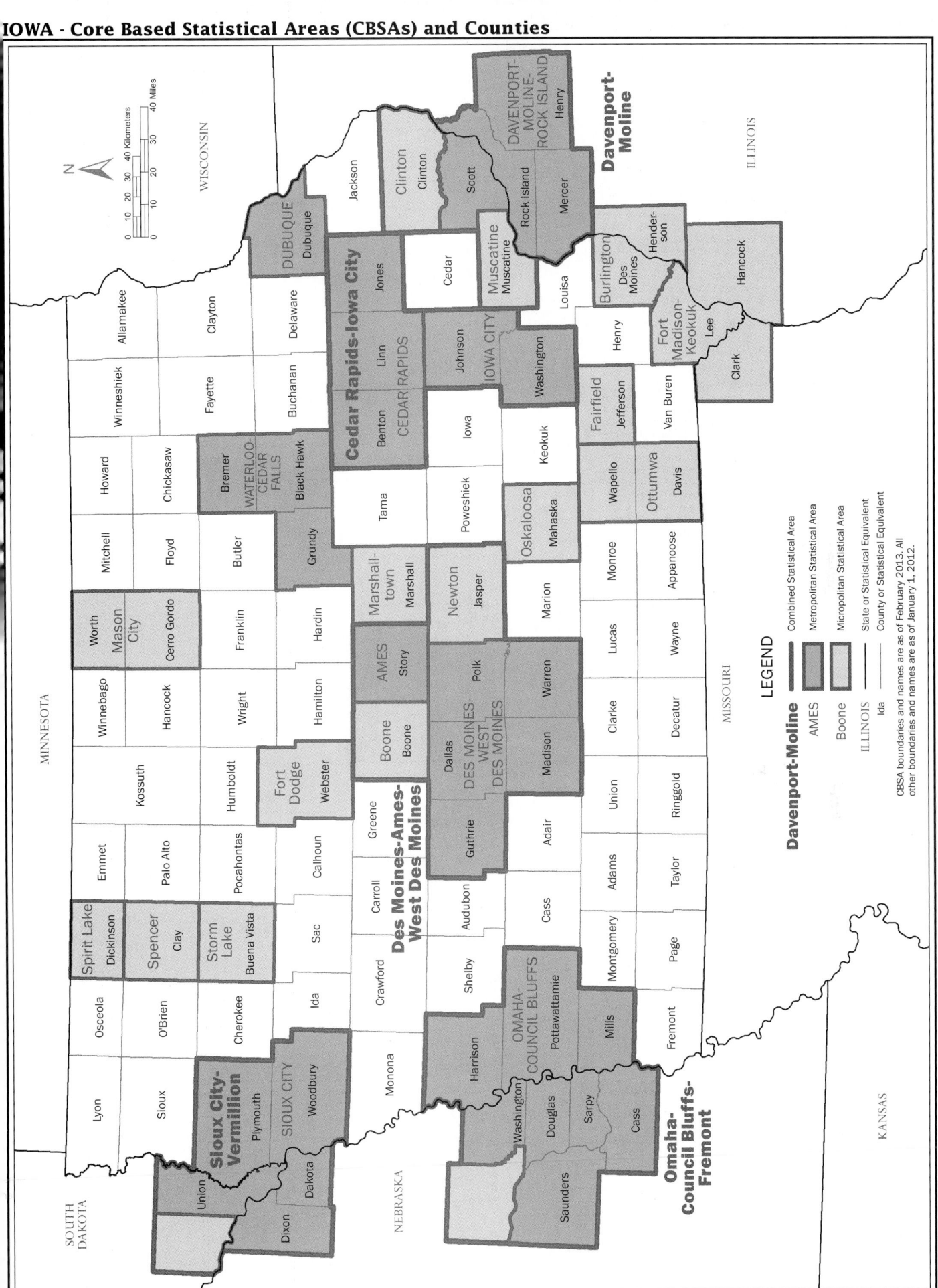

U.S. DEPARTMENT OF COMMERCE Economics and Statistics Administration U.S. Census Bureau

KANSAS - Core Based Statistical Areas (CBSAs) and Counties

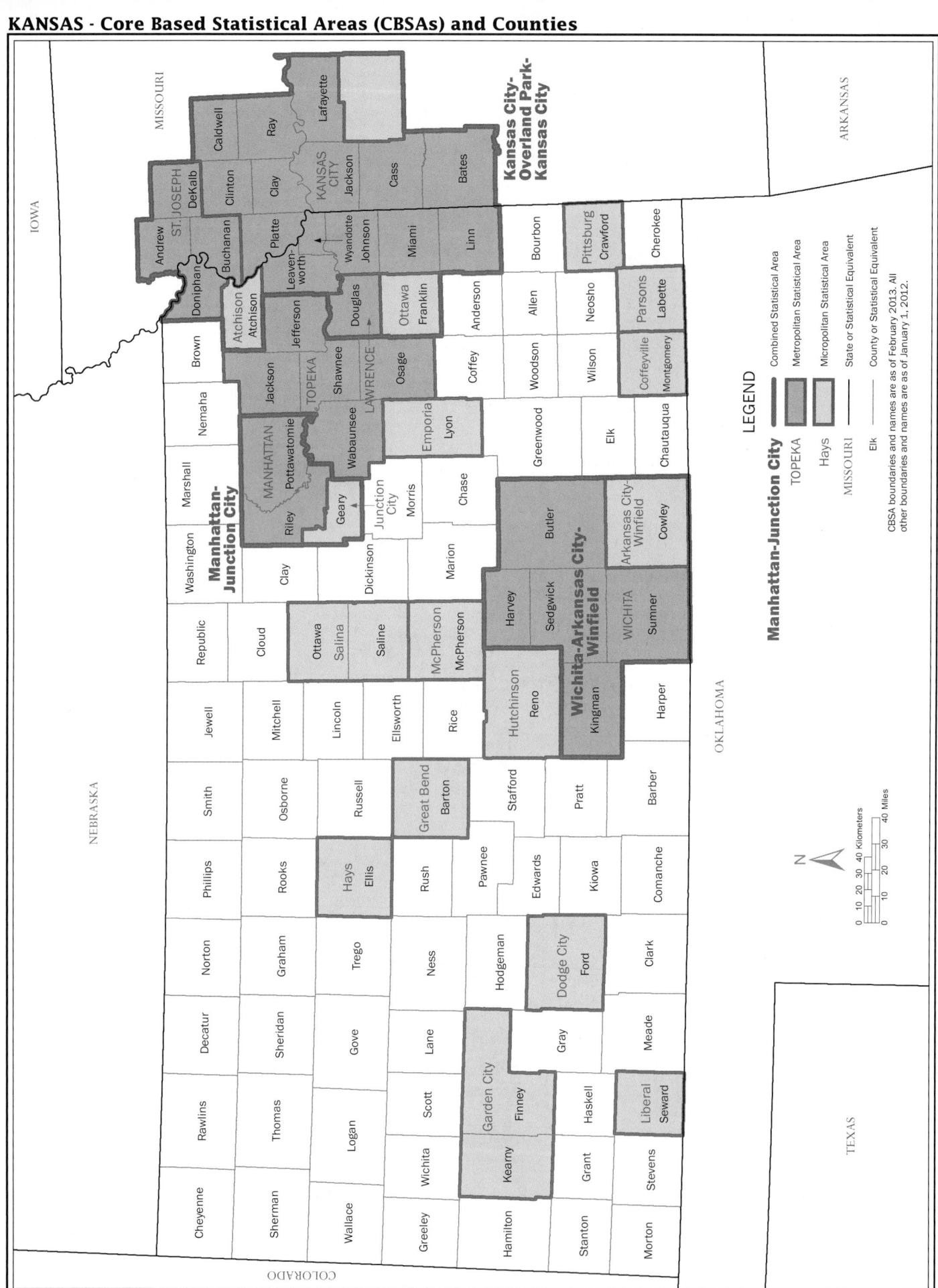

U.S. DEPARTMENT OF COMMERCE Economics and Statistics Administration U.S. Census Bureau

KENTUCKY - Core Based Statistical Areas (CBSAs) and Counties

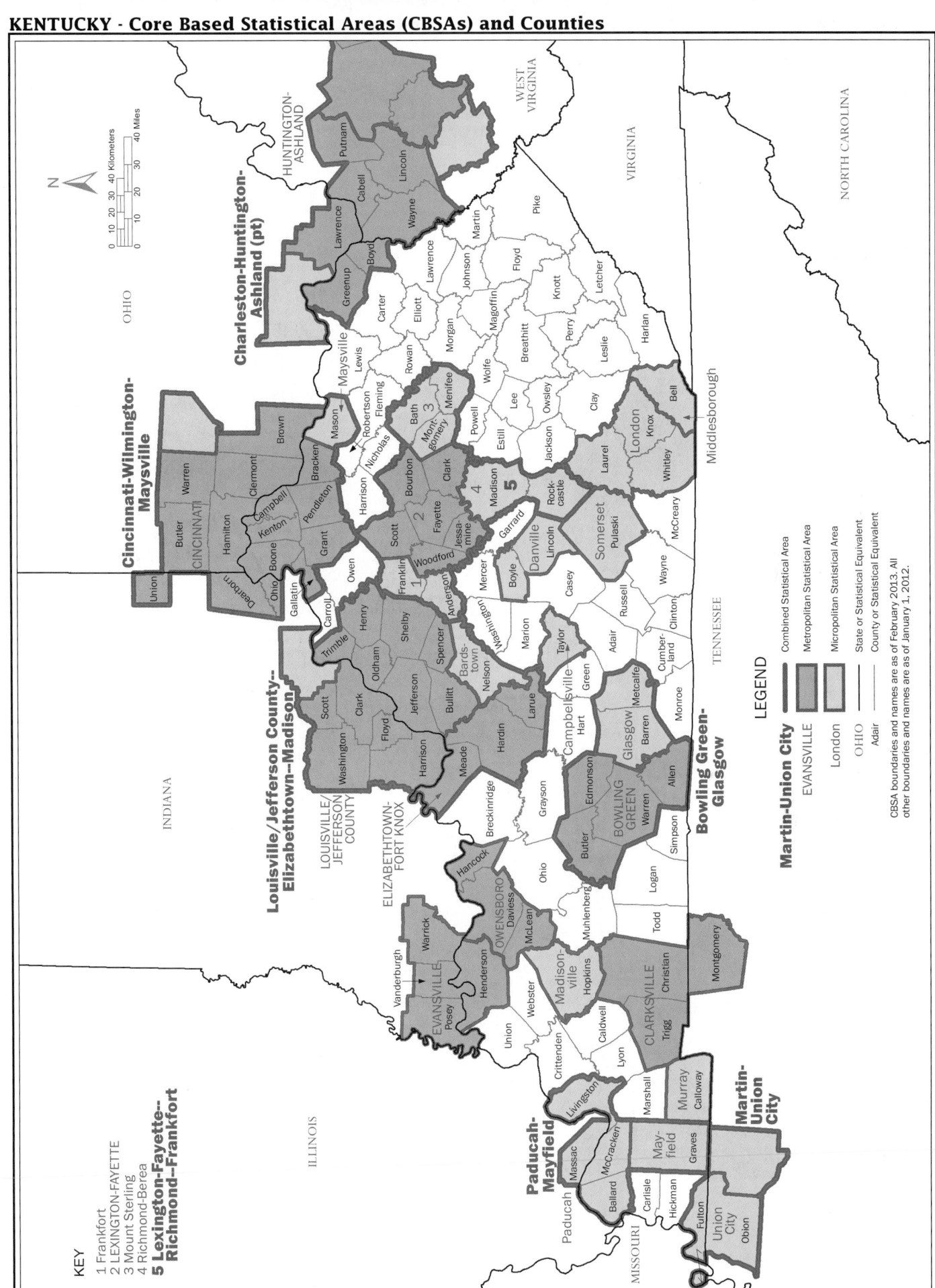

KEY
1 Frankfort
2 LEXINGTON-FAYETTE
3 Mount Sterling
4 Richmond-Berea
5 **Lexington-Fayette--Richmond--Frankfort**

LEGEND

Combined Statistical Area

Metropolitan Statistical Area

Micropolitan Statistical Area

State or Statistical Equivalent

County or Statistical Equivalent

Martin-Union City
EVANSVILLE

London

OHIO

Adair

CBSA boundaries and names are as of February 2013. All other boundaries and names are as of January 1, 2012.

U.S. DEPARTMENT OF COMMERCE Economics and Statistics Administration U.S. Census Bureau

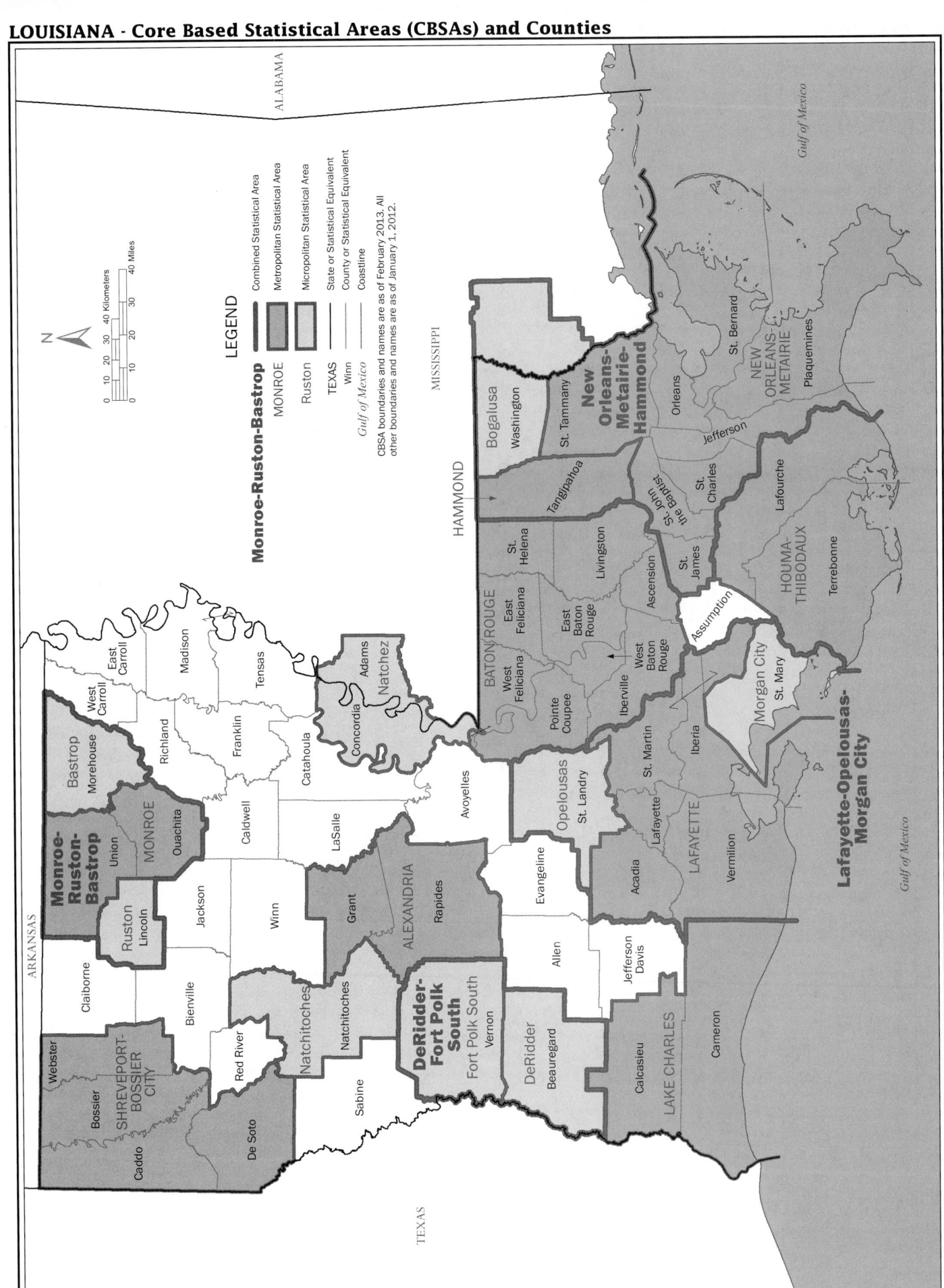

MAINE - Core Based Statistical Areas (CBSAs) and Counties

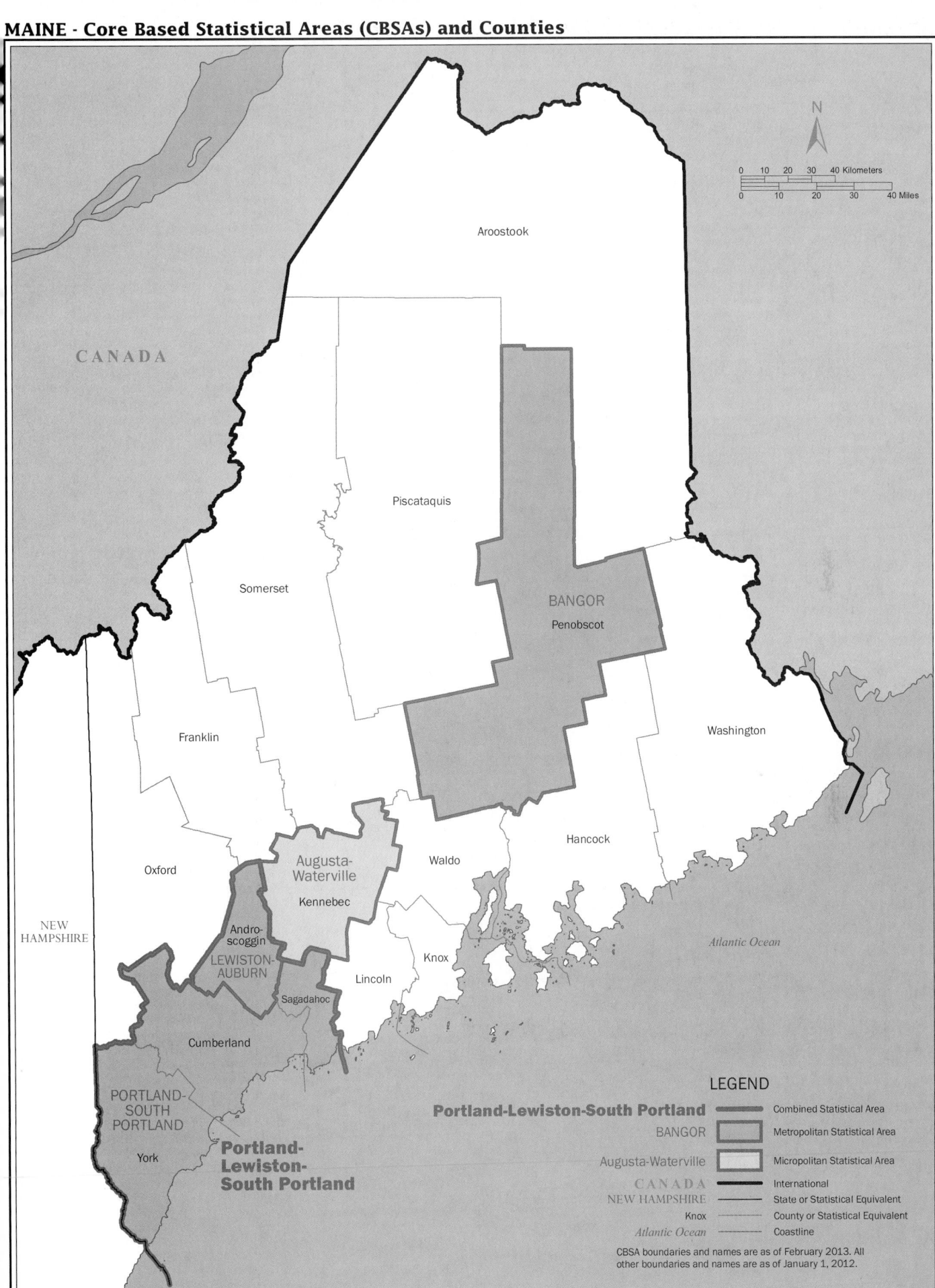

LEGEND

Portland-Lewiston-South Portland	Combined Statistical Area
BANGOR	Metropolitan Statistical Area
Augusta-Waterville	Micropolitan Statistical Area
CANADA	International
NEW HAMPSHIRE	State or Statistical Equivalent
Knox	County or Statistical Equivalent
Atlantic Ocean	Coastline

CBSA boundaries and names are as of February 2013. All other boundaries and names are as of January 1, 2012.

U.S. DEPARTMENT OF COMMERCE Economics and Statistics Administration U.S. Census Bureau

MARYLAND - Core Based Statistical Areas (CBSAs) and Counties

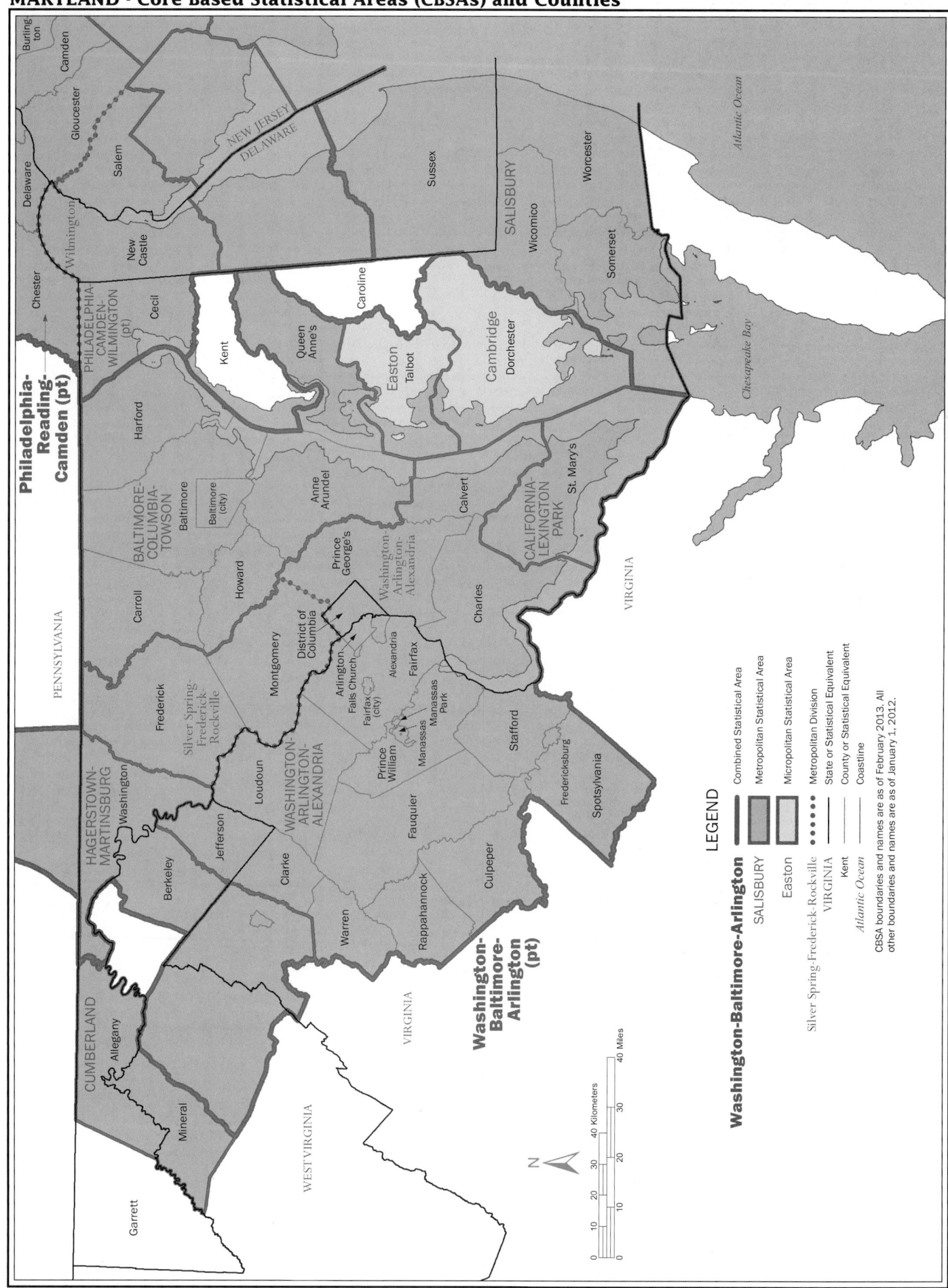

U.S. DEPARTMENT OF COMMERCE Economics and Statistics Administration U.S. Census Bureau

MISSOURI - Core Based Statistical Areas (CBSAs) and Counties

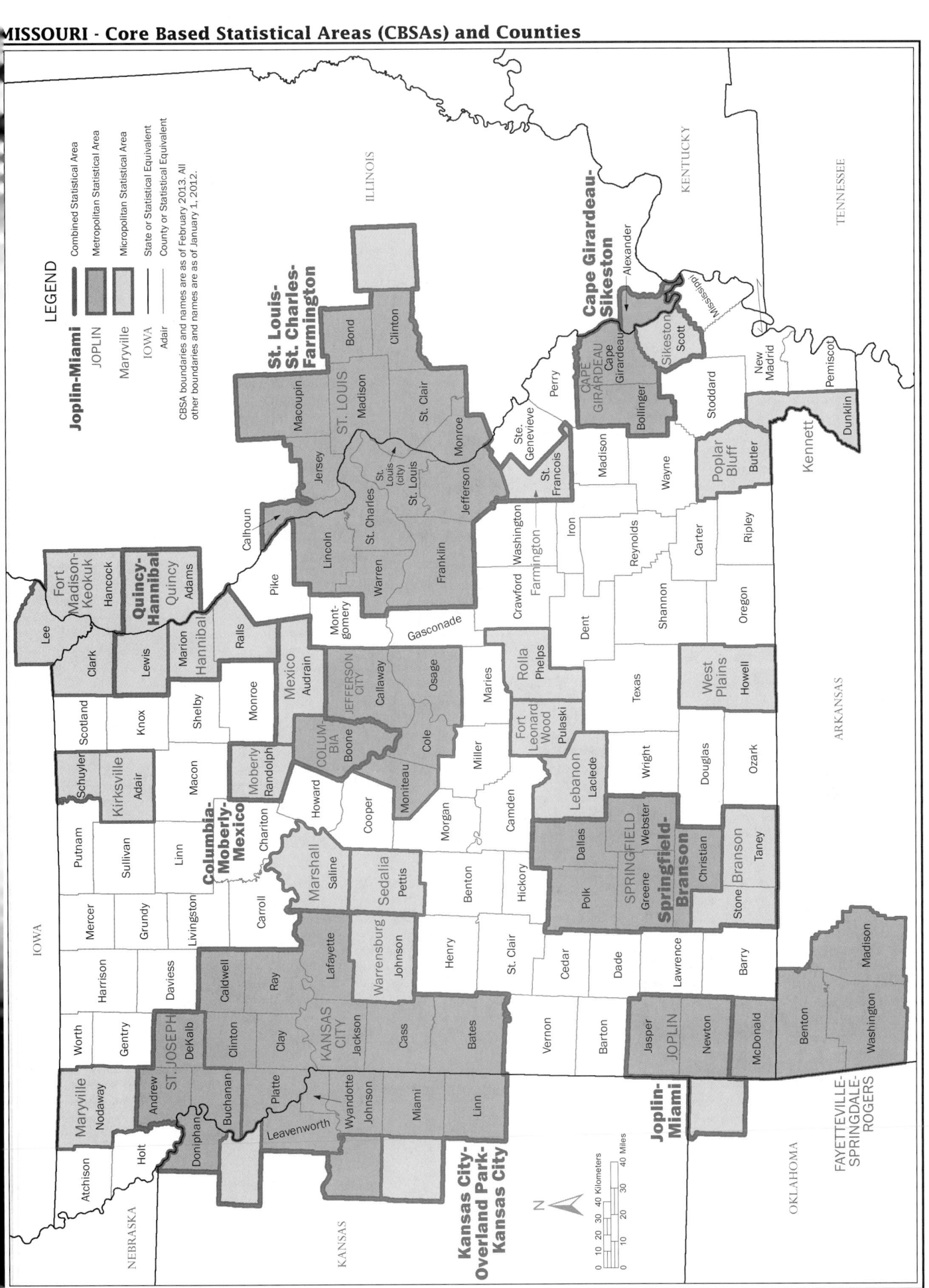

MONTANA - Core Based Statistical Areas (CBSAs) and Counties

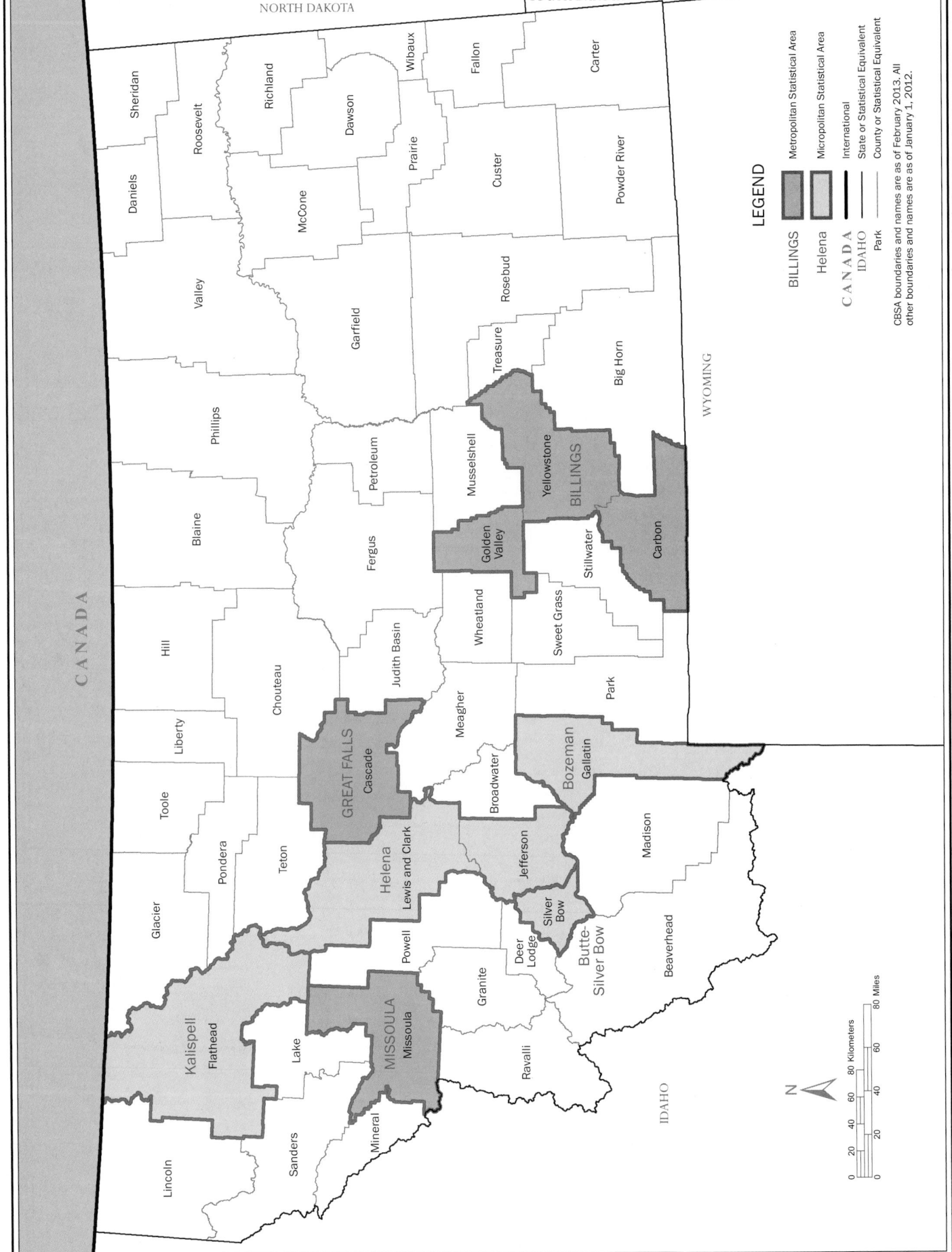

U.S. DEPARTMENT OF COMMERCE Economics and Statistics Administration U.S. Census Bureau

Appendix D

NEBRASKA - Core Based Statistical Areas (CBSAs) and Counties

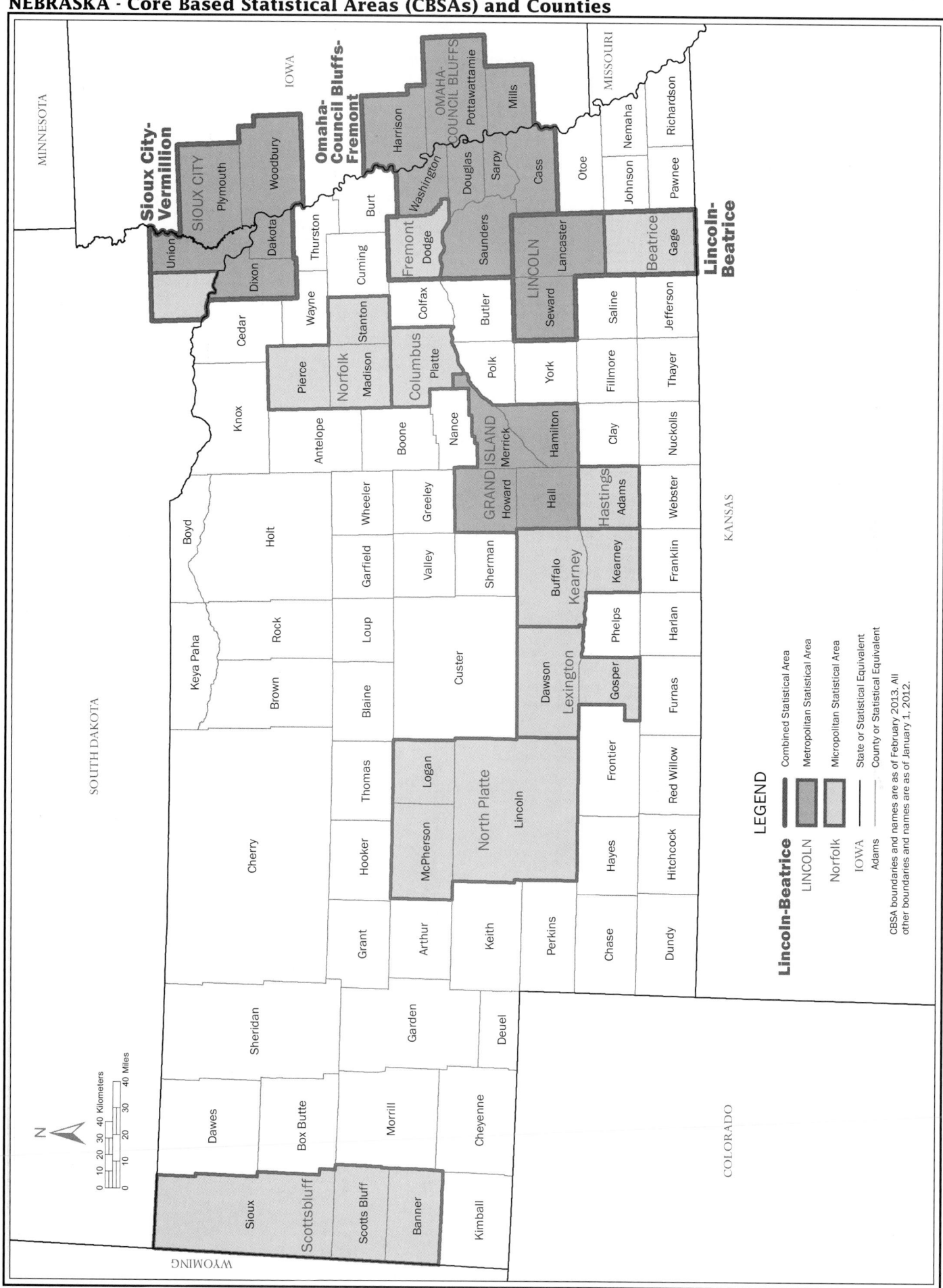

LEGEND

Lincoln-Beatrice Combined Statistical Area

LINCOLN Metropolitan Statistical Area

Norfolk Micropolitan Statistical Area

IOWA State or Statistical Equivalent

Adams County or Statistical Equivalent

CBSA boundaries and names are as of February 2013. All other boundaries and names are as of January 1, 2012.

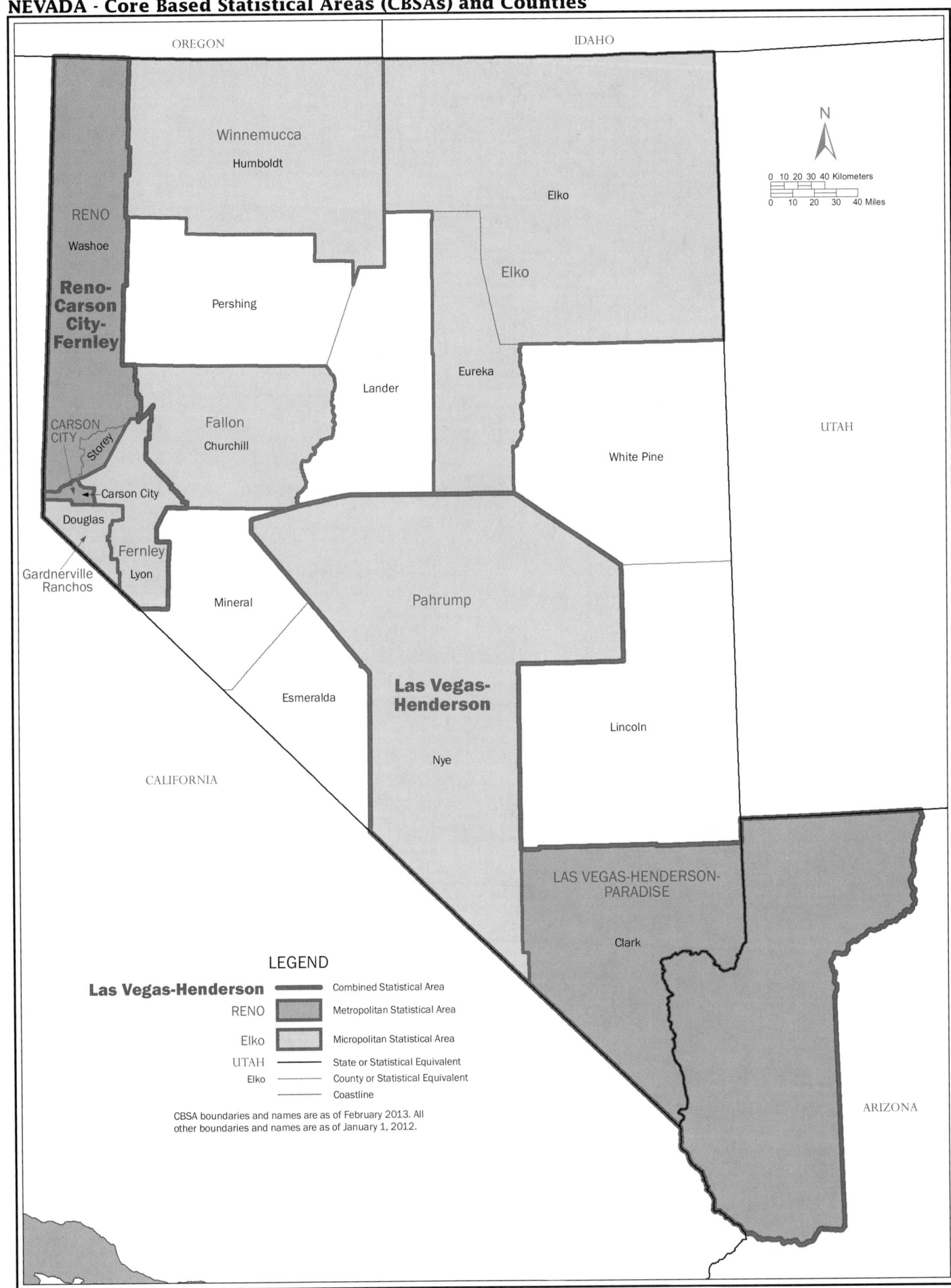

OREGON

IDAHO

N

0 10 20 30 40 Kilometers
0 10 20 30 40 Miles

Winnemucca

Humboldt

Elko

RENO

Washoe

Elko

**Reno-
Carson
City-
Fernley**

Pershing

CARSON
CITY

Storey

Lander

Eureka

UTAH

Fallon

Churchill

White Pine

Carson City

Douglas

Fernley

Gardnerville
Ranchos

Lyon

Pahrump

Mineral

Esmeralda

**Las Vegas-
Henderson**

Lincoln

CALIFORNIA

Nye

LAS VEGAS-HENDERSON-
PARADISE

Clark

ARIZONA

LEGEND

Las Vegas-Henderson ▬▬▬ Combined Statistical Area

RENO ▢ Metropolitan Statistical Area

Elko ▢ Micropolitan Statistical Area

UTAH ▬▬ State or Statistical Equivalent

Elko ─── County or Statistical Equivalent

────── Coastline

CBSA boundaries and names are as of February 2013. All
other boundaries and names are as of January 1, 2012.

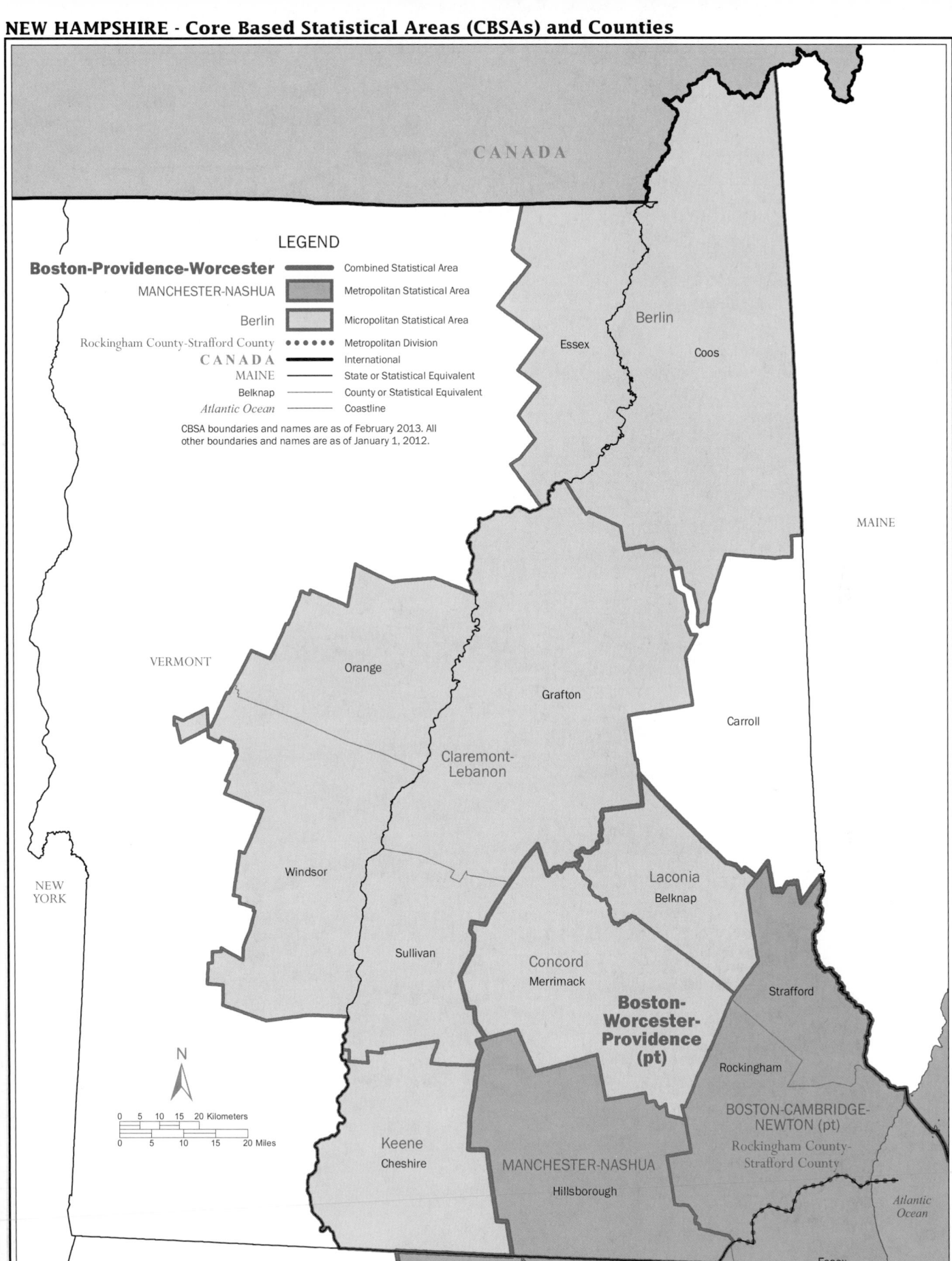

LEGEND

Boston-Providence-Worcester — Combined Statistical Area

MANCHESTER-NASHUA — Metropolitan Statistical Area

Berlin — Micropolitan Statistical Area

Rockingham County-Strafford County ••••• Metropolitan Division

CANADA — International

MAINE — State or Statistical Equivalent

Belknap — County or Statistical Equivalent

Atlantic Ocean — Coastline

CBSA boundaries and names are as of February 2013. All other boundaries and names are as of January 1, 2012.

CANADA

Essex

Berlin

Coos

MAINE

VERMONT

Orange

Grafton

Carroll

Claremont-Lebanon

Windsor

Laconia

Belknap

NEW YORK

Sullivan

Concord

Merrimack

Boston-Worcester-Providence (pt)

Strafford

Rockingham

BOSTON-CAMBRIDGE-NEWTON (pt)

Rockingham County-Strafford County

N

0 5 10 15 20 Kilometers

0 5 10 15 20 Miles

Keene

Cheshire

MANCHESTER-NASHUA

Hillsborough

Atlantic Ocean

MASSACHUSETTS

Essex

Middlesex

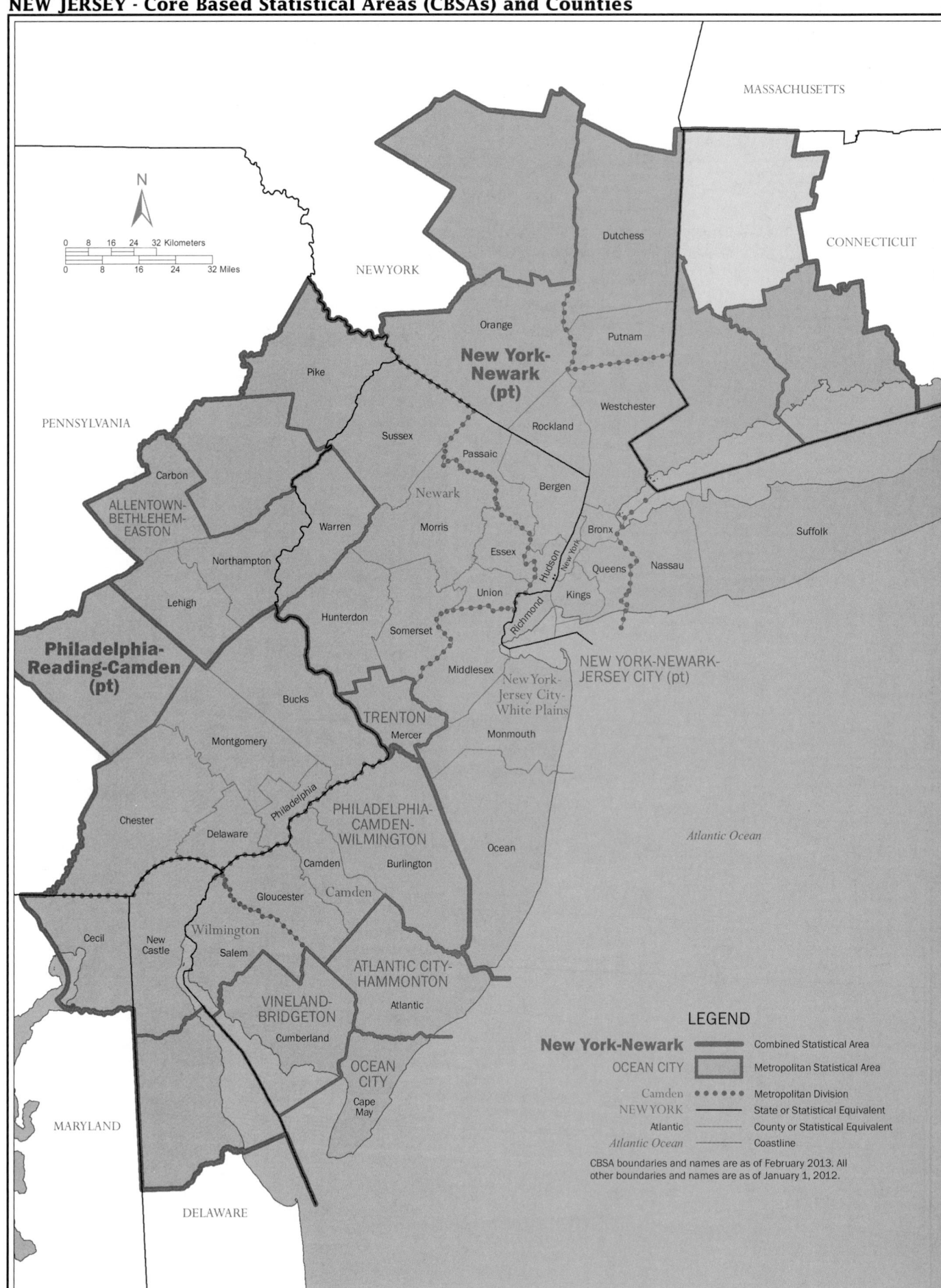

NEW MEXICO - Core Based Statistical Areas (CBSAs) and Counties

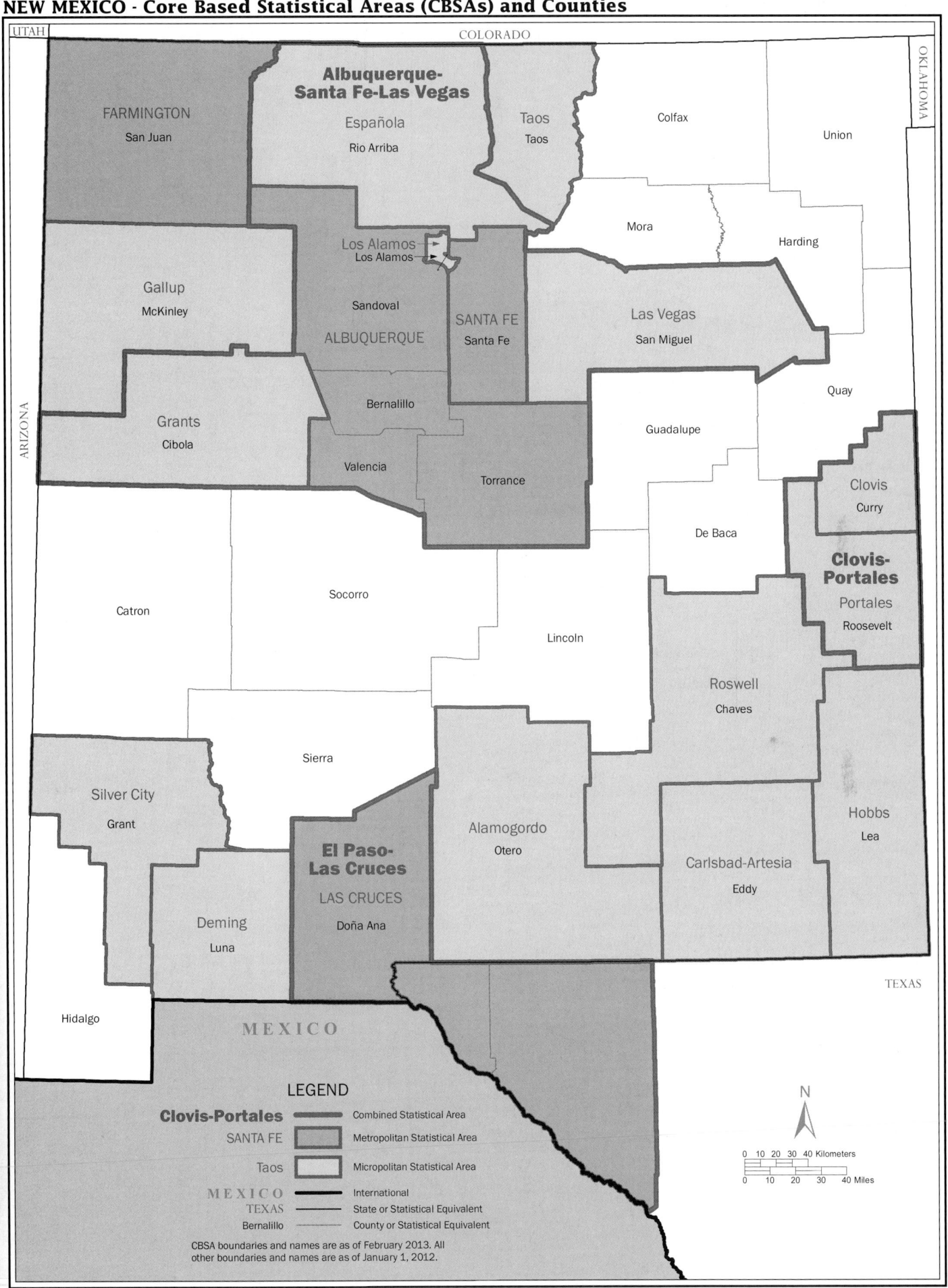

Albuquerque-Santa Fe-Las Vegas

FARMINGTON
San Juan

Española
Rio Arriba

Taos
Taos

Colfax

Union

Los Alamos
Los Alamos

Gallup
McKinley

Sandoval

SANTA FE
Santa Fe

ALBUQUERQUE

Las Vegas
San Miguel

Mora

Harding

Bernalillo

Quay

Grants
Cibola

Guadalupe

Clovis
Curry

Valencia

Torrance

De Baca

Clovis-Portales

Catron

Socorro

Portales
Roosevelt

Lincoln

Sierra

Roswell
Chaves

Silver City
Grant

Alamogordo
Otero

Hobbs
Lea

Deming
Luna

El Paso-Las Cruces

LAS CRUCES
Doña Ana

Carlsbad-Artesia
Eddy

Hidalgo

MEXICO

TEXAS

UTAH

COLORADO

ARIZONA

OKLAHOMA

N

LEGEND

Clovis-Portales	Combined Statistical Area
SANTA FE	Metropolitan Statistical Area
Taos	Micropolitan Statistical Area
MEXICO	International
TEXAS	State or Statistical Equivalent
Bernalillo	County or Statistical Equivalent

0 10 20 30 40 Kilometers
0 10 20 30 40 Miles

CBSA boundaries and names are as of February 2013. All
other boundaries and names are as of January 1, 2012.

U.S. DEPARTMENT OF COMMERCE Economics and Statistics Administration U.S. Census Bureau

NEW YORK - Core Based Statistical Areas (CBSAs) and Counties

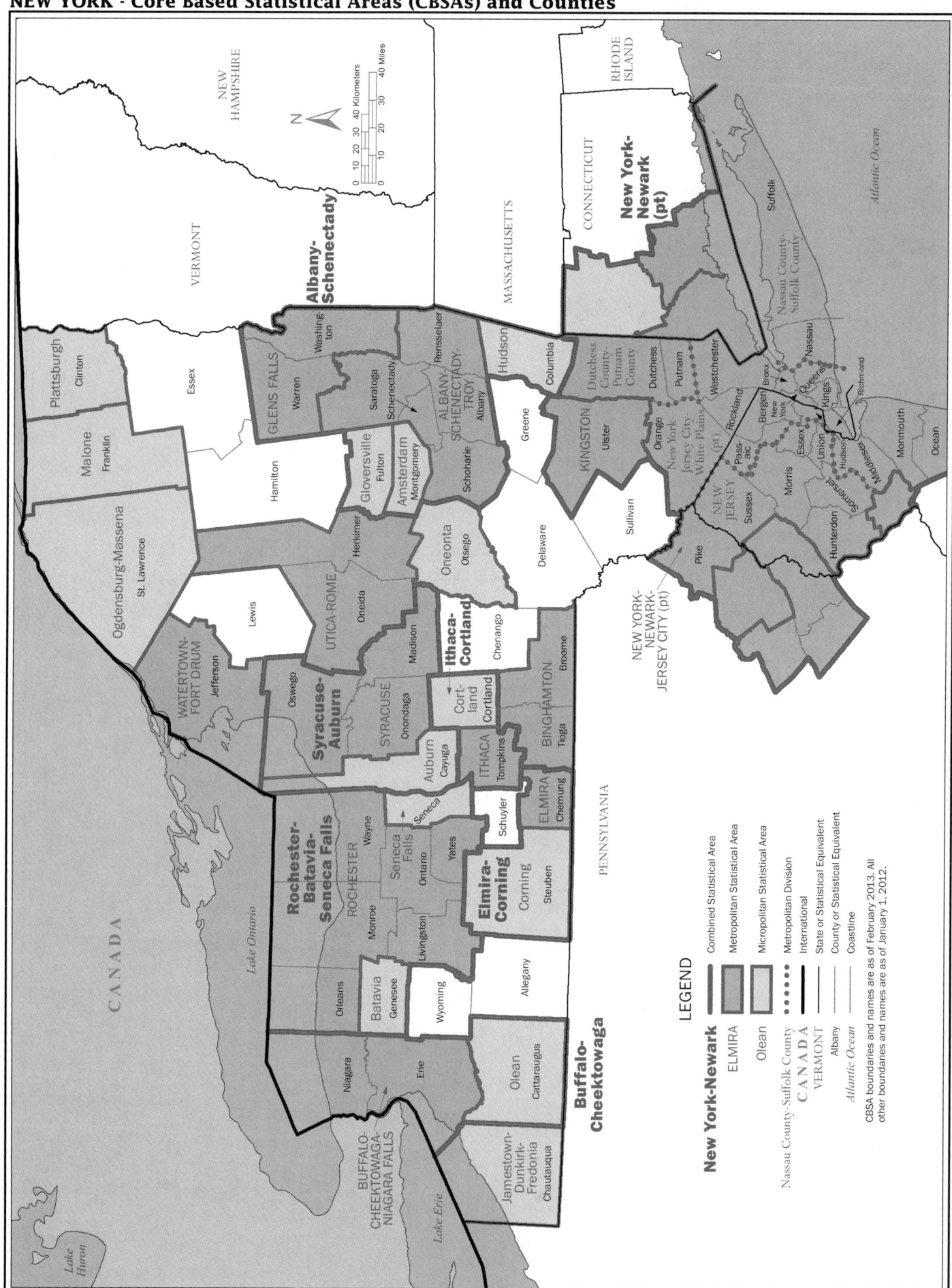

U.S. DEPARTMENT OF COMMERCE Economics and Statistics Administration U.S. Census Bureau

LEGEND

New York-Newark

ELMIRA — Combined Statistical Area

Olean — Metropolitan Statistical Area

Nassau County-Suffolk County — Micropolitan Statistical Area

CANADA — Metropolitan Division

VERMONT — International

Albany — State or Statistical Equivalent

Atlantic Ocean — County or Statistical Equivalent

— Coastline

CBSA boundaries and names are as of February 2013. All other boundaries and names are as of January 1, 2012.

Virginia Beach-Norfolk

VIRGINIA BEACH-NORFOLK-NEWPORT NEWS

Greenville-Washington

New Bern-Morehead City

Rocky Mount-Wilson-Roanoke Rapids

Raleigh-Durham-Chapel Hill

Greensboro—Winston-Salem—High Point

GREENSBORO-HIGH POINT

Fayetteville-Lumberton-Laurinburg

Myrtle Beach-Conway

MYRTLE BEACH-CONWAY-NORTH MYRTLE BEACH

Charlotte-Concord

Asheville-Brevard

Atlantic Ocean

Chesapeake Bay

VIRGINIA

WEST VIRGINIA

KENTUCKY

TENNESSEE

SOUTH CAROLINA

GEORGIA

County/city labels:
Mathews, Gloucester, Poquoson, Hampton, Norfolk, Portsmouth, Chesapeake, Suffolk, Isle of Wight, York, Newport News, James City, Williamsburg, Virginia Beach, Currituck, Camden, Pasquotank, Perquimans, Gates, Chowan, Kill Devil Hills, Dare, Hyde, Elizabeth City, Tyrrell, Washington, Bertie, Hertford, Northampton, Halifax, Warren, Hender-son, Vance, Oxford, Granville, Franklin, Wake, Durham, Person, Caswell, Orange, Alamance, BURLINGTON, Chatham, Rockingham, Guilford, Randolph, Stokes, Forsyth, WINSTON-SALEM, Davidson, Davie, Yadkin, Surry, Mount Airy, Alleghany, Ashe, North Wilkesboro, Wilkes, Alexander, Iredell, Catawba, Caldwell, Boone, Watauga, Avery, Burke, Mitchell, Yancey, Madison, ASHEVILLE, Buncombe, Haywood, Henderson, Transyl-vania, Brevard, Jackson, Cullowhee, Swain, Macon, Graham, Cherokee, Clay, Polk, Rutherford, Forest City, McDowell, Marion, Cleveland, Shelby, Lincoln, Gaston, Mecklenburg, York, CHARLOTTE-CONCORD-GASTONIA, Chester, Lancaster, Union, Stanly, Cabarrus, Albemarle, Rowan, Montgomery, Moore, Pinehurst-Southern Pines, Sanford, Lee, Harnett, Dunn, Johnston, Nash, ROCKY MOUNT, Edgecombe, Wilson, GOLDS-BORO, Wayne, Greene, Pitt, GREEN-VILLE, Martin, Beaufort, Washington, Pamlico, Morehead City, Carteret, NEW BERN, Craven, Jones, Lenoir, Kinston, Duplin, Onslow, JACKSON-VILLE, Pender, WILMINGTON, New Hanover, Brunswick, Columbus, Bladen, Sampson, Cumberland, FAYETTE-VILLE, Hoke, Robeson, Lumberton, Scot-land, Laurinburg, Rich-mond, Rockingham, Anson, Horry

KEY
1 Hickory-Lenoir
2 HICKORY-LENOIR-MORGANTOWN

N

0 10 20 30 40 Miles
0 10 20 30 40 Kilometers

LEGEND

Charlotte-Concord — Combined Statistical Area
ASHEVILLE — Metropolitan Statistical Area
Boone — Micropolitan Statistical Area
VIRGINIA — State or Statistical Equivalent
Ashe — County or Statistical Equivalent
Atlantic Ocean — Coastline

CBSA boundaries and names are as of February 2013. All other boundaries and names are as of January 1, 2012.

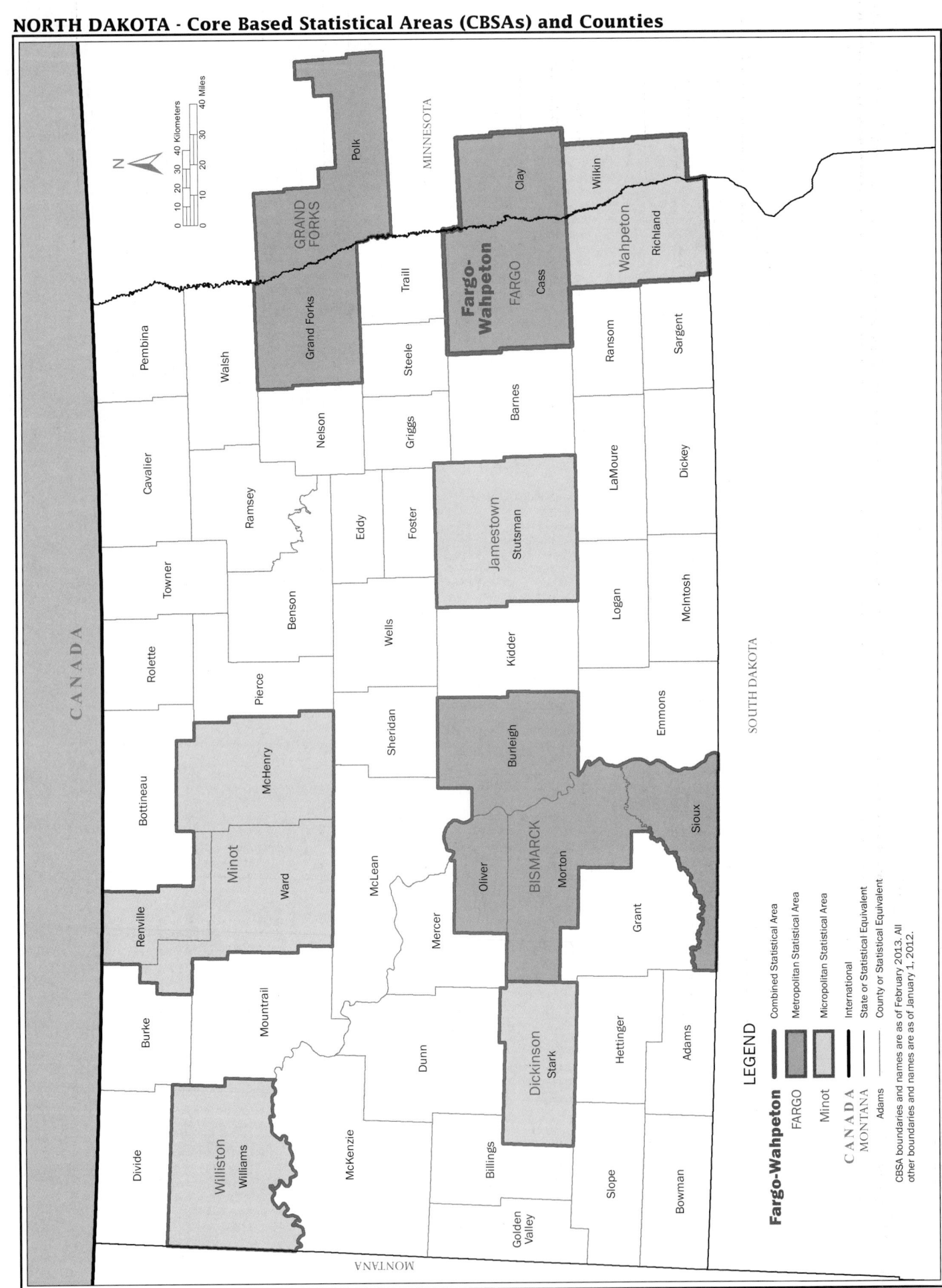

OHIO - Core Based Statistical Areas (CBSAs) and Counties

CANADA

MICHIGAN

PENNSYLVANIA

Lake Erie

Cleveland-Akron-Canton

Toledo-Port Clinton

Williams

Fulton

Lucas

Ottawa

Port Clinton

Erie

Sandusky

Lorain

CLEVELAND-ELYRIA

Cuyahoga

Lake

Geauga

Ashtabula

Ashtabula

Youngstown-Warren

YOUNGSTOWN-WARREN-BOARDMAN

Trumbull

Mercer

Defiance

Defiance

Henry

TOLEDO

Wood

Fremont

Sandusky

Sandusky

Mansfield-Ashland-Bucyrus

Medina

AKRON

Summit

Portage

Mahoning

Paulding

Putnam

Findlay-Tiffin

Findlay

Hancock

Tiffin

Seneca

Norwalk

Huron

CANTON-MASSILLON

Stark

Salem

Columbiana

Lima-Van Wert-Celina

Van Wert

Van Wert

LIMA

Allen

Wyandot

Bucyrus

Crawford

MANS-FIELD

Richland

Ash-land

Ashland

Wooster

Wayne

Pittsburgh-New Castle-Weirton (pt)

Hancock

Brooke

Jefferson

WEIRTON-STEUBENVILLE

Celina

Mercer

Hardin

Marion

Marion

Morrow

Holmes

Tuscarawas

New Philadelphia-Dover

Carroll

Harrison

Ohio

INDIANA

Wapakoneta

Auglaize

Bellefontaine

Logan

Union

Delaware

Knox

Mount Vernon

Coshocton

Coshocton

WHEELING

Belmont

Greenville

Darke

Sidney

Shelby

Urbana

Champaign

Columbus-Marion-Zanesville

COLUMBUS

Licking

Cambridge

Guernsey

Marshall

DAYTON

Miami

SPRINGFIELD

Clark

Madison

Franklin

Zanesville

Muskingum

Noble

Monroe

Preble

Dayton-Springfield-Sidney

Montgomery

Greene

Washington Court House

Fairfield

Perry

Morgan

Marietta

Washington

Parkersburg-Marietta-Vienna

Union

Cincinnati-Wilmington-Maysville

Butler

Warren

Wilmington

Clinton

Fayette

Pickaway

Hocking

Athens

Athens

CINCINNATI

Hamilton

Highland

Chillicothe

Ross

Vinton

Meigs

WEST VIRGINIA

Dearborn

Boone

Kenton

Campbell

Clermont

Brown

Pike

Jackson

Jackson

Point Pleasant

Ohio

Gallatin

Grant

Pendleton

Bracken

Adams

Portsmouth

Scioto

Gallia

Mason

KENTUCKY

Greenup

Boyd

Lawrence

Putnam

Charleston-Huntington-Ashland

HUNTINGTON-ASHLAND

Cabell

Lincoln

Wayne

VIRGINIA

LEGEND

Findlay-Tiffin — Combined Statistical Area

AKRON — Metropolitan Statistical Area

Athens — Micropolitan Statistical Area

CANADA — International

INDIANA — State or Statistical Equivalent

Adams — County or Statistical Equivalent

Lake Erie — Coastline

CBSA boundaries and names are as of February 2013. All other boundaries based names are as of January 1, 2012.

0 10 20 30 40 Kilometers

0 10 20 30 40 Miles

N

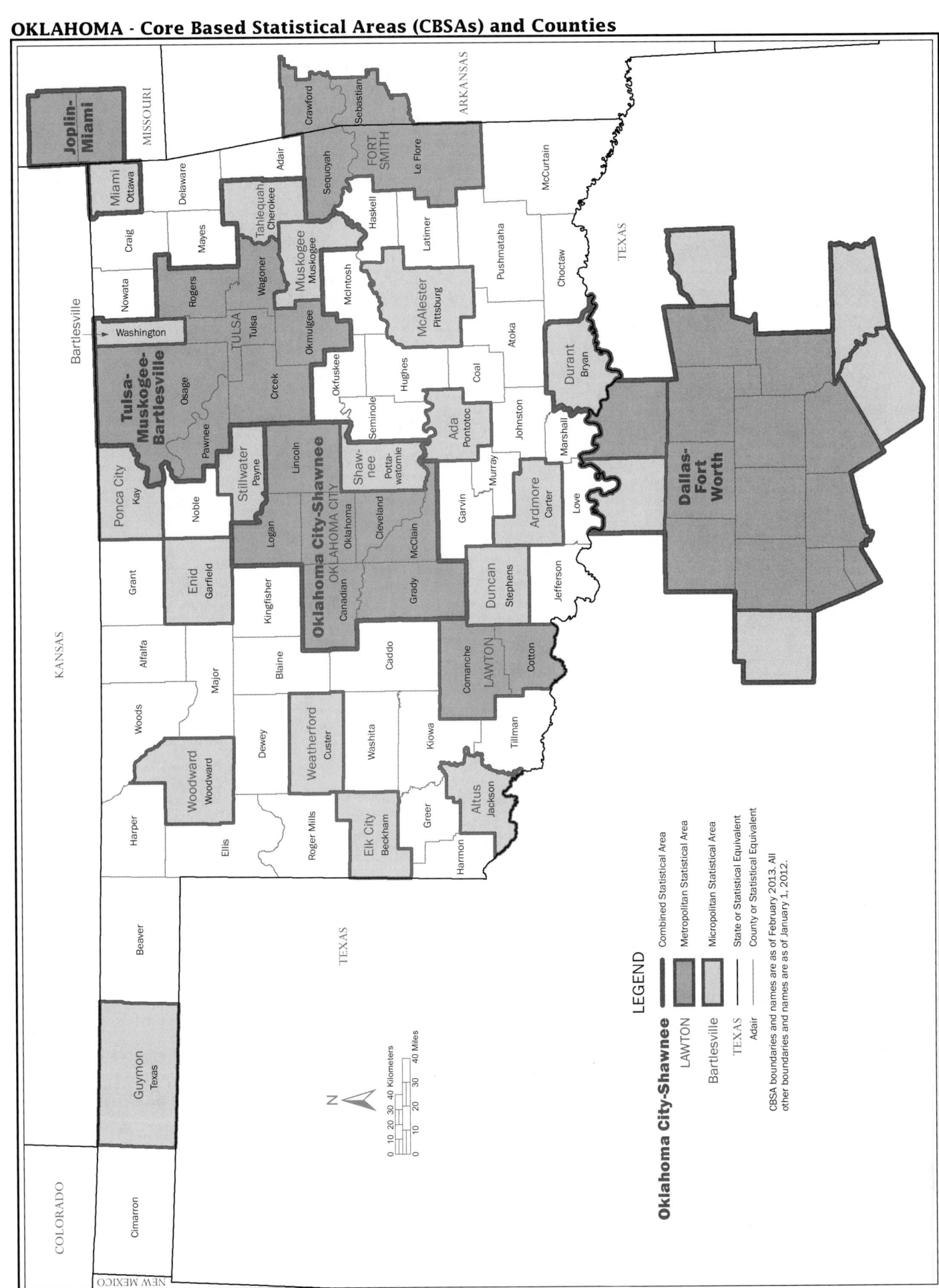

LEGEND

Oklahoma City-Shawnee — Combined Statistical Area

LAWTON — Metropolitan Statistical Area

Bartlesville — Micropolitan Statistical Area

TEXAS — State or Statistical Equivalent

Adair — County or Statistical Equivalent

CBSA boundaries and names are as of February 2013. All other boundaries and names are as of January 1, 2012.

0 10 20 30 40 Kilometers
0 10 20 30 40 Miles

N

OREGON - Core Based Statistical Areas (CBSAs) and Counties

IDAHO

NEVADA

CALIFORNIA

WASHINGTON

Boise City-Mountain Home-Ontario

Wallowa

Baker

La Grande
Union

Hermiston-Pendleton
Umatilla

Morrow

Grant

Harney

Ontario
Malheur

Payette

Gilliam

Sherman

Wheeler

Lake

Bend-Redmond-Prineville

Prineville
Crook

The Dalles
Wasco

Jefferson

BEND-REDMOND
Deschutes

Hood River
Hood River

Klamath Falls
Klamath

PORTLAND-VANCOUVER-HILLSBORO

Skamania

Clark

Multnomah

Portland-Vancouver-Salem

Clackamas

Marion

SALEM

ALBANY
Linn

EUGENE
Lane

Roseburg
Douglas

Medford-Grants Pass

MEDFORD
Jackson

Washington

Columbia

Yamhill

Polk

Benton

CORVALLIS

Astoria
Clatsop

Tillamook

Newport
Lincoln

Coos Bay
Coos

GRANTS PASS
Josephine

Brookings
Curry

Pacific Ocean

LEGEND

Medford-Grants Pass
Combined Statistical Area

ALBANY
Metropolitan Statistical Area

Brookings
Micropolitan Statistical Area

NEVADA
State or Statistical Equivalent

Baker
County or Statistical Equivalent

Pacific Ocean
Coastline

CBSA boundaries and names are as of February 2013. All other boundaries and names are as of January 1, 2012.

N

0 10 20 30 40 Kilometers
0 10 20 30 40 Miles

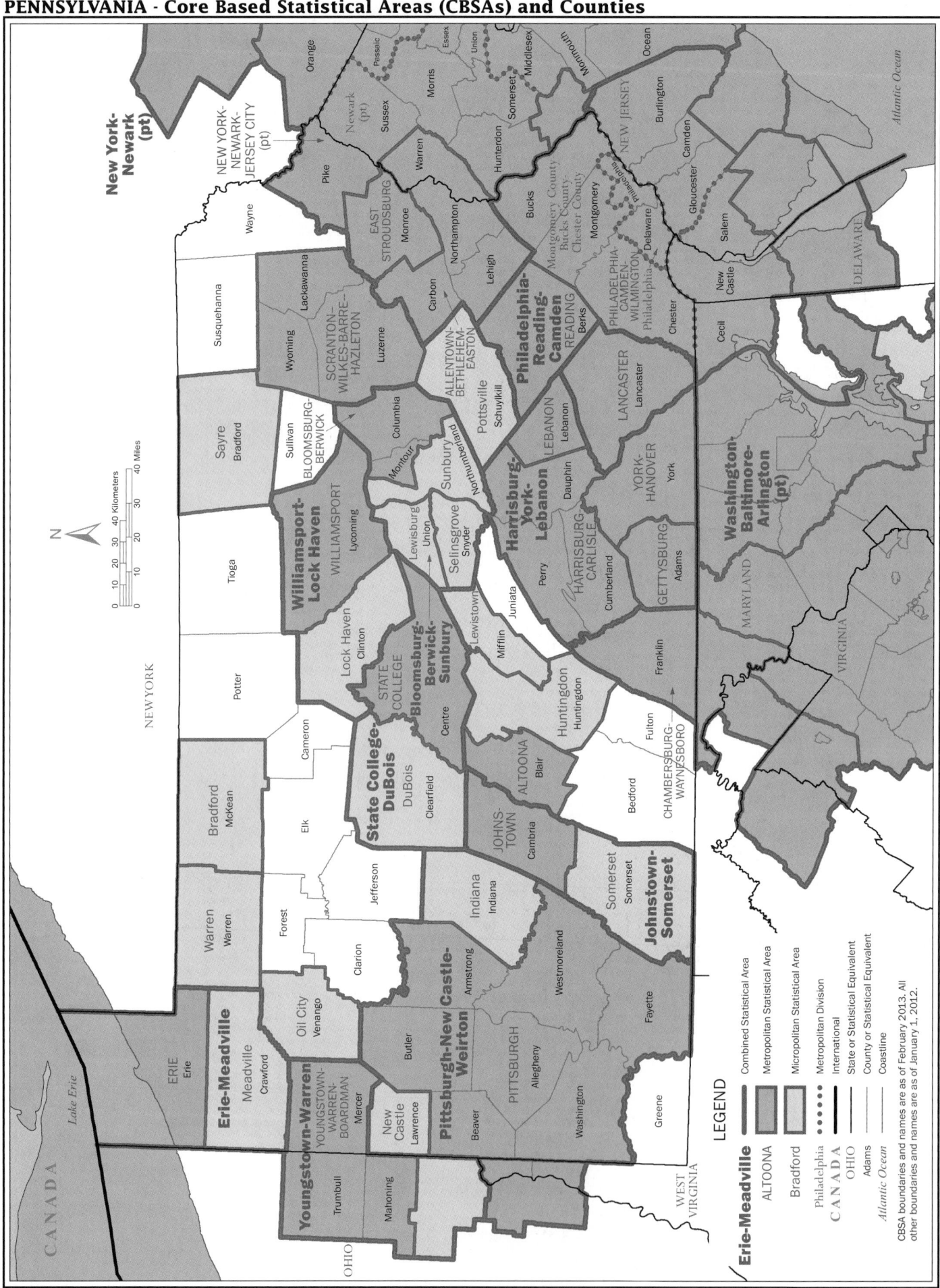

MASSACHUSETTS

Boston-Worcester-Providence (pt)

PROVIDENCE-WARWICK

Providence

Bristol

CONNECTICUT

Kent

Bristol

MASSACHUSETTS

Newport

Washington

N

0 2 4 6 8 Kilometers

0 2 4 6 8 Miles

Atlantic Ocean

LEGEND

Boston-Worcester-Providence	Combined Statistical Area
PROVIDENCE-WARWICK	Metropolitan Statistical Area
MASSACHUSETTS	State or Statistical Equivalent
Bristol	County or Statistical Equivalent
Atlantic Ocean	Coastline

CBSA boundaries and names are as of February 2013. All other boundaries and names are as of January 1, 2012.

SOUTH CAROLINA - Core Based Statistical Areas (CBSAs) and Counties

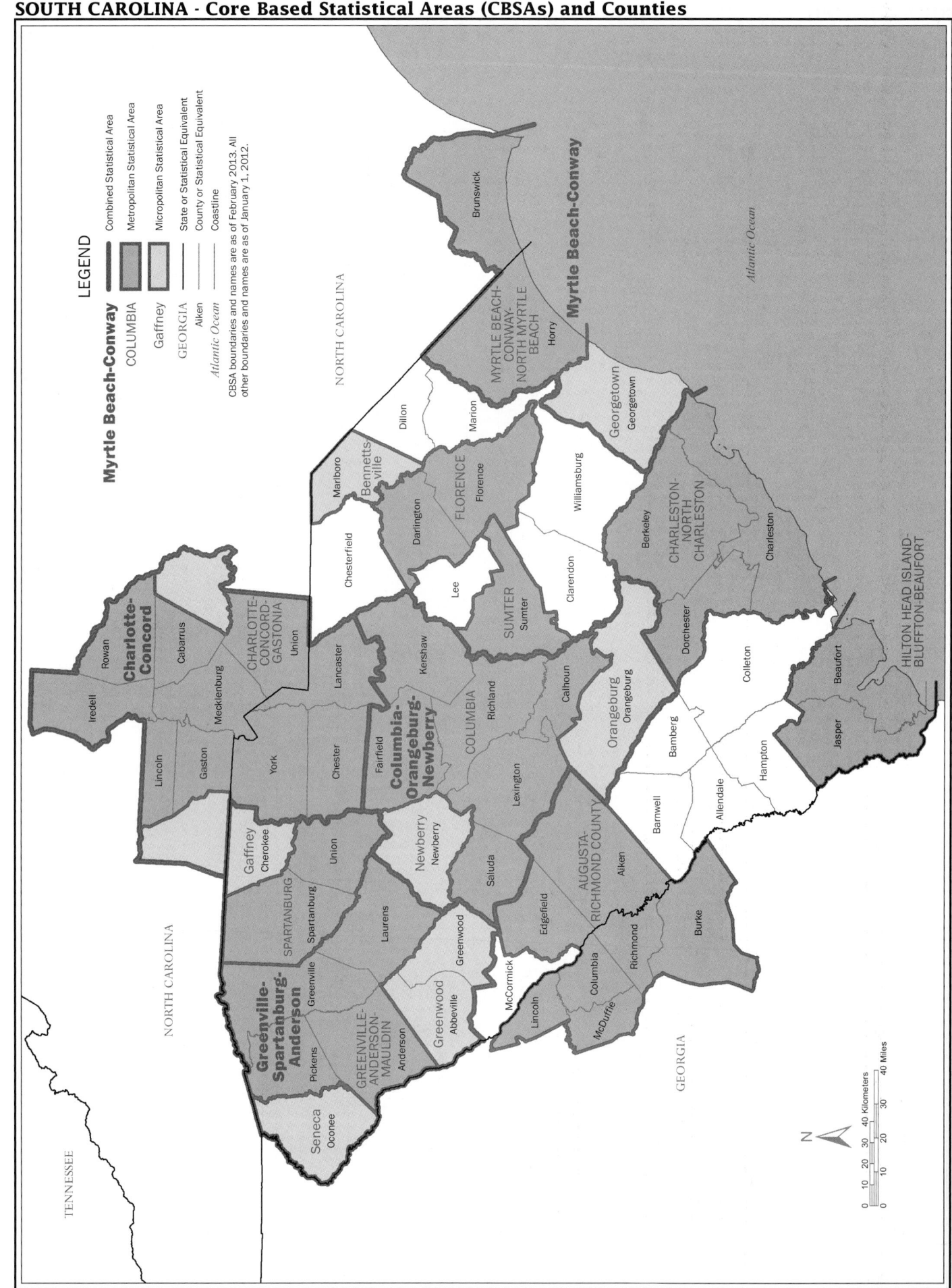

U.S. DEPARTMENT OF COMMERCE Economics and Statistics Administration U.S. Census Bureau

SOUTH DAKOTA - Core Based Statistical Areas (CBSAs) and Counties

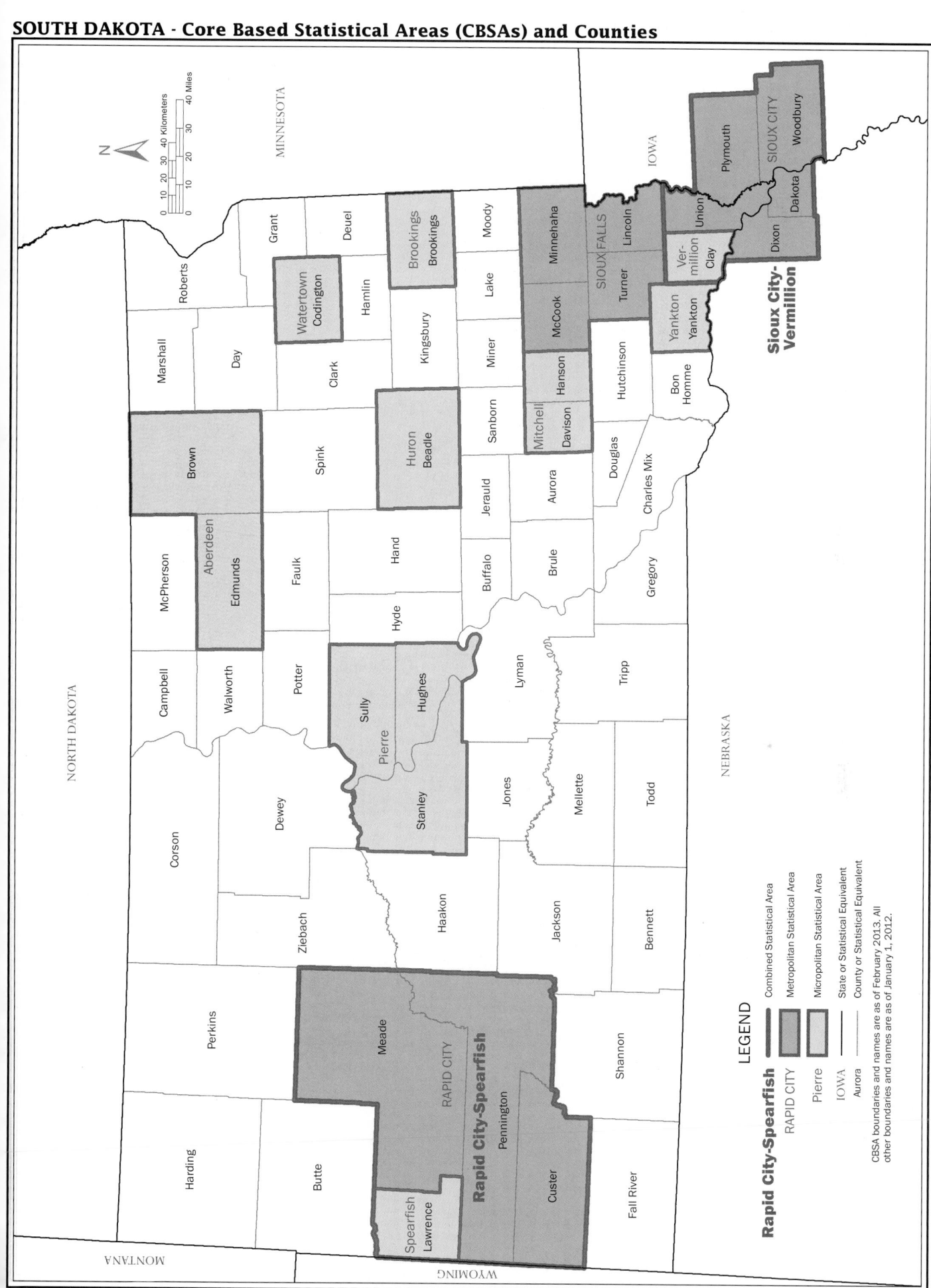

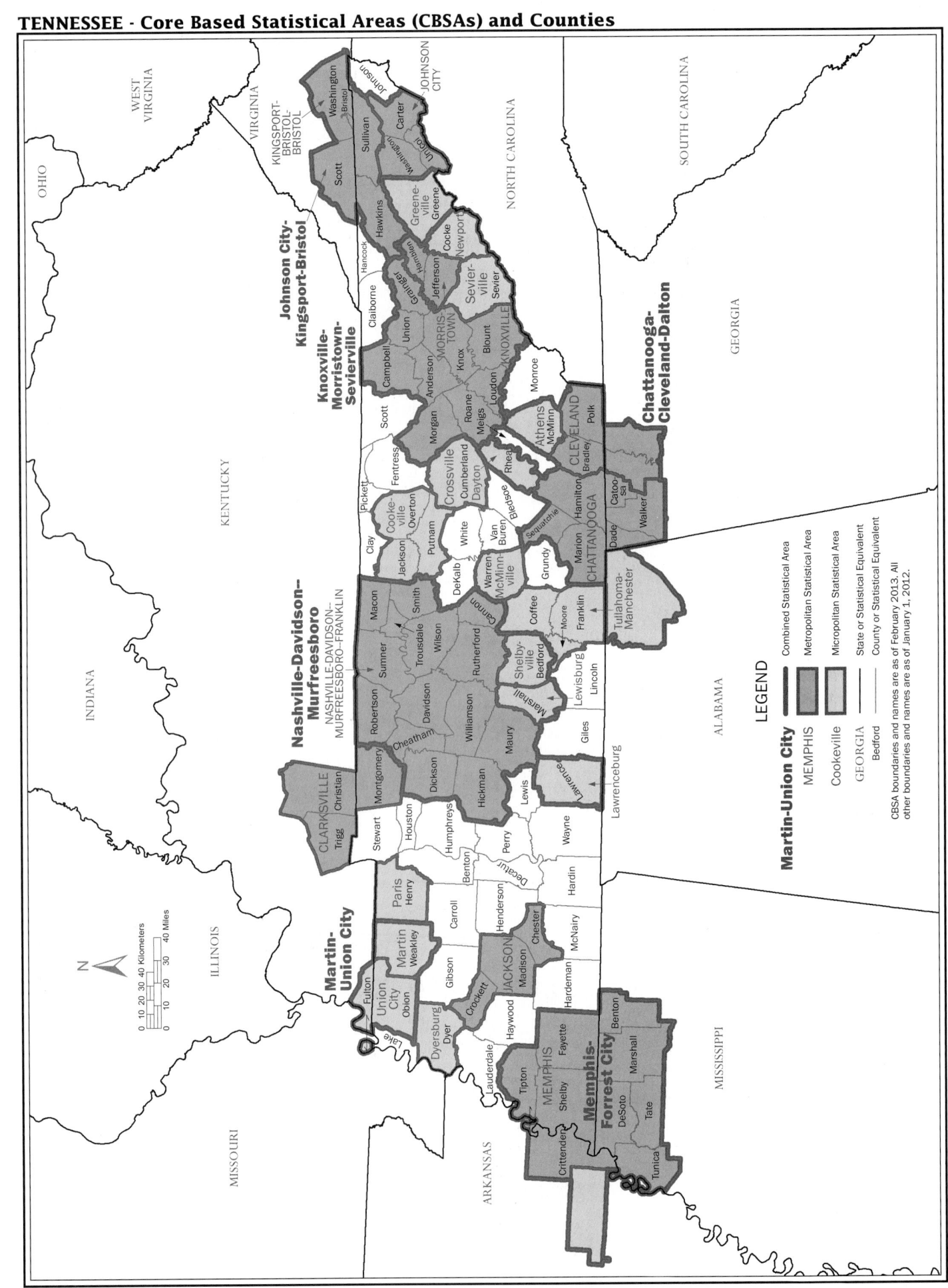

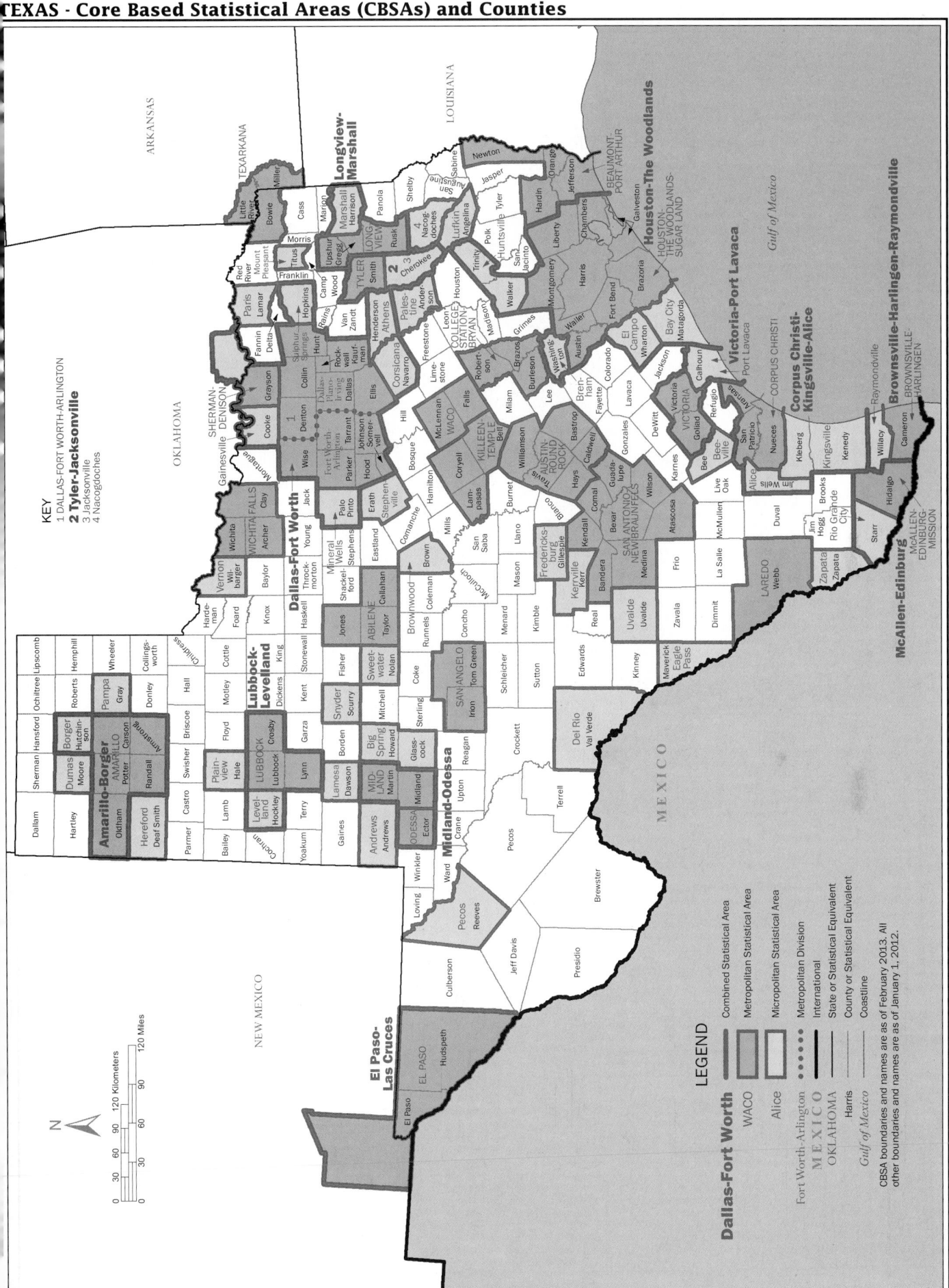

UTAH - Core Based Statistical Areas (CBSAs) and Counties

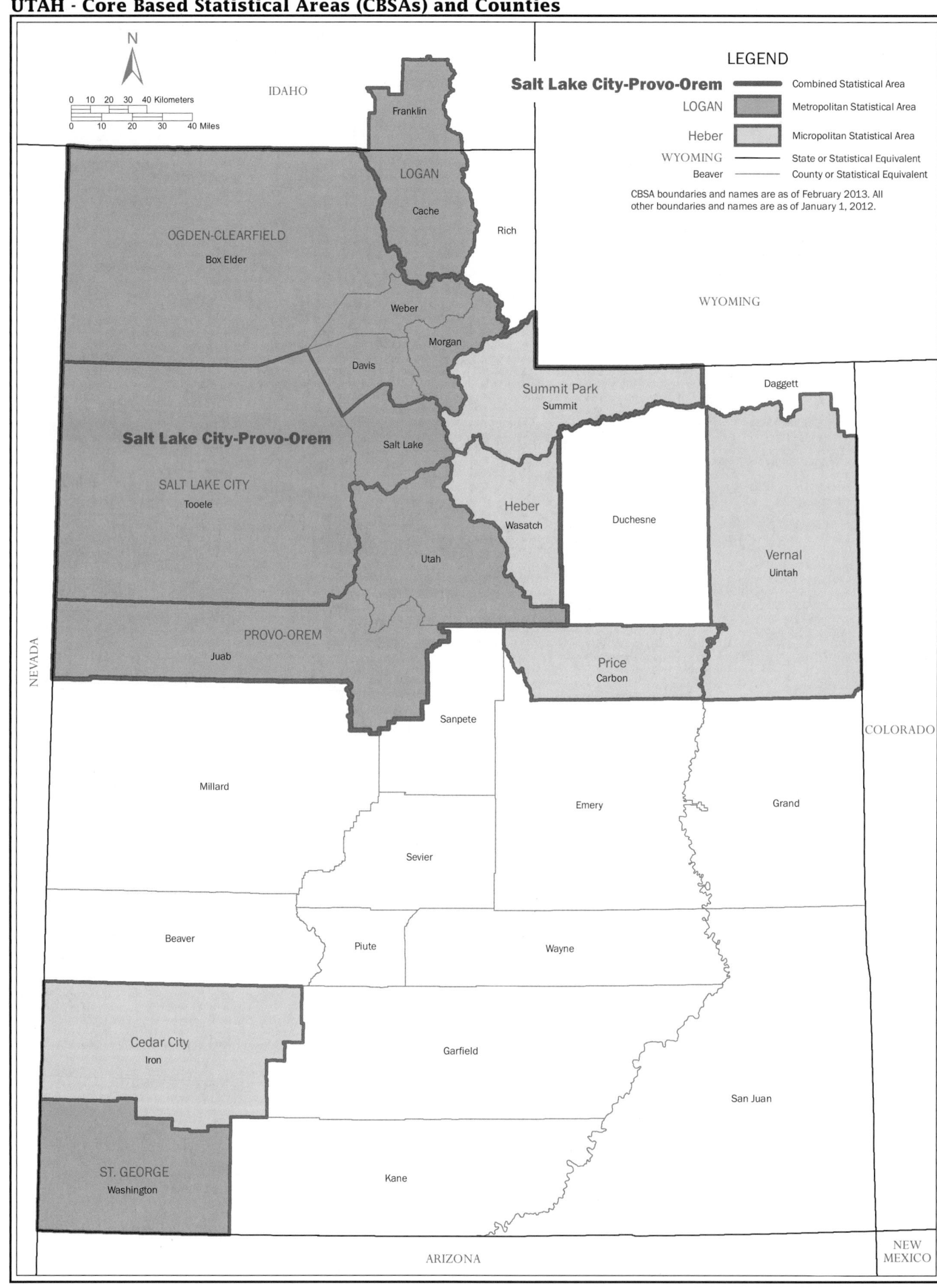

N

0 10 20 30 40 Kilometers
0 10 20 30 40 Miles

IDAHO

Franklin

LEGEND

Salt Lake City-Provo-Orem ▬▬▬ Combined Statistical Area

LOGAN ▨ Metropolitan Statistical Area

Heber ▨ Micropolitan Statistical Area

WYOMING ─── State or Statistical Equivalent

Beaver ─── County or Statistical Equivalent

CBSA boundaries and names are as of February 2013. All
other boundaries and names are as of January 1, 2012.

LOGAN

Cache

Rich

WYOMING

OGDEN-CLEARFIELD

Box Elder

Weber

Morgan

Summit Park

Summit

Daggett

Davis

Salt Lake City-Provo-Orem

Salt Lake

SALT LAKE CITY

Tooele

Heber

Wasatch

Duchesne

Vernal

Uintah

Utah

PROVO-OREM

Juab

Price

Carbon

Sanpete

NEVADA

Millard

Emery

Grand

COLORADO

Sevier

Beaver

Piute

Wayne

Cedar City

Iron

Garfield

San Juan

ST. GEORGE

Washington

Kane

ARIZONA

NEW
MEXICO

N

0 5 10 15 20 Kilometers
0 5 10 15 20 Miles

CANADA

Grand Isle

Franklin

Orleans

BURLINGTON-SOUTH BURLINGTON

Essex

Berlin

Coos

Lamoille

Chittenden

Caledonia

MAINE

Barre

Washington

Addison

Orange

Grafton

NEW YORK

Claremont-Lebanon

NEW HAMPSHIRE

Rutland

Rutland

Windsor

Sullivan

Bennington

Bennington

Windham

LEGEND

BURLINGTON-SOUTH BURLINGTON — Metropolitan Statistical Area

Barre — Micropolitan Statistical Area

CANADA — International

NEW HAMPSHIRE — State or Statistical Equivalent

Addison — County or Statistical Equivalent

CBSA boundaries and names are as of February 2013. All other boundaries and names are as of January 1, 2012.

MASSACHUSETTS

VIRGINIA - Core Based Statistical Areas (CBSAs) and Counties

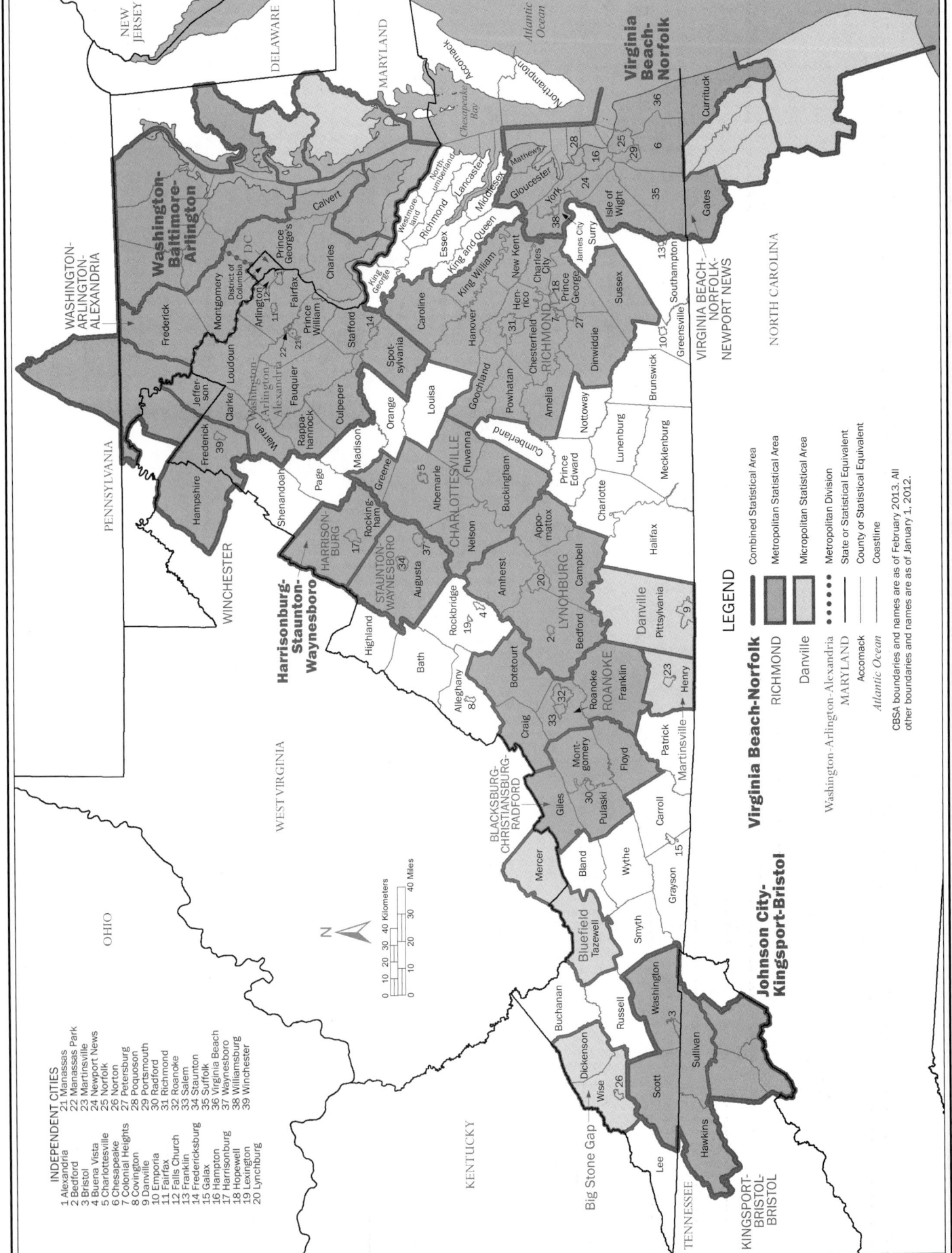

U.S. DEPARTMENT OF COMMERCE Economics and Statistics Administration U.S. Census Bureau

IDAHO

CANADA

LEWISTON
Nez Perce

Spokane-
Spokane Valley-
Coeur d'Alene

Pend
Oreille

Spokane

Pullman-
Moscow

Asotin

Garfield

Pullman
Whitman

Stevens

SPOKANE-
SPOKANE
VALLEY

WALLA WALLA

Columbia

Ferry

Lincoln

Moses Lake-
Othello

Othello
Adams

Walla Walla

Franklin

Moses Lake
Grant

KENNEWICK-
RICHLAND

Benton

LEGEND

Seattle-Tacoma

YAKIMA

Aberdeen

Tacoma-Lakewood

CANADA

OREGON

Adams

Pacific Ocean

Combined Statistical Area

Metropolitan Statistical Area

Micropolitan Statistical Area

Metropolitan Division

International

State or Statistical Equivalent

County or Statistical Equivalent

Coastline

CBSA boundaries and names are as of February 2013. All
other boundaries and names are as of January 1, 2012.

Okanogan

Douglas

WENATCHEE

Chelan

Ellensburg
Kittitas

YAKIMA
Yakima

Klickitat

OREGON

N

0 10 20 30 40 Kilometers
0   10   20   30   40 Miles

BELLINGHAM
Whatcom

MOUNT VERNON-ANACORTES

Skagit

Seattle-Tacoma

SEATTLE-TACOMA-
BELLEVUE

Snohomish

Seattle-Bellevue-Everett

King

Tacoma-Lakewood

Pierce

PORTLAND-
VANCOUVER-
HILLSBORO

Skamania

Oak Harbor

Island

San Juan

Kitsap

Centralia
Lewis

Clark

Multnomah

Portland-
Vancouver-
Salem (pt)

Clackamas

BREMERTON-SILVERDALE

Jefferson

Port Angeles
Clallam

Shelton
Mason

OLYMPIA-
TUMWATER

Thurston

LONGVIEW
Cowlitz

Columbia

Washington

Yamhill

Aberdeen
Grays Harbor

Pacific

Wahkiakum

Pacific
Ocean

WEST VIRGINIA - Core Based Statistical Areas (CBSAs) and Counties

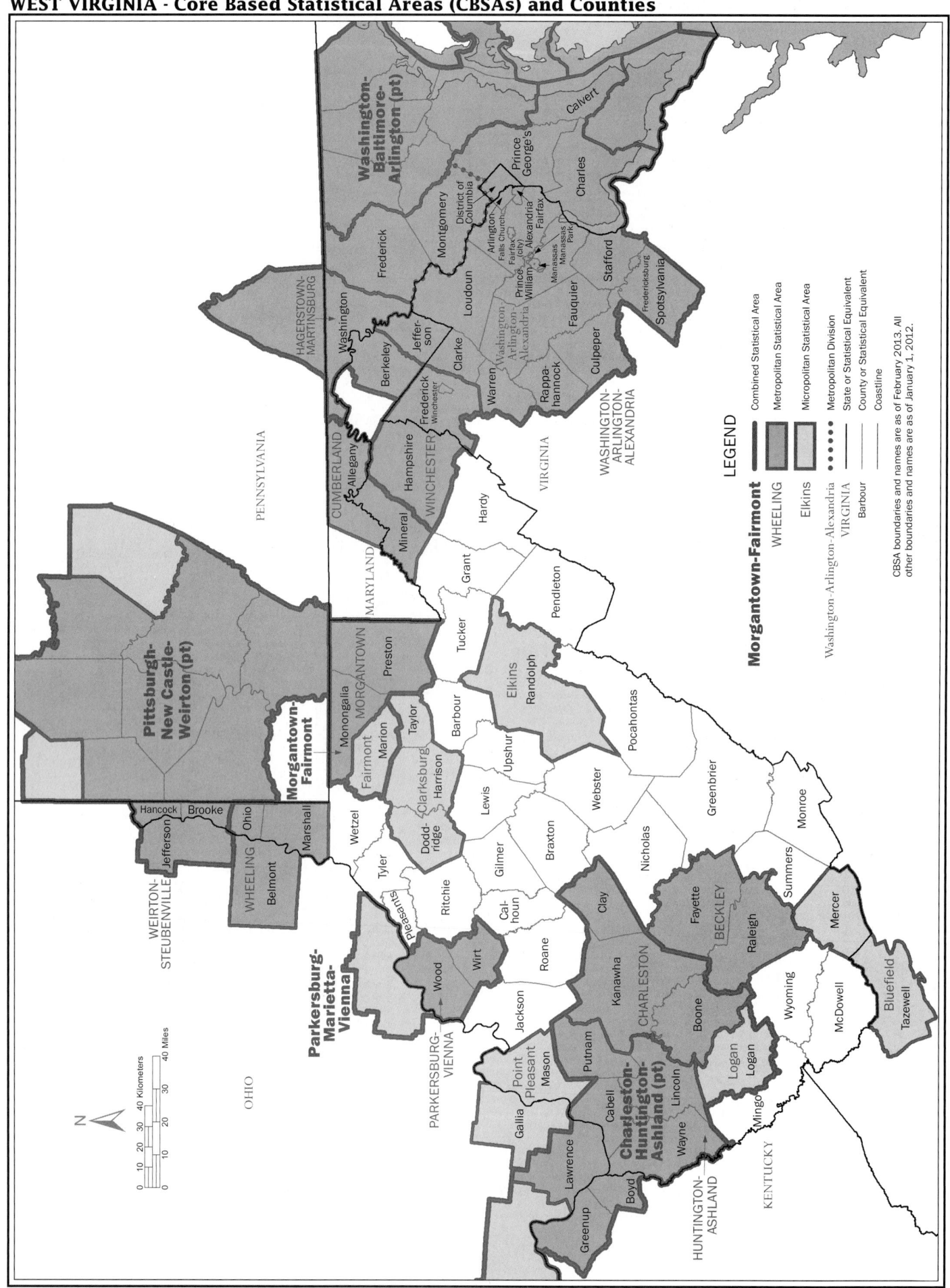

LEGEND

Combined Statistical Area

Metropolitan Statistical Area

Micropolitan Statistical Area

Metropolitan Division

State or Statistical Equivalent

County or Statistical Equivalent

Coastline

Morgantown-Fairmont

WHEELING

Elkins

Washington-Arlington-Alexandria

VIRGINIA

Barbour

CBSA boundaries and names are as of February 2013. All other boundaries and names are as of January 1, 2012.

WISCONSIN - Core Based Statistical Areas (CBSAs) and Counties

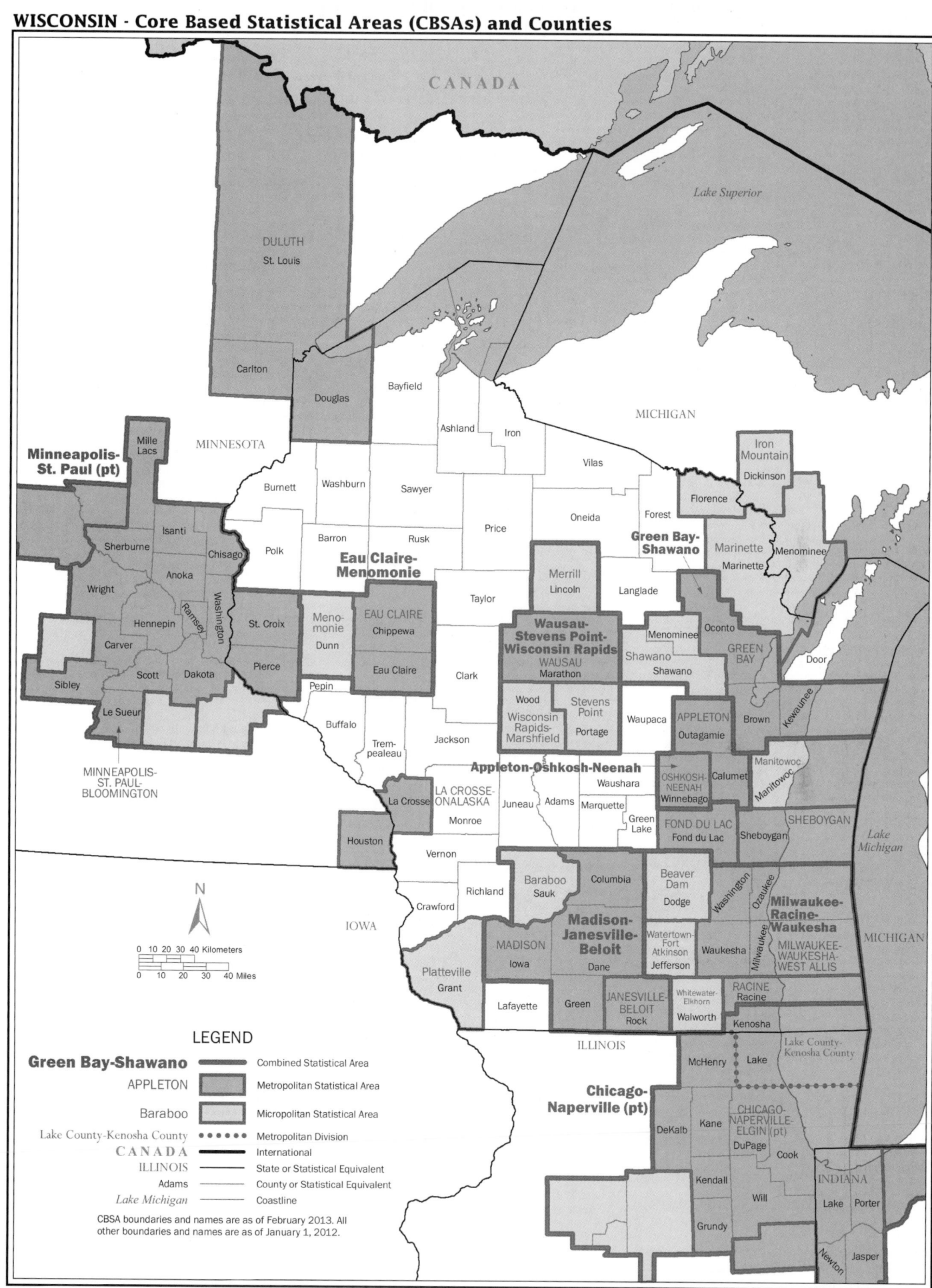

LEGEND

Green Bay-Shawano — Combined Statistical Area

APPLETON — Metropolitan Statistical Area

Baraboo — Micropolitan Statistical Area

Lake County-Kenosha County ••••• Metropolitan Division

C A N A D A — International

ILLINOIS — State or Statistical Equivalent

Adams — County or Statistical Equivalent

Lake Michigan — Coastline

CBSA boundaries and names are as of February 2013. All other boundaries and names are as of January 1, 2012.

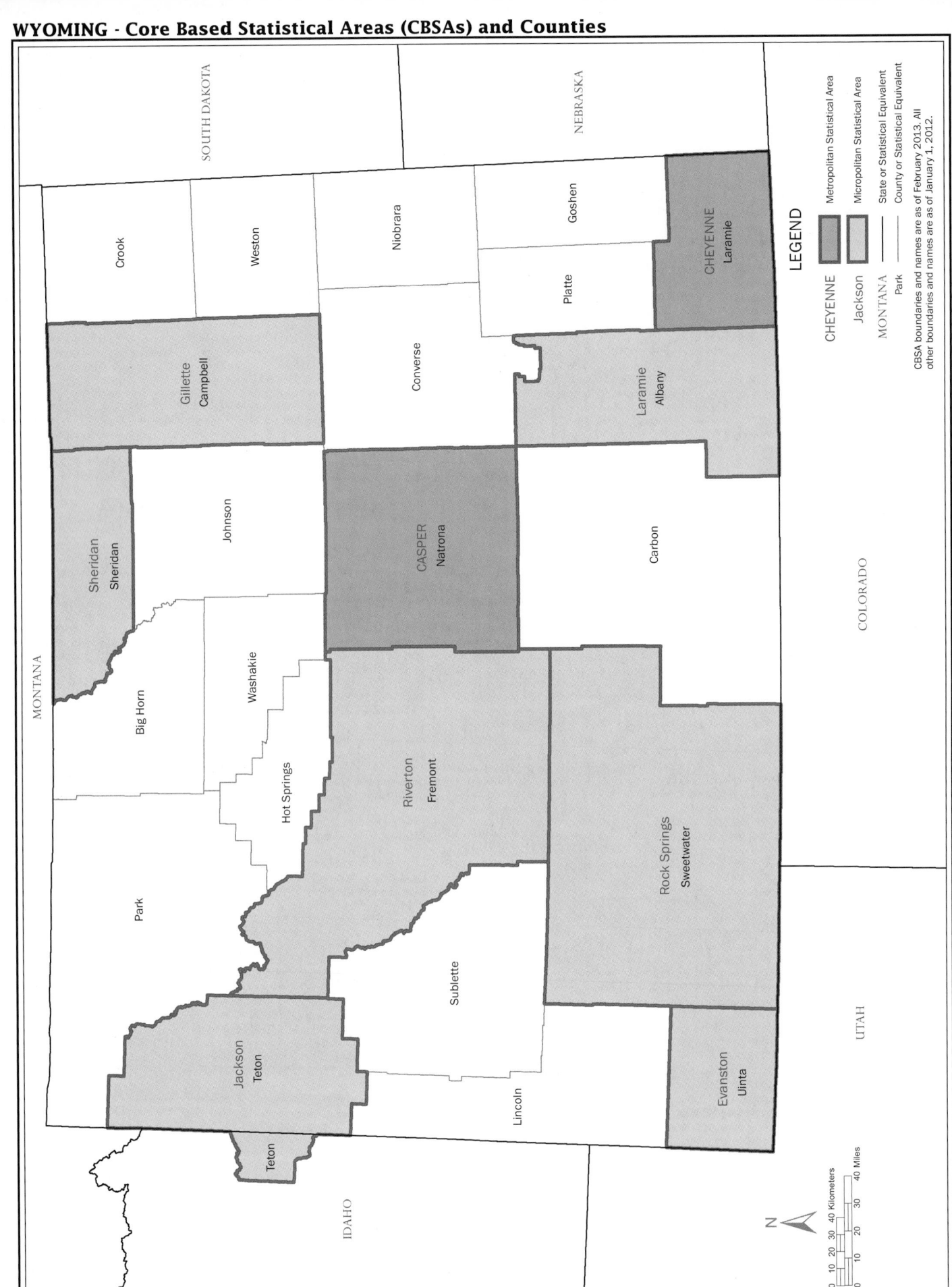

SOUTH DAKOTA

NEBRASKA

Crook

Weston

Niobrara

Goshen

Platte

CHEYENNE
Laramie

Gillette
Campbell

Converse

Laramie
Albany

Sheridan
Sheridan

Johnson

CASPER
Natrona

Carbon

MONTANA

Big Horn

Washakie

Hot Springs

Riverton
Fremont

Rock Springs
Sweetwater

COLORADO

Park

Sublette

Jackson
Teton

Lincoln

Evanston
Uinta

Teton

UTAH

IDAHO

LEGEND

CHEYENNE Metropolitan Statistical Area

Jackson Micropolitan Statistical Area

MONTANA —— State or Statistical Equivalent

—— County or Statistical Equivalent

Park —— Park

CBSA boundaries and names are as of February 2013. All
other boundaries and names are as of January 1, 2012.

N

0 10 20 30 40 Kilometers
0 10 20 30 40 Miles

APPENDIX E
CITIES BY COUNTY

The following table is arranged alphabetically by state. Under each state heading are listed all cities with a 2010 census population over 25,000 along with their component counties and the population in each component.

State Code	Place Code	County Code	Geographic Area Name	2010 Census Population	State Code	Place Code	County Code	Geographic Area Name	2010 Census Population
01			**ALABAMA**	4 779 736	01	78552		Vestavia Hills city	34 033
01	00820		Alabaster city	30 352	01	78552	073	Jefferson County	34 019
01	00820	117	Shelby County	30 352	01	78552	117	Shelby County	14
01	03076		Auburn city	53 380	02			**ALASKA**	710 231
01	03076	081	Lee County	53 380	02	03000		Anchorage municipality	291 826
01	05980		Bessemer city	27 456	02	03000	020	Anchorage Municipality	291 826
01	05980	073	Jefferson County	27 456	02	24230		Fairbanks city	31 535
01	07000		Birmingham city	212 237	02	24230	090	Fairbanks North Star Borough	31 535
01	07000	073	Jefferson County	210 609	02	36400		Juneau city and borough	31 275
01	07000	117	Shelby County	1 628	02	36400	110	Juneau City and Borough	31 275
01	20104		Decatur city	55 683	04			**ARIZONA**	6 392 017
01	20104	083	Limestone County	84	04	02830		Apache Junction city	35 840
01	20104	103	Morgan County	55 599	04	02830	013	Maricopa County	294
01	21184		Dothan city	65 496	04	02830	021	Pinal County	35 546
01	21184	045	Dale County	887	04	04720		Avondale city	76 238
01	21184	067	Henry County	5	04	04720	013	Maricopa County	76 238
01	21184	069	Houston County	64 604	04	07940		Buckeye town	50 876
01	24184		Enterprise city	26 562	04	07940	013	Maricopa County	50 876
01	24184	031	Coffee County	26 139	04	08220		Bullhead City city	39 540
01	24184	045	Dale County	423	04	08220	015	Mohave County	39 540
01	26896		Florence city	39 319	04	10530		Casa Grande city	48 571
01	26896	077	Lauderdale County	39 319	04	10530	021	Pinal County	48 571
01	28696		Gadsden city	36 856	04	12000		Chandler city	236 123
01	28696	055	Etowah County	36 856	04	12000	013	Maricopa County	236 123
01	35800		Homewood city	25 167	04	22220		El Mirage city	31 797
01	35800	073	Jefferson County	25 167	04	22220	013	Maricopa County	31 797
01	35896		Hoover city	81 619	04	23620		Flagstaff city	65 870
01	35896	073	Jefferson County	58 582	04	23620	005	Coconino County	65 870
01	35896	117	Shelby County	23 037	04	23760		Florence town	25 536
01	37000		Huntsville city	180 105	04	23760	021	Pinal County	25 536
01	37000	083	Limestone County	1 521	04	27400		Gilbert town	208 453
01	37000	089	Madison County	178 584	04	27400	013	Maricopa County	208 453
01	45784		Madison city	42 938	04	27820		Glendale city	226 721
01	45784	083	Limestone County	3 453	04	27820	013	Maricopa County	226 721
01	45784	089	Madison County	39 485	04	28380		Goodyear city	65 275
01	50000		Mobile city	195 111	04	28380	013	Maricopa County	65 275
01	50000	097	Mobile County	195 111	04	37620		Kingman city	28 068
01	51000		Montgomery city	205 764	04	37620	015	Mohave County	28 068
01	51000	101	Montgomery County	205 764	04	39370		Lake Havasu City city	52 527
01	57048		Opelika city	26 477	04	39370	015	Mohave County	52 527
01	57048	081	Lee County	26 477	04	44270		Marana town	34 961
01	59472		Phenix City city	32 822	04	44270	019	Pima County	34 961
01	59472	081	Lee County	4 153	04	44270	021	Pinal County	0
01	59472	113	Russell County	28 669	04	44410		Maricopa city	43 482
01	62328		Prattville city	33 960	04	44410	021	Pinal County	43 482
01	62328	001	Autauga County	32 168	04	46000		Mesa city	439 041
01	62328	051	Elmore County	1 792	04	46000	013	Maricopa County	439 041
01	77256		Tuscaloosa city	90 468					
01	77256	125	Tuscaloosa County	90 468					

State Code	Place Code	County Code	Geographic Area Name	2010 Census Population	State Code	Place Code	County Code	Geographic Area Name	2010 Census Population
04	51600		Oro Valley town	41 011	05	41000		Little Rock city	193 524
04	51600	019	Pima County	41 011	05	41000	119	Pulaski County	193 524
04	54050		Peoria city	154 065	05	50450		North Little Rock city	62 304
04	54050	013	Maricopa County	154 058	05	50450	119	Pulaski County	62 304
04	54050	025	Yavapai County	7					
					05	53390		Paragould city	26 113
04	55000		Phoenix city	1 445 632	05	53390	055	Greene County	26 113
04	55000	013	Maricopa County	1 445 632					
					05	55310		Pine Bluff city	49 083
04	57380		Prescott city	39 843	05	55310	069	Jefferson County	49 083
04	57380	025	Yavapai County	39 843					
					05	60410		Rogers city	55 964
04	57450		Prescott Valley town	38 822	05	60410	007	Benton County	55 964
04	57450	025	Yavapai County	38 822					
					05	61670		Russellville city	27 920
04	58150		Queen Creek town	26 361	05	61670	115	Pope County	27 920
04	58150	013	Maricopa County	25 912					
04	58150	021	Pinal County	449	05	63800		Sherwood city	29 523
					05	63800	119	Pulaski County	29 523
04	62140		Sahuarita town	25 259					
04	62140	019	Pima County	25 259	05	66080		Springdale city	69 797
					05	66080	007	Benton County	6 054
04	63470		San Luis city	25 505	05	66080	143	Washington County	63 743
04	63470	027	Yuma County	25 505					
					05	68810		Texarkana city	29 919
04	65000		Scottsdale city	217 385	05	68810	091	Miller County	29 919
04	65000	013	Maricopa County	217 385					
					05	74540		West Memphis city	26 245
04	66820		Sierra Vista city	43 888	05	74540	035	Crittenden County	26 245
04	66820	003	Cochise County	43 888					
					06			**CALIFORNIA**	37 253 956
04	71510		Surprise city	117 517	06	00296		Adelanto city	31 765
04	71510	013	Maricopa County	117 517	06	00296	071	San Bernardino County	31 765
04	73000		Tempe city	161 719	06	00562		Alameda city	73 812
04	73000	013	Maricopa County	161 719	06	00562	001	Alameda County	73 812
04	77000		Tucson city	520 116	06	00884		Alhambra city	83 089
04	77000	019	Pima County	520 116	06	00884	037	Los Angeles County	83 089
04	85540		Yuma city	93 064	06	00947		Aliso Viejo city	47 823
04	85540	027	Yuma County	93 064	06	00947	059	Orange County	47 823
05			**ARKANSAS**	2 915 918	06	02000		Anaheim city	336 265
05	04840		Bella Vista town	26 461	06	02000	059	Orange County	336 265
05	04840	007	Benton County	26 461					
					06	02252		Antioch city	102 372
05	05290		Benton city	30 681	06	02252	013	Contra Costa County	102 372
05	05290	125	Saline County	30 681					
					06	02364		Apple Valley town	69 135
05	05320		Bentonville city	35 301	06	02364	071	San Bernardino County	69 135
05	05320	007	Benton County	35 301					
					06	02462		Arcadia city	56 364
05	15190		Conway city	58 908	06	02462	037	Los Angeles County	56 364
05	15190	045	Faulkner County	58 908					
					06	03064		Atascadero city	28 310
05	23290		Fayetteville city	73 580	06	03064	079	San Luis Obispo County	28 310
05	23290	143	Washington County	73 580					
					06	03162		Atwater city	28 168
05	24550		Fort Smith city	86 209	06	03162	047	Merced County	28 168
05	24550	131	Sebastian County	86 209					
					06	03386		Azusa city	46 361
05	33400		Hot Springs city	35 193	06	03386	037	Los Angeles County	46 361
05	33400	051	Garland County	35 193					
					06	03526		Bakersfield city	347 483
05	34750		Jacksonville city	28 364	06	03526	029	Kern County	347 483
05	34750	119	Pulaski County	28 364					
					06	03666		Baldwin Park city	75 390
05	35710		Jonesboro city	67 263	06	03666	037	Los Angeles County	75 390
05	35710	031	Craighead County	67 263					

Cities by County–*Continued*

State Code	Place Code	County Code	Geographic Area Name	2010 Census Population	State Code	Place Code	County Code	Geographic Area Name	2010 Census Population
06	03820		Banning city	29 603	06	13214		Chino Hills city	74 799
06	03820	065	Riverside County	29 603	06	13214	071	San Bernardino County	74 799
06	04758		Beaumont city	36 877	06	13392		Chula Vista city	243 916
06	04758	065	Riverside County	36 877	06	13392	073	San Diego County	243 916
06	04870		Bell city	35 477	06	13588		Citrus Heights city	83 301
06	04870	037	Los Angeles County	35 477	06	13588	067	Sacramento County	83 301
06	04982		Bellflower city	76 616	06	13756		Claremont city	34 926
06	04982	037	Los Angeles County	76 616	06	13756	037	Los Angeles County	34 926
06	04996		Bell Gardens city	42 072	06	14218		Clovis city	95 631
06	04996	037	Los Angeles County	42 072	06	14218	019	Fresno County	95 631
06	05108		Belmont city	25 835	06	14260		Coachella city	40 704
06	05108	081	San Mateo County	25 835	06	14260	065	Riverside County	40 704
06	05290		Benicia city	26 997	06	14890		Colton city	52 154
06	05290	095	Solano County	26 997	06	14890	071	San Bernardino County	52 154
06	06000		Berkeley city	112 580	06	15044		Compton city	96 455
06	06000	001	Alameda County	112 580	06	15044	037	Los Angeles County	96 455
06	06308		Beverly Hills city	34 109	06	16000		Concord city	122 067
06	06308	037	Los Angeles County	34 109	06	16000	013	Contra Costa County	122 067
06	08100		Brea city	39 282	06	16350		Corona city	152 374
06	08100	059	Orange County	39 282	06	16350	065	Riverside County	152 374
06	08142		Brentwood city	51 481	06	16532		Costa Mesa city	109 960
06	08142	013	Contra Costa County	51 481	06	16532	059	Orange County	109 960
06	08786		Buena Park city	80 530	06	16742		Covina city	47 796
06	08786	059	Orange County	80 530	06	16742	037	Los Angeles County	47 796
06	08954		Burbank city	103 340	06	17568		Culver City city	38 883
06	08954	037	Los Angeles County	103 340	06	17568	037	Los Angeles County	38 883
06	09066		Burlingame city	28 806	06	17610		Cupertino city	58 302
06	09066	081	San Mateo County	28 806	06	17610	085	Santa Clara County	58 302
06	09710		Calexico city	38 572	06	17750		Cypress city	47 802
06	09710	025	Imperial County	38 572	06	17750	059	Orange County	47 802
06	10046		Camarillo city	65 201	06	17918		Daly City city	101 123
06	10046	111	Ventura County	65 201	06	17918	081	San Mateo County	101 123
06	10345		Campbell city	39 349	06	17946		Dana Point city	33 351
06	10345	085	Santa Clara County	39 349	06	17946	059	Orange County	33 351
06	11194		Carlsbad city	105 328	06	17988		Danville town	42 039
06	11194	073	San Diego County	105 328	06	17988	013	Contra Costa County	42 039
06	11530		Carson city	91 714	06	18100		Davis city	65 622
06	11530	037	Los Angeles County	91 714	06	18100	113	Yolo County	65 622
06	12048		Cathedral City city	51 200	06	18394		Delano city	53 041
06	12048	065	Riverside County	51 200	06	18394	029	Kern County	53 041
06	12524		Ceres city	45 417	06	18996		Desert Hot Springs city	25 938
06	12524	099	Stanislaus County	45 417	06	18996	065	Riverside County	25 938
06	12552		Cerritos city	49 041	06	19192		Diamond Bar city	55 544
06	12552	037	Los Angeles County	49 041	06	19192	037	Los Angeles County	55 544
06	13014		Chico city	86 187	06	19766		Downey city	111 772
06	13014	007	Butte County	86 187	06	19766	037	Los Angeles County	111 772
06	13210		Chino city	77 983	06	20018		Dublin city	46 036
06	13210	071	San Bernardino County	77 983	06	20018	001	Alameda County	46 036

State Code	Place Code	County Code	Geographic Area Name	2010 Census Population	State Code	Place Code	County Code	Geographic Area Name	2010 Census Population
06	20956		East Palo Alto city	28 155	06	32548		Hawthorne city	84 293
06	20956	081	San Mateo County	28 155	06	32548	037	Los Angeles County	84 293
06	21712		El Cajon city	99 478	06	33000		Hayward city	144 186
06	21712	073	San Diego County	99 478	06	33000	001	Alameda County	144 186
06	21782		El Centro city	42 598	06	33182		Hemet city	78 657
06	21782	025	Imperial County	42 598	06	33182	065	Riverside County	78 657
06	22020		Elk Grove city	153 015	06	33434		Hesperia city	90 173
06	22020	067	Sacramento County	153 015	06	33434	071	San Bernardino County	90 173
06	22230		El Monte city	113 475	06	33588		Highland city	53 104
06	22230	037	Los Angeles County	113 475	06	33588	071	San Bernardino County	53 104
06	22300		El Paso de Robles (Paso Robles)	29 793	06	34120		Hollister city	34 928
06	22300	079	San Luis Obispo County	29 793	06	34120	069	San Benito County	34 928
06	22678		Encinitas city	59 518	06	36000		Huntington Beach city	189 992
06	22678	073	San Diego County	59 518	06	36000	059	Orange County	189 992
06	22804		Escondido city	143 911	06	36056		Huntington Park city	58 114
06	22804	073	San Diego County	143 911	06	36056	037	Los Angeles County	58 114
06	23042		Eureka city	27 191	06	36294		Imperial Beach city	26 324
06	23042	023	Humboldt County	27 191	06	36294	073	San Diego County	26 324
06	23182		Fairfield city	105 321	06	36448		Indio city	76 036
06	23182	095	Solano County	105 321	06	36448	065	Riverside County	76 036
06	24638		Folsom city	72 203	06	36546		Inglewood city	109 673
06	24638	067	Sacramento County	72 203	06	36546	037	Los Angeles County	109 673
06	24680		Fontana city	196 069	06	36770		Irvine city	212 375
06	24680	071	San Bernardino County	196 069	06	36770	059	Orange County	212 375
06	25338		Foster City city	30 567	06	39220		Laguna Hills city	30 344
06	25338	081	San Mateo County	30 567	06	39220	059	Orange County	30 344
06	25380		Fountain Valley city	55 313	06	39248		Laguna Niguel city	62 979
06	25380	059	Orange County	55 313	06	39248	059	Orange County	62 979
06	26000		Fremont city	214 089	06	39290		La Habra city	60 239
06	26000	001	Alameda County	214 089	06	39290	059	Orange County	60 239
06	27000		Fresno city	494 665	06	39486		Lake Elsinore city	51 821
06	27000	019	Fresno County	494 665	06	39486	065	Riverside County	51 821
06	28000		Fullerton city	135 161	06	39496		Lake Forest city	77 264
06	28000	059	Orange County	135 161	06	39496	059	Orange County	77 264
06	28168		Gardena city	58 829	06	39892		Lakewood city	80 048
06	28168	037	Los Angeles County	58 829	06	39892	037	Los Angeles County	80 048
06	29000		Garden Grove city	170 883	06	40004		La Mesa city	57 065
06	29000	059	Orange County	170 883	06	40004	073	San Diego County	57 065
06	29504		Gilroy city	48 821	06	40032		La Mirada city	48 527
06	29504	085	Santa Clara County	48 821	06	40032	037	Los Angeles County	48 527
06	30000		Glendale city	191 719	06	40130		Lancaster city	156 633
06	30000	037	Los Angeles County	191 719	06	40130	037	Los Angeles County	156 633
06	30014		Glendora city	50 073	06	40340		La Puente city	39 816
06	30014	037	Los Angeles County	50 073	06	40340	037	Los Angeles County	39 816
06	30378		Goleta city	29 888	06	40354		La Quinta city	37 467
06	30378	083	Santa Barbara County	29 888	06	40354	065	Riverside County	37 467
06	31960		Hanford city	53 967	06	40830		La Verne city	31 063
06	31960	031	Kings County	53 967	06	40830	037	Los Angeles County	31 063

State Code	Place Code	County Code	Geographic Area Name	2010 Census Population	State Code	Place Code	County Code	Geographic Area Name	2010 Census Population
06	40886		Lawndale city	32 769	06	48788		Montclair city	36 664
06	40886	037	Los Angeles County	32 769	06	48788	071	San Bernardino County	36 664
06	41124		Lemon Grove city	25 320	06	48816		Montebello city	62 500
06	41124	073	San Diego County	25 320	06	48816	037	Los Angeles County	62 500
06	41474		Lincoln city	42 819	06	48872		Monterey city	27 810
06	41474	061	Placer County	42 819	06	48872	053	Monterey County	27 810
06	41992		Livermore city	80 968	06	48914		Monterey Park city	60 269
06	41992	001	Alameda County	80 968	06	48914	037	Los Angeles County	60 269
06	42202		Lodi city	62 134	06	49138		Moorpark city	34 421
06	42202	077	San Joaquin County	62 134	06	49138	111	Ventura County	34 421
06	42524		Lompoc city	42 434	06	49270		Moreno Valley city	193 365
06	42524	083	Santa Barbara County	42 434	06	49270	065	Riverside County	193 365
06	43000		Long Beach city	462 257	06	49278		Morgan Hill city	37 882
06	43000	037	Los Angeles County	462 257	06	49278	085	Santa Clara County	37 882
06	43280		Los Altos city	28 976	06	49670		Mountain View city	74 066
06	43280	085	Santa Clara County	28 976	06	49670	085	Santa Clara County	74 066
06	44000		Los Angeles city	3 792 621	06	50076		Murrieta city	103 466
06	44000	037	Los Angeles County	3 792 621	06	50076	065	Riverside County	103 466
06	44028		Los Banos city	35 972	06	50258		Napa city	76 915
06	44028	047	Merced County	35 972	06	50258	055	Napa County	76 915
06	44112		Los Gatos town	29 413	06	50398		National City city	58 582
06	44112	085	Santa Clara County	29 413	06	50398	073	San Diego County	58 582
06	44574		Lynwood city	69 772	06	50916		Newark city	42 573
06	44574	037	Los Angeles County	69 772	06	50916	001	Alameda County	42 573
06	45022		Madera city	61 416	06	51182		Newport Beach city	85 186
06	45022	039	Madera County	61 416	06	51182	059	Orange County	85 186
06	45400		Manhattan Beach city	35 135	06	51560		Norco city	27 063
06	45400	037	Los Angeles County	35 135	06	51560	065	Riverside County	27 063
06	45484		Manteca city	67 096	06	52526		Norwalk city	105 549
06	45484	077	San Joaquin County	67 096	06	52526	037	Los Angeles County	105 549
06	46114		Martinez city	35 824	06	52582		Novato city	51 904
06	46114	013	Contra Costa County	35 824	06	52582	041	Marin County	51 904
06	46492		Maywood city	27 395	06	53000		Oakland city	390 724
06	46492	037	Los Angeles County	27 395	06	53000	001	Alameda County	390 724
06	46842		Menifee city	77 519	06	53070		Oakley city	35 432
06	46842	065	Riverside County	77 519	06	53070	013	Contra Costa County	35 432
06	46870		Menlo Park city	32 026	06	53322		Oceanside city	167 086
06	46870	081	San Mateo County	32 026	06	53322	073	San Diego County	167 086
06	46898		Merced city	78 958	06	53896		Ontario city	163 924
06	46898	047	Merced County	78 958	06	53896	071	San Bernardino County	163 924
06	47766		Milpitas city	66 790	06	53980		Orange city	136 416
06	47766	085	Santa Clara County	66 790	06	53980	059	Orange County	136 416
06	48256		Mission Viejo city	93 305	06	54652		Oxnard city	197 899
06	48256	059	Orange County	93 305	06	54652	111	Ventura County	197 899
06	48354		Modesto city	201 165	06	54806		Pacifica city	37 234
06	48354	099	Stanislaus County	201 165	06	54806	081	San Mateo County	37 234
06	48648		Monrovia city	36 590	06	55156		Palmdale city	152 750
06	48648	037	Los Angeles County	36 590	06	55156	037	Los Angeles County	152 750

Cities by County–*Continued*

State Code	Place Code	County Code	Geographic Area Name	2010 Census Population	State Code	Place Code	County Code	Geographic Area Name	2010 Census Population
06	55184		Palm Desert city	48 445	06	60466		Rialto city	99 171
06	55184	065	Riverside County	48 445	06	60466	071	San Bernardino County	99 171
06	55254		Palm Springs city	44 552	06	60620		Richmond city	103 701
06	55254	065	Riverside County	44 552	06	60620	013	Contra Costa County	103 701
06	55282		Palo Alto city	64 403	06	60704		Ridgecrest city	27 616
06	55282	085	Santa Clara County	64 403	06	60704	029	Kern County	27 616
06	55520		Paradise town	26 218	06	62000		Riverside city	303 871
06	55520	007	Butte County	26 218	06	62000	065	Riverside County	303 871
06	55618		Paramount city	54 098	06	62364		Rocklin city	56 974
06	55618	037	Los Angeles County	54 098	06	62364	061	Placer County	56 974
06	56000		Pasadena city	137 122	06	62546		Rohnert Park city	40 971
06	56000	037	Los Angeles County	137 122	06	62546	097	Sonoma County	40 971
06	56700		Perris city	68 386	06	62896		Rosemead city	53 764
06	56700	065	Riverside County	68 386	06	62896	037	Los Angeles County	53 764
06	56784		Petaluma city	57 941	06	62938		Roseville city	118 788
06	56784	097	Sonoma County	57 941	06	62938	061	Placer County	118 788
06	56924		Pico Rivera city	62 942	06	64000		Sacramento city	466 488
06	56924	037	Los Angeles County	62 942	06	64000	067	Sacramento County	466 488
06	57456		Pittsburg city	63 264	06	64224		Salinas city	150 441
06	57456	013	Contra Costa County	63 264	06	64224	053	Monterey County	150 441
06	57526		Placentia city	50 533	06	65000		San Bernardino city	209 924
06	57526	059	Orange County	50 533	06	65000	071	San Bernardino County	209 924
06	57764		Pleasant Hill city	33 152	06	65028		San Bruno city	41 114
06	57764	013	Contra Costa County	33 152	06	65028	081	San Mateo County	41 114
06	57792		Pleasanton city	70 285	06	65042		San Buenaventura (Ventura)	106 433
06	57792	001	Alameda County	70 285	06	65042	111	Ventura County	106 433
06	58072		Pomona city	149 058	06	65070		San Carlos city	28 406
06	58072	037	Los Angeles County	149 058	06	65070	081	San Mateo County	28 406
06	58240		Porterville city	54 165	06	65084		San Clemente city	63 522
06	58240	107	Tulare County	54 165	06	65084	059	Orange County	63 522
06	58520		Poway city	47 811	06	66000		San Diego city	1 307 402
06	58520	073	San Diego County	47 811	06	66000	073	San Diego County	1 307 402
06	59444		Rancho Cordova city	64 776	06	66070		San Dimas city	33 371
06	59444	067	Sacramento County	64 776	06	66070	037	Los Angeles County	33 371
06	59451		Rancho Cucamonga city	165 269	06	67000		San Francisco city	805 235
06	59451	071	San Bernardino County	165 269	06	67000	075	San Francisco County	805 235
06	59514		Rancho Palos Verdes city	41 643	06	67042		San Gabriel city	39 718
06	59514	037	Los Angeles County	41 643	06	67042	037	Los Angeles County	39 718
06	59587		Rancho Santa Margarita city	47 853	06	67112		San Jacinto city	44 199
06	59587	059	Orange County	47 853	06	67112	065	Riverside County	44 199
06	59920		Redding city	89 861	06	68000		San Jose city	945 942
06	59920	089	Shasta County	89 861	06	68000	085	Santa Clara County	945 942
06	59962		Redlands city	68 747	06	68028		San Juan Capistrano city	34 593
06	59962	071	San Bernardino County	68 747	06	68028	059	Orange County	34 593
06	60018		Redondo Beach city	66 748	06	68084		San Leandro city	84 950
06	60018	037	Los Angeles County	66 748	06	68084	001	Alameda County	84 950
06	60102		Redwood City city	76 815	06	68154		San Luis Obispo city	45 119
06	60102	081	San Mateo County	76 815	06	68154	079	San Luis Obispo County	45 119

Cities by County–*Continued*

State Code	Place Code	County Code	Geographic Area Name	2010 Census Population	State Code	Place Code	County Code	Geographic Area Name	2010 Census Population
06	68196		San Marcos city	83 781	06	75630		Suisun City city	28 111
06	68196	073	San Diego County	83 781	06	75630	095	Solano County	28 111
06	68252		San Mateo city	97 207	06	77000		Sunnyvale city	140 081
06	68252	081	San Mateo County	97 207	06	77000	085	Santa Clara County	140 081
06	68294		San Pablo city	29 139	06	78120		Temecula city	100 097
06	68294	013	Contra Costa County	29 139	06	78120	065	Riverside County	100 097
06	68364		San Rafael city	57 713	06	78148		Temple City city	35 558
06	68364	041	Marin County	57 713	06	78148	037	Los Angeles County	35 558
06	68378		San Ramon city	72 148	06	78582		Thousand Oaks city	126 683
06	68378	013	Contra Costa County	72 148	06	78582	111	Ventura County	126 683
06	69000		Santa Ana city	324 528	06	80000		Torrance city	145 438
06	69000	059	Orange County	324 528	06	80000	037	Los Angeles County	145 438
06	69070		Santa Barbara city	88 410	06	80238		Tracy city	82 922
06	69070	083	Santa Barbara County	88 410	06	80238	077	San Joaquin County	82 922
06	69084		Santa Clara city	116 468	06	80644		Tulare city	59 278
06	69084	085	Santa Clara County	116 468	06	80644	107	Tulare County	59 278
06	69088		Santa Clarita city	176 320	06	80812		Turlock city	68 549
06	69088	037	Los Angeles County	176 320	06	80812	099	Stanislaus County	68 549
06	69112		Santa Cruz city	59 946	06	80854		Tustin city	75 540
06	69112	087	Santa Cruz County	59 946	06	80854	059	Orange County	75 540
06	69196		Santa Maria city	99 553	06	80994		Twentynine Palms city	25 048
06	69196	083	Santa Barbara County	99 553	06	80994	071	San Bernardino County	25 048
06	70000		Santa Monica city	89 736	06	81204		Union City city	69 516
06	70000	037	Los Angeles County	89 736	06	81204	001	Alameda County	69 516
06	70042		Santa Paula city	29 321	06	81344		Upland city	73 732
06	70042	111	Ventura County	29 321	06	81344	071	San Bernardino County	73 732
06	70098		Santa Rosa city	167 815	06	81554		Vacaville city	92 428
06	70098	097	Sonoma County	167 815	06	81554	095	Solano County	92 428
06	70224		Santee city	53 413	06	81666		Vallejo city	115 942
06	70224	073	San Diego County	53 413	06	81666	095	Solano County	115 942
06	70280		Saratoga city	29 926	06	82590		Victorville city	115 903
06	70280	085	Santa Clara County	29 926	06	82590	071	San Bernardino County	115 903
06	70742		Seaside city	33 025	06	82954		Visalia city	124 442
06	70742	053	Monterey County	33 025	06	82954	107	Tulare County	124 442
06	72016		Simi Valley city	124 237	06	82996		Vista city	93 834
06	72016	111	Ventura County	124 237	06	82996	073	San Diego County	93 834
06	72520		Soledad city	25 738	06	83332		Walnut city	29 172
06	72520	053	Monterey County	25 738	06	83332	037	Los Angeles County	29 172
06	73080		South Gate city	94 396	06	83346		Walnut Creek city	64 173
06	73080	037	Los Angeles County	94 396	06	83346	013	Contra Costa County	64 173
06	73220		South Pasadena city	25 619	06	83542		Wasco city	25 545
06	73220	037	Los Angeles County	25 619	06	83542	029	Kern County	25 545
06	73262		South San Francisco city	63 632	06	83668		Watsonville city	51 199
06	73262	081	San Mateo County	63 632	06	83668	087	Santa Cruz County	51 199
06	73962		Stanton city	38 186	06	84200		West Covina city	106 098
06	73962	059	Orange County	38 186	06	84200	037	Los Angeles County	106 098
06	75000		Stockton city	291 707	06	84410		West Hollywood city	34 399
06	75000	077	San Joaquin County	291 707	06	84410	037	Los Angeles County	34 399

Cities by County–*Continued*

State Code	Place Code	County Code	Geographic Area Name	2010 Census Population	State Code	Place Code	County Code	Geographic Area Name	2010 Census Population
06	84550		Westminster city	89 701	08	31660		Grand Junction city	58 566
06	84550	059	Orange County	89 701	08	31660	077	Mesa County	58 566
06	84816		West Sacramento city	48 744	08	32155		Greeley city	92 889
06	84816	113	Yolo County	48 744	08	32155	123	Weld County	92 889
06	85292		Whittier city	85 331	08	43000		Lakewood city	142 980
06	85292	037	Los Angeles County	85 331	08	43000	059	Jefferson County	142 980
06	85446		Wildomar city	32 176	08	45255		Littleton city	41 737
06	85446	065	Riverside County	32 176	08	45255	005	Arapahoe County	39 328
					08	45255	035	Douglas County	28
06	85922		Windsor town	26 801	08	45255	059	Jefferson County	2 381
06	85922	097	Sonoma County	26 801					
					08	45970		Longmont city	86 270
06	86328		Woodland city	55 468	08	45970	013	Boulder County	86 240
06	86328	113	Yolo County	55 468	08	45970	123	Weld County	30
06	86832		Yorba Linda city	64 234	08	46465		Loveland city	66 859
06	86832	059	Orange County	64 234	08	46465	069	Larimer County	66 859
06	86972		Yuba City city	64 925	08	54330		Northglenn city	35 789
06	86972	101	Sutter County	64 925	08	54330	001	Adams County	35 777
					08	54330	123	Weld County	12
06	87042		Yucaipa city	51 367					
06	87042	071	San Bernardino County	51 367	08	57630		Parker town	45 297
					08	57630	035	Douglas County	45 297
08			**COLORADO**	5 029 196					
08	03455		Arvada city	106 433	08	62000		Pueblo city	106 595
08	03455	001	Adams County	2 849	08	62000	101	Pueblo County	106 595
08	03455	059	Jefferson County	103 584					
					08	77290		Thornton city	118 772
08	04000		Aurora city	325 078	08	77290	001	Adams County	118 772
08	04000	001	Adams County	39 871	08	77290	123	Weld County	0
08	04000	005	Arapahoe County	285 090					
08	04000	035	Douglas County	117	08	83835		Westminster city	106 114
					08	83835	001	Adams County	63 696
08	07850		Boulder city	97 385	08	83835	059	Jefferson County	42 418
08	07850	013	Boulder County	97 385					
					08	84440		Wheat Ridge city	30 166
08	08675		Brighton city	33 352	08	84440	059	Jefferson County	30 166
08	08675	001	Adams County	33 009					
08	08675	123	Weld County	343	09			**CONNECTICUT**	3 574 097
					09	08000		Bridgeport city	144 229
08	09280		Broomfield city	55 889	09	08000	001	Fairfield County	144 229
08	09280	014	Broomfield County	55 889					
					09	08420		Bristol city	60 477
08	12415		Castle Rock town	48 231	09	08420	003	Hartford County	60 477
08	12415	035	Douglas County	48 231					
					09	18430		Danbury city	80 893
08	12815		Centennial city	100 377	09	18430	001	Fairfield County	80 893
08	12815	005	Arapahoe County	100 377					
					09	37000		Hartford city	124 775
08	16000		Colorado Springs city	416 427	09	37000	003	Hartford County	124 775
08	16000	041	El Paso County	416 427					
					09	46450		Meriden city	60 868
08	16495		Commerce City city	45 913	09	46450	009	New Haven County	60 868
08	16495	001	Adams County	45 913					
					09	47290		Middletown city	47 648
08	20000		Denver city	600 158	09	47290	007	Middlesex County	47 648
08	20000	031	Denver County	600 158					
					09	49880		Naugatuck borough	31 862
08	24785		Englewood city	30 255	09	49880	009	New Haven County	31 862
08	24785	005	Arapahoe County	30 255					
					09	50370		New Britain city	73 206
08	27425		Fort Collins city	143 986	09	50370	003	Hartford County	73 206
08	27425	069	Larimer County	143 986					
					09	52000		New Haven city	129 779
08	27865		Fountain city	25 846	09	52000	009	New Haven County	129 779
08	27865	041	El Paso County	25 846					
					09	52280		New London city	27 620
					09	52280	011	New London County	27 620

State Code	Place Code	County Code	Geographic Area Name	2010 Census Population	State Code	Place Code	County Code	Geographic Area Name	2010 Census Population
09	55990		Norwalk city	85 603	12	14125		Cooper City city	28 547
09	55990	001	Fairfield County	85 603	12	14125	011	Broward County	28 547
09	56200		Norwich city	40 493	12	14250		Coral Gables city	46 780
09	56200	011	New London County	40 493	12	14250	086	Miami-Dade County	46 780
09	68100		Shelton city	39 559	12	14400		Coral Springs city	121 096
09	68100	001	Fairfield County	39 559	12	14400	011	Broward County	121 096
09	73000		Stamford city	122 643	12	15968		Cutler Bay town	40 286
09	73000	001	Fairfield County	122 643	12	15968	086	Miami-Dade County	40 286
09	76500		Torrington city	36 383	12	16335		Dania Beach city	29 639
09	76500	005	Litchfield County	36 383	12	16335	011	Broward County	29 639
09	80000		Waterbury city	110 366	12	16475		Davie town	91 992
09	80000	009	New Haven County	110 366	12	16475	011	Broward County	91 992
09	82800		West Haven city	55 564	12	16525		Daytona Beach city	61 005
09	82800	009	New Haven County	55 564	12	16525	127	Volusia County	61 005
10			**DELAWARE**	897 934	12	16725		Deerfield Beach city	75 018
10	21200		Dover city	36 047	12	16725	011	Broward County	75 018
10	21200	001	Kent County	36 047					
					12	16875		DeLand city	27 031
10	50670		Newark city	31 454	12	16875	127	Volusia County	27 031
10	50670	003	New Castle County	31 454					
					12	17100		Delray Beach city	60 522
10	77580		Wilmington city	70 851	12	17100	099	Palm Beach County	60 522
10	77580	003	New Castle County	70 851					
					12	17200		Deltona city	85 182
11			**DISTRICT OF COLUMBIA**	601 723	12	17200	127	Volusia County	85 182
11	50000		Washington city	601 723					
11	50000	001	District of Columbia	601 723	12	17935		Doral city	45 704
					12	17935	086	Miami-Dade County	45 704
12			**FLORIDA**	18 801 310					
12	00950		Altamonte Springs city	41 496	12	18575		Dunedin city	35 321
12	00950	117	Seminole County	41 496	12	18575	103	Pinellas County	35 321
12	01700		Apopka city	41 542	12	24000		Fort Lauderdale city	165 521
12	01700	095	Orange County	41 542	12	24000	011	Broward County	165 521
12	02681		Aventura city	35 762	12	24125		Fort Myers city	62 298
12	02681	086	Miami-Dade County	35 762	12	24125	071	Lee County	62 298
12	07300		Boca Raton city	84 392	12	24300		Fort Pierce city	41 590
12	07300	099	Palm Beach County	84 392	12	24300	111	St. Lucie County	41 590
12	07525		Bonita Springs city	43 914	12	25175		Gainesville city	124 354
12	07525	071	Lee County	43 914	12	25175	001	Alachua County	124 354
12	07875		Boynton Beach city	68 217	12	27322		Greenacres city	37 573
12	07875	099	Palm Beach County	68 217	12	27322	099	Palm Beach County	37 573
12	07950		Bradenton city	49 546	12	28452		Hallandale Beach city	37 113
12	07950	081	Manatee County	49 546	12	28452	011	Broward County	37 113
12	10275		Cape Coral city	154 305	12	30000		Hialeah city	224 669
12	10275	071	Lee County	154 305	12	30000	086	Miami-Dade County	224 669
12	11050		Casselberry city	26 241	12	32000		Hollywood city	140 768
12	11050	117	Seminole County	26 241	12	32000	011	Broward County	140 768
12	12875		Clearwater city	107 685	12	32275		Homestead city	60 512
12	12875	103	Pinellas County	107 685	12	32275	086	Miami-Dade County	60 512
12	12925		Clermont city	28 742	12	35000		Jacksonville city	821 784
12	12925	069	Lake County	28 742	12	35000	031	Duval County	821 784
12	13275		Coconut Creek city	52 909	12	35875		Jupiter town	55 156
12	13275	011	Broward County	52 909	12	35875	099	Palm Beach County	55 156

State Code	Place Code	County Code	Geographic Area Name	2010 Census Population	State Code	Place Code	County Code	Geographic Area Name	2010 Census Population
12	36950		Kissimmee city	59 682	12	54075		Palm Beach Gardens city	48 452
12	36950	097	Osceola County	59 682	12	54075	099	Palm Beach County	48 452
12	38250		Lakeland city	97 422	12	54200		Palm Coast city	75 180
12	38250	105	Polk County	97 422	12	54200	035	Flagler County	75 180
12	39075		Lake Worth city	34 910	12	54700		Panama City city	36 484
12	39075	099	Palm Beach County	34 910	12	54700	005	Bay County	36 484
12	39425		Largo city	77 648	12	55775		Pembroke Pines city	154 750
12	39425	103	Pinellas County	77 648	12	55775	011	Broward County	154 750
12	39525		Lauderdale Lakes city	32 593	12	55925		Pensacola city	51 923
12	39525	011	Broward County	32 593	12	55925	033	Escambia County	51 923
12	39550		Lauderhill city	66 887	12	56975		Pinellas Park city	49 079
12	39550	011	Broward County	66 887	12	56975	103	Pinellas County	49 079
12	43125		Margate city	53 284	12	57425		Plantation city	84 955
12	43125	011	Broward County	53 284	12	57425	011	Broward County	84 955
12	43975		Melbourne city	76 068	12	57550		Plant City city	34 721
12	43975	009	Brevard County	76 068	12	57550	057	Hillsborough County	34 721
12	45000		Miami city	399 457	12	58050		Pompano Beach city	99 845
12	45000	086	Miami-Dade County	399 457	12	58050	011	Broward County	99 845
12	45025		Miami Beach city	87 779	12	58575		Port Orange city	56 048
12	45025	086	Miami-Dade County	87 779	12	58575	127	Volusia County	56 048
12	45060		Miami Gardens city	107 167	12	58715		Port St. Lucie city	164 603
12	45060	086	Miami-Dade County	107 167	12	58715	111	St. Lucie County	164 603
12	45100		Miami Lakes town	29 361	12	60975		Riviera Beach city	32 488
12	45100	086	Miami-Dade County	29 361	12	60975	099	Palm Beach County	32 488
12	45975		Miramar city	122 041	12	62100		Royal Palm Beach village	34 140
12	45975	011	Broward County	122 041	12	62100	099	Palm Beach County	34 140
12	49425		North Lauderdale city	41 023	12	62625		St. Cloud city	35 183
12	49425	011	Broward County	41 023	12	62625	097	Osceola County	35 183
12	49450		North Miami city	58 786	12	63000		St. Petersburg city	244 769
12	49450	086	Miami-Dade County	58 786	12	63000	103	Pinellas County	244 769
12	49475		North Miami Beach city	41 523	12	63650		Sanford city	53 570
12	49475	086	Miami-Dade County	41 523	12	63650	117	Seminole County	53 570
12	49675		North Port city	57 357	12	64175		Sarasota city	51 917
12	49675	115	Sarasota County	57 357	12	64175	115	Sarasota County	51 917
12	50575		Oakland Park city	41 363	12	69700		Sunrise city	84 439
12	50575	011	Broward County	41 363	12	69700	011	Broward County	84 439
12	50750		Ocala city	56 315	12	70600		Tallahassee city	181 376
12	50750	083	Marion County	56 315	12	70600	073	Leon County	181 376
12	51075		Ocoee city	35 579	12	70675		Tamarac city	60 427
12	51075	095	Orange County	35 579	12	70675	011	Broward County	60 427
12	53000		Orlando city	238 300	12	71000		Tampa city	335 709
12	53000	095	Orange County	238 300	12	71000	057	Hillsborough County	335 709
12	53150		Ormond Beach city	38 137	12	71900		Titusville city	43 761
12	53150	127	Volusia County	38 137	12	71900	009	Brevard County	43 761
12	53575		Oviedo city	33 342	12	75812		Wellington village	56 508
12	53575	117	Seminole County	33 342	12	75812	099	Palm Beach County	56 508
12	54000		Palm Bay city	103 190	12	76582		Weston city	65 333
12	54000	009	Brevard County	103 190	12	76582	011	Broward County	65 333

Cities by County–*Continued*

State Code	Place Code	County Code	Geographic Area Name	2010 Census Population	State Code	Place Code	County Code	Geographic Area Name	2010 Census Population
12	76600		West Palm Beach city	99 919	13	55020		Newnan city	33 039
12	76600	099	Palm Beach County	99 919	13	55020	077	Coweta County	33 039
12	78250		Winter Garden city	34 568	13	59724		Peachtree City city	34 364
12	78250	095	Orange County	34 568	13	59724	113	Fayette County	34 364
12	78275		Winter Haven city	33 874	13	66668		Rome city	36 303
12	78275	105	Polk County	33 874	13	66668	115	Floyd County	36 303
12	78300		Winter Park city	27 852	13	67284		Roswell city	88 346
12	78300	095	Orange County	27 852	13	67284	121	Fulton County	88 346
12	78325		Winter Springs city	33 282	13	68516		Sandy Springs city	93 853
12	78325	117	Seminole County	33 282	13	68516	121	Fulton County	93 853
13			**GEORGIA**	9 687 653	13	69000		Savannah city	136 286
13	01052		Albany city	77 434	13	69000	051	Chatham County	136 286
13	01052	095	Dougherty County	77 434	13	71492		Smyrna city	51 271
13	01696		Alpharetta city	57 551	13	71492	067	Cobb County	51 271
13	01696	121	Fulton County	57 551	13	73256		Statesboro city	28 422
13	04000		Atlanta city	420 003	13	73256	031	Bulloch County	28 422
13	04000	089	DeKalb County	28 292	13	73704		Stockbridge city	25 636
13	04000	121	Fulton County	391 711	13	73704	151	Henry County	25 636
13	19000		Columbus city	189 885	13	78800		Valdosta city	54 518
13	19000	215	Muscogee County	189 885	13	78800	185	Lowndes County	54 518
13	21380		Dalton city	33 128	13	80508		Warner Robins city	66 588
13	21380	313	Whitfield County	33 128	13	80508	153	Houston County	66 224
13	23900		Douglasville city	30 961	13	80508	225	Peach County	364
13	23900	097	Douglas County	30 961	15			**HAWAII**	1 360 301
13	24600		Duluth city	26 600	15	06290		East Honolulu CDP	49 914
13	24600	135	Gwinnett County	26 600	15	06290	003	Honolulu County	49 914
13	24768		Dunwoody city	46 267	15	14650		Hilo CDP	43 263
13	24768	089	DeKalb County	46 267	15	14650	001	Hawaii County	43 263
13	25720		East Point city	33 712	15	22700		Kahului CDP	26 337
13	25720	121	Fulton County	33 712	15	22700	009	Maui County	26 337
13	31908		Gainesville city	33 804	15	23150		Kailua CDP	38 635
13	31908	139	Hall County	33 804	15	23150	003	Honolulu County	38 635
13	38964		Hinesville city	33 437	15	28250		Kaneohe CDP	34 597
13	38964	179	Liberty County	33 437	15	28250	003	Honolulu County	34 597
13	42425		Johns Creek city	76 728	15	51050		Mililani Town CDP	27 629
13	42425	121	Fulton County	76 728	15	51050	003	Honolulu County	27 629
13	43192		Kennesaw city	29 783	15	62600		Pearl City CDP	47 698
13	43192	067	Cobb County	29 783	15	62600	003	Honolulu County	47 698
13	44340		LaGrange city	29 588	15	71550		Urban Honolulu CDP	337 256
13	44340	285	Troup County	29 588	15	71550	003	Honolulu County	337 256
13	45488		Lawrenceville city	28 546	15	79700		Waipahu CDP	38 216
13	45488	135	Gwinnett County	28 546	15	79700	003	Honolulu County	38 216
13	49000		Macon city	91 351	16			**IDAHO**	1 567 582
13	49000	021	Bibb County	90 885	16	08830		Boise City city	205 671
13	49000	169	Jones County	466	16	08830	001	Ada County	205 671
13	49756		Marietta city	56 579	16	12250		Caldwell city	46 237
13	49756	067	Cobb County	56 579	16	12250	027	Canyon County	46 237
13	51670		Milton city	32 661	16	16750		Coeur d'Alene city	44 137
13	51670	121	Fulton County	32 661	16	16750	055	Kootenai County	44 137

Cities by County–*Continued*

State Code	Place Code	County Code	Geographic Area Name	2010 Census Population	State Code	Place Code	County Code	Geographic Area Name	2010 Census Population
16	39700		Idaho Falls city	56 813	17	09447		Buffalo Grove village	41 496
16	39700	019	Bonneville County	56 813	17	09447	031	Cook County	13 644
					17	09447	097	Lake County	27 852
16	46540		Lewiston city	31 894					
16	46540	069	Nez Perce County	31 894	17	09642		Burbank city	28 925
					17	09642	031	Cook County	28 925
16	52120		Meridian city	75 092					
16	52120	001	Ada County	75 092	17	10487		Calumet City city	37 042
					17	10487	031	Cook County	37 042
16	56260		Nampa city	81 557					
16	56260	027	Canyon County	81 557	17	11163		Carbondale city	25 902
					17	11163	077	Jackson County	25 902
16	64090		Pocatello city	54 255	17	11163	199	Williamson County	0
16	64090	005	Bannock County	54 239					
16	64090	077	Power County	16	17	11332		Carol Stream village	39 711
					17	11332	043	DuPage County	39 711
16	64810		Post Falls city	27 574					
16	64810	055	Kootenai County	27 574	17	11358		Carpentersville village	37 691
					17	11358	089	Kane County	37 691
16	67420		Rexburg city	25 484					
16	67420	065	Madison County	25 484	17	12385		Champaign city	81 055
					17	12385	019	Champaign County	81 055
16	82810		Twin Falls city	44 125					
16	82810	083	Twin Falls County	44 125	17	14000		Chicago city	2 695 598
					17	14000	031	Cook County	2 695 598
17			**ILLINOIS**	12 830 632	17	14000	043	DuPage County	0
17	00243		Addison village	36 942					
17	00243	043	DuPage County	36 942	17	14026		Chicago Heights city	30 276
					17	14026	031	Cook County	30 276
17	00685		Algonquin village	30 046					
17	00685	089	Kane County	8 433	17	14351		Cicero town	83 891
17	00685	111	McHenry County	21 613	17	14351	031	Cook County	83 891
17	01114		Alton city	27 865	17	15599		Collinsville city	25 579
17	01114	119	Madison County	27 865	17	15599	119	Madison County	22 573
					17	15599	163	St. Clair County	3 006
17	02154		Arlington Heights village	75 101					
17	02154	031	Cook County	75 101	17	17887		Crystal Lake city	40 743
17	02154	097	Lake County	0	17	17887	111	McHenry County	40 743
17	03012		Aurora city	197 899	17	18563		Danville city	33 027
17	03012	043	DuPage County	49 433	17	18563	183	Vermilion County	33 027
17	03012	089	Kane County	130 976					
17	03012	093	Kendall County	6 019	17	18823		Decatur city	76 122
17	03012	197	Will County	11 471	17	18823	115	Macon County	76 122
17	04013		Bartlett village	41 208	17	19161		DeKalb city	43 862
17	04013	031	Cook County	16 797	17	19161	037	DeKalb County	43 862
17	04013	043	DuPage County	24 411					
17	04013	089	Kane County	0	17	19642		Des Plaines city	58 364
					17	19642	031	Cook County	58 364
17	04078		Batavia city	26 045					
17	04078	043	DuPage County	0	17	20591		Downers Grove village	47 833
17	04078	089	Kane County	26 045	17	20591	043	DuPage County	47 833
17	04845		Belleville city	44 478	17	22255		East St. Louis city	27 006
17	04845	163	St. Clair County	44 478	17	22255	163	St. Clair County	27 006
17	05092		Belvidere city	25 585	17	23074		Elgin city	108 188
17	05092	007	Boone County	25 585	17	23074	031	Cook County	24 032
					17	23074	089	Kane County	84 156
17	05573		Berwyn city	56 657					
17	05573	031	Cook County	56 657	17	23256		Elk Grove Village village	33 127
					17	23256	031	Cook County	33 127
17	06613		Bloomington city	76 610	17	23256	043	DuPage County	0
17	06613	113	McLean County	76 610					
					17	23620		Elmhurst city	44 121
17	07133		Bolingbrook village	73 366	17	23620	031	Cook County	0
17	07133	043	DuPage County	1 571	17	23620	043	DuPage County	44 121
17	07133	197	Will County	71 795					
					17	24582		Evanston city	74 486
					17	24582	031	Cook County	74 486

State Code	Place Code	County Code	Geographic Area Name	2010 Census Population	State Code	Place Code	County Code	Geographic Area Name	2010 Census Population
17	27884		Freeport city	25 638	17	53234		Normal town	52 497
17	27884	177	Stephenson County	25 638	17	53234	113	McLean County	52 497
17	28326		Galesburg city	32 195	17	53481		Northbrook village	33 170
17	28326	095	Knox County	32 195	17	53481	031	Cook County	33 170
17	29730		Glendale Heights village	34 208	17	53559		North Chicago city	32 574
17	29730	043	DuPage County	34 208	17	53559	097	Lake County	32 574
17	29756		Glen Ellyn village	27 450	17	54638		Oak Forest city	27 962
17	29756	043	DuPage County	27 450	17	54638	031	Cook County	27 962
17	29938		Glenview village	44 692	17	54820		Oak Lawn village	56 690
17	29938	031	Cook County	44 692	17	54820	031	Cook County	56 690
17	30926		Granite City city	29 849	17	54885		Oak Park village	51 878
17	30926	119	Madison County	29 849	17	54885	031	Cook County	51 878
17	32018		Gurnee village	31 295	17	55249		O'Fallon city	28 281
17	32018	097	Lake County	31 295	17	55249	163	St. Clair County	28 281
17	32746		Hanover Park village	37 973	17	56640		Orland Park village	56 767
17	32746	031	Cook County	20 636	17	56640	031	Cook County	56 583
17	32746	043	DuPage County	17 337	17	56640	197	Will County	184
17	33383		Harvey city	25 282	17	56887		Oswego village	30 355
17	33383	031	Cook County	25 282	17	56887	093	Kendall County	30 355
17	34722		Highland Park city	29 763	17	57225		Palatine village	68 557
17	34722	097	Lake County	29 763	17	57225	031	Cook County	68 557
					17	57225	097	Lake County	0
17	35411		Hoffman Estates village	51 895					
17	35411	031	Cook County	51 895	17	57875		Park Ridge city	37 480
17	35411	089	Kane County	0	17	57875	031	Cook County	37 480
17	38570		Joliet city	147 433	17	58447		Pekin city	34 094
17	38570	093	Kendall County	9 749	17	58447	143	Peoria County	0
17	38570	197	Will County	137 684	17	58447	179	Tazewell County	34 094
17	38934		Kankakee city	27 537	17	59000		Peoria city	115 007
17	38934	091	Kankakee County	27 537	17	59000	143	Peoria County	115 007
17	41183		Lake in the Hills village	28 965	17	60287		Plainfield village	39 581
17	41183	111	McHenry County	28 965	17	60287	093	Kendall County	2 079
					17	60287	197	Will County	37 502
17	42028		Lansing village	28 331					
17	42028	031	Cook County	28 331	17	62367		Quincy city	40 633
					17	62367	001	Adams County	40 633
17	44407		Lombard village	43 165					
17	44407	043	DuPage County	43 165	17	65000		Rockford city	152 871
					17	65000	201	Winnebago County	152 871
17	45694		McHenry city	26 992					
17	45694	111	McHenry County	26 992	17	65078		Rock Island city	39 018
					17	65078	161	Rock Island County	39 018
17	48242		Melrose Park village	25 411					
17	48242	031	Cook County	25 411	17	65442		Romeoville village	39 680
					17	65442	197	Will County	39 680
17	49867		Moline city	43 483					
17	49867	161	Rock Island County	43 483	17	66040		Round Lake Beach village	28 175
					17	66040	097	Lake County	28 175
17	51089		Mount Prospect village	54 167					
17	51089	031	Cook County	54 167	17	66703		St. Charles city	32 974
					17	66703	043	DuPage County	543
17	51349		Mundelein village	31 064	17	66703	089	Kane County	32 431
17	51349	097	Lake County	31 064					
					17	68003		Schaumburg village	74 227
17	51622		Naperville city	141 853	17	68003	031	Cook County	74 227
17	51622	043	DuPage County	94 533	17	68003	043	DuPage County	0
17	51622	197	Will County	47 320					
					17	70122		Skokie village	64 784
17	53000		Niles village	29 803	17	70122	031	Cook County	64 784
17	53000	031	Cook County	29 803					

State Code	Place Code	County Code	Geographic Area Name	2010 Census Population	State Code	Place Code	County Code	Geographic Area Name	2010 Census Population
17	72000		Springfield city	116 250	18	28386		Goshen city	31 719
17	72000	167	Sangamon County	116 250	18	28386	039	Elkhart County	31 719
17	73157		Streamwood village	39 858	18	29898		Greenwood city	49 791
17	73157	031	Cook County	39 858	18	29898	081	Johnson County	49 791
17	75484		Tinley Park village	56 703	18	31000		Hammond city	80 830
17	75484	031	Cook County	49 236	18	31000	089	Lake County	80 830
17	75484	197	Will County	7 467					
					18	34114		Hobart city	29 059
17	77005		Urbana city	41 250	18	34114	089	Lake County	29 059
17	77005	019	Champaign County	41 250					
					18	38358		Jeffersonville city	44 953
17	77694		Vernon Hills village	25 113	18	38358	019	Clark County	44 953
17	77694	097	Lake County	25 113					
					18	40392		Kokomo city	45 468
17	79293		Waukegan city	89 078	18	40392	067	Howard County	45 468
17	79293	097	Lake County	89 078					
					18	40788		Lafayette city	67 140
17	80060		West Chicago city	27 086	18	40788	157	Tippecanoe County	67 140
17	80060	043	DuPage County	27 086					
					18	42426		Lawrence city	46 001
17	81048		Wheaton city	52 894	18	42426	097	Marion County	46 001
17	81048	043	DuPage County	52 894					
					18	46908		Marion city	29 948
17	81087		Wheeling village	37 648	18	46908	053	Grant County	29 948
17	81087	031	Cook County	37 642					
17	81087	097	Lake County	6	18	48528		Merrillville town	35 246
					18	48528	089	Lake County	35 246
17	82075		Wilmette village	27 087					
17	82075	031	Cook County	27 087	18	48798		Michigan City city	31 479
					18	48798	091	LaPorte County	31 479
17	83245		Woodridge village	32 971					
17	83245	031	Cook County	0	18	49932		Mishawaka city	48 252
17	83245	043	DuPage County	32 949	18	49932	141	St. Joseph County	48 252
17	83245	197	Will County	22					
					18	51876		Muncie city	70 085
18			**INDIANA**	6 483 802	18	51876	035	Delaware County	70 085
18	01468		Anderson city	56 129					
18	01468	095	Madison County	56 129	18	52326		New Albany city	36 372
					18	52326	043	Floyd County	36 372
18	05860		Bloomington city	80 405					
18	05860	105	Monroe County	80 405	18	54180		Noblesville city	51 969
					18	54180	057	Hamilton County	51 969
18	10342		Carmel city	79 191					
18	10342	057	Hamilton County	79 191	18	60246		Plainfield town	27 631
					18	60246	063	Hendricks County	27 631
18	14734		Columbus city	44 061					
18	14734	005	Bartholomew County	44 061	18	61092		Portage city	36 828
					18	61092	127	Porter County	36 828
18	16138		Crown Point city	27 317					
18	16138	089	Lake County	27 317	18	64260		Richmond city	36 812
					18	64260	177	Wayne County	36 812
18	19486		East Chicago city	29 698					
18	19486	089	Lake County	29 698	18	68220		Schererville town	29 243
					18	68220	089	Lake County	29 243
18	20728		Elkhart city	50 949					
18	20728	039	Elkhart County	50 949	18	71000		South Bend city	101 168
					18	71000	141	St. Joseph County	101 168
18	22000		Evansville city	117 429					
18	22000	163	Vanderburgh County	117 429	18	75428		Terre Haute city	60 785
					18	75428	167	Vigo County	60 785
18	23278		Fishers town	76 794					
18	23278	057	Hamilton County	76 794	18	78326		Valparaiso city	31 730
					18	78326	127	Porter County	31 730
18	25000		Fort Wayne city	253 691					
18	25000	003	Allen County	253 691	18	82700		Westfield town	30 068
					18	82700	057	Hamilton County	30 068
18	27000		Gary city	80 294					
18	27000	089	Lake County	80 294	18	82862		West Lafayette city	29 596
					18	82862	157	Tippecanoe County	29 596

State Code	Place Code	County Code	Geographic Area Name	2010 Census Population	State Code	Place Code	County Code	Geographic Area Name	2010 Census Population
19			**IOWA**	3 046 355	20	25325		Garden City city	26 658
19	01855		Ames city	58 965	20	25325	055	Finney County	26 658
19	01855	169	Story County	58 965					
					20	33625		Hutchinson city	42 080
19	02305		Ankeny city	45 582	20	33625	155	Reno County	42 080
19	02305	153	Polk County	45 582					
					20	36000		Kansas City city	145 786
19	06355		Bettendorf city	33 217	20	36000	209	Wyandotte County	145 786
19	06355	163	Scott County	33 217					
					20	38900		Lawrence city	87 643
19	09550		Burlington city	25 663	20	38900	045	Douglas County	87 643
19	09550	057	Des Moines County	25 663					
					20	39000		Leavenworth city	35 251
19	11755		Cedar Falls city	39 260	20	39000	103	Leavenworth County	35 251
19	11755	013	Black Hawk County	39 260					
					20	39075		Leawood city	31 867
19	12000		Cedar Rapids city	126 326	20	39075	091	Johnson County	31 867
19	12000	113	Linn County	126 326					
					20	39350		Lenexa city	48 190
19	14430		Clinton city	26 885	20	39350	091	Johnson County	48 190
19	14430	045	Clinton County	26 885					
					20	44250		Manhattan city	52 281
19	16860		Council Bluffs city	62 230	20	44250	149	Pottawatomie County	146
19	16860	155	Pottawattamie County	62 230	20	44250	161	Riley County	52 135
19	19000		Davenport city	99 685	20	52575		Olathe city	125 872
19	19000	163	Scott County	99 685	20	52575	091	Johnson County	125 872
19	21000		Des Moines city	203 433	20	53775		Overland Park city	173 372
19	21000	153	Polk County	203 419	20	53775	091	Johnson County	173 372
19	21000	181	Warren County	14					
					20	62700		Salina city	47 707
19	22395		Dubuque city	57 637	20	62700	169	Saline County	47 707
19	22395	061	Dubuque County	57 637					
					20	64500		Shawnee city	62 209
19	28515		Fort Dodge city	25 206	20	64500	091	Johnson County	62 209
19	28515	187	Webster County	25 206					
					20	71000		Topeka city	127 473
19	38595		Iowa City city	67 862	20	71000	177	Shawnee County	127 473
19	38595	103	Johnson County	67 862					
					20	79000		Wichita city	382 368
19	49485		Marion city	34 768	20	79000	173	Sedgwick County	382 368
19	49485	113	Linn County	34 768	21			**KENTUCKY**	4 339 367
					21	08902		Bowling Green city	58 067
19	49755		Marshalltown city	27 552	21	08902	227	Warren County	58 067
19	49755	127	Marshall County	27 552					
					21	17848		Covington city	40 640
19	50160		Mason City city	28 079	21	17848	117	Kenton County	40 640
19	50160	033	Cerro Gordo County	28 079					
					21	24274		Elizabethtown city	28 531
19	60465		Ottumwa city	25 023	21	24274	093	Hardin County	28 531
19	60465	179	Wapello County	25 023					
					21	27982		Florence city	29 951
19	73335		Sioux City city	82 684	21	27982	015	Boone County	29 951
19	73335	149	Plymouth County	6					
19	73335	193	Woodbury County	82 678	21	28900		Frankfort city	25 527
					21	28900	073	Franklin County	25 527
19	79950		Urbandale city	39 463					
19	79950	049	Dallas County	6 337	21	30700		Georgetown city	29 098
19	79950	153	Polk County	33 126	21	30700	209	Scott County	29 098
19	82425		Waterloo city	68 406	21	35866		Henderson city	28 757
19	82425	013	Black Hawk County	68 406	21	35866	101	Henderson County	28 757
19	83910		West Des Moines city	56 609	21	37918		Hopkinsville city	31 577
19	83910	049	Dallas County	11 569	21	37918	047	Christian County	31 577
19	83910	153	Polk County	44 999					
19	83910	181	Warren County	41	21	40222		Jeffersontown city	26 595
20			**KANSAS**	2 853 118	21	40222	111	Jefferson County	26 595
20	18250		Dodge City city	27 340					
20	18250	057	Ford County	27 340					

State Code	Place Code	County Code	Geographic Area Name	2010 Census Population	State Code	Place Code	County Code	Geographic Area Name	2010 Census Population
21	46027		Lexington-Fayette urban county	295 803	24	04000		Baltimore city	620 961
21	46027	067	Fayette County	295 803	24	04000	510	Baltimore city	620 961
21	56136		Nicholasville city	28 015	24	08775		Bowie city	54 727
21	56136	113	Jessamine County	28 015	24	08775	033	Prince George's County	54 727
21	58620		Owensboro city	57 265	24	18750		College Park city	30 413
21	58620	059	Daviess County	57 265	24	18750	033	Prince George's County	30 413
21	58836		Paducah city	25 024	24	30325		Frederick city	65 239
21	58836	145	McCracken County	25 024	24	30325	021	Frederick County	65 239
21	65226		Richmond city	31 364	24	31175		Gaithersburg city	59 933
21	65226	151	Madison County	31 364	24	31175	031	Montgomery County	59 933
22			**LOUISIANA**	4 533 372	24	36075		Hagerstown city	39 662
22	00975		Alexandria city	47 723	24	36075	043	Washington County	39 662
22	00975	079	Rapides Parish	47 723	24	45900		Laurel city	25 115
22	05000		Baton Rouge city	229 493	24	45900	033	Prince George's County	25 115
22	05000	033	East Baton Rouge Parish	229 493					
					24	67675		Rockville city	61 209
22	08920		Bossier City city	61 315	24	67675	031	Montgomery County	61 209
22	08920	015	Bossier Parish	61 315					
					24	69925		Salisbury city	30 343
22	13960		Central city	26 864	24	69925	045	Wicomico County	30 343
22	13960	033	East Baton Rouge Parish	26 864					
					25			**MASSACHUSETTS**	6 547 629
22	36255		Houma city	33 727	25	00840		Agawam Town city	28 438
22	36255	109	Terrebonne Parish	33 727	25	00840	013	Hampden County	28 438
22	39475		Kenner city	66 702	25	02690		Attleboro city	43 593
22	39475	051	Jefferson Parish	66 702	25	02690	005	Bristol County	43 593
22	40735		Lafayette city	120 623	25	03690		Barnstable Town city	45 193
22	40735	055	Lafayette Parish	120 623	25	03690	001	Barnstable County	45 193
22	41155		Lake Charles city	71 993	25	05595		Beverly city	39 502
22	41155	019	Calcasieu Parish	71 993	25	05595	009	Essex County	39 502
22	51410		Monroe city	48 815	25	07000		Boston city	617 594
22	51410	073	Ouachita Parish	48 815	25	07000	025	Suffolk County	617 594
22	54035		New Iberia city	30 617	25	07740		Braintree Town city	35 744
22	54035	045	Iberia Parish	30 617	25	07740	021	Norfolk County	35 744
22	55000		New Orleans city	343 829	25	09000		Brockton city	93 810
22	55000	071	Orleans Parish	343 829	25	09000	023	Plymouth County	93 810
22	70000		Shreveport city	199 311	25	11000		Cambridge city	105 162
22	70000	015	Bossier Parish	2 702	25	11000	017	Middlesex County	105 162
22	70000	017	Caddo Parish	196 609					
					25	13205		Chelsea city	35 177
22	70805		Slidell city	27 068	25	13205	025	Suffolk County	35 177
22	70805	103	St. Tammany Parish	27 068					
					25	13660		Chicopee city	55 298
23			**MAINE**	1 328 361	25	13660	013	Hampden County	55 298
23	02795		Bangor city	33 039					
23	02795	019	Penobscot County	33 039	25	21990		Everett city	41 667
					25	21990	017	Middlesex County	41 667
23	38740		Lewiston city	36 592					
23	38740	001	Androscoggin County	36 592	25	23000		Fall River city	88 857
					25	23000	005	Bristol County	88 857
23	60545		Portland city	66 194					
23	60545	005	Cumberland County	66 194	25	23875		Fitchburg city	40 318
					25	23875	027	Worcester County	40 318
23	71990		South Portland city	25 002					
23	71990	005	Cumberland County	25 002	25	25172		Franklin Town city	31 635
					25	25172	021	Norfolk County	31 635
24			**MARYLAND**	5 773 552					
24	01600		Annapolis city	38 394	25	26150		Gloucester city	28 789
24	01600	003	Anne Arundel County	38 394	25	26150	009	Essex County	28 789

State Code	Place Code	County Code	Geographic Area Name	2010 Census Population	State Code	Place Code	County Code	Geographic Area Name	2010 Census Population
25	29405		Haverhill city	60 879	25	76030		Westfield city	41 094
25	29405	009	Essex County	60 879	25	76030	013	Hampden County	41 094
25	30840		Holyoke city	39 880	25	77890		West Springfield Town city	28 391
25	30840	013	Hampden County	39 880	25	77890	013	Hampden County	28 391
25	34550		Lawrence city	76 377	25	78972		Weymouth Town city	53 743
25	34550	009	Essex County	76 377	25	78972	021	Norfolk County	53 743
25	35075		Leominster city	40 759	25	81035		Woburn city	38 120
25	35075	027	Worcester County	40 759	25	81035	017	Middlesex County	38 120
25	37000		Lowell city	106 519	25	82000		Worcester city	181 045
25	37000	017	Middlesex County	106 519	25	82000	027	Worcester County	181 045
25	37490		Lynn city	90 329	26			**MICHIGAN**	9 883 640
25	37490	009	Essex County	90 329	26	01380		Allen Park city	28 210
					26	01380	163	Wayne County	28 210
25	37875		Malden city	59 450					
25	37875	017	Middlesex County	59 450	26	03000		Ann Arbor city	113 934
					26	03000	161	Washtenaw County	113 934
25	38715		Marlborough city	38 499					
25	38715	017	Middlesex County	38 499	26	05920		Battle Creek city	52 347
					26	05920	025	Calhoun County	52 347
25	39835		Medford city	56 173					
25	39835	017	Middlesex County	56 173	26	06020		Bay City city	34 932
					26	06020	017	Bay County	34 932
25	40115		Melrose city	26 983					
25	40115	017	Middlesex County	26 983	26	12060		Burton city	29 999
					26	12060	049	Genesee County	29 999
25	40710		Methuen Town city	47 255					
25	40710	009	Essex County	47 255	26	21000		Dearborn city	98 153
					26	21000	163	Wayne County	98 153
25	45000		New Bedford city	95 072					
25	45000	005	Bristol County	95 072	26	21020		Dearborn Heights city	57 774
					26	21020	163	Wayne County	57 774
25	45560		Newton city	85 146					
25	45560	017	Middlesex County	85 146	26	22000		Detroit city	713 777
					26	22000	163	Wayne County	713 777
25	46330		Northampton city	28 549					
25	46330	015	Hampshire County	28 549	26	24120		East Lansing city	48 579
					26	24120	037	Clinton County	1 969
25	52490		Peabody city	51 251	26	24120	065	Ingham County	46 610
25	52490	009	Essex County	51 251					
					26	24290		Eastpointe city	32 442
25	53960		Pittsfield city	44 737	26	24290	099	Macomb County	32 442
25	53960	003	Berkshire County	44 737					
					26	27440		Farmington Hills city	79 740
25	55745		Quincy city	92 271	26	27440	125	Oakland County	79 740
25	55745	021	Norfolk County	92 271					
					26	29000		Flint city	102 434
25	56585		Revere city	51 755	26	29000	049	Genesee County	102 434
25	56585	025	Suffolk County	51 755					
					26	31420		Garden City city	27 692
25	59105		Salem city	41 340	26	31420	163	Wayne County	27 692
25	59105	009	Essex County	41 340					
					26	34000		Grand Rapids city	188 040
25	62535		Somerville city	75 754	26	34000	081	Kent County	188 040
25	62535	017	Middlesex County	75 754					
					26	38640		Holland city	33 051
25	67000		Springfield city	153 060	26	38640	005	Allegan County	7 016
25	67000	013	Hampden County	153 060	26	38640	139	Ottawa County	26 035
25	69170		Taunton city	55 874	26	40680		Inkster city	25 369
25	69170	005	Bristol County	55 874	26	40680	163	Wayne County	25 369
25	72600		Waltham city	60 632	26	41420		Jackson city	33 534
25	72600	017	Middlesex County	60 632	26	41420	075	Jackson County	33 534
25	73440		Watertown Town city	31 915	26	42160		Kalamazoo city	74 262
25	73440	017	Middlesex County	31 915	26	42160	077	Kalamazoo County	74 262

Cities by County—*Continued*

State Code	Place Code	County Code	Geographic Area Name	2010 Census Population	State Code	Place Code	County Code	Geographic Area Name	2010 Census Population
26	42820		Kentwood city	48 707	26	84000		Warren city	134 056
26	42820	081	Kent County	48 707	26	84000	099	Macomb County	134 056
26	46000		Lansing city	114 297	26	86000		Westland city	84 094
26	46000	045	Eaton County	4 734	26	86000	163	Wayne County	84 094
26	46000	065	Ingham County	109 563					
					26	88900		Wyandotte city	25 883
26	47800		Lincoln Park city	38 144	26	88900	163	Wayne County	25 883
26	47800	163	Wayne County	38 144					
					26	88940		Wyoming city	72 125
26	49000		Livonia city	96 942	26	88940	081	Kent County	72 125
26	49000	163	Wayne County	96 942					
					27			**MINNESOTA**	5 303 925
26	50560		Madison Heights city	29 694	27	01486		Andover city	30 598
26	50560	125	Oakland County	29 694	27	01486	003	Anoka County	30 598
26	53780		Midland city	41 863	27	01900		Apple Valley city	49 084
26	53780	017	Bay County	157	27	01900	037	Dakota County	49 084
26	53780	111	Midland County	41 706					
					27	06382		Blaine city	57 186
26	56020		Mount Pleasant city	26 016	27	06382	003	Anoka County	57 186
26	56020	073	Isabella County	26 016	27	06382	123	Ramsey County	0
26	56320		Muskegon city	38 401	27	06616		Bloomington city	82 893
26	56320	121	Muskegon County	38 401	27	06616	053	Hennepin County	82 893
26	59440		Novi city	55 224	27	07948		Brooklyn Center city	30 104
26	59440	125	Oakland County	55 224	27	07948	053	Hennepin County	30 104
26	59920		Oak Park city	29 319	27	07966		Brooklyn Park city	75 781
26	59920	125	Oakland County	29 319	27	07966	053	Hennepin County	75 781
26	65440		Pontiac city	59 515	27	08794		Burnsville city	60 306
26	65440	125	Oakland County	59 515	27	08794	037	Dakota County	60 306
26	65560		Portage city	46 292	27	13114		Coon Rapids city	61 476
26	65560	077	Kalamazoo County	46 292	27	13114	003	Anoka County	61 476
26	65820		Port Huron city	30 184	27	13456		Cottage Grove city	34 589
26	65820	147	St. Clair County	30 184	27	13456	163	Washington County	34 589
26	69035		Rochester Hills city	70 995	27	17000		Duluth city	86 265
26	69035	125	Oakland County	70 995	27	17000	137	St. Louis County	86 265
26	69800		Roseville city	47 299	27	17288		Eagan city	64 206
26	69800	099	Macomb County	47 299	27	17288	037	Dakota County	64 206
26	70040		Royal Oak city	57 236	27	18116		Eden Prairie city	60 797
26	70040	125	Oakland County	57 236	27	18116	053	Hennepin County	60 797
26	70520		Saginaw city	51 508	27	18188		Edina city	47 941
26	70520	145	Saginaw County	51 508	27	18188	053	Hennepin County	47 941
26	70760		St. Clair Shores city	59 715	27	22814		Fridley city	27 208
26	70760	099	Macomb County	59 715	27	22814	003	Anoka County	27 208
26	74900		Southfield city	71 739	27	31076		Inver Grove Heights city	33 880
26	74900	125	Oakland County	71 739	27	31076	037	Dakota County	33 880
26	74960		Southgate city	30 047	27	35180		Lakeville city	55 954
26	74960	163	Wayne County	30 047	27	35180	037	Dakota County	55 954
26	76460		Sterling Heights city	129 699	27	39878		Mankato city	39 309
26	76460	099	Macomb County	129 699	27	39878	013	Blue Earth County	39 305
					27	39878	079	Le Sueur County	4
26	79000		Taylor city	63 131	27	39878	103	Nicollet County	0
26	79000	163	Wayne County	63 131					
					27	40166		Maple Grove city	61 567
26	80700		Troy city	80 980	27	40166	053	Hennepin County	61 567
26	80700	125	Oakland County	80 980					
					27	40382		Maplewood city	38 018
					27	40382	123	Ramsey County	38 018

Cities by County–*Continued*

State Code	Place Code	County Code	Geographic Area Name	2010 Census Population	State Code	Place Code	County Code	Geographic Area Name	2010 Census Population
37	55000		Raleigh city	403 892	39	16014		Cleveland Heights city	46 121
37	55000	063	Durham County	1 067	39	16014	035	Cuyahoga County	46 121
37	55000	183	Wake County	402 825					
					39	18000		Columbus city	787 033
37	57500		Rocky Mount city	57 477	39	18000	041	Delaware County	7 245
37	57500	065	Edgecombe County	17 524	39	18000	045	Fairfield County	9 666
37	57500	127	Nash County	39 953	39	18000	049	Franklin County	770 122
37	58860		Salisbury city	33 662	39	19778		Cuyahoga Falls city	49 652
37	58860	159	Rowan County	33 662	39	19778	153	Summit County	49 652
37	59280		Sanford city	28 094	39	21000		Dayton city	141 527
37	59280	105	Lee County	28 094	39	21000	113	Montgomery County	141 527
37	67420		Thomasville city	26 757	39	21434		Delaware city	34 753
37	67420	057	Davidson County	26 493	39	21434	041	Delaware County	34 753
37	67420	151	Randolph County	264					
					39	22694		Dublin city	41 751
37	70540		Wake Forest town	30 117	39	22694	041	Delaware County	4 018
37	70540	069	Franklin County	899	39	22694	049	Franklin County	35 367
37	70540	183	Wake County	29 218	39	22694	159	Union County	2 366
37	74440		Wilmington city	106 476	39	25256		Elyria city	54 533
37	74440	129	New Hanover County	106 476	39	25256	093	Lorain County	54 533
37	74540		Wilson city	49 167	39	25704		Euclid city	48 920
37	74540	195	Wilson County	49 167	39	25704	035	Cuyahoga County	48 920
37	75000		Winston-Salem city	229 617	39	25914		Fairborn city	32 352
37	75000	067	Forsyth County	229 617	39	25914	057	Greene County	32 352
38			**NORTH DAKOTA**	672 591	39	25970		Fairfield city	42 510
38	07200		Bismarck city	61 272	39	25970	017	Butler County	42 510
38	07200	015	Burleigh County	61 272	39	25970	061	Hamilton County	0
38	25700		Fargo city	105 549	39	27048		Findlay city	41 202
38	25700	017	Cass County	105 549	39	27048	063	Hancock County	41 202
38	32060		Grand Forks city	52 838	39	29106		Gahanna city	33 248
38	32060	035	Grand Forks County	52 838	39	29106	049	Franklin County	33 248
38	53380		Minot city	40 888	39	29428		Garfield Heights city	28 849
38	53380	101	Ward County	40 888	39	29428	035	Cuyahoga County	28 849
38	84780		West Fargo city	25 830	39	31860		Green city	25 699
38	84780	017	Cass County	25 830	39	31860	153	Summit County	25 699
39			**OHIO**	11 536 504	39	32592		Grove City city	35 575
39	01000		Akron city	199 110	39	32592	049	Franklin County	35 575
39	01000	153	Summit County	199 110					
					39	33012		Hamilton city	62 477
39	03828		Barberton city	26 550	39	33012	017	Butler County	62 477
39	03828	153	Summit County	26 550					
					39	35476		Hilliard city	28 435
39	04720		Beavercreek city	45 193	39	35476	049	Franklin County	28 435
39	04720	057	Greene County	45 193					
					39	36610		Huber Heights city	38 101
39	07972		Bowling Green city	30 028	39	36610	057	Greene County	0
39	07972	173	Wood County	30 028	39	36610	109	Miami County	959
					39	36610	113	Montgomery County	37 142
39	09680		Brunswick city	34 255					
39	09680	103	Medina County	34 255	39	39872		Kent city	28 904
					39	39872	133	Portage County	28 904
39	12000		Canton city	73 007					
39	12000	151	Stark County	73 007	39	40040		Kettering city	56 163
					39	40040	057	Greene County	467
39	15000		Cincinnati city	296 943	39	40040	113	Montgomery County	55 696
39	15000	061	Hamilton County	296 943					
					39	41664		Lakewood city	52 131
39	16000		Cleveland city	396 815	39	41664	035	Cuyahoga County	52 131
39	16000	035	Cuyahoga County	396 815					

Cities by County–*Continued*

State Code	Place Code	County Code	Geographic Area Name	2010 Census Population	State Code	Place Code	County Code	Geographic Area Name	2010 Census Population
39	41720		Lancaster city	38 780	39	77588		Troy city	25 058
39	41720	045	Fairfield County	38 780	39	77588	109	Miami County	25 058
39	43554		Lima city	38 771	39	79002		Upper Arlington city	33 771
39	43554	003	Allen County	38 771	39	79002	049	Franklin County	33 771
39	44856		Lorain city	64 097	39	80892		Warren city	41 557
39	44856	093	Lorain County	64 097	39	80892	155	Trumbull County	41 557
39	47138		Mansfield city	47 821	39	83342		Westerville city	36 120
39	47138	139	Richland County	47 821	39	83342	041	Delaware County	7 792
					39	83342	049	Franklin County	28 328
39	47754		Marion city	36 837					
39	47754	101	Marion County	36 837	39	83622		Westlake city	32 729
					39	83622	035	Cuyahoga County	32 729
39	48188		Mason city	30 712					
39	48188	165	Warren County	30 712	39	86548		Wooster city	26 119
					39	86548	169	Wayne County	26 119
39	48244		Massillon city	32 149					
39	48244	151	Stark County	32 149	39	86772		Xenia city	25 719
					39	86772	057	Greene County	25 719
39	48790		Medina city	26 678					
39	48790	103	Medina County	26 678	39	88000		Youngstown city	66 982
					39	88000	099	Mahoning County	66 971
39	49056		Mentor city	47 159	39	88000	155	Trumbull County	11
39	49056	085	Lake County	47 159					
					39	88084		Zanesville city	25 487
39	49840		Middletown city	48 694	39	88084	119	Muskingum County	25 487
39	49840	017	Butler County	45 994					
39	49840	165	Warren County	2 700	40			**OKLAHOMA**	3 751 351
					40	04450		Bartlesville city	35 750
39	54040		Newark city	47 573	40	04450	113	Osage County	3
39	54040	089	Licking County	47 573	40	04450	147	Washington County	35 747
39	56882		North Olmsted city	32 718	40	09050		Broken Arrow city	98 850
39	56882	035	Cuyahoga County	32 718	40	09050	143	Tulsa County	80 634
					40	09050	145	Wagoner County	18 216
39	56966		North Ridgeville city	29 465					
39	56966	093	Lorain County	29 465	40	23200		Edmond city	81 405
					40	23200	109	Oklahoma County	81 405
39	57008		North Royalton city	30 444					
39	57008	035	Cuyahoga County	30 444	40	23950		Enid city	49 379
					40	23950	047	Garfield County	49 379
39	61000		Parma city	81 601					
39	61000	035	Cuyahoga County	81 601	40	41850		Lawton city	96 867
					40	41850	031	Comanche County	96 867
39	66390		Reynoldsburg city	35 893					
39	66390	045	Fairfield County	910	40	48350		Midwest City city	54 371
39	66390	049	Franklin County	26 157	40	48350	109	Oklahoma County	54 371
39	66390	089	Licking County	8 826					
					40	49200		Moore city	55 081
39	67468		Riverside city	25 201	40	49200	027	Cleveland County	55 081
39	67468	113	Montgomery County	25 201					
					40	50050		Muskogee city	39 223
39	70380		Sandusky city	25 793	40	50050	101	Muskogee County	39 223
39	70380	043	Erie County	25 793					
					40	52500		Norman city	110 925
39	71682		Shaker Heights city	28 448	40	52500	027	Cleveland County	110 925
39	71682	035	Cuyahoga County	28 448					
					40	55000		Oklahoma City city	579 999
39	74118		Springfield city	60 608	40	55000	017	Canadian County	44 541
39	74118	023	Clark County	60 608	40	55000	027	Cleveland County	63 723
					40	55000	109	Oklahoma County	471 671
39	74944		Stow city	34 837	40	55000	125	Pottawatomie County	64
39	74944	153	Summit County	34 837					
					40	56650		Owasso city	28 915
39	75098		Strongsville city	44 750	40	56650	131	Rogers County	2 614
39	75098	035	Cuyahoga County	44 750	40	56650	143	Tulsa County	26 301
39	77000		Toledo city	287 208	40	59850		Ponca City city	25 387
39	77000	095	Lucas County	287 208	40	59850	071	Kay County	25 387

Cities by County–*Continued*

State Code	Place Code	County Code	Geographic Area Name	2010 Census Population	State Code	Place Code	County Code	Geographic Area Name	2010 Census Population
40	66800		Shawnee city	29 857	41	74950		Tualatin city	26 054
40	66800	125	Pottawatomie County	29 857	41	74950	005	Clackamas County	2 862
					41	74950	067	Washington County	23 192
40	70300		Stillwater city	45 688					
40	70300	119	Payne County	45 688	41	80150		West Linn city	25 109
					41	80150	005	Clackamas County	25 109
40	75000		Tulsa city	391 906					
40	75000	113	Osage County	6 136	42			**PENNSYLVANIA**	12 702 379
40	75000	131	Rogers County	0	42	02000		Allentown city	118 032
40	75000	143	Tulsa County	385 613	42	02000	077	Lehigh County	118 032
40	75000	145	Wagoner County	157					
					42	02184		Altoona city	46 320
41			**OREGON**	3 831 074	42	02184	013	Blair County	46 320
41	01000		Albany city	50 158					
41	01000	003	Benton County	6 463	42	06064		Bethel Park municipality	32 313
41	01000	043	Linn County	43 695	42	06064	003	Allegheny County	32 313
41	05350		Beaverton city	89 803	42	06088		Bethlehem city	74 982
41	05350	067	Washington County	89 803	42	06088	077	Lehigh County	19 343
					42	06088	095	Northampton County	55 639
41	05800		Bend city	76 639					
41	05800	017	Deschutes County	76 639	42	13208		Chester city	33 972
					42	13208	045	Delaware County	33 972
41	15800		Corvallis city	54 462					
41	15800	003	Benton County	54 462	42	21648		Easton city	26 800
					42	21648	095	Northampton County	26 800
41	23850		Eugene city	156 185					
41	23850	039	Lane County	156 185	42	24000		Erie city	101 786
					42	24000	049	Erie County	101 786
41	30550		Grants Pass city	34 533					
41	30550	033	Josephine County	34 533	42	32800		Harrisburg city	49 528
					42	32800	043	Dauphin County	49 528
41	31250		Gresham city	105 594					
41	31250	051	Multnomah County	105 594	42	33408		Hazleton city	25 340
					42	33408	079	Luzerne County	25 340
41	34100		Hillsboro city	91 611					
41	34100	067	Washington County	91 611	42	41216		Lancaster city	59 322
					42	41216	071	Lancaster County	59 322
41	38500		Keizer city	36 478					
41	38500	047	Marion County	36 478	42	42168		Lebanon city	25 477
					42	42168	075	Lebanon County	25 477
41	40550		Lake Oswego city	36 619					
41	40550	005	Clackamas County	34 066	42	50528		Monroeville municipality	28 386
41	40550	051	Multnomah County	2 544	42	50528	003	Allegheny County	28 386
41	40550	067	Washington County	9					
					42	54656		Norristown borough	34 324
41	45000		McMinnville city	32 187	42	54656	091	Montgomery County	34 324
41	45000	071	Yamhill County	32 187					
					42	60000		Philadelphia city	1 526 006
41	47000		Medford city	74 907	42	60000	101	Philadelphia County	1 526 006
41	47000	029	Jackson County	74 907					
					42	61000		Pittsburgh city	305 704
41	55200		Oregon City city	31 859	42	61000	003	Allegheny County	305 704
41	55200	005	Clackamas County	31 859					
					42	61536		Plum borough	27 126
41	59000		Portland city	583 776	42	61536	003	Allegheny County	27 126
41	59000	005	Clackamas County	744					
41	59000	051	Multnomah County	581 485	42	63624		Reading city	88 082
41	59000	067	Washington County	1 547	42	63624	011	Berks County	88 082
41	61200		Redmond city	26 215	42	69000		Scranton city	76 089
41	61200	017	Deschutes County	26 215	42	69000	069	Lackawanna County	76 089
41	64900		Salem city	154 637	42	73808		State College borough	42 034
41	64900	047	Marion County	130 398	42	73808	027	Centre County	42 034
41	64900	053	Polk County	24 239					
					42	85152		Wilkes-Barre city	41 498
41	69600		Springfield city	59 403	42	85152	079	Luzerne County	41 498
41	69600	039	Lane County	59 403					
					42	85312		Williamsport city	29 381
41	73650		Tigard city	48 035	42	85312	081	Lycoming County	29 381
41	73650	067	Washington County	48 035					

State Code	Place Code	County Code	Geographic Area Name	2010 Census Population	State Code	Place Code	County Code	Geographic Area Name	2010 Census Population
42	87048		York city	43 718	45	70270		Summerville town	43 392
42	87048	133	York County	43 718	45	70270	015	Berkeley County	3 643
					45	70270	019	Charleston County	1 010
44			**RHODE ISLAND**	1 052 567	45	70270	035	Dorchester County	38 739
44	19180		Cranston city	80 387					
44	19180	007	Providence County	80 387	45	70405		Sumter city	40 524
					45	70405	085	Sumter County	40 524
44	22960		East Providence city	47 037					
44	22960	007	Providence County	47 037	46			**SOUTH DAKOTA**	814 180
					46	00100		Aberdeen city	26 091
44	54640		Pawtucket city	71 148	46	00100	013	Brown County	26 091
44	54640	007	Providence County	71 148					
					46	52980		Rapid City city	67 956
44	59000		Providence city	178 042	46	52980	103	Pennington County	67 956
44	59000	007	Providence County	178 042					
					46	59020		Sioux Falls city	153 888
44	74300		Warwick city	82 672	46	59020	083	Lincoln County	21 095
44	74300	003	Kent County	82 672	46	59020	099	Minnehaha County	132 793
44	80780		Woonsocket city	41 186	47			**TENNESSEE**	6 346 105
44	80780	007	Providence County	41 186	47	03440		Bartlett city	54 613
					47	03440	157	Shelby County	54 613
45			**SOUTH CAROLINA**	4 625 364					
45	00550		Aiken city	29 524	47	08280		Brentwood city	37 060
45	00550	003	Aiken County	29 524	47	08280	187	Williamson County	37 060
45	01360		Anderson city	26 686	47	08540		Bristol city	26 702
45	01360	007	Anderson County	26 686	47	08540	163	Sullivan County	26 702
45	13330		Charleston city	120 083	47	14000		Chattanooga city	167 674
45	13330	015	Berkeley County	8 095	47	14000	065	Hamilton County	167 674
45	13330	019	Charleston County	111 988					
					47	15160		Clarksville city	132 929
45	16000		Columbia city	129 272	47	15160	125	Montgomery County	132 929
45	16000	063	Lexington County	559					
45	16000	079	Richland County	128 713	47	15400		Cleveland city	41 285
					47	15400	011	Bradley County	41 285
45	25810		Florence city	37 056					
45	25810	041	Florence County	37 056	47	16420		Collierville town	43 965
					47	16420	047	Fayette County	0
45	29815		Goose Creek city	35 938	47	16420	157	Shelby County	43 965
45	29815	015	Berkeley County	35 933					
45	29815	019	Charleston County	5	47	16540		Columbia city	34 681
					47	16540	119	Maury County	34 681
45	30850		Greenville city	58 409					
45	30850	045	Greenville County	58 409	47	16920		Cookeville city	30 435
					47	16920	141	Putnam County	30 435
45	30985		Greer city	25 515					
45	30985	045	Greenville County	18 635	47	27740		Franklin city	62 487
45	30985	083	Spartanburg County	6 880	47	27740	187	Williamson County	62 487
45	34045		Hilton Head Island town	37 099	47	28540		Gallatin city	30 278
45	34045	013	Beaufort County	37 099	47	28540	165	Sumner County	30 278
45	48535		Mount Pleasant town	67 843	47	28960		Germantown city	38 844
45	48535	019	Charleston County	67 843	47	28960	157	Shelby County	38 844
45	49075		Myrtle Beach city	27 109	47	33280		Hendersonville city	51 372
45	49075	051	Horry County	27 109	47	33280	165	Sumner County	51 372
45	50875		North Charleston city	97 471	47	37640		Jackson city	65 211
45	50875	015	Berkeley County	0	47	37640	113	Madison County	65 211
45	50875	019	Charleston County	78 393					
45	50875	035	Dorchester County	19 078	47	38320		Johnson City city	63 152
					47	38320	019	Carter County	1 252
45	61405		Rock Hill city	66 154	47	38320	163	Sullivan County	367
45	61405	091	York County	66 154	47	38320	179	Washington County	61 533
45	68290		Spartanburg city	37 013	47	39560		Kingsport city	48 205
45	68290	083	Spartanburg County	37 013	47	39560	073	Hawkins County	2 854
					47	39560	163	Sullivan County	45 351

Cities by County–*Continued*

State Code	Place Code	County Code	Geographic Area Name	2010 Census Population	State Code	Place Code	County Code	Geographic Area Name	2010 Census Population
47	40000		Knoxville city	178 874	48	11428		Burleson city	36 690
47	40000	093	Knox County	178 874	48	11428	251	Johnson County	29 111
					48	11428	439	Tarrant County	7 579
47	41200		La Vergne city	32 588					
47	41200	149	Rutherford County	32 588	48	13024		Carrollton city	119 097
					48	13024	085	Collin County	2
47	41520		Lebanon city	26 190	48	13024	113	Dallas County	49 352
47	41520	189	Wilson County	26 190	48	13024	121	Denton County	69 743
47	46380		Maryville city	27 465	48	13492		Cedar Hill city	45 028
47	46380	009	Blount County	27 465	48	13492	113	Dallas County	44 477
					48	13492	139	Ellis County	551
47	48000		Memphis city	646 889					
47	48000	157	Shelby County	646 889	48	13552		Cedar Park city	48 937
					48	13552	453	Travis County	489
47	50280		Morristown city	29 137	48	13552	491	Williamson County	48 448
47	50280	063	Hamblen County	29 131					
47	50280	089	Jefferson County	6	48	15364		Cleburne city	29 337
					48	15364	251	Johnson County	29 337
47	51560		Murfreesboro city	108 755					
47	51560	149	Rutherford County	108 755	48	15976		College Station city	93 857
					48	15976	041	Brazos County	93 857
47	55120		Oak Ridge city	29 330					
47	55120	001	Anderson County	26 271	48	16432		Conroe city	56 207
47	55120	145	Roane County	3 059	48	16432	339	Montgomery County	56 207
47	69420		Smyrna town	39 974	48	16612		Coppell city	38 659
47	69420	149	Rutherford County	39 974	48	16612	113	Dallas County	37 905
					48	16612	121	Denton County	754
47	70580		Spring Hill city	29 036					
47	70580	119	Maury County	7 023	48	16624		Copperas Cove city	32 032
47	70580	187	Williamson County	22 013	48	16624	027	Bell County	0
					48	16624	099	Coryell County	31 457
48			**TEXAS**	25 145 561	48	16624	281	Lampasas County	575
48	01000		Abilene city	117 063					
48	01000	253	Jones County	5 145	48	17000		Corpus Christi city	305 215
48	01000	441	Taylor County	111 918	48	17000	007	Aransas County	0
					48	17000	273	Kleberg County	0
48	01924		Allen city	84 246	48	17000	355	Nueces County	305 215
48	01924	085	Collin County	84 246	48	17000	409	San Patricio County	0
48	03000		Amarillo city	190 695	48	19000		Dallas city	1 197 816
48	03000	375	Potter County	105 486	48	19000	085	Collin County	46 885
48	03000	381	Randall County	85 209	48	19000	113	Dallas County	1 124 296
					48	19000	121	Denton County	26 579
48	04000		Arlington city	365 438	48	19000	257	Kaufman County	0
48	04000	439	Tarrant County	365 438	48	19000	397	Rockwall County	56
48	05000		Austin city	790 390	48	19624		Deer Park city	32 010
48	05000	209	Hays County	2	48	19624	201	Harris County	32 010
48	05000	453	Travis County	754 691					
48	05000	491	Williamson County	35 697	48	19792		Del Rio city	35 591
					48	19792	465	Val Verde County	35 591
48	06128		Baytown city	71 802					
48	06128	071	Chambers County	4 116	48	19972		Denton city	113 383
48	06128	201	Harris County	67 686	48	19972	121	Denton County	113 383
48	07000		Beaumont city	118 296	48	20092		DeSoto city	49 047
48	07000	245	Jefferson County	118 296	48	20092	113	Dallas County	49 047
48	07132		Bedford city	46 979	48	21628		Duncanville city	38 524
48	07132	439	Tarrant County	46 979	48	21628	113	Dallas County	38 524
48	08236		Big Spring city	27 282	48	21892		Eagle Pass city	26 248
48	08236	227	Howard County	27 282	48	21892	323	Maverick County	26 248
48	10768		Brownsville city	175 023	48	22660		Edinburg city	77 100
48	10768	061	Cameron County	175 023	48	22660	215	Hidalgo County	77 100
48	10912		Bryan city	76 201	48	24000		El Paso city	649 121
48	10912	041	Brazos County	76 201	48	24000	141	El Paso County	649 121

State Code	Place Code	County Code	Geographic Area Name	2010 Census Population	State Code	Place Code	County Code	Geographic Area Name	2010 Census Population
48	24768		Euless city	51 277	48	38632		Keller city	39 627
48	24768	439	Tarrant County	51 277	48	38632	439	Tarrant County	39 627
48	25452		Farmers Branch city	28 616	48	39148		Killeen city	127 921
48	25452	113	Dallas County	28 616	48	39148	027	Bell County	127 921
48	26232		Flower Mound town	64 669	48	39352		Kingsville city	26 213
48	26232	121	Denton County	64 457	48	39352	273	Kleberg County	26 213
48	26232	439	Tarrant County	212					
					48	39952		Kyle city	28 016
48	27000		Fort Worth city	741 206	48	39952	209	Hays County	28 016
48	27000	121	Denton County	7 813					
48	27000	367	Parker County	7	48	40588		Lake Jackson city	26 849
48	27000	439	Tarrant County	733 386	48	40588	039	Brazoria County	26 849
48	27000	497	Wise County	0					
					48	41212		Lancaster city	36 361
48	27648		Friendswood city	35 805	48	41212	113	Dallas County	36 361
48	27648	167	Galveston County	25 510					
48	27648	201	Harris County	10 295	48	41440		La Porte city	33 800
					48	41440	201	Harris County	33 800
48	27684		Frisco city	116 989					
48	27684	085	Collin County	72 489	48	41464		Laredo city	236 091
48	27684	121	Denton County	44 500	48	41464	479	Webb County	236 091
48	28068		Galveston city	47 743	48	41980		League City city	83 560
48	28068	167	Galveston County	47 743	48	41980	167	Galveston County	81 998
					48	41980	201	Harris County	1 562
48	29000		Garland city	226 876					
48	29000	085	Collin County	266	48	42016		Leander city	26 521
48	29000	113	Dallas County	226 608	48	42016	453	Travis County	1 077
48	29000	397	Rockwall County	2	48	42016	491	Williamson County	25 444
48	29336		Georgetown city	47 400	48	42508		Lewisville city	95 290
48	29336	491	Williamson County	47 400	48	42508	113	Dallas County	841
					48	42508	121	Denton County	94 449
48	30464		Grand Prairie city	175 396					
48	30464	113	Dallas County	123 487	48	43012		Little Elm city	25 898
48	30464	139	Ellis County	45	48	43012	121	Denton County	25 898
48	30464	439	Tarrant County	51 864					
					48	43888		Longview city	80 455
48	30644		Grapevine city	46 334	48	43888	183	Gregg County	78 585
48	30644	113	Dallas County	0	48	43888	203	Harrison County	1 870
48	30644	121	Denton County	0					
48	30644	439	Tarrant County	46 334	48	45000		Lubbock city	229 573
					48	45000	303	Lubbock County	229 573
48	30920		Greenville city	25 557					
48	30920	231	Hunt County	25 557	48	45072		Lufkin city	35 067
					48	45072	005	Angelina County	35 067
48	31928		Haltom City city	42 409					
48	31928	439	Tarrant County	42 409	48	45384		McAllen city	129 877
					48	45384	215	Hidalgo County	129 877
48	32312		Harker Heights city	26 700					
48	32312	027	Bell County	26 700	48	45744		McKinney city	131 117
					48	45744	085	Collin County	131 117
48	32372		Harlingen city	64 849					
48	32372	061	Cameron County	64 849	48	46452		Mansfield city	56 368
					48	46452	139	Ellis County	95
48	35000		Houston city	2 099 451	48	46452	251	Johnson County	1 652
48	35000	157	Fort Bend County	38 124	48	46452	439	Tarrant County	54 621
48	35000	201	Harris County	2 057 280					
48	35000	339	Montgomery County	4 047	48	47892		Mesquite city	139 824
					48	47892	113	Dallas County	139 731
48	35528		Huntsville city	38 548	48	47892	257	Kaufman County	93
48	35528	471	Walker County	38 548					
					48	48072		Midland city	111 147
48	35576		Hurst city	37 337	48	48072	317	Martin County	0
48	35576	439	Tarrant County	37 337	48	48072	329	Midland County	111 147
48	37000		Irving city	216 290	48	48768		Mission city	77 058
48	37000	113	Dallas County	216 290	48	48768	215	Hidalgo County	77 058

State Code	Place Code	County Code	Geographic Area Name	2010 Census Population	State Code	Place Code	County Code	Geographic Area Name	2010 Census Population
48	48804		Missouri City city	67 358	48	65600		San Marcos city	44 894
48	48804	157	Fort Bend County	61 755	48	65600	055	Caldwell County	3
48	48804	201	Harris County	5 603	48	65600	187	Guadalupe County	0
					48	65600	209	Hays County	44 891
48	50256		Nacogdoches city	32 996					
48	50256	347	Nacogdoches County	32 996	48	66128		Schertz city	31 465
					48	66128	029	Bexar County	1 157
48	50820		New Braunfels city	57 740	48	66128	091	Comal County	845
48	50820	091	Comal County	47 586	48	66128	187	Guadalupe County	29 463
48	50820	187	Guadalupe County	10 154					
					48	66644		Seguin city	25 175
48	52356		North Richland Hills city	63 343	48	66644	187	Guadalupe County	25 175
48	52356	439	Tarrant County	63 343					
					48	67496		Sherman city	38 521
48	53388		Odessa city	99 940	48	67496	181	Grayson County	38 521
48	53388	135	Ector County	98 270					
48	53388	329	Midland County	1 670	48	68636		Socorro city	32 013
					48	68636	141	El Paso County	32 013
48	55080		Paris city	25 171					
48	55080	277	Lamar County	25 171	48	69032		Southlake city	26 575
					48	69032	121	Denton County	773
48	56000		Pasadena city	149 043	48	69032	439	Tarrant County	25 802
48	56000	201	Harris County	149 043					
					48	70808		Sugar Land city	78 817
48	56348		Pearland city	91 252	48	70808	157	Fort Bend County	78 817
48	56348	039	Brazoria County	86 706					
48	56348	157	Fort Bend County	721	48	72176		Temple city	66 102
48	56348	201	Harris County	3 825	48	72176	027	Bell County	66 102
48	57176		Pflugerville city	46 936	48	72368		Texarkana city	36 411
48	57176	453	Travis County	46 636	48	72368	037	Bowie County	36 411
48	57176	491	Williamson County	300					
					48	72392		Texas City city	45 099
48	57200		Pharr city	70 400	48	72392	071	Chambers County	0
48	57200	215	Hidalgo County	70 400	48	72392	167	Galveston County	45 099
48	58016		Plano city	259 841	48	72530		The Colony city	36 328
48	58016	085	Collin County	254 525	48	72530	121	Denton County	36 328
48	58016	121	Denton County	5 316					
					48	74144		Tyler city	96 900
48	58820		Port Arthur city	53 818	48	74144	423	Smith County	96 900
48	58820	245	Jefferson County	53 814					
48	58820	361	Orange County	4	48	75428		Victoria city	62 592
					48	75428	469	Victoria County	62 592
48	61796		Richardson city	99 223					
48	61796	085	Collin County	28 569	48	76000		Waco city	124 805
48	61796	113	Dallas County	70 654	48	76000	309	McLennan County	124 805
48	62828		Rockwall city	37 490	48	76816		Waxahachie city	29 621
48	62828	397	Rockwall County	37 490	48	76816	139	Ellis County	29 621
48	63284		Rosenberg city	30 618	48	76864		Weatherford city	25 250
48	63284	157	Fort Bend County	30 618	48	76864	367	Parker County	25 250
48	63500		Round Rock city	99 887	48	77272		Weslaco city	35 670
48	63500	453	Travis County	1 362	48	77272	215	Hidalgo County	35 670
48	63500	491	Williamson County	98 525					
					48	79000		Wichita Falls city	104 553
48	63572		Rowlett city	56 199	48	79000	485	Wichita County	104 553
48	63572	113	Dallas County	49 188					
48	63572	397	Rockwall County	7 011	48	80356		Wylie city	41 427
					48	80356	085	Collin County	39 957
48	64472		San Angelo city	93 200	48	80356	113	Dallas County	415
48	64472	451	Tom Green County	93 200	48	80356	397	Rockwall County	1 055
48	65000		San Antonio city	1 327 407	49			**UTAH**	2 763 885
48	65000	029	Bexar County	1 327 381	49	01310		American Fork city	26 263
48	65000	091	Comal County	0	49	01310	049	Utah County	26 263
48	65000	325	Medina County	26					
					49	07690		Bountiful city	42 552
48	65516		San Juan city	33 856	49	07690	011	Davis County	42 552
48	65516	215	Hidalgo County	33 856					

State Code	Place Code	County Code	Geographic Area Name	2010 Census Population	State Code	Place Code	County Code	Geographic Area Name	2010 Census Population
49	11320		Cedar City city	28 857	49	76680		Tooele city	31 605
49	11320	021	Iron County	28 857	49	76680	045	Tooele County	31 605
49	13850		Clearfield city	30 112	49	82950		West Jordan city	103 712
49	13850	011	Davis County	30 112	49	82950	035	Salt Lake County	103 712
49	16270		Cottonwood Heights city	33 433	49	83470		West Valley City city	129 480
49	16270	035	Salt Lake County	33 433	49	83470	035	Salt Lake County	129 480
49	20120		Draper city	42 274	50			**VERMONT**	625 741
49	20120	035	Salt Lake County	40 532	50	10675		Burlington city	42 417
49	20120	049	Utah County	1 742	50	10675	007	Chittenden County	42 417
49	36070		Holladay city	26 472	51			**VIRGINIA**	8 001 024
49	36070	035	Salt Lake County	26 472	51	01000		Alexandria city	139 966
					51	01000	510	Alexandria city	139 966
49	40360		Kaysville city	27 300					
49	40360	011	Davis County	27 300	51	07784		Blacksburg town	42 620
					51	07784	121	Montgomery County	42 620
49	43660		Layton city	67 311					
49	43660	011	Davis County	67 311	51	14968		Charlottesville city	43 475
					51	14968	540	Charlottesville city	43 475
49	44320		Lehi city	47 407					
49	44320	049	Utah County	47 407	51	16000		Chesapeake city	222 209
					51	16000	550	Chesapeake city	222 209
49	45860		Logan city	48 174					
49	45860	005	Cache County	48 174	51	21344		Danville city	43 055
					51	21344	590	Danville city	43 055
49	49710		Midvale city	27 964					
49	49710	035	Salt Lake County	27 964	51	35000		Hampton city	137 436
					51	35000	650	Hampton city	137 436
49	53230		Murray city	46 746					
49	53230	035	Salt Lake County	46 746	51	35624		Harrisonburg city	48 914
					51	35624	660	Harrisonburg city	48 914
49	55980		Ogden city	82 825					
49	55980	057	Weber County	82 825	51	44984		Leesburg town	42 616
					51	44984	107	Loudoun County	42 616
49	57300		Orem city	88 328					
49	57300	049	Utah County	88 328	51	47672		Lynchburg city	75 568
					51	47672	680	Lynchburg city	75 568
49	60930		Pleasant Grove city	33 509					
49	60930	049	Utah County	33 509	51	48952		Manassas city	37 821
					51	48952	683	Manassas city	37 821
49	62470		Provo city	112 488					
49	62470	049	Utah County	112 488	51	56000		Newport News city	180 719
					51	56000	700	Newport News city	180 719
49	64340		Riverton city	38 753					
49	64340	035	Salt Lake County	38 753	51	57000		Norfolk city	242 803
					51	57000	710	Norfolk city	242 803
49	65110		Roy city	36 884					
49	65110	057	Weber County	36 884	51	61832		Petersburg city	32 420
					51	61832	730	Petersburg city	32 420
49	65330		St. George city	72 897					
49	65330	053	Washington County	72 897	51	64000		Portsmouth city	95 535
					51	64000	740	Portsmouth city	95 535
49	67000		Salt Lake City city	186 440					
49	67000	035	Salt Lake County	186 440	51	67000		Richmond city	204 214
					51	67000	760	Richmond city	204 214
49	67440		Sandy city	87 461					
49	67440	035	Salt Lake County	87 461	51	68000		Roanoke city	97 032
					51	68000	770	Roanoke city	97 032
49	70850		South Jordan city	50 418					
49	70850	035	Salt Lake County	50 418	51	76432		Suffolk city	84 585
					51	76432	800	Suffolk city	84 585
49	71290		Spanish Fork city	34 691					
49	71290	049	Utah County	34 691	51	82000		Virginia Beach city	437 994
					51	82000	810	Virginia Beach city	437 994
49	72280		Springville city	29 466					
49	72280	049	Utah County	29 466	51	86720		Winchester city	26 203
					51	86720	840	Winchester city	26 203
49	75360		Taylorsville city	58 652					
49	75360	035	Salt Lake County	58 652					

State Code	Place Code	County Code	Geographic Area Name	2010 Census Population	State Code	Place Code	County Code	Geographic Area Name	2010 Census Population
53			**WASHINGTON**	6 724 540	53	56625		Pullman city	29 799
53	03180		Auburn city	70 180	53	56625	075	Whitman County	29 799
53	03180	033	King County	62 761					
53	03180	053	Pierce County	7 419	53	56695		Puyallup city	37 022
					53	56695	053	Pierce County	37 022
53	05210		Bellevue city	122 363					
53	05210	033	King County	122 363	53	57535		Redmond city	54 144
					53	57535	033	King County	54 144
53	05280		Bellingham city	80 885					
53	05280	073	Whatcom County	80 885	53	57745		Renton city	90 927
					53	57745	033	King County	90 927
53	07380		Bothell city	33 505					
53	07380	033	King County	17 090	53	58235		Richland city	48 058
53	07380	061	Snohomish County	16 415	53	58235	005	Benton County	48 058
53	07695		Bremerton city	37 729	53	61115		Sammamish city	45 780
53	07695	035	Kitsap County	37 729	53	61115	033	King County	45 780
53	08850		Burien city	33 313	53	62288		SeaTac city	26 909
53	08850	033	King County	33 313	53	62288	033	King County	26 909
53	17635		Des Moines city	29 673	53	63000		Seattle city	608 660
53	17635	033	King County	29 673	53	63000	033	King County	608 660
53	20750		Edmonds city	39 709	53	63960		Shoreline city	53 007
53	20750	061	Snohomish County	39 709	53	63960	033	King County	53 007
53	22640		Everett city	103 019	53	67000		Spokane city	208 916
53	22640	061	Snohomish County	103 019	53	67000	063	Spokane County	208 916
53	23515		Federal Way city	89 306	53	67167		Spokane Valley city	89 755
53	23515	033	King County	89 306	53	67167	063	Spokane County	89 755
53	33805		Issaquah city	30 434	53	70000		Tacoma city	198 397
53	33805	033	King County	30 434	53	70000	053	Pierce County	198 397
53	35275		Kennewick city	73 917	53	73465		University Place city	31 144
53	35275	005	Benton County	73 917	53	73465	053	Pierce County	31 144
53	35415		Kent city	92 411	53	74060		Vancouver city	161 791
53	35415	033	King County	92 411	53	74060	011	Clark County	161 791
53	35940		Kirkland city	48 787	53	75775		Walla Walla city	31 731
53	35940	033	King County	48 787	53	75775	071	Walla Walla County	31 731
53	36745		Lacey city	42 393	53	77105		Wenatchee city	31 925
53	36745	067	Thurston County	42 393	53	77105	007	Chelan County	31 925
53	37900		Lake Stevens city	28 069	53	80010		Yakima city	91 067
53	37900	061	Snohomish County	28 069	53	80010	077	Yakima County	91 067
53	38038		Lakewood city	58 163	54			**WEST VIRGINIA**	1 852 994
53	38038	053	Pierce County	58 163	54	14600		Charleston city	51 400
					54	14600	039	Kanawha County	51 400
53	40245		Longview city	36 648					
53	40245	015	Cowlitz County	36 648	54	39460		Huntington city	49 138
					54	39460	011	Cabell County	45 214
53	40840		Lynnwood city	35 836	54	39460	099	Wayne County	3 924
53	40840	061	Snohomish County	35 836					
					54	55756		Morgantown city	29 660
53	43955		Marysville city	60 020	54	55756	061	Monongalia County	29 660
53	43955	061	Snohomish County	60 020					
					54	62140		Parkersburg city	31 492
53	47560		Mount Vernon city	31 743	54	62140	107	Wood County	31 492
53	47560	057	Skagit County	31 743					
					54	86452		Wheeling city	28 486
53	51300		Olympia city	46 478	54	86452	051	Marshall County	276
53	51300	067	Thurston County	46 478	54	86452	069	Ohio County	28 210
53	53545		Pasco city	59 781					
53	53545	021	Franklin County	59 781					

Cities by County–*Continued*

State Code	Place Code	County Code	Geographic Area Name	2010 Census Population	State Code	Place Code	County Code	Geographic Area Name	2010 Census Population
55			**WISCONSIN**	5 686 986	55	72975		Sheboygan city	49 288
55	02375		Appleton city	72 623	55	72975	117	Sheboygan County	49 288
55	02375	015	Calumet County	11 088					
55	02375	087	Outagamie County	60 045	55	77200		Stevens Point city	26 717
55	02375	139	Winnebago County	1 490	55	77200	097	Portage County	26 717
55	06500		Beloit city	36 966	55	78600		Sun Prairie city	29 364
55	06500	105	Rock County	36 966	55	78600	025	Dane County	29 364
55	10025		Brookfield city	37 920	55	78650		Superior city	27 244
55	10025	133	Waukesha County	37 920	55	78650	031	Douglas County	27 244
55	22300		Eau Claire city	65 883	55	84250		Waukesha city	70 718
55	22300	017	Chippewa County	1 981	55	84250	133	Waukesha County	70 718
55	22300	035	Eau Claire County	63 902					
					55	84475		Wausau city	39 106
55	25950		Fitchburg city	25 260	55	84475	073	Marathon County	39 106
55	25950	025	Dane County	25 260					
					55	84675		Wauwatosa city	46 396
55	26275		Fond du Lac city	43 021	55	84675	079	Milwaukee County	46 396
55	26275	039	Fond du Lac County	43 021					
					55	85300		West Allis city	60 411
55	27300		Franklin city	35 451	55	85300	079	Milwaukee County	60 411
55	27300	079	Milwaukee County	35 451					
					55	85350		West Bend city	31 078
55	31000		Green Bay city	104 057	55	85350	131	Washington County	31 078
55	31000	009	Brown County	104 057					
					56			**WYOMING**	563 626
55	31175		Greenfield city	36 720	56	13150		Casper city	55 316
55	31175	079	Milwaukee County	36 720	56	13150	025	Natrona County	55 316
55	37825		Janesville city	63 575	56	13900		Cheyenne city	59 466
55	37825	105	Rock County	63 575	56	13900	021	Laramie County	59 466
55	39225		Kenosha city	99 218	56	31855		Gillette city	29 087
55	39225	059	Kenosha County	99 218	56	31855	005	Campbell County	29 087
55	40775		La Crosse city	51 320	56	45050		Laramie city	30 816
55	40775	063	La Crosse County	51 320	56	45050	001	Albany County	30 816
55	48000		Madison city	233 209					
55	48000	025	Dane County	233 209					
55	48500		Manitowoc city	33 736					
55	48500	071	Manitowoc County	33 736					
55	51000		Menomonee Falls village	35 626					
55	51000	133	Waukesha County	35 626					
55	53000		Milwaukee city	594 833					
55	53000	079	Milwaukee County	594 833					
55	53000	131	Washington County	0					
55	53000	133	Waukesha County	0					
55	54875		Mount Pleasant village	26 197					
55	54875	101	Racine County	26 197					
55	55750		Neenah city	25 501					
55	55750	139	Winnebago County	25 501					
55	56375		New Berlin city	39 584					
55	56375	133	Waukesha County	39 584					
55	58800		Oak Creek city	34 451					
55	58800	079	Milwaukee County	34 451					
55	60500		Oshkosh city	66 083					
55	60500	139	Winnebago County	66 083					
55	66000		Racine city	78 860					
55	66000	101	Racine County	78 860					

APPENDIX F
SOURCE NOTES AND EXPLANATIONS

The following documentation is provided in the order in which items appear in the tables. Internet addresses are provided for the sources of the data. Some of the links refer to the specific data tables. Others provide information about the general data source.

TABLE A—STATES

Table A presents 355 items for the United States as a whole, for each individual state, and for the District of Columbia. The states are presented in alphabetical order.

LAND AREA, Items 1 and 4

Source: U.S. Census Bureau—2017 U.S. Gazetteer Files,
http://www.census.gov/geo/maps-data/data/gazet-teer2017.html

Land area measurements are shown to the nearest square mile. Land area includes dry land and land temporarily or partially covered by water, such as marshlands, swamps, and river floodplains. The 2017 land areas have been aggregated from the counties as listed in the 2017 Gazetteer files.

POPULATION AND COMPONENTS OF CHANGE, Items 2–4, 31–41

Source: U.S. Census Bureau—Decennial Censuses and Population Estimates
https://www.census.gov/programs-surveys/popest.html
https://www.census.gov/programs-surveys/decennial-census/data/datasets.2010.html

The population data for 2017 are Census Bureau estimates of the resident population as of July 1, 2017.

The population data for 1990, 2000, and 2010 are from the decennial censuses and represent the resident population as of April 1 of those years.

The change in population between 2010 and 2017 is made up of (a) natural increase—births minus deaths, and (b) net migration—the difference between the number of persons moving into a particular state and the number of persons moving out of the state. Net migration is composed of internal and international migration.

POPULATION AND POPULATION CHARAC-TERISTICS, Items 5–23 and 45–63

Source: U.S. Census Bureau—Population Estimates and 2016 American Community Survey

https://www.census.gov/programs-surveys/popest.html
http://www.census.gov/acs/www/

Data on age, sex, race, and Hispanic origin are from the Population Estimates program. Data on place of birth are from the 2016 American Community Survey, a nationwide continuous survey designed to replace the long form questionnaire used in previous censuses.

The concept "race alone or in combination " includes people who reported a single race alone (i.e., Asian) and people who reported that race in combination with one or more of the other major race groups (i.e., White, Black or African American, American Indian and Alaska Native, Native Hawaiian and Other Pacific Islander, and Some Other Race). The "race alone or in combination" concept, therefore, represents the maximum number of people who reported as that race group, either alone, or in combination with another race(s).

The sum of the four individual race alone or in combination categories in this book may add to more than the total population because people who reported more than one race were tallied in each race category. In this book, the Asian group has been combined with the Native Hawaiian and Other Pacific Islander group, causing double-counting of persons who identify with both groups. This is especially pronounced in Hawaii.

Data on race were derived from answers to the question on race that was asked of all persons. The concept of race, as used by the Census Bureau, reflects self-identification by respondents according to the race or races with which they most closely identify. These categories are sociopolitical constructs and should not be interpreted as being scientific or anthropological in nature. Furthermore, the race categories include both racial and national origin groups.

The **White** population is defined as persons who indicated their race as White, as well as persons who did not classify themselves in one of the specific race categories listed on the questionnaire but entered a nationality such as Irish, German, Italian, Lebanese, Near Easterner, Arab, or Polish.

The **Black** population includes persons who indicated their race as "Black, African Am., or Negro," as well as persons who did not classify themselves in one of the specific race categories but reported entries such as African American, Afro American, Kenyan, Nigerian, or Haitian.

The **American Indian or Alaska Native** population includes persons who indicated their race as American Indian or Alaska Native, as well as persons who did not classify themselves in one of the specific race categories but reported entries such as Canadian Indian, French-American Indian, Spanish-American Indian, Eskimo, Aleut, Alaska Indian, or any of the American Indian or Alaska Native tribes.

The **Asian and Pacific Islander** population combines two census groupings: **Asian** and **Native Hawaiian or Other Pacific Islander**. The **Asian** population includes persons who indicated their race as Asian Indian, Chinese, Filipino, Japanese, Korean, Vietnamese, or "Other Asian," as well as persons who provided write-in entries of such groups as Cambodian, Laotian, Hmong, Pakistani, or Taiwanese. The **Native Hawaiian or Other Pacific Islander** population includes persons who indicated their race as "Native Hawaiian," "Guamanian or Chamorro," "Samoan," or "Other Pacific Islander," as well as persons who reported entries such as Part Hawaiian, American Samoan, Fijian, Melanesian, or Tahitian.

The Hispanic population is based on a question that asked respondents "Is this person Spanish/Hispanic/Latino?" Persons marking any one of the four Hispanic categories (i.e., Mexican, Puerto Rican, Cuban, or other Spanish) are collectively referred to as Hispanic.

Age is defined as age at last birthday (number of completed years since birth), as of April 1 of the census year.

The **median age** is the age that divides the population into two equal-size groups. Half of the population is older than the median age and half is younger. Median age is based on a standard distribution of the population by single years of age and is shown to the nearest tenth of a year.

The **female** population is shown as a percentage of total population.

The **foreign-born** population includes all persons who were not U.S. citizens at birth. Foreign-born persons are those who indicated they were either a U.S. citizen by naturalization or were not a citizen of the United States. Neither the census nor the American Community Survey asked about immigration status. The population surveyed included all persons who indicated that the United States was their usual place of residence. The foreign-born population consists of immigrants (legal permanent residents), temporary migrants (students), humanitarian migrants (refugees), and unauthorized migrants (persons illegally residing in the United States).

Percent born in state of residence is shown as a percentage of total population.

IMMIGRANTS, Item 24

Source: Department of Homeland Security, U.S. Citizenship and Immigration Services
http://www.dhs.gov/yearbook-immigration-statistics

The number of immigrants by state of intended residence is summarized from the administrative records of the Citizenship and Immigration Services. This information is compiled from immigrant visas and forms granting legal permanent resident status.

An **immigrant** is an alien admitted to the United States as a lawful permanent resident. Immigrants are those persons lawfully accorded the privilege of residing permanently in the United States. They may be newly arrived individuals who were issued immigrant visas by the Department of State overseas, or they may be U.S. residents who were admitted to permanent resident status in 2016 by the U.S. Citizenship and Immigration Services.

HOUSEHOLDS, Items 25–30 and 64–68

Source: U.S. Census Bureau—2016 American Community Survey
http://www.census.gov/acs/www/

A **household** includes all of the persons who occupy a housing unit. Persons not living in households are classified as living in group quarters. A housing unit is a house, an apartment, a mobile home, a group of rooms, or a single room occupied (or, if vacant, intended for occupancy) as separate living quarters. Separate living quarters are those in which the occupants live separately from any other persons in the building and have direct access from the outside of the building or through a common hall. The occupants may be a single family, one person living alone, two or more families living together, or any other group of related or unrelated persons who share living quarters. The number of households is the same as the number of year-round occupied housing units.

The measure of **persons per household** is obtained by dividing the number of persons in households by the number of households or householders. One person in each household is designated as the householder. In most cases, this is the person, (or one of the persons) in whose name the house is owned, being bought, or rented. If there is no such person in the household, any adult household member 15 years old and over can be designated as the householder.

A **family** includes a householder and one or more other persons living in the same household who are related to the householder by birth, marriage, or adoption. All persons in a household who are related to the householder are regarded as members of his or her family. A **family household** may contain persons not related to the householder; thus, family households may include more members than families do. A household can contain only one family for the purposes of census tabulations. Not all households contain families, as a household may comprise a group of unrelated persons or one person living alone. Families are classified by type as either a "married couple family" or "other family" according to the presence of a spouse.

The category **female family householder** includes only female-headed family households with no spouse present.

POPULATION PROJECTIONS, Items 42–44

Source: U.S. Census Bureau—Population Projections Branch
https://census.gov/programs-surveys/popproj/guidance.html

Projections are estimates of the population for future dates. They illustrate plausible courses of future population change based on assumptions about future births, deaths, international migration, and domestic migration. Projected numbers are based on an estimated population consistent with the most recent decennial census as enumerated. The Census Bureau does not have a current set of state population projections and currently has no plans to produce them. This volume includes projections released in 2005, based on the 2000 census. The Census Bureau notes that these projections should be used with caution because population trends may have changed substantially since their release.

HOUSING, Items 69–92

Source: U.S. Census Bureau—2010 and 2016 American Community Survey
http://www.census.gov/acs/www/

Housing data for 2010 and 2016 are from the American Community Survey, a nationwide continuous survey designed to replace the long form questionnaire used in previous censuses. A sample of households is surveyed to provide estimates.

A **housing unit** is a house, apartment, mobile home or trailer, group of rooms, or single room occupied or, if vacant, intended for occupancy as separate living quarters. Separate living quarters are those in which the occupants do not live and eat with any other person in the structure and which have direct access from the outside of the building or through a common hall. For vacant units, the criteria of separateness and direct access are applied to the intended occupants whenever possible. If that information cannot be obtained, the criteria are applied to the previous occupants.

The occupants of a housing unit may be a single family, one person living alone, two or more families living together, or any other group of related or unrelated persons who share living arrangements. Both occupied and vacant housing units are included in the housing inventory, although recreational vehicles, tents, caves, boats, railroad cars, and the like are included only if they are occupied as a person's usual place of residence.

A housing unit is classified as **occupied** if it is the usual place of residence of the person or group of persons living in it at the time of enumeration, or if the occupants are only temporarily absent (away on vacation). A household consists of all persons who occupy a housing unit as their usual place of residence.

Housing cost, as a percentage of income, is shown separately for owners with mortgages, owners without mortgages, and renters. Also shown is the percentage of mortgaged owners and renters who pay 30 percent or more of household income on selected monthly costs. Rent as a percent of income is a computed ratio of gross rent and monthly household income (total household income divided by 12). Selected owner costs include utilities and fuels, mortgage payments, insurance, taxes, etc. In each case, the ratio of housing cost to income is computed separately for each housing unit. The housing cost ratios for half of all units are above the median shown in this book, and half are below the median. Median monthly housing costs divides the monthly housing costs distribution into two equal parts, one-half of the cases falling below the median monthly housing costs and one-half above the median.

Median value is the dollar amount that divides the distribution of specified owner-occupied housing units into two equal parts, with half of all units below the median value and half above the median value. Value is defined as the respondent's estimate of what the house would sell for if it were for sale. Data are presented for single-family units on fewer than 10 acres of land that have no business or medical office on the property.

Median rent divides the distribution of renter-occupied housing units into two equal parts. The rent concept used in this volume is gross rent, which includes the amount of cash rent a renter pays (contract rent) plus the estimated average cost of utilities and fuels, if these are paid by the renter. The rent is the amount of rent only for living quarters and excludes any business or other space occupied. Single-family houses on lots of 10 or more acres of land are excluded.

Substandard units are occupied units that are overcrowded or lack complete plumbing facilities. For the purposes of this item, "overcrowded" is defined as having 1.01 persons or more per room. Complete plumbing facilities include hot and cold piped water, a flush toilet, and a bathtub or shower. These facilities must be located inside the housing unit, but do not have to be in the same room.

Different house includes all people 1 year old and over who, a year earlier, lived in a different house or apartment from the one they occupied at the time of interview.

BUILDING PERMITS, Items 93–95

Source: U.S. Census Bureau—Building Permits Survey
http://www.census.gov/construction/bps/

These figures represent private residential construction authorized by building permits in approximately 20,000 places in the United States. Valuation represents the expected cost of construction as recorded on the building permit. This figure usually excludes the cost of on-site and off-site development and improvements, as well as the cost of heating, plumbing, electrical, and elevator installations.

National, state, and county totals were obtained by adding the data for permit-issuing places within each jurisdiction. These totals thus are limited to permits issued in the 20,000 place universe covered by the Census Bureau and may not include all permits issued within a state. Current surveys indicate that construction is undertaken for all but a very small percentage of housing units authorized by building permits.

Residential building permits include buildings with any number of housing units. Housing units exclude group quarters (such as dormitories and rooming houses), transient accommodations (such as transient hotels, motels, and tourist courts), "HUD-code" manufactured (mobile) homes, moved or relocated units, and housing units created in an existing residential or nonresidential structure.

MANUFACTURED HOUSING UNITS, Item 96

Source: U.S. Census Bureau—Manufactured Housing Survey
https://www.census.gov/data/tables/time-series/econ/mhs/shipments.html

The Manufactured Housing Survey (MHS) is conducted by the U.S. Census Bureau and sponsored by the Department of Housing and Urban Development (HUD). MHS produces monthly regional estimates of the average sales price of new manufactured homes and more detailed annual estimates including selected characteristics of new manufactured homes. In addition, MHS produces monthly estimates of homes shipped to each state.

A manufactured home is defined as a movable dwelling, 8 feet or more wide and 40 feet or more long, designed to be towed on its own chassis, with transportation gear integral to the unit when it leaves the factory, and without need of a permanent foundation. These manufactured homes include multi-wides and expandable manufactured homes. Excluded are travel trailers, motor homes, and modular housing.

BIRTHS AND DEATHS, Items 97–103

Source: U.S. Centers for Disease Control and Prevention, National Center for Health Statistics
https://www.cdc.gov/nchs/data/nvsr/nvsr66/nvsr66_06.pdf
https://www.cdc.gov/nchs/data/nvsr/nvsr67/nvsr67_01.pdf

The registration of births, deaths, and other vital events in the United States is primarily a state and local function. The civil laws of every state provide for continuous and permanent birth and death registration systems. Through the National Vital Statistics System, the National Center for Health Statistics (NCHS) obtains data on births and deaths from the registration offices of each state, New York City, and the District of Columbia.

Birth and death statistics are limited to events occurring during the year. The data are by place of residence and exclude events for nonresidents of the United States. Births or deaths occurring outside the United States are excluded.

Birth and death rates represent the number of births and deaths per 1,000 resident population enumerated as of April 1 for decennial census years and estimated as of July 1 for other years.

Figures for infant deaths include deaths of children under 1 year of age but exclude fetal deaths. The infant death rate is per 1,000 live births.

The rates of almost all causes of disease, injury, and death vary by age. Age adjustment is a technique for "removing" the effects of age from crude rates, in order to allow meaningful comparisons across populations with different underlying age structures. For example, comparing the crude death rate in Florida to that of California is misleading, since the relatively older population in Florida will lead to a higher crude death rate. For such a comparison, age-adjusted death rates are preferable.

The population estimates were developed by the Census Bureau's Population Division using a traditional cohort component method. Starting with a basic population from the 2000 census, each component of population change—births, deaths, domestic migration, and international migration—is estimated separately for each birth cohort by sex, race, and Hispanic or Latino origin.

Age-adjusted rates are calculated by applying the age-specific rates of various populations to a single standard population. In this volume, the standard population is 2000. Beginning in 2003, The Centers for Disease Control and Prevention switched to the year 2000, after many years of using the year 1940 as the standard population for age-adjusted death rates.

PERSONS LACKING HEALTH INSURANCE, Items 104–105

Source: U.S. Census Bureau—American Community Survey

https://www.census.gov/library/publications/2017/demo/p60-260.html

These estimates are from the American Community Survey, an ongoing nationwide survey that is conducted throughout the year. About 250,000 addresses per month receive the ACS. Respondents are asked whether each household member is currently covered (by specific types of health coverage) at the time of interview. The 2013 estimates were the first to use the ACS. Prior year estimates were based on the Annual Social and Economic Supplement (ASEC) of the Current Population Survey (CPS).

Those lacking coverage are the percentage of the population of each state who were not covered by private health plans purchased directly or provided by an employer, Medicaid, Medicare, or military health care.

MEDICARE BENEFICIARIES, Item 106

Source: U.S. Department of Health and Human Services, Centers for Medicare and Medicaid Services
https://www.cms.gov/Research-Statistics-Data-and-Systems/Statistics-Trends-and-Reports/CMSProgramStatistics/Dashboard.html

The Centers for Medicare and Medicaid Services (CMS) administers Medicare, which provides health insurance to persons 65 years old and over, persons with permanent kidney failure, and certain persons with disabilities. Original Medicare has two parts: Hospital Insurance and Supplemental Medical Insurance. In recent years, Medicare has been expanded to include two new programs: Medicare Advantage plans and prescription drug coverage. Medicare Advantage Plans are health plan options that are approved by Medicare but run by private companies. Medicare prescription drug plans can be part of Medicare Advantage plans or stand-alone drug plans.

Persons who are eligible for **Medicare** can enroll in Part A (Hospital Insurance) at no charge, and can choose to pay a monthly premium to enroll in Part B. Most eligible persons are enrolled in Part A, and most enrollees in Part A are also enrolled in Part B (Supplemental Medical Insurance.) This table includes persons who were enrolled in both Part A and Part B during 2017.

Part B beneficiaries can choose to enroll in **Original Medicare**, a fee-for-service plan administered by the Centers for Medicare and Medicaid Services, or in a **Medicare Advantage** plan. Medicare Advantage plans include private fee-for-service plans, preferred provider organizations, health maintenance organizations, medical savings account plans, demonstration plans, and programs for all-inclusive care for the elderly.

The annual Medicare enrollment counts are determined using a person-year methodology. For each calendar year, total person-year counts are determined by summing the total number of months that each beneficiary is enrolled during the year and dividing by 12. Using this methodology, a beneficiary's partial-year enrollment may be counted in more than one category (i.e., both Original Medicare and Medicare Advantage).

CRIME, Items 107–110

Source: U.S. Federal Bureau of Investigation—Uniform Crime Reports
https://ucr.fbi.gov/crime-in-the-u.s/2016/
crime-in-the-u.s.-2016

Crime data are as reported to the Federal Bureau of Investigation (FBI) by law enforcement agencies and have not been adjusted for underreporting. This may affect comparability between geographic areas or over time.

Through the voluntary contribution of crime statistics by law enforcement agencies across the United States, the Uniform Crime Reporting (UCR) Program provides periodic assessments of crime in the nation as measured by offenses that have come to the attention of the law enforcement community. The Committee on Uniform Crime Records of the International Association of Chiefs of Police initiated this voluntary national data-collection effort in 1930. The UCR Program contributors compile and submit their crime data either directly to the FBI or through state-level UCR Programs.

Seven offenses, because of their severity, frequency of occurrence, and likelihood of being reported to police, were initially selected to serve as an index for evaluating fluctuations in the volume of crime. These serious crimes were murder and nonnegligent manslaughter, forcible rape, robbery, aggravated assault, burglary, larceny-theft, and motor vehicle theft. By congressional mandate, arson was added as the eighth index offense in 1979. The totals shown in this volume do not include arson.

In 2004, the FBI discontinued the use of the Crime Index in the UCR Program and its publications, stating that the Crime Index was driven upward by the offense with the highest number of cases (in this case, larceny-theft) creating a bias against jurisdictions with a high number of larceny-thefts but a low number of other serious crimes, such as murder and forcible rape. The FBI is currently publishing a violent crime total and a property crime total until a more viable index is developed.

In 2013, the FBI adopted a new definition of rape. Rape is now defined as, "Penetration, no matter how slight, of the vagina or anus with any body part or object, or oral penetration by a sex organ of another person, without the consent of the victim." The new definition updated the 80-year-old historical definition of rape which was "carnal knowledge of a female forcibly and against her will." Effectively, the revised definition expands rape to include both male and female victims and offenders, and reflects the various forms of sexual penetration understood to be rape, especially non-consenting acts of sodomy, and sexual assaults with objects.

Violent crimes include four categories of offenses: (1) Murder and non-negligent manslaughter, as defined in the UCR Program, is the willful (non-negligent) killing of one human being by another. This offense excludes deaths caused by negligence, suicide, or accident; justifiable homicides; and attempts to murder or assaults to murder. (2) Rape is the penetration, no matter how slight, of the vagina or anus with any body part or object, or oral penetration by a sex organ of another person, without the consent of the victim. Assaults or attempts to commit rape by force or threat of force are also included; however, statutory rape (without force) and other sex offenses are excluded. (3) Robbery is the taking or attempting to take anything of value from the care, custody, or control of a person or persons by force or threat of force or violence and/or by putting the victim in fear. (4) Aggravated assault is an unlawful attack by one person upon another for the purpose of inflicting severe or aggravated bodily injury. This type of assault is usually accompanied by the use of a weapon or by other means likely to produce death or great bodily harm. Attempts are included, since injury does not necessarily have to result when a gun, knife, or other weapon is used, as these incidents could and probably would result in a serious personal injury if the crime were successfully completed.

Property crimes include three categories: (1) Burglary, or breaking and entering, is the unlawful entry of a structure to commit a felony or theft, even though no force was used to gain entrance. (2) Larceny-theft is the unauthorized taking of the personal property of another, without the use of force. (3) Motor vehicle theft is the unauthorized taking of any motor vehicle.

Rates are based on population estimates provided by the FBI. For some states, reporting is not sufficiently complete to be representative of the state as a whole. The FBI has estimated state totals for those states.

ELEMENTARY AND SECONDARY SCHOOL ENROLLMENT, Items 111 and 112

Source: U.S. Department of Education, National Center for Education Statistics—Common Core of Data
http://nces.ed.gov/ccd/elsi/

Data on public school enrollment is from the Common Core of Data 2015-2016 survey. Public school enrollment includes pre-kindergarten through grade 12 and ungraded students. The student/teacher ratio is calculated by dividing the number of students in all schools by the number of full-time equivalent teachers employed by all schools and agencies.

EDUCATIONAL ATTAINMENT, Items 113–116

Source: U.S. Census Bureau—2010 and 2016 American Community Survey
http://www.census.gov/acs/www/

Data on **educational attainment** are tabulated for the population 25 years old and over. The data were derived from a question that asked respondents for the highest level of school completed or the highest degree received. Persons who had passed a high school equivalency examination were considered high school graduates. Schooling received in foreign schools was to be reported as the equivalent grade or years in the regular American school system. Vocational and technical training, such as barber school training; business, trade, technical, and vocational schools; or other training for a specific trade are specifically excluded.

High school graduate or more. This category includes persons whose highest degree was a high school diploma or its equivalent, and those who reported any level higher than a high school diploma.

Bachelor's degree or more. This category includes persons who have received bachelor's degrees, master's degrees,

LOCAL GOVERNMENT EDUCATION EXPENDITURES, Items 117 and 118
Source: U.S. Department of Education, National Center for Education Statistics—Common Core of Data
http://nces.ed.gov/ccd/

Total expenditure for education includes provision or support of schools and facilities for elementary and secondary education. It encompasses instructional, support, and auxiliary services (school lunch, student activities, and community service) offered by public school systems. Retirement benefits paid to former education employees and interest payments are not included. Current expenditure includes all components of total expenditure except capital outlay. Expenditure data are obtained by the Census Bureau through its annual survey of government finances and are supplied to the National Center for Education Statistics (NCES). Current expenditure per student is current expenditure divided by the number of students enrolled. The number of students enrolled is based on an annual "membership" count of students on or about October 1.

NCES uses the Common Core of Data (CCD) Survey system to acquire and maintain statistical data from each of the 50 states, the District of Columbia, and the outlying areas. State education agencies compile and submit data for approximately 94,000 schools and 17,000 local school districts. Typically, this results in varying interpretation of NCES definitions and different record keeping systems, leading to large amounts of missing data for several states; this absence is reflected in the data in this publication.

EXPORTS, Items 119–121
Source: U.S. Department of Commerce, International Trade Administration
http://www.census.gov/foreign-trade/statistics/state/origin_movement/index.html

The data on exports of goods by state of origin are based on the location of the exporter (the principal party responsible for exportation from the United States). Exporters are often intermediaries, so the data do not necessarily represent the states in which the goods were actually produced. The total includes re-exports of foreign goods.

INCOME AND POVERTY, Items 122–133
Source: U.S. Census Bureau—2016 American Community Survey
http://www.census.gov/acs/www/

The data on income were derived from answers to questions which were asked of the population 15 years old and over. **Total income** is the sum of the amounts reported separately for wage or salary income; net self-employment income; interest, dividends, or net rental or royalty income or income from estates and trusts; Social Security or railroad retirement income; Supplemental Security Income (SSI); public assistance or welfare payments; retirement, survivor, or disability pensions; and all other income. Receipts from the following sources are not included as income: capital gains; money received from the sale of property (unless the recipient was engaged in the business of selling such property); the value of income "in kind" from food stamps, public housing subsidies, medical care, employer contributions for individuals, etc.; withdrawal of bank deposits; money borrowed; tax refunds; exchange of money between relatives living in the same household; and gifts and lump-sum inheritances, insurance payments, and other types of lump-sum receipts.

Per capita income is the mean income computed for every man, woman, and child in a particular group. It is derived by dividing the aggregate income of a particular group by the total population in that group. Per capita income is rounded to the nearest whole dollar.

Household income includes the income of the householder and all other individuals 15 years old and over in the household, whether or not they are related to the householder. Since many households consist of only one person, average household income is usually less than average family income. Although the household income statistics cover the past 12 months, the characteristics of individuals and the composition of households refer to the time of enumeration. Thus, the income of the household does not include amounts received by individuals who were members of the household during all or part of the past 12 months if these individuals no longer resided in the household at the time of interview. Similarly, income amounts reported by individuals who did not reside in the household during the past 12 months but who were members of the household at the time of interview are included. However, the composition of most households was the same during the past 12 months as at the time of interview.

Median income divides the income distribution into two equal parts, with half of all cases below the median income level and half of all cases above the median income level. For households and families, the median income is based on the distribution of the total number of households and families, including those with no income. Median income for households is computed on the basis of a standard distribution with a minimum value of less than $2,500 and a maximum value of $200,000 or more and is rounded to the nearest whole dollar.

For **family income**, the incomes of all household members 15 years old and over related to the householder are summed and treated as a single amount. Although the family income statistics cover the past 12 months, the characteristics of individuals and the composition of families refer to the time of interview. Thus, the income of the family does not include amounts received by individuals who were members of the family during all of part of the past 12 months if these individuals no longer resided with the family at the time of interview. Similarly, income amounts reported by individuals who did not reside with the family during the past 12 months but who were members of the family at

Poverty Thresholds for 2016 by Size of Family and Number of Related Children Under 18 Years

Size of family unit	Weighted average thresholds	Related children under 18 years								
		None	One	Two	Three	Four	Five	Six	Seven	Eight or more
One person (unrelated individual):	12,228									
Under age 65	12,486	12,486								
Aged 65 and older	11,511	11,511								
Two people:	15,569									
Householder under age 65	16,151	16,072	16,543							
Householder aged 65 and older	14,522	14,507	16,480							
Three people	19,105	18,774	19,318	19,337						
Four people	24,563	24,755	25,160	24,339	24,424					
Five people	29,111	29,854	30,288	29,360	28,643	28,205				
Six people	32,928	34,337	34,473	33,763	33,082	32,070	31,470			
Seven people	37,458	39,509	39,756	38,905	38,313	37,208	35,920	34,507		
Eight people	41,781	44,188	44,578	43,776	43,072	42,075	40,809	39,491	39,156	
Nine people or more	49,721	53,155	53,413	52,702	52,106	51,127	49,779	48,561	48,259	46,400

Source: U.S. Census Bureau.

the time of interview are included. However, the composition of most families was the same during the past 12 months as at the time of interview.

The **poverty status** data were derived from data collected on the number of persons in the household, each person's relationship to the householder, and the income data. The Social Security Administration (SSA) developed the original poverty definition in 1964, which federal interagency committees subsequently revised in 1969 and 1980. The Office of Management and Budget's (OMB) *Directive 14* prescribes the SSA's definition as the official poverty measure for federal agencies to use in their statistical work. Poverty statistics presented in American Community Survey products adhere to the standards defined by OMB in *Directive 14*.

The poverty thresholds vary depending on three criteria: size of family, number of children, and, for one- and two-person families, age of householder. In determining the poverty status of families and unrelated individuals, the Census Bureau uses thresholds (income cutoffs) arranged in a two-dimensional matrix. The matrix consists of family size (from one person to nine or more persons), cross-classified by presence and number of family members under 18 years old (from no children present to eight or more children present). Unrelated individuals and two-person families are further differentiated by age of reference person (under 65 years old and 65 years old and over). To determine a person's poverty status, the person's total family income in the last 12 months is compared to the poverty threshold appropriate for that person's family size and composition. If the total income of that person's family is less than the threshold appropriate for that family, then the person is considered poor or "below the poverty level," together with every member of his or her family. If a person is not living with anyone related by birth, marriage, or adoption, then the person's own income is compared with his or her poverty threshold. The total number of persons below the

poverty level is the sum of persons in families and the number of unrelated individuals with incomes below the poverty level in the last 12 months. The average poverty threshold for a four-person family was $24,563 in 2016.

The data on **poverty status of households** were derived from answers to the income questions. Since poverty is defined at the family level and not the household level, the poverty status of the household is determined by the poverty status of the householder. Households are classified as poor when the total income of the householder's family in the previous 12 months is below the appropriate poverty threshold. (For nonfamily householders, the person's income is compared with the appropriate threshold.) The income of persons living in the household who are unrelated to the householder is not considered when determining the poverty status of a household, nor does their presence affect the family size in determining the appropriate threshold. The poverty thresholds vary depending upon three criteria: size of family, number of children, and, for one- and two-person families, age of the householder.

Poverty status of children by **family type** is the percentage of children living in that particular type of family that has a family income below the poverty threshold based on family size and composition.

PERSONAL INCOME AND EARNINGS, Items 134–158
Source: U.S. Bureau of Economic Analysis, Regional Economic Accounts
http://www.bea.gov/regional/index.htm#state

Total personal income is the current income received by residents of an area from all sources. It is measured before deductions of income and other personal taxes but after deductions of personal contributions for Social Security, government retirement, and other social insurance programs. It consists of **wage and salary disbursements** (covering all employee earnings, including executive salaries, bonuses, commissions, payments-in-kind, incentive payments, and tips); various types of supplementary earnings, such as employers' contributions to pension funds (termed "other labor income" or "supplements to wages and salaries"); proprietors' income; rental income of persons; dividends; personal interest income; and government and business transfer payments.

Proprietors' income is the monetary income and income-in-kind of proprietorships and partnerships (including the independent professions), and the income of tax-exempt cooperatives. **Dividends** are cash payments by corporations to stockholders who are U.S. residents. **Interest** is the monetary and imputed interest income of persons from all sources. **Rent** is the monetary income of persons from the rental of real property, except the income of persons primarily engaged in the real estate business; the imputed net rental income of owner-occupants of nonfarm dwellings; and the royalties received by persons.

Transfer payments are income for which services are not currently rendered. They consist of both government and business transfer payments. Government transfer payments include payments under the following programs: Federal Old-Age, Survivors, and Disability Insurance ("Social Security"); Medicare and medical vendor payments; unemployment insurance; railroad and government retirement; federal- and state-government-insured workers' compensation; veterans' benefits, including veterans' life insurance; food stamps; black lung payments; Supplemental Security Income; and Temporary Assistance for Needy Families. Government payments to nonprofit institutions, other than for work under research and development contracts, are also included. Business transfer payments consist primarily of liability payments for personal injury and of corporate gifts to nonprofit institutions.

Per capita personal income is based on resident population estimated as of July 1 of the year shown.

Personal tax payments include taxes paid by individuals to federal, state, and local governments. Personal taxes include individual income taxes, estate and gift taxes, motor vehicle license taxes, and personal property taxes. Personal contributions to social insurance ("Social Security taxes") are not included, nor are sales taxes.

Disposable personal income equals personal income less personal tax payments. It is a measure of the income available to persons for spending or saving.

Earnings cover wage and salary disbursements, other labor income, and proprietors' income.

The data for earnings obtained from the Bureau of Economic Analysis (BEA) are based on place of work. In computing personal income, BEA makes an "adjustment for residence" to earnings based on commuting patterns; thus, personal income is presented on a place-of-residence basis.

Farm earnings include the income of farm workers (wages and salaries and other labor income) and farm proprietors. Farm proprietors' income includes only the income of sole proprietorships and partnerships.

Farm earnings estimates are benchmarked to data collected in the Census of Agriculture and the revised Department of Agriculture state totals of income and expense items.

Goods-related industries include mining, construction, and manufacturing. **Service-related** and other industries includes private-sector earnings in forestry, related activities, and other; utilities; transportation and warehousing; information; wholesale trade; retail trade; finance and insurance; real estate and rental and leasing; and services, which includes professional, scientific, and technical services; management of companies and enterprises; administrative and waste services; educational services; health care and social assistance; arts, entertainment, and recreation; accommodation and food services; and other services, except public administration. Government earnings include all levels of government. Industries are categorized under the North American Industry Classification System (NAICS), and are not directly comparable to years prior to 2002.

GROSS STATE PRODUCT, Item 159
Source: U.S. Bureau of Economic Analysis, Regional Economic Accounts
http://www.bea.gov/regional/index.htm#state

Gross state product (GSP) for a state is derived as the sum of gross state product originating in all industries in the state. In concept, an industry's GSP, referred to as its "value added," is equivalent to its gross output (sales or receipts and other operating income, commodity taxes, and inventory changes) minus its intermediate inputs (consumption of goods and services purchased from other industries or imported from other countries). As such, it is often referred to as the state counterpart to the nation's gross domestic product (GDP). In practice, GSP estimates are measured as the sum of distributions by industry of the components of gross domestic income—that is, the sum of the costs incurred (such as compensation of employees, net interest, and indirect business taxes) and the profits earned in production.

SOCIAL SECURITY AND SUPPLEMENTAL SECURITY INCOME, Items 160–162
Source: U.S. Social Security Administration
http://www.ssa.gov/policy/docs/statcomps/oasdi_sc/
http://www.ssa.gov/policy/docs/statcomps/ssi_sc/

Social Security beneficiaries are persons receiving benefits under the Old-Age, Survivors, and Disability Insurance Program. These include retired or disabled workers covered by the program, their spouses and dependent children, and the surviving spouses and dependent children of deceased workers.

Supplemental Security Income (SSI) recipients are persons receiving SSI payments. The SSI program is a cash assistance program that provides monthly benefits to low-income aged, blind, or disabled persons.

Data are as of December of the year shown.

CIVILIAN EMPLOYMENT, Items 163–166

Source: U.S. Census Bureau—2016 American Community Survey
http://www.census.gov/acs/www/
http://www2.census.gov/programs-surveys/acs/tech_docs/code_lists/2016_ACS_Code_Lists.pdf

The data on occupation were derived from answers to questions that were asked of all persons 15 years old and over who had worked in the past 5 years. **Occupation** describes the kind of work the person does on the job. For employed persons, the data refer to the person's job during the previous week. For those who worked two or more jobs, the data refer to the job at which the person worked the greatest number of hours. For unemployed persons, the data refer to their last job. The American Community Survey uses the occupational classification system that was developed for the 2000 census and modified in 2002 and again in 2010. This system consists of 539 specific occupational categories for employed persons arranged into 23 major occupational groups. This classification was developed based on the *Standard Occupational Classification (SOC) Manual: 2010*, published by the Executive Office of the President, Office of Management and Budget.

CIVILIAN LABOR FORCE AND UNEMPLOYMENT, Items 167–171

Source: U.S. Bureau of Labor Statistics—Local Areas Unemployment Statistics
http://www.bls.gov/lau/#tables

Data for the civilian labor force are the product of a federal-state cooperative program in which state employment security agencies prepare labor force and unemployment estimates under concepts, definitions, and technical procedures established by the Bureau of Labor Statistics (BLS). The **civilian labor force** consists of all civilians 16 years old and over who are either employed or unemployed.

Unemployment includes all persons who did not work during the survey week, made specific efforts to find a job during the prior four weeks, and were available for work during the survey week (except for temporary illness). Persons waiting to be called back to a job from which they had been laid off and those waiting to report to a new job within the next 30 days are included in unemployment figures.

PRIVATE NONFARM EMPLOYMENT AND EARNINGS, Items 172–183

Source: U.S. Bureau of Labor Statistics—Current Employment Survey
http://www.bls.gov/ces/#tables

Data for private nonfarm employment and earnings are compiled from payroll information reported monthly on a voluntary basis to the BLS and its cooperating state agencies. More than 350,000 establishments represent all industries except agriculture.

Employment is the annual average of monthly totals of persons who received pay for any part of the pay period including the 12th day of the month. Included are all full-time and part-time workers in nonfarm establishments. Not covered are government employees, proprietors, the self-employed, unpaid volunteers or family workers, farm workers, and domestic workers in households. The data by industry conform to the definitions established in the North American Industry Classification System (NAICS).

Earnings of **production workers** in **manufacturing** industries are derived from reports of gross payrolls and corresponding paid hours. Payroll is reported before deductions of any kinds. Total hours during the pay period include all hours worked (including overtime hours) and hours paid for holidays, vacations, and sick leave.

AGRICULTURE, ITEMS 184–202

Source: U.S. Department of Agriculture, National Agricultural Statistics Service—2012 Census of Agriculture
https://agcensus.usda.gov/Publications/2012/

The Census Bureau took a census of agriculture every 10 years from 1840 to 1920; since 1925, this census has been taken roughly once every 5 years. The 1997 Census of Agriculture was the first one conducted by the National Agricultural Statistics Service of the U.S. Department of Agriculture. Over time, the definition of a farm has varied. For recent censuses (including the 2012 census), a farm has been defined as any place from which $1,000 or more of agricultural products were produced and sold or normally would have been sold during the census year. Dollar figures are expressed in current dollars and have not been adjusted for inflation or deflation.

The term **operator** refers to a person who operates a farm by either doing the work or making day-to-day decisions about such activities as planting, harvesting, feeding, marketing, etc. The operator may be the owner, a member of the owner's household, a salaried manager, a tenant, a renter, or a sharecropper. If a person rents land to others or has land worked on shares by others, he/she is considered the operator only of the land that is retained for his/her own operation. The census collected information on the total number of operators, the total number of women operators, and demographic information for up to three operators per farm.

Government payments consists of direct payments as defined by the 2002 Farm Bill; payments from Conservation Reserve Program (CRP), Wetlands reserve Program (WRP), Farmable Wetlands Program (FWP), and Conservation Reserve Enhancement Program (CREP); loan deficiency payments; disaster payments; other conservation programs; and all other federal farm programs under which payments were made directly to farm operators. Commodity Credit Corporation (CCC) proceeds, amount from state and local federal crop insurance payments were not included in this category.

The acreage designated as **land in farms** consists primarily of agricultural land used for crops, pasture, or grazing. It also includes woodland and wasteland not actually under cultivation or used for pasture or grazing, provided that this land was part of the farm operator's total operation.

Land in farms is an operating-unit concept and includes all land owned and operated, as well as all land rented from others. Land used rent-free is classified as land rented from others. All land in Indian reservations used for growing crops or grazing livestock is classified as land in farms.

Irrigated land includes all land watered by any artificial or controlled means, such as sprinklers, flooding, furrows or ditches, sub-irrigation, and spreader dikes. Included are supplemental, partial, and preplant irrigation. Each acre was counted only once regardless of the number of times it was irrigated or harvested. Livestock lagoon waste water distributed by sprinkler or flood systems was also included.

Total cropland includes cropland harvested, cropland used only for pasture or grazing, cropland on which all crops failed or were abandoned, cropland in cultivated summer fallow, and cropland idle or used for cover crops or soil improvement but not harvested and not pastured or grazed.

Respondents were asked to report their estimate of the current market **value of land and buildings** owned, rented, or leased from others and rented and leased to others. Market value refers to the respondent's estimate of what the land and buildings would sell for under current market conditions.

The **value of machinery and equipment** was estimated by the respondent as the current market value of all cars, trucks, tractors, combines, balers, irrigation equipment, etc., used on the farm. This value is an estimate of what the machinery and equipment would sell for in its present condition and not the replacement of depreciated value. Share interests are reported at full value at the farm where the equipment and machinery are usually kept. Only equipment that was physically located at the farm on December 31, 2012, is included.

Market **value of agricultural products sold** by farms represents the gross market value before taxes and the production expenses of all agricultural products sold or removed from the place in 2012, regardless of who received the payment. It is equivalent to total sales and it includes sales by the operator as well as the value of any share received by partners, landlords, contractors, and others associated with the operation. It includes value of direct sales and the value of commodities placed in the Commodity Credit Corporation (CCC) loan program. Market value of agricultural products sold does not include payments received for participation in other federal farm programs. Also, it does not include income from farm-related sources such as customwork and other agricultural services, or income from nonfarm sources.

LAND USE, ITEMS 203 to 205
Source: U.S. Department of Agriculture, Natural Resources Conservation Service—2012 National Resources Inventory
http://www.nrcs.usda.gov/technical/NRI/

The National Resources Inventory (NRI) has been conducted every five years since 1982. It provides updated information on the status, condition, and trends of land, soil, water, and related resources on the Nation's non-federal lands. Non-federal lands

include privately owned lands, tribal and trust lands, and lands controlled by State and local governments.

The 2012 NRI is based on a sample of about 800,000 locations throughout the United States (excluding Alaska and the District of Columbia). Acreages for federal land and total surface area are established through geospatial processes and administrative records. Total surface area of the contiguous United States is 1,937.7 million acres.

Cropland includes areas used for the production of adapted crops for harvest. Cultivated cropland comprises land in row crops or close-grown crops and also other cultivated cropland, such as hayland or pastureland that is in a rotation with row or close-grown crops. Noncultivated cropland includes permanent hayland and horticultural cropland.

Federally-owned lands include military bases, national forests, wildlife refuges, parks, grassland game preserves, scenic waterways, wilderness areas, monuments, lakeshore, parkways, battlefields, Bureau of Land Management lands, and other federal lands.

Developed land includes any built-up area greater than one fourth of an acre. Built-up areas include residential, industrial, commercial, and institutional land; construction sites; public administrative sites; railroad yards; cemeteries; airports; golf courses; sanitary landfills; sewage treatment plants; water control structures and spillways; other land used for such purpose; small parks (fewer than 10 acres of land) within urban and built-up areas; and highways, railroads, and other transportation facilities that are surrounded by urban areas. Also included are tracts of fewer than 10 acres that do not meet the above definition but are completely surrounded by urban and built-up land, as well as all highways, roads, railroads, and associated rights-of-way outside of urban and built-up areas (including private roads to farmsteads or ranch headquarters, logging roads, and other private roads).

WATER CONSUMPTION, Item 206
Source: U.S. Geological Survey, National Water Use Information Program—2015 Water Use Data
http://water.usgs.gov/watuse/

Every five years, the U.S. Geological Survey compiles national water-use estimates. This volume includes the total fresh and saline water withdrawals for public water supplies expressed as million gallons per day. Estimate of withdrawals of ground and surface water are given for the following categories of use: public water supplies, domestic, commercial, irrigation, livestock, industrial, mining, and thermoelectric power. Only public water supply is included in this volume because the other categories had not been published in time for this book. Public supply refers to water withdrawn from ground and surface sources by public and private water systems for use by cities, towns, rural water districts, mobile-home parks, Native American Indian reservations, and military bases. Public-supply facilities provide water to at least 25 persons or have a minimum of 15 service connections. Water withdrawn by public suppliers may be delivered to users for domestic, commercial, industrial, and thermoelectric-power purposes, as well as to other public-water suppliers. Public-supply water is also used for public services (public uses)—such as pools, parks, and public buildings—and may have unaccounted uses (losses) because of system leaks or such non-metered services as firefighting, flushing of water lines, or backwashing at treatment plants. Some public-supply water may be used in the processes of water and wastewater treatment. Some public suppliers treat saline water before distributing the water. The definition of saline water for public supply refers to water that requires treatment to reduce the concentration of dissolved solids through the process of desalination or dilution.

MANUFACTURES, Items 207–216
Source: U.S. Census Bureau— 2016 Annual Survey of Manufactures
https://www.census.gov/programs-surveys/asm.html

The Annual Survey of Manufactures (ASM) has been conducted annually every year since 1949, except for years ending in "2" and "7," at which time ASM data are included in the manufacturing sector of the Economic Census. The ASM provides statistics on employment, payroll, worker hours, payroll supplements, cost of materials, value added by manufacturing, capital expenditures, inventories, and energy consumption. It also provides estimates of value of shipments for over 1,400 classes of manufactured products. The Annual Survey of Manufactures includes approximately 50,000 establishments selected from the census universe of 350,000 manufacturing establishments.

The **all employees** number is the average number of production workers for the payroll periods including the 12th of March, May, August, and November plus the number of other employees in mid-March. Included are all persons on paid sick leave, paid holidays, and paid vacations during the pay period. Officers of corporations are included as employees, while proprietors and partners of unincorporated firms are excluded.

Payroll figures include the gross annual earnings of all employees on the payroll of operating manufacturing establishments. The definition, which is the same as the one used for calculating the federal withholding tax, includes all forms of compensation, such as salaries, wages, commissions, dismissal pay, bonuses, vacation and sick leave pay, and compensation-in-kind, prior to such deductions as employees' Social Security contributions, withholding taxes, group insurance, union dues, and savings bonds. The total includes salaries of officers of corporations; it excludes payments to proprietors or partners of unincorporated concerns. Also excluded are payments to members of armed forces and to pensioners carried on the active payrolls of manufacturing establishments.

Production workers include workers (up through the line-supervisor level) engaged in fabricating, processing, assembling, inspecting, receiving, storing, handling, packing, warehousing, shipping (but not delivering), maintenance, repair, janitorial and guard services, product development, auxiliary production for the plant's own use (for example, power plant), record keeping, and other services closely associated with these production operations at the establishment covered by the report. Employees above the working-supervisor level are excluded.

The number of production workers is the average for the payroll periods including the 12th of March, May, August, and November.

Not included in this classification are all other employees, defined as non-production employees, including those engaged in factory supervision above the line-supervisor level.

Production worker hours cover hours worked or paid for at the manufacturing plant, including actual overtime hours (not straight-time equivalent hours). The data exclude hours paid for vacations, holidays, or sick leave when the employee is not at the establishment. Production wages represent all compensation paid to production workers.

Value added by manufacture is derived by subtracting the cost of materials, supplies, containers, fuel, purchased electricity, and contract work from the value of shipments (products manufactured plus receipts for services rendered). The result of this calculation is adjusted by the addition of value added by merchandising operations (the difference between the sales value and the cost of merchandise sold without further manufacture, processing, or assembly) plus the net change in finished goods and work-in-process between the beginning- and end-of-year inventories.

Value of shipments covers the received or receivable net selling values; free on board plant (excluding of freight and taxes), of all products shipped, both primary and secondary; and all miscellaneous receipts, such as receipts for contract work performed for others, installation and repair, sales of scrap, and sales of products bought and sold without further processing. Included are all items made by or for the establishments from material owned by it, whether sold, transferred to other plants of the same company, or shipped on consignment. The net selling value of products made in one plant on a contract basis from materials owned by another was reported by the plant providing the materials.

In the case of multi-unit companies, the manufacturer was asked to report the value of products transferred to other establishments of the same company at full economic or commercial value, including both the direct cost of production and a reasonable proportion of "all other costs" (including company overhead) and profit (interplant transfers).

The aggregate of the value of shipments figure for industry groups and for all manufacturing industries includes large amounts of duplications, as the products of some industries are used as materials by others. Estimates as to the overall extent of this duplication indicate that the value of manufactured products exclusive of such duplication (the value of finished manufactures) tends to approximate two-thirds of the total value of products reported in the census of manufactures.

Total cost of materials refers to direct charges actually paid or payable for items consumed or put into production during the year, including freight charges and other direct charges incurred by the establishment in acquiring these materials. It includes the cost of materials or fuel consumed, whether purchased by the individual establishment from other companies, transferred to it from other establishments of the same company, or withdrawn from inventory during the year. Included in this item are cost of parts, components, containers, etc.; cost of products bought and sold in the same condition; cost of fuels consumed for heat and power; cost of purchased electricity; and cost of contract work. Aggregate of total cost of materials and total value of shipments includes extensive duplication, since products of some industries are used as materials of others.

2012 ECONOMIC CENSUS: OVERVIEW, Items 217–308

Source: U.S. Census Bureau
http://www.census.gov/econ/census/about/

The Economic Census provides a detailed portrait of the nation's economy, from the national to the local level, once every five years. The 2012 Economic Census covers nearly all of the U.S. economy in its basic collection of establishment statistics. The 1997 Economic Census was the first major data source to use the North American Industry Classification System (NAICS); therefore, data are not comparable to economic data from prior years, which were based on the Standard Industrial Classification (SIC) system.

NAICS, developed in cooperation with Canada and Mexico, classifies North America's economic activities at two, three, four, and fivedigit levels of detail; the U.S. version of NAICS further defines industries to a sixth digit. The Economic Census takes advantage of this hierarchy to publish data at these successive levels of detail: sector (two-digit); subsector (three-digit); industry group (four-digit); industry (five-digit); and U.S. industry (six-digit). Information in Table A is at the two-digit level, with a few three- and four-digit items.

Several key statistics are tabulated for all industries included in this volume: number of establishments (or companies); number of employees; payroll; and a measure of output (sales, receipts, revenue, value of shipments, or value of construction work done).

Number of establishments. An establishment is a single physical location at which business is conducted. It is not necessarily identical with a company or enterprise, which may consist of one establishment or more. Economic Census figures represent a summary of reports for individual establishments rather than companies. For cases in which a census report was received, separate information was obtained for each location where business was conducted. When administrative records of other federal agencies were used instead of a census report, no information was available on the number of locations operated. Each Economic Census establishment was tabulated according to the physical location at which the business was conducted. The count of establishments represents those in business at any time during 2012.

When two activities or more were carried on at a single location under a single ownership, all activities were generally grouped together as a single establishment. The entire establishment was classified on the basis of its major activity and all of its data were included in that classification. However, when distinct and separate economic activities (for which different industry classification codes were appropriate) were conducted at a single location under a single ownership, separate establishment reports for each of the different activities were obtained in the census.

Number of employees. Paid employees consist of the fulltime and parttime employees, including salaried officers and executives of corporations. Included are employees on paid sick leave, paid holidays, and paid vacations; not included are proprietors and partners of unincorporated businesses. The definition of paid employees is the same as that used by the Internal Revenue Service (IRS) on form 941.

For some industries, the Economic Census gives codes representing the number of employees as a range of numbers (for example, "100 to 249 employees" or "1,000 to 2,499" employees). In this volume, those codes have been replaced by the standard suppression code "D".

Payroll. Payroll includes all forms of compensation, such as salaries, wages, commissions, dismissal pay, bonuses, vacation allowances, sickleave pay, and employee contributions to qualified pension plans paid during the year to all employees. For corporations, payroll includes amounts paid to officers and executives; for unincorporated businesses, it does not include profit or other compensation of proprietors or partners. Payroll is reported before deductions for Social Security, income tax, insurance, union dues, etc. This definition of payroll is the same as that used on IRS form 941.

Sales, shipments, receipts, revenue, or business done. This measure includes the total sales, shipments, receipts, revenue, or business done by establishments within the scope of the Economic Census. The definition of each of these items is specific to the economic sector measured.

CONSTRUCTION, Items 217–221

Source: U.S. Census Bureau—2012 Economic Census (See Overview of 2012 Economic Census prior to Item 217)

The Construction sector (sector 23) comprises establishments primarily engaged in the construction of buildings and other structures, heavy construction (except buildings), additions, alterations, reconstruction, installation, and maintenance and repairs. Establishments engaged in the demolition or wrecking of buildings and other structures, the clearing of building sites, and the sale of materials from demolished structures are also included. This sector also contains those establishments engaged in blasting, test drilling, landfill, leveling, earthmoving, excavating, land drainage, and other land preparation. The industries within this sector have been defined on the basis of their unique production processes. As with all industries, the production processes are distinguished by their use of specialized human resources and specialized physical capital. Construction activities are generally administered or managed at a relatively fixed place of business, but the actual construction work can be performed at one or more different project sites. This sector is divided into three subsectors of construction activities: (1) building construction and land subdivision and land development; (2) heavy construction (except buildings), such as highways, power plants, and pipelines; and (3) construction activity by special trade contractors.

WHOLESALE TRADE, Items 222–226

Source: U.S. Census Bureau—2012 Economic Census (See Overview of 2012 Economic Census prior to Item 217)

The Wholesale Trade sector (sector 42) comprises establishments engaged in wholesaling merchandise, generally without transformation, and rendering services incidental to the sale of merchandise. The wholesaling process is an intermediate step in the distribution of merchandise. Wholesalers are organized to sell or arrange the purchase or sale of (1) goods for resale (i.e., goods sold to other wholesalers or retailers), (2) capital or durable non-consumer goods, and (3) raw and intermediate materials and supplies used in production.

Wholesalers sell merchandise to other businesses and normally operate from a warehouse or office. These warehouses and offices are characterized by having little or no display of merchandise. In addition, neither the design nor the location of the premises is intended to solicit walkin traffic. Wholesalers do not normally use advertising directed to the general public. Customers are generally first reached via telephone, inperson marketing, or by specialized advertising that may include internet and other electronic means. Followup orders are either vendorinitiated or clientinitiated, are usually based on previous sales, and typically exhibit strong ties between sellers and buyers. In fact, transactions are often conducted between wholesalers and clients that have long-standing business relationships.

This sector is made up of two main types of wholesalers: those that sell goods on their own account and those that arrange sales and purchases for others for a commission or fee.

(1) Establishments that sell goods on their own account are known as wholesale merchants, distributors, jobbers, drop shippers, import/export merchants, and sales branches. These establishments typically maintain their own warehouse, where they receive and handle goods for their customers. Goods are generally sold without transformation, but may include integral functions, such as sorting, packaging, labeling, and other marketing services.

(2) Establishments arranging for the purchase or sale of goods owned by others or purchasing goods on a commission basis are known as agents and brokers, commission merchants, import/export agents and brokers, auction companies, and manufacturers' representatives. These establishments operate from offices and generally do not own or handle the goods they sell.

Some wholesale establishments may be connected with a single manufacturer and/or promote and sell that particular manufacturer's products to a wide range of other wholesalers or retailers. Other wholesalers may be connected to a retail chain or a limited number of retail chains and only provide a variety of products needed by that particular retail operation(s). These wholesalers may obtain the products from a wide range of manufacturers. Still other wholesalers may not take title to the goods but act as agents and brokers for a commission.

Although, in general, wholesaling normally denotes sales in large volumes, durable nonconsumer goods may be sold in single units. Sales of capital or durable nonconsumer goods used in the production of goods and services, such as farm machinery, medium- and heavy-duty trucks, and industrial machinery, are always included in Wholesale Trade.

RETAIL TRADE, Items 227–235
Source: U.S. Census Bureau—2012 Economic Census (See Overview of 2012 Economic Census prior to Item 217)

The Retail Trade sector (44–45) is made up of establishments engaged in retailing merchandise, generally without transformation, and rendering services incidental to the sale of merchandise.

The retailing process is the final step in the distribution of merchandise; retailers are, therefore, organized to sell merchandise in small quantities to the general public. This sector comprises two main types of retailers: store and nonstore retailers.

Store retailers operate fixed pointofsale locations, located and designed to attract a high volume of walkin customers. In general, retail stores have extensive displays of merchandise and use massmedia advertising to attract customers. They typically sell merchandise to the general public for personal or household consumption; some also serve business and institutional clients. These include establishments, such as office supply stores, computer and software stores, building materials dealers, plumbing supply stores, and electrical supply stores. Catalog showrooms, gasoline service stations, automotive dealers, and mobile home dealers are treated as store retailers.

In addition to retailing merchandise, some types of store retailers are also engaged in the provision of aftersales services, such as repair and installation. For example, new automobile dealers, electronic and appliance stores, and musical instrument and supply stores often provide repair services. As a general rule, establishments engaged in retailing merchandise and providing aftersales services are classified in this sector.

Nonstore retailers, like store retailers, are organized to serve the general public, although their retailing methods differ. The establishments of this subsector reach customers and market merchandise with methods, such as the broadcasting of "infomercials," the broadcasting and publishing of directresponse advertising, the publishing of paper and electronic catalogs, doortodoor solicitation, inhome demonstration, selling from portable stalls (street vendors, except food), and distribution through vending machines. Establishments engaged in the direct sale (nonstore) of products, such as home heating oil dealers and home-delivery newspaper routes are included in this sector.

The buying of goods for resale is a characteristic of retail trade establishments that distinguishes them from establishments in the Agriculture, Manufacturing, and Construction sectors. For example, farms that sell their products at or from the point of production are classified in Agriculture instead of in Retail Trade. Similarly, establishments that both manufacture and sell their products to the general public are classified in Manufacturing instead of Retail Trade. However, establishments that engage in processing activities incidental to retailing are classified in retail.

Industries in the **Motor Vehicle and Parts Dealers** subsector (441) retail motor vehicle and parts merchandise from fixed point-of-sale locations. Establishments in this subsector typically operate from a showroom and/or an open lot where the vehicles are on display. The display of vehicles and the related parts require little by way of display equipment. Personnel generally include both sales and sales support staff familiar with the requirements for registering and financing a vehicle as well as a staff of parts experts and mechanics trained to provide vehicle repair and maintenance services. Specific industries have been included in this subsector to identify the type of vehicle being retailed. Sales of capital or durable nonconsumer goods, such as medium and heavy-duty trucks, are always included in the Wholesale Trade sector. These goods are virtually never sold through retail methods.

Industries in the **Food and Beverage Stores** subsector (445) usually retail food and beverage merchandise from fixed point-of-sale locations. Establishments in this subsector have special equipment (e.g., freezers, refrigerated display cases, and refrigerators) for displaying food and beverage goods. They have staff trained in the processing of food products to guarantee the proper storage and sanitary conditions, as mandated by regulatory authority.

Industries in the **Clothing and Clothing Accessories Stores** subsector (448) retail new clothing and clothing accessories merchandise from fixed point-of-sale locations. Establishments in this subsector have similar types of display equipment, as well as employees who are knowledgeable regarding fashion trends and who can match styles, colors, and combinations of clothing and accessories to the characteristics and tastes of the customer.

Industries in the **General Merchandise Stores** subsector (452) retail new general merchandise from fixed point-of-sale locations. Establishments in this subsector are unique in that they have the equipment and staff capable of retailing a large variety of goods from a single location. This includes a variety of display equipment and staff trained to provide information on many lines of products.

INFORMATION, Items 236–246

Source: U.S. Census Bureau—2012 Economic Census (See Overview of 2012 Economic Census prior to Item 217)

The Information sector (51) comprises establishments engaged in the following processes: (1) producing and distributing information and cultural products, (2) providing the means to transmit or distribute these products as well as data or communications, and (3) processing data.

The main components of this sector are the publishing industries, including software publishing; the motion picture and sound recording industries; the broadcasting and telecommunications industries; and the information services and data processing industries.

For the purpose of NAICS, the transformation of information into a commodity that is produced and distributed by a number of growing industries is at issue. The Information sector groups three types of establishments: (1) those engaged in producing and distributing information and cultural products; (2) those that provide the means to transmit or distribute these products as well as data or communications; and (3) those that process data. Cultural products are those that directly express attitudes, opinions, ideas, values, and artistic creativity; provide entertainment; or offer information and analysis concerning the past and present. Included in this definition are popular, massproduced products, as well as cultural products that normally have a more limited audience, such as poetry books, literary magazines, or classical records. These activities were formerly classified throughout the existing national classifications. Traditional publishing was in manufacturing; broadcasting in communications; software production in business services; film production in amusement services; and so forth.

Industries in the **Publishing Industries, Except Internet** subsector (511) include establishments engaged in the publishing of newspapers, magazines, other periodicals, and books, as well as database and software publishing. In general, these establishments, which are known as publishers, issue copies of works for which they usually possess copyright. Works may be in one or more formats, including traditional print format, CDROM format, or proprietary electronic networks. Publishers may publish works originally created by others for which they have obtained the rights and/or works that they have created inhouse. Software publishing is included here because the activity (creation of a copyrighted product and bringing it to market) is equivalent to the creation process for other types of intellectual products.

In NAICS, publishing—the reporting, writing, editing, and other processes that are required to create an edition of a book or a newspaper—is treated as a major economic activity in its own right, rather than as a subsidiary activity to printing, which is a manufacturing activity. Thus, publishing is classified in the Information sector, while printing remains in the NAICS Manufacturing sector. In part, the NAICS classification reflects the fact that publishing increasingly takes place in establishments that are physically separate from the associated printing establishments. More crucially, the NAICS classification of book and newspaper publishing is intended to portray their roles in a modern economy—roles that do not resemble manufacturing activities.

Music publishers are not included in the Publishing Industries subsector, but can be found in the Motion Picture and Sound Recording Industries subsector. Reproduction of prepackaged software is treated in NAICS as a manufacturing activity; online distribution of software products is in the Information sector, and custom design of software to client specifications is included in the Professional, Scientific, and Technical Services sector. These distinctions arise because of the different ways that software is created, reproduced, and distributed.

The Information sector does not include products, such as manifold business forms. Information is not the essential component of these items. Establishments producing these items are included in subsector 323, Printing and Related Support Activities.

Industries in the **Motion Picture and Sound Recording Industries** subsector (512) group establishments involved in the production and distribution of motion pictures and sound recordings. While producers and distributors of motion pictures and sound recordings issue works for sale as traditional publishers do, the processes are different enough to warrant placing the establishments engaged in these activities in separate subsectors. Production is typically a complex process that involves several distinct types of establishments engaged in activities, such as contracting with performers, creating the film or sound content, and providing technical postproduction services. Film distribution is often to exhibitors, such as theaters and broadcasters, rather than to a wholesale or retail distribution chain. When the product is in a massproduced form, NAICS treats production and distribution as the major economic activity, rather than as a subsidiary activity to the manufacture of such products.

This subsector does not include establishments primarily engaged in the wholesale distribution of video cassettes and sound recordings, such as compact discs and audio tapes; these establishments are included in the Wholesale Trade sector. Reproduction of video cassettes and sound recordings that is carried out separately from establishments engaged in production and distribution is treated in NAICS as a manufacturing activity.

active membership structure to promote causes and represent the interests of their members. Establishments in this subsector may publish newsletters, books, and periodicals for distribution to their membership.

GOVERNMENT EMPLOYMENT, Items 309–311

Source: U.S. Bureau of Economic Analysis—Regional Economic Accounts
http://www.bea.gov/regional/index.htm#state

Employment is measured as the average annual sum of full-time and part-time jobs. The estimates are on a place-of-work basis. Data for federal civilian employment include civilian employees of the Department of Defense. Military employment includes all persons on active duty status.

STATE GOVERNMENT EMPLOYMENT AND PAYROLL, Items 312–330

Source: U.S. Census Bureau—Annual Survey of Government Employment and Payroll
http://www.census.gov/govs/programs-surveys/apes.html

The annual Survey of Government Employment and Payroll measures the number of federal, state, and local civilian government employees and their gross monthly payroll for March of the survey year for state and local governments and for the federal government.

The survey provides state and local government data on full-time and part-time employment, part-time hours worked, full-time equivalent employment, and payroll statistics by governmental function (i.e., elementary and secondary education, higher education, police protection, fire protection, financial administration, central staff services, judicial and legal, highways, public welfare, solid waste management, sewerage, parks and recreation, health, hospitals, water supply, electric power, gas supply, transit, natural resources, correction, libraries, air transportation, water transport and terminals, other education, state liquor stores, social insurance administration, and housing and community development).

Data have been collected annually since 1957. A census is conducted every five years (years ending in '2' and '7'). A sample of state and local governments is used to collect data in the intervening years. A new sample is selected every five years (years ending in '4' and '9').

State government employees include all persons paid for personal services performed, including persons paid from federally funded programs, paid elected or appointed officials, persons in a paid leave status, and persons paid on a per meeting, annual, semiannual, or quarterly basis. Unpaid officials, pensioners, persons whose work is performed on a fee basis, and contractors and their employees are excluded from the count of employees. **Full-time employees** are persons employed during the pay period to work the number of hours per week that represents regular full-time employment. Included are full-time temporary or seasonal employees who are working the number of hours that represent full-time employment. **Part-time employees** are persons paid on a part-time basis during the designated pay period. Included are

those daily or hourly employees usually engaged for less than the regular full-time workweek, as well as any part-time paid officials. **Full-Time Equivalent employees** is a computed statistic representing the number of full-time employees that could have been employed if the reported number of hours worked by part-time employees had been worked by full-time employees. This statistic is calculated separately for each function of a government by dividing the "part-time hours paid" by the standard number of hours for full-time employees in the particular government and then adding the resulting quotient to the number of full-time employees.

Full-time payroll represents gross payroll amounts for the one-month period of March for full-time employees. **Part-time pay** represents gross payroll amounts for the one-month period of March for part-time employees. Gross payroll includes all salaries, wages, fees, commissions, and overtime paid to employees **before** withholdings for taxes, insurance, etc. It also includes incentive payments that are paid at regular pay intervals. It excludes employer share of fringe benefits like retirement, Social Security, health and life insurance, lump sum payments, and so forth.

Administration combines **Financial administration** and **Other government administration**. **Financial administration includes** activities concerned with tax assessment and collection, custody and disbursement of funds, debt management, administration of trust funds, budgeting, and other government-wide financial management activities. This function is not applied to school district or special district governments. **Other government administration** applies to the legislative and government-wide administrative agencies of governments. Included here are overall planning and zoning activities, and central personnel and administrative activities. This function is not applied to school district or special district governments.

Judicial and legal includes all court and court related activities (except probation and parole activities that are included at the "Correction" function), court activities of sheriff's offices, prosecuting attorneys' and public defenders' offices, legal departments, and attorneys providing government-wide legal service.

Police includes all activities concerned, with the enforcement of law and order, including coroner's offices, police training academies, investigation bureaus, and local jails, "lockups", or other detention facilities not intended to serve as correctional facilities.

Corrections includes activities pertaining to the confinement and correction of adults and minors convicted of criminal offenses. Pardon, probation, and parole activities are also included here.

Highways and transportation includes activities associated with the maintenance and operation of streets, roads, sidewalks, bridges, tunnels, toll roads, and ferries. Snow and ice removal, street lighting, and highway and traffic engineering activities are also included here. Also included are the operation, maintenance, and construction of public mass transit systems, including subways, surface rails, and buses, and the provision, construction, operation, maintenance; support of public waterways, harbors, docks, wharves, and related marine terminal facilities; and activities associated with the operation and support of publicly operated airport facilities.

Public welfare includes the administration of various public assistance programs for the needy, veteran services, operation of nursing homes, indigent care institutions, and programs that provide payments for medical care, handicap transportation, and other services for the needy.

Health includes administration of public health programs, community and visiting nurse services, immunization programs, drug abuse rehabilitation programs, health and food inspection activities, operation of outpatient clinics, and environmental pollution control activities.

Hospitals includes only government operated medical care facilities that provide inpatient care. Employees and payrolls of private corporations that lease and operate government-owned hospital facilities are excluded.

Social insurance administration includes the administration of unemployment compensation systems, public employment services, and the Federal Social Security, Medicare, and Railroad Retirement trusts.

Natural resources and Parks includes activities primarily concerned with the conservation and development of natural resources (soil, water, energy, minerals, etc.) and the regulation of industries that develop, utilize, or affect natural resources, as well as the operation and maintenance of parks, playgrounds, swimming pools, public beaches, auditoriums, public golf courses, museums, marinas, botanical gardens, and zoological parks.

Utilities, sewerage, and waste management includes operation, maintenance, and construction of public water supply systems, including production, acquisition, and distribution of water to general public or to other public or private utilities, for residential, commercial, and industrial use; activities associated with the production or acquisition and distribution of electric power; provision, maintenance, and operation of sanitary and storm sewer systems and sewage disposal and treatment facilities; and refuse collection and disposal, operation of sanitary landfills, and street cleaning activities.

Elementary and secondary education and libraries includes activities associated with the operation of public elementary and secondary schools and locally operated vocational-technical schools. Special education programs operated by elementary and secondary school systems are also included as are all ancillary services associated with the operation of schools, such as pupil transportation and food service. **Also included are the** establishment and provision of libraries for use by the general public and the technical support of privately operated libraries. This category includes classroom teachers, principals, supervisors of instruction, librarians, teacher aides, library aides, and guidance and psychological personnel as well as school superintendents and other administrative personnel, clerical and secretarial staffs, plant operation and maintenance personnel, health and recreation employees, transportation and food service personnel, and any student employees.

Higher education includes state government degree granting institutions that provide academic training above grade 12. This includes persons engaged in teaching and related academic research as well as administrative, clerical, custodial, cafeteria, health personnel, noninstructional employees engaged in organized research, law enforcement personnel, and paid student employees.

STATE GOVERNMENT FINANCES, Items 331–350

Source: U.S. Census Bureau—State Government Finances
http://www.census.gov/govs/state/

Data are from an annual survey conducted by the Census Bureau and pertain to state government fiscal years ending on June 30, except for four states with other ending dates: Alabama and Michigan (September 30), New York (March 31), and Texas (August 31).

The state government finance data presented in this publication may differ from data published by state governments because the Census Bureau may be using a different definition of which organizations are covered under the term, "state government."

For the purpose of Census Bureau statistics, the term "state government" refers not only to the executive, legislative, and judicial branches of a given state, but it also includes agencies, institutions, commissions, and public authorities that operate separately or somewhat autonomously from the central state government but where the state government maintains administrative or fiscal control over their activities as defined by the Census Bureau.

Total **general revenue** includes all revenue except utility, liquor stores, and insurance trust revenue. All tax revenue and intergovernmental revenue, even if designated for employee-retirement or local utility purpose, are classified as general revenue.

Intergovernmental revenue covers amounts received from the federal government as fiscal aid, reimbursements for performance of general government functions and specific services for the paying government, or in lieu of taxes. It excludes any amounts received from other governments from the sale of property, commodities, and utility services.

Taxes consist of compulsory contributions exacted by governments for public purposes. However, this category excludes employer and employee payments for retirement and social insurance purposes, which are classified as insurance trust revenue; it also excludes special assessments, which are classified as non-tax general revenue. Sales and gross receipts taxes do not include dealer discounts, or "commissions" allowed to merchants for collection of taxes from consumers. General sales taxes and selected taxes on sales of motor fuels, tobacco products, and other particular commodities and services are included.

General government expenditure includes capital outlay, a major portion of which is commonly financed by borrowing. Government revenue does not include receipts from borrowing. Among other things, this distorts the relationship between totals of revenue and expenditure figures that are presented and renders it useless as a direct measure of the degree of budgetary "balance" (as that term is generally applied).

Direct general expenditure comprises all expenditures of the state governments, excluding utility, liquor stores, insurance trust expenditures, and any intergovernmental payments.

State government expenditure for **education** is mainly for the provision and general support of schools and other educational facilities and services, including those for educational institutions beyond high school. They cover such related services as student transportation; school lunch and other cafeteria operations; school health, recreation, and library services; and dormitories, dining halls, and bookstores operated by public institutions of higher education.

Health and hospitals expenditure includes health research; clinics; nursing; immunization; other categorical, environmental, and general health services provided by health agencies; establishment and operation of hospital facilities; provision of hospital care; and support of other public and private hospitals.

Highways expenditure is for the provision and maintenance of highway facilities, including toll turnpikes, bridges, tunnels, and ferries, as well as regular roads, highways, and streets. Also included are expenditures for street lighting and for snow and ice removal. Not included are highway policing and traffic control, which are considered part of police protection

Public safety expenditure includes police and correctional institution expenditures.

Public welfare expenditure covers support of and assistance to needy persons; this aid is contingent upon the person's needs. Included are cash assistance paid directly to needy persons under categorical (Old Age Assistance, Temporary Assistance for Needy Families, Aid to the Blind, and Aid to the Disabled) and other welfare programs; vendor payments made directly to private purveyors for medical care, burials, and other commodities and services provided under welfare programs; welfare institutions; and any intergovernmental or other direct expenditure for welfare purposes. Pensions to former employees and other benefits not contingent on need are excluded.

Natural resources, parks, and recreation includes expenditures for conservation, promotion, and development of natural resources (soil, water, energy, minerals, etc.) and the regulation of industries which develop, utilize, or affect natural resources. It also includes the provision and support of recreational and cultural-scientific facilities, such as golf courses, playgrounds, tennis courts, public beaches, swimming pools, play fields, parks, camping areas, recreational piers and marinas, galleries, museums, zoos, botanical gardens, auditoriums, stadiums, recreational centers, convention centers, exhibition halls, community music, drama, and celebrations.

Debt outstanding includes all long-term debt obligations of the government and its agencies (exclusive of utility debt) and all interest-bearing, short-term (repayable within one year) debt obligations remaining unpaid at the close of the fiscal year. It includes judgments, mortgages, and revenue bonds, as well as general obligation bonds, notes, and interest-bearing warrants. This category consists of non-interest-bearing, short-term obligations; inter-fund obligations; amounts owed in a trust or agency capacity; advances and contingent loans from other governments; and rights of individuals to benefit from government-administered employee-retirement funds.

VOTING AND REGISTRATION, Items 351 and 352

Source: U.S. Census Bureau—Current Population Survey
http://www.census.gov/topics/public-sector/voting.html

These estimates are based on the November 2016 Voting and Registration Supplement to the Current Population Survey (CPS).

Voting rates are calculated using the voting-age population, which includes both citizens and noncitizens. Statistics from surveys are subject to sampling and nonsampling error. The CPS estimate of overall turnout differs from the "official" turnout reported by the Clerk of the House of Representatives.

ELECTION STATISTICS, Items 353–355

Source: U.S. House of Representatives, Statistics of the Presidential and Congressional Election of November 8, 2016
http://history.house.gov/Institution/Election-Statistics/2016election/

Election results show the percentage of the total vote cast for the Democratic and Republican candidates, as well as the combined percentage for all other candidates in the 2016 presidential election. This information was compiled by the Office of the Clerk, U.S. House of Representatives and published on February 22, 2017.

TABLE B—STATES AND COUNTIES

Table B presents 199 items for the United States as a whole, each individual state, and the District of Columbia; and every county, county equivalent, and independent city. The counties are presented in alphabetical order within each state, and the states are also presented in alphabetical order. Independent cities, which are found in Maryland, Missouri, Nevada, and Virginia, are placed in alphabetical order at the end of the list of counties for those states. The District of Columbia is included in Table B as both a county and a state. It is also included as a city in Table D.

LAND AREA, Items 1 and 4

Source: U.S. Census Bureau—2017 U.S. Gazetteer Files,
http://www.census.gov/geo/maps-data/data/gazetteer2017.html

Land area measurements are shown to the nearest square mile. Land area is an area measurement providing the size, in square miles, of the land portions of each county.

POPULATION, Items 2–4

Source: U.S. Census Bureau—Population Estimates
https://www.census.gov/programs-surveys/popest.html

The population data are Census Bureau estimates of the resident population as of July 1 of the year shown. The ranks are shown for counties (including independent cities and the District of Columbia).

POPULATION AND POPULATION CHARACTERISTICS, Items 5–19

Source: U.S. Census Bureau—Population Estimates
https://www.census.gov/programs-surveys/popest.html

The concept of race, as used by the Census Bureau, reflects self-identification by persons according to the race or races with which they most closely identify. These categories are sociopolitical constructs and should not be interpreted as being scientific or anthropological in nature. Furthermore, race categories include both racial and national origin groups.

Beginning with the 2000 census, respondents were offered the option of selecting one or more races. This option was not available in prior censuses; thus, comparisons between censuses should be made with caution. In Table B, Columns 5 through 8 refer to individuals who identified with each racial category, either alone or in combination with other races. The estimates exclude persons of Hispanic or Latino origin from all race groups.

The sum of the four individual race alone or in combination categories in this book will often add to more than the total population because people who reported more than one race were tallied in each race category. In this book, the Asian group has been combined with the Native Hawaiian and Other Pacific Islander group, causing double-counting of persons who identify with both groups. This is especially pronounced in Hawaii.

The **White** population is defined as persons who indicated their race as White, as well as persons who did not classify themselves in one of the specific race categories listed on the questionnaire but entered a nationality such as Irish, German, Italian, Lebanese, Near Easterner, Arab, or Polish.

The **Black** population includes persons who indicated their race as "Black, African Am., or Negro," as well as persons who did not classify themselves in one of the specific race categories but reported entries such as African American, Afro American, Kenyan, Nigerian, or Haitian.

The **American Indian or Alaska Native** population includes persons who indicated their race as American Indian or Alaska Native, as well as persons who did not classify themselves in one of the specific race categories but reported entries such as Canadian Indian, French-American Indian, Spanish-American Indian, Eskimo, Aleut, Alaska Indian, or any of the American Indian or Alaska Native tribes.

The **Asian and Pacific Islander** population combines two census groupings: **Asian** and **Native Hawaiian or Other Pacific Islander**. The **Asian** population includes persons who indicated their race as Asian Indian, Chinese, Filipino, Japanese, Korean, Vietnamese, or "Other Asian," as well as persons who provided write-in entries of such groups as Cambodian, Laotian, Hmong, Pakistani, or Taiwanese. The **Native Hawaiian or Other Pacific Islander** population includes persons who indicated their race as "Native Hawaiian," "Guamanian or Chamorro," "Samoan," or "Other Pacific Islander," as well as persons who reported entries such as Part Hawaiian, American Samoan, Fijian, Melanesian, or Tahitian.

The **Hispanic population** is based on a question that asked respondents "Is this person Spanish/Hispanic/Latino?" Persons marking any one of the four Hispanic categories (i.e., Mexican, Puerto Rican, Cuban, or other Spanish) are collectively referred to as Hispanic.

In the census, the Hispanic origin question was placed before the race question and specific instructions indicated that both questions should be answered. These changes were designed to improve accuracy and may affect comparability with data prior to the 2000 census.

Age is defined as age at last birthday (number of completed years since birth), as of April 1 of the census year. The census also asked for the specific date of birth of the respondent, and census procedures used the birth date for deriving age data. For this reason, it is likely that the data have fewer problems than data from censuses prior to 2000, such as the tendency of respondents to round ages or to report their ages on the date the questionnaire was filled out rather than on April 1.

The **female** population is shown as a percentage of total population.

POPULATION AND COMPONENTS OF CHANGE, Items 20–26

Source: U.S. Census Bureau—Decennial Censuses and Population Estimates
http://www.census.gov/main/www/cen2000.html
https://www.census.gov/programs-surveys/popest.html
http://www.census.gov/2010census/data/

The population data for 2000 and 2010 are from the decennial censuses and represent the resident population as of April 1 of those years. The components of change are based on Census Bureau estimates of the resident population as of July 1, 2017. The change in population between 2010 and 2017 is made up of (a) natural increase—births minus deaths, and (b) net migration—the difference between the number of persons moving into a particular area and the number of persons moving out of the area. Net migration is composed of internal and international migration.

Because the 2017 population estimates are based on a model that begins with a national population estimate, the county components of change do not always exactly add up to the difference between the 2010 census population and the 2017 estimates.

HOUSEHOLDS, Items 27–31

Source: U.S. Census Bureau—American Community Survey, 2016 5-year Estimates
http://www.census.gov/acs/www/

A **household** includes all of the persons who occupy a housing unit. (Persons not living in households are classified as living in group quarters.) A housing unit is a house, an apartment, a mobile home, a group of rooms, or a single room occupied (or, if vacant, intended for occupancy) as separate living quarters. Separate living quarters are those in which the occupants live separately from any other persons in the building and have direct access from the outside of the building or through a common hall. The occupants may be a single family, one person living alone, two or more families living together, or any other group of related or unrelated persons who share living quarters. The number of households is the same as the number of year-round occupied housing units.

A **family** includes a householder and one or more other persons living in the same household who are related to the householder by birth, marriage, or adoption. All persons in a household who are related to the householder are regarded as members of his or her family. A **family household** may contain persons not related to the householder; thus, family households may include more members than families do. A household can contain only one family for the purposes of census tabulations. Not all households contain families, as a household may comprise a group of unrelated persons or of one person living alone. Families are classified by type as either a "married-couple family" or "other family," according to the presence or absence of a spouse.

The measure of **persons per household** is obtained by dividing the number of persons in households by the number of households or householders. One person in each household is designated as the householder. In most cases, this is the person (or one of the persons) in whose name the house is owned, being bought, or rented. If there is no such person in the household, any adult household member 15 years old and over can be designated as the householder.

The category **female family householder** includes only female-headed family households with no spouse present.

A nonfamily household consists of a householder living alone or with nonrelatives only. Column 31 shows one-person households as a percentage of all households.

GROUP QUARTERS, Item 32
Source: U.S. Census Bureau—Population Estimates
https://www.census.gov/programs-surveys/popest.html

The Census Bureau classifies all persons not living in households as living in group quarters; this category includes both the institutional and noninstitutional populations. The institutionalized population includes persons under formally authorized, supervised care or custody in institutions, such as correctional institutions, nursing homes, mental (psychiatric) hospitals, and juvenile institutions. The noninstitutionalized population includes persons who live in group quarters other than institutions, such as college dormitories, military quarters, and group homes. This volume includes the total number of persons in group quarters.

DAYTIME POPULATION, Items 33 and 34
Source: U.S. Census Bureau—American Community Survey, 2016 5-year Estimates
http://www.census.gov/acs/www/

Daytime population refers to the number of persons who are present in an area or place during normal business hours, including workers. This can be contrasted with the "resident" population, which is present during the evening and nighttime hours. The daytime population estimate is calculated by adding the total resident population and the total workers working in the area/place, and then subtracting the total workers living in the area/place from that result. Information on the expansion or contraction experienced by different communities between their nighttime and daytime populations is important for many planning purposes, especially those concerning transportation, disaster, and relief operations.

The employment/residence ratio is a measure of the total number of workers working in an area or place, relative to the total number of workers living in the area or place. It is often used as a rough indication of the jobs-workers balance in an area/place, although it does not take into account whether the resident workers possess the skills needed for the jobs available in their particular area/place. The employment/residence ratio is calculated by dividing the number of total workers working in an area/place by the number of total workers residing in the area/place.

BIRTHS AND DEATHS, Items 35–38
Source: U.S. Census Bureau—Population Estimates
https://www.census.gov/programs-surveys/popest.html

The numbers of births and deaths are from the Census Bureau's Population Estimates Program. They represent the total number of live births and deaths occurring to residents of an area as estimated using reports from the National Center for Health Statistics (NCHS) and the Federal-State Cooperative for Population Estimates (FSCPE). The rates measure births and deaths during the specified time period as a proportion of an area's population. Rates are expressed per 1,000 population estimated as of July 1. These numbers and rates do not represent the calendar year, but rather the year-long period ending on July 1.

PERSONS UNDER 65 WITH NO HEALTH INSURANCE, Items 39 and 40
Source: U.S. Census Bureau—Small Area Health Insurance Estimates
https://www.census.gov/programs-surveys/sahie.html

The Small Area Health Insurance Estimates (SAHIE) program develops model-based estimates of health insurance coverage for counties and states. This developmental program builds on the work of the Small Area Income and Poverty Estimates (SAIPE) program. The SAHIE program models health insurance coverage by combining survey data with population estimates and administrative records. These estimates combine data from administrative records, postcensal population estimates, and the decennial census with direct estimates from the American Community Survey to provide consistent and reliable single-year estimates. These model-based single-year estimates are more reflective of current conditions than multi-year survey estimates.

MEDICARE ENROLLMENT, Items 41–43

Source: U.S. Department of Health and Human Services, Centers for Medicare and Medicaid Services
https://www.cms.gov/Research-Statistics-Data-and-Systems/Statistics-Trends-and-Reports/CMSProgramStatistics/Dashboard.html

The Centers for Medicare and Medicaid Services (CMS) administers Medicare, which provides health insurance to persons 65 years old and over, persons with permanent kidney failure, and certain persons with disabilities. Original Medicare has two parts: Hospital Insurance and Supplemental Medical Insurance. In recent years, Medicare has been expanded to include two new programs: Medicare Advantage plans and prescription drug coverage. Medicare Advantage Plans are health plan options that are approved by Medicare but run by private companies. Medicare prescription drug plans can be part of Medicare Advantage plans or stand-alone drug plans.

Persons who are eligible for Medicare can enroll in Part A (Hospital Insurance) at no charge, and can choose to pay a monthly premium to enroll in Part B. Most eligible persons are enrolled in Part A, and most enrollees in Part A are also enrolled in Part B (Supplemental Medical Insurance.) This table includes persons who were enrolled in both Part A and Part B during 2017.

Part B beneficiaries can choose to enroll in **Original Medicare**, a fee-for-service plan administered by the Centers for Medicare and Medicaid Services, or in a **Medicare Advantage** plan. Medicare Advantage plans include private fee-for-service plans, preferred provider organizations, health maintenance organizations, medical savings account plans, demonstration plans, and programs for all-inclusive care for the elderly.

The annual Medicare enrollment counts are determined using a person-year methodology. For each calendar year, total person-year counts are determined by summing the total number of months that each beneficiary is enrolled during the year and dividing by 12. Using this methodology, a beneficiary's partial-year enrollment may be counted in more than one category (i.e., both Original Medicare and Medicare Advantage).

CRIME, Items 44–47

Source: U.S. Federal Bureau of Investigation—Uniform Crime Reports
https://ucr.fbi.gov/crime-in-the-u.s/2016/crime-in-the-u.s.-2016

Crime data are as reported to the Federal Bureau of Investigation (FBI) by law enforcement agencies and have not been adjusted for underreporting or overreporting. This may affect comparability between geographic areas or over time.

Through the voluntary contribution of crime statistics by law enforcement agencies across the United States, the Uniform Crime Reporting (UCR) Program provides periodic assessments of crime in the nation as measured by offenses that have come to the attention of the law enforcement community. The Committee on Uniform Crime Records of the International Association of Chiefs of Police initiated this voluntary national data collection effort in 1930. The UCR Program contributors compile and submit their crime data either directly to the FBI or through state-level UCR Programs.

Seven offenses, because of their severity, frequency of occurrence, and likelihood of being reported to police, were initially selected to serve as an index for evaluating fluctuations in the volume of crime. These serious crimes were murder and nonnegligent manslaughter, forcible rape, robbery, aggravated assault, burglary, larceny-theft, and motor vehicle theft. By congressional mandate, arson was added as the eighth index offense in 1979. The totals shown in this volume do not include arson.

In 2004, the FBI discontinued the use of the Crime Index in the UCR Program and its publications, stating that the Crime Index was driven upward by the offense with the highest number of cases (in this case, larceny-theft), creating a bias against jurisdictions with a high number of larceny-thefts but a low number of other serious crimes, such as murder and rape. The FBI is currently publishing a violent crime total and property crime total until a more viable index is developed. This book includes the crime total, as well as violent crime and property crime rates.

In 2013, the FBI adopted a new definition of rape. Rape is now defined as, "Penetration, no matter how slight, of the vagina or anus with any body part or object, or oral penetration by a sex organ of another person, without the consent of the victim." The new definition updated the 80-year-old historical definition of rape which was "carnal knowledge of a female forcibly and against her will." Effectively, the revised definition expands rape to include both male and female victims and offenders, and reflects the various forms of sexual penetration understood to be rape, especially nonconsenting acts of sodomy, and sexual assaults with objects.

Violent crimes include four categories of offenses: (1) Murder and nonnegligent manslaughter, as defined in the UCR Program, is the willful (nonnegligent) killing of one human being by another. This offense excludes deaths caused by negligence, suicide, or accident; justifiable homicides; and attempts to murder or assaults to murder. (2) Rape is the penetration, no matter how slight, of the vagina or anus with any body part or object, or oral penetration by a sex organ of another person, without the consent of the victim. Assaults or attempts to commit rape by force or threat of force are also included; however, statutory rape (without force) and other sex offenses are excluded. (3) Robbery is the taking or attempting to take anything of value from the care, custody, or control of a person or persons by force or threat of force or violence and/or by putting the victim in fear. (4) Aggravated assault is an unlawful attack by one person upon another for the purpose of inflicting severe or aggravated bodily injury. This type of assault is usually accompanied by the use of a weapon or by other means likely to produce death or great bodily harm. Attempts are included, since injury does not necessarily have to result when a gun, knife, or other weapon is used, as these incidents could and probably would result in a serious personal injury if the crime were successfully completed.

Property crimes include three categories: (1) Burglary, or breaking and entering, is the unlawful entry of a structure to commit a felony or theft, even though no force was used to gain entrance. (2) Larceny-theft is the unauthorized taking of the personal property of another, without the use of force. (3) Motor vehicle theft is the unauthorized taking of any motor vehicle.

Rates are based on population estimates provided by the FBI. The county totals published in this volume were obtained by aggregating individual reporting units within each county. If the population total for the units aggregated was less than 75 percent of the county's population (as estimated by the Census Bureau), the total was not considered representative of the county as a whole and was not published. State and U.S. totals include FBI estimates for those areas, adjusted to include areas that did not report and to correct for underreporting and overreporting, as published in the FBI's *Crime in the United States*.

EDUCATION—SCHOOL ENROLLMENT AND EDUCATIONAL ATTAINMENT, Items 48–51

Source: U.S. Census Bureau—American Community Survey, 2016 5-year Estimates
http://www.census.gov/acs/www/

Data on **school enrollment** are tabulated for the population 3 years old and over. Persons were classified as enrolled in school if they reported attending a "regular" public or private school (or college) during the three months preceding the interview. The instructions were to include only nursery school, kindergarten, elementary school, and schooling which would lead to a high school diploma or a college degree as regular school. The Census Bureau defines a public school as "any school or college controlled and supported by a local, county, state, or federal government." Schools primarily supported and controlled by religious organizations or other private groups are defined as private schools.

Data on **educational attainment** are tabulated for the population 25 years old and over. The data were derived from a question that asked respondents for the highest level of school completed or the highest degree received. Persons who had passed a high school equivalency examination were considered high school graduates. Schooling received in foreign schools was to be reported as the equivalent grade or years in the regular American school system.

Vocational and technical training, such as barber school training; business, trade, technical, and vocational schools; or other training for a specific trade are specifically excluded.

High school graduate or less. This category includes persons whose highest degree was a high school diploma or its equivalent, and those who reported any level lower than a high school diploma.

Bachelor's degree or more. This category includes persons who have received bachelor's degrees, master's degrees, professional school degrees (such as law school or medical school degrees), and doctoral degrees.

LOCAL GOVERNMENT EDUCATION EXPENDITURES, Items 52 and 53

Source: U.S. Department of Education, National Center for Education Statistics, Common Core of Data (CCD), "National Public Education Financial Survey (State Fiscal)", 2013-14 (FY 2014) v.1a; "School District Finance Survey (F-33)", 2013-14 (FY 2014) v.1a;

Expenditures are for elementary and secondary Education which includes prekindergarten through twelfth grade regular, special, and vocational education, as well as cocurricular, community service, and adult education programs provided by a public school system. The financial activities of these systems for all instruction, support service, and noninstructional activities are included

Current spending comprises current operation expenditure, payments made by the state government on behalf of school systems, and transfers made by school systems into their own retirement funds. Current operation expenditures include direct expenditure for salaries, employee benefits, purchased professional and technical services, purchased property and other services, and supplies. It includes gross school system expenditure for instruction, support services, and noninstructional functions. It excludes expenditure for debt service, capital outlay, and reimbursement to other governments (including other school systems).

Current expenditure per student is current expenditure divided by the number of students enrolled. The number of students enrolled is based on an annual "membership" count of students on or about October 1, collected by the National Center for Education Statistics on the Common Core of Data (CCD) agency universe file—"Local Education Agency (School District) Universe Survey."

MONEY INCOME, Items 54–57

Source: U.S. Census Bureau—American Community Survey, 2016 5-year Estimates
http://www.census.gov/acs/www/

Total money income is the sum of the amounts reported separately for wage or salary income; net self-employment income; interest, dividends, or net rental or royalty income or income from estates and trusts; Social Security or railroad retirement income; Supplemental Security Income (SSI); public assistance or welfare payments; retirement, survivor, or disability pensions; and all other income. Receipts from the following sources are not included as income: capital gains; money received from the sale of property (unless the recipient was engaged in the business of selling such property); the value of income "in kind" from food stamps, public housing subsidies, medical care, employer contributions for individuals, etc.; withdrawal of bank deposits; money borrowed; tax refunds; exchange of money between relatives living in the same household; and gifts, lump-sum inheritances, insurance payments, and other types of lump-sum receipts.

Money income differs in definition from personal income (item 62). For example, money income does not include the pension rights, employer provided health insurance, food stamps, or Medicare payments that are included in personal income.

Per capita income is the mean income computed for every man, woman, and child in a particular group. It is derived by dividing the aggregate income of a particular group by the resident population in that group as estimated in the American Community Survey. Per capita income is rounded to the nearest whole dollar.

Household income includes the income of the householder and all other individuals 15 years old and over in the household, whether or not they are related to the householder. Since many households consist of only one person, median household income is usually less than median family income. Although the household income statistics cover the 12 months preceding the interview, the characteristics of individuals and the composition of households refer to the date of interview. Thus, the income of the household does not include amounts received by individuals who were no longer residing in the household at the time of interview. Similarly, income amounts reported by individuals who did not reside in the household during all of the past 12 months but who were members of the household at the time of interview are included. However, the composition of most households was the same during those 12 months as it was at the time of interview.

Median income divides the income distribution into two equal parts, with half of all cases below the median income level and half of all cases above the median income level. For households, the median income is based on the distribution of the total number of households, including those with no income. Median income for households is computed on the basis of a standard distribution with a minimum value of less than $2,500 and a maximum value of $200,000 or more and is rounded to the nearest whole dollar. Median income figures are calculated using linear interpolation if the width of the interval containing the estimate is $2,500 or less. If the width of the interval containing the estimate is greater than $2,500, Pareto interpolation is used.

Income amounts have been adjusted for inflation to represent the final year of multi-year estimates, in this case 2012-2016 estimates. The constant-dollar figures are based on an annual average Consumer Price Index from the Bureau of Labor Statistics. Constant-dollar figures are estimates representing an effort to remove the effects of price changes from statistical series reported in dollar terms. However, the estimates do not reflect the price and cost-of-living differences that may exist between areas.

INCOME AND POVERTY, Items 58–61
Source: U.S. Census Bureau—Small Area Income and Poverty Estimates Program
http://www.census.gov/did/www/saipe/index.html

The annual income and poverty estimates by county are constructed from statistical models that relate income and poverty to indicators based on summary data from federal income tax returns, data about participation in the Food Stamp program, and the previous census. A regression model predicts the number of people in poverty using county-level observations from the current year's American Community Survey (ACS) and administrative records and census data as the predictors. The 2005 estimates were the first to use the ACS. Prior year models were based on the Annual Social and Economic Supplement (ASEC) of the Current Population Survey (CPS). The ACS is a much larger survey than the ASEC, permitting income and poverty estimates based on a single year for many counties, Because of the differences between the two surveys, caution should be used when comparing these estimates with those from earlier years.

The **poverty status** data were derived from data collected on the number of persons in a household, each person's relationship to the householder, and income data. The Social Security Administration (SSA) developed the original poverty definition in 1964, which federal interagency committees subsequently revised in 1969 and 1980. The Office of Management and Budget's (OMB) *Directive 14* prescribes the SSA's definition as the official poverty measure for federal agencies to use in their statistical work. Poverty statistics presented in American Community Survey products adhere to the standards defined by OMB in *Directive 14*.

Poverty thresholds vary depending on three criteria: size of family, number of children, and, for one- and two-person families, age of householder. In determining the poverty status of families and unrelated individuals, the Census Bureau uses thresholds (income cutoffs) arranged in a two-dimensional matrix. The matrix consists of family size (from one person to nine or more persons), cross-classified by presence and number of family members under 18 years old (from no children present to eight or more children present). Unrelated individuals and two-person families are further differentiated by age of reference person (under 65 years old and 65 years old and over). To determine a person's poverty status, the person's total family income over the previous 12 months is compared with the poverty threshold appropriate for that person's family size and composition. If the total income of that person's family is less than the threshold appropriate for that family, then the person is considered poor or "below the poverty level," together with every member of his or her family. If a person is not living with anyone related by birth, marriage, or adoption, then the person's own income is compared with his or her poverty threshold. The total number of persons below the poverty level is the sum of persons in families and the number of unrelated individuals with incomes below the poverty level over the previous 12 months.

PERSONAL INCOME AND EARNINGS, Items 62–83
Source: U.S. Bureau of Economic Analysis, Regional Economic Accounts
http://www.bea.gov/regional/index.htm#state

Total personal income is the current income received by residents of an area from all sources. It is measured before deductions of income and other personal taxes, but after deductions of personal contributions for Social Security, government retirement, and other social insurance programs. It consists of **wage and salary disbursements** (covering all employee earnings, including executive salaries, bonuses, commissions, payments-in-kind, incentive payments, and tips); various types of supplementary earnings, such as employers' contributions to pension funds (termed "other labor income" or "supplements to wages and salaries"); proprietors' income; rental income of persons; dividends; personal interest income; and government and business transfer payments.

Per capita personal income is based on the resident population estimated as of July 1 of the year shown.

Proprietors' income is the monetary income and income-in-kind of proprietorships and partnerships (including the independent professions) and the income of tax-exempt cooperatives.

Poverty Thresholds for 2016 by Size of Family and Number of Related Children Under 18 Years

Size of family unit	Weighted average thresholds	Related children under 18 years								
		None	One	Two	Three	Four	Five	Six	Seven	Eight or more
One person (unrelated individual):	12,228									
Under age 65	12,486	12,486								
Aged 65 and older	11,511	11,511								
Two people:	15,569									
Householder under age 65........	16,151	16,072	16,543							
Householder aged 65 and older	14,522	14,507	16,480							
Three people...............................	19,105	18,774	19,318	19,337						
Four people.................................	24,563	24,755	25,160	24,339	24,424					
Five people	29,111	29,854	30,288	29,360	28,643	28,205				
Six people	32,928	34,337	34,473	33,763	33,082	32,070	31,470			
Seven people..............................	37,458	39,509	39,756	38,905	38,313	37,208	35,920	34,507		
Eight people................................	41,781	44,188	44,578	43,776	43,072	42,075	40,809	39,491	39,156	
Nine people or more	49,721	53,155	53,413	52,702	52,106	51,127	49,779	48,561	48,259	46,400

Source: U.S. Census Bureau.

Dividends are cash payments by corporations to stockholders who are U.S. residents. **Interest** is the monetary and imputed interest income of persons from all sources. **Rent** is the monetary income of persons from the rental of real property, except the income of persons primarily engaged in the real estate business; the imputed net rental income of owner-occupants of nonfarm dwellings; and the royalties received by persons.

Transfer payments are income for which services are not currently rendered. They consist of both government and business transfer payments. Government transfer payments include payments under the following programs: Federal Old-Age, Survivors, and Disability Insurance ("Social Security"); Medicare and medical vendor payments; unemployment insurance; railroad and government retirement; federal- and state-government-insured workers' compensation; veterans' benefits, including veterans' life insurance; SNAP (Supplemental Nutrition Assistance Program, or food stamps); black lung payments; Supplemental Security Income; and Temporary Assistance for Needy Families. Government payments to nonprofit institutions, other than for work under research and development contracts, are also included. Business transfer payments consist primarily of liability payments for personal injury and of corporate gifts to nonprofit institutions.

Personal income differs in definition from money income (items 54–57). For example, personal income includes pension rights, employer-provided health insurance, food stamps, and Medicare. These are not included in the definition of money income.

Earnings cover wage and salary disbursements, other labor income, and proprietors' income.

The data for earnings obtained from the Bureau of Economic Analysis (BEA) are based on place of work. In computing personal income, BEA makes an "adjustment for residence" to earnings, based on commuting patterns; personal income is thus presented on a place-of-residence basis.

Farm earnings include the income of farm workers (wages and salaries and other labor income) and farm proprietors. Farm proprietors' income includes only the income of sole proprietorships and partnerships. Farm earnings estimates are benchmarked to data collected in the Census of Agriculture and the revised Department of Agriculture statistical totals of income and expense items.

Goods-related industries include mining, construction, and manufacturing.

Mining, Quarrying, and Extracting comprises establishments that extract naturally occurring mineral solids, such as coal and ores; liquid minerals, such as crude petroleum; and gases, such as natural gas. The term mining is used in the broad sense to include quarrying, well operations, beneficiating (e.g., crushing, screening, washing, and flotation), and other preparation customarily performed at the mine site, or as a part of mining activity.

The **Construction** sector comprises establishments primarily engaged in the construction of buildings or engineering projects (e.g., highways and utility systems). Establishments primarily engaged in the preparation of sites for new construction and establishments primarily engaged in subdividing land for sale as building sites also are included in this sector.

Manufacturing comprises establishments engaged in the mechanical, physical, or chemical transformation of materials, substances, or components into new products. The assembling of component parts of manufactured products is considered manufacturing, except in cases where the activity is appropriately classified in **Construction**.

Service-related and other industries include private-sector earnings in agricultural services, forestry, and fisheries; transportation and public utilities; wholesale trade; retail trade; finance, insurance, and real estate; and services. Government earnings include all levels of government.

The **Information** sector comprises establishments engaged in the following processes: (a) producing and distributing information and cultural products, (b) providing the means to transmit or distribute these products as well as data or communications, and (c) processing data.

Professional, Scientific, and Technical Services comprises establishments that specialize in performing professional, scientific, and technical activities for others. These activities require a high degree of expertise and training. The establishments in this sector specialize according to expertise and provide these services to clients in a variety of industries and, in some cases, to households. Activities performed include: legal advice and representation; accounting, bookkeeping, and payroll services; architectural, engineering, and specialized design services; computer services; consulting services; research services; advertising services; photographic services; translation and interpretation services; veterinary services; and other professional, scientific, and technical services.

The **Retail Trade** sector comprises establishments engaged in retailing merchandise, generally without transformation, and rendering services incidental to the sale of merchandise.

The retailing process is the final step in the distribution of merchandise; retailers are, therefore, organized to sell merchandise in small quantities to the general public. This sector comprises two main types of retailers: store and nonstore retailers.

Store retailers operate fixed point-of-sale locations, located and designed to attract a high volume of walk-in customers. In general, retail stores have extensive displays of merchandise and use mass-media advertising to attract customers. In addition to retailing merchandise, some types of store retailers are also engaged in the provision of after-sales services, such as repair and installation.

Nonstore retailers, like store retailers, are organized to serve the general public, but their retailing methods differ. The establishments of this subsector reach customers and market merchandise with methods, such as the broadcasting of "infomercials," the broadcasting and publishing of direct-response advertising, the publishing of paper and electronic catalogs, door-to-door solicitation, in-home demonstration, selling from portable stalls (street vendors, except food), and distribution through vending machines. Establishments engaged in the direct sale (nonstore) of products, such as home heating oil dealers and home delivery newspaper routes are included here.

Finance and Insurance comprises establishments primarily engaged in financial transactions (transactions involving the creation, liquidation, or change in ownership of financial assets) and/or in facilitating financial transactions. Three principal types of activities are identified: raising funds by taking deposits and/or issuing securities and, in the process, incurring liabilities; pooling of risk by underwriting insurance and annuities; and providing specialized services facilitating or supporting financial intermediation, insurance, and employee benefit programs.

The **Real Estate and Rental and Leasing** sector comprises establishments primarily engaged in renting, leasing, or otherwise allowing the use of tangible or intangible assets, and establishments providing related services. The major portion of this sector comprises establishments that rent, lease, or otherwise allow the use of their own assets by others. The assets may be tangible, as is the case of real estate and equipment, or intangible, as is the case with patents and trademarks. This sector also includes establishments

primarily engaged in managing real estate for others, selling, renting and/or buying real estate for others, and appraising real estate.

Health Care and Social Assistance comprises establishments providing health care and social assistance for individuals. The sector includes both health care and social assistance because it is sometimes difficult to distinguish between the boundaries of these two activities. The industries in this sector are arranged on a continuum starting with those establishments providing medical care exclusively, continuing with those providing health care and social assistance, and finally finishing with those providing only social assistance. The services provided by establishments in this sector are delivered by trained professionals. All industries in the sector share this commonality of process, namely, labor inputs of health practitioners or social workers with the requisite expertise. Many of the industries in the sector are defined based on the educational degree held by the practitioners included in the industry.

Government includes the executive, legislative, judicial, administrative and regulatory activities of Federal, state, local, and international governments. Also included are Government enterprises: government agencies that cover a substantial portion of their operating costs by selling goods and services to the public and that maintain separate accounts.

Industries are categorized under the North American Industry Classification System (NAICS), and are not comparable to years prior to 2002.

SOCIAL SECURITY AND SUPPLEMENTAL SECURITY INCOME, Items 84–86

Source: U.S. Social Security Administration
http://www.ssa.gov/policy/docs/statcomps/oasdi_sc/
http://www.ssa.gov/policy/docs/statcomps/ssi_sc/

Social Security beneficiaries are persons receiving benefits under the Old-Age, Survivors, and Disability Insurance Program. These include retired or disabled workers covered by the program, their spouses and dependent children, and the surviving spouses and dependent children of deceased workers.

Supplemental Security Income (SSI) recipients are persons receiving SSI payments. The SSI program is a cash assistance program that provides monthly benefits to low-income aged, blind, or disabled persons.

Data are as of December of the year shown.

HOUSING, Items 87–96

Source: U.S. Census Bureau—Population Estimates Program
http://www.census.gov/popest/
Source: U.S. Census Bureau—American Community Survey, 2016 5-year Estimates
http://www.census.gov/acs/www/

Housing data for 2017 are from the Population Estimates Program. Housing unit characteristics for 2012-2016 are from the American Community Survey.

A **housing unit** is a house, apartment, mobile home or trailer, group of rooms, or single room occupied or, if vacant, intended

Similarly, establishments that both manufacture and sell their products to the general public are classified in Manufacturing instead of Retail Trade. However, establishments that engage in processing activities incidental to retailing are classified in Retail Trade.

REAL ESTATE AND RENTAL AND LEASING, Items 143–146

Source: U.S. Census Bureau—2012 Economic Census (See Overview of 2012 Economic Census prior to Item 135)

The Real Estate and Rental and Leasing sector (53) comprises establishments primarily engaged in renting, leasing, or otherwise allowing the use of tangible or intangible assets, and establishments providing related services. The major portion of this sector is made up of establishments that rent, lease, or otherwise allow the use of their own assets by others. The assets may be tangible, such as real estate and equipment, or intangible, such as patents and trademarks.

This sector also includes establishments primarily engaged in managing real estate for others, selling, renting, and/or buying real estate for others, and appraising real estate. These activities are closely related to this sector's main activity. In addition, a substantial proportion of property management is selfperformed by lessors.

The main components of this sector are the real estate lessors industries; equipment lessors industries (including motor vehicles, computers, and consumer goods); and lessors of nonfinancial intangible assets (except copyrighted works).

PROFESSIONAL, SCIENTIFIC, AND TECHNICAL SERVICES, Items 147–150

Source: U.S. Census Bureau—2012 Economic Census (See Overview of 2012 Economic Census prior to Item 135)

The Professional, Scientific, and Technical Services sector (54) is made up of establishments that specialize in performing professional, scientific, and technical activities for others. These activities require a high degree of expertise and training. The establishments in this sector specialize in one or more areas and provide services to clients in a variety of industries (and, in some cases, to households). Activities performed include legal advice and representation; accounting, bookkeeping, and payroll services; architectural, engineering, and specialized design services; computer services; consulting services; research services; advertising services; photographic services; translation and interpretation services; veterinary services; and other professional, scientific, and technical services.

This sector excludes establishments primarily engaged in providing a range of daytoday office administrative services, such as financial planning, billing and record keeping, personnel services, and physical distribution and logistics services. These establishments are classified in sector 56, Administrative and Support and Waste Management and Remediation Services.

MANUFACTURING, Items 151–154

Source: U.S. Census Bureau—2012 Economic Census (See Overview of 2012 Economic Census prior to Item 135)

The Manufacturing sector (31–33) is made up of establishments engaged in the mechanical, physical, or chemical transformation of materials, substances, or components into new products. The assembling of component parts of manufactured products is considered manufacturing, except in cases in which the activity is appropriately classified in the Construction sector. Establishments in the Manufacturing sector are often described as plants, factories, or mills, and characteristically use power-driven machines and materials-handling equipment. However, establishments that transform materials or substances into new products by hand or in the worker's home, and establishments engaged in selling to the general public products made on the same premises from which they are sold (such as bakeries, candy stores, and custom tailors) may also be included in this sector. Manufacturing establishments may process materials or contract with other establishments to process their materials for them. Both types of establishments are included in the Manufacturing sector.

The materials, substances, or components transformed by manufacturing establishments are raw materials that are products of agriculture, forestry, fishing, mining, or quarrying, or are products of other manufacturing establishments. The materials used may be purchased directly from producers, obtained through customary trade channels, or secured without recourse to the market by transferring the product from one establishment to another, under the same ownership. The new product of a manufacturing establishment may be finished (in the sense that it is ready for utilization or consumption), or it may be semifinished to become an input for an establishment engaged in further manufacturing. For example, the product of the alumina refinery is the input used in the primary production of aluminum; primary aluminum is the input used in an aluminum wire drawing plant; and aluminum wire is the input used in a fabricated wire product manufacturing establishment.

Data are included for counties with 500 or more employees in the Manufacturing sector.

ACCOMMODATION AND FOOD SERVICES, Items 155–158

Source: U.S. Census Bureau—2012 Economic Census (See Overview of 2012 Economic Census prior to Item 135)

The Accommodation and Food Services sector (72) consists of establishments that provide customers with lodging and/or meals, snacks, and beverages for immediate consumption. This sector includes both accommodation and food services establishments because the two activities are often combined at the same establishment.

Excluded from this sector are civic and social organizations, amusement and recreation parks, theaters, and other recreation or entertainment facilities providing food and beverage services.

HEALTH CARE AND SOCIAL ASSISTANCE, Items 159–162

Source: U.S. Census Bureau—2012 Economic Census (See Overview of 2012 Economic Census prior to Item 135)

The Health Care and Social Assistance sector (62) consists of establishments that provide health care and social assistance services to individuals. The sector includes both health care and social assistance because it is sometimes difficult to distinguish between the boundaries of these two activities. The industries in this sector are arranged on a continuum, starting with establishments that provide medical care exclusively, continuing with those that provide health care and social assistance, and finishing with those that provide only social assistance. The services provided by establishments in this sector are delivered by trained professionals. All industries in the sector share this commonality of process—namely, labor inputs of health practitioners or social workers with the requisite expertise. Many of the industries in the sector are defined based on the educational degree held by the practitioners included in the industry.

Excluded from this sector are aerobic classes, which can be found in subsector 713, Amusement, Gambling, and Recreation Industries; and nonmedical diet and weight-reducing centers, which can be found in subsector 812, Personal and Laundry Services. Although these can be viewed as health services, they are not typically delivered by health practitioners.

OTHER SERVICES, EXCEPT PUBLIC ADMINISTRATION Items 163–166

Source: U.S. Census Bureau—2012 Economic Census (See Overview of 2012 Economic Census prior to Item 135)

The Other Services, Except Public Administration sector (81) comprises establishments engaged in providing services not specifically categorized elsewhere in the classification system. Establishments in this sector are primarily engaged in activities such as equipment and machinery repairing, promoting or administering religious activities, grant making, and advocacy; this sector also includes establishments that provide dry-cleaning and laundry services, personal care services, death care services, pet care services, photofinishing services, temporary parking services, and dating services.

Private households that employ workers on or about the premises in activities primarily concerned with the operation of the household are included in this sector.

Excluded from this sector are establishments primarily engaged in retailing new equipment and performing repairs and general maintenance on equipment. These establishments are classified in sector 44–45, Retail Trade.

NONEMPLOYER BUSINESSES, Items 167 and 168

Source: U.S. Census Bureau—Nonemployer Statistics https://www.census.gov/programs-surveys/nonemployer-statistics.html

Nonemployer Statistics is an annual series that provides subnational economic data for businesses that have no paid employees and are subject to federal income tax. The data consist of the number of businesses and total receipts by industry. Most nonemployers are self-employed individuals operating unincorporated businesses (known as sole proprietorships), which may or may not be the owner's principal source of income.

The majority of all business establishments in the United States are nonemployers, yet these firms average less than 4 percent of all sales and receipts nationally. Due to their small economic impact, these firms are excluded from most other Census Bureau business statistics (the primary exception being the Survey of Business Owners). The Nonemployers Statistics series is the primary resource available to study the scope and activities of nonemployers at a detailed geographic level.

BUILDING PERMITS, Items 169 and 170

Source: U.S. Census Bureau—Building Permits Survey http://www.census.gov/construction/bps/

These figures represent private residential construction authorized by building permits in approximately 20,000 places in the United States. Valuation represents the expected cost of construction as recorded on the building permit. This figure usually excludes the cost of on-site and off-site development and improvements, as well as the cost of heating, plumbing, electrical, and elevator installations.

National, state, and county totals were obtained by adding the data for permit-issuing places within each jurisdiction. Not all areas of the country require a building or zoning permit. The statistics only represent those areas that do require a permit. These totals thus are limited to permits issued in the 20,000 place universe covered by the Census Bureau and may not include all permits issued within a state. Current surveys indicate that construction is undertaken for all but a very small percentage of housing units authorized by building permits.

Residential building permits include buildings with any number of housing units. Housing units exclude group quarters (such as dormitories and rooming houses), transient accommodations (such as transient hotels, motels, and tourist courts), "HUD-code" manufactured (mobile) homes, moved or relocated units, and housing units created in an existing residential or nonresidential structure.

COUNTY AREA LOCAL GOVERNMENT EMPLOYMENT AND PAYROLL, Items 171-179

Source: U.S. Census Bureau—2012 Census of Governments
https://www.census.gov/govs/programs-surveys/cog.html

These items include data for all local governments (i.e., counties, municipalities, townships, special districts, and school districts) located within the county. The Census of Governments identifies the scope and nature of the nation's state and local government sector; provides authoritative benchmark figures of public finance and public employment; classifies local government organizations, powers, and activities; and measures federal, state, and local fiscal relationships. The Employment component was mailed **March 2012** to collect information on the number of state and local government civilian employees and their payrolls.

Government employees include all persons paid for personal services performed, including persons paid from federally funded programs, paid elected or appointed officials, persons in a paid leave status, and persons paid on a per meeting, annual, semi-annual, or quarterly basis. Unpaid officials, pensioners, persons whose work is performed on a fee basis, and contractors and their employees are excluded from the count of employees. **Full-Time Equivalent employees** is a computed statistic representing the number of full-time employees that could have been employed if the reported number of hours worked by part-time employees had been worked by full-time employees. This statistic is calculated separately for each function of a government by dividing the "part-time hours paid" by the standard number of hours for full-time employees in the particular government and then adding the resulting quotient to the number of full-time employees.

March payroll represents gross payroll amounts for the one-month period of March for full-time and part-time employees. Gross payroll includes all salaries, wages, fees, commissions, and overtime paid to employees **before** withholdings for taxes, insurance, etc. It also includes incentive payments that are paid at regular pay intervals. It excludes employer share of fringe benefits like retirement, Social Security, health and life insurance, lump sum payments, and so forth.

Administration and Judicial and Legal combines **Financial administration**, **Other government administration**, and **Judicial and Legal** activities. **Financial administration includes** activities concerned with tax assessment and collection, custody and disbursement of funds, debt management, administration of trust funds, budgeting, and other government-wide financial management activities. This function is not applied to school district or special district governments. **Other government administration** applies to the legislative and government-wide administrative agencies of governments. Included here are overall planning and zoning activities, and central personnel and administrative activities. This function is not applied to school district or special district governments. **Judicial and legal** includes all court and court related activities (except probation and parole activities that are included at the "Correction" function), court activities of sheriff's offices, prosecuting attorneys' and public defenders' offices, legal departments, and attorneys providing government-wide legal service.

Police and Corrections includes all activities concerned, with the enforcement of law and order, including coroner's offices, police training academies, investigation bureaus, and local jails, "lockups", or other detention facilities not intended to serve as correctional facilities. **Corrections** includes activities pertaining to the confinement and correction of adults and minors convicted of criminal offenses. Pardon, probation, and parole activities are also included here.

Fire protection includes local government fire protection and prevention activities plus any ambulance, rescue, or other auxiliary services provided by a fire protection agency. Volunteer fire-fighters, if remunerated for their services on a "per fire" or some other basis, are included as part-time employees.

Highways and transportation includes activities associated with the maintenance and operation of streets, roads, sidewalks, bridges, tunnels, toll roads, and ferries. Snow and ice removal, street lighting, and highway and traffic engineering activities are also included here. Also included are the operation, maintenance, and construction of public mass transit systems, including subways, surface rails, and buses, and the provision, construction, operation, maintenance; support of public waterways, harbors, docks, wharves, and related marine terminal facilities; and activities associated with the operation and support of publicly operated airport facilities.

Health and Welfare includes Health, Hospitals, and Public welfare. Health includes administration of public health programs, community and visiting nurse services, immunization programs, drug abuse rehabilitation programs, health and food inspection activities, operation of outpatient clinics, and environmental pollution control activities. **Hospitals** includes only government operated medical care facilities that provide inpatient care. Employees and payrolls of private corporations that lease and operate government-owned hospital facilities are excluded.

Public Welfare includes the administration of various public assistance programs for the needy, veteran services, operation of nursing homes, indigent care institutions, and programs that provide payments for medical care, handicap transportation, and other services for the needy.

Natural resources and Utilities includes activities primarily concerned with the conservation and development of natural resources (soil, water, energy, minerals, etc.) and the regulation of industries that develop, utilize, or affect natural resources, as well as the operation and maintenance of **parks**, playgrounds, swimming pools, public beaches, auditoriums, public golf courses, museums, marinas, botanical gardens, and zoological parks. **Utilities, sewerage, and waste management** includes operation, maintenance, and construction of public water supply systems, including production, acquisition, and distribution of water to general public or to other public or private utilities, for residential, commercial, and industrial use; activities associated with the production or acquisition and distribution of electric power; provision, maintenance, and operation of sanitary and storm sewer systems and sewage disposal and treatment facilities; and refuse collection and disposal, operation of sanitary landfills, and street cleaning activities.

Education and libraries includes activities associated with the operation of public elementary and secondary schools and locally operated vocational-technical schools. Special education programs operated by elementary and secondary school systems are also included as are all ancillary services associated with the operation of schools, such as pupil transportation and food service. **Also included are the e**stablishment and provision of libraries for use by the general public and the technical support of privately operated libraries. This category includes classroom teachers, principals, supervisors of instruction, librarians, teacher aides, library aides, and guidance and psychological personnel as well as school superintendents and other administrative personnel, clerical and secretarial staffs, plant operation and maintenance personnel, health and recreation employees, transportation and food service personnel, and any student employees. Also included are any degree granting institutions that provide academic training above grade 12.

LOCAL GOVERNMENT FINANCES, Items 180–193

Source: U.S. Census Bureau—2012 Census of Governments
https://www.census.gov/programs-surveys/cog.html

Data on local government finances are based on result of the 2012 Census of Governments. For each county area, the financial data comprise amounts for all local governments—not only the county government, but also any municipalities, townships, school districts, and special districts within the county. Statistics from governmental units located in two or more county areas are assigned to the county area containing the administrative office.

Revenue and expenditure items include all amounts of money received and paid out, respectively, by a government and its agencies (net of correcting transactions such as recoveries of refunds), with the exception of amounts for debt issuance and retirement and for loan and investment, agency, and private transactions.

Payments among the various funds and agencies of a particular government are excluded from revenue and expenditure items as representing internal transfers. Therefore, a government's contribution to a retirement fund that it administers is not counted as expenditure, nor is the receipt of this contribution by the retirement fund counted as revenue.

Total **general revenue** includes all revenue except utility, liquor stores, and insurance trust revenue. All tax revenue and intergovernmental revenue, even if designated for employee-retirement or local utility purpose, are classified as general revenue.

Intergovernmental revenue covers amounts received from the federal government as fiscal aid, reimbursements for performance of general government functions and specific services for the paying government, or in lieu of taxes. It excludes any amounts received from other governments from the sale of property, commodities, and utility services.

Taxes consist of compulsory contributions exacted by governments for public purposes. However, this category excludes employer and employee payments for retirement and social insurance purposes, which are classified as insurance trust revenue; it also excludes special assessments, which are classified

as non-tax general revenue. Property taxes are taxes conditioned on ownership of property and assessed by its value. Sales and gross receipts taxes do not include dealer discounts, or "commissions" allowed to merchants for collection of taxes from consumers. General sales taxes and selected taxes on sales of motor fuels, tobacco products, and other particular commodities and services are included.

General government expenditure includes capital outlay, a major portion of which is commonly financed by borrowing. Government revenue does not include receipts from borrowing. Among other things, this distorts the relationship between totals of revenue and expenditure figures that are presented and renders it useless as a direct measure of the degree of budgetary "balance" (as that term is generally applied).

Direct general expenditure comprises all expenditures of the local governments, excluding utility, liquor stores, insurance trust expenditures, and any intergovernmental payments.

Local government expenditure for **education** is mainly for the provision and general support of schools and other educational facilities and services, including those for educational institutions beyond high school. They cover such related services as student transportation; school lunch and other cafeteria operations; school health, recreation, and library services; and dormitories, dining halls, and bookstores operated by public institutions of higher education.

Health and hospital expenditure includes health research; clinics; nursing; immunization; other categorical, environmental, and general health services provided by health agencies; establishment and operation of hospital facilities; provision of hospital care; and support of other public and private hospitals.

Police protection expenditure includes police activities such as patrols, communications, custody of persons awaiting trial, and vehicular inspection.

Public welfare expenditure covers support of and assistance to needy persons; this aid is contingent upon the person's needs. Included are cash assistance paid directly to needy persons under categorical (Old Age Assistance, Temporary Assistance for Needy Families, Aid to the Blind, and Aid to the Disabled) and other welfare programs; vendor payments made directly to private purveyors for medical care, burials, and other commodities and services provided under welfare programs; welfare institutions; and any intergovernmental or other direct expenditure for welfare purposes. Pensions to former employees and other benefits not contingent on need are excluded.

Highway expenditure is for the provision and maintenance of highway facilities, including toll turnpikes, bridges, tunnels, and ferries, as well as regular roads, highways, and streets. Also included are expenditures for street lighting and for snow and ice removal. Not included are highway policing and traffic control, which are considered part of police protection

Debt outstanding includes all long-term debt obligations of the government and its agencies (exclusive of utility debt) and all interest-bearing, short-term (repayable within one year) debt obligations remaining unpaid at the close of the fiscal year. It includes judgments, mortgages, and revenue bonds, as well as general obligation bonds, notes, and interest-bearing warrants. This category consists of non-interest-bearing, short-term obligations; inter-fund obligations; amounts owed in a trust or agency capacity; advances and contingent loans from other governments; and rights of individuals to benefit from government-administered employee-retirement funds.

GOVERNMENT EMPLOYMENT, Items 194–196

Source: U.S. Bureau of Economic Analysis—Regional Economic Accounts
http://www.bea.gov/regional/index.htm#state

Employment is measured as the average annual sum of full-time and part-time jobs. The estimates are on a place-of-work basis. State and local government employment includes person employed in all state and local government agencies and enterprises. Data for federal civilian employment include civilian employees of the federal government, including civilian employees of the Department of Defense. Military employment includes all persons on active duty status.

INDIVIDUAL INCOME TAX RETURNS, Items 197–199

Source: U.S. Internal Revenue Servicw, Statistics of Income Program
https://www.irs.gov/uac/soi-tax-stats-county-data-2015

The Revenue Act of 1916 mandated the annual publication of statistics related to "the operations of the internal revenue laws" as they affect individuals, all forms of businesses, estates. nonprofit organizations, trusts, and investments abroad and foreign investments in the United States. The Statistics of Income (SOI) division fulfills this function by collecting and processing data so that they become informative and by sharing information about how the tax system works with other government agencies and the general public. Publication types include traditional print sources, Internet files, CD-ROMs, and files sent via e-mail. SOI has an information office, Statistical Information Services, to facilitate the dissemination of SOI data.

SOI bases its county data on administrative records of individual income tax returns (Forms 1040) from the Internal Revenue Service (IRS) Individual Master File (IMF) system. Included in these data are returns filed during the 12-month period, January 1, 2016 to December 31, 2016. While the bulk of returns filed during the 12-month period are primarily for Tax Year 2015, the IRS received a limited number of returns for tax years before 2015 and these have been included within the county data.

Data do not represent the full U.S. population because many individuals are not required to file an individual income tax return. The address shown on the tax return may differ from the taxpayer's actual residence. State and county codes were based on the ZIP code shown on the return. Excluded were tax returns filed without a ZIP code and returns filed with a ZIP code that did not match the State code shown on the return.

SOI did not attempt to correct any ZIP codes on the returns; however, it did take the following precautions to avoid disclosing information about specific taxpayers: Excluded from the data are items with less than 20 returns within a county. Also excluded are tax returns representing a specified percentage of the total of any particular cell. For example, if one return represented 75 percent of the value of a given cell, the return was suppressed from the county detail. The actual threshold percentage used cannot be released.

Column 197 show the number of returns. Column 198 shows the mean Adjusted Gross Income for the county and column 199 shows the mean income tax (line 56 on Form 1040). for the county.

TABLE C—METROPOLITAN AREAS

Table C presents 199 items for the 382 metropolitan statistical areas (MSAs) and 31 metropolitan divisions in the United States. The metropolitan areas are presented in alphabetical order, and the metropolitan divisions are presented in alphabetical order within the appropriate metropolitan area. For some data items, the metropolitan area data have been aggregated from county data sources.

LAND AREA, Items 1 and 4

Source: U.S. Census Bureau—2017 U.S. Gazetteer Files,
http://www.census.gov/geo/maps-data/data/gazetteer2017.html

Land area measurements are shown to the nearest square mile. Land area is an area measurement providing the size, in square miles, of the land portions of each county.

POPULATION, Items 2–4

Source: U.S. Census Bureau—Population Estimates
https://www.census.gov/programs-surveys/popest.html

The population data are Census Bureau estimates of the resident population as of July 1 of the year shown. The ranks are shown for metropolitan statistical areas, but exclude metropolitan divisions.

POPULATION AND POPULATION CHARACTERISTICS, Items 5–19

Source: U.S. Census Bureau—Population Estimates
https://www.census.gov/programs-surveys/popest.html

The concept of race, as used by the Census Bureau, reflects self-identification by persons according to the race or races with which they most closely identify. These categories are sociopolitical constructs and should not be interpreted as being scientific or anthropological in nature. Furthermore, race categories include both racial and national origin groups.

Beginning with the 2000 census, respondents were offered the option of selecting one or more races. This option was not available in prior censuses; thus, comparisons between censuses should be made with caution. In Table C, Columns 5 through 8 refer to individuals who identified with each racial category, either alone or in combination with other races. The estimates exclude persons of Hispanic or Latino origin from all race groups. Because respondents could include as many categories as they wished, and because the columns refer to the percentage of the population, the total will often exceed 100 percent.

The **White** population is defined as persons who indicated their race as White, as well as persons who did not classify themselves in one of the specific race categories listed on the questionnaire but entered a nationality such as Irish, German, Italian, Lebanese, Near Easterner, Arab, or Polish.

The **Black** population includes persons who indicated their race as "Black, African Am., or Negro," as well as persons who did not classify themselves in one of the specific race categories but reported entries such as African American, Afro American, Kenyan, Nigerian, or Haitian.

The **American Indian or Alaska Native** population includes persons who indicated their race as American Indian or Alaska Native, as well as persons who did not classify themselves in one of the specific race categories but reported entries such as Canadian Indian, French-American Indian, Spanish-American Indian, Eskimo, Aleut, Alaska Indian, or any of the American Indian or Alaska Native tribes.

The **Asian and Pacific Islander** population combines two census groupings: **Asian** and **Native Hawaiian or Other Pacific Islander**. The **Asian** population includes persons who indicated their race as Asian Indian, Chinese, Filipino, Japanese, Korean, Vietnamese, or "Other Asian," as well as persons who provided write-in entries of such groups as Cambodian, Laotian, Hmong, Pakistani, or Taiwanese. The **Native Hawaiian or Other Pacific Islander** population includes persons who indicated their race as "Native Hawaiian," "Guamanian or Chamorro," "Samoan," or "Other Pacific Islander," as well as persons who reported entries such as Part Hawaiian, American Samoan, Fijian, Melanesian, or Tahitian.

The sum of the four individual race alone or in combination categories in this book will often add to more than the total population because people who reported more than one race were tallied in each race category. In this book, the Asian group has been combined with the Native Hawaiian and Other Pacific Islander group, causing double-counting of persons who identify with both groups. This is especially pronounced in Hawaii.

The **Hispanic population** is based on a complete-count question that asked respondents "Is this person Spanish/Hispanic/Latino?" Persons marking any one of the four Hispanic categories (i.e., Mexican, Puerto Rican, Cuban, or other Spanish) are collectively referred to as Hispanic.

In the 2000 census, the Hispanic origin question was placed before the race question and specific instructions indicated that both questions should be answered. These changes were designed to improve accuracy and may affect comparability with 1990 data.

Age is defined as age at last birthday (number of completed years since birth), as of April 1 of the census year. The 2000 census also asked for the specific date of birth of the respondent,

and 2000 census procedures used the birth date for deriving age data. For this reason, it is likely that the 2000 data have fewer problems than data from prior censuses, such as the tendency of respondents to round ages or to report their ages on the date the questionnaire was filled out rather than on April 1.

The **female** population is shown as a percentage of total population.

POPULATION AND COMPONENTS OF CHANGE, Items 20–26

Source: U.S. Census Bureau—Decennial Censuses and Population Estimates
http://www.census.gov/main/www/cen2000.html
https://www.census.gov/programs-surveys/popest.html
http://www.census.gov/2010census/data/

The population data for 2000 and 2010 are from the decennial censuses and represent the resident population as of April 1 of those years. The components of change are based on Census Bureau estimates of the resident population as of July 1 of 2016. The change in population between 2010 and 2016 is made up of (a) natural increase—births minus deaths, and (b) net migration—the difference between the number of persons moving into a particular area and the number of persons moving out of the area. Net migration is composed of internal and international migration.

Because the 2016 population estimates are based on a model that begins with a national population estimate, the county and msa components of change do not always exactly add up to the difference between the 2010 census population and the 2016 estimates.

HOUSEHOLDS, Items 27–31

Source: U.S. Census Bureau—American Community Survey, 2016 1-year Estimates
http://www.census.gov/acs/www/

A **household** includes all of the persons who occupy a housing unit. (Persons not living in households are classified as living in group quarters.) A housing unit is a house, an apartment, a mobile home, a group of rooms, or a single room occupied (or, if vacant, intended for occupancy) as separate living quarters. Separate living quarters are those in which the occupants live separately from any other persons in the building and have direct access from the outside of the building or through a common hall. The occupants may be a single family, one person living alone, two or more families living together, or any other group of related or unrelated persons who share living quarters. The number of households is the same as the number of year-round occupied housing units.

A **family** includes a householder and one or more other persons living in the same household who are related to the householder by birth, marriage, or adoption. All persons in a household who are related to the householder are regarded as members of his or her family. A **family household** may contain persons not related to the householder; thus, family households may include more members than families do. A household can contain only one family for the purposes of census tabulations. Not all households contain families, as a household may comprise a group of unrelated persons or of one person living alone. Families are classified by type as either a "husband-wife family" or "other family," according to the presence or absence of a spouse.

The measure of **persons per household** is obtained by dividing the number of persons in households by the number of households or householders. One person in each household is designated as the householder. In most cases, this is the person (or one of the persons) in whose name the house is owned, being bought, or rented. If there is no such person in the household, any adult household member 15 years old and over can be designated as the householder.

The category **female family householder** includes only female-headed family households with no spouse present.

GROUP QUARTERS, Item 32

Source: U.S. Census Bureau—Population Estimates
https://www.census.gov/programs-surveys/popest.html

The Census Bureau classifies all persons not living in households as living in group quarters; this category includes both the institutional and noninstitutional populations. The institutionalized population includes persons under formally authorized, supervised care or custody in institutions, such as correctional institutions, nursing homes, mental (psychiatric) hospitals, and juvenile institutions. The noninstitutionalized population includes persons who live in group quarters other than institutions, such as college dormitories, military quarters, and group homes. This volume includes the total number of persons in group quarters.

DAYTIME POPULATION, Items 33 and 34

Source: U.S. Census Bureau—American Community Survey, 2016 1-year Estimates
http://www.census.gov/acs/www/

Daytime population refers to the number of persons who are present in an area or place during normal business hours, including workers. This can be contrasted with the "resident" population, which is present during the evening and nighttime hours. The daytime population estimate is calculated by adding the total resident population and the total workers working in the area/place, and then subtracting the total workers living in the area/place from that result. Information on the expansion or contraction experienced by different communities between their nighttime and daytime populations is important for many planning purposes, especially those concerning transportation, disaster, and relief operations.

The employment/residence ratio is a measure of the total number of workers working in an area or place, relative to the total number of workers living in the area or place. It is often used as a rough indication of the jobs-workers balance in an area/place, although it does not take into account whether the resident workers possess the skills needed for the jobs available in their particular area/place. The employment/residence ratio is calculated by dividing the number of total workers working in an area/place by the number of total workers residing in the area/place.

BIRTHS AND DEATHS, Items 35–38

Source: U.S. Census Bureau—Population Estimates
https://www.census.gov/programs-surveys/popest.html

The numbers of births and deaths are from the Census Bureau's Population Estimates Program. They represent the total number of live births and deaths occurring to residents of an area as estimated using reports from the National Center for Health Statistics (NCHS) and the Federal-State Cooperative for Population Estimates (FSCPE). The rates measure births and deaths during the specified time period as a proportion of an area's population. Rates are expressed per 1,000 population estimated as of July 1. These numbers and rates do not represent the calendar year, but rather the year-long period ending on July 1.

PERSONS UNDER 65 WITH NO HEALTH INSURANCE, Items 39 and 40

Source: U.S. Census Bureau—Small Area Health Insurance Estimates
http://www.census.gov/did/www/sahie/index.html

The Small Area Health Insurance Estimates (SAHIE) program develops model-based estimates of health insurance coverage for counties and states. This developmental program builds on the work of the Small Area Income and Poverty Estimates (SAIPE) program. The SAHIE program models health insurance coverage by combining survey data with population estimates and administrative records. These estimates combine data from administrative records, postcensal population estimates, and the decennial census with direct estimates from the American Community Survey to provide consistent and reliable single-year estimates. These model-based single-year estimates are more reflective of current conditions than multi-year survey estimates. The metropolitan area estimates have been aggregated from the county estimates.

MEDICARE ENROLLMENT, Items 41–43

Source: U.S. Department of Health and Human Services, Centers for Medicare and Medicaid Services
https://www.cms.gov/Research-Statistics-Data-and-Systems/Statistics-Trends-and-Reports/CMSProgramStatistics/Dashboard.html

The Centers for Medicare and Medicaid Services (CMS) administers Medicare, which provides health insurance to persons 65 years old and over, persons with permanent kidney failure, and certain persons with disabilities. Original Medicare has two parts: Hospital Insurance and Supplemental Medical Insurance. In recent years, Medicare has been expanded to include two new programs: Medicare Advantage plans and prescription drug coverage. Medicare Advantage Plans are health plan options that are approved by Medicare but run by private companies. Medicare prescription drug plans can be part of Medicare Advantage plans or stand-alone drug plans.

Persons who are eligible for Medicare can enroll in Part A (Hospital Insurance) at no charge, and can choose to pay a monthly premium to enroll in Part B. Most eligible persons are enrolled in Part A, and most enrollees in Part A are also enrolled in Part B (Supplemental Medical Insurance.) This table includes persons who were enrolled in both Part A and Part B during 2014.

Part B beneficiaries can choose to enroll in **Original Medicare**, a fee-for-service plan administered by the Centers for Medicare and Medicaid Services, or in a **Medicare Advantage** plan.

Medicare Advantage plans include private fee-for-service plans, preferred provider organizations, health maintenance organizations, medical savings account plans, demonstration plans, and programs for all-inclusive care for the elderly.

The annual Medicare enrollment counts are determined using a person-year methodology. For each calendar year, total person-year counts are determined by summing the total number of months that each beneficiary is enrolled during the year and dividing by 12. Using this methodology, a beneficiary's partial-year enrollment may be counted in more than one category (i.e., both Original Medicare and Medicare Advantage).

CRIME, Items 44–47

Source: U.S. Federal Bureau of Investigation—Uniform Crime Reports
https://ucr.fbi.gov/crime-in-the-u.s/2016/crime-in-the-u.s.-2016

Crime data are as reported to the Federal Bureau of Investigation (FBI) by law enforcement agencies. The Metropolitan Area numbers in this volume are from *Crime in the United States* and have been adjusted by the FBI to include estimates of areas that did not report. Where the FBI analysts determined that the numbers reflected underreporting or overreporting or other factors that made them unreliable, the numbers have not been included.

Through the voluntary contribution of crime statistics by law enforcement agencies across the United States, the Uniform Crime Reporting (UCR) Program provides periodic assessments of crime in the nation as measured by offenses that have come to the attention of the law enforcement community. The Committee on Uniform Crime Records of the International Association of Chiefs of Police initiated this voluntary national data collection effort in 1930. The UCR Program contributors compile and submit their crime data either directly to the FBI or through state-level UCR Programs.

Seven offenses, because of their severity, frequency of occurrence, and likelihood of being reported to police, were initially selected to serve as an index for evaluating fluctuations in the volume of crime. These serious crimes were murder and nonnegligent manslaughter, forcible rape, robbery, aggravated assault, burglary, larceny-theft, and motor vehicle theft. By congressional mandate, arson was added as the eighth index offense in 1979. The totals shown in this volume do not include arson.

In 2004, the FBI discontinued the use of the Crime Index in the UCR Program and its publications, stating that the Crime Index was driven upward by the offense with the highest number of cases (in this case, larceny-theft), creating a bias against jurisdictions with a high number of larceny-thefts but a low number of other serious crimes, such as murder and forcible rape. The FBI is currently publishing a violent crime total and property crime total until a more viable index is developed. This book includes the crime total, as well as violent crime and property crime rates.

In 2013, the FBI adopted a new definition of rape. Rape is now defined as, "Penetration, no matter how slight, of the vagina or anus with any body part or object, or oral penetration by a sex organ of another person, without the consent of the victim." The new definition updated the 80-year-old historical definition of rape which was "carnal knowledge of a female forcibly and against her will." Effectively, the revised definition expands rape to include both male and female victims and offenders, and reflects the various forms of sexual penetration understood to be rape, especially nonconsenting acts of sodomy, and sexual assaults with objects.

Violent crimes include four categories of offenses: (1) Murder and nonnegligent manslaughter, as defined in the UCR Program, is the willful (nonnegligent) killing of one human being by another. This offense excludes deaths caused by negligence, suicide, or accident; justifiable homicides; and attempts to murder or assaults to murder. (2) Rape is the penetration, no matter how slight, of the vagina or anus with any body part or object, or oral penetration by a sex organ of another person, without the consent of the victim. Assaults or attempts to commit rape by force or threat of force are also included; however, statutory rape (without force) and other sex offenses are excluded. (3) Robbery is the taking or attempting to take anything of value from the care, custody, or control of a person or persons by force or threat of force or violence and/or by putting the victim in fear. (4) Aggravated assault is an unlawful attack by one person upon another for the purpose of inflicting severe or aggravated bodily injury. This type of assault is usually accompanied by the use of a weapon or by other means likely to produce death or great bodily harm. Attempts are included, since injury does not necessarily have to result when a gun, knife, or other weapon is used, as these incidents could and probably would result in a serious personal injury if the crime were successfully completed.

Property crimes include three categories: (1) Burglary, or breaking and entering, is the unlawful entry of a structure to commit a felony or theft, even though no force was used to gain entrance. (2) Larceny-theft is the unauthorized taking of the personal property of another, without the use of force. (3) Motor vehicle theft is the unauthorized taking of any motor vehicle.

Rates are based on population estimates provided by the FBI. If the population total for the metropolitan area was less than 75 percent of the area's population (as estimated by the Census Bureau), the total was not considered representative of the metropolitan area as a whole and was not published. For many of the metropolitan areas, the FBI has estimated violent and property crimes, adjusted to include areas that did not report and to correct for underreporting and overreporting, as published in the FBI's *Crime in the United States*. If a metropolitan area was not included in *Crime in the United States,* it is not included in Table C in this volume.

EDUCATION—SCHOOL ENROLLMENT AND EDUCATIONAL ATTAINMENT, Items 48–51

Source: U.S. Census Bureau—American Community Survey, 2016 1-year Estimates
http://www.census.gov/acs/www/

Data on **school enrollment** and educational attainment were derived from a sample of the population. Persons were classified as enrolled in school if they reported attending a "regular" public or private school (or college) during the three months prior to the survey. The instructions were to "include only nursery school, kindergarten, elementary school, and schooling which would lead to a high school diploma or a college degree" as regular school. The Census Bureau defines a public school as "any school or college controlled and supported by a local, county, state, or federal government." Schools primarily supported and controlled by religious organizations or other private groups are defined as private schools.

Data on **educational attainment** are tabulated for the population 25 years old and over. The data were derived from a question that asked respondents for the highest level of school completed or the highest degree received. Persons who had passed a high school equivalency examination were considered high school graduates. Schooling received in foreign schools was to be reported as the equivalent grade or years in the regular American school system.

Vocational and technical training, such as barber school training; business, trade, technical, and vocational schools; or other training for a specific trade are specifically excluded.

High school graduate or less. This category includes persons whose highest degree was a high school diploma or its equivalent, and those who reported any level lower than a high school diploma.

Bachelor's degree or more. This category includes persons who have received bachelor's degrees, master's degrees, professional school degrees (such as law school or medical school degrees), and doctoral degrees.

LOCAL GOVERNMENT EDUCATION EXPENDITURES, Items 52 and 53

U.S. Department of Education, National Center for Education Statistics, Common Core of Data (CCD), "National Public Education Financial Survey (State Fiscal)", 2013-14 (FY 2014) v.1a; "School District Finance Survey (F-33)", 2013-14 (FY 2014) v.1a;

Expenditures are for elementary and secondary Education which includes prekindergarten through twelfth grade regular, special, and vocational education, as well as cocurricular, community service, and adult education programs provided by a public school system. The financial activities of these systems for all instruction, support service, and noninstructional activities are included Current Spending comprises current operation expenditure, payments made by the state government on behalf of school systems, and transfers made by school systems into their own retirement funds. Current operation expenditures include direct expenditure for salaries, employee benefits, purchased professional and technical

services, purchased property and other services, and supplies. It includes gross school system expenditure for instruction, support services, and noninstructional functions. It excludes expenditure for debt service, capital outlay, and reimbursement to other governments (including other school systems).

Current expenditure per student is current expenditure divided by the number of students enrolled. The number of students enrolled is based on an annual "membership" count of students on or about October 1.

INCOME AND POVERTY Items 54–61

Source: U.S. Census Bureau—American Community Survey, 2016 1-year Estimates
http://www.census.gov/acs/www/

The data on income were derived from responses of a sample of persons 15 years old and over. **Total money income** is the sum of the amounts reported separately for wage or salary income; net self-employment income; interest, dividends, or net rental or royalty income or income from estates and trusts; Social Security or railroad retirement income; Supplemental Security Income (SSI); public assistance or welfare payments; retirement, survivor, or disability pensions; and all other income. Receipts from the following sources are not included as income: capital gains; money received from the sale of property (unless the recipient was engaged in the business of selling such property); the value of income "in kind" from food stamps, public housing subsidies, medical care, employer contributions for individuals, etc.; withdrawal of bank deposits; money borrowed; tax refunds; exchange of money between relatives living in the same household; and gifts, lump-sum inheritances, insurance payments, and other types of lump-sum receipts.

Money income differs in definition from personal income (item 62). For example, money income does not include the pension rights, employer provided health insurance, food stamps, or Medicare payments that are included in personal income.

Per capita income is the mean income computed for every man, woman, and child in a particular group. It is derived by dividing the aggregate income of a particular group by the resident population in that group in the survey year. Per capita income is rounded to the nearest whole dollar.

Household income includes the income of the householder and all other individuals 15 years old and over in the household, whether or not they are related to the householder. Since many households consist of only one person, median household income is usually less than median family income. Although the household income statistics cover the year preceding the survey, the characteristics of individuals and the composition of households refer to the date of the survey. Thus, the income of the household does not include amounts received by individuals who were members of the household during the year if these individuals were no longer residing in the household at the time of the survey. Similarly, income amounts reported by individuals who did not reside in the household during the year but who were members of the household at the time of the survey are included. However, the composition of most households was the same during the year as it was at the time of the survey.

Mean household income is the amount obtained by dividing the aggregate income of all households by the total number of households. The mean is based on the distribution of the total number of households including those with no income. Mean income is rounded to the nearest whole dollar. Care should be exercised in using and interpreting mean income values for small subgroups of the population. Because the mean is influenced strongly by extreme values in the distribution, it is especially susceptible to the effects of sampling variability, misreporting, and processing errors. The median, which is not affected by extreme values, is, therefore, a better measure than the mean when the population base is small.

Median income divides the income distribution into two equal parts, with half of all cases below the median income level and half of all cases above the median income level. For households, the median income is based on the distribution of the total number of households, including those with no income. Median income for households is computed on the basis of a standard distribution with a minimum value of less than $2,500 and a maximum value of $200,000 or more and is rounded to the nearest whole dollar. Median income figures are calculated using linear interpolation if the width of the interval containing the estimate is $2,500 or less. If the width of the interval containing the estimate is greater than $2,500, Pareto interpolation is used.

Income components were reported for the 12 months preceding the interview month. Monthly Consumer Price Indices (CPI) factors were used to inflation-adjust these components to a reference calendar year (January through December). For example, a household interviewed in March 2012 reports their income for March 2011 through February 2012. Their income is adjusted to the 2012 reference calendar year by multiplying their reported income by 2012 average annual CPI (January-December 2008) and then dividing by the average CPI for March 2011–February 2012. However, the estimates do not reflect the price and cost-of-living differences that may exist between areas.

The **poverty status** data were derived from data collected on the number of persons in a household, each person's relationship to the householder, and income data. The Social Security Administration (SSA) developed the original poverty definition in 1964, which federal interagency committees subsequently revised in 1969 and 1980. The Office of Management and Budget's (OMB) *Directive 14* prescribes the SSA's definition as the official poverty measure for federal agencies to use in their statistical work. Poverty statistics presented in American Community Survey products adhere to the standards defined by OMB in *Directive 14*.

Poverty thresholds vary depending on three criteria: size of family, number of children, and, for one- and two-person families, age of householder. In determining the poverty status of families and unrelated individuals, the Census Bureau uses thresholds (income cutoffs) arranged in a two-dimensional matrix. The matrix consists of family size (from one person to nine or more persons), cross-classified by presence and number of family members under 18 years old (from no children present to eight or more children present). Unrelated individuals and two-person families are further differentiated by age of reference person (under 65 years old and 65 years old and over). To determine a person's poverty status, the person's total family income over the previous 12 months is compared with the poverty threshold appropriate for that person's family size and composition. If the total income of that person's family is less than the threshold appropriate for that family, then the person is considered poor or "below the poverty level," together with every member of his or her family. If a person is not living with anyone related by birth, marriage, or adoption, then the person's own income is compared with his or her poverty threshold. The total number of persons below the poverty level is the sum of persons in families and the number of unrelated individuals with incomes below the poverty level over the previous 12 months.

PERSONAL INCOME AND EARNINGS, Items 62–83

Source: U.S. Bureau of Economic Analysis, Regional Economic Accounts
http://www.bea.gov/regional/index.htm#state

Total personal income is the current income received by residents of an area from all sources. It is measured before deductions of income and other personal taxes, but after deductions of personal contributions for Social Security, government retirement, and other social insurance programs. It consists of **wage and salary disbursements** (covering all employee earnings, including executive salaries, bonuses, commissions, payments-in-kind, incentive payments, and tips); various types of supplementary earnings, such as employers' contributions to pension funds (termed "other labor income" or "supplements to wages and salaries"); proprietors' income; rental income of persons; dividends; personal interest income; and government and business transfer payments.

Per capita personal income is based on the resident population estimated as of July 1 of the year shown.

Proprietors' income is the monetary income and income-in-kind of proprietorships and partnerships (including the independent professions) and the income of tax-exempt cooperatives. **Dividends** are cash payments by corporations to stockholders who are U.S. residents. **Interest** is the monetary and imputed interest income of persons from all sources. **Rent** is the monetary income of persons from the rental of real property, except the income of persons primarily engaged in the real estate business; the imputed net rental income of owner-occupants of nonfarm dwellings; and the royalties received by persons.

Transfer payments are income for which services are not currently rendered. They consist of both government and business transfer payments. Government transfer payments include payments under the following programs: Federal Old-Age, Survivors, and Disability Insurance ("Social Security"); Medicare and medical vendor payments; unemployment insurance; railroad and government retirement; federal- and state-government-insured workers' compensation; veterans' benefits, including veterans' life insurance; food stamps; black lung payments; Supplemental Security Income; and Temporary Assistance for Needy Families. Government payments to nonprofit institutions, other than for work under research and development contracts, are also included. Business transfer payments consist primarily of liability payments for personal injury and of corporate gifts to nonprofit institutions.

Poverty Thresholds for 2016 by Size of Family and Number of Related Children Under 18 Years

Size of family unit	Weighted average thresholds	Related children under 18 years								
		None	One	Two	Three	Four	Five	Six	Seven	Eight or more
One person (unrelated individual):	12,228									
Under age 65	12,486	12,486								
Aged 65 and older	11,511	11,511								
Two people:	15,569									
Householder under age 65........	16,151	16,072	16,543							
Householder aged 65 and older	14,522	14,507	16,480							
Three people.............................	19,105	18,774	19,318	19,337						
Four people...............................	24,563	24,755	25,160	24,339	24,424					
Five people...............................	29,111	29,854	30,288	29,360	28,643	28,205				
Six people.................................	32,928	34,337	34,473	33,763	33,082	32,070	31,470			
Seven people.............................	37,458	39,509	39,756	38,905	38,313	37,208	35,920	34,507		
Eight people..............................	41,781	44,188	44,578	43,776	43,072	42,075	40,809	39,491	39,156	
Nine people or more	49,721	53,155	53,413	52,702	52,106	51,127	49,779	48,561	48,259	46,400

Source: U.S. Census Bureau.

Personal income differs in definition from money income (items 54–57). For example, personal income includes pension rights, employer-provided health insurance, food stamps, and Medicare. These are not included in the definition of money income.

Earnings cover wage and salary disbursements, other labor income, and proprietors' income.

The data for earnings obtained from the Bureau of Economic Analysis (BEA) are based on place of work. In computing personal income, BEA makes an "adjustment for residence" to earnings, based on commuting patterns; personal income is thus presented on a place-of-residence basis.

Farm earnings include the income of farm workers (wages and salaries and other labor income) and farm proprietors. Farm proprietors' income includes only the income of sole proprietorships and partnerships. Farm earnings estimates are benchmarked to data collected in the Census of Agriculture and the revised Department of Agriculture statistical totals of income and expense items.

Goods-related industries include mining, construction, and manufacturing. **Service-related** and other industries include private-sector earnings in agricultural services, forestry, and fisheries; transportation and public utilities; wholesale trade; retail trade; finance, insurance, and real estate; and services. Government earnings include all levels of government. Industries are categorized under the North American Industry Classification System (NAICS), and are not comparable to years prior to 2002.

SOCIAL SECURITY AND SUPPLEMENTAL SECURITY INCOME, Items 84–86

Source: U.S. Social Security Administration
http://www.ssa.gov/policy/docs/statcomps/oasdi_sc/
http://www.ssa.gov/policy/docs/statcomps/ssi_sc/

Social Security beneficiaries are persons receiving benefits under the Old-Age, Survivors, and Disability Insurance Program. These include retired or disabled workers covered by the program, their spouses and dependent children, and the surviving spouses and dependent children of deceased workers.

Supplemental Security Income (SSI) recipients are persons receiving SSI payments. The SSI program is a cash assistance program that provides monthly benefits to low-income aged, blind, or disabled persons.

Data are as of December of the year shown.

HOUSING, Items 87–96

Source: U.S. Census Bureau—Population Estimates Program
https://www.census.gov/programs-surveys/popest.html
Source: U.S. Census Bureau—American Community Survey. 2016 1-year Estimates
http://www.census.gov/acs/www/

Housing data for 2017 are from the Population Estimates Program. Housing unit characteristics for 2016 are from the American Community Survey.

A **housing unit** is a house, apartment, mobile home or trailer, group of rooms, or single room occupied or, if vacant, intended for occupancy as separate living quarters. Separate living quarters are those in which the occupants do not live and eat with any other person in the structure and which have direct access from the outside of the building through a common hall.

The occupants of a housing unit may be a single family, one person living alone, two or more families living together, or any other group of related or unrelated persons who share living quarters. Both occupied and vacant housing units are included in the housing inventory, although recreational vehicles, tents, caves, boats, railroad cars, and the like are included only if they are occupied as a person's usual place of residence.

A housing unit is classified as occupied if it is the usual place of residence of the person or group of persons living in it at the time of enumeration, or if the occupants are only temporarily absent (away on vacation). A household consists of all persons who occupy a housing unit as their usual place of residence. Vacant units for sale or rent include units rented or sold but not occupied and any other units held off the market.

Median value is the dollar amount that divides the distribution of specified owner-occupied housing units into two equal parts, with half of all units below the median value and half of all units above the median value. Value is defined as the respondent's estimate of what the house would sell for if it were for sale. Data are presented for single-family units on fewer than 10 acres of land that have no business or medical offices on the property.

Median rent divides the distribution of renter-occupied housing units into two equal parts. The rent concept used in this volume is gross rent, which includes the amount of cash rent a renter pays (contract rent) plus the estimated average cost of utilities and fuels, if these are paid by the renter. The rent is the amount of rent only for living quarters and excludes amounts paid for any business or other space occupied. Single-family houses on lots of 10 or more acres of land are also excluded.

Housing cost as a percentage of income is shown separately for owners with mortgages, owners without mortgages, and renters. Rent as a percentage of income is a computed ratio of gross rent and monthly household income (total household income in the past 12 months divided by 12). Selected owner costs include utilities and fuels, mortgage payments, insurance, taxes, etc. In each case, the ratio of housing cost to income is computed separately for each housing unit. The housing cost ratios for half of all units are above the median shown in this book, and half are below the median shown in the book.

The proportion of **Households that have Internet Access** includes households with internet subscriptions through broadband (cable, fiber optic, or DSL), satellite, cellular data plans, or dial-up, as well as persons who have internet access without a subscription (access provided by a town or university.)

CIVILIAN LABOR FORCE AND UNEMPLOYMENT, Items 97–100

Source: U.S. Bureau of Labor Statistics—Local Area Unemployment Statistics
http://www.bls.gov/lau/#tables

Data for the civilian labor force are the product of a federal-state cooperative program in which state employment security agencies prepare labor force and unemployment estimates under concepts, definitions, and technical procedures established by the Bureau of Labor Statistics (BLS). The civilian labor force consists of all civilians 16 years old and over who are either employed or unemployed.

Unemployment includes all persons who did not work during the survey week, made specific efforts to find a job during the previous four weeks, and were available for work during the survey week (except for temporary illness). Persons waiting to be called back to a job from which they had been laid off and those waiting to report to a new job within the next 30 days are included in unemployment figures.

Table C includes annual average data for the year shown. The Local Area Unemployment Statistics data are periodically updated to reflect revised inputs, reestimation, and controlling to new statewide totals.

CIVILIAN EMPLOYMENT, Items 101–103

Source: U.S. Census Bureau—American Community Survey. 2016 1-year Estimates
http://www.census.gov/acs/www/

Total employment includes all civilians 16 years old and over who were either (1) "at work"—those who did any work at all during the reference week as paid employees, worked in either their own business or profession, worked on their own farm, or worked 15 hours or more as unpaid workers in a family farm or business; or were (2) "with a job, but not at work" —those who had a job but were not at work that week due to illness, weather, industrial dispute, vacation, or other personal reasons.

The **occupational categories** are based on the occupational classification system that was developed for the 2000 census. This system consists of 509 specific occupational categories for employed persons arranged into 23 major occupational groups. This classification was developed based on the *Standard Occupational Classification (SOC) Manual: 2000*, published by the Executive Office of the President, Office of Management and Budget.

Column 102 includes the Management, business, science, and arts occupations category while Column 103 combines the Natural resources, construction, and maintenance occupations and the Production, transportation, and material moving occupations.

PRIVATE NONFARM EMPLOYMENT AND EARNINGS, Items 104–112

Source: U.S. Census Bureau—County Business Patterns
http://www.census.gov/econ/cbp/index.html

Data for private nonfarm employment and earnings are compiled from the payroll information reported monthly in the Census Bureau publication *County Business Patterns*. The estimates are based on surveys conducted by the Census Bureau and administrative records from the Internal Revenue Service (IRS).

The following types of employment are excluded from the tables: government employment, self-employed persons, farm workers, and domestic service workers. Railroad employment jointly covered by Social Security and railroad retirement programs, employment on oceanborne vessels, and employment in foreign countries are also excluded.

Annual payroll is the combined amount of wages paid, tips reported, and other compensation (including salaries, vacation allowances, bonuses, commissions, sick-leave pay, and the value of payments-in-kind such as free meals and lodging) paid to employees before deductions for Social Security, income tax, insurance, union dues, etc. All forms of compensation are included, regardless of whether they are subject to income tax or the Federal Insurance Contributions Act tax, with the exception of annuities, third-party sick pay, and supplemental unemployment compensation benefits (even if income tax was withheld). For corporations, total annual payroll includes compensation paid to officers and executives; for unincorporated businesses, it excludes profit or other compensation of proprietors or partners.

AGRICULTURE, ITEMS 113–132

Source: U.S. Department of Agriculture, National Agricultural Statistics Service—2012 Census of Agriculture
http://agcensus.usda.gov/index.php

Data for the 2012 Census of Agriculture were collected in 2013, but pertain to the year 2012.

The Census Bureau took a census of agriculture every 10 years from 1840 to 1920; since 1925, this census has been taken roughly once every 5 years. The 1997 Census of Agriculture was the first one conducted by the National Agricultural Statistics Service of the U.S. Department of Agriculture. Over time, the definition of a farm has varied. For recent censuses (including the 2012 census), a farm has been defined as any place from which $1,000 or more of agricultural products were produced and sold or normally would have been sold during the census year. Dollar figures are expressed in current dollars and have not been adjusted for inflation or deflation.

The term **operator** refers to a person who operates a farm by either doing the work or making day-to-day decisions about such activities as planting, harvesting, feeding, marketing, etc. The operator may be the owner, a member of the owner's household, a salaried manager, a tenant, a renter, or a sharecropper. If a person rents land to others or has land worked on shares by others, he/she is considered the operator only of the land that is retained for his/her own operation. The census collected information on the total number of operators, the total number of women operators, and demographic information for up to three operators per farm.

The acreage designated as **land in farms** consists primarily of agricultural land used for crops, pasture, or grazing. It also includes woodland and wasteland not actually under cultivation or used for pasture or grazing, provided that this land was part of the farm operator's total operation. Land in farms is an operating-unit concept and includes all land owned and operated, as well as all land rented from others. Land used rent-free is classified as land rented from others. All land in Indian reservations used for growing crops or grazing livestock is classified as land in farms.

Irrigated land includes all land watered by any artificial or controlled means, such as sprinklers, flooding, furrows or ditches, sub-irrigation, and spreader dikes. Included are supplemental, partial, and preplant irrigation. Each acre was counted only once regardless of the number of times it was irrigated or harvested.

Livestock lagoon waste water distributed by sprinkler or flood systems was also included.

Total cropland includes cropland harvested, cropland used only for pasture or grazing, cropland on which all crops failed or were abandoned, cropland in cultivated summer fallow, and cropland idle or used for cover crops or soil improvement but not harvested and not pastured or grazed.

Respondents were asked to report their estimate of the current market **value of land and buildings** owned, rented, or leased from others, and rented and leased to others. Market value refers to the respondent's estimate of what the land and buildings would sell for under current market conditions. If the value of land and buildings was not reported, it was estimated during processing by using the average value of land and buildings from similar farms in the same geographic area.

The **value of machinery and equipment** was estimated by the respondent as the current market value of all cars, trucks, tractors, combines, balers, irrigation equipment, etc., used on the farm. This value is an estimate of what the machinery and equipment would sell for in its present condition and not the replacement or depreciated value. Share interests are reported at full value at the farm where the equipment and machinery are usually kept. Only equipment that was physically located at the farm on December 31, 2012, is included.

Market value of agricultural products sold by farms resents the gross market value before taxes and the product expenses of all agricultural products sold or removed from t place in 2012, regardless of who received the payment. It is equiv alent to total sales and it includes sales by the operator as well a the value of any share received by partners, landlords, contrac tors, and others associated with the operation. It includes value of direct sales and the value of commodities placed in the Commodity Credit Corporation (CCC) loan program. Market value of agricultural products sold does not include payments received for participation in other federal farm programs. Also, it does not include income from farm-related sources such as custom work and other agricultural services, or income from nonfarm sources.

Government payments consists of direct payments as defined by the 2002 Farm Bill;

payments from Conservation Reserve Program (CRP), Wetlands Reserve Program (WRP), Farmable Wetlands Program (FWP), and Conservation Reserve Enhancement Program (CREP); loan deficiency payments; disaster payments; other conservation programs; and all other federal farm programs under which payments were made directly to farm operators. Commodity Credit Corporation (CCC) proceeds, amount from State and local federal crop insurance payments were not included in this category.

WATER CONSUMPTION, Items 133–134

Source: U.S. Geological Survey, National Water-Use Information Program, Estimated Use of Water in the United States County-Level Data for 2015, version 1.0
http://water.usgs.gov/watuse/

Every five years, the U.S. Geological Survey compiles county-level water-use estimates. This volume includes the total fresh and saline withdrawals for public water supplies in 2015, expressed as million gallons per day. Estimate of withdrawals of ground and surface water are given for the following categories of use: public water supplies, domestic, commercial, irrigation, livestock, industrial, mining, and thermoelectric power. Only public water supply is included in this volume because the other categories had not been published in time for this book. The number of gallons withdrawn per person is based on the metropolitan area population in 2015 but the water is not necessarily used locally, providing an indicator of metropolitan areas that serve as major water sources.

Public supply refers to water withdrawn from ground and surface sources by public and private water systems for use by cities, towns, rural water districts, mobile-home parks, Native American Indian reservations, and military bases. Public-supply facilities provide water to at least 25 persons or have a minimum of 15 service connections. Water withdrawn by public suppliers may be delivered to users for domestic, commercial, industrial, and thermoelectric-power purposes, as well as to other public-water suppliers. Public-supply water is also used for public services (public uses)—such as pools, parks, and public buildings—and may have unaccounted uses (losses) because of system leaks or such non-metered services as firefighting, flushing of water lines, ...ckwashing at treatment plants. Some public-supply water ...d in the processes of water and wastewater treatment. ...uppliers treat saline water before distributing the ...efinition of saline water for public supply refers to requires treatment to reduce the concentration of dis-...olids through the process of desalination or dilution.

/12 Economic CENSUS: OVERVIEW, Items ¡35–166

Source: U.S. Census Bureau
http://www.census.gov/programs-surveys/ Economic-census/tables.html

The Economic Census provides a detailed portrait of the nation's economy, from the national to the local level, once every five years. The 2012 Economic Census covers nearly all of the U.S. economy in its basic collection of establishment statistics. The 1997 Economic Census was the first major data source to use the new North American Industry Classification System (NAICS); therefore, data from this census are not comparable to economic data from prior years, which were based on the Standard Industrial Classification (SIC) system.

NAICS, developed in cooperation with Canada and Mexico, classifies North America's economic activities at two, three, four, and fivedigit levels of detail; the U.S. version of NAICS further defines industries to a sixth digit. The Economic Census takes advantage of this hierarchy to publish data at these successive levels of detail: sector (two-digit), subsector (three-digit), industry group (four-digit), industry (five-digit), and U.S. industry (six-digit). Information in Table A is at the two-digit level, with a few three- and four-digit items. The data in Tables B and C are at the two-digit level.

Several key statistics are tabulated for all industries in this volume, including number of establishments (or companies), number of employees, payroll, and certain measures of output (sales, receipts, revenue, value of shipments, or value of construction work done).

Number of establishments. An establishment is a single physical location at which business is conducted. It is not necessarily identical with a company or enterprise, which may consist of one establishment or more. Economic Census figures represent a summary of reports for individual establishments rather than companies. For cases in which a census report was received, separate information was obtained for each location where business was conducted. When administrative records of other federal agencies were used instead of a census report, no information was available on the number of locations operated. Each Economic Census establishment was tabulated according to the physical location at which the business was conducted. The count of establishments represents those in business at any time during 2002.

When two activities or more were carried on at a single location under a single ownership, all activities were generally grouped together as a single establishment. The entire establishment was classified on the basis of its major activity and all of its data were included in that classification. However, when distinct and separate economic activities (for which different industry classification codes were appropriate) were conducted at a single location under a single ownership, separate establishment reports for each of the different activities were obtained in the census.

Number of employees. Paid employees consist of the fulltime and parttime employees, including salaried officers and executives of corporations. Included are employees on paid sick leave, paid holidays, and paid vacations; not included are proprietors and partners of unincorporated businesses. The definition of paid employees is the same as that used by the Internal Revenue Service (IRS) on form 941.

For some industries, the Economic Census gives codes representing the number of employees as a range of numbers (for example, "100 to 249 employees" or "1,000 to 2,499" employees). In this volume, those codes have been replaced by the standard suppression code "D".

Payroll. Payroll includes all forms of compensation, such as salaries, wages, commissions, dismissal pay, bonuses, vacation allowances, sickleave pay, and employee contributions to qualified pension plans paid during the year to all employees. For corporations, payroll includes amounts paid to officers and executives; for unincorporated businesses, it does not include profit or other compensation of proprietors or partners. Payroll is reported before deductions for Social Security, income tax, insurance, union dues, etc. This definition of payroll is the same as that used by on IRS form 941.

Sales, shipments, receipts, revenue, or business done. This measure includes the total sales, shipments, receipts, revenue, or business done by establishments within the scope of the Economic Census. The definition of each of these items is specific to the economic sector measured.

WHOLESALE TRADE, Items 135–138

Source: U.S. Census Bureau—2012 Economic Census (See Overview of 2012 Economic Census prior to Item 135)

The Wholesale Trade sector (sector 42) comprises establishments engaged in wholesaling merchandise, generally without transformation, and rendering services incidental to the sale of merchandise. The wholesaling process is an intermediate step in the distribution of merchandise.

Wholesalers are organized to sell or arrange the purchase or sale of (1) goods for resale (i.e., goods sold to other wholesalers or retailers), (2) capital or durable nonconsumer goods, and (3) raw and intermediate materials and supplies used in production.

Wholesalers sell merchandise to other businesses and normally operate from a warehouse or office. These warehouses and offices are characterized by having little or no display of merchandise. In addition, neither the design nor the location of the premises is intended to solicit walkin traffic. Wholesalers do not normally use advertising directed to the general public. In general, customers are initially reached via telephone, inperson marketing, or specialized advertising, which may include the internet and other electronic means. Followup orders are either vendorinitiated or clientinitiated, are usually based on previous sales, and typically exhibit strong ties between sellers and buyers. In fact, transactions are often conducted between wholesalers and clients that have longstanding business relationships.

This sector is made up of two main types of wholesalers: those that sell goods on their own account and those that arrange sales and purchases for others for a commission or fee.

(1) Establishments that sell goods on their own account are known as wholesale merchants, distributors, jobbers, drop shippers, import/export merchants, and sales branches. These establishments typically maintain their own warehouse, where they receive and handle goods for their customers. Goods are generally sold without transformation, but may include integral functions, such as sorting, packaging, labeling, and other marketing services.

(2) Establishments arranging for the purchase or sale of goods owned by others or purchasing goods on a commission basis are known as agents and brokers, commission merchants, import/export agents and brokers, auction companies, and manufacturers' representatives. These establishments operate from offices and generally do not own or handle the goods they sell.

Some wholesale establishments may be connected with a single manufacturer and promote and sell that particular manufacturer's products to a wide range of other wholesalers or retailers. Other wholesalers may be connected to a retail chain or a limited number of retail chains and only provide the products needed by the particular retail operation(s). These wholesalers may obtain the products from a wide range of manufacturers. Still other wholesalers may not take title to the goods, but act instead as agents and brokers for a commission.

Although wholesaling normally denotes sales in large volumes, durable nonconsumer goods may be sold in single units. Sales of capital or durable nonconsumer goods used in the production of goods and services, such as farm machinery, medium- and heavy-duty trucks, and industrial machinery, are always included in Wholesale Trade.

The metropolitan area table includes only **Merchant wholesalers, except manufacturers' sales branches and offices,** establishments primarily engaged in buying and selling merchandise on their own account. Included here are such types of establishments as wholesale distributors and jobbers, importers, exporters, own-brand importers/marketers, terminal and country grain elevators, and farm products assemblers.

RETAIL TRADE, Items 139–142

Source: U.S. Census Bureau—2012 Economic Census (See Overview of 2012 Economic Census prior to Item 135)

The Retail Trade sector (44–45) is made up of establishments engaged in retailing merchandise, generally without transformation, and rendering services incidental to the sale of merchandise.

The retailing process is the final step in the distribution of merchandise; retailers are therefore organized to sell merchandise in small quantities to the general public. This sector comprises two main types of retailers: store and nonstore retailers.

Store retailers operate fixed pointofsale locations, located and designed to attract a high volume of walkin customers. In general, retail stores have extensive displays of merchandise and use massmedia advertising to attract customers. They typically sell merchandise to the general public for personal or household consumption; some also serve business and institutional clients. These include establishments such as office supply stores, computer and software stores, building materials dealers, plumbing supply stores, and electrical supply stores. Catalog showrooms, gasoline service stations, automotive dealers, and mobile home dealers are treated as store retailers.

In addition to retailing merchandise, some types of store retailers are also engaged in the provision of aftersales services, such as repair and installation. For example, new automobile dealers, electronic and appliance stores, and musical instrument and supply stores often provide repair services. As a general rule, establishments engaged in retailing merchandise and providing aftersales services are classified in this sector.

Nonstore retailers, like store retailers, are organized to serve the general public, although their retailing methods differ. The establishments of this subsector reach customers and market merchandise with methods including the broadcasting of "infomercials," the broadcasting and publishing of directresponse advertising, the publishing of paper and electronic catalogs, doortodoor solicitation, inhome demonstration, selling from portable stalls (street vendors, except food), and distribution through vending machines. Establishments engaged in the direct sale (nonstore) of products, such as home heating oil dealers and home-delivery newspaper routes are included in this sector.

The buying of goods for resale is a characteristic of retail trade establishments that distinguishes them from establishments in the Agriculture, Manufacturing, and Construction sectors. For example, farms that sell their products at or from the point of production are classified in Agriculture instead of in Retail Trade. Similarly, establishments that both manufacture and sell their products to the general public are classified in Manufacturing instead of Retail Trade. However, establishments that engage in processing activities incidental to retailing are classified in Retail Trade.

REAL ESTATE AND RENTAL AND LEASING, Items 143–146

Source: U.S. Census Bureau—2012 Economic Census (See Overview of 2012 Economic Census prior to Item 135)

The Real Estate and Rental and Leasing sector (53) comprises establishments primarily engaged in renting, leasing, or otherwise allowing the use of tangible or intangible assets, and establishments providing related services. The major portion of this sector is made up of establishments that rent, lease, or otherwise allow the use of their own assets by others. The assets may be tangible, such as real estate and equipment, or intangible, such as patents and trademarks.

This sector also includes establishments primarily engaged in managing real estate for others, selling, renting, and/or buying real estate for others, and appraising real estate. These activities are closely related to this sector's main activity. In addition, a substantial proportion of property management is selfperformed by lessors.

The main components of this sector are the real estate lessors industries; equipment lessors industries (including motor vehicles, computers, and consumer goods); and lessors of nonfinancial intangible assets (except copyrighted works).

PROFESSIONAL, SCIENTIFIC, AND TECHNICAL SERVICES, Items 147–150

Source: U.S. Census Bureau—2012 Economic Census (See Overview of 2012 Economic Census prior to Item 135)

The Professional, Scientific, and Technical Services sector (54) is made up of establishments that specialize in performing professional, scientific, and technical activities for others. These activities require a high degree of expertise and training. The establishments in this sector specialize in one or more areas and provide services to clients in a variety of industries (and, in some cases, to households). Activities performed include legal advice and representation; accounting, bookkeeping, and payroll services; architectural, engineering, and specialized design services; computer services; consulting services; research services; advertising services; photographic services; translation and interpretation services; veterinary services; and other professional, scientific, and technical services.

This sector excludes establishments primarily engaged in providing a range of daytoday office administrative services, such as financial planning, billing and record keeping, personnel services, and physical distribution and logistics services. These establishments are classified in sector 56, Administrative and Support and Waste Management and Remediation Services.

MANUFACTURING, Items 151–154

Source: U.S. Census Bureau—2012 Economic Census (See Overview of 2012 Economic Census prior to Item 135)

The Manufacturing sector (31–33) is made up of establishments engaged in the mechanical, physical, or chemical transformation of materials, substances, or components into new products. The assembling of component parts of manufactured products is considered manufacturing, except in cases in which the activity is appropriately classified in the Construction sector. Establishments in the Manufacturing sector are often described as plants, factories, or mills, and characteristically use power-driven machines and materials-handling equipment. However, establishments that transform materials or substances into new products by hand or in the worker's home, and establishments engaged in selling to the general public products made on the same premises from which they are sold (such as bakeries, candy stores, and custom tailors) may also be included in this sector. Manufacturing establishments may process materials or contract with other establishments to process their materials for them. Both types of establishments are included in the Manufacturing sector.

The materials, substances, or components transformed by manufacturing establishments are raw materials that are products of agriculture, forestry, fishing, mining, or quarrying, or are products of other manufacturing establishments. The materials used may be purchased directly from producers, obtained through customary trade channels, or secured without recourse to the market by transferring the product from one establishment to another, under the same ownership. The new product of a manufacturing establishment may be finished (in the sense that it is ready for utilization or consumption), or it may be semifinished to become an input for an establishment engaged in further manufacturing. For example, the product of the alumina refinery is the input used in the primary production of aluminum; primary aluminum is the input used in an aluminum wire drawing plant; and aluminum wire is the input used in a fabricated wire product manufacturing establishment.

Data are included for counties with 500 or more employees in the Manufacturing sector.

ACCOMMODATION AND FOOD SERVICES, Items 155–158

Source: U.S. Census Bureau—2012 Economic Census (See Overview of 2012 Economic Census prior to Item 135)

The Accommodation and Food Services sector (72) consists of establishments that provide customers with lodging and/or meals, snacks, and beverages for immediate consumption. This sector includes both accommodation and food services establishments because the two activities are often combined at the same establishment.

Excluded from this sector are civic and social organizations, amusement and recreation parks, theaters, and other recreation or entertainment facilities providing food and beverage services.

HEALTH CARE AND SOCIAL ASSISTANCE, Items 159–162

Source: U.S. Census Bureau—2012 Economic Census (See Overview of 2012 Economic Census prior to Item 135)

The Health Care and Social Assistance sector (62) consists of establishments that provide health care and social assistance services to individuals. The sector includes both health care and social assistance because it is sometimes difficult to distinguish between the boundaries of these two activities. The industries in this sector are arranged on a continuum, starting with establishments that provide medical care exclusively, continuing with those that provide health care and social assistance, and finishing with those that provide only social assistance. The services provided by establishments in this sector are delivered by trained professionals. All industries in the sector share this commonality of process—namely, labor inputs of health practitioners or social workers with the requisite expertise. Many of the industries in the sector are defined based on the educational degree held by the practitioners included in the industry.

Excluded from this sector are aerobic classes, which can be found in subsector 713, Amusement, Gambling, and Recreation Industries; and nonmedical diet and weight-reducing centers, which can be found in subsector 812, Personal and Laundry Services. Although these can be viewed as health services, they are not typically delivered by health practitioners.

OTHER SERVICES, EXCEPT PUBLIC ADMINISTRATION Items 163–166

Source: U.S. Census Bureau—2012 Economic Census (See Overview of 2012 Economic Census prior to Item 135)

The Other Services, Except Public Administration sector (81) comprises establishments engaged in providing services not specifically categorized elsewhere in the classification system. Establishments in this sector are primarily engaged in activities such as equipment and machinery repairing, promoting or administering religious activities, grant making, and advocacy; this sector also includes establishments that provide dry-cleaning and laundry services, personal care services, death care services, pet care services, photofinishing services, temporary parking services, and dating services.

Private households that employ workers on or about the premises in activities primarily concerned with the operation of the household are included in this sector.

Excluded from this sector are establishments primarily engaged in retailing new equipment and performing repairs and general maintenance on equipment. These establishments are classified in sector 44–45, Retail Trade.

NONEMPLOYER BUSINESSES, Items 167 and 168

Source: U.S. Census Bureau—Nonemployer Statistics
http://www.census.gov/econ/nonemployer/

Nonemployer Statistics is an annual series that provides subnational economic data for businesses that have no paid employees and are subject to federal income tax. The data consist of the number of businesses and total receipts by industry. Most nonemployers are self-employed individuals operating unincorporated businesses (known as sole proprietorships), which may or may not be the owner's principal source of income.

The majority of all business establishments in the United States are nonemployers, yet these firms average less than 4 percent of all sales and receipts nationally. Due to their small economic impact, these firms are excluded from most other Census Bureau business statistics (the primary exception being the Survey of Business Owners). The Nonemployers Statistics series is the primary resource available to study the scope and activities of nonemployers at a detailed geographic level.

BUILDING PERMITS, Items 169 and 170

Source: U.S. Census Bureau—Building Permits Survey
http://www.census.gov/construction/bps/

These figures represent private residential construction authorized by building permits in approximately 20,000 places in the United States. Valuation represents the expected cost of construction as recorded on the building permit. This figure usually excludes the cost of on-site and off-site development and improvements, as well as the cost of heating, plumbing, electrical, and elevator installations.

National, state, and county totals were obtained by adding the data for permit-issuing places within each jurisdiction. Not all areas of the country require a building or zoning permit. The statistics only represent those areas that do require a permit. These totals thus are limited to permits issued in the 20,000 place universe covered by the Census Bureau and may not include all permits issued within a state. Current surveys indicate that construction is undertaken for all but a very small percentage of housing units authorized by building permits.

Residential building permits include buildings with any number of housing units. Housing units exclude group quarters (such as dormitories and rooming houses), transient accommodations (such as transient hotels, motels, and tourist courts), "HUD-code" manufactured (mobile) homes, moved or relocated units, and housing units created in an existing residential or nonresidential structure.

METROPOLITAN AREA LOCAL GOVERNMENT EMPLOYMENT AND PAYROLL, Items 171-179

Source: U.S. Census Bureau—2012 Census of Governments
https://www.census.gov/govs/programs-surveys/cog.html

These items include data for all local governments (i.e., counties, municipalities, townships, special districts, and school districts) located within the metropolitan area. The Census of Governments identifies the scope and nature of the nation's state and local government sector; provides authoritative benchmark figures of public finance and public employment; classifies local government organizations, powers, and activities; and measures federal, state, and local fiscal relationships. The Employment component was mailed **March 2012** to collect information on the number of state and local government civilian employees and their payrolls.

Government employees include all persons paid for personal services performed, including persons paid from federally funded programs, paid elected or appointed officials, persons in a paid leave status, and persons paid on a per meeting, annual, semi-annual, or quarterly basis. Unpaid officials, pensioners, persons whose work is performed on a fee basis, and contractors and their employees are excluded from the count of employees. **Full-Time Equivalent employees** is a computed statistic representing the number of full-time employees that could have been employed if the reported number of hours worked by part-time employees had been worked by full-time employees. This statistic is calculated separately for each function of a government by dividing the "part-time hours paid" by the standard number of hours for full-time employees in the particular government and then adding the resulting quotient to the number of full-time employees.

March payroll represents gross payroll amounts for the one-month period of March for full-time and part-time employees. Gross payroll includes all salaries, wages, fees, commissions, and overtime paid to employees **before** withholdings for taxes, insurance, etc. It also includes incentive payments that are paid at regular pay intervals. It excludes employer share of fringe benefits like retirement, Social Security, health and life insurance, lump sum payments, and so forth.

Administration and Judicial and Legal combines **Financial administration, Other government administration, and Judicial and Legal** activities. **Financial administration includes** activities concerned with tax assessment and collection, custody and disbursement of funds, debt management, administration of trust funds, budgeting, and other government-wide financial management activities. This function is not applied to school district or special district governments. **Other government administration** applies to the legislative and government-wide administrative agencies of governments. Included here are overall planning and zoning activities, and central personnel and administrative activities. This function is not applied to school district or special district governments. **Judicial and legal** includes all court and court related activities (except probation and parole activities that are included at the "Correction" function), court activities of sheriff's offices, prosecuting attorneys' and public defenders' offices, legal departments, and attorneys providing government-wide legal service.

Police and Corrections includes all activities concerned, with the enforcement of law and order, including coroner's offices, police training academies, investigation bureaus, and local jails, "lockups", or other detention facilities not intended to serve as correctional facilities. **Corrections** includes activities pertaining to the confinement and correction of adults and minors convicted of criminal offenses. Pardon, probation, and parole activities are also included here.

Fire protection includes local government fire protection and prevention activities plus any ambulance, rescue, or other auxiliary services provided by a fire protection agency. Volunteer fire-fighters, if remunerated for their services on a "per fire" or some other basis, are included as part-time employees.

Highways and transportation includes activities associated with the maintenance and operation of streets, roads, sidewalks,

bridges, tunnels, toll roads, and ferries. Snow and ice removal, street lighting, and highway and traffic engineering activities are also included here. Also included are the operation, maintenance, and construction of public mass transit systems, including subways, surface rails, and buses, and the provision, construction, operation, maintenance; support of public waterways, harbors, docks, wharves, and related marine terminal facilities; and activities associated with the operation and support of publicly operated airport facilities.

Health and Welfare includes Health, Hospitals, and Public welfare. **Health** includes administration of public health programs, community and visiting nurse services, immunization programs, drug abuse rehabilitation programs, health and food inspection activities, operation of outpatient clinics, and environmental pollution control activities. **Hospitals** includes only government operated medical care facilities that provide inpatient care. Employees and payrolls of private corporations that lease and operate government-owned hospital facilities are excluded.

Public Welfare includes the administration of various public assistance programs for the needy, veteran services, operation of nursing homes, indigent care institutions, and programs that provide payments for medical care, handicap transportation, and other services for the needy.

Natural resources and Utilities includes activities primarily concerned with the conservation and development of natural resources (soil, water, energy, minerals, etc.) and the regulation of industries that develop, utilize, or affect natural resources, as well as the operation and maintenance of **parks**, playgrounds, swimming pools, public beaches, auditoriums, public golf courses, museums, marinas, botanical gardens, and zoological parks. **Utilities, sewerage, and waste management** includes operation, maintenance, and construction of public water supply systems, including production, acquisition, and distribution of water to general public or to other public or private utilities, for residential, commercial, and industrial use; activities associated with the production or acquisition and distribution of electric power; provision, maintenance, and operation of sanitary and storm sewer systems and sewage disposal and treatment facilities; and refuse collection and disposal, operation of sanitary landfills, and street cleaning activities.

Education and libraries includes activities associated with the operation of public elementary and secondary schools and locally operated vocational-technical schools. Special education programs operated by elementary and secondary school systems are also included as are all ancillary services associated with the operation of schools, such as pupil transportation and food service. **Also included are the e**stablishment and provision of libraries for use by the general public and the technical support of privately operated libraries. This category includes classroom teachers, principals, supervisors of instruction, librarians, teacher aides, library aides, and guidance and psychological personnel as well as school superintendents and other administrative personnel, clerical and secretarial staffs, plant operation and maintenance personnel, health and recreation employees, transportation and food service personnel, and any student employees. Also included are any degree granting institutions that provide academic training above grade 12.

LOCAL GOVERNMENT FINANCES, Items 180–193

Source: U.S. Census Bureau—2012 Census of Governments
https://www.census.gov/programs-surveys/cog.html

Data on local government finances are based on result of the 2012 Census of Governments. For each metropolitan area, the data are aggregated from its component counties, and the financial data comprise amounts for all local governments—not only the county governments, but also any municipalities, townships, school districts, and special districts within the county. Statistics from governmental units located in two or more county areas are assigned to the county area containing the administrative office.

Revenue and expenditure items include all amounts of money received and paid out, respectively, by a government and its agencies (net of correcting transactions such as recoveries of refunds), with the exception of amounts for debt issuance and retirement and for loan and investment, agency, and private transactions.

Payments among the various funds and agencies of a particular government are excluded from revenue and expenditure items as representing internal transfers. Therefore, a government's contribution to a retirement fund that it administers is not counted as expenditure, nor is the receipt of this contribution by the retirement fund counted as revenue.

Total **general revenue** includes all revenue except utility, liquor stores, and insurance trust revenue. All tax revenue and intergovernmental revenue, even if designated for employee-retirement or local utility purpose, are classified as general revenue.

Intergovernmental revenue covers amounts received from the federal government as fiscal aid, reimbursements for performance of general government functions and specific services for the paying government, or in lieu of taxes. It excludes any amounts received from other governments from the sale of property, commodities, and utility services.

Taxes consist of compulsory contributions exacted by governments for public purposes. However, this category excludes employer and employee payments for retirement and social insurance purposes, which are classified as insurance trust revenue; it also excludes special assessments, which are classified as non-tax general revenue. Property taxes are taxes conditioned on ownership of property and assessed by its value. Sales and gross receipts taxes do not include dealer discounts, or "commissions" allowed to merchants for collection of taxes from consumers. General sales taxes and selected taxes on sales of motor fuels, tobacco products, and other particular commodities and services are included.

General government expenditure includes capital outlay, a major portion of which is commonly financed by borrowing. Government revenue does not include receipts from borrowing. Among other things, this distorts the relationship between totals of revenue and expenditure figures that are presented and renders it useless as a direct measure of the degree of budgetary "balance" (as that term is generally applied).

Direct general expenditure comprises all expenditures of the local governments, excluding utility, liquor stores, insurance trust expenditures, and any intergovernmental payments.

Local government expenditure for **education** is mainly for the provision and general support of schools and other educational facilities and services, including those for educational institutions beyond high school. They cover such related services as student transportation; school lunch and other cafeteria operations; school health, recreation, and library services; and dormitories, dining halls, and bookstores operated by public institutions of higher education.

Health and hospital expenditure includes health research; clinics; nursing; immunization; other categorical, environmental, and general health services provided by health agencies; establishment and operation of hospital facilities; provision of hospital care; and support of other public and private hospitals.

Police protection expenditure includes police activities such as patrols, communications, custody of persons awaiting trial, and vehicular inspection.

Public welfare expenditure covers support of and assistance to needy persons; this aid is contingent upon the person's needs. Included are cash assistance paid directly to needy persons under categorical (Old Age Assistance, Temporary Assistance for Needy Families, Aid to the Blind, and Aid to the Disabled) and other welfare programs; vendor payments made directly to private purveyors for medical care, burials, and other commodities and services provided under welfare programs; welfare institutions; and any intergovernmental or other direct expenditure for welfare purposes. Pensions to former employees and other benefits not contingent on need are excluded.

Highway expenditure is for the provision and maintenance of highway facilities, including toll turnpikes, bridges, tunnels, and ferries, as well as regular roads, highways, and streets. Also included are expenditures for street lighting and for snow and ice removal. Not included are highway policing and traffic control, which are considered part of police protection

Debt outstanding includes all long-term debt obligations of the government and its agencies (exclusive of utility debt) and all interest-bearing, short-term (repayable within one year) debt obligations remaining unpaid at the close of the fiscal year. It includes judgments, mortgages, and revenue bonds, as well as general obligation bonds, notes, and interest-bearing warrants. This category consists of non-interest-bearing, short-term obligations; inter-fund obligations; amounts owed in a trust or agency capacity; advances and contingent loans from other governments; and rights of individuals to benefit from government-administered employee-retirement funds.

GOVERNMENT EMPLOYMENT, Items 194–196

Source: U.S. Bureau of Economic Analysis—Regional Economic Accounts
http://www.bea.gov/regional/index.htm#state

Employment is measured as the average annual sum of full-time and part-time jobs. The estimates are on a place-of-work basis. The estimates are on a place-of-work basis. State and local government employment includes person employed in all state and local government agencies and enterprises. Data for federal civilian employment include civilian employees of the federal government, including civilian employees of the Department of Defense. Military employment includes all persons on active duty status.

INDIVIDUAL INCOME TAX RETURNS, Items 197–199

Source: U.S. Internal Revenue Servicw, Statistics of Income Program
https://www.irs.gov/uac/soi-tax-stats-county-data-2015

The Revenue Act of 1916 mandated the annual publication of statistics related to "the operations of the internal revenue laws" as they affect individuals, all forms of businesses, estates. nonprofit organizations, trusts, and investments abroad and foreign investments in the United States. The Statistics of Income (SOI) division fulfills this function by collecting and processing data so that they become informative and by sharing information about how the tax system works with other government agencies and the general public. Publication types include traditional print sources, Internet files, CD-ROMs, and files sent via e-mail. SOI has an information office, Statistical Information Services, to facilitate the dissemination of SOI data.

SOI bases its county data on administrative records of individual income tax returns (Forms 1040) from the Internal Revenue Service (IRS) Individual Master File (IMF) system. Included in these data are returns filed during the 12-month period, January 1, 2015 to December 31, 2015. While the bulk of returns filed during the 12-month period are primarily for Tax Year 2014, the IRS received a limited number of returns for tax years before 2014 and these have been included within the county data.

Data do not represent the full U.S. population because many individuals are not required to file an individual income tax return. The address shown on the tax return may differ from the taxpayer's actual residence. State and county codes were based on the ZIP code shown on the return. Excluded were tax returns filed without a ZIP code and returns filed with a ZIP code that did not match the State code shown on the return.

SOI did not attempt to correct any ZIP codes on the returns; however, it did take the following precautions to avoid disclosing information about specific taxpayers: Excluded from the data are items with less than 20 returns within a county. Also excluded are tax returns representing a specified percentage of the total of any particular cell. For example, if one return represented 75 percent of the value of a given cell, the return was suppressed from the county detail. The actual threshold percentage used cannot be released.

Column 197 show the number of returns. Column 198 shows the mean Adjusted Gross Income for the metropolitan area and column 199 shows the mean income tax (line 56 on Form 1040). for the county.

Table D—Cities

Table D present 146 items of data for cities with populations of 25,000 or more at the time of the 2010 census.

LAND AREA, Items 1 and 4

Source: U.S. Census Bureau—2017 U.S. Gazetteer Files,
http://www.census.gov/geo/maps-data/data/gazetteer2017.html

Land area measurements are shown to the nearest square mile. Land area is an area measurement providing the size, in square miles, of the land portions of each county.

POPULATION, Items 2-4

Source: U.S. Census Bureau—Population Estimates
https://www.census.gov/programs-surveys/popest.html

The population data are Census Bureau estimates of the resident population as of July 1 of the year shown.

POPULATION CHARACTERISTICS, Items 5–22

Source: U.S. Census Bureau—American Community Survey 2016 1-year Supplemental Estimates
http://www.census.gov/acs/www/

Data on age, sex, race, Hispanic origin, and place of birth are from the 2016 American Community Survey, a nationwide continuous survey designed to replace the long form questionnaire used in previous censuses.

Data on race were derived from answers to the question on race that was asked of all persons. The concept of race, as used by the Census Bureau, reflects self-identification by respondents according to the race or races with which they most closely identify. These categories are sociopolitical constructs and should not be interpreted as being scientific or anthropological in nature. Furthermore, the race categories include both racial and national origin groups.

On the American Community Survey, respondents were offered the option of selecting one or more races. This option was not available prior to the 2000 census; thus, comparisons between censuses should be made with caution. In this table, Columns 5 through 10 refer to individuals who identified with one specific racial category, while Column 11 includes those who selected more than one race.

The **White** population is defined as persons who indicated their race as White, as well as persons who did not classify themselves in one of the specific race categories listed on the questionnaire but entered a nationality such as Irish, German, Italian, Lebanese, Near Easterner, Arab, or Polish.

The **Black** population includes persons who indicated their race as "Black, African Am., or Negro," as well as persons who did not classify themselves in one of the specific race categories but reported entries such as African American, Afro American, Kenyan, Nigerian, or Haitian.

The **American Indian or Alaska Native** population includes persons who indicated their race as American Indian or Alaska

Native, as well as persons who did not classify themselves in one of the specific race categories but reported entries such as Canadian Indian, French-American Indian, Spanish-American Indian, Eskimo, Aleut, Alaska Indian, or any of the American Indian or Alaska Native tribes.

The **Asian** population includes persons who indicated their race as Asian Indian, Chinese, Filipino, Japanese, Korean, Vietnamese, or "Other Asian," as well as persons who provided write-in entries of such groups as Cambodian, Laotian, Hmong, Pakistani, or Taiwanese.

The **Native Hawaiian or Other Pacific Islander** population includes persons who indicated their race as "Native Hawaiian," "Guamanian or Chamorro," "Samoan," or "Other Pacific Islander," as well as persons who reported entries such as Part Hawaiian, American Samoan, Fijian, Melanesian, or Tahitian.

Some Other Race includes all other responses not included in the "White," "Black or African American," "American Indian or Alaska Native," "Asian," and "Native Hawaiian or Other Pacific Islander" race categories described above. Respondents reporting entries such as multiracial, mixed, interracial, or a Hispanic, Latino, or Spanish group (for example, Mexican, Puerto Rican, Cuban, or Spanish) in response to the race question are included in this category.

Two or More Races. People may choose to provide two or more races either by checking two or more race response check boxes, by providing multiple responses, or by some combination of check boxes and other responses. The race response categories shown on the questionnaire are collapsed into the five minimum race groups identified by OMB, and the Census Bureau's "Some Other Race" category.

The **Hispanic population** is based on a separate question that asked respondents "Is this person Spanish/Hispanic/Latino?" Persons marking any one of the four Hispanic categories (i.e., Mexican, Puerto Rican, Cuban, or other Spanish) are collectively referred to as Hispanic.

The Hispanic origin question was placed before the race question and specific instructions indicated that both questions should be answered.

The **foreign-born** population includes all persons who were not U.S. citizens at birth. Foreign-born persons are those who indicated they were either a U.S. citizen by naturalization or were not a citizen of the United States. The foreign-born population consists of immigrants (legal permanent residents), temporary migrants (students), humanitarian migrants (refugees), and unauthorized migrants (persons illegally residing in the United States).

Age is defined as age at last birthday (number of completed years since birth), at the time of the interview. The American Community Survey also asked for the specific date of birth of the respondent. Both age and date of birth are used in combination to calculate the most accurate age at the time of the interview.

The **female** population is shown as a percentage of total population.

POPULATION CHANGE, Items 23–26

Source: U.S. Census Bureau—Decennial Censuses
U.S. Census Bureau—Population Estimates
http://www.census.gov/main/www/cen2000.html

https://www.census.gov/programs-surveys/decennial-census/data/datasets.2010.html
https://www.census.gov/programs-surveys/popest.html

The population data for 2000 and 2010 are from the decennial censuses and represent the resident population as of April 1 of those years. The data for 2017 are from the Census Bureau's Population Estimates Program and represent the estimated resident population as of July 1.

The change in population from 2000 to 2010 and from 2010 to 2017 is calculated from census data based on city boundaries as they existed in 2000 and 2010, respectively. No attempt was made to adjust the data to reflect boundary changes.

HOUSEHOLDS, Items 27–34

Source: U.S. Census Bureau—American Community Survey, 2016 1-year Supplemental Estimates
http://www.census.gov/acs/www/

A **household** includes all of the persons who occupy a housing unit. (Persons not living in households are classified as living in group quarters.) A housing unit is a house, an apartment, a mobile home, a group of rooms, or a single room occupied (or, if vacant, intended for occupancy) as separate living quarters. Separate living quarters are those in which the occupants live separately from any other persons in the building and have direct access from the outside of the building or through a common hall. The occupants may be a single family, one person living alone, two or more families living together, or any other group of related or unrelated persons who share living quarters. The number of households is the same as the number of year-round occupied housing units.

A **family** includes a householder and one or more other persons living in the same household who are related to the householder by birth, marriage, or adoption. All persons in a household who are related to the householder are regarded as members of his or her family. A **family household** may contain persons not related to the householder; thus, family households may include more members than families do. A household can contain only one family for the purposes of census tabulations. Not all households contain families, as a household may comprise a group of unrelated persons or of one person living alone. Families are classified by type as either a "married couple family" or "other family," according to the presence or absence of a spouse.

A **Married-Couple Family** is a family in which the householder and his or her spouse are listed as members of the same household. The category **female family householder** includes only female-headed family households with no spouse present.

A **Nonfamily Household** includes a householder living alone or with nonrelatives only. Unmarried couples households, whether opposite-sex or same-sex, with no relatives of the householder present are tabulated in nonfamily households.

The measure of **persons per household** is obtained by dividing the number of persons in households by the number of households or householders. One person in each household is designated as the householder. In most cases, this is the person (or one of the persons) in whose name the house is owned, being bought, or rented. If there is no such person in the household, any adult household member 15 years old and over can be designated as the householder.

CRIME, Items 35–38

Source: U.S. Federal Bureau of Investigation—Uniform Crime Reports
https://ucr.fbi.gov/crime-in-the-u.s/2016/
crime-in-the-u.s.-2016

Crime data are as reported to the Federal Bureau of Investigation (FBI) by law enforcement agencies and have not been adjusted for underreporting. This may affect comparability between geographic areas or over time.

Through the voluntary contribution of crime statistics by law enforcement agencies across the United States, the Uniform Crime Reporting (UCR) Program provides periodic assessments of crime in the nation as measured by offenses that have come to the attention of the law enforcement community. The Committee on Uniform Crime Records of the International Association of Chiefs of Police initiated this voluntary national data collection effort in 1930. The UCR Program contributors compile and submit their crime data either directly to the FBI or through state-level UCR Programs.

Seven offenses, because of their severity, frequency of occurrence, and likelihood of being reported to police, were initially selected to serve as an index for evaluating fluctuations in the volume of crime. These serious crimes were murder and nonnegligent manslaughter, forcible rape, robbery, aggravated assault, burglary, larceny-theft, and motor vehicle theft. By congressional mandate, arson was added as the eighth index offense in 1979. The totals shown in this volume do not include arson.

In 2004, the FBI discontinued the use of the Crime Index in the UCR Program and its publications, stating that the Crime Index was driven upward by the offense with the highest number of cases (in this case, larceny-theft), creating a bias against jurisdictions with a high number of larceny-thefts but a low number of other serious crimes, such as murder and forcible rape. The FBI is currently publishing a violent crime total and property crime total until a more viable index is developed. This book includes the total Crime Index, as well as violent crime and property crime rates.

In 2013, the FBI adopted a new definition of rape. Rape is now defined as, "Penetration, no matter how slight, of the vagina or anus with any body part or object, or oral penetration by a sex organ of another person, without the consent of the victim." The new definition updated the 80-year-old historical definition of rape which was "carnal knowledge of a female forcibly and against her will." Effectively, the revised definition expands rape to include both male and female victims and offenders, and reflects the various forms of sexual penetration understood to be rape, especially nonconsenting acts of sodomy, and sexual assaults with objects.

Violent crimes include four categories of offenses: (1) Murder and nonnegligent manslaughter, as defined in the UCR Program, is the willful (nonnegligent) killing of one human being by another. This offense excludes deaths caused by negligence, suicide, or accident; justifiable homicides; and attempts to murder or assaults to murder. (2)) Rape is the penetration, no matter how slight, of the vagina or anus with any body part or object, or oral penetration by a sex organ of another person, without the consent of the victim Assaults or attempts to commit rape by force or threat of force are also included; however, statutory rape (without force) and other sex offenses are excluded. (3) Robbery is the taking or attempting to take anything of value from the care, custody, or control of a person or persons by force or threat of force or violence and/or by putting the victim in fear. (4) Aggravated assault is an unlawful attack by one person upon another for the purpose of inflicting severe or aggravated bodily injury. This type of assault is usually accompanied by the use of a weapon or by other means likely to produce death or great bodily harm. Attempts are included, since injury does not necessarily have to result when a gun, knife, or other weapon is used, as these incidents could and probably would result in a serious personal injury if the crime were successfully completed.

Property crimes include three categories: (1) Burglary, or breaking and entering, is the unlawful entry of a structure to commit a felony or theft, even though no force was used to gain entrance. (2) Larceny-theft is the unauthorized taking of the personal property of another, without the use of force. (3) Motor vehicle theft is the unauthorized taking of any motor vehicle.

Rates are based on population estimates provided by the FBI. If a city is not in the UCR database, or if the population total for the units aggregated was less than 75 percent of the city's population (as estimated by the Census Bureau), the total was not considered representative of the city as a whole and was not published. State and U.S. totals include FBI estimates for those areas.

EDUCATIONAL ATTAINMENT, Items 39–41

Source: U.S. Census Bureau—American Community Survey, 2016 1-year Supplemental Estimates
http://www.census.gov/acs/www/

Data on **educational attainment** are tabulated for the population 25 years old and over. The data were derived from a question that asked respondents for the highest level of school completed or the highest degree received. Persons who had passed a high school equivalency examination were considered high school graduates. Schooling received in foreign schools was to be reported as the equivalent grade or years in the regular American school system.

Vocational and technical training, such as barber school training; business, trade, technical, and vocational schools; or other training for a specific trade are specifically excluded.

High school graduate or less. This category includes persons whose highest degree was a high school diploma or its equivalent, and those who reported any level lower than a high school diploma.

Bachelor's degree or more. This category includes persons who have received bachelor's degrees, master's degrees, professional school degrees (such as law school or medical school degrees), and doctoral degrees.

INCOME, Items 42–49
Source: U.S. Census Bureau—American Community Survey, 2016 1-year Supplemental Estimates
http://www.census.gov/acs/www/

Total money income is the sum of the amounts reported separately for wage or salary income; net self-employment income; interest, dividends, or net rental or royalty income or income from estates and trusts; Social Security or railroad retirement income; Supplemental Security Income (SSI); public assistance or welfare payments; retirement, survivor, or disability pensions; and all other income. Receipts from the following sources are not included as income: capital gains; money received from the sale of property (unless the recipient was engaged in the business of selling such property); the value of income "in kind" from food stamps, public housing subsidies, medical care, employer contributions for individuals, etc.; withdrawal of bank deposits; money borrowed; tax refunds; exchange of money between relatives living in the same household; and gifts, lump-sum inheritances, insurance payments, and other types of lump-sum receipts.

Household income includes the income of the householder and all other individuals 15 years old and over in the household, whether or not they are related to the householder. Since many households consist of only one person, median household income is usually less than median family income. Although the household income statistics cover the twelve months prior to the survey, the characteristics of individuals and the composition of households refer to the date of the interview. Thus, the income of the household does not include amounts received by individuals who were members of the household during all or part of the year if these individuals were no longer residing in the household at the time of the interview. Similarly, income amounts reported by individuals who did not reside in the household during full year but who were members of the household at the time of the interview are included. However, the composition of most households was the same during the year as it was at the time of the interview.

Income of Families – In compiling statistics on family income, the incomes of all members 15 years old and over related to the householder are summed and treated as a single amount.

Median income divides the income distribution into two equal parts, with half of all cases below the median income level and half of all cases above the median income level. For households, the median income is based on the distribution of the total number of households, including those with no income. Median income for households and families is computed on the basis of a standard distribution with a minimum value of less than $2,500 and a maximum value of $200,000 or more and is rounded to the nearest whole dollar. Median income figures are calculated using linear interpolation if the width of the interval containing the estimate is $2,500 or less. If the width of the interval containing the estimate is greater than $2,500, Pareto interpolation is used.

Income components were reported for the 12 months preceding the interview month. Monthly Consumer Price Index (CPI) factors were used to inflation-adjust these components to a reference calendar year (January through December). For example, a household interviewed in March 2012 reports their income for March 2011 through February 2012. Their income is adjusted to the 2012 reference calendar year by multiplying their reported income by 2012 average annual CPI (January-December 2012) and then dividing by the average CPI for March 2006-February 2012. In addition, the 3-year estimates are inflation-adjusted to the final year. However, the estimates do not reflect the price and cost-of-living differences that may exist between areas.

Earnings – Earnings are defined as the sum of wage or salary income and net income from self-employment. "Earnings" represent the amount of income received regularly for people 16 years old and over before deductions for personal income taxes, Social Security, bond purchases, union dues, Medicare deductions, etc. An individual with earnings is one who has either wage/salary income or self-employment income, or both. Respondents who "break even" in self-employment income and therefore have zero self-employment earnings also are considered "individuals with earnings."

HOUSING, Items 50–54
Source: U.S. Census Bureau--American Community Survey, 2016 1-year Supplemental Estimates
http://www.census.gov/acs/www/

The characteristics of occupied housing units are from the 2016 American Community Survey.

A **housing unit** is a house, apartment, mobile home or trailer, group of rooms, or single room occupied or, if vacant, intended for occupancy as separate living quarters. Separate living quarters are those in which the occupants do not live and eat with any other person in the structure and which have direct access from the outside of the building through a common hall. For vacant units, the criteria of separateness and direct access are applied to the intended occupants whenever possible. If that information cannot be obtained, the criteria are applied to the previous occupants.

The occupants of a housing unit may be a single family, one person living alone, two or more families living together, or any other group of related or unrelated persons who share living quarters. Both occupied and vacant housing units are included in the housing inventory, although recreational vehicles, tents, caves, boats, railroad cars, and the like are included only if they are occupied as a person's usual place of residence.

A housing unit is classified as occupied if it is the usual place of residence of the person or group of persons living in it at the time of enumeration, or if the occupants are only temporarily absent (away on vacation). A household consists of all persons who occupy a housing unit as their usual place of residence. Vacant units for sale or rent include units rented or sold but not occupied and any other units held off the market.

A housing unit is **owner occupied** if the owner or co-owner lives in the unit, even if it is mortgaged or not fully paid for. The owner or co-owner must live in the unit and is usually the first person listed on the census or ACS questionnaire.

All occupied housing units that are not owner occupied, whether they are rented for cash rent or occupied without payment of cash rent, are classified as **renter occupied**.

Median value is the dollar amount that divides the distribution of specified owner-occupied housing units into two equal parts, with half of all units below the median value and half of all units above the median value. Value is defined as the respondent's estimate of what the house would sell for if it were for sale. Data are presented for single-family units on fewer than 10 acres of land that have no business or medical offices on the property.

Median rent divides the distribution of renter-occupied housing units into two equal parts. The rent concept used in this volume is gross rent, which includes the amount of cash rent a renter pays (contract rent) plus the estimated average cost of utilities and fuels, if these are paid by the renter. The rent is the amount of rent only for living quarters and excludes amounts paid for any business or other space occupied. Single-family houses on lots of 10 or more acres of land are also excluded.

COMMUTING, Items 55 and 56
Source: U.S. Census Bureau—American Community Survey, 2016 1-year Supplemental Estimates
http://www.census.gov/acs/www/

Means of transportation to work refers to the principal mode of travel or type of conveyance that a worker usually used to get from home to work during the reference week. This question was asked of people who indicated that they worked at some time during the reference week. People who used different means of transportation on different days of the week were asked to specify the one they used most often, that is, the greatest number of days. People who used more than one means of transportation to get to work each day were asked to report the one used for the longest distance during the work trip. The category, "Car, truck, or van," includes workers using a car (including company cars but excluding taxicabs), a truck of one-ton capacity or less, or a van. The category, "**Drove alone**," includes people who usually drove alone to work as well as people who were driven to work by someone who then drove back home or to a non-work destination.

The question on **travel time to work** was asked of people who indicated that they worked at some time during the reference week, and who reported that they worked outside their home. Travel time to work refers to the total number of minutes that it usually took the worker to get from home to work during the reference week. The elapsed time includes time spent waiting for public transportation, picking up passengers in carpools, and time spent in other activities related to getting to work.

COMPUTER AND INTERNET USE, Items 57 and 58
Source: U.S. Census Bureau—American Community Survey, 2016 1-year Supplemental Estimates

http://www.census.gov/acs/www/

The **computer use** question asked if anyone in the household owned or used a computer and included three response categories for a desktop/laptop, a handheld computer, or some other type of computer. Respondents could select all categories that applied.

Another question asked if any member of the household accesses the **internet**. "Access" refers to whether or not someone in the household uses or connects to the Internet, regardless of whether or not they pay for the service. Respondents were to select only ONE of the following choices:

- Yes, with a subscription to an Internet service –This category includes housing units where someone pays to access the Internet through a service such as a data plan for a mobile phone, a cable modem, DSL or other type of service. This will normally refer to a service that someone is billed for directly for Internet alone or sometimes as part of a bundle.
- Yes, without a subscription to an Internet service–Some respondents may live in a city or town that provides free Internet services for their residents. In addition, some colleges or universities provide Internet services. These are examples of cases where respondents may be able to access the Internet without a subscription.
- No Internet access at this house, apartment, or mobile home–This category includes housing units where no one connects to or uses the Internet using a paid service or any free services.

MIGRATION, Items 59 and 60
Source: U.S. Census Bureau—American Community Survey, 2016 1-year Supplemental Estimates
http://www.census.gov/acs/www/

Residence one year ago is used in conjunction with location of current residence to determine the extent of residential mobility of the population and the resulting redistribution of the population across the various states, metropolitan areas, and regions of the country. **Same house** includes all people 1 year old and over who, a year before the survey date, lived in the same house or apartment that they occupied at the time of interview.

The **percent who lived outside** current **county** includes all persons who did not live in their current county 1 year before the interview. However, they may have lived outside their current city but still in the same county.

CIVILIAN LABOR FORCE AND UNEMPLOY-MENT, Items 61–64
Source: U.S. Bureau of Labor Statistics—Local Areas Unemployment Statistics
http://www.bls.gov/lau/#tables

Data for the civilian labor force are the product of a federal-state cooperative program in which state employment security agencies prepare labor force and unemployment estimates under concepts, definitions, and technical procedures established by the

Bureau of Labor Statistics (BLS). The civilian labor force consists of all civilians 16 years old and over who are either employed or unemployed.

Unemployment includes all persons who did not work during the survey week, made specific efforts to find a job during the previous four weeks, and were available for work during the survey week (except for temporary illness). Persons waiting to be called back to a job from which they had been laid off and those waiting to report to a new job within the next 30 days are included in unemployment figures.

Table D includes annual average data for the year shown. The Local Area Unemployment Statistics data are periodically updated to reflect revised inputs, reestimation, and controlling to new statewide totals.

EMPLOYMENT, Items 65–68
Source: U.S. Census Bureau—American Community Survey, 2016 1-year Supplemental Estimates
http://www.census.gov/acs/www/

The **labor force** includes all persons 16 years old and over who were either (1) "at work"—those who did any work at all during the reference week as paid employees, worked in either their own business or profession, worked on their own farm, or worked 15 hours or more as unpaid workers in a family farm or business; or were (2) "with a job, but not at work" —those who had a job but were not at work that week due to illness, weather, industrial dispute, vacation, or other personal reasons.

Full-year, Full-Time Workers includes people 16 to 64 years old who usually worked 35 hours or more per week for 50 to 52 weeks in the past 12 months.

BUILDING PERMITS, Items 69–71
Source: U.S. Census Bureau—Building Permits Survey
http://www.census.gov/construction/bps

These figures represent private residential construction authorized by building permits in approximately 20,000 places in the United States. Valuation represents the expected cost of construction as recorded on the building permit. This figure usually excludes the cost of on-site and off-site development and improvements, as well as the cost of heating, plumbing, electrical, and elevator installations.

National, state, and county totals were obtained by adding the data for permit-issuing places within each jurisdiction. These totals thus are limited to permits issued in the 20,000 place universe covered by the Census Bureau and may not include all permits issued within a state. Current surveys indicate that construction is undertaken for all but a very small percentage of housing units authorized by building permits.

Residential building permits include buildings with any number of housing units. Housing units exclude group quarters (such as dormitories and rooming houses), transient accommodations (such as transient hotels, motels, and tourist courts), "HUD-code" manufactured (mobile) homes, moved or relocated units, and

housing units created in an existing residential or nonresidential structure.

2012 Economic CENSUS: OVERVIEW, Items 72–107
Source: U.S. Census Bureau
http://www.census.gov/programs-surveys/economic-census/tables.html

The Economic Census provides a detailed portrait of the nation's economy, from the national to the local level, once every five years. The 2012 Economic Census covers nearly all of the U.S. economy in its basic collection of establishment statistics. The 1997 Economic Census was the first major data source to use the new North American Industry Classification System (NAICS); therefore, data from this census are not comparable to economic data from prior years, which were based on the Standard Industrial Classification (SIC) system.

NAICS, developed in cooperation with Canada and Mexico, classifies North America's economic activities at two, three, four, and fivedigit levels of detail; the U.S. version of NAICS further defines industries to a sixth digit. The Economic Census takes advantage of this hierarchy to publish data at these successive levels of detail: sector (two-digit), subsector (three-digit), industry group (four-digit), industry (five-digit), and U.S. industry (six-digit). Information in Table A is at the two-digit level, with a few three- and four-digit items. The data in Table D are at the two-digit level.

Several key statistics are tabulated for all industries in this volume, including number of establishments (or companies), number of employees, payroll, and certain measures of output (sales, receipts, revenue, value of shipments, or value of construction work done).

Number of establishments. An establishment is a single physical location at which business is conducted. It is not necessarily identical with a company or enterprise, which may consist of one establishment or more. Economic Census figures represent a summary of reports for individual establishments rather than companies. For cases in which a census report was received, separate information was obtained for each location where business was conducted. When administrative records of other federal agencies were used instead of a census report, no information was available on the number of locations operated. Each Economic Census establishment was tabulated according to the physical location at which the business was conducted. The count of establishments represents those in business at any time during 2002.

When two activities or more were carried on at a single location under a single ownership, all activities were generally grouped together as a single establishment. The entire establishment was classified on the basis of its major activity and all of its data were included in that classification. However, when distinct and separate economic activities (for which different industry classification codes were appropriate) were conducted at a single location under a single ownership, separate establishment reports for each of the different activities were obtained in the census.

Number of employees. Paid employees consist of the full-time and parttime employees, including salaried officers and executive of corporations. Included are employees on paid sick leave, paid holidays, and paid vacations; not included are proprietors and partners of unincorporated businesses. The definition of paid employees is the same as that used by the Internal Revenue Service (IRS) on form 941. For some industries, the Economic Census gives codes representing the number of employees as a range of numbers (for example, "100 to 249 employees" or "1,000 to 2,499" employees). In this volume, those codes have been replaced by the standard suppression code "D".

Payroll. Payroll includes all forms of compensation, such as salaries, wages, commissions, dismissal pay, bonuses, vacation allowances, sickleave pay, and employee contributions to qualified pension plans paid during the year to all employees. For corporations, payroll includes amounts paid to officers and executives; for unincorporated businesses, it does not include profit or other compensation of proprietors or partners. Payroll is reported before deductions for Social Security, income tax, insurance, union dues, etc. This definition of payroll is the same as that used by on IRS form 941.

Sales, shipments, receipts, revenue, or business done. This measure includes the total sales, shipments, receipts, revenue, or business done by establishments within the scope of the Economic Census. The definition of each of these items is specific to the economic sector measured.

WHOLESALE TRADE, Items 72–75

Source: U.S. Census Bureau—2012 Economic Census (See Overview of 2012 Economic Census prior to Item 72)

The Wholesale Trade sector (sector 42) comprises establishments engaged in wholesaling merchandise, generally without transformation, and rendering services incidental to the sale of merchandise. The wholesaling process is an intermediate step in the distribution of merchandise.

Wholesalers are organized to sell or arrange the purchase or sale of (1) goods for resale (i.e., goods sold to other wholesalers or retailers), (2) capital or durable nonconsumer goods, and (3) raw and intermediate materials and supplies used in production.

Wholesalers sell merchandise to other businesses and normally operate from a warehouse or office. These warehouses and offices are characterized by having little or no display of merchandise. In addition, neither the design nor the location of the premises is intended to solicit walkin traffic. Wholesalers do not normally use advertising directed to the general public. In general, customers are initially reached via telephone, inperson marketing, or specialized advertising, which may include the internet and other electronic means. Followup orders are either vendorinitiated or clientinitiated, are usually based on previous sales, and typically exhibit strong ties between sellers and buyers. In fact, transactions are often conducted between wholesalers and clients that have longstanding business relationships.

This sector is made up of two main types of wholesalers: those that sell goods on their own account and those that arrange sales and purchases for others for a commission or fee.

(1) Establishments that sell goods on their own account are known as wholesale merchants, distributors, jobbers, drop shippers, import/export merchants, and sales branches. These establishments typically maintain their own warehouse, where they receive and handle goods for their customers. Goods are generally sold without transformation, but may include integral functions, such as sorting, packaging, labeling, and other marketing services.

(2) Establishments arranging for the purchase or sale of goods owned by others or purchasing goods on a commission basis are known as agents and brokers, commission merchants, import/export agents and brokers, auction companies, and manufacturers' representatives. These establishments operate from offices and generally do not own or handle the goods they sell.

Some wholesale establishments may be connected with a single manufacturer and promote and sell that particular manufacturer's products to a wide range of other wholesalers or retailers. Other wholesalers may be connected to a retail chain or a limited number of retail chains and only provide the products needed by the particular retail operation(s). These wholesalers may obtain the products from a wide range of manufacturers. Still other wholesalers may not take title to the goods, but act instead as agents and brokers for a commission.

Although wholesaling normally denotes sales in large volumes, durable nonconsumer goods may be sold in single units. Sales of capital or durable nonconsumer goods used in the production of goods and services, such as farm machinery, medium- and heavy-duty trucks, and industrial machinery, are always included in Wholesale Trade.

The city table includes only **Merchant wholesalers, except manufacturers' sales branches and offices,** establishments primarily engaged in buying and selling merchandise on their own account. Included here are such types of establishments as wholesale distributors and jobbers, importers, exporters, own-brand importers/marketers, terminal and country grain elevators, and farm products assemblers.

RETAIL TRADE, Items 76–79

Source: U.S. Census Bureau—2012 Economic Census (See Overview of 2012 Economic Census prior to Item 72)

The Retail Trade sector (44–45) is made up of establishments engaged in retailing merchandise, generally without transformation, and rendering services incidental to the sale of merchandise.

The retailing process is the final step in the distribution of merchandise; retailers are therefore organized to sell merchandise in small quantities to the general public. This sector comprises two main types of retailers: store and nonstore retailers.

Store retailers operate fixed pointofsale locations, located and designed to attract a high volume of walkin customers. In general, retail stores have extensive displays of merchandise and use massmedia advertising to attract customers. They typically sell merchandise to the general public for personal or household consumption; some also serve business and institutional clients. These include establishments such as office supply stores, computer and software stores, building materials dealers, plumbing supply stores, and electrical supply stores. Catalog showrooms, gasoline service stations, automotive dealers, and mobile home dealers are treated as store retailers.

In addition to retailing merchandise, some types of store retailers are also engaged in the provision of aftersales services, such as repair and installation. For example, new automobile dealers, electronic and appliance stores, and musical instrument and supply stores often provide repair services. As a general rule, establishments engaged in retailing merchandise and providing aftersales services are classified in this sector.

Nonstore retailers, like store retailers, are organized to serve the general public, although their retailing methods differ. The establishments of this subsector reach customers and market merchandise with methods including the broadcasting of "infomercials," the broadcasting and publishing of directresponse advertising, the publishing of paper and electronic catalogs, doortodoor solicitation, inhome demonstration, selling from portable stalls (street vendors, except food), and distribution through vending machines. Establishments engaged in the direct sale (nonstore) of products, such as home heating oil dealers and home-delivery newspaper routes are included in this sector.

The buying of goods for resale is a characteristic of retail trade establishments that distinguishes them from establishments in the Agriculture, Manufacturing, and Construction sectors. For example, farms that sell their products at or from the point of production are classified in Agriculture instead of in Retail Trade. Similarly, establishments that both manufacture and sell their products to the general public are classified in Manufacturing instead of Retail Trade. However, establishments that engage in processing activities incidental to retailing are classified in Retail Trade.

REAL ESTATE AND RENTAL AND LEASING, Items 80–83

Source: U.S. Census Bureau—2012 Economic Census (See Overview of 2012 Economic Census prior to Item 72)

The Real Estate and Rental and Leasing sector (53) comprises establishments primarily engaged in renting, leasing, or otherwise allowing the use of tangible or intangible assets, and establishments providing related services. The major portion of this sector is made up of establishments that rent, lease, or otherwise allow the use of their own assets by others. The assets may be tangible, such as real estate and equipment, or intangible, such as patents and trademarks.

This sector also includes establishments primarily engaged in managing real estate for others, selling, renting, and/or buying real estate for others, and appraising real estate. These activities are closely related to this sector's main activity. In addition, a substantial proportion of property management is selfperformed by lessors.

The main components of this sector are the real estate lessors industries; equipment lessors industries (including motor vehicles, computers, and consumer goods); and lessors of nonfinancial intangible assets (except copyrighted works).

PROFESSIONAL, SCIENTIFIC, AND TECHNICAL SERVICES, Items 84–87

Source: U.S. Census Bureau—2012 Economic Census (See Overview of 2012 Economic Census prior to Item 72)

The Professional, Scientific, and Technical Services sector (54) is made up of establishments that specialize in performing professional, scientific, and technical activities for others. These activities require a high degree of expertise and training. The establishments in this sector specialize in one or more areas and provide services to clients in a variety of industries (and, in some cases, to households). Activities performed include legal advice and representation; accounting, bookkeeping, and payroll services; architectural, engineering, and specialized design services; computer services; consulting services; research services; advertising services; photographic services; translation and interpretation services; veterinary services; and other professional, scientific, and technical services.

Table D includes only those establishments subject to federal income tax.

This sector excludes establishments primarily engaged in providing a range of daytoday office administrative services, such as financial planning, billing and record keeping, personnel services, and physical distribution and logistics services. These establishments are classified in sector 56, Administrative and Support and Waste Management and Remediation Services.

MANUFACTURING, Items 88–91

Source: U.S. Census Bureau—2012 Economic Census (See Overview of 2012 Economic Census prior to Item 72)

The Manufacturing sector (31–33) is made up of establishments engaged in the mechanical, physical, or chemical transformation of materials, substances, or components into new products. The assembling of component parts of manufactured products is considered manufacturing, except in cases in which the activity is appropriately classified in the Construction sector. Establishments in the Manufacturing sector are often described as plants, factories, or mills, and characteristically use power-driven machines and materials-handling equipment. However, establishments that transform materials or substances into new products by hand or in the worker's home, and establishments engaged in selling to the general public products made on the same premises from which they are sold (such as bakeries, candy stores, and custom tailors) may also be included in this sector. Manufacturing establishments may process materials or contract with other establishments to process their materials for them. Both types of establishments are included in the Manufacturing sector.

The materials, substances, or components transformed by manufacturing establishments are raw materials that are products of agriculture, forestry, fishing, mining, or quarrying, or are products of other manufacturing establishments. The materials used may be purchased directly from producers, obtained through customary trade channels, or secured without recourse to the market by transferring the product from one establishment to another, under the same ownership. The new product of a manufacturing establishment may be finished (in the sense that it is ready for utilization or consumption), or it may be semifinished to become an input for an establishment engaged in further manufacturing. For example, the product of the alumina refinery is the input used in the primary production of aluminum; primary aluminum is the input used in an aluminum wire drawing plant; and aluminum wire is the input used in a fabricated wire product manufacturing establishment.

Data are included for cities with 500 or more employees in the Manufacturing sector.

ACCOMMODATION AND FOOD SERVICES, Items 92–95

Source: U.S. Census Bureau—2012 Economic Census (See Overview of 2012 Economic Census prior to Item 72)

The Accommodation and Food Services sector (72) consists of establishments that provide customers with lodging and/or meals, snacks, and beverages for immediate consumption. This sector includes both accommodation and food services establishments because the two activities are often combined at the same establishment.

Excluded from this sector are civic and social organizations, amusement and recreation parks, theaters, and other recreation or entertainment facilities providing food and beverage services.

ARTS, ENTERTAINMENT, AND RECREATION, Items 96–99

Source: U.S. Census Bureau—2012 Economic Census (See Overview of 2012 Economic Census prior to Item 72)

The Arts, Entertainment, and Recreation sector (71) includes a wide range of establishments that operate facilities or provide services that meet the diverse cultural, entertainment, and recreational interests of their patrons. This sector is made up of: (1) establishments that are involved in producing, promoting, or participating in live performances, events, or exhibits intended for public viewing; (2) establishments that preserve and exhibit objects and sites of historical, cultural, or educational interest; and (3) establishments that operate facilities or provide services that enable patrons to participate in recreational activities or pursue amusement, hobby, and leisure time interests.

Some establishments that provide cultural, entertainment, or recreational facilities and services are classified in other sectors. Excluded from this sector are: (1) establishments that provide both accommodations and recreational facilities—such as hunting and fishing camps and resort and casino hotels—are classified in subsector 721, Accommodation; (2) restaurants and night clubs that provide live entertainment in addition to the sale of food and beverages are classified in subsector 722, Food Services and Drinking Places; (3) motion picture theaters, libraries and archives, and publishers of newspapers, magazines, books, periodicals, and computer software are classified in sector 51, Information; and

(4) establishmentsthat use transportation equipment to provide recreational and entertainment services, such as those operating sightseeing buses, dinner cruises, or helicopter rides, are classified in subsector 487, Scenic and Sightseeing Transportation.

Table D includes only those establishments subject to federal tax.

HEALTH CARE AND SOCIAL ASSISTANCE, Items 100–103

Source: U.S. Census Bureau—2012 Economic Census (See Overview of 2012 Economic Census prior to Item 72)

The Health Care and Social Assistance sector (62) consists of establishments that provide health care and social assistance services to individuals. The sector includes both health care and social assistance because it is sometimes difficult to distinguish between the boundaries of these two activities. The industries in this sector are arranged on a continuum, starting with establishments that provide medical care exclusively, continuing with those that provide health care and social assistance, and finishing with those that provide only social assistance. The services provided by establishments in this sector are delivered by trained professionals. All industries in the sector share this commonality of process—namely, labor inputs of health practitioners or social workers with the requisite expertise. Many of the industries in the sector are defined based on the educational degree held by the practitioners included in the industry.

Excluded from this sector are aerobic classes, which can be found in subsector 713, Amusement, Gambling, and Recreation Industries; and nonmedical diet and weight-reducing centers, which can be found in subsector 812, Personal and Laundry Services. Although these can be viewed as health services, they are not typically delivered by health practitioners.

Table D includes only those establishments subject to federal tax.

OTHER SERVICES, EXCEPT PUBLIC ADMINISTRATION Items 104–107

Source: U.S. Census Bureau—2012 Economic Census (See Overview of 2012 Economic Census prior to Item 72)

The Other Services, Except Public Administration sector (81) comprises establishments engaged in providing services not specifically categorized elsewhere in the classification system. Establishments in this sector are primarily engaged in activities such as equipment and machinery repairing, promoting or administering religious activities, grant making, and advocacy; this sector also includes establishments that provide dry-cleaning and laundry services, personal care services, death care services, pet care services, photofinishing services, temporary parking services, and dating services.

Private households that employ workers on or about the premises in activities primarily concerned with the operation of the household are included in this sector.

In Table D, only firms subject to federal tax are included.

Excluded from this sector are establishments primarily engaged in retailing new equipment and performing repairs and general maintenance on equipment. These establishments are classified in sector 44–45, Retail Trade.

CITY GOVERNMENT EMPLOYMENT AND PAYROLL, Items 171-179

Source: U.S. Census Bureau—2012 Census of Governments
https://www.census.gov/programs-surveys/cog.html

These items include data for municipal governments only. They do not include any special district government entities within the city. The Census of Governments identifies the scope and nature of the nation's state and local government sector; provides authoritative benchmark figures of public finance and public employment; classifies local government organizations, powers, and activities; and measures federal, state, and local fiscal relationships. The Employment component was mailed **March 2012** to collect information on the number of state and local government civilian employees and their payrolls.

Government employees include all persons paid for personal services performed, including persons paid from federally funded programs, paid elected or appointed officials, persons in a paid leave status, and persons paid on a per meeting, annual, semi-annual, or quarterly basis. Unpaid officials, pensioners, persons whose work is performed on a fee basis, and contractors and their employees are excluded from the count of employees. **Full-Time Equivalent employees** is a computed statistic representing the number of full-time employees that could have been employed if the reported number of hours worked by part-time employees had been worked by full-time employees. This statistic is calculated separately for each function of a government by dividing the "part-time hours paid" by the standard number of hours for full-time employees in the particular government and then adding the resulting quotient to the number of full-time employees.

March payroll represents gross payroll amounts for the one-month period of March for full-time and part-time employees. Gross payroll includes all salaries, wages, fees, commissions, and overtime paid to employees **before** withholdings for taxes, insurance, etc. It also includes incentive payments that are paid at regular pay intervals. It excludes employer share of fringe benefits like retirement, Social Security, health and life insurance, lump sum payments, and so forth.

Administration and Judicial and Legal combines **Financial administration, Other government administration, and Judicial and Legal** activities. **Financial administration includes** activities concerned with tax assessment and collection, custody and disbursement of funds, debt management, administration of trust funds, budgeting, and other government-wide financial management activities. This function is not applied to school district or special district governments. **Other government administration** applies to the legislative and government-wide administrative agencies of governments. Included here are overall planning and zoning activities, and central personnel and administrative activities. This function is not applied to school district or special district governments. **Judicial and legal** includes all court

and court related activities (except probation and parole activities that are included at the "Correction" function), court activities of sheriff's offices, prosecuting attorneys' and public defenders' offices, legal departments, and attorneys providing government-wide legal service.

Police and Corrections includes all activities concerned, with the enforcement of law and order, including coroner's offices, police training academies, investigation bureaus, and local jails, "lockups", or other detention facilities not intended to serve as correctional facilities. **Corrections** includes activities pertaining to the confinement and correction of adults and minors convicted of criminal offenses. Pardon, probation, and parole activities are also included here.

Fire protection includes local government fire protection and prevention activities plus any ambulance, rescue, or other auxiliary services provided by a fire protection agency. Volunteer firefighters, if remunerated for their services on a "per fire" or some other basis, are included as part-time employees.

Highways and transportation includes activities associated with the maintenance and operation of streets, roads, sidewalks, bridges, tunnels, toll roads, and ferries. Snow and ice removal, street lighting, and highway and traffic engineering activities are also included here. Also included are the operation, maintenance, and construction of public mass transit systems, including subways, surface rails, and buses, and the provision, construction, operation, maintenance; support of public waterways, harbors, docks, wharves, and related marine terminal facilities; and activities associated with the operation and support of publicly operated airport facilities.

Health and Welfare includes Health, Hospitals, and Public welfare. **Health** includes administration of public health programs, community and visiting nurse services, immunization programs, drug abuse rehabilitation programs, health and food inspection activities, operation of outpatient clinics, and environmental pollution control activities. **Hospitals** includes only government operated medical care facilities that provide inpatient care. Employees and payrolls of private corporations that lease and operate government-owned hospital facilities are excluded.

Public Welfare includes the administration of various public assistance programs for the needy, veteran services, operation of nursing homes, indigent care institutions, and programs that provide payments for medical care, handicap transportation, and other services for the needy.

Natural resources and Utilities includes activities primarily concerned with the conservation and development of natural resources (soil, water, energy, minerals, etc.) and the regulation of industries that develop, utilize, or affect natural resources, as well as the operation and maintenance of **parks**, playgrounds, swimming pools, public beaches, auditoriums, public golf courses, museums, marinas, botanical gardens, and zoological parks. **Utilities, sewerage, and waste management** includes operation, maintenance, and construction of public water supply systems, including production, acquisition, and distribution of water to general public or to other public or private utilities, for residential, commercial, and industrial use; activities associated with the production or acquisition and distribution of electric power; provision, maintenance, and operation of sanitary and storm sewer systems and sewage disposal and treatment facilities; and refuse collection and disposal, operation of sanitary landfills, and street cleaning activities.

Education and libraries includes activities associated with the operation of public elementary and secondary schools and locally operated vocational-technical schools. Special education programs operated by elementary and secondary school systems are also included as are all ancillary services associated with the operation of schools, such as pupil transportation and food service. **Also included are the** establishment and provision of libraries for use by the general public and the technical support of privately operated libraries. This category includes classroom teachers, principals, supervisors of instruction, librarians, teacher aides, library aides, and guidance and psychological personnel as well as school superintendents and other administrative personnel, clerical and secretarial staffs, plant operation and maintenance personnel, health and recreation employees, transportation and food service personnel, and any student employees. Also included are any degree granting institutions that provide academic training above grade 12.

CITY GOVERNMENT FINANCES, Items 117–139

Source: U.S. Census Bureau—2012 Census of Governments
https://www.census.gov/programs-surveys/cog.html

Revenue and expenditure data are included in Table D for municipal governments only. The data do not include funds of any special district governments located in the city. For example, if a city's school district is a separate governmental unit, it is not included.

Total **general revenue** includes all revenue except utility, liquor stores, and insurance trust revenue. All tax revenue and intergovernmental revenue, even if designated for employee-retirement or local utility purpose, are classified as general revenue.

Intergovernmental revenue covers amounts received from other governments as fiscal aid in the form of shared revenues and grants-in-aid, as reimbursements for the performance of general government functions and specific services for the paying government (for example, care of prisoners or contractual research), or in lieu of taxes. It excludes any amounts received from other governments from the sale of property, commodities, and utility services. All intergovernmental revenue is classified as general revenue. Intergovernmental revenue from the state governments includes amounts originally from the federal government but channeled through the state.

Taxes consist of compulsory contributions exacted by governments for public purposes. However, this category excludes employer and employee payments for retirement and social insurance purposes, which are classified as insurance trust revenue. All tax revenue is classified as general revenue and comprises amounts received (including interest and penalties, but excluding protested amounts and refunds) from all taxes imposed by a government. Note that local government tax revenue excludes any amounts from shares of state-imposed and collected taxes, which are classified as intergovernmental revenue.

Property taxes are based on ownership of property and measured by its value. They include general property taxes related to

property as a whole—real and personal, tangible or intangible—whether taxed at a single rate or at classified rates. Also included are taxes on selected types of property, such as motor vehicles or certain or all intangibles.

Sales and gross receipts taxes include "licenses" at more than nominal rates, based on volume or value of transfers of goods or services; taxes upon gross receipts or upon gross income; and related taxes based upon the use, storage, production (other than the severance of natural resources), importation, or consumption of goods. Dealer discounts "commissions," which are allowed to merchants for the collection of taxes from consumers, are excluded.

Total **general expenditure** includes all city expenditure other than specifically enumerated kinds of expenditure, including utility, liquor store, and employee-retirement and other insurance trust expenditures.

Capital outlays are direct expenditures for contract of force account construction or buildings, roads, and other improvements, and for purchases of equipment, land, and existing structures. They include amounts for additions, replacements, and major alterations to fixed work and structures. Expenditures for repair to such works and structures, however, is classified as current operation expenditure.

A major portion of capital outlay is commonly financed by borrowing, while governmental revenue does not include receipts from borrowing. Among other things, this distorts the relationship between the totals presented for revenue and expenditure and renders this relationship useless as a direct measure of the degree of budgetary "balance" (as that term is generally applied).

Public welfare expenditure covers support of and assistance to needy persons; this aid is contingent upon the person's needs. Included are cash assistance paid directly to needy persons; vendor payments made directly to private purveyors for medical care, burials, and other commodities and services provided under welfare programs; welfare institutions; and any intergovernmental or other direct expenditure for welfare purposes. Pensions to former employees and other benefits not contingent on need are excluded.

Highway expenditure is for the provision and maintenance of highway facilities, including toll turnpikes, bridges, tunnels, and ferries, as well as regular roads, highways, and streets. Also included are expenditures for street lighting and for snow and ice removal. Not included are highway policing and traffic control, which are considered part of police protection

Parking facilities include the construction, purchase, maintenance, and operation of public-use parking lots, garages, parking meters, and other distinctive parking facilities on a commercial basis.

Education is mainly for the provision and general support of schools and other educational facilities and services, including those for educational institutions beyond high school. Elementary and secondary education includes the provision of public kindergarten through high school education by local governments. It encompasses instructional, support, and auxiliary services (school lunch, student activities, and community services) offered by public school systems. Higher education consists of all local institutions of higher education.

Health expenditures include outpatient health services other than hospital care, such as public health administration; research and education; categorical health programs; treatment and immunization clinics; nursing; environmental health activities, such as air and water pollution control; ambulance service if provided separately from fire protection services; and other general public health activities, such as mosquito abatement. School health services provided by health agencies (rather than school agencies) are included here. Not included are sewage treatment operations, which are classified as part of sewerage and sanitation. **Hospital expenditures** include financing, construction, acquisition, maintenance and operation of hospital facilities, provision of hospital care, and support of public or private hospitals.

Police protection encompasses expenditures for the preservation of law and order, as well as for traffic safety. It includes police patrols and communications, crime prevention activities, detention and custody of persons awaiting trial, traffic safety, and vehicular inspection.

Sewerage and recreation include sanitary and storm sewers, sewage disposal facilities and services, and other government activities for such purposes. Street cleaning and the collection and disposal of garbage and other waste are also included.

Parks and recreation includes cultural and scientific activities, such as museums and art galleries; organized recreation, including playgrounds and playing fields, swimming pools, and bathing beaches; and municipal parks and special recreation facilities, such as auditoriums, stadiums, auto camps, recreation piers, and boat harbors.

Housing and community development includes city housing and redevelopment projects and the regulation, promotion, and support of private housing and redevelopment activities. Data from Arizona, Kentucky, Michigan, New Mexico, New York, and Virginia generally include municipal housing authorities. Housing authorities for other cities are usually classified as independent governments, and data from them are not included.

Interest on debt is the amount paid for the use of borrowed money.

Total **debt outstanding** is the total of debt obligations remaining unpaid on the date specified. **Debt issued during the year** is the amount of the outstanding debt that was recently borrowed.

CLIMATE, Items 140–146

Source: National Oceanic and Atmospheric Administration
https://www.ncdc.noaa.gov/data-access/
land-based-station-data/land-based-datasets/
climate-normals

All climate data are average values for the 30-year period from 1971 to 2000.

Mean temperatures for January and July were determined by adding the average daily maximum temperatures and the average daily minimum temperatures and dividing by two.

Temperature limits represent average daily minimum for January and average daily maximum for July.

Annual precipitation values are the average annual water equivalent of all precipitation for the 30-year period.

Heating and cooling degree days are used as relative measures of the energy required for heating and cooling buildings. One heating degree day is accumulated for each whole degree that the mean daily temperature is below 65 degrees Fahrenheit (a mean daily temperature of 62 degrees Fahrenheit will produce three heating degree days). Cooling degree days are accumulated in similar fashion for deviations of the mean daily temperature above 65 degrees Fahrenheit.

TABLE E—CONGRESSIONAL DISTRICTS OF THE 115TH CONGRESS

Members of the House of Representatives are for the 115th Congress.

LAND AREA, Items 1 and 3

Source: U.S. Census Bureau—2017 U.S. Gazetteer Files,
http://www.census.gov/geo/maps-data/data/gazetteer2017.html

Land area measurements are shown to the nearest square mile. Land area includes dry land and land temporarily or partially covered by water, such as marshlands, swamps, and river floodplains.

POPULATION, Items 2–3

Source: U.S. Census Bureau—American Community Survey
http://www.census.gov/acs/www/

The population data are estimates from the American Community Survey.

POPULATION AND POPULATION CHARACTERISTICS, Items 4–24

Source: U.S. Census Bureau—American Community Survey
http://www.census.gov/acs/www/

Data on age, sex, race, Hispanic origin foreign-born residents, and percent born in state of residence are from the 2016 American Community Survey.

Data on race were derived from answers to the question on race that was asked of all respondents. The concept of race, as used by the Census Bureau, reflects self-identification by people according to the race or races with which they most closely identify. These categories are sociopolitical constructs and should not be interpreted as being scientific or anthropological in nature. Furthermore, the race categories include both racial and national origin groups.

In Table E, Columns 4 through 8 refer to individuals who identified with each racial category alone, while column 9 includes persons who identified with two or more races.

The **White** population is defined as persons who indicated their race as White, as well as persons who did not classify themselves in one of the specific race categories listed on the questionnaire but entered a nationality such as Irish, German, Italian, Lebanese, Near Easterner, Arab, or Polish.

The **Black** population includes persons who indicated their race as "Black, African Am., or Negro," as well as persons who did not classify themselves in one of the specific race categories but reported entries such as African American, Afro American, Kenyan, Nigerian, or Haitian.

The **American Indian or Alaska Native** population includes persons who indicated their race as American Indian or Alaska Native, as well as persons who did not classify themselves in one of the specific race categories but reported entries such as Canadian Indian, French-American Indian, Spanish-American Indian, Eskimo, Aleut, Alaska Indian, or any of the American Indian or Alaska Native tribes.

The **Asian and Pacific Islander** population combines two census groupings: **Asian** and **Native Hawaiian or Other Pacific Islander**. The **Asian** population includes persons who indicated their race as Asian Indian, Chinese, Filipino, Japanese, Korean, Vietnamese, or "Other Asian," as well as persons who provided write-in entries of such groups as Cambodian, Laotian, Hmong, Pakistani, or Taiwanese. The **Native Hawaiian or Other Pacific Islander** population includes persons who indicated their race as "Native Hawaiian," "Guamanian or Chamorro," "Samoan," or "Other Pacific Islander," as well as persons who reported entries such as Part Hawaiian, American Samoan, Fijian, Melanesian, or Tahitian.

The **Hispanic population** is based on a question that asked respondents "Is this person Spanish/Hispanic/Latino?" Persons marking any one of the four Hispanic categories (i.e., Mexican, Puerto Rican, Cuban, or other Spanish) are collectively referred to as Hispanic.

The **Non-Hispanic White alone** number in Column 11 includes only those persons who were not Hispanic and whose race was "White only."

The **female** population is shown as a percentage of total population.

The **foreign-born** population includes all persons who were not U.S. citizens at birth. Foreign-born persons are those who indicated they were either a U.S. citizen by naturalization or were not a citizen of the United States. The foreign-born population consists of immigrants (legal permanent residents), temporary migrants (students), humanitarian migrants (refugees), and unauthorized migrants (persons illegally residing in the United States).

Percent born in state of residence is shown as a percentage of total population.

Age is defined as age at last birthday (number of completed years since birth).

EDUCATION—SCHOOL ENROLLMENT AND EDUCATIONAL ATTAINMENT, Items 25–27
Source: U.S. Census Bureau—American Community Survey
http://www.census.gov/acs/www/

Data on school enrollment and educational attainment were derived from a sample of the population. Persons were classified as enrolled in school if they reported attending a "regular" public or private school (or college) during the year. The instructions were to "include only nursery school, kindergarten, elementary school, and schooling which would lead to a high school diploma or a college degree" as regular school. The Census Bureau defines a public school as "any school or college controlled and supported by a local, county, state, or federal government." Schools primarily supported and controlled by religious organizations or other private groups are defined as private schools.

Data on **educational attainment** are tabulated for the population 25 years old and over. The data were derived from a question that asked respondents for the highest level of school completed or the highest degree received. Persons who had passed a high school equivalency examination were considered high school graduates. Schooling received in foreign schools was to be reported as the equivalent grade or years in the regular American school system.

Vocational and technical training, such as barber school training; business, trade, technical, and vocational schools; or other training for a specific trade are specifically excluded.

High school graduate or more. This category includes persons who have received a high school diploma or its equivalent, and those who reported any level higher than a high school diploma.

Bachelor's degree or more. This category includes persons who have received bachelor's degrees, master's degrees, professional school degrees (such as law school or medical school degrees), and doctoral degrees.

HOUSEHOLDS, Items 28–33
Source: U.S. Census Bureau—American Community Survey
http://www.census.gov/acs/www/

A **household** includes all persons who occupy a housing unit. (Persons not living in households are classified as living in group quarters.) A housing unit is a house, an apartment, a mobile home, a group of rooms, or a single room occupied (or, if vacant, intended for occupancy) as separate living quarters. Separate living quarters are those in which the occupants live separately from any other persons in the building and have direct access from the outside of the building or through a common hall. The occupants may be a single family, one person living alone, two or more families living together, or any other group of related or unrelated persons who share living quarters. The number of households is the same as the number of year-round occupied housing units.

A **family** includes a householder and one or more other persons living in the same household who are related to the householder by birth, marriage, or adoption. All persons in a household who are related to the householder are regarded as members of his or her family. A **family household** may contain persons not related to the householder; thus, family households may include more members than families do. A household can contain only one family for the purposes of census tabulations. Not all households contain families, as a household may comprise a group of